Crowfoot

Susanna Woodie

Jeanne Sauvé

Victoria Cross

Alex Baumann

Ned Hanlan

Sir Frederick Banting

Tom Thomson

Tom Longboat

Y0-CCL-713

THE CANADIAN ENCYCLOPEDIA

VOLUME III
Pat - Z
INDEX

Hurtig Publishers
Edmonton

Copyright © 1985 by Hurtig Publishers Ltd.
All rights reserved.
No part of this book may be reproduced or transmitted
in any form by any means, electronic, electrical,
mechanical, chemical, optical, or otherwise, including
photocopying and recording, or by any information
storage or retrieval system, without written permission
from the publisher, except for brief passages
quoted by a reviewer in a newspaper or magazine.

Hurtig Publishers Ltd.
10560 – 105 Street
Edmonton, Alberta
Canada   T5H 2W7

Every attempt has been made to identify and credit sources for
photographs. The publisher would appreciate receiving
information as to any inaccuracies in the credits for
subsequent editions.

Canadian Cataloguing in Publication Data

Main entry under title:
The Canadian Encyclopedia

Editor in Chief: James H. Marsh.

ISBN 0-88830-269-X (set). — ISBN 0-88830-270-3
(v. 1). — ISBN 0-88830-271-1 (v. 2). — ISBN
0-88830-272-X (v. 3)

1. Canada – Dictionaries and encyclopedias.
I. Marsh, James H.
FC23.C36 1985   971'.003'21   C84-091250-1
F1006.C36 1985

Designed, typeset and manufactured
in Canada

Patriotes, the name given after 1826 to the PARTI CANADIEN and to the popular movement that contributed to the REBELLIONS OF 1837-38 in Lower Canada. The primarily francophone party, led mainly by members of the liberal professions and small-scale merchants, was widely supported by farmers, day-labourers and craftsmen. Its more distinguished leaders included Louis-Joseph PAPINEAU, Jean-Olivier Chénier and Wolfred Nelson.

Though the Patriotes dominated LOWER CANADA's elected House of Assembly, their adversaries, the merchant bourgeoisie, the aristocracy and the colonial administration, controlled the appointed Legislative Council, which held most of the power. The Patriotes demanded greater power for assembly members, including increased ministerial responsibility and eligibility for appointment to the council. Their demands, put forth in the name of democracy and the right of peoples to self-government, marked a liberal, nationalist and anticolonial ideology.

Some historians state that the Patriotes' political program included a comprehensive economic-development project for all Lower Canada, designed to benefit the majority of its inhabitants and, of course, their representatives. Others argue that, behind a liberal façade, this was really a retrograde and conservative socioeconomic goal. The Patriotes, except for those of 1838, favoured the retention of the SEIGNEURIAL SYSTEM and more readily supported agricultural than commercial interests. By blocking the economic projects of their adversaries, they delayed the development of British capitalism in the colony. But their positions were neither that clear nor that rigid. As social and economic conflict intensified during the 1830s, the party radicalized both its pressure tactics and its goals, though not without some schisms between its moderate and extremist factions.

In 1834 the Patriotes listed their major complaints in the "Ninety-Two Resolutions" sent to the British government. Britain rejected this call for reform and settled the quarrel over subsidies through the Russell Resolutions of Mar 1837, which authorized the governor of the colony to obtain his budgetary estimates without a vote of the Assembly. This decision caused many demonstrations; verbal violence soon gave way to physical violence. The Rebellions of 1837 and 1838 were followed by the torching of Patriotes' homes, imprisonments, exiles, trials and hangings. The failure of the rebellions led to the disappearance of the Parti patriote. Some of its former leaders, however, returned to active politics in the united PROVINCE OF CANADA. *See also* FILS DE LA LIBERTÉ.   FERNANDE ROY

Patronage, political, is the dispensation of favours, eg, public office, jobs, contracts, subsidies, prestige, etc, by a patron (who controls their dispensation) to a client who cannot obtain the job, etc, by other means and who offers in return to vote for the patron's party or to provide money or manpower for electoral campaigning. The patron (eg, a politician) has access to resources which the client (eg, a businessman) could not otherwise obtain, even though the client's economic resources might exceed the patron's. The relationship between patron and client is usually selective and discretionary; the patron does not generally grant favours to all potential clients but picks and chooses among them. The client may be in direct contact with a patron who controls the resource distribution, eg, a minister may reward election organizers by appointing them as office staff, but clients and patrons may also be linked by a go-between. The patron may be an elected member or an election organizer who needs to approach a minister or the prime minister to obtain the favour for the client. The favour may also be obtained via an intermediary, eg, a civil servant or a politician

obeying the orders of a patron. The resources — a job or position, information, prestige, material rewards — may be just as diverse.

Unlike patronage, CORRUPTION is deleterious conduct which gives an individual or group some private advantage thought to be contrary to public interest. Corruption may become part of patronage. For example, it is considered preferable that government contracts go to the lowest bidder; when a client uses influence to win a contract even though his bid is higher than others, it is said that corruption has become part of political patronage. If a minister uses his expense money for personal pleasure, some people will call that corruption, even though it does not involve patronage. Some patronage practices are considered corrupt by intellectuals or journalists but not by politicians and their clients. For example, if an important position is given to a supporter of the governing party, this may be viewed by some as corrupt conduct, but politicians argue that if all applicants are equally competent it is normal to choose a friend over an adversary or stranger. Celebrated controversial examples of patronage (and corruption) include the PACIFIC SCANDAL, in the 19th century, and the Beauharnois Scandal of the late 1920s. In both cases individuals linked with political parties privately benefited from major public-works projects in a manner generally considered excessive and contrary to public interest.

Patronage is defended as a process that makes job, contract and subsidy allocation less expensive and as an antidote to the excessive bureaucratization of government, but others consider it to be a questionable use of public money. Many American observers claim that it can reinforce party unity and discipline among its members, but a good part of the Canadian intelligentsia oppose practices that they think undermine the principles of merit and equal access for all to the benefits of the state. It is difficult not to judge this as a class reaction; the disadvantaged members of society have long approved of (and still approve of) patronage when they have no other access to resources, while the intelligentsia, who have other means of obtaining what they want from the state, oppose patronage. However, as minor patronage, which favours the disadvantaged, declines, patronage favouring the middle and upper classes, eg, contracts and nominations to high positions, is increasing.

Less dramatically and more persistently, political machines have traditionally used patronage to maintain their advantage over rivals. The machines created by the Liberal and Progressive Conservative parties, by the Union Nationale in Québec and by Social Credit in BC existed in every region of Canada until 1960, but since then Parliament and several provincial legislatures have attempted to control political donations and election spending, and laws governing election practices and PARTY FINANCING have been tightened. The PUBLIC SERVICE has also become less vulnerable to patronage and corruption because the merit principle generally governs recruitment and promotion. Where civil servants are unionized, resistance to such practices is even greater. The spread of the WELFARE STATE has increased the number of political measures available to all, with a corresponding decrease in the more personalized and specialized individual relationships. The weakening of family ties and religious culture has also weakened the cultural and social bases for patronage, especially in Roman Catholic or rural areas. The increased ideological content of politics has also helped reduce patronage. Even so, patronage and corruption will never disappear; wherever competing parties have to depend on the support of friends against enemies, they will use patronage to win victory and offer rewards. *See also* CONFLICT OF INTEREST.

VINCENT LEMIEUX

Patsalas, Constantin, choreographer, character dancer (b at Thessaloníki, Greece 1 Aug 1943). Trained in Germany, Patsalas joined the NATIONAL BALLET OF CANADA in 1972, becoming resident choreographer in 1980. His ballets range widely in style from the abstract (*Rite of Spring, Nataraja*) to the romantic (*L'Île inconnue*) or even punk (*Past of the Future*), but his imaginative CHOREOGRAPHY is unified by its uncompromising stylistic faithfulness to the inspiring score, its structural integrity and its inventive exploration of dynamic contrasts in mood and movements.   PENELOPE DOOB

Patterson, Freeman Wilford, photographer (b at Long Reach, NB 25 Sept 1937). Patterson began his photographic career in 1965. An early success was his contribution of 75 colour images to *Canada: A Year of the Land* (1967). Besides freelancing, Patterson helped organize the National Assn for Photographic Art and edited its magazine, *Camera Canada,* for 10 years. In 1973 he cofounded a photography school at Shampers Bluff, NB, but closed it in 1977 to devote himself to his own PHOTOGRAPHY, lecturing and writing. Patterson's 3 books (*Photography for the Joy of It,* 1977; *Photography and the Art of Seeing,* 1979; and *Photography of Natural Things,* 1982) provide considerable information on the technical as well as aesthetic aspects of photography. The texts are illustrated with his own photographs, which reflect his documentary and interpretive approaches to photography.   LOUISE ABBOTT

Patterson, John, meteorologist (b in Oxford County, Ont 3 Jan 1872; d at Clarkson, Ont 22 Feb 1956). Educated at U of T and Cambridge, Patterson returned to Canada in 1910 after serving in India as professor and imperial meteorologist. He designed a pilot-balloon system for studying the upper air and developed a new anemometer and a new barometer for operational use. In 1929 Patterson succeeded Sir Frederic STUPART as director of the national meteorological service, a position he held until 1946. Under his leadership, the service survived the Depression and expanded tenfold to meet wartime needs, providing meteorological services for the new TRANS-CANADA AIRLINES and for the BRITISH COMMONWEALTH AIR TRAINING PLAN and the Home War units. A fellow of the RSC, he as in 1954 the first recipient of the Patterson Medal for distinguished service to METEOROLOGY.   MORLEY THOMAS

Patterson, Walter, army officer, colonial administrator (b 1735? in County Donegal, Ire; d at London, Eng 6 Sept 1798). He served briefly with the British army in America during the SEVEN YEARS' WAR and arrived in Charlottetown in Aug 1770 as the first British governor of the Island of St John (renamed Prince Edward I in 1799). His tenure (1769-87) was remarkable for land speculation and political uproar, but his outstanding legacy was the entrenchment of PEI as a separate political entity. The problems of his new charge were enormous: the total population was but a few hundred; the officers of government were inexperienced; and his administration had no reliable financial basis. Within a few years he had established a rudimentary government including a House of Assembly (1773); and in 1777 he succeeded in securing for the colony an annual grant of £3000. Land speculation proved Patterson's undoing. Through considerable political manipulation, he gained tenuous possession of over 40 000 ha. In the words of Captain John MacDonald, an opponent, he "would have done extremely well, had he known where to stop." Dismissed in 1787, he was stripped of his property by his political adversaries and died in poverty. *See also* LAND QUESTION, PEI.   HARRY BAGLOLE

Patterson, William John, premier of Saskatchewan 1935-44 (b at Grenfell, Sask 13 May

1886; d at Regina 10 June 1976). First elected to the Saskatchewan legislature in 1921, the popular, though prudent, Patterson became the first Saskatchewan-born premier when he succeeded James GARDINER in 1935. Although he inherited a formidable political machine, Patterson provided uninspiring leadership during the Depression and then WWII. The CO-OPERATIVE COMMONWEALTH FEDERATION, meanwhile, broadened its base of support by playing down government ownership in favour of government planning. In June 1944 the CCF under T.C. DOUGLAS won a decisive victory, reducing the once powerful Liberal Party to 5 seats. Patterson resigned as Liberal leader in 1946 and subsequently served as the province's lieutenant-governor 1951-58. He was the first person in the province's history to hold both posts of premier and lieutenant-governor.   W.A. WAISER

Pattison, James Allen, entrepreneur (b at Saskatoon 1 Oct 1928). Pattison was raised in Vancouver. He became a used-car salesman in 1952 and in 1961 he invested his savings in a General Motors dealership, which he built into one of the largest in western Canada. In 1967 he acquired Neon Products, a national manufacturer and lessor of signs. Since then he has purchased over 50 other companies including airlines, soft-drink producers and magazine distributors. Although the recession of 1982-83 led to cutbacks and layoffs in a number of his companies, his business empire had assets of over $400 million in 1982. In 1984 he was chairman of 2 crown corporations: Expo 86 and BC Place, a huge urban-renewal project in Vancouver.

CHRISTOPHER G. CURTIS

Pattullo, Thomas Dufferin, politician, businessman, public servant, premier of BC (b at Woodstock, Ont 19 Jan 1873; d at Victoria 30 Mar 1956). Though best known as premier of BC during the 1930s, Pattullo had a long, varied career before that. He worked for the Woodstock *Sentinel* and in 1896 became editor of the Galt *Reformer.* His father's Liberal Party connections gained him the position of secretary to J.M. WALSH, commissioner of the Yukon Territory, in 1897. Pattullo worked in government service in Dawson City until 1902, becoming acting assistant gold commissioner. He then formed a business partnership in real estate and insurance, and for a time was a member of the Dawson City council. In 1908 he moved to Prince Rupert to open a branch office. He was alderman and mayor of the town, and in 1916 was elected to the BC Assembly, becoming minister of lands in the new Liberal government. After the Liberals' defeat in 1928, he became leader of the Opposition. Revitalizing the party, he led it to victory 1933 and became premier. Faced with the tremendous economic and social problems of the GREAT DEPRESSION, Pattullo was innovative in extending the role of government. His frustration with the limitations of provincial power led to a battle with Ottawa that resulted in a reappraisal of Canadian federalism. After an inconclusive 1941 election, he rejected a coalition with the Conservatives and was rebuffed by his own party. Defeated in 1945 in his old riding of Prince Rupert, he retired to Victoria.   ROBIN FISHER

Reading: Margaret A. Ormsby, "T. Dufferin Pattullo and the Little New Deal," *Canadian Historical Review* 43 (1962); Martin Robin, *The Rush for Spoils: The Company Province* (1972) and *Pillars of Profit: The Company Province* (1973).

Paul, Robert, figure skater (b at Toronto, 2 June 1937). A specialist in pairs skating, Paul started skating with Barbara WAGNER in 1952, and in 1954 they placed 3rd in the N American championships. In 1957, over 16 days, they won the Canadian, N American and world championships and held them for the next 3 years. They won the gold medal at the 1960 Squaw Valley, Calif, Olympics, the first non-Europeans

to win the pairs event. After 1960 they continued to skate together on the professional circuit. The partnership was dissolved in 1964, and Paul became a skating choreographer and coach in the US.   BARBARA SCHRODT

Paula Ross Dance Company, founded in the mid-1960s, incorporated 1973, is one of the few Canadian dance groups with a clearly defined movement style and artistic point of view. Despite many difficult years of financial and organizational problems, Paula Ross has created a large repertoire of work reflecting her personal vision and her commitment to social and political issues. She received the Jean A. Chalmers Award for Choreography in 1977, and her company has toured Canada.   GRANT STRATE

Paull, Andrew, Squamish leader, organizer, lobbyist (b at Squamish, BC 6 Feb 1892; d at Vancouver 28 July 1959). Born into a prominent family in the Durieu system at Mission Reserve No 1, Burrard Inlet, Paull was educated at the reserve school and became a longshoreman. Secretary of his band, he was interpreter for the royal commission of 1913 to 1916. A member of the executive of the Allied Tribes of BC, he testified before a special joint committee in Ottawa in 1927. At home he organized bands and orchestras, athletic events, beauty contests, employment services and labour groups. In 1942 he joined the Native Brotherhood of BC, becoming its business manager, but in 1945 he broke with it and formed the North American Indian Brotherhood. In the late 1940s he testified before parliamentary committees considering Indian Act revisions, memorizing long portions of documents.   E. P. PATTERSON II

Pauta Saila, sculptor (b at a hunting camp on the W coast S Baffin I, NWT Dec 1917). Technically skillful on paper or in stone, Pauta is known particularly for his "dancing bears," powerful, somewhat abstract sculptures of upright polar bears. The son of Saila, an important Inuit leader, Pauta grew up on his father's immense SW Baffin hunting territory and knows the habits of polar bears from close observation. He lives with his second wife, well-known graphic artist Pitaloosie, at Cape Dorset, and some 40 of his own drawings have been published as prints. Widely exhibited, his best-known work may be his massive *Bear,* executed in 1967 during the International Sculpture Symposium in High Park, Toronto, and now at the McMichael Collection at Kleinburg, Ont.

DOROTHY HARLEY EBER

Pavelic, Myfanwy Spencer, painter (b at Victoria 27 Apr 1916). Largely self-taught, Pavelic's talent was noticed early by Emily CARR, who arranged an exhibition of her work in 1934. From 1944 to 1960 she spent much time in New York. The abstract art so prevalent there made her challenge her own style. However, the human figure remained her prime interest and her mature style is dominated by humanistic and meditative tendencies. In 1983 the British National Portrait Gallery accepted Pavelic's portrait of Yehudi Menuhin to hang in its permanent collection. She was the first Canadian-born artist to be so honoured. Pavelic was one of the founding members of the Society of Limners (1971), a Victoria group of artists who take their name from the travelling journeymen painters of the Middle Ages.   KATHLEEN LAVERTY

Pawley, Howard Russell, politician, premier of Manitoba (b at Brampton, Ont 21 Nov 1934). Raised in a Methodist home, Pawley moved to Winnipeg at age 17 and was educated at Manitoba Teachers Coll, United Coll and Manitoba Law School. First elected as MLA for Selkirk in 1969, he was reelected in 1973, 1977 and 1981. In Premier Edward SCHREYER's NDP administration, Pawley held the portfolios of minister

Howard Pawley, who was elected premier of Manitoba in Nov 1981 *(courtesy Canapress).*

of municipal affairs (1969-76) and attorney general (1973-77). After the Schreyer government's defeat, Pawley served in opposition and was elected permanent leader of the NDP of Manitoba in Nov 1979. He led his party to victory in the Nov 1981 election. The most controversial action by the Pawley government during its first term was the introduction of a resolution entrenching French-language rights in the constitution and providing for the extension of French-language services within the provincial public service. Never a charismatic or forceful personality, Pawley has encouraged a team approach and a willingness to consult widely.

PAUL G. THOMAS

Pawnbroking People in need of quick cash loans may bring personal items, eg, clocks, musical instruments and pieces of jewellery, to a pawnbroker as collateral. If the loan is not repaid within a specified time, the pawnbroker may sell the item. Thus, pawnshops operate as lending institutions and as retail stores.

The procedure of pawning an item is similar across Canada. A pawnbroker inquires how much an individual is hoping to borrow. If the item is acceptable to the pawnbroker, a quick appraisal is done. Many pawnshops have trained gemologists on staff to appraise precious stones. The pawnbroker names the amount he is willing to lend and issues a pawn ticket to the customer. The loan is usually up to 25% of the value of the merchandise but may be as low as a few dollars. The item may be reclaimed at any time within the loan period marked on the ticket by full repayment of the loan, plus INTEREST and nominal service and storage charges. Pawnshops are, in fact, frequented by a cross section of Canadians. Part of the appeal of this avenue of acquiring ready cash is that no explanation is required regarding why the money is needed.

Because human need, greed and desperation are intrinsic to this trade, pawnbroking has had a colourful past and some murky connotations. Unscrupulous lenders were known in the past to strip desperate clients by accepting clothes, shoes, false teeth and glass eyes; to charge usurious interest rates; or to sell someone's cherished possession almost as soon as he or she had pledged it and left the shop. As well, some thieves saw pawnshops as places to dump stolen goods.

However, pawnbroking in Canada today is so well regulated that nearly all risks — both to borrowers and shoppers — as well as some of the drama have disappeared. A federal Pawnbrokers' Act was passed in 1886, and more recently various provincial laws concerning pawnbroking have come into effect. In general, the areas that are regulated include the safekeeping of objects left as collateral; the level of interest rates that may be charged; the length of time pledged items must be kept before being sold (usually one year); and requirements for municipal licensing. Local police usually monitor pawnbroking businesses by checking the pawnbrokers' daily records of transactions against lists of stolen goods.

Though pawnshop merchandise is often still a grab bag of odd items, pawnbrokers in Canada, for practical and economic reasons, are more selective, some specializing only in precious metals. Approximately 80% of the items placed are redeemed by their owners.

RUTH DANYS

Pay Television Although undertaken experimentally in Etobicoke, Ont, between 1960 and 1965, pay television as a major venture was licensed only in Mar 1982, after a decade of debate. Promoted for many years by the CABLE TELEVISION industry for its moneymaking potential, pay television had been opposed by established broadcasters who feared the competition, by telephone companies who resisted cable's proliferation of services and technological advance, and by cultural nationalists. The CANADIAN RADIO-TELEVISION AND TELECOMMUNICATIONS COMMISSION, in 1975 and again in 1978, having undertaken inquiries as to the desirability of introducing pay TV to Canada, concluded that inauguration was "premature." The CRTC believed pay TV would simply constitute another channel for American programming and would undermine the financial base of Canadian broadcasting (see BROADCASTING, RADIO AND TELEVISION; TELEVISION PROGRAMMING).

Nonetheless, under request from the federal Dept of Communications in 1979, the CRTC initiated a third inquiry, the Therrien Committee, which duly reported in 1980, recommending that a competitive industry be authorized. The Dept of Communications, with a mandate broader than the cultural objectives of the CRTC, has viewed pay TV as a means of stimulating satellite usage and furthering development in HIGH TECHNOLOGY industries. Therrien's recommendations were accepted by the government and the CRTC.

In 1982 the CRTC inaugurated a discretionary, pay-per-channel pay-television industry in the private sector. At one stroke 6 services were licensed — a national general-interest service (in English and French), 3 regional general-interest channels, a performing arts service, and a regional multilingual service. Subsequently, additional regional channels were authorized. For all but the multilingual licensee, progressively increasing time and revenue quotas were imposed to be allocated to Canadian programming. However, the CRTC chose not to regulate dealings between the pay companies and either program suppliers or exhibitors (cable companies); likewise, the retail price to the subscriber was left unregulated. In Feb 1983 the pay services became operational, utilizing SATELLITES to deliver programming to cable systems, which in turn billed subscribers about $16 per month for a single channel (see SATELLITE COMMUNICATIONS).

Controversies soon broke out anew, however. First Choice, the national, general-interest licensee, announced in Jan 1983 a joint venture with an American production company whereby $30 million in "adult" films would be produced to help meet Canadian regulatory obligations. Thousands marched and wrote letters to the CRTC in protest (see PORNOGRAPHY); the commission then requested the industry to draw up guidelines for self-regulation. In the spring of 1983 it became apparent that licensees could fulfil their programming obligations through "scaffolding," eg, by flowing through preproduction revenues from US sources and counting these as contributions for regulatory purposes.

During 1983-84 the industry faced severe shakedowns as projected subscriptions did not materialize. The arts network, C-Channel, collapsed after 17 weeks; Star Channel, the Atlantic regional licensee, eventually was shut down; the French-language regional service, TVEC, merged with First Choice which was itself refinanced and taken over by a film production/distribution company. Nonetheless, in 1984 a new round of licensing took place as "specialty" channels, which were to combine ADVERTISING and subscriber fees, were authorized for satellite delivery to cable systems.

Pay TV is a radical departure from historic broadcasting policy. First, the industry has no publicly owned or nonprofit oriented component; indeed, a competitive structure was immediately introduced with a view to giving market forces important play. Second, highest priority was accorded to increased diversity in production sources and viewing options, to be contrasted with the cultural and political goals heretofore dominant. Finally, with these decisions, it is apparent that communication policy is being formulated increasingly with a view to stimulating COMMUNICATIONS TECHNOLOGY and that cultural concerns respecting the nature of the programming are in decline. ROBERT E. BABE

Reading: CRTC, Committee on Extension of Service to Northern and Remote Communities [Therrien Committee], *The 1980's: A Decade of Diversity — Broadcasting, Satellites and Pay-TV* (1980); J. Meisel, "An Audible Squeak: Broadcast Regulation in Canada," in *Cultures in Collision: The Interaction of Canadian and US Television Broadcast Policy* (1984); R.B. Woodrow and K.B. Woodside, eds, *The Introduction of Pay TV in Canada* (1982).

Pays d'en Haut [French "up country" or "upper country"] was an expression used in the FUR TRADE to refer to the area to which the VOYAGEURS travelled to trade. In the days of NEW FRANCE it referred to what is now NW Québec (except the King's Posts), most of Ontario, the area W of the Mississippi and S of the Great Lakes and beyond to the Canadian prairies. Later usage was limited to the prairies and today *pays d'en haut* is used in Québec to refer to the NW part of the province.

Pea (*Pisum sativum*), annual VEGETABLE of the legume family. The species originated in central and western Asia, where wild types still exist and can be crossed with cultivated varieties. In Canada, English peas (sweet or garden peas) are used for canning and freezing; edible-podded peas (sugar, snow or chinese peas) are grown for the pod, which is tender and fibre free when harvested at an early stage and are much less important commercially. Some cultivars (commercial varieties) are pole type, grown mainly on trellises; others are dwarf type, used primarily by the canning industry. Peas are a cool-season crop. Seed germination is good at 5-10°C; optimum growth is obtained at 15-20°C. The sugar in the grains is rapidly converted into starch when harvest time temperatures are too high. Sweet peas are harvested by machines which cut, shell and size the grains. The canning industry requires small, tender peas; tendrometers, instruments measuring grain tenderness, determine the time to harvest. Bigger grains are acceptable for freezing. ROGER BÉDARD

Pea, Field (*Pisum arvense*), hardy annual belonging to the legume family. Field peas, among the oldest of cultivated CROPS, originated in India, were carried to Europe in prehistoric times and introduced to the New World in the 1600s. The field pea, a viny climbing PLANT, occurs in dwarf, medium and tall types. Some cultivars (cultivated varieties) have branching stems. Leaved types have alternate leaves with 1-3 pairs of leaflets ending in one or more tendrils; semileafless and leafless types also occur. The reddish purple flowers are borne in the leaf axils, either singly or in 2 or 3 racemes (flowering structures). The cylindrical pod varies in

length (2.5-12.5 cm), is yellow-green to green in colour, and contains 2-10 seeds. Field peas are planted 5-8 cm deep, in rows 30-60 cm apart, at a seeding rate of 130-200 kg/ha, depending on seed size. They require 90-160 days to mature and 40-100 cm of rainfall during the growing season. Field peas are grown in temperate regions worldwide; however, their susceptibility to PLANT DISEASES could limit further development as a field crop. Field peas are grown for their high-protein seed, used in soups, dhal, livestock feed and flour. Canada produces approximately 75 000 t of field peas annually, primarily for export. P. McVETTY

Peace, Order and Good Government, introductory phrase of section 91 of the CONSTITUTION ACT, 1867, generally stating the scope of the legislative jurisdiction of Parliament. In the eyes of some of the FATHERS OF CONFEDERATION, this clause was a general power enabling Parliament to enact laws on matters not specifically conferred upon the provinces, ie, on "residuary" matters. When examining a particular law to ascertain which legislature had jurisdiction, it became necessary to review the 2 lists of enumerated powers, including the provincial power to legislate in the matters of "property and civil rights in the province". In the 1920s the power of this provision was emasculated by Lord Haldane's interpretation of it as an "emergency" power, an interpretation rejected by Lord Simon in the 1946 Prohibition case. The Supreme Court of Canada has, since 1949, done much to revive the clause, particularly through such references as the ANTI-INFLATION ACT REFERENCE.

It can now be stated with some certainty that the opening words of s91 have both a residuary and an emergency function. Parliament can invoke the residuary function of the words "peace, order and good government" when the subject matter of legislation is a genuinely new matter not included within any of the enumerated heads of ss91 and 92 and is of national dimension or importance. This is somewhat of a departure from the "dimensions" doctrine of the 1960s in which the general power was interpreted to mean federal jurisdiction over local matters that have assumed a national dimension. The emergency function can be invoked by Parliament to legislate matters which are normally under provincial jurisdiction, but which because of their perceived magnitude or nature are sufficiently critical to require a national or regional legislative response. The exercise of the emergency power by Parliament holds in suspension the normal distribution of powers set out in the Constitution Act, 1867; in these instances it is crucial that the legislation be temporary. For example, during WWI Parliament enacted the WAR MEASURES ACT which empowered the government to make regulations on almost any subject.

The provinces have proposed reforms of the peace, order and good government clause and it is likely that consideration will be given to them. *See also* RUSSELL CASE; AERONAUTICS REFERENCE; LABOUR CONVENTIONS REFERENCE. A.A. McLELLAN

Peace Movement In 1983, with East-West relations at their lowest point in 2 decades, the Mennonite Central Committee (Manitoba) published a directory listing more than 100 Canadian peace organizations. The directory is itself a reflection of the growing concern in Canada about the nuclear arms race between the Soviet Union and the US, which together possess the vast majority of the world's nuclear weapons. Peace research, public education, seminars, demonstrations and lobbying campaigns directed at politicians have become common activities of the diverse peace groups. In general, they want Canada to play a stronger role internationally in pressing for DISARMA-

MENT and a strong UNITED NATIONS collective security strategy rather than the military alliances' policy of deterrence, which has fostered an open-ended arms race.

The peace movement of the 1980s is different from an earlier movement in Canada at the end of the 1950s and in the early 1960s. At that time a national debate, and protests, occurred over the acquisition of nuclear weapons for Canadian forces (*see* BOMARC MISSILE CRISIS) and the atmospheric testing of nuclear weapons. In 1957 the first Pugwash Conference of scientists was held in Pugwash, NS. The Canadian Campaign for Nuclear Disarmament was formed and organized some marches. The VOICE OF WOMEN began to hold an annual Mothers' Day vigil. The Canadian Peace Research Institute was founded. The QUAKERS and MENNONITES, traditionally dedicated to peace, spoke out. World Federalists advocated a stronger UN. Canadian Pugwash, the Canadian Peace Research Institute and the World Federalists of Canada all have international affiliations. The Canadian Peace Congress, which had close links to the COMMUNIST PARTY OF CANADA, was also active. These groups were narrowly based, labelled "left-wing" and dismissed by a general public that continued to think of peace as that state of security resulting from superiority over the Soviet bloc in the possession of arms.

Though the Canadian government did renounce the production of nuclear weapons, Canada has maintained its participation in NATO, which relies on nuclear weapons to deter an attack even by conventional forces. In 1979, to counter the Soviet buildup of intermediate nuclear missiles targeted at western Europe, NATO adopted a "two-track modernization" program: 572 Cruise and Pershing II missiles were to be deployed in 5 European countries, starting in 1983; and throughout the period leading up to deployment, negotiations between the USSR and the US were to take place to reduce the nuclear level. When deployment started, the Soviets broke off negotiations. This alarming atmosphere, in which no end to the arms race was in sight, gave rise to a renewed peace movement in Canada, as in Europe and the US. This movement was more broadly based. New organizations of physicians, scientists, educators, lawyers, artists and many other occupations were formed. The Voice of Women and the World Federalists continued to be active (*see also* WOMEN'S INTERNATIONAL LEAGUE FOR PEACE AND FREEDOM). Throughout, the mainstream peace movement has been nonviolent in philosophy and practice.

The peace movement of the 1980s is not a unified structure, but a loose network of uncoordinated groups. However, there are 2 bodies — Project Ploughshares and Operation Dismantle — that have taken a leading role as catalysts for the movement (*see* ECUMENICAL SOCIAL ACTION). Sponsored by the Canadian Council of Churches in 1976, Project Ploughshares, with local affiliates in more than 20 locations, has developed a national campaign of research, education and publications on the problems of disarmament and development both in Canada and internationally. Its major programs include actions to make Canada a nuclear weapon-free zone; a special study of the impact of US defence procurement on Canadian defence expenditures; the presentation of briefs to the government and parliamentarians; and conferences, seminars and workshops throughout Canada. Operation Dismantle, founded 1977 by T. James Stark, has developed the concept of a world referendum on disarmament, which the organization is pressing the UN to support. The global referendum is described as "a radical nonconfrontrational vehicle" through which ordinary people throughout the world could express themselves directly on the goal of balanced, general disarmament. In 1982 and 1983, a referendum on disarmament was voted on in 191 Canadian municipalities by more than one million Canadians, 76.2% of whom supported balanced disarmament.

The activities of the peace groups in Canada have undoubtedly helped to develop public opinion, which now supports a verifiable Soviet-American freeze on the testing, production and deployment of all nuclear weapons and delivery systems. But this opinion had not solidified to the extent of stopping the Canadian government from allowing the US to conduct a test in Canada, in early 1984, of the air-launched "Cruise" missile delivery system. The government position was that NATO solidarity compelled participation in the "modernization" program to which Canada had already given its consent. Canada has been deeply divided on the "Cruise" testing issue and, with the newly developed peace groups leading the way, in opposing Canada's involvement in the escalating nuclear arms race. Many Canadians want the arms buildup to stop, but they are ambivalent about where Canada's duty, in the interests of security, lies. Though the peace movement has been unable to resolve this ambivalence, it has awakened an important segment of the public to the issue of nuclear war. Its presence has also contributed to the recent creation of 2 bodies: Parliamentarians for World Order, a nongovernmental group of over 50 Canadian MPs and senators linked to similar groups in more than 30 countries; and the Canadian Institute for International Peace and Security, an independent but government-financed body dedicated to doing research and providing information to Canadians. DOUGLAS ROCHE

Reading: E. Regehr and S. Rosenblum, eds, *Canada and the Nuclear Arms Race* (1983).

Peace River, Alta, Town, pop 5907 (1981c), inc 1919, is located at the junction of the PEACE and Smoky rivers, 485 km NW of Edmonton. It takes its name from nearby Peace Point, where Cree and Beaver Indians settled a territorial dispute. The strategic location at the river junction was first used as a base by Alexander MACKENZIE on his western journey (1793). Later, buffalo hides were brought by trail from Ft Edmonton and transported upstream to New Caledonia. The junction was an important ferry crossing, and the Edmonton, Dunvegan and BC Ry crossed the river in 1915. Missions were founded in 1879 and 1887, and Rev J. Gough Brisk dramatically showed the area's agricultural potential by winning the world wheat championship at the Chicago Exposition (1893). By 1913 a permanent settlement was emerging on the present townsite, known up to 1916 as Peace River Crossing. Today the town is the distribution and administration centre for the area. Local tourist attractions include Peace River Museum, the remnants of Mackenzie's Fort Fork (1792-93), the grave of H.F. "Twelve Foot" Davis and nearby Queen Elizabeth Prov Park. ERIC J. HOLMGREN

Peace River, 1923 km long, is one of the principal tributaries of the MACKENZIE R system. Formerly, the Peace was formed by the juncture of the Finlay R from the N and the Parsnip R from the south. Today the 2 rivers have been dammed near Hudson Point and have swelled to form WILLISTON LK. The Peace flows from the E arm of the lake, cuts through the Rocky Mts and is joined by the Halfway and Beatton rivers from the N and the Pine R from the S. Just E of the BC-Alberta border it is joined by the Pouce Coupé. It cuts a deep gash, up to 11 km wide, across the northern Alberta prairie. It is an ancient course; dinosaur tracks have been uncovered along its banks. At the town of PEACE RIVER, it is joined by the Smoky R and swings abruptly N, meandering to near Ft Vermilion, where it turns E and, joined by the Wabasca R, flows into WOOD BUFFALO NATIONAL PK and pours into the Slave R, whence its waters are carried to the Mackenzie.

Alexander MACKENZIE wintered in the river's upper reaches 1793. Other traders, including Peter POND, may have preceded him; traders certainly followed and the river was a major freight route up to 1826. Five different forts, dating from 1805-06, were built at various times around the location of modern FORT ST JOHN, and Simon FRASER built a strategic post at Hudson's Hope (1805), the head of navigation. The valley of the Peace is fertile; it is the northernmost commercially important agricultural region of N America. The great Gordon M. Schrum hydroelectric power station near Hudson's Hope was built 1968-80 and at 2.4 MW is the third largest in Canada; nearby Peace Canyon station generates another 0.7 MW. JAMES MARSH

Peace River Lowland, a gently rolling lowland without clearly defined outer boundaries, extends E of the ROCKY MTS on both sides of the PEACE R, sloping downward to the E. Although it is often called a "lowland," the landform region is part of the high plains of western Alberta. The higher hills in the foothills E of the

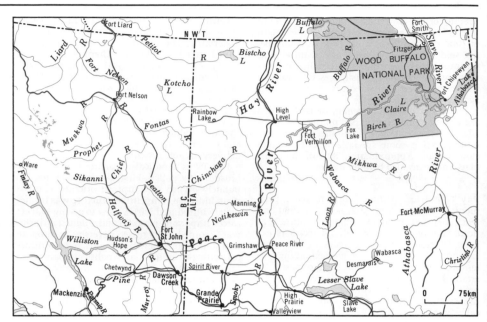

Autumn harvest, Peace River, Alta. The Peace River Lowland is the most northerly grain-growing area of N America (*photo by V. Claerhout*).

Rockies in northeastern BC have elevations of about 1000 m and the plain W of Lk ATHABASCA is about 300 m above sea level. Local landform features are illustrated by several flat-topped, erosional-remnant hills that rise a few hundred metres above the broad, gently sloping valleys. In contrast, the Peace R and its immediate tributaries are deeply entrenched about 200 m into the lowland in the western section causing significant land-transportation obstacles. However, to the E the steep-sided banks of the Peace R floodplain have decreased in height to about 70 m W of Ft Vermilion.

Most of the Peace R Lowland was covered by an aspen-poplar forest when the area was occupied by the BEAVER (Athapaskans) prior to European exploration and settlement in the 19th century. Spruce trees grew on the upper slopes, which were underlain by less-fertile grey-wooded soils. Many of the broad valleys, particularly in the western section, had tall, prairie grass vegetation cover and were underlain by more fertile and darker-coloured soils. Agricultural settlers who moved into the region early in the 20th century tended to occupy the grassy areas where less forest had to be removed prior to cultivation.

The climate of the lowland is a little more favourable for agriculture than other parts of N-central Alberta. Because the Rocky Mts are lower W of the region, Pacific air masses can cross over with less modification, resulting in about 38 to 45 cm of annual precipitation, more than in E-central Alberta. However, cold air masses from the NW may cover the area at any time, causing the average annual frost-free season to vary greatly from year to year and from place to place. An average frost-free season of about 110 days is recorded in the agricultural areas near the Alberta-BC boundary.

Fur traders penetrated this forest environment at the end of the 18th century and encouraged the Indians to trap for furs. Fur-trading posts opened and closed throughout the area, such as at Rocky Mountain Fort (est 1798), Fort Dunvegan (1805) and FORT ST JOHN (1806). Pioneer agricultural settlers reached the area at the beginning of the 20th century as part of the general settling of the northern fringes of the prairies and parklands of the Canadian Interior Plains. Settlement accelerated after a railway reached PEACE RIVER in 1915 and extended to GRANDE PRAIRIE in 1916. These settlers found a physical environment that compared favourably with that of central Alberta, but they were hampered by lack of accessibility and distance of markets. By 1981 cultivated land in the western part of the area totalled 1 727 000 ha in Alberta and 377 000 ha in northeastern BC. Though most of the area still remains under forest cover, some of which is being used for lumber and pulpwood, its underground resources of petroleum and natural gas are being more widely explored and utilized. J. LEWIS ROBINSON

Peacekeeping, the usual term applied to UNITED NATIONS military operations. Because of L.B. PEARSON's role in the SUEZ CRISIS of 1956 and the Canadian role in the UN Emergency Force he helped create, Canadians tended to look on peacekeeping with a proprietary air. When the UN Charter was drafted in 1945 it included elaborate provisions for the maintenance of collective security. But the COLD WAR blocked every attempt to institutionalize a UN force, and the UN had to rely on improvisation. This was first evident in Apr 1948 when the UN authorized the employment of military observers in Kashmir and when it repeated this action the next month along the Arab-Israeli borders. Military observers could watch the movements of armies, supervise cease-fires and the local civilians and generally bring calm to an area. That was the theory, and it usually proved workable. Canada provided 8 officers for the UN force in Kashmir and after 1953 it sent 4 officers to the Palestine force as well as Gen E.L.M. BURNS, who took command in Feb 1954.

This type of UN peacekeeping was markedly different from that practised in the KOREAN WAR. There, because the USSR fortuitously was boycotting the Security Council when the crisis arose in late June 1950, the US was able to organize a "police action" to resist the N Korean invasion. Much more typical, even if not under the UN, was the Canadian role on the International Commissions for Supervision and Control in Vietnam, Laos and Cambodia. These commissions (usually called International Control Commissions, or ICCs) were set up by the Geneva Conference of 1954 on a "troika" model, with a communist state (Poland), a Western state (Canada) and a neutral (India). The task was important, since the ICCs had responsibility for relocating populations, supervising elections and watching the new boundaries. The manpower commitment was relatively heavy, however, as almost 100 bilingual officers and a substantial number of external affairs officials were required for what proved to be a notably thankless task. In Cambodia and Laos there was initally some success, but the Vietnam ICC bogged down in futility as the war there spread out of control in the 1960s.

But in 1956, when the Suez Crisis arose, Canadians eagerly seized on the opportunity for UN service. The UN had quickly become involved when Britain and France co-operated with Israel in an assault on Egypt. The Canadian interest was to minimize the harm done to the Western alliance by the Anglo-French aggression, and Canadian Secretary of State for External Affairs Pearson, working with UN Secretary-General Dag Hammarskjöld, produced the idea of a peacekeeping force to stabilize the situation and to permit the withdrawal of the attackers. To assist, Pearson offered a battalion of The Queen's Own Rifles. The United Nations Emergency Force (UNEF) came into being quickly, but the Egyptians, to Canada's surprise, objected to the presence of Canadians. The uniforms, the regimental name and the Canadian flags all seemed very similar to those of the British invaders and, the Egyptians argued, their people would not understand. In the end a compromise was struck: Canadian service and supply troops, vital to the success of the UN force, would replace the infantry. This experience played its part in convincing Pearson that Canada needed its own symbols; it also won him the Nobel Peace Prize.

After Suez, Canadians came to feel that peacekeeping was their métier. This was evident in July 1960 when a newly independent Congo erupted in violence. The Diefenbaker government was reluctant to participate when the UN asked for signallers and other troops, but public opinion forced the government's hand. Peacekeeping popularity had been established, and

there was no hesitation in 1962 when Canada sent a small number of men to West New Guinea (Irian Jaya), or in the next year when servicemen went to Yemen for service with a UN observer mission. A much larger commitment followed in 1964 when the UN intervened to separate Greeks and Turks in Cyprus. Canadian Secretary of State for External Affairs Paul MARTIN was instrumental in creating the Cyprus UN force.

But the heyday of peacekeeping was over. Some critics were already beginning to complain that peacekeeping merely rendered situations static and did nothing to resolve them. Others worried about costs and casualties, and fretted over often unclear mandates. The death blow came in 1967 when President Nasser ordered the UNEF out of Egypt, and then ordered the Canadian force to withdraw. Another Arab-Israeli war followed. The expulsion of the Canadians amounted almost to a national humiliation, a reaction that was not eased by charges that Canadians in the ICC had been spying for the US. The idea of peacekeeping had helped to reinforce a mythos of Canada as an impartial and acceptable observer, but now peacekeeping quickly dropped out of favour in Canada. Although Canadian servicemen still participate in UN peacekeeping, since 1967 it has seemed a chore rather than an opportunity. *See* MIDDLE POWER; PEACE MOVEMENT. J.L. GRANATSTEIN
Reading: L.B. Pearson, *Mike,* vol 2 (1973); A. Taylor et al, *Peacekeeping* (1968).

Peach (*Prunus persica,* ROSE family), most widely grown of stone fruits, is native to China and was introduced to Europe 2000 years ago. Peaches are now grown in temperate zones, worldwide. They were an important crop in Ontario by the 1880s and in BC by the 1890s. Peach trees are 3-5 m tall with long, narrow, pointed leaves, single, pink flowers, and fruits (5-8 cm diameter) with light fuzz. Fuzzless peaches are called nectarines. When ripe, varieties grown for the fresh market (in Canada, 80%) have sweet, juicy flesh; those for processing (20%) have firm, almost rubbery flesh adapted to mechanical handling.

In Canada peach trees are short-lived (10-20 years), beginning to bear fruit at 2-3 years. The least cold hardy of stone fruits (injured or killed by winter temperatures below -23°C), their culture is limited to southern BC and southern Ontario. Peaches thrive where summer temperatures are high. The season extends from July to Sept; growers plant 12 or more varieties, ripening at different times. In the semiarid valleys of BC, irrigation is essential for commercial culture. In Ontario, orchards are normally cultivated until July; a cover crop is then established to absorb surplus soil nitrogen, to slow tree growth and thus aid in hardening off for winter and to hold snow to protect the roots. In BC a permanent sod cover is usually established and orchards are not cultivated. Orchards are baited in fall and trees are painted with repellants to discourage injury from animals. Peaches are susceptible to various insect pests, mites, nematodes and PLANT DISEASES. Raw peaches are high in vitamin A. In 1980, 45 136 t were produced, with a farm value of $18.5 million.
R.E.C. LAYNE

Peachey, James, painter, surveyor (probably b in Eng; d in Martinique? 24 Nov 1797). He was an officer in the British army, attached to the surveyor general of Canada, Samuel HOLLAND (around 1781), and the staff assigned to settle the LOYALISTS. He was later deputy surveyor general. He is best known for his watercolour sketches of contemporary events, such as the arrival of the Loyalists along the St Lawrence R. He also illustrated *The Book of Common Prayer — translated into the Mohawk language by Joseph Brant* (1787). It is assumed he died during an epidemic in the West Indies. JAMES MARSH

Pear (genus *Pyrus*), common name for over 20 species of fruit-bearing and ornamental TREES of the ROSE family. The genus is indigenous to Europe and Asia. The European pear (*P. communis*), which produces buttery, juicy and aromatic FRUIT, is the most widely grown. In Canada, commercial pear production is limited to regions with a mild winter climate, including the OKANAGAN VALLEY, BC; southern Ontario, and NS. In other regions, hybrids of the Ussurian (*P. ussuriensis*) and European pears are grown in home gardens. Pear varieties are asexually propagated by grafting on seedling rootstocks. Bartlett, the most important variety, is marketed fresh and as canned halves and baby food. Anjou and Bosc varieties are marketed only as fresh fruit — Anjou all year with the use of controlled-atmosphere storage methods. Kieffer was once important in the canning industry but recently its use has declined. Fire blight is especially troublesome in warm, humid regions of Ontario. Pear Psylla is a sucking insect which produces a sticky ooze; a black fungal growth develops on the ooze, disfiguring the fruit. In 1980, 39 405 t of pears were produced, with a farm value of $11.2 million. H.A. QUAMME

Pearce, Joseph Algernon, astrophysicist (b at Brantford, Ont 7 Feb 1893). Together with J.S. PLASKETT, the first director of the Dominion Astrophysical Observatory in Victoria, BC, Pearce demonstrated that the sun is two-thirds from the centre of our galaxy and rotates in 220 million years. He studied radial velocities of O- and B-type stars, catalogued the observable B stars and found that 40% are double stars, and estimated the temperatures and dimensions of representative giant eclipsing double stars. Director of the Dominion Astrophysical Observatory 1940-52, Pearce was active in the International Astronomical Union, the Royal Astronomical Soc of Canada (president, 1940) and the American Astronomical Soc (vice-president, 1944-46). Elected a fellow of the Royal Soc of Canada in 1931, he was president in 1949. Pearce was a major in the Canadian forces in WWI, and is a Freemason and an enthusiastic philatelist. K.O. WRIGHT

Pearce, William, surveyor, civil servant (b near Port Talbot, Canada W 1 Feb 1848; d at Calgary 3 Mar 1930). Pearce journeyed W as a public-land surveyor for the federal Dept of the Interior in 1874 and was promoted superintendent of mines in 1884. Responsible for resource development and land use, Pearce was particularly concerned with arid-land administration and developed the federal irrigation and grazing policies in southern Alberta. In 1899 he joined the CPR to advise the company on its vast irrigation and settlement scheme. Pearce also helped establish Canada's national parks system. DAVID H. BREEN

Pearkes, George Randolph, soldier, politician (b at Watford, Eng 26 Feb 1883; d at Victoria 30 May 1984). He immigrated to Canada in 1906, homesteaded in Alberta, and then joined the RNWMP. He enlisted in the 2nd Canadian Mounted Rifles in 1915 and by 1918 commanded the 116th Battalion, CEF. One of the most decorated Canadian officers, he remained in the army, commanded the 1st Canadian Infantry Division in the UK (1940-42) until appointed general officer commanding, Pacific Command. His support of CONSCRIPTION led him to resign in 1945 to enter federal politics as a Conservative. He became minister of national defence (1957-60) during a critical period when production of the AVRO ARROW aircraft was halted, the Bomarc missile introduced, and the use of atomic warheads by Canada's armed forces hotly debated. Appointed lieutenant-governor of BC in 1960, he retired in 1968. R.H. ROY

Pearson, John Andrew, architect (b at Chesterfield, Eng 22 June 1867; d at Toronto 11 June 1940). Pearson, in partnership with Frank Darling, built up one of the most successful architectural practices in Canada. Trained at Sheffield, Pearson immigrated to Canada in 1888. In 1893 he was employed by Darling and Sproatt of Toronto and this firm, which became Darling and Pearson in 1893, endured until 1923. Darling and Pearson were best known for their bank designs and large office buildings designed in the grand classical manner of the École des beaux-arts. In 1916 Pearson designed with J. Omer MARCHAND the new PARLIAMENT BUILDINGS in Ottawa. JANET WRIGHT

Pearson, Lester Bowles, "Mike," statesman, politician, public servant (b at Newtonbrook, Ont 23 Apr 1897; d at Ottawa 27 Dec 1972). Pearson was Canada's foremost diplomat and formulated its basic post-WWII foreign policy. A skilled politician, he rebuilt the Liberal Party and as prime minister strove to maintain Canada's national unity. Son of a Methodist parson, Pearson spent his childhood moving from one parsonage to another before enrolling in history at U of T. With the outbreak of WWI, he enlisted in the Canadian Army Medical Corps and in 1915 was shipped to Greece to join the Allied armies fighting the Bulgarians. After 2 years of stretcher-bearing, he transferred to the Royal Flying Corps in England. His military career came to a sudden end when he was run over by a London bus and invalided home.

After taking his BA at U of T in 1919, Pearson was undecided on a career. He tried law and business, won a fellowship to Oxford, and was hired by U of T to teach history, which he combined with tennis and coaching football. Pearson also married and soon had children. Finding a professor's salary insufficient, he joined the Department of External Affairs. By 1928 he had trained himself as a perceptive observer and an able writer, both useful qualities in his work. Pearson quickly attracted the attention of his deputy minister, O.D. SKELTON. In 1935 he was sent to London as first secretary in the Canadian High Commission, giving him a front-row seat as Europe drifted towards WWII. He was profoundly influenced by what he saw and thereafter attached great importance to collective defence in the face of dictatorships and aggression. In 1941 Pearson returned to Canada. He was sent to Washington as second-in-command at the Canadian Legation in 1942, where his easy-going personality and personal charm made him a great success, particularly with the press. In 1945 he was named Canadian ambassador to the US and attended the founding conference of the UNITED NATIONS at San Francisco.

Lester Pearson addressing the United Nations Assembly in March 1957, after the Israeli agreement to withdraw from captured Egyptian territory. Pearson won the Nobel Peace Prize for his efforts to bring peace to the Middle East (*courtesy United Nations*).

In Sept 1946 Pearson was summoned home by PM KING to become deputy minister (or under secretary) of external affairs. He continued to take a strong interest in the UN but also promoted a closer political and economic relationship between Canada and its principal allies, the US and the UK. Pearson's work culminated in Canada's joining NATO in 1949. He strongly supported a Western self-defence organization, although he hoped that its existence would persuade the USSR that aggression would be futile. By the time NATO was in place, Pearson had left the civil service for politics. In Sept 1948 he became minister of external affairs and subsequently represented Algoma East, Ont, in the House of Commons. As minister, he helped lead Canada into the Korean War as a contributor to the UN army and, in 1952, served as president of the UN General Assembly, where he tried to find a solution to the conflict. His efforts displeased the Americans, who considered him too inclined to compromise on difficult points of principle. Pearson's greatest diplomatic achievement came in 1956, when he proposed a UN peacekeeping force as means for easing the British and French out of Egypt. His plan was implemented, and as a reward he received the Nobel Peace Prize in 1957.

By then Pearson was no longer in office. He and the ST. LAURENT government were widely blamed for not standing by Britain in 1956. The Liberals were defeated, St. Laurent resigned as leader, and at a convention in Jan 1958 Pearson defeated Paul MARTIN to become leader. The Liberals faced a minority Conservative government under John DIEFENBAKER and in his first act as leader Pearson challenged Diefenbaker to resign and turn the government over to him. Diefenbaker ridiculed the idea and in the subsequent general election the Liberals were reduced to 49 of the 265 seats in the Commons. Pearson began the slow task of rebuilding the party. With the assistance of parliamentary debaters such as Paul Martin and J.W. PICKERSGILL and party workers such as Walter GORDON, Mitchell SHARP, and Maurice LAMONTAGNE, he re-established the Liberals as a national party and in the 1962 general election raised the party's total to 100 seats. In 1963 the Diefenbaker government collapsed over the issue of nuclear weapons and in the subsequent election the Liberals won 128 seats to form a minority government. Pearson took office 22 Apr 1963. His government was expected to be more businesslike than Diefenbaker's but proved instead to be accident-prone in aborting its first budget. Much of Parliament's time was spent in bitter partisan and personal wrangling, culminating in an interminable FLAG DEBATE of 1964. In 1965 Pearson called a general election but again failed to secure a majority. In the next year the MUNSINGER scandal erupted with even more partisan bitterness. The year 1965 marks a dividing line in his administration, as Finance Minister Walter Gordon departed and Jean MARCHAND and Pierre TRUDEAU from Québec became prominent in the Cabinet. Pearson's attempts in his first term to conciliate Québec and the other provinces with "co-operative federalism" and "bilingualism and biculturalism" were superseded by a firm federal response to provincial demands and by the Québec government's attempts to usurp federal roles in international relations. When, during his centennial visit, French President Charles de Gaulle uttered the separatist slogan "Vive le Québec libre" to a crowd in Montréal, Pearson issued an official rebuke and de Gaulle promptly went home. In Dec 1967 Pearson announced his intention to retire and in Apr 1968 a Liberal convention picked Pierre Trudeau as his successor.

For all its superficial chaos, the Pearson government left behind a notable legacy of legislation: a Canada Pension Plan, a universal medicare system, a unified armed forces, a new flag,

a revised transport act, and a new approach to the problem of Canada's disadvantaged regions through the Department of Regional Economic Expansion. Not all of these initiatives proved fruitful and some were costly, but they represented the high point of the Canadian WELFARE STATE that generations of social thinkers had dreamed about. In retirement Pearson worked on a study of international aid for the World Bank and on his memoirs.   ROBERT BOTHWELL
Reading: Robert Bothwell, *Pearson* (1978); L.B. Pearson, *Mike,* 3 vols (1972, 1973, 1975).

Pearson, Peter, film and TV director (b at Toronto 13 Mar 1938). He graduated from U of T and held various production roles at CBC TV 1961-66, including work on the celebrated "This Hour Has Seven Days." He studied film in Rome, was president of the Directors' Guild of Canada, 1972, and chairman of the Council of Canadian Filmmakers, 1973. As a free-lance director and producer with the CBC and National Film Board, he has won a number of Canadian film awards (eg, for *The Best Damn Fiddler From Kaladar to Calabogie, Saul Alinsky Went to War* and the feature *Paperback Hero*), and made numerous documentaries, short subjects and commercials. In 1983 he began working for the Canadian Film Development Corporation, after teaching film at Queen's U for a year.   JOHN L. KENNEDY

Peat, partially decomposed organic matter made up principally of decayed *Sphagnum* MOSS, together with other aquatic plants, GRASSES or SEDGES. Peat is formed slowly by the decay of vegetation under anaerobic (oxygen-deficient) conditions. Canada's extensive peat bogs developed since the last GLACIATION, about 10 000 years ago (*see* SWAMP, MARSH AND BOG). At all stages of development peat contains about 95% water by weight. The high water content has always been the main barrier to its extensive exploitation as an ENERGY source; however, dried peat has been one of the traditional fuels in places where bogs are of high quality and easily accessible (eg, Ireland).

Peatlands cover approximately 12% of Canada's land surface. Much of the resource is located in inaccessible northern areas but significant deposits occur in the Atlantic provinces, southern Québec and Ontario. This peat could be used for energy production, particularly in areas lacking other energy resources; however, at present, Canadian peat is recovered exclusively for horticultural purposes. Interest in peat fuel has increased recently; one study on peat-fired ELECTRIC-POWER GENERATION concluded that peat was economical, compared with oil-fired or coal-fired stations, in NB. HYDRO-QUÉBEC has studied the feasibility of peat-fired power stations and has been considering plant gasification to replace diesel generation on Ile d'Anticosti. Newfoundland is developing a peat bog to determine the practicality and cost of transporting fuel peat on the island. Peat-burning tests have been conducted at a Grand Falls, Nfld, pulp and paper mill. Newfoundland is also interested in the potential of small, peat-fired generators in isolated communities. The 1981 House of Commons Special Committee on Alternative Energy and Oil Substitution concluded that peat could be "a significant alternative energy opportunity" for Canada. A particularly attractive option would be to produce methanol from peat-derived synthesis gas; the methanol could substitute for PETROLEUM products as a portable liquid fuel.

Perhaps one reason that peat development has been slow in Canada has been the lack of experience with the resource. In Europe, extensive research and development programs exist and the technology of harvesting and using peat is well developed. World peat resources (those over 50 cm thick) are estimated at some 145 billion t dry weight, with an energy equivalent of about 63.5 billion t of oil. The USSR has the largest reserve; Canada's resource, second largest in the world, is about one-sixth that of the USSR. More than 6000 MW of the USSR's ELECTRIC POWER, equivalent to over 6% of Canada's electrical generation, is peat fired, and about 4.5 million t of peat are produced annually for home heating. Finland has several peat-burning power stations which produce electricity and provide steam and hot water for district heating. Ireland obtains about one-third of its electric power from 7 peat-fired generating stations, which consume about 56% of Ireland's annual peat harvest of 5 million t. The NATIONAL RESEARCH COUNCIL OF CANADA has established a Peat Program designed to define Canada's peat resources, develop harvesting and utilization technology, assess and reduce environmental impacts and develop carbon-added products.

Peat bogs differ from other types of wetlands in that they are nourished almost entirely from rainwater. Their surface is a continuous carpet of *Sphagnum* moss which supports a layer of grass and shrubs and, occasionally, trees. In Canada peat bogs may be tens of kilometres across but generally are much smaller. A peat bog is made up of layers, the top layer being living bog vegetation; the second, very young peat; the third, of varying thickness, becomes darker and denser with depth until the black colour and puttylike consistency of mature peat is encountered. Because peat occurs on the surface rather than below ground, its removal is unlikely to cause environmental problems. However, care is needed during and after harvesting to ensure that harvested bogs do not become muddy wastelands.

Peatlands usually require several years of preparation before production can begin. The bog must first be surveyed to determine the quantity and quality of the resource, drainage requirements and access routes. The second step is drainage: because peat is 95% water, it cannot support heavy machinery; removal of as much moisture as possible is essential. A network of drainage ditches begins the process; the ditches are deepened as the bog consolidates. This stage normally takes 5-7 years and reduces the bog's water content to about 90%. After drainage, the bog is levelled to facilitate drying and mechanical handling. The final step is building a network of light railways over the bog's surface for handling and transporting the peat. The bog is then ready for decades of harvesting, typically at a rate of a few centimetres per year, as the surface dries.

Harvested peat can be marketed in 3 forms. Sod peat is made by a large cutting machine which dredges peat from all depths of the bog, mixes it and forms it into sods. The sods are all of similar quality and can compete in the marketplace with other industrial fuels. Milled peat is scraped from the surface of the bog in the form of a course powder. After drying, milled peat can either be burned (eg, in power stations), or processed into briquettes. About one-fifth of the energy in peat is lost when it is processed into small, tightly packed briquettes, used primarily for home heating. *See* BIOMASS ENERGY.
                                    ROBERT BOTT

Peavey, a lever for handling logs, invented in 1858 by a Maine blacksmith as a simple refinement of the earlier canthook, greatly facilitating the downriver timber drive. Each peavey carried a thumblike hook near the base of its handle. It was generally about 25 cm longer than the 100 cm canthook and its distinctive spiked tip gripped the log more securely than did the iron ferrule and jutting toe of the canthook. *See* TIMBER TRADE HISTORY.   GRAEME WYNN

Peckford, Alfred Brian, teacher, politician, premier of Newfoundland (b at Whitbourne, Nfld 27 Aug 1942). Peckford was first elected to the House of Assembly on 24 Mar 1972. In 1973 he was a special assistant to Frank MOORES; in 1974 minister of municipal affairs and housing; and in 1976 minister of mines and energy. In 1977 he asserted Newfoundland's ownership of offshore petroleum resources and regulated the conditions for exploration by oil companies. By 1978 exploration companies were using drilling permits from both the Newfoundland and federal governments. His stand gained widespread public support and enabled him to win his party's leadership in Mar 1979. In that year and in 1982 he won election by offering a future of prosperity based on the successful control and management of Newfoundland's resources. His efforts to secure greater provincial control were marked by jurisdictional disputes with the federal government. In *The Past in the Present* (1983), Peckford presented his perspectives on the past mismanagement of natural resources and put forward suggestions for Newfoundland's social and economic direction. Following a stormy campaign, he was re-elected in 1985 with a reduced majority.   MELVIN BAKER

Peden, William J., "Torchy," cyclist (b at Victoria, BC 16 Apr 1906; d at Chicago, Ill 25 Jan 1980). As a youth, Peden participated in several sports and was a nationally ranked swimmer. A member of Canada's cycling team at the 1928 Amsterdam Olympics, he afterwards won several important races in Europe. He turned professional in 1929 and joined the Six-Day racing circuit, achieving acclaim in N America and Europe. A large man, he was a crowd favourite during the heyday of this unusual sport. He won 38 of 148 races between 1929 and 1948, a record that stood until 1965.   J. THOMAS WEST

Pediatrics is that branch of medicine concerned with the child, its development, care and diseases. As a specialty in Canada it originated with the development of hospitals for children. The first, the Hospital for Sick Children, was founded, in Toronto, in 1875 and by 1919 had established an international reputation. The Montreal Children's Hospital (at the Montreal General) was established in 1903, and the Winnipeg Children's Hospital in 1909. To these centres, in the 1920s, came eager, well-trained pediatricians such as Alan Brown (Toronto), Alton Goldbloom (Montréal) and Gordon Chown (Winnipeg). As a result of the emphasis in pediatric medicine on nutrition, hygiene, and immunization against the serious infections that beset children, child mortality rates from infectious diseases dropped dramatically. The Canadian Paediatric Society was founded in 1923, to promote "the advancement of knowledge of the physiology, pathology, psychology and therapeutics of infancy and childhood." The society, which has since expanded its role, maintains close liaison with the American Academy of Pediatrics. In the 1950s some surgeons began to specialize in pediatric surgery; the Canadian Association of Paediatric Surgeons was founded in 1967 and maintains close ties with the Canadian Paediatric Society.

Internationally recognized Canadian pediatricians include Bruce Chown in Rh immunization; Robert A. Usher and Paul Swyer for the care of the newborn; Charles Scriver and F. Clark Fraser in genetics; John D. Keith and Richard D. Rowe in cardiology; and Henri J. Breault for the development of containers with safety caps for toxic medications. Other specialists are raising the standards of care and expanding research in such diverse fields as neonatal medicine, developmental pediatrics, the care of the handicapped child and intensive care for critically injured children.

                                    WILLIAM C. TAYLOR

Pedlar, a derogatory term used in the days of the FUR TRADE by HUDSON'S BAY COMPANY men to describe any trader from Québec, and later any trader from the NORTH WEST COMPANY, who "peddled" his goods to the Indians by taking them to their encampments rather than having the Indians transport their furs to the trading post.   JOHN ROBERT COLOMBO

Peel, Paul, figure painter (b at London, Canada W 7 Nov 1860; d at Paris, France 11 Oct 1892). Trained first at the Pennsylvania Academy of Fine Arts in Philadelphia with the great American figure painter Thomas Eakins, Peel studied at the Royal Academy Schools in London and at the École des beaux-arts in Paris. His sentimental studies of children, such as *The Tired Model* (1889) and *After the Bath* (1890), are widely admired. He was one of the first Canadian painters to portray nude figures, as in his delicately erotic *A Venetian Bather* (1889). His small impressionistic sketches achieve a remarkable freshness; his large canvases have a slicker, more finished surface. Peel spent most of his working life in Paris. During a brief return to Canada in 1890, the low prices his work brought at a Toronto auction caused him considerable grief.   JOAN MURRAY

Pegahmagabow, Francis, Anishnabe (Ojibwa) chief, Indian rights advocate, war hero (b at Shawanaga, Ont 9 Mar 1889 into the Caribou clan; d at Parry I, Ont 5 Aug 1952). A WWI hero, Pegahmagabow became a vocal advocate for Indian rights and self-determination. He was promoted lance corporal in 1915 and was awarded the military medal and 2 bars for his excellence as sniper and scout in the battles of Ypres (1916), Passchendaele (1917) and Amiens (1918). He was twice elected chief of the Parry I Ojibwa band. Throughout his life he eloquently fought with his pen against transgressions of Indian treaty rights.   FRANZ M. KOENNECKE

Peguis, Saulteaux chief (b near Sault Ste Marie, Ont c1774; d at Red River, Man 28 Sept 1864). Although a prominent leader of his own people, Peguis became famous for his role in aiding the Selkirk settlers. Upon their arrival at Red River in 1812, he defended them, showed them how to subsist from the country, and later assisted the survivors after the SEVEN OAKS INCIDENT. Peguis and his wife were baptized by Anglican missionaries in 1840 and took the names William and Victoria King, their children adopting the name of Prince. Although he remained friendly with whites, Peguis later became disillusioned because of trespassing on his reserve and violations of his 1817 treaty with Lord SELKIRK.   HUGH A. DEMPSEY

Peigan form the largest of the 3 tribes of the BLACKFOOT NATION. Their name is a corruption of the word *apiku'ni,* meaning "badly tanned robe." They were known to fur traders as the Muddy River Indians. The official spelling of the tribe's name in Canada is Peigan; in the US it is Piegan. Of Algonquian linguistic stock, they speak the same language as the BLOOD and BLACKFOOT, with only slight dialectal variations. The Peigan once occupied a vast hunting ground which ranged along the foothills from Rocky Mountain House to Heart Butte, Montana, and extended eastward onto the plains. By the mid-19th century they had moved farther S to an area encompassing the Teton R and Marias R in Montana and the Milk R region in Alberta. They also travelled as far N as Ft Edmonton and E to the present Alberta-Saskatchewan border.

Because of the tribe's large size, the Peigan eventually divided into 2 smaller groups, the N and S Peigan, although they often travelled together and were so intermingled that a clear division was impossible. The population of the 2 groups ranged between 3000 and 5000 persons, reaching a low of 2500 after the 1837 smallpox epidemic. In 1870 the population of the S Peigan was 3240 and the N Peigan 720. The Peigan were a nomadic, buffalo-hunting tribe

(*see* BUFFALO HUNT), with complex religious and warrior societies. Their enemies included the Crow, Shoshoni, Nez Percé, DAKOTA and ASSINIBOINE tribes.

In 1855 the N and S Peigan were prominent signers of a treaty with the Americans, but by 1877 the southern group had already settled on a reservation in Montana, so only the N Peigan signed Treaty No 7 with the Canadian government. They selected a reserve near Pincher Creek, Alta. In later years the S Peigan adopted the official title of Blackfeet Indians of Montana, and the N Peigans in Canada simply called themselves Peigan. Their reserve provides some opportunities for farming and ranching, although the tribe has faced the common problems of integration and disruption of their social and cultural life (*see* INDIAN RESERVE). Efforts have been made to establish small industries on the reserve and many Peigan have sought employment away from the area. By the 1980s the population of the reserve in Canada had grown to almost 2000 persons. *See also* NATIVE PEOPLE: PLAINS and general articles under NATIVE PEOPLE.   HUGH A. DEMPSEY
Reading: Hugh A. Dempsey, *Indian Tribes of Alberta* (1979).

Péladeau, Pierre, publisher (b at Outremont, Qué 11 Apr 1925). He studied philosophy at U de M and law at McGill. After graduating from McGill (1950), he bought a suburban Montréal newspaper. In 1952 he added 4 other papers, and in 1964 founded the daily *Le Journal de Montréal,* later adding *Le Journal de Québec.* In 1984 he was president and principal owner of Québecor, the major newspaper chain in Québec, which owns, in addition to the dailies mentioned, some 27 weeklies, 8 printing plants and book-publication and film-development divisions. In 1980 Québecor had 46.5% of the circulation of all francophone papers in Canada. Péladeau is also a director of the Caisse de dépôt et placement du Québec.   JORGE NIOSI

White pelican (*artwork by John Crosby*).

Pelican (Pelecanidae), family of large water BIRDS with long, flat bills, expandable throat pouches, and 4 toes connected by a web. Six species occur worldwide; 2 in Canada. The white pelican (*Pelecanus erythrorhynchos*) nests locally in the western provinces. The brown pelican (*P. occidentalis*), a marine species of the southern US, is a casual visitor to the BC coast. Characterized by a 32-36 cm orange bill, adult white pelicans weigh 4.8-8.2 kg and have black-tipped wings, spanning 2.4-2.9 m. Flying pelicans form a line and, together, alternate between flapping and gliding flight. In flight, the head is drawn back, bill resting on the breast. White pelicans nest, colonially, on islands in remote lakes. Approximately 2200 pairs nest on Primrose Lk, Sask; most colonies contain fewer than 150 pairs. Nonbreeders frequent lakes away from breeding sites. Isolation during nest building and incubation is critical, as adults may abandon nests if disturbed. A gregarious, slow-maturing bird, the white pelican feeds from the water surface, trapping prey in

the expandable lower bill and pouch. Birds often co-operate to drive prey into shallow water. Although often regarded as predators of game fish, pelicans subsist primarily on coarse fish (perch, suckers, minnows and stickleback). The belief that pelicans carry fish in the pouch is false; prey are swallowed and regurgitated to young.   PHILIP H.R. STEPNEY

Pellan, Alfred, painter (b at Québec City 16 May 1906). In 1923, while Pellan was still a student at Québec's École des beaux-arts (1920-25), the National Gallery of Canada purchased his painting *Corner of Old Quebec.* Pellan also won the first government of Québec fine-arts scholarship in 1926, enabling him to study in Paris where he remained until 1940. There the colour in Pellan's still lifes and figure studies became more intense, his linear rhythms more fluid, his images more abstract. Pellan's most outstanding achievement during his Paris sojourn was winning first prize at the 1935 exposition of mural art. When he returned to Canada because of WWII he settled in Montréal. Although work he brought from Paris received acclaim during exhibitions in 1940 at Québec and Montréal, Pellan's cubist and surrealist art was considered too avant-garde and he sold little. To survive, he taught at Montréal's École des beaux-arts 1943-52. His objections to the restrictive, academic philosophy of its director, Charles Maillard, resulted in Maillard's resignation in 1945 and a more liberal atmosphere there.

In the mid-1940s Pellan began illustrating poetry books and designed costumes and sets for the theatre. During this period he developed his mature style. He was increasingly drawn to surrealism; his imagery became more erotic and his always strikingly coloured paintings larger, more complex and textured. His refusal to be affiliated with any particular school of art led to the formation in 1948 of Prisme d'yeux, a group of artists whose manifesto called for an art free of restrictive ideology.

In 1952 Pellan received an RSC grant and moved to Paris, living there until 1955, when he became the first Canadian to have a solo exhibition at the Musée national d'art moderne. On his return to Canada, numerous exhibitions and mural commissions established his reputation nationally.   REESA GREENBERG
Reading: G. Lefebvre, *Pellan* (1973); Reesa Greenberg, *The Drawings of Alfred Pellan* (1980).

Alfred Pellan, *Self-Portrait* (*courtesy Alfred Pellan*).

Pellatt, Sir Henry Mill, capitalist (b at Kingston, Canada W 16 Jan 1859; d at Toronto 8 Mar 1939). Pellatt was educated at Upper Canada Coll and had a distinguished athletic career before joining his father's brokerage firm. He was active in the development of hydroelectric projects at NIAGARA FALLS, Ont, and in the transmission and distribution of power in Toronto, until the provincial government created the Ontario Hydro-Electric Power Commission and nationalized many of the private companies. He was also active in several transportation companies and in the organization of the Canadian General Electric Co. He took a keen interest in the Canadian militia. His eccentric stone mansion, Casa Loma, has become a Toronto landmark. He was created KB in 1905.   T.D. REGEHR

Pelletier, Gérard, journalist, labour and social activist, politician, diplomat (b at Victoriaville, Qué 21 June 1919). One of 8 children of a working-class family, Pelletier was educated at the Séminaire de Nicolet, Collège Mont-Laurier and the U de M. He was secretary-general of Québec's Jeunesse étudiante catholique 1939-43 and field secretary of the World Student Relief organization in Geneva, 1945-47. After touring Argentina, he and his wife Alexandrine returned to Montréal where he became a reporter for *Le DEVOIR* 1947-50. His reporting of the 1949 ASBESTOS STRIKE brought him the position of director of *Le Travail*, the organ of the Confédération des travailleurs catholiques du Canada. In 1961 he left to become editor of *La PRESSE*; after a prolonged strike in 1964 the owners of *La Presse* fired him for his radical editorial views. His radical ideas developed during the war when he was influenced by the French social catholics, especially the personalist philosophy of Emmanuel Mounier and the review *Esprit*. He was inspired, with several colleagues, including Pierre Elliott TRUDEAU, to found CITÉ LIBRE. Through *Cité libre* and Radio-Canada, Pelletier and the others denounced the socially regressive and antidemocratic practices and policies of the DUPLESSIS regime as well as the clericalism of the Quebec Catholic Church. They advocated using the state and dynamic labour organizations to create a modern, democratic and pluralistic Québec society. Pelletier's SOCIAL DEMOCRACY contributed to the reemergence of ideological pluralism in Québec during the 1950s.

When that ideological pluralism and Confederation were threatened by the rise of SEPARATISM in the 1960s, Pelletier, Trudeau and his longtime friend in the Catholic labour movement, Jean MARCHAND, decided to enter federal politics in 1965. Pelletier served as secretary of state for external affairs (1968-72) and minister of communications (1972-75) in the Trudeau administration. He helped formulate the federal government's response to the growing crisis in Québec/Ottawa relations. He pursued this goal as Canadian ambassador to France, 1975-81, and then became ambassador to the UN, 1981-84.   MICHAEL D. BEHIELS

Pelletier, Wilfred, or Baibomsey, meaning "traveller," Odawa wise man, philosopher, author (b Wikwemikong Reserve, Manitoulin I, Ont 16 Oct 1927). His voice is expressive of the unity of all terrestrial life with the Earth, and with his quiet eloquence he can inspire listeners of different ages and backgrounds. Especially interested in education, he believes that there are better ways of learning than traditional Western methods, and he was active in the Rochdale College experiment in alternative learning in Toronto in the late 1960s. He served as codirector of the Nishnawbe Institute, an Indian cultural and educational project, and has been involved with a network of Indian elders concerned with the application of traditional Indian wisdom to 20th-century problems.   JOHN BENNETT

Pelletier, Wilfrid, conductor, pianist, administrator (b at Montréal 20 June 1896; d at New York City, NY 9 Apr 1982). He played a major role in the formation of Québec musical life, especially in the field of lyric theatre (opera) and with young people. He studied with Mme François Héraly (piano, solfeggio, harmony), Alfred LALIBERTÉ (interpretation) and Alexis Contant (harmony, composition) in Canada, and with Charles-Marie Widor (composition) and Camille Bellaigue (lyric repertory) in Paris. He held at different times the positions of rehearsal pianist for French repertory, and assistant conductor, artistic director and regular conductor of the Metropolitan Opera of New York. His many Canadian activities include the creation of the Matinées symphoniques pour la jeunesse (1935), the Montréal Festivals (1936) and the Conservatoire de musique du Québec à Montréal (1943). He was also first artistic director of the orchestra of the Société des concerts symphoniques de Montréal (1935-40), artistic director of the Québec Symphonic Orchestra (1951-66), director of musical education for Québec's Ministry of Cultural Affairs (1961-67), a founder of the Société de musique contemporaine du Québec (1966) and national chairman of JEUNESSES MUSICALES DU CANADA (1967-69). Pelletier was awarded the medal of the Canada Council (1962) and the medal of the Canadian Music Council (1975) and made a companion of the Order of Canada (1968).

HÉLÈNE PLOUFFE

Pelly Bay, NWT, Hamlet, pop 257 (1981c), is located on the eastern Arctic coast, 1312 air km NE of YELLOWKNIFE. The seal-dependent way of life of the Netsilingmiut Inuit of the area was untouched by the whaling and trapping periods that affected other areas of the North. Although first European contact came in 1829, it was not until 1935 that a white settler came to reside in the community (named for HBC governor Sir John Pelly). In the late 1970s a small commercial char fishery and fine ivory carving have come to supplement the hunting-trapping economy of local residents.

ANNELIES POOL

Pembroke, Ont, City, seat of Renfrew County, pop 14 026 (1981c), inc 1971, located on the OTTAWA R at the confluence of the Indian and Muskrat rivers, 158 km NW of Ottawa. Peter White, a retired naval petty officer who had served under Admiral Nelson and on Lk Ontario in the War of 1812, settled here 1828. The early communities, known as Campbellton and Mirimichi, became Pembroke in honour of Admiralty Secretary Sidney Herbert, son of the earl of Pembroke. Long associated with the lumber trade, the city currently produces veneers, plywood, matches, boxes and office furniture. It was the site of pioneering experiments in telephones and commercial lighting. The Pembroke Lumber Kings hockey club has won numerous championships. CFB PETAWAWA is located nearby. Pembroke has a bridge link over the Ottawa R to Québec.   K.L. MORRISON

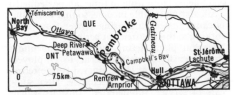

Pemmican [Cree *pimikan*, meaning "manufactured grease"] dried meat, usually BISON, pounded into coarse powder and mixed with an equal amount of melted fat, and occasionally saskatoon berries or other edibles. Cooled and sewn into bison-hide bags in 41 kg lots, pemmican could be stored and shipped with ease to provision FUR-TRADE personnel. Peter POND is credited with introducing this vital food to the trade in 1779, having obtained it from the CHIPEWYANS in the Athabasca region. Later, posts along the Red, Assiniboine and N Saskatchewan rivers were devoted to acquiring pemmican from the Plains Indians and MÉTIS. Pemmican was also made and used outside the region, eg, by the Royal Navy, which provisioned several arctic expeditions with beef pemmican made in England.   JOHN E. FOSTER

Penfield, Wilder Graves, neurosurgeon, scientist (b at Spokane, Wash 26 Jan 1891; d at Montréal 5 Apr 1976). He was founder and first director of the Montreal Neurological Inst and established the "Montreal procedure" for the surgical treatment of epilepsy.

Having obtained a B Litt from Princeton in 1913, Penfield attended Merton College, Oxford. There he was influenced by 2 great medical teachers, Sir William OSLER, who became his lifelong hero, and the eminent neurophysiologist Charles Sherrington, who introduced him to experimental investigation of the nervous system. After graduating with an MD from Johns Hopkins in 1918, he served as surgeon to the Presbyterian Hospital (affiliated with Columbia) and to the New York Neurological Inst 1921-28. His studies in 1924 with the Madrid neurohistologist Pio del Rio-Hortega provided him with metallic staining techniques that yielded new information on the glia, the supporting cells of the nervous system. In 1928 he learned from the German surgeon Otfrid Foerster the method of excising brain scars to relieve focal epilepsy. That year he moved with his neurosurgical partner, William Vernon Cone, to work at Montréal's Royal Victoria Hospital, where they became associated with neurologist Colin K. Russel. In 1934, supported by the Rockefeller Foundation, the government of Québec, the City of Montréal and private donors, Penfield founded the Montreal Neurological Inst, which rapidly became an international centre for teaching, research and treatment related to diseases of the nervous system. He was to be its director until 1960.

Epilepsy became Penfield's great teacher. His surgical studies yielded reports on brain tumours, the pial circulation, the mechanisms of headache, the localization of motor, sensory and speech functions, and the role of the hippocampus in memory mechanisms. Epilepsy arising in the temporal lobe of the brain assumed special importance because of the re-excitation of past experiences that occurred when the cortex was stimulated during surgery. Some of the modern theories of separable function of the 2 cerebral hemispheres were built upon his findings. His concept of centrencephalic seizures arising from deep midline portions of the brain had an important impact on the understanding of the relationship between the brain's structures and consciousness. Penfield's work brought him many high honours both within Canada and abroad. His scientific papers and the handbooks and monographs he wrote with associates became standard reference works on the function of the human brain.

In the last 15 years of his life Penfield enjoyed a second career as a writer of historical novels and medical biography. He devoted himself to public service, particularly in support of university education, and became first president of the Vanier Inst of the Family. He was widely known for promoting early second-language training. His writings from this period include *The Mystery of the Mind* (1975), summarizing his views on the mind/brain problem, and *No Man Alone* (1977), an autobiography of the years 1891-1934.

Penfield's most lasting legacy was the foundation and the establishment by endowment of the Montreal Neurological Inst. This neurological hospital integrated with a brain-research complex continues to provide a centre where both basic scientists and physicians study the brain and has served as a model for similar units throughout the world. To Penfield the brain and the nervous system represented the most important unexplored field in the whole of science. "The problem of neurology," he wrote, "is to understand man himself." WILLIAM FEINDEL

Pension, lifetime payment by a government or employer in consideration of past service after individuals have retired from employment because of age or disability or because they have reached some specified age; this payment may be continued, at the same or a reduced level, to the individual's spouse or other survivors. Public pension plans, which include the federal OLD AGE PENSION (Old Age Security Programs or OAS), the Guaranteed Annual Supplement (GIS) and the CANADA PENSION PLAN or QUÉBEC PENSION PLAN (CPP or QPP), cover all the population or virtually all the labour force. Public plans are schemes for intergenerational transfers. The pensions they provide to the retired and the elderly are financed by taxes levied largely on the younger population. Private pension plans, which cover people working for a particular employer or a group of employers, include government-employee plans. Under private plans contributions are invested to be made available (augmented) at a later period. Any element of transfer in private plans is incidental.

Public Pensions The first national social-security system for old age pensions was established by German Chancellor Otto von Bismarck in 1889. By 1925, most European states had enacted similar schemes. In 1935 the American Social Security Act, a pay-as-you-go system with only a relatively small fund built up to cover fluctuations in the ratio of payments to taxes, was passed. During and after WWI the movement in Canada for a "mother's pension," fuelled by a similar movement in the US and by the development of federal war-service pensions and social-insurance benefits for widows, was opposed by private charitable institutions on the grounds that public pensions would encourage dependency. However, in 1920 the BC legislature passed a Mother's Pension Act which allowed women to apply for a small, assured monthly income for themselves and for their children under the age of 16. But in 1931 the government tightened the eligibility qualifications and cut back the services to mothers. The inclusiveness of pension plans for mothers in other provinces varied, as did the generosity of the allowances provided.

Under Canada's first public pensions legislation, the Old Age Pension Act (1927), the federal government reimbursed provinces for 50% of the cost of pensions up to $20 per month that were paid by the provinces, after a means test, to persons aged 70 or more. In 1931 the federal share was increased to 75%, but the plan only became national in 1937 when all provinces adopted compatible legislation (*see* SOCIAL SECURITY). The level of benefits and other provisions were adjusted until 1951 when the Act was replaced by the Old Age Security Act, under which $40 monthly was paid to everyone aged 70 or over who passed a residence test. By 1963 the amount had risen to $75.00. With the introduction (1965) of the CPP and QPP, which are compulsory plans based on earnings, 91% of the labour force was covered and provision was made for the gradual reduction from 70 to 65 years of age for eligibility for OAS benefits. The CPP and QPP (phased in over 10 years) are financed by taxes levied on the employee and employer, and the resulting revenues are segregated from the general tax revenues. The revenues from these plans comprise 25% of average individual pensionable earnings; they also include survivor and disability benefits. The GIS, designed to ensure, with the OAS, a minimum socially accepted income for the aged, was also introduced in 1966. The GIS is reduced by $1 for every $2 of non-OAS income. The original maximum supplement for individuals was $40 of OAS payment per month. By 1982 it was $233.89 per month (OAS was $239.73) and was not available if non-OAS income exceeded $5600 (the rates are different for married couples). The OAS and GIS are financed from general tax revenues. The CPP and QPP, GIS and OAS have been tied to the CONSUMER PRICE INDEX (CPI) with a maximum annual change of 2%. By Jan 1974 all 3 pensions were fully indexed to the CPI; the OAS and GIS are adjusted quarterly, the CPP and QPP annually.

Private Pensions Even before the 19th century, governments provided pensions for disabled veterans and for war widows. Pension plans for public servants, which replaced various ad-hoc payments, were instituted in the last half of the 19th century. The GRAND TRUNK RAILWAY introduced the first private-sector employee plan in 1874, but the Labour Commission criticized the GTR for compelling its employees to pay 80% of the cost of their own benefits and for requiring them to waive their rights to any disability or death allowances, even if these resulted from company negligence. The coverage of private-sector plans established by railways and financial institutions has been expanded into other areas of the economy but it is still partial and a matter of public concern. It has been suggested that the private plans should be made compulsory, with a transfer of pension credits between employers, or that both the level of earnings covered by the CPP and QPP and the proportion of such earnings awarded as a pension be increased. Benefits in employer pension plans are calculated by various formulas — final earnings, career average earnings and flat benefits. Under a final earnings formula, a pension is based upon the contributor's length of service and average earnings in the final years of employment, eg, 5 years or on the best average earnings over a limited period; typically such a formula would result in a pension equal to one-sixtieth of average annual earnings just before retirement, multiplied by years of service. Career average earnings uses a similar formula. According to the flat benefits formula, the pension is calculated as a specific number of dollars for each year of service. In addition there are money-purchase plans where the benefits obtained depend on contributions over time and on the rates of return on these contributions. Although, for taxation and regulation purposes, the latter are generally considered as pension plans, they resemble savings plans because no pension formula exists and because payments are limited to the accumulated value of contributions. An important example of individual savings plans for retirement purposes are Registered Retirement Savings Plans. Legislation providing for them was enacted in 1957, and individual contributions up to a maximum that has been altered from time to time can be deducted in calculating taxable income, so that individuals can transfer purchasing power from their working to their retirement period.

Pension plans define the conditions under which pension benefits accrue to employees whose employment is terminated before retirement. Employees may be eligible, after some years of service, for deferred pensions, calculated according to their years of employment and average earnings, and payable when they reach retirement age. In other cases employees may be permitted to withdraw from pension plans and to have their individual contributions (accumulated at some specified rate of interest) returned. Because pension rights for workers who change employers could be lost, most provinces require that at a minimum pension benefit must be vested in an employee who has reached 45 years of age and worked for 10 years. In such cases the employee's pension contributions are locked in and cannot be withdrawn (subject to certain exemptions) from the plan. These provisions have helped mobile workers; but deferred pensions are related to past earnings which may be substantially below the individual's earnings at retirement. In addition, many years of employment could still slip through the safety net of these provisions, and there are proposals for earlier vesting. The CANADIAN COUNCIL ON SOCIAL DEVELOPMENT reported that of the 2.8 million (40% of the working population) persons covered by private pension plans in 1970, about 40% were employed by government or by crown corporations, so that nearly 70% of those employed by private companies were not receiving coverage. The Canadian Labour Congress estimated that of those covered only 4-10% collect benefits because many employees quit their jobs before they can collect.

Pension Funds Employers must have sufficient funds to pay private pensions. When they were first established, benefits under private plans were often financed out of the employers' current incomes, but a guaranteed payment required that contributions be set aside each year to build up a fund adequate to cover the payment of promised pensions. Legislation now requires that private plans be funded in this way. The cost of the eventual pension earned by employment in the present depends on factors such as rates of return on investment and future earnings that can only be estimated now. Changes either in benefits or contributions might be required from time to time to meet funding standards. American legislation also requires funding for private plans, but in some European countries, eg, France, the plans are operated on a pay-as-you-go system, with only minimum reserves being kept, possibly because they are compulsory for employees in a geographical area or broad industrial sector. The pensions are guaranteed by the contributions of all workers even though the particular enterprise for which a pensioner has worked may have gone out of business. Technically, these plans, though private, resemble public plans; the compulsory contributions are similar to taxes that result in transfers.

Pensions and Inflation INFLATION in the 1970s and 1980s has highlighted one of the problems of funded private pension plans. If benefits are tied to final earnings (and the importance of such provisions has increased), then the initial pensions benefit tends to be protected against inflation because earnings keep up with inflation, but its real value can be quickly eroded during retirement. With inflation of 8% over 15 years an unindexed pension for $1.00 is worth 32¢. Very few plans outside the public-sector pensions are indexed to the CPI. Funds may be invested in bonds, equities, mortgages and even real estate, but no particular real rate of return over any period of time in an uncertain world is assured. Interest rates tend to rise during inflationary periods and there have been proposals to adjust nominal pensions by the excess of interest earned over some inflation-free rate, eg, 3 percent. This would be an improvement over the current situation, but would not necessarily guarantee the real value of pensions. Expansion of the scope of public pensions is supported because they, with taxes based on current earnings, are protected against inflation. A potential weakness of public plans is the possible increase in the ratio of workers to pensions because of demographic changes (*see* AGING), which could increase the burden of pension taxes on workers and possibly lead to a dilution of the real value of pensions.

A. ASIMAKOPULOS

Pentecostal Movement in Canada was begun by EVANGELICAL Christians who believed that the world was ripe for a spiritual revival and therefore organized prayer services. Many early Pentecostals were from HOLINESS CHURCHES, and held that the faithful must be sanctified by the Holy Spirit after they had been saved. After learning that a revival had begun under W.J. Seymour in Los Angeles, some Canadian evangelicals travelled there to participate. The first report on 9 Apr 1906 emphasized the signs of the revival, especially the initial sign of speaking in other languages when the believer had been filled with the Spirit. This message of the "baptism of the Holy Spirit" was accepted first at the Hebden Mission on Queen St in Toronto. Soon ANGLICANS, MENNONITES, Roman Catholics and METHODISTS were joining those from evangelical and holiness denominations in affirming that they, like Christ's apostles on the first Christian Pentecost (Acts 2), had spoken in other, unlearned languages, as evidence of this "second blessing." In time it became accepted that "speaking in tongues" was the pre-eminent sign of the baptism of the Holy Spirit.

Hostility from home churches and the need to share their experiences led the revivalists to form an umbrella structure. The Pentecostal Missionary Union was formed 1909, initially for missionary purposes. Some leaders were reluctant to formalize the movement into an organization, either because they regarded ecclesiastical governance as man-made, or because they feared the intransigence of their old-church hierarchies. By 1917 Pentecostals found that they needed to be a registered society in order to obtain building permits for churches, orphanages and schools. This fact, combined with the existence of government regulations for missionaries sent abroad and the need for doctrinal and disciplinary structure within the movement, led to the formation of a number of associations. These centered on doctrinal issues (eg, Apostolic Church of Pentecost, which rejected trinitarianism), ethnic identity (eg, German Pentecostal Church) or locale (eg, Pentecostal Assemblies of Newfoundland). The largest Pentecostal church, with a present-day membership of 134 000, received its charter in 1919 as the Pentecostal Assemblies of Canada, although for a time it was organically part of the Assemblies of God, the largest US group. In 1981 there were 300 000 active members in Canadian Pentecostal Churches (1981c). Canada's best-known Pentecostal was Ontario evangelist Aimee Semple MCPHERSON, who moved to Los Angeles and established the International Church of the Foursquare Gospel, and whose dramatic preaching style and colourful life drew much publicity. Pentecostals have also been successful in using television to propound their ideas, as *100 Huntley Street* shows. *See also* CHARISMATIC RENEWAL.   EARLE WAUGH

Penticton, BC, City, pop 23 181 (1981c), inc 1948, is nestled between Okanagan and Skaha lakes in S-central BC. Originally called by the Indians *Phthauntac* ("ideal meeting place") and later *Pen-tak-Tin* ("place to stay forever"), it was visited by David Stuart in 1811 and Alexander Ross in 1812. The brigade trail passed by the site 1812-48. The first orchards appeared in the 1890s; the Southern Okanagan Land Co provided irrigation in 1905. A town was formed in 1906. Transportation via rail to Okanagan Landing and stern-wheelers to Penticton had been in place since 1892. The Kettle Valley Ry linked the town to CROWSNEST PASS and HOPE by 1915. Tourism started with the opening of the Hope-Princeton highway in 1949 and increased with completion of the ROGERS PASS section in 1962. The opening of the Peach Bowl convention centre (1965) firmly established the city's year-round attractions.

The city of Penticton, located in the southern Okanagan Valley of BC (*photo by Dennis Laing/Reflexion*).

The 2 largest sources of employment are the service industries and trade. Agriculture, forestry, tourism, manufacturing, mining and the retirement industry are also important. Since the 1960s Penticton has led the province in the production of mobile prefabricated houses. The wine industry is growing. Industrial and population growth, however, is leading to a substantial loss of agricultural land (20%, 1971-76). A good climate, excellent beaches on 2 lakes and developing ski hills have increased tourist interest in Penticton.   WILLIAM SLOAN

Pentland, Barbara Lally, composer (b at Winnipeg 2 Jan 1912). One of the first Canadian composers to use avant-garde techniques, she studied at the Juilliard School of Music, New York C, and the Berkshire Music Center, Mass. Through her high-quality compositions for piano, orchestra, chamber ensemble and voice she has helped introduce 2 generations of Canadians to modern music. She taught at the Toronto Conservatory of Music from 1943 to 1949 and UBC from 1949 to 1963. Honours include a doctorate from U of Manitoba 1976 and the Diplôme d'honneur bestowed by the Canadian Conference of the Arts 1977. Her compositions, some of them commissioned and 17 recorded, are performed all over the world and have been featured on many radio programs, particularly the CBC. They include *News* (1970), her reaction to violence as reported in the media; *Disasters of the Sun* (1976, text by Dorothy LIVESAY), expressing her fight against male domination; *Music of Now,* a series of 3 books that introduced young pianists to the modern sounds; and her best-known composition, *Studies in Line* (1941), a set of 4 piano pieces that reflect different kinds of linear motion.   TIMOTHY J. MCGEE

Reading: Sheila Eastman and Timothy J. McGee, *Barbara Pentland* (1983).

Pépin, Clermont, composer, pianist, professor, administrator (b at St-Georges-de-Beauce, Qué 15 May 1926). First taught composition by Claude CHAMPAGNE, Rosario Scalero and Arnold Walter, he won the 1949 Prix d'Europe as a pianist and studied composition, theory and piano in Paris. He taught at the Montréal Conservatory of Music, of which he was director 1967-72, and also at the Québec Conservatory of Music. He was VP (1966-70) and president (1981-83) of CAPAC, and national president of JEUNESSES MUSICALES DU CANADA (1969-72). His major works include *Guernica,* a symphonic poem; *Quasars, Symphonie No 3; La Messe sur le monde, Symphonie No 4; Cycle Eluard;* and a series of works called *Monade.* In 1982 he composed *Trio No 2* for violin, cello and piano (commissioned by Radio-Canada) and in 1983 completed *Implosion, Symphonie No 5* (commissioned by the Montréal Symphony Orchestra). He won the 1970 Prix de Musique Calixa-Lavallée and in 1980 founded les Éditions Clermont-Pépin. Fascinated with new techniques in writing music, he was one of the founders in 1965 of a study

group about the future, the Centre d'études prospectives du Québec, of which he became president.   HÉLÈNE PLOUFFE

Pepin, Jean-Luc, academic, politician (b at Drummondville, Qué 1 Nov 1924). Educated at U of Ottawa and U of Paris, Pepin later taught political science at U of O. Elected as a Liberal to the House of Commons in 1963, he held several Cabinet posts between 1965 and 1972 under PMs PEARSON and TRUDEAU. Defeated in 1972, Pepin was engaged in business 1973-75, and in 1975 became chairman of the ANTI-INFLATION BOARD. In 1977 Trudeau made him cochairman, with John ROBARTS, of a task force on CANADIAN UNITY. Returning to politics 1979-84, Pepin served as minister of transport 1980-83 and then as minister of state in the Dept of External Affairs. An engaging and informal speaker, Pepin was known for his ability to tackle difficult issues, including abolition of the CROWS NEST PASS AGREEMENT rates, which occupied him as minister of transport.   ROBERT BOTHWELL

Pepin, Marcel, labour leader (b at Montréal 28 Feb 1926). After completing an MA in industrial relations at Laval (1949) he worked for the Fédération nationale de la métallurgie. Secretary general of the Confédération des syndicats nationaux from 1961, he succeeded Jean MARCHAND as president in 1965, promising a war on POVERTY. During his 10-year presidency the CSN became more and more radical as its leaders promoted an independent and socialist Québec. Pepin helped create the Common Front, an organization of all public- and para-public-sector unions that invoked a general strike in 1972. Robert BOURASSA's government sent him and other union leaders to jail for refusing to comply with back-to-work legislation. Pepin has been a member of Québec state corporations such as the Société générale de financement and the Caisse de dépôt et de placement. He was an ardent supporter of the PARTI QUÉBÉCOIS. In 1973 he became president of the Confédération mondiale du travail.   MICHAEL D. BEHIELS

Pepper (*Capsicum annuum*), perennial plant, cultivated as an annual, and belonging to the NIGHTSHADE family. Native to tropical America, peppers were widely disseminated after Columbus's discovery of America; some botanists now claim that some species are native to southern Asia. Some botanical varieties crossbreed naturally and many cultivars (commercial varieties) exist. Most pepper plants are well branched, 35-80 cm tall, with smooth, glossy, oblong-to-ovate leaves. They bear either erect or drooping fruits. Immature fruits of all types are green. Depending on variety, mature fruits are mostly red or yellow, and sweet or hot. Most fruits are puffy regardless of shape; all types have a central core with attached seeds. Peppers are started under glass, 8-10 weeks before transplanting, after all risk of frost is past. They require 55-80 days to mature in the field. Across Canada, common INSECT PESTS are potato aphids, flea beetles; in SW Ontario, European corn borer, pepper maggot and green peach aphid. Major PLANT DISEASES are damping-off, bacterial leaf spot, viruses and *Verticillium* wilt. Peppers, high in vitamins A and C, are eaten fresh or cooked, or used to produce condiments, pickles, sauces, etc. Varieties have been developed for Canada's different climatic regions. Commercial production is confined to the favoured climatic areas, eg, southern Ontario and BC. Statistics for Canada as a whole are unavailable. Ontario's production in 1980 was worth $1.97 million.   V.W. NUTTALL

Pepper, George Douglas, painter (b at Ottawa 25 Feb 1903; d at Toronto 1 Oct 1962). He studied under J.E.H. MACDONALD and J.W. Beatty in Toronto, and then in Paris and Italy (1924-25). He was strongly influenced by the GROUP OF SEVEN and his sense of line and rhythmic pattern produced many works in the 1920s and 1930s sympathetic to the Group's approach to Canadian landscape. Still, he forfeited none of his own originality in arrangement and perspective, as in *Totem Poles, Kitiwanga* (1930). Pepper served as an official war artist in WWII and helped illustrate many subsequent publications about the war. He painted several commissions for the Canadian government and on its behalf spent 3 months with his wife, artist Kathleen Daly, studying Inuit art in the eastern Arctic in 1960. Pepper taught at the Ontario College of Art and the Banff School of Fine Arts. He was a founding member of the Canadian Group of Painters (1933) and was elected to the Royal Canadian Academy of Arts in 1957.   ERIK J. PETERS

Pepperrell, Sir William, commander in chief of New England forces at LOUISBOURG (b at Kittery Point, Maine 27 June 1696; d there 6 July 1759). Reared in his father's counting house, the most successful in colonial Maine, trading in fish and lumber to the W Indies and England, he became a popular member of the Massachusetts Bay House of Representatives as an assemblyman and as a member of council (1727-59). He was selected to command the New England forces at the 1745 siege of Louisbourg, after a long career as a militia colonel, but his skills in business were unsuited to the military task. The capitulation of the fortress brought him a colonelcy in a newly raised regiment of foot and a baronetcy, both unique achievements, until then, for an American. His regiment formed part of the Louisbourg garrison, though he resided in Boston. Promoted maj-gen in 1755, he led his regiment in the abortive campaign against Fort Niagara. In 1757 he served briefly as acting governor of Massachusetts.
JULIAN GWYN

Percé, Qué, City, pop 4839 (1981c), inc 1970, is located 750 km NE of Québec City on the shore of the Gulf of ST LAWRENCE. The neighbouring villages of Barachois, Bridgeville, Cap-d'Espoir and St-Pierre-de-la-Malbaie were amalgamated in 1970; the old town itself has a population of about 1500. Its magnificent location attracts many visitors from around the world. Percé takes its name from PERCÉ ROCK, which dominates the area. Dozens of species of birds flock in the thousands to Bonaventure Island Conservation Park, a few kilometres offshore. Percé's history is as old as that of NEW FRANCE. Jacques CARTIER arrived there in 1534, and European fishermen used the bay as a haven in the 16th and 17th centuries. Missionaries have served this fishing port since 1673, although the mission was destroyed in 1690 by English troops and no one lived there again until the Conquest. With the arrival of the LOYALISTS, Percé became

The spectacular Percé Rock is the most famous landmark on the Gaspé Peninsula and attracts visitors from around the world (*photo by Al Williams*).

more active. Until the end of the 19th century, the local economy depended almost exclusively on fishing, but the region then began to attract tourists and the economy is now based largely on tourism and fishing. Leading Québec and Canadian artists have made the town a centre of artistic activity.   ANTONIO LECHASSEUR

Percé Rock, Qué, monolith in the GASPÉ peninsula, 750 km E of Québec City, near its namesake, the town of PERCÉ. This island-peninsula, once attached to the shoreline, is of an impressive size: 510 m long, 100 m wide and 70 m high. Its name derives from the fact that the sea has pierced holes in its structure to form archways. According to some, there were once 4 arches, but only one large opening, 30 m wide, exists today. Enigmatic and fascinating, immortalized by artists, poets and writers, Percé Rock is one of the major tourist attractions of Québec and Canada, and is an important bird sanctuary.
ANTONIO LECHASSEUR

Fourteen species of perch occur in Canada, including the yellow perch (*Perca flavescens*) shown here, which is a common sport fish (*artwork by Claire Tremblay*).

Perch Although perch is the common name for several distantly related species of FISH, it properly refers to members of the perch family (Percidae), order Perciformes, class Osteichthyes. Perches are small- to medium-sized, carnivorous, bottom-dwelling, freshwater fishes usually with long, rounded, laterally compressed bodies and 2 dorsal fins. The swim bladder is usually reduced or absent; eyes are conspicuous; dorsal, anal and pelvic fins are spined. In N America, true perches are confined, originally, to the area E of the Rocky Mts, but some species have been introduced to the West.

In Canada, 14 species of true perches occur, including the yellow perch, the WALLEYE and sauger, and 11 darters (genera *Ammocrypta, Etheostoma, Percina*). Darters are very small fish, few being longer than 8 cm. They are most common in Ontario; no species are native W of the Rocky Mts. The yellow perch (*Perca flavescens*) is the one most commonly thought of as "perch." It is distinguished from other members of its warm- to cool-water community by its short, stubby, hunch-backed body; 2 dorsal fins, of which the first has spiny rays; rather large mouth; bright yellow to green eyes; and lateral pattern of 7 green to brownish, tapered bars over a bright yellow to greenish undercoat. It spawns in spring (Apr-May) in southern Canada, as late as July in the North. No nest is built, but the unique, transparent, gelatinous, accordion-folded strings of eggs are looped over vegetation. These strings can be as long as 2 m and as heavy as 1 kg, and contain an average of 23 000 eggs. The large numbers of almost transparent young are significant in the diets of other important fishes. The largest adult yellow perch are usually 20-30 cm long, weighing 170-340 g. Specimens as large as 35 cm have been taken in eastern Canada, and one taken in Québec weighed almost 2 kg. Individuals can survive to 9 years of age. This N American species has a wide native distribution in Canada, from NS (excluding Cape Breton I), across Ontario, northward through most of Manitoba, Saskatchewan and Alberta, southern BC (introduced) and N to

Great Slave Lk, NWT. Both young and adults form schools of 50-200 individuals, making them attractive to anglers and commercial fishermen.

Yellow perch are regularly hosts to parasites such as yellow grub (in flesh) and blackspot (on skin), neither of which infect humans. Less frequently, perch carry the broad tapeworm, which can infect humans if raw or poorly cooked fish are eaten. In Canada, this species is classed as a sport and commercial fish. In spring, numerous larger individuals, migrating to spawning grounds, attract anglers. The white, flaky, very tasty flesh makes yellow perch a prominent commercial species in the Great Lakes. The commercial catch in Canada in 1980 was 6526 t, yielding to fishermen a value of $9 million.   E.J. CROSSMAN

Peregrine Falcon (*Falco peregrinus*), crow-sized, long-winged BIRD OF PREY, generally acknowledged to be the swiftest bird (attaining speeds of over 320 km/h). The name, which means wandering, is well suited to this species, represented by 18 races and found breeding on every continent (except Antarctica). Adults are dark blue-grey to blue-black above with dark bars on a salmon to white breast and belly. They have either very dark cheeks or moustachelike markings on the side of the head. Immature birds have brownish plumage with darker, longitudinal stripes on the breast. Both sexes have similar plumages, although males frequently have much paler breasts. Males (tiercels) are about one-third smaller than females (falcons).

The peregrine preys almost exclusively on bird species in most parts of its range (coastal and inland cliffs). Normally, 3-5 eggs are laid on a cliff ledge in a slight depression scraped out of earth or gravel by the female. There is little or no nest. Eggs are incubated, mainly by the female, for about 33 days. The male's role is primarily to protect the territory and provide food for the female and young. When young are half grown, the female may help provide food. Young leave the nest at about 5 weeks but remain nearby and depend on parents for food until they can hunt for themselves. Shortly thereafter, the birds leave the nesting area and begin MIGRATION. The first year is very difficult for young. Band-recovery information indicates that only about 1 in 4 lives to return to the breeding grounds. Whether peregrines migrate depends on food supply and climatic conditions. The Canadian tundra peregrine (*F. peregrinus tundrius*) winters as far S as southern S America, whereas the W coast peregrine (*F. p. pealei*) is essentially non-migratory. The third race breeding in Canada is the endangered anatum peregrine (*F. p. anatum*), which bred across Canada wherever adequate food and nesting habitat were available. These birds wintered from the southern US through Central America into northern S America. The anatum peregrine has declined to near extinction in most of the breeding range. The decline is well documented and studies indicate that the principal cause was reproductive failure resulting from contamination by PESTICIDES (especially DDT) which cause eggshell thinning. The bird has become a symbol of the problems resulting from misuse of the ENVIRONMENT. In Canada and the US, specific conservation programs have been very successful and many young anatum peregrines, bred in captivity, are being released in the wild annually. *See* WILDLIFE CONSERVATION AND MANAGEMENT; ENDANGERED ANIMALS. R.W. FYFE

Perehudoff, William, painter (b at Langham, Sask 1919). Though he has lived most of his adult life in Saskatoon, he left the Prairies as a young man to study art. He explored mural painting at the Colorado Springs Fine Art Center (1948-49), then studied with French Cubist Amédée Ozenfant in New York. Ozenfant's purism and insistence on "significant form" impressed Perehudoff deeply. The notion of stripping a painting down to its essentials is the core of his developed work 30 years later. Perehudoff's knowledge and ambition were expanded by his travels in the US and Europe in 1952. He married Dorothy KNOWLES in 1952 and they returned to western Canada, where he earned his living as a commercial artist. U of Sask's summer artists' workshops at Emma Lake influenced him during the period 1957-68, notably those led by American critic Clement Greenberg (1962) and painter Kenneth Noland (1963). Their respect for his work encouraged his development of large-scale, abstract painting. Perehudoff's continuing preoccupations are with colour, surface and texture. His work has evolved through complex orchestrations of shifting, transparent bands of colour, to his most recent textured areas of intense, saturated hues. He has exhibited widely in Canada, the US and Europe, and is regarded by many as the heir to Jack BUSH as Canada's most important colour painter.

Pérez Hernández, Juan Josef, naval officer, explorer (b c 1725 at Majorca, Spain; d 2 Nov 1775 off Calif). Pérez served as a pilot and marine officer in Spain's Pacific trade between Mexico and the Phillipines and in the Spanish expansion into Alta California. He was curious about the unknown northern coastline and his request to explore it coincided with the Spanish government's desire for information on Russian penetration southward. In 1774 he sailed aboard the frigate *Santiago* with orders to reach at least 60°N lat. Pérez was the first European to explore the Queen Charlotte Is and to approach Nootka Sound, but unfavourable weather prevented him from landing to take formal possession for Spain. Although he reached only about 55°30′ lat and left some missions unfulfilled, he collected important data that served future Spanish mariners. Pérez was second officer in the 1775 expedition commanded by Bruno de Hezeta, but he died at sea.   CHRISTON I. ARCHER

Periglacial Landform, a feature resulting from the action of intense frost, often combined with the presence of PERMAFROST. Periglacial landforms are restricted to areas that experience cold but essentially nonglacial CLIMATES. The term was proposed by Walery von Lozinski in 1909 to describe frost weathering conditions in the Carpathian Mts of Central Europe. Subsequently the concept of a "periglacial zone" developed, referring to the climatic and geomorphic conditions of areas peripheral to the Pleistocene ice sheets and GLACIERS. Theoretically, this zone was a TUNDRA region extending as far S as the TREELINE. Modern usage encompasses a wide range of cold, nonglacial conditions, regardless of their proximity to glaciers in time or space. Periglacial environments exist not only in high latitudes and tundra regions but also in areas S of the treeline and in high altitude (alpine) regions of temperate latitudes.

Approximately 50% of the LAND surface of Canada currently experiences periglacial conditions (intense frost action, the presence of permafrost, or both). All gradations exist between environments in which frost action processes dominate and where all or a major part of the landscape is the result of such processes, and those in which frost action processes are subservient to others. Some complicating factors are the varying susceptibilities of different rock formations to frost action and the fact that there is no perfect correlation between areas of intense frost action and areas underlain by permafrost. Large areas of northern Canada have only recently emerged from the late Wisconsinan GLACIATION, and periglacial processes currently serve to modify their glacial landforms. In areas that have experienced longer histories of nonglacial conditions, eg, northern interior YT, NW BANKS

The distinctive polygons are the result of winter contraction cracks that have become infilled with ice formed from percolating summer meltwater (*photo by Stephen J. Krasemann/DRK Photo*).

ISLAND and other high-arctic islands, landscapes are more likely to be in equilibrium with current periglacial conditions. Processes unique to periglacial environments include formation of permafrost, development of thermal contraction cracks, thawing of permafrost (formation of thermokarst), and formation of wedge and injection ICE. Other processes, not necessarily restricted to periglacial regions, are important because of their high magnitude or frequency in cold, nonglacial environments. These include ice segregation, seasonal frost action and various forms of instability and rapid mass movement. Nearly all frost-action processes operate in conjunction with the freezing of water.

The most distinctive periglacial landforms are those associated with permafrost. The most widespread, tundra polygons formed by thermal-contraction cracking, divide the ground surface up into polygonal nets 20-30 m in dimension. Water often penetrates the cracks to form ice wedges several metres deep and up to 1-2 m wide near the surface. In drier environments mineral soil infills the cracks and sand wedges result. Ice-cored hills (PINGOS) are a less widespread periglacial landform. Pingos form when water moves to the freezing plane under a pressure gradient that may be hydraulic or hydrostatic in nature. Pingos are not typical of all periglacial landscapes but result from specific geomorphic and hydrologic conditions that severely limit their occurrence. Other aggradational landforms such as palsas and peat plateaus are usually associated with ice segregation rather than injection. Ground-ice slumps, thaw lakes and irregular depressions (thermokarst) resulting from the melt and EROSION of ice-rich permafrost constitute a further group of unique, permafrost-related periglacial landforms.

Many periglacial phenomena result from frost wedging and the cryogenic weathering of exposed bedrock. Frost wedging is associated with the freezing and expansion of water which penetrates joints and bedding planes. The details of cryogenic weathering are still poorly understood. Coarse, angular rock debris (block fields), normally attributed to frost wedging or cryogenic weathering, occur widely over large areas above the treeline and in the arctic islands. In

addition, frost-heaved bedrock blocks and extensive talus (scree) slopes are common. Angular, frost-shattered rock protuberances (tors) may stand out above the debris-covered surfaces, reflecting more resistant bedrock. These are most frequent in SEDIMENTARY ROCKS, especially in the arctic islands (eg, SOMERSET ISLAND); however, in the unglaciated interior of the YT (Klondike Plateau) tors are formed on very old and extremely resistant metamorphic rocks. Flat, erosional surfaces (cryoplanation terraces) are sometimes associated with tors but can also occur independently.

Agents of transport include frost creep, the ratchetlike movement that occurs when soil, during a freeze-thaw cycle, expands normally to the surface and settles in a more nearly vertical direction; and solifluction, the slow downslope movement of water-saturated debris. Where solifluction occurs on or above frozen ground, it is termed gelifluction. Solifluction lobes, sheets and terraces are especially well developed above the treeline and below sites of perennial snowbanks.

The small-scale relief of periglacial regions is characterized by various patterned ground phenomena. These are often related to cryoturbation, the lateral and vertical displacement of soil that accompanies seasonal or diurnal freezing and thawing. The most widespread are nonsorted circles or nets, typically 1-2 m in diameter and up to 0.5 m high. In the Mackenzie Valley, they occur over extensive areas, wherever fine-textured and poorly drained sediments exist. In Keewatin, morphologically similar forms caused by density differences in saturated sediments are termed "mud boils." A wide range of nonsorted and sorted forms of patterned ground are described from other parts of northern Canada, and no single explanation is applicable to all. *See* PHYSIOGRAPHIC REGIONS.

HUGH M. FRENCH

Reading: Hugh M. French, *The Periglacial Environment* (1976).

Periwinkle, common name for any of the edible intertidal SNAILS of the genus *Littorina*. Periwinkles are represented by 6 species in Canadian coastal waters. *Littorina littorea*, the common periwinkle, was introduced in 1850 to the East Coast from western Europe where it is a popular food. The northern yellow periwinkle (*L. obtusata*) is another Atlantic coast species, which is usually found associated with rockweeds. *Littorina scutulata*, the checkered periwinkle, is a dominant species in British Columbia's coastal intertidal region, where it nestles among BARNACLES in upper littoral zones. Where its southern range extends into California, *L. scutulata* is in competition with the eroded periwinkle, *L. planaxis*. Species of *Littorina* usually occupy the upper reaches of the rocky intertidal zones where they graze on encrusted algal material by means of a radula, a ribbonlike organ covered by many hundreds of minute teeth. This feeding device emerges from a snoutlike head which supports a pair of tentacles each bearing a single eye. The littorines are a relatively advanced group of prosobranch gastropod MOLLUSCS with separate sexes and internal fertilization. Some species release pelagic egg cases from which larvae hatch; others brood their eggs, giving birth to larvae or little snails.   PETER V. FANKBONER

Perjury A witness in a judicial proceeding who knowingly gives false evidence with intent to mislead the judge or jury commits the crime of perjury. If a person knowingly makes a false statement under oath outside a judicial proceeding he or she would also be guilty of an offence.   VINCENT M. DEL BUONO

Perkins, Simeon, merchant, diarist (b at Norwich, Conn 24 Feb 1735; d at Liverpool, NS 9 May 1812). He arrived in Liverpool in 1762 and rapidly became the leading local merchant, dealing in fish and lumber, building sawmills and small vessels, and developing a trade with New England and the W Indies. During the AMERICAN REVOLUTION he invested profitably in several Liverpool privateers. His ability, integrity and charity resulted in a long civic career in local administrative and judicial offices. He also held high rank in the militia. He served as MLA for Queen's County 1765-99 and, although his attendance was intermittent, he was quietly effective. His diary (1766-1812), published in 5 volumes by the CHAMPLAIN SOCIETY, and his home, now a museum, are valuable records of a man whose career reflects NS's economic, social and political beginnings. LOIS KERNAGHAN

Reading: C.B. Fergusson, *Early Liverpool and its Diarist* (1961).

Perley, Moses Henry, lawyer, naturalist, author (b at Maugerville, NB 31 Dec 1804; d off Labrador coast 17 Aug 1862). An avid sportsman and natural historian, Perley became the leading authority on NB's resources in the mid-19th century. In 1842 he prepared a report on the province's Indian reserves — the basis for its 1844 Indian Reserve Act. He was active in forming the Saint John Mechanics' Institute in 1838 and the Provincial Assn in 1844, was provincial emigrant agent 1843-48 and in 1854 published a *Handbook.. .for Emigrants.* In 1846 and 1848 he prepared reports on possible railway routes. He published a report on trees (1847) and 1848-49 reports on NB's fish and the fisheries of the Gulf of ST LAWRENCE and Bay of FUNDY. He collected information used in RECIPROCITY treaty (1854) negotiations and in 1855 became a fishery commissioner. W.A. SPRAY

Permafrost, ground remaining at or below 0°C continuously for at least 2 years. It may consist of cold, dry earth; cold, wet, saline earth; icy lenses and masses; or ice-cemented earth or rock. Although GLACIERS fit this definition, they are a special case dealt with elsewhere. Most permafrost includes ice cement, lenses or masses that result from the freezing of the bulk of subsurface water. At most surface temperatures some capillary water will be unfrozen. Saline water in soil freezes below 0°C; hence, unfrozen permafrost occurs below parts of the shores of the Arctic Ocean and in cold brine pockets in the ground. If the ground is dry, no ice will be present despite the temperature. In permafrost regions, the upper layer that undergoes seasonal freezing and thawing is called the active layer. Below this lies the permafrost, the upper surface of which is called the permafrost table. Permafrost is mapped as follows: where over 80% of the ground is underlain by permafrost, it is continuous; 30-80%, discontinuous, with the rest being unfrozen talik; under 30%, sporadic. Taliks occur beneath water bodies and where water flows through the ground, keeping it warm. Permafrost is produced by a sub-zero winter heat flux in the ground which is greater than the above-zero summer heat flux. Its development is favoured by high latitude and altitude, by long, cold winters and thin winter snow cover. Cold-air drainage in mountain valleys or through rock caves may cause pockets of permafrost in the sporadic zone.

Permafrost underlies 20-25% of the Earth's LAND area, including about 99% of Greenland, 80% of Alaska, 50% of the USSR, 40-50% of Canada and 20% of China. The greatest thicknesses in Canada are over 1000 m at high elevations in parts of Baffin and Ellesmere islands, ranging down to 60-90 m at the southern limit of the continuous permafrost zone. Active layer thicknesses range from under 10 cm in Ellesmere to 15 m at high altitudes in the mountains of SW Alberta on the outer margin of continuous permafrost. The coldest ground temperatures in permafrost worldwide are found on ELLESMERE I

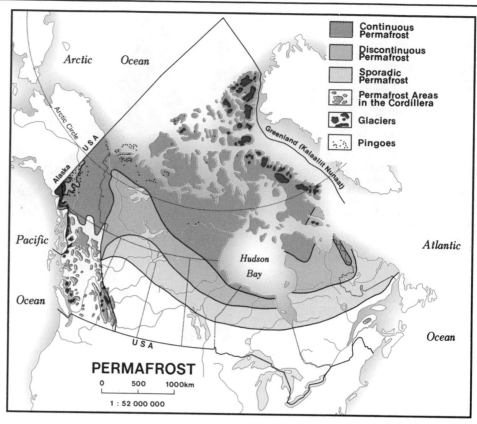

Continuous Permafrost

Discontinuous Permafrost

Sporadic Permafrost

Permafrost Areas in the Cordillera

Glaciers

Pingoes

PERMAFROST

0 500 1000km

1 : 52 000 000

(about -15°C). The permafrost in Canada developed largely after the last GLACIATION, and its distribution adjusts to small CLIMATE CHANGES. Thus the continuous permafrost zone extended to S of Fort Norman in the mid-19th century. A 4°C warming of the winter air temperature resulted in the migration of its southern boundary nearly to Inuvik. Since 1940, a 2°C cooling in the mean winter temperature has resulted in the boundary moving southwards to Arctic Red R. Similar changes can be demonstrated in alpine areas and in Alaska, northern USSR, etc.

The ice in permafrost may be interstitial or segregated, and is concentrated in the few metres immediately below the permafrost table. Water tends to move through the pores to the freezing plane, resulting in ice contents as high as 1600% by weight of the mineral matter in some silts and peats in low-lying areas, eg, the Mackenzie Delta. The segregated ice may be in isolated masses, in distinct lenses parallel to the surface or in wedges tapering downwards. Distinctive landforms are associated with permafrost (*see* PERIGLACIAL LANDFORM). The ice wedges form a polygonal pattern and are the result of winter contraction cracks that have become infilled with ice from percolating summer meltwater. In dry areas, sand may fill in the cracks, forming sand wedges within the permafrost table. On steep slopes, high ice content may permit unconsolidated deposits to move slowly downslope as rock glaciers. In taliks, the freezing of water may cause the localized growth of PINGOS, ice-cored mounds up to 100 m high. Localized ice segregation in wet lowlands can form mounds domed up by small lenses of ice (palsas). Seasonal freezing in the active layer can cause the turning up of stones, heaving of the ground, and sorting of coarse and fine rock material. These seasonal changes also cause physical weathering of the bedrock and can reduce mudstones to silts, eg, along the Dempster Hwy in Rat Pass, NWT. The sorting processes can form patterned ground in only 5 years. Thawing of the permafrost often results in subsidence where ice was present and also in the formation of thaw lakes or hummocky terrain. This ter-

rain, called thermokarst, can be induced by human activities.

The presence of ice and the consequences of an alteration in the thermal regime make economic development of permafrost terrain difficult. All materials, except gravels or clean sand, heave or become unstable during seasonal freezing and thawing. Normal agriculture is impossible over permafrost because of subsidence, while heated structures must be separated from the frozen ground by adequate insulation. Paved roads or runways increase summer heating and require a suitable insulating subgrade. Even a slight alteration of the vegetation cover may cause thermokarst subsidence. Artificial refrigeration of the ground is too expensive for all except special cases, which is why the Alaska oil PIPELINE is placed on supports in permafrost areas. Water supplies are difficult to obtain except where natural springs or deep lakes occur. Sewage disposal is a major problem. Construction of dams for HYDROELECTRICITY requires special techniques, as do mining and drilling for oil and gas. The elasticity of ice reduces the effectiveness of explosive charges. Ice-rich ore is more difficult to process because it must be thawed. Drilling without disturbing the environment is practically impossible in Canada. STUART A. HARRIS

Reading: R.J.E. Brown, *Permafrost in Canada* (1970); G.H. Johnston, *Permafrost Engineering Design and Construction* (1981); A.L. Washburn, *Geocryology* (1979).

Permanent Joint Board on Defence, a Canadian-American advisory body established Ogdensburg, NY, 18 Aug 1940, by PM Mackenzie King and US Pres F.D. Roosevelt. This meeting, which took place at Roosevelt's suggestion in a period of crisis in WORLD WAR II, inaugurated an era of intimate military ties. The PJBD first met 26 Aug 1940, and had its greatest influence from then until Dec 1941, when the US entered the war. Consisting of 2 national sections, each composed of a chairman (usually a civilian) and representatives of the armed forces and foreign service, the board studies joint defence problems and offers recommendations to the respective governments. Although now only one of a number of agencies for Canadian-American military co-operation, it continues as an arena for frank and informal exchange of views and information. NORMAN HILLMER

Perrault, Jean-Pierre, modern dancer, choreographer (b at Montréal 16 Feb 1947). He started dance training at 17 in Montréal with Jeanne Renaud and Peter Boneham, continuing his studies in Europe and New York City. In 1972 he became co-artistic director of Le GROUPE DE LA PLACE ROYALE, Ottawa. His creative explorations with Le Groupe were nontraditional and often controversial. He attempted to break the barriers between the arts by using dancers as singers and musicians to produce an integrated work of art. Still closely associated with the company, he resigned the co-directorship in 1981 to work as an independent choreographer and teacher.
JILLIAN M. OFFICER

Perrault, Pierre, film director, poet (b at Montréal 29 June 1927). After working for Radio-Canada, he codirected the series "Au pays de Neufve-France" and then made a début in film at the NFB with Michel BRAULT in *Pour la suite du monde* (1963), a classic of direct cinema. Still with the NFB, he directed *Le Règne du jour* (1966) and *Les Voitures d'eau* (1968), which form a trilogy with the 1963 film. He then turned to 2 controversial issues, Québec separatism (*Un Pays sans bon sens* 1970) and the fate of the Acadians (*L'Acadie, l'Acadie* 1971). These were followed by series on the Abitibi region: *Un Royaume vous attend* (1975), *Le Retour à la terre* (1976), *Gens d'Abitibi* (1980), *C'était un québécois en Bretagne, madame* (1977); and American Indians: *Le Goût de la farine* (1976), *Le Pays de la terre sans arbre ou le Mouchouânipi* (1980). In 1982 his film about hunting (*La Bête lumineuse*) had an enormous emotional impact on Québec audiences. He then chose Saint-Malo, France, birthplace of Jacques CARTIER, as the setting for *Les Voiles bas et en travers* (1983). A major director of realist cinema, Perrault is a master of words and a skillful interpreter of the human soul. PIERRE VÉRONNEAU

Perry, Aylesworth Bowen, police officer (b at Violet, Ont 21 Aug 1860; d at Ottawa 14 Feb 1956). As commissioner of the NWMP, Perry transformed the police from a romantic frontier force into a modern national police force. A member of the first class at RMC, Kingston, Ont, Perry joined the police as an inspector in 1882, served with the Alberta Field Force during the NORTH-WEST REBELLION in 1885, and was placed in command of the police in the Yukon in 1899. As commissioner 1900-23, Perry modernized the force's equipment and methods. During WWI, departures to serve overseas weakened the force and the creation of provincial police forces in Alberta and Saskatchewan reduced its responsibilities. The future of the force was in doubt, but it proved its usefulness in controlling postwar unrest, and Perry was made responsible for reorganizing the force as the ROYAL CANADIAN MOUNTED POLICE. A.B. McCULLOUGH

Persaud, Trivedi Vidhya Nandan, anatomist (b at Pt Mourant, Guyana 19 Feb 1940). Educated at Rostock, E Ger (MD 1965), and U of W Indies, Kingston, Jamaica (PhD 1970), Persaud has received international acclaim for his research in embryology, teratology and pathology. He was editor of the *West Indian Medical Journal*, 1970-73, and president of the Canadian Assn of Anatomists, 1981-83. Author of several medical books, notably *Prenatal Pathology*, he also has edited *Advances in the Study of Birth Defects* (7 vols). He has published more than 120 scientific papers. He was elected a fellow of the Royal College of Pathology (London) in 1984.
KEITH L. MOORE

Person, Clayton Oscar, scientist, educator (b at Regina 16 May 1922). Educated at Saskatoon,

Alberta and overseas, Person has worked at U Man, U of A and UBC. He is recognized internationally as an authority on the genetics of host-parasite relations. His writings have made a major contribution to the development of a rigorous theoretical basis for our understanding of how the genetic structure of parasitic populations interacts with that of their host populations. His theoretical methods have been applied widely in the practical management of parasitic diseases in agriculture and forestry. In 1971 he was elected a fellow of the RSC; in 1981 he was awarded the BC Science Council's gold medal and was elected fellow of the American Phytopathological Soc; in 1982 he received the RSC's Flavelle Medal. A.J.F. GRIFFITHS

Persons Case In 1928, the SUPREME COURT OF CANADA unanimously decided women were not "persons" who could hold public office as Canadian senators. The terms of the CONSTITUTION ACT, 1867, and the historical incapacity of women to hold office under common law barred the suit of Henrietta Muir EDWARDS and her companion Alberta suffragettes. In 1929 the British Privy Council reversed the decision and called the exclusion of women from public office "a relic of days more barbarous than ours."
DAVID A. CRUICKSHANK

Perth, Ont, Town, seat of Lanark County, inc 1850 (village), 1854 (town), pop 5655 (1981c), located on the Tay R, 83 km SW of Ottawa. It was laid out 1816 as a backwoods military settlement intended to provide experienced militiamen for the defence of the inland water route linking the Ottawa R and Lk Ontario. Perth was joined to the RIDEAU CANAL by a separate canal, putting the settlement in touch with the flow of commerce through this "backdoor" to Upper Canada. Among the earliest settlers were several hundred from Perth, Scotland, and so the village received its name. Cheese making has always been an important local industry. In 1893 a local cheese weighing 9900 kg and measuring 1.8 m high and 8.56 m around was sent to the Chicago World's Fair. Perth has an economy based on light industry and in the summer hosts many vacationers who are attracted to the surrounding lake country. Many beautifully preserved 19th-century buildings remain, eg, the neoclassical Lanark County Courthouse (1843) and the Hotel Imperial, built before 1850 and still in use. DANIEL FRANCIS

Pesticide Substances used to control pests include insecticides (for control of INSECTS), fungicides (for disease-causing FUNGI), herbicides (for WEEDS), rodenticides (for RODENTS), avicides (for BIRDS), piscicides (for FISH) and nematicides (for NEMATODES). Insecticides, fungicides and herbicides are the most widely used. More than 400 pesticides are now registered for use in Canada; they are formulated as liquids, dusts, wettable powders, aerosols and granules.

Pesticides include a wide range of synthetic and natural substances. Relatively few pesticides existed before WWII: insecticides were primarily salts of arsenic or fluorine or plant-derived products such as nicotine, pyrethrum and rotenone; fungicides were primarily based on MERCURY, COPPER or SULPHUR; herbicides included PETROLEUM oils, sulphuric acid, some arsenites and SALT. After WWII, many synthetic compounds became available, the first of these being DDT for insect control, the phenoxy herbicides (eg, 2-4-D) for weed control, and captan and a series of dithiocarbamates for control of fungal diseases of plants.

Toxicology
Pesticides now available differ widely in their toxicity to different forms of life. The term LD_{50}, used to indicate toxicity, refers to the dosage of the pesticide (expressed as milligrams per kilo-

gram of body weight) required to kill 50% of a test population. The RAT is the most common animal used for determining LD_{50} values but the MOUSE and the RABBIT are also usually tested. If a pesticide is intended for wide usage, it is also usually tested on birds and fish. Each pesticide is selective in its toxicity, being highly toxic to some organisms and much less so to others. Within a class of compounds, however, toxicity varies widely, from 10 or fewer milligrams per kilogram to several thousand mg/kg.

The nature of the toxicity of pesticides differs between different classes of substances. In general, insecticides are more toxic to warm-blooded animals than are herbicides or fungicides, but some of the older fungicides, such as mercury and the arsenite herbicides, are also highly toxic to mammals and birds. Many insecticides act on the nervous system of insects and, although less toxic to warm-blooded animals, act on the nervous system of these organisms as well. Some newer classes of insecticides have been developed that act on processes found in insects but not in mammals, eg, compounds that interfere with the molting process in insects or that affect hardening of the cuticle. With the exception of mercury, most of the fungicides are not very toxic to warm-blooded animals because they are toxic to systems in fungi that are quite different from those found in mammals and birds. This is true also of most herbicides. Over time, target species develop resistance to specific pesticides and dosages have to be increased or new pesticides developed.

Registration and Use
Because pesticides are toxic, their use is carefully controlled and, in Canada, pesticides may be sold only after they have been registered by Agriculture Canada. The registration process is comprehensive and includes a review of the toxicology of the product, a demonstration that the product is effective for the pest for which it is intended and the nature of the treatment needed to control the problem. The registration process permits a pesticide to be registered only for specific uses, which are detailed on the label that accompanies the pesticide when it is sold. One or more of the many pesticides available are used on practically every CROP grown in Canada and the use, particularly of herbicides, is increasing rapidly each year. Insecticides are also used widely to control insects around the home and for control of MOSQUITOES, BLACK FLIES and pests on livestock. Fungicides are used extensively in building materials, paint and disinfectants, and for the treatment of timbers (eg, railway ties, telephone posts) to prevent decay.

Problems
Although pesticides have been widely adopted by Canadians for pest control, a number of concerns have been raised. In the 1950s and early 1960s, a number of environmental problems were found to be related to the extensive use of pesticides. These problems included contamination of water with resulting fish kill; reproductive effects in birds (eg, the PEREGRINE FALCON); and direct toxicity to some birds in areas where large-scale spraying operations were carried out. Research identified the problem pesticides and these have been restricted in use or banned. More recently, concern has been expressed that pesticides may cause long-term health effects and there is significant controversy about whether or not they should be used. There is little evidence that the pesticides now in use are likely to cause significant health effects when used properly and each is extensively tested for long-term effects before it is registered. Prudence dictates, however, that all pesticides be used with caution and that care be taken to avoid overexposure. *See* PLANT DISEASE. F.L. McEWEN
Reading: F.L. McEwen and G.R. Stephenson, *The Use and Significance of Pesticides in the Environment* (1979).

Petawawa, Canadian Forces Base Occupying 30 770 ha along the Ottawa and Petawawa rivers, 166 km NW of Ottawa, it was created (1905) as an eastern Ontario summer-training militia camp. Built astride historic fur-trading routes, it had roles in both world wars as a major military staging and training base, especially for the artillery and engineers, and as an internment centre. During the GREAT DEPRESSION there were relief camps here. After 1945 it became a permanent regular military-unit establishment. Designated "Camp Petawawa" in 1951, it underwent substantial military expansion and urban growth. Renamed CFB Petawawa 1966, the base has a total population of 3500 military and 1950 civilian personnel, with 5000 dependants. Its annual budget of over $100 million makes it economically important to nearby PEMBROKE and surrounding areas. At present it is the home of the elite Airborne Unit, the Special Service Force.

R.G. HAYCOCK

Peterborough, Ont, City, inc 1905, seat of Peterborough County, situated on the Otonabee R, about 40 km N of Lk Ontario and 110 km NE of Toronto. With a population of 60 620 (1981c; 58 111, 1971c), it is the largest city on the Trent-Severn Waterway and the regional centre for the KAWARTHA LAKES cottage country.

Settlement and Development. Peterborough was named in 1826 for Peter Robinson, who directed the settlement of a large number of Irish immigrants in the area. Its history has been tied to the waterways and forests, and to its proximity to Toronto. The site, at one end of the long portage to Lk Chemung, was well travelled by the Mississauga Indians and their forebears, and was visited by Samuel de CHAMPLAIN 1615. Under European settlement, Peterborough quickly emerged as the administrative centre for the region N of Rice Lk, particularly with the Robinson settlement and the creation of the Col-

The locks on the Trent-Severn waterway at Peterborough are the highest lift-locks in the world (*photo by Kim Patrick O'Leary*).

borne Dist in 1842. It was incorporated as a town 1850. The development of Red Fife WHEAT in the area was an important contribution to Canada's agriculture, but timber was the main source of wealth for more than half a century. By the 1870s Peterborough was Ontario's principal timber producer, shipping over 100 million board ft to American wholesalers annually. The subsequent development of hydroelectricity along the Trent system (before Niagara Falls), together with generous municipal bonuses and concessions, attracted large manufacturers, including Edison Electric (later Canadian General Electric) and Quaker Oats. Associated with the city have been literary figures such as Catharine Parr TRAILL, Robertson DAVIES and Margaret LAURENCE; the capitalists Sir Joseph FLAVELLE and George A. COX, who began his financial career here; and Lester B. PEARSON, who attended school here.

Cityscape Peterborough features the rolling hills of a major drumlin field. Its 19th-century

prosperity shows in 2 impressive blocks of pre-Confederation buildings, which include locally quarried stone buildings from the 1830s and several stately residences. The engineering marvels of the world's highest lift lock, the Centennial Fountain, and the architecturally acclaimed TRENT U reflect continuing change. By contrast, the nearby petroglyphs and Serpent Mounds probably date back a thousand years.

Population Peterborough's population doubled every 2 decades before WWI thanks to the lumber economy and manufacturing, and the 1904 annexation of Ashburnham (pop 2000e) as the city grew from 4611 (1871c) to 18 360 (1911c). The modest growth since then has been more rapid than elsewhere in eastern Ontario (except Ottawa) because of manufacturing expansion. The city's unique quality is its demographic averageness — by religion, occupation and ethnicity — making it a bellwether riding provincially and federally and a favourite site for consumer market testing.

Economy and Transportation In addition to manufacturing, the economic impact of educational institutions, insurance companies, shopping plazas and tourist attractions has been strong in the past decade. Mixed agriculture remains a feature of the area. Peterborough is on the Trans-Canada Hwy and has convenient access to Hwy 401. Until recently, it was well served by railways, starting with the Grand Trunk Ry and the CPR's first main line from Toronto to Montréal.

Government and Politics The city's municipal history has been marked by fiscal restraint since the railway failures of the 1850s. For 80 years after 1861 a Town Trust Commission managed its finances. Peterborough has usually favoured a ward system and has resisted provincial efforts to abandon the township/county system for regional government.

Cultural Life The city's vigorous cultural life

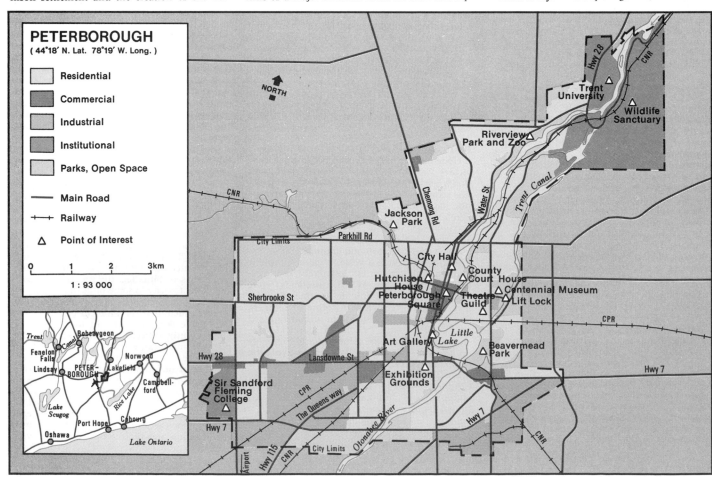

PETERBOROUGH
(44°18' N. Lat. 78°19' W. Long.)

Residential
Commercial
Industrial
Institutional
Parks, Open Space

Main Road
Railway
Point of Interest

0   1   2   3km
1 : 93 000

features a symphony orchestra, a theatre guild and professional companies, public and private art galleries, and the Centennial Museum. It has a winter carnival (Snowfest) and summer Arts and Water Festival. Home of the Peterborough canoe, it has won national titles in junior hockey (Petes), lacrosse and synchronized swimming. The city hosted the 1980 Ontario Summer Games.　　　　　　　　　　ELWOOD JONES

Reading: R. Borg, ed, *Peterborough, Land of Shining Waters* (1967); A.O.C. Cole, ed, *Illustrated Historical Atlas of Peterborough County 1825-1875* (1975).

Peters, Arthur, lawyer, premier of PEI (b at Charlottetown 29 Aug 1854; d there 29 Jan 1908), brother of Frederick PETERS. Called to the PEI Bar in 1878, Peters was first elected to the Assembly in 1890 as a Liberal. Appointed attorney general in 1900, he became premier 29 Dec 1901 and died holding office. He is remembered as a stout defender of fair terms for PEI within CONFEDERATION.　　　　　　PETER E. RIDER

Peters, Frederick, lawyer, premier of PEI (b at Charlottetown 8 Apr 1852; d at Prince Rupert, BC 29 July 1919). A brother of Arthur PETERS, Frederick was elected to the assembly in 1890 as a Liberal and became premier 22 Apr 1891, serving until resigning on 27 Oct 1897. He retained his seat until 1899 although he moved to Victoria, BC, in 1897. He practised law there until 1911 when he was appointed city solicitor, and after 1916 city clerk, of Prince Rupert. During his premiership the 2 legislative chambers were merged into a single assembly.　　PETER E. RIDER

Peterson, Leonard Byron, playwright (b at Regina 15 Mar 1917). This prairie Norseman who has lived in Toronto since the outbreak of WWII is unquestionably Canada's most prolific playwright, with well over 1000 radio and TV original scripts and adaptations to his credit. His first CBC radio play was produced in 1939, and *They're All Afraid,* a controversial "Stage 44" production, brought fame to him and producer Andrew ALLAN, winning the top award at the Columbus, Ohio, American Broadcasting Festival, as did his *Joe Katona* in 1961. His innovativeness and versatility in form and social concern as well as his humanism in content are illustrated by such plays as *Burlap Bags* (1946), a precursor of Absurd Theatre, and *The Great Hunger* (1960), an Inuit play frequently studied in high schools and universities. A cultural activist, Peterson cofounded Playwrights Co-op in 1972.　　　　　　ROTA HERZBERG LISTER

Peterson, Oscar E., jazz pianist (b at Montréal 15 Aug 1925). Peterson began his career after studies with Lou Hooper and Paul de Marky. He was a radio performer heard locally in Montréal on CKAC by 15, and nationally on the CBC by 20. He played with Johnny Holmes's dance band in 1948-49 at the Alberta Lounge with his own trio before making a remarkable debut in Sept 1949 at Carnegie Hall, New York. He then pursued his career internationally but maintained his home in Canada: in Montréal until 1958, thereafter in Toronto. Peterson has recorded over 80 albums under his own name in the US and Germany and made many as accompanist to Lester Young, Louis Armstrong, Coleman Hawkins and others. He has been host for TV series in London (BBC), Vancouver (CTV) and Toronto (CBC).

Peterson's extravagantly skillful piano technique has drawn both praise and criticism. Full-blown and joyous, his approach to jazz, without offering innovation, is in the mainstream 1940s tradition of which he has become the outstanding proponent, working in trio and solo contexts. He has composed several jazz themes, as well as the extended *Canadiana Suite* (1963) and *African Suite* (1979), and the score for the Canadian film *The Silent Partner* (1977). Winner of many popularity and critics' polls, Peterson re-

The internationally acclaimed jazz pianist Oscar Peterson in his home studio (*courtesy Canapress*).

ceived Grammy awards in 1975, 1979 and 1980 and became an officer in the Order of Canada in 1973.　　　　　　　　　MARK MILLER

Petitclair, Pierre, dramatist (b 12 Oct 1813 at St-Augustin de Portneuf, Qué; d at Pointe-au-Pot, Labrador 15 Aug 1860). He is author of the first play published by a native French Canadian, apart from dramatized political dialogues, *Griphon, ou la vengeance d'un valet* (1837). This work was never performed, but his 2 other extant plays were staged in Québec C with considerable success: *La Donation* (1842), a 2-act play visibly influenced by melodrama, and *Une partie de campagne,* first performed in 1857 and published posthumously (1865). The latter play is a satirical depiction of the dangers of aping English ways, and is the first stage text to make use of rural Québecois speech.　　　　L.E. DOUCETTE

Petite Rivière, NS, UP, pop 281 (1981c), is located on the Petite R, about 13 km SW of LAHAVE. The name ("little river") was given by CHAMPLAIN. Its Micmac name was *Simkook.* French settlers brought by de MONTS founded the settlement about 1632. The community was based on farming and fishing, while the settlers also hunted to supplement their diets. Agriculture and fishing remain the main industries, though various support industries, such as lumbering, are carried on. Petite Rivière attracts many summer visitors, drawn by its nearby sandy beaches and quiet, peaceful scenery.
　　　　　　　　　　JEAN PETERSON

Petrie, Robert Methven, astronomer (b at St Andrews, Scot 15 May 1906; d at Victoria 8 Apr 1966). Brought to Canada by his parents in 1911, Petrie became interested in astronomy at high school and was encouraged by J.S. PLASKETT. After studying at UBC and Michigan, he joined the Dominion Astrophysical Observatory, Victoria, in 1935, when Plaskett retired, and stayed there (except while in the RCN during WWII) for the rest of his life, becoming director in 1951 and the last Dominion Astronomer in 1964. His studies of spectroscopic binaries and the motions and distances of hot B-type stars won international acclaim. When he died, he was planning the construction of a very large Canadian telescope. He was the first Canadian astronomer to become a VP of the International Astronomical Union (1958-64).　　　A.H. BATTEN

Petro-Canada, a federal CROWN CORPORATION created by statute on 30 July 1975, and given a broad legislative mandate to expedite PETROLEUM EXPLORATION and development in Canada, to acquire imported oil supplies, and to engage in a broad program of energy research and development. The company's sole shareholder is the Crown and its officers report to the minister of energy, mines and resources. Established with an initial appropriation of $1.5 billion in equity and debt capital, Petro-Canada expanded rapidly during its first 6 years of operation, acquiring the Canadian assets of 4 foreign-owned multinationals. By 1983 the company had esti-

mated assets of over $8 billion, making it one of the largest petroleum corporations in Canada. Although it was nearly turned over to the private sector by the Conservative government of Joe CLARK in 1979, the company remains an agent of the national government and has performed a number of functions as an instrument of public policy, eg, investing in higher-risk energy ventures such as frontier exploration and oil-sands development, and has been used by the government to gauge the turbulent international market. Nationally the company has 9000 employees and is headquartered in Calgary. *See also* ENERGY POLICY.　　LARRY R. PRATT

Petrochemical Industry, which produces chemicals using OIL AND NATURAL GAS as major raw materials, occupies an important position in Canada's MANUFACTURING and consuming sectors. Oil and natural gas are composed primarily of hydrocarbons. Most petrochemicals, except SULPHUR, contain hydrogen or carbon or both. Petrochemicals can be converted into thousands of industrial and consumer products, including PLASTICS, paints, RUBBER, fertilizers, detergents, dyes, TEXTILES and solvents. The industry consists of 2 major divisions. The primary petrochemical industry produces basic CHEMICALS, such as ethylene, from oil or gas. The secondary industries convert the basic petrochemicals into materials that may be directly used by other industries.

Canada's standard of living is dependent to a significant degree on domestic petrochemical production. The availability of economic petrochemicals allows the domestic production of numerous items that would be more costly if imported. The Canadian industry is growing more rapidly than its counterparts in Europe, Japan and the US, which are the dominant world producers. FOREIGN INVESTMENT is attracted to Canada because abundant energy resources can be profitably upgraded to supply growing world needs.

History in Canada

Many compounds now considered petrochemicals were formerly made from wood and COAL. By the late 19th century, a wood-based industry made methanol, acetic acid and other products. In 1901 an industry began in Shawinigan, Qué, making acetylene and related chemicals from coke and limestone. Following WWI, Shawinigan Chemicals expanded to make vinyl resins, now an integral part of the petrochemical industry. Canadian research played a key role in the development of this important class of plastics and adhesives. The discovery of oil in Lambton County, Ont, in 1857 eventually led to a petrochemical industry that replaced the one established on acetylene. Within 7 years, 27 small oil refineries were established in Petrolia, Ont. Abraham GESNER, one of Canada's industrial pioneers, was responsible for major technological breakthroughs in refining oil. Early efforts were aimed at producing lamp and stove oil, but as automobile use grew, refineries were adapted to produce TRANSPORTATION fuel. The new refinery processes also produced hydrocarbon mixtures suitable for petrochemical raw material (feedstock) but these were little exploited before WWII.

The outbreak of WWII made Canada an important petrochemical producer for the Allied war effort. Polymer Corporation Ltd (now Polysar) was established by the federal government in 1942 at Sarnia, Ont, to make synthetic butadienestyrene rubber. St Clair Processing Corp Ltd (a subsidiary of Imperial Oil Ltd) and Dow Chemical of Canada Ltd built plants nearby to make the petrochemicals for the synthetic rubber process. Also in 1942, Alberta Nitrogen Products began production of ammonia from natural gas at Calgary, Alta. These efforts spawned the modern Canadian industry.

The Modern Industry

After the war, the industry grew to supply the increasing demand for synthetic consumer products. The first industry-owned chemical plant based on oil was built at Sarnia by Dow in 1947, to produce polystyrene, a widely used plastic. Manufacture of many other chemical products soon developed at Sarnia including antifreeze, polyethylene, solvents and detergent materials. Montréal also grew as a petrochemical centre, especially after 1957, when Union Carbide Canada Ltd launched ethylene chemicals and polyethylene operations. The industry in Sarnia and Montréal still relies heavily on feedstocks from oil-refining plants. Meanwhile a gas-based industry was developing in Alberta. Canadian Industries Ltd established the first Canadian polyethylene plant near Edmonton in 1953, using ethane extracted from natural gas by Imperial Oil. The ethane-based industry remains the cornerstone of Alberta's petrochemical production, but the oil-based counterpart has grown since its beginning in 1953.

Location of Plants Today, most petrochemical plants are located near oil-producing and oil-refining centres or near natural-gas sources and transmission pipelines. They are concentrated in Ontario, Québec and Alberta, but plants are also present in most other provinces. Petrochemical plants are costly, some requiring more than $300 million to build. The asset value of Canadian petrochemical plants totalled nearly $7.6 billion in 1983. New additional investments of over $1 billion a year have been made recently.

Ownership Many multinational petrochemical companies have established Canadian subsidiary companies and operations. These tend to be dominated by foreign shareholders, although Canadians also hold equity in some of the subsidiaries. Some major petrochemical companies, such as Novacor Chemicals and Polysar, are controlled by Canadian shareholders. Joint ventures between foreign-controlled and Canadian-controlled companies are important to the industry in Sarnia and Montréal. Canadian investment is increasing, though the industry is dominated by two-thirds or more foreign ownership.

Economic Status Annual sales of petrochemicals exceeded $5 billion in Canada in 1982, about 40% of the value of all chemical shipments. The sales volume represents 2.7% of all manufacturing sales and 1.6% of the GROSS NATIONAL PRODUCT. The industry is growing at a much faster rate than the GNP and manufacturing in general. Products based on natural gas account for the greatest growth, especially in Alberta.

Nearly 66% of petrochemical production was consumed domestically in 1982 but exports are increasing. Most new plants were built with significant export business in mind; because their output exceeds Canadian needs, they are referred to as world scale. Since 1980, Canada has exported more petrochemicals than it has imported, but imports exceed $1 billion a year. Exports are more than $1.5 billion annually, of which over half goes to the US. Other large markets include Japan and other Pacific nations, Europe and S America. Imports, mainly chemicals for which the Canadian market is too small to warrant domestic production on an economic scale, come mostly from the US.

Costs In 1981 the industry consumed about 5% (280 trillion Btu) of Canada's oil and gas production, 19% of that used by all industry. Purchases of energy and feedstocks are the largest operating costs of a petrochemical plant, typically 50%. Other major costs are related to equipment and maintenance services.

Work Force The industry employs over 18 000 persons in jobs ranging from equipment operators to research scientists. Wages and salaries average more than 10% higher than for other manufacturing sectors. Productivity per worker is high because of the large investment in equipment. Plants normally operate 24 hours a day so that equipment can run continuously. The largest union in the industry is the Energy and Chemical Workers Union, although a significant number of workers are nonunionized.

Technology Petrochemical technology employs high pressures and temperatures, requiring sophisticated ENGINEERING and equipment in order to use energy efficiently. Most modern technology has been developed at great expense in laboratories run by multinational firms and located outside Canada. However, Canadian research efforts have resulted in notable discoveries, such as Du Pont Canada's development of linear-low-density polyethylene (a plastic resin) at Kingston and Sarnia in the 1960s. This product is becoming the preferred material for flexible packaging. Funds spent on petrochemical research in Canada are small compared with other industrialized nations, averaging less than 2% of industry sales. Most of these funds are generated by industry.

Government Control Federal and provincial controls on pricing and supply of oil and gas constitute the major government influence on the industry. The domestic industry maintains that, for it to be competitive, its raw material costs must be lower than world averages. Setting oil and gas prices that are acceptable to both industry and government has been a perennial subject of negotiation. Governments offer little direct aid to the industry, but have invested in joint ventures to spur growth and increase Canadian ownership. Exportation of certain primary petrochemicals requires approval by the National Energy Board; otherwise, normal trade regulations apply.

Environmental Status The industry has made great strides in controlling unwanted emissions; compared with other resource industries, its emissions are low per unit of output. Emissions are generally gaseous and can arise from production processes, handling and storage. Provincial regulations establish maximum emission levels that are complied with by the use of well-designed and well-maintained equipment. The industry does not generate large volumes of contaminated water.

Associations Although there is no petrochemical industry association in Canada, companies are members of the Canadian Chemical Producers' Assn (Ottawa), which represents most large industrial chemical manufacturers. The Chemical Institute of Canada (Ottawa) and its affiliate, the Canadian Society for Chemical Engineering, are important bodies for professional development. Trade publications include *Canadian Chemical Processing, Canadian Petroleum* and *Corpus Chemical Report,* all published by Southam Communications Ltd; *Nickles Daily Oil Bulletin,* published by Southam Communications Ltd; and *Oilweek,* published by MACLEAN HUNTER LTD. MICHAEL LAUZON

Petroleum Since its first commercial exploitation in the 1850s, petroleum has become the major ENERGY source of Canada and the industrial world. Petroleum is the mixture of complex hydrogen and carbon compounds, known as hydrocarbons, found in the Earth's crust. Most of these compounds are the FOSSIL remains of prehistoric forests and seabeds and can be thought of as fossilized BIOMASS. If fossil hydrocarbons are very high in carbon content and in solid form, they are classified as COAL. Petroleum, however, can occur in a solid or viscous-liquid form, known as BITUMEN, or in liquid and gaseous forms, crude oil and natural gas, respectively. The main hydrocarbon groups in petroleum are paraffins, naphthenes and aromatics, with minor amounts of oxygen, nitrogen and sulphur compounds. Except for rare deposits of exceptionally pure natural gas or crude oil, most petroleum requires processing to make it useful.

Although petroleum is occasionally found seeping out of surface rocks, most is recovered by drilling deep wells. Crude oil, the unrefined liquid found in underground reservoirs, can vary in appearance from a thin, colourless liquid composed primarily of naphtha, to a heavy, black, gummy substance with a high asphalt content. These forms require relatively complex processing. Most oil is intermediate between these extremes and can be industrially refined and distilled into a wide range of combustible fuels, PETROCHEMICAL feedstocks and lubricants.

Natural gas, a colourless, odourless, combustible mixture of methane, ethane, butane and propane, is often found associated with crude-oil deposits, as well as in separate commercial deposits or "fields." Much of the natural gas found in the foothills of the Rocky Mts in Alberta contains a significant proportion of hydrogen sulphide and is called "sour" gas. This poisonous, colourless, foul-smelling, corrosive gas necessitates extra precaution in drilling, and the hydrogen sulphide must be removed to make the natural gas suitable for domestic or industrial use. The removal yields a valuable by-product, elemental SULPHUR.

Bitumen, also known as asphalt or tar, is a dark brown-to-black mixture of oil, asphaltine and resin, which has lost its more volatile compounds through evaporation and oxidation. When found mixed with sedimentary particles, as in the vast Athabasca oil-sand deposits in northern Alberta, it is called tar sand or oil sand. Complex processing is required to produce usable oil from bitumen.

Most oil or gas does not form within the reservoir in which it is found. It migrates, often over great distances, from a "source rock," a sediment rich in organic matter, to the petroleum reservoir, usually a porous SEDIMENTARY ROCK. Oil can be generated from any organic material, eg, fish, marine plants, terrestrial plants and animals. A primary source of organic material is marine ALGAE. These minute, one-celled organisms form the bulk of plant life in the world's oceans. They are ideally situated for preservation in deep oceans because of their planktonic (ie, free-floating) existence. When they die, algae sink to the seafloor where they are buried within silts and clays. Since burrowing organisms (which consume plant material in shallow water) are not present, the algal material gradually builds up to form an appreciable part (1-2%) of the total sediment. Bacterial action releases oxygen from this organic material, further concentrating the hydrogen and carbon molecules required to produce petroleum.

Petroleum formation can begin almost as soon as the organic-laden silt becomes buried. Carbon-14 datings of such silts in the Gulf of Mexico have yielded ages of as little as 500 years. Conversely, investigations of certain types of oil fields have shown oil and gas accumulating millions of years after the deposition of the source rock. Alberta's LEDUC oil field is found in carbonate rocks of Devonian age, deposited 350 million years ago, yet the formation of oil in Devonian source rocks did not occur until they were buried to a sufficient depth in the Cretaceous period, more than 250 million years later.

Major Canadian Basins A sedimentary basin is a large downwarp of the Earth's crust in which sediment (weathered rock debris and chemical precipitates) has accumulated. Oil and gas accumulations are always found in, or associated with, sedimentary basins. Canada possesses 40 basins, covering 47% of the land surface and continental slopes, that are capable of containing hydrocarbons. Only a few of these

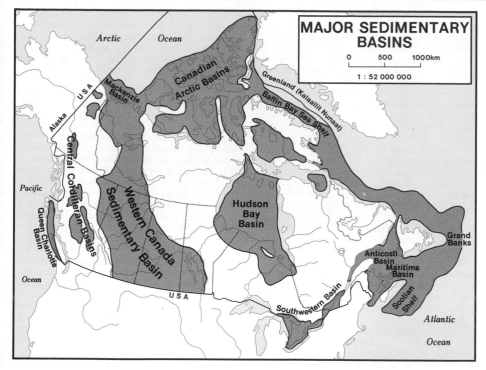

MAJOR SEDIMENTARY BASINS

0   500   1000km

1 : 52 000 000

covered in southwestern Ontario in 1857. Early explorers used the presence of oil seeps on the surface to locate their targets. In Alberta, Canada's largest oil-producing province, gas was first discovered in Medicine Hat in 1904 and oil at Turner Valley in 1910. Major discoveries in western Canada were sporadic until after WWII, when renewed oil industry activity led to the discovery of the Leduc oil field in 1947. Since then the industry has played a major role in Canada's development. Some of Canada's major petroleum deposits, usually identified by the age of the sediments and the place first discovered, include the Cretaceous Pembina oil field, the Devonian Bonnie Glen, Leduc, Norman Wells, Redwater and Wizard Lake oil fields, the Cretaceous Athabasca oil sands, the Cretaceous Suffield gas field and the Cretaceous and Triassic Deep Basin gas fields, all in Alberta. As of Dec 1980, Canada had produced 1555 million m³ of oil and 42 exajoules of gas, or 67% of known recoverable oil reserves in Canada (estimated at 2314 million m³) and 31% of total known gas reserves (estimated at 137 exajoules).

Ownership and Development To regulate and control the exploration and development of petroleum resources in Canada, the disposition of all oil and gas rights is controlled by various levels of government. The federal Dept of ENERGY, MINES AND RESOURCES is responsible for all federal crown acreage, which is primarily situated N of the 60th parallel and in offshore waters. Each provincial government also has a separate energy RESOURCES ministry to regulate all provincial crown acreage. The federal Dept of Indian Affairs and Northern Development acts on behalf of status Indians for all reservation land. Each government department periodically posts land sales in parts of the area for which it is responsible. The rights to explore and develop oil and gas on leases or licences are purchased by sealed bid in an open auction. The highest bidder purchases the exclusive rights to lease the land for a given period (usually 3-10 years) during which time it is allowed to explore for oil and gas in a manner established by the authorities.

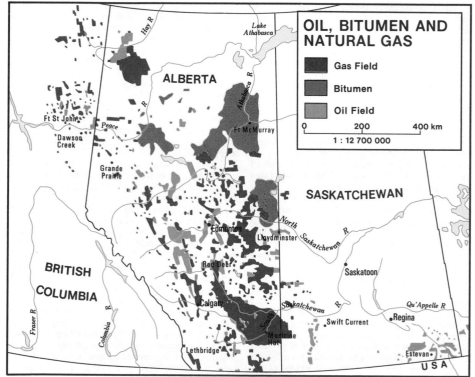

OIL, BITUMEN AND NATURAL GAS

■ Gas Field

■ Bitumen

■ Oil Field

0   200   400 km

1 : 12 700 000

Imperial Oil Leduc No 1 Well, Leduc Oil Field, the day the well blew, 13 Feb 1947 (*courtesy Provincial Archives of Alberta/H. Pollard Coll*).

basins, situated on land, now actually produce oil or gas. Canada's greatest potential for future sources of hydrocarbons lies offshore in the Arctic and off the East Coast. The major producing basin in Canada is the Western Canada Sedimentary Basin, situated beneath Alberta, northeastern BC, southern Saskatchewan, SW Manitoba and the western NWT. It extends from the Arctic Sea southeastwards across the N American continent to the Gulf of Mexico. It is a virtual textbook of natural history, recording the geological, environmental and biological events that have occurred on the N American continent over the last 600 million years (*see* GEOLOGICAL HISTORY). The Canadian part of the basin covers 1 815 000 km².

Other major Canadian sedimentary basins in-

clude the Hudson Bay Basin (970 000 km²), beneath Hudson Bay; the Mackenzie and Banks basins, beneath the BEAUFORT SEA (131 000 km²); the Canadian Arctic Basins, covering most of the arctic islands but excluding Baffin I (1 721 000 km²); the Baffin Bay and Labrador Sea shelves, off the East Coast (780 000 km²); the SCOTIAN SHELF and the GRAND BANKS, south of Nova Scotia and Newfoundland (900 000 km²); and the Anticosti and Maritimes basins in the Gulf of St Lawrence (340 000 km²). Programs by private industry and government are now under way to discover and exploit the vast natural resources in the Beaufort Sea, the arctic islands, the Scotian Shelf and the East Coast off Labrador and Newfoundland.

Oil and Gas Production Oil was first dis-

If petroleum is discovered, the lease owner can apply to develop and exploit the accumulation. Regulatory bodies (eg, the Energy Resources Conservation Board in Alberta) ensure that any petroleum accumulation discovered is removed from the ground in such a way as to reclaim the maximum possible amount of oil. If no petroleum is discovered, the lease is allowed to expire, and rights to oil and gas revert to the crown.

The federal government also maintains the right to establish exploration agreements on federal crown lands without public notice if it feels that it is in the public interest (eg, in expensive frontier exploration) or that there is a need to act quickly. Freehold lands are lands in which the mineral and surface rights were granted to individuals or large companies (eg, the HUDSON'S BAY COMPANY). In the late 19th century, large tracts of freehold land were distributed to pioneers in western Canada and to the CANADIAN PACIFIC RAILWAY. The oil and gas rights to freehold lands can be bought and sold privately by the individual or company, but the province or federal government regulates their exploitation.

Government Regulations The petroleum industry plays an important role in the energy sector of the Canadian economy. Because Canada only produces part of the oil necessary to meet its consumption requirements, large amounts must be imported. Price and supply fluctuations of imported oil affect the stability of the Canadian economy. To reduce this dependence on foreign oil, the federal government announced a comprehensive package of legislation, the National Energy Program, in 1980. The NEP established a price structure and revenue-sharing agreement and was intended to ensure petroleum-industry stability and to redistribute the costs of petroleum consumption throughout Canada. It also established incentives to conserve energy, increase Canadian ownership of the petroleum industry, expand exploration in Canadian frontier areas and develop alternatives to oil consumption. The intended outcome of the program was to establish eventual total energy self-sufficiency in Canada. Ottawa, the provinces and the petroleum industry were engaged in heated debate over the NEP, and the program has been revised considerably, particularly since the Conservative electoral victory of Sept 1984 (*see* ENERGY POLICY; NATIONAL ENERGY BOARD).   GORDON COPE

Petroleum Exploration and Production
There is a saying in the petroleum industry that "oil is found in the minds of men." Even with the most sophisticated scientific techniques, finding hidden petroleum deposits involves a large measure of creative interpretation. Until a hole is drilled, the existence of oil or gas is theoretical; "dry" holes are common even in established production areas. Once the resource is found, its value also depends on the "minds of men": exploration and production are expensive endeavours, worthwhile only when society needs the oil or gas badly enough to pay for it. The existence of buried petroleum had been known for many centuries, but people did not start drilling for oil until the middle of the 19th century. At that time a shortage of whale oil coincided with the invention of techniques for refining "rock oil" into lamp oil. Since then, demand for oil and gas has periodically surged and slumped, and so have prices and exploration activity.

Geology and Geophysics The Earth's surface often provides the field geologist with clues to what lies below. The hints may be obvious: seepages of oil and gas, or outcroppings of SEDIMENTARY ROCK or FOSSILS exposed in a tilted layer of rock on a mountain. That layer of rock might once have been the flat bottom of an ancient sea

which, through millions of years and constant movements of the Earth's crust, was folded, tilted and exposed (*see* PLATE TECTONICS). The clue is important: accumulations of oil and gas are often found in rock strata that are folded or tilted to some degree. However, the rocks that may contain traps for reservoirs of oil and gas are often thousands of metres below the surface, sometimes covered by a fairly horizontal plain. Aerial photographs and topographical maps can be useful in determining the underground landscape, and the science of geophysics can be even more helpful in mapping the depths beneath the surface.

Geophysics studies physical properties of rocks (eg, magnetism, resistivity, radioactivity). The geophysicist's tools include a magnetometer and a gravimeter, which are used to identify rock types. Both instruments were developed in the 1800s and have continually been improved since that time. Deeply buried sedimentary rocks are often very dense and contain high concentrations of IRON and other materials detectable by a magnetometer. Differences in the pull of gravity of various rocks, measured by the gravimeter, can also help identify the locations of certain rock types beneath the surface.

Another geophysical tool, the seismograph, can virtually compose pictures of underground rock formations. The seismograph works on the principle of sound-wave transmission. As sound waves travel downwards through layers of different types of rocks, they are reflected back to the surface. Differences in wave intensity and travel time provide information about the different types and structures of rocks through which the waves travel. At the surface, the sound waves are recorded by geophones, sensitive recording devices that are connected to computer equipment. Computers are used to produce the "pictures," ie, seismographs in which the geophysicist can "see" the structural composition of the rocks far below.

Drilling The only way to prove what lies in buried rocks is to drill a well. Even with modern GEOLOGY and geophysical techniques, drilling remains risky. An exploratory or "wildcat" well in an area that has not been drilled before faces high odds against success: perhaps one of 7 or even 10 exploratory wells finds commercial accumulations of oil or gas. To be commercially viable, a well must be able to produce enough oil or gas to justify the costs of drilling and placing it on production. In wildcat areas the first exploratory wells are often drilled as tests; they are not expected to yield oil or gas. Such wells, however, produce valuable information about the nature of the rocks and their oil and gas potential. In frontier areas, such as the BEAUFORT SEA or off Canada's East Coast, a series of widely separated exploratory wells is needed to determine the potential of a particular area. If exploratory wells establish the presence of producible quantities of oil or gas, "development" wells are drilled to define the size and extent of the

Dome Petroleum drilling activities in the Beaufort Sea (*courtesy Canapress*).

field. In development drilling the odds for success are higher: perhaps 6 or 7 successful wells for every 10 drilled. But the element of risk is still present: there may not be enough oil or gas to be commercially attractive; or the technology required to produce oil or gas may be too expensive.

The exploration industry in Canada has gone through "booms and busts," ups and downs that have little to do with the amount of oil or gas left to be found. The level of exploration activity is determined largely by the balance between supply and demand. For example, the NORMAN WELLS oil field in the NWT was first discovered in 1920, but it was then considered too remote to be of interest to southern Canada. A modest amount of oil was refined there to meet regional demands. It was not until the mid-1970s that decreasing supplies and increasing oil values made large-scale development at Norman Wells worthwhile. Technology also can have an impact on exploration activity. For example, extensive exploitation of the large volumes of heavy oil in the LLOYDMINSTER area was dependent on the development of enhanced recovery techniques.

There is a certain romantic air about drilling, perhaps a result of the risk, or of the movies and TV programs that show burly men wrestling with heavy equipment, gushers blowing in and wells blowing out. In today's drilling industry, however, the emphasis is on sophisticated technology. Skills and knowledge are more important than brawn. Blowouts have almost been eliminated by improvements in drilling equipment and knowledge.

In the early years of Canada's petroleum industry, wells were not drilled but punched with cable tools. On a cable tool rig, a heavy bit with a chiseled edge was suspended on a line of rope or wire cable. The hole was made through the constant raising, lowering and pounding of the bit into the earth. By the late 1920s, most drilling operations were using rotary drilling equipment, which was more efficient, drilling deeper and faster.

Today, drilling is accomplished by a bit at the end of lengths of steel pipe. Each piece of pipe is about 9 m long and is added, a length at a time, by threading onto the next piece of pipe. The bit, drill collars (which add weight to the bit) and lengths of pipe are called the drilling "string." The whole string is turned by a rotating platform, the rotary table. The revolving bit cuts and grinds through rock formations, lubricated and cooled by drilling fluid, commonly called drilling "mud," a mixture of water or oil, clay and chemicals. A deep-rated drilling rig, which might be used to drill holes 5000 m deep, is composed of much heavier, larger and stronger equipment than one used to drill shallow wells (eg, 1000 m deep). For offshore drilling, rigs generally are permanently mounted on barges or platforms so they can be towed from well site to well site. Some offshore drilling rigs are mounted on specially designed ships which move under their own power.

Drilling operators constantly monitor the progress of a well so that decisions about completion or abandonment can be made quickly. Throughout the drilling operation, the rock cuttings are examined for traces of hydrocarbons. If the well is judged a dry hole, it will be plugged with cement and abandoned. However, if the tests show promise, the well will be "completed." The first step in completion is the installation of production casing, tubular steel pipe that is cemented in place down the length of the well bore. After this process, the drilling rig is usually removed from the well and a truck-mounted service rig is moved into place. In fracturing, or fracing, materials are pumped down the well under high pressure to prop open cracks in the reservoir rock so that the oil or gas can move more freely through the formation. Formations that years ago might have been considered capable of only minimal production now achieve good production rates through completion practices that, with better prices for oil and gas, are worth implementing.

Production Years ago, reservoirs were often damaged and depleted early because of poor production practices. Natural gas, often produced along with crude oil, was ignited and flared away. Today, as crude oil and natural gas, their products and by-products become more valuable, optimizing recovery has become more important.

Natural gas generally flows to the surface through its own pressure; thus, a natural-gas wellhead is usually composed of only a series of chokes and valves to control flow. The wellhead structure is called a "Christmas tree." Crude oil, which typically contains some natural gas or solution gases, is sometimes produced through its natural pressure, but most crude oil wells in Canada require some method of lifting the oil to the surface. Pumping equipment is known by various names including "pump jack," "horsehead pump" and walking beam. Only about 25% of the oil would be recovered from a typical reservoir by natural means or primary recovery techniques. Enhanced-recovery techniques permit production of more oil from many reservoirs. The most common enhanced-recovery method, water injection, involves injecting water into the oil-bearing formation; the water forces the oil toward the producing well bore. Such techniques can result in recovery rates that exceed 80% of the oil in place.

Transportation In a country as large as Canada, the transportation of oil and gas from areas of supply to areas of demand is a very important aspect of the petroleum industry. In western Canada's oil and gas producing provinces, long trains of tank cars are a common sight. They carry everything from asphalt (produced from heavier crude oils and used for paving roads) to propane, butane and other liquid and gaseous products of crude oil and natural gas. Many of these tank cars are headed east, to industrial centres where the petroleum products and by-products are used in a great variety of MANUFACTURING processes (*see* CHEMICAL INDUSTRIES). Before the 1950s, railway and truck transport were the only methods of transporting oil and gas across Canada, but since then PIPELINES have carried most of Canada's oil and gas production to areas of consumption. Just as the construction of railroads was essential to the early development of Canada, pipelines became an integral part of Canada's industrial growth midway through the 20th century.

Refining Gasoline, diesel fuel and jet fuel are the most obvious petroleum products, but the list of manufactured products includes everything from insecticides to shampoo and plastic. The processes that result in these products are often complex, but all are based on separating crude oil's various components into useful by-products, which can be in solid, liquid or gaseous forms.

Refining begins with "boiling" crude oil past its evaporation point. In a process called distillation, the various by-products are separated according to their boiling points. The basic hydrocarbon streams include gasoline, middle distillates (diesel and heating fuels) and residues (industrial fuel and asphalt). Gasoline, lubricants and some other products must be blended and improved with chemical additives to produce finished products with desired characteristics. Refineries may also produce heating fuels, heavy industrial fuels and feedstocks for the PETROCHEMICAL INDUSTRY.

Regulation The marketing of crude oil, natural gas, their products and by-products is complex. Various regulations, both federal and pro-

vincial, govern all aspects of production and sales. Although the provinces have jurisdiction over the oil and gas produced within their boundaries, the federal government has the ultimate jurisdiction over oil and gas pricing, transmission and sales, both domestic and export. The federal and provincial governments share the revenues of producing companies through taxes and royalties. The right to revenue sharing and regulation has been a topic of dispute among federal and provincial governments, as has the question of who actually owns the oil and gas, particularly in offshore waters (*see* ENERGY POLICY). The NATIONAL ENERGY BOARD is the regulatory body of the federal government with authority to establish prices and export allocations.   ANNE MCNAMARA

Petroleum Industries find, develop, transport, process and market petroleum. They transform BITUMEN, OIL AND NATURAL GAS from raw resources extracted from the ground into useful products such as gasoline, kerosene, heating fuel, plastics and fertilizers. As petroleum has become the critical ENERGY resource of this century, governments have become more and more intimately involved in the operations of the petroleum industries. Compared to other industries, most sectors of the petroleum business are very capital intensive (ie, they require a high proportion of machinery and equipment relative to their labour force) and typically involve higher financial risks. The profitability and level of activity in the industries vary enormously, depending on PETROLEUM SUPPLY AND DEMAND, and they are often termed "boom-and-bust" businesses. A small number of large, vertically integrated companies engage in all activities, from initial PETROLEUM EXPLORATION AND PRODUCTION to the final retail sale of petroleum products. Most of the Canadian integrated companies are subsidiaries of multinational oil companies based in the US, the UK and the Netherlands, although the federal crown corporation PETRO-CANADA, created by Parliament in 1975, now rivals the size and scope of the foreign-controlled "majors." There also are more than 600 smaller companies that have specialized in one or more sectors; most of these "independents" are Canadian owned.

The Canadian petroleum industry began in Ontario in 1857, when James Miller WILLIAMS found oil in a well in Enniskillen Township, near the town later named Oil Springs. The well, known as Williams No 1, set off an oil-exploration boom that established southwestern Ontario as a significant oil-production area during the late 19th century. About 18 small refineries were built to convert the oil into buggy-wheel grease and kerosene lamp fuel, which were the major uses of oil until the spread of the automobile in the early 20th century. The oil and products were transported by wagons, railways, barges and leaky, wooden PIPELINES; most retail sales were made by general stores. Hundreds of drillers, producers, shippers, refiners and retailers competed in a boom-and-bust atmosphere until 1880, when several refiners merged to form IMPERIAL OIL. In 1898 John D. Rockefeller's Standard Oil Trust acquired control of Imperial Oil for $350 000, and Imperial remained a subsidiary of Standard Oil of New Jersey when the trust was split up by US authorities in 1911. Standard of New Jersey, later renamed Exxon, is still the world's largest oil company and still owns 69% of Imperial.

In 1914, when the Royal Navy was worried about the security of its oil supplies, the Canadian government decided to issue crown oil leases only to Canadian- and UK-controlled companies. Imperial Oil circumvented this regulation by acquiring freehold leases from private mineral owners (mainly the CANADIAN PACIFIC RAILWAY and the HUDSON'S BAY COMPANY) in

Alberta's refineries produce gasoline, diesel and aviation fuels; an Edmonton refinery is shown here (*courtesy Petroleum Resources Communication Foundation*).

western Canada and by setting up a subsidiary with majority Canadian ownership to exploit oil on crown leases. As a result, Imperial became a major developer of oil discoveries at Turner Valley, Alta, in 1910 and at NORMAN WELLS, NWT, in 1920. UK-based companies, eg, Royal Dutch Shell and Anglo-Persian Oil (later renamed British Petroleum), expanded their interests in Canada after 1914.

In 1946 domestic wells supplied only 10% of Canadian oil consumption. Canadian companies, eg, Canadian Oil (under the White Rose brand), McColl-Frontenac, British-American, Royalite and Home Oil, reached significant size in the first half of this century mainly as refiners and marketers of oil imported from the US. Then, on 13 Feb 1947, Imperial Oil discovered the major oil field at LEDUC, Alta, beginning the modern era of western Canadian oil production. A takeover spree by foreign companies in the 1950s and 1960s left virtually all of Canada's integrated oil companies controlled by multinational majors. By the early 1970s over half of the Canadian oil business (whether measured by assets, revenues or retail sales) belonged to units of the 7 biggest multinationals, the "seven sisters": Exxon, Royal Dutch Shell, British Petroleum, Mobil, Texaco, Gulf and Standard Oil of California. In 1973 foreign-controlled companies took in about 90% of petroleum revenues in Canada (*see* FOREIGN INVESTMENT).

Since the 1950s foreign ownership had been a growing concern of economic nationalists, consumer groups, socialists, some Canadian oilmen and independent fuel retailers. In 1959, after 2 ROYAL COMMISSIONS urged greater government control of the petroleum industries, Parliament created the NATIONAL ENERGY BOARD to oversee and regulate imports, exports, pipelines and other interprovincial oil and gas activities in Canada (although the NEB did not actually set pipeline tariffs until 1978). Provincial authorities, eg, the Alberta Energy Resources Conservation Board, also regulated the petroleum industries. But the federal government only acted to restrict foreign ownership after Oct 1973, when the Arab oil embargo set off a quadrupling of world oil prices.

The Foreign Investment Review Act of 1974 and the establishment of Petro-Canada in 1975 marked the first efforts to curb the domination of the multinationals, but these were not the first instances of government participation in the petroleum industry. During WWII the government operated a crown company called Wartime Oils and joined the US in building a pipeline from Norman Wells to the West Coast. In 1967 the government established PanArctic Oils Ltd to explore for oil and gas in the arctic islands. It was a joint venture, Ottawa owning 45% and private companies 55%. The provinces also were active in the petroleum business: Alberta Gas Trunk Line Co (now NOVA, AN ALBERTA CORPORATION) was set up by the Alberta government in 1955 to organize gas-gathering pipelines in the province; the equity was then sold to Canadian investors. Another Alberta oil and gas entity, the ALBERTA ENERGY COMPANY, was formed in 1975; 50% of the equity was sold to the public and 50% retained by the Alberta government. Provincial oil corporations also have been established by BC, Sask, Man, Ont, Qué, NS and Nfld. However, Petro-Canada is the only one to become fully integrated: its coast-to-coast operations now include research and development, exploration and production, pipelines, refineries and retail outlets. In 1983 the federal oil company had 6601 employees, $8.2 billion in assets and $4.1 billion in revenues. Its reported asset value was slightly larger than that of Imperial Oil, although Imperial had more than twice as many workers and twice as much revenue. Petro-Canada grew mainly by buying assets from Atlantic Richfield (US controlled, 1976), Pacific Petroleums (US, 1978), Petrofina (Belgian, 1981) and BP Canada (UK, 1982).

The foreign-owned multinationals have made substantial contributions to the Canadian petroleum industries. Except for a few brief periods (eg, the mid-19th century, 1969-74 and again in 1983) Canada has imported more oil than it has exported. The world resource base, tanker fleets and marketing expertise of the multinationals delivered most of these imports relatively cheaply and efficiently. The majors provided much of the training in management and technical skills that allowed Canadians to operate their own companies, including Petro-Canada, and to sell their expertise abroad. The giant companies' financial strength enabled them to carry on long-term, expensive PETROLEUM RESEARCH AND DEVELOPMENT projects, including the oil-sands processing, offshore and arctic oil exploration, enhanced oil recovery, sour-gas processing, oil and gas transportation, refinery technologies and computer systems. These companies still account for a large proportion of petroleum R&D spending. The multinationals provided much of the financing for projects (eg, oil-sands plants, pipelines, refineries) that might have been too big and too risky for Canadian capital markets.

Whatever the merits of the multinationals' prominence, the structure of the petroleum industries was altered fundamentally when world oil prices quadrupled in 1973-74 and again when they nearly tripled in 1979. The first concern each time was to ensure adequate oil supplies for Canada, and government-to-government deals undermined the trading power of the oil majors. Government attention then shifted quickly to the enormous new revenues created by higher prices. Since 1973 the federal government has controlled oil and gas prices in Canada, generally maintaining them at levels well below the equivalent world oil price. (The Conservative government of Brian Mulroney indicated its intention to bring oil prices to world level in 1985.) Taxes and royalties diverted 60% of oil revenues to federal and provincial treasuries and to programs designed to cushion consumers from the full impact of world prices. After bitter debate in 1974-75 between the federal and Alberta governments, the federal oil policy remained intact, but a much different policy was adopted for natural gas. Historically low gas prices were allowed to rise rapidly, and less than 40% of gas revenues were funnelled to taxes and royalties. At the same time, tax provisions allowed investors to get substantial write-offs for investment in oil and gas drilling. The combination of high prices, big profit potential and generous tax breaks set off a huge gas-exploration boom in western Canada in the late 1970s. Canadian companies (eg, DOME PETROLEUM, Nova, Sulpetro) soared to prominence. Meanwhile the majors were saddled with many less-profitable oil investments and were effectively barred from new corporate acquisitions by the Foreign Investment Review Act.

The second major reshaping of the petroleum industries came in Oct 1980, when the federal Liberal government announced a sweeping National Energy Program (NEP). The policy further increased the federal taxation of petroleum revenues and took away the tax write-offs that had encouraged drilling in the 1970s. Instead, a so-called Petroleum Incentive Program (PIP) paid grants to petroleum drillers depending on their Canadian-ownership level and on the location of the wells. The highest PIP grants, up to 80% of actual spending, went for wells drilled in frontier areas by companies more than 75% Canadian owned; there would be no PIP grants at all for companies less than 50% Canadian owned drilling in the provinces. The NEP was substantially modified in 1981 and 1982 after harsh criticism from the petroleum-producing provinces in western Canada and from the petroleum industries. The NEP, combined with the 15% drop in world oil price 1982-83, led to a sharp decline in petroleum activity in western Canada and to the cancellation of several proposed MEGAPROJECTS in the Alberta oil sands. However, exploration activity continued in frontier areas such as the BEAUFORT SEA, the arctic islands and the East Coast offshore from Newfoundland and Nova Scotia. The NEP also encouraged Canadian companies to acquire the Canadian operations of foreign oil companies. Amid slumping world oil prices and a general economic recession, the debt-financed takeovers caused financial crises for many of the Canadian oil companies. Nonetheless, Canadian-controlled companies, including Petro-Canada, increased their share of petroleum revenues from 13% in 1977 to 19% in 1980 and 28% in 1983. In late 1984, the newly elected Conservative government planned to revamp the NEP.

The petroleum industries employ roughly 260 000 people in Canada, of whom about 125 000 are engaged in marketing, which includes heating-fuel deliveries and the operation of more than 20 000 retail gasoline outlets. Most integrated companies have their head offices in Toronto and base their marketing operations there. Exploration and production directly employ about 40 000; another 60 000 are employed in associated service industries and equipment manufacturing. Most of these operations have their headquarters in CALGARY, although the exploration activities now extend to the farthest extremities of Canada. Refinery operations, employing about 15 000, are scattered across Canada, but the main refining centres are EDMONTON, SARNIA and MONTRÉAL. Petroleum transportation, mainly by pipeline companies based in Calgary, Vancouver and Toronto, provides another 20 000 jobs in Canada.

In 1983, according to the federal Petroleum Monitoring Agency, the Canadian petroleum industries made capital expenditures of $9.5 billion in Canada and another $0.8 billion abroad. The industries had total revenues of $56.5 billion and reported profits of $1.5 billion. The companies paid out $1.2 billion in dividends to shareholders. From 1976 to 1982 the petroleum companies accounted for between one-fifth and one-third of all profits reported by Canadian nonfinancial corporations. *See* ENERGY POLICY.   ROBERT BOTT

Reading: Carl E. Beigie et al, *The Canadian Oil Industry in Context* (1981); David Crane, *Controlling Interest: The Canadian Oil and Gas Stakes* (1982); Peter Foster, *The Blue-Eyed Sheiks: The Canadian Oil Establishment* (1980).

Petroleum Research and Development
Research has always been the backbone of the petroleum industry. Bringing crude oil, BITUMEN or natural gas to the surface presents major technological problems and, once recovered, there is little use for the RESOURCE in its raw state. When the industry was first established in Canada about 1850 in the region of Oil Springs, southwestern Ontario, its main product was asphalt.

Soon after, a Nova Scotia physician-geologist, Abraham GESNER, developed a technique for producing kerosene, a high-quality illuminating oil, initially from coal and later from petroleum. This development laid the groundwork for the petroleum-refining industry. Technology for drilling and production of crude oil was developed in the oil fields around Petrolia and Oil Springs, Ont, in the latter half of the 19th century. Notable early developments were spring-pole percussion drilling and a jerker-rod pumping system still in use in southern Ontario fields. The expertise of the Petrolia drillers was used abroad in the development of oil fields in Java, Galicia, Germany and Hungary. In 1884 a German chemist, Herman Frasch, was hired by IMPERIAL OIL to study petroleum-refining problems. He developed a process for the removal of SULPHUR from kerosene that solved the odour problems of Canadian kerosene and enabled it to compete with products made from low-sulphur Pennsylvania crude. This development initiated the use of CHEMISTRY in improving the quality of petroleum products.

The first Canadian petroleum-related laboratory was established by the federal government in Ottawa in 1910 as the Fuels Testing Station of the Dept of Mines, now the Energy Research Laboratories of the Dept of ENERGY, MINES AND RESOURCES. In 1921 the Alberta government established the forerunner of the ALBERTA RESEARCH COUNCIL, a body that has been intimately involved in petroleum, COAL and bitumen research. The first industrial research laboratory was established by Imperial Oil in Sarnia, Ont, in 1924, when R.K. Stratford was hired as a research chemist and later appointed director of the technical and research department. This laboratory is currently the largest petroleum research centre in Canada. In 1949 Imperial Oil formed a production research division in Calgary, now the research department of Esso Resources Canada Ltd. Imperial also initiated geophysical and geological research and development in exploration technology in the early 1950s; most major exploration companies now maintain programs in applied research in earth science. Canadian Oil Sands (later Syncrude Canada) set up its research operations in Edmonton, Alta, in 1958 to support its proposed oil-sands mining and upgrading plant. Shell Canada Ltd established a research centre in Oakville, Ont, in 1962, and in Calgary, Alta, in 1982. Gulf Canada Ltd opened laboratories in Sheridan Park, Ont, in 1964. PETRO-CANADA initiated research operations in Calgary soon after its formation in 1975. The GEOLOGICAL SURVEY OF CANADA conducts geological and geophysical research at the Institute of Petroleum and Sedimentary Geology in Calgary and at the BEDFORD INSTITUTE OF OCEANOGRAPHY in Dartmouth, NS. In addition to these government and industry operations, substantial research into petroleum recovery is carried out in centres associated with the universities of Alberta and Calgary, notably the Petroleum Recovery Institute and the Computer Modelling Group. In Canada, in 1982, there were about 1500 people involved in petroleum research and development.

Much of the research carried out in these laboratories is associated with the solution of problems directly related to Canadian conditions, although the solutions have often been applied worldwide. Manufacture of high-quality lubricants from Canadian crudes, which may contain waxy components, sulphur and other impurities, has resulted in the development of extraction, dewaxing and hydrotreating processes now used in many countries. Sulphur-asphalt paving mixtures and fuels and lubricants designed to operate under harsh, winter conditions are other examples of Canadian-developed products. Since Canada has extensive deposits of heavy crude and oil sands in Alberta and Saskatchewan, many laboratories are involved in researching methods of recovery and upgrading of bitumen to produce high-quality synthetic crudes. In the 1970s and 1980s the increase in world crude prices, accompanied by the decline in production of conventional oil and gas in Canada, led to an increase in research studies aimed at CONSERVATION and efficient use of natural resources. As well as methods to increase recovery of hydrocarbons from conventional oil fields, research has resulted in such developments as fuel-saving lubricants, high-efficiency fuel oil and natural-gas burners, and the use of alcohol fuels to extend gasoline supplies. New techniques, such as the building of artificial islands and ice-resistant drilling platforms, have been developed for hydrocarbon exploration in Canada's northern and offshore frontier areas (see OCEAN INDUSTRIES). Another significant area of research is in reservoir engineering, which uses computer modelling and other techniques to determine why oil accumulates in the way it does. The rapidly changing conditions in the petroleum industry and the incentives to achieve self-sufficiency ensure that R&D will remain an important part of Canada's petroleum industry (see INDUSTRIAL RESEARCH AND DEVELOPMENT). *J.L. TIEDJE*

Petroleum Supply and Demand Petroleum demand reflects ENERGY use in society and is usually forecast by projecting recent trends in economic growth, energy consumption, petroleum technology and prices. The supply of petroleum available to meet those demands depends on 2 factors: reserves in the ground and the productivity of those reserves. The total in-place reserves of crude oil, natural gas or BITUMEN are less important than the recoverable reserves. "Proved" reserves are the estimated quantities that analysis of geological and engineering data demonstrates, with reasonable certainty, to be economically recoverable from known reservoirs, under existing economic and operating conditions. They increase as new discoveries are made, concurrently decreasing as they are exploited. "Unproved" reserves are estimated quantities that might be economically recoverable from known deposits but with a lower degree of certainty. A less certain category is "speculative" reserves, which are not yet discovered but which general geological and engineering judgement suggests might eventually be found or become economically recoverable. The sum of proved, unproved and speculative reserves is termed "future potential recovery" and, when added to cumulative production, results in estimates of "ultimate potential recovery." "Productivity" is the estimate of the maximum practical rate at which oil or gas can be produced, having regard to existing proved reserves and facilities, the rate at which proved reserves will grow and new facilities be installed, and economic, political and other relevant factors.

Oil reserves are classified as "conventional" if the oil is produced through well bores by ordinary production methods. "Synthetic" oil results, for example, from upgrading bitumen or from COAL LIQUEFACTION. Production of conventional Canadian oil has exceeded the rate of additions to proved reserves since the early 1970s. Consequently, proved reserves have declined to some 800 million m³. Some 1900 million m³ have been produced to date indicating an initial proved reserve of some 2700 million m³. This is about one-quarter of the 10-14 billion m³ that most authorities consider to be Canada's ultimate potential recovery. Canadian synthetic oil currently comes from bitumen recovered from the Alberta oil sands. Some authorities restrict proved reserves of synthetic oil to production recoverable during the reasonable producing life of existing facilities. Other estimates include all volumes of synthetic oil recoverable from

oil sands considered economically attractive for development. Thus, synthetic-oil proved reserves estimates range from some 230 to 3900 million m³. The ultimate potential recovery of synthetic oil is difficult to speculate about because huge deposits exist although only a small fraction is being developed. Ultimate potential recovery will depend on future technology and the economics of recovering and upgrading bitumen to synthetic oil. Estimates currently range from 1 billion m³ to 40 billion m³. In Canada growth in proved reserves of natural gas has exceeded for many years the rate of production. Proved reserves are currently some 2600 billion m³ and, when coupled with production to date, indicate initial proved reserves of some 3950 billion m³. Estimates of ultimate potential recovery for natural gas in Canada range from some 12 to 15 trillion m³. For both natural gas and conventional oil, a major portion of Canada's future potential recovery is expected from frontier regions, such as the BEAUFORT SEA and the eastern Continental Shelf (see OCEAN INDUSTRIES). Most proved reserves are in the Western Canada Sedimentary Basin, the source of current production.

Canada's total productivity of conventional and synthetic oil has declined over the past decade to some 220 000 m³ per day. Productivity is expected to decline during the next few years, then return to almost current levels by about 1991. Natural-gas production has increased somewhat over the past decade but is much lower than existing productivity, which, in turn, is expected to grow in future. Much of this growth will come from proved reserves that are not now being produced; hence this forecast is less uncertain than that for oil.

Canadian per-capita demands for oil and natural gas have been among the highest in the world (see ENERGY IN SOCIETY). This rate partly results from Canada's severe climate, but also from its high standard of living and the relatively low energy prices that prevailed until the 1970s. Canadian requirements for oil products, which include conventional and synthetic oil and condensate (a gas by-product and oil substitute), increased steadily through most of the early 1970s but recently declined as a result of CONSERVATION measures, slower economic growth and higher petroleum prices. The decline is expected to continue during the next decade with demand dropping from a current level of some 250 000 m³/day to about 230 000 m³/day by 1991. Demand for natural gas over the same period has generally increased and most authorities forecast a substantial growth in future (from 130 million m³/day to 190 million m³/day within a decade) because of the ongoing price advantage of natural gas over oil and the efforts to substitute gas for oil.

Domestic sources have supplied most of Canada's oil and natural gas, although an increasing portion of oil has been imported. Net imports of oil now comprise less than 5% of total requirements, although Canada was a net exporter of oil prior to 1974. All gas requirements have been met with Canadian production. Despite Canada's need to import some foreign oil, there are still exports of light and heavy oil for which there is not sufficient Canadian refinery capacity or markets located near sources of supply. Total oil productivity is expected to continue to fall modestly short of Canadian demand throughout the next decade. The shortfall, which must be made up by imports, has been as great as 30 000-40 000 m³/day, but has declined to less than 10 000 m³/day. Gas productivity is expected to continue to exceed demand, leaving a surplus for possible export. Imports and exports of oil and natural gas are a function of Canadian demand, available productivity and government ENERGY POLICY. Imports come predominantly from Venezuela and Saudi Arabia. Natural-gas surpluses have been exported to

the US throughout the past decade, and there is increasing scope for exports of liquefied natural gas. *GERALD L. DE SORCY*

Petrolia, *see* SARNIA.

Petun ("Tobacco") were an Iroquoian-speaking people, closely related to the HURON, who lived in the region of COLLINGWOOD, Ont, in the early to mid-16th century. The name Petun was applied to these people by the French, and refers to the fact that they were particularly noted for cultivating tobacco. At the time of European contact, the Petun occupied from 8 to 10 villages located below the Niagara Escarpment along the SW margin of Georgian Bay. Their precontact population is uncertain, but appears to have numbered several thousand.

The Petun differed little from the Huron, who lived one day's journey to the NE. It appears from historical accounts and archaeology that the Petun were of relatively recent origin, having been formed in late prehistoric times by a union of groups of Iroquoian-speakers moving west from HURONIA and other Iroquoian groups from the areas that are now Toronto or Hamilton. They maintained trading relationships with the NEUTRAL and Huron, and with the Algonquian-speaking OTTAWA and Nipissing. They were destroyed or dispersed along with the Huron by the IROQUOIS in 1649. The surviving Petun joined with the refugee Huron and made extensive journeys through the midwestern US. They eventually settled in the 1850s in Oklahoma where descendants of both groups now reside under the name *Wyandot,* a form of the original Huron name for themselves.

The Petun are historically recorded as consisting of 2 tribes, the Wolves and the Deer, each comprising one principal village and several lesser villages or hamlets. The villages were palisaded, occupied year-round and contained numerous LONGHOUSES. The population subsisted by cultivating corn, beans and SQUASH, as well as by hunting and fishing. The Petun are one of the lesser known native groups, partly because they were not numerous, but primarily because they were overshadowed in 17th-century European attention by the larger and politically more important Huron Confederacy. *See also* NATIVE PEOPLE: EASTERN WOODLANDS and general articles under NATIVE PEOPLE. *PETER G. RAMSDEN*

Reading: B.G. Trigger, *The Children of Aataentsic: A History of the Huron People to 1660* (1976).

Pewee, *see* FLYCATCHER, TYRANT.

Pewter, essentially an alloy of the same metals as bronze (COPPER and tin), was probably discovered during the Bronze Age. From the early 17th century until the mid-19th century, pewter was a favourite metal for domestic flatware (spoons, forks) and small serving, pouring, eating and drinking vessels. In pure form, pewter is a mixture of approximately 80% tin and 20% copper. Where guild systems prevailed, as in England, contents were controlled and cast vessels often marked by the maker. In N America, raw tin was not readily available and pewterers depended on scrap pewter for their metal. Such scrap pewter, melted and recast into new objects, was commonly adulterated or "bulked-up" with lead, minimally with pieces requiring hardness (eg, spoons, forks) but to a proportion of as much as one-third for nonwearing objects (eg, organ pipes, candle molds).

Since pewter is a soft metal, objects in daily use had a short lifespan, estimated at 5 years, before requiring melting and recasting. Two-piece manufactured bronze molds were commercially available for casting common vessels, and pewterers formed their own molds for others. In Canada a few older religious orders in Québec, notably the Congrégation de Notre Dame, still use pewter and own several spoon and plate molds used for periodic recasting.

Both French and English pewter was in common use during the French regime, and many spoons and segments of porringers, bowls and plates have been excavated at early habitation sites from Louisbourg to Montréal. Although there is no documentary evidence of commercial pewtering during this period, examples of unmarked pewter have been found which were undoubtedly local castings or recastings. Later inhabitants of NEW FRANCE and early British North America appear to have used imported pewter almost exclusively. Recasting, particularly of spoons, was a regular practice. The bronze or home-carved wooden molds were often engraved or chiselled to leave handle decorations in relief. These pewterwares were not maker marked and do not bear punch stamps, as does much English and American pewter. Marked and identifiably Canadian pewter does not appear until the early 19th century and then was limited to Montréal and Québec. Present evidence indicates that pewtering in Canada never developed as a major craft industry, possibly because, by the 1830s, pewter was being replaced as a tableware by inexpensive imported English ceramics and steelware. It is probable that the first substantial settlement of Canada came slightly late for the widespread use of domestic pewterware.

Few Canadian pewterers have been identified from markings on pewterwares. Chief among them was Thomas Menut of Montréal, who produced primarily spoons and forks punched with a large "T.M." and a beaver motif. His working dates appear to have been principally from about 1810 to 1820, extending into the 1850s. He was succeeded by his son Jean-Baptiste Menut, who is listed as a Montréal pewterer in 1857-58, and again in 1868. Jean-Baptiste Menut used the mark of a spread-winged angel, flanked by his initials "I.M." A few Montréal and Québec silversmiths also appear to have been part-time pewterers. A small number of existing pieces are known with small "Montréal" punchmarks, identical to those used on the silver of the Arnoldis, Robert Cruikshank, Salomon Marion and Paul Morand. None of this "Montréal"-stamped pewter has corresponding marker's stamps. David Smellie of Québec City, operating from 1780 to 1827, is also known to have made a small quantity of pewter. Britannia ware, a hard pewter manufactured by spinning in molds and finishing on lathes, is not known to have been produced in Canada. D.B. WEBSTER

Phalarope (family Scolopacidae), sandpiper-like SHOREBIRD, highly specialized for aquatic life. Phalaropes' legs are flattened laterally and toes have lobed flaps on sides and small webs at bases. Phalaropes swim jerkily, in tight circles, picking at food (aquatic invertebrates and larval fishes) stirred up by the small currents they create. They are often seen far out at sea. Females do the courting and after egg laying usually abandon their mates, leaving them to incubate eggs and care for young. Three species occur in Canada. Red phalarope (*Phalaropus fulicaria*) has circumpolar range. It usually breeds in small colonies near coastal freshwater pools; in Canada, from western Hudson Bay to northern Ellesmere I. Nests are cup-shaped depressions, often concealed by grasses domed over the 4 eggs (greenish buff with dark brown markings). This species may winter on the Indian Ocean. Wilson's phalarope (*P. tricolor*), the largest species, wades and walks more frequently than the other 2, and has reduced lobes and webs on its toes. Found only in N America, it breeds mainly in the prairies and locally in Ontario and Québec, often nesting with black terns. The nest, a scrape near shallow water, is lined with grass by the male. Wilson's phalaropes winter mainly in Argentina. The red-necked phalarope (*P. lobatus*),

the smallest phalarope, breeds in the low Arctic of the New and Old worlds. In Canada, it nests from Labrador to the southern YT. It migrates mainly along the coast and winters in seas of the Southern Hemisphere. S.D. MacDONALD

Pharmaceuticals Industry The pharmaceutical industry began more or less with the Industrial Revolution. The first laboratories were extensions of dispensaries where galenic drugs (herb and vegetable medicines) were prepared. A few drug manufacturers were established in Europe in the early 19th century: in France, Joseph Pelletier in Paris; in Germany, Friedrich Ludwig Koch in Oppenheim, Merck in Darmstadt and Riedel in Berlin. One of the first drugs produced industrially was quinine (from cinchona bark), which was extracted in much the same way as plant dyes. Later, the synthesis of aniline-based dyes (ie, synthetic organic dyes) provided the impetus for the MANUFACTURING of certain drugs. In N America the pharmaceutical industry probably began in Philadelphia in 1786, although it did not produce on a truly industrial scale until the 19th century.

E.B. Shuttleworth, first dean of the Ontario College of Pharmacy, founded a laboratory in Toronto in 1879, later known as Dow Pharmaceuticals. Charles E. Frosst opened a laboratory in Montréal (1899) to produce elixirs, syrups and tonics. The company established by the Wyeth brothers in Philadelphia in 1860 opened a branch in Montréal in 1883. Duffield, Parke and Co (later Parke-Davis) was founded in Detroit in 1866 and established an office and laboratory in Windsor, Ont, in 1887. The Rougier laboratories opened in 1901 in Montréal, followed by those of Frank W. Horner in 1912 and those of Ayerst, McKenna and Harrison in 1925. CONNAUGHT LABORATORIES was established in the Department of Hygiene at University of Toronto in 1914.

Before WWI the effective pharmacopoeia contained only about 20 products, including plant extracts such as opium, digitalis, aloe and quinine, and synthetic chemicals such as ether, phenobarbital, aspirin, certain arsenicals and some heavy metal salts. These products were manufactured by a number of small laboratories in industrialized countries. WWI sparked a drug crisis in N America because, despite its nascent pharmaceutical industry, the US still depended heavily on Germany for new and synthetic products.

Pharmaceutical research burgeoned in Europe and in N America between the wars. Several important new drugs were discovered, some in industrial laboratories, eg, organic mercurial diuretics, sulphonamides and phenytoins. The discovery of INSULIN by Frederick G. BANTING and Charles H. BEST in 1921-22 was a scientific breakthrough and a landmark in the history of medicine and pharmacy in Canada. The commercial production of insulin was confined to the Connaught Laboratories and, in the US, mainly to the Eli Lilly company. During these years several multinational corporations established subsidiaries in Canada. The pharmaceutical industry experienced its most rapid growth in the 1950s but, after the problems with thalidomide, development was modified by increased control by the Food and Drug Directorate (now the Health Protection Branch or HPB) of Health and Welfare Canada.

The federal government first legislated pharmaceutical products in the Inland Revenue Act of 1875, which became the Adulteration Act in 1884 and, in 1885, the Act respecting the Adulteration of Food, Drugs and Agricultural Fertilizers. Thirty-five years later, this Act became the Food and Drugs Act, which received only minor amendments until 1962. Certain European companies began to market the sedative and pain reliever thalidomide in the early 1960s. Pregnant

women who took the drug gave birth to babies with congenital malformations of the limbs. Under public pressure, the HPB imposed much stricter standards on drug manufacturers to avoid such incidents. These measures are laid out in the 1962 amendments to the Act. Since then the HPB has extended its jurisdiction to areas such as marketing authorization, all forms of advertising, and the distribution of samples to doctors. It has also developed the Drug Quality Assessment Program to inform members of the health professions about lower-priced drugs manufactured and distributed by more than one company. The Canadian drug industry was also affected in 1969 by the coming into force of Bill C-102, which modified the protection given by patents and allowed patented pharmaceuticals to be imported into Canada.

Canada's pharmaceutical industry is the world's 12th largest, producing about 2% of the drugs on the world market. In 1979 it employed 16 433 persons in 144 establishments; the value of its manufactured products was over $1 billion. It ranked 46th among Canadian industries in after-tax profits. Its fuel and electricity consumption was a modest $10.3 million in 1979 and its plants are not a major source of pollution. Most pharmaceutical houses in Canada today are branches of foreign multinationals. Eighty are located in Ontario and 50 in Québec. Almost all are privately owned. One CROWN CORPORATION owns a few plants. Two laboratories which produce vaccines, Connaught Laboratories and INSTITUT ARMAND-FRAPPIER, receive government subsidies.

Operation of a Pharmaceutical Laboratory

Under a director of research, the heads of chemical laboratory groups conduct research in various fields of human or animal pathology in order to discover new therapeutic agents (antibiotics, tranquillizers, anticonvulsants, etc). Work may be guided by the study of molecules, the activity of which is already known, or may start from the synthesis of molecules that do not exist in nature. Several derivatives of a single molecule are prepared and submitted to an analytical laboratory to determine structures and purity of preparation. In some cases, extracts from plant or animal tissue are used. These extracts are decomposed to isolate the active substance, which is later synthetically reproduced.

Pharmacological screening consists of a battery of tests on laboratory animals designed to reveal a drug's pharmacological activity. A drug that tests positively is put through more rigorous and specific tests and, if these too are positive, is further examined for possible toxicological and teratological (ie, malformation causing) effects. If a drug passes all tests, a pharmaceutical formula is developed that maximizes its activity in the organism. At this stage a report containing all data about the substance is submitted to the HPB, which may then authorize clinical testing of the substance on humans. The laboratory's medical director then draws up a protocol plan for the experiment, which is carried out by clinical pharmacologists at hospitals or institutes. If tests are conclusive, the laboratory's director submits a statistical analysis of results and requests permission from the HPB to market the drug. Many obstacles can appear while the new drug is being perfected; thus the failure rate is high. It is estimated that only one substance in 10 000 passes all stages successfully; the others are abandoned, either because they have no (or insufficient) therapeutic effect or because they are found to be toxic or to cause fetal malformations.

If the clinical tests meet its requirements, the HPB authorizes use of the drug for specific conditions. The drug is distributed to health professionals, along with instructions for its use and details of its properties, contraindications, undesirable effects and dosages. Marketing of the drug is followed by a surveillance program in which the drug is monitored for rare side effects that may have escaped detection during clinical testing. When the HPB has given its approval, the new drug must be submitted to provincial ministries of health for approval by therapeutic committees. The drug is then entered in the *Compendium of Pharmaceuticals and Specialties* (CPS); it may later also be entered in one of the large national pharmacopoeias (USP, BP, etc). Canada does not have its own pharmacopoeia.

The pharmaceutical industry is subject to more stringent purity and sterility requirements than most other industries. Painstaking precautions must be taken to avoid contamination by dust or vapours that may alter drug composition. The preparation of distilled water for injections, for example, requires no less than 25 operations. In addition to inspections by HPB representatives, production facilities of large laboratories are closely watched by their own quality-control services. All raw materials, all drugs in various stages of production and all batches of finished products are analysed so that their identity may be confirmed and their purity and stability determined.

Training

The development of the pharmaceutical industry has resulted in scientists being trained not only in synthetic medicinal chemistry and analytical chemistry but also in pharmacology, toxicology and teratology. Universities have added new disciplines to their teaching programs; industry, through the Pharmaceutical Manufacturers Assn of Canada, has provided funds to the Canadian Foundation for the Advancement of Clinical Pharmacology to set up training programs. The handbook of clinical pharmacology research activities in Canadian universities listed 86 entries in 1981. Universities offered training programs in 5 departments, which could accept 15 researchers for one- or 2-year training periods. The pharmaceutical industry in Canada allocates some $75 million annually to research and development of new products. The importance of industrial research in pharmacy is shown in that, between 1935 and 1949, 52% of all new drugs were discovered in industry laboratories; 34% came from universities and affiliated research institutes. Between 1950 and 1960, the industry's share increased to 69% and reached 91% between 1960 and 1969.

Patents

In most industrialized countries, inventions are protected by PATENT from duplication or imitation for 17 years. The US, the UK and Japan are considering extending this period to 20 years or more for pharmaceuticals. In 1969 consumer-group pressure moved the Canadian government to pass Bill C-102, allowing pharmaceuticals, even patented ones, to be imported or duplicated in order to encourage competition and lower prices. A study by the Canadian Institute of Economic Policy shows that, since this Act went into effect, the price of products falling within its purview dropped from 93% to 74% of the US price.

Manufacturers of pharmaceutical specialties felt that their rights were being violated and protested to the federal government. They pointed out that R&D on a new drug extends over much of the 17 years during which the drug is protected by patent and that, in 1981, they had invested up to $80 million in R&D. They argued that they should have exclusive rights to sales to recoup their investment, and they emphasized that the short-term savings might create considerable losses in the long run by discouraging capital investment in Canadian pharmaceutical research. In addition, trained researchers might be deprived of job opportunities.

Generic manufacturers (ie, those selling drugs without a trademark registration) are obliged to pay patent holders royalties of only 4% of the sales price of their products. These establishments operate on a limited budget since they do not have to maintain research laboratories and rarely offer post-sale documentation or information services. Generic drugs are registered in provincial formularies where they help to lower the cost of health insurance (although the pharmaceutical cost of prescription drugs is only 5% of the total insurance cost). When several similar drugs are registered in the formulary, provincial health-insurance administrations reimburse the cost of the lowest-priced drug or the average between the most and least expensive drugs. Thus, substitution of a less costly generic drug for a specialty or brand-name product is an officially recognized and sanctioned practice.

The current trend in the Canadian pharmaceutical industry is amalgamation of large laboratories into even larger enterprises to reduce expenses. This trend will probably continue and small independent companies probably will disappear. Canadian subsidiaries may well be limited to manufacturing and distributing drugs developed elsewhere. Manufacturers of generic products will see a boom. If not repealed, the Act changing patent protection may eliminate pharmaceutical research in the Canadian industry, creating an even greater dependence on foreign innovations and making it more difficult for pharmacologists and other Canadian scientists to work in Canada.

Associations

The Pharmaceutical Manufacturers Assn of Canada, fd 1914, brings together firms active in the research, development, manufacturing and marketing of prescription drugs and over-the-counter products. In 1970 the Council for the Accreditation of Pharmaceutical Manufacturers Representatives (CAPMR) was founded to develop the technical knowledge of such representatives and thus improve the quality of their presentations to the medical profession. The Pharmaceutical Advertising Advisory Board (PAAB), est 1975, is an independent agency that monitors pharmaceutical advertising and has adopted a code of advertising ethics. The Proprietary Assn of Canada, formed in 1896, consists of manufacturers of drugs whose formulae are revealed to the government but not to the public.

Publications

The *Compendium of Pharmaceuticals and Specialties* is published annually in both official languages by the Canadian Pharmaceutical Assn. It contains papers on the drugs most frequently used in Canada, based on information provided by manufacturers and other sources. It contains a medical guide, a therapeutic index, a section on the identification of pills and capsules according to their appearance and identi-code number, and a list of poison-control centres. The provincial ministries of health annually publish a list of drugs for which they reimburse the elderly or those receiving social assistance. The monthly magazines *Drug Merchandising* and *Canadian Food and Drug Product News* provide the latest news on production and the commercial aspects of the Canadian pharmaceutical industry. *Canadian Research* reports research work conducted in industry and elsewhere. *Le Pharmacien* is written for French-speaking pharmacists.

M.R. DUFRESNE

Pharmacy, the act or practice of preparing, preserving, compounding and dispensing drugs. Louis HÉBERT, one of the first settlers of New France, was a pharmacist from Paris. From the time he settled in Québec (1617) until 1750, when the first medical legislation by Intendant François BIGOT was promulgated, there was little regulation of the health professions in New France. For the next 120 years, efforts to obtain more specific and effective legislation for the control of drug distribution were integrated into medical regulations and were largely ineffectual. A number of pharmacists' organizations were formed in both Upper and Lower Canada during this time in an attempt to establish pharmacy legally as a profession. These groups were short lived; there was no permanent national organization of Canadian pharmacy until the Canadian Pharmaceutical Assn was founded in 1907.

Until Confederation, 1867, efforts by pharmacy organizations to obtain appropriate regulation by federal legislation were unsuccessful. With the creation of the provinces of Québec and Ontario, pharmacy Acts were passed (in 1870 and 1871, respectively) granting self-government to the profession. These Acts served as models for the rest of Canada; each province has now passed similar legislation to regulate the practice of the profession within its borders. Under this legislation, the professional association issues the licences to practise and supervises the conduct of its members.

Nevertheless, significant differences exist from province to province. Registration in any province qualifies a pharmacist to practise also in the Yukon and the NWT, but not in other provinces, because the requirements of each province must be met separately. In response to this situation, the Pharmacy Examining Board of Canada was formed in 1963 under federal statute to establish academic qualifications acceptable to participating provincial licensing bodies.

Pharmacists no longer learn their profession through an apprenticeship system. In Newfoundland students attend a certificate program in the College of Trades and Technology; all other provinces require pharmacists to obtain a baccalaureate degree in pharmacy for licensure. Faculties of pharmacy are located at Dalhousie, Université de Montréal, Laval, U of T, U of Manitoba, U of Saskatchewan, U of Alberta and UBC. Courses in basic biological and physical sciences are a required prerequisite to professional pharmacy courses and the program of studies that includes supervised practical experience. Research has become important in the pharmacy colleges because advances in drug therapy arise primarily from work carried out in industry and the universities. All Canadian faculties of pharmacy provide graduate work at the master's and doctoral level for students seeking careers in teaching, research, industry, hospital pharmacy and other specialized areas.

Twenty-five percent of Canadian pharmacies are large establishments (frequently part of chain stores and franchise operations), selling a variety of merchandise in addition to providing prescriptions and health needs.

The professional practice of pharmacy has changed dramatically over the years. Pharmacists now dispense a vast array of complex, potent and specific medicinal agents (the federal government has enacted regulations dealing with the quality, safety and efficacy of therapeutic agents, and specifying the terms under which certain potent and addictive drugs must be handled). The preparation of these pharmaceuticals requires special techniques of formulation and analysis that are available more efficiently and economically in the elaborately equipped laboratories of industry; therefore, most of the pharmaceuticals dispensed today are obtained by the pharmacist in the finished form. The pharmacist's role has changed from that of compounder to that of a supervisor of drug regimens and a consultant to the other health professions and to the public on drug usage. This transition was initially developed in hospitals, where it is now well established. More recently, this concept of clinical pharmacy has been extended to ambulatory patients. The community pharmacist has frequent contact with patients receiving medication and is thus able to provide against drug interactions, toxicities, side effects, allergic reactions and other untoward responses. Most pharmacies today maintain a patient-record system, usually computerized, to help the pharmacist follow the progress of drug treatment.   MERVYN J. HUSTON

Pheasant (Phasianidae), family of BIRDS, with plumage ranging from metallic blue, green and burnished copper to cryptic patterns of browns, greys and black. Coloured wattles (fleshy protuberances) or vivid, bare skin adorn the head, and the tail may be highly modified for display, most notably in the peafowl (genus *Pavo*). The family is related to the families of fowls which include GROUSE, turkeys, QUAILS and the red junglefowl (*Gallus gallus*), presumed ancestor of all domestic POULTRY. Pheasants are henlike in form, some with sharp spurs on their longish, strong legs. Many species may be bred in captivity; wide-scale introductions outside their native habitats (Asia and Japan) have occurred. Hence, some species may survive although destruction of their habitats threatens extinction. Of the 48 pheasant species, at least 16 are endangered. In Canada, the introduced ring-necked pheasant (*Phasianus colchicus*) is a permanent resident. It is most successful in milder areas, notably southern Ontario and BC. *See* GAME BIRDS.   S.D. MACDONALD

The ring-necked pheasant (*Phasianus colchicus*) is found mainly in milder areas, notably of Ontario and BC (*photo by Wayne Lankinen/DRK Photo*).

Philately, *see* STAMP COLLECTING.

Philipps, Richard, governor of Nova Scotia 1717-49 (b in Pembrokeshire, Wales c 1661; d at London, Eng 14 Oct 1750). Although he spent little time in NS (1720-22, 1729-31), his dealings with the Acadians in 1730 had a strong effect on subsequent events. Ceded by France in 1713, the province was populated by a French-speaking people who refused to take the normal oath of allegiance, and was barely held by a tattered garrison at ANNAPOLIS ROYAL. Sent out to demonstrate British authority but powerless to force the issue, Philipps administered a modified oath and apparently promised verbally that the Acadians would not have to bear arms against France. Other officers had made a similar concession but Philipps was the governor; fortified with the memory of his word, the Acadians maintained a general neutrality for 25 years. Their success, however, contributed to their unpreparedness when they faced Gov Charles LAWRENCE's ultimatum in 1755 and were subsequently deported (see ACADIA).

Philipps went home for good in 1731. British authorities remained inattentive to Nova Scotia until the late 1740s; and the practical governor, his counsels largely unheeded, spent his last years living on his allowances in London.
    MAXWELL SUTHERLAND

Phillips, Walter Joseph, artist (b at Barton-upon-Humber, Eng 25 Oct 1884; d at Victoria 5 July 1963). Phillips's early art training was undertaken in opposition to his father's wishes. He immigrated to Winnipeg in 1913, where he was appointed art master at St John's Technical High School. There he learned etching from a colleague, Cyril Barraud, and printed on the school's press. As a means of introducing colour to his prints he began experimenting with the Japanese method of woodblock printing, producing his first complete print in 1917. Not only a fine technician, Phillips was an acute observer of his environment. His images of Canada were widely distributed and collected. He also published a number of print portfolios and illustrated several books. In 1943 he moved to Banff, where he taught and painted in watercolour.
    JUDY GOUIN

Phillips, William Eric, financier, industrialist (b at Toronto 3 Jan 1893; d at Palm Beach, Fla 26 Dec 1964). In Europe at the outbreak of WWI, Eric Phillips joined the British army, winning both the DSO and the Military Cross, and becoming a lieutenant-colonel. After the war he served in Poland before leaving the army in 1920. He married the daughter of R.S. MCLAUGHLIN and established his own company, W.E. Phillips Ltd, in Oshawa, Ont, in 1922. In 1940 C.D. HOWE recruited him to head Research Enterprises Ltd, making optical glass, range finders, binoculars and radar components. Between 1940 and 1946 Research Enterprises sold $220-million worth of equipment. At the end of WWII, Phillips joined E.P. TAYLOR in ARGUS CORP, becoming chairman of this investment firm. In 1945 he was appointed chairman of the board of governors of U of T and became known for strong and decisive management of the business and financial affairs of the university.
    ROBERT BOTHWELL

Philosophy, originally the love of wisdom in all its forms, both practical and theoretical. Sometimes a philosopher is thought of as a sage, a person of insight and good judgement, who shows equanimity in adversity. An individual may have a philosophy of life — a general view of the world, a life plan and a set of policies to guide action. Similarly, there may be a philosophy for any sphere of thought or activity — a basic theory and policies for it.

But over the centuries philosophy evolved into a special, technical discipline, comprising at its core: (1) *logic*, which studies principles for correct reasoning and inference; (2) *epistemology* (theory of knowledge), concerned with standards for reasonable belief and the attainment of truth; (3) *metaphysics*, the study of being as such and related notions such as existence, appearance and reality; the most basic or general categories of thought (eg, "thing," "property," "possibility," "time"); and principles of general order (eg, determinism: every event has a cause); (4) *ethics* (including social and political philosophy), which deals with values and the good, right and wrong action, obligations and rights, justice and ideal social and political arrangements. In addition, there are many "philosophies of such and such," in which the logical, epistemic, metaphysical and ethical problems of a field (science, religion, art, history, education, etc) are studied. Finally, some philosophers study the history of philosophy, interpreting, explaining, comparing and criticizing previous philosophical work.

Before WWII there were few philosophers in Canada, and they were separated by geography and sometimes language; they most often worked in or under the influence of a denominational religious institution; and many of them devoted themselves mainly to teaching, historical scholarship, or the development of the thought of a particular "school" (eg, Thomism, objective idealism). Nevertheless, there were significant philosophies in Canada in this period.

After 1950 Canada's growing wealth, a population boom and a new interest in culture and education led to significant change. (The Massey Royal Commission on NATIONAL DEVELOPMENT IN THE ARTS, LETTERS AND SCIENCES, the CANADA COUNCIL and the Parent Royal Commission of Inquiry on Education in Québec, 1962-64, were important milestones.) With the rapid growth of universities, the number of philosophers grew and they became increasingly professional and secular. They often devoted themselves to esoteric technical problems, made no pretense of being sages and had little communication with the public. But changes in communications and travel, the founding of professional institutions (eg, the Canadian Philosophical Association, 1957; the journals *Dialogue*, 1962, and *The Canadian Journal of Philosophy*, 1971) and personal encounters at conferences, eg, LEARNED SOCIETIES, helped to develop a professional community. Relative harmony and some fruitful interaction between the 2 linguistic groups have been created by the existence of a bilingual journal, the CPA policies of passive bilingualism and rotation of offices between Francophones and Anglophones, and the growing common interest in secular philosophy. Three recent trends suggest a rapprochement between professional interests and those of the public: a revival of political philosophy; an interest in normative and applied ethics (eg, MEDICAL ETHICS); and the development of Québecois and CANADIAN STUDIES.
    JOHN T. STEVENSON

Philosophy Before 1950

French Canada In New France, as elsewhere in the New World, the teaching of philosophy was initially the responsibility of the church. Philosophy was taught regularly from 1665 at the Jesuit College in Québec, which, like such colleges in France, followed the dictates of the Jesuit teaching philosophy as set out in the *Ratio Studiorum*. In 2 years the college's few students took a course in logic consisting of the second book of Aristotle's *Organon, On Interpretation*, and the first 2 books of *The Prior Analytics*. The entirely Aristotelian physics program included the 8 books of the *Physics, On the Heavens*, and the first book of *On Coming to Be and Passing Away*. Metaphysics was also Aristotelian and the ethics course followed *The Nicomachean Ethics*. As often as possible, professors made reference to medieval philosopher St Thomas Aquinas (c 1224-74). In the hierarchy of the liberal arts in the Middle Ages, philosophy was the servant of theology (*ancilla theologiae*). Until 1759 the same was true in Québec, where philosophy appeared in the program as a basic prerequisite to theology for students aspiring to the priesthood.

Interrupted by the British military conquest, the teaching of philosophy was resumed in 1770 in 5 colleges. This new start led to the 1835 publication of the first Canadian philosophy textbook, the *Institutiones philosophicae ad usum studiosae juventutis*, by Abbé Jérôme DEMERS of the SÉMINAIRE DE QUÉBEC. Professors, by then more numerous and mostly of Canadian origin, based their teaching on Charles Rollin's *Traité des études* (rev ed 1845), according to which the purpose of philosophy was to establish a moral structure and to forearm youth against unbelief. Unbelief was seen to stem from the Protestant Reformation, the writings of French philosopher René Descartes (1596-1650), Denis Diderot's *Encylopédie* (1751-80) and the impact of the American and French revolutions (1776 and 1789) in a province where from 1764 printed material was becoming more widely available. The teaching of philosophy was therefore a controversial activity, and new ideas and new objections to those ideas appeared: the origin of ideas and of certainty, immortality of the soul and the existence of God, ATHEISM, the origins of political power and the highest form of government. After Descartes and the Enlightenment, one had either to accept or to oppose the rules of reason.

It was this challenge that lay at the root of a philosophical controversy (1833-34) centered on the French philosopher Félicité de Lamennais (1782-1854) and the publication of Abbé Demers's textbooks. At issue were the establishment of certainty against Cartesian doubt in the teaching of logic, refutation of the Enlightenment's atheism in metaphysics and moral philosophy, and the affirmation that political power came from God, not from the sovereignty of the people.

Limited to objection and refutation until around 1840, the teaching of philosophy was subsequently characterized by a quest for affirmative philosophical theses, and by a frantic search for an authority and for a "Catholic philosophy" that found its ultimate expression in Pope Leo XIII's encyclical, *Aeterni Patris* (1879), on the restoration of Christian philosophy. It was in this context that Thomism appeared, so long to be considered synonymous with French Canadian philosophy. By 1879 the philosophy of St Thomas Aquinas had provided solutions to the basic, traditional problems in the teaching of philosophy. Certainty was henceforth the product of reason based on faith and no longer troubled by doubt. In ethics the hierarchy of purposes justified God's priority over man, the spiritual over the temporal and church over state, thus providing the philosophical basis of the ULTRAMONTANISM that dominated French Canadian society.

Thereafter the teaching of philosophy was rigidly standardized by means of a single baccalaureate examination at the end of the classical course in all colleges and a single philosophy textbook used in all colleges. The philosophical uniformity of this instruction by manual was disrupted at the beginning of the century by the "social question." INDUSTRIALIZATION (capital, labour, strikes) and URBANIZATION confronted the Thomist world with new problems (*see* SOCIAL DOCTRINE) and often justified the preparation and adoption of new manuals.

Philosophy took new strides after 1920 when it was introduced into the universities. A faculty of philosophy was founded 1921 at U de Montréal; Dominican monk Ceslas-Marie Forest was dean there, 1926-52. In Québec City, the École supérieure de philosophie (fd 1926) of Laval U became a faculty in 1935, and the Belgian Charles DE KONINCK was director 1939-56. The early development of the teaching of philosophy in the universities drew support from the general expansion of the universities and the increasing importance of philosophical studies in Rome and Louvain.

Its real development occurred, however, following another papal pronouncement, *Deus Scientiarum* (1931), which favoured science as the bastion of faith and resulted in a reorganization of faculties of philosophy. At Laval the faculty had an equally Aristotelian and Thomist approach, as may be seen from professors' publications and the subjects of theses and articles in *Laval théologique et philosophique* (1945-). In Montréal, Latin was abandoned as the language of instruction in 1936, and day courses established in 1942 doubled in number by 1948. Theses incorporated a Thomist approach until around 1948, whereas the history of philosophy was predominant as the faculty was becoming more and more secularized.

French Canadian studies in medieval history and philosophy were probably the most important international contributions made in those fields until around 1950. The exceptional contribution made by Franciscans was belittled and in 1927 even became the subject of a heated debate in Thomist circles between the future Cardinal VILLENEUVE and the great Franciscan medievalist, Father Ephrem Longpré. In Ottawa

in 1930 the Dominicans founded the Institute of Mediaeval Studies, which moved to Montréal in 1943. It was affiliated with U de Montréal. There was much philosophical activity and discussion after 1930 with the publications of de Koninck, Hermas Bastien, Fathers Louis-Marie Régis, Louis Lachance, Patrice Robert, Julien Péghaire and Arcade Monette, and the organization of philosophical societies such as La Société de philosophie de Montréal (fd 1924) and the very formal Académie canadienne Saint Thomas d'Aquin (1930-45).

After 1930 a new generation that included Étienne Gilson (in Toronto) and Jacques Maritain took over from the old guard and moved into the editorial ranks of new journals and of the *Journées thomistes* (1935 and 1936) organized for the young generation. Between the 1929 crash and the 1948 REFUS GLOBAL, Maritain, the catalyst in philosophical debates (with de Koninck) and ideological controversies (over Pétainism), became an important source of inspiration before the arrival of Emmanuel Mounier, Christian and atheistic existentialism, and phenomenology. YVAN LAMONDE

English Canada Philosophy took root in English Canada with the founding of the first universities in Nova Scotia and what is now Ontario. (By 1860 Canada, with a population less than 2 million, had 12 universities.) Most philosophers teaching at these universities came from Britain, especially Scotland. They were trained primarily as clergymen, but philosophy comprised a large part of their education. It soon became apparent to these newcomers to Canada that the practice of teaching the Scottish sermon was not suited to the rapidly diversifying student population. Many students from rural backgrounds were beginning to suspect, because of ever-present hardships, claims made about God as saviour and protector. The students would have to be convinced through reason and sound argument that moral behaviour was preferable to amoral behaviour; the individual had a place in this new wild land; nature could be productive and still be protected; advanced scientific and evolutionary theories could take their place alongside theology and the idea of God; religion could make sense in the face of natural disasters; and in a town with many religious factions a clergyman could give a sermon that offended no one and offered meaning and purpose to tired and harassed parishioners. The philosophers who faced these formidable tasks adjusted to the demands of the environment and tirelessly undertook to educate the future clergy, teachers, circuit preachers and civil servants of Canada.

On the surface, Canada's culture is a conglomerate of differing actions and attitudes towards events and institutions. The philosophers saw that a single set of meanings (interpretations) for these events and institutions could not easily be imposed upon groups of people spread far apart without considerable force and pressure to conform to this particular "way of thinking." People had immigrated for many reasons, often to escape from rigid and uniform ideas. If freedom of thought was to have meaning, another basis of Canadian culture had to be established. And so the philosophers looked to "reason."

Through reason we assign meanings to events and defend ourselves from encroachment on meanings around which we structure our lives. Canadian philosophers were not alone in their concern with the nature and uses of reason, but their interpretations gave a distinctive base for a unifying cultural identity. A kind of philosophical federalism was being developed.

Three basic themes concerned the first philosophers in English Canada: the philosophical basis of religion, the idea of nature, and the philosophical examination of political ideas and systems. In the late 19th and early 20th

centuries some scholars, such as John WATSON at Queen's U, published on all 3 themes. George BLEWETT, U of Toronto, concerned himself with the idea of nature and its relation to God. However, philosophy in Canada was not confined to these themes. Richard Maurice BUCKE, a psychiatrist in London, Ont, wrote about evolutionary spirituality. John Macdonald, U of Alberta, published on the philosophy of education. Herbert Leslie STEWART, a Maritimer, had interests ranging from CALVINISM to the work of German philosopher Nietzsche. Rupert LODGE, a Plato scholar at U of Manitoba, tackled questions about ethics, business and education.

The seeds of respect, tolerance and a commitment to explore all sides of a problem before suggesting solutions were truly being sown by Canadian philosophers such as Lodge. He believed that there may never be a right answer to a question and that any problem exists in a context. Although his writings seem biased towards idealism and the importance of preserving valued ideas, not just progressing materially at any price, he still presented the viewpoints of the pragmatist and the realist on any problem he approached in his later books. At U of T, George BRETT emphasized the importance of history in understanding man's nature, and spearheaded the "Toronto school of intellectual history," which dominated philosophy there until the late 1950s. John Irving, U of T, turned that historical vision upon the first 100 years of philosophy in Canada and published the first assessment of "Canadian" philosophy. He also wrote on science, values and the SOCIAL CREDIT movement in Alberta.

The need to come to grips with religious claims and the advance of science was pressing. Industrialism, increased control over nature, and continued progress in the creation and distribution of wealth seemed to have given humans many powers previously associated with God. The geographical circumstances and the diverse population of Canada worked against the likelihood of there being an established church (*see* ANGLICANISM), which might provide answers to the rapid changes. Catholic philosophers sought solutions in the writings of Aquinas. The establishment in Toronto of the Institute of Mediaeval Studies (1929; papal charter 1939, when it became the Pontifical Institute of Mediaeval Studies) was testimony to the devotion and scholarship of these pioneers in Catholic thought.

For Protestants there was no clear strategy. The first philosophy book written in English Canada was *Elements of Natural Theology* (1850) by James BEAVEN. Wishing to connect religion with scientific developments, Beaven focused on law, order and structure in the universe as evidence of a rational being, or God; because the laws of the universe work together, the universe is intelligible as a whole. If "God" is what we mean by the source of intelligibility, argued Beaven, then the close relation between man and God remains intact. Major works of philosophy and religion were published by Watson, an acknowledged expert on German philosopher Immanuel Kant. In *Outline of Philosophy* (1908) and *The Interpretation of Religious Experience* (1910-12) Watson examined thoroughly the historical arguments for and against God's existence, and he proposed a metaphysical system to explain existence that drew correlations between reason, God, and a concept from idealism, developed by German philosopher G.W.F. Hegel, called the "Absolute." In "The Invisible Church," a chapter in *The Interpretation of Religious Experience*, Watson anticipated the uniquely Canadian UNITED CHURCH and foresaw its ultimate integration into Canadian life as a social agency of rational morality. He published 8 books and over 200 articles. His sophisticated work was well known in the US and Britain.

At McGill U, John Clark MURRAY, in *A Handbook of Psychology* (1885) and *An Introduction to Ethics* (1891), pursued metaphysical problems to give both man's increasing power and God's will places in the rational explication of what exists. Murray spent many hours giving public lectures and writing newspaper articles about the plight of the working class, and he was energetic and fearless as Canada's earliest philosophical feminist. Murray was not Canada's only public philosopher: both Stewart and Irving later became lecturers on CBC Radio. At U of T George Paxton YOUNG, who wrote on ethics and mathematics and openly challenged the doctrines of his church, like Murray had a devoted following.

The relation between God and man was highlighted by Dalhousie U's William LYALL in *Intellect, the Emotions, and the Moral Nature* (1855). Man is a part of nature, argued Lyall, and to violate nature is indirectly to violate man. Blewett, a farm boy from southern Ontario, wrote *The Study of Nature and the Vision of God* (1907) and *The Christian View of the World* (1912), concluding even then that the environment was in danger from man's waste and neglect. Blewett also believed reason to be the basis of all possible experience and all freedom, and he argued that a notion of a community of rational spirits was more fundamental than one of individual beings. The idea of community as the key to survival was becoming well entrenched in a developing, but still mainly rural, Canadian society.

Two distinctive features of Canadian society as a political entity are its many-faceted pluralism in language, culture, religion, geography, educational theory and values; and a strong commitment to tradition among its diverse communities. The French and Scots brought with them centuries-old patterns of social organization. LOYALISTS came firmly committed to old ways, having rejected new political experiments in the US. Philosophers interested in political theory had to find ways to create a conceptual basis for politics while surrounded by distinct and occasionally warring factions. Once again they focused on reason as a mediator and discovery tool.

Watson's *The State in Peace and War* (1919) emphasized the need to see progress in a historical context. New social orders could not be invented willy-nilly. People progress from experience to experience, and reason must interpret the present in relation to the past. Mistakes would be inevitable in the gradual move from theoretical to real equality. Watson was undoubtedly conservative. Brett was equally reserved; in *The Government of Man* (1913) he emphasized the need for historical understanding of problems more than the need for solutions. Still, neither philosopher believed that the state was rational and beyond challenge.

Murray faced the Industrial Revolution and concomitant social disruptions directly. In 1887 he completed *The Industrial Kingdom of God* (published posthumously, 1981), in which he openly discussed Karl Marx and Henry George, communal planning, strikes and the advantages and disadvantages of capitalism. Its Victorian prose did not hide its radical elements, a fact that may have had something to do with its remaining in manuscript form for almost 100 years. Murray believed that rational assessment of existing institutions would lead to positive change.

If political philosophy in Canada leaned to the left, it did so with reserve. The philosophers believed that men would be changed, not by rational assault but by rational exchange. It would be a slow, arduous task to create the just society, but along the way society would be more stable, less violent, less prone to fall prey to radical innovations and quick solutions. Government, if not always loved, needed at least to

be understood. Dissension would be inevitable, but the dismantling of creditable institutions as an alternative would result in much more stress and disruption. The role of reason, as interpreter and key to compromise, was critical to Canada's philosophers; what they envisaged was much like the Canada we know today: orderly and reticent, but an international example of the value of discussion, tolerance and democracy. The philosophers in English and French Canada were scholars first. But a thorough examination of their works reveals as much about the national character of Canadians and Canadian culture as about the eternal questions of philosophy.   ELIZABETH A. TROTT

Historical Scholarship

A major subdiscipline of philosophy in Canada for many years was and remains historical scholarship in philosophy. This includes discovering and editing texts written by philosophers of the past, writing expository and explanatory commentaries on them and discussing them in an evaluative, critical or even polemical way. Why might historical work of this sort be more important for philosophy than for another discipline, such as physics? A variety of answers have been given. For some, philosophy is concerned with enduring questions, the answers to which can best be sought in a timeless "dialogue" with great thinkers, past or present. For others a perennial philosophy, as good for today as for yesterday, has already been created; we can only understand, refine, interpret and apply it to our own time. According to both views, philosophy is only accidentally historical; it is essentially universal and timeless. The contrary view claims that time, place and circumstance do make a difference for the correctness of philosophical questions posed, answers given and standards of evaluation used. Some believe there are patterns of growth, development and progress in philosophy, others do not; but both agree that philosophy varies with historical context. In spite of these and other differences, there is a consensus that some knowledge of the classical texts is important in philosophical education and that scholarly work on them is a worthy enterprise.

In Canada the emphasis on this type of scholarship has been accentuated by religious, political and institutional circumstances. As late as the 1960s, many philosophers, both anglophone and francophone, worked in institutions with some religious affiliation. They conducted their work in an ideologically sensitive atmosphere, and there were often expectations about how the enterprise would be conducted. The study of the history of philosophy provided an acceptable way of introducing a cosmopolitan element into the climate of opinion.

At U of T a widely shared belief in the importance of a historical approach to the humanities, and a teaching program that reflected that conviction, led to the development of the so-called "Toronto school of intellectual history." George BRETT was one of its dominant figures. His own work was historical and frequently interdisciplinary. His main contribution, *A History of Psychology* (3 vols, 1912-21), presented the philosophical theories of mind that served as the historical context for the later development of scientific PSYCHOLOGY. Subsequent department heads Fulton H. Anderson and Thomas A. GOUDGE continued, in many respects, the tradition of the "school." In the early 1980s attempts were being made to renew it through a new generation of promising scholars. Much good work in the history of philosophy has come from inheritors of this tradition. It includes work in classical Greek philosophy by G.M.A. Grube, John Rist, David Gallop, T.M. Robinson and Reginald Allen (*see* CLASSICS); on figures of the 16th, 17th and 18th centuries by Brett, Anderson, Robert McRae, D.P. Dryer, David Savan,

C.B. Macpherson and David Gauthier; and on the 19th century by Emil Fackenheim and John Robson. The work done by these and other academics has had considerable influence both in Canada and abroad.

An influence at least as great has stemmed from another Toronto institution. The (Pontifical) Institute of Mediaeval Studies was a Canadian development in the revival of medieval philosophy following the papal encyclical *Aeterni Patris*. The influence of French philosopher Etienne Gilson was keenly felt in the institute, and with it came an emphasis on careful editing and study of original texts, an effort to understand them in their proper contexts, and an interest in both their classical antecedents and their early modern descendants. Anton Pegis, Joseph Owens and Armand Maurer have been important figures in the institute's research and teaching. A similar institution was the Institut d'études médiévales, founded in Ottawa in 1930.

In Québec, important academic figures working in this Catholic tradition were Louis Lachance, Charles de Koninck, Benoît Lacroix and Vianney Décarie. Although the influence of the church tended to restrict study of heterodox or progressive doctrines, there was an interest among younger thinkers in French philosophers such as Maurice Blondel, Henri Bergson, Emmanuel Mounier, Gabriel Marcel and especially Jacques Maritain. By the 1960s the search for alternative ideological models intensified, and there was a growing interest in Nietzsche, Freud, Marx and such 20th-century movements as existentialism and phenomenology. Students of philosophy applied lessons from these new models in "radical" periodicals such as PARTI PRIS and LIBERTÉ. Gradually the diversification of interests was followed by increasingly sound scholarship. Good work was done in the more traditional areas by such scholars as Yvon Lafrance, Léonce Paquet and Luc Brisson, and some excellent work by, among others, Olivier Réboul on Kant, François Duchesneau on Leibniz and Guy Lafrance on Rousseau, Bergson and Durkheim. The higher standards are reflected in the pages of *Philosophiques* (1974-), the official periodical of the Société de philosophie du Québec.

In English Canada there has been a relative decline since the late 1960s in the influence of Toronto institutions. Scholarship has become so widespread — and so diversified in its authors, subjects and institutional affiliations — that it is almost invidious to single out examples. In any case, one need not turn now to Toronto (or to Montréal's Raymond Klibansky, Alastair McKinnon or Charles Taylor) to find notable historical scholarship: one can find it in Calgary, Guelph, Waterloo, Peterborough or Fredericton. And the works studied range, in origin, from ancient Greece and India to the modern Germanys and France and, in subject matter, from the intricacies of late medieval logic to the global sweep of Hegel's system. It may be more useful to note other recent trends.

First, Canadian scholars participate extensively in international networks in which the results of individual studies are exchanged and evaluated. Second, there is the development of important international publishing projects centered in Canada, often involving several institutions, eg, publication of the collected papers of Bertrand Russell, from material in the Russell Archives at McMaster U, Hamilton; interdisciplinary projects in Toronto, one to produce an edition of the work of John Stuart Mill and another the writings of Erasmus; and an edition of C.S. Peirce's work involving U of Waterloo. Third, there is the introduction of computer technology to facilitate the production of research instruments, eg Alastair McKinnon's Kierkegaard concordance, the concordance of the Gerhard edition of Leibniz's work being produced under the direction of Robert McRae, and the Bibliography of Philosophy in Canada Project, 1790-1976 .

Finally, there is an expanding interest in philosophy as practised in Canada. Francophone philosophers have taken the lead, as is demonstrated in the pioneering work of Roland Houde, the solid historical work of Yvan Lamonde and the important writing of Maurice Lagueux on the impact of Marxist thought on Québecois ideology during the 1960s. Similar historical self-examination has excited less interest in anglophone Canada, but valuable contributions have been made by pioneer John Irving, historians Carl Berger and Brian McKillop and philosophers Leslie Armour and Elizabeth Trott. JOHN T. STEVENSON AND THOMAS MATHIEN

Ethics, Social and Political Philosophy

English Canada In English Canadian philosophy since 1950 a strong point has been the study of values, including ethics (what, if anything, makes an action right or wrong?), social and political philosophy (what principles should be used to assess social groups and political institutions?), and philosophy of law (what standards are inherent in law, and what is their relation to moral rules?). Some of this work arises from reflection on important figures in the history of ethics, especially on the work of Hobbes, Hume, Kant, Hegel and Marx. Such work has often led to original insights into major normative issues. Nevertheless, most work in this period has been more problem centered than historical. The predominant approach has been in the English "analytical" tradition, rather than in the manner of current European philosophy. The main work here can be conveniently divided into 3 areas: metaethics, theoretical ethics and politics, and applied philosophy.

Metaethics, the most abstract of these, received the greatest attention through the 1960s. The primary concern was with the meaning and meaningfulness of moral claims, eg, as explored in Francis Sparshott's *Enquiry into Goodness and Related Concepts* (1958). A further issue has been the relation between self-interest and morality, with some, like Gauthier, arguing that self-interest grounds morality, but most, like Kai Nielsen, rejecting this claim and the view of morality implicit in it. A major focus has been what David Braybrooke labels "the ethopolitical intersection," where the philosophy of history and the social sciences intersects social and political philosophy. Outstanding work has been done by Braybrooke, Donald Brown, Charles Taylor, Jonathan Bennett and Gerald Cohen in differentiating scientific and normative accounts of human behaviour; for the normative approach they have developed criteria for rational and moral action. Debate continues in metaethics on the most fundamental questions, in particular over the extent to which definitive standards can be provided to resolve moral, political and legal disputes.

At the second level, theory construction, Canadian philosophers have been active. Much of their theorizing has been piecemeal, concentrating on testing rival theories on central aspects of the moral life, eg, interpersonal relations, emotions, punishment, rights, and legal and moral obligations. There have also been larger-scale efforts defending the main theories in contention: utilitarianism, individual rights and Marxism. These theories supply different answers to the question of whether the demands of justice are essentially negative (leave others alone) or are also positive (those in easy circumstances must help those in need). Since the mid-1970s there has been increasing polarization in political philosophy towards Marxist collectivism or libertarian individualism; defenders of the status quo have been less vocal, perhaps having turned their attention to the third area.

This is the area of applied philosophy. Up to the mid-1970s most philosophers were concerned with metaethics and theory construction. They wrote principally for other philosophers and had little contact with academics in other disciplines or with the general public. But now most philosophy departments offer courses in biomedical ethics, business and professional ethics, and moral, political and legal problems. There has been increasing contact with nonphilosophers working in related areas in jointly taught courses, interdisciplinary meetings, and the establishment of institutes (such as the Westminster Institute for Ethics and Human Values in London, Ont) and societies (such as the Canadian Section for Philosophy of Law) to study leading moral issues.

Philosophers increasingly have brought their theoretical insights to bear on practical problems such as native rights, discrimination against women, moral education, nuclear energy and war. A fine example is Wayne Sumner's utilitarian *Abortion and Moral Theory* (1981). Philosophers have also been turning their attention to specifically Canadian problems, as evidenced in the 1979 discussions of CONFEDERATION and SOVEREIGNTY-ASSOCIATION. Doubtless the 1982 Constitution with its CANADIAN CHARTER OF RIGHTS AND FREEDOMS will also receive philosophical attention. Such attention to Canadian problems may come to differentiate Canadian work in political and legal philosophy from work done elsewhere. Two recent anthologies in theoretical and applied ethics are Stanley French's *Philosophers Look at Canadian Confederation* (1979) and Wesley Cragg's *Contemporary Moral Issues* (1983).

Although the emphasis on applying philosophy has grown in recent years, always implicit in specific applications are normative theories and metaethical positions. Philosophers are adept at making these implicit views explicit and providing searching criticisms of them. But this means that philosophers are inevitably led back to fundamental questions about the status and justification of moral, political, social and legal rules. MICHAEL MCDONALD

French Canada During the 1950s in French Canada, work in the field of ethics and social and political philosophy continued to be based essentially on the Aristotelian-Thomist tradition and to respect the social doctrine of the Roman Catholic Church. University and college courses in ethics and social philosophy conveyed the principles of Christian morality and the church's social doctrine as expressed in papal encyclicals. There was still only limited interest in political philosophy and the philosophy of law, these subjects generally being included in the teaching of social philosophy. Although little philosophical research was published, there were exceptions, such as Louis Lachance's studies of justice and law in the writings of Aristotle and Aquinas.

The end of the decade marked a new era. Pluralism entered the scene as the scholastic and systematic tradition declined, and the new generation of philosophers pursued the history of thought and comparisons between various schools of philosophy and value systems. Philosophy echoed the QUIET REVOLUTION: Marxist and existentialist values became the vehicle for changes in the content of, and general approach to, philosophical research and teaching. Some sociopolitical philosophers probed the basic structures and values of Québec society and conducted research on cultural issues, power structures and ideologies. Important works in this area included Fernand Dumont's *Le Pouvoir dans la société canadienne-française* (1966); *Le Lieu de l'homme* (1968); and *La Vigile du Québec, octobre 1970: l'impasse?* (1974). During this period an ideology research group, led by Claude Savary, was founded.

In the 1970s, publications on social and political philosophy increased in number and became more diversified. Personal essays and popular publications included the works of thinkers involved in social and political issues in Québec, such as Jacques Grand'Maison's *Une société en quête d'éthique* (1977), *Un nouveau contrat social* (1980) and, the essay by Michel Morin and Claude Bertrand, *Le Territoire imaginaire de la culture* (1979). The more academic essays deal mainly with forms of political power; they include the works of Joseph Pestieau and, in *La Confédération canadienne* (1979), the reflections of a group of philosophers. Maurice Lagueux's *Le Marxisme des années soixante* (1982) won the Governor General's Award for nonfiction.

Studies devoted to the sociopolitical ideas of the major philosophers are more common and include the works of Olivier Reboul on Kant, Leo-Paul Bordeleau on Blondel, Jean-Guy Meunier on Marx, Guy Lafrance on Bergson, Durkheim and Rousseau, and Jean Roy on Hobbes. The philosophy of history, a subject of growing interest, is dealt with by Roberto Miguelez in *Sujet et histoire* (1974). Similarly the philosophy of law, a relatively new field, is the subject of Georges Legault's *La Structure performative du langage juridique* (1977).

Ethics and social and political philosophy have also been discussed at conferences on political issues or on the relationship between philosophy and law. Interest in interdisciplinary studies has recently grown, particularly in those relating to economics, law and the social sciences. Similarly, studies on cultural issues are coming to the fore, particularly since the founding of the Institut québécois de recherche sur la culture. This interest appears to be a feature of the new philosophy of French Canada, and clearly indicates closer links between philosophical activities and society at large.

GUY LAFRANCE

Logic, Epistemology, Philosophy of Science

English Canada Logic is studied as formal deductive science (part of mathematics, including computer applications); a tool for investigating problems in the structure of reasoning (valid argument, semantics, hypothetical reasoning); and that part of philosophy dealing with exact analysis of difficult concepts. In the last 3 decades philosophers in English Canada have made contributions to logic in all these areas. Bas Van Fraassen has developed a formal semantics for logic; William Harper, a probability semantics and a theory of preference and utility; Hans Herzberger, a theory of preference ordering; and Alasdair Urquhart, a semantics for relevance logics. Brian Chellas has dealt with modal logics, William Rozeboom with various technical problems in philosophical semantics. Van Fraassen and Charles Morgan have done studies of probability semantics; Anil Gupta and Herzberger have investigated the semantics of truth and paradoxes; John Woods has written on relevance and on paradoxes.

Epistemology (theory of knowledge) studies the nature and extent of human knowing. It relates to psychology, cognitive science and the arts. Work in philosophy of psychology has been done by Patricia and Paul Churchland, by Roland Puccetti and by Zenon Pylyshyn, director (1983) of the Centre for Cognitive Science at University of Western Ontario. An accessible work combining epistemological and other philosophical concerns is A.H. Johnson's *Experiential Realism* (1973).

The most comprehensive form of epistemology is investigation of scientific knowledge to try to determine its theoretical structure and its place in human culture. Philosophers in Canada have made important contributions in philosophy of biology, including work on evolutionary theory by Thomas Goudge and Michael Ruse; philosophy of physics, especially of quantum mechanics, involving work in logical interpretation of the theory (Jeffrey Bub and William Demopoulos), the modal interpretation (Van Fraassen), and other aspects of quantum theory (Clifford Hooker, Edwin Levy and Leslie Ballentine). Other philosophers of physics include Mario Bunge, whose work ranges from technical philosophy of physics to science policy, Roger Angel (relativity physics) and Robin Giles (empirical treatment of thermodynamics). Some philosophers have begun to develop theories of science based on its history. Canadians have been active contributors in this venture, and they include Robert E. Butts (Whewell, Kant, historical methodology), Robert McRae (Leibniz), William Shea (Galileo), John Nicholas (Kuhnian anomalies), Jagdish Hattiangadi, James Brown and Andrew Lugg (methodology, evolutionary epistemology, the distinction between pseudoscience and science); and Ian Hacking (probability theory). Others are working on philosophy of the social sciences. They include Charles Taylor, who wrote *The Explanation of Behaviour* (1964); David Braybrooke (general problems), Frank Cunningham (objectivity) and Jonathan Bennett (rationality). William Dray writes on philosophy of history, and coedited *Substance and Form in History* (1981). Other problems in epistemology and philosophy of science have been studied by Fred Wilson, Alex Michalos and Brian Cupples.

A basic problem in 20th-century philosophy is that of the status of those things science postulates as existing: electrons, quarks and other objects unobservable by normal means. Scientific realism is the view that such objects exist; but realism is a disputed theory. Two major Canadian contributions to the debate are Van Fraassen's *The Scientific Image* (1980) and Paul Churchland's *Scientific Realism and the Plasticity of Mind* (1979).

Canada supports work in logic, epistemology and philosophy of science in many ways. International prominence in a major scientific and scholarly field is not easy to obtain, but in recent years Canada has achieved that presence at a level of excellence.   ROBERT E. BUTTS

French Canada Between 1950 and 1960 in French Canada, the teaching of philosophy at the university level continued to be dominated by neoscholasticism. Researchers involved in other areas, including Hugues Leblanc and Roland Houde, pursued their careers in the US. From 1960 to 1970 Thomism progressively disappeared and the universities recruited a few specialists, such as Michel Ambacher and Jerzy Wojciechowski, who favoured research on contemporary themes. Visits to francophone universities by thinkers such as Paul Ricoeur, Georges Canguilhem, Jean-Blaise Grize and Alan Montefiore, and the growing influence of European epistemologists such as Gaston Bachelard and Jean Piaget and analytical philosophers such as J.L. Austin, resulted in the emergence of new problematics and led some students to complete their training in Europe. After 1970 there were more exchanges with European researchers and a growing interest in Anglo-American problematics. At the same time a number of young researchers, trained in the philosophy of science and in epistemology and logic, secured university positions and provided growing support for specialized research.

Works on logic and the history of logic include those of Yvon Gauthier, Serge Robert, Daniel Vanderveken, Louis Valcke, Jaromir Danek and François Lepage; and on the philosophy of language, those of Gilles Lane, Jean-Paul Brodeur, Jacques Poulain, Ghyslain Charron, Jean-Guy Meunier, Claude Panaccio and Guy Bouchard. The most notable research in the combined field of logic and philosophy of language is being conducted in formal semantics and the theory of acts of language.

The common element linking general epistemology researchers, such as Jean Theau, François Duchesneau, Maurice Gagnon, Normand Lacharité, Robert Nadeau and Serge Robert, lies in analysis of the formation and transformation processes of science. It is striking that, in the various projects undertaken in this field, the purely structural analysis of scientific theories is replaced by consideration of the historical development of the disciplines.

The philosophy of mathematics is probed in the research of Charles Castonguay and Gauthier. Works by R. Bernier, Paul Pirlot, Camille Limoges and Duchesneau deal with the current problematics of the philosophy of biology in relation to the historical transformation of concepts and theories. Contemporary physical theories preoccupy Gauthier and Georges Hélal. The basics of physics and mathematics figure prominently in Gauthier's original research, under the label "constructivism." Constructivism is an analysis of the constructive dimension in the language of scientific theories, and thus contrasts with realism, which suggests that theories describe a reality independent of the constructing linguistic agent.

The vast social-science field is being investigated by Maurice Lagueux, Roberto Miguelez and Nadeau in history; Charron and J.N. Kaufmann in psychology; Fernand Dumont, Lagueux and Kaufmann in economics; Georges Legault and Brodeur respectively in law and criminology; and Fernand Dumont, Panaccio, Kaufmann, Meunier, Claude Savary and Josiane Ayoub in ideological theory.

F. DUCHESNEAU AND R. NADEAU

Metaphysics and Philosophy of Religion

Metaphysics includes the study of claims about what is ultimately real and important. Philosophy of religion is concerned with religious views of reality and with the evaluation and understanding of religious practice. Philosophers of religion and metaphysicians have faced 2 difficult challenges since 1950: acceptance of the sciences, especially physics, as the basic model of knowledge, and the preoccupation of philosophers with the theory of meaning. The study of reality is not the domain of any one science, and it has frequently been suggested that propositions about "reality" are too vague to be capable of scientific verification and are therefore possibly meaningless. Metaphysicians have been accused of twisting language into unintelligible shapes, and the major religions of endorsing world views that science cannot substantiate and that at times clash with "scientific" world views. Despite vigorous attacks on religious belief (eg, by Kai Nielsen in *Scepticism*, 1973), the tendency in Canada has been to seek ways in which the disputes can be resolved, and religious belief saved and made intelligible. The results may be divided into 7 groups.

First, F.W. Waters in *The Way In and the Way Out* (1967) and Alastair McKinnon in *Falsification and Belief* (1970) suggest similarities between science and religion: both involve fallible and limited attempts to apply fundamental principles. But these principles are not themselves uncertain. Thus, McKinnon argues, the scientist, committed to the principle that the world has an order, and the Christian, committed to belief in God, must try to show that experience and life become intelligible through reasonable application of the principle concerned.

Secondly, there have been attempts to revivify parts of the idealist philosophy dominant in English Canada until WWII. "Idealism" has had many meanings, but the Canadian idealists' central tenet was that all reality formed a unified, rational whole. They suggested that science and religion were not antithetical but part of a larger rational system and that there was a natu-

ral order to human affairs. These concerns were complicated by developments in science (such as quantum physics) that suggested chance elements in reality; by a growing gap between scientists' and religious believers' characterizations of the world; and by theories that suggested that meanings (interpretations) were arbitrary. In response, Lionel Rubinoff, in *Collingwood and the Reform of Metaphysics* (1970), argued in support of British philosopher R.G. Collingwood that our world views, scientific and otherwise, must be seen in the context of the presuppositions with which humans approach the world. Metaphysical systems and religious world views can be seen as intelligible if they are taken to be accounts of the way the human mind is able to see the world at different times. Science also reflects this historical process. In the course of history, these changing views begin to reveal a pattern, which Rubinoff called the "transcendental structure of reality," ie, a structure that appears through but ultimately leads beyond the immediacies of human experience. Part of the science-religion-metaphysics controversy has had to do with theories of logic, meaning and truth that were tailored to scientific knowledge. In *The Rational and the Real* (1962), *The Concept of Truth* (1969) and *Logic and Reality* (1972), Leslie Armour argued that these notions of logic, truth and meaning are specialized subforms of more embracing notions. The more embracing notions make possible many traditional metaphysical and religious ideas.

A third group, including Thomas Goudge and Charles de Koninck, has sought to build within the structure of science. Goudge's *The Ascent of Life* (Governor General's Award, 1961) makes few explicit claims about metaphysics or religion, but meticulously examines parts of biological theory and exposes a number of points at which conceptual possibilities remain open. De Koninck, in *The Hollow Universe* (1960), insists that the scientific world view is an abstract and hollow shell that must be filled by concrete experience in order to make sense. A.H. Johnson, in a series of books including *Whitehead's Theory of Reality* (rev ed 1962), reflects British philosopher Alfred North Whitehead's attempt to move from the scientific world picture to a more embracing structure by showing where the scientific structure needed metaphysical support. Johnson's theories, expounded chiefly in *Experiential Realism* (1973), continue his attempt to achieve an ultimate theory of reality through an adequate understanding of experience.

A fourth group, drawing inspiration from St Thomas Aquinas, searches for demarcation lines between science and theology and for a way to understand religion as rational. Louis-Marie Régis describes in *Epistemology* (1959) his view of the forms and limitations of science. Joseph Owens, in *An Interpretation of Existence* (1968), defends Aquinas's notion that being is capable of a measure of general characterization and that it is both active and intelligible. In *L'Éducation à la liberté* (1978; tr *Education for Freedom*, 1982) Jean-Louis Allard offers an account, which follows the philosophy of Jacques Maritain, of the way fundamental principles become intelligible through the ordering of one's life. Reactions against details of this philosophy include André Dagenais's *Vingt-quatre défauts thomistes* (1964) and *Le Dieu nouveau* (1974).

A fifth group is that of the many English-speaking philosophers who have worked within "analytic" philosophy, a tradition much influenced by Austrian Ludwig Wittgenstein and the British Bertrand Russell, G.E. Moore, Gilbert Ryle and J.L. Austin. Kai Nielsen uses this philosophy to question the foundations of religion and metaphysics. Alistair M. Macleod developed in *Paul Tillich* (1973) a strong negative critique of attempts to answer what Tillich called *the* question of being. Macleod urges that

Tillich is confused in thinking there is one central "mystery of being," but stops short of arguing that no metaphysical or religious world views can ever be justified.

Despite the frequent hostility of the analytic tradition to metaphysics and religion, many Canadian analytic philosophers have sought to find room for religious expression. In *Survival and Disembodied Existence* (1970) Terence Penelhum calls into question the meaningfulness of some widely held religious beliefs, but his *Rationality and Religion* (1971) leaves possibilities for religious discourse. Donald Evans, after close association with the new analytic philosophy during which he wrote *The Logic of Self-Involvement* (1963), developed his own defence of religious experience in *Struggle and Fulfillment* (1979) and *Faith, Authenticity and Morality* (1979). Pierre Lucier, in *Empirisme logique et langage religieux* (1976), assesses the strengths and impact of the analytic movement.

Frequently, analytic philosophers have used language analysis to sustain essentially "humanistic" positions against claims of "determinists" in psychology and history who have believed that free human action is unintelligible or impossible. A branch of philosophy known as "action theory" is concerned with analysis of the language with which human actions are described. Donald Brown, in *Action* (1968), carefully analysed such language and suggested that we cannot easily convert talk about human action into talk about events figuring naturally in the sciences. Similarly, William Dray argues in *Laws and Explanation in History* (1957) that explanations of human history cannot be reduced to the form of scientific laws.

Sixth, German phenomenologists and French existentialists had a substantial influence in Canada. Emil Fackenheim shows these influences in *Metaphysics and Historicity* (1961) along with those of Hegel and of 19th-century German philosophy in general. The most extensive work in this genre in French Canada is *Existant et acte d'être* (1977-80) by Benoit Pruche, who also draws heavily on Aquinas and Aristotle.

Concern with the idea of the self and the attempt to build a philosophical anthropology (ie, a theory of the nature of man) are strong in works such as those of Jacques Croteau, whose *L'Homme: sujet ou objet* (1981) develops ideas from European phenomenology against a background influenced by Aquinas and Maritain. In *La Genèse du concept du soi* (1980) René l'Ecuyer ties experimental psychology to ideas from a diverse group of philosophers, raising many issues that concerned the existentialists. In *The Art of Art Works* (1982) Cyril Welch applies other aspects of that tradition to our understanding of art and of the ways in which that understanding transforms reality. Existentialism and phenomenology have been criticized as well, eg, by F. Temple Kingston in *French Existentialism* (1961).

Finally, there has been a return to the rationalist metaphysics best represented by 17th- and 18th-century philosophers such as Leibniz and Spinoza. This movement, generally using modern logical and analytic techniques, has been led by John Leslie and Helier J. Robinson. The rationalists had urged that one must start with questions about what is logically possible rather than what seems to exist. They were guided by the principles that everything has an explanation and that whatever does not exist fails to do so because it is prevented from existing by something else. Leslie's *Value and Existence* (1979) argues for the reintroduction of principles of value into these discussions. In *Renascent Rationalism* (1975), which is also an attempt to make experience intelligible, Robinson admits that we cannot tell whether or not a god outside the world exists, but he believes that we can tell, for instance, that a god exists in some sense within the world.   LESLIE ARMOUR

Conclusion

Philosophers ask universal questions, but do philosophical answers have national characteristics? The question whether there is, could be, or should be a Canadian (or Québecois or western) philosophy is a vexed one. The following main positions in the debate can be distinguished. (1) The notion of a "Canadian philosophy" (or any other local one) is an absurdity. For philosophy, by definition, transcends the local and particular; it is transhistorical and transcultural. (2) There could be a Canadian philosophy, as there is German or American philosophy, but no such development, more or less unified, more or less distinctive, has taken place in Canada. (3) There could develop a Canadian philosophy, but such a development would be evil. For it would reflect the prejudices, oppressions and divisiveness of nationalism, when the world's survival and individual freedoms depend on the development of a cosmopolitan outlook. (4) A philosophy is a set of ultimate presuppositions (categories, principles and values) for imposing "meaning" (interpretation, explanation and significance) on experience. Philosophy is a key element in, and is as variable as, culture itself. Insofar as there is a Canadian (or Québecois) culture, there is some sort of Canadian (or Québecois) philosophy. This view may be combined with either the view that different presuppositions are incommensurable and cannot themselves be judged as true or false, good or bad, or the view that presuppositions can be judged not only "internally" as appropriate to, or well integrated in, a culture, but also "externally" as good, correct, true, etc. (5) Philosophies are ideologies that reflect the economic base and class divisions of a society; they are usually a form of "false consciousness" that serves the ruling class as an instrument of oppression. Insofar as Canada (or a region) has a distinctive economy and class structure, it will have a distinctive philosophy. Such a philosophy should be exposed and replaced by a "scientific" (eg, Marxist) analysis. (6) The intellectual historian can discern philosophical interests, themes, trends and schools that arise in the development of a country or region, and can correlate these with both international developments and the exigencies of the local situation. Partial explanation of philosophical change can be given in terms of these factors "external" to philosophy, but evaluation of the truth and acceptability of philosophical claims depends upon objective, transcultural standards. That is, the history of philosophy in Canada — and it may have had a distinctive development — is one thing, but the evaluation of it as correct or good is quite another.

One should distinguish questions of (a) possibility, (b) fact or actuality, (c) desirability or acceptability. Whether a national or regional philosophy is possible depends on one's definition of "philosophy." The bad faith or inconsistency to be avoided here is to admit the possibility of, eg, American philosophy and to deny the possibility of Canadian (or Québecois) philosophy. Matters of fact depend upon careful historical inquiry which, on this question in Canada, is still in its infancy. Questions of desirability or acceptability depend upon extended, rational philosophical debate. It may well be easier to argue in favour of national or regional particularity in social and political principles or policies — for here circumstances do alter cases — than for such diversity in logical, epistemic and metaphysical matters. *See also* INTELLECTUAL HISTORY.   JOHN T. STEVENSON

Reading: L. Armour and E. Trott, *The Faces of Reason* (1981); D. Braybrook, "The Philosophical Scene in Canada," *Canadian Forum* 53, 636 (Jan 1974); T.A. Goudge, "Philosophical Literature, 1910-1960" and "Philosophical Literature, 1960-1973," in C. Klinck, ed, *Literary History of Canada,* vols 2 and 3, respectively (rev ed 1976); Roland Houde, *Histoire et philosophie au Québec (1979);* J.A.Irving and A.H. Johnson, "Philosophical Literature 1910-1964," in C. Klinck, ed, *Literary History of Canada,* vol 1 (1965); M. Lagueux, *Le Marxisme des années soixante* (1982); Y. Lamonde, *Historiographie de la philosophie au Québec 1853-1970* (1972) and *La Philosophie et son enseignement au Québec (1956-1920)* (1980); A.B. McKillop, *A Disciplined Intelligence* (1979).

Phips, Sir William, adventurer, colonial governor (b near Kennebec, Maine 2 Feb 1650/51; d at London, Eng 18 Feb 1694/95). Knighted for recovering a sunken treasure ship off Haiti in 1686-87, Phips captured and plundered PORT-ROYAL 19 May 1690 and later that year brought 32 ships and over 2000 militiamen before QUÉBEC. His summons to surrender elicited Gov FRONTENAC's response that he had no answer "save from the mouths of my cannon." The attack was haphazard and disastrous and Phips made sail for Boston. Despite his defeat, he was named first royal governor of Massachusetts in 1692. He was summoned to England in 1694 to answer charges of maladministration but died before the investigation was completed.
                                    JAMES MARSH

Phlox (Polemoniaceae), family of flowering PLANTS ranging from leafless annual HERBS to small TREES and vines. Most species occur in N America, particularly in the western desert and in dry, cold regions. About 300 species are known worldwide. The genus *Phlox* is the best-known member of the family; 11 species occur in Canada. Wild blue phlox (*P. divaricata*), found in eastern Canadian open woodlands, blooms in May. In western Canada, *P. hoodii* (moss phlox) and *P. diffusa* (spreading phlox) form mats of colour ranging from white to bright mauve and pink in open prairie grassland and in foothill regions of the Rockies, Apr-June. Tall, vibrantly coloured summer-flowering phlox, derived from eastern N American *P. paniculata,* one of the most popular garden perennials in Canada, is often used for island beds or as border plants. Many flower colours are available and most produce a sweet fragrance during the July-Sept flowering period. Sweet William, a traditional garden plant in Canada, was developed from *P. maculata* (native from Québec to Virginia) and is a popular cut flower.   ROY L. TAYLOR

Photography The invention of photography was not a sudden discovery, but rather the result of an evolution of knowledge in chemistry and optics. Investigations into the light sensitivity of silver salts carried out by Johann Heinrich Schultze in 1727, and the use of a *camera obscura* as a tool to render perspective accurately, developed the components necessary for photography. The actual creation of a photographic image required the receptive mind of the 19th-century world, radically changed by the innovations of the Industrial Revolution. In 1839, 2 photographic processes were announced. In France, Louis Daguerre succeeded in securing a unique image on a silver-plated copper plate, resulting in one of the first photographic processes, the daguerreotype. At the same time in England, William Talbot developed a negative/positive process on paper, in which the term "calotype" referred to the negative, "salted paper print" to the positive. Both processes had distinct characteristics: in the daguerreotype everything was equally defined and minutely detailed whereas in the salted paper print broad masses and soft focus were emphasized.

Through the 19th-century press network and individual couriers, the daguerreotype and the calotype became known around the world, although initially the daguerreotype enjoyed greater success since it was not restricted by patent except in England. News of the remarkable discoveries reached the Canadian public in the spring of 1839. The *Québec Gazette,* the Toronto *Patriot* and the *Halifax Colonial Pearl* reported on

Clergyman, early photograph by Seth Park (*courtesy Public Archives of Canada/C-55366*).

the daguerreotype and on Talbot's "new art of sun painting." Itinerant daguerreotypists set up studios in suitable hotel rooms or stores with skylights and produced likenesses of their clients, or "patients" as they were sometimes called. The task was arduous: long exposure times, bad weather, erratic temperatures and difficult working conditions contributed to the low success rate of the early photographers. Few identified images have survived. Records in Canadian journals identify 2 Americans, Halsey and Sadd, who set up studios in Montréal and Québec late in 1840 and a Mrs Fletcher in Montréal in 1841, probably the first woman photographer in Canada. Thomas Coffin Doane was one of the few successful daguerreotypists in Montréal. He visited Newfoundland in 1843 in partnership with William Valentine and secured some portraits, but he is best known for his daguerreotypes of Lord ELGIN and family and of Louis-Joseph PAPINEAU. He also received an honourable mention award at the Paris Exhibition of 1855, along with Eli J. Palmer. In Toronto several studios flourished for short periods of time, but their output is now lost. However, from 1847 until about 1870 Palmer produced daguerreotypes and the popular *cartes de visite*, small photographic images glued to stiff cardboard and used as calling cards or bound in photo albums for future generations.

The original *carte de visite* was popularized in France by André Adolphe Disdéri, who photographed Napoleon III in 1859 and mass-produced the image on small cards. Prominent leaders and the rising middle class rushed to portrait studios to acquire portraits of themselves. Duplication was greatly improved by the introduction of the wet collodion process, developed by an Englishman, F. Scott Archer, in 1851. The procedure gave a clear negative on glass and, by contact printing, a finely delineated positive. The salted paper print was superseded by the albumen print, a positive on paper with a different application of the emulsion. Like Talbot's process, it had the potential of unlimited copies, yet it retained an admirable clarity of detail. The calotype was never used extensively in Canada, but by the 1860s the daguerreotype had been eclipsed. The wet collodion process improved speed and reproduction, but by modern standards it was difficult. The operator had to coat the plate, then expose and develop it before the emulsion had dried and lost sensitivity. Nevertheless, in the 19th century it facilitated photographic activity. In 1851 Lovell's *Canadian Directory* cited only 11 daguerreo-

typists; by 1865 the *Canada Classified Directory* listed more than 360 photographers.

The most famous was William NOTMAN, who exercised his influence in Halifax, Saint John, Montréal, Ottawa, Toronto and in the US. In 1858 he documented the construction of the Victoria Bridge in Montréal, the longest tubular bridge in the world. Conscious of history and the importance of the ceremony, in 1860 he recorded the royal visit of the Prince of Wales to inaugurate the bridge and was appointed photographer to the Queen. He also roamed the streets looking for interesting subjects. Pioneering the use of the magnesium flare in Canada, he recreated in his Montréal studios many indigenous scenes which represented the 4 seasons. Portraits, *cartes de visite*, cabinet cards and stereographs were his bread and butter. By the 1870s Notman, his sons, and a large staff turned out 14 000 negatives each year. Notman also excelled in composite photographs, where each image was made from several individual pictures, cut out, pasted onto a painting and rephotographed. An ambitious montage of the Skating Carnival in 1869 was made from about 300 single photos. James Inglis was also known for his composite images. Cabinet cards were a larger version of the *cartes de visite* and were collected with enthusiasm from 1868 until WWI. Stereographs had a long history. The apparatus for the production of a stereographic image was a camera with 2 lenses separated by the same distance as human eyes. It produced 2 nearly identical images which, when looked at through a stereo-viewer, fused into one image and gave the impression of the third dimension. "No home without a stereoscope" was the claim of the London Stereoscopic Co, and images from around the world graced the drawing rooms of the middle class. Given the bulky equipment, imperfect lenses and slow exposure speeds, events in motion were extremely difficult to photograph. They were not commercially viable, and there are few extant views from this period, though 2 are remarkable for their instantaneity: a photograph taken by Inglis at Thomas D'Arcy MCGEE's funeral procession in Montréal in 1868, and an anonymous photograph taken at the Feu de joie in front of the Parliament buildings the same year.

Albums of views were popular in the 19th century. Probably the first photographer to publish a series of mounted photos was Samuel McLaughlin who, in 1858-60, produced *The Photographic Portfolio*, views of Québec and the surrounding area. His best-known image is *The Ice*

Boat, a scene on the St Lawrence framed by the Québec Citadel. In 1861 he became the official government photographer, commissioned to photograph the construction of the Parliament Buildings. In keeping with the grandeur of the project, McLaughlin used mammoth plates, sometimes as large as 27" x 36". Despite the unwieldy wet collodion process, he succeeded in producing 24 negatives of various sizes in 1861.

Alexander Henderson was a photographer of merit and specific vision; his photographs are characterized by a sense of space relative to the Canadian landscape and a sense of time and season. They were published in *Canadian Views and Studies, Photographed from Nature*, a series of albums which appeared in the mid-1860s. Portraits from the Québec studio of Ellisson and Co were notable for their directness, strength and power, and contrasted with the elaborate studio backdrops typical of other mid-19th-century portrait photographers. As well as large portraits, Ellisson produced *cartes de viste* of local dignitaries in Québec.

Initial photographic activity was restricted to the settlements in Upper and Lower Canada. In the 1850s the westward trek began, stimulated by the discovery of gold in BC, by an effort to protect isolated communities from American expansion, and by government interest in trade and commerce. The efforts of 19th-century photographers to record the land and overcome the difficulties of an unfriendly environment were heroic and stubborn. One of the first was Humphrey Lloyd HIME, who accompanied the government Assiniboine and Saskatchewan Exploring Expedition to survey the West for future settlement and exploration. His photographs of prairie topography are stark in their simplicity and economical in their vision, and were published in *The London Illustrated News*. In 1871 Benjamin Baltzly, a Notman employee, accompanied the Geological Survey of Canada party led by Alfred Selwyn to the West.

With the opening of BC, the pioneering spirit of some photographers took hold and was fired by the gold rush of the 1850s and 1860s — prime photographic material. Charles Gentile accumulated historically important photos of the Leech River gold flurry in 1864. The Englishman Frederick Dally photographed the Cariboo goldfields and Barkerville, a boom town. According to newpaper reports, he did "wonderful face work" — presumably portraits. Another Englishman, George Robinson Fardon, documented Vancouver I; his photographs and his panoramic views of Victoria, composed of several small prints carefully matched to give the impression of a panorama, were exhibited at the International Exhibition in London in 1862. Francis G. Claudet, son of the celebrated French daguerreo-

The colourful Breakneck Steps, on Little Chaplain St, were one of Québec City's most popular photographic scenes. Stereo albumen print, c1870, by Ellisson & Co (*courtesy National Gallery of Canada*).

reotypist, Antoine Claudet, arrived in BC in 1859 as chief assayer for BC. He photographed at least 2 albums of views, though not all the photographs were taken by him. Photographers often bought or accumulated photos and published them under their own name, thereby making the task of identification difficult. Some of the plates taken by Dally were eventually acquired by Richard and Hannah Maynard, 2 of the most successful photographers in BC. In 1862 Hannah Maynard established a portrait studio in Victoria; Richard Maynard learned the trade from her and was responsible for a number of views of the province in the 1870s and 1880s.

By the late 1870s the mass-produced gelatine dry plate was in common use and photographers no longer suffered the trials of preparing their own plates on the spot. Dry plates became standard material on government survey expeditions, including a British expedition to reach the North Pole. Through blinding snowstorms this team managed to travel to the farthest point ever reached by an expedition, and 2 members, Thomas Mitchell and George White, secured more than 100 plates, at least one at -45°C. With technical improvements, instantaneous photography became a fact. Compact cameras came on the market and photographers could maneuvre with greater facility. Photographs of the North-West Rebellion in 1885 were made by Capt James Peters. Using a camera equipped with a magazine to facilitate changing plates after each exposure, Peters managed to get some images from horseback during the battle.

In 1888 George Eastman invented the hand camera and Kodak became an immediate success. The camera was loaded with film capable of 100 exposures. Once the film had been exposed, the camera with the film still inside was returned to Kodak. The film was removed, processed, positive prints made, a new roll of film put into the camera, and the whole thing returned to the sender. "You press the button, we do the rest" was honest advertising. As the number of amateur photographers increased rapidly, photo clubs were formed which in turn produced some distinguished photographers. The Toronto Amateur Photographic Assn was organized in 1888 and, as the Toronto Camera Club, began to hold exhibitions by 1891. In 1905 Sidney Carter, an associate member of Photo Secession, founded the Toronto Studio Club designed after England's Linked Ring, which, though it existed for only one year, espoused the virtues of the overtly manipulated image.

Photography had been criticized as a mechanical medium which ignored the intervention of the photographer. In an effort to give visual evidence of the nonmechanical hand of man, many advocates of the manipulated image appeared. Simultaneously, there were the champions of the straight, unretouched image as a true manifestation of the medium. The dichotomy between pictorialism or manipulated image and purism or straight photography echoed the difference between the calotype and daguerreotype. As photography asserted itself at the turn of the century, pictorialists also emerged strongly.

Diverse processes were used by pictorialist photographers to achieve their objectives: gum bichromate, cyanotype and bromoil transfer all allowed the gesture of the brush stroke to show as the emulsion was applied to a paper support. In a less obvious manner, without resorting to alternative processes, photographers also threw the image out of focus to obtain tone and an ethereal atmosphere rather than finely delineated details. In the first decades of the 20th century, Harold Mortimer-Lamb, a British engineer who had a close association with Carter and the Toronto Camera Club, and John VANDERPANT, a Dutchman who settled in Vancouver,

produced romantic soft-focus portraits and concentrated on the effects of light and shadow, mass and tone. By the 1930s, Vanderpant's style was changing and he began to investigate the potential of straight photography. He exhibited widely in international salons and achieved recognition from photographers in the US. In 1926 Vanderpant and Mortimer-Lamb opened a gallery together, featuring a studio and art and antique galleries. The association was short-lived, but the gallery continued and occasionally served as a showcase for members of the Group of Seven.

In 1934 the National Gallery of Canada inaugurated the first annual Canadian International Salon of Photographic Art, which marked the beginning of its involvement with the medium. Until the outset of WWII the gallery organized travelling exhibits. The Canadian Government Motion Picture Bureau had a still-photo division shortly after WWI, a tradition continued by its successor, the NATIONAL FILM BOARD, founded in 1939. Initially, this sector was set up to provide visual material for various government departments, and later expanded into a photo bank for newspapers and journals across the country. An active editorial group supplied weekly photo stories to Canadian and foreign publications.

With government recognition of the value of documentary photography, photojournalism flourished in Canada. William James and Arthur Goss were both active before 1914 and produced significant collections. One of the first sustained efforts to document military events occurred during WWI. The Canadian War Records Office was established in 1916 by Max AITKEN (Lord Beaverbrook). One of its tasks was to secure photographs from the front in order to obtain a permanent and vivid impression of what was happening. The Englishman William Ivor Castle was appointed official Canadian photographer and went to France in 1916; he came back with some of the first photographs to be widely circulated (they went on a 2-year tour in Canada and the US). Photos of men scrambling over the top of the trenches were acclaimed as accurate portrayals of men at war. In fact, it appears they were taken during combat training or staged far from the front line and later cropped to eliminate any unwarlike paraphernalia. Other more instantaneous photos were taken by William Rider-Rider, another Englishman appointed by the War Records Office, at major battles involving Canadians from 1917 until the end of the war.

The rise of the picture magazine also provided an outlet for photojournalists. Although the Toronto *Star Weekly* had a tentative start in the early 1930s, the *Montreal Standard* and the Winnipeg *New World* were the first to commission the photo essay in the 1940s. A *Montreal Standard* photographer, Henri Paul, a Frenchman living in Montréal, was well known for his coverage of the THÉÂTRE DU NOUVEAU MONDE; he was one of the first photographers in Canada to use the 35 mm camera, well suited to the needs of reportage. *Weekend* took over from the *Montréal Standard* in the 1950s and became a national magazine in competition with the *Star Weekly*. Between them they hired photographers Kryn TACONIS, John REEVES, John deVisser, Lutz Dille, Michel LAMBETH, Walter CURTIN, Chris Lund, John Max and Yousuf KARSH. Karsh, a well-known and popular portrait photographer, established a studio in Ottawa in 1932; using dramatic studio lighting and classical poses, he photographed many contemporary leaders and celebrities.

A dramatic increase in photographic activity occurred in the late 1960s. The National Film Board began a publishing program and established a photo gallery in Ottawa. It collected work from contemporary Canadian photog-

Yousuf Karsh (left) working with his assistant in his Ottawa studio, Nov 1957 (*courtesy Public Archives of Canada/PA-1166770/National Film Board/Chris Lund*).

raphers, organized travelling exhibitions and prepared support material such as catalogues and slide-tape shows. In 1967 the NATIONAL GALLERY, under the direction of James Borcoman, began an international photo collection, particularly of historical works. The PUBLIC ARCHIVES OF CANADA houses a collection of Canadian documentary photographs from the mid-19th century to the present. These 3 government institutions attempt to provide an overview of national and international photographic representation, without overlap or competition.

Photography has yet to be accepted by galleries and museums as equal to other art forms. Except for the National Gallery, no other major gallery in Canada employed a full-time curator of photography in 1983. Individual exhibitions arranged by guest curators, however, have been well received by the public in many cities, and the Winnipeg Art Gallery has been endowed with funds for a photography collection. Since 1973 the CANADA COUNCIL has provided program and operating funds to several artist-run spaces specializing in photography; grants are also made to individual photographers and to galleries for particular exhibitions.

In 1967 a group of photographers began the monthly bilingual magazine *Foto Canada*, which was printed in gravure and reflected a high standard of photography in Canada. Unfortunately, financial support for the magazine waned after a year and it ceased publication. In the 1970s *Impressions* presented a variety of photographic work. The bilingual magazine *OVO* has been published quarterly since 1970 in Montréal, and promotes photography as a means of communication and social improvement. *Photo Communiqué* has been published since 1979 and attempts to provide an information exchange among members of the photographic community. Also promoting Canadian photography is *Camera Canada*, published by the National Association for Photographic Art. Two books published by the National Film Board under the direction of Lorraine Monk, *Canada: A Year of the Land* (1969) and *Between Friends* (1976), attracted a good deal of public attention.

Among photographers who rose to prominence in the late 1960s and 1970s were Nina Raginsky, who gained recognition for her straightforward and subtly hand-tinted portraits of West Coast individuals; Gabor SZILASI, for his portraits and interiors of rural Québec; Tom GIBSON and Charles GAGNON, painters who took up a camera and walked the streets; Lynne Cohen, who photographed interiors which reflect contemporary taste; Freeman Patterson, who found romance in the landscape of the East; Robert Minden, who documented Doukhobors and Japanese Canadians in the West; and Orest Semchishen, who recorded the western landscape and vernacular architecture. Also important were Geoffrey James, Robert Bourdeau, David McMillan and Sam Tata.

The West and the East in Canada have their

differences, which relate to the light, the lay of the land and the different tempos in the various cities. Vancouver photographers rely on diffused light from the Pacific waters; the inhabitants of the Rockies focus their attention on the anomalies between breathtaking landscape and contemporary living. The prairie terrain serves as a minimal backdrop for western towns and specific industrial forms. Toronto takes its impetus from the US and splays out in all directions. Photographers from Québec respect the political dimension and record urban and rural phenonema with the eye of a sociologist. The Maritimes provide source material for introspection through isolation. Photography in Canada is now open-ended. The impact of 35 mm cameras on photography continues with the introduction of newer, small, light, automatic, self-loading and self-focusing 35 mm cameras and new reliable, fast-speed films. With curiosity about the medium expanded, the territory is fertile, ready for countless experiments and inventive minds. KATHERINE TWEEDIE

Reading: A. Birrel, *Benjamin Baltzly; 1871* (1978); *Canadian Perspectives: A National Conference of Canadian Photography* (1979); R. Greenhill and A. Birrell, *Canadian Photography 1839-1920* (1979); R. Huyda, *Camera in the Interior: 1858, H.L. Hime, Photographer* (1975).

Physical Education, a branch of the educational curricula of every province in Canada, which originated with a variety of forms of activity and concepts such as drill, calisthenics, gymnastics, physical training and physical culture. The modern term, "physical education," denotes a subject area of deliberate or systematic physical training undertaken in the classroom or during regular school hours, rather than an all-encompassing concept which might include all forms of games and interscholastic or extracurricular sport undertaken within educational institutions.

Because EDUCATION is under provincial jurisdiction, the history of physical education varies from province to province. Those involved in education in central Canada were responsible for early leadership and initiative in the area, particularly the first chief superintendent (minister) of education in Ontario, Egerton RYERSON. After frequent trips to Europe in the 1840s to study various educational systems, Ryerson attempted to infuse new, practical subjects such as music, art and physical education into the existing curricula of schools in Canada West.

Education in the mid-19th century was grounded in the classics (Latin, Greek) and directed mainly at the sons of well-to-do families who attended PRIVATE SCHOOLS and secondary or "grammar" institutions. Ryerson sought to rebuild the educational pyramid from its base, the elementary or "common" schools.

In Europe physical training was entrenched in institutional systems of exercise, such as the Ling system in Sweden, the Danish system and the German gymnastics or "Turnverein" societies, but Canada had no such tradition. When in 1852 Ryerson published a series of articles on "Physical Training in Schools" in his administrative mouthpiece, *The Journal of Education for Upper Canada,* (complete with woodcut diagrams), he was effectively advocating the inclusion of physical training into the schools. Prior to 1880, only 17% of Ontario's teachers received some form of pedagogical preparation and only the Toronto Normal School, the province's main teacher-training centre, could boast any facility for teaching physical training of any kind. However, the Normal School's first instructor of physical training, Col Henry Goodwin, a retired drill instructor, probably taught only army drill and calisthenic exercises to the few prospective teachers who did enrol. The only physical training manual available for teachers from the education office was a military drill manual.

BALANCING BAR. INCLINED BOARD.

TRIANGLE. BACKBOARD.

The introduction of physical exercise into public schools in the 19th century was intended to train the physical as well as the moral faculties of children. Different activities were prescribed for boys and girls, who were perceived to have different abilities. From a Toronto Dept of Public Instruction book, 1857 *(courtesy Ontario Institute for Studies in Education, Library)*.

Ryerson's advocacy of some form of physical training and the militaristic threats of the American Civil War during the 1860s resulted in the entrenchment of drill and rigid calisthenics as forms of physical education in schools. During the last third of the 19th century, the French Catholic and English Protestant schools in Québec followed the military drill precedent with some apparatus gymnastics introduced to Montréal schools through Mr Frederick Barnjum, the proprietor of a Montréal gymnasium and McGill's first physical education instructor. The idea of training and disciplining the body through military drill was also adopted in the Maritimes, where military instructors were hired to teach physical education classes. In the western provinces, which were being settled in the late 19th century, drill and calisthenics were the only forms of physical training employed by interested teachers or school boards; nowhere in Canada were play, games or sports accepted as legitimate aspects of the curriculum.

By the turn of the century, with the movement in many provinces toward compulsory public education and mandatory systems of teacher training, curricula (at least in theory) became more standardized. Of great importance in this regard was the development and widespread availability of teaching manuals which provided, in effect, written guidelines for lesson plans in many subject areas. In physical education, teaching manuals contained sections on physical education instructional material. In addition, early textbooks, eg, Blackie's *Sound Bodies for Boys and Girls* in New Brunswick and Houghton's *Physical Culture* in Ontario, both published in the late 1880s, offered lesson plans for teachers in drill, calisthenics and gymnastics. Ministerial reports on numbers of students in each subject area reflected dramatic increases in the number of students taking physical training, concomitant with the availability of these manuals and textbooks.

The first national program of physical education, the Strathcona Trust, was implemented in 1909 in elementary and secondary schools through a joint venture among provincial departments of education and the federal departments of militia. Sir Frederick W. BORDEN, the minister of militia, persuaded Canadian railway magnate and philanthropist Sir Donald SMITH (Lord Strathcona) to donate $500 000 to be used for the initiation and sponsoring of national programs of physical training and military drill in Canadian schools. The principal sum was invested, and the accrued interest financed the program. The Strathcona Trust sponsored 3 syllabuses or manuals that were widely used in Canadian schools; it systematized physical education as a regular subject of instruction and it encouraged teacher training in physical education. Departments of education, however, relied totally upon the trust and offered very little substantive or financial incentive to promote physical education further. Because the system was militarily based, it did not evolve in concert with American and European trends in physical education, which were directed at the inclusion of play, games and sport to complement the systematic training of the body.

Female educators, led by McGill University's physical director Ethel Mary Cartwright, were vociferous in their opposition to the militaristic nature of the Strathcona Trust and its advocated "physical jerks," which ran contrary to the child's natural inclination toward play. Women teachers of physical education were first taught at the Margaret Eaton School of Physical Culture (originally the Margaret Eaton School of Literature and Expression) in Toronto and at the McGill School of Physical Education; they received diplomas in physical education by taking courses in anatomy, physiology, hygiene, first aid, sports instruction, etc.

Although the last Strathcona Trust syllabus, published in 1933, included a full section on play and games, the actual teaching of classes remained rigid, formal and discipline-oriented. Dr Arthur Stanley Lamb, the director of physical education at McGill University and the proclaimed "father" of physical education in Canada, fought the Strathcona Trust system at every opportunity. Lamb sought to instill a new form of physical education by creating a national physical education professional association in 1933: the Canadian Physical Education Association, renamed, in 1947, the Canadian Association for Health, Physical Education and Recreation. Combined with the first university degree programs in physical education in Canada — U of T (1940), McGill (1945), UBC and Queen's (1946), and Western Ontario (1947) — the Canadian Association worked to inculcate sports and games in the curriculum, to teach students through physical education instead of disciplining them by it, and to make physical education a recognized, significant part of the curriculum. (In the 1920s and 1930s some universities required all students to take a minimum number of hours of physical training classes or to participate in the intramurals or intercollegiate athletics.) In the latter regard, the National Physical Fitness Act, passed by the federal government in 1943, was an important catalyst in promoting teacher training in physical education at universities across Canada. Under the Act $250 000 was offered to each province on a grant-matching basis, to encourage the development of physical education.

Modern concepts of physical education have achieved considerable recognition in a short period of time. Supported by a sport-conscious public, by media attention to physical fitness and by programs such as PARTICIPaction, physical education is firmly established in all levels of education from primary grades through to university degree programs. *See also* SPORTS HISTORY. DON MORROW

Reading: F. Cosentino, *A History of Physical Education in Canada* (1971); M.L. Van Vliet, ed, *Physical Education In Canada* (1965).

Physical Geography is that branch of GEOGRAPHY concerned with describing and analysing the distribution of physical elements of the environment interpreting environmental systems located at or near a boundary between atmosphere, lithosphere (rigid part of the Earth's crust), biosphere or hydrosphere (the Earth's water); and determining the resilience of such systems to human activities at or near the Earth's surface. In Britain and France, GEOMORPHOLOGY is commonly a subfield of physical geography. In N America, it is frequently seen as a branch of GEOLOGY. Both traditions are found in Canadian universities.

The roots of physical geography in Canada lie in scientific exploration. In the 17th and early 18th centuries, explorers provided descriptions of local and regional physical geographies, but the first substantial contribution was that of David THOMPSON. He carefully surveyed the terrain, made regular meteorological and astronomical observations and discussed the hydrology and ecology, in addition to assessing the resource potential and cultural and settlement characteristics of the Canadian West. Thompson's map of western Canada (1814) was a milestone in the development of physical geography in Canada (see CARTOGRAPHY). The FRANKLIN Expedition (1819-22) included John Richardson whose geological and physiographic interpretation of the Mackenzie R valley and the Arctic coast was the first in a long tradition of northern physiographic studies.

Establishment of the GEOLOGICAL SURVEY OF CANADA (GSC) in 1842 marked a further stage. The PALLISER EXPEDITION (1857-60), sponsored by the Royal Geographical Society, and the Hind-Dawson Expedition (1857-58), supported by the Government of Canada, generated information on climatic, vegetation, geological and landform contrasts in the Canadian West. Henry Y. HIND documented the overwhelming influence of GLACIATION on Canada. In this period Somerville's *Physical Geography*, the first book to be so titled, appeared in England (1848) and Herschel made the first reference to physical geography in the *Encyclopaedia Britannica* (1853). Much of the information generated by scientific exploration in Canada was incorporated into European physical geography. During the 1860s the Meteorological Service of Canada was organized; in 1870 the responsibilities of the GSC were extended to the western interior. Sensitive descriptions of the physical environment of Canada ensued and meteorological networks were extended through western and northern Canada. By 1894 John MACOUN had discussed the FORESTS of Canada and their distribution and, in 1914, some of the first integrated SOIL survey work in Canada was organized by the newly established Ontario Agricultural College at Guelph. Regular reports on FLOODS were published by the Department of the Interior, Dominion Water Power Branch, from the 1890s.

In 1915 the first Canadian university-level course in physical geography was established in the Department of Geology and Mineralogy at UBC. A course in meteorology and climatology was added in 1920. In 1922, the name of the department was changed to Geology and Geography. In 1921, E. Miller, the first geography-trained geography instructor in Canada, was appointed to the Faculty of Social Science at U de Montréal to teach physical and human geography. Later in the 1920s and the 1930s, extended visits by J. Brunhes and R. Blanchard from France made Montréal the Canadian centre of academic geography. In 1935 Griffith TAYLOR became founding head of the first full department of geography in Canada, at U of T.

By 1950 general courses in physical geography were offered at UBC, Laval, McGill, McMaster, U de Montréal, U of T and U of Western Ontario, but a change in the degree of emphasis on physical geography within geography departments had taken place. This change derived primarily from the increasing dominance in Canadian geography departments of US-trained academic geographers, who came from a SOCIAL SCIENCE tradition. By 1980 there were 41 university geography departments in Canada, of which 19 had more than 15 faculty members. In these larger departments, 121 professors (30% of the total) were physical geographers; of these, 40% could be classified as geomorphologists, 24% as climatologists, 22% as biogeographers and 14% as hydrologists. Of the departments, 13 had research and teaching activities in all 4 subfields of physical geography (UBC, Calgary, Simon Fraser, Guelph, McMaster, Ottawa, Queen's, Toronto, Waterloo, McGill, Montréal, Sherbrooke, and Memorial). Thirteen also offered MSc programs in some aspect of physical geography (Alberta, UBC, Calgary, Simon Fraser, Guelph, McMaster, Queen's, Toronto, Western, York, McGill, Montréal and Sherbrooke).

Applications The federal-government departments in which most physical geographers have found employment provide an indication of the range of applications of physical geography: Atmospheric Environment Service; Division of Building Research, National Research Council; GSC, Energy, Mines and Resources; Indian Affairs and Northern Development; Inland Waters Directorate and Lands Directorate, Environment Canada. Educational, private consulting and provincial governmental agencies are also major employers of physical geographers. Physical geographic expertise may be applied to problems associated with PERMAFROST, snow, GLACIERS, mountain environments, urban climates, SOLAR ENERGY, CLIMATE CHANGE, LANDSLIDE and flood hazards, terrain analysis and environmental planning. The range of technologies employed to acquire and manipulate data include REMOTE SENSING, infrared and satellite photography, computers (analysis), etc.

Institutions and Journals The International Geographical Union (IGU) is one of 18 member unions of an International Council of Scientific Unions (ICSU). Canada is one of 86 member nations of the IGU. In the 1980-84 term, Canada, in physical geography, provided one VP and 2 commission chairmen, elected by the General Assembly. The union has 5 commissions and 8 working groups concerning physical geography. Within Canada, the Canadian Assn of Geographers (CAG), the Québec Assn of Geographers, the Royal Canadian Geographical Soc, the Québec Geographical Soc and the Canadian Committee for Geography of the IGU form the national foci for most geographers. Physical geographers are also involved in the Canadian Geoscience Council (as representatives of CAG), the Canadian Meteorologic and Oceanographic Soc, the Canadian Quaternary Assn, the Québec Quaternary Assn and the Geological Assn of Canada, among others.

The scientific journals in which most physical geography research is published include *The Canadian Geographer, Canadian Geographic, Canadian Journal of Earth Science, Géographie physique et quaternaire, Atmosphere-Ocean, Cahiers de géographie de Québec, Revue de géographie de Montréal, Albertan Geographer* and *Ontario Geography*. A new journal, *Operational Geographer*, sponsored by the Canadian Assn of Geographers, will attract contributions on applied aspects of the work of physical geographers. OLAV SLAYMAKER

Physical Oceanography, branch of OCEANOGRAPHY that studies the physical processes occurring in the open OCEAN and in COASTAL WATERS through investigations of ocean currents, OCEAN WAVES, TIDES, distribution of physical properties (eg, temperature, salinity), thermodynamics of seawater, behaviour of SEA ICE and ICEBERGS, and the PHYSICS of sound and light in the ocean. Typically, field measurements are carried out to determine how the ocean behaves and to develop theoretical or numerical models, the results of which can be tested against observed evidence. Laboratory scale models (large tanks) are also used.

The earliest significant physical oceanographic study carried out in Canada was the Canadian Fisheries Expedition (1914-15). The expedition, planned jointly by the Norwegian director of fisheries, J. Hjort, and E.E. Prince, Dominion commissioner of fisheries and chairman of the Biological Board of Canada, studied the physical and chemical oceanography of the Gulf of St Lawrence. In 1928 H.B. HACHEY became the first physical oceanographer at the Atlantic Biological Station, St Andrews, NB. N.B. Carter and J.P. TULLY (in 1930 and 1931, respectively) were appointed to the Biological Station at Nanaimo, BC. WWII gave an impetus to physical oceanography studies. In 1942 Tully was seconded to the navy to improve the sonar detection methods of submarines. Today, physical oceanography studies are carried on at government institutes (BEDFORD INSTITUTE OF OCEANOGRAPHY; Institute of Ocean Sciences) and universities. See ARCTIC OCEANOGRAPHY.
ALLYN CLARKE AND PETER SMITH

Reading: G.L. Pickard, *Descriptive Physical Oceanography* (1979).

Physics is the study of matter and radiation, the space-time continuum that contains them, and the forces to which they are subject. Physics may be experimental, observing the behaviour of matter and radiation under various conditions, using increasingly sophisticated instruments, or theoretical, using mathematical tools to construct models, to formulate laws governing observed behaviour and to indicate (on the basis of these models and laws) promising avenues for further experimentation. The terms macroscopic and microscopic (or, more accurately, submicroscopic), and "classical" and "modern," refer to aspects of physics characterized by different scales in the phenomena studied. Macroscopic or classical physics deals with matter in bulk, as solids, liquids or gases. The closely interrelated fields of mechanics (based on Newton's laws of motion), heat (ie, thermometry and calorimetry), thermodynamics, classical electricity and magnetism (based on discoveries by Coulomb, Ampere, Faraday and Maxwell), and some aspects of statistical physics, lie in the domain of classical physics. Submicroscopic or modern physics studies the detailed structure of matter: atoms, molecules, electrons, nuclei, nucleons and various so-called "elementary particles," many of which are unstable and very short-lived.

The transition from classical to modern physics involved recognition of the existence in nature of a number of fundamental constants, which have since been measured with ever greater precision. Thus the speed of light in a vacuum is now known to 0.004 parts per million (c = 299 792 458 m/s). Other fundamental constants, such as e (the charge of an electron), m (its mass), M (the proton mass) and h (Planck's constant), have all been measured to a precision of a few parts per million. In classical physics, radiation (eg, visible light, radio waves) is treated as continuous waves characterized by a wavelength and a frequency. Modern physics introduced the concept of discrete bundles of energy, called quanta, associated with the waves and, shortly thereafter, discovered that under certain conditions the subatomic units of matter exhibit a wavelike behaviour. To deal with this behaviour a new mode of mathematical description, known as quantum mechanics, has been developed.

Finally the pair of terms basic and applied

represents an arbitrary division of physics into 2 broad areas, the boundary between which shifts continually. Michael Faraday's basic studies of the relation between electricity and magnetism have led to the applied field of ELECTRICAL ENGINEERING. The basic studies in nuclear physics by Ernest RUTHERFORD at McGill at the turn of the century eventually resulted in CANDU nuclear power reactors. Basic studies in SPECTROSCOPY, such as those of Canada's Nobel laureate Gerhard HERZBERG, underlie lasers, atomic clocks, and the NATIONAL RESEARCH COUNCIL OF CANADA's daily TIME signal on CBC Radio.

GEORGE M. VOLKOFF

History in Canada

The history of physics in Canada involves the development of undergraduate and graduate studies and research in universities, research in government institutions and in private industry.

Universities The first professors of natural philosophy (physics combined with MATHEMATICS) were appointed at Dalhousie University in 1838 and at King's College (later University of Toronto) in 1843. Professorships were established at Dalhousie (1879), Toronto (1887) and McGill (1890). The professors were occupied primarily by teaching, doing little original research; however, the European discoveries of the 1890s (X rays, radioactivity, electrons, etc) inspired Canadian professors to become active in the development of their subject. Especially prominent were Ernest Rutherford (McGill) and J.C. MCLENNAN (U of T). Establishment of graduate programs with research followed. Until after WWI, U of T and McGill were the only Canadian universities granting PhDs in physics. However, especially after WWII, many universities set up comprehensive graduate study and research programs. Between 1974 and 1981, 674 PhDs in physics were awarded by 30 universities (about 31% at Toronto).

The early slow growth of physics research was largely the result of financial difficulties. Establishment in 1916 of the National Research Council of Canada promoted the development of SCIENCE through scholarships for graduate students and apparatus grants to professors. Financial assistance from federal and provincial government sources increased, especially after WWII. In 1980 the NATURAL SCIENCES AND ENGINEERING RESEARCH COUNCIL took the place of NRC as the main federal granting agency.

Dalhousie can probably lay claim to the first meaningful research by a physics professor. J.G. MACGREGOR was appointed in 1879 and, during the next 20 years, published some 50 papers and memoirs. H.L. Bronson, department head from 1910 to 1956, inspired many students, including G.H. Henderson (radioactivity, pleochroic halos) and W.J. Archibald (theoretical physics), to take up careers in physics.

McGill got off to an excellent start with H.L. Callendar and E. Rutherford as Macdonald professors of physics. Important discoveries in radioactivity and nuclear physics were made by Rutherford and numerous assistants, some of whom (eg, H.M. TORY, J.A. Gray, H.L. Bronson, R.W. BOYLE) played vital roles in the development of science in other parts of the country. Nuclear physics at McGill culminated in 1949 in establishment of the Radiation Laboratory with the first cyclotron in Canada. This development was due chiefly to J.S. FOSTER, world-renowned for his work on the Stark effect. The Radiation Laboratory was headed by R.E. Bell for many years and the present nuclear physics group includes J.M. Robson. In the 1920s, L.V. King did outstanding work in mathematical physics. D.A. KEYS and A.S. Eve initiated early work on geophysics and, somewhat later, J.S. Marshall, on atmospheric physics. McGill was the first Canadian university to develop a theoretical phys-

ics group and has produced numerous theorists with international reputations.

J.C. McLennan was director of the physics laboratory at U of T from 1906 to 1932. His first researches were on atmospheric conductivity and cathode rays, but he shifted to atomic spectroscopy with the advent of the Bohr atom in 1912. Optics and spectroscopy have continued to be one of the main interests of the department with M.F. Crawford, H.L. WELSH, Elizabeth J. Allin and, since 1965, B.P. STOICHEFF as leader of a large laser group. In the 1920s McLennan, G.M. Shrum and others built a helium liquefier, the first in N America, for work on metals and solidified gases at low temperatures; this type of work is still actively pursued. During this early period, E.F. BURTON supervised research in colloid physics and, in 1941, he and his students built the first high-resolution electron microscope in N America. In the late 1920s L. Gilchrist began work in geophysics which later, under J. Tuzo WILSON, became one of the largest research groups in the department. In the 1960s a program in atmospheric physics was inaugurated. Extensive work was begun in high-energy particle physics in the early 1960s in nuclear physics with K.G. McNeill and A.E. Litherland, and in medical biophysics with H.E. JOHNS. Until the 1960s, theoretical physics was chiefly the concern of the department of applied mathematics which included J.L. Synge and L. Infeld. However, with appointment of J. Van Kranendonk in 1958, a strong theoretical section, embracing most of the branches of modern physics, was set up in the physics department.

UBC and McMaster were founded early in this century and demonstrated a remarkable rise in scientific productivity in the 1940s. At UBC the change resulted from the appointment of G.M. Shrum (head 1938-61) and others (including G.M. Volkoff, M. Bloom, R.D. Russell and J.B. Warren) which made possible a broad spectrum of teaching and research in many branches of physics. In the 1970s, UBC became the site of TRIUMF (Tri-University Meson Facility), one of the most important nuclear facilities in Canada. McMaster became an important centre of Canadian science following appointment of H.G. THODE in 1940. His work on mass SPECTROSCOPY and isotope abundances led to intensive work on various aspects of nuclear physics by M.W. Johns, H.E. Duckworth, B.N. Brockhouse and others. In 1957 a research reactor was set up, the first university reactor in the Commonwealth, followed, in the 1970s, by a particle-accelerator laboratory with extensive facilities. McMaster has achieved prominence in other research fields; eg, spectroscopy (A.B. McLay), solid state physics, biophysics and theoretical physics (M.H. Preston, J. Carbotte). Research is interdisciplinary (eg, in the Institute for Materials Research with J.A. Morrison as director).

R.W. Boyle became professor of physics at University of Alberta in 1912 and began extensive research in ultrasonics. Somewhat later, S. Smith and R.J. Lang began important work in optics and spectroscopy. Research has gradually broadened to include geophysics (J.A. Jacobs), solid state, nuclear, medical and theoretical physics (A.B. Bhatia, W. Israel).

At Laval, Québec City, Italian physicist F. Rasetti began a new era in physics teaching and research (1939-47). Rasetti was followed by his friend E. Persico (1947-50) and J.L. Kerwin, P. Marmet, A. Boivin and others. Main areas of research are optics, atomic and molecular physics, nuclear and theoretical physics. Like Laval, Université de Montréal has greatly increased its contributions to Canadian physics in the last 30 years. The 2 main areas of research are nuclear and plasma physics and associated theory, developed by P. Demers, P. Lorrain and others.

The department at Manitoba was begun by F. Allen who made applications of physics to

physiology. After WWII, active work on nuclear physics was begun by R.W. Pringle and expanded rapidly by B.G. Hogg and others. More recently, A.H. Morrish has instituted important work on magnetic materials. The department at Saskatchewan developed during the long headship (1924-56) of E.L. Harrington. Upper atmospheric research, begun by B.W. Currie in 1932, led to the present Institute of Space and Atmospheric Studies with an international reputation. In the period 1935-45, Gerhard Herzberg worked on atomic and molecular structures. In the 1950s the department gained renown with its betatron in photonuclear physics and radiation therapy, including development of a cobalt-60 unit by H.E. Johns and others. Plasma physics is also an important field of study. The younger western universities, Victoria, Simon Fraser and Calgary have rapidly developing physics departments.

Queen's University Kingston, and University of Western Ontario have made notable contributions to physics. Research and graduate work at Queen's was initiated by A.L. Clark in the 1920s. Nuclear physics research was begun by J.A. Gray and continued with B.W. Sargent, A.T. Stewart and others. Other fields of research are optics (initiated early by J.K. Robertson), microwave spectroscopy and solid state physics. At UWO rapid development of research began in the 1940s with a RADAR program. The work begun by R.C. Dearle, G.A. Woonton and others was continued by P.A. Forsyth, culminating in the Centre for Radio Science (1967), which studies problems in atmospheric and ionospheric physics. Nuclear research has made considerable progress, especially in the scattering of positrons (J.W. McGowan). The University of Waterloo was established in the late 1950s. The physics department immediately embarked on a program of research in experimental and theoretical solid state physics, with connected areas in laser physics and MICROWAVE spectroscopy. Geophysics and biophysics are also studied. York University has a Centre of Research for Experimental Space Sciences (CRESS) with R.W. Nicholls as director. The Universities of Ottawa, Windsor, Guelph and Carleton (with its particle physics program under E.P. Hincks) have promising futures. Concordia, L'École Polytechnique de Montréal and the Universities of Sherbrooke, New Brunswick, St Francis Xavier and Memorial conduct advanced studies in physics.

Physics staff members and graduates played an important role in both world wars. In WWI J.C. McLennan became director of experimental research for the British Admiralty and also organized production of helium from Canadian natural-gas wells; R.W.-Boyle conducted ultrasonic experiments in the Admiralty antisubmarine division. In WWII university staffs were in danger of being completely depleted by requests for assistance from NRC and other government and national defence organizations. In addition, several universities gave concentrated courses in physics and electronics to enlisted personnel destined to operate radar and signal devices in army, navy and air force.

Federal Research The NRC has played a major role in physics research. In 1928, NRC established laboratories in Ottawa including a Division of Physics with R.W. Boyle as director. The division expanded very rapidly after the outbreak of WWII; areas of study important to the war effort included nuclear physics, submarine detection and minesweeping devices, aerial photography and range finders. To implement results in optics and radar, Research Enterprises Ltd was set up as a CROWN CORPORATION. A large part of the physics staff dispersed at the end of the war; however, things began to improve with the appointment in 1948 of Herzberg and introduction in 1949 of a program of postdoctoral assistants with one- or 2-year terms. Applied physics became a separate division (1955), under L.E. Howlett. The spectroscopy section of the pure physics division rapidly attained world renown with the work of Herzberg, A.E. Douglas, D.A. Ramsay, T. Oka and others. In the 1970s the spectroscopy section was incorporated in ASTRONOMY and astrophysics in the Herzberg Institute of Astrophysics. The solid state section under D.K.C. MacDonald (1951-63) also attained renown. After establishment of the Herzberg Institute, the divisions of physics and applied physics were reunited. Sections of this division include electric and time standards (C.C. Costain), high-energy physics (E.P. Hincks) and solid state science (Z.S. Basinski).

In 1942 a British-Canadian atomic energy project, under NRC administration, was begun in Montréal, leading to the building of NRX, a heavy-water uranium research reactor, which began operation in 1947 at Chalk River, Ont. In 1952 administration of the project was transferred to ATOMIC ENERGY OF CANADA LTD. In 1957 a much larger reactor, NRV, came into operation, and an MP Tandem Van de Graaf accelerator was installed. The aim of this program was to develop research reactors for nuclear experimentation and NUCLEAR-POWER reactors for generation of electricity. W.B. LEWIS was in charge of research. Many Canadian physicists have been involved in the project, including G.C. Laurence, B.W. Sargent, J.M. Robson (neutron decay), R.E. Bell, B.N. Brockhouse (neutron scattering), E.P. Hincks (cosmic rays) and A.E. Litherland.

Other federal research establishments include the Defence Research Board, which has maintained stations for naval research at Halifax and Esquimalt, BC, an armament research and development establishment (CARDE) at Valcartier, Qué, and a telecommunications establishment (with J.H. Chapman) at Ottawa.

Provincial Research Physics-related research is carried out by many of the 8 provincial research organizations, the oldest being the ALBERTA RESEARCH COUNCIL (est 1921). The hydroelectric corporations of most provinces have research facilities relating to ELECTRIC-POWER GENERATION and transmission, the largest being that of HYDRO-QUÉBEC.

Industrial Research Compared with other industrialized nations, Canada shows a rather low level of INDUSTRIAL RESEARCH AND DEVELOPMENT. Many of the better industrial laboratories doing physics-related research have been set up as Canadian subsidiaries of American companies. For example, the Radio Corporation of America maintained for many years the RCA Canadian Research and Development Laboratories Ltd (under M.B. Bachynski from 1958); in 1976 a large part of its work was taken over by MPB Technologies Inc, with Bachynski as president and director. The Xerox Research Centre of Canada Ltd is a recent example of an American firm locating a part of its research in Canada. Bell-Northern Research Ltd (with D.A. Chisholm as chairman and president since 1977) is doing excellent work. H.L. WELSH

Subfields

Physics has been divided into various subdisciplines unified by the basic laws of mechanics and quantum mechanics, thermodynamics, etc.

Theoretical Physics Physics proceeds by the constant interplay between experimentation and the conceptual interpretation of the results. Until late in the 19th century the 2 often went hand in hand; early 19th-century physicists often engaged in both activities. With the development of increasingly sophisticated techniques of experimentation on the one hand and of mathematical analysis on the other, and with a rapid acceleration of the acquisition of knowledge in the 20th century, specialization became more general and theoretical physics, the evo-

lution and theoretical exploitation of rapidly changing concepts, emerged as a more or less distinct discipline. The division of physicists into the categories "theoretical" and "experimental" has now become almost universal. A distinction must be made between "theoretical physics" and "mathematical physics," the former being characterized by a preoccupation with concepts and models of the physical world and the latter with the evolution of mathematical technique per se.

The modern revolution in physics stems from 3 major developments of the late 19th and early 20th centuries. The first was the refinement of the science of thermodynamics, by 19th-century American mathematician Willard Gibbs, into a general theory which has become one of the conceptual foundations of modern physics. The next involved the formulation of the general theory of relativity by Albert Einstein in 1917. This theory laid the basis for the first scientific COSMOLOGY by integrating gravity, the principal motor of the cosmos, into the very structure of space and time. The third was the development of an integrated and coherent quantum theory by Einstein, Niels Bohr, Arnold Sommerfeld, Louis De Broglie, Erwin Schrödinger, Werner Heisenberg and others. Quantum theory permits understanding of the subatomic structure of matter.

The 20th-century developments began in Europe, primarily Germany and Great Britain. The American continent, with its emphasis on technology and an empirical tradition, contributed only modestly. The rise of European fascism caused a mass emigration from Europe to the US and refugees (eg, Einstein, Fermi, Wigner, Bethe) propelled American physics, in the space of a generation, into a position of world leadership in theoretical physics.

In Canada, where the empirical tradition had been firmly established by Rutherford and others, theoretical physics was almost nonexistent until after WWII. Only at U of T had Leopold Infeld, a refugee from Poland, working in a new department founded by the Irish theorist J.L. Synge, laid the groundwork for a new school. The enhanced prestige of theoretical physics resulting from its dramatic contributions to the winning of the war created the conditions for the rapid expansion of theoretical physics in the universities. By 1957 a theoretical physics division was created within the Canadian Assn of Physicists. The balance between theoretical and experimental physics is now much the same as in the US, and important contributions are being made by Canadian theorists in all domains. P.R. WALLACE

Upper Atmosphere and Space Physics deals with the physical behaviour of matter in regions beginning about 60 km from Earth's surface and extending to the far reaches of the solar system. In such regions a near vacuum exists. Most of the material present is in the plasma state, ie, the electrons are separated from the parent atoms and thus produce an "electrified fluid," which is easily influenced by electric and magnetic forces. Near Earth, streams of charged particles from the SUN distort Earth's magnetic field to form a vast region called the magnetosphere, within which complex interactions take place between the electrons, ions and electric and magnetic fields. A visible result of these processes is the NORTHERN LIGHTS.

The first explorers in northern Canadian waters recognized that frequent gross compass errors were the result of magnetic disturbances that were somehow linked to the Northern Lights. The first organized attack on the problem was made by expeditions from Europe during the first International Polar Year (1882-83). By the time of the Second International Polar Year (1932-33), Canadian groups were able to participate in the study of auroral phenomena. Fol-

lowing WWII there appeared new spectroscopic instruments of sufficient sensitivity to permit analysis of the rapidly changing auroral luminosities, and new radio and radar devices that permitted direct study of auroral ionization. By that time, it had become apparent that radio communications in northern Canada were adversely affected by ionospheric disturbances. Finally, during the International Geophysical Year (1957-58), Canadian scientists came to the forefront of this area of research. In 1957 a research rocket range was established at Churchill, Man, initially under US sponsorship. It has provided the stimulus for the development of a Canadian "family" of research rockets, the Black Brants. Such rockets can place an instrument directly in the region of interest, albeit for only a few minutes. Satellites make it possible to take continuous measurements over weeks or years.

Stimulated by Canadian radio studies of the ionosphere, a joint US-Canada program led to 4 Canadian-made scientific satellites: Alouette 1 in 1962, Alouette 2, 1965; ISIS 1, 1969; ISIS 2, 1971. These satellites provided a wealth of new information about the structure of the ionosphere, the precipitation of energetic charged particles into the high-latitude atmosphere, the global distribution of auroras and phenomena of the magnetosphere. Today, Canadian scientists are active in several international co-operative programs making use of satellites, the US Space Shuttle and interplanetary space probes. The Canadian program focuses on tracing the energy flow from the solar particle stream through many intermediate processes to heating of the atmosphere. For such global studies international co-operation is mandatory. P.A. FORSYTH

Earth Physics studies the solid Earth and its atmosphere and oceans. Although LAND, sea and air are often studied in isolation by separate disciplines (geophysics, OCEANOGRAPHY, METEOROLOGY), modern investigations are often intensely multidisciplinary. The physics of the solid Earth encompasses both academic and applied aspects. The questions, "how and of what was Earth formed" and "what physical and chemical processes control its evolution," remain at the forefront of current research. Perhaps the most important scientific advance in the past century of geophysical enquiry has been the dramatic verification of the hypothesis of continental drift, achieved since 1965. This PLATE TECTONICS theory received support from the geophysical methods of seismology and geomagnetism (see GEOLOGY). These methods are also employed, with considerable practical success, in exploring the near-surface crustal region of Earth for economically important deposits of PETROLEUM and base metals. Electrical methods, many of which have been developed in Canadian laboratories, have proven to be particularly suited to the discovery of MINERAL deposits. These methods include electromagnetic induction, induced polarization and direct current resistivity measurements. Other geophysical techniques that are of major industrial significance include seismic reflection and refraction SURVEYING, and potential field methods based on analyses of minute variations in Earth's gravitational and magnetic fields. In all these areas Canada has played a leading role in developing and implementing new methodology.

The atmospheric sciences, often considered together under meteorology, are also characterized by a multifaceted collection of applied and fundamental concerns, including questions regarding the detailed processes through which precipitation (rain, hail and snow) is formed; the potential negative effects of increases in carbon levels in the atmosphere; the sensitivity of the atmosphere to small changes in insolation and to changes in stratospheric concentrations of ozone and the oxides of nitrogen; and the assessment of air quality, especially relating to the problem of ACID RAIN. Considerable recent progress has also been made in understanding the planetary-scale hydrodynamics of the atmosphere, through the use of detailed mathematical models implemented on the largest digital computers available. Practical by-products of this fundamental research include the numerical weather prediction models routinely employed to make twice-daily forecasts. Canada's Atmospheric Environment Service has played a leading role in developing and improving such models.

The science of oceanography has many similarities to both solid Earth geophysics and meteorology. Physical oceanographers study the waves and currents of all spatial and temporal scales that characterize the motions of the sea in the major ocean basins. Chemical oceanographers study the composition of the sea and, more recently, have begun to employ measurements of trace-element concentrations to reveal the patterns of oceanic circulation. Biological oceanographers are concerned with the life systems that the oceans sustain. The necessity for acquiring improved understanding of the oceans has been made particularly clear by recent and unsuccessful United Nations attempts to formulate a LAW OF THE SEA that would control exploitation of the mineral wealth of the ocean floors. This economic incentive and that provided by large-scale offshore programs of drilling for subsurface deposits of hydrocarbons have enhanced traditional concerns about the sea as a source of food.   W.R. PELTIER

Optics The Greek word *optikes* originally meant the study of the eye and vision. Today, optics encompasses the whole spectrum of electromagnetic waves, radio waves, microwaves, infrared, visible light, ultraviolet, X rays and gamma rays. Classical optics dealt mainly with lenses, mirrors, gratings and instruments made with them. Such artifacts can be designed and analysed using the classical (ie, geometrical and wave) theories of light. The main proponents of geometrical theory were Johannes Kepler (German astronomer) and Sir Isaac Newton (English physicist and mathematician). This theory assumes that a light source emits light rays, which propagate rectilinearly in a homogeneous medium. When the medium changes, the rays are reflected, refracted or both. Pinhole cameras and shadows of objects cast by light beams demonstrate the truth of this theory. The main proponent of wave theory was Christian Huygens (Dutch scientist). It assumes that a light source emits waves that travel out in spheres; at any moment, every point on a wavefront acts as a new secondary source emitting new wavelets. The optical phenomena of interference, diffraction and polarization can be studied by this theory. Optics has always been an extremely important component in spectroscopy, which has played a vital role in the study of atoms and molecules. In Canada, Gerhard Herzberg won a Nobel Prize (1971) for work in molecular spectroscopy.

Optics was revitalized and revolutionized by the invention of the maser and LASER by Charles Townes (American physicist), N.G. Basov and A.M. Prokhorov (Soviet physicists), winners of the 1964 Nobel Prize for physics for their work in this field. The first laser was built by Theodore Maiman (American physicist) in 1960. The main types of lasers are (according to the lasing materials used) solid, liquid, dye, gas and semiconductor. Extreme high-intensity pulses can be produced by transversally excited atmospheric carbon dioxide (TEA-CO_2) lasers. The Canadian Defence Research Establishment, Valcartier, Qué, was among the important pioneers and inventors of TEA-CO_2 lasers. Canada has a few laser-manufacturing companies, including internationally renowned Lumonics Inc.

Among the latest developments in optics is fibre optics. Optical waves can propagate inside optically transparent fibres by total internal reflection. The diameters of the fibres may be a few micrometres (single mode) to a few hundred micrometres (multimode). Because of their high frequencies, optical waves in the visible and near infrared regimes can carry far more information than electrical currents in metal wires. Canada is one of the leaders in fibre optics. Much research is done at the Communications Research Centre. Commercially, Bell-Northern Research and Canada Wire and Cable are the leading Canadian companies. The world's first fibre-optic, cable-television, digital super trunk system was installed in London, Ont. Some other early Canadian systems were installed at Dept of National Defence headquarters, Ottawa (1976), downtown Montréal (1977), Toronto (1978) and Vancouver (1979). Two recent and very advanced systems were the Calgary-Cheadle (Alta) and the Elie-St Eustache (Man) projects.   JOHN W.Y. LIT

Atomic and Molecular Physics is concerned with understanding the physical nature of atoms and molecules and with observing and understanding processes involving a small number of atoms and molecules, which may or may not be electrically charged. The emphasis on the small number of particles distinguishes atomic and molecular physics from solid state physics, statistical mechanics and thermodynamics, and plasma physics. The subject has diffuse borders with many branches of physics, CHEMISTRY and astrophysics. The ultimate aim of atomic and molecular physics is to establish the physical laws that govern observed atomic and molecular processes. At present, it is generally believed that all known phenomena are compatible with the laws of quantum mechanics and quantum electrodynamics. While many elegant verifications of these laws have been obtained for simple physical systems, the quantitative application to more complex systems is limited by mathematical and computational difficulties.

The term electronics was first used to describe the branch of physics that evolved from the discovery of the electron by English physicist J.J. Thomson in 1897. The subject then involved the determination of the fundamental properties of individual electrons (eg, charge, mass, magnetic moment) and the properties of free electrons in vacuum tubes. Today the term has a wider connotation, embracing the study, design and application of devices (eg, electronic tubes, transistors, integrated circuits) the operation of which depends largely on the characteristics and behaviour of electrons. Electronics plays a key role in COMMUNICATIONS and computers.

Spectroscopy is concerned with the interaction between matter and radiation. Historically the subject started in the visible region of the spectrum and was primarily concerned with the emission and absorption spectra of atoms. Today the subject embraces the complete electromagnetic spectrum and is concerned with atoms, molecules and charged species in the gas, liquid and solid phases. The emission or absorption of radiation by a system accompanies a transition between 2 energy levels or quantum states of the system and gives information on the nature of these quantum states (*see* CHEMISTRY SUBDISCIPLINES). The spectrum of a substance is probably its most characteristic single property; this fact underlies the widespread use of various forms of spectroscopy in qualitative and quantitative analysis.   D.A. RAMSAY

Nuclear and Particle Physics The atomic nucleus is a small, dense object containing nearly the entire mass of the atom. The existence of the nucleus was demonstrated by E. Rutherford in 1911, but an understanding of its composition came only with English physicist James Chadwick's discovery of the neutron in 1932. The ex-

istence of the neutron provided the key to understanding the nucleus as a composite body, formed of neutrons and protons. The neutrons and protons (referred to as nucleons) are bound in the tiny nuclear volume by a force that is very strong (ie, much stronger than the energies involved in binding atoms to form a molecule) and of very short range. The most important manifestations of nuclear energy are found in the processes of NUCLEAR FUSION and fission, in which a fraction of the internal nuclear energy is transformed into kinetic energy, which ultimately appears as heat (*see* NUCLEAR-POWER PLANTS). A chemical element has a characteristic number of nuclear protons but nature permits a certain latitude in the number of neutrons that may bind to the protons, under the influence of the strong force. The differing neutron numbers give rise to what are known as isotopes. Several isotopes of a chemical element may be absolutely stable, but the remainder manifest an instability called radioactive decay. Some radioisotopes occur naturally in the heavy elements and many more have been produced artificially. Many radioisotopes are valuable in medicine and industry.

A nucleus may have a number of distinct excited states, differing from one another by discrete amounts of internal nuclear energy. Such states undergo radioactive transformation under the perturbing effects of internal electromagnetic interactions or the very feeble, but significant, weak interaction. These excitations and transformations have been much studied as a means of understanding the complexities of the strong nuclear force. Although the structure of a nucleus is explicable in terms of just 2 particles, scores of other subatomic particles have been observed, studied and classified. These particles are grouped in 3 families: baryons, mesons and leptons. The lepton family is characterized by its insensitivity to the strong interaction; the most notable attribute of the baryon and meson families is their affinity for the strong interaction. Baryons and mesons appear to have an important internal structure of their own: the baryon family is believed to be formed of different combinations of 3 fundamental constituents, known as u, d and s quarks; the meson family is formed by the binding of 2 constituents, a quark and an antiquark. The quarks are thought to be permanently confined or bound and hence unobservable as free particles. The quark hypothesis received strong support in 1974 and 1977 with the discoveries of massive long-lived mesons, known as psi and upsilon mesons, formed by the binding of heavy quarks, called c and b, with their respective antiquarks. A very important concept in particle physics is the unified theory of weak and electromagnetic interactions. According to this theory the weak interaction is associated with particles about 100 times more massive than the proton. These particles are expected to be observed in the large electron-positron and proton-antiproton colliding beam machines now in operation or construction in Europe and the US.   D.G. STAIRS

Condensed Matter Physics studies the fundamental, microscopic properties of matter in the solid and liquid phases, and their technological uses. Condensed matter physics is an outgrowth of solid state physics that blossomed in the post WWII period. Most research was done on crystalline materials, in which the atoms are in ordered positions, especially semiconductors. The discovery of the transistor revolutionized electronics. It is now at the heart of modern communications and SPACE TECHNOLOGY, computers, commercial electronic devices and microelectronics. Solid state physics evolved into condensed matter physics in the 1970s in Canada. There is strong affinity between the properties of liquids and solids, and between techniques used to investigate them. There are similarities between the disordered (amorphous or glassy) materials and liquids. There is a parallel between superfluids, which flow without friction, and superconductors, in which electrical currents flow without losses, at low temperature. These co-operative phenomena, which implicate all particles in unison, have applications in computers, electric-power transmission and public transport (superconducting motors and levitation). Liquid-crystals (eg, watch displays) have properties of both the liquid and solid.

Condensed matter physics calls on a host of experimental techniques such as microwave, optical, X ray, magnetic resonance, neutron and electron spectroscopies, thermal, acoustic, magnetic and electrical probing. It is also strongly dependent on theoretical techniques such as quantum mechanics and statistical physics. It is a broad and diversified field that blends into most other fields of physics and chemistry, biology, engineering and medicine. The Canadian effort in condensed matter is quite substantial, in 1980 involving over 400 full-time equivalent physicists. Canada played a leading role in development and use of neutrons and positrons to probe condensed matter. There is now considerable interest in using unusual but promising materials, such as layered solids (eg, graphite) and polymer conductors, in batteries, and organic conductors and superconductors. The conversion of light to electricity and the storage of energy (eg, solar heat, hydrogen) in materials are of practical interest. The acoustic microscope, which uses ultrasonic waves instead of light, shows great promise. LAURENT G. CARON

Plasma Physics American chemist Irving Langmuir was the first to make systematic studies on electrical properties of ionized gases or plasmas. Atoms or molecules in a gas become ionized when bombarded by energetic particles or irradiated by short-wavelength electromagnetic waves. In general, a plasma contains equal amounts of positive and negative charges and maintains electric neutrality. An ionized gas is appropriately called a plasma if there are a sufficiently large number of electron-positive ion pairs in a characteristic sphere (Debye sphere) and the space occupied by the gas is much larger than the Debye length. A plasma is a good electric conductor because of the presence of highly mobile free electrons. In a fully ionized plasma, electric conductivity rapidly increases with the temperature, but is practically independent of the density of the plasma electrons.

Plasmas can be found in such engineering devices as glow discharge tubes, mercury vapour rectifiers, fluorescent lamps and gas lasers. Plasmas in these devices are initiated and maintained by electrical discharge through neutral gases. Ionization, however, is maintained by plasma electrons themselves, which can acquire a temperature of several thousand degrees. Tube walls, usually glass, do not melt since gases are extremely rarefied.

Plasmas can be found in nature. LIGHTNING is caused by an electric discharge or breakdown among clouds or between clouds and Earth. Air, being a good electric insulator otherwise, becomes a plasma and provides conduction paths for electric currents. Auroras, another example of a natural plasma, occur when Earth's upper atmosphere becomes ionized when exposed to solar radiation. More importantly, stars, and nebulae are all in the plasma state with energy released through the nuclear fusion process.

A plasma greatly modifies the nature of electromagnetic waves. For example, shortwave radio, out-of-sight communication is possible because of wave reflection by the ionospheric plasma. Self-generation of plasma waves (instability) is largely the result of intrinsic temperature difference between an energetic plasma and its environment. A plasma tends to establish thermal equilibrium through thermal and

particle diffusion which can be greatly enhanced by plasma instabilities, and often jeopardizes plasma confinement in nuclear-fusion devices. However, plasma instabilities have also been utilized as various microwave sources.
A. HIROSE

Societies

The Canadian Assn of Physicists, the national society of Canadian physicists, has a membership of over 1800 individuals and 30 corporations. CAP was founded in 1945 and incorporated in 1951. It publishes a bimonthly bulletin, *Physics in Canada,* and holds an annual 3-day congress for discussion of current research. Congresses take place at selected university campuses across the country. Since 1945, the Canadian Assn of Physicists Medal has been awarded annually for distinguished achievement in physics and, since 1970, the Herzberg Medal for outstanding achievement by a physicist not more than 38 years of age. Through its Educational Trust Fund, the association arranges and finances lectures throughout Canada, and conducts an annual program of physics examinations and awards for high-school students (provincially) and for undergraduates (nationally). From time to time, CAP produces special reports on the state of physics in Canada, the latest being a major review titled *On Future Research Opportunities for Physics* (1982) for NSERC. Canada's national physics journal is the *Canadian Journal of Physics.*

Many physicists are members of the Association canadienne-francaise pour l'avancement des sciences. ACFAS was established in 1923 for the advancement of science in Québec and in French-speaking communities of N America. With a membership of over 2500, ACFAS holds an annual congress attended by 2000 researchers and students, who gather to hear approximately 1000 scientific papers.

Most Canadian physicists are also active members of the many scientific societies in physics and astronomy that form the American Institute of Physics (AIP). For example, the American Physical Society has over 1000 Canadian members; the Optical Society of America (OSA), over 350. There is a large Canadian representation in the American Assn of Physics Teachers (AAPT), and in the more general American Assn for the Advancement of Science (AAAS). An appreciable number of Canadian physicists are enrolled in the Physical Society of London and in the European Physical Society. Canadian physicists have taken an active part in international organizations, eg, the International Council of Scientific Unions and the International Union of Pure and Applied Physics (a member of ICSU). IUPAP promotes international co-operation in physics, and international agreements on the use of symbols, units, nomenclature and standards. Canadian participation on these and other world bodies is co-ordinated through the Office of International Relations of the NRC. Individual universities have also made agreements for specific programs of study and research. Scientific exchanges have permitted collaboration of many groups in nuclear and particle physics research, making use of the costly accelerators at national laboratories in Europe, the US and Canada (AECL and TRIUMF).

Canadian physicists have been honoured by both national and international bodies. Physicists who have served as presidents of the ROYAL SOCIETY OF CANADA include G. Herzberg, H.E. Duckworth, J.T. Wilson, L. Kerwin and R.E. Bell. One of the oldest and foremost scientific organizations worldwide, the Royal Society, was founded in 1662 in London, England, to improve natural knowledge. In the past decade, a number of Canadian physicists have been made Fellows of the Royal Society, including Z.S. Basinski, R.E. Bell, B.N. Brockhouse, A.E. Douglas,

G. Herzberg, W.B. Lewis, A.E. Litherland, M.H.L. Pryce, D.A. Ramsay, B.P. Stoicheff, H.L. Welsh and J.T. Wilson. BORIS P. STOICHEFF

Physiographic Regions Physiography originally meant "the study of natural phenomena" but later usage limited its application to PHYSICAL GEOGRAPHY in particular and, more recently, to landforms alone. The latter usage makes the word redundant, as GEOMORPHOLOGY is the universally accepted term for the study of landforms; nevertheless, in many works about physiographic regions, only landforms are considered. Physiographic regionalization is here defined as the process by which regions with relatively homogeneous physical geography are delimited. The 4 elements, land, air, water and vegetation, in distinctive combinations, define the physiographic regions of Canada. Geologic structure (*see* GEOLOGICAL REGIONS), relief attributes of land, the distribution of continuous PERMAFROST (a measure of broad-scale atmospheric and hydrologic effects) and the position of the TREELINE (a significant vegetation boundary) are the criteria used in the following physiographic regionalization. Combinations of these generate the major physiographic regions of Canada: Arctic Lands, Cordillera, Interior Plains, Hudson Bay Lowland, Canadian Shield Forest Lands, St Lawrence Lowlands and Appalachia. These regions have broadly homogeneous physical geographic characteristics and differences between them are visible from a jet travelling at 10 000 m altitude or from satellite images (*see* REMOTE SENSING). Areas quoted for these regions are the land areas and do not include adjacent continental shelves or bodies of ocean water within Canada's territorial limits. Certain parts of Canada may be properly classed in 2 regions (eg, arctic portion of the Canadian Shield).
OLAV SLAYMAKER

Arctic Lands

The Canadian Arctic Lands lie N of the treeline and cover 2.6 million km², or 26% of the country (including the Arctic Coastal Plains, the Innuitian Region, Arctic Lowlands and part of the Canadian SHIELD). Except on the Canadian Shield, where much bare ROCK is exposed, the mainland TUNDRA is a closed mat with up to 900 species of vascular plants. The richness of tundra vegetation decreases towards the Pole. The islands S of Parry Channel (now Viscount Melville Sound, Barrow Str and Lancaster Sound) are rock and moss surfaces; the Queen Elizabeth Is are a desert of mainly bare rock and soil with patch vegetation on moist sites. Freshwater lakes and rivers are ice-free June-Oct in the S, July-Aug in the N; they are ice-covered for the rest of the year. Slightly more than half the precipitation falls as snow which, in a treeless zone, is greatly affected by wind. Snow is moved over the surface, drifted into hollows and becomes hard packed, with wave and ripple forms related to prevailing wind directions. The NW and the High Arctic are dry with annual precipitation averaging 10 cm. The central Arctic receives 20-30 cm; S Baffin and N Québec, up to 50 cm.

Several thousand years of cold CLIMATE have created a condition of perennially frozen ground (permafrost), in which GROUNDWATER occurs as ice in crystals, lenses and layers up to tens of metres thick. In some areas, rock may be frozen but it contains no ice. Permafrost may be tens of metres thick in the S increasing to more than 500 m in the NW islands. Each summer the top, active layer may melt down from a few centimetres to a metre or more. Associated with permafrost is the formation of patterned ground (surface circles, ovals, polygons and stripes). Tundra polygons, a tortoise-shell pattern of cracks up to 30 m apart with ice wedges below the cracks, cover many thousands of square kilometres. Other distinctive PERIGLACIAL LAND-

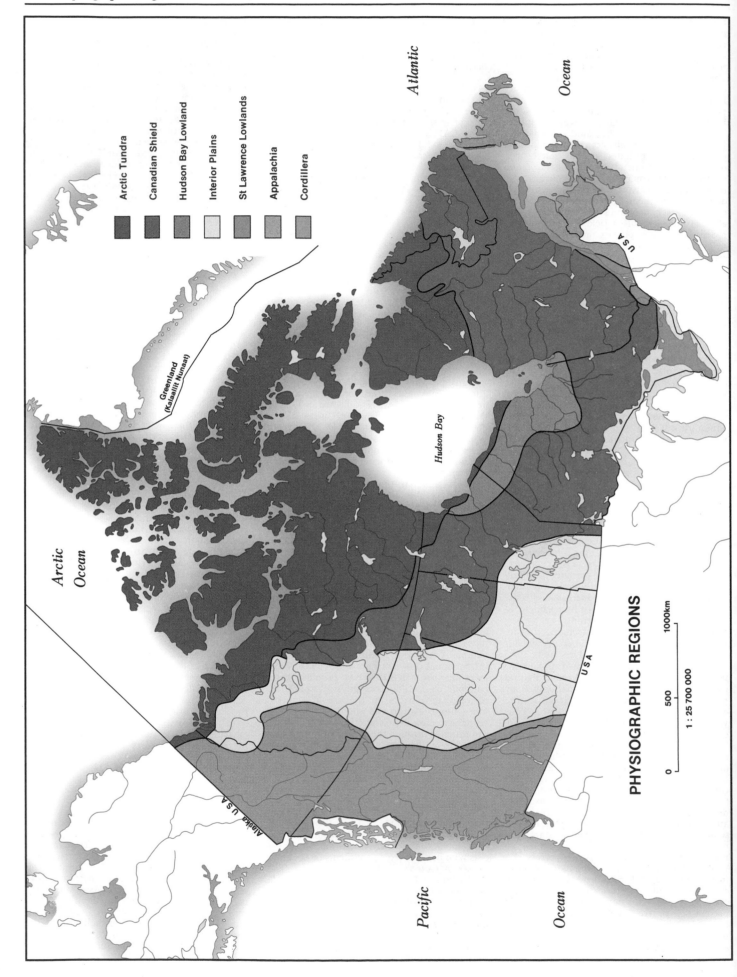

Arctic Tundra
Canadian Shield
Hudson Bay Lowland
Interior Plains
St Lawrence Lowlands
Appalachia
Cordillera

Atlantic

Ocean

Greenland
(Kalaallit Nunaat)

Arctic
Ocean

Hudson Bay

USA

Alaska U.S.A.

Pacific

Ocean

PHYSIOGRAPHIC REGIONS

1 : 25 700 000

0   500   1000km

FORMS are PINGOS, over 1500 of which have been counted near the Mackenzie Delta.

Land surfaces owe their character, in part, to the underlying GEOLOGY. The mainland E of Great Bear and Great Slave lakes, the Ungava Peninsula and most of Baffin I are part of the Canadian Shield. These ancient rocks have been much changed through GEOLOGICAL HISTORY and have been glaciated to form an upright saucer with the centre flooded by Hudson Bay. The eastern rim, extending from Labrador N along Baffin I and into Ellesmere I, is a mountainous zone with elevations 1500 m and higher in the N, and a fjorded coast. This zone possesses GLACIERS covering about 5% of the Arctic's surface. The zone between the Shield and the Western Cordillera is a Paleozoic plain (570-225 million years old) gently sloping from 500 m elevation downwards to the Arctic Ocean. The islands are mostly of SEDIMENTARY ROCKS which form plains, uplands and hills. The rock layers are mainly flat-lying in the S but have been folded, then eroded, in the ARCTIC ARCHIPELAGO. Surface elevations rise from near sea level in the NW to approach the high mountain rim in the E. The many channels among the ISLANDS may be caused by faulting, or may be fault-controlled and further deepened by riverine EROSION and GLACIATION.   JOHN K. STAGER

Cordillera

This region is part of the MOUNTAIN system that extends the length of the Pacific Coast of N and S America. The Canadian part of the Cordillera is about 800 km wide, and extends northwestward from 49° N for over 2000 km to the Alaska border at 141° W. Most of the Cordillera lies within BC and YT, but it also extends into southwestern Alberta and NWT. The total area covered by this physiographic region is 1.6 million km² (16% of Canada). The Cordillera includes plateaus, valleys and plains as well as rugged mountains. The most continuous mountain chains form high rims along the SW and SE sides of a belt of varied terrain. The Eastern system consists of sedimentary rocks that have been tilted, faulted and folded. The Interior system's mountain ranges and dissected plateaus are underlain by folded sedimentary and volcanic strata, by metamorphic rocks and numerous, small IGNEOUS intrusions. In the Western system, the Coast Mts consist of a mass of interlocking igneous intrusions and metamorphic rocks, but the outermost mountains are geologically similar to the Interior system.

The oldest recognizable feature of the Cordilleran landscape is the gently rolling upland of its interior plateaus. This ancient surface was sculpted by erosion many millions of years ago. Since then, it has been uplifted, partly buried by lava flows, dissected by river erosion and modified by glaciers. The most widespread landforms and surface deposits of the Cordillera date from the glaciations of the past million years. South of 61° N, only the highest mountain peaks projected above the Cordilleran ice sheet. Farther north, extensive parts of the YT and the NWT were too dry for glacier formation, although very cold. In the glaciated areas landforms such as cirques and U-shaped valleys are common in the mountains and along the edges of higher plateaus. Features such as striations, DRUMLINS, ESKERS and till plains are widespread on plateaus and plains. Valleys and lowlands commonly contain thick silts and clays that were deposited in ice-dammed lakes during glacier melting, and sands and gravels that were deposited by meltwater streams.

During the 12 000 years of postglacial time, rivers have formed terraces, alluvial fans, floodplains and deltas (see RIVER LANDFORM). Valley sides have been modified by rockfalls, debris flows, LANDSLIDES, soil creep and snow AVALANCHES. Periglacial landforms are present above treeline. In the south, permafrost exists beneath

Rock outcrops in the Manitoba tundra (*photo by Barry Griffiths/Network*).

only the highest, windswept ridge crests, but northward it becomes lower and, in the central and northern YT, occurs at all elevations. Volcanic activity has occurred sporadically at scattered locations in the western and interior systems up to the present. Some eruptions occurred during glaciation. The youngest lava flows and cinder cones are only a few hundred years old; these eruptions are described in Indian legends.

The Cordillera encompasses a great variety of climates because of its great latitudinal extent, its location between the Pacific Ocean and the continental interior, and its rugged terrain. Several significant effects of climate are visible in the natural landscape. Heavy rain and snow on the Coast Mts give rise to luxuriant forests and maintain extensive snowfields and glaciers at relatively low elevations. The altitudinal treeline and the snowline rise eastward as snowfall decreases, and descend northward as temperature declines. Differences in climate caused by elevation in any particular area are reflected by altitudinal vegetation zones. The highest of these is the alpine tundra. In the semiarid valleys of the Interior system, the lowest vegetation zone is grassland.

The Cordillera as a whole is distinguished by its mountainous and irregular topography, and its great variety of climates, soils and vegetation. Many aspects of its physiography, including steep slopes, natural hazards and severe climate, restrict land use by humans. Other features, such as FORESTS, grasslands, lakes and rivers, and varied scenery, are natural RESOURCES. *See* KARST LANDFORM.   J.M. RYDER

Interior Plains

The Canadian Interior Plains extend from the 49th parallel to the Arctic Ocean, between the Canadian Shield and the Cordillera. They cover 1.8 million km², or 18% of Canada's land surface. The regional topography is largely determined by flat-lying sedimentary rocks. An uneven surface of SAND AND GRAVEL, deposited by rivers flowing from the Rocky Mts, was superimposed on this sedimentary substratum. Deposition was followed by periods of erosion associated with uneven uplift which resulted in the carving of the surface into isolated uplands. In addition to these erosional remnants, the relatively uniform slope of the southern portion of the region is broken into 3 levels by the Manitoba Escarpment and the Missouri Coteau. The

Cattle grazing on the foothills near the Rocky Mts (*photo by Richard Harrington*).

Manitoba Plain lies below the Manitoba Escarpment at elevations under 400 m. It is the lowest and flattest of 3 PRAIRIE steps. The underlying Paleozoic rocks (600-225 million years old) are covered by a mantle of glacial drift, overlain in most areas by glacial lake silts and clays. The Saskatchewan Plain, the dip slope of the Manitoba Escarpment, is covered almost entirely by glacial deposits, largely hummocky MORAINE, with lesser amounts of large, flat areas of former glacial lakes, which are lower and smoother than the Alberta Plain to the W. Surface elevations range from 460 to 790 m, reaching 915 m in hillier areas. West of the Missouri Coteau is a gradual slope upwards to the foothills of the Rocky Mts. This third step, the Alberta Plain, has a bolder, more varied relief. Hummocky moraine is once again a dominant component of the landscape. More striking are the BADLANDS, formed from the severe dissection of soft, underlying rocks in the more arid region. The Alberta Plateau, N of the Athabasca R, is virtually a continuation of the plain to the S. It is a ring of plateaus with summits from 760 to 970 m, separated by the wide valleys of the Peace, Fort Nelson and Hay rivers. North of the Peace R, the plateau surface forms a disconnected escarpment overlooking the Great Slave Plain. Widespread distribution of glacial lake deposits is the most striking feature in the plateau area; till plains and hummocky moraines are also common. The northern Interior Plains, comprised largely of peat-covered till plains below 300 m in elevation, stretch from the Alberta Plateau to the Arctic Ocean.

Rolling prairie in Grasslands National Park, Sask (*photo by Brian Milne/First Light*).

The Interior Plains are characterized by grassland vegetation (prairie) under semiarid climatic conditions in the S. This grassland gives way to a parkbelt region, to the N and E, under slightly cooler temperatures and higher precipitation. As this trend continues northward, a coniferous forest predominates. Finally, through the northern extension of the Interior Plains, forest gives way to treeless tundra.   D.F. ACTON

Hudson Bay Lowland

This land area of 320 000 km² (3.5% of Canada's land surface) is only 40% of a sedimentary basin in the middle of the Canadian Shield, 60% of which lies beneath HUDSON BAY and JAMES BAY. Apart from the Sutton Ridges in the NE of the lowland, the bedrock terrain is completely masked by a mantle of glacial and marine sediments associated with the advance and retreat of ice during the last glaciation. The inland edge of the lowland (about 180 m high) coincides approximately with the highest level of marine inundation which followed the disappearance of glacial ice from Hudson Bay about 7500 years ago. In the western part of the lowland, landform subdivisions tend to parallel the Shield edge and coast. Nearer the Shield are found streamlined hills of glacial till, which were formed beneath ice moving SW from Hudson Bay towards Manitoba. These have not been totally masked by younger marine deposits and, thus, give the surface a corrugated appearance.

Closer to the coast, where the marine mantle is thicker, vast level plains with thick PEAT accumulations and innumerable ponds are typical. These plains contrast with terrain in a wide zone (50-80 km) inland of the coast. There, scores of parallel, gravel beach ridges were thrown up by storm waves during the last 5000-6000 years, as sea level fell in response to rapid uplift of Earth's crust. This zone is characterized by dry, forested, low ridges separated by boggy depressions. At the coast the almost level offshore zone is exposed at low tide as marshy and muddy flats, often strewn with glacial boulders (*see* SWAMP, MARSH AND BOG). At present, sea level is still falling at approximately 60 cm/100 years, continually exposing more of the offshore zone. In the eastern lowland, flooding by marine waters was immediately followed by readvance of the ice sheet margin approximately along longitude 86-87° W. This caused molding of the marine deposits into more prominent, streamlined hills.   I.A. BROOKES

Canadian Shield Forest Lands

The Shield proper (area 4.6 million km²) covers 46% of Canada's land surface (including freshwater lakes and arctic islands). If the Arctic Shield is excluded, this remains the largest physiographic region in Canada, comprising 32% of the land surface. It is a vast, saucer-shaped region: the rim on its S, E and NE sides like that of a soup plate; the centre a sedimentary rock basin, the southern fringe of which underlies the Hudson Bay Lowland. The Shield is composed of crystalline Precambrian rocks formed during several phases of mountain building between 3.5 and 1 billion years ago. In the last billion years it has remained a relatively stable bulwark, unaffected by the PLATE TECTONIC movements which have impinged on it to form the mountainous fringe of Canada. The stability of the Shield has allowed denudation to level its surface, giving it characteristic level or undulating skylines. The southeastern and eastern borders have been uplifted in the relatively recent geological past as a result of tectonic movements associated with the opening of the Atlantic Ocean. Glacial erosion had little effect, except along the eastern rim.

Approximately half of the Shield is classified as upland. Extending from NW Québec through N Ontario, Manitoba and Saskatchewan to NW Keewatin and E Mackenzie districts, NWT, this terrain (200-500 m elevation) is upland only by virtue of its elevation above the Hudson Bay Lowland and the Interior Plains which border it. Bedrock relief of only 50-60 m has been smoothed by a thin mantle of glacial till and sediment deposited in glacial lakes. The eastern Shield is dominated by plateaus between Hudson Bay and the Gulf of St Lawrence. Elevations increase from 300 m near the coasts to 900 m in central Labrador-Nouveau Québec. Relief of 150-300 m is caused by incision of valleys into the higher terrain. At several places over the Shield, uplands and plateaus are broken by belts of hills, in which relief increases because of dif-

Shield country near Goose Bay, Labrador (*photo by Freeman Patterson/Masterfile*).

The Laurentian Highlands, part of the plateau and dissected southern rim of the Canadian Shield in Québec, have been a centre of outdoor recreation since the 1890s (*photo by John deVisser*).

ferential erosion of linear geological structures formed in former mountain belts. Examples are the Labrador and Port Arthur hills. The high, rugged terrain along the E and SE rim of the Shield is classified as highland. In Baffin I and northern Labrador it stands at 800-1500 m and possesses rolling plateau surfaces which are deeply dissected by glacial troughs, giving a fjordlike aspect to those coasts. Highlands N of St Lawrence R stand at 500-900 m with isolated summits at 1000-1200 m in terrain which is more dissected, with few plateaus.

The 2 extensive shield zones, E and W of Hudson Bay, were the centres of ice sheet outflow during the last glaciation (from 100 000 to 6000 years ago). The central parts of these zones show unorganized terrain mantled with till and pocked with irregular, shallow lake basins. Around these, glacial scouring of the bedrock is more obvious, with occasional ice-molded till hills and many eskers marking the courses of subglacial rivers, and large moraines marking pauses in retreat of the ice front across the Shield. The periphery of these 2 core areas is marked by more level terrain which was flooded by lakes and seas during ice retreat.   I.A. BROOKES

St Lawrence Lowlands

The Lowlands (180 000 km², 1.8% of Canada's land surface) lie between the Shield to the N and the Appalachian Region to the E and SE, and are broken into 3 subregions.

West St Lawrence Lowland This subregion lies between the Shield and Lakes Huron, Erie and Ontario. The West St Lawrence Lowland consists of a limestone plain (elevation 200-250 m) which is separated by a broad, shale lowland from a broader dolomite and limestone plateau, W of Lk Ontario. This plateau is bounded by the NIAGARA ESCARPMENT. From the escarpment the plateau slopes gently SW to Lakes Huron and Erie (elevation 200 m). Glaciation has mantled this subregion with several layers of glacial till, the youngest forming extensive, undulating till plains, often enclosing rolling drumlin fields. Prominent moraines on the western plateau and N of Lk Ontario mark temporary pauses in the retreat of glacial lobes, between 14 500 and 12 500 years ago. Level clay and sand plains, which were deposited in glacial lakes, fringe the present lakes.

Central St Lawrence Lowland This subregion has undulating topography, developed on sedi-

mentary rocks beneath the lowland, which is largely masked by glacial and marine deposits. The 7 Monteregian Hills (eg, Mont Royal), which are aligned approximately W-E between the Shield W of Montréal and the Appalachians, stand at 200-400 m. Along the Shield and Appalachian fringes of the lowland, sandy terraces (elevation up to 200 m) were deposited in the CHAMPLAIN SEA which flooded the newly deglaciated lowland approximately 12 500 years ago. These have been eroded by postglacial streams to form more broken terrain. The low, gently hummocky, Drummondville moraine trends SW from near Québec City to near the Vermont border.

East St Lawrence Lowland This subregion widens from the lower St Lawrence estuary into the Gulf of St Lawrence and narrows again to the NE at the Str of Belle Isle. There are small, isolated low plateaus and plains along the N shore of the Gulf of St Lawrence, eg, Mingan Is; a coastal plain at less than 100 m in NW Newfoundland; and a larger, undulating plateau at 100-200 m with a central spine at 300 m on Anticosti I. These fragments have a smooth terrain influenced by flat or gently dipping sedimentary bedrock. Surface conditions may be barren and dry, or boggy, depending on surface slope and the influence of coastal winds.   I.A. BROOKES

Appalachian Region

The Appalachian Region (360 000 km², about 2% of Canada's land surface) lies between the St Lawrence Lowlands to the NW and the Atlantic Continental Shelf to the E and SE. Like other mountain regions, its terrain is a mosaic of uplands and lowlands, the characters, boundaries and shapes of which reflect the complexity of rocks and structures inherited from tectonic movements between 480 and 280 million years ago. Since then, denudation has removed several kilometres of rock, revealing once deeply buried structures. At the same time, regional uplift has maintained smooth-topped uplands and highlands on stronger rocks, while weaker rocks have been fashioned into lowlands and plains. Highlands and mountains are disposed in a Z-shaped belt, from the Québec border with Vermont and New Hampshire, northeastwards to Gaspésie, then southwestwards across NB, and continuing NE north of the Bay of Fundy to Cape Breton I. Thence, broken by Cabot Str, the belt continues along the high, western spine of Newfoundland. These highlands reach over 1200 m in central Gaspésie (Mt Jacques Cartier, 1268 m). In western Newfoundland and northeastern NB summits stand at 600-800 m; elsewhere in the region, this highland belt is flanked by uplands at 300-600 m in Québec, northwestern NB, southern and eastern Newfoundland, and southern NS. Except in southern NS, the uplands share with the highlands smoothly undulating skylines and deeply cut valleys.

In eastern NB, PEI, Îles de la Madeleine, northern NS and the triangular Newfoundland Central Lowland, weak rocks have allowed the development of plains and lowlands. In Newfoundland and southern NS, terrain strongly resembles that of the Shield, with extensive, glacially smoothed bedrock plains, patchily covered with bouldery till and dotted with irregular lakes. In the rest of the region, even highland and mountain zones show only locally severe glacial erosion, particularly in valleys crossing the "grain" of the terrain. Glacial deposits are thicker there and, although mostly sandy and infertile, locally they may be good soil parent materials. With deglaciation, between 14 000 and 10 000 years ago, crustal uplift was sufficiently great to exceed sea-level rise in the central and northern zones of the Appalachian Region, so that a coastal fringe exhibits raised marine terraces which often provide pockets of arable land. In the S, bordering the Atlantic Ocean, sea-level rise has exceeded uplift along this submerging coast with rocky headlands and irregular bays. Sea level continues to rise at up to 30 cm/100 years.   I.A. BROOKES

Reading: J.B. Bird, *The Natural Landscapes of Canada* (1978).

Piano Manufacturing The piano is a keyboard instrument which produces sound by means of strings, stretched over a soundboard, which vibrate when struck by a hammer. The decisive invention is generally attributed to Bartolomeo Cristofori about 1709. The piano has developed from a softer-sounding, delicate, wood-framed instrument to one which is sonorous and sturdily constructed, the frame reinforced with cast iron and steel. The shape of the piano has evolved from earlier square or rectangular designs to the contemporary horizontal, wing-shaped grands, and the uprights.

By the late 18th century, pianos were imported from Europe for sale in Canada. This was a costly practice, and often the instrument's sensitive mechanism suffered during transit. As the demand for pianos increased during the early 19th century, a few skilled British and German immigrant craftsmen began to build pianos in the workshops where they also carried out the business of piano tuning and repair. From these small beginnings in Québec City, Montréal and Toronto grew a major domestic and export industry, which flourished especially from the 1880s to the 1920s. At some point during this period there existed close to 100 companies or craftsmen involved in the manufacture of pianos or their accessory parts. Firms such as HEINTZMAN AND CO LTD, R.S. Williams, Mason & Risch, Karn, Lesage, Gerhard Heintzman, Martin-Orme, Mendelssohn, Rainer, Weber, Nordheimer, Bell, Pratte, Sherlock-Manning, to name but a few, provided excellent quality, prize-winning pianos at reasonable costs. Except for a few firms, the industry was centered in southern Ontario and the Montréal region but pianos were readily available through retailers across the country.

Many factors brought about the decline of the piano manufacturing industry, notably the increasing popularity of alternative forms of home entertainment, such as the phonograph and the radio, and the effects of the GREAT DEPRESSION. As the economy stabilized in the 1930s and 1940s, renewed interest in piano purchasing was served by 7 surviving companies (Lesage, Quidoz, and Willis in Québec, Sherlock-Manning, Heintzman, and Mason & Risch in Ontario, and Edmund in BC). The advent of tele-

vision and sophisticated home sound systems, the introduction of cheaper, mass-produced Japanese pianos, and the durability of existing Canadian pianos, however, caused a decrease in sales and the closure of more firms. In 1984, 3 manufacturers remained in Canada: Heintzman Ltd (now owned by the Sklar Manufacturing Co) in Hanover, Ont; Sherlock-Manning (now owned by lifelong employees of the firm) in Clinton, Ont; and Lesage Pianos Ltd (owned by the original family) in Ste-Thérèse, Qué. *See also* MUSICAL INSTRUMENTS.   FLORENCE HAYES

Picard, Gérard, labour leader, (b at Stratford-Centre, Qué 27 May 1907). After completing a law degree at Laval, he was a journalist for *L'Évènement* and *L'Action catholique* in Québec C during the early 1930s. Secretary-treasurer, then secretary general of the Confédération des travailleurs catholiques du Canada, he succeeded Alfred CHARPENTIER as president in 1946. Under his leadership the CTCC became more militant, as in several bitter and prolonged postwar strikes, including the 1949 ASBESTOS STRIKE and the violent 1952-53 strike of Louiseville textile workers that almost precipitated a province-wide general strike. During the 1950s the CTCC devoted itself to democratizing the workplace through co-management, profit sharing and co-ownership, and it was one of the few organizations to oppose the policies and practices of the Union Nationale government of Maurice DU-PLESSIS. In 1961 the CTCC became the Confédération des syndicats nationaux. Picard encouraged union activists to partake in political action. In 1959 he joined the Québec wing of the CCF, and in 1961 helped found the New Democratic Party, becoming its first associate president. In the mid-1960s he was appointed to the Canadian Council of Industrial Relations.
MICHAEL D. BEHIELS

Pichon, Thomas, alias Thomas Tyrell, colonial official, spy, author (b at Vire, France 30 Mar 1700; d at St Helier, Jersey 22 Nov 1781). Seeking advancement after an unrewarding career in Europe, Pichon arrived at LOUISBOURG in 1751 as the governor's secretary and at FT BEAUSÉJOUR in 1753 as chief stores clerk. Enticed by financial promises, he began spying for the neighbouring British garrison at Ft Lawrence. He passed along information, encouraged Acadian neutrality, discouraged French defence schemes, and generally facilitated the British capture of Beauséjour in 1755. He moved on to Halifax, then London, and in 1760 published a reliable but uneven history of Cape Breton. Although condemned for ambition, avarice, treason and moral dissipation, Pichon remains an intriguing figure in early Canadian history.   LOIS KERNAGHAN

Pickard, George Lawson, oceanographer, educator (b at Cardiff, Wales 5 July 1913). Following military service with the RAF during WWII Pickard came to Canada in 1947. He was professor of physics at UBC 1947-79 and director of the Institute of Oceanography there 1958-79. He began the studies of water properties and circulation that have provided much of our understanding of the OCEANOGRAPHY of BC's fjords and estuaries. His expertise in fjord studies later took him to study in Chile and NZ. As a teacher and administrator, Pickard was influential in the development of marine sciences in western Canada; his textbooks on physical oceanography have received worldwide circulation.
P.H. LeBLOND

Pickerel, common name for 3 closely related, carnivorous, soft-rayed, freshwater fishes in the PIKE family (Esocidae). In parts of Canada, the name is applied, erroneously, to the WALLEYE. The name is derived from an English diminutive of pike. Pickerel occur naturally only in eastern N America. The group consists of 2 species: *Esox niger,* chain pickerel; *E. americanus,*

Chain pickerel (*Esox niger*) (*courtesy National Museums of Canada/National Museum of Natural Sciences*).

divisible into 2 forms, redfin pickerel, which grows to 35 cm, and the slightly smaller grass pickerel. In Canada, one or more species occur in limited portions of the territory from southern NS to Ontario, inhabiting smaller, warm waters (eg, ponds, small streams, bays of lakes). Only the chain pickerel, growing to about 50 cm long and 1.4 kg, is of any consequence as a sport fish.   E.J. CROSSMAN

Pickersgill, John Whitney, public servant, politician, historian (b at Wycombe, Ont 23 June 1905). "Clear it with Jack" was the Ottawa watchword through the KING and ST. LAURENT eras, a testimony to Pickersgill's extraordinary influence. He was raised on a poor Manitoba farm and secured a good education at U of Manitoba and Oxford thanks to his great abilities — and an extraordinary mother. He taught history at Wesley College, Winnipeg, 1929-37, and then joined the Dept of External Affairs. Quickly shifted to the PMO, Pickersgill assisted King and St. Laurent on virtually all aspects of policy and politics. In 1952 he became clerk of the Privy Council and the next year secretary of state. He held 2 portfolios in the PEARSON government and was appointed president of the Canadian Transport Commission when he left politics in 1967. Pickersgill's historical studies of the King-St. Laurent years are important.   J.L. GRANATSTEIN

Reading: J.L. Granatstein, *The Ottawa Men* (1982); J.W. Pickersgill, *My Years with Louis St. Laurent* (1975).

Pictographs and Petroglyphs, prehistoric paintings executed with the finger in red ochre (pictographs), and carvings (petroglyphs) incised, abraded or ground by means of stone tools upon cliff walls, boulders and flat bedrock surfaces. They have been discovered throughout Canada. "Rock art" constitutes Canada's oldest and most widespread form of artistic expression, and is part of a worldwide genre of prehistoric art which includes the cave paintings of Spain and France. No foolproof method for the precise dating of rock art has been discovered, other than speculative association with stratified, relatively datable archaeological remains. While the tradition of rock art was no doubt brought into Canada by the earliest Indians some 25 000 years ago, it is most unlikely that examples of antiquity will ever be found.

Rock art in much of Canada is linked with shamanism, a widespread religious tradition in which the SHAMAN's major tasks are healing and prophesy, along with the vision quest; and with the search for "helping" spirits. Several broad regions of rock-art "style areas" have been distinguished. The petroglyph sites in KEJIMKUJIK

Indian petroglyphs near Peterborough, Ont (*photo by John deVisser*).

NATIONAL PARK in NS reveal a unique, small-scale and fine-line style that has been attributed to the MICMAC. The Canadian SHIELD, extending from the St Maurice R in Québec to N Saskatchewan, has many pictograph sites, while petroglyphs are confined to the S. The Peterborough petroglyph site in southern Ontario has several hundred images of humans, animals, birds, snakes, turtles and boats. Here, as at many sites in the Shield, there are no pictorial boundaries such as frames or groundlines. Nor is there any evidence of a deliberate grouping of images. Aesthetic order is in accord with nature, and images are often integrated with the numerous hollows, crevices and seams of the rock itself. Pictograph sites are less extensive in scale and contain fewer image clusters. Although sites at Bon Echo Provincial Park in southern Ontario and at Lake Superior Provincial Park near Wawa, Ont, are well known, the majority of pictograph discoveries have been made in Quetico Park and at Lake of the Woods in NW Ontario.

Despite the lack of rock surfaces on the prairies, petroglyphs and pictographs are an important prehistoric art form of southern Saskatchewan and Alberta. Many pictographs have been found on isolated boulders and rocky outcrops along the foothills near Calgary, and there is an extensive series of small-scale petroglyphs incised on the sandstone bluffs of the MILK R in southern Alberta. They depict typical prairie Indian subject matter, mythological motifs such as THUNDERBIRD or shaman figures, and sometimes give evidence of European contact: horses, men bearing shields and guns, battle scenes with camp circles dotted with tipis, and a wheeled cart.

Some of the most intriguing images of Canadian rock art are painted on cliffs in interior BC. Those near Keremeos are probably abstractions of the spirits the shaman encountered in his visions. The BC coast has several petroglyph sites, though the few pictograph sites are probably more recent. Stylistically, West Coast rock art is unique in Canada, often showing form and subject-matter linkages with the later historic art of the 19th century. Outstanding sites are located primarily on Vancouver I — Nanaimo Petroglyph Park and Sproat Lake — but sites have been discovered as far N as Prince Rupert and along the Nass and Skeena R system.

Only 2 rock-art sites have been discovered in the Canadian Arctic. At Qajartalik on a rocky outcrop in the Joy Bay region, Ungava, for example, a clustering of 44 human faces has been attributed to the prehistoric DORSET CULTURE. *See also* INDIAN ART; INUIT ART.   JOAN M. VASTOKAS

Reading: Nancy-Lou Patterson, *Canadian Native Art* (1973); Joan M. and Romas Vastokas, *Sacred Art of the Algonkians: A Study of the Peterborough Petroglyphs* (1973).

Picton, Ont, Town, pop 4361 (1981c), inc 1837, seat of Prince Edward County, a peninsula of rolling farmland and sand beaches which juts out into Lk Ontario about 160 km E of Toronto. Located on an arm of the B of Quinte, Picton developed as a harbour and distribution centre for the surrounding countryside. It was originally settled by LOYALISTS in the 1780s and was first named Hallowell. During the 1820s the introduction of steamboats made the harbour more accessible to lake traffic. An adjacent village called Picton was laid out, and the 2 were amalgamated as Picton in 1837. Sir Thomas Picton was a British officer in the Napoleonic Wars who died at the Battle of Waterloo. For 2 years, 1833-35, Sir John A. MACDONALD practised law here. Picton has remained a small lake port and service centre for an agricultural hinterland.
      DANIEL FRANCIS

Pictou, NS, Town, pop 4628 (1981c), inc 1878, shire town of Pictou County is located on Pictou harbour adjacent to Northumberland Str and the Gulf of St Lawrence. The traditional centre of Scottish settlement in the Maritimes, it was first occupied by Micmac. Visited by French fur traders and missionaries, and later the site of a land grant to the Philadelphia Co (1762), its settlement followed the arrival of some 200 highland SCOTS on the HECTOR in 1773. By the early 19th century, it was an active and free port, shipping timber to Great Britain. Sawmills, foundries, tanneries, biscuit making and flour milling supported the export trade. Shipbuilding brought further prosperity. Scottish-styled stone houses and commercial buildings are still prominent on Water Street. Pictou Academy, founded in 1809 by Thomas MCCULLOCH signalled the end of Anglican-dominated education in NS. J.W. DAWSON, McGill's first principal, was an academy graduate. Late 19th-century growth focused on port functions connecting northern NS to PEI, the Magdalen Is and Cape Breton I, but Pictou's isolated location eventually brought decline. Nearby towns were better situated to develop the county's coal and iron-ore resources. Railways and highways bypassed the town. Today, Pictou benefits from an administrative role, some marine industries and tourism based on its rich Scottish heritage.   L.D. MCCANN

Pidgeon, George Campbell, Presbyterian and United Church minister (b at Grand-Cascapédia, Qué 2 Mar 1872; d at Toronto 15 June 1971). After being ordained (1894) and earning his DD from Presbyterian Coll, Montréal, Pidgeon served churches in Montréal, Streetsville, Ont, and Toronto. He taught practical theology at Westminster Hall, Vancouver (1909-15), then served Bloor St United Church, Toronto, from 1915 until his retirement in 1948. From 1949 until 1960 he wrote a religious column for the Toronto *Telegram*. Pidgeon led the Presbyterian Church into the union of 1925 and was unanimously elected the first moderator of the UNITED CHURCH OF CANADA. During his long and distinguished career, he was a staunch supporter of temperance and home mission work and helped promote the World Alliance of Reformed Churches, the Canadian Council of Churches and the World Council of Churches. He was chief spokesman of the United Church and its embodiment to the country and to the Christian community.   NEIL SEMPLE

Pidgeon, Lloyd Montgomery, chemist (b at Markham, Ont 3 Dec 1903). After studies at McGill under Otto MAASS (1927-29) and Oxford (1929-31), Pidgeon joined the NATIONAL RESEARCH COUNCIL in Ottawa, initally working on electrochemical problems. During this period he developed his well-known process for the production of magnesium metal of high purity (*see* METALLURGY). Because of the demand for magnesium during WWII, 6 magnesium plants were built throughout N America. In Canada, his discovery led to the formation of Dominion Magnesium Ltd, which he joined in 1941 as director of research. In 1943 Pidgeon was appointed professor and head of the dept of metallurgical engineering at U of T. There he built a strong graduate school in metallurgy of worldwide reputation. Although he was a chemist by background, his appreciation of the physics of metals led to the growth of physical metallurgy within his department. Under Pidgeon's leadership, the department expanded into materials science in 1965, thus catalyzing creation of a Materials Research Interdisciplinary Group within the Faculty of Applied Science and Engineering.   J.M. TOGURI

Pierce, Lorne Albert, publisher, editor, writer (b at Delta, Ont 3 Aug 1890: died at Toronto 27 Nov 1961). Editor in chief of RYERSON PRESS 1920-60, Pierce championed Canadian writers and writing for over 40 years. He attended Queen's Union Theological Seminary, NY; New York U; Victoria College, Toronto; and United Theological College, Montréal. He was ordained a Methodist minister in 1916. Pastoral work, in Ottawa and elsewhere, and wartime army service preceded his association with Ryerson Press in 1920, briefly as literary adviser, then as editor. Pierce typified the enthusiastic nationalism of English Canada in the 1920s: he launched the important Ryerson Chapbook poetry series, the pioneering Makers of Canadian Literature volumes of criticism, and the textbook series, The Ryerson Books of Prose and Verse.

Pierce's own writings include studies of William KIRBY and Marjorie Pickthall, a critique and an anthology of Canadian literature, and editions of the poetry of Pickthall and Bliss CARMAN. In 1926 he established the Lorne Pierce Medal of the RSC for literary achievement and in 1927 the Edith and Lorne Pierce Collection of Canadian Literature at Queens. He was prominent in the Canadian Authors' Assn, the Canadian Bibliographical Soc, the Canadian Writers Foundation, the ROYAL ONTARIO MUSEUM and the Art Gallery of Toronto (ART GALLERY OF ONTARIO). In 1940 he was a founder of what became the Canadian Hearing Soc, a by-product of his own deafness.   SANDRA CAMPBELL

Pigeon (Columbidae), large family (300 species) of BIRDS, many of which are called doves, distributed throughout temperate and tropical areas worldwide. Species vary from sparrow size to that of a female turkey. Many are plainly attired but some Old World, tropical species are strikingly coloured in green, red, orange or purple. All are characterized by a plump body with short neck, small head and short, slender bill with a fleshy, naked area at its base. All drink by immersing the bill and sucking up water. Vocalizations are mostly cooing sounds. Six species are known in Canada. The mourning dove (*Zenaida macroura*) inhabits open woods, groves and farmland transcontinentally, extending to northern Manitoba and Saskatchewan, but restricted to extreme southernmost parts on both coasts. Band-tailed pigeon (*Columba fasciata*) prefers open woods, edges and openings in southwestern BC. Wild populations of rock dove (*C. livia*), a widely domesticated Eurasian species, are common in cities, towns and farmland across Canada. The PASSENGER PIGEON (*Ectopistes migratorius*) is now extinct. All but rock dove are migratory but some mourning doves winter in southern Canada.   W. EARL GODFREY

Pika, common name for smallest members of order LAGOMORPHA, which also includes RABBITS and HARES. Pikas are like guinea pigs in size and shape, have relatively short legs, no external tail and almost circular, prominent, external ears. They are distributed discontinuously along the W coast of N America and throughout Asia and European Russia. They are known by various names including cony and rock rabbit, the latter referring to the fact that N American and some Asian pikas occur only in rocky habitats. Two species are known in Canada; 18 worldwide. Rocky Mountain pika (*Ochotona princeps*) is found throughout the Rocky Mts in BC and Alberta. Collared pika (*O. collaris*) is found in northern BC and throughout YT and Alaska. Pikas are versatile feeders, eating most plants in their habitat. As they do not hibernate, pikas gather cuttings of preferred plants, cure them in sheltered, sunny places, and store them among rocks for winter use. Pikas are diurnal and both Canadian species are colonial. Within a colony, individuals tend to occupy exclusive home ranges but during breeding season, male and female ranges overlap. Breeding generally occurs twice, in spring and summer; 2-6 offspring are born per litter. Although of no direct economic value to man, pikas are an important source of food for many furbearing mammals.
      M.L. WESTON

Northern pike (*Esox lucius*), which inhabits warm to cool lakes and rivers, is a commercial as well as a sport fish (*artwork by Claire Tremblay*).

Pike, common name for the group of 5 species of predaceous freshwater FISH with elongated snouts, sharp teeth, cylindrical bodies and forked tails, belonging to family Esocidae, order Salmoniformes, class Osteichthyes. Northern pike (*Esox lucius*) is circumpolar in distribution; Amur pike (*E. reicherti*) is native to Siberia and China; MUSKELLUNGE (*E. masquinongy*) and PICK-EREL (*E. niger* and *E. americanus*) are confined to N America. Pikes are lie-in-wait predators, rushing on prey from cover, capturing it sideways, then returning to cover to turn the victim around and swallow it head first. The northern pike is the fish most commonly thought of as "pike." It is a large, soft-rayed fish with an oval body and a large, flattened head with duck-billed snout, well armed with large teeth. The single dorsal fin and the anal and caudal (tail) fins are close together. The northern pike is distinguished by a pattern of horizontal rows of bean-shaped, yellow spots on a green to brown background, 4-6 pores on the underside of each lower jaw, and the presence of scales over the whole of the cheeks and half of the gill covers. Pike spawn in early spring (Apr-May); adults often move towards spawning grounds under the ice. No nest is built; no parental care is provided. Adults eat other fishes almost exclusively. Reproductive capability is achieved at 2-4 years of age. Specimens are known to exceed 24 years of age, 1-1.5 m in length and 14-20 kg in weight. The N American angler record fish, caught in 1940, was 133.3 cm long and weighed 20.92 kg. The record for Canada, caught in Saskatchewan in 1954, weighed 19.39 kg. The northern pike occurs throughout Canada, except in the Maritimes, Gaspé, most arctic coastal areas and all but the NE corner of BC. This species inhabits warm to cool lakes, rivers and large ponds, usually in association with aquatic vegetation. The northern pike is subject to cancerous lymphosarcoma and to a disease called red sore. Pike carry parasites known as yellow grub (in the flesh) and blackspot (on the skin) which cannot infect humans and are killed when the pike are properly cooked. In certain locations, pike carry the broad tapeworm, which can be transferred to humans. Northern pike is a commercial fish as well as a sport fish. It ranks fourth, by weight, of fish taken annually in Saskatchewan. In 1980, the total Canadian commercial harvest was 4301 t, with a value to fishermen of $2.4 million.   E.J. CROSSMAN

Pilgrimage, journey to a sacred place for religious or spiritual purposes. There are several sites in Canada which attract many Canadian and foreign pilgrims. Foremost are the CATHOLIC shrines of Québec, the oldest being the church of STE-ANNE-DE-BEAUPRÉ, some 30 km NE of Québec City. During construction of the first shrine on this site in 1658, the miraculous cure of a workman was reported. Other cures followed, and the shrine soon became renowned for miracles. Pilgrims and patrons came flocking, among them Anne of Austria, mother of Louis XIV of France. Today the stone basilica attracts over 250 000 pilgrims per year. The principal gather-

ing is on the feast of St Anne (July 26). A more recent shrine which now enjoys great popularity is St Joseph's Oratory on Mount Royal, Montréal. The pious Brother ANDRÉ, a member of the Order of the Holy Cross and a devotee of St Joseph, built the first small chapel to the saint in 1904. A stone crypt was added in 1917. A basilica with a capacity of 5000, begun in 1922, now stands on the site. The annual volume of pilgrims today exceeds 3 million, with the largest gatherings on May 10 and Labour Day.

Ste-Anne-de-Beaupré and St Joseph's Oratory attract pilgrims because of their fame as sites of miracles. The saints of these shrines are now popularly believed to be effective intercessors, taking the pilgrim's message to God. The long racks of crutches and canes, braces and corsets discarded by pilgrims are seen to bear testimony to the many healing miracles that have occurred. For those who do not seek a miracle, the shrines offer objects of devotion for prayers. At St Joseph's the devotee can inspect relics of Brother André's life, observe the permanent exhibition on the lives of saints or follow a footpath through the Stations of the Cross (14 images representing the stages of Christ's suffering and crucifixion).

Another shrine to St Anne at LAC STE ANNE, Alta, attracts large numbers of native Indians from across Canada to a pilgrimage of several days culminating on July 26, the saint's day. Healing is an important feature of this pilgrimage as well.

Canadians also travel outside Canada to centres sacred to the various religions represented in our population. Thousands of Muslims (*see* ISLAM) annually make the *hajj* (pilgrimage) to Mecca and Medina in Saudi Arabia, places made holy through their importance in the life of the prophet Muhammad. Christians make pilgrimages to Rome, Canterbury, Lourdes, Fatima and many other shrines. Muslims, Christians and JEWS all journey to Jerusalem for their devotions. HINDUS and BUDDHISTS visit the many shrines of India. Through their journeys the faithful renew connections with the global centres of their religions and with their coreligionists throughout the world, strengthening their communities' international bonds. In return, the religious communities in Canada are revitalized.

Pilgrimage was formerly a difficult, dangerous austerity from which the pilgrim could not be sure of returning. Although today the sacred journey may appear to resemble a package tour more than a spiritual exercise, it is still an important feature of popular religion. In an uncertain and sorrow-laden world, there is magnetism in places where the divine is believed to manifest itself in a living, active, miraculous form to heal the sick, soothe the troubled and ease the burden of the faithful. This is likely to ensure that pilgrimage remains popular.

E. ALAN MORINIS

Reading: P. Boglioni and B. Lacroix, eds, *Les Pèlerinages au Québec* (1981).

Pilot, Robert Wakeham, painter (b at St John's 9 Oct 1898; d at Montréal 17 Dec 1967), stepson of painter Maurice CULLEN. Pilot's best pictures are moody views of the St Lawrence R, such as *Quebec from Levis*, and seascapes of NS and NB. Pilot is also widely recognized as the painter of snow-covered Rockies that contributed to the prevailing view of Canada as a country of blue and white peaks with pink and purple shadows. He studied in Paris (1920-22), then returned to work with William BRYMNER, Edmond DYONNET, and Cullen in Montréal. His later oils, sketches and murals had a stiff literal quality, but his work was well received. He was elected associate of the Royal Canadian Academy of Arts in 1925, and was president 1952-54.

ANNE McDOUGALL

Pimlott, Douglas Humphreys, conservationist, wildlife biologist, ecologist, environmentalist (b at Quyon, Qué 4 Jan 1920; d at Richmond Hill, Ont 31 July 1978). A founder of the modern environmental movement in Canada, Pimlott advocated the conservation of wolves as predators with a rightful place in nature. He eliminated the wolf bounty in Ontario and launched conservation programs in Europe where only a few wolves remained. He was also one of the first spokesmen in the 1970s for protecting the northern Canadian environment. Pimlott directed a number of Canadian environmental organizations, founded the Canada-US Environmental Council and chaired an international wolf specialist group. He taught at U of T and published many professional articles and books, including *The Ecology of the Timber Wolf in Algonquin Park* (repr 1978), and *Oil Under the Ice* (1976), which he coauthored.   MONTE HUMMEL

Pine (genus *Pinus*), evergreen CONIFERS for which the Pinaceae family is named. The 80-90 species occur in the Northern Hemisphere; 9 in Canada. Most are TREES but some are shrubs. Long, needlelike leaves are found in clusters of 2-8 (rarely one) on dwarf shoots. Seed cones are woody, often with sharp spines on scales. Each scale bears 2, usually winged, seeds, maturing the year after POLLINATION. Most are either "soft" pines with 5 needles per shoot or "hard" pines with 2-3 per shoot. The most familiar soft pines are western white pine (*P. monticola*) of BC, and eastern white pine (*P. strobus*), east of Manitoba. Others include limber pine (*P. flexilis*) and whitebark pine (*P. albicaulis*) of the western mountains. Hard pines include ponderosa pine (*P. ponderosa*) and lodgepole pine (*P. contorta*) in the West, jack pine (*P. banksiana*) in the boreal forest, red pine (*P. resinosa*) and pitch pine (*P. rigida*) in the East. Eastern white pine provides a very valuable softwood which was exported from New France as early as 1700, and used in the colony and later by the British for construction and shipbuilding. As a group, pines are still the most common Canadian conifers and yield lumber, pulp and paper. *See* FORESTRY; TIMBER TRADE HISTORY; VEGETATION REGIONS.

JOHN N. OWENS

Jack pine (*Pinus banksiana*), with male flowers (left) and cones (*artwork by Claire Tremblay*).

Pine Pass, elev 874 m, crosses the continental divide NW-SE in northeastern BC. The Pine R rises southwest of the pass then flows NW to meet the Peace R, near Fort St John. The most northerly and lowest of the 6 highway passes through the ROCKY MTS, it was known by whites as early as 1806, when one of Simon FRASER's men deserted and travelled this way. Joseph Hunter "rediscovered" the pass in 1877 as a possible CPR route. Hart Hwy crosses it, linking Prince George and Dawson Creek. GLEN BOLES

Pine Point, NWT, Town, pop 1861 (1981c), inc 1974, is located 10 km inland from the S shore of GREAT SLAVE LK, 190 air km S of YELLOWKNIFE. The discovery of lead-zinc deposits near this mining town were closely related to the KLONDIKE GOLD RUSH. In 1898 prospectors, heading overland to the Yukon, met a party of DENE who had musket bullets and fish weights, fashioned from local metal. Originally the metal deposits were considered uneconomic because they lack silver. But in the early 1920s the deposits began to be considered for their lead-zinc content alone. Further exploration took place in 1948 and Pine Point Mines, owned by Cominco Ltd, was formed in 1951. Production finally started in 1965 and the mine workers and their families now live in a modern, planned town that was built by the company from 1962 to 1965.
ANNELIES POOL

Pingo, ice-cored hill typically conical in shape, growing and persisting only in PERMAFROST. "Pingo" is of Inuit origin and was first used by the botanist A.E. PORSILD (1938) to describe the ice-cored hills typical of the Mackenzie Delta. Subsequently, the term has been widely adopted elsewhere in Canada, Alaska and Greenland. In the USSR the equivalent is *bulganniakh,* of Yakut origin. Pingos range from a few metres to several tens of metres in height. The greatest concentration (about 1450) and some of the largest in the world occur in the Tuktoyaktuk area of the Mackenzie Delta. Two of the best known are Ibyuk, 50 m high and about 1000 years old, and Aklisuktuk ("the one that is growing"), first sketched by the explorer John RICHARDSON in 1848. Other concentrations occur in the interior of the YT, along the western coastal plains of the northern YT and Alaska, and on BANKS ISLAND. Pingos grow through the freezing of water which moves under a pressure gradient to the site of the pingo. If water moves from a distant, elevated source, the pingo is a hydraulic-system pingo (eg, open-system pingos of Alaska, the YT and Greenland). If water moves under hydrostatic pressure resulting from local permafrost aggradation, then the pingo is a hydrostatic-system pingo (eg, closed-system pingos of the Mackenzie Delta and Banks I). The latter type typically forms in recently drained lake basins or drainage channels. Field studies by J.R. Mackay in the Mackenzie Delta indicate that pore water expulsion and the accumulation of subpingo water lenses can lead to rapid pingo growth (0.1-0.5 m/year), especially in the initial stages. HUGH M. FRENCH

Pingo on Tuktoyaktuk Peninsula, NWT. The pingo's unique shape is caused by the force of freezing water (*photo by Fred Breummer*).

Pinky Schooner, ancient type of vessel adapted to a primitive sloop or schooner rig in the British N American colonies and widely used in the Maritime provinces until the early 1900s. Often less than 14 m long, they were cheap to build and ideally suited for fishing. The distinctive upward sweep of the bulwarks protected the outside rudder and gave shelter to the man at the tiller — an obvious advantage to the exposed head of most colonial ships. "Pinks" were popular in NS for mackerel jigging and were used in the WAR OF 1812 as privateers. Today the pink is occasionally seen as a cruising yacht. The origin of the name is unknown. JAMES MARSH

Pinsent, Gordon Edward, actor, writer (b at Grand Falls, Nfld 12 July 1930). Diversely talented, he began his successful career as an actor in Winnipeg where he joined John HIRSCH's Theatre 77. He appeared in many stage roles in Winnipeg, Toronto and at the STRATFORD FESTIVAL, and performed on radio and TV, including the title role in the notable CBC TV series *Quentin Durgens MP* (1966-69). Newfoundland settings and characters are important in his writings. Pinsent, who is responsible for many of his own best roles, wrote the screen play and the musical version of *The Rowdyman* (film released 1972), playing the charming and irresponsible character in both. *The Rowdyman* was published as a novel in 1973 and was followed by *John and the Missus* in 1974. He also adapted the latter for the stage, playing the leading role at NEPTUNE THEATRE in Halifax. He created and appeared in the CBC series *A Gift to Last*, for which he received an ACTRA Award in 1979. His Canadian film appearances include *Who Has Seen the Wind* and *Silence of the North*. JAMES DeFELICE

Pioneer Life As each new area of Canada was opened to European settlement, pioneers faced the difficult task of building homes and communities from the ground up. Pioneer life revolved around providing the basic necessities of existence in a northern wilderness — food, shelter, furnishings, clothing and fuel — and adapting familiar institutions (churches, schools, local government, and the web of social manners and customs) to new conditions. Some pioneer settlers brought personal belongings, including furniture, kitchen utensils, books and ornaments; some settled on land prepared by COLONIZATION COMPANIES or within reach of villages or towns. For most, however, and especially before roads, canals and railways provided communication and transportation of goods, pioneering on all Canada's frontiers meant isolation, deprivation and hardship, success being measured by sheer survival. Yet, usually within a few years, primitive pioneering was followed by relative comfort, and the prospect of security and even prosperity for one's children. Thus, persistence, optimism, thrift, resourcefulness and the acceptance of unremitting hard work became character traits valued by succeeding generations long after pioneer conditions had passed.

Pioneer houses varied with local building materials and the newcomers' origins and means, but all had to be designed to withstand Canada's long, cold winters. A settler's first house was typically a one-room structure made of logs, fieldstone, spruce poles or prairie sod (*see* LOG HOUSES; SOD HOUSES). Frame or brick houses with partitions, second storeys, glass windows and shingled roofs signalled the end of pioneering, as the original dwelling became a stable. Furniture would often be homemade, eg, the chair made from a barrel described by Catharine Parr TRAILL in *The Female Emigrant's Guide* (1855). Also homemade were the cloth for blankets and clothing; carpets to cover unplaned wood floors; pails and children's toys. The mending of boots, harness and tinware might await an itinerant tradesman. Providing fuel for the huge fireplaces, usually the dwelling's only source of heat, was a constant chore; timber, although plentiful in many areas, had to be felled, trimmed, cut into lengths and carried home.

Pioneer diet depended on local produce and was generally nourishing but monotonous. Diaries and travellers' accounts (*see* EXPLORATION AND TRAVEL LITERATURE) tell of pork served 3 times a day, month in and month out, varied only by coarsely ground meal cakes, stewed dried apples or preserved small fruits and berries, and potatoes and other root vegetables. But game, fish and wildfowl were abundant in most places, and home gardens, dairy cattle and domestic fowl soon led to a more rounded and appetizing menu.

The characteristic CO-OPERATIVE principle that found expression in community work parties ("bees"), whether for house building, barn raising, clearing fields or making quilts, was reflected in local organization as well as in relations between the sexes. A church might serve Presbyterians in the morning and Methodists at night; a school district would speedily be formed, with the teacher being paid by local assessment and "boarded around" in the community. Settlers worked together to build roads, to attract tradesmen and small industry, and generally to promote the prosperity of their district.

Although pioneers on fur-trading, lumbering, mining and ranching frontiers were usually single men, women joined in the settlement of NEW FRANCE in the 17th and 18th centuries, of the MARITIMES and UPPER CANADA from 1760 to 1860, and throughout the prairie HOMESTEADING era, 1870-1914. Women's work was essential to the comfort and long-term success of a farm operation, and Canadian immigration and the DOMINION LANDS POLICY encouraged family life as a guarantee of social stability and a larger population. Pioneer women worked tirelessly for their family's material and cultural betterment, and although they suffered loneliness and hardship, their courage and strength gave them a place of respect in Canadian life. SUSAN JACKEL

Reading: E.C. Guillet, *Pioneer Days in Upper Canada* (1933); J.G. MacGregor, *North-West of Sixteen* (1958); A.Y. Morris, *Gentle Pioneers* (1966); L. Rasmussen et al, comp, *A Harvest Yet to Reap* (1976); Catharine Parr Traill, *The Backwoods of Canada* (1836).

Pipeline is a line of pipe with pumps, valves and control devices for conveying liquids or gases. Pipelines became extremely important in Canada after the discovery of oil at LEDUC, Alta (1947), for moving oil and gas from western Canada to Ontario, BC and the US. However, pipeline construction has been politically controversial since the first Pipe Line Act was passed (1949). Debate has raged about almost every major line concerning routes (the shortest routes between producers and markets sometimes cross the US), costs, estimates of reserves, federal-provincial jurisdiction, FOREIGN INVESTMENT, native LAND CLAIMS, and exports to the US. Intense controversy surrounded the Interprovincial Pipeline, TRANSCANADA PIPELINE (*see* PIPELINE DEBATE) and the proposed MACKENZIE VALLEY PIPELINE. Nevertheless, the present Canadian pipeline system is the second longest in the world (196 000 km), ranking after the US (670 000 km) and ahead of the USSR (175 000 km estimated). Several lines are brilliant engineering feats. The Transmountain Pipeline traverses the Rocky Mts and crosses 72 rivers and streams. Alberta has the most developed system, with 84 600 km, followed by Ontario with 48 700 km, Saskatchewan with 27 900 km, BC with 21 900 km, Manitoba with 8000 km, and Québec with 4200 km. In total, 155 300 km carry gas and 39 700 oil.

Structure of the System The Canadian pipeline network consists of 3 basic parts: gathering systems, trunk lines and distribution systems. The gathering system transports a mixture of oil, gas and sometimes water from the wells to col-

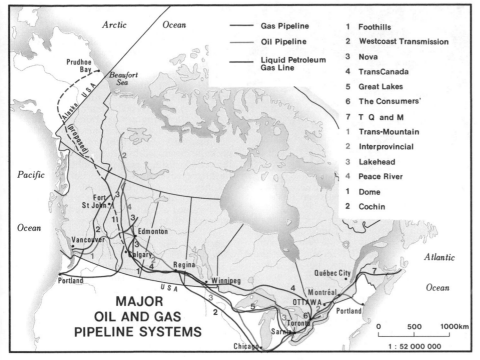

—— Gas Pipeline	1 Foothills
—— Oil Pipeline	2 Westcoast Transmission
—— Liquid Petroleum Gas Line	3 Nova
	4 TransCanada
	5 Great Lakes
	6 The Consumers'
	7 T Q and M
	1 Trans-Mountain
	2 Interprovincial
	3 Lakehead
	4 Peace River
	1 Dome
	2 Cochin

MAJOR OIL AND GAS PIPELINE SYSTEMS

0   500   1000km

1 : 52 000 000

lection points such as a gas-processing plant or treating facility where the water is removed and the oil and gas are separated. Most gathering lines are located in the West. The trunk or main pipelines move oil or gas at high pressures over long distances through large-diameter pipes, from the collection points to the market centres. Energy to overcome friction is supplied by pump or compressor stations spaced at roughly 100 km intervals. As markets expand, the capacity of trunk lines is increased by installing parallel lines (loops) and adding more pumps or compressors. Natural gas is withdrawn from the trunk line and delivered to the consumer via the distribution system. This part of the system is the longest of the 3 and is about equally distributed between East and West. Typically, the pipes in this system have a small diameter and are operated at low pressure. In the case of oil, trunk lines supply the refineries which, in turn, distribute the products to the retailer by truck or product pipelines. Product pipelines are able to move more than one product at the same time by pumping batches of each commodity sequentially. Most of these lines are located near population centres although one, the Cochin line (Edmonton to Ontario), crosses much of the country.

Regulations The design, construction and operation of all portions of the system are subject to governmental regulations and must conform to accepted engineering, environmental and safety standards. In 1959, the federal government delegated the regulation of pipelines to the NATIONAL ENERGY BOARD. The NEB issues export permits, sets pipeline tariffs, and occasionally appoints a commission to examine a particular issue, as for the Mackenzie Valley Pipeline. In addition, all pipelines must conform to the regulations of each province through which they pass, and public hearings are held to present evidence and concerns.

Technology Most pipelines are constructed of steel, although plastic and aluminum are sometimes used in natural-gas distribution networks. Steel pipelines are formed by welding 20 m sections of pipe together. The welds are x-rayed, the pipe is wrapped with protective coating and then buried. Small-diameter plastic lines are commonly "plowed in" instead of being laid in a trench. Here the plastic pipe is unreeled from a large spool through a special plow pulled by a

large tractor. This method is quick and causes little surface disturbance. All pipelines, regardless of type, are inspected and pressure tested before being used. The usual depth of burial is about 1.5 m for large pipes and slightly less for small pipes, although the Interprovincial crosses the Straits of Mackinac at depths exceeding 70 m. Canada is the world leader in winter pipeline construction, having developed unique trenching machines and welding techniques.

Operation of pipelines is often directed by computer from a remote control room, continuously monitoring the pressure, flow and energy consumption throughout the line. The computer can perform leak-detection calculations quickly and initiate remedial action such as closing emergency valves, shutting off pumps and alerting repair crews. As a further precaution, periodic tests are made to ensure the safe operation of lines. Occasionally, wax and foreign material are removed from oil lines by "pigging." A pig is a bristle-covered cylinder

Pipeline being laid across the Chalk R, near Petawawa, Ont, by TransCanada PipeLines (*photo by Jim Merrithew*).

which is pushed through the pipeline by the fluid pressure, moving the wax in front of it. "Smart pigs" are equipped with sensors and recorders so that the inside of the line can be inspected for corrosion and weak spots.

Future Technology No major breakthroughs are expected in land-based pipelines; however, the Canadian climate imposes 2 serious problems for underwater piping systems: pack ice and icebergs. In the high Arctic islands, pipelines must be trenched through the pack ice before being laid on the ocean floor. Large-scale tests are now underway to develop this technology. Icebergs, both off the East coast and in the Arctic, leave gouges in the ocean bed up to 50 m deep as they approach the shoreline. Since these gouges are deeper than pipelines can currently be buried under water, new technology must be developed to overcome this problem. *See also* ENVIRONMENT and MEGAPROJECT.   J.T. RYAN

Pipeline Debate, 8 May-6 June 1956, one of the most famous confrontations in Canadian parliamentary history. Liberal Minister of Trade and Commerce C.D. HOWE decided that a PIPELINE to carry natural gas from Alberta to central Canada was a national necessity. Howe argued that it must run entirely in Canada and deliver to Canadian consumers. The project required very large sums of capital and specialized products and expertise. In 1954 Howe put together TRANSCANADA PIPELINES, a private syndicate of Canadian and American businessmen; temporary predominance of the Americans raised charges that the pipeline was a sellout to American interests. After many vicissitudes, a bill to authorize the pipeline and provide a loan for part of its construction was introduced in May 1956. Social Credit supported it, but the CCF and the Progressive Conservatives attacked the bill from every angle. The CCF preferred public ownership; the Conservatives objected to what they saw as American control. But these substantive concerns were overshadowed by the procedural issue of CLOSURE, by which the Liberals placed a strict time limit on debate. As they and the Opposition knew, laying the pipe had to begin by early June or nothing could be done until the next year. The government charged obstruction and the Opposition charged dictatorship, but the bill passed. A 3700 km pipeline was completed from Burstall, Sask, to Montréal by Oct 1958, and TransCanada became a principally Canadian-owned company. The debate, however, discredited Howe and the Liberals, and contributed to their defeat in the 1957 general election.

ROBERT BOTHWELL

Pipes, William Thomas, lawyer, politician, premier of NS (b at Amherst, NS 15 Apr 1850; d at Boston, Mass 7 Oct 1909). Pipes, a leading figure in the NS Liberal Party, held various Cabinet posts and was premier between 1882 and 1884. During the provincial election of 1886 he created consternation within party circles, referring to Premier FIELDING's secession from the Confederation campaign as "the putrid carcass of repeal." In part his opposition reflected his attachment to the industrial development of his home town of Amherst. At his death, Pipes was a director of Amherst Boot and Shoe Manufacturing Co, a large shareholder in the Rhodes Curry Co, director and secretary of the Nova Scotia Lumber Co and attorney general of the province.

COLIN D. HOWELL

Pipit, common name for some BIRDS of the family Motacillidae, which also includes wagtails. The family, comprising 54 species, occurs worldwide except on some oceanic islands. Only 3 species occur regularly in Canada: yellow wagtail (*Motacilla flava*), water pipit (*Anthus spinoletta*) and Sprague's pipit (*A. spragueii*). These small passerines (perching birds) range in length from 12 to 22 cm. Plumage varies from black, grey or brown, to olive or yellow and may be plain or streaked. Outer tail feathers are often white. The bill tends to be long, slender and pointed. Legs and toes are often long; the hind toe is elongated in most species. These birds are mainly terrestrial and habitually "wag" their tails when on the ground. They feed primarily on insects, spiders and small mollusks. They are gregarious, particularly out of breeding season. The nest is a cuplike, sometimes domed, structure built on the ground, in rock cavities, walls or trees. Parents share incubation of the 2-7 speckled eggs and feeding of young. Pipits and wagtails have simple, repetitive songs, often delivered in flight, sometimes very high above the ground. HENRI OUELLET

Piracy, seizure and robbery of craft at sea or in the air, has played only a slight role in Canada's history. In 1612 Peter EASTON, an English pirate, embarked on a series of raids on English, French and Portuguese fishing fleets in Newfoundland harbours from Trinity Bay to Ferryland; he inflicted little injury but caused an estimated £20 400 damage. Much of Canada's piracy centres on tales of buried booty. A fabulous treasure ascribed to William Kidd (hanged in 1701) is reputed to be buried on OAK I, off Nova Scotia's S shore. More certain is the June 1720 attack on Trepassey, Nfld, by Bartholemew ROBERTS, the most successful corsair of piracy's Golden Age. Roberts captured 22 merchant ships and 4 vessels and sank a few fishing boats. Proceeding to the Grand Banks, he captured 6 French vessels. Roberts, who during his 4-year career captured 400 ships, was apprehended in 1722 by ships of the Royal Navy off West Africa.

Halifax has been the site of 2 piracy trials. In 1809 Edward and Margaret Jordan and a sailor named Kelly were tried for seizing the *Three Sisters*, previously owned by Jordan, and for murdering a number of the crew. The vessel's master, John Stairs, threw himself overboard on a hatch cover upon which he floated 4 hours before being picked up by an American fisherman. Margaret and Kelly were acquitted, but Edward Jordan was found guilty of murder and piracy and was hanged on 23 Nov 1809. His tarred and chained corpse was gibbeted at the entrance to Halifax Harbour.

In 1843 Capt George Fielding and his son sought passage home to England from Peru. Sailing from Valparaiso on the barque *Saladin,* Fielding successfully persuaded some crew members to seize the vessel and murder 6 shipmates. Under Fielding's command the *Saladin,* with a valuable cargo of guano, copper and silver, a chest of dollars and several money letters, set course for Newfoundland. So terrified of Fielding were his fellow conspirators that they threw him and his son into the sea. The *Saladin* went aground near Country Harbour, NS. The crew members were charged with piracy, a charge that was later changed to murder. Two were acquitted because they had not taken part in the murders and were deemed by the court to have been unwilling partners in the death of the Fieldings. The other 4 were hanged 30 July 1844 on a knoll where Victoria General Hospital now stands. JOHN G. LEEFE

Pitcher Plant, common name for family (Sarraceniaceae) of insectivorous perennial PLANTS. The family is restricted to N and S America. It occurs chiefly in eastern N America where 9 native species of genus *Sarracenia* occur. The pitcher (ascidium) is a modified leaf. Lined with downward-pointing bristles, it prevents insects attracted by nectar from escaping. These insects drown in water in the bottom of the tube and are decomposed by bacterial action or by an enzyme. The plant assimilates some of the nutrients; however, the many micro-organisms inhabiting the bottom of the ascidium probably benefit most. The purple pitcher plant (*S. purpurea*), the only species native to Canada, grows

The insectivorous purple pitcher plant (*Sarracenia purpurea*) is found in bogs from Newfoundland to Saskatchewan and is the provincial floral emblem of Newfoundland (*photo by Bill Ivy*).

in bogs from Newfoundland to Saskatchewan. Its rot-resistant leaves are purple veined or completely green. This plant flowers May-June, producing a solitary, drooping, purple flower. Newfoundland adopted it as its PROVINCIAL FLORAL EMBLEM in 1954. The plants grow from seeds; seedlings may be transplanted in a garden, terrarium or any very humid, acidic location. Pitcher plants belonging to different families occur in Asia (Nepenthaceae) and SW Australia (Cephalotaceae). *See* CARNIVOROUS PLANTS. CÉLINE ARSENEAULT

Pitfield, Peter Michael, civil servant, senator (b at Montréal 18 June 1937). Although Pitfield came to Ottawa in 1959 to work for Conservative Davie FULTON, he became closely identified with Pierre TRUDEAU and the Liberals after 1968 and became Canada's most prominent and sometimes controversial civil servant. In 1975 he became clerk of the Privy Council and secretary to Cabinet and profoundly influenced the policies and processes of government. PM Joe CLARK dismissed Pitfield, but he was reinstated when Trudeau returned in 1980. Though he chose to sit as an independent, his appointment to the Senate in 1982 was accompanied by widespread accusations of favouritism. JOHN ENGLISH

Peter Pitseolak, an Inuk camp leader, recognized the passing of traditional Inuit life and strove to record it in photographs, writing and art (*courtesy McCord Museum/McGill University*).

Pitseolak, Peter, photographer, artist, writer (b at Nottingham I, NWT Nov 1902; d at Cape Dorset, NWT 30 Sept 1973). A camp leader, he recognized early that traditional INUIT life was disappearing and strove to record its passing, writing diaries, notes and manuscripts, drawing Inuit customs and legends, and photographing the life around him. He took his first photograph in the 1930s for a white man who was afraid to approach a polar bear and, in the early 1940s, while living in Cape Dorset working for fur traders, he acquired a camera from a Catholic missionary. With help from his wife Aggeok, he developed his first pictures in a hunting igloo, using as a safelight a 3-battery flashlight covered with red cloth. He photographed over a 20-year period, and after his death more than 1500 negatives, images increasingly valued as an insider's record of the final moments of Inuit camp life, were purchased from his widow for the National Museums of Canada. A fine artist, he is credited too with Cape Dorset's earliest contemporary works on paper: watercolour drawings executed in 1939 for John N.S. Buchan, later 2nd Baron Tweedsmuir, at the time a fur trader with the Hudson's Bay Co. Shortly before his death, Pitseolak put down in Inuit syllabics the story of his early life (published in 1975 as *People from Our Side*, with oral biography by D. Eber) and an account of near disaster among the ice floes (published in 1977 as *Peter Pitseolak's Escape from Death*, D. Eber, ed). *See* INUIT ART. DOROTHY HARLEY EBER
Reading: D. Bellman, ed, *Peter Pitseolak (1902-1973)* (1980).

Pitseolak Ashoona, graphic artist (b on Nottingham I, NWT 1907; d at Cape Dorset, NWT 28 May 1983). She is known for lively prints and drawings showing "the things we did long ago before there were many white men" and for imaginative renderings of spirits and monsters. She began working in the late 1950s after James HOUSTON started PRINTMAKING experiments at Cape Dorset. She created several thousand drawings reflecting her love and intimate knowledge of traditional INUIT life. Talent ran in her family. She was married in 1922 to Ashoona, a capable hunter who died young, and their sons Kumwartok QAQAQ and KIUGAK Ashoona and daughter Napadive Pootoogook also became artists. Highly articulate, she told her story in the illustrated oral biography *Pitseolak: Pictures out of My Life* (from recorded interviews by D. Eber, 1971), which became an NFB animated documentary. She was elected a member of the Royal Canadian Academy of Arts in 1974. *See* INUIT ART. DOROTHY HARLEY EBER

Place des Arts, Montréal's major performing-arts complex, consists of 3 halls. Salle Wilfrid-Pelletier, originally named Grande Salle when it opened in 1963, is the largest, with a seating capacity of 2963. Designed by Montréal architects Affleck, Desbarats, Dimakopoulos, Lebensold, Michaud and Sise, the structure is made of reinforced concrete and a roof of steel. It is the home for the ORCHESTRE SYMPHONIQUE DE MONTRÉAL, and the Opéra du Québec and Les GRANDS BALLETS CANADIENS have performed there. Edifice des Théâtres, comprising 2 halls, one built on top of the other, was opened in 1967. The upper Théâtre Maisonneuve accommodates 1290, and the lower Théâtre Port-Royal, 823. This part of the complex was designed by Montréal architects David, Barott, Boulva, Dufresne and opened in time to showcase EXPO 67 events. Many international stars of music, theatre and dance have appeared at Place des Arts, including Maria Callas and Vladimir Horowitz. FREDERICK A. HALL

Place Ville Marie, Montréal (architects I.M. Pei, with Ray Affleck, 1956-65), was developed as an entire city block by CN Real Estate. This cruciform (cross-shaped) 45-storey tower, grand plaza and lower office buildings, designed by an internationally famous US architect, helped to set new standards for architecture in Canada in the 1960s. It confirmed for Montréal the importance of the below-ground pedestrian walkway system (which had its origins in CN's Central Station). Shops, restaurants and cinemas are located below the plaza, and are reached by generous square wells providing daylight as well as access. The tower's smooth aluminum and glass surface and crisp unadorned geometric form demonstrate Pei's adherence to the mainstream of 20th-century modern design.

MICHAEL McMORDIE

Place-names To many Canadians the name CANADA reveals strength, generates pride and reflects much of this land's rugged character and its resourceful people. Happily, the name is derived from the land itself, for Jacques CARTIER in 1535 noted that the Huron and Iroquois applied the designation "*kanata*," meaning a cluster of dwellings, to the present site of Québec City. The name clearly impressed Cartier, for "Canada" appears in the Saguenay and Gaspé regions on the various maps compiled shortly after his historic voyages. For a number of years the name Québec ("narrow passage" in the Algonquian languages) was assigned to the French territory from the Gulf of St Lawrence to the Ohio River and the British adopted "Province of Québec" as the name of British lands or territories in present-day Ontario and Québec, 1763-91. By 1791 the name Canada was restored to the area of present southern Québec (Lower Canada) and southern Ontario (Upper Canada); from 1841-1867, these divisions, united as the Province of Canada, were known as Canada East and Canada West. In the 1860s numerous patriotic and clever suggestions were made to identify the new country being created from the union of the provinces of Canada, NS and NB; fortunately a designation with substantial heritage was assigned to the "one Dominion under the name of Canada."

Besides Québec, 3 other provinces and one territory have names of native origin. Ontario is often reported to mean "handsome lake," but such a vague description is not really in keeping with native naming. Dr Henry Scadding (1813-1901) suggested in 1862 that Ontario is more likely derived from the name used by the Seneca Indians for themselves, *Entouhonorons* ("the people"), with the present spelling of the lake's name appearing on mid-17th-century maps. Manitoba, first given to the lake, is said to be derived from the roaring noise ("strait of the spirit") at the narrows of Lake Manitoba. Saskatchewan comes from the Cree for "swift flowing river." Yukon means "great river" in Kutchin and was first noted (as "Youcan") by John Bell (1799-1868) in 1846.

Newfoundland may be the oldest European name in continuous literary and cartographic use, dating from a letter of 1502. Nova Scotia could have come down in history as simply New Scotland, but the form in the Latin text of Sir William Alexander's grant of 1621 was fortunately preserved as a distinctive name. New Brunswick was chosen in 1784 to honour King George III (1760-1820), who was descended from the House of Brunswick. Canada's smallest province was known as "Isle de Saint Jean" to the French, and then St John's Island from 1759-98, when its present name — Prince Edward Island (for the duke of Kent then in command of troops in Halifax) — was chosen to reduce the confusion among various places called St John's and Saint John. Unfortunately, neither St John's, Nfld (possibly named on 24 June 1497), nor Saint John in NB (named by royal charter in 1785 after the river discovered by de MONTS and CHAMPLAIN on 24 June 1604) has deemed it wise to effect a change to resolve toponymic confusion. British Columbia dates from 1858 when Queen Victoria selected it in preference to New Caledonia. The Columbia River had been named in 1792 by the American explorer, Robert Gray, for his ship. The word "British" was added to distinguish the province from the S American country, Colombia. Queen Victoria's son-in-law, the marquess of Lorne, suggested Alberta in 1882 for a district of the then North-West Territories in honour of his wife, Princess Louise Caroline Alberta. Lake Louise was also named for her.

The names that are, on the whole, truly unique to Canada are those applied by the original peoples of Canada who spoke a multitude of tongues, from Cree and Micmac in the E to Blackfoot and Haida in the W and to Chipewyan and Inuktitut in the N. Most of their names describe an outstanding physical characteristic of each feature, others reflect a significant incident or relate to some activity. Some denote Indian bands or tribes, often as they were known in a language of a neighbour, friend or foe. So rarely was a personal name applied that such names in the official records, eg, Muskoka and Donnacona, are probably company titles or designations given by white settlers. In many instances meanings of names are unreliable, and frequently the language source is uncertain. Well-known names relating to physical characteristics include Niagara ("thunder of waters"), Restigouche ("fine river"), Gaspé ("end place"), Nepisiguit ("rough waters"), Mississauga ("large outlet"), Saguenay (probably, "water flows out"), Nipissing ("little body of water," in contrast to the Great Lakes), Chicoutimi ("end of deep water"), Timiskaming ("deep water"), Caughnawaga ("rapids"), Athabasca ("where there are reeds"), Kamloops ("meeting of the waters"), Keewatin ("north wind"), Minnedosa ("swift water") and Winnipeg ("murky water"). Names associated with occupancy or the tribes themselves include Ottawa ("traders"), Toronto ("meeting place"), Kitimat ("people of the snow"), Kootenay ("water people"), Penticton ("always place," ie, permanently settled), Nanaimo ("big strong people") and Assiniboine ("cook by placing hot stones in water"). Names such as Iroquois Falls, Sioux Lookout, Stony Plain, Cree Lake, Algonquin Park, Lake Erie, Indian River and Eskimo Point reflect communal names. Kelowna means "grizzly bear," Aklavik, "place of bear" and Tuktoyaktuk, "reindeer that looks like caribou." Inuvik, "place of man," was assigned in 1958 to the new town set up to replace Aklavik. Saskatoon was named for a wild berry found in abundance by the first settlers in 1882. Some of Canada's most interesting and evocative names are really translations of the aboriginal designations of the present places or associative features, eg, Medicine Hat, Moose Jaw, Yellowknife, Peace River, Qu'Appelle River, Swift Current, Thunder Bay, Battle River, Red Deer, Crowsnest Pass and Grand-Mère.

Virtually every province has a city, town or village named after Queen Victoria. The most widely known, Victoria, BC, was given in 1843 to the Hudson's Bay Company fort. In 1882 the marquess of Lorne gave the Queen's Latin title, Regina, to the capital of what was then the North-West Territories, replacing the Indian Wascana and its English derivative, Pile O'Bones. Victoria's consort is recalled in Prince Albert. Royalty is reflected in names such as Queen Elizabeth Foreland adjacent to Baffin Island, for Elizabeth I, to Queen Elizabeth Islands in the Arctic Archipelago, for Elizabeth II. Annapolis Royal was named in 1710 for Queen Anne, replacing PORT-ROYAL, established in the area in 1604 by de Monts and Champlain. George III was honoured in Georgetown (PEI), Kingston, Prince George and Lancaster Township (Ont); his wife, Charlotte, in the adjoining Charlottenburgh Township; and their children, beginning with the duke of Cornwall, in adjacent townships. Charlottetown was named for Queen Charlotte. Fredericton was named for their son in 1785. The city of Guelph was named by John Galt in 1827 for the British royal family. In 1906 the name of Prince Rupert was chosen after a national competition was sponsored by the Grand Trunk Pacific Ry. The last major island in the Canadian Arctic was discovered in 1948, and the name of the newly born Prince Charles was assigned to it. Non-British royalty honoured include King Christian of Denmark in the name of an island in the Arctic, Prince Gustaf Adolf of Sweden in a sea in the Arctic Ocean, and King Louis XIV of France in LOUISBOURG.

Many of the same reasons (respect, allegiance, hope for continued financial support) for using royalty names applied to the practice of honouring noted political leaders, government officials, military commanders, etc. Examples include Richelieu River (duc de Richelieu, 1585-1642), Ile d'Orléans (duc d'Orléans, son of Françis Ier) and Churchill River (duke of Marlborough, 1650-1722). Churchill Falls in Labrador was named for Winston Churchill. Perhaps regrettably, Hamilton River, named in the early 1800s for Sir Charles Hamilton, was changed to Churchill River by provincial legislation; now 2 major Canadian river systems have the same name. Among British political leaders, the duke of Wellington, the earl of Chatham (William Pitt), the earl of Halifax (George Montagu Dunk) and the earl of Beaconsfield (Benjamin Disraeli), have been honoured several times. Brandon derives its name from Brandon House, a Hudson's Bay Company post established in 1793 and named for the duke of Brandon, a company shareholder.

There has been a trend away from honouring foreign leaders, one of the last being John F. Kennedy, whose name was assigned in 1964 to a mountain in the Yukon. Great military leaders, eg, Montcalm and Wolfe had their names applied to a number of places; Robert Monckton was honoured in the name Moncton (efforts to respell it in the 1920s were sharply rejected); Jeffrey Amherst (1717-97), the victor at Louisbourg, in Amherst (NS) and Amherstburg (Ont); Isaac Brock (1769-1812), the hero of the War of 1812, in Brockville; Garnet Wolseley, leader of the Red River Expedition in 1870, in Wolseley (Sask); and Horatio Herbert Kitchener, after whose death at sea in 1916 Berlin (the centre of German immigration in southwestern Ontario) was renamed Kitchener. Among exploration promoters honoured were Sir Felix Booth, a London distiller, in the name, Boothia Peninsula, and Axel Heiberg and Amund and Ellef Ringnes, patrons of Sverdrup's expedition at the turn of this century, in the names of islands adjacent to Ellesmere Island.

Cabot Strait, Mont Jacques-Cartier, Baffin Bay, Davis Strait, Frobisher Bay, Hudson Bay, James Bay, Juan de Fuca Strait (BC) and Vancouver Island are names that recall the early explorers, although in Juan de FUCA's case the voyage may be apocryphal. Labrador and Bras d'Or Lake can be traced to John Cabot's contemporary, the Portuguese explorer, João Alvares FAGUNDES. Some of those who first mapped and described much of the interior of the country are remembered in Lake Champlain (Samuel de Champlain), Mackenzie River (Alexander Mackenzie), Fraser River (Simon Fraser), Thompson River (David Thompson) and Dawson and Dawson Creek (George M. Dawson).

Prominent Canadian political leaders, statesmen, industrialists and scientists have often been honoured in Canada's place-names. Numerous features commemorate John A. Macdonald, Wilfrid Laurier, Robert Borden and Mackenzie King. In recent years the names Mount Louis St. Laurent and Mount Lester Pearson have been given to mountains in BC's Premier Range, and Lake Diefenbaker has been assigned to a huge reservoir on the South Saskatchewan River. The earl of Dalhousie, Sir Guy Carleton and Sir John Sherbrooke are among governors general widely honoured; since Confederation, numerous places and features have been named for their successors, from the earl of Dufferin and Earl Grey to Roland Michener. The official naming of Mount Michener in 1979 with Michener present was a rare event in Canada's toponymic history. Georges P. Vanier is remembered in many features and places.

Personal names of local developers, community founders and settlement promoters have provided an extensive source for Canadian names. Hamilton was named for George Hamilton (1787-1835), Timmins for Noah Timmins (1867-1936), Lloydminster for Rev (later Bishop) George Lloyd (1861-1940), Joliette for Barthélemy Joliette (1787-1850) and Lethbridge for William Lethbridge (1824-1901). Forenames as well as surnames have been used for placenames, eg, Peterborough (Peter Robinson), Belleville (Arabella Wentworth Gore) and Orangeville (Orange Lawrence) in Ontario, Melville (Charles Melville Hays) in Saskatchewan, Raymond (Raymond Knight) in Alberta and Rossland (Ross Thompson) in BC. At one time the assigning of personal names was done quite liberally, eg, Kirkland Lake, was named in 1907 after a secretary in the Ontario Department of Mines. In recent years the approval of personal names has been stringently controlled by the names authorities in all the provinces and territories.

A distinctive characteristic of Canada's toponymy, especially in Québec, is the profusion of saints' names; the 1978 Québec gazetteer records over 2200 of them. Many of the hagionyms not only recall specific saints but were also the forenames of certain community founders, missionaries and priests. They include Saint-Hyacinthe, for Hyacinthe Delorme who purchased the seigneury there in 1753, Saint-Lambert, for Raphael Lambert Closse, a 17th-century merchant in the Montréal area, Saint-Jean-sur-Richelieu, for Jean Phélypeaux, a French minister of marine, and Sainte-Thérèse, for Thérèse de Blainville. Others across Canada include St Albert for Fr Albert Lacombe (1827-1916); St Thomas for Thomas Talbot (1771-1853), who developed a large part of southwestern Ontario; St Marys for Mary Strachan Jones, daughter of Bishop John Strachan; and St Catharines for Catharine Hamilton, the mother of Hamilton's founder. Religious naming extends to the Ile Jésus, Maniwaki ("place of Mary"), Trinity Bay, Conception Bay and Bay of Gods Mercy.

From the Avalon Peninsula in the E to New Westminster on the W, Canada's linguistic mosaic preponderantly reflects Anglo-Celtic influences. Calgary traces its roots to the Isle of Mull in Scotland; Edmonton to the suburbs of London. Ontario has a multitude of Anglo-Celtic names, eg, Renfrew, Pembroke, Sudbury, Windsor, Woodstock, Dublin, Listowel, Stratford, Brampton; as does Québec, eg, Hull, Windsor, Thetford-Mines, Thurso, Armagh, Bedford, Buckingham; and the Atlantic provinces, eg, Truro, Windsor, Perth-Andover, Newcastle, Kensington. Evidence of the French as the first Europeans to occupy large parts of Canada is not only evident in Québec, where 80% of the names are of French origin, but in every one of the provinces and territories — Rideau River, Point Pelee, Lake Superior and Sault Ste Marie in Ontario, Portage la Prairie (Man), Lac la Ronge (Sask), Lac La Biche (Alta), Cariboo (BC), Liard River (BC, Yukon, NWT) Bay of Fundy (NB, NS), Minas Basin (NS), Cape Breton (NS); and in Newfoundland, Port aux Basques, Notre Dame Bay, Strait of Belle Isle. Montréal is generally thought to be a variant of Jacques Cartier's "Mont Roiall," although there may have been an Ital-

ian influence in the choice of the name. Names transferred from other countries include Dresden and New Hamburg (Germany), Gimli (Iceland), Delhi and Lucknow (India), Zurich (Switzerland), Florence (Italy), Brussels (Belgium), Warsaw (Poland), Odessa (Ukraine), Moscow (Russia), Ladysmith (South Africa), Corunna (Spain). The personal names of settlers and early postmasters from European countries provide a fascinating array of community names from languages other than English and French, but few of them are widely known beyond their own immediate regions.

Several of Canada's names reflect classical origins, eg, Acadia given by Verrazano in 1524 to suggest a land of rustic peace, Avalon Peninsula assigned by Sir George Calvert in the early 1600s, Sarnia given by Sir John Colborne in 1839 for the Roman name of Guernsey, and Athens named in 1888 to replace the prosaic Farmersville, but perhaps the commonest type of name in Canada is descriptive, either of physical characteristics or of fauna, flora or minerals. Examples are Percé, Trois-Rivières, Rivière-du-Loup, Glace Bay, Midland, North Bay, Sturgeon Falls, Broadview, Grande Prairie, Cobalt, Asbestos, Petrolia, Val-d'Or, Gypsumville, Coppermine River, Whitehorse (referring to rapids in the Yukon River resembling a horse's mane) and Old Man on His Back Plateau, Rivière Qui-Mène-du-Train, Pinchgut Tickle, Cape Gargantua and Giants Castle. Newfoundland's share of unusual names include Joe Batt's Arm, Come By Chance, Little Seldom, Happy Valley, Pick Eyes, Bareneed, Hearts Delight, Bay d'Espoir (meaning "hope" but pronounced "despair") and Lushes Bight. Ecum Secum is in NS and Peekaboo Corner is in NB. In Québec there is Saint-Louis-de-Ha!Ha!, the expression "ha ha" implying "dead end" or "one way." Punkeydoodles Corners near Kitchener, Ont, presumably derives from a mispronunciation of Yankee Doodle. Flin Flon is derived from a character in the novel *The Sunless City* — Josiah Flintabbatey Flonatin. Saskatchewan has Eyebrow and Elbow; Alberta, Hairy Hill and Pincher Creek; BC has Kleena Kleene, Bella Bella, Horsefly. Snafu Creek in the Yukon recalls an indelicate WWII expression assigned by army engineers who also baptized Tarfu Creek; Sons of the Clergy Islands, Old Lady's Ghost Creek and Man Drowned Himself Lake are all in the NWT. Some names have resulted from a single incident or unusual circumstance. Lachine, Qué, dates from 1688 when La Salle failed to reach China. In NB, when land grants across a lake in 1784 were considered as impossible to attain as the perfection ascribed to Utopia, the lake was appropriately named Lake Utopia. Kicking Horse Pass in the Rockies was named for an 1858 incident when James Hector was kicked by one of his packhorses. Lindsay, Ont, was named for an assistant surveyor who died after being accidentally shot while doing a street survey there in 1834.

In 1905 the adjoining places of Keewatin, Norman and Rat Portage provided initial letters for Kenora. Arvida, now part of the city of Jonquière, Qué, was bestowed in honour of Arthur Vining Davis, an official of the Aluminum Company of Canada. Noranda, Qué, was derived from "North Canada," the name of the mining company established there in 1922. In Saskatchewan, Robert Kerr, a CPR traffic manager, is remembered in Kerrobert. Castlegar, BC, is derived from Castle Gardens, a former immigration centre in New York; the community's railway station reminded the namer of the New York structure. National and international literary figures have been commemorated in a number of place-names, from Shakespeare and Haliburton in Ontario to Carlyle and Lampman in Saskatchewan. In the Yukon, Stephen Leacock and Robert Service have been memorialized in

the names of mountains. Gravenhurst, Bracebridge and Nokomis are derived from literary characters or places.

The problem of duplication of names, eg, Trout River, Wolf Lake and Mud Lake, has frequently bothered map users. Although some efforts have been made to change some of the more common names and to discourage the use of such names in the future, arbitrary substitution by authorities has usually not been successful, especially when local people have been ignored in the process. The best-known example was the change of Castle Mountain to Mount Eisenhower in 1946. During the following 30 years, several efforts were made to reverse this decision. Late in 1979, the federal and Alberta authorities agreed to restore Castle Mountain, and assigned the name Eisenhower Peak to its most prominent summit. Attempts to change names considered by authorities to be repugnant have usually not been supported locally. In 1826 there was an effort to replace Pugwash (NS) with Waterford, but fortunately the former, of Micmac origin, was retained. In Ontario the residents of Swastika have resisted attempts to change their name, given in 1906 as a reflection of a good luck charm. Residents of Strassburg, Sask, and Berlin, Ont, were given little choice in being assigned the new names: Strasbourg and Kitchener. In recent years, Galt, Hespeler and Preston have had the common name Cambridge, Ont, superimposed, and Fort William and Port Arthur have been amalgamated to form Thunder Bay. The derivation or meanings of some names in Canada are disputed, eg, Barrie (Ont), The Pas (Man) and Mount Robson (BC), and in many cases the records are not clear. While most of Canada's 350 000 official names will endure unchanged, a number will undoubtedly be modified by political and cultural pressures, and by geographical reality and local usage. Many geographical features are still unnamed, at least officially. The official names records expand at the rate of about 25 000 new names a year so that by the end of the century there may be nearly a million names on record. *See also* CANADIAN PERMANENT COMMITTEE ON GEOGRAPHICAL NAMES; MINERAL NAMING.

ALAN RAYBURN

Reading: G.P.V. and H.B. Akrigg, *1001 British Columbia Place Names* (1973); R. Coutts, *Yukon Places and Names* (1980); P. Ham, *Place Names of Manitoba* (1980); W.B. Hamilton, *The Macmillan Book of Canadian Place Names* (1983); N. and H. Mika, *Places in Ontario,* 3 vols (1977-83); Alan Rayburn, *Geographical Names of Prince Edward Island* (1973) and *Geographical Names of New Brunswick* (1975); E.R. Seary, *Place Names of the Avalon Peninsula of the Island of Newfoundland* (1971); E.T. Russell, *What's in a Name: The Story Behind Saskatchewan Place Names* (1980); Captain J.T. Walbran, *British Columbia Coast Names, 1592-1906: Their Origin and History* (1909 repr 1977).

Placentia, Nfld, Town, pop 2204 (1981c), inc 1945, is located on PLACENTIA BAY on the W coast of the AVALON PENINSULA. The site, called *Plaisance* by the French, was a BASQUE fishing station in the late 1500s. The name may derive from Plasencia, a town in Salamanca, Spain. After the French claimed Newfoundland in 1624, Plaisance became the first official French colony on the island. It remained the French capital of Newfoundland, guarding French fishing activities, until the Treaty of Utrecht, 1713. It was defended by a number of forts and was the base for French raids on English settlements on the Avalon Pen in 1696, 1705 and 1709. After 1913 Placentia became a British stronghold and further fortifications were erected until the garrison was withdrawn in 1811. With its wide beaches and strategic location, Placentia grew as an important fishing and trading centre in the 1800s, but became heavily dependent upon employment at the nearby Argentia Naval Base, built 1940-41. Since the phase-down of the base in 1969 and 1974, employment has depended on the fishery and tourism attracted by the town's historic buildings and Castle Hill National Historic Pk (since 1968).   J. E. M. PITT AND R. D. PITT

Placentia Bay, from the French *plaisance,* is a large, deep bay formed by Newfoundland's Burin Pen to the W, and the SW AVALON PENINSULA to the E. From Ferryland Head in the W and CAPE ST MARY'S 90 km E, the bay runs 125 km to its head, the Isthmus of Avalon. Ringed with coves and harbours, the bay has 2 extensive islands, Merasheen and Long, formerly populated, which divide the bay into channels to the N. Once utilized by Dorset Eskimo and the BEOTHUK, the fine fishing grounds were probably first frequented by BASQUES and French in the 1500s; by 1662, when PLACENTIA became Newfoundland's French capital, French fishermen occupied the bay, as modern place-names still attest. After the TREATY OF UTRECHT, 1713, English use and settlement slowly followed in Placentia B. Today the principal settlements are in the Burin-MARYSTOWN area and in the vicinity of Placentia and ARGENTIA, once the location of a major US military facility and now the terminus of a CN Marine ferry service to NS. Fishing, shipbuilding and services are now the main employers, though there was once a large oil refinery at COME BY CHANCE.   ROBERT D. PITT

Plamondon, Antoine, painter (b at Ancienne-Lorette, Qué 29 Feb 1804; d at Neuville, Qué 4 Sept 1895). After a 6-year apprenticeship with Joseph LÉGARÉ, Plamondon left for Europe in 1826. He studied in Paris under J.B. Paulin Guérin, official painter to King Charles X. Returning to Québec in 1830, he specialized in portraits of the bourgeoisie and copies of religious works. In 1838 the Literary and Historical Soc of Québec awarded him a medal for his portrait *Zacharie Vincent, le dernier des Hurons,* which was bought by Lord DURHAM, and the following year he exhibited in the House of Assembly his famous Stations of the Cross intended for Notre-Dame de Montréal. In 1841 he painted 3 remarkable portraits of nuns, including *Soeur Saint-Alphonse.* He taught drawing in various educational institutions, and counted Théophile HAMEL among his disciples. A fervent polemicist, Plamondon frequently wrote to the newspapers to argue his pictorial ideas and attack his rivals. In 1851, a year after winning a first prize with his *Chasse aux tourtes* at the Exposition de Québec, he moved his studio to Neuville, about

Antoine Plamondon, *Self Portrait* (1882) (*courtesy Musée du Séminaire de Québec/Pierre Soulard*).

30 km upstream from Québec. There he continued painting until the 1880s, turning out a stream of religious paintings of uneven quality and portraits copied from photographs. His long career was crowned in 1880 when he was named founding VP of the Royal Canadian Academy of the Arts.   JOHN R. PORTER

Plamondon, Joseph-Marcel-Rodolphe, tenor, teacher (b at Montréal 18 Jan 1876; d there 28 Jan 1940). After cello and voice training in Montréal and early success as a church soloist, Rodolphe Plamondon continued his musical education in France. Prior to WWI he appeared frequently in opera roles. However, his reputation rests primarily on his proficiency as a concert and oratorio soloist, which kept him in constant demand with Europe's leading choirs and orchestras until the late 1920s. Plamondon's concerts often included music by Canadian composers. In 1925 and 1926 he made several recordings of French songs. Plamondon's singing tours brought him to Canada only rarely, but he returned to Montréal permanently in 1928 and taught there until his death.

BARCLAY McMILLAN

Plankton [Gk *planktos,* "drifting"] plants and animals, phytoplankton and zooplankton, respectively, that float freely or drift with currents in oceans, freshwater ponds and LAKES. At present, phytoplankton is considered to include members of 3 kingdoms (Monera, Protista, PLANT); zooplankton contains members of 2 kingdoms (Protista, ANIMAL). Unattached and having weak powers of independent movement, plankton contrast with organisms that are benthic (attached to or living in bottom sediments) or nektonic (active swimming). They are usually microscopic, although some zooplankton (eg, JELLYFISH) may be several metres long. Planktonic food chains are the basis of the aquatic ecosystem. At the lowest level are phytoplankton, primary producers able to use SOLAR ENERGY, carbon dioxide and water to photosynthesize organic matter. Smaller zooplankton, feeding on phytoplankton, represent the second, "grazing" trophic level (herbivores). Larger zooplankton, feeding on the smaller zooplankton, represent the third trophic level (predators or carnivores).

Plant, member of a large and diverse group of organisms sharing certain common features, but difficult to separate absolutely from all other living things (*see* BIOLOGY). Two characteristics stand out because of the sharp contrast with ANIMALS. Plants are primarily autotrophs (self feeders), using light energy from the sun to synthesize organic molecules from inorganic precursors (photosynthesis). They are stationary organisms and obtain their energy while fixed in one place. These properties are reflected in the structure of a typical land plant which is organized into 2 basic systems, shoot and root. The shoot system (stem and leaves) grows upward into the light and is the site of photosynthesis; the root system penetrates the soil, anchors the plant and absorbs necessary water and minerals. Both systems are potentially unlimited in growth, thus providing for the immobile plant a means of adjustment to the environment. This open-ended growth pattern results from the functioning of regions of continued growth (meristems) at the tip of each shoot and root. Meristems originate in early embryonic development. The fertilized egg (zygote) develops into many cells which, like those of the animal embryo, begin to specialize for a function in the adult body. Two groups of cells remain unspecialized or embryonic (ie, capable of continued cell division). These become the first shoot and root apical meristems. The shoot apical meristem initiates stem tissues, produces outgrowths that develop into leaves and initiates primordia

of lateral branches just above the leaf axil (junction of leaf and stem). With suitable stimulation, the shoot apical meristem may be transformed to give rise to a flower, inflorescence or cone, thus relinquishing its capacity for unlimited growth. The root apical meristem initiates root tissues and a protective covering over itself (root cap). It forms no appendages comparable to leaves or branches; branch roots arise internally, emerging some distance behind the root tip.

Cell Structure
A plant's immobility is readily understood when its cells are examined. Unlike animal cells, each plant cell is enclosed in a boxlike wall, the main structural component of which is cellulose. Furthermore, the walls of adjacent cells are held together by a cementing substance (but intercellular spaces occur frequently, especially where several cells meet at their edges). All plant cells have a relatively thin, outer primary wall, capable of extension during cell growth. Certain supporting and conducting cells have an inner, often relatively thick secondary wall which is incapable of growth. The secondary wall does not cover the primary wall completely but is interrupted by small pits or by more extensive gaps. Clearly, nerve and muscle tissues, the bases of animal motility, could not be constructed of such cells. The meristems continually add new, functionally active cells at the growing tips, apparently accomplishing the result achieved in animals by cell turnover. Thus, there is a steady replacement of leaves as the shoot grows and of absorbing root hairs near the root tip.

Inside the cell wall, the protoplasmic contents are bounded by a differentially permeable membrane, like that surrounding the animal cell. Plants lack an organized nervous system but have plasmodesmata connecting almost all living cells. These are fine strands of protoplasm (bounded by membrane) that extend through the primary wall and provide cell-to-cell continuity. When a secondary wall is present, plasmodesmata are restricted to the pits. The cytoplasm (generalized cell protoplasm) contains a nucleus and several organelles of diverse structure and function. Conspicuous among these are plastids, which in photosynthetic tissues contain chlorophyll and are known as chloroplasts. A further, distinctive characteristic of plant cells is the presence of fluid-filled vacuoles bounded by a membrane similar to the cell membrane. Small and often numerous in immature cells, they enlarge and fuse during cell growth so that a single, central vacuole, sometimes traversed by cytoplasmic strands, occupies most of a mature cell.

Types of Cells
Plant cells have many different forms, but those encountered in vascular plants fall into a few classes.

Parenchyma cells are roughly equidimensional in shape, have only thin primary walls and carry on most of the plant's metabolic activities (eg, photosynthesis, storage).

Collenchyma cells also retain active protoplasmic contents, but are elongated with thickened primary walls, often unevenly distributed around the cell's circumference. They combine support with flexibility.

Sclerenchyma cells have thick secondary walls and provide rigid support. When mature they are usually dead, containing no protoplasmic contents. Elongated sclerenchyma cells are called fibres; more nearly equidimensional ones are sclereids.

Conducting cells of the xylem (water-transporting tissue) are tracheids and vessel cells. Both are dead at maturity and have secondary walls (either a continuous wall with pits or in the form of rings, spirals or a network). Tracheids are elongate and spindle shaped. Water

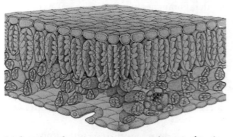

Leaf section of sugar maple (*Acer saccharum*), showing the epidermis ("skin"), the inner food-producing cells (mesophyll), a food-and-water-carrying vascular bundle ("vein"), and a pore (stoma) whose size is controlled by the surrounding guard cells (*courtesy National Museums of Canada/National Museum of Natural Sciences*).

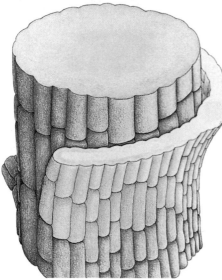

Section through the stem and a leaf of cord moss (*Funaria hydrometrica*) (*courtesy National Museums of Canada/National Museum of Natural Sciences*).

passes between them through pits or other gaps in the secondary wall. Vessel cells vary from elongate to barrel shaped and are superimposed one above the other to form vessels. The end walls of a vessel cell are perforated, leaving no barrier to water flow within the limits of a vessel.

Sieve elements are conducting cells of the phloem (tissue that transports organic solutes). Unlike xylem elements, these are living cells, but the protoplasm has undergone substantial alteration (usually including loss of nucleus). In flowering plants, sieve elements are superimposed to form sieve tubes and are connected by plates through which enlarged intercellular connections extend.

Epidermal cells form a surface barrier against water loss. They resemble parenchyma but the outer wall is often thickened and impregnated with cutin. A layer of cutin, the cuticle, is also deposited on the outer surface. Certain epidermal cells are modified in shape and function as guard cells for the stomata (minute openings on leaf or stem surfaces). Others may form unicellular or multicellular outgrowths (hairs or trichomes).

Cork cells are dead when mature, have walls modified by deposition of suberin and reduce water loss.

Tissues and Organs

The diverse cells of the plant body are organized into tissues, some relatively homogeneous, others more complex. On the basis of structure and function, tissues may be grouped into 3 systems: vascular (conducting) system; dermal (protective) system; and fundamental (metabolic) system. These systems occur, in somewhat different configurations, in each major plant organ (root, stem and leaf).

In the root, the vascular system consists usually of a central core of xylem, with radiating ridges, and phloem, located in troughs between the ridges. Around the phloem is a layer of parenchyma (pericycle) in which branch roots originate. Surrounding the pericycle is the endodermis, cells of which have a band of suberized material in the transverse and radial walls that restricts the passage of materials into or out of the vascular system. Tissues inside the endodermis are sometimes referred to as the stele. The fundamental system is represented by the parenchymatous cortex and sometimes by a core (pith) in the centre of the xylem. The cortex is bounded by the epidermis. In a zone just behind the root's growing region, certain epidermal cells extend outward in projections (root hairs) which are extremely important in absorption from the soil. The root cuticle is usually very thin, particularly in the absorbing region.

In the stem of SEED PLANTS the vascular system consists of interconnected bundles of xylem and phloem, the phloem outside the xylem. These bundles are continuous with the vascular supply of the leaves, and one or more diverge into each leaf at the level of its node (point of attachment to stem). In dicotyledons (plants with 2 embryo leaves), the bundles form a ring around a central pith; in monocotyledons (plants with one embryo leaf), they are scattered throughout the centre of the stem, embedded in fundamental tissue. The cortex is often photosynthetic. The stem is bounded by an epidermis with stomata.

In the leaf, the petiole (stalk that supports leaf) contains one or several vascular leaf traces embedded in fundamental tissue, which often includes collenchyma. In the blade (lamina) the vascular system is subdivided into a network of veins and veinlets serving all parts of the photosynthetic tissue. The fundamental system (mesophyll) is composed of chloroplast-containing parenchyma with extensive intercellular spaces. Often one or 2 layers of columnar cells, the palisade layer, occur just below the upper epidermis and above the more open, spongy mesophyll. Stomata are usually more numerous in the lower epidermis. The veins traversing the mesophyll are surrounded by a compact layer of parenchyma, the bundle sheath, often associated with substantial amounts of collenchyma (sclerenchyma in larger veins).

Secondary Growth

Although an entire plant body can be formed by the shoot and root apical meristems, a substantial supplement is often provided by additional or secondary meristems, especially in TREES and shrubs. The vascular cambium and cork cambium contribute additional tissues to the vascular and dermal systems, respectively, a further example of cell replacement by addition. The vascular cambium is a layer of meristem situated between the xylem and phloem. By longitudinal division of its cells parallel to the surface of the stem or root, it forms secondary xylem or wood to the inside and secondary phloem to the outside. In trees and shrubs this activity may continue for years. Wood is one of Canada's major natural RESOURCES. In herbaceous plants cambial activity is greatly restricted, or absent (in most monocotyledons). Even without a cambium, plants such as palms and tree ferns can build up a massive body and maintain a long life span. The continued expansion of the vascular system internally cannot be long contained by the epidermis, the rupture of which would have serious consequences if the dermal system were incapable of replacement. However, the cork cambium, located near the surface, produces a periderm (bark) composed largely of suberized cork cells which restrict water loss.

Lenticels, which perforate the periderm with loose, spongy parenchyma, accomplish aeration. These openings are not controlled, but may be sealed by development of cork and reopened by further production of spongy tissues.

T.A. STEEVES

Reading: W.A. Jensen and F.B. Salisbury, *Botany: An Ecological Approach* (1972).

Plant Classification Popular classification usually divides living beings into PLANTS and ANIMALS and, sometimes, microbes. Scientific classification long followed a similar system, with 2 principal kingdoms: the animal order and the vegetable order. Plants and plantlike organisms (eg, fungi, algae) were those lacking complex sensory organs and organs of locomotion, and capable either of making their own food from inorganic elements or of absorbing it directly from the surrounding environment. This system is outdated; biologists now generally divide living beings into 5 kingdoms: Monera, Protista, FUNGI, Plantae and Animalia. These kingdoms are themselves organized into super kingdoms: Prokaryota and Eukaryota. Prokaryotes are single-celled organisms lacking membrane-bound organelles (Monera); eukaryotes are composed of cells with membrane-bound nuclei (the other 4 kingdoms). Thus, true plants are multicellular and eukaryotic, contain pigments responsible for fixing light energy, have rigid cell walls and reproduce sexually.

There are probably some 600 000 species of plants and plantlike organisms, and a classification system is needed to give order to this diversity. Specialists in classification of living beings (systematists or taxonomists) have developed a hierarchical system to classify organisms in increasingly generalized groupings, according to common characteristics. The super kingdom is the most general grouping and is divided into increasingly narrow categories down to the species level. Species may be subdivided into subspecies, varieties and forms. The sugar maple is thus classified as follows: super kingdom–Eukaryota; kingdom–Plantae; division–Anthophyta; class–Magnoliopsida; subclass–Rosidae; order–Sapindales; family–Aceraceae; genus–*Acer*; species–*Acer saccharum* Marsh.

The name of a species is always a binomial, giving the name of the genus (here, *Acer*) and a specific epithet (*saccharum*). The species designation is followed by the name, usually abbreviated, of the first person to name the species in question: for sugar maple, the American botanist Humphrey Marshall (1722-1801). Plant names obey a set of rules (eg, that scientific names be in Latin) which make up the International Code of Botanical Nomenclature. The classification of living beings is not fixed; it is modified and improved through research. Modern classification depends on data from CHEMISTRY, BIOCHEMISTRY, cytology, PALEONTOLOGY, MOLECULAR BIOLOGY, embryology, etc, as well as on traditional morphological and anatomical details, and attempts to build a system that reflects the evolutionary history and relationships of plants. *See* entries under individual species; ALGAE; BLUE-GREEN ALGAE; BOTANY; CLUB MOSSES; MUSHROOMS AND PUFFBALLS; LIVERWORTS; VEGETATION REGIONS.

PIERRE MORISSET

Reading: Lyman Benson, *Plant Classification* (1979); H.J. Scoggan, *The Flora of Canada*, 4 vols (1978).

Plant Disease can decrease the economic, aesthetic and biological value of all kinds of plants. Plant pathology (phytopathology) is the study of the nature, causes, prevention and socioeconomic aspects of plant diseases. Plant diseases are recognized by symptoms such as necrosis (death of cells or tissues), chlorosis (yellowing), wilting (shoot and leaf drooping), rot, dwarfing, tumefaction (formation of gall or localized swelling), bronzing, damping-off (plant toppling), etc. Plant diseases are separated into nonparasitic (noninfectious, nontransmissible) and parasitic (infectious) diseases.

Nonparasitic diseases are caused by improper environmental conditions such as deficiencies and excesses of nutrients, biological toxicants, adverse soil and weather conditions, and pollutants. Deficiencies of mineral nutrients (nitrogen, phosphorus, potassium, boron, calcium, copper, iron, magnesium, manganese, molybdenum, sulphur and zinc) can induce some diseases in all kinds of crops. Diseases caused by pollutants can also be found. Air pollutants from combustion include sulphur dioxide and fluorides; those from photochemical reactions include complex nitrates and ozone. In addition, some toxic chemicals occur naturally.

Most plant diseases are caused by parasitic FUNGI, bacteria, mycoplasma, spiroplasma, viruses, viroids, nematodes and protozoa. In addition, some plants (eg, dodders, MISTLETOES) can parasitize other green plants.

Fungi are microscopic or macroscopic threadlike organisms which lack the photosynthetic pigment, chlorophyll, and which bear reproductive structures (usually spores). Thousands of fungi cause approximately 100 000 diseases in green plants including rusts, smuts, powdery mildews and ergot of cereals; blights of potatoes and tomatoes; scab of apples; heart rots of trees; downy mildew of tobacco, damping-off of seedlings, etc.

Bacteria, Mycoplasma and Spiroplasma are simple cells which lack chlorophyll and which usually reproduce by cell division. Mycoplasma can be considered as simple forms of bacteria which lack cell walls. Spiroplasma are mycoplasmalike cells with a spiral structure. In nature, mycoplasma and spiroplasma are essentially dependent upon leafhoppers for their dispersal. In some cases, bacteria can also be disseminated by insects but may also be dispersed by splashing rain, wind, contact, etc. A few hundred species of bacteria attack plants.

Viruses and Viroids represent the simplest form of parasitic entities. Viruses are made up of proteins and nucleic acids; viroids, of unprotected ribonucleic acids. They are considered molecular parasites, using host components for the replication (ie, multiplication) of their infectious nucleic acids. A few hundred plant viruses cause diseases known as tobacco, cucumber or tomato mosaics, potato leafroll, raspberry ringspot, tulip flower breaking, barley yellow dwarf, etc. Several viroids cause diseases such as potato spindle tuber, cucumber pale fruit, hop and chrysanthemum stunt, etc. Viroids and some viruses are transmitted by contact. Many viruses are disseminated in nature by arthropod vectors (eg, APHIDS, leafhoppers, THRIPS, white flies, mealy bugs, MITES); some are also transmitted by nematodes and soil-borne fungi.

Nematodes (eg, eelworms) are nonsegmented INVERTEBRATE animals. Most plant-parasitic nematodes cause root galls, rots and lesions and can severely retard root growth. Some nematodes feed on plants with their stylets (spears). Nematodes produce eggs and larvae which undergo several molts before becoming plant-pathogenic adults. Nematodes are also troublesome because they can act as very efficient vectors of 2 groups of plant viruses.

Protozoa are primitive forms of microscopic animals. A few species have been associated with some plant diseases.

Control

Because of the economic losses (billions of dollars worldwide each year) resulting from plant diseases, control measures are commonly used. Exclusion is prevention of the entry of a pathogen into an area by plant quarantines, certification programs, voluntary or mandatory inspection and pathogen-free production of plant material. Eradication is accomplished by removal of the pathogen hosts, by crop rotation and by heat or chemical treatment of the soil harbouring the pathogen. Protection methods depend primarily on chemical PESTICIDES such as fungicides, bactericides, nematicides, fumigants and insecticides (against insect vectors). However, some plant pathogens (eg, viruses and viroids) cannot be chemically suppressed because these agents multiply so intimately with the plant cells. Some cultural practices (eg, early and shallow seeding, fertilization) can also protect the plants against the disease-causing agents or conditions. Genetic manipulation is the best overall control method, when stable resistance or tolerance genes are easily found and incorporated into the plant's hereditary material. Many agronomically important crops have resistance or tolerance genes against several fungal and viral diseases. Biological control measures and integrated pest-management approaches represent promising avenues in the search for effective and safe control of plant diseases. These methods involve using natural predators against the disease-causing organism (*see* INSECT, BENEFICIAL).

Research in Canada

Because of the importance of FORESTRY operations and the AGRICULTURE AND FOOD system to Canada's economy, control of plant diseases has been a major focus of research (*see* AGRICULTURAL RESEARCH AND DEVELOPMENT). Forest stands and extensive hectarages seeded to a single crop, because they are both monoculture systems, are particularly vulnerable to damage from disease pathogens. The cost of such losses, however, is difficult to estimate. For example, in a 2-year study completed by Agriculture Canada's London Research Centre, crop losses caused by insects, disease and weeds in potato, rutabaga and onion crops were 64%, 88% and 100%, respectively. Cost of such losses, based on 1981 farm value of these crops, would have been $29.9 million, $5.3 million and $12.8 million. Research into the eradication or control of plant diseases takes place in federal and provincial government laboratories, university faculties or colleges of agriculture and forestry and some private companies. Because many horticultural plants begin as transplants from US nurseries, the possibility of introducing disease-causing organisms in these plants presents special problems.   ALAIN ASSELIN

Reading: G.N. Agrios, *Plant Pathology* (1980).

Plante, Jacques, hockey goaltender (b near Mont Carmel, Qué 17 Jan 1929). He began playing goal for a factory team in Shawinigan and played junior for Québec Citadels before turning professional with Montreal Royals at age 22. He played several games with MONTREAL CANADIENS during the 1953 playoffs and the final 17 games of the regular 1953-54 season, becoming Montréal's regular goalie 1954-55. He was the first goalie to win the VEZINA TROPHY 5 straight seasons (1955-56 to 1959-60), and after an off-year in which he was injured, he won the Vezina again in 1961-62, as well as the HART TROPHY (most valuable player). He was traded to New York Rangers in 1963 after bouts of asthma had gained him a reputation for being undependable, but retired after only 1½ seasons. He returned to the NHL with St Louis 1968-70, sharing the Vezina with Glenn Hall in 1968-69 and, playing perhaps his best hockey ever, with Toronto 1970-73 and briefly with Boston in 1973. He finished his playing career with Edmonton Oilers (WHA) 1974-75 and coached Québec Nordiques 1973-74.

Plante played goal with superb technical ability and with drama and flair. He was famous in the sport for roving beyond his net, and after being struck in the face with a puck 1 Nov 1959 he was the first goalie to wear a protective mask regularly. In 17 NHL seasons, Plante played 837 regular season and 112 playoff games and compiled a 2.37 regular season and 2.16 playoff goals-against average, with 82 regular season and 14 playoff shutouts.   JAMES MARSH

Planter, a term which usually designated, from the 1600s to the 1800s, an independent fisherman who owned his own "fishing," room or "plantation," on the coast of Newfoundland, and perhaps several large, inshore fishing boats. He employed other fishermen and might act as a local merchant or as middleman for a larger firm. Usually a permanent resident of Newfoundland, or LIVEYER, he might, like the BYE-BOAT keeper, frequently return to Britain or retire there (*see* FISHERIES HISTORY). In more recent times, applied to the Labrador fishery, the term was nearly synonymous with STATIONER.
                ROBERT D. PITT

Plants, Native Uses Over a thousand plant species were used traditionally by Indian and Inuit peoples. These species, ranging from ALGAE to CONIFERS and flowering PLANTS, provided food, medicine and materials; and played an important role in native language, ritual and mythology. Many species remain important in today's native cultures. The study of direct interrelationships between humans and plants is called ethnobotany. In Canada systematic ethnobotanical studies have been few, but with contributions from researchers in various disciplines, much has been learned. The roles of plants in traditional cultures are summarized below.

Food Plants Cultivation of food crops was practised by native Canadians, before the arrival of Europeans, only in southern Ontario and the St Lawrence Valley. Crops included the "three sisters" — corn, beans and squash — as well as sunflowers, tobacco and, possibly, Jerusalem artichoke. Over 500 species of wild plants provided foods for native peoples in Canada. Some of these foods are similar to those eaten today: root and green vegetables, fruits, nuts, seeds and MUSHROOMS. Others, eg, some types of LICHENS, marine algae and inner bark tissues of some trees, are not normally part of the modern diet. Plants were also used as sweeteners, flavourings and beverages. Many wild plants provided more than one type of food. Today, maple

Agnes Edgar, a Bella Coola, gathering Indian medicines, 1976 (*photo by Dorothy Kennedy*).

Examples of Food Plants of Canadian Native Peoples*

Food Type	Plants
root vegetables	balsamroot; blue camas bulbs, cattail rhizomes; groundnuts, Indian breadroot, wild onions; spring beauty corms; wapato tubers
green vegetables	cactus stems; cow parsnip shoots; dock leaves; fiddleheads; fireweed shoots; lamb's-quarters; milkweed shoots; nettle shoots; seaweeds; thimbleberry shoots
fleshy fruits	bearberries; blackberries; blueberries; buffaloberries; wild cherries; cloudberries; wild crabapples; cranberries (bog, highbush and rock); crowberries; currants; elderberries; gooseberries; huckleberries; wild plums; raspberries; rose hips; salal berries; saskatoon berries; strawberries
grains, nuts, seeds	acorns; balsamroot seeds; beech nuts butternuts; hazelnuts; hickory nuts; black walnuts; wild rice
inner bark tissues	alder; aspen; birch; cottonwood; hemlock; pine; spruce
beverages	wild bergamot; coniferous trees (except yews and yellow cedar); Labrador tea; wintergreen
flavourings, sweeteners	wild ginger; licorice fern; maple sugar and syrup; pepperroot; sassafras

* Note that many of these require special preparation, eg, peeling or cooking

syrup, wild rice and many wild fruits are enjoyed by native and non-native Canadians.

Medicinal Plants Plants were an important component of native medicine. Curing of disease and maintenance of health were usually carried out by herbal specialists. Although administering herbal medicines was sometimes associated with ritual and "magic," and in many cultures herbal curing and magical curing were virtually inseparable, the specialists were not necessarily shamans who invoked supernatural powers in healing. Sometimes, special curative and spiritual organizations existed, eg, the Ojibwa *Midewiwin* (grand medicine society) in which initiates passed through stages, eventually learning the ritual and herbalism for curing disease.

More than 500 plants were used in native medicine. These were administered as herbal teas, preparations to be chewed and swallowed, poultices, or inhaled vapours, although a variety of more exotic modes of application (eg, pouring a concoction in patient's ear) were also

Examples of Some Pharmacologically Valid Native Medicines

Plant	Use/ Preparation	Native group	Medicinal principle
balsam fir	colds/inhale vapours	many groups	monoterpenes— nasal stimulants
cascara	constipation/ tea from bark	western groups	anthracenes— cathartics
gold-thread	mouth sores/ tea from roots	Iroquois & others	alkaloid— antibacterial
kinni-kinnick	kidney ailments/tea from branches	Okanagan	glycoside & other compounds— diuretic
red oak	diarrhea/tea from bark	Maliseet	tannins— astringents
poplar	back pain/ tea from roots	Ojibwa	salicin— analgesic

used. Any part of a plant, alone or in combination with other HERBS, could be prescribed.

Although native herbal cures have been alternately rejected as superstition or embraced as cure-alls, an objective assessment by medical authorities indicates that treatments of certain ailments (eg, wounds, skin sores, gastrointestinal disorders, coughs, colds, fevers and rheumatism) were rational and effective. In many cases, pharmacological constituents of plants can be correlated with the native application. A famous example is the curing of CARTIER'S men of scurvy (winter 1535-36). They were treated by natives of Hochelaga with a conifer tea of high vitamin C content (probably eastern white cedar). For other plants, the "ritual" or "magical" element may be more important, an example being the use of spiny or thorny plants as protective agents to ward off "spirits" associated with illness and death. This approach was probably effective for psychosomatic ailments, and it may have improved the outlook of patients with organic complaints as well. Native practitioners were skilled in selection, preparation and dosage of herbal medicines. The reader is cautioned that many plant species used as medicines are highly poisonous and should not be used except under qualified supervision.

Some Plant Materials Used by Canadian Native Peoples

Type of Material	Plants
wood	alders; ash; cedars (red, white); wild cherries; cottonwood; crabapple; Douglas fir; elm; true firs; hawthorn; hickory; juniper; maples; oaks; oceanspray; pines; saskatoon; spruces; yew
bark, in sheets	white birch; red cedar; cottonwood; true firs; balsam poplar; pines; spruces
stem, root, bark and leaf fibres	basswood bark; cattail leaves; cedar bark, branches, roots; bitter cherry bark; Indian hemp stems; bull kelp stipes; nettle stems; sedge leaves; spruce roots; tule stems; willow bark, branches
gums, resins	cottonwood buds; Douglas fir; true firs; pines; spruces; hemlocks
dyes, pigments	alder bark; butternut bark, roots; hemlock bark; Indian paint fungus; Oregon grape bark, roots; puccoon roots, wolf lichen
scents	true fir boughs; Indian consumption plant seeds; juniper boughs; lovage roots; sagebrush; sweetgrass
absorbents	cedar bark, shredded inner; grass, dried; Sphagnum moss
abrasive	scouring rushes
lining, wrapping	fern fronds; skunk cabbage leaves; thimbleberry leaves

Utility Plants Various plant materials, from several hundred different species, were used by Canadian native peoples. Woods were of prime importance as fuels, and as major components of utilitarian items: buildings, dugout canoes, boxes, totem poles and implements (eg, paddles, digging sticks, spear shafts, bows, arrows, snowshoe frames, etc). Sheets of bark, especially birch, were made into containers and canoes. Bark was also used to cover roofs and line storage pits. Fibrous tissues from stems, roots, bark and leaves served for twine, rope and weaving materials for baskets, mats and clothing. Tree resin was used as glue and waterproofing. Plants provided dyes and pigments, scents, absorbent materials, abrasives, linings and wrappings, insect repellents, toys and recreational items, and personal adornment.

Conclusion Plants have provided varied and abundant resources for native peoples for thousands of years. A vast traditional knowledge of plant foods, medicines and materials has enabled Indian and Inuit peoples to thrive in Canada's diverse environments. Many plants they depended on have been adopted into our modern life-style. Others have potential as nutritional supplements, future food resources, and sources of new pharmaceuticals and other useful compounds. *See* individual species entries.

NANCY J. TURNER, J.T. ARNASON, R.J. HEBDA
AND T. JOHNS

Reading: A.F. Szczawinski and Nancy J. Turner, *Edible Wild Plants of Canada*, vols 2-4 (1978-80).

Plaskett, John Stanley, astronomer (b at Hickson, UC 17 Nov 1865; d at Esquimalt, BC 17 Oct 1941). Born on a farm, Plaskett joined the Edison Co in Schenectady, NY, and Sherbrooke, Qué. Foreman of the workshop in the dept of physics at U of T in 1890, he enrolled as a student in 1895 and graduated in 1899. In 1903 Plaskett joined the astronomical branch of the Dept of the Interior, Ottawa, helping to design and construct instruments for the new Dominion Observatory. He observed a solar eclipse in 1905 and did important work on radial velocities of stars. His proposal for a large telescope was approved and the 72-inch (1.8 m) telescope (then the world's largest) was completed in 1918 at Victoria, BC. Plaskett became director, working on spectroscopic binaries (a massive one that he discovered still bears his name) and galactic structure (with J.A. Pearce). In 1984 Minor Planet No 2905 was named Plaskett in honour of J.S. Plaskett and his son H.H. Plaskett, also an astronomer. A.H. BATTEN

Plasticiens, Les In the mid-1950s, following the excitement generated by the AUTOMATISTES, many Québec artists felt a need to return to a more controlled and ordered style of PAINTING. This sentiment was noticeable in the recent work of Fernand LEDUC, a loyal follower of Paul-Emile BORDUAS and automatism from the beginning. Leduc now felt that automatism had unconsciously held on to a dated concept of pictorial space by maintaining the dichotomy of object and background. A new pictorial movement was launched with the 1955 publication of the *Manifeste des plasticiens.* Drafted by critic and painter Rodolphe de Repentigny (who signed his paintings with the pseudonym Jauran) and countersigned by Louis Belzile, Jean-Paul Jérôme and Fernand Toupin, it was quite different from the REFUS GLOBAL, which had appeared in 1948. The *Manifeste des plasticiens* encouraged young Québec artists to follow the example of the pioneers of abstract art, in particular that of Mondrian. The Plasticiens preferred a strict use of 2-dimensional space in their paintings. In 1956, Guido MOLINARI (Noirs et Blancs) and Claude TOUSIGNANT (Monochromes) proposed even more radical departures: 2-dimensional surfaces, reversible spaces and the series concept. The Plasticien movement remained a force in the Québec art community; artists such as Yves GAUCHER, Jacques Hurtubise and Charles GAGNON, though not directly associated with this school, were influenced by it. Only with the rise of postmodernism at the end of the 1960s did the Plasticien movement give way to a new avant-garde in the Québec art world. FRANÇOIS-MARC GAGNON

Reading: D. Burnett and M. Schiff, *Contemporary Canadian Art* (1983); J. Russell Harper, *Painting in Canada* (1977).

Plastics-Processing Industry Plastics are based on giant molecules (polymers) which have a structure so ordered that they can be shaped at elevated temperatures and pressures, ie, these long-chain polymers exhibit "plastic flow" when heated. They are often modified with other materials (eg, plasticizers, fillers, stabilizers) before being processed in the molten state. Certain "thermosetting" polymers are subject to irrevocable chemical changes (curing or cross-linking) so that once shaped they are infusible. The "thermoplastic" types (notably polyethylene, polyvinyl chloride, polypropylene, polystyrene) can be recycled because they do not lose their ability to flow when remelted.

The forming of plastics into film, pipe, bottles and a myriad of molded shapes is estimated to involve well over 60 000 people in Canada. Shipments by plastic fabricators totalled $5 billion in 1981. Some of the major processors include Leco Inc, Toronto; Union Carbide Canada Ltd, Toronto; Grandview Industries Ltd, Toronto; Canadian General-Tower Ltd, Cambridge, Ont; Tarxien Co Ltd, Ajax, Ont; and Plastomer Inc, Barrie, Ont. This manufacturing activity has defied easy classification because the output (from bathtubs to wire and cable insulation) is more often than not an integral part of another industrial operation. Where the plastic part is a component of a larger assembly (eg, automobiles, TV sets), the same blurring of industrial categories occurs. Many producers of durable goods operate plastics-processing equipment on their own premises. In contrast to the manufacture of the resins, usually undertaken by multinationals strong in polymer technology, the fabricating of plastics products is often guided by entrepreneurs. The most successful of these are generally members of the Society of Plastics Engineers (SPE) and the Society of Plastics Industry (SPI).

The equipment, whether the property of the approximately 1800 independent establishments or "captive" to a particular assembly line, has increased in sophistication and size over the last century. In 1881 a Toronto cabinetmaker began laminating cellulose nitrate (ie, celluloid) sheet onto piano and organ keyboards. The advent of phenolformaldehyde polymers in 1909-1910 (products in which Lawrence Redmond, a chemist born in Petrolia, Ont, had a pioneering role) paved the way for compression-molding presses.

Not until thermoplastic cellulose acetate, initially a material employed for coatings and fibres, was recognized as an exellent molding compound, did processors accept the injection-molding machine. The injection system entails melting the polymer and forcing the molten material under high pressure into closed-mold cavities. In 1931 French Ivory Products of Toronto, making cellulose acetate caps for toothpaste tubes, operated the first injection-molding machine in N America. The molding of cellulosics had limited application but, in the next 30 years, processors learned to work with new materials: nylon, polyvinylchloride, polystyrene, polyethylene and polypropylene came out of the laboratory before 1960. Today a mold is designed to exploit the particular properties of a wide range of thermoplastics. Cost is of major importance; therefore, most injection-molded products are formed from so-called "commodity" resins, ie, those polymerized from relatively low-priced PETROCHEMICALS (eg, ethylene, styrene, propylene, vinyl chloride). For certain high-performance parts requiring toughness, special electrical properties, or resistance to elevated temperatures or similar "hostile" environments, the molder is likely to choose one of several engineering resins (eg, nylon, polyphenylene oxide, polycarbonate, acetals, terephthalates).

Polyethylene is the most ubiquitous of thermoplastics; in 1981 Canadian consumption of the various grades exceeded 496 000 t. Polyethylene is popular because it can be extruded through a shaping die to form a thin film. Film products such as milk pouches, bread bags, grocery sacks and garbage bags have transformed the flexible packaging industry. Vinyl films have a place in meat packaging and household wraps; polypropylene film is displacing paper and cellulose film for many types of overwraps.

The weathering characteristics of polyvinyl chloride have made it a popular material for other extrusions as well. Vinyl pipe is gaining ascendancy over metal, asbestos, clay and concrete for water and sewer lines, electrical conduits and ducts. Vinyl competes with aluminum and wood for house siding. Vinyl extruded "profiles" make excellent sashes and thermal breaks for windows. Other plastics vie for a part of the pipe market. Most homes are now equipped with drain, waste and vent pipes extruded from a styrenic compound. Industrial effluent pipe is normally extruded from polyethylene. Farmland is often reclaimed with the help of polyethylene (or polypropylene) corrugated drain tubing.

Either extrusion or injection molding is a necessary step in another plastics process, in which a parison (round hollow tube) is formed for subsequent blow molding. The parison is put between 2 halves of a mold and expanded with air pressure into a blown part. Bottles, drums and other hollow containers are made quite economically by this process. Polyethylene bottles are favoured for packaging detergents, bleaches and a wide range of other products. Vinyl bottles most often hold hair shampoos. *See* CHEMICAL INDUSTRIES.   CHARLES LAW

Plate Tectonics is the theory describing motions of Earth's crust and part of the underlying mantle. It states that large fractures divide the Earth's brittle surface layer into a few large and many smaller rigid plates, and that forces in the hot, deformable interior very slowly move these plates about relative to one another. These movements are considered the principal cause of geological change. Over GEOLOGICAL HISTORY they have opened and closed OCEAN basins, raised MOUNTAINS, facilitated accumulation of MINERAL and petroleum deposits, and influenced EVOLUTION and CLIMATE CHANGE. Friction between plates prevents steady motion and stores energy that is intermittently released in sudden movements, causing EARTHQUAKES. Most VOLCANOES erupt close to plate boundaries.

Past Theories Early scientists assumed that the Earth's major features were fixed. The discovery of the Americas showed that the opposite coasts of the Atlantic or, more precisely, the edges of the continental shelves have similar shapes and seem once to have fitted together. At that time the Earth was believed to be only about 6000 years old; therefore, it was thought that any separation must have occurred as the result of cataclysmic events at the time of creation.

During the 19th century, geologists argued that to provide time for the great thicknesses of SEDIMENTARY ROCK to have accumulated, the Earth must be older than 6000 years, perhaps hundreds of millions of years old. Conversely, physicists argued that the Earth was losing heat to space and that, since no adequate sources of internal energy were known, it must be cooling. They pointed out that, even if the Earth had been red-hot when formed, it would have cooled to its present temperature in a few tens of millions of years at most. They also held that the ensuing contraction would have squeezed the surface and uplifted mountains. In 1896 the discovery of radioactivity led to the realization that radioactive elements are widespread in common rocks and provide a heat source for the Earth. It also permitted development of methods to determine the Earth's age (about 4.6 billion years). In 1908 American geologist Frank B. Taylor proposed that the continents are slowly moving about and that their collisions give rise to mountains. Almost immediately Alfred Wegener, a German meteorologist, proposed that 200 million years ago a single supercontinent, Pangea, had broken apart and that since then the continents had been moving separately through the ocean floors like ships. Opponents rightly objected that he had not provided a cause or enough supporting evidence. At a large conference held in 1926, authorities strongly rejected Wegener's ideas. A few supporters held out in areas where evidence for drift was strongest, eg, the Alps and South Africa. In the latter, A.L. du Toit proposed that Pangea had broken into Gondwanaland in the S and Laurasia in the N before fragmenting into the existing continents.

Plate tectonics is a modified version of the theory of continental drift. The essential difference is that the latter theory assumed that each continent was propelled separately through stationary ocean floors. According to plate tectonics, continents do not form individual plates but are incorporated with sections of ocean floor in larger, moving plates constituting the surface of the Earth.

Seismology and Earth's Interior In the early 20th century too little was known about the ocean floors and the planet's interior to allow the development of any clear idea of how the Earth behaved. Nothing has done more to increase knowledge about and understanding of the planet than the study of seismology (*see* GEOLOGY). Earthquakes were familiar but little understood until, in the late 19th century, the Emperor of Japan invited John Milne from England to study them. Milne and his contemporaries produced the first satisfactory seismographs, the first worldwide network for reporting earthquakes and a theory to explain earthquake waves. Seismographic studies revealed the general pattern of the Earth's internal structure. Visualized as a boiled egg, Earth's shell is a cool, brittle crust of the visible rocks; the white, a far thicker mantle of denser rocks, white-hot and deformable, but solid; the yolk, a core rich in liquid iron. The existence of a readily deformable layer at a depth of a few tens of kilometres beneath the surface is well illustrated by the depression of north-central N America beneath the load of GLACIERS during the recent ICE AGES and the uplift of the land since the ice sheets melted (*see* GLACIATION). This uplift has left beaches raised by hundreds of metres around the shores of the Great Lakes and Hudson Bay. If the surface can move up and down through hundreds of metres, the interior must be deformable and it follows that, if the surface layer is ruptured, the pieces may be able to move horizontally as well. Improvement in recording of earthquakes enabled the French Rothés, father and son, and the Americans B. Gutenberg and C.F. Richter to show that most earthquakes closely follow the principal mountains and island areas around the Pacific Ocean and the Himalayan and Alpine ranges across Eurasia.

Ocean Floors The collection of information about the ocean floors began in the mid-19th century, when Commodore M.F. Maury, US Navy, made soundings across the Atlantic Ocean. These soundings revealed that the central part is much shallower than the rest. The CHALLENGER EXPEDITION (1872-76) showed this centre to be part of a great ridge along the axis of the ocean. Later expeditions found shallow mid-ocean areas in other oceans and located deep trenches off some continental coasts and on the convex side of island arcs. In the 1920s the Canadian geologist R.A. Daly advocated a mobile Earth and in 1930, in England, A. Holmes suggested that radioactive heating causes convection currents to rise within the Earth beneath the mid-ocean ridges, uplifting them and spreading out in either direction to descend beneath mountain ranges. Unfortunately, until instruments were developed to permit detailed study, too little firm evidence was available at that time to permit acceptance of these ideas.

Starting with the echo sounder in the 1930s, the period during and since WWII has seen rapid development of instruments for studying the ocean floors. In 1956 M. Ewing and B.C. Heezen of Columbia University, using data much of which they had collected, noticed that the axial belt of earthquakes coincided with the crest of known mid-ocean ridges. Observing the continuity of the earthquake belts, they speculated that the ridges were also continuous. By 1960 they had proved this. They also established the existence of the Earth's greatest mountain system, winding its way for 60 000 km down the axis of the Atlantic Ocean, around South Africa to the middle of the Indian Ocean, whence one branch follows the Gulf of Aden into the Red Sea and another passes S of Australia and New Zealand to cross the Pacific and join the San Andreas Fault at the head of the Gulf of California. The ridge rises to form islands such as Iceland, the Azores and Easter I.

Great Faults Californian oceanographers observed that the crest of the ridge was offset, as much as hundreds of kilometres, by fracture zones which resembled faults, but appeared to end abruptly. Similar, smaller fractures were soon found in other ridges, notably in the equatorial Atlantic. These mysterious submarine features added fuel to arguments about huge faults recognized on land, eg, in 1924 by C.H. Stockwell alongside Great Slave Lk. In 1946 geologists in Scotland and New Zealand proposed that huge faults with offsets over 100 km crossed those countries, beginning and ending in the sea. In 1953 California geologists proposed an even greater offset along the San Andreas Fault which began in the Gulf of California and ended in the Pacific off Cape Mendocino. These discoveries posed a problem for believers in a rigid Earth, because they could not explain such large offsets or how such large faults could be terminated.

Rock Magnetism That some pieces of rock, usually of an iron ore (magnetite), are naturally magnetized was known to the ancients and led to the invention of the mariner's compass. Early in this century it was shown that many rocks are weakly magnetized and retain their direction of magnetism permanently. It was supposed that they had acquired direction when formed, but the first investigations proved puzzling and only slowly were 3 causes of irregularity discovered. First, the North GEOMAGNETIC POLE has moved a few hundred kilometres across northern Canada since it was discovered 150 years ago. It is now agreed that the magnetic poles and field are slowly moving about the geographical poles of rotation. Thus, to determine the former latitude (relative to the geomagnetic pole) of any place, many measurements must be made upon a series of nearly contemporaneous lava flows or strata, and the average taken. Secondly, the Earth's magnetic field varies in strength and periodically dies away to zero, before starting up in the reverse direction. This results in a reversal of the poles so that the north pole becomes a south pole and vice versa. Fortunately, each reversal is complete and no intermediate positions occur. Reversals occur at irregular intervals varying from a few thousand to millions of years; many reversals have been dated. Third, some rocks have been altered or do not hold their original magnetization; these produce irregular results.

Development of Plate Tectonic Theory By the mid-1950s these problems were understood and reliable magnetic directions were available from rocks of different ages from different parts of the world. These data revealed a fourth cause for changes in the direction of magnetization in rocks. At a symposium held in Tasmania in 1956, it was established that on any continent the apparent magnetic latitude changes systematically with increasing age of the rocks. This al-

teration strongly suggested that steady continental motions had occurred and that these motions agreed with the evidence from geology and the fit of the continents across the Atlantic. The symposium inaugurated a change of opinion which, over the next 2 decades, converted most earth scientists to a belief in continental movement, although a precise mechanism had still to be found. In 1960 H.H. Hess elaborated on Holmes's idea of convection currents. He suggested that such a current is rising beneath the mid-ocean ridge crossing the Pacific Ocean, and that it splits the crest apart creating fresh ocean floor, while the ocean floors on either side are carried away to sink beneath the mountain and island areas along the Pacific coasts. In 1963 Canadians L.W. Morley and A. Larochelle first showed that long lines of magnetic anomalies in the Atlantic form parallel stripes situated symmetrically along both sides of the ridge crests. They realized that the magnetic stripes were caused by the natural reversals in the Earth's magnetic field. Their ideas seemed so strange that 2 reputable journals rejected their paper; however, later that year, Englishmen F. Vine and D.H. Matthews made similar observations in the Indian Ocean which they also interpreted as the result of reversals in the Earth's field.

Their paper was ignored until, 2 years later, a plot of earthquake locations was superimposed on a magnetic map of the N American Pacific coast which R.G. Mason of England had made. This superimposition showed that linear magnetic anomalies could be interpreted to show the existence of 3 small, spreading ridges off BC, forming an extension to the main mid-ocean ridge system and connected to it by the San Andreas Fault. Hence, the spreading of the ridge system controls motions on the faults. When Vine saw the results, he pointed out that the time scale of reversals established in California could be used to date reversals on the ocean floor off BC. Hence, the date of commencement and the rate of spreading of the ridges off BC had been established. The behaviour of these ridges also determined the date of the start of motion and the rate and direction of movement in the San Andreas Fault with which the ridges connect off Cape Mendocino, Calif.

This result was quickly accepted and applied by Vine and scientists at Columbia University and in California to interpret magnetic anomalies and date the ocean floors. The oldest part is near the Mariana Arc in the western Pacific where the floor is a little under 200 million years old. Clearly, the oceans are being constantly renewed. In contrast, the continents contain small areas of rocks as much as 3800 million years old. This discovery also led to an explanation of the behaviour of great faults and their relation to spreading ridges. For example, in the equatorial Atlantic, the mid-ocean ridge does not follow the same curved shape as the adjacent coasts of Brazil and Africa, but is broken into a series of steps. It seems that, as soon as continents separate, the ridge breaks up into alternating segments of 2 kinds. Spreading segments form at right angles to the direction of separation of the continents and new lava flows up along them. They are joined by shearing segments (ie, transform faults) parallel to the motion of the continents.

When these large faults were first discovered, it was assumed that they would extend for great distances, but actually they stopped abruptly. In 1965 J. Tuzo WILSON pointed out that, because of the formation of new crust, the surface area of the Earth in such localities is increasing; hence, the laws of ordinary geometry cease to apply and faults are of a special type called transform. These faults extend, are active and produce earthquakes only between spreading segments; they stop abruptly at either end. The direction of

motion on transform faults is the reverse of that in faults occurring in regions of unchanging surface area. These discoveries showed that Earth's surface is divided into rigid segments, changing shape only at boundaries; hence, the name "plate tectonics" was coined. Evidence from magnetism, seafloor spreading and faulting has made it difficult not to accept the theory.

Because the Earth is not believed to be changing appreciably in size, the spreading of the mid-ocean ridges with its accompanying growth of new ocean floors must be balanced by a return somewhere of older crust into the interior. This occurs especially off the coasts surrounding the Pacific Ocean, where the ocean plates are bent down beneath the overriding continental plates producing deep trenches — except where rapid sedimentation from adjacent coasts fill the trenches. K. Wadati and H. Benioff showed that most of the world's large earthquakes occur beneath circum-Pacific island arcs and mountains. The patterns traced by the foci of numerous earthquakes form parts of vertical cones that reach the surface in the trenches and extend to depths of 700 km. They mark the zones of contact between the overlapping plates. The disturbance caused by the sinking plates produces melting and lava rises to form the arcs of volcanic islands.

F.C. Frank explained the conical zones and circular surface trenches and arcs by pointing out that, if part of the surface of a sphere is pushed inwards, the depression tends to be circular (as when one pinches a soft tennis ball). This theory holds in East Asia where the crustal layer forming the Pacific plate is advancing over the underlying mantle and sinking under the continental Eurasian plate, which is stagnant relative to the interior. The theory fails where S America is advancing over the interior and over the stationary Nazca plate, which is not free to move but is forced down following the outline of the continental coast. The trenches follow the coast and the zone of deeper earthquakes is irregular.

Continents are less dense than ocean floors and, like a granitic scum, cannot readily be overridden. Where 2 continental blocks (eg, India and the rest of Eurasia) have met, closing a former ocean that lay between them, the collision piles up mountains and plateaus. It appears that, from time to time, such collisions halt or change the direction and motion of plates.

Present System of Plates The surface of the Earth is now broken into 6 or 7 major plates: the African, Antarctic and Eurasian plates each contain one continent; the Pacific plate none; the Indian and American plates 2 each, but some separate the N and S American plates. There are many smaller plates. All plates grow by the formation of new oceanic crust along mid-ocean ridges. They slide past one another along transform faults and they overlap and absorb crust beneath island areas and growing mountains. The pattern is slowly, but ceaselessly, changing. Most changes are gradual, but occasional reorganization takes place. No parts of the Atlantic or Indian oceans are more than 180 million years old; the Red Sea and Gulf of Aden are about 10 million years old; the East African rift valleys are younger still and are only beginning to open. This progression of age and width suggests a cycle of growth in oceans but, since the Earth is most unlikely to be expanding, it must be complemented by a progression of shrinking oceans. Coasts of Pacific Ocean and Mediterranean Sea are overriding their respective basins and, in the Himalayan region, India has closed the Tethys Sea and collided with the rest of Eurasia. These reductions represent the later stages of what K. Burke and W. Kidd have called the Wilson cycle of ocean history.

In 1930 H. Cloos drew attention to the associations of faults, earthquakes and volcanoes along the Rhine and East African rift valleys. Volcanism and domal uplift are greatest at triple points, eg, in Ethiopia where the Red Sea, Gulf of Aden and rift valleys meet, and at Sinai where the Red Sea and gulfs of Aden and Aqaba meet. The Red Sea appears to join these 2 places. In Africa there are many domed uplifts with volcanoes, called hot-spots, and the rift valleys appear to join some of them. This fact suggests that oceans start to form where rifts have connected a succession of volcanic hot-spots (or uplifts) and that these fractures spread to form widening oceans. Hot-spots form on continents and in oceans. Some, like the islands of Hawaii, are isolated, as are some on continents; others, like Iceland, the Azores, St Paul Rocks and Tristan da Cunha, lie along mid-ocean ridges. Both types have associated trails of extinct and progressively aging volcanic islands or submarine ridges: in the first case, a single trail; in the second, a double trail, which, in the case of Tristan, forms the Walvis and Rio Grande ridges. At the shoreward ends of these 2 ridges, volcanic rocks 130 million years old crop out on the coasts of Africa and S America. This evidence supports the views that, at that date, a single volcanic hot-spot formed in Gondwanaland, linked by rift valleys to other hot-spots. These hot-spots and rifts, which determined where the Atlantic Ocean would form, have remained active. Hot-spots may represent the tops of columns of heated rock rising through the mantle to carry off the Earth's surplus heat.

Earlier Cycles of Ocean and Mountain Building The present oceans mark only the last part of a cycle that began when Pangea broke apart; however, there is no marked change in the types of rocks observed before and after that 200-million-year-old event, although the Earth's age is great and radioactive heating continuous. Thus, it is likely that the supercontinent of Pangea existed only briefly, and that oceans had opened and closed in many places and at many times earlier. Paleomagnetism and geology indicate that this has been happening regularly since near the start of Proterozoic time (2500 million years ago). Rocks older than that, from Archean time, are different; therefore, the Earth's behaviour must have been different.

The Himalayan and Ural mountains are thought to be uplifts formed where continents collided. If the 2 sides of the Atlantic are reassembled, it is evident that the Scandinavian, Scottish, Appalachian and Moroccan mountains once formed part of a single chain which came together to close a proto-Atlantic 400 million years ago, then, 200 million years later broke up to help form the present Atlantic. In that case, it may be that not hot-spots but the concentration of radioactive elements in the mountain belts caused the oceans to form.

Consequences of Tectonic Movement The evidence that continents have often collided and separated has provided an explanation for the transfer of living forms that evolved on one continent to another continent, and shows that all continents are in effect mosaics of many fragments. The movement of continents has also affected climates and caused periodic ice ages. In some configurations of continents, ocean currents flow between the warm equatorial regions and the cold polar regions, distributing heat and giving rise to equitable climates. If one continent becomes isolated, with currents flowing around and not towards it (eg, modern Antarctica), that continent loses much heat, the world's climates are uneven and an ice age results.

Vast deposits of copper ores have been worked on Cyprus for thousands of years and the surrounding rocks have recently been shown to be typical of those formed on ocean floors. Beginning in 1977, great hot springs or jets of ex-tremely hot water rich in minerals were observed along the crests of some spreading mid-ocean ridges. These jets are surrounded by mineral deposits, which they precipitated on emerging. It is now believed that many ore deposits were formed in the oceans and later uplifted, and that these juvenile waters from the interior are a major factor in creating ore bodies and in modifying ocean GEOCHEMISTRY (*see* OCEAN MINING).
J. TUZO WILSON

Reading: J. Tuzo Wilson, *Continents Adrift and Continents Aground* (1976).

Platinum (Pt), heavy, greyish white metallic element that melts at 1769°C. It occurs with the other platinum group metals: palladium, iridium, rhodium, osmium and ruthenium. Platinum does not easily enter into chemical combination with other elements and is soluble only in hot aqua regia (mixture of nitric and hydrochloric acids). The usual natural form is native platinum, in which platinum is alloyed with small amounts of other platinum metals, appreciable amounts of iron and, often, copper, nickel or silver. It is usually found in small grains and scales, and occasionally in irregular masses and large nuggets. Initially platinum was recovered from placer deposits, but it has become possible to recover it from platinum-bearing ultrabasic rocks. Platinum is a rare, precious metal, valued at up to $1000 per troy ounce. Modern knowledge of the metal dates from the 16th century when it was discovered in S America by Spaniards who named it *platina* ("little silver"). South Africa and the Soviet Union are the main suppliers, with Canada 3rd, producing about 6% of world supplies in 1981 — most of it drawn from masses of nickel-copper ores from the Sudbury Basin. Platinum is intrinsically valuable and is used in jewellery, but its greatest use is in catalytic converters controlling emissions from automobile exhausts and in rhenium catalysts used to break down crude oil. Platinum's inertness makes it the choice metal for pacemaker electrodes placed in the human heart. Much of the world's platinum is hoarded in bank vaults.

Palladium, lightest of platinum-group metals, has the lowest melting point of the group (1552°C). Palladium is more reactive chemically than other platinum metals and is, therefore, known in more compound mineral forms than any other platinum-group metal. In the nickel-copper ore bodies of the Sudbury Basin, palladium forms about 45% of the platinum-group metals. In the USSR it forms about 65% and in the Merensky Reef of South Africa about 26%. Palladium is used as a component in brazing alloys. It gives colour and hardness to white gold used in jewellery. Palladium and palladium-rich alloys are widely used for electrical contacts, especially those that must operate at small contacts and low voltages, eg, telephone switching relays.
S.A. HAMILTON

Plaunt, Alan Butterworth, organizer, broadcaster, journalist (b at Ottawa 25 Mar 1904; d there 12 Sept 1941). Born of a wealthy lumbering family, he devoted his life to national unity, public broadcasting, economic reform and pacifism. As cofounder in the 1930s, with Graham SPRY, of the Canadian Radio League, Plaunt was instrumental in mobilizing popular and political support for public broadcasting. He was a leading force in the league until his appointment to the original board of governors of the CBC (1936-40). A member of the LEAGUE FOR SOCIAL RECONSTRUCTION (1933), he helped draft the Regina Manifesto. He founded the New Canada Movement in 1933 and, as coproprietor with Spry of the *Farmers' Sun* (1932-35), used the paper to advance the movement's causes, namely a "new deal" for rural peoples. In the late 1930s he helped organize the Neutrality League to promote pacifism and political neutrality for Canada.
ROBERT E. BABE

Plaut, W. Gunther, rabbi, author (b at Münster, Germany 1 Nov 1912). He left Germany, where he was raised and educated, to escape the Nazis. Immigrating to the US, he studied to become a Reform rabbi at the Hebrew Union College in Cincinnati, Ohio. He was Jewish chaplain in the American forces 1943-46, and has held reform pulpits at Chicago (1939-48), St Paul, Minn (1948-61) and Toronto's Holy Blossom Temple (1961-77) where he became senior scholar in residence in 1978. His most important scholarly works include *The Rise of Reform Judaism* (1965) and *The Torah: A Modern Commentary* (1981); the latter, a 17-year project, supports the school of modern biblical scholarship. Hence, he has parted company with traditional Talmudists, placing himself firmly within the secular Jewish camp. He has published one collection of short stories, *Hanging Threads* (1978). Rabbi Plaut writes a weekly column for the *Canadian Jewish News* and writes frequently for the *Globe and Mail*. Although many orthodox Jews do not accept his religious views, he has still managed to earn himself the position of chief spokesman of the Canadian Jewish community. *See* JUDAISM.
SHARON DRACHE

Playing-Card Money, government notes made of playing cards, first circulated in NEW FRANCE in 1685 when ships failed to arrive at Québec with coin. They became legal tender and after 1700 were redeemed in set amounts annually for bills of exchange on the treasury. They were abolished in 1720 following France's state bankruptcy but re-established in 1730. The quantity of these new cards issued was strictly limited, and they were therefore less a factor in inflation during wartime than was the uncontrolled issue of other fiduciary paper (orders, receipts, bills of exchange) which was lent respectability by the success of cards.
DALE MIQUELON

Plessis, Joseph-Octave, archbishop of Québec (b at Montréal 3 Mar 1763; d at Québec City 4 Dec 1825). After his ordination in 1786, Plessis served as secretary to 3 bishops and as parish priest at Québec. Chosen coadjutor in 1797, he became bishop in 1806, and in 1819 was named first archbishop of Québec by Rome though never recognized as such by the British government. A small, corpulent man, Plessis was ambitious, methodical and a realist with a flair for diplomacy. He co-operated with the British colonial authorities in civil matters while resisting their efforts to weaken and dominate the church. He urged Canadians to support the British during the War of 1812, and in 1817 he was appointed to the Legislative Council of Lower Canada. He opposed a plan for state-controlled education but encouraged the establishment of Catholic primary education in the parishes. Plessis maintained the church's position in the struggle for the social leadership of Lower Canada between the British colonial government and a rising Canadian bourgeoisie. Though his clergy were too few to meet all the pastoral needs in the parishes, Plessis deliberately channelled a significant number of young ecclesiastics into classical and clerical education, a policy which eventually halted the persistent decline in clerical recruitment. Largely through Plessis's efforts, the Roman Catholic diocese of Québec, then including all the BNA colonies except Newfoundland, was divided into a number of administrative units, the basis of today's diocesan organization.
JAMES H. LAMBERT

Pleure pas, Germaine (1965), by Claude Jasmin, one of the most accessible and poetic contributions to "the joual debate" in the French Canadian novel, narrates the journey of Gilles Bédard and his family from Montréal to Gaspé. Escaping from drink and debt, hunting the rapist who killed his daughter, and visiting his wife's parents, Gilles is caught between the desire for revenge and his innate capacity for love. He is freed by a case of mistaken identity in a dénouement that blends New Testament imagery with political engagement. Reflecting Gilles's point of view, the narrative is structured around the names of rest-stops on the journey of discovery, using JOUAL to communicate the complex predicament of a simple man. The title, a line from Roger LEMELIN's *Au Pied de la pente douce* (1944), situates the novel against earlier experiments with joual. MICHÈLE LACOMBE

Plouffe, Les (1948), a novel by Roger LEMELIN in which the author's expansive comic gift offers an insider's view of Québec's working-class Lower Town district. Spanning WWII, the saga of the Plouffe family presents unforgettable characters within a social-realist tradition — the sensitive Ovide, wavering between religion and romance; the prankish Guillaume, a local sports hero; Cécile, a sour spinster; and many others. The imbroglios of Ovide's ambitious journalist friend Denis Boucher, the protagonist of Lemelin's first novel, lead to trouble for all in a community faced with censorship, conscription and militant Catholic trade unions. Populated by streetcar conductors, newspaper typographers, meddlesome priests and nosy neighbours, Lemelin's fiction gently satirizes and celebrates a blend of American and Catholic influences in local popular culture. Translated by Mary Finch as *The Plouffe Family* (1950), the story was made into French and English CBC television series in the 1950s and a film by Gilles CARLE in 1980. MICHÈLE LACOMBE

Plover, common name for family (Charadriidae) of SHOREBIRDS with 2 subfamilies: Charadriinae, including true plovers and surfbirds; and Vanellinae, including lapwings. Of the 63 species occurring worldwide, 10 are found in Canada. These include the northern lapwing (*Vanellus vanellus*), an occasional visitor to eastern Canada. Killdeer, semipalmated, black-bellied and lesser golden plovers (*Charadrius vociferus, C. semipalmatus, Pluvialis squatarola, P. dominica*, respectively) are the most widely distributed species in Canada. Common ringed plovers (*C. hiaticula*) breed in NE arctic Canada; piping plovers (*C. melodus*) from SE central Alberta to Manitoba, in the Maritimes and, until recently, Ontario; and mountain plovers (*C. montanus*) in SE Alberta and probably SW Saskatchewan. Plovers have plump bodies, short necks and short bills, which are expanded near the tip. Although none are brightly coloured, many have strongly marked plumage patterns of black, white and brown that are conspicuous in flight. Because invertebrate prey are located visually, plovers have relatively large eyes and good eyesight. True plovers are characterized by tapering wings. Many species have one or more breast bands; most have melodious calls. Lapwings are much larger than true plovers and are recognizable by their broad, rounded wings. Some have feather crests or wattles of skin on the face and spurs on the wings, features that are important in courtship displays and territory defence. Most plovers are gregarious outside the breeding season, gathering in flocks of several hundreds to thousands. They fly strongly and migrate from coastal, winter feeding areas on bays and estuaries, N to breeding sites in remote arctic regions. Nests are a shallow scrape in the ground with little or no lining. Usually 4 eggs are laid (range 2-4). Chicks are down-covered on hatching and leave the nest soon after they are dry. Normally, parents share incubation (21-30 days) and guarding of chicks. All plovers use elaborate distraction displays, such as the "broken wing" display, to lure predators away from eggs or young. A.J. BAKER

Plum, common name for certain members of genus *Prunus* of the ROSE family, which produce a smooth-skinned, elliptical, heart-shaped, oblong, ovate or round FRUIT with a flat seed. About 18 plum species are horticulturally important, including the European plum (*P. domestica*), which probably originated in the Caspian Sea area; Japanese plum (*P. salicina*), of Chinese origin; cherry plum (*P. ceracifera*), native to SE Europe or SW Asia; and *P. nigra* and *P. americana*, of Canadian and American origin respectively. In N America, plum growing began towards the end of the 18th century. European plums were first brought to the Maritimes by French colonists; Japanese plums were introduced to N America around 1870; and domestication of native species began around 1850. European and Japanese plums are hardy only in milder areas of Canada and are grown commercially in BC, Ontario and NS. The native species lack size and quality but hardy hybrids have been developed that have excellent fruit quality and are relatively winter hardy. Most plums produced in Canada are for the fresh market. The main varieties are Bluefre, Bradshaw, Burbank, Early Golden, Italian, Peach, Shiro and Stanley. Common INSECT PESTS are red mite, curculio, scale, aphid, maggot and lesser peach tree borer. The main diseases are brown rot, black knot and leaf spot. In 1980, 9492 t of plums and prunes were produced in Canada, with a farm value of $3.6 million. G. TEHRANI

Plummer, Arthur Christopher Orme, actor (b at Toronto 13 Dec 1929), great-grandson of PM Sir John ABBOTT. He apprenticed with the Montréal Repertory Theatre and made his professional debut in 1948 with Ottawa's Stage Society, performing over 100 roles with its successor, the Canadian Repertory Theatre. Performances in Bermuda led to a US tour of *Nina* (1953) and Broadway recognition in *The Lark* (1955) and as Marc Antony in the American Shakespeare Festival's 1955 inaugural season. Other notable New York City engagements include the musical *Cyrano* (1973), for which he won a "Tony" Award, and Iago in *Othello* (1981). In 1961 he appeared at Stratford-upon-Avon, Eng, as Richard III while alternating in London as Henry II in *Becket*. At Canada's STRATFORD FESTIVAL he has played Henry V, Hamlet, Aguecheek, Mercutio, Leontes and Macbeth, as well as other roles. Among his many movies are *Stage Struck* (1957), *The Sound of Music* (1965), *Oedipus the King* (1967), *Waterloo* (1970), *The Man Who Would Be King* (1975), *The Silent Partner* (1978) and *Murder By Decree* (1979). His work on television includes *Little Moon of Alban* ("Emmy" nomination 1958), *Hamlet at Elsinore* (BBC 1965) and *Riel* (CBC 1979). DAVID GARDNER

Pocket Gopher (Geomyidae), family of medium-sized, solitary, nonhibernating, subterranean RODENTS. About 31 species occur in N and Central America, 2 in Canada. The northern pocket gopher (*Thomomys talpoides*) lives in southern Manitoba, Saskatchewan and Alberta, and in south-central BC. The larger plains pocket gopher (*Geomys bursarius*) barely extends into Canada via the Red River Valley, Man. Pocket gophers have a round body, small eyes, short ears and tail, and large, curved claws on the forefeet for digging. Their short fur is grey to brown and can lie in any direction. They carry food or nesting materials in fur-lined, external cheek pouches, which they empty with their forefeet. The mouth closes behind ever-growing, gnawing teeth, enabling the rodent to harvest underground vegetation and excavate networks of tunnels in prairies and mountain meadows without ingesting earth. The fan-shaped mounds they raise are burrow exits, and are usually closed with round, earthen plugs. Each year 1-2 litters of 2-11 young are raised in deep tunnels. Pocket gophers damage crops but also aerate soils and bring nutrients to the surface. J. MARY TAYLOR

Pocket Mouse, small, jumping RODENT of the N American family Heteromyidae. The 75 species of Heteromyidae are adapted to desert and semidesert environments. Three live in Canada: olive-backed and Great Basin pocket mice (*Perognathus fasciatus, P. parvus*, respectively) and Ord's KANGAROO RAT. Pocket mice occur in the dry western plains and the basin between the Rocky Mts and the BC coastal range. They are greyish above with white underparts. Pocket mice have large hindlimbs and smaller front limbs, all 4 used in jumping. The tail, almost as long as head and body together, serves as a prop, particularly when the animal feeds in its characteristic sitting position. Food is carried to the burrow in external, fur-lined cheek "pockets." Stored food enables pocket mice to survive winter, alternating between dormant and feeding periods. Insects and plants complement the primarily granivorous diet. Pocket mice can survive long periods without water and are nocturnal. Mating occurs in Apr; the gestation period is 3-4 weeks; 2 litters are produced, each averaging 4-5 young. The relatively scarce olive-backed pocket mouse, the smallest rodent in Canada, measures about 12.5 cm. Except for killing weeds, it has little economic value. The much larger and more common Great Basin pocket mouse causes considerable damage to cereal crops. JEAN FERRON

Podborski, Steve, alpine skier (b at Toronto 25 July 1957). On skis at age 2, he began racing at 10 and joined the Canadian alpine ski team in 1973. His international downhill racing performances as a key member of the "Crazy Canucks" improved steadily, despite a serious knee injury in 1976, up to his first World Cup win in 1979 (at Morzine, France). In 1980 his Olympic bronze medal in the downhill provided one of only 2 Canadian medals. In 1982 he won 3 consecutive World Cup downhills, skiing with extreme technical skill, particularly on the tough icy courses he preferred. His strength, skill and daring were particularly apparent in the 3rd victory, where his winning speed of 166 km/h was the fastest ever recorded at Kitzbühel, Austria. In 1982 he combined 3 more wins with consistent top placings to become the first non-European winner of the World Cup downhill championship title. During 10 years of international racing he won 8 World Cup races to become the most successful Canadian male skier to date. MURRAY SHAW

In 1982 skier Steve Podborski became the first non-European to win the World Cup downhill championship (*courtesy Canapress*).

Poetry in English Addressing the poets of the classical, European tradition in *Quebec Hill* (1797), J. MacKay asks: "Ye who, in stanzas, celebrate the Po,/Or teach the Tyber in your strains to flow,/How would you toil for numbers to proclaim/The liquid grandeur of St. Lawrence' Stream?" Besides pointing to a major concern of pre-Confederation poetry — the representation in European verse forms of the Canadian physical and social landscapes — MacKay's question anticipates similar concerns in much later Canadian poetry, suggesting the continuity that exists through poetry written in Canada from the earliest to the most recent times.

It is convenient to divide pre-Confederation poetry, somewhat arbitrarily, but justifiably, into two chronological categories: poetry written before 1825 and that written between 1825 and 1867. Before 1825 the verse written in what would become Canada (primarily in Lower Canada, Nova Scotia and New Brunswick) was largely dominated by neoclassical models. Among the major influences on the poetry of this period were the heroic couplets of English poets Alexander Pope and Oliver Goldsmith and the blank verse of James Thomson's *The Seasons* (1726-46), a poem with evident application to a land with Canada's seasonal variations. Whereas the relatively fluid and continuous form of blank verse seems to have been a fitting vehicle for such subjects as the sublime spectacle of Niagara Falls and the "liquid grandeur" of the St Lawrence, the rational order of the heroic couplet was a formalistic means by which the early poets affirmed and reflected a sense of governance in their environment and in themselves. After 1825 the influence of romanticism (which had been present in Canada earlier, just as neoclassicism would continue to be felt later) came increasingly to be evident in Canadian poetry. The result was that from the 1820s writers turned to such poets as Byron, Wordsworth, Shelley and Thomas Moore for their models. Frequently employed forms now were *ottava rima* (for satire), the Spenserian stanza (for framing picturesque scenes and momentary insights) and the sonnet. Also in evidence after 1825 were the romantic narrative and the "dramatic poem" (Adam Kidd, "Preface," *The Huron Chief and Other Poems*, 1830), genres that were appropriate to the depiction of emotionally and spiritually complex issues, conflicts and quests. By 1864 there was enough Canadian verse in various forms to enable Edward Hartley Dewart (although ignoring material from before 1825) to produce *Selections from Canadian Poets* (1864) — the first anthology of Canadian poetry in English and the only one before Confederation. The anthology's division into poems "Sacred and Reflective," "Descriptive and National" and "Miscellaneous" (a category that includes pieces entitled "Heroes," "Childhood," "Twilight," "Taapookaa — A Huron Legend," "Glimpses of Highland Superstitions" and "The Beech-Nut Gatherer") indicates the emphasis and content of pre-Confederation poetry.

Practically all the verse of this period was written by amateur poets, men and women who did not attempt to make their living as writers but wrote to occupy "a few leisure hours" (Thomas Cary, "Preface," *Abram's Plains*, 1789). Like Cary, these amateurs usually produced only one poem of note that they published in a newspaper, as a pamphlet or in a slim volume with "Other Poems." Yet the recreational products of these amateurs were not merely belletristic amusements written to beguile the time between sermons, mess dinners, harvests, household duties and other employments; the early poets aimed to describe the aesthetic and economic attractions of Canada, to chronicle the achievements of their colonial society, to warn their readers of life's moral pitfalls, and to express the spiritual and cultural aspirations of sensitive people in a new land. All these things are attempted in what is probably the most important treatment of pioneer life (in Nova Scotia) from the early period: *The Rising Village* by Oliver GOLDSMITH (grand-nephew of the Irish author of the more famous *The Deserted Village*, 1770). The publication history of *The Rising Village* — as a pamphlet in 1825 in England, in excerpts that year in *The Canadian Review* (Montréal) and finally "with Other Poems" in 1834 in Saint John — also runs the gamut of available possibilities. Throughout the pre-Confederation period there were poets such as Jacob Bailey, Charles HEAVYSEGE and Charles SANGSTER, whose poetic output would fill several substantial volumes and might have permitted them to make a living by writing poetry if the population had been larger.

As in the case of prose, the Maritimes — where many LOYALISTS had settled — were the centre of poetic activity prior to 1825. Long before the Loyalist influx, John Hayman had celebrated Newfoundland as a settlers' paradise in *Quodlibets* (1628); and in the pre-Loyalist period Henry ALLINE wrote his accomplished *Hymns and Spiritual Songs* (2 vols, 1782-86). With the Loyalists and their descendants such as Bailey (author of several Hudibrastic satires), Jonathan ODELL and Joseph Stansbury (whose *Loyal Verses* . . . appeared posthumously in 1860), Joseph HOWE and Goldsmith came the flowering of early pre-Confederation poetry. This took the form of a body of work that treats of both the present and future of the Maritimes and the present and past in the US.

Not all poetic activity before 1825 occurred in the Maritimes: in 1690 Henry KELSEY had written a versified description of the prairies and in 1825 James Lynn Alexander published a dramatic narrative, *The Wonders of the West*, centered on Niagara Falls. Between these years the poems of Cary, MacKay, John Hood Burwell (*Talbot Road*, 1818) and numerous others attest to the existence of poetic activity in what is now Québec and Ontario, as do 2 later poems by John RICHARDSON, *Tecumseh* (1828) and *Kensington Gardens* (1830).

An important node of activity around 1825 was Montréal, the home of several flourishing newspapers and periodicals (*see* LITERARY MAGAZINES). A number of poems and volumes were published there in the 1820s, including the suggestively similar Byronic imitations of Levi Adams (*Jean Baptiste*, 1825) and George Longmore (*The Charivari*, 1826), which remain interesting for their satire, depictions of life in Canada and poetic accomplishment. Adam Kidd's *The Huron Chief* is among the more adroit of the Montréal publications, but the work of William Hawley, Margaret Blennerhasset and Ariel Bowman will also repay the sympathetic reading (demanded by all pre-Confederation poetry) that is attentive to its combination of imported form and local subject. With the founding of the *Literary Garland* (1838-51), the longest-running pre-Confederation periodical, Montréal's position as a literary centre was consolidated. In the *Garland* appeared the work of such poets as Rosanna (Mullins) LEPROHON. And from Montréal publishers in the late 1830s and 1840s came such works as Standish O'GRADY's *The Emigrant* (1841), with its frank descriptions of the Canadian environment.

Although numerous volumes of interest, including the *Sonnets* (1855) and *Jephthah's Daughter* (1865) of Charles Heavysege and *Canadian Ballads* (1858) of Thomas D'Arcy MCGEE, were published in Montréal in the 1850s and 1860s, other centres, particularly Toronto in Canada West, were publishing their share of poetry. Charles Sangster, who had published *The St. Lawrence and the Saguenay and Other Poems* in New York in 1856, saw his *Hesperus* (1860) published in both Montréal and his native Kingston; Alexander MCLACHLAN had his works, including *The Emigrant and Other Poems* (1861), published in Toronto, and William KIRBY's *The U.E.: A Tale of Upper Canada* (1859) was printed in Niagara-on-the-Lake. The long, narrative poems of Heavysege, Sangster, McLachlan and Kirby have been subjected to closer critical scrutiny than most pre-Confederation poems, probably because the grandeur of their design does much to compensate for their unevenness of execution.

Several poetic productions of the pre-Confederation period did not appear in print until after 1867, when the natural self-examination of the new nation prompted the publication of Howe's *Poems and Ballads* (which included *Acadia*), Kirby's *Canadian Idylls* and Leprohon's *Poetical Works*, volumes belonging, in form and approach, to an earlier era. That era produced a quantity of poetry which, though only sporadically distinguished by real talent and too frequently characterized by acquiescent imitativeness, cannot be dismissed as devoid of interest for later readers or of significance for Canadian culture.

D.M.R. BENTLEY

Poetry in English, 1867-1918

The honour of publishing the first volume of verse in the newly confederated Canada belongs to Charles MAIR, whose *Dreamland and Other Poems* appeared in 1868. Negligible as verse, the volume gained interest when Mair escaped after being captured by Louis RIEL during the RED RIVER disturbances of 1869-70. His *Tecumseh: A Drama* followed in 1886, and although its blank verse is pedestrian and untheatrical, Mair's attempt to interpret Canadian subject matter in a traditionally heroic manner gives the play a certain power.

Far more promising, though notoriously uneven, is the work of Isabella Valancy CRAWFORD, whose *Old Spookses' Pass, Malcolm's Katie, and Other Poems* was published at her own expense in 1884. She lived a lonely, frustrated life in Peterborough and Toronto, with few literary contacts, but at its best her poetry is remarkable for presenting the Canadian landscapes with an almost Blakean visionary power, often containing diction and imagery derived (not altogether accurately) from Indian life and tradition. "Malcolm's Katie," a long and somewhat melodramatic narrative poem of love and deception set against a background of logging and pioneering, is remembered for passages of vivid scenic description, whereas shorter poems, especially "The Camp of Souls," "Said the Canoe" and "The Dark Stag" employ seasonal and elemental imagery with colourful intensity.

The "Confederation Poets," so called because they were born within a decade of Confederation, were in no way a cohesive group. They did, however, lay firm foundations for a tradition of Canadian poetry — a tradition, moreover, that attracted attention beyond the boundaries of Canada. Their early work was naturally imitative (following British and, to a lesser extent, American models), but they gradually developed a modestly distinctive native style. Charles G.D. ROBERTS, who later became well known for his animal stories, set an example with *Orion and Other Poems* (1880). This volume displays considerable technical skill; it concerns itself, however, with "alien matters in distant regions." His next book, *In Divers Tones* (1886), makes more conspicuous use of Canadian subjects, and contains the well-known "Tantramar Revisited," whereas *Songs of the Common Day* (1893) includes a series of descriptive sonnets that evoke the landscapes of his native New Brunswick. Unfortunately, his later poetry, written mainly in the US and Europe, only fitfully maintains the promise of his earlier work.

His cousin and fellow Maritimer, Bliss CARMAN, became known as much for his personality as for his poetry. He is the most lyrical of the group, and his more characteristic poems envelop a simple, romantic story or theme in a wealth of evocative, though vague, imagery. His collaboration with American poet Richard Hovey in *Songs from Vagabondia* (1894) and its sequels gave him a reputation for wandering Bohemianism. The title poem of his first volume, *Low Tide at Grand Pré* (1893), is probably his best.

The other members of the group were products of Ontario. Archibald LAMPMAN was inspired to devote himself to poetry after reading Roberts's *Orion*. He spent his short working life as a postal clerk in Ottawa, and his poems are for the most part close-packed melancholy meditations on natural objects, emphasizing the calm of country life in contrast to the restlessness of city living. Limited in range, they are nonetheless remarkable for descriptive precision and emotional restraint. Although characterized by a skillful control of rhythm and sound, they tend to display a sameness of thought. Best known are "Heat" from *Among the Millet* (1888) and the nightmarish "City of the End of Things" from *Alcyone* (1899).

Duncan Campbell SCOTT, who did much to popularize Lampman's poems after his early death, worked as a civil servant in the Dept of Indian Affairs and derived much of the inspiration for his poetry from official trips into northern Ontario. He communicates a vivid sense of the northern landscape, and in poems such as "The Onondaga Madonna" in *Labor and the Angel* (1898) and "The Forsaken" in *New World Lyrics* (1905) writes poignantly about the decline of the Indian way of life. "The Height of Land," in *Lundy's Lane* (1916), a meditation on human culture and the mystery of life in a symbolically appropriate setting, is a central poem which brings together Scott's major poetic and philosophical preoccupations. Also loosely · associated with the Confederation Poets was Wilfred Campbell, who proved most successful when writing about the "lake region" of western Ontario.

The generation of Canadian poets that began to publish at the turn of the century was more varied in approach but noticeably less distinguished. Pauline JOHNSON daughter of a Mohawk father and an English mother, achieved popularity as a poet and reciter; her poems about Indian life and legend possess a facile charm but little permanent value. William Henry DRUMMOND became extremely popular on the publication of *The Habitant and Other French-Canadian Poems* (1897), but the dialect he employed, though considered amusing in its time, now reads as unpleasantly condescending. Robert SERVICE aimed at verse rather than poetry, and celebrated the worlds of trapping, ranching and the KLONDIKE GOLD RUSH. Volumes such as *Songs of a Sourdough* (1907, containing "The Shooting of Dan McGrew," for which Service is best known) and *Rhymes of a Rolling Stone* (1912) were popular for their strong stories and emphatic rhythms. Francis Sherman and Marjorie Pickthall both wrote poems that combine technical competence with an eloquent lyricism but lack originality and depth. They are minor figures who could offer little more than a civilized conventionality. These poets failed to match the work of their immediate predecessors, and the achievement of the Confederation Poets remained unchallenged until the emergence of E.J. Pratt after WWI.　　　　　　　　　　　　　W.J. KEITH

Poetry in English, 1918-60

The first rather tentative experiments in 20th-century poetic technique began in 1914. The earliest evidence of this activity came from the pen of poet and popular novelist Arthur STRINGER, who that year presented his free-verse collection *Open Water*. A truly consistent expression of modernist principles did not occur, however, until a configuration of circumstance and career brought F.R. SCOTT, A.J.M SMITH and Leon Edel to McGill University. In 1925 Smith and his associates (who later included A.M. KLEIN and Leo KENNEDY) launched the *McGill Daily Literary Supplement* (1924-25; followed by the *McGill Fortnightly Review*, 1925-27), in which they published poems in the modern manner and articles on contemporary trends. At the same time the CANADIAN FORUM (est 1920 in Toronto), with a wider cultural focus, promoted debate on current art and the quality of Canadian criticism. It featured a series of articles and statements by young writers and critics comparing the old poetry with the new, thus claiming the attention of the informed reader and laying the groundwork for a vigorous Canadian criticism. Felix Walter, E.J. PRATT and Dorothy LIVESAY, to name a few, were part of this debate.

The early 1930s were not a good time for the new poetry. The GREAT DEPRESSION dampened creative activity in some poets and drove others into political action. The better-known, older and more conservative poets continued to publish, but the new movements, with the exception of Kennedy's *The Shrouding* (1933), were still not accepted. In 1936 the situation changed with the appearance of the first serious offering of the new poetry in a pioneer anthology called *New Provinces*. Its publication had been orchestrated — with difficulty — by Scott, who had assembled poems by Pratt and Robert Finch of Toronto with those of Smith, Kennedy, Klein and himself. A bold and forward-reaching introduction by Smith was set aside as too provocative, and was replaced by the moderate tones of Scott's tiny "Preface." The anthology sold very few copies. That year also, W.E. Collin, a professor of French at University of Western Ontario, published *The White Savannahs*, the first collection of criticism of contemporary poetry from the modernist point of view. It admirably complemented *New Provinces*. The modernist credo — rejecting past poetic practice, discarding the norms of punctuation, typographical conventions and traditional verse forms and cultivating new subject matter, which drew on the modern city with its variousness, its social ills, its machinery, its politics, its intellectual predisposition for the new in art, its ironies, tensions and structural complexities, and its new vocabulary — pointed in a fresh direction. But the gestures of 1936 were not exclusively modernist. That year the Canadian Authors' Association established *Canadian Poetry Magazine*, which soon became identified with a more traditional poetic line. The CAA, in which Pratt took a strong hand, stood adamantly for a more conventional approach to poetry.

When WWII broke out, Canadian poetry appeared to be firmly set in 2 camps, the modern and the traditional, although the conservative group was much more successful in reaching its audience and in finding publishers for its work. The war seemed to provide a new impetus for poetry, chiefly in the surge of activity involving little magazines, which had suffered during the economically troubled 1930s. In 1941 *Contemporary Verse*, a periodical of eclectic taste edited by Alan Crawley, began to publish in British Columbia. In Montréal in 1942 F.R. Scott joined forces with newly arrived Patrick Anderson to launch a group publication called *Preview* (1942-45), which was intended to keep the writing of a poetry workshop before its readers. Within a few months a newer generation of writers with a more realistic bent and a stronger political tone gave notice of itself in Montréal with a mimeographed little magazine called *First Statement* (1942-45). This group, headed by John SUTHERLAND, included Irving LAYTON and Louis DUDEK, and its poetry would be character-ized by stronger social concern and a more direct sense of urban experience. In *First Statement* were published articles and reviews on literature in which the issue of national identity in Canadian writing found voice. Out of this group and its periodical there developed a modest series of books published under the First Statement imprint and featuring the early work of Layton, Anderson, Raymond SOUSTER and Miriam WADDINGTON. The group also published the important anthology of this generation, *Other Canadians* (1947). The SMALL PRESS movement in Canada was truly established, and now helped to focus attention on, and to pull together, the work of solitary spirits who had been writing modernist poetry. Dorothy Livesay, Raymond Knister, R.G. EVERSON and W.W.E. Ross had made their mark as early as the 1920s and 1930s, but the real momentum for modern poetry would be supplied by the little magazines (*see* LITERARY MAGAZINES) and small presses, and the collective action that they were able to generate. *First Statement* did not function only as a vehicle for the work of a group of like-minded writers. It was as much a little magazine in the classical sense, an outlet for new critical thinking on Canadian writing and a centre for activity destined to supply the motive force for a little press. It would later provide the energy to fuel the pivotal little magazine *cum* LITERARY PERIODICAL, *Northern Review* (1945-56).

The years of WWII, when writers were traumatized by mass slaughter and the destruction of much that was prized by civilization, also witnessed an unusual burgeoning of Canadian poetry. In 1942 Ralph Gustafson scored an international coup with his *Anthology of Canadian Poetry*, which carried English Canadian poets to a large readership under the prestigious imprint of Penguin Books. Gustafson's selection included writing not only by poets who had by now become familiar (Scott, Klein, Smith, Kennedy, Pratt and Finch), but also by the relatively unknown Livesay, P.K. PAGE and Earle BIRNEY. In 1943 Gustafson was guest editor of No 113 of Harold Vinal's quarterly *Voices*, in which the new names to appear were Anderson, Layton and Souster. A "pattern of notice" had begun to develop, as a result of which modern Canadian poetry was being recognized in its own right through being featured in a number of significant international magazines. *Poetry: A Magazine of Verse* (Chicago) had featured a "Canadian Number" in Apr 1941. It bore the mark of the cautious taste of E.K. BROWN, who in 1936 had initiated the annual review of Canadian writing under the "Letters in Canada" section of UNIVERSITY OF TORONTO QUARTERLY; his selection for *Poetry* reached back to Duncan Campbell Scott and forward to Livesay, F.R. Scott, Finch, Kennedy and Anne Marriott. The issue also featured Brown's essay, "The Development of Poetry in Canada, 1880-1940," which foreshadowed in its scope and approach his important study, *On Canadian Poetry* (1943). This book complemented, almost as opportunely as *The White Savannahs* had done with *New Provinces* in 1936, the Canada-US publication of A.J.M. Smith's milestone anthology, *The Book of Canadian Poetry* (1943). Smith's book is distinguished by his high critical standards and by a controversial introduction that segregated the Canadian moderns into "The Native Tradition" and "The Cosmopolitan Tradition." Smith's classification anticipated a split in Canadian poetry which occurred in the second half of the 20th century between a poetry deriving from the large framework of ideas, structures and literary influences of Britain as the mother country, and a poetry written in the language of Canadians, based on an outlook and experience peculiar to this country, and showing a N American sensibility.

At the end of the war, *Preview* merged with *First Statement* to form NORTHERN REVIEW, under the editorship of John Sutherland. But the modernists soon began to draw apart. The critical quarrel between the "cosmopolitans" and the "natives" grew sharper. The late 1940s and early 1950s were grim years for Canadian poetry. Publishers other than The RYERSON PRESS were painfully modest in their efforts, nor were the poetry magazines doing much. FIDDLEHEAD was active in Fredericton, *Northern Review* and the *Canadian Forum* in central Canada, *Contemporary Verse* in Vancouver, while *Canadian Poetry Magazine* functioned nationally. But the mood was one of disillusionment, even of failure. It was as if the momentum of the war years had spent itself completely.

The renewal began in 1952 with the appearance of a new mimeographed poetry magazine, *Contact* (1952-54). It was the brainchild of Raymond Souster of Toronto, who had aligned himself during the 1940s with *First Statement;* he had served his own little-magazine apprenticeship by editing *Direction* (1943-46) from an RCAF base in the Maritimes, and by producing 6 issues of *Enterprise* in Toronto in 1948. Prompted by a desire to challenge the conservative drift that had become apparent in Sutherland's thinking, Souster, egged on and joined by Dudek and Layton, launched *Contact*. The new direction taken in Canada was similar to a shift towards the new poetry taking place in Europe and the US in the second half of the century. The 1950s also saw the emergence of the ideas of Marshall MCLUHAN, who coedited the magazine *Explorations* (1953-59), and the establishment of Northrop FRYE as a major critic and literary theorist.

Frye's work had a major effect on certain young Canadian poets. In 1949 *The Red Heart*, a collection of poems written by James REANEY, a student of Frye, won the Governor General's Award and marked the beginning of the "mythopoeic school" in Canadian poetry. This movement included others influenced by Frye, such as Jay MACPHERSON, Eli MANDEL, D.G. JONES and later Margaret ATWOOD.

Contemporaneously, and through the effort of *Contact*, there appeared Contact Press (1952-1967), which became an important publisher of Canadian poetry. Created in order to give young poets a chance to publish, despite seeming indifference on the part of commercial publishers, Contact Press produced the work of Dudek, Layton and Souster, and gave a start to many of the poets who went on to create the poetry of the 1960s and the 1970s. Atwood, George Bowering, Al Purdy, Alden Nowlan, Mandel and Phyllis Webb, Gwendolyn MacEwan, John Newlove, Frank Davey and Ron Everson all published under its imprint. The press also kept in touch, through the translations of Gael Turnbull and Jean Beaupré, with the contemporary poets of French Canada.

As the 1950s progressed the poetry scene began to change rapidly once again. In 1954 Fred COGSWELL began to publish a series of chapbooks called Fiddlehead Poetry Books, which featured Purdy and Nowlan, among others. In 1956 TAMARACK REVIEW was established by Robert Weaver. Dudek launched the McGill Poetry Series, in which the first books of Leonard COHEN and Daryl Hine appeared. Canadian poetry was becoming diverse, and with the help of a general popularization of the arts, poetry was on the verge of finding a broad audience. In this it was helped by the sudden popularity of coffeehouses, the marriage of jazz to poetry, the new vogue for public readings and the effects of McLuhan's message which confirmed the importance of the reading as a happening and supported the idea of the concrete in poetic self-expression. The poet had "gone public," and no one succeeded better at projecting a popular persona than Irving Layton, who boldly and outrageously carried poetry to its Canadian audience. In 1959 Layton, who had hammered at the insensitivity of the public and had been misunderstood and neglected by the critics, broke through with his collection *A Red Carpet for the Sun* to win the Governor General's Award. A new phase had begun.   MICHAEL GNAROWSKI

Poetry in English, 1960-1980s

A Red Carpet for the Sun marks both an end and a beginning: it established Layton as a major poet and marked the ascendancy of second-generation modernism in Canada. The Layton of *Red Carpet* is an interesting mixture: essentially traditional in form, yet popular in content and often aggressively colloquial in speech. The attitude to poetry he championed, along with his Contact Press colleagues Louis Dudek and Raymond Souster, triumphed in the years to come, but although he continued to publish voluminously his influence has proved slight beyond winning poets the right to use all aspects of language. The important advances or transformations in art tend to be formal, and Layton is essentially conservative in form. Far more important for the possibilities it presented, in Canada as well as in the US, was *The New American Poetry, 1945-1960*, edited by Donald Allen; it affected the writing of at least one generation of Canadian poets, bringing up to date the open forms promoted by William Carlos Williams after Ezra Pound. Here the contemporary N American voice clearly challenged the traditional British one; if, as some critics argue, Canadian poets only shifted from one colonial master to another, at least the accent now belonged to their own continent.

The early 1960s saw the emergence of many new poets. One of the most important was Al PURDY, an older poet who had been steadily learning his craft throughout the 1950s. With *Poems for All the Annettes* (1962) he achieved a unique personal voice which contained the lessons of modernism, yet was determinedly Canadian, even regional (central Ontario, United Empire Loyalist, mid-20th century). In *The Cariboo Horses*, which won the Governor General's Award in 1965, Purdy consolidated his poetic: here was a colloquial, quizzical, wide-ranging and engaging bumbler who somehow articulated the Canadian presence as never before. Although not as popular as Leonard Cohen, whose *The Spice Box of Earth* appeared in 1961, Purdy became a more important model to younger poets, for his laconic, open-ended, mytho-colloquial yarns suggested formal possibilities previously barely recognized in Canada.

Meanwhile, excellent young poets began to publish during the early 1960s: Margaret Atwood, John Robert COLOMBO, Gwendolyn MACEWEN and Joe ROSENBLATT in Toronto; George BOWERING, Frank DAVEY, Lionel Kearns, Daphne Marlatt, John NEWLOVE and Fred Wah on the West Coast; Alden NOWLAN on the East Coast. Atwood and MacEwen, the first of a growing number of fine female poets, neatly divided the literary terrain between them: the former was restrained, ironic and modernist; the latter exuberant, mythic, passionate and romantically postmodernist in sensibility. Bowering, Davey, Kearns, Marlatt and Wah were associated with the poetry newsletter *Tish* and with the new poetics championed in *The New American Poetry* by such writers as Robert Creeley, Robert Duncan, Denise Levertov, Charles Olson and Jack Spicer. The *Tish* group was more cohesive than most associations of writers. This had both advantages and disadvantages. The *Tish* poets gave each other support and criticism, but they also generated a certain paranoia: they felt they were ignored while poets in the rest of Canada felt ignored by them. These feelings did not dissipate until the mid-1970s.

It seems obvious, in retrospect, that what happened in Vancouver in the early 1960s has deeply influenced Canadian poetry. Although not part of the *Tish* group, writers as different as John Newlove, Gerry Gilbert and bill BISSETT were also writing there; bp NICHOL came from Vancouver, although he has done most of his writing in Toronto; Pat LANE came there with Barry McKinnon later in the decade; UBC began its creative-writing program; and a number of poets of different persuasions found positions at Simon Fraser. Vancouver became and remained a hotbed of poetic activity. Older poets, too, were excited by all this energy: Earle Birney's *Selected Poems 1940-1966* revealed, in its revisions and typography, how taken he was by the formal concepts of the New American poets, as did Dorothy Livesay's first new collection in over a decade, *The Unquiet Bed* (1967). In Edmonton, Eli Mandel, earlier identified with the "Frye school," won the Governor General's Award for *An Idiot Joy* (1967), a book announcing a new directness in his poetic speech that later books would push even further.

Some later critics argued that the lessons taught by Olson and the others were a form of American imperialism, but this was to miss the point. As Marlatt put it: what these poets taught about language and "composition by field" was "one of those crucial developments one has to come to terms with in some way. And to ignore it or try to divide it off as simply a regional American phenomenon" would be absurd. Moreover the charge that Canadian writing incorporating these lessons would somehow prove not fully Canadian was simply "ridiculous." Indeed, one of the basic tenets of the new poetics was that poetry must be rooted in the place of its imagining. Purdy taught the same lesson, for no matter how far he travelled, his language and perceptions were rooted in the harsh Loyalist "Country North of Belleville" to which he always returned.

Alongside the influence of "composition by field" poetics, such eastern US poets as Robert Lowell and Sylvia Plath, as well as older Canadians such as F.R. Scott, Birney, Livesay and Ralph Gustafson, also made an impression on younger writers. Essentially modernist, they did not have the profound impact of *The New American Poetry* and certain contemporary European influences, yet they demonstrated that a contemporary Canadian poetry was possible. Then in 1965 Phyllis WEBB published *Naked Poems*, reinventing the long poem in Canada along the lines of contemporary poetics. Its impact has continued to be felt; its suites of brief lyrics present with exquisite craft the same lessons concerning language and seriality of composition as do the American works. Transformed into something new, rich and strange, the long poem emerged as perhaps the most important poetic genre in Canada in the 1960s and 1970s.

If there are important outside influences on contemporary writing, there was also a renewed Canadian nationalism associated with the Centennial of 1967, which asserted itself in the appearance of a number of small presses dedicated to the publication of the new writing. Whereas Contact Press had stood almost alone in the 1950s (with Fred Cogswell's Fiddlehead Books), by the late 1960s there were the House of Anansi and Coach House Press in Toronto, Oberon Press in Ottawa and Talonbooks in Vancouver. Since that time, other little presses have arisen and often fallen throughout the country. Without their industry and commitment to the new Canadian poetry, much of the excitement and discovery of recent years would never have occurred. In one of its final acts, Contact Press published *New Wave Canada* (1966), edited by Raymond Souster. Of the 17 poets represented there, at least 8 — Daphne Buckle (Marlatt), Victor Coleman, Gerry Gilbert, Robert Hogg, David McFadden, bp Nichol, Michael ONDAATJE and Fred Wah — have been influential innovators;

David Cull, David Dawson, E. Lakshmi Gill and George Jonas have all continued to write and publish; which leaves only 4 who have given up poetry. Shortly after the publication of *New Wave Canada*, the triumph of the young poets was certain. In 1966 Margaret Atwood's first full-length collection, *The Circle Game*, won the Governor General's Award. By 1968 Nelson Ball, Wayne Clifford, Dennis Lee, Tom Marshall, bissett, Coleman, Hogg, Lane, McFadden, Marlatt, Nichol, Ondaatje, Rosenblatt and Wah had all published first books, most with small presses.

In 1970 the Governor General's Awards confirmed the place of the new writing in Canadian culture: all 3 awards for writing in English went to experimental works. In prose and poetry, Michael Ondaatje won for his long collage poem, *The Collected Works of Billy the Kid*, while bp Nichol won for 4 books, including a box of minimalist visual poems, *Still Water*, and an anthology of "concrete poetry," *The Cosmic Chef*. All these books were published by small presses. Although visual "concrete poetry" had appeared in the work of bissett, Nichol and others in the early 1960s, *The Cosmic Chef* clearly signalled its importance as an experimental form to a wide range of writers. Bissett and Nichol had also begun to experiment with "performance" or "sound" poetry, chants and chantlike structures, ways of breaking down intellectual meaning in order to involve audiences with more basic emotional connections to the poet's voice. In 1970 Nichol, Steve McCaffery, Paul Dutton and Rafael Barreto-Rivera formed The Four Horsemen, Canada's first sound-poetry ensemble. During the 1970s other ensembles formed and performed across Canada — the Cold Mountain Group in Montréal, Owen Sound in Ontario, Re:Sounding in Alberta — as did many solo performers. Other forms of experimentation include various kinds of "found poetry" and "homolinguistic translation" — the translation of texts in a language into new texts in the same language by a variety of methods. What these experimental forms share is a fascination with potentialities of language.

- While the newer poets were making their presence felt, many older writers continued to work with undiminished, even renewed, vigour. In 1972 Livesay published her *Collected Poems: The Two Seasons*. In 1974 Gustafson won the Governor General's Award for *Fire on Stone*. One feature differentiating the contemporary period from earlier ones is that the younger writers do not feel the need utterly to displace the old. Instead a very broad range of writing continues to appear. This breadth is signalled not only by continued output by, and recognition of, older and more traditional writers, but by the variety of approaches taken by new poets. For example, in 1973 alone, first books appeared by John Thompson, a learned, highly symbolic poet; Tom Wayman, a post-Purdy narrative poet; and Christopher Dewdney, a complex and stringent explorer of language-centered poetics.

In the 1970s, there was a resurgence of REGION-ALISM, a shift away from Toronto as the centre of culture. The West Coast, protected by the mountains from both the harsh climate and the cultural assumptions of the rest of Canada, had always been a place unto itself. But now the Prairies asserted their identity, especially as the import of the poetry of Robert KROETSCH and Andy Suknaski made itself felt. Purdy's influence was important here, for his narrative line and colloquial speech provided a means for Prairie poets to tell their own stories (a method that has recently degenerated into a standard "Prairie-anecdotal" form that is too often banal and prosaic). As poets appeared in the Prairie West so did regional publishing houses: NeWest Press in Edmonton, Thistledown Press in Saska-

Poet Michael Ondaatje has won the Gov Gen's Award for *The Collected Works of Billy the Kid* and *There's a Trick with a Knife I'm Learning to Do* (photo by Ron Watts/First Light).

toon, Turnstone Press in Winnipeg and, more recently, Longspoon Press in Edmonton. In Montréal, which had been active in the 1940s and 1950s, a number of poets, including Richard Sommer, Artie Gold, Ken Norris and Stephen Morrissey, many of them associated with Véhicule Press, created new excitement. In the Atlantic provinces, many young writers appeared to bolster the Fredericton group centered on Alden Nowlan and *Fiddlehead* magazine. Most of these poets are not known nationally, since they have been published by presses unable to promote their books across the country (*see* AUTHORS AND THEIR MILIEU). One major exception is Don Domanski, whose visionary poems were published by Anansi.

In the early 1980s, many of the new poets and presses of the early years of the period appeared to be as well established as they could hope to be. The differences between now and then are many, however, and include funding by the Canada Council and various provincial arts councils, which have provided generous support for writers and presses. Although good new poets continue to appear, eg, Erin Mouré, Sharon Thesen, David Donnell and Roo Borson, they are not making the great steps into new poetics that were made by the generation of the early 1960s; instead, they are building on the poetic accomplishments of that earlier period. The ongoing poem by bp Nichol, *The Martyrology* (up to Book 6 in 1984), is an important long poem, and a wide variety of poems in extended forms have appeared; one of them, Stephen Scobie's *McAlmon's Chinese Opera*, won the Governor General's Award in 1980. Many small presses, seen originally as antiestablishment, have become entrenched and necessary parts of our culture. Coach House Press, for example, which began by publishing only new and experimental authors, published D.G. Jones's Governor General's Award-winning *Under the Thunder the Flowers Light Up the Earth* (1977) and Phyllis Webb's extraordinary return after more than 10 years' silence, *Wilson's Bowl* (1980). In the mid-1980s poetry of every kind was healthy

all across Canada. If perhaps too many mediocre poets were being published, that was a small price to pay for an active and lively culture. Poetry is still the one form of literature where, finally, the language is served most selflessly. While it remains in good health, the prospects for Canadian culture as a whole are good.

DOUGLAS BARBOUR

Reading: E.K. Brown, *On Canadian Poetry* (rev ed 1944); Frank Davey, *From Here to There* (1974); Louis Dudek and Michael Gnarowski, eds, *The Making of Modern Poetry in Canada* (1967); Carl F. Klinck, ed, *Literary History of Canada* (2nd ed, 1976); Tom Marshall, *Harsh and Lovely Land* (1979); William Toye, ed, *The Oxford Companion to Canadian Literature* (1983); George Woodcock, ed, *Colony and Confederation* (1974) and *Poets and Critics* (1974).

Poetry in French Satirical and epigrammatic verse in French appeared in 18th-century Québec NEWSPAPERS, but only 2 poets writing before 1820, both Frenchmen, deserve mention. Joseph Quesnel (1746-1809), captured at sea off Halifax in 1779, later settled near Montréal and wrote songs, poems and plays. Joseph Mermet (1775-1828?), sent to Canada with DE MEURON troops to help repel the American invasion of 1812, wrote dozens of poems, including a description of Niagara Falls and an account of the French Canadian victory at the BATTLE OF CHÂTEAUGUAY (1813).

The first volume of verse (1830) published by a French Canadian contained didactic poems by Michel Bibaud (1782-1857), among them satires on avarice, envy, laziness and ignorance. By that time the new "classical colleges" were producing young men with political aspirations and literary interests. The French romantic poets Lamartine and Hugo were being read and imitated by the future historian François-Xavier GARNEAU and Québec's future prime minister, Pierre-Joseph-Olivier CHAUVEAU. Before 1850, however, poetry was primarily a political weapon or an elegant diversion, and poems were printed only in newspapers and magazines.

After 1850 poets became more numerous, and can be grouped in 3 "generations." The first, born in the 1820s, includes Joseph Lenoir, author of exotic oriental fantasies and of skillful verse translations of Burns, Longfellow and Goethe; Louis-Joseph-Cyprien Fiset, who wrote long narrative poems on Canadian historical subjects or on the emigration crisis (*see* FRANCO-AMERICANS); and the most competent versifier of this group, Octave CRÉMAZIE, who, before his self-imposed exile for bankruptcy in 1862, became the unofficial bard of French Canada with his poems on international topics (Crimean War, unification of Italy), the glories of the French regime in Canada and the obligations of the living to the dead.

But Lenoir died prematurely, Crémazie left Canada and Fiset abandoned poetry for law. A new generation of poets, born during the 1830s and associated with the literary movement of 1860, succeeded them. Alfred Garneau (1836-1904), self-effacing son of the historian, left some 60 poems attesting to his sensitivity and his wide knowledge of French poetry. Léon-Pamphile Le May, librarian of the Legislative Assembly of Québec, published almost a dozen collections of poems, including a verse translation of Longfellow's EVANGELINE. Le May's best-known volume, *Les Gouttelettes* (1904), consisted entirely of the new sonnet form although his themes — religion, friendship, patriotism, the beauties of rural nature — remained those of his youth, and linked the 1860 movement with regionalism in early 20th-century Québec. The most important poet of this generation was Louis FRÉCHETTE, author of Québec's first volume of lyric poetry (*Mes loisirs*, 1863) and of the most important collection of narrative poems published in 19th-century Québec (*La Légende d'un peuple*, 1887). He was also the first Québec poet to be honoured by the French Academy (1880), and the first to publish a collected edition (3 vols, 1908) of his own verse.

After Confederation took Parliament to Ottawa in 1867, the 1860 literary movement in Québec City languished until 1875, when a new generation of poets, born about 1850, began to publish. Nérée Beauchemin (1850-1931), an obscure country doctor in Yamachiche, wrote tastefully of the joys of rural life in poems that were not collected until 1897. William Chapman (1850-1917) was a youthful admirer of Fréchette, but later turned against his idol, denouncing him as a plagiarist. Chapman's most successful collections were those he published in France early in the 20th century (*Les Aspirations*, 1904; *Les Rayons du nord*, 1909), which depicted a colourful Canadian northland peopled by VOYAGEURS, trappers and lumberjacks. The most original of this last generation of romantic poets was Eudore Évanturel, whose one slim volume, *Premières poésies* (1878), was attacked by the enemies of its prefacer, Joseph Marmette; Évanturel, discouraged, never returned to his whimsical accounts of flirtations and his witty personifications of Canadian seasons.

Between 1830 and 1895, some 50 Québec poets published about 100 collections of verse. Their work was frequently inspired by the French romantics, but, unlike their models, 19th-century Québec poets neglected the themes of passionate love, individualism or pantheism, preferring patriotic, social, historical or religious subjects. Yet their experiments with versification were varied: in their youth Fréchette and Le May attempted dozens of verse forms. Gradually sonnets and 6-line stanzas became the accepted lyric forms, whereas alexandrine (12-syllable) rhyming couplets were used in narrative poems. The period 1830-95 was thus one of poetic apprenticeship. There were no great poets and no outstanding works, but considerable imitation, adaptation and experimentation. A poetic tradition was being created, a reading public being formed.   DAVID M. HAYNE

Poetry in French, 1896-1930

The École littéraire de Montréal (fd in 1895) concentrated on purifying the French language and seeking out new forms of literary expression. The movement, which survived into the 1930s, lived through a period marked by the emergence of rural poetry (the "terroir" school) and the "art for art's sake" (Parnassian) movement.

The École's first 5 years culminated in the publication of its first collection, *Les Soirées du Château de Ramezay* (1900), followed by Émile NELLIGAN's *Poésies* in 1904. Nelligan, the youngest member of the group, created a remarkable collection of poetic works over a 3-year period (1896-99). Strongly influenced by Paul Verlaine, Charles Baudelaire, Georges Rodenbach, Maurice Rollinat, Edgar Allen Poe, José de Heredia and Leconte de Lisle, he had a gift for imagery and music, successfully mastered the sonnet and the rondeau and plunged with determination into the depths of his troubled soul to create a sad, delirious and sometimes hallucinatory poetry. His "Romance du vin" and "Vaisseau d'or" describe his destiny as an artist and bear witness to his marvellous mastery of verse.

After 1900, the symbolist dream crumbled. The École sought to evoke "the soul of the people," in the words of Charles GILL, whose *Cap Éternité* (1919), the fragments of a Dantesque fresco, reflects the trends of that period. Some poets, among them Louis-Joseph Doucet, Lionel Léveillé, Hector Demers and Albert Ferland (author of *Le Canada chanté*) devoted themselves to nationalist poetry. The review *Le Terroir* lasted scarcely a year, and its 10 issues were published in book form in 1910.

Some members of the École concentrated on poetry with a philosophical bent: Jean Charbonneau (*Les Blessures*, 1912); Alphonse Beauregard (*Les Forces*, 1912; *Les Alternances*, 1921); and Jean-Aubert Loranger (*Les Atmosphères*, 1920; *Poèmes*, 1922), the last enriching his meditation on man with oriental and unanimist influences. The school's third collection, *Les Soirées de l'école littéraire de Montréal* (1925), contained the works of 10 poets. Around 1930 the École disbanded, but a few collections were still published: Charbonneau's *La Flamme ardente* (1928), Gonzalve Desaulniers's *Les Bois qui chantent* (1930) and Joseph Melançon's *Avec ma vie* (1931).

The rural theme continued to develop. The fields, rivers, forests and villages of this poetry carried an often nostalgic tune, echoing the early settlers' songs. This tradition was a carry-over from the previous century. The young poets of Crémazie's era, strongly attached to the homeland, suddenly found themselves at the dawn of the 20th century. The rural theme became the leitmotif of all Blanche Lamontagne-Beauregard's poetry, her second collection, *Par nos champs et nos rives* (1917), being a striking example. Rural poetry is found in the works of Alphonse Désilets (pseudonym, Jacquelin), eg, *Heures poétiques* (1910), *Mon pays, mes amours* (1913) and *Dans la brise du terroir* (1922). Jules Tremblay, an intimist poet, took up rural poetry in *Arômes du terroir* (1918), his fourth collection. Émile Coderre (pseudonym Jean Narrache) created a sort of dialectic poetry in *Quand j'parl'tout seul* (1933), but the best rural poets were without doubt Nérée Beauchemin and Alfred DESROCHERS. Beauchemin wrote 2 collections evocative of Canadian history and life in Trois-Rivières: *Les Floraisons matinales* (1897) and *Patrie intime* (1928). DesRochers is noted for his startling vision of reality and his mastery of sonnet, rondeau, madrigal, chanson, acrostic, ode and elegy. The life of early settlers, vigorous thought and masterly art dominate DeṣRochers's *L'Offrande aux vierges folles* (1928) and *À l'ombre de l'Orford* (1930). With its powerful epic flavour, his poem "Hymne au vent du nord" is a landmark in the history of rural poetry.

The "art for art's sake" movement began in Québec in 1895 with the exotic sonnets of Arthur de Bussières. Although Alfred Garneau, Émile Nelligan, Jules Tremblay, Guy Delahaye, René Chopin and Marcel Dugas all practised symbolism, they also occasionally indulged in Parnassian art. The best representative of art for art's sake in Québec was lawyer Paul MORIN. Sonorous vocabulary, striking imagery and exotic landscapes are all found in his *Paon d'émail* (1911) and *Poèmes de cendre et d'or* (1922). The short-lived review, *Le* NIGOG (1918), launched a Parnassian movement which rapidly faded when it ceased publication.

At the beginning of the century, there emerged many poets who had little or no attachment to any particular school. An example is Louis Dantin (pseudonym Eugène Seers), the author of philosophical poetry and a literary critic, but above all, the person who revealed Nelligan's poetry to Montréalers in 1902. Also worthy of mention are the paralytic poet, Albert Lozeau, whose nostalgic landscape is found throughout his collections, *L'Âme solitaire* (1907) and *Le Miroir des jours* (1912); and Antonio Desjardins, author of *Crépuscules* (1924). Most important is Robert Choquette, whose first 3 collections, *À travers les vents* (1925), *Metropolitan Museum* (1931) and *Poésies nouvelles* (1933), are permeated by a visionary force and probe the destiny of modern man.

Between 1895 and 1930 Québec poetry dealt with a wide range of experiences. Beginning with the romantic tradition, it soon evolved toward symbolist poetry, later the "terroir" movement, and lastly the Parnassian school. Having turned away from traditional forms, it moved slowly toward free verse.   PAUL WYCZYNSKI

Poetry in French, 1930-1970

In poetry, as in other matters, change was often resisted in Québec: Clément Marchand (*Les Soirs rouges*, 1947) and Alphonse Piché (*Remous*, 1947) attempted new themes while adhering to traditional forms. Simone Routier (*Les Tentations*, 1934) adopted free verse but without any other advance. The mercurial François Hertel (*Axes et parallaxes*, 1941), a Jesuit and for over a decade a leading cultural figure, did much to encourage a climate of change; yet his intellectual poems failed to acknowledge the realities of Québec's future. The real vanguard in poetry at this time consisted of 4 rather isolated poets: Hector de Saint-Denys GARNEAU, Anne HÉBERT, Rina LASNIER and Alain GRANDBOIS.

Garneau published only one collection in his lifetime, *Regards et jeux dans l'espace* (1937). A second collection, *Les Solitudes*, appeared posthumously in his *Poésies complètes* (1949). Living in seclusion, Garneau devoted himself to poetry and to an increasingly difficult spiritual journey. His poems, written in rigorously controlled free verse, have a magical quality, expressing anguish and joy with equal simplicity and beauty.

In Hébert's *Les Songes en équilibre* (1942) the poet becomes a priest-magician with a social function. Hébert's psychological explorations reached the collective unconscious in *Le Tombeau des rois* (1953), in poetry pared to the bone. In the second half of *Poèmes* (1960) she entered a new phase, addressing Québec (or humankind) with epic generosity of line and spirit.

Beginning with *Images et proses* (1941), Lasnier wrote principally on religious themes. Though her early work is too intellectual to be of lasting interest, in *Escales* (1950), *Présence de l'absence* (1956) and later volumes her poetry is an impassioned plunge into contradictions wherein darkness and light come to coexist. Other women poets of this period include Medjé Vézina (*Chaque heure a son visage*, 1934), Jovette Bernier (*Les Masques déchirés*, 1932), Cécile Chabot (*Vitrail*, 1939) and Jeannine Bélanger (*Le Visage dans la roche*, 1941).

Grandbois became the most influential of the new poets, but his influence was primarily among the younger poets who came to dominate the 1960s. *Les Îles de la nuit* (1944) was a breath of fresh air, treating the poet's obsessive world travels, and conveying a sense of the cosmic and of human fraternity, as well as an unconstrained eroticism. The poems were fragmented and often surrealistic, yet thoroughly accomplished, as were the volumes that followed: *Rivages de l'homme* (1948) and *L'Étoile pourpre* (1957).

During the "Dark Years" of the rule of Premier Maurice DUPLESSIS (1944-60), an important minority of poets chose surrealistic modes of expression. Most had ties with the visual arts or jazz. REFUS GLOBAL (1948), a revolutionary cultural manifesto by painter Paul-Émile BORDUAS, included poems by Claude Gauvreau (*Brochuges*, 1957), whose work consisted of strangely meaningful nonsense words. Roland GIGUÈRE was an accomplished painter, engraver and typographer as well as a major poet. His poems, brought together in *L'Âge de la parole* (1965), are in revolt against anything that might suppress or sterilize life. Gilles Hénault sought "signs" in the remote past, among native peoples and in the collective unconscious as encountered in dreams. His 3 volumes of poetry are collected in *Signaux pour les voyants* (1972). Other poets whose writings touched upon surrealism include Yves Préfontaine (*Boréal*, 1957), an editor of LIBERTÉ; Marie-Claire BLAIS (*Pays voilés*, 1963), better known for her novels; and Claude Péloquin (*Jéricho*, 1963). Foremost was jazz musician Paul-Marie LAPOINTE, whose "automatiste" method of writing (*see* AUTOMATISTES) was akin to jazz improvisation. Only his first volume, *La Vierge incen-*

diée (1948), is truly surrealistic, but it contains the basic themes of all his poetry — justice for mankind, sexual freedom and the liberating power of love — expressed through repetition and inventory, and with great musicality. In later works, brought together in *Le Réel absolu* (1971), individual rebellion becomes collective revolution.

Though a gradual shift was taking place toward politicized poetry, many poets continued to write within their personal worlds. Éloi de Grandmont (*Plaisirs*, 1953) wrote charming verses celebrating the pleasures of love. Sylvain Garneau (*Les Trouble-fête*, 1952) lived in an adolescent dreamworld, pure yet disturbing, before killing himself in his early twenties. Gilles Constantineau (*Simples Poèmes et ballades*, 1960) portrayed an intimate world illuminated with striking perceptions and happiness. Luc Perrier (*Du temps que j'aime*, 1963) precisely evoked the strange poetry of daily existence. At the opposite extreme, Suzanne Paradis (*Pour les enfants des morts*, 1964) poured out her ardent will to live, affirming a powerful feminine mystique and expanding it to affect all areas of life.

The publication in 1958 of *La Poésie et nous*, consisting of essays by Hénault, Préfontaine, Michel Van Schendel, Jacques BRAULT and Wilfrid Lemoine, signalled the development of indigenous poetic theories. During the 1940s the magazines, *La Nouvelle relève* and *Gants du ciel*, had helped introduce the ideas of the French avant-garde. By the 1960s it was clear that the ideas most relevant to Québec were those emerging within the province itself. The magazines *Liberté* and PARTI PRIS fostered a vigorous exchange of literary and political thinking. Publishing houses were equally important, especially les Éditions de l'hexagone (fd in 1953).

During the 1960s Québec experienced a sudden growth in collective self-awareness and political ferment (*see* QUIET REVOLUTION). FRENCH CANADIAN NATIONALISM and the arts began to seem inseparable, justifying and stimulating each other. Although much nationalist writing was little more than propaganda, a surprising amount achieved the highest poetic quality, as did Brault's *Mémoire* (1965). Brault, like Paul-Marie Lapointe and many others of the period, belonged to the Hexagon movement, which consisted of essentially nationalist poets. At the centre of the movement, and principal force behind les Éditions de l'hexagone, was the energetic and charismatic Gaston MIRON. After *Deux Sangs* (1953), which he published with Olivier Marchand, Miron refused to collect his own poems until 1970, though he was a gifted poet and performer.

The theme of the land was a constant in the poetry of the 1960s, which gradually pulled away from the pan-Canadian perspective offered in Pierre Trottier's *Le Combat contre Tristan* (1951). The St Lawrence R became a national symbol. Pierre Perrault celebrated its islands in *Toutes isles* (1963), and Gatien Lapointe's effusive poetry reached its highest expression in *J'appartiens à la terre/Ode au Saint-Laurent* (1963). Van Schendel's *Poèmes de l'Amérique* (1958) was a reaction to the violence of modern America, but his *Variations sur la pierre* (1964) conveyed a sense of being reborn in Québec. Nationalist themes entered the powerful writing of Fernand OUELLETTE in *Le Soleil sous la mort* (1965), a title suggestive of national regeneration. That idea is made explicit in Andrée Maillet's *Le Chant de l'Iroquoise* (1967). In addition, although Paul CHAMBERLAND's *Genèses* (1963) may suggest a solitary spiritual struggle, that struggle is made concrete and collective in his *Terre Québec* (1964), a work of unfailing intensity and originality.

Language, affecting both the form and the content of Québec poetry, was the most important nationalist theme of all. Whether as JOUAL or as a "legitimate" dialect of French, Qué-

bec French was long a source of humiliation. As that humiliation was confessed, probed and held up for redress, the language gradually became a national birthright; for poets, *le parler québécois* became a vivid mode of expression as well as a symbol both of the nation and of the very enterprise of poetry. Fernand Dumont published a group of poems entitled *Peuple sans parole* (*Liberté*, 1965), and Yves Préfontaine published *Pays sans parole* (1967). Language dominated the poems of the future PARTI QUÉBÉCOIS culture minister, Gérald Godin (*Les Cantouques*, 1966). Most famous is Michèle Lalonde's *Speak White* (1974), a bitterly ironic poem first recited in 1968.

By the end of the 1960s the nationalist, populist phase of Québec poetry was coming to an end, though Lalonde carried it to the extreme in *Défense et illustration de la langue québécoise* (1979). Poets like Luc Racine (*Les Dormeurs*, 1966) and Raoul Duguay (*Ruts*, 1966) began to argue for more concern with pure writing and less with messages. As though it had proven its worth after a decade or more of activism on a common front, poetry now could afford to turn inward, to adapt to individual interests in the mundane or the metaphysical.   ROD WILLMOT

Poetry in French, 1970-80s

This decade is marked by a shattering of the ideological, nationalist and humanist unity that permeated the poetry of the 1960s. Although the break is not complete, the young generation of poets turned away from the "poésie du pays" movement exemplified by Gaston Miron's *L'Homme rapaillé* (1970) and adopted surrealism and its Québec variant, automatism. The works of Paul-Marie Lapointe, Claude Gauvreau, Roland Giguère and Gilles Hénault, all born between 1920 and 1930 and affiliated with surrealism, have been republished and widely read. The new poetry is not a simple extension of this trend, but reflects a mentality. It is the radical rebuttal of all social and cultural institutions and the values associated with them, and is critical of the dogmatic unity inherent in "la belle poésie."

The avant-garde finds its most coherent expression in the poetry of the group associated with *Les Herbes rouges*. Inspired more by the theories of the French avant-garde than by those of the American counterculture found in poets like Denis Vanier and Lucien Francoeur, the journal *Les Herbes rouges* is in fact a publishing house which has issued 100 or so brochures over a 10-year period. The influence of Nicole Brossard figures prominently in its publications. Two of her collections, *Suite logique* and *Le Centre blanc* (1970), set the tone for the decade: disjointed syntax, preoccupation with the irrational (desire, the body, loss of the senses, madness) in a reflective and critical manner. Roger Des Roches and André Roy follow the trend set by *Les Herbes rouges*, while François Charron tends to depart from it through the use of parody and a return to lyricism.

The poetry of this period generally rebels against the previously dominant telluric and cosmic-inspired lyricism, an exception being the mystical-cosmic utopia created by Paul Chamberland in *Demain les dieux naîtront* (1974). Elsewhere, private life and the urban world are dominant. This poetry of everyday existence is expressed in the work of Michel Beaulieu, particularly in *Variables* (1973) and in *Anecdotes* (1977), which uses analytical language to convey modern man's drift through his body, desires and memory. For Juan Garcia and Alexis Lefrançois, private life becomes the focal point for the metaphysical experience of experimentation and purification; the concisely expressed individualism of Gilbert Langevin (*Mon refuge est un volcan*, 1978) is a scathing denunciation of modern society. By contrast, Michel Garneau

and Pierre Morency affirm the "torrential" and "amorous" energy of the individual. Finally, 2 poets of the Hexagone generation, Jacques Brault, in *L'en-dessous l'admirable* and *Poèmes des quatre côtés* (1975), and Fernand Ouellette in *Ici, ailleurs, la lumière* (1977), undertake an inner journey and react against the more superficial aspects of the modern world.

The major poetic movement of the latter part of the decade is linked to the modernism of *Les Herbes rouges*. Inspired by Brossard's reflection on the imaginary, this new movement places great importance on feminist concerns. Madeleine Gagnon's *Pour les femmes et tous les autres* (1974), Brossard's *La Partie pour le tout* (1975) and France Théorêt's *Bloody Mary* (1977) are the first examples of "feminist writing" to challenge patriarchal symbolism and develop fiction documenting the history and experiences of women. This trend appears to be leading poetry toward less revolutionary forms and to a fusion with other literary genres, particularly narrative writing and the essay, examples being the works of Yolande Villemaire and Suzanne Jacob. At the end of the decade, there was evidence of a "new imagination" and a "new readability" embodied in *Les Passions du samedi* (1979) by André Roy, the neo-lyricist writing of François Charron, the transparency of Philippe Haeck and, at another level, that of Marie Uguay. The resounding success of *Estuaire*, a journal published since 1976, publishing houses like Éditions du Noroît, poet Gatien Lapointe's Écrits des forges, and the production of works at Éditions de l'hexagone all attest to the continuity and diversity of Québec poetry in the early 1980s. However, despite these successes, poetry has lost some of its influence on the cultural life of Québec.   PIERRE NEPVEU

Reading: Réginald Hamel et al, *Dictionnaire pratique des auteurs québécois* (1976); M. Lemire, ed, *Dictionnaire des oeuvres littéraires du Québec*, 4 vols (1980-84); L. Mailhot and Pierre Nepveu, eds, *La Poésie québécoise* (1981).

Point Pelée National Park (est 1918) is a 17 km long peninsula jutting abruptly into LK ERIE. The southernmost tip of Canada's mainland, it is on the same latitude as Rome and northern California. The climate is somewhat warmer than in the rest of Canada and many species found in the park are typical of southern areas. The park sits atop a deposit of sand up to 70 m thick left by glacial meltwaters on a submerged limestone ridge. Over the centuries a thin but rich soil has formed, supporting a lush deciduous forest of such exotic species as shagbark hickory, sassafras and hackberry, one of Canada's few remaining stands of Carolinean forest. A boardwalk gives access to the marshlands comprising much of the park. REPTILES and AMPHIBIANS abound and several species rare elsewhere in Canada, such as the fox snake and spotted turtle, thrive. Point Pelée is best known

Point Pelée National Park occupies a 17 km peninsula jutting into Lk Erie. It is Canada's finest bird-watching site – over 100 species have been sighted on one day (*courtesy Parks Canada*).

as Canada's finest BIRD WATCHING spot. Located on the crossroads of 2 major MIGRATION flyways, over 100 species can sometimes be seen in a day. Over 300 species have been recorded in the park. Point Pelée is a day-use park. Its fragile environment permits hiking, canoeing, swimming and bird watching. LILLIAN STEWART

Poirier, Anne-Claire, film director, producer (b at St-Hyacinthe, Qué 6 June 1932). She joined the NFB in 1960, eventually going into film direction, which had been essentially a male preserve. Her first full-length film, *De mère en fille* (1968), dealt with the physical and emotional experience of pregnancy. In 1973 Poirier produced the "En tant que femmes" series which offered female film producers their first organized platform for expression. In this series, Poirier directed *Les Filles du roy* (1974) and *Le Temps de l'avant* (1975), the latter a sensitive study of the abortion issue. She then produced the powerful *Mourir à tue-tête* (1979), a film about rape. *La Quarantaine* (1982) deals with the critical fifth decade of a person's life. PIERRE VÉRONNEAU

Poison Ivy (*Toxicodendron*), small genus of woody perennial PLANTS of cashew family (Anacardiaceae), closely related to and sometimes classified with the SUMACS (genus *Rhus*). The name most commonly refers to *T. rydbergii*, found from southern BC to the Atlantic provinces but also refers to *T. radicans* subspecies *radicans*, occurring in southern NS and *T. radicans* subspecies *negundo*, in southern Ontario. The plants spread by underground stems. Most are small shrubs (0.5-1 m tall); others are vinelike plants, 15 m or longer, supported by aerial roots. Shrubby forms are sometimes called poison oak. Leaves have 3 leaflets, shiny, somewhat concave, entire or coarsely toothed or lobed. Greenish yellow berries turn white and remain on plants all winter. They are found in various habitats (eg, sandy or gravelly soils, dunes, talus slopes) but generally prefer calcareous places. Dermatitis can develop on contact with any plant part throughout the year (especially spring and summer), even from smoke from fires containing it. Skin blisters develop, exuding liquid if broken. Washing with strong soap helps; juice of jewel weed (*Impatiens capensis*) is also supposed to be effective. *See* PLANTS, NATIVE USES; POISONOUS PLANTS. J.M. GILLETT

Poisonous Plants Most major groups of PLANTS contain species that can produce toxic reactions ranging from discomfort, through organ damage, to death. Poisons may be assimilated by being eaten, inhaled, or absorbed through the skin. Nontoxic plants and plant products may cause simple physical damage followed by infection. Toxic reactions are caused by compounds that may be produced by plants or absorbed from soil. Alkaloids (bitter-tasting, semialkaline substances containing nitrogen) occur throughout plants in soluble organic acid salts. Polypeptides and amines are organic substances containing nitrogen. Glycosides are compounds that break down to form sugars and toxic aglycones. Oxalates occur as soluble or insoluble salts. Insoluble calcium salts are irritants that are deposited in kidneys. Resins or resinoids irritate muscle tissue. Phytotoxins or toxalbumins (protein molecules acting as enzymes) break down natural proteins, causing ammonia accumulation and protein deficiency. Many plants take up minerals (eg, copper, selenium, lead, molybdenum, nitrates or nitrites) from soils in sufficient quantities to cause poisoning.

Allergies Many people are sensitive to plant substances. Airborne material (eg, FUNGI spores, soil ALGAE, pollen grains, etc) causes hayfever. Pollen, the most serious problem, is seasonal. Early flowering trees cause reactions in spring. A midsummer peak is caused primarily by GRASS species. In autumn, a peak is caused

Principal Poisonous Plants of Canada (fungi and algae excluded)

Common Name	Scientific Name	Distribution	Notes
almond (bitter)	*Prunus amygdalus dulcis*	cultivated, ornamental	seeds rich in glycosides; inedible
almond (sweet)	*Prunus amygdalus amara*	cultivated	seeds edible
apricot	*Prunus armenica*	cultivated	seeds rich in glycosides; inedible
black cherry	*Prunus serotina*	Ont to NS	glycosides in leaves and fruit stones
bracken fern	*Pteridium aquilinum*	southern Canada	toxic to cattle and horses
buttercup	*Ranunculus*	45 species in Canada	plant acrid in taste, or even toxic
castor bean or castor oil plant	*Ricinus communis*	ornamental	all parts, especially seeds, poisonous to children
chokecherry	*Prunus virginiana* var *melanocarpa* var *virginiana*	BC and Alta eastern provinces	all have high levels of cyanogenetic glycosides (cause cyanide poisoning)
columbine	*Aquilegia*	throughout Canada	flowers toxic to humans
Daphne	*Daphne mezereum*	ornamental shrub	all parts, especially berries, poisonous to children
death camas	*Zygadenus elegans* *Z. venenosus*	across Canada BC, Alta and Sask	steriod alkaloids responsible for death of sheep
dogbane	*Apocynum*	southern Canada to YT	milky juice toxic
dumbcane	*Dieffenbachia maculata*	ornamental house plant	oxalate crystals can cause tongue swelling and block breathing, danger to children especially
false azalea	*Menziesia ferruginea*	western mountains	
false hellebore	*Veratrum viride*	alpine	poisonous to grazing animals; European species used medicinally and as insecticide
foxglove	*Digitalis purpurea*	weed escaped from gardens in BC and eastern Canada	medicinal plant once; overdose very dangerous as contains cardiac or steroid glycosides
groundsel	*Senecio jacobaea*	weed	causes Pictou disease of cattle in NS
horsetail	*Equisetum, especially Equisetum arvense*	throughout Canada	toxic to cattle and horses
ivy	*Hedera helix*	ornamental	leaves poisonous
Jack-in-the-pulpit	*Arisaema triphyllum*	eastern Canadian wet woods	irritation, swelling about mouth; contains oxalates (like all members of Arum family)
larkspurs	*Delphinium*	3 species in West, some cultivated species	toxic to man or animals
lily of the valley	*Convallaria majalis*	cultivated and garden escapes	all parts poisonous, especially underground stem; contain glycosides similar to digitalis
locoweeds	*Oxytropis* and *Astragalus*	arctic, alpine and prairie	poisonous to animals
lupines	*Lupus*	28 species, most southern Sask to BC; also cultivated and garden escapes	untreated seeds poisonous to livestock
milkweed	*Asclepias*	over 12 species; 2 from BC to Man, others from Man to Nfld	milky latex poisonous to livestock; fortunately unpalatable
monkshood or aconite	*Aconitum columbianum* *A. nagellus*	BC cultivated	toxic to man or animals
mustard family (includes horseradish, etc)	*Cruciferae family*	cultivated or woody	contain varying quantities of mustard oil; if grazed in quantity can poison cattle, sheep, swine
nightshade	*Solanum*	across Canada	poisonous alkaloids in many species
oleander	*Nerium oleander*	ornamental pot plant	contains cardiac glycosides; all parts extremely toxic to humans or livestock
peach	*Prunus persica*	cultivated	pits and tree parts rich in glycosides
pin cherry	*Prunus pensylvanica*	southern Canada	bright red, acid fruit recognized by 2 small glands at base of leaf blade
poinsettia	*Euphorbia pulcherrima*	sold as pot plant	especially dangerous to children
poison hemlock	*Conium maculatum*	roadsides, fields, ditches	cattle poison
poison ivy	*Toxicodendron rydbergii* *T. radicans*	BC to Atlantic provinces eastern provinces	causes dermatitis
poison sumac	*Rhus vernix*	eastern provinces	causes dermatitis

Principal Poisonous Plants of Canada (fungi and algae excluded)

Common Name	Scientific Name	Distribution	Notes
poppy	*Papaver*	mostly gardens	hallucinogenic; opium poppy unlawful to grow
precatory or jequirity bean	*Abrus precatorius*	seeds imported from tropics as beads by tourists	importation illegal; made into necklaces; chewing one bean can be fatal
rhubarb	*Rheum*	cultivated, occasionally escapes	blade of leaf can be fatal; stalk safe; contains oxalates
Saint-John's-wort	*Hypericum perforatum*	weedy in eastern Canada and BC	causes photosensitivity in livestock
sheep laurel or sheepkill	*Kalmia angustifolia*	woods or bogs Lab to central Ont	leaves eaten in spring when other grazing scarce; can poison animals
snow-on-the-mountain	*Euphorbia marginata*	garden subject; occasionally weed	especially poisonous to children
spurges	*Euphorbia*	all weedy	milky sap can cause blisters
trapper's tea	*Ledum glandulosum*	BC to Alta	twigs, leaves and flowers toxic
water hemlock	*Cicuta maculata, C. bulbifera*	wet habitats throughout southern Canada	dahlialike root very poisonous to cattle; death within hours
water parsnip	*Sium suave*	wet places	cattle poison
white snakeroot	*Eupatorium rugosum*	eastern Canadian woodlands	causes trembles in livestock
wild lettuce	*Lactuca scariola*	weed	early growth harmful to grazing animals
yew	*Taxus brevifolia T. canadensis T. cuspidata,*	BC southern Man to Nfld ornamental	foliage, bark or seeds toxic to man or animals

by herbaceous plants, chiefly spiny-pollened ragweed (3 species of genus *Ambrosia*) in Canada. The Atlantic provinces, BC, Saskatchewan, northern Ontario, Québec and Manitoba are relatively free of ragweed. Allergies rarely kill.

Dermatitis Several plants (eg, POISON IVY, poison sumac and primrose) cause skin irritation (redness, itching or blisters). Cultivated *Cyclamen* (primrose family) also causes reactions in some people, severity depending on degree of contact and individual susceptibility. Contact with stinging nettle (*Urtica*), woodnettle (*Laportea*) and stem hairs of some species of Avens (*Geum*) can cause temporary discomfort.

Internal Poisoning Poisoning cannot occur unless plants, or parts of them, are consumed. People can avoid them, but animals left to graze native range may eat them. Internal poisoning depends upon type and quantity of plant eaten, the condition and age of person or animal and other factors.

Mechanical Injury While not poisonous, certain plants cause physical injury followed by secondary infection. Hawthorn (*Crataegus*), rose (*Rosa*) and blackberry (*Rubus*) have prominent thorns. The West Coast Devil's-club (*Oplopanax horridus*) is spiny throughout and forms thickets. Barbs of grasses such as wild barley (*Hordeum*), brome grass (*Bromus*), wild rye (*Agropyron*) and needle-grass (*Stipa*) can stick in the throat of an animal. Cocklebur (*Xanthium*) has prickly fruits. Mullein (*Verbascum*), crimson and rabbit-foot clovers (*Trifolium*) can form hair balls in the stomach. *See* individual species entries.

J.M. GILLETT

Reading: John M. Kingsbury, Poisonous Plants of the US and Canada (1964).

Pokemouche, NB, UP, pop 341 (1981c), rural area of Inkerman, pop 4455 (1981c), is located 15 km S of CARAQUET, close to the centre of the Acadian Pen (S of CHALEUR BAY). The marshy lagoon at the mouth of the Pokemouche R prevents port development, but Pokemouche was important in land and river communications. Two MICMAC village sites, 3 campsites and 3 portages were in this area. The first European settlers were ACADIAN refugees arriving in 1797. English ex-soldiers and many Irish settlers followed after 1800, but French influence is now dominant.

The lumber industry that flourished after 1825 declined around 1860, and the labour force is now mostly employed in farming or in service industries. The nearby airport, opened 1978, has improved communications. SHEILA ANDREW

Polanyi, John Charles, chemist, professor (b at Berlin, Ger 23 Jan 1929), son of scientist and philosopher Michael Polanyi. He is widely recognized and honoured for his brilliant research on the dynamics of chemical reactions, his views on science policy and his dedication to achieving a rational approach to nuclear disarmament. He was educated in Manchester, Eng, where his family had settled after leaving Germany in 1934. Following postdoctoral research at NRC and Princeton, he was appointed lecturer at University of Toronto in 1956 and professor of chemistry in 1962. Development of his discovery in 1958 of the emission of infrared radiation from newly formed molecules has led to new levels of understanding of the nature of chemical transformations. One result, subsequently confirmed by experiment, was his prediction of the conditions necessary for a chemical laser. D.J. LE ROY

Polar Bear (*Ursus maritimus*), large, white BEAR with long, narrow head and very small ears. Polar bears inhabit ice and coastlines of arctic seas, mostly in Canada, but also in Alaska, USSR, Norway's Svalbard I and Greenland. In Canada, polar bears are found in coastal regions of both territories, Manitoba, Ontario and arctic Québec. James Bay region is the southern limit of their range. Unlike most other bears, polar bears remain active during winter, hunting and travelling on sea ice. They eat mainly seals, hunted by waiting beside a breathing hole in the ice. In summer, the breakup often forces them to live on land where they eat various foods, including waterfowl, berries, marine vegetation and even smaller polar bears. Females become fertile every second year. In late fall, the pregnant female builds a den in a large snowdrift, where cubs are born. The family stays there until Mar, when a move to sea ice occurs and the mother begins hunting. Twins are the rule (range 1-3). Cubs stay with the mother for over a year. Polar bears breed in spring with embryo implantation delayed until fall; hence, cubs are extremely small (about 1 kg) at birth. Adult males, however, can weight 650 kg; females, 350 kg. BRIAN KNUDSEN

Poles In 1795 Russia, Prussia and Austria partitioned the territories of Poland. The assimilation of Polish territories, as well as religious persecution and a poor economy, inspired the emigration of the Poles. The majority of the first Polish newcomers to Canada did not arrive directly from Poland. The first Polish immigrant arrived in Canada in 1752. Two other Poles reportedly in Canada in 1776 were August F. Globenski, an army surgeon of the Hesse-Haynau regiment, and Leveright Pinze, a surgeon of the auxiliary forces from Brunswick. Karol Blaskowitz, a captain-cartographer of the British army, arrived in 1802 and Aleksander E. Kierzkowski, an engineer who became politically active in the St Hyacinthe riding in 1867, arrived in 1841. Among the Swiss regiments that fought at Fort Barrie in 1812, there were about a dozen Poles from former Napoleonic

The polar bear (*Ursus maritimus*) inhabits the ice and coastlines of the Canadian Arctic as far south as James Bay (*photo by Fred Breummer*).

legions. Sir Casimir GZOWSKI, a prominent civil engineer, railway builder and social activist, arrived from the US in 1842. Izaak Helmuth, from Warsaw, Poland, came via England and was one of the founders of University of Western Ontario.

Migration The major periods of Polish immigration to Canada were 1858-94 (1000), 1895-1913 (119 600), 1920-39 (55 500), 1946-56 (62 000) and 1957-82 (42 000). The first 2 waves included many family groups from villages and small towns of Austrian-occupied territory. Hardworking, religious peasants, many received land grants from the government or bought lots in Manitoba, Saskatchewan and Alberta where they built farms. Others worked on railroad construction or in the coal mines. The second generation often moved to larger settlements or towns where they opened small businesses.

The immigrants of 1920 to 1939 arrived from an already independent Poland and settled (at least until 1931) primarily on the Prairies. Until 1945 Winnipeg had the largest Polish community. The first after 1945 wave of immigrants (over 50% of whom settled in Ontario) consisted largely of former soldiers of the Polish armed forces who had fought in Western Europe, former inmates of Nazi concentration or forced-labour camps and political REFUGEES from communist Poland. From 1957 to 1981, immigrants again arrived directly from Poland. The latest wave was motivated by the deep economic and political crisis in Poland.

Settlement Patterns With the exception of one homogeneous group from German-occupied territory, which arrived in 1858 and settled in Renfrew County, Ont, the Polish newcomers frequently homesteaded (eg, in Manitoba around Springfield, St Clement's, Brokenhead, Lac du Bonnet, Whitemouth, Gimli, Bifrost, Glenella, Rosedale, McCreary and Dauphin) close to already established Ukrainian farmers who were often from neighbouring villages in Poland. A widespread movement of immigrants to larger centres started in the 1930s. There were 254 485 Poles living in Canada in 1981. The largest Polish communities are, in descending order, in Toronto, Winnipeg, Montréal, Edmonton, Hamilton, Vancouver and St Catharines. Lesser concentrations live in Calgary, Ottawa, Kitchener, London, Sudbury, Regina, Saskatoon, Thunder Bay, Windsor and Oshawa. Eighty-eight percent of the Poles in Canada live in urban areas.

Economic Life The first Polish immigrants helped settle the prairies of Manitoba, Saskatchewan and Alberta and made up a large percentage of the labour force in mines, in the forest industry and in public works. The second generation and the post-WWII immigrants were more financially secure, with professional experience and technical qualifications. They opened their own enterprises, occupied executive positions in industry, and were prominent in social and health services and in higher education.

Social and Community Life The majority of Poles are Roman Catholic, but there are also Lutherans and United Church members. A separate Polish Catholic Church, which is not affiliated with the Roman Catholic Church, has parishes in various cities (*see* CATHOLICISM). Parishes formed the first organizational units, providing a framework for community and social life. Lay organizations appeared in towns only shortly before WWI. The 1930s marked the appearance of social clubs that helped maintain Polish customs and traditions, as did the Polish government through its consulates. Polish credit unions were created across Canada. The first, the St Stanislaus Credit Union, was organized in Toronto; it is now the largest financial institution of its kind in N America, with capital assets of

$80 million. In the mid-1950s women formed a self-contained and independent organization (the Federation of Polish Women in Canada) concerned with cultural and political issues. Various folk groups or dance ensembles surfaced at different times and in different communities.

The Catholic Church has played a very important role in the life of the Polish nation, especially in difficult times. For many immigrants in the past it provided the sole contact with their native country and its culture. The priests were advisers, defenders, spokesmen, religious leaders and community leaders. Catholics in Polish communities still observe the customs of Christmas, Lent, Holy Week and Easter.

The first Polish newspaper, which appeared in Winnipeg in 1904, was short-lived. The second attempt, *Gazeta Katolicka* (*Catholic Gazette*), was founded in Winnipeg in 1908. The Polish press in Canada today is very active and includes several different publications, some of them running 10 000 copies.

Polish writers and poets include Louis DUDEK, W. Iwaniuk, B. Czaykowski, Florian Smieja, J. Ihnatowicz, A. Busza, and the late Zofia Bohdanowicz and Danuta Bienkowska. Artists include Mary Schneider, Krystyne Sadkowska, E. Koniuszy, S. Katski, E. Chruscicki, T. Jaworska, G. Staron, M. Ciechomska, B. Michalowska, H. Hoenigan and J. Lubojanska.

Education The first 2 phases of Polish immigration included numerous illiterate peasants, but later immigrants were generally well educated. The children were sent to public schools, but a network of part-time Polish-language schools was also established. Most of the latter are affiliated with the Polish Teachers Federation.

Ethnic identification is fully realized only within groups directly connected with Polish organizations or parishes. The Polish Congress encompasses some 160 independent organizations whose membership varies from a few dozen to a few thousand people. According to the 1981 census, Polish was the mother tongue of 127 970 people, of whom only about 7% belong to ethnic organizations.

Politics Until 1980 the majority of Poles voted Liberal in federal elections. Candidates of Polish origin have always been supported by their ethnic constituents. Stanley Haidasz, born in Toronto of Polish parents, was the first Polish Liberal MP. He later became minister for multiculturalism in the Trudeau government and the first Polish representative in the Senate. There were 3 ministers of Polish origin in the Saskatchewan NDP government until its defeat in 1982. A small group of Polish communists had been quite active during the GREAT DEPRESSION, especially in Winnipeg, Timmins, Sudbury, Hamilton, Toronto and Montréal. Their paper, *Kronika Tygodniowa* (*A Weekly Chronicle*), still appears in Toronto in small runs.

Group Identification The feeling of unity among Polish Canadians has been expressed primarily in support of the Polish nation. Political and financial support for Poland was strong during WWII, when Poland was under German occupation, and later when the communist government attempted to suppress the church. An extensive "Help for Poland" program established in Canada after Oct 1956 has recently been revived. Contact with the motherland remains vivid through Polish-organized travel tours, family visits and language courses for the young. National pride was reinforced by the election of Pope John Paul II, the choice of Czeslaw Milosz in 1980 for the Nobel Prize for Literature and the selection of Lech Walesa in 1983 for the Nobel Peace Prize.

The Polish Canadian Research Institute, established in 1956, conducts studies on Poles in Canada. It has an extensive library and archives

and publishes its research (over 17 volumes have appeared in English so far). The institute cooperates with associate scientific centres both in Canada and Poland, provides scholarships and assistance to young researchers and organizes lectures. The Polish Scientific Institute, headquartered in Montréal, provides information on Poland's history and Polish ethnic groups abroad. In addition, 3 foundations have been established to assist Polish schools and cultural life.   BENEDYKT HEYDENKORN

Reading: Benedykt Heydenkorn, *The Organizational Structure of the Polish Canadian Community* (1979); R.K. Kogler, *The Polish Community in Canada* (1979); W.B. Makowski, *History and Integration of Poles in Canada* (1967); H. Radecki and Benedykt Heydenkorn, *A Member of a Distinguished Family: The Polish Group in Canada* (1976); V. Turek, *Poles in Manitoba* (1967); L.K. Zubkowski, *The Poles in Canada* (1968);

Police The primary function of police is to preserve order (sometimes referred to as "keeping the peace") between people within a community. Ideas about what this order is may be widely shared within a community or they may be imposed by a dominant group.

Type of Police When the authority under which police operate is public, eg, a municipality, public POLICING exists; when the authority is private, eg, a large corporation, it is called private policing (also referred to as private security to avoid confusion with the public police). Public policing is usually carried out by a full-time police force, but sales staff and apartment superintendents are frequently required to engage in private policing as part of their jobs. In 1981, according to estimates of police strength in Canada, there were 53 897 public police and some 50 000 specialized private police. About 66% of private police, referred to as "in-house security," work directly for the authorities on whose behalf they police. The remainder, "contract security," act for companies who provide security services for hire.

History and Development Prior to the 19th century, public policing was the responsibility of the ordinary citizenry and private policing was the norm. The Industrial Revolution disrupted the traditional police structures, leaving a gap that government filled in the early 19th century by developing the modern public police. This "new police" model was also adopted in Canada. Canadian municipal policing was modelled primarily on the London Metropolitan Police, whereas the NORTH-WEST MOUNTED POLICE (now the ROYAL CANADIAN MOUNTED POLICE) was modelled on the more militaristic Royal Irish Constabulary. Even in Québec, where the French influence is of obvious importance, public police are organized on the British model.

There are signs that the organization of policing may be reverting to its earlier forms. The public police are relying less frequently on their own resources and are increasingly involving the public directly in policing through community-based programs such as "block parents" (which encourages parent participation in making their neighbourhoods safer for their children) and "neighbourhood watch." In some cases, public police forces and governments have hired private police agencies to do a variety of tasks, including patrolling, which they had previously undertaken themselves. In addition, corporations have become increasingly active in providing their own police, eg, to maintain order in areas such as commercial shopping malls.

Methods Policing operates by fostering voluntary compliance with the desired order, by forcibly insisting on it, or both. As physical force is the ultimate coercive resource available to police, the instruments of force they most commonly use (eg, the billy club and the handgun) have come to symbolize the police. However, police in Canada usually rely on voluntary compliance, and when they do rely on force it may only be as an implicit or overt threat of force. Another central feature of police work is INTELLIGENCE GATHERING. This function has shaped the organization of the police. For example, the traditional grid system of patrol was developed to extend the net of police surveillance as widely as possible.

Police surveillance is constantly frustrated by the institutions of PRIVACY, which restrict where and how the police may seek information. For example, public police on patrol are largely limited to public places. Therefore they must routinely patrol public streets, although crimes usually occur in private places. Private police, as agents of the owners of private property, usually have greater routine access to private property.

Many of the changes in the structure of public policing are a result of attempts by police to deal with the restriction of the institutions of privacy. For example, 2-way radios, telephones and automobiles are used in an attempt to provide a quick response to members of the public. These devices take advantage of the citizen access to private places. Similarly, the recent use by the public police of "team policing," in which a team of police officers remains in an area and works together to police it, is largely a strategy to improve policing intelligence.

The tension between privacy and police intelligence is an essential feature of policing. It creates pressures on police to circumvent legal and social restrictions on their power. This tension is greatest for political police, such as Canada's Security Service, who can seldom use evidence of wrongdoing to legitimate intrusions into privacy.

Sources of Police Powers Police powers derive from the power resources at the disposal of the authorities on whose behalf they act. Where the authority is the STATE this capacity is ultimately physical force, because access to such force is an essential characteristic of state power. Where the authority is private, the resources to which police have access vary considerably. In educational communities, for example, they include sanctions such as the denial of library privileges and the withholding of educational certificates. Similarly, in economic communities the sanctions will tend to be economic in character, eg, loss of pay or credit privileges. In private policing the threat of physical force may underlie other sanctions because the private police may be able to draw on the assistance of the public police. In addition, they may be able to act themselves as agents of government, eg, by exercising citizen powers of arrest or by acting as special constables, a status that is used to extend some police powers to a few private police.

Safeguards The law (both the general law, especially the Canadian CRIMINAL CODE, and provincial Police Acts) limits police power by defining the circumstances in which the police may act. These limits may be overridden by legislation giving the police "special powers" in particular circumstances. The most extraordinary example in Canada is the WAR MEASURES ACT, invoked during the 1970 OCTOBER CRISIS in Québec.

Authorities to whom police are responsible may restrict the police in other ways. The public police are bound by departmental regulations. Private police may also be bound by internal regulations, such as the terms of management-labour agreements.

All restrictions on police power are characterized by the fact that they limit the extent to which the police can legitimately intrude upon the privacy of others; the institutions of privacy thus help determine police power boundaries.

Police Deviance and Accountability When police disregard the restrictions placed on their exercise of power they expose themselves to possible sanctions. Traditional legal sanctions have not been effective in controlling police deviance because of the problems of securing evidence that will stand up in a court (in the case of criminal charges) and because of the costs involved (where civil remedies are pursued). Thus the sanctions most often used against police misconduct are internal disciplinary procedures, but the use of such remedies has raised accusations of "cover up" and has resulted in considerable political pressure to establish independent bodies to hear complaints against the public police. Although such boards have been established in a few jurisdictions, they rely on the public police to undertake investigations and have been criticized for lack of independence.

In addition, several commissions of inquiry have been established by governments over the last decade to investigate allegations of public police misconduct (see INQUIRY INTO CERTAIN ACTIVITIES OF THE RCMP). While these inquiries have led to few criminal charges being laid against the police, they have resulted in significant changes in the way complaints against the police are handled and in internal disciplinary procedures.

In many cases the news media have initially reported the allegations and lobbied for an inquiry. The press, however, while acting as an important watchdog over the public police, has until recently been less attentive to abuses on the part of private police.

Comparative Jurisdictions of Public Police Forces Under the Constitution, responsibility for public policing is primarily a provincial matter. In exercising this responsibility, the provinces have, through provincial Police Acts, followed the British tradition and delegated the responsibility for public policing to municipalities when they are large enough to take it on. Nonetheless, provinces exercise considerable control over policing by paying part of the cost of municipal policing and by penalizing municipalities that fail to maintain standards. In most provinces this supervision is undertaken by a police commission established to avoid at least the appearance of direct governmental control over the public police. In addition, at the municipal level many towns and cities have established police boards to oversee the operation of the public police. Most municipal police forces, however, are governed directly by municipal councils or their committees.

The provinces not only provide provincial police for those areas that fall outside municipal jurisdiction but also support and co-ordinating services such as police training, criminal intelligence and forensic facilities.

Although the federal government does not have primary constitutional responsibility for policing, the federal police force, the RCMP, headquartered in Ottawa, is the largest single police force in the country and operates at both the municipal and provincial level in all provinces — except Ontario and Québec — and in the Yukon and the NWT. RCMP involvement in policing at the provincial and municipal levels arises because the RCMP contracts to provide policing services to the provinces and municipal jurisdictions. In addition to acting as a contract agency for policing in Canada, the RCMP provides services to all Canadian public police forces. The 2 most important services are the Canadian Police Information Centre, which provides information on such matters as criminal records, and the Canadian Police College, which provides advanced police training.

Apart from federal, provincial and municipal police, governments in Canada authorize other forms of police with legal powers which, while limited to specific areas or specific groups of people, or both, are not unlike those of the public police. The Harbour Police, Military Police and Railway Police are examples.

C.D. SHEARING AND P.C. STENNING

Reading: R. Ericson, Reproducing Order: A Study of Police Patrol Work (1982); W. and N. Kelly, Policing in Canada (1976); W. McGrath and M. Mitchell, eds, The Police Function in Canada (1981).

Policing The police in Canada are an armed paramilitary force charged with the general responsibility of social control. The ROYAL CANADIAN MOUNTED POLICE, federal descendants of the North-West Mounted Police, exist and operate under federal statute and contract their services to 8 provinces (only Ontario and Québec have their own provincial police forces); other Canadian police forces are governed by provincial legislation. Police-science texts characteristically refer to the police functions of preventing crime, crime detecting and the apprehending of offenders, keeping order and protecting life and property — all of which may be summarized as order maintenance and law enforcement. The latter is the most publicized and romanticized of police activity. The police are expected to control disruptive social deviance, especially violations of formal law, but maintaining social order involves other activities as well, including the monitoring of deviant actions not explicitly illegal, surveillance and crowd control. By responding to deviance, intervening and pressing charges on behalf of the public or by ignoring offences, the police participate in the definition of social norms or moral standards, as exemplified by their selective enforcement of PORNOGRAPHY violations. The police enjoy considerable discretionary power in Canada that can be used by the political authorities on whom the police depend for financial support (see INQUIRY INTO CERTAIN ACTIVITIES OF THE RCMP). For example, between the wars police were often used in strikebreaking. Their intervention in the WINNIPEG GENERAL STRIKE in 1919 probably saved the RCMP from contemplated disbandment. INTELLIGENCE GATHERING, or security, a responsibility of the RCMP that will probably be transferred to a federal intelligence agency, is another controversial and ambiguous area of policing and a matter of public dispute.

Traffic or civic bylaw enforcement and general order maintenance comprise the bulk of police work, 20-30% of which is directly related to crime control. The remainder is devoted to random patrol, traffic control and clerical work. etc. Motor patrol (either one or 2 persons) is the major police activity. The Metropolitan Toronto Police Force has 2-person patrol units; foot patrol is common on only a small number of downtown city beats. Detective and CRIMINAL INVESTIGATION by specialized personnel is also important, although most legal violations are handled by uniformed officers. Police intervene in domestic crises and conduct searches for missing persons. These activities, difficult to measure and evaluate, are not highly regarded by the police, who define their role in relation to crime control and evaluate their efficiency and justify their budgets on the basis of crime-related policing.

Vancouver and Calgary have decentralized their police service in an attempt to make them more responsive to community needs, reorganizing them into team and zone policing, respectively. In both systems 12-50 men working under a staff sergeant will be assigned for several years to neighbourhood or sub areas of a city. Calgary describes zone policing as an attempt to encourage better relations between police and citizens and to enlist community help in solving problems.

All police forces in Canada are public agencies, responsible to either one or all municipal, provincial and national civil authorities. Most large Canadian cities maintain local municipal police forces (in BC several municipal forces as well as the RCMP are under contract). Numbers of police in Canada are increasing proportionately more rapidly than the total population, reflecting the effects of urbanization and the elaborate demands on police for services ranging from law enforcement to emergency health care and traffic control. In 1962 there were 1.7 police employees per 1000 population, including 1.5 sworn police officers. By 1977 the figures had risen to 2.8 and 2.3, respectively. The largest proportion was in Québec, with 3.0 per 1000 in 1977, and in the territories, 5.5 per 1000 in the Yukon and 5.3 in the NWT. Policing cost each Canadian $28 in 1971 and $40 in 1976 (in 1971 dollars). The largest municipal force is the Metropolitan Toronto Police, followed by the Montréal Urban Community Police Force. In 1977 the former employed 7177 persons, including 866 civilians and 598 sworn police officers. Calgary employed 1086 police employees in 1977, including 190 civilians. Toronto and Calgary expenditures for police in 1977 totalled, respectively, $156 746 968; and $31 921 000. Police salaries in major Canadian cities and for the Royal Canadian Mounted Police are similar; Montréal, Toronto and Vancouver establish the standards against which other police associations bargain. By the 1980s, a first-class constable in major Canadian cities received $20 000-$23 000. In 1981 the RCMP agreed to a salary for recruits of $20 650; after 4 years constables receive a maximum salary of $27 400. All Canadian police forces, except the RCMP, which is not unionized, use COLLECTIVE BARGAINING. Only in NS, NB, Manitoba, Saskatchewan and BC can police legally strike.

Recruitment and Training There is no standard training for Canadian police, although major regional training centres exist in the Maritimes, Québec, Ontario and BC. Training standards vary; a formal period of basic recruit training lasts only an average of 12 weeks. The national Canadian Police College in Ottawa, managed by the RCMP, offers courses in specialized areas, eg, police management for selected police officers from across Canada. The RCMP offer 22 weeks of basic training at the Regina depot. Recruit selection also varies, although high-school diplomas are generally preferred and sometimes compulsory. A very small number of university graduates, comprising from 0 to 12% of a police force, are recruited to serve as career police officers, but for a senior officer position no formal education beyond grade 10 or 11 is required. Because police forces have tended to recruit persons primarily from the working class, white, male population, police forces are not broadly representative of the experiences and attitudes of the Canadian population. In the past decade broadly based recruitment has been emphasized in an attempt to develop police forces more responsive to the population and more capable of investigating and discerning WHITE-COLLAR CRIME, eg, computer fraud. Training is aimed more at prevention than reactive enforcement. Public pressure for a more publicly representative force has increased, particularly in Toronto, with its concentration of immigrants, and there has also been an attempt to recruit members of minority groups. The RCMP has recruited and trained native Indian police in the western provinces, but they have been given "special" constable status only, limiting their responsibilities to specific tasks. The RCMP also employs "specials" for responsibilities such as airport security. However, although Canadian police forces have been under pressure to recruit more women and better educated persons, male high-school graduates still comprise the bulk of recruits. For example, in 1977 women comprised only 1.7% of sworn police personnel in Canada, compared to 2.7% in the US and 7.3% in Britain.   D. FORCESE

Political Campaign, an organized effort to secure the nomination and ELECTION of those seeking government office. In a system of represen-

tative democracy, electoral campaigns are the primary means by which parties (*see* PARTY SYSTEM) and candidates communicate and by which voters are informed of a party's or candidate's views. In Canada, political campaigns take place at the federal, provincial and municipal levels of government (*see* LOCAL ELECTIONS). Federal campaign practices are regulated by the Canada Elections Act (*see also* ELECTION EXPENSES ACT; ELECTORAL SYSTEMS). At the provincial and municipal levels, campaign practices are regulated by analogous provincial legislation.

The conduct of political campaigns in Canada has evolved gradually as a result of nearly 2 centuries of experience, as well as the adaptation of British (and, to a considerable extent, American) practices to the needs of a parliamentary federation with 2 official languages, a severe climate and a relatively small population spread over half a continent. Technological developments, such as television and air transport, and socioeconomic changes have dramatically influenced the evolution of campaign practices in recent years. Federal and provincial campaigns are quite similar. Municipal campaigns do not usually involve parties, but in other ways they resemble federal and provincial campaigns.

Early History of Campaigns Because representative institutions were established in the British N American colonies of Lower Canada, Upper Canada, Nova Scotia and New Brunswick before the end of the 18th century, political campaigns in Canada have a long history. Early campaigns preceded the establishment of organized political parties and were therefore largely a series of individual efforts in the constituencies. Until RESPONSIBLE GOVERNMENT was established in the middle of the 19th century, the governor of each colony, as the appointed representative of the Crown, frequently intervened in electoral campaigns to ensure the election of members who would co-operate with him and who would make the necessary funds available to his administration.

Once responsible government was achieved, recognized government and opposition leaders sat in the legislature and attempted to co-ordinate the campaigns of their respective followers to elect as many of them as possible. With Confederation in 1867, campaigns had to be extended over a vast geographical area, but the general election campaigns of 1867, 1872 and 1874 were conducted in a highly decentralized manner and largely followed the rules and practices that the various provinces had inherited from pre-Confederation days.

The most striking difference between these early campaigns and their modern counterparts was that early campaigns did not culminate in a single polling day. Elections were spread over several weeks, with different constituencies voting on different days. This enabled the government to schedule the polling in its safest ridings at an early date to create a bandwagon effect that might persuade voters in more doubtful ridings to support the government candidates. Opposition strongholds would be left to the last so as not to discourage supporters of the government. Party leaders and other notables often were candidates in more than one constituency so as to be sure of retaining a seat. Within each constituency, voting might extend over 2 days. Voting was by a show of hands rather than by secret ballot, and bribery and intimidation were therefore a common and more or less accepted aspect of campaigns. The small size of the electorates facilitated a more personal approach to campaigning than is possible today. Skillful politicians such as Sir John A. MACDONALD knew most of their supporters by name. In the federal election of 1867 an average of fewer than 1500 votes was cast in each constituency.

The federal election campaign of 1878 was in some respects the first modern campaign. Virtu-

ally all candidates represented one of the 2 recognized parties, LIBERAL or CONSERVATIVE. The parties were clearly differentiated on issues of policy that were extensively discussed during the campaign, and the Conservative victory could be regarded as a mandate to implement that party's policies of tariff protection and rapid completion of the transcontinental railway. Virtually all constituencies voted on the same day and a secret ballot was used for the first time. This was also the first election in which candidates were required to appoint an official agent and to file a statement of their campaign expenditures. The most important procedures followed by future campaigns were largely established in 1878.

Strategies, Issues and Leaders Modern electoral campaigns are carefully planned and coordinated efforts requiring lengthy preparation and centralized control. The leader of a political party appoints a campaign committee with a campaign director reporting to the leader. Specific persons are responsible for various aspects of the campaign, eg, fund raising, advertising, travel arrangements, relations with the media and the measurement of PUBLIC OPINION. In the Liberal Party it is customary to run a virtually separate campaign in Québec with its own autonomous organization reporting directly to the national leader. In the Conservative Party and the NEW DEMOCRATIC PARTY the campaign in Québec is merely a part of the overall national effort although this may change for the Conservatives as a result of their large majority in Quebec in the 1984 federal election.

Planning is somewhat easier for the party that controls the government because the PRIME MINISTER normally determines the date of the election. The election date will be selected to maximize the effectiveness of the governing party's campaign and will thus be influenced by economic conditions, by the government's popularity and the progress of its legislative program through PARLIAMENT. However, this important advantage is lost when an election is precipitated by the loss of a vote of confidence in the HOUSE OF COMMONS. In such cases (eg, the federal elections of 1926, 1963, 1974 and 1980) the governing party loses this advantage.

Political campaign strategies must take into account the fact that Canadians display widely varying degrees of affiliation with particular political parties. Each party seeks to mobilize its own supporters, to secure the votes of those who are leaning in its direction, and to persuade as many as possible of the uncommitted. Governing parties emphasize their accomplishments in office and announce initiatives designed to attract uncommitted voters. Opposition parties attack the government's record and make promises to do better if elected. The issues in election campaigns emerge out of the interaction between government and Opposition. However, not all campaigns have been characterized by well-defined issues. Partly for this reason, and partly because Canadian parties are not sharply differentiated by ideology, campaigns emphasize the personal characteristics and presumed capabilities of the party leaders. Campaign strategies are designed to acquaint voters with the leaders and to convince voters of their attractiveness; they may or may not include overt attacks on the leaders of other parties.

General election campaigns that appear to have been dominated by particular issues include those of 1878 (*see* NATIONAL POLICY), 1891 (commercial RECIPROCITY with the US), 1896 (MANITOBA SCHOOLS QUESTION), 1911 (reciprocity again), 1917 (CONSCRIPTION), 1926 (the constitutional powers of the governor general, *see* KING-BYNG AFFAIR), 1957 (the government's imposition of CLOSURE during the PIPELINE DEBATE), 1963 (nuclear weapons), 1974 (WAGE AND PRICE CONTROLS) and 1980 (ENERGY POLICY). Most of these issues were promoted and emphasized by the Opposition, more than by the government, and most of the campaigns listed ended with the defeat of the governing party. In the majority of campaigns in which the opposition parties failed to generate a dominating major issue, the governing party was reelected. The governing party usually prefers to emphasize its competence and overall record rather than a specific issue.

Virtually all campaigns have emphasized leadership, a fact sometimes deplored by those who would prefer a more intellectual and rational approach to politics. This is not a new phenomenon, as former slogans attest: "The Old Man, The Old Flag, and The Old Party" (used for Macdonald's last campaign in 1891), "Let Laurier Finish His Work" (1908), "King or Chaos" (1935) and "It's Time for a Diefenbaker Government" (1957). The leader referred to in the slogan won the election in each case.

In early campaigns the ability of the leaders and their "image" to influence the voters was largely indirect and was dependent on the persuasive powers of local candidates and of newspapers that supported the leader. As a result of modern transportation and communication, party leaders are better known to the voters. Macdonald and his Liberal opponents, Alexander MACKENZIE and Edward BLAKE, campaigned only in southern Ontario. Sir Wilfrid LAURIER, in 1917, was the first party leader to visit the western provinces during a campaign. W.L. Mackenzie KING failed to visit Québec, his party's major stronghold, during his successful campaign in 1921. Today, leaders of national parties are expected to campaign in every province, and planning the leader's itinerary during the 2 months of the campaign is a major activity of the campaign committee. Up to and including John DIEFENBAKER, party leaders relied mainly on the railways for their travel arrangements, but today they use specially chartered aircraft. At each stop on the tour the leaders promise new policies of particular interest to the locality.

Media, Advertising and Polls Electronic communications have made it possible for voters to hear and see party leaders without leaving their homes. Nationwide radio broadcasts by party leaders were first used in the campaign of 1930 and television was first employed in the campaign of 1957. In each case an opposition leader who was particularly effective in employing the new medium won the election.

Television tends to keep voters at home in the evening and has made it impossible, as well as unnecessary, to attract large numbers of them to political meetings. Party leaders still address large rallies in the hockey arenas and auditoriums of the major cities, but nowadays such events are attended mainly by reporters, television cameramen and persons directly involved in the party's local campaign. Those in the latter category are usually brought to the rally by chartered bus to ensure that empty seats will not be seen by voters viewing the event on television.

Political advertising is now an essential feature of any campaign. Modern advertising techniques were first applied to political campaigns before WWII. Today, advertising agencies help shape the campaign strategies of the parties, and advertising experts such as Dalton CAMP and Keith DAVEY have served as influential advisers to Canadian politicians. Slogans, leaflets, posters, lapel buttons and other paraphernalia, as well as newspaper advertisements and the tapes and films made available to the electronic media, seek to create the desired "image" of the party, its leaders and its policies. In recent campaigns, about one-half of all advertising expenditure has been devoted to television.

Modern campaigning has also been affected

by the development of scientific techniques for sampling and measuring public opinion. The periodic measurements of party standings by independent polling organizations are reported in the media and may affect the timing of elections and create a bandwagon effect during the campaign, similar to the effect of nonsimultaneous voting prior to 1878. The parties themselves employ pollsters (whose findings are normally not published) to identify areas of strength and weakness and to discover the voters' attitudes towards leaders, candidates, issues, policies and events.

Campaigning in the Constituencies Television, air transport and modern techniques of measuring and manipulating public opinion have all tended to increase the importance of centralized organization in a national or provincial campaign. Nonetheless a strong local campaign at the constituency level, co-ordinated with the central campaign, is still necessary for electoral success.

Local campaigns are primarily the responsibility of the candidate, the official agent and the campaign manager. The main objectives are to introduce the candidate to as many voters as possible, to identify the voters who are likely to support the candidate and to ensure that those voters actually vote. The first objective is accomplished mainly by having the candidate visit voters in their homes, although in industrial and mining centres it is also customary to visit the factories and mines where many voters are employed. Community associations in middle-class neighbourhoods often sponsor debates among the local candidates, but it is widely believed that only voters who have already made up their minds attend them (*see* ELECTORAL BEHAVIOUR).

Identifying the committed vote was easy in the stable rural communities and small towns of Macdonald's and Laurier's Canada. Among the heterogeneous and mobile populations of modern metropolitan agglomerations it can only be accomplished by an army of canvassers who attempt to visit each household at least once during the campaign. On election day the same persons will check periodically to ensure that friendly voters have actually voted, and may provide transportation to the polling place as an inducement.

Local campaigns, now generally honest and fair, were not always so. In rural areas it was once common to bribe voters with food, alcoholic beverages and money. In the larger cities, particularly in Montréal before the QUIET REVOLUTION, there were many instances of impersonating voters, placing fictitious names on the voters' lists, stealing ballots and intimidating the other party's volunteers by the threat or use of violence. Stricter regulation of campaigns and a more affluent and sophisticated electorate have brought about the virtual disappearance of such practices. However, the manipulation of the electorate through advertising and the frequency with which campaign promises are ignored after the election continue to raise questions about the quality of the democratic process.
GARTH STEVENSON

Reading: J.M. Beck, Pendulum of Power (1968); André Bernard and Bernard Descôteaux, Québec: Elections 1981 (1981); Dalton Camp, Gentlemen, Players and Politicians (1970); John Meisel, The Canadian General Election of 1957 (1962); Howard R. Penniman, Canada at the Polls (1981); Jeffrey Simpson, Discipline of Power (1981).

Political Economy is the study of the relationship between POLITICS and ECONOMICS. Economists study the workings of the economic system, while political scientists study the workings of political systems, the nature of government and the STATE, the functioning of political parties and the participation of citizens in decision making. To political economists, the notion that a phenomenon can be "purely political" or

"purely economic" is wrongheaded. For example, it is difficult to analyse the role of the corporation in the economy without understanding the political system in which it functions. Political science and economics must also be studied together to understand how income and wealth are distributed, how economic priorities are established, etc. A political economist examines the cultural, constitutional and political context within which economic developments occur, but also analyses the nature of the productive system in a given society and the social relationships that interact with it. Political economy as a discipline predates the separate study of economics and POLITICAL SCIENCE. Today the special area of study of political economists is the meeting point of the 2 newer disciplines.

Most Canadian scholars in the field agree that the preeminent Canadian political economist was Harold INNIS. He studied the FUR TRADE, the building of the railways, the relationship between the extraction of staple products and the nature of the Canadian state, and theorized about the interaction between the means of communications and systems of government.

Contemporary Canadian political economists have built on the work of Innis. They have concentrated on the relationship of the Canadian economy and the Canadian state with the economies and states of other more powerful countries, principally Britain and the US, but have also examined subjects such as the formation of the bourgeoisie and working class, the "national question" in Québec, industrialization and natural resources.
J. LAXER

Political History is the study of the processes, activities and institutions of GOVERNMENTS, the influences on them and the individuals involved with them. Political historians traditionally examined and documented the deeds of monarchs and prime ministers, of politicians and parties, of governments and related institutions. More recently, however, political historians and political scientists have been preoccupied with broader questions linked to the exercise of power within society, such as the attempts of interest groups to determine policies, the circulation of ideas and ideologies and their influence in the political arena, and the impact of increasing intervention by governments in society (*see* POLITICAL SCIENCE). While political biography has remained important for understanding and explaining our political history, it has been supplemented by examinations of nearly every facet of Canadian political life. In the process our perception of Canada's political evolution has had to be adjusted to encompass such things as the views of working people, the role of women in society, the impact of social and political reform movements, etc. The horizons of political history have been broadened forcibly in the historians' effort to understand and explain the practice of power within Canadian society. Thus Canadian political history no more than begins with the study of politicians and parties.

The modern political historian attempts to find and follow the various threads of Canadian life — economic, social and cultural — that have affected Canadian politics through time and bear on the historian's understanding of political events. Certain issues have been of perennial concern to Canadian politicians and are of current interest to historians. For example, Canada is a vast, resource-rich but lightly populated land which, especially after the mid-19th century, invited politicians to build platforms around programs of national economic expansion. For Sir John A. MACDONALD and Sir Wilfrid LAURIER, this meant industrializing central and eastern Canada through PROTECTIONISM, while colonizing the West through railway construction and massive IMMIGRATION. For John DIEFEN-

BAKER, economic expansion signified support for the opening of Canada's NORTH.

Political parties have long used economic themes as a means of uniting Canadians. CONFEDERATION, for instance, was promoted as, among other things, a solution to BRITISH NORTH AMERICA's economic woes. But economic questions have often bitterly divided Canadians. For example, policies of "national" development, such as the protective tariff, could be presented to the people as good for everyone, not merely for the manufacturer who was being offered a more or less captive market. But the tariff was also denounced by opposing parties as bad for everyone outside the industrialized communities of central Canada. Railways were necessary to open up the nation and to further trade, but questions as to how many, whether they should be privately or publicly owned, and what the state's railway policy should be have divided Canadians and influenced political decisions (see RAILWAY HISTORY). The many potentially divisive economic issues have been at the heart of most federal-provincial disputes (see FEDERAL-PROVINCIAL RELATIONS). A large and diverse territory also fostered the growth of regional economies whose interests have been exceedingly difficult to harmonize (see REGIONAL ECONOMICS). The exploitation of natural resources was promoted as certain to enrich the entire country, but when it has come time to divide up the profits, national unity has always been sorely taxed. It is scarcely surprising that Canadian economic and political unity has obsessed federal politicians. Federal parties, to gain power, have had to build coalitions of classes and regional interest groups whose goals are often contradictory. Moreover, provincial governments have seen themselves as more attuned to local and regional interests and thus often obliged to defend those interests against federal intrusion.

Other influences on political development, and therefore of interest to political historians, include RELIGION, once the primary factor affecting the citizen's vote. Issues such as the denominational schools questions (see CATHOLICISM; SEPARATE SCHOOLS) and TEMPERANCE have often been the subject of acrimonious political debate. As education came to be seen as a necessity, politicians at all levels had to elaborate policies to reform traditional institutions, revamp curricula, train teachers, and increase funding and access to educational institutions. INDUSTRIALIZATION made it necessary to protect workers and improve working conditions, and governments had to intervene increasingly in disputes between workers and employers. The spectre of UNEMPLOYMENT made it necessary to define policies that would not only alleviate misery but also support workers' buying power for economic reasons. URBANIZATION changed the needs of Canada's population. Citizens' health became an important question, and governments began to assume an active role in improving medical and hospital care and facilitating access to it. Some debates have centered on housing, URBAN AND REGIONAL PLANNING, municipal and regional organization, child care, WOMEN IN THE LABOUR FORCE, consumer protection and CRIME. Lobbies and interest groups developed to promote specific policies.

POPULATION characteristics have also greatly influenced Canadian politics. The existence of a French-speaking minority constituting about 30% of Canada's population, largely concentrated within Québec, has had special implications for the debate on Canadian unity. Indeed, many French Canadian spokesmen have perceived the interests of their society as being clearly different from the interests of Canada as a whole. For them, Canadian unity has meant assimilation and the destruction of the foundations of French Canadian culture (see FRENCH CANADIAN NATIONALISM). On the other hand, the "two nations" (DEUX NATIONS) debate, with roots in the mid-19th century (see DURHAM REPORT) and one of the most controversial themes in Canadian politics during the 1960s and 1970s, has tended to becloud the cultural heterogeneity of English-speaking Canada. Politicians have usually found it easier to unite French Canada than English Canada around a cause. Indeed, outside of war, there has been no issue powerful enough to unite a large majority of English-speaking Canadians. Regional, provincial, social and ethnic differences have proven to be stronger, in most cases, than a common LANGUAGE that for many has not even been the mother tongue (see ETHNIC LANGUAGES).

It is impossible to study Canadian political history without recognizing the great strength of Canada's economic and social links with Britain and later with the US (see COMMONWEALTH; CANADIAN-AMERICAN RELATIONS). As long as most Canadians were of British origin, ties with the mother country, notably in wartime, remained close. But as Canadians whose bonds with Britain were distant or nonexistent became a majority, Canada came increasingly to define itself by reference to its N American setting. The influences of such events as the American abrogation of RECIPROCITY in 1866 and the AMERICAN CIVIL WAR have been great. Economic links with the US became much more important in the 20th century; the tariff debate and the question of reciprocity have to a certain extent given way since the 1960s to problems associated with FOREIGN INVESTMENT and foreign control of Canadian INDUSTRY. Canada's cultural independence has been at issue as well. In the 1920s Canadians were already reading American magazines, listening to American radio and watching American movies. Later their leisure hours included more and more American television. In the 1960s and 1970s Canadian university students were often taught by American professors, but in the early 1980s indigenous Canadian political history studies and HISTORIOGRAPHY were again on a firm footing, with a greater breadth of vision and variety of approaches than ever before.

For broad surveys of Canadian political history, see NEW FRANCE; ACADIA; PROVINCE OF QUEBEC; UPPER CANADA; LOWER CANADA; PROVINCE OF CANADA; ATLANTIC PROVINCES; MARITIME PROVINCES; PRAIRIE WEST; and separate articles on each province and territory, as well as entries on FUR TRADE; FISHERIES HISTORY; AGRICULTURE HISTORY; and HISTORY SINCE CONFEDERATION. The many articles dealing wholly or in part with political themes include CONQUEST; LOYALISTS; RESPONSIBLE GOVERNMENT; REPRESENTATIVE GOVERNMENT; REPEAL MOVEMENT; PACIFIC SCANDAL; NATIONAL POLICY; URBAN REFORM; WOMEN'S SUFFRAGE; GREAT DEPRESSION; EXTERNAL RELATIONS and others. Canada's involvement in a number of domestic conflicts and international wars has been determined and directed largely at the political level, and these conflicts have affected other political events; see SEVEN YEARS' WAR; WAR OF 1812; REBELLIONS OF 1837; RED RIVER REBELLION; NORTH-WEST REBELLION; SOUTH AFRICAN WAR; WORLD WAR I; WORLD WAR II; and KOREAN WAR. There are, as well, numerous other areas of concern which can affect the understanding of Canadian political history, including CONSTITUTIONAL HISTORY; INTELLECTUAL HISTORY; SOCIAL HISTORY; and WORKING-CLASS HISTORY.

RICHARD JONES AND MICHAEL BEHIELS

Reading: J.M. Beck, *Pendulum of Power* (1968); R. Cook with J. Saywell and J. Ricker, *Canada* (1964); Paul Fox, *Politics: Canada,* 4th ed (1977); J.L. Granatstein and P. Stevens, ed, *A Reader's Guide to Canadian History 2: Confederation to the Present* (1982); E. McInnis, *Canada: A Political and Social History* (rev ed 1982). W.L. Morton, *The Kingdom of Canada* (1963), and ed, The Canadian Centenary Series.

Political Participation may describe any voluntary act to influence elections or public policy (see PRESSURE GROUP). It may be as simple as casting a ballot or it may mean running for office; it may be intended to influence the broad outlines of policy, or it may be very specific, eg, seeking benefits for an individual (see PATRONAGE). It may even be illegal (see CONFLICT OF INTEREST; CORRUPTION). Paying taxes would not usually be regarded as political participation, but refusing to do so can be a political act. Striking over wages or working conditions, while usually voluntary, is not considered a form of political participation, although some strikes are explicitly political, eg, the widespread protest, 14 Oct 1976, against the Anti-Inflation Board measures (see also WINNIPEG GENERAL STRIKE).

The frequency of political participation depends on several factors. About 90% of Canadians eligible to vote have done so at least once. In national ELECTIONS, turnout is typically just over 75% of those registered (considerably higher than in the US, where it is about 55%); turnout in provincial elections is usually slightly lower, although the opposite is true in Québec and some other provinces (see ELECTORAL BEHAVIOUR). Municipal turnout is usually the lowest of all. In both provincial and national elections, turnout has increased gradually since 1945. Participation falls off sharply for more difficult activities during POLITICAL CAMPAIGNS. According to sample surveys, about one person in 5 tries to persuade a friend to vote for a particular party or individual, and about one in 6 attends a rally or meeting and displays a lawn sign or bumper sticker. Between 5% and 10% of the population canvass, help to mail campaign literature, make campaign-related telephone calls, or act as election-day drivers or scrutineers. Fewer than one in 20 give money to a party or a candidate (see PARTY FINANCING) or belong to a party. Fewer still run for office or engage in illegal political activities.

Costs of political participation for individuals are usually more psychological than monetary, although some political acts obviously cost money. Political participation usually requires social and bureaucratic skills, a mastery of language and an ability to process information, and is therefore most powerfully influenced by levels of education (see CLASS AND POLITICS). Other differences in political involvement, such as those between occupation or income groups, partly reflect such differences in levels of education, although these differences can be offset by experience. For example, whatever their education, older citizens are more active than younger ones. Skills developed through nonpolitical experiences, eg, in the BUREAUCRACY or voluntary associations, are often useful to political participation. Women, who were enfranchised for national elections in 1918 and who have traditionally been excluded from those social roles that encourage political learning, are politically less active than men; however, as they have accumulated political experience, women have sometimes moved into roles formerly reserved for males. Sex differences in political activity count for less among the younger age groups and the more highly educated.

The benefits of political activity are as important a determinant of its frequency as are the costs. For example, people are more likely to vote and engage in other campaign activities when a race is close than when it is one-sided. Some occupation groups are more affected by government decisions than others and so are more likely to act politically whatever the cost of the act. PUBLIC SERVICE employees, whose incomes depend on political decisions, vote at a significantly higher rate than other citizens, although legally they cannot participate in certain other political actions. Farmers, whose incomes are greatly affected by government price and supply management decisions, are much more active than other groups with similar income and education levels.

Levels of political activity vary greatly across provinces, partly reflecting the competitiveness of the PARTY SYSTEM. Alberta, with its one-sided national and provincial elections, has the lowest electoral turnout in Canada. PEI and NS, with closely competitive 2-party systems, have the highest turnouts. In Québec, participation is greater in the highly competitive provincial elections than in the typically one-sided federal ones up to 1984. In rural Saskatchewan, democratically managed co-operatives are major producers and consumers; members acquire skills that are transferred to politics, and this involvement, combined with the competitiveness of the province's party system, raises participation in Saskatchewan politics to levels far exceeding those of Alberta.

Some political actions generate social benefits for the individual, regardless of their effects on policy or on the outcome of an election. Canvassing and committee-room work, because they provide opportunities to meet people, are popular among those who particularly enjoy the company of others. Donating money requires few social skills; displaying a lawn sign or bumper sticker requires neither money nor highly developed social skills, but does require sufficient commitment to a party or a candidate to withstand possible criticism from neighbours. Survey evidence suggests that the overlap between different kinds of action is weak. A person is more likely to engage in the same action in both provincial and federal elections than to engage in more than one action within either type of election.

Some observers argue that the present participation level of Canadians is sufficient. Survey evidence suggests that low-level participants care and know little about politics and often have a weak grip on democratic values. Others argue that participation is valuable in itself and ought to be encouraged, and that participation is the best teacher of democratic values; the relatively weak democratic commitment of those who do not participate is largely a consequence of their exclusion from political life, even if the exclusion is self-willed.

Any attempt to increase participation should either increase the benefits or reduce the costs of political action. Increased benefits might include changes in electoral law or in tax rules. The ineffectiveness of individual votes and campaign efforts in one-sided constituencies could be averted by a shift to an electoral formula of proportional representation, although other, undesirable consequences might result. Allowing tax credits for contributors to parties or candidates can transform a cost of participation into a benefit, which is precisely what has occurred in national elections and in many provinces in recent years. Individuals now contribute more money to Canadian parties than ever before. Increases in education levels, however, have not produced corresponding increases in participation, in spite of the positive association at any time between educational attainment and participation. The principal agents for reducing the cost of participation in campaigns must be political parties themselves, eg, by more active recruitment of volunteers. According to survey evidence, many more citizens are willing to work in campaigns than are asked. But the increased importance of electronic mass media in campaigns indicates that parties are substituting capital for labour rather than the reverse. Legislation to restrict party access to media might force the parties to seek voluntary assistance but might also infringe upon other political freedoms. Perhaps the most effective means of encouraging participation in campaigns and other political arenas lies in the democratization of activities that are not commonly regarded as political.

RICHARD JOHNSTON

Political Protest is the kind of political activity, eg, demonstrations, strikes and even VIOLENCE, usually but not always undertaken by those who lack access to the resources of organized PRESSURE GROUPS, or by those whose values conflict sharply with those of the dominant ELITE. Sometimes a protest centres around a specific issue or set of issues; at other times it is concerned primarily with the general grievances of such groups as ethnic or linguistic minorities, farmers, women or youth. Political protests may arise from any sector of society, and they reflect either left-wing or right-wing ideology.

When protest movements resort to extra-parliamentary means of expression, the STATE usually responds with repression, with some form of symbolic accommodation, or a mixture of both. Where the leadership of a protest movement is itself middle class, accommodation is often facilitated by some form of co-optation of the leadership into the political process. In such cases, the protest movement itself tends to become institutionalized as a new organized interest group which participates, however uneasily, in the process. Sometimes such movements themselves evolve into political parties organized around their particular protest issue or issues, become contestants in the electoral and parliamentary processes, and more or less abide by the established rules of the game. At other times, protest movements are met by repression and become violent, resorting to TERRORISM or civil insurrection. Some movements have tried to steer a middle course between violence and co-optation by carrying out peaceful civil disobedience.

Protest movements in Canada, which were concerned particularly with the economic grievances of farmers and workers, erupted in the early part of this century. Farmers adopted various tactics to bring their grievances to the attention of the Canadian state, culminating in farmers' protest parties which won office in Ontario, Alberta and Manitoba, and became briefly the second-largest party in the House of Commons after the 1921 federal election. In office, however, the farmers behaved very like the previous Conservative governments.

The protests of workers in 1919 against low wages, poor working conditions and the refusal of employers to recognize unions resulted in the WINNIPEG GENERAL STRIKE. The government responded with repression. Another important protest movement early in the century was the WOMEN'S SUFFRAGE movement which engaged in widespread agitation. The grant of adult female suffrage in federal elections (1918) resulted in a decline of this early feminist movement, which had concentrated its energies on the issue of the vote.

The GREAT DEPRESSION of the 1930s, with the consequent misery of unemployment and economic collapse, sparked many protest movements, several of which, radical or socialist in nature, challenged the dominant values of private enterprise. The CO-OPERATIVE COMMONWEALTH FEDERATION was founded to give political direction to many of these movements, while the COMMUNIST PARTY OF CANADA offered a yet more radical form of expression. Police repression against radical protest, especially strikes, and marches and demonstrations of the unemployed, such as the ON TO OTTAWA TREK of 1935 (which resulted in a bloody riot in Regina), were common. There were also populist right-wing protest movements, grounded in the ideology of FASCISM, in the 1930s, especially in Québec (see also KU KLUX KLAN).

During WWII there was a widespread and popular protest movement in Québec against the imposition of CONSCRIPTION by the federal government. This movement, which led to the formation of a political party, the Bloc populaire, encountered a certain amount of repression, but was sufficiently popular to force the federal government to delay imposing conscription until 1944.

During the 1960s, political protest became a familiar part of the political process (see HIPPIES; NEW LEFT). Antiwar demonstrations against nuclear weapons and the Vietnam war; student and youth protests; feminist movements; protests against racial discrimination; protests by community associations against urban redevelopment schemes; and protests against attacks on the environment imparted a new and more clamorous tone to Canadian politics. Perhaps the most serious protest movement of this decade was the movement for independence in Québec, which assumed several forms. The FRONT DE LIBÉRATION DU QUÉBEC, a violent and revolutionary wing, used bombings and terrorism. In October 1970 the kidnapping of a British diplomat and the kidnapping and later murder of Québec Cabinet minister Pierre LAPORTE led to the imposition of the WAR MEASURES ACT. With the virtual disappearance of the violent separatist movement, a moderate, constitutional wing devoted to independence for Québec grew stronger around the PARTI QUÉBÉCOIS, which came to provincial office in 1976 (see SOVEREIGNTY-ASSOCIATION), an instance of a protest movement that was sufficiently respectable and institutionalized to become the government of a province.

The WOMEN'S MOVEMENT remains an important protest movement in Canada. Women's groups, although diverse, have become a permanent source of protest and pressure on a wide spectrum of issues. Environmental and ecological groups (see GREENPEACE) have also continued to exercise pressure over issues such as ACID RAIN and the dangers of nuclear power and industrial POLLUTION. Native groups have become increasingly vocal. In the 1980s the antinuclear peace movement mobilized large numbers of protesters across Canada, especially against the testing in Canada of the American Cruise missile. More traditional sources of protest have also continued: labour unions mounted the largest demonstration on Parliament Hill in Canadian history in 1982 to protest against high INTEREST rates and UNEMPLOYMENT; farmers have mounted protests against farm foreclosures and against changes in the CROW'S NEST PASS AGREEMENT (see NATIONAL FARMERS UNION).

Another feature of protest movements in the late 1970s and early 1980s has been the emergence of widespread right-wing and populist (see POPULISM) protests. Protest campaigns against bilingualism and metrification, the movement for western SEPARATISM and the movement against ABORTION (eg, the Pro-Life Campaign) have all shown that protest movements are no monopoly of the political left.

Protest movements are now a normal part of the political process. They offer an opportunity for groups with a grievance to dramatize their

Former agriculture minister Eugene Whelan confronting angry dairy farmers, 1976 (*courtesy Canapress*).

views and seek to win wider support. In some cases, where marginal groups have been shut out of the political process, frustration breeds violence, which in turn brings on repression. In other cases, protests have been successful enough to win wide acceptance and have been met with accommodation. The dangers of cooptation for relatively successful protest groups are considerable, as are the dangers of electoral success for protest movements that evolve into protest parties; in the latter instance the original cause may itself become a victim of success.

REG WHITAKER

Political Science has been defined as the systematic study of government processes by the application of scientific methods to political events, but this rather narrow definition has been questioned by those who believe that power and its organization in human relations is the subject matter of political science, and power is a phenomenon that may be studied in forms of human association other than the state. Toward the middle of the 20th century, a narrower interpretation of power — that it leads to control over processes through which public decisions are made — gained popularity, although it is important to distinguish political from other kinds of decisions, eg, those in corporations. Another fundamental starting point for political analysis is the study of how scarce resources are allocated among competing groups of persons, how support is acquired and maintained for human projects. Politics exists because people do not always agree about what the community should be doing, or about how things should be done; politics is about the rules that are agreed upon for resolving conflict and about how these rules are accepted, even by those who disagree with the decisions made. It can also be about the breakdown of these rules and about revolutionary changes in political organization.

Political science is the systematic development of our knowledge and understanding of politics. Before the 20th century, what we now call political science tended to be philosophy, political history or the study of constitutional law — the latter 2 involving the description of political institutions. These 3 areas continue as aspects of modern political science, but they have evolved together into a separate, specialized, academic discipline.

Political philosophy is primarily concerned with the study of political ideas, eg, the place and order of values, the meaning of terms such as "right," "justice" and "freedom" often in the context of their times. Written political philosophy originated with the Greeks (philosophy meaning "love of wisdom," and politics, which referred to the activity of the city). Socrates, Plato and Aristotle were primarily interested in the nature of justice. Plato applied philosophy to the question of what is best, or what ought to be done in politics. Aristotle, comparing and classifying different forms of government, asked as well: "How does politics actually work?" Plato's question led to the tradition of political philosophy or political theory, and political philosophers are still concerned with political values. Aristotle's question led to the tradition of the scientific or empirical investigation of politics, which is concerned first of all with facts and with how to draw useful conclusions from factual observations about how political institutions actually function.

If philosophy began with the Greeks, medieval and more modern notions of law derive from the Romans and the more ancient Hebrew tradition of a covenant. In 1159, in *Policratus*, John of Salisbury compared the physiology of the body to that of the state; in *Summa Theologica*, the 13th-century theologian and philosopher Thomas Aquinas described man as naturally political and the state as a natural institution.

Aquinas assumed that the universe was inherently orderly, and that in law and politics, like everything else, the world moved from imperfection to perfection. Machiavelli, in the early 16th century, is often credited as the first modern political theorist; his credo was "For how we live is so far removed from how we ought to live, that he who abandons what is done for what ought to be done will rather learn to bring about his own ruin than his preservation." Hobbes, Locke and Rousseau, Montesquieu, Burke, Mill and Hegel among others all contributed to the literature of political philosophy. Marx, originally a follower of Hegel, decried philosophers for merely interpreting the world and not trying to change it, and claimed that he had taken a scientific approach to the world. By the end of the 19th century, it is often said that ideology had replaced political philosophy.

Contemporary political science owes its development to the 19th and early 20th centuries' enthusiasm for the SOCIAL SCIENCES, which was stimulated by the rapid growth of the natural sciences. The major change characterizing the growth of political science as a field of study is an emphasis on analysis. Instead of simply describing the formal rules and procedures involved in political institutions, eg, how a bill travels through Parliament to enactment, modern political science is equally interested in analysing the processes involved, how people actually behave.

Political Science in Canada In Canada political science is also an academic discipline. Departments of political science, or political studies, exist in some 45 universities, as well as in community colleges. Canadian political scientists are engaged in extensive research on the various aspects of politics and publish their findings in books, specialized academic journals, research reports and other forms of scholarly communication. Political science at Canadian universities dates to the late 19th century; originally it was strongly connected to constitutional law and to economics. The latter connection is somewhat distinctively Canadian, reflecting perhaps Canada's status as a developing nation with a strong concern with economic questions. At University of Toronto, which dominated political science until the mid-20th century, political scientists were colleagues of economists in a department of political economy. The first professional association, established permanently in 1929-30, was the Canadian Political Science Association, a joint venture with economists. Its official journal, another joint venture, the CANADIAN JOURNAL OF ECONOMICS AND POLITICAL SCIENCE, existed until 1967, when separate associations and separate journals were created.

Although Queen's, McGill, Dalhousie and later the universities of Saskatchewan and BC also taught political science, until after WWII academic departments were very small, faculty were poorly paid and political science (along with the social sciences in general) had little prestige. As late as 1950, there were only 30 political scientists in all Canadian universities. The 1940s, however, witnessed a coming-of-age of Canadian political science. The publication of major books by R. McGregor DAWSON, J.A. Corry, Alexander Brady and H.McD. Clokie indicated that indigenous Canadian scholarship in political science concerned with the study of Canadian political institutions was now possible, separate from economics or constitutional law.

In the 1960s, Canadian universities underwent a dramatic expansion. New universities sprang up and older institutions expanded their faculties and their offerings. Political science, gaining in prestige along with the other social sciences, shared in this rapid growth. By the early 1970s, there were about 30 times more

political scientists teaching at Canadian universities than there had been in 1950; according to a survey of the Canadian Political Science Association, in 1979 there were 687 political scientists with permanent teaching positions in 45 universities. Sixteen percent of these were located in Québec, and 14% were in French-language or bilingual departments. This does not include the political scientists who became public servants, politicians, journalists, lobbyists, consultants, researchers and advisers to various organizations, or high-school or community-college teachers.

During the 1960s, English Canadian political science was strongly influenced by American political science. Because the relatively small departments and small graduate programs of the 1950s had not produced a sufficient number of graduates to fill all the new positions created by expansion, Canadian universities turned to the relatively better-developed American political-science departments and a large number of American political scientists were recruited throughout the 1960s. By the end of the 1960s, nearly 50% of faculty members in political-science departments in Canada were non-Canadian by birth. The influence of American schools, American concepts and models and American authors and journals was very strong at a crucial period in the development of Canadian political science.

At the same time the so-called "behavioural revolution," an attempt (originating in the US) to make political science as scientific as possible, gained precedence. Value judgements were to be excluded. Political facts that could be given numerical values and that could be systematically analysed were called "hard data." For example, with voting, representative samples of electorates are drawn up, questionnaires administered and sophisticated statistical techniques applied to the results. Not all aspects of politics, however, are as easily quantified, nor is there any real basis for a science of politics exactly comparable to the hard sciences. Political scientists are themselves part of what they study and not detached observers. Within the discipline, during the 1960s, a major controversy concerned with the limits of this behavioural revolution erupted. Some political scientists claimed that the scientific study of politics alone was legitimate; others argued for the continuation of more traditional ways of looking at politics, claiming that political facts could not be separated entirely from political values. This conflict has now moderated considerably. Behaviourism is generally accepted as a legitimate but not exclusive part of the study of politics. Political science in Canada is varied and pluralist in its approaches.

During the 1960s and 1970s, French-speaking political scientists were influenced by different forces. In Québec social sciences were relatively underdeveloped and very much in the shadow of religious influence before the 1960s. The first political-science faculty in Québec was created at Laval in 1954, followed by a major expansion throughout Québec universities in the 1960s. However, American political science did not influence the development of the discipline in Québec as strongly as it did in English Canada. New positions in political science faculties were filled primarily by Québécois, but most of their graduate training was in France. European influences on political science were much more marked in Québec than in English Canada. Marxism was one such influence, and there was a greater emphasis on ideas and on political ideology. Another major difference in Québec was that the growth of Québec political science coincided with the QUIET REVOLUTION. As a result of the rapid rise of Québec nationalism and the debate over the constitutional future of Québec in (or out of) Canada, political science enjoyed a more central position than it held in English Canada. Political scientists became major participants in public debates and Québec political scientists are consequently more engaged politically than their English Canadian counterparts.

There is both autonomy and collaboration in the relations between the English- and French-speaking political-science communities. A separate francophone association was established in the early 1960s (first called the Société canadienne de science politique, since 1978 it has been known as the Société québécoise de science politique). The *Canadian Journal of Political Science/Revue canadienne de science politique* is a bilingual journal with editors and contributors drawn from both communities. A separate French-language journal, *Politique,* is also published by the Société québécoise. The Société holds separate annual meetings, although many francophone political scientists hold joint membership in the Canadian Political Science Association, and participate in its meetings as well.

Fields of Study There are a number of fields of study within the discipline of political science. Political theory is either about the explicit study of values (sometimes still called political philosophy) or about the methodology of political inquiry. The latter is concerned with more technical questions, such as the construction of hypotheses, deductive and inductive logic, the use of statistical tests. Political theory in this sense is a much more specialized field than political philosophy, which sometimes spills over into debates over democracy, liberalism, conservatism, socialism or federalism. Sometimes public debates invoke the concepts developed by political philosophers — as in the debate over independence for Québec or the new Canadian constitution — although rarely in a form that political philosophers would recognize.

A second subfield is comparative politics, practitioners of which compare political forms, institutions, values and processes in different countries. This is a vast field encompassing a considerable amount of detailed information about many countries. Comparative politics has also evolved more specialized branches, eg, area studies, which focus on particular groups of nations and geographic regions such as Latin America, Africa, the Soviet Union. Political developments are concerned with the problems of developing nations. In political-science departments in Canadian universities, the study of Canadian politics not surprisingly forms a distinct subfield in itself, as does Québec politics in Québec universities. Within this field provincial and municipal politics are also studied. International relations focuses on the interrelationship of states, diplomacy, foreign and defence politics, war and international organization. Yet another subfield is PUBLIC ADMINISTRATION, primarily the study of BUREAUCRACY. Public policy focuses attention on the process of policy formation.

An important subfield unique to Canadian political science is POLITICAL ECONOMY, which is both a subfield of study and an approach to politics in itself. It attempts systematically to relate economic, social and political factors together, partly a reflection of the older Canadian connection between economic history and the study of politics, but also a reflection of the influence of Marxist analysis and of a recent trend to more interdisciplinary research, wherein politics is linked with economics, sociology and history in particular.

At annual meetings of the Canadian Political Science Association and the Société québécoise de science politique, scholarly papers are presented from all the subfields. The *Canadian Journal of Political Science/Revue canadienne de science politique,* and *Politique* publish articles from all of them as well. There are also more specialized journals, such as *Canadian Public Adminis-*

tration (sponsored by the Institute of Public Administration), *Canadian Public Policy, International Journal, Studies in Political Economy, Canadian Journal of African Studies, Recherches sociographiques.* Canadian and Québec political scientists publish in journals edited abroad. Canadian political science is well respected internationally in a number of fields, particularly in the area of political theory. R. WHITAKER

Politics broadly refers to any or all conflicts among human beings over the allocation of power, wealth or prestige, when interests are pursued by means other than the use of physical violence. According to a more optimistic view, politics are an essential means by which collective goals can be achieved through peaceful co-operation. Narrowly the term describes activities associated with GOVERNMENT and the STATE. The state serves the purpose of managing conflicts and imposing solutions that are binding on all individuals and groups subject to its authority. To be viable, a state must enjoy unchallenged authority over a particular territory and population.

There are many schools of thought in POLITICAL SCIENCE concerning the role of the state. David Easton, a Canadian-born political scientist of international renown, has defined the role of the state as "the authoritative allocation of values." Marxists, however, interpret politics as class conflict and consider the state the institution that reflects and expresses the common interests of the dominant SOCIAL CLASS. Pluralists define politics as competition among organized groups and interests, the state being the neutral referee that imposes generally acceptable solutions. Other observers view politics as the conflict among ELITES who manipulate the masses as a means of pursuing their own ends.

Politics have existed in Canada for thousands of years, although political authority among the native peoples before the arrival of Europeans differed significantly from that which exists in a modern state. In the narrower sense politics probably began under the French regime and certainly no later than the latter part of the 18th century, when elected legislatures were established in Upper Canada, Lower Canada, Nova Scotia and New Brunswick.

Politics in the Canadian state usually include activities associated with the federal, provincial and municipal levels of government, as well as the relations among these 3 levels of government. Political activities among these levels of government involve legislative, executive and judicial institutions, the administrative departments and agencies of government, and political parties and interest groups.

A large proportion of the events reported and commented upon by the news media involve politics (*see* POLITICS AND THE MEDIA). Most Canadians can identify the PRIME MINISTER, the PREMIER of their own province and other leading participants in the political process, and the vast majority of adult Canadians participate in politics by voting in elections. The academic study of politics is called political science but other subjects, eg, history, geography and sociology, also involve the study of politics.

The term "politics" is sometimes associated in people's minds with the cynical manipulation of PUBLIC OPINION, the trading of favours for political support, and the enrichment of politicians and their friends at the expense of society (*see* CORRUPTION). While such activities no doubt exist, they are only a small part of the substance of politics. GARTH STEVENSON

Reading: Paul Fox, *Politics: Canada* (5th ed, 1982); R. Van Loon and M. Whittington, *The Canadian Political System* (3rd ed, 1981).

Politics and the Media Much of what Canadians know about their political leaders, party politics or public policy comes from the media

— especially television, radio and newspapers — the primary information link between the Canadian population and the political sphere. The media try to explain the government's goals and policies, helping to mobilize and reinforce public support necessary for effective political action, but they also focus attention on controversial policies, expose corruption and hold politicians accountable to public opinion. In reporting on politics, the media help select the issues that are to receive public attention and help shape the public agenda.

The free flow of a meaningful account of political events and issues is necessary for the public's understanding of politics, the formation of PUBLIC OPINION and the public's participation in the political process. The freedom of the media from political interference; the vitality of the media and the way they conduct their political functions; the way freedom of the media is reconciled with the pressures of the commercial system that finance media institutions; and the openness of the government in providing information all influence the health and vigour of Canadian democracy.

During the 19th century, there were bitter struggles between newspaper editors and political authorities. In 1835 the Joseph HOWE libel trial in Halifax established important precedents about the right of the press to criticize the authorities (*see* LAW AND THE PRESS; NEWSPAPERS). In the 20th century the Supreme Court of Canada has supported press freedom in a number of cases. In the 1938 ALBERTA PRESS ACT REFERENCE the Supreme Court ruled that attempts by the Social Credit government in Alberta to curb press criticism were unconstitutional; in Québec, the PADLOCK ACT was used as an instrument of CENSORSHIP for 20 years until it was ruled unconstitutional in 1957. Censorship was also practised in WWI and WWII and during the OCTOBER CRISIS in 1970 (*see* WAR MEASURES ACT).

There are restraints on the flow of information about government in every society. Canada's governmental process tends to be more secretive and closed. The public's "right to know" is often sacrificed to the penchant of the government to conduct business away from the glare of publicity. In 1982 Parliament partly corrected this situation with the enactment of the Access to Information Act (*see* FREEDOM OF INFORMATION). In 1982 Canada's new Constitution provided guarantees for freedom of expression, including freedom of the press and other media of communications. The CANADIAN CHARTER OF RIGHTS AND FREEDOMS guaranteed formal recognition to a tradition of press freedom that evolved, despite occasional serious setbacks, over 150 years.

Economics and Free Press While Canada's media are part of the machinery of POLITICS, they are generally operated for profit. (The major exception is the CANADIAN BROADCASTING CORPORATION). Daily newspapers and privately owned broadcast operations have been among the most profitable business enterprises in Canada. The pursuit of profits, however, has led to the growth of newspaper chains and the virtual disappearance of newspaper competition. Of Canada's nearly 100 newspaper cities, only 6 have more than one daily. Of the 117 dailies, 88 are owned by 12 companies. Two chains, SOUTHAM Newspapers Inc and THOMSON Newspapers, sell 6 out of 10 English papers produced each day; one Québec chain, Québecor, controls nearly half of the French-language circulation. In broadcasting, some companies own daily newspapers and broadcast stations in the same cities. The Royal Commission on Newspapers (Kent Commission) reported in 1981 that the extensive concentration of newspaper ownership that exists in Canada is "entirely unacceptable" for a democratic society: "too much power is put in too few hands and it is power without accountability." The commission called for federal government intervention to curb the power of chains and make the operation of newspapers more democratic and responsible, although critics charged that the proposals would increase the potential for political interference in news operations (*see* MEDIA OWNERSHIP).

Changing Role of Media in Politics Canada's press became deeply involved in politics around 1820 when the economies of the British N America colonies could support a competitive newspaper system through advertising, subscriptions and print jobs. By focusing attention on politics, newspapers helped to politicize the population and mobilized public support for democratic institutions, especially RESPONSIBLE GOVERNMENT. In the latter part of the 19th century, press and politics were so entwined that Canada's leading journalists were often politicians. At the CHARLOTTETOWN CONFERENCE of 1864, which led to Confederation, 23 of the 98 delegates were journalists (*see* JOURNALISM). Furthermore, newspapers helped spur the growth of political parties while political patronage helped finance newspapers. In the early 1900s technological changes in newspaper production and the changing interest of advertisers led to a new relationship between press and politics. Newspaper competition declined and there was less party attachment. The introduction of radio in the 1920s and television in the 1950s revolutionized the mass communications industries. By 1984 there were more television sets than households and twice as many radios as people. Canadians, who spend 6 hours watching television for every hour of newspaper reading, regard television as the most important and reliable news medium. Television has become the great battleground for public opinion in the struggle for political power. However, the transmission of political electoral information tends to be dictated by the medium, ie, television may have helped expose more Canadians to politics than ever before, but it has done so at the cost of oversimplifying complex issues. Election campaigns are increasingly run for the news media and there is much less concern with convincing live audiences on the hustings. Political leaders crisscross the country to provide television filming opportunities in the right places, and great emphasis is placed on the "images" portrayed by the party leaders in formal television debates. Party campaign strategies are aimed at effective use of media. Public opinion surveys are used to help parties decide the acceptable image and to determine party platforms.

Media and Nationhood It is often said that Canada's mass meida — especially electronic communication — help build Canada's national identity without erasing the multiple cultural and linguistic dimensions of society. It is for this reason that Canadian governments have played a dynamic role in shaping the broadcast media. Canada has been a world leader in the application and development of new COMMUNICATIONS TECHNOLOGY. It is possible, however, that technology has not helped to bridge major communication gaps in Canada's heterogeneous society. For example, the French and English media provide very different accounts of Canadian political developments. The French media generally support Québec nationalism; the English media are closely tied to the American media and broadcast enormous amounts of American TELEVISION PROGRAMMING. This and other evidence indicates that in some ways Canada's media have in fact been principal agents of denationalization and have not necessarily contributed in major ways to a national identity.

ARTHUR SIEGEL

Reading: F. Peers, *The Public Eye: Television and the Politics of Canadian Broadcasting, 1952-1968* (1979); P. Rutherford, *The Making of the Canadian Media* (1978); Arthur Siegel, *Politics and the Media in Canada* (1983); B. Singer, ed, *Communications in Canadian Society* (2nd ed 1983).

Bee on a foxglove (*photo by V. Claerhout*).

Pollination is the transfer of pollen (each grain an immature reproductive structure) from male to female parts of SEED PLANTS. It may occur by nonbiological means, eg, water or wind, or by biological agents, eg, animals. Pollination is vital to AGRICULTURE. Successful production of FORAGE CROPS, VEGETABLES and FRUITS is dependent on INSECT pollination. Insect pollinators are also important in reproduction of native plants and regeneration of vegetation as well as being aesthetically pleasing. *See* BEEKEEPING; PALYNOLOGY.

Pollution was viewed initially as the unsightly mess or visible environmental damage resulting from careless disposal of various materials. Most commonly, pollution was seen as the dirty scum on rivers or lakes, or the grey and yellow smog in the skies over cities. These relatively obvious problems (confirmed by dead fish floating on waters or irritation of eyes and throats on particularly smoggy days) were considered local concerns which would be cleaned up by reducing emissions from sewer pipes and smokestacks, thus giving the environment time to absorb and purify materials. Dilution was considered the solution to pollution.

Scientific research increasingly has shown that pollution also includes odourless and colourless chemicals that remain in soil, air and WATER long after the materials they were used in have disappeared. Pollution now also includes chemicals that were not carelessly dumped but are gradually sprayed on farmland as fertilizers and PESTICIDES, others from inside pressurized spray cans, and others plastered on walls and ceilings as asbestos fireproofing. Problems caused by these pollutants can take over 20 years to develop, as exemplified by the fatal lung disease asbestosis, caused by exposure to asbestos dust. Problems are now known to be widespread. ACID RAIN that kills fish in Ontario lakes comes largely from AIR POLLUTION emitted by smokestacks hundreds of kilometres away in Ohio. Snow falling in the Canadian Arctic includes chemicals from Japan. Scientists have also discovered that some chemicals which are not harmful alone bond with other chemicals to create new and dangerous pollutants.

Pollution is now recognized to include more than just substances. It can take the form of excessive NOISE, causing damage to hearing; heat discharged as hot water from power plants, destroying aquatic life; electronic transmissions (eg, microwaves, X rays), damaging human tissue. Scientists are still unsure how much exposure to many modern pollutants is dangerous to humans and other living matter. In some cases, no exposure may be the only safe exposure. Our ENVIRONMENT now appears as a garbage dump filling up to overflow with invisible additives. In a strict sense, pollution can be defined as the release of any material or energy that may cause immediate or long-term harmful effects to the natural environment. On that basis, very little can be used or thrown away without consideration of its long-term effects. Thus, pollution involves all products and processes we use except those proven not to be harmful.

Pollution arises largely from the sheer volume of throwaway material created to meet the needs of the Earth's rapidly expanding population. Much of the world is already at the limit of unconsidered and uncontrolled growth of both products and their effects as pollutants. In one day the average Canadian citizen discards about 2.5 kg of solid garbage. Almost 7000 L of fresh water are needed per Canadian per day. This average person throws away more than 10 000 bottles and 17 500 cans during a lifetime. Residents of Metropolitan Toronto discard a total of 87 000 t of plastic per year in municipal garbage (*see* WASTE DISPOSAL).

To meet the demands of consumer society growth in the 1950s, many new and unnatural chemicals were developed for use in manufacture of food and drugs, etc. More than 60 000 chemical compounds are now used commercially in Canada; another 1000 are developed annually. About 15 000 drug products are sold in Canada; over 1500 flavourings, many of them synthetic, are permitted in foods (*see* FOOD ADDITIVES). Many synthetic chemicals do not decompose through natural biological processes (eg, the action of sunlight, heat and cold, bacteria). They slowly leak out into the environment, contributing to the steady accumulation of potential pollutants in land, air, water, vegetation and our bodies.

The pesticide DDT provided an early example of the danger of bioaccumulation. Millions of kilograms of DDT were used to kill insects in N America, until scientists discovered that the chemical was accumulating in insect-eating birds. The pesticide accumulated to the point of damaging the birds' eggs; thus, for example, the PEREGRINE FALCON came close to extinction. DDT was banned in Canada by 1971, but its chemical components are still found in soil and water and in migrant birds returning from Central and South American countries which still use DDT. Thousands of other chemicals have yet to be considered.

Pollution is now studied in laboratories and evaluated medically for its cancer-causing potential, longevity (often hundreds of years) and volumes (usually microscopic). The scientific danger level of "one part per million," roughly equal to a drop of pollution in a barrel of water, has entered common parlance. Many chemicals that Canadians have accepted, tasted, worked with and relied on since the 1950s are now suspected to be "toxic" or deadly.

The 1970s was a period of awakening to the reality of the costly effects of pollution resulting from industrial by-products. This recognition was based on scientific investigations and frightening, sometimes painful, experience. For example, in northern Ontario hundreds of residents along the English-Wabigoon river system have lost their jobs as commercial fishermen, their community stability and their expectation of a long and healthy life because of invisible, poisonous MERCURY in the fish. The mercury was dumped as waste material by a local paper mill before 1970, but will remain a danger in the water and fish for another century. In New Brunswick, although several children have died, residents continue to be exposed to aerial spraying with a pesticide designed to kill forest insects and protect the forest industry. At Port Hope, Ont, thousands of tonnes of slightly radioactive wastes, dumped years earlier, were removed from beneath houses, schools and stores to lessen the danger of cancer developing among citizens. In Toronto, public clinics are held to test the blood of residents of some neighbourhoods for low levels of LEAD dust from nearby factories, which could lead to nervous disorders and learning disabilities.

Pollution poisoning is increasingly becoming a risk and a concern to Canadians, especially in urban areas. When most of the chemicals were developed, research on their long-term impacts was minimal. Through ignorance or greed, many industries long ignored the obvious pollution they were creating by dumping wastes into the public environment. As the SCIENCE COUNCIL OF CANADA pointed out in its scathing 1977 report "Policies and Poisons," governments were for too long ill-equipped to measure pollution and too hampered by red tape and political compromise to tackle polluters. Heightened public awareness of pollution dangers and public pressure on governments and industries are changing these attitudes. Public opinion surveys show that environmentalism and pollution fighting are now consistently important concerns of Canadians. Pollution is no longer perceived as a simple choice between halting pollution or shutting down the polluting factory. Jobs are created by cleaning up and protecting the environment. Waste materials can be recycled instead of dumped, thus saving companies' money. The cost of cleaning up and preventing pollution is far less than that of repairing environmental and health damage, or losing an environmental resource forever.

Science and citizens are working in 2 directions: in laboratories, studying new and existing chemicals for subtle but long-lasting consequences for the environment; and in legislation, writing new laws to ensure proper cleanup of existing problems and prevention of new ones (*see* ENVIRONMENTAL LAW). Prevention accomplishes far more in the long run than belated reaction. More money is required for scientific research and technologies to reduce pollution and promote recycling. Producers and consumers will pay more for safer, less wasteful products, but these measures will reduce long-term economic and social impacts.

Water Pollution Polluted water can destroy valuable commercial and sports FISHERIES, make vital supplies of drinking water unfit for human and animal consumption and damage a recreational and aesthetic resource of unmeasurable value to all Canadians (*see* WATER POLLUTION; WATER TREATMENT). Sewage wastes exceed millions of gallons per day for most Canadian cities; by itself this flow would vastly exceed the capacity of local rivers or lakes for dilution and neutralization. The algae choke out other vegetation on lake and river bottoms, often causing bad odours and tastes and creating a breeding ground for disease-bearing bacteria. In the 1960s Lk ERIE became clogged and its beaches strewn with foul algae; a huge portion of this shallow lake became effectively "dead." Complex pollutants such as dissolved and suspended metal particles (eg, arsenic, lead, cadmium) and chemicals (ranging from oils to acids) washed into the waters with city grit and dirt pose greater problems. Many of these invisible particles are toxic to aquatic life and, when they accumulate in water and fish, can be harmful to humans consuming either. In 1981 Canadian scientists discovered, for the first time, very small amounts of one of the most deadly man-made chemicals, Dioxin TCDD 2,3,7-8, in the Great Lakes. Dioxin is a byproduct of agricultural chemical production and the degradation of industrial wastes. As little as a droplet of the pure chemical is deadly in thousands of litres of water. Researchers are only beginning to consider the problems which would be involved in the protection and purification of Great Lakes water for human consumption if Dioxin concentrations increased. The ultimate solution will require expensive barriers to stop leaks from chemical dumps, and bans on chemical products containing compo-

nents which degrade into Dioxin. Some such products are disappearing from use in industry, homes and farms, but more research is needed to identify all sources.

Land Pollution Industrial and urban waste dumping, poor agricultural practices and mineral exploitation all produce pollutants that reduce or destroy the ability of soil to sustain healthy plant life. Many of these pollutants are ultimately transferred to water bodies, but en route they can sterilize, poison and erode the soil. Millions of tonnes of industrial chemicals, in liquid form, and commercial and residential garbage, particularly in a semisolid form, are disposed of annually in open pits, giant holes and artificial mountains across Canada (*see* SOLID WASTES; WASTE DISPOSAL). Even with daily efforts to cover the garbage with layers of dirt, these "sanitary landfills" cause aesthetic problems, odours and health risks. The gradual disintegration and decomposition of garbage also releases potentially dangerous chemical pollutants into surface and underground water supplies. Carefully designed dumps can reduce seepage, but many municipalities lack conveniently situated disposal sites.

Incineration of garbage can substantially reduce the volume to be buried, but adds its own risks of air pollution. Recycling and reduction of unnecessary packaging can significantly reduce the volume of garbage before incineration or landfill disposal. Disposable plastic packaging, for example, comprises 36% of plastic materials produced for society. At present, almost one third of commercial-residential garbage is paper; 20% glass and metal; 17% food wastes. Recycling and source reduction are becoming important industries as people realize that pollution is best prevented by reducing the use of source materials.

Other sources of land pollution include poor AGRICULTURAL SOIL PRACTICES and logging, which expose the bare topsoil to wind and water EROSION, or excessive use of chemical fertilizers and pesticides, which gradually accumulate in soil and reduce crop growth or make crops unsafe for human consumption. Polluted soil which lacks vital minerals and microorganisms to hold it together is also more subject to erosion. Erosion can lead to enormous accumulations of salt in rivers and streams, blocking the flow of water and making it unsuitable for aquatic life.

Industrial liquid wastes of highly toxic composition are another critical source of pollution in Canada (*see* HAZARDOUS WASTES). In Ontario an estimated 35-70 million L of the total 350 million L of liquid industrial wastes produced annually are considered hazardous. At present, there are almost no fully safe sites and systems operating in Canada to handle these wastes. These liquids pose high risks of long-lasting pollution of underground and surface water supplies if they leak out of garbage dumps where they are often discarded. Most of these liquids can be first reduced in volume by filtering out useful chemicals for reuse, then neutralized by adding other chemicals, or destroyed in specially built high-temperature furnaces. Finally, they can be converted into permanently solid wastes that will not leak or decompose when buried in special sites.

Air Pollution is the accumulation in the atmosphere of substances that can endanger health or otherwise damage materials or living matter. Air includes a wide range of substances produced by natural and man-made sources; most of these substances have not accumulated to obviously harmful levels. The major source of these pollutants is the burning of carbon-based fuels (eg, coal, oil, natural gas), which produces invisible potential pollutants. These can cause local, regional and worldwide pollution problems, either as individual chemicals or in combination. Smog, for example, is a combination

of nitrogen oxides, hydrocarbons and carbon monoxide, which, under the action of sunlight and water, are blended together into pollutants such as ozone, which irritates human lung tissue and damages vegetation; aldehydes, which irritate human eyes and skin; and acids, which damage human tissue and buildings. A weeklong smog in London, England, in 1952 caused more than 4000 deaths and prompted enactment of new limits on the burning of coal in city factories and homes. On a global scale, carbon monoxide resulting from combustion converts to carbon dioxide and permanently accumulates in the Earth's upper atmosphere.

In Canada, particulate or gritty air pollution has been reduced by installation of filters on smokestacks and by better-tuned automobiles. But automobiles, fossil-fueled power plants, factories and mineral smelters all produce other air pollutants which can reach levels threatening to human health when local weather conditions allow them to accumulate. These local episodes require industry to reduce operations until weather improves, ie, until the local smog is diluted by fresh winds. Even when local conditions appear clean and safe, regional accumulations of pollutants can pose other problems. Acid rain, for example, is caused by the accumulation of nitrogen and sulphur oxides, which blow long distances, gradually changing to nitric and sulphuric acids in the moist air and falling as acid rain, snow and grit.

In Canada, controls have been introduced on most major types of air pollution. Technologies are being developed to reduce fossil-fuel emissions further but, over a longer period, a significant reduction in consumption of these fuels is necessary. The problem of air pollution will ultimately be solved by development of less-polluting energy sources, not by pollution controls.

The pollution outlook for Canadians for the next 20 years is murky. Despite the vast size of the country, most people live in cities, where pollution problems are concentrated. Ultimate solutions to pollution require major changes in what we produce, use and throw away. Pressures for these changes will increase and the costs of changes will be more readily shared when people realize that everyone shares the risks.   ROSS HOWARD

Reading: Donald Chant, ed, *Pollution Probe* (1970); Ross Howard, *Poisons in Public: Case Studies of Environmental Pollution in Canada* (1980).

Pollution Probe Foundation Pollution Probe was established in 1969 to provide education and advice on ways to restore and preserve the Canadian environment. It became the Pollution Probe Foundation (a registered charity) in 1971, and has successfully addressed a wide range of environmental issues, including ACID RAIN, PESTICIDE abuse, FOOD ADDITIVES, industrial-waste reduction and recycling, WATER POLLUTION, toxic chemicals and energy CONSERVATION. The foundation also operates Ecology House, an urban demonstration of energy and resource conservation in downtown Toronto, and publishes *Probe Post: Canada's Environmental Magazine*. The organization is governed by a 20-member board of directors. Financial support comes from individuals, corporations, charitable foundations, sale of publications and services and a Canada-wide membership. While the foundation has been instrumental in establishing a number of other environmental public-interest groups, it now has no connection with any other organization of similar name.   COLIN F.W. ISAACS

Polo is a game that originated in Persia, and over the centuries spread throughout Asia. It was discovered in the mountainous areas of northern India by British army officers during the 19th century and was organized in its modern form. It is now played chiefly in ranching areas and in countries where the traditions of wealthy horsemen prevail. An international handicap system gives each player a rating for purposes of competition.

Polo was first played in Canada in 1878 by British garrison officers stationed in Halifax. The game was more widely played in western Canada, however, and by 1889 weekly matches were organized in Victoria between garrison teams and British naval officers. Alberta was a centre of polo activity, with the NORTH-WEST MOUNTED POLICE providing much of the initiative for organization. Clubs were formed in Calgary and High River in the 1890s, and by the turn of the century in Toronto and Montréal. The first Canadian polo tournament was held in Toronto in 1903. In 1905, the High River team won both the Canadian and American championships. Between the world wars, Vancouver, Victoria and Kamloops, BC, were strongholds of polo in the West, and Montréal the leading city in the East. But after WWII, the sport almost died out entirely. In the early 1950s it was revived in Vancouver and Victoria; and in the 1960s clubs in southern Alberta banded together to form the Calgary Polo Club, now the strongest polo organization in Canada. Competition in the West is usually with teams from the US. In Toronto, the most popular form is arena, or indoor, polo. BARBARA SCHRODT

Pommier, Hugues, priest, missionary, painter (b in Vendôme, France *c*1637; d in France Dec 1686). He sailed for Canada in 1663, stopping first briefly in Placentia, Nfld, and then working as a missionary throughout NEW FRANCE. Bertrand de Latour, in 1761, claimed that Pommier "prided himself on being a painter, producing many pictures; no one liked them; he hoped his talents would be better appreciated in France; he had no luck there either." This severe judgement explains why no painting can be attributed to him with certainty. The retouched portrait of Mother Catherine de Saint-Augustin and the *Martyres des pères jésuites*, both in the Hôtel-Dieu in Québec, are attributed to him but are probably not his work. He evidently returned to France in 1678.
FRANÇOIS-MARC GAGNON

Pond, Peter, fur trader (b at Milford, Conn 18 Jan 1739/40; d there 1807). In 1775, with proverbial Yankee shrewdness, Pond moved from the area SW of the Great Lakes, where he had been trading for most of the previous decade, to focus on what is now the Canadian West, which proved a much richer territory. In 1778 fellow traders chose him to take goods from the lower Saskatchewan R into the Athabasca country, which they had heard of from the Indians. He accomplished the difficult journey, wintering on the Athabasca R and doing an extremely good trade. In 1779 he received one share in the partnership that brought together the trading interests of Benjamin FROBISHER and Simon MC-TAVISH. He returned to the Athabasca country in 1783-84, and again from 1785 to 1788 as a partner in the NWC. Having been implicated in the murder of 2 competitors, he left the FUR TRADE under a cloud. He went back to the US, probably to his birthplace. The map of the North-West that Pond drew in 1784-85, based on his own exploration and Indian reports, is the earliest to depict what is now called the Mackenzie Basin. He subsequently prepared other versions of the map and wrote an account of his early adventures, a work that radiates the energy and enormous confidence that drove him.
JANE E. GRAHAM

Pondweed, common name for members of the family Potamogetonaceae [Gk *potamos,* "river"], which consists of the genus *Potamogeton.* Formerly, pondweeds were classified as family Zosteraceae, along with several other genera, eg,

Ruppia (ditch-grass), *Zannichellia* (horned pondweed) and *Zostera* (eelgrass or grass-wrack). All these have representatives in Canada and are now generally regarded as distinct families. Pondweeds grow submerged in fresh or, occasionally, brackish water. The genus *Zostera* is a true marine aquatic and, in Canada, *Z. marina* is widely distributed on both the E and W coasts. *Potamogeton* species are perennial, herbaceous PLANTS anchored in the mud at the bottom of shallow lakes and ponds by underground stems (rhizomes). The leaves, varying considerably in shape, are arranged alternately and all may be submerged or some may float. The flowers are small, often borne in elongated clusters that may be submerged, allowing for POLLINATION by water, or emergent from the water for wind pollination. Pondweeds are widely distributed, but a majority of the approximately 100 species occur in the N temperate region. About 30 species occur in Canada, several extending into arctic areas.

Pontbriand, Henri-Marie Dubreil de, sixth bishop of Québec (b at Vannes, France Jan 1708; d at Montréal 8 June 1760). Educated by the Jesuits and Sulpicians, appointed bishop of Québec in 1740, Pontbriand arrived in Aug 1741, determined to remedy the abuses of episcopal absenteeism. He visited the religious institutions, parishes, missions and reserves of his vast diocese 1741-44 and again 1749-52. After the fall of Québec in 1759 he urged conciliation with Gen James MURRAY. He died before Montréal capitulated, leaving New France without a spiritual leader in her darkest hour.
CORNELIUS J. JAENEN

Pontiac, chief of the OTTAWA (b 1720?; d at Cahokia [Ill] 20 Apr 1769). He may have served with the French and Indian forces that defeated Maj-Gen Edward Braddock at FORT DUQUESNE (1755). He later was able to organize Indians discontented with the English regime, arranging a series of secret meetings among the SENECA and other groups. In spring 1763 he ignited hostilities, leading an alliance of OTTAWA, HURON, Potawatomis and OJIBWA against Ft Detroit and capturing a contingent of 46 English soldiers at Pt Pelee. Detroit was held under siege, and the uprising spread throughout the PAYS D'EN HAUT, as Michilimackinac, Ft Sandoské, Ft St-Joseph, Ft Miami and others fell to the widening alliance. On July 29 at Bloody Run, Pontiac's forces routed an encampment of 260 reinforcements heading for Detroit. Pontiac's direct control was limited to the warriors around Detroit, but even that group disintegrated as the Potawatomis and Huron left, and even the Ottawa deserted to winter hunting grounds. A series of peace treaties was signed in July 1765, with the prestigious Pontiac a key signatory. He insisted that the Indians were not surrendering their land by making peace. Those still hostile to the English turned against him, expelling him from his own village. He led a wandering life until murdered by a Peoria assassin. JAMES MARSH

Pope, James Colledge, entrepreneur, landed proprietor, land agent, politician, premier of PEI (b at Bedeque, PEI 11 June 1826; d at Summerside, PEI 18 May 1885). Second son in a family prominent in PEI business and politics, he participated in several types of business and was PEI's third-largest shipowner of the 19th century. He entered politics as a Tory in 1857, and served as premier 3 times: 1865-67 (Conservative), 1870-72 (coalition) and Apr-Sept 1873 (Conservative). As premier he called upon troops to quell TENANT LEAGUE disturbances in 1865, negotiated purchase of the Cunard estate in 1866, commenced construction of a railway in 1871, and led the Island into Confederation on 1 July 1873. He was elected one of PEI's first 6 federal MPs. He was minister of marine and

fisheries in John A. MACDONALD's government 1878-82. Burdened with illness and anxiety arising out of business losses, he died in greatly reduced circumstances. IAN ROSS ROBERTSON

Pope, Maurice Arthur, engineer, army officer, diplomat (b at Riviére du Loup, Qué 9 Aug 1889; d at Ottawa 20 Sept 1978). Son of Sir Joseph Pope and grandson of Sir Henri T. Taschereau, he was a strong nationalist who believed that Canadians must respect the traditions of both founding peoples. He joined the Royal Canadian Engineers in 1915 and served overseas in the CANADIAN EXPEDITIONARY FORCE. Remaining in the army, he became vice-chief of the General Staff (1941), senior Canadian Army member of the PERMANENT JOINT BOARD ON DEFENCE (1942), chairman of the Canadian Joint Staff Mission, Washington (1942-44), and military staff officer to PM Mackenzie KING. He was ambassador to Belgium (1950-53) and Spain (1953-56). His memoirs, *Soldiers and Politicians,* were published in 1962. STEPHEN HARRIS

Pope, William Henry, lawyer, journalist, politician, judge (b at Bedeque, PEI 29 May 1825; d at St Eleanors, PEI 7 Oct 1879). Born into a family important in the economic and public life of PEI, he became a lawyer after study in London. Like many other Island lawyers, he served as a land agent, and in 1854 made his name from a controversial real-estate transaction in which he and 3 associates made more than £10 000 at the expense of his employer. He was editor of the colony's leading Tory newspaper, the *Islander,* 1859-72. Elected to the Assembly in 1863, he enthusiastically supported union of the British colonies in N America. His position being unpopular, he left the Cabinet in 1866 and did not contest subsequent elections. As the colony's most tenacious advocate of CONFEDERATION, however, he continued to promote the Island's union with Canada. When this was accomplished in 1873 under the leadership of his younger brother, James Colledge POPE, the government of Sir John A. MACDONALD appointed him judge of the Prince County Court.
IAN ROSS ROBERTSON

Poplar, short-lived, deciduous, hardwood TREE of genus *Populus* of the willow family, widely distributed in the N temperate zone. The genus includes ASPENS and cottonwoods. In N America, they grow from TREELINE to northern Mexico. Forty species occur worldwide; 5 are native to Canada. Aspen (*P. tremuloides*) and balsam poplar (*P. balsamifera*) occur across Canada. Hybrids and introduced poplars, eg, white or

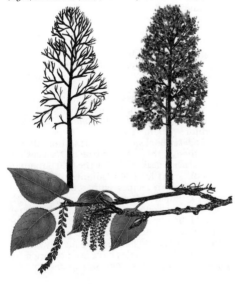

Balsam poplar (*Populus balsamifera*), with male flowers (right) and fruits (left) (*artwork by Claire Tremblay*).

silver-leaved poplar (*P. alba*) and black poplar (*P. nigra*), are planted as ORNAMENTALS and windbreaks. Leaves are simple, alternate, roundish and toothed. Bark of young trees is smooth, yellowish green, becoming grayish green to brownish and furrowed. Male and female flowers are clustered in drooping catkins on separate trees. Wind-pollinated flowers appear before leaves; seed matures as leaves develop. Seeds are tipped with long, silky down (cotton) for wind distribution. The widespread, shallow root system facilitates regeneration by "suckers" on cutover and burned land. Abundant suckers allow single trees to produce copses of clones with identical characteristics (eg, early leafing or late retention of autumn colour). Rapid growth makes poplars useful for reclamation. In ideal conditions, pulpwood is produced in 10 years, small sawlogs in 15 and veneer stock in 20. Infertile hybrids that produce no "cotton" have been cloned for ornamental plantings. Natural hybridization is common and causes difficulty in defining species.

Popular Literature in English, writing which has shown wide and continued acceptance, measured by sales, frequent imitation, adaptation to other cultural forms and general commercial success. The word "popular" is meant as a synonym for "successful," not as an antonym for "serious." Certain books are carefully tailored by authors and publishers to capture the attention of a wide range of potential readers.

In Canada, whether published in paperback or cloth editions or both, trade or general books are considered to have had satisfactory sales if they have sold 1500 copies (poetry, play), 3000 (first novel) or 7000 (political commentary); at double these figures the publisher may have a BEST-SELLER. Arguably the best-selling Canadian author of all time is Arthur HAILEY, many of whose novels, such as *Hotel* (1965) and *Airport* (1968), have sold millions of copies each. Popular, nonfiction authors such as Pierre BERTON, Farley MOWAT and Peter C. NEWMAN, who write serious books of particular interest to Canadians, enjoy hardcover sales of 75 000-150 000 copies per title. As substantial as such figures may seem, they pale in comparison with the sales record of *Coles Notes*. This series of study aids in monograph form (over 400 titles since 1947) has sold over 40 million copies worldwide.

Reference Books A number of notable, single-volume sources of Canadian information are revised and updated at intervals. The Government of Canada has compiled, irregularly since 1867, its official statistical record called *Canada Year Book*. Commercial publishing houses have brought out 2 volumes with some overlap in coverage: *Canadian Almanac & Directory* (since 1847) and *The Corpus Almanac of Canada* (since 1966; in 2 volumes since 1981). More compact is *Quick Canadian Facts*, over one million copies of which have been sold since 1946. Other annual tomes are *Canadian Who's Who* (1910-), with some 8000 biographies of prominent living Canadians, and *Canadian Books in Print* (issued since 1967), which lists about 24 000 Canadian books (over 10% of which are new each year). A specialized, single-volume reference work is *The Oxford Companion to Canadian Literature* (1983), general editor William Toye.

Cookbooks Books of recipes traditionally sell well, although this was not true of *The Cook Not Mad; or Rational Cookery* (1831), the first Canadian cookbook (or at least "Canadianized," for it reprints American recipes with some "Canadian content"), which was not reprinted until 1972. Probably more copies of *Canadian Cook Book* have been sold than have those of any Canadian competitor. It was originally compiled by Nellie Lyle Pattison in 1923 and has been frequently revised and enlarged. Large sales have been reported for more recent titles: *The Laura Secord Canadian Cook*

Book (1966); Elizabeth Baird's *Classic Canadian Cooking* (1974); and numerous collections by Mme Jehane Benoît, particularly *Enjoying the Art of Canadian Cooking* (1974) and *New and Complete Encyclopedia of Cooking* (1978). The regional cookbook, such as Edna Staebler's *Food that Really Schmecks* (1968), is a staple in the fast-changing world of contemporary CUISINE.

Romantic Fiction Romantic novels are usually published only in mass-market, paperback editions. What such novels may lack in depth and sophistication, they more than make up in their strong appeal to a devoted N American readership that seems to be predominantly female. The field of romantic fiction is less interesting for literary than for social, psychological and commercial reasons. The world's largest publisher of romantic fiction is Harlequin Books, founded in Winnipeg in 1949 and located in Toronto since the 1960s. Having found a market for reprints of romantic novels, the company discovered the successful formula of commissioning the novels, some 65 000 words in length; it now issues about a dozen each month. Many are set in hospital wards or gothic castles. A Harlequin romance invariably has a happy ending.

At least 3 Canadian women authors have found success writing commercial romantic fiction. Novelists such as Joy Carroll, Joy Fielding and Charlotte Vale Allen have been called, by literary columnist Beverly Slopen, "paperback princesses," because their works, perhaps modelled on those of American popular novelist Jacqueline Susann, have sold many thousands of copies apiece. But the country's most prolific author of romantic and other popular fiction is a man: between 1962 and 1978, under various pseudonyms, W.E. Dan Ross wrote 342 novels. Some of the westerns were signed "Dan Roberts"; some of the nurse stories "Jane Rossiter." As "Marilyn Ross," he wrote *Barnabas Collins* (1968), on which the ABC-TV "soap opera" *Dark Shadows* was based. Many of Ross's novels are "gothics," set in dark castles where defenceless heroines await a menace in the form of dark, mysterious strangers.

Mysteries Common to stories of intrigue and espionage, detective novels and thrillers, is the notion that a mystery is about to be revealed. In the past, Canadian addicts of mystery fiction have not required that their mysteries be Canadian in locale or character. The earliest Canadian work in this genre was probably James DE MILLE's *The Cryptogram* (1871), which followed by 3 years the English writer Wilkie Collins's *The Moonstone*, which it resembles. Two turn-of-the-century writers with Canadian connections, Grant Allen and Robert Barr, enjoyed large Anglo-American readerships. Allen's *An African Millionaire* (1897) and especially Barr's *The Triumphs of Eugène Valmont* (1906) — with a French detective not unlike the later Hercule Poirot — are important in the history of world detective fiction.

Three residents of the US who were born in Canada — Hulbert Footner, Frank L. Packard and Arthur STRINGER — also contributed to the genre. The first detective in Canadian fiction, November Joe, "detective of the woods," was created by Englishman H. Hesketh Prichard in *November Joe* (1936). Although they lived in California for many years, Margaret Millar (who was born in Canada) and her husband Ross Macdonald (who was raised here) wrote many novels, some with Canadian characters and settings.

Howard Engel, in the series that begins with *The Suicide Murders* (1981), has created what many regard as the first truly Canadian private investigator in fiction: Benny Cooperman, who is something of a *schnook*, works in the small city of Grantham (modelled on St Catharines, Ont). Other writers who have contributed notable

novels to the genre are Hugh GARNER (*The Sin Sniper*, 1970), Ian Adams, Shaun Herron, Donald MacKenzie, Larry Morse, Philippe van Rjndt and Sara Woods. Michael Richardson edited *Maddened by Mystery: A Casebook of Canadian Detective Fiction* (1982), which includes 13 stories, a historical introduction and a list of over 100 Canadian fictional sleuths.

"The Great Detective" is a CBC-TV series starring actor Douglas Campbell as John Wilson Murray, a real-life Toronto police inspector, who wrote *Memoirs of a Great Detective* (1905), the factual basis of the fictional series. Of related interest is The Bootmakers of Toronto, fd 1972 as the Canadian counterpart to Britain's Baker Street Irregulars to study the Sherlock Holmes "canon." The Arthur Conan Doyle Collection of the Metropolitan Toronto Library was opened in 1971 and has the world's largest public collection of books relating to Doyle's detective.

Fantastic Fiction Unreflective people who are content with their value systems and unenthusiastic about scientific research and technological development are unlikely to place a premium on fantastic fiction, ie, fantasy fiction, weird fiction and science fiction, which emphasizes the impact on man and society of imaginative, supernatural and innovative values, respectively. Such reasoning has been used to explain Canadians' lack of awareness of their own fantastic tradition. The relative weakness of the periodical and BOOK PUBLISHING industry has meant the importation rather than the creation of mass-market genre fiction. Nevertheless, well over 1000 books in the fantastic vein have been written by Canadians or have been set in Canada by foreign authors. Two landmark novels are James De Mille's *A Strange Manuscript Found in a Copper Cylinder* (1888), an adventure set in a polar world of inverted values, and Frederick Philip GROVE's *Consider Her Ways* (1947), a satiric fantasy about sentient ants who maintain that their society is superior to man's.

A celebrated contributor to the so-called Golden Age of science fiction, A.E. Van Vogt, was born in Manitoba and wrote over 600 000 words of fantastic fiction (including his classic novel about a persecuted mutant, *Slan*, 1946) before settling in California. The distinguished anthologist of speculative literature, Judith Merril, reversed the migration and settled in Canada. Her donation of 5000 books and periodicals to the Toronto Public Library in 1970 formed the nucleus of The Spaced Out Library, which was created under the direction of former chief librarian Harry Campbell. In 1982, with holdings totalling 22 000 items, this was the world's largest public collection of such literature.

Two contemporary novelists command particular attention. Phyllis GOTLIEB, in her stories and especially in such novels as *Sunburst* (1964), writes with sympathy about humans and aliens in societies in which ESP is a fact. Richard Rohmer, in a series of near-future thrillers beginning with *Ultimatum* (1973), has found a wide readership for descriptions of disasters extrapolated from present social unrest.

Distinctive Canadian contributions to the fantastic genres include novels set in the Arctic, notably *Sick Heart River* (1941) by John BUCHAN (Baron Tweedsmuir) and *The Time Before This* (1962) by Nicholas Monsarrat (a South African novelist who spent several years in Canada); and novels concerned with Québec nationalism, such as Jules-Paul TARDIVEL's *Pour la patrie* (1895, tr *For My Country*, 1975) and William Weintraub's *The Underdogs* (1979). Brian MOORE has written science fiction (*Catholics*, 1972), fantasy fiction (*The Great Victorian Collection*, 1975) and weird fiction (*The Mangan Inheritance*, 1979). Hugh MACLENNAN's *Voices in Time* (1980) is a remarkable, near-future story deeply rooted in contemporary social and spiritual problems.

Authors who write exclusively in the field

of the fantastic in Canada include Michael G. Coney, William Gibson, Terence M. Green, Crawford Kilian, Donald Kingsbury, Edward Llewellyn, Spider Robinson, Charles R. Saunders and Andrew Weiner. Authors of outstanding fantastic novels for younger readers (*see* CHILDREN'S LITERATURE) include Pierre Berton, Monique Corriveau, Christie Harris, Monica Hughes, Suzanne Martel, Ruth Nichols and Mordecai RICHLER. The standard anthology is *Other Canadas* (1979), edited by John Robert COLOMBO, which includes a short bibliography and a critical commentary.

JOHN ROBERT COLOMBO

Popular Literature in French, an urban phenomenon born in the industrialization of the turn of the 20th century, includes many types of writing: adventure and historical NOVELS, detective and spy stories, romantic novels, even "morally uplifting" literature (lives of saints, apologias, or the *Journal* of Gérard Raymond). In 1923 publisher Edouard Garand decided to fight the success of the American "dime novel" in Québec by bringing out a collection of his own. The series, called "Le Roman canadien," published monthly novels by, among others, Jean Féron, Ubald Paquin and Alexandre Huot that glorified patriotism and conservative ideology. A craze for weekly 32-page serials was born in 1941 with the series *Les Aventures policières d'Albert Brien, détective national des Canadiens-français.* In 1948 Imprimerie Judiciaire alone published 8 series. Between 1947 and 1966, Pierre Saurel (pseudonym of Pierre Daigneault) published, through that same company, 934 *Aventures étranges de l'agent IXE-13, l'as des espions canadiens.* The sentimental novel did not pay off as handsomely. From 1940 to 1960, *Les Plus Belles histoires d'amour,* with its sermons on the virtues of marriage, family, suffering and submission, was practically the only series aimed at women. Today, although Canadian Harlequin romances (published in French under the name "Colombine") are popular, foreign multinationals control the market in this genre. The 250 000 photo-romances bought every month in Québec are also foreign, usually Italian, in origin. Television, the growing popularity of the paperback and foreign book dumping have all combined to kill off local production. The specialized collections of detective stories are at their last gasp. Only Québec/Amérique still publishes a series of popular detective novels, "Le Manchot," the work of the prolific Saurel.

Fantasy and Science Fiction In 19th-century Québec newspapers and magazines, short stories mixed the natural with the supernatural, never setting them in opposition to each other — the main criterion of fantasy. Fantasy, itself more than a genre, is woven right into a story, and today Jacques FERRON, Anne HÉBERT, Jacques BENOÎT and Michel TREMBLAY all add elements of fantasy to works that are otherwise not fantastic. Science fiction was flourishing in English-speaking countries long before it was developed in Québec. Despite a few series — *IXE-13* for one — and the occasional publication of a novel, it took the QUIET REVOLUTION and the new emphasis on science to give Québec science fiction a boost. Some authors (eg, Louky Bersianik, François Barcelo) use the genre as a pretext for speculation or social criticism; others (eg, Jean Tétreau, Emmanuel Cocke) play at it as dilettantes.

Authors who devote themselves to science fiction or fantasy (Esther Rochon, Elisabeth Vonarburg, Jean-Pierre April, Michel Bélil, Daniel Sernine and René Beaulieu) appeared with, or after, the magazines *Requiem* (fd 1974, renamed *Solaris* 1979), which organized writing workshops, a story competition and an annual convention, "Boréal"; and *Imagine. . .,* publishing only science fiction. There are also 2 specialized collections: "Nuits d'encre" (fantasy), published

by Desclez, and "Chroniques du futur," from Le Préambule. There is an effort underway to make Québec science fiction regularly available, as it was with the Volpek (Yves THÉRIAULT) and Unipax (Maurice Gagnon) series published by Lidec in the 1960s.

Comic Strips Unlike the other forms of popular literature, comic strips appeared in Québec at the same time as they did elsewhere. Raoul Barré first published "Pour un dîner de Noël" in 1902 in *La Presse.* That paper fought with *La Patrie* for control of the market. "Le Père Ladébauche" by *La Presse* editorial cartoonist Albéric Bourgeois was one of the few strips to withstand the syndicates which, after 1910, began providing the world's newspapers with their daily comics. "Onésime," by Albert Chartier, first appeared in 1944 in the *Bulletin des agriculteurs,* and his "Seraphin illustré" (an adaptation of C.H. GRIGNON's *Un homme et son péché*) followed, 1951-70; "Ti-Prince," a sequel to "Seraphin," began in *Bonnes soirées* in 1955. Apart from these, the Québec comic strip, until the end of the Quiet Revolution, consisted of *Histoire en images* (1919-36), published by the ST JEAN-BAPTISTE SOCIETY, and the Fides comics for schoolchildren (1944-65, *François, Claire, Hérauts*). These moralizing strips were usually foreign in origin. With few exceptions, daily papers would not give space to Québec comics.

The comic-strip boom coincided with the student and counterculture explosion of the late 1960s. The Chiendent group (1968), led by Claude Haeffely and André Montpetit, encouraged the creation of strips, and *Le Magazine Maclean* and *Perspectives* published the first ones. Pierre Dupras, *Québec-Presse* cartoonist, published a few collections in 1970 and 1971. Some short-lived magazines burst on the scene: *BD, L'Hydrocéphale Illustré, L'Écran.* Robert Lavaill and Léandre Bergeron had a smash hit with their *Histoire du Québec.* In 1972 the publishing house L'Hydrocéphale Entêté started the cooperative Les Petits Dessins, which in 1974 turned out 6 daily strips for the newspaper *Le Jour.* It did not last long. In 1973 *La Presse* ran 2 Québec comic strips daily: "Les Microbes" by Michel Tassé and "Rodolphe" by Bernèche.

Québec comic strips then divided into 2 main tendencies. The information bulletin and publishing house, BDK, and *Prisme* and *Baloune* magazines (the latter the heir to *Mainmise*) encourage experiments outside the usual rigid commercial format. *Croc* magazine has published humorous comic strips since 1979 and, in 1982, put out several books by Réal Godbout and Jacques Hurtubise. *Cocktail* (1981-82) ran classic as well as Québec strips.

But commercial publishers are also looking for new readers. Some of them (Mondia, Mirabel) want to take over part of the market, which is now 95% foreign controlled. Since 1973, books based on children's programs (*Capitaine Bonhomme, Bobino et Bobinette*) have been flooding the market. *La Presse* cartoonist Jean-Pierre Girerd has tried comic strips (*On a volé la Coupe Stanley*) with little success. In 1981 Henri Desclez, who had been editor in chief of *Tintin* magazine and later worked for Éditions Héritage (which published "Nic et Pic" by Serge Wilson and Claude Poirier; "Monsieur Petitbois" by Bastien) produced a series of comics, the first volume being *Atlantic City* by Cedric Loth and Pierre Montour. Nevertheless, it is still difficult and expensive for Québec publishers to succeed in the field. *See* LITERATURE IN FRENCH; SHORT FICTION IN FRENCH.

BENOÎT MELANÇON

Reading: Alexandre Amprimoz, "French Language Science Fiction and Fantasy," in *A Bibliography of Canadian Science Fiction and Fantasy* (1979); "La bande dessinée kébécoise" in *La Barre du jour,* nos 46-49 (winter 1975); Victor-Levy Beaulieu, *Manuel de la petite littérature du Québec* (1974).

Popular Music Attempting to succeed in the "big time" while trying to maintain an indigenous cultural identity has placed many Canadian popular singers and musicians at cross-purposes. Living directly in the shadow and glare of the US, the world's most imposing entertainment machine, has defined this condition. Canadians often believed they had to "sound American" in order to "make it," and, owing to Canada's proximity to the US, many have assimilated popular American styles. However, in recent years Americans have embraced a number of singers whose styles are identifiably Canadian. Canadian Francophones face a double bind; maintaining a viable career is dependent upon reflecting regional realities, thus virtually eliminating American acceptance.

In the first half of the century, Canada's wide open spaces and sparse population made the nation's popular music (often COUNTRY AND WESTERN MUSIC) regional in character. Radio was the only existing link, but listeners living near the US border often preferred American broadcasts of that country's popular bands and orchestras. It was probably Guy LOMBARDO & His Royal Canadians, originally from London, Ont, who put Canada on the musical map — but only because of the orchestra's name, as there was nothing inherently Canadian about his mellifluous dance style.

The advent of Canadian television in 1953 spurred the modest beginnings of a national "star system," basically a string of smooth, if somewhat bland, singers who emulated American crooners. Among the most prominent were Wally Koster; Giselle McKenzie; vivacious blonde JULIETTE ("our pet"); Robert GOULET, who went on to Broadway and movies; Tommy AMBROSE and Alan Blythe, who became successful television producers on both sides of the border; and country singer Tommy HUNTER, who 25 years later was more popular than ever and whose TV series was the only non-US country music production to be aired in N America.

The rock 'n' roll era that began in 1955 brought 3 Canadian harmony groups into prominence: the Four Lads, who counted the innocuous "Standing on the Corner" among their dozen US "Top 40" hit records; the Diamonds, with 15 hits, including "Little Darlin'," a "whiteified" adaptation of the popular black "do-wop" street-corner style, and the Crew-Cuts.

The first Canadian pop superstar was Ottawa's teenage sensation Paul ANKA. Son of a Lebanese restaurant owner, he knocked on doors in Los Angeles and New York for 3 years before he struck gold in 1957 with "Diana," a dittie about an older babysitter. He was 16. He differed from other greasy-haired teen stars because he wrote his own songs and aimed to be accepted in the same circles as Frank Sinatra (for whom he wrote "My Way" in 1968). With over 40 American hits, more than 400 of his songs recorded, records in French, Italian and German, royalties in the millions from songs, commercials and theme music (including "The Tonight Show"), and regular performances at the Las Vegas-Atlantic City showcases, he has succeeded in his goal. Anka still retains his Canadian citizenship. Indeed, career longevity — and the ability to avoid the pitfalls of fame — has become a major characteristic of numerous Canadian pop stars.

Canadian singers, songwriters and musicians played a major role in the FOLK MUSIC boom of the early 1960s and its subsequent "folk-rock" hybrid. IAN AND SYLVIA'S "Four Strong Winds" was one of the most performed songs of the folk movements and, in its cool yet impassioned way, the first lyric to explore the Canadian temperament, borne of wide open spaces. The duo was also the first to introduce 2 songs, "Early Morning Rain" and "For Lovin' Me," by Gordon

LIGHTFOOT. Lightfoot's understated lyric style, delivered in clipped southern Ontario tones, has since graced over a dozen best-selling albums and 6 hit songs. "The Canadian Railroad Trilogy" superbly portrayed the nation's growing pains while "Wreck of the *Edmund Fitzgerald*," about an ill-fated ore ship, was the only piece of authentic history to find massive radio airplay in 1976. Lightfoot has performed with the same musicians for many years and retains a loyal international following.

While Lightfoot has continued living in Canada, others fled what they termed deaf ears: Zal Yanovsky became a driving force behind the "good-time" band The Lovin' Spoonful; Denny Doherty harmonized with the millions-selling Mamas and the Papas; Andy Kim wrote the 8-million selling "bubble gum" classic "Sugar Sugar" and sold 3 million copies of "Rock Me Gently" internationally; and David CLAYTON-THOMAS became lead singer of Blood, Sweat and Tears.

The most influential singer-songwriters were Joni MITCHELL and Neil YOUNG, who became integral parts of the Los Angeles music scene. Mitchell reflected the Canadian qualities of tolerance and acceptance in "Both Sides Now," which has been recorded by hundreds of singers. Her collection of albums (including "Court and Spark," "Blue") are lyrically and musically idiosyncratic (influenced as much by JAZZ as folk) and arguably the most adventurous by any female over the past 15 years. Young, formerly of folk-rocking Buffalo Springfield and counter-culture favourites Crosby, Stills, Nash & Young, has claimed his stake in desultory songs about loss of innocence and alienation, and cynicisms about America. His style is best summed up by album titles "Everybody Knows This Is Nowhere" and "Rust Never Sleeps."

No other group reflected such devotion to N American roots, regions and traditions as did The BAND. The 4 southern Ontarians and their Arkansas drummer forged their solidly eclectic style over 10 years barnstorming the continent with rockabilly singer Ronnie HAWKINS and folk-rock-poet Bob Dylan. Their first 2 albums, issued in 1968-69, came as a breath of fresh air in the hectic "blow-your-mind" rock scene of the time. Their finely crafted, intelligent songs were filled with a plethora of characters — rugged rural folk, pioneers, adventurers, colourful urban types — and atmospheric settings. Their music was pure Americana: rock 'n' roll, country, rhythm & blues, folk and church music. Clearly The Band's upbringing — close to the US, yet tempered by Canadian distance — was the major factor in the remarkable quality of their music. "Acadian Driftwood," conveying the Acadian's plight more graphically than any history book, is ample proof of The Band's unique place in pop. After 7 acclaimed albums, they performed a gala farewell concert in 1976, resulting in *The Last Waltz*, widely regarded as the best pop film ever.

The lack of support by Canadian radio, resulting in the painful fact that Canadians had to achieve success abroad to gain respect at home, prompted the CANADIAN RADIO-TELEVISION AND TELECOMMUNICATIONS COMMISSION into adopting regulations requiring AM radio stations to play at least 30% of records that were in some way Canadian. Although the US was still the barometer of success, the CRTC rulings did provide a solid national base for many singers and bands.

Anne MURRAY was the first star of the CRTC era. Her 1970 multi-million-selling "Snowbird" set forth a clean, clear, crisp style that has made her the most popular female "middle-of-the-road" singer since then. She has had over a dozen hits, sold millions of albums, won Grammy awards in both pop and country categories, and her TV specials are aired internationally.

The 1970s and 1980s marked the coming of age of Canadian rock groups, most fitting the popular formulas of lightning and thunder combined with indefatigable touring. The GUESS WHO were the pioneers; among their 14 hit discs was 1970s "American Woman," which jeered at the Vietnam War and American racial tensions. Bachman-Turner Overdrive followed with a more basic, "blue-collar" view of life. The STAMPEDERS' jaunty "Sweet City Woman" became number one internationally. The most popular group over the past 10 years was RUSH, whose high-pitched excursions into cosmic mythology ("New World Man") and space-age life-styles have sold over 15 million albums worldwide. LOVERBOY emerged in 1981 with textbook examples of how to blend popular rock components into a commercially effective, but hardly original, style. Other international successes were achieved by April Wine, who travelled more miles across Canada than any other group; Mahogany Rush, whose guitarist Frank Marino sounded uncannily like the late Jimi Hendrix; singer-guitarist Aldo Nova; the sexually ambiguous and provocative ROUGH TRADE; dance-oriented Martha and the Muffins; rocker Bryan Adams; and "heavy-metal" outfits Saga, Triumph, Streetheart and CHILLIWACK. Many of the above acts capitalized on the popular 1980s "video clip" phenomenon that set their sounds to televised images. Also worth noting are the dance music successes of Gino Soccio (whose 1979 album "Outline" sold over one million copies worldwide) and Lime, and the "easy listening" discs of Frank Mills.

Despite the recent glut of rock groups, Canada's most individualistic voices remain singer-songwriters. Bruce COCKBURN grew from introspective folksinger of the early 1970s to embrace rock, jazz and reggae styles, painting pastoral scenes as well as sociopolitical statements. Murray MCLAUCHLAN delivered good-natured, workingman's folk-rock. Dan Hill sold 4 million copies of his excrutiatingly sensitive "Sometimes When We Touch" in 1977. Poet Leonard COHEN set his disquietingly romantic works to song ("Suzanne," "Bird On A Wire"), selling over a million albums internationally, yet strangely few in N America. American expatriate Jesse Winchester, now a Canadian, wrote superbly subtle songs ("Brand New Tennessee Waltz") that have been recorded by many others. Classic rock 'n' roller Michel Pagliaro was the only Canadian to earn "gold" singles in both English and French. Kate and Anna McGarrigle garnered an international following for songs, in both languages, that embrace traditional folk, gospel, ragtime and pop ("Heart Like A Wheel," "The Work Song").

Québec's Popular Music reflects its people's struggle for survival amid Anglo-American culture, as well as the struggle to be competitive with American styles and market appeal. Much of the province's best and most successful music is inherently regional in character, yet this quality often inhibits its appeal in the rest of Canada, the US and France. It is relatively easy to garner "star" status in Québec yet, increasingly, singers and musicians have guarded against "overexposure," thus putting strains on viable career-development in a limited marketplace.

Cultural and political struggles were best defined by the "chansonniers" of the 1950s and 1960s, who sang poetry to the accompaniment of music in the folk and European music hall traditions. Leading the way was Félix LECLERC, whose plaintive emotional style was recognized first in France in 1951. He blended pithy statements of Québécois sentiment with pointed reflections of cultural and political alienation, survival, exploitation and the "boss." His songs remain evergreen and today Québec's popular music awards bear his first name. His success also cleared the way for Raymond Lévesque (with "Quand les hommes vivront d'amour,"

1956) and, towards the turn of the decade, for a new wave of chansonniers reflecting the transition from a Québec society dominated by Duplessis and the Catholic church to the QUIET REVOLUTION of the 1960s asserting Québec's identity.

The most influential artist of the early 1960s was Gilles VIGNEAULT from Natashquan, whose people's traditions, pride and worries were conveyed in lively, almost theatrical songs. Vigneault's passionate "Mon Pays" became Québec's anthem for the late 1960s; his more banal "Gens du pays" accompanied the Parti Québécois' rise to power in the 1970s.

Others to emerge were Claude LÉVEILLÉE, a sophisticated singer-pianist whose "Pianos mécaniques" was recorded by France's Edith Piaf; the subtle, soft-spoken Claude Gauthier; fiery Pauline JULIEN, Vigneault's leading interpreter, whose passion was often matched with vitriol; Jean-Pierre Ferland, a romantic whose "Jaune" was the first double-album ever released by a Canadian; Monique LEYRAC, Georges Dor and Clémence Desrochers, who blended song with monologue. This wave of singer-songwriters was accompanied by the rise of the "boîtes à chanson" ("song boxes"), frequented by students, artists, intellectuals and some future politicians.

However, a totally different form of music was making its impact on the population at large. The explosion of the Québec record industry, spurred by the Beatlemania phenomenon, was largely founded on translated versions of Anglo-American hits; this success, in turn, provoked rock and pop original material. The tabloid press covered such local stars as Pierre Lalonde, Donald Lautrec, Michel Louvain, Michèle Richard, Johnny Farrago, Renée Martel, Renée CLAUDE, Tony Roman (the province's most flamboyant producer), and child-singer René Simard, who a decade later appeared with younger sister Nathalie, both selling over half a million albums. By far the most talented stars of this regional pop were Ginette Reno, whose best-selling albums (300 000) included "Je ne suis qu'une chanson" (1982), and Michel Pagliaro, a master of classic rock and pop styles, who created the rollicking anthem "J'entends frapper" ("I Hear Knocking").

The gap between intellectuals and populists was bridged in 1968 by Robert CHARLEBOIS, then an "enfant terrible" because of his raucous use of JOUAL, Québec's street slang rife with anglicisms. Backed by rock and jazz musicians with space-age sounds, he proclaimed Québec's independence from — and attraction for — N America. His albums broke sales records for a solo artist and eventually he gained stardom in France.

Charlebois' success spurred a mini-explosion in the homegrown RECORDING INDUSTRY, resulting in a wave of rock bands of all descriptions. Beau Dommage parlayed clean harmonies and pop music clichés with picturesque breezy postcard greetings from Québec. Their debut album sold over 200 000 copies, a record for any Canadian group in its native market. Their competitors, Harmonium, were entrenched in "peace-and-love" styles, eventually swelled with a grandiose cosmic sound.

Other popular groups included Ville Emard Blues Band, an 18-member "musical cooperative" (comprised mainly of accompanists of the stars) that offered differing musical excursions and spurred offshoots, such as progressive-rockers Contraction (the only group to issue French and English versions of the same album) and Toubabou's Afro-Québec rock. The first and longest-lasting group was Offenbach, specializing in a rough-hewn blues-rock sound ("Câline de blues"). Two members of this group eventually formed Corbeau. In 1984 Offenbach and Corbeau were the only financially stable groups in Québec; the prohibitive costs of operating a rock group in a relatively small market signalled the return of the solo singer.

Easily the most spectacular star singer has been Diane Defresne, whose flamboyant performances and perfectionist recordings gave her a consistency unmatched in Québec after the mid-1970s. Other voices included Diane Tell, a singer-songwriter in a jazzy soft-pop mold; the pristine Fabienne Thibeault; Nanette Workman, an American émigrée whose dynamic style made her dance-oriented recordings sparkle; and Claude Dubois, whose simple romantic album "Sortie" is a classic. Serge Fiori, former leader of Harmonium, has intermittently continued his musings, as have Marie-Claire and Richard Séguin. Daniel Lavoie was the first Québecois to spend $100 000 on album production, and Céline Dion out-sold everyone with her brand of family-oriented youthful schmaltz. Two singers stand out: Michel Rivard, ex-leader of Beau Dommage, whose well-tempered odes to Québec life are matched by immaculate musical taste; and Plume Latraverse, whose ribald, sometimes scatological, and always razor-sharp humour provides the best portrait of Québec society. JUAN RODRIGUEZ

Reading: M. Melhuish, *Heart of Gold* (1984); Juan Rodriguez, *Profiles in Canadian Music* (1985); R. Yorke, *Axes, Chops & Hot Licks* (1971).

Population The settlement of Canada by Europeans resulted from the agricultural and Industrial Revolution in western Europe and the subsequent expansion of European population that began during the 17th century. The French were among the early explorers of the New World and their establishment of NEW FRANCE was primarily the consequence of their political and military concerns, the search for natural wealth and the Roman Catholic Church's interest in converting the native people. Environmental conditions were harsh and the survival of early settlements depended to a great extent on the continuing flow of traders, soldiers, priests and administrators from France. In 1665 the population of New France was just 3215. As was typical of early settlements, most of the inhabitants were single and male, but increasing numbers of settlers arriving from France ultimately established a population capable of sustaining itself through natural increase. During the next 100 years, birthrates ranged from 50-65 births per 1000 population and produced a sufficient excess of births over deaths for the population to reach 70 000 in 1775, after the British had won political control from the French at the end of the SEVEN YEARS' WAR. Rapid population growth continued and the non-French population increased dramatically under the impetus of the migration of British Empire LOYALISTS from the American colonies after the Revolution and increasing IMMIGRATION from Europe. By 1867 the population was about 3.3 million.

Population growth was alternately stimulated and depressed by recurring fluctuations in economic conditions and immigration. The economy was depressed at Confederation and EMIGRATION consistently exceeded immigration during the last 4 decades of the 19th century. Population would have declined had it not been for the high levels of fertility that still characterized the population towards the end of the century. Crude birthrates varied between 45 and 36 births per 1000 population, while death rates declined moderately from 21 to 18 deaths per 1000 during this period.

At the turn of the century, with both fertility and mortality rates declining, high natural increase combined with the heavy immigration of the early 1900s to boost the average annual rate of growth for the country to a high of 3%. Unsettled times followed WWI, culminating in the GREAT DEPRESSION of the 1930s. By 1941 growth rates had declined to 1%, but the long-term

decline in fertility was interrupted by the approach of WWII and a period of increasing political and economic activity. During the postwar period, both immigration and birthrates were greatly stimulated by the unexpectedly high level of economic development. Canada's average annual rate of growth reached 2.8% during the BABY BOOM of the late 1940s and the 1950s. By the beginning of the 1960s, a weakening economy and continuing social change brought an end to the unprecedented postwar growth; the consistent decline in birthrates was relatively unaffected by fluctuations in the economy. During the early 1960s, immigration was encouraged by changes in IMMIGRATION POLICY. Long-standing restrictions based on racial and ethnic origins were removed and selection criteria were introduced based on education, occupational skills and LABOUR-FORCE needs, but despite this the average annual growth rate by 1966 had declined to 1.7%. During the 1970s it declined further to 1.3%. Notwithstanding worsening national and global economics, the same numbers of immigrants (1.4 million) arrived between 1971 and 1981 as between 1961 and 1971 (only slightly less than the numbers that had arrived during the decade of the baby boom). In 1978 Canada introduced annual global ceilings on admissible numbers of immigrants to achieve better control over the continuing influx of immigrants. These ceilings are now established after consultations with provincial governments on national economic goals, regional conditions and standing commitments to family reunification and REFUGEE resettlement.

Canada is one of the 3 main immigrant-receiving nations in the world; its ratio of immigrants to population during the latter half of the 1971-81 decade was one of the highest. From 1976 to 1981, immigration averaged about 121 000 annually and, in spite of continuing high levels of unemployment in 1982, Canada publicly committed itself to maintaining immigration ceilings of between 135 000 and 145 000 for the 3-year planning period ending in 1984.

Natural Increase and not immigration, however, has been the major factor in the nation's growth for more than 100 years. Since 1871 Canada's population increased by almost 21 million, about 80% of which can be attributed to an excess of births over deaths. As birthrates were declining during this period, the positive contribution by natural increase largely reflected the improvement in the general quality of life

Population of Canada and Components of Change: Canada, 1851-1981

(Source: Employment and Immigration Canada, *1980 Immigration Statistics;* and Statistics Canada, Vital Statistics annual reports, 1977 to 1980)

Decade	Population Total: (End of Decade)	Natural Increase: Births – Deaths (000s)	Net Immigration (000s)
-1851	2 436 297	–	–
1851-1861	3 229 633	641	152
1861-1871	3 689 257	651	-191
1871-1881	4 324 810	723	- 87
1881-1891	4 833 239	714	-206
1891-1901	5 371 315	718	-180
1901-1911	7 206 643	1 120	716
1911-1921	8 787 949	1 230	351
1921-1931	10 376 786	1 360	229
1931-1941	11 506 655	1 222	- 92
1941-1951	14 009 429[1]	1 972	169
1951-1961	18 238 247	3 148	1 081
1961-1971	21 568 311	2 703	724
1971-1981	24 343 180	1 920	855

[1] Includes Newfoundland

and concomitant decline in the death rate. The low annual rate of natural increase of 0.8% in 1981 is characteristic of industrialized and urbanized populations that have experienced the demographic transition from high to low levels of vital rates. While considerably below the global average of 1.7%, the current rate is about the same as that for the US and significantly above those for the western and northern European countries, 0.1% and 0.2% respectively.

Mortality levels have been declining since the latter part of the 18th century, but the decline has been more pronounced since 1867. The major gains in life expectancy have been attributed more to improved nutritional levels, personal hygiene and better housing than to medical science or improved medical services. The gradual elimination of infectious and parasitic diseases as major causes of death has significantly increased life expectancy for Canadians. The most dramatic improvements have resulted from reductions in infant mortality rather than gains for the older population, and women have benefited more from these improvements than have men. In 1931 the number of years a person could expect to live at birth under prevailing mortality conditions was 60.0 for males and 62.1 for females. By 1976 life expectancies at birth had reached 70.19 and 77.48 years respectively, reflecting gains of 17% and 25% for males

Components of Population Growth: Natural Increase and Net Immigration, 1881-1981

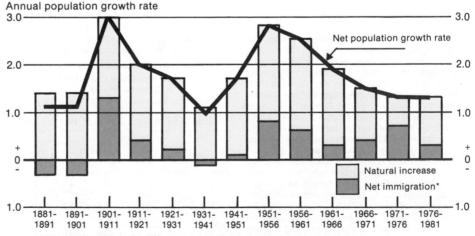

Source: George, M.V., *Population Growth in Canada, Catalogue 99-701. 1981 Census of Canada, Catalogue 99-901.*

* Net immigration is the difference between immigration and emigration.

Selected Measures[1] of Mortality and Fertility: Canada, 1921-1981
(Source: Statistics Canada, Vital Statistics, 1977 and 1981)

Year	Crude Death Rate	Infant Mortality Rate	Crude Birth Rate	Gross Reproduction Rate
1921	10.6	88.1	29.3	1.712
1931	10.1	84.7	23.2	1.555
1941	10.0	59.7	22.4	1.377
1946	9.4	46.7	27.2	1.640
1951	9.0	38.5	27.2	1.701
1956	8.2	31.9	28.0	1.874
1961	7.7	27.2	26.1	1.868
1966	7.5	23.1	19.4	1.369
1971	7.3	17.5	16.8	1.060
1976	7.3	13.5	15.7	0.887
1981	7.0	9.6	15.3	0.829

[1] Selected measures of mortality and fertility:

Crude Death Rate: The number of deaths per 1000 population in a given year

Infant Mortality Rate: The number of deaths to infants under 1 year of age per 1000 live births in a given year

Crude Birth Rate: The number of live births per 1000 population in a given year

Gross Reproduction Rate: The average number of daughters that would be born to a woman during her lifetime if she passed through her child-bearing years conforming to the age-specific fertility rates of a given year

and females respectively. Overall life expectancy for Canadians in 1981 was 74 years, as it was in the US. This was exceeded in only a few countries, eg, Norway and Sweden (75 years), and Iceland (76 years), which had the highest reported life expectancy of any country in 1981.

Improvements in living conditions and in the STANDARD OF LIVING have drastically altered the health concerns and medical-care problems of Canadians. The current major causes of death are the degenerative diseases (cancer, cardiovascular), diseases caused by stress and deteriorating environmental conditions. During the 1970s, cardiovascular and heart diseases accounted for almost 33% of all deaths; infant deaths accounted for only 2% in 1981.

Fertility Before the 19th century, fertility levels in N America were as high, or higher, than present levels in many of the world's lesser developed countries. As Canada developed and living conditions improved, birthrates declined steadily from their early levels of around 50 births per 1000 population. By the 1920s the crude rate had dropped below 40 and by 1937 had reached 20 births per 1000 population. WWII revived the economy and reversed the declining trend in birthrates; they reached a high of 28.9 in 1947 and again in 1954 before resuming the long-term historical decline beginning in the 1960s. By 1978, and again in 1981, Canada's birthrate reached a low of 15.3 births per 1000 population.

The significance of declining birthrates for future population growth is more evident in the gross reproduction rate (GRR), which reveals how many female children women may expect to have on the average if they live through their reproductive years experiencing the age-specific fertility rates of a given year. The GRR for Canadian females had dropped from a rate of 1.7 in 1921 to 1.3 in 1937, before increasing to 1.9 in 1959 at the end of the postwar baby-boom years. The rate again dropped sharply and by 1972 the GRR of 0.98 was below the replacement level. By 1981 the rate had reached 0.83 and women were even less likely than before to produce enough daughters to replace themselves. Continuation of such low fertility levels for an indefinite period would eventually lead to an actual decline in Canada's population, provided there was no significant revival of immigration.

In the past, Canada's birthrates have been somewhat higher than those of the US, with almost identical patterns. N American birthrates have tended to be somewhat higher than those reported for northern and western European countries, but slightly below the average for countries of eastern Europe. In contrast, birthrates for most of the lesser developed regions of the world were more than twice that of Canada's in 1981.

Population Characteristics Relatively greater numbers of young adult men than women immigrated to Canada in the early years. Following the heavy immigration during the first decade of the 20th century, the census of 1911 reported 113 males for every 100 females living in Canada. Since 1921 the ratio of males to females has gradually declined for the country as a whole, reaching parity shortly after the 1971 census. The AGING of the population, with longer life expectancies for females, and the increasing proportion of women among arriving immigrants have continued to erode the sex ratio. In 1981 there were only 98 males for every 100 females.

The numbers of males, however, still exceed those of females in the more rural areas and in the West and North. Alberta's sex ratio in 1981 was 104 in favour of males, but it was highest in the Yukon and the Northwest Territories where the number of males per 100 females was 111 and 110 respectively. In contrast, relatively more women are found in the larger urban centres where they have been attracted by greater employment opportunities. In 1981 the sex ratios for the Toronto and Montréal Census Metropolitan Areas were 96 men to 100 women and 94 men to 100 women respectively. The number of males per 100 females varies significantly by age group and between rural and urban areas. Sex ratios at birth are consistently about 106 in favour of males, but the relative number of males compared to females gradually declines with increasing age. For the population over 85 years, there were only 49 males per 100 females in 1981. As recently as 1971, no age group in the rural population had a sex ratio less than 100, while for urban populations both the age group between 20-24 and that over 45 had fewer men than women.

Age Composition Canada's population has gradually aged as the importance of immigration has waned and birthrates have declined. By 1951 the average (median) age had increased to 27.8 years before the unprecedented birthrates of the 1950s lowered the median age to 25.6 years in 1966. Between 1976 and 1981 however the median age of the population increased from 27.8 to 29.6 years. The relative size of the young dependent population (those under 15 years of age) regained its 1901 level of 34% in 1961, before dropping sharply to 22.5% in 1981. During the same period, the percentage of Canada's population 65 years of age and over almost doubled, to 9.8%. Canada's population has shifted from an "early mature" status in 1881, when 4.1% of the population was 65 and over,

Selected Population Characteristics: Canada, 1901-1981
(Source: Statistics Canada, 1971 and 1981 Censuses of Canada; and Dominion Bureau of Statistics, Censuses of Canada, 1901 to 1961)

Year	Males per 100 Females	Average (Median) Age	Percent under 15 Years	Percent 65 Years and over	Percent Population Foreign-born
1901	105	22.7	34.6	5.0	13.0
1911	113	23.8	33.1	4.5	22.0
1921	106	23.9	34.5	4.7	22.3
1931	107	24.7	31.7	5.5	22.2
1941	105	27.0	27.8	6.7	17.5
1951	102	27.8	30.4	7.7	14.7
1961	102	26.5	34.0	7.6	15.6
1971	100	26.4	29.5	8.1	15.3
1981	98	29.6	22.5	9.8	16.1

to, since 1979, an "aged" population, signifying that the proportion of those 65 years of age and over exceeded the 8% criterion established by the UN. As the baby-boom generation ages and if levels of fertility remain low, the relative numbers of the latter group will continue to show significant increases.

While the relative size of the young, dependent population was quite similar to that in the US and the northern and western European countries, the proportions of those aged 65 and over for most European countries were somewhat higher, ranging from 14% in Denmark, Norway, France and the UK, to 16% in Sweden. By contrast, the least economically developed countries in the world have proportions of population under 15 years of age and over 65 years that approach 50% and 2% respectively.

Native and Foreign-Born Population Variations in immigration and the natural increase of the native-born population have altered the relative size and importance of the native-born and foreign-born population over the years. When colonization by the French first began, the native-born were the native Indians and Inuit, and the foreign-born were the European explorers, traders, military and government personnel, priests, missionaries and settlers. The native Indian population was hard pressed to survive in the face of the European encroachment and by mid-20th century their numbers were estimated to be fewer than they had been when New France was first established. During the interim period, the native-born population was greatly augmented by the children of the European immigrants and tended to grow more rapidly through natural increase than the foreign-born population did through additional immigration. Because the native Indian population had great difficulty in maintaining their numbers, their long-term survival was seriously threatened. It was not until the 1930s that they began to show consistent increases and by 1971 the combined populations of native Indians and Inuit reached 313 000. During the decade of the 1970s, their population increased by 32%, reaching 413 000 by 1981.

Just before Confederation, the foreign-born population accounted for 21% of Canada's total. Emigration during the late 1800s reduced the proportion to 13% in 1901, but the heavy immigration of the early 1900s boosted their relative size to 22% between 1921 and 1931. The native-born population grew more rapidly during the Depression and early war years, but heavy postwar immigration reinforced the numbers of foreign-born in Canada. While birthrates declined after the postwar baby boom, immigration continued to add to the foreign-born population, raising its relative size from 14.7% in 1951 to 16.1% in 1981.

The countries of origin of Canada's foreign born have both established and altered the cultural nature of Canadian society. Its bicultural nature is a consequence of the early settlement by the French and subsequent acquisition of military and political control by the British, after which most immigrants came from the British Isles, the US and Europe. Between 1881 and 1891, the proportion of arriving immigrants originating in the UK varied between 21% and 37%, while those from the US varied between 46% and 76%. In 1871, 84% of the foreign-born had been born in the UK. As the character of immigration has shifted, particularly after WWII, the proportion dropped to 36% (1971) as immigration from other European countries, notably Germany and Italy, increased.

The main birthplace of those born outside of Canada is still Europe, but the proportion born in Europe decreased from 80% in 1971 to 67% in 1981. At the same time, those born in the US declined from 9% to 8%. Reflecting the significant changes in Canada's immigration sources in recent decades, Asian-born immigrants more than tripled in numbers to about 543 000 between 1971 and 1981, increasing their proportion of the foreign born from 5% to 14%. Those born in Latin America and the Caribbean increased from 3% to 7%, while those born in other countries increased from just under 3% to 4% in 1981. Regardless of the future levels of immigration to Canada, world conditions will continue to maintain pressure for immigration from non-European sources. Canada's population, particularly in its more highly urbanized areas, can be expected to increase in its ethnic and cultural diversity as it responds to these pressures in the future. It is estimated that on 1 Jan 1984 Canada's population exceeded 25 million.

WARREN E. KALBACH

Reading: Warren E. Kalbach and W.W. McVey Jr, *Demographic Bases of Canadian Society* (1979).

Populism now ordinarily refers to political movements and ideas based on a strong faith in the ability of ordinary people to act together politically despite potentially serious class, racial, regional or religious cleavages. Populist movements generally support DECENTRALIZATION of economic and political power believing that such power should be spread among individuals or among regional and local governments. Politicians may be described as populists, although their party may not be a populist movement. René LÉVESQUE, leader of the PARTI QUÉBÉCOIS, former mayor of Toronto John Sewell, and John DIEFENBAKER have all been labelled populists. "Populists" were originally supporters of the Peoples' Party in the US, which enjoyed considerable electoral success during the agrarian revolt of the 1890s. In Canada populist parties developed during the depression after WWI, when farm organizations entered federal and provincial politics. The PROGRESSIVE PARTY (1920) under T.A. CRERAR, a Manitoba leader, became the second-largest party in the House of Commons after the 1921 election but refused to form the Opposition. The populist UNITED FARMERS OF ALBERTA (UFA), under Henry Wise WOOD, and the UNITED FARMERS OF MANITOBA (UFM) formed governments in their respective provinces.

North American agrarian populist movements have traditionally polarized into left and right; in Canada the divergent CO-OPERATIVE COMMONWEALTH FEDERATION (CCF) and SOCIAL CREDIT were both formed during the 1930s. Left-wing populists usually attempted to organize an explicit farm-labour alliance. They criticized corporate capitalism, the railways, mining companies, manufacturing trusts and financial institutions. They demanded that government generate countervailing power by nationalization if necessary, and undertake extensive welfare-state reforms. Left-wing populism typically emerged as an extension of co-operative societies and frequently had strong links to congregationally based Protestant sects. Right-wing populists typically attacked both the power of banks to limit the money supply and raise the price of credit, and "big government." They were less interested in democracy and more authoritarian, and their religious ties were often with evangelical Christianity.

Social Credit, founded by William ABERHART, a charismatic radio evangelist, inherited agrarian group support from the UFA, which had allied itself with the socialist CCF. Aberhart expounded the British theory that the GREAT DEPRESSION could be cured by providing people with an appropriate increase in purchasing power: social credit. In 1935 Aberhart became premier of Alberta. In 1962 Social Credit elected 26 MPs in Québec under Réal CAOUETTE, but no strong national consensus emerged. The CCF, in its Regina Manifesto, committed itself to public ownership of industry, and to government planning. In the 1940s it enjoyed widespread national support.

The Liberal government adopted CCF programs supporting the expansion of the welfare state and the maintenance of full employment. In Saskatchewan, under T.C. DOUGLAS, the CCF came to power (1944) and pioneered many social-insurance programs that later became national and launched numerous CROWN CORPORATIONS in new industries. After allying with the Canadian Labour Congress in 1961, the CCF was renamed the NEW DEMOCRATIC PARTY.

The popularity of populist movements has varied directly with the level of effort ordinary people make in realizing political reforms. When high, such movements flourish; when low, they wilt. Also, the administrative competence of many populist governments has been poor, because pure populist movements have lacked access to an administrative elite. The administratively competent (such as the CCF in Saskatchewan) were hybrid alliances of a populist movement with a cadre of professional administrators. In search of a more stable existence, leaders of populist movements may transform them into political parties representing well-organized interest groups. Social Credit in Alberta achieved such a relationship with the major oil companies that invested heavily in the province following oil discoveries at Leduc in 1947; the CCF did likewise with organized labour after 1961. Ultimately the importance of populism is to insist that "democracy matters": that people can play a far more active role in government than the passive one of choosing among alternative rulers at infrequent elections.

JOHN RICHARDS

Porcupine Of the world's 23 species, only the North American porcupine (*Erethizon dorsatum*) occurs in Canada, throughout mainland forests and thickets. Canada's second-largest RODENT (up to 18 kg and 103 cm long, including a 30 cm tail) has a stout, black-and-white body bearing 30 000 sharp, slightly barbed quills (up to 8 cm long) on upperparts and tail. When cornered, a porcupine erects its quills and lashes its tail. Quills are easily dislodged from the porcupine's skin, but cannot be thrown. Mammal predators (eg, fishers, wolverines) avoid them by flipping the porcupine over to attack unprotected underparts. Slow-moving porcupines are vulnerable to automobiles and fires. One young is born 7 months after fall mating. It soon walks and climbs, is weaned within 10 days, and leaves its mother by fall. Porcupines are usually nocturnal and do not hibernate. Usually solitary, they sometimes share good dens or feeding areas. They eat bark, buds, leaves and twigs of trees and other plants. Food, cut by 4 chisel-shaped incisors, is ground by 16 ridged cheek-teeth. Some trees are damaged but extensive harm to forests is rare. Porcupines gnaw tools and other salty objects, wooden buildings and occasionally damage corn or alfalfa.

DONALD A. SMITH

Porkeater [French, *mangeur de lard*], in the parlance of the FUR TRADE, was a derogatory term for a VOYAGEUR hired by the NORTH WEST COMPANY who made only the short run between Montréal and GRAND PORTAGE (and not into the North-West) and whose staple diet was pork, unlike the WINTERER, or *homme du nord*, who made do with fish and PEMMICAN. Later it came to refer to any voyageur who was a newcomer to the North-West.

JOHN ROBERT COLOMBO

Pornography For most of Western cultural history, pornography has been defined loosely as "material depicting erotic behaviour and intended to cause sexual excitement." The word derives from the Greek *pornographos*, meaning "the writing of prostitutes." Sexually explicit materials have likely circulated in one form or another — sketches, photos, poetry, novels, lantern slides — since the mid-19th century in Canada. In the last half of the 20th century the industry aimed at the distribution and sale of pornography has experienced a remarkable boom. In 1972, 8 so-called "girlie" magazines were available on Canadian newsstands; by 1982, 32 such magazines were marketed. In this same decade in N America, the pornography industry in magazine, film and video form grew from a $5 million to an estimated $7-billion-a-year enterprise. The rapid growth in COMMUNICATIONS TECHNOLOGY has helped create new vehicles for pornography. The development of video technology, in particular, has made it possible for consumers of pornography to circumvent public venues (eg, commercial movie theatres) and to lease video tapes and equipment for home use. Images depicting graphic sex have proliferated in advertising and rock video.

The traditional definition of pornography generally embraced all erotic materials and graphic depictions of sex. The definitions of these matters changed in a community over time and have been used to ban materials that have later been deemed acceptable. Recently, concern has grown as mainstream pornography has become more aggressive and preoccupied with coercion and violence in conjunction with sexuality. There are currently several different approaches to defining pornography. One argues that a clear definition of pornography is not possible, that what is considered pornographic is a matter of taste and that one person's erotica is another person's pornography. From another perspective, *Playboy* is considered to be on one end of a continuum while child pornography, bestiality and sex fused with violence are on the other end; the difference between the materials and hence of their deleterious effects is considered a matter of degree. According to this view it is meaningless to lump an advertisement for designer jeans in the same category as sado-masochistic depictions. A third perspective, held by most feminists, defines pornography as the images of overt domination and coercion of women. According to this view images in which women are consistently depicted as victims encourage or at least condone actual violence against women. The first organized Canadian protest on these grounds occurred in 1977 in Toronto, when a group of women protested against the film *Snuff*, which purported to show the actual murder of a woman. In 1982 in BC a group of Vancouver women (Women Against Pornography) mounted a determined protest campaign when Red Hot Video, a chain that leased "hard-core" videos, gang-rape tapes and other violent pornography, opened 15 new outlets in 3 months. In 1983 numerous women across Canada angrily opposed the plans of a Canadian pay-television network to broadcast programs developed by Playboy. The proliferation of pornography has prompted the founding of at least one national group, the Canadian Coalition Against Media Pornography.

While more recently the demands for legislation directed against pornography have focused on the premise that pornography is linked to sexual crimes, Canadian obscenity legislation was originally framed on the assumption that pornography corrupts morals. Section 159 of the Criminal Code provides that it is an offense to distribute materials "a dominant characteristic of which is the undue exploitation of sex, or of sex and any one of the following subjects, namely crime, horror, cruelty and violence." It has been argued that under this provision Canadian courts have paid more attention to sexually explicit materials than to the more threatening violent materials that critics see as dangerous to the mental health and physical safety of women. As a result, the Liberal government commissioned (1983-84) a study — the so-called

Fraser Committee — to study this and other related issues and, in addition, introduced a Bill in the House of Commons (1984) which, among other things, redefined obscenity in such a way as to avoid the existing linkage between sex and violence, thus allowing violent or degrading materials, in themselves, to be regarded as obscene. The change in the federal government in Sept 1984 and anticipation of the Fraser Report late in 1984 has stalled action on the bill.

The discussion of pornography and how to regulate it in a democracy invariably raises difficult questions. Those who demand legislation to eradicate pornography make the point that the objectification of women for commercial purposes is attitudinally harmful to society, but it is very difficult under this premise to distinguish the various degrees of objectification, and therefore degrees of harm. A second, and critical, problem is that the abolition of pornography is a form of CENSORSHIP, which must be balanced against the constitutionally protected rights of free expression. From the feminist perspective, these individual rights of free expression must be balanced against the human rights of those they believe are victimized by pornography, as well as the societal effects of such victimization. *See also* OBSCENITY; WOMEN'S MOVEMENT. SUSAN COLE

Reading: D. Copp and S. Wendell, *Pornography and Censorship* (1983).

Porpoise, *see* DOLPHIN AND PORPOISE.

Porsild, Alf Erling, botanist, northern explorer (b at Copenhagen, Denmark 17 Jan 1901; d at Vienna, Austria 13 Nov 1977). Assistant botanist 1922-25 at the Danish Biological Station, Greenland, he was hired (with his brother Robert) by the Canadian government in 1926 to investigate reindeer grazing in arctic Canada and Alaska. In 1936 he was appointed acting chief botanist of the National Museum of Canada. He served as Canadian consul to Greenland 1940-43. Returning to the National Museum, he was chief botanist 1946-67. He was the author of over 100 publications and his botanical collections included about 80 new species. His honours included an MBE and fellowship in the RSC. W.J. CODY

Port Alberni, BC, City, pop 19 892 (1981c), inc 1912, amalgamated with Alberni 1967, is located in central VANCOUVER I, 195 km N of Victoria, at the head of Alberni Inlet, a deep W-shore inlet that almost divides the island. The Alberni inlet was named after Don Pedro Alberni, the Spanish officer in command of the Nootka outpost during the Spanish occupation 1789-95. HBC employees led by Adam Horne started fur trading with the region's Indians, the Coast SALISH and NOOTKA 1850-59. The English shipping firm Anderson and Co erected a sawmill 1860 in Alberni as it was surrounded by good timber and the inlet offered easy access. Pioneers came to the area to farm and mine and many eventually turned to logging and operating small sawmills.

Lumbering has always been Port Alberni's most important industry. It has the largest forestry complex on the island and one of the largest in the world, and also benefits from the manufacture and servicing of forestry-related equipment. The lumber industry has helped make Port Alberni the third-largest port by volume in BC. Fishing and mining are important. In 1978 Port Alberni's average personal income ranked 4th out of 100 Canadian cities and was the highest in BC.

Port Alberni has a marina in the heart of the city, 2 golf courses, the Echo Centre (library, museum, pool and meeting complex), the Rolin Art Centre and the J.V. Clyne Bird Sanctuary. Della Falls — the highest in N America — are within hiking distance. Important geological features in the area are Mt Arrowsmith (summer hiking and winter skiing) and 2 large freshwater lakes, Sproat and Great Central. ALAN F.J. ARTIBISE

Port Arthur, *see* THUNDER BAY.

Port au Choix, Nfld, Town, pop 1311 (1981c), inc 1966, is located on the W side of the Great Northern Pen. Its name derives from the Basque *Portuichoa,* "little harbour." Two major archaeological sites have been investigated at Port au Choix. The first, excavated during the 1950s, is a large site of DORSET Eskimo culture dating between about 200 and 600 AD. It consists of a group of rectangular winter house remains and outdoor hearths suggesting year-round use. The many tools, weapons, ornaments and other objects were used to define "Newfoundland Dorset Culture," now thought to represent a variant of the more general Middle Dorset period in Newfoundland and Labrador. The second Port au Choix site was a large cemetery from which the Maritime ARCHAIC tradition was defined. The tools, weapons, religious and other objects discovered, along with more than 100 skeletal remains, indicate a people whose way of life was attuned to the coastal resources of Newfoundland between 2000 and 1200 BC. Because of its great historical and cultural value, Port au Choix is the location of a national historic park commemorating aboriginal occupations of the site. In recorded history, Port au Choix was a major BASQUE fishing station in the 1500s and an important French station on the FRENCH SHORE from the 18th to the late 19th century, when the site was settled by Newfoundland and English fishermen who vigorously asserted their right to settlement on this disputed coast. The modern town is a fish-processing and fish-collecting centre, which serves as a regional services centre for several smaller settlements to the N.
JANET E.M. PITT, ROBERT D. PITT AND JAMES A. TUCK

Reading: James A. Tuck, *Ancient People of Port au Choix* (1976).

Port au Port Peninsula is a roughly triangular peninsula with 130 km of rocky coastline but no harbours, joined to SW Newfoundland W of STEPHENVILLE. It was named *Ophor portu,* "port of rest," by the BASQUES. An eroded highland with hills to the S and sloping lowlands on the N side, the once heavily forested peninsula is bounded by Port au Port Bay, the Gulf of ST LAWRENCE and St George's Bay, and terminates in Cape St George in the S and fingerlike Long Point 50 km N. Scattered settlement occurred around the peninsula's shores by the mid-1800s, though it continued as part of the FRENCH SHORE until 1904. The population represents a more varied ethnic and linguistic mix than is commonly found in Newfoundland, with the highest proportion of French-speaking settlement on the island (15%). Since 1971 the peninsula has been designated insular Newfoundland's only bilingual district. The economy has been based on fishing, woodcutting and limestone mining (c 1900-1960) at Aguathuna. From 1940 to 1966, many people in the peninsula's more than 20 small communities were employed at the US military base in Stephenville. Piccadilly Head Prov Pk is located on the NE shore.
JANET E.M. PITT

Port Colborne, Ont, City, pop 19 225 (1981c), inc 1966, located on Lk ERIE at the S port of entry to the WELLAND CANAL. The settlement was founded 1833 with the construction of the canal, and changed as the waterway was enlarged. The largest lock on the canal is located here; at

421 m it is one of the longest in the world. The town also benefited from its location on the Welland Ry, and the Buffalo and Lake Huron (now CN) Ry. Industries associated with the canal include servicing, flour mills, repair and breakup of vessels, lake fishing, marinas and limestone quarrying. The city has an important nickel refinery. The harbour is man-made, and some intensive agriculture occupies reclaimed marshland. JOHN N. JACKSON

Port Coquitlam, BC, City, pop 27 535 (1981c), inc 1913, is located on the Pitt and Fraser rivers, 27 km E of VANCOUVER, of which it is a satellite. It is bounded on the N and W by the Dist of Coquitlam. Indians originally settled at the mouth of the Coquitlam (meaning "salmon") R, known for its abundant fish. An industrial area around the CPR's new Pacific Coast Terminal became the city of Port Coquitlam. WWI cut short the hope of extensive trade after the opening of the Panama Canal. Prior to and during WWII, most of the work force was employed in railways, but after WWII, metal, rubber and iron-casting industries, TUNGSTEN refining, boat building and gravel operations were established and the population grew to 3200 in 1951, 8100 in 1961 and 19 500 by 1971. The city has encouraged industrial and commercial development in recent years, devoting 125 ha to industrial use, with a further 120 ha held in reserve. Much land in the surrounding district is devoted to dairy, poultry and fruit farming. In recent years a downtown revitalization program has begun.
ALAN F.J. ARTIBISE

Port Dover, Ont, Town, inc 1954, located on Lk ERIE at the mouth of the Lynn R, 60 km from Hamilton. A Neutral village was originally on the site. Jesuit priests François Dollier de Casson and René de Galinée landed here 1669 and claimed the land around Lk Erie for French King Louis XIV. In 1804 a gristmill was built and a small hamlet developed, named after Dover, Eng. This was destroyed by invading American troops during the WAR OF 1812, but the village recovered and developed as an agricultural centre and lake port. Blessed with a good harbour, it was home port to a large commercial fishing fleet. In 1974 it was amalgamated with several other communities to create the city of NANTICOKE. DANIEL FRANCIS

Port Hardy, BC, District Municipality, pop 5075 (1981c), area 3965 ha, inc 1966, is located on the NE coast of Vancouver I, 390 km by road N of Nanaimo. Its harbour is the largest and most sheltered on the north island. The economy is based on the nearby Island Copper Mine, logging, fishing and a cannery. Tourism has become a growing industry after completion of the Island Hwy and ferry service to Prince Rupert in the late 1970s. ALAN F.J. ARTIBISE

Port Hood, NS, UP, pop 701 (1981c), is located on NORTHUMBERLAND STR on Cape Breton I, 30 km SW of Inverness. It was named *Ragweamkek* ("sandbar") by the Micmac, Juste-au-Corps by the French and Port Barrington before 1775, when Samuel Hood, later a viscount, was honoured. The French built vessels here for their Newfoundland trade and quarried stone for LOUISBOURG and forts in the French West Indies. Early French settlers reported coal deposits, but these have been mined with disappointing results. The area prospered 1850-71 with the fishery, but declined following the expiration of a treaty with the US. Federal government programs in the 1960s have helped the industry develop to its most prosperous state. JANICE MILTON

Port Hope, Ont, Town, pop 9992 (1981c), inc 1834, located on Lk Ontario at mouth of the Ganaraska R, 60 km E of Toronto. The site originally was an Indian village named Cochingomink. It was a fur-trade post from 1778, and was named for a time Smith's Creek after Peter Smith, a trader. In 1817 citizens chose the name Port Hope, for Col Henry Hope, former lt-gov. Long a manufacturing and regional commercial centre, its main street is one of the best preserved from late 19th-century Ontario. It is now a centre for uranium refining and the manufacture of machinery, tools, plastics and rubber. Trinity College School, fd 1865, is one of the oldest private schools for boys in Canada. K.L. MORRISON

Port Moody, BC, City, pop 14 917 (1981c), inc 1913, lies at the head of Burrard Inlet, some 20 km E of Vancouver. It was named for Col Richard Moody, the BC land commissioner who selected the site for New Westminster. A heavily industrialized community within the Coquitlam area, with a bulk-loading terminal for deep-sea vessels, Port Moody is also a residential suburb of Vancouver. The manufacture of lumber, plywood and other forest products is important to the local economy. A restored 1908 CPR station houses a local history collection, including early CPR track-laying equipment. ALAN F.J. ARTIBISE

Port Refuge is a small bay on the S coast of Grinnell Pen, DEVON I, in the High Arctic. It was named by Sir Edward Belcher in 1853, when it provided shelter from moving ice to his expedition in search of Sir John FRANKLIN. Archaeology has shown that this bay has been occupied sporadically over the past 4000 years. Four distinct Paleoeskimo occupations between about 2000 BC and 1000 AD have been recognized, as well as a THULE-culture Inuit occupation of about 1200 to 1400 AD. Prehistoric hunters were attracted to this area by the presence of an offshore polynia, where currents maintained open water for most or all of the year and which supported a concentration of sea mammals. The area is of interest to ARCHAEOLOGY since most of the prehistoric occupations of the High Arctic islands are represented at sites on the beaches surrounding Port Refuge. *See also* PREHISTORY. ROBERT McGHEE

Port-Royal (now ANNAPOLIS ROYAL, NS), est 1605 by François Gravé, Sieur du Pont, and Samuel de CHAMPLAIN on the N shore of the Annapolis Basin near the mouth of the Annapolis R. The *habitation* consisted of buildings grouped around a central courtyard. The garden became the first European experimental seed plot in N America. During the winter of 1606-07 Champlain organized the ORDRE DE BON TEMPS, the first social club in N America, and it was here that the first theatre event in Canadian history took place in 1606 — Marc LESCARBOT's *Le Théâtre de Neptune en la Nouvelle-France.* Hopes for a prosperous colony were disappointed, however, and the site was abandoned in the summer of 1607.

The colony was re-established in 1610 by one of the original colonists, BIENCOURT DE POUTRINCOURT, but the *habitation* was destroyed 3 years later by English freebooter Samuel Argall. In 1628 William Alexander established a settlement there, but in 1632 French claims to the

Champlain's drawing of the habitation at Port-Royal, from *Les Voyages* (1613) *(courtesy National Library of Canada/Rare Book Division).*

Paul Kane's *White Mud Portage, Winnipeg River* (c1851-56), shows an Indian brigade portaging rapids on the Winnipeg R *(courtesy National Gallery of Canada).*

area were again recognized. Although the buildings were rudimentary, Port-Royal remained the earliest European settlement of any permanence in N America N of St Augustine, Florida. The first dikes were built on the marshes before mid-century and the concentration of troops and administration around the fort was the only compact village in ACADIA. The farmers lived in relative poverty, compared to elsewhere in Acadia, though they developed small orchards and were able to provide cattle, sheep and wheat for export to the fortress of LOUISBOURG. When retaken by the English in 1654, Port-Royal had a population of about 200; at the time of the CONQUEST (1759-60) it was about 350. In 1938-39 the federal government reconstructed the *habitation* and in 1940 created Port-Royal Habitation National Historic Park. *See* ANNAPOLIS ROYAL; HISTORIC SITE. ROBERT S. ALLEN

Portage, a way by land around an interruption in a water route. Until the early 19th century most inhabitants of what is now Canada travelled mainly by water. Alexander MACKENZIE and Simon FRASER demonstrated that it is possible, by portaging 100 times, to canoe from the St Lawrence to the Arctic or Pacific oceans.

The first trails around waterfalls and rapids were often made by moose. Then Indians used the same paths, carrying their marvellously light birchbark CANOES. The organized FUR TRADE required the transport of heavy goods. VOYAGEURS were expected to hoist 2 packs (*pièces*), each weighing about 41 kg. The first was slung on the back with a TUMPLINE across the forehead and the second was placed on top. It was fatiguing work, usually done at a slow jog to reduce the strain on the back. On a long portage, the voyageurs would dump loads at *poses* every kilometre or so and go back for more loads. Two or 4 voyageurs would combine to carry the North or Montréal canoes, and when heavy YORK BOATS came into widespread use in the 1820s, portages were often equipped with rollers.

Packhorses were used on the trail to Ft Assiniboine and across the Athabasca Pass. Oxcarts were needed for the heavier freight on PORTAGE LA LOCHE and at Ft Smith. In eastern Canada, canals and roads improved and supplemented water routes. At Niagara and between Montréal and the Richelieu R, early "portage railways" were a partial answer to transport needs (*see* RAILWAY HISTORY). The GRAND TRUNK RY in the 1850s and the CANADIAN PACIFIC RY in the 1880s marked the shift to continuous land transport across southern Canada. C.S. MACKINNON

Portage La Loche (Methye Portage), in present-day northern Saskatchewan, was the longest PORTAGE (20 km) in the regular FUR TRADE, traversing the height of land between the Hudson Bay watershed with the Arctic watershed. It lies between Lac La Loche (the top of the CHURCHILL R system) on the SE and the CLEARWATER R (which flows into the Athabasca R) on the NW. *Methy(e)* is Cree for burbot (*see* COD); after long use, this name was gradually supplanted by the French term for the same fish, *loche* (or *lotte*). Peter POND explored this traditional Indian route in 1778, and soon NOR'WESTERS were portaging canoes and outfits into the rich Athabasca area. The system was later reorganized by the HUDSON'S BAY COMPANY: in 1823 the Athabasca brigade left its YORK BOATS at the NW end of the portage, carried the fur packs across and embarked in other boats which were waiting for them at the SE end. In 1826 the more distant Mackenzie R brigade simply exchanged furs for supplies with the La Loche brigade coming from the SE. In the early years local Indians were hired to help portage the heavy loads. By the 1850s, packhorses and ox-carts had come into use, and over 100 tonnes could be portaged annually. After 1886, this route was displaced by one that led northward from Edmonton via ATHABASCA Landing. *See* ATHABASCA LANDING TRAIL. C.S. MACKINNON

Portage la Prairie, Man, City, pop 13 086 (1981c), inc 1907, situated 85 km W of WINNIPEG, is an important regional service centre for the flat but highly fertile soils of the surrounding Portage Plains. Fort la Reine was built in the vicinity by LA VÉRENDRYE in 1738, but voyageurs gave the locality its name. After 1794 both the NWC and HBC maintained trading posts at the portage, but permanent white settlement began only after 1851, when the Reverend Cockran established a mission there. In 1867-68 the still tiny settlement became the capital of Thomas Spence's short-lived "colony" of Manitobah. After the Pacific Railway reached there in 1880, the population grew rapidly, and the town was incorporated. Since then, Portage la Prairie has weathered boom and depression, building suc-

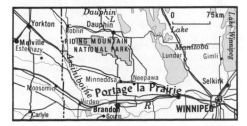

cessfully on its accessibility and exceptional agricultural resource base to become one of the most prosperous communities in Manitoba.

Food-processing industries employing some 1000 people are a mainstay of the economy. Along with handling the district's traditional grain and field crops, Portage la Prairie industries now process such diverse products as mushrooms, soups, frozen foods and cocktail onions. There are also large cold-storage facilities, as well as the Manitoba Research Council's Food Products Development Centre. Location on the TRANS-CANADA HWY and the CPR and CNR main lines has attracted a variety of nonfood-related businesses to the city's modern industrial park. Important government-operated facilities include the Canadian Forces Base nearby.

H. JOHN SELWOOD

Porter, John Arthur, sociologist (b at Vancouver 12 Nov 1921; d at Ottawa 15 June 1979). Regarded by many as Canada's leading sociologist, he published his most important work, *The* VERTICAL MOSAIC in 1965. Porter's chief concerns were equality of opportunity and the exercise of power by bureaucratic, economic and political elites in Canada. He had a profound influence on students, some of whom have become leading social scientists and carry on his work. A graduate of London School of Economics, Porter spent most of his scholarly career at Carleton U where he was teacher, department chairman, dean and academic vice-president. Porter was also visiting professor at Harvard and U of T. Shortly before his death he put together what he regarded as his 10 most significant essays in a volume entitled *The Measure of Canadian Society: Education, Equality, and Opportunity* (1979).

FRANK G. VALLEE

Portuguese explorers were among ·the first Europeans to see Canadian soil. It is believed that Diogo de Teive (1452), João Vaz Corte-Real (1470), João FERNANDES and Pedro de Barcelos (1493) touched on the eastern coast of Canada, and conclusive evidence exists about explorations by Miguel and Gaspar CORTE-REAL, who were lost in Newfoundland waters in 1501 and 1502, respectively. That Portuguese subsequently fished for cod on the GRAND BANKS is attested to by numerous place names. Labrador, likely from the Portuguese *lavrador* ("small landowner or farmer") indicates that the Portuguese knew of this territory. During 5 centuries of intermittent contact, however, only a handful of Portuguese fisherman settled on the Atlantic coast. The Portuguese in New France were descended from a few families founded by immigrants of 1668 and later.

From a trickle in the 1940s (some 200) Portuguese immigration to Canada increased rapidly after 1953. Immigrants arrived from the Azores (comprising 70% of Portuguese immigration to Canada) and Madeira archipelagoes and from continental Portugal. Many of the 1950s arrivals were recruited to work in rural and isolated locations in Canada, but soon established themselves in the larger cities. Between 1951 and 1957, 8115 persons immigrated; between 1958 and 1962, 16 731; between 1963 and 1967, 32 473; and between 1968 and 1973, 54 199. Portuguese immigrated for the same reasons many other nationalities immigrated — economic opportunity, underemployment at home and a desire to escape political oppression. By 1981 the Portuguese community of 188 105 comprised less than 1% of the Canadian population.

Migration and Settlement Portuguese is the mother tongue for 164 615 Portuguese Canadians (1981 census). Most Portuguese Canadians reside in Ontario (69%), followed by Québec (15%), BC (8.5%) and the Prairie provinces (7.5%). They usually live in urban centres. Almost 48% of the population of Canada who re-

port Portuguese as the mother tongue live in Toronto, primarily in city-core areas, a residential pattern evident also in Montréal. The centre with the highest percentage of Portuguese relative to the total urban population is CAMBRIDGE, Ont. Winnipeg and Vancouver also have settlements of several thousand Portuguese. The only rural concentrations of Portuguese (fruit farmers) are in the southern Okanagan Valley of BC.

Social and Cultural Life For the first generation of Portuguese, community cultural life was largely bound up with popular entertainments, eg, soccer matches, dances, picnics and music. Recreational activities were sponsored by clubs with Portuguese regional affiliations, or with particular parish congregations or Portuguese political parties. Today, Portuguese formal culture and language is taught in after-hours schools and in various schools and universities across Canada where numbers permit.

Many of the first generation prefer to attend social activities in Portuguese, but this is not true for their Canadian-educated children. Economic advances followed urbanization. Most of the labourers first worked in Canada as farmhands or railway labourers. When they transferred to the cities, they sought out janitorial, construction and factory work. Women were employed as cleaners or as textile or food-processing workers. During the 1960s, increasing numbers of families opened variety and clothing stores, fish shops, bakeries and restaurants. The minority with secondary education often became realtors, travel agents, or driving-school instructors, or provided other services for the community members. By the 1970s a second, Canadian-trained generation included high-school teachers, lawyers, social workers, engineers and civil servants. Many more entered semiskilled and skilled trades.

Most Portuguese are Roman Catholics, but recently some have converted to other Christian denominations, eg, Pentecostal, Baptist and Seventh Day Adventist.

Group Maintenance The first generation of Portuguese are concerned to maintain their *Portuguesismo* "Portugueseness" — but regional loyalties to the Portuguese area of origin are equally compelling. At the local level emphasis on individual and family economic advances, heightened by class distinctions based on education and ways of life, induces rivalries which serve as a barrier to community-wide co-operation. Among the second generation, intermarriage with a non-Portuguese spouse occurs occasionally. Several Portuguese newspapers have been published in Toronto, Montréal, Winnipeg and Vancouver.

DAVID HIGGS AND GRACE M. ANDERSON

Reading: Grace M. Anderson and David Higgs, *A Future to Inherit: The Portuguese Communities of Canada* (1976).

Post, Sandra, golfer (b in Oakville, Ont 4 June 1948). She became Canada's first female professional golfer in 1968 and won the Ladies Professional Golf Assn Championship at Sutton, Mass, during her rookie year. She won 8 official LPGA events 1968-83 and $746 714 in prize money — more than any Canadian professional, male or female, had ever won. Post's finest year came in 1979, when she won $178 750 and 3 tournaments for second place on the LPGA money list. That year she won the LOU MARSH TROPHY as Canada's athlete of the year. She had won the Canadian junior girls championship 1964-66, and when she decided to turn professional, she moved to Florida, where she could practise year-round. That determination, coupled with her success, eventually encouraged more Canadian women to try professional golf. By 1984, 7 women in addition to Post held LPGA tour playing cards.

LORNE RUBENSTEIN

Postage Stamps The first adhesive postage stamps were issued in Great Britain on 6 May 1840 as part of the innovative postage scheme proposed by Sir Rowland Hill in 1837. Prepayment of postage by the use of stamps was a practice quickly adopted by many countries. The provinces of Canada followed the lead of Britain beginning with Upper and Lower Canada, NS and NB (1851), Nfld (1857), BC (1860) and PEI (1861). With Confederation, all of the provinces ceased to issue their own stamps and used the Dominion of Canada general issue. Newfoundland continued to issue its own postage stamps until it too joined the Confederation (1949).

Design of Stamps Canada's first stamp was the Three-Pence Beaver designed by Sir Sandford FLEMING. It was issued 23 Apr 1851, and was the world's first pictorial stamp. Stamps prior to this depicted either the head of the ruler or some other official device. Until the post WWII period most Canadian stamps were designed by staff artists of the various security printers under contract to the Post Office. In the 1950s, however, more emphasis was placed on design, and the policy of inviting designs from individual artists was begun. Since 1969, stamps have been chosen on the advice of a Stamp Advisory Committee made up of competent people from the visual arts, printing and philately. The present committee is headed by the chairman of the board of the CANADA POST CORPORATION. Subjects and design proposals are examined by the Stamp Advisory Committee and a stamp program is recommended to the minister responsible for the Canada Post Corporation.

Stamp Printing Stamps have a monetary value and are produced only by security printers under very strict control. The production methods must be difficult to duplicate in order to prevent forgery. Almost all Canadian stamps issued before 1967 were printed by an engraving process. In this process the design is engraved in actual size in reverse on a block of steel called the master die. During this process various prints are made to show progress; these trial prints are called "die proofs." When a die proof is approved by Canada Post, the die is hardened and impressions of the design are transferred to a hardened steel roller. The impressions are then rolled into a steel plate, curved to fit modern rotary presses. A recent modification of this process involves the transfer of the plate impressions to a plastic sheet which is then used to produce an electrolytically deposited duplicate used for printing. In the late 1960s the techniques of multi-coloured offset lithography were sufficiently developed to use this process in stamp production. Since then Canadian stamps have been unrestricted in their use of colour, giving stamp designers far greater flexibility than when confined to the one-colour or 2-colour process. Two kinds of paper have been used: laid paper and wove paper. The use of these printing methods

The Three-Pence Beaver, designed by Sandford Fleming, was Canada's first postage stamp (*courtesy Canada Post Corporation*).

and papers has given Canada unusual variety and beauty in stamps.

Usage Canadian postage stamps are used strictly for postage purposes. Some countries, notably Britain, have their stamps inscribed "postage and revenue," thus validating them for both postal and excise use. In Canada special stamps are made available for excise purposes by both federal and provincial governments. *See also* STAMP COLLECTING.   K. ROWE

Postal Strikes, CUPW Since 1965 the Canadian Union of Postal Workers (previously Canadian Postal Employees Assn) has been involved in approximately 18 major disputes over several complex issues. The strike between 22 July and 9 Aug 1954, one of the largest Canadian "wildcat" strikes, the largest involving government employees, and one of the first nationwide strikes, played an important role in gaining collective bargaining rights for civil servants. The 1968 strike and the 1970 work-to-rule campaign were mainly the result of wage grievances; the latter secured an increase above the Trudeau government's guidelines. Strikes in the 1970s centered on wages and the threats posed by automation. Demands included legal guarantees of job security and maintenance of existing job classifications, as well as firm controls over the use of casual and part-time employees. In 1974 and 1975 CUPW, under Joe DAVIDSON, undertook long, bitter strikes which turned public opinion against it. In 1976 and 1977 postal service was disrupted by a series of illegal regional strikes: the union claimed that changes were being made without the promised consultation. A national strike in 1978 met with back-to-work legislation: union president Jean-Claude Parrot was jailed for refusing to comply, and relations became strained between the union and the CANADIAN LABOUR CONGRESS. There was a strike-free settlement in 1980, but in June 1981 workers struck over demands which included one for 17 weeks' paid maternity leave. CUPW became the first federal civil service bargaining unit to win this concession.

On 16 Oct 1981 the post office became a CROWN CORPORATION, something CUPW had been urging in the hope that it would streamline negotiations by placing the union under the Canada Labour Code. The corporation inherited a bitter legacy of mistrust, and although many problems remained unresolved, negotiations brought a new agreement without a strike in 1985.

C.D. CHORNIAWY

Postal System, a network of postal facilities serving people in all parts of Canada, of transportation services linking post offices, and thousands of people dedicated to transmitting mail. It is a service used for personal, social and commercial purposes. Co-operation between postal systems transcends political differences and makes it possible to exchange mail almost anywhere in the world. About 7 billion pieces of mail are handled by Canada's more than 8500 postal facilities each year.

Post Offices The Gateway postal plant near the international airport in Mississauga, Ont, covers 10 ha under one roof and is one of 30 mechanized postal plants in Canada. In addition to these large, mechanized sortation plants there are about 400 staff post offices in urban communities large enough to warrant a letter-carrier service and about 2000 semi-staff post offices in smaller communities. Nearly 3500 revenue post offices serve villages and rural areas; traditionally, their postmasters and assistants are paid from postal revenues. Seasonal post offices are set up to accommodate people during the busy vacation season in certain areas.

Postal stations are an extension of the main post office and provide the basic services. Sub-post offices are found in stores and businesses for the convenience of the public. In these the

Mail sorting, Toronto, c1925 (*courtesy Public Archives of Canada/PA-129707/Province of Ontario Picture Bureau/Post Office Dept Coll*).

owner of the business acts as the postmaster and provides a postal clerk as necessary. In rural areas of a certain density a rural delivery service is provided. In some cases group mail boxes may be set up at convenient points where customers can pick up their mail. Lock boxes are also provided in urban locations. Mail may be sent to a specific address or by general delivery to a post office to be picked up by the addressee.

Postal History Early commerce required a means of exchanging information as well as goods and services. The growth of empires required a speedy and reliable system for issuing orders and receiving and responding to reports. Using a system of relay posts, ancient Egypt was able to send messages quickly over long distances. The Romans, with fast horses and good roads, were able to assure next-day delivery up to 170 miles by post. The next great improvement came with the development of steam vehicles in the 19th century. The railways carried mail over 500 miles in a day. In the 20th century, aircraft carry mail thousands of kilometres a day, and recently with electronic facsimile transmittal by satellite, mail has been sent around the world in only a few hours. The modern postal system began in England with the introduction of the adhesive POSTAGE STAMP by Rowland Hill in 1837. Hill also devised uniform postage-rate schedules based on weight, rather than size, and made prepayment of postage both possible and practical. The British government adopted Hill's system in May 1840 and its use quickly became worldwide.

Significant Developments in Canada When the French arrived in N America in the 16th century, messages were carried among the native people by swift and trusted messengers. The French adopted the practice of using canoes between settlements along the St Lawrence R. In 1734 a road was opened between Québec and Montréal and a special messenger was appointed to carry official dispatches. He also carried messages for a fee. At intervals along the route "Post Houses" with a "Maître de poste" were set up to receive messages and fees and to provide conveyance to the next post. In 1753 Benjamin Franklin was appointed deputy postmaster general for the British colonies. In 1755 Franklin organized the first regular monthly mail packet service between Falmouth, Eng, and New York and opened the first official post office in Canada in Halifax, NS, to link Halifax with the Atlantic colonies and the packet service to England. A post office for local and outgoing mail had been started by Benjamin Leigh in Halifax in Apr 1754.

After the Treaty of Paris in 1763, Franklin established a post office in Québec City with subsidiaries in Montréal and Trois-Rivières. A Scottish immigrant, Hugh Finlay, became postmaster. A monthly courier service by way of Lk Champlain connected Montréal with New York and the Atlantic packet service. In 1774 Franklin was dismissed because of his sympathy with the American revolutionary cause, and Finlay became deputy postmaster general for the northern colonies. By 1775 the mails were being

seriously disrupted by the revolutionaries, and because of the threat to the couriers' lives Finlay stopped the inland service. Peace returned in 1783 and on 7 July 1784 Hugh Finlay became the deputy postmaster general for Canada. The revolution brought a major immigration of LOYALISTS to Canada and a demand for improved postal services. Early in 1784 Finlay hired a courier, Pierre Durand, to pioneer a Canadian route to Halifax from Québec City through 1000 km of forest. The round trip with the mail took 15 weeks.

By 1851 there were deputy postmasters general in NS, NB and Canada, but the British government still administered the postal system. The provincial deputies were convinced that they could operate the system more efficiently and petitioned Queen Victoria for a transfer of authority. The queen's approval was gazetted on 22 Feb 1851 and became effective 5 Apr 1851. From then until Confederation, the provinces co-operated in providing the mail service required, with W.H. Griffin, secretary in charge, reporting to the Honourable James Morris, postmaster general of the Province of Canada. The new decentralized, co-operative arrangement lived up to the expectation of its advocates. Rates were reduced and volumes doubled in the first year of provincial co-operation.

In 1853 the Grand Trunk Railway ran from Québec City to Sarnia; the Great Western from Niagara to Detroit through Hamilton; the Central Canada Ry, from Brockville to Ottawa; and the Northern Ry, from Toronto to Collingwood. They all carried mail. Postal clerks began sorting and distributing the mail en route on the Niagara-to-London, Ont, run in 1854. By 1857 there were specially equipped cars called railway post offices, and the railway mail service had reduced the delivery time for a letter from Québec City to Windsor, Ont, from about 10 days to a dependable 49 hours. By 1863 the trial period for the travelling post offices was over and an order-in-council established the standards for their use on the Grand Trunk Railway 12 Aug 1863.

The post office was one of the first federal-government departments formed after Confederation and took over the postal service on 1 Apr 1868. A year later Timothy EATON, an enterprising Toronto merchant, established the first mail-order system. As the Canadian Pacific Ry stretched across the prairies, a railway post office, addressed "End of the Line," moved with it, bringing banking, money-order and mail-order facilities to the settlers. On 28 June 1886 another railway mail car left Montréal and arrived in Port Moody, BC, on July 4. It began a national mail service which for 75 years was the envy of the world. Free letter-carrier delivery service was introduced in Montréal on 1 Oct 1874. Free rural mail delivery began between Hamilton and Ancaster, Ont, on 10 Oct 1908. Captain Brian Peck flew the first official Canadian air mail from Montréal to Toronto 24 June 1918. Two weeks later, Katherine Stinson, Canada's first woman air-mail pilot, flew mail from Calgary to Edmonton. Prepaid, stamped air mail was flown between Haileybury, Ont, and Rouyn, Qué, 21 Sept 1924, reducing mail time between these remote northern mining towns from weeks to a few hours.

On 4 Oct 1927 the first contract air-mail service commenced between Lac du Bonnet, Bisset and Wadhope in Manitoba. The post office also began an experimental air service (1927) to meet the ocean liners at Rimouski and fly the mail to Québec, Montréal and Ottawa. This service continued until 1939. In Dec 1929 air mail between Ft McMurray and Aklavik linked the NWT with the postal system and established a postal service 480 km within the Arctic Circle. An air-mail contract helped finance Trans Canada Air-Lines in 1937. On 1 Mar 1939 a daily air-mail service between Montréal and Vancouver began. It was extended to the Maritimes in Jan 1940. On 1 July 1948 Canada became the first country in the world to introduce domestic "all-up" service. First-class mail was carried by air at regular postage rates.

Technological Change In the 19th century steamboats and trains made it possible to carry more mail quickly over long distances, at the same time sorting it en route, thus eliminating some of the dead time and post-office handling. Mechanization of the postal transportation system brought a tremendous improvement in speed and reliability. In the 1920s the introduction of conveyor belts, elevators and gravity-feed systems greatly reduced the time and labour required to move mail within the post offices. The introduction of the all-up air-mail service, the improvement in paved roads and TRUCKING services and a railroad strike in 1950 brought about the rapid decline of the railway mail service and shifted its sortation load back into the post offices. Air mail also increased the public's expectations of the postal service. People now anticipated delivery at the speed of the airplane.

Distribution systems became more complicated as the nation grew and became urbanized and as the composition of the mail changed. Then, in the mid-1960s, the annual examinations on distribution skills and rules and regulations were dropped, and the speed and efficiency of the manual memory sortation declined. To meet this problem the simplified alphabetic sortation, used at Christmas, was extended. It required less training, but more people, overtaxing crowded facilities and equipment. The obvious need was to mechanize the sortation process itself.

Canada Post first sought to simplify and streamline existing work methods and make the best of existing facilities through work simplification, measurement and standardization. This led to mechanizing the steps of the sortation process. A British-designed mechanical segregating, facing and cancelling machine called Sefacan was introduced in Winnipeg, and a sortation machine from Holland, called the Transorma, was installed in Peterborough in the 1950s. The early machines were noisy and inefficient, and in 1970 Canada Post chose a proven Belgian Coding System and Letter Sorting Machine, and Japanese-designed, high-speed Culler-Facer-Canceller and Optical Character Reader equipment. Canada now has the most mechanized and potentially efficient postal system in the world.

The Postal Process When a person deposits a letter in the red mailbox on the corner, the box is cleared at a scheduled time and the letter is taken by truck to the main post office where parcels, large envelopes and metered mail are separated out and the rest is sent to be cancelled. Mail addressed to the community in which it was posted is sorted by street names into letter-carrier routes or sent to postal stations for the letter carriers, who sort it by street and house number for delivery. The letter carrier takes about 16 kg at a time in his bag. The rest is taken by truck to relay boxes at convenient places along the letter carrier's route. Large parcels are delivered by drivers. Mail addressed to places outside the community is sorted, packaged and sent to the country, city or distribution centre for that address. There it is sorted again and turned over to the letter carriers or rural mail couriers for delivery to the addressee.

Starting in Ottawa in 1972, the post office installed equipment to mechanize the sortation process. The system is based on a 6-character postal code which forms the last line of every address. This postal code is made up of alphabet letters and numbers, arranged in the order ANA NAN. The first group, ANA, represents a geographic area; the second group, NAN, is a local

code that may identify a street, an apartment building or a group of rural post offices. Mail brought into a Letter Processing Plant (LPP) is unloaded, dropped onto a conveyor and taken to a bag shake-out machine. There it is shaken out and taken by a conveyor to a culling station where oversize, undersize and nonacceptable articles are removed to be sorted manually. The mail then goes to a Culler-Facer-Canceller (CFC) where it is culled again if it does not meet machine standards of size and thickness. The machine then faces up the remainder and the stamp is located by a photoelectric cell that triggers its cancellation. Letters are then stacked in coded trays and sent to a temporary storing system from which a computer dispatches them to the next step according to a scheduling program.

The next step may be an Optical Character Reader (OCR), which locates and reads typed or printed codes and applies a coloured-bar code that actuates a Letter-Sorting Machine (LSM). As many as 20 000 letters an hour can be sorted into the LSM's destination bins. Addresses that cannot be identified by the OCR are rejected and sent to the Group Desk Suite (GDS) where the code is read by an operator who keys the coloured-bar code onto the letter by hand. Uncoded or indecipherable coded letters are rejected at the GDS and sent to manual sorters. Both the OCR and the GDS take care of the primary sortation of the mail and add the bar codes for the final sortation by the LSM. Mail that does not meet the standards, or bear the code legibly printed, has to be separated out of the main flow. Large envelopes or magazines, called flats, are sent to Flat-Sorting Machines (FSM) for processing. Small parcels and small objects such as hotel keys also have their own sorting system. An operator indicates their postal code to a computer, which directs them to a mechanism that sorts them to their destination. Standard mail, parcels, large envelopes or manually sorted mail come together in a consolidation area where mail for a particular destination is assembled and packaged for transport by conveyor or fork lift to the dispatching dock. Local mail goes out to the postal stations by shuttle trucks for delivery. Forward mail goes by truck to other post offices or to the Air-Mail Facility (AMF) for shipment to other cities or countries by air.

The Universal Postal Union, an international organization, facilitates the exchange of mail between nations. It is a forum in which countries can discuss and work out problems that interfere with the free flow of mail among them. It originated in Berne, Switzerland, in 1874, and Canada became a member in 1878. The Universal Postal Union is a specialized agency of the United Nations, made up of 165 member countries comprising a single postal territory. Freedom of transit for postal items is guaranteed throughout the union territory. Canada is also a member of the Postal Union of the Americas and Spain (PUAS) and of the Conference of Commonwealth Postal Administration (CCPA), and has played an active role in all of these organizations.

Canada Post Corporation Canada Post became the Canada Post Corporation on 16 Oct 1981. Deputy Postmaster General J.C. Corkery was replaced by President R. Michael Warren, reporting to a board of directors chaired by Judge R.J. Marin. The assistant deputies were replaced by executive vice-presidents and vice-presidents, and the CROWN CORPORATION was reorganized along divisional lines. COLLECTIVE BARGAINING is, under the rules of the Canada Labour Code, administered by the Canada Labour Relations Board and the federal Dept of Labour. Canada Post Corporation had more than 62 000 regular full-time and part-time employees in 1981. About 97% were members of its 27 bargaining units, represented by 8 unions, the largest of which was the CANADIAN UNION OF POSTAL

WORKERS representing about 24 000 inside mail-processing and counter staff; and the Letter Carriers' Union of Canada, with about 20 000 truck drivers and letter carriers; the Canadian Postmasters and Assistants Assn, representing 9500 rural postmasters and assistants; the Assn of Postal Officials of Canada, representing more than 4000 postal operations supervisors; the Public Service Alliance of Canada, representing about 6000 maintenance and administrative staff; the Professional Institute of the Public Service of Canada, with about 175 computer specialists, engineers and other professionals; the International Brotherhood of Electrical Workers, representing about 70 electrical and electronic workers; and the Economists, Sociologists and Statisticians Assn with 20 members.

Canada Post Corporation is in competition with a number of forces. Its survival depends on the restoration of a speedy and reliable postal service. Its future lies in co-operative ventures such as Priority Post, with links to the International Express Mail network; Telepost, with links to CNCP Telecommunications; and Intelpost, with links to Teleglobe Canada and the world. More information about the Postal System can be obtained from the National Postal Museum in Ottawa and from the Corporate Communications Branch of the Canada Post Corporation.   H. GRIFFIN

Reading: W. Boggs, *The Postage Stamps and Postal History of Canada* (1974); Canada Post, *Postal Service Down the Centuries* (1974); S.M. McDonald, *The Posts in Canada to 1776* (1975); W. Smith, *History of the Post Office in British North America* (1920).

Potash refers to potassium compounds and potassium-bearing materials, the most common being potassium chloride (KCl). Potassium is one of 14 elements essential to plant life and, with nitrogen and phosphorus, makes up mixed fertilizers. About 94% of world potash consumption is in fertilizers, with small amounts used in manufacturing soaps, glass, ceramics, chemical dyes, drugs, synthetic rubber and explosives. The term potash comes from the pioneer practice of extracting potassium fertilizer (K_2CO_3) by leaching wood ashes and evaporating the solution in large iron pots. As early as 1767, potash from wood ashes was exported from Canada, and exports of potash and pearl ash (potash and lime) reached 43 958 barrels in 1865. There were 519 asheries in operation in 1871. The industry declined in the late 19th century when large-scale production of potash from MINERAL salts was established in Germany. In 1943 potash was discovered in Saskatchewan in the process of drilling for oil. Active exploration began in 1951 and by 1958 the Potash Company of America began MINING from a flat-lying bed 1 km underground. In June 1962, International Minerals and Chemicals Corp (Canada) Ltd completed a mine shaft to a depth of 1030 m near ESTERHAZY, Sask, now the world's largest potash mine. In 1964 Kalium Chemicals Ltd opened the world's first potash solution mine near Regina, at a depth of 1585 m. By 1970, 9 mines were in operation in Saskatchewan, with a total capacity of 6.8 million t K_2O equivalent. Potash sales were unable to keep up with this growth rate: less than 3.5 million t were sold in 1969. By January 1970 prorationing of production to market demand was introduced by the Saskatchewan government to stabilize the price. These regulations were in force until demand caught up to supply. From 1977 to 1979 the Saskatchewan government bought 4 mines and created the Potash Corporation of Saskatchewan (PCS) to run them. By 1980, PCS accounted for 40% of provincial mining capacity.

Western Canada's potash deposits occur in the prairie evaporite formation underlying a broad, northwesterly trending belt extending across and beyond south-central Saskatchewan (*see* GEOLOGICAL REGIONS). Reserves recoverable by conventional underground mining are estimated at a minimum of 14 billion t; those available for solution mining may be 3 times as large. Significant reserves occur in formations of the Windsor group in NB (about 400 million t), where 2 mines are to be brought into production by 1984. Canada and the USSR each produce about 25% of the world's potash. The USSR uses most of its own; Canada contributes over 40% of world supplies. Canada developed from an importer of potash in 1961 to a production of 7.2 million t valued at $1.05 billion in 1981. Exports contributed $1 billion to Canada's BALANCE OF PAYMENTS.   G.S. BARRY AND W.E. KOEPKE

Potato (*Solanum tuberosum*), herbaceous annual of the NIGHTSHADE family, which produces tubers at the end of underground stems. Potatoes are an important VEGETABLE crop, with total production slightly greater than wheat. The principal cultivars (commercial varieties) grown in Canada for table stock and processing are Superior (early), Norchip (mid-season), Kennebec (main crop) and Russet Burbank (late). Tubers are about 80% water; the remainder contains useful amounts of minerals, vitamins B_1, and C, carbohydrate and protein. Eight hundred grams of potatoes and one egg will supply the daily protein requirements of a 70 kg human. A cool-season plant, the potato originated in the Andes and is now grown in temperate regions worldwide. Taken to Spain by conquistadores in about 1500 AD, it remained a botanical curiosity for some 200 years before being recognized as a useful food source. Potato cultivation spread slowly across western Europe and, thence, to Britain and N America. The greatest production and highest yields occur in eastern Europe and the USSR, where much of the crop is used to produce starch, alcohol and animal feed. In Canada the greatest production is still in the eastern provinces. The crop is produced by planting seed pieces, whole tubers or portions of larger tubers weighing 40-60 g. Total Canadian production is about 2.5 million t, grown on about 108 000 ha: PEI, 24 000 ha; NS, 1600 ha; NB 21 500 ha; Qué, 19 000 ha; Ont, 14 600 ha; Man, 16 600 ha; Sask, 700 ha; Alta, 6600 ha; and BC, 3000 ha. Crop value varies from year to year but averages $300 million. Exports of seed and table stock, mostly from PEI and NB, total about $30 million. A roughly equal amount is imported from the US.   G. ROWBERRY

Potlatch, a highly regulated event common to all Northwest Coast Indian cultures (*see* NATIVE PEOPLE: NORTHWEST COAST). The potlatch validated status and established claims to names, powers and privileges, thereby confirming the social structure of traditional native society organized by lineage, clan and tribe. Wealth, in the form of utilitarian goods and prestige items, was accumulated in order to bestow it on others and thereby affirm rights and privileges. Potlatches were given to celebrate initiation, mourning, investiture of chiefs, etc, in a continuing series of reciprocal exchanges between and within groups. A great potlatch was many years in the making, might last for several days, and would involve feasting, spirit dances, theatrical demonstrations and distribution of gifts. A federal government ban on potlatches, 1884-1951, was detrimental to NORTHWEST COAST INDIAN ART and culture.   RENÉ R. GADACZ

Reading: H.G. Barnett, *The Nature of the Potlatch* (1968); P. Drucker and R. Heizer, *To Make My Name Good* (1967).

Potts, Jerry, or *Ky-yo-kosi,* meaning "Bear Child," scout, guide, interpreter (b at Ft McKenzie, US 1840; d at Fort MacLeod, Alta 14 July 1896). Of Blood Indian and Scots parentage, he became famous among the BLACKFOOT as a great warrior and hunter. Hired by NWMP Commissioner G.A. FRENCH, Potts led the police to the notorious whisky post Ft Whoop-up. He also directed them to an island in the OLDMAN R where they constructed FORT MACLEOD. Hero to the Blackfoot Confederacy and a special constable in the NWMP, Potts educated each group about the other and ensured friendly relations. His influence with the Blackfoot helped to get Treaty No 7 signed and assure that his people remained neutral during the NORTH-WEST REBELLION of 1885.   D. BRUCE SEALEY

Reading: D. Bruce Sealey, *Jerry Potts* (1980).

Potvin, Damase, journalist, writer (b at Bagotville, Qué 16 Oct 1879; d at Québec C 9 June 1964). After studies at the Petit Séminaire de Chicoutimi in 1903, Potvin entered the novitiate of the White Fathers of Africa in Algiers. He returned to Chicoutimi in 1905 and began his long career in journalism as founder and editor of *Le Travailleur*. Over the next few years he worked for several newspapers as well as publishing an agricultural novel *Restons chez nous!* (1908). In 1910 he became parliamentary correspondent for *L'Evenement*, was made head of Associated Press in Québec in 1912 and head of the Québec Press Gallery in 1915, as well as publishing a political novel *Le "Membre"* (1916). He founded the Société des arts, sciences et lettres de Québec with some friends, among them Alonzo Cinq-Mars, and in 1918 helped found *Le Terroir*, the society's journal, in which he published some 500 articles and reviews. A second rural novel *L'Appel de la terre* appeared in 1919. Moving from *L'Evenement* to *Le Soleil* in 1920, he left the latter in 1925 for *La Presse*, and continued to write for it into the 1960s. During his long career he appeared in more than 150 national and foreign periodicals, published 36 books (including some that dealt with forgotten historical figures and numerous works on different areas of Québec). In 1945 he joined the Québec Dept of Public Instruction. His many honours and distinctions included the Prix David in 1938. He perfected the format of the agricultural novel and deeply influenced authors of this kind of book.   AURÉLIEN BOIVIN

Poultry Farming Poultry are domesticated birds kept for their meat or eggs. Common varieties in Canada are chickens (*Gallus gallus* or *G. domestica,* family Phasianidae), turkeys (*Meleagris gallopavo,* family Phasianidae), ducks (*Anas platyrhynchos, Cairina moschata,* family Anatidae) and geese (genus *Anser,* family Anatidae). In 1980 there were over 93 million hens and chickens on farms across Canada: Ont had 32.1 million; Qué, 21.0 million; Alta, 10.6 million; BC, 9.8 million; Man, 7.3 million; Sask, 5.3 million; NS, 3.5 million; NB, 2.3 million; Nfld, 1.1 million; PEI, 264 000. In the same year, there were almost 9.5 million turkeys in Canada: Ont had 3.8 million; Qué, 2.2 million; Alta, 1.3 million; Man, 962 000; BC, 566 000; Sask, 432 000; NS, 127 000; NB, 72 000; PEI, 7000; Nfld, 3000. The most recent available figures for the duck and goose populations show that in 1976 Man had 251 000; Ont, 230 000; Alta, 168 000; Sask, 106 000; Qué, 100 000; BC, 18 000; PEI, 6000; NS, 3000; NB, 2000; Nfld, 1000. In 1981 Canadian per capita consumption averaged 18.9 dozen eggs (12.9 kg), 18.8 kg of chicken, 4.1 kg of turkey and 0.4 kg of ducks and geese. Sale of poultry and eggs contributed over $1.2 billion to Canada's 1981 total farm-cash receipts. Foundation breeders have developed hybrid strains of chickens specifically for commercial egg and meat production; to a lesser degree, the same has been done for turkey meat production; very little breeding work has been done on WATERFOWL. Foundation breeders must keep pure bloodlines for crossing; however, most purebreds are kept as a hobby by poultry fanciers or exhibition poultrymen. The only world-class foundation breeding companies located in Canada are Shaver Poultry Breeding Farms Ltd, Cambridge, Ont, and Hybrid Turkeys Ltd, Kitchener, Ont. However, nearly all foundation breeders worldwide sell parent stock to franchised hatcheries in Canada which, in turn, supply commercial stock to Canadian poultry producers.

Chickens The basic egg-producing breeds are White Leghorn and Rhode Island Red. The commercial layer is white feathered and weighs about 1.8 kg. Most lay white-shelled eggs, but brown-shelled egg layers are gaining in general popularity and efficiency of production. Laying chickens produce 265-280 eggs during the 13-14 months they are in lay. They are expected to produce one dozen eggs for every 1.64 kg of feed. White Plymouth Rock females are used in crosses with other breeds (eg, Cornish, New Hampshire) to produce meat-type birds sold as broilers or roasters. The commercial bird is white feathered, fast growing, vigorous and well fleshed. Chicken broilers are generally slaughtered when 47 days old, at a liveweight of 1.77 kg. They require 888 g of feed to produce 1 kg liveweight. The Shaver chicken, developed in Canada, is used for both egg and meat production. Other popular stocks include Dekalb (egg), Hyline (egg or meat), Hubbard (meat), Arbor Acres (meat), Ross (egg or meat) and Babcock (egg).

Turkeys Most commercial turkeys are white feathered, vigorous, fast growing and plump. Turkey broilers are slaughtered at 13-14 weeks, when they weigh 4.44 kg (females) or 6.50 kg (males). They require 1.06 kg of feed to produce 1 kg liveweight. Tonnage turkeys are slaughtered at 21 weeks when they weigh at least 1.10 kg. They require 1.30 kg of feed to produce 1 kg liveweight. The Broad Breasted Bronze and the White Holland turkeys were used to develop the modern varieties Hybrid (in Canada) and Nicholas (in US).

Ducks and Geese Pure breeds and crosses are the sources of commercial stock. The White Pekin is the most popular meat duck; the Rouen, Aylesbury and Muscovy are used to a limited extent. A few Indian Runner and Khaki Campbell ducks are kept for egg production in Canada. The 3 most popular breeds of geese are Embden, Chinese and Toulouse.

Poultry farms may be classed as producers of eggs, chicken meat, turkey, waterfowl or game and exotic birds. Production of eggs, chicken meat and turkey is regulated federally (Agricultural Products Marketing Act) and provincially (AGRICULTURAL MARKETING BOARDS). Federal agencies allocate production quotas to the provinces, remove market surpluses and regulate import and export of products. Provincial boards allocate production quotas to producers, set prices, advertise the product and deduct board levies from producers for operating costs. The general strategy is to ensure that each province is self-sufficient. Waterfowl and the relatively new GAME BIRD and exotic bird production have little control and few statistics are available.   JOHN P. WALKER

Poundmaker, Cree chief (b in central Saskatchewan *c* 1842; d at Blackfoot Crossing, Alta 4 July 1886). Although he was the son of a Stoney, his mother's brother, Big Child, was a leading chief of the Eagle Hills Cree. In 1873 Poundmaker became influential when he was adopted by CROWFOOT, head chief of the Blackfoot. In 1876 he opposed Treaty no 6, but finally accepted it and 2 years later was recognized as a chief. During the NORTH-WEST REBELLION of 1885, Poundmaker's followers ransacked the abandoned village of Battleford and placed the fort under siege. A short time later, Col W.D. OTTER led a military force to "punish" the Indians, but when they attacked Poundmaker's camp near Cut Knife Hill they were forced to retire under heavy fire. Although Poundmaker had not taken part in the fight, he did prevent the warriors from pursuing the retreating army. At his

subsequent trial for treason-felony, Poundmaker protested his innocence but was sentenced to 3 years in prison. After serving only a
year he was released, broken in spirit and
health, and died a few weeks later while visiting his foster father on the Blackfoot Reserve.
HUGH A. DEMPSEY

Poussière sur la ville (1953), a novel by André
LANGEVIN, dramatizes, with the simple structural
elegance of Greek tragedy and the complex tone
and perspective of modern existentialist literature, the failure of a marriage. The setting of
Macklin, an industrial town modeled after
Thetford-Mines, Qué, and dominated by dreary
winter weather, grey asbestos dust and garish
neon lights, encloses the narrator's despair and
inability to communicate, pitted as he is against
repressive community standards. A city boy, Dr
Alain Dubois recalls his unlikely marriage to
the passionate Madeleine; his ambivalence
about her affair with Richard Hétu, broken up
by the parish priests; and finally her suicide, reinforcing his decision to remain in Macklin to
practise medicine — an act of compassion and
revenge. Awarded the Prix du Cercle du livre de
France, the novel was translated by John Latrobe and Robert Gottlieb as *Dust over the City*
(1955). MICHÈLE LACOMBE

Poverty One of the fundamental problems in
estimating the number of poor people is agreeing on a definition of poverty. How badly nourished, housed and clothed, how much insecurity and stress, and how much withdrawal and
powerlessness must people suffer before they are
considered or feel poor? It is one task to describe
the conditions of poverty, but establishing an
objective measure is more difficult. The 2 distinct and opposing methods ("absolute" and "relative") used to establish the basic level of income
that defines poverty are evidence that the definition and measurement of poverty is an exercise in values and politics, ie, society's beliefs
about poverty and its causes largely determine
the way poverty is defined and measured. The
absolute approach is based on the belief that
poor people only require the absolute necessities
of life, eg, substandard housing and the bare essentials of food and clothing, and that these can
be objectively established. This view stems from
the belief that poverty is an individual's own
doing and should not be rewarded or encouraged by the provision of adequate levels of social
assistance. Although the absolute approach and
the income levels or poverty lines resulting from
it are not used in practice for measuring poverty
in Canada, the levels of income provided by provincial and municipal authorities for welfare
recipients ensure only absolute (ie, substandard)
levels of living.

In the relative approach, the absolute notion
that poverty can be objectively defined without
reference to prevailing community standards is
rejected. A poor Canadian household exists in
the context of a highly interrelated, well-to-do
Canadian community; therefore the economic,
social and political functioning of that household is relevant. Two well-known national
measures based on the relative approach are
those developed by the national, nonprofit
social organization, the Canadian Council on
Social Development (CCSD), and the special Senate committee on poverty. The CCSD poverty
line is based on average Canadian family income, and a family is defined as poor if its income is less than 50% of average family income.
Adjustments are then made for family size. The
poverty line established by the Senate is similar
although it uses post-tax (disposable) income.
The calculation of the line is more complex, but
the final effect is to produce a poverty line set at
about 56% of the level of average Canadian family income.

If either the CCSD or Senate lines (and not

Slum dwelling in Toronto, Ont, 14 August 1913 (*courtesy City of Toronto Archives/Series 11-94*).

those of STATISTICS CANADA) are used as indicators
of the poverty rate, there has been no decline in
poverty since 1969, which also suggests (correctly) that the relative distribution of income in
Canada has remained unchanged. The CCSD
and Senate lines do not adjust the poverty line
for rural-urban residency, taking the view that
there is no significant difference between rural
and urban areas in the cost of purchasing the necessities for a basic standard of living.

The leading relative standard, however, is
that employed by Statistics Canada. Canada is
one of the few countries to take an annual survey of the poor, and the Statistics Canada approach has become by common usage the "official" measure of poverty, although it has never
been accorded this status formally. For its annual survey, Statistics Canada begins with an income line based on the actual share of income
that an average Canadian family devotes to
food, clothing and shelter purchases (thus the
amount of income allotted to poor families is
related to the expenditure standards of the community), and then adds 20% to this share. Any
family that must spend more than this share of
its income on food, clothing and shelter, has so
little discretionary income left that it lives in
"straitened circumstances." As the living standard of the average Canadian household has
risen over time, so has the poverty line, in order
to maintain a relationship with living standards. Statistics Canada adjusts its income line
for family size, and according to whether the
household is located in an urban or rural setting. The poverty line for rural households is
about 25% lower than that for urban households. Statistics Canada refrains from calling its
income measures poverty lines, preferring to label them "low-income cut offs."

The actual calculation of the number of people who are poor is conducted each spring
through a questionnaire survey covering a representative sample of approximately 40 000 Canadian households (excluding native households on reserves). Among the many questions
asked in the survey is the total amount of income received in the previous year. Income is
defined to include wages, interest payments,
government TRANSFER PAYMENTS, pension income
and some income in "kind" such as free room
and board given to farm workers. The family is
defined as all people sharing a dwelling and
related by blood or marriage.

After the income data is collected for the sample, and projections made for the Canadian population as a whole, family and individual incomes are ranked according to whether they fall
above or below the poverty lines. Statistics Canada publishes the results of its income survey in
such a way that it is possible to determine how

many individuals and families are poor, as well
as the characteristics of these households.

A major shortcoming of this type of poverty
survey is that it produces a "snapshot" of poor
households for that year only. In preceding or
succeeding years, it is not known whether the
same or different households registered poverty
incomes. Unfortunately, this is a serious omission because it is almost certainly the length of
time that a person or household suffers such an
income that leads to poverty conditions. In the
annual survey, no distinction is made between
the university student with a temporary low income, and the single-parent mother or disabled
person who has been living on a poverty income
for years with little prospect of escaping. Nonetheless, this survey does provide much information on how many and which types of people
suffer from poverty.

The method chosen to define poverty will determine how many Canadian households are officially considered poor in any one year. Statistics
Canada, in its annual report on low incomes,
has estimated that 869 000 families (13.2%) and
998 000 unattached individuals (37.4%) have
low incomes in Canada (1982). Female-headed
single-parent families comprise 31% of poor
families; indeed, this type of family faces a 47%
chance of being poor. The aged comprise 32% of
the total of poor unattached individuals; elderly
females face a 60% chance of being poor. Data
for native people and the disabled are not systematically collected, but the consensus among
experts is that these groups face above-average
chances of being poor. Among low-income
families in Canada it is important to note that
53% are headed by a person in the labour force.
These families are frequently referred to as the
"working poor" because they rely primarily on
employment earnings, not public assistance, for
their income. The other 47% of all poor families
("welfare poor") rely primarily on some form of
public assistance for support.

As measured by Statistics Canada, the rate of
family poverty declined from 21% in 1969 to
13% in 1982. However, since about 1973, the
family rate has stabilized around the 12-13%
level. The most likely cause for this arrested
decline is the prolonged economic slump in virtually all Western industrialized economies. The
resulting UNEMPLOYMENT has made it difficult for
an increasing number of families to earn adequate incomes. Among unattached individuals,
the decline in poverty has not been so marked.
It fell from 43% (1969) to 37% (1982). Most of the
decline has taken place in recent years, primarily as a result of gradual improvements in
government-funded income retirement programs. Since a large fraction of unattached individuals are aged, improvements in programs
such as the CANADA (OR QUÉBEC) PENSION PLAN, OLD
AGE PENSION, Guaranteed Income Supplement,
Spouses Allowance and some provincial income
supplement programs have helped more elderly
to escape complete poverty.

There have been noticeable shifts since 1969
in the composition of poor households. For example, poverty is less regionally concentrated.
In 1969 a family in the Atlantic provinces had
almost 3 times the chance of being poor as did a
family in Ontario, but by 1982 the poverty rate
for families in Ontario was 11%, and for those
in the Atlantic provinces 17%. Regarding the elderly in 1969, families headed by a person 65
years of age or older constituted 30% of all poor
families, but by 1982 this had dropped to 11%.
On the other hand, female-headed families constituted 18% of all poor families in 1969, but
35% by 1982. The shift in the composition of
poverty among families has been so dramatic
that poverty is less strongly associated with old
age than with being female. The combination of
sex and age yields an even gloomier prognosis,
as elderly women face a 60% poverty rate.

Poverty has also been "urbanized," ie, in 1969 just over 50% of all poor families were rural dwellers, but by 1982 this share has declined to 21%. In the largest cities (500 000 population or more), the proportion of poor families increased from 16% (1969) to 41% (1982).

Official measures of poverty in Canada date only to the 1960s, when poverty became a public issue. Much of the concern was generated by the appalling living conditions under which many of Canada's native people and elderly lived, and by large regional income disparities. This sudden "discovery" of poverty contradicted the vision of affluence prevailing in the post-WWII era. In 1964 the US launched its "war against poverty" and Canada began a more quiet campaign of study and legislation in an effort to understand better the causes of and remedies for poverty. The federal PRIVY COUNCIL OFFICE established (1965) a group of specialists to study and encourage greater federal-provincial co-operation in combatting poverty. In the same year the Company of Young Canadians (CYC) was created to help co-ordinate and stimulate local self-help efforts to overcome poverty. Although the CYC was later disbanded, it was a precursor of federal government programs such as Opportunities for Youth (OFY), the Local Initiatives Program (LIP) and Canada Works which attempted to provide employment and reduce poverty through local initiative efforts.

In 1968 Statistics Canada released a study on the incomes of Canadians that became the basis for defining and measuring low incomes in Canada. In the same year, the ECONOMIC COUNCIL OF CANADA (ECC) shocked the nation by using this new low-income measure to estimate the extent of poverty in Canada. It concluded that 27% of the Canadian population lived in poverty. In 1968, partly because of these findings, the influential Special Senate Committee on poverty, chaired by David CROLL, began its cross-country hearings and investigations. Its widely publicized report, released in 1971, reiterated much of what had been revealed in the ECC's report and proposed a guaranteed annual income program to eliminate poverty in Canada. Another influential commission created during this period, headed by Claude Castonguay, also released its report following a massive examination of social security in Québec. This commission also advocated (among many recommendations concerning health care, income security, employment and social services) a guaranteed annual income. The concern with poverty during the 1960s, particularly its disturbing presence among affluence, also led to several significant new pieces of antipoverty legislation. Negotiations between the provinces and the federal government, which began in 1964, resulted in the introduction of the Canada and Québec pension plans, which were based on the recognition that the private pension system did not provide adequate coverage to low-income retired workers and their families. In conjunction with these new pension plans, the Guaranteed Income Supplement Program, which assured all low-income aged a basic income support level, was implemented. The Canada Assistance Plan (CAP) was also introduced in 1966. A comprehensive social-assistance program, it replaced the many piecemeal cost-shared programs that the federal and provincial governments had begun entering into as far back as 1927. As well as providing a major source of funds for the disabled, blind and unemployed, the CAP assisted other low-income persons as well, including the working poor. Also brought into federal cost sharing under CAP were a wide range of SOCIAL SERVICES, including DAY CARE, family counselling, visiting homemaker and CHILD WELFARE services. Exponents of CAP claimed it would allow for the expenditure of funds to the needy who could not

secure sufficient aid, ie, it was a promise to use public funds to prevent, and not just respond, to poverty. In practice, however, CAP maintained the earlier tradition of only responding to poverty.

Another innovation in social service provision was the implementation in 1968 of the Medical Services Act (Medicare), which provided free access to a basic level of health care for all Canadians (see HEALTH POLICY).

During the 1970s and early 1980s, most legislative activity either represented slight improvements to, or cutbacks in, earlier legislated programs. The UNEMPLOYMENT INSURANCE Act was amended in 1971 to provide more extensive coverage to the unemployed as well as to the sick. The Child Tax Credit of 1978 extended federal benefits to families with children in a manner that was most beneficial to low-income families. Several provinces instituted income-tested payments to the aged, while Saskatchewan, Manitoba and Québec introduced programs that provided assistance to the families of the working poor. But the comprehensive federal-provincial review of Canada's social-security system conducted in the mid-1970s failed in its central purpose to establish a guaranteed annual income, and the 1980s have been marked by budget cuts on income provision and social services directed towards the poor.

The concern and legislation of the 1960s also raised the question of why there were so many poor people in a country as rich as Canada. In the prevailing ethos, poverty is perceived and treated as an individual, not a social problem, ie, individuals who are poor have themselves to blame. Therefore, it is not a country's total wealth that is relevant, but how that country distributes its wealth. A society can distribute its wealth under the laissez-faire or free-enterprise economic system, according to which people are presumed to get out of the marketplace what they put in, ie, those that put in very little or nothing get little or nothing back, and those that work at home for their lifetimes also receive nothing directly. Theoretically a society can also distribute its wealth through a collective or socialist system under which the fruits of economic production are distributed according to need. The economic and income distribution system in Canada has evolved and is still evolving from the precepts of 19th-century capitalism, although government involvement in the income distribution process ensures that those in need and those without economic means do receive some assistance. Thus the Canadian system is generally described as mixed. Most wealth is distributed through a market-based economic system, under which ownership of resources and well-paying jobs are the keys to an adequate share of the country's economic benefits. Those who are unable to find a decent place within this market system — women, the elderly, disabled persons, those with poor skills and native people — must rely on some combination of assistance from family, social organizations and government, but because individuals are held responsible for their inability to benefit from the economic system, the amount of aid is generally small and extended begrudgingly.

The plight of women and the relationship of women with the labour force have a unique history. Historically, it was accepted that women belonged in the home, where they received no direct income for their labour. If the male breadwinner leaves the household or dies, there is little provision under the Canadian legal and economic system for the woman, and she is particularly vulnerable if there are young children in her care. Divorced, separated and widowed women thus become prime candidates for poverty. On the other hand, WOMEN IN THE LABOUR FORCE are discriminated against in the labour market. On average women earn about 60% of

the income of the average male worker because women have not had access to the same type of training and advancement opportunities as men; they are placed in lower-paying, lower-skilled jobs, and they frequently receive less pay than men for jobs that are identical. Consequently, women working in the labour force are not ensured of a life out of poverty, particularly if they are single parents.

Low-income households can be subclassified as either welfare poor or working poor. The former tend to be people who cannot produce, or who are believed to be incapable of producing at a level high enough to make them attractive as employees. Single-parent mothers, who are not necessarily expected to take employment while they are caring for their young children, are a large group in this category, as are native people, although in their case the reasons for their situation are complicated by the long history of PREJUDICE AND DISCRIMINATION they have suffered at the hands of Canada's non-native population.

The welfare poor depend for most of their assistance on CAP. To rely almost exclusively on the social assistance benefits provided by provincially administered plans (plus federal family allowances and child tax credits, where applicable) guarantees a poverty income. Averaging across Canada, provincial social assistance (welfare) rates provide 60% of official poverty-line income.

The working poor includes itinerant workers who are always on the margin of the labour force. They are frequently the last hired and the first laid off, but even when they are employed they work for low wages and poor benefits, are seldom able to accumulate savings, and rarely qualify for benefits such as sickness insurance, health and dental plans, private pensions and paid vacations. Their life is marked by extreme economic insecurity. The fact that about 50% of the working poor actually work year-round should put to rest the timeworn belief that people can always work their way out of poverty, but the persistence of this belief has led to a situation in Canada where the social security system provides very little comprehensive assistance to the working poor while they are working, even though they are only earning poverty incomes.

DAVID P. ROSS

Reading: David P. Ross, *The Canadian Fact Book on Poverty,* 1983 (1983).

Powell, Ray Edwin, "Rep," business executive (b at Table Grove, Ill 7 Dec 1887; d at Montréal 9 Nov 1973). Educated at U of Ill, Powell served in the US army during WWI. He then joined Alcoa, the Aluminum Co of America, and in 1928 came to Canada, becoming a VP of the ALUMINIUM CO OF CANADA (Alcan), a subsidiary of Aluminum Ltd. From 1937 to 1957, Powell was Alcan's president, overseeing an extraordinary expansion in the company's business. Because ALUMINUM was a vital war material, Powell was able to use loans from the British, American and Australian governments and tax arrangements with the government of Canada to expand his company's facilities along the Saguenay R. Between 1937 and 1944, Alcan's assets increased 500%. Alcan expanded again in the early 1950s, establishing a power development and smelter at KITIMAT, BC. Under Powell, Alcan moved from being an American subsidiary to becoming an independent Canadian company.

ROBERT BOTHWELL

Powell, William Dummer, chief justice of Upper Canada (b at Boston, Mass 1755; d at Toronto 6 Sept 1834). Powell went to England with his family in 1776; he revisited Boston only after the AMERICAN REVOLUTION, in a vain attempt to claim his father's confiscated estates. Called to the English Bar, in 1779 he moved to Montréal to practise law. A spokesman for Loyalists' dissatisfaction with the QUEBEC ACT, he lobbied unsuccessfully for an elected assembly and wrote the report that induced Guy CARLETON, Baron Dorchester, to set up 4 new administrative districts in what was soon to become Upper Canada. In 1789 he was appointed the first judge of the Court of Common Pleas for the district of Hesse, with headquarters at Detroit. In 1794 he became a judge of the Upper Canadian Court of King's Bench and in 1807 a member of the Executive Council. An able lawyer and a conscientious administrator, he rose to become in 1816 Speaker of the Legislative Council and chief justice, the first permanent resident of the province to hold that office. His most controversial case was the trial of Robert GOURLAY. He retired in 1825.   S.R. MEALING

Powell River, BC, District Municipality, pop 13 423 (1981c), area 410 ha, inc 1955, is located on the E side of the Strait of GEORGIA, 140 km NE of Vancouver. It is bounded on the E by the Smith Mt Range, Powell Lk and Haslam Lk, and enjoys a mild climate year-round, moderated by the warm current of the strait. Named for Israel Wood Powell, BC Indian superintendent in the 1880s, the original settlement was a pulp and paper-milling centre. The region's economy is based on forest industries, in particular the pulp and paper operations of MACMILLAN BLOEDEL LTD, the largest source of employment. The climate and scenery make Powell River and its hinterland an attractive summer resort area. Saltwater and freshwater fishing and boating are important activities. Inauguration in 1965 of an automobile ferry from Comox, on Vancouver I, has boosted tourism.   ALAN F.J. ARTIBISE

Power, Charles Gavan, "Chubby," lawyer, politician (b at Sillery, Qué 18 Jan 1888; d at Québec C 30 May 1968). Power was seriously wounded in WWI and won the Military Cross for gallantry. He denounced military "brass hats" ever after. He was MP for Québec S (his father's seat) 1917-55, when he went to the Senate. The popular MP was brought into Mackenzie KING's government — despite the PM's legitimate doubts about Power's temperance — on the advice of Ernest LAPOINTE. Power was minister of pensions and national health 1935-39, and postmaster general 1939-40, but his greatest contribution came as minister of national defence for air, 1940-44, when he fought to promote the interests of RCAF personnel serving under British command and to create Canadian squadrons in NW Europe. Blunt and emotional, he opposed CONSCRIPTION for service abroad and therefore resigned from the Cabinet in 1944. His memoir, *A Party Politician* (1966), is among the best by a Canadian politician.   NORMAN HILLMER

Power Corporation of Canada, controlled by Paul DESMARAIS, is a large diversified company engaged in NEWSPAPERS, financial services, pulp, paper and packaging. Through its subsidiary, Gesca Ltée, Power publishes 4 daily newspapers, including *La Presse*. In addition, Gesca has 2 separate book-publishing operations. Its financial services include controlling interest in the Great-West Life Assurance Co, Montreal Trustco Inc and the Investors Group. The company's pulp, paper and packaging interests are held in Consolidated-Bathurst Inc, a major Canadian pulp and paper firm. Total assets of all operations associated with Power Corporation exceeded $12.7 billion in 1983, with revenues exceeding $4 billion.   PETER S. ANDERSON

Powwow, a traditional Indian celebration, in the same category as religious ceremonies, festivals, dances, rodeos and athletic contests, at which Indians and Inuit participate throughout N America. These intertribal events are open to tourists, and native art and craft objects are often sold.   RENÉ R. GADACZ

Prairie French explorers had no precise word for the large N American grasslands, but the term *prairie* [Fr, "meadow"] implied that it was an open, grass-covered, treeless landscape. The Canadian prairies occupy the southern parts of Alberta, Saskatchewan and Manitoba and comprise a nearly semicircular arc resting on the 49th parallel and extending through Calgary, Edmonton, North Battleford, Yorkton and Winnipeg. The region is the northern extremity of a vast grassland region extending almost to the Gulf of Mexico. Prairie, often considered a featureless flatland, actually contains great diversity: from broad plains to rolling hills and plateaus, often dissected by beautiful valleys and escarpments. While GRASSES dominate the natural vegetation, prairie flowers such as violets, daisies, crocus and goldenrod add to its beauty. The prairie is also the natural habitat of PRAIRIE DOG, BISON, COYOTES, grasshoppers, gophers, prairie chickens, songbirds, deer and antelope. Extremes of CLIMATE typify the prairies: cold winters, hot summers, a wet season followed by a period of DROUGHT or very dry conditions. The severity of drought increases with distance from the forest margins. Periods of above and below average conditions are common and tend to be cyclical. The prairies are believed to have been uninhabited until the introduction of the horse to N America enabled Indian tribes to use the vast herds of buffalo. The highly fertile prairie soils induced settlers from Europe, eastern Canada and the US to move into the region to farm and ranch in the latter part of the 19th century. Native prairie grasses have been largely replaced by another grass, WHEAT, the major component of western Canadian agriculture. In Canada, the word prairie is also used to refer to the 3 provinces of Manitoba, Saskatchewan and Alberta (*see* PRAIRIE WEST). *See* GRASSLANDS NATIONAL PARK; PHYSIOGRAPHIC REGIONS.   D.F. ACTON

Prairie Dog, highly gregarious, diurnal, terrestrial SQUIRREL that lives in colonies or "towns." It is very vocal and one call, a bark, prompted its generic name *Cynomys* [Lat, "dog mouse"] and its common name. Prairie dogs have receded in distribution as a result of deliberate exterminations because, although they aid soil by their excavations, they compete with domestic livestock for green plants. Of 4 species, only black-tailed prairie dog (*Cynomys ludovicianus*) extends into Canada (near Val Marie, Sask). It is pinkish-brown above, whitish below, with short ears and short, black-tipped tail. Adults weigh 1-1.5 kg. Prairie dogs remain close to elevated bare mounds that surround the mouths of their burrows, using them for vantage points. Their habit of sitting upright has given them the name "picket pin." One litter (4-5 young) is born each spring in a nesting chamber 4-5 m below the surface. Deep chambers are also used during extreme winter conditions. Prairie dogs do not hibernate, but use body fat accumulated in autumn when food is scarce.   J. MARY TAYLOR

Prairie Farm Rehabilitation Administration This agency was established by the federal government in 1935 in the midst of a prolonged and disastrous DROUGHT to deal with the problems of soil EROSION (and related SOIL-CONSERVATION problems) and lack of WATER resources for agricultural development. Emergency programs instituted to deal with the devastating drought included on-farm dugouts for the conservation of water for livestock, strip farming to prevent extensive soil drifting, seeding of abandoned land for community pastures, and extensive tree-planting projects to protect against wind-induced soil erosion. The PFRA's soil-conservation role was transferred to another agency in 1946, but work in the area of water development continued. The PFRA has been heavily involved in large-scale water development and conservation programs, including the St Mary River Irrigation Project, the Bow River Irrigation Project and the South Saskatchewan River Irrigation Project. There are few prairie communities which have not benefited from its activities. Today the agency is involved in the operation of 4 programs: Rural Water Development, Community Pastures, Tree Nurseries and Engineering Services.   J.C. GILSON

Prairie West, the "western interior" of Canada, bounded roughly by Lk Superior and the Rocky Mts, the 49th parallel of latitude and the low Arctic. It was peopled in 5 great eras: the migration from Asia, probably 20-40 000 years ago, produced a native population of 20-50 000 by about 1640; several thousand European and Canadian fur traders followed by several hundred British immigrants, between 1640 and 1840, created dozens of small outposts and a few European-style settlements, the largest being the RED RIVER COLONY; the third wave, 1840s-90s, consisted chiefly of Canadians of British heritage; the fourth and by far the largest was drawn from many nations and occurred 1897-1929, with a hiatus 1914-22 associated with WWI; and the fifth, drawn from other Canadian provinces and from around the world, commenced in the late 1940s and has continued with fluctuations to the present. Throughout the last century, the region has also steadily lost residents, as a result of migration to other parts of Canada and the world.

The first immigrants moved between resource zones according to the dictates of the season, the fortunes of the hunt, and diplomatic relations with neighbouring groups. In the 18th century they utilized European trade goods such as axes and knives, and were affected by some European innovations, particularly the gun and the horse, but they remained in control of their domestic economies and diplomatic alliances. Native autonomy was lost in the 19th century, partly through population pressure from eastern N America and partly because of the destruction of the single, crucial element in the plains economy — the buffalo (*see* BISON; BUFFALO HUNT). Seven INDIAN TREATIES were negotiated in the 1870s between the Canadian government and the natives of the western interior, exchanging native sovereignty over the land for government promises of economic assistance, education and the creation of reserves for native people. Thus, in a few short decades, prairie natives became wards of the state.

From the European perspective, the early history of the western interior was the story of FUR-TRADE competition. The English HUDSON'S BAY COMPANY, fd 1670, traded from posts on Hudson Bay until competition forced it to establish inland houses in the 1770s. The French and later the NORTH WEST COMPANY, with Montréal as headquarters, created an extensive post network that was pushed into the Prairie West by the LA VÉRENDRYES in the 1730s, and extended by Peter POND in the 1770s and Alexander MACKENZIE, 1789-93. Deadly competition finally forced the merger of the HBC and the NWC in 1821. The restructured HBC ruled the fur trade and the region for another 5 decades.

Some traders established liaisons with native women. Their offspring, whether French-speaking (Métis) or English-speaking ("mixed bloods" or country born) were sufficiently numerous by the early 19th century to constitute the largest group in the Red River Colony and an important component of fur-company operations. They led the defence of local interests against incoming speculators when outside interest in the region quickened in the 1840s-60s. Canada eventually secured sovereignty over RUPERT'S LAND, but only after the 1869-70 RED RIVER REBELLION led by Louis RIEL resulted in significant revisions to the terms allowing the region's entry into CONFEDERATION.

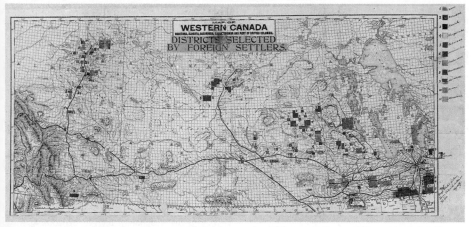

Map showing by various colours the areas selected by "foreign" (ie, non-British) settlers c 1900 (courtesy *Public Archives of Canada/NMC-17557*).

Because of the federal government's great powers and because of PM J.A. Macdonald's decision to retain control of western lands, the policy framework for development was created in Ottawa. Decisions taken between 1870 and 1874 on the dispatch of the North-West Mounted Police, the square survey (*see* CARTOGRAPHY; DOMINION LANDS POLICY), the policy on HOMESTEADING and immigration recruitment activities remained cornerstones of prairie history for 2 generations. Crucial decisions on tariff policy and the CANADIAN PACIFIC RAILWAY followed, 1879-80. The region was to become an agricultural hinterland, built upon international IMMIGRATION and the family farm, and integrated with a growing manufacturing sector in central Canada. The failure of the 1885 NORTH-WEST REBELLION and the passage of the Manitoba Schools Act and other language legislation in 1890 made plain that the defining elements of prairie society were henceforth to be Protestant, English speaking, and British. The creation of Saskatchewan and Alberta in 1905 (*see* AUTONOMY BILLS) seemed to demonstrate that the British tradition of peaceful evolution from colony to self-governing state had been fulfilled.

New forces at work in the Prairie West around 1900 made complacency inappropriate. Social leaders were troubled by the arrival of hundreds of thousands of non-British immigrants who placed great strains upon prairie institutions during the next few decades. The newcomers, on the other hand, relinquished much of their traditional culture as they helped to build the new West. Scandinavians and Germans assimilated quickly; MENNONITES, JEWS and UKRAINIANS sought to retain more of their cultural heritage, and eventually helped to create a multicultural definition of Canada; HUTTERITES remained isolated from the larger community; and some other religious groups — notably a few DOUKHOBORS and Mennonites — preferred to leave the region rather than accommodate to its norms. By the 1950s the Prairies were far closer to a British Canadian model than to that of any other culture.

Political institutions, too, underwent severe testing in the early 20th century. A wide gap between the wealthy and the poor produced real tension. In cities such as Winnipeg and Calgary, luxurious homes in segregated residential areas, exclusive clubs, colleges and social events, and the concentration of political and economic power in the hands of a few were signs that a ruling class was evolving. By contrast, the squalor of slum areas such as Winnipeg's North End, some frontier construction camps, and resource towns such as Lovettville and Cadomin, Alta, suggested that a class struggle was in the making. The intensity of labour-management con-

flicts, especially in Winnipeg (*see* WINNIPEG GENERAL STRIKE) and the Alberta coal towns, should be seen in this context.

A full-scale class struggle did not develop in the early 20th century for 3 reasons. The first was the relative openness of the agricultural frontier: the availability of homesteads undercut the militancy of many camp and mine workers by offering a ready alternative, a modest living and hope for the future. At this early stage, the future of agriculture was too uncertain to permit the existence of firm class identities among farmers. Second was the development of a professional middle class: the teachers, doctors, social workers and journalists belonged neither to the business elite nor to the working class, and simultaneously tempered the crudeness of the economic decision makers while offering aid and hope to the workers. The third factor working against class formation was the GREAT DEPRESSION. So devastating was the combination of drought, international trade crisis, commodity price declines and the disappearance of local investment that prairie society went into prolonged stasis. Ethnic hostility, serious in the late 1920s (*see* KU KLUX KLAN), dissipated in the face of this more serious crisis. Political expressions of anger were channelled into either the moderate CO-OPERATIVE COMMONWEALTH FEDERATION or Alberta's variant of the SOCIAL CREDIT movement. The Prairie West entered WWII poorer and more united than at any time since 1900.

After 1940 a remarkable shift in prairie fortunes occurred. Wealth flowed into the region as OIL and POTASH, as well as URANIUM and other minerals, diversified an economy that had once relied on WHEAT. Improvements in agriculture, which ranged from larger equipment to fertilizers, herbicides and new plant strains, increased productivity, reduced the size of the work force and hastened the departure of farm children to urban centres; prairie farms in 1981 numbered half the 1941 total. Accompanying the economic gains was a significant change in material culture. Television, cars, airplanes and universities brought the Prairie West closer to a growing global cultural consensus. Social issues within the region increasingly resembled those in other nations: the indigenous peoples' renaissance, an international political and cultural phenomenon, was an important development; the growing gulf between fundamentalists and modernists in the Christian churches was part of an international trend; and political debates about the fate of the region, as in other nations, were grounded upon local perceptions of MULTINATIONAL CORPORATIONS and the global balance of power. Similarly, social change assumed an international cast: the remarkable changes in the family that accompanied widespread birth control, higher employment rates for women, higher divorce rates and increases in life span

were evident in the Prairie West and around the N Atlantic world. Prairie art also became international: though rooted firmly, even self-consciously, in local images, prairie artists, novelists and performers in theatre and dance found their context, their standards and their audience in an international rather than a local or regional community. The Prairie West, 1940s-80s, became a neighbourhood of the N Atlantic industrial capitalist world. GERALD FRIESEN

Reading: Gerald Friesen, *Prairie Road* (1984); J.A. Lower, *Western Canada* (1983).

Pratt, Edwin John, poet, professor, critic (b at Western Bay, Nfld 4 Feb 1882; d at Toronto 26 Apr 1964). Son of a Methodist minister, Pratt grew up in a succession of Newfoundland outports, completing his schooling at the Methodist Coll, St John's. After teaching for 2 years he became a candidate for the Methodist ministry in 1904, serving a 3-year probationship before entering Victoria Coll, U of T, where he studied mainly theology and psychology. Ordained in 1913, he never served as a regular minister, teaching psychology at U of T before being appointed to the department of English at Victoria Coll in 1920, where he taught until retirement in 1953.

Pratt began publishing poetry in 1914, but made no notable impression until *Newfoundland Verse* (1923). Thereafter in a dozen volumes of varied poetry, from *The Witches' Brew* and *Titans* in 1926 to *Collected Poems* in 1958, he established himself as the foremost Canadian poet of the first half of the century. Recipient of many honours, he was elected to the Royal Soc of Canada in 1930, and awarded its Lorne Pierce Medal for poetry in 1940. Books of his poetry won Gov Gen's Awards in 1937, 1940 and 1952. In 1946 he was made a CMG by King George VI. From 1936 to 1943 he was editor of *The Canadian Poetry Magazine*.

Pratt's poetry frequently reflects his Newfoundland background, though specific references to it appear in relatively few poems, mostly in *Newfoundland Verse*. But the sea and maritime life are central to many of his poems, both short (eg, "Erosion," "Sea-Gulls," "Silences") and long, such as *The Cachalot* (1926), describing duels between a whale and its foes, a giant squid and a whaling ship and crew; *The Roosevelt and the Antinoe* (1930), recounting the heroic rescue of the crew of a sinking freighter in a winter hurricane; *The Titanic* (1935), an ironic retelling of a well-known marine tragedy; and *Behind the Log* (1947), the dramatic story of the N Atlantic convoys during WWII. Themes from science and technology also appear frequently in his work, and during the 1930s his poems manifested much concern with contemporary economic and social problems; *The Fable of the Goats* (1937) was an antiwar poem written on the eve of WWII. In *Brébeuf and His Brethren* (1940) and *Towards the Last Spike* (1952), Pratt turned to specifically Canadian, historical, heroic themes, in the former recounting with accuracy and vivid depiction the martyrdoms of the Jesuit missionaries to HURONIA in the 17th century, and in the latter giving a dramatic account of the building of the CPR.

Pratt presents a generally realistic, unsentimental view of life, often tinctured with humour and irony. The qualities he most values and celebrates are courage, self-sacrifice, loyalty and defiance of oppressors. A major poet, he is, nevertheless, an isolated figure, belonging to no school or movement and directly influencing few other poets of his time. DAVID G. PITT

Reading: Sandra Djwa, *E.J. Pratt: The Evolutionary Vision* (1974); David G. Pitt, ed, *Critical Views on Canadian Writers: E.J. Pratt* (1969) and *E.J. Pratt: The Truant Years 1882-1927* (1984); E.J. Pratt, *Collected Poems,* ed N. Frye (1958); John Sutherland, *The Poetry of E.J. Pratt: A New Interpretation* (1956); Milton Wilson, *E.J. Pratt* (1969).

Memorial Window (1982), original signed screenprint by Christopher Pratt (*courtesy Mira Godard Gallery/Christopher Pratt*).

Pratt, John Christopher, painter, printmaker (b at St John's 9 Dec 1935). He was encouraged by his wife Mary PRATT to study at the Glasgow School of Art (1957-59) and at Mount Allison (1959-61), where he worked with Alex COLVILLE. He then taught at Memorial before deciding to paint full-time in 1963. He is well known for his realistic and curiously intense studies with typically eastern Canadian settings, purged of all extraneous detail. He focuses on realistic images drawn from recollection (many of his memories evoke physical environments). Through Pratt's eyes, Newfoundland looks like another country, Russia perhaps or Siberia — a stark land of sharp contrasts. His architectural studies are equally trim and lacking in sentimentality. All his work projects a mood of aloneness and stark, austere beauty, the simple facts of life. His figure subjects suggest the same hauntingly remote but sturdy reality. Sometimes their shy sensualism can be disturbing in the midst of Pratt's focus on a quiet existence. Along with Colville, he is one of the greatest classicists of contemporary Canadian PAINTING.

JOAN MURRAY

Pratt, Mary, (née West), painter (b at Fredericton 15 Mar 1935). For subject matter Mary Pratt uses things found in the kitchen of her home at St Mary's Bay, Nfld: baked apples or cod fillets on tin foil, eviscerated chickens on a Coca-Cola box, 2 lunch pails. Some of her earlier paintings have a whimsical mood; some of her later ones, ambitious figure works in a large format, such as a moose carcass hanging in a service station, are more sombre. But her kitchen imagery is what has established her reputation. Pratt paints with care. Her training has been long in the making. She took her first colour lessons from her mother, Katherine E. MacMurray. Then she studied at Mount Allison (1953-56) with Alex COLVILLE, Lawren Phillips Harris, and drawing master Ted Pulford, graduating in 1961. Often

Many of the subjects in Mary Pratt's paintings are things found in the kitchen of her home, such as *Christmas Turkey* (1980), oil on board (*courtesy Robert McLaughlin Gallery, Oshawa*).

she works from slides, a recent tendency in international art which relates her to American photo-realists such as Richard Estes, Chuck Close and Ben Schonzeit. But unlike their work, her domestic images recall old masters like Chardin. She is married to painter Christopher PRATT.

JOAN MURRAY

Pre-Dorset Culture, 2000-500 BC, represents the first occupation of arctic N America by Paleoeskimos. These people, probably related biologically and culturally to the INUIT, seem to have crossed Bering Strait from Siberia shortly before 2000 BC and then spread rapidly across arctic Canada and Greenland. Lacking much of the technology that allowed the more recent Inuit to adapt to arctic conditions, they nevertheless developed a successful way of life based on the hunting of seals and other small sea mammals, caribou, muskoxen and small game. They lived in temporary settlements of tents and perhaps snowhouses. Their tools and weapons had remarkably small cutting edges chipped from stone, which has led archaeologists to refer to Pre-Dorset and the related Denbigh Flint Complex in Alaska as the "Arctic Small Tool tradition." Pre-Dorset developed into DORSET CULTURE *c* 500 BC. *See also* PREHISTORY. ROBERT McGHEE

Reading: Robert McGhee, *Canadian Arctic Prehistory* (1978).

Prehistory The first human occupants of Canada arrived during the last ICE AGE, which began about 80 000 years ago and ended about 12 000 years ago. During much of this period almost all of Canada was covered by several hundred metres of glacial ice. The amount of water locked in the continental GLACIERS caused world sea levels to drop by over 100 m, creating land bridges in areas now covered by shallow seas. One such land bridge occupied what is now the Bering Sea, joining Siberia and Alaska by a flat plain over 1000 km wide (*see* BERINGIA). Across this plain moved large herbivores such as CARIBOU, MUSKOXEN, BISON, HORSE and mammoth, and at some time during the ice age these animals were followed by human hunters who had adapted their way of life to the cold climates of northern latitudes.

There is continuing argument regarding the time of the first immigration to the New World. It was long thought that humans could not have reached the American continents until the end of the ice age, that prior to the last major ice advance, 25 000 to 15 000 years ago, human cultures in the Old World had developed neither technologies capable of living in the cold arctic conditions of NE Asia nor watercraft capable of crossing the open water of a flooded Bering Strait. Recent research indicates, however, that man had reached Australia across a wide stretch of open sea by at least 30 000 years ago, and that as long as 200 000 years ago the Paleolithic (Old Stone Age) occupants of Europe were living under extremely cold environmental conditions and may have had watercraft capable of crossing the Strait of Gibraltar. It is theoretically possible, therefore, that humans could have reached N America from NE Siberia at any time during the past 100 000 years.

Paleoindian Period During the past few decades, several New World archaeological sites have been claimed to date to the period of the last ice age. The earliest widespread occupation that is universally accepted by archaeologists, however, begins only 12 000 years ago. Much of Alaska and the Yukon Territory remained unglaciated throughout the ice age, probably because of a dry climate and insufficient snowfall (*see* NUNATAK). Joined to Siberia by the Beringian Plain, and separated from the rest of N America by glaciers, these regions, called Beringia, were essentially part of Asia. The environment was a cold TUNDRA, although spruce forests were present at least during interstadial or nonglacial pe-

riods, and supported a wide range of animals. Archaeological finds along the OLD CROW BASIN in the northern Yukon have been claimed to indicate the presence of Paleolithic hunting populations in the period 25 000 to 30 000 years ago; however, all these objects have been found in redeposited sediments, many of them may have been manufactured by agencies other than man (such as carnivore chewing or ice movement), and the age of the few definitely man-made artifacts has been questioned.

The archaeological site of the earliest accepted occupation by man is BLUEFISH CAVES in N Yukon. Here, in 3 small caves overlooking a wide basin, have been found a few chipped stone artifacts in layers of sediment containing the bones of extinct FOSSIL ANIMALS, which radiocarbon dating indicates have an age of at least 10 000 to 13 000, and possibly 15 000 to 18 000 years ago (*see* GEOLOGICAL DATING; GEOLOGICAL HISTORY; PALEONTOLOGY). The artifacts include types similar to those of the late Paleolithic of NE Asia, and probably represent an expansion of Asian hunting peoples across Beringia and Alaska into northwestern Canada. We do not know whether people similar to those who occupied the Bluefish Caves expanded farther into N America. A relatively narrow ice-free corridor may have existed between the Cordilleran glaciers of the western mountains and the Laurentide ice sheet extending from the Canadian SHIELD, or such a corridor may have opened only after the glaciers began to melt and retreat about 15 000 years ago (*see* GLACIATION). No early sites have been found along the route of this corridor in the western NWT and Alberta, but by 12 000 years ago some groups had penetrated to the area of the western US and had developed a way of life adapted to hunting the large herbivores that grazed the grasslands and ice-edge tundras of the period.

By about 11 000 years ago some of these PALEOINDIANS, as they are known to archaeologists, began to move northward into Canada as the southern margin of the continental glaciers retreated. Environmental zones similar to those found today in arctic and subarctic Canada shifted northward as well. In many regions the ice front was marked by huge meltwater lakes (eg, Lk AGASSIZ), their outlets dammed by the glaciers to the N, surrounded by land supporting tundra vegetation grazed on by caribou, muskoxen and other herbivores. To the S of this narrow band of tundra were spruce forests and grasslands, and the Paleoindians probably followed the northern edge of these zones as they moved across Canada. Paleoindian sites are radiocarbon dated to around 10 500 years ago in areas as far separated as central Nova Scotia and northern BC. The largest sites yet found in Canada are concentrated in southern Ontario, where they are clustered along the southern shore of Lk Algonquin, the forerunner of the present Lk Huron and Georgian Bay (*see* GREAT LAKES). By about 10 000 years ago Paleoindians had probably occupied at least the southern portions of all provinces except Newfoundland. Most sites are limited to scatters of chipped stone artifacts, among them spearpoints with a distinctive channel or "flute" removed from either side of the base to allow mounting in a split haft. Such "fluted points" are characteristic of early Paleoindian technologies from Canada to southern S America, and serve to define the first widespread occupation of the New World about 9000 to 12 000 years ago.

Because very little inorganic material is preserved on archaeological sites of this period, it is difficult to reconstruct the way of life that the Paleoindians followed. In the dry western regions of the US, where sites are better preserved, they appear to have concentrated on hunting large herbivores, including bison and mammoths. In Canada we can only speculate that Paleoindians preyed on the caribou herds of the E and the bison herds of the northern plains, as well as fishing and hunting small game. Coastlines were well below present sea level, so any evidence of Paleoindian use of coastal resources has been destroyed by the later rise in sea level.

While the Paleoindians occupied southern Canada, the continental glaciers melted rapidly and disappeared by about 7000 years ago. A warmer climate than the present existed until about 4000 years ago, and the environments of the country diversified as coniferous forest, deciduous woodland, grassland and tundra vegetation became established in suitable zones. The ways of life of the Paleoindians occupying these environmental zones became diversified as they, and later immigrants from Siberia, adapted to the conditions and resources of local regions. The development over time of the various cultures of prehistoric native peoples is therefore best described on a regional basis.

West Coast There is little evidence that the classic "fluted point" Paleoindian cultures penetrated the coastal regions of BC and the earliest occupants of the area appear to have been related to other cultural traditions. About 9000 to 5000 years ago the southern regions were occupied by people of the Old Cordilleran tradition, whose sites are marked by crude pebble tools made by knocking a few flakes from heavy beach cobbles and by more finely made lanceolate projectile points or knives chipped from stone. No organic material is preserved on these sites, but their locations suggest that these people were adapted primarily to interior and riverine resources, gradually making greater use of marine resources.

The northern and central coast was occupied by people of the early Coast Microblade tradition who also used pebble tools but lacked lanceolate points. Microblades are small razorlike tools of flint or obsidian made by a specialized technique developed in the Old World and were widely used during this period in Alaska and NW Canada. It is suggested that these people entered BC from the N and that they were related to Alaskan groups who may have crossed the Bering land bridge shortly before it disappeared.

It is unclear how either of these 2 groups were related to those who occupied the West Coast after 5000 years ago, but it seems likely that both contributed to the ancestry of the later occupants. At about 5000 years ago a major change occurred in coastal occupation. Whereas earlier sites were all relatively small, indicating brief occupations by small groups of people, large shell middens characterize most of the more recent sites. Stabilization of sea levels probably resulted in increased salmon stocks, which in turn allowed people to store more food and live a more sedentary life in coastal villages that were occupied for years or generations. Animal bones and bone tools have been preserved in the shell middens and artifacts of wood or plant fibre in occasional waterlogged deposits, allowing archaeologists to reconstruct a more complete picture of the way of life of these people than of earlier occupants of the region.

Artifacts recovered from the earliest sites indicate an efficient adaptation to the coastal environment. Barbed harpoons for taking sea mammals, fish hooks, weights for fish nets, ground slate knives and weapon points, and woodworking tools that could have been used for the construction of boats occur on coastal sites of the period. Waterlogged sites have produced examples of basketry, netting, woven fabrics and wooden boxes similar to those known from the historic period. By about 3500 years ago there is evidence that this adaptation was beginning to lead to the development of the sophisticated societies known from the historic NORTHWEST COAST. Burials that show differential treatment in the number of grave goods for members of the community, as well as the appearance in some regions of artificial skull deformation, suggest the existence of the ranked societies with which these practices were later associated. The high incidence of broken bones and skulls among male burials, coincidentally with the appearance of decorated clubs of stone or whalebone, suggests the development of a pattern of warfare. Social organizations based on status and wealth may also account for the appearance at this time of numerous art objects, personal ornaments such as beads, labrets and earspools, and exotic goods indicating widespread trade networks to the interior and the south. In the Gulf of Georgia region, the Locarno Beach (35-2500 years ago) and the Marpole (25-1500 years ago) phases are seen as a local cultural climax, producing evidence of a richer culture than that which existed in the area in more recent times (*see* INDIAN ART).

A similar situation appears to have characterized most coastal regions during the past 1500 years. This interpretation is based on the decline of the sculpted stone artwork that characterized the preceding period, perhaps indicating only a change from art in stone to art in wood and woven fabrics, which are poorly preserved archaeologically but were highly developed by the historic occupants of the region. This period produces the first definite evidence for occupation of the large plank-house villages characteristic of the historic period, and of major earthworks and defensive sites indicating an increase in warfare. Stone pipes mark the introduction of TOBACCO, the only agricultural crop grown in the area in prehistoric times. Building on the adaptational base developed over the previous 3000 years, the people of the past 1500 years developed the various tribal traditions and ways of life of the historic Northwest Coast Indians (*see* NATIVE PEOPLE).

Intermontane Region The valleys and plateaus of interior BC are characterized by diverse environments, ranging from boreal forests through grasslands to almost desert conditions. The prehistoric cultures of the area were correspondingly diverse and this variety, combined with the lack of sufficient archaeological research in the region, results in an unclear picture of the prehistory of the area.

Finds of Paleoindian projectile points and other artifacts indicate that the earliest occupants of the area came from the plains, adapting their grassland bison-hunting way of life to the pursuit of bison, wapiti and caribou in the intermontane valleys. Little is known of these people, but the skeleton of one man who died in a mudslide near Kamloops is radiocarbon dated to about 8250 years ago and is thus the earliest well-dated human skeleton known from Canada. Analysis of the composition of the bones indicates that this man lived primarily on land animals rather than on the salmon of the Thompson R. Between 8000 and 3000 years ago the area appears to have been occupied by various groups who manufactured and used microblades and who are thought to have been related to the microblade-using peoples of the N coast or of the Yukon interior. The riverine location of many microblade sites suggests that these groups were developing adaptations based on the salmon resources of interior rivers, but little else is known.

A major change in the occupation of the region began about 3000 years ago, with the introduction of semisubterranean pithouses from the Columbia Plateau to the south. Pithouse villages grew larger through time, indicating a more efficient economy and an increasingly sedentary way of life. As in the coastal areas to the W, the appearance of exotic trade goods (shells), stone sculpture and differential burial patterns is interpreted as evidence of more complex societies in which ranking was based on

A lanceolate-triangular stone point, a small-stemmed point and a stemmed point from the Klo-kut site, Old Crow, YT (*courtesy National Museums of Canada/National Museum of Man/K75-946*).

wealth and display. Over the past 3000 years cultural influences from the West Coast, the plains and the Columbia Plateau combined to form the cultures of the various interior people of BC.

Plains and Prairies The northern plains and prairies of central Canada, like no other region of N America, provided an environment in which the Paleoindians of 10 000 years ago were able to continue their way of life with relatively little alteration until the time of European contact. As the large herbivores of the ice age became extinct in the early postglacial period, these people transferred their pursuit to the various species of now-extinct bison that occupied the grasslands. Although heavily dependent on bison, Paleoindians and their later descendants must also have been hunters of smaller game and gatherers of plant foods where available. They almost certainly developed techniques of communal hunting involving ambush or the driving of bison to hunters armed with spears and darts thrown with throwing boards. ARCHAEOLOGY knows these people primarily through the chipped flint spearpoints that they used. By about 9000 years ago their fluted projectile points had been replaced by lanceolate or stemmed varieties characteristic of the late Palaeoindian Plano tradition. Between approximately 9000 and 7000 years ago the Plano people developed a widespread and apparently efficient bison-hunting adaptation across the northern plains, and by at least 7000 years ago caribou hunters using spearpoints obviously related to those of the Plano tradition had pushed northward to the Barren Lands between Great Bear Lake and Hudson Bay.

The following 2 millennia, between approximately 7000 and 5000 years ago, are poorly known on the northern plains. This period saw the climax of the postglacial warm period or altithermal, and it is suggested that heat and drought reduced the carrying capacity of the grasslands so that the area was occupied by fewer bison and consequently by fewer bison hunters. Sites around the fringes of the plains, and some sites in the plains area itself, show continuing occupation, and the development of spearpoints with notches for hafting. Such points are characteristic of the following Middle

Prehistoric period (approximately 5000 to 2000 years ago), during which various groups developed more efficient communal bison hunting techniques, including the use of pounds and jumps over which the bison were driven.

The past 2000 years saw the introduction to the plains area of various influences emanating from the eastern woodlands and from the Mississippi and Missouri valley peoples to the S. During the early first millennium A.D. small chipped stone arrow points began to replace the spearpoints of earlier times, and the introduction of the bow must have increased hunting efficiency. Pottery cooking vessels and containers, of types similar to those in use to the E and S, were used. Burial mounds were constructed in some regions, especially in southern Manitoba, and exotic trade goods indicate contacts with the farming people of the Missouri Valley. Although most of the northern plains was beyond the limit of prehistoric agriculture, relatively small-scale farming was attempted in the more southerly regions.

The westward push of European settlement in the 18th century caused a rapid acceleration of change in prehistoric plains life, as tribes from the eastern woodlands began to move westward onto the grasslands. Horses, which had gradually spread northward from the Spanish settlements in the American SW, reached the Canadian plains about 1730, causing a revolution in aboriginal techniques of hunting, travelling and warfare. For the next 150 years, until the disappearance of the bison in the late 19th century, the Canadian plains and prairies saw the development of a way of life that must have been dramatically richer, more nomadic and varied than that of earlier occupants of the area.

Eastern Woodlands Early Paleoindian hunters using fluted spear points had occupied southern Ontario, and probably the St Lawrence Valley, by at least 10 000 years ago. With the draining of the large ice-edge lakes and seas of the region, the extinction of the ice-age fauna, and the establishment of coniferous forests, the environments of these regions changed dramatically during the following 2 millennia. The next occupation of the region was by late Paleoindians using artifacts similar to those of the Plano tradition, which developed on the plains to the W. The best evidence for Plano occupation comes from the northern shores of Lks Superior and Huron, but Plano-related sites are known from the upper St Lawrence Valley and as far E as the Gaspé Peninsula. These eastern Plano people of some 9000 to 7000 years ago were probably big-game hunters who were heavily dependent on caribou, the predominant herbivore in the subarctic forests of the period.

The following millennia, with warmer climates and the establishment of deciduous forests, saw the development of ARCHAIC cultures. The Archaic label is applied to cultures throughout eastern N America that show adaptations to the utilization of local animal, fish and plant resources, and which are consequently much more varied than the widespread but relatively uniform Paleoindian cultures that preceded them. These adaptations probably allowed increases in the populations of many areas, and greater social complexity is suggested by complex burial practices and the existence of long-distance trade. The Archaic stage is also marked archaeologically by the development of new items of technology: stemmed and notched spear points and knives, bone harpoons, ground stone weapon points and woodworking tools (gouges, axes), and in some areas tools and ornaments made from native COPPER.

The Canadian Shield area of central and northern Québec and Ontario was occupied at this time by groups belonging to the Shield Archaic culture. They apparently developed about 7000 years ago out of northern Plano cultures

such as those which occupied the Barren Grounds west of Hudson Bay or those known from northwestern Ontario. Since the acid forest soils of the region have destroyed all organic remains, we know relatively little of their way of life. From the locations of their camps, however, they were probably generalized hunters heavily dependent on caribou and fish. Although pottery and other elements were introduced from the S over the past 3000 years, marking the Woodland period of local prehistory, it seems likely that the Archaic way of life remained relatively unchanged and was much like that of the Algonquin peoples of this area at the time of European contact and the beginning of the FUR TRADE.

The deciduous forest areas to the S supported denser populations than did the spruce forests to the N and saw the development, about 6000 years ago, of the Laurentian Archaic, probably from earlier Archaic cultures of the area. These people were generalized hunters and gatherers of the relatively abundant animal and plant resources of the region. Exotic materials, such as copper and marine shells, most often found as grave goods in an elaborate burial ceremonial, indicate extensive trade contacts to the S, E and W.

The appearance of pottery, introduced from areas S of the Great Lakes between 3000 and 2500 years ago, is used archaeologically to mark the beginning of the Woodland period. As in the regions to the N, the initial Woodland period probably saw few changes in the general way of life of local peoples. During the following centuries, however, there is evidence of continuing and expanding influence from the S, including an elaborate mortuary complex involving mound burial, which appears to have been transferred, or at least copied, from the Adena and Hopewell cultures of the Ohio Valley. The most important introduction was agriculture, based on crops that had been developed in Mexico and Central America several millennia previously, and which had gradually spread northward as they were adapted to cooler climatic conditions.

The first crop to appear was maize, which began to be cultivated in southern Ontario about 1500 years ago and was a major supplement to a hunting and gathering economy. The early maize farmers occupied relatively permanent villages of multifamily wood and bark houses, often fortified with palisades as protection from the warfare that appears to have intensified with the introduction of agriculture. By 1350 AD beans and squash were added to local agriculture, providing a nutritionally balanced diet that led to a decrease in the importance of hunting and gathering of wild foods (*see* PALYNOLOGY; PLANTS, NATIVE USES). At the time of European contact this agricultural life-style was characteristic of the Iroquoian peoples who occupied the region from southwestern Ontario to the middle St Lawrence Valley. It is the only region of Canada in which prehistoric agriculture was established as the local economic base, and was the area of greatest aboriginal population density. The late prehistoric Iroquoians lived in villages composed of large multifamily LONGHOUSES, with some of the larger communities containing more than 2000 people. Wide-ranging social, trade and political connections spanned their area of occupation, as a complement to the warfare which occupied much of their attention. These patterns intensified with the appearance of Europeans and European trade goods during the 17th century, and eventually led to the destruction of the Canadian Iroquoians during the mid-17th century at the hands of their Iroquois neighbours to the south of Lk Ontario.

East Coast Paleoindians had occupied the Maritime provinces by at least 10 000 years ago, but evidence of their presence is slight as sea lev-

els were much lower than at present and only traces of interior camps can be found above present sea level. The same problem restricts our knowledge of early Archaic sites, although we can probably assume that there was continuous occupation throughout this period as there was in the Eastern Woodlands area to the west. The best evidence of early Archaic occupation is found in the Strait of Belle Isle area of Labrador, where initial occupation occurred before 8000 years ago and is marked by chipped stone artifacts suggesting a late Paleoindian/Archaic transition. The coastal location of these early Archaic sites suggests a maritime adaptation, an interpretation reinforced by the 7500-year-old burial mound at L'ANSE AMOUR BURIAL SITE in which was found a toggling harpoon, a walrus tusk and an artifact of walrus ivory. The term Maritime Archaic is applied to these people and their descendants.

Coastal hunting and fishing allowed Maritime Archaic people to expand to far northern Labrador by 6000 years ago, and to Newfoundland by about 5000 years ago. For the following 2000 years they were the primary occupants of these areas, developing a distinctive maritime way of life with barbed harpoons, fishing gear, ground-slate weapons and ground-stone woodworking tools. They also elaborated a mortuary complex in which large cemeteries were used over considerable lengths of time, the burials accompanied by large numbers of grave goods and heavily sprinkled with red ochre. Cemeteries of this type are found in the Maritime provinces and New England. Similarities in burial traditions, artifacts and the physical type of the skeletons suggest relationships to the contemporaneous Laurentian Archaic of the Eastern Woodlands, and it seems likely that Laurentian people occupied some regions of the Maritime provinces.

Between 4000 and 2500 years ago the Maritime Archaic people were displaced from most of coastal Labrador by a southward expansion of Paleoeskimos from the Arctic, and by other Archaic groups moving eastward from the Shield area and the St Lawrence Valley. The Dorset Paleoeskimos also occupied Newfoundland for about a millennium, beginning about 2500 years ago. With the withdrawal of the Paleoeskimos from Newfoundland and all but northern Labrador about 1500 years ago, these areas were reoccupied by Indians who were probably ancestral to the Labrador Naskapi and Newfoundland BEOTHUK. We do not know whether these were the descendants of earlier Maritime Archaic people, or of other groups that moved to the area at a later time.

In the Maritime provinces to the south of the Gulf of St Lawrence the past 2500 years saw the introduction of ceramics from the S and the W. The possible extent of other cultural influences is suggested by the 2300-year-old Augustine burial mound in New Brunswick, which duplicates the Adena burial ceremonialism of the Ohio Valley and includes artifacts imported from that region. Early in this period local groups apparently began to develop a more sedentary way of life, as shell middens began to accumulate in some coastal regions. Evidence from these sites indicates a generalized hunting and fishing way of life, utilizing both coastal and interior resources. This life-style was characteristic of Atlantic Canada at European contact, and the sites dating to the past 2000 years almost certainly represent those of the ancestral MICMAC and MALISEET peoples.

Western Subarctic The forest and forest-tundra area between Hudson Bay and Alaska is, archaeologically, one of the least-explored regions of Canada. Although the far NW of the region has produced evidence of extremely early human occupation, later developments are only vaguely known.

In the area to the W of the Mackenzie R there is thought to be evidence of 2 distinct early postglacial occupations dating between roughly 11 000 and 7000 years ago. One is by groups related to the Paleoindians of more southerly regions, and marked by lanceolate spearpoints. Probably the earliest Paleoindians to occupy the area used fluted points, since a few such artifacts are known from Alaska and the Yukon Territory; however, these finds have not been dated earlier than the fluted point sites to the south, so it is still uncertain whether they represent the original movement of Paleoindians to the S or a subsequent return movement northward. Somewhat more recent occupations are marked by spearpoints which relate either to the late Paleoindian Plano tradition of the northern Plains, or to the Old Cordilleran tradition of BC and the western US. The second major occupation is by groups related to the Paleoarctic tradition of Alaska, a people whose microblade technology is derived from eastern Asia and who are thought to have crossed the Bering Land Bridge.

It is unclear at present how these early occupations relate to those of the Northern Archaic, which was present in the area from about 6000 to at least 2000 years ago. This culture is characterized by notched spearpoints and other elements of apparent southern origin, but at least the early sites of the period also produce microblades, and microblades may have been in use in some regions until close to the end of this period. Neither is it known how the Northern Archaic relates to the ancestry of the Athapaskan-speaking peoples who occupied interior NW Canada. Definite ancestral Athapaskan sites can be traced for only about the past 1500 years in this area. This may represent an intrusion of Athapaskans from elsewhere, or continous development out of the Northern Archaic of earlier times.

The earliest occupation of the region between Mackenzie R and Hudson Bay was by Plano-tradition people who moved into the Barren Grounds from the S shortly before 7000 years ago. Notched spearpoints and other types of stone tools from at least 6000 years ago led to the definition of the Shield Archaic tradition. It seems that the Shield Archaic developed locally out of Plano culture, rather than representing an intrusion of people from the S, and there was little change in the way of life followed by local groups. The Barren Grounds continued to be occupied by Shield Archaic Indians until about 3500 years ago when, perhaps in response to climatic cooling that caused the treeline to shift southward, the region was taken over by Paleoeskimos from the Arctic coast (*see* CLIMATE CHANGE). This occupation lasted for less than 1000 years, when Indians using various forms of lanceolate and stemmed spearpoints, and later arrow points, reoccupied the territory. The origin of these Indian groups is not clear, but they probably moved into the Barren Grounds from the S and W, and may have arrived at various times between 2500 and 1000 years ago. At least the more recent of these prehistoric groups were ancestral to the Athapaskan-speaking occupants of the historic period, who led a caribou-hunting way of life not greatly different from that of the Plano and Shield Archaic peoples of much earlier times.

Arctic The coasts and islands of arctic Canada were first occupied about 4000 years ago by groups known as Paleoeskimos. Their technology and way of life differed considerably from those of known American Indian groups and more closely resembled those of eastern Siberian peoples. Although there is disagreement among archaeologists on the question of Paleoeskimo origins, it seems likely that the Paleoeskimos crossed Bering Strait from Siberia, either by boat or on the sea ice, shortly before 4000 years ago, and rapidly spread eastward across the unoccu-

pied tundra regions of Alaska, Canada and Greenland. These early occupants seem to have preferred areas where they could live largely on caribou and muskoxen, but were also capable of harpooning seals and in some areas adapted to a maritime way of life. Early Paleoeskimo technology, based on tiny chipped flint tools including microblades, was much less efficient than that of the historic INUIT occupants of the region. There is no evidence that they used boats, dogsleds, oil lamps or domed snowhouses, as they lived through most or all of the year in skin tents heated with fires of bones and scarce wood. Nevertheless, between 4000 and 3000 years ago they occupied most arctic regions and had expanded southwards across the Barren Grounds and down the Labrador coast, displacing Indian occupants.

After about 2500 years ago the Paleoeskimo way of life had developed to the extent that it is given a new label, the DORSET culture. There is slight evidence that the Dorset people used kayaks and had dogs for hunting if not for pulling sledges; soapstone lamps and pots appear, as well as semipermanent winter houses banked with turf for insulation. Dorset sites are larger than those of their predecessors, suggesting more permanent occupation by larger groups, and in some regions it is apparent that the Dorset people were efficient hunters of sea mammals as large as walrus and beluga. A striking art form was developed in the form of small carvings in wood and ivory (*see* INUIT ART). It was the Dorset people who, around 2500 years ago, moved southward to Newfoundland and occupied the island for about 1000 years.

The Dorset occupation of arctic Canada was brought to an end about 800 years ago, with the movement into the area of THULE culture Inuit from Alaska. Over the preceding 3000 years the ancestors of the Inuit, who were probably descended from Alaskan Paleoeskimos, had developed very efficient sea-mammal hunting techniques involving harpoon float and drag equipment, kayaks and large, open skin boats from which they could hunt whales. The Thule movement across the Arctic, during a relatively warm climatic period when there was probably a decrease in sea ice and an increase in whale populations, occurred rapidly. Travelling by skin boat and dogsled, by 1200 AD they had established an essentially Alaskan way of life over much of arctic Canada and displaced the Dorset people from most regions. In Greenland and probably in the eastern Canadian Arctic they soon came into contact with the Norse who had arrived in Greenland about 980 AD. Norse artifacts have been recovered from several Thule sites.

The Thule way of life, characterized by summer open-water hunting and the storage of food for use during winter occupation of permanent stone and turf winter houses, became more difficult after 1200 AD as the arctic climate cooled, culminating in the Little Ice Age of 1600 to 1850 AD. During this period many elements of their way of life had to be changed, and the Thule people either abandoned portions of the Arctic or rapidly adapted to the new conditions. It was during this late prehistoric period that much of the culture of the historic Inuit was developed.   ROBERT MCGHEE

Reading: J. Jennings, *Prehistory of North America* (1968) and, ed, *Ancient Native Americans* (1978); Robert McGhee, *Canadian Arctic Prehistory* (1978); J.A. Tuck, *Newfoundland and Labrador Prehistory* (1976); J.V. Wright, *Six Chapters of Canada's Prehistory* (1976), *Ontario Prehistory* (1972) and *Quebec Prehistory* (1979).

Prejudice and Discrimination Ethnic and racial prejudice usually refers to an unsubstantiated negative prejudgement of individuals or groups because of their ethnicity, race or religion (*see also* RACISM). Discrimination is the exclusion of individuals or groups from full par-

ticipation in society because of their ethnicity, race or religion. Prejudice (an attitude) and discrimination (behaviour) are usually linked, but are distinct phenomena. In a vicious circle, prejudice frequently leads to discriminatory behaviour while discrimination reinforces or creates social and economic inequalities that then reinforce prejudices.

Prejudice arose early in the contact between native peoples and the European colonizers who came to N America in the 17th and 18th centuries. The European view of native peoples was complex and ambivalent, ranging from seeing them as "noble savages" to soulless barbarians. While there were significant differences in French-native and British-native relations in pre-Confederation Canada, in both cases the economic interests of the FUR TRADE helped to cement a tolerable working relationship between the colonizers and the native peoples until large-scale settlement led to a deterioration in relations, as Indians became an impediment rather than an aid to economic development. As a result of European settlement during the 1700s and 1800s, of the British CONQUEST in 1759-60 and of the geographical isolation of Indians, NATIVE-WHITE RELATIONS gradually became less important than the relations between the colonizing powers. The economic, political, social and religious co-operation and rivalries between British and French settlers shaped much of Canada's development from the 1750s to the present. Prejudice and discrimination existed on both sides. Because the 2 groups shared a technologically based Western culture, the nature of their relationship and the kinds of prejudice and discrimination that characterized it were considerably different than those that characterized Indian-white relations.

By far the largest group of non-British, non-French and non-natives in Canada at the time of Confederation, 1867, were the GERMANS, who had little trouble being accepted in Canadian society. Their arrival had been within the context of British colonial policy; they were seen as energetic and conservative, and they were isolated and scattered.

BLACKS, however, encountered significant prejudice in the pre-Confederation era. Although there were many opponents to it, SLAVERY existed in New France and British N America. By the 1860s, the 40 000 blacks in Canada included descendants of black slaves in New France, black Loyalists, Jamaican Maroons, black American refugees from the WAR OF 1812, and black fugitives who came to Upper Canada to escape slavery in the US.

Many white Canadians opposed slavery on moral grounds and assisted refugees from the US, but many others feared the influx of black settlers, seeing them as backward, ignorant, immoral, criminal and an economic threat. Blacks were treated primarily as a source of cheap labour. Following the final abolition of slavery throughout the British Empire in 1833, blacks were victims of fewer legal barriers, but nonetheless faced a great deal of social prejudice.

The numbers of people of other than British, French or native origin remained small until the end of the 19th century, when large numbers of immigrants arrived in Canada, settling primarily in the West. Most English-speaking Canadians saw this non-British and non-French immigration primarily as a way of speeding Canada's economic development. Others, however, worried about the social impact of non-British immigration and labour, feared economic competition and opposed an open-door IMMIGRATION POLICY. French Canada opposed it on the grounds that such a policy would further erode the status of French Canada within Confederation. Most English-speaking Canadians shared prejudices concerning the comparative desirability of immigrant groups.

Head tax certificate of Ma Ton Hang. Measures such as the head tax were used to limit Asian immigration (*courtesy Chinese Canadian National Council*).

During the late 19th and early 20th centuries, the belief in progress and white superiority was taken for granted throughout the Western world. Bolstered by pseudo-scientific ideas of race, derived from SOCIAL DARWINISM, English-speaking Canadians believed that the Anglo-Saxon peoples and British principles of government were the apex of biological EVOLUTION and that Canada's greatness depended on its Anglo-Saxon heritage (*see* IMPERIALISM). Their assessment of a group's desirability, therefore, varied almost directly with the degree to which its members conformed to British culture and physical type. British and American immigrants were regarded as the most desirable, followed by northern and western Europeans, central and eastern Europeans and then by JEWS and southern Europeans. Close to the bottom of the pecking order were the pacifist religious sects, the German-speaking HUTTERITES and MENNONITES and the Russian-speaking DOUKHOBORS, who were invariably lumped together by public officials and the general public. Their social separatism made their assimilation problematic, their thrift and industry made them strong economic competitors, and their pacifism raised doubts about their commitment to Canada. Last were the blacks and the Asian immigrants — the CHINESE, JAPANESE and SOUTH ASIANS — who were considered inferior and unassimilable. Chinese immigration was curbed by a "head tax" and was stopped altogether by the Chinese Exclusion Act of 1923. A "gentlemen's agreement" was arrived at with Japan in 1908, restricting the number of Japanese immigrants. Orders-in-council banned immigration from India in 1907. Blacks were informally denied entry from 1910. The government also introduced restrictive immigration laws in 1906, 1910 and 1919 to control European immigration.

Between 1896 and WWII, French Canadian nationalists charged that large-scale immigration (particularly since little of it was French speaking) was a British Canadian plot to undermine the status of French Canada. Immigration was not as significant a public issue in Québec as it was in Ontario and the West because so few immigrants settled there. However, by 1914 the Jewish community of Montréal was the victim of strong anti-Semitism, much of it stemming from the religious bias of FRENCH CANADIAN NATIONALISM. Jews were depicted as exploiters, as threats to Christian morality and civilization, and as symbols of the evils of internationalism, liberalism, bolshevism, materialism and urban life. Public controversies involving both the French and British in Montréal emerged over the Jews' place in the denominationally based school system and over Sunday-closing legislation. Antagonism to Jews was expressed in occasional cemetery desecrations and street fights. The French Canadian hostility to Jewish immigration was paralleled by the hostility of ultra-Protestants in English-speaking Canada to Catholic immigrants from Europe, who were regarded as subservient tools of Rome and poten-

tial political allies of the French Canadian Catholics.

The ethnic stereotypes of turn-of-the-century Canada emphasized the peasant origins of central, eastern and southern Europeans and Asians, depicting them as poor, illiterate, diseased, morally lax, politically corrupt and religiously deficient. The alleged predilection of central and southern Europeans for drink, violence and crime, and of the Chinese for drugs, gambling and white women were powerful and popular images with the dominant society. Opprobrious ethnic slurs were widely used in the pre-1950s era.

Prior to WWII, extensive patterns of social, economic and political discrimination against non-Anglo-Saxons developed throughout Canada. Northern and western Europeans encountered relatively little discrimination compared to Jews and those from central and southern Europe, while nonwhites, especially in BC, suffered a pervasive pattern of discrimination that affected almost every aspect of their lives. Discrimination was one of the factors that led to the transference of the ethnic "pecking order" of immigration policy to a VERTICAL MOSAIC of occupations and incomes — the British on top and so on down to the Chinese and blacks who occupied the most menial jobs. Non-British and non-French groups had very little economic power, and they did not even begin to make any significant inroads into the middle echelons of politics, education or the PUBLIC SERVICE until after WWII (*see* ELITES).

The most widespread legalized pattern of discrimination occurred against Asians in BC, where anti-Asian sentiment was endemic from the 1850s to the 1950s. Asians were regarded as alien, inferior and unassimilable. Organized labour claimed that Asians took jobs from whites and lowered living standards for all workers because they were willing to work for less money than white workers. Asians were excluded from most unions, and as a matter of policy employers paid Asian workers less than others.

Because of discriminatory legislation and social practices in BC, Chinese, Japanese and South Asians could not vote, practise law or pharmacy, be elected to public office, serve on juries or work in public works, education or the civil service. Public opinion on Asian immigration was expressed on several occasions in violent anti-Chinese and anti-Asian riots, the most serious being in Vancouver in 1887 and 1907. Various attempts were also made by anti-Asian groups to exclude Asians from public schools, to restrict the sale of land to Asians and to limit severely the number of licences issued to Japanese fishermen. In 1892 and 1907 smaller scale anti-Chinese riots occurred in Alberta; and Québec, Nova Scotia and Saskatchewan passed legislation prohibiting white women from working in restaurants, laundries and any other business owned by Chinese or Japanese.

Blacks also faced a widespread pattern of discrimination in housing, employment and access to public services during the late 19th century and early to mid-20th century. They had difficulty being served in hotels and restaurants, and in being admitted to theatres and swimming pools, and were on occasion forced into segregated schools, particularly in Nova Scotia and Ontario where they were most concentrated. The discrimination against blacks occasionally erupted into violence. In both world wars, armed forces units were reluctant to accept blacks, Chinese, Japanese and South Asians, although some from each group did eventually serve.

The levels of prejudice and discrimination against nonwhite minorities only reached comparable levels for white immigrants during the periods of intense NATIONALISM generated by war. During WWI, Germans and immigrants

from the Austro-Hungarian Empire were victims of intense prejudice and persecution. "Enemy aliens" were dismissed from their jobs. Some were placed under police surveillance or in INTERNMENT CAMPS. Their language schools and many of their churches were closed; their newspapers were first censored and then gradually suppressed; and during crisis periods of the war, rioting soldiers and civilians attacked the premises of German clubs and German-owned businesses. Loyalty and cultural and linguistic uniformity were assumed to be synonymous, and Prairie provincial governments abolished bilingual schools and classes. The UNION GOVERNMENT disenfranchised "enemy aliens" who had become Canadian citizens after March 1902.

Opposition to the pacifist religious sects also intensified during the war, eventually leading to the 1919 order-in-council (rescinded during the 1920s) that specifically barred the entry of members of these groups into the country. From 1919 to 1953, Doukhobors in BC were denied the right to vote and this prohibition was extended to the federal level from 1934 to 1955. The return of WWI veterans and the postwar economic depression brought hostility toward these pacifist sects to a peak and contributed to anti-radical "nativism," ie, the conviction that immigrant political radicals posed a threat to Canadian national life. Slavic immigrants were no longer perceived as "stolid peasants," but as dangerous revolutionaries. The connection between immigrants and radicalism in the public's mind was strengthened by the WINNIPEG GENERAL STRIKE. One of the measures passed by the federal government to end the strike was a bill providing for the deportation of foreign-born Canadian citizens under certain circumstances. Veterans and radical Slavic workers clashed in violent labour incidents across western Canada in 1919 as veterans asserted what they saw as their priority right to jobs.

By the early 1920s, central, southern and eastern European immigrants were officially classified among the "nonpreferred" and restricted categories of immigrants. In the mid-1920s, however, in response to public pressure, the federal government loosened restrictions on immigration from Europe as a way of promoting economic development. The federal government allowed the railways to import more than 185 000 central and eastern Europeans and Mennonites as farmers, farm labourers and domestics during the late 1920s. The new wave of immigration reawakened prejudices. Organizations such as the KU KLUX KLAN (KKK), the Native Sons of Canada and the ORANGE ORDER criticized the new immigrants as a threat to Canada's "Anglo-Saxon" character. Several of these organizations, particularly the KKK, also opposed Catholic immigrants. The Klan began organizing in Montréal, Ontario, BC and Manitoba in the early 1920s, and its membership in Saskatchewan in the late 1920s reached 20 000. The Klan organized boycotts of Catholic businessmen, intimidated politicians who seemed sympathetic to French or Catholic interests, opposed federal immigration policy, opposed Catholic schools and the alleged Catholic influence in public schools, and tried to prevent interracial and Catholic-Protestant marriages. The Klan was sufficiently powerful in Saskatchewan to contribute to the defeat of the Liberals in the 1929 provincial election.

Because Anglo-Saxon workers demanded, and often received, priority in obtaining and keeping jobs, a large proportion of non-Anglo-Saxons were forced onto relief during the GREAT DEPRESSION. Central and eastern Europeans suffered covert discrimination in the administration of relief, while Chinese were victims of open discrimination in relief administration in BC and Alberta. The federal government, in the

Immigration Act, provided for deportation of non-Canadian citizens on relief. Government officials took advantage of the law to reduce their relief rolls.

A vicious circle of prejudice and discrimination became further entrenched during the 1930s. The discrimination that non-Anglo-Saxons encountered led them to support radical political movements, eg, communism (see COMMUNIST PARTY) and FASCISM, and this reinforced discrimination against them. Between 1930 and 1935, Prime Minister R.B. BENNETT used deportation as a way of thwarting support for the communists. In labour conflicts in western Canada and Ontario during the Depression, a predominantly non-Anglo-Saxon work force was frequently pitted against an Anglo-Canadian management that attempted to destroy labour solidarity and discredit the strikers by stressing their foreign origins.

During the 1930s, patterns of social discrimination against Jews (eg, informal residential restrictions, quotas in university professional schools and exclusion from elite social clubs, beaches and holiday resorts in Montréal, Toronto and Winnipeg) were extended by fascist groups into a vicious and virulent anti-Semitism, which also influenced immigration policy. Canada closed its doors to Jewish immigrants at the time when they desperately needed refuge from Nazi persecution in Europe.

During WWII Germans, Italians, and members of pacifist sects encountered hostility. Popular prejudice against the Doukhobors, strong in rural BC during the 1920s and 1930s, was reinforced by wartime attitudes. In 1942 the Alberta government passed a law banning all land sales to Hutterites for the duration of the war; from 1947 to 1972 it legislated restrictions on the amount of land Hutterite colonies could own and on the areas of the province in which they could expand.

Hostility toward Japanese Canadians both before and during the war, was sustained, widespread and intense, especially in BC. Waves of anti-Japanese feeling, each of several months duration, swept BC in 1937-38, 1940 and 1941-42. The assault by Japan's navy on Pearl Harbour ignited the most violent hostility towards Japanese Canadians. Following a federal government order of 24 Feb 1942 that all Japanese must evacuate the Pacific coast area, some 22 000 Japanese Canadians were relocated to the interior of BC and to other provinces, where they continued to encounter racial prejudice. The government sold their property to preclude their return at the end of the war. Towards the end of the war the government also encouraged the Japanese to seek voluntary deportation to Japan, and after the war it proceeded with these deportation plans. Intense pressure from civil-rights groups finally led to the dropping of the deportation orders (1947), to a partial compensation for property losses, and an end to the restrictions that prevented Japanese from returning to the coast (1949).

Nevertheless a number of developments during and after the war undermined certain prejudices against various minority groups. Groups such as the Chinese and UKRAINIANS won a new respectability through their support for the war effort. The involvement of all levels of society in wartime industries undermined social barriers, and revulsion against Hitler and Nazism also eventually extended to a reaction against Hitler's concept of a superior race and against public expressions of anti-Semitism.

Canada's signing of the UNITED NATIONS charter in 1944 and the Universal Declaration of Human Rights in 1948 brought Canada's discriminatory policies into glaring focus. Following intense lobbying by Asian groups and an increasingly sympathetic white public, Asians were finally given the vote (South Asians and Chinese in 1947, Japanese in 1949) and the ban on Chinese and South Asians was repealed, although only wives and children of Canadian citizens were eligible for immigration.

The immigration that began after 1945 was still biased in favour of Europeans, although the government allowed a small quota of immigrants from India, Pakistan and Ceylon (1951). The post-WWII immigrants were better accepted, partly because a large proportion were educated and skilled. Probably the most important factor in accounting for a new tolerance towards immigrants in the 1950s and 1960s (exemplified and encouraged by the passage of provincial HUMAN RIGHTS bills and codes, the passage of the federal CANADIAN BILL OF RIGHTS (1960), and the establishment of both provincial and federal human rights commissions) was the undermining of the intellectual assumptions and social respectability of Anglo-Saxon racism. This resulted from a revulsion against Hitler's racism, the decline of the UK as a world power, and the growth of the American civil-rights movement, among other factors. The prosperity of the 1950s and 1960s facilitated the upward socioeconomic mobility of second- and third-generation non-Anglo-Saxons and helped weaken the fairly rigid relationship between class and ethnicity.

The postwar acceptance of immigrants in Montréal (the destination of most immigrants settling in Québec) was complicated by their tendency to choose English rather than French as the language of instruction for their children, and strong political pressure was brought to bear to force immigrants to send their children to French-speaking schools (see LANGUAGE POLICY).

International pressures for ethnic tolerance and human rights and the continuing need for skilled workers at a time when immigration from Europe was declining led in 1962 and 1967 to the introduction of new immigration regulations that allowed significant numbers of nonwhites from the Third World, particularly from Hong Kong, India and the West Indies, to enter Canada (see CANADA-THIRD WORLD RELATIONS). The influx during the 1970s reawakened latent fears and hostilities toward nonwhite immigrants. The negative sentiments reached a crescendo during the 1975 national debate on the federal governments's Green Paper on Immigration. The group now singled out frequently for racist attention are immigrants of South Asian origin who have come to Canada not only from India, Pakistan and Bangladesh, but from East Africa, the West Indies and other parts of the world. Between 1974 and 1977, South Asian immigrants in various Canadian cities were victims of vandalism and assaults. West Indian immigrants in Toronto and Montréal have complained of job and housing discrimination and of police harassment.

Sociological studies reveal that the relation between the ethnic hierarchy, which has such a long history in Canada's immigration policy, and the class system, is still a reality in Canada, although the ethnic pecking order has been removed from Canadian immigration law and is more difficult to maintain in the class system because of changing attitudes and because discrimination in jobs and housing has been made illegal by human-rights legislation.

HOWARD PALMER

Premier Because of the shared framework of CABINET government, the office of provincial premier is similar to that held by Canada's PRIME MINISTER. The policy direction and management of the provincial governments is visibly dominated by their premiers. Though this capability has been eroded by the increased scope of provincial government activity, premiers remain in every sense the "first" ministers.

The constitutional powers of the LIEUTENANT-GOVERNORS as the representatives of the Crown for the provinces are ordinarily exercised solely on the advice of the premier. Other provincial Cabinet members therefore owe their appointments to the premier and may be removed or shuffled between ministries at the premier's discretion. Party or other sociopolitical interests may determine the choice of Cabinet colleagues, but the specific composition of the Cabinet is decided by the premier. He may hold a government portfolio of his own, as well as the title of president of the Executive Council. The growth in staff support for the premiership in the form of policy and public relations advisers has directly added to the commanding position of the office itself. The appointments of deputy ministers as the administrative heads of government departments and those of the heads of government corporations are also generally subject to the premier's approval.

The premier shapes the conduct and decisions of Cabinet and speaks for the government, regardless of the departmental responsibilities of other ministers. Although a provincial general election is not called without some Cabinet discussion, a lieutenant-governor will dissolve a Legislative Assembly only on the advice of the premier.

In addition to his authority as head of government, a premier possesses an additional source of power as the head of the governing political party. His selection as party leader through the trials of a party LEADERSHIP CONVENTION is the first step on the road to premiership. This confirms a personal power base within the party unrivalled by any other party member. Since the image of party leader is a prime determinant of voting behaviour, leadership status is further enhanced by the electoral victory that propels a party into government office. Successive victories add to this source of power.

The growth in the importance of FEDERAL-PROVINCIAL RELATIONS in the making of Canadian public policy has also enhanced the personal status of the premiers. Federal-provincial and interprovincial meetings of first ministers on a broad range of policy issues have made such as Premiers Richard HATFIELD of NB, Brian PECKFORD of Newfoundland and Peter LOUGHEED of Alberta known to more people outside than within their own provinces.

It should be emphasized that the sources of authority and prestige establish only the potential for strong political leadership in the office of premier. The realization of this potential will in large part depend on the propensity and ability of the individual premier to utilize the power of his office. NORMAN J. RUFF

Reading: R. Cheffins and R. Tucker, *The Constitutional Process in Canada* (2nd ed, 1976).

Prent, Mark George, sculptor (b at Montréal 23 Dec 1947). Prent works with plastics such as polyster resin, fibreglass epoxies and found objects. His works are extremely realistic. His subjects are mostly human figures treated in an exaggerated manner (eg, a male nude figure, mouth open as if screaming, encased in a block of ice set upright in a freezer) and are never attractive in the superficial sense. Sometimes there is a certain ironic humour in his work. He has often worked on a large scale, creating 3-dimensional, extremely detailed, room-sized environments. Prent's subject matter is considered disturbing by many and a great deal of sensation surrounds it. In exhibitions of his work in 1970 and 1972, The Isaacs Gallery in Toronto was charged "with displaying disgusting objects," contrary to the Criminal Code of Canada. Both charges were dismissed. AVROM ISAACS

Prerogative Powers, defined as "the residue of discretionary or arbitrary authority which at any given time is legally left in the hands of the

CROWN." Originating in common law from practices developed through centuries, the sovereign delegates them to the GOVERNOR GENERAL on advice from the federal Cabinet, and to the lieutenant-governors through the governor-in-council. They include appointment and dismissal of the prime minister, and the summoning, proroguing and dissolving of Parliament in accordance with ministerial advice, parliamentary practice and constitutional remedies for unusual emergencies, such as electoral deadlock or a premier's death.   FRANK MACKINNON

Presbyterian and Reformed Churches All Christian churches of the "Reformed" tradition derive from the 16th-century Protestant Reformation and from CALVINISM. They function through a system of presbyterian or representative elected courts, rising from the congregational session to presbytery to synod, and from the Presbyterian Church in Canada to the annual General Assembly. Although French Calvinists (HUGUENOTS) shared in the early FUR TRADE, non-Catholics were generally barred from New France until the British CONQUEST. Early Scottish and other settlers brought Presbyterianism to the Maritimes and central Canada in the late 18th century. Attempts by Scottish, Irish and American churches to organize congregations in the colonies and efforts to found an indigenous Canadian Presbyterian church all failed, but by the early 19th century branches of the Church of Scotland and its smaller "Secessionist" offshoots had been established. Their complex relations, caused by disagreements about church-state connections, were further confused in 1844 when some colonial members of the C of S started "Free" churches in sympathy with the Free Church Disruption in Scotland, which also stemmed from church-state disputes.

In 1860 and 1861, respectively, the Secession and Free churches in the Maritimes and in central Canada formed 2 regional unions. In 1875 these and the remnants of the C of S combined to form the Presbyterian Church in Canada, which the 1891 census showed to be the Dominion's largest Protestant denomination. Before WWI the new church expanded rapidly in the West and added missions in China, Korea, Taiwan and India to older ones in the Caribbean and New Hebrides. These foreign missions included large medical and educational operations that employed hundreds of Canadians. In that same period Canadian Presbyterians, both lay and clergy, actively supported the ideals of the SOCIAL GOSPEL movement in crusades for moral and political purity, TEMPERANCE and social justice.

By the opening of the 20th century the combination of nationalism, a co-operative climate in religion, and the expansionist spirit of the major Canadian Protestant denominations led the Presbyterian Church to seek union with other Protestant bodies in a single Canadian church. This movement was opposed by a Presbyterian minority, and when the UNITED CHURCH OF CANADA was formed in 1925 about one-third of all Presbyterians (chiefly in Montréal and Southern Ontario) refused to join. Those who continued as Presbyterians lost most of their educational and charitable institutions and home and foreign missions. Since 1925, the total of members and adherents (proportionately wealthier and better educated than the national average) has remained almost constant at about 700 000 (1981c), making the Presbyterian Church the fourth-largest denomination in Canada.

Because of the corporate structure of Presbyterianism individual leadership is not especially evident in church life, but the church has numbered among its members such well-known Canadians as the vocal nationalist G.M. GRANT, principal of Queen's U, 1877-1902; PM Mackenzie KING; novelist Charles W. GORDON (Ralph Connor); George BROWN, publisher of the *Globe*;

Canada's first woman senator, Cairine WILSON; Thomas MCCULLOCH, pioneer NS educator; and Ontario's long-time premier, Oliver MOWAT. The Presbyterian Church in Canada retains its Calvinist and Scottish heritage in its organization and church life, emphasizing the central role of preaching and scripture reading, and severe simplicity in worship and church decor. Nevertheless, it has abandoned harsher elements in Calvinist theology and practice, such as double predestination and rigid sabbatarianism (sabbath observance). Although linked historically most closely to Scotland, the Presbyterian Church contains ethnic congregations of French and Swiss, Hungarians, Koreans and Chinese. It maintains active connection with such co-operative Christian bodies as the World Council of Churches, the World Alliance of Reformed Churches, and the Canadian Council of Churches.

In Canada the Reformed tradition is also represented by Dutch Calvinists. LOYALIST members of the colonial Dutch Reformed Church were absorbed by Presbyterian groups after the WAR OF 1812, but a later schism in the DRC (Reformed Church in America after 1867) produced the Christian Reformed Church (headquarters in Grand Rapids, Mich), which established several mission congregations in the Canadian West before 1920. In the 15 years following WWII, when nearly 150 000 Dutch migrated to Canada, Canadian CRC membership increased by more than 30 000 to reach 62 000 in 1961, and new congregations were formed in Ontario and BC. There are also 4 smaller Dutch Calvinist bodies — the Protestant Reformed Church, the Canadian Reformed Churches, the Free Reformed Churches of N America, and the Netherlands Reformed Congregations — all dating from the 1950s and from the same wave of Dutch immigration. Older members of these ethnic churches preserved their Dutch heritage through their religion, but Canadian-born members accommodate more easily to Canadian life-styles.
                                    JOHN S. MOIR

Reading: John S. Moir, *Enduring Witness* (1974).

Prescott, Ont, Town, pop 4670 (1981c), inc 1851, located 18 km E of Brockville on the St Lawrence R. The site was strategically located at the head of navigation above the former St Lawrence rapids. The French built Fort de Lévis nearby in 1760, and the town was founded 1810 by LOYALISTS under Major Edward Jessup, and named for Governor-in-Chief Robert PRESCOTT. Ft Wellington was built here during the WAR OF 1812 and used as the base for an attack on Ogdensburg, NY. The blockhouse (1838) has been restored and made part of Fort Wellington National Historic Pk. The stone windmill (1822), which served as a makeshift fort for rebels during the bloody Battle of the Windmill, has been preserved nearby. The town produces paper cartons, clothing, hardware, electronic components and plastic pipe. The weekly newspaper is the *Journal*.   K.L. MORRISON

Prescott, Robert, soldier, colonial administrator (b in Lancashire, Eng *c*1726; d at Rose Green, W Sussex, Eng 21 Dec 1816). He joined the British army in 1745 and saw service during the SEVEN YEARS' WAR at Louisbourg in 1758. He was appointed aide-de-camp to General Jeffery AMHERST in 1759 and took part in the advance on Montréal the following year. He later served in the AMERICAN REVOLUTION in the W Indies. Briefly governor of Martinique (1794-95), Prescott was appointed governor-in-chief of the Canadas, NB and NS and commander of forces in British N America in 1796. Although governor-in-chief until 1807, he spent only 3 years in Canada. Prescott was noted for stubbornness and irascibility but was not without skill. His decisive and judicious manner, however, was not enough to help him resolve the difficulties

he faced in LOWER CANADA, especially those related to land affairs. He was recalled in 1799.   DAVID EVANS

Press Gallery, *see* PARLIAMENTARY PRESS GALLERY.

Presse, La Montréal NEWSPAPER started in 1884 by William-Edmond Blumhart and other conservatives in opposition to *Le Monde*, edited by Hector LANGEVIN, and its support for John A. MACDONALD. Under the ownership of Trefflé Berthiaume its editorial orientation became liberal, 1899-1904, but with the Berthiaume-Du Tremblay family, 1906-55, it was generally conservative. After Paul DESMARAIS bought the paper in 1955, its editors have been liberal: Jean-Louis Gagnon (1958-61), Gérard PELLETIER (1961 to 1965), Roger Champoux (1965-69), Jean-Paul Desbiens (1969-72), Roger Lemelin (1972-80) and Roger Landry (1980-). Daily circulation was 14 000 in 1896, 64 000 in 1900, 121 085 in 1913, 147 074 in 1940, 285 787 in 1962, and 225 000 in 1984 (323 000 on Saturday). Its content has always been diversified, with excellent coverage of both national and international news. In the early 1980s the weekly supplement *Plus* included reports from the Third World. The influence of *La Presse* is growing in intellectual and business circles, especially since Michel Roy became the main editorialist in 1982.
           ANDRÉ DONNEUR AND ONNIG BEYLERIAN

Pressure Group, also known as interest group or lobby, is an organization that seeks to influence public policy to promote its own interest. The term "lobbyist" was coined in honour of 17th-century favour seekers who loitered in the lobbies of the British Parliament. The proliferation of some pressure groups is so extensive, their size so large and their organization so sophisticated that they virtually constitute another arm of government. Ironically, Canadians tend to disapprove of lobbying and refuse to realize its importance, while governments, which certainly do realize its influence, do not acknowledge the fact publicly. For example, over 50% of 703 Canadian firms studied in 1978 had been in contact with federal political leaders and bureaucrats, and 42% had made individual representations to federal-government departments, boards and commissions. The proportion of large firms (over 500 employees) that made individual representations to government (55%) was almost twice that of small firms (28.2%). Examples of powerful lobbies are the industry-financed CANADIAN TAX FOUNDATION, the commercial banks, the Canadian Federation of Agriculture, the CANADIAN MEDICAL ASSOCIATION, the automobile, steel, rubber, chemical and energy industries, which act alone or through their trade associations, eg, the Business Council on National Issues (an association of chief executive officers of large Canadian corporations formed in 1977 to co-ordinate business participation in the policy-making process), the CHAMBER OF COMMERCE and the CANADIAN MANUFACTURERS' ASSOCIATION. The Institute of Association Executives, which in Ottawa alone has 304 members, constitutes a virtual lobby of lobbyists.

Lobbying can take the form of a mass-media campaign or paid advertisements that oppose or support a particular policy, informal meetings with senior bureaucrats, or the presentation of a brief to a parliamentary committee. Lobbying in Canada, however, described as the process "of keeping things pleasant, dull and controlled" is usually characterized by private, informal meetings with influential advisers and Cabinet ministers. The closeness of these lobbyists to the politicians and bureaucrats sometimes results in charges of CONFLICT OF INTEREST. Successful lobbies are almost always well financed, cohesive and stable, and their leaders, many of whom are ex-MPs, tend to represent causes favourably regarded by politicians and civil servants. Lobbies facilitate the process by which leaders of the ruling party and senior bureaucrats arrange policy with business-community representatives. They usually maintain permanent offices near the capital and their leaders frequent important clubs and associations. The less successful groups are not usually well financed. Their leaders do not generally belong to the elite and they are often organized around a single issue, while others soldier on for years, defending small or lost causes. Exceptions include the federally funded Public Interest Advocacy Centre, which represented consumer interests in the debate over Bell Canada's rate increases, and Energy Probe, which despite its low budget (it receives 70% of its funding from donations) is respected for its scrupulous research. However, it is frequently unable to afford attendance at public regulatory hearings.

Because legislative decision making in Canada is highly centralized and party discipline is strong, the rivalries between legislators cannot be easily exploited. However, the same monopoly of power that allows the Cabinet to ignore pressure groups' demands also allows it to respond to them. The development of legislation usually follows a certain sequence. First, the need for policy change is perceived, then the policy proposal is developed, frequently with interest-group representatives, and circulated within government, eg, the PRIME MINISTER'S OFFICE and CENTRAL AGENCIES. It is then sometimes sent to the media, to experts and occasionally to provincial governments, before it is circulated to more government departments. At this point the policy may also be reviewed by pressure groups. Before amendments or new statutes are introduced into Parliament the proposal is reviewed by a COMMITTEE, whose opinions are confirmed or modified by Cabinet; the bill is drafted by the Department of Justice, considered by another Cabinet committee, confirmed by Cabinet and signed by the Prime Minister. But to be effective, legislation must be implemented, for which purpose public servants enjoy great discretion and power. Furthermore the impact of legislation is often determined by the interpretation of the courts. Because the legislative process, particularly policy initiative, is controlled in practice by the BUREAUCRACY, interest groups often express their opinions or provide information to public servants as well as to Cabinet. But interest groups can also exert their influence on parliamentary committees, whose suggestions regarding modifications of a bill are often confirmed by Cabinet; on the Senate, which can wield influence through the powerful Banking Committee; and on backbenchers, who may someday become Cabinet members, although it is generally acknowledged that once a bill has reached Parliament it is more difficult to influence the government's intentions.

Despite the conclusions of the Royal Commission on CORPORATE CONCENTRATION that farm, labour and other interest-group organizations are successful in affecting government policy, many such groups are excluded from any effective role by the power of powerful, recognized interests and bureaucrats to inhibit organizational efforts of groups that do not share accepted attitudes. If a group's representatives do not enjoy confidential intimacy with senior civil servants and Cabinet ministers, they resort to other tactics to excite the attention of the government, but tactics such as protest rallies underline their marginal political status. Among experienced lobbyists such tactics, although they are becoming more common, are considered illegitimate. Consumer, environmental and labour groups are also less successful, not only because they are socially and ideologically further from government but because they are trying to facilitate, not prevent, change.

Disputes between federal and provincial governments have helped powerful interests play off one level of government against another. Groups with strong regional interests, eg, the western oil and gas industry, have successfully mobilized their provincial governments in their cause against the federal government and other regions of Canada. It is when pressure groups do not pursue the same goals that the big battles are waged. The petroleum-pricing issue of the 1970s and early 1980s pitted the oil industry and the governments of producer provinces against the manufacturing industries in central Canada and the Ontario government. United big-business interests successfully prevented an effective strengthening of the Combines Investigation Act, which the Trudeau government had pledged to reform when it came into office. The same lobby also prevented reform of the TAXATION system, despite the recommendations of the Carter Commission. Generally, pressure groups in Canada have reinforced the status quo, but then for the most part they are the status quo.   HUGH G. THORBURN

Prevost, Sir George, soldier, administrator, governor-in-chief of Canada (b in New Jersey 19 May 1767; d at London, Eng 5 Jan 1816). Prevost was a captain of foot in the British army by 1784. In the Napoleonic Wars he saw service primarily in the West Indies as commander on St Vincent (1794-96), lieutenant-governor of St Lucia (1798-1802) and governor of Dominica (1802-05). Appointed in 1808 lieutenant-governor of Nova Scotia, Prevost became governor-in-chief of British N America and commander of British forces in N America in 1811. He was a suitable choice to take over the administration of Québec, given his ability to speak French, and demonstrated talents in colonial administration. As commander of the British forces during the WAR OF 1812, Prevost was held responsible for the failure to take Plattsburgh, NY, in 1814, which resulted in his recall to England in 1815. He died before an inquiry could be held.
DAVID EVANS

Price, Frank Percival, carillonneur, campanologist, composer (b at Toronto 7 Oct 1901). The first non-European graduate of the renowned Beiaardschool for carillonneurs in Mechelen, Belgium, Price became Canada's first Dominion carillonneur when the instrument he helped design for the Peace Tower of the Parliament Buildings in Ottawa was installed in 1927. Devoted to bells and their music, he became an international authority on campanology, initiating reforms and innovations in design and performance practice. From 1939 to 1972 he taught at U of Michigan, Ann Arbor, where he was also university carillonneur. A brilliant recitalist, Price has played carillons the world over. He is a prolific composer and arranger, and has contributed many hundreds of works to his instrument's repertoire.   BARCLAY McMILLAN

Price, William, entrepreneur (b at Hornsey, Eng 17 Sept 1789; d at Québec C 14 Mar 1867). An enterprising lumber and timber merchant, William Price, "the father of the Saguenay," developed a business empire that extended throughout the Saguenay, St Lawrence and Ottawa river areas. At age 14 Price became an employee of Chistopher Idle, a prominent London businessman. Six years later he was sent to the Québec branch of the British firm as a clerk, becoming manager of the office in 1815. In 1820 he became a partner in Montréal, Québec and London. The William Price Company at Québec specialized in exporting timber. Price reinvested profits from this trade, which by 1833 had grown to over 100 shiploads per year, in sawmills, timber limits and financing lumber and timber operations and eventually bought out his partners, forming William Price and Sons

in 1855. At his death the company continued under the management of his sons. *See* TIMBER TRADE HISTORY   CHRISTOPHER G. CURTIS

Price, Sir William, lumber merchant, manufacturer (b at Talca, Chile 30 Aug 1867; d at Kenogami, Qué 2 Oct 1924). The grandson of William PRICE, young Price was educated at private schools in Québec and England before entering the family firm, Price Bros and Company, in 1886. In 1889 he became president, managing-director and owner. Rejuvenating the then tottering company, he used its huge timber limits and capital resources to move into the developing paper industry. Price bought the pulp mill at Jonquière, using its pulp to produce cardboard and then paper. As he concentrated on supplying the American newsprint market, his Kenogami-Jonquière establishment became the largest Canadian producer of newsprint and revived the economic fortunes of the Saguenay. Price was a Conservative MP for Québec W 1908 to 1911. Associated with many Québec business enterprises, he was a strong imperialist and raised 2 companies for the SOUTH AFRICAN WAR. He was accidentally killed while inspecting his timber limits at Kenogami.   CHRISTOPHER G. CURTIS

Prime Minister, the chief minister and effective head of the executive in a parliamentary system, normally the leader of the majority party in the HOUSE OF COMMONS. If there is no majority, the PM is the leader of that party most likely to win support from other parties in the House. In Canada the title is usually reserved for the head of the federal government while the term PREMIER is normally (but not always) used to designate the head of the executive branch of a provincial government. Formally a PM is appointed by the GOVERNOR GENERAL who has little discretion in the matter, except in a crisis such as the death of the incumbent PM. Although the position and responsibilities of office are not defined in any statute or constitutional document, the PM has always been the most powerful figure in Canadian politics. He controls the party, speaks for it, and after appointment to office has at his disposal a large number of PATRONAGE appointments with which to reward party faithful. The PM appoints and dismisses all members of CABINET and allocates their responsibilities. As chairman of Cabinet, he controls the agenda and

Prime Ministers of Canada 1867-1985		
	Party	*Dates of Administration*
Sir John A. Macdonald	C[1]	1 Jul 1867 – 5 Nov 1873
Alexander Mackenzie	L[2]	7 Nov 1873 – 9 Oct 1878
Sir John A. Macdonald	C	17 Oct 1878 – 6 Jun 1891
Sir John J.C. Abbott	C	16 Jun 1891 – 24 Nov 1892
Sir John Sparrow Thompson	C	5 Dec 1892 – 12 Dec 1894
Sir Mackenzie Bowell	C	21 Dec 1894 – 27 Apr 1896
Sir Charles Tupper	C	1 May 1896 – 8 Jul 1896
Sir Wilfrid Laurier	L	11 Jul 1896 – 6 Oct 1911
Sir Robert Laird Borden	C	10 Oct 1911 – 12 Oct 1917
Sir Robert Laird Borden	U[3]	12 Oct 1917 – 10 Jul 1920
Arthur Meighen	U	10 Jul 1920 – 29 Dec 1921
W.L. Mackenzie King	L	29 Dec 1921 – 28 Jun 1926
Arthur Meighen	C	29 Jun 1926 – 25 Sep 1926
W.L. Mackenzie King	L	25 Sep 1926 – 6 Aug 1930
Richard Bedford Bennett	C	7 Aug 1930 – 23 Oct 1935
W.L. Mackenzie King	L	23 Oct 1935 – 15 Nov 1948
Louis St. Laurent	L	15 Nov 1948 – 21 Jun 1957
John G. Diefenbaker	C	21 Jun 1957 – 22 Apr 1963
Lester Bowles Pearson	L	22 Apr 1963 – 20 Apr 1968
Pierre Elliott Trudeau	L	20 Apr 1968 – 4 Jun 1979
Charles Joseph Clark	C	4 Jun 1979 – 3 Mar 1980
Pierre Elliott Trudeau	L	3 Mar 1980 – 30 Jun 1984
John Napier Turner	L	30 Jun 1984 – 17 Sep 1984
Martin Brian Mulroney	C	17 Sep 1984 –

[1] Conservative
[2] Liberal
[3] Unionist

discussions at meetings. He appoints the members of Cabinet committees and is chairman of the Priorities and Planning Committee. Because of these factors and the convention of party solidarity, the PM has great influence over the activities and agenda of PARLIAMENT. He also enjoys a special relationship with the CROWN, as he is the only person who can advise the governor general to dissolve Parliament and call an election. In recent years the PM has chosen a personal staff to advise him on policy. This enables him to have a direct influence on policy discussions and committee decisions, making it highly unlikely that any policy proposal not meeting his approval will be put into effect. Political reality, various conventions and the CONSTITUTION do limit the power of the PM. He must always be wary of offending the various regions of the country and must be able to conciliate competing factions within the party and the Cabinet and throughout Canada. He must also be able to delegate authority without losing control. This requires rare qualities and few prime ministers, if any, have been generously endowed with all of them. W.A. MATHESON

Reading: R.M. Punnett, *The Prime Minister in Canadian Government and Politics* (1977).

Prime Minister's Office (PMO), a central agency that came into its own in the late 1960s. It differs from its counterparts in that it is staffed with temporary political appointees rather than full-time, career civil servants and has no statutory base, its budget being a component of the estimates for the PRIVY COUNCIL OFFICE. The PRIME MINISTER determines the PMO's organization and role; its functions derive from his political responsibilities as leader of his party rather than as head of government, though in practice the division between these responsibilities is not clear, thereby providing opportunities for the PMO to trespass on the more purely administrative preserves of other CENTRAL AGENCIES. It is responsible for press and public relations, the PM's large correspondence, his speaking engagements, etc; it advises on candidates for appointment to the numerous order-in-council appointees, eg, directorships on CROWN CORPORATIONS, members of regulatory commissions, on which the PM's recommendation is essential and decisive; it maintains contact with the party's officials outside the legislature and with the party caucus in the legislature; it generally serves as a listening post and a "gatekeeper" determining which matters will be brought to the PM's attention and ensuring that the political dimensions of public policies are not overlooked by the permanent bureaucracy. There is potential for overlap and competition with the Privy Council Office. The expansion of the personnel and functions of the PMO under PM Pierre TRUDEAU was a clear reflection of the increasingly dominant role of the PM, as both head of government and head of party. J.E. HODGETTS

Reading: C. Campbell and G. Szablowski, *The Superbureaucrats: Structure and Behaviour in Central Agencies* (1979); B.G. Doern and P. Aucoin, eds, *The Structures of Policy-Making in Canada* (1971).

Prince, Edward Ernest, fisheries biologist (b at Leeds, Eng 23 May 1858; d 10 Oct 1936). Educated at St Andrews, Cambridge and Edinburgh universities, Prince was a disciple of W.C. McIntosh of St Andrews, a leading fishery scientist. In 1893 he was appointed commissioner of fisheries. He immediately advocated a marine scientific station for Canada through the RSC, of which he became a fellow, and through the British Assn for the Advancement of Science meeting in Toronto in 1897. When Parliament appropriated $7000 for establishment of the station in 1898, Prince became director and chairman of its board of management. In 1912 this became the Biological Board of Canada and in 1937 the Fisheries Research Board — a unique

and successful Canadian experiment in the administration of research by a body with a majority of university scientists working with representatives of government and industry. Prince was chairman until 1921. A.W.H. NEEDLER

Prince, Richard Edmund, sculptor (b at Comox, BC 6 Apr 1947). Prince has been making conceptual sculpture since his studies at UBC (1971). He has developed a provocative style that intentionally forces the viewer's participation either physically or visually in a sequence of causes and effects. His early work centred on trying to depict forces, such as gravity, that have been largely ignored in Western art. The sculptures are well-executed models that use found objects encased in a box. They create, with a touch of humour, a miniature environment that implies levels of meaning. KATHLEEN LAVERTY

Prince, Thomas George, soldier (b at Petersfield, Man 25 Oct 1915; d at Winnipeg 25 Nov 1977). He worked at various unskilled jobs until he joined the Royal Canadian Engineers in 1940. With the Canadian Parachute Battalion (1943), he fought at the Battle of Anzio, Italy, and was awarded the Military Medal. After the invasion of southern France he was recommended for the French Croix de Guerre and was awarded the American Silver Star. He was elected chairman of the Manitoba Indian Assn in 1946 and lobbied to improve knowledge in Ottawa of Indian needs. In 1950 he joined the Princess Patricia Canadian Light Infantry and fought with the UN forces in Korea. Unable to fit into civilian life after the war he did odd jobs to supplement a small army pension. D. BRUCE SEALEY

Reading: D. Bruce Sealey and Peter Van de Vyvere, *Thomas George Prince* (1981).

Prince Albert, Sask, City, pop 31 380 (1981c), inc 1904, is located on the N SASKATCHEWAN R 140 km N of Saskatoon. It is an agricultural service centre and the gateway to northern Saskatchewan. The city is governed by a mayor and 8 aldermen. A provincial agency, the Local Government Board, oversees municipal financing.

Named for Queen Victoria's consort, Prince Albert was founded 1866 as a Presbyterian mission. Its character changed dramatically with the selection of a route through the valley of the N Saskatchewan for the transcontinental railway. Prince Albert grew rapidly, but the boom collapsed when the CPR adopted a more southerly route. After the turn of the century the city embarked on a scheme to harness nearby La Colle Falls, in the confident expectation that cheap electric power would attract industry. These dreams were never realized, however, and the project brought Prince Albert to the verge of bankruptcy. For 4 decades the city marked time, but resource development and the growth of tourism at nearby Prince Albert National Park since 1945 have revived its economy.

The majority of the population is native born, and nearly half is British in origin. People of French, Ukrainian and German ancestry form sizable groups as well. The largest religious denominations are Roman Catholic, United Church, Anglican, Lutheran and Presbyterian.

The Prince Albert Pulp Co is the city's largest employer. At peak production its mill employs

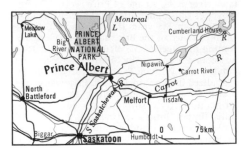

450; another 500 are engaged in timber harvesting operations. Prince Albert is served by 2 airlines, branches of the CPR and CNR and one bus line. The city is served by one English-language TV station, a radio station and a daily newspaper, the Prince Albert *Daily Herald*. Three prime ministers have represented Prince Albert in the House of Commons: Wilfrid LAURIER, Mackenzie KING and John DIEFENBAKER.
J. WILLIAM BRENNAN

Reading: G.W.D. Abrams, *Prince Albert: The First Century, 1866-1966* (1966).

Prince Albert National Park (est 1927) is located 200 km N of Saskatoon and covers 3874 km². It is characterized by boreal forests, prairie grasslands and clear lakes. Eskers, drumlins, glacial lakes, moraines, meltwater channels and other glacial features mark the land. The cabin and grave of Grey Owl (Archibald BELANEY) are located in the PARK beside Ajawaan Lk, where he spent the last 7 years of his life. The park is rich in the wildlife he fought to protect. Elk, moose and deer browse in the trembling aspen forests; wolves and caribou roam the forests of jack pine, larch and balsam fir; badger and a herd of 20 bison inhabit the prairie meadows and fescue grasslands. Park waterways harbour beaver, the animal most closely associated with Grey Owl. Over 195 bird species have been seen; white pelicans and double-crested cormorants nest on an island in the park. Commercial facilities and accommodation are available in nearby Waskesiu, Sask. LILLIAN STEWART

Prince Charles Island, 9521 km², 130 km long and 100 km wide, is the largest island in FOXE BASIN, W of BAFFIN I. It is an outcrop of a coast of postglacial marine deposition, and exhibits the characteristics of this kind of topography, having monotonously straight, flat coasts with a shallow offshore zone. The shore consists of wide mud flats, littered with boulders and crossed by occasional watercourses, and passes imperceptibly to the inland tundra marshes. The maximum elevation is only 73 m; local relief generally is in the order of 10 m or less. The island remained undiscovered until a 1948 RCAF aerial survey. DOUG FINLAYSON

Prince Edward Island, Canada's seventh and smallest province, is affectionately referred to by its people as "the Island." Known to its earliest settlers, the MICMAC, as *Abegweit* ("cradle in the waves"), the province has other names that highlight aspects of its history and character: the "Garden of the Gulf," the "Million-Acre Farm," the "Cradle of Confederation" or, less eloquently, "Spud Island." Situated in the Gulf of St Lawrence and separated from NS and NB by the shallow Northumberland Strait, the Island has a crescent shape and extends for 224 km, with a width ranging from 4 to 60 km. The Island makes up only 0.1% of the Canadian land mass, and although the population is only 0.5% of the Canadian total, it is the most concentrated in the country, with over 21 persons per square kilometre. In spite of its high density the Island is the most rural province in the nation as only 36.3% of the population is classed as urban. The Island's deep red soil has always been its most striking feature and important resource and together with the sea has been the mainstay of the population since the early 18th century. The Island was described by Jacques CARTIER in 1534 as "the fairest land that may possibly be seen." The 15 km of water between the Island and the Canadian mainland has helped develop and maintain a strong sense of distinctiveness in the province, which continues to cherish its rural past while facing the unsettling challenges of the 20th century.

Although designed to reflect its reliance on Great Britain, the province's crest — 3 small oak trees beneath the shelter of a larger oak — and its motto — *parva sub ingenti* ("the small under the protection of the great") — also aptly describe the position of the province in the Canadian Confederation.

Land and Resources

Geology Prince Edward Island's insular status is of relatively recent origin in geological terms. An enormous sedimentary basin underlying the present Gulf of St Lawrence was laid down by freshwater streams that drained ancient highlands. The surface geology of the Island is of more dramatic origin. The ice ages left an imprint on the land, especially during the late Pleistocene period between 75 000 and 15 000 years ago. When the last glaciers receded, uncovering what is now PEI, glacial debris and the marks of glacial scouring were left on the exposed land, which began gradually to assume its present character. Because of lower ocean beds and land depressed by the glaciers' weight, the Island was connected to the mainland by a low plain covering much of the present Northumberland Strait. As ocean levels rose with the melting of the glaciers, and as the land rebounded, the crescent shape of the Island emerged about 5000 years ago.

Surface The present land surface of the Island ranges from nearly level in the W, to hilly in the central region and to gently rolling hills in the E. The highest elevation is 142 m in central Queens County. The Island's predominant reddish brown sandy and clay soils are occasionally broken by outcroppings of sedimentary rock, most commonly a red-coloured sandstone or mudstone. The heavy concentrations of iron oxides in the rock and soil give the land its distinctive reddish brown hue.

The coastline is deeply indented by tidal inlets. The N shore of the Island, facing the Gulf of St Lawrence, features extensive sand-dune formations. These shifting sands pose problems for fishermen by clogging harbour entrances, but they provide a haven for summer tourists. The shoreline of the Island generally alternates between headlands of steep sandstone bluffs and extensive sandy beaches. Many of the Island's harbours have been created by dredging tidal runs and are usable only by vessels of shallow draught, such as inshore fishing boats. A few natural harbours, such as those of Summerside, Charlottetown, Georgetown and Souris, provide access and shelter for larger vessels.

Because the Island has only small ponds, few significant rivers and generally low elevation, waterpower has not been developed. In the last century numerous gristmills and sawmills used the limited hydropower available, but few survive today. Lacking hydroelectric capability, the Island has been forced to rely on fossil fuels to generate power and on electrical power transmitted from NB via submarine cable.

Little is left of the original forests of the Island; 3 centuries of clearing for agriculture and shipbuilding, as well as fire and disease have radically transformed them. Only 100 years ago the upland areas of the province were forested with beech, yellow birch, maple, oak and white pine. Today, most of the woodlands have deteriorated into a mixture of spruce, balsam fir and red maple, which cover over 241 000 ha of the province.

Climate The Island climate is moderate. Winters are long but relatively mild, springs are late and cool. Summers are cool and marked by prevailing SW breezes. Average mean temperatures are approximately -7°C in Jan and Feb and 18°C in July. The Island is relatively free of fog year-round, unlike neighbouring provinces. Annual precipitation averages 112 cm, ensuring adequate groundwater supply. The waters of both the Gulf of St Lawrence and Northumberland Strait are warmer in summer than the coastal waters of NS and NB, although in

Prince Edward Island

Capital: Charlottetown
Motto: Parva Sub Ingenti ("The small under the protection of the great")
Flower: Lady's slipper
Largest Cities: Charlottetown, Summerside
Population: 122 500 (1981c); rank tenth, 0.49% of Canada; 36.3% urban; 53.8% rural nonfarm; 9.8% farm; 21.6 per km² density; 3.6% increase from 1976-81; Jan 1984e pop, 124 600
Languages: 96.6% English; 3% French; 0.4% Other
Entered Confederation: 1 July 1873
Government: Provincial — Lieutenant-Governor, Executive Council, Legislative Assembly of 32 members; federal — 4 senators, 4 members of the House of Commons
Area: 5660 km²; 0.1% of Canada
Elevation: Highest point — Queen's County (142 m); lowest point — sea level
Gross Domestic Product: $990 million (1982e)
Farm Cash Receipts: $161.4 million (1982)
Value of Fish Landings: $41.391 million (1983 prelim total); $35.841 million (1982 total)
Electric Power Generated: 11 404 MWh (1983)
Sales Tax: 10% (1984)

winter ice covers both the strait and the gulf, and ICEBREAKERS are needed to keep shipping lanes open. Drift ice is often found in Island waters as late as the latter part of May, causing difficulty for fishermen and slowing the arrival of spring.

Resources The 2 major resources of the Island are the soil and the sea. Mineral resources have not been discovered in commercial quantities although trace deposits of coal, uranium, vanadium and other minerals exist. Since 1940, drilling has revealed the existence of natural gas beneath the seabed off the NE part of the province, but no commercially exploitable finds have been made. Mining to date has been restricted to open-pit removal of sand and gravel, but the latter is of low quality and in insufficient quantities to meet even local demand.

Agriculture, based on the rich soil and temperate climate of the province, is the most important primary resource industry. Most Island soils are coarse-textured sandy loams with a very low stone content. In general the soil is moderately acidic and it is common practice periodically to add lime to the soil to reduce the acidity. Close to 50% of the Island's land has been identified as being highly productive and upwards of 90% of the entire province is potentially farming land. Although the area actually in agricultural production has dropped in recent years, some land is still being cleared, especially for high value crops such as potatoes and tobacco. Fishing, especially for lobster and cod, is the second important resource industry of the Is-

Sea view, PEI, showing the Island's distinctive and fertile red soil (*photo by Freeman Patterson/Masterfile*).

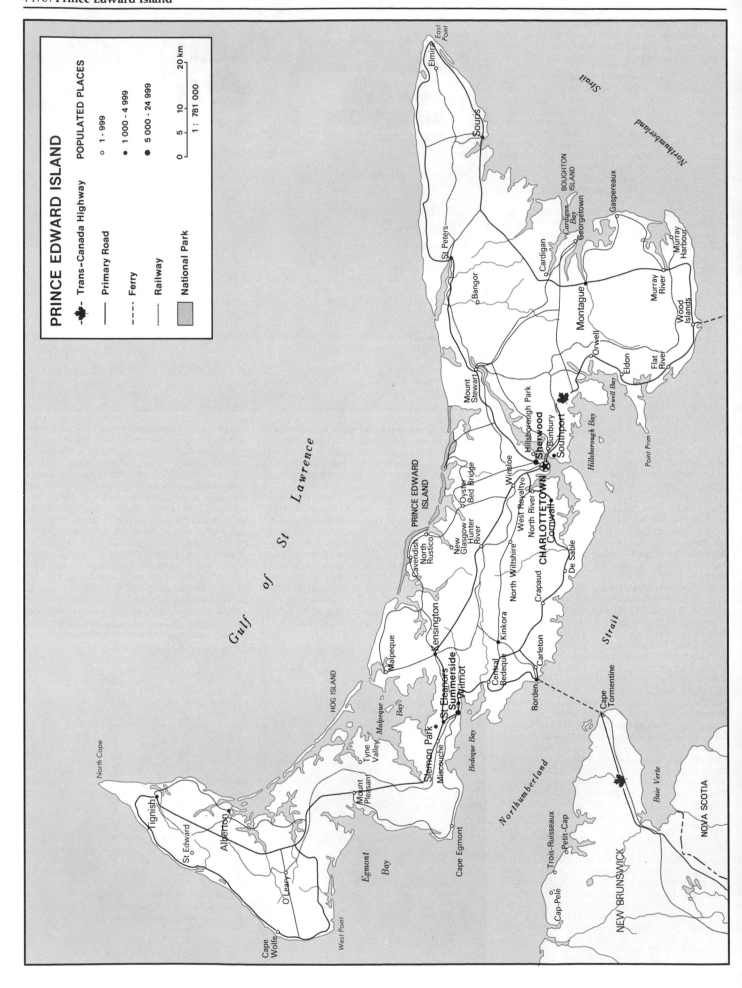

PRINCE EDWARD ISLAND

POPULATED PLACES

○ 1 - 999
● 1 000 - 4 999
● 5 000 - 24 999

Trans–Canada Highway

Primary Road

Ferry

Railway

National Park

1 : 781 000

0 5 10 20 km

land. A supplementary shellfish fishery includes scallops, oysters, clams and lately mussels. Forestry is relatively undeveloped on the Island, because of the depleted state of the woodlands and lack of effective management of the remaining resource. There have, however, been some attempts to improve the quality of the forest cover. Since 1945, through exploiting the appeal of PEI's unspoiled landscape and sandy beaches, tourism has emerged as a major industry. It has not been an unmixed blessing; often it has brought inappropriate and random development, dependence on low seasonal wages and loss of land to off-Island owners.

Conservation Conservation has become a major concern of government and of public interest groups in the province. Overcropping, extensive mechanization, reliance on chemical fertilizers and removal of hedgerows had led to considerable wind and water erosion of some of the Island's best land. It is estimated, for example, that up to 5 t of soil per ha can be eroded from an unprotected, plowed field in one year. This soil erosion has also led to heavy siltation of the creek and river systems, turning many streams, navigable in the last century, into shallow and unusable creeks. Another major concern has been the purchase of large tracts of land by nonresidents for recreation or development and by vertically integrated business for farming. Both problems led to the establishment of a Royal Commission on Land Use and Ownership and to the subsequent creation of a Provincial Land Use Commission, which regulates zoning, ownership and development questions. Groups such as the PEI Nature Trust have attempted to bring public attention to many of PEI's imperiled natural areas, but most of the land is privately owned and is vulnerable to inappropriate development, misuse or unwitting neglect.

People Prince Edward Island is the most culturally homogeneous province of Canada. The population is overwhelmingly British in origin, with roughly 12% of Acadian descent. Small communities of Dutch, Lebanese and Micmac also exist. The Micmac can trace their ancestry to Indian tribes that inhabited the Island as far back as 8000 to 10 000 years ago, although the Micmac, a branch of the Algonquians, actually came to the Island within the last 2000 years. Although left only with small parcels of land of poor quality and suffering from disease and high unemployment, the Micmac population has remained relatively steady. The majority of the Acadian population can be traced to several hundred Acadians who escaped deportation at the time of the British occupation of the Island following the fall of LOUISBOURG in 1758. Today the group numbers approximately 15 000, and there are large numbers of this population sharing common surnames. ENGLISH, SCOTS and IRISH arrived in the late 18th and early 19th centuries and by 1861 the population had grown to just over 80 000. Thereafter growth slowed and after 1891 natural increase was unable to keep up with the number of Islanders leaving, especially for New England. Most of the other ethnic groups in the population are the result of immigration in the last 40 years. The 1950s and 1960s were periods of slow population growth as Islanders continued to leave the province in search of economic opportunities elsewhere. The last decade has seen a small balance of inmigration, and this, combined with natural increase, has allowed growth to the 1981 level of 123 000. Within this population, however, the percentage of those over 65 years of age has steadily increased and the government has indicated some concern about this shift in the population makeup.

Urban Centres CHARLOTTETOWN, the capital city, is the largest urban centre of the province, with a population of 15 282 in 1981. Growth in the capital region has been most notable in the

Gathering Irish moss at Tignish on Prince Edward Island's northern tip (*photo by Richard Vroom*).

suburbs, and if the populations of the 7 smaller communities bordering Charlottetown were included the population was just over 30 000 (1981). Charlottetown is the only incorporated city in the province and is the seat of most government offices, the provincial university and the Confederation Centre theatre and art gallery. At one time the city was a major port, but in recent years the number of vessels entering has declined significantly, although efforts by several agencies have resulted in regular visits by summer cruise liners. In 1984 the federal Department of Veterans Affairs was moved to the city, resulting in an increase in federal government employees in the area.

The next largest urban centre is SUMMERSIDE in the western part of the Island, which with its surrounding communities houses approximately 12 000 people. Summerside's principal economic bases are agricultural service industries, government offices and the nearby Canadian Forces Base. Other population centres in Prince County include Kensington (1143), Alberton (1020) and Tignish (982). In King's County, Montague (1957), Souris (1413) and Georgetown (737) are the major towns. Like other parts of Canada, PEI has seen a shift from rural to urban population and many smaller villages have declined in size.

Labour Force In 1983 the labour force of Prince Edward Island numbered 55 000, but unemployment is a chronic problem with the rate rarely falling below 10% in recent years. Wage rates and per capita income for Islanders are near the lowest in Canada and personal income is only 70% of the national average. Transportation difficulties, lack of natural resources, and high energy costs make the outlook for the expansion of the provincial labour force remote, despite the development plans of both provincial and federal governments.

Language and Ethnicity The overwhelming majority (94%) of the Island's population reported English as their mother tongue in 1981. Although approximately 12% of the Island's population is of Acadian descent, only 5% of the total population reported French as their mother tongue. Attempts are being made to preserve and expand the use of French. One of the 5 regional school districts is French, and the St Thomas Aquinas Society, an influential cultural group, actively promotes Acadian language and culture. The native language of most of the

highland Scots who came to the Island in the 18th and 19th centuries has fared less well. Gaelic is virtually extinct, because of school systems that rewarded English speakers.

According to the 1981 census, 77% of the Island's population is British, primarily highland Scots, followed by Irish, English and lowland Scots. Acadians constitute about 12% of the population, and those listed as British *and* French constitute a further 5%. Dutch, Lebanese, Scandinavian and native Indian represent 2%; a small but vigorous Micmac population of 440 is concentrated at Lennox I on the N shore and at Scotchfort on the Hillsborough R.

Religion There are almost equal numbers of Protestants and Catholics in PEI. The United Church is the largest Protestant group, followed by the Presbyterian, Anglican and Baptist churches. Small but rapidly growing evangelical groups are also active, and there is a tiny Jewish community. Until recently religion has played an important role in Island life. Bitter struggles over religion and education were not resolved until the era of Confederation.

Economy

The economic history of PEI has been dominated by geography. In the 18th and 19th centuries its insularity was a benefit. Produce and manufactured goods had to travel only short distances before they could be loaded aboard cheap water transportation and the forests of the Island provided the resources for SHIPBUILDING, which became a major industry in the mid-1800s. The prosperity of the Island was further reinforced by the RECIPROCITY Treaty of 1854 that led to increased export of agricultural products to the US. At the time of Confederation trade links were well established along the Atlantic seaboard and with the United Kingdom. However, the shift of focus after 1873 towards central Canada and western expansion, together with changes in technology, left the Island — which had been a relatively strong economic partner in Confederation — in a weakened condition that has persisted to this day. PEI was ill-equipped for the industrial age. It lacked coal and water resources essential to industrial development, and the cost and availability of transportation proved to be a difficulty that has not been completely overcome. What industries had existed on the Island were soon crushed by larger and more efficient plants in central Canada, but at the same time the NATIONAL POLICY provided no protection or markets for the Island's natural products. The change in technology was most strongly felt in the shipbuilding industry. As the wooden sailing ship was replaced by steam vessels constructed of iron and steel, the entire industry died, having neither the raw materials nor the capital to make such a fundamental shift. Although there was more of a stagnation in the economy than an absolute decline, by the early 1950s the per capita income in PEI was just over 50% of the national level and the outlook for the future was bleak.

The post-WWII development of what amounted to a new National Policy has had the most profound impact on the Island. Income support programs, human-services programs and new federal-provincial fiscal policy have dramatically altered the Islanders' way of life. Attempts to alleviate regional disparities by using forced economic growth have caused a social revolution. Certainly personal income levels have risen substantially, and markedly better health and educational facilities have been established. The Federal-Provincial Comprehensive Development Plan, begun in 1969, has been central to much of this development. This new period of development through government intervention has not been an unmixed blessing. Increasing dependence has been the principal cost. By 1981 federal spending amounted to 67% of the gross domestic product of PEI. If the provincial government's funding is included, by 1981 total government spending amounted to 87% of the gross domestic product. At the same time, the number of persons engaged in primary industries has declined sharply and the number of government and related jobs increased. Facing a heavy burden of fixed costs to support social programs and the new infrastructure, it is unlikely that the province will be able to undertake significant initiatives. The outlook in the private sector is not encouraging. For example, per capita investment in the province, as a percentage of the Canadian average, dropped from 70% in 1971 to 42% in 1981. If the province is to develop a secure and less dependent economic future, clearly some new directions must be sought. Obviously a solution to the transport and energy problems is essential, together with a fresh look at ways of utilizing the primary resources of the province.

Agriculture In the last 30 years there have been major changes in agriculture on Prince Edward Island. As late as 1951 over 90% of all farms on PEI had horses for a total of 21 000 animals. Today, workhorses are rarely seen, and fields used to produce the huge amount of forage for these animals have been turned to other uses. The number of farms has dropped from 10 137 in 1951 to 3154 in 1981. At the same time the area in farms has been reduced by 37% although in recent years the area used as cropland and pasture has remained stable. The size of the average farm has increased from 44 ha in 1951 to 92 ha in 1981, but owing to heavy investment in equipment needed in larger farms the margin of profit for Island farmers has been reduced from approximately 50% to 25%; thus a producer has to sell twice as much to have the same net income. Total farm cash receipts in 1983 were $181 million. Of this total the largest single crop was POTATOES, which earned over $71 million. Potatoes flourish in the soil and climate conditions found in Prince Edward Island. About 20 000 ha are planted annually and the average yield is about 25 t per ha. Three-quarters of this yield is high-grade seed potatoes that are exported to more than 15 countries. Table stock is either sold fresh in eastern Canada and the US or processed into french fries and other potato products. There are about 1100 dairy farms in the province with a total of 22 000 dairy cattle, which produce 95 million litres of milk annually. Eighty percent of this is processed into milk products, such as evaporated milk, most of which are exported. In 1983 the cash receipts from dairy products totaled over $26 million. Cattle are also raised for beef. Although recent fluctuation in beef prices has resulted in uneven production, Island farmers sent about 30 000 cattle to slaughter per year between 1978 and 1983, and in 1983 the receipts from cattle and calves amounted to $23 million. Almost as important is the production of hogs, which are raised on a commercial scale by about 700 farmers. TOBACCO has been produced on Prince Edward Island since 1959 and although faced with high energy costs, a crop sensitive to unpredictable weather, and a high labour requirement, it has been successful, with the 1979 crop, for example, exceeding 2579 t and selling for over $7.6 million.

The provincial and federal governments have put in place a large number of programs to halt the exodus of farmers from the land and to increase farm incomes, and they have met with some degree of success, but the high cost of entering the industry remains a problem. Both levels of government are active in agricultural research and Agriculture Canada maintains a large research facility in Charlottetown. A new Atlantic Veterinary College being constructed on the campus of University of Prince Edward Island is expected to have a significant impact on both animal and aquatic research that will be of benefit to the fishing industry.

Industry Tourism, construction, primary-resource-related manufacturing, and services are the major industries of PEI. Of these TOURISM has grown most in the last 2 decades, although growth has stopped and in 1983 the number of tourist parties was lower than in any of the preceding 6 years. The Island still attracts over 600 000 tourists annually and in 1983 this group spent over $50 million. Since the 1960s the government has been deeply involved in the promotion of industry and in the construction and operation of attractions and accommodations. Attempts have been made to divert tourists from the central part of the Island, which is dominated by Prince Edward Island National Park, to eastern and western parts of the province, which have benefitted less from the tourist dollar. A major problem is the shortness of the season, which consists of only 8 to 10 weeks in July and August. Government has been promoting attractions and activity in other seasons, and the recent openings of new hotel and convention complexes are part of the attempt to promote year-round tourism. The major attraction remains the fine warm sandy beaches along the 1800 km of shoreline. Golf, deep-sea fishing and horse racing are among the sports available for tourists. In the last decade government and private developers attractions have established a number of "heritage" attractions, including sites operated by the Prince Edward Island Museum and Heritage Foundation.

Manufacturing in the province is dominated by fish- and farm-product processing. This area grew rapidly until 1979, but since then has declined as expansion in product lines has not offset the closure of some major plants. In 1983 some 4000 were employed and the dollar value of goods shipped in that year was $275 million. One of the development strategies explored by the government in the Comprehensive Development Plan was the establishment of manufacturing plants in industrial parks, but many of the attempts to introduce non-food-related manufacturing have failed. The last 2 decades have seen increased employment in the service sector and both the federal and provincial governments are major employers with over 7000 persons on government payrolls in 1983.

Forestry Although forestry was a principal industry in the 1800s, it has since declined dramatically. About 37% of the province is covered

Cavendish Beach, PEI (*photo by Richard Vroom*).

by woodland, 99% of which is privately owned. Most of the best timber was harvested in the 19th century and over 80 000 ha have regenerated in inferior species of little commerical value. Today, forests are being reconsidered as a source of both fuel and lumber for provincial use. Many Island homes are now being heated at least in part by wood fuel, and the number will likely increase as costs of fuel oil and electricity continue to rise.

Fisheries In 1982 there were just over 3000 fishermen and helpers in the province. Almost all of the 1485 vessels used were small inshore boats, most of which were employed in the lobster fishery but were converted to other forms of fishing when the seasonal lobster fishery was closed. The fishery also provided seasonal employment in processing plants for up to 2000 workers. Fish landings in 1982 had a value of $35.8 million, but when processing, outfitting and vessel construction are included, the contribution to the provincial economy was estimated to exceed $80 million. Lobster is by far the most valuable species, with 1982 landings of 5493 t, having a value of $22.8 million. Other shellfish, including scallops and the famous Malpeque oysters, added a further $4 million to the industry. Fishing for the giant bluefin tuna has become an important attraction for sportfishermen from around the world, but the species is also fished commercially. Groundfish such as cod, hake, flounder and redfish and pelagic species such as herring and mackerel are also caught in the Island's waters, accounting for a value of $7.3 million in 1982. An important industry in the western part of the Island is the harvesting of IRISH MOSS, a marine plant that, when processed, yields carrageenin, an emulsifying and stabilizing agent used in many food products.

Transportation Because PEI is an island, transportation is a major problem. At present the island is serviced by 2 ferry systems. CN operates a year-round service from Borden, PEI, to Cape Tormentine, NB, for passengers, motor vehicles and railcars; icebreaking ferries are used in winter. Northumberland Ferries, a private company heavily subsidized by the federal government, operates between Wood Islands, PEI, and Caribou, NS, from April to November, closing when ice and weather become severe. The province is also connected to major Canadian centres by daily air routes operated by both Eastern Provincial Airways and Air Canada. There has been recurring interest in a fixed crossing to the mainland. A popular proposal in

the late 19th century was for a tunnel under Northumberland Strait. As recently as the late 1960s, work was actually begun on a causeway but abandoned in favour of the negotiation of the Comprehensive Development Plan. In recent years the deterioration of the province's railway system has been a cause for concern. As operation of branch lines has become less economical, CN has drastically reduced services. Opposition to these cutbacks has been strong, especially from farmers who market their produce via the rail system. The road network within the province has been substantially improved and now almost all primary and secondary routes are paved, which has greatly increased the use of road transportation in the shipping of primary and manufactured products.

Energy Energy costs are one of the most serious problems facing PEI. Electrical energy is the most expensive in Canada. In 1982, for example, a kWh of electricity in PEI cost 11.85¢. In Québec the same electricity cost 3.2¢, and in NB 4.5¢. All power is either generated in oil-fixed thermal plants or imported via submarine cable from NB. Since there is no potential for large-scale hydroelectrical development, alternative energy sources such as wind, solar and wood-fired generators are being investigated. As yet, none of these alternatives has been proved to have the required capacity, despite successful small-scale applications. The reduction of energy costs is certain to be a major topic of future interprovincial and federal-provincial negotiation.

Government and Politics

Government and politics are closer to the people in PEI than in any other province. Its 123 000 people have a full range of federal, provincial and municipal institutions. As a result, constituencies are small, politicians familiar, and a sense of informality pervades the political process. The basic structures of provincial government are similar to those of other provinces, but there are important distinctions arising from the size and political history of the province. Government was established in PEI by order-in-council in 1769, but it was not until the post-Confederation period that the modern structure and practice of government emerged. There is a lieutenant-governor appointed by the governor general for a 5-year term. The Executive Council, or Cabinet, usually consists of 10 members responsible for single or multiple departments and is headed by the premier. The Legislative Assembly has 32 representatives, with one councillor and one assemblyman drawn from

Lieutenant-Governors of Prince Edward Island 1873-1984

	Term
W.C.F. Robinson	1873-78
Robert Hodgson	1878-79
Thomas H. Haviland	1879-84
Andrew A. Macdonald	1884-89
Jedediah S. Carvell	1889-94
George W. Howlan	1894-99
P.A. McIntyre	1899-1904
D.A. MacKinnon	1904-10
Benjamin Rogers	1910-15
Augustine C. Macdonald	1915-19
Murdock Mackinnon	1919-24
Frank R. Heartz	1924-30
Charles Dalton	1930-33
G. Des Brisay Deblois	1933-39
Bradford Lepage	1939-45
Joseph A. Bernard	1945-50
T. William L. Prowse	1950-58
F.W. Hyndman	1958-63
William J. MacDonald	1963-69
J. George MacKay	1969-74
Gordon L. Bennett	1974-80
Joseph A. Doiron	1980-

Premiers of Prince Edward Island 1873-1984

	Party	Term
J.C. Pope	Conservative	1873
L.C. Owen	Conservative	1873-76
L.H. Davies	Liberal	1876-79
W.W. Sullivan	Conservative	1879-89
N. McLeod	Conservative	1889-91
F. Peters	Liberal	1891-97
A.B. Warburton	Liberal	1897-98
D. Farquharson	Liberal	1898-1901
A. Peters	Liberal	1901-08
F.L. Haszard	Liberal	1908-11
H. James Palmer	Liberal	1911
John A. Mathieson	Conservative	1911-17
Aubin E. Arsenault	Conservative	1917-19
J.H. Bell	Liberal	1919-23
James D. Stewart	Conservative	1923-27
Albert C. Saunders	Liberal	1927-30
Walter M. Lea	Liberal	1930-31
James D. Stewart	Conservative	1931-33
William J.P. MacMillan	Conservative	1933-35
Walter M. Lea	Liberal	1935-36
Thane A. Campbell	Liberal	1936-43
J. Walter Jones	Liberal	1943-53
Alexander W. Matheson	Liberal	1953-59
Walter R. Shaw	Conservative	1959-66
Alexander B. Campbell	Liberal	1966-78
W. Bennett Campbell	Liberal	1978-79
J. Angus McLean	Conservative	1979-81
James M. Lee	Conservative	1981-

each of 16 constituencies; Charlottetown elects 4 members and Summerside 2. Most of the constituencies are rural and small, many having no more than 2000 voters. In 1983 the government departments consisted of Energy and Forestry, Community and Cultural Affairs, Agriculture, Industry, Justice, Health and Social Service, Education, Finance and Tourism, Fisheries and Labour, and Transportation and Public Works. The judicial system consists of the Supreme Court, which has Estates, Family and Trial divisions and which sits on Appeals *en banc*, Provincial Courts and the Small Claims Court. There are no county courts in the province.

Local Government There are 3 levels of municipal government in the province: city, town and community. Charlottetown (inc 1855) is the only city, governed by a mayor and councillors, elected for 2-year terms. The 8 towns are Parkdale, Alberton, Borden, Georgetown, Kensington, Montague, Souris and Summerside, the largest and oldest. In 1983 there were 75 incorporated communities. The towns are governed by mayors and councillors and the communities by elected commissioners.

Federal Representation The Island is represented by 4 members of Parliament, elected from the ridings of Egmont, Malpeque, Hillsborough and Cardigan, and 4 senators. When PEI entered Confederation in 1873 it was entitled to 6 members, but declining population relative to the rest of Canada reduced this figure to 5 in 1892 and 4 in 1904, and by 1911 it was entitled to only 3 members. After vigorous protests, the BNA Act was amended in 1915, stating that no province should have fewer members of Parliament than senators. Thus, PEI was guaranteed its current 4 seats.

Public Finance Total provincial expenditures as of 31 Mar 1983 were $390 million. The largest departmental budget was education with $95.6 million, but health and social services, hospitals, and transportation and public works all exceeded $38 million each. Debt charges amounted to $51 million. In the same year, provincial revenues amounted to $373.9 million, 52% of which came from the federal government, $121.7 million in direct equalization payments. The dependence of the Island on federal funding is underlined by the fact that expenditures by the federal government, including payments to individuals, were more than one and one-half times the provincial budget.

Health The Island is reasonably well served by hospital and health facilities, especially since the introduction of a provincial health-care plan in the late 1960s, providing nonpremium medical and hospital services. The largest hospital is the new Queen Elizabeth Hospital in Charlottetown. There are 8 smaller hospitals in the province, with a total bed capacity for all Island hospitals in 1983 of 739. In 1983 there were 138 practising physicians in the province, a ratio of 1.11 physicians per 1000 people. As in other provinces, health-care costs have risen sharply in the last 10 years. For example, the cost of physicians' services rose from about $4.3 million in 1974 to $18.8 million in 1983, a cost per capita rise from $37 to over $110. Hospital costs rose in similar fashion from $102 per capita in 1974 to $331 per capita in 1983.

Politics The emergence of fairly stable political parties in PEI was a product of the 1870s. From that time to the present the Liberal and Conservative parties have dominated the electoral scene. Although a provincial NDP organization exists, and the CCF/NDP has run candidates in both provincial and federal elections since the 1940s, no third-party candidate has ever come close to gaining a seat in the legislature. When PEI entered Confederation it had a bicameral legislature, an upper house or council elected by property owners, and an assembly elected by universal male suffrage. As provinces moved in the late 19th century to abolish upper houses, a unique compromise emerged in PEI. A single Legislative Assembly was created in 1893, but for each constituency there was one candidate designated a councillor and one an assemblyman. Property owners elected the councillor and all males the assemblyman. Persons holding property in more than one riding could vote in each riding, a system that led to all manner of obvious abuses. This property qualification was maintained until 1963, and the practice of electing a councillor and an assemblyman from each district continues to the present. The franchise was extended to women in 1922. Because the population is almost equally split between Roman Catholics and Protestants a practice developed of ensuring that opposing candidates in provincial elections faced a coreligionist, but in recent years this tradition has weakened. Owing to the small size of constituencies and the nearly even division of political allegiances, elections tend to be decided by narrow margins. Each vote is important, and candidates stay in touch with their constituents, especially when patronage is to be distributed. The introduction of the secret ballot in 1913 reduced the impact of patronage but by no means eliminated it. Political issues have tended to be relatively low key. Governments more often change because the party in power has grown tired and it "is time to give the other guys a chance." Politics has become relatively more sophisticated in the past decade; television advertising and the emergence of "image" as an important factor have affected PEI as they have other provinces.

Education

The educational system of PEI has undergone revolutionary changes in the last decade. The public school system originated in the Free Education Act of 1852, which authorized the establishment of autonomous school districts based on local communities. Each of the 475 districts was entitled to a one-room school, usually offering grades one through 10. The school districts were governed by local boards, who collected taxes, hired teachers and organized volunteer services. Along with the church and the general store, schools became focal points in each community. This system served the Island well in the 19th and early 20th centuries, but began to show serious deficiencies by the 1920s and 1930s. Inadequate facilities, lack of opportunities to study beyond grade 10 (except for a fortunate few who could attend high school in Charlottetown) and poorly paid, underqualified teachers all began to reach public attention. By 1956 per capita expenditures for elementary and secondary education were the lowest in Canada — $92 compared with the $279 Canadian average — and by the 1960s the local schools, while providing an essential focus of community life, had fallen far behind Canadian educational norms.

The Comprehensive Development Plan provided the vehicle and the rationale for transforming the Island educational system. Beginning in 1970 the many small school districts were replaced by 5 regional boards, and the process of closing schools and building new, consolidated institutions began. In 1971 there were 245 schools; by 1979 there were 70. New regulations requiring university degrees for teachers were introduced, and teachers' salaries rose from an average of $5724 in 1971 to $28 166 by 1983. The facilities and opportunities available to Island students improved immeasurably as a result of the consolidation process. Yet much of the interaction of home and school and the cohesiveness of local communities has been lost.

In 1981-82 there were just over 28 000 children enrolled in the public school system. Expenditure on education has increased almost as dramatically as the number of schools has dropped, rising from $30.6 million in 1974 to $89.5 million in 1982.

Higher education in PEI began with the creation of Prince of Wales College (1834) and St Dunstan's University (1855). These 2 institutions remained small and separated along religious lines until they amalgamated as University of Prince Edward Island in 1969. This university was established as another phase of the Development Plan; it offers undergraduate programs in arts, science, education and business administration and will soon offer degrees in veterinary medicine. Approximately 1800 full-time and part-time students are enrolled. Holland College, created in 1969, is responsible for a wide range of vocational and occupational training programs at several locations throughout the province.

Cultural Life

The rich cultural heritage of Prince Edward Island developed as an integral part of the community partially because of the relative isolation of the province. Even within the province there was little communication between the Acadian communities in the western part of the Island and the predominantly Scots communities in the SE. Although the French language and Acadian culture have been strengthened in recent years, the Gaelic language has all but disappeared. Because of threats to the cultural life of the province many groups have emerged in recent years supporting aspects of the Island's cultural heritage. The provincial government's Department of Community and Cultural Affairs assists these groups and funds a wide variety of activities. The PEI Museum and Heritage Foundation, for example, not only administers historic sites, but is also active in collecting and interpreting material culture. The PEI Council of the Arts, a recently formed group, also assists and encourages local cultural development. Both Holland College and U of PEI are vital contributors to the contemporary cultural life of the Island.

Arts The Confederation Centre of the Arts was built as a memorial to the FATHERS OF CONFEDERATION in 1964 to mark the 100th anniversary of the CHARLOTTETOWN CONFERENCE. The centre is a major arts complex with theatres, an art gallery and a public library. The gallery has a fine collection of Canadian Art and features a large collection of the works of Robert HARRIS, a portraitist of the late 19th and early 20th century

A Meeting of the School Trustees (c 1885), oil on canvas, by Robert Harris, Prince Edward Island's best-known artist. The paper on the desk is inscribed "Roll/Pine Creek School/Kate Henderson/Teachers" (courtesy National Gallery of Canada).

whose most notable work is the group portrait of the Fathers of Confederation. The theatre is home to the Charlottetown Summer Festival, a showcase of Canadian musical theatre. Recent years have seen the growth of community theatre productions across the province. Summer stock theatres operate in the communities of Victoria and Georgetown. At present there is an active artistic community on the Island and in addition to the Confederation Centre Gallery there are several other private and public galleries. While the province has been the home or birthplace of a large number of popular or academic writers, none is so well known as Lucy Maud MONTGOMERY, author of ANNE OF GREEN GABLES. Most of Montgomery's stories are set on the Island and each year thousands of visitors come to the Island to see places mentioned in her books or associated with her life.

Communications PEI is served by an English-language CBC radio station and by English- and French-language CBC television. The CTV television network also covers the Island but is not produced locally. Two private radio stations broadcast in Charlottetown and one operates in Summerside. Cable television systems operate in all Island population centres, offering a wide range of programs, mostly of US origin. There are 3 daily newspapers published in the province: the *Guardian* (morning) and the *Patriot* (evening) in Charlottetown and the *Journal-Pioneer* in Summerside. The liveliest newspapers are the weekly *Eastern Graphic* published in Montague and the *West Prince Graphic* published in Alberton. *La Voix acadienne* is a French-language weekly produced in Summerside.

Historic Sites Of PEI's many important historic sites, the best known is Province House, the location of the Charlottetown Conference of 1864. Government House, the residence of the lieutenant-governor, is a fine early 19th-century building, which has been carefully refurbished. Other sites include Green Gables, the L.M. Montgomery home at Cavendish, and heritage sites operated by the Museum and Heritage Foundation at Port Hill, Basin Head and Orwell Corner. A visitor can appreciate much of the Island's architectural heritage by simply walking in the older areas of Charlottetown or Summerside, or by driving along the country roads. Many fine examples of both rural and urban buildings from the last century are still intact and functional.

History

The first inhabitants of Prince Edward Island were the precursors of the Micmac. These native people may have occupied sites on PEI as much as 10 000 years ago by crossing the low plain now covered by Northumberland Strait. Occupation since that time has most likely been continuous, although there are some indications that there may have been seasonal migrations to

hunt and fish on the Island as well. The Micmac have inhabited the area for the last 2000 years.

Exploration The first European to record seeing the Island was Jacques Cartier, who landed at several spots on the N shore during his explorations of the gulf in the summer of 1534. Although there was to be no permanent settlement for almost 200 years, the harbours and bays were known to French and BASQUE fishermen, but no trace of their visits has survived.

Settlement French settlement of the Island (then known as as Île St-Jean) began in the 1720s with the colony being a dependency of Île Royale, although a small garrison was stationed near what is now Charlottetown. Settlement was slow with the population in 1748 reaching just over 700. However, with increasing British pressure on the Acadian inhabitants of Nova Scotia culminating in the decision to expel them in 1755, the population of the Island was significantly increased. Some 5000 settlers were on the Island at the fall of LOUISBOURG in 1758 but the British quickly forced all but a few hundred to leave, even though the colony was not ceded to them until the TREATY OF PARIS, 1763.

Under the British administration the name of the Island was anglicized to the Island of Saint John. This was the first of the new possessions to benefit from a plan to survey all of the territory in N America. Surveyor General Samuel HOLLAND was able to provide detailed plans of the Island by 1765. He had divided it into 67 townships of 20 000 acres each. Almost all of these were granted as the result of a lottery held in 1767 to military officers and others to whom the British government owed favours. With the exception of small areas surrounding the land allotted for towns, there was no crown land. The proprietors were required to settle their lands to fulfil the terms of their grants, but few made an effort to do so. As a result the Island had vast areas of undeveloped land, yet those who wished to open up farms often had to pay steep rents or purchase fees. Some proprietors refused to sell land at all and settlers found that they had no more security of tenure than they formerly had as tenants in England or Scotland. Further, the costs of the administration of the Island were to be borne by a tax paid by the proprietors on the land they held. This was often impossible to collect, and efforts made by the local government to enforce the terms of the grants were usually overruled by the British government under the influence of the landowners, most of whom never set foot in the colony. The LAND QUESTION was the dominating political concern from 1767 until Confederation. Confrontation between the agents of the proprietors and the tenants frequently led to violence, and attempts to change the system were blocked in England. During the 1840s the government was able to buy out some of the landowners and make the land available for purchase by the tenants, but funds available for this purpose were quickly exhausted.

In spite of these difficulties the population grew from just over 4000 in 1798 to 62 000 around 1850. Although there was an influx of LOYALISTS after the American Revolution the majority of the newcomers were from the British Isles. Several large groups were brought from Scotland in the late 1700s and early 1800s by landowners such as Captain John MacDonald and Lord SELKIRK, and by 1850 the Irish represented a sizable proportion of the recent immigrants.

Colonial Government After 1758 the Island had been governed as part of Nova Scotia, but in 1769, following representations made by the proprietors, a separate administration was set up complete with governor, lieutenant-governor, Council and Assembly. In 1799 the name of the colony was changed by the Assembly to Prince Edward Island to honour a son of

This pencil and ink drawing by Robert Harris illustrates events on election day in Charlottetown in the late 19th century (*courtesy Confederation Centre Art Gallery and Museum*).

King George III stationed with the army in Halifax at the time. With rapid growth in the second quarter of the 19th century, demands came for more effective control over the affairs of the colony by the elected Assembly. Although the concept of representative government had been accepted since 1773 the administration was still dominated by the appointed Executive Council. In 1851 RESPONSIBLE GOVERNMENT was granted to the colony and the first elected administration under George COLES took office. The period was not a politically stable one, however, for in the next 22 years a total of 12 governments were in office. The land question continued unresolved and in addition matters such as assistance to religious schools divided the population.

Confederation The Charlottetown Conference of 1864, the first in a series of meetings leading to Confederation, was held in the colony, and it marked the beginning of a period of political change that would leave a deep imprint. The meeting had been called to discuss maritime union, but when visiting representatives from Canada began to promote a larger union the original proposal failed to capture the imagination of Islanders. When the other British North American colonies joined in the new federation in 1867, few people in PEI regretted not being part of the union. The aloofness of the Islanders, however, could not last for long. A massive debt incurred by the Islanders in building a railway running from one end of the colony to the other, combined with pressures from the British government and Canadian promises, pushed the Island into Confederation in 1873. The enticements held out by the Canadians included an absorption of the colony's debt, year-round communication with the mainland, and the provision of funds with which the colony could buy out the proprietors and end the land question. Although few Islanders displayed much enthusiasm, most accepted the union as a marriage of necessity.

Post-Confederation The post-Confederation period brought severe blows to the Island's economy and population as new technology, the National Policy and other forces combined to reduce the Island's prosperity. Although the province reached a population level of 109 000 in 1891, the lure of employment in western and central Canada and in the US led to a drain on

the population, which had slipped to 88 000 by the time of the GREAT DEPRESSION. Dominion-provincial relations dominated the political sphere as the Island sought to increase its subsidy from Ottawa, retain the level of political representation it had enjoyed at Confederation, and finally establish the continuous communication with the mainland that had been promised in 1873. Throughout the first half of the 20th century the economy of the province was stable, with only slight changes in both farming and fishing. By the mid-1960s, however, the situation had changed considerably. The number of farmers and fishermen had dropped and the economy, which had lagged behind that of the rest of Canada, was in serious trouble. The 20th century has forced Islanders to give up more and more of their cherished independence, but it has also brought with it better lives for almost all Islanders, at least in material terms. Education, health and social support programs, higher incomes and greater mobility have had a price, but it is one that most Islanders have been willing to pay. Though Islanders might still regard the rest of the world as being "from away," they are also securely a part of Canada.   S. ANDREW ROBB AND H.T. HOLMAN

Prince George, BC, City, pop 67 559 (1981c), inc 1915, is situated in the geographical centre of BC at the junction of the NECHAKO and FRASER rivers, 784 km NE of VANCOUVER. The first white person in the region was Alexander MACKENZIE, who passed through on his journey to the Pacific coast in 1793. Simon FRASER also passed the site in 1806 during his exploration of the Fraser. The next year he established a trading post for the North West Co at the confluence of the Nechako and Fraser rivers and named it Fort George after George III of England. From 1814 Fort George, which was not closed until 1915, was on the Brigade Trail from Stuart Lk in the N to the forts in the S. It remained outside the area settled during the gold rush of the 1860s, though the main party of the OVERLANDERS led by R.B. McMicking passed that way on their way down the Fraser to

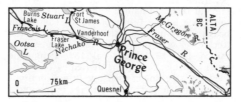

the Cariboo goldfields in 1862. Settlement in the region was negligible until the land boom during construction of the Grand Trunk Pacific Ry (now part of CNR) 1908-20. For a period various neighbouring townsites vied for dominance, with the railway townsite eventually winning out. The town's name was changed to Prince George after a referendum held during the first civic election (1915). Growth of the city was slow until after WWII when a booming forest industry brought prosperity and rapid growth to the region. Between 1961 and 1981 Prince George grew from a rough mill town to the major manufacturing, supply and government administration centre for N-central BC. By 1980 the city had 3 pulp mills and 17 producing sawmills.

Prince George is also an important transportation centre. It is a subdivisional point on the Jasper/Prince Rupert CNR line and an important station for the BC Ry, formerly the Pacific Great Eastern Ry (PGE). For many years it was the northern terminus for the PGE, until the line was extended into northern BC. The city is a major highway junction and the airport is served by both Pacific Western and Canadian Pacific airlines.   JOHN STEWART

Prince of Wales Island, 33 338 km², eighth largest in the ARCTIC ARCHIPELAGO. Composed almost entirely of sedimentary bedrock formations, its northern part is hilly, reaching up to 415 m; the rest is gently undulating. The vegetation is sparse polar desert and semidesert, but well-vegetated broad valleys occur, especially in the E. Muskoxen are common, mainly in the NE. Peary caribou are also common, especially in the N. The shores of the island were explored during the FRANKLIN SEARCH expeditions in 1851 under Capt T.H. Austin and in 1852 under William Kennedy.   S.C. ZOLTAI

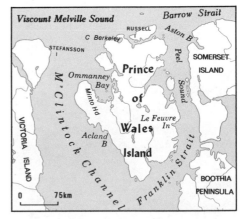

Prince of Wales Strait is situated in the ARCTIC ARCHIPELAGO between the uplands of western VICTORIA I and the E coast of BANKS I. About 275 km long and generally about 20 km wide, its depths reach 160 m at the southern end and become progressively shallower towards the northern entrance. The NE-SW orientation prevents prevailing winds from driving heavy pack ice down the strait, which is primarily covered with locally formed ice that breaks up more readily, leaving a reasonably clear channel. Linking Viscount Melville Sound and Amundsen Gulf, the strait is one of 4 possible routes in the NORTHWEST PASSAGE and was first surveyed by a land party led by McClure in 1850, though it was not navigated until the RCMP patrol of Sgt LARSEN in 1944 (*see* ST. ROCH). It has since become the preferred route of large vessels making the passage.   DOUG FINLAYSON

Prince of Wales Trophy is awarded annually to the team finishing first in the Prince of Wales Conference of the NATIONAL HOCKEY LEAGUE. It was donated by the Prince of Wales to the NHL in

1924. From 1927-28 to 1937-38 it was presented to the first-place team of the American Division, and from 1938-39 to 1967-68 to the team finishing first in the NHL overall. It became a divisional trophy again after expansion in 1967-68, going at first to the East Division and now to the Prince of Wales Conference. JAMES MARSH

Prince of Wales's Fort (Ft Churchill) In 1686 HUDSON'S BAY COMPANY men sailed into the CHURCHILL R, but it was not until 1717 that James Knight built a permanent post there, about 11 km from the mouth. Two years later it was named Prince of Wales's Fort. The company was interested not only in furs, but also in establishing a whaling industry. Fear of a sea attack by the French led the HBC to construct a stone fort that would command the entrance to Churchill R. By Aug 1731 tradesmen had picketed the fort, which was 91.4 m square, on Eskimo Point. The walls of the original ramparts were completed in 1739, and the following year HBC Gov Richard Norton moved to the new site. Work on the fort appears to have been practically continuous until 1771. In Aug 1782, 3 French ships and about 300 men, under command of the comte de Lapérouse, arrived at the mouth of the Churchill R. The fort was easily captured; its masonry was poor and Samuel HEARNE, governor of the fort, had insufficient men to operate its 42 guns. Hearne and the men were taken prisoners. Before sailing, Lapérouse spiked the cannon and blew up the buildings. Hearne returned in 1783 to build a post farther up the river. Ft Prince of Wales was left until 1934-35 when the Canadian government had the cannon dug up and remounted and the walls repaired. Today the partially restored fort is one of the main tourist attractions in CHURCHILL, Man. *See* HISTORIC SITE. SHIRLEE ANNE SMITH

Prince of Wales's Fort, later called Ft Prince of Wales, was first established in 1717. Restoration work was begun 1934-35 and the fort is now a tourist attraction (*courtesy Hudson's Bay Company Archives/R.V. Oleson*).

Prince Patrick Island, 15 848 km², is the farthest W of Canada's Arctic QUEEN ELIZABETH IS. Topographically, it is a low-elevation, dissected plateau that rises gently from an exceptionally low coast to a maximum elevation in the SE of only 200 m. It lies within the Sverdrup Basin geological structure and consists of thick beds of Upper Devonian deposits, dipping at a shallow angle to the SW. During the Tertiary, the island was uplifted and faulting occurred. The area is still seismically active, and tectonic movement

along the faults appears at surface as fissures and small scarps. A thin strip of sand and gravel deposits of nonglacial origin was laid down along the island's Arctic Ocean coastline during the early Pleistocene. The island was named for Prince Arthur William Patrick, duke of Connaught, governor general 1911-16.
DOUG FINLAYSON

Prince Rupert, BC, City, pop 16 197 (1981c), inc 1910, is situated on Kaien I, at the mouth of the SKEENA R in the Coast Mtn range of the NORTHWEST COAST of BC, 1520 km by road NW of Vancouver (720 km by air) and 730 km W of Prince George. Kaien I was once the meeting place of the TSIMSHIAN and HAIDA and the city has preserved numerous relics of its native past. The western terminus of Yellowhead 16 Hwy and, as a seaport, a link between the US, Vancouver and Alaska, it is the industrial, commercial and institutional centre for BC's northwest.

Prince Rupert (named for the first HBC governor) was envisioned in the early 1900s as the western terminus of the Grand Trunk Pacific Ry and as a rival of Vancouver as Canada's Pacific outlet, but the hoped-for boom never materialized. The fishing industry became important to the city's economy after WWI. During WWII the port became a shipbuilding centre and was used by the American army as a transportation base for men and materials to Alaska, the Pacific Is and the Far East. New interest in the coalfields of northeastern BC and strategies to speed up grain movement to the Prairies' Pacific Rim markets have affected the city and led to the construction of new terminal facilities. In addition, Prince Rupert is the most important fish-landing port on the N coast, headquarters for the vast Prince Rupert Forest Dist and the terminus of the BC and Alaska ferry systems.
ALAN F.J. ARTIBISE
Reading: P. Bowman, *Prince Rupert* (1973); R.G. Large, *Prince Rupert: Gateway to Alaska* (1960).

Princess Sheila According to popular accounts, Sheila Na Geira Pike was an Irish princess captured and married by a naval-officer-turned-pirate, Gilbert Pike, in the early 17th century. Her adventurous husband established a homestead in Carbonear, Conception Bay, where Pikes today recount tales of their beautiful, proud and aristocratic ancestor. Throughout Newfoundland, she is sometimes associated with various weather conditions such as Sheila's Brush.
CAROLE H. CARPENTER

Princeton, BC, Town, pop 3051 (1981c), inc 1951, is located at the junction of the Tulameen and Similkameen rivers, 70 km W of Penticton. Originally known as Vermilion or Red Earth Forks, it was also called Similkameen and Allisons. It became a stop on the pack trail from Fort Colvile to Fort Hope after the OREGON TREATY. John Fall Allison established a ranch 1859 and lived there until 1900, discovering coal and copper in the area. James DOUGLAS had a townsite laid out 1860 and named it in honour of a visit to Canada by the Prince of Wales. The region boasts a long mining history, starting with the Rock Creek gold rush in the 1860s. Copper was mined 1878-1957 and coal 1898-1950. The nearby Nickle Plate Mine at Hedley benefited the town. Opening of the Hope-Princeton highway in 1949 helped to offset mine closures and a

brewery shutdown in 1961. Princeton contains many promising copper properties and coal and low-grade iron ore. Tourism and agriculture supplement mining, and a large sawmill opened in 1976. WILLIAM A. SLOAN

Print Industry, the process of producing multiple copies or reproductions, is traditionally associated with a printing press, but may also describe photographic or electrostatic copier processes of duplication. In the 20th century the print medium has become but one part of a complex and rapidly changing COMMUNICATIONS process. Within its own area, printing is allied with the graphic arts industry, which involves preparation, actual press work and finishing procedures.

Prior to the printing process, of putting impressions on paper, foil, plastic or cloth, there are pre-press procedures such as design, artwork, layout, creation of type or graphics, film and platemaking, and press makeready. In the past all these processes were done by hand or camera. Today, type is set by microcomputer phototypesetters and can be produced in negative or positive film as an automatic process. It can be stored and retrieved from magnetic tape or discs, and manipulated into any form. Pagination systems can combine halftone or line graphics, type and page layout in a single process. Little handwork is done after the creation of the written script or the artist's finished work. The newer equipment can combine these elements into a page, produce a printing plate automatically, and send the information by wire or SATELLITE to any distant point. The GLOBE AND MAIL national edition is transmitted by satellite to locations across Canada, where it is printed and distributed. CABLE TELEVISION connections and videotex are augmenting or replacing print in many areas as a means of transmitting information (*see* TELIDON).

There are 4 major printing processes: the letterpress, or relief printing method, in which printing areas are raised above nonprinting areas and the impression is made directly from the inked raised surface to the substrate or paper; the planographic, or offset, lithographic system, in which the image and nonimage areas lie on the same plane but are distinguished by application of the principle that grease and water do not mix; the intaglio or gravure system, by which the image is engraved into the cylindrical or flat plate surface, then inked and printed on to the substrate; the screenprinting or serigraphy process, in which ink is pushed through a screen to the substrate. In recent years, other methods of producing multiple copies from one master have been developed: flexography, a raised image system using rubber plates and aniline inks; electrostatic printing, either in a photocopier or through a fine screen; and jet ink printing, in which tiny globules of ink are jetted on to the substrate, often prompted by a computer or magnetic tape. Laser beam printing is now commercially successful, and electro-erosion printing is a strong probability for the future.

Beyond the press are the bindery or finishing procedures, many of them in-line with the press as a continuing operation. These steps could include folding, stitching and trimming on computerized cutters or cutting equipment on-press; or they may involve punching, perforating for tearaway, fan folding as in business forms, collating many signatures, round-cornering, adding carbon sheets, varnishing, laminating and embossing.

History Wooden handpresses (flatbed or "common" presses) imported from the US or Great Britain introduced printing to eastern Canada in the 1750s and were replaced only in the 1830s in large centres by the iron Washington handpress. The first known press was established in Halifax by Bartholomew Green, Jr, of Boston in 1751; his partner, John Bushell, launched the first Canadian newspaper, the *Halifax Gazette*, in 1752. Following the outbreak of the American Revolution, in 1776, a large number of skilled LOYALIST printers arrived from New England, and by the mid-1780s there were presses in Saint John and Charlottetown. In Québec City the 2 most important printing pioneers were William Brown and Thomas Gilmore, who founded the *Quebec Gazette* in 1764. In addition to the newspaper, the printing shop produced calendars, order forms and eventually pamphlets and books. Fleury Mesplet, who had learned the printing trade in France, brought the first press to Montréal in 1776. Initially, he produced religious works, but in 1778 began publishing the *Montreal Gazette (Gazette du commerce et littéraire)*. After John Graves SIMCOE was appointed lieutenant-governor of Upper Canada in 1791, he convinced Louis Roy, a French Canadian, to establish his press in Newark [Niagara-on-the-Lake], the capital of the province. Although Roy's stay was brief, he started the province's first paper, the *Upper Canada Gazette*, in 1793. Because there was little commerce in Canada, printers relied heavily on newspaper subscriptions, government patronage (the printing of proclamations and laws) and the church (the production of countless tracts that arose from the religious controversies of the era).

It was missionary zeal that introduced printing to the West. In 1841 Methodist pastor James EVANS compiled a system of syllabic signs for the Cree language. When he was unable to get financing for a printing press, he cut molds in wood, melted the lead linings of old tea boxes into characters, constructed a handpress and, using ink made of soot, printed his book on birchbark. Commercial printing in the RED RIVER COLONY began in 1859 when William Buckingham and William Coldwell began publishing the *Nor'-Wester*. Printing in BC originated with the founding of the *Victoria Gazette* in 1858. Its presses also printed various government proclamations. In 1878 Patrick Laurie founded the *Saskatchewan Herald* in Battleford, and in 1880 Frank OLIVER took a press by oxcart from Winnipeg to Edmonton and began publication of the *Edmonton Bulletin*. The first press arrived in Dawson, YT, in 1897 to print the *Caribou Sun*.

Until the 1830s, printers in Canada looked to the US or Great Britain for their presses and ink, type and paper supplies. The cylinder press, for example, developed in the US in the 1830s, was adopted during the next decade by large circulation NEWSPAPERS in Canada. George BROWN bought the first such press in Canada West for his *Globe* in Aug 1844. Paper was first made in the Toronto area from rags in 1826 by Eastwood and Skinner, and Alexander Buntin is credited with introducing the groundwood process to N America in his Valleyfield mill. The Montreal Type Foundry (TTF) opened in the 1830s and, until it closed 40 years later, was among the earliest producers of type in Canada and a supplier of both imported and domestic presses. In 1887 the Toronto Type Foundry (TTF) was established, an indication that the centre of the printing industry had moved from Montréal to Toronto, and by 1898 had branches across the country from Halifax to Vancouver. The TTF used American matrices exclusively, and it was only in 1967 that Carl DAIR created Cartier, the first Canadian-designed type face (*see* GRAPHIC DESIGN). Of the few manufacturers of printing presses in Canada, none were as commercially successful or long lived as Westman and Baker of Toronto. Producing Gordon presses (invented by the American G.P. Gordon in 1858) from 1874 to 1922, the business also manufactured a wide variety of printers' and bookbinders' equipment which was distributed nationwide. Two models of Linotype machine were built in Canada, the first manufactured by the Linotype

Co in Montréal in 1891 and the second by the Canadian-American Linotype Co Ltd of Toronto after it acquired the Montréal firm. Both models were exported to Australia, S America and S Africa in competition with Mergenthaler Linotype of the US.

As print shops proliferated between 1810 and 1830, printers' societies or unions were formed in Québec City, Montréal, Hamilton and Toronto. In 1832, for example, a group of 24 journeymen printers set up the York Typographical Society to fight for better conditions; the union failed after bitter struggles, but was revived in 1844 and, as the Toronto Typographical Union, is today the oldest trade union in Canada. At first these unions represented workers who set type, ran letterpresses, or did hand bindery, but as new equipment was introduced and typesetting and presswork became increasingly mechanized, the unions began to represent specific crafts, so that by the late 19th century there were unions of pressmen, compositors, stereotypers, mailers and bookbinders. By 1900 they had created federations such as the Toronto Allied Printing Trades Council in the larger cities. In 1892 John Bayne MACLEAN founded the *Canadian Printer and Publisher* as a monthly magazine, designed as the official organ of the Canadian Press Assn.

The final 3 decades of the 19th century saw a great number of technological changes in printing in Canada. W.A. Leggo and G.E. Desbarets of Montréal are credited with having invented the halftone process of graphic reproduction in 1871 and, although others have also claimed this honour, there is no doubt that these Canadians played an important role in its development. In 1873 the weekly *Grip* was founded and became the first paper to make its own engravings. Its production manager, Samuel Moore, left the company in 1882 to found Moore Business Forms to make and sell the carbon flipover Paragon Sales book. In 1905 *Grip* made the first 4-colour plates in Canada, and thereafter consumer MAGAZINES saw a greater use of colour in advertising and illustrations.

Contemporary Developments Commercial printing, publishing and printer-publishing have enjoyed an unspectacular but steady growth in the years following WWII. In the industry that Statistics Canada calls Print, Publishing & Allied Industries (which includes platemaking, typesetting and trade bindery companies), the number of establishments grew from 3650 in 1970 to 4639 in 1982. The number of employees increased from 84 041 to 106 588, with wages and salaries of $2.28 billion. Selling value of shipments swelled from $1.5 billion to $6.76 billion. At the same time, many "instant printing" shops have opened, and industries not concerned with printing have established in-plant printing and finishing plants, now a substantial part of the print supply business. Consequently the number of commercial printing plants have shown little increase, slowed to some extent by amalgamations and acquisitions by larger companies and the development of institutional and government printing plants.

Canada makes a great deal of paper, much of it in the form of newsprint exported to the US and the Caribbean, but it also imports many fine papers (*see* PULP AND PAPER INDUSTRY). Most ink used in Canadian printing, publishing and package houses, including in-plant shops, is made in Canada. Two companies, one in Québec and one in Cambridge, Ont, design and manufacture business forms, presses and decollators. An Ontario company creates and manufactures folding, inserting, high-speed imprinting and paper-cutting machines. Nearly all this production is exported, mainly to Europe, Asia and the US. A small computer invented in Toronto will convert noncomputer cutters and guillotines to automated computer operation. A domestic

market has been created, but exports will account for the majority of business. Some labelling equipment is also manufactured in Canada. In 1974 Mitel Corporation was established in Kanata, Ont, to invent and distribute microelectronic devices for electronic communications, and was the first to develop complete in-house publishing using laser (Xerox 9700). The Mitel systems have been adopted worldwide and are used by many US manufacturers in the production of communications systems.

In 1981 Canada exported graphic arts machinery, parts and supplies worth $37.3 million. Imports in this category to Canada from all other countries were valued at $295.4 million. In the years 1982 to 1987 it is estimated that Canada will import more than $1.75 billion in printing and subsidiary graphic equipment, parts and supplies. *See also* ALMANACS; BOOK PUBLISHING; PRINTMAKING.   WILLIAM FORBES

Reading: Canadian Printer and Publisher (May 1967); L.B. Duff, *Journey of the Printing Press across Canada* (1937); A. Fauteux, *The Introduction of Printing into Canada* (1930); J.N. Field et al, eds, *Graphic Arts Manual* (1980); J. Gibson and L. Lewis, ed, *Sticks and Stones: Some Aspects of Canadian Printing History* (1980); H.P. Gundy, *Early Printers and Printing in the Canadas* (1964); V. Strauss, *The Printing Industry* (1967); M. Tremaine, *Early Printing in Canada* (1934).

Printmaking, which encompasses the production of images by any one of the numerous processes of intaglio, relief, planographic and screenprinting techniques, has a long and complex history in Canada. Both the evolution of printmaking techniques and artistic innovation on the N American continent play major roles in this history, but the records of these developments are scattered, rare and often nonexistent.

There seems to have been little demand for printed images in New France, and what was needed for educational or religious purposes was invariably imported from Europe. Certainly no examples remain of any Canadian-produced prints from the French regime in Canada up to 1760. The earliest printmaking coincided with British attempts to conquer Canada in the mid-1750s and was closely related to the printed word. In 1751 a printing press was established at Halifax, but it was a flatbed type, imported from Britain or the American colonies and was incapable of printing images other than small vignette woodcuts used for advertising or announcements. With the end of the SEVEN YEARS' WAR in 1763 England sought to colonize its newly won territories by encouraging skilled tradesmen to emigrate from Europe and America. Among these immigrants were some from southern Germany who had the knowledge and ability to make prints. The result was the appearance of a woodcut *View of Halifax* in the *Nova Scotia Calender* of 1777 published by an Alsatian émigré to Halifax, Anthon Henrich. He published similar and more elaborate woodcuts in succeeding decades in both English- and German-language versions of his calendar, as did another German émigré, Christopher Sauer (or Sower), whose prints were issued in New Brunswick calendars published in Saint John from 1786 onwards. Unfortunately, this early

Printing and Allied Industries, 1982		
Province	Establishments	Shipments ($)
Newfoundland	26	24 731 000
PEI	10	2 324 000
NS	86	75 534 000
NB	55	46 625 000
Québec	1 269	1 909 296 000
Ontario	20 008	3 359 969 000
Manitoba	172	246 939 000
Sask	125	111 412 000
Alberta	404	473 549 000
BC	478	506 662 000
YT & NWT	6	2 218 000

woodcut tradition did not outlast the 18th century, since it was only a sideline to the more serious venture of book and ALMANAC publications.

Instead, artistic impetus and public approbation for the art of printmaking grew in the region of Québec City, the centre of the British Empire in the northern half of the continent. Here British officers and officials were headquartered, and lively interest in the arts, expressed primarily in watercolour sketching, was maintained (*see* TOPOGRAPHIC PAINTING). Many military artists (most notably Thomas Davies, Edward Walsh and George Fisher) brought topographic sketches back to England to be engraved and published prior to the WAR OF 1812, but there were also a few experiments in etching and engraving carried out by officers while stationed in Canada. James PEACHEY, a member of the surveyor general's staff, executed a small copperplate etching of the MONTMORENCY FALLS in 1779, of which only the plate itself exists. George HERIOT, deputy postmaster general of British N America, a prolific artist and author of several English publications illustrated with his own works relating to Canada, also experimented with etching. Heriot was associated with Samuel and John Neilson, the publishers of the *Quebec Magazine,* in which one of Heriot's etched and aquatinted views appeared in 1792. The Neilsons made the first serious attempt to establish professional printmaking in Canada in that year by importing a rolling or intaglio press and hiring the German émigré printer J.G. Hochstetter to produce a series of views, portraits and allegorical prints for their publications in the early 1790s. The Neilson press was probably responsible for a number of single-sheet broadsides and other prints that appeared during this decade, but by the turn of the century such productions had virtually ceased. For the next decade, no work in professional printmaking seems to have taken place, evidently because Canada had neither the population nor the prosperity to support such activity before the War of 1812. Newfound wealth brought about by a war economy, a rising tide of immigration, and an enriched national fabric derived from the conflict with the US would all combine to allow artistic developments to flourish in the second decade of the 19th century. In the interim, various professional and amateur artists were experimenting with printmaking for their private amusement or satisfaction, including William von Moll BERCZY, Elizabeth SIMCOE and Judge Alexander Croke, an Admiralty court official in Halifax, all of whom made Canadian-inspired etchings that have survived to the present day.

The next phase of professional printmaking occurred in Halifax where Robert Field, an English-born artist resident since 1808, executed and published an etching copied from his full-length oil portrait of Lt-Gov Sir John Sherbrooke in 1816. The print was probably produced on an intaglio press owned by Charles W. Torbett, a local printer specializing in books and maps, who also executed portrait prints, club certificates and book illustrations. His press was probably the one on which a set of 4 coloured aquatint etchings showing views of public buildings in Halifax was printed in 1819 by John Elliott Woolford, official draftsman to Lord Dalhousie, Sherbrooke's successor.

Though Halifax after 1815 was the new centre for printmaking developments, tentative renewals of the art were occurring in Lower Canada. A few prints were published between 1815 and 1820 by isolated firms specializing in jewellery or metalware engraving, but not until the mid-1820s did professional printers establish themselves. In Québec, D. Smillie & Sons were patronized by the local elite after setting up in business in 1822 or 1823, while Montréal by 1829 saw the beginning of the long career

in printmaking and publishing of Adolphus Bourne. Apparently never an active printer himself, Bourne worked in conjunction with a number of artists and engravers, including William S. Leney, Robert A. Sproule, Charles Crehen and John Murray, in producing over 50 separately issued prints (etchings, engravings and lithographs) before Confederation.

Amateur work in printmaking by military artists continued and was stimulated by the decision of the British government in 1807 to purchase the rights to Aloys Senefelders's lithographic process for use in its official establishments throughout the empire. By 1824 Québec City had a press, and lithographic prints of both a public and private nature were widely produced and diffused by the 1830s. Lithography represented a great advance for would-be printmakers because it was easy to operate the press and to copy images. Lithography would become the dominant type of printmaking in Canada from the 1840s onwards, but it was not introduced professionally until 1831, when Samuel O. Tazewell, an English-born printer who had emigrated to Kingston, built himself a press and sought out local varieties of limestone for use in his operations. Tazewell, after producing an image of the Chaudière bridges in Ottawa in Jan 1832, moved to York [Toronto] in hopes of becoming the province's official printer. There he produced several single-sheet prints for sale and worked in conjunction with the artists George D'Almaine and Henry Bonnycastle until his hopes for official patronage were dashed in the politics of the day. In 1835 he retired to St Catharines to resume his former occupation as a watch and clock repairman, and apparently never printed again.

Other printers, including Bourne, Hugh Greene and George Matthews of Montréal, and Napoleon Aubin of Québec City, rapidly followed Tazewell's example in printing and publishing lithographic views and portraits in the late 1830s and 1840s. Matthews worked with the artist James Duncan to produce a set of 6 lithographed views of Montréal in 1843, following Bourne's format of a set of engraved views published 13 years earlier, while Aubin published prints of local politicians and celebrities, St-Jean-Baptiste Society dinners and a portrait of Bishop LAVAL.

In the Maritimes the proximity of the great printmaking centre of Boston had a strong influence on local development. As artists such as William Eagar and Mary G. Hall took their work to Boston to be lithographed in the mid-1830s, interest in printmaking withered, not to be revived until the late 1850s. The same was not true of Toronto, which in the 1840s saw a rapid expansion in the field. The most prominent enthusiast was Scottish-born Hugh Scobie, who set up business in 1838. Working with several artists, including John Gillespie, John HOWARD and Sandford FLEMING, and in partnership with John Balfour from 1846 to 1850, Scobie published a number of beautiful and well-received prints until his early death in 1853. Another pioneer was John Ellis, an English printer who opened a shop in 1843, publishing lithographic views until his retirement in 1868 (*see also* PRINT INDUSTRY).

By the 1850s many large printing companies had been established in Toronto, Montréal, Québec City, Ottawa and elsewhere. Technological developments such as the steam-driven rotary press, colour lithography and wood engraving stimulated the demand, production and market for prints to prodigious levels, but the quality of these prints was generally inferior. Thus, an artist like Cornelius KRIEGHOFF, in seeking a printer who could reproduce his pictures, turned first to a firm in Munich, and then in New York, to carry out the work. Paul KANE found the Toronto firm of Fuller & Benecke (or Bencke) able

to produce a remarkably beautiful multiple colour woodblock print of his *Death of Big Snake.* Kane did not repeat this exciting achievement and the firm soon failed, a victim of economic circumstances and the trend towards the industrialization of printing techniques.

Canadian artists were becoming increasingly frustrated with their role in printmaking in the 1860s and 1870s, as commercial concerns, technological innovations and the advent of photography reduced them to the status of craftsmen, especially in the larger centres of Montréal and Toronto. At the same time, they were becoming more conscious of their place within Canadian society. Native-born artists were also learning from immigrants about a new attitude towards printmaking that had developed in Great Britain and France. Known as the "Etching Revival," the movement was espoused by artists such as Alphonse Legros and the American James Whistler. These men began to treat the print, not as a method of reproducing images created in other mediums or solely as an illustration, but as a work of art unto itself, of which the artist was not only the designer but also the maker of the plate, the printer and the publisher. This radical new direction also involved the concept of limited editions of prints, each numbered and signed by the artist and able to stand on its own merit. As these ideas spread and artists elsewhere, including in Canada, took them up, a dichotomy arose between the fine-art print and the reproductive or commercial print that remains the case even today.

Early Canadian manifestations of the movement occurred among Canadian artists studying abroad. Among the first was Elizabeth Armstrong Forbes, who studied with the Art Students League in New York before going on to London, Munich and Brittany, where she began etching at Pont Aven in 1882. Her example influenced such artists as Charles Henry White, who studied with Whistler in England, and Clarence GAGNON, who went to Paris in 1904 and in the next 5 years developed an international reputation as an etcher/artist. Regrettably, none of these artists had much influence in their native country; Forbes and White both remained abroad, while Gagnon abandoned etching upon his return to Canada in 1909, although he gained a considerable reputation as a painter.

In Canada a number of events occurred that also gave an impetus to fine-art printmaking. The publication of *Picturesque Canada* in 1882, which featured the work of a number of American artists as well as employing several Canadians, including J. Henry Sandham, Lucius O'BRIEN and John A. FRASER, had a twofold effect: it demonstrated the potential of the print medium as a means of displaying the beauty of the Canadian landscape; and it evoked a conscious desire among Canadian artists to train themselves in the skills of fine-art printmaking. The relative neglect of the print medium by the Royal Canadian Academy and the Ontario Society of Artists also had an effect. As the ideas of the "Etching Revival" spread, it was inevitable that its influence would be felt in Canada, particularly in Toronto, where the Assn of Canadian Etchers was formed in 1885. The association was made up of several British émigré artists, including Arthur Cox, William Cruikshank and Thomas Mower Martin, as well as the younger Canadian artists William W. Alexander, Henry S. Howland and William J. Thomson. As an organization, they sponsored an exhibition of their work and of earlier European masters; it failed because of financial problems and public indifference but set the example for the development of similar artists' groups in Toronto. In 1886 the Toronto Art Students' League, loosely based on similar American and English artists' societies, was formed with the purpose of meeting once a week for life study and composition classes. The league lasted until 1904, and included printmakers William J. Thomson, John Cotton, later known for his exquisite aquatints, W.W. Alexander, Alfred H. Howard and William D. Blatchly, as well as artist/illustrators John D. Kelly, Charles M. Manly, R. Weir Crouch, Charles W. JEFFERYS and Fred Brigden. The league provided a congenial atmosphere for artistic endeavour, and was a training ground for younger artists and a means by which international artistic trends could be diffused within the Canadian art community. Many members were commercial artists with F. Brigden Ltd and Grip Ltd, where their skills were translated into GRAPHIC DESIGN, and several of them eventually left Canada to work elsewhere: David F. Thomson and Norman Price pursued successful commercial careers in the US, as did C.W. Jefferys and David MILNE, who, however, later returned; Milne's drypoint engravings constituted an outstanding body of work, some of the finest printmaking ever produced in Canada. Arthur C. Goode and A.A. Martin went to England and founded the Carlton Studio, which was to develop into that country's dominant commercial art studio.

The Toronto Art Students' League had several offshoots, notably the Mahlstick Club, 1889-1903, and the Little Billee Sketch Club, 1898-99. Its most important successor, however, was the Graphic Arts Club, founded in 1904 by the artists Jefferys, Manly, Brigden, Kelly, Robert Holmes, Thomas G. Greene, John W. Beatty, who would later become a teacher at the ONTARIO COLLEGE OF ART, and Albert H. Robson, art director at Grip Ltd, which would later employ Tom THOMSON, J.E.H. MACDONALD and other GROUP OF SEVEN artists. In 1924, on the occasion of its first public exhibition, the Graphic Arts Club was incorporated as the Canadian Society of Graphic Art. This organization became the primary artists' group in Canada by the 1940s, with a nationwide membership that included Ivor Lewis, Eric Aldwinckle, Miller BRITTAIN, Carl SCHAEFER, Nicholas Hornyansky and H. Eric Bergman (see also ARTISTS' ORGANIZATIONS).

Toronto continued to be the centre for fine-art printmaking in the first 2 decades of the 20th century, owing mainly to the effort of William Thomson to gain wider public acceptance for the medium. He found a powerful friend in Sir Edmund WALKER, whose influence resulted in the pivotal loan exhibition of prints and drawings at the Art Gallery of Toronto in 1912, with an accompanying catalogue. Further annual exhibitions at the gallery from 1914 to 1917, and the decision of other art bodies, notably the Art Assn of Montréal, the Ontario Society of Artists and the Royal Canadian Academy, to recognize printmaking as a legitimate art form on its own, contributed to the foundation in 1916 of the Society of Canadian Painter-Etchers/Engravers. This society, with Thomson as its first president, drew artists from across the country, including Herbert Raine of Montréal, Henry Ivan Neilson of Québec, who was to form and become the first president of the Québec Society of Artists in 1920, and Walter J. Phillips of Winnipeg.

Developments in printmaking in western Canada deserve much closer examination than they have so far received. Although numerous artists recorded views of the West throughout the 19th century, prints based on their work were generally published elsewhere. Little is known of the early developments in printmaking, but by 1882, a steam cylinder and a chromolithographic press had been established in the *British Colonist* office in Victoria. The Montréal firm of Bishop Printing and Engraving Co established an office in Winnipeg in 1883, and was soon followed by other eastern firms such as Brigdens. By 1900 there were several commercial firms of printers in business across the West. Serious developments in printmaking, how-

ever, only occurred with the arrival in Winnipeg just prior to WWI of the English-born artists Cyril J. Barraud, Hubert V. Fanshaw and Walter PHILLIPS, and of H. Eric Bergman from Germany. Cyril Barraud taught Phillips etching and sold him a press before returning to England in 1915 and becoming a war artist. In 1919, as part of the Canadian War Memorials Exhibition, Barraud, in conjunction with Caroline Armington, Gerard De Witt and Gyrth Russell, published a series of drypoints and etchings of Canadian battle scenes. During and after the war Phillips and Bergman began developing national reputations for their work in etching and wood engraving, and both joined the Society of Canadian Painter-Etchers/Engravers. Phillips also began experimenting with colour woodblock printing, a medium in which he became internationally recognized by the late 1920s. In 1925 Phillips, Bergman and the Scottish-born Alexander Musgrove formed the Manitoba Society of Art, which also included the Canadian-born Lionel LeMoine FITZGERALD, better known for his paintings than his delicate etchings and drypoints.

By the 1940s printmaking was firmly established as a fine-art medium in Canada. Many printmakers were able to live comfortably from the sale of their work, while others had taken up prestigious positions as teachers in the field. Among the latter were the painter Edwin HOLGATE, also reputed for his woodcuts, who was an instructor at the École des beaux-arts in Montréal; Frederick Haines, who became the principal of the Ontario College of Art in 1932; and Ernest LINDNER, an Austrian-born émigré who came to Canada in 1926 and in 1935 became an instructor at the Saskatoon Technical College where he experimented in linoleum and linocut printing. Lindner was a forerunner of developments to come, as etching and wood engraving gave way to other print processes in the 1930s and 1940s.

Colour screenprinting (or serigraphy) was introduced into Canada in the 1920s by the Toronto commercial firm of Sampson-Matthews, and gradually gained acceptance as a fine-art medium in the hands of artists such as Leonard Brooks. Lithography also enjoyed a renaissance in the 1940s after falling into disfavour at the end of the 19th century. Together with linocuts, lithography and screenprinting would come to dominate post-WWII developments. They were peculiarly suited to the next generation of Canadian artist/printmakers, who continued the traditions of their predecessors in absorbing international trends and ideas and adapting them to the Canadian art scene. JIM BURANT

Contemporary Printmaking

Printmaking in Canada received wider public acclaim in the mid-1950s following an international rediscovery of the artistic and aesthetic challenges of prints. National and international print exhibitions flourished and Canadian prints won recognition in prestigious international shows. Modern prints differ from earlier ones in their style and subject matter, larger scale, use of more colour, combination of several techniques, and photographic processes.

Contemporary developments occurred first and were most pronounced in Montréal, already a centre for printmaking and teaching. Artist and teacher Albert Dumouchel inspired print artists Peter Daglish, Richard Lacroix, Robert Savoie, Serge TOUSIGNANT, Vera Frenkel, Pierre Ayot, Ghitta CAISERMAN-ROTH, Janine Leroux-Guillaume and Roland GIGUÈRE. The painter Yves GAUCHER pursued printmaking intensively after studying with Dumouchel. From 1960 to 1964 Gaucher created only prints, experimenting with uninked or minimally inked, heavily embossed intaglio prints. In the late 1950s Toronto painter Harold TOWN devoted his

energies to lithography, creating exceptional "single autographic prints," unique accretions of various printing techniques, including stencil, linocut and overprinting. In the 1950s and 1960s Jack NICHOLS's black-and-white lithographs impressed the public and critics with a disciplined, yet modern, approach and strong images disclosing humanity's anguish and melancholy. Other early, innovative artists include Moe Reinblatt, Gilbert Marion, Walter Bachinski, James Boyd, Tobie STEINHOUSE, Aba BAYEFSKY, Richard Gorman and David Partridge. Image makers first and foremost, these influential artists were uninhibited about experimenting with new approaches, materials, printing procedures or uses of paper, setting the stage for creative explorations of traditional techniques.

The sincere interest in prints in Québec and Ontario was evidenced by the national print societies, whose membership came largely from eastern Canada. The societies provided printmakers with professional standards, a congenial artistic climate and exhibition opportunities. The Canadian Society of Graphic Art and the Society of Canadian Painter-Etchers/Engravers amalgamated in 1976, forming the Print and Drawing Council of Canada. Toronto's Ontario College of Art played a significant role in educating successive generations of printmakers.

Printmaking was not well established in western Canada. Although Gordon SMITH set up lithographic and silkscreen facilities at the Vancouver School of Art in the mid-1940s and, with Orville Fisher, Bruno BOBAK and Alistair BELL, created prints in the late 1950s, the art community was small. Victoria's early print artists include Herbert Siebner and Pat Martin BATES. Known internationally, Bates has set an example for younger artists seeking to further their reputation through international, open-juried exhibitions; like Gaucher, she has experimented with uninked surfaces, which developed into perforated *estampille* prints. Calgary's Maxwell BATES and John Snow became self-taught pioneers in lithography after rescuing 2 discarded presses in 1953; Bates's figurative prints are expressive, Snow's lyrical. Through John K. Esler's teaching and artistic efforts, printmaking blossomed in Calgary, which became a major print centre. Serigraphy was introduced to Edmonton in 1948 by George Weber. Presses were unavailable in Saskatchewan before 1965, although Eli BORNSTEIN brought serigraphy to Saskatoon in 1955.

The renewed interest in prints was manifested through the growth of print exhibitions, commercial galleries specializing in prints, university printmaking facilities, graphic workshops and a lessening of prejudices toward innovations like the collagraph, serigraphy and mixed techniques. The relative ease of shipping prints allows printmakers to participate in exhibitions throughout the world. Canadian print societies, public art galleries and educational institutions organize shows exclusively for prints. Unique exhibition opportunities have been provided by the Canadian Printmakers' Showcase and the Burnaby Print show (both now defunct), annual shows such as Graphex and Concours d'estampe et de dessin québecois, or the biennial exhibitions of the Print and Drawing Council of Canada. The first commercial galleries specializing in print, Agnes Lefort (1950) and Galerie 1640 (1961), opened in Montréal. In Toronto, Dorothy Cameron, who opened her gallery in 1959, organized an important print exhibition in 1965 to demonstrate that the best contemporary Canadian printmaking compares with the best printmaking anywhere. Toronto's Gallery Pascal opened in 1963.

Canadian university print departments are now among the leaders in the world and have greatly stimulated printmaking in Canada. As enrolment increased and fine-arts departments

Pulling a Kenojuak print at the Cape Dorset print shop, Cape Dorset, NWT (*photo by John deVisser*).

were developed in the 1960s, printmaking equipment was acquired and technically competent and aesthetically aware instructors were hired. Print workshops emerged to relieve the high cost of equipment and to provide a stimulating and creative environment for print artists. These shops may offer equipment rental, collaboration with a professional printer and publication of print editions. Although Roland Giguère founded Editions Erta in 1949, publishing deluxe editions that included prints, the first contemporary workshops in Montréal were L'Atelier libre de recherches graphiques (1964) and La Guilde graphique (1966), founded by Richard Lacroix. Montréal's GRAFF, established by Pierre Ayot in 1966, is active with working printmakers, demonstrations for school children, print courses for adults and an annual auction. The Grand Western Canadian Screen Shop was founded in Winnipeg in 1968 by Bill Lobchuk; many artists now working across Canada began their work there.

In 1976 Rudolf Bikkers founded Editions Canada in London as a publisher where artists worked closely with the printers throughout the production process. Ontario's major printshops are Open Studio (1970) and Sword Street Press (1978). At Open Studio artists may print their own images or work with a professional printer, but Sword Street Press offers only the latter option. Open Studio has attracted and influenced artists and printers from all of Canada. Other workshops are located in St Michael's, Nfld; Québec City, Trois-Rivières and Val-David, Qué; and in Halifax, Winnipeg, Calgary and Vancouver.

Contemporary Print Artists have been very successful in international competitions and are often better known abroad than in Canada. David BLACKWOOD's subject matter is rooted in his Newfoundland birthplace. His large etchings of fishermen, sealers and their families depict human relationships and humanity's battle with the elements. Technically traditional, Blackwood's etchings are credited with attracting many collectors to purchase prints. Jo Manning renders nature in a contemporary manner in her linear black-and-white etchings. Ed Bartram's colour viscosity etchings of the boldly textured rocks of Ontario's Precambrian Shield area are a continuation of earlier Canadian landscape interpretations, intimately linking content and process.

During the 1960s it was common for several techniques to be used in a single print, as may be seen in the abstracted landscapes by Roslyn Swartzman and Anne Meredith Barry who combine embossing or collagraphy in etchings or serigraphs. Serigraphy, the youngest of the traditional techniques, has gained popularity, its clear-cut shapes and flat colours being most appropriate for works of the pop, op, hard-edge or minimal art styles. Prints by Harry Kiyooka, Tony Tascona and Rita LETENDRE are examples of such uses. Although pop art never had a large Canadian following, artists associated with GRAFF, especially Ayot, use serigraphy for their witty pop prints. Works by Winnipeg's Bill Lobchuk, Don Proch and E.J. Howorth incorporate the prairie landscape tradition into flat, partially drawn, partially photographic images. Images by Maritimer Jim Hansen, relying on line and incorporating handwritten words, are first drawn on acetate, then photomechanically transferred to screens.

Painters Gordon Smith and Toni ONLEY have used prints, particularly serigraphs, to bring their art to a larger audience. Both have explored nonobjective or abstract subject matter but are artistically strongest in personal depictions of West Coast landscapes. Newfoundlander Christopher PRATT's high realist works use subject matter from everyday life: crisp clapboard houses, quiet interiors or harmonious seascapes. In Pratt's serigraphs, superimposed layers of colour achieve subtle chromatic and textural effects. Ann McCall and Lauréat Marois have also created outstanding realistic serigraphs.

Photography has long been used in commercial screenprint processes. During the 1970s, especially, artists such as Michel Leclair began to explore photographic techniques creatively. At Open Studio, founder Richard Sewell incorporates serigraphy, lithography, photography and even 3-dimensional imagery in his highly original prints; Judy Gouin uses her own landscape photographs, often incorporating unusual vantage points and reflections, as the basis for her prints. In Ottawa, Leslie Reid uses photoserigraphy and photolithography for her monochromatic naturalistic works.

Serge Tousignant, who worked with Dumouchel, pursues formal explorations of space and favours serigraphy and photomechanical processes. Walter Jule and Lyndal Osborne of University of Alberta, using different imagery and techniques, explore the possibilities of mixed media in their art and teaching. Unlike many technically excellent print artists, Jule is able to join technique and content without rendering his imagery subservient to his technical virtuosity. Carl Heywood, principally known for his lithographs and serigraphs incorporating a variety of photographic techniques, depicts his subject matter realistically but incorporates symbolic references.

Lithography became the most popular technique in the 1970s. Such artists as Don Holman, Bob Evermon, Charles Ringness and Edward Porter came to Canada from successful American lithographic workshops. Teaching in Halifax, Porter has contributed to contemporary awareness of lithography, as have Maritime artists Frank Lapointe and Roger Savage. Printmakers Jack Cowin and Charles Ringness work in Saskatchewan, Ringness making serigraphs or lithographs on which he applies drawing and collage. John Will combines many separate realistic images in a larger one, and frequently includes clever words or sentences. Evermon often presents his nonobjective lithographs, with their beautiful, coloured transparent washes, as diptychs. Otis Tamasauskas has mastered the subtleties and forcefulness of both lithography and intaglio, and his abstract compositions cover the complete surface of the paper.

Never exclusively a printmaker, Jennifer Dickson has had a significant influence on the visual-arts scene through her art and her teaching. With Irene Whittome, she was a pioneer of photographic techniques in etching, and continues to combine these methods with serigraphy, embossing or painting.

Relief printing, the oldest print technique, has not experienced the same revival as other techniques; nevertheless, relief artists such as Pierre-Léon Tétreault, René Derouin and Noboru Sawai excel. Tétreault's more recent print work is in wood, both relief and engraving, but he is also known for the offset lithographs that he produced at Gaston Petits's workshop in Japan in the mid-1970s. A student of Japanese techniques, Derouin blends the oriental and occidental and produces highly stylized, richly coloured contemporary images, some of conventional size, others very large. Primarily an etcher, Sawai intriguingly contrasts the firm linear qualities of occidental copper etching with the softly coloured, oriental-style woodcut. The 2 cultures also figure in his unique subject matter: engraved images based on paintings by European old masters are contrasted with woodcuts depicting oriental erotic encounters.

Printmakers are conscious of their paper, ensuring that the paper's texture is appropriate for the image and that the composition is correctly placed on the sheet. Some artists, however, have become interested in other aspects of paper. Helmut Becker makes his own printing paper; Paul Lussier makes multiples out of paper; and Betty Davison, reconstituting rag paper into pulp, creates cast paper prints, which are then hand coloured.

Some printmakers, like other artists, are experimenting with new technology (*see* ART, CONTEMPORARY TRENDS). Artists not primarily known as print artists have also contributed to printmaking. By exploring the print medium, either independently or with a professional printer, these artists have achieved more exposure for their own works and for prints. Contemporary Canadian prints do not exhibit a national style or subject matter, though in both temperament and preoccupation distinct regional characteristics may be discerned (*see also* PAINTING). In general, however, printmaking in Canada is the product of an individual artist's creativity and aesthetics.   BENTE ROED COCHRAN

Reading: M. Allodi, *Printmaking in Canada* (1980); J. Russell Harper, *Early Painters and Engravers in Canada* (1970).

Prior, Edward Gawler, mining engineer, businessman, premier of BC (b at Dallaghgill, Eng 21 May 1853; d at Victoria 12 Dec 1920). In 1873 Prior immigrated to Vancouver I, BC, and worked for a mining company in Nanaimo. Appointed inspector of mines in 1877, he returned to business in 1883, becoming manager of E.G. Prior, the leading hardware and machinery business in BC. Elected an MP he lost his seat in 1900 because of violations of the Electoral Act. Returning to provincial politics he became minister of mines in 1901 and premier in 1902. Dismissed in 1903 following a charge of conflict of interest, he remained an MLA until his defeat in 1904. Appointed lieutenant-governor in 1919, he died in office.   SYDNEY W. JACKMAN

Reading: Sydney W. Jackman, *Portraits of the Premiers* (1969).

Prison, as a term meaning a place in which people are kept in captivity, covers a variety of institutions in Canada. Jails, increasingly called detention or remand centres, are used to incarcerate persons awaiting trial or those sentenced for short terms. Traditionally the responsibility of municipalities or counties in most provinces, they are now part of the correctional system that also includes reformatories (correctional centres) for those sentenced to less than 2 years. Sentences of 2 years and over are served in federal penitentiaries that are part of the Correctional Services of Canada, administered through the federal ministry of the solicitor general. The division is based only on length of sentence. Constitutionally, criminal law is federal, but offences are listed not only in the Canadian Criminal Code and other federal statutes but also in numerous provincial statutes (*see* CRIME). Offences arising from federal statutes may be served in provincial institutions and vice versa.

Institutions for juveniles, commonly called training schools, are under provincial jurisdiction. A new Young Offenders' Act received Royal Assent in July 1982 and was, in part, proclaimed in 1983. This Act applies to persons, from age 12 (the new age of criminal responsibility) to age 17 inclusive, charged with offences arising from federal statutes. The provinces will have to pass separate legislation on provincial offences for this age group.

Historical Developments In the early 1800s, prisons were essentially jails attached to courthouses. They were used for holding debtors for the civil process and to a lesser extent for holding accused persons awaiting trial. The first large prison, opened in Kingston, Upper Canada (June 1835) was designated to serve Upper and Lower Canada by the Act of Union in 1840. By 1867, Saint John, NB, and Halifax, NS, also had penitentiaries and in 1880 Dorchester penitentiary was built in the Maritimes. The penitentiaries of St Vincent de Paul, Qué (1873), Stony Mountain, Man (1876), New Westminster, BC (1878), and Prince Albert, Sask (1911) completed the chain of fortress-like prisons across Canada. In 1930 another opened in Collins Bay, Ont.

The development of provincial prison systems depended on the size and change of populations, as well as on resources. Sentencing patterns also varied provincially, influenced by the number and kinds of available institutions. By 1982 there were about 25 000 prisoners in Canada on any given day, 10 000 of whom served sentences in federal penitentiaries. Admissions over one year are much higher and amounted, in Ontario alone, to about 50 000 sentenced prisoners. After remaining fairly stable in the 1970s the number of prisoners began to grow again at the beginning of the 1980s, despite the increase in other sentencing options, eg, PROBATION, community service orders, restitution and fines.

The debate about prisons as institutions of punishment began with their inception. Prisons originated partly because it was no longer possible to banish offenders, and partly as a result of public abhorrence of the infliction of bodily pain and the exposure of offenders to public ridicule and shame, although stigma remains one of the essential elements not only of conviction and punishment but even of official accusation. Penitentiaries (meant to lead the offender to penitence through isolation, silence and religious instruction) and reform institutions (meant to reform deficiencies in the character of criminals) reflected the values of their society. Work followed penitence as the major condition for salvation, but it was the work regime, often involving meaningless tasks and submission to rules, that was important. An emphasis on training and education to "upgrade" the social position of offenders came next, followed by focus on rehabilitation and treatment and in the 1970s emphasis on due process — prisoners' rights and administrative fairness. Because almost all offenders are eventually released, it is highly questionable whether the expenditure of over $41 000 annually per inmate makes much sense. It is now generally conceded that prisons exist because we do not know what else to do. Various groups, including the Quakers, who were instrumental in trying to make prisons places of humanitarian reform, have demanded their abolition.

Programs Kingston penitentiary, opened with great hopes of solving the problem of crime and criminals, was plagued by dissension, corruption and inhumanity from the beginning. The first major investigation, the *Brown Report* (1849), is full of cases like that of Peter Charboneau, a 10- or 11-year-old child lashed 57 times in 8½ months for offences including staring, winking and laughing. Although there have been major changes in the handling of prisoners as well as in the administration of the institutions, the problems and the reports continued. The last major one, the *MacGuigan Report* (1977), was conducted by the Sub-Committee on the Penitentiary System in Canada of the Standing Committee on Justice and Legal Affairs.

A diversity of institutions, generally classified as maximum, medium and minimum according to their security measures, as well as work camps and Community Release Centres now exist. Programs are still modelled on the traditional beliefs in penitence (moral improvement), education, work and rehabilitation, but life in most prisons is essentially characterized by making time pass. Riots and hostage taking, although widely publicized, are remarkably rare events considering the tensions created by a rigidly controlled environment.

Relationship to Community Although generally isolated from the community, prisons depend on it for even a semblance of purpose and proper functioning. A network of interest groups with a variety of programs inside and outside the institutions has grown up around prisons, eg, the John Howard and Elizabeth Fry societies, halfway houses, prison visitors and self-help groups. Citizens in general, however, tend to know little and seem to care less about who is in prison, what happens there and what happens to people after they leave.
                                                    JOHANN W. MOHR

Prisoners of War (POWs), those captured by the enemy while fighting in the military, a byproduct of relatively sophisticated warfare. In primitive fighting, prisoners were rarely taken, the vanquished being tortured (often ritualistically) or killed. The concept of permanent enslavement of a defeated enemy developed, and from that the idea of ransom in the case of the rich or powerful. These options were practised by the indigenous inhabitants of N America, and all, except ritualistic torture, by the early European settlers. By the end of the 18th century, however, most communities had accepted the principle of simply quarantining prisoners, either by confining them or paroling them in some fashion. Such were the usual practices in the Anglo-French wars, the AMERICAN REVOLUTION and the WAR OF 1812.

International rules to govern the treatment of POWs were first formulated at Geneva in 1864 and refined at The Hague in 1899 as part of a broader codification of the rules of war. Canadians taken prisoner during the SOUTH AFRICAN WAR had little need of these rules, since the Afrikaners, fighting a guerrilla campaign for most of the war, had no facilities for holding prisoners. After being relieved of their weapons, equipment and supplies, prisoners were usually released.

The Hague Convention was revised in 1907, and the 2818 men of the CANADIAN EXPEDITIONARY FORCE taken prisoner during WORLD WAR I, as well as the 2005 German POWs held in Canada, were treated in accordance with the revisions. But in Europe there were many complaints that the spirit of the convention was not observed. In 1929 a Geneva Convention relating specifically to the Treatment of Prisoners of War was negotiated through the LEAGUE OF NATIONS. Prisoners were to be treated humanely, subject to the need to secure them. A prisoner need only give his captors his name, rank and number; he might be required to work but must not be assigned to work with direct military implications.

In WORLD WAR II about 8000 Canadians became German POWs and were generally treated in accordance with the Geneva Convention. Two glaring exceptions were the execution of some participants in a mass escape attempt from *Stalag Luft* III in Mar 1944 and the manacling of British and Canadian prisoners in Oct 1942 as a reprisal for the temporary tying up of German prisoners taken at DIEPPE and in a minor British commando raid. The British retaliated by shackling some of their prisoners and asked the Canadians to do likewise. Canada acquiesced and some Germans were handcuffed until the British and Canadian governments decided in Dec 1942 that retaliation was counterproductive. The Germans continued shackling until Nov 1943, but long before that most of the prisoners were only manacled while on parade.

Among the 30 000 German and Italian POWs held in Canada during the war, Luftwaffe Oberleutnant Franz von Werra distinguished himself as "the one that got away," escaping from a train near Prescott, Ont, the night of 23-24 Jan 1941, crossing into the US, and subsequently returning to Germany. He was later killed in action. Others escaped but did not succeed in recrossing the Atlantic; one, at least, got to Mexico. Several POWs were murdered by their fellow prisoners for not conforming to Hitlerian standards of conduct.

Thirty-two Canadians were taken POW during the KOREAN WAR and treated harshly, neither N Korea nor the People's Republic of China being signatories to the revised Geneva Convention of 1949. Efforts were made to "brainwash" them in attempts to alter their political perceptions; none died in captivity. Canadian soldiers were briefly used to guard POWs after a rising of N Korean and Chinese POWs in a UN prison camp on KOJE-DO in May 1952. *See also* INTERNMENT.   BRERETON GREENHOUS

Reading: D.G. Dancocks, *In Enemy Hands* (1983); J. Melady, *Escape from Canada!* (1981); K. Burt and J. Leasor, *The One That Got Away* (1956);

Privacy In a primarily rural society, such as 19th-century Canada, privacy was basically a territorial concept. Today, privacy tends to be defined not only territorially but as the right of individuals to determine when, how and to what extent information about themselves is to be communicated to others. When Canadians refer to "invasion of privacy" they may include electronic camera surveillance and unapproved computer record-linking of personal information. It is the marriage of data files and the computer that poses the greatest threat to privacy (*see* COMPUTERS AND SOCIETY).

Government intervention has primarily been directed at giving individuals access to personal information held by government. However, the same legislation also gives to third parties in certain situations the right of access to personal information about other people, and creates exemptions allowing individual access to some personal information.

Federal legislation regarding privacy includes the 1982 Privacy Act (which supplanted and reinforced provisions regarding privacy in the Canadian Human Rights Act of 1977) and the 1974 Protection of Privacy Act, which allows wiretaps under certain conditions.

Québec has enacted a privacy and access to information law as well; and BC in 1968, Manitoba in 1970, and Saskatchewan in 1974 have passed enabling legislation recognizing legal causes of action for invasion of privacy, but these laws have been described as "unused and unusable."

The Québec Charter of Rights (but not the Canadian Charter of Rights and Freedoms) also contains a right to privacy clause. In 1981 the joint committee on the Constitution defeated an amendment that would have provided for "freedom from unreasonable interference with privacy, family, home, and correspondence."

Personal privacy is protected under other federal and provincial statutes as well. For example, the federal Statistics Act prohibits disclosure of personal statistical information, and Ontario's fair credit-reporting legislation allows access to personal credit records and provides some rights to correct inaccurate information. Another level of privacy protection is provided by the courts, which hear cases argued on grounds such as trespass and theft, but there is no recognizable legal right to sue on the grounds of privacy invasion. The federal government has introduced proposals for amendments to the CRIMINAL CODE to protect individuals against the misappropriation and misuse of personal information stored on computers.

Canadians became aware of extensive violations of privacy through the controversy surrounding the use of SOCIAL INSURANCE NUMBERS (SIN) and the federal Commission of INQUIRY INTO CERTAIN ACTIVITIES OF THE RCMP (McDonald Commission). SIN were developed as a administrative registration number for social-security programs. The use of social insurance numbers, however, both in the public and private sectors, has now become a means of identifying individuals. SIN are used, for example, to register PEI babies as well as some amateur hockey teams. This has raised concerns about the potential abuse of SIN as a means of linking together much personal information stored in files and computer banks. No direct parliamentary action has been taken to restrict SIN usage but individuals are no longer required to divulge their SIN to cash Canada Savings Bonds coupons. The McDonald Commission learned that the RCMP had enjoyed unauthorized access to personal information about thousands of Canadians and had opened files on 800 000 Canadians. The commission also learned of RCMP infringements on personal privacy through the use of wiretapping, break and entry, and mail openings.

The vulnerability of Canadians to invasion of privacy was also made evident in 1983, when the public learned that Revenue Canada claimed many sweeping powers of access to personal information, and demanded unrestricted access to certain municipal financial data banks.

Governments and law enforcement officials are not the only violators of personal information. In the early 1980s the Ontario Commission of Inquiry into the Confidentiality of Health Information (Krever Commission) learned that certain insurance representatives were impersonating medical officers to obtain medical information about claimants.

The greatest threat to personal privacy lies in the growing reliance on information machines with their immense and quick capacity for record-linking and transmitting data. With the advent of electronic banking, shopping and mails, information about an individual's employment and financial and health status and personal habits can be easily recorded and traded (*see* INFORMATION SOCIETY).

Problems arise when the computers storing personal information can be surreptitiously entered by third parties and when the terminal containing the information is not located in Canada (for example, medical insurance information about many Canadians is stored in Boston).

Unlike some European countries, Canada has no legislation to restrict and protect the access to and distribution of personal information on Canadians held in computers abroad.

Canadians are increasingly aware of how delicate is their personal control over information about themselves. In a 1984 Gallup of 1071 adults, 68% said they did not believe there was any real privacy in Canada, because the government could learn anything it wanted to learn about any individual.   KEN RUBIN

Private Presses are dedicated to the art of fine printing and, as the name implies, are usually operated by individuals who normally perform or oversee all aspects of production: selecting the text, designing, typesetting, illustrating, printing (on fine handmade papers) and binding the book. More often than not, the book becomes an art object in itself. This production in limited editions (it can go from one copy to a few hundred copies, often numbered and signed by the author and the artist) is intended for the book lover.

The concept of private presses originated in Europe at the end of the 19th century. In England, William Morris founded the Kelmscott Press in 1891. He dreamed of recreating the art of the *incunabula* — a tradition of fine-book printing prevailing before 1500 — and conceived new types, commissioned hand-made papers with his own imprints, and used parchment for his most precious productions. The emphasis, however, was on the use of types and page design. He gave birth to a tradition which was to influence English Canadian and American hand printers for years. In France, bibliophiles were more interested in lavishly illustrated books. In 1875 Manet produced 8 lithographs to illustrate Mallarmé's translation of Edgar Allan Poe's "The Raven," the text occupying another 8 pages. A new tradition was born, that of the "livre d'artiste," a concept that has permeated French Canada's private presses, the emphasis there being on PRINTMAKING rather than fine printing. Few exceptions are to be found, although the situation is slowly changing in English Canada where Charles Pachter (who studied in Paris) has produced some magnificent albums, the twelfth of which, *The Journals of Susanna Moodie* (1980), comprises 30 poems by Margaret ATWOOD and 30 serigraphs by Pachter. A few Ontario artists have taken that route, including Brender à Brandis of Brandstead Press (Carlisle, Ont), Elizabeth Forrest of Greyn Forest Press (Toronto) and Soren Madsen of Mad-Ren Press (Toronto), whose books are fine examples of well balanced, imaginative book design. For most of their books both Pachter and Madsen have created their own handmade papers.

Research on the history of private presses in Canada has only begun, and knowledge is still fairly fragmented. Claudette Hould, in *Répertoire des livres d'artistes au Québec, 1900-1980*, has catalogued 249 titles from private presses in Québec, 195 of them published between 1970 and 1980. Marilyn Rueter (in David B. Kotin and Marilyn Rueter, *Reader, Lover of Books, Lover of Heaven*) and Maureen Bradbury (in *News From the Rare Book Room* 17 and 18, U of A) have indexed hundred of titles from some 50 publishers, most of which appeared after 1960.

The 1950s, however, had marked a turning point, with the founding in Montréal of Editions Erta (1949) by Roland Giguère, poet and printmaker, and in Thornhill, Ont, Gus Rueter's Village Press (1957). They were the first hand printers who themselves executed all aspects of book production. Others, like J. Kemp Waldie of Golden Dog Press (Toronto) and Louis Carrier (Montréal), had, in the early 1930s, published under their imprints good examples of fine printed books, but these were usually printed commercially.

Private printing in Canada is flourishing. The

One of the great rarities in modern Canadian literature is Margaret Atwood's *Speeches for Doctor Frankenstein*, designed and printed by Charles Pachter in 1966. Only 15 copies were made, from linen and cotton, and the illustrations were printed in various combinations from blocks of wood and linoleum, silk screens and certain found objects (*courtesy of the artist and Bruce Peel Special Collections Library/U of A*).

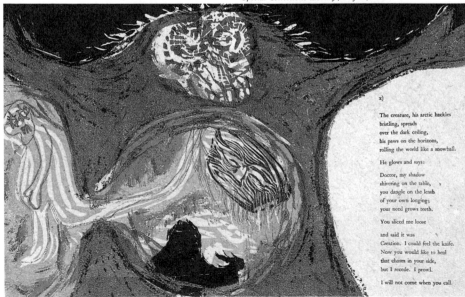

The creature, his arctic hackles
bristling, spreads
over the dark ceiling,
his paws on the horizons,
rolling the world like a snowball.

He glows and says:

Doctor, my shadow
shivering on the table,
you dangle on the leash
of your own longing;
your need grows teeth.

You sliced me loose

and said it was
Creation. I could feel the knife.
Now you would like to heal
that chasm in your side,
but I recede. I prowl.

I will not come when you call.

foundation of the Guild of Hand Printers (Toronto, 1959) and publications in their *Wrong-fount* series have been instrumental in stimulating private printers' production of well-wrought books. Similarly, the Alcuin Society (Richmond, BC, fd 1965) brings finely printed books to its membership and provides them with the periodical *Amphora*, devoted to the art of fine printing. Many private-press proprietors have contributed to the publications of both these societies, eg, Wil Hudson (Vancouver), Gus Rueter, W. Craig Ferguson of Basement Cage Press (Kingston), John Robert COLOMBO of Hawkshead Press (Kitchener and Toronto) and Purple Partridge Press (Kitchener and Toronto), William Rueter of Aliquando Press (Toronto), Roger Asham (Toronto and Tillsonburg) and Peter Dorn of Heinrich Heine (Don Mills and Kingston), to name but a few.

In Québec the driving force came from the artistic milieu, and many contributors were printmakers who commissioned master hand printers, such as Pierre Guillaume, for their typography. Among some 75 private presses, a handful have produced half the books indexed to date: Éditions Erta, Éditions de la guilde graphique, Éditions Graffones, Michel Nantel, Éditions du songe, Arts global and, more recently, Éditions du Noroît.

In addition to their excellence in design, private presses, like little magazines, often publish first editions of poems and prose by major Canadian writers (*see also* SMALL PRESSES).

JEAN-MARCEL DUCIAUME

Private School Fee-supported educational institutions at the primary and secondary level not under direct government control have existed in Canada from the earliest years of white settlement to the present day. Until the 1830s, most schooling was private. Today, although the private schools' proportion of total enrolment is very small (5%), their appeal to Canadian society continues to give them significance.

During the first centuries of settlement, EDUCATION was still considered the responsibility of the family and the church (*see* EDUCATION, HISTORY OF). Local clerics or parents taught some children to read and write. Other children attended schools founded by enterprising individuals as private ventures, and yet others remained illiterate. A handful of grammar schools and denominational institutions also existed. A *collège classique*, or academic SECONDARY SCHOOL for boys, was founded by the Jesuits in Québec City in 1635. King's College School, also restricted to boys, was begun by an Anglican missionary cleric in Nova Scotia in 1789.

The movement away from a reliance on private education began in the early 19th century with the growing recognition that all children, not just a select few, should receive some formal education. The governments of British N America began assisting some existing schools and created new ones, mainly at the elementary level.

The emergence of free public educational systems did not, however, spell the demise of all private schooling. By the terms of the CONSTITUTION ACT, 1867, education was placed under provincial control with the intention that patterns of schooling officially recognized prior to Confederation should remain in place. Québec, Ontario, and later Saskatchewan and Alberta accepted Catholic and nondenominational Protestant schools (under certain conditions) within their provincial systems. Manitoba did so originally but in 1890 defied legal rulings to join the Maritime provinces and BC in supporting a single nondenominational public system (*see* MANITOBA SCHOOLS QUESTION).

The private schooling that remained differed among the provinces. All Catholic schools in the Maritimes, in Manitoba after 1890, and in BC,

were in effect still private. So were all schools, in whatever province, that were affiliated with other religious denominations. Ontario's acceptance of Catholic schools into its public system originally included only those at the elementary level, but has now been extended through grade 13. Moreover, Catholic classical colleges, still the principal form of secondary education in Québec, retained their private status even while becoming provincially subsidized. Not surprisingly, when the first federal statistics on private education were compiled in the 1920s, it was determined that the proportion of children in school who were being educated privately varied from about 10% in Québec to 3-5% in provinces where Catholic schools were excluded from public systems to 1-2% in the remaining provinces.

As well as retaining a religious function, private education continued to play a role in class differentiation. Early tuition-free public systems centered on the elementary level, which meant that families desiring more advanced schooling for their offspring had to be able to afford a private institution or the fees of a public secondary school. The identification of private education with socioeconomic status was reinforced by developments in Great Britain, where during the second half of the 19th century the middle and upper classes had opted almost exclusively to retain their traditional commitment to private education, treating the emerging state system as a visibly inferior alternative serving only families unable to afford anything better. Numerous boys' and girls' schools in the Maritimes, Ontario and Québec, many of them established as Anglican or other Protestant denominational institutions, began consciously to identify with their British counterparts and to take on a distinct class character. Toronto's Upper Canada College, for instance, began terming itself "the Eton of Canada."

Additional schools on the British model also appeared, both in eastern Canada and in BC. There, a massive influx of British middle-class settlers, who arrived during the halcyon years of Canadian immigration preceding WWI, provided both the organizational impetus and the clientele to sustain several dozen new schools adhering to the principles and practices of British private education. It has been primarily the existence of schools in this British tradition that has prompted such general assessments of Canadian private education as that by John PORTER in *The Vertical Mosaic:* "The acquisition of social skills and the opportunities to make the right contacts can be important reasons for the higher middle classes to send their children to private schools."

Several important shifts in private education occurred in the decades following WWII. Increasing prosperity and a general mood of egalitarianism encouraged governments to upgrade public systems. Some private schools found it difficult, even impossible, to compete with higher teacher salaries, updated curricula and improved physical facilities, particularly in the sciences. Others fought back. Private schools in the British tradition abandoned the self-appellation "private," with its implication of exclusivity and private profit, in favour of "independent," which was thought to suggest most of the schools' nonprofit status and their independence from government control. The Roman Catholic Church undertook a major fundraising campaign to improve and expand private schools under its control.

The recovery of private education was facilitated by the appearance of a new dynamic. Of the immigrant groups entering postwar Canada, DUTCH Calvinists most keenly felt that existing public systems did not serve their special needs and so established their own "Christian" schools. Concentrated in areas of Dutch settlement in Ontario, Alberta and BC, Christian schools have been characterized by a very strong moral and religious base. In addition, the widespread dissatisfaction of the 1960s and early 1970s brought a proliferation of alternative schools focusing on the uniqueness of the individual child; however, most of them soon disappeared or became part of public systems (*see* EDUCATION, ALTERNATE). From the 1950s onward, both new and older private schools began lobbying their provincial governments for financial assistance to allow them to compete more equitably with public systems. Success eventually came in Alberta, Québec, BC and Manitoba, and in Saskatchewan at the secondary level. In these provinces private schools meeting designated standards of personnel, curriculum and facilities receive an annual per capita grant out of public monies. In contrast, Québec's classical colleges were integrated into the province's public system in the late 1960s.

The growing conservatism which has characterized the 1970s and early 1980s across N America has had its effect on private education. Enrolments have risen steadily from 2.5% of all children in school in 1970-71 to 4.1% in 1980-81 and an estimated 4.9% in 1984-85. Ironically the importance of provincial funding to this growth is questionable, for proportions have more than doubled in Ontario (2.1% in 1970-71 to 4.7% by 1984-85) where schools receive no assistance, while they have grown by just over half in Alberta and BC, where schools do receive assistance (1.3% to 1.9% and 3.9% to 5.6%). Rather, it would seem, the search for more traditional values and disillusionment with the public system have turned many families both toward existing private schools and toward a new, second variety of Christian school. Generally small independent entities, affiliated with local evangelical churches, these Christian schools have proliferated largely as a result of the development in the US of self-directed, highly religious curriculum packages, the best known being Accelerated Christian Education, which can be purchased individually as pupils enroll.

Private schools have appealed and will continue to appeal to a minority of Canadians who are convinced that their children's special needs outweigh the benefits accorded by participation in the common socialization experience that is public education. A few private schools offer training in such specialized areas as dance and remedial education at a more intensive level than is generally available in the public system. Adherents to a variety of denominations believe that education must be more firmly based in morality and in religious belief than is possible within a single public system that serves pupils of all faiths and backgrounds. Of the 800 or more private schools existing across Canada in the early 1980s, about 33% are Catholic, 33% Calvinist or evangelical Christian and perhaps 200 are affiliated with other denominations.

As well, the tendency of many private schools, particularly the 50 or more schools in the British tradition, to focus on traditional academic subjects leading to university entrance, appeals to many families, including recent immigrants who want to ensure their children's integration into Canadian society. Even at Upper Canada College, the private school most often cited as maintaining the generational continuity of Canada's social and economic elite, 33% of the pupils enrolled in 1982 came from families who had arrived in Canada since WWII. More generally, the appeal of private education may simply be that because access is restricted by fees, by academic entrance examinations or some combination of factors, the desire to partake increases on the assumption that the product offered must almost by definition be superior to that freely available. JEAN BARMAN

Privateering, government licensing of private vessels to wage war against enemies of the state. In Canada this commenced with Samuel Argall's attack in 1613 on PORT-ROYAL, Acadia. English privateers, operating out of harbours in New England and Newfoundland, included the KIRKE brothers who captured Québec in 1629. French privateers operated out of Port-Royal, LOUISBOURG and many isolated harbours, and included Pierre Le Moyne d'IBERVILLE, who in 1696-97 captured and burned St John's and terrorized several coastal communities in Newfoundland. From 1756 to 1815 British privateers sailed from Halifax, Liverpool, Shelburne, Annapolis Royal, St Andrews and Saint John, cruising as far S as Venezuela. Britain's embroilment in numerous wars presented no shortage of conflicts in which privateersmen could become involved.

A cruise began when merchants invested risk capital. Usually a merchant vessel was converted, although infrequently a ship was specially built. A privateering licence (letter of marque) was acquired from the governor and the vessel was fitted out appropriately. Privateersmen received no salary, but rather signed aboard in the hope of sharing prize money. Although most came home, many were buried abroad or consigned to the ocean in canvas sacks with cannonballs at their feet. A captured vessel and its cargo were sent before the Court of Vice Admiralty in Halifax and, if judged to have been legally taken, were sold at public auction. During the WAR OF 1812 the *Liverpool Packet* sent some 50 vessels before the court. The judge and court officials received commissions, and further proceeds were shared among each vessel's owners, its captain and crew, and the "informer" (as the captor was termed).

Privateering from Canadian ports ceased in 1815 with the TREATY OF GHENT, although it was not ended by international convention until the Declaration of Paris in 1856. Privateering was more than an economic activity, for it provided a means of defence and offence managed at the local level, much like the Canadian militia (*see* ARMED FORCES). It is not inappropriate to suggest that herein lay the seeds of the Royal Canadian Navy.   JOHN G. LEEFE

Reading: John G. Leefe, *The Atlantic Privateers* (1978).

Privy Council, common name for the Queen's Privy Council of Canada, established under the Constitution Act, 1867, to advise the Crown. Privy councillors are appointed for life by the governor general on the prime minister's recommendation, and include the chief justice of the Supreme Court, provincial premiers, former and present federal CABINET ministers, and speakers of the House of Commons and Senate. The Cabinet, which has no statutory basis, acts formally as the Privy Council through ORDERS-IN-COUNCIL issued in the name of the governor-in-council.   J.E. HODGETTS

Privy Council Office (PCO), prime minister's government department headed by the clerk designated (since 1940) secretary to the Cabinet.

Perhaps the most important and certainly the most senior of the CENTRAL AGENCIES of government, the PCO's pre-Confederation roots can be traced to the position of the clerk of the executive council of the Province of Canada; under the CONSTITUTION ACT, 1867, the PCO was only responsible for preparing and registering ORDERS-IN-COUNCIL. In fact no specific statutory basis for most of its functions exists; the bulk of its activities are conducted pursuant to the unwritten, conventional authority of the PRIME MINISTER and the Cabinet. It can be said that the PCO is the prime minister's administrative agency, with the clerk of the PCO essentially serving as his permanent deputy minister.

From 1940 on, the PCO has provided the secretarial functions not only for the full Cabinet but for the numerous Cabinet committees created in response to the mounting burdens on the political executive. It co-ordinates the activities of Cabinet and Cabinet committees and acts as a liaison with government agencies and departments on Cabinet matters; it examines, edits and registers statutory regulations and arranges for their publication, and it traditionally advises the prime minister on those senior appointments in the public service not under the purview of the Public Service Commission. It has also exercised independent political initiatives, eg, in 1978 it was revealed that the PCO had initiated RCMP scrutiny of PARTI QUÉBÉCOIS financing (*see* INQUIRY INTO CERTAIN ACTIVITIES OF THE RCMP).

In 1974 Parliament created the Federal-Provincial Relations Office, which assumed some of the responsibilities previously under the PCO. During the administration of PM Pierre TRUDEAU, the PCO was criticized by those who object to the growing power of the executive. *See* PRIME MINISTER'S OFFICE.   J.E. HODGETTS

Reading: C. Campbell and G.J. Szablowski, *The Super-bureaucrats* (1979); J.L. Granatstein, *The Ottawa Men* (1982).

Pro Pelle Cutem [Lat, "a skin for a skin"], the official motto of the HUDSON'S BAY COMPANY, was adopted soon after the company received its charter in 1670. Both the origin and the interpretation of the motto have been much debated. It may be an adaptation of *pellem pro pelle* (Job 2:4, usually translated "skin for skin") or of *pro cute pellem* (Juvenal, *Satires* 10.192, "a hide in place of a skin"). The motto is often taken to mean "[animal] skins obtained at the cost of [human] skin."

Probation and Parole Probation, in law, is a correctional method under which a convicted offender is given a suspended sentence and released under supervision, rather than being sentenced to PRISON terms. It has come to be recognized as a judicial device for providing another chance for first offenders. The theory of probation derives from a long-standing tradition in Anglo-American courts to suspend judgement in certain cases. In practice it originated with John Augustus, a Boston shoemaker, who through his interest in the TEMPERANCE cause agreed to supervise the behaviour of an offender in lieu of a prison term. By the time he died Augustus had made himself responsible for nearly 2000 offenders. In Canada, probation is an exclusively provincial jurisdiction. Probation services, which exist in all provinces, are responsible for preparing presentencing reports that focus on the accused's background. The reports may suggest that the offender make restitution to the victim and may identify specific skills that the accused possesses that could be incorporated into a community service order. The report may also recommend that the offender be required to take treatment for alcohol or drug problems or to accept a psychiatric referral (*see also* JUVENILE DELINQUENCY). Although authorities concerned with the legal and sociological

aspects of law enforcement agree that probation is more effective and less expensive for the rehabilitation of most offenders than institutional confinement, relatively few countries adhere to the principles on which its success depends: careful selection of suitable cases, suspension of sentence for offenders selected for probation, supervision by trained personnel, release of the probationer at the end of the specified time contingent on satisfactory behaviour or revocation of probation if the contrary is true.

As a judicial process probation is a function of the court. Parole, however (derived from the Fr, *parole d'honneur*, "word of honour," meaning particularly the pledge of a prisoner of war not to try to escape or bear arms, in return for conditional freedom), is an executive process, a function of an administrative body or board. The National Parole Board, under the authority of the solicitor general of Canada, reviews parole requests made by inmates of federal penitentiaries and provincial prisons if there is no provincial board (provincial boards in Québec, Ontario and BC handle parole requests from prison inmates in their provinces). During the first one-sixth of a sentence no consideration is given to parole; for the period of one-sixth to one-third of a sentence the individual is eligible for day parole consideration; for the period one-third to two-thirds consideration may be given to full parole; and for two-thirds to expiry most individuals are released on mandatory supervision.

Before CAPITAL PUNISHMENT was abolished, those serving a life sentence could be considered for release after serving 7 years, but in July 1976 the law changed to provide mandatory life imprisonment for first- and second-degree murder. Those convicted of first-degree murder are ordinarily ineligible for parole until 25 years have been served, although there is a possibility of judicial review after 15 years. For those convicted of second-degree murder the judge must determine how many years must be served before the individuals can be considered for parole; to be eligible for parole an individual must have served more than 10 but not more than 25 years. The main criteria for deciding whether parole will be granted are the plans for the post-liberation period, the severity and frequency of the inmate's delinquent behaviour and his character. Supervision of parolees is entrusted to federal or provincial correctional services, or to private-sector agencies, eg, John Howard Society, Salvation Army, Native Counselling, Elizabeth Fry Society, or to individuals, eg, a police officer, an elder in an Indian band or a volunteer. Offenders may receive full parole or be granted day parole for a specific period of time. Halfway houses are available as an intermediate step between prison and freedom.

A number of Exchange of Service Agreements exist between the federal government and the provinces providing for respective correctional services to house individuals who would normally be serving time in federal or provincial correctional centres. Transfers may be made from either the province to the federal authority or vice versa. In addition, Canada has 24 international agreements providing for the exchange of prisoners.   GUY LEMIRE

Procedural Law, legal rules governing the process for settlement of disputes. In contrast, SUBSTANTIVE LAW sets out the rights and obligations of members of society. Procedural law brings substantive law to life and enables rights and duties to be enforced and defended. Because procedural law qualifies substantive law it is sometimes referred to as "adjectival" law.
    K.G. McSHANE

Prochain Épisode is Hubert AQUIN's first novel (1965). Its nameless narrator, like the author, turns his adventures into a spy thriller in order

Privy Council chamber in the East Block of the Parliament Buildings, Ottawa (*photo by Jim Merrithew*).

to pass the time while he is detained in the psychiatric ward of a Montréal prison, pending trial for an unspecified revolutionary crime. The psychological thriller develops into a suspenseful confession with suicidal overtones as the individual quest for revolution fails: confronted with H. de Heutz, his enemy and double, in a Swiss chateau, the narrator cannot bring himself to kill this man, a fellow art-lover. The beautiful and elusive K stalks through the novel, possibly a double agent, certainly an allegorical symbol for the protagonist's long-lost love, the Québec nation. Acclaimed by both critics and radicals during the QUIET REVOLUTION, *Prochain Épisode* is a densely allusive, poetic text, containing a self-referential postmodern theory of art and language. It was translated by Penny Williams in 1967.   MICHÈLE LACOMBE

Proclamation of 1763 (Royal Proclamation of 1763), 7 Oct 1763, provided boundaries and governments for the territories acquired by Britain through the TREATY OF PARIS, Feb 1763. The PROVINCE OF QUEBEC was created out of part of what had been NEW FRANCE; its boundaries ran from Labrador's St John R westward to Lk Nipissing, southward to 45°N lat, eastward to the N shore of Baie des Chaleurs, and northward at the W end of Ile d'ANTICOSTI to the starting point. Labrador, the Gulf of ST LAWRENCE, Ile d'Anticosti and the Magdalens were given to Newfoundland; NS acquired Île St Jean [PEI] and Île Royale [Cape Breton]; and the vast interior N and W of rivers draining into the Atlantic, except HBC territory, became an Indian territory where settlement and alienation of land was forbidden and where traders could operate only under licence. A governor and council were to administer Québec until conditions permitted an assembly to be elected and English laws and courts were to be introduced.

The Québec provisions of the proclamation became effective in Aug 1764, ending 4 years of military rule. Problems became apparent immediately: the reduction of New France to this "contemptible fragment" broke the province's traditional links with the interior Indians and the fur trade, and with the eastern inshore fisheries. The expected strengthening and integration of the Québec economy into the British system did not occur. American settlers were not diverted into Québec from their westward flow, and the expected swamping of the French Catholic population by the English, and the resultant assimilation, did not occur. The proclamation did not mention language, religion, land tenure or the French CIVIL CODE, and the promised elected assembly did not materialize, a circumstance that angered the British and American merchants who had become accustomed to such democratic institutions. Finally the proclamation further alienated the Thirteen Colonies. In 1774, after several years' deterioration, the Proclamation of 1763 was replaced by the QUEBEC ACT.   NANCY BROWN FOULDS

Proctor, Henry, army officer (d at Bath, Eng 31 Oct 1822). Proctor entered the British army on 5 Apr 1781 and was serving in Canada with the 41st Regiment when war with the US broke out in 1812. As commander of the western front, he led a force of regulars and Indians to victory over Gen Winchester at Au Raisin R Jan 1813. Reversals in May and July forced a retreat, however, and in Oct 1813 Proctor was defeated by Gen Harrison at MORAVIANTOWN. Proctor was court-martialled and suspended for 6 months without pay. Maj-Gen Henry Proctor is often confused with the younger Henry Adolphus Procter (1787-1859) who served in Canada during the War of 1812 as a major in the 82nd Regiment and later rose to the rank of lt-gen.   CARL A. CHRISTIE

Progressive Conservative Party, *see* CONSERVATIVE PARTY.

Progressive Party was formed when Ontario and prairie farmers on the Canadian Council of Agriculture united with dissident Liberals led by Thomas CRERAR, who resigned from the federal Cabinet in 1919 opposing high tariffs. In Nov 1918 the CCA had proposed a "New National Policy" of free trade, nationalization (particularly of railways) and direct democracy. Under Crerar the Progressive Party permanently broke the 2-party pattern of federal politics in the 1921 election: it won 65 seats in the West, Ontario and NB, and was the second-largest party in Parliament. However, it was unable to act cohesively when facing the new minority Liberal government. Many party members were former Liberals who wanted only to shift their old party to free trade. Others wanted a more radical party. Although public support dropped in the 1925 and 1926 elections, agrarian revolt and the Progressive Party had transformed Canadian politics. The more radical members joined the CO-OPERATIVE COMMONWEALTH FEDERATION in 1932 and others linked with the CONSERVATIVE PARTY in 1942.   PETER A. RUSSELL

Prohibition was an attempt to forbid by law the selling and drinking of intoxicating beverages. It was enacted in Prince Edward Island and Nova Scotia before WWI and in the remaining provinces during the war, and was later confirmed by referenda. In Mar 1918, as a wartime measure, the federal government stopped the manufacture of liquor and its importation into provinces where purchase was illegal; in the early 1920s importation was again cut off by provincial plebiscites. Though seen as a patriotic duty and a sacrifice to help win the war, prohibition was also the culmination of generations of effort by TEMPERANCE workers to close the bars and saloons, which were the sources of much drunkenness and misery in an age before social welfare existed. The fight against "demon rum" was connected to other reforms of the time, including the WOMEN'S SUFFRAGE movement.

The provincial temperance Acts varied, but in general they closed legal drinking establishments and forbade the sale of alcohol for beverage purposes and its possession and consumption except in a private dwelling; in some provinces native wines were exempt. Alcohol could be purchased through government dispensaries for industrial, scientific, mechanical, artistic, sacramental and medicinal uses. Distillers and brewers and others properly licensed could sell outside the province.

Although enforcement was difficult, drunkenness and associated crimes declined significantly. However, illicit stills and home-brewed "moonshine" proliferated. Much inferior booze hit the streets, but good liquor was readily available since its manufacture was permitted after the war. Bootlegging (the illegal sale of alcohol as a beverage) rose dramatically, as did the number of unlawful drinking places known as "speakeasies" or "blind pigs." One way to drink legally was to be "ill," for doctors could give prescriptions to be filled at drugstores. Scandalous abuse of this system resulted, with veritable epidemics occurring during the Christmas holiday season.

A dramatic aspect of the prohibition era was rum-running. By constitutional amendment, the US was under even stricter prohibition than was Canada from 1920 to 1933: liquor legally produced in or imported into Canada was exported legally under Canadian law to its "dry" neighbour. SMUGGLING, often accompanied by violence, erupted in border areas and along the coastlines. Cartoons showed leaky maps of Canada with Uncle Sam attempting to stem the alcoholic tide.

Prohibition was too short-lived for real success. Opponents maintained that it violated Brit-

CITIZENS AWAKE AND ACT

The righteous tone of the Prohibition movement is illustrated in this cartoon from an early 20th-century prohibitionist newspaper, the *Pioneer*.

ish traditions of individual liberty; and settling the matter by referendum was an aberration from Canadian parliamentary practice. Québec rejected it as early as 1919 and became known as the "sinkhole" of N America, but the province was popular with tourists and its government reaped large profits from the sale of booze. In 1920 BC voted "wet," followed by Manitoba and Alberta in 1923 and Saskatchewan in 1924. When the Ontario Temperance Act was finally replaced in 1927 by the new Liquor Control Act, which established legal sale of alcoholic beverages through government stores, almost all of Canada had rejected "the noble experiment" in favour of "government control."

GERALD HALLOWELL

Promyshlennik, Russian (chiefly Cossack) free-lance exploiter of natural resources, notably furs. Like the COUREURS DE BOIS, *promyshlenniki* had a sure instinct for rivers, forests and terrain. They travelled in bands, sharing resources and profits. Pathfinders of Russian empire, they were active in the fur trade on the NORTHWEST COAST from the 18th until the early 19th century. They were forerunners of the Russian American Fur Company (chartered 1799).   BARRY M. GOUGH

Pronghorn (*Antilocapra americana*), small, trim ungulate, the last surviving species of a once abundant and diverse subfamily (Antilocaprinae) of American ruminants. Although sometimes called pronghorn antelope, it is not a true antelope. The species reflects the harsh predator regimes under which American ungulates evolved, for no MAMMAL is more fleet of foot. The extinct American cheetah probably helped shape the pronghorn, as did the erratic prairie environment with its grass fires, blizzards, droughts and floods. These factors re-

Pronghorn (*Antilocapra americana*), last surviving species of a once abundant subfamily of American ruminants. It is extremely fleet of foot (*photo by Stephen J. Krasemann/DRK Photo*).

sulted in a highly social, short-lived species, which possesses a large brain, indicative of adaptability and learning. Sexes move together and readily travel hundreds of miles to avoid bad winter conditions or vacate burned-over areas. Its very high reproductive rate permits rapid restoration of losses from catastrophic kills by blizzards, drowning or fire. Like other plains ungulates, pronghorns have strongly patterned coats. Males and females are similar in size and appearance. When bucks shed horn sheaths after mating season, they assume female form and become difficult for predators to detect. In mating season, bucks are territorial in some populations, harem herders in others. Pronghorns are unusual because males shed the horn sheath annually, unlike bovids in which the sheath is permanent. In 1900, they were near extinction, but the CONSERVATION and management of pronghorns has been successful. Rigorous protection and reintroduction have made them common in the western US. SW Saskatchewan and SE Alberta are the northern fringe of the pronghorns' distribution. VALERIUS GEIST

Property Law The popular notion of property as something owned encourages the conception of property rights as absolute and indefeasible, but property in the legal sense is more accurately regarded as the aggregate of legal rights of individuals with respect to objects and obligations owed to them by others and guaranteed and protected by government. Ownership of property is classified as "private" (property owned by an individual or individuals) or "public" (property owned by some form of government unit).

Property law is also classified under COMMON LAW, as real or personal. Real property (or realty) is land, any buildings on that land, any mineral rights under the land, and anything that is attached to the land or buildings that can be considered permanently attached. Personal property (sometimes known as "chattels") includes any property that is not real property. The dichotomy between real and personal property derives from early English law, under which property was considered "real" if the courts could restore to the dispossessed owner the thing itself rather than simply awarding damages as compensation for its loss.

Origin and Development of Canadian Property Law Property law, for all common law provinces, originated in England. The laws were established at various times, eg, in Nova Scotia and New Brunswick in 1758, PEI in 1763, Ontario in 1792, Newfoundland in 1832, BC in 1858 and the 3 Prairie provinces in 1870. The Constitution Act, 1867, allocated legislative power over property and civil rights to the provinces. Thus general property law, including succession law and matrimonial property law (*see* FAMILY LAW), may only be enacted by the provincial legislatures. However, certain kinds of property (eg, bills of exchange and promissory notes, patents, copyrights and interest for the use of money) are within federal legislative competence. Parliament may incidentally affect property rights through legislation regulating interprovincial or international trade and commerce, through its power of taxation and through its power of expropriation for federal purposes. Nevertheless, general property law is the preserve of the provincial legislatures.

The development of property law has generally been gradual and unspectacular. In the latter part of the 19th century, Canadian provinces and territories enacted statutes that permitted married women to hold property separate from their husbands. Prior to this time, on marriage a woman's personal property was vested in her husband. Separate property for a married woman permitted the matrimonial home to be held in joint tenancy and during the 20th century this has become popular.

In the 19th century, the succession law of real property became the same as that for personal property. The rule of primogeniture, ie, inheritance by the eldest son, gave way, where there was no will, to a sharing of land among the spouse and children in the same way that personal property could be shared. In 1910 Alberta and Saskatchewan, following the example of New Zealand, became the first provinces to enact legislation restricting the power to leave property by will (respectively, the Act Respecting the Rights of Married Women in the Estate of their Deceased Husbands and the Act to Amend the Devolution of Estates Act). Gradually, all the common-law provinces enacted legislation, called testators' family maintenance or dependants' relief legislation, that empowered a judge to set aside a will if the maker of the will had failed to provide adequate maintenance for a spouse or other dependants.

In 1973, in the MURDOCH CASE, the Supreme Court of Canada held that an Alberta rancher's wife whose marriage had broken down was not entitled to a share in the ranch, which was registered in the husband's name, even though she had worked hard to make the ranch a success. The patent unfairness of the law, graphically illustrated by this case, resulted in a profound change in matrimonial property laws throughout the common-law provinces in the 10 years following the decision. Provincial legislation now permits a judge to order a division of property after a marriage has broken down to achieve fairness between spouses no matter who owns the assets. There has also been a corresponding response by the courts, and property law concepts have been modified to achieve fairer results. In the *Rathwell* case, the Supreme Court of Canada, in order to prevent unjust enrichment by the title-holding husband, resorted to the constructive trust as a remedial device to prevent such unjust enrichment occurring from the contributions made to the acquisition of assets by the wife. In *Pettkus v Becker,* the same concepts leading to an equal division of assets were applied between an unmarried man and woman who had been living together for approximately 20 years, where the contribution of the woman enabled the man to acquire assets.

The property laws of the common-law provinces are generally similar, but one area in which the real property law does differ is in the system of recording the ownership of land. In the Atlantic provinces and in southern Ontario, there is a deed registration system and in the 4 western provinces and in northern Ontario there is a land titles or Torrens system. Under the deed registration system, individuals establish ownership to land derivatively through their predecessors in title. Theoretically, to establish ownership they should trace the title to the original grant of the land from the Crown. In southern Ontario, it is necessary now to show a good root of title dating back 40 years. Under the land-titles system or Torrens system, named after Sir Robert Richard Torrens who developed the system in South Australia, the state registers all lands within its jurisdiction by listing who owns them and who has claims against them. Under this system, prospective purchasers need only be concerned with who the register says is the owner and not with whether there is a good root of title. The Council of Maritime Premiers has created an agency to develop and implement a unified land registration system to replace the existing deed registration system. In northern Ontario and parts of southern Ontario a modified Torrens system has been adopted modelled on that in western Canada.

Types of Property reflect the economic and social aspects of society. INDUSTRIALIZATION introduced new forms of property rights in factories and machines. The growth of joint-stock companies, the forerunners of modern corporations,

created new property rights in the form of bonds and shares. Recently the nature of property rights has been transformed by the tendency of modern governments to draw in revenue and power and to pour forth money, benefits, services, contracts, franchises and licences. This government largesse may replace the traditional forms of wealth and new rules will be required to protect individuals from arbitrary government action. It has been suggested that property should no longer be defined solely as the right to exclude all others from the use or benefit of something, but should also comprehend the right not to be excluded from the use or benefit of the achievements of the whole society.

Property and the Charter of Rights Although the Canadian Charter of Rights and Freedoms does not expressly provide for the protection of property rights, property rights are created and are therefore protected by common law and by statute law, although both can be changed by legislation. Any constitutional guarantee should recognize that property is a social institution that must be constantly remolded. A great jurist has warned that an absolute right of property would result in the dissolution of society. The importance of this warning can perhaps be best illustrated by considering a person who buys a gun. The property rights that this person acquires in the gun cannot extend to permission to use the gun in any way. Similarly, landowners should not be permitted to pollute the air and water because this would lessen the enjoyment and property values of adjacent owners and because of the moral obligation to pass on to succeeding generations a habitable planet. Property rights may therefore be modified to respond to new threats to the environment. There is no preordained harmony between private rights and public welfare; society will always face the dilemma of how to combine efficient use of resources with effective regulation in the interests of all society.

Property Law in Quebec

In the widest sense, the law of property in Quebec comprises the principles regulating the ways in which all kinds of property may be disposed of and acquired, ie, all the mechanisms and transactions by which property circulates. In a narrower sense, Quebec property law is concerned with defining what constitutes property. In fact, anything with a financial value (ie, anything that constitutes wealth) can be defined as property, and such a definition would embrace any right assessable in monetary terms and not merely rights in things ("real rights") or indeed those things themselves. Traditionally, however, property law is limited to the realm of real rights in intangible or corporeal things.

Quebec property law is firmly rooted in the French CIVIL LAW tradition and derives, therefore, from Roman law. Anglo-American common law has had little influence on its institutions (except for the mechanism of the TRUST and a number of security devices). Quebec law, like French law, has historically attached the greatest importance to land and rights in land as objects of wealth. Indeed, feudal landholding (the SEIGNEURIAL SYSTEM) was finally abolished in Quebec in 1854, a necessary reform before the civil law itself could be codified in a modern form (1866). Land in Quebec, whether once held in seigneurial tenure under the French regime or whether granted by the Crown (since 1763), is now in all cases held by individuals in a "free" tenure, ie, it is held of the Crown as absolutely as possible.

The Quebec Civil Code contains the fundamental principles of property law applicable to private persons. Since 1866 it has been supplemented by much ancillary legislation regulating new forms of property (such as hydraulic power) and controlling the use of property in view of contemporary concerns (such as environmental hazards and cultural heritage). The code nonetheless enshrines 2 fundamental tenets of Quebec property law: the right of private property (private ownership of lands and goods) and, as a corollary, the free circulation of such property. The code itself regulates private property in this sense, whereas statutory legislation regulates Crown or public and municipal property to which special rules apply.

More technically, Quebec civil law views all types of property either as "immovable" (land and its appurtenances, and all rights in land) or as "movable" (physically movable objects as well as claims for money and performances under contracts and obligations in general). This distinction is the thread that runs throughout Quebec law and it is the basis for many of the different legal technicalities attached to various properties. For example, rights of all kinds in land are subject to official recording in the land titles registration system, whereas rights in movable property are not.

Rights in things (technically "real rights") can be divided into 3 broad categories. Individuals may have either a right of ownership, ie, the right in their own property; a right in the thing belonging to another, ie, a right less than ownership but nonetheless composed of some of the prerogatives associated with ownership; or a right in the form of claim by a creditor to seize and sell a debtor's property to satisfy an unpaid debt.

Ownership, the most complete real right, is the right of using, enjoying and disposing of things in the most absolute manner provided no use is made thereof contrary to law or regulation. Ownership is an "exclusive" or individual right and, as a concept, is unitary. Thus, the law discourages 2 or more persons from owning the same property jointly (with certain notable exceptions such as of condominiums and aspects of property relations between married persons). Nor does the civil law admit the distinction, known to the common law, of legal and equitable ownership, eg, property shared between a trustee and a beneficiary of a trust. And, because ownership is viewed as exclusive and individual, the general policy of the law is that rights less than ownership vested in other persons are normally limited in time so that the full integrity of the prerogatives attaching to ownership itself is preserved.

The rights in the second category — rights in things of which someone else is the owner — carry some of the prerogatives of ownership but are less complete than the right of ownership. The right of "usufruct" is the right of possessing, using and enjoying the property (movable or immovable) of another, subject to the obligation of restoring the property (or sometimes its equivalent in money) at the end of the period of enjoyment. This scheme (or variations thereof) is often encountered in the context of estate planning. "Emphyteusis" is the right, under a long-term lease of land belonging to another, whereby the lessee agrees to make improvements in return for the right to enjoy the land as owner for the period specified. It is used principally in connection with large urban development projects. "Real servitudes" are rights of various kinds linking 2 lands whereby one land (or landowner) is subject to specified obligations or services in favour of the other, such as rights of view or of passage or the obligation not to build a wall above a certain height.

In the third category of rights, a creditor may have a right over the property of his debtor enabling him to seize and sell the property, under the authority of the court, if the debtor is unable to pay his debt. The property subject to seizure by the creditor may previously have been transferred into the possession of the creditor or may have remained in the possession of the debtor. These various security devices in

Quebec are known either as privileges, ie, rights attaching to the movable or immovable property of the debtor that have been created by law to secure a wide and varied list of creditors' claims; or as "hypothec," the right of the creditor to seize and sell the immovable property (land, buildings) of his debtor made liable to secure the debt by contract. The hypothec is the civil law equivalent of the MORTGAGE in common-law Canada.

It is not certain in Quebec law to what extent it may be open to private persons to create, under the principle of freedom of contract, real rights or rights of property other than those already laid down in the civil code or in ancillary legislation. The most commonly used property rights are now provided for in these sources.

GORDON BALE AND JOHN E.C. BRIERLEY

Prospecting Exploration for new MINERAL RESOURCES began with the first use of metal (COPPER) about 7000 years ago. In N America indigenous peoples used native copper before the arrival of Europeans in at least 2 areas: the southern shore of Lk Superior and the mouth of the COPPERMINE R, NWT. The first organized mineral exploration by Europeans in what is now Canada was led by Martin FROBISHER in his 3 expeditions to Baffin I (1576, 1577 and 1578). Although his first expedition was directed primarily to finding a NORTHWEST PASSAGE to Asia, the much larger, privately financed, programs of 1577 and 1578 were largely prompted by the hope of finding gold ore. The program was a failure and the supposed gold ore brought back seems to have been schist or gneiss containing sparkling mica. The next recorded prospecting venture, near the present harbour of St John's, Nfld, was instigated by Sir Humphrey GILBERT. In 1583 Gilbert brought out a Saxon miner, named Daniel, who prospected the shores and reported silver. No commercial deposits of any mineral were found, however, and both Gilbert and Daniel were lost on the return voyage.

There is little evidence of prospecting in the early French settlements of eastern Canada (see DIAMONDS OF CANADA) and not much by the employees of the Hudson's Bay Co. The exception was Samuel HEARNE, employed by the HBC at Prince of Wales's Fort near the present port of Churchill, Man, who undertook a cross-country expedition to find the source of the native copper used by members of a northern Indian tribe. In 1771, after 2 unsuccessful attempts, Hearne reached the source of the copper on the banks of the Coppermine R near the Arctic Ocean. Apart from these expeditions, there was little deliberate search for metals in Canada from 1600 to 1800, except for a general alertness for mineral deposits shown by traders and trappers in their wilderness travels, especially through the Precambrian SHIELD. LEAD was found near the Ottawa R and on the E shore of Lk Timiskaming. The first discovery of copper to reach commercial production was at Bruce Mines on the N shore of Lk Huron; production began in 1847-48. SILVER was found at SILVER ISLET, on the N shore of Lk Superior, in 1868. The copper-nickel deposits of Sudbury were discovered by chance, in the early 1880s, as a result of railway construction in the area.

Founding of the GEOLOGICAL SURVEY OF CANADA (1842) and of the geological departments of the Ontario Bureau of Mines (1891) and the Québec Department of Colonization and Mines (1898) encouraged prospecting in these provinces. The Porcupine area, first noted as favourable for GOLD mineralization by W.A. PARKS in his report to the Ontario Dept of Mines (about 1900), became the scene of a GOLD RUSH in 1909. In 1903 silver was discovered at Cobalt, Ont, and in the following 2 decades the area became the world's largest silver producer. In the meantime, prospecting had progressed from the West Coast into

Northern Ontario prospector's camp, *c* 1900 (*courtesy Ontario Northland Transportation Comm*).

the valleys and mountains of BC. Placer gold first attracted prospecters N from earlier gold rushes in the western US in the mid-19th century. In 1896 discovery in the YT of placer gold on the Klondike R and its tributaries led to the most extensive gold rush in Canadian history (*see* KLONDIKE GOLD RUSH). In BC, prospecting for lead, silver and copper followed that for gold. Several base-metal mines were active by the end of the 19th century, including the Sullivan Mine near the Slocan R, which is still one of the largest producers of lead and silver.

During this period, prospecting, aided by the GSC, was carried on in the Eastern Townships of Québec, S of the St Lawrence R. Placer gold had been found in the area earlier but had reached only limited production. By the end of the 19th century, interest had extended to copper and, later, to ASBESTOS. In northern Québec, copper was first noted in the Chibougamau area in 1870, but it was 25 years before this discovery resulted in widespread prospecting. The turn of the century also saw vigorous prospecting for gold in eastern NS that resulted in the establishment of many small-scale producers. By 1920, prospecting was active in some parts of all provinces (except PEI) and, since the end of WWII, has occupied a significant part of Canadian expenditures on natural RESOURCES.

Aids to Prospecting

Geology Until after WWII, prospecting in Canada and elsewhere depended essentially on the use of the pick and shovel, guided by some knowledge of GEOLOGY. Prospectors chose areas for exploration aided by geological maps prepared and distributed by the GSC and by geological departments in the various provinces. Mineral deposits in Canada occur in 3 main areas: the mountainous belt of BC and the YT affected by the Cordilleran folding from 230 to 50 million years ago; the Precambrian Shield, extending from the Labrador Coast W to northern Saskatchewan and N to the Arctic coast, which has rocks and periods of folding and intrusion dating from over 3 billion to 570 million years ago; and southeastern Qué, NB, NS and Nfld, all of which were affected by the Appalachian folding of 470-320 million years ago. Each area has its own mineral characteristics and prospecting targets.

Geophysics Since 1946 there has been an increasing use of geophysical techniques (*see* PHYSICS). This trend has coincided with an increased proportion of MINING exploration conducted by companies and syndicates, as compared with that by individuals or small groups of prospectors. The first application of geophysics was the design and use of the dip needle and its successor, the magnetometer. The latter instrument, first developed in Sweden in the latter part of the 19th century, measures the relative magnetic attraction of different parts of the Earth's surface (*see* GEOMAGNETIC POLE). Magnetite (magnetic iron oxide) gives the strongest magnetic pull of any mineral, but sulphide-nickel ore also has above-average magnetic intensity and, under soil or rock covering, presents a suitable target for the magnetometer. In Canada, Thomas Edison, the American inventor, was the first recorded user of the magnetometer on nickel. Near Sudbury, Ont, shortly after WWI, he noted a strong magnetic anomaly between 2 known copper-nickel deposits on the projection of the same geological contact, but in an area covered by a thick layer of gravel. The shaft sunk on the indicated location did not go deep enough and it was not until some years later that deeper investigations proved the existence of the ore body that had given the magnetic indication. The magnetometer was also used before WWI in areas known to have IRON formations in Ontario and Québec. Its use became widespread in the 1930s, both for the direct indication of magnetic ores and in tracing geological contacts under surface covering.

Geophysics was also applied to prospecting, beginning in Canada in the late 1920s, for measurement of natural, weak electric currents that flow between rock formations with different electrical charges and, especially, in the vicinity of metallic sulphide bodies that are being oxidized by weathering processes near the surface. The use of electrical measurements then moved to the introduction of artificial direct currents and the measurement of their concentration along conductive zones such as would be provided by a metallic sulphide vein. A further stage was the introduction into the ground of an alternating current to cause the formation of secondary electromagnetic fields, around natural conductors such as metallic ore bodies. These fields can then be measured by receiving coils. These developments took place prior to WWII, but it was not until the 1950s that the use of electromagnetic methods began to play a major role in mining exploration. At this time, both magnetic and electromagnetic equipment were installed in aircraft and used in systematic air surveys. Geophysics began to be responsible for a significant proportion of new metal discoveries. The airborne magnetometer measures and records the magnetic pull of the ground directly below it. Airborne electromagnetic methods involve equipping the aircraft with a transmitting coil that projects a primary electromagnetic field into the ground below the aircraft, and a receiving coil that picks up secondary electromagnetic fields that are initiated in conductive bodies. The first discovery in Canada of an ore body by means of airborne electromagnetic methods was the one that became the Heath-Steele Mine, NB, in 1952. From 1950-59, 19 of a total of 59 discoveries resulted initially from indications collected by airborne geophysical methods. The most important such discovery took place in 1963, and became the Kidd Creek Mine, N of Timmins, Ont.

Airborne geophysical methods cannot define the location of a conductor or magnetic body with sufficient accuracy to allow direct testing by drilling. Normally, when an anomaly is noted by airborne techniques and selected for investigation, a ground party is sent in to prospect the area by conventional methods and confirm, by ground geophysical techniques, the airborne indications. Airborne geophysics is most suitable in relatively level areas covered by glacial overburden, eg, much of the Precambrian Shield. Prospecting in the mountains of BC and the YT has depended less on the use of airborne geophysics but, even here, the technique is being increasingly employed.

With the growing interest in URANIUM following WWII, instruments to measure radioactivity, such as the Geiger counter or scintillometer, became important prospecting aids.

Many discoveries, especially in the Athabasca area of Saskatchewan, have resulted from tracing trains of radioactive boulders, plucked from their source by GLACIERS in the Pleistocene ICE AGE and distributed in a rough line in the direction of the ice movement. Measurement of the radioactivity of waters of lakes overlying radioactive deposits has also led to discoveries. Radioactive measuring techniques have become increasingly accurate and sensitive. The use of radioactive measurements from aircraft is now routine and the GSC, in collaboration with some provincial surveys, has carried out such surveys in a reconnaissance fashion over large areas of the Precambrian Shield. These surveys indicate broad areas with above-average radioactivity and have aided prospectors in their search for uranium. Since uranium ores are commonly difficult to recognize by sight, most discoveries of the metal have resulted from radioactive measurements.

Geochemistry The application of GEOCHEMISTRY has aided conventional prospecting increasingly since 1960. The technique involves chemical analysis of samples of the silts along rivers and streams, of sediments in lake bottoms and of surface soils at selected intervals. Geochemical prospecting techniques are most suitable in unglaciated areas or in mountainous regions; therefore, their application in Canada lagged behind that in tropical countries, except in BC and the YT where their use has resulted in the discovery of a number of large, low-grade copper deposits of the porphyry class (*see* IGNEOUS ROCK). In the Precambrian Shield areas, the use of geochemistry as a prospecting tool has been slower to develop but there, too, as a result of greater sensitivity in analysis and the obtaining of samples by probing through the glacial covering, its use is increasing, particularly in following up airborne geophysical indications. Geochemical sampling can be used by individual prospectors more easily than can most geophysical techniques.

Associations In 1932 the Prospectors and Developers Assn was formed. Its membership includes individual prospectors using conventional methods and geologists, geophysicists and geochemists involved in mining exploration for corporations or governments. The association meets once a year (usually in Toronto), sponsors a technical program, issues informative literature to its members throughout the year, and deals with the appropriate ministries of the federal and provincial governments.   D.R. DERRY
Reading: M. Zaslow, *Reading the Rocks* (1975).

Prostitution is generally defined as the practice of providing sexual services for money, but because it requires a buyer and a seller it can more appropriately be defined as the practice of exchanging money for sexual services. Heterosexual prostitution (men as the buyers and women as sellers) is most common; homosexual prostitution also exists, but on a much smaller scale.

The buying and selling of sex has been organized through street prostitution, brothels and call-girl operations. Throughout the 1800s, prostitution in Canada was organized around brothels. The houses were grouped together, often sharing their neighbourhood with taverns in the poorer parts of town. In Ottawa and Québec City the brothel districts were in the "lower towns"; in Saint John, Halifax, and in Kingston, Ont, they were near the docks; Montréal and Toronto each had a couple of districts. The brothels in Saint John and Halifax provided gambling in addition to sex and alcohol, and were known to be some of the most financially successful houses in the first half of the 19th century.

As the first wave of settlers moved west, the sexual exploitation of Indian women by white men became commonplace. The North-West

Mounted Police (NWMP) reported that Indians brought their wives and daughters to the river flats below Lethbridge, Alta, for the purpose of prostitution, and in 1886 the traffic in Indian women became a national scandal involving employees of the Indian affairs department.

In 1880 the federal government decided to regulate against the prostitution of Indian women and "An Act to Amend and Consolidate the Laws Respecting Indians" was introduced. The Act prohibited keepers of bawdy houses from allowing Indian women to work as prostitutes on their premises. Four years later the Act was amended to state specifically that keepers of "tents and wigwams," as well as houses, fell within the bawdy house provisions. This was done to ensure that native Canadians could be convicted of being brothel keepers.

With the development of the transcontinental railways, there was a mass migration westward at the turn of the century. Unlike the earlier settlers who had been mainly farm families, these migrants were mostly single men, either bachelors or husbands who had temporarily left their wives and families at home. This mass migration of single men upset the normal male-female ratio and created an environment in which prostitution flourished.

Brothels were established within convenient distance of the railway stations and unless they or their inmates came to the attention of social or moral reformers, who then exerted pressure on the authorities, little was done to close them. The authorities were inclined to feel that prostitution had to be tolerated because it could not be eradicated. On occasions when the NWMP did take action, it was usually for reasons other than a mere violation of the prostitution laws. Such reasons included arguments that prostitution was having a damaging effect on the Indians or on the railway construction projects, or evidence that brothel inmates were involved in other criminal activities. Local police across the Prairies followed the NWMP policy and prosecuted brothel owners and inmates only when something worse than "illicit sex" was brought to their attention.

It was the parishioners and clergy of the Anglo-Saxon Protestant churches who took the least tolerant view of the existence of brothels. In some instances they mounted crusades to wipe out the traffic in women; in others they demanded that the women be driven out of town. Most often, however, since the brothels were regarded more as adjuncts to the liquor trade than as evils in themselves, the attention of the crusaders was directed toward combatting the evils of alcohol.

Public pressure to do something about prostitution was not always directed at the police or the politicians. On some occasions it was directed at the municipal authorities. Evidence suggests that this tactic may have been more successful, for between 1851 and 1881 many municipalities passed bylaws suppressing houses of prostitution, prostitutes, inmates and frequenters.

From 1890 on, legal repression made it more difficult to operate brothels, and streetwalking became a much more common type of prostitution. Prostitutes became dependent on middlemen, especially pimps. Brothels (sometimes organized as massage parlours) and call-girl operations (often disguised as escort services) still exist today, but street prostitution is the most visible form of prostitution and receives the most attention. Yet it has been estimated that only a small proportion of the prostitute population is engaged in street prostitution (estimates range from 10% to 33%). A significant number of the prostitutes who work the streets and other public places are juveniles; about 50% of these are young men engaged in homosexual prostitution.

Legislation and Enforcement Prostitution itself has never been a crime in Canada. However, various activities associated with it, eg, street solicitation, the operation of bawdy houses, procuring, and living off the avails of prostitution, have been and still are illegal. The earliest legislation grew out of general vagrancy statutes that were designed to remove indigents and other undesirables from the streets. Lower Canada (Québec) enacted a comprehensive statute dealing with prostitution in 1839. Police were authorized to apprehend "all common prostitutes or night walkers wandering in the fields, public places or highways, not giving a satisfactory account of themselves." Persons "in the habit of frequenting houses of ill-fame" could also be arrested if they failed to give a satisfactory account of themselves. In 1858 this legislation was extended to the United Province of Canada.

In 1867 Parliament passed an Act Respecting Vagrants that condemned all vagrants and disorderly persons to a maximum of 2 months in prision, a fine of $50, or both. Vagrants were defined as including all common prostitutes wandering in the streets and persons in the habit of frequenting bawdy houses who could not give a satisfactory account of themselves; all keepers of bawdy houses; and all persons who lived off the avails of prostitution. Only women were charged as prostitutes under this Act, and prostitution remained a status offence (one in which specific offensive behaviour is not a prerequisite for detention) until 1972 when the vagrancy law was repealed in response to a recommendation by the Royal Commission on the STATUS OF WOMEN IN CANADA, and because of pressure from women's groups and civil liberties groups. It was replaced by a soliciting law: "Every person who solicits any person in a public place for the purpose of prostitution is guilty of an offence punishable on summary conviction." The words "every person" were intended to prohibit both males and females from soliciting, but courts of appeal differed about whether a male could be a prostitute and about whether a client could be charged with soliciting. In 1978 the BC court held that a male could be a prostitute but that a client could not be charged with soliciting; in the same year the Ontario court held that a male could not be a prostitute (because dictionary meanings of prostitutes only dealt with females) but a that customer could be charged with soliciting. In 1978 the Supreme Court of Canada held that "soliciting" means conduct that is "pressing or persistent," and it later stated that "pressing and persistent" means repeated soliciting of the same person. According to the same judgement, a car is not a public place.

Subsequent growth in the visibility of street prostitution in middle-class residential neighbourhoods has reopened the debate regarding prostitution legislation. The debate has focused on the validity of the municipal bylaws (enacted in Montréal, Calgary, Vancouver, Niagara Falls and Halifax) and on proposals to amend the soliciting section of the Criminal Code. The first issue was resolved in 1983 when the Supreme Court of Canada (in *Westendorp* v *The Queen*) found the Calgary bylaw to be invalid and ULTRA VIRES of the city of Calgary. The debate over the amendments, however, is still raging.

Representatives of the police, citizens' group and municipal governments have been lobbying the federal government to strengthen the soliciting section of the Criminal Code so that it will apply both to customer and prostitute; to redefine "public place"; and, most importantly, to reword the legislation so that soliciting need be neither pressing nor persistent to constitute an offence. Women's groups and civil-liberties groups, as well as groups organized around the rights of prostitutes, are opposed to this amendment on the grounds that it would so expand the soliciting section that it would amount to a return to the old vagrancy law. These groups have been pressuring the federal government to remove both the soliciting and the bawdy house sections from the Criminal Code on the grounds that they cause more social harm than they prevent.

In 1983 an amendment to the Criminal Code provided that both male and female persons could be charged as prostitutes, but this amendment did not deal with the cloudy issue of the prosecution of clients nor did it resolve the public debate. Somewhat later in 1983, a proposal to amend the soliciting section of the Criminal Code was tabled in the House of Commons. It was worded to ensure that the offence can apply to anyone who solicits, whether this be a prospective customer or prostitute, and to include within the definition of a "public place" a motor vehicle in or on a public place. Because the status quo regarding pressing or persistent behaviour would not be effected by this proposal, it will not serve to still the public debate even if passed into law. In the meantime, enforcement strategies continue to focus on the selling and not the buying of sex; even in those jurisdictions that provide for the prosecution of the client, most prosecutions for soliciting are undertaken against prostitutes.

Community attitudes have always governed the approach taken to prostitution. Parliamentarians have been pressured to amend the laws, municipalities have been encouraged to enact bylaws, and from time to time police have been pressed by public sentiment to enforce the laws against prostitution by closing brothels and arresting streetwalkers. Suppression has usually been spasmodic and ineffective; once brothels were closed or prostitutes driven from the streets, the public would turn its attention elsewhere, the brothels would reopen, the prostitutes would return and law enforcement officers would permit prostitution to exist until another public protest.

Three main approaches have been taken historically toward prostitution in Canada — regulation, prohibition and rehabilitation. Proponents of regulation believed that prostitution resulted from the different sexual needs of men and women. They felt that prostitution should be recognized as a necessary social evil and regulated to contain its worst side effects, eg, the spread of SEXUALLY TRANSMITTED DISEASE and the traffic in women. Proponents of prohibition believed that prostitution should be eradicated, and wanted criminal law to serve as a tool to root out all forms of prostitution activities. Those in favour of the third approach believed that individual prostitutes should be rehabilitated. Feminists, social reformers and government officials all vigorously debated which approach was preferable, and each approach was tried in some form or other. All of these legislative schemes, either as provided in law or as enforced, were interlaced with class, race and, most significantly, sex discrimination. They were doomed to failure because they did not address the major causes of prostitution, which are deeply rooted in social inequality, in a longtime double standard of sexual morality as applied to men and women, and in the general inability of society to satisfy the sexual needs of men and women.

In recent years a fourth approach has been taken toward prostitution, that of abolition. Abolitionists consider prostitution to be a personal choice and hence a private matter between consenting adults. Their aim is to eradicate the objective conditions that lead people into it and to ensure that those profiteering from the prostitution of others are penalized. They want activities between prostitute and customer decriminalized, arguing that this is the best way to prosecute profiteers. FRAN SHAVER

Reading: F. Finnegan, *Poverty and Prostitution* (1979); James H. Gray, *Red Lights on the Prairies* (1971); J. James et al, *The Politics of Prostitution* (1977); E. McLeod, *Women Working: Prostitution Now* (1982); R. Symanski, *The Immoral Landscape* (1981).

Protectionism, government policies that shield domestic production (and producers) from foreign competition. For example, a Canadian tariff of 15% on an automobile that costs $5000 in a foreign country means that a tax (CUSTOMS duty) of $750 will be levied on the car when it is imported to Canada. The Canadian price will be $5750, and Canadian producers of similar vehicles who can operate profitably at a price of $5750, but not $5000, will be able to compete with imports in the Canadian market. Producers dependent on protection cannot normally export, since their costs are above world prices, and they therefore depend almost entirely on the home market. (The effect of the 1965 CANADA-US AUTOMOTIVE PRODUCTS AGREEMENT is that automobiles produced in Canada can be exported to the US, although the price in Canada is higher.)

Economic analysis shows that economic losses from a tariff exceed its benefits. Theoretically, a tariff is wasteful because it leads to a substitution of higher-cost home production for lower-cost imports; if tariffs were repealed, manpower and capital in protected industries would shift to other employments, at home or abroad, and everyone, in their role as consumers, would gain from lower prices. Owners having to change the employment of their resources would suffer losses: landowners and shareholders in the contracting industries would lose more as owners than they would gain as consumers; specialized workers in the contracting industries would probably face retraining or lower-paying jobs; and others would bear the "transitional" costs of reorganizing their economic lives. Probably the many net winners would each gain a relatively small amount, while the relatively few net losers would suffer fairly heavy losses. Nevertheless, in principle it should be possible for a government to compensate losers and still produce a net social "profit" by repealing tariffs.

The debate about protectionism has revolved around attempts to find an intellectually respectable rebuttal to the economic argument, but none has been found. Public discussion of protectionism would be better if its proponents would argue that, although it involves economic costs, these are outweighed by noneconomic benefits. The intriguing question is why virtually all governments have passed laws known to reduce their citizens' economic well-being.

Protectionist policies may confer benefits that cannot be bought in the marketplace, such as increased military security, a larger population and more diversified production, and a heightened sense of national identity. These vague contentions cannot be definitively refuted, but they seem not to fit the Canadian situation. The defence argument is largely irrelevant in countries of small populations. Belief in the virtues of size and diversification, although given no credence by economists, seems widely shared by politicians. Voters may view size and diversification as matters of national pride, in which case the "diversification" argument merges with the "national identity" argument. In Canada, arguments for protectionism are generally not supported by residents in 8 provinces who observe that the tariff diversifies production mainly in Ontario and Québec.

A second explanation may be that political dynamics almost ensure protectionist policies. Politicians are likely to support tariffs where the "protectionist" vote is concentrated, and ignore tariffs or pay lip service to "free trade" elsewhere. Even voters who would gain by repeal may vote against it in compassion for those "vested interests" whose lives would be disrupted. But this explanation is not fully satisfying. Practical techniques exist for compensating the losers from a change in government policies, so that the "compassion" argument loses force; and the "vote-getting" argument begs the question of why a political party could not promise both to raise the standard of living by phasing out tariffs and to adopt policies to ease the transition. A third possible explanation for protectionism suggests some deep psychological or biological "imperative" compelling people to favour domestic producers and protect production in the "home territory."

Although the British North American colonies had relied upon relatively low tariffs on specific commodities for government revenues, the first coherent Canadian system of protection was established well after Confederation. Sir John A. MACDONALD won the 1878 general election largely on the strength of the NATIONAL POLICY, a policy of ECONOMIC NATIONALISM designed to protect Canadian businesses against competition from lower-cost US firms. Since that time, although the 1911 general election was contested over the question of free trade with the US (see RECIPROCITY), protectionism in some form has always been part of Canada's international economic relations.

After WWII Canada signed a General Agreement on Tariffs and Trade (GATT) that obligated member nations to reduce tariffs and other barriers to trade by multilateral negotiations. GATT has been effective in reducing tariff rates, but not in reducing "nontariff barriers." Indeed, the decline of tariffs has been accompanied by a growth of other barriers, including import quotas; threats of quotas or other measures that induce foreigners to accept "voluntary export restraints" when shipping specific goods to Canada; administrative protection, by which customs officers restrict or impede the entry of imports; and many other policies ranging from exchange controls to health and safety regulations. Canada can perhaps claim to have pioneered another form of protection: "content" provisions, which make it easier for firms to import when they produce in Canada a certain proportion of the content of the goods they sell. Content provisions have been applied to automobile firms since 1926 and are also used in the broadcasting industry.

Since WWII, several tariff substitutes have been adopted by Canadian provinces in a pronounced movement to "provincial protectionism." Marketing boards have been established to raise the incomes of certain farmers (notably milk, egg and poultry producers) by restricting provincial production, and by persuading the national government to apply tariffs to imports from abroad and "production quotas" to all provinces. Provincial governments also favour provincial producers in letting government contracts by accepting "domestic" bids even if they are higher than bids from other provinces. Recently some provinces have required firms bidding for contracts to abide by "provincial-content" rules, and some have required that particular industries give priority in hiring to applicants who reside (or perhaps were born) in the province.

The phenomenon of provincial protectionism, and the suspicion that there would also be municipal protectionism if it were feasible to restrict trade between cities — as it was in the Middle Ages when local protectionism flourished — suggests that protectionism is not simply a matter of national economic diversification or national identity. See FOREIGN INVESTMENT; INTERNATIONAL TRADE.

JOHN H. DALES

Reading: John H. Dales, *The Protective Tariff in Canada's Development* (1966); Economic Council of Canada, *Looking Outward* (1975).

Proulx, Maurice, priest, filmmaker (b at St-Pierre-de-Montmagny, Qué 13 Apr 1902). Born into a farming family, he entered Séminaire de Québec in 1924 and was ordained in 1928. Though trained in agronomy after his ordination, Proulx developed an interest in filmmaking and used it to record the colonization of the Abitibi and other regions of Québec in the 1930s. His most famous film, the feature-length *En pays neuf* (1934-37), offers an extraordinary testament to the settlement of the Abitibi area, but he also made 36 other films for the provincial government and for industry between 1934 and 1961, mostly on agriculture, tourism and religion. He retired in 1966. His films were acquired for preservation by the Québec government in 1977.

PETER MORRIS

Provancher, Léon, priest, naturalist (b in the parish of Bécancour, Qué 10 Mar 1820; d at Cap-Rouge, Qué 23 Mar 1892). While still simply a country priest, Provancher came to the attention of scholars and the public when he published *Flore du Canada* (1862) and launched a magazine, *Le Naturaliste canadien* (1868). After taking up residence in the small village of Cap-Rouge in 1872, Provancher devoted his remaining years to natural history. His *Faune entomologique du Canada*, describing over 1000 new insect species, principally Hymenoptera, made him known to naturalists around the world. A prolific author, his works included *Traité élémentaire de botanique* (1858), *Le Verger canadien* (1862), *Histoire du Canada* and *De Québec à Jérusalem* (1884). In 1888 he founded *La Semaine religieuse de Québec*. His brooding temperament, virulent polemics and strict ultramontane convictions made Provancher stand out among the intellectuals of Québec. A true scholar, but without a following, he left a rich legacy of contributions to science.

RAYMOND DUCHESNE

Provigo Inc, with head offices in Montréal, is a holding company involved in the wholesale and retail distribution of foodstuffs, tobacco, drugs and general merchandise. Provigo began operations in Québec in 1961 and has since expanded to Ontario, the West and the Maritimes. In 1981 it acquired the Québec assets of DOMINION STORES LIMITED. Through its subsidiaries it is also active in the US. As of Jan 1984 it had annual sales or operating revenue of $3.9 billion (ranking 16th in Canada), assets of $660 million (ranking 112th) and 11 264 employees. Its major shareholders are the CAISSE DE DÉPÔT ET PLACEMENT DU QUÉBEC (27%) and Sobey Stores Ltd (15%).

DEBORAH C. SAWYER

Province House, Halifax, built between 1811 and 1818 to house Parliament, the courts and the public service, is a sophisticated example of the influence of the Palladian style on Canadian architecture. Each floor of the building is clearly set off, and the central vertical part of the main facade is emphasized by 6 Ionic columns supporting a large triangular pediment decorated with coats of arms. In the lateral sections, 2 pilasters also support small pediments. The placement of the decorative elements, the openings, the pilasters and the columns show a rare atten-

Province House facade, Halifax, NS. Built 1811-18, it is the finest example of Palladian architecture in Canada (*courtesy Parks Canada/Heritage Recording Service*).

tion to harmony and symmetry. Tradition has it that John Merrick designed the building, but the name of Richard Scott is also frequently mentioned. Province House is the most noteworthy example of Palladian architecture in Canada.

NATHALIE CLERK

Province of Canada This union of the former provinces of UPPER CANADA and LOWER CANADA stemmed from the DURHAM REPORT of 1839, after an imperial mission to investigate REBELLIONS OF 1837 in both Canadas. Lord DURHAM proposed a united province to develop a common commercial system, and particularly to complete canals on the St Lawrence. No less important, a combined Canada would have an overall English-speaking majority, thereby controlling the divisive forces Durham saw in largely French LC, and making it safe to grant the RESPONSIBLE GOVERNMENT he also advocated. Britain agreed to union, though not yet to the principle of responsible government. In 1840 the British Parliament passed the ACT OF UNION, which went into force 10 Feb 1841, establishing a single government and legislature. But whereas Durham advocated basing representation on population, counting on British immigration steadily to increase an existing Anglo-Canadian majority, the Act of Union provided equal representation for each of the Canadas in the new parliament, even though British UC then had a considerably smaller population: some 480 000, to 670 000 in LC, of whom about 510 000 were French Canadians. The French element would thus be underrepresented, and safely submerged from the start. Yet the device of equal representation had an unforeseen result. The old Canadas, each with its separate history, society and culture, virtually remained equal, distinct sections inside one political framework. They were now Canada West and Canada East geographically, but even the names Upper and Lower Canada survived in popular and some official use. The Union Act had embedded dualism in the very constitution, resulting in dual parties, double ministries and sectional politics.

As the Union began, French Canadians well realized its purpose was to submerge them. But a rising liberal leader, Louis LAFONTAINE, saw the advantage of an alliance with Canada W Reformers to seek responsible government. French Canadians would then share in ruling the United Province, maintaining themselves as a people, while co-operating with Anglo-Canadian allies. Hence LaFontaine readily responded to overtures from leading Canada W Reformers Francis HINCKS and Robert BALDWIN. Hincks, a Toronto journalist and shrewd strategist, was already backing Baldwin's campaign for responsible rule, centered on the British principle of responsible government. Its adoption in Canada would mean that governments would depend on elected parliamentary majorities. Baldwin and LaFontaine built up a powerful Reform alliance behind this principle. In Sept 1842 they won admission to the government, essentially compelling Gov Gen Sir Charles BAGOT to reconstruct his ministry because of the weight of parliamentary support behind them. On 26 Nov 1843 they and other party colleagues resigned, claiming they could not take responsibility for appointments by a new governor, METCALFE, that they had not advised. But in a succeeding Tory-Conservative ministry, William DRAPER, acting virtually as a party premier, freely managed patronage himself to help stay in power. In fact, he held on until May 1847, thus furthering responsible government in practice even before its full acceptance.

A shift in imperial policy finally brought full acceptance. In 1846, Britain's repeal of the CORN LAWS signalled a movement towards FREE TRADE, ending a centuries-old pattern of imperial trade controls and protective duties. It no longer saw much need to withhold internal self-government from its more politically advanced colonies. Lord ELGIN came to Canada as governor general in 1847, instructed to implement responsible rule. Early in 1848, after Reformers swept elections in both Canadas, Henry Sherwood's Tory-Conservative ministry resigned, and Elgin at once called on Reformers to form a government. Responsible rule was plainly confirmed when in March an all-Reform Cabinet took office under LaFontaine as premier (he had the larger following) with Baldwin as co-premier. There was still a severe testing to come. In Canada trade was at a low ebb, the newly completed St Lawrence canals half used. Tory English merchants of Montréal blamed the problem on the loss of imperial tariff protection, although world depression spreading since 1847 was a deeper cause. In the thriving earlier 1840s, moreover, expanding farm and lumber frontiers, canal building, and rising towns had readily absorbed a surge in British immigration; but now, when times were hard and frontier expansion was halting against the margins of the rugged Canadian Shield, a new tide of Irish immigrants poured in — destitute and typhus-infected, fleeing famine in their homeland. Amid these strains, the Reform ministry brought in the 1849 REBELLION LOSSES BILL.

Meant to compensate damages suffered in the LC Rebellion of 1837-38 (Upper Canadians had already settled their claims), the bill seemed vital social justice to French Canadians — proof also that responsible government could work for them. Canada E's British Tories, however, saw it as a blatant rewarding of rebels. The Reform-dominated legislature, meeting in Montréal, passed the bill over heated protests; but Tory-Conservatives still looked to a British governor to refuse his assent. Elgin did not: the measure had been recommended by a responsible ministry with support of the parliamentary majority. All the strains in Montréal burst forth in the MONTRÉAL RIOTS. Yet Elgin and his ministers rode out the storm, which subsided after a few wild days in Apr. Then in Oct the ANNEXATION manifesto appeared in the city, urging union with the US. It proved only a bitter, passing gesture. The mass of French Canadians saw colonial self-rule to be working; eastern Tories drew back; while in Canada West, apart from a few radicals, Reformers and Conservatives held firm to British connections. Responsible government survived its first test.

By 1850, depression had given way to an era of rapidly expanding world trade. Grain and timber production rose. The St Lawrence canals were bustling; Montréal merchants soon forgot annexationism. And with increasing British and American capital available, Canadian entrepreneurs took eagerly to railway building. Tracks linked Montréal to ice-free Portland, Maine, on the Atlantic, and Toronto to the Upper Great Lakes at Collingwood. A line from the Niagara to the Detroit rivers, via Hamilton, connected with rails to New York at one end and Chicago at the other, and soon extended to Toronto as well. Above all, the GRAND TRUNK, chartered 1853, built a transprovincial route connecting the lower St Lawrence by way of Québec, Montréal and Toronto to Sarnia, Ont. This first great railway boom subsided after 1857 in another world depression. The Grand Trunk in particular, overpromoted and extravagantly built, was left deep in debt, blighted with political deals and scandals. Nevertheless, rail lines had remade Canada, breaking inland winter isolation, vastly improving long-range transport, and focusing development on major towns. Railway-connected factory industries grew, notably in Montréal, Toronto and Hamilton, which rapidly advanced in urban size, wealth and complexity.

An anonymous lithograph depicting London, Canada West, c1850 (courtesy Public Archives of Canada/C-40810).

The 1854 RECIPROCITY Treaty with the US stimulated growth by giving Canadian grain and lumber free access to American markets. It also tied Canada far more closely to the American economy; the US decision in 1865 not to renew reciprocity spurred Canadian efforts to seek economic integration with other BNA provinces. Yet the same decade also brought a Canadian protective tariff, promoted by the very rise in provincial industry. In 1858 duties were raised enough to shelter manufactures effectively, though this was "incidental" protection — incidental to needs for revenue made pressing by heavy public debt incurred from lavish railway grants. Duties were lowered again in 1866. Still, the tariff of 1858 was a foretaste of the later high-tariff NATIONAL POLICY, and signified the increasingly close ties between government and business in an era of advancing large-scale capitalism.

Meanwhile, since the early 1850s, other factors had been steadily disrupting the Union's political life. Around 1850, left-wing Reform elements had emerged, the PARTI ROUGE in Canada E, the CLEAR GRITS in Canada W, advocating fully elective democracy and an American-style written constitution. In 1851 Baldwin and LaFontaine gave up combating radicalism in their own ranks and left politics. Their chief lieutenants, Francis Hincks and Augustin Morin, took over the ministry, which at first looked more secure as radical ardour waned in an atmosphere of widespread enthusiasm for railway promotion. But soon freshly divisive issues loomed, chiefly concerning public education and church-and-state relations. Predominantly Protestant Canada W widely believed in nondenominational public schools and rejected state-connected and supported religion. Largely Catholic Canada E, where mainstream French Liberals had made increasing links with the Catholic hierarchy, widely upheld denominational schools and church-state ties. More specifically, French Canadian votes backed bills in Parliament to enlarge the rights of state-aided Catholic schools in Canada W. Many Upper Canadians came to feel that their own interests were being thwarted by unchecked French Catholic power. Moreover, the census of 1851-52 revealed that the western section now had the greater population, and so was underrepresented, while paying the larger share of taxes. The strenuous editor of the powerful Toronto Globe, George BROWN, entered the Legislative Assembly as a Reform independent to battle for "justice" for Canada W. In 1853 he proposed representation by population to give the western section its full weight in seats. His initial attempt got nowhere; but it began a sharpening sectional struggle over REP BY POP: sought by Upper Canadians to overcome "French domination," fought by French Canadians to prevent their being submerged in the Union anew.

On 22 June 1854 the Hincks-Morin ministry fell. The old Reform alliance had crumbled under sectional strains. In its stead, a new ruling Liberal-Conservative COALITION appeared, which combined the moderate Liberals of Hincks and

Morin with Tory-Conservative forces, among whom a Canada W politician from Kingston, John A. MACDONALD, was rapidly gaining stature. This broad coalition managed to abolish both the old CLERGY RESERVES and the SEIGNEURIAL SYSTEM. Brownites, Clear Grits and Rouges, left in the cold, called the Conservative-oriented combination "unprincipled." Actually, it rested on essential agreement between the major parties: on railway and business development, maintenance of the Union, and defence of the French Canadian place within it. Furthermore, the coalition shortly came under the command of another outstanding Canadian partnership: that of John A. Macdonald, easygoing but brilliantly resourceful, and George-Etienne CARTIER, a formidable party manager and Montréal Grand Trunk lawyer. Under them, the CONSERVATIVE PARTY of the future gradually took shape. On the other side, Brown and the Clear Grits, earlier adversaries, moved together. On 8 Jan 1857 a party convention at Toronto hailed a rebirth of UC Reform, as Brownites, Grits and some returning moderate Liberals adopted a platform calling for rep by pop, nonsectarian education and acquisition of RUPERT'S LAND, which had lately attracted attention from both Toronto's businessmen, keen to expand their city's trade domain westward, and agrarians eager for new land frontiers. The resulting Brownite-Grit party powerfully consolidated Canada W sectionalism, while its stress on farmers' rights and hostility to big railway interests and expensive government had a long political future as well.

There followed an incessant struggle between Macdonald-Cartier conservatism and Brownite liberalism, loosely allied with the limited Rouge eastern group under A.A. DORION. In Aug 1858 a Brown-Dorion government lasted just 2 days (see DOUBLE SHUFFLE). The returning Conservatives now took up BNA federal union to answer Canada's troubles, urged on by Alexander GALT, a leading Montréal financier, who joined the ministry. Yet the other provinces proved uninterested, and general federation was soon laid aside. In Nov 1859 at another Reform convention, Brown moved his Grits behind a dual federation of the Canadas (already suggested by Dorion), which as quickly failed in Parliament. While both sides had now adopted the federal principle as a way out of sectional disruption, neither was actually ready for it, and rows over rep by pop returned.

In May 1862, the Macdonald-Cartier forces were defeated on a costly Militia Bill, a response to border tensions roused by the AMERICAN CIVIL WAR. A moderate Reformer, Sandfield MACDONALD, tried to keep the Union running by double majority, requiring majorities for government measures from both halves of the province. Sandfield's principle failed though he hung on until early 1864, when John A. Macdonald returned, to be defeated in 3 months. Elections and government shifts had achieved nothing in the equal balance of sectional forces. By June 1864, with the United Province plainly deadlocked, Brown made a crucial offer to back a government willing to remake the Union. Negotiations between Macdonald, Cartier, Galt and Brown led quickly to an agreement to seek general federation and include the North-West, or a federation of the Canadas if that failed. The first aim would not fail. Brown and 2 Liberal colleagues joined the ministry, and the "GREAT COALITION" took up the federation cause with the other BNA colonies. The outcome was the scheme for CONFEDERATION and the BRITISH NORTH AMERICA ACT of 1867. Throughout the shaping of the confederation plan Canadian representatives had played commanding roles, especially John A. Macdonald. When it went into force on 1 July 1867, the day of the old Canadian Union was over, scarcely mourned amid bright aspirations for the future. Before the Union ended, its Parliament endorsed the federal scheme with both English and French majorities in 1865, and in 1866 drafted constitutions for the successor provinces of Québec and Ontario. The United Province had gone through much and achieved much. But its final achievement lay in Confederation itself.   J.M.S. CARELESS

Reading: J.M.S. Careless, The Union of the Canadas (1967) and Brown of the Globe (1959); D.G. Creighton, John A. Macdonald: The Young Politician (1952); W.L. Morton, The Critical Years (1964).

Province of Quebec, 1763-91 At the end of the SEVEN YEARS' WAR, Great Britain organized the territories that were confirmed as its possessions by the TREATY OF PARIS, 1763. By the Royal PROCLAMATION OF 1763, the Province of Quebec was created out of the inhabited portion of NEW FRANCE, taking the shape of a quadrilateral on each side of the St Lawrence R and stretching from Lk Nipissing and the 45th parallel to the Saint John R and Ile d'Anticosti. These boundaries were modified by the QUEBEC ACT (1774) to include the fishing zone off Labrador and the Lower North Shore and the FUR-TRADE area between the Ohio and Mississippi rivers and the Great Lakes. The TREATY OF PARIS, 1783, pushed the boundary farther N. The "old province of Quebec," to use historian A.L. Burt's expression, ceased to exist when it was divided into 2 separate colonies, LOWER CANADA and UPPER CANADA, following the CONSTITUTIONAL ACT of 1791.

Since many of the province's inhabitants were, or had been, employed by fur-trade companies and merchants, their geographic universe was not limited to these official boundaries; it stretched westward to include the PAYS D'EN HAUT and the North-West, the source of the colony's main export. The fur trade had been virtually destroyed during the war and then hobbled first by PONTIAC's revolt and later by the restrictions imposed by British authorities. It took nearly a decade to revive the trade, but the traders eventually occupied the previous French territory. Then, following the example set by Peter POND, they explored and exploited new areas. By 1789, when Alexander MACKENZIE descended the Mackenzie R to the Arctic Ocean, the entire North-West, from Lk Superior to the Rockies, had been linked to the Province of Quebec through the activities of the VOYAGEURS and fur traders. During the period 1763-91 Montréal merchants drained off most of the furs from the SW. Competition from New York and Albany was gradually eliminated by the 1768 decision to return to the colonies the regulation of the fur trade and by the 1774 annexation of the Ohio territory to the province. That region had ties with Montréal even after the 1783 treaty, since Britain retained the posts S of the Great Lakes until 1796 (*see* JAY'S TREATY).

Although the fur trade was vital for the province and its commerce with Britain, it was not the main domestic economic activity. Agriculture, especially the growing and preparation of wheat products, occupied the largest number of people and supplied the local market. Surpluses increasingly allowed food to be exported to the W Indies and Britain. Industrial production at the artisan level supplied domestic needs and the smaller needs of the fur trade.

The domestic market should not be underestimated: as a result of a high birth rate the population more than doubled, from nearly 70 000 in 1775 to nearly 144 000 in 1784 and over 161 000 in 1790. Migration played little part in this growth. Seven thousand people left the St Lawrence Valley after the CONQUEST, and the expected British immigration did not take place. The number of "old subjects" was very small — some 500 in 1766 and perhaps 2000 in 1780. Their number grew significantly only after the AMERICAN REVOLUTION, when LOYALISTS arrived in significant numbers — the 1784 census

A View of Château Richer, watercolour by Thomas Davies, depicts rural life in the Province of Quebec, 1787 (*courtesy National Gallery of Canada*).

listed some 25 000. The Loyalists settled mainly in the SW part of the province, which later became Upper Canada [Ontario].

The British, many of whom were merchants and officials, had influence and position out of proportion to their numbers. The governors, James MURRAY, Guy CARLETON and Frederick HALDIMAND, were responsible for the province; they and their entourages (which often, in fact, included Francophones) therefore held social as well as political power. The merchants, with the advantage of credit in London, soon controlled commercial relations with the mother country. At first supported by the military authorities and helped by francophone voyageurs, they acquired in less than 2 decades the lion's share of the fur trade. They established the NORTH WEST COMPANY, which took an increasingly larger share of the trade and was, by 1790, the most powerful fur-trade organization in the Province of Quebec.

The administrators and merchants often failed to see eye to eye. The merchants even managed to have Murray, the first governor, recalled. The dispute with Murray centered on the application of British law and the creation of an Assembly, as provided for in the Proclamation of 1763. The merchants felt that these institutions were essential to the anglicizing of the colony and the protection of British interests. They perceived and defined these interests as those of Britons resident in the colony. But both Murray and Carleton defined British interests as the interests of the British Crown, and they therefore felt that their main task was to avoid any threat to the Crown's possession of the colony. Given the style of government adopted during the period of military occupation (1760-63), the lack of British immigration and the growing unrest in the Thirteen Colonies, the governor had no choice but to try to win over the majority of the population. Major portions of the Proclamation were set aside and "new subjects" were appointed to official positions.

In 1774 Carleton, who was determined to preserve a military base of operations in N America, obtained the passage of the Quebec Act. It fell far short of pleasing the merchants, who wanted an Assembly, even though it strengthened their monopoly on the fur trade to the south. The governor hoped the Act would win the support of the francophone elite. Murray had already gained the collaboration of the Roman Catholic clergy (*see* CATHOLICISM). The death of Bishop Henri-Marie Dubreil de PONTBRIAND in 1760 had left the church without a bishop to run its affairs and ordain new priests; moreover, funds were desperately short and war-destroyed buildings had to be replaced. Murray therefore made himself the champion of the church and was instrumental in bringing about the 1766 consecration in France of Jean-Olivier Briand as the new bishop of Québec. The Quebec Act allowed the free practice of the Catholic faith, re-established the COUTUME DE PARIS in civil matters and restored property rights to the church and SEIGNEURS. A council was created and the aboli-

tion of the Test Oath allowed Catholics to enter public office.

But these conciliatory measures failed to have the desired effect. The habitants showed little enthusiasm for British interests, especially during the American invasion of 1775-76. Nevertheless, for various reasons, they also failed to side with the revolutionaries. And so Carleton's strategy had partial success: the province remained British.

The sociopolitical structure created by the Quebec Act failed to survive the consequences of war. It was upset by the arrival of the Loyalists, and this increase in British population greatly strengthened the merchants' position and intensified their conflict with the governor. The British authorities asked Carleton (now Lord Dorchester) to suggest a solution to the problem. In order to satisfy, at least partially, the merchants and the Loyalists without angering the Francophones, in 1791 London produced a revised Quebec Act and a new constitution, which included the creation of a House of Assembly. The new provinces of Lower and Upper Canada were created, with Lower Canada retaining many of the institutional forms of the Province of Quebec.

The 30 years following the Conquest are of major importance to the understanding of Canadian history. The economic structure of the St Lawrence Valley remained almost unchanged: 2 economies coexisted, one commercial and oriented towards the mother country, the other agricultural and artisanal, and oriented toward the local market. These 30 years were marked on one hand by the intention, explicitly expressed in 1763, to anglicize the colony, and on the other hand by the need to come to terms with changing circumstances on the N American continent. During those 30 years, 2 ethnic groups came together, anticipating many of the points of contact, co-operation and tension that characterized much of subsequent Canadian history. By 1791 the process of anglicization proposed in 1763 was no longer practicable, and the francophone culture would survive.   G. ALLAIRE

Provincial Floral Emblems Floral emblems are generally selected from among the flora of the country, nation, state, territory or province

Floral Emblems of Canada		
Canada	sugar MAPLE *Acer saccharum*	1867
Alberta	prickly or wild ROSE *Rosa acicularis*	1930
BC	Pacific DOGWOOD *Cornus nuttallii*	1956
PEI	showy LADY'S SLIPPER *Cypripedium reginae* replaced by pink lady's slipper *C. acaule*	1947 1965
Manitoba	prairie crocus or CROCUS ANEMONE *Anemone patens*	1906
NB	purple VIOLET *Viola cucullata*	1936
NS	MAYFLOWER *Epigaea repens*	1901
Ontario	white TRILLIUM *Trillium grandiflorum*	1937
Québec	Madonna LILY *Lilium candidum*	1963
Saskatchewan	western red or prairie lily *Lilium philadelphicum*	1941
Newfoundland	PITCHER PLANT *Sarracenia purpurea*	1954
NWT	MOUNTAIN AVENS *Dryas integrifolia*	1957
YT	FIREWEED *Epilobium angustifolium*	1957

that they are meant to represent. Tradition dictates that the plant selected be popular and commonly found throughout the region. Floral emblems may thus differ from coats of arms or flags, since the latter are more symbolic in nature (*see* HERALDRY). For historical reasons, however, a nonindigenous plant or one linked to the founding nation, an industry or a particular landscape may be chosen. The entire plant or only the flower may be represented. The latter is a true floral emblem. The emblem may also be the leaves or branches of a tree. Some countries have both a floral and a tree emblem. Some emblems are adopted officially or legally, others are unofficially recognized by the people for historic, religious or other reasons.

The table on page 1498 lists the floral emblems of Canada and its provinces and territories, along with the dates on which they were adopted (by Act of the provincial or territorial legislature). Because they are known by various common names, French and English, the scientific names, given in italics, are most accurate. *See* EMBLEMS OF CANADA; EMBLEMS, PROVINCIAL AND TERRITORIAL. CÉLINE ARSENEAULT

Provincial Government Under Canada's federal system, constitutional power is shared between the federal government and 10 provincial governments. The provincial governments are primarily responsible for public schooling, health and social services, highways and LOCAL GOVERNMENT (through municipalities), but overlapping and, at times, conflicting regional and national interests have stretched provincial concerns across virtually every area of Canadian public policy. Each province is free to determine levels of provincial public services and each provincial government has been true to its regional economic and cultural interests in its own fashion. Generalizations about provincial activities such as "province building" or "policy convergence" therefore do not always stand up to close scrutiny, and it is easier to cite the exceptions than frame universal rules. The CONSTITUTION ACT, 1867, which outlined the DISTRIBUTION OF POWERS between the provinces and the central government established a federal union in Canada (*see* FEDERALISM), but not a perfect or ideal federal state. Preoccupied with nation building, the FATHERS OF CONFEDERATION designed the original constitutional arrangements with a bias toward a strong central government. The powers of the federal government to disallow provincial statutes within one year of their passage (*see* DISALLOWANCE); to appoint provincial lieutenant-governors; to declare provincial works to be for the general advantage of Canada or 2 or more provinces; to appoint judges of superior, district and county courts (*see* JUDICIARY); and to enjoy broad lawmaking powers all confirm the intended junior status of provincial governments. However, the evolution of Canadian society, despite the centralizing swings occasioned by the 2 world wars and the economic depression of the 1930s, has long eroded this early sense of provincial subordination. Although not all contemporary provincial governments are as assertive as those of Québec or Alberta, most claim a more equal partnership with Ottawa.

CONFEDERATION was predicated on a primary role for the central government in the promotion of an economic union and in the stimulation of national economic expansion through the development of transportation links (railways, harbours and canals) and other forms of public-policy support (*see* RAILWAY HISTORY), but by the 1880s the momentum behind nation building had slowed and was soon overtaken by the assertion of provincially based political and economic attachments. Other elements that helped enhance the status of provincial governments included the political leadership of such

provincial spokesmen as Oliver MOWAT, Honoré MERCIER and William FIELDING; PM LAURIER'S more sympathetic attitude towards the provinces; the development, in various provinces, of resource-based economic interests (*see* RESOURCE RIGHTS); and the emergence of a provincial bias in the decisions of the JUDICIAL COMMITTEE OF THE PRIVY COUNCIL on the distribution of powers. The provincial governments always played some role in their own regional economic development through public investment in transportation and the growth of their public education systems; the expansion of these activities and the later growth of social welfare, health and hospital programs have changed the original conception of the functions and the jurisdictions of provincial governments.

Legislative Power Under the Constitution Act, 1867 (s92), the powers of the provincial legislatures were carefully circumscribed. The legislatures were granted specific jurisdiction in 16 subject areas. In s91 powers were granted to Parliament in 29 areas, but these powers were intended for "greater Certainty" in the application of Parliament's more comprehensive (and controversial) residual power to make laws for the PEACE, ORDER AND GOOD GOVERNMENT of Canada in relation to all matters not assigned exclusively to the provinces. The scope of provincial legislative power was broadly defined in the final subsection of their grant of powers as "generally all matters of a merely local or private Nature in the Province." Other enumerated areas include property and civil rights, the management and sale of provincially owned public lands, hospitals, municipal institutions, local works and undertakings, the incorporation of companies with provincial objectives, the solemnization of marriage and the administration of justice. Provincially established courts enforce both civil and CRIMINAL LAW. Under s93, education is an exclusive provincial responsibility, subject to certain qualifications. Under s95 agriculture and immigration are matters of concurrent jurisdiction but with federal paramountcy, ie, if there is conflicting legislation, the federal government prevails. The control of public lands and provincial ownership of natural resources has proved to be of particular importance, but the most significant interpretations of the constitution regarding provincial rights have been in the area of property and civil rights. These interpretations have protected provincial jurisdiction against encroachment and have provided specific support for provincial government regulation of labour relations, marketing and business contracts.

Provincial taxing powers are limited to direct TAXATION within the province, ie, personal and corporate income taxes, consumer taxes and certain property taxes. From their jurisdiction over the management and sale of public lands, timber and ownership of natural resources, the provinces derive authority for the principal source of nontax revenues. According to a 1982 constitutional amendment (92A), the provinces were granted an unrestricted taxing power ("any mode or system") in the natural-resource field. This amendment, which clarified and expanded provincial legislative and taxing powers over nonrenewable resources, forestry resources and electrical energy, was designed to resolve the constitutional difficulties posed by revenue raising that strayed into the indirect tax field. Although the federal government still retains the power to disallow a provincial statute, it has not done so since 1943. Any federal Cabinet that contemplated using disallowance today would encounter significant political difficulties. A LIEUTENANT-GOVERNOR's power to reserve a bill passed by a provincial legislature for action by the governor general can similarly be regarded as a relic of an earlier age of intergovernmental relations. The last reservation, which occur-

red in Saskatchewan in 1961, went against an 80-year-old understanding that this power would only be exercised on instructions from the governor general, and the bill was subsequently approved.

Since 1867 there have been only 6 constitutional amendments directly affecting the powers of all provincial legislatures. The amendments of 1940, 1951 and 1964 transferred powers to Parliament with the agreement of the provinces; those of 1930, 1931 and 1982 expanded provincial powers. The 1940 amendment of s91 (subs2A) secured exclusive federal government jurisdiction for a national UNEMPLOYMENT INSURANCE scheme. In 1951 the addition of s94A permitted national OLD AGE PENSIONS with concurrent jurisdiction under provincial paramountcy. This section was further broadened to include supplementary benefits in 1964 to provide for the introduction of the CANADA PENSION PLAN. Québec was the only province to OPT OUT of this agreement. The Constitution Act, 1930, under which natural-resource powers were transferred to the western provinces, was the first constitutional amendment to increase the jurisdiction of a province. In the following year, the STATUTE OF WESTMINSTER gave powers to both provincial and central governments to repeal British colonial statutes. Despite concerted provincial demands for an expansion of their jurisdictions during the constitutional reform conferences of the late 1960s and 1970s, the Constitution Act, 1982, made only one direct change in provincial jurisdiction — the addition of s92A.

Provincial Government Activities Levels of government expenditure only partly reflect the range of provincial government activity, but they do underscore the role the provinces play in the provision of public goods and services and in the making of transfer payments to individuals. Since 1926, total government expenditures for all governments has risen from 16% to over 40% of the GROSS NATIONAL PRODUCT (GNP) in the 1980s. In this time, provincial government expenditures (excluding intergovernmental transfers) have risen from 3% to nearly 13% of GNP and those of their municipalities from 7% to 9%. Government expenditures, including federal government spending for income-security payments and regional assistance programs, are of special significance for the less prosperous of the Atlantic provinces. Their provincial government expenditures as a proportion of provincial gross domestic products are double those of the other 6 provinces.

Provincial expenditures are primarily in the fields of hospital and medical care, education, income maintenance and other social services. The participation of all provincial governments in federal-provincial, shared-cost arrangements for hospital insurance and medicare (*see* HEALTH POLICY) has helped ensure nationwide standards of service, despite some differences in their modes of financing and program coverage. In contrast, the retention of a high degree of provincial autonomy in the provision of elementary and secondary education and the accommodation of religious and linguistic cleavages has resulted in a variation in SCHOOL SYSTEMS.

Over 50% of total provincial government revenues are derived from personal income taxes, general sales taxes, natural-resource revenues and returns from their investments. The relative importance of these sources varies for each province because of differing taxation policies as well as the wide variations in their economic bases. The government of Alberta derives over 50% of its revenue from its oil and natural-gas resources and as of 1984 was the only province that did not levy a general retail sales tax. In Québec, personal income tax accounts for nearly 33% of provincial revenue, while in the Atlantic provinces at least 25% of revenue is derived from EQUALIZATION PAYMENTS from the federal government. Since 1962 the joint occupancy of the income-tax fields by both the federal and provincial governments has been governed by a series of 5-year fiscal and tax-collection arrangements. Under the current 1982-87 agreement, the federal government collects personal income taxes for 9 provinces (excluding Québec) and corporation income taxes for 7 provinces (excluding Alberta, Ontario and Québec).

The growth of provincial activities has not only been marked by a full exploitation of their direct tax and other revenue-raising powers, but also by federal government encouragement and financial assistance. Federal conditional shared-cost programs in social assistance and other provincial areas of provincial jurisdiction, plus unconditional grants in the form of equalization payments, have all contributed to the expansion and maintenance of provincial public services. Since 1977 the federal Established Program Financing arrangements have resulted in a greater degree of provincial autonomy through the substitution of more unconditional fiscal transfers and cash payments for the medicare, hospital insurance and post-secondary education grant programs.

Expenditure on social services may account for the largest proportion of provincial government spending, but it is only one dimension of a far wider range of government intervention. Regulatory activity and programs for economic development conducted by a variety of provincial government agencies and CROWN CORPORATIONS pay an equally important role in provincial life. Workers' compensation, labour relations, agricultural marketing, energy and public utilities are all, for example, regulated by provincial agencies. All provinces have publicly owned development corporations or other agencies, akin to the Saskatchewan Economic Development Corporation, which provide assistance, loans and other incentives for the expansion and diversification of their economies, and often compete with each other, with varying degrees of success. Other provincial crown corporations, particularly those responsible for the generation of electrical power, are also important in provincial economics. Both ONTARIO HYDRO and HYDRO-QUÉBEC, for example, have assets of more than $23 billion and sales of over $3.5 billion. The rapid growth in the number of provincial crown corporations has been one of the most striking aspects of the recent expansion of provincial activities. Nearly 50% of the more than 200 such corporations were established during the 1970s.

Government Institutions Distinctive patterns of economic and social development have produced wide variations in provincial political life and provincial PARTY SYSTEMS, but all provincial government institutions and the political conventions that shape their operation are closely modeled after the British parliamentary tradition and the practice of Cabinet government, and reflect the principles of RESPONSIBLE GOVERNMENT. The Crown is represented through the office of lieutenant-governor. Provincial public policymaking and administration is controlled by an executive council, ie, a Cabinet, comprising ministers of the Crown and headed by a PREMIER. A provincial legislature is defined, for lawmaking purposes, as being composed of the lieutenant-governor and the provincial Legislative Assembly in the same way that the central Parliament is composed of the Crown, SENATE and HOUSE OF COMMONS. In ordinary usage, however, the term legislature refers only to the Assembly. The 4 provinces of Québec (1867-1968), New Brunswick (1867-92), Nova Scotia (1867-1928) and Manitoba (1871-76) originally had bicameral legislatures made up of an elected Assembly and an appointed Legislative Council. PEI also had a bicameral legislature but

with an elected council which was absorbed into the lower chamber in 1893. Today, all have a unicameral system composed of a single elected chamber. Appointments to Cabinet are ordinarily made from members of the political party that holds the majority of seats in the Legislative Assembly. The further requirement that the premier and Cabinet maintain the support of the majority in the legislature is a principle of responsible government that had been formally acknowledged in 1848 by the colonial antecedents of the 4 original provinces.

Office of the Lieutenant-Governor Provincial government is carried out in the name of the Crown; the lieutenant-governor of the province acts as the Crown's representative in all areas of provincial jurisdiction and in the exercise of any related prerogative powers. The lieutenant-governors appoint and may dismiss the provincial premiers and the members of their Cabinets. They summon, prorogue and dissolve the provincial legislatures and assent to provincial legislation in the name of the Crown. The lieutenant-governors still retain a power to withhold or reserve a bill for consideration of the central government. These latter powers are presumed dormant, if not entirely unexercisable. In practice the lieutenant-governor's constitutional responsibilities are circumscribed by the conventions of responsible government and conducted on the advice of the premier and Cabinet. The discretionary powers enabling a lieutenant-governor to act alone in the appointment or dismissal of a premier or dissolution of the provincial Legislative Assembly remain potentially important, however, should there be any uncertainty about who commands the support of the majority in the Assembly. If a premier or Cabinet acted in a way that was unquestionably contrary to any constitutional conventions, the office of lieutenant-governor might also be used to protect those fundamental principles.

The lieutenant-governors are appointed by the federal Cabinet on the advice of the prime minister, with little participation from the provincial governments in the selection process. Their salaries are fixed and paid by Parliament and before 1892 they were regarded as federal officers. The Judicial Committee of the Privy Council ended any suggestion of subordinate status for the lieutenant-governors — and by extension for the provincial legislatures — when it held the appointment to be an act of the Crown and the office to be as much the representative of the Crown for all the purposes of provincial government as the office of governor general was for Canada.

Premiers and Cabinets Provincial premiers ordinarily hold the position of president of the Executive Council, and enjoy the same pre-eminent status as head of their provincial governments as the PRIME MINISTER holds in relation to his CABINET colleagues. Virtually all Cabinets have assignments for such policy areas as health, education, labour and manpower, social services, energy, environment, natural resources (forests, lands or mines), economic development, agriculture, highways and transportation, tourism and recreation, justice (ATTORNEY GENERAL), finance, municipal affairs and consumer protection. The Atlantic provinces and Québec have specific fisheries portfolios. Others, such as the minister for the status of women in Québec, the ministers of international trade in Alberta and Québec, and the ministers for northern affairs in Ontario, Saskatchewan and Manitoba, express the particular policy commitments of a province. Both Ontario and Québec have also experimented with horizontal portfolios that combine responsibilities for policy development and co-ordination in broadly defined areas (eg, social development and resources development) under a single minister.

In 8 provinces there is a specific assignment of responsibilities for intergovernmental relations — in some instances a position held by the premier. In 1984 the average size of the provincial Cabinets was 21 members — the largest was Alberta with 30, the smallest was PEI with 10.

Since 1960 the increasing size of the provincial Cabinets and attention to improved policy planning and co-ordination has spawned the growth of Cabinet COMMITTEE systems. These typically include a central policy or management board/planning and priorities committee, and a treasury board (for financial, personnel, and general government management policy). This development has in turn given rise to the introduction of provincial Cabinet secretariats which provide administrative and professional assistance.

Legislatures The provincial Legislative Assemblies (known as the House of Assembly in Nova Scotia and Newfoundland and the National Assembly in Québec) are significant institutional expressions of the central values of Canadian democracy. As in other parliaments, the making of provincial law requires that the government's legislative proposals (bills) move through the formal state of first reading, second reading and detailed review in committee stage, and a final third reading before receiving assent by the lieutenant-governor. The BUDGETARY PROCESS also requires that the legislature annually approve the funds required for government programs and that expenditures are to be only for those purposes authorized by the Legislative Assembly. In practice there is rarely room for independent action by the legislature in the lawmaking process. The party loyalty of individual members of the Assembly, the power of the party leadership to maintain discipline, and the government's control of the timetable of the Assembly ensure that the work of the Legislative Assembly is determined by the premier and Cabinet. With the modern emphasis on executive government, the lawmaking powers of the Cabinet and of its individual ministers is considerable. The weight of government business undermines the backbencher's right to sponsor private member's bills, and few such bills advance beyond second reading and even fewer become law. The general rule that only the government may initiate spending and taxing proposals is strictly interpreted to curtail such initiatives. MINORITY GOVERNMENTS are rare in the provinces, but one-party dominance of the Assembly has historically been common. The Conservative Party of Ontario has enjoyed the longest period of uninterrupted government office (from 1943 to the present), but currently the Alberta Conservatives have secured the greatest level of electoral success with their capture of over 90% of the seats in the Alberta legislature in the 3 successive general elections of 1975, 1979 and 1982.

Despite the power of the government within the Legislative Assembly, the debates on the various stages of a bill, question period and the other scheduled opportunities for debates on public policy, together with the other work of the members in representing and servicing their constituents, help ensure some measure of accountable government. The premier and members of the Cabinet are generally challenged, in the Assembly, to answer for their direction and management of provincial affairs, and the reporting of the proceedings through the media exposes the government to public scrutiny. All provinces, save for PEI, publish a HANSARD report of their debates and proceedings and both Saskatchewan and Québec have instituted full television coverage.

In 1984 the provincial legislatures varied in size from 32 members in PEI to 122 in Québec and 125 in Ontario. Newfoundland and Nova Scotia both had 52 seats; BC and Manitoba, 57;

New Brunswick, 58; Saskatchewan, 64; and Alberta, 79 seats. Two members are elected from each provincial riding in PEI, and BC also has a varying number of dual-member electoral districts. All other provinces have single-member ridings.

Judged by the number of days spent sitting in debate, the provincial legislatures are less active than the House of Commons. Over the past 20 years, however, their sessions have increased in length and are generally more productive in their legislative output than their counterpart in Ottawa. In 1983, for example, the PEI legislature met for just 40 days, but 5 other provincial legislatures sat for 90 or more days. The average number of public statutes passed by the Legislative Assemblies between 1979 and 1983 was twice that passed by the House of Commons. This may in part reflect the more crowded agendas of provincial governments but is also attributable to the smaller-sized legislature and to greater Cabinet control. All provincial legislatures have a standing-committee system and at times use ad hoc special or select committees to investigate particular areas of public policy. The Québec National Assembly has particularly strong committees, but elsewhere the roles and resources of committees are more limited than in Ottawa. The total remuneration (including salary and tax-free allowances) of ordinary private members of the legislatures varied from $20-30 000 in PEI, Newfoundland, Nova Scotia and Saskatchewan, to $31-40 000 in Alberta, Manitoba, New Brunswick and BC, and over $45 000 in Ontario and Québec.

The growth in the scope and quality of provincial government activities has been accompanied by a considerable increase in the numbers of provincial government employees who provide the managerial, clerical and manual skills required for the provision of provincial services. In Dec 1982 the total number of provincial departmental employees reached 303 000; a further 159 000 were employed in provincial government enterprises and over 93 000 others in boards, commissions, agencies and institutions. Combined with the employees of municipalities, hospital and school boards, they comprise 75% of the total number of public employees in Canada. In recent years, the measures taken by provincial governments to restrain the growth of their expenditures have centered in large part on the containment of salary and wages expenditure and the reduction of the size of their public services.   NORMAN J. RUFF

Provincial Marine By 1748, during the WAR OF THE AUSTRIAN SUCCESSION, French and British naval strength had become so thinly stretched that the N American colonies of each nation had developed auxiliary naval forces. The "sea militia" concept of New England spread to Nova Scotia, and in 1759 Capt Joshua Loring, a Bostonian seconded from the Royal Navy, built a flotilla to support the British army's advance up Lk CHAMPLAIN. It formed the nucleus of a provincial marine that survived on the Great Lakes until the WAR OF 1812. When UPPER CANADA became a separate province in 1791, Lt-Gov SIMCOE had attempted to strengthen its marine force by issuing his own commissions to officers serving on Lakes Ontario and Erie. Provincial armed vessels performed various duties on the coasts, lakes and rivers of several provinces, but UC's marine had the most important role when war broke out. Composed mostly of merchant seamen and soldiers, particularly of the Royal Newfoundland Regiment, the UC force was not a match for professional seamen of the US Navy until the RN took over in 1813. Five UC warships, on Lk Ontario and 6 on Lk Erie, with another building on each lake before the RN started further construction, met the test of battle. Subsequently, various forms of naval militia

sprang up from time to time in BNA. In the REBELLIONS OF 1837 some RN officers on half pay and other volunteers formed an ad hoc force to destroy the American vessel CAROLINE, being used by W.L. MACKENZIE's supporters, and thereby exacerbated relations with the US. The Naval Brigade of the UC Militia existed for a few troubled years, but neither this nor later forms of naval militia in BNA approached the provincial marine in form or importance. *See also* ARMED FORCES.   W.A.B. DOUGLAS

Prowse, Daniel Woodley, judge, publicist, historian (b at Port de Grave, Nfld 12 Sept 1834; d at St John's 27 Jan 1914). Educated in St John's and Liverpool, Eng, Prowse was called to the Newfoundland Bar in 1859. He practised law and served as a member of the Legislative Assembly between 1861 and 1869, when he was appointed a judge of the Circuit Court and later of the Central District Court. An experienced if sometimes eccentric justice and indefatigable publicist of Newfoundland, he was a prolific journalist in local, American and British journals and wrote *Manual for Magistrates in Newfoundland* (1877), *Newfoundland Guide Book* (1905) and *A History of Newfoundland* (1895), still the most comprehensive general history of the Island and the first to be written "from the English, Colonial, and Foreign Records." G.M. STORY

Prus, Victor Marius, architect (b at Minsk Mazowiecki, Poland 24 Apr 1917). Educated at Warsaw Technical U (1939), he served with the Polish forces in the Middle East and with the RAF during WWII. He studied at U of Liverpool and practised in London, immigrating to Canada in 1952. After research with Buckminster Fuller at Princeton he set up practice. With his wife Maria Fisz Prus and various associates he has designed outstanding buildings that are characterized by an appropriate "ambience" — in his view the "ultimate objective" in architecture. His principal works include Rockland Shopping Centre (Massey Medal), Savoie Apartment Bldg and Palais de Congrés in Montréal; RCAF Memorial, Trenton; Grand Théâtre and Conservatory of Music in Québec City; and Canada/France Astronomical Observatory in Hawaii.   NORBERT SCHOENAUER

Psychiatry is the branch of medicine concerned with disorders of the mind (or mental illnesses), and a broad range of other disturbed behaviours, including behavioural and emotional reactions to physical disease, life stresses and personal crises; personality problems; and difficulties with coping, adjustment and achievement.

Psychiatrists are physicians, and in Canada they need to have passed the fellowship examination of the Royal College of Physicians and Surgeons of Canada, or, in Québec, to have obtained the specialist's certificate of the Professional Corporation of Physicians. The examination is preceded by 4 years of postgraduate training in a recognized training centre. The program seeks to ensure that graduate psychiatrists are expert in the application of those medical, surgical, biological, psychological and social factors relevant to the diagnosis, treatment and management of psychiatric disorders. All postgraduate trainees must register with a university and plan their programs in collaboration with the director of the residency program at the university. Of the 4 years of approved training, 3 must be spent in intensive learning that provides both basic clinical experience and theoretical instruction.

The areas of skill and knowledge which must be covered in basic psychiatric training in Canada include basic patterns of disease; historical trends in psychiatry; normal and abnormal psychosexual development; contributions of biological, psychological and sociocultural

sciences; child and adolescent psychiatry; mental retardation; genetics; theories of personality and psychopathology; psychiatric assessment; psychiatric emergencies; psychophysiological disorders; psychosocial reactions to illness; psychiatric syndromes; treatment methods (eg, psychopharmacology, behaviour modification, psychotherapies, social therapies); community psychiatry; geriatric psychiatry; forensic psychiatry; psychiatric research and research methods. Each Canadian medical school now offers postgraduate training programs in psychiatry; in 1981 over 350 psychiatrists were enrolled across Canada in such programs.

Psychiatry, in common with other mental-health professions, specializes in psychotherapy. In psychotherapy (often confused with psychoanalysis) a professionally trained person establishes a clinical relationship with a patient for the purpose of modifying symptoms, changing behaviour or promoting personality growth. There are many kinds of psychotherapy which differ in their emphasis upon restructuring attitudes, changing emotional responsiveness or modifying behaviour directly (supportive and re-educative psychotherapies are also used to deal with behavioural problems not strictly classified as mental illness, such as vocational, school or marriage problems). Psychoanalysis, a term coined by Freud to characterize his system of free association, dream interpretation of resistance, and transference, is not widely practised in Canada, where relatively few psychiatrists are trained in its methods. Biological treatments, eg, drugs and electroconvulsive therapy, supplement psychotherapeutic approaches to treatment by psychiatrists.

Psychiatric Disorders The overall knowledge about mental illness is greater than usually assumed, although specific measures for diagnosis have not yet been found. In an examination of a patient, the psychiatrist enquires into the personal, medical, and family history of the patient and into the history of the complaint; notes the patient's behaviour, speech, mood, perceptions; observes the stream, form and content of thought; and tests memory, awareness of time, place and person, and abstract thinking. Throughout the world the *International Classification of Disease* (ICD) is used to classify mental disorders. The third edition of the *Diagnostic and Statistical Manual of Mental Disorders* (DSM-III), developed in the US, provides specific criteria for diagnosis.

Psychosis embraces disorders characterized by behaviours that are often unrealistic and incomprehensible to observers. The main subdivision is between organic and functional psychoses (the latter are subdivided into schizophrenia and affective disorders). Organic psychoses are diseases associated with impaired brain tissue function, and are characterized by loss of memory, disorientation, and behaviour changes usually associated with later life. Most are due to degenerative diseases, eg, Alzheimer's disease. Arteriosclerosis (hardening of the arteries) causes only a small proportion of dementias. Between 5% and 10% of those over 65 years of age may develop dementia at some time.

Schizophrenia, often a lifetime disease, is characterized by impaired thinking, delusions and hallucinations, limited emotional response, lack of drive and poor judgement, but not, contrary to popular opinion, a "split personality." Many believe that this disorder is to some extent inherited, that it is influenced considerably by social environment, and that biochemical brain disturbances are involved. Drug treatment has markedly improved the outlook for patients.

Depression Affective disorders include bipolar (mania and depression) and unipolar (only depression) depressions. While 10% of the population suffer from some symptoms of depression, only 0.2% suffer a major affective disorder at any one time. Depressions are episodic, rather than chronic. Bipolar depression, (which includes manic phases) generally begins in the 20s and 30s and affects men and women equally; unipolar disorders, which appear mainly in the 50s and 60s, are more frequent in women. SUICIDE is a considerable risk among severely depressed patients, 15% of whom may die. Treatments include antidepresssant drugs, electroconvulsive treatment and lithium carbonate.

Neuroses (anxiety, mild depression, insomnia, loss of appetite, fatigue, irritability, poor concentration and hypochondriasis) are extremely common short-lived disorders and are usually treated by family doctors with psychotherapy and drugs. Some longer lasting disorders require consultation with specialists.

Personality Disorders are disorders that are characterized by permanent and limited patterns of behaviour, ineffective functioning and difficulty with interpersonal relationships.

Hospital Services By the 1940s most persons with major mental illnesses were being treated in mental hospitals remote from their communities and other health services. In the early 1950s, half of all mental-hospital patients were in isolated mental institutions; 75% of these patients had been hospitalized for more than 5 years and were more likely to leave the hospital by dying than by discharge. Few services were available outside the mental hospitals.

The advent of effective drug treatment for mental illnesses helped patients in hospitals re-enter the community and reduced the need for both long- and short-term hospitalization. Effective drugs for psychiatric treatment were introduced around 1953 and are now widely used in the medical treatment of mental illness by family physicians as well as psychiatrists. There are now 34 mental hospitals in Canada (annual cost of services: $374 million), with 19 000 staff. There are about 40 000 patients admitted each year, half of whom remain for less than 1 month. The use of mental-hospital beds (for patients staying in hospital less than 1 year) generally ranges from 1 per 2000 population in Nova Scotia to below 1 per 15 000 population in Saskatchewan.

The number of "long-stay" (over 1 year) patients in mental hospitals decreased from 46 000 in 1956 to 14 000 in 1978, the year this system ended. The number of new patients requiring long-term hospitalization is decreasing each year. Substantial numbers of those still remaining in mental hospitals could be appropriately treated in out-patient, day-treatment and residential settings. Studies of the needs of patients currently hospitalized in BC, Ontario and NB have repeatedly shown that 40-60% need not remain in hospital for treatment, but adequate services and accommodation for these patients in the community do not exist.

In some cities — Victoria, Calgary, Regina, Saskatoon, St Catharines, Windsor and Sherbrooke — mental hospitals are not greatly used. Seriously ill patients, as well as less disturbed patients, are treated in general hospital psychiatric units close to their communities. These are "psychiatric oases" in which psychiatrists based in general hospitals treat most of the patients requiring hospitalization. There are currently more admissions to general hospital psychiatric units than to mental hospitals. The number of general hospital psychiatric units grew from 45 in 1958 to over 164 in 1981. In comparison with other countries, Canada has a relatively high ratio of general hospital psychiatric beds; in 1981 there were 23 general hospital psychiatric beds per 100 000 population.

Provincial HEALTH POLICY as well as the needs of patients determine the kinds of services provided. The marked regional variation in the use of mental hospitals and general hospital psychiatric units across Canada results mainly from differences in the way services are organized, rather than from clinical differences in patients.

Personnel There are some 2200 psychiatrists in Canada; 60% of them are engaged in private practice. About 33% completed their medical training outside Canada. The majority of psychiatrists work in the metropolitan centres, while 7% practise in communities with a population of under 50 000. The vast majority of psychiatrists are men, but with the recent influx of women into medical schools, this is changing. The majority practise general psychiatry, but there is some subspecialization into child psychiatry, geriatric psychiatry, forensic psychiatry, liaison psychiatry, behaviour therapy, family therapy, sexual counselling, psychoanalysis and research. Private psychiatrists render services comprising 3.5% of medicare costs. On the average, full-time psychiatrists spend 28 hours a week (80% of their clinical time) in psychotherapy; the remaining 20% of their time is spent in office consultations and hospital visits.

The case load of psychiatrists varies greatly, depending not only on the amount and type of psychotherapy practised, but on the length of treatment. In some Canadian centres, 50% of psychiatrists' time is taken up with long-term patients who comprise one-eighth of the case load. The average private psychiatrist in some provinces sees 250-350 patients a year.

Within the Canadian health-care system, family physicians, psychiatrists in private practice, community mental-health clinics, psychiatric units in general hospitals and public mental hospitals provide treatment for mental illness. Most patients with mental disorders can be treated by family doctors, without consultation with a psychiatrist. During any year, about 10% of adults may see a family physician for psychiatric problems; another 2% may consult a private psychiatrist or mental-health clinic. At least another 10% of the population annually seek help from church, social or psychological services for personal problems or other crises.

There has been a large-scale increase in the number of psychiatrists in private practice and in the provision of psychotherapy by family physicians. In 1982 the ratio of psychotherapy hours by psychiatrists varied regionally from 41 to 93 hours per 1000 Canadians. During 1982-83, 5.5% ($225 million) of Canadian medicare fee-for-service expenditures were for psychotherapy and counselling services by physicians. This ranged from 4% to 5.3% across the country. Over 40% of these services were provided by family physicians. Between 1972 and 1982, the number of psychotherapy and counselling services by family physicians increased from 57 to 146 per 1000 Canadians, and costs for these services increased from 2.6% to 5.6% of family physician costs.

Canadian Contributions to Psychiatry Canada has contributed significantly to the field of psychiatry. Canadian mental-health services have been fostered by unique medicare and hospital insurance programs which provide comprehensive universal medical coverage for mental illness. The 1964 Royal Commission on Health Services stated that medicare should not discriminate in coverage for the diagnosis and treatment of psychiatric conditions. Therefore, there is no restriction or discrimination on the extent or duration of psychiatric treatment by family physicians or by psychiatrists.

Saskatchewan has been an international leader in changing psychiatric services. In this province, psychiatric services are no longer based in mental hospitals, but in regional general hospital psychiatric units. Comprehensive community care systems enable patients to complete treatment near their homes, and they also promote follow-up and continuity of care.

Canada has also been a leader in the development of general hospital psychiatric units and in the development of day and night hospitals. The concept of partial hospitalization for persons not requiring 24-hour hospital care, but requiring daily contact, supervision or medication, originated in Montréal and has spread to many countries.

The Canadian Mental Health Association's 1963 publication *More for the Mind* emphasized the need for a number of changes: integration of mental-health services within general health services; regionalization; decentralization of psychiatric services from the provincial government to regional agencies; and co-ordination of psychiatric services for patients through all phases of their illness. These basic principles were reflected in the goals advocated in every subsequent review of psychiatric services in Canada.

Major contributions were made to the development of psychiatry by D.E. Cameron (a leader in psychiatric research in Canada who was instrumental in promoting the development of day hospitals); G.B. CHISHOLM (former director-general of medical services of the Canadian Army in WWII and first director-general of the World Health Organization); C.B. Farrar (founder of the first Canadian postgraduate training program in psychiatry, former head of the department of psychiatry at U of T and editor of the *American Journal of Psychiatry* for 34 years); C.M. HINCKS (founder of the Canadian National Committee for Mental Hygiene, which is now the Canadian Mental Health Association, and director of both the Canadian and US committees for Mental Hygiene in the 1930s); D.C. Meyers (founder of the first general hospital psychiatric unit in Canada in 1906); and A.B. Stokes (former chairman of the department of psychiatry at U of T who helped in the development of the Clarke Institute of Psychiatry). Textbooks on psychiatry by Canadians include the 1980 publication *A Method of Psychiatry*, and the 1981 publications *Précis pratique en psychiatre* and *Psychiatrie clinique: approche contemporaire*.

Problems and Prospects Despite the advances made by psychiatry, there is still much dissatisfaction with psychiatric services. Nearly every province, in reviewing its mental-health services since the late 1970s, has found that the goals described by the Canadian Mental Health Association 20 years ago have not been met. Unfortunately, adequate treatment as early and as continuously as possible, and with as little dislocation and as much social re-establishment as possible, is not yet available. The increase of psychiatric staff, facilities and programs is offset by an expanding demand for additional psychiatric services. Increasingly, many psychiatrists have changed their role, spending less time as consultants to other physician and assuming more responsibility for the primary care of patients with mental illness, particularly those persons with "relative" as opposed to "absolute" need, ie, persons with neuroses and adjustment reactions that are less disabling, for whom working or social capacity is maintained and for whom psychotherapy or social treatment could be provided by family physicians or by individuals in specialized nonmedical mental health disciplines. However, the psychiatric treatment of patients with long-term schizophrenic and major depressive disorders is still inadequate. ALEX RICHMAN

Reading: J.S. Tyhurst et al, More for the Mind (1963); J. Marshall, Madness: An Indictment of the Mental Health Care System in Ontario (1982).

Psychology [Gk, *psyche* "spirit" and *logos* "study"], literally "the study of the spirit or soul." The term seems to have been used for the first time by Melanchthon in the 16th century. Originally, the subject was part of PHILOSOPHY and its roots can be traced to antiquity. Sir Francis Galton (1822-1911), a half cousin of Charles Darwin, is generally acknowledged as the founder of individual psychology as a branch of science, but whether it should be classified as a biological or social science was a contentious issue among scholars until 1960, after which time it was increasingly described as a behavioural science, ie, the science of the behaviour of organisms. It is considered a science because it seems to constitute, by means of the scientific method, a body of organized knowledge, the purpose of which is to describe, explain, predict and in some cases influence behaviour. "Behaviour" includes conduct and internal processes (thoughts, emotional reactions, feelings, etc), that may be inferred from external actions.

Psychology is an applied science because it attempts to solve concrete problems. Because it is so inclusive, it encompasses many specialities. These include experimental psychology, characterized by laboratory experiments in the investigation of areas such as sensation and perception, learning and memory; physiological psychology, the study of the physical basis of behaviour, particularly how the brain and the rest of the nervous system (which is affected by a wide variety of factors, eg, heredity, diet, drugs, etc) function in activities perceived as characteristic of man and other animals; developmental psychology, the study of factors influencing the development of behaviour from infancy to old age (see GERONTOLOGY); social psychology, which studies the relations between the group and the individual; clinical psychology, which is concerned primarily with the diagnosis and treatment of emotional disorders; counselling psychology, which, although similar to clinical psychology, is primarily concerned with helping emotionally balanced individuals having difficulty deciding vocational and educational goals, etc; educational psychology, concerned with behavioural problems in school; industrial psychology, the study of human factors in industry and organization; personality psychology, the study of personality traits; and cognitive psychology, the study of the higher mental processes, eg, processes or perception, language, intelligence, imagery, creativity, etc.

It is generally believed that psychology belongs to the family of behavioural sciences which includes SOCIOLOGY, ANTHROPOLOGY, etc, but in its research and application it maintains close ties with BIOLOGY and the health sciences.

Psychology in Canada The developement of psycology in Canada paralleled that in Europe and the US. Courses were taught during the first half of the 19th century in moral and mental philosophy. Thomas MCCULLOCH apparently taught the first psychology course in eastern Canada in 1838 at Dalhousie University, but the field did not really grow until the last half of the 19th century. In 1855, William LYALL, who taught in Halifax, wrote the first basic psychology text to be published in Canada.

In 1879 Wundt opened the first psychology laboratory in Leipzig, and psychology distinguished itself from philosophy and become a science. Ten years later one of Wundt's students, James Mark Baldwin, who taught in Toronto, founded the first psychology laboratory in Canada. In the 1920s, independent departments of psychology began to appear: — one at McGill, directed by W.D. Tait, and one at Toronto, led by E.A. Bott. After 1940, other departments of psychology began to separate from philosophy and take on independent stature. The same process occurred somewhat later in western Canada. J.M. McEachran, who in 1909 became professor of philosophy in Alberta, may be called the first psychologist in a western university. After that, teaching and research in psychology developed in the other universities, but once again it was

not until the 1940s that the psychology departments became autonomous and were truly separated from philosophy.

Although psychology in the francophone universities followed a similar path, it was the result of different influences. The anglophone universities based their view of man on a mixture of Scottish realism and British idealism, but the francophone universities were dominated by Catholic Thomist philosophy. Of the first francophone psychology departments, one was founded in 1941 in Ottawa by R.H. Shevenel and the other in 1942 in Montréal by N. Mailloux. These departments retained a Roman Catholic orientation for some time and stressed clinical and applied research. Basic research began to develop at the end of the 1950s and is today as well developed as that of the anglophone universities. Psychology has developed very rapidly in Canada in the last 2 decades and departments of psychology now exist in the great majority of Canadian universities.

Psychology and Its Applications Parallel with its development as an academic discipline, psychology, since the beginning of the 20th century and especially since the 1950s, has grown dramatically as an applied science. At the beginning of the century, A. Binet in France developed the first intelligence test. The development in the US of tests to select soldiers during WWI established psychology's credibility as a science with practical applications. Today, psychology is applied in every field of human activity.

Contrary to widespread belief, psychologists do not work exclusively with people suffering from mental illness or from serious problems of adaptation. Generally, psychologists apply their knowledge to solve or prevent behavioural, cognitive and affective problems. For example, some psychologists concentrate on the design of control panels for sophisticated equipment to ensure machines are well adapted to the characteristics of their users; some are concerned with problems of adaptation in school, the work place, etc, and, with the people involved, try to establish organizational structures and ways of interaction that will facilitate study or work; others try to alter behaviours and life-styles that cause or accompany the development of psychosomatic problems, eg, ulcers and allergies.

Scientific and Professional Associations Like many other disciplines in Canada, psychology owes much of its development and vitality to various scientific and professional associations. In Canada the most influential, the Canadian Psychological Association, was established in 1939 to bring Canadian psychologists together, a role previously filled by the American Psychological Association, founded in 1892 as a continental organization. The imminence of a war in which Canada was likely to be involved much sooner than the US sparked the establishment of the Canadian organization. During WWII, the CPA was instrumental in legitimizing psychology as an applied science. In 1941 the NATIONAL RESEARCH COUNCIL was the first federal organization to give a research grant in psychology for one of a long series of projects undertaken by the CPA. With its annual conference, its various study committees, its political lobbying and its 3 publications, *The Canadian Journal of Psychology, The Canadian Journal of Behavioural Science* and *Canadian Psychology,* the CPA is still the most important of all national organizations of psychologists.

Provincial associations, however, also play an important role. Under the Canadian Constitution the provinces are responsible for the standards of accreditation and practice in the professions. One or more associations exist in each province. The 2 oldest, the BC Psychological Association, established 1938, and the Association de psychologie du Québec, established 1944 and since transformed into the Corporation profes-

sionnelle des psychologues du Québec, each publishes one or more scientific or professional journals.   LUC GRANGER

Ptarmigan are distinguished from other members of the GROUSE subfamily by their all-white wings. Like other grouse, they are well adapted to cold environments, eg, nostrils are hidden by feathers, body feathers have a long, downy aftershaft that increases insulation, and toes are feathered. Ptarmigan are the only birds with snow-white winter plumage. Summer plumage is mottled brown. Willow ptarmigan (*Lagopus lagopus*) and rock ptarmigan (*L. mutus*) are the only grouse native to both Old and New Worlds. Willow ptarmigan has circumpolar distribution. In Canada, it occupies higher western mountain elevations and tundra habitats as far N as Melville I. Rock ptarmigan, the most northern grouse, prefer habitats higher and drier than those of willow ptarmigan. Both are strong fliers but rock ptarmigan are more migratory, moving from high latitudes to escape the dark arctic winter. White-tailed ptarmigan (*L. leucurus*), the smallest grouse, lacks the black tail common to the other 2. It is found only in N America, occupying windswept upper slopes of the western mountains year-round. Its high-pitched, cackling scream contrasts to the guttural calls of the others. All ptarmigan nest on the ground, laying 6-10 cryptically marked eggs. Incubation is by females; males frequently abandon their territories at this time. Male willow ptarmigan usually remain and may assist in raising chicks, a trait not found in most grouse. Ptarmigan are important GAME BIRDS. *See* ANIMALS IN WINTER.   S.D.MACDONALD

Public Administration has no generally accepted definition. The scope of the subject is so great and so debatable it is easier to explain than define. Public administration is both a field of study, or a discipline, and a field of practice, or an occupation. There is much disagreement about whether the study of public administration can properly be called a discipline, largely because it is often viewed as a subfield of 2 other disciplines — POLITICAL SCIENCE and administrative science (or administration).

In Canada the study of public administration has evolved primarily as a subfield of political science. Knowledge of the machinery of government and of the political and legal environment in which public administrators work is essential to understanding the political system. Also, public administrators play an important role by providing policy advice to elected politicians and by active involvement in the making, enforcement and adjudication of laws and regulations. As a subfield of administrative science, public administration is part of the generic process of administration. The broad field of administration is divided into public, business, hospital, educational and other forms of administration. The similarities between these forms of administration are considered to be greater than their differences. There is, however, increasing recognition of public administration as a separate field of study, which is reflected in the creation within universities of schools of public administration which take a policy-management approach combining elements of the 2 earlier approaches with an examination of public policy. Public administration is taught as an interdisciplinary but integrated subject by political scientists, economists, sociologists and others.

No single date or event clearly marks the beginning of the study of public administration in Canada. The multivolume work *Canada and Its Provinces* (1914) by A. Shortt and A.G. DOUGHTY covered the practice of public administration and several books written by R. MacGregor DAWSON between 1919 and 1933 made an enduring contribution to the field. The first degree program in public administration was established at Dalhousie U by Luther Richter and R.A. Mackay in 1936. Carleton College (now Carleton U) had its first graduates in 1946, and in 1952 that university founded its School of Public Administration. There are now schools or faculties of public administration at Dalhousie, UQAM, U of Ottawa, Carleton, Queen's, Scarborough Coll (U of T), York, Brock, U of Manitoba and U of Winnipeg (combined), Regina, U of Alberta and U of Victoria. Beginning in the early 1950s, significant contributions to the literature on Canadian public administration were made by such prominent scholars as Roch Bolduc, J.E. Hodgetts, J.R. Mallory, D.C. Rowat and Malcolm Taylor.

Public administration is a relatively new but vigorous and important field of study. The increasing number of people who study it are — or would like to be — employed by a federal, provincial or municipal government. Even public employees who are trained in law, engineering, medicine, etc, often study public administration to help them understand and perform management tasks. Job opportunities exist in regular government departments and in government agencies, boards and commissions. If the scope of public administration is broadly defined, it also includes such occupational categories as hospital and educational administration. Among the many fields of work in public administration are the broad areas of personnel management, financial management, regulation and policy analysis. The major institution or society in the field of public administration is the Institute of Public Administration of Canada, a national organization and a learned society of public employees from all levels of government and university teachers. It sponsors seminars, conferences and publications, including the learned journal *Canadian Public Administration*.   KENNETH KERNAGHAN

Reading: Kenneth Kernaghan, ed, *Public Administration in Canada* (1985).

Public Archives of Canada is one of Canada's oldest and most important archival institutions. As the national keeper of Canada's documentary unpublished records, the Public Archives houses material from many sources, relating to all aspects of Canadian life. An order-in-council (1872) appointed an officer in the Dept of Agriculture to be responsible for historical documents of national significance. This marked the beginning of Canada's first federal ARCHIVES. In 1903, the head of the archives was given the additional responsibility of selecting and preserving valuable records of the federal government. An Act of Parliament (1912) transformed the archives into a separate department, the Public Archives.

Collections now comprise millions of documents, such as copies of early French and British records relating to the colonial regime in Canada, files from all federal government departments and agencies, as well as rare books, maps and atlases, medals and photographs. Correspondence and other papers of individuals and private societies, films, TV programs, sound recordings and computer-generated records are also included. The archives preserves these materials and provides consultation facilities to make them accessible to researchers from government, universities, the media, or citizens interested in history and genealogy. To reach the general public, the archives produces brochures, slides, microfiches and reference books, and organizes exhibitions that highlight its diverse holdings and illustrate the country's development. The archives also plays an important role in government administration by assisting federal departments and agencies in using efficient records management systems, in ensuring that papers created in the course of administration are systematically destroyed when no longer needed, and that valuable documents are preserved and eventually transferred to its permanent collections.
                    PUBLIC ARCHIVES OF CANADA

Public Art is commissioned for a specific public space by an individual or a group. Parks, government buildings, banks, schools, churches, hotels, stations, head offices and restaurants are some of the settings for displaying immobile works, created on site or on the basis of scale models, with the composition, dimensions and proportions blending into and gaining meaning from the surroundings. The artist may work closely with the architect and, if required, with a team of craftsmen, to attain the desired unity. The theme of the particular artwork may relate to the function of the building or environment it enhances. Public art is often produced for celebrations or propaganda, commemorative and educational purposes. The decorative function may be coupled with a political, social or religious message that represents the ideology of the group or individual who commissioned it.

Among native people in N America many tribes produced an elaborate public art, particularly in the form of wood carvings. This art served both a social and ritual function (*see* INDIAN ART; INUIT ART; NORTHWEST COAST INDIAN ART).

During the French regime the most common form of public art was SCULPTURE. Paintings, mostly imported, were small and adaptable to different settings, and only Frère LUC designed paintings that blended with the architecture of the retables. In 1686 Intendant Bochart de Champigny had the bronze bust of Louis XIV erected in Place Royale, Québec City. Intersections were decorated with statues of saints in niches of corner buildings, and these ornaments helped to identify particular streets. Monumental sculptures, mostly carved in wood, graced the facades of churches, such as Ste-Famille (Ile d'Orléans) or Cap-Santé (Portneuf), and the retables on the main altar were rich in gilded statues, bas-reliefs and paintings. One of the most beautiful examples, executed by Pierre-Noël Levasseur and members of his workshop, is found in the Ursulines' Chapel in Québec City. In the 18th and 19th centuries sculptors expanded into the field of naval sculpture and made the names of Québec and Maritime shipyards and shipowners known throughout the Atlantic world. The tradition of religious and naval sculpture was maintained during the 19th century by members of the BAILLAIRGÉ family in Québec and by the workshops of QUÉVILLON and his competitors in the Montréal region (*see* ART; RELIGIOUS BUILDING).

These early examples were tied to French cultural traditions and marked the presence of a royal and Catholic power. Changes brought about as a result of the Conquest were mainly iconographic. The new political power was less demonstrative, and GOVERNMENT BUILDINGS were surmounted by British arms. The major example of this change in political power is a stone column dominating the city of Montréal, constructed in 1808 to celebrate Admiral Nelson's victory over Napoleon. In 1828 a stone obelisk was dedicated in Québec City to the memory of Generals Montcalm and Wolfe. It became the first of similar austere monuments in Canada commemorating valour in death.

The flourishing economy, growing population and arrival of itinerant immigrant artists in the colony led to a proliferation of public artworks. In the 19th century, ephemerals were popular, works such as triumphal arches, allegorical chariots, and posters (*see* PAINTING). Artists Louis Dulongpre, Joseph LÉGARÉ and, later, Alfred PELLAN all produced theatre sets.

Mural painting was inspired originally by foreign artists, chiefly from Italy and Germany. The earliest documented example of a painted décor, designed as a whole and created on site in collaboration with the architect, were the columns and vault of Notre-Dame in Montréal in the years following 1828. In 1844, reflecting a growing secularization in art in Canada, Andrew Morris produced the allegories of Commerce and Agriculture for Montréal's legislative building. In Europe the Nazarenes and pre-Raphaelites encouraged public art, an influence absorbed by the Canadian Catholic clergy during their frequent trips abroad. Immigrant artists such as Lamprecht at St Romuald Church, the Mulleir brothers at Gésu in Montréal and Luigi Cappello in the Montréal region left evidence of their ability to create an entire iconographic program in proportion to the ARCHITECTURE for which it was designed. In sculpture, Italian artists introduced to Canada a taste for elaborate funeral stelae and monuments, often decorated in relief bronze or figures in the round (*see* TOMBSTONES). The Montréal firm of Carli and Petrucci was a leader in the eastern Canadian market at the end of the 19th century.

Gradually, Canadian artists took over the market for mural painting as major programs for commemorative monuments encouraged the development of their careers. A rich iconographic decoration was planned for the façade of the Québec legislative building, though work was delayed until 1890, when Louis-Philippe HÉBERT produced sculptures of Frontenac, Elgin, Salaberry, Wolfe, Montcalm, Lévis and the groups *Halte dans la forêt* and *Pêche au nigog*. Napoléon BOURASSA, who completed his training in Italy and France, was the pioneer Canadian muralist, the architect and decorator of Notre-Dame-de-Lourdes in 1883 and founder of a studio where Hébert and many mural painters were trained. The decoration by 5 young artists of the Sacré-Coeur Chapel in Notre-Dame in Montréal marked the domination by Canadian artists of mural art. Charles HUOT and Ozias LEDUC continued well into the 20th century to develop Canadian themes directly related to the setting. With political evolution came a greater awareness of history, and local historical societies, historians and genealogists multiplied. The number of historical figures and events that had to be marked increased rapidly and fathers of the new Canadian nation such as George-Etienne Cartier and John A. Macdonald were celebrated in many monuments (*see* Robert HARRIS).

In Toronto in 1899 George A. REID designed a series for the lobby of the new City Hall depicting the establishment of settlements in Upper Canada. Although this project was not completed, he left several important murals in Toronto, among them those of the Earlscourt Library and the auditorium of Jarvis Collegiate Institute. Like most mural artists in Canada at that time, Reid did not use the fresco technique, but mounted the painted canvas on the wall.

In Europe and the US, at the turn of the century, vast construction projects featuring sculpture monuments, murals, mosaics and stained-glass windows were popular. In 1898 the Toronto Guild of Civic Art was established and, after 1895, the Royal Canadian Academy of Arts sometimes devoted a room during its annual expositions to mural painting (*see* ARTISTS' ORGANIZATIONS).

As a relatively peaceful country, Canada had few war memorials. The WAR OF 1812 was commemorated by a heroic statue of Isaac BROCK placed atop a tall classical column at Queenston Heights, Ont. The SOUTH AFRICAN WAR was commemorated by George W. Hill in Montréal (Lord Strathcona Memorial) and W.S. Allward in Toronto. After 1918, and again after 1945, private donations and public funds provided considerable revenues for artisan-founders and sculptors. Cities and public buildings were decorated with commemorative plaques, busts, standing figures, or even depictions of soldiers in combat, generally surmounted by an allegory of Victory, such as the eloquent monument in Confederation Square in Ottawa.

Fountains and monuments celebrating historical or contemporary figures provided subjects for beautiful works by artists such as E.O. Hahn, Alfred LALIBERTÉ and Elizabeth WYN WOOD. The architect/sculptor John M. LYLE integrated many allegorical reliefs based on Canadian iconography into his buildings.

The industrial growth that Canada experienced during WWI resulted in the construction of numerous public buildings by the private sector (head offices, hotels, banks), many of which included murals. Some artists used this technique only sporadically (Charles COMFORT, Arthur LISMER), but others such as Gustav Hahn, Guido Nincheri or Frederick Challener made it the focal point of their career. In 1923 and 1924 the RCA organized 2 competitions in mural art. In 1924 a group of 10 artists were commissioned to decorate St-Anne's Church in Toronto.

This trend toward decorating large surfaces was encouraged by the art schools and a number of striking works were produced before and after the Depression, though, unlike the US, Canada had no public art projects to provide work for artists. Among the rare examples of these years was the construction and decoration of the Chalet du Mont-Royal, noteworthy less for the quality of the paintings than for the effort to renew an historical iconography based on facts, rather than myths.

The applied art professions evolved slowly in Canada. The main development came after 1960, and glazing, ceramics, weaving and glassmaking are now represented in public art. Many auditoria, exhibition centres, university campuses and airports are integrating the arts with architecture in new ways. Weavers such as Mariette Rousseau-Vermette and Micheline BEAUCHEMIN, respectively, made stage curtains for the Place des Arts in Montréal and the National Arts Centre in Ottawa. Jordi Bonet produced ceramic and bronze murals and doors for many theatres and public places, and encircled the main hall of the Grand Théâtre in Québec City with a relief that was as controversial as it was inspired.

EXPO 67 in Montréal, the sad fate of "Corridart" during the 1976 Olympic Games, and the construction and enlarging of the Montréal and Toronto subway systems all provided occasions for the production of public artworks. Collaborations between architects, engineers and artists helped integrate light and movement in these settings, illustrating the new relationships between man and his environment. Public art, however, is often seen as mere decoration. The federal government, paralysed in its role as commissioning or buying agent by its elaborate administrative committees, has lost sight of the relationships between art and public space. In this respect the commissions for the major airports and acquisitions for the national capital are nothing but a very sad apogee. One example of a successful collaboration between public art and architecture, in breadth, scope and sensitivity, is the work of sculptor Anne KAHANE at the Canadian Embassy at Islamabad, Pakistan.

In an effort to revitalize, support and sometimes disguise urban space, a "city walls" campaign was begun by many communities in the early 1970s. Supported by private business and government assistance projects, these murals were of uneven quality and were intended only as ephemera.

The concept of public art is often limited to an invitation to decorate a building just prior to its opening. A few provinces legislate that part of the budget for the construction of public buildings is to be assigned to the integration of works of art, and architects and artists co-operate from the start of the project. The dominant concept in large corporations is all too often that of commissioning a well-known artist to produce a "decorative" work that will impress visitors as soon as they enter the vestibule, and perhaps also the boardroom. Even if architects give all their attention to the treatment of space, it is up to the artists, in co-operation with them, to provide the elements that, fused with the architecture, help users identify with the space and make it their own. LAURIER LACROIX

Public Debt Governments finance their expenditures by taxing and borrowing. They sometimes raise money from the public or from institutions by selling securities, eg, bonds. The accumulated total of all such government liability is called the "public debt." The interest and principal on the portion of public debt held by nonresidents must usually be paid in foreign currencies, which must be earned and which represent debits on Canada's BALANCE OF PAYMENTS. Long-term debt, eg, that due in 10 years or more, is usually in the form of bonds; short-term debt indicates a maturity date of less than 5 years. Direct obligations comprise securities issued by government itself; contingent obligations comprise securities issued by government corporations, eg, funds for corporations such as the CNR and Ontario Hydro are raised by bonds issued by them and guaranteed by the respective governments.

In 1867 Canada's debt was $94 million and it grew slowly until 1915. WWI pushed the figure to $2.4 billion, it rose to $5 billion during the Great Depression and to $18 billion by the end of WWII. From 1977 to 1983 the net federal debt in the public accounts increased from $34.6 to $119.5 billion. As a proportion of GROSS NATIONAL PRODUCT (GNP) the "debt ratio" grew from 18% to 34% between 1977 and 1983. This "net debt" is the difference between gross debt (unmatured government bonds, bills, notes and other liabilities) and certain recorded financial assets of the federal government, eg, cash, investments and loans. Basically, changes in net debt equal budgetary deficits or surpluses, and the federal government's total net debt at any time therefore equals its accumulated overall deficit since Confederation.

The federal government's debt can also be measured as the difference between its liabilities to other sectors of the economy and its financial assets (claims on those sectors); net federal liabilities measured in this way equalled only $76 billion (1982), compared to $95 billion on the public accounts basis. The difference of $19 billion was "owed" to the federal government by itself. On the same basis, the debt of provincial and local governments in 1982 was about $23 billion, most of which will finance capital expenditures expected to benefit future generations who will bear much capital outlay cost in debt service charges.

However, although the public debt has increased as a proportion of GNP, it is relatively much smaller than it was in the 1950s and early 1960s. In 1983 net federal debt (public accounts basis) was only 34% of GNP compared to 36% in 1964 and 52% in 1952, and inflation has lessened the real value of the outstanding debt (by over $6 billion in 1980), although this is not reflected in government accounting. Nevertheless the management of the federal debt, an important aspect of MONETARY POLICY, has become more difficult in recent years, mainly because the average life of government debt instruments has shortened so that the government constantly has to roll over its debt through campaigns, the issuing of new treasury bills, etc. Although, for all governments together, real public debt has been retired since 1979, freeing resources for other purposes, constant activity in the financial markets has created concern that private borrowers will be crowded out. Also, because of shorter maturities of government debt, debt service charges are more vulnerable to interest rate variations. The average rate of interest on unmatured debt rose from 7.5% in 1977 to 11.1% in 1983, consequently interest on the public debt charges rose to $17 billion by 1983, or about 18% of total federal expenditures, compared to only 11% in 1977, exacerbating the federal deficit problem. From one viewpoint, the substantial part of the deficit attributable to the higher debt charges induced by INFLATION and the resulting high interest rates is simply a transfer to compensate bondholders for the loss in the real value of their bonds, but their loss is government gain, roughly offsetting the higher debt costs. From another viewpoint, deficits do not reflect high inflation-related interest rates, but rather cause both inflation and high interest rates. R.M. BIRD

Public Expenditure refers to government spending. From an average of 23% of GROSS NATIONAL PRODUCT (GNP), 1947-51, total government expenditure rose to an average of 44% of GNP, 1980-83. Over the 1947-83 period as a whole, total government expenditures as measured in the national accounts (a comprehensive series of statistics) rose 96% faster than GNP to a peak of 46% of GNP in 1983. For many economic purposes, however, the total size of government expenditures is less significant than its components. The division between transfer expenditures, which shift private income from one person to another, and exhaustive expenditures, which use goods and services for government activities proper, is particularly important. In the 1970s, 79% of the increase in public expenditure was attributable to transfers and only 21% to expenditures on goods and services, and by 1983 transfer expenditures accounted for over 52% of all government spending.

The relative prices of the goods and services that government purchases must also be taken into account. In real terms, the relative expansion of government spending as a proportion of GNP from 1947 to 1982 was 59%, not 70%. Since 1970 the proportion of real goods and services produced in the economy that is used by the government sector in the course of its activities has actually declined by about 10%. In contrast, transfer payments in real terms have increased slightly during this period, largely owing to a significant liberalization of the family allowance and unemployment insurance.

Fifty percent of the postwar increase in government expenditure is accounted for by expenditures on health, education and welfare. Since 1970 government expenditures on education actually declined in relation to GNP, but in the 1960s public-health spending rose substantially, largely in substitution for private expenditures, however, since total health expenditures in relation to GNP changed relatively little. In the 1970s only expenditures on social welfare, mainly in the form of large cash-transfer programs, continued to expand significantly until the end of the decade.

Provincial and local governments are responsible for almost all educational and health expenditure. Over the postwar period the federal government expenditures accounted for only 9% of the total growth in government expenditures, compared to 86% for the provincial-local sector (including hospitals). The remaining 5% is accounted for by the CANADA PENSION PLAN and the separate, but closely related, QUÉBEC PENSION PLAN. In 1980 the federal government was responsible for only 40% of total government expenditures (excluding intergovernmental transfers) — a proportion that has changed little since the mid-1960s.

The decline in federal defence spending freed resources that financed the expanding provincial-local health and education sectors. At the same time, programs such as OLD AGE PENSION, FAMILY ALLOWANCES and UNEMPLOYMENT INSURANCE, which were financed by a considerable increase in taxes, in the end appear to have redistributed income among Canadians only slightly because so many of the taxes were paid by the same broad groups that received the transfers. *See also* PUBLIC FINANCE.   R.M. BIRD

Public Finance, both a name for government finance — the way governments secure and manage their revenues — and the name of a branch of ECONOMICS that studies the entire sector of the economy. Government finances its expenditures through TAXATION, the borrowing of funds by the public sector (*see* PUBLIC DEBT) and the printing of money (*see* MONETARY POLICY). This article is concerned with the pattern and role of government expenditures.

The relative importance of government expenditures in the Canadian economy has risen almost continually over the past 50 years, from 10% of the GROSS NATIONAL PRODUCT (GNP) in the late 1920s to 47.3% of GNP in 1982. This rise has reflected a gradual trend which was interrupted by WWII when government expenditures reached a peak of 45% of GNP, largely because of the war effort. Of the 1982 percentage, 20.8% can be accounted for by federal government expenditures, 17.5% by provincial governments and 8.9% by local governments.

Total government expenditures are of 2 fundamentally different types — those on goods and services, and those on TRANSFER PAYMENTS. Government expenditures on goods and services represent the diversion of productive resources from the private sector to governments (only these expenditures are included in the GNP), while transfer payments (*see* INTERGOVERNMENTAL FINANCE) financed by taxes represent the shift of purchasing power from one group of individuals to another.

In 1982 expenditures by all levels of government on goods and services was 24.7% of GNP (a figure similar to that of 1970 but somewhat higher than the early postwar figure of 14%) of which the federal government was responsible for only 5.7%, the remainder being divided roughly equally between provinces and municipal governments, and largely comprising expenditures for education and health. Government expenditure on transfers (about 20% of GNP) accounted during the 1970s for roughly 80% of the growth in government expenditures. In 1970 only 13% of GNP comprised transfer payments; in 1983 the proportion was almost 20%. This rapid growth resulted primarily from the expansion of FAMILY ALLOWANCE and UNEMPLOYMENT INSURANCE payments (*see* SOCIAL SECURITY).

Rationale for Government Expenditures In mixed economies such as Canada's, the private sector is generally viewed as the "engine of growth" and is left to undertake those activities for which its profit-oriented behaviour is theoretically suited. The public sector is made responsible for tasks the value of which it is felt, should not be judged solely on the basis of whether they will generate profit. Economists usually identify 5 different components which comprise the rationale for public-sector intervention into the markets of the economy, but the rationale for public expenditures is not always economic in nature.

Provision of Public Goods The goods produced and sold by the private sector are called "private goods" (eg, food, clothing, shelter). "Public goods" by their very nature (eg, defence, general government, justice, external affairs, police protection, penal services, communications) provide services to many or all households si-

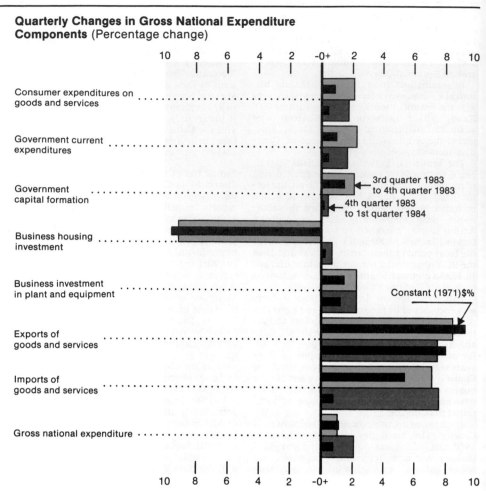

Quarterly Changes in Gross National Expenditure Components (Percentage change)

Source: Catalogue 13-001, Statistics Canada.

multaneously. These goods could not be provided by markets, so they must be provided collectively. Some are provided by the federal government, others by provincial or local governments.

Externalities Another type of goods, closely related to public goods but providing significant benefits to persons other than those who would purchase them, is referred to as "externalities." Although these goods could be produced and sold through markets, those purchasing them would lack the incentive to purchase the amounts that would be warranted by the social benefit generated by their consumption. For example, the benefit to an individual of purchasing an inoculation against a communicable disease would be significantly less than the benefit to society as a whole; the individual benefits from his or her own safety from the disease, while others in society benefit from the reduction in the risk that the person will spread the disease. Individuals acting out of self-interest would not have an incentive to consume the socially desirable amount or would not procure it because it was unpleasant, which is one reason children are forced by regulation to obtain immunization before they can go to school.

Governments encourage the production and consumption of externalities in 2 ways. On the one hand, the private sector may be left to undertake these activities while being encouraged by subsidies (or tax concessions) to involve itself more fully than it would otherwise choose to do. For example, assistance is provided to encourage INDUSTRIAL RESEARCH AND DEVELOPMENT, manpower training and regional development. On the other hand, the government may simply assume responsibility for the provision of goods, for example, certain health services and

education at all levels. There is some dispute over whether the public provision of such goods is always appropriate.

Natural Monopolies Some goods, eg, those provided by UTILITIES and by the transportation or communications industries, can be provided more cheaply by one or a few large firms rather than by several competing small firms. However, if the private sector was allotted sole responsibility for the provision of these goods according to the criterion of profitability, prices could be set too high and outputs too low, because no effective competition would exist to induce firms to provide services to consumers at the lowest possible price. In response to these "natural monopolies," governments may create public or CROWN CORPORATIONS, eg, Air Canada, the CBC and the CNR (*see* PUBLIC OWNERSHIP; ECONOMIC REGULATION).

Income Redistribution Governments also transfer incomes among persons, partly because the distribution of income would be far more unequal if it was controlled only by the private sector. Income is redistributed partly through the tax structure and partly through transfers to low-income earners. These transfers can include welfare schemes operated by provincial and local governments (but financed 50% by the federal government under the Canada Assistance Plan), family-allowance payments by the federal government, and income-related pension payments by federal and provincial governments; but they can also include transfers that incidentally redistribute income, having been designed for other reasons.

Some transfer payments (social-insurance schemes) are designed to supplement an individual's income at times of abnormally low earnings or abnormally high expenditures. Un-

Government Gross General Expenditure
Percentage Distribution, 1980-81
Source: *The National Finances, 1983-84* (Toronto:
Canadian Tax Foundation, 1984), Table 4-4 P. 40

| | Consolidated Expenditure | | |
	Federal	Provincial Local	Total
Social services	35.9	12.7	22.2
National defence	9.1	—	3.7
Health	0.7	19.6	11.9
Debt charges	13.5	8.7	10.7
Transportation and communications	7.7	8.6	8.2
General services	6.4	6.8	6.6
Education	0.6	22.7	13.7
Resource conservation and industrial development	12.4	5.2	8.2
Protection of persons and property	2.2	5.3	4.0
Foreign affairs and international assistance	2.0	—	0.8
Research establishments	2.0	0.1	0.9
Transfers to own enterprises	2.6	1.3	1.8
Labour, employment and immigration	1.4	0.2	0.7
Recreation and culture	1.0	3.3	2.4
Regional planning and development	0.2	0.9	0.6
Housing	1.8	0.6	1.1
Environment	0.5	3.8	2.4
Other	—	0.2	0.1
Total	100.0	100.0	100.0

employment insurance represents income transfers made by the federal government to persons temporarily out of work; WORKERS' COMPENSATION payments are made by provincial governments to those who have ceased working because of injury incurred on the job; public PENSION payments, including the universal payments by the federal government to all persons over the age of 65 and payments made by the federal government to the retired and disabled under the contributory CANADA PENSION PLAN or QUÉBEC PENSION PLAN, are transfers to persons who have lost income because of retirement. These pension payments are partly related to past earnings and contributions and are made to contributors and to their surviving dependents. The federal government also makes transfers to war veterans. Another type of social insurance covers medical care and hospitalization; payments to cover both are made on behalf of all residents and are financed jointly by the federal and provincial governments.

The CONSTITUTION ACT, 1867, outlines the expenditure responsibilities of the federal and provincial governments (*see* DISTRIBUTION OF POWERS). Generally, expenditures for services (eg, defence, trade and commerce, external affairs, the money and banking system, criminal law, penitentiaries, postal service, fisheries, unemployment insurance, and a number of lesser matters which tend to affect residents in more than one province) are designated as federal responsibilities, while those primarily affecting residents within a province are allocated to the provinces. In turn the provinces themselves delegate certain responsibilities to the municipalities within their jurisdiction.

The provincial governments' most significant spending responsibilities are health, education and welfare. The provinces administer the system of hospitals and health care; provide primary, secondary and post-secondary education; and administer social programs, including the welfare and social services provided under the Canada Assistance Plan, a program jointly financed by the federal and provincial governments. Provinces are also responsible for natural resources within their boundaries, the administration of justice, property and civil rights, local works and transportation, municipalities and other matters of a purely provincial or local nature.

The provinces tend to delegate to the municipalities responsibility for providing local services such as garbage pickup, fire and police protection, water and sewage, maintenance of local streets and recreational facilities. The municipalities also help in the local administration of provincial programs such as primary and secondary education, welfare assistance and hospitals (*see* LOCAL GOVERNMENT).

Finally, there are areas, eg, agriculture and immigration, in which both the federal and provincial governments may exercise concurrent power. One other important area of joint responsibility is that of OLD AGE PENSIONS. A constitutional amendment in 1951 permitted the federal government to enact old-age pension legislation, provided it did not affect the operation of provincial old-age pension legislation.

All of these designated responsibilities of the federal and provincial governments give rise to government expenditures. The largest categories are social services, education and health, which together comprise almost 50% of total government expenditures. The majority of social service expenditures are made by the federal government, of which old-age security and unemployment-insurance transfer payments comprise over 50%. Sizable amounts are also accounted for by the Canada Pension Plan, family allowances and the Canada Assistance Plan.

Much of the provincial and local government social-service expenditures result from welfare programs jointly funded by federal and provincial governments under the Canada Assistance Plan. Education is a major responsibility of the provincial and local governments; they finance all primary, secondary and post-secondary education, although the latter has been partly financed by federal-provincial transfers. Again, health expenditures are the responsibility of the provincial government, but the financing of medical and hospital insurance is assisted by federal government transfers.

The federal government is also responsible for large interest payments on the national debt, which makes up 13.5% of federal expenditure (*see* FOREIGN INVESTMENT). Provincial and local governments also spend a considerable amount (8.7% of expenditures 1980-81) on interest payments on their debt.   ROBIN W. BOADWAY

Public Health is concerned with the overall physical and MENTAL HEALTH of the community. Interest in public health was fostered by the poor health standards that prevailed in the overcrowded cities of the Industrial Revolution. In the 19th and early 20th centuries, public health was concerned with quarantine measures and emphasized improved sanitation and vaccination campaigns that were initiated in an attempt to control major infectious DISEASES. Today, public health is concerned with education, counselling about living habits, some infectious disease control, the safeguarding of the well-being of children and, through government health insurance and HOSPITAL grants, the provision of medical care.

Canada followed Great Britain's lead in public health reform during the 19th and early 20th centuries. Reformers agitated for environmental solutions to the high mortality rate which particularly afflicted children. Sanitation campaigns to clean up housing and streets were underway in the major eastern Canadian cities by the late 19th century. Water and milk supplies were also sanitized; after the turn of the century pasteurized milk was introduced into Toronto and Montréal in an effort to curtail the spread of bovine tuberculosis, a major cause

Cover illustration depicting the fight against smallpox in Montréal, 1876, with Mayor Hingston as St George slaying the dragon (*courtesy Public Archives of Canada/ C-64647*).

of crippling in children. School (and to some extent preschool) children were immunized against acute diseases such as smallpox and diphtheria or were monitored for more chronic afflictions such as tuberculosis and eye infections. Although hospital beds were available, most sick care took place in the home.

Under the CONSTITUTION ACT, 1867, jurisdiction over health was roughly divided between the federal and provincial governments. The Dominion was given jurisdiction over border quarantine and the provinces were given responsibility for hospitals. The jurisdictional authority of municipalities varied in scope from province to province and even from city to city. All 3 levels of government initiated new tasks in health reform, the nature of which was often decided by the personal interests of the officials in charge. For example, the federal government assumed control of the leper lazaretto in New Brunswick in 1880, largely in response to agitation by the federal deputy minister of agriculture. In 1896 responsibilities under the Constitution Act were renegotiated, but although the great majority of previously unmentioned functions were placed under the jurisdiction of the provinces, health provisions in Canada would remain haphazard for some years to come.

The first great attempt at administrative reform was spurred by the post WWI Spanish flu EPIDEMIC of 1918-19, which killed 50 000 Canadians (*see* INFLUENZA). Conscious of a need to rebuild its population, especially should there be a return to hostilities, governments were also gravely concerned about SEXUALLY TRANSMITTED DISEASES, which caused sterility and produced defective offspring, and about "feeblemindedness," which prevented those born from being of service to their country.

Like many other nations at this time, Canada established its first federal department of health in 1919. The new department was created to take charge of all the old federal health functions, largely to do with quarantine and standards for food and drugs, and to co-operate with the provinces and with voluntary organizations in campaigns against venereal disease (VD), tuberculosis and "feeblemindedness," and to promote child welfare. It funded a chain of VD clinics across the country and began a public education program about child care. Tuberculosis and feeblemindedness were mainly handled by the provinces and voluntary organizations. In 1929 the Department of Health became the Department of Pensions and National Health; it provided, in particular, health services for war veterans.

The GREAT DEPRESSION caused a crisis in Canada's health system. The demands on all levels of government exceeded the resources available. Furthermore, the voluntary organizations and the medical profession, which traditionally provided some free services, were equally hardpressed. Canadian governments were faced with an impoverished population that needed more health care but could not pay for it. Because the federal govermnet reduced the funds available for health care, the onus fell on the provinces, municipalities and voluntary organizations to take up the slack. Some regions of Canada fared better than others; Québec could rely on the ministrations of its religious communities, Ontario negotiated a system of care with its doctors, and Saskatchewan introduced a clinic program. However, by 1939 the federal government was forced to increase its own activities in the field of health.

WWII brought about a revival of the campaigning spirit regarding health. In 1941 PM Mackenzie King summoned a Dominion-Provincial Conference to discuss the Rowell-Sirois royal commission's recommendations regarding public health, and a health-insurance plan. The actual proposal for a nationwide system of health insurance foundered, however, at the Dominion-Provincial Conference of 1945-46, partly because of opposition from the provinces and from the medical profession and partly because wartime prosperity had helped Canadians forget depression and want. Instead, the federal government turned its attention towards the provision of health through welfare (see HEALTH POLICY; WELFARE STATE). The federal health department (which in 1944 had changed again to the Department of National Health and Welfare), now turned its concern to the standard of living rather than the standard of health. The provinces were expected to assume responsibility for initiatives in medical care in aid of which the federal government established a series of health grants.

In 1968 Canada embarked upon a federal cost-sharing program that allowed all Canadians in all provinces to take part in a national health-insurance scheme, an indication that medical care would be provided through subsidized private medical practice rather than through public clinics and that the era of public health, as understood at the time of its great triumphs, had ended. Public health is now concerned primarily with the health of individual members of the public. Education and immunization campaigns still exist, but many environmental battles have been won. New challenges have arisen in the fields of genetic and deteriorative diseases and these offer much smaller scope for sweeping health reform. Medical treatment and medical research offer the best hope for solutions to these diseases and efforts of government and of the voluntary organizations have shifted in that direction. However, there is still need to ensure that expensive medical treatment and research are utilized in a cost-efficient manner. The much-publicized skyrocketing health costs of the 1970s and 1980s have moved public health in the direction of community health. Now a recognized field of instruction in medical and nursing schools alike, community health is an attempt to combine the medical, social and behavioral sciences to provide the best of medical science tempered by an assessment of society's real needs. These curative measures are supported by campaigns aimed at undermining the social causes of ill health, such as ALCOHOLISM, drug abuse, SMOKING and inadequate exercise (see FITNESS; DRUG USE, NONMEDICAL).

In its move towards community health, Canada is following a worldwide trend towards more economic and productive use of the fruits of medical science.

JANICE DICKIN MCGINNIS

Public Opinion, a term popularized by Jacques Necker, Louis XVI's financial minister, who wrote that public opinion influenced the behaviour of investors on the Parisian financial markets. In England Jeremy Bentham insisted that public opinion was a significant force for the social control of misrule and an important basis of democracy. In ancient societies, only among the Greeks did public opinion develop any potency. Public opinion in Europe was frequently considered the weapon of the middle class, the class that "wears black coats and lives in good homes" against the established order. Tocqueville, observing the role of public opinion in the US in 1835, wrote "the majority raises formidable barriers around the liberty of opinion" and "I am not the more disposed to pass beneath a yoke because it is held out to me by the arms of a million of men."

There is no accepted definition of public opinion, although it is now part of daily vocabulary, especially that of politicians and journalists. It is generally defined as a collection of individual opinions on an issue of public interest. It does not necessarily refer to values or beliefs because opinions are more unstable and less focused. Attitude and opinion are frequently used interchangeably, but attitude is conventionally regarded as a more fundamental generalized predisposition, while opinion is a specific manifestation of underlying attitudes. When an event occurs, people form, discuss and then modify or strengthen their attitudes and public opinion is the result. Opinion is often characterized by direction, intensity, breadth and depth.

Long before systematic measures of opinion developed, it was noted that public opinion appeared to equal more than the sum of individual opinions, which led scholars observing crowd behaviour to speculate on the existence of a group mind, although the concept, at least in social science, was discarded for lack of empirical evidence. Some 20th-century social scientists postulate that the relation of individual opinions to each other results in a form of organization. Despite the lack of research on the internal structure of public opinion, some public-relations practitioners see their task as that of transforming individual attitudes into a collectivity that can exert influence. The biggest users of public-opinion research are business and industry. Newspapers, magazines, broadcasters and political parties also use polls to gather opinions.

Measuring Public Opinion Public opinion is measured by questionnaires. The population under study is quite large, so a sampling, taken to represent the entire population, is generally used. This is the public-opinion poll, and its validity depends on the quality of the questions and of the sample taken. Efforts to measure public opinion began in the early 19th century. Some American newspapers, in an attempt to calculate the outcome of an upcoming election, asked their readers to send in their straw votes, which the paper then compiled and published. The practice became widespread during the early 20th century, especially as a result of the activities of the *Literary Digest*, which carried out national polls from 1910 to 1936. The election of 1936, however, was a disaster for this kind of poll. Despite a massive sample of 2.4 million mailed-in ballots, the *Digest* underestimated the election of Franklin Roosevelt by 19.3%, largely because the poll ignored a significant section of the electorate. However, newcomers to the field, notably George Gallup, accurately predicted the results. In Canada the first Gallup polls appeared in the early 1940s and now occur monthly. They are conducted by the Canadian Institute of Public Opinion. Each month the CIPO surveys the opinions of about 1000 Canadians. Gallup polls use statistical inference, estimating the attributes of an entire population

from one sample. Many questions are asked and they vary from poll to poll. Gallup does ask the same questions at intervals over several years, allowing the evolution of public opinion to be traced. On the other hand, as a general rule the relatively large number of respondents unable to express an opinion clearly are presumed to have the same preferences as those that can. The presentation of results can also be misleading. A national sample used to measure voting intentions must appropriately represent demographic categories of age, sex, rural or urban residence, occupation, income, education and religious or ethnic affiliation. Like most national-opinion surveys, Gallup polls use a combination of the quota-stratified method, which involves choosing characteristics of the population to be sampled, determination of the proportion of the population with such characteristics, and the assignment of quotas to interviewers; and the area-probability method, which involves choosing characteristics of a population to be studied, dividing the country into "areal" units, eg, counties, rural municipalities, cities, etc, arbitrarily dividing these units into area segments, selecting a certain number of dwelling units in each segment and selecting the adults (or eligible voters) to be interviewed.

The Gallup organization claims a 4% margin of error for final election results. However, this polling error, expressed as an unweighted percentage-point average (obtained by dividing total percentage-point error by the number of categories of parties), does not reflect polling competence. For example, in 1957 the average error was 3.5%, but the forecast error was 53%, or about 1 million votes. Even when, in 1962, the average polling error was only 1.5%, the disparity between the error expressed in actual votes (446 000) and the leading party's plurality of 8000 votes was very large. Between 1945 and 1974, in 11 federal elections, the CIPO accurately predicted the percentages of votes cast for party categories in only 7 of 44 instances, and in the case of the 2 major parties the institute grossly overestimated Liberal strength in 1957 and 1965. In recent provincial elections, polling sponsored by newspapers and conducted by private organizations has increased dramatically. In many cases the polls attempt to forecast proportional vote distributions and not actual constituency outcomes. Usually a random provincial sample is consulted through telephone interviews. Some of these studies, eg, those of the Centre de recherches sur l'opinion publique, conducted during the 1970 and 1973 Québec elections, succeeded in predicting election trends only in a general manner.

Many politicians and observers have claimed that polling strongly influences the opinions it seeks to measure. It has been suggested that polls can cause voters to change their minds in order to be on the winning side, that weaker parties benefit as a result of an underdog effect, and that polls discourage voting by many who feel the results are foregone. There is no clear evidence to substantiate any of these theories, although corporate leaders, media executives, politicians and civil servants are often powerfully influenced themselves by survey results. The literature on voting behaviour indicates that the psychology of voting is very complex and includes many determinants. Generally, citizens in democracies appear to tolerate polling errors or the use or misuse of polls by the media. After the 1970 Québec elections, evidence suggested that certain newspapers had flagrantly misrepresented pre-election survey results. In response 9 Montréal polling organizations, to forestall an outright ban on certain polling activities such as exists in BC, recommended an elaborate set of rules to control media presentation of results. Federally, the Barbeau Committee on Election Expenses recommended no poll results be published during any pre-election period. A private member's bill to the same effect was tabled in the House of Commons in 1970, but no such proposals have been passed.

In fact Canadian political parties have used polls with increasing frequency, as have Canadian government agencies, royal commissions, task forces and other policy-oriented groups. The Liberal, Progressive Conservative and New Democratic parties all regularly commission surveys for their private use. The Conservative government of Ontario uses external and domestic polling organizations extensively. New techniques of motivational and mass-attitude analysis are deployed at national, provincial and constituency levels. These surveys are conducted not only by conventional polling specialists but by sociologists and social psychologists as well. The newer survey methods are costly, which may affect competition between parties. The motivation behind the polling, for some politicians, also suggests a preoccupation with image projection, a tendency for party leaders to dominate in elections and consequently in decision making, and a tendency to negotiate or bargain with voters, rather than persuade them. However, researchers claim that some leaders have always sought to follow or manipulate public opinion and always will, and also point to many cases where minority viewpoints have ultimately become the prevailing opinions of the public. For obvious reasons some politicians view published pre-election surveys with scorn, reflected in Mr Diefenbaker's famous comment, "Every morning when I take my little dog, Happy, for a walk, I watch with great interest what he does to the poles." ANDRÉ BLAIS

Public Ownership, government provision of goods and services, the commercial or business activities of the STATE. Although the boundaries between the public and private sectors have been blurred by governments' expanding role in the economy, public ownership generally refers to enterprises, wholly or partially government owned, which sell goods and services at a price according to use. According to this definition, government-owned railways, airlines, and utilities are examples of public ownership, but hospitals, highways and public schools are not. In Canada the latter are provided by the state but are financed primarily by general government revenues, not by fees paid by individuals in relation to the quantities of goods or services produced. Such a definition, though not absolute, does distinguish public ownership from private ownership and other sorts of state activity.

Although many Canadians probably believe private enterprise dominates their economy, public ownership is important at all 3 levels of Canadian government. For example, in 1984 the federal government owned AIR CANADA, Canada's largest airline; CANADIAN NATIONAL RAILWAYS; the CANADIAN BROADCASTING CORPORATION and PETRO-CANADA; as well as coal and uranium mines, aircraft factories and financial institutions. Provincial public ownership is very diverse. Not only are most provinces involved in the generation and transmission of electricity (see UTILITIES), the retail sale of liquor and the provision of financial services to farmers and small businesses; but telephone service in the Prairie provinces, railways in BC, Alberta and Ontario, steel mills in Québec and NS, automobile insurance in several provinces, and energy companies in most provinces are also publicly owned. Public ownership is also important in Canadian municipalities where it may include the provision of urban transportation, water, electricity and, in a few cases, notably Edmonton, telephone service. Although the election of NEW DEMOCRATIC PARTY provincial governments

has led to greater public ownership, Canadian governments do not resort to it out of political ideology. Public ownership, which generally supplements private enterprise and the market, is used to promote economic growth through the provision of economic infrastructure, to achieve federal and provincial control over certain firms and industries, to maintain employment and to promote national security. Private enterprise has not always been willing or able to provide important goods and services in such a large, sparsely populated country. The threatening presence of the US, the need to extend important services over vast distances, and regional and cultural forces have played a large role in determining the use of public ownership.

However, public ownership has not been uncontroversial in Canada. Public ownership of hydro in several provinces, the nationalization of automobile insurance in BC and Manitoba, and the creation and growth of Petro-Canada are a few of the government actions that evoked conflict about government's role in the economy. The effectiveness of Canada's burgeoning public-enterprise sector has been seriously questioned. Some interests now argue that public ownership has been too widely extended in Canada, a common prescription being the "privatization" (return to private ownership) of a number of publicly owned firms. Public ownership also has many supporters and defenders. It remains an important policy instrument for Canadian governments of diverse persuasions.

Public ownership in Canada has been achieved in several ways. Occasionally governments have created new firms, or less frequently they have acquired or nationalized, private ones. The NATIONALIZATION of industries such as potash in Saskatchewan, asbestos in Québec and hydroelectric power in Ontario has been very controversial. However, the owners of firms that have been nationalized normally received financial compensation. Public ownership is generally administered through the form of a CROWN CORPORATION, but a publicly owned industry need not be in corporate form. Government departments may also administer state-owned businesses. Recently, governments have employed "mixed" corporations that involve, in varying degrees, public and private ownership within a single firm. The ALBERTA ENERGY COMPANY, a firm owned jointly by the Alberta government and many individual Canadian investors, is a good example of a mixed enterprise. But the political and economic effectiveness of such enterprises remains undetermined. A. TUPPER

Public School Public schools are free, state controlled, tax supported and nonsectarian and are funded by provincial and local taxes (although federal funds, transferred through provincial governments, may be directed into public schools in special cases). Provincial political authority alone determines their aims and controls their curriculum, textbooks and standards, and authorizes who may serve in them as teachers and administrators. (Although local SCHOOL BOARDS construct and manage public schools they do so within powers delegated by provincial governments.) SEPARATE SCHOOLS and tax-supported denominational schools are a special kind of public school for citizens of either Catholic or Protestant faith, although usually of the former. Children are required by law to attend school for a minimum of 10 years from the age of 6, although they may be excused from attendance at a public school if they receive other, equivalent education.

Public Service, also known as the civil service, is the public BUREAUCRACY comprising, in Canada, departmental organizations that support the political executive in the development, implementation and enforcement of government

policies. It includes some 50 departmental organizations (and more than 200 000 employees) normally established by Acts of Parliament designating the positions of minister, the political head, and the senior official or deputy head, and outlining the powers, duties and functions of the organization. Generally the administrative machinery is designed to support the individual and collective responsibilities of ministers to Parliament. Nondepartmental organizations — CROWN CORPORATIONS, CENTRAL AGENCIES, regulatory commissions and ADMINISTRATIVE TRIBUNALS — are also part of the public service.

By convention, the prime minister selects ministers and assigns to them statutory responsibilities, although their formal appointment is made by the governor general. The Cabinet theoretically directs the public service in its application and enforcement of current policies and the development of new ones, and is responsible to the legislature for the administration of it. Cabinet committees and the PRIME MINISTER'S OFFICE have in recent years been used to counter independent policy making within the public service, but the Cabinet secretariat, the PRIVY COUNCIL OFFICE (PCO) are themselves all part of the bureaucracy. The effectiveness of the budgetary process designed to control bureaucratic financial expenditures is also questionable, because the Treasury Board Secretariat (TBS) is part of the bureaucracy as well.

Cabinet is supported in the co-ordination of government policies and in the direction and management of the public service by central agencies, by departments such as finance, justice and external affairs, which have traditionally been major central policy departments, and by policy secretariats such as the ministries of state for economic development and social development, which co-ordinate departmental activites in these policy sectors. Particular government policies and programs are developed and implemented by a large number of program departments, eg, agriculture, national health and welfare, national defence, labour, employment and immigration, and transport. There is also a small group of departments, such as public works and national revenue, that provide common administrative services for other government departments.

The rights and responsibilities of public servants are outlined in statutes such as the Public Service Employment Act, the Canadian Human Rights Act, the Official Languages Act, the Public Service Staff Relations Act and the regulations and directives passed under the authority of these Acts. Appointment to the public service and subsequent career advancement are based on the merit principle, which, although not defined in legislation, is generally considered to be "the selection of the most qualified candidates competing for a position based on their relative knowledge, experience and abilities, without discrimination or favouritism." It is administered through the merit system, which includes the regulations, policies, procedures and directives related to the recruitment, hiring and promotion of public servants and which has been adapted to changing circumstances. For example, after the OFFICIAL LANGUAGES ACT (1969) was passed, bilingualism became an element of merit in the staffing of positions. Moreover, efforts to increase the participation of individuals from underrepresented or disadvantaged groups, eg, women, francophones, native peoples and handicapped persons, have involved special recruitment and staffing measures. Equal opportunity programs have been directed at removing discriminatory practices in recruitment and promotion and affirmative programs have attempted to increase the participation of individuals from these groups directly.

The convention of political neutrality in the public service is maintained by the principle of appointment on the basis of merit rather than on political affiliation. The traditional separation of politics and administration and of the anonymity of public servants theoretically meant public servants could remain neutral in supporting the government in power, but in recent years the recognition that politics, policy and administration are interrelated has modified the convention. As part of their job, public servants are involved actively in developing policy and are often expected to explain these policies to the public on their minister's behalf.

Political rights of public servants are restricted to voting and other forms of passive participation, eg, attending political meetings and contributing funds to political parties. They are legally forbidden to criticize government policy publicly or to disclose confidential information. Public servants wishing to seek a nomination and contest an election for national or provincial office must apply for a leave of absence without pay, which may be denied if it conflicts with job responsibilities, but they are allowed to take an active part in elections at the municipal level.

COLLECTIVE BARGAINING in the public service provides the majority of its employees (not those in managerial or confidential capacities, or members of the RCMP or Armed Forces) the right to belong to public-service unions and to participate in a process of joint determination of salary and compensation benefits. The employer, represented by Treasury Board, retains the right to determine the classification of positions, standards of discipline and other conditions of employment. The Public Service Staff Relations Board, which administers the Public Service Staff Relations Act, determines bargaining units and agents, hears complaints of unfair practices and is generally responsible for the administration of collective bargaining legislation that falls under the Act. It reports to Parliament through a minister, the president of the PCO, who does not sit on the Treasury Board. Bargaining is between Treasury Board and its representatives and certified bargaining agents representing employees. Dispute settlement options include binding arbitration and conciliation, which sometimes allow the right to strike. Collective bargaining, like other rights of public servants, is granted by Parliament and may be changed or withdrawn by that same authority; parliamentary action to legislate striking public servants back to work or to impose wage controls may modify collective bargaining processes.

Responsibility for personnel management is divided between departmental organizations, Treasury Board and the PUBLIC SERVICE COMMISSION. Public servants are employees of their department and the public service as a whole. The Treasury Board has overall responsibility for personnel management policies and represents the employer in collective bargaining, but the Public Service Commission, under the Public Service Employment Act (1967), establishes staffing criteria for departments and assists them in training and development. It exercises full authority for appointments to senior executive positions except at the deputy-minister level. It hears appeals on appointments, investigates allegations of discrimination, decides on cases of political partisanship and audits staffing actions of departments. Established to rid the public service of political patronage, it has remained an independent central staffing agency dedicated to guarding the merit principle.

Provincial Variations The basic structure and organization of provincial public services are similar to that of the federal government; in recent years provincial public-service activities in areas such as social services, education and resource development have grown significantly.

The recruitment of a large number of skilled employees has led to the reform of personnel management practices and the development of professional public services. The role of provincial public-service commissions in staffing and training employees varies widely. Collective bargaining systems have also been introduced at the provincial level but again there are variations in the rights accorded employees in each province. In some provinces, public servants do not have the right to strike. AUDREY D. DOERR

Public Service Commission The Civil Service Commission (CSC) was established in 1908 under the Civil Service Amendment Act, which introduced the principle of merit as established by competition. The Civil Service Act of 1962 preserved the independence of the CSC and the Public Service Employment Act of 1967 reaffirmed the merit principle and changed the name of the CSC to Public Service Commission. The powers and duties of the PSC are to appoint qualified persons, to hear appeals against staffing actions, to make decisions on allegations of political partisanship, and to investigate allegations of discrimination. The commission reports directly to Parliament, though the president of the Privy Council usually represents the commission in the House. *See* PUBLIC SERVICE.

Public-Service Unions The public sector is one of the most highly unionized in Canada. Approximately 80% of those public-sector employees eligible for collective bargaining are covered by collective agreements, compared with only 25% in the private sector. Most municipal employees belong to the 290 000-member CANADIAN UNION OF PUBLIC EMPLOYEES (CUPE), and had bargaining rights similar to those in the private sector until 1982-83, when many provincial governments moved to restrict these rights. Health-care workers in some provinces are denied the right to strike. Provincial employees, largely represented by affiliates of the 242 000-member National Union of Provincial Government Employees (except in Québec and New Brunswick), are covered by more restrictive legislation. Most school, health-care and social-service employees bargain with a variety of boards and agencies that administer primarily provincial-government monies. New Brunswick unions bargain directly with the province. In Québec a coalition of militant public-sector unions representing members of the CONFEDERATION OF NATIONAL TRADE UNIONS, the Québec Federation of Labour and the Québec Teachers' Corporation bargains directly with the province.

Most federal government employees belong to the 160 000-member Public Service Alliance of Canada, and have had bargaining rights since passage of the 1967 Public Service Staff Relations Act. This Act, however, severely limits the provisions that unions may negotiate. The smaller Canadian Union of Postal Workers (25 000 members) is considered the most militant (*see* POSTAL STRIKES; CUPW) and has bargained such breakthroughs as paid maternity leave, premium pay for weekend work and the right to bargain on technological change.

All of these public-sector unions have evolved from docile employee associations into genuine trade unions. All except the CNTU and the QTC are affiliated with the CANADIAN LABOUR CONGRESS, where public-service employees now make up more than half the membership. Professional unions in the public sector — eg, nurses, teachers, academics, engineers — have largely remained independent. But even these groups have recently become militant and have frequently struck.

Great expansion occurred in public-sector programs and services from 1965 to 1975, and a tremendous upsurge in union membership allowed many employees to obtain limited bargaining rights. After 1975, limited economic growth resulted in cutbacks in many government programs. Bargaining rights were curtailed by Wage-control legislation and limitations on the right to strike. Employees designated "essential" were prohibited from striking, and others were subjected to special legislation to terminate their legal strikes. The result was a sharp increase in public-sector strikes. Several union leaders were jailed during this period for defying back-to-work legislation. In recent years it has become increasingly difficult for unions to defend their members. Up to 1982, public-employee unions faced a choice: to revert to being benevolent associations, playing the limited role that they had prior to the advent of collective bargaining, or to become militant political organizations in order to win back the bargaining rights they enjoyed in the 1965-75 period. By 1983-84 repressive legislation and huge services cutbacks forced public-sector unions to take the militant route, eg, the Operation Solidarity strikes in BC in the autumn of 1983. GILBERT LEVINE

Public Works, Canada, Department of, est 1867 by an Act of Parliament. Before that time public works were carried on in the Province of Canada by the commissioner of public works, who controlled canals, harbours, lighthouses, roads and bridges, public buildings, etc. The department manages real property for the federal government and provides construction and maintenance of government departments, institutions and agencies. Responsibilities include construction of wharves, piers, roads, bridges and improvement of harbours. The Dominion Fire Commission is responsible for protection of life and property on government premises. The department also administers all expropriation activities of the federal government and is responsible for the CANADA MORTGAGE AND HOUSING CORPORATION and the NATIONAL CAPITAL COMMISSION. The department's 1984-85 budget was $1.3 million.

Publications, Royal Commission on, est Sept 1960 to examine the impact of foreign publications in Canada on domestic periodicals, with particular emphasis on questions of competition and national identity. It is also known as the O'Leary Commission for its chairman, Grattan O'LEARY. The commission's recommendation that the deduction from income tax of advertising expenditures aimed at the Canadian market but appearing in a foreign publication be eliminated became law 16 years later, when Bill C-58, the so-called "Time-Reader's Digest Act," was proclaimed despite the aggressive lobbying campaign of *Time* magazine in particular against the proposed legislation. The commission's only other claim to fame was that it employed P. Michael Pitfield as its secretary in one of his first official capacities. RICHARD STURSBERG

Pubnico, NS, UP, pop 173 (1981c), is located 30 km SE of YARMOUTH, at the head of Pubnico Harbour. Several communities around the harbour share the name, from Lower East to Lower West Pubnico, and their populations total about 2600. The name evolved through many variations of the Indian word *pogocoup* ("land from which the trees have been removed to fit it for cultivation"). Philippe D'Entremont founded Pubnico on a grant from his friend Charles de La Tour in 1651 or 1653. In 1755 the ACADIANS were expelled from NS, but many later made their way back. Today the D'Entremont surname survives in a large part of Pubnico's population. Shipbuilding was for some time a major industry in this area, acting as a support for trade in nearby Yarmouth. Both E and W Pubnico depend economically on fishing and farming, the region being famous for its lobsters during the winter season. Several small boatbuilding yards produce the famous Cape Sable Island fishing boat. JEAN PETERSON

In contrast to his contemporaries, Inuk artist Pudlo incorporates modern technology, as in his *Aeroplane* (*courtesy West Baffin Eskimo Co-operative, Cape Dorset, NWT*).

Pudlo Pudlat, graphic artist (b at Kamadjuak Camp, Baffin I, NWT 4 Feb 1916). One of the most original contemporary Inuit artists, Pudlo began drawing in the early 1960s after he had moved to CAPE DORSET, NWT, leaving a semi-nomadic life of seasonal hunting and fishing behind him. His preferred medium is a combination of acrylic wash and coloured pencils. In contrast with most of his contemporaries, Pudlo has included in his imagery icons of the modern technology that has brought such profound changes to the Canadian North. In his work, airplanes, helicopters and telephone poles enter into strange interactions with the arctic landscape and its animals. A muskox rider lassoing an airplane or a loon steering a motorboat are examples of his juxtapositions. In many ways Pudlo's work symbolizes the paradoxes of the encounter between 2 cultures. *See* INUIT ART.
MARIA MUEHLEN

Puffball, *see* MUSHROOM.

Puffin, common name for 3 species of medium-sized SEABIRDS of the AUK family. Most commonly, the name refers to the Atlantic puffin (*Fratercula arctica*), about 33 cm long, with a distinctive triangular bill, red with a bluish grey base. Puffins are highly colonial in breeding season, usually nesting in burrows in grassy slopes or flattish ground, sometimes in rock crevices and boulder skree. They first breed when 4-5 years old, a pair normally remaining together for entire breeding life. The single, white egg is incubated by both parents for about 42 days. The chick is fed small fish for 6-7 weeks. Both adults and immatures winter offshore, but where they spend the 7-8 months before returning to the colony is poorly known. Atlantic puffins breed along both coasts and on many islands of the N Atlantic. Their N American breeding range centers on Newfoundland and Labrador coasts. The N American breeding population is estimated at about 338 000 pairs; almost 70% nest on 4 islands in Witless Bay, SE Nfld. Populations in Gulf of St Lawrence-New England states area and in NE Atlantic have de-clined considerably since 1900, probably because of human persecution, variation in food availability, and oil pollution. Horned (*F. corniculata*) and tufted puffins (*Lunda cirrhata*) occur in the Bering Sea and N Pacific Ocean. Both breed in coastal colonies from eastern Siberia and NW Alaska S to the Aleutian Is and SE Alaska. Tufted puffins also breed in BC, Washington, Oregon and California. D.N. NETTLESHIP

Pugsley, William, lawyer, politician, premier and lieutenant-governor of NB (b at Sussex, NB 27 Sept 1850; d at Toronto 3 Mar 1925). A prominent political figure in NB in the early part of the 20th century, Pugsley was a tough politician who employed patronage blatantly to win support for the Liberal cause. He served as Speaker of the House, solicitor general and attorney general before becoming premier in 1907. He resigned after a few months to enter the federal Cabinet as minister of public works. Following a term as lieutenant-governor, 1918-23, he was appointed commissioner of the settlement of war claims in Ottawa, a position he held until his death. ARTHUR T. DOYLE

Pugwash, NS, UP, pop 648 (1981c), is located 65 km NW of TRURO, at the mouth of the Pugwash R. It takes its name from the Micmac *Pagwechk* ("shallow water" or "shoal"). Cyrus EATON, multi-millionaire industrialist and humanitarian, opened his summer home here for a "Thinkers' Conference" where statesmen, philosophers and businessmen could discuss issues of world concern. These successful international meetings, known as "Pugwash Conferences," have since been held around the world, and Pugwash is internationally known as "the Global Village." Famous as well are its annual Gathering of the Clans and Fisherman's Regatta; many of its street signs are bilingual — English and Gaelic. Shipbuilding and fishing were major industries in the 19th century, but declined with the advent of the steamship and railway. A vast salt mine, opened 1957, is a major employer. Today, Pugwash also supports a commercial fishery, as well as numerous businesses and artisans.
JANICE MILTON

Pukaskwa National Park (est 1971, 1888 km²) is SHIELD country, an ancient plateau of granite and gneiss riddled with lakes and dissected by tumbling rivers. The park is bracketed on the W by the coastline of Lk Superior, an impressive stretch of massive headlands and boulder beaches. In this wilderness roam moose, black bear, woodland caribou, wolves and smaller species adapted to the northern forest of black spruce, jack pine and white birch. The "Pukaskwa Pits" are evidence of early habitation by OJIBWA Indians. The purpose of these carefully arranged boulders remains a mystery. In the 17th century European explorers came, soon to be followed by fur traders and the logging industry. Today, Pukaskwa challenges the modern explorer to paddle its turbulent spring rivers and hike the rugged hills. Commercial accommodation is available in nearby Marathon, Ont. LILLIAN STEWART

Pulp and Paper Industry comprises MANUFACTURING enterprises that convert cellulose fibre into a wide variety of pulps, papers and paperboards. About 95% of their fibre comes from wood from Canadian FORESTS, the balance from wastepaper and a very small quantity of linen and cotton rags. Wood is reduced to fibre by mechanical means or by cooking in chemicals. The fibres are then mixed with water, adhering to one another as the water is removed by pressure and heat. This is the fundamental principle of papermaking, discovered by the Chinese nearly 2000 years ago and brought to Spain by the Moors, probably during the 12th century.

Papermaking today is a large, capital-intensive industry, characterized by high-speed machines and complex systems of control for manufacturing to close tolerances thousands of products vital to education, communications, marketing, packaging, construction, etc. Canada today ranks second to the US in pulp and paper manufacture, and first in pulp and paper exports. It has about 140 pulp, pulp and paper, and paper mills, every province except PEI having at least one.

Pulp and paper production in recent years has been valued at some $11 billion annually and has accounted for 3-3.5% of the GROSS NATIONAL PRODUCT. Exports of around $9 billion have comprised about 10% of total Canadian exports. The industry is the largest of Canada's manufacturing industries, with about 85 000 workers in mills and offices, some $2.4 billion paid in wages and salaries and some $5.5 billion in value added by manufacture. Furthermore the industry makes a net contribution to Canada's BALANCE OF PAYMENTS of some $8 billion, larger than that of any other Canadian industry.

The first Canadian paper mill was built in 1805 at St Andrews, Qué, by 2 entrepreneurs from New England. It produced printing, writing and wrapping papers for sale mostly in the growing markets of Montréal and Québec City. Sites chosen for early mills were on rivers or streams, which provided water necessary for papermaking processes and waterpower to run machinery. Waterways also provided a convenient means of transporting raw materials (rags) to the mill and finished goods to markets. Throughout the 19th century, pulp and paper was largely a domestic industry, serving the gradually increasing needs of Canadians. As literacy spread and commercial and industrial activity quickened, the need for cultural and packaging papers grew. Many new mills were established along the Great Lakes — St Lawrence system and its tributaries and in the Maritimes. For many centuries the traditional source of cellulose fibre for paper manufacture had been cotton and linen rags. The full potential of a Canadian pulp and paper industry based on a vast forest resource began to be realized only after the discovery of how to make paper from wood (around 1850). The first chemical wood-pulp mill in Canada was built in 1864, at Windsor Mills, Qué. Wood pulp then gradually displaced rag pulp for most uses, and the era of modern papermaking began.

Two developments, both occurring within a relatively short period, moved Canada onto the world papermaking stage. The first, in the 1890s and early 1900s, was the prohibition of exports of pulpwood from crown lands, applied by provincial governments. The second was the removal of the US tariff on newsprint in 1913. These actions stimulated large investments in Canadian pulp and papermaking for foreign markets and set the industry on the course it has followed ever since. By the end of WWI, Canada had already become the world's largest exporter of pulp and paper.

Each subsequent decade of the industry's history has had its particular flavour. Rapid growth took place in the 1920s, especially in northwestern Ontario and the St-Maurice Valley, Ottawa Valley and Lac Saint-Jean regions of Québec. Mills were sited in northern locations that offered hydroelectric power potential as well as spruce stands. Establishment of a mill frequently necessitated development of a townsite such as KENORA, Ont (*see* RESOURCE TOWNS). Expansion was followed by the worldwide depression of the 1930s, when some companies went bankrupt and most others were in very serious financial straits. WWII brought a return to higher levels of activity and even some expansion as European wood-pulp supplies that had formerly served the US market became unavailable. The postwar economic boom arrived in the late 1940s, continuing almost uninter-

The tufted puffin (*Lunda cirrhata*) is found in the Bering Sea and N Pacific Ocean (*photo by Lyn Hancock*).

rupted through to the late 1950s. Pulp and paper companies, by now fully restored to financial health, refurbished their manufacturing operations, steadily raised shipments and exports and, for a number of years, ran at maximum capacity.

With the 1960s came the greatest surge of expansion in the industry since the 1920s. It occurred everywhere, but the pacesetter was BC. Canadian and foreign interests, spurred by provincial governments eager for new industrial investment, scrambled to participate as large areas of public forestland were made available. Sixteen new mills opened between 1965 and 1970, mostly for the production of bleached kraft pulp for world markets. The 1970s were a turbulent period for the industry, marked by greatly intensified competition in international markets, periods of worldwide overcapacity, a deep recession in mid-decade, large changes in currency exchange rates, rapidly rising inflation throughout the industrial world and a decline in the competitiveness of the Canadian economy as a whole. Nevertheless, as the decade ended, devaluation of the Canadian dollar had helped restore the competitive strength of the pulp and paper industry, and large programs of mill modernization were underway in every region.

The early 1980s brought other abrupt changes: a deep recession and sharp cutbacks in pulp and paper production were followed, in early 1983, by the beginnings of economic recovery and the prospect of substantial future growth in worldwide use of pulp and paper. This prospect was accompanied by the knowledge that the Canadian industry would continue to face intense competition in all its traditional markets. In quantity, Canada's pulp and paper shipments now total about 21 million t: about 40% is newsprint, of which Canada has been the world's largest producer for over 50 years; about 36% is wood pulp, for further processing into paper and paperboard; 24% is a wide variety of packaging papers and boards, book and writing papers, tissue and sanitary papers and building papers and boards.

Some 77% of Canadian production is exported; 23% is used in Canada. The largest export market has for many years been the US, which now absorbs about 51%. Western Europe takes about 14%; Japan some 4%; all other world markets together about 8%. Nearly 90% of exports consists of newsprint and wood pulp, which have entered the major world markets duty free for many years. Historically, other papers and paperboards have encountered tariffs around the world and, partly for this reason, have been manufactured largely for use within Canada. Although this situation is now changing to some extent, as a result of successive rounds of multilateral tariff reductions negotiated through the GATT, newsprint and wood pulp remain the export staples of the Canadian industry.

The pulp and paper industry uses about 85 million m³ of wood annually: over 90% is SPRUCE, FIR, PINE and other softwoods; the balance is hardwoods. Over the past 20 years the most significant development in the industry's fibre requirements has been the tremendous increase in the use of wood chips, reject lumber and other wood residues from sawmills. Such residues now account for about half of all wood used in Canadian pulp and paper mills, as compared with around 10% in the early 1960s. This development has meant a more complete and efficient use of the forest resource and has stimulated greater integration of pulp and paper and lumber manufacture.

Québec accounts for the largest share of total production, about 35%; BC and Ontario each have about 23%; and the Atlantic and Prairie provinces together have some 19%. Most mills

Pulp logs in the river at the Great Lakes Forest Products, Ltd, plant at Dryden, Ont (*photo by Jim Merrithew*).

are located in communities near the forests from which they draw their chief raw material; some that purchase pulp for conversion into finished products or use mostly wastepaper have been built in the large metropolitan areas. About 70% of Canada's pulp and paper is manufactured by companies that are controlled in Canada; some 23% comes from companies controlled in the US; and 7%, from companies controlled elsewhere. Canadian ownership is largely via the private sector. There has been some public-sector ownership by provincial governments or their agencies in Québec, Manitoba and Saskatchewan, but this amount represents only some 10-15% of the industry's total manufacturing capacity. The major Canadian companies are Abitibi-Price Inc, British Columbia Forest Products Ltd, Canadian Forest Products Ltd, CIP Inc, Consolidated-Bathurst Inc, Domtar Pulp & Paper Products Group, Great Lakes Forest Products Ltd, MacMillan Bloedel Ltd.

The pulp and paper industries of Canada and the other large producing regions of the world (eg, the US, Europe, Japan) have traditionally shared information on technological development. Hence, the major advances in wood harvesting, pulping and papermaking during the 20th century have tended to result from research work in several countries. Canada has participated fully in these developments and has had a very important role in some of them, such as the chemical-recovery system used in alkaline pulping, which stimulated the growth of the kraft pulp industry all over the world; improved pulp-bleaching techniques, which opened new markets for many papers and paperboards; and twin-wire forming, one of the most significant developments in the papermaking process since the invention of the Fourdrinier machine in the first decade of the 19th century (*see* CHEMICAL ENGINEERING). Scientific research is carried out by a number of Canadian pulp and paper manufacturers and the industry also carries on co-operative research through the Pulp and Paper Research Institute of Canada and the Forest Engineering Research Institute of Canada, both situated in Pointe-Claire, Qué. The industry makes large capital expenditures on air and water POLLUTION abatement; in recent years, $150-300 million annually. Mill effluent losses have been reduced substantially: suspended solids per tonne of production has dropped by 86%; biochemical oxygen demand, by 65%.

GORDON MINNES

Pulse Crops are members of the legume family, seeds or plant parts of which are edible. Pulses have taproots with the potential to form symbiotic associations with nitrogen-fixing *Rhizobium* bacteria. The fruit is a pod containing one to several seeds, which are high in carbohydrate, protein and, in some instances, oil. Pulses are primarily warm-season annuals, requiring 40-100 cm of precipitation annually. Of the pulses of economic importance, chickpeas and SOYBEANS originated in China; common BEANS and lima beans in Central and S America; cowpeas, LENTILS, mung beans and PEAS in India;

and FABA BEANS and mung beans in central Asia. Worldwide, soybeans are the most important pulse crop grown. Canada produces significant quantities of common beans, faba beans, lentils, peas and soybeans.   P. MCVETTY

Pumpkin, common name for SQUASH with large, orange fruits. In N America the term most commonly refers to those fruits of *Cucurbita pepo*, which are picked after the rind has hardened but before the first frost. In Europe, the word is used for various squashes, eg, *C. maxima*. Pumpkins have little economic importance in Canada and the US, being used mainly for making pies and for jack-o'-lanterns during the Halloween season.   ROGER BÉDARD

Purcell, Jack, badminton player (b at Guelph, Ont 24 Dec 1903). He was famous as a lanky, lithe athlete with a wide repertoire of badminton strokes and tremendous court presence. In the 1920s he won numerous Ontario titles and was Canadian singles champion in 1929 and 1930 before turning professional in 1932. Professional play was of the barnstorming, challenge variety. After defeating top professionals from Canada, England and the US, he was acclaimed in 1933 the professional champion of the world, retaining his title until retirement in the early 1940s. Canadian sportswriters chose Purcell in 1950 as one of the outstanding Canadian athletes of the half century. JOHN J. JACKSON

Purcell, James, architect (*fl* St John's 1841-58). Purcell arrived in ST JOHN'S from Cork, Ire, 1841 to superintend the building of the Roman Catholic cathedral and departed 1858 following his bankruptcy. Apparently the principal architect in the capital at the time, he designed for both the Catholics (St Bonventure's College 1858) and the Anglicans (Christ Church at Quidi Vidi 1842; a rejected design for the Anglican cathedral 1842). His most significant work is the Colonial Building, constructed in the classical revival style 1847-50.   SHANE O'DEA

Purcell String Quartet The Vancouver-based PSQ was founded in 1969 by 4 Vancouver Symphony Orchestra principals, Norman Nelson and Raymond Ovens (violins), Simon Streatfeild (viola) and Ian Hampton (cello). The ensemble was joined in 1969 by Philippe Etter (viola) and in 1979 by Sydney Humphreys and Bryan King (violins). The quartet has toured, broadcast and recorded extensively in Canada. International appearances have included London, New York and San Francisco. The PSQ was quartet-in-residence at Simon Fraser U (1972-82). It has commissioned or given premiere performances of numerous Canadian works.   MAX WYMAN

Purdy, Alfred Wellington, (b at Wooler, Ont 30 Dec 1918). Al Purdy is one of a group of important Canadian poets — Milton ACORN, Alden NOWLAN and Patrick LANE are others — who have little formal education and whose roots are in Canada's working-class culture. He was brought up in Trenton, Ont, educated at Albert Coll, Belleville, but did not attend university. During the Depression, he rode the rods to Vancouver and worked there several years at various manual occupations. In WWII he served in the RCAF, and after the war — until the late 1950s — he worked as a casual labourer in Ontario. Eventually he settled in Ameliasburgh, the small Loyalist community celebrated in his poems. By the early 1960s Purdy was able to support himself by free-lance writing, poetry reading and periods as writer-in-residence at various colleges. He has been a restless traveller throughout Canada (including the High Arctic) and around the world, and all these journeyings have been reflected in his writing.

Like other writers who live by their craft, Purdy has worked in a variety of genres: radio and TV plays, book reviewing, travel writing,

Poet Al Purdy has sought to bring into poetry a sense of Canada's past. He was awarded the Gov Gen's Award for *The Cariboo Horses (courtesy Canapress).*

magazine features. He has edited anthologies, particularly of younger poets, and also a collection of essays entitled *The New Romans* (1968), which revealed his deep Canadian nationalism. But it is poetry, written and read, that is Purdy's essential mode. He has written it since he was 13, and by 1982 had published 25 volumes. The evolution of his verse shows an interesting progression from the conservatively traditional lyrics of his first collection, *The Enchanted Echo* (1944), to the open, colloquial and contemporary style of his later years, which began to emerge in his fourth collection, *The Crafte So Longe to Lerne* (1959).

Important factors in Purdy's poetic liberation from his early dependence on moribund romantic models were the humour and the anger he began to introduce, a characteristic style and form with relaxed, loping lines and a gruff, garrulous and engaging poetic persona. Purdy was at the heart of the 1960s movements that set Canadian poets wandering the country, reading their poems to large audiences. There is no doubt that this experience helped him to develop a poetry more closely related to oral speech patterns than his 1940s apprentice poems. The influence of readings on his work is one aspect of the close contact between experience and writing in Purdy's work. He has been described as a "versifying journalist," and some of his books have in fact been poetic accounts of journeys, such as *North of Summer* (1967), based on a trip to the Arctic, and *Hiroshima Poems* (1972), on a visit to Japan. Many of the poems such books contain were written during the journeys, as if entries in a diary. In them the interval between experience and creation is brief, which leads to an uneven-

ness of tone, though the best of Purdy's travel poems are superb examples of their kind. Purdy travels in time as well as in space. His poems reveal the generalist erudition that is acquired by a self-taught man with a passion for reading, and he has sought especially to bring into poetry a sense of Canada's past, of the rapid pattern of change that has made much of Canada acquire the quality of age in so brief a history. Few Canadian poets have evoked our past as effectively as Purdy in poems like "The Runner," "The Country North of Belleville," "My Grandfather's Country," "The Battlefield of Batoche" and the long verse cycle for radio that he wrote about the Loyalist heritage, *In Search of Owen Roblin* (1974).

Among the most successful of Purdy's many volumes are *Poems for All the Annettes* (1962), *The Cariboo Horses* (1965), which won him the Gov Gen's Award, *Sex & Death* (1973), which won him the A.J.M. Smith Award, and *The Stone Bird* (1981), which Purdy considers his best book. There are 2 important selections of his verse, *Being Alive* (1978) and *Bursting into Song* (1982), which between them contain all his memorable poems except those in *The Stone Bird*. Purdy's oral presentation of his poems, essential for a full understanding of his work, is preserved in the CBC recording, *Al Purdy's Ontario.*

GEORGE WOODCOCK

Reading: George Bowering, *Al Purdy* (1970).

Purple Martin (*Progne subis*), largest (14.4-14.9 cm) and most urbanized of Canadian SWALLOWS, is the northernmost representative of an otherwise tropical New World genus. Martins extend into Canada in NB, southern Ontario and adjacent Québec, the southern prairies (NW to Peace R) and southwestern BC (from which it may now be gone). They are migratory and formerly nested in tree cavities, but now largely in nesting box colonies around human settlements. Males are dark, glossy purplish black with blackish wings and tail; females and young, dark blue and grey. Martins feed almost entirely on flying insects and generally forage higher than other swallows.

A.J. ERSKINE

Pursh, Frederick, botanist (b Friedrich Traugott Pursch in Grossenhain, Saxony 4 Feb 1774; d at Montréal 11 July 1820). At age 25 Pursh left Dresden to try his luck in the New World. After working in the Baltimore and Philadelphia gardens, he became the collector for the rich naturalist Benjamin Smith Barton. On behalf of Barton and several other wealthy botanists, Pursh explored the eastern US from North Carolina to Vermont 1806-11. He also examined the specimens brought back by explorers Lewis and Clark. Pursh went to England with his notes and collections and found there the support and resources that allowed him to publish his main work, the *Flora Americae Septentrionalis* (1814). Despite major errors, it was an important contribution to knowledge of N American flora. Having for a while hoped to join Lord SELKIRK's Red R expedition, Pursh settled in Montréal to prepare a flora of Canada. In 1818 he explored ANTICOSTI I but his specimens were destroyed in a fire the following winter. Discouraged and reduced to poverty, Pursh died at age 46.

RAYMOND DUCHESNE

Purvis, Arthur Blaikie, industrialist (b at London, Eng 31 Mar 1890; d at Prestwick, Scot 14 Aug 1941). At the age of 20 Purvis joined Nobel's Explosives Co of Glasgow, which became part of Imperial Chemical Industries of London. It was as an employee of ICI that Purvis was sent to Canada to be president and managing director of Canadian Industries Ltd, one of Canada's most technologically advanced companies. A liberal-minded employer, with broad views on social and economic questions, he was appointed chairman of the National Employment Commission (1936-38) by PM Mackenzie KING, but the 2 clashed over the commission's recommendation that the federal government should bear all relief costs and responsibility for the unemployed. In WWII the British government (not the Canadian) made Purvis head of the British Supply Council in charge of British purchases in N America. Purvis reconciled himself with King, but quarrelled repeatedly with Lord Beaverbrook [Max AITKEN], the British minister of aircraft production. Purvis was killed in an air crash en route to the US.

ROBERT BOTHWELL

Put-In-Bay, site of a battle fought between British and American naval forces on 10 Sept 1813 during the WAR OF 1812, in the SW portion of Lake Erie. Both fleets were newly built of green lumber, and both experienced technical problems. The American ships were superior to the British in tonnage, weight and broadsides, and number of seamen; the bold American commander, Oliver Hazard Perry, made effective tactical use of his advantages. After determined and gallant resistance by Robert Barclay of the Royal Navy, the British fleet was forced to surrender. The Americans controlled Lake Erie for the rest of the war. But the British were still able to provision their posts on the upper lakes by creating a new route via York [Toronto], Lake Simcoe, Georgian Bay and Lake Huron.

ROBERT S. ALLEN

Puttee, Arthur, printer, editor (b at Folkestone, Eng 25 Aug 1868; d at Winnipeg 21 Oct 1957). Puttee was Manitoba's first Labour MP, as member for Winnipeg 1900-04. He had immigrated to N America in 1888, settling in Winnipeg 3 years later, where he was especially influential as publisher 1899-1918 of *The Voice.* In this labour weekly, Puttee popularized his reforming ideas, emphasizing the links between "labourism" in Canada and the philosophy of labour representation in Britain. However, political opponents charged that behind him lurked unnamed "revolutionists" and "assassins," accusations that led to his defeat in the 1904 general election. Puttee was an advanced Liberal, not a socialist, and won his seat in 1900 only after soliciting important Liberal support and promising Winnipeg electors that he would not vote down war credits for South Africa. Himself a critic of alleged "Industrial Workers of the World methods" during WWI, Puttee was replaced by younger and more radical leaders and played no major part in the 1919 WINNIPEG GENERAL STRIKE, whose seed he had nonetheless helped sow.

ALLEN SEAGER

Pyrite, *see* GOLD; IRON ORE.

Qaqaq Ashoona (also known as Kaka), sculptor (b 19 Aug 1928). Elder son of Inuk artist PITSEOLAK ASHOONA, Qaqaq is a central figure in this remarkable creative family which includes brothers KIUGAK and Kumwartok (sculptors), sister Napatchie (graphic artist) as well as wife Mayureak (sculptor and graphic artist) and son Ohitok (sculptor). A reserved man with traditional values, Qaqaq has for most of his life chosen not to reside in the modern settlement of CAPE DORSET, NWT, preferring instead to maintain a year-round camp nearby on the land. He began his artistic career at about age 18, and his sculpture is acclaimed for the sense of monumentality and strength he imparts to animal and human subjects alike. *See* INUIT ART.
MARIE ROUTLEDGE

Qitdlarssuaq, Inuk leader (b at Cape Searle, NWT; d near Cape Herschel, NWT 1875). He led an epic migration from Baffin I to northern Greenland. A powerful *angakkuq* (SHAMAN) he was so respected that more than 50 Inuit followed him far into unknown territory as he escaped vengeance for murder. The journey took many years and he navigated, it is said, partly by spiritual flights, leaving his body and examining the terrain ahead. After spending several years with the Polar Eskimos, to whom they introduced the kayak, the bow and arrow, and the fish spear, Qitdlarssuaq and his followers set out for their homeland, but the old leader died along the way. The survivors returned to Greenland, where their descendants still live, and where the story has become important in local tradition.
JOHN BENNETT

Quadra Island, 269 km², is situated at the N end of the Str of GEORGIA between VANCOUVER I and mainland BC, opposite CAMPBELL RIVER. The forested island, about 35 km long, forms the E side of Discovery Passage, a narrow, treacherous ship channel leading N out of the strait. Four small communities are dotted around its coast. It was named after 18th-century Spanish naval explorer BODEGA Y QUADRA.
DANIEL FRANCIS

Quail, name most commonly applied to an Old World species, *Coturnix coturnix*, of chickenlike BIRDS, which migrate seasonally in vast flocks and have long been an important human food source, eg, for the Israelites in the wilderness. New World quail are the only members of the PHEASANT subfamily native to N America. New World quail are not migratory. Some are adapted to desert habitats and can survive indefinitely without water if succulent food is available. In Canada, 3 species are found: California quail (*Callipepla californicus*) and mountain quail (*Oreortyx pictus*) in the mildest parts of southern BC; northern bobwhite (*Colinus virginianus*) in southern Ontario and introduced elsewhere. The northern bobwhite is the best-known species and, in the US, is the most widely hunted GAME BIRD. Unlike the other 2, it lacks an ornamental crest.
S.D. MacDONALD

Quakers (properly The Religious Society of Friends), a body of Christians that arose out of the religious ferment of mid-17th century Puritan England. Founder George Fox (1624-91) was the son of a Leicestershire weaver. The popular name, "Quakers," may have arisen from Fox's admonition to his followers, "Tremble at the Word of the Lord." Persecuted at home, many Quakers emigrated to the N American colonies. In the late 17th century, Quaker "Publishers of Truth" visited Newfoundland, but it was not until the mid-18th century that Quaker whalers from Nantucket established permanent settlements in Nova Scotia. In the 19th century more Quakers settled in what is now southern Ontario, where they established meetinghouses and schools. By 1860 there were over 7300 Quakers in Canada, mostly in Canada W. The number then declined to about 1000, a strength

that has been maintained to this day, mainly through new members. Throughout the 19th century, Quakers were a religious community identified by a distinctive faith and form of worship, and by special marriage customs, dress, forms of speech and "testimonies" against SLAVERY, CAPITAL PUNISHMENT and war. In the 20th century, Quakers in Canada have been active in the Christian antiwar movement (*see* PACIFISM; PEACE MOVEMENT) and in opposition to capital punishment. This witness has been carried out principally by the Canadian Friends Service Committee, Toronto. Today, Quaker groups are found in many Canadian cities, parts of a worldwide Society of Friends.
DAVID L. NEWLANDS

Reading: Arthur G. Dorland, *A History of the Society of Friends (Quakers) in Canada* (1927).

Qu'Appelle River, 430 km long, rises in Lk DIEFENBAKER and meanders generally E across southern Saskatchewan, joining the ASSINIBOINE R just E of the Manitoba border. The broad, tranquil river valley is rich agricultural land, and is famous for the berries that grow on the moist, north-facing slopes. At Ft Qu'Appelle the river widens into a chain of pleasant lakes bordered by parks. The charming name comes from a Cree legend. A young man heard someone call his name as he crossed one of the valley lakes. He replied "Who calls?" (*Qu'appelle*), but only his echo answered. He realized later it was his bride-to-be, calling him at the instant of her death.
JAMES MARSH

Quarrying Industry The quarrying of natural stone is an important industry in Canada, with commercial production in all provinces except PEI and Saskatchewan. The value of all stone quarried in 1983 was nearly $314.5 million, representing a total production volume of over 67 million t. Quarrying is taking stone (nonmetallic MINERAL matter of which ROCK consists) from a large open excavation or pit by cutting, digging or blasting. Solid stone is removed by the method best suited to each deposit, including sawing by various modes, drilling and blasting.

The Qu'Appelle River valley is rich agricultural land famous for the berries that grow along the river's north-facing slopes (*photo by Richard Vroom*).

Quarried stone is handled with mechanical equipment appropriate to the operation, eg, draglines, loaders, conveyors, forklifts and trucks. Crushed stone, which is mechanically produced, consists of irregular broken pieces of rock, usually screened or sized to meet particular specifications and needs. Dimension stone is custom cut or shaped specifically for use as building blocks, components or panels. It may be rough cut, sawn smooth, textured or polished, and is selected for strength, durability and appearance. Many quarries produce stone for ornamental dimensional building stone and monuments as well as crushed stone for construction, industrial and other purposes. Often these quarries are owned and operated by companies associated with the CONSTRUCTION INDUSTRIES.

The principal types of stone quarried in Canada are LIMESTONE, granite, sandstone and marble. Limestone accounts for 75% of the total volume both in tonnage and value. Granite accounts for over 20% of the annual total. By comparison, output of marble and sandstone is relatively small. Limestone quarries are widely distributed in Canada and economics usually dictate that sources nearest the largest markets become volume producers on the largest scale. Québec produces nearly half of Canada's annual quarry production; Ontario accounts for over a third; the balance comes mainly from British Columbia.

Today, nearly 90% of all stone produced is crushed and used by the construction industries: for concrete and asphalt aggregates, as a stabilizing base material in road building, for rubble and riprap used for fill and embankment reinforcement, as railway ballast, as roofing granules, and as chips for stucco and terrazzo. Industry consumes about 8% of annual quarry production. The CHEMICAL INDUSTRIES use crushed limestone in the neutralizing of acids; in the extraction of aluminum oxide from bauxite; in the manufacture of soda ash, calcium carbide, calcium nitrate and carbon dioxide; in PHARMACEUTICALS; in the manufacture of dyes, rayons, paper, sugar and GLASS; and in WATER TREATMENT. Limestone is used in METALLURGY as a fluxing material to cleanse impurities from molten metal. Pulverized limestone is used extensively by industry as a filler and extender for CEMENT and as a whiting used in CERAMICS, PLASTICS, floor coverings, insecticides, paper, wood putty, paints and other commodities. Limestone is used in the manufacture of fertilizer, and has other agricultural applications. About 2% of all stone quarried in Canada is used as dimension stone or ornamental building stone. Most prominent are the granites of Québec and the limestones of Ontario, Québec and Manitoba. Perhaps the best known of the latter is Manitoba Tyndall Stone, an attractively mottled dolomitic limestone quarried near Winnipeg.

In 1983 the value of stone exported from Canada was about $34 million, some 10% of total production. By comparison, total imports in 1983 were about $32.6 million. The quarrying industry is directly influenced by the construction industry: a decline in the latter causes reduced demand for building materials. In addition, an increasing trend towards stricter environmental controls could limit or even close many quarries, particularly those near larger urban centres, where dust and noise create objections and where extensive rehabilitation of spent pits may be required. This trend could ultimately lead to regional shortages of certain products and higher costs for others. I.B. BICKELL

Quartz, *see* SILICA.

Quastel, Judah Hirsch, professor of neurochemistry (b at Sheffield, Eng 2 Oct 1899). Quastel is a founder of modern neurochemistry. During 1927-28, he put forward the active-centre hypothesis of enzyme action, leading to his discovery of the principle of competitive inhibition of an enzyme by a substrate analogue. He pioneered the use of suspensions of *E. coli* for systematic biochemical studies of the living cell, and coined the term "phenylketonuria" in studies of mental defect. His contributions to the study of membrane transport processes include the original demonstration of the necessity of sodium ion in the active, energy-assisted process. A professor at UBC since 1966, he has received the RSC Flavelle Medal and the Gairdner Researcher Foundation Award, and is a companion of the Order of Canada. He has published more than 370 scientific papers and several books.   SHAN-CHING SUNG

Québec, Canada's largest province, is partly detached from the rest of Canada by Hudson Bay, and faces both Europe and the heart of N America. Representing 15.5% of the surface area of Canada, the province occupies some 1.5 million km², an area 3 times the size of France and 7 times that of Great Britain. A distance of 1700 km separates towns in the Gaspé region of the province's eastern extremity from Ville-Marie in the NE. Québec has common borders with Ontario, New Brunswick and Newfoundland and is currently embroiled in a dispute with Newfoundland over the exact location of the Labrador boundary (*see* LABRADOR BOUNDARY DISPUTE). Québec still refuses to recognize the boundary established by the British Privy Council in 1927, though it was recognized in the CONSTITUTION ACT, 1982. Québec also neighbours on 4 American states: Maine, New Hampshire, Vermont and New York. The word "Québec" comes from an Algonquian word meaning "where the river narrows." It first appeared on a map in 1601 to designate the present site of Québec City. Until the royal PROCLAMATION OF 1763, the word was used only for the city, but it now applies to the entire province.

Québec is more than a province; it is the national territory and home of over 90% of Canadians of French origin. It is the only French territory in N America (apart from the islands of ST PIERRE AND MIQUELON) and has one of the largest francophone communities outside France. Forming a distinct society within the Canadian community, Quebeckers consider themselves one of Canada's 2 founding peoples. Their language, traditions, culture and institutions set Québec apart from all other provinces.

Land and Resources

Québec is composed of 3 major geological regions. The Canadian SHIELD, covering 80% of the province, is a vast plateau with many lakes, rivers and forested areas, extending over all of northern Québec. To the S lies the ST LAWRENCE R valley and lowlands, where 90% of the population is concentrated. This is the most fertile and developed region. Finally, on the S bank of the St Lawrence, between Québec City and Lk Champlain, lies the Appalachian region, part of a very old mountain chain, extending from Newfoundland to Alabama.

Geology and Relief The St Lawrence Lowlands region was the first settled by French colonists. Its location on the St Lawrence R permitted easy travel and the land was arable. Wedged between the Appalachians and the Shield, this land is composed of a series of broad terraces sloping gently toward the river. With an average elevation of 150 m, the area has fertile soil and a pleasant environment. On the other hand, only about 5% of the Shield is arable land, most of which is located in the lower section, known as the Laurentides or LAURENTIAN HIGHLANDS. The Laurentides cover half of southern Québec N of the St Lawrence. The southern extension of the Laurentides is dotted with villages that have become summer and winter resort areas. N of the Laurentides lie the great coniferous forests, the

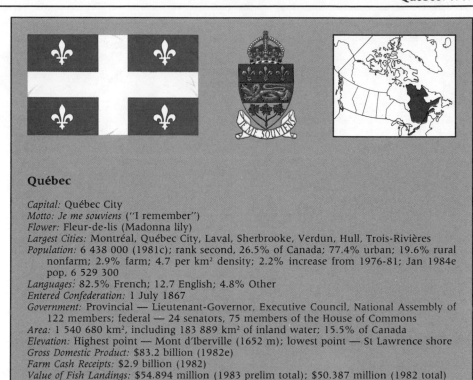

Québec

Capital: Québec City
Motto: Je me souviens ("I remember")
Flower: Fleur-de-lis (Madonna lily)
Largest Cities: Montréal, Québec City, Laval, Sherbrooke, Verdun, Hull, Trois-Rivières
Population: 6 438 000 (1981c); rank second, 26.5% of Canada; 77.4% urban; 19.6% rural nonfarm; 2.9% farm; 4.7 per km² density; 2.2% increase from 1976-81; Jan 1984e pop, 6 529 300
Languages: 82.5% French; 12.7 English; 4.8% Other
Entered Confederation: 1 July 1867
Government: Provincial — Lieutenant-Governor, Executive Council, National Assembly of 122 members; federal — 24 senators, 75 members of the House of Commons
Area: 1 540 680 km², including 183 889 km² of inland water; 15.5% of Canada
Elevation: Highest point — Mont d'Iberville (1652 m); lowest point — St Lawrence shore
Gross Domestic Product: $83.2 billion (1982e)
Farm Cash Receipts: $2.9 billion (1982)
Value of Fish Landings: $54.894 million (1983 prelim total); $50.387 million (1982 total)
Electric Power Generated: 110 565 906 MWh (1983)
Sales Tax: 9% (1984)

resource base of a major pulp and paper industry. The third area, the Appalachian region, consists of a succession of small mountain formations intersected by arable plateaus and plains. The EASTERN TOWNSHIPS, the meeting point of the US and Québec, are the heart of this region, and the area in which the first LOYALIST immigrants settled after their flight from the US. Overall, Québec has a fairly even elevation, half of the province lying between 300 and 600 m and only 7% above 600 m. Mt Iberville, in northern Québec, is the highest point at 1526 m. In southern Québec, Mt Jacques Cartier in the Gaspé region rises to 1248 m.

During the Quaternary period, the entire province was covered with glaciers. Their gradual retreat began some 15 000 years ago in the Appalachians. This retreat was accompanied by the formation of a vast inland sea, the Champlain Sea, which covered a large portion of Québec between what are today Québec City and Montréal. This deglaciation was partly responsible for the worn and rounded relief that characterizes Québec, as well as for the many lakes that dot the province.

Flora and Fauna Québec flora have had a relatively short time to evolve. The glaciers, which did not disappear until fairly recently, were followed by a cold climatic period. Consequently, present vegetation was born essentially from the northward movement of vegetation originally found along the US border. Climate has thus been the determining factor for the province's vegetation (*see* VEGETATION REGIONS). Generally, as one moves N, the variety, size and number of plant species decline. N of the 56th parallel, the arctic tundra is characterized by a lack of forest covering. Here are lichens and mosses, as well as peat bogs broken up by rocky outcroppings. This desolate landscape is the habitat of certain animal species that are particularly well adapted to the northern climate — the polar bear, fox and arctic hare.

The taiga, the transition zone between the arctic tundra and the boreal forest to the S, covers hundreds of square kilometres between the 52nd and 56th parallels. Although this is an essentially nonforested zone, a few trees are found in more sheltered areas. These are most often stunted species mixed with dwarf shrubs and trees. Here lichens form a carpet, soaking up water at night and crackling in the heat of the day. Herds of caribou, which move N over several hundred kilometres to calve, form the largest group of cervidae in Québec. The George R herd alone numbers approximately 280 000. The boreal forest covers a large part of the Canadian Shield. Unlike the boreal forests of the Rockies or Alps, it has very little vegetation. Only fir and spruce survive, along with a few tamarack and pine. Lakes and rivers are numerous and abound with trout and other fish.

Dominating the Ottawa Valley, St Lawrence Lowlands, Appalachians and Lac Saint-Jean areas, the temperate forest is composed essentially of maple, ash, beech and oak. The broad, deciduous leaves of these trees change colour in the autumn. The temperate forest is the habitat for large herds of deer, Ile d'ANTICOSTI alone accounting for some 60 000 head. A large herd of some 75 000 moose is concentrated in the Laurentide region and in the heart of the Chics-Chocs mountains in the interior of the Gaspé Peninsula. Coyotes, wolves, mink and even a few lynx also inhabit this region.

Since the St Lawrence provides a route to the interior, a number of sea mammals have become permanent or seasonal inhabitants of Québec waters, eg, several thousand beluga whales in the estuary, as well as seals, killer whales and blue whales. There are about 120 species of freshwater fish, about one dozen of which live in salt water but spawn in fresh water. These include salmon, smelt and eel. Pike, all types of trout, yellow perch, black bass and yellow pike are found throughout the area.

Québec has some 350 species of birds, only 5-7% of which winter in the province. Birds of prey such as the merlin, sparrowhawk and eagle owl all winter in Québec and inhabit the boreal forest. A little farther S live buzzards, gyrfalcons and several nonmigratory birds such as the herring gull and the Lapland bunting. Populated areas contain the greatest variety of birds, such

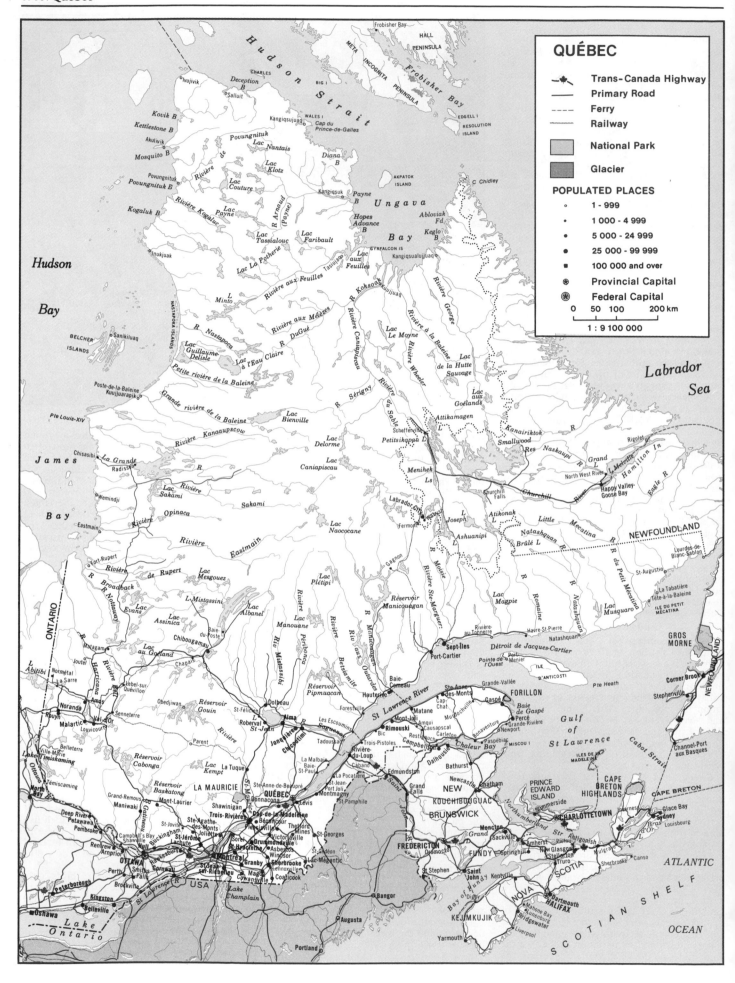

QUÉBEC

Trans-Canada Highway
Primary Road
Ferry
Railway

National Park
Glacier

POPULATED PLACES
○ 1 – 999
· 1 000 – 4 999
• 5 000 – 24 999
● 25 000 – 99 999
■ 100 000 and over
⊛ Provincial Capital
◉ Federal Capital

0   50   100   200 km
1 : 9 100 000

as crows, starlings, finches and swallows. In the summer months, the waters are inhabited by Canada geese and snow geese. Their southward migration signals the advent of winter.

Québec is a paradise for SPORTFISHING and HUNTING. In 1979 salmon fishing alone drew close to 30 000 fishermen to the Ungava, North Shore, Ile d'Anticosti and Gaspé regions. In the same year, hunters killed 2075 deer, 8202 moose and 2446 caribou.

Waterways The St Lawrence R is undoubtedly Québec's most important geographical feature. Flowing over 3600 km at a rate of 8776 m^3/s, it ranks with the great rivers of the world. Inland waters drain 284 898 km^2. These lakes and rivers, purportedly more than one million in number, represent an area larger than half of France. Québec's waterways can be divided into 3 major watersheds, the St Lawrence R, estuary and gulf being the largest. Its main tributaries to the S are the RICHELIEU, Yamaska, CHAUDIÈRE and Matapédia, and in the N the ST-MAURICE, SAGUENAY, MANICOUAGAN and OTTAWA. Major hydroelectric projects have created large reservoirs such as the one in the Manicouagan R, which will have a capacity of 800 m^3 upon completion. The Gouin dam along the St-Maurice controls a water flow of 878 m^3. More than any other Canadian province, Québec owes its development to its rivers, particularly the St Lawrence, which has been celebrated by poets and songwriters and is part of Québec's collective imagination. The St Lawrence is Québec's central nervous system, the main transit way for its exports and imports. Although big and magnificent the St Lawrence has always presented serious problems to navigation. Between Québec City and Montréal the fairway is tortuous and often quite narrow. To reach the Great Lakes canals had to be built, and it is only recently with the opening of the ST LAWRENCE SEAWAY that the river has realized its full potential. But periodically this direct link between the Great Lakes and the Atlantic has not benefited Montréal, which can no longer claim to be Canada's entry point to the world.

Eight of the 19 largest rivers in Québec flow into the JAMES BAY and HUDSON BAY Basin. This area contains so many lakes that from the air it is hard to tell whether land or water predominates. Since 1973 the area's vast potential, particularly around the Nottaway, Rupert and Eastmain rivers, has been harnessed as part of the largest hydroelectric project in Canada, under the authority of the James Bay Development Corporation. The first phase of this JAMES BAY PROJECT alone will add 9 billion kW to Hydro-Québec's production. The third watershed is UNGAVA BAY, whose major rivers are the KOKSOAK and the Caniapiscau. Here lies the Chubb, or Ungava Crater, a lake 3.3 km in diameter which was created by a meteorite and has no tributaries or draining rivers. Major lakes in the Ungava area include the MISTASSINI (2336 km^2), EAU CLAIRE (1383 km^2) and SAINT-JEAN (1350 km^2), which lies at the end of the Saguenay R in the heart of a major settlement which Quebeckers affectionately call the "Kingdom of the Saguenay".

Climate Québec's CLIMATE is severe and irregular. Because of the province's relatively moderate relief, air masses circulate freely. Neither the Canadian Shield nor the Appalachians is a large enough natural obstacle to block these air currents. Peripheral marine currents can thus have a direct effect on temperatures. The cold Labrador Current, which moves southward and disappears near Newfoundland, causes cool East Coast summers. The Gulf Stream, moving northward along the East Coast, has virtually no effect on Québec's climate. In winter the prevailing winds blow from the interior towards the ocean, cancelling out any possible effects of this warm current. In summer, however, ocean winds often bring humid heat waves. In short,

Baie-St-Paul, a typical Québec community on the St Lawrence R (*photo by Karl Sommerer*).

N winds prevail when it would be more pleasant if they were coming off the ocean, and vice versa. Another feature of Québec's climate is the sometimes stormy meeting of cold, dry air masses from the N and W with warm, humid currents from the S. In winter the meeting of these fronts causes a great deal of snow to fall over the entire province. In summer, humidity and heavy rainfalls take the place of snow.

Quebeckers like to claim that spring and autumn do not exist. Summers lengthen in the S, where most of the population resides. In the plain of Montréal, summer light and a higher number of frost-free days create an environment that is not only more favourable to agriculture but also quite enjoyable. With its blazing colours, autumn is often the most breathtaking season around Québec City and Montréal, along the Richelieu, and in Mauricie and the Eastern Townships. Winter, however, is the season that has most influenced Québec society. It has taken 4 centuries to tame and conquer it. Today, it is no longer synonymous with hardship and isolation but has become a season with its good points as well: skiing, skating and skidooing. Also, without winter there would be no HOCKEY, which Quebeckers consider their national sport.

Resources Although abundant natural resources gave Québec an early comparative advantage in raw material extraction, this advantage has not produced a balanced economic development. Distant markets, the small percentage of francophone managers in extraction companies, and a lack of economic planning have meant that natural resources are extracted in Québec but processed outside the province. The province nevertheless has over 75% of Canada's ASBESTOS reserves, 24% of its GOLD, 40% of its IRON ORE, 63% of its TITANIUM, 79% of its COLUMBIUM and 89% of its lithium. Some of these reserves represent a large portion of the world supply: 36% of asbestos, 11% of titanium, 6% of iron and 5% of columbium.

Québec's subsoil contains a number of other industrial minerals such as PEAT, limestone, silica, granite and mica. With the exception of peat, however, these products have been mined only to meet the primary needs of local markets. Although Québec is not mining uranium at the moment, it is believed to have great potential in this area. In building materials such as stone, cement, sand and lime, the Québec construction industry is largely self-sufficient. In 1979 these products were worth $432 million.

Environmental Protection Like all societies, Québec produces a considerable amount of solid wastes (180 million t annually) which, when introduced into the ecosystem, become pollutants. To these solid wastes must be added 150 million L of toxic liquid wastes from factories, mines and farms. Since 1977, open-air dumps have been banned and must be replaced by underground waste-disposal sites. A toxic material recycling centre was constructed recently N of Montréal.

ACID RAIN, which threatens almost all of Québec's lakes and forests, is the most worrisome air-pollution phenomenon. Many groups and associations are fighting to protect the environment and have successfully urged the Dept of the Environment to impose strict regulations on water and air pollution. Huge de-pollution programs are under way, notably for the rivers around Montréal.

Population and Society

France took a long time to establish its roots on the shores of the St Lawrence. There were scarcely 100 inhabitants in 1627 and only 3418 by 1666. The period between 1608 and 1760 witnessed the arrival of only 10 000 immigrants in all: 3500 soldiers, 1100 women, 1000 prisoners, 3900 volunteers and 500 free men. Three centuries later, these 10 000 colonists had grown to approximately 10 million people, of which half still live in Québec and the rest in New England and in some areas of Canada, especially in Ontario. The unique Québec culture results solely from the perseverance of these first colonists, for after 1760 there was virtually no French immigration.

Land Settlement Québec's land was settled in a unique fashion, in the rows, or rangs, of the SEIGNEURIAL SYSTEM. This method had enormous impact not only on the distribution of the HABITANTS, but also on their social organization. The colonists built their farm buildings along the rivers, which were the only thoroughfares navigable by canoe in summer and by sled in winter. Each colonist's land was therefore necessarily very narrow (200 to 250 m wide) but 2000 to 2500 m long. The same pattern was repeated behind the first row — some municipalities had over 10 rows. The system had a number of advantages: co-operation for defence, the relative ease of plowing a short section of road in winter, and the encouragement of sociability and community initiatives. People helped each other, and when it was time to marry off daughters or sons, people looked to their neighbours first.

Thus, each row became an individual social entity, obliging each person to share but also to be relatively independent because of the scattered population. With time, certain habitants developed their own areas of expertise, schools were created and businesses opened. They gathered in villages built around their church. Only the Eastern Townships, which were originally colonized by loyalist immigrants, were not settled in this manner.

Population Growth and Distribution Under the French regime, Québec's population grew very slowly. More than 50 years after the founding of QUÉBEC CITY, it had grown to only 2500, compared to a population of 80 000 in the American colonies. By 1760 Québec's population had reached only 65 000. Because of a very high birthrate, one of the highest in the world (65 per 1000 inhabitants), the population increased very quickly. By 1791 Lower Canada had a population of over 160 000. By this time, however, the major change was the presence of 20 000 Anglophones (12.5% of total population), some of whom had been forced to flee the US during the American Revolution. They were welcomed by British authorities who wished, among other things, to anglicize their new colony. These new arrivals joined with a rising tide of SCOTS, ENGLISH and IRISH immigrants. Many settled in Montréal and Québec City, or SE of Montréal in the Eastern Townships, where they benefited from generous concessions and organized themselves on the TOWNSHIP system. For a time, Montréal even had a majority of anglophone inhabitants.

By 1871 Québec's population had reached 1.2 million, 20% of whom claimed to be of British origin. This increase had been mainly owing to a birthrate that was much higher than anywhere else in Canada. Despite this, the proportion of Quebeckers in Canada had already begun to drop, from 43% in 1866 to 30% in 1926. Today, it is around 26%.

At the time of Confederation, 1867, only 20% of the population of Québec lived in cities, chiefly in Montréal, which then had 90 000 inhabitants, and Québec City, which had 58 000. These figures increased rapidly as the province became industrialized. In 1901, 36% of the population lived in cities, and by 1921 the figure had grown to 52%. Montréal continued to grow and in 1930 had almost one million inhabitants. Over 30% of all Quebeckers (half of Québec's urban population) lived on the island of Montréal. Today, over 80% of the population may be considered urban, giving Québec the second-largest urban population after Ontario (84%). Only 3% of the entire population live on farms.

With 60% of Québec's total population, the region of MONTRÉAL is by far the most populated area of Québec. It is followed by the Quebec City region with 16%. Less than 5% of the population is found in the 8 other regions (Lower St Lawrence, Saguenay-Lac Saint-Jean, TROIS-RIVIÈRES, Estrie, the Outaouais, the Northwest and the North Shore).

Since 1950, and even more rapidly since 1960, Quebec's birthrate has been decreasing steadily, stabilizing in 1979 at around 16 per 1000 inhabitants, a rate now lower than that in the rest of Canada. Considering the systematic emigration that has taken place since the 1970s, this low growth rate raises a number of worrisome issues. By 1981 Montréal was no longer Canada's largest city, having lost that position to Toronto.

Labour Force In 1979, 5% of Québec's labour force was concentrated in the primary sector (compared to 12% in 1961), 28% in the secondary sector (35% in 1961) and 67% in the tertiary sector (54% in 1961). Since then, this development of the tertiary sector has slowed down somewhat, and by 1982 an estimated 65% of the population was employed in tertiary industries.

Québec's very high UNEMPLOYMENT rate has not dropped below 8% since 1975. It has been increasing steadily, reaching 10% in 1980 and 14% at the low point of the economic recession in 1982-83. Certain regions such as Abitibi-Témiscamingue, the Lower St Lawrence and Mauricie are especially hard hit, with rates 20% higher than the Québec average. The very rapid increase in the active work force, from 1.9 million to 2.8 million between 1963 and 1978, is the main reason for high unemployment. Between 1977 and 1980, 65 000 new jobs were created annually, thus stabilizing or even reducing the unemployment rate in 1982.

Although Québec continues to be marked by major regional disparities in favour of Montréal, opportunities have equalized somewhat since 1971. This process has resulted more from a reduction in Montréal's advantages than from any noticeable improvement in the situation of the regions.

Language and Ethnic Groups Québec is the only region in N America where French is the language of the majority. In 1981, 82.4% of Québec's inhabitants claimed French as their mother tongue. Approximately 11% of Quebeckers are of British origin, a percentage which has steadily declined from the mid-19th century when the British represented 25% of the total Québec population. About 7% of Quebeckers have neither English nor French as the mother tongue. However, since the vast majority of this group have made English their language of usage, it is generally estimated that about 16% of Québec's population is English speaking. Traditionally, eastern Europeans and ITALIANS were the most important ethnic groups. Since 1960 they have been joined by PORTUGUESE, Haitians, GREEKS and various SOUTHEAST ASIAN groups which have all contributed in giving Québec a multicultural atmosphere.

This assimilation of over 85% of new arrivals to Québec into the anglophone group, coupled with the rapid decline in the birthrate of francophone families, has led every Québec government since 1969 to pass legislation guaranteeing the survival and growth of the French language in Québec. Since the adoption of BILL 101 in 1977, French has been the sole official language of Québec. Despite their opposition to this legislation, anglophone Quebeckers benefit from a complete school system, including 3 universities, a number of newspapers, radio and television stations, hospitals and many kinds of cultural institutions, making them the best-served ethnic minority in Canada. Recognizing the important role of ethnic groups in Québec society, the government has recently renamed its Dept of Immigration the Dept of Immigration and Cultural Communities.

Religion Statistics on church attendance aside, religion has always occupied a special place in Québec society. Although Quebeckers have long since stopped defining themselves as a Catholic society, religion and language helped them stay together as a group after the Conquest of 1760 and throughout the entire English colonial regime. For a long time, the parish was Québec's major social structure and the clergy one of the principal local elites through its control over educational and health-related structures.

The Roman CATHOLICISM has the largest number of adherents among Quebeckers (87%), followed by the Anglican Church (3%), the United Church (3%), Judaism (2%) and the Greek Orthodox Church (1%). Analysis by ethnic group provides some interesting results: although 97% of Quebeckers of French origin officially claim to be Catholics, only 88% of Catholics are of French origin. This reveals the existence of sizable Catholic communities other than the French, chiefly among Quebeckers of Irish, Italian and German origin.

Social Institutions It is essentially language and culture that distinguish Quebec's society from any other. Over time, these distinctions have led to the establishment of social institutions that have made Québec a distinct society within the Canadian community. Québec's legal and judicial system occupies an important place among these institutions. Québec is governed by the CIVIL CODE, developed from the old French laws, rather than from COMMON LAW. Consequently, relationships between individuals, societies and groups are based on principles different from those in the rest of Canada.

Québec's distinctiveness in this respect is evident in the way its social services are integrated, combining medical and social assistance with a network that provides services for children, the sick, the aged and anyone who has a particular need. This network is the responsibility of a government department, and comprises 1280 establishments, including 246 hospital centres, 942 reception centres and 65 local community-service centres. Québec's social-benefits program, established in 1965, differs from those in the rest of Canada. An agency of the Québec government sets and collects premiums and administers benefits. Also established in 1965, the Caisse de dépôt et placement administers funds received from depositors such as the Régie des rentes, the Régie de l'assurance-automobile and the Commission de la santé et de la sécurité au travail. With a 1983 revenue of $1.8 billion, the caisse has become one of the major economic powers in Québec and Canada.

The existence of a charter of human rights and a consumer protection Act (both the most comprehensive in Canada), a legal-aid and small-claims-court system, a well-established network of day-care centres, a unique auto-

View of Montréal from the St Lawrence R (*photo by Kennon Cooke/Valan*).

mobile insurance system and a distinct income-security and family-allowance system all show the autonomous nature of Québec society.

Economy

Québec has a highly industrialized and relatively diversified economy. With an immense territory abounding in natural resources and located near developed and inhabited regions, and with a young and well-trained labour force, Québec has an economy that has not yet reached its full potential. The problems assailing it since WWII have not yet been solved and tend to mask the progress that has been made. These problems include its outdated industrial structure, stubborn regional disparities, the lack of co-operation among the various sectors of the economy and the small degree of control that francophone Quebeckers exert over the main levers of their economic development.

A number of these problems have historical roots. Although New France's small population was scattered over a large area and received little attention from France, it was able to maximize its resources and make the most of the land. The FUR TRADE was the basis of the colony's economy. In fact the desire to control this trade was at the root of the Franco-British rivalry to dominate the colonization of N America. However, the enormously profitable and risky fur trade was never the settlers' only economic activity. Contrary to the popular image of colonists as COUREURS DE BOIS, 80% of settlers lived permanently on their farms; hence their name "habitants." By 1750 it was clear that New France had chosen to become a colony of settlers. Montréal, Trois-Rivières and Québec City already had fairly large populations. Fishing was profitable and there were enough mills and bakeries to produce a surplus for export. In 1743 the FORGES SAINT-MAURICE produced 175 000 kg of iron, and there were already some shipyards in operation.

The British takeover was both beneficial and catastrophic for the Québec economy — beneficial because everything had to be reconstructed after the ravages of war. Agricultural production resumed; increased demand stimulated forest exploitation; and fishing, iron-ore mining and fur trading all expanded considerably because of an injection of new capital and the opening of new markets.

Between 1800 and 1815, a new economy was being established in Québec, one from which, to all practical purposes, French Canadians were excluded. At that time a primitive economic system requiring only the support of a few financiers and abundant manpower was replaced by a system that heralded an industrial revolution. Large landowners and adventurer merchants began to dwindle in number, to be succeeded by a generation of great entrepreneurs, who were dynamic, decisive and eager to free themselves of the restrictions imposed by outmoded political and legal structures.

Although the period between 1820 and 1880 was the golden age of the Québec economy, it was deceptively so. Montréal was Québec's economic centre. It was here that large transportation projects were planned. The canal system, completed in 1848, enabled ships to go all the way to the Great Lakes without taking the Ottawa R route. By 1860, 3000 km of railway had already been built across the various British colonies. Forest exploitation and shipyards profited from the European and Anglo-American wars. Agriculture became an industry. From 1880, however, Québec became a victim of its own success. The NATIONAL POLICY inaugurated in 1879 established a true Canadian common market, a powerful foil to the American market to the S. Sheltered by these protectionist barriers, new markets developed in the West and the country's manufacturing industry moved toward Ontario, which by 1900 was the centre of

51% of Canadian manufacturing production, as compared to Québec's 32%.

By 1860 Québec already had a viable industrial sector, notably in the textile, shoe, railway, food, clothing and wood sectors. At the turn of the century, natural resources provided new possibilities but also required foreign capital, American and British for the most part, to develop the new resources of hydroelectricity, pulp and paper mines and chemical industries (aluminum principally). Foreign investment and control became the rule of the day and it was only after 1960 that a succession of Québec governments began to play an active role in the economic development process. By nationalizing private electricity companies in 1962, establishing many CROWN CORPORATIONS and showing a genuine willingness to support small and medium enterprises — the backbone of the Québec economy. All Québec governments since 1960 have aimed at the dual goal of a more Québec-controlled economy and a more dynamic Québec economy.

Agriculture Between 1961 and 1977, Québec's share of total Canadian agricultural production dropped from 15.8% to 12.4%. A number of factors contributed to this relative decline. Owing to its geographical position, Québec has only 6.8 million ha of arable land, of which just 2.2 million ha have been upgraded and only 800 000 ha are located in a favourable climate. Speculation and urban growth reduced this already small area by another 100 000 ha between 1971 and 1975. The family nature of most farms has also constituted a serious obstacle to the efficiency of production.

Although $10-billion worth of food was sold on the Québec market in 1982, Québec agricultural production was able to meet only 60% of the province's consumption needs. Too many processing plants (over 1200), a lack of product variety, low productivity and a marketing structure vulnerable to the giants in the field have all impeded the adaptation of Québec's agricultural sector. The preponderance of milk and dairy products is another complication, consumption of these products having dropped by 45 kg per capita between 1972 and 1977.

Since the early 1970s, agriculture has revived and has produced promising results. The Agricultural Land Protection Act, passed in 1978, now protects Québec's best farmland. Between 1926 and 1981, harvest insurance and stabilization insurance plans, as well as a considerable increase (from $116 million to $238 million) in allocations to various assistance programs have caused a 22% rise in the per capita gross domestic product in the agricultural sector. The agricultural sector grew in real terms by 27% from $716 million to $1505 million. In the coming years, the Québec government intends to increase the province's self-sufficiency in food by 60%, by giving top priority to grain cultivation, horticulture and beef production. With only 7% of its food production destined for external markets, Québec agriculture is particularly sensitive to fluctuations in the domestic market.

Industry In 1980 the Québec manufacturing sector comprised about 10 000 plants, 30% of the Canadian total. In 1978 these plants declared a total production value of $33 billion, 25% of the Canadian total, as compared to 51% for Ontario and 10% for BC. Today, this sector employs 525 000 people, one-quarter of whom are women. Most of Québec's labour force (51%) works in plants employing between 50 and 500 persons (19% of all establishments).

Five groups of industries form the core of Québec's manufacturing sector and account for 60% of plants and 53% of jobs: clothing and textiles (20%), food and beverages (10%), paper and related products (9%), metal products (8%) and wood products (6%). Seventy percent of Québec's plants are located in the Montréal region.

Forests With its 500 000 km² of forests, Québec has the third-largest area of forestland in Canada after Ontario and BC. Over 90% of this land is provincially owned. About 300 000 km² are accessible productive forests, three-quarters of this being located in the Saguenay-Lac Saint-Jean, Abitibi and North Shore regions where it has always constituted the backbone of regional economic development. Québec harvests around 28 million m³ of wood each year, more than 90% of it conifer, and has an annual production potential of 40 million m³. Most cut wood is used for lumber (66%) and pulp manufacturing (33%). Over 275 plants employing 12 000 people are involved in forest operations. Since 1978 a vast REFORESTATION program has been under way and over 32 million saplings have been planted annually.

The PULP AND PAPER INDUSTRY is one of the most important in Québec, which is among the 10 leading producers in the world and the second-largest exporter of newsprint in Canada. With its 60 plants, this sector employs close to 32 000 workers, who produce over 40% of Canada's pulp and paper. Timber, wood pulp and newsprint together comprise 20% of Québec exports, accounting for $1.5 million in 1978. One-third of these forest-based exports go to the US.

Since the early 1970s, the lumber industry has been particularly active. In 1979 it produced 3.4 million t of wood chips and 3.2 billion feet of boards. Exports, which in 1960 totalled barely 5% of that of pulp and paper, reached 40% by 1980. In 1978 there were 366 sawmills and workshops with 16 000 employees.

Fishing With only 5000 full-time fishermen and catches valued at around $40 million, the maritime fishery contributes relatively little to Québec's employment and gross domestic product, although in certain regions, notably in the GASPÉ Peninsula it plays a significant role. Between 1970 and 1976, the volume of catches decreased dramatically from 125 000 to 37 000 t. Improved resource management and the extension of Canadian jurisdiction to 322 km has since helped increase this figure to 72 000 t, but Québec landed only 6.2% of the total catch of all the maritime provinces. Of the Québec catch, 70% were groundfish, 13% ocean fish and 17% various molluscs and crustaceans.

Since 1978 Québec has implemented a plan to upgrade fishing. It has established a modernization program to replace many of the fleet's 2700 boats under 13 m long with larger ones. The Québec fleet has only 250 boats of from 13 to 20 m in length and only 27 boats of more than 20 m.

Domestic consumption is not very high. Quebeckers do not eat much fish, and the lack of local production in many sectors (molluscs and crustaceans) means that the balance of trade has increased very little since 1979 ($79 million in 1982 compared to $73 million in 1979). Cod, Norway haddock and sole, the main fish caught in Québec, represent about 70% of the total catch.

Energy In the late 1970s, the total net energy available for consumption was around 34 million petroleum-equivalent t. Of the total energy used between 1970 and 1979, the percentage of petroleum dropped from 74% to 66% and that of coal from 3% to 1%; natural-gas consumption increased from 4% to 7% and electricity from 19% to 25%.

Montréal and Service Activities Fewer than one dozen N American cities are larger than metropolitan Montréal. Unlike other cities of comparable size, however, MONTRÉAL is much closer to its hinterland, which includes the rest of the province, part of the Maritime provinces and part of the New England states. Montréal has the infrastructure appropriate to a major financial metropolis — a stock exchange — and is the headquarters of 4 chartered banks and 3 major Canadian trust and life-insurance companies. In 1978, 85 000 people were employed in the financial sector, which has enjoyed an annual rate of growth of 8.5% since 1971. The metropolitan region is the location of 70% of Québec's manufacturing research firms and 90% of its research personnel. Montréal has developed particularly in the space and aeronautics industry (Pratt and Whitney, Canadair, Spar Aerospace, CAE Electronics), telecommunications (Northern Telecom, Marconi), energy (Hydro-Québec) and transportation (Bombardier, Deutz Diesel). The head offices of over 1200 companies are located in Montréal and employ some 100 000 persons. About 110 of these head offices belong to firms with over 1000 employees. Consulting engineering firms are particularly important to Québec's economy. Three of the world's major corporations are Québec owned, and Québec alone employs 13 000 of the 24 000 Canadian workers in this sector — more than Germany, Australia, France or Sweden. A number of large construction projects such as EXPO 67, the 1976 OLYMPIC GAMES, Mirabel Airport and Montréal's subway system enabled Montreal's 228 consulting engineering firms to grow at an annual rate of 22% between 1967 and 1977. In 1980 these firms took in a total of $480 million in fees, 42% of which came from outside Québec, particularly from the Middle East, Africa and Latin America.

First with BILL 22, then with BILL 101, recent Québec governments have shown a desire to emphasize the French nature of the city and accelerate the promotion both of the French language and of francophone managers. The city's cosmopolitan character, its intense cultural and artistic life, its reputation for good food and the quality of urban life all contribute to Montréal's great appeal.

Transportation Montréal is one of the hubs of the Canadian and American transportation networks, thanks to the St Lawrence Seaway and the head offices of Air Canada, Canadian National and many transportation companies, including over 50% of the Canadian aeronautics and space industry.

Québec is well equipped for automobile transportation, having 126 000 km of roads, including 2200 km of highway and over 3 million licensed vehicles in 1979. There are about 1000 trucking firms, employing about 28 000 workers, and sharing about $1 billion in annual revenue. The industry's main problems are long distances, often troublesome regulations, a lack of capital and excessive operating costs. A plan to help this sector has been in effect since 1982. Despite the fact that Montréal was the base from which Canada's epic CANADIAN PACIFIC RAILWAY was constructed, the railway network is least developed in Québec. The ratio of kilometres of rail per 1000 inhabitants is only 1:4 in Québec, compared to 3:3 for Canada as a whole and 2:1 for Ontario. Railway companies have invested barely 15% of their capital in Québec, with the result that the province's railway system has declined steadily since 1960.

In international shipping, Québec's 18 ports handled about 97 million t of cargo in 1979. Major ports are SEPT-ILES, Port Cartier, Montréal and Québec City. In 1978 about 30 ports handled 335 million t of coastal trade cargo. Paradoxically, while the opening of the St Lawrence Seaway contributed to the rapid development of North Shore ports, it also helped establish Ontario ports of entry on the Great Lakes for Canada's international trade. With the seaway, the port of Montréal lost its privileged position. It now handles only 6% of freight passing through Canadian ports, as compared to Vancouver's 10%.

Québec has 3 international airports: Dorval, Mirabel and Québec City. The small increase in air traffic has delayed plans to develop Mirabel, which was to have been Québec's main airport and one of the major airports in Canada. The 2 Montréal airports have handled 18% of Canadian passengers, compared to Toronto's 31%. Twenty-five percent of all air freight passes through Montréal and 38% through Toronto. In 1979, 66% of the 2.7 million passengers who used Québec's airports passed through Dorval and Mirabel. The other large airports are those of Québec City (14%) and Sept-Iles (4%).

Government and Politics

Initially a French colony, Québec was later administered directly by British authorities. In 1841 it became part of a legislative union, and in 1867 a member of the Canadian federation. The evolution of Québec's institutions has thus not been marked by any legal discontinuity.

Central Political Institutions Québec, like all constitutional regimes of British tradition, has no rigid division of legislative and executive functions among its various agencies. Its political system is based on co-operation rather than on a separation of powers. The Assemblée nationale, formerly known as the Legislative Assembly, represents Québec citizens directly and is composed of one member from each of the province's 122 ridings. Each riding has about 34 000 voters. The Assemblée nationale passes laws in areas over which Québec has jurisdiction. The LIEUTENANT-GOVERNOR is the Queen's representative in Québec. Although his role is purely symbolic, in certain extreme cases he or she may be called upon to settle an issue. As the sovereign's direct and personal representative, the lieutenant-governor ensures the continuity of government. Although technically a federal public servant, the lieutenant-governor's actions are in fact governed by the directives of Québec's Conseil executif, also called the Conseil des ministres, which is composed of the premier ministre (PREMIER) and his ministers. It is the Conseil executif that decides on the general orientation of government action. It expresses its will through draft bills and *décrets*. The 25 or so Cabinet ministers are appointed by the premier and are bound by the principle of ministerial solidarity.

Since the 1970s, major reforms have transformed the operations of these central bodies. The Assemblée nationale's rules of procedure were modernized and adapted to Québec's circumstances: a total of 18 parliamentary standing committees have been established and debates are now televised. The Conseil executif is operating more and more with the assistance of departmental standing committees, each headed by a minister of state. A priorities committee provides better planning and a treasury board, headed by a minister, is responsible for formulating and implementing the government's financial policies.

Legal Institutions Québec's judicial system has 2 levels: lower-court powers are shared by a number of courts, but there is only one Court of Appeal. Québec courts interpret and apply Québec law, and a large part of federal law. The federal Parliament has not fully exercised its constitutional right to create courts in order to ensure that its laws are implemented. The lower-court hierarchy has 7 components: 1) Justices of the peace have jurisdiction in criminal matters such as minor crimes, infractions of federal and provincial laws and of certain municipal regulations. 2) Municipal courts may be created by town councils to decide how municipal regulations should be implemented. They are presided over by judges appointed by the Québec government. 3) Juvenile courts are presided over by 42 judges appointed by the Québec government and have jurisdiction in certain civil and criminal matters involving juveniles. 4) Courts of Sessions of the Peace are presided over by 64 judges who deal mainly with criminal matters in urban areas. 5) The Provincial Court is composed of 149 judges and its jurisdiction extends throughout Québec in less important civil matters and for municipal and school taxation issues. 6) The Superior Court has 107 judges appointed by the federal government and acts as a common-law trial court. 7) The Court of Appeal is composed of 15 judges who are also appointed by the federal government.

Municipal Institutions Under the CONSTITUTION ACT, 1982, the Québec government has authority to organize and administer its municipal institutions. Québec has over 1600 municipalities, of which 1271 are rural, 260 urban and 71 townships. All fall under the Municipal Code and the Towns and Cities Act. Some of the larger cities, such as Québec City and Montréal, also have their own charters specifying their status. Québec has 2 urban communities, Montréal and Québec City, and one regional community, the Outaouais; all 3 have jurisdiction over their assessment, development, public transportation, taxation and public safety provisions.

Since 1978 Québec's municipalities have been extremely active. Municipal tax reforms for the first time granted a large degree of financial autonomy and a more solid tax base to the municipalities. The Agricultural Land Protection Act has saved large areas of land from urban expansion and obliged municipalities to plan their development more carefully. Finally, regional county municipalities have been established to pool certain community services outside the larger urban centres.

Public Finance The Québec government derives its revenue from 2 sources: taxes levied under Acts passed by the Assemblée nationale, and transfer payments received from the federal government in accordance with fiscal arrangements and agreements on established programs. In 1981-82 the Québec government's revenues totalled $17.4 billion, of which $8.4 billion (48%) came from income and commodities taxes, $3.1 billion (18%) from various taxes on consumer goods (tobacco, retail sales, fuel), $982 million (6%) from copyrights, permits and fines, and $382 million (2%) from transfers from crown corporations. Transfer payments from the federal government were in the order of $4.5 billion (26%).

In 1982-83 expenditures roughly totalled $23 billion, distributed roughly as follows: social services $8.6 billion, education and culture $7.5 billion, government $4.7 billion, and resources, industries and transportation $2.5 billion.

Intergovernmental Relations Québec has 75 representatives in the federal House of Com-

Lieutenant-Governors of Québec 1867-1984	
	Term
Narcisse-Fortunat Belleau	1867-73
René Édouard Caron	1873-76
Luc Le Tellier de Saint-Just	1876-79
Théodore Robitaille	1879-84
Louis François-Rodrigue Masson	1884-87
Auguste-Réal Angers	1887-92
Joseph-Adolphe Chapleau	1892-98
Louis-Amable Jetté	1898-1908
Charles-Alphonse-Pantaléon Pelletier	1908-11
François-Charles-Stanislas Langelier	1911-15
Pierre-Laurent-Damase-Evariste LeBlanc	1915-18
Charles Fitzpatrick	1918-23
Louis-Philippe Brodeur	1923-24
Narcisse Perodeau	1924-29
Jean-Lomer Gouin	1929
Henry George Carroll	1929-34
Esioff-Léon Patenaude	1934-39
Eugène-Marie-Joseph Fiset	1939-50
Gaspard Fauteux	1950-58
J. Onésime Gagnon	1958-61
Paul Comtois	1961-66
Hugues Lapointe	1966-78
Jean-Pierre Côté	1978-84
Gilles Lamontagne	1984-

mons and 24 members in the Senate. The federal and Québec authorities co-ordinate their activities, not without difficulty, through about 100 joint committees and a number of federal-provincial conferences. It is in international relations, however, that Québec has distinguished itself. In 1871 Québec opened 2 offices abroad and, in 1882, a trade officer was appointed to France. Closed shortly after, these "foreign" offices received a new lease on life in 1961 when the first Department of Intergovernmental Affairs was created. Québec delegations have been established in the US, France, Italy, Belgium, Venezuela, Great Britain and elsewhere. Co-operative agreements link Québec to a number of countries, particularly France. Québec is also a member of the Agence de coopération culturelle et technique, which is composed of the major francophone countries.

Politics Since 1960 Québec politics have been characterized by change and affirmation. The election of Premier Jean LESAGE's Liberal government in June 1960 set in motion what is commonly known as the QUIET REVOLUTION. The principal manifestations of this revolution were increased government intervention, cleaner political ethics and an affirmation of a distinct political personality for Québec. The UNION NATIONALE's return to power in 1966 under Premier Daniel JOHNSON accelerated the movement to create a true national Québec state. Between 1970 and 1976, the Liberal Party under Premier Robert BOURASSA consolidated some of the gains made during the Quiet Revolution and gave the province new direction in health insurance and legal reform, and in economic development by making the decision to harness the hydroelectric potential of the rivers that empty into James Bay.

The election of a PARTI QUÉBÉCOIS government in Nov 1976 brought to the fore one of the still-unresolved issues in Québec society — the province's relations with the rest of Canada. Firmly convinced that Québec had to be considered as a separate society, the government of Premier René LÉVESQUE proposed to Quebeckers a new contract of association with the rest of Canada. Known as SOVEREIGNTY-ASSOCIATION, this proposal called for political equality between Québec and Canada as well as a close economic, trade and military association between both communities.

In the referendum of 20 May 1980, 60% of the voters rejected this proposal, although within the francophone community itself the split was closer to 50-50. Most citizens preferred the federal prime minister's solemn promise of renewed FEDERALISM. However, in face of the threat that this renewal posed for the autonomy and distinct nature of Québec, Quebeckers re-elected the Parti Québécois in April 1981. Subsequently the Québec government, supported by the official opposition in the Assemblée nationale, opposed the federal government's proposed CANADIAN CHARTER OF RIGHTS AND FREEDOMS and constitutional amending formula. It did not manage to prevent this bill from being passed, however, and the issue of political relations between Québec and the rest of Canada remains unresolved (*see* CONSTITUTION, PATRIATION OF).

Education

Beginning in the mid-17th century, primary schools in the major cities of New France — Québec City, Montreal and TROIS-RIVIÈRES — were run by male and female religious orders. Secondary education began with the establishment of the Collège de Québec in 1635, which from 1680 on also offered a number of more advanced courses, notably in law, mathematics and surveying. After the arrival of the Loyalists and British immigrants, a complete English-language school system, from nursery school to university, was established and financed by government in the same way and according to the same criteria as the French-language system.

Major Reforms Until the mid-1960s, the French-language education system was highly decentralized, with local school boards responsible for day-to-day operations and the Roman Catholic Church dominating those state bodies that decided on programs and curricula. The Parent Commission on Education changed this situation. In 1960 the Québec government made education its priority — a priority that arose from the need to increase the public's general level of education and to produce highly qualified manpower. This educational reform had 5 principal goals: 1) Universal access to secondary education through the establishment of regional school boards and a network of high schools. 2) Creation of COLLÈGES D'ENSEIGNEMENT GÉNÉRAUX ET PROFESSIONNELS (CEGEPs), the intermediate level between secondary school and university that provides broader access to post-secondary studies while preparing students for university by offering advanced job-related technical training. 3) Creation of the UNIVERSITÉ DU QUÉBEC system, which offers university training in all regions of Québec. 4) Establishment of the Department of Education, which has become the ultimate authority on education issues. 5) Use of active teaching techniques focused on students and their needs, on promotion by subject and on decompartmentalization. An initial evaluation in the mid-1970s revealed that while the major objectives of accessibility, democratization and modernization had been met, a number of grey areas still remained. Some of these included improvement in the quality of education, special attention to certain disadvantaged groups and greater parent participation in school management. These areas have become the system's new priorities.

Administration The Québec primary- and secondary-school system is based on a mixture of linguistic and religious criteria. The 31 Protestant school boards administer 268 schools, 48 of which are French-language institutions, and the 213 Catholic boards control 2370 schools, 162 of which are English-language schools. The CEGEP system includes 40 francophone and 4 anglophone colleges, one of which administers 3 campuses. These colleges are in fact corporations and are managed by boards of directors.

The university system comprises 7 universities, 3 of which are English-language institutions. The Université du Québec, the largest institution, has full-scale campuses at Montréal, Chicoutimi, Hull and Rouyn-Noranda and 5 affiliated research institutions.

In 1980, 1.2 million students were enroled in Québec's primary and secondary schools, a decline of 17% from 1974. In that same year, however, 134 186 students were registered in colleges, an increase of 18%. The universities had over 100 000 full-time and 90 000 part-time students. The primary, secondary and college systems are financed entirely by the provincial government, which also finances up to 75% of the costs of private schools. Today, government contributions to these 3 levels of education exceed $4 billion. Subsidies represent about 80% of the $1 billion that the government provides for university financing.

Culture

Culture is one of the most dynamic elements in Québec society. It is chiefly through its culture, which has now reached maturity, that Québec has been able to stand as a distinct society both in Canada and throughout N America. Today, Québec exports its culture, as Québec LITERATURE IN FRENCH is studied in a number of countries. Québec's painters and sculptors are known worldwide and its television is recognized as one of the best.

Rural and folk traditions were so dominant until 1950 that no one could have expected the cultural explosion of the 1960s. In the 1950s, however, artists and intellectuals began to show their dissatisfaction with the monolithic society that was characterized by an obsession with survival and the status quo. After 1960 the old beliefs began to crumble. Naturally, Québec artists found themselves in the forefront of this movement to define a new identity. The term "Québécois" began to replace "French Canadian" and confirmed this new cultural surge. Following the flood of change that occurred in the 1960s, the 1970s were years of consolidation marked by the emergence of various groups — women, regional communities, cultural minorities. The creation of the Ministry of Cultural Affairs (1961) helped give institutional foundation to this cultural development. Today, with a budget of $142 million, Québec is a leader in governmental support of cultural endeavours.

The Arts Québec, particularly Montréal, is a very productive centre for theatre. During February 1981 alone, for example, 50 theatrical productions were taking place in Montréal, of which 27 were by Québec authors and 14 were original creations. Montréal has 8 established companies with their own premises, traditions and government grants, as well as about 85 relatively active and truly innovative troupes.

All the other major Québec cities also have permanent or semiprofessional groups that have developed original theatre productions independently of Montréal. In the summer, over 50 troupes present plays in Québec's major resort areas, and occasionally foreign troupes from New York, Paris or Brussels appear in Québec theatre.

Québec has one symphony orchestra in Québec City and another in Montréal (see ORCHESTRE SYMPHONIQUE DE MONTRÉAL). In addition to these 2 pillars of Québec's musical world, there are the Société de musique contemporaine du Québec,

Premiers of Québec 1867-1984

	Party	Term
Pierre-Joseph-Olivier Chauveau	Conservative	1867-73
Gédéon Ouimet	Conservative	1873-74
Charles-Eugène Boucher de Boucherville	Conservative	1874-78
Henri-Gustave Joly de Lotbinière	Liberal	1878-79
Joseph-Adolphe Chapleau	Conservative	1879-82
Joseph-Alfred Mousseau	Conservative	1882-84
John Jones Ross	Conservative	1884-87
Louis Olivier Taillon	Conservative	1887
Honoré Mercier	Liberal	1887-91
Charles-Eugène Boucher de Boucherville	Conservative	1891-92
Louis-Olivier Taillon	Conservative	1892-96
Edmund James Flynn	Conservative	1896-97
Félix-Gabriel Marchand	Liberal	1897-1900
Simon Napoléon Parent	Liberal	1900-05
Jean-Lomer Gouin	Liberal	1905-20
Louis-Alexandre Taschereau	Liberal	1920-36
Joseph-Adélard Godbout	Liberal	1936
Maurice Duplessis	Union Nationale	1936-39
Joseph-Adélard Godbout	Liberal	1939-44
Maurice Duplessis	Union Nationale	1944-59
Paul Sauvé	Union Nationale	1959-60
J. Antonio Barrette	Union Nationale	1960
Jean Lesage	Liberal	1960-66
Daniel Johnson	Union Nationale	1966-68
Jean-Jacques Bertrand	Union Nationale	1968-70
Robert Bourassa	Liberal	1970-76
René Lévesque	Parti Québécois	1976-

the McGill Chamber Orchestra, the Ladies' Morning Club, the Montréal Opera, and various conservatories, music schools and medieval music ensembles.

Montréal has a privileged role in the FILM industry as the commercial meeting place of American and European films. It is therefore not uncommon to see the most recent American, French, Italian and Japanese films playing simultaneously. In addition to repertory theatres, Montréal has 150 commercial cinemas. In 1980 the local film industry produced 19 full-length feature films, either through private producers in co-operation with foreign companies, through the NATIONAL FILM BOARD (whose headquarters are in Montréal) or through television corporations. Notable Québec directors include Gilles CARLE and Claude JUTRA.

In 1979, 3128 books were published in Québec. POETRY, the NOVEL and the ESSAY are particularly well-developed genres. Songwriters and singers, such as Gilles VIGNEAULT, Félix Leclerc, Robert CHARLEBOIS, Pauline JULIEN, and the operatic bass Louis QUILICO, are recognized well beyond Québec's borders. Dance, mime, sculpture, singing and crafts are also forms of cultural expression in which Quebeckers excel.

Communications In 1981 Québec had 175 television stations, compared to Ontario's 140. French-language stations include Radio-Canada, Radio-Québec and TVA, while on the English-language side there are the CBC, CTV and American stations. In addition, there are 176 cable networks reaching about 45% of the market, and 115 radio stations, of which 14 broadcast in English and 4 are multilingual. Québec has 10 French-language and 2 English-language daily newspapers, 210 weeklies, 148 periodicals and 24 ethnic publications.

Heritage Since the mid-1960s, interest in preserving and developing Québec's cultural heritage has increased considerably. The Ministry of Cultural Affairs and local historical societies have been the prime movers in this area. In Québec City, major archaeological projects have revitalized a number of sites, including Place Royale, which is a genuine recreation of an architectural ensemble that dates from the French regime, and the QUÉBEC CITADEL. In Montréal, Vieux Montréal (Old Montréal) is a city within a city. Over 300 archaeological sites have been documented throughout the province. This search for the sources of Québec culture is part of Quebeckers' desire to understand and establish their roots more firmly in N America.

Old houses and hotels on Rue St-Denis, Québec City (*photo by Kim Patrick O'Leary*).

History

Although explorers in the 16th century had found many large Iroquois villages in the lower St Lawrence Valley (eg, STADACONA, HOCHELAGA), these settlements had vanished by the time the first colonists arrived in the 17th century. About 4000 MONTAGNAIS-NASKAPI lived along the N shore of the St Lawrence, and the first permanent contacts were established with these people and a firm alliance established by Samuel de CHAMPLAIN with the HURON. Farther N, the Cree had very little contact with the first settlers.

French Colonization Jacques CARTIER landed in Gaspé on 14 July 1534, where he officially took possession of the land in the name of the king of France. The following year, he returned and went as far as Stadacona [Québec C] and Hochelaga [Montréal]. However, the first settlement was not established until Champlain established the village of Québec in 1608. The colony's beginnings were hampered by France's lack of interest in a permanent colony of settlers. By 1628 the colony still had only 76 settlers, all in Québec, which was little more than a trading post. By 1640 the population had grown to 300, and it was not until the end of the IROQUOIS WARS that NEW FRANCE could truly be said to exist. By 1666 the population had reached 3418.

From the outset, the colony's social organization was different from that of the mother country. The divisions among social classes were much less rigid. The seigneurs had privileges, of course, but these were not inherited; like the settlers, they were merchants, farmers and soldiers. From 1686, wars with the English colonies increased but were interrupted by relatively long periods of peace. These recurring conflicts against an enemy superior in numbers seriously hindered the colony's development. Peace came in 1713 with the TREATY OF UTRECHT, but New France was cut off from Acadia, Newfoundland and the lands around Hudson Bay. After scarcely one generation of peace, war with England resumed. It was an uneven battle between 65 000 French settlers, backed by an indifferent French government, and some one million English colonists supported by the Royal Navy. In 1759 a British expeditionary force took Québec City, and the following year Montréal. The end of the era of New France broke the colony's natural development, particularly since most of the political and commercial leaders returned to France.

British Colonization and Confederation In order to secure the co-operation of its new subjects, the first English governors allowed the French to keep their language and religion, although they excluded Catholics from administrative positions. The QUEBEC ACT (1774), which attempted largely to reinstate the former boundaries of New France (to the great annoyance of the American colonies), effectively reinforced the power of the seigneurs and the clergy, who became convenient allies for the aristocratic British governors, who rejected the demands of the new English merchants for an elected assembly.

In order to satisfy recent Loyalist immigrants, the CONSTITUTIONAL ACT, 1791, divided the colony into 2 provinces, UPPER and LOWER CANADA, each administered by a governor, a legislative council and a legislative assembly. The British merchants in Montréal had a difficult time accepting the fact that they were to be isolated in a province with a French-speaking majority. Political battles multiplied, and in 1837 Louis-Joseph PAPINEAU, Jean-Olivier Chénier and Wolfred Nelson led a revolt. Poorly led and lacking arms, the PATRIOTES were crushed by the British authorities, who restored peace at the price of political repression (*see* REBELLIONS OF 1837).

In the still-famous DURHAM REPORT, Lord Durham advocated the creation of an English majority by massive immigration and through the anglicization of French Canadians in areas where they were a minority. Thus, section 41 of the ACT OF UNION stated that English would be the only language of the new united PROVINCE OF CANADA and that Canada East [Québec], with a much larger population than Canada West [Ontario], would have the same number of elected representatives and would have to repay a large share of Canada West's debt.

The economic crisis that forced 40 000 French Canadians to emigrate to the US between 1840 and 1850 (*see* FRANCO-AMERICANS) and the continuing political crisis stemming from inadequate political structures raised the issue of the survival of the French Canadians who, for the first time in their history, had no political recourse of their own. When English Canadian political leaders proposed the idea of a federal pact to break the impasse, French Canadian opinion was divided. Those following the lead of George-Etienne CARTIER accepted the federal solution because it gave Québec control over language, religion and civil law, which were considered to be the foundations of French Canada. A mixture of more liberal and progressive elements favoured a looser federation, where provincial rights would be more explicit and guaranteed, so as to counter the status of inferiority that the new Constitution would impose on Québec. Lastly a third, much smaller, group proposed outright independence for Québec. With the militant support of the clergy and English-speaking commercial elites from Montréal, the federal proposal won out (though with some difficulty, and without any consultation with the people, as the proposal's opponents had demanded). On 1 July 1867 Québec, a former French and British colony, became a Canadian province.

Modern Québec At the time of Confederation, 1867, Québec was a poor province, particularly ill equipped to step into the Industrial Revolution. Cities were small and few — Montréal (90 000 inhabitants), Québec City (58 000) Trois-Rivières (6000) and Sorel (4700). Farming was at subsistence level and most companies were small. Larger manufacturing companies were located only in Montréal and were owned almost exclusively by Anglophones. The resources of the new government of Québec were sorely limited: 60% of its $1.5-million budget came from the federal government, which also had tight control over provincial legislation because of its authority to appoint the lieut-gov and to disallow certain provincial laws (*see* DISALLOWANCE). The only avenue of intervention that remained was to colonize distant regions. Thus the Gaspé Peninsula, the Lac Saint-Jean region and the Laurentides were opened up to settlers. Despite this movement, between 1850 and 1900, 500 000 Quebeckers left for the US, while thousands of others moved to the western provinces where they formed small francophone settlements (see FRENCH IN THE WEST).

Culturally and intellectually, this is one of the saddest periods in Quebec's history. The provincial government was unable to handle the new responsibilities of a modern state (education, health, colonization) and the federal government was preoccupied with Ontario's industrial development and with opening up the West. As a result, the church took charge of the educational and health needs of Quebeckers. Uninterested in questioning the established authorities and the excesses of INDUSTRIALIZATION, and wary of new ideas, the Québec church was more concerned with maintaining its privileged position than with helping Quebeckers enter the 20th century. It extolled the virtues of rural life, cautioned against the evils of the city and the dangers of education and preached the need to accept one's lot in life. The surge in the American economy around 1896 also impeded the development of Québec's economy. Between 1900 and 1910 the manufacturing production volume increased by 76%. By the time a second industrial revolution took hold in 1920, Québec was in a very good position to follow the movement. This time it was not iron and steam that propelled the revolution but electricity and nonferrous metals such as copper, aluminum and nickel. Industries that exploited Québec's natural resources replaced light industry. External markets, good lines of communication and large sources of capital were more important than the domestic market or qualified manpower.

Between 1920 and 1940, the face of Québec changed. Whereas in 1920 agriculture still accounted for 37% of Québec production, compared to 38% for manufacturing and 15% for forestry, by 1941 manufacturing accounted for 64%, mining for 10% and agriculture for 10%. This accelerated industrialization caused classic transformations to take place in Québec society — urbanization, a higher standard of living and a better-educated population. It was English and then American capital that stimulated this economic surge. In addition, the priority given to the export of natural resources obscured the fact that the archaic manufacturing sector was still founded on labour-intensive but relatively unproductive industries such as textiles and shoes.

In politics, this period was marked by the long reign of the Liberal Party, which remained in power from 1897 with Premier F.G. MARCHAND until the fall of Adélard GODBOUT's government in 1936. For much of this same period, the federal Liberals were also in power in Ottawa. It was the time of "red in Québec, red in Ottawa" and of a tacit alliance between businessmen and politicians. The former suggested projects, the latter granted railway subsidies, authorized road building and passed special legislation, handing out patronage and favours of all kinds. The Conservative Party, so powerful in Québec in the 19th century, was but a shadow of its former self after the CONSCRIPTION crisis of 1917.

The GREAT DEPRESSION in the 1930s challenged both this course of development and the primacy of the Liberal Party. The economic crisis was accompanied by a moral crisis; for the first time, individuals and groups condemned the political, cultural and economic inferiority to which they believed French Canadians had been subjected by Confederation and by Canadian business. There was talk of social renewal, NATIONALIZATION and economic change aimed at reappropriating natural resources. In 1936 Maurice DUPLESSIS and the new UNION NATIONALE Party won the election by taking 76 of the 90 seats.

Swept into power by a desire for change, Duplessis hastened to direct his action toward an increased conservatism that represented the disparate interests of a number of groups — traditional elites, foreign capitalists, rural people and the Catholic hierarchy. Temporarily removed from power in 1939, he returned in 1944. He died in 1959 and his party was defeated in the 1960 elections.

During its long reign, the Duplessis regime faced 2 major problems: the federal government's desire to centralize all major economic, social and cultural authority in Ottawa and the problems engendered by the new economic order established in 1945. Duplessis was somewhat successful in blocking Ottawa's centralist aims by establishing a corporate income tax in 1947 and a personal income tax in 1953 and by refusing certain federal programs in areas under provincial jurisdiction. He was less successful, however, in the social and economic spheres. By refusing federal subsidies, Duplessis protected the autonomy of the Québec political system but also deprived it of precious resources. Even today, historians disagree on the causes of this marked backwardness in Québec society between 1945 and 1960. Would it have been better to overlook Québec's distinct social and cultural character and to allow the federal government to organize its development? Was the conservatism of the Union Nationale the consequence of federal centralism?

Opposition to the Duplessis government came particularly from intellectual, academic and union groups. The new generation of university graduates were beginning to question the traditional elites. They condemned the government's absence from major areas of concern. Teachers questioned the clergy's hold on the education system. Magazines such as CITÉ LIBRE, and one newspaper in particular, Le DEVOIR, spearheaded the socioeconomic opposition. The deaths of Maurice Duplessis and his successor Paul SAUVÉ, a few months later, made it easier for the Liberals to come to power on 22 June 1960. This election was to change the course of Québec and of Canadian history. It was the beginning of the Quiet Revolution.

The New Québec This period, neither revolutionary nor quiet, was marked from the outset by the new government's will to build a modern administration capable of countering all the backward influences that had assailed Québec for a century. This desire to act on all fronts made the period from 1960 to 1966 appear extremely frenetic. Public finances were reorganized and control measures instituted. The Parent Commission of Inquiry completely overhauled the educational system. The Société générale de financement was formed to take care of weaknesses in the private sector, and the Conseil d'expansion économique (Economic Development Council) was established to lay the foundation for an economic plan. Four new departments were created, including those dealing with education and cultural affairs.

For the first time, trade unionism penetrated the public service. In 1962, following an election fought on this theme, the government nationalized private electricity companies. Between 1945 and 1963, Québec's budget grew from $96 million to $851 million. Economic expansion was so great between 1961 and 1966 that the unemployment rate dropped from 9.2% to 4.7%. Increasing control exerted by the Québec government began to cause more serious conflicts with the federal government. In Oct 1961 Premier Lesage inaugurated the Maison du Québec (Québec House) in Paris and signed co-operation agreements with France. Since then, Québec has established 16 delegations on 3 continents. Ottawa became concerned about Québec's desire to act autonomously on the international scene, even though this action was

limited to sectors which, according to the constitution, were under provincial jurisdiction. Numerous conflicts ensued between the 2 governments after 1960, as a result of dissatisfaction with federal-provincial tax agreements, which were considered to be unfavourable to Québec.

Between 1960 and 1965, the federal government, anxious to show Quebeckers that the federal system could accommodate a renewed Québec, made a number of compromises with the Québec government by transferring part of the tax base to the province.

While negotiating these special agreements, Ottawa created the Royal Commission on BILINGUALISM AND BICULTURALISM. In its preliminary report in 1965, the commissioners concluded that Canada was in the throes of a serious crisis, one which, they said, could be resolved only when Quebeckers were convinced that they could exist both individually and collectively in equality and mutual respect with the rest of the country. The Union Nationale's return to power after the 1966 election marked the beginning of a fundamental realignment of Québec's political forces. Re-elected with a majority of seats, but only 41% of the popular vote compared to the Liberal's 47%, the Union Nationale, this time led by Daniel Johnson, was forced to continue in the tradition of the great reforms of the Quiet Revolution. Already on shaky ground with its more conservative electorate, the party lost its leader in Sept 1968. Jean-Jacques BERTRAND took over as leader and as Québec's premier, but his leadership was contested within party ranks. The government was accused of fence-sitting, of being neither sufficiently nationalist nor federalist. The Québec Liberal Party, led by Robert Bourassa, was clearly federalist and in 1967 rejected the sovereignty-association proposal submitted by René Lévesque. Lévesque left the party and founded the Mouvement souveraineté-association which, in the autumn of 1968, joined with one of the small existing separatist parties to become the Parti Québécois. Soon afterwards the Rassemblement pour l'indépendence nationale, the major separatist group, chose to fold and join the Parti Québécois. Between 1967 and 1970, Canadian political representatives joined in an important round of constitutional negotiations. At the Victoria Conference in the summer of 1971, an agreement in principle was reached on an amending formula and on the inclusion of a charter of rights in the new constitution. In the end, Québec's new Liberal government, elected the previous spring, withdrew its support because the Victoria agreement provided for no transfer of legislative powers between the 2 levels of government — a priority for Québec since 1965.

In October 1970 the government had to face a major political and social crisis when, after a campaign of terrorist bombings, the FRONT DE LIBÉRATION DU QUÉBEC (FLQ) kidnapped a British diplomat, James Cross, and a Québec minister, Pierre LAPORTE, who was later killed by his abductors. The federal government proclaimed the WAR MEASURES ACT, which provided for the suspension of civil liberties. Hundreds of Quebeckers were held for questioning and then released, but no charges were laid. Subsequent inquiries (McDonald Commission, Cliche Commission) revealed that the Royal Canadian Mounted Police were conducting burglaries and other illegal activities at the time.

Aided by the improving American economy, Robert Bourassa's Liberal government (which had been elected in 1970) was easily able to surmount these difficulties and was re-elected in October 1973. The PARTI QUÉBÉCOIS, which in the 1970 election had received 24% of the popular vote but only 7 seats (6% of the total), this time obtained 30% of the popular vote, though only 6 seats. Despite this imbalance in the electoral system, the PQ was still the official Opposition.

Much of the political debate and turmoil of the 1960s and 1970s centered on the issue of Québec sovereignty. Jacques Parizeau, finance minister in the PQ government, was an outspoken advocate of sovereignty and resigned in 1984 to protest his party's softening on the issue (*photo by Bernard Brault/Reflexion*).

From 1973, the energy crisis, rampant inflation and increased unemployment created a new and more difficult situation for the government, which also had to face militant trade unions and many strikes in public services. Events such as the campaign by the Association des gens de l'air du Québec to use French in Québec air space, and the stir caused by the implementation of Bill 22, which gave priority to the French language, only aggravated the political climate.

On 15 November 1976 the Parti Québécois swept to victory and immediately undertook or completed some major reforms: automobile insurance, the charter of the French language, control of the financing of political parties, agricultural zoning, and dental insurance for children. During the government's first mandate, Québec's economic situation improved, as shown by the creation of 6500 new jobs annually between 1977 and 1980. The PQ government suffered a major defeat, however, in the 1980 referendum. In the meantime the Liberal Party, headed since 1978 by Claude RYAN, former editor of *Le Devoir*, completely revamped its political thinking and practices. Financed directly by contributions from its supporters, open to ideas and to participation, and proposing a new federalism, the Liberals appeared about to win the next election. Nevertheless the Québec electorate accepted on good faith the PQ's promise to shelve its sovereignty-association proposal, and on 13 April 1981 the party handily won re-election. Lévesque's late 1984 announcement that the next provincial election would not be fought on the issue of Québec sovereignty encountered resistance among PQ members and led to the resignation of several Cabinet ministers. However, at a Jan 1985 party convention, the majority of delegates supported Lévesque.

The Parti Québécois and the Liberal Party both rejected the decision by the federal and provincial governments to impose on Québec a new constitution that restricted the powers of the Assemblée nationale. Following his election defeat and because of this united stand with the Québec government, Ryan was forced to resign his position in Aug 1982 and was replaced in 1983 by Robert Bourassa, the former premier. Québec

was at the time hard hit by the economic crisis, which raised the unemployment rate to 17% and thus negated much of the progress made since 1976.

Québec politics shifted dramatically during the Sept 1984 federal election when 58 of 75 seats went to the Conservative Party led by Baie Comeau's Brian MULRONEY. Subsequently, federal-provincial relations seemed to improve with the spirit of co-operation between Mulroney and Lévesque.   DANIEL LATOUCHE

Quebec Act (An Act for making more effective Provision for the Government of the Province of Quebec in North America) was a British statute which received royal assent 22 June 1774 and became effective 1 May 1775. The Act enlarged the boundaries of the PROVINCE OF QUEBEC to include Labrador, Ile d'Anticosti and the Magdalens on the E, and the Indian territory S of the Great Lakes between the Mississippi and Ohio rivers on the W. The colony was to be governed by a governor and 17 to 23 appointed councillors; an elected assembly was not provided. Religious freedom was guaranteed for the colony's Roman Catholic majority, and a simplified Test Oath, which omitted references to religion, enabled them to enter public office conscientiously (*see* CATHOLICISM). The Act established French civil law and British criminal law and provided for continued use of the SEIGNEURIAL SYSTEM.

Framed largely by Gov Sir Guy CARLETON, the Quebec Act has been variously interpreted. It was an attempt to rectify some of the problems created by the royal PROCLAMATION OF 1763, which dramatically reduced the size of NEW FRANCE, provided an untouchable Indian territory out of the vast western interior and promised an elected assembly. It was also an attempt to deal more fairly with the colony's French Catholics, perhaps with a view to ensuring their loyalty in the event of troubles with the American colonies, and it effectively guaranteed the survival of the *ancien régime* society in N America. Territorial expansion was a recognition of Montréal's role in the continental economy, and it returned to the Québec economy its traditional links with the fisheries and interior FUR TRADE. American settlers were enraged when Québec acquired the

Indian territory, which they perceived to be theirs by right; they considered the Quebec Act one of the "Intolerable Acts" which contributed to the outbreak of the AMERICAN REVOLUTION. Anglophone members of Québec's population, although pleased with the territorial expansion, were dissatisfied that an elected assembly was not provided for.

The Quebec Act became less effective when LOYALISTS began arriving in the colony after 1783. It was replaced by the CONSTITUTIONAL ACT, 1791, which created UPPER CANADA and LOWER CANADA.   NANCY BROWN FOULDS
Reading: Hilda Neatby, *The Quebec Act* (1972).

Québec Bridge Disasters Construction on the Québec Bridge, 11 km above QUÉBEC CITY, began in 1900. On 29 Aug 1907, when the bridge was nearly finished, the southern cantilever span twisted and fell 46 m into the St Lawrence R. Seventy-five workmen, many of them Caughnawaga Indians, were killed in this, Canada's worst, bridge DISASTER. An inquiry established that the accident had been caused by faulty design and inadequate engineering supervision. Work was resumed, but on 11 Sept 1916 a new centre span being hoisted into position fell into the river, killing 13 men. The bridge was completed in 1917. *See* BRIDGES.   HUGH A. HALLIDAY

Québec Citadel, a military FORTIFICATION built 1820-31 in Québec City. According to a number of 19th-century authors, including Charles Dickens, the Citadel, which crowns a 100 m escarpment named Cap Diamant, made Québec the "Gibraltar of N America." It was built when Québec was Canada's main port, and its purpose was to protect the city from attack from the St Lawrence R below and from the Plains of Abraham to the W. It could also serve as a last refuge for the garrison if the city were captured by an enterprising enemy. The Citadel replaced or incorporated defence works built during the French regime, eg, the western rampart (still in existence opposite the National Assembly). After the CONQUEST, 1759-60, the British considered this rampart inadequate; by the early 19th century, they completed construction of the present ramparts, encircling the Upper Town Cliff and also built the 4 MARTELLO TOWERS on the Plains of Abraham. Designed by British engineers on a classical model, the Citadel was somewhat anachronistic, given the recent evolution of European military architecture. It was

Wreckage of the first Québec Bridge, which collapsed 29 Aug 1907, killing 75 men (*courtesy Public Archives of Canada/PA-109481 Dominion Bridge Co Ltd*).

Citadel, Québec City (*photo by J.A. Kraulis*).

begun in 1820 and completed in 1831. The garrison provided most of the labour. Although the Citadel was designed as an arms, munitions and supplies depot as well as a barracks, only part of the 1000-man garrison was lodged there. Soldiers were also billeted in Artillery Park and in the Jesuit Barracks (the site of the present city hall).

After the mid-19th century, improvements in weaponry, particularly the introduction in 1856 of more precise and longer-range rifled artillery, led the British military authorities to modify their defence system substantially. Military fortifications were then located farther from the city centre. During the AMERICAN CIVIL WAR the threat of an American invasion encouraged the military to construct 3 forts between 1865 and 1871 on the heights of Pointe-Lévis across the river from Québec. None of these structures was ever subject to assault (other than by tourists).

The British military departed Québec in 1871. The Citadel served as headquarters for one of the artillery schools of the Canadian Army and became the headquarters of the Royal 22nd Regiment during WWI. Lord DUFFERIN was the first governor general to make the Citadel a viceregal residence and persuaded local politicians to save the old French walks from destruction.

YVON DESLOGES

Reading: André Charbonneau, Yvon Desloges and Marc Lafrance, *Québec: The Fortified City* (1982).

Québec City, Qué, capital of the province of QUÉBEC, is located on the N shore of the ST LAWRENCE R where it meets the Rivière St-Charles. Here the St Lawrence narrows to a width of just over 1 km and navigation is made difficult by a group of islands, the largest of which is the Ile d'ORLÉANS. Cap Diamant, a promontory with an elevation of about 100 m dominates the site and was used effectively as a fortification, earning Québec City the name "Gibraltar of America." The town successfully repulsed assaults by Sir William PHIPS in 1690 and a large American force in 1775-76. The name "Québec" is probably drived from an Algonquian word meaning "narrowing of the river."

Metropolitan Québec City includes, among its largest municipalities, Sainte-Foy (pop 68 883), Charlesbourg (pop 68 326), Beauport (pop 60 447), LÉVIS (pop 17 895) and Loretteville (pop 15 060).

Settlement Prior to the arrival of the Europeans, the site of Québec City was occupied by Indian hunters and fishermen for several thousands of years. In 1535 Jacques CARTIER discovered a fairly large Iroquoian village, STADACONA, whose 1000 or so inhabitants lived from fishing, hunting and the cultivation of corn. Sometime between 1543 and 1608, when Samuel de CHAMPLAIN arrived at the site, the Stadaconans had disappeared and been replaced by the occasional nomadic Algonquians, likely MONTAGNAIS-NASKAPI. Cartier wintered near Stadacona in 1535-36 and returned in 1541-42, spending a difficult winter at Cap-Rouge, a few kilometres upriver, before heading home with barrels of worthless minerals (*see* DIAMONDS OF CANADA). ROBERVAL spent the following winter at Cap-Rouge, but failure of these early expeditions diminished French interest in the area and a permanent settlement was not established until 1608 when Champlain founded a trading post. The post was captured by the KIRKE brothers in 1629, but was restored to the French by the Treaty of St Germain in 1632.

Development Québec City's strategic location on the St Lawrence R determined the nature of its development. In the age of sail, it held a dominant position as a port of entry and exit for oceangoing vessels. It quickly became the transfer port for domestic and foreign trade (especially furs and timber) and the arrival and departure point for travellers and immigrants to N America. From the beginning, its location made Québec City a political, administrative and military centre.

The long delay in establishing a rail link to the city, the technological developments in oceangoing vessels enabling them to bypass the city and sail directly to MONTRÉAL, and finally the shift of population and the economy westward, tended to reduce Québec City's importance in the mid-19th century. Despite repeated efforts, the city was unable to maintain its earlier position as a focus of economic production and trade, and it gradually became a provincial and regional administrative centre. However, over the past quarter century, the considerable growth of the provincial government has accelerated the growth of the city and its suburbs and

Population: 166 474 (1981c); 576 075 (CMA)

Rate of Increase (1971-81): (City) −10.5%; (CMA) 14.9%

Rank in Canada: Eighth (by CMA)

Date of Incorporation: 1833

Land Area: 89.1 km²

Elevation: Citadelle 98 m

Climate: Average daily temp, July 19.2°C, Jan −11.6°C; Yearly precip 1088.6 mm; Hours of sunshine 2016 per year

has given added emphasis to the relative importance of its administrative function. The city has also continued to develop as a centre for TOURISM.

Cityscape In the 17th century, the inhabitants of Québec City first occupied the narrow strip of land between the promontory and the port (Lower Town) and then the promontory itself, following in the wake of the religious institutions and colonial administration that occupied Upper Town. This expansion was strongly influenced by the construction of and improvements to the town's FORTIFICATIONS, which were established mainly in the Upper Town but also along the banks of the river (*see* QUÉBEC CITADEL). The fortifications and military barracks occupied a considerable area and restricted the establishment of a residential civilian population, which was already limited by the development of religious institutions (the Bishop's Palace, the cathedral, the seminary, colleges and convents, the HÔTEL-DIEU and the Château St-Louis). Lower Town was for many years the residential and commercial centre. Both parts form the core of the old city, which is still well preserved and has been partially reconstructed as part of the Place Royale project.

At the end of the French regime, Lower Town stretched along the port toward the Intendant's Palace, to the N of the promontory. During the 19th century, the town broke out of its fortified confines and stretched westwards on the promontory, along the shores of the Rivière St-Charles and to the foot of the N face of the promontory. These new parts of town were often built hastily and of wood, and fell victim to a number of major fires (St-Roch, 1845; St-Sauveur, 1866, 1870 and 1889; St-Jean-Baptiste, 1845, 1876 and 1881). The result was major reconstruction and improved protective infrastructures (water supply, fire-fighting services, etc).

Growth to the W and N of the city has been even more substantial in the 20th century, particularly since the 1950s. The small parishes in outlying areas grew quickly as residential and commercial suburbs: Sillery, Sainte-Foy, Charlesbourg, Cap-Rouge, Ancienne Lorette, etc. Although the downtown area was quite radically transformed with the appearance of private and governmental buildings and a few major hotels, the historic character of the old city has been largely preserved and the modern

Roof tops of Place Royale, a partial reconstruction of the old city at the end of the French regime (*photo by Barry Griffiths/Network*).

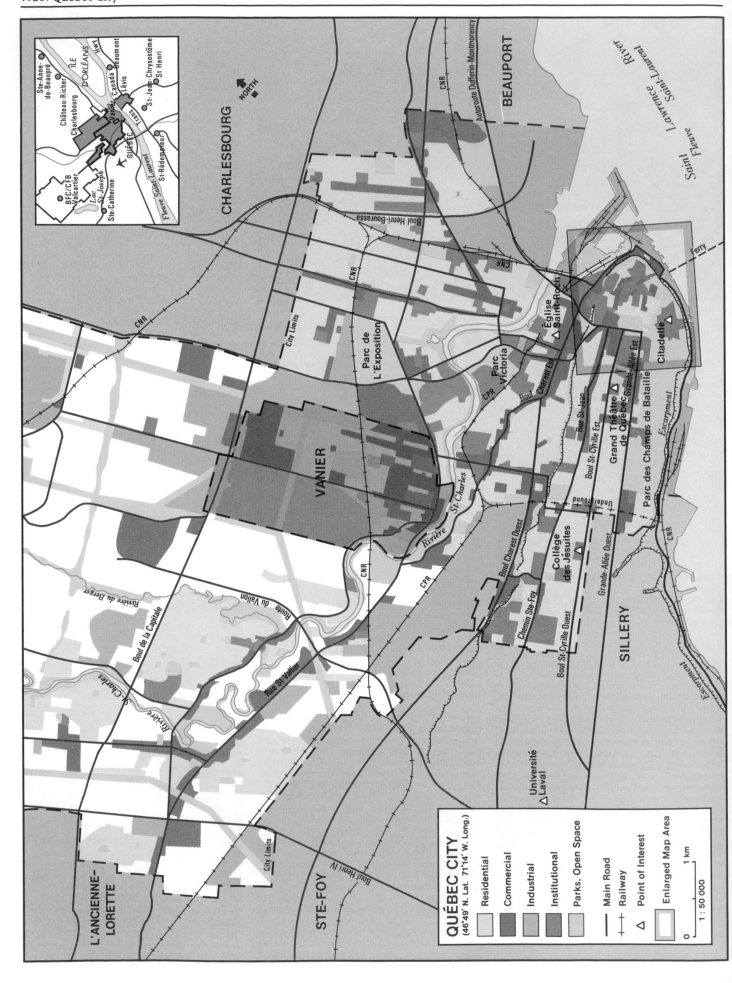

QUÉBEC CITY
(46°49′ N. Lat. 71°14′ W. Long.)

Residential
Commercial
Industrial
Institutional
Parks, Open Space

— Main Road
+ Railway
△ Point of Interest
Enlarged Map Area

1 : 50 000

0   1 km

CHARLESBOURG

BEAUPORT

VANIER

SILLERY

STE-FOY

L'ANCIENNE-LORETTE

Saint Lawrence River / Fleuve Saint-Laurent

Autoroute Dufferin-Montmorency

Boul Henri-Bourrassa

Parc de L'Exposition

Parc Victoria

Église Saint-Roch

Citadelle

Grand Théâtre de Québec

Grande-Allée Est

Parc des Champs de Bataille

Escarpment

Rue St-Jean

Boul Charest Est

Boul St-Cyrille Est

Collège des Jésuites

Boul Charest Ouest

Chemin Ste-Foy

Grande-Allée Ouest

Boul St-Cyrille Ouest

Université Laval

Underground

Rivière St-Charles

Rivière St-Charles

Boul de la Capitale

Rivière du Berger

Route du Vallon

Rue St-Vallier

City Limits

Boul Henri IV

CNR

CPR

Ferry

Ste-Anne-de-Beaupré

Château-Richer

ÎLE D'ORLÉANS

Beaumont

St Henri

St-Jean-Chrysostôme

St-Rédempteur

Lévis

Vanier Canada

Charlesbourg

BFC/CFB Valcartier

Lac St-Joseph

Ste-Catherine

Fleuve Saint-Laurent

Québec

Trans Canada HWY

NORTH

buildings blend quite well with the characteristic landscape of Québec City: the promontory, fortifications, Château Frontenac, Parliament Buildings, Rivière St-Charles, the Port and the Québec Bridge.

Population Although Québec City was the capital of the French empire in N America in the days of NEW FRANCE, for many years it was little more than a large village. In 1608 it had 28 inhabitants and by the time of the CONQUEST in 1759-60 its population only slightly exceeded 8000. Growth was rapid in the first half of the 19th century and by 1861 it numbered 60 000 inhabitants. The growth resulted from the economic expansion associated mainly with the TIMBER TRADE and the important political and administrative activities centered in the city. It was also the entry and transit port for the substantial annual influx of immigrants heading towards Upper Canada and the rest of N America. In some years the city's population doubled during the summer, causing many attendant problems such as EPIDEMICS and drunkenness.

As a result of the gradual but significant slowdown in the timber trade and SHIPBUILDING in the second half of the 19th century, the population of Québec City remained relatively stable until the early 20th century. In fact, the Lower and Upper Town experienced a decline as people moved to the new areas, particularly St-Roch. The overall population increase in a 40-year period, 1861-1901, was only 14.7% (60 000 to 68 840). Besides experiencing unfavourable economic conditions, the old city lacked residential space; only with the amalgamation of small outlying municipalities did its population begin to grow at the beginning of the 20th century. Metropolitan Québec City nevertheless grew more rapidly from the 1950s until the end of the 1970s. In the early 1980s this growth

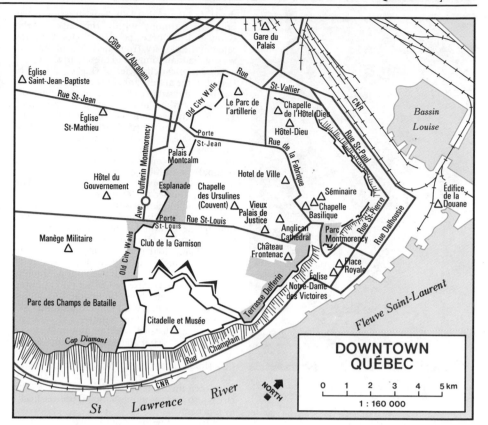

DOWNTOWN QUÉBEC

0 1 2 3 4 5 km

1 : 160 000

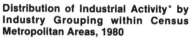

Distribution of Industrial Activity* by Industry Grouping within Census Metropolitan Areas, 1980

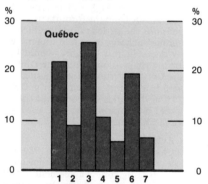

Industry groupings
1. Food and beverage and tobacco products industries
2. Leather, textile, knitting mills and clothing industries
3. Wood, furniture and fixtures, paper and allied and printing, publishing and allied industries
4. Machinery, transportation equipment and electrical products industries
5. Primary metal and metal fabricating industries
6. Rubber and plastic products, petroleum and coal products and chemical products industries
7. Non-metallic mineral products and miscellaneous manufacturing industries.

* Industry activity based on the average of percentage shares of the value shipments of goods of own manufacture, total value added and total number of employees for each of the selected metropolitan areas.

Source: Figure II, Catalogue 31-209, Statistics Canada.

again slowed, partly as a result of stabilization of growth in the province overall.

Prior to the Conquest, Québec City's population had been French. But in the early 19th century this changed with the influx of British immigrants. In 1851 the city's population was 41% British and other groups, a figure that rose to 51% in 1861. This high proportion dropped rapidly as immigration to Québec City stopped and as many British immigrants moved to other parts of Canada and to the US. By 1871 the percentage of non-Francophones had dropped to 31.5%, by 1921 to 10%, and by 1981 to 4%, both for the city itself and the metropolitan area. Thus, Québec City regained its essentially French character, which continues to this day.

Economy, Transportation and Labour Force The early economy of Québec City was directly dependent upon its activities as a transit port for basic products exported to Europe (furs, cereals and lumber) and for imported manufactured products. The considerable expansion of this trade enabled Québec to maintain a relatively competitive position with Montréal as the major trading centre of the province until the mid-19th century. At that time, the commercial position of Québec City was seriously affected by the decline in the timber trade and the shift from raw timber to lumber, the development of railway networks that bypassed Québec (the GRAND TRUNK RY OF CANADA passed on the S shore opposite the city), the weakness of Québec City's hinterland, the dredging of the St Lawrence between Québec and Montréal, the expansion of economic relations with the US, and the impact of technological change on trade and transportation (see TECHNOLOGY). Montréal rapidly acquired a dominant position in the second half of the 19th century in trade and finance, transportation and industry.

The Québec City middle class, which was already declining in numbers, attempted to maintain its position but failed. It struggled to attract transcontinental railways, such as the Quebec, Montreal, Ottawa and Occident Ry (which was the first railway to reach Québec City in 1879), the National Transcontinental Ry and the Cana-

dian Northern, and to have them adopt Québec City as their ocean terminal. Efforts were also made to have the 2 shores of the river connected by a bridge. The Québec Bridge, still the largest cantilevered bridge in the world, was built between 1899 and 1917, but experienced serious construction difficulties in 1907 and 1916 (see QUÉBEC BRIDGE DISASTERS). The bridge actually helped promote the circulation of products to ports farther east. A second bridge, the Pierre Laporte, was built in 1970. It is a suspension bridge, several hundred metres longer than the earlier one.

In the middle of the 19th century, Québec City went through an industrial revolution (see INDUSTRIALIZATION), particularly in the FOOTWEAR INDUSTRY, which gradually became the largest source of employment for the region. However, the city was unable to maintain growth in its manufacturing sector and the footwear industry declined in the 1920s. Even though various other concerns appeared and disappeared and offered employment to a significant number of people, they did not manage to diversify the city's industrial base. These enterprises included shipbuilding, breweries, textiles and clothing, pulp and paper and, more recently, the Ultramar refinery. Most jobs in Québec City are concentrated in public administration, defence and the service sector, as well as trade and transportation; only 9% of jobs in 1981 were in manufacturing. Québec City benefits from its status as the provincial capital and the regional administrative and services centre. It also attracts large numbers of tourists.

Government and Politics From 1765 to 1833 and from 1835 to 1840, Québec City was administered by a commission of justices of the peace appointed by the governor and composed largely of landowners, French Canadian professionals and British merchants. The commission was responsible for ensuring that the orders of the Legislature of LOWER CANADA were respected. Following pressure from the local population, Québec City received its first municipal charter in 1833. This lasted until 1835 and a second was issued in 1840. These charters established an

Bird's-Eye View of Countryside Around Quebec City (1664), looking eastward. The Beaupré shore is to the left, the Ile d'Orleans centre, the S shore between Pointe Lévis and Berthier to the right, and Québec City in the foreground. The city's strategic location on the St Lawrence R determined its development. In the age of sail, it held a dominant position as a port of entry for trade and immigration (*courtesy Bibliothèque Nationale, Paris*).

elected municipal council with the power to adopt regulations in their area of jurisdiction. From 1833 to 1856 and 1870 to 1908 the mayor was elected by the reeves and councillors, and then directly by citizens (property owners and tenants) by secret ballot from 1856 to 1870 and after 1908. The number of reeves, councillors and districts changed on many occasions as a result of amalgamations, in particular those of St-Sauveur (1889), St-Malo (1908), Limoilou (1909), Montcalm (1913), Notre-Dame-des-Anges (1924), Les Saules (1969), Duberger (1970), Neufchatel (1971) and Charlesbourg Ouest (1973). Currently, 21 councillors are elected by universal suffrage. Since 1970 the urban community of Québec City has included 23 municipalities on the N shore, and is responsible for urban planning, public transit, building regulations, property evaluation and industrial and tourist promotion.

The role played by Québec City as a "national" capital until 1840 (and subsequently 1851 to 1855 and 1859 to 1865 during the Union period) and as a provincial capital since 1867 has given it a special relationship with national, provincial and municipal politicians — so much so, in fact, that with the exception of a few businessmen prior to 1870, most Québec City mayors have also been involved in political careers at higher levels before, after and even during their mandates. One of the most famous mayors of Québec City, Simon-Napoléon PARENT (1894 to 1905) was also premier of Québec 1900 to 1905.

Cultural Life Québec City remains the major centre of French culture and the seat of the only francophone government in N America. In addition to conserving these traditions, it has managed to maintain a greater cultural homogeneity than Montréal, the other major pole of the French culture. Its teaching institutions include the SÉMINAIRE DE QUÉBEC (1668) and UNIVERSITÉ LAVAL (1852). Until 1920 the latter was the only francophone university in Québec; its satellite campus in Montréal, founded in 1876, became

the U de Montréal (1920). This situation often produced acrimony within the ranks of the clergy and in Québec political circles. Long located in the old city, from the 1950s on the university gradually moved to the suburbs.

The historical character of Québec City is reflected in the architecture of the old city, which has been the subject of major restorations and has become the site of exceptional museums. The municipal, provincial and federal governments have combined their efforts to restore Place Royale, Artillery Park and the fortifications (Citadel, walls, gates, S shore forts), the Old Port, the Voûtes du Palais, the Musée du Séminaire, a number of private religious museums, and the Musée de la Civilisation. The Musée du Québec (1934) contains collections of ancient and modern works and is part of a large urban park, the Plains of Abraham, or Parc des Champs de Bataille (1908), which commemorates the battle leading to the fall of the city and of New France to the British army in 1759. There is also a zoological garden in Orsainville, N of the city, an aquarium near the Pont de Québec, and the Grand Théâtre de Québec (1971), home to the Québec Symphony Orchestra.

A number of downhill and cross-country ski centres, including Mont Sainte-Anne and Lac Beauport, are located within a few minutes of Québec City. After having excellent minor hockey league teams for many years, Québec City finally entered the realm of major league hockey with the QUÉBEC NORDIQUES (1972), who have been members of the NHL since 1979. The city is also host to an international peewee hockey tournament.

Tourists and residents are attracted by a number of popular events: the Québec Carnival (since 1954), the Summer Festival each July, and a number of major anniversaries, including the 300th in 1908, the 375th in 1983 and the 450th anniversary of Cartier's arrival (1534-1984).

Of Québec's many literary figures, mention should be made of Roger LEMELIN, whose novels depict the working-class districts of the city. Québec City has 3 TV stations, one of which is English, a number of radio stations, and 2 daily newspapers, *Le Soleil* and the *Journal de Québec.*

MARC VALLIÈRES

Reading: M. Lafrance and D.T. Ruddel, "Physical Expansion and Socio-Economic Segregation in Quebec City," in G. Stelter and A. Artibise, eds, *Shaping the Urban Landscape* (1982); G.A. Nader, *Cities of Canada,* vol 2 (1976).

Québec Conference, 10-27 Oct 1864. At the earlier CHARLOTTETOWN CONFERENCE, representatives from the 3 Maritime colonies and the PROVINCE OF CANADA had agreed on a scheme for the federation of BRITISH NORTH AMERICA. On Oct 10, 33 delegates, including 2 from Newfoundland, met in Québec City to formulate a detailed plan for union. The Maritime delegates were drawn from government; Canada was represented by its Cabinet, which set the agenda, proposed the resolutions and dominated the conference. Canadian PM Sir E.P. TACHÉ acted as chairman. Voting was by colony; Canada was given 2 votes. The greatest controversy was over the composition of PARLIAMENT: only PEI disagreed that members of the HOUSE OF COMMONS should be elected on the basis of representation by population, but the distribution of seats in the SENATE led to a prolonged dispute. The financial arrangements proposed by Alexander T. GALT also precipitated considerable discussion. The distribution of powers between federal and provincial governments was settled with comparative ease and followed the outline suggested by John A. MACDONALD and Oliver MOWAT. The delegates completed their work and adjourned Oct 27. Their conclusions were embodied in 72 resolutions, which became the focus of the CONFEDERATION debates. Although the Québec Resolutions were formally adopted only by the

Province of Canada, they formed the basis of the BRITISH NORTH AMERICA ACT, which created the new Dominion of Canada. *See* FATHERS OF CONFEDERATION.

P.A. BUCKNER

Québec Nordiques, hockey team. An original World Hockey Association (WHA) franchise (1972), the Nordiques surfaced as a league power in 1975 when they advanced to the WHA finals. They won the championship in 1977 and two of their stars, Marc Tardif and Réal Cloutier, won the last 4 WHA scoring titles (1976-79). In 1976 the Carling O'Keefe Brewery became majority team shareholders for approximately $2 million. The 1979 WHA-NHL merger saw the Nordiques playing in the 15 264-seat Colisée de Québec (in Québec City) as members of the Adams Division. Their best performance to date was in 1982, when, with the help of brothers Peter, Anton and Marian Stastny, they eliminated their provincial rivals, the MONTREAL CANADIENS, and then the Boston Bruins en route to the Prince of Wales conference final.

DEREK DRAGER

Quebec, North Shore and Labrador Railway was built by the Iron Ore Co of Canada to carry ore from the mines at the Knob Lk region near the Québec-Labrador boundary to SEPT-ÎLES, where it could be transferred to ships. Construction began in 1950, greatly aided by BUSH FLYING as heavy equipment and supplies were flown to inland work points. The single-track 570 km railway was built to extremely high standards in anticipation of the loaded ore cars carrying over 10 million tonnes of ore per year. The railway was completed from Sept-Îles to SCHEFFERVILLE, Qué, in 1954 at a cost of $120 million.

JAMES MARSH

Québec Pension Plan (QPP), established in 1966, is the counterpart for the Québec labour force of the CANADA PENSION PLAN. The plan has the same rate of contributions, maximum pensionable earnings, retirement pensions and annual escalation of benefits, but the QPP flat-rate components of disability and surviving spouses' benefits are higher. The QPP allows women to exclude from the formula used to calculate pensions the periods during which they were at home in charge of a child under 7 years of age. Women in this category would be eligible for higher pensions under the QPP than under the CPP. QPP funds are deposited with the Caisse de depôt et placement du Québec. About 75% of the funds were invested (1981) in bonds issued or guaranteed by Québec, 13% in equities and 5% in mortgages. A. ASIMAKOPULOS

Québec Referendum, called by the Parti Québécois (PQ) government on 20 May 1980 to ask the people of Québec for a mandate to negotiate, on an equal footing, a new agreement with the rest of Canada, thus honouring the promise it had made in 1976 to hold a REFERENDUM before making any radical change in Québec's status. The concept of SOVEREIGNTY-ASSOCIATION was rejected by about 60% of voters, although it is estimated about 50% of the francophones supported it. The PQ leadership maintained that sovereignty remained the only viable option for Québec, and would someday win majority support. The federalist side, organized into one group as required by the law governing the referendum, was led by Claude RYAN. Prime Minister TRUDEAU, in an official statement near the end of the referendum campaign, persuaded a number of the Québecois that a rejection of the *péquiste* option would lead to negotiations for a new Canadian FEDERALISM. The intense negotiations between the federal government and the provinces began after the referendum but broke down when all 10 provinces rejected the proposals made by the federal team, although later many of the provinces (not Québec) agreed to them. Despite their defeat in the referendum,

the *péquiste* government won re-election in 1981 with a marked increase (9%) in the popular vote.
R. HUDON

Québec Seminary, see SÉMINAIRE DE QUÉBEC.

Québec Shoe Workers' Strike, properly a lockout, 27 Oct-10 Dec 1900, the first direct intervention in a labour conflict by Québec Catholic clergy and the first step toward the creation of Catholic unions (*see* CONFEDERATION OF NATIONAL TRADE UNIONS). Unionized boot and shoe workers had grown too militant to suit Québec manufacturers, who closed their factories, planning to keep them shut until the workers quit their unions. But the 4000 workers directly affected resisted. Finally the conflict was submitted by mutual consent to the arbitration of Archbishop Bégin. His decision, pronounced 14 Jan 1901, recognized the workers' right of association, but insisted that passages in the union constitutions that contravened the principles of "honest and just ends" and "means consistent with the standards of morality, honesty and justice" be revised by an ecclesiastical committee. The committee modified the overly radical passages to conform to the SOCIAL DOCTRINE of the church and recommended that a chaplain attend all union meetings. Québec unions thus acquired their church affiliation.
JACQUES ROUILLARD

Québec Since Confederation Confederation opened the way to a permanent settlement of a political problem that Canada had faced for several decades — the existence of a French Canadian nation in what had now become, through immigration, a predominantly English-speaking country. The solution that had begun to take shape with the Act of Union of 1840 (*see* PROVINCE OF CANADA) took on its definitive form with CONFEDERATION in 1867, and there would be few challenges to it in the century that followed. Confederation confirmed French Canadians as a minority, but gave them in return — in addition to bilingualism in federal institutions — provincial status for their heartland, the former LOWER CANADA. They were a majority in Québec, the new province, securely in control of their own cultural and social development. But this political reorganization was only one of the fundamental changes that Québec society was undergoing at the time.

The Late 19th Century For a long time, writers concerned with Québec's development characterized it as a traditional society, largely closed to the changes occurring elsewhere in N America, and described Québec as a peasant society, emphasizing its stability, arguing that at bottom its characteristics changed little between the 18th and mid-20th centuries. In the 1960s, however, new historical research began to show that Québec was a much more complex society, constantly evolving and with phases of apparent stability between periods of rapid transformation. Québec participated in the major developments that characterized the Atlantic world between 1815 and 1930: large-scale population movements and increasing INDUSTRIALIZATION and URBANIZATION in which respects the second half of the 19th century was a pivotal period.

This can be seen first by looking at developments in demography. The ethnic composition of Québec's population changed significantly over the 19th century. Heavy immigration from the British Isles occurred between 1815 and 1860; in 1867 a quarter of Québec's 1.2 million people traced their roots to the British Isles (mostly to Ireland) while three-quarters were of French origin. Around 1870, however, this large wave of immigration ended.

Meanwhile, French Canadians were also increasing rapidly in number because of their high birth rate. In Québec's older rural areas they soon became too numerous and farmers'

children had to look for jobs elsewhere. A French Canadian who wanted to be a farmer had to go to a distant colonization zone in Québec where the soil was typically poor and living conditions were difficult. The colonist was isolated and the deficiencies of his marginal farm forced him to work in the forest as a lumberjack to make ends meet. Few rural Quebecers were attracted by the new colonization regions, and most, regarding even the long hours of factory work as preferable to the life of a colonist, went to urban areas instead.

The textile mills of New England needed cheap and plentiful labour, which they found in the Québec countryside. In the late 19th century emigration to the US became a mass movement (*see* FRANCO-AMERICANS); it is estimated that between 1850 and 1930 almost a million French Canadians left Québec for American destinations. The rural population surplus also stimulated the emergence of industries in Québec itself. This was one of numerous reasons for the growth of industry in Québec, others being the expansion of the Canadian domestic market, railway construction, and the Canadian government's economic policies — especially the protective tariff of 1879 (*see* NATIONAL POLICY).

Industrialization in Québec during this period occurred in two stages. The first, in the mid-19th century, was concentrated primarily in Montréal. That city's industrial structure was also strengthened in the second stage, in the 1880s, but during this period industry grew in many small and middle-sized cities and towns as well, especially Québec City and the urban centres of the Eastern Townships.

Industrialization in Québec was based mainly on light manufacturing, employing plentiful, underpaid labour and producing goods for immediate consumption, such as shoes, textiles and food. There was also some heavy industry, linked to the transportation sector and concentrated in Montréal.

Industrialization increased the process of urbanization, and by the end of the 19th century a third of all Quebecers lived in cities and towns. The most significant urban and industrial growth took place in Montréal, where half of Québec's industrial production was concentrated and almost a quarter of all Quebecers lived in 1901.

Nevertheless the majority of Québec's population was still in rural areas, where subsistence was beginning to yield to more commercial forms of agriculture. The farmers were weaned from their traditional attachment to grain cultivation and started to concentrate on dairy farming and the production of more specialized, market-oriented commodities. This change took place slowly, and its pace varied widely from region to region.

As a result of the period's economic growth, a new bourgeoisie emerged. Unlike the bourgeoisie of the previous period, whose interests were purely commercial, this class also invested in transportation, the financial sector and industrial corporations. It was drawn overwhelmingly from the English and Scottish groups, and was concentrated in Montréal, Canada's leading economic centre. It controlled the major economic institutions that operated Canada-wide, such as the powerful BANK OF MONTREAL (fd 1817). French Canadians were almost completely absent from the upper level of the bourgeoisie. At the same time, however, there arose a class of French-speaking businessmen with a much more local or regional economic base. They actively exercised a share of political power in Québec and established specifically French-speaking institutions, eg, banks, business periodicals and chambers of commerce.

Industrialization also led to the formation of a working class. In Montréal, Québec City and the smaller industrial centres, Quebecers who

had left farms to become workers lived under difficult conditions: low wages, long working hours, poor housing conditions, a high death rate and widespread seasonal unemployment. French Canadian workers had the fewest skills and had to be satisfied with the lowest-paying jobs. This was especially true of women, whose numbers were increasing in the textile, clothing, shoe and tobacco industries. The growing importance of the working class was confirmed by the rise of the labour movement in the 1880s and 1890s (*see* WORKING-CLASS HISTORY). The trade union movement quickly became dominated by 2 American organizations, the KNIGHTS OF LABOR and the American Federation of Labor, which established affiliates in Canada. During this period, only a small proportion of Québec's workers — primarily the most highly skilled ones — belonged to these unions.

This period was marked politically by the domination of the Conservative Party which, except for brief intervals, held power in both Ottawa and Québec. After the death of George-Etienne CARTIER in 1873, the party was gradually eroded by quarrels between its ULTRAMONTANE and moderate wings. Between 1867 and 1897 Québec had 10 premiers: 8 Conservatives, including P.J.O. CHAUVEAU (1867-73) and J.A. CHAPLEAU (1879-82), and 2 Liberals, one of whom was Honoré MERCIER (1887-91).

The Roman Catholic Church (*see* CATHOLICISM) was a powerful social force. It controlled the public education system, and through its network of parishes and religious associations it exercised tight control over people's morals. The rapid numerical growth of the clergy and religious communities, starting in the mid-19th century, was evidence of the church's vitality and its power in society. Nevertheless the church was not ubiquitous and all-powerful. Despite its success in the social and cultural spheres, it was less effective in the political and economic realms. The clergy did not have the power to stop industrialization or immigration to the US. And although the clergy did try to dominate Québec's politicians, to the point of supporting the formation of a Catholic party in 1871, it was unable to control government institutions. Many priests were openly hostile to the Liberal Party, but the Liberals, under federal leader Wilfrid LAURIER and provincial leader Honoré Mercier followed a strategy of softening their radicalism and increased their support among the population.

Although rural life was still a major feature of late-19th-century Québec, the province's social and economic development was parallel to that of other parts of N America that were becoming industrialized. There were still significant differences of language and culture between Québec and the rest of the continent. In addition, French Canadians were not masters of Québec's economic development; they occupied a secondary economic position and were much more likely to be workers than employers.

1896-1930 In the first 30 years of the 20th century, Québec experienced strong economic growth and the pace of the changes that had marked the previous period quickened. Industrialization and urbanization continued: by WWI half the population lived in cities and towns, and this proportion grew to 60% by 1931.

To an increasing extent, Montréal was Québec's metropolis, and in 1931 Greater Montréal accounted for 35% of the province's population. The city's industrial growth was remarkable: new industries developed while some old ones increased production substantially to meet the demand caused by Canada' rapid economic growth. Through its railway systems, large banks and many commercial and industrial corporations, Montréal became the metropolitan centre for the development of western Canada. Canadian wheat was exported to Europe from its harbour. It remained Canada's leading industrial centre, and accounted for two-thirds of the value of Québec's manufacturing production.

At the same time the Québec countryside was being changed by a new kind of industrialization based on the exploitation of natural resources. Industries linked to hydroelectric and forest resources (pulp and paper, aluminum, chemicals) developed quickly in former colonization zones, such as the St Maurice Valley and the Saguenay-Lac Saint-Jean region. Immigration to the US slowed, although it remained substantial until the 1930s.

As concentration in the industrial and banking sectors increased early in the century, economic power increasingly became centralized in the hands of a few Montréal capitalists, almost all of them English Canadian; the French Canadian bourgeoisie was reduced to a marginal position and increasingly limited to local institutions and traditional sectors. However, it maintained a strong political presence, especially at the provincial level.

But the vast majority of French Canadians could choose only farming or factory work. The situation of Québec farmers improved as the trend towards specialization and market orientation continued up to WWI. In the 1920s Québec farmers tended to come out of their traditional isolation and join together in associations and co-operatives (see UNITED FARMERS OF QUÉBEC; CO-OPERATIVE MOVEMENT).

In the cities and towns, French Canadian workers had to compete with a new wave of immigrants who came increasingly from continental Europe. The largest ethnic group that was neither French nor British consisted of eastern European Jews, and Italians were a distant second. In the second half of the 19th century, the proportion of French Canadians in Québec's population had increased from 75% to 80%, and it remained at this level through the early part of the 20th century. The proportion represented by the British group, however, declined to 15% by 1931, while people of neither French nor British origin accounted for almost 6%. At the same time, ethnic diversity was a phenomenon that was increasingly limited to Montréal Island, where people of French origin represented only 60% of the population.

As they had in the late 19th century, French Canadian politicians and businessmen strongly supported Québec's industrial development. The provincial Liberal Party, in power from 1897 to 1936, was solidly behind big business and the entry of American capital in the new resource-based industries. Premiers F.G. MARCHAND (1897-1900), S.N. PARENT (1900-05), Lomer GOUIN (1905-20) and L.A. TASCHEREAU (1920-36) all pursued programs of modernization. However, a group of intellectuals and members of the liberal professions, led in turn by Henri BOURASSA and Abbé Lionel GROULX and calling themselves nationalists, reacted by trying to resist rapid industrialization, and especially the sale of natural resources to foreigners. The nationalists' opposition to large-scale industrialization received considerable support from the Catholic clergy, which was alarmed at the massive rural exodus and the rapid urbanization of the population. However, the clergy was not rejecting outright a process over which it had no control; instead, it developed a new strategy of establishing organizations to make it possible to dominate the new economic and social order from within. For example, the clergy promoted the establishment of Catholic unions, which were especially active in Québec's smaller industrial towns. However, these new unions largely failed to take root in Montréal, and, despite clerical support, only a quarter of all unionized workers in Québec belonged to Catholic unions in the late 1920s, the great majority remaining with the big US-based international unions.

Throughout the period, 2 opposing conceptions of Québec society confronted each other. The first, which can be called the liberal ideology, was upheld by businessmen and most politicians. Emphasizing economic growth and the idea of progress, it placed a high value on the individual and free enterprise. Its representatives believed that the well-being of the nation would flow from the individual progress of its members, and that economic growth was the only road Québec could take. Since they took the position that individual progress would lead to collective progress, they also believed that better education was the path to an improved economic situation. At the same time, they favoured modernizing Québec's economic and social structures.

Opposed to the liberal ideology was the deeply traditionalist clerical-nationalist ideology, which suggested that the French Canadian collectivity would achieve national well-being by withdrawing into itself and returning to rural life and traditional French Canadian and Catholic values. Upheld by nationalist intellectuals and many clergymen, this ideology was opposed to almost everything foreign. It was forcefully expressed in a number of publications and in sermons and speeches. It was much more explicit and more fully articulated than was the liberal ideology, and hence historians and sociologists long maintained that it was Québec's dominant ideology. However, the real situation was much more complex. Despite the resistance of clerical-nationalist ideologues, industrialization continued and increasing numbers of Quebecers left their farms to live in cities and towns. A return to traditional rural society was a dream that did not come true.

Socialist ideological currents were very important in Europe at the time, but they occupied only a marginal position in Québec. Some representatives of the labour movement became involved in politics, but they were closer in their thinking to the British Labour Party than to European socialists.

The rise of Québec nationalism, moreover, posed the question of Québec's place in Confederation. While Laurier was prime minister, French Canadians felt that they held some power. In fact, they witnessed the reduction of their educational and linguistic rights throughout various parts of the country, despite the vigorous battles fought by the nationalists. The nationalists' real political setback, however, the election of a Conservative government to Ottawa in 1911 — and especially the CONSCRIPTION crisis of 1917 — served to highlight the isolation of Québec, which henceforth bound its fortunes to those of the Liberal Party.

1930-45 The GREAT DEPRESSION of the 1930s appeared to be a partial vindication of the clergy and the nationalist intellectuals who had long been predicting that the liberal model of society would fail. The area of Québec most seriously affected was Montréal. Because Montréal was Canada's leading port, it suffered substantial unemployment when international trade and Canadian exports collapsed. In addition, its industries were hurt as a result of decreased domestic consumption. Montréal teemed with tens of thousands of unemployed people living on public assistance.

All over Canada, traditional solutions based largely on private charity proved inadequate to cope with the Depression. Governments had to intervene. Provincial governments were overwhelmed and appealed to Ottawa, which participated financially in assisting the unemployed. This intervention by the federal government in social policy led to a rethinking of Canadian federalism in the form of the Rowell-Sirois Commission. It also marked the beginning of a long process of centralization favouring the federal government, which had a considerable

impact on Québec. WWII, during which Ottawa intervened extensively in economic management, played a determining role in this respect. During the Depression and the war, the idea of more systematic government intervention, based on Keynesian economic policies, was gradually accepted. In a federal system such as Canada's, however, such a development raised a fundamental question: which level of government should be in charge of the regulatory instruments that are established? In general, English Canadians believed that this is properly the responsibility of the federal government, which should provide for equality of opportunity from coast to coast. By contrast, most French-speaking political thinkers and politicians in Québec were opposed to concentrating power in Ottawa's hands in this way, on the grounds that it threatened the autonomy that French Canadians had gained through the existence of a provincial government over which they had majority control. The question seemed especially complicated in Québec's case because most Québec representatives in Ottawa, the Liberals who were in power 1935-57, supported federal centralization. During the war the federal government could impose its own solution, but once the war was over the issue reappeared, as vexatious as ever. As a result, the recent history of Québec — and of Canada as a whole — has been marked by federal-provincial struggles.

In the economic disorder brought about by the Depression, there were many challenges to the prevailing political and social system. Although communist and socialist groups grew substantially in Canada during the 1930s, they had little success in recruiting French Canadians, among whom left-wing traditions were very weak. In Québec, only immigrants and English-speaking intellectuals in Montréal were attracted to these groups. Among French Canadians, nationalist and traditionalist movements enjoyed new popularity instead, and new groups emphasizing nationalism and corporatism had considerable success at the ballot box.

Their success was short-lived, however, as the ideological effervescence of the 1930s was calmed by the war. In Québec the war was synonymous with a return to prosperity and full employment. Quebecers actually profited from the war — although they were reluctant to pay the price for their new prosperity. Thousands of French Canadians joined the Canadian Army to fight in Europe, but in its culture and operation the Canadian Army was a profoundly anglophone institution and held little attraction for French-speaking Quebecers. Nationalist leaders portrayed the war as something foreign that did not concern French Canadians, so that intense resistance to Canadian military participation in Europe, and especially to conscription, developed in Québec. In 1942 Ottawa held a Canada-wide plebiscite on the question of conscription. An overwhelming majority of Quebecers voted against compulsory military service, whereas a majority of English Canadians in the other provinces voted in favour of it; a deep national cleavage ensued.

The war also had highly significant long-term social consequences, which manifested themselves both concretely and in attitudes. Quebecers who served in Europe came into contact with different cultures and ways of life. Thousands of women worked in factories as part of the war production system, and even if many returned to traditional family life after the war this exposure would have long-term effects. But the impact of the war was probably felt most strongly by rural Quebecers. They were increasingly integrated into the industrial capitalist economy, as many of them left the countryside to work in factories while others introduced changes that made their farms much more productive. Meanwhile, war propaganda, the increasing availability of radio and improved communications all tended to bring rural Quebecers into the broad current of modernization that had been felt in Québec for several decades but had not reached all parts of the province in equal measure.

The Duplessis Era, 1945-60 After the war Québec entered another period of rapid economic growth. It was conspicuous in the natural resource sector, where it was stimulated by American demand. Its most spectacular manifestation was the opening up of the North Shore of the St Lawrence and the far north of the province, New Québec, to mining development. But growth was also visible in the manufacturing and service sectors. Québec underwent a new wave of urbanization, its standard of living improved substantially, and Quebecers had greater access to the consumer society of N America. By 1960 farmers represented only a small minority of Québec's economically active population.

Québec's population grew substantially. The numbers of births increased and remained at a high level until the early 1960s. Immigration, which had almost stopped in the 1930s and during the war, resumed. The many newcomers came from the British Isles as before, but also — and in greater numbers — from southern Europe, especially Italy. Montréal became even more cosmopolitan, and by 1961 Italian Quebecers constituted the largest ethnic group of neither French nor British origin.

Economic growth also had significant social effects. It brought about the rise of a new middle class made up of highly skilled workers, executives, managers and teachers. This group increasingly favoured a modernization of Québec's social and political structures, in which traditionalism and social control by the church played too large a role. The gap between socioeconomic reality and the needs of the population on the one hand, and the traditionalism that characterized Québec's institutions and structures on the other, was increasingly evident.

Throughout the postwar period the Québec government was dominated by the UNION NATIONALE party under Maurice DUPLESSIS. Maintained in power by Québec's most traditional elements, political corruption and an outdated electoral map, Duplessis ran a conservative, narrow-minded government with no overall vision of society. While the need for a wide range of reforms was ever more strongly felt, the Union nationale effectively delayed them.

The Duplessis government used Québec nationalism to justify its policies. Its nationalism was traditionalist and conservative, emphasizing the classic themes of religion, language and the rural character of French Canada. It resisted the federal government in the name of provincial autonomy. At the same time, the federal government represented a new and reform-oriented brand of liberalism which attracted many young French Canadian intellectuals, who described this period in Québec's history as the era of the "Great Darkness." Moreover, the federal government was led by a French Canadian, Louis ST. LAURENT, who had strong backing from the Québec electorate. Thus, much of that electorate simultaneously supported 2 first ministers of opposing orientations.

The Duplessis period was especially difficult for the trade union movement, which came into conflict with the antiunion policies of the government. A number of strikes, especially the ASBESTOS STRIKE of 1949, had wide repercussions. There were also changes within the unions themselves: the Catholic unions became more secular and radical (*see* CONFEDERATION OF NATIONAL TRADE UNIONS; UNION CENTRALS, QUÉBEC), and the merger of the 2 American trade union congresses, the American Federation of Labor and the Congress of Industrial Organizations, (*see*

AFL-CIO), led to a similar reorganization among their Québec affiliates.

The Quiet Revolution and After Some of Québec society's institutions — especially the educational system, the social services and the administrative arm of the provincial government — were increasingly ill suited to the postwar world. When Duplessis died in 1959, it was the signal for the start of a new era, known as the QUIET REVOLUTION. The political and ideological heritage of the Duplessis era was liquidated with a speed that indicated how little it corresponded to contemporary socioeconomic realities. The provincial Liberal Party, led by Jean LESAGE (1960-66), proceeded to modernize government institutions, the school system and social services. This direction was followed, though less spectacularly, by subsequent governments: the Union Nationale of Daniel JOHNSON (1966-68) and Jean-Jacques BERTRAND (1968-70), the Liberal Party of Robert BOURASSA (1970-76) and the PARTI QUÉBÉCOIS of René LÉVESQUE (1976-). Québec society also broke with a much longer historical tradition by becoming declericalized: religious observance declined, the clergy decreased in numbers and the church lost its former hold on social services and, more generally, on people's attitudes.

But the Quiet Revolution, which lasted roughly from 1960 to 1966, also represented the persistence of long-term trends in the development of Québec society. The effects of industrialization, urbanization and the growth of the service sector, all of which had been in process for a long time, were fully felt in the 1960s and 1970s. Other trends continued: a rising standard of living, the emergence of a new middle class and new elites, and a higher level of education.

While postwar prosperity brought benefits to Francophones, it also made them see much more clearly the extent of ethnic discrimination. In the workplace, French Canadians were limited to subordinate jobs, while in Montréal department stores and the public arena in general their language held second place to English. A new form of nationalism emerged. Unlike Duplessis's nationalism, it was essentially reformist and demanded a change in Québec's position in Confederation. This new nationalism manifested itself in a number of different tendencies. There were the Liberals, who favoured autonomy for Québec but remained federalists; the independence movement, which grew in size and credibility during the 1960s; and the socialists, working within a newly strong trade union movement and in intellectual circles, who wanted to go beyond reformism.

Major struggles for power took place in Québec in the 1960s and 1970s between old and new elites and between Francophones and Anglophones. Especially noteworthy were battles over language, the economy and politics.

The struggle on the language front was aimed at having French, the language of the majority, fully recognized as Québec's primary language. One major objective was to integrate Quebecers of neither French nor British origin into the French-speaking majority, and this engagement was fought on the battleground of the language of education. The goal of making Québec French was achieved in stages, and at each stage it encountered resistance from non-francophone groups. In the late 1960s the language struggle was fought in the streets, but it later found its way into Québec's National Assembly and, more generally, the forum of public debate. Three language laws were passed by 3 different provincial governments between 1969 and 1977. Step by step, these pieces of legislation increased the pressure in favour of French, widened its recognition as Québec's official language and made its use compulsory. The third of these laws, known as BILL 101 or the Charter of the French Language, went well beyond the ed-

ucational field. It was aimed not only at bringing more children into French schools but also at making all of Québec society French, and dealt with corporations, professional services, public signs, etc. By 1980 French was spoken and recognized everywhere in the province.

Another struggle was over the question of economic power. One government objective was to introduce changes into the workplace so that French Canadians would have better jobs and career opportunities in the private sector. Another goal was to support and assist French Canadian businessmen and the companies they owned so that they would grow and gain a larger share of the market. A third aim was to have large Canadian and international corporations which operated in the province take Québec's specific needs increasingly into account. And a final objective was to make the Québec government a major partner with private enterprise in Québec's economic development. In the 1960s and 1970s French Canadians made considerable economic progress. The growth of new French Canadian financial groups was significant, as was the increasing intervention of the Québec government in the economy through such publicly owned corporations as HYDRO-QUÉBEC and the CAISSE DE DÉPÔT ET PLACEMENT. These successes, however, were counterbalanced by the weakening of Québec's economic position in Canada as a whole as the country's economic centre of gravity moved westward. Toronto replaced Montréal as Canada's metropolis and many companies moved their head offices or manufacturing operations to Ontario.

The third struggle was over political power within Canada. Throughout the 1960s and 1970s there were continuing attempts to increase Québec's influence in Confederation and revamp the division of powers between the 2 levels of government. The Québec government's goal was to stem the tide of federal centralization and to make itself the government with primary responsibility for French Canadians. The debate over the constitution was clearly one of the major themes of the 1960s and 1970s. It was marked by provocative statements and battles over protocol and appearance, and also by discussions, negotiations and federal-provincial conferences. Québec's firm self-assertion during the Quiet Revolution was followed by a period of federal resistance to the provinces' desire to increase their autonomy; the new federal stance became explicit when P.E. TRUDEAU came to power in Ottawa in 1968.

This long political conflict, which mobilized much of Québec's energy for two decades, culminated in two defeats for Québec: advocates of Québec independence were the losers in the 1980 referendum, and the adoption of the new Canadian Constitution in 1982 represented a defeat for those who supported a stronger Québec within Confederation. The political struggle led only to increased federal centralization and the confirmation of Québec's minority status in Confederation.

In fact, however, the position of Québec with respect to the federal government appeared to be improving. Under Trudeau (1968-79 and 1980-84) there were more Québecois than ever before in Cabinet, and federal institutions adopted a far more pronounced bilingual stance. But these circumstances depended on the influence of Québec representatives in the Liberal Party, and in 1984 the number of Francophones in administrative posts remained low — particularly at the senior levels.

In addition, there were conflicts internal to French Canadian society. The growing strength of the trade union movement during the 1960s led in the next decade to serious confrontations between the major union federations and the provincial government. At the same time there were profound tensions within the new French Canadian middle class, which had grown up gradually in the postwar period and occupied centre stage during the 1960s and 1970s. There was relative unanimity during the Quiet Revolution, but afterwards deep divisions appeared — politically, with the polarization between the Liberal Party and the Parti Québécois, and socially, with the tensions between trade union leaders and provincial government administrators. In late 1984 René Lévesque announced that, while sovereignty-association would continue to be supported, he would not fight the next election on the issue of Québec independence. Several prominent Cabinet ministers resigned in protest; however, Lévesque retained the party's support at a convention held in Jan of 1985.

Although the province enjoyed a higher standard of living, serious inequalities continued to characterize Québec society. There were regional inequalities, as Montréal flourished while other regions remained underdeveloped, and social inequalities, as Québec's unemployment rate was substantially higher than the Canadian average and many of its citizens lived in poverty. Awareness of these problems was much greater in the 1960s and 1970s than it had been previously, and demands for a change in the situation were increasingly heard.

Québec society in the 1980s is thus a complex society, in which numerous tensions prevail and people disagree on social goals, policies and the interpretation of the past. The 1980 referendum provided evidence that French Canadians are divided into 2 groups of almost equal size. This is not a new phenomenon. Rather, it is historically based and can only be understood by looking anew at the long-term changes Québec society has undergone.   PAUL-ANDRÉ LINTEAU

Quebecair, with headquarters in Dorval, Qué, is a regional airline that began in 1946 as the Rimouski Aviation Syndicate. This company became Rimouski Airlines in 1947, merged with Gulf Aviation to create Quebecair in 1953, and acquired Matane Air Service, Northern Wings (now Regionair) and Northern Wings Helicopters in 1965. Quebecair now operates scheduled passenger flights in Québec, western Labrador and Ontario, and offers domestic and international group charters. The company has about 900 employees. Its major shareholder is the Québec government, which assumed control in 1981. Financially the airline has not fared well: in 1982 it lost $21.6 million, and in 1983, $18 million. The airline is now owned by the province of Québec.   DEBORAH C. SAWYER

Quebecor Inc, controlled by Pierre PÉLADEAU, publishes 2 French-language morning tabloids, *Le Journal de Montréal* and *Le Journal de Québec,* with a combined 1983 circulation of 402 601, and 29 regional and popular weeklies in Québec (circulation 472 000). Its interests in English-language NEWSPAPERS include the *Sunday Express* (western Québec and eastern Ontario) and The Winnipeg Sun Ltd, publisher of the *Winnipeg Sun* and the *Winnipeg Magazine.* Other publishing interests include *Filles d'aujourd'hui* and *Vivre,* trade magazines and a book-publishing division. Quebecor operates 10 printing plants; *Messageries dynamiques,* one of the largest publications distribution networks in Québec; *Trans-Canada,* a distributor of records and cassettes serving mainly the Québec market; and is shareholder in Premier Choix/First Choice PAY TELEVISION in Québec. In 1983 Quebecor's total assets were $76 million, with revenues of $221 million.   PETER S. ANDERSON

Queen Charlotte Islands, named for the wife of King George III, lie off the N coast of BC. They include about 150 islands in a scimitar-shaped archipelago 250 km long. Graham and Moresby

The Queen Charlotte Is are a biologically unique area, containing some plants that are also found only in Japan or Ireland and several unique subspecies of mammals and birds *(photo by Tom W. Parkin/Pathfinder).*

Is comprise the bulk of the 9033 km² area. The islands are separated by 45-130 km of open water (HECATE STR) from the mainland islands, making the Charlottes among the most isolated islands in Canada. Also unique is the absence of a continental shelf off the steep western ramparts of Moresby I.

Archaeological evidence indicates that man has lived on the Charlottes for at least 6000 years. Juan PÉREZ was the first European to sight the islands (1774). They were visited by James COOK in 1778 and named by Capt James Dixon in 1787 after his ship the *Queen Charlotte.* At that time the HAIDA nation populated the islands and probably numbered over 6000. Since then white man's diseases drastically lowered the Haida to about 588 individuals in 1915, the most dramatic drop for any tribe recorded in the province. The present population of all peoples on the Charlottes totals about 5700. Until recently, most people were loggers (huge spruce and cedar), fishermen (salmon and groundfish) or miners (iron and gold) in the towns of Masset, Port Clements, Skidegate, Queen Charlotte, Sandspit and Tasu. Today geologists, biologists and recreationists come to study and enjoy the rugged mountain scenery (peaks up to 1200 m) along the western backbone of the islands, spectacular fjords, seabird and sea lion colonies, dark giant Sitka spruce and cedar forests, and remnants of decaying Haida TOTEM POLES.

Recently, geologists have documented that the Charlottes were formed by the movement of huge plates under the Pacific Ocean from the region of the South Pacific to their present location. Biologists have determined that, unlike most of Canada, much of the Charlottes escaped glaciation. This, coupled with the islands' isolation, has resulted in the Charlottes becoming a biologically unique area in Canada. There are numerous plants here found either only on the Charlottes or in distant lands such as Japan or Ireland. All the native land mammals and 3 kinds of birds are subspecifically unique, with the black bear being the largest in N America. The absence of some predators has permitted the Charlottes to become the home of almost half a million pairs of nesting seabirds.

The old Haida village of Ninstints, on Skungwai I, has been made a World Heritage Site of UNESCO. Its spectacular totem poles are now being protected from the elements as part of a collection of world treasures. All these natural features are attracting tourists in swelling numbers. Naikoon Provincial Park has vast beaches and huge bogs for hikers. The S Moresby area, with its outstanding totem poles, marine life, hot springs, forests and mountain scenery, is unrivalled in Canada as a place to explore by water.   BRISTOL FOSTER

Queen Elizabeth Islands, NWT, group of islands in the Canadian ARCTIC ARCHIPELAGO lying N of a great hydrographic trench composed of (E to W) LANCASTER SD, Barrow Str, Viscount Melville Sd and M'Clure Str. The islands form a triangle at the northern tip of Canada, with ELLESMERE I at the apex and DEVON, CORNWALLIS, BATHURST, MELVILLE and PRINCE PATRICK across the base. The islands are further grouped as the Parry Islands (Prince Patrick, Melville, MACKENZIE KING, Borden, Bathurst and Lougheed) and the Sverdrup Islands (ELLEF RINGNES, AMUND RINGNES, AXEL HEIBERG, CORNWALL and Meighen). The total area of land in the group (about 425 000 km²) is roughly equivalent to one of the Prairie provinces. About one-fifth of the land is covered with land ICE, with the largest mass on Ellesmere and concentrations on Devon and Axel Heiberg. Ice caps and glaciers cover a greater area than elsewhere in the North, owing to the cooler, shorter summers and the widespread uplands.

The islands consist of Cambrian to Upper Devonian rocks formed during the late Silurian period (*see* GEOLOGICAL HISTORY) and again in the late Devonian. As a result of intense folding and erosion the islands are characterized by folding mountains. In the eastern islands (Ellesmere, Axel Heiberg and Devon) remnants of the folds rise to 2600 m — the highest point in eastern N America lies in northern Ellesmere. Elsewhere the land is lower, much of it formed of horizontally embedded sediments, or peneplains. Spectacular cliffs rise above Lancaster Sd on Devon I. Melville I is largely formed of an erosion platform of folded rocks, although the Raglan Range in the NW approaches 915 m. The islands along the NW margin generally lie below the 150 m contour.

The islands have long been known and occupied by INUIT. Their European discovery may be attributed to William BAFFIN, who sailed the coasts of Baffin Bay in 1616. However, they were not rediscovered until 1818, when John Ross confirmed their existence. In 1819 Parry sailed to Melville I, naming Devon, Cornwallis, Bathurst and Byam Martin. The exploration of the islands at the turn of the century in effect completed the geographical discovery of N America. From 1898 to 1902 a Norwegian expedition led by Otto SVERDRUP surveyed the N coast of Devon, S and W coasts of Ellesmere, Axel Heiberg, King Christian and the Ringnes islands. In 1916-17 Vilhjalmur STEFANSSON found Brock, Borden and Meighen islands. The islands remain remote and, except for weather and research stations, uninhabited. It is known that there is oil and gas in the area, primarily in the Sverdrup Basin. The islands were named in 1953 for Queen Elizabeth II.   JAMES MARSH

Reading: M. Zaslow, ed, *A Century of Canada's Arctic Islands* (1981).

Queen Elizabeth Way, connecting Toronto with Niagara Falls and Fort Erie, Ont, was Canada's first 4-lane, controlled-access superhighway. Using the latest concepts in streamlined design, the highway was built to overcome local traffic bottlenecks and to open the province to US motorists entering via the Peace Bridge at Fort Erie. Construction began in the early 1930s on the Toronto-Burlington section, first called the Middle Road. The highway was officially opened by Queen Elizabeth, queen consort of King George VI, at St Catharines, 7 June 1939. Four lanes of pavement were completed to Fort Erie in 1956.   ROBERT M. STAMP

Queen's Counsel (QC), title conferred on lawyers by the CROWN; also King's Council (KC) when the sovereign is a king. Originally awarded to those considered worthy to argue cases for the Crown, in many provinces it has lost its distinction, being awarded to most practitioners of generally 10 years or more standing who conform politically to the government in office. The title can be conferred by either the provinces or the federal government. Duties no longer attach to the rank, which entitles holders to seniority within the profession and to wear a silk BARRISTER gown.   K.G. McSHANE

Queen's Plate, a stakes race for thoroughbred horses, was first run on 27 June 1860. It was given royal assent by Queen Victoria in 1859. In 1918 and 1919, to retain its perpetuity during WWI, the 59th and 60th runnings were staged as features of a Red Cross Horse Show in Toronto, the only racing held those 2 years. Thus, it is the oldest uninterrupted stakes race on the continent. (The Kentucky Derby's inaugural was held 1875.)

Politicians lobbied to hold the race in their constituencies in the early years. It was raced in Ontario at Toronto, Guelph, St Catharines, Whitby, Kingston, Barrie, Woodstock, Picton, London, Hamilton and Ottawa before it settled permanently, with the Queen's approval, in Toronto in 1883. In its early years the race's atmosphere resembled that of a country-fair meet. Two or 3 heats, or trials, were run to select a winner. It was claimed that the race attracted a "rowdy" crowd, and there were charges of fixed races.

The race was called the Queen's Plate until 1902, the year after Victoria's death, when it became the King's Plate (after Edward VII). It

reverted to the former name upon the ascension of Elizabeth II in 1952. George VI (with his queen consort Elizabeth) was the first reigning monarch to attend the race, at Woodbine racetrack, Toronto, in 1939. Elizabeth II and Prince Philip attended the 100th running in 1959. The race was confined to Ontario-bred horses until 1944, when it was opened to 3-year-olds foaled in Canada. The race's distance varied from a mile to 2 miles until 1957, when it was fixed at a mile and a quarter. At that distance, the race record is 2:02, set in 1960 by E.P. TAYLOR'S Victoria Park. The renowned NORTHERN DANCER, a Kentucky Derby and Preakness winner, and the world's leading sire in 1982, won in 2:02:1 in 1964.

Plate winners earn a gift of 50 guineas from the monarch. But the little purple bag of coins contains not guineas but sovereigns. Minting of guineas was discontinued by George III, whose forebear, George I, instituted the royal gift of 50 guineas for thoroughbred race winners, a tradition that remains today.

Queen's Quarterly, fd 1893 at Queen's U, largely on the initiative of Queen's president, G.M. GRANT, is the oldest of Canadian scholarly journals. At first contributors were chosen mainly from the Queen's faculty, but in 1928 it became open to national and even international contributors. It also began to publish fiction and poetry. In the 1930s the stories of F.P. GROVE appeared in its pages, and the *Quarterly* launched Sinclair ROSS as a writer. Its real flowering began in the 1950s during the brief editorship of Malcolm ROSS, who actively sought to bring the *Quarterly* into contact with the current growth in Canadian writing. Since that time the work of many of Canada's best writers has appeared in its pages, including that of fiction writers Rudy WIEBE, Sheila WATSON, W.P. Kinsella, Hugh HOOD and John METCALF, and that of poets Margaret ATWOOD, Irving LAYTON, Al PURDY, George BOWERING, John GLASSCO, F.R. SCOTT, A.J.M. SMITH and Tom Wayman. The *Quarterly* has continued to publish scholarly articles in many disciplines and has maintained an extensive section of book reviews.   GEORGE WOODCOCK

Queen's University, Kingston, Ont, was founded 1841. Queen's today is a nondenominational and coeducational university with students from all parts of Canada, the US and some 60 other countries. Nine out of 10 Queen's students live away from home; thus, most "live Queen's" 24 hours a day. This commitment no doubt contributes to the strong loyalty of graduates and students — the famous Queen's spirit.

Queen's has 13 faculties and schools ranging in age from the original faculty of arts and science (est 1842), to the faculty of industrial relations (1983). The affiliated Queen's Theological College prepares students for the UNITED CHURCH ministry. Queen's is also a major research university in almost every aspect of health sciences, engineering, basic sciences, humanities and social sciences. It has centres and institutes devoted to transportation, resource development and intergovernmental relations. It is the home of the government- and industry-supported Canadian Microelectronics Corporation. Facilities on campus include one of Canada's finest university libraries. Queen's Archives houses one of the most notable and widely used nongovernmental collections of Canadian historical materials in the country.

Queen's roots run deep in the history and life of Canada. It is located in one of Canada's historic cities, and modern buildings blend with old limestone buildings to provide a distinctive campus. "Cha Gheill" (a Gaelic battle cry which is part of the school song), freshmen tams and tartans, and a small theological college are the only apparent reminders of Queen's College, established by the PRESBYTERIAN Church of Canada in association with the Church of Scotland "on the old Ontario strand" in 1841. On Oct 16 Queen's received a royal charter from Queen Victoria, for whom the new college was named. Classes began on 7 Mar 1842 in a rented building with 2 professors and 10 students. It was intended primarily as a college to train young men for the ministry, but denominational ties progressively diminished. In 1912 Parliament, by amending the charter, completed the separation of church and university. Thus the college became Queen's University at Kingston, an independent institution controlled primarily by its graduates who, through the years, have conscientiously honoured their convocation pledges "to maintain a generous loyalty to the university."

Queenston, Ont, a quiet residential village in the town of NIAGARA-ON-THE-LAKE. Founded at the N end of the Niagara portage in the 1780s, and named for the Queen's Rangers stationed there, the village prospered on trade and a ferry crossing to Lewiston, NY — an important route of pioneer immigration. The house in which Laura SECORD overheard American troops planning to attack has been restored as a pioneer museum. Brock's Monument (1853) commemorates the British victory over American invaders at the Queenston Heights (1812); beneath it lies the tomb of Gen Sir Isaac BROCK. To the S are the 2 massive Sir Adam Beck generating stations. *See* NIAGARA HISTORIC FRONTIER.   JOHN N. JACKSON

Quesnel, BC, City, pop 8240 (1981c; 10 000 1982e), inc 1928, is located at the junction of the Quesnel and Fraser rivers in central BC, 625 km NE of Vancouver. It takes its name from the river and lake (to the SE) named by explorer Simon FRASER after NWC clerk Jules Maurice Quesnel, his companion on his 1808 journey of discovery down the Fraser R. Settlement began in 1860 when the area became the best access into the Cariboo goldfields. For many years Quesnel was a steamboat landing for shipping to and from the goldrush town of BARKERVILLE to the E. The log HBC store, built in 1866, is still standing today. Farm settlement increased before WWI, and the Pacific Great Eastern Ry, now called the BCR, reached Quesnel in 1921, opening up the region's rich forest reserves. Forestry, mining and agriculture (mostly ranching) are the major industries today, with some oil and gas exploration. Quesnel is the gateway to Barkerville Historic Park and Bowron Lake Provincial Park.   JOHN R. STEWART

Quesnel, Louis-Joseph-Marie, merchant, composer, poet, playwright (b at Saint-Malo, France 15 Nov 1746; d at Montréal 3 July 1809). Canada's first opera composer arrived here quite by chance. While captain of a French vessel carrying munitions to the Americans in 1779, Quesnel was captured by the British and taken to Québec where Governor HALDIMAND granted him a safe conduct. He set up a fur-trading and wine-import business at Boucherville, near Montréal. Missing the sophisticated entertainments of France, Quesnel began to write and compose. Many poems and several plays survive intact, but from his musical remnants only the opera *Colas et Colinette*, first performed in Montréal in 1790, can be restored. Using the surviving vocal and second-violin parts, composer Godfrey RIDOUT reconstructed the opera in 1963. The charming period piece has been published, performed and recorded.   BARCLAY McMILLAN

Enrolment: Queen's University, 1982-83 (Source: Statistics Canada)			
Full-time Undergrad	Full-time Graduate	Part-time Undergrad	Part-time Graduate
9 752	1 590*	3 192	481

* Includes medical interns and residents

Quévillon, Louis-Amable, woodworker, sculptor, architect (b at St-Vincent-de-Paul [Laval, Qué] 14 Oct 1749; d there 11 Mar 1823). He began his career as a woodworker in St-Vincent-de-Paul in the early 1770s. Working mainly in the Montréal region, he was hired by about 40 parishes to do carvings and decorate their churches with gilding, silvering and marbling. At the turn of the century he penetrated the market around Québec C where he worked in various churches. Throughout his career Quévillon trained apprentices, and his studio, which employed 14 sculptors, companion sculptors and apprentices in 1818, produced a great number of works, many of which have been lost to fire. An altarpiece remains in the church at Verchères and some of his church furniture is found in museums in Québec, Montréal and Ottawa. *See* SCULPTURE; RELIGIOUS BUILDING.

NICOLE CLOUTIER

Quiet Revolution (Révolution tranquille) was a period of rapid change experienced in Québec from 1960 to 1966. This vivid, yet paradoxical, expression was first used by an anonymous writer in the *Globe and Mail.* Although Québec was a highly industrialized, urban and relatively outward-looking society in 1960, the UNION NATIONALE Party, in power since 1944, seemed increasingly anachronistic as it held tenaciously to a conservative ideology and relentlessly defended outdated traditional values. In the election of 22 June 1960 the Liberals broke the hold of the Union Nationale, taking 51 seats and 51.5% of the popular vote as compared to the latter's 43 seats and 46.6% of the vote. Under Jean LESAGE the Québec Liberal Party had developed a coherent, wide-ranging reform platform. The main issue of the election was indicated by the Liberal slogan, "It's time for a change."

In 2 years the Lesage government managed to carry out or plan many reforms. Everything came under scrutiny, everything was discussed; a new age of open debate began. The government attacked political patronage and changed the electoral map to provide better representation for urban areas. To reduce the size of secret electoral funds, it limited authorized expenditures during election periods. It also lowered the voting age from 21 to 18. Lesage attempted to put the public purse in order by promoting a dynamic provincial budget and by raising loans. From 1960-61 to 1966-67, the budget grew from $745 million to $2.1 billion. The spectacular development of government institutions and the vastly increased role of the state in the province's economic, social and cultural life unleashed forces that would have major consequences.

The pressures exerted by the BABY BOOM generation, which had now reached adolescence, created a dramatic situation and pushed Québec's weak educational system to the breaking point. The government introduced new legislation on education and established a commission of inquiry on education, which was chaired by Mgr Alphonse-Marie Parent. The resulting Parent Report tackled the entire system. In recommending the creation of a department of education, it questioned the role of the Catholic Church, which controlled the public Catholic school system. The church resisted recommended changes, but without success. The Parent Report contributed significantly to creating a unified, democratic, modern school system accessible to the entire population.

The desire to modernize was also evident in the social sphere. Upon taking power, the government decided to participate in the federal-provincial hospital-insurance program. In 1964 it introduced 3 major pieces of legislation: an extensive revision of the labour code; Bill 16, which abolished a married woman's judicial handicap by which her legal status was that of a minor; and a pension plan.

The government's most spectacular accomplishment in economics was the nationalization of private electricity companies, an idea that was promoted in 1962 by René LÉVESQUE, minister of natural resources. The government decided to go to the electorate on this issue, and on 14 Nov 1962 the Liberals won again, with 56.6% of the vote and 63 seats. The many objectives of nationalization included standardizing rates across the province, co-ordinating investments in this key sector, integrating the system, encouraging industrialization, guaranteeing economic benefits for the Québec economy through a buy-Québec policy, and making the sector more French in nature. HYDRO-QUÉBEC not only met most of these objectives but became a symbol of success and a source of pride for Quebeckers. Another major success was the creation in 1965 of the CAISSE DE DÉPÔT ET PLACEMENT DU QUÉBEC. The caisse was made responsible for administering the assets of the QUÉBEC PENSION PLAN, which rapidly grew to several billion dollars.

The *maîtres chez nous* ("masters in our own house") philosophy that permeated the government and its reforms was bound to have an influence on FEDERAL-PROVINCIAL RELATIONS. The Lesage government demanded a review of federal policy and won a major victory following a stormy first ministers' conference in 1964. Lesage forced the federal government to accept Québec's withdrawal from several cost-sharing programs and to compensate Québec fiscally. The issue of special status arose when Québec was the only province to win acceptance of the right to withdraw. It was perhaps to calm the anxieties of English Canada and to show his good will that in 1964 Lesage agreed to the proposal for repatriating and amending the constitution by a method known as the Fulton-Favreau formula. However, because of the extreme reactions of various nationalist groups within the province, Lesage had to withdraw his support and to dissociate himself from the other 10 governments that had accepted the formula.

The Québec government also sought to stake out international rights. In 1961 it opened the Maisons du Québec in Paris, London and New York. However, when Québec signalled its intention to sign cultural and educational agreements with France, Ottawa intervened, asserting that there could be only one interlocutor with foreign countries.

These federal-provincial quarrels raised the question of the place of Québec and French Canadians in Confederation. In 1965, for instance, the Royal Commission on BILINGUALISM AND BICULTURALISM noted that "Canada, without being fully conscious of the fact, is passing through the greatest crisis in its history. The source of the crisis lies in the Province of Quebec." FRENCH CANADIAN NATIONALISM, which was becoming more and more Québécois in nature, was exacerbated by this crisis. The number of separatist groups increased; some of them adopted more extreme positions and the FRONT DE LIBÉRATION DU QUÉBEC began to indulge in TERRORISM. At the same time, other Francophones worried about this growth of nationalism. Among them were Jean MARCHAND, Gérard PELLETIER and Pierre Elliott TRUDEAU, who joined the federal Liberal Party and were elected to Parliament in 1965.

When the Québec Liberals again faced the electorate in 1966 they were confident of re-election. But the Union Nationale had renewed its image and attracted dissatisfied individuals among conservatives, nationalists and those who had voted CRÉDITISTE in the federal election. The party still had a solid base in the rural areas that were left largely untouched by the Quiet Revolution. On June 5 the Union Nationale won 56 seats against the Liberals' 50. However, the Liberals obtained 47% of the popular vote whereas the Unionistes, led by Daniel JOHNSON, obtained only 41%.

For 2 decades the Quiet Revolution has been the major reference point used by all Québec governments who have held power since the Liberal defeat in 1966, a fact which illustrates the importance of this episode in Québec's history.

RENÉ DUROCHER

Reading: R. Jones, *Community in Crisis* (1972); S.M. Trofimenkoff, *The Dream of Nation* (1983).

Quilico, Louis, baritone, teacher (b at Montréal 14 Jan 1925). Quilico studied in Rome (1947-48), returning to Montréal to study (1948-52) with Lina Pizzolongo whom he soon married. He completed his studies (1952-55) at Mannes College in New York. His professional stage debut (1954) in Canada was with the Opera Guild of Montréal and though he won the Metropolitan Opera Auditions of the Air, his New York debut in 1955 was with the New York City Opera. His first official appearance with the Metropolitan Opera did not take place until 1973. During his long and respected operatic career Quilico sang in major roles with most of the important operatic companies throughout Europe and N America. As a teacher at U of T since 1970, Quilico helped to develop several important young singers, including his son Gino. Quilico was awarded the 1965 Prix de musique Calixa-Lavallée and in 1975 he was made companion of the Order of Canada.

MABEL H. LAINE

Quill & Quire is a magazine of the Canadian book trade. It is read chiefly by publishers, booksellers, librarians, writers and educators. Founded by the Seccombe family in 1935, it was a monthly magazine serving stationers and booksellers. By 1971, the year in which the magazine was purchased by Michael de Pencier, president of Key Publishers, it had shifted its emphasis to the book trade alone. Since 1972 the magazine has grown in size and scope. Its regular features include a book-review section, spring and fall publishers' announcements, author profiles, industry statistics, and in-depth features on magazine and BOOK PUBLISHING, government policy, BOOKSELLING and librarianship. Its paid circulation is 7000. Twice annually, *Quill & Quire* issues the *Canadian Publishers Directory,* and in the fall it produces *Books for Everybody,* a gift catalogue for consumer distribution.

SUSAN WALKER

Quill Lakes, comprising 2 connected lakes, Big Quill and Little Quill, totalling 611 km², elev 152 m, are located 146 km N of REGINA and 152 km E of SASKATOON. Both lakes are fed by numerous small streams, creeks and lakes, and they drain in a southeasterly direction, via the meandering Whitesand R, eventually emptying into the ASSINIBOINE R. The lakes are shallow, and very salty owing to the mineral-laden streamflow into them. The resulting salt flats are a noticeable feature of the shoreline and restrict vegetation in the area to the hardiest shrubs. The lakes are named for the many feathers (quills) shed by the migrating birds that stop over here. The nearby Slovenian village of Quill Lake (est 1905) is on the CNR line.

DAVID EVANS

Quillwork included decorated buckskin clothing, birchbark boxes, pipestems, knife sheaths and medicine bags. The Indians had 4 methods of using dyed porcupine quills — sewing, weaving, wrapping, pushing into tiny bark perforations — though sewing was the most common method. Quills were moistened to make them pliable and flattened by drawing them between the teeth or over the thumbnail. Thin strips of sinew were used as thread. In the east, tanned hide was always used as the base and background on which designs, often floral, were traced. Among the western CREE, quills woven with sinew strands without a hide background

Eastern Ojibwa or Ottawa pouch made from tanned skin and decorated with porcupine quillwork, sewn with sinew (*courtesy National Museums of Canada / National Museum of Man*).

and then attached to the article were almost always of geometric design. *See* INDIAN ART.

RENÉ R. GADACZ

Quilt, bedcover consisting of 2 layers of cloth separated by a soft substance (eg, unwoven cotton or wool). To keep the filling from shifting, the 3 layers are tacked together, ie, tied with pieces of yarn or sewn, usually in a pattern, by running seams through all the layers. This tacking process is called quilting. This method of providing warm bedcovers has been used in Europe and northern Asia for centuries, and quilts were first made in Canada in the late 18th century when settlers from the UK and the US began to arrive.

There are 2 types of quilts: wholecloth, ie, the top layer consists of a single piece of cloth; and patchwork, either pieced or appliquéd. In a pieced quilt, the top consists of many small pieces or patches seamed together, edge to edge, which may or may not form a pattern; in an appliquéd quilt, small pieces of cloth are sewn onto a single large foundation cloth to form a

Contemporary stitched quilt (*courtesy Canadian Crafts Council / Elsie Blaschke*).

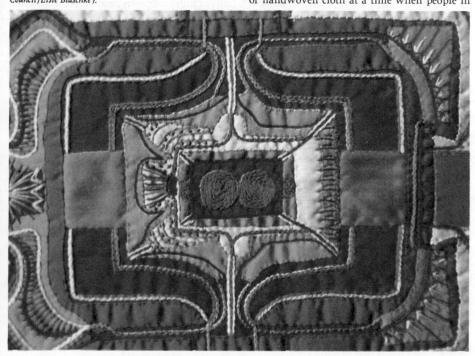

pattern. Both types may be made as an allover pattern or may be assembled in units (called blocks), which are then seamed together to form a whole.

Because pieced quilts required the least outlay of cloth, which was scarce and expensive in early Canada, this method was commonly used to make everyday quilts. Quilts made for special occasions (eg, marriage) were often of the appliquéd type and were passed from one generation to another. As a result, more appliquéd quilts have survived, although fewer were made. A woman might make many quilts in her lifetime, but often only her treasured, fancy marriage quilt survives. Quilts made for special uses were always made in traditional patterns, unlike everyday quilts, which tended to be truer expressions of the women of the period. Hence, everyday quilts include some of the finest and most interesting examples of art.

The art of making patchwork quilts achieved its zenith in N America. One reason for this development was the important part that quilt making (ie, the "quilting bee") played in Canadian social life in the 19th century. When a women had accumulated several quilt tops, she would invite a group of women to her house to help her quilt them. They would tack the bottom layer, the filling and the top layer onto a rectangular wooden frame, and several women working together did the quilting. In the evening, the men would join the women for a party, and girls would often meet their future husbands. Only one or 2 women worked on very finely quilted bedcovers because it was felt that too many workers created an unevenness in the stitching. Very fine, even stitching is a skill achieved by practice, the result of a woman's learning to sew as a child and sewing every day of her life. A young woman was expected to have made 12 everyday quilts for her marriage. After she became engaged, she would prepare a fancy quilt to be used on her marriage bed.

Warm bedding was very important in Canada because of the severe winters. Scraps of worn clothing and blankets were used to make the first patchwork quilts. Because of the scarcity of cloth, the early establishment of a home clothmaking industry was of prime importance. This process involved clearing land to grow flax for linen and acquiring sheep for wool.

Thus women in Canada began to make quilts of handwoven cloth at a time when people in

other countries were discontinuing its use. Hence a distinctive Canadian quilt developed, the patchwork woolen quilt made in both simple and elaborate patterns. The designs were strong and simple, making use of diamonds, triangles, rectangles and squares. The cloth was usually home dyed with vegetable dyes.

The 2 main influences affecting Canadian quilt styles were the American and the European. Settlers coming from the US during the late 18th and early 19th centuries brought with them the distinctive styles that had been developed in that country during the first hundred or more years of settlement. At the same time, immigrants from England, Ireland and Scotland brought their own styles, ones that had not changed much during the previous century. A quilt showing British influence often consists of an embroidered or appliquéd square, surrounded by borders of patchwork. Women coming to Canada from middle-European countries lacked a strong tradition of making quilts but were accustomed to making woven bedcovers. Because of Canada's climate, greater warmth was necessary and was achieved by making whole cloth quilts of handwoven, unused material, often with a woven pattern of checks or stripes. Women in Québec did not make quilts until a late date, when quilts became popular elsewhere. Frequently, they continued to use English names for their patterns.

The women of the 19th century lived in a world in which the seasons and cycles of life dominated their lives and the themes of the quilts reflect this fact. By the late 19th century, pattern books were circulated and, except in isolated communities, people began to follow patterns fashionable at the time. The old countries had long-established traditions of naming quilts; this practice resulted in descriptive names varying little from one area to another. In contrast, there was a tremendous exuberance in the naming of quilts in Canada. Quilt names vary a great deal from region to region, and the new ones sometimes have little relation to the old. Many names reflect rural humour at its best: Old Maid's Ramble, Toad in the Puddle, Swallow on the Path, Duck's Foot in the Mud, Corn and Beans, Hole in the Barn Door.

By 1930 the tradition of making quilts as part of the daily routine had come to an end, except in a few rural areas. Around the middle of the 20th century there was a revival of interest in making quilts for use as decorative bedspreads rather than as utilitarian bedcovers. These large quilts, made of springy materials, look quite different from the old ones. Modern women interested in maintaining the old tradition of quilt making have formed quilting guilds in urban areas. Although bedding was a daily chore, most women took the trouble to make their quilts aesthetically pleasing. Women of artistic sensibilities found such creativity stimulating, and it was one of the few ways in which a woman in the 19th century could express herself.

RUTH McKENDRY

Quimper, Manuel, naval office, explorer (fl 1790). At the outbreak of the NOOTKA SOUND CONTROVERSY Quimper and 6 other young naval lieutenants were transferred from Europe to bolster Spain's Pacific strength. In 1790 he commanded the captured British vessel *Princess Royal* during the expedition to reoccupy Nootka Sound. In June he was ordered to explore and trade in Juan de Fuca Str. Quimper visited Chief WICKANANISH at Clayoquot Sound and then explored harbours and bays around present-day Victoria. Later he crossed the strait to explore Puerto Nuñez Gaona (Neah Bay), which became the second Spanish post on the Northwest Coast. In 1791 Quimper sailed the *Princess Royal* to Hawaii and the Philippines to return the vessel to its British owners.

CHRISTON I. ARCHER

R v Coffin In the summer of 1953 the bodies of 3 American hunters were found in a Gaspé forest. Wilbert Coffin, a local prospector, was charged with and convicted of the murder of one of them, Richard Lindsay. Almost from the beginning, the case was controversial; it was charged that Coffin had not received a fair trial and that the Québec government had applied pressure on police and crown prosecutors to obtain an immediate conviction because of concern over possible loss of American tourist trade. Largely because of public concern, the federal Cabinet ordered a special reference to the SUPREME COURT OF CANADA, which upheld Coffin's conviction. He was hanged on 10 Feb 1956.

Notwithstanding the Supreme Court's ruling, the controversy did not diminish and various books continued to claim that Coffin was innocent and had been the victim of unprofessional conduct by police and prosecutors. The Québec government appointed a royal commission in 1964 (the Brossard Committee) to investigate the accusations. The commission report concluded there was no evidence of wrongdoing on the part of the prosecutors or police officers and that Coffin had received a fair trial.

To lawyers the Coffin case is an important decision on evidence dealing with rules relating to hearsay evidence, leading questions and contradiction of one's own witness, but the Coffin case is important as well in any debate over CAPITAL PUNISHMENT, in which it is inevitably cited in support of the argument for abolition.
A. PRINGLE

R v Olson In the summer of 1982, Clifford Robert Olson was arrested for the murder of 11 children. He entered guilty pleas to the charges of murder, but it was later revealed that the attorney-general of BC had agreed to a proposal by Olson that $100 000 be held in trust for Olson's wife and infant son in return for Olson's help in finding 6 missing bodies and providing information on 4 bodies already discovered. Reports of the deal sparked bitter controversy across the country over the ethics of a criminal benefiting from his crimes and over police payment for information. The debate raised questions about the propriety of deals made with any criminal, including payment for information and withdrawal of charges in return for information or evidence. It has been argued that such inducements could lead to the creation of "professional witnesses" who are involved in crimes and yet benefit from them. Although the SUPREME COURT OF CANADA held in *R v Wray* (1970) that payment for evidence was legal, there has been a growing demand for attorneys-general to establish ethical guidelines for such payment. The case may establish a CIVIL LAW precedent, because the families of the victims have successfully pursued actions against Olson, his wife and the lawyer administering the trust fund for compensation for the deaths of the children. An appeal has been filed against that decision which might result in having this issue eventually determined by the Supreme Court of Canada.
A. PRINGLE

R v Truscott In 1959, 14-year-old Steven Truscott was convicted in adult court of the murder of 12-year-old Lynn Harper. Few cases in Canadian legal history have created so much controversy. In the book *The Trial of Steven Truscott* (1966), Isabel LeBourdais strongly asserted that Truscott was innocent. Citing inconsistencies in the evidence and what she believed was questionable medical testimony, LeBourdais suggested that the evidence did not support a conviction and that the emotions surrounding the case precluded the possibility that Truscott could receive a fair trial. Because of public interest in the case, in 1967 Parliament took the unusual step of referring the case to the SUPREME COURT OF CANADA for a further review. The court upheld

the conviction, but nevertheless the controversy surrounding the case remains. After serving 10 years of a life sentence, Truscott was released on parole, still asserting his innocence. The case sparked discussion of the law governing juvenile offenders, of CAPITAL PUNISHMENT and of methods of presenting evidence to a jury.
A. PRINGLE

Rabbit, common name for some MAMMALS of order Lagomorpha. The young, born in fur-lined nests, are naked, blind and helpless in contrast to the well-developed young of HARES. Gestation lasts 26-30 days, with 2-7 young per litter and, usually, 3-4 litters per year. Young are nursed for 16-22 days and leave the nest after about 2 weeks. Family units are often formed, lasting up to 7 weeks. Females frequently mate within 2-3 days after the birth of a litter, while still nursing. Female rabbits are usually larger than males. In Canada, both native rabbits belong to genus *Sylvilagus*. The eastern cottontail (*S. floridanus*), found in southern Ont, Qué and Man (introduced to BC), is small (average weight 1.2 kg) and is active at dawn, dusk and night. Nuttall's cottontail (*S. nuttalli*) is found in parts of BC, Alta and Sask. This smaller, paler version of eastern cottontail inhabits arid sagebrush areas. Both species form important links in the food chain and are often hunted for food and sport by man. The common or Old World rabbit (*Oryctolagus cuniculus*), the ancestor of our domestic rabbit, has proved valuable in many ways, eg, for food, for laboratory research and as pets. Some local, wild populations exist in various parts of the country, but these are largely released domesticated rabbits rather than true Old World rabbits.
M.L. WESTON

Rabbit Farming in Canada is not the highly organized, market-oriented industry typified by the POULTRY, HOG or BEEF sectors. Originally, N American rabbit production was developed to supply felt-hat manufacturers; meat production was secondary. With the changing population base after WWII, the demand for rabbit meat has been increasing in Canada. Rabbit farms may specialize in meat production, fancier or breeding stock production or research animal production. Statistics Canada does not record rabbit meat production; volume varies because of the volatile nature of the industry and the influence of large foreign imports. Estimated annual consumption in Canada is 50 g per capita (in France, 5 kg). Fanciers or hobbyists account for a measurable amount of production and tend to remain in production regardless of financial returns. Production of rabbits for research establishments is conducted under contract and is the most profitable aspect of rabbit raising. Some provinces provide inspection services to maintain and certify standards of health for these rabbits.

Farm size varies but the average commercial production unit has 100-150 does. New Zealand White is the most popular breed, followed by Californian. Some attempts are made to capitalize on the body size of Flemish Giant; however, this breed generally has low reproduction performance.

Rabbits produce low-fat meat and have the best meat-to-bone ratio of any meat-producing animal except turkeys. The high labour input of rabbit-meat production, coupled with unsteady markets, allows only a small profit margin, even for efficient producers. Marketing is a serious industry problem. Large chain stores insist on a constant flow of product, a demand difficult to meet because of the high summer, low winter production. Limited killing facilities for rabbits often force long haulage of live animals for processing and encourage farm-gate marketing, which further disrupts supply. The future for rabbit-meat production is promising because rabbits consume a high forage diet and do not compete with humans for food. Furthermore, on a given amount of ALFALFA, a doe can produce almost 5 times as much meat as a beef cow. The industry will have to improve technology to reduce labour costs, develop effective disease-control measures, regulate supply and improve the quality of the hide for effective use.
JOHN R. HUNT

Rabinowitch, David, sculptor (b at Toronto 6 Mar 1943). Like his twin brother Royden RABINOWITCH, he first came to national attention as a member of the artistic community in London, Ont, around Greg CURNOE, celebrated in the National Gallery of Canada's exhibition, *The Heart of London* (1968). He has since produced one of the most challenging bodies of work in recent contemporary SCULPTURE. He shares minimalism's interest in exploring the demands made by sculpture within the space and time of its interaction with the viewer. His "Romanesque" sculptures, constructions of flat steel masses whose horizontal extension is counterpointed by vertical holes bored through each mass, present themselves as fields of perception in which the appearance of the sculpture depends on the position of the perceiver. A series of independent appearances follow one another as the viewer moves around the sculpture. It is as if the world dissolves into an irreconcilable, if related, succession of unique appearances. The possibility of unity is known because all the material facts of the sculpture are always present, but it is a product, not of experience, but of intellect or desire. Rabinowitch moved to New York in 1972 and has taught at Yale U 1974-75 and at Düsseldorf 1984.
ROALD NASGAARD

Rabinowitch, Royden, sculptor (b at Toronto 6 Mar 1943). One of Canada's truly original contributors to modern SCULPTURE, he began his career in London, Ont, during the 1960s (as did his twin brother David RABINOWITCH) and moved to New York in the 1970s. He has exhibited widely, especially in Europe. Although Rabinowitch's early work showed characteristics of minimalism, his sculpture is also a critique of it — as it is of most other nonfigurative sculpture (which he contends has been based on assumptions about space that are too mechanical, abstract and visual). Typical of his style is the group of works titled "Handed, Limited and Numbered Manifolds" — low, ground-hugging constructions, each composed of a single polygonal steel plate bent to form a series of angled planes (the manifold), on top of which, aligned with the edges, are other steel plates (the limits) on the right or left, depending on whether the individual sculptures are left- or right-handed. Although purely abstract, the sculptures evince the principal properties of the human body that apply to its orientation in space.
ROALD NASGAARD

Raccoon (*Procyon lotor*), only Canadian member of the Procyonidae (a primarily tropical New World family of carnivores). Raccoons are distinguished by their black facial mask and ringed tail, and vary from almost black to light brown. They weigh 5-12 kg (maximum 22-26 kg). Raccoons are found in northern Alta, southern BC and Sask, central Man and Ont, southern Qué and the Maritimes. Raccoons have a nest only when nursing young. Breeding begins at one year. Usually 3 kits are born, in Mar-May after 63-65 days gestation. Young become independent in autumn. Raccoons are omnivorous, and manipulate but do not wash their food. They have sensitive hands used in foraging, eg, in capturing crayfish, etc. They may foul their nest when adult. They are agile climbers and strong but reluctant swimmers. Raccoons can whistle, shriek, chatter, click their teeth, snarl, growl and make other sounds. They coexist with man in urban areas and, with sufficient food, will remain active all winter. Young raccoons make good pets but become independent and antisocial when mature. Their pelts were used to make overcoats. Their flesh is edible if the scent glands are removed. C.S. CHURCHER

Raccoon (*Procyon lotor*) (artwork by Claire Tremblay).

Racism The disagreement among scholars over the meaning of "race" does not extend to its derivative, racism; there is virtual agreement that racism refers to the doctrine that some races are innately superior or inferior to others. Because racism indiscriminately includes groupings such as religious sects, linguistic groups and cultural groups under its concept of "race" it can be regarded as a virulent form of ethnocentrism (the belief that one's own ethnic group is superior to others). Racism is based upon the assumption that organic, genetically transmitted differences between human groups are intrinsically related to the presence or absence of certain social, psychological or cultural traits of that group. It is also predicated on the false assumption that human beings are naturally and permanently comprised of separate, pure races (eg, mongoloid, caucasoid), and that the physical, mental and cultural qualities of each group are determined by its supposed genetic constitution.

Individual racism is a belief by one individual about another person's "racial" inferiority. Institutional racism exists when the political, economic and social institutions of a society operate to the detriment of a specific individual or group in a society because of their alleged genetic makeup. Cultural racism is the expression of the superiority of a socially defined race's culture over that of another race.

Racism does not derive from the fact that races or groups of individuals in a society are different, but from the social meaning attributed to these differences by society. It is not a study of race or of the present inequality of certain groups in society, but is an assertion that inequality is absolute and unconditional.

Racism as we know it originated in the 16th and 17th centuries with the spread of capitalism and later social Darwinism. Racism is also a formal doctrine whose contemporary intellectual notions are derived from the 1853 *Essai sur l'inégalité des races humaines* by Joseph Arthur, Comte de Gobineau. In the 20th century this doctrine was promoted by H.S. Chamberlain, the English-born German publicist. Racism in Canada from 1800 to 1945 was reflected in restrictive IMMIGRATION POLICIES and practices regarding nonwhite immigrants, particularly the CHINESE, BLACKS and JEWS, and by the treatment of native peoples. Today certain groups, eg, the KU KLUX KLAN and the Western Guard promulgate racist beliefs in various parts of the country.

Over the past 20 years the federal and provincial governments have implemented legislation to combat racism, eg, the creation of Human Rights Commissions, and the positions of ombudsman and commissioner of official languages. *See also* PREJUDICE AND DISCRIMINATION. J.S. FRIDERES

Reading: H.D. Hughes and E. Kallen, *The Anatomy of Racism: Canadian Dimensions* (1974).

Racoon, 26-gun British sloop of war sent to seize Astoria, the American PACIFIC FUR COMPANY post at the Columbia R mouth, and to establish an outpost there during the WAR OF 1812. When the vessel, under Capt William Black, arrived 30 Nov 1813, Astoria had already been purchased by Nor'Westers led by John George McTavish. On Dec 13, Black claimed the country for King George III, naming the post Ft George. The TREATY OF GHENT provided for a return to the *status quo ante bellum;* since Black had claimed the territory as a conquest of war, Astoria was returned to the US. The voyage of the *Racoon* constituted official government support for Canadian FUR-TRADE interests and initiated co-operation between fur traders and the Royal Navy on the NORTHWEST COAST. J.W. SHELEST

Racquetball, one of the newest and most popular sports in N America today, is played indoors on a 4-wall court 20 ft (6 m) wide, 40 ft (12 m) long and 20 ft high. The 2½ in (6.35 cm) rubber ball must be returned to the front wall before it bounces twice, and floor, ceiling and walls are in play. Only 50 000 people played in 1970, whereas nearly 3 million participants were claimed by the mid-1970s. The game probably derived from paddleball, invented in the 1930s and transformed by a Connecticut squash professional into "paddle-racquets," in which a short-handled, gut-string racquet is used. The first National Paddle Racquets Tournament (1968) attracted the attention of media and businessmen, and within a year the International Racquetball Assn was formed.

The Canadian Racquetball Assn was incorporated in 1971, and considerable growth has occurred, particularly in the western provinces. Edmonton has been described as "North America's Racquetball City" and the U of A has hosted many championships. Private clubs now exist in several cities, as do racquetball facilities in colleges and YMCAs. Two landmarks in 1976/77 were a grant for racquetball from Sport Canada, and grants-in-aid to 2 racquetballers from the federal government. Some Canadian players, such as Wayne Bowes and Lindsay Myers, have competed with success in the US, where there is a lucrative professional circuit, and similar opportunities are still developing for this fitness-inducing sport in Canada. GERALD REDMOND

Radar (*radio detection and ranging*), device that obtains information about an object of interest (eg, its distance, position) by emitting an electronic signal and observing the echo returned from the object. The key elements of radar systems are the transmitter, receiver and data-processing unit. Radars use radio-frequency transmissions, first described theoretically by J.C. Maxwell in 1864. Radio waves are part of the electromagnetic spectrum, as is visible light. H.R. Hertz provided practical demonstration of Maxwell's theory and, in 1888, actually performed radio-wave-reflection experiments. In 1900 Nikola Tesla suggested that moving targets should be observable through radio-frequency shifts (predicted by C.J. Doppler in 1842 for waves in general). The first patent for a rudimentary radar was issued in Germany in 1904. It required the threat of WWII to motivate real progress. In 1934 Robert Watson-Watt proposed to the British goverment the principle of aircraft detection by ground-based pulsed radar. By spring 1935 an experimental system had proved successful, leading to construction of the British Home Chain. Five stations facing Europe were operational in 1938. The system is credited with making the decisive difference in the Battle of Britain.

Development of radar exploded during WWII, aided by high-level technical exchange agreements among the Allies. Scientists at the NATIONAL RESEARCH COUNCIL OF CANADA participated, and A.E. COVINGTON in 1946 used surplus radar research equipment to construct Canada's first radio telescope (*see* OBSERVATORY). The range and sensitivity of radars were constantly improved and smaller units were built for shipborne and airborne use. In 1935 radars worked at wavelengths of 25 m; by 1940, at 10 cm, thus initiating microwave radar. The critical development was that of the cavity magnetron by John T. Randal and Henry A. Boot of Birmingham U (1939-41). The device was capable of generating microwave pulses at up to 500 kW and permitted construction of small but, for the time, very accurate radars. Development of radar by the Allies was considered classified information during WWII. Therefore, wavelengths received code names, still recognized today: L-band (25 cm), S-band (10 cm), C-band (5 cm), X-band (3 cm) and K-band (1 cm). Shorter waves are used by "millimetre radars."

Operation Radar devices emit energy within a beam shaped by the radiating antenna. The beam-limited radiated energy propagates in range at the speed of light. When it strikes an object, a small fraction of the energy is reflected back, to be received by the radar. The echo arrives at a time delay after transmission; delays are usually very short (for terrestrial radars) and are measured in microseconds. Since the speed of light is known, each microsecond (0.000001 second) of delay corresponds to 150 m in range. The ranging pulse must be short and powerful to detect reliably several small, closely spaced objects, such as aircraft in formation. These properties are specified by the range resolution (usually given in metres) and the sensitivity (usually given in m²); both factors are "better" for smaller numbers. A good radar may be described as "high resolution" because it is able to separate targets only a few metres apart.

Air-defence technician operating a radar set (*courtesy Canadian Forces*).

Types of Radars Today there are many radar systems, from the speed-measuring units used by police forces (costing a few thousand dollars each) to VRM, the Venus Radar Mapper (costing approximately $350 million). VRM, approved by NASA in 1983, is expected to yield a radar map of that planet, based on a SATELLITE system, by 1988. Military applications, especially surveillance, targeting, guidance, navigation and EARLY WARNING, are the most important uses. Canada and the US continue to co-operate in the area of ballistic missile defence. For example, BMEWS (Ballistic Missile Early Warning System) has major radar electronics and antennae sited in Canada's North, yet the system's data-processing centre is an underground control centre in Colorado, which has access to the information from many other systems, including AWACS (Airborne Warning and Control System). In the civilian area, the most important application is in air-traffic control. Ship navigation and maritime vessel traffic-management radars are essential for safe operations on Canada's waterways. Other applications include weather and storm-centre tracking, atmospheric sounding and radar ASTRONOMY.

Radar Remote Sensing Since 1976 Canada has developed a world-recognized reputation in certain radar techniques, taking a lead in the application of radar to observation and monitoring of vast areas. In addition to routine mapping of ice in the Arctic and North Atlantic by airborne radar, Canada benefited from the US Seasat, an experimental satellite (July-Oct 1978) that carried the first imaging radar into Earth orbit. This was an L-band, high-resolution system, capable of sweeping out a continuous image 100 km wide. The instrument was a synthetic-aperture radar (SAR), the operating principles of which are closely related to holography. The data could be processed optically from the image. Canada developed the first digital processor for such data; MacDonald, Dettwiler and Associates of Vancouver published the first image in Nov 1978. This technology continues to set the world standard. Airborne and spaceborne SAR radar technologies are areas of active development in Canada and promise to contribute to RESOURCE MANAGEMENT. *See* SONAR.   R.K. RANEY

Raddall, Thomas Head, historical novelist (b at Hythe, Eng 13 Nov 1903). Raddall was brought as a boy to Nova Scotia, the province about which he was to write in a score of books, fictional and non-fictional. In an age of public appetite for magazine fiction, Raddall first made his name as a short story writer; his debut collection, *The Pied Piper of Dipper Creek and Other Tales* (1939), won his first Gov Gen's Award (1943). But larger renown awaited him as a historical novelist, particularly with *His Majesty's Yankees* (1942) and *The Governor's Lady* (1960). Yet his most highly regarded book was not historical but drew on his own experiences as a Sable Island radio operator after WWI: *The Nymph and the Lamp* (1950). His history, *Halifax, Warden of the North* (1948, Gov Gen's Award), has remained the most popular of his non-fictional books. His autobiography, *In My Time* (1976), reflects the agonizingly slow development of Canadian literary life since the 1920s.   DOUG FETHERLING

Radio Broadcasting, *see* BROADCASTING.

Radio Drama, English-Language The production of radio dramas in Canada began in 1925 when the Canadian National Railways Radio Dept began broadcasting plays. The national broadcasting networks, CNR, CRBC and CBC, have been in the forefront of radio-drama production and experiment, and have provided audiences and training for many Canadian theatre professionals.

The radio play shares the usual dramatic qualities of drama on the stage and in films and television, with this primary difference: the absence of the traditional visual resources of drama. Reliance on sound alone to communicate has forced the creators of radio drama to refine the available sound techniques: voice, music, sound effects and the control and mixing of sounds. Canadian radio drama has been in the vanguard of these developments, achieving flexibility in the representation of scenes and scene transitions, original music and depiction of character.

The first regular drama series in Canada was the CNR Drama Dept's "CNRV Players," produced from Vancouver by Jack Gillmore 1927-32. The productions included Shakespeare, adaptations from American and European plays and from fiction, and some original Vancouver dramas. The first national series of Canadian radio plays was the "Romance of Canada," 24 plays based on Canadian history, written by Merrill DENISON and produced in 1931-32 in CN Radio's Montréal studios. Tyrone Guthrie directed the first 14 plays, and Rupert Caplan and Esmie Moonie produced the second season. Another pioneer radio-drama series, the "CKUA Players," was produced by Sheila Marryat throughout the 1930s from CKUA, the station of U of Alberta, over a network of western stations.

The CN Radio network was nationalized in 1932 and became the Canadian Radio Broadcasting Commission (*see* BROADCASTING, RADIO AND TELEVISION). In 4 years the CRBC increased the number of weekly national-network radio-drama series to 17, under its program director Ernest BUSHNELL. Rupert Caplan's "Radio Theatre Guild" was the best-known national drama series, including original Canadian, American and European plays. Popular too were Don Henshaw's "Forgotten Footsteps" and the serial "Youngbloods of Beaver Bend." In Nov 1936 the CRBC was reorganized as the CANADIAN BROADCASTING CORPORATION. Its first supervisor of drama, Rupert Lucas, continued the development of drama offerings: Shakespeare and the classics, adaptations from fiction, documentaries and original radio plays. He established regional weekly drama series in Winnipeg, Toronto, Montréal and Vancouver. With the beginning of WWII the CBC Drama Dept series became important instruments of war education and publicity, and the project of centralizing prestige radio drama was begun.

With the appointment of Andrew ALLAN in 1943 as national drama supervisor, the golden age of Canadian radio drama began, with productions of original Canadian plays challenging the previous domination of theatre by British and American professionals. In Jan 1944 Allan introduced a new national play-anthology series, the weekly "Stage" series from Toronto. With its balanced mix of ambitious original Canadian plays and the best of the classical and modern American and European dramas, "Stage" attracted large national audiences. It became in effect our national professional theatre, setting the pace for the regional CBC drama series, completed by the Halifax series in 1947.

That same year another CBC national drama series was established in Toronto, "CBC Wednesday Night," which included international plays and some original Canadian dramas. Four senior drama producers shared its direction: Andrew Allan, Rupert Caplan, Esse W. Ljungh and J. Frank Willis.

This CBC network of major national and regional drama series was the primary showcase for the best of Canadian and world drama, as well as a training ground for many Canadian theatre professionals. Among the well-known writers for the national series were Fletcher Markle, Len Peterson, Joseph SCHULL, Mac Shoub, Lister Sinclair, Gerald Noxon, Alan King, Mavor MOORE, Hugh Kemp and W.O. MITCHELL. In the period 1944 to 1961 an estimated 6000 plays were produced in over 100 CBC series across the country; more than half of them were Canadian originals.

CBC television, with its own drama series, arrived in 1952, and began to wean audiences away from radio drama (*see* TELEVISION DRAMA). The growth of the legitimate stage in the 1950s in Canada had a similar effect, especially the STRATFORD FESTIVAL, which many CBC drama professionals helped to establish. The pace of CBC drama production did not slacken, however, until the mid-1960s. The second-generation CBC producers, notably John Reeves and Gerald Newman, began new experiments in radio-drama forms and techniques. "Stage" and "Wednesday (later "Tuesday") Night" continued well into the 1970s, and radio-drama production from all regions has continued to the present.

Things have come full circle in the 1980s. Audiences in Canada and the US are rediscovering "talking radio," the radio of ideas and of drama. The CBC now produces an increasing number of drama series. "Audience" and "Celebration" are series reminiscent of "Wednesday Night," while the new flagship series of original Canadian plays is "Sunday Matinee." There is even a popular mystery-fantasy series, "Nightfall."

Few of the more than 3000 original Canadian radio plays have been published, though they represent the largest single group of Canadian dramas. The official script archives of CBC radio plays is the Centre for Broadcasting Studies, Concordia U, Montréal. Many sound versions of the broadcasts are at the National Film, Television and Sound Archives, Public Archives of Canada, Ottawa. Specialized script collections exist, notably at U of Calgary, McMaster, and the Manuscript Division, PAC. *See also* RADIO PROGRAMMING.   HOWARD FINK

Reading: A. Allan, *A Self Portrait* (1974); Howard Fink, *Canadian National Theatre on the Air, 1925-61, CBC-CRBC-CNR Radio Drama in English: A Descriptive Bibliography and Union List* (1983) and "North American Radio Drama," in *Radio Drama,* ed, Peter Lewis (1981); A. Weir, *The Struggle for National Broadcasting in Canada* (1965).

Radio Drama, French-Language Radio drama in Québec is of 2 kinds, *radioromans* (serials or "soap operas") and *radiothéâtre* (radio plays).

The radio serial took its form from the theatre and its structure and length from the novel. When radio came to Québec, theatre was still considered somewhat heretical and novels frivolous if not outright immoral (*see* THEATRE, ENGLISH-LANGUAGE; THEATRE, FRENCH-LANGUAGE). Moreover the French Canadian press had not published many indigenous serialized novels. The immediate success of the first broadcast serial, Alfred Rousseau's "L'Auberge des chercheurs d'or" (CKAC, Jan 1935-June 1938), inspired other writers and commissions. In 1937 Edouard Baudry launched "Rue principale" on CKAC, which ran for 22 years. Fall 1938, when 4 series went simultaneously on air, marked the beginning of the golden age, which lasted more than 20 years and created in Québec a phenomenon that was as much sociocultural as literary.

Between 1939 and 1960 there were 10-15 serials a day on Québec airwaves, averaging 3 hours daily, excluding comedy skits (more than 100) and episodic and historical dramas (120 and over 90, respectively). The accumulated repertoire of 71 radio serials equalled 260 000 typed pages, or several hundred printed volumes and almost 13 000 hours of programming. Some 30 Québec writers were involved in varying degrees with this radio genre 1935-65, including Paul Gury, responsible for 15 years of "Rue principale" and all 14 years of "Vies de femmes"; Aliette Brisset-Thibaudet, who for 11 years wrote the weekly half hour, "Ceux qu'on aime"; and Claude-Henri GRIGNON, who for 23 years supplied the daily half hour of "Un Homme et son péché." Though there were some translations or adaptations of American soap operas, more than 75% of the serials were original Québec works, most of them by young authors. Some, such as Roger LEMELIN's "La Famille Plouffe" or Grignon's "Un Homme et son péché," had been preceded by a published novel, but used the novel as a springboard for entirely new situations.

Three stations in particular, CKAC, CBF and CKVL, broadcast radio serials at prime time to hundreds of thousands of listeners. The daily scheduling of these serials, usually 15 minutes long, created a ritual of tuning in. The serial genre is limited in scope and remained stable over the years, a mixture of popular novels and romances. The tone was usually melodramatic, sometimes comic, occasionally lighthearted. The topics were rooted in the realist tradition and reflected Québec family mores. Jeered at by intellectuals, the genre was exploited until it was threadbare. Some serials, however, deserve inclusion in literary history, especially those of Robert Choquette ("Le Curé de village," "La Pension Velder," "Métropole") and of Henri DEYGLUN ("Les Secrets du docteur Morhange"). Television killed radio serials (*see* TELEVISION DRAMA). Their numbers began to decline in the late 1950s, and gradually they disappeared from Québec airwaves, despite a fleeting revival on CKVL in 1974.

Radio plays were not as popular in Québec as radio serials, but they played an important role in Québec cultural life. Chronologically, plays preceded the serials, since CKAC created the first program, "Le Théâtre de J.-O. Lambert," in Nov 1933. Radio plays took over from stage theatre, which had been hard hit by the Depression. In 35 years, 80 anthology series were broadcast on Québec AM stations, and provided a living for writers and actors. The genre increasingly detached itself from written theatrical tradition to exploit the different possibilities of the microphone. At first, authors adapted novels, short stories or works from repertory theatre ("Le Théâtre N.G. Valiquette," "Le Théâtre lux français," "L'Atelier"), a custom used throughout the history of radio plays, especially on CBF. Public radio broadcast 26 foreign-play series, including "Radio-Théâtre" (1939-40), "Le Théâtre classique français" (1940), "Théâtre" by Radio-Collège (1941-50), "Sur toutes les scènes du monde" (1953-70), "Théâtre populaire" (1950) and "Petit Théâtre" (1966-67). In addition, there were 10 programs, such as "Le Radiothéâtre de Radio-Canada," which presented both adaptations and original Québec plays. Many great works of international theatre, from the classics to the avant-garde, were mounted by talented producers. These adaptations were the first efforts of young authors like Marcel DUBÉ, Louis Pelland, Hubert AQUIN and Yves THÉRIAULT.

These original Québec radio dramas were a small part of the total amount of material broadcast, but they played an essential cultural role. They were a training ground for many young French Canadian playwrights and helped form a body of Québec theatrical works. More than 1500 radio plays may be listed, the work of more than 200 authors. Each week, for 20 years, at least one original Québec play was broadcast. In the 1950s up to 4 new works were aired each week. From 1930 to 1970, 44 original Québec series were presented on the province's AM stations. CKAC's first series was "Le Théâtre de chez nous," which was broadcast 1938-47 and in which Henri Letondal played a major part. Robert Choquette was the first important author to present a series of theatrical radio works (CRCM, 1934). CBF put its first Québec theatrical series on the air in 1944 ("Entrée des artistes"), followed by such programs as "L'Equipe aux quatre vents," "Les Voix du pays," and "Le Théâtre des nouveautés." The most important program, because of its experimental nature, was

"Les Nouveautés dramatiques," produced by Guy BEAULNE 1950-62, which launched many authors. Among the 58 who worked on it were Yves Thériault, Marcel Dubé, Louis-Georges Carrier, Marcel Cabay, François Moreau, Jacques GODBOUT, Jacques Languirand, Félix LECLERC and Robert Gadouas. More than 320 plays were presented in this series.

A wide variety of Québec plays was produced for radio, ranging from psychological to street theatre, via character comedies, social satire, melodrama and surrealism. Different types were given priority, depending on the era and the station, but they were almost always indigenous plays, raising Québec problems, using Québec language and destined for a Québec audience. It was definitely popular theatre, as the names of some of the series clearly show.

During the 1960s, plays, like the serials, deserted the AM airwaves. Since then drama has been found almost exclusively on television. The only remaining bastion of radio drama is the FM network of Radio-Canada, with such series as "Escales" and "Premières."

GÉRARD LAURENCE

Reading: R. Legris, *Robert Choquette: romancier et dramaturge de la radio-télévision* (1977); Legris and P. Pagé, "Le Théâtre à la radio et à la télévision au Québec," in *Archives des lettres canadiennes*, vol 5, *Le Théâtre canadien-français* (1976).

Radio Programming Radio has proven an extremely flexible medium. The technology of BROADCASTING enabled the radio producer to reach much larger audiences than was usually possible for the journalist. The reliance on sound alone liberated radio producers from many of the constraints that have restricted their counterparts in visual media. The costs of production are much lower. The expectations of the audience are not so demanding. The radio producer can experiment with an array of program types to activate the listener's imagination or engage his mind. Consequently, radio has played many roles in society to meet the changing needs of the public.

Over the past 60 years, radio programming has gone through 3 distinct stages. Radio shifted from being a novelty to becoming a mass medium between 1920 and 1940. During the 1920s, the small, low-power Canadian stations filled their abbreviated schedules with all manner of cheap, live productions: music, comedy, drama, education, preaching, news or poetry or story reading, nearly all of which was amateurish. Audiences preferred the more polished products of American radio and at the end of the decade, 80% of the programs listened to were American. In 1929, 2 stations in Montréal and Toronto became affiliates of American networks.

The solution seemed to lie in the organization of Canadian networks. The pioneers were commercial enterprises intent on self-promotion. By 1930 Canadian National Railways was offering a few hours a week of high-quality French and English programming on its own and independent stations across the country: symphony, chamber and folk music; original drama and operas; children's tales; grain price reports and even health talks. There were national broadcasts sponsored by Imperial Oil and the Canadian Pacific Railways. What killed these initiatives was the arrival in 1932 of public broadcasting, to which the government granted a monopoly of network broadcasting. The Canadian Radio Broadcasting Commission created the initial national service which was much expanded after 1936 by the new CANADIAN BROADCASTING CORPORATION. Indeed, the CBC organized separate French- and English-language networks using its own stations and private affiliates.

By the end of the 1930s listeners could already enjoy a wide range of programs. Much

American material was available because of the widespread use of recorded popular music and transcribed programs, because of the service of a few Canadian affiliates of American networks, and because of the CBC itself, which offered popular, sponsored American programs in the evening hours. American daytime soap operas such as "Ma Perkins" and "Big Sister," and evening comedy shows such as "Amos 'n' Andy" and "Fibber McGee & Molly" were enormously popular. Private radio broadcast much live programming in the form of big-band music from hotels, adult and children's drama, and talk or commentary shows. The CBC carried more and more national programs: hockey broadcasts, variety shows such as "The Happy Gang" from Toronto, dance-band programs like Mart Kenny's group from Vancouver, the farm family drama "The Craigs," and round tables and forums. Even so, public radio was still too novel to attract large and devoted audiences, except in Québec where the appeal of its French-language programming was enormous.

The war years changed the situation. Suddenly a vital instrument of propaganda, the CBC developed a balanced schedule of programs to inform, inspire and entertain the mass audience as well as more select publics. The first initiative was the creation of a special news department, which supplied eager listeners with bulletins and reports on the war effort abroad and at home. News was supplemented with talks and education: the famous "Citizen's Forum" and "Farm Forum," war-related mini-series such as "Let's Face the Facts" and "Arsenal of Democracy," and the French network's "Radio-Collège." Much effort was put into developing musical programming, such as "Les Joyeux Troubadors," "Victory Parade," and feature variety broadcasts studded with American stars for the assorted Victory Loan drives. The CBC's most memorable achievements, however, were in the field of RADIO DRAMA. Many series were linked to the war, such as the "Theatre of Freedom," "Fighting Navy," "L for Lanky" and "Soldier's Wife" (a soap opera sponsored by the Wartime Prices and Trade Board!). In a different vein was the "Stage" series of radio plays, many of them written by Canadian playwrights, begun by Andrew ALLAN in 1944 for discriminating listeners. In order to carry the wealth of Canadian and American entertainment, the CBC launched a second, evening-only network in English Canada, the "Dominion," to supplement the full-day "Trans-Canada" network.

The success of the war years had inaugurated the golden age of Canadian radio. Radio news and views were able to attract a huge cross section of listeners, much to the chagrin of NEWSPAPERS and MAGAZINES. Programs like "Les Idées en marche" probed topics which ranged from child discipline to price control, and from the St Lawrence Seaway to Canada's international policies. CBC broadcasts of serious music and opera made the networks renowned as the great sponsors of high culture. The many plays of producers like Allan, Esse W. Ljungh, Rupert Caplan and J. Frank Willis made the CBC a national theatre for English Canada. In 1947 the CBC began its grand experiment in highbrow radio, "CBC Wednesday Night": 3 noncommercial hours under the general direction of Harry Boyle which offered up opera, musicals, classical and original plays, even documentaries, and won enormous fame among the intellectual and artistic communities in Canada.

The networks, of course, were able to capture much larger audiences for their regular coverage of Canadian sports, notably HOCKEY, which bolstered one of the few Pan-Canadian sources of identity in the country. In French Canada the CBC produced some extraordinarily popular forms of light entertainment: serial drama (*see* RADIO DRAMA, FRENCH-LANGUAGE) like "Un homme et son péché" (which sometimes won an 80% share of the listening audience), programs specializing in the FOLK MUSIC and FOLK DANCE of Québec like "Soirée à Québec," and talent shows such as "Nos futures étoiles." Even in English Canada the CBC had some very popular variety and comedy shows, notably "The Happy Gang" and "The Wayne and Shuster Show." There were also specialized programs for minority audiences: the schools, the regions, women ("Lettre à une canadienne"), children ("Maggie Muggins"), farmers ("Le Choc des idées") and the religious minded ("National Sunday Evening Hour"). Between 1945 and 1955 the CBC was a central institution serving and nurturing many aspects of the country's culture.

Yet the CBC was only one among a number of sources of radio programming. A survey of one broadcast week in April 1949 showed that the radio scene boasted a range of different styles of programming because of the mix of CBC-owned outlets, privately owned network affiliates and 36 independents. The amount of British material broadcast was miniscule. Canadian-originated programs might be dominant throughout the broadcast day on the public outlets and in the evening hours on all but the independent stations; but Canadian listeners could enjoy American records and programs at any time, especially on private stations, making the US the single most important source of programming in English Canada. The top shows in the ratings were usually American. What was called "local live" programming — news, sports, entertainment, religion and talks — persisted, notably on the independent stations where over one-third of evening air time was devoted to such offerings. Yet imported popular music had become the most common program ingredient, except on CBC's French network which still devoted much air time to "serious" music. The CBC's own stations supplied a varied and Canadian brand of programming, notable for the number of sustaining (noncommercial) shows, which explained why the corporation was perceived as a Canadian version of the British Broadcasting Corporation. But the programming of the major private stations, even the CBC affiliates, was designed on the American model to attract large audiences and more advertising revenue. In English Canada then, radio was bringing listeners into closer contact with the cultural mainstream of the US.

The arrival of Canadian television in 1952 spelled disaster for radio's golden age. As Canadian families acquired television sets, evening radio lost money, listeners and eventually programs. Variety stars Johnny WAYNE and Frank SHUSTER, Don MESSER and his Islanders, and others shifted to television. The popular American hits had been taken off the air by the end of the decade. The radio play series was retired. The CBC officially recognized the change in radio's significance by closing down the Dominion network in 1962.

If radio had lost family and evening audiences, it swiftly regained stature as the companion of the individual. Assisting that renaissance was the spread of transistor radios and car radios which enabled consumers to listen when they pleased and in solitude. Private radio made the transition with ease, actually increasing its ad revenue by two-thirds during the 1950s. Programs as such disappeared in the new radio format, which emphasized the continual playing of recorded music interspersed with newscasts and commercials and hosted by disc jockeys who changed every few hours. The exceptions were broadcasts of sporting events and the new "open line" or phone-in programs, both legacies of the tradition of live radio. More and more stations came to specialize in a particular brand of music: "middle-of-the-road," "easy listening," "rock" and eventually "country." This kind of

formula programming succeeded on the rising FM stations as well. The Canadian Radio-Television Commission did promulgate various regulations to ensure a minimum of Canadian content on AM and to differentiate programming on FM. American music remained the staple, however, because it was so obviously popular with listeners. As early as 1967 private stations had captured over three-quarters of the radio audience. The listening peaks were now in the early morning and in the late afternoon.

The CBC was much slower to adapt to the times. Up to the late 1960s its schedule continued to look old-fashioned, filled with short, distinct programs. First in English Canada, eventually in Québec, audience levels plummeted, suggesting that the network was irrelevant to the needs of listeners. Finally, after 1971, the CBC scrapped the old daytime program format and added 7 hours a day of morning and late afternoon information programs. New talk and discussion shows like "As It Happens," "Aux 20 heures," "This Country in the Morning" and "Présent à l'écoute" were launched on the AM networks. Revamped programs in popular music, arts, drama and criticism remained, especially in the evening hours. Likewise the CBC established its FM stereo network to offer listeners a chance to indulge their taste for high culture, particularly classical music and sophisticated learning. These changes were complemented by the elimination of all advertising in 1975.

The renaissance of CBC programming almost doubled the audience share of the network's own stations in English Canada between 1967 and 1977. "This Country in the Morning" (later "Morningside") and "As It Happens" won substantial numbers of fans. CBC radio gained a N American reputation as a showcase of excellence. Nonetheless, the revival did not seriously challenge the dominance of independent radio in French or English Canada, where network outlets (private as well as public) had captured only 20% and 25%, respectively, of the potential audience in 1977.

Little has changed in recent years. The growing popularity of FM radio, the increased availability of American signals via cable, the experiment of an "all-news" FM service, the re-emergence of radio networking, and the arrival of rock video on television in the US may alter the shape of the radio scene in time. At present, however, radio remains the grand music box (even CBC radio, where 40% of AM broadcasting and 65-70% of FM broadcasting is devoted to music), dispensing a range of sounds to serve a variety of different tastes. *See also* COMMUNICATIONS IN THE NORTH; COMMUNICATIONS IN QUÉBEC; EDUCATIONAL BROADCASTING; MUSIC BROADCASTING. PAUL RUTHERFORD

Reading: P. Audley, *Canada's Cultural Industries: Broadcasting, Publishing, Records and Film* (1983); D. Jack, *The Story of CFRB* (1977); B. McNeil and M. Wolfe, *Signing On: The Birth of Radio in Canada* (1982); A.E. Powley, *Broadcasting from the Front* (1975); S. Stewart, *A Pictorial History of Radio in Canada* (1975); P. Stursberg, *Mister Broadcasting: The Ernie Bushnell Story* (1971).

Radish (*Raphanus sativus*), hardy annual or biennial VEGETABLE belonging to the Cruciferae family. Roots are mostly rounded with a red exterior and white, acrid flesh. Originating in Eurasia, radishes were prized by the Egyptians and Greeks. Commercial varieties now include Red Prince, Champion, French Breakfast and White Icicle. Radishes are a cool-season, fast-germinating crop. Outdoors, they require 25-35 days from seeding to table; winter types, 50-60 days. Radishes tolerate light frosts and are seeded 1 cm deep as soon as soils are workable in spring; precision seeders provide accurate spacing for commercial crops. With skillful management and cool, moist soils, seeding every 10-14 days provides radishes from Apr to Sept

(early Nov in SW Ontario). Growth checks by heat or drought result in inedible, hot, tough roots. Flea beetles, cabbage-root maggots and damping-off require control. Appreciated for their crisp, texture and mild, tangy flavour, radishes are high in potassium and a good source of vitamins A and C. Production figures for Canada are unavailable; however, in 1980 Ontario produced 5549 t (on 561 ha), worth $2.7 million.
V.W. NUTTALL

Radisson, Pierre-Esprit, explorer, fur trader (b in France 1636; d at London, Eng June 1710). This shrewd opportunist was valued for his knowledge of Indian life and N American geography. He followed his half sister to Trois-Rivières in 1651 and observed the IROQUOIS as their adopted captive 1652-53 and with the Jesuit mission to the Onondaga 1657-58. In 1659 he was taken on an unlicensed fur-trading expedition to Lks Superior and Michigan by his sister's husband, Médard Chouart DES GROSEILLIERS. In the lands beyond they found a "great store of beaver" and heard of "the Bay of the North Sea" that gave direct access to the region. After the governor of New France punished them for this expedition, the partners went to Boston to arrange a voyage to Hudson Bay. In 1665 they sailed to England, where their plan of bypassing the St Lawrence R to reach the interior fur-producing region found backers. The NONSUCH's voyage 1668-69 proved that the plan was practical and profitable. After the HUDSON'S BAY CO was incorporated in 1670, Radisson established its Nelson R post and served as guide, translator and adviser.

Their "dissatisfaction" with the company and a generous offer from the French secretary of state, Jean-Baptiste Colbert, led the brothers-in-law to desert to France in 1674. With a wife in England, Radisson was never fully trusted. As Canada's governor would not employ him, Radisson was a French navy midshipman 1677-79. In 1682 the Compagnie du Nord engaged him to challenge the English traders in Hudson Bay. Radisson destroyed rival posts and established Ft Bourbon on the Nelson R. When the governor of Canada taxed their furs and released a ship they had captured, the brothers-in-law sought restitution in France. They failed because Colbert, their patron, was dead. Radisson returned to England in 1684, and despite the losses he had caused, the HBC re-employed him, hoping to profit by "his great Experience & dexterity." He had his nephew surrender Ft Bourbon and its contents to the company. Radisson was chief director of trade at Ft Nelson 1685-87. With a price on his head in Canada, he retired with his family to Westminster [London], Eng, where he completed the narrative of his voyages. *See also* FUR TRADE. PETER N. MOOGK

Radium (Ra), rare, radioactive metal found in naturally occurring URANIUM (about 1 part radium to 3 million parts uranium). It was discovered in 1898 by Pierre and Marie Curie and G. Bémont who chemically treated pitchblende, a uranium ore obtained as a by-product from a silver mine in Bohemia. Most of the world's radium has come from the Shinkolobwe mine in what is now Zaire (beginning 1921), and the Port Radium mine in the NWT (beginning 1933). The high-grade pitchblende concentrates were treated at radium refineries at Oolen, Belgium, and PORT HOPE, Ont, respectively. Both mines closed in the late 1930s, but were reopened in the early 1940s as sources of uranium. Radium was recovered as a by-product of uranium at the Port Hope refinery until 1953. The most important use for radium has been to destroy cancer cells. Radium compounds, sealed in tubes or needles, were implanted in patients at cancer sites. Radium has also been employed industrially, eg, in luminous paint used in watches and instruments. However, there is now little demand for radium as radioisotopes such as COBALT-60 can be processed more cheaply and are more effective than radium in most applications.   R.M. WILLIAMS

Rae, John, trader, explorer (b in Orkney Is 30 Sept 1813; d at London, Eng 22 July 1893). An expert boatman, swimmer and climber, Rae qualified as surgeon in 1833, entered the HBC and was posted to Moose Factory. In 1846-47 he explored the coast W from Fury and Hecla straits to Boothia Isthmus, and in 1848 he accompanied Sir John RICHARDSON on a search for Sir John FRANKLIN. In 1851, with the same purpose, he searched the western, southern and eastern shores of VICTORIA I; much was original discovery. From an 1853-54 exploration, he brought back the first authentic tidings of the Franklin disaster. He spent his later life in London. Rae was supremely gifted in arctic survival, living off the country in comparative comfort and security. But he lacked a proclivity for self-advertisement, and his modesty permitted Vilhjalmur STEFANSSON to appropriate the honours owing to him.   L.H. NEATBY

Rae-Edzo, NWT, Hamlet, pop 1878 (1981c), is located near the N arm of GREAT SLAVE LK, 106 km NW of YELLOWKNIFE. It comprises the traditional Dogrib DENE community of Rae and the government settlement of Edzo. Today the largest Dene community in the NWT, Rae was originally a trading post, established 1790. The area had been the traditional hunting grounds for the Dogrib for centuries. Edzo, about 24 km from Rae, was constructed by the government 1965 as an alternative site to Rae, which offered poor drainage. However, most of the Dogrib preferred to remain at the original site and today still pursue hunting and trapping from there. Edzo has a small cluster of houses occupied mainly by NWT government employees.
                                          ANNELIES POOL

Raft Once the spring timber drive reached the main rivers, the timber was assembled into rafts for transportation to the shipping port. On the Ottawa, Saint John and Miramichi rivers, rafts comprised several "cribs" or "joints," each about 20 sticks secured in an ingenious 2-layer wooden frame. On the St Lawrence, "drams," larger frames secured with withes (sapling "ropes"), were used. Both types varied greatly in size. On the Saint John, rafts of 12-140 joints came downriver in the 1830s, but the largest were on the St Lawrence and probably contained 2000-2500 t of timber. *See* TIMBER TRADE HISTORY.   GRAEME WYNN

Raginsky, Nina, photographer (b at Montréal 14 Apr 1941). Educated at Rutgers, Raginsky turned to photography seriously in 1964. She worked first in black and white, but later began to sepia-tone and hand-colour her prints. Since 1972 Raginsky has been an instructor at the Emily Carr College of Art, formerly Vancouver School of Art. Her work has appeared in solo and group exhibitions in Canada and the US and in various magazines and books, including those of the National Film Board's *Image* series, *Canada: A Year of the Land* and *Between Friends*. She is best known for her frontal, full-figure portraits, particularly of eccentric or whimsical personalities.   LOUISE ABBOTT

Ragweed, annual or perennial PLANT of genus *Ambrosia*, family Compositae or Asteraceae. Fifteen species are native to N America; 3 occur across Canada: common ragweed (*A. artemisiifolia*), perennial ragweed (*A. coronopifolia*) and giant ragweed (*A. trifida*). Ragweed pollen is the most prevalent cause of hay fever in Canada, and common ragweed can also cause dermatitis. Common ragweed, the most abundant, is an erect, hairy-stemmed, coarse, annual herbaceous plant, 5-200 cm high, usually with deeply

divided, dark green leaves. Greenish, male flowers with obvious yellow stamens are borne in clusters along an erect stalk. One-seeded fruits (achenes) occur singly or in clusters, and are found at bases of upper leaves. It is an abundant WEED in cultivated fields, open disturbed areas and along roadsides, especially in southern Ontario and Québec. Giant ragweed, also an annual, can reach 5 m in height. It is more common on moist, partly shaded, disturbed sites.   PAUL B. CAVERS

Rail, common name for some members of the rail family (Rallidae) which also includes COOTS and GALLINULES. About 132 species occur worldwide; 44 are confined to islands or archipelagos; 13 are extinct. Many of the flightless forms may have evolved on isolated islands. In N America, rails are generally tawny coloured, or with grey-brown stripes or bars. They are hen-shaped and secretive, rarely seen but often heard. Rails probe soft mud for snails, clams, crustaceans, insects and small frogs and pick plant material from the ground. They fly hesitantly, with legs dangling, and quickly drop back into the marsh where their strong legs and long toes serve them well. In Canada, the sora (*Porzana carolina*) and yellow rails (*Coturnicops noveboracensis*) breed in almost every province. Virginia rails (*Rallus limicola*) have a westward breeding range similar to that of yellow rails but do not occur as far N, except in Alberta. They also nest in southern BC. King (*R. elegans*) and clapper rails (*R. longirostris*) occur, rarely, in southeastern Canada. Nests are woven baskets of marsh plants, sometimes roofed with plant stalks. Clutches contain 5-12 buff eggs (smaller species lay the larger clutches).   E. KUYT

Railway History The development of steam-powered railways in the 19th century revolutionized TRANSPORTATION in Canada and was integral to the very act of nation building. The early Canadian technology was imported from England, where experiment during the Industrial Revolution led from wooden tracks to iron rails and flanged wheels.

Mining railways, used to carry ore and coal from pitheads to water, were introduced to England early in the 17th century — the motive power being provided by horses. A primitive railway of this type may have been used as early as the 1720s to haul quarried stone at the fortress of LOUISBOURG. An incline railway of cable cars, powered by a winch driven by a steam engine, was used in the 1820s to hoist stone during the building of the QUÉBEC CITADEL. Another railway was used during the building of the RIDEAU CANAL to carry stone from the quarry at Hog's Back [Ottawa].

Steam locomotion, together with the low rolling friction of iron-flanged wheels on iron rails, enabled George Stephenson (the first of the great railway engineers) to design and superintend the building of the Liverpool and Manchester Railway (1830), which began the railway age in England. By 1841 there were some 2100 km of rail in the British Isles and by 1844 the frenetic promotion of railways aptly called "The Mania" was underway. Many of the lasting characteristics of the railway were established in this early stage: steam locomotion, the standard gauge (1.435 m) and the rolled-edge rail (bellying out on the underside for strength).

Early Railways Railway fever came a little later to British N America, which had a small population and much of its capital tied up in the expansion of its CANALS AND INLAND WATERWAYS. Nevertheless, it did not take long for politicians and entrepreneurs to realize the potential benefits. The PROVINCE OF CANADA (1841) was an enormous country. Its roads were poor and its waterways were frozen for up to 5 months per year. The first railway actually built in Canada was the CHAMPLAIN AND SAINT LAWRENCE RAILROAD

from Laprairie on the St Lawrence R to St Johns on the Richelieu R. Backed by John MOLSON and other Montréal merchants, the line opened officially 21 July 1836. Built as a "portage" between Montréal and Lk Champlain, in fact the railway carried little freight. The first railway in the Maritimes was the Albion Mines Railway, built to carry coal from Albion Mines some 9.5 km to the loading pier at Dunbar Pt (near Pictou, NS), opened 19 Sept 1839. The MONTREAL AND LACHINE RAILROAD (opened 1847) was another short (12 km) line built to supplement water transportation.

More ambitious was the ST LAWRENCE AND ATLANTIC RAILROAD, promoted initially by John A. Poor of Portland, Maine, and Alexander Tilloch GALT. The dual purpose of the line was to provide Montréal with a year-round ocean outlet and Portland with a hinterland. Promotion of the railway set a pattern often repeated later. In the initial enthusiasm, Montréalers subscribed £100 000 but paid up only 10% of that amount. Galt raised another £53 000 in England and mortgaged his land company to get the project moving. But it was the GUARANTEE ACT, 1849, sponsored in the Canadian legislature by Galt's friend Francis HINCKS, that ensured the railway's completion. The Act guaranteed interest of not more than 6% on half the bonds of a railway longer than 75 miles (120 km). A similar collaboration lay behind the GREAT WESTERN RAILWAY, begun in Oct 1849 and completed from Niagara Falls to Windsor, Canada W, in Jan 1854. In this case Conservative politician and businessman Allan MACNAB arranged for partners in Canada and the US, persuaded the legislature to proffer a loan of £200 000, and profited mightily himself.

The most ambitious pre-Confederation railway project in Canada was the GRAND TRUNK RAILWAY — a bold attempt by Montréal to capture the hinterland of Canada West and traffic from American states in the Great Lakes region. The GTR aroused great anticipation, but Canadians had neither the money nor the technicians to build it. The success of Hincks and other promoters in raising money for the GTR and other railway projects was largely due to their determination and the seemingly unbounded enthusiasm of British investors for railways. By the time it was completed from Sarnia to Montréal in 1860, the GTR was £800 000 in debt to the British banks of Baring Bros and Glyn Mills. Edward Watkin, sent out by head office to reorganize the railway, declared the GTR "an organized mess — I might say a sink of iniquity." In 1862 the Grand Trunk Arrangements Act put an end to the annual government handouts to the GTR by injecting new capital. The contempt and hostility with which the GTR began to be viewed by the public matched in intensity the early enthusiasm for its potential.

The financial difficulties experienced by all early railways forced massive public expenditures in the form of cash grants, guaranteed interest, land grants, rebates and rights-of-way. In return, the railways contributed to general economic developments, and the indirect bene-

The *Toronto* was the first locomotive manufactured in Ontario. On 16 April 1853, it was moved out of the shop to permanent track on Front St, Toronto (*courtesy Canadian National*).

fits for business and employment were clearly large. Unlike canals, railways extended into new territories and pushed the agricultural and timber frontiers westward and northward. The effect of railways on emerging urban centres was crucial and dramatic. Toronto's dominant position in S-central Ontario was clearly established by its connections with the Great Western and its central place on the GTR (neither of which it had done much to help build) and tapped the northern hinterland via the Ontario, Simcoe and Huron Railway (completed to Collingwood, Georgian Bay, in 1855), Toronto, Grey and Bruce Railway (completed to Owen Sound, Georgian Bay, in 1873), and Toronto and Nipissing Railway (extended to Lk Simcoe 1877).

The railways played an integral role in the process of INDUSTRIALIZATION, tying together and opening up new markets while, at the same time, themselves creating a demand for fuel, iron and steel, LOCOMOTIVES AND ROLLING STOCK. The pioneer wood-burning locomotives had huge appetites, and "wooding-up" stations were required at regular intervals along the line. The first locomotive built in Canada, in 1853, was made by James Goode of Toronto (the *Toronto No 2* of the Ontario, Simcoe and Huron). Entrepreneurial talents invested in the manufacture of almost everything that went into the operation of the railway, and consequently railways had a positive effect on levels of employment. Some small towns became in fact railway service and maintenance centres, with the bulk of the population dependent on the railway shops; eg, the Cobourg Car Works employed 300 workers in 1881. The railway also had a decisive impact on the physical characteristics of Canadian cities, since the tracks, the yards and the stations became central urban features, around which industries and hotels were built in ways that made the railway a central feature of the urban landscape. The railway greatly stimulated ENGINEERING, particularly with the demand for BRIDGES and TUNNELS. Canadians contributed a few inventions, notably the first successful braking system (W.A. Robinson, 1868) and the rotary snowplough (J.W. Elliott, 1869; developed further by O. Jull), which made possible safe, regular travel in Canadian winters. The great Canadian railway engineer Sir Sandford FLEMING devised his famous zone system of time to overcome the confusion of clocks varying from community to community along the rail routes.

Dramatic bluff on the Kaslo & Slocan Railway, 1900. The line hauled ore from Sandon to Kaslo on Kootenay Lake. Many passengers disembarked and followed the train around the bluff (*courtesy Vancouver City Archives/ CVA2-99*).

The Transcontinentals The second phase of railway building in Canada came with CONFEDERATION, 1867. As one historian has put it, "Bonds of steel as well as of sentiment were needed to hold the new Confederation together. Without railways there would be and could be no Canada." In fact, the building of the INTERCOLONIAL RAILWAY was a condition written into the Constitution Act, 1867. Because political considerations often overrode economic realities (eg, in the circuitous routes the Intercolonial and other railways took to avoid American territory), and because of the grand scale of the new nation, government assistance was crucial. The Intercolonial was owned and operated by the federal government and was largely financed with British loans backed by imperial guarantees. Despite the badgering of commissioners determined to make political advantage, Sandford Fleming built the Intercolonial to the highest standards and completed it by 1876.

In 1871 BC was lured into Confederation with the promise of a transcontinental railway within 10 years. The proposed line — 1600 km longer than the first US transcontinental — represented an enormous expenditure for a nation of only 3.5 million people. Two syndicates vied for the contract, and it was secretly promised to Sir Hugh ALLAN in return for financial support for the Conservatives during the closely contested 1872 election. The subsequent revelation that Allan was largely backed by American promoters and that he had sunk $350 000 into the Conservative campaign brought about the government (*see* PACIFIC SCANDAL). The contract with the CANADIAN PACIFIC RAILWAY Co, headed by George STEPHEN, was signed 21 Oct 1880. Macdonald's controversial decision in favour of an expensive all-Canadian route seemed to be vindicated during the NORTH-WEST REBELLION; how would the American government have reacted to Canadian troops moving across American territory? The "Last Spike" was driven 7 Nov 1885 and the first train left Montréal June 1886, arriving in Port Moody, BC, July 4. Completion of the railway was one of the great engineering feats of the day and owed much to the indefatigable supervision of William VAN HORNE and the determination of Macdonald.

Though ostensibly a private enterprise, the CPR was generously endowed by the federal government with cash ($25 million), land grants (25 million acres), tax concessions, rights-of-way, and a 20-year prohibition on construction of competing lines on the Prairies that might provide feeder lines to US railways. Whether or not the country received adequate compensation for this largess has been hotly debated ever since. However, the CPR was built in advance of a market and by a very expensive route through the SHIELD of northern Ontario. It had a profound effect on the settlement of the PRAIRIE WEST, and new cities, from Winnipeg to Vancouver, virtually owed their lives to the artery. Other western towns were strung out along the railway like beads on a string.

The flood of immigrants to the Prairie West after 1900 and the dramatic increase in agriculture soon proved the CPR inadequate, and a third phase of railway expansion began. Numerous branches sprouted in the West, of which the most notable was the CANADIAN NORTHERN RAILWAY, owned by the 2 bold entrepreneurs Donald MANN and William MACKENZIE. The Canadian Northern grew by leasing and absorbing other lines and constructed new links to Regina, Saskatoon, Prince Albert and Edmonton, and pushed on through the YELLOWHEAD PASS. It was linked to the East, with its main eastern terminus at Montréal, and also operated mileage in eastern Québec and the Maritimes. Though sometimes portrayed as rapacious promoters, Mackenzie and Mann built their railway to serve western needs that were not being met by

the CPR, and they invested most of their own fortunes in the enterprise. Nevertheless, the railway received public assistance of one-quarter billion dollars, most of it in the form of provincial and federal bond guarantees.

Meanwhile, the formerly aloof Grand Trunk was finally roused, under the leadership of Charles M. HAYS, to take part in western railway expansion, enthusiastically encouraged by PM LAURIER. Mutual jealousies precluded logical co-operation between the GTR and Canadian Northern, and the federal government itself undertook to build a line from Winnipeg to Moncton (the National Transcontinental Railway) and to lease it to the GTR on completion. The GTR's subsidiary, the GRAND TRUNK PACIFIC, undertook to build the more profitable line westward from Winnipeg. The NTR was built through the empty expanse of northern Québec and Ontario in hopes of encouraging development there; beginning in 1906, it was completed in 1914 at a cost of $160 million. The GTP began construction in 1905 and was completed in 1914 through the Yellowhead Pass and along the spectacular SKEENA R valley to PRINCE RUPERT, BC.

The ill-planned proliferation of railways (about half of the track now in operation was built between 1890 and 1914) proved disastrous. Rumours of outrageous patronage in the building of the NTR were later confirmed. The Canadian Northern and GTP were constantly begging aid from the public purse. WWI delivered the knockout blow — ending immigration and stifling the flow of British capital. In confusion and frustration PM BORDEN called a royal commission, headed by Sir Henry Drayton and British financier W.M. Acworth, which recommended (May 1917) "immediate nationalization of all railways of Canada except for American lines and the CPR... that the Intercolonial... National Transcontinental, the old Grand Trunk, the Grand Trunk Pacific and the Canadian Northern be brought together into one system, to be owned by the people of Canada." The name CANADIAN NATIONAL RAILWAYS was authorized for this conglomeration in 1918, but organization was not completed for 5 years.

The period after formation of the CNR was essentially one of consolidation, although several lines were pushed into northern frontiers. The HUDSON BAY RAILWAY, beginning at a line built by Mackenzie and Mann to The Pas in 1906, was finally opened to traffic in 1929. The Pacific Great Eastern began pushing uncertainly into the interior of BC in 1912 and was completed from Squamish to Quesnel by 1921, but only reached Prince George and Dawson Creek in the 1950s. Northern Alberta Railways (owned jointly by CNR and CPR) ran lines from Edmonton N to Grande Prairie and to Dawson Creek by 1931. Perhaps the most successul of these ventures was the ONTARIO NORTHLAND Railway, which reached James Bay in 1932. Owned by the Ontario government, the railway led directly to a fantastic mining boom in the Timmins-Porcupine area as well as to the emergence of the giant PULP AND PAPER INDUSTRY. The QUEBEC, NORTH SHORE AND LABRADOR RAILWAY, completed in 1954, provided access to the massive iron-ore deposits of the deep interior of Québec and Labrador. The Great Slave Railway was opened in 1965 between Roma, Alta, and Hay River, NWT.

Did the railways achieve the ends expected of them? Did they repay the large infusions of public money? A final accounting can likely never be done, particulary in trying to judge the satisfaction of nationalistic and long-term economic goals. Regulation of the railways (now the responsibility of the CANADIAN TRANSPORT COMMISSION) and freight-rate agreements (notably the CROW'S NEST PASS AGREEMENT) have been highly controversial, and very different views have been taken by western farmers and the railway companies on these issues (*see* TRANSPORTATION REGULATION). At the same time, the railwaymen — from Fleming and Van Horne to Allan, Mann, Mackenzie, Stephen and Lord SHAUGHNESSY — have been among the most prominent figures in Canadian history, evoking by turns admiration for their outstanding engineering feats and contempt for their perceived bleeding of the public purse. The building of the transcontinentals perhaps provided for Canada the closest approximation of a heroic age. *See also* RAILWAYS, CONTEMPORARY. JAMES MARSH

Reading: Pierre Berton, *The National Dream* (1969) and *The Last Spike* (1971); R. Chodos, *The CPR: A Century of Corporate Welfare* (1973); A.W. Currie, *The Grand Trunk Railway of Canada* (1957); W.K. Lamb, *History of the Canadian Pacific Railway* (1977); R.F. Legget, *Railways to Canada* (1973); N. and H. Mika, *Railways of Canada* (1972); T.D. Regehr, *The Canadian Northern Railway* (1976); G.R. Stevens, *History of the Canadian National Railways* (1973); A. Tucker, *Steam Into Wilderness* (1978); B.J. Young, *Promoters and Politicians* (1978).

Railway Safety Each year in Canada there are thousands of railway accidents. Most are minor and cause little damage and only a slight delay to the train. Some, however, result in injury, loss of life and substantial property damage. In 1982 there were 4983 "accidents" reported to the CANADIAN TRANSPORT COMMISSION. Only one-quarter were classified as "train" accidents, the rest were "normal industrial accidents." Train accidents resulted in 146 deaths and 628 injuries. Most of the fatalities were occupants of automobiles involved in grade-crossing accidents; 18 were railway employees; none were passengers. Most of the injuries involved railway employees. Although there are individual years which do not fit the trend, the safety of Canadian railways has improved steadily. The number of accidents, deaths and injuries has declined since 1960 in spite of a vast increase in freight traffic, and they are minor compared to highway casualties.

The most famous railway accident in recent years was the 1979 "Mississauga Derailment." There were no injuries, but the accident involved leaking chlorine cars and forced the evacuation of 250 000 nearby residents. This, and a rash of similar accidents, served to focus public attention on railway safety, especially the problems of handling dangerous goods in urban areas. The ensuing Commission of Inquiry conducted by Mr Justice Samuel Grange made a number of sweeping recommendations with respect to equipment design and inspection and train-operation procedures intended to decrease the potential for further derailments, especially for trains handling dangerous cargo such as poisonous or explosive gas. Many of these recommendations were subsequently imposed on the railways by the Transport Commission. The commission itself has also conducted extensive investigations of railway safety, major derailments and collisions, and imposed further standards.

While such standards have an impact on the possibility — and extent of damage — of derailments, collisions and other types of accidents, nearly 20% of all railway accidents, and most of the deaths, are at grade crossings, where driver behaviour plays an important factor. A complete but expensive solution for this type of accident is grade separation (overpass or underpass). There is an ongoing federal-provincial program to install signals and barriers at busy crossings. CHARLES SCHWIER

Railway Station Rail service began in Canada in 1836 with the opening of the CHAMPLAIN AND SAINT LAWRENCE RAILROAD east of Montréal. The new TRANSPORTATION system required a new building type: stations to accommodate the passengers and freight that it carried.

No information has survived on stations for the first Canadian railways, if indeed there were

Railway station, Churchill, Man (*courtesy Provincial Archives of Manitoba*).

stations; the earliest ones known are the "road stations" built between 1855 and 1857 for the GRAND TRUNK RAILWAY's line from Montréal to Toronto and Sarnia. Most, such as the station at St Marys Junction, were small rectangular one-storey stone buildings with broad-eaved gabled roofs and round-arched windows and doors; those at Kingston and Belleville had a second storey within a mansard roof. The designer may have been Grand Trunk chief engineer A.M. Ross or Thomas S. SCOTT, the future federal chief architect who served for a time as architect to the railway. A number of the early Grand Trunk stations were of frame construction, as were those built in 1867 for the INTERCOLONIAL RAILWAY's route from Truro to New Glasgow, NS, and likely designed by Sir Sandford FLEMING. The 5 shingled "way stations" on this route combined passenger and freight facilities and had a separate long platform.

The CANADIAN PACIFIC RAILWAY used a number of station types and designers for its transcontinental route. Several stations, such as the one at Peterborough, Ont (architect Thomas Charles Sorby, 1883), were built of brick, with the passenger waiting room separate from the freight shed and the stationmaster's quarters located above the waiting room. This arrangement became the basis for standard plans subsequently adopted by the CPR and other lines and continued well into the present century. In several early western CPR stations the passenger and freight facilities were joined by a covered platform. The Vancouver station (Paul Marmette, 1886, frame construction) followed this plan, as did stations at Calgary (1893, in stone) and Banff, Alta (1889, log construction), both designed by Edward Colonna.

Windsor Station, Montréal, built 1888-89 in the château style with Romanesque detail (*photo © 1984 Hartill Art Associates*).

Urban stations, many of them terminals, were much larger than stations along the line and were designed in the fashionable architectural styles of the time. Toronto's second Union Station (E.P. Hannaford, 1871-73) was an Italianate design with 3 tall mansard-roofed towers; the Intercolonial's North Street Terminal in Halifax (Dept of Public Works, 1874-77) displayed a fine Second Empire design; and the CPR's Windsor Station in Montréal (Bruce Price, 1888-89) was in the Richardsonian Romanesque style (*see* ARCHITECTURAL STYLES). All featured large train sheds of utilitarian iron or steel construction located behind the passenger building.

Many stations were designed in the years before WWI, and 20th-century designs generally continued the styles developed in earlier years. The station at Smith, Alta, built in 1914 for the Edmonton, Dunvegan and British Columbia Railway, has a low freight shed alongside a gabled 2-storey passenger wing similar to CPR stations of a generation earlier, and is typical of smaller stations built by most lines. Many railways had a series of standard designs that were repeated in various locations, particularly on the Prairies. The Union Station in Winnipeg (Warren and Wetmore, 1911) and Toronto's third Union Station (Ross and Macdonald, Hugh G. JONES and John M. LYLE, 1915-20) continued the practice of using fashionable "high" styles for urban stations, in both instances beaux-arts classicism. The Toronto station is notable for its grand concourse and its effective use of levels to separate functions.

Modernism was first applied to station design with the erection of the CANADIAN NATIONAL RAILWAY's Central Station in Montréal (John Schofield, 1938-43). The deceptively simple brick structure also became the core of an extensive commercial development, culminating in the PLACE VILLE MARIE office complex (I.M. Pei and Associates, 1956-65).

After 1960, many railway stations were demolished. The numerous line abandonments and the elimination of passenger service from many surviving lines, combined with the need to renew aging building stock, brought about a wave of station removal. The few new stations built generally used simple contemporary design, as in the CN stations at Dorval, Qué, and Kingston, Ont. In other communities, stations were removed and replaced with small, standard shelters (eg, CP Rail at Arnprior, Ont, 1981).

Public interest in the preservation of unusual railway stations has resulted in a number being reused as museums (eg, High River, Alta), some as community facilities (eg, Theodore, Sask) and others as integrated transportation facilities (eg, Regina). The former Ottawa station is now a conference centre. The railways are beginning to co-operate with communities wishing to retain unused stations, although removal of stations continues at a rapid pace. *See also* TOURISM.

HAROLD D. KALMAN

Railways, Contemporary In the 4 decades following WWII, Canada's 2 major railways became major conglomerates, among the largest companies in Canada. In 1983 railway activity accounted for 22% of CP's $12.8 billion revenues (but contributed 63% of total net income). CP's railway assets were $3.5 billion of a total of $17.6 billion. CN had revenues of $4.6 billion in 1983, 82% earned from railway operations. Of CN's 6.8 billion assets, 50% are railway related. Between them, CP and CN account for nearly 90% of the Canadian railway business. The balance is handled by 30 regional and short-line carriers. In addition, both CP and CN have subsidiary railways in the US, own major trucking operations and have considerable other investments.

In general terms, the railway network is much the same in the 1980s as it was in the 1940s, although many independent railways have become part of the CP or CN systems. Total length in 1981 was 92 414 km, compared to 90 221 km in 1945. Many thousand km of low-density branch lines have been retired, but there has also been considerable new-line construction, particularly in northern Québec, Alberta and BC. During the 1950s and 1960s a number of major resource railways were completed. The Pacific Great Eastern (now the BRITISH COLUMBIA RAILWAY) has had a construction program extending over several decades to serve mining and timber areas in northern BC. The Great Slave Lake Railway was built by CN to serve mining and timber areas in northern Alberta and the NWT. The QUEBEC, NORTH SHORE AND LABRADOR RAILWAY was completed in 1954 to haul iron ore to Sept-Îsle, Qué, on the N shore of the St Lawrence R.

Passenger Transportation The post-WWII era saw a contraction in the railway share of passenger transportation as the AUTOMOBILE and airplane became dominant (*see* AVIATION). In 1945 the railways carried 55.4 million passengers (including commuters), accounting for 20% of their revenue. Ten years later passengers had fallen to 27.2 million, accounting for less than 10% of revenue; in spite of both major railways having invested in new fleets of passenger equipment. In 1980 fewer than 16 million passengers were carried. This decrease, coupled with inflation, led to losses on almost all passenger-train runs.

This decline was one of the problems addressed in 1959-61 by the MacPherson Royal Commission. Noting the advantages of the automobile and airplane, the commission recommended that uneconomic passenger trains be discontinued, with provision of a subsidy during a transitional period. This recommendation was adopted in the 1967 National Transportation Act, which provided for a federal subsidy of 80% of the losses sustained by passenger trains which were retained in the public interest. Even with this provision, during the 1960s and 1970s many of Canada's passenger trains were withdrawn and the number of stations served was gradually reduced as many trains became express or semiexpress. Over this period the railways, especially CN, undertook various initiatives, such as the Red-White-and-Blue discount fares introduced in the 1960s, to improve passenger service, but with limited success. Although there was some resurgence of passenger traffic, the subsidies grew.

In 1977, at a time when annual passenger

subsidies had increased to more than $200 million, a new step was taken with the formation of VIA RAIL CANADA, INC, a crown corporation which assumed responsibility for most passenger trains, operating them under contract with the federal government. VIA owns only the trains and employs only some of the staff. The remainder of its services it purchases from the railways at cost. VIA has introduced service improvements and new equipment such as the LRC (Light Rapid Comfortable) train. In 1982 there were over 7 million passengers; the cost to government, however, was $450 million. Although traffic had increased, the number of cities served was reduced in 1981 as 20% of VIA's runs were cut. A number of these trains were restored by the new government early in 1985. Most of Canada's railway passenger service is provided in the densely populated Québec-Windsor corridor. Coast-to-coast service is provided with 2 daily Montréal-Maritime trains, a daily Montréal-Toronto-Calgary-Vancouver train, and a Winnipeg-Edmonton-Vancouver train. A few regional services are also provided. GO Transit, an agency of the Ontario government, began running commuter trains in the Toronto area in 1967, using CN and CP tracks. A similar arrangement started in Montréal in 1984.

Freight Transportation Freight, especially bulk commodities, has become the dominant railway service. Freight ton-miles increased from 63.4 billion in 1945 to 160.5 billion in 1981. The principal commodities which account for this increase are iron ore (via 2 new railways, the Québec, North Shore and Labrador and the Québec Cartier in northern Québec) and coal, sulphur and potash (in western Canada). Other major freight commodities include grain, forest products, chemicals, petroleum, and automobiles and automobile parts. Among them, they account for more than 75% of total Canadian freight shipments. High-value, manufactured goods traffic has not grown as fast as bulk traffic, but, contrary to popular belief, the railways have not lost all of this traffic to trucks (*see* TRUCKING INDUSTRY). With the advent of intermodal services — containers and piggyback — there has been a resurgence of manufactured goods traffic on the railways since the early 1970s.

The railways have withdrawn from the "small package" freight market, leaving it to their trucking or express subsidiaries. Many rail shipments are multiple carload lots, much of it in unit trains. For the most part, freight stations in smaller cities have been closed and low-density branch-lines abandoned. A number of uneconomic branch lines have been retained in the public interest. Losses on these lines are paid for from federal funds. In 1983 such payments amounted to $259 million, 90% of which was for grain-dependant lines. In areas still served by rail, orders are placed with regional carload centres rather than with a local agent.

Substantive changes have occurred in the reg-

A VIA Rail turbo near Port Hope, Ont (*courtesy National Film Board/Photothèque*).

ulation of freight movements. As a result of the MacPherson Royal Commission recommendations in 1961, railway freight rates were deregulated in the National Transportation Act of 1967. Rather than seeking the permission of the CANADIAN TRANSPORT COMMISSION to alter freight rates, the railways are now free to set rates as competition dictates and have only to publish increases 30 days in advance. Protection for shippers without alternate means of transportation is afforded by a provision of the Act which limits rates to 250% of long-run variable costs. Protection for other carriers from predatory pricing by the railways is provided by a minimum rate set at variable cost. In addition, section 23 of the Act stipulates the disallowance of any rate that is "not in the public interest." This new regulatory philosophy came after a long period of freight-rate complaints set off by a postwar cycle of inflation, railway wage increases and freight-rate increases. This cycle made freight rates one of the political issues in the late 1950s, culminating in a federal government rollback of rates and payment of a subsidy in the summer of 1959.

After deregulation, freight rates did not increase substantially until the inflation and fuel crisis of the mid-1970s. Even then, freight-rate increases did not keep pace with general price levels. With the exception of the Crow grain rates and a brief flurry of activity during the start of the inflationary period of the 1970s, railway freight rates have ceased to be the issue they once were (*see* CROW'S NEST PASS AGREEMENT).

Modernization The period since WWII has been a time of modernization and technical change for the railways. The most visible of the early steps to modernization was the conversion from steam to diesel-electric power. While there already existed an electrified line in Montréal, nearly all of the railways' 4400 locomotives in 1945 were steam engines, although many were oil- rather than coal-fired. Conversion to diesel-electric, which had a cost advantage in labour, fuel and maintenance, began in the late 1940s. In 1950, 91% of Canadian trains were pulled by steam engines; by 1960, steam engines accounted for only 1.4%. Steam engines were used sporadically for excursion service until the early 1980s.

The diesel engine was less expensive to operate, and more powerful and flexible. In the 1980s the bulk of the locomotive fleet was made up of 3000-hp units which could go 800 to 1000 kilometres without servicing. Larger trains with multiple locomotives could be operated. Firemen were no longer required, and the need to change or service steam locomotives every 150 to 200 kilometres was eliminated. Both these developments created labour difficulties in the 1950s and led to a decreased importance of many small towns which had been railway division points. The typical freight train of the 1980s may have over 100 cars pulled by 3 or 4 locomotives, with a 4-man crew, running nonstop between major terminals.

The diesel also replaced the few electric railway lines in Canada, except the Deux Montagnes commuter run in Montréal. Electric traction was used on the 11 km Carol Lake railway extension of the Quebec, North Shore and Labrador Ry. In 1984 British Columbia Ry electrified its new 135 km Tumbler Ridge Branch Line for coal haulage.

There have also been changes in freight cars. The 40-foot boxcar, long the standard of the industry and capable of carrying 40 to 50 tons, has been replaced by larger cars and special purpose cars. In the 1980s much of the bulk freight is handled in 100-ton (91 t) cars. The railways have an increasing number of unit trains which were dedicated to specific services and move directly from shipper to consignee without intermediate classification. Between 1945 and 1980 such innovations allowed the railways to increase the amount of freight carried while reducing the number of employees required by 32%, and to offer freight rates which have increased far below inflation rates.

Other, less visible, technological changes adopted by the railways since the 1940s include the use of Centralized Traffic Control, microwaves and radios for train control, modern metallurgy and continuous welded rails, automated rail-laying machinery, automatic car identification and the application of computers in all aspects of the railway business.

CHARLES SCHWIER

Reading: Canadian Institute of Guided Ground Transport, *An Overview of Railway Transportation in Canada* (1985); H.J. Darling, *The Politics of Freight Rates* (1980); W.G. Scott, *Canadian Railway Freight Pricing: Historical and Current Perspectives* (1984).

Railways, Track and Yards Railway track is the assembly of the 5 basic components, rail, ties, fastenings, ballasts and subgrade, over which trains run. Rails are rolled steel lengths bolted or welded together to form the running surface for trains. The tie, usually wood or concrete, is the transverse member of the railway track structure to which the rails are fastened; it provides proper gauge and transmits the stresses through the ballast. Fastenings for wooden ties are spikes driven into the tie through holes in the metal plate on which the rail rests; the head of the spike grips the rail base; for concrete ties the rail rests on a polymer pad and can be secured by various patented clip systems. Ballast is selected rock material placed on the roadbed to hold the track in place. The subgrade, usually good quality soil, further distributes the track loading into the ground to provide a stable base.

A turnout or switch is the device used to divert trains from one track to another. Trackage can be divided into 2 categories: line and yards. The line is the running portion of the railway. A yard is a system of tracks for making up trains, sorting and storing cars, maintaining rolling stock and other activities. At major terminals, large classification yards are used to facilitate the sorting of freight cars. Often a hump is located at one end of the classification yard and freight cars are rolled down by gravity to various tracks to make up trains.

The objective in railway design is to select the route that will give the most economical combination of construction costs and operating expenses. There are 2 basic restraints to train performance, curvature and gradient. Curvature limits speed and leads to high maintenance costs for track and rolling stock. Gradient increases the requirements for locomotive horsepower and leads to an increase in fuel consumption and braking. Single-track routes are also a major limiting factor in performance, because of the delays that occur unless trains moving in opposite directions meet at the designated passing tracks with perfect timing.

Railway traffic control is provided by means of a signal system. The basic element in most railway signal systems is the block, a length of track to which entrance is governed by signal indicators, usually coloured lights. In the Automatic Block Signal System (ABS), block signals are activated by the presence of a train in the block, or the position of track turnouts (switches). Though ABS provides collision protection, it does not provide a means of authorizing train movements — a severe limitation for a single-track or even a double-track railway with trains of varying speeds. This problem can be overcome by Centralized Traffic Control (CTC), by means of which a dispatcher at a central control panel can actuate all power-equipped turnouts for a certain segment of track. Thus the dispatcher can control the routing of trains either meeting or overtaking. The dispatcher can

Aerial view of the CN Symington yards in Winnipeg, Man (*courtesy National Film Board/Phototheque*).

also monitor track-mounted detection devices for hot wheel bearings, dragging equipment, broken wheels and shifted loads. Computer-aided dispatching can be used on congested lines. One of the innovations in some other countries is in-cab signalling. By means of coded track circuits the status of track-side signals is continually displayed in the locomotive cab. An extension of in-cab signalling is Automatic Train Control (ATC). With ATC, the locomotive automatically responds to reduced speed requirements or is automatically stopped if the engineer does not respond. A further refinement of ATC is an on-board control unit that computes the train's braking distance and controls the train's speed to maintain a safe braking distance between trains. JEFFERY YOUNG, CANADIAN INSTITUTE OF GUIDED GROUND TRANSPORT

Rain is liquid precipitation — precipitation being liquid and solid WATER that condenses in and falls from the atmosphere. A typical raindrop is about 2 mm in diameter (range, 0.5-5 mm). Almost all rain-producing CLOUDS are formed as a result of upward motion of air charged with water vapour. Such motion produces cooling and subsequent condensation into water droplets and ICE crystals. Normally the crystals melt before reaching the ground. In Canada rain is usually an event of the warm season. Rainfall is sometimes classified according to the process responsible for the initial lifting of the air. Cyclonic rainfall occurs when moist air converges and lifts in low-pressure (cyclone) areas. This process accounts for much of Canada's rainfall. Central US lows, entering Canada somewhere between Manitoba and Québec, are of major environmental significance because they pass through the industrial heartland of the US and frequently bring ACID RAIN. Frontal rainfall results from lifting of warm air on one side of a frontal surface (zone separating air masses of dissimilar characteristics) over colder, denser air on the other side. Convective rainfall, caused by warmer air rising in colder surroundings, is sometimes associated with thunderstorms. Orographic rainfall occurs when moist air is lifted over mountains.

For synoptic purposes, rain is classified as slight if it falls at a rate less than 0.5 mm/h; moderate if the rate is 0.5-4 mm/h; heavy if the rate is greater than 4 mm/h. The heaviest rainfall in Canada occurs along the BC coast, where annual precipitation can exceed 2500 mm. Canada's one-day record rainfall of 489 mm fell at UCLUELET on Vancouver I (6 Oct 1967). The second zone of high rainfall is the Maritimes. Average annual precipitation in parts of NS and Newfoundland exceeds 1500 mm. Occurrences of heavy rainfall in other parts of Canada are frequently associated with the extratropical phase of hurricanes: Hurricane Hazel dumped more than 178 mm of rainfall in 24 hours in parts of southern Ontario (15-16 Oct 1954). Arctic regions receive the least rainfall, followed by the southern prairies and the deep valley systems of interior BC. But even in these areas, isolated very heavy rains are not uncommon.

For example, 17.8 mm fell in 5 minutes in Winnipeg (14 July 1968). The benefits of rainfall are considerable. Rain is a major vehicle through which Canada's freshwater resources are renewed. In many parts of the country, especially in the prairies, crop yield is closely related to amount and timing of rainfall during the growing season. But very heavy rainfall can cause flash FLOODS and washouts. L.C. NKEMDIRIM

Rainbow, coloured arc that occurs when sunlight shines onto falling raindrops and is refracted, then reflected back towards the observer. In this process, each drop acts as a tiny prism, splitting the SUN's rays (according to wavelength) into their component colours. One of the reflected bundle of rays is much more intense than the rest and emerges at an angle of 42° to the direction of incoming sunlight. The strong reflections from each drop of similar size reinforce each other and a visible image of the sun's spectrum appears as an arc (ie, a primary rainbow). Occasionally, sunlight and rainfall may be intense enough to produce a second, fainter rainbow above or beyond the first. The secondary rainbow results from 2 internal reflections of light in raindrops and occurs at an angle of 50° (compared to the one internal reflection and 42° angle of primary rainbows). As rainbow formation requires that the sun be visible in some part of the sky while RAIN is falling in another, rainbows are seldom seen during extensive frontal-type rains but are restricted to THUNDERSTORMS and light showers. Because of the angle requirement, they are also more likely to be observed during or just after late afternoon showers. Rarely, the light of the full MOON may be bright enough to produce a rainbow arc from a night shower. J. MAYBANK

Rainbow, a light cruiser serving in the Royal Navy from 1891 until 1910, when the Canadian government purchased the ship for the new Royal Canadian Navy. After its arrival at ESQUIMALT, BC, 7 Nov 1910, its duties included training and fisheries patrol. In July 1914 its appearance persuaded the KOMAGATA MARU to leave Vancouver harbour. From Aug 1914, when powerful German cruisers briefly appeared in the NE Pacific, until early 1917, *Rainbow* performed defensive patrols. It was sold for scrap in 1920. ROGER SARTY

The light cruiser *Rainbow* served in the RCN 1910-20. It is shown here (front) during the *Komagata Maru* incident, July 1914 (*courtesy Vancouver Public Library/6229*).

Rainmaking Rainfall is vitally important to mankind and many techniques have been used to induce it. In ancient times, bonfires were built to appease the gods. In Napoleonic Europe, cannons were fired during cloudy weather. North American Indians performed elaborate dances. Unfortunately, it is unlikely that any such techniques had more than psychological value. Scientific rainmaking or rainfall enhancement began in 1946 when American scientists Vincent Schaefer and Bernard Vonnegut discovered, in independent studies, that it was possible to cause supercooled CLOUD droplets (those below 0°C) to freeze into ICE crystals by introducing dry ice (solid carbon dioxide, with a temperature of -72°C) or silver iodide crystals into cloud.

In natural rain formation, cloud droplets develop as water vapour ascends and rapidly reach equilibrium at a diameter of 5-20μ. Ultimately a million or more such droplets are needed to produce an average raindrop. Although these cloud droplets can combine and grow by collision, this is an unusual and inefficient process in temperate latitude clouds. Instead a highly efficient process involving ice crystals and supercooled water droplets is the dominant process by which rain is formed in Canada.

By freezing cloud droplets directly (through the injection of dry ice pellets), it is possible to induce ice-crystal growth, eventually leading to rainfall. Silver iodide operates in a more subtle fashion. Its molecular crystalline dimensions are very similar to those of an ice crystal. Consequently, when silver-iodide particles contact supercooled cloud droplets, they cause the water molecules to align themselves like ice molecules and the droplet freezes.

In Canada modern rainmaking began in 1948 with a federal government experiment that used dry ice dispersed into clouds to stimulate rainfall. Under appropriate conditions, rainfall did result. However, the classic question with all rainmaking activities is, What would have happened if man had not intervened? The results of this project were questioned since a randomly selected control population of unseeded clouds was not available for comparison with the population of seeded clouds. Nonetheless, in spite of scientific uncertainties, the 1950s saw a blossoming of rainmaking activities on the prairies for agricultural purposes, and in eastern Canada for forestry and hydroelectric power. Silver iodide was the seeding agent, dispersed variously from ground-based and airborne generators. These operations were not designed as scientific experiments, and later analyses were inconclusive; when compared with precipitation averages, small increases and small decreases in precipitation were found.

In 1959 one of the first of a series of international statistical rainmaking experiments was mounted by the federal government in NE Ontario and NW Québec. The outcome of this 4-year experiment on large-scale storm systems was an overall 2.5% decrease in rainfall. This decrease was not statistically significant and could have been the result of chance. However, an operational rainmaking project in the Lac SAINT-JEAN area, Qué, was perceived by residents as having been very successful — so successful, in fact, that "Operation Umbrella" was mounted and mothers petitioned the Québec government for vitamins for their children because of lack of sunshine. In 1965 the Québec minister of natural resources ordered all rainmaking activities in the province to cease.

Rainmaking declined throughout Canada during the 1960s and 1970s, although some projects continued sporadically in Nfld, Ont and Alta. By the mid-1970s revolutionary advances in techniques to observe cloud and precipitation particles from aircraft resulted in a federal 4-year single cumuliform cloud-seeding experiment in NW Ontario and the NWT. While the sample of clouds seeded was small, strong evidence was found for the possibility of initiating a precipitation process if the cloud did not dissipate in the 20 minutes following seeding. Clouds in NW Ontario were found to be short-lived and not susceptible to seeding; clouds in the NWT were long-lived and reacted positively.

Similar results have been found in other countries. However, the international scientific community is still cautious about whether rainmaking works. There is not a good general answer: the success of rainmaking probably depends on a variety of geographical and meteorological parameters that science has yet to delineate.

A.J. CHISHOLM

Rainy Lake, 932 km² (741 km² in Canada), elev 338 m, is located in rough woodlands astride the Ontario-Minnesota border, 240 km W of Lk SUPERIOR. It discharges into the Rainy R, which flows W along the border to LK OF THE WOODS. Originally inhabited by Cree and Assiniboine, the irregularly shaped lake was first visited by a European in 1688. The explorer Pierre LA VÉRENDRYE ordered a post built at the western end in 1731. The lake was located on the well-travelled FUR-TRADE ROUTE to the northwest. Later, logging and the pulp-and-paper industry were important. FORT FRANCES, the lake's main settlement, is located at a waterfall where the river leaves the lake. DANIEL FRANCIS

Rainy River Burial Mounds, archaeological sites on the Canadian bank of the river, were built by the Laurel and Blackduck peoples between the early Christian era and the early historic period. Most of them are low, broad structures, but one, at the Long Sault Rapids, is 34 m in diameter and 7 m high. Both within the mounds and in pits below are clusters of human bones and, occasionally, rich assortments of grave furniture. Clay pots filled with food for the departing spirits were placed in the grave; shell, bone and copper beads were scattered across the graves; and the whole was then sprinkled with red ochre. In the historic period, although articles of European manufacture replace many native artifacts, the burial pattern remains ancient and aboriginal. *See also* ARCHAEOLOGY; PREHISTORY. W.A. KENYON

Ralston, James Layton, lawyer, politician (b at Amherst, NS 27 Sept 1881; d at Montréal 21 May 1948). A WWI battalion commander with a reputation for bravery and competence, Ralston was twice minister of national defence, 1926-30 and 1940-44. Intense, scrupulously honest, an able representative of the political interests of the Maritime provinces, he was a stalwart in PM Mackenzie KING's WWII Cabinet, serving briefly as minister of finance, 1939-40, before becoming defence minister. Depite a tendency to become mired in administrative detail, he was a fine judge of generalship and a devoted defender of Canada's fighting men. King forced Ralston's resignation in 1944 because of his outspoken support of overseas CONSCRIPTION.

NORMAN HILLMER

Ramezay, Claude de, officer, acting governor of NEW FRANCE (b at La Gesse, France 15 June 1659; d at Québec C 31 July 1724). An officer in the TROUPES DE LA MARINE, he arrived in Canada in 1685. He served as governor of Trois-Rivières 1690-99, as commander of the Canadian troops 1699-1704, and as governor of Montréal 1704-24 (except for the period 1714-16 when he was acting governor of the colony during VAUDREUIL's absence). During much of this time he was also involved in the FUR TRADE and lumber business. The magnificent Château de Ramezay, which he built in 1705-06, still stands in Montréal.

MARY MCDOUGALL MAUDE

Ramezay, Jean-Baptiste-Nicholas-Roch de, officer (b at Montréal 4 Sept 1708; d at Blaye, France 7 May 1777), son of Claude de RAMEZAY. He rose through the ranks of the TROUPES DE LA MARINE in New France, serving in the West and in Acadia, until becoming in 1758 king's lieutenant at Québec C, the senior military post in the town under the governor. In Sept 1759, operating under instructions from Governor VAUDREUIL given the night of MONTCALM's defeat on the Plains of Abraham, petitioned by the townspeople, and advised by a council of war, he negotiated terms for the capitulation of the town. These were signed by the British on Sept 18 and he surrendered Québec C to them the next day.

MARY MCDOUGALL MAUDE

Ranching History Ranching developed where physical and climatic features combined to provide sufficient natural grassland for livestock — primarily BEEF CATTLE but also sheep — to graze relatively independently year-round. It began in the BC interior in the late 1850s, and was encouraged by markets created by the GOLD RUSHES. Livestock was brought in from the western US to the mild, sheltered Cariboo and Chilcotin areas and the Thompson and Nicola river valleys. Ranching expanded quickly into other British Columbia valleys, the Rocky Mt foothills and eventually into the CYPRESS HILLS and semiarid plains of southeastern Alberta and southwestern Saskatchewan.

Still a centre of the contemporary beef cattle industry, the heartland of the old ranching frontier was the foothill country of of southwestern Alberta, where the sheltered, well-watered valleys and the CHINOOK winds which bare the hills of winter snow combine to make it one of the continent's preferred stock-raising areas. After 1874 the NORTH-WEST MOUNTED POLICE provided the 2 essentials of an incipient range-cattle industry: a small local market and security for open grazing. The police were soon joined by Joseph MacFarland, an Irish-American frontiersman, and George Emerson, an ex-Hudson's Bay man, who drove in small herds from Montana. At the same time in the Bow R valley W of Ft Calgary, George and John MCDOUGALL established a herd near their mission at Morleyville [Morley, Alta]. Numerous policemen joined the ranching fraternity when their terms of enlistment expired, thus forming a distinctive core about which the industry developed and helping to define its emerging social character. The British-Canadian orientation of the ranching frontier was reinforced by the arrival of Englishmen attracted by the great publicity accorded in Britain to N American cattle ranching. They typically described themselves as "gentlemen" and came generally from the landed classes, with sufficient capital to establish their own ranches.

Access to distant markets was assured when the CANADIAN PACIFIC RAILWAY reached the prairies in the early 1880s, and interest in ranching grew dramatically. Led by Montréal capitalist and stock breeder Sen Matthew Cochrane, Canadian businessmen vied to obtain the grazing leases provided through the DOMINION LANDS POLICY. The lure of being able to ship cheaply grown western beef to the rapidly expanding British market and cashing in on the "beef bonanza" led Cochrane and others to organize the great cattle companies that soon dominated the Canadian range: the Cochrane, Bar U, Oxley and Walrond ranches in Alberta, the '76, Hitchcock and Matador ranches in Saskatchewan, and the Douglas Lake, Gang and Empire Valley ranches in BC.

The railway, however, also brought the threat of general settlement, especially in Saskatchewan and Alberta, and an accompanying grid of barbed wire fences. Ranchers were determined to keep the "sodbusters" out and settlers were equally bent on penetrating the grazing leases. Finally the government yielded to the overwhelming demand for open settlement: in 1892 the ranchers received 4 years' notice that all old leases restricting HOMESTEAD entry would be cancelled. But the powerful cattle compact argued that the ranching regions were too dry for cereal agriculture. Recognizing that the upper hand was with those who controlled the water supply, cattlemen persuaded Ottawa to protect the cattle industry by setting aside major springs, rivers and creek fronts as public stock-watering reserves. Most choice sites thus became inaccessible to settlement, and the ranchers' hegemony continued.

After the election of Wilfrid Laurier's Liberals (1896) the cattlemen faced a government committed to unrestricted settlement. Convinced that dryland agricultural techniques were surmounting the obstacle of moisture deficiency, the Liberals began to auction off the elaborate system of stock-watering reservations. The spirited defence of the ranchers' cause by stock growers' associations, and strong beef markets, only slowed the decline of the industry. Soon in full retreat before the rush of homesteaders who settled on even the most marginal lands in southern Alberta and Saskatchewan, the faltering cattle kingdom was dealt the ultimate blow by nature. Whereas homesteaders had enjoyed years of above-average rainfall, the winter of 1906-07 was without the accustomed chinook, bringing stock losses in the thousands for many large-scale ranchers.

The passing of the great cattle companies in Alberta and Saskatchewan brought a new generation of local ranchers, including A.E. CROSS of the A7 and George LANE of the Bar U, to prominence. At the same time the predominantly American origin of most dryland settlers, and heavy WWI enlistments and casualties sustained by the British-Canadian population, combined to change profoundly the social character of the ranch country. Nonetheless, during the war ranchers' fortunes began to improve: their political party had returned to power in Ottawa, beef prices were buoyant and the return of a dry cycle caused settlement in the region to ebb. A decade later the ebb became a flood and the out-migration of thousands of drought-driven refugees in the 1930s brought grudging recognition that the cattlemen had pioneered, and would carry on, an enterprise especially suited to semiarid environments. *See* ANIMAL AGRICULTURE.   DAVID H. BREEN

Reading: David H. Breen, *The Canadian Prairie West and the Ranching Frontier 1874-1924* (1983); E. Gould, *Ranching* (1978); D.C. McGowan, *Grassland Settlers* (1975).

Rand, Ivan Cleveland, judge, labour and international arbitrator, educator (b at Moncton, NB 27 Apr 1884; d at London, Ont 2 Jan 1969). He achieved prominence in labour relations for his development, in the 1945 FORD MOTOR COMPANY labour dispute, of the RAND FORMULA for dealing with closed union shops; in international affairs for his leading role in the UN Special Committee on Palestine (1947); as a jurist for his uncompromising civil-libertarian and natural-rights orientation on the Supreme Court of Canada (1943-59); and as educator as inaugural dean of Western's Faculty of Law (1959-64). The frugal, principled, eloquent and often brusque son of a Baptist railway mechanic, Rand was committed to judicial activism in pursuit of social justice, a commitment encouraged at Harvard under mentor Louis D. Brandeis, and in a frontier litigation practice at Medicine Hat, Alta (1913-20). After working as a lawyer in Moncton (1920-24) and a brief foray into politics as Liberal attorney general of NB (1924-25), Rand was corporate counsel to the Canadian National Ry (1926-43). He was elevated to the Supreme Court by the Mackenzie KING government, and his judicial profile later led to his appointment to various royal commissions.   G. BLAINE BAKER

Rand Formula, a form of union security whereby an employer deducts a portion of the salaries of all employees within a bargaining unit, union members or not, to go to the union as union dues ("checkoff"). It was named for a 1946 decision handed down by Mr Justice Ivan RAND of the Supreme Court of Canada while he was arbitrating the WINDSOR STRIKE. The original formula was based on the assumption that the union is essential for all workers and must be responsible for them. Two interrelated provisions following from this assumption guaranteed the union the financial means to carry out its programs, and established the financial penalties for employees and unions engaging in

work stoppages or illegal strikes. For employees, these sanctions could consist of daily fines and loss of seniority; for the union the suspension of union dues. Collective agreements have spread a modified Rand Formula throughout Canada, and some provinces have given it legal force. *See* LABOUR RELATIONS.   GÉRARD DION

Randazzo, Peter, dancer, choreographer (b at Brooklyn, NY 2 Jan 1943). He joined the Martha Graham company in 1962 and went on to create roles in several of her works. In 1968 he left to cofound TORONTO DANCE THEATRE with Patricia BEATTY and David EARLE. The most prolific choreographer of the TDT triumvirate, Randazzo has observed close movement ties with his great teacher. His style, distinctively sharp, angular and staccato, is best seen in his dramatic earlier works. Later choreographies have revealed a darkly comic side and relied more on pure movement for their impact.   GRAHAM JACKSON

Random Island, 235 km², is an irregularly shaped island running 40 km E-W and 14 km N-S, situated in a deep western indentation of TRINITY BAY, Nfld. Its name may come from the Old English *randon,* "disorderly," referring to the sea. The heavily forested island is separated from the mainland by Smith Sound to the N, Northwest Arm and Random Sound to the SE. Dominated by Baker's Peak, 166 m, on its NE tip, Random I has massive beds of red shale and limestone on the NW side that supported brick factories at Elliot's Cove and Snooks Harbour from the late 1800s. The 9 communities that now ring the island were founded in the mid-1800s by fishermen. Today the island is connected to insular Newfoundland by the Hefferton Causeway.   JANET E.M. PITT

Rankin Inlet, NWT, Hamlet, pop 1109 (1981c), is located on the W coast of HUDSON BAY, 1150 km E of YELLOWKNIFE. Named after Rankin Inlet (discovered by John Rankin, on which it sits, the community was established as a mining centre in 1955 by North Rankin Nickel Mines. When the mine closed in 1962, the mostly Inuit residents suffered a serious setback. Today the economy has recovered with a successful fishery and a booming Inuit craft industry. It is also a key government, transportation and communications centre.   ANNELIES POOL

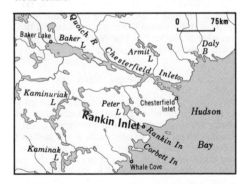

Rape Until it was amended in 1982 the Criminal Code contained the offence of rape. The offence required proof that a man had sexual intercourse with a woman other than his wife, without her consent. It was punishable by up to life imprisonment.

The offence of rape, perhaps more than any other offence, demonstrated the tensions arising in CRIMINAL LAW from conflicting principles: the presumption of innocence (and thus, the requirement that the Crown prove all of the elements of the offence beyond a reasonable doubt) and the need to protect potential victims and punish offenders. The emotional and traumatic nature of the trial (which might include cross-examination of the complainant about her prior sexual conduct with the accused and others), ag-

gravated by the feelings of shame and degradation suffered by a rape victim, may have contributed to the fact that rape was an under-reported crime. Sometimes the accused was a "friend" or relative which led to the imposition of even greater pressure upon the complainant.

With the passing of Bill C-127, Parliament has abolished the offence of rape, replacing it with the offences of sexual assault. There are 3 categories of such assault: basic sexual assault, ie, sexual touching or sexual intercourse without consent, punishable by up to 10 years imprisonment; sexual assault with a weapon or threatened violence, punishable by up to 14 years in prison; and aggravated sexual assault, in which the victim is wounded or disfigured, punishable by up to life imprisonment. The distinction between men and women, in that only men could commit rape, has been abolished, since sexual assault is a crime which either sex can commit; spousal immunity has been ended, ie, sexual conduct between spouses must now be consensual; proof of vaginal penetration by the penis is no longer a requirement, and so failing to report the crime within a matter of hours (and certainly a day) will no longer be fatal to the Crown's case because of insufficient evidence as it previously might have been; and the doctrine of recent complaint has been abolished so that failure to complain at the first reasonable opportunity will no longer lead to a comment to the jury that may harm the complainant's credibility.   MARGARET A. SOMERVILLE

Rapeseed, *see* CANOLA.

Raphael, William, painter (b in W Prussia 1833; d at Montréal 15 Mar 1914). A graduate of the Berlin School of Art, Raphael came to Canada in 1860, bringing academic status, as well as striking apricot colours, to his genre painting of the Montréal harbour and market life. The elegance and precision of his townspeople waiting by the docks is also found in his portraits in the Parliament Bldg (Ottawa). He painted wild winter storms and wolves, and was included in *Picturesque Canada* (1882). By 1904 he was giving drawing and painting classes in Montréal and was appointed a member of the Council of Arts and Manufacturers of Québec.

                   ANNE McDOUGALL

Rapson, William Howard, chemical engineer, professor, consultant (b at Toronto 15 Sept 1912). After 12 years of research at the Canadian International Paper Co, Hawkesbury, Ont, he returned to U of T where he had received his doctorate in chemical engineering in 1941. In addition to teaching, research and administration at the university, he became consultant on the manufacture and application of chemicals for the pulp and paper industry. From his research came new methods of bleaching woodpulp that enabled pine wood to be used for strong, white paper for the first time and gave Canada important advantages in export trade. He also invented processes for the manufacturing industry. In recent years he turned his attention to the amelioration of water pollution by woodpulp mills. A fellow of the RSC, he has been honoured in Canada and abroad.   MORRIS WAYMAN

Rasminsky, Louis, banker (b at Montréal 1 Feb 1908). Rasminsky played a major role in creating the post-WWII international monetary system. He attended U of T and London School of Economics, specializing in the study of money. In 1930 he joined the Economic and Financial Section of the League of Nations in Geneva, Swit, and by 1939 had established a high reputation. In 1940 he became a member of the Foreign Exchange Control Board, Ottawa, organizing its research and statistics section, and by 1942 he was alternate chairman. Much of his time was devoted to producing a "Canadian plan" for an international monetary system. In meetings before and during the conference at Bretton Woods, NH, in 1944, Rasminsky's plan was thoroughly studied and partially accepted. After WWII Rasminsky rose through the BANK OF CANADA hierarchy to become governor in 1961. He headed the bank for 11 years, carefully shepherding monetary policy through difficult times.   J.L. GRANATSTEIN

Reading: J.L. Granatstein, *The Ottawa Men* (1982).

Raspberry, *see* BERRIES, CULTIVATED; BERRIES, WILD.

Rat, common name for certain MAMMALS of order RODENTIA. Three species occur in Canada, the bushy-tailed wood rat (*Neotoma cinerea*) of the Cricetidae family being the only native. The Eurasian black rat and brown or Norway rat (*Rattus rattus, R. norvegicus,* respectively), of the Muridae family, were introduced to N America by man. The bushy-tailed wood rat, which may grow to 50 cm long, has a long, hairy tail and long, soft fur. It inhabits the CORDILLERA of western N America from the YT to New Mexico. It is solitary and nocturnal, feeds chiefly on vegetation, and scavenges around cottages. In Canada, it produces one litter annually (averaging 3-4 young). Black and brown rats have short, straight-haired coats and scaly, hairless tails. The brown rat is the larger, growing to 68 cm. Both species inhabit populated areas, black rats being found only along the BC coast, brown rats, in almost every inhabited region of Canada. These species are gregarious. The black rat, an excellent climber, inhabits lofts and roofs of houses or farm buildings. Brown rats mainly burrow. Both are prolific, reproducing throughout the year, mainly spring through autumn. The brown rat produces from 3-12 (usually 5) litters annually, each averaging 9 young. These omnivorous rats eat food produced by humans, transmit disease and may even attack sleeping humans. They damage homes, transmission wires and drains.   JEAN FERRON

Rattenbury, Francis Mawson, architect (b at Leeds, Eng 11 Oct 1867; d at Bournemouth, Eng 28 Mar 1935). As a young architect, he left England for BC (1892) where he won the competition to design Victoria's Legislature Buildings. He won other government contracts to design various BC courthouses and designed homes for numerous wealthy clients. During the KLONDIKE GOLD RUSH he established 2 companies to carry men and supplies to the goldfields, but both had failed by 1899 and he returned to architecture. As architect for the Bank of Montreal he designed banks in Rossland, Nelson and New Westminster, and as house architect for the CPR he designed Victoria's Empress Hotel. One of his last works in BC was the Crystal Garden in Victoria. Rattenbury's abilities as an architect have been questioned; he was known more for his grand schemes than the aesthetics of his architecture. His reputation fell after he left his wife and appeared publicly with his mistress, Alma Victoria Clarke Dolling Pakenham. They left Victoria for England about 1930; their life together soon disintegrated, and in 1935 Alma and her young lover, George Stoner, were charged with Rattenbury's murder. After being acquitted Alma committed suicide. Stoner was sentenced to life imprisonment but was later released.   DAVID R. ELLIOTT

Rattlesnake, common name for 31 species of venomous viperid SNAKES in the genera *Crotalus* and *Sistrurus,* found from southern Canada to S America. Characteristic features include a broad, triangular head with movable fangs, a stout body and a "rattle" made up of unmolted, modified scales, each of which once capped the tip of the tail. The buzzing sound produced by rapidly vibrating the tail is believed to act as a defensive warning to intruders. Rattlesnakes are pit vipers, ie, have a heat-sensing pit on either side of the face. Three species are native to Canada: the

Three species of rattlesnake are native to Canada, including the massasauga rattlesnake (*Sistrurus catenatus*). (*photo by Mary W. Ferguson*).

western rattlesnake occurs in arid grasslands of Saskatchewan, Alberta and BC; the timber rattlesnake (probably extirpated in Canada) and massasauga rattlesnake are restricted to southern Ontario. Rattlesnakes often hibernate communally in rocky outcrops. Mating occurs in late summer; fertilization takes place the following spring. In early fall 5-10 live young are born. Females reproduce only every 2-3 years. Diet consists mainly of rodents, other small mammals and birds. The venom used to kill prey is a mixture of neurotoxins and hemotoxins (affecting nerve and blood tissues, respectively) delivered through the fangs. Rattlesnakes rarely strike humans, unless provoked or accidentally stepped on. The bite can cause painful swelling, muscular paralysis and tissue destruction, and may result in death. Less than 2% of all snakebites in N America are fatal if given medical attention. The incidence of snakebite in Canada is low.   J. MALCOLM MACARTNEY

Raudot, Jacques, intendant of NEW FRANCE, 1705-11 (b 1638; d at Paris, France 20 Feb 1728). He was related to the powerful Pontchartrain family and had had a distinguished legal career when he and his son Antoine-Denis RAUDOT were jointly appointed to the intendancy (with only Jacques salaried). Leaving finance largely to his son, Raudot concentrated his attention on the administration of justice and public order, attempting to bring in reforms of the seigneurial and judicial systems, education, agriculture and the militia. Though sociable and cultured, he had an emotional nature and was quick to take affront. He had a low opinion of Canadians in general and resented Governor VAUDREUIL's preeminent position. The last years of his term he spent unproductively feuding with the governor.   MARY McDOUGALL MAUDE

Raudot, Antoine-Denis, intendant of NEW FRANCE, 1705-10 (b 1679; d at Versailles, France 28 July 1737). He had begun a career in the ministry of marine when he and his father Jacques RAUDOT were jointly appointed INTENDANT. Intelligent and rational in approach, Antoine-Denis devoted his energies to the colony's economy, depressed because of a glut of beaver on the European market. He wanted to improve the economic base by developing agriculture, fishing and lumbering. His most imaginative proposal, outlined in a lengthy 1706 memoir, was to establish a new city on Cape Breton I to act as an entrepôt for the French empire, which by its location would ease the transportation problems between France and her colonies. Unable to achieve any such solution because of the ongoing WAR OF THE SPANISH SUCCESSION and because of his father's feud with Governor VAUDREUIL, he requested a recall and went on to a successful career in France.   MARY McDOUGALL MAUDE

Raven, black bird with a purplish lustre, belonging, like the CROW, to genus *Corvus.* Ravens are similar to crows in appearance but larger, with heavier bills. Throat feathers are pointed and elongated. Ravens are scavengers and in-habit mountainous and wild hill country and seacoasts in both forested and unforested regions. The common raven (*C. corax*), a fierce and crafty bird, is found in both the Old and New Worlds. It is the only raven native to Canada and breeds from the High Arctic islands (Prince Patrick I, southern Ellesmere I) across to Nfld, but is absent from central Alta, SW Man and central and southern Sask. The only other N American raven, the chihuahuan raven (*C. cryptoleucus*), is restricted to the southwestern US and Mexico. Ravens nest, in single pairs, on cliff ledges and in cavities, sometimes in trees. Evidence suggests that pairs mate for life. Ravens are majestic fliers and aerobatic displays seem to be involved in their courtship rituals. Their long lives, uncanny intelligence and fearlessness have given them a unique place in native mythology.   LORRAINE G. D'AGINCOURT

Raven Symbolism The Indians of the Northwest Coast had numerous origin myths which explained, for example, how daylight began or why summer and winter alternate. The principal character in many of these myths is a powerful trickster, Raven, who is known to different tribes under various names. On the northern part of the coast, Raven was the most popular crest figure. In the south he was valued as a guardian spirit. Possessors of this spirit are fine hunters who enjoy special ease in killing game. Raven combined the characteristics of good and evil, and for his mischief he was turned black forever. The HAIDA, TLINGIT and TSIMSHIAN had moieties they called Raven.   RENÉ R. GADACZ

Rawson, Donald Strathearn, limnologist (b at Claremont, Ont 19 May 1905; d at Saskatoon 16 Feb 1961). His doctoral dissertation (U of T, 1929) on the bottom fauna of Lk Simcoe was a model for ecological limnology for 20 years. His studies of Great Slave and Athabasca lakes opened those lakes to rational exploitation. He pioneered the study of Rocky Mountain lakes and was active on the prairies and Canadian Shield. His definition of the influence of lake basin on lake productivity is the basis of the widely used "morphoedaphic index" to estimate potential fish yield. He joined the faculty of U of Sask in 1928 and became head of biology in 1949.   J.R. NURSALL

Ray, FISH with cartilaginous skeleton, closely related to sharks and belonging to order Rajiformes, subclass Elasmobranchii. The order includes sawfishes, guitarfishes, sting rays, electric rays, mantas and skates. Rays occur widely in world oceans, with some also inhabiting tropical or subtropical estuaries. Skates of genus *Raja* are the most common batoid fishes in temperate and cool seas of higher latitudes. There are about 400 species of batoids, some 100 of which are skates of genus *Raja.* In Canada, there are 17 species of batoid fishes in Atlantic waters, 8 in Pacific waters. Skates of genus *Raja* are the most common, comprising 13 species in Atlantic and 6 in Pacific waters. Electric and sting rays also occur occasionally off both coasts. Rays are flattened dorsoventrally, the body appearing disclike. The pectoral fins are attached to the side of the head. The mouth, nostrils and 5 pairs of gill slits are located on the white lower surface. A pair of spiracles occurs on the upper surface behind the eyes. The skin may be smooth or variously covered with short spines. The tail is usually elongate and whiplike. Species vary greatly in size, from a disc width of about 30 cm in small forms up to 6 m and 1300 kg for the mantas. Rays swim by an undulating motion of the pectoral fins or by a winglike flapping of the whole fin. Most rays feed primarily on bottom organisms, which they crush with their specialized grinding teeth. Skates are oviparous, depositing each large egg in a horny capsule, but most other rays bear living young. Rays are of little commercial importance. Skates are processed and marketed for food in Europe but in Canada they are a by-catch used mainly for fish meal and only occasionally eaten.　　W.B. SCOTT

Ray, Carl, artist, author (b at Sandy Lk, Ont 18 Jan 1943; d at Sioux Lookout, Ont 26 Sept 1978). After his schooling he became a trapper, logger and gold miner. He contracted tuberculosis and continued his painting as therapy. A superb draughtsman, Ray was capable of painting in several different styles and media. His work stands out in the flat 2-dimensional Anishnabe (Ojibwa) school for the implied third dimension he gave each creature and for the graceful curves and original compositions. His influence is evident in the work of many Anishnabe artists today. Universally admired, he was, with Norval MORRISSEAU, one of the first native Ontario artists to defy tribal taboos and depict the sacred legends. Ray was commissioned to work on the Indians of Canada Pavilion at EXPO 67. Editor of *Kitiwin*, the Sandy Lk newspaper, he was co-author and illustrator of *The Sacred Legends of the Sandy Lake Cree* (1971).　　MARY E. SOUTHCOTT

Raymond, Louis-Marcel, botanist, man of letters (b at St-Jean, Qué 2 Dec 1915; d at Montréal 23 Aug 1972). He was a disciple and co-worker of Brother MARIE-VICTORIN at the Jardin Botanique in Montréal, and the literary quality of his scientific writing made it enjoyable to people outside the scientific community. Educated at U de M, he worked at the Jardin Botanique from 1943 until his retirement in 1970 at age 54. He wrote at least 240 scientific works and another 500 literary articles. His *Esquisse phytogéographique du Québec* (1950) is the only provincial phytogeographical study and was for 25 years the principal work on the subject. His treatises on the *Cyperaceae* (the sedge family) of different countries are basic reference works. For the last 2 years of his life he worked on a botanical history of Canada. Raymond was interested in reintroducing poetry into theatre, and his *Le Jeu retrouvé* (1943) is a panorama of French history between the wars.　　BERNARD BOIVIN

Rayner, Gordon, painter (b at Toronto 14 June 1935). Renowned for his manipulation of painting materials, Rayner has been called "the carpenter" of contemporary Canadian art. He learned his craft from his father, a landscape painter, and worked in various commercial art firms, including Wookey, Bush and Winter with Jack BUSH. An exhibition of William RONALD's work at Toronto's Hart House turned his attention to abstraction. Rayner's early 1960s work, with its juxtaposed materials, experiments in canvas shape and sense of humour, reflects the neo-dada mood then prevalent in Toronto. In time he became a sumptuous painter of Canadian landscape, especially the area around Magnetawan, Ont. His cityscapes reflect his home on Toronto's Spadina Ave. Rayner's work boldly ricochets from one concern to another, even within the same PAINTING, though his inventions are united by his broad touch and spectacular sense of colour.　　JOAN MURRAY

Razilly, Isaac de, naval captain, knight of Malta, colonizer, and lieutenant-general in Acadia (b at Château d'Oiseaumelle, Touraine, France 1587; d at La Hève, Acadia 1635). In 1626, after naval service in various parts of the world, Razilly wrote an influential memorandum to Cardinal Richelieu on French sea power and the need for the expansion of French colonies in N America. In 1632 he was selected to lead an expedition to re-establish the colony of ACADIA after 3 years of Scottish occupation. With his headquarters at La Hève and an establishment of some 300 soldiers and colonists, Razilly worked effectively to consolidate the French hold on Acadia until his unexpected death in 1635.　　JOHN G. REID

Razorbill (*Alca torda*), medium-sized (about 42 cm long) member of the AUK family. Head, neck and upperparts are black, with a narrow white line extending from the base of the laterally flattened bill to the eye; underparts are entirely white. Razorbills breed in loose groups on sheltered sites in rock crevices or under rock slabs and boulders. They first breed at 4-5 years. The one egg produced is incubated for 34-39 days. The chick is fed small fish by the parents for about 18 days and then leaves the colony for the sea, accompanied by one parent. Razorbills winter offshore. They breed along both coasts of the N Atlantic; in N America, mainly in small colonies throughout Atlantic Canada with most of the population centered in southern Labrador. The northernmost colony in Canada is in Digges Sound at the eastern entrance to Hudson Bay and there may be small groups off southeastern Baffin I. The total world breeding population, estimated at about 300 000 pairs, is one of the smallest of any auk. Recently, substantial reduction in numbers has occurred throughout its range, probably because of mortality from oil spills.　　D.N. NETTLESHIP

Razutis, Al, filmmaker, videographer, holographer, professor (b at Bamberg, W Germany 28 Apr 1946). Razutis moved to Vancouver from the US in 1968. His interest in the garish and vivid imagery of popular media, his desire to produce strong sensations through his art and his willingness to deal with political issues tie him more closely to American West Coast filmmakers than to other Vancouver film artists, such as David RIMMER. A brilliant technician, Razutis was one of the first experimental filmmakers in Canada to use the optical printer and the video synthesizer. In 1983 he was continuing to revise and release new titles in his 2 epic series, *Amerika*, a study of the effects of "a media-excessive culture," and *Visual Essays: Origins of Film*.　　R. BRUCE ELDER

Read, John Erskine, lawyer, judge (b at Halifax 5 July 1888; d at Toronto 23 Dec 1973). A Dalhousie professor (and dean) of law in the 1920s, Read was present during the formative years of the Dept of External Affairs, which he served as legal adviser 1928-46, and the International Court of Justice at the Hague, where he was a judge 1946-58. In External Affairs, Read acted for Canada in disputes such as the I'M ALONE case, seizing opportunities to extend Canada's legal independence, and rose to be deputy undersecretary of state. An expert in constitutional and international law, progressive in his views, he wrote *The Origins and Nature of the Law* (1955) and *The Rule of Law on the International Plane* (1961).　　NORMAN HILLMER

Read, Ken, alpine skier (b at Ann Arbor, Mich 6 Nov 1955). He was raised in Calgary and began skiing at 3 and competing at 8. First selected to the World Cup Team in 1974, he opened the 1975 season with a victory in the downhill at Val d'Isère, the first World Cup win by a Canadian male. With 4 further World Cup victories, he became a key member of the "Crazy Canucks" downhill team which took Europe press by storm in the late 1970s. He won 5 consecutive Canadian national championships 1975-80 (the 1977 race was cancelled).　　MURRAY SHAW

Real Estate can refer to land itself (real property), including what grows or is built on land; ownership of real property (*see* ESTATE); and the real-estate business, ie, brokers, agents, builders, developers, property managers, mortgage lenders, investors, consultants and investment advisers or appraisers.

Real estate is commonly classified as residential (eg, houses, condominiums, duplexes, cottages), rural (eg, farms and ranches), commercial (income-generating, eg, shopping centres, apartments, office or industrial buildings) or institu-

tional (eg, churches, schools, hospitals or airports). Land without improvements is regarded as residential, rural, commercial or institutional according to its intended use. Real estate is characterized by immobility, by durability (the availability of services or income over a long period) and uniqueness (no 2 properties are identical), as well as by a special body of laws and legal institutions. Real-estate values tend to fluctuate, increasing during periods of (and in regions experiencing) rapid economic growth and remaining stable or declining during periods of (and in regions experiencing) slow economic growth. The durability of real estate contributes to the price fluctuations. For example, a small change in the rents of an apartment building may have a significant impact on its value. Values may also fluctuate as a result of the slow adjustment of supply to a change in demand, and they are sometimes magnified through speculation (demand or supply arising from expectations of further price changes). Improvements to one property generally affect the value of another, and transaction costs are high (commissions, legal and appraisal fees, financing, surveying and registration costs). For residential properties the commission alone often amounts to 6% or 7% of the selling price.

It is common for vendors to use a real-estate agent to assist with the sale. The property is then generally listed for sale with a real-estate company (listing agent) that handles marketing, advertising, open houses, placement of signs, etc. The listing agent often co-operates with other real-estate companies, through a multiple-listing service, whereby a member firm may list properties to be sold by other members, as well as sell properties listed by others. The firm finding a purchaser becomes the selling agent. Both listing and selling agents are agents of the vendor, who pays the commission when the property changes hands. Normally, no commission is payable if the deal does not close. If more than one company is involved in the transaction, the commission is shared among them, often equally, but unequal splits are also common. The companies in turn share with the sales people involved. It is common for the actual transfer and registration, as well as all legal documents, to be handled by a lawyer. The term "deal pending" refers to a property being sold with one or more conditions of the sale yet to be satisfied, eg, a mortgage to be arranged.

The comparatively high value of real estate would put it beyond the reach of most people were it not for mortgages. The security of real estate enables financial institutions to lend a substantial portion of the value of the property, making ownership possible with a limited amount of owner equity (nonmortgaged portion of value). This, however, also makes real-estate values dependent on mortgage rates, which also cause price fluctuations.

Ownership rights originally extended from the centre of the earth to the sky, but are now generally limited to surface rights only. In Canada, subsurface rights, particularly mineral rights, are usually reserved by the Crown, even where the real estate is privately owned. Air rights are also held by the Crown. In addition, government also retains the right to tax, expropriate, escheat (inherit in the absence of heirs) and regulate (through land-use and zoning laws, building, health and fire codes, or rent controls) (*see* PROPERTY LAW). Property title in many provinces is registered in the local land-titles office and provides proof of ownership. Real estate can be owned individually or collectively, by corporations, co-operatives, partnerships, syndicates, etc.

Real estate is formally referred to by its legal description, eg, in cities, towns and hamlets by lot, block and plan. Condominiums (high-rise, row house or office) are described by unit number and condominium plan. In rural areas land is referred to by sections, townships, ranges and meridians.

In 1981 the total value of all mortgage loans outstanding in Canada was $149 billion; the total value of new mortgage loans placed was $13.6 billion; and the total value of all building permits issued in that year (which conveys approximately the value of additions to the stock of buildings and other improvements, but does not include the value of land upon which the improvements are being built) amounted to $18.7 billion.

Housing starts are an important economic indicator and construction expenditures play a major role in the economy. The annual total of housing and housing-related expenditures generally amounts to close to 20% of GNP. The total value of all real-estate sales completed through Multiple Listing Systems in Canada during 1983 amounted to $15.9 billion. There were 205 009 total transactions by some 55 000 members of the Canadian Real Estate Association. The total amount of property tax collected in 1980 was $9.8 billion, compared to $46.9 billion for income tax. A number of universities (eg, UBC, Laval) offer degree programs in real estate and urban and land economics. There are also a number of journals devoted to real estate.

CHRISTIAN T.L. JANSSEN

Reading: M. A. Goldberg and P. Chinloy, *Urban Land Economics* (1984).

Real Wages are estimates of money or nominal wages that have been adjusted to take into account their effective purchasing power or command over goods and services. The actual calculation of real-wage estimates involves dividing an estimate of money income (hourly, weekly or annual wages) by an index of consumer prices for the region being considered. The CONSUMER PRICE INDEX is a weighted sum of the percentage change in the price of commodities commonly bought by households compared to a particular base year.

From 1870 to 1950 real hourly wages of wage earners increased by over 346% — an annual average rate of 1.9%. The change did not occur at a constant rate: variations between periods are caused by cyclical factors that influence the demand of businesses for labour and the price level faced by consumers. Over the longer run, however, the fundamental determinant of the growth rate of real wages is the productivity of labour, which itself is determined by the skills of the labour force, CAPITAL FORMATION by business, and technological change.

Canadian weekly money and real wages experienced an increase of 370.3% from 1961 to 1981. This change largely reflected a high rate of INFLATION, particularly during the late 1960s and throughout the 1970s. But real weekly wages 1961-81 did increase slightly faster than the long-term (1870-1950) rate for hourly wages.

Estimates of national real wages can be somewhat misleading as a measure of individual economic well-being. The tendency toward a diminishing work week must be taken into account. In 1870 the standard work week in manufacturing was 64.0 hours; by 1967 it was down to 40.8 hours and in 1982 the average work week was 37.7 hours. This decline in the length of the work week means that the change in hourly real wages tends to overestimate the growth of weekly real incomes. UNEMPLOYMENT is also neglected. Even though real wages rose during the GREAT DEPRESSION, high levels of unemployment meant that expected real incomes (real wages weighted by the probability of employment) probably declined significantly. Finally, in the Canadian context an emphasis on national real wages also conceals differences in real wage levels and trends between regions.

M.B. PERCY

Reaney, James Crerar, poet, playwright, children's writer, professor, literary critic (b at Easthope, near Stratford, Ont 1 Sept 1926). Reaney has been engaged in an energetic program of "rousing the faculties" by holding up the shaping mirror of literary forms to life in Canada, particularly in southwestern Ontario. His first book, *The Red Heart* (1949), won the first of his 3 Gov Gen's Awards. In 1951 he married poet Colleen Thibaudeau. Reaney's poetry, which includes *A Suit of Nettles* (1958), *Twelve Letters to a Small Town* (1962) and the collected *Poems* (1972), has earned him a reputation as an erudite poet at once deriving structures from metaphor, mythology and a cosmopolitan literary tradition while deeply rooted in a regional sense of place.

In 1960 Reaney moved from Winnipeg to London, Ont, to teach in the English dept at Western. In a shift of emphasis from poetry to the public and communal form of drama, he wrote *The Killdeer and Other Plays* (1962), *Colours in the Dark* (1969), *Listen to the Wind* (1972), *Masks of Childhood* (1972) and plays for children. More recently, in such plays as *Wacousta, The Canadian Brothers* and his landmark trilogy *The Donnellys*, Reaney has combined archival research, poetry, elements of romance and melodrama, mime and myth to tell the central stories and legends of Ontario.

CATHERINE ROSS

Rebellion Losses Bill, modelled on Upper Canadian legislation, was introduced by Louis LAFONTAINE in Feb 1849 to compensate Lower Canadians whose property had been damaged during the Rebellions of 1837-38. LaFontaine saw the bill as the means both to gain justice for French Canadian claims to equality in the legislative union and to block the growing influence of Louis-Joseph PAPINEAU; his Tory opponents regarded it as payment for disloyalty. (In fact, because it was difficult in any given instance to determine which side in the conflict had caused the damage, some rebels, as well as those who remained loyal to the government, were compensated for losses.) Over heated Tory opposition, the legislation became law on 25 Apr 1849. Gov Gen Lord ELGIN was attacked by an English-speaking mob in Montréal and the Parliament buildings were burned (*see* MONTRÉAL RIOTS). For a short period the Montréal merchants, feeling the effects of an economic depression, advocated ANNEXATION to the US. However, Elgin was supported by the British government, and the concept of RESPONSIBLE GOVERNMENT was confirmed.

DAVID MILLS

Rebellions of 1837 took place in both Upper and Lower Canada. In LOWER CANADA the rebellion was in large part an expression of FRENCH CANADIAN NATIONALISM. The 1830s was a period of widespread economic distress fueled by an agricultural crisis and overpopulation, and of increasing tension between the French Canadian majority and the British minority, which was rapidly growing through immigration. When Britain refused to surrender control over all provincial revenues or to remodel the executive and legislative councils, Louis-Joseph PAPINEAU and the PATRIOTE Party leaders became disillusioned with the imperial connection. In 1834 the Assembly embodied its program in 92 Resolutions; the British Parliament responded with the Russell Resolutions in Mar 1837, rejecting the Assembly's demands and giving the executive authority to use provincial revenues. During the summer of 1837 patriote agitation increased, and in Nov many patriote leaders were arrested; others took refuge in the countryside. On Nov 23 government forces were repulsed by the patriotes at St-Denis. But the ill-organized, poorly equipped, and badly led rebels were crushed 2 days later at St-Charles and finally, after fierce resistance under Chenier's leadership, at St-Eustache. Papineau and some of the patriote leaders fled to the US, several

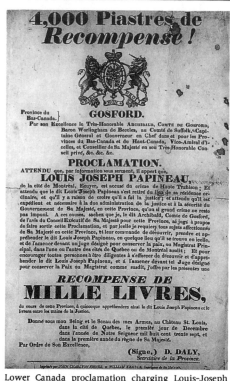

Lower Canada proclamation charging Louis-Joseph Papineau with high treason (*courtesy Public Archives of Canada/C-54741*).

hundred insurgents were wounded or killed, many more were captured, and the Constitution was suspended. The new governor, Lord DURHAM, issued an amnesty for most of the prisoners. In Nov 1838 a second outbreak led by Dr Robert Nelson and Dr Cyrille Côté was also easily controlled; 12 participants were executed and 58 others transported to Australia.

Initially the UPPER CANADA rebellion was a more limited affair. Although there was considerable discontent with the network of officials (the FAMILY COMPACT), and with provincial land-granting policies and the favouritism shown to the Church of England (*see* CLERGY RESERVES), most of the population did not want a rebellion. In 1836 Lt-Gov Sir Francis Bond HEAD assisted the conservatives in winning a majority in the Assembly, thereby playing into the hands of the radicals. When Head sent all the troops in the colony to LC, a group of radicals, led by William Lyon MACKENZIE, prepared a draft constitution declaring independence, and gathered N of Toronto in preparation for an armed attack. On Dec 5 some 800 rebels bearing rifles, staves and pitchforks marched S on Yonge St, but a group of militia and volunteers dispersed the rebels. Dr Charles Duncombe led a second futile insurrection near Brantford. Only 2 rebels, Samuel LOUNT and Peter MATTHEWS, were executed, but Canadian refugees in the US, including the erratic Mackenzie, organized raids across the border (*see* HUNTERS' LODGES), with the assistance of American sympathizers, and created an atmosphere of fear and uncertainty which led to more executions and deportations.

The causes and consequences of the rebellions have remained controversial. Some writers have seen the LC rebellion as a sudden burst of anger and indignation unleashed by Russell's Resolutions; others as a logical outcome of a long political conflict. Still others emphasize the immediate economic and social tensions that beset LC in the 1830s. In UC the controversy revolves around the extent to which the rebellion was a historical accident precipitated by Mackenzie. The relationship between the 2 outbreaks also remains problematical. The short-term results were the destruction of the influence of the radicals in both colonies, as well as Durham's appointment and his recommendations for RESPONSIBLE GOVERNMENT (*see* DURHAM REPORT) and the union of the Canadas.   P.A. BUCKNER

Reading: G. Craig, *Upper Canada* (1963); Jacques Monet, *The Last Cannon Shot* (1967); F. Ouellet, *Social and Economic History of Québec, 1760-1850,* (tr 1980).

Recession, technically, 2 or more successive quarters of declines in real GROSS NATIONAL PRODUCT, calculated by adjusting for price changes. For example, if GNP increases by 12% and the price level by 8%, real GNP has risen by 4%. Recessions are caused by a decline in one or more of the components of aggregate demand for goods and services — consumer expenditure, business-investment expenditure, government expenditure or exports. Investment expenditure is the most volatile component. In a recession the demand for the products of most businesses declines, causing a fall in sales, production and employment. Recessions can usually be halted by expansionary monetary policy, which involves increasing the money supply, thus reducing interest rates and making credit easier to obtain, or by expansionary FISCAL POLICY, which involves increased government expenditure. One reason for the reduced severity of recessions after WWII is the effect of built-in stabilizers (mechanisms that automatically increase government expenditure in downturns and reduce it in upturns), eg, unemployment insurance. A depression is a severe recession.   W.C. RIDDELL

Reciprocity, a mutual reduction of duties charged on goods exchanged between Canada and the US. The movement toward reciprocity began 1846-50 in Canada West and the Maritime colonies, particularly New Brunswick. Its earliest major advocate in Upper Canada was William Merritt. British diplomats negotiated in Washington without success before 1852, when a dispute developed over the rights of American fishermen in British coastal waters in N America. Both governments became anxious for a comprehensive settlement to dispose of the reciprocity and the fisheries issues. The Reciprocity Treaty was finally signed by BNA Gov Gen Lord ELGIN and US Secretary of State William Marcy, 6 June 1854. It was accepted by the US Congress in Aug. The treaty's principal provisions were the admission of American fishermen to the Atlantic coastal fisheries of BNA, a similar privilege to British North American fishermen in US coastal waters N of 36°N lat, and the establishment of free trade in a considerable list of natural products. Trade between the US and the colonies increased sharply after 1854, although other factors such as the Canadian railway boom and the effects of the AMERICAN CIVIL WAR (1861-65) were largely responsible.

At first the treaty was popular in both countries, but owing to a combination of political and economic factors it became unpopular in the US. Abrogated by the US, it ceased to be operative on 17 Mar 1866. Canadians continued to desire renewal, and John A. MACDONALD, George BROWN, Charles TUPPER and others made pilgrimages to Washington without success. A notable disappointment was Macdonald's failure to have a large measure of reciprocity included in the 1871 TREATY OF WASHINGTON. In the 1880s an extensive free-trade arrangement, called "commercial union" or "unrestricted reciprocity," was advocated by Erastus Wiman, Richard Cartwright and others, but protectionist and pro-British sentiments brought about the rejection of these proposals during the 1891 general election. The last major attempt at reciprocity was negotiated in 1911 by the Liberal government of Sir Wilfrid LAURIER. The Reciprocity Agreement, to be implemented by concurrent legislation, provided for free trade in natural products and the reduction of duties on a variety of other products. The agreement was accepted by the US Congress but repudiated by Canadians, who ousted the Liberals in the general election of 21 Sept 1911. After 1911 reciprocity played a less prominent part in CANADIAN-AMERICAN RELATIONS. In 1935 the Mackenzie King administration negotiated a treaty which was much less sweeping in its removal of trade barriers than that of 1854. Renewed in 1938, it was suspended in 1948 after participation of both countries in the General Agreement on Tariffs and Trade (GATT).   D.C. MASTERS

Reading: J.B. Brebner, *North Atlantic Triangle* (1945); D.C. Masters, *The Reciprocity Treaty of 1854* (2nd ed, 1963).

Recollets, *see* CHRISTIAN RELIGIOUS COMMUNITIES.

Reconstruction, the process of readjustment to a peacetime economy following WWII. Many believed the end of the war would mean a return to the economic depression of the 1930s, with falling production and widespread unemployment. When the Mackenzie KING government established a Department of Reconstruction in 1944, however, it turned the department over to C.D. HOWE, one of the most optimistic men in the cabinet. Howe believed there would be a shortage of goods at war's end rather than a surplus, and he concentrated on reconversion of factories to civilian and consumer production, while stimulating the construction industry to make up for building lost since the onset of the GREAT DEPRESSION. Howe's program was very successful; government regulations were largely abolished, and Canada was returned to a free-enterprise economy.
                    ROBERT BOTHWELL

Recording Industry Sound recordings were first manufactured in Canada in 1900 by the Berliner Gramaphone Co in Montréal, from masters recorded by the company's European and US companies. Berliner's first Canadian recording artist was French Canadian baritone Joseph Saucier. Before 1960 nearly all records sold in Canada were of non-Canadian performers; however, a steady growth in the production and sale of records by Canadians resulted from the worldwide boom in the record industry as popular music became a major cultural force in the late 1960s. This trend was augmented by a radio broadcast ruling implemented in 1970 by the CRTC (now CANADIAN RADIO-TELEVISION AND TELECOMMUNICATIONS COMMISSION) which required that AM broadcasters play a minimum of 30% Canadian material in a week. To qualify as "Can con" (Canadian content), a recording must be Canadian in 2 of the 4 following criteria: music, artist, production or lyrics (known as the MAPL code). While there were many attempts to start Canadian-owned record companies during the 1960s, few survived prior to the implementation of the "Can con" rulings.

Retail sales of records in Canada in 1981 were valued at approximately $600 million. Canadian-owned companies accounted for about 9% of those sales. The other 91% of the market was held by a handful of multinational companies, but only 9% of their releases were Canadian, while 45% of the recordings released by Canadian-owned firms were "Can con." Because of the limited size of the domestic market, Canadian companies depend on foreign income for a significant portion of their earnings. In general, inadequate investment capital, poor marketing skills and lack of a viable independent distribution network in Canada are the primary causes for the market imbalance and the slow pace at which the market share for independents is increasing.

Figures compiled for 1981 indicate that the recording industry accounts for roughly 12 000 employees in Canada, with roughly 65% in retail, 5% in distribution and 30% in production (including the creative artists — composers, songwriters and performers). Because of a tariff imposed on the physical form (disc or tape), the manufacturing of foreign-originated works is largely done in Canada. The creative work itself is not taxed, in conformity with international agreements.

In 1981, 80% of the recordings sold in Canada were in the "popular" music category — rock and middle-of-the-road. In descending order, the remaining sales were in classical, jazz, country/folk and children's recordings. Examples of internationally known Canadian performers are RUSH, LOVERBOY, and Saga (in the rock idiom); Anne MURRAY, Gordon LIGHTFOOT and René Simard (in middle-of-the-road genres); Maureen FORRESTER, Glenn GOULD, Kenneth GILBERT, Liona BOYD, André GAGNON, Jon VICKERS and Anton KUERTI (in the classical field); Oscar PETERSON, Hagood HARDY and the Boss Brass (in jazz); and chansonniers Pauline JULIEN and Félix LECLERC.

The CBC has played an important role in recording Canadian classical artists and compositions. The first album was issued in 1945 but it was not until the early 1970s, when it became clear that the CBC's listeners were anxious to hear more of the performances that were available on radio and TV, that they offered records for sale to the public. Within 10 years, the CBC has become the largest manufacturer and distributor of Canadian classical recordings. It also produces records in the folk, electronic, jazz, pop and children's fields.

In Canada, the performer is paid in the form of royalties on records sold. Publishers and composers are paid from "mechanical" royalties, a fixed fee paid for each record manufactured. Mechanical royalties are collected on behalf of artists and publishers by the Canadian Mechanical Reproduction Rights Agency (CMRRA) and the Administration du droit de reproduction mécanique des auteurs, compositeurs et éditeurs (SDRM). Performance royalties are paid to composers and publishers for the use of the music for public broadcast purposes, such as radio or TV broadcasts. Performance royalties are collected and disbursed by 2 associations in Canada: the Composers, Authors and Publishers Assn of Canada (CAPAC) and the Performing Rights Organization of Canada (PROCan). The entire payment scheme is dictated by the Copyright Act of Canada and by negotiated agreements between rights holders and record companies (*see* COPYRIGHT LAW).

Trade associations are active in the recording industry. The multinationals (and some of the larger independents) are represented by the Canadian Recording Industry Assn (CRIA); the independent sector by the Canadian Independent Record Production Assn (CIRPA) and the Assn du disque et de l'industrie du spectacle québecois (ADISQ); and publishers by the Canadian Music Publishers Assn (CMPA). These associations deal with industry-wide issues, including home taping, which drains estimated millions from the industry each year; generating private sector investment; a viable government cultural and economic policy; and understanding and adapting to new technologies, such as compact digital audio discs, electronic music jukeboxes and music videos.

The Juno Awards (est 1964) are the awards presented annually by the Canadian recording industry. There are a variety of categories in the fields of performance, production and composition, and awards are made on the basis of record sales over a 14-month period. Since Québec performers were infrequently included in the Junos, the ADISQ introduced its own awards in 1979. *See also* CHAMBER MUSIC; COUNTRY AND WESTERN MUSIC; FOLK MUSIC; JAZZ; ORCHESTRAL MUSIC; POPULAR MUSIC.   CANADIAN INDEPENDENT
RECORD PRODUCTION ASSOCIATION

Reading: Encyclopedia of Music in Canada (1981); E.B. Moogk, *Roll Back the Years/En remontant les années* (1975).

Red Bay, Nfld, Community, pop 316 (1981c), inc 1973, is located on the Str of Belle Isle, off Labrador's S coast. Named for its prominent red cliffs, it was one of 2 major BASQUE whaling stations established in the 1540s. After research into Spanish documents and archaeological finds on Saddle I and under water, Red Bay was designated a historical site 1978-79. A sunken whaler, *San Juan*, one of the oldest-known and best-preserved shipwrecks of the post-medieval period, yielded information about some of the estimated 2000 men who caught and processed whales at Red Bay at the peak of the fishery. By 1983 several other sunken ships had been discovered in the area. The community, settled by Newfoundland fishermen from CONCEPTION BAY by the early 1800s, originally alternated between winter and summer sites, but now occupies the former summer harbour year-round. Red Bay was the site of the first co-operative store in Labrador, the second such venture in the colony.　　JANET E.M. PITT AND ROBERT D. PITT

Reading: Selma Barkham, "The Basques: Filling a Gap in Our History Between Jacques Cartier and Champlain," *Canadian Geographical Journal,* vol 96, no 1 (Feb-Mar 1978) 8-19.

Red Cross Society The International Committee of the Red Cross is an independent institution recognized by international law. There are Red Cross or related societies in 131 countries. The League of Red Cross Societies (est 1919) co-ordinates relief to disaster areas. The world Red Cross movement was founded in Geneva, Swit, by Henri Dunant, who organized help for the wounded at the Battle of Solferino in 1859. A book he wrote about the carnage he witnessed stirred a worldwide sensation. His work resulted in the signing of the Geneva Convention (in 1864), which provided for the neutrality of medical personnel in war and humane treatment of the wounded. He shared the first Nobel Peace Prize in 1901. The famous red cross symbol (the reverse of the Swiss flag) was adopted to identify and guarantee the safety of relief workers.

The founder of the Red Cross movement in Canada was Surgeon-Major (later Maj-Gen) George Sterling Ryerson. He accompanied the militia force sent to quell the NORTH-WEST REBELLION in 1885 and used a makeshift red cross to protect his horse-drawn ambulance. This flag (now in the Metropolitan Toronto Library) was flown during the Battle of BATOCHE, 9-12 May 1885. In 1896 Ryerson organized a Canadian branch (Toronto) of the British Red Cross Society which, in 1898, raised money for relief of combatants in the Spanish-American War and in 1899 distributed medical supplies during the SOUTH AFRICAN WAR.

In 1909 the federal government passed the Canadian Red Cross Society Act, which established the society as a corporate body. During WWI the society raised $35 million in relief, shipped supplies overseas, maintained 5 hospitals in England and one in France, and provided recreation huts and ambulance convoys. After the war, outpost hospitals were set up in isolated areas and in 1927 the International Committee recognized the CRC as an independent national society. During WWII the society contributed volunteer services and $125 million in goods and money, followed in later years by veterans' services and overseas services for orphaned children and refugees.

The Canadian Red Cross supervises a number of programs, including the Blood Transfusion Service (est 1947), which accepts blood from over one million donors each year. The Water Safety Service trains instructors who implement the program in all parts of Canada. Volunteers provide transportation and recreational facilities for veterans, hospital outpatients, the aged and the disabled, and contribute articles of clothing for victims of disaster. The CRC is made up of 10 provincial divisions and 700 branches, with headquarters in Toronto.

Red Crow, Blood chief (b on Belly R, Alta *c*1830; d near Stand Off, Alta 28 Aug 1900). Head chief of the BLOOD tribe, Red Crow was one of the prominent leaders whose support was required for the peaceful settlement of the West. Born of a long line of chiefs, he became a noted warrior before succeeding to the chieftainship of his branch of the BLACKFOOT nation in 1870. He greeted the NORTH-WEST MOUNTED POLICE as friends when they came west in 1874, and, because of his trust in them, 3 years later he signed Treaty No 7. When he settled on his reserve (the largest in Canada), he pursued self-sufficiency for his people, introducing ranching and stressing the importance of education. At the same time, he remained a strong proponent of native customs and religion.　　HUGH A. DEMPSEY

Reading: Hugh A. Dempsey, *Red Crow, Warrior Chief* (1980).

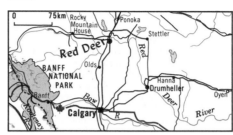

Red Deer, Alta, City, pop 46 393 (1981c), inc 1913, is located on the RED DEER R, 150 km S of Edmonton. The Cree applied the name "Elk" to the river, but Scottish settlers appear to have confused elk with the red deer of their homeland. The original settlement began 1882 where the old Calgary-Edmonton Trail crossed the Red Deer R. During the Riel Rebellion (1885) the Canadian militia constructed Fort Normandeau at this site. The post was then used by the NWMP until 1893. In 1891 the settlement moved 7 km downstream to a site on the newly constructed Calgary-Edmonton Ry (now part of the CPR). Around the turn of the century, the community experienced a surge of growth as a huge number of settlers flooded into the area to take up homesteads.

Red Deer developed primarily as an agricultural service and distribution centre, an activity enhanced by its location midway between Calgary and Edmonton, in the centre of a very fertile mixed-farming district. It became a major divisional point of the CPR in 1907, and in 1911 the Alberta Central and Canadian Northern railways entered the town. The provincial institution for the care of the mentally handicapped, currently known as the Michener Centre, established 1922, has had a great impact on the community. After WWII, with the discovery of significant oil and natural-gas fields in the area, Red Deer entered a prolonged boom. In the late 1950s it may have been the fastest-growing city in Canada.

The petroleum service industry became an increasingly important part of Red Deer's economy. After a lull in growth in the early 1970s, another boom accompanied the construction of world-scale petrochemical plants E of the city at Joffre and Prentiss. Currently, Red Deer is a modern city with excellent recreational and cultural facilities, a college, a large regional healthcare centre, and extensive convention and exhibition facilities. It is also the centre of the parkland district of central Alberta. Attractions are the award-winning city hall (1961) and St Mary's Church (1968).　　MICHAEL DAWE

Reading: G.C. Parker, *Proud Beginnings: A Pictorial History of Red Deer* (1981); K. Wood, *A Corner of Canada* (1966).

Red Deer River, 740 km, is glacier-fed by streams from Mt Drummond and Cyclone Mt in the Rockies of Banff National Park, Alberta. It flows E then S to join the S SASKATCHEWAN R just inside Saskatchewan. Its 44 500 km² basin includes mountains, foothills and semiarid prairies; recognized white-water courses occur on its wilder upper reaches. On its lower portion, 300 km are lined by famous scenic badlands containing dinosaur fossils, examples of which may be seen in the Tyrell Museum (Drumheller, Alta) and DINOSAUR PROVINCIAL PARK, a UNESCO World Heritage Site. The city of RED DEER is a major industrial (petrochemicals) user of water, along with irrigation and water-diversion schemes.　　IAN A. CAMPBELL

Red Ensign (often "Canadian Red Ensign"), the recognized flag of Canada until 1965 when it was replaced by the maple leaf design. Based on the ensign flown by British merchant ships, the Canadian Red Ensign is a red flag with a Union Jack in the upper corner next to the staff and the Canadian coat of arms in the fly. The Red Ensign, bearing the appropriate coats of arms, is now the official flag of Ontario and Manitoba (*see* EMBLEMS OF CANADA).　　JOHN ROBERT COLOMBO

Red River, 877 km long (to the head of the Sheyenne R), rises in Lk Traverse on the Minn-S Dak border, as the Bois de Sioux R, joins the Otter Tail R and flows directly N past Fargo and Grand Forks, crossing the Canadian border between Pembina, N Dak, and EMERSON, Man. It receives its major tributary, the ASSINIBOINE, at the "forks" in WINNIPEG and enters Lk Winnipeg through a labyrinth of channels. As the last glacier receded, the river actually flowed S; today, it flows N across a flat plain, rich in topsoil left by the glacial Lake AGASSIZ. Though in time of drought (eg, 1934) the river can virtually dry up, a late spring thaw after heavy snow can cause it to spill over its shallow banks onto the plain, with disastrous effect. The flooding threat is made worse because the river flows S to N, meaning the upper reaches thaw before the lower river.

The river was discovered (1734) by the LA VÉRENDRYE expedition; a French post, Ft Maurepas, was built on the delta that year and Ft Rouge (1738) at the forks. Retired voyageurs and their Métis offspring settled along the river, but systematic farming only began with the SELKIRK colonists (1812). The river was the heart of the RED RIVER COLONY; farms were laid in narrow strips along the riverbanks for irrigation and easy

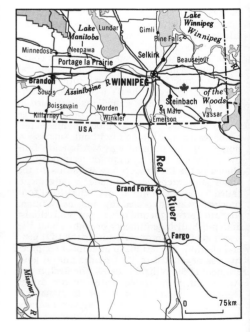

transport. By 1831 enough wheat was being grown to provision part of the HBC operation. The MENNONITES (1870s) were the first to farm the prairie, away from the river. Key settlements on the river were Upper and LOWER FT GARRY, Selkirk and, after 1865, the growing town of Winnipeg. The N-S flow of the river encouraged commerce with the US, but this attraction lessened with the arrival of the railway from Canada. Works to prevent flooding began as early as 1844, but the major project began after the devastating flood of 1950, which drove 100 000 people from their homes and inundated 15 000 farm buildings and businesses. The Red River Floodway, a wide channel 47 km long, diverts floodwaters around Winnipeg. The river's name is a translation of the French Rivière Rouge (about 1740), which in turn is a translation of the Cree *Miscousipi*, "red water river." The river takes its red colour from the clay deep in its trench.   JAMES MARSH

Red River Cart Likely originating in both French and Scottish traditions, the Red River cart was constructed entirely of wood and was tied together with leather. It was easily repaired and was wonderfully adapted to prairie conditions; its 2 high, deeply dished wheels made it stable, and it could be drawn through mud and marsh. Wood and leather produced an ear-piercing squeal audible for kilometres. The cart was buoyant and could be floated across streams, yet it was strong enough to carry loads as heavy as 450 kg. Two shafts attached to the axle were strapped to a pony or ox.

The Red River cart was first used by the MÉTIS to bring meat from the buffalo hunt and later in farm work. By the 1850s organized brigades of carts were making the 885 km journey from Ft Garry to St Paul, Minn, and by the 1860s some 600 carts were making 2 round trips annually, carrying some 270-360 kg each. The most important long-distance cart road was the Carlton Trail from Ft Garry to Ft Ellice and Ft Carlton (on the N Saskatchewan R) and on to Ft Edmonton. For several years into the 1860s about 300 carts made one trip per season from the RED RIVER COLONY, carrying trade goods and furs. The carts were gradually replaced by the steamboat and ultimately the railway.   JAMES MARSH

Red River Colony, settlement on the Red and Assiniboine rivers in what is now Manitoba and N Dakota, fd 1812 by the earl of SELKIRK. From 1801 Selkirk had sought British support for settlement in the region occupied by the HUDSON'S BAY COMPANY, but not until he and his family had gained control of the company in 1810 did his scheme become practical. In 1811 the company granted Selkirk some 300 000 km² in the Winnipeg Basin, which he called ASSINIBOIA. Under Miles MACDONELL, Selkirk's choice as governor, an advance party was sent from Scotland to Hudson Bay in July 1811, and finally arrived on the Red R on 29 Aug 1812. A second group joined them in Oct. Macdonell established his base near the junction of the Red and Assiniboine rivers (now downtown WINNIPEG) with a subsidiary centre 130 km S at Pembina (N Dak). The settlers had difficulty becoming self-sufficient, and only the assistance of resident NORTH WEST COMPANY traders and local freemen enabled them to survive. Naturally bellicose and fearing that new settlers would strip the area of food supplies, Macdonell attempted to monopolize the region's provision trade through the "Pemmican Proclamation" of 8 Jan 1814, by which he prohibited the export of provisions from the region. This threat to the NWC's trans-continental transportation system which took provisions, especially PEMMICAN, from the area to supply its canoe brigades, led 'the NOR'WESTERS and their MÉTIS allies to retaliate. In early 1815 the Nor'Westers seduced many colonists back to Canada by promising better land. Macdonell

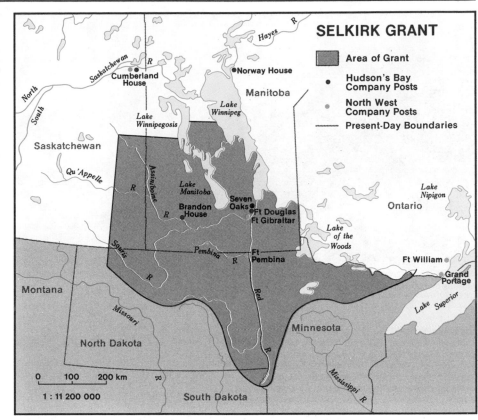

SELKIRK GRANT

- [shaded] Area of Grant
- ● Hudson's Bay Company Posts
- ○ North West Company Posts
- —— Present-Day Boundaries

1 : 11 200 000

was arrested, the remaining inhabitants withdrew, and the settlement was burnt. Later that year the colony was reoccupied under Colin Robertson, and Robert SEMPLE replaced Macdonell as governor. Continual complaint with the NWC led in 1816 to the SEVEN OAKS INCIDENT, after which the Nor'Westers again evacuated the colony. Meanwhile, Selkirk had recruited new settlers among the DE MEURONS, discharged mercenary soldiers, and was leading this group to Red River when he learned of Seven Oaks. On Aug 13 he seized the NWC's FORT WILLIAM, which lay on his route, and on 10 Jan 1817 sent a force to retake Ft Douglas. When Selkirk finally arrived that July, he distributed land and restored the settlers' confidence, promising them schools and clergymen. Roman Catholic priests arrived in 1818, but not until 1820 did a Protestant missionary come, and he was Anglican rather than Gaelic-speaking Presbyterian, a source of grievance to the Scots settlers for years.

After 1817 the environment became the major threat to the infant colony. Locusts devastated the crops in 1818 and 1819, and the greatest known flood of the Red R virtually destroyed the settlement in 1826. After Selkirk's death in 1820 his executors administered the colony, and sought to reduce expenses by ending settlers' subsidies and refusing to recruit new European immigrants. Population growth came largely

A group of Métis carters, camped with their Red River carts on the trail to St Paul, Minn, 1858 (*courtesy Minnesota Historical Society/405*).

through the retirement of fur traders and their native families to the colony, encouraged after 1821 by the newly amalgamated HBC's draconian reduction of the number of its employees. On 4 May 1836 Assiniboia was transferred to the HBC by Selkirk's family and administrative confusion ended.

Population grew slowly but steadily, composed largely of Métis (French-speaking Roman Catholics) and "mixed-bloods" or "country-born" (English-speaking Protestants), the former slightly more numerous than the latter. Despite continual conflicts over language, religion and class, a promising multiracial society was developing. The roots of its problems were economic, because of the colony's isolation. The HBC attempted to control commerce, although its limitations were made clear by the HBC's prosecution in 1849 of Pierre-Guillaume Sayer for illicit fur trading: the outcome was, in effect, free trade for the Métis. Perhaps equally critical was the inability of the colony to provide suitable employment for an increasingly literate population, leading the younger generation to become extremely restive. When in the wake of CONFEDERATION (and without consultation with the colony's inhabitants or guarantees of their rights) arrangements were made to transfer the colony and RUPERT'S LAND to Canada, the stage was set for the RED RIVER REBELLION. The colony was reluctantly admitted to Canada as the province of Manitoba, its boundaries limited to the existing areas of settlement N of 49° lat.
        J.M. BUMSTED

Reading: W.L. Morton, *Manitoba* (2nd ed, 1967).

Red River Rebellion (also known as Red River Resistance), a movement of national self-determination by the MÉTIS of the RED RIVER COLONY in what is now Manitoba, 1869-70. The settlement was after 1836 administered by the HUDSON'S BAY COMPANY and populated mainly by people of mixed European and Indian blood. Slightly over half were francophone (Métis), slightly under half anglophone ("country-born"). The inhabitants were continually in conflict with the HBC, particularly over trading

Painting by F.A. Hopkins showing the *Red River Expedition* (1870) (*courtesy Public Archives of Canada/C-2775*).

privileges. By the 1850s the company's rule was under attack from Britain, Canada and the US, and by the 1860s it had agreed to surrender its monopoly over the North-West, including the settlement. Arrangements were negotiated to transfer sovereignty to Canada. During the lengthy bargaining period, Canadian and American settlers moved in, and their pretensions led the mixed bloods to fear for the preservation of their land rights and culture. Neither the British nor the Canadian government made serious efforts to assuage these fears, negotiating the transfer of RUPERT'S LAND as if no population existed there. Mixed-blood concerns were exacerbated by Canadian attempts to resurvey the settlement in defiance of existing occupancy, and by the appointment of Canadian annexationist William MCDOUGALL as the territory's first lieutenant-governor. In late 1869 Louis RIEL emerged as the Métis spokesman. He recognized that his people must work with the more reticent anglophone mixed-bloods to satisfy their grievances. While local HBC officials maintained a studied neutrality, Métis opposition late in 1869 caused the Canadian government to refuse to take over the territory on 1 Dec 1869 as had been agreed. This encouraged Riel's insurgents, who had already prevented McDougall from entering the settlement; they seized Upper Ft Garry and fought against supporters of Canada. Representatives of the settlers were summoned to an elected convention, which in Dec proclaimed a provisional government, soon headed by Riel. In Jan 1870 Riel gained the support of most of the country-born in a second convention, which agreed to form a representative provisional government to negotiate with Canada the terms of entry into CONFEDERATION. Armed conflict persisted over the winter, but Riel seemed in control until he made the colossal blunder of court-martialling and executing a prisoner, Ontario Orangeman Thomas SCOTT. Although the Canadian authorities were still willing to deal with Riel, they later seized upon the Scott case as a reason for refusing to grant an unconditional amnesty.

The legislative assembly of the provisional government organized the territory of ASSINIBOIA in Mar 1870 and enacted a law code in Apr. Although the Canadian government recognized the "rights" of the people of Red River in negotiations in Ottawa that spring, the victory was limited. A new province called Manitoba was created by the MANITOBA ACT, its territory severely limited to the old boundaries of the settlement, whereas the vast North-West remained firmly

in Canadian hands. Even within Manitoba, public lands were controlled by the federal government. Mixed-blood land titles were guaranteed and some 607 000 ha were reserved for the children of mixed-blood families, but these arrangements were mismanaged by subsequent federal governments. The Métis nation did not flourish after 1870 in Manitoba. There was no amnesty for Louis Riel and his lieutenants, who fled just before the arrival of British and Canadian troops in Aug 1870. Although the insurrection had ostensibly won its major objectives — a distinct province with land and cultural rights guaranteed — the victory was hollow. The Métis soon found themselves so disadvantaged in Manitoba that they moved farther W, where they would again attempt to assert their nationality under Riel in the NORTH-WEST REBELLION of 1885.   J.M. BUMSTED

Reading: W.L. Morton, "Introduction," *Alexander Begg's Red River Journal* (1956); G.F.G. Stanley, *The Birth of Western Canada* (1936).

Red Tory, popular term describing Canadian Conservatives who favoured an interventionist state and feared the increasing influence of the US upon Canada. To Gad Horowitz, Canada's SOCIALISM developed from the conservative ideology of the LOYALISTS, who rejected liberal individualism and believed in an organic state where each part bore responsibility for the welfare of the whole. George GRANT, a self-described "red Tory," believed he was part of a tradition essential to the distinctiveness of Canada in N America. Conservative interventionism is now more easily explained by political needs than by philosophy. "Red Tory" is used to refer loosely to the left wing of the CONSERVATIVE PARTY.

JOHN ENGLISH

Redistribution describes both the allocation of seats in the HOUSE OF COMMONS and the procedure for drawing specific constituency boundaries within a provincial allocation (*see* ELECTORAL SYSTEMS; ELECTIONS). The current mechanism for the former is the latest in a continuing series of attempts to construct a system that will reasonably reconcile a number of very different interests and principles. Formalized in the Representation Act (1974), its basic provision is that the number of seats in the Commons, and their allocation, will be adjusted following each decennial census. The starting point is Québec, which was allocated 75 seats in 1974 with an additional 4 seats to be added in each subsequent redistribution. Dividing the current population of Québec by its allocation produces a quota, which in turn, when divided into the populations of the "large provinces" (those with a population of more than 2.5 million), de-

termines their appropriate number of seats. For the "small provinces" (those with a population under 1.5 million) a quotient is reached by dividing the total population of all the small provinces according to the preceding census by their total number of seats at the last redistribution; this quotient, divided into the current population of each small province, determines its current allocation. The provision that no province can have fewer seats in the Commons than its SENATE entitlement ensures that, despite the formula, PEI will have at least 4 seats. For the "intermediate provinces" (those with a population of between 1.5 and 2.5 million) the quotient is the total of the current small province populations divided by their new allocation of seats. The intermediate provinces' number of seats at each redistribution is increased by half the difference between its previous allocation and the figure arrived at by dividing its present population by the quotient. In all these allocations, remainders are ignored. A quite separate provision gives 2 seats to the NWT and one to the Yukon.

The actual drawing of individual constituency boundaries within a provincial allocation is governed by the Electoral Boundaries Readjustment Act (1964), which not only provided for a long-overdue redistribution of federal constituencies, but entrusted responsibility for redistribution to a set of independent boundary commissions — one in each province. Previously this task had been undertaken by Parliament, with mixed results, including overt gerrymandering (the deliberate manipulation of constituency boundaries to give the maximum partisan advantage to one party). Under the 1964 Act, new boundary commissions are to be set up after each decennial census, and the process is now bound up with the regular reallocation of seats to the provinces. The principle of redistribution in the 1964 legislation was population. The total population of a province was divided by its allocation of seats to produce its provincial electoral quota. The commissions were then to proceed on the basis that "the population of each electoral district in the province . . . shall correspond as nearly as may be to the electoral quota for the province." Although a commission could depart from a strict application of this rule where necessary, no commission could propose an electoral district in which the population departed from the provincial electoral quota by more than 25% either way. The interpretation and application of these principles have produced long and bitter debates. Members of Parliament may object to, but may not overrule, commission proposals. The timing of a redistribution is such that more than 3 years can elapse (as was the case in the 1984 federal election) from the publication of the census, through the allocation of seats to the provinces and the setting up of the commis-

	1976 (1971 census)	1982 (1981 census)
"Large provinces"		
Québec	75	79
Ontario	95	105
BC	—	33
"Intermediate provinces"		
BC	28	—
Alberta	21	27
"Small provinces"		
Nfld	7	8
NS	11	12
NB	10	10
Manitoba	14	15
Saskatchewan	14	14
PEI	4	4
NWT	2	2
Yukon	1	1
Total	282	310

sions, to the final proclamation of the new boundaries. TERENCE QUALTER

Reed, George Robert, football player (b in Mississippi 2 Oct 1939). Reed was a slashing, determined fullback with the SASKATCHEWAN ROUGHRIDERS 1962-75. He set 44 Canadian Football League records, including 16 116 yards gained, 137 touchdowns, 11 seasons of over 1000 yards, and 300 passes caught for 2772 yards. A CFL allstar 9 times and Schenley outstanding player in 1965, he was also president of the CFL Players' Assn. He began the George Reed Foundation for the Handicapped and his contributions as a citizen of Saskatchewan were recognized by the province in 1973. FRANK COSENTINO

Reeves, John, judge (b probably at London, Eng c1752/53; d there 7 Aug 1829). He studied at Oxford and was called to the bar in 1779. In 1791 he became "chief judge" of a new temporary court of civil jurisdiction instituted to correct a defect that had been revealed in Newfoundland's existing judicial system. In this capacity he was in Newfoundland from 10 Sept to 1 Nov 1791. In 1792 he became "chief justice" of another temporary court, "the supreme court of judicature of the island of Newfoundland," and again visited his jurisdiction. In 1793, on the basis of his advice, permanent judicial reforms were legislated for Newfoundland. In the same year Reeves published his *History of the Government of the Island of Newfoundland*. This pitted local residents against English West Country merchants involved in the Newfoundland trade, a theme to which later historians would frequently return. Though transient, Reeves's connection with Newfoundland was nevertheless influential, both judicially and intellectually. PETER NEARY

Reference Books, see POPULAR LITERATURE; ENCYCLOPEDIAS; ENCYCLOPEDIA OF MUSIC IN CANADA; DICTIONARY OF CANADIAN BIOGRAPHY; DICTIONARY; NATIONAL ATLAS OF CANADA.

Referendum, the referring of a political question to an electorate for direct decision by general vote. Deriving from the Latin, *ad referendum,* meaning that which must be taken back or that which must be submitted to an assembly, its roots lie in ancient Rome where the vote of the plebes ("plebiscite") invested the emperor with his position. Referendum and plebiscite are often used interchangeably. Referendums do not easily fit in with the traditions of British parliamentary practice and are inherently polarizing, even impassioning, processes and thus risky undertakings for political parties. Nevertheless, for many observers a referendum is a useful and inherently democratic device that provides a precise answer from the population to a specific measure. Referendums have taken place since the 15th century in Switzerland. In France and other European countries the practice was used in the 18th century but did not spread widely until the second half of the 20th century. Australia uses them for constitutional amendments and some American states and municipal legislatures use them for policy and constitutional issues.

As the Canadian experience demonstrates, referendums may be constitutional or simply legislative, or they may have a nonlegislative function of arbitration. They may have binding power on the government or be merely consultative in nature and may be initiated either by the government or by the people. The latter take place at the local or regional rather than national level. In Canada, referendums exist at the municipal level, but the federal government has held only 2: a legislative one, in 1898, on prohibition and an arbitrative one, in 1942, on CONSCRIPTION. In neither case were they binding. The latter, called a plebiscite, was more dramatic

than the former. The Liberal government of Mackenzie KING asked Canadians if they were in favour of releasing the government from any obligations arising out of past commitments restricting the methods of raising men for military service. Over 60% of the voters replied yes; the others, no. In Québec, however, 71% voted no — virtually the entire francophone population. In the other provinces the no vote was less than 30%.

In 1948, 2 important constitutional referendums in Newfoundland were held on the issue of union with Canada. The first failed to give an absolute majority to any of the 3 options: confederation with Canada, responsible government as it existed in 1933, or commission of government for 5 years. But a second vote, held a month later on July 2, resulted in a slim majority (52.3%) for confederation. The QUÉBEC REFERENDUM (constitutional) of 20 May 1980 was the most recent in Canada. In it, 60% of the voters refused to give the Parti Québécois government a mandate to negotiate SOVEREIGNTY-ASSOCIATION with the rest of Canada. VINCENT LEMIEUX

Reforestation, the re-establishment of a FOREST where an earlier one existed. Afforestation means starting a forest where there was none. Reforestation (or regeneration) may occur naturally over time or may result from the artificial introduction of seeds or plants. Natural regeneration will nearly always take place eventually; artificial reforestation reduces the time required, improves the spacing of seedlings, controls the species mix and allows the establishment of faster-growing, healthier seedlings from genetically improved seed orchards. During the first three-quarters of the 20th century in Canada, too much logged or burned forest was left to regenerate naturally; the result was that a great deal of land was unsatisfactorily reforested. As awareness of this problem grew, more efforts were directed to artificial reforestation. This process begins with collection and storage of seed. Seed may be sown directly, but more commonly seedlings grown in nurseries are planted in spring or fall. Seedlings grow better when planted near the area in which the seed originated. The site may be prepared for planting by burning off unwanted debris or by scarification (stirring up of surface soil). Most seedlings planted in Canada are native species, but occasionally "exotics" or new species are tried. M.F. PAINTER

Reform Movement in Upper Canada The rapid development of UPPER CANADA after the WAR OF 1812 produced social and economic tensions which were translated into politics through such issues as the expulsion of Robert GOURLAY, the ALIEN QUESTION, the Anglican monopoly of the CLERGY RESERVES and education, and TORY domination of patronage. A varied group, calling itself the Reform movement and including the Baldwins, the BIDWELLS, William Lyon MACKENZIE, John Rolph and Egerton RYERSON, presented opposition to the dominant FAMILY COMPACT. By 1828 the Reformers formed a majority in the assembly, but their program was blocked in the Tory-dominated councils.

During the early 1830s the Reform movement split. Moderates, led by Robert BALDWIN, were committed to the British Constitution, the imperial connection and the concept of a stable, hierarchical society; they simply wanted to enlarge the ruling elite through the introduction of RESPONSIBLE GOVERNMENT. Radical reformers increasingly demanded the application of republican principles to create a social and economic democracy modelled on the US; they also sought greater colonial independence. Mackenzie led a third, extreme faction.

In 1836 Baldwin entered the executive council but Lt-Gov Sir Francis Bond HEAD refused to accept responsible government. The admin-

istration resigned and the moderates were squeezed out of the political process. Mackenzie's group, devastated in the subsequent election, became more revolutionary but were crushed in the REBELLIONS OF 1837. The moderates, led by Baldwin and Francis Hincks, re-emerged as a potent political force in the United PROVINCE OF CANADA, and the nonrevolutionary radicals sank into oblivion. DAVID MILLS

Refugees, those who flee their home countries to escape persecution or danger. Canada is a country of immigrants — a country, most Canadians believe, with a long tradition of welcoming refugees and dissidents from all over the world. This, at least, has been part of the Canadian mythology. The first great wave of immigrants to arrive in Canada, the United Empire LOYALISTS, is widely regarded as Canada's first refugee contingent. But as Gerald Dirks points out in *Canada's Refugee Policy,* most were not refugees, but British settlers who preferred their old flag to the new American one. Among them were some legitimate refugees, mostly QUAKERS, MENNONITES and other nonconformists who, fearing persecution by the new American government, fled northwards. Before 1860 thousands of fugitive American slaves arrived in Canada, and the public recognition given Canada as the final stop on the UNDERGROUND RAILROAD reaffirmed to many that this country was indeed a sanctuary for the oppressed and the enslaved. An estimated 60 000 BLACKS came to Canada. It was perhaps not much of a haven, because as soon as they could (after the Emancipation Proclamation and the end of the AMERICAN CIVIL WAR) most of these ex-slaves returned home.

Over the next generation, 2 groups of refugees, Mennonites and DOUKHOBORS, arrived from Russia. Both found life under the tsars intolerable and were anxious to leave. The Canadian government, desperately searching for immigrants — especially agriculturalists — to settle the West, was just as anxious to have them. Indeed, until the 1930s GREAT DEPRESSION, almost any immigrants except blacks and Asians could come to Canada. Among the millions who arrived were obviously numbers of refugees, but no special arrangements were made for them.

A major test of Canada as a refuge for the oppressed occurred in the 1930s as German JEWS begged for admission to any country. Many nations suffering far worse economic distress than Canada were nonetheless much more receptive. While Canada grudgingly accepted some 4000 of these refugees, the US welcomed 240 000, Britain 85 000, China 25 000, Argentina and Brazil over 25 000 each, and Mexico and Colombia some 40 000 between them. But xenophobia and anti-Semitism permeated Canada, and there was little public support for, and much opposition to, the admission of refugees.

This attitude did not change until after WWII. With Europe full of "displaced persons" (a newly minted term to describe an old phenomenon, the refugee), Canada became much more receptive, largely because of a booming economy and a desperate need for manpower. Hundreds of thousands of DPs came to Canada, their journeys often subsidized by the Canadian government. Indeed, Canada now began to play an increasingly active role in the UNITED NATIONS refugee organization.

In 1956 Canada was put to the test again; this time however, it did not fail. Within months of the Hungarian uprising against the Soviets, the government succumbed to much domestic pressure, especially from ethnic and religious groups, and announced that it would accept a large number of HUNGARIAN refugees. Almost 38 000 arrived. The Canadian government was pleased; not only did these refugees bring some badly needed skills, but they provided the Western world with a not-to-be-missed opportunity of embarrassing the USSR. In 1968, 11 000 CZECHS, following the Soviet invasion of their country, settled in Canada. Most were highly skilled and rapidly integrated into Canadian society. In 1972 Canada accepted 5600 highly trained and educated Ugandan Asians who were fleeing the notorious regime of Idi Amin. Like the Czechs they quickly began making important contributions to Canada.

A more controversial group of refugees were the American war resisters ("draft dodgers"), who fled across the border to escape service in the Vietnam War. Though some returned home after the war, many took up new lives in Canada. Most controversial of all, however, were the Chilean and other LATIN AMERICAN refugees forced out of Chile by the Sept 1973 overthrow of Salvador Allende's Marxist government. Fearing that most of these political refugees were too left-wing, and not wishing to alienate either the American or new Chilean rulers, the Canadian government took only a small number. This is in sharp contrast to Canada's humanitarian behaviour during the Vietnamese "boat-people" crisis of the late 1970s. Touched by the plight of the hundreds of thousands who escaped the communist regime by taking to the high seas in leaking, unsafe boats, many Canadians offered to sponsor their journey to Canada, and the government admitted some 75 000 refugees. A 1978 amendment to the Immigration Act made it possible for the first time for refugees to apply for admission as immigrants. Refugees had previously been permitted into Canada only by special orders-in-council. Their future admission would now depend less on Canada's political and economic vagaries. Although by 1983 the government had not determined its precise definition of a refugee, Canada has agreed to accept the comprehensive definition of the United Nations Commission on Refugees. The Immigration Act (1976) refers to a refugee as one who "by reason of a well-founded fear of persecution for reasons of race, religion, nationality, membership in a particular social group or political opinion" is outside his own country and cannot, or fears to, return there. *See* IMMIGRATION.   IRVING ABELLA

Refuş global, a manifesto written by painter Paul-Emile BORDUAS, poet Claude GAUVREAU, Bruno Cormier (later a psychoanalyst), dancer Françoise Sullivan and painter Fernand LEDUC; signed by the 15 members of the AUTOMATISTES; and published (400 copies) in Montréal on 9 Aug 1948. Borduas wrote the main essay, from which the manifesto's title was taken, and 2 other texts. *Refus global* not only challenged the traditional values of Québec society but proposed the "refusal" of any ideology that hampered creative spontaneity. The manifesto referred to the strong need for liberation and "resplendent anarchy," and depicted the coming of a new hope. That was enough to cause the authorities to have Borduas removed from his post at the Ecole du meuble, where he had been teaching since 1937. The press echoed the government and largely condemned the manifesto. *Refus global* had far more than artistic impact in Québec; it served as a benchmark for the emergence of a new pluralism in the province.
          FRANÇOIS-MARC GAGNON

Regan, Gerald Augustine, lawyer, politician, premier of NS (b at Windsor, NS 13 Feb 1928). He was elected MP in 1963 and leader of the NS Liberal Party in 1965. His vigorous tactics did much to undermine the Smith Conservative government and secure a Liberal minority government in 1970, followed by a solid victory in 1974. As premier, he espoused such undertakings as a new steel complex at Gabarus, industrialization and a superport at the Strait of Canso, harnessing the tides of the Bay of FUNDY,

and development of the offshore oil and gas resources. Before any came to fruition, his government was defeated by John BUCHANAN's Conservatives in 1978, mainly because of the large increase in domestic energy costs resulting from more expensive foreign oil. Re-elected to the Commons in 1980, he served as minister of labour and minister of state for international trade.   J. MURRAY BECK

Regiment, a body of troops composed of squadrons, batteries, or companies, and often divided into battalions for military operations. A single-battalion regiment numbers 300-1000. In Canada the meaning of the term "regiment" is complex. Infantry regiments are administrative parent organizations that raise one or more battalions for service. Armoured regiments are normally battalion-sized units, though they may have both regular and reserve force components and administrative elements. The artillery organizes its batteries into regiments, but it also traditionally calls the entire artillery branch a regiment. Engineer and communication regiments are also battalion sized.

Armoured and infantry regiments are the centre of collective pride for their members and maintain close "family" relationships. For artillery and others, the branch rather than the individual regiment is the traditional family focus. In Canadian practice, a regiment's "lifetime" is the number of unbroken years of existence, though disbanded units (and their customs and battle honours) can be perpetuated by others with a proven connection. Armoured and infantry regimental precedence is determined largely by this seniority. In Europe, prior to the 16th century, the basic organization raised for battle was the company. Companies came to be grouped into regiments under a single superior officer for recruiting, training and administration. Regiments soon developed their own insignia and customs, and became the focus of esprit de corps. In battle array such groupings were called battalions, and this term then often was used interchangeably with regiment. Later, Revolutionary France structured each of its regiments permanently into 3 battalions. This practice became common, but never universal.

French settlers in Canada very early formed a militia (*see* ARMED FORCES), organized into companies from each parish. These companies worked together in battalions as the need arose. The first regiment to serve in Canada was the CARIGNAN-SALIÈRES REGIMENT, which arrived in 1665, but almost all its troops returned to France after 3 years. Until the SEVEN YEARS' WAR the militia and the regular infantry serving in the colony, TROUPES DE LA MARINE, were responsible for defence. Only in 1755, on the eve of war, did the French regular army return when battalions from 8 regiments arrived at Louisbourg and Québec. That war also brought to Canada the British regular army, which had previously garrisoned Nova Scotia and Newfoundland. After the CONQUEST the British retained and built upon the French militia organization, adding their own military heritage. When the Americans marched against Québec in 1775, the garrison consisted only of 2 weak British regular battalions, 2 composite battalions of militia and the Royal Highland Emigrants. This last, eventually 2 battalions, was a British unit raised locally for full-time service in N America. It was the first of a number of colonial regular or "fencible" regiments. The AMERICAN REVOLUTION resulted in the resettlement of members of American LOYALIST regiments in Upper Canada and New Brunswick. Such units as Butler's Rangers, settled at Niagara, provided veteran leaders for the militia in later years. As Britain's difficulties with Revolutionary France grew, the authorities again made use of fencible regiments. From 1793 to 1802 the Royal Nova Scotia Regiment, the Royal

Canadian Volunteers and the Queen's Rangers were on full-time service in Nova Scotia, Lower Canada and Upper Canada respectively.

The WAR OF 1812 was fought, on the British side, by regular regiments, some fencible units and the militia. By this time the militia of Upper and Lower Canada was organized into regiments based upon counties, with one or more from each county as population allowed. It was impractical to call out all the inhabitants of an area for lengthy periods. Instead, in LC portions of the militia were embodied into service battalions, whereas in UC only the "flank companies" (a term for the 2 elite companies in a regular 10-company battalion) were trained and equipped. The Battalion of Incorporated Militia, which figured prominently in several battles, was really a Canadian full-time regiment made up of volunteers from such flank companies.

The Canadian regimental system changed substantially with the MILITIA ACTS of 1846 and 1855. The "lifetime" of Canada's oldest present-day regiments officially begins with volunteer units created under these Acts. A few semi-official units already in existence gained official status. For instance, the York Dragoons, since 1822 part of the West York Regiment of Militia, were gazetted in 1847 as the 1st Toronto Independent Troop of Cavalry, and eventually became The Governor General's Horse Guards. The Royal Regiment of Canadian Artillery traces its continuous existence from field batteries formed 1855. Initially the volunteer cavalry and infantry were organized only as troops and companies. However, threats of war with the US and invasion by the FENIANS in the 1860s demonstrated the need for larger units. The 1st Battalion, Volunteer Militia Rifles of Canada, was formed 1859, and is today The Canadian Grenadier Guards. By Confederation most of the force was consolidated into such numbered battalions. The Canadian system was extended to the Maritimes in the Militia Act of 1868 and absorbed volunteer regiments already in existence there.

The regular Canadian army came later. The first permanent units, Schools of Gunnery formed 1871, still exist as batteries in the Royal Canadian Horse Artillery. Three companies of the Infantry School Corps, established 1883, were the beginnings of The Royal Canadian Regiment. The Cavalry School Corps, also begun in 1883, was the nucleus for The Royal Canadian Dragoons. During the SOUTH AFRICAN WAR The Royal Canadian Regiment formed 2 new battalions. The 2nd Battalion went overseas and the 3rd relieved British troops at Halifax. Both were disbanded after the war. Several battalions of Canadian Mounted Rifles were raised for war service and also were disbanded upon their return. Donald SMITH, Lord Strathcona, privately raised Strathcona's Horse for South Africa. This was later perpetuated in the permanent force as Lord Strathcona's Horse (Royal Canadians).

In 1900 all militia infantry battalions were renamed as regiments, although most retained only one battalion. The organization created for WWI was very different. The CANADIAN EXPEDITIONARY FORCE was composed of new numbered infantry battalions, artillery batteries and other arms and services. Militia regiments served only as recruiting bases, and in many cases a regiment raised more than one overseas battalion. There were a few exceptions, eg, Princess Patricia's Canadian Light Infantry, which was formed primarily from British ex-soldiers settled in Canada; it fought for a year in the British army before joining the Canadian Corps in France. Other units remained outside the Corps. The Canadian Cavalry Brigade, composed of The Royal Canadian Dragoons, Lord Strathcona's Horse (Royal Canadians), the Fort Garry Horse and the Royal Canadian Horse Artillery, served throughout the war with the British army. (The

Royal Newfoundland Regiment also fought with the British since Newfoundland was not then part of Canada.) After the war Canada disbanded the CEF units, but decided that existing regiments would perpetuate wartime battalions with which they were most closely associated in order to preserve their battle honours. At the same time, names replaced numbers in regimental titles. Two new regiments joined the permanent force: PPCLI and the Royal 22nd Regiment ("Vandoos"), the latter a French-speaking unit that had served with distinction as a CEF battalion. A 1936 reserve force reorganization converted several regiments from one role to another. Six infantry regiments became "tank," and others became "machine gun," previously a separate corps. Later, cavalry generally converted to "armoured" (tank or armoured car) regiments.

In WWII the army mobilized the Active Service Force from existing regiments. Individual units fought from HONG KONG to NW Europe. Artillery batteries, until then brigaded for tactical purposes, were combined permanently into regiments. A unique Canadian-American unit, the First Special Service Force, was formed, organized along American regimental patterns.

The regular force greatly expanded in the 1950s for the KOREAN WAR and NATO service. Additional infantry battalions formed a new regiment, The Canadian Guards, and regular components of 2 existing reserve regiments, The Queen's Own Rifles of Canada and The Black Watch (Royal Highland Regiment) of Canada. Other reserve regiments such as The Loyal Edmonton Regiment (4th Battalion, Princess Patricia's Canadian Light Infantry) became reserve battalions of the remaining regular infantry regiments. New artillery regiments and a signal regiment were raised. Two reserve armoured regiments, the 8th Canadian Hussars (Princess Louise's) and The Fort Garry Horse, also raised regular components. Tight defence budgets and reduced manpower in the 1960s led to a smaller army in the unified Canadian Armed Forces. The Canadian Guards disappeared, as did the regular components of some other units. In order to broaden francophone representation in the forces, 2 new regular regiments were formed, the 12e Régiment blindé du Canada and the 5e Régiment d'artillerie légère du Canada. The Canadian Airborne Regiment was also created.

The following armoured and infantry regiments, in order of precedence, were active on the order of battle in 1983. An asterisk (*) indicates both regular and reserve components, listed separately. *Regular Armour:* The Royal Canadian Dragoons; Lord Strathcona's Horse (Royal Canadians); *8th Canadian Hussars (Princess Louise's); *12e Régiment blindé du Canada. *Militia Armour:* The Governor General's Horse Guards; *8th Canadian Hussars (Princess Louise's) (Militia); The Elgin Regiment; The Ontario Regiment; The Queen's York Rangers (1st American Regiment); Sherbrooke Hussars; *12e Régiment blindé du Canada (Milice); 1st Hussars; The Prince Edward Island Regiment; The Royal Canadian Hussars (Montreal); The British Columbia Regiment (Duke of Connaught's Own); The South Alberta Light Horse; The Saskatchewan Dragoons; The King's Own Calgary Regiment; The British Columbia Dragoons; The Fort Garry Horse; Le Régiment de Hull; The Windsor Regiment. *Regular Infantry:* *The Royal Canadian Regiment; Princess Patricia's Canadian Light Infantry; *Royal 22e Régiment; The Canadian Airborne Regiment. *Militia Infantry:* Governor General's Foot Guards; The Canadian Grenadier Guards; The Queen's Own Rifles of Canada; The Black Watch (Royal Highland Regiment) of Canada; Les Voltigeurs de Québec; The Royal Regiment of Canada; The Royal Hamilton Light Infantry (Wentworth Regiment); The Princess

of Wales' Own Regiment; The Hastings and Prince Edward Regiment; The Lincoln and Welland Regiment; *The Royal Canadian Regiment; The Highland Fusiliers of Canada; The Grey and Simcoe Foresters; The Lorne Scots (Peel, Dufferin and Halton Regiment); The Brockville Rifles; The Lanark and Renfrew Scottish Regiment; Stormont, Dundas and Glengarry Highlanders; Les Fusiliers du St-Laurent; Le Régiment de la Chaudière; *Royal 22e Régiment; Les Fusiliers Mont-Royal; The Princess Louise Fusiliers; The Royal New Brunswick Regiment; The West Nova Scotia Regiment; The Nova Scotia Highlanders; Le Régiment de Maisonneuve; The Cameron Highlanders of Ottawa; The Royal Winnipeg Rifles; The Essex and Kent Scottish; 48th Highlanders of Canada; Le Régiment du Saguenay; The Algonquin Regiment; The Argyll and Sutherland Highlanders of Canada (Princess Louise's); The Lake Superior Scottish Regiment; The North Saskatchewan Regiment; The Royal Regina Rifle Regiment; The Rocky Mountain Rangers; The Loyal Edmonton Regiment (4th Battalion, Princess Patricia's Canadian Light Infantry); The Queen's Own Cameron Highlanders of Canada; The Royal Westminster Regiment; The Calgary Highlanders; Les Fusiliers de Sherbrooke; The Seaforth Highlanders of Canada; The Canadian Scottish Regiment (Princess Mary's); The Royal Montreal Regiment; The Irish Regiment of Canada; The Toronto Scottish Regiment; The Royal Newfoundland Regiment.

M.V. BEZEAU AND O.A. COOKE

Reading: Canada., Army Headquarters, Historical Section., *The Regiments and Corps of the Canadian Army* (1964); George F.G. Stanley, *Canada's Soldiers* (1954).

Regina, Sask, capital and commercial and financial centre of the province, is situated 160 km N of the US border. The city is set in a wide, level alluvial plain.

Settlement Regina, named for Queen Victoria — mother-in-law of then Governor General the marquess of Lorne — was founded in 1882 and made capital of the North-West Territories in 1883. The town was a creature of the CPR, which determined the location of the townsite, near the meandering Pile O' Bones (Wascana) Cr, and influenced Regina's street layout and land-use patterns.

Development Regina grew slowly at first, reaching a population of 2250 by 1901, but thereafter its fortunes improved dramatically. Named provincial capital when Saskatchewan was formed in 1905, Regina grew quickly, and by 1911 numbered over 30 000 inhabitants. The boom mentality of the period survived the destruction wrought by a 1912 tornado, but an economic depression in 1913 and the outbreak of WWI temporarily halted the city's growth. Economic conditions remained unsettled after the war, and Regina continued to mark time. Not until the mid-1920s did prosperity return, as the population leaped from 34 400 to 53 200 in the decade, but then a decade of drought and depression reduced life in Saskatchewan to bare subsistence. When better times returned for the province's farmers after 1939, Regina's economy began to revive as well. Since WWII the city has experienced steady, though unspectacular, growth, with the primary spurt in the 1950s, when the population grew by 57%.

Population: 162 613 (1981c); 164 313 (CMA)

Rates of Increase (1971-81): (CMA) 16.6%

Rank in Canada: Sixteenth (by CMA)

Date of Incorporation: 1903

Land Area: 110.6 km²

Elevation: 575 m

Climate: Average daily temp, July 19°C, Jan -17°C; Yearly precip 292 mm rainfall, 1148 mm snowfall; Hours of sunshine 2286 per year

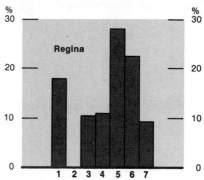

Distribution of Industrial Activity* by Industry Grouping within Census Metropolitan Areas, 1980

Industry groupings
1. Food and beverage and tobacco products industries
2. Leather, textile, knitting mills and clothing industries
3. Wood, furniture and fixtures, paper and allied and printing, publishing and allied industries
4. Machinery, transportation equipment and electrical products industries
5. Primary metal and metal fabricating industries
6. Rubber and plastic products, petroleum and coal products and chemical products industries
7. Non-metallic mineral products and miscellaneous manufacturing industries.

* Industry activity based on the average of percentage shares of the value shipments of goods of own manufacture, total value added and total number of employees for each of the selected metropolitan areas.

Source: Figure II, Catalogue 31-209, Statistics Canada.

Cityscape Reginans have transformed the cheerless prairie into a city of shaded parks and streets. Wascana Centre, surrounding manmade Wascana Lk, is a unique 920 ha area in the heart of Regina, within which may be found the stately Legislative Building (1912) and other provincial government offices, UNIVERSITY OF REGINA, the Museum of Natural History and the Saskatchewan Centre of the Arts. Interest in town planning dates from 1913 when Thomas Mawson was engaged to prepare a plan for Regina; completed in 1921, it was never implemented. The city's first town-planning bylaw, passed 1927, established 6 land-use zones.

Population Regina's population has more than doubled since WWII, in part through immigration from outside the province, but more from a general population shift from farm to city within Saskatchewan. The majority of citizens are native-born and nearly half are British in origin. People of German, Ukrainian and Scandinavian ancestry form large groups as well, and during the last 2 decades many native people have come to the city. The largest religious denominations are Roman Catholic, United Church, Lutheran, Anglican and Greek Orthodox.

Economy and Labour Force Regina is surrounded by a rich wheat-growing plain on which its economy is largely dependent. The city is the most important retail, distribution and service centre in southern Saskatchewan. Within a 40 km radius, Regina currently serves a retail trade population of 160 000, and within a 240 km radius a wholesale trade population of 500 000. The headquarters of the SASKATCHEWAN WHEAT POOL, the world's largest grain-handling co-operative, is located here.

The provincial government continues to be a major factor in the urban economy. The number

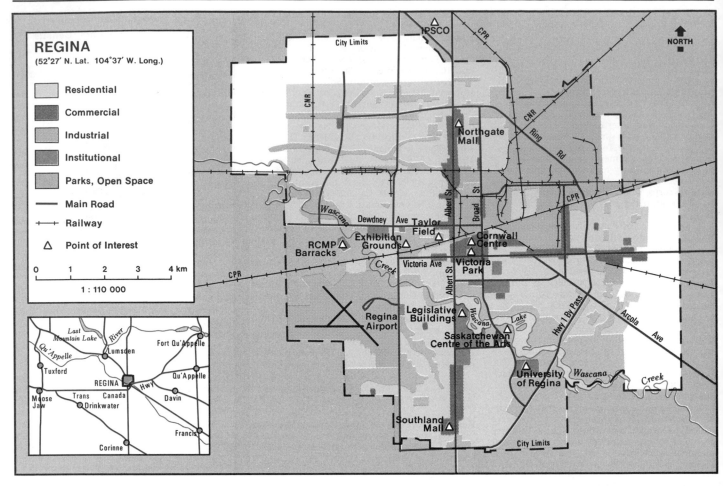

REGINA
(52°27' N. Lat. 104°37' W. Long.)

- Residential
- Commercial
- Industrial
- Institutional
- Parks, Open Space
- —— Main Road
- +—+— Railway
- △ Point of Interest

0 1 2 3 4 km

1 : 110 000

of government and crown corporation employees has grown steadily since 1945, and they have been accommodated in new high-rise office buildings that have dramatically altered the city's skyline. The most significant federal government presence is the RCMP, whose training facilities have been located in Regina since 1882. In recent decades Regina has also diversified its economy, the principal new developments being in cement, paper products and steel fabricating. In 1980 Regina accounted for 34% of the total value of manufacturing activity in Saskatchewan.

Transportation Regina is located on the TRANS-CANADA HWY, on the main line of the CPR and on a branch line of the CNR. Four airlines and 2 bus lines serve the city.

Government and Politics Regina is governed by an elected mayor and 10 aldermen, each of the latter representing a specific "division" or ward. The ward system, first introduced in 1906, was abolished in 1914. It appeared again 1934, only to be abandoned 2 years later. The present wards were established 1974. The powers of city council are set out in The Urban Municipality Act, and a provincial agency, the Local Government Board, oversees municipal financing. Public and separate (Roman Catholic) school boards administer Regina's 2 tax-supported elementary and high-school systems.

Cultural Life Regina's educational facilities include University of Regina, the Wascana Institute of Applied Arts and Sciences and the Regina Plains Community College. The Regina Symphony Orchestra is one of the city's most distinguished cultural institutions. The Norman Mackenzie and the Dunlop art galleries have substantial permanent collections and feature many travelling exhibitions. The Globe Theatre has gained a national reputation for its professional theatre productions.

Regina is served by 2 English-language and one French-language TV stations, 8 radio stations and one daily newspaper, the *Leader-Post*. The pride of the city, and indeed of the whole province, is the SASKATCHEWAN ROUGHRIDERS, a Canadian Football League team that plays at Taylor Field.　　　　J. WILLIAM BRENNAN

Reading: E.H. Dale, ed, *Regina: Regional Isolation and Innovative Development* (1980); E.G. Drake, *Regina: The Queen City* (1955).

Regina Five is the name given to the artists included in the 1961 National Gallery of Canada's circulating exhibition, "Five Painters from Regina," which represented the work of Kenneth LOCHHEAD, Arthur MCKAY, Douglas Morton, Ted Godwin and Ronald BLOORE. Young painters (b 1925-33) from Ontario and the Prairie provinces who had studied in Canadian and international centres before settling in Regina, these artists, along with painter Roy Kiyooka and architect Clifford Wiens, who shared a common commitment to their work, became part of the small but active artistic community of Regina.

In 1961 Bloore, who as director of the Norman Mackenzie Gallery since 1958 had brought national and international exhibitions of art to Regina, organized the May Show that was to form the basis for the exhibition that Richard Simmins of the National Gallery arranged to travel across Canada. The bold, nonfigurative paintings (often featuring a central or all-over image) in this exhibition represented a new direction for abstract painting in Canada and reflected aesthetic concerns similar to those of contemporary American art. Several factors contributed to this burst of mature creative expression in a previously isolated cultural centre. Primarily there was the Regina School of Art at University of Saskatchewan and its faculty. In 1955 its director, Lochhead, with fellow faculty member, McKay, initiated the Emma Lake Artists Workshop, a series of professional workshops held for 2 weeks each year in August. In early years, visitors included Joe Plaskett, Jack SHADBOLT and Will Barnet. For future members of the Regina Five, the 1959 visit of American artist Barnett Newman provided a catalyst. Three years later American critic Clement Greenberg had a significant impact on a number of western artists, including Lochhead. In the next decade 3 of the Five left Regina to pursue their careers as painters and teachers. *See also* PAINTING.　　　　JOYCE ZEMANS

Regina Manifesto, *see* CO-OPERATIVE COMMONWEALTH FEDERATION.

Regina Riot, *see* ON TO OTTAWA TREK.

Regional Development Planning is undertaken by governments at all levels with the aim of improving the well-being of people in areas where there is concern about present and future living conditions. Economic conditions normally receive the greatest attention, but economic problems (such as high rates of unemployment, low income levels or lack of investment opportunities) are closely associated with a broad range of physical and social problems. These include substandard health and housing conditions, inadequacies in physical infrastructure (eg, water supplies, waste disposal, transport facilities), environmental pollution and degradation, and deficiencies in educational and recreational services and in social services of all kinds. A planned program of regional development normally attempts to treat these problems comprehensively (*see* URBAN AND REGIONAL PLANNING).

Canada has a long history of development programs of many kinds, the most notable being the system of income transfers among the provinces that followed from the Rowell-Sirois report of 1940. Yet the federal government did not adopt an integrated approach to the problem of regional disparities until 1969, when the Dept of Regional Economic Expansion (DREE) was established. DREE's chief purpose was to help create employment opportunities, but 2 levels of need were recognized. The first related to "designated regions" where unemployment was high but the infrastructure for development was already in place; here, grants were provided to firms willing to invest in new or expanded manufacturing plants. The second were "special areas" where infrastructure was not available, and social facilities and services were lacking as well. For these areas, DREE adopted comprehensive programs that included the development of industrial parks, vocational training, the construction of new housing, the provision of a wide range of health and social services, and the creation of jobs, which could be in service industries or in manufacturing. Both types of program were funded and administered as federal-provincial partnerships, although the federal government bore a larger proportion of costs in the poorer provinces.

Beginning in 1973, in response to criticisms that the regional development programs were too much under central control, the provincial governments were given more autonomy over the design and implementation of projects supported by DREE. Then, in 1982, most of DREE's programs were moved to a Dept of Regional Industrial Expansion (DRIE) in the Ministry of Trade and Commerce. A new Ministry of Economic and Regional Development was created at this time to co-ordinate federal government actions to generate beneficial regional impacts. With the national economy performing badly, it came to be argued that regional development could not be effective unless well-thought-out development strategies had first been formulated at the national and provincial levels. If regions were left to compete with one another for limited opportunities, it was feared that Canada would fail to develop an international comparative advantage in such emerging fields as communication electronics or northern transport equipment (*see* COMMUNICATIONS TECHNOLOGY; TRANSPORTATION IN THE NORTH).

These swings in federal government policy reflect a fundamental disagreement about the proper approach to regional development in Canada. For their part, provincial governments have shown little enthusiasm for the idea of national strategies or plans. In general, provincial governments have seen regional development planning as their responsiblity, on the grounds that they are closer to the problem areas than any national agency and have a better understanding of regional needs and priorities. Certainly the various provincial governments have instituted a wide variety of development programs of their own over the years, and are likely to continue to do so.   DOUGLAS WEBSTER

Reading: Economic Council of Canada, *Living Together: A Study of Regional Disparities* (1977); R. Matthews, *The Creation of Regional Dependency* (1983); P. Phillips, *Regional Disparities* (rev ed 1983); C. Weaver and T.I. Guntin, "From Drought Assistance to Mega-Projects: Fifty Years of Regional Theory and Policy in Canada," *Canadian Journal of Regional Science* 5 (spring 1982); D. Webster, "Developmental Planning: State of the Art and Prescription," in W.T. Perks and I.M. Robinson, eds, *Urban and Regional Planning in a Federal State: The Canadian Experience* (1979).

Regional Economics is concerned with understanding and explaining the geographic configuration of the economy, particularly regarding industrial location, regional development, urbanization, migration, land use, etc. The first major works devoted to theories of location for economic activity appeared, chiefly in Germany, at the turn of the century. As a field of study, regional economics has flourished in most industrialized nations, including Canada;

it has much in common with economic geography and the new field of regional science in its emphasis upon both economic principles and the role of spatial relationships. Courses on it are offered by most Canadian universities.

The Distribution of Economic Activity in Canada Economic activity in Canada is highly localized. Ontario has, since 1910, regularly accounted for about 40% of the national total of income and production, although the percentage declined slightly during the 1970s. Ontario's gross domestic product (GDP) in 1980 was $113.4 billion, roughly comparable to Sweden's. Ontario accounts for 50% of Canadian manufacturing, economic activity being highly concentrated in southern Ontario from Windsor to Oshawa. Corporations headquartered there, chiefly in Toronto, controlled over 50% of Canadian production in 1977 and over 50% of the assets of Canada's major financial institutions.

Québec's economy, with a GDP of $69 billion (1980), has since 1910 accounted for about 25% of Canada's income and production, but its share of the national total has been declining since the 1970s. The Montréal region accounts for about 45% of Québec's income and production, making it Canada's second major business centre. Corporations headquartered there controlled about 25% of Canada's production and close to 35% of the assets of Canada's major financial institutions. The 1170 km corridor from Windsor, Ont, to Québec City has sometimes been referred to as the economic heartland of Canada, representing, during the early 1970s, over 55% of Canada's population, generating over 60% of its income and production, and accounting for over 70% of its manufacturing employment.

Manitoba, Saskatchewan, Alberta and BC, with a combined GDP of about $100 billion, accounted in 1980 for roughly 33% of Canada's GDP and for 35% of Canadian personal income. BC's domestic income and product have been increasing since 1910 and Alberta's energy-based economy grew dramatically in the 1970s. Vancouver and, more recently, Calgary, although they do not yet rival Montréal and Toronto, have become important corporate and financial centres. Since the GREAT DEPRESSION, Manitoba's and Saskatchewan's shares of national income have decreased steadily; Manitoba's gradually, Saskatchewan's erratically, reflecting the volatility of its wheat-based economy. The position of Winnipeg as the traditional manufacturing and service centre of the Prairies is now challenged by Edmonton and Calgary. Newfoundland, NS, NB and PEI generated a combined GDP of $13.6 billion in 1980, accounting for 4.5% of the national total. The economies of NS, NB and PEI have declined steadily over the last century. They represented 3.5% of the national GDP in 1980, compared to 16.2% in 1890. The decline (which has slowed significantly in recent decades) is often blamed on the NATIONAL POLICY following Confederation and technological changes in shipbuilding. The growth of personal income in the Atlantic provinces has generally followed the national average since 1961.

Regional Income Disparities The continuing disparity between the Atlantic region and the more affluent parts of the nation, particularly Ontario and BC, remains Canada's principal regional economic problem. In 1980, personal income per inhabitant in Ontario, Alberta and BC was about 70% higher than in Newfoundland, 50% higher than in NB and PEI and 33% higher than in NS. Per capita income in Québec has also remained systematically below the national average. However, per capita income in Québec was 31% below that of Ontario in 1961 but only 13% below in 1980. The improvement can be attributed partly to efforts begun in Québec in the early 1960s to raise the educational level of its population (traditionally among the lowest in

Canada). With the dramatic decline in birthrates and increasing number of women workers, the proportion of the population in the LABOUR FORCE (and of working age) has risen substantially. On the other hand, the encouragement of French language and culture in Québec has probably had an economic cost, reflected in the decline of Montréal as a business centre. Income disparities between the Prairie provinces and the rest of Canada are reflected in alternate patterns of divergence and convergence and severe fluctuations in per capita income, the result of dependence upon primary production (wheat, oil, natural gas, potash) and levels of demand, which are often determined by uncontrollable natural and international factors. Saskatchewan's relative per capita income changes erratically, 59% of the national average in 1941, 107% in 1951, 71% in 1961 and 91% in 1980. In Manitoba, where there is a stronger manufacturing base, per capita income, since 1956, has tended to remain below the national average. In 1980 Alberta ranked above Ontario and BC in having a per capita income above the national average.

Following the international oil crisis of 1973-74, corporate and other business income from oil production increased sharply. Most of this "windfall" income was generated in Alberta. Income generated in one region may flow to another in the form of federal government transfer payments, eg, EQUALIZATION PAYMENTS, unemployment benefits, or in interest, dividends and profits accruing to investors outside the region (*see* INTERGOVERNMENTAL FINANCE). The outflow from Alberta to other regions of Canada (1982-83) was about $8 billion. From the mid-1970s the federal government and energy-producing provinces (especially Alberta) were in conflict over the right to regulate, tax and redistribute energy profits. The surge of revenues from energy production upset the traditional regional balance in which Ontario was the senior "have" province and chief contributor to federal transfer schemes. For the fiscal year 1980-81, Ontario's autonomous capacity to raise revenues (based purely on its own residents) had fallen below the national average while Alberta's had risen to well over twice the national average. Only the revenue potentials of Saskatchewan and BC (1980-81) were above the national average, although still well below those of Alberta. But the economic history of the Prairies amply demonstrates the fragility of resource-based prosperity.

Causes of Regional Income Disparity Differences in income per person between regions may exist at any time because of variations in employment, wage rates, investment income or income from government transfer schemes. In Canada, where about 70% of personal income is derived from wages and other labour income, employment and wage rates are by far the most important factors.

The uneven distribution of jobs in Canada is measured by variations in the portion of each province's employed population, which is based on the proportion of the population of working age (15-64 years old), the percentage of the working-age population in the labour force and the unemployment rate. The proportion of the population of working age has traditionally been lower in Atlantic Canada than elsewhere, partly as a result of EMIGRATION; labour-force participation rates have also remained low while unemployment rates have remained high. Thirty-five percent of Newfoundland's population was employed in 1980 compared to 54% of Alberta's, which largely accounts for the disparity in per capita income.

Regional differences in wage rates may result from differences in labour productivity and in industrial structure. The traditionally high level of per capita income in BC largely reflects high wages. However, because of influences such as unionization, labour mobility, social legislation and the growth in public-service employment, a national trend towards wage equalization exists. Wage rates in Québec and Ontario, for instance, were roughly equivalent in 1980. Many economists maintain that high wages may actually reduce employment opportunities in regions where they are not warranted by labour productivity. The regional disparities of employment and wages can be partly attributed to comparative advantages of location. The first areas to develop, because of natural or historical advantages, will often continue growing as the necessary markets, institutions and infrastructures are created. The St Lawrence Valley was developed because of its unique transportation advantage and agricultural potential. By building canals, roads and other infrastructures, settlers enhanced this initial natural advantage so that even before Confederation the combined populations of Québec and Ontario were already considerably larger than that of the Maritimes.

Canada's internal market is small by world standards; one plant or office often serves the entire country. The centre of that market is clearly situated in southern Ontario and southwestern Québec. The Maritimes and the Prairie provinces were poorly located for serving the Canadian market. Modern industry and offices often require services, skills and infrastructures only found in large cities, and Atlantic Canada possesses no large urban metropolis of international calibre. Halifax cannot compare, as a business and financial centre, to Winnipeg, Calgary or Edmonton. The lack of waterways on the Prairies confounds the difficulty of reaching major markets and constitutes a special handicap to industrial development.

The position of the US as Canada's chief trading partner and source of foreign investment since WWI has benefited some regions more than others. Southern Ontario benefits not only from its access to the Great Lakes but also by its proximity to the major industrial zones of the American Midwest, of which it has in many ways become an extension — the development of an automobile industry in Windsor, across the river from Detroit, is perhaps the most obvious example. American investment is heavily concentrated in Ontario, and Toronto is the centre for US-controlled head offices. The integration of Canada into the N American economy has undoubtedly increased the isolation of Atlantic Canada, whose economic links with the UK were traditionally stronger than those of other regions. In more recent years the growth of the Pacific Rim economies (Japan, China, California) has significantly benefited BC and, to some extent, Alberta.

The human element is the most elusive in regional development. Migration has a decisive impact on the quality of human resources in a region. Low-income regions in Canada are often locked into a cycle of decline because the most dynamic and educated people of working age emigrate.

The resources of BC and Alberta help account for their past and recent growth. BC's high wages and productivity are the result partially of its forest resources, but also of its advantageous location and skilled labour force and Vancouver's role as an emerging industrial and business centre. The Atlantic provinces are handicapped not only by the lack of competitive, high-quality, natural resources, but by disadvantages of location and a history of decline. Natural-resource exploitation alone, however, rarely constitutes a sufficient basis for sustained economic growth. In Canada, as elsewhere, industrial and office-location patterns have had more lasting impact in determining the emergence and persistence of regional income disparities.

Regional Economic Policies Since Confederation Canadian economic policy has been influenced by regional considerations. National policies have important repercussions, intentional and unintentional, at the regional level, often creating tensions between the provinces and the federal government and between the individual provinces. In recent years regional policies specifically directed at low-income areas have been developed.

Canada's protective tariff structure, a legacy of John A. MACDONALD's National Policy, designed to encourage Canadian industrialization, primarily benefited the manufacturing areas of Québec and Ontario, providing them with a captive market. Canada's tariff policies continue to grieve Atlantic Canada and the West, where consumers feel they are subsidizing the protected industries of central Canada and stifling the development of their own regions. On the other hand, Québec and Ontario have financed and continue to subsidize Canada's elaborate transport network linking the less accessible regions to major markets. The Maritime Freight Act (1927) provides for subsidies to reduce freight rates for rail shipments moving from points E of Lévis, Qué, to the rest of Canada. The subsidy has since been raised and extended to commercial trucking. Freight rates on grain shipments out of the Prairies were kept artificially low from the turn of the century by the CROW'S NEST PASS AGREEMENT (agreement was modified in 1984) and Prairie wheat farmers are assisted in the transport and marketing of their output by multiple subsidy schemes and by the Winnipeg-based Federal Wheat Board.

With Canada's long tradition of state enterprise, subsidies and regulation, the effect of state intervention, including fiscal and monetary policy, immigration and procurement, is difficult to evaluate. Federal ENERGY POLICY, for example, has become controversial. Before the 1972 to

1974 oil crisis, energy policy favoured the oil-producing provinces because of the so-called Borden Line (1961), which divided Canada into 2 oil-marketing zones at the Ontario/Québec border. West of the line no imported oil could be refined or sold; foreign oil and its by-products were limited to the market east of it. The then more expensive western oil was ensured a captive market, including Ontario, but the expansion of the Montréal-based (and more easterly based) oil-refining and petrochemical industry was hampered by artificial limitation of its market at the Québec and Ontario borders. From 1973 until the mid 1980s, the National Energy Policy has tended to favour oil-consuming provinces by keeping internal oil prices below international levels and by redistributing a significant portion of western oil royalties. Late in 1984, the Mulroney government indicated it intended to allow domestic oil prices to match world prices.

Canada's comparatively generous system of TRANSFER-PAYMENT programs, comprising transfers both to other governments and to individuals (unemployment benefits, family allowances, pensions), accounted for about 50% of the federal budget during the late 1970s. Income differences in early 1980s would appear much greater if transfer income to individuals were excluded from personal income calculations. Newfoundland's income per person, for example, would fall from 66.9% to 55.7% of the national average. Without transfer payments, the level of regional income disparity in 1982 would be about the same as it was in 1961, implying the improvement in Atlantic Canada's income position may be more the result of money transfers than of real improvement in the region's economy. Specific programs to encourage the development of low-income areas were established in 1962 under an Area Development Agency. In 1969 it was replaced by the Department of Regional Economic Expansion (DREE), which in 1982 was divided into the Department of Regional Industrial Expansion and the Ministry of State for Economic and Regional Development. DREE administered a new Regional Development Incentives Act, which provided grants, special depreciation allowances and loans to encourage the location of firms in designated areas. DREE also entered into General Development Agreements with the provinces, which included infrastructure programs, mineral exploration, industrial restructuring incentives, rural development schemes, etc. The Cape Breton Development Corporation is an example of the type of undertaking in which DREE has participated. Regional policies have clearly benefited smaller regions, especially in the more depressed zones of Atlantic Canada. On the other hand, it is by no means certain, considering the scale of DREE's intervention (1.2% of the federal budget) and the effects of other national policies, that area-directed regional policies have profoundly altered the pattern of regional development in Canada.

Regional problems and policies similar to those on the national level may be found within almost every province. For example, within Ontario disparities in per capita income and employment levels between the industrialized south and the less developed north are as distinctive as they are between provinces. In Québec, per capita income and employment levels in the Abitibi and Gaspé regions have remained considerably below those of the greater Montréal regions. In NS the Halifax and Cape Breton regions are, respectively, fairly prosperous and economically depressed; in the western provinces and in Québec a clear difference exists between the richer urbanized southern regions and the sparsely populated northern areas. Most provinces have developed their own regional policies and objectives, often independently of

Personal Income Per Capita, by Province, 1926-1982
(Relative to the National Average; Canada = 100)
(Source: Statistics Canada, Provincial Economic Accounts)

Province	1926	1931	1936	1941	1946	1951	1956	1961	1966	1971	1976	1980	1982	Excluding transfer income* (1982)
Newfoundland	–	–	–	–	–	48.2	53.5	58.2	59.9	63.6	68.5	64.0	66.9	55.7
PEI	56.1	51.4	55.6	46.9	58.2	54.4	58.7	58.8	60.1	63.7	68.6	71.0	69.4	60.5
Nova Scotia	67.8	75.9	79.6	77.1	85.9	69.1	71.9	77.5	74.8	77.4	78.8	79.1	78.6	74.4
New Brunswick	64.8	67.2	67.4	63.9	75.2	67.0	65.9	67.8	68.9	72.2	75.6	71.1	71.9	65.3
Québec	84.6	94.9	92.1	86.6	81.5	83.9	86.1	90.1	89.0	88.8	93.0	94.5	93.8	90.5
Ontario	114.4	127.9	125.5	129.4	115.7	118.3	117.8	118.3	116.9	117.0	109.0	107.0	107.9	110.9
Manitoba	108.4	90.7	92.4	92.8	102.9	100.8	96.9	94.3	91.9	94.0	93.7	89.5	93.5	93.8
Saskatchewan	101.8	44.9	58.0	59.3	96.1	107.1	93.5	70.8	92.9	80.3	99.6	91.0	96.4	95.4
Alberta	113.7	77.9	76.3	80.0	107.8	111.0	104.6	100.0	100.0	98.9	102.6	111.6	109.1	112.9
British Columbia	122.1	129.9	131.9	120.9	114.9	119.2	121.1	114.9	115.9	109.0	109.1	111.3	107.6	108.2
Yukon & NWT	–	–	–	–	–	86.7	129.8	96.6	80.7	86.8	91.9	102.9	101.5	105.7

* Transfer income (excluded in the last column) comprises items such as unemployment benefits, family allowances and other social-welfare related payments.

the federal government; eg, Québec has established location subsidies, infrastructure investments, preferred loans, etc.　　　MARIO POLÈSE
Reading: Economic Council of Canada, *Living Together: A Study of Regional Disparities* (1977); H. Lithwick, *Regional Economic Policy: The Canadian Experience* (1978); P. Phillips, *Regional Disparities* (1978).

Regional Government is a structure created by the provinces, in particular Ont and Qué, BC and Alta, under which municipalities are regrouped under a regional administration. Except in Alberta, regional governments have been created by the superimposition of a geographically larger level of government over existing municipalities to make certain municipal functions more economical and establish a tax base sufficient to enhance local services or create new ones. The most comprehensive reform occurred in Ontario, which in 1969 began to replace COUNTY governments (in place since 1849) with a system of 11 larger regional municipalities, which were assigned extensive responsibilities for land-use planning, water and sewerage, solid waste disposal, policing, transportation, social services and public health. The regions included CITIES, suburbs and rural TOWNSHIPS at the lower level. Regional councils comprise delegates from the lower-tier municipalities. Similar reforms took place in Québec for the regional communities centered on Montréal, Hull and Québec City. In BC a 2-tier system of 29 regional districts covering the province and focusing upon urban centres was created by statute in 1965, although the districts came into existence only at the minister's discretion. Few local boundaries were changed. The Greater Vancouver Regional District, the most developed region, is a type of METROPOLITAN GOVERNMENT. In 1967 it took over long-standing regional agencies providing water, sewerage and drainage services, later adding responsibilities such as regional parks, hospital financing and labour relations.　　　JAMES LIGHTBODY
Reading: C.R. Tindal, *Structural Changes in Local Government: Government for Urban Regions* (1977).

Regionalism may refer to the distinctive local character of different parts of the world or to a people's perception of and identification with such places. The concept is rarely applied, for example, to differences between parts of a city or to those between continents or countries. Rather, it is usually used as an intermediate scale. In Canada the term has acquired a particular vogue as a result of many recent tensions between national and more local economic, institutional and emotional attachments. Generally the phrase "Canadian regionalism" refers broadly to the vitality of regional differences within Canada.

That regionalism is an inescapable component of society, economy and politics in Canada is hardly surprising; a national organization was imposed over a vast territory and scattered different peoples little more than 100 years ago. The nature of Canadian settlement and the spatial structure of the Canadian economy have ensured the persistence of a complex regional texture alongside the increasingly standardized late 20th-century technology, the functionally integrated economy and the national sentiments that are also part of Canadian life.

Canadian settlement developed within confined spaces characteristically bounded on the N by inhospitable land, and to the S by the US, between which are the discontinuous patches of land capable of supporting more than a handful of people. European settlers arrived early in the 17th century when a few fishermen were left behind in rockbound Newfoundland harbours. Simultaneously, a few French settlers occupied the marshlands of the Bay of Fundy, and more began to farm the narrow borders of cultivable land along the St Lawrence R. Much later, Irish,

Scots and English, propelled by Highland clearances, Irish famine or the technological and demographic changes of early 19th-century industrialization, filled up the Ontario peninsula and the fishing harbours, the lumber camps and the meagre agricultural patches of Atlantic Canada (*see* IMMIGRATION). The descendants of all these settlers soon faced a common predicament. The patches of settlement were small, their agricultural possibilities circumscribed, and as numbers multiplied in still rural preindustrial societies, there was soon a shortage of land. The pioneer fringe ran into rock. Until the end of the 19th century, there was no western safety valve, only the granitic Canadian SHIELD and other already settled patches of British America. The surplus young faced the choice of striking N into rock and spruce or S into the US. In Atlantic Canada, Québec and Ontario, most went S where they were absorbed into a larger America; N of the border, local societies that now exported people bypassed the mixing effects of the migrations they had launched. Only when the CANADIAN PACIFIC RAILWAY reached Winnipeg in 1881 did Canada really acquire a West, but one that would be cut off to French Canadians by the Protestant outburst over Louis RIEL and by the collapse in Manitoba of French educational and linguistic guarantees. Although Ontario would be better represented there, the Canadian Prairie was settled over a short generation before WWI by migrants from eastern Canada, immigrants directly from the British Isles and from the northern fringe of the late 19th- and early 20th-century peasant migration to America from central Europe, and with a wave of American settlement moving northward along the eastern flank of the Rockies. In BC the mix was different again; much less of continental Europe, a good deal of Ontario, something of Atlantic Canada and, on the Pacific Ocean, elements from the Orient.

This was how the patches of arable land between an implacable North and the US were settled. There was no continuous, expansive Canadian experience with the land. Settlement proceeded in patches. One patch would fill up, then people would emigrate, S more often than N because the US was more inviting than the Shield. Until the last century, there was no settlers' West. The next Canadian patch was inaccessible or occupied, and when a West finally did open the eastern settlements would be partially represented and much diluted there. The process of Canadian settlement had imparted striking discontinuities. Canada did not expand westward from an Atlantic beginning. Different patches were settled at different times by people of different background who depended on different technologies and economies.

This pattern of settlement sharply differentiated the Canadian experience from the American. There the land was perceived as a garden as readily as wilderness, and it attracted far more settlers and focused European dreams. There eastern seaboard beginnings could migrate westward to desert margins over 3000 km inland that were the first major environmental obstacle to an expanding agrarian civilization. There the West was a lure for 300 years. As different streams from the initial settlements along the colonial seaboard, augmented by newcomers from Europe, moved westward, different ways met and substantially merged. As it gathered momentum in the late 18th and early 19th centuries the American occupation of an essentially welcoming land had the capacity to mold different peoples into a relatively homogeneous culture as it spread them over an astonishing area. But in Canada, where all of this was checked by the physical limits of settlements, the country's underlying structure was disjointed and discontinuous.

The spatial structure of the Canadian econ-

omy also worked to strengthen Canadian regionalism. In the late 19th century an industrial technology with the capacity to integrate the bulky products of a large area within a single market was superimposed on the patches of Canadian settlement. Such spatial integration could create metropolitan centres where there were clear economies of agglomeration and distribution, and extensive resource and market hinterlands. Railways and factories would impose this economic structure on Canada; the only issues were at what scale and in what direction. The decision to create a Canadian market was implicit in Confederation and explicit in the NATIONAL POLICY that followed it. Protected by tariffs from the US, the metropolitan centre (*see* INDUSTRIAL STRATEGY) stabilized in the St Lawrence-Great Lakes lowland where most of the market was located and where there was optimal overall access to the hinterlands to the E and W. The rest of the country would consume the manufactures of the core, and would supply it with some raw materials. This structure could be intensified by public or private policy, eg, by changing freight rates, but given the pattern of Canadian settlement at Confederation and the character of industrial economy, it followed in all essentials from the decision to create a Canadian market. Canadian settlements achieved a considerable functional economic integration; most secondary industry and associated financial institutions were concentrated in Montréal or around the western end of Lk Ontario, resource-based primary industries were scattered across the land, and core and periphery were linked by growing commercial and financial networks.

Economically, such integration encouraged sharp regional specialization, reflected, for example, in the Prairie wheat economy. Emotionally it laid the basis for strikingly different regional perceptions of Canada. Those at the core tended to feel expansive about the country on which their economy relied and over which their institutions exerted much influence, although French Canadians, who worked in the factories but did not own them, would have no entrepreneurial enthusiasm for a transcontinental country and a good deal of cultural suspicion of it. But for most English speakers in the core a British Canada from sea to sea, which would reinforce their traditions as it expanded their markets, seemed authentic and just. On the other hand, those on the peripheries would be suspicious of the core, their suspicion stemming from a sense that local circumstances were controlled from afar, and from the conviction that by being forced "to sell cheap and buy dear" they were subsidizing central Canada and absorbing the cost of Confederation. What was a National Policy in central Canada could easily be interpreted by the Maritimes as Upper Canadian imperialism, and in the West as the manipulation of James and Bay streets. From a Prairie or Maritime vantage point, the "Big Interests" and "Special Privilege" lived in central Canada.

The pattern of Canadian settlement and the tensions between core and periphery inherent in a national economy are sufficient to account for a strikingly regional Canada, but factors such as distance, the varied physical geography of a vast land and, in many parts of Canada, the considerable, growing presence of native peoples, also contributed. Canadian regionalism has not always expressed itself in the same fashion, however. Since Confederation regional feelings have been associated with local settlements, with substantial parts of provinces (eg, Cape Breton I), with provinces, and with such amorphous, poorly defined territories as the Maritimes, central Canada and the West. Among these, the provinces are now the primary exponents of the country's fragmented structure. Settlements that once provided definition and defence for traditional ways have been overridden by modern transportation and communications, while the STATE has assumed a growing symbolic and practical importance. In this situation, the Canadian province, with its constitutionally defined power, tends to replace both the local settlements that no longer define Canadian life and the broader but amorphous regions that have no clear political definition. It is this simplified and thereby politically more powerful regionalism that increasingly confronts the concept and the sentiment of Canada.

The consolidation of regional sentiment in the provinces occurred while governments were assuming a larger role in Canadian life and while the evolution of the Canadian economy was changing the significance of some of the terms of the BRITISH NORTH AMERICA ACT (now CONSTITUTION ACT 1867). Provincial governments have played a growing role in the economy, and the province a growing role in Canadian feeling. Many activities that were once organized at different regional levels are now organized provincially. Simultaneously, federal power has increased as Ottawa has expanded its services and its economic presence. The result of this growth of provincial and federal governments is an increasingly polarized debate between national and more regional conceptions of Canada that is also a debate between 2 levels of government. The political consolidation of regionalism in provincial governments is felt across the country, but is probably most obvious in Québec. The culture of a French-speaking, Roman Catholic people was once defended by the local community, by a variety of nationalistic societies, and above all by the Roman Catholic Church. For some, the clearest defence of culture was a rural life and a high birthrate, and from this perspective the provincial government could do little more than encourage colonization. In recent years government has assumed the defence of culture; many French-speaking Québecois have concentrated on increasing the political power of the Québec government. The protection of the French language, a central element of the regional variety of Canada, has become an essentially political issue dependent on different conceptions of federal and provincial responsibility. The economy is an even more pervasive source of federal-provincial conflict. The location of oil and coal fields and the growing economic importance of the Pacific basin have challenged economic assumptions held by Canadians for almost 100 years. Core and peripheries seem to have come unstuck and in a country like Canada it takes only the possibility of this change to raise the ghosts of 100 years of spatial tension. For some provinces it seems their turn has come — as long as the natural momentum of different circumstances is left to run its course. But if federal political power resides in the core, and if the Constitution Act leaves ample opportunity for federal influence on resource policy, then the economic advantages of the peripheries can be compromised by the protective instincts of the core, which accounts for the aggressiveness of western provinces and Newfoundland over resource control. As long as the federal government is elected in central Canada, as it is likely to be, a conflict over the spatial economy is immediately translated into a conflict between different levels of government.

Canadian regionalism is now most vigorously promoted by provincial politicians and is most stridently expressed in federal-provincial debate, but underneath this rhetoric lies the far more subtle regional texture of Canadian life. It is expressed in the distinctive landscapes of farm and village, of camp and city, across the breadth of Canada. It is expressed in different accents and different memories of different pasts. It is expressed in the ways of life associated with different resource-based economies in different physical settings. It is expressed in the relationships of towns to different hinterlands and to different positions in the urban system. And it is expressed most sensitively throughout Canadian painting and literature (*see also* FEDERALISM).   R.C. HARRIS

Regionalism in Literature Geographer Cole Harris describes the inhabited part of Canada as "an island archipelago spread over 4000 east-west miles.... Different islands were settled at different times within different technologies and economies by people from different backgrounds." Throughout Canada's history this concept has been a powerful alternative to the idea of a homogeneous nation spreading from sea to sea. To the writer, Northrop FRYE argues, the concept is essential: "What affects the writer's imagination...is an environment rather than a nation.... Regionalism and literary maturity seem to grow together."

But in 1943, E.K. BROWN suggested in *On Canadian Poetry* that REGIONALISM threatened the growth of a Canadian literature, "because it stresses the superficial and peculiar at the expense, at least, if not to the exclusion, of the fundamental and universal." The main achievement of Canadian literature before WWII was finding the vocabulary, and some sense of appropriate forms, to articulate authentically a new place. Given the power of the imperial language and its literary tradition, the accomplishment was great, but could in itself only be "superficial." Those early writers committed to naming the details of a new world inevitably emphasized a local area. T.C. HALIBURTON, our first humorist, was regional in his recording of the dialects and folkways of pre-Confederation Nova Scotia; Charles G.D. ROBERTS depicted the New Brunswick landscape, particularly in *Songs of the Common Day* (1893); D.C. SCOTT evoked several northern settings in his narratives of Indian life. The popular romance, which dominated Canadian fiction until 1920, encouraged the more sentimental side of regionalism, with quaint peculiarities of mannerism or costume to provide relief from the didacticism and melodrama. Gilbert PARKER's historical romances are unusual in suggesting a connection between setting and character. Ralph Connor (C.W. GORDON) animated his best-selling, fictionalized sermons with the local colour of Glengarry and the Canadian West.

Regional literature in the more precise sense is tied to the conventions of realism because it attempts to distinguish accurately the features of a clearly definable region, either rural or closely linked to the land. In its fullest achievement such regional literature, as the works of Thomas Hardy and William Faulkner show, is not synonymous with surface detail and pedestrian style, but with profound exploration of the shaping influence of particular regions on individual lives.

Anticipated by D.C. Scott's connected short stories *The Village of Viger* (1896), by Sara Jeannette DUNCAN's finely detailed picture of Brantford in *The* IMPERIALIST (1904), and by Stephen LEACOCK's humorous insights in SUNSHINE SKETCHES OF A LITTLE TOWN (1912), literary regionalism firmly established itself in Canada in the 1920s, particularly in Frederick Philip GROVE's suite of essays, *Over Prairie Trails* (1922), and his novels *Settlers of the Marsh* (1925) and FRUITS OF THE EARTH (1933). Other western writers more inclined to the romance, such as Martha Ostenso, Robert Stead and Frederick Niven, contribute to an identification of literary regionalism and the Prairies in this period. In LITERATURE IN FRENCH, the interest in *le terroir*, associated with the École littéraire de Montréal in the late 19th century, continued strongly into the 1930s; comparison of Louis HÉMON's MARIA CHAPDELAINE (1916) with *Trente arpents* (1938) by Ringuet (Philippe PANNETON) shows the same shift from sentimentalism to realism that took place in LITERATURE IN ENGLISH.

Until 1940, however, even Grove's frequently ponderous prose and the nostalgia implicit in *le terroir* justify Brown's view of the inherent weakness of regionalism. But Sinclair ROSS's AS FOR ME AND MY HOUSE (1941) demonstrated that Canadian literature could be intensely concerned with regional landscape and social structure, and that it could also be challenging in its shrewd use of form and language. Certainly much of the most interesting Canadian fiction of the next 15 years is confidently regional: Emily CARR's KLEE WYCK (1941), W.O. MITCHELL's WHO HAS SEEN THE WIND (1947), Hugh MACLENNAN's *Each Man's Son* (1951), Ernest BUCKLER's *The Mountain and the Valley* (1952), Ethel Wilson's *Hetty Dorval* (1947) and SWAMP ANGEL (1954), and Charles Bruce's *The Channel Shore* (1954). More recently Margaret LAURENCE's Manawaka, Alice MUNRO's Jubilee and, in drama, James REANEY's SouWest O have become favourite places in Canadian literature. Except for Edward McCourt's *The Canadian West in Fiction* (1949; rev 1970), sustained critical comment on literary regionalism did not appear until the early 1970s when a proliferation of studies and anthologies began to change the direction of Canadian studies. The concurrent decentralization of political power in the 1970s was reflected in various stimuli to the growth and awareness of regional literatures: the development of provincial arts councils or departments of cultural affairs, the creation of academic courses and centres for regional studies, the organization of many conferences with regional emphases, and the appearance of dozens of LITERARY PERIODICALS with pronounced regional loyalties.

A fantastic, or burlesque, or even anti-regional regionalism emerged as a significant extension of regional fiction, especially in the works of such writers as Sheila WATSON, Robert KROETSCH and Jack HODGINS. Meanwhile, many regional SMALL PRESSES, from Breakwater in St John's, Nfld, to Oolichan in Lantzville, BC, appeared to promote the growth of regional poetry, in which the connection between region and realism continues to be strong. Al PURDY's fusing of artifacts, stories and voices of particular regions has been extremely influential. Canadian regional poets, as various as Alden NOWLAN, Don Gutteridge, Andrew Suknaski, Glen Sorestad and Peter Trower, find inspiration in Purdy's casual combining of historical processes and the immediately local.

In the 1980s writers and critics have been developing a different approach to region, one that is conceptually broader and theoretically more focused. A connection to place and land remains important, but the multitude of historical, economic, ethnic and linguistic regions which comprise Harris's archipelago are shifting or destroying the boundaries of the traditional regions (Atlantic, Québec, Ontario, Prairies, British Columbia, North), which have too simplistically shaped the understanding of Canada's literary regionalism.   LAURIE RICOU

Reading: W. Westfall, "On the Concept of Region in Canadian History and Literature," *Journal of Canadian Studies* 15, 2 (1980); George Woodcock, *The Meeting of Time and Space* (1981).

Régis, Louis-Marie, priest, Thomist philosopher (b at Hébertville, Qué 8 Dec 1903). Régis is one of the most productive Catholic philosophers in Canada and one of the few whose work is well known in both languages. He was educated chiefly at Dominican colleges in St-Hyacinthe, Qué; Hainault, Belgium; and Ottawa; though he also studied briefly at Oxford, Cologne and Paris. He has taught in Montréal and Ottawa. Of his some 60 books and articles, the best known are *St. Thomas and Epistemology* (1946) and *Epistemology* (1959). The latter, widely used in Catholic colleges and universities, emphasizes and theorizes about the importance of scientific knowledge.   LESLIE ARMOUR

Regulation 17, *see* ONTARIO SCHOOLS QUESTION.

Regulatory Process All levels of government in Canada are involved in regulation. Because many activities in Canada are regulated (eg, airline routes, the types and prices of service provided by telecommunications companies, the number of taxicabs in a municipality and how much they may charge), regulatory systems must be tailored to particular needs. However, certain standard models of regulatory agencies have been widely adopted. In the early 1980s there was growing concern over regulatory reform, partly in the form of "deregulation" (though not in as concerted a way as in the US) and in proposals and actions that have led to more, or expanded, regulation.

Regulatory Agencies There are 3 main types of regulatory agency: self-governing bodies, which regulate the conduct of their own members; independent government agencies and boards; and regular line departments headed directly by ministers, which regulate specified industries and activities. Familiar examples of self-governing bodies include the professions, eg, LAW, MEDICINE and ACCOUNTING, which are empowered by provincial legislatures to determine their own requirements for admission and to discipline members who do not adhere to prescribed standards of professional conduct. With self-governing bodies, regulators are drawn from the professions themselves. Government regulatory agency members, on the other hand, are appointed by government. Called commissions (eg, Canadian Transport Commission), boards (eg, Nova Scotia Board of Public Utility Commissioners) or tribunals (eg, Ontario Commercial Registration Appeal Tribunal), these agencies derive their authority from the legislature, and no regulatory agency has any more authority than that expressly delegated to it by the legislature (*see* ADMINISTRATIVE LAW).

An occupational safety branch of a provincial Department of Labour that decides and enforces employment safety standards is an example of a departmental regulatory agency. Certain agencies may appear more independent than they really are; eg, the FOREIGN INVESTMENT REVIEW AGENCY (FIRA) assessed the benefits of foreign investments but in reality only advised the federal Cabinet, which made the actual decisions. In many fields of public policy (eg, energy, communications) often all 3 types of regulatory agency are in existence.

If the members of an agency are appointed for fixed terms with tenure (unlike other civil servants who may be reassigned at any time) and if the agency has a separate and distinct existence outside of any government department, then it is an independent regulatory agency. A typical agency of this type is the CANADIAN RADIO-TELEVISION AND TELECOMMUNICATIONS COMMISSION (CRTC), which regulates the Canadian broadcasting system and the federal telecommunications carriers. It has its own staff and office complex and is completely separate from the federal Department of Communications. Although these types of agency are created by the legislatures and are answerable to them and rely on them for operating funds, they are still, when compared to a branch of a government department, relatively independent. Independence, however, is rarely absolute, in that the Cabinet or a particular minister (or both) may often issue directives to a board and has the power to appoint regulators and approve their budgets.

Policy Formulation and Implementation In-

dependent regulatory agencies characteristically operate in an open manner, though the degree of openness varies greatly. Their procedures are designed to allow for some degree of public participation. In a typical proceeding a company will apply either for an increase in the rates it charges customers or for a licence for some procedure. Notice of this application will appear in the government's official gazette and possibly in local newspapers so that interested persons may attend a public hearing to state their support or disapproval of the applications. The agency then renders a decision. Such procedures may be appropriate for specific decisions, but may not be suitable for determining broader policy issues. Here a somewhat different procedure is often used. Notice is given of a proposed new policy rule and interested persons are invited to comment. There may or may not be an informal public hearing.

Regulators will often discover that they must fill a policy gap. When legislatures create regulatory agencies, they often leave it to the regulator to develop rules that give specific meaning to broad legislative standards. For example, a regulator may be instructed to issue licences for commercial trucking operations where "public necessity and convenience" indicate that licences should be issued. Another regulator may issue airline routes "in the public interest" or allow only "just and reasonable" rates to be charged to telecommunications consumers, phrases so vague that regulators will feel obliged to outline precisely the applicable criteria, which in effect means they are making policy and exercising considerable discretionary power. Theoretically, in the Canadian system of government, only elected officials make major policy decisions because they alone are politically accountable and may be voted out of office for unpopular policies. But the broad statutory language employed not only allows but in practice requires regulators who are appointed to determine major policies about, for example, trucking and air transportation and telecommunications. Consequently, it is often suggested that the Cabinet be given authority to issue binding policy directives to the independent regulatory agencies. Indeed, in the case of some agencies, this power already exists. This provision often creates dual standards of political accountability that are not always wholly compatible, since one provision ensures greater immediate political accountability through elected ministers whereas the other seeks to provide opportunities for direct public participation in policymaking.

Evaluation of Regulatory Process Professional self-regulation is usually in the best interests of a profession but not necessarily of the public. Self-regulating bodies need to be continually scrutinized by both the public and by legislatures. The major need in departmental regulation is for increased access, for both the public and elected legislators, to precise information. Unless the public has access to information, it cannot hold regulators accountable. Where regulation is by way of an independent agency, it is essential that opportunities for public participation exist and are acted upon; otherwise such agencies tend to be influenced by the industries they are supposed to regulate. The ultimate evaluation of regulatory agencies is not only based on the process used but is also dependent upon the often — indeed usually — conflicting underlying values that govern the purposes that regulation in particular sectors is supposed to serve.   H.N. JANISCH

Reading: G.B. Doern, ed, *The Regulatory Process in Canada* (1978).

Reichmann family, real-estate developers. In 1984 the family comprised 3 brothers, Albert, Paul and Ralph, their wives and their mother Renée. Born in Hungary, the Reichmanns

moved to Austria, France, Spain and Morocco before arriving in Canada in 1956. They started their business career in Montréal, where they bought Olympia Floor and Wall Tile. In the 1960s they moved into real estate, and in 1969 incorporated Olympia and York, a private enterprise entirely controlled by the family. In 1962 they moved into office-tower development. Their real-estate company started operations in the US in 1976 and is now one of the largest developers in New York City. In 1980 they bought English Property Corp, one of the largest British developers, and also bought a 50.1% interest in Brinco Ltd. In 1981 they paid $502 million for Abitibi-Price Inc, the world's largest newspaper producer. Olympia & York also has investments in Royal Trust, Hiram Walker Resources and several other large Canadian companies. It is now the world's largest developer, with assets between $4 and $5 billion and operations in Canada, the US, the UK and France. It remains a private company.   JORGE NIOSI

Reid, Daphne Kate, actress (b at London, Eng 4 Nov 1930). She studied at the Royal Conservatory of Music, Toronto, and trained with Uta Hagen, New York. She first appeared at Hart House Theatre and made her professional debut with Muskoka's Straw Hat Players. By 1962 this warm and vulnerable performer had starred in London, Eng, at the STRATFORD FESTIVAL and in New York, and since then has divided her time between the US and Canada. She has been nominated for an Emmy Award as Queen Victoria (*Disraeli* 1963) and 2 "Tonys" (*Dylan* 1964 and *Slapstick Tragedy* 1966). Honours in Canada include ACTRA and Dora Mavor Moore Awards in 1980 and 1981. Some Stratford Festival roles have been Juliet's Nurse (1960), Lady Macbeth (1962), Chekhov's Mme Ranevskaya (1965) and Fonsia in *The Gin Game* (1980). She has played also at Stratford, Conn (1969, 1974), the SHAW FESTIVAL (1976) and the NATIONAL ARTS CENTRE (1983). In addition to frequent TV appearances, she has been in a number of feature films, including *The Andromeda Strain, A Delicate Balance* and *Atlantic City.*   DAVID GARDNER

Kate Reid, stage and screen actress, portraying women's advocate Nellie McClung in a 1978 CBC television drama (*courtesy Public Archives of Canada/PA-120142*).

Reid, Escott Meredith, diplomat (b at Campbellford, Ont 21 Jan 1905). A graduate of U of T and Oxford, Reid concentrated on Canadian foreign policy and neutrality after he became national secretary of the Canadian Institute of

International Affairs in 1932. In 1938 he joined the Dept of External Affairs; he served in Washington (1939-41, 1944-45), in Ottawa where he helped shape air transport policy, and in San Francisco and London where he worked on the creation of the UN. Lester PEARSON's chief aide, 1946-49, Reid was instrumental in devising the idea of a collective security alliance of Western democracies, which culminated in NATO. Thereafter, his career led to New Delhi and Bonn, to the International Bank for Reconstruction and Development, and to Glendon College, York U, as first principal. Reid's own important writings on politics and diplomacy include *Time of Fear and Hope* (1977) and *Envoy to Nehru* (1981).   J.L. GRANATSTEIN

Reid, George Agnew, painter (b at Wingham, Canada W 25 July 1860; d at Toronto 23 Aug 1947). Reid brought Parisian Academy precision to emotional genre paintings of his own Ontario country people. Trained at the Central Ontario School of Art, Toronto (1879), the Pennsylvania Academy (1883), and the Julian and Colarossi academies, Paris, and the Prado, Madrid (1888-89), Reid turned from portraiture to genre, as in *The Foreclosure of the Mortgage* (1893), making his name with these successful narrative pictures. He was elected to the Royal Canadian Academy of Arts in 1889, and was principal of the Central Ontario School of Art and Design (later Ontario Coll of Art) 1912-18. He also did murals and private and public commissions, including Toronto City Hall. In 1944 he presented 459 paintings to the Ontario government.

    ANNE MCDOUGALL

George Agnew Reid, *The Call to Dinner* (1887), oil on canvas (*courtesy McMaster U Coll*).

Reid, Richard Gavin, farmer, politician, premier of Alberta 1934-35 (b at Aberdeenshire, Scot 17 Jan 1879; d at Edmonton 17 Oct 1980). Reid served in the British Royal Army Medical Corps in the SOUTH AFRICAN WAR 1900-02 and sought his fortune in Canada in 1903. Following interludes of lumbering in Ontario and farming near Winnipeg, Reid moved to a homestead S of Mannville, Alta. One of the successful UNITED FARMERS OF ALBERTA candidates in the 1921 provincial election, Reid held several portfolios over the next 13 years. When Premier John E. BROWNLEE resigned in 1934, Reid was selected as his successor and sworn in as premier, president of the Executive Council and provincial secretary on 10 July 1934. Despite bringing in innovative debt adjustment legislation, Reid and his government were placed in an impossible political position facing, on the one hand, UFA executive preference for the new Cooperative Commonwealth Federation and, on the other hand, the strong appeal to farmers of William ABERHART's Social Credit proposals. The UFA government was swept from office in the 1935 election.   CARL BETKE

Reid, Sir Robert Gillespie, bridge and railway builder, financier (b at Coupar Angus, Scot 1842; d at Montréal 3 June 1908). He worked briefly in Australia as a contractor and then came to Canada (1871). His fame in Canada as a bridge builder comes from his construction of the Lachine bridge across the St Lawrence R at Montréal, the bridge at Sault Ste Marie and the International Bridge over the Niagara R. Reid became involved in the building of the CPR and constructed difficult sections of the line along the N shore of Lk Superior. In 1890 he contracted to build railways for the Newfoundland government. Within 6 years, Reid's line had crossed the Island, and thereafter he developed telegraphs, steamships and natural resources. Reid, and later his sons, controlled communication and transportation systems on the Island through Reid-Newfoundland Co until the Nfld government took over in 1923.   DAVID EVANS

Reid, William Ronald, Bill, sculptor (b at Vancouver 12 Jan 1920). An internationally recognized HAIDA artist, Reid is frequently credited with the revival and innovative resurgence of Northwest Coast Indian arts in the contemporary world. Son of a Haida mother and a Scots-American father, Reid was a teenager before he knew of his native heritage. He studied jewellery and engraving at Ryerson, Toronto, in 1948, and at the Central School of Design in London, Eng, in 1968. He began investigating the arts of the Haida in 1951 and later was involved with the creation of a monumental sculpture for UBC, *Haida Village,* eventually becoming a recognized authority on Haida art and life. Among his major works are the 4.5-ton cedar sculpture *Raven and the First Humans* in UBC's Museum of Anthropology (1980) and a bronze killer whale sculpture, *The Chief of the Undersea World,* for the Vancouver Aquarium (1984). He was awarded the MOLSON PRIZE in 1977.   CAROL SHEEHAN

Reindeer, see CARIBOU.

Reindeer Lake, 6651 km², elev 337 m, max length 233 km, located on the border between northeastern Saskatchewan and northwestern Manitoba, is the second-largest lake in Saskatchewan and ninth largest in Canada. An irregularly shaped lake, it has a heavily indented shoreline and contains numerous small islands. On its E shore is the community of Kinoosao, at its N end Brochet, Man, and at its S end, Southend, Sask. It drains mainly to the S, via the Reindeer R and a controlled weir, to the CHURCHILL R and thence E to Hudson Bay. In the N it drains partly to Lk ATHABASCA via the Cochrane R and WOLLASTON LK. Fishing is an important industry in the area, and sportfishermen are drawn by its clear and deep waters. The name of the lake appears to be a translation of the Indian name.

    DAVID EVANS

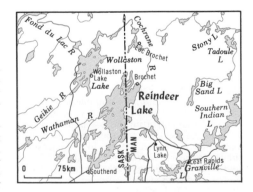

Relève, La, monthly magazine fd 1934 in Montréal by Paul Beaulieu, Robert CHARBONNEAU and Claude Hurtubise. The magazine published 103 issues before its demise in 1948, the first 48 as *La Relève* and the rest as *La Nouvelle Relève.* Major Québec contributors included Robert Élie, Roger Duhamel, Saint-Denys GARNEAU and Jean Le Moyne, and later Guy Frégault, Berthelot Brunet and others; among the major French ones were Daniel-Rops, Jacques Maritain, Emmanuel Mounier and Georges Bernanos. The original objective was to establish an "independent, national and Catholic" group to work towards correcting the sad lack of art, literature and philosophy in the country. The main themes were the economic crisis of the 1930s, perceived as a crisis of civilization; revolution, ie, the transformation of society in accordance with a Mounier-inspired "personalist" and communal belief system (*see* CITÉ LIBRE); CATHOLICISM, the best way to establish a new social consensus modelled on the Christian Middle Ages; art and literature as a means of spiritual development; marriage and the family, values badly needed in a chaotic world. The magazine explored these subjects with great openness of spirit — something that set it apart from other nationalist and traditionalist publications. However, edited by young bourgeois Montréalers with no financial worries, it was also highly idealistic: its articles frequently posed general questions about contemporary civilization, but ignored the real problems then facing Québec society. It had little social, economic or political impact, but it did make a significant contribution to the world of ideas. *See* LITERARY PERIODICALS IN FRENCH.

    JACQUES PELLETIER

Religion [Lat *religio,* "respect for what is sacred"] may be defined as the relationship between human beings and their transcendent source of value. In practice it may involve various forms of communication with a higher power, such as prayers, rituals at critical stages in life, meditation or "possession" by spiritual agencies. Religions, though differing greatly in detail, usually share most of the following characteristics: a sense of the holy or the sacred (often manifested in the form of gods, or a personal God); a system of beliefs; a community of believers or participants; ritual (which may include standard forms of invocation, sacraments or rites of initiation); and a moral code.

In Canada the principal religion is CHRISTIANITY, to which 90% of the population claims adherence (1981c). Before European settlement the native peoples practised a wide variety of religions (*see* NATIVE PEOPLE, RELIGION). Many native individuals and groups were converted to Christianity through missionary work that began in NEW FRANCE, but in recent years there has been a revival of native religions in a number of regions. During the 19th century, and boosted particularly by 20th-century immigration, numerous other traditions have come to Canada. By the early 1980s JUDAISM, BUDDHISM, SIKHISM, HINDUISM, ISLAM and the BAHA'I FAITH were well represented. The various traditions can be contrasted according to whether their sense of the sacred is focused on historic events (Judaism, Christianity, Islam, Sikhism and the Baha'i Faith) or on the natural cycle and rhythms of life (Hinduism, Taoism and, to some extent, Buddhism). But such contrasts overlook the fact that similar phenomena are found across traditions.

In the academic study of religion, Christians have generally been among the leaders, and therefore Christian usages and definitions of the descriptive vocabulary of religious studies tend to dominate discussions of the subject, as do Christian views of what constitutes religion. In N America this tendency has been influenced most strongly by Protestant Christianity. The Protestant Reformation of the 16th century marked a reaction initiated against priestly religion by scholars such as Martin Luther (*see* LUTHERANS) and John Calvin (*see* CALVINISM), who studied the Bible in its original languages of Hebrew and Greek, rather than in Latin translation. Following St Paul, Luther stressed what God does for humanity through Christ, rather than how human beings prove themselves for

God, with the result that faith (trust in God's action), rather than ritual (human routines), became the touchstone of what Protestants regarded as true religion. The preachers, rather than the priests, became the leaders in Protestantism, basing the Christian message on the prophetic tradition of the Hebrew Bible and summarizing it in set creeds. Consequently, to most N Americans religion has come to mean a system of beliefs. Since Christians are theists (believers in a personal god), their central belief has been in God as creator, redeemer and judge of the world.

In recent centuries, partly under the impact of the prophetic emphasis on personal faith and social justice, Christians and Jews influenced by the PHILOSOPHY of Immanuel Kant have emphasized the moral life as the key to true religion. Consequently, a full account of religion in our culture typically refers to moral codes, as well as cultic practices and creedal affirmations, as equally necessary components of any organized religion.

The contrast between the cultural compromises of different churches and "true religion" (considered as true faith, moral probity or purified ritual) means that, in the case of Christianity and other major religious movements such as Buddhism, one has to distinguish between the cultural forms associated with a religious tradition and its "critical edge"; this is usually derived from its otherworldly perspective, or from contrasting the ideal life portrayed in its scriptures with the historical practices of different congregations. Allowing for both aspects, one may then see religion as the present interplay between past and future: ie, between traditional faith and ultimate hope in the life of individuals and communities. For instance, Christianity includes a range of practices, organizations and expectations of a life where God's will is fully realized (defined by many as heaven); Buddhism includes the ordinary customs of the monks and laity with respect to life in this world (*samsara*), and the expectation of ultimate bliss (*nirvana*). One reason that traditional religion is thought to be contradicted by secular culture is that the secular outlook makes no allowance for any ultimate hope resting on expectations not bound by historical circumstance. As religion loses its hold on its sacred reference it seems to lose its reason for being.

Christian views have tended to dominate discussions of religion, but in the academic study of the subject the impact of the SOCIAL SCIENCES has led to a more functional approach to the data. As anthropologists have made us more familiar with so-called primal traditions, including those of native N American peoples, scholars of religion have had to reconsider emphases and choice of categories. For instance, where a culture is shaped without a codified scripture (such as the Bible) and without official creeds, the meaning of different rituals is typically carried by myths relayed orally from generation to generation. Scholars have tended to fasten on cosmogonic myths (myths of creation) as the religiously significant ones. However, the most significant myths may remain concealed from researchers: the SHAMANS or tribal seers and medicine men who perform the rituals often keep secret their most sacred traditions, which relate the ways of the group's ancestors to the ordeals of tribal life. Analysis of such traditions uses the contrast between the religious and the secular, since the sacred is equally secular ("this-worldly") in these traditions. By "sacred" is meant whatever is of foundational value in a given society, its point of reference for bringing order out of chaos. Through myth and ritual the symbolic system of values is often tied to specific events and places, so that within any given group we find sacred mountains, sacred trees and rivers, sacred plants, etc.

The functional approach to religion can be used also in analysing the literary religious traditions that rely on written scriptures. For instance, the importance of Mt Zion or Jerusalem in Judaism, Rome in CATHOLICISM, and the river Jordan in revivalist Protestant sects indicates the importance of sacred places and times in Judaeo-Christian culture, as does the close association of Christmas and Easter with winter and spring festivals. One consequence of the use of social-science methodology in the study of religion is that a given people's profession of faith is now much less likely to be taken at face value than it was when its leaders controlled the study of religion. (For instance, the hierarchical structure of the Catholic and major Protestant churches, with its identification of God as Heavenly Father, may be viewed by some as a set of myths and rituals serving to reinforce male supremacy, rather than as a response to divine revelation.)

At the same time, a functional approach teaches us to look beyond the confines of formally organized religious groups for the full picture of religion. In modern Canada, a complete analysis would look to rituals associated with Hockey Night in Canada and the GREY CUP, as well as with the Hebrew Bible, when the discussion turns to our foundational values. Among our sacred places, in popular imagination, may be the NORTH, as the horizon of our sense of identity, and the ST LAWRENCE R, as the locus of early European settlements. In this connection it is worthy of note that the parliamentary system, as contrasted with the American presidential and congressional system, so far has not fostered a nationalistic civil religion in Canada such as the one sociologist Robert Bellah has identified in the US. Quasi-religious creeds, codes and cults exist in such contemporary movements as MARXISM and feminism (*see* WOMEN'S MOVEMENT), as these develop articulated traditions and criticize the compromises of present culture in the name of some ultimate hope. Only an assumption that religion necessarily means belief in God or supernaturalism prevents us from including such movements under the heading "religion."

As various Asian traditions have been introduced to N America through IMMIGRATION, one indirect consequence has been the development of NEW RELIGIOUS MOVEMENTS. Some of these are actually ancient, but are newly transplanted and attractive to Westerners disaffected with the secularism of Judaism and Christianity (eg, Hare Krishna, which has its roots in Hinduism). Other groups represent a fusion of Christian and Asian motifs (eg, the Unification Church, which combines Christian with Korean ideas). Still others (eg, Scientology) are the invention of individuals who gain a following by using traditional philosophies to meet secular aspirations. So far, these movements are known to us mostly through the functional analyses of social scientists or the apologetic claims of converts. While traditional, organized religious practice may seem to be on the decline, fascination with the occult and esoteric rituals seems to be on the rise in N America. This suggests to some scholars that some form of religious behaviour is typical of all human societies, even when formal religion is repudiated.

Religion as a mode of human behaviour often reflects an awareness of human weaknesses. Much religious imagery is based on the projection of human fears concerning death and social decay onto the symbols of ultimate power. In the name of religion, wars have been started, minorities persecuted and social inequalities such as apartheid perpetuated. At the same time, religion as a response to the deepest spiritual values in the universe has been the motive for major reform movements in history. Spiritual and moral leaders such as Gotama Buddha, Jesus, Confucius, Socrates, Muhammad and Mahatma Gandhi have directly or indirectly inspired the abolition of slavery and the caste system, and the alleviation of ignorance and disease. One way to account for the paradox is to contrast extrinsic and intrinsic motivations in religion, following psychologist Gordon Allport. Extrinsic motivation involves the use of religious institutions for other purposes, social or economic. Intrinsic motivation involves living by such commands as those to love strangers and to seek justice for widows and orphans. By and large, the priestly caste views religion positively. The prophetic traditions view religion with suspicion.

Finally, it is useful to distinguish among magic, science and religion. Magic uses formulae supposed to effect changes willed by manipulative individuals. Science uses formulae or laws to explain general physical processes. Religion reflects ancestral wisdom and a spirituality which brings one to terms with one's personal destiny. In so-called primal societies, such distinctions are less frequently made. With the increasing complexity of, and emphasis on specialization in, the industrial world, the significance of such distinctions is beginning to be recognized. As it is, many critics have come to accept that science and religion need not conflict and that magical practices can be found in all cultural modes, including religion. PETER SLATER

Religious Studies

English Canada Important in the early history of many Canadian universities and colleges, religion has continued to make a contribution, especially in seminaries. Seminaries were established to teach ministers and full-time church workers the particular doctrines of their denomination. Christianity was seen as the one true religion, and the denominational formulation of Christian doctrine was regarded as authoritative. Seminaries with their residences were frequently attached to universities, and their degrees were usually given the status of university degrees. A few general religion courses, eg, in biblical literature or church history, were offered for the arts and science faculties by seminary staff; all other teaching was confessional. Many university faculty suspected seminary staff of clericalism, anti-intellectualism and proselytism. Whether these concerns were justified or not, seminaries and theology departments were far more interested in the Judaeo-Christian tradition than in religion in general.

Around 1960 a distinction was made between confessional and academic studies of religion. This provided the philosophical prerequisite for new departments of religious studies at McMaster U, Sir George Williams U [Concordia] and UBC, located in faculties of arts and science without denominational ties. An academic approach was taken to religious studies as an intellectual discipline.

The Canadian Society for the Study of Religion (CSSR) was established 1965 to supplement 3 existing societies: Canadian Society of Biblical Studies, Canadian Society of Church History and Canadian Theological Society. The academically oriented CSSR was the first society connected with religion to join the LEARNED SOCIETIES and to adopt bilingualism. In 1970 the 4 societies formed the Canadian Corporation for Studies in Religion/Corporation canadienne des sciences religieuses. In 1971 CCSR began publication of *SR: Studies in Religion/Sciences religieuses*, which succeeded the *Canadian Journal of Theology*. CCSR also publishes various series of books.

By 1980 most universities and many colleges offered religious studies programs treating the major world religions, and sacred languages such as Hebrew and Sanskrit. Opportunities for graduate work have developed in many provinces. Graduates become university and college

Religious Affiliation: Percentage of Total Population
(Source: derived from Statistics Canada, 1981 census)

	Christian:		Orthodox	Jewish	Islamic	Hindu	Sikh	Buddhist	No. Religion
	Catholic	Protestant*							
Canada	47.3	41.2	1.5	1.2	0.4	0.3	0.3	0.2	7.3
BC	19.8	54.7	0.9	0.5	0.5	0.3	1.5	0.4	20.5
Alta	27.7	56.0	2.2	0.5	0.8	0.3	0.3	0.3	11.5
Sask	32.4	58.3	2.4	0.2	0.1	0.1	**	0.1	6.2
Man	31.5	56.6	2.1	1.5	0.2	0.2	0.2	0.2	7.3
Ont	35.6	51.8	2.0	1.7	0.6	0.5	0.2	0.2	7.1
Qué	88.2	6.4	1.2	1.6	0.2	0.1	**	0.2	2.1
NB	53.9	42.9	0.1	0.1	**	0.1	**	**	2.8
NS	37.0	58.0	0.3	0.2	0.1	0.1	**	0.1	4.0
PEI	46.6	50.5	**	0.1	0.1	0.1	**	**	2.6
Nfld	36.3	62.6	**	**	**	0.1	**	**	1.0
NWT	40.3	52.0	0.4	**	**	**	**	**	6.4
YT	24.2	53.3	0.1	0.1	**	**	0.2	0.3	19.5

* Includes Anglicans
** Below 0.05% of region's population

instructors, or teachers in high school social studies and world religions classes. Although most offerings still emphasize biblical studies and Christian thought, there is a serious effort to present all world religions. This is especially important, given the pluralistic nature of contemporary Canadian society.

Wilfred Cantwell Smith (b 1916) stands out in the academic study of religion in Canada. A Presbyterian minister and an Islamic specialist, in 1951 he organized McGill U Institute of Islamic Studies to foster academic, interreligious dialogue. In 1964 Smith became Director of Harvard U's Centre for the Study of World Religions. Returning to Canada in 1973, he developed a religious studies department at Dalhousie U. Smith has emphasized the cumulative history and the personal faith experience of each religion. His books, known worldwide, include *The Meaning and End of Religion* (1963), *Belief and History* (1977) and *Towards a World Theology* (1981). Traditional Christian theology's assumption that it has a monopoly on divine grace and salvation is, in Smith's view, morally wrong, and must give way to thinking which allows that God is active in other traditions as well.

French Canada In French Canada, the academic study of religion was long totally identified with the study of theology as practised in seminaries for the formation of clergy. However, various phenomena and events of the QUIET REVOLUTION era (1960-66) helped break that monopoly and speed the introduction of a new tradition in religious study. This new approach to the religious phenomenon had been known in Europe for a century, mainly under the German name *Religionswissenschaft*. In Québec it takes a number of names: human sciences of religion, sciences of religion, religious sciences, religiology. The *Guide to Religious Sciences in Canada* (1972) listed 13 university-level institutions (including U de Moncton, Laurentian U and U of Ottawa) teaching theology or religious sciences in French Canada. Nine of them concentrate largely or exclusively on theology.

French Canadian scholars participate in the activities of the CCSR and have also founded a section within the Association canadienne française pour l'avancement des sciences (a francophone counterpart to the learned societies) called "Sciences of Religion," which holds a conference each May.

Francophone theologians belong to the Société canadienne de théologie, of which most members are from Québec. In 1944 the francophone exegetes formed the Association catholique des études bibliques au Canada, which holds an annual conference. ACEBAC did a translation of the New Testament in 1953; in 1982 it was reissued, with commentaries, by Bellarmin in Montréal.

French-language Canadian journals devoted to the scientific study of religion include *Sciences religieuses* and the *Cahiers du centre de recherche en sciences de la religion* of Laval. Francophone theologians publish in magazines such as *Science et esprit, Laval théologique et philosophique, Église et théologie* and *Sciences pastorales*. *Cahiers éthicologiques* follows research being done in ethics by the religious sciences department at U du Québec à Rimouski.

The importance of the Christian tradition in the formation of Québec society and its growing religious pluralism augur well for the development of theology and the science of religion. *See* BIBLE SCHOOLS; SUNDAY SCHOOLS.

HAROLD COWARD AND ROLAND CHAGNON

Religious Building Canadian religious architecture began with the arrival of the first missionaries to NEW FRANCE. The Recollets and Jesuits, who arrived in 1615 and 1625, respectively, built mission chapels, sometimes using Indian construction techniques. They later replaced these buildings with more solid timber structures. Early in the 17th century, religious orders also built chapels and small churches for the colony's settlers. Like mission chapels, the construction of these buildings was simple and basic, initially of wood and later of stone.

Later in the 17th century, under Jesuit influence and with the arrival of more artisans and builders trained in France, certain traditional features of religious architecture were used to construct churches in Québec City and Montréal. These were built in the shape of a Latin cross, with steeples where the nave and transept met. The Jesuit church in Québec City (1666, destroyed 1807) was a striking example of this classical French monumental architecture. The first bishop of Québec City, François de LAVAL, was instrumental in spreading this style to small villages by encouraging and supervising the construction of many stone churches adapted and simplified from French architectural models.

During the first half of the 18th century, the king's engineer, Gaspard-Joseph CHAUSSEGROS DE LÉRY prepared all plans for a second cathedral in Québec City and designed a new facade for the parish church in Montréal. Small rural churches built by local people when new parishes were established illustrate the originality and quality of the general architectural tradition of French Canada. Physically and symbolically the parish church was the community's most important building. Until the early 19th century, 3 models were used to construct these churches: the Jesuit Latin cross design; the Recollet plan, consisting of a broad nave with a narrower semicircular apse; and the even simpler MAILLOU plan, consisting of a nave ending with a semicircular apse. With its fieldstone walls and arched openings, the Saint-François church (1734-36) on Ile d'ORLÉANS, built according to the Recollet plan, is representative of these small parish churches

with very plain exteriors. However, the rich ornamentation (*see* SCULPTURE) inside many of these churches contrasts sharply with their austere exteriors. The superlative quality of this ornamentation can be seen in the interior of the Ursuline Convent chapel in Québec City, carved by Noël and Pierre-Noël Levasseur (1734-39).

The arrival and establishment of a new, mainly Anglican and British, society brought major developments to Canadian architecture after 1750. In various parts of eastern Canada, churches were built in a Palladian style which was closely associated with the Anglicans and had been popular in England and America since the beginning of the 18th century. Features of the Palladian style include symmetry, order and a restrained classical vocabulary. St Paul's in Halifax (1750) was the first Anglican church in Canada and was modelled on the Marylebone Chapel (1721-22) in London, designed by the Palladian architect James Gibbs. Similarly, Québec City's Holy Trinity Cathedral (1800-04) drew its inspiration from Gibbs. These new buildings, as well as the arrival of skilled workers from England or the US, helped spread the Palladian style and its variants, particularly in Québec and the Atlantic colonies. Many little wooden churches of various denominations in NS and NB incorporated Palladian elements, notably the wide pediment gracing the facade, the venetian window in the apse, the vaulted openings and the classical ornamentation around the main door.

LOYALIST immigrants arriving in the late 18th century introduced a new type of church to the Atlantic provinces, used particularly by the Congregationalists. Primarily a meeting place, this type of wooden building (eg, Barrington's Meeting House in NS) is designed like a 2-storey private home where part of the floor is removed to provide a high room with a gallery for sermons and prayer meetings.

The Palladian style did not affect traditional religious architecture in Québec until the 1820s and even then its greatest influence was on exterior ornamentation. The architect François BAILLAIRGÉ was most successful in integrating the decorative aspect of the new Palladian architectural style into Québec churches. Through his *Précis d'architecture* (1828), Abbé Jérome DEMERS was also instrumental in spreading new ideas among a generation of builders. At the beginning of the 19th century, with the encouragement of Abbé Conefroy, the Recollet, Jesuit and Maillou plans were abandoned in favour of the 17th-century Jesuit Latin-cross format, which combined the first 2 plans. From the 1820s until the 1860s interest in classical architecture shifted from the Renaissance era to more ancient times, thereby giving certain features of church facades (columns, pillars, entablature) new importance. This neoclassical period was exemplified in Québec between 1830 and 1840 by the work of the architect Thomas Baillairgé. In certain cases the influence of Greek architecture was expressed simply through decorative details on the church's facade. On other occasions, however, the church design was modelled on a Greek temple, an example being St Andrew's Church (1831) in Niagara-on-the-Lake.

The construction of the NOTRE DAME CHURCH in Montréal (1823-29) marks an important moment in Canadian architectural history. For almost the next century, the Gothic revival style was closely associated with religious architecture for all denominations throughout Canada. This was not immediately accepted, particularly in eastern Canada where it had to coexist with a well-established classical tradition. Yet Gothic revival began to flourish in the 1840s, when there was a trend toward realism and archaeological authenticity particularly suited to religious architecture. The Ecclesiologists, a group

High altar, Notre-Dame Cathedral, Montréal (*photo by G.J. Harris*).

Interior of the Cathedral Marie Reine du Monde, Montreal (*photo © 1984 Hartill Art Associates*).

of English theologians who from 1839 promoted a renewal of religious architecture, encouraged builders of Anglican churches to return to the plan of medieval Catholic churches, based on a nave flanked by aisles, surmounted by galleries and facing the chancel. From then on, the chancel became a focal point. Each component of the interior plan was henceforth expressed in the exterior of the building. Toronto's St James's Cathedral (1849-53), Fredericton's CHRIST CHURCH CATHEDRAL (1846-53) and St John the Baptist Cathedral (1848-80) in St John's, are examples of this desire to follow medieval models.

It was not as easy for the Gothic revival style to become established in Québec as in other regions because there the classical tradition was already closely associated with Catholic architecture. Thus, in reaction to the construction of the Anglican Christ Church Cathedral (1857-59) in Montréal, a Gothic revival building, Mgr Ignace BOURGET had the St-Jacques Cathedral (1875-85) built on the model of St Peter's in Rome. Bourget, who in this way sought to dissociate the Catholic faith from the Gothic revival style, opened the way for an intense interest in Neobaroque architecture between 1870 and 1880.

The Gothic revival style's evolution toward High Victorian Gothic was most powerfully expressed in Ontario in the work of Henry Langley, who built Anglican, Methodist, Baptist and Catholic churches for over 40 years. Just as this style began to wane in eastern Canada, it became popular in the West. The side tower, wide roof and massive proportions of St Paul's Cathedral (1895, Regina), and the vertical proportions and ornamentation of St John-the-Divine Cathedral (1912, Victoria), are characteristic of the Gothic revival style. At the same time, small churches were also incorporating some striking features of the Gothic revival style. This "Carpenter's Gothic" (when done in wood) style is found in such eastern Canadian churches as St John's Anglican (about 1840) in Lunenburg, NS, and the United Church in MALPÈQUE, PEI (about 1870). In Ontario, one group of small churches uses contrasting coloured bricks to accentuate the picturesque aspects of certain Gothic revival details, particularly around the windows. The Crown Hill United Church (about 1880) exemplifies this trend. In Ontario, Manitoba and Saskatchewan other simply constructed small churches retained only the Gothic revival arched windows and central tower added to the facade. Examples of this are St Clement Anglican (1860-61) in Sel-

kirk, Man, and St James Anglican (about 1909) in Star City, Sask. In the extreme west, many wooden mission churches made picturesque use of certain Gothic revival details. The facade of the Holy Cross mission church (about 1905) in Skookumchuk, BC, has many such features, and the one in Fort Good Hope in the NWT (1864-82) contrasts a fairly conventional exterior with a richly decorated interior.

Between 1880 and 1890, some architects abandoned the Gothic revival for a new architectural mode popular in the US. They built large churches whose rustic masonry and wide, rounded openings expressed the Romanesque revival influence. The Metropolitan United Church (1890-91) in Victoria is an example. Also at this time, a number of architects adopted an auditorium layout, particularly for Methodist and Presbyterian churches. Generally speaking, the plans of 19th-century Catholic and Anglican churches were similar in that they were rectangular, with the altar in the centre of the sanctuary. The interior of Anglican churches was usually plainer than that of Catholic churches. Methodist and Presbyterian churches were also very sparsely decorated, but had the pulpit as the focal point. Other religious groups, such as the Congregationalists, Unitarians, Seventh-Day Adventists and Baptists, also constructed very simple meeting places.

In the last quarter of the 19th century, a number of immigrant groups from Scandinavia and Russia settled in the West, bringing their architectural traditions with them. The Ukrainian immigrants who settled in Manitoba and Saskatchewan constructed churches reminiscent of the Byzantine style, with their cruciform plan, barrel-vaulted nave, dome-shaped belltowers and coloured interior ornamentation.

At the beginning of the 20th century, under the influence of the École des beaux-arts in Paris, architects moved away from the 19th-century emphasis on the picturesque, historical models and stylistic details, and gave more thought to layout, composition, proportions and overall organization. Church plans began to be designed on a system of axes; with new emphasis on the nave. Using the composition principles of the École des beaux-arts, churches continued to be built in the Gothic revival, classical, baroque or Romanesque styles — eg, the Catholic cathedral in St Boniface, Man (1908), was built in the Romanesque tradition, and the one in Gravelbourg, Sask (1919), reveals the neobaroque influence. The influence of the École des beaux-arts marked the end of the era when architects turned to the past for inspiration and models. Nineteenth- and early 20th-century churches, because of their size and symbolic importance for each community, best illustrate the contribution of these important architectural currents.   NATHALIE CLERK

St Paul's Church, Halifax, NS (*courtesy Parks Canada/ Heritage Recording Service*).

Modern Religious Building

Churches and temples built in Canada during the post-WWII period occupy an important place in Canadian religious architecture. In urban areas, where population increased the most, more churches were built than in all previous periods combined. Most of these new churches were built in suburbs and reflect the character of their neighbourhoods, with their widely dispersed population and small-scale buildings. The number of parishioners was often small and the budget restricted. Because most worshippers had to drive to church, parking lots became essential. These physical problems reduced the importance of the church in the cityscape and left an ambiguous image of this type of building. A more fundamental problem arose from the redefining of churches. Though architects and their clients recognized the need to renew religious architecture, they were uncertain of what form the change should take. Their uncertainty was compounded by the debate over the role of religion in the modern world. Following fiery debates held in Europe between the 2 wars, various Canadian cities (Toronto 1956, 1961, and Vancouver, 1960) hosted seminars on church construction. Was a church to be a house of God or a house of man? Should it be a shelter for the faithful to pray and hear the word of God? Is it a refuge for meditation, or should it be more a part of everyday life? The interior arrangement was affected as well by the redefining of liturgical functions. The locations of the baptistry, the altar and other liturgical places were influenced by the symbolism enshrouding them. Though construction of churches (some of which are also community centres) attests to the continuing evolution of liturgy and religious conception, many modern churches have limited architectural interest, and from 1970 on very few churches were being built.

While theologians tried to define the nature and role of the church, architects were trying to renew the design of the church and convince their clients of the need for these changes. Until WWII it was accepted that churches were built in one of the historical styles. This usually meant Gothic revival in English Canada and one of the classical styles in Québec. However, in the mid-1930s new forms began to appear in church architecture just as in secular architec-

Anglican church at Frobisher Bay, NWT, built to resemble an igloo (*photo by Karl-Heinz Raach*).

ture. St James's Anglican Church (1935), Vancouver, by London architect Adrian G. Scott, appears to mark the beginning of the modern movement on the Pacific coast. The Greek-cross plan and the barrel vaults of this concrete church give a Byzantine effect to the interior, but the extreme starkness highlights the geometry of the forms. On the outside, the rectilinear recesses of the portal and the large, smooth, stuccoed surfaces of the geometric masses indicate the influence of functionalist architecture, and the prismatic forms of the upper parts are reminiscent of art deco. Scott's associates were Sharp and Thompson, local architects who built Vancouver's Crown United Church during the same period. The narrow windows capped with mitre arches, such as those of St James's, are a compromise between the pointed arch of Gothic architecture and the geometrical forms of the international style. The cubic mass of the church and its stucco covering are further evidence of the entrenchment of the modern style in BC.

During the same period, religious architecture in Québec was influenced by Dom Bellot, a French Benedictine monk who came to Canada for the first time in 1934. Inspired by medieval architecture, Dom Bellot had devised a structural system of polygonal arches for reinforced concrete and parabolic arches for brick. As early as 1935-36, examples of both types were built: St-Jacques, of concrete, in Montréal (G. Gagnier) and Ste-Thérèse-de-Lisieux, of brick, in Beauport (A. Dufresne). They marked the beginning of a 20-year trend that gave Québec a distinctive, if only moderately modern style in religious architecture.

After 1950, the difference between churches in Québec and those elsewhere in Canada began to fade. Two styles in particular grew in popularity. In the first category are churches with horizontal roofs or very slight slopes, such as the small Anglican church in Montréal, St Cuthbert's (1946-47), by Lasserre. The churches in the second category have very steeply sloped roofs and low lateral walls. Many of these have a laminated wood structure. In both styles the structure determines both the exterior shape and the interior space. This rationalism, particularly

Precious Blood Church, St-Boniface, Man, designed to resemble an Indian tipi (*photo by Henry Kalen*).

stark in churches of the first category, was criticized for not inspiring uplifting feelings in the congregation. To solve the problem, one device was to give the slopes of the roof an excurved profile in order to increase the effect of ascension, as in Westminster Presbyterian Church (Salter and Allison) in Barrie, Ont. Another device was the piercing of the ridge of the roof, sometimes along its entire length, in order to provide the interior with a skylight, as in Scarborough's West Ellesmere United Church (E. ZEIDLER). Some churches, for example, St-Raphaël in Jonquière (St-Gelais and Tremblay) and Notre-Dame-des-Champs in Repentigny (D'Astous and Pothier), combine the 2 devices.

At the beginning of the 1960s, it became more common in Catholic churches to replace the longitudinal plan by the central plan. The resolution of the Vatican Council to encourage the participation of the congregation in the mass popularized this plan, which created a close relationship between the congregation and the altar. These churches, some of which are the most expressive of all postwar religious architecture, are in general low, with a single roof over the choir and the nave. Examples of this architecture can be found across the country; for example, St-Jean-Baptiste-de-la-Salle, Montréal (Lemay and Leclerc), St John Brébeuf, Winnipeg (Libling, Michener and Associates) and ST MARY'S in Red Deer, Alta (Cardinal). There are also several Manitoba churches by Étienne Gaboury in this category (*see* ARCHITECTURE).

It must be noted that during the 1960s a number of architects attempted to renew the styles of churches of the oriental rites, though continuing to respect their architectural traditions. Most examples are to be found in Ukrainian churches, such as Holy Family in Winnipeg and St Michael's in Tyndall, Man (Zuk). The cupolas which give the traditional churches their distinctive silhouette are recalled in the elegant geometric shapes which at the same time respect the nature of the wood or concrete of which they are built. Another example of this is Montréal's Greek Orthodox Cathedral (Affleck, Desbarats, Dimakopoulos, Lebensold, Sise), which respects the Byzantine tradition with its concrete cupola set on a rectangular nave plan.

CLAUDE BERGERON

Reading: N. Tardif-Painchaud's *Dom Bellot et l'architecture religieuse au Québec* (1978).

Religious Communities, *see* BUDDHISM; CHRISTIAN RELIGIOUS COMMUNITIES; NEW RELIGIOUS MOVEMENTS.

Religious Festivals Each major religion practised in Canada has, in addition to its own system of beliefs, a way of marking the passage of time and commemorating sacred events. Two main measures are used to establish years and their internal division: the solar cycle (including the length of days, of the seasons and of entire years) and the lunar cycle (linked especially to the definition of months).

Hinduism Hindu tradition boasts a plethora of festivals dated according to several luni-solar calendar systems. The proper date for a given festival involves complicated calculations resolving the cycles of the sun and the moon. The 4-day New Year festival, *Divali*, falls in Oct/Nov. Krishna, a popular Hindu diety, is honoured in the carnival atmosphere surrounding the festival of *Holi*, in Mar. Lord Rama is honoured at the spring equinox, *Rama-navami*, Mar/Apr, and the goddesses Sarasvati and Lalita are worshipped along with family ancestors at the autumnal equinox, Sept/Oct. Two nativities are celebrated in Aug/Sept, in the Hindu month of *Bhadrapada*, those of Lord Ganesha and Lord Krishna. A *puga* (worship service) is conducted with appropriate *mantras* (prayers) to the deity whose feast day it is. Specific elements of local Indian folk tradition animate the occasion.

Buddhism Buddhist festivals commemorate the historical Buddha, the founders of particular Buddhist movements, and Buddhist teachings as embodied in the cycle of nature. Canada's Japanese community follows the Jodo Shinshu school of Buddhism. Their dating system places the birth of the Buddha on Apr 8, which is celebrated as *Wesak*, or *Hanamatsuri* (Flower Festival); his enlightenment, upon which the core of Buddhist teaching is based, is celebrated on Dec 8 as *Bodhi* day; and Feb 15, *Nirvana* day, celebrates his death which, tradition suggests, occurred in Nepal in 486 BC. The Jodo Shinshu movement was founded by Shinran Shonin (1173-1262). Festivals commemorate his birth on May 21 and his death on Jan 16. At the spring and fall equinoxes most Buddhists celebrate Devotion day. These focus on the Buddha's teaching, called the 6 perfections, which lead to a balanced life like the universe at the equinox. The greatest festival among Japanese Buddhists is *O-Bon* (July/Aug). Devotees visit cemeteries and perform various rites to commemorate family ancestors.

The Theravada tradition of Buddhism common among SOUTHEAST ASIANS is marked by 2 major festivals. *Vaisakha*, the full-moon festival in May, commemorates the birth, enlightenment and death of the Buddha; *Vas* (Lent), the period of monastic enclosure beginning in July, is preceded by a festival and culminates in a grander Lent-end festival in Oct. In addition, Theravada Buddhists celebrate *Dharma-chakka*, a day commemorating Buddha's proclamation of his "gospel," on the full moon in July. *Dharma-vijaya* celebrates the missionary work carried out by Indian Emperor Asoka which spread the faith to Sri Lanka.

Sikhism Sikh festivals are rooted in the historical development of the faith. They include the birth and martyrdom of the key gurus (teachers): Guru Nanak's and Guru Gobind Singh's birthdays, and Guru Arjun Dev's and Guru Tegh Bahadur's martyrdom. A major festival marks the founding of the Sikh brotherhood, the *Khalsa*, on Apr 13.

Judaism The Jewish festival year begins with the carnival celebration at the feast of *Purim*, 14 of Adar (falling in Feb/Mar). It commemorates the biblical account of Esther and her role in rescuing the Jewish community from Persian oppression. *Pesach* (Passover, or the Feast of Freedom) focuses on the freeing of the Jews from exile in Egypt. It lasts 8 days beginning on the 15 of Nisan (Mar/Apr), and is celebrated largely through a ritual meal in the home. In May/June, 6-7 of Sivan, *Shavuoth* (Feast of Weeks) commemorates God's giving of the Torah to Moses on Mt Sinai. *Rosh Hashanah* (New Year) falls in Sept/Oct. Preparation involves 10 days of penance followed by a 2-day celebration. *Yom Kippur* (Day of Atonement) is the holiest of all festivals except *Shabbat*. It involves a day of rigorous fasting and collective penitential prayers. Five days later an ancient harvest festival is combined with a commemoration of the Israelites' 40-year sojourn in the wilderness prior to settlement in Palestine. *Sukkot* (Feast of Tabernacles, or Booths) lasts 8 days, falling in Sept/Oct. The final reading of a cycle in the Jewish Scripture is marked by *Simchat Torah*, Sept/Oct, accompanied by expressions of delight in the revelation embodied in the Hebrew Bible. *Hanukkah*, an 8-day Dec festival of lights, commemorates the struggle for liberty under the Maccabees against the Syrian-Greek rulers of Palestine in 168 BC. Technically a minor feast, it has become prominent in N America because of its proximity to Christmas. The greatest of Jewish festivals is *Shabbat* (Sabbath, or Saturday), the final day of the week, when the Creator's rest from his labours is celebrated.

Christianity The festivals of Christian traditions follow 2 calendars, the Julian, devised in 46 BC by Julius Caesar, and the Gregorian, a reformed calendar introduced by Pope Gregory XIII in 1582. A portion of the ORTHODOX CHURCH continues to follow the Julian calendar, which runs approximately 13 days behind the Gregorian. Christmas, which in the Gregorian calendar falls on Dec 25, celebrates the birth of Jesus Christ, after a 4-week preparation period called Advent. Epiphany (Jan 6) commemorates Jesus' baptism and, for some, the visitation of the Magi after the nativity. Easter, which is the greatest feast in Christianity, is a series of rituals marking the suffering, death and resurrection of Christ. It is dated following the Jewish lunar calendar as the first Sunday after the full moon following the spring equinox (Mar/Apr). Lent, a 40-day period of penitential preparation, begins with Ash Wednesday and culminates on Palm Sunday a week before Easter Sunday.

Ascension day, a major feast 40 days after Easter, marks Christ's last earthly appearance and is named for his ascension to God the Father. The cycle of feasts following Easter is closed with Pentecost Sunday 50 days after Easter when, tradition teaches, the Holy Spirit descended upon the disciples and the church was formed.

Many Protestant churches celebrate a founder's day, eg, Reformation Sunday (closest to Oct 31), commemorating Martin Luther's formal protest in 1517 against Roman Catholic practice and belief.

Islam The Islamic year is lunar, and 11 days shorter than the solar year. Muslims celebrate the Great Festival or Feast of Sacrifice, *'Id al-Adha,* at the end of the annual pilgrimage to Mecca. It consists of several rites focusing on the sacrifice of a consecrated animal at Mina, near Mecca. The founding of the city of Mecca and the devotion to monotheism of Abraham and his son Ishmael are commemorated. The little festival, *Id-al-fitr* (festival of fast-breaking) ends the 28-day fast of *Ramadan,* the ninth month. It begins with the appearance of the new moon. The followers of Shi'ite Islam have an additional festival called after the first Islamic month, *Muharram,* in which it occurs. A passion play commemorates the martyrdom of Husain, the son of Ali and grandson of the Prophet Muhammad. This occurred on the 10th of Muharram, 61 AD (10 Oct 680 AD) when he died in a battle with the Damascus caliphs. *See* HINDUISM; BUDDHISM; SIKHISM; JUDAISM; CHRISTIANITY; ISLAM.

DAVID J. GOA

Religious Music may be said to have begun in Canada with the arrival of the first settlers, but the indigenous peoples used music in a religious context prior to the 16th century. The first Christian service of which we have a record was a mass sung at Brest (Bonne Espérance Harbour) in Labrador on 14 June 1534. Missionaries in the early 17th century soon found that the Indians' love of music could be a powerful factor in their conversion to CHRISTIANITY. They were easily taught the simpler forms of church music. In 1610 the converts sang the *Te Deum* at the baptism of the Micmac chief Membertou and his tribe at PORT-ROYAL. The so-called "Huron Carol" is a relic of these times — a French Christmas tune wedded to Huron words. There is some doubt about both dates and authenticity, but the first religious composition to have been written in Canada may well have been the Prose from the *Office de la Sainte Famille,* attributed to Charles-Amador Martin, which dates from about 1700. The JESUIT RELATIONS contain many references to church music, both choral and instrumental. It is known that there was an organ in the Jesuit Chapel in Québec City by 1661 (*see also* NEW FRANCE).

There is a disappointing lack of references for the first half of the 18th century, although there are collections of polyphonic music in libraries in both Montréal and Québec City dating

from this period. By 1775 the picture becomes clearer. English-speaking settlers had brought the Church of England and Protestant observances with them, choirs had been established (eg, St Paul's Church, Halifax, in the 1760s), and churches in a few towns had organs (eg, Montréal, Québec City, at both the Roman Catholic and Anglican cathedrals, and Halifax). There are references to a continuing tradition of sung high masses and vespers in the Roman Catholic Church, while the Church of England and other congregations relied more on the singing of psalms (metrical versions, almost certainly), hymns and, occasionally, anthems (*see also* ANGLICANISM; CATHOLICISM).

The early years of the 19th century saw a growth of choral activity in the East and a gradual spread westward across the country. The popularity of the singing school movement gave an impetus to this development. Trained church musicians appeared on the scene. Most importantly, these years saw the start of what was to be, by the latter years of the century, a flood of publications devoted to church music. *Le Graduel romain* was published in Québec in 1800, Stephen Humbert's *Union Harmony* appeared in Saint John in 1801, Mark Burnham's *The Colonial Harmonist* in Port Hope, Ont, in 1832, and, in Toronto, William Warren of St James's Cathedral published *A Selection of Psalms and Hymns* (music edition in 1835). The greater availability of published materials encouraged the formation of choirs in smaller centres and facilitated the introduction of a repertoire based on a European heritage, particularly in the Church of England (to become the Anglican Church of Canada in 1955). Vested choirs appeared, eg, at Holy Trinity Cathedral in Québec City in 1804, though Toronto had to wait until 1868 for its first surpliced choir, at Holy Trinity Church. Anglican choirs at this time led their congregations in the singing of metrical psalms and hymns and often sang, as anthems, adaptations from the works of the great composers (eg, Handel, Haydn and Mozart, Beethoven and Rossini). The appearance of *Canadian Church Psalmody* in 1845 paved the way for the use of Anglican chant for the psalms.

Roman Catholic Church music in the 19th century also reflected a European heritage. Though factual evidence is hard to discover, some choirs did sing music by Haydn, Beethoven, Rossini and Gounod. Music by Canadian composers J.C. Brauneis, Jr, and Antoine DESSANE was also available, though this may not have been known outside of Québec. The papal *motu proprio* of 1903 ordered a return to the renaissance ideals of unaccompanied polyphonic music and restored the pre-eminence of Gregorian chant. In Catholic churches around the world this order made for a glorious period of good music, reverently sung.

A parallel development in the early years of the 20th century had an immense effect in the Anglican Church. Cheap editions of liturgical music by the great masters of the Tudor and Jacobean period in England facilitated a return to simple, uncluttered music and fostered a similar style of composition. However, the music of Stainer, Barnby, Gounod, Spohr, Simper and Maunder still had a stranglehold, especially in smaller towns and churches.

Meanwhile, the Protestant churches had been moving slowly towards a form of worship in which music, both congregational and choral, could take a larger part. BAPTIST, METHODIST and CONGREGATIONAL churches had always allowed the organ, and eventually PRESBYTERIAN churches welcomed its inclusion in their service. Even quite small churches acquired instruments and formed choirs, and began to undertake the singing of an anthem. Large churches gave their choirs visibility and gowned them and finally began to spend money on them; often there

would be a paid quartet of professional singers, who not only led the choir but also sang solos. This type of organization also spread to Anglican churches. Better choirs, in addition to leading Sunday services, now undertook to perform oratorios, or extracts from them, in almost concertlike circumstances. The first oratorio performance in a Canadian church is known to have been given in 1769 in St Paul's Church, Halifax, though we do not know what was sung. In the Protestant churches a mixed choir was the norm, often with a junior choir of children of both sexes. All-male choirs of men and boys were common in larger Roman Catholic and Anglican churches.

By the mid-20th century, in the Roman Catholic Church, choirs were occasionally all-male but more often mixed, were sometimes vested but mostly unvested in rear galleries, sang a repertoire spiced with Palestrina, but based more often on 18th- or 19th-century settings, and used plainsong with varying degrees of success. These choirs were almost never paid, and frequently the posts of organist and choirmaster were divided. In the Anglican Church, choirs were either mixed or all-male (the latter showing a decline in numbers from 1950 onwards), were almost always vested, and sat in choir stalls in a chancel area. The repertoire was largely English in origin but drawn from a wide range of periods. Some members of the choir might be paid, and the organist-choirmaster was often well trained. The typical Protestant church would have a senior mixed choir and a junior choir. It was always visible, often sitting in curved stalls behind the minister, and was gowned. Its repertoire is hard to characterize but would have a leaning towards 19th- and early 20th-century English music, with some American and Canadian compositions. The qualifications of the choir director and organist could vary greatly with the affluence of the church. Organs were often large.

Developments in the 1960s and 1970s changed the pattern of religious music in Canada. Vatican Council II of 1963, while specifically recommending the continuing use of Gregorian chant, was taken by many Roman Catholic clergy as giving them "carte blanche" to do away with Latin, Gregorian chant and polyphony in one clean sweep. The use of vernacular texts, and a new spirit of liturgical experimentation, led to a "popular" style of church music. "Song leaders," armed with microphones, are now the arbiters of sacred music, though there are pockets of resistance.

In the Anglican Church, change has not been so widespread or so sudden. Many clergy, however, have copied the Roman Catholic reforms and, fortified with new texts as alternatives to the Book of Common Prayer, have seen congregational participation as the only goal of church music. This trend has resulted in some parishes in so-called "folk masses," hymns in "pop" style, and the downgrading of choirs and organs. In some areas change has been minimal, and in other churches sympathetic pastors and musicians have compromised so as to make effective use of the vast heritage of church music.

Modern change is harder to describe in the Presbyterian and United churches. Traditionally, these denominations relied less on forms and texts from a missal or prayer book, so the shift to contemporary texts has not been a potent force. Nevertheless, styles of acceptable church music have changed in response to movements in the Roman Catholic, Anglican and Evangelical churches.

The Lutheran Church dates from the 18th century in Canada and in 1983 was the fifth-largest denomination. As its members have come from a wide variety of countries, there has been a lack of tradition in the form of service. The US is the major source for hymnbooks, service music and anthems. Choirs are active, almost exclusively amateur, and church musicians have generally been trained in the US.

Music plays a central role in the SALVATION ARMY's ministry, particularly hymn singing with or without band accompaniment. Choirs are formed both to lead services and to give concerts.

"Gospel" music has an important teaching and persuasive role in Evangelical churches (see EVANGELICAL AND FUNDAMENTALIST MOVEMENTS). A soloist is normally featured, with choir and an instrumental group providing a back-up. The fact that televised services are an integral element in this ministry has an effect on styles of presentation.

Jewish religious music in Canada is divided between traditional chants, some of great antiquity, sung by the cantor, and more modern music (often late 19th-century in style) sung by choir or congregation, or both. Canadian cantors have studied with older European-trained cantors or have trained in the US. Music is seen as a vital part of synagogue worship, in both Orthodox and Reform traditions, though only Reform synagogues admit the use of the organ (see JUDAISM).

Other Christian denominations that have strong musical traditions, both based on European practice, are the various MENNONITE churches and the Greek Orthodox Church.

All denominations have produced composers of church music. The name of Healey WILLAN stands out. English-trained, he wrote mostly for the Anglican Church in a wide variety of forms but his music has been sung in Roman Catholic, United, Presbyterian and Lutheran churches and has been used in both England and the US. Earlier musicians wrote for the church, particularly in Québec for the Roman Catholic Church, but it is doubtful that their works are much heard these days. Other composers who should be mentioned include W.H. Anderson, Alfred Whitehead, Bernard Naylor, Keith Bissell, Ben Steinberg and Srul Irving Glick.

Publication of religious music in Canada, while in no way equalling the volume in the US, has continued, though the British legacy of many of the churches with choirs means that much music is imported. Western Music Company Ltd, Frederick Harris Music Co Ltd and Gordon V. Thompson Ltd are particularly active in English-language music. Most of the major denominations have their own Canadian hymnbooks (see HYMNS).

Many of the larger churches in Canada have issued recordings of their choirs, thus enabling them to reach a wider audience. Several organizations exist to assist choirs and choirmasters to achieve better standards, particularly the various provincial choral federations, the Royal School of Church Music, and the Royal Canadian College of Organists.   GILES BRYANT

Reading: Encyclopedia of Music in Canada (1981); H. Kallmann, A History of Music in Canada, 1834-1914 (1960).

Remembrance Day, honouring the war dead, is a legal holiday observed throughout Canada on Nov 11. It commemorates the armistice that ended WWI at 11:00 AM of that day in 1918. Originally called Armistice Day — as it continues to be known in Newfoundland — it was merged with Thanksgiving Day from 1923 to 1931, when it was renamed Remembrance Day and its observation reverted to Nov 11. The symbol of this day is the poppy of Flanders, replicas of which are distributed by the ROYAL CANADIAN LEGION. Characteristic of Remembrance Day are patriotic and memorial ceremonies on steps of cenotaphs and other war monuments in Canada and throughout the COMMONWEALTH.

JOHN ROBERT COLOMBO

Remittance Man, a term once widely used, especially in the West before WWI, for an immigrant living in Canada on funds remitted by his family in England, usually to ensure that he would not return home and become a source of embarrassment.   JOHN ROBERT COLOMBO

Remote Sensing means "sensing" at a distance or, more specifically, deriving data or information about Earth's surface or the atmosphere by observing reflected or emitted electromagnetic radiation. The oldest remote-sensing instrument is the photographic camera, which has a long history of use in making observations of Earth from aircraft and, more recently, spacecraft. The earliest recorded air photo in Canada was taken of the HALIFAX CITADEL, from a BALLOON at an altitude of about 1450 feet (442 m), by Captain H. Esdale, Royal Engineers, in Aug 1883. Aerial photography and air-photo interpretation were developed during WWI for military intelligence and after the war were applied to mapping (see CARTOGRAPHY). The first Canadian air-mapping photograph was taken in 1923. By 1963, 97% of the country had been photographed in black and white.

Since the 1960s, colour aerial photography has been used extensively for AGRICULTURE and FORESTRY. The first photograph from space was taken from the NASA Gemini III spacecraft in 1965. Since then, space photography has been acquired on Gemini, Apollo and Skylab missions. The electromagnetic spectrum extends in a continuum from microwave wavelengths of 0.1-100 cm through infrared, visible, ultraviolet and X-ray to gamma-ray wavelengths (measured in billionths of a metre). Photographic film can be used to sense only a small region of this spectrum, ie, mainly the visible region. Remote-sensing instruments use nonvisible regions of the spectrum as well; this technology has improved enormously man's ability to manage the world's RESOURCES and environment.

Instruments Photographic films sensitive to the infrared spectral region (0.7-0.9 μm) were developed during WWII for camouflage detection. Infrared photography is now regularly used for measuring plant vigour and detecting stress caused by disease or lack of moisture and for terrain mapping. Films are not sensitive to wavelengths beyond the near infrared region; thus, for other wavelengths, nonphotographic sensors must be used. The infrared line scanner detects radiation in the thermal infrared band (3-14 μm) and produces an image in which the brightness of an object in the scene is related to the temperature of the object. This technique is used from aircraft to measure heat loss through the roof of buildings caused by poor insulation, to trace effluents from power plants and sewers into rivers and lakes, to detect incipient FOREST FIRES and to locate water supplies by detecting where underground streams empty into the ocean. It is used from spacecraft to map temperature distribution in water bodies.

The camera and the infrared scanner have one serious shortcoming as remote-sensing instruments: they cannot see through clouds. RADAR, which operates in the microwave region of the spectrum, can provide all-weather, night-and-day remote-sensing information. For earth surveying, SLAR (Side-looking Airborne Radar) and SAR (Synthetic Aperture Radar) are used. SAR produces radar images of high resolution by using special processing techniques and is the radar most suitable for use on SATELLITES.

The first satellite designed specifically for remote-sensing purposes was ERTS 1 (later named Landsat 1), launched 23 July 1972. It was followed by Landsat 2 in Jan 1975 and Landsat 3 in Mar 1978. Landsat 4, which carries a unique new sensor, was launched in July 1982. These satellites travel in a polar orbit and carry instruments which sense the energy reflected from a 180 km wide swath underneath the satellite path. They provide complete coverage of Earth every 16-18 days. Data is transmitted from the satellite to ground stations, where it is recorded on magnetic tape for conversion to image (photographic) form or for computer analysis.

In Canada, data from these satellites has been received, recorded and distributed to users from a station at Prince Albert, Sask, since 1972. The information has been used for purposes as diverse as measuring the vigour and acreage of crops, determining present land use and changes, mapping water depth and oil spills and other pollutants in lakes and oceans, mapping of snow and ice distribution, geological structures and forest clear cut and burns, making studies of EROSION, assessing the effect of engineering projects on aquatic vegetation and revising topographic maps.

Seasat was a short-lived satellite (June-Oct 1978) that carried 5 sensors for use in measuring oceanographic parameters (eg, ocean-surface temperature, surface wind speed and direction, wave height). This satellite was of particular interest to Canada because one of the 5 sensors was a SAR, which demonstrated the usefulness of spaceborne radars in measuring ice distribution in the Canadian Arctic as an aid to shipping and offshore exploration.

Weather satellites (eg, the NOAA, TIROS and NIMBUS series) carry instruments primarily for use in METEOROLOGY, but have also produced useful information on ice distribution and water-surface temperature. The NIMBUS-7 satellite carries an instrument that is used primarily for measuring sedimentation and chlorophyll levels in water.

A number of nations and agencies are now planning a new generation of remote-sensing satellites for launch from 1984 to 2000. These vehicles will carry sensors with improved performance, including higher resolution (up to 10 m), more and different spectral bands and stereoscopic viewing capability.

Data Analysis The power of remote sensing as a means of providing information for RESOURCE MANAGEMENT and environmental monitoring is greatly enhanced by the use of computer techniques. Images can be processed by computer to overlay a map or another image accurately, thereby permitting the updating of maps and the detecting of changes such as those caused by forest depletion or engineering projects (eg, MEGAPROJECTS). Another computer technique allows "themes," such as water, crops, summer fallow or forest-fire burns, to be identified and displayed cartographically and the area of each theme to be computed. This technique has been used in Canada for computing potato acreages and forest-fire burn areas. Using still another technique, images are processed to make features of interest easier to identify visually. For example, variations representing different rangeland conditions are accentuated to assist in range management.   E.A. GODBY

Landsat image of the Canada-US border, showing the difference in land-use practices in Alberta, top (rangeland), and Montana (intensive farming) (*courtesy Canada Centre for Remote Sensing*).

Renaud, Jacques, novelist, poet (b at Montréal 10 Nov 1943). Associated in the 1960s with the radical journal PARTI PRIS, Renaud also worked as a journalist and TV researcher for Radio-Canada. Active in the Réseau de résistance, an underground independentist group that preceded the FRONT DE LIBÉRATION DU QUÉBEC, Renaud is best known as the author of the novella *Le Cassé* (1964), a violent story replete with fractured and anglicized "joual," considered the best fictional work produced by the publishing house of *Parti pris*. A 2nd edition of *Le Cassé* (1977) added several short stories and the "Journal du Cassé," dealing with the impact of and controversies surrounding that publication. *En d'autres paysages* (1970) is a novel that attempts to wed realism and fantasy, and points to his later interests in esotericism and orientalism, evident in *Le Fond pur de l'errance irradie* (1975) and *Le Cycle du scorpion* (1979), *La Colombe et la brisue éternité* and *Clandestine(s) ou la tradition du couchant* (1980) — the latter mixing occultism with political violence.   B.-Z. SHEK

Renfrew, Ont, Town, pop 8283 (1981c), inc 1895, located on Bonnechere R, 100 km W of Ottawa. The first settlers were timber squatters; Scottish settlers followed, the most prominent being John Lorne McDougall, the first store owner and later a member of Parliament, whose mill (1855) is now a museum. About 1848 the site received its present name, for Renfrew, Scotland, ancestral home of the Stuarts. In 1850 Sir Francis Hincks offered free water sites to those who would build mills, and a boom followed. The town was first prominent for lumber, butter making and textiles. Now it produces magnesium alloys, clothing, office equipment and aerospace products. Financed by wealthy mine-owner Ambrose J. O'Brien, the famed Renfrew Millionaires ruled hockey for several years in the early 20th century.   K.L. MORRISON

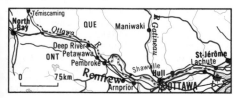

Rennie, Man, UP, pop 98 (1981c), is located 110 km E of Winnipeg, at the western boundary of the 2735 km² Whiteshell Provincial Park, of which it is the headquarters. One of Manitoba's most popular recreation areas, the park stretches along the Manitoba-Ontario border from the TRANS-CANADA HWY N to the Winnipeg R. Named after the British engineering family that designed and built the London Bridge, Rennie became a coal and water station for CPR locomotives 1880, and later housed construction shops and a station for the Grand Trunk Pacific. In 1884 the area was incorporated into Manitoba. Whiteshell Forest Reserve was created 1931, and ranger headquarters were established at Rennie 1941. The park has wild-rice lakes, waterfowl staging areas, the deepest lake in Manitoba (the meteor-created West Hawk), hydroelectric plants, mining sites and Laurel Culture petroforms (Indian boulder mosaics dated 500 BC to AD 800). Rennie is adjacent to the Alfred Hole Goose Sanctuary, a breeding and staging site for giant Canada geese, a species once thought to be extinct.   D.M. LYON

Rep by Pop "representation by population," demanded by citizens of Canada West to replace equal representation of the 2 Canadas in the PROVINCE OF CANADA after 1850, when Canada West gained a growing population lead over the largely French-speaking eastern section. It led to sectional breakdown by 1864; the ultimate remedy was federal government within CONFEDERATION.   J.M.S. CARELESS

Repeal Movement In 1867 many Nova Scotians were reluctant to endorse CONFEDERATION. In the elections of Sept 1867 anti-Confederates captured 36 of 38 seats in the local legislature, and 18 of 19 seats in the Dominion Parliament. Opposition to Confederation was based on the conviction that Nova Scotia was a maritime community with a natural affinity to Britain and historical ties with New England. Confederation meant a reorientation of its commercial life towards the interior of the continent, an unattractive prospect for those whose prosperity was based upon international commerce and the sailing ship. Britain was unwilling to allow Nova Scotia to secede, however, and when Joseph HOWE accepted the inevitable, agreeing to enter Sir John A. Macdonald's government in return for an increased provincial subsidy in 1869, the anti-Confederate protest collapsed.

In 1886 the secession movement re-emerged, led by Liberal premier William S. FIELDING. Campaigning on the issue of repeal and stressing the need for increased subsidies to the province, Fielding's party won 29 of 38 seats in the provincial elections that year. The bulk of support for secession came from those areas most closely tied to the traditional maritime economy and the international shipping trades. Opposition to repeal was strongest in those parts of the province which were beginning to industrialize, particularly in coal mining areas and towns along the INTERCOLONIAL RAILWAY, which linked Nova Scotia to the continental interior. This second repeal movement quickly collapsed when the Conservative Party won 14 of 21 seats in Nova Scotia during the federal election of Feb 1887.   COLIN D. HOWELL

Repentigny, Marie-Jeane-Madeleine Legardeur de, dite de Sainte Agathe (1698-1739), remembered because of the "lamp which is never extinguished," a lamp burning at the foot of the statue of Notre-Dame du Grand Pouvoir in the Ursuline convent in Québec City. Madeleine entered the convent after the death of her soldier fiancé, according to official accounts, but legendary tradition remembers her as having an Indian lover, who was killed by a sentry when she tried to help him escape from imprisonment. After entering the convent, she had difficulty in maintaining her vocation, but succeeded through prayer to the Virgin Mary. In gratitude, a legacy ensured that the lamp would burn at the foot of the statue in perpetuity.
                                NANCY SCHMITZ

Reppen, John Richard, Jack, artist, painter (b at Toronto 17 July 1933; d there 2 June 1964). Studying design at the Ontario Coll of Art in the evening, he was a free-lance cartoonist for the Toronto *Star* 1952-64 and art director for the Prudential Insurance Co, Toronto, 1952-62. From 1959 he devoted himself to his painting, exhibiting regularly in solo and group shows, and created several murals on commission. Travel — to Mexico (1961, 1963) and northern France (1962) — was an important source of Reppen's imagery. His best works have a strong feeling for surface and texture, with an almost relief quality, being often built on a matrix of gesso, with collage elements and incised surfaces.   JOYCE ZEMANS

Representative Government, government elected, in part at least, by the people. In colonies settled by the English, it was long recognized that, although the Crown might institute governments, the inhabitants could be legislated for and taxed only by a legislature in which they were represented, or by the British Parliament itself. In conquered colonies the Crown might legislate as it pleased; however, once colonies were promised or granted an assembly, that privilege could be taken away only by Parliament. In Nova Scotia, the governors' commis-

sions after 1719 looked to the establishment of an assembly, and the first elective assembly in what is now Canada met on 2 Oct 1758 in Halifax. Because of the difficulty of communications, the Crown granted PEI a separate government in 1769 and an elective assembly in 1773. In 1784, following the influx of LOYALISTS, New Brunswick was separated from Nova Scotia and given representative institutions. In 1832, after considerable debate in Britain, the governor of Newfoundland was instructed to summon an assembly.

Elsewhere today's representative institutions rest on statutes. The conquered colony of Canada was promised an assembly, but the British Parliament passed the QUEBEC ACT of 1774, establishing rule by governor and council. Hence the Crown lost its power to legislate for the province. A second British statute, the CONSTITUTIONAL ACT of 1791, created Upper and Lower Canada, each with an assembly; a third, the ACT OF UNION of 1840, reunited the 2 Canadas and established their Parliament; and a fourth, the BRITISH NORTH AMERICA ACT of 1867, created Québec and Ontario and laid the foundation of their present assemblies. The colony of Vancouver's I possessed an assembly, 1856-58, but the present form of legislature in BC stems from that of the elective assembly constituted under British authority before Confederation. Intended for the post-Confederation period, it was first elected in 1871.

In 1870 the Canadian Parliament created Manitoba out of former HBC lands, granting it representative institutions. When the validity of the MANITOBA ACT was questioned, the British Parliament the following year empowered the Canadian Parliament to create provinces out of the same lands. The old North-West Territories received a fully elective assembly in 1886 by federal statute, (see NORTH-WEST TERRITORIES ACT), before the creation of the provinces of Alberta and Saskatchewan with the usual elective assemblies, again by federal statute, in 1905 (see AUTONOMY BILLS). Parliament established the Yukon in 1898 and made its territorial council fully elective in 1908; the NWT Council, constituted in 1905, became partly elective in 1951 and fully elective in 1974. If history is a guide, these territorial councils are the forerunners of provincial assemblies. *See also* PROVINCIAL GOVERNMENT.   J. MURRAY BECK

Reptile, class of VERTEBRATE animals derived from AMPHIBIANS and ancestral to BIRDS and MAMMALS. Reptiles are primarily tetrapod (4-legged), but with legs lost in SNAKES and some LIZARDS. Epidermal scales cover the outside skin, providing protection from injury and drying. Dermal scales (in underlayer of skin) are best developed in turtles, fusing to each other and to the ribs dorsally to form the shell. Crocodilians, tuatara and some lizards also have dermal scales. Epidermal scales are modified to form the horns of the horned lizard and rattles of rattlesnakes. Modern reptiles are mainly relatively small, active forms. The largest, the marine leatherback turtle, may weigh up to 680 kg. Reptiles have lungs, not gills. Some turtles can supplement their oxygen supply through pharyngeal breathing to stay underwater for extended periods. The reptile heart is 3-chambered, except in crocodilians, which have a 4-chambered heart. Skin glands are almost entirely missing, but many reptiles excrete a foul musk for protection, or more pleasantly scented secretions for sexual attraction. One group of lizards and several groups of snakes have labial poison glands in the upper jaw.

The key to reptile success in invading the land was the amniote egg with a protective shell and embryonic membranes. The shell is permeable, so must have some environmental moisture, but is much more resistant to desiccation than the

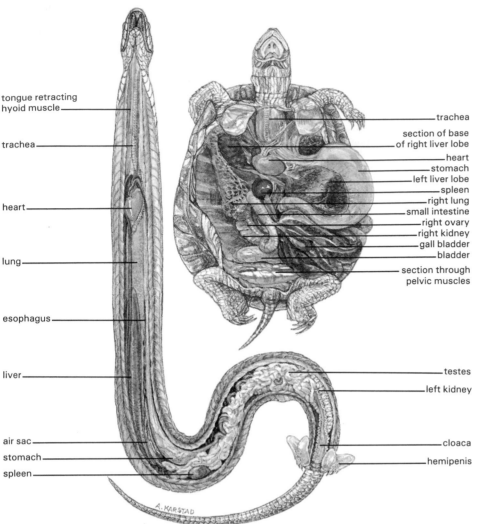

tongue retracting
hyoid muscle

trachea

heart

lung

esophagus

liver

air sac

stomach

spleen

trachea

section of base
of right liver lobe

heart

stomach

left liver lobe

spleen

right lung

small intestine

right ovary

right kidney

gall bladder

bladder

section through
pelvic muscles

testes

left kidney

cloaca

hemipenis

A. KARSTAD

Internal organs of a snake (left) and turtle (*artwork by A. Karstad Schueler*).

amphibian egg. Eggs are usually buried in loose soil or sand, or deposited in rotting vegetation. Tuatarans, crocodilians and turtles lay eggs. Many lizards and snakes do also, but many evolutionary lines hold the eggs within the mother, and the young are born after hatching. Like amphibians, reptiles are ectothermic, ie, have a relatively low metabolic rate and depend largely on external heat to attain the temperature at which they function best. Most reptiles maintain preferred temperatures by alternately basking and seeking shelter. Although reptiles are most abundant in the tropics, turtles, snakes and lizards are fairly successful in temperate climates. By hibernating in cold months they avoid having to eat just to maintain their body temperature and can use proportionally more food energy for growth and reproduction.

Although reptiles are not as diverse as in the Mesozoic (225-65 million years ago), the dominant modern group, the squamata, is very successful. There are 3307 species of lizards, 135 of amphisbaenians and 2267 of snakes. Turtles (222 species), crocodilians (22) and tuatara (1) are less diverse. Lizards, snakes and turtles have worldwide distribution in both tropical and temperate areas. Crocodilians are largely tropical although they invade the fringes of the temperate zone.

In Canada 40 species are native: 10 turtles, 5 lizards and 25 snakes. Southwestern Ontario and grassland valleys of southern BC have most species. No reptiles occur on the tundra and few species in the boreal forest. All are postglacial immigrants. The common garter snake, the

most northerly ranging species, reaches Fort Smith, NWT, and the southern coast of James Bay. Reptiles are not economically important in Canada, except as predators, such as the rodent-consuming snakes. Turtles are trapped and sold as food, mainly in the East, most apparently going to US markets. Garter snakes are collected, particularly in Manitoba, for sale to universities for laboratory dissection. Fatal bites from rattlesnakes are rare and Canada's 3 restricted species do not represent a general hazard to people or livestock.
F.R. COOK

Reading: F.R. Cook, *An Introduction to Canadian Amphibians and Reptiles* (1984).

Research, Provincial Organizations All provinces except Newfoundland and PEI have provincial research organizations functioning to promote economic development through the application of modern TECHNOLOGY to regional INDUSTRY. The first to be established was what is now the ALBERTA RESEARCH COUNCIL (1921); the latest, the CENTRE DE RECHERCHE INDUSTRIELLE DU QUÉBEC (1969). Most are CROWN CORPORATIONS, but the MANITOBA RESEARCH COUNCIL operates essentially as a government branch and the BRITISH COLUMBIA RESEARCH COUNCIL is an independent, nonprofit society. The organizations co-operate with other agencies in federal programs. The NOVA SCOTIA RESEARCH FOUNDATION CORPORATION and NEW BRUNSWICK RESEARCH AND PRODUCTIVITY COUNCIL may be expanded to serve the entire Atlantic region. The organizations fulfil their mandates by a combination of free advice to small business, advice to government, and contracted, nonprofit short-term research and longer-term investigations. Emphasis varies according to provincial needs and the activities of other pro-

vincial agencies. All have achieved expertise in fields appropriate to regional resources, varying from textiles by the ONTARIO RESEARCH FOUNDATION to uranium by the SASKATCHEWAN RESEARCH COUNCIL. Although some economists criticize the emphasis on small business, most agree that the provincial research organizations play a vital role in helping Canadian industry keep pace with technological developments. *See* INDUSTRIAL RESEARCH AND DEVELOPMENT; SCIENTIFIC RESEARCH AND DEVELOPMENT.
MARTIN K. MCNICHOLL

Research Stations, Agricultural For almost a century, agricultural research has been among the dominant SCIENTIFIC RESEARCH AND DEVELOPMENT activities in Canada. The federal government assumes a leading role in AGRICULTURAL RESEARCH AND DEVELOPMENT, operating a coast-to-coast network of experimental farms, research stations and research institutes.

On 2 June 1886 Parliament passed An Act Respecting Experimental Farms and Stations, which established 5 experimental farms: the Central Experimental Farm at Ottawa, serving Ontario and Québec; and branch farms at Nappan, NS; Brandon, Man; Indian Head, North-West Territories (now Indian Head, Sask); and Agassiz, BC. The program was aimed at improving livestock, DAIRY products, field CROPS, FRUITS, VEGETABLES, fertilizers and seeds, and at controlling PLANT DISEASES, INSECT PESTS and WEEDS. The Veterinary Branch was responsible for the control of animal diseases.

William SAUNDERS was the first director of the Dominion Experimental Farms system. Under his direction the experimental farms developed earlier and more productive WHEAT varieties and helped western Canada become one of the world's great wheat-growing regions. His son, Charles SAUNDERS, became the first Dominion cerealist in 1903. He and his staff obtained early wheats from Russia, India, Australia and other regions in which climatic conditions approached those of Canada. Through hybridization and plant selection, they developed several new varieties. The most significant early success occurred when Charles Saunders co-operated with the staffs of the experimental farms at Indian Head and Brandon to develop Marquis, a wheat variety with a very desirable combination of plant and kernel characteristics. It set a new quality standard (still observed today) as a bread-making wheat. Marquis became available in 1909 and by 1920 accounted for 90% of western Canada's nearly 7 million ha of spring wheat, and for nearly 5 million ha in the US.

Research scientists have continued to protect Canada's crop-production capability by helping overcome current and anticipated agricultural problems in Canada's many SOIL and CLIMATE regions. Programs are designed to determine the best conditions for producing approximately 30 crops (including cereals, oilseeds and forage, horticultural and field crops); develop new and improved varieties of crops and breeds of animals; overcome hazards caused by diseases, insects and weeds; understand problems associated with soil fertility, EROSION and WATER use; improve crop-management techniques and animal feeding and management through biological and engineering research; and develop new and improved methods for the preparation and preservation of foods.

Federal involvement in research has grown with the expansion of Canadian agriculture. In 1983 Agriculture Canada had 44 research establishments: 11 designated as experimental farms, 28 as research stations and 5 as national research centres or institutes. In addition, there were 17 specialized substations, eg, a rangeland substation at Manyberries, Alta, and a substation specializing in soil problems at Vegreville, Alta. Research establishments vary greatly in size and degree of specialization, but all have 2 mandates: to develop and implement programs to serve regional needs; and to contribute to national objectives and goals of the Research Branch of Agriculture Canada and other departmental functions. Each experimental farm operates under the guidance of a nearby larger research station.

Research provides many benefits to agricultural producers, consumers and AGRIBUSINESS. The efforts of over 850 scientists employed by Agriculture Canada support and strengthen Canada's success as a food-producing nation. Canada's network of federal research establishments is recognized as unique in the world, and is renowned for its accomplishments. Experimental farms and research stations and institutes are located across the country.

National Research Institutes, with headquarters in Ottawa, include the Biosystematics Research Institute, Chemistry and Biology Research Institute, Engineering and Statistical Research Institute, Food Research Institute and Land Resource Research Institute.

Atlantic Region has its institutional headquarters in Halifax. Research stations are located at St John's, Nfld; Kentville, NS; Charlottetown, PEI; and Fredericton, NB. Experimental farms are located at Nappan, NS, and Buctouche, NB.

Québec Region, with headquarters in Montréal, has research stations at Ste-Foy, St Jean and Lennoxville and experimental farms at La Pocatière, Normandin and L'Assomption.

Ontario Region, with headquarters in Ottawa, oversees research stations at Vineland, Delhi, Harrow and Ottawa. Experimental farms are located at Kapuskasing, Thunder Bay and Smithfield. There is an animal research centre at Ottawa and a research centre at London. The Central Experimental Farm, which is now located within Ottawa's city limits, has continued to expand since its establishment nearly 100 years ago. It now covers 500 ha and includes experimental fields; ornamental, vegetable and herb gardens; a tropical greenhouse; an ARBORETUM; show herds of dairy cattle, beef cattle, horses, sheep and swine; and an agricultural museum; as well as research laboratories and facilities. The farm attracts over 100 000 visitors each year.

Western Region, with headquarters in Saskatoon, serves BC, Alta, Sask and Man. In Alberta, research stations are located at Lethbridge, Lacombe and Beaverlodge; in Saskatchewan at Swift Current, Saskatoon, Melfort and Regina; and in Manitoba at Winnipeg, Brandon and Morden. Experimental farms are located at Fort Vermilion, Alta; and Indian Head, Sask.

Pacific Region, with headquarters in Vancouver, serves British Columbia. The research stations are located at Summerland, Kamloops, Vancouver, Agassiz and Saanichton (Sidney). An experimental farm is located at Prince George. D.G. HAMILTON

Reserve Force of Canada comprises part-time members of the ARMED FORCES whose role is to augment and support the Regular Force. Compulsory universal military service for early settlers eventually became part-time, volunteer soldiering. This reserve ("militia") tradition remained the dominant feature of Canadian military service, despite the evolution of a regular permanent land force; not until the 1950s did the regular components outnumber the reserves. The Royal Naval Canadian Volunteer Reserve was formed 1914, although there had been naval companies in colonial militias long before. The Canadian Air Force, est 1920, was almost entirely an air militia until the 1924 formation of the Royal Canadian Air Force, which had its own reserve component from the beginning.

The present Reserve Force is made up of 4 parts: the Primary Reserve, the Supplementary List, the Cadet Instructors List and the Canadian Rangers. The Primary Reserve is divided into the Naval Reserve, the Militia, the Air Reserve and Communication Reserve; all are composed of volunteers who train evenings, on weekends or at short camps. The Supplementary List consists of those who have left the Regular Force or Primary Reserve but are still available if needed. The Cadet Instructors List comprises Reserve Force officers whose primary duty is the supervision, administration and training of CADETS. The Canadian Rangers, whose special contribution is expert local knowledge, are reservists in sparsely settled areas of the country.

NORMAN HILLMER AND O.A. COOKE

Reservoir, a pond or LAKE designed to store WATER and to improve its availability for offstream, primarily consumptive, uses (irrigation, municipal and industrial purposes) and instream, largely nonconsumptive, uses (power and recreational developments, FLOOD control, wildlife habitat improvement). Reservoirs may be constructed by enhancing the holding capacity of a natural basin or creating a new one, through construction of a dam at the outlet of a lake or on a RIVER. They cause an obvious change in the water-storage area upstream from the dam and in the water depth. Reservoirs are usually classified by 3 basic physical characteristics: depth, flooded area and volume of water stored. Multipurpose reservoirs may have several design levels, each planned to ensure a usable pond of water. Thus, in addition to its normal full supply level (FSL), a reservoir may have a conservation storage level (ie, level at which a flood-control reservoir is held before and after floods), a flood storage level (maximum desirable level during floods) and a dead storage level (level below which water may not be withdrawn for consumptive uses).

Before construction, reservoir sites are subjected to detailed hydrologic studies to determine their ability to meet the needs of potential users. Studies are usually carried out monthly, using estimated or recorded historical stream flow to evaluate the project's performance under DROUGHT and flood conditions. The results may be used to develop reservoir operating plans to prevent unanticipated shortages. A reservoir used for municipal purposes is usually designed to have no shortages. When uses are such that shortages may be inconvenient, but will not cause severe economic hardship, reservoirs are often designed to allow for some shortages in critically dry periods, to permit more efficient use to be made of available water in most years. Often 2 or more reservoirs are used in combination to maximize the water supply potential of a DRAINAGE BASIN. The improvement achievable by adding one or more reservoirs to an existing system may be evaluated before construction.

Water evaporates from the surface of reservoirs when they are not covered by ICE. These losses may be estimated and the reservoir's net evaporation calculated by subtracting precip-

itation from evaporation. The volume of reservoir losses caused by net evaporation is then calculated by multiplying net evaporation by the reservoir's surface area. When the addition of further storage capacity fails to increase significantly the yield of the reservoir (usually because the additional water stored evaporates before it can be used), the project is at its optimum storage capacity and further storage increases will be wasted.

Reservoirs have spillways to divert excess water during above-normal periods. The spillway's capacity is based on the economic losses and potential loss to human life that would occur as a result of failure. Where the potential exists for downstream loss of life, extensive property damage or both, spillways are designed to carry the largest flood that may be expected to occur on the river at that site. After construction a reservoir should be operated to co-ordinate consumptive, recreational and power uses with downstream releases to maintain predetermined levels of minimum flow. Thus, its operational plan will establish monthly reservoir levels, regulated discharge and diversions.

Several changes occur to the environment adjacent to a reservoir. A new lake is created providing an additional recreational area, but the preexisting river is destroyed and the area at the river's edge that provided shelter to animals and birds is lost. The river downstream from the reservoir usually has lower peaks and higher low flows. Colder water is released from the reservoir and fish must adjust to the new environment or emigrate. However, there is often an increase in volume and diversity of fish in the reservoir itself, resulting in a net gain to the fishery. The overall water quality in the reservoir and downstream tends to improve because the reservoir acts as a mixing bowl, averaging out normal seasonal fluctuations. The clarity of downstream water also improves as the river's sediment load is trapped by the reservoir. This process often has an adverse affect on the channel below the reservoir as the river's streambed erodes. Similarly, at the upstream end of the reservoir, the capacity of the inlet channel is usually decreased by sedimentation. R.B. GODWIN
Reading: B. Henderson-Sellers, *Reservoirs* (1979).

Resolute, NWT, UP, pop 168 (1981c), is located on the S coast of CORNWALLIS I, 1561 air km NE of YELLOWKNIFE. It was named for a ship which wintered here in 1850, but its development began in 1947 with the construction of a joint US-Canadian weather station. In 1955, Inuit families from other areas were relocated to the area to take advantage of the island's game resources. These included Idlouk, whose camp is pictured on the Canadian $2 bill. Today the community is a key transportation, communications and administrative centre. ANNELIES POOL

Resource Management usually refers to the responsibility of governments to ensure that natural resources under their jurisdiction are used wisely or conserved. "Wise use" excludes unnecessary waste and, in the case of renewable resources, implies that their use will be constrained to provide a sustained use in the future. Where the use of a resource conflicts with other natural resources, eg, where FORESTRY operations interfere with the spawning of salmon, sound resource management implies that policies will recognize the desirability of multiple uses and place restraints on single purpose uses that are detrimental to other resource values. Sometimes governments decide that the best policy is to preserve natural resources from all consumptive uses. Ecological reserves maintaining lands indefinitely in their natural state are one method of preserving such resources.

The use of a natural resource often raises conflicts among individuals and groups with special interests in the resource. Conflicts may arise

Principal Reservoirs in Canada				
Reservoir	River	Province	Total Storage Capacity*	Year Completed
Lk St Lawrence	St Lawrence	Ont	808	1958
Cross Lk-Cedar Lk	Saskatchewan	Man	9 643	1965
Williston Lk	Peace	BC	70 309	1967
Daniel Johnson	Manicouagan	Qué	141 851	1968
Diefenbaker Lk	S Saskatchewan	Sask	9 868	1968
Mactaquac Lk	Saint John	NB	913	1968
Abraham Lk	N Saskatchewan	Alta	1 768	1972
Kinbasket Lk	Columbia	BC	24 670	1972
Wreck Cove	Wreck Cove	NS	126	1978
Hinds Lk	Humber	Nfld	305	1980

* In millions of cubic metres

among industrial users of FORESTS, MINERALS and FISH plus the recreation industry, which depends on lakes, streams and forests, and naturalists who advocate wilderness preservation and conservation of wildlife. Such clashes may occur at levels ranging from the broad scale (industry versus wilderness) to conflicts between industries (dams versus forestry), between recreation users (snowmobilers versus hikers) or between naturalists and their objects of study (eg, when too much disturbance interferes with nesting). In Canada native peoples whose aboriginal rights have not yet been recognized claim special natural-RESOURCE RIGHTS based on their historic relationship with the land (*see* LAND CLAIMS).

These conflicts and others require careful management strategies by governments. In Canada government ownership of natural resources provides the foundation for management strategies and policies. The 4 original provinces in Confederation retained ownership and control of their natural resources. British Columbia and Prince Edward Island also retained ownership of natural resources on joining the union. When Manitoba, Alberta and Saskatchewan were formed out of the North-West Territories, natural-resource ownership was retained by the federal government, in part to provide revenues to support colonization and the construction of the transcontinental railway. In 1930 a constitutional amendment transferred ownership and control of what remained of the publicly owned natural resources from the federal government to the Alberta, Saskatchewan and Manitoba governments. Hence, in Canada publicly owned natural resources now belong to the provinces, although jurisdiction over migratory birds and fish is largely federal. In the NORTH, the natural resources in the YT and the NWT remain under the control of the federal government. Conflicting claims of the federal and provincial governments to resources in the offshore regions have been settled in favour of the federal government by a March 1984 decision of the Supreme Court of Canada. In many regions of Canada, both onshore and offshore, native peoples have unsettled aboriginal claims.

In the earlier years provincial governments followed policies that permitted outright alienation of farm and urban lands and even of forest and wildlands. More recently, particularly in western Canada and the North, government policy has been to grant only limited tenures of forest and mineral lands. Thus, governments function as landlords of forestry and oil companies and, to a lesser extent, of mining companies. Consequently, provincial and federal natural-resource management in these cases is dual in nature; a government acts as an owner/landlord and as a regulator of resource use.

As owner/landlord, a provincial government may become a joint developer with industry. In this capacity, the government's management policies may be to stimulate investment and jobs (as in the northeast coal development in BC), to maximize rents and royalties (eg, of publicly owned oil and gas resources), to maintain a sustained yield (eg, in forests and FISHERIES) or to influence the structure of industry participation (eg, the "Canadianization" of the PETROLEUM INDUSTRY).

As regulator, a government controls natural-RESOURCE USE through statutes authorizing resource management by various departments, branches and agencies. In Canada constitutional powers are divided between the national and provincial governments by the CONSTITUTION ACT, 1982. Provincial legislatures are authorized to enact laws for the management and sale of natural resources and for the regulation of primary production; the Parliament of Canada is given legislative power to regulate coastal and inland fisheries and interprovincial and export trade in natural-resource commodities. Each level of government may tax natural-resource revenues. Consequently, while a province may adopt and enforce resource management policies, these policies must be consistent with national policies adopted by Parliament. These overlapping powers and responsibilities lead to conflicts between the provincial and national governments over such matters as markets, pricing and sharing of natural-resource revenues, and may sometimes hamper broad-scale management. Intergovernmental conflicts are further complicated in urban areas, where municipal governments may own the land. In the past, natural-resource statutes created a variety of single resource management entities, designating a separate department or branch for each individual resource, eg, the federal fisheries department, a provincial mines and minerals department, a provincial forest service or a provincial wildlife branch. Government departments in the natural-resources sector now usually have broader mandates and require policies that recognize the multiple demands on resources. Integrating strategies such as regional resource planning and multiple-use task forces are used more frequently in an effort to accomplish more coordinated resource management, and environmental impact assessments and public hearings on resource uses and projects are now common.

These trends in government are largely a consequence of the emergence of professional natural-resource planners and managers. With specific education and training in natural-resource management programs, these professionals are widely employed in industry, government and consulting firms. New statutory requirements for formal assessment and review of development projects that may impose adverse impacts on the ENVIRONMENT contribute to a climate in which wise natural-resource use is no longer taken for granted. Concerns about the finite nature of resources, about the possibility of irreversible harm to the environment and about gaining economic efficiency and optimum benefit from resource use will place ever higher demands on these professionals.

While much attention has been paid to multiple-use and social cost/benefit questions, much more could be accomplished if certain inherent features of natural-resources management are recognized and if research strategies can be more specifically directed to management priorities. Resource management is now characterized by high degrees of uncertainty about causes and effects, about mitigative measures and about the costs and benefits of different means of resolving resource use conflicts. For example, ACID RAIN is widely recognized as a major threat to the global environment, but great difficulty is experienced in getting experts and political leaders to agree on mitigative and remedial programs, even between neighbouring countries like Canada and the US. These uncertainties call for research priorities that focus on key unknowns, and management strategies that are designed to provide more adaptive and flexible means of coping with the future. The importance of natural resources in the economy and life of Canadians is so great that better resource management practices should be a matter of national priority.   ANDREW R. THOMPSON

Resource Rights Natural-resource development has played a major role in Canada's economy and continues to be a focus of national concerns. While these concerns have centered on ENERGY POLICY during the past decade, water resource management may be the issue of the 1990s. Other resource sectors such as fishing, forestry and mining also present difficult policy choices as Canadians face the issues of conservation, environmental protection, unemployment, and the maintaining of markets in a competitive world.

The right to develop resources (or to choose not to develop them) is, in the first instance, a right of ownership. Under the common law of Canada, the basic rule is that the ownership of land carries with it the right to harvest renewable resources, such as crops, trees, fish and wildlife, and also the right to extract nonrenewable resources such as coal, minerals and oil. Originally, governments in Canada gave individuals ownership of this type when crown land grants were made to settlers and developers, but new policies emerged around the turn of the century whereby governments gave only restricted ownership rights to resource developers. Mining leases and limited cutting rights began to replace outright grants of mineral and forestlands. In the case of agricultural lands, homesteaders of crown grants were not granted rights to minerals such as coal, oil and gas under their land. The government claimed ownership of minerals and gave only restricted development rights (by means of leases) to companies conducting exploration for minerals such as petroleum and natural gas. In western Canada today, provincial governments are by far the largest owners of undeveloped natural-resource rights; as well, they are the landlords of the oil, mineral and forest companies that enjoy exploration and development rights. In northern Canada and in the offshore regions, the federal government enjoys such ownership.

Under the CONSTITUTION ACT, 1867, the original provinces of Confederation retained ownership of crown lands and resources within their boundaries. When BC and PEI joined Confederation in 1871 and 1873, respectively, they too retained ownership of natural resources. But when the Prairie provinces were created (Manitoba in 1870, Alberta and Saskatchewan in 1905) a new and controversial policy emerged. In these provinces, ownership of natural resources was retained by the federal government to provide funds for colonization and railway building. Not until 1930, after a sometimes bitter political struggle, were natural-resource rights transferred by the federal government to the Prairie provinces. By this time, most of the agricultural lands had been transferred into private ownership; but because the federal government had reserved mineral rights when disposing of land in the prairies and had granted restricted tenures the Provincial governments inherited a rich treasure house of resource rights under the 1930 transfer. It is as a consequence of these rights that Alberta grants oil and gas leases and receives oil and gas royalties; that Manitoba can develop vast hydroelectric power resources to sell in the US; and that Saskatchewan controls uranium and potash reserves of worldwide significance.

The mineral and petroleum resources of northern Canada and the offshore regions of the East and West coasts remain under the ownership and control of the federal government and provide a huge potential for development. The federal government has also passed legislation that provides for the issuing of exploration rights and production licences, under which developers must meet expenditure commitments and pay royalties when commercial production begins. The Canada Oil and Gas Act, 1980-81-82, establishes a federal regime for petroleum resources that is intended to increase Canadian ownership in petroleum companies and to ensure Canadian benefits in terms of jobs and the procurement of goods and services.

Ownership is not the only determinant of resource rights. Just as the owner of a business is subject to federal, provincial and municipal legislation setting out how the business must operate, so companies that acquire resource rights from the federal and provincial governments are subject to legislated requirements, eg, laws to protect the environment, laws providing for employee safety, or taxation laws. Obviously, resource rights acquired by an owner often clash with these legislated requirements. In a BC case, the court held that restrictions placed on operations in a provincial park were so severe as to amount to expropriation of mining rights that had been granted before the park was established. In result, the holder of the mining rights was entitled to compensation.

The classic Canadian example of conflict between resource ownership rights and restrictive legislation occurred in the 1970s when federal legislation (the Petroleum Administration Act) was perceived by the western provinces as an unconstitutional interference with provincial resource ownership rights. In particular, federal threats to establish unilaterally the wellhead prices for petroleum and natural gas, and new federal taxes levied on these resources, were seen as direct interference with the rights claimed by these provinces to sell their resources on such terms as they saw fit and to receive royalties at rates they would determine. These conflicts were temporarily resolved by agreement between the federal and provincial governments during the constitutional debates of 1981. A new section of the CONSTITUTION ACT, 1982, purports to clarify the extent to which provinces may manage their resources, giving them exclusive power to make laws dealing with the development, conservation and management of nonrenewable resources and forestry resources, and to regulate the rate of primary production from these resources. Parliament has paramount jurisdiction to regulate interprovincial and export trade in natural resources, and both levels of government are given full powers of taxation. The federal-provincial conflict over petroleum supply, pricing and taxation may erupt again when the current agreements expire in 1986.

There are other areas of conflict over the ownership and control of natural resources in Canada. There is conflict between the US and Canada over alleged discrimination against foreign investors under Canada's National Energy Program (1980), and claims by the US lumber industry that Canadian lumber competes unfairly in US markets because of alleged subsidies given to the Canadian industry by the federal and provincial governments. Boundary disputes between Canada and the US affect fisheries and petroleum development in offshore waters on the East and West coasts and in the projection seawards of the Alaska-Yukon boundary.

Within Canada, native people have land claims to natural resources made pursuant both to treaties and to aboriginal LAND CLAIMS in nontreaty areas. In the northern territories, claims to regional self-government are accompanied by claims to ownership rights over northern natural resources. In the offshore regions, a longstanding dispute between the federal government and the coastal provinces concerning ownership and jurisdiction has recently been resolved in favour of the federal government in a decision of the Supreme Court of Canada concerning conflicting Newfoundland and federal claims to the Hibernia oil field (*see* HIBERNIA CASE).

Issues involving resource rights also surface from time to time in relation to such matters as the regulation of fishing, the protection of the environment, the control of the air waves and the management of watersheds. A recent report cites the need for an interjurisdictional agreement covering the Mackenzie R drainage basin before developments such as hydroelectric dams in Alberta and BC are allowed to proceed.

Canada is a large country with bountiful natural resources. Its size and its federal system of government (*see* FEDERALISM) explain why natural resources play such an important role in the Canadian economy and why government poli-

cies are so significant and so likely to be contentious. In these circumstances, it is a continuing national challenge to manage natural resources co-operatively and wisely.

ANDREW R. THOMPSON

Resource Towns, or "new towns," are the small isolated communities built around resource-based industries and transportation — mining towns, mill towns, railway towns, fishing villages, etc. Examples include GRAND FALLS, Nfld (pulp and paper); GLACE BAY, NS (coal); Black's Harbour, NB (fish packing); Murdochville, Qué (asbestos); Copper Cliff, Ont (nickel); Snow Lake, Man (copper, zinc); Drayton Valley, Alta (oil); and KITIMAT, BC (aluminum). These communities are very common in Canada; eg, in 1971, about 1 million Canadians lived in 636 resource communities across Canada.

Resource development has long been recognized as a significant factor in shaping patterns of Canadian development. It has been argued that all Canadian urban growth ultimately depends on the production of staple products. Resource towns have been important agencies in this process of staple exploitation. Government involvement in the exploitation of natural resources during recent decades has helped improve the quality of life in these towns, which are the most unstable and precarious of Canadian communities, and will remain so unless a more comprehensive approach to their planning is adopted.

In some respects Canadian resource towns resemble similar towns throughout the world, ie, towns based on the extraction or processing of resources such as minerals, forest products and hydroelectric power. Characteristically the resource town is an adjunct of an industrial enterprise, lacking control over its own economic development. The economic base is controlled by outside corporations or governments who determine the nature and extent of the extractive or processing activity and thereby determine the size of the local work force and the degree of local prosperity or growth. Because raw materials are usually shipped elsewhere, often outside Canada, for processing, most resource towns are excluded from the ultimate economic benefits derived from the resources. Boom and bust fluctuations depend on the vagaries of the international market for resources, or upon government or corporate decisions, and not on local initiative. Recurring fluctuations generate feelings of insecurity and impermanence in the community, feelings accentuated in mining towns by the knowledge that the resource base will eventually be exhausted.

Resource towns are also characterized by the simplified occupational structure inherent to them. The middle class is relatively weak, and usually includes only a small group of managers, merchants and professionals who are oriented, as far as careers are concerned, to organizations outside the town. Workers often migrate between resource towns in search of employment. Several factors discourage the development of a diversified economy which would generate a more heterogeneous work force. Isolation from major markets, relatively high wages paid by resource industries, and high development costs combine to prevent the influx of secondary industry. One result is that the male-female ratio in resource towns is usually slanted heavily in favour of men, since there are fewer employment opportunities for women. Another result is that most (but not all) resource towns remain small; only a few are over 10 000 in population. Therefore, they share many of the features of any small town, regardless of its economic base. A final common characteristic is physical appearance. Although recently built resource towns tend to resemble the new suburbs of large cities, older towns are generally

unattractive, ramshackle communities with a townscape dominated by a mine or mill.

While Canadian resource towns have a great deal in common both with each other and with towns in other countries, it is possible to delineate several distinctive characteristics. One basic distinction involves the origins of the population. The industrial population of many of the resource towns of the Atlantic provinces and Québec is drawn from the surrounding fishing, lumbering and agricultural population. In sharp contrast, the work force and management of the resource towns of Ontario and western Canada are drawn from populations remote from the town or from outside the country. "New towns" created in largely uninhabited areas have no physical or cultural rural connections.

A second major distinction is based on the decision-making process involved in creating and maintaining the community. Some towns are the products of decisions made by a single company or a government; others represent the outcome of a number of decisions made by a number of companies or by the residents of the community itself. The 2 types of towns which result are service and supply towns (eg, SUDBURY, Ont), which sometimes begin as boom towns, and company towns (eg, TÉMISCAMING, Qué), which are generally small, static communities closely attached to one industry's operation.

The physical appearance of resource towns depends, as does function, on who is responsible for planning and building the town. Chronologically the shaping of the towns has reflected the approach to URBAN AND REGIONAL PLANNING that has been current in Canada at specific periods. Three generations of resource towns have been built since Confederation: 1867-1920, privately built towns, eg, COBALT, Ont; 1920-39, holistically built towns, eg, KAPUSKASING, Ont; and since 1945, comprehensively planned, third-generation towns, eg, Kitimat, BC.

The modernization of some of the larger service centres and the designs of some of the new towns dramatically illustrate the advances made in resource-town building since the first-generation towns appeared in the 19th century. But regardless of the sophistication of recent planning concepts, the basic problems facing resource towns remain unresolved. Many have a limited lifetime, and prospects for activity and growth beyond the initial function seldom materialize. In some cases the resources simply run out; or perhaps market conditions change, or an international corporation moves its operation to another country. Mines or plants close and the town eventually dies. Hundreds of Canadian communities have disappeared in this way and the process continues. In other cases the industrial plants become obsolete. But in both cases the future remains uncertain and fluctuations between boom and bust plague attempts for orderly, long-term community development (*see also* COMPANY TOWN). ALAN F.J. ARTIBISE

Reading: R.T. Bowles, ed, *Little Communities and Big Industries* (1982); Rex Lucas, *Minetown, Milltown, Railtown* (1971); I.M. Robinson, *New Industrial Towns on Canada's Resource Frontier* (1962); Alan F.J. Artibise and Gilbert A. Stelter, *Canada's Urban Past* (1981).

Resource Use Since prehistoric times, the inhabitants of what is now Canada used vegetation and animals for food, clothing and shelter. They fashioned implements and ornaments from MINERALS and, after the arrival of Europeans, used furs for trading. The FISHERIES were the first resource to be systematically exploited by Europeans. As early as the 16th century, BASQUES from France and Spain pursued WHALES in the Gulf of St Lawrence. Early in the 16th century, French fishermen took COD on the GRAND BANKS. Early resource exploitation, like exploration, was peripheral to attempts to find a NORTHWEST PASSAGE to the Orient. During his voyage into the Gulf of St Lawrence in 1534, Jacques CARTIER traded furs with the Micmac. By the late 1500s, French fishermen who sailed annually to the Grand Banks conducted a lucrative trade in furs. The FUR TRADE helped stimulate colonization as short-term monopolies on the St Lawrence fur trade were granted in return for promises to settle colonists there. From the arrival of Samuel de CHAMPLAIN to the days of Jean TALON, the colony in NEW FRANCE depended almost exclusively on the fur trade. The establishment in 1608 of a trading post at the Indian village of Stadacona (later QUÉBEC CITY) provided a base for the trade, which eventually extended into the continental interior. This settlement, together with Tadoussac, Trois-Rivières and later Montréal became the object of regular visits from Indians bearing furs.

The first organized attempt at processing resources came with the arrival in 1665 of the Intendant Jean Talon, who established various "manufactories" that used agricultural products to satisfy the settlers' needs and launch revenue-producing export industries. Large numbers of farm animals were introduced to New France. Wool from sheep and hides from cattle provided clothing and shoes. Talon encouraged the growing of hemp, barley and hops and the production of tar. Wood and tar were used for SHIP-BUILDING in a yard on the banks of the St-Charles R. Hemp was used to make rigging for sails. With the hops and barley, beer was made in the "King's brewery" located near the shipyard. Surplus agricultural products, fish, wood and beer were exported to the West Indies on locally built ships. Talon also recognized that COPPER, LEAD, iron and COAL were potential sources of wealth for the colony. There was considerable PROSPECTING activity, but these efforts failed to discover minerals that could be exploited with the limited MINING technology of the time.

The impetus for exploitation of most resources was lost after Talon departed. Even the fur trade became more difficult as fur reserves were depleted and the French were forced to travel to Indian villages to trade. The departure of men for the woods (COUREURS DE BOIS) depleted the agricultural labour force and farming declined. Processing of minerals was stopped in 1704 when Louis XIV ordered the colonies not to compete with industries in France. This edict limited colonial economic activity to sending raw materials back to France and was a harbinger of the "further processing" issue, a principal concern in the 20th-century exploitation of Canada's resources. Thus, early in the 18th century, furs again became the principal economic resource of New France. Following the British CONQUEST (1760), the trade flourished until the middle of the 19th century and declined rapidly thereafter.

The exploitation of Canada's MINERAL RESOURCES began before the arrival of Europeans. The Inuit and Indians used and traded copper implements (see COPPER INUIT; PREHISTORY). In 1604 an exploration party under Champlain found native copper at Cap d'Or, NS. IRON ORE was one of the first minerals mined in Canada. Around 1670, deposits were found in swampy areas near Trois-Rivières. By the 1740s, Canada's first ironworks, the FORGES ST-MAURICE at Trois-Rivières, was turning out top-quality cast-iron stoves, pots, kettles, bullets and cannon for settlers and the military. Samuel HEARNE journeyed N in search of copper. He was to be disappointed, despite being the first white man to reach the Arctic Ocean overland. In 1770 Jesuit fathers experimented with native copper found at Point Mamainse on the N shore of Lk Superior. However, copper mining in Canada began with the discovery that led to the establishment of the Bruce Mine in the Algoma district of Ontario in 1847. Although reports of SILVER deposits dated back to the voyages of Cartier, the first accurate

account was that of Pierre, Chevalier de TROYES, a French military commander who recorded finding a silver-bearing vein of ore on the eastern shore of Lk Timiskaming in 1686. The first commercial deposit was discovered in 1868 at SILVER ISLET, a tiny rock island in Lk Superior, about 30 km E of Thunder Bay. The first discovery of GOLD in Canada, in the sands of the Fraser R (1858), led to the Cariboo GOLD RUSH (1860). Further discoveries were made in Nova Scotia and Ontario. The KLONDIKE GOLD RUSH began in 1896. Gold rushes had a profound effect on the development of BC, and on the opening of the Yukon and North-West Territories to settlement.

Much of the exploration of western Canada was the result of the quest for beaver pelts. Simon FRASER led the traders of the NORTH WEST COMPANY into what is now BC in the early part of the 19th century. The railway later opened the mineral riches of the West to exploitation. Railways also brought pioneer farmers who began to reap the rich agricultural potential (see AGRICULTURE HISTORY). The explorers had opened up the vast reaches of the West and NORTH and later scientists and surveyors (particularly from the GEOLOGICAL SURVEY OF CANADA) would gather useful details of terrain and resources. The old fur-trading posts of the Hudson's Bay Co and North West Co were quickly transformed into settlements.

Canada's Contemporary Resource Status

In the 1980s, over a century after the beginning of INDUSTRIALIZATION in Canada, this country remains primarily a supplier of raw materials for the MANUFACTURING industries of other nations (eg, the US, Japan, EEC countries).

Minerals Canada is a leading producer of economic minerals. Wealth generated by these mineral resources is an important foundation of the Canadian economy and mineral prospecting and extraction continue to accelerate the northward advance of Canada's population and economic activity. Discoveries of silver at Cobalt and nickel at Sudbury, Ont; gold in the YT, iron in Québec and Labrador, and nickel in Manitoba, extended the boundaries of civilization and established new communities (see NORDICITY; RESOURCE TOWNS). Minerals provide construction materials for dams, highways and office buildings; yield metals for stainless steel, automobiles and electric wires; supply fuel for NUCLEAR POWER PLANTS; furnish products that insulate homes, remove ice and snow from streets, carry water supplies and fertilize the soil; and provide raw materials for JEWELLERY and Inuit carvings.

With the world's second-largest land area, Canada ranks third (behind the US and the USSR) in value and diversity of nonfuel mineral production. Canada is the world's largest mineral exporter, shipping more than 80% of its mineral production abroad. In the mid-1980s over 60 commodities were being produced from about 270 mines, 230 mills, 16 smelters and 15 refineries across Canada. In 1983 about 84 000 people were directly employed in mining and a further 88 000 in smelting and refining activities, well below the peak levels of the mid-1970s. Economic recession and stagnation caused closure of many mines in the early 1980s. The production value of Canadian mines in 1983 was $12.3 billion, 3.2% of the nation's GROSS NATIONAL PRODUCT. Metals accounted for $7.2 billion; nonmetals $1.9 billion; coal $1.3 billion; structural materials $1.7 billion. In 1983, basic mineral output ($12.3 billion), plus refined metal and other fabricated metal products, resulted in a total output of $40.4 billion.

Canada leads the Western world in ASBESTOS, NICKEL, POTASH, ZINC and NEPHELINE-SYENITE production, and is the second-largest producer of gold, GYPSUM, URANIUM, MOLYBDENUM and COLUMBIUM. Nonfuel minerals account for about 15% of total Canadian exports. Canadian minerals

are exported to more than 90 countries. In 1983 mineral exports amounted to $12.9 billion. The US took 60%, importing $6.3 billion worth of fabricated minerals and $1.4 billion in raw minerals; Japan's purchases of $1 billion accounted for 7.7%. About one-half of Canada's nonferrous mine production leaves the country in a relatively unprocessed form. Shipment of minerals represents about 60% of railway freight, and half of all cargoes loaded at Canadian ports and of St Lawrence Seaway and Great Lakes shipping traffic.

Oil and Natural Gas Although oil was first collected in Ontario as early as the 1850s, the Canadian PETROLEUM INDUSTRY came of age with the Leduc discovery in Alberta in 1947. In the early 1980s, oil dominated Canada's energy consumption, accounting for more than 40% of energy fuels. Transportation consumed about 45% of Canada's oil, principally as motor gasoline. Residential and farm uses comprise about 15%; other industrial sectors 14%; nonenergy uses 11%; electric-power generation 4%; commercial and government uses 6%; and the refining process 7%.

Early in the 1980s, demand for oil products began to decline as a result of substitution and CONSERVATION practices, higher prices and a slowdown in economic activity (see ENERGY POLICY). This decline created a surplus of refining capacity, particularly in eastern Canada. The economic downturn also slowed the growth of gas-processing facilities. In 1983 Canada produced an average of 230 200 m³/day of crude oil and equivalent hydrocarbons, an increase of 5.8% from the 1982 level. Production of synthetic oil (from oil-sands and other petroleum-upgrading facilities) averaged 29 200 m³/day, a 29.8% increase from 1982 levels of 22 500 m³/day (see BITUMEN). Gas plant production of ethane, butane and propane averaged 35 800 m³/day, an increase of 2.6% from 1982 levels. After 7 years as a net importer of crude oil, Canada registered a positive trade balance in 1983, exporting 46 600 m³/day and importing 39 320 m³/day. These exports contributed to an overall trade surplus of 39 000 m³/day for crude, refined petroleum and liquefied petroleum gases. In 1983, domestic refinery production of 266 000 m³/day exceeded domestic demand of 235 900 m³/day. Gas export sales averaged 55.3 million m³/day in 1983, about 43% of authorized export volumes. Domestic sales dropped by 1.8% to 123.6 million m³/day. Canada had a net trade surplus in 1983 of $262 million in crude oil, $1.0 billion in oil products and almost $4.0 billion in natural gas, giving a total favourable energy trade balance of $8 billion, a significant slice of the nation's overall trade surplus of $15.1 billion.

Canada's conventional oil reserves in southern areas declined steadily during the 1970s and 1980s. It is hoped that explorations in frontier and offshore areas will halt this decline. Preliminary reserve estimates for 1983 by the federal energy department were 1069 million m³. Estimated remaining reserves of marketable natural gas in conventional producing areas at the end of 1982 were 19.86 x 10¹¹ m³ with another 6.05 x 10¹¹ m³ in frontier regions of the Mackenzie Delta and arctic islands, for a total reserve of 25.9 x 10¹¹ m³.

The bulk of Canada's petroleum-refining capacity was established between 1948 and 1958. Canada now ranks eighth among refining nations, but falling demand is creating temporary overcapacity and has led to the closing of some refineries. Gas-processing output, including pipeline gas, propane, butanes, pentanes and sulphur, also declined. Refineries produce about one-third gasoline, one-third middle distillates (eg, light heating oil, diesel oil, jet fuel) and 16% heavy fuel oil. Other products include liquified petroleum gas, PETROCHEMICAL feedstocks, aviation gasoline, asphalt, petroleum coke and lubricating oil.

Forest Resources FORESTS cover over one-third of Canada's land area, dominate the landscape and have been a significant factor in settlement and economic development. Forest resources provided an early basis for industrialization and they continue to be an important element in the economic and social life of every province. Forests also serve as the backdrop of a multi-billion dollar recreation and tourism industry. The economic, social and environmental benefits of Canada's forests make them perhaps the nation's most valuable resource. Canada has about one-tenth of the world's productive forest area: some 44% (4.4 million km²) of Canada's total area is forestland, with a wood volume of 23 billion m³. Of the total area, the 1981 National Forest Inventory classified about 2.2 million km² as capable of producing crops at regular intervals. Of the total wood volume, about 19.6 billion m³ is classified as gross merchantable timber. Softwoods comprise about 80% of this amount. The most important issue facing the forest sector in the last quarter of the century is timber supply. For more than 150 years virgin timber was harvested, with nature left to replenish the supply. Forestry in the 1980s reached a critical transition stage where thoughtless cutting had to yield to systematic forest renewal.

The principal sectors in Canada's forest industry are the LUMBER AND WOOD INDUSTRIES and the PULP AND PAPER INDUSTRY. The total value of shipments in 1983 was some $25 billion. Forest products constitute 12.5% of all manufactured goods in Canada (as high as 30% in NB and 45% in BC). Forest industry exports in 1983 totalled about $13 billion and imports $1.2 billion. However, as with most resource commodities, forest products slumped during the economic stagnation of the early 1980s, only recovering to 1980 levels in 1983. FORESTRY accounts for about 14% of the labour force, 20% of new investment in Canadian manufacturing, 13% of the value of manufacturing shipments and 14% of Canada's total export earnings in 1983.

Canada's forest industry has relied heavily on exports. Canada accounts for one-quarter of total world trade in manufactured wood products. It ships half the bleached kraft (strong paper or board) grades of wood pulp, two-thirds of the newsprint and 40% of the softwood lumber. The long-term competitive strength of the industry is based largely on the softwood timber species. The industry faces strong competition for export markets, particularly from the US. Canada's share of world exports of forest products declined from 25% in 1961 to 20% in 1982. This reduction has involved pulp and paper products and results from the increased export capabilities of developing countries and established producers (eg, the US, Scandinavia).

Agricultural Land Many would consider Canada's agricultural lands our most significant resource. Of Canada's land area of almost 923 million ha, only about 14% has any agricultural capacity whatever and only 5%, or about 46 million ha, is free of severe physical limitations to agricultural productivity. Alberta, Saskatchewan and Manitoba contain 70% of Canada's prime agricultural land. Ontario has 16%; however, this figure includes over one-half of Canada's best farmland. One of the most serious problems facing Canadian agriculture is a loss of soil fertility resulting in large part from poor cropping and AGRICULTURAL SOIL PRACTICES. It is estimated that some prairie soils have lost as much as 50% of their productive potential; substantial amounts of land in Ontario and Québec have undergone permanent and irreversible decreases in productivity. Serious SOIL CONSERVATION efforts are needed to prevent further deterioration and to improve soils, where possible.

The AGRICULTURE AND FOOD system accounts for

about one-sixth of all of Canada's economic activity, but this proportion is much higher in areas such as the southern Prairie provinces and the FRUIT belts of BC and Ontario. In 1981 Canadian agricultural production had a farm-gate value of about $18.5 billion: livestock and products accounted for 48%; field and horticultural CROPS 52%. The marketing of CEREALS, most OIL-SEEDS, eggs, POULTRY, milk, TOBACCO and sugar beets is controlled by various national and provincial AGRICULTURAL MARKETING BOARDS. In 1980 agriculture and related industries provided employment for 750 000 people; however, in 1981 fully 39% of farmers were also engaged in some form of off-farm labour. Canada has consistently been a net exporter of agricultural products: exports ($8.8 billion) exceeded imports ($5.6 billion) by $3.2 billion in 1981. Grains and oilseeds account for 80% of exports; other major exports include live animals, meats and DAIRY products. Imports include fresh fruits and vegetables, nuts, sugars, fibre, etc. The agricultural surplus has represented up to 89% of Canada's net merchandise trade balance. MAURICE CUTLER

Resources are those aspects of the natural environment that humans value and from which we produce goods and services. This definition demonstrates that, although natural resources originate in the natural environment, they are in a very real sense "created" by humans. Human values and abilities determine which parts of the environment societies use and benefit from. Resource and environmental systems are highly interconnected and both continuously change in character. Change is usually accelerated by human use. Because of the interconnections, impacts beyond the particular resource being used are common. In fact, use of some resources may preclude use of others. Human decisions, as well as natural processes, cause resources to change over time (*see* BIOGEOGRAPHY; ecosystems). These changes may decrease or increase resource supply and may be rapid or slow.

Classes

Resources may be classified according to various criteria, including information and availability, and temporal, spatial and ownership characteristics.

Information and Availability Three general classes of resources (potential, conditional and current) are distinguished on the basis of information known about them and their availability. A potential resource is one which is only thought to exist (ie, positive information is still lacking); a conditional resource is known to exist but its availability for use depends upon a number of conditions; a current resource has met all conditions and is in use and yielding benefits. Progression of a resource from potential to current status occurs as information about it increases and preproduction conditions are met. This transformation may take a long time and, until it is complete, few benefits flow to society. For example, initial information from geological and geophysical SURVEYING may indicate that a particular area has mineral potential. More information may suggest that a deposit exists and further elaborate and expensive exploration may confirm the deposit. A potential resource has become a conditional one. Additional information is needed to determine the extent and quality of the deposit; then other specific conditions must be met before production can begin.

The first condition is that suitable TECHNOLOGY is available to produce and process the mineral in marketable form. Next, a decision must be made as to whether production is economically feasible, ie, whether economic benefits outweigh costs sufficiently to warrant financial risks. At this stage, production, processing and transport costs are assessed in relation to the expected market price. Political and legal condi-

tions must also be met. These arise from non-market concerns and the relative importance different governments place upon them. Recent concerns have included environmental degradation, health hazards and financial returns to governments (*see* SOCIAL IMPACT ASSESSMENT). If these conditions are fulfilled, production may commence, thus creating a current resource. The process is reversible. The resource will revert from current to conditional status if preproduction conditions change sufficiently to make use no longer feasible.

Temporal Characteristics Resources that regenerate in short periods of time (eg, months, years, decades) or that are characterized by repeated occurrence are classed as renewable. WATER, plants and animals are generally considered renewable resources; their regenerative capabilities are measured in months for water supply, years for animal stocks and decades for FOREST stands. These varied time periods pose different management problems for users. Furthermore, the regenerative capacity of some renewable resources can be partially or completely removed by changes in habitat (eg, fish, as the result of WATER POLLUTION), harvesting to the point of extinction (eg, overhunting of game species) or habitat destruction resulting from poor harvesting techniques (eg, EROSION caused by overcutting of a forest).

Most renewable ENERGY resources rely upon atmospheric processes that occur repeatedly but are subject to cycles and periodical changes; thus, the potential for regeneration is not always met. Solar radiation, for example, is "renewable" in the sense that, except at high latitudes, the sun rises and sets daily, but direct solar radiation is available only intermittently, between night and day and between cloudy and clear periods. Similarly, wind blows only intermittently. Thus, although these 2 resources occur repeatedly and are attractive as potential energy sources, they pose management problems (*see* SOLAR ENERGY; WIND ENERGY).

The great advantage of renewable resources is that they can yield continuous benefits if managed properly, a process requiring a high degree of knowledge of life cycles, controlled harvesting and habitat protection. For example, once an oceanic fish stock is discovered, data must be obtained about its size and life cycle and the distance over which it moves, although the information-gathering process is difficult and time consuming. Such information is necessary because fish are mobile and regarded as common property, and therefore, catch limits are needed to ensure the stock's ability to reproduce itself. Establishment of some limits requires a high level of information on population dynamics, movement patterns and habitat characteristics. Poor management can convert a renewable resource to nonrenewable status, or necessitate intensive rehabilitation efforts.

Nonrenewable resources are those that cannot be regenerated in a human life span. Minerals are the best example of this class, but there are others. Land, for example, is not used consumptively as are minerals, but on balance the land area of Canada is not likely to be increased, except for possible reclamation of wetlands. SOIL is also nonrenewable in that it forms slowly and some uses are consumptive (eg, when it is removed to make way for buildings or transportation facilities). When managed well, soil can sustain biomass production for long periods.

Spatial Characteristics The 2 spatial aspects of resources that influence their use are mobility and concentration. Mobile resources include air, water and wildlife. Control over the use and management of mobile resources is complicated because they may move widely and be subject to many influences. They may cross jurisdictional boundaries (eg, national or provincial borders) or move into areas of no specific jurisdiction (eg, the OCEANS). Concentrated resources such as minerals and RIVERS occupy relatively confined spaces in comparison with dispersed resources such as forests and agricultural land. The degree of concentration sometimes determines whether a resource moves from conditional to current status because costs of use increase with wider dispersion.

Ownership Characteristics Some resources are privately owned by individuals or firms (eg, farmland); others are owned by governments, and rights to their use are allocated by licence, permit, etc (eg, forests, minerals, water). Others, called common property resources, are not owned at all (eg, fish, atmospheric elements). Common property resources attract users, each of whom tries to maximize benefits from them; consequently, they may quickly become degraded or exhausted. This class of resource raises special management problems. Access to common resources through private property may also be contentious.

Provincial Resource Profiles

The table Renewable Resources, shows the proportion in each province of land with high capability for AGRICULTURE (20 551 000 ha for Canada), hunted wildlife (117 028 000 ha for Canada) and recreation (5 864 000 ha for Canada) as recorded by the Canada Land Inventory, and the total Annual Allowable Cut of timber (276 million m³ for Canada), as estimated by the Forest Management Institute. For agriculture, wildlife and recreation, only the area with the highest capability classes (Classes 1 and 2) are tabulated. Quantitative data for other renewable resources such as waterpower and climatic characteristics either are not available on a comparable basis for the provinces or are contained elsewhere in this volume (*see* ELECTRIC-POWER GENERATION; REGIONAL ECONOMICS).

The table Mineral Production tabulates the average production in 3 recent years (1979-81) of major mineral commodities, ie, base metals (LEAD, ZINC, COPPER), ferrous metals (iron), alloys

---

Renewable Resources
(Percentage of National Total)
(Source: W. Simpson-Lewis et al,
Environment Canada, Ottawa, 1979;
Proceedings of the Canadian Forest Congress, 1980)

| | \multicolumn{3}{c}{Area With High Capability For} | Forest Productivity |
	Agriculture	Wildlife	Recreation	Annual Allowable Cut
Nfld	0.0	5.7	10.0	2.0
PEI	1.3	0.0	1.1	0.0
NS	0.8	1.7	1.3	1.4
NB	0.8	3.7	2.3	5.0
Qué	4.5	16.0	29.3	14.8
Ont	21.3	7.1	23.6	23.8
Man	13.1	8.8	3.0	2.8
Sask	33.4	21.9	6.5	3.0
Alta	22.5	20.6	2.7	10.2
BC	2.3	14.5	20.2	36.0

(NICKEL), precious metals (GOLD, SILVER), nonmetals (ASBESTOS, POTASH, sulphur) and energy commodities (URANIUM, COAL, OIL AND NATURAL GAS).

British Columbia has rich and varied resources. Most notable are the coniferous forests of the coast and central interior, the dispersed basemetal deposits and the coal and natural-gas resources of the E and NE. The PEACE and COLUMBIA rivers have been developed for HYDROELECTRICITY and considerable potential remains, particularly in the north (eg, LIARD and STIKINE rivers). Other major rivers (eg, FRASER, SKEENA) and many smaller streams are the spawning grounds of SALMON which, with herring, groundfish and crustaceans, support a large FISHING industry. Mountainous landforms and an extensive coastline provide habitats suitable for a variety of wildlife and considerable opportunity for outdoor recreation of many kinds. High-quality agricultural land is limited to the SW corner of the province and small strips in valley locations in the interior.

Yukon and the Northwest Territories, covering almost 40% of Canada (and constituting most of Canada's NORTH), have a harsh winter CLIMATE and short summers, resulting in limited plant growth. The eastern parts contain TUNDRA; some of the mountains are permanently ice covered. South of the TREELINE, particularly in the Yukon and in the Mackenzie River Basin, extensive areas are covered with forests of low productivity. Despite limiting environmental conditions, the territories support large populations of terrestrial and marine wildlife. Wildlife stocks are important sources of food and FUR for the native populations. Many special areas of unique environmental character afford valuable recreational and scientific opportunities. Much of the resource base (especially in minerals) is classed as potential or, at best, conditional. Base-metal resources have been developed in western sections and geological conditions suggest considerable potential. Most attention, however, is being given to exploration for PETROLEUM in the Mackenzie Delta, Beaufort Sea and the northwestern arctic islands.

Alberta consists mainly of 2 major geological areas, the Western Sedimentary Basin and the Rocky Mts. Large resources of fossil fuels (coal, oil and gas) exist beneath the surface of the former, while substantial areas of high-quality agricultural land cover the surface in the southern half of the province. Aridity limits agricultural productivity in the SE. The Rocky Mts contain large coal resources, the headwaters of many rivers and spectacular mountain and lake scenery, offering dramatic opportunities for outdoor recreation. Forested areas across central Alberta provide a modest forest resource.

Alberta's resources of conventional oil (lowviscosity oil that flows to the surface in its natural condition) have been heavily used and pro-

duction is declining. There are also very large deposits of heavy oil (ie, oil too viscous to come to the surface without special production techniques) and, in the tar sands, BITUMEN. These expensive "conditional" oil resources are in production to some extent, but large-scale development depends on economic and technological factors. Collectively, these energy resources make Alberta the fossil-fuel storehouse of Canada.

Saskatchewan The natural-resource base of Saskatchewan consists of the largest area of high-quality agricultural land in Canada, extensive and productive wildlife habitat (particularly for WATERFOWL), major deposits of potash and uranium, and significant supplies of petroleum and coal. Saskatchewan is Canada's primary wheat-growing area and a major producer of other grains and field CROPS. Boreal and mixed forest areas provide a modest forest resource. After 1962 Saskatchewan became the world's largest exporter and second-largest producer of potash. Large uranium resources in northern areas make the province the second-largest producer in Canada, while in the S strip-mined lignite coal is used extensively for thermal-power generation. In addition, Saskatchewan shares with Alberta a portion of the Lloydminster heavy and conventional oil fields.

Manitoba has a mixed resource base, including a variety of metallic minerals, hydroelectric power potential, and a significant area of good quality agricultural land. Nickel is the major mineral produced, with copper, lead, zinc and precious metals mined locally in significant quantities. Some northward-flowing rivers have already been developed for hydroelectricity (eg, NELSON R); others have large potential for development (eg, CHURCHILL R). Manitoba's current production of oil is small, but a promising hydrocarbon area has been identified along the southern border. The fish stocks of Lakes Winnipeg and Manitoba, significant areas of wildlife habitat and locally important forest resources all add to the variety of Manitoba's resource base.

Ontario is the largest market for resourcebased goods and services in Canada. However, with the important exception of fossil fuels, the province's own renewable and nonrenewable resources are large. The province ranks third, after Saskatchewan and Alberta, in area suitable for agriculture; however, southern Ontario alone has over 50% of Canada's Class 1 agricultural land, which, coupled with favourable climate, provides a resource base for productive and varied crops and livestock. In central and northern Ontario the forest cover contributes almost 25% of the national allowable cut and supports a major forest-product industry. Many of the more accessible forested areas and numerous lakes and streams afford extensive opportunities for outdoor recreation. The outstanding water resources of the GREAT LAKES and the ST LAWRENCE R offer major transportation routes, sources of hydroelectricity and recreational opportunities. Ontario lacks significant amounts of conventional fossil fuels and is only moderately endowed with industrial minerals (except SALT); however, northern Ontario is a storehouse of other minerals. The province leads Canada in production of nickel, uranium, zinc, gold and silver, and is second to BC in production of copper.

Québec has the greatest developed and potential hydroelectric resources in Canada. Many rivers running off the Canadian SHIELD into the ST LAWRENCE LOWLANDS and JAMES BAY have been harnessed to provide a large renewable source of energy, which helps compensate for the lack of fossil fuels. The St Lawrence R affords an important transportation route. Extensive areas of fresh water (in lakes and rivers) offer considerable opportunity for both outdoor recreation

---

Mineral Production
(Percentage of National Total)
(Source: Dept of Energy, Mines and Resources, Ottawa, 1981-82)

	Nfld	PEI	NS	NB	Qué	Ont	Man	Sask	Alta	BC	YT	NWT
Lead	1.7	—	1.0	21.5	—	2.0	0.1	—	—	28.6	23.3	21.8
Zinc	4.7	—	0.2	19.5	6.7	26.4	4.3	0.5	—	7.3	9.8	20.6
Copper	0.9	—	—	1.6	12.9	32.0	8.7	0.8	—	40.8	1.3	0.1
Iron	51.0	—	—	—	35.5	12.3	—	—	—	1.2	—	—
Nickel	—	—	—	—	—	77.4	22.6	—	—	—	—	—
Gold	0.6	—	—	0.4	30.9	35.7	2.8	0.7	0.2	15.5	4.5	8.7
Silver	0.9	—	—	14.5	5.3	34.5	2.5	0.5	—	23.6	13.1	5.1
Asbestos	5.0	—	—	—	87.8	—	—	—	—	7.2	—	—
Potash	—	—	—	—	—	—	—	100.0	—	—	—	—
Sulphur	—	—	—	0.8	0.9	5.5	—	—	87.5	5.3	—	—
Uranium	—	—	—	—	62.2	—	—	37.8	—	—	—	—
Coal	—	—	6.8	1.2	—	—	—	16.2	46.4	29.4	—	—
Oil	—	—	—	—	—	0.1	0.7	10.7	85.7	2.6	—	0.2
Natural gas	—	—	—	—	—	0.4	—	1.5	87.5	10.6	—	—

and wildlife habitat. Good quality agricultural soils are limited, but Québec ranks third (after BC and Ontario) in the productivity of its extensive forested area. Important mineral resources include asbestos (the production of which is only exceeded by that of the USSR), iron, gold and some base metals.

The Atlantic Provinces Even with the relatively large size of Newfoundland, the Atlantic provinces collectively cover a land area that is less than any of the remaining 6 provinces. Much of the area is made up of islands and peninsulas, which give easy access to the FISH and CRUSTACEAN RESOURCES of the Gulf of St Lawrence and the Continental Shelf of the western Atlantic, the location of Canada's largest fishing industry (see COASTAL WATERS; FISHERIES; OCEAN INDUSTRIES). Other important renewable resources include forests (particularly in NB and Nfld), relatively small areas of productive land (eg, PEI, the Annapolis Valley of NS) and hydroelectric resources, particularly in Labrador and in the Bay of Fundy (see TIDAL ENERGY). The extensive coastlines provide many opportunities for seasonal outdoor recreation. The mineral-resource base may be divided into onshore and offshore. Onshore there is a large base-metal resource in northern NB, iron in Nfld and GYPSUM and salt in NS. The only significant onshore fossil-fuel resources are coal deposits in Nova Scotia's Cape Breton area. Offshore, the Continental Shelf has a significant potential for oil (particularly off Nfld) and gas (off NS).

Opportunities and Challenges

The economic development of Canada has been based to a great extent upon a large and varied endowment of resources, availability of foreign capital and access to export markets (see FOREIGN INVESTMENT). When compared with other countries, both the magnitude and variety of resources available remain a major national advantage. Large stocks of many wildlife species and major freshwater and marine fish populations exist. Canada is second to the USSR in the volume of standing softwood timber and the area of land suitable for agriculture is extensive. Similarly, the volume of standing and running water is greater than in most countries. Because of Canada's vast landmass and the variety of geological conditions, many and varied mineral deposits await discovery (see GEOLOGICAL REGIONS). In addition, many areas with special environmental characteristics offer opportunities for a variety of outdoor recreational, educational and scientific activities. All of these resources, with the important exception of minerals, are renewable.

Some emerging challenges must be addressed if Canada is to continue to benefit from this large and varied resource base. First, heavy use has been made of the most accessible and highest-quality resources. For example, the best agricultural lands have been cultivated for many decades; the best timber has been harvested; the most accessible oil fields have passed their peak output. Consequently, attention must be directed to maintaining productivity of the land, replacing harvested trees and finding other supplies of oil (see SOIL CONSERVATION). For renewable resources, this process will require significant improvements in the knowledge of the processes that control plant growth so that an intensive-regenerative style of RESOURCE MANAGEMENT will replace extensive extraction. For nonrenewable resources, active exploration programs must be maintained and new technologies developed. Such technologies are required to increase the efficiency of resource extraction and use, and for work in areas that are relatively inaccessible with hostile, but often sensitive, environments (see NORTH; NORDICITY).

A second challenge is an increasing competition among RESOURCE USES, resulting from population growth and a widening variety of potential uses, particularly near urban centres. For example, a tract of forestland may have logging potential, or mining capability or be suitable for a park or WILDLIFE PRESERVE. Similarly, an area of Class 1 agricultural land near an urban centre could be used for agriculture, as the site of an airport or for a housing development. Conflicts about uses of resource complexes are growing and, if full benefits are to be derived from the resource endowment, ways must be found to resolve such conflicts quickly and fairly. In particular, risk to human welfare and environmental quality must be assessed thoroughly and levels established in which the costs are both acceptable and realistic.

Third, if resources are to continue to contribute substantially to Canadian economic development, they must be able to compete in world markets. Access to these markets depends on price, quality and reliability of supply. Thus, some aspects of export marketing, such as a transportation infrastructure, must be provided at high efficiency. But perhaps of greatest importance is the need for a balance between competitiveness, on the one hand, and the maintenance of a high income level, social services and environmental quality on the other (see CONSERVER SOCIETY).   J.D. CHAPMAN

Responsible Government, loosely used to mean a government responsible to the people, as popular rule is naturally conceived to be. Properly, however, as used by those who gained it in Canada, it meant a government responsible to the representatives of the people, ie, an executive or cabinet collectively dependent on the votes of a majority in the elected legislature. This key principle of responsibility, whereby a government needed the confidence of Parliament, originated in established British practice. But its transfer to British N America gave the colonists control of their domestic affairs, since a governor would simply follow the advice (ie, policies) of responsible colonial ministers, except in imperial matters. Moreover, this control was enlarged by degrees, so that Canadians through governments based on elected parliaments gradually acquired a general command of their own political concerns, thereby achieving national self-direction without revolution.

The idea of responsible government was taken up in the 1830s in BNA largely by loyal admirers of the British model, who sought it both to remedy discontent with unyielding local oligarchies (see FAMILY COMPACT; CHÂTEAU CLIQUE; COUNCIL OF TWELVE) and to keep the provinces securely, though freely, within the Empire. Radicals such as William Lyon MACKENZIE and Louis-Joseph PAPINEAU preferred American elective patterns, but Joseph HOWE in Nova Scotia and Robert BALDWIN in Upper Canada showed far better comprehension — better even than Lord DURHAM, an influential advocate of responsible government — since they realized that an organized party system was vital. Howe in Nova Scotia, and Baldwin and Louis LAFONTAINE in the PROVINCE OF CANADA, built up strong, moderate Reform parties to gain responsible government, and by 1848 saw it fully operating, accepted by a Liberal, imperial Britain. It then was granted to other eastern colonies: PEI in 1851, NB in 1854 and Nfld last, in 1855, and as western provinces emerged in CONFEDERATION they too obtained it.   J.M.S. CARELESS

Restigouche, Qué, IR, pop 1091 (1981c), is located in the GASPÉ Peninsula at the mouth of the RESTIGOUCHE R (spelled Ristigouche in Qué). A bridge links it to CAMPBELLTON, NB. Before the Europeans arrived, the Gaspé and present-day northeastern NB belonged to the MICMAC, an Algonquian family of hunters and fishers. The name originated with the Micmac *Lustagooch*, perhaps meaning "good river." In the 1750s the ACADIANS began to settle the area and, on 8 July 1760, Restigouche was the site of the last battle between the French and British during the SEVEN YEARS' WAR. The French lost 3 ships during that battle to the superior military tactics of the British. After colonization by whites, the Micmac territory gradually diminished to the size of the present reserve. A mission dedicated to St Anne was built in 1745 and served by the Capuchin order. One member, Father Pacifique, produced the Gospels and a dictionary in the Micmac language. Parks Canada is developing an interpretation centre for the Battle of Restigouche.

ANTONIO LECHASSEUR

Restigouche River, 200 km long, rises in the highlands of northwestern New Brunswick as the Little Main Restigouche R. Fed by its tributaries Kedgwick, Patapédia and Matapédia flowing S from Gaspé, and Upsalquich flowing N from central NB, it flows northeasterly towards the towns of RESTIGOUCHE and CAMPBELLTON where it broadens into a wide estuary. At DALHOUSIE it empties into Chaleur Bay on the Gulf of ST LAWRENCE. From the confluence with the Patapédia to Chaleur Bay, the river forms the boundary between NB and Québec. Together with its tributaries, the Restigouche drains a large area of northern NB and Gaspé, a land of timber resources and great scenic grandeur. The name derives from the Micmac word *Lustagooch*, likely meaning "good river." The river is famous for its run of ATLANTIC SALMON.   JAMES MARSH

Restrictive Trade Practices Commission, est 1952 as a court of record by the Combines Investigation Act. The commission responds to applications by the director of investigation and research by holding a hearing at which evidence is presented by the director and the persons involved. An order may be issued prohibiting the trade practice. The commission reports to the minister of consumer and corporate affairs.

Retail Trade, sales of goods or services to consumers for personal or household use. Consumer spending through the retail trade accounts for 60% of the GROSS NATIONAL PRODUCT of Canada and employs over one million people. Statistics Canada recognizes some 185 000 retail outlets in Canada, primarily shops, car dealers, supermarkets and department stores, but the number does not include street vendors, farmers' markets, roadside stands or the growing UNDERGROUND ECONOMY. There is also a great variety in the methods by which the selling takes place: over the counter, by vending machines, door-to-door or telephone canvassing, mail order and others. In 1983 Canadian retail sales totalled $106.2 billion, with Alta (at $4805), Ont (at $4474) and Sask (at $4392) the leading per capita spenders. Ontario remained the largest market (37.1%); Qué (24.3%) and BC (11.5%) followed.

There are 2 broad categories of retail-trade organization: retail chains, which operate 4 or more stores in the same kind of business under the same ownership, and independent retailers operating 1 to 3 stores. Chains dominate combination grocery and meat stores (71.5%), variety stores (75.7%), general merchandise stores (79.1%) and shoe stores (64.8%). Independent retailers tend to dominate motor-vehicle dealers (98.7%), service stations (80%), pharmacies (79.1%), sporting-goods stores (89.1%) and flower shops (95.8%). Chains possess enormous buying power and rank among the most powerful corporations in Canada. For example, George Weston Ltd, a supermarket chain which includes Loblaws, had $7.8 billion in sales (1983), employed 60 000 people and ranked 5th among Canadian corporations. Steinberg, Canada Safeway and Dominion ranked 24th, 25th and 33rd, had combined sales of another $9 billion and employed among them 76 000 people.

Chain-store operations are highly concentrated. In 1979 chains with annual sales volumes in excess of $5 million (some 245 organizations) accounted for over 95% of total chain sales. Those chain organizations with annual sales of over $100 million (32 firms) accounted for over 64% of all chain-store sales. In 1980 chain stores were most important in the class of department stores — where they represented 100% of sales; they were least important in motor-vehicle dealers where they accounted for only 1.2% of sales in the same year. Other important types of chain-store operation include jewellery stores (49.1%), book and stationery stores (51.1%) and family shoe stores (69.3%).

Department Stores are huge emporiums selling a wide variety of goods. THE T. EATON CO of Toronto (fd 1869) was one of the first stores anywhere to offer a wide variety of goods on a large scale, and along with Simpsons it initiated mail-order sales in Canada. Department stores grew in popularity after WWI; by 1930 there were roughly 25 to 30 in Canada. The number has not grown significantly since then, but by 1980 department stores accounted for some 12% of total retail sales. The HUDSON'S BAY CO, with its subsidiaries Simpsons and Zeller's, had over $4 billion in sales (1983), employed 45 000 and ranked thirteenth among Canadian corporations. The HBC, Simpsons-Sears ($3.1 billion in sales) and T.E. Eaton Co ($2 billion) have a combined market share of 75%. (Simpsons-Sears, owned by HBC and Sears Roebuck, comprises 72 retail and over 1200 catalogue stores — Sears is the name given to the former, Simpsons-Sears designates the latter.) The concentration of department stores largely depends on urbanization and disposable income, and therefore accounts for a much higher percentage of retail sales in Ontario than in the Atlantic provinces, Québec or Saskatchewan. The first *hypermarché*, or superstore (over 3500 m²) opened in Montréal in 1973.

Direct Selling takes place through a number of channels, eg, mail ordering, door-to-door selling, sales directly to employees and house-party sales. Home deliveries of milk and bread, newspapers, magazines, books, aluminum doors and windows, etc, make up the largest proportion. In 1977 there were 662 vending-machine firms with 105 587 machines in factories, institutions, offices, hotels and restaurants. Sales amounted to $286 million, of which 43% was cigarettes, 18% coffee and 15% soft drinks.

Retail Prices are used to calculate changes in the cost of living. The CONSUMER PRICE INDEX (CPI) measures percentage change over time in the cost of purchasing a constant or equivalent "basket" of goods and services typical of a particular group of private households — both families and individuals — living in cities of 30 000 or more in a specific period. Food, housing, household operation, household furnishings and equipment, clothing, transportation, health and personal care, recreation and similar activities, tobacco and alcohol are included in the index. The index is usually stated in relative terms, 1971 being equal to 100. The index has increased dramatically from 138.5 in 1975 to 175.2 in 1978, to over 200 in 1982. Retail prices were therefore more than twice as high in 1982 as they were in 1971.

Shopping Centres More of the retail trade in Canada is taking place in various types of shopping centre. A shopping centre is a group of retail stores and consumer service outlets which is planned and developed as a unit and which must have a minimum of 5 stores and a major "anchor" tenant such as a supermarket or a department store. There are 3 basic types of shopping centre: neighbourhood centres (5-15 retail stores), community centres (16-30 retail stores) and regional centres (more than 30 retail stores). Regional shopping centres are the most important, not simply because of their size but be-

The indoor skating rink at West Edmonton Mall, the largest shopping centre in N America (*photo by Roman Spalek/Reflexion*).

cause they are quickly changing the urban landscape in Canada, replacing the traditional downtown central business districts. (West Edmonton Mall, with more than 425 stores — reputedly the largest mall in the world — has caused controversy for its impact on a previously residential neighborhood.) They have strongly influenced the movement of population from urban to suburban areas and have restructured much of retail trade. A retailer in a shopping centre must learn new management skills and conform to the behaviour of retailers in the centre. The growth of shopping centres has had and will continue to have a direct impact on small independent businesses that are unable to compete or thrive within them (*see* SMALL BUSINESS). Shopping centres have also affected the variety of choice by excluding many small retail establishments. Unfortunately, Statistics Canada has not compiled data on shopping centres since 1973; their importance can be indirectly calculated by the sales data for department stores within the 12 metropolitan areas. Sales are divided between downtown and shopping centres. In 1978, 52.2% of the department stores were in the 12 major metropolitan areas and these stores accounted for 68.5% of the total dollar volume of department stores. Within these same areas, department stores accounted for approximately 66% of metropolitan department-store sales. Shopping centres across Canada resemble one another because the same major chains rent space in them. This results partly from their aggressive behaviour in seeking out centres and partly from their participation in the development and management of the centres. There may in the future be a resurgence of opportunities for local developers to offer space to new and diverse types of retail operations. Although the number of regional shopping centres has probably reached a peak in Canada, development of the other 2 types will undoubtedly continue.

Retail Employment Retailing in Canada is a major source of employment, although retail positions are generally poorly paid. Despite the general strength of the labour movement in Canada, attempts to organize retail workers in any systematic way have been quite unsuccessful. This is partly because of the nature of retail jobs, which do not require highly developed skills, and because of the transience of retail employees. But it is also a consequence of efforts by major Canadian retailers to discourage UNIONS. With the shift to self-service and open stores, the role of retail employees has generally been reduced to taking orders. Major retailers are currently implementing new systems to increase labour productivity, including centralized "cashpoints" and computer applications throughout store operations.

The retail employment pool is one of the most fickle. Students, younger women and older people move in and out of the retail trade in response to economic needs in general and to

seasonal needs, eg, extra money for Christmas. Often neither time nor resources are available to develop a trained selling staff. Other jobs in retailing include buying and merchandising, store operations (especially those related to operation and maintenance of the physical plant), personnel management, accounting, and control of operations.

Despite the trend toward bigness, retailing is still an area where individuals can gain a foothold in business. It has been a traditional means by which many immigrants have established themselves. The retail store often provides employment for the family while simultaneously serving specific markets. These establishments will always be important because of their flexibility and their ability to respond to particular market opportunities. They will always offer substantial competition to the larger, more sophisticated, types of retailers.

Retail Merchandising Practices and Regulation Choosing a product assortment and displaying it, establishing a price level, developing a promotional program and creating a store "image" are 4 aspects of merchandising. Regulation of retail trade not only protects the consumer from unfair merchandising practices, discriminatory prices, and unfair and misleading promotion and advertising, but also encourages competition among retail firms (*see* COMPETITION POLICY). The federal Combines Investigation Act theoretically regulates agreements, eg, mergers, among competitors, and restrains trade among retailers. Under the Act misleading price advertising is illegal. The Act is administered by the Dept of Consumer and Corporate Affairs, which is responsible for problems arising from misleading advertising and hazardous products, and for packaging and labelling. The department, along with similar provincial agencies, develops and distributes materials designed to help consumers become more informed shoppers. Individual provinces have also passed consumer protection laws regarding selling practices. Two of the most comprehensive Acts concerning retailing are found in BC and Québec. The Deceptive Trade Practices Act in BC lists 18 deceptive practices and is designed to curtail the "sharp" practices of sellers; the Québec legislation passed in 1971 includes provisions aimed at preventing advertising directed toward children and gives consumers the right to inspect and obtain credit records. The general principle of *caveat vendor* ("seller beware") holds in Canada, ensuring that retailers are cautious in the development of specific merchandising activities.

Development Retail trade in Canada developed along relatively specialized product lines, replacing the trading posts or general stores which had characterized retailing until the turn of this century. Single-line stores, particularly in population centres, developed for specific product groups such as drugs, food and hardware. Other areas were and still are to some degree served by mail order. In the last 20 years stores of all types have begun to practise mass merchandising in a movement toward high-volume, low-margin operations. Supermarkets began to sell, along with food items, a range of products including automotive supplies, clothing, hardware and pharmaceutical items. Department stores began to sell automotive accessories and repairs, "health foods" and services such as banking, insurance and travel. Discount operations in Canada offered a wide range of products — in contrast to those in the US which offered only narrow lines — and also expanded service operations. The control of the market by a limited number of firms is increasing. In general merchandise, the HBC controls about 11% of the market. In department-store sales, the HBC, with its subsidiaries Zeller's and Sears (Simpsons-Sears Ltd), and T.E. Eaton Co, have a combined market share of more than 75%. The same concentration exists in food retailing. The 5 dominant food chains — Loblaws, Dominion, Canada Safeway, Steinberg's and A & P — control about 60% of the market.

Retail trade is subject to fluctuations and change. In both the general merchandise and food areas, new competition appears to be coming from specialty stores. As in Europe and the US, telephone and television retailing will probably become common in the future. The rapid growth in the variety and sophistication of consumer demand is affecting retail change, as are shifts in population and even tourism. Patterns of consumption vary across Canada; in provinces such as Alberta and BC, where population and income increased in the 1970s and early 1980s, more money became available for retail purchases. Patterns vary also according to age and the number of children; younger people tend to be more receptive to new products and new forms of retailing. Within Canada expenditures are influenced by ethnic diversity and even by the weather. *See also* WHOLESALE TRADE.

RONALD SAVITT

Revelstoke, BC, City, pop 5544 (1981c; 9682, 1982e), inc 1899 and reincorporated 1981 when the city boundaries were extended to include Big Eddy district, South Revelstoke and Arrow Heights. It is situated on the COLUMBIA R between the Selkirk and Monashee mountains, 415 km by road W of Calgary, Alta. The area was first settled in the mid-1800s and by the 1870s was known as "Big Eddy" and "Second Crossing" (of the Columbia R). The original townsite, laid out in 1880, was named Farwell after a surveyor. In 1886 the new CPR station just to the W was named Revelstoke after Lord Revelstoke, whose British bank had invested in the CPR. Mining and the railway spurred the community's growth. In 1899 Revelstoke became the mountain divisional centre for the CPR, and for many years it was the western entrance to the old Big Bend Hwy along the Columbia R through the Selkirk Mts. Today the CPR remains an important employer, along with mining, forestry, tourism and the new Revelstoke Dam.

JOHN R. STEWART

Revenue Canada Until WWI the federal government financed its operations from indirect taxes, customs duties and excise taxes. Direct TAXATION was introduced in 1916 through an excess business-profits tax and in 1917 by income tax. The Dept of National Revenue was established 1927 to assess and collect duties and taxes, control the international movement of persons and goods, provide Canadian industry with protection under the customs law and administer the statutes of other government departments and agencies where they concern the international movement of persons and goods. The department has 2 sections: Taxation, and Customs and Excise, which has 3 branches — Customs Programs, Customs Field Operations and the Excise Branch.

Revolutionary Industrial Unionism, a broad international movement dedicated to organizing all workers into single, unified labour organizations designed to overthrow the capitalist system by striking, and, in contrast with more orthodox socialism, communism or social democracy, to establish direct workers' control over economic and political life through unions and workers' councils. Its best expression in Canada was the ONE BIG UNION (1919-56), a coalition of INDUSTRIAL WORKERS OF THE WORLD sympathizers, socialists and trade unionists. Unlike the IWW (fd 1905) and the communist-sponsored Workers' Unity League (1929-36), the OBU was wholly indigenous. Although preaching the general strike as a means to destroy capitalism, and fiercely denouncing the flaws of the parliamentary system, it did not eschew political action.

In general, revolutionary unionism in Canada reflected an eclectic reading of syndicalist (doctrine by which workers seize control of the economy and government by direct means, eg, a strike) and socialist theory, and was appropriate to the diverse traditions and complex needs of its constituency. Canadian revolutionary unionism, in contrast to its British, German and even American counterparts, failed to make significant inroads into mass production industries (in theory its main targets). But until the 1930s it had solid backing in the forest and mining sectors, an influence still felt in such unions as the steelworkers and woodworkers. It also attracted support from groups who felt estranged from the political-economic establishment on the one hand and the established labour movement on the other: non-English-speaking immigrants, farm workers, the unemployed. Finally, specifically within the OBU, revolutionary unionism briefly embraced skilled workers.

The American-based IWW was very active in western Canada, 1906-14, and its influence was felt in the increasingly militant activities of established trade unions. It attracted particular attention by closing down the giant CANADIAN NORTHERN RAILWAY construction project in the Fraser Canyon in 1912, when about 7000 callously treated immigrant workers struck under its aegis. The strike was forcibly suppressed, and authorities agreed that the IWW was to be infiltrated and, if possible, destroyed. On 28 Sept 1918 the IWW was declared unlawful and most of its sympathizers went underground.

Briefly after WWI it seemed that revolutionary unionism would seriously challenge or even destroy traditional patterns of industrial relations and union organization in Canada. War difficulties, including the bitter debate over CONSCRIPTION, induced a deep cleavage between eastern and western union leaders. The militant BC Federation of Labour crossed swords continually with the majority ("eastern") bloc of the TRADES AND LABOR CONGRESS. In the heated atmosphere of 1917 and 1918 when one of BCFL's executive officers, Albert "Ginger" Goodwin, was killed by a Dominion Police constable, supporters of secession from TLC gained the upper hand in BCFL. The Canadian government only offered workers a royal commission in the spring of 1919 to discover the causes of industrial unrest. Many unionists simply boycotted the proceedings. The OBU was still organizing when the workers its leaders claimed to represent rose independently. The rebellion hinged upon the WINNIPEG GENERAL STRIKE, May-June 1919, but it included the shutdown of the Alberta coal industry by miners and foremen, a mass walkout by several thousand Chinese and Japanese mill workers in the BC Lower Mainland and a general strike in Amherst, NS. Government, employers and international union leaders generally collaborated in the ensuing repression. After the Winnipeg strike the OBU's chance for a takeover in the labour movement had passed.

During the 1920s, many of the IWW's and OBU's former sympathizers drifted into the COMMUNIST PARTY OF CANADA or the "Left Wing" in the TLC unions. Best known was J.B. MCLACHLAN from Glace Bay, NS, who was jailed for his efforts in the 1923 CAPE BRETON STRIKES. This experience contributed to the zeal with which McLachlan and countless others engaged in the last attempt to build a "revolutionary union central" in Canada in the 1930s: the Workers' Unity League. The WUL had originated in the Communist International and the Communist Party, but it evolved into a genuine workers' unity league, especially during 1932-34 when the party's leadership was incarcerated in Kingston Penitentiary. In 1933 a bona fide delegate convention saw significant revisions to the League's constitution and the election of J.B. McLachlan as president.

The WUL, like the IWW and the OBU, failed to build a stable membership of more than a fraction of TLC affiliates, but it mobilized over 50 000 workers in strikes. The WUL's penetration of central Canada's factory belt was a new departure in revolutionary unionism, and a signal of a force in Canadian industrial life that gained major momentum after the WUL was gone. The WUL's high point was 1934 when its militants led no less than 109 strikes. Many Canadians remember the accompanying violence: 3 coal miners killed at Estevan in 1931; alleged sabotage in the Crowsnest Pass in 1932; army machine-gun carriers in Stratford in 1933; brass knuckles and machine guns on the Vancouver docks in 1935. The WUL fought for immediate demands, such as the "work and wages" sought by the 1935 ON TO OTTAWA trekkers. Its politics were not revolutionary. An entire slate of WUL supporters was elected to town council in Blairmore, Alta, in 1933, ousting the incumbent group of alleged grafters and strikebreakers.

Revolutionary industrial unionism in N America did not really die during the Depression; rather, its advocates were co-opted into the orthodox political left or into the pragmatic Congress of Industrial Organizations. The WUL militants merged with the international unions in 1936. Fate was not kind to the revolutionary unionists in Canada, but the situation can be favourably contrasted with that in Europe, the movement's birthplace, where by 1940 any revolutionary unionists left in Italy, Germany, Spain or the USSR were behind the barbed wire of the dictators. *See* WORKING-CLASS HISTORY.

ALLEN SEAGER

Revue d'histoire de l'Amérique française, La was founded in 1947 by Lionel GROULX, professor of history at U de Montréal. At first the RHAF was devoted to the history of French colonization in America — not just the history of French Canada, but also French efforts at colonization in the US, the Caribbean and S America. The development of the RHAF cannot be separated from the evolution of francophone historiography in Québec. It was started at the same time as the history departments of the only 2 Québec francophone universities of the day, U de Montréal and Laval U. It quickly became the favoured vehicle for communications among francophone specialists in Canadian and QUÉBEC HISTORY. It is now the major review devoted to Québec history (though it also accepts some articles on other topics). The RHAF is published quarterly by the Institut d'histoire de l'Amérique française, which selects the members of its editorial committee.

JEAN-CLAUDE ROBERT

Rexton, NB, Village, pop 928 (1981c), inc 1966, is located in southeastern NB, at the mouth of the Richibucto R. At the close of the AMERICAN REVOLUTION, several LOYALIST refugees received land grants here in an area where Acadian families were already located. From 1790 the Richibucto R attained new importance with the establishment of milling operations supplied by the abundant white pine along its bank. By the 1820s a substantial SHIPBUILDING business had evolved under the leadership of John Jardine. In 1842 the shipbuilding partnership of Holderness and Chalton founded Rexton, then called Kingston, after its namesake in England. Today, its principal economic activities remain a blend of farming and fishing for the local population. Rexton is the birthplace of Andrew Bonar LAW, who became prime minister of Great Britain. His father's farm on the banks of the Richibucto is now a historic attraction.

ROGER P. NASON

Reynolds, Leslie Alan, sculptor (b at Edmonton 16 May 1947). Like many contemporary sculptors, Alan Reynolds works in a "constructivist" idiom. His initial work in wood was encouraged in 1973 by American sculptor Michael Steiner, whose influence suited Reynolds's personal vision. In the mid-1970s Reynolds worked with large blocks of laminated wood that resembled walls. Later in the decade he exploited arrangements of flat sheets, often in complex, tablelike configurations. He turned to welded steel early in the 1980s, partly because of the structural limitations of wood. He adapted his vision to the new material with surprising speed and was soon producing sculptures of cylinder and tub shapes with attached lips and rims fused into the surfaces. As a result, the works inclined towards the expressive devices of functional pottery and traditional sculptural modelling. His art has had a considerable influence on younger sculptors in Edmonton.

TERRY FENTON

Rhinoceros Party, founded (1963) by a group of humorists led by Montréal doctor Jacques Ferron to poke fun at federal election campaigns. First fielding candidates for 1964 by-elections, it has participated in every subsequent general election. Eighty-nine candidates (across Canada) represented the party in the federal election of 1984; it received 99 207 votes, 0.790% of the total votes cast. ANDRÉ BERNARD

Rhinoceros Party meeting in Vancouver, 1979 (courtesy Canapress).

Rhodes, Edgar Nelson, lawyer, politician, premier of NS (b at Amherst, NS 5 Jan 1877; d at Ottawa 15 Mar 1942). A distinguished politician, he began his career as a lawyer in Amherst in 1902. While serving as the federal Conservative member for Cumberland 1908-21, he became Speaker in 1917 and a member of the Privy Council in 1921. He then moved to provincial politics, sitting as the Liberal-Conservative member for Hants County 1925-30 and occupying the offices of premier and provincial secretary. His tenure was brief but is remembered for decisive legislative action. Rhodes resigned to become federal minister of fisheries under R.B. BENNETT and the member for Richmond-W Cape Breton. He held the finance portfolio 1932-35 and was then named to the Senate.

LOIS KERNAGHAN

Rhododendron [Gk, "red tree"], a large genus (700 species) of the heath family (Ericaceae) found in the Northern Hemisphere; 4 species are native to Canada. The genus contains both rhododendrons, usually evergreen, and azaleas, which are deciduous. Rhododendrons range from creeping shrubs to medium-sized TREES, with saucerlike to bell-shaped flowers (white, pink, red, mauve, purple, yellow to orange). Rhododendrons possess a wide range of leaf types, all simple, often leathery, and frequently covered with soft hairs (indumentum) or scales. Larger-leaved species frequently exhibit very tight enrolling of leaves during freezing weather, an adaptation that prevents water loss. Indian azalea (single- and double-flowered), derived from *R. simsii*, is sold as a pot plant at Christmas. Many variously coloured outdoor hybrids have been produced. Species and hy-

brids are significant ORNAMENTALS in Canadian gardens, particularly in milder coastal regions. Most rhododendrons are propagated by cuttings. ROY L. TAYLOR

Rhubarb (genus *Rheum*), common name for about 50 species of cool-season herbaceous perennial PLANTS belonging to the BUCKWHEAT family and originating in central Asia. Common rhubarb (*R. rhabarbarum* or *R. rhaponticum*) was probably the first to be cultivated, initially as a source of purgative drugs from the powdered root. It was established as a food plant in Europe in the mid-18th century and now grows throughout Canada. Considerable hybridization has occurred to produce the present commercial cultivars. Leaves are poisonous; the edible portion is the elongated petiole (leafstalk), which may be harvested for immediate use or for processing (canning, freezing, pie filling). Dormant plants may be dug in early winter for "forcing" in heated, darkened buildings, where the delicate petioles are produced. Forced rhubarb is grown commercially in Ontario. Rhubarb is relatively free from pest and disease problems.

ARTHUR LOUGHTON

Richard, Joseph-Henri-Maurice, "Rocket," hockey player (b at Montréal 4 Aug 1921). He was seriously injured in his last 2 years of amateur hockey and his first year (1942-43) with MONTREAL CANADIENS, but collected 32 goals in his first full season. In 1944-45 he scored 50 goals in 50 games — long hockey's most celebrated record. Richard's fierce competitiveness and scoring heroics made him the most exciting player of his generation and a national hero among Québécois. He led the league in goals 5 times and won the HART TROPHY in 1947, but the scoring title eluded him. He excelled above all under pressure; in playoffs he scored 3 goals in a game 7 times, 4 goals in a game twice, and in 1944 all 5 goals in a 5-1 triumph over Toronto. He also scored 83 game-winning goals, still a record. Richard possessed a short temper and seldom refused a challenge or left an attack unanswered. In March 1955 he struck Boston Bruin player Hal Laycoe with his stick and attacked a linesman who intervened. His suspension for the rest of the year by NHL president Clarence Campbell was considered an outrage by Montréal fans. Campbell was attacked at the Montréal Forum on St Patrick's Day and the violence spilled into the streets in the worst sports RIOT in Canadian history. It was indicative of the passionate devotion Richard inspired. His career ended in 1960 after he suffered a severed tendon. His 544 goals in regular-season play was an NHL record on his retirement and in 1984 still ranked him sixth in NHL history; his 82 goals in Stanley Cup play was still a record in 1985.

JAMES MARSH

Maurice "Rocket" Richard in one of his typical assaults on the opposition goal. He was the greatest scorer of his generation (courtesy Canada's Sports Hall of Fame).

Richards, Charles Dow, lawyer, politician, premier of NB (b at Southampton, York County, NB 12 June 1879; d at Fredericton 15 Sept 1956). Initially a schoolteacher, Richards was admitted to the bar at age 33. Before becoming premier and attorney general in 1931 he was Conservative house leader in the provincial Assembly and minister of lands and mines under J.B.M. BAXTER. His 12-year administration, in the depths of the Great Depression, instituted public bidding on crown land and fishing rights. He was appointed to the Supreme Court in 1943 and was chief justice from 1948 to 1955. He is best remembered not so much as a politician but as a dignified scholarly lawyer and distinguished judge. ARTHUR T. DOYLE

Richardson, Ernie, curler (b at Stoughton, Sask 1931). He gained world acclaim as skip of the famous Richardson Rink, probably the best known in Canadian curling history. In 1959 at Québec this family group of 2 brothers (Ernie and Garnet) and 2 cousins (Arnold and Wes), all Richardsons, became the youngest team to win the Brier. Noted for aggressive, take-out play, they went on to win 4 Briers in 5 years, 4 Scotch Cups for the world championship, and numerous other championships and titles. Ernie Richardson has also written several books on curling. GERALD REDMOND

Richardson, James Armstrong, Sr, merchant, financier (b in Kingston, Ont 21 Aug 1885; d in Winnipeg 27 June 1939). Educated at Queen's, in 1906 Richardson entered the family firm of James Richardson and Sons, grain exporters, becoming VP in 1912 and president in 1919. He was a director of many companies, including the CPR, the Canadian Bank of Commerce, International Nickel, the Great West Life Assurance Co, National Trust and Canadian Vickers and was also president and member of the Winnipeg Grain Exchange and several Canadian and American boards of trade. JORGE NIOSI

Richardson, James Armstrong, Jr, grain merchant, politician (b at Winnipeg 28 Mar 1922), son of James A. RICHARDSON, SR. After studying at Queen's and serving in the RCAF as a Liberator Bomber pilot patrolling the N Atlantic, Richardson joined the family firm of James Richardson and Sons in 1945 and was chairman and executive officer 1966-68. He was elected Liberal MP for Winnipeg S in June 1968 and appointed minister without portfolio in July. Minister of supply and services 1969-72, he was reelected in the 1972 general election and was appointed minister of national defence. He resigned from Cabinet in 1976, over the government's language policy, and sat as an Independent 1978-79, when he returned to the family firm and became a director. JORGE NIOSI

Richardson, Sir John, arctic explorer, naturalist (b at Dumfries, Scot 5 Nov 1787; d at "Lancrigg," Eng 5 June 1865). After qualifying as a member of the Royal College of Surgeons in 1807, Richardson enlisted in the Royal Navy. Retired on half pay in 1815, he studied mineralogy under Robert Jameson, professor of natural history, U of Edinburgh, and obtained his MD in 1816. He joined both overland Franklin expeditions (1819-22 and 1825-27) as surgeon and naturalist, and commanded a search party looking for Sir John FRANKLIN (1848-49). Richardson's 1851 book on his own arctic searching expedition contains a summary of his previous work on the physical geography of present northwestern Canada as well as a geological map. His reputation as an accomplished naturalist rests largely on his contributions to the *Flora Boreali-Americana* and the 4-volume *Fauna Boreali-Americana*. Richardson presented what probably was the first GEOLOGY course in British N America to Franklin's officers at Great Bear Lk in the winter of 1825-26. W.O. KUPSCH

Richardson, John, soldier, writer (b at Queenston, Upper Canada 4 Oct 1796; d at New York 12 May 1782). Richardson's most enduring work, WACOUSTA; OR, THE PROPHECY (1832) is set at the time of PONTIAC's uprising and relates a complex story of betrayal, disguise and slaughter. Reginald Morton, the renegade Scot turned Indian leader, Wacousta, comes to represent the author's perception of the terror and savagery lurking in the Canadian wilderness. The smoother villain, Colonel De Haldimar, demonstrates how much repression, hypocrisy and cold-blooded evil is possible within the civilized garrison. As a youth, Richardson had fought in the WAR OF 1812 alongside TECUMSEH. His attempts to pursue successfully a career first as a soldier and then as a Canadian writer and journalist came to nothing. Except for his incomplete history, *The War of 1812* (1842), his other works remain of slight value. Departing from Canada about 1849, he sought a literary career in New York where he died impoverished. *Wacousta,* however, remains in print in an abridged version. Adapted for the stage in its own day, it was also dramatized by James REANEY in 1979.

DENNIS DUFFY

Richelieu, Rivière, or Richelieu R, almost 130 km long, flows from Lake Champlain in the US northward to the St Lawrence R near Lac St-Pierre. Located in the southeastern corner of Québec, the river is often referred to in two parts — the Upper and Lower Richelieu ("le Haut et Bas Richelieu"). The southern portion of the river, the Upper Richelieu, is bordered by the cities and towns of ST-JEAN-SUR-RICHELIEU, IBERVILLE, Chambly, Beleoil and Mont St-Hilaire. A set of rapids extends from Saint-Jean to CHAMBLY. Thereon the Lower Richelieu continues its course through smaller, albeit perhaps more picturesque communities such as St-Charles-sur-Richelieu, St-Denis and St-Ours. The Lower Richelieu then extends to the mouth or junction of the river with the St Lawrence at the city of SOREL.

The Rivière Richelieu has played a prominent role in the historical development of Québec. Originally inhabited by Iroquois, Huron and Algonquin, Samuel de CHAMPLAIN navigated its water shortly after his arrival in 1608. Throughout the French regime the Richelieu, named after Cardinal Richelieu, was of great military importance. The French established numerous forts along it, including Isle-aux-Noix (Fort Lennox), Fort St-Jean, Fort Ste-Thérèse, Fort St-Louis (Fort Chambly) and Fort de Richelieu (Sorel). Owing to the fertile nature of the land and its defences, French Canadian farmers settled here. Following the British Conquest, 1759-60, and the American Revolution, British military and LOYALIST settlers joined the area's local populations. Benedict ARNOLD's invasion of British N America included the capture of British forts along its route. Several uprisings of the REBELLION OF 1837-38, including the battles at ST-DENIS and ST-CHARLES, took place along its shores.

The Richelieu was of significant economic importance in the 19th century. In 1843-44, the Chambly Canal was constructed, bypassing the rapids and making the river transport of such products as wood, pulp, hay and coal from the US to Montréal more direct. Consequently the regional centres of Sorel and St-Jean grew and were incorporated as towns in the 1850s. The construction of railway lines from the US to Montréal in this same period, however, contributed to the eventual decline of the river's traffic. The economic influence of the region thus changed from commerce to industry in the later 19th and 20th centuries. The Richelieu R valley nonetheless retains some importance as an agricultural base, yielding some of the province's finest produce, as well as maintaining a military and industrial presence. A division of Parks Canada's Québec region deals solely with the Richelieu R valley and conducts archaeological excavations at FORT CHAMBLY, Fort Lennox and supervises the operations of the Chambly Canal.

KATHLEEN LORD

Richler, Mordecai, writer (b at Montréal 27 Jan 1931). One of Canada's foremost novelists, a controversial and prolific journalist, and an occasional scriptwriter, Richler was educated at Sir George Williams Coll, Montréal. After a 2-year stay in Paris and Spain (1951-52), he took up residence in England in 1954, returning to live in Montréal in 1972. Richler securely established himself as an accomplished novelist with the publication of The APPRENTICESHIP OF DUDDY KRAVITZ (1959). A scintillating portrait of a young Montréal-Jewish entrepreneur, the novel is characterized by an energizing authorial ambivalence and a contrast between the comic and the pathetic, by rich dramatic scenes, by a lively narrative pace, and by a comprehensive depiction of the protagonist as Montréaler, Jew and individual. Richler's earlier novels, *The Acrobats* (1954), *Son of a Smaller Hero* (1955) and *A Choice of Enemies* (1957), are essentially apprenticeship pieces portraying young, intense protagonists absorbed with finding proper values in a corrupt world.

Richler's considerable talent for the comic is displayed in *The Incomparable Atuk* (1963), a zany piece on Canadian nationalism, and in *Cocksure* (1968), a comical-satirical account of the difficulty of adhering to traditional values in a world gone mad. *St. Urbain's Horseman* (1971) and *Joshua Then and Now* (1980) are ambitiously conceived novels that incorporate and go beyond the settings, characters and concerns of the preceding novels. *St. Urbain's Horseman* examines the personal, professional and ethnic experiences of a 37-year-old man subjected to intense, contradictory feelings, who, Richler has stated, is "closer to me than anybody else." *Joshua Then and Now* employs a complex pattern of flashbacks to explore the possessive nature of the past, the ironical inversions caused by the passage of time, and the sad aspects of mutability. *Jacob Two-Two Meets the Hooded Fang* (1975) tells of the difficulties experienced by the young child in an adult world.

Richler has published over 300 journalistic pieces in a wide range of publications in Canada, the US and Britain. He published selections in *Hunting Tigers Under Glass* (1968), *The Street* (1969), *Shovelling Trouble* (1972), *Notes on an Endangered Species* (1974) and *Home Sweet Home: My Canadian Album* (1984). His periodic ventures into scriptwriting, which he approaches with less fervour than his journalism, have produced such scripts as *Life at the Top* (1965), *The Apprenticeship of Duddy Kravitz* (1974) and *Fun with Dick and Jane* (1977). His many awards include a Gov Gen's Award (1972), a Screenwriters Guild of America Award (1974) and a Ruth Schwartz Children's Book Award (1976). VICTOR RAMRAJ

Richmond, BC, District Municipality, pop 96 154 (1981c), area 16 807 ha, inc as a township 1879, is located adjacent to and S of VANCOUVER and W of NEW WESTMINSTER. It comprises 2 large islands, Lulu I and Sea I, and several smaller ones in the delta of the FRASER R. The 2 main islands are protected by 64 km of dikes skirting the 3 arms of the Fraser R. Richmond is governed by a mayor and 8 aldermen.

History The area's first inhabitants were Coast SALISH, though they mainly visited the islands on fishing trips. In 1861 Col R.C. Moody, in surveying southern BC and selecting townsites on the Fraser R, named Sea I and Lulu I, the latter after an American actress called Lulu Street. Hugh McRoberts became the first settler in 1862, purchasing 648 ha on Sea I. He called his farm Richmond View after his former home in Australia — perhaps the origin of the present name. A slow but steady migration of farmers to the islands began and by 1879 the area had 30 families. During this period the port of Steveston developed to take advantage of salmon at the mouth of the Fraser R. At one time it boasted 49 canneries. The first bridge connecting Richmond with the mainland was built 1889 and by 1902 a railway link existed. With improved connections over the years, Richmond has become primarily a residential area within Greater Vancouver. Vancouver International Airport was built on Sea I in 1931. The JAPANESE have played an important role, especially in the fishing and canning industry. Today there are more than 2000 Japanese in Richmond, and Steveston is one of the largest Canadian centres of Japanese culture.

Economy In its early years, Richmond's agriculture and fishing made it Vancouver's "bread basket." Two large fish-processing plants in Steveston and Richmond's rich alluvial farmlands continue to be productive, but the district has become increasingly residential. Today the largest employer is the international airport. Proximity to the US along Hwy 99 has also made tourism important.

Townscape The most popular landmark in Richmond is the Minoru Chapel, built 1890 and restored 1968 as a historic site to commemorate the official "twinning" of Richmond and Pierrefonds, Québec. The Steveston Salmon Festival is held on 1 July. ALAN F.J. ARTIBISE
Reading: B. Richards, *Exploring Richmond* (1979); L.J. Ross, *Richmond: Child of the Fraser* (1979).

Richmond and Lennox, Charles Lennox, 4th Duke of, soldier, administrator, governor-in-chief of Canada (b Eng 9 Sept 1764; d near Richmond, UC 28 Aug 1819). After an undistinguished career in the British army, he sat as an MP in the British House of Commons 1790-1806 until he inherited the dukedom of Richmond. After serving as lord lieutenant of Ireland 1807-13, he was appointed governor-in-chief of British N America in 1818. The year after his arrival in Canada, Richmond set out on a tour of the area's internal communications and defences. Bitten by his pet fox, he developed rabies and died suddenly. DAVID EVANS

Ricker, William Edwin, fishery and aquatic biologist (b at Waterdown, Ont 11 Aug 1908). Ricker is widely recognized as Canada's fore-

Novelist Mordecai Richler has received the Gov Gen's Award twice (*photo by Martha Kaplan*).

most fishery scientist. Through his work with the Fisheries Research Board of Canada and the Pacific Biological Station in Nanaimo, BC, he has achieved world acclaim for original contributions in the study of fish population dynamics and many other aspects of biological research fundamental to fisheries management. Educated at U of T, he joined the FRB and then was professor of zoology at Indiana U 1939-50 before returning to the FRB. During his career, Ricker authored over 200 publications. He is best known for *Computation and Interpretation of Biological Statistics of Fish Populations* (1975) and for his development of new concepts of the relationship between parent fish stock size and the number of resulting progeny: *Stock and Recruitment* (1954). Both publications have been widely used in the management of national and international fisheries important to Canada and both won him awards from the North American Wildlife Soc. He is noted as a limnologist for his theories on lake circulation and in the field of entomology as a world authority on Plecoptera, or stoneflies. Self-taught in Russian, he has done much to create an awareness of Soviet fishery science in the Western world through translations and by publishing a *Russian-English Dictionary* for students of fisheries and aquatic biology (1973). Ricker was elected fellow of the RSC 1956 and has received many awards and medals as well as 2 honorary degrees.

K.S. KETCHEN

Ricketts, Thomas, soldier, pharmacist (b at Middle Arm, White Bay, Nfld 15 Apr 1901; d at St John's 10 Feb 1967). Ricketts enlisted in Sept 1916, left for Europe early in 1917, and was wounded late that year. He was awarded the Victoria Cross for action near Ledgeham, Belgium, on 14 Oct 1918, the youngest winner of the award in the British army and the only recipient from the Newfoundland Regiment.

RALPH DALE

Riddell, Walter Alexander, scholar, public servant (b at Stratford, Ont 5 Aug 1881; d in Algonquin Park, Ont 27 July 1963). He served as deputy minister of labour in Ontario before joining the International Labour Organization in Geneva in 1920. In 1925 he became Canadian advisory officer at the League of Nations. A strong believer in collective security, he acted without instructions in 1935 in proposing oil sanctions against Italy, which had invaded Ethiopia. Repudiated by PM KING's government in this "Riddell incident," he was subsequently posted to Washington and New Zealand. He became professor of international relations at U of T and published a memoir, *World Security by Conference,* and books on international relations.

ROBERT BOTHWELL

Rideau Canal, 200 km long, links the Ottawa R at Ottawa with Lk Ontario at Kingston. Conceived as the major component of an alternative route for military purposes between Montréal and Kingston, the canal was first proposed as the War of 1812 drew to its close. Construction started (1826) to the design, and under the direction, of Lt-Col John BY. About 50 dams were necessary to control the water levels at rapids on the Rideau and Cataraqui rivers. The 47 locks in use raise vessels 83 m from the Ottawa R to the portage channel at Newboro, whence vessels descend 54 m to Lk Ontario at Kingston. The canal was built in virgin forest, all work being done by hand, and caused great hardship to its Irish labourers, many of whom died of malaria. Finished in 1832 after 5 summer working seasons, with up to 2000 men being employed by the Royal Engineers and appointed contractors, the canal ranks among the greatest early civil-engineering works of N America. By located his headquarters at the junction of the Ottawa and Rideau rivers, and started a small settlement,

first named Bytown in his honour but renamed Ottawa in 1855. Although it carried freight and passengers in small steamboats for a century, the Rideau Canal was never economically viable, and is now used entirely by pleasure craft. Its stone walls, ponds and bridges have preserved a quiet beauty along its course through the city of Ottawa, and in the wintertime it provides one of the world's most famous skating rinks. Its 150th anniversary of service was celebrated during the summer of 1982.

ROBERT LEGGET

Rideau Hall, located in Ottawa, is the residence of the GOVERNOR GENERAL. The original stone house was built in 1838 by Thomas MacKay, contractor on the Rideau Canal, on his 100 acre estate overlooking the Ottawa and Rideau rivers. MacKay designed the house himself, in the style of a Regency villa. In 1864 the MacKay estate was leased to be used as the temporary residence for the governor general and the villa was enlarged by 3 or 4 times, 1865-68, during the residency of Lord Monck. The house was finally purchased by the government in 1868 for $82 000, and a conservatory and iron gates were added.

Rideau Hall, the governor general's residence, shown in 1880 (*courtesy Public Archives of Canada / C-3884*).

Rideau Lakes, 65 km², elev 123 m, mean depth 12.3 m, is a commonly used collective name for 3 lakes: Big Rideau, Upper Rideau and Lower Rideau. They are located near the height of land on the RIDEAU CANAL system between Kingston and Ottawa in eastern Ontario. Their natural drainage is to the NE, by way of the Rideau R through the town of SMITHS FALLS. Located on the Frontenac axis of the Canadian SHIELD, the lakes are studded with islands and their surrounding shores are rocky. They are used almost entirely for recreational activities such as boating and cottaging; their common sport fish are largemouth and smallmouth bass, northern pike, lake trout and yellow perch. The waterway through these lakes was originally an Indian canoe route. The intent of making it navigable for larger craft was strategic. Col BY built the canal 1826-32, primarily to provide access from Montréal to Kingston for troops and supplies, along a route that would be free of risk from American attack. The name of the lakes is derived from a waterfall at the mouth of the Rideau R that early French explorers named for its resemblance to a curtain.

FREDERICK M. HELLEINER

Reading: K.M. Wells, *Cruising the Rideau Waterway* (1965).

Rideout, Patricia Irene, contralto (b at Saint John 16 Mar 1931). An opera singer, concert soloist and recitalist, Rideout has performed extensively across Canada. The interpreter of many roles from the standard repertoire, among them Suzuki in *Madama Butterfly,* Bianca in Britten's *The Rape of Lucretia* and Mercedes in *Carmen,* she has also participated in the premieres of several operas by Canadian composers. Performances in major choral works with most of Canada's leading orchestras and choral societies have won her much acclaim. She is a fine and committed performer of contemporary music and has introduced N American and European audiences to many new Canadian works, including Bruce MATHER's *Madrigals III,* written for her. Several of these performances of new music have been recorded.

BARCLAY McMILLAN

Riding Mountain National Park (est 1929, 2970 km²) is located 272 km NW of Winnipeg, perched almost 500 m above the PRAIRIE on the Manitoba Escarpment. The park is a rolling landscape of mixed forests and grasslands dotted with lakes, streams and bogs. In many ways, the park is a blend of Canada's North, West and East with elements of the boreal forest, prairie and mixed deciduous woods present. Within its varied habitats, 233 species of birds, 60 kinds of mammals and at least 10 species of reptiles and amphibians thrive. Bison, elk, moose, wolf, beaver, black bear and white-tailed deer are the park's largest denizens. Cree and Assiniboine first entered the park area, which they favoured for hunting, 1200 years ago. By 1800 the highland was surrounded by fur-trading posts. Later, local settlers used the park's resources for timber, cattle grazing, hunting and recreation. Riding Mountain provides facilities for tent and recreational-vehicle camping, and over 300 km of hiking and riding trails are available.

LILLIAN STEWART

Ridout, Godfrey, composer, teacher, writer, conductor (b at Toronto 6 May 1918; d there 24 Nov 1984). A student of Peaker, Mazzoleni, Kilburn and WILLAN, Ridout began teaching at the Toronto Conservatory of Music in 1940. At the Faculty of Music, U of T, from 1948 until his retirement in 1982, he guided some of Canada's best-known musicians. He was music director (1949-58) of the Eaton Operatic Soc in Toronto and long associated with the Toronto Gilbert & Sullivan Soc. His compositions, ranging from chamber music and symphonic pieces to scores for radio drama and film, are professional and tuneful. His interest in Healey Willan, the English Edwardian composers and in church music was evident in his works for voice and orchestra.

MABEL H. LAINE

Riel, Louis, Métis leader, founder of Manitoba, central figure in the NORTH-WEST REBELLION (b at Red River Settlement [Man] 22 Oct 1844; d at Regina 16 Nov 1885). Riel was educated at St-Boniface and studied for the priesthood at the Collège de Montréal. In 1865 he studied law with Rodolophe La Flamme, and he is believed to have worked briefly in Chicago, Ill, and St Paul, Minn, returning to St-Boniface in 1868.

In 1869, the federal government, anticipating the transfer of Red River and the North-West from the HBC to Canadian jurisdiction, appointed William McDOUGALL as lieutenant-governor of the new territory and sent survey crews to Red River. The Métis, fearful of the implications of the transfer, wary of the aggressive Anglo-Protestant immigrants from Ontario, and still suffering economically from the grasshopper plague of 1867-68, organized a "National Committee" of which Riel was secretary. Riel's education and his father's history marked him out as an obvious leader. The committee halted the surveys and prevented McDougall from entering Red River. On Nov 2 Ft Garry was seized, HBC officials offering no resistance. The committee then invited the people of Red River, both English and French speaking, to send delegates to Ft Garry. While they were discussing a "List of Rights" prepared by Riel, a group of Canadians, led by John Christian SCHULTZ and John Stoughton Dennis, organized an armed resistance. Meanwhile, the federal government postponed the transfer, planned for Dec 1 and Dennis and McDougall returned to Canada. When Schultz and his men surrendered to Riel, he imprisoned them in Ft Garry, issued a "Declaration of the People of Rupert's Land and the Northwest," and on Dec 23 became head of the "provisional government" of Red River. The Canadian government sent special commissioners "of goodwill" to Red River: Abbé J.B. Thibault, Col Charles de Salaberry and Donald A. SMITH, chief representative of the HBC in Canada. Smith persuaded Riel to summon a general meeting, at which it was decided to hold a convention of 40 representatives of the Settlement, equally divided between English and French speakers. Its first meeting was Jan 26. The delegates debated a new "List of Rights" and endorsed Riel's provisional government. The Canadian prisoners taken in Dec were released (some had escaped earlier) and plans were made to send 3 delegates to Ottawa to negotiate the entry of Red River into CONFEDERATION.

Meanwhile a force of some of the Canadians who had escaped, mustered by Schultz and surveyor Thomas SCOTT and led by Canadian militia officer Charles Boulton, gathered at Portage la Prairie, hoping to enlist support in the Scottish parishes of Red River. The appearance of this armed force alarmed the Métis who promptly rounded them up and imprisoned them again in Ft Garry. The Métis convened a court martial at which Boulton was condemned to death. Smith intervened, however, and the sentence was remitted. But, at a court martial presided over by Riel's associate, Ambroise Lépine, the obstreperous Scott was sentenced to death. This time Smith's appeals were rejected and Scott was executed by firing squad on 4 Mar 1870.

Bishop A.A. TACHÉ of St-Boniface, summoned from the 1870 Ecumenical Council in Rome, reached Red River 4 days after Scott's death, bringing a copy of the federal proclamation of amnesty which he believed included any actions up to that date. Taché persuaded Riel's council to free all prisoners and send the delegates to Ottawa. Despite opposition from the Orange Lodges of Ontario, of which Thomas Scott had been a member, Riel's delegates obtained an agreement, embodied in the MANITOBA ACT passed 12 May 1870, and the transfer was set for 15 July. In addition, the federal government agreed to a land grant of 1 400 000 acres (566 580 ha) for the Métis and to bilingual services for the new province. Other than verbal assurances, there was no specific mention of the amnesty, however.

To reassure Ontario and support administration of the new lieutenant-governor A.G. Archibald, the federal government sent a military force to Red River under Col Garnet WOLSELEY in the summer of 1870. Though the "Red River Expedition" was supposed to be "a mission of peace," Riel had reason to fear its arrival and fled to the US. Later he returned quietly to his home at St-Vital and, when the province was threatened with a FENIAN raid from the US in the autumn of 1871, offered a force of Métis cavalry to Archibald.

In Ontario, however, Riel was widely denounced as Thomas Scott's "murderer" and a reward of $5000 was offered for his arrest. In Québec he was regarded as a hero, a defender of the Roman Catholic faith and French culture in Manitoba. Anxious to avoid a political confrontation with the 2 principal provinces of Canada, Sir John A. MACDONALD tried to per-

Even after a century, Métis leader Louis Riel's execution excites political debate, especially in Québec and Manitoba (*courtesy Provincial Archives of Manitoba*).

suade Riel to remain in voluntary exile in the US, even providing him with funds. But, encouraged by his friends, Riel entered federal politics. Successful in a by-election in 1873 and in the general election of 1874, Riel went to Ottawa and signed the register but was expelled from the House on a motion introduced by the Ontario Orange leader Mackenzie BOWELL. Although re-elected, Riel did not attempt to take his seat again. Meanwhile Ambroise Lépine was arrested, tried and condemned to death for the "murder" of Thomas Scott. Subsequently, his sentence was commuted to 2 years' imprisonment and loss of political rights. In Feb 1875 the federal government finally adopted a motion granting amnesty to Riel and Lépine, conditional on 5 years' banishment from "Her Majesty's dominions."

Shortly after, Riel suffered a nervous breakdown and was admitted to hospital at Longue Pointe (Montréal) as "Louis R. David," and later transferred to the mental asylum at Beauport, Qué, as "Louis La Rochelle." Always introspective by nature and strongly religious, Riel became obsessed with the idea that his was a religious mission — to establish a new N American Catholicism with Bishop BOURGET of Montréal as Pope of the New World. Released in Jan 1878, he spent some time in Keeseville, NY, and then set out for the Upper Missouri region of Montana territory where he engaged in trade, joined the Republican Party, became an American citizen, and married a Métis, Marguerite Monet, *dit* Bellehumeur. In 1883 he became a schoolteacher at St Peter's mission on the Sun R and in June 1884 was asked by a group of Canadian Métis to help them obtain their legal rights in the Saskatchewan valley.

Early in July Riel and his family reached BATOCHE, the main centre of Métis settlement in Saskatchewan. He conducted a peaceful agitation, speaking throughout the district and preparing a petition. Sent to Ottawa in Dec, Riel's petition was acknowledged and the federal government promised to appoint a commission to investigate and report on western problems.

Early in 1885, however, Riel encountered opposition in Saskatchewan because of his unorthodox religious views, old memories of Thomas Scott's execution, and his reiteration of his personal claims against the federal government (which he estimated at $35 000) which suggested self-interest as the motive behind his political activity. His exasperation mounted and

he began to contemplate direct action. But 1885 was not 1870 when Wolseley had taken several months to lead a military force to Ft Garry. By 1885 the North-West Mounted Police had been established and a railway to the West almost completed. Nevertheless, convinced that God was directing him, and seeing himself as the "Prophet of the New World," on March 19 Riel seized the parish church at Batoche, armed his men, formed a provisional government and demanded the surrender of Ft Carlton. The ensuing fighting lasted scarcely 2 months before Riel surrendered.

On 6 July 1885, a formal charge of treason was laid against him and on 20 July his trial began at Regina. His counsel proposed to defend him on the grounds of insanity but Riel repudiated that defence and, in the face of damning statements by his cousin, Charles Nolin, who had opposed him in 1870 and deserted him in 1885, the jury found him guilty. However, they recommended clemency. The verdict was appealed to the Court of Queen's Bench of Manitoba and to the Judicial Committee of the Privy Council. Both appeals were dismissed, but public pressure, particularly from Québec, delayed execution pending an examination of Riel's mental state. The 3 examining physicians found Riel excitable but only one considered him insane. Owing to questionable excisions, the official version of the report did not reveal any difference of opinion and the federal Cabinet decided in favour of hanging. Riel was executed at Regina 16 Nov 1885. His body was sent to St-Boniface and interred in the cemetery in front of the cathedral.

Politically and philosophically, Riel's execution has had a lasting effect on Canadian history. In the West, the immediate result was to depress the lot of the Métis. In central Canada, FRENCH CANADIAN NATIONALISM was strengthened and Honoré MERCIER came to power in Québec in 1886. In the longer term Québec voters moved from their traditional support of the Conservative Party to the Liberal Party led by Wilfrid LAURIER. Even after a century, Riel and his fate excite political debate, particularly in Québec and Manitoba. Riel's execution has remained a contentious issue even today and demands have been made for a retroactive pardon. *See also* RED RIVER REBELLION.   GEORGE F.G. STANLEY

Reading: P. Charlebois, *The Life of Louis Riel* (1975); W.M. Davidson, *Louis Riel* (1955); T.E. Flanagan, *Louis "David" Riel: Prophet of the New World* (1979) and *Riel and the Rebellion, 1885 Reconsidered* (1983); the several volumes edited by Projet Riel Project to be published 1985-86 will contain all the known writings of Louis Riel; J.K. Howard, *Strange Empire* (1952); George F.G. Stanley, *Louis Riel* (1963).

Rigler, Frank Harold, biologist (b at London, Eng 9 June 1928; d at Montréal 26 June 1982). Educated at U of T, in 1957 he returned from postdoctoral study in England to the zoology department there. A world authority in aquatic biology, he directed an important Canadian contribution to the International Biological Program, a study of Char Lk in the High Arctic. In 1976 he moved to McGill's biology department as chairman and professor. Rigler believed that good science required sound philosophy and taught its importance to a generation of students. He was alarmed by environmental degradation and his advocacy of a more applicable ecology crystallized a long tradition in Canadian freshwater research that stresses practical theory based on observation rather than precepts; his later work on eutrophication control is an example. In his honour the Society of Canadian Limnologists instituted the F.H. Rigler Memorial Lectures in 1984.   ROBERT PETERS

Rimmer, David, filmmaker, photographer (b at Vancouver 20 Jan 1942). His experimental film works (primarily 1968-75) are generally held to exemplify a distinctive West Coast tradition distinguishable from the Toronto school, but, although definable differences do generally distinguish experimental filmmakers on the West Coast of the US from those in New York, the evidence is against making such distinctions in Canada. Many of Rimmer's films (*Surfacing on the Thames* 1971, *Seashore* 1971, *Watching for the Queen* 1973) are no less austere, have no more surface polish and are no more contemplative than the films of Torontonians Michael SNOW and Joyce WIELAND, and most are produced using rudimentary rather than advanced technologies. Rimmer's experimental films are painstakingly careful examinations of how film constructs the illusions of movement, depth, continuity and audience presence at the situation depicted. In 1979 Rimmer released *Al Neil*, an innovative performance documentary, and he has been working mainly in that genre since. However, in 1980 he completed *Narrows Inlet*, a delicate study of the sea and landscape near Vancouver.   R. BRUCE ELDER

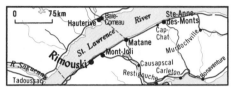

Rimouski, Qué, City, pop 29 120 (1981c), inc 1869, is located on the S shore of the ST LAWRENCE R, 300 km NE of Québec City. Greater Rimouski, with 50 000 inhabitants, is the most populous area of eastern Québec. The charming city is built on 3 levels, in the shape of an amphitheatre. A seigneury was granted here in 1688, but it was not settled until 1696. In the 18th century, agriculture and seasonal fishing were the only occupations, but the area experienced some growth when Québec City merchants, including William Price, began to develop the forest resources and built several sawmills. The parish of St-Germain was established 1829; a courthouse was added 1857 and a bishop's seat in 1867. The arrival of the railway made the town a centre for expansion into the GASPÉ and Matapédia. Its economy was based on the forest industry and services such as trade, teaching and government and church administration. After a terrible fire in 1950, the town experienced more rapid growth. It became the regional capital when several federal and provincial government departments opened offices to serve the Lower St Lawrence and the Gaspé. Today the economy is based largely on long-standing activities: schools, a university and health and social services. The town is now a major centre for oceanographic research.   ANTONIO LECHASSEUR

Rindisbacher, Peter, painter (b at Eggiwil, Upper Emmenthal, Switz 12 Apr 1806; d at St Louis, Mo 13 Aug 1834). Allegedly a Swiss army drummer boy, Rindisbacher immigrated with his family to the RED RIVER COLONY in 1821. He painted views of the HBC forts along the route from York Factory to the colony, leaving the only visual record of them, and the earliest pictorial record of the country W of the Great Lakes. He spent 5 years in the colony, contributing to family support by selling paintings of prairie and Indian life to HBC officers. Some of these, described as "taken by a gentleman on the spot" in 1823 and 1824, were lithographed and published in London, Eng, in 1824 and 1825. In 1826, repeated hardships finally drove the family to the US. Rindisbacher died at age 28, just as he was gaining success as a portrait artist.   JAMES MARSH

A War Party at Fort Douglas, watercolour by Peter Rindisbacher, who left the only pictorial record of the forts en route to the Red River Colony (*courtesy Royal Ontario Museum*).

Ringwood, Gwendolyn, née Pharis, playwright (b at Anatone, Wash 13 Aug 1910; d near Williams Lake, BC 24 May 1984). Ringwood was western Canada's regional dramatist par excellence. Her prairie tragedy, *Still Stands the House* (1939), is one of the most frequently anthologized and performed Canadian plays. A pioneer of western community theatre, she began her career as secretary to the U of A Extension director of drama, and wrote and produced her first stage play, *The Dragons of Kent*, in 1935 when she was registrar of the new Banff School of Fine Arts. She polished her playwriting skills at U of N Carolina drama dept, where she wrote numerous folk plays, culminating in *Dark Harvest*. She received the Gov Gen's Award for outstanding service to Canadian drama (1941), and published the first volume of collected plays in 1982 by a Canadian dramatist. The Gwen Pharis Ringwood Civic Theatre (1971), Williams Lake, BC, is named for her.   ROTA HERZBERG LISTER

Riopelle, Jean-Paul, painter, sculptor (b at Montréal 7 Oct 1923). An original member of the AUTOMATISTES, he is the most internationally acclaimed Canadian painter of the 20th century. While a student of Paul-Émile BORDUAS at the École du Meuble, Riopelle met with other artists to discuss surrealism, political radicalism and psychoanalysis. In 1946 he exhibited in Montréal along with Borduas and several others, marking the inception of the Automatistes on Canadian soil and the first show in Canada by a group of abstract painters. Under the influence of surrealism, with its emphasis on the "liberation of the human spirit," Riopelle moved from figurative painting to the gestural abstractions for which he is now famous. After WWII, against the growing standardization and depersonalization of industrial capitalism, Riopelle's paintings were characterized by personal improvisation and "raw" gestures that attested to the uniquely human process by which they were made. To increase the spontaneity of his art, he used several experimental techniques: supple gestural brushstrokes (1946-49); the controlled drip technique of squeezing paint directly from the tube onto the canvas (*c*1950); and, in the early 1950s, the use of the palette knife to create mosaiclike surfaces of paint — a hallmark of his later style.

Riopelle went to Paris in 1947, participated in

the Automatiste exhibition at the Galerie du Luxembourg, and signed the surrealist manifesto *Ruptures inaugurales*. International recognition came quickly. He was singled out by critic Michel Tapié and surrealist leader André Breton. In 1948 Riopelle returned briefly to Montréal where he signed REFUS GLOBAL, the cover of which featured one of his ink drawings. After returning to Paris in 1948, Riopelle increasingly gained recognition. A high point of this fame came in 1962 when Riopelle was given the UNESCO Award. He was honoured in 1963 with a retrospective exhibition at the Art Gallery of Ontario.   DAVID L. CRAVEN

Reading: David L. Craven and Richard Leslie, "The Automatic Paintings of Jean-Paul Riopelle," *Artscanada* 240/241 (1981) and "Jean-Paul Riopelle's Art of Affirmation," *Artscanada* 248/249 (1982).

Riot Under the Criminal Code (s64), an unlawful assembly is created when 3 or more persons, with intent to carry out any common purpose, assemble in such a manner or conduct themselves in such a fashion as to cause persons in the neighbourhood of the assembly to fear, on reasonable grounds, that the persons assembled or others reacting to the assembly will disturb the peace tumultuously. A riot is defined (s65) as an unlawful assembly that has in fact begun to disturb the peace tumultuously. The term "riot" is often used to describe the behaviour of people who are intending to use collective violence to achieve some unlawful aim. Technically, however, the term riot can include street parades, boisterous parties and demonstrations that have been held to be unlawful assemblies. If there is evidence that the peace has been disturbed tumultuously, these activities fall within the definition of a riot. Everyone who takes part in a riot is guilty of an indictable offence and liable to imprisonment for 2 years.

Where a riot involving 12 or more people is in progress, a justice, mayor, sheriff or deputy sheriff is authorized to order the rioters to disperse in the name of the queen. Failure to do so within 30 minutes, or hindering or obstructing the person who is making the proclamation (ie, "reading the Riot Act") is yet another offence, with punishment of up to life imprisonment. The proclamation has been used a number of times in Canadian history, eg, in Montréal in 1832 when a riot ensued during a by-election and in

Winnipeg during the WINNIPEG GENERAL STRIKE of 1919.

Many social scientists agree that collective violence of the sort labelled "riot" should be conceived of as a collective act of resistance to established authority and perceived injustice, but others argue that the notion of "riot" is not a legitimate concept but an ideological one used by those in power to denigrate resistance to their authority. Within the legal system, the term "riot" has a much broader meaning and is not necessarily linked to a notion of resistance to authority or perceived injustice. CLIFFORD SHEARING

Ritchie, Albert Edgar, diplomat (b at Andover, NB 20 Dec 1916). A Rhodes scholar who worked for the British government and UN in the 1940s, Ritchie was a member of the Dept of External Affairs, 1944-46, 1948-80. His expertise was economics, his judgement and integrity impeccable. He was assistant undersecretary, 1959-64, and deputy undersecretary, 1964-66, before serving in the department's 2 top posts: ambassador to Washington 1964-70 and undersecretary 1970-74. A companion of the Order of Canada, he was appointed ambassador to Ireland in 1976. ANNE HILLMER

Ritchie, Charles Stewart Almon, diplomat, author (b at Halifax 23 Sept 1906). Ritchie joined the Dept of External Affairs in 1934, rising to assistant (later deputy) undersecretary, 1950-54. Restless in Ottawa, he escaped to Germany as ambassador 1954-58, and subsequently held the top posts in Canada's diplomatic service — ambassador to the UN 1958-62, to the US 1962-66, to NATO and the EEC, 1966-67, and high commissioner to the UK, 1967-71. Ritchie had grown up wanting to be an author, and he kept diaries from an early age. Four volumes have been published since his retirement: *The Siren Years* (1974; Gov Gen's Award), *An Appetite for Life* (1977), *Diplomatic Passport* (1981) and *Storm Signals* (1983). The diaries, like the man, are cool, elegant, cyncial about human nature but generous to individuals. NORMAN HILLMER

Ritchie, Eliza, educator, feminist (b at Halifax 20 May 1856; d there 5 Sept 1933). Ritchie graduated from Dalhousie in 1887 and 2 years later obtained her PhD from Cornell, probably the first Canadian woman to secure a doctorate. After further study at Leipzig, Germany, and Oxford she taught at Wellesley College, Mass. In 1901 she returned to teach philosophy at Dalhousie. A strong suffragist, she quickly joined sisters Mary and Ella in leadership positions in the Victoria School of Fine Art, the VON and the local Council of Women. With Agnes DENNIS and Edith ARCHIBALD she dominated the feminist movement in Halifax until the end of WWI. She showed tact in working with other women, was noted for the clarity of her writing style, and displayed a commitment to a Maritime region. Her appointment to the Dalhousie board of governors in 1919 was hailed as another first in Canada. Her publications include *The Problem of Personality* (1889) and *Songs of the Maritimes* (1931). ERNEST R. FORBES

Ritchie, Octavia Grace, married name England, physician, educator (b at Montréal 16 Jan 1868; d there 1 Feb 1948). Though a brilliant student, she was at first refused admission to McGill, but Principal Sir J.W. DAWSON relented when Donald A. SMITH provided $50 000 for women's education there. In 1888, as the first female valedictorian at McGill, she boldly but unsuccessfully demanded admission to the Faculty of Medicine. Having then entered Kingston Women's Medical Coll, she later transferred to and graduated from Bishop's, becoming the first women to receive a medical degree in Québec (1891). Following study abroad she was appointed assistant gynecologist at Western Hospital, Montréal, and demonstrator in anatomy at Bishop's. She remained in practice and continued to be active in local, national and international groups promoting humanitarian causes and women's rights. MARGARET GILLETT

Reading: Margaret Gillett, *We Walked Very Warily: a History of Women at McGill* (1981).

Rivard, Lucien, convicted drug smuggler (b at Montréal? 1915?). An underworld figure of no great consequence, he was arrested in Montréal in 1965 on narcotics charges filed by US authorities. While fighting extradition, he escaped from jail after obtaining a garden hose "to flood the skating rink" on a spring evening with the temperature above freezing. Allegedly, Rivard used the hose to climb the wall and was at large for 4 months. During that time, charges of bribery connected with the escape created a scandal for the federal Liberal government. A royal commission looked into the "Rivard affair" and criticized Minister of Justice Guy FAVREAU, who resigned. Rivard was extradited to the US. Convicted of smuggling narcotics, he was sentenced to 20 years in prison. He served 9 years, and was then deported back to Canada. BILL CAMERON

River, a course of WATER, usually growing in volume between its source and its terminus in an OCEAN, a LAKE or another river. A stream or riverlet is smaller but the volumes involved are not closely defined. Most rivers have continuous although variable flow, but some may have no flow in very dry or very cold seasons. Streams, especially in drier and colder regions, are more prone to no-flow periods and many are intermittent. Rivers and streams with large GROUNDWATER inflow are usually less variable in flow than those dependent on surface runoff. Only GLACIATION has had more impact than running water in the shaping of the Earth's landforms.

The many features that make rivers different from one another can be grouped in the following categories: hydrologic regime, ICE regime, major geomorphological setting and dominant channel processes, channel materials and stability and channel dimensions. Almost all Canadian rivers are characterized by variable runoff that may be modified by extensive natural storage in lakes and muskeg. Similarly, most Canadian rivers are affected by ice during winter, except on the BC coast. Most rivers and streams in Canada occupy well-defined channels that they have developed since the last ICE AGE (within the last 6000-14 000 years for most areas). Several regions have experienced extensive glacial rebound, which has affected the present course of major rivers. Some are "misfit" in large spillway channels that were formed by glacial meltwaters. Rapids and WATERFALLS separating stretches of marshes and lakes occur where rock formations resistant to erosion are present, especially in SHIELD and CORDILLERAN regions (see PHYSIOGRAPHIC REGIONS). They are less common in areas of deep drift deposits and softer rock, as in the Interior Plains, where channels are more regular in gradient. Some rivers with heavy sediment loads are locally braided and many divide into distributary channels in DELTAS.

The rivers originating in Canada discharge approximately 98 000 m³/s (cubic metres per second) of flow to the ocean, ie, about 8% of world river discharge. The ST LAWRENCE and MACKENZIE rivers, each with approximately 10 000 m³/s, rank 16th and 17th among world rivers, 2nd and 3rd in N America. The Amazon is over 20 times as large as our largest river; the Mississippi about 75% larger. The St Lawrence and Mackenzie rivers are approximately equal in annual flow and arguments about which is larger depend upon semantic differences, such as where in the St Lawrence estuary the water becomes brackish, and if the Peel and other tributaries of the Mackenzie Delta, entering below where the main channel divides, should be counted. The

Principal Rivers and Their Basins

Drainage basin and river	Drainage area (km²)	Mean discharge (m³/s)
Pacific Ocean		
Columbia	155 000[a]	2 890
Fraser	233 000	3 620
Nass	20 700	892
Porcupine	55 700	368
Skeena	54 900	1 760
Stikine	49 200	1 080
Yukon	298 000[a]	2 360
Other	228 000	11 100
Arctic Ocean		
Back	107 000	612
Mackenzie	1 787 000	9 910
Other	1 663 000	5 890
Hudson Bay		
Albany	134 000[a]	1 420
Arnaud	49 500	654
Attawapiskat	50 200	626
Aux Feuilles	42 500	575
Churchill	298 000	1 270
Eastmain	46 400	909
George	41 700	881
Grande Rivière de la Baleine	42 700	665
Harricana	29 300	473
Hayes	108 000	694
Kazan	71 500	566
Koksoak	133 000	2 420
La Grande Rivière	97 600	1 720
Moose	109 000	1 440
Nelson	1 132 000[ab]	2 830
Nottaway	65 800	1 130
Rivière à la Baleine	31 900	581
Rupert	43 300	878
Severn	101 000	722
Thelon	142 000	804
Winisk	67 300	694
Other	1 173 000	8 950
Atlantic Ocean		
Aux Outardes	19 100	399
Churchill	79 800	1 620
Manicouagan	45 800	852
Moisie	19 200	490
Natashquan	16 100	422
Petit Mécatina	19 600	524
Saguenay	88 100	1 760
Saint John	55 400[a]	1 100
St Lawrence	1 026 000[a]	10 100
St Maurice	43 300	731
Other	624 000	15 400
Summary		
Arctic Ocean	3 557 000	16 400
Atlantic Ocean	2 036 000[a]	33 400
Gulf of Mexico	29 500[a]	25
Hudson Bay	4 010 000[ab]	30 900
Pacific Ocean	1 095 000[a]	24 100
	10 730 000[a]	105 000[a]

[a] including areas in the US
[b] including internal drainage

Mackenzie Basin is wholly Canadian and is 3.5 times as large as the Canadian portion of the St Lawrence Basin (see DRAINAGE BASINS). The Mackenzie (to the head of the Finlay R in BC) is the longest river in Canada (4241 km), followed by the St Lawrence (3058 km), Nelson (2575 km), Churchill (1609 km) and Fraser (1368 km). Tributaries such as the Saskatchewan (1939 km), Peace (1923 km), Ottawa (1271 km), Athabasca (1231 km) and Liard (1115 km) are also very long.

Almost 75% of Canada is drained northward to the Arctic Ocean, Hudson Bay and Hudson Str. According to data of the early 1970s, this northward drainage involved almost half (47.9%) of the total flow of Canada's rivers. Drainage to the Pacific (10.2% of the area) accounted for almost one quarter of the flow (23.5%); drainage to the Atlantic (15.2% of the area), for over one quarter (28.5%). A very small area is drained southward in the Missouri-Mississippi Basin. More recent measurements show that the earlier estimates for northern and Pacific regions and for Canada as a whole were too conservative, and that northern values especially might be increased substantially (possibly as much as 20% for some basins). Upward revisions might be expected as better, longer-term data become available. Canada has abundant freshwater supplies and, although regional shortages will be experienced, national shortages are unlikely.

Most of the rivers and streams of Canada have snowmelt regime patterns of flow. Winter snows, subject to very little evapotranspiration loss, provide the peak flows on melting in Mar-Apr in southern lowlands and in May-June, extending into July in higher mountain and northern areas. Summer RAINS are greater than winter snowfall in most regions but much of the rain is lost to evapotranspiration in summer and streamflow response is smaller (see CLIMATE). Some rivers at lower elevations in Pacific coastal areas have rainfall-based peaks of flow in midwinter. Glacier meltwater flows peak in midsummer but this pattern is not dominant for most of the larger mountain rivers. Natural storage in groundwater aquifers, lakes and marshes results in reduced peaks and more equable flow.

Artificial storage behind dams has contributed to major regime modification (see RESERVOIR). Much of the storage change is for HYDROELECTRIC power production and winter flow enhancement is widely present. Storage for peaking power purposes may result in low flows at night and on weekends and major surges in flow during periods of peak demand. Such flow modification, as on the Kananaskis R, Alta, may conflict greatly with recreation, WILDLIFE CONSERVATION and other objectives. Storage for irrigation purposes is usually for mid- to late-summer periods when natural flow is declining.

The larger Canadian rivers have some natural lag in flow because of the size of their basins and the distances travelled by streamflow to downstream stations. Most have been modified in regime and sometimes volume by artificial storage and diversion. Interbasin transfers, largely for hydroelectric power and irrigation, and growing diversions for urban, industrial and other uses have affected many rivers but the greatest impacts have been from the discharge of pollutants (see POLLUTION). Natural processes contributing dissolved and suspended materials to rivers and streams have always resulted in striking regional and seasonal differences in water quality. Canadian shield rivers tend to be low in sediment, dissolved solids, calcium carbonate and turbidity; PRAIRIE rivers are relatively high in each. Man has added, directly and indirectly, to these substances and chemical, physical and biological changes in water bodies have been apparent in many areas. Rivers and streams have been used as convenient means of WASTE DISPOSAL. The capacity of these water bodies to assimilate waste has been widely and carelessly exceeded. Most industrial, municipal, agricultural and mining waste disposal can be controlled at the source (see WATER TREATMENT). Nonpoint pollution such as that from the atmosphere (eg, ACID RAIN), storm sewers and ill-defined sources is more difficult to control. Good progress is being made in treatment of some wastes but the development of new chemical compounds is rapid; fortunately public awareness of new hazards is growing. See separate entries on rivers listed on accompanying table.

A.H. LAYCOCK

River Landform, feature resulting from the movement of WATER on the Earth's surface. In a geological context, flowing water is the most important external process shaping the Earth's surface. RIVER landforms may be depositional, eg, floodplains, river terraces, alluvial fans, pediments and DELTAS; or erosional, eg, the valleys, canyons and sculptured BADLANDS that provide some of Canada's most impressive scenery. River processes are especially important in regions ranging through semiarid, subhumid, humid, to very wet, but even in arid regions rare cloudbursts may accomplish a significant amount of geomorphic work. In the classic era of GEOMORPHOLOGY, which ended around 1950, fluvial (river) landforms were studied in the context of W.M. Davis's cycle of EROSION. The cycle concept is a simplistic but pedagogically effective way of looking at landscape development in a humid, temperate CLIMATE where river action dominates landscape sculpture (eg, southern Canada). Davis's theory states that, after initial uplift of a landmass, the landscape passes sequentially through the stages of youth, maturity and old age. Youth is characterized by V-shaped valleys and irregular gradients; maturity by long valley slopes, meandering streams and floodplain development; old age by sluggish streams, broad floodplains, oxbow LAKES and low hills called monadnocks. Such a landscape is shaped essentially through a combination of fluvial and slope-forming processes, leading eventually to the formation of a flat erosion surface or peneplain, close to sea level. Peneplanation may be followed by uplift, resulting in the initiation of a new cycle of erosion. Uplift before the cycle is completed leads to stream rejuvenation, entrenchment and stepped erosion levels. Valley morphology commonly reflects the controlling influence of bedrock GEOLOGY. Other important models in fluvial geomorphology have been proposed by Walther Penck (Germany) and L.C. King (South Africa). King's model emphasizes the role of pediment formation and pediplanation in semiarid climates. Modern research is exploring new conceptual approaches in the interpretation of fluvial landforms.

Fluvial activity has played a dominant role in shaping large segments of the Canadian landscape. The scenario is complex because most regions shaped by rivers now also bear the imprint of Quaternary GLACIATION. Many of the magnificent valleys that now dissect the CORDILLERA were formed by stream rejuvenation and entrenchment during Tertiary uplift (65-2.5 million years ago), eg, the Fraser, Thompson and Okanagan valleys in the Fraser-Nechako Plateau, BC. Some Cordilleran river valleys were also partly infilled with glacial/glaciofluvial detritus during the ICE AGES (2.5 million – 10 000 years ago), but subsequent postglacial downcutting has left a series of high-level river terraces, eg, Bow R, Alta. Terracing of valley fills is also common in central and eastern Canada.

The flattish PRAIRIES were formed by the long-continued deposition of rock waste eroded from the Cordillera by easterly flowing streams (with some contribution from glacial deposition). The modern streams that traverse the prairies (eg, Saskatchewan) are shallowly entrenched in youthful/early mature valleys to a maximum depth of several hundred metres. In some dry parts of Alberta the incision of streams into Cretaceous sediments (140-65 million years old) has created a badlands topography, as at Drumheller.

Most of the Canadian SHIELD had been bevelled by erosion/planation surfaces long before the advent of the Quaternary ice ages. The preglacial drainage patterns were deranged during the ice ages and valleys were buried under glacial drift, leaving a legacy of lakes. Some of the buried valleys are now being re-excavated by modern stream action. In central Canada, before the onset of the ice ages, the lowland area now occupied by the Great Lakes was drained by normal river systems. The present Great Lakes owe their origin to glaciation. Where Lk Erie now drains into Lk Ontario via the Niagara R, waters flow over an ESCARPMENT of Silurian rocks (425-395 million years old) giving rise to Niagara Falls and the downstream gorge. Farther E the waters drain from Lk Ontario into the St Lawrence R, where in the picturesque THOUSAND ISLANDS stretch the headward-cutting river has scoured an irregular Precambrian rock plain (an erosion surface over 600 million years old).

With its extensive coastline and many rivers and lakes, Canada has its share of deltaic landforms, eg, the deltas of the Mackenzie, Fraser and Red rivers (Lk Winnipeg).

Modern quantitative geomorphology considers fluvial landforms in an open-systems context. The fundamental unit, the DRAINAGE BASIN, is considered an open system with inputs (eg, rainfall, solar energy), throughputs and outputs (river flow, sediment) of energy and matter. The morphology of landforms within the basin develops as a process-response or internal adjustment to the varying inputs and outputs. This conceptual approach also involves the idea of systems equilibrium: if inputs and outputs remain appreciably constant, the morphology of the landscape should assume a time-independent form in which the ridges (of more resistant rock/structure) downwaste at the same rate as the river valleys. Drainage-network analysis, first introduced by the American R.E. Horton in 1945, is part of quantitative fluvial geomorphology. Networks can be considered under such headings as pattern (eg, dendritic, rectangular) and composition, the latter involving a study of the mathematical relationships between stream orders, lengths, numbers, gradients and valley slopes. The modern approach to fluvial systems, including landforms, emphasizes stream hydrology; hydraulic geometry of stream development; stream patterns (straight, meandering and braided); ice regimes; river mechanics and fluid turbulence; processes of erosion, transportation and deposition (scour-and-fill); bed-form development; and rates of basin denudation (sediment yields). In the field of applied geomorphology, quantitative criteria for the aesthetic comparison of riverscapes have also been devised for environmental impact assessment in connection with river development projects. Interpretation of the wide range of fluvial forms is important for the identification of desirable crossing locations for highways, pipelines and railways and for the prediction of bank stability and ice-jam locations. Finally, fluvial geomorphology has important implications for the exploration of placer deposits, and for water-management studies, flood control and river-basin management in general. See PHYSIOGRAPHIC REGIONS. ALAN V. JOPLING

Riverview, NB, Town, pop 14 097 (1981c), inc 1973, is situated on the Petitcodiac R opposite MONCTON. Formed by the amalgamation of the villages of Bridgedale, Gunningsville and Riverview Heights with the town of Coverdale, it is the product of the post-WWII growth of Moncton, to which it has been connected by bridge since the 1870s. Riverview is the largest municipality in Albert County, an area known for its gypsum and oil-shale resources and as the site of FUNDY NATIONAL PARK. Although boasting an industrial park, Riverview is mainly residential and the bulk of the populace finds employment in Moncton. DEAN JOBB

Rivière-du-Loup, Qué, City, pop 13 459 (1981c), inc 1874 under the name Fraserville, is located 200 km E of Québec City on the ST LAWRENCE R. Built at the mouth of the river of the same name, it sits on land that belonged to the former seigneuries of Rivière-du-Loup, de Verbois and du Parc, awarded in 1673 to Charles Aubert de La Chesnaye, the richest trader in New France. Rivière-du-Loup's development owes much to its location at the entrance to the Temiscouata Valley and portage. In 1783 the British administration built a military route through the town to facilitate communications with the other English colonies. Rivière-du-Loup became a major railway centre in the last 40 years of the 19th century, a terminal of the GRAND TRUNK RY (1860) and a departure point for the INTERCOLONIAL (1870) and the Temiscouata Ry (1887-88). The forestry, pulp and lumber, and tourist industries have been major factors in its economic development, especially after closure of the railway repair shops. The city still benefits from seasonal seaway links with the N Shore. Today, it has become a service-industry town, with emphasis on commerce, teaching and public administration. A paper mill employs several hundred people.   ANTONIO LECHASSEUR

Roads and Highways To a greater extent than most countries, Canada depends for its social, economic and political life on efficient communication and transportation.

History Canada's first highways were the rivers and lakes used by the native people, travelling by canoe in summer and following the frozen streams in winter. The water network was so practical that the explorers, settlers and soldiers followed the example of the Indians. There was negligible road development before the beginning of the 19th century, and the first graded road in Canada, built (1606) by Samuel de CHAMPLAIN, was a 16 km military road from PORT-ROYAL to Digby Cape, NS. By 1734 Québec City and Montréal were linked by a road and a carriage could be driven the 267 km in 4½ days. In the early days of NEW FRANCE, roads and bridges were the responsibility of a crown-appointed chief inspector, a system retained by the British until 1832. Roads were divided into 3 classes: main roads, 7.2 m wide; connecting roads to farms, 5.4 m wide; back roads, built on orders of the seigneurs (*see* SEIGNEURIAL SYSTEM).

Early roads in British North America were built out of military necessity, eg, the 60-km Yonge Street from York to Lk Simcoe (1796) blazed by the Queen's Rangers, commanded by Col John Graves SIMCOE, and Dundas Street from York to London, safely inland from Lk Erie. The concern of the state for roads set an early pattern. As early as 1801, the NB Assembly made regular grants for road construction. In 1793 an Act of the first Parliament of Upper Canada placed all roads under the supervision of overseers, called pathmasters, and required settlers to work 3 to 12 days each year on the roads. An appropriation for roads was made in 1804, a munificent £1000, doubled 12 years later. These early roads complemented rather than replaced water transport. Mostly little more than cleared paths, a few were planked or "corduroy" (made of logs laid side by side). Nevertheless, they provided valuable inland transportation (especially in winter), reduced costs and opened new areas to settlement.

Travel by road in early Canada was difficult and often hazardous. The roads were so bad that most people preferred horseback or walking rather than vehicle transportation. Settlers' vehicles were usually homemade and crude, wheels were cut from the round trunks of huge oak trees. Later came the Conestoga wagons for carrying heavy loads (some were 30 feet long, drawn by 6-horse teams) and then 4-wheeled buckboards. The elite of the new cities and towns of Lower Canada had the Caléche (open carriages) and the wealthy of Upper Canada and the Maritimes drove buggies. The stagecoach era began at the start of the 19th century and lasted more than 50 years. With it, in 1805, came the toll road and the turnpike trusts. Some of the turnpike companies controlled greater or lesser stretches of road, and the countryside was a network of toll roads for more than a century. On

Between Kingston and York, watercolour by James Cockburn (*courtesy Public Archives of Canada/C-12632*).

some roads even a traveller on foot was charged a penny. In recent years some provincial governments have revived the idea to help finance costly projects, such as the Laurentien Autoroute north of Montréal. Some international crossings also charge tolls. At the peak of the stagecoach era, regular services for passengers and mail were being run between all major cities and towns and into the US. But travel was still an adventure in clumsy, uncomfortable vehicles, ranging from open wagons to ungainly carriages hung on leather springs. In winter they were mounted on runners and some carried wood stoves for warmth. The stagecoach era waned with the coming of the RAILWAYS, and as the network of rails spread roads were used only for local travel. Trunk roads deteriorated as maintenance expenditures were cut. With vast investments in railways, there was virtually no road building.

BC's first road, from Esquimalt to Victoria, was built (1854) by sailors of the Royal Navy. Four years later gold was discovered at Hope and hordes of prospectors poured through the Fraser and Thompson river valleys all the way to the Cariboo. A road was needed to serve the boom towns that had sprung up. Royal Engineers and private contractors, recruiting out-of-luck miners as their work force, drove the 616 km CARIBOO ROAD through in 3 years at a cost of $2 million. It was one of the wonders of its age, blasted out of mountainsides, crossing gorges on suspension bridges and hanging over precipices on timbered trestles.

Road development came more slowly to the Prairies. There was little need for roads at first; the early pioneers used Indian trails and over these rumbled the RED RIVER CARTS and the settlers' covered wagons — "prairie schooners." Crossings at rivers were provided by fords or ferries. Most of the development of the Prairies took place through the railway, with roads providing local transportation. The road system in the North-West Territories, which included present-day Alberta and Saskatchewan, was administered from Regina from the early 1880s until the provinces were formed in 1905. The development of natural resources spurred road construction, first in Manitoba and later in the newer provinces.

Transportation development of the North received great impetus from the building of the

ALASKA HIGHWAY during WWII. Like early roads it was built for military reasons, but it provided an economic link between the YT and the Peace R country. The 614 km Mackenzie Highway began as a winter road in 1938 and was completed to Hay River on the shore of Great Slave Lk after WWII and to Yellowknife in 1961. The cost-sharing Roads to Resources Program, unveiled in 1958, was designed to exploit the resources of the North, and the volume of traffic has increased yearly as supplies, machinery and mining equipment are moved north and minerals, fish and furs south (*see* TRANSPORTATION IN THE NORTH).

Automobile The modern highway system dates from the introduction of the internal-combustion engine some 20 years after Confederation. In 1898 John Moodie of Hamilton brought a one-cylinder Winton "horseless carriage" from the US and 6 years later Canada's AUTOMOTIVE INDUSTRY was born — a Ford assembly plant in Windsor, Ont. In 1907 there were 2131 cars registered in Canada, and by the outbreak of WWI there were more than 100 000 vehicles. Some efforts were made to improve inadequate roads and streets. In 1915 Ontario completed the construction, begun 5 years earlier, of a concrete highway from Toronto to Hamilton, the first in that province and one of the longest intercity concrete roads in the world. Canada's first provincial Dept of Highways had been created by Québec (1914). Two years later Ontario, which had had a provincial Instructor in roadmaking attached to the Dept of Agriculture since 1896, formed its separate highways department.

Through the 1920s cars became cheaper and their numbers multiplied; registration of motor vehicles increased from 408 790 to nearly 1.25 million by the end of the decade. Good roads associations, national and provincial, led the crusade for improved road travel, and expenditures on roads by all governments tripled. By 1930 the annual outlay was $94 million. Methods and technology for building roads improved as horse-drawn scrapers and graders gave way to steam power for shovels and rollers. However, road building in most provinces ceased and maintenance was reduced during the Great Depression and WWII as men and materials were urgently needed in the war effort. The few good paved roads that had been built were almost completely destroyed by heavy wartime traffic, particularly in industrial areas. The "Last Spike" of the Canadian Pacific Railway was driven in 1885, but 61 years passed before a motor vehicle was driven across Canada. Brigadier R.A. Macfarlane and Kenneth MacGillivray made the journey (1946) in 9 days from Louisbourg, Cape Breton, to Victoria, BC. This was 4 years before the TRANS-CANADA HIGHWAY was started.

Post-WWII Development Burgeoning road development in Canada and around the world left virtually no facet of economic or social life unchanged. With increasing efficiency and improving technology, road builders constructed highways and streets to accommodate automotive traffic. Expenditures soared from $103.5 million (1946) to $1.5 billion (1966) and to $4.1 billion (1982). Between 1946 and 1966 the number of motor vehicles increased from 1.6 million to 7 million; by 1982 there were over 14 million. In 1946 there were 28 982 km of paved rural highways and some 10 000 km of paved urban roads and streets. By 1966, this total had risen to 148 987 km, nearly two-thirds of which were rural highways. By 1982 the total road mileage, paved and unpaved, was 391 792 km. These changes left a deep imprint on the Canadian landscape, ripping through the wilderness and transforming the urban environment with expressways, interchanges, and suburban sprawl and ribbonlike development along the high-

View of the David Thompson Highway by Lake Abraham, Alta (*courtesy National Film Board/Photothèque*).

ways. Rural life was also transformed, as the farmer could enjoy the amenities of city living. Trucks delivered necessities; livestock, fruit, vegetables and other agricultural products were quickly conveyed to market (*see* TRUCKING INDUSTRY).

Engineering Early traffic laws were very simple, concerned mostly with the marking of roads in winter by evergreen branches set in the snow. Later, sleigh bells on harness were used to warn of approaching vehicles when visibility was poor. Canada made 2 early notable contributions to N American road transportation. Highway numbering was introduced (1920) in Manitoba, replacing the identifying coloured bands painted on telephone poles. In Ontario an engineer experimented (1930) with dotted white lines down the centre of a road. Within 3 years they had become standard throughout the continent. Traffic engineers, experienced in planning and electronics, were eagerly sought by municipalities in the 1940s and 1950s to help untangle the traffic snarls. In 1956 the Canadian Good Roads Assn established a Council on Uniform Traffic Control Devices and 3 years later published the first manual of standard signs, signals and pavement markings. The association also launched a program of scholarships to help overcome the shortage of engineers qualified to use new techniques such as photogrammetry and computer programming. Postgraduate studies began in Canada as University of Alberta offered the first degree in road engineering (1956).

Jurisdiction Under the CONSTITUTION ACT, 1867, the provinces were given almost complete responsibility for the building of roads. The federal government did not become involved until 1919 when the Canada Highways Act provided $20 million toward the cost of improving and building roads over a 5-year period. In 1981-82 the federal contribution would be $230 million, less than 6% of a total road expenditure of $4.1 billion. In 1981-82 the provinces paid $3.9 billion, part of which came from municipalities. Revenues from users — provincial motor-fuel taxes, the federal excise tax on gasoline, vehicle and driver licence fees, street-parking revenue and fines — were never enough to cover expenditures. Large sums came from consolidated revenue with the logic that efficient highway transportation benefited the entire economy. Alberta was the first province to levy a gasoline tax (1922) of 2 cents a gallon.

In addition to its earlier large financial contributions to the Trans-Canada Highway and the Roads to Resources Program (1958), the federal government is responsible for roads in the Yukon, NWT and national parks; and makes grants through the Department of Regional Economic Expansion and other projects. Street systems in cities, towns and villages are the responsibility of the municipalities, though sometimes subsidized by the provinces. In the peak years of urban freeway development, the high costs frequently brought provincial and municipal governments together in cost-sharing agree-

ments. Each year many kilometres of new roads are added to the highway system. The escalating costs of equipment, materials and manpower for replacement, repairs and maintenance of older roads mean higher budgets.

Canadians prize their mobility and, not content to store their cars in the winter as their grandfathers did, they demand all-weather roads. The cost of snow removal therefore adds millions of dollars to maintenance budgets. Canadians are among the most mobile people on Earth. In 1982 the odometers of their more than 14 million vehicles ran up more than 100 billion miles of road travel.   C.W. GILCHRIST

Roads and Transportation Association of Canada Founded (1914) as the Canadian Good Roads Association, later incorporated by Act of Parliament, the association has had a strong influence on highway development and technology. One example is the TRANS-CANADA HIGHWAY, the culmination of many years of campaigning. In 1970 the name was changed to Roads and Transportation Assn because of its increasing involvement in other transportation modes. The association's members include the federal, all provincial and many municipal governments, carriers and suppliers of transportation goods and services, planners, builders and the academic community. CGRA organized Canada's first national conference (1955) on road safety, from which came the Canada Safety Council. In 1956 it established the Council on Uniform Traffic Control Devices and 3 years later published a manual of standard signs, signals and pavement markings. In 1963 it published a Manual of Geometric Design Standards for Canadian Roads and Streets. In its nearly 70 years the association has conducted and published more than 100 technical studies and research projects. Since 1952 it has awarded up to 8 scholarships annually for postgraduate studies in transportation sciences. A technical information resource centre maintains computer links with international data banks.   C.W. GILCHRIST

Robarts, John Parmenter, politician, premier of Ontario (b at Banff, Alta 11 Jan 1917; d at Toronto 18 Oct 1982). He moved to London, Ont, in 1931 and graduated from U of Western Ontario in 1939. After naval service in WWII, during which he was mentioned in dispatches, he completed law studies at Osgoode Hall. Returning to London, he was elected an alderman in 1950 and an MPP in 1951. He entered the Cabinet in 1958 and was appointed minister of education in 1959; on 8 Nov 1961 he was sworn in as premier. A staunch advocate of individual freedom, he also defended provincial rights from centralist initiatives of the Canadian government and Canada from separatist threats in Québec. He was thus placed in the middle of Canadian constitutional struggles. In 1967 he chaired the Confederation of Tomorrow Conference. On his retirement in 1970, he joined a number of boards of large corporations, served as chancellor of U of Western Ontario and later of York U, chaired a royal commission on Metropolitan Toronto (1975-76) and cochaired with J.L. PEPIN the Task Force on CANADIAN UNITY (1977-79). In 1981 he suffered a series of strokes while travelling in the US. After a lengthy program of rehabilitation, he took his own life on 18 Oct 1982.   ALLAN K. MCDOUGALL

Reading: Jonathan Manthorpe, *The Power & the Tories* (1974).

Robb, Frank Morse, inventor, designer, business executive (b at Belleville, Ont 28 Jan 1902). After studying at McGill, Morse Robb set out in 1926 to develop a church organ with modest demands on space and upkeep. The following year he demonstrated a trial Wave Organ in Belleville, a trailblazing electronic instrument featuring 12 rotating shafts, one for each note in the chromatic scale, on which were mounted

discs edged in the shape of photographed soundwaves. Patents were obtained in 1928 and later improvements were applied, including experiments with a touch-sensitive keyboard. At least 16 Robb Wave Organs were built, among them a 2-manual, 32-pedal note organ in 1934. Demonstrations were given at department stores and at a 1936 Toronto concert, and musicians and critics were warm in their praise. Attempts to fund commercial production failed, however, and the discouraged inventor gave up the project in 1938. He joined his brother's mechanical packing company in Montréal and invented devices for the packing of guns, later becoming VP of the company. He has won acclaim also as a designer of sterling silver articles. *See also* ELECTROACOUSTIC MUSIC.   HELMUT KALLMANN

Robbery is one of the earliest and most serious felonies and was once punishable by death. Robbery is a serious, indictable offence under the Canadian CRIMINAL CODE (s302), punishable by life imprisonment. Basically robbery consists of 2 elements: the theft or extortion of property, and the use of a weapon, violence or threats of violence. In order to constitute robbery, however, rather than the separate offences of theft and assault, these elements must be linked; either the element of violence must be used for the purpose of taking the victim's property, or the 2 elements must be proximate in time. Although neither physical harm to the victim nor actual use of a weapon is essential to the crime, these factors may be considered in imposing sentences. *See* BURGLARY.   LEE PAIKIN

Robbins, John Everett, educator, diplomat (b at Hampton, Ont 9 Oct 1903). He taught school in Saskatchewan for 3 years before entering U of Man. He later gained a PhD from U d'Ottawa. He served in the Educational Division, Dominion Bureau of Statistics, Ottawa 1930-52, becoming director in 1936. In 1952 he was appointed editor-in-chief of the new *Encyclopedia Canadiana*, a 10-volume work whose publication he supervised for the next 8 years. In 1960 he went to Brandon U as its president and in 1969 was appointed Canada's first ambassador to the Vatican. Robbins was active in founding and directing a number of national cultural and educational societies, such as the Canadian Assn for Adult Education, Canadian Library Assn, the Social Science and Humanities research councils and the Canadian Writers' Foundation.   D.M.L. FARR

Roberts, Bartholomew, pirate (b in Pembrokeshire, Wales *c*1682; d 10 Feb 1722). Called "the Puritan pirate" because he forbade excessive immoral conduct on board his ships, he is believed to have captured more than 400 vessels. Having appeared off the coast of NS in June 1720, he made for Trepassey, Nfld, where in a pre-dawn raid with a single ship he captured 22 vessels. He sacked the town and then sailed N along the shore, preying on shipping and settlements and recruiting men for his crew. After he quit Canadian waters he made for the African coast. He was killed in an engagement with a British ship off Cape Lopez; most of his surviving crewmen were executed or sentenced to slavery. His death marked the end of the "golden age" of PIRACY.   EDWARD BUTTS

Roberts, Sir Charles George Douglas, poet, animal-story writer (b at Douglas, NB 10 Jan 1860; d at Toronto 26 Nov 1943). As author of *Orion and Other Poems* (1880), Roberts inspired Bliss CARMAN (his cousin), Archibald LAMPMAN and D.C. SCOTT and became a prominent member of the so-called "poets of Confederation." At his death he was regarded as Canada's leading man of letters. The son of a clergyman, he was brought up in New Brunswick, near the Tantramar marshes and in Fredericton. He attended UNB (1876-79), and then worked as a school-

Poet and animal story writer Charles G.D. Roberts in military uniform during WWI (*courtesy Public Archives of Canada/PA-7764*).

teacher at Chatham and Fredericton (1879-83), as editor of *The Week* (1883-84) and as professor at King's College, Windsor, NS (1885-95).

His finest poetry was produced in these early years, appearing in *In Divers Tones* (1886) and *Songs of the Common Day* (1893), and he was elected fellow of the Royal Society of Canada (1890). Financial pressure forced him to turn his main attention to fiction. Then, in 1897, he moved to New York, and subsequently lived apart from his wife and family. He wrote a number of novels and historical romances, but his most successful prose genre was the animal story, in which he drew upon his early experience in the wilds of the Maritimes. He published over a dozen such volumes between *Earth's Enigmas* (1896) and *Eyes of the Wilderness* (1933). In 1907 he left for Europe, where he continued to write, though interrupted by service in WWI. His return to Canada in 1925 led to a renewed production of verse with *The Vagrant of Time* (1927) and *The Iceberg and Other Poems* (1934). Roberts was a popular figure at this time. He lectured throughout Canada and in 1935 was knighted.

Roberts is remembered for creating in the animal story, along with Ernest Thompson SETON, the one native Canadian art form. His early descriptive and meditative poetry ("Tantramar Revisited," "The Potato Harvest," "The Sower") recreates his Maritimes years with vivid sensitivity. Although he never fulfilled his early poetic promise, he laid a foundation for future achievements in Canadian verse. W.J. KEITH
Reading: W.J. Keith, ed, Charles G.D. Roberts: Selected Poetry and Critical Prose (1974); C.G.D. Roberts, The Last Barrier, and Other Stories (1958) and King of Beasts, and Other Stories (1967).

Roberts, William Goodridge, painter (b at Barbados, W Indies 24 Sept 1904; d at Montréal 28 Jan 1974), nephew of Sir C.G.D. ROBERTS. He trained at Montréal's École des beaux-arts 1923-25 and New York's Art Students League 1926-28, beginning a lifelong commitment to modernism. The first resident artist at Queen's U (1933-36), he then moved to Montréal, joining John LYMAN's Eastern Group and, in 1937, becoming founding member of the Contemporary Arts Soc. He taught at the School of Art and Design 1930-49, except for service as a war artist 1943-45. By the early 1950s, he had national

prominence through his participation in numerous Canadian and international exhibitions, and in 1952 was one of 4 artists in Canada's first official participation at the Venice Biennale. He became the first artist-in-residence at UNB in 1959. In 1969 he was given a retrospective exhibition by the National Gallery of Canada, then unusual for a living artist. Roberts was the first Canadian painter to treat landscape, the figure and still life with equal emphasis. Because of his empathy for his subjects, the power of his painting rests in the ambiguity between the real and the painted. SANDRA PAIKOWSKY

Robertson, Bruce Richard, swimmer (b at Vancouver 27 Apr 1953). A specialist in the butterfly stroke, Robertson established himself as a world-class swimmer at the 1972 Munich Olympics, where he won the silver medal in the 100 m butterfly and swam on the 3rd-place Canadian 4 x 100 m medley relay team. His greatest achievement was winning the 100 m butterfly race at the World Aquatic Games in Belgrade (1973) — the first world championship swimming performance by a Canadian in over 60 years. Robertson also swam on the 3rd place 4 x 100 m medley relay team there. At the 1974 Commonwealth Games in New Zealand he won 2 gold, 2 silver and 2 bronze medals. In 1973 he was named male athlete of the year.
BARBARA SCHRODT

Robertson, James, Presbyterian minister (b at Dull, Scot 24 Apr 1839; d at Toronto 4 Jan 1902). Robertson emigrated to Woodstock, Canada W, in 1855 and after teaching school entered U of T, serving in its militia company at the battle of Ridgeway (1860). Following theological studies at Princeton Seminary, he became a minister in rural Ontario in 1869. In 1874 he moved to Winnipeg and in 1881 was appointed superintendent of Presbyterian mission work in the North-West. Under Robertson, "the Presbyterian bishop," 4 congregations grew to 141, in addition to 226 missions serving 1130 points.
JOHN S. MOIR

Robertson, James Wilson, dairyman, educator (b at Dunlop, Scot 2 Nov 1857; d at Ottawa 20 Mar 1930). Robertson farmed in Ontario from 1875 to 1886, when he became professor of dairying at the Ontario Agricultural Coll. As the Dominion government's dairy commissioner 1890-1904, he was influential in developing the cheese industry, especially in eastern regions unable to produce wheat as cheaply as the new prairie farms. He became the first principal of the Macdonald Coll of Agriculture, affiliated with McGill, in 1905 and was chairman of the influential Royal Commission on Technical Education (1909-13). Robertson's later career is obscure. Although honoured for his cheese work with the CMG in 1905, he lost the Macdonald principalship in 1910. Except for postwar work in 1919 on food supplies for Europe, he held

Goodridge Roberts, *Reclining Nude* (1961), oil on masonite (*courtesy Mrs Joan Roberts*).

no university or governmental appointments after 1913. DONALD J.C. PHILLIPSON

Robertson, John Ross, newspaper publisher, philanthropist (b at Toronto 28 Dec 1841; d there 31 May 1918). He was the son of a Scottish-born merchant. After attending Toronto's Upper Canada College, where he published a student paper, he founded the evening *Telegram*, which became the voice of working-class, conservative, Orange Toronto. Known as "the old lady of Melinda Street," it was the bitter rival of the Liberal *Toronto Star*. Robertson was a Tory maverick whose keen interest in local history led him to compile and publish the several volumes of *Landmarks of Toronto and Canada*. His own notable collection of Canadiana was left to the Toronto Public Library. Toronto's Hospital for Sick Children also benefited enormously from his wealth. The *Telegram* was continued by his heirs until sold in the 1930s. It ceased publication 1971.
Reading: R. Poulton, The Paper Tyrant (1971).

Robertson, Norman Alexander, public servant, diplomat (b at Vancouver 4 Mar 1904; d at Ottawa 16 July 1968). Well educated at UBC, Oxford and the Brookings Inst, he joined the Dept of External Affairs in 1929. He drew the attention of PM KING and O.D. SKELTON when he worked out trade policies during the Depression, and in 1941 became undersecretary. Aided by Lester PEARSON and Hume WRONG, Robertson directed Canadian diplomacy during WWII along new and untried paths — with great success. His postwar service saw 2 terms as high commissioner in London (1946-49, 1952-57), where he dealt with financial problems and the SUEZ CRISIS, one year (1957-58) in Washington as ambassador, and a second term as undersecretary (1958-64), where his deeply held antinuclear convictions reinforced those of Howard Green, his minister, and helped bring about the collapse of the DIEFENBAKER government in 1963. In his last years he was a professor at Carleton.
J.L. GRANATSTEIN
Reading: J.L. Granatstein, A Man of Influence (1981).

Robertson, Robert Gordon, public servant (b in Davidson, Sask 19 May 1917). Gordon Robertson was educated at U of Sask, Oxford and U of T before joining the Dept of External Affairs in 1941. He worked in the Prime Minister's Office and subsequently as a member of the Cabinet secretariat before becoming deputy minister of northern affairs and national resources (1953-63). Promoted clerk of the Privy Council and Cabinet secretary (1963-75), Robertson was admired for his mental clarity and his efficiency; he was the most influential public servant of his day. He was secretary to the Cabinet for federal-provincial relations 1975-79, and participated in the constitutional review. After his retirement, he became president of the newly formed Institute for Research on Public Policy in Ottawa. ROBERT BOTHWELL

Roberval, Qué, City, pop 11 429 (1981c), inc 1976, located on the SW shore of Lac SAINT-JEAN is the county seat for Lac St-Jean Ouest (1892) and headquarters for the judicial district of Roberval (1912). Named for France's lieutenant-general in Canada in the 16th century, Roberval was founded in 1855 and grew rapidly after 1888 when the Québec-Lac Saint-Jean railway company (amalgamated into the CNR in 1917) decided to make the town its Saint-Jean terminal. A navigation centre for the lake and an internationally renowned summer resort until the early 20th century, Roberval also had a few sawmills. The Ursulines built their provincial convent here in 1882. A hospital was added in 1918. Since then, Roberval has been the service centre of the area and since 1955 has yearly hosted the prestigious swim, the International Crossing of Lac Saint-Jean. MARC ST-HILAIRE

Roberval, Jean-François de La Roque, Sieur de, French lieutenant-general in Canada (b in France c1500; d in Paris 1560). A courtier of noble descent, he received a royal commission as lieutenant-general of Canada 1541, despite being a Protestant convert. He was set in command over explorer Jacques CARTIER, who had already made 2 expeditions to Canada and who sailed again that May. Roberval, delayed by shortage of funds and equipment, set out Apr 1542. By that time Cartier had decided to abandon his settlement at Charlesbourg-Royal [Cap-Rouge, Qué]. The 2 expeditions met in the harbour of St John's, Nfld, going in opposite directions. Roberval, with a party of around 200, re-occupied Cartier's settlement. The ensuing winter was disastrous, the colonists' morale being undermined by climate, disease and internal disputes. After some weeks exploring in the direction of HOCHELAGA [Montréal] during the summer of 1543, the surviving colonists abandoned the colony and returned to France. The expedition's failure ended any immediate prospect of colonization of Canada and brought Roberval financial ruin. He was killed with other Protestants in a Paris street affray at the start of the French Wars of Religion.
JOHN G. REID

Reading: H.P. Biggar, ed, *A Collection of Documents Relating to Jacques Cartier and the Sieur de Roberval* (1930).

Robichaud, Louis Joseph, lawyer, politician, senator (b at St-Antoine, NB 21 Oct 1925). Educated at Sacré Coeur U and Laval, he practised law and was elected MLA for Kent County in 1952. Elected leader of the NB Liberal Party in 1958, he led it to victory over Hugh J. FLEMMING, 1960, and served as attorney general, 1960-65, and minister of youth, 1968. The first Acadian elected premier, he introduced far-reaching social reforms through the centralizing Programme of Equal Opportunity. His Liberal government modernized liquor laws, abolished the Hospital Premium Tax, passed an Official Languages Act, established U de Moncton, increased Acadian administrative influence, and encouraged the mining and forest industries. In 1970 the Liberals were defeated by Richard HATFIELD and Robichaud resigned as party leader and MLA in 1971 to become chairman of the Canadian section of the INTERNATIONAL JOINT COMMISSION. In 1973 he was appointed to the Senate, where he continued to support bilingualism and national unity.
DELLA M.M. STANLEY

Robin, American (*Turdus migratorius*), largest and best-known member of THRUSH family in Canada. It is widely distributed in Canada, the northern limit of its range being the TREELINE. It is migratory in most parts, but may winter or attempt to winter in southern parts of most provinces. The American robin is a graceful, primarily terrestrial bird with a black head, black and white streaks on the throat, grey back, blackish tail and wings, reddish orange breast, and white abdomen. Sexes differ little in size (22-28 cm long). Males are more brightly coloured than females. Young have the same general appearance as adults but, like all thrushes, are heavily marked with conspicuous dark spots on underparts. The American robin is a good singer. It has adapted to humans in inhabited areas and is relatively tame; in remote areas, it avoids them. Nests are usually built a few metres from the ground in trees or bushes. The nest is a large structure of grass, twigs and small stems, crudely assembled around a cup of mud lined with finer grasses. The female incubates 4 bluish green eggs for 12-13 days; the male assists with feeding young. Robins frequently have 2 broods in southern parts of Canadian range. They feed extensively on insects, insect larvae and earthworms but also consume fruits and berries in season and are considered pests in many areas.

Robins have many natural enemies, eg, birds, snakes, predatory mammals (eg, domestic cats). The term robin also applies to several other thrushes not closely related to the American robin and birds of other families.
HENRI OUELLET

Robinson, Clifford William, lawyer, businessman, premier of NB (b at Moncton, NB 1 Sept 1866; d at Montréal 27 July 1944). In 1897 Robinson was elected mayor of Moncton and a member of the provincial Assembly. After serving as Speaker of the House and provincial secretary he became premier in 1907. A year later his government was defeated. He served as minister without portfolio and minister of lands and mines in the provincial Liberal government from 1917 until 1924, when he was appointed to the Senate.
ARTHUR T. DOYLE

Robinson, Sir John Beverley, lawyer, politician, judge (b at Berthier, LC 26 July 1791; d at Toronto 31 Jan 1863). He was enrolled at the school of John STRACHAN and made a lifelong friend of the Tory Anglican cleric. Appointed acting attorney general in 1813, he became solicitor general after the war and left for England to finish his legal studies. When he returned, he was reappointed attorney general. In 1820 Robinson was elected to the Assembly; he was government spokesman until 1828. As a member of the FAMILY COMPACT, he was a staunch defender of the imperial connection, an established Church of England and a social hierarchy headed by a chosen elite. He incurred the wrath of reformers and opponents, such as Robert GOURLAY, whom he prosecuted, and he played a leading role in depriving American settlers of their property and political rights, defining them as "aliens." Nevertheless, Robinson promoted economic development and had an outstanding judicial career. He was appointed chief justice in 1829, Speaker of the Legislative Council and president of the Executive Council. During the trials of the Upper Canadian rebels in 1838, he banished 25 men and had Samuel LOUNT and Peter MATTHEWS executed. Critical of Lord DURHAM's report, Robinson favoured union of all British N America. He had little political influence after 1841.
DAVID MILLS

Robinson, Laurence Clark, Larry, hockey player (b at Winchester, Ont 2 June 1951). He was a first-round selection for the MONTREAL CANADIENS in the 1971 NHL draft and, after a year and a half in the American Hockey League, was called up to play on the Canadiens' 1973 STANLEY CUP winning team. The tall redhead became the anchor of a great defence corps, leading Montreal to 4 more Cups (1976-80). He has won the JAMES NORRIS MEMORIAL TROPHY (1977, 1980), the CONN SMYTHE TROPHY (1978) and 3 NHL all-star awards.
DEREK DRAGER

Robinson, Peter, merchant, developer, immigration superintendent (b in NB 1785; d at Toronto 8 July 1838). Until 1822 he was active in the development of Yonge St in the Newmarket and Holland Landing area. Linked with his brother, John Beverley ROBINSON, in the FAMILY COMPACT, he served in the Upper Canadian assembly (1817-24) and, as commissioner of crown lands, on the legislative and executive councils (1827-36). Robinson is best remembered as the founder of PETERBOROUGH, Ont, which took its name from him. He supervised 2 settlements of southern IRISH immigrants assisted by the Colonial Office, one based at Sheppard's Fall (later ALMONTE, Ont) in 1823, the other at Peterborough in 1825. As commissioner of crown lands he employed land agents across the province. From 1829 to 1933, his agents, under the local authority of Sir John COLBORNE, assisted indigent immigrants to settle in townships in the Peterborough area, in Nottawasaga Bay, and in Adelaide and Warwick townships, W of London, Ont.
WENDY CAMERON

Roblin, Dufferin, businessman, politician, premier of Manitoba 1958-67 (b at Winnipeg 17 June 1917). After attending U of Man and U of Chicago and wartime service in the RCAF, "Duff" Roblin first won election to the Manitoba legislature in 1949, as an Independent Conservative, for the riding of Winnipeg S. Grandson of Sir Rodmond P. ROBLIN, the province's vigorously partisan premier 1900-15, he challenged the avowedly nonpartisan government of Douglas CAMPBELL, and after extricating the Conservatives from the government coalition in 1951, won the party leadership in 1954 and defeated the Campbell government in 1958. The Roblin administration was one of the most active in Manitoba history, upgrading highways, creating provincial parks, building the Greater Winnipeg Floodway (derided at the time as "Duff's Ditch"), modernizing hospitals and welfare agencies, consolidating schools and expanding post-secondary facilities, restoring the use of French in education and initiating a shared-services program for private schools, promoting urban renewal, co-ordinating Winnipeg's municipalities with a metropolitan structure, launching northern power and mining projects, and establishing numerous agencies to assist private economic development. On this record, his government won re-election in 1959, 1962 and 1966. In Nov 1967 Roblin resigned as premier to contest the federal leadership of the PC Party, but lost to Robert STANFIELD. In the 1968 federal election he was defeated in Winnipeg S Centre, a casualty of "Trudeaumania." After a term as executive with Canadian Pacific Investments, he established a security firm in Winnipeg. In 1978 he was appointed to the Senate where he served on committees considering constitutional and Senate reform. On the latter, he proposed that the Senate be elected. Roblin is significant as an exponent of classic conservatism, in the John A. MACDONALD tradition, advocating an active government role in social reform.
THOMAS PETERSON

Roblin, Sir Rodmond Palen, businessman, premier of Manitoba 1900-15 (b at Sophiasburg, Canada W 15 Feb 1853; d at Hot Springs, Ark 16 Feb 1937). Roblin, of Dutch Loyalist stock, completed his education at Albert Coll, Belleville, Ont. When he arrived in Winnipeg in late May 1877, he turned his hand to various business endeavours in Carman and in Winnipeg and to local politics. On his second attempt, he won election as an Independent MLA in 1888. The paramount issue of the day was the "monopoly clause" of the CPR charter that gave the railway a stranglehold on western transportation. Roblin, as a strong provincial rights advocate, gave his full support to the GREENWAY government's struggle to overturn the monopoly, but he was hostile to Greenway's scheme for bringing the Northern Pacific Ry into Manitoba without rate control and to his government's failure to forward the plan for a railway to Hudson Bay. With the sudden death of John NORQUAY, the Conservative leader, in late 1889, Roblin's prominent and effective opposition to Greenway's railway policy made him a popular choice as the new Conservative chief. In the dramatic session of 1890, Roblin denounced Greenway's repudiation of his government's recent guarantees to the Catholic minority not to disturb the language and school laws of the province. But Greenway weathered the storm and retained power for the rest of the decade.

After 10 years in and out of politics, Roblin succeeded Hugh John MACDONALD as premier in 1900. He assumed the portfolio of railways himself and made a startling agreement with the Canadian Northern whereby the railway completed an alternative route to the Lakehead and vested control of rates in the provincial government. Roblin always considered this his greatest achievement. Under Roblin the province bought out the Bell Telephone Co, created a successful government telephone system, and established the first effective public utilities commission in the nation. His attempt to institute a publicly owned system of grain elevators, in response to farmers' demands, was a disastrous failure, but his government did introduce a workmen's compensation law as well as corporation taxes.

The Roblin "machine," as it was called, played an important role in the federal RECIPROCITY election of 1911 that turned out the LAURIER Liberals. With Robert BORDEN's Conservatives in Ottawa, the boundaries of Manitoba were finally extended and the premier became Sir Rodmond, a not unconnected series of events.

While Roblin was not directly implicated in the scandal surrounding the building of the new legislature that brought down his government in 1915, he shared in the political odium and resigned to return to business. ED REA

Reading: H.R. Ross, *Thirty-Five Years in the Limelight: Sir Rodmond P. Roblin and his Times* (1936); W.L. Morton, *Manitoba: A History* (1957, 2nd ed 1967); James A. Jackson, *The Centennial History of Manitoba* (1970).

Robotics The term "robot," derived from the Czech word *robota,* meaning "labour" or "work," was introduced into literature in 1921 by playwright Karel Capek in his play *R.U.R. (Rossum's Universal Robots),* about a multinational company that produced mechanical workers. The word is now used for multifunctional machines capable of replacing workers on assembly lines. In contrast to their automaton ancestors of the 17th and 18th centuries or the "androids" of futuristic novels, industrial robots, designed according to the tasks they are to perform, have no need to imitate human form. But, unlike previous machine tools, robots are programmable and so may carry out varied tasks in varying environments, or different tasks in succession. Born of the marriage of machine tools and computers, robotics has developed largely thanks to cybernetics. Cybernetics is the comparative study of the automatic control systems of the brain and of mechanical and electrical devices. One of the simplest examples of such a device is a thermostat control. Cybernetics developed from military research of the 1950s, and cybernetic devices are also known as servo-controlled systems. According to the Robot Institute of America's definition of a robot (as a reprogrammable, multifunctional manipulator designed to move material, parts, tools or specialized devices through variable programmed motions for the performance of various tasks), there were only 18 000-20 000 true robots functioning in the world in the early 1980s. Some 14 500 of them were in Japan and fewer than 250 in Canada.

Robson, John, journalist, politician, premier of BC (b at Perth, UC 14 or 15 Mar 1824; d at London, Eng 29 June 1892). Coming to BC in 1859, Robson established the New Westminster *British Columbian* in 1861. In 1869 he moved to Victoria and became editor of the *Daily British Colonist,* a position he held until becoming paymaster for CPR surveyors in 1875. Robson was an eloquent advocate of representative and RESPONSIBLE GOVERNMENT and of CONFEDERATION, joining his rival Amor DE COSMOS in the "Confederation League" in 1868. He served on the New Westminster Council (1863-67), in the Legislative Council of BC, and in the Legislative Assembly (1871-73, 1882-92). In 1883 he became provincial secretary and minister of finance and agriculture in the cabinet of William SMITHE and, after the death of A.E.B. DAVIE in 1889, headed the government. His administration was noted for giving bonuses to railways, attempting to check undue exploitation of natural resources, redistributing legislative seats and promoting immigration.
PATRICIA E. ROY

Robson, Mount, elev 3954 m, the highest mountain in the Canadian ROCKY MTS, is located 72 km NW of Jasper townsite, 10 km SW of the Continental Divide. There is much speculation about its name, but it was probably named originally after Colin Robertson, an officer of the HBC post at St Marys in the Peace R country. Its heavily glaciated northern slopes drop steeply to Berg Lk. A high escarpment of the S side falls off 2969 m to Kinney Lk. The highly prized first ascent was claimed earlier, but the first complete ascent was made July 1913 by guide Conrad Kain and W.W. Foster and A.H. MacCarthy. Foster and MacCarthy both later climbed Mt LOGAN. The mountain is now climbed by several very challenging routes.
GLEN BOLES

Rock, natural aggregate of one or more MINERALS and, sometimes, noncrystalline substances. Rocks are the solid matter forming the Earth's crust. Description and classification of rocks is the subject of petrography; their genesis and evolution, the subject of petrology. The 3 major rock types, classified according to their origin, are IGNEOUS, SEDIMENTARY and metamorphic. *See* GEOLOGY; GEOLOGICAL HISTORY.
C.M. SCARFE

Rock and Mineral Collecting is a hobby, an avocation and a profession, attracting Canadians of all ages from all parts of the country and from every educational, economic and social level. Rocks are collected from outcropping rocks and pits, quarries and other man-made openings in rock, from mine-waste dumps and from river, lake and ocean shores. Now mainly a leisure-time activity, collecting was a preoccupation born of necessity for the first collectors, the native peoples, who searched for waterworn fragments of nephrite jade, copper, flint and soapstone and fashioned them into weapons and tools. Nor is it solely a recreational pursuit for today's professional collectors and mineral dealers who have transformed a hobby into a full-time occupation.

Collectors are generally self-taught, learning as they examine, break and sample the rocks around them. Field experience is supplemented by courses on PROSPECTING, GEOLOGY or MINERAL and rock recognition offered by universities, colleges, high schools and government institutions. Collectors fall into categories: some collect minerals from a particular locality or mineral group; others restrict their specimens to "micro" sizes, collecting crystal specimens that reveal their perfect geometrical forms only through the microscope; species collectors aim to assemble a collection representing each of the nearly 3000 mineral species known. Many collectors, particularly in the West, focus on collecting specimens suitable for the lapidary arts, ie, those that can be cut, carved and polished into ornamental objects.

Information available to collectors includes hobby-oriented books on mineralogy, geology and lapidary arts; guidebooks describing collecting sites in Canada, published by the GEOLOGICAL SURVEY OF CANADA, some provincial geological departments and collectors themselves; geological reports and maps published by government agencies; and mineral and rock kits available from government mines departments and mineral dealers. Equipment is minimal: prospector's pick, collecting bag or baskets, hand magnifier, safety glasses and hiking boots. More advanced collectors may use ultraviolet lamps, geiger counters and microscopes. There are some 200 mineral/lapidary dealers across the country.

Transportation is generally a combination of automobile and foot travel. Jeep or boat, floatplane or helicopter are used to reach more inaccessible collecting sites. In some cities, eg, Winnipeg and Montréal, urban transportation takes collectors to local sites. An estimated 15 000 collectors are members of the 125 organized mineral, rock or lapidary clubs in Canada.

Club activities (eg, field excursions, lapidary workshops, lectures) foster interest in minerals, rocks and gems. In fact, many of today's mineralogists and geologists were introduced to their fields through membership in a mineral club. The most visible activity of clubs or federations of clubs (eg, the Gem and Mineral Federation of Canada) is the annual mineral or gem show where members display their mineral, rock or FOSSIL collections and the gems and ornaments fashioned from them. There are dealer booths, demonstrations on lapidary techniques and excursions to local collecting sites.

Hundreds of collectors have no club affiliation. Each year their numbers swell by the influx of tourist/collectors from the US and abroad. They come individually or in organized club trips to collect from Canada's unique and classic localities, which have furnished specimens to the world's foremost museums. Most of the world's mineral collections, including Canada's National Mineral Collection, have been enriched by specimens collected by amateurs. These self-taught collectors, past and present, hobbyist and professional, have forged a link with the professional mineralogist and geologist, enriched their leisure time and made a unique contribution to our knowledge of the minerals and rocks around us. ANN P. SABINA

Rockslide, a type of LANDSLIDE common on high, steep ROCK slopes, which occurs when a mass of rock moves quickly downslope. When the mass moves through the air, the movement is a rockfall. If the upper part of the mass initially rotates outwards, the movement is better described as toppling. Subsidence, downward movements of rock into closed depressions in the ground, may result from the collapse of natural underground openings called CAVES and is typical of KARST LANDFORMS. Sliding describes the motion of a mass that remains undeformed except along its base. In slides, a rupture surface separates the displaced mass of rock from the rock over which it moves. Numerous small falls from a cliff of hard rock produce a talus or scree, an accumulation of loosely packed rock fragments sloping outward from the cliff. Such a landform is sometimes popularly called a rockslide. This entry, however, concentrates on slope movements in rock.

Rock slope movements occur in mountainous regions or where EROSION or excavation has exposed the rock. They are known throughout the Canadian CORDILLERA and along rocky coastlines and in deeply cut river valleys in eastern Canada. Rockslides also occur in artificial excavations, in cuts for roads or excavations for mines and quarries. Movements can vary in size from the fall of a single block less than 1 m³ to slides of whole mountainsides involving many millions of cubic metres. Larger slides may travel kilometres in a few minutes; the FRANK SLIDE lasted about 100 seconds and transported some boulders 2 km. Such high velocities have caused catastrophic rockslides to be called rock avalanches by analogy with the rapid downslope movements of snow AVALANCHES.

Natural weaknesses often control the shape and location of rockslides. Sedimentary rocks, like those at Frank and at Brazeau Lk, have surfaces of weakness separating the layers of sediment (or beds) from which the rocks were formed. If the sedimentary rocks are later compressed and folded into MOUNTAIN chains, the beds are tilted to steep angles. Valleys eroded through the mountains by rivers or glaciers may expose a surface of weakness sloping into the valley, and a typical Rocky Mt rockslide can then take place. COAL MINING at the base of Turtle Mt may also have contributed to the Frank Slide. A contemporary official report commented that, although destructive landslides were common in the Alps, they were very un-

Some Historic Rockslides

Site	Date	Volume (m³)	Damage
Rubble Creek, BC	1855?	25 million	unknown
Frank, Alta	29 Apr 1903	30 million	c76 fatalities; town destroyed
Brazeau Lk, Alta	July 1933	5 million	telephone line
Hope, BC	9 Jan 1965	47 million	4 fatalities; 2.5 km of road

common in the Canadian Rockies. This comment suggests that there may have been an artificial cause for the slide.

Recent research has mapped the debris of hundreds of rockslides, comparable in size to the Frank Slide, throughout the Cordillera. These prehistoric slides and those at Brazeau Lk, Hope and Rubble Creek clearly have natural causes. Processes that destroy cohesion or bonding across potential rupture surfaces can trigger rock slope movements. For example, water infiltrating the rock mass may freeze and expand, lengthening natural cracks along the growing rupture surface. At Hope, shaking caused by an EARTHQUAKE may have triggered the slide. Rupture may have occurred at Rubble Creek when debris or freezing obstructed the large springs that at present flow from the scarp of the slide. In limestones, like those at Frank, karst processes are often active in dissolving rock along bedding planes, effectively removing the natural glue holding the rock mass together. A number of different processes may contribute to a single rock-slope movement.

Large rockslides rarely occur without such precursors as cracking of the ground at the crown of the slide, or bulging of the ground surface above the toe of the rupture surface. SURVEYING systems have been designed to monitor slopes so that work in any excavations around the gradually accelerating, displaced rock mass may continue until slope failure approaches. Movements can be reduced by decreasing gravitational forces disturbing the rock mass through off-loading the head of the slide or by draining water from it. Resistance to movement can be increased by loading the foot of the slide or by artificially reinforcing the rupture surface. Modern ENGINEERING practice can eliminate loss of life and movable property from rock-slope movements. Careful exploration before construction can identify dangerous sites for permanent structures and lead to their relocation or redesign. D.M. CRUDEN

Rockwood, Man, Rural Municipality, pop 6332 (1981c), area 1156 km², located N of Winnipeg; it includes the communities of Stony Mountain, Grosse Isle, Argyle, Balmoral, Gunton and Komarno. Stonewall and Teulon are separate corporate entities. Stony Mountain was a haven from RED RIVER floodwaters for early traders and later for Red River colonists. Homesteading began in the 1860s; during the 1870s settlers included Ontarians, Americans, Red River colonists and British immigrants. Scandinavians settled at Norris Lk and Teulon; Ukrainians at Komarno. Mixed farming was the main activity, but several brickyards and quarries were established at Balmoral, Gunton, Stonewall and Stony Mountain. Agriculture remains central today, with the communities functioning as service centres. Industries include a rocket plant near Stonewall and a federal fish hatchery/research station close to Balmoral. A federal prison has been at Stony Mountain since 1874. D.M. LYON

Rocky Mountain House National Historic Park, near Rocky Mountain House, Alta, a HISTORIC SITE commemorating a series of FUR-TRADE posts built 1799-1864 by the NWC and the HBC near the junction of the Saskatchewan and Clearwater rivers. The posts were established to form a link between the eastern supply routes and the Pacific Slope fur trade, and it was intended that they would promote trading relations with the KOOTENAY of eastern BC. The posts were in the territory of the BLACKFOOT Confederacy, which opposed trade with the Kootenay, so they failed in their intended purpose. Instead, Rocky Mountain House became the centre for sporadic trade with the Blackfoot. Despite HBC attempts to close the post, Blackfoot pressure kept it in operation until 1875. Little remains except 2 restored chimneys from the last establishment. Created a national historic park, the site is being developed by Parks Canada, which maintains a small interpretation centre there.
C.J. TAYLOR

Rocky Mountain Trench is a great valley extending 1400 km NW through BC from Montana to the Liard Plain just S of the Yukon Territory. Its floor is 3-20 km wide and 600-1000 m in elevation. The trench is mainly demarcated by the wall-like slopes of major mountain ranges — the ROCKY MTS on the E and the COLUMBIA, Omineca and CASSIAR mountains on the W. The northern half of the trench is very straight and trends more northerly than the southern half, which is slightly sinuous to arcuate. Prior to construction of hydroelectric dams in eastern BC and NW Montana, 7 major rivers occupied different parts of the trench. Now all but the Fraser and Kechika empty into reservoirs (eg, WILLISTON LK) covering large areas of the valley floor. The trench is bordered along much of its length by faults and is an ancient zone of crustal weakness, perhaps a former continental margin. Its present form is a product of faulting and of erosion and deposition by rivers and glaciers during the Cenozoic period.

The southern trench is an important transportation and communication corridor and a popular tourist and recreation area. Mining, forestry and agriculture are important sources of employment. Numerous towns and settlements dot the area, the largest being CRANBROOK, KIMBERLEY and GOLDEN. Archaeological surveys have shown that native Indians have inhabited the trench for thousands of years. The first NWC explorers and trappers came into the region in the early 19th century, followed by settlers of European stock. The discovery of placer gold in the Kootenay Valley in 1864, the completion of the CPR main line (1885) and the opening of the Sullivan Mine at Kimberley (1910) helped spur population growth in the southern trench, as have recent economic diversification and improvements in the road system. The northern trench remains largely undeveloped and sparsely inhabited. JOHN J. CLAGUE

Rocky Mountains are the northern segment of a large mountain system widely known for its vistas of spacious subalpine valleys and rugged, exposed rock faces. In Canada they extend 1200 km from the American borders of BC and Alberta to the LIARD R Basin, flanked on the W by a distinct trench and on the E by rolling foothills. The Canadian Rockies of song, film, painting and postcard, however, are in the Park or Main ranges, near the rail and highway routes through 2 mountain passes. These and other passes mark the southern boundary between BC and Alberta.

KICKING HORSE PASS was chosen in 1881 for the CPR link between the Prairies and coastal BC. Castlelike mountain resorts built on the rail line at BANFF (1888) and LAKE LOUISE, Alta, have become all-season recreation centres for BANFF NATIONAL PARK's many alpine attractions, which attract over 3 million visitors annually. Development of the YELLOWHEAD PASS area, SW of Edmonton, followed the same pattern, adding railway lines (1915), JASPER NATIONAL PARK (est 1907), the town of JASPER (1911) and a resort hotel. Four adjoining national parks (Banff, Jasper, Kootenay and Yoho) form the largest body of mountain parkland in the world. Throughout this area the Rockies form NW-trending waves of sedimentary rock lifted by vast thrust faults in the Tertiary age (less than 58 million years ago) and eroded by glaciers. Magnificent mountain forms, commonly higher than 3050 m, include castellate, matterhorn, sawtooth and dipping strata peaks. The highest is Mt ROBSON, BC.

To the S, in the CROWSNEST PASS area of the Boundary Ranges, a railway line begun in 1896 opened Rocky Mt coal to underground mine development. Open-pit mines near SPARWOOD and Elkford, BC, have greatly expanded the area's coal production since the 1960s. The southern Alberta foothills of the Rockies have been a RANCHING centre since the 1870s. Natural-gas drilling has progressed into foothill country in recent decades.

N of the Kakwa R, the Rockies are entirely in BC. They subside to modest heights (maximum 2542 m), with rounded, often timbered summits and little evidence of glaciation. The forest industry followed highway (1952) and railway (1958) construction NE from PRINCE GEORGE. Open-pit coal mines opened at Quintette and Bullmoose mountains in the BC foothills in 1983. The higher Muskwa Ranges, N of the Peace R, are penetrated by the ALASKA HWY, but remain undeveloped. PETER GRANT

Roddick, Sir Thomas George, surgeon, medical administrator, politician (b at Harbour Grace, Nfld 31 July 1846; d at Montréal 20 Feb 1923). A McGill medical graduate, he introduced Joseph Lister's antiseptic system to Montréal in 1877, a system that greatly reduced infections after surgery. He was the first chief surgeon of the Royal Victoria Hospital in Montréal, professor of surgery and dean of medicine of McGill. His greatest achievement came in 1912 with the creation of the Medical Council of Canada which provided a system of common examinations throughout the provinces for those seeking a licence to practise medicine. This followed 18 years of patient and tireless effort, including 8 years as an MP (1896-1904). In recognition of this and other services, he was knighted in 1914. EDWARD H. BENSLEY

Rodentia, largest and most common order of MAMMALS, including 34 families, 354 genera and 1685 species. In Canada, 68 of the 151 species of terrestrial mammals are rodents (including representatives of 10 families). They are characterized by having upper and lower incisors specialized for gnawing. These grow continuously from living pulp. Because the front surface, composed of enamel, is harder than the rear surface, the latter wears faster, creating a chisellike edge. As there are no canines, a large gap occurs between the incisors and the 2-5 cheek teeth. When the cheek teeth are in use, the incisors do not meet, and vice versa. Hence the jaw can crush food in a backward and forward, as well as a sideways motion. The hairy lips close in the gap behind the incisors, permitting some rodents to gnaw or excavate without filling the mouth with debris. Rodents are primarily herbivorous, eating parts of trees, grasses and herbaceous plants. Some (eg, deer mice and red squirrels) are omnivorous, also eating animal matter, eg, insects. Rodents range in size from 10 g (olive-backed pocket mouse) to 35 kg (beaver).

Their broad spectrum of evolutionary adaptations allows rodents to occupy diverse habitats. Aquatic rodents (eg, beaver) have feet webbed for swimming. Saltatorial rodents (eg, jumping mice) have hindlimbs and tails elongated for rapid movement in open habitats. Fossorial or digging rodents (eg, pocket gophers) have fore-paws modified for tunnelling in soil. Arboreal rodents, eg, squirrels, have hooked claws adapted to climbing. Gliding rodents, eg, flying squirrels, have a skin fold between forelimbs and hindlimbs that allows them to glide rapidly between trees. The behaviour patterns of rodents are equally diverse. Some species (eg, deer mice) are nocturnal, some (eg, most squirrels) are diurnal, and some (eg, *lemmings, voles*) are active night and day. Some form large colonies (eg, black-tailed prairie dogs); others are solitary (eg, red squirrels). Some (eg, beavers) are monogamous; others (eg, Richardson's ground squirrels) are polygamous. To cope with the Canadian winter, many rodents (including chipmunks, ground squirrels, marmots, jumping mice) hibernate; others (eg, beavers, voles) remain active throughout the year. Reproductive behaviour depends largely on size. Small species tend to mature quickly, breed several times through the year, produce large litters, and live less than one year. Larger rodents show the opposite trends and generally live longer than one year.

Humans derive direct benefit from fur-bearing rodents (eg, beavers, which also check stream erosion by their dams) and from domesticated *rats* and mice used for biological research. Indirect benefit is obtained from species that serve as food for game and fur mammals. However, rodents also compete with man for resources. Some, eg, meadow voles, may injure or kill shrubs and trees by girdling (chewing a ring around the bark). Some, especially the introduced brown rat and house mouse, may consume standing or stored grain crops. Rodents may also be carriers of human diseases, eg, bubonic plague, tularemia and scrub typhus. *See* individual species entries.   R. BOONSTRA

Reading: Peter W. Hanney, Rodents: Their Lives and Habits (1975).

Rodeo means roundup, or the gathering of livestock (usually cattle or horses) to be counted, inspected and branded; as a sport it refers to the public spectacle in which the dynamic elements of a roundup are presented as a cowboy competition: bronc riding, bull riding, steer wrestling, calf and steer roping (with more recent additions such as barrel racing, chuckwagon racing and wild-cow milking), as seen in such annual events as the CALGARY STAMPEDE. The name originates in the Spanish verb *rodear*, "to go around," or the Latin verb *rotare*, "to turn." Currently drawing spectators to cowboy contests coast to coast, rodeo is generally associated with life "in the West," the first major official Canadian rodeo being assembled 2 Sept 1912, as "The Last and Best Great West Frontier Days Celebration," at Calgary. Rodeo in N America owes its origin to a variety of historical traditions and entertainment forms. In the 16th century, *vaqueros*, Mexican herdsmen, used *la reata* (rope), clothed themselves in *chaperajos* (leggings) and tended hardy Spanish cattle from the backs of wiry N African riding stock. The 1847 diaries of travelling Irish military captain Mayne Reid provide perhaps the earliest rodeo documentation of *vaqueros* roping and throwing steers in the streets of Santa Fe, New Mexico Territory. These fiesta antics, transposed to cattle-driving communities such as Cheyenne (Wyoming Territory), Pecos City (Texas) and the pre-1900 ranches of what later became Alberta, fostered rodeo in its purest form.

In the Canadian West, broncobusting was considered sport at the Military Colonization Company ranch, and rope-throwing competitions were commonplace at the Fort Macleod Agricultural Fair in the 1880s. At the Walrond corral, John Ware is credited with some of the earliest exhibits of steer wrestling in 1892. The first Canadian rodeo was held in Raymond, Alta, in 1903. But it was not until the American

show-business phenomenon of the "Wild West Show" came to Canada in the early 1900s that spectators paid to see cowboy stunts. Former American cowpuncher Guy Weadick is responsible for promoting Wild West Shows in Canada, and in 1908 took his idea for an annual frontier day celebration, "pioneer reunion" and cowboy competition for world championship titles, to Calgary. With help from local politicians and businessmen, Weadick amassed over $100 000 for the first Calgary Stampede in 1912. It was a 6-day pageant and rodeo attracting more than 40 000 spectators a day, as well as legendary cowboys of the day — including some of Pancho Villa's bandits — in pursuit of $20 000 in prizes and world titles. WWI stalled the momentum of rodeo competition, but the Victory Stampede at Calgary (1919) revived cowboy contests in Canada permanently. Rodeo became an annual international event at Calgary in 1923 with a combined exhibition and stampede.

Rodeo's popularity sparked the growth of rodeo organizations in the 1930s, first with the Rodeo Assn of America (which represented primarily rodeo managers). In 1936, at an RAA rodeo in the Boston Gardens, Canadian and American cowboys broke the stranglehold that circuit managers had on rodeo purses when they staged a boycott; rodeo's first strike by professional cowboys succeeded in winning for competitors a greater percentage of the gate and precipitated the formation of the Professional Rodeo Cowboys' Assn in the US and the Canadian Rodeo Cowboys' Assn, founded 1944.

Despite periodic incursions to rearrange rodeo competition along team-sport lines, the basic premise of individual human strength and precision against animal and clock has remained. Bull riding, pitting a rider's balance and stability against a one-ton Brahma bull's instinct to remove the cowboy from its back, officially entered rodeo competition in 1921. Saddle-bronc riding dates back to a time when the livelihood of some working cowboys was broncobusting. Bareback riding began as a sideshow in rodeo, when younger cowboys earned mount money in exhibition rides aboard particularly ornery unbroken horses; the 1950s saw bareback riding gain the legitimacy of the other 2 riding events. Calf roping is one rodeo event still practised on the ranch, but in the artificial setting of the rodeo arena it reaches near perfection; when a barrier in front of a horse and rider is released by a bolting calf, the contestant runs down the calf, throws it to the ground and ties any 3 feet; fastest time wins. The other timed rodeo event, steer wrestling (originally known as bulldogging), moved from the Wild West Shows to the first rodeos as a cowboy's test of strength in bringing down a running steer by leaping from a moving horse, locking onto the steer's horns and twisting it to the ground; in the earliest rodeos, the bulldogger had to finish the maneuvre by taking the steer's lower lip in his own teeth. While world-championship titles in early rodeo were usually awarded to the winners of year-end competitions, such as the Pendleton Round-up in Oregon, the Cheyenne Frontier Days in Wyoming or the Calgary Stampede in Alberta, championships are currently determined by a cowboy's prize-money accumulation at season's end; that is, at the National Finals Rodeo in Oklahoma City or the Canadian Finals Rodeo in Edmonton. Among Canadians who have achieved international success as world champions in rodeo are Pete Knight (Crossfield, Alta) 4-time saddle bronc champ between 1932 and 1936; Nate Waldrum (Strathmore, Alta) bareback champ in 1933; Carl Olson (Calgary, Alta) saddle bronc champ in 1947; Marty Wood (Bowness, Alta) saddle bronc champ in 1958, 1964 and 1966; Winston Bruce (Calgary, Alta) saddle bronc champ in 1961; Kenny McLean (Okanagan Falls, BC) saddle bronc champ in 1962; Mel

Hyland (Surrey, BC) saddle bronc champ in 1972; Jim Gladstone (Cardston, Alta) calf roping champ in 1977; and Cody Snyder (Redcliff, Alta) first Canadian to win the world bullriding championship in 1983.   TED BARRIS

Reading: Ted Barris, *Rodeo Cowboys: The Last Heroes* (1981); B. Berry, *Let 'Er Buck! The Rodeo* (1971); C. Eamer and T. Jones, *The Canadian Rodeo Book* (1882); D.K. Hall, *Rodeo* (1976); B. St. John, *On Down the Road* (1977).

Rogers, Edward Samuel, inventor, broadcasting pioneer (b at Toronto 21 June 1900; d there 6 May 1939). Son of a wealthy businessman, Rogers was obsessed with radio from childhood. At 13 he won a prize for the best amateur-built radio in Ontario, and in 1921 was the only Canadian to win an American competition for low-power broadcasts across the Atlantic. His alternating-current radio tube, perfected in 1925, revolutionized the home radio-receiver industry throughout the world. Before Rogers, home receivers had to run on direct current from rechargeable acid-filled batteries: the 25- or 60-cycle hum of alternating-current mains electricity was often louder than radio signals. Rogers's amplifying tube eliminated this problem, making mains-powered home radios practical for the first time. With his father, he founded the Rogers Majestic manufacturing company and established several broadcasting companies, including station 9RB (later CFRB, Toronto) named for the "Rogers Batteryless" system. His son **Edward Samuel** (b at Toronto 27 May 1933) heads ROGERS TELECOMMUNICATIONS LIMITED.   DONALD J.C. PHILLIPSON

Rogers, Norman McLeod, scholar, politician (b at Amherst, NS 25 July 1894; d at Newtonville, Ont 10 June 1940). Educated at Acadia and Oxford, Rogers interrupted his studies to serve in WWI. He was professor of history at Acadia, 1922-27, private secretary to PM KING, 1927-29. Although a professor of political science at Queen's, 1929-35, Rogers kept his connections with King, authoring a campaign biography, *Mackenzie King* (1935). Elected to Parliament for Kingston, Ont, in 1935, he became minister of labour and the leading progressive liberal in the Cabinet. Appointed minister of national defence in 1939, he died the next year in a plane crash.   ROBERT BOTHWELL

Rogers, Otto Donald, painter, sculptor (b at Kerrobert, Sask 19 Nov 1935). One of Canada's foremost contemporary practitioners of colour-field painting and constructivist steel sculpture, Rogers was encouraged to pursue an artistic career by Wynona Mulcaster while attending Saskatoon Teachers' Coll (1952-53). He attended U of Wisconsin (1953-59). Upon his return to Saskatoon (1959), he was appointed to the faculty of U of Sask, serving as head of the art dept 1973-77. In 1960 Rogers adopted the BAHA'I FAITH. Since then he has lectured and written extensively on this religion emphasizing its importance to his art. While recognizing the spiritual element, some critics claim that the prairie environment is equally important in his work.   NORMAN ZEPP

Rogers, Robert, author, army officer (b at Methuen, Mass 8 Nov 1731; d at London, Eng 18 May 1795). A versatile frontiersman, Rogers ably led colonial Rangers during King George's War (1744-48; *see* WAR OF THE AUSTRIAN SUCCESSION) and the SEVEN YEARS' WAR. But he had a knack for getting into trouble through prodigal spending habits, drinking and gambling. He was tried by court-martial at Montréal in 1768 for alleged treason and overspending, but acquitted. During the AMERICAN REVOLUTION, Rogers was distrusted and imprisoned by Gen George Washington and then raised and commanded the LOYALIST Queen's (later King's) Rangers. His most significant achievements are literary. While in London in 1765 he published his wartime *Journals* and *A*

Concise Account of North America. Ponteach, or, The Savages of America was published in London in 1766, a critical portrayal of British colonists' exploitation of Indians.   ROTA HERZBERG LISTER
Reading: J.R. Cuneo, *Robert Rogers of the Rangers* (1959).

Rogers Pass, elev 1323 m, in BC's Selkirk Mtns, was named for A.B. Rogers (1829-89) hired by the CANADIAN PACIFIC RY to find a route through this range. Rogers reached the pass via the S fork of the Illecillewaet R May 1881. The following year he approached from the E to satisfy his employers that the Selkirks could be breached. During 1885 and 1886 the railway was built through the pass at great expense. Over 6.4 km of snowsheds (31) were built to protect trains, trackage and workmen from avalanches (the area receives up to 15 m of snow each winter). The CPR soon after built Glacier House, a world-renowned hostelry just W of the pass. After much damage and loss of life from avalanches, the 8 km Connaught Tunnel was pushed through below the pass (1916). A longer tunnel is now being constructed to cut down track grades in the pass. The all-weather TRANS-CANADA HWY opened over the pass 1962. An extensive avalanche safety program is carried out in the pass area.   GLEN BOLES

Rogers Telecommunications Limited (RTL), controlled by the Edward S. ROGERS family, is one of the world's largest CABLE-TELEVISION holding companies, with subsidiary interests in radio broadcasting and entertainment services. Rogers Cablesystems Inc, controlled by RTL, operates several cable-television systems in Canada (1 316 000 subscribers in 1983), the US (461 100) and Ireland (110 000), and provides a variety of services including special programming, interactive television, security monitoring and PAY-TELEVISION services. Its principal Canadian operations are located in Vancouver, Victoria, Calgary, Toronto and southern Ontario. RTL's other holdings include CFTR-AM and CHFI-FM in Toronto and stations in Sarnia and Leamington, Ont, and an interest in cellular radio. Total assets for Rogers Cablesystems were $914 million in 1983, with revenues of $364 million.   PETER S. ANDERSON

Roller Skating is a sport with a wide range of recreational and competitive aspects. Artistic competition is closely related to ICE SKATING and includes figures, freestyle, pairs and dance events. Speed skating includes both individual and relay races. Roller hockey started as roller polo in the 1880s and is now played with a ball or puck; ball hockey is organized as an international roller sport. The use of plastic urethane wheels and sealed precision bearings, both adapted from skateboards, produced a skate that gives a smooth ride on outdoor surfaces and stimulated the roller-skating boom of the 1970s.

The roller skate was developed in Holland in the 18th century, with wooden spools attached to strips of wood. Today's 4-wheel arrangement was satisfactorily produced in 1863. Roller-skating facilities were built in the 1880s in Toronto and Montréal. In 1884, skating started in Chatham, Ont, which within a year had become one of the foremost roller-skating centres in the world. Speed skater George Berry, of Chatham, became the Canadian roller-skating champion in 1884 and in the next year won the N American championship and was acclaimed world champion. WWI signalled the end of competitive skating, but a revival in the 1930s stimulated events such as the 5-day roller-skating derby held at the CANADIAN NATIONAL EXHIBITION in 1940. The Canadian Roller Skating Assn was formed in 1961 and became the Canadian Federation of Amateur Roller Skaters in 1973. Canada sent a team to the World Artistic Roller Skating Championships for the first time in 1976, placing 5th among 19 countries. In 1979, these championships were held in Montréal. The CFARS organizes national championships in figures, freestyle and overall categories, at 3 levels for boys and girls and 6 for men and women.
    BARBARA SCHRODT

Rolph, John, barrister, physician, politician, educator (b at Thornbury, Eng 4 Mar 1793; d at Mitchell, Ont 19 Oct 1870). Educated in England, he practised law and medicine in Upper Canada from 1821, operating medical schools in 1824-25 in St Thomas and from 1832 in York [Toronto]. By 1828 he shared leadership of the REFORM MOVEMENT with M.S. BIDWELL and the BALDWINS. A secretive, 11th-hour supporter of William Lyon MACKENZIE's ill-fated REBELLION OF 1837, he fled to Rochester, NY. He returned in 1843 to reopen his medical school, which soon flourished. An ineffectual member of the Hincks-Morin ministry, 1851-54, he severely disappointed his ultra-reform (CLEAR GRIT) supporters. Thereafter, he concentrated on running his school. By eloquently defending American settlers' rights and opposing special privileges for the Church of England, Rolph contributed greatly to the rising popularity of the constitutional reform movement before 1837 and did more than anyone before the 1860s to provide first-class medical training in the province.
    DAVID R. KEANE

Romaine, Rivière, 496 km long with a 14 349 km² basin, rises (elev 760 m) in the Québec-Labrador lacustrine plateau, 45 km SW of the CHURCHILL R, and forms part of the Québec-Labrador boundary N of the 52nd parallel. Near its head, it crosses Lac Brûlé. The Montagnais frequently used it in their annual migrations to the Labrador coast, for there are only 15 km of lakes and portages before it joins the Churchill Basin. The river's last 35 km flow through a vast postglacial delta, on the shores of which sits Havre-Saint-Pierre (pop 3200), terminus of Hwy 138 and of the 40 km railway that joins Québec Iron and Titanium on Lac Allard with the coast. Hydro-Québec sees great hydroelectric power potential on this river. "Romaine" is a French deformation of the Montagnais word *uramen,* which means "red ochre."   JEAN-MARIE DUBOIS

Roman, Stephen Boleslav, mine executive (b at Velky Ruskov, Slovakia 17 Apr 1921). Roman immigrated to Canada in 1937, working as a farm labourer before joining the Canadian Army in 1942. Discharged in 1943, he became interested in the stock market, organized several natural-resources ventures, and in 1953 acquired a interest in a uranium prospect that formed the basis of Denison Mines Ltd. As president and later chairman of Denison, Roman expanded and diversified his firm and was periodically involved in controversies on nuclear politics and FOREIGN INVESTMENT. An outspoken advocate of private enterprise, Roman sued PM TRUDEAU and Energy Minister J.J. Greene because Ottawa tried to block the sale of Denison shares to an American controlled firm. Roman was twice unsuccessful as a federal PC candidate. With Eugen Loebl he wrote *The Responsible Society* (1977).   JOSEPH LINDSEY

Roman Catholic Church, *see* CATHOLICISM.

Romanians In 1878 Romanian independence from the Ottoman Empire was recognized. Many Romanians were living in provinces (Transylvania and Bukovina) then part of the Austro-Hungarian Empire, and it was from these provinces, particularly the latter, that many Romanians emigrated to Canada, although they had been preceded by individual priests from Bucharest sent to the early settlements of Canada. They were motivated by a wish to escape living under a foreign government, a desire to own land, and general economic conditions. Most of the early immigrants were peasants and by 1895 they were arriving by the thousands. By 1914 there were 8301 Romanians in Canada; in 1921 the number was 13 470, though these figures are tentative since many immigrated from regions which were not part of Romania until 1918, and others came from Hungary, Austria and Russia.

Early settlements were founded at Regina, Limerick, Dysart, Kayville, Flintoft and Canora (Sask); Inglis (Man); and Boian (Alta). Because French has traditionally been the second language of Romania, many Romanians were attracted to Québec where they established themselves in Montréal. Between 1921 and 1929, many new immigrants arrived to join relatives and friends, so by 1931 there were some 29 000 Romanian Canadians. After WWII a significant number of Romanians immigrated to Canada, mainly professionals who settled in cities. The current number of Canadians of Romanian origin is about 22 485.

Most Romanians belong to the Romanian ORTHODOX CHURCH (the first such church in N America was the Church of St Nicholas, built in Regina in 1901). Many parishes are attached to a youth group which is a branch of American Romanian Orthodox youth. Mutual benefit and cultural organizations have existed at some time in most communities, many part of an American organization — the Union and League of Romanian Societies of America. Two Romanian-language newspapers are published in Canada: *Ecouri Romanesti* (*Romanian Echoes*) and *Curantul Romanesc* (*The Romanian Voice*). Lively homeland religious and social events centre around rural churches.

Ethnic consciousness has decreased considerably among descendants of the early immigrants, accelerated by the high educational level and wide dispersal of the post-WWII immigrants. Fewer than 30% of Romanian Canadians now speak Romanian.   G. JAMES PATTERSON
Reading: G. James Patterson, *The Romanians of Saskatchewan* (1977).

Romantic Fiction, *see* POPULAR LITERATURE.

Ronald, William, né Smith, painter (b at Stratford, Ont 13 Aug 1926). Ronald's abstract expressionism influenced an era in Canadian art; he was the catalyst who organized PAINTERS ELEVEN, the first abstract PAINTING group in Ontario, in 1953. His gift lies in his work's spontaneity, dynamism and energy and in his natural talent for handling paint. After studies at the Ontario Coll of Art with Jock MACDONALD, Ronald went to New York in 1952 where he briefly attended Hans Hofmann's School. In the mid-1950s, after travelling frequently between Toronto and New York, he moved to New York. He was influenced by the fragmentary, explosive painting of Willem de Kooning, but by contrast created large central images with a background horizon line, painted in a savage technique. In 1957 he had his first exhibition in the Samuel Kootz Gallery with whom he remained until 1963. In the mid-1960s he returned to Canada. Because of a 1967 mural commission at the NATIONAL ARTS CENTRE in Ottawa, Ronald's style evolved into a more hard-edged format prophetic of the 1970s in Canadian art. Through the

William Ronald, *Slow Movement* (1953), casein and duco on masonite (*courtesy Robert McLaughlin Gallery, Oshawa*).

years he has maintained his interest in automatic painting using a vocabulary of symbols, often central images, that interest him. He has also had a career as a broadcaster; he was host for the CBC radio program *As it Happens* (1969-72) and for a TV variety show about the arts, *The Umbrella* (1966-67).   JOAN MURRAY

Roncarelli v Duplessis In 1946, Maurice DUPLESSIS, then premier and attorney general of Qué, caused the Liquor Commission chairman to revoke the liquor licence of Frank Roncarelli, a Montréal restaurant owner, so ruining the restaurant. Roncarelli was innocent of all misconduct, but the authorities thought him troublesome because he (legitimately) provided bail for many JEHOVAH'S WITNESSES charged (groundlessly, as the Supreme Court later held) with supposed offences resulting from the distribution of religious pamphlets attacking Roman Catholicism (see SAUMUR V CITY OF QUÉBEC). The Supreme Court (1959) held the premier had committed a civil wrong and ordered him personally to pay damages.   STEPHEN A. SCOTT

Rondeau Provincial Park (48 km²) provides environmental protection and recreation on one of 3 peninsulas jutting S into Lk ERIE. It lies 120 km E of Windsor and 115 km SW of London. The peninsula was formed in late geological time by currents in Glacial Lk Erie that converged and deposited sediment that accumulated in a succession of sandbars. The processes of deposition and erosion have continued and the cuspate sandspit is continuously changing in size and shape. It has been colonized successively by grasses, oaks and white pines and, finally, by some shade-tolerant species (eg, sugar MAPLE, American beech). In addition, plants such as tulip and sassafras, normally occurring much further S, are found, as are some 125 herbaceous plants considered rare in Ontario (eg, species normally associated with tall-grass PRAIRIE). Eighteen species of orchids flourish in Rondeau. Over 30 mammal species have been observed in the park, including white-tailed deer, opossum and grey fox. Amphibians and reptiles (eg, turtles, toads, fox snakes) are well represented. Rondeau is renowned for birdlife: 323 species have been recorded; 124 have nested in the park; and 80% of all species found in Ontario have been seen here, including the rare prothonotary warbler.

The NEUTRAL exploited the area's fish, game and plant resources. The English recognized the timber and harbour potential, bought the land and, in 1795, declared it Ordnance Land, reserved for government purposes. Thereafter, it was used for naval purposes, exploited for timber, waterfowl, fur bearers and fish and, in the late 1800s, developed for hotels and tourism. In 1894 it became Ontario's third provincial park. There has been an increased emphasis in recent years on nature protection.   JOHN S. MARSH

Ronning, Chester Alvin, diplomat (b at Fancheng [Xiangfan], China 13 Dec 1894; d at Camrose, Alta 31 Dec 1984). He spent his early years in China and in northern Alberta. He served in the Royal Flying Corps (1918), but upon completion of courses at U of A and U of Minn, he returned to China as a teacher (1922-27) until being named principal of Camrose Lutheran College. While principal (1927-42), he was (1932) an MLA in the UNITED FARMERS OF ALBERTA government and active in the CO-OPERATIVE COMMONWEALTH FEDERATION. After leading an RCAF intelligence unit (1942-45), Ronning entered the Dept of External Affairs, serving in China (1945-51), in Ottawa (1951-54), as ambassador in Norway (1954-57), as high commissioner in India (1957-64), and also as a member of the conference on Korea in Geneva (1954) and on Laos (1961-62). He undertook special missions to Hanoi (1965 and 1966) to attempt to mediate

during the Vietnam War. Ronning was an untiring advocate of the recognition of the People's Republic of China and of its admission to the UNITED NATIONS. His knowledge of China and his friendship with such Asian leaders as Zhou Enlai made him an invaluable go-between.
          B.L. EVANS

Root Crops The important temperate zone root crops are sugar BEET, CARROT, red RADISH, PARSNIP, TURNIP and RUTABAGA. Horseradish (a CONDIMENT CROP) and KOHLRABI are minor but locally important crops. All are cool-season biennials grown from seed (except horseradish, which is grown from root cuttings), thriving in deep, friable soil and suitable for long-term storage. Sugar beets, important in Alberta and Manitoba, belong to the same species as red beets, mangelwurzel and Swiss chard. Carrots, important in Ontario and Québec, are a valuable source of vitamin A. Parsnips are similar to carrots in production practices but seedlings are very slow to emerge and require a long growing season. Radish is a quick-growing crop, needing as little as 3 weeks from seeding to harvest. Several crops can be grown in a season. Almost all are eaten raw in salads. Red beets are grown mostly in home and market gardens for fresh use, although some are grown commercially for canning. Rutabagas and turnips are very similar, except that turnips are much smaller and the tops can be eaten as "greens." They are important in Ontario and to a lesser extent Québec.   G. ROWBERRY

Rose, common name for members of genus *Rosa* of the rose family (Rosaceae). This large family, comprising more than 100 genera and 2000-3000 species, includes PLANTS as diverse as strawberries, almonds and pears. The genus *Rosa* comprises over 100 species of erect, climbing or trailing shrubs, plus cultivars. About 14 species are native to Canada, and many introduced species have become established. The prickly rose (*R. acicularis*), the largest and most widespread wild rose in Canada, is found from Québec to BC and S to Virginia and New Mexico. This 1-1.5 m high shrub forms thick bushes that spring from underground shoots. It grows mainly in open, sunny areas. Its stems have slender spines and, in June, bear usually a single, delicately scented,

The prickly rose (*Rosa acicularis*) is the largest and most widespread wild rose in Canada; it is Alberta's provincial floral emblem (*photo by Al Williams*).

pale or dark pink flower, 5 cm in diameter. The edible rose hips, which make excellent jams and jellies, are also enjoyed by birds. Since 1930 the prickly rose has been the PROVINCIAL FLORAL EMBLEM of Alberta, where it grows abundantly. It is easily grown in sandy soil. Cultivated roses have been popular ORNAMENTALS since ancient times. Most ornamental roses are hybrids of Old World species.   CÉLINE ARSENEAULT

Rose, Cultivated Roses have been cultivated from very early times, but little is known of their origin. Modern garden roses began with the introduction of the first hybrid tea rose in 1867. Today, roses are classified as hybrid tea (large flowered), floribunda (cluster flowered), grandiflora (large-cluster flowered), miniature, shrub, climbing and rambling types; however, these classifications are being changed because of recent introductions of different flowering types. In Canada rose breeding has concentrated primarily on developing hardy roses with better flowers for colder areas (eg, the prairies); however, except in SW coastal BC, most roses still require winter protection. Three early rose breeders were prairie nurserymen. In recent years, Agriculture Canada's research stations in Ottawa and Morden, Man, have introduced a number of excellent garden roses, some closely resembling the popular hybrid teas and floribundas. Roses will grow in most well-drained soils but prefer a fertile loam in an open location with at least 6 hours of sunlight. They flower from early summer to late fall, depending on climate. All roses require a low-nitrogen, balanced fertilizer during the early growing season and frequent watering. Some shrub roses form large, colourful seed heads (hips) and their leaves may turn red in fall. Common garden pests, frequent on most roses, can be controlled chemically. Black spot and mildew diseases are difficult to control; selecting resistant varieties helps avoid these problems. Statistics are unavailable on the value of roses to the Canadian greenhouse and nursery industries. However, in 1982, almost 38 million roses were produced for sale as cut flowers in Canada, and nearly 627 000 rose plants were grown for sale. A further, undetermined number were imported from the US and Europe.

Rose, Fred, union organizer, politician (b Fred Rosenberg at Lublin, Poland 7 Dec 1907; d at Warsaw, Poland 16 Mar 1983). Rose moved with his parents to Montréal. In the 1930s, as a member of the Young Communist League, he organized unions of unemployed and unskilled workers. He was arrested in 1929 and again in 1931 at a meeting of the unemployed, and was convicted and sentenced to a year for sedition. In the 1943 by-election in Montréal-Cartier he was elected to the House of Commons as a Labour Progressive. He was re-elected in 1945, the only MP elected as a communist in Canadian history. In 1946 he was arrested in the first Cold War spy trials and sentenced to 6 years in the penitentiary for communicating official secrets to a foreign power.   MERRILY WEISBORD

Rose, Sir John, politician, banker, diplomat (b at Turriff, Scot, 2 Aug 1820; d at Langwell Forest, Scot 24 Aug 1888). He immigrated to Canada in 1836 and became a prominent corporation lawyer in Montréal. Elected to Legislative Assembly of the PROVINCE OF CANADA in 1857, he was appointed solicitor general for Canada E in the Macdonald-Cartier administration. Chief commissioner of public works 1859-61, he resigned and sat as a private member and spokesman for the Protestant minority of Canada E 1861-67. Considered John A. MACDONALD's closest friend, he was minister of finance 1867-69 and responsible for the Dominion's first banking legislation. He moved to London as an investment banker in 1869 and served as a quasi-official representative of the Canadian government in England. He undertook the preliminary negotiations with the US that led to the TREATY OF WASHINGTON, 1871, and was involved in setting up the original CPR syndicate in 1880. A well-known figure in English society and a financial adviser to the Prince of Wales, he was created baronet in 1872.

D.M.L. FARR

Rosenblatt, Joseph, poet, artist, editor (b at Toronto 26 Dec 1933). He achieved prominence as a concrete and sound poet but some of his best work is lyrical, drawn from his proletarian and Jewish background. He has published 12 books of poetry, (including *Bumblebee Dithyramb* (1972), *Sleeping Lady* (1980) and *Brides of the Stream* (1983)), winning the Gov Gen's Award for *Top Soil* (1976). As an artist he has created phantasmagoric drawings of the animal kingdom, offering a unique vision of humanity. He has published one art book, *Dr Anaconda's Solar Fun Club* (1978). His limited-edition drawing portfolio, *Snake Oil* (1978), contains many satirical literary references. As editor of the Toronto quarterly *Jewish Dialogue*, Rosenblatt has encouraged new literary talent. He was president 1983-84 of the League of Canadian Poets.

SHARON DRACHE

Rosenfeld, Fanny, "Bobbie," track and field athlete, sportswriter (b in Russia 28 Dec 1903; d at Toronto 14 Nov 1969). Canada's woman athlete of the half century, she entered international athletics in 1928, the year women were first admitted to the Olympic Games. She held Canadian records in the running and standing broad jump and in the discus; at the 1928 Amsterdam Olympics she took the silver medal in the 100 m dash and was lead runner for the women's 4 x 100 relay team that won in a record time of 48.2 sec. Rosenfeld was also joint holder of the 11-sec, 100-yard world record.

TED BARRIS

Ross, Alexander, fur trader, author (b in Morayshire, Scot 9 May 1783; d at Red River [Man] 23 Oct 1856). Immigrating to Canada as an adult, he taught school for a few years. In 1810 he joined the Pacific Fur Co as a clerk serving variously at Ft Astoria, Ft Okanagan, Ft George and Ft Nez Percés for the NWC and then the HBC. He retired to Red River in 1825 where he became sheriff of Assiniboia, commander of the volunteer Corps, captain of the police, magistrate, commissioner and court examiner. He wrote several fur-trade classics: *Adventures on the Columbia River* (1849), *The Fur Hunters of the Far West* (1853) and *The Red River Settlement* (1856). He was married to an Okanagan Indian "princess," and several of their children played important roles in Manitoba's history. In his last book, Ross saw Red River as a civilized island in a barbarous wilderness, but despaired as to its future and that of its mixed-blood inhabitants.

FRITS PANNEKOEK

Ross, Sir George William, politician, premier of Ontario 1889-1905 (b near Nairn, Ont 18 Sept 1841; d at Toronto 7 Mar 1914). After some years as a teacher, school inspector and journalist, Ross was elected to the House of Commons for W Middlesex. On his defeat in the federal election of 1883, he joined Sir Oliver MOWAT's Ontario Cabinet as minister of education. Ross rationalized and improved the public school system, while grappling with bitter public controversies over language and religion in Roman Catholic separate schools and over the financing of the provincial university at Toronto and the denominational colleges. He succeeded Arthur Sturgis HARDY in the premiership in 1899, but his government was defeated in 1905. After leading the Opposition for 2 years, he accepted appointment to the Senate where he was Liberal

leader from 1910 until his death. A noted orator, Ross also published books and pamphlets, including the autobiographical *Getting Into Parliament and After* (1913).

WENDY CAMERON

Ross, James, capitalist (b at Cromarty, Scot 1848; d at Montréal 20 Mar 1913). A professional engineer, Ross was associated with the construction of numerous railways and was manager of construction of the mountain division on the main line of the CPR. In the 1890s, he and other promoters undertook reorganization, electrification and expansion of the street railways in Toronto and Montréal, and subsequently in other cities in Canada, the US, the UK, Mexico, S America and the Caribbean. In 1901 he undertook a major and controversial reorganization of the Dominion Coal Co and the Dominion Iron and Steel Co. He was a patron of several art societies and donated substantial sums to various hospitals. He became an avid yachtsman, and his yacht *Glencairn* won several racing trophies.

T.D. REGEHR

Ross, Sir James Clark, naval officer, polar discoverer (b in Scot ? 15 Apr 1800; d at Aylesbury, Eng 13 Apr 1862). Best known for antarctic researches (1839-43), Ross did his polar voyaging chiefly in the Canadian Arctic. He journeyed there 4 times as an officer under William Edward PARRY and twice under his uncle, John Ross. With the latter he explored the northern shore of King William I and located the N Magnetic Pole in 1831. Ross was employed by both officers in magnetic research, in which he became expert. He retired after the antarctic expedition, but was called back to command the 1848-49 arctic expedition to rescue Sir John FRANKLIN. He discovered Peel Sound, but the expedition miscarried because of a severe winter.

L.H. NEATBY

Ross, James Sinclair, writer (b at Shellbrook, Sask 22 Jan 1908). Ross is one of Canada's most respected writers, in particular for his acclaimed novel, *As for Me and My House*. Shortly after Ross was born, his family separated, and "Jimmy" was raised by his mother. He left school at 16 to join the Royal Bank of Canada as a clerk at Abbey, Saskatchewan. Banking became his lifelong career. He wrote in his spare time, and in 1934 his first story, "No Other Way," was published in London, Eng. Like most of Ross's fiction, it is set on the Canadian prairies. There ensued a productive period of storywriting for small Canadian magazines. The best-known stories, "The Painted Door," "A Field of Wheat" and "The Lamp at Noon," have been much anthologized. Several were later collected as *The Lamp at Noon and Other Stories* (1968). Their well-crafted structures and precise images have brought many readers to appreciate Ross's work. In them, he presented a theme that remained a preoccupation: intellectual isolation. Ross was little known to the Canadian or international public until his first novel, *As for Me and My House*, was published in New York in 1941. It was immediately hailed as superior, with its insight into the barren existence of Horizon, Sask. Often perceived as a gloomy portrait of rather miserable people, the book has surprising moments of humour and satire. The theme of triumph over the stultifying effects of small-town life and the Depression is its greatest strength and what differentiates it from *Main Street*, the Sinclair Lewis novel with which it is often compared. Its psychological penetration guarantees its place in modern Canadian literature. Ross's next 2 novels, *The Well* (1958) and *Whir of Gold* (1970), failed to make much critical impact. His novella called *Sawbones Memorial* (1974), however, is a technical tour de force, relying more on dramatic than narrative technique. It consists of a series of dialogues and interior monologues in which the history of the town and most of its

inhabitants is powerfully recreated. Upon retirement from the Royal Bank in 1968, Ross moved to Greece and then to Spain. Ill health prompted his return to Canada in 1980.

KEN MITCHELL

Ross, John Jones, physician, politician, premier of Québec (b at Ste-Anne-de-la-Pérade, Lower Canada 16 Aug 1833; d there 4 May 1901). A rather dull and uninspiring man, Ross was premier 23 Jan 1884 to 25 Jan 1887. His Conservative government refused to take a position on the Louis RIEL affair, leading to its defeat late in 1886 by the new PARTI NATIONAL of Honoré MERCIER. In an attempt to keep the Conservatives in power, Ross resigned in favour of L.O. TAILLON; defeated in the House, Taillon resigned and Mercier became premier. PM John A. MACDONALD rewarded Ross with an appointment to the Senate.

DANIEL LATOUCHE

Ross, Malcolm, humanist, educator (b at Fredericton 2 Jan 1911). As editor of the New Canadian Library series, Ross gave Canadian readers the benefit of the enthusiasm and discrimination that made him an outstanding teacher at universities from Manitoba to Trinity, Queen's and Dalhousie. His books and articles began with work on the 17th century (*Milton's Royalism* 1943, 1970); he moved to universal issues (*Poetry and Dogma* 1954, 1969) and to critical assessment and anthologies of Canadian writings (*Our Sense of Identity* 1954 and *The Arts in Canada* 1958). As officer and policymaker on the Canada Council, the Royal Society of Canada, and the Humanities Assn of Canada, he has been a benign force in Canadian culture.

ELIZABETH WATERSTON

Ross Farm, at New Ross, NS, 28 km N of Chester, dates from 1816, when Capt William Ross led 172 disbanded soldiers into the NS interior to establish an agricultural settlement. Focusing on the family dwelling called Rosebank Cottage, Ross Farm consisted of tillage, pasture and woodland, and remained the home of the Ross family until 1970, when the New Ross Dist Museum Soc and NS Museum undertook its development as a living museum of NS's agricultural heritage. Today, ploughs pulled by oxen, and grain harvested by sickle and scythe, illustrate the last century's farm technology and the significance of NS's role in the development of Canadian agriculture. Local crafts such as barrel making and woodworking are demonstrated. Period buildings include a blacksmith's shop, cooperage, stave mill and 100-year-old schoolhouse.

DEBRA MCNABB

Rossiter, Roger James, biochemist, neurological scientist (b at Glenelg, Australia 24 July 1913; d at Helsinki, Finland 21 Feb 1976). Rossiter pioneered studies of the nervous system's chemical composition and was prominent in the development of BIOCHEMISTRY in Canada. Educated in Australia and at Oxford, he trained as a medical scientist under Sir Rudolph Peters. During WWII Rossiter conducted army research on malaria and burn injuries and studied malnutrition in repatriated prisoners of war. He emigrated to London, Ont, in 1947 as head of UWO dept of biochemistry, where he later became dean of graduate studies and vice-president. Rossiter established an active research group which rapidly acquired an international reputation for studies on brain biochemistry. Over the years his work led to elucidation of lipid components in the nerve myelin sheath and processes involved in formation or degradation of these key structural elements in relation to development or to degenerative diseases of the nervous system.

W.C. MCMURRAY

Rossland, BC, City, pop 3967 (1981c), inc 1897, is located 7 km SW of TRAIL at the base of Red Mt. Copper-gold mines were discovered on Red Mt 1890 by Joe Bourgeois and Joe Moris. The city was named after Ross Thompson, an early settler, and was changed from Thompson to Rossland in 1894 by postal authorities. It had 8000 inhabitants by 1897, and was connected by rail with Trail, site of a large smelter. Mining boomed until 1916, then continued sporadically until 1930. In the 1960s MOLYBDENUM mining was opened on Red Mt; it continues intermittently. The city functions mainly as a service centre for mining and as a place of residence for Cominco employees in Trail. The development of skiing facilities at Red Mt is the most promising means for expanding the local economy.

WILLIAM A. SLOAN

Rothstein, Aser, physiologist (b at Vancouver 29 Apr 1918). He has contributed enormously to the fields of cellular physiology and toxicology. A graduate of UBC, he obtained his PhD at U of Rochester, NY, in 1943. He performed pioneering experiments introducing the use of radioisotopes in the biological sciences. Rothstein's research has been mainly related to the transport of substances across biological membranes. His contributions include the identification of the protein responsible for anion transport in red blood cells. He was president of the Soc for General Physiologists and chairman of the Cell Physiology Commission for UNESCO. He has been director of the Research Institute of the Hospital for Sick Children (Toronto) since 1972.

SERGIO GRINSTEIN

Rouges, *see* PARTI ROUGE.

Rough Trade, an internationally popular Toronto-based rock group, was founded in 1974 by vocalist Carole Pope (1982 Juno Award, Top Female Vocalist) and guitarist/keyboardist Kevan Staples. Rough Trade is best known for songs "All Touch" and "High School Confidential." Other members in 1983 included Jorn Anderson, Howard Ayee and David McMorrow.

JOHN GEIGER

Roughing It in The Bush: or, Forest Life in Canada, by Susanna MOODIE (London, 1852; Toronto, 1871), is Moodie's best-known book, and has been variously described as a novel, a romance, a diary and a history. Its subject, less elusive than its form, is Moodie's experience as an immigrant who settled with her husband near Peterborough, Canada West. Unlike the account by her sister, Catharine Parr TRAILL, of the settler's experience, Moodie's opens with a grim warning to prospective emigrants that Canada is not the Eden it is widely promoted to be in England, and that the settler's lot is a harsh one. Moodie's tone is more sombre than her sister's, but her descriptions of place and character are more imaginative, alloying the documentary with the fictional; and the personality she presents is more complex. Moodie's character inspires Margaret Atwood's fine book of poems, *The Journals of Susanna Moodie* (1970). NEIL BESNER

Round Table Movement, an organization devoted to the study of British Empire problems and the promotion of imperial unity, fd 1909 in London, Eng. Branches were quickly established in Canada, South Africa, Australia and New Zealand and for the next 10 years the movement played an important role in imperial affairs. Its primary concerns were to involve the Dominions in defence and foreign policy decision making so they would be able more readily to assert their nationhood, and to ensure the greater strength and continued unity of the British Empire. Its efforts to achieve imperial federation failed, partly because leading Canadian members, Arthur Glazebrook, Joseph FLAVELLE, John WILLISON, George WRONG and Vincent MASSEY, did not favour imperial union. The movement helped, however, to publicize the ideal of a COMMONWEALTH of free "British" nations.

JOHN KENDLE

Rousseau, Jacques, botanist, ethnobiologist, ethnohistorian (b at St-Lambert, Qué 5 Oct 1905; d at Lac Ouareau, Qué 4 Aug 1970). Explorer of the Québec-Labrador peninsula and of eccentric regions in Québec, skilled in many natural and "human" sciences, and possessed of an encyclopedic knowledge, he produced close to 550 publications. He was founder and first secretary (1930-46) of L'Association canadienne-française pour l'avancement des sciences. He received his doctorate in science from U de M, and later became a director of its Botanical Institute (1944-56). Because of his interdisciplinary competence he was the first director of the National Museum of Man in Ottawa (1956-59). His written work (observation notes, diary, reviews, articles), including numerous articles on the "Amerindiens" — a concept now in use in ethnological writings — demonstrate rare observational skills and original views. His writings reveal a breadth of scientific knowledge and are masterpieces of interdisciplinary writing, though his innovating talents were not fully recognized in his lifetime. His edition of Pehr KALM's 1749 *Voyage* was completed by Guy Béthune and Pierre Morisset and published in 1977.

MARC-ADÉLARD TREMBLAY

Roussil, Robert, sculptor (b at Montréal 1925). He studied fine arts with the Association artistique of Montréal, and from 1958 to 1978 lived in Tourettes-sur-Loup, France. In 1952 he suggested the idea of international sculpture symposiums in Vienna. Thus, in the early 1960s, he participated in international sculpture symposiums, such as in Yugoslavia and in Montréal. Roussil's sculptures, both gigantic and miniature, express a fundamental and consistent theme: life regenerating in joy, sensuality, eroticism and love; and his principal subjects are man and bird. He uses the intrinsic structural qualities of his materials (iron, cast-iron, gold, copper, stone, clay, wood) to produce works ranging from representational allusion to abstraction (*Couple réuni*, limestone, no date). His work is characterized by slender forms and solid mass, curved edges and conical surfaces, holes and rings.

LOUISE BEAUDRY

Roux, Jean-Louis, theatre director, writer, actor (b at Montréal 18 May 1923). A doctor's son, Roux completed his classical studies at Collège Sainte-Marie and then enrolled in medicine at U de M (1943-46). During WWII Ludmilla Pitoëff came to Montréal from New York with her theatre company (including Yul Brynner) and, in 1942, was invited to mount a production with the Compagnons de Saint-Laurent, *L'Échange;* Roux played a major role that time and played again for Pitoëff in 1946 with Jean GASCON in *Phèdre* and *Le Pain dur*. That year, war being over, Roux received a study bursary and, upon Pitoëff's invitation, decided to give up medicine and study theatre in Paris for 3 years.

Returning from abroad, in 1949 Roux joined Éloi GRAMMONT to establish the Théâtre d'essai, which gave place to the THÉÂTRE DU NOUVEAU MONDE (July 1951); they produced Grammont's *Un fils à tuer* (1949) and Roux's *Rose Latulippe* (Feb 1951). After the production of *Un fils à tuer* in Montréal, Roux had gone back for a while to Paris to work as a professional actor (1949-50). He played later in the TNM's first production (9 Oct 1951), *L'Avare*, along with Grammont, Gascon, Georges Groulx, Guy Hoffmann, Ginette Letondal, Denise Pelletier and others who would remain Roux's close associates for many years, during which time he produced approximately 40 of the TNM's productions and occupied the positions of secretary general (1953-63) and artistic director (1966-81). Roux wrote and produced the play *Bois-Brûlés* (1967), translated some of the plays performed by the TNM, and has written radio and TV scripts for

Artistic director of the Théâtre du nouveau monde (1966-81), Jean-Louis Roux has to his credit more than 100 roles. He has staged many plays and has directed and participated in numerous productions in major cities in Canada and abroad (*courtesy Canapress*).

Radio-Canada. He has played several famous TV roles, including a part in *Septième nord* and *Les Plouffe*, and a few roles in motion pictures, such as Jean Beaudieu's *Cordélia*, Fernando Arrabol's *L'Empereur du Pérau* and Tony Richardson's *Hotel New Hampshire*. He served as president of the Société des auteurs, administrative secretary and later president of the Centre canadien du théâtre, and was on the executive committee of the Institut international du théâtre. His honours include the Victor-Morin award in 1969 and the MOLSON PRIZE in 1977. In 1981 Roux was appointed director general of the National Theatre School.

ANDRÉ G. BOURASSA

Rouyn-Noranda, Qué, City, pop 25 991 (1981c), is the largest centre in the Abitibi-Témiscaming region and its administrative capital. It comprises 2 municipalities, both of which were established after the discovery of COPPER and GOLD deposits at the Noranda mine in the mid-1920s. Noranda (pop 8767) was created by NORANDA MINES LTD in 1926. The town limits are those of the company's mining properties on the W shore of Lac Osisko. At the time, Noranda was considered a model northern mining town. For many years, it was completely controlled and administered by Noranda Mines, formed in 1922 to exploit one of the richest copper and gold deposits ever found in Canada. The name "Noranda" is a combination of the words "North" and "Canada." Today's vast mining empire, Noranda Mines Ltd, grew from the mine which operated 1927-66. The smelting plant, one of the largest in Québec, is still in operation.

Rouyn (pop 17 224) is located on the other shore of Lac Osisko. It became a town in 1927 and a city in 1948. Its name honours Jean-Baptiste de Rouyn, a captain in Montcalm's Royal-Rousillon regiment in New France. Rouyn was originally a large mining village inhabited by a mixture of prospectors, miners, adven-

turers and merchants drawn by the gold rush that erupted in 1922 after discovery of the Noranda mine deposits. Rouyn is still a lively city.

Rouyn-Noranda is the heart of a rich mining region where over 20 copper and gold mines operated for several decades. Five mines are still in operation nearby. Since the 1960s Rouyn-Noranda has established its role as the administrative capital and service centre of the Abitibi-Témiscamingue region.   BENOÎT-BEAUDRY GOURD

Rowan, William, ornithologist (b at Basle, Swit 29 July 1891; d at Edmonton 30 June 1957). After biological studies at University Coll, London, Eng, he became lecturer in zoology at U of Manitoba in 1919 and contributed to ornithological works in Manitoba and Ontario, participating in founding the Natural History Soc of Man. He moved to Edmonton in 1920, founding the U of A dept of zoology, which he headed until retirement in 1956. Though active in naturalist and sportsmen groups, he was best known for his scientific research. Rowan's experiments on the influence of photoperiod on bird hormones, determining the timing of migration, are widely cited as a milestone in ornithological history, and resulted in his being presented with the RSC's Flavelle Medal. His banding studies were also extensive. Later he turned his attention to cyclic population fluctuations in birds and mammals. His artistic prowess was exemplified by several exhibits in Canada and England, and by the selection of his crane drawing for a postage stamp. His assistant, Robert Lister, has portrayed Rowan's eccentric genius in a book based on his diaries, *The Birds and Birders of Beaverhills Lake* (1979).   MARTIN K. McNICHOLL
Reading: W. Rowan, *The Riddle of Migration* (1931).

Rowe, John Stanley, botanist, ecologist (b at Hardisty, Alta 11 June 1918). Educated at U of A, Nebraska and U of Man, Rowe worked as a forest labourer and schoolteacher in BC and then as a research officer on the prairies with the federal Department of Forestry from 1948 to 1967, when he became professor of plant ecology at U of Sask. In his work on the ecology of boreal forest, tundra and peatlands, Rowe insisted on broad long-term conceptual approaches to resource questions, an approach reflected in his many scientific and popular articles. His 1959 treatise (rev 1972), *Forest Regions of Canada,* is a key source for foresters, biologists and land managers. An active participant in the International Biological Program and on the Canadian Forestry Advisory Council, he received the Canadian Forestry Achievement Award in 1972.   MARTIN K. McNICHOLL

Rowing is a sport of propelling boats or specially designed racing shells with oars on water. Shells are usually classified for either sculling (2 oars, or sculls, one in each hand) or rowing (one oar, held by both hands). Sculling shells include the single, double and quadruple, used by 1, 2 and 4 people respectively. Rowing shells include the pair (with or without coxswain), 4s (with or without coxswain) and an 8 (with coxswain).

Racing shells are lightweight, slender but strong craft with hulls less than 3 mm thick and commonly made of mahogany, cedar, fiberglass or carbon fibre; their frames are made of lightweight hardwood. Shells are equipped with sliding seats and with "shoes" attached firmly to the frame that allow the seated rower to slide forward into a powerful crouch position at the start of the stroke, place the oar in the water and then push off the foot supports, extending the legs and pulling on the oar(s) with the arms and back. This power phase of the rowing motion is very similar to the action of a weightlifter who squats to pick up a heavy weight. Oars vary in length, weight and blade design, according to their use for rowing or sculling, the strength and size of the rower and individual preference. The

shafts are hollow for lightness and the oar is balanced so as to be light in the hands of the rower.

Rowing as a sport began at least as far back as 450 BC. There are artistic and written representations linking the sport to many ancient civilizations, including the Greeks, Romans, Egyptians and Japanese. England, however, was the birthplace of modern rowing equipment and regattas as we know them today. Perhaps the oldest sculling race was instituted on the R Thames in 1715 by the Irish comedian Doggett; one can find references to regattas on the Thames by the 1770s. The sport was introduced to Canada gradually as Englishmen emigrated to the N American colonies in the early 19th century. One of the earliest recorded regattas in Canada occurred 10 Aug 1816 in St John's harbour, Nfld. The ST JOHN'S REGATTA, perhaps the oldest continuous sporting event in N America, commenced in 1818 at Quidi Vidi Lk and is still rowed in fixed-slide, 6-man boats that are considerably heavier and slower than the swift racing shells used today in national and international competitions. In the 1820s, the rowing clubs of Halifax, comprising mainly garrison and naval personnel, dominated maritime regattas. In the 1840s, rowing clubs and regattas appeared in the Ontario communities of Toronto, Brockville, Monkton and Cobourg. By this time Canadian oarsmen were competing increasingly against British and American oarsmen in regattas in Halifax, Toronto, Boston, Philadelphia, Chicago and other centres. To the end of the 19th century, and into the 20th, many Canadian scullers and crews gained international fame, in both amateur and professional races. In the later 1860s, George Brown, a fisherman of Herring Cove, NS, raced successfully against the best scullers in Canada, the US and Britain. In the 1870s and 1880s, Toronto sculler Edward (Ned) HANLAN won Canadian, American and English titles, including 7 all-comers matches that were the equivalent of world championships. He has been Canada's most acclaimed oarsman and was widely hailed as Canada's first national sporting hero.

Four oarsmen from Saint John, NB (Price, Ross, Hutton, Fulton), won Canada's first world championship on 7 July 1867 in Paris, France, and were afterwards called the "Paris Four." Other Canadian greats include Bob Pearce, the Australian winner of the 1932 Olympics single sculls, who became a Canadian titleholder in 1933; Jake Gaudaur, of Orillia, Ont, world titlist in 1896; and Toronto scullers Lou Scholes and Joe WRIGHT, Sr. The Vancouver Rowing Club has had a long and glorious tradition, commencing in 1888. Different crews of one of the club's world-class coaches, Frank Read, figured in numerous international victories between 1954 and 1960, including COMMONWEALTH and PAN-AMERICAN GAMES gold medals and 3 Olympic medals, one gold and 2 silver. The 1956 Olympic

Men's heavy eights rowing team with gold medals won at the 1984 Los Angeles Olympics (*courtesy Athlete Information Bureau/Service Information-Athlètes*).

gold-medal four of Don Arnold, Walter d'Hondt, Lorne Loomer and Archie MacKinnon, all UBC students, achieved probably the largest victory margin of any crew in the modern games. The 1964 Olympic gold-medal pair, from the UBC-Vancouver Rowing Club, of Roger Jackson and George Hungerford was coached by 2 disciples of Read — Glen Mervin, from the 1960 Olympic silver-medal 8, and David Gillanders, who assisted Read for many years. In the last decade, much of Canada's international success has come from junior and senior women's crews at world championships and the 1976 Olympics. Tricia Smith, Betty Craig and Susan Antoft have each won silver medals in world championships 1978-81, as well as many other international awards. Women's rowing was first introduced to the Olympics in 1976 in Montréal.

Canada's best performance ever occurred at the Los Angeles Olympic Games, where 6 medals were won. For the first time in Canadian Olympic history the men's 8-oared crew won the gold medal in a classic stroke-for-stroke duel with the US crew. Olympic silver medals were won in both the women's coxed 4 and by the pair without coxwain rowed by Tricia Smith and Betty Craig. Bronze medals were won by Robert Mills in the men's single, by the men's quadruple sculls, and by the women's double sculls of Daniele and Silken Laumen.

Whereas the Olympic Rowing Basin in Montréal and the courses at St Catharines, Ont, and Burnaby Lake, BC, are rated as international-class courses, Canadian clubs from Vancouver I to Newfoundland row on rivers, lakes, ocean inlets and any type of water. The premier regatta in N America is the Royal Canadian Henley Regatta at St Catharines, 100 years old in 1982. Each year there is also a national championship for schoolboys. In 1880 the Canadian Assn for Amateur Oarsmen was created, one of the earliest sports governing bodies in Canada. Made up of clubs from across Canada, the association is responsible for the rules governing Canadian rowing. Since 1974, it has staged national championships for men, women, lightweights, youths and Masters. The association has its offices at the National Sport and Recreation Center in Vanier, Ont, and is served by full-time professional technical and administrative personnel.
ROGER JACKSON
Reading: J. A. Carver, *The Vancouver Rowing Club* (nd); R. S. Hunter, *Rowing in Canada Since 1848* (1933); P. King, *Art and a Century of Canadian Rowing* (1981).

Rowsell, Harry Cecil, veterinarian, animal-care specialist (b at Toronto 29 May 1921). After serving in the Canadian Navy 1941-45, he became a veterinarian (U of T, 1949) and later conducted several years of research on cardiovascular diseases and thrombosis as part of a McMaster-Ontario Veterinary Coll team. He was the first chairman of veterinary pathology at the Western Coll of Veterinary Medicine, U of Sask 1965-68, and first executive secretary of the Canadian Council of Animal Care 1968. Rowsell has a strong national and international reputation in the care of domestic, wild and laboratory animals and birds of all types, but in particular in experimental animal care. His efforts have resulted in dramatic improvements in the treatment of experimental animals in Canada and abroad. *See* VETERINARY MEDICINE.   R.G. THOMSON

Roy, Camille, priest, professor, literary critic (b at Berthier-en-Bas, Qué 22 Oct 1870; d at Québec City 24 June 1943). Though largely outmoded today, Roy's work was representative of his generation. After studies at Laval and the Sorbonne, Roy taught philosophy and then rhetoric at the Petit Séminaire de Québec 1894 to 1918 and French literature at Laval 1896-1927. Preoccupied with the survival of the French language in Canada, he helped found the Société du parler français (1902), pioneered the teaching of French Canadian literature at Laval (1902) and published the first *Manuel d'histoire de la littérature canadienne-française* (21 editions, 1907-62). His critical articles, which appeared in magazines 1902-33 and have been collected in 10 volumes, encouraged pastoral novels and reflected a classical ideal, though one open to romanticism. Tutor in the Petit Séminaire de Québec 1918-23, founder of the École normale supérieure (1920), rector of Laval (1924-27, 1929, 1932-38), dean of the Faculté des lettres (1939-43), both in print and at conferences he argued for development of a national educational system oriented towards social action. Received into the RSC 1904, he won the Prix David 1924 (*À l'ombre des érables*) and the gold medal of the Académie française in 1925.   LUCIE ROBERT

Roy, Fabien, politician (b at St-Prosper, Qué 17 Apr 1928). He was elected the Ralliement créditiste MNA for Beauce in 1970, and was re-elected in 1973 under the Parti créditiste banner and in 1976 under that of the Parti national populaire, which he had founded the previous year with former Liberal minister Jérôme Choquette. He was largely responsible for the party's acceptance of nationalist and progressive ideas. In Apr 1979 he was chosen interim leader of the federal Social Credit Party. He was elected as this party's MP for Beauce in 1979, but was defeated in 1980, thereafter working for several economic development organizations in the Beauce region.   DANIEL LATOUCHE

Roy, Gabrielle, writer (b at St-Boniface, Man 22 Mar 1909; d at Québec City 13 July 1983). Winner of the Gov Gen's Award (1947, 1957, 1978) and of many other literary distinctions in Canada and abroad (Lorne Pierce Medal 1947; Prix Duvernay 1956; Prix David 1971), Roy was one of the most important Canadian writers of the postwar period. The youngest of 8 children of a francophone family in St-Boniface, Roy lived in Manitoba until 1937. She was profoundly influenced by the prairie landscape and by the cosmopolitan world of the immigrants who settled in western Canada in the early 20th century. Her studies completed, she taught school for 12 years, first in isolated villages and then in St-Boniface, where she also did some theatre with the Cercle Molière. In the summer of 1937, she taught in northern Manitoba and after that went to Europe. It was during the 2 years she spent in France and England that she began to write.

The approaching war forced her to return to Canada in 1939. She chose to live in Montréal, where she became a free-lance journalist and began writing *Bonheur d'occasion.* Published in 1945, this novel, which describes working-class life in the early war period, won the Prix Fémina in Paris and the Literary Guild of America Award in New York. Translated into more than 15 languages (*The Tin Flute* in English), it brought Roy literary fame. In 1947 she was the first woman to be admitted to the RSC. She married Dr Marcel Carbotte that same year.

During a subsequent stay in France, she wrote a second book based on her memories of the Canadian West. *La Petite Poule d'eau* (1950) was later magnificently illustrated by painter Jean-Paul LEMIEUX. Upon returning to Canada, Roy settled in Québec City. She continued to write about the solitude of modern man (*Alexandre Chenevert,* 1954), the obsessive preoccupations of the artist (*La Montagne secrète,* 1961, inspired by the life of painter René Richard), the conflict between the values of progress and those of tradition (*La Rivière sans repos,* 1970), the poetry of nature (*Cet été qui chantait,* 1972), immigration and travel (*Un Jardin au bout du monde,* 1975; *De quoi t'ennuies-tu, Eveline?* 1982), and particularly about her own youth (*Rue Deschambault,* 1955; *La Route d'Altamont,* 1966; *Ces enfants de ma vie,* 1977). Roy

Gabrielle Roy, one of the most important Canadian writers of the postwar period, was brought to fame by *The Tin Flute (courtesy Globe and Mail, Toronto).*

also published stories for children (*Ma vache Bossie,* (1976); *Courte-Queue,* 1979) and a volume of articles and essays (*Fragiles lumières de la terre,* 1978).

Written in a simple, uncluttered style, the works of Roy today have a vast public, both in Canada (where almost all her books have been translated into English) and abroad. The central theme of her work is that of humanity in pain and solitude, but redeemed by the love implicit in creation and by hope for a world in which all men are reconciled.   FRANÇOIS RICARD

Roy, Philippe, physician, diplomat (b at St-François, Qué 1 Feb 1868; d at Ottawa 10 Dec 1948). Educated at Laval, Roy practised medicine in Québec C, and after 1897, in and around Edmonton, where he worked to promote the interests of the FRENCH IN THE WEST. He was a senator 1906-11 and then a pioneer in Canada's foreign service: commissioner general at Paris, France, 1911-28; and the first envoy extraordinary and minister plenipotentiary in Paris, 1928-38. As commissioner general, with a princely 1911 salary of $8000 plus $5000 expenses, Roy advanced Canadian commercial interests. As minister, he had full diplomatic privileges, the second Canadian (after Vincent MASSEY in Washington) to have such status.   NORMAN HILLMER

Royal Alexandra Theatre designed by John LYLE and built in Toronto in 1907 at a cost of $750 000 by a group of prominent businessmen headed by Cawthra Mulock, is one of the few surviving large professional theatres found in numerous Canadian cities at the turn of the century. In 1963 it was purchased by the Toronto entrepreneur "Honest Ed" Mirvish and restored to its Edwardian beauty at a cost of $500 000. With a seating capacity of 1497, the Royal Alex is noted for its large proscenium stage, excellent acoustics and intimacy between performers and audience. Although it has staged a few Canadian works, including John WEINZWEIG's ballet *Red Ear of Corn* and the revues *My Fur Lady* and *Spring Thaw,* the theatre has been a touring house for drama, musicals, opera and dance, particularly from Britain and the US.   ANTON WAGNER

Royal Bank Award for Canadian Achievement honours a Canadian citizen or person

living in Canada "whose outstanding accomplishment makes an important contribution to human welfare and the common good." The award was established in CENTENNIAL YEAR, 1967, and consists of $100 000 and a gold medal. The selection committee is composed of 7 distinguished Canadians and is independent of the ROYAL BANK. Recipients include Wilder PENFIELD, C.J. MACKENZIE, Cardinal Paul Emile LÉGER, Morley CALLAGHAN, Arthur ERICKSON, R. Keith DOWNEY and Baldur STEFANSSON, Northrop FRYE, Georges Henri LÉVESQUE and Hugh MACLENNAN.

Royal Bank of Canada, with head offices in Montréal, is the largest Canadian chartered bank. It started around 1864-69 as the Merchants Bank of Halifax, and its present name was adopted in 1901. The bank established its first branch outside Canada in Bermuda in 1882, and between 1903 and 1925 grew by absorbing other banks, including several in the Caribbean. Today the bank provides a full range of financial services. It has long been a pioneer in home mortgages and holds over $6.5 billion in mortgages. The first bank to install computers, it has over 95% of all customer accounts on-line. It was also the first bank to expand services to the Arctic. It operates 1568 branches and is the fourth-largest bank in N America in assets and deposits. In 1982 it acquired Canadian Acceptance Corp, which is now a wholly owned subsidiary. As of Oct 1983, it had $9.5 billion in annual sales or operating revenue, assets of $84.6 billion and 38 687 employees. The shares are widely held.   DEBORAH C. SAWYER

Royal Canadian Legion originated in several small associations of ex-soldiers that banded together throughout Canada during WWI. The first national organization, the Great War Veterans Association, was established Apr 1917 and by 1919 was the largest such group in Canada. By the mid-1920s, internal problems, a decline in membership and the emergence of rival associations brought the movement near collapse. In 1925 Field Marshal Earl Haig, founder of the British Empire Service League, visited Canada and encouraged all Canadian veterans to unite in one organization. In 1926 the GWVA and other groups amalgamated to form the Canadian Legion of the BESL. The new Legion grew steadily during the 1930s and expanded rapidly during and immediately after WWII. It concentrated on the re-establishment of veterans, advising them on pensions and other benefits available from the federal government. In 1960 the organization was renamed the Royal Canadian Legion.

The Legion continues to serve veterans by bringing their concerns to the attention of the government. The association's primary aim since 1915 has been service to the veteran and his dependants, although it now engages in many public and community service activities, helping to remind Canadians of those who have served their country in war. Each province is organized as a command, and in 1983 the Legion, with headquarters in Ottawa, had several hundred branches in Canada with over 500 000 members.   GLENN T. WRIGHT
Reading: C. Bowering, *Service* (1960).

Royal Canadian Mint, *see* MINTING.

Royal Canadian Mounted Police, with an establishment of over 20 000, the national force that provides policing in all provinces and territories except Ontario and Québec. The RCMP maintains 8 crime-detection laboratories, a computerized police information centre in Ottawa and the Canadian Police College. Liaison officers are posted in 27 foreign capitals. This large, sophisticated force had small, temporary beginnings. In the late 1860s when Canada was negotiating the acquisition of RUPERT'S LAND, the government faced the problem of how to administer these vast lands peacefully. Hudson's Bay Co rule had been almost without incident because the fur trade brought only a handful of Europeans, and those few did not compete economically with the native population. If not handled properly, the expected large influx of settlers might result in the kind of violence occurring in the American West. Apart from the cost in lives on both sides, the Canadian government could not contemplate the expense of a major Indian war, which might easily bankrupt the country or provide the expansionist US with an excuse to move in.

In the British Empire the burden of maintaining public order fell upon the courts, backed up by the military. The British government had some experience with centralized police forces in India and Ireland, however, and the forces there were unquestionably effective. PM Sir John A. MACDONALD adopted the Royal Irish Constabulary as the model for Canada. Until the western lands were occupied by settlers who understood traditional institutions, a paramilitary police force would hold the line. In 1869 William MCDOUGALL, sent out as first Canadian lieutenant-governor of the North-West Territories, carried instructions to organize a police force under Capt D.R. Cameron. Half the men were to be local Métis. These plans had to be shelved when the RED RIVER REBELLION of 1869-70 led to the creation of the province of Manitoba. Under the BRITISH NORTH AMERICA ACT, law enforcement was a provincial responsibility.

Not until 1873, when Ottawa created an administrative structure for the remainder of the Territories, was the idea of a police force revived. Parliament passed an Act in May establishing a force, and in Aug 150 recruits were sent W to winter at Ft Garry; the following spring another 150 joined them. The new mounted force, which gradually acquired the name NORTH-WEST MOUNTED POLICE, was armed with pistols, carbines and a few small artillery pieces. The red tunic, adopted from the British Army, gained great symbolic significance among the Indians. The commanding officer was given the title "Commissioner." There was an assistant commissioner and 2 officer ranks, superintendent and inspector; noncommissioned ranks were staff sergeant, sergeant, corporal and constable. Lt-Col George Arthur FRENCH, commander of the Permanent Force gunnery school at Kingston, was first commissioner.

In June 1874 the combined force marched W. Its destination was present-day southern Alberta, where whiskey traders from Montana were reportedly operating among the Blackfoot. After a gruelling march of over 2 months the force arrived and warned off the traders. Asst Commissioner James F. MACLEOD with 150 men established a permanent post at Ft Macleod. Part of the remaining half had been sent to Ft Edmonton and the rest under the commissioner returned E to Ft Ellice (near St-Lazare, Man). The following year FT WALSH, in the Cypress Hills, Ft Calgary and Battleford were established. A network of posts and patrols was thus begun, and extended year by year until it covered the territories.

For a decade and a half the NWMP concentrated on establishing close relations with the Indians. The police helped prepare the Indians for treaty negotiations and mediated conflicts with the few settlers. Their success is indicated by the signing of treaties covering most of the southern prairies in 1876 and 1877, by their reluctance to use the force of arms before 1885 and by the small number of Indians who participated in the NORTH-WEST REBELLION that year. Growing unrest in the early 1880s because of the disappearance of the buffalo and crop failures in the Saskatchewan valley led to an increase to

North-West Mounted Police lancers at Ft Walsh, Sask, 1878 *(courtesy Public Archives of Canada/C-18046A).*

500 men in 1882. But this did not keep pace with the force's growing responsibilities. CPR construction had drawn the police into a limited role even in southern BC. They repeatedly warned Ottawa of the growing possibilities of violence, but the warnings were ignored and the rebellion took its tragic course. Belatedly the government increased the NWMP to 1000 men and appointed a new commissioner, Lawrence W. Herchmer, to modernize the force.

Herchmer improved training and introduced a more systematic approach to crime prevention, thus preparing the police to cope with the large increase in settlement after 1885. As memories of the rebellion faded, criticisms began. The Opposition reminded the Government that the NWMP had been intended to disappear when the threat of frontier unrest had passed. The NWMP's demise seemed certain with the election of Wilfrid Laurier's Liberals in 1896; their election platform had called specifically for the dismantling of the NWMP. In power the Liberals quickly discovered intense opposition in the West to their plan. By the mid-1890s, too, the NWMP had begun moving north; in 1895, 20 men had gone to the Yukon to cope with the KLONDIKE GOLD RUSH and within 3 years 250 were stationed there. At about the same time operations were being extended northwards along the Mackenzie R, with posts and patrols reaching the Arctic coast by 1904.

The permanence of the Mounted Police was tacitly accepted by all parties by the early 20th century. When Alberta and Saskatchewan were created in 1905 the RNWMP (the "Royal" added 1904 in recognition of distinguished service by many NWMP men in the SOUTH AFRICAN WAR) was, in effect, rented to the provinces. During WWI security and intelligence operations, previously negligible, became central. But contracts to police Alberta and Saskatchewan were cancelled in 1917, partly because Commissioner A. Bowen PERRY believed their PROHIBITION laws were unenforceable; and when the end of hostilities reduced the need for security work the future of the Mounted Police was very uncertain.

Late in 1918 President of the Privy Council N.W. Rowell toured western Canada to seek opinion on the force's future. In May 1919 he reported to Cabinet that the police could be absorbed into the army or expanded into a national police force. The latter course chosen, in Nov 1919 legislation merged the RNWMP with the Dominion Police, a federal force est 1868 to guard government buildings and enforce federal statutes. The name became Royal Canadian Mounted Police, and headquarters was moved to Ottawa from Regina. The 1920s saw expansion of the RCMP into the arctic islands, and in

1928 the ST. ROCH became a floating detachment in the Far North. In southern Canada the force's principal activities were enforcement of liquor and narcotics laws and security and intelligence work. The latter reflected widespread public fear of subversion that had been fueled by the Russian Revolution in 1917 and the WINNIPEG GENERAL STRIKE of 1919. Saskatchewan renegotiated its policing agreement in 1928 and Alberta followed in 1931, thus beginning a return to more normal police duties for the force.

In Aug 1931 Maj-Gen Sir James H. MACBRIEN became commissioner and nearly doubled the force from 1350 to 2350. In 1932 the force took over provincial policing in Alta, Man, NB, NS and PEI and absorbed the Preventive Service of the National Revenue Dept. Before MacBrien died in office in 1938 he had established a policy of sending several members of the force to universities each year for advanced training, opened the first forensic laboratory in Regina and organized an aviation section. An RCMP Reserve was established in 1937 and the following year the police began preparations for the expected war. When WWII began the RCMP was fully prepared to protect strategic installations, and in fact no acts of sabotage were recorded. Nazi sympathizers were rounded up for INTERNMENT. Despite suspicions about Russian espionage, the RCMP was as surprised as most Canadians by the revelations of Igor GOUZENKO in 1945.

The heightened international tensions of the COLD WAR era that the Gouzenko case inaugurated ensured that security and intelligence work would continue to be a major preoccupation for the Mounted Police. These activities attracted almost no public attention until the mid-1960s, when Vancouver postal clerk George Victor Spencer was discovered to have been collecting information for the USSR. The tacit agreement among politicians that security matters were not subjects of open debate was shattered when John Diefenbaker's Conservative Opposition attacked the Pearson government for mishandling the case. In retaliation the Liberals revealed details of a scandal involving a German woman named Gerda MUNSINGER, whose ties to some Conservative Cabinet ministers and Russian espionage agents had apparently been ignored by the Diefenbaker government. A Royal Commission on Security was appointed in 1966 as a result of these cases and reported in 1968. The commission's recommendation that a civilian intelligence agency replace the RCMP was rejected by the new prime minister, Pierre Trudeau.

By 1969 the rise of separatism in Québec had produced a major shift in security and intelligence operations from a foreign threat to a perceived threat within the country. The OCTOBER CRISIS of 1970 with the kidnapping of James Cross and the murder of Pierre Laporte added enormous impetus to undercover antiseparatist operations in Québec. The RCMP was subsequently discovered to have engaged in such illegal activities as burning a barn and stealing the membership list of the PARTI QUÉBÉCOIS. These revelations raised fundamental questions about the place of the police in the state. Are there situations in which the police can break the law? Who is ultimately answerable if they do? To help answer these questions the Royal Commission of INQUIRY INTO CERTAIN ACTIVITIES OF THE RCMP was appointed under Mr Justice David McDonald. The commission again recommended removing intelligence operations from the RCMP to a civilian agency; legislation to create such an agency, the Canadian Security Intelligence Service, was proclaimed on 1 July 1984.

The postwar period also saw a continued expansion of the RCMP's role as a provincial force. In 1949 they assumed responsibility for provincial policing in Newfoundland and in 1950 absorbed the BC provincial police. In 1959 the most serious conflict over the split federal-provincial control of the force took place. A loggers' strike in Newfoundland led the superintendent in charge of the RCMP there to ask the provincial attorney general to request 50 reinforcements from Ottawa. Justice Minister E. Davie Fulton refused and Commissioner L.H. Nicholson resigned in protest. The question of which level of government controls the RCMP in a given set of circumstances remains vague. It has been a source of tension between the federal and provincial governments, occasionally leading to threats by the latter to cancel their RCMP contracts and establish provincial police.

Since 1945, 3 areas of criminal investigation have occupied a large and growing portion of the force's time: organized crime, narcotics and commercial fraud. The first 2 are closely linked, and from the late 1940s onward there was growing evidence that illegal drug traffic was controlled by Canadian branches of American crime syndicates or "families." In 1961 the RCMP established National Crime Intelligence Units across the country to gather information on organized crime and improve co-operation with other police forces. Similarly, growing numbers of securities frauds and phony bankruptcies led the RCMP to establish Commercial Fraud Sections, with specially trained personnel, beginning in 1966.

Ceremony and symbolism have always been important to the Mounted Police. Their original scarlet tunics were chosen because they represented a legacy of good relations between the British Army and the Indians. Canadian governments since the 1880s have used the force as a national symbol. The early riding drills developed quickly into exhibitions of horsemanship set to music. Thus the origins of the famous Musical Ride can be traced back to the 1870s. Although the mounted training once required of all recruits has long since disappeared, the Musical Ride remains an enormously popular public attraction in Canada and elsewhere. The symbolic importance of the "Mounties" may help to explain why they have retained their popularity in spite of adverse publicity of recent years.   R.C. MACLEOD

Reading: Ronald Atkin, *Maintain the Right* (1973); Nora and William Kelly, *The Royal Canadian Mounted Police* (1973); R.C. Macleod, *The North-West Mounted Police and Law Enforcement* (1976).

Royal Commission On Canada's Economic Prospects (Gordon Commission) The idea for this royal commission was based on a draft article by Walter Gordon in 1955 questioning the validity of a number of the government's economic policies, particularly the question of selling control of Canada's natural resources and business enterprises to foreigners. Gordon was then asked if he would mind if the government took over the idea for a royal commission, and if he would act as chairman.

With the help of Douglas LePan, the commission's brilliant director of research, a research staff of 24 full-time and 15 part-time members was assembled, mostly from universities. Gordon and LePan planned the work to be covered for the commission. Thirty-three studies were undertaken, each of which was published separately.

Because this was the first time that any country had attempted such a comprehensive undertaking, there was a great deal of public interest in the commission's work and its hearings were well reported in the press. A recurrent theme throughout was the concern felt about the acquisition by foreigners, mostly American, of Canadian resources and business enterprises. This issue was well aired.

The commission completed its work and agreed upon its conclusions within the 18 months it had set for itself. Its conclusions were summarized in a preliminary report of 3 Dec 1956. The final report was not completed until Nov 1957.

In its 2 reports, the commission made some long-term forecasts for the next 25 years (broken into 5-year intervals), about the population growth, the size of the labour force, and the probable development of different sections of the economy. Most of these various estimates were remarkably close to the actual results.

The commission also submitted over 50 proposals and suggestions, nearly all of which have since been incorporated in legislation or adopted administratively. The principal exceptions were its proposals respecting FOREIGN INVESTMENT.

In conclusion, it can be stated that the work of the Gordon Commission gave Canadians confidence about the future prospects for their country and encouraged businessmen to think and plan ahead.   WALTER GORDON

Royal Commissions, once described by a member of Parliament as costly travelling minstrel shows, are a form of official inquiry into matters of public concern. They descend from the British monarch's prerogative power to order investigations, said by some to have been exercised first by King William I when he commanded the preparation of the Domesday Book, though the Commission on Enclosures initiated by Henry VIII in 1517 is a more likely prototype of contemporary royal commissions. Closely related to the royal commissions and often hard to distinguish from them are several other kinds of public inquiry, eg, commissions of inquiry, TASK FORCES, and investigations established by departments and other agencies under statutory powers of the Inquiries Act, first passed by Parliament in 1868.

At the federal level royal commissions, task forces and commissions of inquiry are appointed by ORDER-IN-COUNCIL under Part I of the Inquiries Act, while departmental investigations are launched under Part II, but the distinction makes little difference in the functioning of these bodies since they all enjoy the power conferred by the Act to conduct investigations by subpoenaing witnesses, taking evidence under oath, requisitioning documents and hiring expert staff. Royal commissions have the added lustre of being created under the imprint of the Great Seal of Canada while departmental investigations may stem from any one of at least 87 federal statutes that confer powers of inquiry with or without reference to the Inquiries Act. Aside from these minor distinctions royal commissions are no more regal than other kinds of inquiries.

Despite their unexceptionality, however, an air of superiority still clings to royal commissions. The public takes them more seriously than other sorts of investigations and governments tend to reinforce the myth by preferring to appoint royal commissions to examine the gravest matters of concern, eg, FEDERAL-PROVINCIAL RELATIONS, health services, BILINGUALISM AND BICULTURALISM, CORPORATE CONCENTRATION, financial management and accountability, government organization, TAXATION, energy, and economic union and development prospects for Canada. Task forces, on the other hand, have generally been regarded as more prosaic work crews composed of knowledgeable practitioners rather than eminent luminaries. Often appointed by government departments, they have been assigned to examine such practical matters as PRIVACY and computers, IMMIGRATION procedures, retirement income policy, labour market development, FISHERIES POLICY, and sports. However, while it would be tempting to conclude that task forces, departmental investigations and nonroyal commissions are used to probe particular, well-focused problems while royal commissions are devoted to more sweeping national issues, this simple dividing line cannot always be drawn. Some task forces have dealt with broad and important Canadian issues such as housing and urban development, gov-

RCMP Musical Ride (*photo by J.A. Kraulis*).

ernment information, and the structure and foreign ownership of Canadian industry. At the same time royal commissions have sometimes been used to tackle specific issues like disasters (both public and personal), ranging from the burning down of the Parliament Buildings and riots in Halifax to judicial and ministerial indiscretions. In fact there is little rhyme or reason to the appellations of investigations because they have frequently been appointed haphazardly and their titles applied rather indiscriminately. The Pepin-Robarts inquiry into national unity called itself a task force when it might well have been a royal commission. The McDonald INQUIRY INTO CERTAIN ACTIVITIES OF THE ROYAL CANADIAN MOUNTED POLICE had the dimensions of a royal commission. The probe into the loss of the drill rig Ocean Ranger was changed from a commission into a royal commission. In view of this confusion it is not surprising that the Law Reform Commission has recommended that the term "royal commission" be abandoned altogether.

Since Confederation there have been close to 450 federal commissions of inquiry with and without the royal title, more than 1500 departmental investigations, and an undetermined number of task forces. As stated earlier, royal commissions tend to be used either to secure advice upon some important troublesome general problem or to investigate a specific contentious incident but critics allege that royal commissions are often established to give a besieged government an excuse to do nothing while a protracted investigation cools the public's temper. Hence the frequency of royal commissions varies from decade to decade; a greater number are usually created during times of crisis, growth and adjustment.

The cost of having several such acts of national introspection operating simultaneously is not inconsiderable. Though the number of actual commissioners employed in any given inquiry may not be great, ranging from one to the 13 on the (Donald) Macdonald investigation into development prospects, the inclination in recent years to hire a proliferation of high-paid legal counsel and massive research staffs over long periods of time has cost the public a great deal. The most extensive and expensive royal commission until 1982 was the McDonald inquiry into the RCMP which ran for 4 years and cost $10 million. The royal commission on economic union and development prospects may well establish a new record with its $21.8-million budget. However, it was also given a 3-year deadline within which to report, indicating that governments are less willing to pay indefinitely for royal commissions.

On balance royal commissions and other forms of inquiry probably do more good than harm. At least they are necessary from time to time to flush out misfeasance and malfeasance and to examine matters of major public concern. Some royal commissions have produced significant reports, eg, the Rowell-Sirois report on federal-provincial financial relations, Massey on the arts, and Dunton-Laurendeau on bilingualism and biculturalism furnished the documentation for continuing public debate and for some policymaking.

Each province has its own Inquiries Act under which it conducts investigations similar to Ottawa's. Although it is difficult to draw comparisons, because even less academic study has been devoted to provincial bodies than to federal, it appears that the provinces have not tended to use royal commissions as often as has Ottawa. Québec conducted 91 commissions and committees of inquiry from Confederation to 1972 while Ontario appointed 177 royal commissions and commissions of inquiry between 1867 and 1978. The most popular subject for investigation in the 10 provinces has been edu-

cation. From 1787 to 1978 there were 367 inquiries into education, of which 127 were royal commissions.

Various alternatives to royal commissions and other forms of inquiry have been discussed recurrently, including the increased use of legislative committees and white papers, which are simply studies and proposals put out tentatively by government departments for public discussion prior to possible action. But legislatures and the House of Commons do not have sufficient time and objectivity to examine many issues and while the Senate may have the time, the public would probably not accept its views upon a controversial matter as readily as it would receive the opinions of a royal commission headed by a judge or another prominent figure. PAUL FOX

Royal Conservatory of Music of Toronto (until 1947, known as Toronto Conservatory of Music) offers preparatory and professional instruction, administers a nationwide system of practical and theoretical examinations, and operates an annual summer school, featuring a wide range of courses and workshops for teachers. The RCMT has had a significant influence on Canadian music through its recital series, publications and special projects.

The conservatory was founded by Edward Fisher in 1886, and in the following year opened with 200 students and 50 teachers. By 1892 it was organized into 2 departments: the Academic Dept catered to young students and amateurs; the Collegiate Dept offered professional training to teachers and performers. In this period conservatories prepared students for examinations conducted by the universities. Originally associated with University of Trinity College, TCM affiliated with U of T in 1896.

Under the energetic leadership of Augustus VOGT (principal, 1913-26), the conservatory established a national network of examination centres. By 1921 U of T had assumed control of the conservatory and, after absorbing all rival schools (with the exception of the Hambourg Conservatory), enjoyed a position of pre-eminence by the late 1920s. Ernest MACMILLAN (principal, 1926-42) added prestige through annual performances of the TCM choir and revised the examination curricula by incorporating more rigorous requirements in aural skills and theory. In 1944 the Frederick Harris music publishing company was donated to the university, with profits to be used for conservatory scholarships and bursaries.

A modern phase of professional training commenced when diploma programs were offered in a new Senior School (1946). Activities within its opera division eventually led to formation of the CANADIAN OPERA COMPANY. Returned servicemen and students from all parts of Canada participated in these new opportunities for advanced study; concurrrently, the university initiated a degree in school music. Sir Ernest MacMillan, Ettore Mazzoleni and Arnold WALTER were prominent in these postwar developments which produced a new generation of Canadian performers, composers and teachers.

The conservatory has survived several administrative reorganizations and, even with the recent growth of music in universities, has successfully made major accommodations in its teaching operations. In 1983 it had a staff of 250 full-time teachers, 10 000 students and conducted 70 000 examinations across Canada.
J. PAUL GREEN

Royal Flying Corps, formed 13 Apr 1912 to fulfill a perceived need, common before WORLD WAR I in European countries, to participate in the expanding field of AVIATION. It comprised a military wing, a naval wing (later the ROYAL NAVAL AIR SERVICE) and a flying school; duties

included reconnaissance, bombing, observation for the artillery, co-operation with the infantry in attacking enemy positions, supply drops and observation for the Royal Navy. When WWI began, Canada did not have its own air force and, until the RFC established training camps in Canada in Jan 1917, the only way for a Canadian to become a war pilot was to enlist in the regular forces and try to transfer to the air service, or to travel at his own expense to England and attempt to enlist directly. It is impossible to determine the exact number of Canadians who joined the RFC, but it is estimated that over 20 000 Canadians had joined the British flying services by the end of WWI. Many of these became pilots, among them the Canadian "aces" Lt-Col W.A. BISHOP, Lt-Col R. COLLISHAW, Lt-Col W.G. BARKER, Maj D.R. MACLAREN and others. The RFC joined with the RNAS to become the Royal Air Force on 1 Apr 1918. GLENN B. FOULDS
Reading: S.F. Wise, *Canadian Airmen and the First World War* (1980).

Royal Military College of Canada, Kingston, Ont, was founded in 1874; since the 1970s RMC has offered bilingual instruction. The college opened 1 June 1876 with 18 cadets, staffed by British military officers and one Canadian civilian. Queen Victoria conferred the title "Royal" in 1878. The first class graduated on 2 July 1880. Before WWI most ex-cadets took up civilian professions, especially engineering, and 4 graduates received commissions annually in the British army. After 1919 RMC was staffed by Canadians, the first Canadian commandant being Maj-Gen Sir Archibald Macdonnell. Graduates were required to serve in either the active forces of the Crown or the Canadian Militia. The RMC engineering course was recognized as a qualification to practise the profession; certain Canadian universities and provincial law societies accepted RMC graduates to take degrees or diplomas in a final year. Many former cadets held high military rank during WWII. RMC closed in 1942 but was reopened in 1948 as one of the tri-service Canadian Service Colleges (CSC). From 1954 the Regular Officers Training Plan (ROTP) required all CSC graduates to take a regular commission, but a small Reserve Entry was reestablished in 1961. From 1959 RMC granted degrees, and graduate courses were added in 1964. Women students were first admitted in 1979. RMC is now administered as part of the Canadian MILITARY AND STAFF COLLEGES under the Dept of NATIONAL DEFENCE. RICHARD A. PRESTON

Enrolment: Royal Military College of Canada, 1982-83 (Source: Statistics Canada)			
Full-time Undergrad	Full-time Graduate	Part-time Undergrad	Part-time Graduate
754	37	65	24

Royal Naval Air Service The naval wing of Britain's ROYAL FLYING CORPS became the RNAS on 23 June 1914. In WWI it was far more than the envisaged auxiliary force for the navy, being responsible at various times for air defence of Britain and support of land operations in Flanders, Gallipoli (Gelibolu, Turkey), parts of the Middle East, and E Africa. It pioneered strategic bombing but was not prominent in naval operations until 1918, when it played a major part in the war against German U-BOATS. Together with the RFC it became part of the Royal Air Force on 1 Apr 1918. Prominent among the 936 Canadians known to have served in the RNAS were R.H. "Red" Mulock, later a pioneer of Canadian civil aviation, Lloyd S. Breadner, Robert LECKIE, and W.A. CURTIS. W.A.B. DOUGLAS

Royal Ontario Museum in Toronto is now the second-largest museum building in N America (65 030 m²) and one of the most modern and best equipped in the world. The ROM was established by an Act of the Ontario legislature in 1912. The original building, now the west wing, was officially opened in 1914 by the duke of Connaught, governor general of Canada. In 1933, 2 new sections were opened, an east wing facing Queen's Park and centre block connecting the 2 wings to form an H-shaped main building with north and south courtyards. In the next few decades, 2 independent buildings were added to the museum complex as a result of generous donations: the Sigmund Samuel Canadiana Building, a few blocks S of the main building, and the McLaughlin Planetarium, adjoining the main building.

In 1978 a $60-million renovation and expansion project was initiated when work began on the complete renovation of the main building and construction of a 9-floor curatorial centre building in the south courtyard. Construction of the 6-floor terrace gallery building in the north courtyard began in 1980. The 2 new buildings are linked to the main building by skylighted atria, so that a harmonious integration of the old and the new is achieved. The renovated and expanded main building reopened to the public in Sept 1982.

Collections When it opened in 1914, the ROM was an amalgamation of 5 separate museums, each with its own director. In 1955 the 5 museums were reorganized into 3 divisions (art and archaeology, geology and mineralogy, and zoology and palaeontology), all reporting to one director. The collections are now the responsibility of 9 science departments (Botany, Entomology, Ichthyology and Herpetology, Invertebrate Palaeontology, Invertebrate Zoology, Mammalogy, Mineralogy and Geology, Ornithology and Vertebrate Palaeontology) and 9 art and archaeology departments (Canadiana, Egyptian, Ethnology, European, Far Eastern, Greek and Roman, New World Archaeology, Textile and West Asian). Many of the collections, or individual items within them, are of world significance. The science departments are rich in type specimens, the scientifically accepted specimen from which a new species or mineral has been described. The Chinese collections are internationally known, particularly the bronzes, oracle bones and tomb figurines, which comprise the largest aggregation outside China. The Greek and Roman collections are the largest and most representative in Canada. The museum holds the only comprehensive Canadian collection of Egyptian material and the largest textile and costume collections in Canada. A large percentage of the museum's 6 million artifacts and specimens form research collections available to visiting scholars from around the world. In addition, these materials are loaned to cultural and educational institutions for study and public display.

Gallery Displays, Exhibitions and Public Programs About 1 million people visit the museum annually. New galleries and exhibit areas are continually being developed and, when they are all in place, the expanded main building will offer more than 18 580 m² of exhibits. Displays are also housed in the Sigmund Samuel Canadiana Building and the McLaughlin Planetarium. Galleries in the new museum are being organized in 7 clusters: Canadiana, Earth Sciences, European, Far East, Mediterranean World, New World, and Life and Palaeontological Sciences. In these clusters, each display is related to the next, and all form part of an integrated whole to facilitate orientation and comprehension. In addition, there is a theme gallery called Mankind Discovering, a hands-on Discovery Gallery and several areas for rotating exhibits. The new exhibition hall is designed for travelling exhibitions of international significance, including those organized by the museum. The museum offers many public programs: lectures and films, demonstrations, concerts, dramatic per-

formances, special events and the identification of specimens and artifacts for the public. The Members' Volunteer Committee conducts a variety of programs, including public tours of the galleries, walking tours of the city, bus tours of Ontario and world tours to all parts of the globe, led by expert museum staff.

Through travelling exhibits, "museumobiles," a discovery van, a speaker's bureau and resource boxes and travelling cases for schools, the Dept of Extension Services provides museum experiences to more than half a million people each year in hundreds of different communities in Ontario and across Canada. In addition, the teaching staff in the Dept of Education Services gives lessons in the galleries to over 150 000 students during an average year.

Research The work of the curatorial staff in the field and in sophisticated laboratories of the curatorial centre provides the solid academic base for all public activities of the museum. Archaeology departments conduct field excavations in many parts of the world; eg, in Belize, Egypt, the Middle East and Canada (*see* ARCHAEOLOGY; MEDITERRANEAN ARCHAEOLOGY). The science departments provide consultations to a variety of international, national and provincial agencies. Several members of the curatorial staff are world authorities in their fields, and members in the science departments have been recognized by having newly discovered animals or minerals named in their honour. An impressive number of general interest and scholarly publications produced each year by the ROM record and share the results of museum research with both the academic community and the general reader.   DAVID A. YOUNG

Royal Prerogative of Mercy The federal Cabinet has the power to pardon anyone who has been convicted of a criminal offence. The pardon can be free or conditional. The effect of a free pardon is that the person is deemed never to have committed the offence for which they were convicted. The SOLICITOR GENERAL of Canada has the responsibility for receiving requests for pardons for criminal offences. V. M. DEL BUONO

Royal Society of Canada, the senior national organization of distinguished Canadian scholars in the arts and sciences. Its aim is the advancement of learning and research in Canada. Founded in 1882 under the auspices of the Gov Gen the marquess of Lorne, it comprised some 80 French- and English-speaking members (fellows) prominent in fields from geology to literature. In time, other LEARNED SOCIETIES emerged for specific disciplines; but the "mother society" that brought together the whole range of scholarly interests kept to the fore, and election by its membership as a Fellow has remained a prized professional honour. With other interested parties, the Royal Society pressed successfully over the years for the creation of the PUBLIC ARCHIVES OF CANADA, NATIONAL MUSEUMS, the NATIONAL GALLERY, the NATIONAL RESEARCH COUNCIL for the sciences, the Historic Sites and Monuments Board and the NATIONAL LIBRARY. Today the society upholds standards of excellence through its medals and prizes for achievements in literature (both French and English), history, chemistry, biology and much more. It holds annual conferences and organizes interdisciplinary regional, national and international symposia on current topics of importance, the results of which are often published, as are the *Transactions* of its annual meetings. The organization now operates in 3 large units: L'Academie des lettres et des sciences humaines, the Academy of Humanities and Social Sciences, and the Academy of Science. All 3 meet jointly part of the time, as well as separately, thus maintaining the Royal Society's basic purpose of uniting the widespread specialized interests of Canada's scholarly community.   J.M.S. CARELESS

Royal Tours in what is now Canada began when Albert Edward, Prince of Wales (later Edward VII) officially visited British North America in 1860. During a 2-month tour of Newfoundland, the Maritimes and Canada, highlighted by the opening of Montréal's Victoria Bridge and the laying of the cornerstone for Ottawa's Parliament buildings, the prince was honoured as a visible symbol of monarchy and empire. The next major royal tour was that of the duke and duchess of Cornwall and York (later George V and Queen Mary) in 1901. This was the first transcontinental tour, and demonstrated the "steel of empire" significance of the CPR. The popular Edward, Prince of Wales (later Edward VIII), made official tours of Canada in 1919 and 1927 in addition to private visits to his Alberta ranch. In May and June 1939 King George VI and Queen Elizabeth made the first visit of a reigning monarch to Canada. The extensive tour was planned to solidify Canadian support for Britain on the eve of WWII and it succeeded admirably as ecstatic crowds poured forth pro-British sentiments. Princess Elizabeth made her first royal visit to Canada in 1951. During her reign as Elizabeth II royal visits became fairly frequent, thus losing some of the mystique they once possessed in English Canada. The Queen's symbolical associations have been less popular in Québec, where at one time French Pres Charles de Gaulle was given what amounted to a royal welcome in Québec City. PM John TURNER's request that Queen Elizabeth delay her visit to avoid the political campaigning of the summer of 1984 caused a mild controversy.   ROBERT M. STAMP

Royal Trustco Ltd, with head offices in Ottawa, is a Canadian holding company incorporated in 1978 to become the parent of the Royal Trust group of companies. It carries on trust, financial, real-estate and deposit services in Canada, the US and overseas. In 1982 it had sales or operating revenue of $1.4 billion, assets of $10.6 billion (ranking 9th among banks and financial institutions in Canada) and 8697 employees.
DEBORAH C. SAWYER

Royal William, the first Canadian ship to cross the Atlantic almost continuously under steam power. It was built by Messrs Black and Campbell and launched on 27 Apr 1831 by Lord and Lady Aylmer at Québec. The steam engines were made and installed in Montréal. It made several trips between Québec and the Atlantic colonies in 1831, but was quarantined because of the cholera epidemic in 1832 and the owners lost some £16 000 on the venture. It left Pictou on 18 Aug 1833 with 7 passengers and a load of coal and arrived at Gravesend after a 25-day passage. The *Royal William* was eventually sold to the Spanish navy.   JAMES MARSH

Royal Winnipeg Ballet is the second-oldest ballet company in N America and the oldest surviving company in Canada. The RWB had its origins as a ballet club, organized in 1938 by 2 immigrant English dance teachers, Gweneth LLOYD and Betty FARRALLY, who had moved to Canada at the invitation of friends. The club made its first public appearance in June 1939 as part of a pageant planned for a visit to the city by King George VI and Queen Elizabeth. The group was not seen by the royal party but danced 2 brief ballets on prairie themes, *Grain* and *Kilowatt Magic*, both choreographed by Lloyd. The club became the Winnipeg Ballet in 1941 and operated semiprofessionally, making occasional tours out of town, until turning professional in 1949. In 1953 it became the first company in the British Commonwealth to be granted a royal charter (London's Sadler's Wells company did not become the Royal Ballet until 1956), but it almost collapsed in 1954 as the result of a disastrous fire in which the company's entire stock of costumes, original music, choreographic scores and sets was destroyed. Following the fire, the company was directed by a succession of individuals until being taken over in 1958 by Arnold SPOHR, a former principal dancer and choreographer with the company and architect of its rise to international success in the 1960s and 1970s. Spohr built a compact touring ensemble dancing a widely diverse repertoire, performing everything with what became characterized as a "prairie freshness." The company's first resident choreographer was Brian MAC-DONALD, and it was on his works of the late 1960s that the company's first major successes, in the US and Europe, chiefly rested. However, Spohr was tireless in searching out new choreographic talent, and along with the work of Macdonald and Norbert VESAK, he showcased the work of such internationally acclaimed choreographers as the Argentinian Oscar Araiz, John Neumeier from Germany (who gave the company its first full-length work, his highly original version of *Nutcracker*), and the Venezuelan Vicente Nebrada. In the early 1980s Spohr began to introduce more full-evening works in the classical style, such as Rudi van Dantzig's *Romeo and Juliet*, as showcases for the exceptional talents of the company's first international star, Evelyn HART, who took the women's solo gold medal at the Varna International Ballet Competition (1980). In 1982 Spohr's "courage, determination, organizational skills and singular artistic taste" earned him one of the highest accolades of N American dance, the *Dancemagazine* award. The RWB is a member of the Canadian Assn of Professional Dance Organizations.   MAX WYMAN

Rubber Products Industry consists of establishments primarily engaged in MANUFACTURING rubber tires, tubing, hose, belting, washers and gaskets, weather stripping, boot and shoe findings, tapes, etc. The 134 large and small rubber manufacturers in Canada share annual sales of more than $2 billion. The industry directly employs 40 000 people; tens of thousands of additional jobs exist among suppliers and marketers of rubber products, and in the TRANSPORTATION and service sectors. In 1984 the industry had an investment of nearly $1.5 billion in plants and equipment, over half of which had been invested in the preceding decade.

The first European to record rubber in action was Christopher Columbus. While exploring Haiti in 1492, he noticed native boys playing with a ball that bounced. Upon investigation, Columbus found that it was made from the milky-white sap (latex) of a certain type of tree. When exposed to air, the sap darkened, hardened and could be bounced. No real effort was made to use rubber commercially until the 1760s when experimenters in France found it could be dissolved by turpentine and ether. Seventy years later in Scotland, Charles Macintosh began waterproofing garments. Around the same time the English chemist Joseph Priestley found that the substance would rub out pencil marks, hence the name "rubber". Thomas Hancock, an English coach-maker, discovered that rubber could be shredded and pressed into a soft, pliable block. In 1839 the American inventor Charles Goodyear discovered vulcanization, a process by which the rubber compound is cured at high temperatures, using sulphur. Although various rubber-yielding trees were discovered growing wild in Central and S America, the best source was the Brazilian rubber tree, *Helvea brasiliensis*. Seedlings were smuggled from Brazil in 1876 and brought to England. Ultimately plantations were set up in Malaya and other southeast Asian countries, allowing control of the quality of supply of raw natural rubber.

The first Canadian production of rubber articles probably began at Dominion Rubber (now Uniroyal Ltd) in Montréal in 1854. The leading product of the rubber industry, the pneumatic tire, was developed in 1888 by J.D. Dunlop of Belfast, Ireland. Much of rubber-production's growth stems from the development of the bicycle and AUTOMOBILE; the first car tire made in Canada was produced in 1895 by Dunlop Canada Ltd. Progress was slow and, at the turn of the century, 13 Canadian firms were producing about $1.6-million worth of rubber clothing, footwear and elastic goods annually. Goodyear Canada Inc took over the Durham Rubber Co in Bowmanville, Ont, around 1910 (originally Durham had been the Bowmanville Rubber Co and dated from 1887). Firestone Canada Inc set up its first Canadian plant in Hamilton in 1920. B.F. Goodrich Canada Inc was established by the takeover of the Ames Holden Co in Kitchener in 1925. General Tire Canada Ltd began manufacturing in 1978 when it purchased Mansfield-Denman-General in Barrie. The latter company had been formed in 1965 and, until then, had operated under the name of Mansfield Rubber Co, which had produced its first tire in 1955. Michelin Tires (Canada) Ltd opened its first Canadian tire-manufacturing facility at Granton, NS, in 1971.

During WWII Japanese occupation of the natural-rubber-producing countries of Asia created a critical situation. The rubber industry, working closely with the federal government, pushed forward a crash program to produce synthetic rubber. The program eventually resulted in the formation of Polymer Corp (now Polysar Ltd), Sarnia, Ont, one of the world's foremost manufacturers of "raw" synthetic rubbers. Today, about 68% of the rubber used in Canadian industry is synthetic (*see* PETROCHEMICAL INDUSTRY).

In 1984 the industry exported $7.4-million worth of passenger tires to many countries around the world and imported $4.8-million worth. However, although automobile tires are its single most important product, rubber has many other uses. Even in the automotive market, rubber is used for much more than just tires: there are over 200 rubber items in the average car, including wiper blades, engine mounts, door and window weather stripping, fan belts, radiator hose, foot pedals, etc. The industry produces many other rubber products for the agriculture, FOOTWEAR, TEXTILE and CONSTRUCTION INDUSTRIES. The industry is concerned in developing energy-saving products, eg, radial passenger tires that wear longer and reduce gas consumption by about 10% over conventional tires. Most of the industry is represented by the Rubber Assn of Canada.   APRIL J. MacDOUGALL

Rubenstein, Louis, figure skater (b at Montréal, Canada E 23 Sept 1861; d there 3 Jan 1931). One of Canada's finest all-round athletes, Rubenstein was Canadian figure-skating champion 1883-89. In 1890 in St Petersburg, Russia, he won the unofficial world championship, displaying an unmistakable mastery of figures and free skating. President of the Int Skating Union of America 1907-09, Rubenstein was also active in the administration of several sports. He was an accomplished bowler and cyclist, president of the Canadian Wheelmen's Assn for 18 years, and president of the Montréal Amateur Athletic Assn 1913-15. Rubenstein was a partner in the family firm of silver platers and manufacturers, and was a Montréal alderman 1914-31.

BARBARA SCHRODT

Rugby is an amateur game played by 2 sides of 15 players who carry, kick and pass (forward passes are not permitted) an oval-shaped ball. Players score points by touching the ball over the opponents' goal line (a try) or by kicking it over the crossbar (a goal). Ball-carrying and running games have existed since before the Middle Ages and the story that William Webb Ellis invented the modern game at Rugby School in England, hence the name rugby football, has

Rugby was introduced to Canada around 1823 by British garrison troops and members of the Royal Navy (*photo by Ted Grant/Masterfile*).

been largely refuted. Rugby football was distinguished from association football (SOCCER) in 1863 and the Rugby Football Union was formed in 1871. British settlers, garrison troops and members of the Royal Navy probably introduced the game to Canada from 1823 onwards and fostered its development in many parts of the country, especially in Halifax, Toronto and Montréal. F. Barlow Cumberland and Fred A. Bethune first codified rules for rugby football in Canada in 1864 at Trinity College, Toronto, and the first Canadian game of rugby took place in 1865 in Montréal when English regiment officers and civilians, mainly from McGill University, engaged in competition. Clubs across Canada were established after this and organized contests ensued: Montreal FC (1868), Halifax FC (1870), Winnipeg FC (1879) and Vancouver RFC (1889) are notable examples. In 1874 Harvard and McGill universities played the first international rugby match in N America, and thenceforth N American varieties of rugby began to evolve. Separation between the English and N American types of football occurred in 1882 with the formation of the Canadian Rugby Football Union; the English game fell under the control of individual provincial rugby unions before eventually operating under the Rugby Union of Canada from 1929 to 1939 when it was curtailed by WWII. It re-formed in 1965 and was renamed the Canadian Rugby Union in 1967.

While British immigrants and military personnel initially fostered rugby's development, touring teams to and from Canada also helped to promote the game by demonstrating its international appeal. A Canadian team first toured the British Isles in 1902, and since that time representative teams have visited Japan, England, Wales and Argentina. Overseas national teams visiting Canada have included Japan, England, Australia, the British Lions, New Zealand, Fiji and Wales. Provincial, club and schoolboy teams have competed against overseas opponents since 1908 when a BC representative side lost 2 games against the New Zealand All-Blacks in California. Most tours in this category have taken place after 1960 when the Rugby Tours Committee was formed. BC remains the stronghold of rugby in Canada, although the game is played in all 10 provinces. The Carling Cup, emblematic of the national championship, was first won by BC in 1958, and although dormant between 1959 and 1966, the championship was retained by the BC team until Ontario won its first championship in 1971. A junior interprovincial championship was inaugurated in 1976; this development, along with improved coaching (via the CRU's national coaching program) has greatly increased rugby's popularity in Canada.   DAVE BROWN

Rugs and Rug Making A hooked rug is made by pulling loops of yarn or rag strips up through a loosely woven foundation cloth, usually burlap, using a tool like a crochet hook. Eventually, these loops of different kinds of material in a variety of colours create a design — pictorial, floral or geometric — which covers the whole foundation and forms a sturdy mat. In the mid-19th century when hooked rugs were first made, floor covering was a luxury in Canada. The wealthy might have an imported oriental rug or perhaps could afford commercial loom-woven carpeting. Others might make (or have made) a *catalogne* rug, consisting of a weft of rag strips woven on a widely spaced warp of cotton string. The hooked rug solved the problem of covering cold floors cheaply and was the final stage in the recycling of hand-me-down clothing. Very little 19th-century everyday clothing is left in Canada: cloth was too precious to waste and much of it ended up in QUILTS or on the floor (*see* CLOTHING). It is probable that rug hooking developed independently and simultaneously in several centres: Québec, the Maritimes and New England. Hooked rugs were made in much greater numbers in the eastern half of the continent than in the western half since, by the time the Canadian West was settled, store-bought floor coverings had become available.

The most immediately recognizable of Canadian rugs are those from the Grenfell missions in Newfoundland and Labrador. Grenfell rugs have been made since 1913, when Sir Wilfred and Lady GRENFELL industrialized the local mat-making activities. Standard patterns (eg, dogsleds, flights of geese, polar bears) were reproduced on burlap, and then the rugs were hooked by local women. The rugs were sold widely through churches to raise money for medical missions. Grenfell mats, which are still produced today using chemically dyed synthetic fabrics in place of the original natural fibres and vegetable dyes, have always been extremely finely hooked and look almost like needlepoint. Browns and greens predominate in the early rugs, which contained much burlap yarn, as well as underwear and stockings collected on the mainland and donated to the missions. The fine workmanship of the rugs of Cheticamp, NS, is also legendary. The Cheticamp rug industry was established by Lillian Burke at the instigation of Mrs Alexander Graham Bell, who was impressed with the possibility of establishing a homecraft industry in Cape Breton.

Unlike quilts, which are often treasured within a family and passed from one generation to the next, old hooked rugs are usually orphans whose family history has been lost. It is rare to find a very old rug whose maker is known. However, one famous rug hooker was Emily CARR, who made rugs to supplement the income she earned from her boardinghouse. Many rugs designed by the artist Georges-Édouard Tremblay can be identified. As part of the Québec CRAFT revival, these rugs were copied in his Pointe-au-Pic studio from Tremblay's landscape paintings by local women working under his direction; the rugs were often hooked from heavy cotton yarn and featured a wide black edging around a snow scene.

In 1868 Edwards Sands Frost, a Maine tin peddler, devised a series of zinc cutouts that allowed him to mass-produce stenciled patterns on burlap for rug hooking (an early version of paint by number). Other companies also entered the market. By the mid-1890s Garrett's of New Glasgow, NS, was producing *Bluenose* rug patterns. In 1894 Wells and Richardson of Montréal published patterns in its *Diamond Dye Rug Books* ("Do not sell your rags to the travelling rag-gatherer; save them and work them up into handsome and useful Rugs and Mats"). By 1905 Eaton's was advertising *Monarch* hooked rug patterns in its catalogue, and in the early years of the century Hambly and Wilson of Toronto also produced patterns on burlap.

Pattern rugs are still made today, but the most impressive rugs have always been those devised by women from their own materials and visions. Many old Canadian hooked rugs are sur-prisingly eloquent. They speak of economy, individuality and utility. Women incorporated into these rugs generations of clothing and memory-laden cloth — the very fabric of their lives.   MAX ALLEN

Rule, Jane Vance, writer (b at Plainfield, NJ 28 Mar 1931). Educated at Mills College, Calif, and University College, London, Eng, Rule moved to Vancouver in 1956. She was assistant director at International House, UBC (1958-59) and lectured in English and creative writing at UBC (1959-76). In 1976 she moved to Galiano I, BC. Rule is an acute observer of social and emotional relationships, homosexual and heterosexual, and writes about them with refreshing candour. Her novels include *Desert of the Heart* (1964), *This Is Not for You* (1970), *The Young in One Another's Arms* (1977) and *Contract with the World* (1980). She has also written short stories (*Themes for Diverse Instruments,* 1975; *Outlander,* 1981), many essays and a study of lesbian writers, *Lesbian Images* (1975). Her most recent book is a prose collection entitled *A Hot-Eyed Moderate* (1984).   JEAN WILSON

Rule of Law, an underlying constitutional principle requiring government to be conducted according to law and making all public officers answerable for their acts in the ordinary courts (*see* ADMINISTRATIVE LAW). The principle was perhaps first formally enunciated by Bracton (1250), a judge and early writer on English law, who declared, "The King himself however ought to be not under man, but under God and under the law, for the law makes him king." The term was coined by the English legal scholar Dicey, in his *Introduction to the Study of the Law of the Constitution* (1885).   STEPHEN A. SCOTT

Rundle, Robert Terrill, Methodist missionary and circuit clergyman (b at Mylor, Eng, 11 June 1811; d at Garstang, Eng, 4 Feb 1896). Sent as a Methodist missionary to the Saskatchewan country in 1840, he arrived at Fort Edmonton on 18 Oct 1840. Although it remained his headquarters until 1848, he spent several winters at Lesser Slave Lake Fort and Fort Assiniboine, and a few springs and summers at Rocky Mountain House and Gull Lake. Twice, in 1841 and 1847, he went south, deep into Blackfoot country. In 1844 he went past the first ranges of the Rockies, where he saw the mountain that today bears his name. He became a master of the Cree language, having learned CREE SYLLABICS devised by James EVANS; his journals record the adjustments made to the syllabary in the early years. Rundle was less than successful at establishing permanent missions. Only in 1848 was Pigeon Lake started by his follower, Benjamin Sinclair. After his return to England, Rundle served at various circuits until his retirement.   FRITS PANNEKOEK

Rupert, Rivière de, 763 km long to the head of Témiscamie, rises in Lk MISTASSINI in central Québec and follows a twisted course through a series of lakes and across a flat coastal plain to discharge into southeastern JAMES B. Cree have inhabited its banks for centuries. English navigator Henry HUDSON wintered at the mouth in 1610-11. In 1668 the ship *Nonsuch* made its historic voyage to the spot that led to the creation of the Hudson's Bay Co and the beginning of the fur trade in Hudson Bay. The company's first post was built at the river's mouth and for many years it was a main artery of the trade, carrying traders and Indians between the coast and the fur-rich interior. Rupert House, an Indian settlement, is still located near the site of the original post. Prince Rupert was the first governor of the HBC.   DANIEL FRANCIS

Rupert's Land On 2 May 1670 Charles II of England granted to the HUDSON'S BAY COMPANY a large portion of N America, named Rupert's Land in honour of Prince Rupert, the king's cousin and the company's first governor. This grant comprised the entire HUDSON BAY drainage system, which in modern geographical terms included northern Québec and Ontario N of the Laurentian watershed, all of Manitoba, most of Saskatchewan, southern Alberta and a portion of the NWT. The company was to have a monopoly and complete control of the territory. The HBC first established FUR-TRADE posts around James and Hudson bays. In 1774 Samuel HEARNE established the first western inland post at CUMBERLAND HOUSE [Sask]. By 1870 there were 97 posts within the territory. HBC fur traders were responsible for many early travels, explorations and cartography in Rupert's Land.

By the 1850s the Canadian movement to annex Rupert's Land was gaining momentum, and provision was made in the BRITISH NORTH AMERICA ACT for its admission into Canada. The company agreed to surrender its territory on 19 Nov 1869, and royal assent was given 23 June 1870. In exchange for Rupert's Land, the HBC received £300 000, certain land around its posts and some 2.8 million ha of farmland in what are today the Prairie provinces.

SHIRLEE ANNE SMITH

Rural Society, English Canada Rural society is made up of people, their institutions, socioeconomic activities and beliefs. In Canada, rural society has been shaped by geographic and cultural diversity and by population mobility. Canada was settled in a series of westward movements; this pattern created dispersed rural communities differentiated by their dependence on primary production (agriculture, FORESTRY, fishing or MINING), ethnic mix and time of settlement. ACADIAN communities in the Atlantic region are 150 years older than are settlements in Alberta; landholding divisions in Lower Canada (*see* SEIGNEURIAL SYSTEM) are distinct from the "quarter sections" of the prairies. Both factors affect the layout of communities and the formation of rural society. Wars, depressions, technological advancement and URBANIZATION have all affected established communities. Thus, in contemporary rural society, local and regional diversity is strong. However, when compared to urban society, rural society retains a firm sense of solidarity and difference.

Canadian rural society has been influenced by 4 consecutive phases of population mobility: rural settlement, labour migrations, depopulation and return migration. Early mobility was always westward and towards the frontier. Labour migrations were also westward, eg, the movements of workers who manned the threshing crews on western grain farms in the early part of this century (*see* HARVEST EXCURSIONS). The third and longest phase, rural out-migration, began at the beginning of the century and persisted until the 1970s. People, mainly rural youth, left farms, villages and towns to seek jobs, education and a better way of life in Canada's growing urban centres. This migration was also partly the result of the modernization of rural primary industries and the consequent dislocation of the labour force. The farm population fell from under 3 million in 1951 (about 21% of Canada's population) to just over one million in 1981 (about 4%). The fourth phase saw a return flow of people from urban to rural areas in the 1970s, a movement that created large-scale commuting between rural areas and

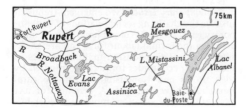

large cities. Evidence from the 1981 census suggests that this return migration to rural areas has slowed down.

Role of Technology and Urbanization Technological change has profoundly affected the composition of rural society. Mechanization in the primary industries has led to constant rationalization of production, with reduced need for manual labour and increased demand for technically skilled operators. Technology and scientific methods have changed the nature of farming from an independent way of life to a highly technical production system dependent upon high-cost inputs (eg, chemical fertilizers, fossil fuels) and more sophisticated knowledge of farm finance and management. Farming has become a business and farmers are referred to as "producers," a term that reflects their specialized production orientation. Farm size increases have accompanied technological change and caused many slow and many far too rapid adopters to leave the land. Farm amalgamation and loss of families have caused economic viability problems for local service centres. Small towns and villages have also suffered from technological change because modern equipment and materials tend to be produced and distributed from cities and processing of foodstuffs now takes place in major cities.

The values of rural society have been profoundly influenced by URBANIZATION. Agricultural fundamentalism — the inherent belief in the virtue of working the land to provide for self and family — developed into a form of "agrarianism," extolling the value of country life while combining the ethics of hard work and frugality to produce a food surplus. Herein lie the origins of the family farm, based on concepts of ownership and independence. Agrarianism upheld the belief in the full-time family farm and laid the basis for subsequent disapproval of the part-time operations that characterize many farming arrangements in Canada today.

Urbanization brought many benefits to rural society, such as automobiles, electrification, the "party line" and modern homes. It also introduced some new values, which often conflicted with those of small-town life, where roles and responsibilities were governed by sex, age and wealth. Many small towns have continued to have 2 communities, the established and the poor. Rural society has tolerated diversity but, in so doing, has often ignored the poor. Failure, once defined by unemployment, poverty and sickness, has been complicated by urbanization, which over time has raised expectations and needs that have not been met by governmental agencies because of the problem of providing services to small rural places. These problems are being addressed by an expanding volunteer network of informal support groups.

Urbanization is particularly evident in the rural-urban fringe. A backflow of migrants from the city to surrounding rural areas has caused many changes, including conflicts with locals over "rights to farm," on the one hand, and community expansion on the other. Ex-urbanites may object to farm noises and smells; locals object to the demands made on the municipality by newcomers. Curiously the value conflicts are often the reverse of what might be expected: many ex-urbanites hold firm conservationist principles, whereas locals often favour progress and development.

Rural Institutions The traditional rural institutions of church, school and family have been affected not only by technology and urbanization but also by internal rationalization. Although the rural church, which was ubiquitous in rural Canadian settlements by 1900, has declined in numbers and significance, it still plays an important role in family life and continues to draw many of its ministers from farm and

Manitoba farm (*photo by Bob Anderson/Masterfile*).

countryside. The rural church tends to be more fundamental in doctrine and social in function than its urban counterpart (*see* EVANGELICAL AND FUNDAMENTALIST MOVEMENTS). In recent years, many new variations of CHRISTIANITY have been established in rural areas.

Rural education changed rapidly in the 20th century. The basic shifts in attendance, curriculum and location, particularly from local school house to the central facility, has had a profound effect on rural society. The shift provided standard educational opportunities, and central schooling also helped prepare rural youth for out-migration by detaching youngsters from their local environment. Changing production technology and the growth of AGRIBUSINESS has required special training in agriculture, forestry and mining. Rural society has become role-specific in the workplace, even on the farm, because of the changing forces in education.

The most enduring institution of rural society is the farm family, a unit of socioeconomic organization that has persisted from pioneer settlement to the modern era of industrial farming. Although the number of farm families has shrunk consistently, the essential feature of the unit has remained intact: family control over land, labour and capital. In order to finance large modern farms, families can incorporate and share the benefits of limited liability and increased access to capital (*see* FARM LAW). Farm families have, in the 1980s, been subject to considerable stress resulting from the cost-price squeeze, high debt load and high interest rates. The rural family has survived the trend of decline in the extended family and has adapted to new household formations. Rural families are smaller than they were (3.2 persons as opposed to 4.1 before WWII) but still have a preponderance of males (117 men per 100 women). The ethics of mutual aid, co-operation, hard work over long hours and community involvement still characterize rural family life and help to explain its survival in the face of ex-urbanite and tourist incursions, which have introduced new trends and values into many areas (*see* CO-OPERATIVE MOVEMENT).

Contemporary Issues Two emergent trends illustrate the changing social relations of contemporary rural society. Women have become more active in the formal labour force and are an accepted part of the decision-making process in many rural economies formerly dominated by men. Roles and responsibilities in the rural household have changed. A demand for DAY CARE, rural transportation, more and better human services and job opportunities for women reflect a changing work ethic and an acceptance of occupational pluralism. Rural women are dealing with stress in the family, are capable of rapid occupational mobility and are adept at acquiring new skills. Women are also forming new organizations to voice their opinions and needs.

The second contemporary feature is the AGING of the rural population. Demographically, rural Canada is already a mature society: more than 13% of its population is over 65 years of age, while the national average remains at 10.1%. The elderly in rural areas are not evenly distributed. In rural towns (population size 1000 to 2500), the elderly average over 20% of the population; on farms and in the rural nonfarm sector, less than 10%. This pattern suggests that in their senior years, people from both farm and city retire to villages and towns. The growing number of seniors is a newfound strength in rural society. Many seniors are active, join volunteer services, more often can pay for their own needs and bring vitality as well as wisdom to rural communities. Inevitably, they also have special needs (eg, medical care), the servicing of which will form the core of social policy in rural areas in the latter part of the 20th century. *See* AGRICULTURE AND FOOD.　　　TONY FULLER

Reading: G.D. Hodge and M.A. Qadeer, *Towns and Villages in Canada* (1983); G. Schramm, ed, *Regional Poverty and Change* (1976); M.-A. Tremblay and W.J. Anderson, eds, *Rural Canada in Transition* (1970).

Rural Society, Québec Québec has often been identified with rural life, an identification based more on myth than fact. In 1890 Québec, like Ontario, was 90% rural, but by 1931 the majority of Québec's population was urban and by 1956 less than half the rural population worked in agriculture. In 1962 barely 4.2% of the province's work force was employed in agriculture, the smallest percentage of any Canadian province.

The view of Québec as a backward, rural society originated primarily with Québecois themselves, rather than with others outside the society. After the mid-19th century, a form of NATIONALISM developed in Québec which insisted that the best way to preserve the heritage of language and faith was to develop a strong, well-integrated rural society. Since the city was viewed as the stronghold of the English and of Protestants, the French Canadian who went there risked the loss of both language and faith. In the countryside, according to this ideology, Québecois could control their economic and cultural future and, above all, their existence as a people. This analysis by Abbé GROULX and others led to the conviction that the future of Québec was both agricultural and rural. The ruralist ideology persisted until the end of the 1950s and until the mid-1960s in the case of the agricultural associations (eg, l'Union catholique des cultivateurs (UCC) and agricultural CO-OPERATIVES). It disappeared only when the proportion of the work force engaged in agriculture dropped below 10% and more than 75% of the total population was urban. The QUIET REVOLUTION and then the PARTI QUÉBÉCOIS gave rise to a new nationalism which defined Québec as an urban, industrial society (which might even become the first post-industrial society).

Whatever the definition provided by outsiders and by its own leaders, rural Québec (agricultural and nonagricultural) has changed a great deal since the early 20th century. Until the end of the 1930s, Québec agriculture was overwhelmingly subsistence farming. Production was diversified so that farmers could feed their own families. Production techniques were rudimentary and were passed on from generation to generation. After 1910 Québec agriculture discovered the DAIRY INDUSTRY and almost every farm had its herd, the milk being sold to butter and cheese factories and the whey being used in the production of pork. However, dairy and pork production were not considered specializations but rather sidelines which brought in cash, used to buy goods which could not be produced on the farm. There were certain exceptions to this situation (notably in the Montréal plain area), but generally speaking, subsistence farming prevailed until WWII (see AGRICULTURE HISTORY).

During the war, the demand for pork and eggs was so great that the normal rules of supply and demand practically ceased to operate: farmers could sell everything they produced at excellent prices. For the first time, they became specialists who earned substantial incomes. But the situation was short-lived and normal market forces prevailed again after the war. Those farmers who had used their wartime earnings to modernize were able to face postwar competition and thrive. Most, however, had purchased consumer goods and had no capital to compete successfully in increasingly mechanized agricultural production. To maintain the standard of living to which they had become accustomed, farmers abandoned agriculture, either moving into the city or working in the forests, where demand for labour was high. Thus, in less than 15 years, more than three-quarters of all farms were abandoned, the farmhouse itself often being moved into a village. At the same time, agricultural production rose dramatically. Those who continued farming did so more effectively than ever and transformed their farms into modern agricultural enterprises. In 1980 Québec's agricultural production was being carried on by about 20 000 farmers, whose individual farms were often worth over $1 million.

Farming organizations underwent a similar transformation. The UCC, which had been primarily an educational organization, became the Union des producteurs agricoles (UPA), bringing together farmers in specialized unions and setting up production offices. Small milk co-operatives united to produce giant co-operatives (Granby being the largest) which entered international markets. The federated co-operative developed control of successive stages of production, distribution and marketing (ie, vertical integration), especially in the area of animal production. Active integration also occurred among private companies.

The nonagricultural rural world has also been transformed. Traditionally, it consisted of craftsmen or day labourers who were few in number (10% of the rural population) and had very little influence. Since 1956 the prolifera-

tion of professional forestry workers and the increase in transportation activities and small factories has caused the nonagricultural proportion of the rural population to skyrocket to 90%. Formerly homogenous and virtually egalitarian (only day workers formed a kind of proletariat), Québec's rural social hierarchy is much more complex today. At the top are civil servants and those in the quasi-public sector (eg, teachers, social workers, inspectors) with steady, high incomes. These are followed by farmers and small businessmen, then by labourers with fairly stable employment and, finally, by people on welfare, many of whom are former farmers or lumberjacks. Labourers and those on welfare constitute by far the largest group and live in relative POVERTY. This endemic poverty has contradictory effects on the school population: while it results in a high number of dropouts after primary or during secondary school, those who do not drop out work harder at the CEGEP (COLLEGE D'ENSEIGNEMENT GÉNÉRAL ET PROFESSIONNEL, ie, senior matriculation) level than do their urban counterparts. The dropout's future is limited to work in the forest or the rural day-labour force, and rural poverty is thereby perpetuated.

The most profound rural transformation has been rural urbanization. Most of the functions previously carried out locally have been transferred to small cities which have become regional capitals. Some primary and all secondary schools, major stores, credit institutions, recreational facilities and medical and social services are now located in urban centres. The youngest members of the rural population are in daily contact with the city; the oldest visit at least once a week, more often 2 or 3 times. This physical contact is reinforced by the daily intrusion of the city through the mass media, especially television. In sociological terms, the life-style of rural people closely resembles that of city dwellers. The only significant difference is that the ruralist lives in a less densely populated region, where rural culture is barely a memory, if not folklore. See CHILDHOOD, HISTORY OF; FAMILY; FRENCH CANADIAN NATIONALISM; QUÉBEC SOCIETY; INTELLECTUAL HISTORY. GÉRALD FORTIN

Rush, rock band formed in the Toronto area 1974, has received popular and critical acclaim with a series of innovative and complex albums including "Moving Pictures" (1981). In 1980 and 1981 Rush led readers' polls in British rock-trade publications. Geddy Lee, Alex Lifeson and Neil Peart continue their success with platinum record sales and sold-out concert tours.

JOHN GEIGER

Rush (Juncaceae), family of herbaceous PLANTS consisting of 8 genera and about 300 species. They are essentially temperate, and are usually found in wet habitats. Six genera with about 10 species occur only in the Southern Hemisphere. The 2 largest genera, the common rush, *Juncus* (225 species), and the wood rush, *Luzula* (80 species), are widely distributed throughout the Northern Hemisphere, though not entirely restricted to it. They are represented in Canada by about 50 and 15 species, respectively, and are found all across the country, including the High Arctic. Most rushes are grasslike, often with sheathing basal leaves, which are sometimes reduced to the sheaths alone. The flowers are small and rather drab. The family is geologically old, dating from the Cretaceous (140-65 million years ago). The rushes (or reeds) of the Bible are not rushes at all but *Cyperus papyrus,* a member of the SEDGE family. *See* GRASSES.

Rush-Bagot Agreement In 1816 US Secretary of State James Monroe proposed to British Foreign Secretary Lord Castlereagh that the 2 countries should agree to limit naval armaments on Lks Ontario and Champlain to 1 ship each, and 2 each on the Upper Lakes. In 1817

notes were exchanged between Acting Secretary of State Richard Rush and Sir Charles Bagot, British minister in Washington. Since naval disarmament of the lakes was virtually complete after 1817, the Rush-Bagot Agreement is frequently cited as the diplomatic origin of the friendly international border. In fact, only naval power was affected, for the US and Britain continued to build land FORTIFICATIONS along the border for the next half century. D.N. SPRAGUE

Russell, Andy, writer, conservationist (b near Lethbridge, Alta 8 Dec 1915). He was a high-school dropout, who trapped for a living in the Depression and then went to work for bighorn-sheep guide Bert Riggall. Russell's intimate knowledge of the wilderness led him to write about it, and he sold his first major article to *Outdoor Life* in 1945. Award-winning books include *Grizzly Country* (1967), *Horns in the High Country* (1973), *Adventures with Wild Animals* (1977) and his autobiographical *Memoirs of a Mountain Man* (1984). He produced *Grizzly Country* and 2 other feature-length films for international lecture tours, contributing significantly to the understanding of these solitude-loving animals. He received the Crandall Award for Conservation in 1977. JOHN PATRICK GILLESE

Russell, Edward, Ted, teacher, magistrate, politician, writer (b at Coley's Point, Nfld 27 June 1904; d at St John's 16 Oct 1977). Russell's writings, combining philosophical wisdom and ingenious wit, drew on his experiences in rural Newfoundland: as a teacher, as a magistrate after the Depression and as a director of co-operatives before Confederation. In 1949 he joined the first provincial Cabinet under J.R. SMALLWOOD, but resigned in 1951 following a disagreement over economic policy. His stories were broadcast on CBC radio 1953-62 as "The Chronicles of Uncle Mose." He wrote and read approximately 600 six-minute scripts as well as 8 radio plays — all centered on the fictitious outport Pigeon Inlet. Many of the stories have been published in *The Chronicles of Uncle Mose* (1975), *Tales from Pigeon Inlet* (1977) and in *The Best of Ted Russell, Number 1* (1982). Also in print is his best-known radio play *The Holdin' Ground* (1972) and a biography by Elizabeth Russell Miller, *The Life & Times of Ted Russell* (1981).

ELIZABETH RUSSELL MILLER

Russell, John Alonzo, architect, educator (b at Hinsdale, NH 28 Oct 1907; d at Winnipeg 28 Dec 1966). A prominent figure in the arts in Winnipeg, he came to U of Man in 1928 with degrees in architecture from Massachusetts Institute of Technology. He became director of the U of Man School of Architecture in 1946 and dean of the Faculty of Architecture in 1963. His involvement with the lively arts as director and designer included design of sets and costumes for the Winnipeg (later ROYAL WINNIPEG) Ballet and Little Theatre Group (predecessor to Manitoba Theatre Centre). WILLIAM PAUL THOMPSON

Russell, Loris Shano, paleontologist, (b at Brooklyn, NY 21 Apr 1904). Raised in Alberta, he was director of the Royal Ontario Museum of Palaeontology from 1946 until 1950, when he joined the National Museum of Canada (chief, Zoology Section, 1950-56; director, Natural History, 1956-63; and acting director, Human History 1958-63). He was then appointed chief biologist at ROM and professor of geology at U of T. Russell's discoveries concerning dinosaurs and early mammals have been particularly important; he was the first to suggest that dinosaurs might have been warm blooded. He has also made original and fundamental contributions to the history of lighting and the antiquities of early Americans, and has published over 100 scientific papers, many popular articles and several books, including *A Heritage of Light* (1968). He retired in 1971, but has continued his fieldwork in western Canada and his research in the evolution of mammals. *See* DINOSAUR HUNTING IN WESTERN CANADA. WILLIAM E. SWINTON

Russell, Robert Boyd, labour politician (b at Glasgow, Scot 1888; d at Winnipeg 9 Sept 1964). Russell was the most prominent personality associated with the 1919 WINNIPEG GENERAL STRIKE. Subsequently charged with seditious conspiracy, he was convicted and sentenced to a 2-year prison term, the harshest treatment meted out to any accused. Russell was on the strike committee as an officer of the International Assn of Machinists, but as leading spokesman for the ONE BIG UNION in Winnipeg, his presence helped convince authorities that the strike was a tentative revolution. The Socialist Party and the OBU tried but failed to return him to Parliament for Winnipeg N in Dec 1921. Ironically, votes cast for the Communist Party candidate, Jacob Penner, helped ensure defeat of the country's most notorious "Bolshevik." Russell's long and stormy career in the labour movement lasted over 50 years. In 1956 the last remnants of the OBU joined the newly organized Canadian Labour Congress. Russell continued as executive secretary of the Winnipeg District Council until ill health forced him to retire in 1962. Long after he ceased to be a "threat," Russell was showered with honours and accolades by the CLC, Manitoba Prem Duff ROBLIN and others as a "Father of Labour in Western Canada." ALLEN SEAGER

Russell Case (1882) Charles Russell was a tavern owner in New Brunswick who challenged the constitutionality of the Canada Temperance Act because it interfered with provincial licences, property rights and revenues. The federal government claimed power to regulate trade and commerce in liquor and a general power over PEACE, ORDER AND GOOD GOVERNMENT. The British Privy Council, in its first major review of federal powers under the CONSTITUTION ACT, 1867, upheld the general power of the federal government to pass temperance laws and have them adopted by local option. The power was confirmed in *Attorney General for Ontario v Canada Temperance Federation.* D.A. CRUICKSHANK

Russians are the largest single linguistic group among the Slavic nations and the dominant nationality in the USSR, comprising about 50% of the total population of 268 million. The 1981 Canadian census indicated that there are only 49 435 Canadians of Russian descent. Except for the relatively concentrated and unified DOUKHOBORS (numbering about 15 000), the members of this aging, rapidly assimilating ethnic group tend to be scattered throughout the country. However, their contribution to the arts, sciences and professions in Canada has been far greater than their numbers would indicate.

Migration and Settlement The first Russians in Canada were fur hunters, who operated among the Queen Charlotte Is and at Nootka Sound in the 1790s, and several officers on detached service with the British navy, who were based at Halifax 1793-96. Russians settled Russian America (now Alaska) in the 18th century, but Russian aspirations to the Pacific coast were curtailed by the 1824 and 1825 conventions with the US and Great Britain, which confined Russian America to the present Canada-Alaska boundary. Official restrictions have usually hindered emigration from Russia. Most early immigrants to Canada from Russia arrived in groups, through special arrangement. Between 1874 and 1880, nearly 8000 German MENNONITE colonists from southern Russia settled in Saskatchewan, and in 1899, 7500 Doukhobors settled in Canada, aided in Russia by Tolstoy and in Canada by Professor James Mavor and Clifford SIFTON, then minister of the interior. Beginning in the 1890s, several thousand Russian JEWS emigrated, seeking relief from ghetto life

and the pogroms of western Russia. Small Russian communities were established in Montréal, Toronto, Windsor, Timmins, Winnipeg, Vancouver and Victoria. Most of the early immigrants were peasants who found work in various industries. After WWI many of the one million Russians (the majority of them agricultural and industrial labourers) fleeing the effects of the Russian Revolution sought admission to Canada, but few were successful. Many Russian intellectuals, on the other hand, preferred to settle in Europe. Men willing to work as farm labourers, loggers and miners were preferred immigrants in Canada, but those who managed to establish themselves in their own professions did outstanding work in many fields. Leonid I. Strakhovsky (1898-1963) pioneered Slavic studies at U of T. Boris P. Babkin (1877-1950) resumed his career in gastroenterology at Dalhousie and McGill universities. Nicholas, Vladimir, Alexis and George IGNATIEFF, the 4 sons of Count Paul Ignatieff, the last minister of education under Tsar Nicholas II, made important contributions to engineering and government. Some Russians joined the Canadian MACKENZIE-PAPINEAU BATTALION which fought on the Republican side during the Spanish Civil War.

The Great Depression and WWII virtually halted immigration of all nationalities, but between 1948 and 1953 a significant number of Russians immigrated to Canada, including some who had originally left Russia and settled in Europe and some who found themselves in Germany after the war either because they opposed Stalin or because they had been sent there as forced labour. Both groups were generally young, well educated, urban oriented and aware of their Russian heritage. After 1953 Russian immigration declined severely (in the early 1970s the average number of immigrants per year from all of the Soviet Union was only 230), although the Soviet government began at that time to allow the emigration of some Jews.

BC has the largest population of Russian origin, largely because of Doukhobor settlement; next are Ontario, Alberta and Saskatchewan.

Social and Cultural Life Although Russian Canadians claim affiliation with a diversity of churches (in order of numbers: the United Church of Canada, Russian Orthodox Church, Roman Catholic), the ORTHODOX CHURCH is still the traditional centre for the most vocal and active of those claiming Russian origin or descent. There are some 40 Russian Orthodox parishes in Canada; half belong to the Russian Orthodox Church Abroad and the remainder to the Orthodox Church in America, which includes in its membership many non-Russian churches which also follow the Byzantine rite. One of the oldest Russian Canadian parishes is that of the Church of Saints Peter and Paul (an Orthodox Church of America member) founded in Montréal in 1907.

Within the Russian community a broad spectrum of political organizations have been formed. During the 1930s, some Russian Canadians were drawn to the Russian Farmer-Worker Clubs. Closed by government order in 1939, they gave rise to the Federation of Russian Canadians (FRK) in 1942. The FRK organized some 15 branches in various Canadian cities and published the newspaper *Vestnik* (*Herald*), still the only Russian newspaper in Canada. In 1944 the FRK had about 4000 members; by 1949, after the spy trials of Igor GOUZENKO, membership dropped to 2270 and by the 1980s to less than 800.

The most active Russian organization in Toronto is the Russian Cultural Society (est 1950). An anticommunist organization, it publishes a journal, *Russkoe slovo v Kanade* (*Russian Word in Canada*), and operates a centre for social and cultural activities. A small Literary Circle (1949), a

Drama Circle, and the "Sovremennik" Publishing Association (1960) which publishes the literary journal, *Sovremennik* (*Contemporary*), are also active. Cultural groups, eg, Ottawa Chekhov Soc (1974), have been founded in other cities as well.

Education Although Russian immigrants have eagerly entered their offspring in Canadian schools, some older immigrants have favoured the establishment of schools by church groups (the 2 largest are in Montréal and Toronto) and clubs for after-hours instruction in Russian language and culture.

National Minorities The immigration of Russians has been less than that of some of the minority peoples of the Soviet Union. Soviet UKRAINIANS emigrating as displaced persons after 1945 have joined earlier immigrants from Austria and Poland to make up Canada's third most numerous ethnic element. THE BYELORUSSIANS in Canada, chiefly from pre-WWII eastern Poland, are now thought to number about 60 000. There are also smaller numbers of ESTONIANS, LATVIANS and LITHUANIANS, as well as Georgians and ARMENIANS. RICHARD A. PIERCE

Rutabaga (*Brassica napus*, Napobrassica Group), herbaceous biennial VEGETABLE belonging to the Cruciferae family and grown as a ROOT CROP in all provinces. Rutabaga has many other names, eg, *chou de Siam* in French and Swede turnip in English. The rutabaga originated in northern Europe and was introduced to N America around 1805. Related to the TURNIP, rutabagas differ in the root (round, elongated), flesh (thick, yellow) and foliage (broad, smooth, down covered). Rutabagas are easily cultivated in cool, moist climates and grow best in heavy clay soils. Seeds are usually sown in the last 2 weeks of June; principal harvest occurs in Oct and Nov. Rutabagas can be stored for 7-8 months at 0°C and 95% humidity. Major cultivation problems are boron mineral deficiencies (causing brown heart); clubroot, a FUNGUS disease which develops in acidic soils; and mosaic, a VIRUS spread by insects, especially plant lice. Cabbage flies lay their eggs on the plant at the soil line and emerging larvae bore holes in the root. Cultivars (commercial varieties) include Laurentian and one of its offshoots, the York, which is immune to most strains of clubroot. HUGUES LeBLANC

Rutherford, Alexander Cameron, lawyer, politician, premier of Alberta (b near Osgoode, Carleton County, Canada W 2 Feb 1857; d at Edmonton 11 June 1941). In 1905 he became the first premier, treasurer and minister of education of the newly created province of Alberta. His administration promoted public education, a public telephone system and railway expansion. Though leader of a powerful Liberal majority in the legislature, he was forced to resign in 1910 over allegations of incompetence and personal interest in his government's agreement to insure the bonds of the Alberta and Great Waterways Ry. Although found innocent of personal interest, a disillusioned Rutherford became increasingly identified with the Conservative Party. Following his defeat in the 1913 provincial election he returned to his Edmonton law practice. He served as chancellor of U of A 1927-41. His fine library of Canadiana now belongs to the university's Rutherford Library.

DOUGLAS BABCOCK

Rutherford, Ernest, Baron Rutherford of Nelson, physicist (b at Nelson, NZ 30 Aug 1871; d at Cambridge, Eng 19 Oct 1937). Although not a Canadian citizen, Rutherford made some of his most fundamental discoveries at McGill and is considered the greatest experimental physicist of the century. He graduated from Canterbury College, Christchurch, in 1895, winning the 1851 Exhibition Scholarship, and went to Cambridge to work in the Cavendish Laboratory under J.J. Thomson. When he came to McGill in 1898 as Macdonald Professor of Physics, Rutherford

Ernest Rutherford, considered the greatest experimental physicist of the 20th century, had a profound influence on Canadian science during his tenure at McGill U (*courtesy Public Archives of Canada/C-18230*).

had begun studying radioactivity at Cambridge and his work at the Macdonald Physics Building, then one of the best equipped laboratories anywhere, was subsidized by William MACDONALD himself. Rutherford's main contribution was his elaboration in 1902 of the disintegration theory of the atom, a theory that completely transformed the understanding of radioactivity. The results of his work at McGill are synthesized in *Radio-Activity* (1904, rev 1905). At McGill Rutherford was assisted by future Nobel Prize winner Frederick Soddy who coauthored the revolutionary papers on radioactivity. In 1904 Rutherford received the Rumford Medal of the Royal Soc of London given to the author of the most important discovery of the preceding 2 years. He complained about his isolation from the great scientific centres of Europe, however, and in 1907 accepted a post at Manchester. One year later he won the Nobel Prize in chemistry for his work at McGill. In 1911 Rutherford made another fundamental discovery: the nucleus of the atom. In 1919 he succeeded Thomson as head of the Cavendish Laboratory, attracting students from all over the world, including many young Canadians. Knighted in 1914 and created baron in 1931, Rutherford kept in touch with his former students and colleagues in Canada; McGill named its physics laboratories after him.   YVES GINGRAS

Rutherford, John Gunion, veterinarian, administrator (b at Mountain Cross, Scot 25 Dec 1857; d at Ottawa 24 July 1923). A graduate of the Ontario Veterinary College 1879, he practised in Woodstock, Ont, and in the US and Mexico, and settled in Portage la Prairie, Man, 1884. He became veterinary inspector of Manitoba in 1887 and was an MLA 1892-96 and MP 1897-1900. He was appointed chief inspector of Canada (later veterinary director general) 1902 and Dominion livestock commissioner 1906. Rutherford's greatest contribution was in upgrading the veterinary profession and its associations. He was president of the American Veterinary Medical Assn 1908-09 and was instrumental in raising the standards of education at OVC and having it taken over by U of T and the Ontario government.   R.G. THOMSON

Ryan, Claude, journalist, politician (b at Montréal 26 Jan 1925). He ran *Le* DEVOIR 1964-78 and strongly influenced public debate during the QUIET REVOLUTION in Québec. Ryan was national secretary of Action catholique 1945-62 and chaired the Ministry of Education's adult-education study committee 1962-63. Admired for his careful analyses and clear positions, he helped make *Le Devoir* one of the most respected and influential newspapers in Canada. In 1978 he was chosen to succeed Robert BOURASSA as leader of the Québec Liberal Party and entered the National Assembly the next year as the member for Argenteuil. He campaigned actively for the *Non* side against Premier LÉVESQUE in the referendum on Québec SOVEREIGNTY-ASSOCIATION, but his participation was eclipsed by that of PM TRUDEAU. His party was defeated in the 1981 election and, despite the democratic reforms and intellectual revival that he brought to the Liberal Party, his leadership was seriously questioned and he resigned in the fall of 1982. However he has remained an MNA, taking a vigorous part in debates on educational questions.
DANIEL LATOUCHE

Ryan, Thomas F., businessman, sports promoter (b 1872; d 1961). He introduced the first 10-pin BOWLING alley in Canada and attracted many prominent businessmen and professionals to his downtown Toronto facility. To meet complaints that the heavy ball was causing arm strain among his genteel clientele, Ryan introduced a smaller ball for a game called duckpin and had his father whittle down 5 pins to match. He invented a new scoring system and introduced his game either in 1908 or 1909. He later added the finishing touch — the rubber collar still familiar around the belly of the pin. Ryan neglected to patent his invention and saw no financial gain from it, except in his own alley.   JAMES MARSH

Rye, common name for members of the genus *Secale* of the GRASS family (Gramineae); grown as a cereal grain. Both annual and perennial forms exist, but only one species, *S. cereale,* is of economic importance, ranking seventh among the world's major food and feed crops. Winter rye, sown in early fall, is far more common than spring rye. Rye probably originated in Asia Minor and spread throughout Europe as a contaminate of WHEAT, which it resembles. It was brought to N America by European immigrants. Additional introductions were made by government agencies in programs to provide cultivars adapted to Canadian conditions. Rye grain is borne on a terminal spike 10-15 cm long. The alternately arranged spikelets produce 2 or 3 kernels. Kernels are generally greenish blue in colour but can range from light tan to dark brown, depending on the cultivar. In N America, rye is used primarily as an animal feed. The FUNGUS disease "ergot" (*Claviceps purpurea*) is its most serious PLANT DISEASE, and caution should be exercised when feeding ergoty rye. Canadian production averaged 475 000 t annually (1972-81): 52% was exported (chiefly to Japan, Netherlands and UK); 27%, fed to livestock; 16%, used by the DISTILLING INDUSTRY; and 2%, used as food (bread and breakfast foods). Rye is the hardiest of all cereal crops and is important in areas subject to cold and drought, eg, drier regions of Alta and Sask, where it has been used to control soil erosion.   D.S. McBEAN

Ryerson, Adolphus Egerton, Methodist minister, educator (b in Charlotteville Twp, Norfolk County, UC 24 Mar 1803; d at Toronto 18 Feb 1882). A leading figure in 19th-century Ontario education and politics, Ryerson was born into a prominent Anglican, Loyalist family, but was converted and ordained in 1827 in the Methodist Episcopal Church. He helped found and edited the *Christian Guardian* (1829), founded Upper Canada Academy (1836) and become first

Egerton Ryerson, Methodist minister and strong-willed advocate of universal and compulsory education (*courtesy Ontario Archives*).

principal of Victoria College (1841). He first came into prominence in 1826 when he spearheaded an attack on the assumptions and prerogatives of the Church of England, which claimed to be the official church of the colony and exclusive beneficiary of the CLERGY RESERVES. Ryerson emerged as the leading Methodist spokesman and a major figure in the Reform cause. He used the press to promote Methodism and continued as an influential political adviser for the rest of his life. He was president of the Methodist Church of Canada 1874-78.

During the Rebellions of 1837, Ryerson was in England but used his influence to oppose William Lyon MACKENZIE's radical philosophy and violent methods. During the 1840s he continued his active role in politics and, much to the anger of his Reform allies and many Methodists, supported Gov Charles METCALFE against Robert BALDWIN and LAFONTAINE in 1844. He appeared to have joined the Tories whom he had opposed for nearly 20 years.

In 1844 he was appointed superintendent of education for Canada W, continuing in this office until retiring in 1876. He believed that education should be universal and compulsory, and had to be religious and moral if it was to improve the individual and help society progress. Culminating in the School Act of 1871, Ontario gained a first-rate primary and secondary school system based on these principles. Ryerson also promoted denominational universities as the pinnacle of the educational process. During his long career, he wrote numerous pamphlets and texts, as well as several works on the history of the province and an important autobiography.

Ryerson based his long and active public career on a consistent, yet often misunderstood, political outlook. He blended a staunch loyalty to British-Canadian institutions and a conservative mistrust of radicalism with a liberal optimism in mankind, adding a deep and abiding religious commitment. He trusted that through religion and education man could fashion his own improvement and the natural, gradual evolution of society. During his early career, when politics in Upper Canada were polarized by Tory and Reform controversy, Ryerson was condemned for not belonging neatly to either camp. However, he fit naturally into the moderate, Liberal-Conservative alliance that predominated after the mid-1850s and in fact helped create its ideological framework through the educational system he fostered. Arrogant and strong willed, he never backed away from controversy, combining strong administrative talents, tireless energy, an anti-partisan spirit and a keen sense of what was best for his province.

NEIL SEMPLE

Reading: Neil McDonald and Alf Chaiton, eds, *Egerton Ryerson and His Times* (1978).

Ryerson, Stanley Bréhaut, historian, COMMUNIST PARTY OF CANADA leader (b at Toronto 12 Mar 1911). After attending Upper Canada Coll and U of T he studied at the Sorbonne, Paris (1931-34), where he encountered European communist politics. He was a member of the Central Committee of the Communist Party of Canada 1935-69 and Québec provincial secretary 1936-40. He moved to Toronto in 1943 as the new Labour Progressive Party's education director and managing editor of its *National Affairs Monthly.*

During the difficult Cold War years 1949-54, Ryerson was party organizational secretary. In 1959 he took responsibility for the Toronto edition of *World Marxist Review,* and became chairman of the Marxist Studies Centre, Toronto; he was editor of *Marxist Quarterly* 1961-69. Ryerson's "people's history" — *The Founding of Canada: Beginnings to 1815* (1960) and *Unequal Union: Confederation and the Roots of Conflict in the Canadas, 1815-1873* (1968) — is still widely read. A pioneering aspect of Ryerson's scholarship from the late 1930s has been his contribution to the Québec/Canada national debate.

The entry of Warsaw Pact tanks into Czechoslovakia in 1968 precipitated Ryerson's departure from the party; he resigned in 1971. He joined the history department of UQAM in 1970 and throughout the 1970s was an important resource to a new generation of Québec and Canadian Marxist scholars.   GREGORY S. KEALEY

Ryerson Polytechnical Institute, Toronto, Ont, was founded 16 Sept 1948 as Ryerson Institute of Technology. The institute is situated on historic St James Square, where the Toronto Normal School was established in 1852 by Egerton RYERSON, chief superintendent of education for Upper Canada. In 1941 teacher education was shifted to another site to make room for a Royal Canadian Air Force training centre. From 1945 to 1948, the buildings served the Training and Re-establishment Institute, which offered trades training to returning war veterans. Ryerson Institute of Technology began offering 2-year trades-oriented programs, but by the early 1950s, it had developed 3-year diploma programs with a significant academic component.

The 1963 Ryerson Act created the autonomous Ryerson Polytechnical Institute, with its own board of governors. The Act was amended in 1971 to empower Ryerson to grant degrees in addition to its diplomas. Today, as a full member of the Council of Ontario Universities, Ryerson offers 34 career-oriented programs in arts, applied arts, business, community services and the technologies. Twenty-six of these lead to degrees of bachelor of applied arts, bachelor of technology or bachelor of business management. The program range includes applied computer science, architecture, journalism, radio and television arts, business administration, fashion design, theatre arts, aerospace engineering, chemical engineering and social work.

B. BEATON

Enrolment: Ryerson Polytechnical Institute, 1982-83 (Source: Statistics Canada)			
Full-time Undergrad	Full-time Graduate	Part-time Undergrad	Part-time Graduate
8 872	—	10 885	—

Ryerson Press, The, was founded as a publishing company in 1829 by the Methodist Church in Toronto. Called the Methodist Book Room, it issued denominational publications and general books until William Briggs took over as book steward in 1879. Briggs developed a coherent policy of using revenue from the sale of foreign (agency) books to publish Canadian writers such as Charles G.D. ROBERTS, Wilfred CAMPBELL and Catherine Parr TRAILL. The name Ryerson Press was adopted 1919 in honour of its illustrious first editor, Egerton RYERSON. Lorne PIERCE assumed editorial control in 1922. He built up a profitable line of school texts and encouraged the careers of promising writers such as F.P. GROVE, Earle BIRNEY and Louis DUDEK. The sale of the press by the United Church of Canada to the American company McGraw-Hill in 1970 caused consternation among those believing Canadian ownership essential to an independent BOOK PUBLISHING industry.   JAMES MARSH

Ryga, George, playwright, novelist (b at Deep Cr, Alta 27 July 1932). Raised in a Ukrainian farm community in northern Alberta, Ryga received little formal education, but over the last 20 years has established himself as a prominent Canadian writer. He was catapulted to fame with *The Ecstacy of Rita Joe and other Plays* (1970), his depiction of the plight of Indians as they struggle to come to terms with a society that incites them to rebellion while blanketing them with bureaucratic indifference. His other plays and 2 novels, *Hungry Hills* (1963) and *Ballad of a Stone-Picker* (1966), also explore the problems of self-doubt, alienation and personal unfulfilment. While stridently critical of society, Ryga's writings are not without humour. His works include *Captives of the Faceless Drummer* (1972), *Night Desk* (1976), *Seven Hours to Sundown* (1977), *Beyond the Crimson Morning* (1979) and *Two Plays: Paracelsus and Prometheus* (1982).   DAVID EVANS

Sable Island horses, named for the island they inhabit, closely resemble the Spanish barb and the Acadian horse, a common working horse in the early Atlantic provinces (*photo by John deVisser*).

Saanich Peninsula, BC, forms part of the Nanaimo Lowlands, along VANCOUVER I's E coast. It extends from SIDNEY in the N to VICTORIA in the S, is 20 km long and averages 4 km in width; 90% of its perimeter is fronted by sea. The dominant geographical features are Mt Newton and Saanich Inlet. Elevations in the area range from sea level to just over 305 m (Mt Newton), but generally the peninsula is of relatively low relief, rare for the rugged BC coastline. Land on the peninsula is arable and the climate is the mildest in Canada. These qualities, necessary for agriculture, also encourage residential development, and Saanich residents face an almost inevitable urban and suburban encroachment as Metropolitan Victoria grows. Agricultural activity is declining, and land that was formerly forest, pasture or cultivated field is being given over to residential and commercial uses. Besides Sidney and Victoria, the peninsula is organized into 3 other municipalities — Saanich, Central Saanich and North Saanich.

The first inhabitants of Saanich were Indians of the Coast Salish tribe. It is estimated there were about 2000 natives in the area in 1850, most of whom lived at "Sanitch" at Cordova Bay. The name Saanich comes from an Indian word meaning "good" or "fertile" soil. In 1852 Sir James DOUGLAS bought a large section of Saanich from the Indians. In 1858 the land was surveyed and marked into 40 ha allotments; in 1859 the electoral district of Saanich was created. The arrival of the railway gave Saanich a great boost.

During the past several decades agricultural activity on the peninsula has been declining, owing to rising land values and taxes, quarantine restrictions and competition from mainland and California producers. Nevertheless, many full-time and part-time farms show sufficient annual profit to justify their operation. Industrial activity is limited and localized, the most important industries being transportation and tourism. Three ferry terminals on the peninsula provide transportation links to mainland BC and Washington state.   ALAN F.J. ARTIBISE

Sabine, Sir Edward, soldier, scientist (b at Dublin, Ire 14 Oct 1788; d at Richmond, Eng 26 June 1883). He fought along the St Lawrence R in Upper and Lower Canada in 1813-14, and then, within the army, went on to a distinguished career in science. In 1819-20 he made geophysical contributions to PARRY's arctic expedition on the *Hecla*. In 1828 he became one of 3 scientific advisers to the Admiralty and, working through that body as well as through the Royal Soc and the Royal Artillery, promoted international geomagnetic studies, particularly magnetic observations in Canada. The Toronto magnetic observatory owed its survival in part to his representations. He persistently sought global interrelations between different geophysical phenomena. He was president of the Royal Soc of London 1861-71 and of the British Association for the Advancement of Science in 1852.
    TREVOR H. LEVERE

Sable Island, NS, is the only emergent part of the outer continental shelf of eastern N America, situated 300 km ESE of Halifax. Shaped like an open crescent, 38 km long and 1.5 km wide at its widest point, it narrows at both ends to W and E Spits, which continue offshore as shallow submerged bars. It stands on broad Sable I Bank of the SCOTIAN SHELF and consists of 2 parallel sand-dune ridges separated by a discontinuous, linear depression. The northern dune ridge is the bulkier, rising to 26 m; the narrower southern ridge rises to 12 m. Sable I has been evolving as a barrier island during the past several thousand years of postglacial time as the sea level has slowly risen over the continental shelf. Southerly storm waves have driven sands from the seabed onto the S shore. Currents related to the Gulf Stream cause a NE drift of beach material

along this shore, slowly extending the island in that direction. Along the northern shore, the Belle Isle Current shifts sand more slowly southwestwards. The dune ridges were built by winds behind the northern and southern beaches, but are eroded by linear blowouts during intense northwesterly winter storms. A comparison of charts of the island made over the last 200 years shows that the northern and southern ridges were broken in the 1760s, and that after closure in the early 19th century, the central depression was occupied by a lake that has progressively shrunk in size due to drifting sand and plant colonization. Lk Wallace, 5.5 km long, is the present shallow remnant of this lake in the western part of the island. The dunes are stabilized by marram grass or low shrub cover, except for extensive blowout areas in the E and W.

Never permanently settled, Sable I has, however, seen temporary occupation by shipwrecked sailors, transported convicts, pirates and wreckers. The first recorded shipwreck was of one of Sir Humphrey GILBERT's ships in 1583. In 1598 the marquis de La Roche landed 40 convict settlers on the island. Only 12 survived to be rescued in 1603. Manned lighthouses were established in 1873, but were automated in the 1960s. Canadian government weather- and navigation-station personnel comprise the only inhabitants, but visits are made by maintenance personnel, ecologists and geologists. Exploratory drilling for oil and gas was undertaken here in the mid-1970s, but has since been concentrated offshore.

Natural fauna include terrestrial insects, freshwater aquatic life in Lk Wallace, birds and seals. Birds are mainly common sea and beach birds such as gulls and sandpipers, but the Ipswich sparrow is unique to the island, nesting nowhere else. Gray and harbour seals are present in the thousands, the gray being a permanent resident, the harbour seal a summer visitor. Over 200 horses roam Sable I, the descendants of groups introduced at various times, and have genetically reverted to an ancestral type of domestic horse. The island's name derives from its sandy composition, being named *Isola della rena* on the first map of New France (about 1550) by Jacopo Gastaldi.   I.A. BROOKES

Reading: H.L. Cameron "The Shifting Sands of Sable Island," *The Geographical Review* 60 (1965).

Sable Island Horses, often referred to as ponies, are not really small; stallions weigh 270-360 kg and stand about 14 hands (140 cm) at the withers (shoulders). Mares are a little smaller, averaging about 40 kg less. The HORSES, named for the island they inhabit, exhibit great variability in form and colour but their most obvious, common characteristics are the stallions' long, flowing manes and tails. They most closely resemble the Spanish barb, a small, tough horse that originated in N Africa, and the Acadian horse, the common working horse of the Atlantic provinces from 17th to 19th centuries. The population organizes itself into family herds of 5-6 horses (stallion, one or more mares and their young). Most foals are born May-June and remain in the family herd for about 2 years. When young males leave, they run with other males in loose bachelor herds until they can attract mares and establish their own family herd. The horse population on the island varies between 150 and 400, averaging around 250. Even without human interference, population fluctuates radically, with periods of growth followed by dieoffs of up to 200 horses in one winter. The animals that die are usually older horses with worn teeth that, in seasons of short food, are unable to gather sufficient nourishment to resist severe, late-winter weather. Attempts to feed starving horses have failed but, even if they had succeeded, would only have postponed the deaths until the following winter.

It is often stated that the ancestors of Sable Island horses were survivors of some of the hundreds of ships that have been wrecked there. However, most evidence indicates that they were introduced purposely by Andrew Le Mercier of Boston, in the middle of the 18th century, along with cattle, hogs and sheep in the course of an unsuccessful attempt to start a farming settlement. At the beginning of the 19th century, a series of lifesaving stations were established on SABLE ISLAND to aid crews of ships wrecked there and the horses were used for riding and as draught animals. The lifesaving establishment continued until the middle of this century and several attempts were made in this period to improve the quality of the wild horses by introductions of new breeding stock. Surplus horses were rounded up periodically and sent to the mainland for sale. Since 1947, no horses have been exported from the island and they are now protected by the Department of Transport, which administers the island. The Sable Island herd is by no means unique in eastern N America: similar feral horse populations occupy the French island of Miquelon, south of Newfoundland; Bird Shoal and Shackleford Bank, off North Carolina; and Chincoteague I, Virginia.   A.R. LOCK

Reading: Barbara Christie, *The Horses of Sable Island* (1980).

Sackville, NB, Town, pop 5654 (1981c), inc 1903, situated 50 km SE of Moncton on the shore of the Bay of FUNDY, near the NS border. Best known as the home of MOUNT ALLISON U (fd 1839), Sackville overlooks the wide expanse of the Tantramar Marshes, which inspired the poetry of its most famous son, Sir Charles G.D. ROBERTS. The area was first settled in the 1670s by the ACADIANS, who built dikes to reclaim its rich farmland from the sea. After the Expulsion of 1755, these lands were taken up by immigrants from New England and Yorkshire, Eng. By the mid-19th century, Sackville was a thriving port, with local shipbuilders supplying the sailing

vessels needed to send farm produce and lumber to markets in Britain and the W Indies. Construction of the INTERCOLONIAL RY through the town (1870) bolstered its position as a commercial centre. With the end of the age of sail in the Maritimes after 1900, the port closed and commerce declined. Two large stove foundries, established in the mid-1800s, are still in operation, and together with the university employ most of the local work force. Sackville is a town of fine old homes and tree-shaded streets, dominated by the red sandstone buildings of the university. DEAN JOBB

Sadlermiut Inuit (or Sallirmiut) were the inhabitants of 3 islands in Hudson Bay: SOUTHAMPTON (Salliq), Coats and Walrus. The original Sadlermiut were annihilated by disease in 1902-03. Their origins, population, development of culture and cause of their decline (from some 200 to 58), prior to their demise, are unknown. The present-day Sadlermiut came mostly from Aivilik (Repulse Bay) and Baffin I and are not directly related to their predecessors. Fragmentary excavations and the notes found in journals of explorers and whalers have excited considerable curiosity, as Sadlermiut, in appearance, behaviour, language and material culture, seem to have been significantly different from the relatively homogeneous peoples of the W coast of Hudson Bay. Three hypotheses have been suggested to account for this: that Sadlermiut were direct descendants of DORSET Eskimos, who preceded the bearers of THULE culture in the area; that they were Thule Inuit whose culture developed idiosyncratically because it was isolated from the mainland Thule culture; and that they were carriers of Thule culture who were both isolated from the mainland and in contact with Dorset people, so that they and their culture derive from both roots, through intermarriage and cultural borrowing. This last hypothesis would account for the mixture of Dorset and Thule traits that characterize the archaeological remains of the Sadlermiut.

The Sadlermiut were isolated from the mainland Inuit; they lived for most of the year in stone and sod houses, and hunted seal, walrus, whales, polar bear and caribou, supplemented with fish and birds. Though they were in contact with whalers between 1860 and 1903, they were not as involved in whaling and trapping as were the mainland Inuit. *See also* NATIVE PEOPLE: ARCTIC. JEAN L. BRIGGS

Safdie, Moshe, architect (b at Haifa, Israel 14 July 1938). Educated at McGill, Safdie had the unique opportunity of building his student thesis as Habitat for EXPO 67 in Montréal. This work was carried on from his Montréal practice, begun in 1964. Other designs have been for Jerusalem, Tehran, Puerto Rico and US sites. In 1984 his most important Canadian project was the new National Gallery, Ottawa. Safdie has written extensively on his work, has taught at McGill and in Israel, and in 1978 became director of the urban design program at Harvard. Prefabricated cellular multi-unit housing is a concern of Safdie's, from Habitat to lighter and more economical later versions. All create diverse, irregular, informal groupings by the sensitive arrangement of repeated units. The images created recall medieval hill towns of Europe and the densely packed traditional cities of N Africa and the Middle East. MICHAEL McMORDIE

Safety Standards, documents or codes which describe characteristics or usage for products, materials and services, are intended to protect citizens from the hazards of technology. A safety standard may specify how to test a hockey helmet for resistance to blows to ensure that it protects the wearer, or how to design an electric coffee pot that does not present the danger of electrocution. Several thousand standards

are currently in use in Canada. Standards are published by sector and government organizations specializing in this field and grouped in the National Standards System, co-ordinated by the Standards Council of Canada. The work of standardization begins when public hazards are recognized and involves field and laboratory studies. Standards are written up by experts who volunteer their time to standards-writing organizations. Current standards are reviewed and revised periodically to keep pace with advancing technology. Standards prepared, published and revised in this fashion are known as consensus standards; their final acceptance depends on substantial agreement among the experts.

Unless made obligatory by law, standards are applied voluntarily by those concerned. Laws making standards mandatory often refer to specific consensus safety standards, rather than specifying detailed technical requirements. Safety standards relating to a specific subject may be collected into volumes, called codes, which are usually drawn up in a way that would allow governments to adopt them for legal use. Several codes have gained wide recognition in Canada, notably the National Fire Code, the National Building Code, the Canadian Electrical Code, the Boiler Code, the Canadian Welding Code and the Code for Hospital Operating Room Safety. The National Labour Code also includes safety legislation.

The National Fire Code sets out the requirements for safe maintenance of buildings after their occupation. Drawing heavily on American and, to a lesser extent, on Canadian standards, this code establishes standards for fire prevention, fire fighting and life safety in buildings in use; for prevention, containment and fighting of fires that start outside buildings and may present a hazard to a community; and for vehicles used to transport flammable and combustible liquids. The National Building Code is essentially a set of minimum regulations for the safety of buildings with reference to public health, fire protection and structural sufficiency (*see* BUILDING CODES AND REGULATIONS). Complementing the National Fire Code, it establishes standards for fire safety during construction of new buildings or reconstruction of old ones. The code also sets out specifications for use, occupancy and design of buildings; requirements for the prevention of damage caused by wind, water and vapour; and regulations for heating, ventilation, air conditioning and plumbing. Finally, it sets out requirements for precautions that must be taken for the safety of the public in the vicinity of construction sites. Provincial and territorial governments exercise jurisdiction over fire and construction safety in Canada and each has adopted, wholly or in part, the 2 national codes.

Electricity posed great danger of electrocution when it first came into public use. Over the years a collection of Canadian electrical safety standards has been assembled into what is now known as the Canadian Electrical Code, a completely Canadian product acclaimed in many parts of the world. Published by the Canadian Standards Association (CSA), the code is consulted by engineers and inspectors responsible for electrical installation in all buildings and engineering structures. Each province requires that all electrical appliances sold within it comply with the code's specifications and bear a mark certifying this compliance.

One of the earliest matters to receive attention in the field of safety standards was the control of boilers and other pressure vessels. When they were first used in steam engines for the propulsion of boats early in the 19th century, pressure vessels often exploded. Today the Boiler Code, published by the Canadian Standards Association, promotes the safe use of such vessels. Relying heavily on the American Boiler Code

(first issued in 1914), it presents information for the design of pressure vessels and requirements for their construction, testing and regular inspection. Provincial and territorial governments rely on the Boiler Code for development of laws affecting the safety of pressure vessels.

Establishment of standards in the medical field is fairly recent. With new developments in MEDICINE the medical and engineering professions began to work closely together to develop standards, eg, for metallic surgical implants. In co-operation with representatives of industry and medicine, CSA published a Code for Prevention of Explosions or Electric Shock in Hospital Operating Rooms. This code, which specifies safety features in operating theatres (especially safety from danger of explosions caused by anaesthetics), is widely used across Canada. Certain requirements in the medical field are of international interest. For example, steel bottles containing compressed gases needed by hospitals must be safe and readily connectable to other hospital equipment; the screw couplings on these containers are a matter of lively international study. The federal government, through the Health Protection Branch of Health and Welfare Canada, plays an active role legislating standards in the medical field. In close co-operation with those concerned, it regulates medical devices (eg, cardiac pacemakers, contraceptive devices, disposable insulin syringes). Close liaison is always maintained with industry since a product cannot be sold until it is approved by the federal department.

Safety standards often bear an international flavour, as in the TRANSPORTATION field. Many standards used in Canada originated in other countries or with international organizations, eg, the International Organization for Standardization and the International Electrotechnical Commission, in both of which the Standards Council of Canada is actively involved. Most international marine safety standards are developed by the Inter-Governmental Maritime Consultative Organization of the United Nations. Canada is represented on this organization by marine and fire research experts. Documents resulting from this work are used as guidelines by the federal government, which legislates all aspects of international transportation. The International Civil Aviation Organization, with headquarters in Montréal, performs similar functions in the field of aviation. Nationally, transportation is administered by the federal government, with some areas delegated to provinces and territories. The Motor Vehicle Safety Act, Motor Vehicle Tire Safety Act, National Transportation Act, Railway Act, Canada Shipping Act and Aeronautics Act govern most federal transportation issues. The Acts are exhaustive and specify everything from requirements for automobile windshields and mirrors to aircraft speed limits. R.L. HENNESSY

Sagebrush (genus *Artemisia*), bitter, aromatic PLANT or shrub of the family Compositae or Asteraceae. They include annual, biennial and perennial plants. More than 100 species are known, chiefly from arid regions of the Northern Hemisphere. Fifteen species are native to Canada; 7 others are introduced (2 European, 4 Eurasian and one from Aleutian Is). The greatest variety of native sagebrushes occurs in the western mountains, where species that range from Alaska to California and Colorado are found. Several species range across the prairies and 2 species are transcontinental in Canada. Sagebrushes grow on dry plains, hills and rocky slopes. Flower clusters, aggregations of heads that are usually loose and nodding and sometimes spikelike, appear in summer and autumn. Each head is a disc of few or many tubular florets. Fruit is small, hard and dry. Many sagebrushes are highly variable, and hybridization occurs freely. The genus includes wormwoods and tarragon. The common name derives from the characteristic, sagelike odour, and the genus is named for the Persian Queen of Caria, Artemisia. *See* PLANTS, NATIVE USES.

Saguenay Provincial Park (under development), now includes strips of land (288 km²) on either side of the SAGUENAY R, from Baie des Ha! Ha!, near Chicoutimi, to the confluence with the St Lawrence at TADOUSSAC. The Laurentide plateau lies southward; the Valin massif, dissected by the Ste Marguerite R valley, northward. Impressive sand dunes and beaches are found at Tadoussac. Climate and vegetation vary with altitude, the lower areas being dominated by maple and yellow birch; the plateau, by white birch and fir. The marine fauna is especially noteworthy, including 238 INVERTEBRATE species and 54 fish species (notably salmon). In the 19th century, the pine forests were exploited, some settlement and farming occurred and tourism developed. Today the park is divided into preservation, ambience and service zones. The park and adjacent villages provide camping and hotel accommodation and opportunities for hiking, picnicking, boating, whale watching and, in winter, skiing.   JOHN S. MARSH

Saguenay River, 698 km long to the head of the Péribonca R, issues from Lac SAINT-JEAN in the LAURENTIAN HIGHLANDS of Québec. It has a DRAINAGE BASIN of 88 100 km² and a mean discharge of 1760 m³/s. It discharges from the lake through 2 channels, which join some 10 km from the lake near ALMA. The majesty, power and stark beauty of the river are legendary. From CHICOUTIMI to the ST LAWRENCE R the river flows through a deep gash in the Precambrian rock, 1500 m wide and 240 m deep, lined with precipitous cliffs rising 460 m above the river. The lower Saguenay is a FJORD gouged by the glaciers of the last ice age, 10 000 years ago. As the ice receded, the sea invaded; tidewaters still surge as far as Chicoutimi, rising and falling as much as 6 m at the equinox. Near Chicoutimi the fresh, warm waters of the tributaries float in layers over the cold, salty brine beneath. The deep Saguenay waters are the breeding grounds of the BELUGA WHALE and the shallower waters near the confluence with the St Lawrence are rich in capelin and shrimp, attracting porpoise, finback, humpback, pilot and even blue whales. The dramatic scenery of the river, particularly the formidable Cap Trinité (518 m) — on which was built a huge statue of the Virgin Mary in 1881 — and Cap Éternité (549 m) at the mouth of Rivière Éternité, has drawn tourists since the 1850s.

The Saguenay was once the corridor of a trading network extending beyond the height of land to Lac MISTASSINI and beyond to JAMES BAY. TADOUSSAC, at the confluence with the St Lawrence, was a meeting point of the Algonquian

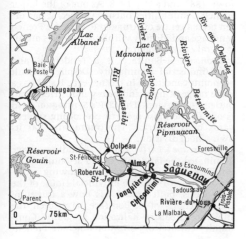

Cargo on the Saguenay. Flowing through a deep gash in the Shield, the river is tidal as far as Chicoutimi (*photo by Anne Gordon/Reflexion*).

peoples of the SHIELD and the Iroquoians of the St Lawrence Valley. Jacques CARTIER visited the river mouth in 1534 and eagerly gathered tales of a rich "Kingdom of Saguenay" in the river's watershed. The "kingdom" was fantasy, and the journey upriver was not made until Jesuit missionary Jacques Dequen went as far as present-day Chicoutimi in 1647; Father Albanel reached Lac Saint-Jean in 1671-72. Pierre Chauvin established the first trading post in Canada at Tadoussac in 1600, and the river remained an avenue for the FUR TRADE and later the TIMBER TRADE into the 19th century. Agricultural settlement began in 1838 with the founding of La Baie. Industrialization began with the building of a sawmill at Chicoutimi in 1842; the Chicoutimi pulp mills were opened in 1898.

The great power of the river and its tributaries has made the Saguenay Valley one of the industrial centres of Québec. The first power station was opened in 1925 at Isle Maligne (336 000 kW). The huge dam at Shipshaw (717 000 kW) was built during WWII to feed the gigantic ALUMINUM smelter at Arvida (now JONQUIÈRE). Generating stations at Chute-à-Caron (180 000 MW) on the Saguenay and at Chute à La Savanne (187 000 MW), Chute des Passes (742 000 MW) and Chute du Diable (187 000 MW) on the Péribonca R also supply pulp and paper mills at Chicoutimi, Jonquière and LA BAIE.   JAMES MARSH

Sailing Ships Canada's early history occurred during the great age of sail, when sailors "under canvas" crossed the Atlantic in expeditions of trade, colonization and exploration. By the mid-19th century Canada had become a major seafaring nation. Canada's ports were crowded with sailing vessels, shipbuilding yards flourished, and Canadian ships sailed every major ocean and visited every major port doing the world's business. In Canada's age of sail (1800-75) over 4000 ships, each exceeding 500 tons burthen, were built in Canada. In 1878 Canadian-registered ships numbered 7196 and totalled 1 333 015 tons. Among the nations, Canada stood fourth in seagoing tonnage.

What accounts for this phenomenal Canadian contribution of "tall ships?" Canada had an abundance of good timber — tamarack, spruce and especially pine — near to shipyards, which were established in secure harbours and river mouths. Canada also possessed good ship designers and shipwrights, and Canadian builders were able to sell their vessels to US, British, Norwegian and other seaborne traders. Canadian vessels were given the highest quality rating — 14 years A 1 — by the marine insurer Lloyd's of London.

Canadian ships were built at numerous locations. The first lumber carrier, the *Columbus*, 3690 tons, was built at Ile d'Orléans in 1824. The 2459-ton W.D. LAWRENCE, launched at Maitland, NS, in 1874, was the largest wooden full-rigger built in Canada. Other famous ships of this period include the MARCO POLO, launched at Saint John in 1851, which made her name trading to

Australia during the gold rush; the square-rigger *Canada*, 2137 tons, launched at Kingsport, NS, in 1891, which ended her worldwide trading career in 1926; and the square-rigger *City of Toronto*, built on the Great Lakes. Canadian ports constructed a variety of smaller commercial craft. Victoria, eg, built sealing vessels; ports on the St Lawrence built one- or 2-masted traders; Atlantic yards built whalers, sealers, and fishing and trading schooners such as the BLUENOSE; York and Mackinaw built boats for specific needs determined by geography (*see* YORK BOAT).

Canada also built naval ships. The 3-decker HMS *St Lawrence*, launched at Kingston in 1814, displaced 2304 tons and carried 112 guns and 1000 men. HMCS *Venture*, built in NS in 1937, was a 3-masted schooner for officer training. At important centres from Halifax to the lower Great Lakes, smaller naval vessels were built, maintaining shipbuilding traditions dating from La Salle's GRIFFON, launched on the Great Lakes in 1679, and the British brig *Ontario*, launched at Oswego in 1755.

Canada's age of sail came to an end gradually with the introduction of steam propulsion and iron hulls, masts and yards. Paddle steamers came first to the St Lawrence in 1809, to the Great Lakes in 1817, and to the Pacific coast in 1835 (*see* STEAMBOATS AND PADDLE WHEELERS). In 1831 the Québec-built ROYAL WILLIAM became the first merchant ship to cross the Atlantic primarily under steam. Canada's shipbuilding industry made the transition to steam and iron, but the 200-year age of Canadian ships under canvas was rapidly coming to an end, and with it came the nostalgia of an age when Canada was known for its great sailing ships. *See also* MARITIME SHIPPING HISTORY TO 1900; SHIPBUILDING AND SHIP REPAIR; SHIPPING.   BARRY GOUGH

Reading: T.E. Appleton, *Usque Ad Mare: A History of the Canadian Coast Guard and Marine Services* (1968); C.A. Armour and T. Lackey, *Sailing Ships of the Maritimes* (1975); L.R. Fischer and E.W. Sager, *Merchant Shipping and Economic Development in Atlantic Canada* (1982).

Ste-Agathe-des-Monts, Qué, Town, pop 5641 (1981c), inc 1915, is located in the Rivière Nord Valley on the shore of magnificent Lac des Sables. Called the "Metropolis of the Laurentides," it is the region's oldest tourist centre. The peak of Mont Sainte-Agathe, accessible by chair lift, offers a panoramic view of the lake and surrounding mountains. From 1849 to 1861, 27 families colonized the area, followed by 35 others from 1861 to 1865. In the 19th century, Sainte-Agathe had only a few sawmills, but the construction of the Montreal and Occidental Ry in 1892 (replaced by the CPR in 1900) encouraged tourism and the development of the hotels that have become the region's economic mainstay. Today, most employment is in commerce, the service sector and hotels. Resortgoers triple the local population.   CLAUDINE PIERRE-DESCHÊNES

St Albans Raid, one of several incidents heightening tensions between Great Britain and the US during the AMERICAN CIVIL WAR. On 19 Oct 1865 a party of Confederate agents based in Canada raided the town of St Albans, Vt. After looting the banks they fled back to Canada, where 13 were arrested and held for extradition. Their release on a technicality by a Montréal police magistrate aroused consternation on both sides of the border. Incidents such as this helped to create tension along the border which led in the British colonies to a climate of fear conducive to CONFEDERATION.   ERNEST R. FORBES

St Albert, Alta, City, pop 31 996 (1981c), inc 1977, is located along the NW city boundary of EDMONTON. Founded 1861 by Father Albert LACOMBE as an Oblate mission, it was named by Bishop A. Taché after Lacombe's patron saint. The log chapel built on the high ground N of the Sturgeon R was enlarged and became the first cathedral in what is now Alberta. The mission was a refuge for some 700 MÉTIS and Indians during a devastating smallpox epidemic in 1870. The mission later became Oblate headquarters and the bishop's residence. St Albert grew into a city providing services for the extensive farming area N of Edmonton, and recently population has increased greatly as the city has become a dormitory for the adjacent capital. St Albert has preserved much of its missionary past. The mission buildings still stand, and the original log church, encased in a brick shell, is now Father Lacombe Museum. The bishop's residence has also been restored, and the tombs of Father Lacombe and Bishop Vital GRANDIN lie in the crypt of the modern church. The city has resisted the political encroachment of its growing neighbour.   ERIC J. HOLMGREN

St-André-Est, Qué, Village, pop 1293 (1981c), inc 1958. Lying mostly on the E bank of the Rivière du Nord several km from its junction with the OTTAWA R, this small town (formerly St-André d'Argenteuil) received Scottish settlers around 1800. A plaque marks the site of the first paper mill in Canada (built by New England immigrants in 1903). One of Québec's most powerful hydroelectric stations was built c1960 on the Long Sault rapids at nearby Carillon. Sir John ABBOTT, Canada's first native-born prime minister, was born here in 1821.   GILLES BOILEAU

St Andrews, Man, Rural Municipality, pop 7990 (1981c), inc 1880, area 70 523 ha, stretches from a boundary 8 km N of Winnipeg to Winnipeg Beach and Netley Marsh at the southern tip of Lk Winnipeg, and includes Lockport, Petersfield, Clandeboye and several resort communities on the W shore of Lk Winnipeg. Selkirk, Winnipeg Beach and Dunnottar are separate corporate entities. The Saulteaux settled in the Netley Cr area 1795. Red R colonists and HBC employees followed in the early 1800s, as did Anglican and Presbyterian ministers who founded some of western Canada's earliest churches and schools. LOWER FORT GARRY (1830) was a HBC provision and retail centre, a military garrison and industrial complex. By the early 1900s, German, Ukrainian and Polish homesteaders moved into the RM, Winnipeg Beach became a resort community (1903) and the St Andrews Locks opened to facilitate navigation over rapids on the Red R (1910). The RM is one focus of preservation/conservation activities by the federal and provincial governments. St Andrews Airport N of Winnipeg, a satellite of Winnipeg International, is one of the busiest facilities of its kind in Canada.   D.M. LYON

St Andrews, NB, Town, pop 1760 (1981c), inc 1903, is located at the mouth of the ST CROIX R in the SW corner of NB. Its earliest occupation was likely by the Passamaquoddy who had seasonal hunting camps here. By the 1760s a few New England settlers had established themselves here. However, it was not until the closing months of the AMERICAN REVOLUTION that a major influx of LOYALIST civilian refugees gave the site a new status. With the arrival of the Penobscot Assn, as they were called, in Oct 1783, the town of St Andrews was formally laid out. For nearly 50 years it remained a principal shipping port for the lucrative trade with the West Indies, but by 1850 economic stagnation hit the area. In the late 1800s, St Andrews was rediscovered by the developing tourist traffic from New England and central Canada. Commonly referred to as St Andrews-By-The-Sea, it remains today a popular N American tourist attraction for its historic architecture, scenic harbour and outstanding Algonquin Hotel.   ROGER P. NASON

Ste-Anne-de-Beaupré, Qué, Town, pop 3292 (1981c), inc 1855, located on the N shore of the St Lawrence R 35 km E of QUÉBEC CITY, is known worldwide for its shrine, a pilgrimage site attracting over one million visitors yearly. In 1658

Basilica of Ste-Anne-de-Beaupré, which dates from 1926 (*photo © Hartill Art Associates*).

Étienne Lessard, one of the first settlers, ceded some land for the construction of the first wooden chapel dedicated to Ste Anne, who was especially venerated in NEW FRANCE. Built too close to the river, it was damaged by the tides and rebuilt in 1661 at the foot of the slope. It was replaced by a stone church in 1676. Enlarged several times, the church welcomed thousands of pilgrims during almost 2 centuries. It was demolished in 1872 and replaced by the first basilica, which was destroyed by fire in 1922. The present Roman-style basilica dates from 1926. Its treasures include sacred 18th-century vases engraved by goldsmiths (among them François Ranvoyzé and Laurent Amyot) and a large collection of ex-votos (*see* VOTIVE PAINTING). The north chapel, built in 1878, holds several works saved from the demolition of the old church, including the 1696 steeple. The altars were designed by Charles Vézina 1702-28; the crucifix and wooden chandeliers were sculpted by François-Noël Levasseur in 1779; the pulpit, put into place in 1807, shows the talents of François BAILLARGÉ. L'Historial, the sanctuary museum, has 17th- and 18th-century religious paintings, including 2 attributed to Frère LUC.
       CLAUDINE PIERRE-DESCHÊNES

St Anns, NS, UP, pop 22 (1981c), is located in the Cape Breton Highlands on St Anns harbour, 34 km W of SYDNEY. The French established a fort and fishing base here in 1609. When they left Cape Breton after the fall of LOUISBOURG in 1758, industrious Scots, under the leadership of Rev Norman MCLEOD, settled here. A large shipbuilding industry was established, but sharply declined when McLeod and his followers emigrated to New Zealand in the mid-1800s. Fishing, farming and, later, a plaster quarry supported the remaining residents. The only Gaelic college outside of Britain was founded at St Anns in 1938. Students may learn Gaelic language, music, dance and customs. Traditional Scottish crafts and handwoven tartans are made here. The college is home to the annual Gaelic Mod and to the Giant Angus McAskill Highland Pioneers Museum. Visitors may find personal effects of the famous giant Angus MCASKILL and other pioneers.   HEATHER MacDONALD

St Anthony, Nfld, Town, pop 3107 (1981c), inc 1945, is located near the top of the Great Northern Pen. Originally called St-Antoine, it was a French fishing station settled by Newfoundlanders in the mid-1800s. With a superb natural harbour, St Anthony is at the crossroads of shipping and fishing routes serving the Str of Belle Isle and the Labrador coast. Dr Wilfred GRENFELL, on behalf of the Royal National Mission to Deep Sea Fishermen, in 1900 chose St Anthony as the site for a small hospital that would later become the headquarters of the International Grenfell Assn, founded by Grenfell in 1914. St Anthony's history since 1900 has been dominated by the work of the mission, the centre of a far-reaching medical and social-services network serving a large area of northern Newfoundland,

Québec and Labrador. Other sources of employment have included a radar base (built 1951), a series of fish plants (beginning in 1944) and an airport built in 1957 and replaced with a multimillion-dollar facility in 1983.
       JANET E.M. PITT AND ROBERT D. PITT
Reading: Sir Wilfred T. Grenfell, *A Labrador Doctor* (1948).

St-Benoît-du-Lac, Qué, a Benedictine abbey of the Congregation of St-Pierre de Solesme (France), est 1914, is located on the shores of Lac Memphrémagog, 40 km SW of SHERBROOKE. The monks are the sole inhabitants (65, 1981c) of this place, which has an area of 2.27 km² and no municipal structure. The present abbey, a lovely piece of architecture in pink granite, was designed by Dom Paul Bellot, a Benedictine monk who arrived in Canada in 1937. This famous architect of religious buildings also created the dome of St Joseph's Oratory in Montréal. His remains lie in the abbey cemetery. The monks spend their time in prayer, meditation, study, Gregorian chant, manual labour and agriculture. They make and sell cheeses under the names Ermite and St-Benoît. A hostelry welcomes people who wish to make a religious retreat.   CLAUDINE PIERRE-DESCHÊNES

St-Boniface, Man, pop 43 465 (1981c), former city and historic French community, now within the jurisdiction of the metropolitan government of the city of WINNIPEG (est 1972), is located on the banks of the Red and Seine rivers in eastern Winnipeg. With St Vital, it forms one of 6 community areas in the Unicity government. Four councillors represent St-Boniface-St Vital on Winnipeg City Council.

History Fur traders and European mercenaries hired by Lord Selkirk to protect his fledgling RED RIVER COLONY were among the area's first settlers. With the founding of a Roman Catholic mission (1818), St-Boniface began its role in Canadian religious, political and cultural history — as mother parish for many French settlements in western Canada; as the birthplace of Louis RIEL and fellow Métis who struggled to obtain favourable terms for Manitoba's entry into Confederation; and as a focus of resistance to controversial 1890 legislation to alter Manitoba's school system and abolish French as an official language in the province. Early educational, cultural and social-service institutions were started by religious orders, including the Sisters of Charity of Montréal (Grey Nuns) who arrived in 1844. The Collège Universitaire de St-Boniface, a founding college of University of Manitoba, and St Boniface General Hospital grew from these institutions. The early economy was oriented to agriculture. Union Stockyards, developed 1912-13, became the largest livestock exchange in Canada and focal point for a meatpacking and -processing industry. By the early 1900s, numerous light and heavy industries were established. St-Boniface incorporated as a town 1883 and a city 1908. As one of the larger French Communities outside Québec, it has often been a centre of struggles to preserve French language and identity within Manitoba's multicultural environment.

Economy St-Boniface is a residential and retail/industrial community. Despite difficult economic conditions in recent years, it still has a wide range of light and heavy industries, retail outlets and services. The CNR's Symington Yard is one of the most modern car-sorting switchyards in N America. The community has its own school division.

Townscape Early church buildings have dominated the landscape of old St-Boniface. St-Boniface Basilica was rebuilt following a disastrous fire in 1968. The Provincial House of the Grey Nuns, built 1846-47, is now a museum. Older sections of St-Boniface have been the subject of urban revitalization programs. Community cultural organizations include French-language radio and TV stations; *La Liberté*, a weekly newspaper; the Centre Culturel Franco-Manitobain, an arts centre; and performing arts groups such as Le Cercle Molière and Les Danseurs de la Rivière Rouge.   D.M. LYON

Reading: R.C. Wilson, ed, *Saint-Boniface, Manitoba, Canada 1818-1968* (1967).

St Catharines, Ont, City, pop 124 018 (1981c), inc 1876, former seat of Lincoln County, centre for the Regional Municipality of Niagara 1970-83, lies S of Toronto across Lk Ontario (111 km by road), 19 km from the international boundary. Its hinterland is the eastern section of the Niagara Peninsula, and the city contains 40.8% of the population in the St Catharines-Niagara Census Metropolitan Area (124 018 out of 304 353; 1981c). Located near the NIAGARA ES-CARPMENT and in the Niagara fruit belt, its urban character has been influenced strongly by the backcloth of the WELLAND CANAL.

Settlement When the area was settled by LOY-ALISTS in the early 1780s, an agricultural centre emerged, known variously as Shipman's Corners or The Twelve. It was named St Catharines after the wife of Robert Hamilton (whose son George founded nearby Hamilton), a merchant at QUEENSTON on the Niagara portage, who constructed a storehouse on Twelve Mile Cr and deeded land for the first (Anglican) church, now St Georges.

Development The Welland Canal (1829) and an associated raceway (1830) introduced mills, shipyards and metal and machinery manufacture. Mineral springs with medicinal properties made St Catharines famous as a spa. The town was served by the Great Western and Welland railways and, with power from the locks, the NIAGARA R and De Cew Falls, manufacturing evolved from domestic goods and the carriage trade to automobile production and accessories,

Population: 124 018 (1981c); 304 353 (CMA*)
Rate of Increase (1971-81): (City) 13%; (CMA) 0.3%
Rank in Canada: Tenth (by CMA)
Date of Incorporation: City 1876
Land Area: 94.4 km²
Elevation: 180.4 m
Climate: Average daily temp, July 21.7°C, Jan -4.3°C; Yearly precip rain 672.1 mm, snow 1227 mm; hours of sunshine 2404 per year

* Includes Niagara Regional Municipality

wineries, canning factories and paper companies. Leading entrepreneurs have included William Hamilton MERRITT, MP, merchant and founder of the Welland Canal; Dr William Chase, the mineral springs; Hiram S. Leavenworth, publisher; W.B. Burgoyne, founder of the St Catharines *Standard;* Louis SHICKLUNA, ship manufacturer; and Dr Theophilus Mack, founder of the General and Marine Hospital and Canada's first school of nursing.

Cityscape Three nodes exist: downtown, where a major E-W road crossed Twelve Mile Cr (the Welland Canal); Port Dalhousie, the northern entrance to the canal; and Merritton where the canal was crossed by the Great Western Ry. The downtown, ennobled by a curving main street with a near-continuous facade of 19th-century buildings, contains numerous "T" junctions and a radial system of former Indian roads. Because of the canal valley, growth moved N from this area, and later suburban expansion has extended the city from the escarpment to Lk Ontario and into the Niagara fruit belt. Manufacturing is dispersed along present and former canals, railway and highway locations. Though the downtown has attracted new office complexes, its retail capability is now secondary to the PEN Regional Centre; numerous

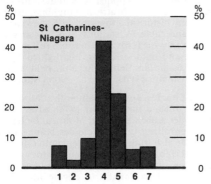

Distribution of Industrial Activity* by Industry Grouping within Census Metropolitan Areas, 1980

Industry groupings
1. Food and beverage and tobacco products industries
2. Leather, textile, knitting mills and clothing industries
3. Wood, furniture and fixtures, paper and allied and printing, publishing and allied industries
4. Machinery, transportation equipment and electrical products industries
5. Primary metal and metal fabricating industries
6. Rubber and plastic products, petroleum and coal products and chemical products industries
7. Non-metallic mineral products and miscellaneous manufacturing industries.

* Industry activity based on the average of percentage shares of the value shipments of goods of own manufacture, total value added and total number of employees for each of the selected metropolitan areas.

Source: Figure II, Catalogue 31-209, Statistics Canada.

other plazas, neighbourhood centres and strip commercial development also offer substantial competition. Open space includes the escarpment, lake beaches, river-canal valleys and city parks.

Population With a 13% increase from a 1971 population of 109 722, the city shows a broad ethnic mix; primarily of British origin (55%), but with substantial Italian (10%), French (8%) and German (7%) components. Religious affiliation is 57% Protestant and 34% Roman Catholic (CMA, 53% and 39%).

Economy and Labour Force Manufacturing (1978c) included 135 establishments with 15 759 employees, $316 million in wages and salaries, and shipments valued at $1397 million with a value added of $705 million. Four establishments employ two-thirds of this labour force, with GENERAL MOTORS being the largest. In spite of new companies and the expansion of some older ones, total employment in manufacturing has declined. Expanding service industries include the commercial and government sectors.

Transportation St Catharines is a district transportation centre, on the main land routes between SW Ontario and the American border. It features the Welland Canal with wharfage; main-line passenger and freight railway services; the QUEEN ELIZABETH WAY and Hwy 406; Niagara District Airport, with a 1524 m runway (but no passenger service); interurban routes; and limousine services to Toronto and Buffalo airports.

Government and Politics One of 12 municipalities in the Regional Municipality of Niagara, St Catharines is governed by a mayor elected at large and 12 aldermen from 6 wards. Its parks and libraries, an historical museum and municipal planning are city responsibilities. A downtown association fosters business

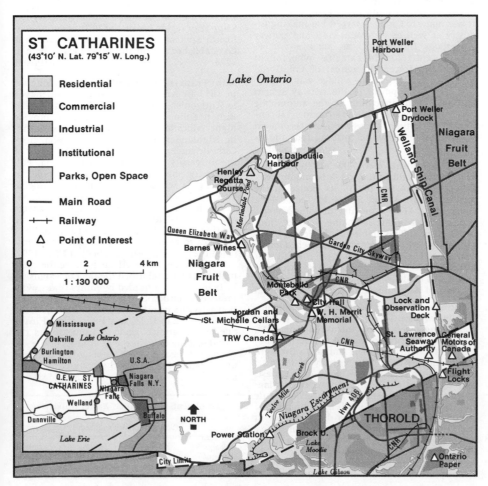

ST CATHARINES
(43°10′ N. Lat. 79°15′ W. Long.)

- Residential
- Commercial
- Industrial
- Institutional
- Parks, Open Space
— Main Road
+++ Railway
△ Point of Interest

0   2   4 km
1 : 130 000

Lake Ontario

Port Weller Harbour
Port Weller Drydock
Niagara Fruit Belt
Welland Ship Canal
CNR
Port Dalhousie Harbour
Henley Regatta Course
Martindale Pond
Queen Elizabeth Way
Barnes Wines
Niagara Fruit Belt
Garden City Skyway
Montebello Park
City Hall
Jordan and St. Michelle Cellars
W. H. Merrit Memorial
TRW Canada
Lock and Observation Deck
St. Lawrence Seaway Authority
General Motors of Canada
Flight Locks
CNR
Twelve Mile Creek
Niagara Escarpment
Hwy 406
Power Station
Brock U.
Lake Moodie
THOROLD
City Limits
Lake Gibson
Ontario Paper

Mississauga
Oakville   Lake Ontario
Burlington
Hamilton
U.S.A.
Q.E.W. ST. CATHARINES
Niagara Falls N.Y.
Niagara Falls
Welland
Buffalo
Dunnville
Lake Erie

NORTH

improvement. Public and separate school boards are elected at large.

Cultural Life Educational and cultural facilities include a Crippled Children's Centre, the Niagara College of Applied Arts and Technology and BROCK U; live theatre, a symphony, art gallery and historical museum; daily newspaper; radio and cable TV stations; and folk arts and grape and wine festivals. There is a full range of indoor and outdoor sports, highlighted by the Royal Canadian Henley Regatta, held at Port Dalhousie since 1903.   JOHN N. JACKSON

Saint-Charles, Joseph, painter (b at Montréal, 9 June 1868; d there 26 Oct 1956). After studying under Abbé Chabert in Montréal he left for Paris, enrolling in the École des beaux-arts in 1885. He also studied under Benjamin Constant, Jules Lefebvre and Jean-Paul Laurens, and spent some time at Rome's École des beaux-arts. He returned to Canada to devote himself to teaching and to art, and around 1890 he executed 3 large canvases for the Sacré Coeur chapel of Notre-Dame in Montréal. In 1906 he painted *La Présentation de la Vierge au Temple* for the chapel of the Grand Séminaire de Montréal. His career as a teacher of design began with the Conseil des Arts et Manufactures, continued at U de M and then at Montréal's École des beaux-arts. From 1942 Saint-Charles was the most famous portraitist of his day. Through his studio passed the leading politicians, ministers and senators, judges, governors, bankers, businessmen and indeed the most beautiful women of contemporary Québec society.   MICHEL CHAMPAGNE

St-Charles-sur-Richelieu, Qué, Village, pop 401 (1981c), inc 1924, is located on the Rivière RICHELIEU, NW of SAINT-HYACINTHE. It was built on land belonging to the St-Charles seigneury (granted 1698). In the early 19th century, the village flourished from trade associated with river transportation. It played an important role in the REBELLIONS OF 1837: the Confédération des Six-Comtés was formed there on October 23. The PATRIOTES fought against British troops on Nov 25 and were defeated. Like many places in the Lower Richelieu region, Saint-Charles experienced a decline in the second half of the 19th century. Towards the end of the century, one of the village's activities was the transportation of oats to New York City for use as feed for tramway horses. In the 20th century, bypassed by the major rail and road systems, it once again became a farming village dominated by the dairy industry.   SYLVIE TASCHEREAU

St Clair, Lake, 1114 km², elev 175 m, 6 m deep, the smallest of the GREAT LAKES, is bordered by the province of Ontario to the E and the state of Michigan to the W. Almost circular in shape, it has a length of 42 km and maximum width of 38 km. Sulpician missionaries Dollier de Casson and Bréhant de Galinée traversed the lake in 1670. In 1679 LA SALLE, becalmed in the lake on the feast day of Ste Claire, christened the lake (and river) in her honour.

Lk St Clair is connected to Lk HURON by the ST CLAIR R and is drained into Lk ERIE by the DETROIT R. Its most important Canadian tributary is the Thames R. The farmlands surrounding the lake are among the most productive in N America. The cities of WINDSOR, Ont, and Detroit, Mich, are located at the SW end of the lake. As part of the ST LAWRENCE SEAWAY, Lk St Clair and the river serve as a major transport route for commercial shipping vessels. Because of the many industries and large population in the area, pollutants have markedly influenced the quality of the lake's water. Its once-prosperous commercial fisheries are closed because of MERCURY poisoning. However, the lake remains an important recreational facility and has the largest concentration of boats and harbours of any of the Great Lks.   MARIE SANDERSON

St Clair River, 64 km long, flows in a southerly direction, connecting Lk HURON in the N with Lk ST CLAIR in the S, and forms the international boundary between Canada and the US. Its northern portion has an average width of 0.8 km and depth of 8-18 m. In the S a delta called the St Clair Flats has formed, creating many channels and islands. The French were the first to explore and name the St Clair R. SARNIA is the most important centre, deriving its industrial base from large petroleum refineries and petrochemical plants. The banks of the St Clair are also home to many Canadian and American cottagers.   MARIE SANDERSON

St Croix River, 121 km long, rises in the Chiputneticook Lks and flows SE to Passamaquoddy Bay, forming part of the border between NB and Maine. It was discovered (1604) by the French, and DE MONTS built the first settlement in Acadia on Isle Sainte-Croix at the river's mouth. The site was chosen for its central position, good anchorage and ease of defence. The winter was cruel; there was no fresh water or firewood on the island. Of the 80 colonists, 36 died of scurvy. The next summer the houses were dismantled and moved to PORT-ROYAL, a more salubrious spot across the Bay of FUNDY. The river was to serve as part of the boundary between British territory and the US, but its location was in dispute until an excavation found the remains of de Monts's camp and conclusively identified the river (1797).   JAMES MARSH

St-Denis, Qué, Village, pop 861 (1981c), inc 1903, is located on the Rivière RICHELIEU, 30 km N of ST-HYACINTHE. It took its name from the St-Denis seigneury, granted in 1694 to Louis de Gannes, Sieur de Falaise, and named in honour of his wife, Barbe Denis. In the early 19th century, St-Denis was a major centre for grain shipments to Québec City. It also had business dealings with Montréal and was the fastest-developing centre in the lower Richelieu region. It was home to Canada's largest hat-making industry as well as to several craft and pottery workshops. During the REBELLION OF 1837 it became a centre for the PATRIOTES who fought against and forced the retreat of Col Gore's troops. In retaliation, the village was burned. The later development of the railway system and subsequent invention of the automobile caused St-Denis to decline as a commercial centre. In this century, it has once again become an agricultural centre with a thriving dairy industry.   SYLVIE TASCHEREAU

St Elias, Mount, elev 5489 m, the second-highest mountain in Canada, a boundary peak between Alaska and the YT, is located in the St Elias Range, 43 km SW of Mt LOGAN. First sighted in 1747 by a member of Vitus BERING's Russian Expedition, its name derived from nearby Cape St Elias, named by the Bering Expedition. In 1781 Capt James COOK attached an elevation of 5517 m, astonishingly close to that officially accepted today. The first successful ascent was made by a large Italian party led by the duke of Abruzzi in July 1897.   GLEN BOLES

St Elmo's Fire, blue or reddish glow accompanying an electrical discharge from a pointed conducting object in an intense electric field. Caused by collision ionization and recombination of air molecules, it is similar to the light from a neon sign. In the vicinity of THUNDERSTORMS, it has been seen at night on the masts and rigging of ships, aircraft propellers, flagpoles and church steeples, and even on cattle horns or the hands and heads of mountaineers. While remaining attached to the conductor, it may move along it and can last for many minutes. Frequently a hissing or fizzing sound is heard. There is speculation that Moses observed it in the burning bush on Mt Sinai; Shakespeare refers to it in *The Tempest;* and it was

reported by early explorers of Canada. Sailors viewed it as a sign of the imminent end of bad weather. The name St Elmo is a corruption of St Erasmus, the patron saint of Mediterranean sailors. English sailors call it the corposant or cormazant, from Span or Ital *corpo santo,* "holy body" or "saint's body."   E.P. LOZOWSKI

St-Eustache, Qué, Town, pop 29 716 (1981c), inc 1835, is located at the junction of the Rivière du Chêne and the Rivière des Mille-Îles, 30 km W of MONTRÉAL. The village was born when the owner of the seigneury of Rivière du Chêne gave the mill enough land in 1770 to build a church. The village is now an important residential suburban town. The main signs of local and regional history are the mill in the centre of town and the parish church (built, respectively, 1762 and 1780). This village was the site of a fierce battle during the REBELLIONS OF 1837 as Chenier and the PATRIOTES barricaded themselves in the church, priest's house and convent. Nearly 100 Patriotes were killed and the British troops put the village to the torch. An important regional centre, with half of its territory farmland, St-Eustache has doubled its population every decade since 1951.   GILLES BOILEAU

St-Félicien, Qué, Town, pop 9058 (1981c), inc 1976, is located at the mouth of the Rivière Chamouchouane on the W shore of Lac SAINT-JEAN. Founded in 1865, the colony of St-Félicien soon became a prosperous agricultural parish. Agriculture and lumber dominated its economy until WWII. The National Transcontinental (CNR) reached here in 1917. The town profited from the Chibougamau-Chapais mining boom of the 1950s, since nearly all the copper extracted from Chibougamau and Chapais (280 km NW of Lac Saint-Jean) left the region via St-Félicien. The transportation was at first by road (opened in 1949), then by train (1959). In 1960 local citizens founded the Zoo St-Félicien, which has become a major attraction in Saguenay-Lac Saint-Jean region because of its innovative zoological approach (nature paths). The Donohue Co established a pulp and paper factory here in 1978.   MARC ST-HILAIRE

Saint Francis Xavier University was founded in 1853 in Arichat, Cape Breton, and moved to Antigonish, NS, in 1855. Although founder Bishop Colin MacKinnon wished to provide higher education facilities for the Roman Catholic Highlanders in eastern Nova Scotia, non-Catholic students and faculty have been part of the university almost since its inception. Full university powers were conferred in 1866. In 1883 a girls' school and academy was founded, later to become Mount St Bernard College. Through its affiliation with St FX, degrees were granted in 1897 to 4 women, and thus it became the first coeducational Catholic institution in N America to grant such degrees. St FX also initiated the first engineering school in NS in 1899.

Well known for its efforts to serve the community, St FX established the Dept of Extension in 1928. This was headed by Moses COADY, who preached a philosophy of self-help. The extension activities were augmented in 1959 with the establishment of the Coady International Institute, which attracts students from around the world seeking to learn the techniques of the ANTIGONISH MOVEMENT. St FX offers a full range of undergraduate degrees and some graduate programs.   R.A. MACLEAN

Enrolment: Saint Francis Xavier University, 1982-83
(Source: Statistics Canada)

Full-time Undergrad	Full-time Graduate	Part-time Undergrad	Part-time Graduate
2 419	53	263	45

St-François, Rivière, 280 km long, drainage basin 10 630 km², is located in southern Québec. Named in 1635 in honour of François de Lauzon, eldest son of the fourth governor of New France, it was called *Alsiganteku*, "river where people no longer live," by the ABENAKI. From Lac St-François, 48 km NW of Lac MÉGANTIC, the river flows in a SW direction via Lac Aylmer toward LENNOXVILLE and SHERBROOKE, where it branches NW and flows into Lac ST-PIERRE, 19 km NE of SOREL. The river rises in the forested Appalachian region and, joined by the Rivière Magog at Sherbrooke, reaches the ST LAWRENCE LOWLANDS in the agricultural region N of DRUMMONDVILLE. Sherbrooke and Richmond are affected by its spring floods. As early as 1690, the river was used by the Abenaki and the French for attacks on the British in New Hampshire.

JEAN-MARIE DUBOIS AND PIERRE MAILHOT

St-Georges, Qué, Town, pop 10 342 (1981c), inc 1907, metropolis of the Beauce region, is located SE of Québec City on the CHAUDIÈRE R at its junction with the Famine R. Its first inhabitants, the ABENAKI called it *sartigan*, "the shady place." This same name was given to the dam built upstream in 1967 to protect the town from spring flooding by the Chaudière. (Designed to hold back ice, it was the first dam of its type in Canada.) The first colonists came during the French regime to settle on the seigneury ceded to Aubert Gallion. The American invasion of 1775 led to British regular troops occupying the Beauce and to the presence of many English families in Sartigan. In 1807 a German named George Pozer bought the seigneury, settled there with 189 compatriots, and gave his name to the area. Population increased with the opening of the Kennebec route, linking the Beauce with New England in 1830. The town is located in a major forestry area and so its main economic activities are wood related: sawmills, prefabricated homes, and furniture. CLAUDINE PIERRE-DESCHÊNES

St Hubert Mission, located some 16 km SW of Whitewood, Sask, originated from the settlement of a group of titled French and Belgian nobility that apparently sought to escape from unacceptable economic, social and political changes in their homelands. In the mid-1880s the representative of a wealthy Frenchman bought land in the area and commenced farming operations. His home, called La Rolanderie, was named after the estate of his employer in France and became synonymous with the name of the district until about 1890 when a church was built and the parish of St Hubert was founded. The "French Counts," as they were known locally, arrived in the years before the turn of the century and initiated a series of ill-conceived, and ultimately unsuccessful, business and farming ventures that included sheep ranching, the cultivation of sugar beets and the operation of a cheese factory. Even after the departure of the French nobility after 1905, St Hubert retained its unique character as a French-speaking, Catholic community deriving its identity from the parish church and its colourful history. GARTH PUGH

St-Hyacinthe, Qué, City, pop 38 246 (1981c), inc 1857, is situated in the St Lawrence R plain on the Yamaska R, about 45 km E of Montréal. From the beginning, St-Hyacinthe has been a commercial and service centre for a thriving agricultural region, known for its impressive religious and educational institutions.

History The history of St-Hyacinthe began with the granting in 1748 of a seigneury which was purchased in 1753 by Hyacinthe Delorme. In 1795 the present site, farther upstream than the original settlement, became the seigneury's focal point because of the potential for hydropower of an abrupt drop there in the riverhead. A village quickly developed as a market and

communications centre, serving the needs of the immediate region and of the other parishes that later appeared farther upstream. A college for boys was founded in 1811; a convent for girls in 1816; a hospital in 1840. In 1848 a railway was opened to Longueuil, across from Montréal. The next year the line reached Richmond, then SHERBROOKE and Portland to the E and LÉVIS to the N, opposite QUÉBEC. But industrial development was slower than anticipated. Manufacturing did not become dominant until the 1870-1900 period, when St-Hyacinthe became one of Québec's main textile-production centres.

In 1831 the village had some 1100 inhabitants. By 1851 the population had reached 3113; 4% were of British origin, the highest such percentage ever recorded. With a population of 9210 in 1900, St-Hyacinthe was one of Québec's 6 most populous smaller centres. Development in the 20th century was slower. The figure of 37 500 in 1976 reflects the inclusion of several municipalities.

Economy Still the centre for one of Québec's thriving agricultural regions, St-Hyacinthe is well situated on rail and road networks. Although Montréal is far enough away to prevent St-Hyacinthe from becoming a suburb, its economic competition is considerable. A diversified industry, however, now has a stabilizing effect on the city.

Cityscape St-Hyacinthe is relatively flat, like the level country surrounding it. A lower town, site of the first buildings, follows the low edge of a meandering curve of the Yamaska R. The public buildings — churches, educational institutions and so on — are noteworthy, as are the parks and green spaces and some magnificent homes built at the turn of the century. Regional market gardeners still bring their produce to market in the "lower town." In the SW are the School of Veterinary Medicine, associated with U de M, and the Institute of Agricultural Technology. JEAN-PAUL BERNARD

Saint-Jean, Lac, Qué, 1350 km², elev 98 m, 63 m deep, is located in S-central Québec, 170 km WNW of the St Lawrence R, into which it flows via the SAGUENAY R. The lake is the centre of a shallow glacial pan and is fed by dozens of little rivers, the most important being (W to E) the Chamouchouane, the Mistassini and the Péribonca to the N and the des Aulnaies, Métabetchouane and the Ouiatchouane to the S. It is lined by various towns, among them ALMA, DOLBEAU, MISTASSINI, ROBERVAL and ST-FÉLICIEN.

Called Piékouagami ("flat lake") by Indians, the lake was named after the patron saint of Jean Dequen, a Jesuit missionary and the first European to reach its shores (1647). Local Indians (Kakouchak and Mistassini) began trading with the Europeans at TADOUSSAC in the 16th century. Later, Lac Saint-Jean was made part of the King's Domain (1674), land reserved for trapping and farmed out to interested parties; a first trading post was built at Métabetchouane in 1676. The FUR TRADE dominated the region's economy until the 19th century, when colonization started in the Saguenay (1838) and then in the Lac Saint-Jean region (1849). Settlement was intense until the early 20th century, with settlers recruited from Québec, the US and even Europe. The economy was mainly based on agriculture and forestry until WWII. Co-operative dairy farming and cattle raising are still very important activities.

Industrial development began with 19th-century sawmills, continued with pulp mills (the first, at Val-Jalbert, opened in 1902), paper mills (after 1925) and aluminum plants (1943), and was greatly encouraged by the construction of hydro stations at Alma (1925) and on the Péribonca R (1954-60). Lac Saint-Jean also has a flourishing summer resort industry. Ever since the railway reached Roberval (1888), SPORTFISHING (landlocked salmon and walleyed pike) have drawn thousands of enthusiasts yearly, along with vacationers who enjoy the lake's beaches. A major swimming event, the International Crossing of Lac Saint-Jean between Péribonka and Roberval, has been held yearly since 1955. Péribonka also houses the Musée Louis-Hémon, commemorating the trip made to Lac Saint-Jean by the author of *Maria Chapdelaine* (1913).

MARC ST-HILAIRE

St-Jean-Baptiste Society (Société Saint-Jean-Baptiste), French Canadian patriotic association fd 24 June 1834 by journalist Ludger Duvernay, who wanted to stimulate a nationalist spirit among his compatriots and encourage them to defend their linguistic and cultural heritage. Gradually, branches were established throughout Québec and in francophone communities elsewhere in N America. Placed under the patronage of St John the Baptist, the society has always organized special activities, originally with religious overtones, for June 24 (the saint's day), a legal holiday in Québec since 1922. The society distributes prizes for artistic and literary merit, and since the 1920s has sponsored annual parades on June 24 with themes such as "Homage to the Patriots of 1837." It has engaged in various financial activities and has produced numerous briefs and resolutions on subjects of nationalist, linguistic and constitutional interest to Francophones. Early in the 20th century the society gave both monetary and moral support to Francophones in Ontario, where bilingual education had been abolished. Its attention later shifted away from francophone minorities outside Québec, and in the 1960s it became principally concerned with Québec nationalism. Since the 1960s, the society's activities have become largely secularized. RICHARD JONES

St-Jean-sur-Richelieu, Qué, Town, pop 35 640 (1981c), inc 1858, is located on the shores of the upper RICHELIEU R, some 40 km SE of Montréal. Across the river is the smaller, adjoining site of Iberville, long known as St-Jean, and popularly as St-Jean d'Iberville.

St-Jean originated as one of a series of forts along the Richelieu during the French regime. After the American Revolution, numerous LOYALISTS joined the local families. Through the 19th century, St-Jean became increasingly French Canadian and Catholic. Politically, it was a Liberal stronghold; one of its inhabitants, Félix-Gabriel MARCHAND, became premier of Québec in 1897. Railways and canals were introduced early in the region to accommodate a thriving commercial trade between Canada and the US and to avert the cumbersome rapids just below St-Jean. In 1836 the first railway line in Canada, the CHAMPLAIN AND ST LAWRENCE RAILROAD, connected St-Jean and La Prairie. The Chambly Canal was finished around 1844. Owing to the success of rival railway interests and a failure to achieve industrial growth, however, the town declined in the latter 19th century.

In the 20th century, several large industries (notably American multinationals) were attracted by generous incentives and the CN and CP rail routes. The decline of secondary manufacturing over the last decade or so, however, has contributed to increasing unemployment in the region. St-Jean has experienced physical growth in recent years. Tall buildings have begun to dot an otherwise flat landscape. The original town, "Vieux Saint-Jean," is experiencing a cultural rejuvenation. KATHLEEN LORD

St-Jérôme, Qué, City, pop 25 123 (1981c), inc 1881, is located on the Rivière du Nord, 40 km NW of MONTRÉAL. From the 1834 creation of the first parish to its 1881 elevation to the status of town, the village of St-Jérôme lived primarily on forestry and agriculture. From 1882 on, the Rolland Co ran one of the oldest paper mills in Canada here. A regional metropolis situated where the Rivière du Nord leaves the Laurentians, St-Jérôme dominates the entire Lower Laurentians. The bishopric, courthouse and CEGEP give the town an administrative function as well as industrial and commercial ones. Its parish priest 1868-91 was the legendary Antoine LABELLE, the determined apostle of colonization whose efforts led to the creation of several dozen Laurentian parishes and the development of the huge territory between St-Jérôme and Mont-Laurier.   GILLES BOILEAU

Saint John, NB, City, largest city in New Brunswick, is located at the mouth of the SAINT JOHN R on the Bay of FUNDY.

Settlement Saint John's earliest known inhabitants were the Micmac and later the Maliseet. Samuel de CHAMPLAIN arrived at Saint John harbour on 24 June 1604 — the feast of St John the Baptist — and gave the river its name. No permanent settlement was attempted until 1630 when Charles de LA TOUR constructed a fort (Ft La Tour) at the site of present-day Saint John. In 1701 the newly appointed French governor of ACADIA, Jacques-François de Brouillan, destroyed the fort and consolidated his forces across the bay at Port-Royal. Not until the 1730s did Acadians from other parts of the Bay of Fundy begin resettling along the river. By 1749 ownership of the territory surrounding Saint John was in dispute between England and France, and in the ensuing struggle the Acadian deportations were carried out from the mid-1750s to the early 1760s. The old French fort was rebuilt by the English in 1758 and renamed Ft Frederick, but it was destroyed in 1775 by the Americans. Finally, in 1778, the English erected Ft Howe on a hill above Portland Point.

The beginnings of permanent English settlement occurred in the 1760s with the arrival from Boston of James Simonds and James White, each of whom established dwellings at the foot of present-day Fort Howe Hill. These pre-Loyalist 18th-century merchants traded with the Indians and the garrison, and formed ties with the British at Halifax. In 1783 this harbour community greatly expanded when LOYALIST refugees settled on the E side of the harbour in Parr Town, on the W side in Carleton, and on the N in Portland. In 1785 Carleton and Parr Town were incorporated, taking the name Saint John — the first incorporated city in what is now Canada. NEW BRUNSWICK was made a separate province in 1784 and Saint John served briefly as the provincial capital before the capital was moved upriver to FREDERICTON.

Development The city's early economy emerged through the TIMBER TRADE, trading and SHIPBUILDING. Quickly growing in prominence as a port, Saint John's lumberyards supplied square timber, and later sawn lumber, to Great Britain and the West Indies; its shipyards produced vessels (as early as 1770) that transported the forestry products and also became export commodities themselves. Many of the city's shipbuilders, such as Angus MACKAY, and ships, such as the MARCO POLO, became internationally famous. Equally significant, the waterfront pro-

Population: 80 521 (1981c); 114 048 (CMA)
Rate of Increase (1971-81): (CMA) 6.6%
Rank in Canada: Twenty-third (by CMA)
Date of Incorporation: 1785
Land Area: 321 km²
Elevation: 36 m (highest point Ben Lomond Mt 237 m)
Climate: Average daily temp, July 16.7°C, Jan -6.5°C; Yearly precip 1305.6 mm; Hours of sunshine 1819 per year

duced the city's largest labour union, which by 1911 affiliated with the International Longshoremen's Assn.

From the 1820s through the 1840s thousands of immigrants — SCOTS and especially IRISH — altered the city's ethnic and religious composition. By 1849 tensions between Protestants and Catholics resulted in riot and loss of life. During this mid-century period, the city's economy of "wood, wind and sail" was challenged from the outside by the newer technology of steam and iron. In addition, it was visited by a host of economic woes. From 1860 to 1880 Saint John began to be deeply affected by the end of the protected British market for colonial timber, the slackening in demand for wooden ships and a general decrease in trade. These conditions were worsened by an international depression that was underway by early 1874 and by a disastrous fire in 1877 that left the city's business district, most of its waterfront and much of its residential area in ashes. To these calamities were added the adverse consequences of Confederation (1867), as the arrival of the INTERCOLONIAL RY (1876) brought Saint John's manufacturers into competition with those from central Canada, to the long-term disadvantage of Saint John.

Population The city's demographic profile reflected these political and economic shocks. Although in 1871 Saint John remained the largest

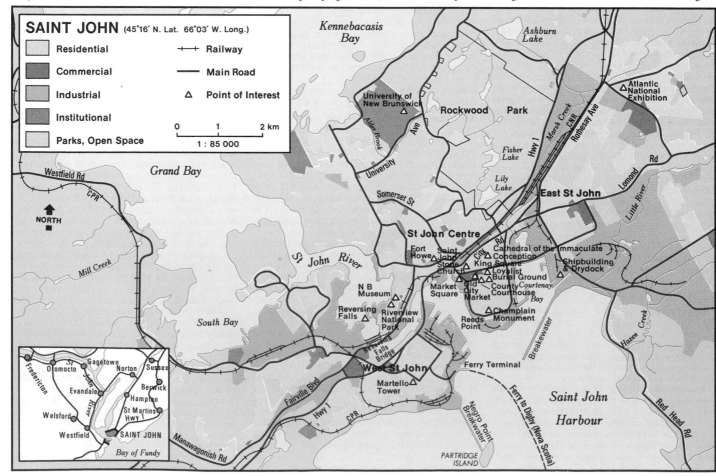

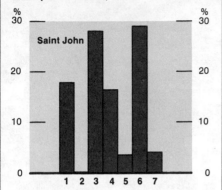

Distribution of Industrial Activity* by Industry Grouping within Census Metropolitan Areas, 1980

Saint John

Industry groupings

1. Food and beverage and tobacco products industries
2. Leather, textile, knitting mills and clothing industries
3. Wood, furniture and fixtures, paper and allied and printing, publishing and allied industries
4. Machinery, transportation equipment and electrical products industries
5. Primary metal and metal fabricating industries
6. Rubber and plastic products, petroleum and coal products and chemical products industries
7. Non-metallic mineral products and miscellaneous manufacturing industries.

* Industry activity based on the average of percentage shares of the value shipments of goods of own manufacture, total value added and total number of employees for each of the selected metropolitan areas.

Source: Figure II, Catalogue 31-209, Statistics Canada.

urban cluster in the Atlantic region, as early as the 1860s population growth had begun to stagnate. During the 1870s and 1880s, local newspapers succinctly captioned the process of outmigration to the "Boston States" as "the exodus." Only in 1901 did there appear to be a modest reversal, an improvement due in part to an influx from the Saint John R communities into the city and the revitalization of the world economy after the mid-1890s. By this time western Canadian wheat fields were poised to replace New Brunswick's forests as a primary export hinterland of the port. Throughout the 1880s Saint John's civic and business leaders had lobbied Ottawa to secure a niche for their city in the emerging Canadian system of cities. To this end, they invested substantially in the modernization of the waterfront and convinced the CPR to establish a terminus at the port in 1889. The adjacent town of Portland became part of the expanding city that same year. Thus, by 1900 Saint John's leaders were beginning to find a role within Canada by depending on water-based transport, to which had been added the railway. Saint John's newly constructed grain elevators became the "winter spout" for Canada's wheat. The traffic generated by the outbreak of WWI contributed to this new winter port prosperity. After the war, however, a severe economic decline continued through the Great Depression.

Government Following WWII Saint John, a city containing some of the oldest and worst housing in N America, embarked on a process of urban renewal. Efforts to modernize the city's streetscape were accompanied by changes in its administration. With the exception of the period from 1912 to the mid-1930s, when Saint John was administered by a Commission government, the city's municipal structure for most of its history consisted of a mayor and council. In 1963 the city adopted a council-manager form of government, wherein authority and political responsibility continued to rest with mayor and council, but administrative responsibility was centralized through a manager appointed by council. In 1967 the city expanded to include the city of Lancaster, the parish of Lancaster and part of the parish of Simonds. Greater access from within the city to outlying areas was achieved in the 1970s with the construction of a substantial throughway system incorporating a new Harbour Bridge.

Economy Since WWII Saint John's economic profile has maintained an emphasis on its traditional industries through freight diversification at the port, revitalization of the shipbuilding industry, and expansion of the pulp and paper mills. The development of the tourist industry is a recent addition, encouraged by the downtown construction of swimming facilities for the 1985 Canada Summer Games, as well as of track-and-field facilities at the expanding Saint John campus of UNB.

Cityscape The cityscape is largely dominated by the harbour and the river. The well-known Reversing Falls are located about 1 km from the centre of town. At high tide the ocean waters surge upstream through a narrow chasm, reversing the rush of river water through the gorge at low tide. The 1980s has witnessed a major city centre renewal pivoting on Market Square, where a section of waterfront has been preserved and embellished to include indoor and outdoor malls, a trade and convention centre, and a new hotel. This development has proceeded with the emerging utilization of a few late Victorian edifices providing some examples of gentrification. City-wide enthusiasm for the enhancement of Saint John's cultural life was demonstrated in the successful Bi-Capitol Project to secure a theatre facility — an acquisition at once recalling the city's rich 19th-century theatre history and its present-day rejuvenation. Thus, Saint John welcomes its third century by celebrating its past and anticipating its future through preservation and renewal of its architectural heritage and expansion of its recreational and educational facilities.

ELIZABETH W. McGAHAN

Reading: D.G. Bell, *Early Loyalist Saint John* (1983); J. Fingard, *Jack in Port* (1982); Elizabeth W. McGahan, *The Port of Saint John* (vol 1, 1982).

Saint John River, 673 km long, rises in northern Maine and flows NE into the forests of Madawaska County to EDMUNSTON, where it is joined by the Madawaska R and turns SE, forming much of the border between Maine and NB. Its DRAINAGE BASIN covers 55 400 km², of which some 20 000 km² is in the US, and it has a mean discharge of 1100 m³/s. It receives its chief tributary, the Tobique R, and swings E south of WOODSTOCK. Called *Oo-lahs-took*, "goodly river," by the MALISEET who lived along its banks, it is generally tranquil, except for cataracts at GRAND FALLS (25 m) and Beechwood (18 m), both of which have been harnessed for hydroelectric power.

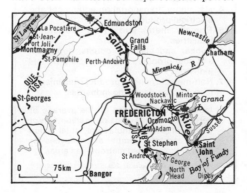

The river flows E past FREDERICTON and ORO-MOCTO, gradually widening and trending southward through a beautiful valley — one of the most fertile areas of Canada. On the lower course, numerous long, low islands have been formed by silt and molded by the current. Near the city of SAINT JOHN the river enters Long Reach, a narrow lake, and receives the Kennebecasis R from the NE. At Saint John the powerful Bay of FUNDY tides throw the river back through a narrow gorge called Reversing Falls. De MONTS and CHAMPLAIN anchored in Saint John harbour and named the river 24 June 1604, the feast day of St John. LA TOUR built a fort at the river's mouth 1631, but it was not until the LOYALISTS arrived in 1783 that significant settlement came to the valley. In the early 19th century, timber was driven from Madawaska, over Grand Falls, to Saint John, which became one of the most prosperous ports in British N America.

JAMES MARSH

St John's, capital and largest city of Newfoundland, is located on the eastern side of the AVALON PENINSULA of SE Newfoundland. Its landlocked harbour is approached through a long, narrow channel and is protected by the high hills on which the city is built. The origin of the name St John's is not known, but its use appears on a 1519 Portuguese map by Rienel as "Rio de San Johem" and later, in a 1527 letter by the English seaman John Rut, as the "Haven of St John's." According to popular folklore, however, the city takes its name from the feast of Saint John the Baptist and the discovery of Newfoundland for England on 24 June 1497 by the Italian discoverer Giovanni Caboto (John CABOT).

Settlement The harbour was frequented by European fishermen by the early 1500s, and by 1583, when Sir Humphrey GILBERT arrived in St John's to declare Newfoundland officially an English colony, settlement had developed on the central and eastern sections of the N side of the harbour. In 1832 St John's became the seat of government when Newfoundland was granted a colonial legislature by England; in 1888 it received its own municipal council.

Development Its strategic geographical location at the centre of the English migratory fishery on the Grand Banks made St John's a rendezvous for European fishermen and, after 1700, the natural focus for imperial administration and defence on the Island. As the cod fishery grew during the 18th century, St John's changed from a fishing town into a growing commercial centre for Newfoundland's increasing resident population. Although destroyed by fires in 1816, 1817, 1819, 1846 and 1892, St John's was rebuilt each time in a haphazard manner, with building regulations being stringently enforced only in the business district near the harbour. After 1870 small manufacturing industries were established in the capital. A dry dock was opened at the port 1882, and in 1897 the city became the headquarters for the trans-island railway which had been completed across Newfoundland by Canadian railway entrepreneur Robert Reid. After 1900 an improved coastal boat service to the outports further enhanced the preeminence of St John's.

Poor world markets for Newfoundland fish following WWI led St John's into a recession which was further worsened by the GREAT DEPRESSION. Prosperity returned during WWII with the arrival in Jan 1941 of the US armed forces to build Ft Pepperell and other military facilities in the capital. The resultant construction boom continued after 1946 with the building of new suburbs and the large infusion of federal funds after Confederation (1949). St John's became more dependent after 1949 on public-sector employment; at the same time it lost its traditional role as the fish-export centre of Newfoundland with the withdrawal from the salt-

Population: 83 770 (1981c); 154 820 (CMA)

Rate of Increase (1971-81): (CMA) -5%

Rank in Canada: Seventeenth (by CMA)

Date of Incorporation: 1888

Land Area: 83 km²

Elevation: 141 m (Torbay weather station)

Climate: Average daily temp, July 15°C, Jan -3.9°C; Yearly precip 1513.6 mm; Hours of sunshine 1458 per year

fish trade of major city mercantile firms, which chose to concentrate on a growing wholesale consumer trade.

The port of St John's has thus been transformed from an import-export centre into an import-service centre, as much of the port's revenue is now generated from supplying and repairing the local and international fishing fleet. The city has excellent air and road connections with both the rest of the province and the Canadian mainland. Close proximity to oil discoveries on the Grand Banks now holds the potential for the city's substantial economic and physical development.

Cityscape Until 1964, when the federal government completed a 915 m wharf along the N side of the harbour, the major feature of the St John's landscape in the harbour-front business district was the numerous private finger piers that jutted out from the merchants' warehouses on the S side of Water St. The city's streets ran in an E-W direction and parallel to the harbour. Before Confederation the streets were narrow and winding, reflecting the city's system of land tenure. With much of the land in the main commercial-residential area owned by British absentee landlords, the government was financially unable, following the 1846 and 1892 fires, to acquire land to create straight, wide streets in a gridiron pattern. After the creation of the St John's Housing Corp in 1944, new planned suburbs were built in the valleys W, N and NE of the principal settlement. Industry was spread throughout the adjacent harbour area. Since the 1960s, new suburban industrial parks have been created to accommodate existing industry and the further economic activity to be generated by offshore oil development.

Early St John's architecture in the 16th and 17th centuries was in the tilt, or log-cabin, form. Before the 1846 fire the Georgian style of the hip or cottage roof predominated among the 2½-storey frame buildings. This style was then gradually replaced by the Gothic revival and the more significant International Second Empire, which was especially dominant after the 1892 fire. Notable 19th-century buildings include the colonial building (classic revival), the Roman Catholic basilica (Romanesque), and the Anglican cathedral (Gothic revival), designed by the English architect Gilbert Scott. Since the mid-1960s the city's skyline has been gradually undergoing change as several new hotel, bank and office buildings have been completed.

Population St John's experienced slow growth until the Napoleonic Wars, when substantial Irish Roman Catholic immigration increased the population from 3742 residents (1796) to 10 018 (1815). After 1832 natural increase and the migration of outport residents to the capital combined to produce steady growth and a compact, ethnically homogeneous community of Irish and British stock. Though Roman Catholics ceased to form a majority of the city's population after 1911, their influence in the social, cultural and political life of St John's was well entrenched. The steady population increase had produced serious social problems of public health, housing and unemployment that were only partly relieved by immigration to the northeast US and Canada. The city's population doubled 1946-71 as large numbers of people

came to St John's to participate in new employment opportunities in the civil-service and service sectors. Since 1971 St John's has experienced a decline, as many residents have moved to MOUNT PEARL and other new suburbs outside city boundaries. St John's population is still predominantly Anglo-Saxon and Irish.

Economy The entry after 1949 of cheaper Canadian manufactured goods into Newfoundland caused the city's industries to collapse and thereby reduced the volume of commercial activity at the port. The completion of a paved

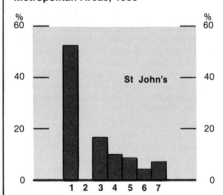

Distribution of Industrial Activity* by Industry Grouping within Census Metropolitan Areas, 1980

St John's

Industry groupings

1. Food and beverage and tobacco products industries
2. Leather, textile, knitting mills and clothing industries
3. Wood, furniture and fixtures, paper and allied and printing, publishing and allied industries
4. Machinery, transportation equipment and electrical products industries
5. Primary metal and metal fabricating industries
6. Rubber and plastic products, petroleum and coal products and chemical products industries
7. Non-metallic mineral products and miscellaneous manufacturing industries.

* Industry activity based on the average of percentage shares of the value shipments of goods of own manufacture, total value added and total number of employees for each of the selected metropolitan areas.

Source: Figure II, Catalogue 31-209, Statistics Canada.

St John's was destroyed by fire several times in the 19th century and was rebuilt each time in a haphazard manner *(photo by John deVisser).*

highway across the Island (1965) enabled mainland distributors to bypass St John's and use CORNER BROOK and CHANNEL-PORT AUX BASQUES to send their goods to Island centres. The growth since 1949 of a large civil service supported by the federal, provincial and municipal governments has been the key to the expansion of the city's labour force and to the stability of its economy, which supports a sizable retail, service and business sector.

Government and Politics The city was governed by the colonial government until 1888, when it received a limited form of self-rule with authority over the water supply, streets, sewers, parks, the fire brigade and building regulations. The city was governed by different councils or commissions composed of government-appointed members and elected officials until 1916, when a fully elective form of municipal council was settled on. In 1921 a comprehensive bill, drafted by the commissioners who had administered the city 1914-16, was passed by the legislature. This 1921 Act and its subsequent amendments by the legislature are the basis of today's St John's city government. In 1969 the number of elected councillors was increased from 6 to 8, and in 1981 a partial ward system was adopted, giving St John's 4 councillors elected at large and 4 elected on the basis of a ward system. There is no regional government in the St John's metropolitan area, but the city council does have representation on the St John's Metropolitan Area Board, a provincially appointed and subsidized board (est 1963) which is responsible for municipal supervision and services in revenue-weak communities on the outskirts of St John's.

Cultural Life St John's has most of Newfoundland's social, educational and religious institutions. The Benevolent Irish Society and the Convent of the Order of Presentation Sisters date from 1806 and 1833, respectively. Until the province undertook a rural high-school building program in the 1950s, the city's denominational high schools provided educational instruction for outport residents. The city is also the site of MEMORIAL UNIVERSITY, the College of Trades and Technology, and the College of Fisheries, Navigation, Marine Engineering and Electronics. Also found here are the Newfoundland Museum, the Arts and Culture Centre, and the Signal Hill National Pk, which contains Cabot Tower, conceived in 1897 to commemorate the 400th anniversary of Newfoundland's dis-

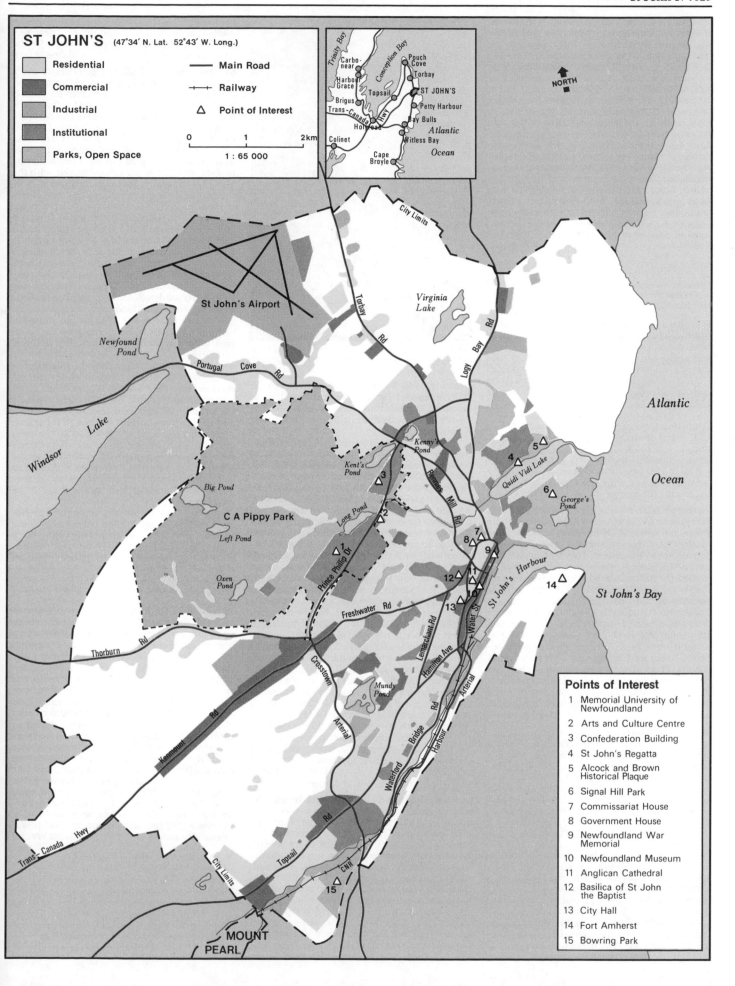

ST JOHN'S (47°34' N. Lat. 52°43' W. Long.)

- Residential
- Commercial
- Industrial
- Institutional
- Parks, Open Space

—— Main Road
+—+—+ Railway
△ Point of Interest

0   1   2km

1 : 65 000

Points of Interest

1 Memorial University of Newfoundland
2 Arts and Culture Centre
3 Confederation Building
4 St John's Regatta
5 Alcock and Brown Historical Plaque
6 Signal Hill Park
7 Commissariat House
8 Government House
9 Newfoundland War Memorial
10 Newfoundland Museum
11 Anglican Cathedral
12 Basilica of St John the Baptist
13 City Hall
14 Fort Amherst
15 Bowring Park

covery and Queen Victoria's Diamond Jubilee. Opened 1900, the tower was the site the following year for Guglielmo Marconi to receive the first transatlantic wireless message. In 1919 the city was the start of the first transatlantic non-stop airplane flight, when Sir John Alcock and Arthur Brown flew to Ireland.

St John's has 2 large newspapers, 2 TV stations and several radio stations. The city has a long tradition in sports; the annual ST JOHN'S REGATTA, held on the first Wednesday in Aug, dates from the 1820s and is the oldest continuous sporting event in N America. St John's was the site of the 1977 Canada Summer Games, which left the city with improved sporting facilities. Since 1978 the city has celebrated June 24 as a civic holiday in honour of Newfoundland's discovery in 1497.   MELVIN BAKER

Reading: Melvin Baker, *Aspects of Nineteenth Century St. John's Municipal History* (1982); P. Copes, *St. John's and Newfoundland: An Economic Survey* (1961); G.A. Nader, *Cities of Canada,* 2 vols (1975-6); S.J.R. Noel, *Politics in Newfoundland* (1971); Shane O'Dea, *The Domestic Architecture of St. John's* (1974); Paul O'Neill, *The Story of St. John's, Newfoundland,* 2 vols (1975-6); J.R. Smallwood, ed, *The Book of Newfoundland,* 6 vols (1937-75); R.E. Pearson, *Atlas of St. John's, Newfoundland* (1969).

St John's Regatta, believed to be the oldest continuing sporting event in N America, is a ROWING race over a 2.6 km course in long, fixed-seat shells carrying 6 oarsmen. The first race may have taken place 22 Sept 1818 on Quidi Vidi Lk, which lies just N of St John's harbour and Signal Hill. Another race was recorded in 1828 or 1829. The Prince of Wales, later Edward VII, visited and offered £100 to the winner. Times improved in the late 19th century, and in 1901 a crew from Outer Cove set a record time, 9 min, 13 sec, that was not broken until 1981. After a suspension during WWI, the regatta resumed in 1918 and has continued since. A lively carnival is held during the regatta, often overshadowing the rowing.   JAMES MARSH

St Joseph Island lies at the E entrance of the St Marys R in the North Channel connecting Lks HURON and SUPERIOR, about 30 km SE of Sault Ste Marie, Ont. It was first settled briefly after the destruction of Huronia in 1649 by fugitive Huron and their Jesuit missionaries, who named it. In 1796 the British Army built Fort St Joseph on the SW corner of the island, at the time the most westerly military post in Canada. It became a rendezvous for traders and Indians, and though it was destroyed in the War of 1812 its remains are visible and have been preserved as a National Historic Park. Agricultural settlement occurred late in the 19th century. Today the island is a tourist and farming centre, producing garden produce, livestock, butter and maple sugar for a local market. A bridge connects it to the mainland across St Joseph Channel, a principal navigation route.   DANIEL FRANCIS

St. Laurent, Louis Stephen, lawyer, politician, prime minister (b at Compton, Qué 1 Feb 1882; d at Québec City 25 July 1973). Born into a poor family, St. Laurent was fluently bilingual, became a prominent lawyer and, in 1914, a law professor at Laval. During the 1920s and 1930s he was a successful corporation lawyer and served as batonnier of the Québec Bar and president of the Canadian Bar Association (1930-32). In 1937-40 he was a counsel to the Rowell-Sirois Commission. In Dec 1941 St. Laurent was approached by PM KING to become minister of justice. He had no political experience but felt it was his duty to accept, and in Feb 1942 he was elected to the House of Commons representing Québec E. Alone among Liberal ministers from Québec, he was not pledged to oppose CONSCRIPTION and supported King in 1944 when he imposed it for overseas service. King was grateful and, impressed with St. Laurent's logical mind, made him secretary of state for external

Louis St. Laurent, 12th prime minister of Canada (*courtesy Public Archives of Canada/Bill and Jean Newton, Ottawa*).

affairs in 1946. St. Laurent represented Canada at international conferences and the UN. He promoted Canadian membership in NATO, believing that Canada must help resist Communist expansion.

As King's choice to succeed himself, a selection ratified by a Liberal convention, St. Laurent became prime minister on 15 Nov 1948. He headed a Cabinet of exceptional competence, including Lester PEARSON in external affairs, C.D. HOWE in trade and commerce, Douglas Abbott in finance and Brooke CLAXTON in national defence. Old-age pensions were extended; hospital insurance was enacted; equalization payments among the provinces were approved; and Newfoundland formally joined Canada. Abroad, Canada garrisoned troops in Europe under NATO and sent forces to fight for the UN in Korea. St. Laurent's grandfatherly appearance and his government's record caused the Liberals to be re-elected in 1949 and 1953 with overwhelming majorities. In 1954 a successful round-the-world trip seemed to tire St. Laurent; thereafter, observers noticed that he seemed removed from events around him. During his last year in office the Liberals suffered reversals in public opinion, partly as a result of the PIPELINE DEBATE in 1956. In June 1957 St. Laurent's government was defeated by John DIEFENBAKER'S PCs, and in Jan 1958 he retired from public life, returning to his law practice in Québec. St. Laurent was much admired for his decisiveness, patriotism and sharp mind, and was held in great personal affection by those who worked with him.   ROBERT BOTHWELL

Reading: D.C. Thompson, *Louis St. Laurent* (1967).

St Lawrence and Atlantic Railroad, the world's first international railway, was inaugurated on 18 July 1853. The purpose of the railway was to provide Montréal, Sherbrooke and other Québec towns with access to an ice-free Atlantic port. The original plan was to build the line to Boston, but promoters in Portland, Maine, succeeded in persuading Canadians that their city was preferable. Construction of the broad-gauge railway began in 1846, but was beset by financial troubles. The section from Longueuil, Qué, to the Richelieu R was completed in Nov 1847 and the Canadian and American sections were joined in 1853 at Island Pond, Vermont. A ferry boat connected Montréal to the

railhead at Longueuil. Upon completion the Canadian section was sold, and the American section leased, to the GRAND TRUNK RAILWAY. *See also* RAILWAY HISTORY.   JAMES MARSH

St Lawrence, Gulf of, a large (250 000 km²), roughly triangular inland sea receiving on average 11 000 m³/s of fresh water from the ST LAWRENCE R at its NW apex, is connected to the Atlantic by the Str of Belle Isle at the NE and CABOT STR at the SE corners. The deep Laurentian Channel extends from the St Lawrence estuary near TADOUSSAC, Qué, through the Cabot Str to the edge of the continental shelf. To the S lie the Iles de la MADELEINE and PRINCE EDWARD ISLAND, with the extensive Magdalen Shallows in between. N of the channel is Ile d'ANTICOSTI. Additional sources of fresh water include the SAGUENAY R and other N shore rivers, plus smaller amounts from NB and Newfoundland. Much of the runoff is entrained in the Gaspé Current, flowing along the S shore of the estuary, out onto the Magdalen Shallows and eventually around the northern tip of CAPE BRETON I to form the Nova Scotian Current. The physical and biological effects of this fresh water are detectable as far away as the Gulf of Maine. Newfoundland Shelf water enters the gulf on the eastern side of Cabot Str, drifts NE along the W coast of Newfoundland and, coupled with a westerly drift along the N shore, completes a large counterclockwise gyre in the surface circulation. Deep inflow of Atlantic water through Cabot Str compensates for the net outflow of surface waters. Winter cooling and contributions from the Labrador Shelf via Belle Isle Str result in significant ice cover (and associated navigational hazards) in the gulf for at least 3 months each winter. Economically the gulf, with the St Lawrence River and ST LAWRENCE SEAWAY, forms a transportation corridor to the heartland of industrial N America, carries away its waste products, and still yields about one-quarter of Canadian fish landings, both by weight and value.

Before European contact, the gulf was frequented by nomadic Indian tribes, such as the MICMAC, who came seasonally to fish. The N shore was inhabited by INUIT, whose fierce opposition long prevented safe harbour. Jacques CARTIER explored the gulf in 1534, but was likely preceded in the area by BASQUE fishermen (*see* RED BAY).   P.C. SMITH AND R.J. CONOVER

St Lawrence Hall, built in 1850, was designed as a multipurpose building containing shops and a farmers' market on the ground level and a number of elegant meeting rooms and reception halls on the upper floors. For many years it was the centre of cultural and political life in Toronto, hosting many balls, receptions, concerts and lectures. John A. MACDONALD, George BROWN and the world renowned soprano Jenny Lind all appeared here. Designed by William THOMAS of Toronto, the architecture reflected the influence of the Renaissance style, with its raised portico over an arcaded base, but reinterpreted in a distinctly Victorian manner. Its richly carved ornamentation, picturesque skyline, and the eclectic incorporation of a French mansard roof were typical of contemporary architectural tastes. By the 1870s more modern theatres, concert halls and ballrooms had been built and St Lawrence Hall fell into decline. In 1967 it was extensively restored.   JANET WRIGHT

St Lawrence Islands National Park (4 km²), Canada's smallest national PARK comprises 19 granite islands and 85 islets scattered from Brockville to Kingston, Ont. The park islands are the summit of ancient hills of the Frontenac Axis, a strip of Precambrian granite connecting the Canadian SHIELD with the Adirondack Mts in New York State. After the retreat of glaciers, the hills were flooded by the newly formed St Lawrence R, resulting in the THOUSAND ISLANDS riverscape. From barren, lichen-covered rock to lush, deciduous woodlands, the park's islands support varied plant and animal life. Many species are typical of regions far to the S and occur nowhere else in Canada. Indians hunted and fished in the area. Explorers, fur traders and missionaries passed this way, but the scant soils did not attract settlers until the late 1770s, when LOYALISTS took up land. During the War of 1812 the area was a vital military route. Later it became a haven for boaters and cottagers. In 1904, as more islands became cottage sites, the government decided to set some aside as a national park. A campground is situated at Mallorytown Landing and overnight camping is available on some larger islands. LILLIAN STEWART

St Lawrence Lowland, 46 000 km² (5000 km² in the US), is a plain along the ST LAWRENCE R between Québec City in the E and Brockville, Ont, in the W, including the Ottawa R valley W to Renfrew, Ont. It is 450 km long W to E and 1000 km wide in the W half, narrowing to 35 km at Québec; an arm extends 130 km S into the Lake CHAMPLAIN valley. Altitude ranges from 15 m above sea level along the St Lawrence R NE of Montréal to 150 m along the borders with the Laurentian Mts to the N, the Adirondacks to the S and the gradual transitions to the Appalachians in the SE and the Precambrian SHIELD of Ontario in the W. Tributaries of the St Lawrence that drain the lowland from the S are the Chateauguay, RICHELIEU, Yamaska, St-François, Nicolet, Bécancour and CHAUDIÈRE rivers, and from the N, L'Assomption, Maskinonge, ST-MAURICE, Batiscan and Ste-Anne rivers. Tributaries of the OTTAWA R crossing the lowland are the S Nation, Rideau, Mississippi, Madawaska and Bonnechere rivers.

The large-scale topographic features are the result of subaerial weathering and erosion by rivers, during the last 100 million years, of the nearly flat-lying early Paleozoic sedimentary rocks of the lowland. The rocks from oldest (lowest) to youngest (uppermost) are sandstone, dolomite and limestone and shale; their age ranges from 520 to 480 million years. These sediments are in a basin surrounded by older, more resistant crystalline rocks. Below the sedimentary rocks is an ancient surface of moderate relief that was eroded on the older (1000-million-year) Precambrian rocks.

The lowland is dominated by the Monteregian Hills, a series of isolated mountains in a belt about 20 km wide extending E from Montréal to the Appalachians. They are, from W to E, Mts Royal (231 m), St-Bruno (213 m), St-Hilaire (404 m), St-Gregoire (229 m), Rougemont (366 m), Yamaska (411 m), Shefford (518 m) and Brome (548 m). All are erosional remnants of igneous intrusions of early Cretaceous age (95 to 135 million years ago). Whether any volcanoes existed above the intrusions is unknown because no direct evidence remains. Igneous dikes and sills radiate from the Monteregian Hills, and some support terraces around the mountains, and form parts of the Lachine Rapids in the St Lawrence R. Hills of Precambrian crystalline rocks project through the sedimentary rocks of the lowland 30-50 km W of Montréal at the Oka Hills (260 m), Rigaud Mtn (213 m) and a hill near St Andrews East (137 m). An estimated 800-1200 m of rock has been eroded from the lowland in the last 100 million years. The N boundary is an eroded fault-line scarp in many places. The lowland is part of a rift valley originating in Cretaceous times, and is a region of high EARTHQUAKE probability where major damage can be expected; during historical times about 10 major earthquakes have occurred in each century.

The details of the lowland's present landscape are the result of the last continental glaciation, followed by marine submergence, emergence and, finally, river erosion and deposition. Evidence of early glaciation has been obliterated by later ones, but deposits exposed in valleys near Lac St-Pierre indicate that an early interval of weathering and deposition of river gravels was followed by at least 2 episodes of glaciation. These were separated by the St-Pierre nonglacial interval during which peat and lake sediments accumulated. This interval lasted from about 70 000 to possibly 34 000 years ago. The last major glacial advance covered the region prior to 18 000 years ago. This ice sheet eventually retreated with minor readvances, intermittently uncovering the S and SW parts of the lowlands, which then were inundated by proglacial lakes. Residual glacier ice obstructing the St Lawrence Valley near Québec disintegrated 13 000 years ago and the sea flooded the region, forming a body of water known as the Champlain Sea. From 13 000 to 10 000 years ago the St Lawrence Lowland rose rapidly (as much as 20 m/century) in response to the disappearance of the ice mass. The highest relict strandlines of the Champlain Sea are now 230 m above sea level on the N side of the lowlands and 75 m lower on the S side. The sea withdrew 9500 years ago and for a short time a lake with a surface at 40 m (present elevation) occupied the central part of the basin. It drained when the St Lawrence R eroded its channel past Québec deeper, and the present course of the river became established around 6500 years ago.

Much of the St Lawrence Lowland is underlain by clay deposited in the Champlain Sea. It is as thick as 60 m along the N side near the former glacier-margin source and becomes progressively thinner until it virtually disappears. When subjected to excessive water percolation from rain or snowmelt, the clay becomes unstable and often subsides in earth-flow landslides, which have caused much loss of life and property. The W and S parts of the lowland are underlain by glacial deposits (till) rather than marine clay. Wave action has removed the silt and clay from the till, leaving behind sand and gravel, so that beach deposits are common on the hills in this region. Around the margins of the lowland are numerous sand and gravel beaches, spits and bars representing former water levels. Fossils are abundant in Champlain Sea deposits, including foraminifera, molluscs and vertebrates such as seals and whales, and indicate that these waters were similar to those of the present Labrador coast and Gulf of St Lawrence.

In the lower, central part of the lowland, areas of sand N and E of Montréal are remnants of former deltas of the Ottawa and St Lawrence rivers. Low terraces covered by river sands occur in the E part of the lowland. Some of the sand has been formed into dunes; locally these have elongated sharp crests as high as 18 m and are called "*crêtes de coq.*" The eolian sand is stabilized by vegetation. Along the Ottawa and St Lawrence rivers from Ottawa to Lac St-Pierre are troughlike abandoned river channels as wide as 2 km, with banks as high as 10 m. On the plain E of Montréal, roughly parallel to the St Lawrence, are ridges of bouldery sand 1.5-4.5 m high and 30 m wide, which appear to be material transported and pushed up by floating river ice during the river's early stages. The ridges have provided excellent building sites and road locations, and many rural communities are built on them. Much of the lowland is good agricultural land. Its clay has been used for brick and tile manufacture, and the sand and gravel deposits are exploited for road metal and construction material. The rocks of the lowland have been quarried for building stone, silica, cement, lime, crushed stone and concrete aggregate and for making brick and tile. The lowland was occupied by Iroquoian-speaking people at the time of its discovery by Jacques CARTIER in 1535. The farmlands were settled in the pattern of narrow strips fronting on the river, characteristic of the SEIGNEURIAL SYSTEM. Industry began near Trois-Rivières where bog iron was exploited in 1737. The St Lawrence Lowland now cradles the largest part of the population of Québec. J.A. ELSON

St Lawrence River, grand river and estuary, which together with the GREAT LAKES forms a hydrographic system that penetrates some 4000 km into N America. The river proper, about 1197 km long, issues from Lk Ontario, flows NE past Montréal and Québec City to the Gulf of ST LAWRENCE, from about 44° N lat near Kingston to about 50° N lat near Sept-Îles. The river's DRAINAGE BASIN covers some 1 million km², of which 505 000 km² is in the US, and its mean discharge of 10 100 m³/s is the largest in Canada. Its greatest tributary, the OTTAWA R, drains some 140 000 km², the SAGUENAY R about 88 000 km², the MANICOUAGAN R about 45 000 km², the ST-MAURICE R some 43 000 km² and the RICHELIEU R about 22 000 km². In geological terms, the St Lawrence is a young river, whose bed is a deep gash in the Earth's crust exposed some 6000 years ago as the glaciers receded.

The route of the explorers and main axis of NEW FRANCE, the river figured prominently in Canada's early history, and it remains the focus of settlement for much of the province of Québec. It is still the most important commercial waterway in Canada, as well as a source of electric power and natural beauty. The St Lawrence forms much of the southwestern outline of the Canadian SHIELD, which encroaches the river at QUÉBEC CITY. At Cap-Tourmente, 40 km below Québec, the LAURENTIANS rise 570 m above the river and follow its course past Les Eboulements (775 m), where they begin to retreat inland, to the Saguenay. The S bank is generally lower, although the Appalachians approach the river at Matane and, continuing eastward, form the tableland of GASPÉ.

Course The westerly limit of the river itself has been set at Everett Pt, Lk Ontario. The section from KINGSTON to MONTRÉAL is called the International Rapids, as sudden drops in the riverbed create a series of rapids. The river begins as an extended arm of Lk Ontario, choked with numerous islands, beginning with Wolfe I and including the THOUSAND ISLANDS near Gananoque, Ont. It trends NE past Brockville, Prescott and Morrisburg to Cornwall, where it broadens to form Lake St Francis. The Beauharnois Canal now carries shipping safely past the former rapids of Lachine and Les Cèdres to another widening of the river, Lac St-Louis, SW of Montréal. The Ottawa joins the mainstream through channels to Lac St-Louis and over a NE route via Lac des Deux Montagnes, Rivière des Mille-Îles and Rivière des Prairies. The various channels at the confluence form the archipelago on which the city of Montréal is built. The port of Montréal has been developed since the 19th century by dredging and canals.

From Montréal to TROIS-RIVIÈRES, the river is generally calm and unaffected by tides. A number of long, narrow islands continue to divide the mainstream and a large cluster, similar to the group at Lk Ontario, lies at the mouth of the Richelieu R at Sorel. The river broadens into Lac St-Pierre, some 15 km wide, and narrows again at Trois-Rivières, at the mouth of the St-Maurice R. From here to Québec, the freshwater flow becomes reversible with the tides. The river constricts at Québec where a promontory commands the entire upper course. The military value of the site was appreciated long before European settlement began. Past Québec the river divides to encircle Ile d'ORLÉANS and steadily widens to 15 km at Cap-Tourmente, almost 25 km at Île-aux-COUDRES. The water becomes brackish and tides are high.

Near the mouth of the Saguenay R, the river-

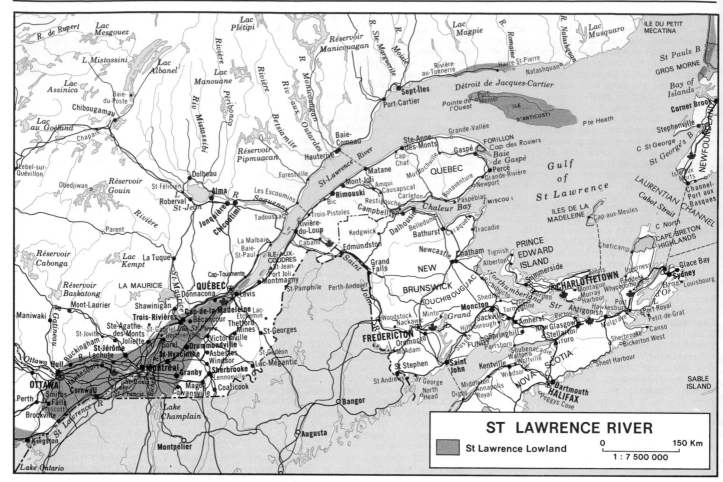

ST LAWRENCE RIVER

St Lawrence Lowland

0   150 Km

1 : 7 500 000

bed drops dramatically from 25 m to 350 m, forming a drowned valley in the lower estuary. The freshwater flow, mingles with cold arctic saltwater. The town of TADOUSSAC sits on a terrace of sand and clay at the confluence, but the rugged Precambrian N shore is sparsely settled. The S shore of the estuary, which forms a great curve towards Gaspé, is more open towards its hinterland, and major roads, including the TRANS-CANADA HIGHWAY, head inland from Rivière-du-Loup, Trois-Pistoles, Rimouski and Matane.

At Pointe-des-Monts, about 70 km E of Baie-Comeau and the mouth of the Manicouagan R, the N shore turns dramatically NNE for about 100 km to Sept-Îles, near the mouth of the MOISIE R. The river doubles in width to over 100 km, forming a deep, broad submarine valley, in which strong currents pour in from the gulf along the N shore and sweep counterclockwise back to the E. The saline water of the estuary discourages ice, and the port of SEPT-ILES is open year-round, despite its northerly location. According to the royal PROCLAMATION OF 1763, a line from the mouth of Rivière St-Jean on the N shore past the W tip of Ile d'ANTICOSTI to Cap des Rosiers on Gaspé marks the end of the river and the beginning of the gulf.

River Life Over the course of the river, the vegetation varies from deciduous, mixed and coniferous forest to taiga. There are sandbank grasses in the freshwater course, and seaweed and other saltwater plants in the middle and maritime estuary. Fish include smelt, sturgeon and herring. Beluga whales inhabit the lower course, on which walrus was once also abundant. Massive flocks of migratory birds use the sandbanks or river reefs as seasonal stops, including most of the world's greater snow geese, which nest on the tidal marshes at Cap-Tourmente.

Sedentary Indian groups — likely Iroquoian

— were settled at the present sites of Québec [STADACONA] and Montréal [HOCHELAGA] at the time of Cartier's first explorations in 1535. They had inexplicably disappeared by the time CHAMPLAIN founded Québec in 1608, possibly dispersed by the nomadic Montagnais, Etchemin and Algonquin, with whom the French established a lucrative trading alliance. Jacques CARTIER had discovered the river in 1535, with the help of Indian guides who took him past Anticosti, which he had believed was a peninsula. He built 2 transient camps near Stadacona in 1535 and 1541, but it was not until 1608 that the French foothold was secure.

The St Lawrence R provides almost the only riverine entrance to the heart of the continent, and French explorers and traders used it to establish a colonial empire that stretched beyond Lk Superior. By 1760 most of the riverbank from Québec to Montréal was patterned with the long, narrow strips of the SEIGNEURIAL SYSTEM, with the seigneury of Beaupré marking the eastern limit of settlement. The river system was suited to the carriage of buoyant softwood logs, and in the 19th century the river became the main artery of the TIMBER TRADE. Montréal and Québec C grew into major commercial centres, as wheat and flour from UPPER CANADA were carried down the river. Under the leadership of the NORTH WEST CO, the fur traders pushed the "Empire of the St Lawrence" all the way to the basin of the Mackenzie R. Donald CREIGHTON and others have argued that the E-W axis of the St Lawrence, which provided a counterpoise to the N-S affinity offered by much of the continent's geography, helped make possible the future nation of Canada. Today, with the development of the ST LAWRENCE SEAWAY, the river links a vast area of Canada and the US with the rest of the world. It is still, as Cartier called it, "the great river of Canada." *See also* ST LAWRENCE LOWLAND.   JAMES MARSH

St Lawrence Seaway–Great Lakes Waterway is the system of waterways linking the 5 Great Lakes and the St Lawrence R with the Atlantic Ocean. The digging of shallow canals along the St Lawrence R began as early as 1783. The first canal around Niagara was opened 1829, and the first lock at Sault Ste Marie in 1855. By 1900 there was a complete system of shallow canals from Lk Superior to Montréal. Between 1912 and 1932, the WELLAND CANAL was gradually deepened, but the US was a reluctant partner in a larger scheme, leaving a treaty signed in 1941 unratified by the Senate for 8 years. A threat by the Canadian government in 1951 to build a seaway entirely in Canadian territory brought about a final agreement in 1954. The Seaway was opened to commercial traffic 1 April 1959, but the official opening came 26 June 1959, attended by PM John Diefenbaker, Pres Dwight D. Eisenhower and Queen Elizabeth II.

Construction of the Seaway was a monumental engineering and construction feat. On the St Lawrence R-Lk Ontario section, which is often thought of as the whole Seaway, the Canadian government built 2 canals and 5 locks around the Soulanges and Lachine Rapids, and the US built a canal and 2 locks around the International Rapids. Together, the 7 locks lift a westbound vessel about 65 m between Montréal and Iroquois, Ont. Between Lk Ontario and Lk Erie, the Welland Canal circumvents the turbulent Niagara R. Its 8 locks lift a westbound vessel about 100 m over a distance of 43.5 km. Between Lk Erie and Lk Huron, the US deepened the Detroit R, St Clair R and Lk St Clair. The St Mary's R Canal links Lk Huron and Lk Superior. Each of its 4 parallel locks, on the US side of the St Mary's R, lifts a westbound vessel the 6.5 m required to bypass the St Mary's Falls. Together, the waterway permits vessels of up to 222.5 m long, 23.1 m wide, and a maximum draft of 7.9

m to sail from Montréal to Duluth, Minn, on the western extremity of Lk Superior. The project included 7 new locks, a control dam at Iroquois, and a major binational hydroelectric development at Cornwall, Ont, and Massena, NY. Major bridge and tunnel construction was required at Montréal, Beauharnois, Cornwall and Massena. The creation of Lk St Lawrence, the headpond of the hydroelectric power dam, simplified construction, but it flooded occupied land along the river and forced the relocation of highways and railways. Over 500 dwellings and 6500 people were moved to higher ground. Parts of the towns of Iroquois and Morrisburg were relocated and several smaller communities were eliminated, to be replaced by 2 new communities, Ingleside and Long Sault. The Canadian St Lawrence Seaway Authority operates the Welland Canal and the 5 Canadian locks on the St Lawrence system. The 2 locks in the US are operated by the St Lawrence Seaway Development Corp. The 4 US locks on the St Mary's R are operated by the US Corps of Engineers. A smaller lock (18.3 m) on the Canadian side of the St Mary's R is operated by Parks Canada.

The massive expenditure of public funds on the Seaway has not been without opposition.

The original St Lawrence section of the Seaway cost Canada $330 million and the US $130 million. Canada has paid a further $300 million to improve the Welland Canal. The huge debt, interest and operating costs could not be covered under existing financial arrangements, and in 1977 a change in legislation converted the Seaway Authority debt to equity held by Canada and required that, revenues cover all costs. The huge investment in the Seaway has been seen as an unfair subsidy by railways and E coast ocean ports. Shippers, in turn, oppose increased tolls. However, maintenance and operating costs have been recovered in most years, and an additional $600 million spent by the 2 countries for a hydroelectric plant has been recovered by the sale of electricity.

The Seaway has had a major economic impact on Canada and the US. It provides economical freight rates for bulk commodities and makes an important contribution to the basic industries of Canada and the US. The Seaway made possible the exploitation of the vast IRON ORE deposits of Québec and Labrador, and turned Canada from an importer to an exporter of iron ore. In 1983, 45.1 million t of cargo moved through the St Lawrence section of the Seaway, in contrast with the annual average of about 11 million t moved in the 1950s. Of the volume of cargo moving through the Seaway in the 1980s, between 48% and 56% was grain, about 25% was iron ore, 15% was other bulk cargo and another 7% was general cargo or finished goods (most imported iron and steel products). Coal moving to Ontario steelmills and ELECTRIC-POWER GENERATING stations was important cargo on the Welland Canal (*see* LAKE CARRIERS). GORDON C. SHAW

Saint-Marcoux, Micheline Coulombe, née Coulombe, composer, teacher (b at Notre-Dame-de-la-Doré, Qué 9 Aug 1938; d at Montréal 2 Feb 1985). Her teachers included Claude CHAMPAGNE, Clermont PÉPIN and Pierre Schaeffer. A cofounder of the Groupe international de musique électroacoustique de Paris (1969) and the Montréal percussion ensemble Polycousmie (1971), she has played a role in contemporary music. *Regards* (1978), a synthesis of her research, reveals a desire to rediscover sound in its pure state: live instrumentation is combined with recorded sequences without amplification. The work is characterized by the importance of the spatial parameter, as is *Moments* (1977), which is true musical theatre. HÉLÈNE PLOUFFE

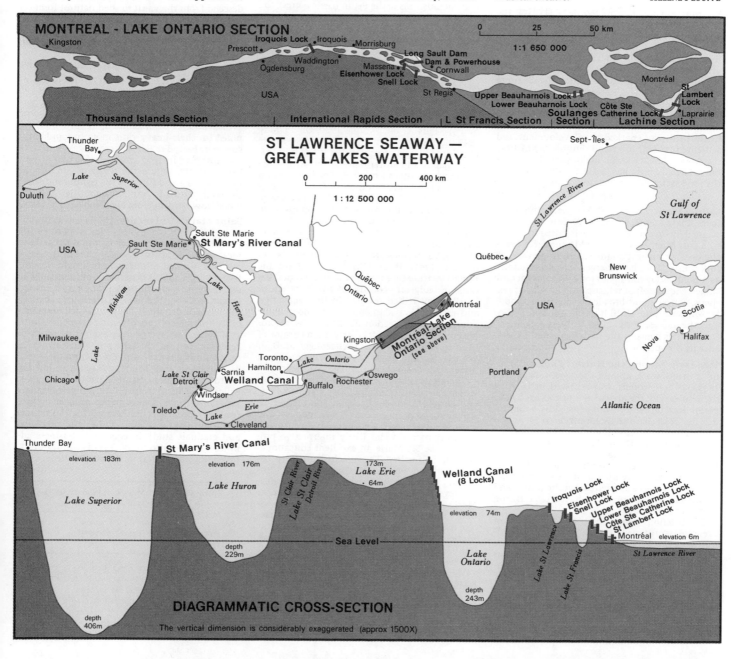

St Margaret's Bay, 70 km², is a small inlet of the Atlantic Ocean on the SE coast of Nova Scotia, 40 km W of HALIFAX. It is a favourite summer resort area, noted especially for its relatively warm surface water, sandy beaches and ideal sailing conditions for small craft. The region also hosts a sizable tourist trade. Peggy's Cove, for instance, a tiny fishing village on the eastern side of the bay, is said to be the most photographed spot in the province. The name stems from a name bestowed on the area by CHAMPLAIN: Le Port Sainte-Marguerite. In the early days smugglers were frequent visitors to the bay, selling contraband goods, including oil and fish. However, the primary industry was and remains fishing. In the late 1960s and early 1970s St Margaret's Bay was used by marine scientists from the BEDFORD INSTITUTE OF OCEANOGRAPHY in Dartmouth, NS, as a field laboratory for studying the physical and biological processes underlying the productivity of COASTAL WATERS. Among the scientists' conclusions were that the observed counterclockwise circulation in the bay helps flush the bay waters every 10 to 30 days and that wind mixing in the surface layers controls primary-production efficiency.

P.C. SMITH

Ste-Marie, Qué, Town, pop 8937 (1981c), inc 1855, is located on the Rivière CHAUDIÈRE. Situated on lowlands suitable for agriculture, Ste-Marie is one of the oldest settlements in the Beauce region. Built on part of the seigneury given in 1736 to Thomas-Jacques Taschereau, it was inhabited by colonists from the Beaupré shore and from Ile d'ORLÉANS. During the 19th century, Ste-Marie retained its agricultural importance, but progressively became a regional service centre as the construction of the Quebec Central railway sparked the development and settlement of its hinterland. From 1880 to 1940 the wood industry was a major part of its economy. The city now has prosperous industries in the food sector and in metalworking.

CLAUDINE PIERRE-DESCHÊNES

Sainte-Marie, Buffy, folksinger, songwriter (b at Piapot Reserve, Sask 20 Feb 1941). Orphaned by Cree parents, she was raised in the US by a part Micmac family, and in the early 1960s she became an important figure in New York folk music. Since her emergence internationally as a bold social commentator and idiosyncratic singer, she has often returned to Canada for festivals, concerts and broadcasts. Her most popular songs include "Until It's Time for You To Go" and the protest song, "The Universal Soldier." Other songs concern the native peoples' experience in N America.

MARK MILLER

Ste Marie Among the Hurons Roman Catholic mission work among the HURON, begun in 1615 by the Recollets, was renewed in 1634 by the Jesuits with the arrival of 3 priests led by Superior Jean de BRÉBEUF and assisted by 5 domestics. In 1638 Jérôme LALEMANT arrived as the new superior; by 1639 there were 13 fathers active among the Huron and PETUN. Lalemant planned an agriculturally self-sufficient, fortified missionary centre, centrally located in HURONIA, with easy access to the canoe route to Québec. It was to serve as a retreat for the priests and ultimately to become the nucleus of a Huron Christian community.

Construction began in 1639, 5 km SE of present-day MIDLAND, Ont. The structure, dedicated to the Virgin Mary, was named Sainte Marie, or Nostre Dame de la Conception. At its busiest in 1648 it housed 19 priests, 4 lay brothers, 23 donnés, 4 boys, 7 domestics and 8 soldiers. By the late 1640s, besides their missions to the Huron (St Joseph), the Jesuits at Ste Marie also had missions to the Petun (Les Apôtres), the Nipissing (St Esprit), the OJIBWA and OTTAWA (St Pierre) and some Algonquian bands along Georgian Bay (St Charles).

In 1648 the Iroquois began a series of devastating attacks on the Huron and a year later on the Petun (see IROQUOIS WARS). Five Jesuit fathers lost their lives: Antoine Daniel (4 July 1648), Brébeuf (16 Mar 1649), Gabriel Lalemant (17 Mar 1649), Charles Garnier (7 Dec 1649) and Noël Chabanel (8 Dec 1649); all were canonized by Pope Pius XI on 29 June 1930. On 15 May 1649 the mission was withdrawn, and Ste Marie was burned by its occupants lest it fall into Iroquois hands and suffer desecration. A new Ste Marie was built and occupied for one year on Christian I in Lake Huron. With further defeats of the Huron and Petun, and following a severe winter famine, the mission was removed to Québec on 10 June 1650.

Exploratory excavations at Ste Marie were conducted as early as 1855 by Father Felix Martin, S.J. Serious archaeological work began in June 1941, directed by K.E. Kidd for the Royal Ontario Museum and the Jesuit order. Because of budgetary constraints the work ended in 1943, but it had resulted in the excavation and meticulous documentation of most of the mission's central section. Excavation was completed 1947-51 by Wilfrid Jury, then curator of the Museum of Indian Archaeology at U of Western Ontario. In 1964 reconstruction began under Dr Jury for the Ontario government.

The reconstruction has drawn considerable scholarly criticism because Jury's archaeology, and therefore his justification for the reconstruction, have not been made public, and because Kidd's work was ignored. Nevertheless the workmanship and lively interpretive program make Ste Marie an excellent educational and tourist facility. The attached museum begins with an outline of conditions in 17th-century France and proceeds to trace the historical development of Québec, the mission at Ste Marie and life among the Huron. The site is enhanced by a good research library and archaeological laboratory. Although not part of the Ste Marie complex, the adjacent Martyr's Shrine, built 1926 and operated by the Jesuits, attracts PILGRIMS and evokes the spirituality that motivated the founding of Ste Marie. *See* CHRISTIAN RELIGIOUS COMMUNITIES; SAINTS.

C.E. HEIDENREICH

St Mary's Bay, on the S coast of Newfoundland's AVALON PENINSULA between PLACENTIA B and Trepassey B, runs 65 km NE to Colinet Harbour from its mouth between St Shotts and Point Lance, 32 km NW. The bay branches into long harbours and inlets towards its head, with deep indentations cut into its eastern shore. Great Colinet I, 8 km long, is situated at the centre of the bay. Though the climate is better at the head, the 2 principal settlements, Branch and St Vincent's, are towards the bay's mouth, nearer the fine Atlantic fishing grounds. The bay was a traditional French fishing ground until the TREATY OF UTRECHT 1713 after which the coasts were gradually settled by English and Irish. With good forests in the N, the bay saw logging operations in addition to the fishery and some fur trapping. Today the primary occupation of the sparsely populated bay is still fishing.

ROBERT D. PITT

St Mary's Church, Red Deer, Alta (designed by Douglas CARDINAL, completed in 1968), the first building to bring Cardinal wide attention, established themes that have continued through his subsequent work. On a bare suburban site, the church creates a dominating presence by its size, flowing forms and the height of the upward sweeping walls. The interior explains the unfamiliar shape; the entrance wall spirals inward past a circular baptistery to shield a broad, shadowed sanctuary under the downward billowing concrete vault. Two concrete cylinders descend from the vault to shed natural light on the altar and tabernacle areas. The church is a demanding building, the forms unexpected but evocative of things ancient and deep-rooted, both incongruous and appropriate.

MICHAEL McMORDIE

St Mary's River, one of the largest in Nova Scotia, flows into the Atlantic Ocean at a point 190 km E of HALIFAX. It offers excellent opportunities for SPORTFISHING, especially for ATLANTIC SALMON and sea trout. Salmon, in particular, are noted for their heavy runs in spring and early summer. Early French fur traders gave the river its name and in 1655 established a post at Fort Sainte Marie, where the town of Sherbrooke now stands. In addition to the fishing industry, the river is used to transport quantities of pulpwood downstream from Sherbrooke. P.C. SMITH

Saint Mary's University, Halifax, was founded in 1802 to provide higher learning to young Catholic men. Founder Rev Edmund BURKE, later vicar apostolic of Nova Scotia, worked tirelessly but with limited resources to maintain the college. In 1852 the NS Assembly confirmed its legal status in perpetuity, but St Mary's existed precariously for the next half century. In 1913 the Irish Christian Brothers assumed responsibility for the college, directing its affairs until 1940 when they were succeeded by the Society of Jesus (Jesuits). In 1970 the province transferred responsibility for the university from the Archdiocese of Halifax to an independent and lay board of governors. Saint Mary's is now a coeducational institution offering undergraduate programs in arts, science and commerce; preprofessional programs in engineering, medicine, law, dentistry and architecture; and theology, and graduate study in education, business administration, astronomy, history, philosophy, psychology and Atlantic Canada Studies.

COLIN HOWELL

Enrolment: Saint Mary's University, 1982-83 (Source: Statistics Canada)			
Full-time Undergrad	Full-time Graduate	Part-time Undergrad	Part-time Graduate
2 737	81	1 215	213

St-Maurice, Rivière, 563 km long, rises upstream from the GOUIN RÉSERVOIR, 200 km W of Lac SAINT-JEAN, Québec. It drains a basin of 16 700 km². After its confluence with the Manouane R, it feeds the Blanc Reservoir and then takes in the Vermillon, Trenche, Croche, Mattawin and Mékinac rivers. It forms a delta at its

Ste Marie Among the Hurons, Ont, located on the Wye R, east of Midland, is a reconstruction of Ontario's first European community (*photo by Odesse*).

outlet into the St Lawrence R, at TROIS-RIVIÈRES – CAP-DE-LA-MADELEINE.The upper St-Maurice flows through a steeply banked valley marked by glacial erosion. Its angular course is controlled by faults in the Precambrian rocks. Its bed is bordered with alluvial terraces and, downstream from LA TUQUE, cuts through transversal moraines and marine clays. The lower St-Maurice begins at the exit from the Laurentides, at Grandes-Piles. With a rate of discharge of 900 m³/s, it runs through ancient sediments and, in places, through the sedimentary rocks of the St Lawrence platform. It is harnessed at Grand-Mère, Shawinigan Falls and La Gabelle.

The river was a route of human penetration. Several paleo-Indian sites, dating from the 2nd to 17th centuries, have been discovered. In 1535 Jacques CARTIER called it Rivière de Fouez. The delta's 3 channels occasioned the name of the city of Trois-Rivières, founded in 1634 by La Violette to promote the fur trade. The name St-Maurice came in 1668, from the given name of Maurice Poulin de La Fontaine. The iron ore of the marshes of the lower St-Maurice area were exploited at the historic site of Vieilles-Forges and in other foundries from 1737 until 1908 (see FORGES ST-MAURICE). The upper St-Maurice was explored in 1828. Hydroelectric energy and floating log booms made possible the establishment, 1890-1900, of pulp and paper mills and chemical industries in Grand-Mère and SHAWINIGAN. On the upper St-Maurice, the Attikamek live in the villages of Manouane, Weymontachingue and Obedjiwan. SERGE OCCHIETTI

Saint Paul University, *see* UNIVERSITY OF OTTAWA.

St Peter's, NS, UP, pop 669 (1981c), is situated between St Peter's Inlet and St Peter's Bay on the S shore of Cape Breton I. Nicholas Denys established a fortified fishing and trading post here in 1650. It was also used to supply LOUISBOURG with wood. After the fall of the fortress in 1758, LOYALISTS settled here among the remaining French. Farming and fishing were the main activities until 1869, when St Peter's Canal was opened. St Peter's then became important to sailing ships using the 0.8 km long canal as the safest and most efficient route between the Cape Breton interior and the Atlantic Ocean. Today, St Peter's is a quiet village with a few tourist attractions, including a national park and a historic blacksmith shop. The canal is now used mainly by pleasure craft. HEATHER MACDONALD

St Peters, PEI, Village, pop 335 (1981c), 53 km NE of Charlottetown, is located at the head of St Peters Bay. The picturesque village was named after the comte de St-Pierre, who in 1720 was granted control over the Island by French authorities. As in the past, the economy of the surrounding area is dependent upon fishing and farming. St Peters's importance declined after the demise of the shipbuilding industry in the late 19th century. Today the more centrally located village of Morell is the area's important commercial centre. W.S. KEIZER

Saint-Pierre and Miquelon, French islands in the Gulf of ST LAWRENCE, 20 km SW of Burin Peninsula, Newfoundland. Miquelon (215 km²) was once 2 islands. In the mid-1700s, an isthmus formed to Langlade in the S from sand collecting in the wrecks that had foundered on the reefs and sandbars between the islands. The treacherous waters between Langlade and Saint-Pierre were up to 1900 called Gueule d'Enfer — "the Mouth of Hell." Since 1816 alone, 674 shipwrecks have been recorded. About 5600 of the total population of 6200 live on the smaller island of Saint-Pierre, where the capital town of the same name is located.

The islands were likely discovered (about 1520) by Portuguese navigator FAGUNDES, and were claimed formally for France by Jacques

CARTIER 14 years later. They were originally settled by 30 BASQUE and Norman fishermen in 1604, but were uninhabited in 1713 when Britain claimed them under the terms of the TREATY OF UTRECHT. The claim was relinquished under the TREATY OF PARIS, 1763, and France resettled the islands with 350 Acadians who had been deported to France. Britain attacked and captured the islands during the AMERICAN REVOLUTION and again in 1793. France resumed control permanently with the Treaty of Ghent, 1814, resettling the islands with French refugees and some 700 Newfoundlanders.

The rocky islands are barren, except for scrubby yews and junipers, a thin volcanic soil, and dirt removed from ships' ballast. However, the islands have provided France with a station near the richest fishing grounds in N America. By 1866, 4000 French fishermen were coming annually from St Malo, France, to fish in a fleet of 200 schooners. The fleet was devastated in 1904, when France lost its rights to the FRENCH SHORE. During Prohibition, Saint-Pierre was a storage base for Canadian liquor companies and a centre of illegal trade to the US. Today, France is determined to maintain its presence on the islands and spends some $25 million there annually; the per capita aid paid to the islands is the highest in the world. Fishing is still important, as trawlers haul 20 000 tonnes of cod a year from the gulf alone. In recent years, a serious dispute has arisen between France and Canada, as Canada extended its exclusive fishing zone to 15 km (1964) and then to 220 km (1977). France retaliated with a 220 km claim of its own, and the 2 claims are obviously in conflict. JAMES MARSH

St-Quentin, NB, Village, pop 2334 (1981c), inc 1966, located in northern NB in the highlands between the Restigouche and MIRAMICHI rivers and tributaries of the SAINT JOHN R. Originally called Five Fingers, for a local brook, it became Anderson Siding in 1910 after the manager of the newly completed INTERNATIONAL RY, and changed to St-Quentin in 1920 after the WWI battle in France. Early settlers followed the railway construction, established potato farms, sawmills and forest-related industries that still predominate. A major fire destroyed much of the village in 1919. The population is predominately French speaking (98%). A multidisciplinary high school, community college and public library serve the surrounding district. The village is the entrance to Mt Carleton Campground and Resource Park in an area noted for fishing and hunting. BURTON GLENDENNING

St. Roch, wooden schooner powered by sails and an auxiliary engine, launched in N Vancouver in Apr 1928 for ROYAL CANADIAN MOUNTED POLICE operations in the Arctic. Under the command of Sgt Henry A. LARSEN, it sailed 23 June 1940 from Vancouver to traverse the Northwest Passage. Taking a treacherous southerly route through the arctic islands, it was trapped in the ice for 2 winters and did not reach Halifax until 11 Oct 1942. It was the second vessel, after Roald AMUNDSEN's *Gjoa*, to traverse the NORTHWEST PASSAGE, and the first to make the voyage W to E. The *St. Roch* returned to Vancouver by a more northerly route, through LANCASTER SOUND and Barrow Str, in only 86 days (22 July-16 Oct 1944). This voyage made it the first vessel to negotiate the passage both ways. The exploits of the *St. Roch* strengthened Canadian sovereignty

in the Far North. It was purchased by the city of Vancouver in 1954 and permanently berthed at the Maritime Museum. The federal government declared the *St. Roch* a national HISTORIC SITE in 1962. ROGER SARTY

Ste-Scholastique, Qué. Made a parish in 1834, the village of Sainte-Scholastique ceased to exist when land was expropriated in 1969 for the construction of Mirabel Airport. It then became part of the new city of MIRABEL. This former agricultural village in the NW area of the plain of Montréal was, from 1857-1924, the chief town of the judicial district of Terrebonne. Several famous trials were held in its courthouse. A few km S of the village on the Belle R, 4 windmills long dominated communal life; one, the old Sulpician manor built in 1802, still recalls that historic age. When it merged with Mirabel, the village had some 900 inhabitants. Thereafter its life was completely changed by the enormous airport. GILLES BOILEAU

St Stephen, NB, Town, pop 5120 (1981c), is located on the eastern bank of the ST CROIX R in southwestern NB. The site was first occupied during the AMERICAN REVOLUTION by a small band of enterprising settlers in search of timber resources for a mill operation. In 1784 they were joined by elements of the Port Matoon Assn, a group composed mainly of disbanded soldiers from the American conflict. Endowed with excellent facilities for prosecuting the timber trade, St Stephen rapidly developed into a prosperous shipping and shipbuilding centre on the Bay of FUNDY for much of the 19th century. Industrial expansion in the latter half of that century saw the rise of a cotton mill in nearby Milltown, soap and axe factories, and Ganong Bros Ltd, still an international candy manufacturer. In 1973 St Stephen was amalgamated with nearby Milltown to form St Stephen-Milltown (pop 1739, 1981c). ROGER P. NASON

St Thomas, Ont. City, seat of Elgin County, pop 28 165 (1981c), inc 1881, located in SW Ontario, 29 km S of London. In 1803 Thomas TALBOT began to place settlers on a large tract of land he owned N of Lk Erie. St Thomas, est *c*1810, was the capital of the settlement and was named for the eccentric founder of the backwoods colony, who governed it for 50 years. Originally an agricultural centre, it became an important railway town at the turn of the century; by 1911 it was on 7 different rail lines. Today it has an economy marked by diversified light industry. In 1824 the first medical school in Ontario was established there by Charles DUNCOMBE and John Rolph. Nicknamed "The Garden City," it has public parks well known for the their brilliant floral displays. DANIEL FRANCIS

Saint Thomas University, *see* UNIVERSITY OF NEW BRUNSWICK.

Saint-Vallier, Jean-Baptiste de La Croix de Chevrières de, second bishop of Québec, founder of the Hôpital Général at Québec (b at Grenoble, France 14 Nov 1653; d at Québec City 26 Dec 1727). Saint-Vallier was bishop of Québec 1688-1727. He impressed the clergy with his zeal and endless activity, but his arrival 31 July 1688 was followed by 16 years of crisis as the autocratic bishop sought to combat drunkenness, immodest dress, blasphemy, dancing, immorality and profiteering, while encouraging family devotions, church attendance and payment of tithes. He promoted missions in Acadia, Louisiana and Illinois. In a short time, however, he fell out with Governor FRONTENAC (over the performance of *Tartuffe*), with the military, cathedral chapter, Recollets, Jesuits and almost the entire diocese. In return, his adversaries denounced his writings, *Catechism* (1702) and *Ritual* (1703), as heretical, and little effort was made to gain his release when he was captured and imprisoned in England. The harsh internment for 5 years, illness and his ascetic behaviour destroyed his health, and in 1713 he gave up his palace to live in the Hôpital Général, donating his fortune to the poor and selling even his shoes and bed. Despite his faults, Saint-Vallier was a pious man and he undoubtedly contributed to the consolidation of the early Catholic church in America. CORNELIUS J. JAENEN

Saints The first N Americans to be canonized (29 June 1930) in the Catholic Church were the 8 Jesuits martyred by Iroquois in Huronia in the 1640s: Jean de BRÉBEUF, Noël Chabanel, Antoine Daniel, Charles Garnier, René Goupil, Isaac JOGUES, Jean de La Lande and Gabriel Lalemant. Their collective feast day is Oct 18. The first candidate for sainthood born in Canada was Marie-Marguerite d'YOUVILLE (1701-71, beatified 3 May 1959), founder of the Grey Nuns.

During the papacy of John Paul II, who somewhat simplified the canonization process, 7 more Canadians have been canonized or beatified: Marguerite BOURGEOYS (1620-1700, canonized 31 Oct 1982), founder of the Congrégation de Notre-Dame; Brother ANDRÉ, né Alfred Bessette (1845-1937, beatified 23 May 1982) of the Congrégation de la Ste Croix, who was instrumental in the building of St Joseph's Oratory in Montréal; Bishop François de Montmorency LAVAL of Québec City (1623-1708, beatified 22 June 1980), the first Canadian bishop; Mother MARIE DE L'INCARNATION (Marie Guyart) (1599-1672, beatified 22 June 1980), the first Ursuline superior in Canada; Mother MARIE-ROSE, née Eulalie Durocher (1811-49, beatified 23 May 1982), founder of the Soeurs de saints noms de Jésus et de Marie; Kateri TEKAKWITHA (1656-80, beatified 22 June 1980), the first Indian candidate for sainthood; and Mother Marie-Léonie, née Alodie-Virginie Paradis (1840-1912), founder of the Petites Soeurs de la Ste-Famille and the first to be beatified on Canadian soil (during the papal visit on Sept 1984).

To be beatified a person must be shown to have died a martyr's death or lived a life of heroic virtue; beatification bestows the title "Blessed" and authorizes public veneration of the individual within a restricted area, such as the home country. The next step, canonization (the official recognition of sainthood), follows after a prescribed number of subsequent miracles have been attested, and extends the right of public veneration through the whole Catholic Church.

By the early 1980s canonization causes had been begun for at least 17 others. From the Edmonton area there were Bishop Vital Justin GRANDIN of St Albert (1829-1902) and Brother Anthony Kowalczyk, OMI (1866-1947); from The Pas, Man, Bishop Ovide Charlebois (1862-1933), apostolic vicar of Keewatin; and from Ottawa, Elisabeth Bruyère (1818-76) of the Soeurs de la charité d'Ottawa. Those from Montréal were Mother Émilie Gamelin (1800-51), founder of the Soeurs de la Providence; Jérôme Le Royer de La Dauversière (1597-1659); Jeanne MANCE (1606-73); and Mother Marie-Anne (Marie-Esther Blondin) (1809-90) of the Soeurs de Sainte-Anne. From St-Hyacinthe, Qué, were Elisabeth Bergeron (1851-1936) of the Soeurs de St-Joseph and Bishop Louis Zépherin Moreau of St-Hyacinthe

(1823-1901), and from Trois-Rivières, Frédéric Jansoone, OFM (1838-1916). Five candidates were from Québec City: Mother Marie-Catherine de St-Augustin (Catherine de Longpré) (1632-68) of the Hospitalière de la miséricorde de l'Ordre de St-Augustin; Mother Marie de Ste-Cécile de Rome (Dina Bélanger) (1897-1929) of the Congrégation de Jésus et de Marie; Father Alfred Pampalon, CSsR (1867-96); Gérard Raymond (1912-32); and Father Marie-Clément Staub (1876-1936), founder of the Soeurs de Ste-Jeanne d'Arc. Causes were being considered or had already begun for the following as well: Marie de la Ferre (1592-1652); Father Eugène Prévost; Mother Caouette; and Bishop Ignace BOURGET. JOHN RASMUSSEN

Saison dans la vie d'Emmanuel, Une, (1965), by Marie-Claire BLAIS, is a darkly lyrical vision of Québec, an act of revolt distinguished by its black humour. Employing multiple viewpoints and blurring reality with nightmare, Blais narrates events surrounding the winter birth of Emmanuel, sixteenth child of a peasant family. The perspective of his indomitable grandmother Antoinette frames the novel, itself dominated by the autobiographical manuscripts of Emmanuel's brother Jean Le Maigre, an adolescent friar and tubercular genius. The lives and deaths of Emmanuel's siblings, like the themes of incest and corrupt monastic life, constitute an allegory of insularity and ignorance as well as a literal response to cold and hunger. Acclaimed by American critic Edmund Wilson in his preface to Derek Coltman's translation, *A Season in the Life of Emmanuel* (1966), the novel won numerous prizes at home and abroad, and has been translated into a dozen languages. MICHÈLE LACOMBE

Salaberry, Charles-Michel d'Irumberry de, soldier (b at Beauport, Qué 19 Nov 1778; d at Chambly, Lower Canada 27 Feb 1829). A protégé of the duke of Kent, he was commissioned in the British army in 1794, and served in Ireland, the W Indies and the Low Countries during the Napoleonic Wars. Returning to Lower Canada in 1810, he became aide-de-camp to Maj-Gen de Rottenburg. Promoted in the militia 1813, he raised and commanded a troop of Canadien VOLTIGEURS during the WAR OF 1812, repelling an American force and in 1813 turning back another numerically superior American advance on Montréal at the BATTLE OF CHÂTEAUGUAY. Salaberry was retired on half pay in 1815 and was made a Companion of the Bath 2 years later. In 1818 he was appointed to the legislative council of Lower Canada. DAVID EVANS

Salamander, common name for most members of the tailed AMPHIBIA (order Caudata). About 340 species are known worldwide; 19 are native to Canada. Salamanders are found mainly in the temperate regions of the Northern Hemisphere but also occur southward to northern Africa, Iran and northern Burma and to northern S America. In Canada, salamanders occur from the Maritimes to BC and N to central Labrador and northern BC; none have been recorded from Newfoundland. Salamander species vary in size, from 3.9 cm to 180 cm. One of the largest salamanders in Canada is the 43 cm aquatic mudpuppy (*Necturus maculosus*); the smallest is the 5-9 cm four-toed salamander (*Hemidactylium scutatum*). A Chinese giant salamander lived in captivity 52 years and certain species of newts 30 years; however, the life span of some of the smaller species may vary from one to a few years.

Most salamanders resemble LIZARDS and are sometimes erroneously referred to as lizards. However, salamanders lack scales and claws and have moist, glandular skin; true lizards (class Reptilia) have claws and a dry, scaly, cornified skin. All adult salamanders found in Canada have 4 legs; 3 species in southeastern US

Aquatic mudpuppy (*Necturus maculosus*), one of the largest salamanders found in Canada (*courtesy National Museums of Canada/National Museum of Natural Sciences/Charles Douglas*).

have front legs only. Hence, salamanders differ from the limbless, tropical caecilians of the amphibian order Gymnophiona. Salamanders have tails, and teeth in both jaws; thus, they differ from the third group of amphibians, the FROGS, which lack tails and lower teeth. Salamanders can pick up vibrations but are unable to hear. They are generally voiceless, although some utter faint squeaks. Salamanders have 2 nostrils connected to the mouth, eyes often with movable lids, mouth with fine teeth, tongue often protrusible, skeleton largely bony, 3-chambered heart with 2 auricles and one ventricle, and body temperature dependent on environment. They breathe by gills, lungs, mouth lining and skin, sometimes in combination, sometimes separately. Fertilization may be external or internal (internal in all Canadian species). When internal, the male deposits jellylike capsules of sperm; the female picks them up in the lips of the cloaca (chamber through which eggs pass). The eggs are fertilized as they are expelled. All Canadian species lay eggs, the number laid and incubation period varying with each species. Some species deposit eggs in fresh water in a jellylike mass attached to vegetation (mole salamanders); others, under stones in moist places along brooks (dusky salamanders); others, use damp, rotted logs (redback salamanders). Some species of mole salamanders go to ponds, ditches and lakes in early spring to

Salamanders of Canada

Common Name	Scientific Name	Range
yellow spotted salamander	*Ambystoma maculatum*	western Ont to PEI
Jefferson salamander	*A. jeffersonianum*	SW Ont
smallmouth salamander	*A. texanum*	extreme SW Ont
tiger salamander	*A. tigrinum*	southern BC, Man, Sask, Alta, SW Ont
long-toed salamander	*A. macrodactylum*	BC
northwestern salamander	*A. gracile*	western BC
blue-spotted salamander	*A. laterale*	eastern Canada
dusky salamander	*Desmognathus fuscus*	southern Qué and NB
two-lined salamander	*Eurycea bislineata*	Ont, Qué, Lab and NB
four-toed salamander	*Hemidactylium scutatum*	Ont to NS
spring salamander	*Gyrinophilus porphyriticus*	southern Qué
eastern newt	*Notophthalmus viridescens*	Ont to PEI
roughskin newt	*Taricha granulosus*	BC
mudpuppy	*Necturus maculosus*	Qué, Ont, Man
eastern redback salamander	*Plethodon cinereus*	Ont to PEI
western redback salamander	*P. vehiculum*	southern BC
Eschscholtz's salamander	*Ensatina eschscholtzi*	southern BC
clouded salamander	*Aneides ferreus*	Vancouver I, BC
Pacific giant salamander	*Dicamptodon ensatus*	southwestern BC

lay eggs, while stream and woodland species may not deposit until summer. Water-hatching young breathe through gills and may retain these for several years before transforming into adults. Land-hatching young resemble adults.

The species of salamanders found along streams and brooks are known as stream salamanders; those around springs and spring-fed brooklets, as spring salamanders; in wooded areas, as woodland salamanders. The mole salamanders are so-called because they burrow under logs or into the earth. The mudpuppy spends its entire life in water. Larvae and, usually, adult red-spotted newts live in water, but in most parts of their range after the young grow legs they leave the water and spend a year or more on land. At this stage, they are referred to as efts.

All salamanders are carnivorous: larger ones consume earthworms and adults and larvae of many insects; smaller species eat small insects, insect larvae and various small invertebrates. Larvae eat tadpoles, smaller salamander larvae and aquatic invertebrates. Salamanders are probably beneficial to FORESTRY and AGRICULTURE as they consume injurious INSECT PESTS. Fishes, frogs, snakes, turtles, birds and mammals are natural predators. When caught, many salamanders are able to break off their tails. The tail continues to twitch for a short time, allowing the salamander to escape as the pursuer is decoyed into seizing the tail. Salamanders are able to regenerate the tail, but the regenerated part is usually shorter than the original. Most species have mildly poisonous glands in the skin that can cause irritation to some animals; newts, particularly the western species, have strong secretions.

Since they are unable to survive heavy freezing and must burrow in the earth or under leaf litter where frost does not penetrate, terrestrial species hibernate during colder months. Most aquatic species are probably active year round. Most nonaquatic salamanders are active at night, usually during wet or damp periods; dry air and warm sun would quickly dehydrate them. During the spring breeding season, mole salamanders may be found moving at night across highways to ditches and ponds, where they can be observed with the aid of a flashlight. If sticks or rocks are gently turned over along or in a rocky brook or around a spring, stream salamanders and spring salamanders may often be discovered. If moss is carefully removed from rotted logs and stumps, woodland salamanders can be found in moist, wooded areas during the day. A certain number of salamanders are collected each year by scientific institutions for research and by individuals for terrarium pets. Mudpuppies are taken for use in university and high-school biology courses; their capture is regulated in Manitoba. At present, no comprehensive law exists in Canada to protect salamanders; however, as they consume insect pests, protection would be justified.   S.W. GORHAM

Salish, Coastal, see BELLA COOLA; NORTHERN GEORGIA STRAIT COAST SALISH; CENTRAL COAST SALISH.

Salish, Interior Lillooet, Shuswap, Thompson and Okanagan are the 4 native Indian groups in the interior of BC (although Okanagan territory extends into Washington state) who speak languages belonging to the Interior Salish division of the Salishan language family.

Lillooet are divided into 2 main groups, linguistically, culturally and geographically: Upper or Fraser R Lillooet, mainly in the vicinity of the town of LILLOOET on the Fraser R; and Lower or Mt Currie Lillooet, mainly around the community of Mt Currie in the Pemberton Valley. Use of the word "Lillooet" is confusing, as the term actually applies to the Mt Currie people only, who call themselves *LEEL'-wat-OOL'* ("the real, original Lillooet"). The Fraser R Lillooet people refer to themselves as *STLA'-tlei-mu-wh;* they and the Mt Currie people speak slightly different dialects of the same language, known in English as "Lillooet." A third group of Lillooet is marginally recognized: the Lakes Lillooet who live in the vicinity of Seton and Anderson lakes, situated midway between Upper and Lower Lillooet territory.

The Lillooet belong to the Plateau culture area (*see* NATIVE PEOPLES), although the Lower Lillooet were strongly influenced by adjacent Northwest Coast cultures. There are about 3500 Lillooet living on INDIAN RESERVES ranging from Skookumchuck and Mt Currie to Anderson Lk and Seton Lk and from Lillooet, Bridge River and Fountain up the Fraser R as far as Pavilion (which was a Shuswap village until the early 1900s).

Just N of the town of Lillooet is the largest late 20th-century Indian fishery on the Fraser R. Every summer, hundreds of Indian people gather to dip-net sockeye salmon from the turbulent waters. The fish are filleted and hung on covered racks to dry in the warm winds. Indians throughout BC and Washington state travel to Lillooet to barter for this delicacy.

The term "Shuswap" is an anglicization of the native word these people call themselves. The Shuswap are the northernmost Interior Salish group of the Plateau culture area. Formerly their territory was vast, extending from the Rocky Mts in the E to the Fraser R in the W, and ranging from Williams Lk in the N to Armstrong in the S. Shuswap villages are located near the numerous lakes in their territory and in the valleys of the N and S Thompson rivers and their tributaries, as well as along the Fraser R. Today there are approximately 4000 Shuswap Indians living on Indian reserves throughout this large area.

Although the Thompson refer to themselves by the native term *in-thla-CAP'-mu-wh* (sometimes spelled "Ntlakapamux"), they have come to be known as Thompson, after the name of the river that flows through their territory.

The Thompson are divided into 2 main groups: Lower Thompson, extending along the Fraser R canyon from just S of Lytton to an area just S of Spuzzum; and Upper Thompson, consisting of 4 subgroups in an area extending from Lytton and up the Fraser R to about 20 km below Lillooet, and including the Thompson R drainage system from its mouth upriver to Ashcroft, and the Nicola R drainage, including a large area around Merritt. Originally the Merritt and Nicola rivers area had been occupied by the NICOLA-SIMILKAMEEN Athapaskan, but by the late 1800s Thompson and Okanagan had taken over their territory. Today there are about 3500 Thompson living on Indian reserves throughout this territory, but centered mostly in Lytton and Merritt.

The Interior Salish living throughout the OKANAGAN VALLEY and along the Similkameen R are known as Okanagan, although they form part of a larger group now known as "Okanagan-Colville" by some linguists and anthropologists. Okanagan-Colville territory occupies 72 500 km² in S-central BC (70%) and NE Washington state (30%).

The native term *in-seel-ick-CHEEN* refers to all those people who speak the Okanagan-Colville language. In BC this language is known in English as "Okanagan," and in Washington state it is most often called "Colville." There are 7 dialect divisions of the Okanagan-Colville language, of which 3 are (or were, in the case of "Lakes") in BC. "Northern Okanagan" refers to the dialect spoken by Indians living in the vicinity of Okanagan Lk and along the Okanagan R drainage system, and "Similkameen Okanagan" refers to the dialect spoken by Indians living along the Similkameen R (territory formerly occupied by the Nicola-Similkameen Athapaskans). The "Lakes" dialect was formerly spoken by those Indians living along the Upper and Lower Arrow Lks, but by about 1870 these people had moved S across the border and were later allotted land on the Colville Indian Reservation. In 1983 there were about 2500 Okanagan living on Indian reserves in the vicinity of Vernon, Westbank, Penticton, Keremeos and Oliver.

Interior Salish Culture Lillooet, Shuswap, Thompson and Okanagan subsistence was based on a combination of fishing, hunting and gathering of plant foods. The quest for food was regimented by an annual cycle that took groups of people to various localities, the choice of which was determined by the availability of resources.

During the winter months Interior Salish lived in villages consisting of clustered semi-subterranean dwellings known as pit houses. Here they existed on the provisions they had prepared and preserved at other times of the year. These pit houses were constructed in circular holes dug about 2 m deep and about 8 m in diameter. The rafters forming the conical roof of each pit house were thickly insulated with earth and grass to protect the people inside from the cold. Sometimes rectangular or conical tule-mat lodges were used as winter homes by the Interior Salish, but such dwellings were most often used during warmer months.

The basic political unit of Interior Salish society, the village, was governed communally. Within each village there were a number of leaders or chiefs known for their proficiency in such skills as fishing, hunting, war or oratory. However, all adult males had the same rights and responsibilities and took part in decision making. Men and women had clearly defined roles: men hunted, fished and manufactured tools from bone, wood and stone; women prepared food, wove baskets and mats, tanned animal hides for clothes, and looked after small children.

As preparation for adulthood, each child underwent a "vision quest" by training alone in the mountains to receive a guardian spirit power. Such spirit power guided and protected initiates throughout their lives and gave them special skills or supernatural strength or vision. Some guardian spirits were more powerful than others, bestowing upon the receiver the ability, for example, to heal the sick. Every year, through special songs and dances during winter ceremonials, the relationship with guardian spirits was renewed.

Contact with Non-Indians The first contact that Interior Salish had with Europeans occurred in 1793 when Alexander MACKENZIE made his overland journey to the Pacific and met groups of Shuswap near the northernmost extremities of their territory. In 1808, when Simon FRASER descended the river later named after him, he encountered Shuswap, Lillooet and Thompson. The first encounter of Okanagan-speaking Indians in BC with Europeans took place in 1811 in the Arrow Lks area, when David THOMPSON, an explorer for the North West Co, was searching for new supplies of furs.

Beginning in the 1870s, Interior Salish lands were surveyed, Indian reserves were established, and the LAND CLAIMS dispute (which continues to the present time) began. Out of the struggle for recognition of Indian rights there emerged several prominent Interior Salish leaders, notably Chief Michelle of the Thompson, Chief Chillihitza of the Okanagan, Chief David of the Shuswap and, most recently, Chief George Manuel, also a Shuswap. *See also* general articles under NATIVE PEOPLE.

DOROTHY KENNEDY AND RANDY BOUCHARD
Reading: C. Hill-Tout, *The Salish People,* 4 vols (1978); V.F. Ray, *Cultural Relations in the Plateau of Northwestern America* (1939).

Salmo, BC, Village, pop 1169 (1981c), inc 1946, is located on the Salmo R at its junction with Erie Cr, 40 km S of Nelson and 40 km E of Trail.

Known as Salmon River before the Grand Coulee Dam cut off salmon migration (salmo is the zoological generic term for salmon), it lay on the route of the first prospectors to the Nelson area 1862-87. By 1897 a number of mines were operating in the area, and lumbering developed as an associated industry. Since 1972 several mines, accounting for most of the town's production, have shut down, as well as a forest-products operation. Completion of the Creston-Salmo Hwy link in 1963 opened some potential for Salmo as a service centre.   WILLIAM A. SLOAN

Salmon, family of FISH, Salmonidae [Lat *salire,* "to leap"], with soft fin rays, short dorsal fin, adipose (fatty) fin, and teeth in the jaws. The family includes salmon, TROUT and CHAR of the subfamily Salmoninae, the GRAYLINGS of the subfamily Thymallinae and the WHITEFISHES of the subfamily Coregoninae. Salmonids are native to north temperate and subarctic waters. However, because of their tremendous sport-fishing appeal, they have been introduced to all continents except Antarctica. Five genera of Salmoninae are recognized. Two are Eurasian, *Brachymystax* and *Hucho.* Three are found in both hemispheres, including Canada: *Salmo,* the trouts and the ATLANTIC SALMON; *Oncorhynchus,* the PACIFIC SALMON; and *Salvelinus,* the chars. Salmoninae differ from other salmonids in having well-developed teeth in large jaws, and small scales. There is one genus of subfamily Thymallinae (*Thymallus*) and 3 of subfamily Coregoninae (*Stenodus, Prosopium* and *Coregonus*), all in Canada. Grayling and whitefish have weak teeth and larger scales. All salmonids spawn in fresh water, usually in streams; many, especially Pacific salmon, are anadromous, ie, spend their adult lives in the ocean, returning to their native streams to spawn. Unlike other salmonids, Pacific salmon die after spawning. Salmonid eggs, large compared to those of most other fish, vary from yellowish pink to orange-red. Females maintain streamlined head shape throughout life; in many species, males develop a pronounced hook, called a kype, in the jaw before spawning. Salmonids are famous for their ability to home precisely to their place of birth to spawn, and for their fighting and jumping when angled.

In Canada, combined sport and commercial values make the salmonids the most economically important group of wild animals. In 1980 the value of the commercial Pacific salmon industry alone was over $289 million. By 1983 this value had dropped to $104 million due to a decline in the catch of high priced species. Pacific salmon also support a huge sport fishery which increased significantly 1980-84 although it is probable this increase cannot be sustained in the future. The trouts, including Atlantic salmon, have a large sport fishery and a small but growing commercial AQUACULTURE industry. The chars are important as sport fish and support a small commercial industry and subsistence fishery, especially among native peoples of northern Canada. There is a small sports fishery for grayling, primarily in the North. The whitefishes support a commercial fishery in central Canada and a subsistence fishery of considerable importance to native people in the North.   E.D. LANE

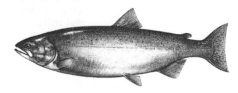
Chinook salmon (*Oncorhynchus tshawytscha*), the largest species of salmon (*courtesy National Museums of Canada/ National Museum of Natural Sciences*).

Salmon Arm, BC, District Muncipality, pop 10 780 (1983e), is located at the head of the SW arm of Shuswap Lk, also called Salmon Arm, 525 km E of Vancouver and 110 km E of Kamloops. Best known for its fruit and dairy farming and as a vacation spot, the area was settled relatively recently. It was originally the home of Shuswap Indians. A GOLD RUSH in the 1860s brought prospectors into the region briefly, but exploration did not begin until 1871 when a route was surveyed for the CPR. Settlement came in the late 1880s with the railway, mixed and fruit farming, and logging and lumbering. Settlement boomed from 1905 to 1912 — the year it was incorporated as a city. Today lumber, tourism, fruit and dairy farming and provincial and federal government agencies are the major employers. A satellite campus of Okanagan College is located here, and the municipality has a museum, a historical society and an active theatre group with a winter and summer season.
JOHN R. STEWART

Salmonella, genus of bacteria of the family Enterobacteriaceae, members of which are commonly found in the intestinal tract of humans and other animals. It is named after D.E. Salmon, the American bacteriologist who described it in 1885. For almost 100 years salmonellae have been recognized as important in causing food-borne disease and water-borne disease. The salmonellae can be divided into 3 groups based on host preference. Those primarily adapted to humans include the typhoid and paratyphoid organisms that have long incubation periods (10-21 days), cause high fever, invade the bloodstream, require a slow convalescence, and have a higher proportion of carriers (ie, asymptomatic victims who excrete the organism) than salmonellae in other groups. Those primarily adapted to animal hosts include *S. choleraesuis* (pigs), *S. dublin* (cattle) and *S. pullorum* (chickens). Only the first 2 serotypes are significant for human illness. Salmonellae not adapted to any specific host include the more than 1700 serotypes with the potential for causing human salmonellosis, a form of gastroenteritis. *S. typhimurium* is the serotype causing most salmonellosis in Canada and other countries. Diarrhea, abdominal cramps, fever, nausea and vomiting occur 8-48 hours after consumption of as few as 100 organisms. Patients typically recover after a few days, but infants and elderly persons can be seriously ill and occasionally may die.

Salmonellosis probably costs Canadians $40-160 million (1984 dollars) annually in total medical care and economic loss. Increased foreign trade and travel have brought in serotypes from other countries and the increased demand for highly processed animal products and interprovincial distribution have made salmonellae widespread in the Canadian environment (eg, in 1982 about 60% of poultry carcasses contained the organism). Foods associated with salmonellosis in Canada have been turkeys, chickens, salami, products made with cracked eggs, chocolate candy, pepper and cream pies. Salmonellae are difficult to eliminate from the environment and, once they come in contact with suitable food, can multiply rapidly, provided the temperature is suitable. Prevention of illness depends on decreasing the source of the organism (eg, salmonellae-free animal feed), reducing the chances of cross-contamination in the processing plant or kitchen, and not allowing growth to take place by keeping the food either cold (4°C or less) or hot (60°C or more).
EWEN TODD

Salt Neither sodium nor chlorine can exist alone in natural form, but together they form the stable compound sodium chloride (NaCl), or common salt, known to geologists as halite. Salt crystallizes as colourless cubes. In 1866, Samuel Platt drilled for oil near Goderich, Ont. Although oil eluded him, he struck a thick bed of clean, white salt, part of the geological formation now known as the Michigan Basin, which underlies much of southwestern Ontario. In western Canada, salt beds extend in a broad belt from southwestern Manitoba to northern Alberta. The Atlantic provinces are underlain by a sedimentary basin containing thick pockets of salt. Underground deposits of rock salt are recovered either by conventional room and pillar MINING, with subsequent milling and refining at the surface, or by the brine method, where water is injected into deposits at depth and the resulting saturated solution is pumped to the surface. Salt is an essential part of the human and animal diet, aiding digestion, but over-consumption is widely held to be a cause of hypertension and heart disease. It is used as a seasoning and in curing meats and preserving fish. Manufacture of salt is one of the oldest chemical industries and salt was used as currency in ancient times. Canada is the world's largest per capita consumer of salt, largely because it is widely used to improve winter driving conditions (it melts ice and snow). The CHEMICAL INDUSTRY uses NaCl to manufacture chlorine, caustic soda and soda ash, which are used in the production of soaps, fibres, PETROCHEMICALS, etc. Canada ranks 7th among world producers and could easily supply the total Canadian requirement, but the expense of transporting such a high-bulk product over great distances makes trade, particularly with the US, more economical in some areas. However, exports are consistently higher than imports.   HELEN R. WEBSTER

Salter, Robert Bruce, orthopedic surgeon (b at Stratford, Ont 15 Dec 1924). One of the most widely travelled and best-known orthopedic surgeons in the English-speaking world, Salter has taught in 30 countries and is recognized for innovative methods of orthopedic treatment, including the Salter operation for children and young adults with congenitally deformed or diseased hips. Appointed to the Hospital for Sick Children in Toronto in 1955, he became chief of orthopedic surgery in 1957 and surgeon in chief in 1966. In 1976 he became senior orthopedic surgeon and project director of the hospital's research institute and head of orthopedic surgery at U of T. In the late 1970s he originated the method of stimulating cells to produce cartilage by continuous passive motion. He has written over 100 articles in scientific journals and a textbook on the musculoskeletal system. His honours include the Gairdner International Award for Medical Science.   J. KNELMAN

Saltspring Island is the largest of the GULF ISLANDS, a group lying in the Str of Georgia off the SE corner of VANCOUVER I, BC. Before the arrival of Europeans, several Indian groups gathered a variety of foods among the islands. The first permanent settlers were black immigrants from the US who arrived in the 1850s and began one of the earliest agricultural communities in the region. The island became known for its sheep, fruit and dairy products. Today it has a permanent population of about 4000, with many more enjoying its beautiful coastal waters each summer. Ganges, a harbour on the E coast, is the largest town in the Gulf Is. Bruce Peak, at 690 m the highest mountain in the group of islands, towers above the W coast. The island is named for brine pools in its interior.   DANIEL FRANCIS

Salut Galarneau! (1967), by Jacques GODBOUT, is cast in the first person as the diary of François Galarneau, a working-class rebel who owns and operates a hot-dog stand in the Montréal suburb of Ile-Perrot. Interweaving the story of his "failed" personal life, narrated piecemeal and randomly, and his "naïve" observations about his society, conveyed by the author with satiric insight and poetic power, Galarneau's diary is begun as a pastime suggested by his mistress but soon acquires the resilient humour of an existential act. Jilted and feeling increasingly alienated from his surroundings, the hot-dog king immures himself behind a brick wall of his own fabrication, but finally cannot resist keeping a ladder, if only to renew his supply of notebooks. A warm and witty allegory of Québec and of the artist's role in Québec society, *Salut Galarneau!* won the Governor General's Award and was translated by Alan Brown as *Hail Galarneau!* (1970). MICHÈLE LACOMBE

Salvation Army "Soup to Salvation" was the response of disaffected METHODIST preacher William Booth in 1865 to "the bitter cry of outcast London." From it emerged the Salvation Army, dedicated to the physical and spiritual reclamation of lost humanity: "soup" soon included men's hostels, women's shelters, farm colonies and similar institutions; "salvation" was preached along Methodist lines by an army of officers — with flags, bands and war songs — seeking out their congregations in the slums. By century's end the Army had become a permanent feature of English society and had invaded many other countries as well. The Army came to Canada in 1882. Introduced by such zealots as Mr and Mrs William Freer (Toronto) and Jack Addie and Joe Ludgate (London), Army Corps sprang up in every major Ontario town. By 1886 the corybantic religion was being practised from Victoria to St John's, although its unusual methods of worship — "hallelujah joy-jigs," free-and-easy meetings, noisy open-airs — raised considerable ire and resulted in some legal battles. But eventually, through persistent social welfare work, the Army won nationwide respect. In 1886 the Rescue Home for "fallen" girls opened in Toronto, followed by similar homes in Winnipeg, Montréal and Victoria. In 1891 the Army opened its first Prison Gate Home to house and rehabilitate released prisoners, and soon children's shelters, prison farms and men's hostels were added. In 1904 the first Grace Hospital opened in Winnipeg; in 1905 an Army officer became the first Dominion Parole Officer; that year the Army's first emigrants sailed from England and by 1914 more than 150 000 had settled in Canada under its sponsorship.

Today the Army maintains its dual social and evangelical purpose. It is a recognized church, with some 120 000 members who, though less evangelical than their forebears, still espouse a Methodist theology with strong adherence to teetotalism and withdrawal from "worldliness." Bands and timbrels still make feet tap and hearts stir. The Social Wing offers language classes for new Canadians, new development programs on behalf of the CANADIAN INTERNATIONAL DEVELOPMENT AGENCY, parole supervision, Harbour Light centres for alcoholics, Sunset lodges, Grace hospitals, fresh air camps for underprivileged children, drug addiction counselling and a willing hand in times of need. The Army's motto still is "With heart to God, and hand to man." R.G. MOYLES
Reading: R.G. Moyles, *The Blood and Fire in Canada* (1977).

Samson, first locomotive in N America to burn coal and the first to run over all-iron rails. Built in New Shildon, Eng, it was shipped to Pictou, NS, to haul coal from the Albion Mines 9.6 km over a tramway to Dunbar Point on Pictou Harbour. The railway, built of cast-iron rails believed to be the first rails manufactured in N America, was officially opened 19 Sept 1839. The *Samson* was one of 3 locomotives and it was in service for nearly 30 years. Exhibited at the Chicago World's Fair in 1893, it was eventually returned to NS and is on display in New Glasgow. JAMES MARSH

Samuel, Lewis, merchant, philanthropist (b at Kingston upon Hull, Eng 1827; d at Victoria 10 May 1887). He founded the organized Jewish community of Toronto, and was a prime mover in establishing in 1856 the first synagogue in Canada W — the Toronto Hebrew Congregation (now Holy Blossom Temple). An orthodox Jew, he served almost continuously as its president 1862-80, fighting to maintain traditional practices, then under attack from reformers. With his brother Mark and A.D. Benjamin, he operated a wholesale metals firm, M. & L. Samuel, Benjamin and Co, which exported a variety of Canadian raw materials in exchange for gas chandeliers, metals, chemicals, glass and marble. An enthusiastic supporter of the British connection, he belonged to the Sons of England Benefit Soc and the St George's Soc. He also served as president of the Mechanics' Institute, precursor of the Toronto Public Library, in the late 1870s. STEPHEN A. SPEISMAN
Reading: Stephen A. Speisman, *The Jews of Toronto* (1979).

Sand and Gravel, unconsolidated, granular mineral materials produced by the natural disintegration of ROCK caused by weathering. The terms sand, gravel, clay and silt relate to grain size rather than composition. Sand is material passing a number 4 (4.76 mm) sieve and remaining on a number 200 (74 μm) sieve. Gravel is granular material remaining on a number 4 sieve and ranging up to about 9 cm. Material finer than 200 mesh is called silt or clay, depending on the particle size. Sand and gravel are used as fill, base and finish material for highway construction, coarse and fine aggregates in concrete and asphalt production, and fine aggregates in mortar and concrete blocks. They are also used as backfill in mines, along with cement and mill tailings. Sand is also used in the manufacture of glass, pottery and bricks and in water filtration. "Sandy" soils are favourable to certain types of agriculture. Deposits are widespread throughout Canada and large producers have established plants as close to major consuming centres as possible. In addition to large aggregate operations, usually associated with some phase of the CONSTRUCTION INDUSTRY, many small producers serve local markets. Exploitation is generally by power shovel or loader and trucks or conveyor systems; processing consists of washing, crushing and screening. Production in Canada, valued at nearly $550 million, contributed about 1.7% to the GNP in 1981. *See* CEMENT INDUSTRY. D.H. STONEHOUSE

Sandon, BC, Ghost Town, pop 4 (1983e), is located in the Slocan Valley, West Kootenay, 13 km E of New Denver. Known as the "Silver City of the Slocan" when a prosperous mining community, it was once the centre of one of the richest silver-lead producing regions in the province. Set in a narrow gulch, split by a fast-flowing creek and surrounded by high, steep mountains, it was vulnerable to avalanches, fire and floods. But the mountains contained silver-lead mines, the base of its economy and source of its origin in 1892. Founded by prospectors, the small camp was made the terminus of 2 railway branch lines in 1895 and boomed in 1896. It was incorporated as a city 1898, peaked in 1900 (pop 2000) and disincorporated in 1920. During WWII it was a relocation centre for Japanese from the coast. For the few remaining residents, the end came in 1955 when the creek overflowed, causing much damage. A few buildings remain; one is now a museum. Though some mines are still being worked, most of the mine employees live elsewhere. C.M. YOUNG

Sandpiper, common name for family (Scolopacidae) of SHOREBIRDS that includes true sandpipers, SNIPE, TURNSTONES, WOODCOCKS, curlews (*see* ENDANGERED ANIMALS), dunlin, godwits, knots, sanderling, surfbirds, tattlers, yellowlegs and

willets. Typical sandpipers have been classified recently in a separate tribe, Calidridini (23 species). Species commonly seen in Canada include spotted, solitary, semipalmated, white-rumped and pectoral sandpipers (*Actitis macularia, Tringa solitaria, Calidris pusilla, C. fuscicollis, C. melanotos,* respectively) and dunlin (*C. alpina*). Sandpipers are distinguished from PLOVERS by their proportionately longer and thinner bills, elongated legs, cryptically coloured plumage, and hind toe (in all but sanderling, *C. alba*). They range in size from the 21 g least sandpiper (*C. minutilla*) to the 200 g great knot (*C. tenuirostris*). True sandpipers breed at high latitudes in the Northern Hemisphere and undertake long MIGRATIONS, wintering in Australia, New Zealand, Asia, Africa and S America. After breeding season they gather in flocks of one or more species. In flight these flocks are remarkable for the precision with which they wheel and turn. The alternate flashing of white ventral plumage and grey dorsal plumage seems to confuse BIRDS OF PREY by making it difficult to single out an individual for attack. Sandpipers have various soft calls that have earned them the popular name "peeps" in N America. No other group of birds has such diverse breeding systems. Most sandpipers are monogamous, laying 1-2 clutches per breeding season; some (eg, dunlin) are polyandrous with different males incubating successive clutches laid by one female; others (eg, pectoral and white-rumped sandpipers) are polygynous with one male mating with more than one female. A clutch usually contains 4 eggs (range 2-5). Incubation takes 18-32 days, depending on species. Young leave the nest soon after hatching. Like plovers, sandpipers guard young and often use distraction displays to lure predators away from eggs or chicks. A.J. BAKER

Sangster, Charles, editor, poet (b at Kingston, UC 16 July 1822; d there 9 Dec 1893). Sangster's first job was with the Ordnance in Kingston. Simultaneously he held a position with the local *British Whig*. In 1849 he became full-time editor of the Amherstburg *Courier* but soon returned to the *Whig* as subeditor. At this time he published his first poetry, in the *Literary Garland*, followed by publication of his only 2 volumes, *The St Lawrence and the Saguenay and Other Poems* (1856) and *Hesperus and Other Poems and Lyrics* (1860).

With his appointment to the Ottawa Post Office (1868) Sangster's life became characterized by overwork, ill health and scant literary output. He published 16 poems during the 1870s, most of which display a distraught, melancholy introspection. Between his 1886 retirement and his death he laboured on revised editions of his 2 volumes and prepared 2 others, *Norland Echoes and Other Strains and Lyrics* and *The Angel Guest*. His poetry distinguishes him as a lover and keen observer of the natural world. He displays overwhelming passion in some poems and equally extreme melancholy in others. Whatever his mood he is consistently and intensely serious and deeply religious. MARLENE ALT

Sanikiluaq, NWT, Hamlet, pop 383 (1981c), is located on the BELCHER ISLANDS in HUDSON BAY, 2092 air km SE of YELLOWKNIFE. The original INUIT inhabitants of the barren Belcher Islands were expert kayak men. Because there were few caribou, they made frequent use of bird skins for clothing. The first European in the area was Henry HUDSON, who sighted the islands in 1610. Today the Inuit residents of Sanikiluaq have an economy based on domestic fishing, trapping and the production of distinctive soapstone carvings. ANNELIES POOL

Sapir, Edward, anthropologist, linguist, essayist (b at Lauenburg, Ger 26 Jan 1884; d at New Haven, Conn 4 Feb 1939). A brilliant anthropologist, Sapir pioneered studies of language and culture and of the psychology of culture. He was the first chief of the GEOLOGICAL SURVEY OF CANADA's division of anthropology, the only professional base for anthropological research in Canada 1910-25.

While he was training at Columbia under Franz BOAS, anthropology and linguistics were in their early stages of professional maturity. Sapir brought to this formative period a scope of interest, expertise and depth of intuition that are unequalled. He combined an extraordinarily fine analysis with an awareness of the vital unity of all aspects of communication and culture and of the essentially human nature in which all languages and cultures are firmly rooted. For him, anthropology did not describe the exotic, but rather rediscovered, in a new idiom, the normal, the human. His book *Language* (1921) presents to general readers and specialists alike the scope, nature and cultural contributions of speech and writing; it is still authoritative. He left Canada for university posts in 1925, but his career was cut short by illness and his major work, to have been titled "The Psychology of Culture," was never written. He published over 400 articles, reviews and poems, and international recognition came during his lifetime. He was a fascinating teacher, and his writings have inspired later generations of scholars with the central importance of understanding the human condition as a historical whole.   R.J.PRESTON

Reading: D.G. Mandelbaum, ed, *Selected Writings of Edward Sapir in Language, Culture, and Personality* (1949) and *Edward Sapir: Culture, Language and Personality: Selected Essays* (1958).

Sapp, Allen, artist (b at Red Pheasant IR, Sask 2 Jan 1929). As a child, his favourite activity was drawing and sketching. He moved from the Plains Cree reserve to N Battleford, Sask, in 1960 to pursue a career as a professional artist. In 1966 Dr A.B. Gonor arranged for him to be tutored by Wynona Mulcaster of Saskatoon. Many regard Sapp as one of Canada's foremost native painters because of the sense of melancholic emotion that infuses his paintings. His paintings portray the Plains Cree people in their daily activities of the 1930s and 1940s. He sees his people as poor, but with a sense of awareness about themselves.   JOHN ANSON WARNER

Reading: John Anson Warner and Thecla Bradshaw, *A Cree Life: The Art of Allen Sapp* (1977).

Allen Sapp, *Where I Used to Live* (1969), acrylic on canvas (*courtesy Glenbow Museum/Allen Sapp*).

Sarah Binks, by U of Manitoba professor Paul Hiebert, was published 1947 in Toronto. Sarah Binks, the Sweet Songstress of Saskatchewan, holds in thrall the hearts of those for whom she has immortalized the "Saskatchewanesque" voice in Canadian letters. Sarah's accomplishments are legend: founder of the influential "geo-literary" school of Canadian verse; creator of such heart-rending lyrics as "Hiawatha's Milking"; winner of Saskatchewan's highest poetic honour — the Wheat Pool Medal — for her epic "Up From the Magma and Back Again"; dead, tragically young, of mercury poisoning from a cracked thermometer. Hiebert judiciously traces the complex and subtle interweaving of

Binksian Life and Art; his definitive biography memorializes the imperishable power, beauty and grace of the Binksian oeuvre. Long, loud may she sing.   NEIL BESNER

Sarcee, an Athapaskan or DENE tribe whose reserve adjoins the SW city limits of Calgary. Their name is believed to have originated from a Blackfoot word meaning boldness and hardiness. The Sarcee people call themselves *tsúùt'inà,* translated literally as "many people" or "every one (in the tribe)." Following the signing of Treaty No 7 in 1877, the Sarcee moved to their present 280 km² reserve (*see* INDIAN RESERVE).

According to legend, the Sarcee split from a northern tribe, probably the BEAVER, and moved to the plains, where they have maintained close contact with the BLACKFOOT, CREE and STONEY. Their acculturation to the Plains culture distinguishes them from other northern Dene people, but they have retained their Athapaskan language. Capt PALLISER estimated the Sarcee population at 1400 during his journey of 1857 to 1860. Epidemics of smallpox (1837), scarlet fever (1864) and other diseases as well as wars reduced the number to 400-450 by the time they settled on the reserve. By 1924 the population had decreased to about 160. In 1980 there were about 730 on the reserve (including some non-Sarcees).

Sarcee with travois (*courtesy McCord Museum, McGill University*).

When Diamond JENNESS visited the reserve in 1921 the tribe consisted of 5 bands: Big Plumes, Crow Childs, Crow Chiefs, Old Sarcees and Many Horses. Before they were confined to the reserve, each BAND, led by a chief, camped in TIPIS and hunted along the edge of the forest during the winter. During summer all bands met in the open prairie to hunt buffalo, collect berries and engage in ceremonies, dances and festivals (*see* BUFFALO HUNT; SUN DANCE). The Sarcee believed in supernatural power that could be obtained through a vision or dream and enshrined in a medicine object (beaver bundle, pipe bundle) or a tipi painting (*see* MEDICINE BUNDLE). The quest for supernatural power, for bravery (men) and chastity (women) was highly valued. Marriages were usually arranged by the family and the gifts exchanged reflected family status.

Well-known leaders include Chief Bull Head, who reluctantly signed Treaty No 7, and Chief David Crowchild, a distinguished contemporary leader. The band is governed by an elected chief and counsellors. Though Sarcees have in recent years taken an active part in modern industries, and in cattle raising and real estate, efforts are being made to revive the traditional culture and life-style. The Sarcee Culture Program records historical, folkloric and linguistic material. Although many people attend one of the 2 churches (Anglican and Catholic) on the reserve, and children attend public or separate schools in Calgary, they observe native ceremonies and feasts, such as the Beaver Bundle Ceremony (spring), the Rock Pile Feast (summer) and the Christmas Powwow. Their annual Indian Days celebration draws people from across the continent, and their participation has become an integral part of the CALGARY STAMPEDE. *See also* NATIVE PEOPLE, PLAINS and general articles under NATIVE PEOPLE.   EUNG-DO COOK

Reading: D. Jenness, *The Sarcee Indians of Alberta* (1938).

Sardine, name applied to various small fishes packed in oil. The true sardine from France, Spain and Portugal is usually the young pilchard. In Canada small HERRING are used.

Sarnia, Ont, City, pop 50 892 (1981c), inc 1914, is located at the convergence of the St Clair R and Lk Huron, 100 km W of London. A railway tunnel beneath the St Clair, car ferries and a highway bridge from nearby Point Edward connect Sarnia with Port Huron, Mich. Sarnia is a petrochemical centre and the southern terminus of an oil pipeline from Alberta. Its government is of the city-manager type, with mayor and council elected every 3 years.

History Father HENNEPIN recorded that La Salle's expedition lay becalmed near here in 1679. Some 120 years later French settlers began to arrive. After the crown settlement with local Ojibwa in 1827, an English-speaking community formed, called The Rapids until 1836 when it was named Port Sarnia after Sarnia Township. Sir John Colborne is said to have named the township Sarnia because that is the Latin name for Guernsey where he had been governor before his appointment to Canada. "Port" was dropped from the name when the town was incorporated in 1857. In 1858 the GREAT WESTERN RY extended its line from London to Sarnia and ran ferries across the St Clair. The GRAND TRUNK RY put a line into Point Edward in 1859. When the St Clair Tunnel opened in 1891, the car ferries stopped running for some years, and Point Edward declined as a rail centre.

Primitive oil refining started in Sarnia after the first commercial oil well on the continent went into production in 1858 at Oil Springs, 36 km SE. In 1898 Imperial Oil Co moved to Sarnia from Petrolia, 26 km SE, and built a refinery. During WWII Polymer Corp, now Polysar, built a synthetic-rubber plant here. In its wake numerous petrochemical plants were built, the latest being Petrosar, opened in 1978. The population of 18 000 before Polysar was almost tripled in the next decade. In 1951 the city annexed part of Sarnia Township and all of the St Clair Indian Reserve.

Economy The PETROCHEMICAL INDUSTRY depends on oil and gas from Alberta, local salt, abundant fresh water and the Great Lks shipping facilities. Products include gasoline, fuels, components for plastics and textiles, rubber, chemicals and insulation. During peak construction in the 1970s, the work force numbered over 7000; it is now about 2200. The city lies in an agricultural district, and because of its location attracts tourists.

Townscape The shores of Sarnia Bay, an inlet of the St Clair R formerly devoted to lumbering and salt wells, were changed by dredging and filling in 1927 to provide for grain elevators. Docks are accessible to the largest ships on the lakes. Most public buildings are recent, including the public library, which houses over 300 pieces of Canadian art. Sarnia was the home of Alexander MACKENZIE, first Liberal prime minister of Canada.   JEAN ELFORD

Sarrazin, Michel, surgeon, physician, naturalist (b at Nuits-sous-Beaune, France 5 Sept 1659; d at Québec C 8 Sept 1734). He came to NEW FRANCE in 1685 and the following year was appointed surgeon-major to the colonial regular troops. He later studied medicine in France for 3 years and returned to Québec in 1697 as king's physician.

Keenly interested in natural history by this time — he had been introduced to BOTANY by scientist Joseph Pitton de Tournefort — he spent the next 30-odd years collecting specimens of plants and minerals, and dissecting and reporting on Canadian animals and natural life to Tournefort and other members of the Académie royale des sciences of Paris. Sarrazin became a corresponding member of the Académie in 1699. He was the first to collect and catalogue plant specimens systematically and his HERBARIUM, which did not survive, may have reached 800 in number. Duplicates of most are found, however, in various collections in Paris. *See* FLORAS and BOTANICAL JOURNALS.   BERNARD BOIVIN

Saskatchewan is the only province with entirely man-made boundaries; it lies between the 49th and 60th parallels of latitude, bordered by the US and the Northwest Territories; and between long 101° 30' and 102°W and 110°W, bordered by Manitoba and Alberta. It was created from the North-West Territories in 1905, at the same time as Alberta, and shares with that province the distinction of having no coast on salt water. The name, which was first used officially for a district of the North-West Territories in 1882, is derived from an anglicized version of a Cree word denoting a swiftly flowing river, which appears in a variety of spellings in early records. When the prairie region was being made into provinces, the largest part of the old district bearing the name was incorporated into the new province. Saskatchewan, unlike the 3 provinces immediately E of it, is still the same size as it was when created: in round numbers, 1225 km long, 630 km wide across the S, and 445 km across the N. Its area is 651 900 km² , of which 12% is fresh water.

Land and Resources

The Precambrian SHIELD, running diagonally SE across Saskatchewan, from above 57° latitude to almost 54°, covers approximately the northern third of the province. The Shield is characterized by rugged rock exposures and many lakes, and includes a sandy region S of Lk Athabasca. South of the Shield, also diagonal from W to E, is the area commonly called the "grain belt," level or gently rolling plains marked by fertile soils that make Saskatchewan one of the world's great wheat producers. On the western boundary and across the SW corner is another plains region of generally higher altitudes, with rolling and hilly terrain distinct from that of the grain belt. In the extreme SW the province shares with Alberta the CYPRESS HILLS, the highest point of land in Canada E of the Rocky Mts. Much of Saskatchewan's landscape consists of undulating slopes, unlike the flat horizons featured in the stereotyped image of the Prairies.

Geology Large areas of Saskatchewan once formed the bottom of a sea that departed millions of years ago. In geological terms much of the modern landscape is relatively young, having been shaped during the quaternary era, ie, within the last million years. The oldest formations, the Precambrian, predated the sea, and there is evidence of impressive mountain ranges that eroded over time into the plains characteristic of today. Erosion, molten and other uprisings, the ebb and flow of the sea and its attendant water courses all contributed in different geological eras to the development of the formations in which are now found the grain belt, gas and oil fields, and deposits of salt, clays, coals, potash and other valuable minerals. The main geological influence of the quaternary era in Saskatchewan was GLACIATION, which variously polished and scarred substantial areas of exposed rock, and left rich sediments elsewhere. The glaciers moved SW across the land, leaving behind lakes that at their largest covered most of the province, and marking the landscape with

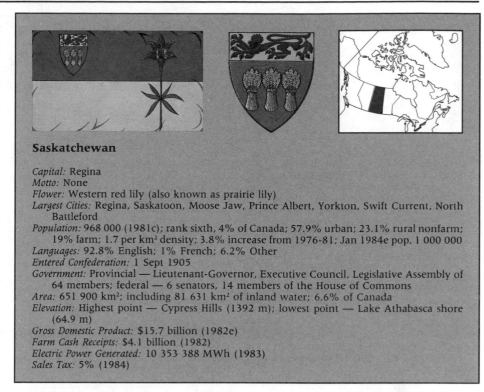

Saskatchewan

Capital: Regina
Motto: None
Flower: Western red lily (also known as prairie lily)
Largest Cities: Regina, Saskatoon, Moose Jaw, Prince Albert, Yorkton, Swift Current, North Battleford
Population: 968 000 (1981c); rank sixth, 4% of Canada; 57.9% urban; 23.1% rural nonfarm; 19% farm; 1.7 per km² density; 3.8% increase from 1976-81; Jan 1984e pop, 1 000 000
Languages: 92.8% English; 1% French; 6.2% Other
Entered Confederation: 1 Sept 1905
Government: Provincial — Lieutenant-Governor, Executive Council, Legislative Assembly of 64 members; federal — 6 senators, 14 members of the House of Commons
Area: 651 900 km²; including 81 631 km² of inland water; 6.6% of Canada
Elevation: Highest point — Cypress Hills (1392 m); lowest point — Lake Athabasca shore (64.9 m)
Gross Domestic Product: $15.7 billion (1982e)
Farm Cash Receipts: $4.1 billion (1982)
Electric Power Generated: 10 353 388 MWh (1983)
Sales Tax: 5% (1984)

drumlins, eskers and moraines that are still visible, some of them more readily from the air. (The buildings on U of Saskatchewan's campus are made largely of multicoloured stone deposited by the glaciers.) At one time or another the glaciers touched all of Saskatchewan except for two small pockets of high land in the extreme S, which still have flora and fauna showing significant variations from their counterparts in the rest of the province. The last glaciers melted in the S approximately 23 000 years ago, and further N as recently as 12 000 years ago.

Surface Generally inhospitable to agriculture because of the climate and thin soil, the northern third of the province is marked by swamp and muskeg, lichened rock, and forest characteristic of the Shield. The altitudes of the grain belt drop markedly from W to E, and from S to N; levels of 600 and 900 m above sea level, common in the W and S, slope to 150 and 300 m in the E and N, causing the province's extensive river systems to flow to Hudson Bay. The soils permit agricultural settlement in what is roughly the southern half of the province; in the northern half the climate is inimical to the use of what little arable land there is. The cultivated areas of the southern portion depend on a variety of soils, predominantly brown and black, whose texture ranges from loamy sands to clays.

Saskatchewan's natural vegetation is divided from N to S into 6 fairly distinct zones, all of which cross the province diagonally SE. A band of subarctic forest tundra exists along the northern boundary, and S of that is a broad region of northern coniferous forest, with a third band of mixed woods below that. The northern agricultural belt is aspen parkland, the central is midgrass prairie, and the southernmost is short grass prairie. Each of the 6 zones corresponds roughly to particular soil deposits. Soil erosion is a continuing problem in the province, the broad river systems providing one type, the winds, so well known that they are a familiar element in prairie literature, creating another.

Water A superficial view of maps of Saskatchewan suggests that the province has an abundance of WATER, both on the surface and in aquafers occurring at varying depths, and in important ways the abundance is real. The province is drained by parts of 4 major basins,

the Mackenzie and Churchill in the N, the Saskatchewan and Qu'Appelle-Assiniboine in the S. The larger aquafers are estimated to be capable of yielding about 10% of the annual flow of the South SASKATCHEWAN R. But aquafers can be tapped only through technology that may be expensive, with individual wells generally not large producers; and much of the most accessible surface water is in the N, where agricultural settlement is minimal.

Both agriculture and industrial development (particularly the production of potash) require large amounts of water, and Saskatchewan is heavily dependent on river flows and precipitation, neither of which is amenable to provincial control. The river systems in the agricultural sector utilize water that comes mainly from snow melt in the Rocky Mts, and snowfall there is subject to wide variations. Precipitation within the province is similarly unreliable, and what does arrive may suffer high rates of evaporation. A characteristic feature of the Saskatchewan farming landscape is the dugout, a large excavation designed to catch the spring runoff from the fields.

Annual precipitation in the province varies enormously, both for the province as a whole and for the differing zones within it. The celebrated drought of the 1930s was intensive and widespread, but it was most severe in the S and diminished northwards into the parkland. The average annual precipitation runs from a few centimetres to 60 or more, the fall generally becoming increasingly heavy from the SW to the NE. Irrigation, although the province's terrain in many areas seems adaptable to it, has not progressed far beyond the experimental stage; much was expected from the elongated Diefenbaker Lake backed up behind the Gardiner Dam on the South Saskatchewan R, but irrigation developments have been small.

Climate The climate of Saskatchewan can in one year include many extremes. Three main climatic zones, corresponding roughly to the main zones of vegetation, cross the province, and range from cold snowy areas in the N, which have brief summers, through more moderate areas in the grain belt, to semi-arid steppes in the SW. Jan temperatures below -50°C and July temperatures above 35°C have been re-

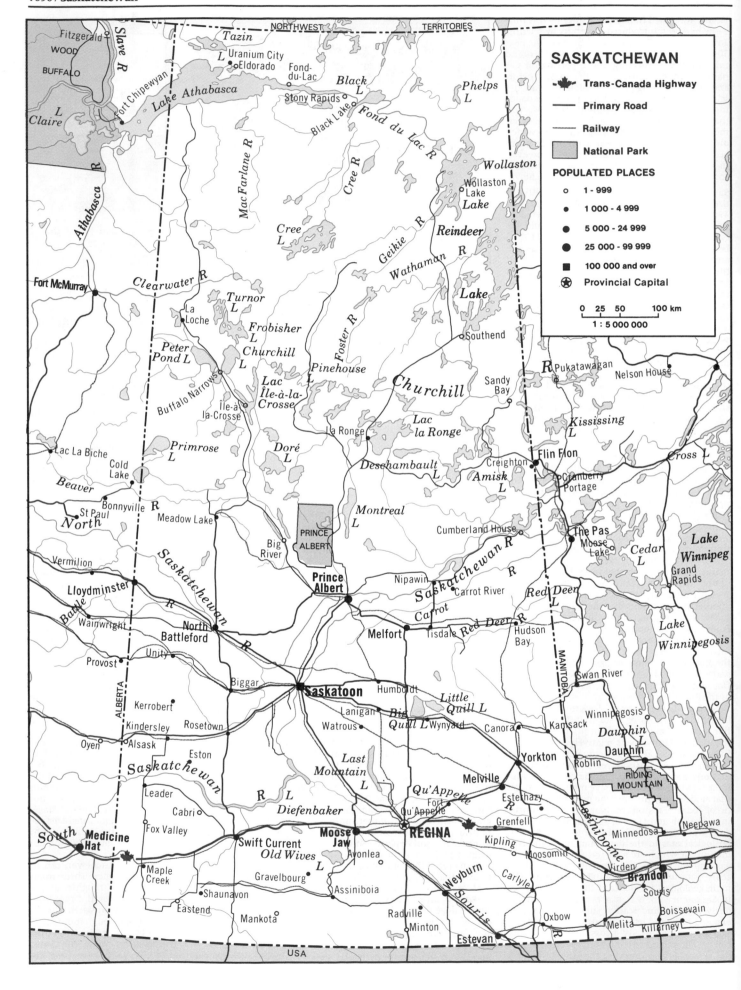

SASKATCHEWAN

- Trans-Canada Highway
- Primary Road
- Railway
- National Park

POPULATED PLACES
- ○ 1 – 999
- • 1 000 – 4 999
- ● 5 000 – 24 999
- ⬤ 25 000 – 99 999
- ■ 100 000 and over
- ✪ Provincial Capital

0 25 50 100 km
1 : 5 000 000

corded, as have Jan temperatures well above freezing and July temperatures well below. Days free of frost can number from 60 to over 100 in any year. In the arable sections the last spring frost usually comes in early June, and the first in autumn in early September. The relatively short growing season profoundly affects what agriculture can produce in Saskatchewan, for grains are sensitive to frost from germination until harvest. In one sense the number of frost-free days is a misleading indicator of the growing season, as the province's northern setting also produces in the summer early sunrises and late sunsets. In the grain belt, on June 21, the sun rises before 5 am and sets after 9:30 pm. For the same reason winter days are short: on Dec 21 sunrise is after 9 am and sunset at 5 pm. Blizzards in winter and thunderstorms in summer are common features of the climate, and the southern half of the province is occasionally visited by tornadoes. Saskatchewan's climate is often given part of the credit for the province's vigorous communal and co-operative life, the long winters allegedly obliging the population to provide offsetting social developments. Winter also produces a unique export: disproportionately large numbers of gifted hockey players.

Resources Soils and water are the fundamental resources of any heavily agricultural region, but to them in recent decades have been added increasingly important discoveries and developments of a non-agricultural nature. The most spectacular of these have been in minerals. Saskatchewan in the early 1980s ranked fifth among the provinces in mineral production, its wealth in metallic resources, although abundant elsewhere in Canada, was generally negligible. But the province contains immensely valuable deposits of POTASH and URANIUM, whose use depends on factors beyond provincial jurisdiction, and of fossil fuels that can to some degree be refined and consumed locally. Saskatchewan contains Canada's largest potash resources, and ranks second in uranium and petroleum. It has significant deposits of fuels, especially natural gas, and clays.

The forest resources are limited by soil and climate, but even so over half the province is wooded, and roughly one-third of the stands yields a harvest; Saskatchewan ranks eighth among provincial forest inventories, and it has more soft than hard woods. In dry years losses from fire are high, not only in the immediate destruction of potential pulp and lumber, but in the loss of habitat for wildlife, which variously supports recreational and commercial fishing, trapping and other hunting, which in the N are essential to the native peoples. Saskatchewan's mammals include most of those familiar on the Canadian landscape, although two of the largest in the W are rarely sighted; the COUGAR is still seen, but evidence of the GRIZZLY BEAR has all but disappeared. The province is a main flyway for an abundance of waterfowl and songbirds, and supports a lush insect life that both impedes and helps agriculture. The wildlife is a major factor in attracting hunters and fishermen, and the province usually ranks around fifth in the value of wild pelts taken. The commercial freshwater fisheries, although valuable locally where they exist, are among the smallest in Canada.

Conservation Saskatchewan has for decades assumed that CONSERVATION principles applied not just to "natural resources" but to human as well, and its government pioneered in publicly supported medical care, advanced labour legislation, and the protection of civil rights. Human occupations have led to further conservation of such essentials as water, and the province is the chief beneficiary of a major federal statute, the Prairie Farm Rehabilitation Act, which with amendments has since 1935 facilitated the transformation of the agricultural landscape

Potash plant at Esterhazy, Sask (*photo by Richard Vroom*).

through the creation of dams and dugouts. The need for conserving water on the prairies is a subject about which there can be little serious disagreement, and federal policy is supplemented by related provincial policies.

The conservation of most other natural resources is more controversial. Hunters, for example, may be willing to accept bag limits on waterfowl, to ensure the continuation of hunting; but the maintenance of large flocks may also mean that some farmers have to tolerate substantial destruction of grain each fall. Pesticides and herbicides are necessary for large crops of weed-free grain, and their use is officially encouraged; but the chemicals used sometimes show up in disturbing quantities in foods consumed by humans and livestock. Even that most traditional of prairie conservation policies, leaving arable fields idle in summerfallow to reduce weeds and conserve moisture, has been shown to be in important ways more wasteful than continual cropping from the soil. The inevitable tensions brought by modern technology have not prevented Saskatchewan from adopting comprehensive programs aimed at preserving its environment. Lookout towers and patrol aircraft in the N, controlled harvesting of wildlife everywhere, game preserves, fish hatcheries, and bird sanctuaries are all familiar parts of provincial life.

People

Evidence of aboriginal occupation of Saskatchewan can be traced to at least 10 000 BC, when hunters followed the migratory herds of bison, leaving behind arrowheads and ashes. The first European explorers, most of them seeking routes of the fur trade, appeared late in the 17th century, and were in time joined by more scientific travellers who expanded knowledge of the area throughout the 19th century. Actual settlement was preceded in most sections by the establishment in 1873 of the North-West Mounted Police, and thereafter homesteaders, attracted by land that was all but free, poured in at an accelerated rate. The census of 1881 revealed 19 114 inhabitants, that of 1911, 492 432, and that of 1931, 921 785. Thereafter the population levelled off and even declined considerably, partly because WWII drained off people to the armed forces and industrial plants elsewhere; after 1961 the population fluctuated between 920 000 and 955 000 and the census of 1981 revealed the largest population yet, 968 313; by 1984 the population was estimated to be 1 028 965. The first immigrants naturally chose to live in farming areas, and most residents still live in the southern half of Saskatchewan. But towns and villages were always necessary as supply depots for farm implements and related service industries, and with the rise of non-agricultural production rural areas have steadily lost population to urban ones.

Urban Centres Saskatchewan has no metropolitan centre, but its urban population grew from a negligible early beginning to 60% by 1981, while the rural farm population declined from a dominant position to less than a quarter of the total. Even so, only 2 cities are of even moderate size: REGINA (1984 estimated population 172 340) and SASKATOON (170 748), with MOOSE JAW (35 118), PRINCE ALBERT (32 957), North Battleford (14 702), SWIFT CURRENT (15 772), and YORKTON (15 895) following far behind. The cities are joined by a grid of E-W, N-S highways, and each serves a surrounding rural area as a market town and shipping centre. Regina and Saskatoon, especially, serve respectively as southern and northern economic "capitals," containing the wholesale houses that provide surrounding retailers with the multitude of consumer goods necessary to the late 20th century. Prince Albert, as the province's most northerly city, performs a special function as a "gateway to the north," of particular importance as the point of departure for recreational and forest areas. Despite its large urban population, Saskatchewan's vast expanses of open landscape, combined with the conspicuous architecture of GRAIN ELEVATORS in the villages and towns, continue to convey the impression of a predominantly agricultural province.

Labour Force Saskatchewan's labour force (400 000 in 1978) has naturally reflected the changes in the provincial economy, as urban workers have steadily replaced farmers and their helpers. Union organization began around the turn of the century in Moose Jaw and Regina, principally among skilled tradesmen in printing and railways; but the development of the economy did not encourage influential union activity of the kind familiar in heavily industrialized communities. The largest single unions of the 1980s are not primarily of steelworkers or automobile makers, but of teachers and public servants, although unions are active in such areas as the retail and wholesale trades, and in oil and potash. Provincial governments under the CCF and NDP were perceived as being particularly friendly to organized labour.

Although the province was one of the chief sufferers during the GREAT DEPRESSION and drought of the 1930s, the technology of later decades has been more conducive to sustaining its labour force. One factor is that Saskatchewan has been an exporter of labour to other provinces, but whatever the reasons the province in the early years of the 1980s, in sharp contrast to the 1930s, had one of the lowest unemployment rates in Canada. Saskatchewan also has one of the highest proportions of married women in the labour force.

Language and Ethnicity Modern Saskatchewan has a population over 90% of whose members, when asked about Canada's official languages, claimed to speak English only, with less than 1% speaking French only, and only 5% speaking both; less than 2% spoke neither official language. The same population, however, offered a striking variety of mother tongues, the languages first spoken in the home, and in the 1980s over 15% learned a mother tongue other than English or French. The current situation in the province is in marked contrast to the beginnings. When the settlement of Saskatchewan began in earnest, residents of French origin slightly outnumbered those of British, but both comprised less than 11% of the population; almost all the rest were aboriginal peoples. The influx of settlers brought few new French (migration from Québec to the West was considered by some influential clergy to be a form of exile), but large numbers of British and other Europeans whose descendants, in one or two generations, also became English speaking. The result was that by 1981 citizens of French origin had dropped to barely 6% of the population, ranking behind the British (40%), German and Austrian (20%), Ukrainian (10%) and Scandinavian (7%). Below those of French origin numerically were Russian, Polish, native Indian and Dutch. Significant numbers of people of Asian origin began to appear in the 1970s and 1980s.

The high ratio of British to French has had important implications for provincial policies on language and education, for English has always been unquestionably the dominant language, and those interested in the teaching of other languages, or in conducting regular schooling in other languages, always faced formidable obstacles. The use of French was at one time confined to primary courses, and in 1931 French was prohibited as a medium of instruction; other languages fared less well. In the 1960s, however, the province began to take a more relaxed view towards French in the schools, and public schools teaching the regular curriculum in French began to appear. Saskatchewan, paradoxically, has not since the 1920s had a population at least half British in origin: the last census to show the British at 50.8% was that of 1926.

Religion Religion in Saskatchewan has always been connected with language and ethnicity, as the incoming settlers naturally tended to congregate in communities where they hoped to practise their religion, and if possible have their children educated in their own language. The largest Protestant denomination in modern Saskatchewan is the United Church (32% of adherents), followed closely by the Roman Catholic (26%). Considerably smaller are the Lutheran and Anglican (about 10% each), and then the Ukrainian Catholic, Greek Orthodox, Mennonite, Presbyterian and Baptist, ranging from 4% down to less than 2%. The advent of television gave numerous fundamentalist religions access to the population, and in the 1980s they appeared to be the most rapidly growing churches.

Throughout the province's history, religious groups have been active in expressing their views on such varied social issues as prohibition, immigration, education and the language used in schools. Religious factors lie behind the division of the province's public schools into Protestant and Roman Catholic systems, and a particularly bitter confrontation occurred in the late 1920s when the KU KLUX KLAN took the lead in inflaming the electorate over religious sym-

Cannington Manor church, Saskatchewan. The community was established in 1882 when Capt Edward Pierce opened an agricultural college for the sons of wealthy Englishmen. The town gradually disappeared after it was bypassed by the CPR in 1901 (*photo by John deVisser/Masterfile*).

bols (specifically Catholic) in the schools. The Conservative party was perceived at the time to have Klan support, and hence some Catholic voters thereafter were thought to be supporters of the party's opponents; but in 1982 the party, led by a Roman Catholic, won an overwhelming victory.

Economy

Saskatchewan's economy, since settlement began, has been heavily dependent on influences that lie outside the province's boundaries. The earliest inhabitants of the area, nomads and hunters, were able to rely on creatures as indigenous as themselves. The earliest settlers, when favoured with good weather, were able to produce grains, and especially wheat, in far larger quantities than they could consume, and from the start of the modern era the province has been an exporter of a few staples, often unprocessed, to markets throughout the world. Commonly the province has had little control over the transportation of its own products, or the financing of it, and that situation did not change as wheat was supplemented by natural gas, petroleum and potash. A high percentage of the consumer goods used in Saskatchewan, on the other hand, from canned food to automobiles and farm implements, come from outside. A recurring feeling among sections of the population is that the province's economy is the victim of outside forces that are not always benign.

That feeling provides one reason for the remarkable success of the CO-OPERATIVE MOVEMENT in Saskatchewan, through which citizens have banded together to satisfy numerous economic needs. Saskatchewan contains nearly 20% of all the co-operative associations in Canada, with individual memberships numbering well over a third of the population. The co-operatives are found in virtually every segment of the retailing and distributing trades, and in many service industries; in 1982, 40% of the population belonged to 1329 associations whose total business ran into the billions of dollars.

Agriculture Although non-agricultural production constitutes over half of Saskatchewan's annual output, agriculture remains the largest single industry. The settled era began almost exclusively as a farm economy, with nearly 460 000 hectares planted to wheat in the year

of the province's creation, yielding 26 million bushels. With setbacks occasioned by the depression years of the 1930s, when drought helped reduce all rural activities, and WWII, when some overseas markets for wheat almost disappeared, wheat acreage has grown steadily throughout the province's history, and now annually approaches 7 million hectares. Saskatchewan is incomparably the largest wheat producer in Canada, and one of the largest in the world: in 1982 the province grew 16 438 t of wheat (compared with barely half that amount in the other provinces combined). The province is also a leader in the production of rapeseed (794 t in 1982) and rye (381), and is always among the largest producers of oats (956), barley (3636), flaxseed (234), and forage crops and pasturage for livestock, which, since they do not all enter the market, are harder to measure. The province's livestock industry, though not comparable to its grains, always an important element in the agricultural economy, farms reporting significant sales of cattle and hogs constituting roughly one-fifth of the number reporting significant wheat sales.

Like all modern agricultural economies, Saskatchewan's is characterized by a diminution in the number of farms and a growth in the size of those surviving. Saskatchewan has the smallest proportion of small to moderate sized farms in Canada, while those yielding annual sales of $15 000 or more number barely 40 000. The same dwindling number of farms continues to provide one of the country's largest markets for farm vehicles and machinery, and the total net income from farming of Saskatchewan's farmers remains the largest in Canada: $1184 million in 1982.

Industry Saskatchewan is not in a conventional sense a manufacturing centre, commonly ranking eighth or ninth in the value of shipped goods of its own manufacture; in 1982 those goods totalled $2.4 billion. Manufacturing establishments, most of them employing fewer than 100 workers, numbered 764 in 1981. Most manufactured goods that are exported go to other parts of Canada. Saskatchewan's industrial economy has always been affected by the relatively small provincial market. What the province produces well it produces in enormous quantities. The Saskatchewan internal market is in many ways more economically served by imports. While a number of attempts were made to establish major industries (Regina obtained an automobile assembly plant in 1928), the province was in the wrong location, and with the wrong resources, to share in the huge industrial expansion of WWII. Non-agricultural production in the 1980s was larger and more varied than it had ever been, but Saskatchewan was still a long way from posing a threat to central Canada as an industrial heartland.

Mining From the 1950s the development of mining in Saskatchewan was almost as spectacular, though not as conspicuous, as that of agricultural settlement half a century earlier. In 1950 the total value of all mineral production was barely $34 million, of which nearly 80% was of metals, mostly copper and zinc; 15% fuels, mostly coal; and most of the rest was sodium sulphate. By the 1980s mining ranked second to agriculture as a contributor to the province's production; the three largest items, oil, potash and uranium, had been of negligible importance in 1950. Crude petroleum accounted for 3.3% of all mineral production in 1950, approximately 50% annually in the 1980s. In 1982 the province exported 3 790 m³ of crude oil to the rest of Canada, and 4241 m³ to the US. In 1950 no potash was mined; it accounted for over 30% of mineral production annually in the 1980s. 1982 potash exports totalled $742.9 million. In 1950 uranium was not being mined; by the 1980s one large mine had already been, in economic terms, worked out, but remarkably

Saskatchewan is Canada's foremost wheat-growing area and one of the great wheat-growing regions of the world (*photo by Brian Milne/First Light*).

rich deposits remained elsewhere. By the 1980s uranium accounted for over 15% of annual mineral production, and in 1982 Saskatchewan produced 3 491 000 kg ($250.5 million) of the metal. Those rising statistics were offset by another relevant factor: in regard to both capital invested and gross production, none of the big 3 prairie minerals employs large labour forces.

Forestry Forestry does not provide one of Saskatchewan's largest industries, although where it exists it is of great local significance. The rapid opening of the prairies for settlement created a demand for building materials, not just for farm buildings but also for railway ties and telegraph poles; the closer settlement moved to the northern forest, the more local wood could be used. Pulpwood, which utilizes smaller growth than lumber, was cut for export as early as the 1920s, but the province's first pulp mill was not built until the 1960s, and then with substantial assistance from the government.

Saskatchewan wood in the 1980s is used for lumber, particle board and plywood, poles and fence posts, and pulp, but the total cut, in statistical terms, makes a minor contribution to the province's economy. In 1980, for example, Saskatchewan's exports of lumber outside Canada were valued at only $28 million, barely 1% of grain exports, and 3% of those of potash. The forest industries are nonetheless sufficiently active that Indian leaders frequently express concern over the damage caused to wildlife habitat.

Fisheries Fisheries rank well below forestry as a contributor to the province's economy, competing for rank with wildlife trapping and fur farming, for an annual production of $3-4 million, chiefly in walleye, whitefish, lake trout and pike. Three-quarters of the commercial activity is in the north, while in the grain belt a fairly common sight is the rainbow trout dugout, a licensed artificial pond in which individual farmers, several hundred a year, raise fish for their own use. In 1977, 2243 commercial licences were issued for fishing in over 200 lakes. Of unknown commercial value, but significant to the tourist industry, is the province's rich supply of game fish and edible wild animals. From 5% to 10% of the sportfishing and hunting licences issued annually go to visitors, most of them from neighbouring American states.

Finance Farming and mining both require a great amount of capital, and Saskatchewan has always had to supplement what it could create with heavy inflows from financial centres elsewhere. No major Canadian bank or trust company has its head office in the province, and the provincial government routinely floats loans in American money markets. The net public debt outstanding in Mar 1983 was over $4 billion; total liabilities amounted to approximately the same.

In 1979 there were 378 branches of chartered banks throughout the province, each village serving a farming area ordinarily having one. It is part of the province's traditional beliefs that banks exploit as well as serve those in debt to them; this response, together with the citizens' confidence in co-operative ventures, led to a widespread network of credit unions, in effect banks owned by their own local customers. In 1981 there were 227 chartered credit unions, with 576 135 members (nearly half the provincial population) and assets of $2.8 billion.

The provincial government pioneered in its own financial enterprises when in 1944 the legislature passed the Government Insurance Act. The Saskatchewan Government Insurance office handles most kinds of property insurance, including fire, and is particularly involved in automobile insurance, in which Saskatchewan also pioneered in 1944 by making it compulsory. Profits from the public insurance operations are reinvested whenever possible within the province. In 1982 the insurance office's assets were over $329 million, over half of which was in bonds of the province and its municipalities.

Transportation Saskatchewan is peculiarly vulnerable to transportation problems. The least difficult usually are in air transport, for the province is served by the usual network of major and minor airlines, none of which are involved in moving its bulkiest products. In the north, where some communities are readily accessible only by air, unpredictable weather is the worst factor to be dealt with. On the surface, on the other hand, the long distances between points, the absence of navigable waters, and the sheer quantities of wheat and potash to be hauled make both highways and railways of overwhelming importance. Potash can be moved directly from the mines to the railways, but grains must be carried by truck from each farm before entering the elevator for subsequent shipment by rail.

Main railway tracks in Saskatchewan comprise the second largest total in Canada (over 13 000 km), only Ontario having more. Saskatchewan roads under provincial jurisdiction are the longest in Canada per capita, and when municipal responsibilities are added, many of which include rural roads essential to farms, the province's road total is in absolute terms the longest in Canada: over 200 000 km. Railways are under federal jurisdiction, but roads and highways are provincial: a major item in every provincial budget, vying for position behind health and education, is transportation. Combined provincial and municipal expenditures on roads in 1983 were over $192 million. A special problem of Saskatchewan transportation, often vexatious enough in itself but also entirely beyond the province's jurisdiction, arises from work stoppages elsewhere in the system. Saskatchewan farmers are aware that they are landlocked; it is a hazard of their occupation that their grain is sometimes held up by labour-management disputes in ports far away.

Energy Generously endowed with real and potential sources of energy, Saskatchewan exports what it does in forms other than electricity. Through the Saskatchewan Power Corporation, established in 1949 out of a provincial commission 20 years older, the province generates large amounts of power in conventional ways, but not nuclear, and neither imports nor exports significant quantities. Domestically the governmental agency enjoys a monopoly over power production and natural gas distribution; and farms, homes and mines are supplied at rates that compare favourably with those elsewhere. The province's total installed capacity for generating electricity in 1982 was 2261 megawatts. Nearly 23% of the electricity produced in 1982 was from hydroelectric plants, and the long lines of transmission towers from sites in the north are conspicuous on the landscape. Thermal units producing power are primarily fired by coal, which accounts for nearly 74% of the provincial total, and natural gas provides almost all of what comes from neither hydro nor coal. Generation from oil is negligible, but oil still heats many homes, particularly in rural areas. Urban homes are more likely to be warmed by natural gas, piped to each one by the power corporation.

Government and Politics

The government of Saskatchewan in form resembles that of the other provinces. The executive consists of the lieutenant-governor and an executive council called the Cabinet, which in the name of the Crown exercises the real powers of government, with the aid of a public service organized into departments and crown corporations. The legislature is unicameral, and its members are elected in 64 single-member constituencies; the support of a majority of the members of the legislature is necessary for the continued life of a Cabinet. The leader of the majority is the premier, and his Cabinet colleagues are ministers, each with assigned responsibilities; the leader of the opposition is paid as if he were a minister. The province's judicial system is the usual hierarchy, with a Court of Appeal and a Court of Queen's Bench at the summit, and provincial courts (formerly magistrate's courts) below. The federal authority appoints all judges except those of provincial courts.

The parliamentary tradition is strong, and Saskatchewan is unique among the western provinces in that its legislature has never supported coalition governments for prolonged periods, nor been dominated by one party to the virtual exclusion of an opposition. Even during the life of the lone coalition, the Co-operative Government of 1929-34, the largest single party was the opposition. Since 1905, when the assembly had 25 members of whom 3 had urban seats, to 1982, when the asembly's 64 members included 27 urban seats, there has always been,

Lieutenant-Governors of Saskatchewan 1905-83	
	Term
Amédée Emmanuel Forget	1905-10
George William Brown	1910-15
Richard Stuart Lake	1915-21
Henry William Newlands	1921-31
Hugh Edwin Munroe	1931-36
Archibald Peter McNab	1936-45
Thomas Miller	1945
Reginal John Marsden Parker	1945-48
John Michael Uhrich	1948-51
William John Patterson	1951-58
Frank Lindsay Bastedo	1958-63
Robert Leith Hanbidge	1963-70
Dr Stephen Worobetz	1970-76
George Porteous	1976-78
Cameron Irwin McIntosh	1978-83
Fred W. Johnson	1983-

even though sometimes small numerically, a vigorous opposition. A second major tradition of government in Saskatchewan depends on a blurring of the line between public and private sectors: the government, no matter what party was in power, has not only encouraged citizens to develop co-operatives that competed with private enterprise, but has not hesitated to go into business itself, as in the creation of a telephone system and a power corporation.

Local Government Saskatchewan has developed its own municipal system, in which townships and counties are not known as governing units, although a measured area may be called a township. There are urban municipalities (in 1978, 11 cities, 135 towns and 346 villages) and rural (299), the latter having been created originally through provincial policy rather than local demand. There are also 10 unincorporated local improvement districts in the southern half, and much of the north, where population warrants it, receives municipal services through provincial initiatives. The municipal governments provide the usual housekeeping facilities: streets, police, water, sewage disposal, hospitals, in the urban areas; roads, help with problems of drainage, weed control, in the rural. Municipal governments, often reluctantly, also collect taxes for other local spending authorities, the largest of which are school districts. Total municipal revenues in 1983 were $525 million; expenditures were $516 million. The Saskatchewan Urban Municipalities Association and the Saskatchewan Association of Rural Municipalities are respected political forces.

Federal Representation Saskatchewan has never loomed large in numbers in Parliament, but its representatives have included many notably vocal individuals. The province usually has at least one Cabinet member at Ottawa, and two prime ministers, King and Diefenbaker, sat for Saskatchewan seats for prolonged periods. One federal minister, James GARDINER, held a portfolio (Agriculture) for a longer consecutive period than any other individual in Canadian history.

The province entered Confederation with 4 senators, which rose to 6 in 1915, where it has stayed. Its Commons delegation has never exceeded 8.6% of the total membership (in 1925-35, when it had 21 MPs) and is now, barring a constitutional amendment, pegged at 14 in a House whose total membership will rise after each census. On one occasion (1952), when the rules for dividing parliamentary seats among the provinces would have dropped Saskatchewan's share from 20 to 15, a change was enacted to drop it to 17 only. The influence of the province's parliamentary representation has never depended primarily on numbers, but on the quality of those elected.

Public Finance Governmental expenditures in Saskatchewan, as elsewhere, grew rapidly af-

ter WWII and in 1981 for the first time passed $2 billion. The main sources of taxation in 1982 were individual income tax (20% of the consolidated fund budgetary revenue), sales tax (13%), gasoline tax (5%), and corporation income tax (4%). The Saskatchewan Heritage Fund provided another 24% and receipts from other governments (almost all of them from federal sources) 23%. The Heritage Fund, established in the 1970s and drawing its income from nonrenewable resources, received 64% of its income from oil and 22% from potash. The total provincial revenue from all sources in 1982 was $2.7 billion. The main expenditures were in public health (25% of the total), education (21%), social services (13%), municipal affairs (9%), and highways (7%).

Health Public health policies in Saskatchewan predate the province's creation in 1905, but the province nonetheless pioneered in comprehensive extensions of health care. The hospital services plan, which became effective in 1947, provided universal hospital care insurance throughout the province: every qualified citizen has since 1947 been provided with a card assuring hospital care when needed, at public expense. The hospital plan provided part of the foundation for universal prepaid medical care, as did the establishment of a medical faculty and teaching hospital at the University of Saskatchewan. Medicare was enacted in 1961 and inaugurated in 1962, after considerable tension between the government and the medical profession, which resulted in many doctors withdrawing their services for a month. Since 1962 the hospital and medicare plans have been supplemented by a dental plan (1974) and a prescription plan (1975). In the 1980s the dental plan was not universal, but limited to categories of school children, and the prescription service was not fully prepaid, but imposed a standard dispensing fee for each prescription.

Politics The lively partisan traditions of Saskatchewan are reflected in its election results: in 20 general elections to 1982, the winning party won over 50% of the vote in only 10, and 4 of those occurred when only 2 parties existed. The Liberals were chosen to form the first administration in 1905, and won the first 6 elections handily, although always facing opposition groups with considerable support. The Liberals' early successes, in keeping with the mores of the day, produced a public service weighted with patronage appointments, an issue used against the party in 1929. The basic issue of the 1929 election, however, about which a vast ill-feeling was generated, turned on the use of the schools for religious purposes, and a loose coalition of Conservatives, Progressives and Independents defeated the government. The Co-operative government then formed fell in turn a victim to drought and depression, and not one of its candidates was elected in 1934. After another decade of Liberal rule, the province in 1944 elected North America's first socialist government, in the CO-OPERATIVE COMMONWEALTH FEDERATION, or CCF. The CCF (known later in Saskatchewan as the CCF-NDP and finally as the NEW DEMOCRATIC

Premiers of Saskatchewan 1905-83		
	Party	Term
T. Walter Scott	Liberal	1905-16
William M. Martin	Liberal	1916-22
Charles A. Dunning	Liberal	1922-26
James G. Gardiner	Liberal	1926-29
James T. M. Anderson	Conservative	1929-34
James G. Gardiner	Liberal	1934-35
William J. Patterson	Liberal	1935-44
Thomas C. Douglas	CCF/NDP	1944-61
Woodrow S. Lloyd	CCF/NDP	1961-64
W. Ross Thatcher	Liberal	1964-71
Allan E. Blakeney	NDP	1971-82
D. Grant Devine	Conservative	1982-

PARTY) lasted 20 years, after which the Liberals returned for the years 1964-71. The NDP came back for 1971-82, and in 1982 the Progressive CONSERVATIVES, who had all but disappeared between 1934 and the 1970s, won their first victory in their own right.

The volatility of the Saskatchewan electorate is less evidence of a capacity to swing from left to right than it is of the parties' practices in rarely differing fundamentally in what they offer. The CCF was plainly the furthest left of the parties, with the Liberals and Conservatives on the right; but the Liberals after 1964, for example, did not dismantle the health and welfare policies or the public enterprises of the preceding CCF, which had in turn built on foundations laid by the Liberals. In a similar way, the province's relations with Ottawa, generally good, have depended primarily not on which parties were in power in each place, but on the provincial government's perception, regardless of its partisan outlook, of the province's needs.

Education

The province inherited the beginnings of a public school system, as well as the idea for a university, from its territorial days. The rapid expansion of the population during the early settlement gave to the provision of teachers and schools a sense of urgency felt almost everywhere, and the upgrading of inadequately trained teachers and the replacement of makeshift premises were major preoccupations of Saskatchewan's first years. Many of the teachers at the start came from provinces to the east, but the new province created Normal Schools, whose work was in 1927 supplemented by a College of Education at the UNIVERSITY OF SASKATCHEWAN; in due course the College absorbed the Normal Schools. The university itself was established in 1909, with a solitary faculty of arts, a teaching staff of 5, and 70 students. The university entered the 1980s with 14 faculties, a teaching staff of 1000, and over 12 000 students. In 1974 UNIVERSITY OF REGINA was created out of the Regina campus of University of Saskatchewan. In 1982 it had over 4000 students. The universities are non-sectarian, although they have affiliated theological colleges. A striking feature of Saskatchewan's public and high school systems is that both Protestant and Roman Catholic systems are public, ie, they are managed by separate elected boards of education and financed by taxes collected by the relevant municipal authority. In the 1970s a series of community colleges, emphasizing non-academic post-secondary education, was also begun.

The basic instruments of educational policy are two related departments of government, Education and Continuing Education, which usually have the same minister. Locally the chief unit is the school district, whose elected board is in effect a municipal council with a single responsibility, schools. The schools are financed primarily by local taxes and provincial grants; education annually provides one of the largest items in the provincial budget. In 1982-83 Saskatchewan had 201 692 students in public schools, and 2590 in private, not counting several thousand in federal institutions, the latter chiefly for Indian and Inuit peoples.

Cultural Life

Much of the artistic energy of the indigenous peoples went into artifacts connected with the hunt, and the making of decorated leather clothing and moccasins has survived. There are petroglyphs on outcrops at Roche Percée, in the southeast. The Europeans brought their own crafts with them, and the significance of handicrafts in Saskatchewan's development is reflected in the seriousness with which they are still taken. When in 1948 the Saskatchewan Arts Board was created, the first governmental body of its kind on the continent, it treated crafts from the start as art forms, and the provincial crafts exhibition held each summer under official auspices is a highlight of the cultural year. The arts board is an independent organization that encourages and funds a wide variety of artistic endeavours, and it reports through the minister of culture and youth. The board has a valuable collection of work by provincial artists; its expenditures in 1982 were $1.9 million.

Arts Individual Saskatchewan artists have excelled in every branch of the arts. Musicians raised in the province have gone on to national and international fame, including performances with leading orchestras and opera companies. Visual artists of both Indian and European origin have earned outstanding reputations. The province's rich deposits of clays have given rise to an unusually active community of ceramicists. Many Saskatchewan artists, like their fellow Canadians generally, have had to leave home to find listeners and viewers, but the domestic scene continues to be extremely active. There are symphony orchestras in Regina and Saskatoon, and the universities there have well-developed arts departments. Workshops for singers, writers, painters et al are available to large numbers of participants, and the Emma Lake campus of University of Saskatchewan becomes each summer a camp for artists. Publishing also flourishes, and one house, the property of the Wheat Pool's weekly newspaper, is a successful commercial enterprise specializing in prairie works.

Communications Absentee ownership is a striking characteristic of the media in the province, but since all the outlets in both print and broadcasting have to cater to local communities the effect of so much external ownership is not conspicuous. Only the major cities support daily newspapers, and smaller centres are served by journals published less frequently, most of them weeklies. Several articulate magazines of literary or political bent struggle constantly for existence, and there are also periodicals that express the particular interests of Indian and Métis associations. A variety of learned journals emanate from the universities.

Radio is as important in the north as the telegraph was formerly throughout the Prairies. Few communities in the 1980s, however remote, are beyond the reach of radio, and the national services of the CBC are distributed through stations in Regina and La Ronge, the latter one of the most northerly villages accessible by road. Television signals, their distribution facilitated by microwave towers and satellite stations, reach all the settled areas and cable TV, beginning in the late 1970s, widened the range of domestic outlets and also, for the first time, made programs originating in the United States available to most viewers in Saskatchewan.

Historic Sites Saskatchewan's native peoples, as their awareness of their common aspirations grew in the 1970s and 1980s, found a renewed interest in their history. The descendants of the European settlers, whose occupation was so recent, were also sensitive to their past. The province is dotted with national and provincial historic sites, the most northerly of them marking early missions, the rest variously celebrating fur posts, the first newspaper, Mounted Police depots, colonies of settlers, old trails, the founding of a grain growers' organization, or a steamship landing. Hundreds of local histories were written around the province's diamond jubilee in 1980, most of them with the help of the Saskatchewan Archives Board, a co-operative university-government venture established in 1945. Between the records around the historic sites and those of the homestead applications and the land titles office, more detailed information is available about Saskatchewan since its European settlement than about most places.

History

The earliest human inhabitants of the area that became Saskatchewan, who left almost no written records, were Indians grouped roughly from N to S as follows: 3 tribes of the Athapaskan linguistic group, the CHIPEWYAN and, to the west of them, the SLAVEY; 2 tribes speaking Algonquian, the CREE and, W and S of them, the BLACKFOOT; 2 tribes of the Siouan group, the ASSINIBOINE and, W of them, the Gros Ventres. Each of the 3 main language groups occupied approximately a third of the area, those in the N depending heavily on caribou and moose as a staple food, those in the southern third (ie, that part which is now the agricultural belt) on the buffalo. All of them had a considerable influence in providing place and geographical names throughout the province.

To this day some of the northern Indians have limited contact with people of European descent. Others, especially those close to waterways, were in contact with whites as early as 1690 when Henry KELSEY, an employee of the Hudson's Bay Company, followed the Saskatchewan R west to the area that is now Prince Albert and then proceeded S into the plains. Thereafter exploration continued throughout the 18th and 19th centuries, and by 1870 not only were the main water routes well known, but the prairie was crisscrossed by well-worn trails, some of whose routes are still visible from the air.

Exploration The earliest European explorers travelled the prairies for no more laudable reason than moneymaking: the felt hat was fashionable in the late 17th century, and the best felt came from beaver. Even before the first fur traders the plains were well known to many, for the various Indian tribes moved about following the migrations of caribou and buffalo herds, and the boundaries of the regions occupied by the main tribes were never clearly defined. Paradoxically, the Indians are rarely thought of as explorers, perhaps because they had different motives from the Europeans, but also because they did not need maps and left no records.

The Europeans, once they had discovered the usefulness of the plains for their purposes, wasted little time in moving in. The HUDSON'S BAY COMPANY was two decades old when Kelsey first saw the Saskatchewan in 1690. The first native N American of European descent, LA VÉ-

Provincial legislative building, Regina, Sask (*photo by John deVisser*).

RENDRYE, traversed the area in 1741, and he was followed by several more of English extraction, of whom the best known is probably Peter POND. None penetrated north of the Churchill R until 1796, when David THOMPSON reached Lk Athabasca. At that time little was known of the southern third of the province, but in 1800 Peter FIDLER crossed the area using the S Saskatchewan. The primary interest of most of the early explorers was exploitation of the fur resources, and that, unfortunately, often included exploitation of the aboriginal peoples. Not all the Indians cared about the fur trade, the Plains Cree especially having few opportunities for trapping. Indians who were in the trade often became increasingly dependent on one particular fort or post — by the late 18th century such settlements dotted the fur-bearing areas — and often also on alcohol, which was used shamelessly as an element in competition between white traders.

Not all exploration had selfish motives, and men interested in the land and the environment entered the region a century behind the traders. The best known of the early observers were Sir John FRANKLIN and Dr John RICHARDSON, between 1819 and 1827, and John PALLISER, 1857-58; and coincidentally with the PALLISER EXPEDITION, which was British, the Province of Canada despatched Henry HIND with a colleague to assess agricultural possibilities. By the middle of the 19th century the domination of the prairies by the fur trade was being threatened.

Settlement A sequence of events in the 19th century determined that the Prairies were to be settled primarily by peoples of European ancestry. The foundation was laid by the acquisition of Rupert's Land from the HBC and its subsequent transfer to Canada shortly after Confederation. A series of treaties with the Indians, beginning in 1871, established the natives on reserves in a manner that suggested that the rest of the land was for somebody else. The treaties were negotiated with the help of the North-West Mounted Police, an adaptation to the plains of a European institution. The defeat of the Métis under RIEL in 1885, in a rebellion in which land was a major issue, meant among other things that the Métis were not the chosen people. Concurrently with this period Parliament in 1872 passed the first Dominion Lands Act, a provision for homesteaders, and an Act to stimulate immigration. In 1882-83 the first railway lines crossed the area, in a southern route through Regina and Moose Jaw. The prerequisites for orderly immigration and settlement were thus all in place well before 1900.

The impact of their combined influence shows dramatically in the statistics. In 1885 the population of the area was 32 097, of whom half were British and 44% were Indian. Three censuses later, in 1911, the population was 492 432, of which half was still British, but the Indians had dropped to 2.4%. The British element by then had consolidated its hold on familiar political institutions: the principles of responsible government, which held the Cabinet responsible to a majority of the legislature, had been settled in 1897. Provincial status, first sought in 1900, came in 1905, and with it the relevant apparatus of parliamentary government. The province's size and shape were important; although many leading prairie politicians favoured one large western province, the federal authorities always insisted that the western plains were too large to be made into a single constitutional entity. Depending on where one settled its northern boundary, such a province could have been the largest in Canada, a potential economic threat to the central heartland. In any event, in 1905 the federal government retained in federal hands the jurisdiction over crown lands in Saskatchewan.

Alienation of the land which, shortly after 1905, included over 6 million hectares for railway grants and 1.6 million for the support of schools, proceeded for settlement in a generally northwesterly direction, most of the arable area being occupied by the 1930s. The pattern of settlement itself profoundly affected the nature of Saskatchewan society. Identifiable groups of immigrants, varying from English people desiring to set up a temperance colony to DOUKHOBORS escaping persecution with the aid of Leo Tolstoi and the Society of Friends, established communities that in the 1980s still reflected their origins. Time, social mobility and intermarriage have blurred the lines separating the original settlements, but many parts of the province were still discernibly French and German, Ukrainian and Scandinavian, Hutterite and Mennonite.

Development Immigration en masse into Saskatchewan had ended at least temporarily by the 1930s, although a high turnover in the population did not stop. A population of barely a million can absorb only limited numbers of artisans, artists and other professionals, and the province's modern history is marked by the steady departure of energetic people born and educated in Saskatchewan. Sometimes, as in the two world wars, thousands left over a short period to enlist or work in war industries, and many did not return. At the same time, migration inwards of trained people did not end, as the universities grew and industries attracted professionals and administrators.

The maturing of the population meant also a slackening of the hold of the English-speaking Protestant establishment on political institutions. In the early years, citizens of non-British origin did not often seek election to Parliament or the assembly, and were even more rarely elected. By the 1970s people with names that were recognizably continental European were working successfully at all levels of politics and administration, often attaining high office. In earlier times religion or national origin frequently decided how sides were chosen over such varied issues as languages in the schools, women's suffrage, or prohibition; and similar divisions can still occur over, for example, abortion. But in the 1980s citizens of every origin are more likely to be found on both sides of most controversies.

Economically the most significant single event of Saskatchewan's modern history was the transfer of jurisdiction over crown lands to the province in 1930. Without that authority, the province was still able to become a great agricultural producer and it would still have been able to make the remarkable contribution to the war effort that it did from 1939 to 1945. But with it the province did not merely have access to lucrative sources of taxation; it also had new sources of power which affected its influence within Canada in the 1970s and after, and gave it, despite its small population, a formidable voice in national affairs. Wheat, once the plains were settled, was always a large factor in Canada's international dealings. In modern Saskatchewan wheat has been joined by potash and several forms of precious energy. The province's economy since the drought and depression decade of the 1930s has shown an impressive capacity for diversification in both agricultural and non-agricultural production. In all that it has been assisted by a sequence of lively and progressive governments supported and trusted by a lively and progressive electorate.

NORMAN WARD

Readings: John H. Archer, *Saskatchewan: A History* (1980); D.H. Bocking, ed, *Pages from the Past: Essays on Saskatchewan History* (1970); G. Friesen, *Prairie Road* (1984); Edward McCourt, *Saskatchewan* (1968); J. Howard Richards and K.I. Fung, *Atlas of Saskatchewan* (1969).

Saskatchewan Legislative Building, Regina, was built 1908-12, following the plans of Montréal architects Edward and William MAXWELL.

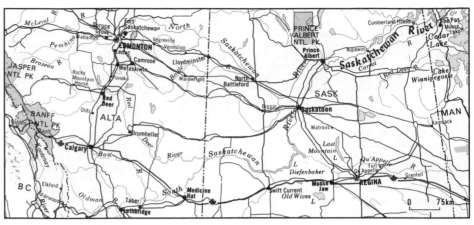

The symmetrical design of the facades, the classical details and the interior all show the influence of the beaux-arts style, an architectural movement that deeply marked Canadian public ARCHITECTURE of this era. Divided into 5 sections, the facade has in its central section a huge portico consisting of Doric columns and a pediment. The floor plan, in the shape of a Latin cross, is based on a system of axes housing the building's major functions.   NATHALIE CLERK

Saskatchewan Research Council (SRC) After an unsuccessful attempt to form a research council in 1930, the Saskatchewan government established SRC in 1947. The council served primarily as an agency for grants and scholarships to university researchers until 1954; its mandate then expanded to include independent research in natural and management sciences directed towards improving the provincial economy. Its own laboratories opened in 1958, expanding in 1963. Special expertise has developed in slurry pipelines, uranium-ore genesis, GROUNDWATER management and various aspects of AGRICULTURE. Council members are appointed by the Lieutenant-Governor-in-Council from government, industry and the universities. Laboratories, including the Canadian Centre for Advanced Instrumentation, are located at Innovation Place on UNIVERSITY OF SASKATCHEWAN's Saskatoon campus. Over 240 staff members, in 5 divisions, report to an executive director. Almost half of the council's funding comes from provincial contracts and grants; most of the remainder from industry; some from federal contracts. In addition to conducting and funding research, SRC issues free technical advice to small businesses, informs the public on SCIENCE POLICY issues and, advises the government.   MARTIN K. MCNICHOLL

Saskatchewan River, 1939 km long, formed by the confluence of the North Saskatchewan (1287 km) and the South Saskatchewan (1392 km) rivers about 50 km E of PRINCE ALBERT, Sask. The system of waters has a combined length greater than the St Lawrence R and drains much of the western prairie. The N Saskatchewan rises in the COLUMBIA ICEFIELD at the foot of Mt Columbia and flows E to ROCKY MOUNTAIN HOUSE, where it takes in the Clearwater R, on through EDMONTON, Alta, where its valley has been preserved as parkland, and then past North Battleford and Prince Albert. The river cuts a deep, wide valley in the prairie, and like all prairie streams carries a heavy load of silt. The S Saskatchewan is formed in southern Alberta by the junction of the BOW and OLDMAN rivers. It flows E past MEDICINE HAT, Alta, then NE into Saskatchewan, past SASKATOON, and continues a course roughly parallel to the N Saskatchewan to the confluence some 130 km upstream. The S Saskatchewan has been dammed about 100 km S of Saskatoon, creating a long broad reservoir, called DIEFENBAKER LK, that provides hydroelectric power and irrigation for SW Saskatche-

wan. From the confluence, the river continues nearly 600 km eastward through Tobin Lk and Cumberland Lk, Sask, into Manitoba, where it trends SE past THE PAS and into CEDAR LK. The waters of the Saskatchewan enter Lk WINNIPEG at Grand Rapids and are carried to Hudson Bay by the NELSON R.

Called *Kisiskatchewani Sipi,* "swift-flowing river," by the Indians, Henry KELSEY (1690) and the LA VÉRENDRYE family (1741) were the first Europeans to see it. The modern rendering of the name was adopted in 1882 when part of the present-day province was made a district of the NWT. The section between Grand Rapids and CUMBERLAND HOUSE (built in 1774 by Samuel HEARNE), was hotly contested by the HBC and NWC. From Cumberland House to Edmonton, there are no rapids that could not be lined up or run down, although shifting gravel bars are a menace. This was a much-travelled route of the HBC traders and made Edmonton an early focal point of trade. The southern branch carried traders SW to Wyoming and into the Rockies by Bow Pass. In years when the sovereignty of the Northwest was in question, the Saskatchewan made possible an E-W highway tying the area to English commercial enterprise on Hudson Bay and, via the Great Lakes, to Canadian interests centered in Montréal.   JAMES MARSH

Saskatchewan Roughriders, FOOTBALL team. They were founded as the Regina Rugby Club in 1910, adopting the Roughrider nickname in 1924 and becoming the Saskatchewan Roughriders in 1948. Until 1936 they were the West's dominant team, winning 16 championships. Although defeated in their 7 early GREY CUP attempts (1923, 1928-32, 1934), the Roughriders won respect for western football, introducing the forward pass to the Grey Cup in 1929 and scoring the West's first Grey Cup touchdown in 1930. Except for a 1951 Cup loss to Ottawa, they did not return to the national final until the 1960s. Calling Regina's Taylor Field (named in 1946 for first-decade quarterback N.J. "Piffles" Taylor) home, the community-owned Roughriders were led by quarterback Ron LANCASTER and indomitable running back George REED into 11 consecutive Western Conference finals (1966-1976) and 5 Grey Cup appearances (1966, 1967, 1969, 1972, 1976), their sole victory occurring over Ottawa in 1966.   DEREK DRAGER

Saskatchewan Sports Hall of Fame, in Regina, captures the rich sports history of the province. It was established in 1966 to honour outstanding athletes, championship teams and sports personalities. Its present location, the old land titles building, is protected as a heritage site by the province. The hall features pictures and information on the inducted individuals and teams, and a collection of artifacts, trophies and memorabilia related to the history of sport in the province. It is open to the public 7 days a week.   MARGARET J. SANDISON

Saskatchewan Wheat Pool, Canada's largest grain-handling company and largest farmer-owned co-operative, began operations in 1924. Its purpose was to market WHEAT in an orderly and stable manner directly to importers, rather than through the grain exchange and futures markets (see GRAIN HANDLING AND MARKETING). Returns were "pooled" and divided annually among members after expenses were paid (a function assumed by the CANADIAN WHEAT BOARD upon its formation in 1935). The company originally contracted with existing elevator companies to handle grain delivered by members. In 1926 it purchased the Saskatchewan Co-operative Elevator Co and its 451 elevators and 4 terminals. By 1928-29 the Pool owned 970 elevators and was handling 158 million bu (57.5 million hL) of wheat annually. The Pool was an early casualty of the GREAT DEPRESSION, falling deeply into debt, but it emerged after WWII as the foremost organization of its kind in Canada.

In 1984 the Pool operated 595 country elevators as well as 5 export terminals in Thunder Bay and one in Vancouver. It sells fertilizer and other farm supplies, markets livestock, publishes the *Western Producer* newspaper (circulation 140 000) and has published books since 1954 under the name Western Producer Prairie Books. It is also involved in oilseed crushing and processing. Equally important are the Pool's activities in public policy. Its elected officials lobby all levels of government for policies favourable to agriculture and are involved in international farm-policy discussions. The Pool ranked 36th among Canadian corporations (1983) with sales of $2.3 billion; it employed 4082 and was wholly owned by its 70 000 farmer members. JAMES MARSH

Saskatoon, second-largest city in Saskatchewan, is situated in rolling parklands on the banks of the northward-flowing S SASKATCHE-

Population: 154 210 (1981c)
Rate of Increase (1971-81): (CMA) 22%
Rank in Canada: Nineteenth (by CMA)
Date of Incorporation: 1906
Land Area: 138.5 km²
Elevation: 480 m
Climate: Average daily temp, July 18.8°C, Jan -18.7°C; Yearly precip 352.6 mm; Hours of sunshine 2403 per year

WAN R, 235 km (by air) NW of REGINA. It serves as regional centre for the northern prairies and for central and northern Saskatchewan.

Settlement The 2 Gowen sites give evidence that hunting tribes were here 6000 years ago. Stratified settlement sites at Tipperary Cr indicate regular winter habitation by Indians. The region was occupied primarily by Cree and Métis, with Sioux at Moose Woods. White settlement began when the area was chosen for a Temperance colony by a Toronto society. John Lake's survey party selected an E bank site 1882, and the first settlers arrived 1883.

Development Arrival of a railway from Regina in 1890 caused the commercial centre to shift to the flatter W bank. The new community appropriated the name Saskatoon (from the Cree word for a local red berry), while the original settlement became Nutana. A third, Riverdale, arose S of the railway yards. All 3 incorporated as villages (1901-05) and in 1906 combined to form the city of Saskatoon. During the ensuing 7 years, Saskatoon became a hub of western Canada's railway network and underwent a boom, becoming a major distributive centre and, in 1907, gaining the provincial university. Inflated land values and overambitious land-subdivision schemes resulted, and a trade recession (1913) brought a "bust." Not until 1919 did growth recommence, to be stunted anew by the

Depression years. Only after WWII did significant development resume. During the 1950s, a healthy farm economy and population shift from the countryside made Saskatoon one of Canada's fastest-growing cities. The opening of potash mines nearby and of uranium mines in northern Saskatchewan meant continuing expansion during the 1960s and 1970s. New manufacturing plants opened. Development resumed a steadier rate since world demand for uranium declined.

Cityscape Located on glacial deposits within the meander belt of a large river, Saskatoon has an attractively variable topography, with oxbow lakes (Moon and Pike) providing recreational opportunities close by. The river is spanned by 7 bridges, including the Traffic Bridge (1907) and the new 42nd-Street Bridge, which completes a ring road. Prominent on the low W bank are the château-style Bessborough Hotel, St John's Anglican and St Paul's Roman Catholic cathedrals and Knox United Church. Attractive residences and university buildings line the higher E bank. Notable buildings from the boom period include the land titles office and CPR station; among new structures are the Centennial Auditorium and Provincial Building.

The city acquired a land bank through forfeiture of holdings during 2 depressions. Development is under tight control, reinforced by agreements with the surrounding RM of Corman Park. Citizen action during the early 1970s brought establishment of the Meewasin Valley Authority to conserve the riverbank.

Population Initially, settlement was from eastern Canada and the British Isles, but later immigrants came from most parts of Europe, notably Ukraine and Scandinavia. Changing agricultural practices caused a progressive population shift from prairie farms into the city; and boundary expansion, notably the incorporation

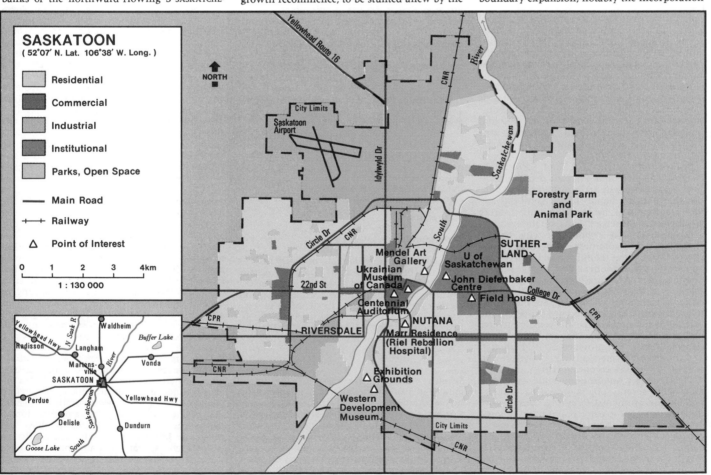

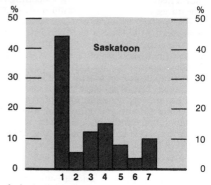

Distribution of Industrial Activity* by Industry Grouping within Census Metropolitan Areas, 1980

Saskatoon

Industry groupings

1. Food and beverage and tobacco products industries
2. Leather, textile, knitting mills and clothing industries
3. Wood, furniture and fixtures, paper and allied and printing, publishing and allied industries
4. Machinery, transportation equipment and electrical products industries
5. Primary metal and metal fabricating industries
6. Rubber and plastic products, petroleum and coal products and chemical products industries
7. Non-metallic mineral products and miscellaneous manufacturing industries.

* Industry activity based on the average of percentage shares of the value shipments of goods of own manufacture, total value added and total number of employees for each of the selected metropolitan areas.

Source: Figure II, Catalogue 31-209, Statistics Canada.

Looking north at the downtown core of Saskatoon, showing 6 of the 7 bridges that span the South Saskatchewan R (*courtesy Saskatoon City Hall*).

of the town of Sutherland (1956), also added citizens. Recent features are rapid growth in the native Indian population and the arrival of East Indians, Filipinos and Vietnamese.

Economy and Labour Force Saskatoon serves a total trading area with a pop of 500 000. It is a centre for health and education services, commercial banking, food processing, mining and manufacturing, and research. The largest employers are the university, the city and Intercontinental Packers Ltd.

Transportation The CNR and CPR retain freight yards here and Via Rail operates minimal passenger services. The airport handles national and international flights. Local bus services are operated by the city, long-distance service by Saskatchewan Transportation Co.

Government and Politics The city charter (1906) specified a commission government, the city's officers being the mayor and at least one appointed commissioner. The strong rule of Commissioner C.J. Yorath (1913-21) gave permanency to this system, much criticized initially. In early aldermanic elections, men voted in each ward where they owned property. The ward system was abolished and female suffrage was introduced in 1920. The ward system was reintroduced by the province in 1973, though not approved by voters until 1979. At present, each of 10 wards elects one alderman.

The city has 3 standing committees of aldermen, plus several others including citizens, notably the Municipal Planning Commission; these are advisory to council and have no separate authority. Relations between the civic and provincial governments are defined by the Urban Municipalities Act (1984). Their fiscal relationships include extensive revenue sharing and unconditional grants.

Cultural Life The UNIVERSITY OF SASKATCHEWAN and its associated religious colleges, Kelsey Institute, Saskatoon Region Community College and the Co-operative College of Canada, are the city's key educational institutions. Important also are the Ukrainian Museum of Canada, Western Development Museum, Mendel Art Gallery and John G. Diefenbaker Centre. There are a daily newspaper (*Star-Phoenix*) and a weekly agricultural paper (*Western Producer*), 3 TV and 6 radio stations and a publishing house (Western Producer Prairie Books). Ethnic organizations operate through the Saskatoon Multicultural Council. The Yevshan Ukrainian Folk-Ballet is the most prominent among numerous dance groups; there are theatres, a symphony orchestra, an opera group, a folk-music coffeehouse and a jazz society. Sports facilities include the Arena, the Field House, Gordie Howe Park and the Harry Bailey Aquatic Centre. There are, among other sports, football, baseball, fastball, hockey, curling, soccer and cricket teams.

A. MARGARET SARJEANT AND
WILLIAM A.S. SARJEANT

Reading: S.P. Clubb, *Saskatoon: The Serenity and the Surge* (1966); W.P. Delainey, J.H. Duerkop and William A.S. Sarjeant, *Saskatoon: A Century in Pictures* (1982); Delainey and Sarjeant, *Saskatoon: The Growth of A City* (1975), I; D. Kerr and S. Hanson, *Saskatoon: The First Half-Century* (1982); B. Peel and E. Knowles, *The Saskatoon Story 1882-1952* (1952).

Saskatoon Berry, *see* BERRIES, WILD.

Sasquatch [Salish, "wild man" or "hairy man"], the name of the mysterious, apelike creature said to inhabit the remoter regions of the Pacific Northwest. In northern California the giant creature is called "Big Foot." Evidence for the existence of the Sasquatch in BC and Alberta is based on references in Indian legend and myth, in passages from journals kept by early travellers and on sightings reported in modern times.
JOHN ROBERT COLOMBO

Satellite, Artificial The Space Age was inaugurated in 1957 by the launching of Sputnik 1; in 1962 Alouette 1 signaled Canada's entry into this era. Canada's early interest in the use of space is not accidental. The country's vast area and sparse population militate against establishment of viable COMMUNICATIONS systems using traditional terrestrial techniques (eg, telephone lines, microwave systems). Communica-

tions satellites are not distance sensitive and, from a single location, can provide service over large areas. Recognition of this potential led to the establishment in 1969 of Telesat Canada as a purveyor of satellite communications on a viable commercial basis. Since then, 7 Anik-series satellites have been launched.

Canada is endowed with generous natural resources, many of them located in remote areas. Identification, exploitation and management of these resources (eg, mineral deposits, petroleum, forests, agricultural lands) can be greatly assisted by resource satellites, eg, the US Landsat series which Canada has used since 1972 and the Radarsat system which is in the planning stages in Canada. WEATHER satellites also provide increasingly reliable information upon which many activities (including resource exploration) depend. Because of its size and position, Canada is an area where weather systems affecting much of the planet are generated and developed. It is thus important that Canada participate in developing weather-information systems. Since 1963 Canada has been receiving and analysing data from the American NOAA and GOES satellites.

Briefly defined, a satellite is a body that revolves about another; thus, the MOON is a satellite of Earth; Earth, a satellite of the SUN. Objects which are lofted into space by man and which continue to revolve around Earth or another planet are referred to as "artificial" or "man-made" satellites. The track repeatedly described by the satellite is called its orbit. Orbits can be relatively low, with an altitude of 200-300 nautical miles and an orbit period of 90-100 minutes for one revolution (eg, those of early US manned flights or the current Shuttle). The forces that keep a satellite aloft can be likened to those affecting an object twirled around at the end of a string: the object's velocity creates a force which tends to propel it away from the source of its initial impulse; the string, like gravity, tends to draw it back towards the source; the 2 forces create a balance which causes the object to remain in a given trajectory (orbit).

The time required for one revolution increases with the height of the orbit. Eventually, an orbital altitude is found at which the satellite takes exactly 24 hours per revolution. Then, if the satellite is moving in the same direction as Earth's rotation and if it remains above the equator (ie, its orbital plane is the same as that of Earth), it will appear to remain immobile above a certain spot on the equator and will be referred to as a geosynchronous or stationary satellite.

Most communications satellites are stationary. Such a satellite may be used without requiring constant changes in the pointing of the user's antenna. One disadvantage, a minor one in many applications, is the lack of coverage over the poles. Polar coverage can be improved by using satellites with orbits inclined relative to the equator; at 90° inclination a polar orbit is described. Such orbits are not only useful in providing polar coverage but, since the satellites are in motion relative to Earth's surface, they will travel, through successive orbits, over Earth's entire surface. These moving satellites are thus useful for the REMOTE SENSING of natural resources, ice and ocean conditions, etc, but they require highly sophisticated antenna systems on the ground to locate and follow them.

The useful lifetime of a satellite can range from a few months to 7-8 years or more. This lifetime rarely depends on the quality of the mission-related equipment; usually, it is limited by the amount of fuel on board or, in some cases, by degradation of solar cells or loss in battery capacity. Fuel is expended to change or correct orbit or to change the attitude (ie, direction) of the satellite relative to the Earth or the sun, etc. Even nominally "stationary" satellites can slowly move from their initial positions under the influence of sun, moon, planets, particle bombardment, etc. Corrections are made by activating small jets or nozzles.

The most advanced technologies from many fields of knowledge contribute to the success of today's relatively sophisticated space systems, and yet the Space Age is in its infancy. Many novel and ambitious concepts, some still found only in the pages of science fiction, are attracting the attention of the scientific community and of industry and social scientists. The 1990s will probably see the realization of large space stations and improved means of transport between Earth and space. J.R. MARCHAND

Satellite Communications In 1945 Arthur C. Clarke proposed that a man-made Earth SATELLITE could be used for communication by radio microwaves between distant locations on Earth. The satellite would be positioned in space at an altitude of about 35 900 km so that its speed of revolution around the Earth would be the same as the speed of the Earth's rotation. This synchronous satellite would always appear in the same place in the sky. It would be in geostationary orbit.

Characteristics A typical satellite consists of a number of repeaters (transponders), each of which provides a large capacity communication channel. Each transponder has a receiver tuned to a frequency channel that has been allocated for uplink communication signals from Earth to the satellite; a frequency shifter to lower the received signals to a downlink frequency; and a power amplifier to transmit signals back to Earth. The communication capacity of a satellite is determined by the number of transponder channels and the volume of communication that can be transmitted on each channel. Although this varies from one type of satellite to another, the most commonly used satellite in 1984 has 12 transponders. Each can carry a colour TV signal or at least 1200 telephone voice signals in one direction. Each new generation of satellites tends to have increased communication capability.

The transmitting and receiving stations on Earth (earth stations) range in size from sophisticated, expensive stations that send and receive all types of communication signals to relatively simple and less costly stations (dish-shaped TV antennas) used only to receive television signals. The size and cost of Earth stations depend upon the power built into the satellite, as well as the frequencies used. The stronger the signal from the satellite, the smaller and less costly the receiving station. Direct Broadcast Satellites (DBS) are designed specifically to minimize the size and cost of TV reception.

Satellites have significant advantages over other modes of transmission such as cable and land-line microwave for certain kinds of communication. The cost of transmission is independent of geographical terrain or distance, as long as both sender and receiver are within line of sight of the satellite (about one-third of the Earth's surface). Communication links can be extended to remote areas that could not otherwise be reached. Satellites are less costly for transmission over extremely long distances — especially for relatively small volumes of communication. A communication signal can be sent to any number of reception points simultaneously, making satellites ideal for television and other forms of point-to-multipoint communication. Satellites are also extremely flexible because the sending and receiving points can be changed on short notice to meet changes in demand. Although satellites are used for voice communication, they are considered to be qualitatively inferior to land-line transmission systems because of the delay (almost 0.3 second) required for the signal to travel to the satellite and return to Earth. Echoes of a speaker's voice are heard 0.6 second after speaking. When echo suppressors are used they sometimes cause the speech of the other party to be clipped.

History The earliest satellite communication experiments were sponsored by the US government. Under project SCORE (Signal Communication by Orbiting Relay Equipment), the first communication satellite was launched by the National Aeronautics and Space Administration (NASA) on 18 Dec 1958 and worked for 13 days. Echo I, launched 12 Aug 1960, was a passive satellite that simply reflected signals sent from ground transmitters back to Earth. Telstar, launched 10 July 1962, was the first active satellite with a microwave receiver and transmitter. The first synchronous satellite, Syncom I, was launched on 14 Feb 1963; it failed after a few days and was followed by a more successful version, Syncom II, on July 26. During this period, the USSR also began a program of satellite experimentation, soon followed by Canada.

The US Congress passed the Communication Satellite Act in 1962, creating the Comsat Corporation with a monopoly on US international satellite communication. An International Satellite Organization (Intelsat) was created in Aug 1964 when 11 Western countries agreed to establish a global satellite communication system. By the early 1980s more than 100 countries were members of Intelsat. It had earth stations in about 150 countries and had successfully launched 24 satellites. (Not all of these satellites continue to be used since the average useful life of a communication satellite is about 8-10 years.)

Within the Soviet bloc, satellite communication is managed by an organization called Intersputnik. By 1980 the Soviets had launched 14 synchronous satellites (Stationar) and at least 75 Molniya satellites, placed in elliptical orbits to serve the far north, where synchronous satellites would be below the horizon.

Canadian Developments On 29 Sept 1962 Canada's first satellite was launched into orbit by NASA, making Canada the third nation in space. Alouette I was designed and built by the Defense Research and Telecommunications Establishment (now the Communications Research Centre), and was used for scientific experiments in the ionosphere. From 1963 to 1969 Canada participated in a joint experimental program with the US called ISIS (International Satellites for Ionospheric Studies). A major objective of this program was to transfer the skills and knowledge developed by government scientists and technicians in the early phase of space communication activity to private industry. RCA Victor, DE HAVILLAND AIRCRAFT and Spar Aerospace were the major companies participating (*see* SPACE TECHNOLOGY).

By 1967 the prime Canadian objective had shifted from scientific experimentation to applications, with emphasis on domestic TELECOMMUNICATIONS and surveys of natural resources. In 1969 Parliament created Telesat Canada to operate a domestic commercial satellite system. Anik A-1 was launched in Nov 1972, followed by Anik A-2 in April 1973, when Canada became the first country to employ satellites for domestic COMMUNICATIONS. A third satellite, Anik A-3, was launched in May 1975. The Anik A system used satellites originally developed by Hughes Aircraft of the US for the Intelsat IV program. Two Canadian companies, Spar Aerospace and Northern Telecom, were subcontractors. Each satellite had 12 transponder channels in the 6/4 GHz band. Over 100 earth stations were installed across Canada.

An experimental communication satellite system, the Communication Technology Satellite (CTS), named Hermes, was developed parallel to the commercial system. The main objective was the opening up of the higher radio frequency 14/12 GHz band that has been allocated for the exclusive use of space communication services. However, the higher frequencies required new technical systems and components, and higher satellite power levels to compensate for the expected increase in signal attenuation, caused primarily by rainfall. The development of new components and the increased weight made necessary by higher power levels meant that major expenditures would have to be incurred on an unproven satellite. Since private firms were unwilling to take these risks, the federal government undertook the project. The Hermes program (1970-80) was a Canada-US collaborative effort: the Dept of Communications was responsible for the design, construction and operation of the spacecraft; NASA provided the launching and other specialized space facilities, and developed a high-power transmitting tube. Use of the satellite was shared equally. The European Space Research Organization (ESRO) joined the program in 1972 with the objective of flight-testing some components designed for a future European satellite.

Hermes was launched on 17 Jan 1976, the most powerful communications satellite at that time, and the first to operate in the 14/12 GHz band. The exclusive use of the frequency band and the higher power of the transponders made possible the use of parabolic (dish) antennas as small as 0.6 m in diameter, especially suited for direct broadcasting of television signals to homes. The Hermes program also included experiments in tele-health, tele-education, community communications, delivery of administrative services, and scientific applications. In addition to experiments conducted over Canada and the US, Hermes was used to demonstrate direct broadcasting in Peru, Australia, and Papua New Guinea. The latter 2 demonstrations were conducted after moving the satellite to a different orbital position over the Pacific. New components developed in government laboratories, such as Field Effect Transistor amplifiers, were subsequently transferred to private industry and are now commonplace in commercial satellites. Major Canadian contractors for Hermes included Spar Aerospace, RCA Ltd, and SED Systems.

NASA launched Anik B for Telesat Canada in Dec 1978. It had 12 commercial radio frequency channels in the 6/4 GHz band and 4 experimental channels in the 14/12 GHz band. The experimental channels were leased to the Dept of Communications for field trials continuing from the Hermes program. Anik D-1 was launched on 26 Aug 1982. It was a replacement

Hermes communications satellite (*courtesy National Research Council / Dept of Communications*).

for the aging Anik A and B satellites. Anik C-3 was placed in orbit in Nov 1982 by the US space shuttle *Columbia*. It has 16 channels, operates in the 14/12 GHz band, and represents a major step toward direct satellite broadcasting to small, rooftop receiving antenna dishes. A second satellite in the same series was launched in Apr 1983 and a third planned for 1984. These new satellites will operate with 4 regional beams across Canada, producing television signals of sufficient strength that they can be received on smaller 1.2-1.8 m rooftop receiving dishes.

With the completion of the Hermes program, government development activity has focused on the Remote Manipulator System (RMS) or the CANADARM for use in the American Space Shuttle Program. Current experimentation is also directed toward the use of satellites for mobile communications. This is made difficult because of the problem of placing satellite microwave antennas on moving vehicles. The first commercial mobile satellite service was to ships at sea. The Marisat system was established in 1976, and the International Maritime Satellite Organization (IMARSAT) in 1979. Canada, with several other countries including the US, France and the Soviet Union, participates in the SAR-SAT program directed to use satellite technology for locating aircraft and ships in distress. Spar Aerospace is designing and building specialized transponders for 3 US Tiros weather satellites under this program. By the 1990s Canada expects to have completed its mobile MSAT, which will further reduce the size of satellite receiving dishes. Considerable research and development is now focusing on radar satellites.

Long-term Implications Despite many technical accomplishments, satellites have not provided the benefits to Canadians that were anticipated. Telesat has become a member of Telecom Canada, the consortium of Canadian telephone companies, and has severely restricted access to its system (*see* TELEPHONES). Telesat's public stock shares were never issued, leaving dominant control of Telesat with the telephone companies. A high proportion of satellite capacity has gone unused. The 1984 satellite was launched into a "parking orbit" because Telesat will have no use for it, at least for several years. Telecommunication service to the North has improved, but many locations do not have satellite service. Television service to the North has expanded by providing northerners with access to television programs of southern Canadian and US stations, but little has been done to promote communication from or between northern communities, or in the languages of native Canadians (*see* COMMUNICATIONS IN THE NORTH).

Similarly, satellites, especially direct broadcast satellites, have increased dramatically the number of US television signals that Canadians can receive. But this has had detrimental effects on the Canadian television and FILM production industries. In 1980, for entertainment/drama programs, only 4% of the programs available were Canadian (*see* TELEVISION PROGRAMMING). Satellites have promoted a wider choice of TV programs for Canadians, but they have not promoted increased opportunities for Canadian expression through its mass media (*see also* CABLE TELEVISION; PAY TELEVISION).

Many countries that do not yet have satellites are concerned that the new technology might be detrimental to both sovereignty and the preservation of national cultures. The expansion of satellite systems in the future will be accompanied by discussion at both national and international levels directed to methods of obtaining the benefits of satellites while avoiding the potential disadvantages. WILLIAM H. MELODY

Reading: Dept of Communications, *Direct-to-Home Satellite Broadcasting for Canada* (1983) and *The Canadian Space Program: Five Year Plan C80181-84185* (1980); *In Search* 4, No 2 (1979), articles by J. Chapman, R. Dohoo, W. Melody; I. Paghis, "Hermes (The Communications Satellite), Its Performance and Applications," *Proceedings of the Royal Society of Canada, Twentieth Symposium* (1978); Science Council of Canada, *A Space Program for Canada*, Report No 1 (1967).

Saturday Night began its life in 1887 under the editorship of E.E. Sheppard. It was initially published weekly in newspaper format, and literally went on sale at 6 PM Saturday. There was a dedicated snobbishness about the magazine as it sought readers among Toronto's high society, but as the desire for circulation and ADVERTISING grew, the snobbishness turned toward a critical and opinionated review of life with a heavy Canadian content. During the 1920s, most notably when Hector Charlesworth was editor, the message was optimism and conservatism, a faithful reflection of the Canadian mood. The magazine first became a genuine critical success when B.K. Sandwell became editor in 1932. Sandwell, who stayed at the helm until 1951, was a man of strong interests, most notably in civil libertarian questions, and he made *Saturday Night* a force. He found good writers on politics and the arts, gave space to profiles of Canadian leaders in government and the arts, and published splendid photographic portraits. By the late 1930s *Saturday Night* had built its advertising lineage to the third largest in N America.

Once Sandwell was gone, *Saturday Night* entered a long decline. Arnold Edinborough was editor for most of the decade after 1958, but it was not until Robert FULFORD became editor in 1968 that *Saturday Night* began to find its critical niche. Under Fulford's lead, the magazine gave ample space to the arts (notably Fulford's film reviews published under the pseudonym of Marshall Delaney) and presented long and sometimes brilliant political reportage, often by Christina McCall. Over the years, *Saturday Night* has featured short stories and poems. It was here that authors such as Dennis LEE and Margaret ATWOOD received their first national exposure.

There were serious financial problems through the 1970s, and in the 1980s *Saturday Night* hovered uneasily between liberal trendiness and serious coverage of the Canadian scene. The life of a general magazine is perilous at best, but *Saturday Night* has a century of survival behind it. Circulation in 1983 was 143 043 per month. *See also* MAGAZINES.   J.L. GRANATSTEIN

Sauger, *see* WALLEYE.

Sault Ste Marie, Ont, City, seat of Algoma Dist, pop 82 687 (1981c), popularly called the "Soo," inc as town 1887 and city 1912, located adjacent to the rapids of the St Mary's R between Lks SUPERIOR and HURON and across the river from the American settlement of the same name. The Algonquian tribes who originally occupied the site called it Bawating ("place of the rapids") and valued it for its control of the upper Great Lks water routes and as a source of abundant whitefish and maple sugar. Etienne BRÛLÉ was probably the first European to visit the area (1622). The site is called Sault (Fr, "falls") de Gaston on Champlain's map of 1632. It became Ste-Marie du Sault when a Jesuit mission was established 1668. The NORTH WEST CO built a post here 1783, developed the fishery as a major food source for the fur trade and dug the first canal past the rapids in 1798. Charles Ermatinger's house, built 1814-23, the oldest stone house in Canada W of Toronto, survives from that period. The original canal was destroyed in the WAR OF 1812, but lake and ocean shipping, with cargoes of grain and iron ore, now bypasses the rapids through a Canadian canal, opened in 1895, and 4 American locks that regularly handle more traffic than any comparable system in the world.

Industrial development was initiated by American-born businessman Francis Clergue who built an electric-power plant and pulp mill, the Algoma Steel Co (1900) and the Algoma Central Ry (1899-1914), which runs to iron-ore reserves nearby. Clergue went into bankruptcy and the Ontario government was forced to step in and rescue some of the businesses. Algoma Steel Co is still the major economic force in the area, employing at peak some 9000 workers. The Soo is Canada's second-largest steel producer after Hamilton, Ont. The forests of the Algoma region also support 2 pulp-and-paper companies in the city. The Ontario Air Service, centered here, maintains the world's largest fleet of planes for fighting forest fires. In its position as a focal point for E-W transportation routes, Sault Ste Marie has become an important regional centre for federal and provincial services, recreation and tourism and post-secondary education.

DAVID D. KEMP

Saumur v City of Québec The Supreme Court, by a 5-4 majority, upheld (1953) the province of Québec's power, challenged by JEHOVAH'S WITNESS Laurier Saumur, to authorize municipalities to prohibit distribution, without police permission, of all publications in the streets. But one majority judge held that, by an Act guaranteeing "free exercise and enjoyment of Religious Profession and Worship," the Québec legislature had precluded application of such bylaws to religious publications; on narrow grounds, the court barred Québec City's interference with

Witnesses' pamphleteering, which had been characterized by harsh attacks on Roman Catholicism. John DIEFENBAKER supported the Witnesses' petition for a Bill of Rights, which became the Canadian Bill of Rights (1960). *See* RONCARELLI V DUPLESSIS.   STEPHEN A. SCOTT

Saunders, Albert Charles, lawyer, politician, judge, premier of PEI (b at Summerside, PEI 12 Oct 1874; d there 18 Oct 1943). Saunders, having completed 4 terms as mayor of Summerside, became the Liberal Party leader in 1923, winning the 1927 election by supporting continued liquor prohibition. In 1931 he became a provincial Supreme Court judge.   LEONARD CUSACK

Saunders, Sir Charles Edward, public servant, plant breeder (b at London, Ont 2 Feb 1867; d at Toronto 25 July 1937), third son of William SAUNDERS. He selected, tested and introduced Marquis wheat to the Canadian West, the foundation for the large commercial production of high-quality bread wheat in Canada. Like his 4 brothers, Charles assisted his father in his many varied interests of plant hybridization, entomology and music. Charles was the least robust of them all but perhaps had the highest standards in everything he did. Educated at U of T and Johns Hopkins U, he was a professor of chemistry at Central U, Ky, in 1892-93 and then devoted 1894-1903 to the study of music and teaching of voice. In 1903 his father, recognizing the value his meticulous standards and perseverance could bring to plant breeding, appointed him to the Experimental Farms Service as experimentalist. (The title became cerealist in 1905 and Dominion cerealist in 1910.)

Saunders immediately applied scientific methods to his new task and spent summers selecting individual heads of wheat from breeding material that previously had been selected in mass. From a cross of Hard Red Calcutta by Red Fife, made in 1892 by his brother A.P. Saunders, a new variety, Markham, resulted. Markham did not produce uniform offspring, however, even though many plants had desirable characteristics. Saunders carefully selected individual heads from early plants having stiff straw. He emphasized that seed from each plant was grown separately with no mixing of strains. Selection was rigorous, only the top lines being kept. He determined which lines had strong gluten by chewing a sample of kernels and intro-

Sir Charles Edward Saunders, plant breeder who developed Marquis wheat (*courtesy Public Archives of Canada/ C-9071*).

duced the baking of small loaves to measure volume. The best strain was named Marquis. In 1907 all surplus seed was sent to Indian Head, Sask, for further testing.

According to Saunders, the response of Marquis to Saskatchewan conditions was phenomenal. It was a week earlier than Red Fife, produced high yields and made excellent bread. Marquis remains the standard for bread making. Its introduction in 1909 meant that wheat could be grown confidently in Saskatchewan and Alberta, where Red Fife frequently matured too late and was damaged by frost. By 1920, 90% of the wheat grown in western Canada was Marquis and a large acreage was grown in the US. Saunders also applied his single-line selection methods to barley, oats, peas, beans and flax and introduced several new excellent varieties of each kind of crop.

In 1922, after 19 years as a plant breeder, Saunders suffered a physical breakdown and resigned his position. He went to Paris where he studied French literature at the Sorbonne for 3 years. He returned to Ottawa but moved to Toronto in 1928. He was knighted in 1934. He continued to lecture on both Marquis wheat and the French language. Music was his major consolation until his death.   T.H. ANSTEY

Saunders, Margaret Marshall, writer (b at Milton, NS 13 Apr 1861; d at Toronto 15 Feb 1947). She moved with her family to Halifax at age 6. At 15 she attended boarding school in Edinburgh, then studied French at Orléans. On her return home she taught school for a short time. Her first novel, a romance, *My Spanish Sailor,* was published in 1889. She wrote *Beautiful Joe* (1894), the story of an abused dog, for an American Humane Soc competition. It won first prize and became a best-seller, was translated into more than 14 languages and was reportedly the first Canadian book to sell more than a million copies. Saunders travelled widely in the US, setting her children's stories of domestic animals and birds in the locales she visited. Her romantic novels include *Esther de Warren* (1927), her own favourite, based on her experiences in Scotland. In 1914 she moved to Toronto. In the 1920s she and her sister toured Canada and the US giving illustrated lectures. A woman of charm and humour, she had an ever-growing interest in humanitarian concerns (especially regarding children) and the treatment of animals. Her stories of pets, while sentimental and didactic, are gracefully written and entertaining.   LORRAINE McMULLEN

Saunders, William, druggist, naturalist, agriculturalist (b at Crediton, Eng 16 June 1836; d at London, Ont 13 Sept 1914). Saunders established the Experimental Farms Service (now Research Branch) of the federal Dept of AGRICULTURE. He moved with his family from England to Canada in 1848 and apprenticed as a druggist, opening his own store in 1855. His concern about insects attacking pharmaceutical plants led him to help found the Entomological Soc of Canada in 1863. An avid gardener and orchardist, he introduced many new varieties of fruit. In 1874 he was made a fellow of the American Assn for the Advancement of Science; he was president of the Ontario College of Pharmacy 1879-82, as well as of the Huron and Erie Mortgage Co; in 1881 he became a fellow of the RSC; and in 1882 he was president of the Fruit Growers' Assn of Ontario. In 1886 Parliament passed legislation establishing the Dominion Experimental Farms and Stations, partly based on Saunders's report of his 1885 investigation of US stations, and he was appointed director. He pursued his new task with vigour, personally selecting sites for each of the original 5 farms, choosing staff and continuing his interests in cereal breeding, horticulture and forestry. He commenced the wheat-breeding program that resulted in his son Sir

Charles Edward SAUNDERS's development of Marquis, the variety that opened the Canadian West. He received honorary degrees from Queen's and U of T; his many technical writings are in Dept of Agriculture libraries.   T.H. ANSTEY

Sauvé, Jeanne-Mathilde, née Benoît, journalist, politician, governor general of Canada (b at Prud'homme, Sask 26 Apr 1922). Educated at Notre-Dame du Rosaire Convent, Ottawa, and U of O, she was national president of the Young Catholic Students Group 1942-47. In 1948 she married Maurice SAUVÉ and began a distinguished career as a free-lance journalist and broadcaster in Montréal. She was first elected as a Liberal MP from Montréal in 1972. From 1972 to 1979 she served successively as minister of state for science and technology, minister of the environment and minister of communications. On 14 Apr 1980 Sauvé became the first woman to be Speaker of the House of Commons. As Speaker she was criticized for lack of control over the turbulent House, but her sweeping reforms of the administration of the Commons were generally acclaimed. She was sworn in as governor general of Canada on 14 May 1984 — the first woman to hold the post.
                HARRIET GORHAM

Jeanne Sauvé, the first woman in Canada to be appointed governor general (*courtesy Canapress*).

Sauvé, Joseph-Mignault-Paul, premier of Québec (b at St-Benoît, Qué 24 Mar 1907; d at St-Eustache, Qué 2 Jan 1960). Though he was premier for only a short time, Sept 1959 to his death, he inaugurated a period of major political and social change for Québec. A member of the reserve from 1931 he served overseas during WWII, and was second-in-command of the Fusiliers de Mont-Royal during the Normandy landing. Promoted brigadier in 1947 he was also able to maintain an active political career throughout. Elected Conservative member of the Québec legislature for Deux-Montagnes during the 1930 by-elections, he was defeated in 1935, but played an important role in the creation of the UNION NATIONALE party and was repeatedly elected for that party from 1936 to 56. He was chosen successor to Maurice DUPLESSIS and quickly served notice that things would not be the same by pronouncing a single word that became famous throughout Québec: *Désormais* ('henceforth'). Sauvé's "hundred days" are seen as the start of the QUIET REVOLUTION because they brought new life and settled several matters that were "on hold," including hospital insurance and university subsidies.   DANIEL LATOUCHE

Sauvé, Maurice, economist, politician, businessman (b at Montréal 20 Sept 1923). Maurice Sauvé received his PhD from U of Paris in 1952 and returned to Montréal to work for the Canadian and Catholic Confederation of Labour. In 1955 he served on the Royal Commission on

Canada's Economic Prospects. A Liberal, he was closely associated with the construction of the economic base for Québec's QUIET REVOLUTION. In 1962 he was elected to the House of Commons and served as minister of forestry and rural development 1964-68. Leaving politics for business, he joined Consolidated Bathurst Inc and held a number of directorships. He is married to Jeanne SAUVÉ.   HARRIET GORHAM

Savage, Alfred, veterinarian, teacher, researcher (b at Montréal 10 Aug 1889; d at Winnipeg 14 Jan 1970). After serving in the Canadian Army Veterinary Corps 1915-19, he became professor of animal pathology at U of Man 1921-64. He was also head of the dept of animal pathology and bacteriology 1930-45 and dean of agriculture 1933-37, and was animal pathologist for the Manitoba Dept of Agriculture 1937-57. Savage conducted early investigations of semen evaluation and agglutination tests for brucellosis, and developed surgical instruments and improved techniques for anesthesia. He was an outstanding lecturer and teacher, and was influential in the formation of the Canadian Veterinary Medical Assn, of which he was president 1951-52.   R.G. THOMSON

Savage, Anne Douglas, painter (b at Montréal 27 July 1896; d there 25 Mar 1971). Best known during her lifetime as a pioneer in teaching children's art along progressive lines, Anne Savage's paintings were initially strongly influenced by the GROUP OF SEVEN. Her paintings later showed a lyrical quality of their own, characterized by muted colour, sound rhythm and a late-in-life foray into abstraction. Trained by William BRYMNER, she was a member of the Beaver Hall Hill group and president of the Canadian Group of Painters (1949, 1960). Savage also taught at Baron Byng High School 1922-48 and had a far-reaching influence on pupils such as artists Tobie STEINHOUSE, Alfred Pinsky and Leah Sherman, who founded the Concordia fine-arts department.   ANNE McDOUGALL

Savard, Félix-Antoine, priest, writer, educator (b at Québec C 31 Aug 1896; d there 24 Aug 1982). After spending his childhood and youth in the Saguenay, Savard discovered and fell in love with the Charlevoix region, which he called Québec's metaphysical county. Ordained a priest in 1922, he started teaching the humanities. He subsequently became curate of several parishes and founding curé of St-Philippe-de-Clermont. He also was active in colonizing the Abitibi region in the 1930s. During these years of pastoral work, Savard's knowledge of humanism deepened through an intensive study of Greek, Latin and French authors of the medieval and classical periods, as well as his contemporaries Mistral, Claudel and Valéry.

In 1937 MENAUD, MAÎTRE-DRAVEUR was published and assured Savard a place among the leading authors of his time. His novel moves like an epic poem in which symbol, image and metaphor abound; its vibrant character, a truly mythical hero, is presented against the magnificent Charlevoix landscape and the cyclical unfolding of the seasons, and his suffering and tragic end provide a grave and urgent warning to future generations.

From the 1940s Savard was closely associated with Laval. Dean of its faculty of arts for 7 years, he taught literature and played an important role in FOLKLORE discoveries and research. He was elected to the RSC in 1945 and to the Académie canadienne-française in 1954. A masterful and often highly controversial speaker, Savard spent most of his active retirement in his chosen region of St-Joseph-de-la-Rive, in Charlevoix.

Savard devoted his life to writing. He published 3 collections, mainly composed of poetry and prose: *L'Abatis* (1943), *Le Barachois* (1959), *Le Bouscueil* (1972); 2 plays, *La Folle* (1960) and *La*

Dalle-des-morts (1965), and narrative works in the form of short stories and parables, eg, *La Minuit* (1948) and *Martin et le pauvre* (1959). He also was the author of personal notebooks, journals and memoirs in which, while he promotes and defends keeping faith with sacred national traditions, he reveals himself to be an artist in words, a sculptor of form, always searching for new images and finding pleasure in the language.

But it is *Menaud, maître-draveur,* a work that took 30 years to complete, that firmly established his literary renown. It was published in 5 versions (3 of which are distinctly different). It remains a fine example of a patiently crafted, successful literary work.   RÉJEAN ROBIDOUX

Savile, Douglas Barton Osborne, botanist, ecologist (b at Dublin, Ire 19 July 1909). After studies at McGill (1933, 1934), Savile began a career with the federal Dept of Agriculture (1936) while studying for his doctorate at U of Mich (1939). His interdisciplinary approach is shown by his wide range of publications on taxonomy, ecology and parasitology of fungi, vascular plants, birds and mammals, including expertise on bird flight. Much of his botanical research was conducted in the Arctic, with a 3-year interlude in coastal BC, eventually resulting in a monograph, *Arctic Adaptations in Plants* (1972). A 1962 monograph on collection and care of plant specimens remains popular with botanists. Savile rose through various government positions to the post of principal mycologist (1957), becoming emeritus research associate of the Biosystematics Research Inst upon "retirement" in 1975.   MARTIN K. McNICHOLL

Sawchuk, Terrence Gordon, hockey goalkeeper (b at Winnipeg 28 Dec 1929; d at New York 31 May 1970). He played junior hockey in Winnipeg and Galt, Ont, turning professional at age 17 with Omaha. He joined Detroit Red Wings 1951 and won the CALDER TROPHY (best rookie). Acrobatic, fearless, he had exceptional reflexes and for the first 5 years of his career played brilliantly, winning the VEZINA TROPHY (fewest goals allowed) 3 times, recording 56 shutouts and allowing fewer than 2 goals a game. However, physical and psychological strains shattered his health and career. He suffered nervous exhaustion, arthritis, mononucleosis, severe back injuries, innumerable cuts, as well as a collapsed lung in a car accident. He was traded from team to team and briefly regained his former glory with TORONTO MAPLE LEAFS, sharing the Vezina Trophy 1965 and leading the team to a Stanley Cup victory 1967 with spectacular play. He compiled 103 shutouts, a record unlikely to be surpassed. He died of injuries suffered accidentally in a scuffle with teammate Ron Stewart.   JAMES MARSH

Sawfly, common name for members of INSECT order Hymenoptera, which resemble wasps and are characterized by the lack of a marked constriction between first and second abdominal segments. Common name is derived from the sawlike ovipositor used by females to slit open host plant and lay eggs. In Canada sawflies are found everywhere, especially in boreal regions. About 10 000 species are known worldwide; about 600 in Canada. Larvae and most adults are herbivorous; adults of some species feed partly on other insects. Their plant-feeding habit may make sawflies important defoliators; however, surprisingly few species are recognized as regular threats to crops and forests. Most species feed on plants of little economic importance (eg, willows, sedges, wild grasses) or show irregular population explosions of limited extent. Larvae are caterpillarlike, but distinguished from true caterpillars by having smooth prolegs (false legs) on abdomen. Most species reproduce bisexually; in some, males are rare or unknown and reproduction is by parthenogenesis (development of offspring from unfertilized eggs).   HENRI GOULET

Sawmill, a common feature of 19th-century eastern Canadian landscapes. Early sawmills were simple structures: water-powered and cheaply built, usually with a single reciprocating blade and a hand-operated ratchet carriage to feed logs into the blade. They were used for cutting local logs for local consumption. Sawing was slow: a day's work might produce 500 boards. Built alongside or in conjunction with a gristmill and near a blacksmith shop, such mills might be the focus of a rising village, though work was seasonal and often part-time.

Far more significant were the fewer, larger mills cutting logs for export. Equipped with gang saws and ancillary machinery, they produced better lumber faster. After 1840 new technologies increased their size and efficiency. Circular saws were used for edging and trimming. The continuous-cutting band saw largely replaced the reciprocating gang after 1890. Rollers and log chains moved material through the mill quickly. Steam power, increasingly common after mid-century, meant faster, more continuous cutting and locational freedom. Electric lighting reduced the fire hazard of night work. In 1830 a large mill might have produced 7500 m/day; by 1850, 18 000 m was unexceptional; in 1900 the figure might be 180 000 m. Massive investment lay behind these increases, and with it came concentration in fewer locations and the preeminence of a relatively small number of firms. See TIMBER TRADE HISTORY.   GRAEME WYNN

Saxifrage, common name for several herbaceous PLANTS of family Saxifragaceae, primarily genus *Saxifraga* [from Lat *saxifragus*, "stonebreaking," describing the ability of roots to burrow into rocks via cracks]. Thirty-three species occur in Canada; 370 worldwide. Some Canadian species, eg, *S. aizoides* and *S. oppositifolia*, are circumpolar and are also found in Iceland, Spitzbergen, northern Europe and Siberia. Most Canadian saxifrages are found in western alpine regions from the YT to BC and Alberta. Flowers, mostly small, commonly white or yellow, are borne as terminal clusters on hairy stalks. Plants form tufted, spreading cushions, frequently giving striking patches of colour. *S. oppositifolia* (purple mountain saxifrage), forming low mats covered by cup-shaped, rosy-purple flowers, is among northernmost growing plants (found on Ellesmere I). Other well-known Canadian members of the family include genera: *Ribes* (currants and gooseberries), *Philadelphus* (mock orange), *Mitella* (mitrewort or bishop's cap) and *Tiarella* (false mitrewort or foam flower). Introduced plants include *Bergenia* (elephant ear) with deep pink flowers.   PATRICK SEYMOUR

Scadding, Henry, clergyman, scholar (b at Dunkeswell, Eng 29 July 1813; d at Toronto 6 May 1901). Educated at Upper Canada College and St John's College, Cambridge, Scadding became a Church of England clergyman in 1838. After teaching for several years at Upper Canada College, he was appointed by Bishop John STRACHAN to be rector of the newly built Holy Trinity Church 1847, where he remained until 1875. Throughout his life, Scadding was a strong supporter of Strachan. He produced numerous pamphlets and articles, but his passion for Toronto's history dominated: in 1873 he produced *Toronto of Old*; in 1884 he and J.C. DENT published *Toronto, Past and Present.* In 1891 he and G. Mercer Adam wrote *Toronto, Old and New.* Scadding's house is now a Toronto landmark.   VICTOR RUSSELL

Scale Insect, highly specialized INSECT belonging to order Hemiptera, suborder Homoptera, superfamily Coccoidea. Scale insects are diverse in habit and structure. Females are wingless, legless and obscurely segmented, have poorly developed eyes and antennae, and may be protected by a waxy, cottony or hard, scalelike covering. Males are tiny, lack mouthparts, and are short-lived. Crawlers, the first juvenile stage, are mobile and function in dispersal. Most species are 0.5-2.0 mm long, but one measures over 25 mm. Many cause serious damage to plants. In Canada, major pests include oyster-shell scale, pine needle scale, and San José scale; they are controlled by predators, parasites, insecticides and fumigants. Cottony maple scale, which occurs throughout the US and Canada, was introduced from Europe. Some species are beneficial: one produces lac, from which shellac is made; several have been dye sources; one produces Indian wax, used for medicinal purposes; another produces China wax, formerly used for candles.   A.M. HARPER

Scallop, bivalve (hinged shell) MOLLUSC of sub-order Pectinina. Scallops are found in all seas. Their rounded or fan-shaped SHELLS are among the most beautiful and colourful of mollusc shells. Larger species are fished worldwide. Scallops usually lie free on the bottom, or may be attached to a solid object by byssal threads (tough filaments secreted by the scallop) or cementlike substance. Many species are present in all Canadian seas, but only sea scallops (*Placopecten magellanicus*) occur in sufficient numbers to be trawled off the East Coast. Weathervane scallops (*Patinopecten caurinus*) are sporadically present on the West Coast but are usually too scarce to fish. Other species, taken recreationally on the Pacific coast, include red scallop (*Chlamys rubida*) and large rock scallop (*Hinnites giganteus*). Iceland scallop (*C. islandica*) is taken in small numbers on the East Coast; attempts are being made to introduce bay scallop (*Argopecten irradians*) to PEI.
                                          FRANK R. BERNARD

Shucking scallops off Digby, NS (*photo by Harold V. Green/Valan*).

Scammell, Arthur Reginald, teacher, writer (b at Change Is, Nfld 12 Feb 1913). He taught school in outport Newfoundland 1932-39 and in Montréal 1942-70, retiring in 1970 to St John's. At age 15 he wrote what was to be his most famous poem, "The Squid-Jiggin' Ground," featuring a wonderful collection of characters participating in a traditional Newfoundland outport activity. A collection of his prose and verse, *My Newfoundland*, appeared in print in 1966 and on record in 1973; the latter featured Scammell reciting and singing his own works.   JAMES G.G. MOORE

Scarlett, Earle Parkhill, physician (b at High Bluff, Man 27 June 1896; d at Calgary 14 June 1982). He received his BA from U of Man in 1916 and then served in WWI with the Canadian Machine Gun Corps, was gassed in 1917 and severely wounded in 1918. After medical studies at U of T and practice in the US, he joined the Calgary Associate Clinic in 1930 and was a leading Calgary physician until he retired in 1958. A writer of elegance, he was author of over 450 papers, a collection of which, edited by C.G. Roland, was published as *In Sickness and in Health* (1972). A man of culture, he was chancellor of U of A, 1952-58. His honours include doc-

torates from U of T, U of A and U of Calgary; he was one of the most loved and respected Canadians of his time.   WALTER H. JOHNS

Schaefer, Carl Fellman, artist, teacher (b at Hanover, Ont 30 Apr 1903). A vigorous yet sensitive interpreter of rural southern Ontario scenery, Schaefer is typical of regionalist Canadian artists who chose to concentrate on agrarian and social rather than wilderness themes during the 1930s. His best work was inspired by the farm environment of his native Grey County. He studied at the Ontario Coll of Art 1921-24, where his teachers included Arthur LISMER and J.E.H. MACDONALD. His introduction to northern Ontario came in 1926 with a canoe trip to the Pickerel and French rivers, but he was forced by the Depression to reestablish himself and his family at Hanover, where he took up watercolour painting. His first "Hanover period" (1932-42) was marked by a transition from a decorative and geometric to a starkly realistic, occasionally allegorical approach to landscape and still life. His experience as an official war artist with the RCAF (1943-46) darkened his vision, but by the 1950s he was again painting in a broad, lyrical spirit in the countryside around Hanover and in neighbouring Wellington and Waterloo counties. Schaefer began teaching in 1930 and taught at OCA 1948-70. He has received numerous awards and honours and was active in art societies of his time.   ROBERT STACEY

Schafer, Raymond Murray, composer, writer, educator (b at Sarnia, Ont 18 July 1933). R. Murray Schafer has earned an international reputation for his musical compositions, innovative educational theories and outspoken opinions. His early career led him in 1956 from Toronto to Austria and England and back to Canada in 1961, where he became artist-in-residence at Memorial (1963-64) and SFU (1965-75). Since 1975 he has lived on a farm near Bancroft, Ont.

Schafer first drew wide attention through his radical experiments in elementary music education in the late 1960s, which resulted in a series of imaginative educational booklets and several compositions designed for performance by youth orchestras and choirs. His intense interest in soundscape ecology led to his forming the WORLD SOUNDSCAPE PROJECT (1971), an organization devoted to the critical study of the social and aesthetic aspects of the sonic environment. His musical compositions reveal many concerns, ranging from themes of alienation and political oppression to a fascination with eastern mysticism and the sounds of the environment. His recent music reflects a strong sense of Canadian identity, one man's response to the Canadian landscape and his search for the myth without which, as he wrote in 1983, the nation dies.   ALAN M. GILLMOR

Schefferville, Qué, Town, pop 1997 (1981c), inc 1955, is located between Knob and Pearce lakes, in the heart of the Québec-Labrador peninsula, 576 km N of SEPT-ÎLES. Father Louis Babel, on a mission to the MONTAGNAIS-NASKAPI 1866-70, made a map of the Ungava region showing mineral-rich areas. In 1895 a Montréal geologist, A.P. LOW, did detailed survey and mapping

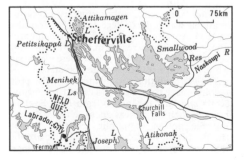

work showing the presence of major iron-ore deposits in the Knob Lk region. In 1938 the research results of a Laval geologist, J.A. Retty, attracted the interest of financiers, and in 1942 the Hollinger North Shore Exploration Co won some land concessions. In 1950 the QUEBEC NORTH SHORE AND LABRADOR RY, a subsidiary of Iron Ore Co of Canada, started building a rail line to Knob Lk. The first shipment of minerals arrived in Sept-Îles in 1954. Schefferville, built in 1953 by the Iron Ore Co, was named by Prem Maurice DUPLESSIS in honour of Mgr Lionel Scheffer (1903-66), first bishop of Labrador.

The area's economic activity basically depends on its IRON ORE. Initial reserves were estimated at 420 million t; the company yearly extracted about 8 million t. In 1979 iron production at Schefferville topped $282 million, but in 1983 Iron Ore Co ceased operations completely, causing the near shutdown of the town.
                              CLAUDINE PIERRE-DESCHÊNES

Schneider, Julius Gustav Albert, Bert, boxer (b at Cleveland, Ohio 1897). Schneider's family moved to Montréal when he was 9 and he took up boxing in high school. He later joined the Montréal Amateur Athletic Assn and became its welterweight champion. Slim in the legs but heavily muscled in the upper body, he was not a stylish boxer. A mixer and scrapper, he capitalized on his ability to move quickly. He was chosen for the 1920 Canadian Olympic team, though still an American citizen, and won the welterweight title. After 75 professional fights he joined the US Border Patrol. He eventually retired to Montréal.   J. THOMAS WEST

Schneider, William George, scientist, scientific administrator (b at Wolseley, Sask 1 June 1915). Schneider received his BSc and MS from U of Sask (1937, 1939) and his PhD from McGill (1941). From 1943 to 1946 he was employed by the Woods Hole Oceanographic Institute, leaving it to join the NATIONAL RESEARCH COUNCIL (1946-80). There he was successively director of the division of pure chemistry (1963-65), vice-president, scientific (1965-67) and president (1967-80). Since 1980 he has been a chemical consultant. He has published extensively in molecular forces, critical phenomena, ultrasonics, nuclear magnetic resonance and organic semiconductors. He has also received many honours and awards, including fellowship in the Royal Soc (London), the RSC and the Chemical Inst of Canada.   LEO YAFFE

Schofield, Francis William, veterinarian, teacher, researcher (b at Rugby, Eng 15 Mar 1889; d at Seoul, S Korea 12 Apr 1970). Schofield joined the faculty of the Ontario Veterinary Coll in 1910. He was a teacher and missionary in Korea 1916-19, and returned there in 1955 at retirement. From 1924 to 1956 he was professor of veterinary pathology at OVC. He was nationally and internationally known for his research in animal disease, in particular sweet-clover poisoning of cattle, infections in young animals and viral mink enteritis. An outstanding lecturer and teacher, he provided philosophy and religion with his teaching, and demonstrated his profoundly intuitive intellect through excellent oratorical ability and a sense of the dramatic.   R.G. THOMSON

School Boards, groups of elected (with exceptions) members of a community to whom the provinces have delegated authority over some aspects of education. There are about 900 school boards in Canada, although the number is steadily decreasing as small jurisdictions are combined into larger ones. A variety of publicly supported school boards exist, generally organized according to either religion or language or both. The 2 largest groups of school boards are the public boards, providing schools open to all children, and the separate boards, providing educational services for children of Roman Catholic parents. In sparsely populated areas and in the territories schools are operated directly by the provincial or federal governments; in these places there are school committees but no formally elected school boards.

The degree to which local school boards, as opposed to the provincial governments, control education is an important issue. Local boards are primarily responsible for personnel matters and for providing facilities and supplies. For example, local boards may hire any professional personnel they wish, although the provinces require that such personnel have completed a certain amount of specific training. Local boards have the power to dismiss teachers (they rarely do so) for just cause if proper procedures are followed. Teachers can generally appeal a dismissal to a board of reference, established by, but independent of, the minister of education and the local school board. Unless the provincial authorities revoke the teaching certificate, however, the teacher can be hired by another board or rehired by the first. There is some shared authority with the province in many other areas, eg, curriculum, textbook selection and courses of study. In curriculum, for example, guidelines are produced by the provincial authorities. Within these guidelines, however, the boards can exercise wide discretionary powers. Sometimes provincial rules, regulations and statutes are ignored, sometimes they are interpreted liberally. Provincial governments generally produce lists of approved books as well and local boards may choose to use them, may approve others, or may ask for the approval of others. It seems that generally boards can prohibit the use of books not approved by provincial authorities. School boards have taxing powers, although in all jurisdictions the provincial treasury provides a major amount of funding. Local boards are legislated by various statutes and regulations.

School business is conducted primarily at school-board meetings, which are scheduled regularly, usually once or twice a month. By law, these are open meetings to which the public is invited; the meetings are run by a chairperson, generally elected by other trustees for a one-year term. Professional staff are also involved in the meetings. Usually the chief executive officer (most commonly the superintendent) submits information for the board's consideration. While the audience is seldom very large (unless a controversial issue arises), it is not uncommon for delegations from the community to appear and present opinions or arguments about various issues, and representatives from the media are often in attendance. It is only the elected trustees, however, who vote on any motion or business before the board.

School-board operation in Canada is distinguished by the use of committees to work out the details of the business. Occasionally members of the public are appointed as well, although this is usually only true for special committees established to study some major problem. Large boards sometimes have more than 20 committees, which are responsible for a variety of areas such as curriculum, personnel, salary negotiations, long-range planning and special education. There is a slight trend toward reducing the number of committees and some boards use only 2 — one for business concerns and one for academic concerns.

According to conventional wisdom, school boards establish policy and administrators carry it out. In reality, the situation is much more complex. While the board has final authority in matters not affected by provincial regulation, most issues are debated by a variety of interest groups and the final policy is the result of extensive consultation. Teachers, for example, are highly organized and often influence a board's policy decisions, as do parents and taxpayers.

Although each school board is uniquely a part of a local community, school boards in general discuss the same issues and carry out similar tasks across the country. Usually a great amount of effort is expended approving and spending the budget, which can run into several hundreds of millions of dollars. In connection with the budget, the board negotiates regularly, often annually, with various categories of staff about salary and work conditions, except in certain provinces, eg, New Brunswick and Québec, where bargaining is conducted by provincial authorities.

Language instruction, special education, curriculum versus enrichment programs, multiculturalism, technical versus liberal education, the role of computers and computer technology, and problems associated with declining enrolments are all issues with which school boards must contend.

School boards have formed provincial organizations in each province for purposes of communication, in-service training and effective representation to the legislatures. The Canadian School Trustees Association is the national organization, with offices in Ottawa.

School boards are a phenomenon rather peculiar to Canada and the US. Some other countries, such as Britain, have school committees, but these are really subgroupings of municipal bodies. Other countries, eg, Australia, have no local governing bodies at all but are administered from the central governments. While often criticized for inefficiency, parochial points of view and lack of expertise in educational technology, school boards are among the most democratic of our institutions, responsive to local demands and close to the people. They provide a lively and sometimes vibrant vehicle for grass-roots participation in educational policies and practice. EDWARD S. HICKCOX

School Facilities have been an integral part of SCHOOL SYSTEMS since the beginning of European settlement in the early 17th century. The first schools were established shortly after the French settled Québec in 1608. The few *petits écoles* organized by the Roman Catholic clergy and other missionaries in French Canada to teach reading, writing, arithmetic and religion appear to have been the first and, for many decades, the only schools in Canada.

Because the parish priest was often the initial organizer and only teacher until a lay person or someone from a teaching order could be recruited from France, these early schools were located close to the local church. The earliest schools probably reflected notions about function and structure that the clergy and settlers had brought with them from their native regions, especially Normandy, Île-de-France and Poitou. Glass and other fittings were not available in Canada at this time and during the winter months the poorly lit rooms could only be used a few hours each day. Only the larger centres, such as Québec and Trois-Rivières, had substantial buildings; most were one-room schools that were small in comparison to the one-room schools of the present century, because population concentrations were small and the finished building materials required considerable manual labour. The only secondary education available was at the Collège de Québec, founded in 1635. As the culturally isolated French Canadian population increased in the 17th and 18th centuries, schools opened where there was a parish priest and a suitable building available.

The prerevolutionary "planters" and the postrevolutionary LOYALISTS who came first to Nova Scotia and later to Ontario from New England brought their own ideas about schools, including the notion of public sectarian schools financed from the sale of crown lands; an idea that was repeated later throughout the upper St Lawrence-Great Lakes region and even later in western Canada. The New Englanders also wanted to establish SECONDARY SCHOOLS, or grammar schools, as they had already done in Boston, Salem and other prosperous New England coastal towns. Among the first of such schools were King's College, the Halifax Grammar School, the College of New Brunswick and Prince of Wales College in PEI.

The architecture of school buildings in the 19th century varied considerably. In Québec City, Trois-Rivières and Montréal, school buildings developed according to a "French Provincial" style. The SÉMINAIRE DE QUÉBEC and College de Montréal are well-known examples. In Halifax and Windsor, NS, they represented the "American Colonial" style, as evident in Kings College and the Halifax Grammar School (*see* ARCHITECTURAL STYLES). In contrast, the school facilities in the small, remote frontier settlements were the simplest buildings that would serve the purpose, and authorities used whatever local skills and materials were available at the time. In many cases these buildings were nothing more than log cabins or sheds. During the early 19th century, tiny wooden schools were still being built in frontier settlements, such as those begun by the Hudson's Bay Company on the N Saskatchewan R in 1808 for the children of company employees, but in the older and larger communities more substantial schools, including some secondary schools, were being constructed. Generally, these buildings facilitated learning only in the sense that they provided relatively comfortable shelter and the larger of them organized students into groups of manageable size and levels of achievement.

The simple buildings of earlier times began to disappear in the second half of the century as architects imitated American or British schools, with their impressive neoclassical entrances. Brick and stone were widely used even where they could not be obtained locally. Furnishings, equipment and books were distributed from rapidly growing commercial centres such as Montréal and Toronto; some were imported. School sites, or school grounds as they were usually called, were cleared and leveled so that school gardens could be planted and playgrounds could be reserved. Unfortunately, inside these massive buildings the plan was often the same. The larger schools generally had a corridor running down the center of each of the 2- or even 3-storey buildings with identical classrooms on both sides, a design pejoratively referred to as an "egg carton." The typical classroom was a large squarish compartment with a high ceiling and a raised platform at one end for the teacher's desk. The intention was no doubt to awe the students by the sheer scale of their surroundings and by the importance attached to education.

In the first quarter of the 20th century, the number of schools increased at a phenomenal rate as the population of Canada mushroomed from 5.3 million in 1901 to approximately 9 million in 1926. During this period, compulsory attendance legislation was stringently enforced wherever possible and recalcitrant families were obliged to send their children to school. As an example of the increase in school building activity, the number of school districts in the new province of Saskatchewan increased from 896 to 3702 from 1905 to 1915, a large proportion of which operated only a one-room rural elementary school. Such a demand for one-room schools developed that THE T. EATON COMPANY advertised what amounted to school building kits in the Winnipeg edition of their 1917-18 catalogue. These kits contained school building plans along with the necessary lumber, nails, fittings and other materials. The school became the ubiquitous public building on the Canadian landscape.

The traditional one-room schoolhouse of rural Canada, c1900-25 (*courtesy Ontario Archives*).

Most schools of the first quarter of this century consisted largely of classrooms, corridors and cloakrooms. However, attempts were made to improve their appearances, especially in rural Ontario. The Ontario Department of Education's *Plans for Rural School Building* commented that "everyone connected with school work should endeavour to improve school architecture so that the present buildings, which are devoid of architectural beauty, should be replaced within the next generation by modern structures."

Little improvement was made during the GREAT DEPRESSION or WWII, though as a result of the emerging "human relations" approach in various disciplines, the heavy wood and iron desks that had been bolted to the floor were replaced by lighter materials so that children no longer had to be seated in rows but could be arranged in rings, blocks and other patterns to facilitate various instructional techniques.

Some of the school buildings in use through WWII were either physically or functionally obsolete, or both, by 1951. Many of the older buildings needed substantial repair or replacement. Furthermore, because of farm consolidation and mechanization, and in some cases farm abandonment, population drifted from rural to urban areas leaving many small schools virtually empty while tending to overcrowd schools in the larger towns and cities. Simultaneously, the consolidation of small school districts and the accompanying school busing and other school services required that larger, more centralized buildings be provided. A special feature of this period was the separation of elementary and high-school students in small towns, villages

The larger "consolidated" school of the late 19th and early 20th centuries classified students according to age, achievement and sex. The school bus was already part of school life (*courtesy Public Archives of Canada*).

and farming areas, for it created a need for large central or regional high schools.

Different approaches to instruction and new approaches to the planning of educational facilities originating in the US and western Europe also helped render the old "egg carton" schools obsolete. A large study of educational facilities (SEF) undertaken by the Toronto Metropolitan Board of Education was used in school planning across Canada. Fresh ideas about organizing students for instruction, including small and large group instruction, team teaching, differentiated staffing, individualized instruction and continuous progress, required flexible space and sophisticated support functions. This period also marked the beginning of the democratization of architecture: buildings were designed for public use and with public advice. The use of educational specifications ("Ed Spec"), prepared after consultations with teachers and others who might be affected by the new facilities resulted in flexible but complex school buildings with specialized learning spaces for sciences, languages, home economics, industrial arts and occasionally others. A new and radical type of building, the "open-area" or "open-plan school," was the most controversial innovation through the 1970s and beyond. These schools had few enclosed spaces and the floor plan was organized around a learning resource centre, or library, with teaching stations and services areas surrounding it. Soon there were complaints by teachers about noise, confusion and inadequate wall space for display purposes; consequently, second and third generation open-area schools were modified to include more closed spaces, including a few traditional classrooms.

Many of the new high-school facilities of this era still contained the traditional classrooms and science laboratories, but also included new features. Larger more diversified instructional resource centres replaced the small school libraries. Gymnasiums were expanded to meet official standards and to accommodate more activities. In some instances swimming pools were added to the facilities. Specialized facilities such as language laboratories, cafeterias and guidance centres became regular features. Consequently the new high school became a very complex and very costly public facility that attracted more use by the general public.

During this period of economic and population growth, Canadian architects produced some notable examples of modern architecture, including some distinctive educational buildings. Most of the educational showpieces were

buildings at post-secondary institutions, particularly some of the newer universities such as SIMON FRASER UNIVERSITY, UNIVERSITY OF LETHBRIDGE and TRENT UNIVERSITY, but a few exemplary school buildings were also designed, eg, the Mayland Heights Elementary School in Calgary designed by architect Gordon Atkins, and Douglas CARDINAL's Cumberland Elementary School at La Ronge, Sask. The floor plan of the latter is shaped like an Indian Chief's ceremonial headdress and has a kindergarten room with one-way glass so that mothers may monitor the initial adjustment of their children to the classroom.

During this period school sites began to attract attention again. The old school garden virtually disappeared, but playgrounds were retained and recreational facilities and landscaping were added. While provincial governments and boards of education might have suggested or even imposed limits on the size of all school sites, some of the high schools built during this period had campus settings, including improved facilities for football, soccer, and track and field.

As a result of spending restraints, fewer new schools are being built in the 1980s. Provincial departments and school boards have settled for a "no frills" approach. Energy efficiency has also become a major concern. Furthermore, with so many comparatively new schools being closed because of decreasing enrolments, boards of education are reluctant to build new facilities except where long-term need can be clearly demonstrated. For this century at least, the golden age of school construction seems to have passed.   ALLAN GUY

School Systems In all modern societies, the young are educated within schools which are generally part of systems organized by the state. The schools within these systems are universal, compulsory, publicly controlled and tax supported. The state not only finances the schools but determines their goals and values. In independent nonsystem schools, the parents and not the state pay for the cost of educating the students.

Constitutional and Political Context The Canadian education system has been shaped by the federal nature of the country. The CONSTITUTION ACT, 1867, allotted exclusive responsibility for education to the provinces (exceptions are noted in subsections of the constitution), stating that "in and for each province, the Legislature may exclusively make laws in relation to education." In exercising its sovereign power with respect to education, each province has developed a distinctive system of education. Provincial power over education is only restricted with respect to the rights of denominational schools that existed at the time the province entered Confederation (s93 says nothing about language rights; s33 speaks of language rights but significantly not in relation to education). Under the Constitution, the rights guaranteed to schools by a province when it joined Confederation may not be abrogated by the province, although the powers of the provinces to do as they see fit regarding education have been strengthened by historical and political precedents. For example, Manitoba has denied or abridged the denominational rights of minorities in its school systems in contravention of those constitutional provisions regarding educational rights of minorities, but arguably it has not contravened the provisions of the Constitution regarding language rights. (Unfortunately, religious and language rights, scrupulously held apart in the Constitution, are not so conveniently separated in people's lives.)

The systems of education established by the provinces are public and most often nonsectarian, ie, they are open to all citizens. A SEPA-

Standardization and conformity have been heavily emphasized in school systems. Here, all pupils sit in rows, hands in the same position. Each student has drawn the same boat (*courtesy Public Archives of Canada*).

RATE SCHOOL is a special kind of public school open to those of a minority religious faith, usually Catholic. Tax-supported separate schools exist in Ontario, Saskatchewan, Alberta, the Yukon and the NWT. Québec has a dual confessional system divided between Protestants and Catholics, and Newfoundland has an exclusively denominational system that recognizes several religious groups for the purpose of organizing school systems. Recently, in Newfoundland, the major Protestant groups joined together in the larger centres to establish amalgamated school systems. The result is that Newfoundland's system is becoming similar to that of other provinces, in which the major dividing line is between public nonsectarian schools and Catholic separate schools. BC has a nondenominational system of schools. In addition to these formal mechanisms for recognizing religion as a basis for organizing educational systems, some provinces make informal arrangements that accomplish the same ends. For example, in NS some schools are designated as serving Catholic students.

Although the provinces are primarily responsible for education, the federal government also has responsibilities in this area, for example, for the education of Indian and Inuit children, and for the education of children of members of the Canadian Armed Forces. The federal government also provides subventions to the provinces to support post-secondary education, adult labour training, official SECOND LANGUAGE INSTRUCTION and cultural development activities, and is drawn into education through its jurisdiction over external affairs. When the Organization for Economic Cooperation and Development surveyed Canadian education in the mid-1970s, the voice of the federal goverment joined those of the provinces in preparing a statement about the problems, priorities and needs of Canadian education.

The Expansion of Educational Systems in Canada The rapid growth of Canada's population, which by 1981 had reached more than 24 million, strained educational systems considerably. To meet new demands across the country both for more education and for new kinds of education, these systems had to grow both quantitatively and qualitatively. By the 1982-83 school year, there were nearly 5 million students in Canadian pre-elementary, elementary and secondary schools and another 722 000 students in post-secondary institutions. The number of students overall had increased by 50% from 1951: the increase in the number of post-secondary students was even larger. These increases were caused by the BABY BOOM and the influx of immigrants between 1945 and 1960. By the mid-1980s, the number of students in the education systems other than post-secondary had declined because of falling birthrates and reduced immigration.

From the 1950s to the 1970s, Canadians spent generously on their school systems. Standards for training teachers were increased and enormous amounts of capital was invested in buildings and equipment. Salaries of teachers and administrators rose steadily, the ratio of students to teachers dropped markedly, and the curriculum and the organization of schools were continually modified to increase their scope and effectiveness. During this period of expansion, some observers claimed that contemporary education was long on quantity but short on quality. "So little for the mind" was the stinging phrase critic Hilda NEATBY used to argue that the expanded system at the secondary levels had abandoned traditional values and the fundamentals of education. On the other hand, the view that there was nothing much wrong with Canadian education that a great deal of money, properly applied, could not cure was supported by surveys of the resources, personnel and facilities devoted to education. For example, Statistics Canada reported in 1951 that 15% of elementary teachers had not met the minimum requirements of secondary-school graduation followed by a year of professional training; 40% of secondary teachers did not have a university degree and professional training, and at the university level 15% of teachers had no more than a bachelor's degree.

During the years of expansion, massive resources were directed into educational systems, resources that helped ensure, by the 1960s and 1970s, that virtually all those who could benefit from schools were in educational systems. The systems provided increasingly complex and diversified programs, and students were taught by more experienced, better trained and better paid teachers. Participation rates are still high, particularly in western Canada and Ontario. In 1982-83, 99-100% of Canadian elementary-school-age children were in elementary schools, 85% of secondary-school-age children were in secondary schools and 22% of university-age students were attending post-secondary institutions. Fifty-nine percent of this last group were in universities.

Organization and Structure of Systems Canadian educational systems provide successive programs for children from ages 3 and 4 in nursery schools and kindergartens, and on through elementary and secondary schools. Education is compulsory from ages 6 for about 10 years and covers the elementary grades and most — but usually not all — of high school. Public-school systems may provide one or more years of education prior to grade one. This service is now quite common in urban schools, but there are also many private kindergartens and nursery schools that operate under varying, but usually nonrestrictive, provincial supervision. Elementary schools often offer 8 grades of study (50% of the provinces have junior-high schools) and secondary another 4, but this pattern varies considerably among the provincial school systems. The length of high school varies as well, eg, in some provinces students graduate after grade 11, in others after grade 13. Newfoundland's schools are organized on a 6-2-3 plan; in Québec it is 6-5, in BC, 7-5 or 7-3-2; and in Ontario, 8-4 or 8-5. The view reflected in most provincial systems of education is that all children are entitled to a period of 12 to 14 years of publicly funded schooling.

Provincial authorities govern all educational systems within their boundaries, but sharp differences exist even among the systems of a single province with regard to administrative structures. The years of public, compulsory education are administered by SCHOOL BOARDS whose members are elected and who have the power to levy taxes against local property. Post-secondary institutions, on the other hand, while funded from the public treasury, are established by charter, are governed by appointed boards and with the general exception of community colleges are relatively autonomous, although some provincial governments have now moved to create unified ministries that are responsible for education at all levels of schooling, including the post-secondary sector.

The Financing of Education Constitutionally, only the federal and provincial governments enjoy the authority to levy taxes for the support of public services, but provincial governments have delegated certain taxing powers to local authorities, the most important of which is the real-property tax. Traditionally, elementary- and secondary-school costs were met by municipal authorities through property taxes while universities were funded through private sources, including tuition fees. The growth of the system after WWII destroyed this pattern as the demand for education expanded rapidly and costs skyrocketed. In 1947 total expenditure on education exceeded $1 billion for the first time; for 1983-84 it totalled about $32 billion. From 1950 the cost of education rose from 2.5% of GROSS NATIONAL PRODUCT to 7% by 1970, and 7.5% by 1981-82.

A colonial statistician estimated in 1882 that it cost parents about $10.00 annually in fees to keep a child in school and that this was more than most parents could afford. By 1981 the average amount spent in Canada per full-time student was $3848.60. In that year, Québec spent the highest amount per pupil, at $5235, and Newfoundland the lowest, at $3055. However, although citizens in the Atlantic provinces appear to spend generally less on education than citizens in other provinces, they spend a larger part of their incomes on education, since their average income is less than that in other provinces.

Most of the money spent on education in Canada is public money. Less than 5% of Canadian children attend PRIVATE SCHOOLS (where the cost is borne largely by fees), but some provincial governments — notably Québec, Manitoba, Saskatchewan, Alberta and BC — provide some financial support to private schools. The decision to fund private institutions with public money represents a crack in the monolith of public education. Strong voices in Canadian society are opposing the vision of a universal, free and compulsory school system. For those who oppose public-school systems, values (and money to support them) are the heart of the educational question. These critics demand the right to pursue their own values through education, but with the model of the publicly supported common school vividly before them, they now demand public money to pursue private values through private schools. They wish to educate only those who choose their values, raising the spectre of one of Egerton RYERSON's critics who complained that he was under no obligation to educate "every brat on the street." The opinion that private money is better spent than public money has also been resurrected, allied once again to the view that "that which costs nothing is likely to be valued at nothing." These ideas challenge the fundamentals of a public-school system.

The Future of Educational Systems in Canada At the end of the postwar period, larger numbers of children were in school and were there for longer periods of time, and comprehensive and diversified programs had been designed to serve their needs and interests. In some deep sense Canadians have always shown faith in their institutions, otherwise they would not have built such elaborate and costly systems of education. Despite the fact that major questions are being asked about the Canadian school systems, that there are declining enrolments, a sharper competition for the funds that support the systems and a declining faith in the value of education itself and in the policies and programs that shape it, the systems as a whole represent an enduring and substantial achievement. A relatively small proportion of school-age children in Canada attend private and independent schools. The majority's choice in this matter bespeaks an extraordinary and continuing faith in the idea of common schools based on compulsory attendance and public tax support.

School Trustee, member of a board of education elected (a few are appointed) for terms ranging from 2 to 4 years. Membership varies from 5 to more than 20 on some large boards. There are roughly 6000 to 8000 trustees in Canada; the number is decreasing in accordance with a trend toward fewer boards. Most SCHOOL BOARDS pay a stipend to trustees, from a few hundred dollars to more than $10 000 in wealthy jurisdictions. Most boards include a number of professional people and business executives. Increasingly, in recent years, educators (from other jurisdictions) have become trustees and it is not uncommon to have students elected. The majority of trustees are men. Although it is commonly held that school trustees are not politically oriented, the governance of education is a political process and many trustees move on to higher office in municipal, provincial and federal politics.   EDWARD S. HICKCOX

Schreiber, Charlotte Mount Brock, née Morrell, painter (b at Woodham, Eng 1834; d at Paington, Eng 1922). Schreiber was the only female charter member of the Royal Canadian Academy in 1880 and was the only woman elected full academician until 1933. She studied in London, Eng, and exhibited at the Paris Salon and at the Royal Academy, London. She moved to Canada in 1875 when she married Torontonian Weymouth Schreiber. She painted figures, landscapes and genre in a sentimental Victorian manner. *The Croppy Boy*, oil on canvas, was her RCA diploma piece and she exhibited regularly at the RCA until her return to England in 1898. She was one of the first female book illustrators in Canada and 3 children's books with Schreiber illustrations were published in Toronto. She was the sole woman on the board of the Ontario School of Art and Design (later Ontario Coll of Art). Ernest Thompson SETON was her protégé.   DOROTHY FARR

Schreyer, Edward Richard, politician, premier of Manitoba, governor general of Canada 1979-84, diplomat (b at Beauséjour, Man 21 Dec

1935). Educated at United College and U Man he became the youngest member of the Manitoba legislature at age 22. He served there 1958-65 and in the federal Commons 1965-69. He swept to the leadership of the Manitoba NEW DEMOCRATIC PARTY in 1969 and within months was premier. It was a Schreyer-dominated government: moderate, honest, mildly progressive. An advocate of bilingualism and a strong central government, he got along well with PM Pierre TRUDEAU. It was Trudeau who named Schreyer governor general, rescuing him from an unhappy period as Manitoba Opposition leader, 1977-78. He was determined as head of state to speak his mind and to democratize the office. He and his popular wife Lily made RIDEAU HALL more accessible to ordinary Canadians and travelled prodigiously. But a governor general's words, he discovered, were easily misunderstood and he was forced to tailor his speeches accordingly. He caused political controversy by hesitating before allowing PM Joe CLARK to call an election in 1979, and by suggesting that he might have dissolved parliament if Trudeau had attempted to impose his constitutional proposals unilaterally in 1981-82. In 1984 Schreyer was appointed Canadian high commissioner to Australia.   NORMAN HILLMER

Schull, Joseph, historian (b at Watertown, S Dakota 6 Feb 1906; d at Montréal 19 May 1980). Schull grew up in Moose Jaw, Sask, and began writing professionally after WWII, primarily as a radio dramatist and journalist, though his first book publications were as a poet. Work on the official history of the Royal Canadian Navy in the war (*The Far Distant Ships,* 1950) led him to many other commissioned histories, including *100 Years of Banking in Canada: A History of the Toronto-Dominion Bank* (1958) and *Edward Blake* (1975-76), an impressive 2-vol biography of the 19th-century Liberal leader commissioned by Blake's old law firm. *Laurier: The First Canadian* (1965) is a first-rate political biography. Other works include *Rebellion: The Rising in French Canada 1837* (1971), a concise and readable narrative, as well as works for children.   DOUG FETHERLING

Schultz, Sir John Christian, businessman, medical practitioner, politician (b at Amherstburg, UC 1 Jan 1840; d at Monterey, Mexico 13 Apr 1896). Schultz settled at the RED RIVER COLONY in 1861. He practised medicine but increasingly occupied himself with furs, retail trade and real estate. During 1865-68 he was owner of the *Nor'-Wester,* and in its columns attacked the "tyranny" of the HUDSON'S BAY CO. He became the leader of the small but noisy Canadian party which demanded annexation to Canada and which roused Métis fears. Imprisoned by Louis RIEL's provisional government 7 Dec 1869, Schultz escaped 23 Jan 1870 and later made his way to Ontario where he and others of the CANADA FIRST movement raised Protestant ire over the execution of Orangeman Thomas SCOTT. No mention was made of the deaths of Hugh Sutherland and Norbert Parisien for which Schultz and others were responsible. Shrewd and acquisitive, Schultz became a wealthy businessman. He was an MP 1871-82, a Senator 1882-88 and lieutenant-governor of Manitoba 1888-95. A figure of controversy, he played a key role in the troubles of 1869-70 and left a legacy of bitterness.   LOVELL CLARK

Science, the rational study of nature, rose to prominence in European civilization at almost the same time as the first European EXPLORATION of what is now Canada and was, from the beginning, an element in those explorations. From the time of John CABOT, scientific navigation and GEOGRAPHY were essential to enable explorers to reach and penetrate Canada. During the 19th century and, more particularly, the 20th century, science, increasingly closely linked with TECHNOLOGY, assumed a central place

in Canadian life and culture, providing the basis of national wealth and well-being.

The practical uses of science have always been foremost in Canada. From the earliest times, scientific observers noted and catalogued the natural RESOURCES of the country. The Jesuit missionaries, the first organized group with both a scientific education and an interest in nature, sent back to Europe reports of the new land (*see* JESUIT RELATIONS). From the mid-17th century, they taught general science in Québec and trained navigators. During the following century, the Jesuits were joined by civil and military authorities with a taste for science. Physicians J.F. Gaulthier and Michel SARRAZIN, the marquis de la Galissonière and engineer Michel Chartier de Lotbinière, made forays into BOTANY and GEOLOGY, but their contributions were transient; after 1759, only the Jesuit-inspired education survived. A procession of foreign visitors, such as Pehr KALM, André Michaux, Capt John PALLISER and J.J. Bigsby, noted Canada's geology, botany and ZOOLOGY well into the 19th century. The native Canadian development of science did not begin until the early 19th century, with the coming of colleges, government agencies and locally sponsored expeditions. Important contributors such as Adam Henry Bayfield, Lt Frederick Baddeley, Capt Richard Bonnycastle, Lt Edward Ashe and Capt John Lefroy were British military men with an appetite for science. As the British military presence in Canada diminished during the second half of the century, Canadian-born and educated men, both professional and amateur, replaced them and gave Canadian science its own flavour. The structure of modern Canadian science began to form during the last quarter of the century, slower to develop than its American counterpart, and while similar in many ways is distinguishable from it. One major difference, which retains much of its original impact, is the strong role of government in Canadian science.

Government Involvement Because of Canada's small population, few universities and industries, government has long been an important supporter of science. The PROVINCE OF CANADA took the lead in 1842 by creating the GEOLOGICAL SURVEY OF CANADA under Montréal-born William (later Sir William) LOGAN. Modelled on the British survey and American state surveys, it was intended to be a short-lived project aimed at the discovery of economic MINERALS, but so vast was Canada and so adroit were Logan, his colleagues and successors that the survey has survived to the present as the second-oldest national survey in the world, and one of the most distinguished. Although the survey was officially limited to Upper and Lower Canada, Logan's assistant, Alexander Murray, who became provincial geologist in Newfoundland, and Logan's correspondents in the Maritimes, such as Charles Hartt and G.F. Matthew of Saint John, and James Robb and Loring BAILEY of Fredericton, ensured, before Confederation, the foundations of a systematic study of Canadian geology. After 1867, the survey was faced with the exploration of virtually all the territories now comprising Canada. A succession of visionary directors, such as A.R.C. SELWYN, George M. DAWSON, Albert P. LOW and Reginald Brock nurtured the survey into a large and multifaceted organization. The collections of the survey, first housed in Logan's home, evolved into the National Museum (now NATIONAL MUSEUM OF NATURAL SCIENCE), by the 1890s. The more economic aspects of geology called forth the creation of different organizations such as the federal Mines Department (1907). Some provinces had moved earlier, eg, NS had established a Commissioner of Mines before Confederation, and Ontario set up a Bureau of Mines in 1891. After the turn of the century, most provinces maintained government bureaus devoted to MINING.

Governor General Edward Schreyer reading the Speech from the Throne during the opening of Parliament in Ottawa. Her Excellency Lily Schreyer is on the right (*courtesy National Film Board/Photothèque*).

The imperial government initiated little in science beyond creating the Toronto Magnetic Observatory in 1840 as a link in an international chain of institutions for the study of geomagnetism. On the British withdrawal of support in 1853, the provincial government assumed its operation. The small astronomical OBSERVATORY in Québec, built in 1850 to provide TIME for shipping, and small observatories in Saint John, Montréal and Kingston were linked together with Toronto by the federal Dept of Marine and Fisheries in the 1870s as the Canadian Meteorological Service, which survives as the Atmospheric Environment Service (see CLIMATOLOGY). The Dept of the Interior pursued practical ASTRONOMY in the 1880s as part of the transcontinental railway surveys. The need for a permanent observatory for geographic and timekeeping purposes led to establishment of Ottawa's Dominion Observatory, which opened in 1905. Not only was the observatory an important centre for practical astronomy, but also the birthplace of Canadian astrophysics, in the hands of J.S. PLASKETT and his colleagues. As a result of Plaskett's efforts, the Dominion Astrophysical Observatory, which briefly possessed the world's largest telescope, commenced work in 1918. It has remained one of the most important international astrophysical centres.

Federal government scientific programs nearly always grew from practical and economic considerations. Because AGRICULTURE was so central to the 19th century economy, the Central Experimental Farm was founded in Ottawa in 1886 under the direction of William SAUNDERS (see RESEARCH STATIONS). The staff, including the Dominion Cerealist, Entomologist, Chemist and others, were responsible for new varieties of CROPS and for pest control. The Experimental Farm system rapidly opened branches across the country. The Dept of Agriculture's research staff has, during the present century, carried on the traditions of research of the pioneers such as John MACOUN, William and Charles SAUNDERS, C.J.S. BETHUNE, Frank Shutt and others.

Zoological research was initiated by the government in the mid-19th century with Pierre FORTIN's fisheries studies in the Gulf of St Lawrence; by 1899, the Marine Biological Station at St Andrew's, NB, directed by E.E. PRINCE, was in operation, followed by a number of other marine stations (see OCEANOGRAPHY). The Biological Board of Canada, first appointed in 1912, oversaw this research; by 1937 it had become the Fisheries Research Board. The Canadian Conservation Commission, established in 1909 and dismantled in 1921, took a wider view of Canada's natural heritage. Contemporary government agencies for the natural sciences, mostly grouped within the departments of Environment and Agriculture, consume the largest portion of the federal science budget.

The most important government initiative in science was the appointment, in 1916, of the Honorary Advisory Council for Scientific and Industrial Research, a group similar to the British wartime scientific advisory council. It soon became the NATIONAL RESEARCH COUNCIL. Obtaining its own laboratories for industrial research in 1932, the NRC, under the leadership of such men as H.M. TORY, C.J. MACKENZIE and E.W.R. STEACIE, expanded to become one of the most diversified and successful governmental research organizations in the world. Before WWII, its endeavours were largely in aid of INDUSTRIAL RESEARCH AND DEVELOPMENT, but, with a ten-fold increase in staff during and after the war, its work branched into many new fields including RADAR, NUCLEAR ENERGY, aeronautics and radio astronomy (see DEFENCE RESEARCH). Its pure science component continues to be strong, complementing applied research in TRANSPORTATION, northern environments, ENERGY, building technology, materials science and CHEMISTRY. Along

with its laboratory work, the NRC has, since its early days, been a primary contributor to university science with its grants, scholarships and fellowships. From a modest $13 000 in 1918, its subventions grew to nearly $70 million annually by the early 1970s. More recently, research and educational grants for the sciences have been disbursed by the NATURAL SCIENCES AND ENGINEERING RESEARCH COUNCIL of Canada and by the MEDICAL RESEARCH COUNCIL.

Other government agencies, such as the Defence Research Board, the departments of National Defence, Communications, Transport and others, have, since 1945, become important in Canadian science. One branch of the NRC wartime operation, the nuclear research at CHALK RIVER, Ont, grew into the crown corporation, ATOMIC ENERGY OF CANADA LTD (1952) which, with ONTARIO HYDRO, a world leader in electrical technology since early in the century, developed the CANDU reactor. The reactor employs Canada's natural uranium and Canadian-manufactured heavy water. Another crown corporation, the Polymer Corp, has been an important leader in the PETROCHEMICAL INDUSTRY. The provinces have also participated in science: beginning with the precursor to the ALBERTA RESEARCH COUNCIL in 1919 and the ONTARIO RESEARCH FOUNDATION in 1928, nearly all the provinces have created more modest versions of the NRC (see RESEARCH, PROVINCIAL ORGANIZATIONS).

Education Early EDUCATION in Canada was in private or church hands and, although elementary MATHEMATICS appeared in all curricula, elementary science was rare. From the 1840s, provincially supported schools included only a smattering of science. During the latter part of the 19th century, the prevailing ideology of science education held that only natural history was suitable for children, they being unable to grasp the complexities of physical science. This view, then also current in Britain and the US, has survived almost to the present; biological studies, complemented by environmental studies, remain the core of elementary science. Ontario SECONDARY SCHOOLS led the way in science courses as a preparation for university matriculation examinations. The church-run classical colleges of Québec, following the original French pattern, taught science to few students and only in the last 2 years. By the mid-19th century, the francophone student was as knowledgeable in science as an anglophone liberal arts student in a 3- or 4-year college program. The curriculum froze, however, and the gap between anglophone and francophone science education continued to grow. Dissatisfaction in the state-supported universities and the conservatism of the church-run colleges combined to produce a widespread debate in the late 1920s and early 1930s led, on the scientific side, by Université de Montréal biologist Frère MARIE-VICTORIN and Université Laval chemist Adrien Pouliot. Progress was slow and science began to take its proper place in the secondary curriculum in Québec only in the 1960s.

Science teaching in Canadian universities was a mixture of various elements, with the Scottish and American predominating. From the founding until after the turn of the 20th century, most of the small liberal arts colleges offered general science as part of a general education. For most of the century, 2 reasons for teaching science were commonly given: science aided the student in learning to think logically, and it exhibited to the student the wonders of God's creation. Little thought was given to preparing future scientists, and those Canadians who became professionals had either to resort to schools overseas (usually German or American) or to virtually train themselves with the help of sympathetic professors. The state of science was such, however, that practical work in geology, botany or zoology required far less formal training than it

would a century later. Typically, 2 professors, one for natural history and geology, the other for PHYSICS, chemistry and perhaps astronomy, covered the entire range of science. Laboratory practice was unknown until the present century.

The few 19th century universities to develop curricula beyond the introductory level were those possessing ENGINEERING or medical faculties. McGill, Toronto and, to a lesser extent, Dalhousie, New Brunswick and Queen's, were the sources of science graduates and employers of the best-known academic scientists. McGill, under the inspired leadership of paleontologist Sir William Dawson, and Toronto, with the physicist James LOUDON as president, moved away from the liberal arts tradition to more professionally oriented education during the last 2 decades of the 19th century. This modernization included the creation of specialized degrees (the Bachelor of Science, BSc), research laboratories for chemistry, physics, biology and engineering, larger staffs and the adoption of the earned doctorate (PhD). The science PhD, an earlier German innovation, required independent research on the part of the student rather than preparation for examinations. American schools adopted doctoral programs from 1876 but Toronto did not award its first, to J.C. MCLENNAN, until 1900. McGill followed soon after and was quickly emulated by others, such as Queen's, where engineering had developed in the 1890s. This modernization was costly and was borne, in most cases, by provincial authorities eager for economic benefits of scientific training. McGill, object of the private philanthropy of Peter Redpath and Sir William C. MACDONALD, was able to create excellent laboratory facilities and, consequently, could attract a younger generation of scientists such as Ernest RUTHERFORD, Frederick Soddy and Otto Hann, who would become international stars after their Canadian apprenticeships.

Despite the lack of funds, books, laboratories, research students and understanding on the part of college councils and provincial legislatures, several college teachers distinguished themselves in their researches. Among them were the natural historian James Robb, biologist and geologist L.W. Bailey and astronomer W.B. JACK in UNB; geologist William Dawson, biologist J.F. Whiteaves and geologist Frank ADAMS at McGill; mathematician Nathan Dupuis and botanist George LAWSON at Queen's (later at Dalhousie); chemist Henry CROFT, at U of T. They were largely self-made scientists and were superseded by a better-educated generation which created the science education format which, with changes, still exists.

In Canada's colleges and universities created before WWI, science evolved slowly from the liberal arts tradition to the research-oriented system. The universities created after the war, particularly the western provincial universities in Saskatchewan, Alberta and BC, included science and technology as a core. A strong influence in the West was H.M. Tory, a McGill mathematician and physicist and later president of the NRC, who was not only the outstanding institution builder of the interwar years but also one convinced of the importance of science in the university curriculum. The western schools were thus able to attract first-rate staffs, including physicist Gordon Shrum (a co-worker of Sir John McLennan's at Toronto) at UBC, chemist John SPINKS and astrophysicist Gerhard HERZBERG at Saskatchewan, and physicist R.W. BOYLE at Alberta.

The end of WWII signaled a massive influx of students, the availability of many young scientists who had been involved in the war effort and greater financial resources from governments. These developments led to a new phase in university science, one devoted to larger faculties, new specialties and facilities and, from the 1960s, a stronger emphasis on the importance of science for society. Older schools became centres of excellence: Western Ontario became noted for biomedical research, SPECTROSCOPY and astronomy, McMaster for nuclear science and engineering, Manitoba for agricultural science and biology. At the same time, the tremendous increase in students and interest in higher education during the 1960s and 1970s resulted in establishment of new universities, distinguished from the outset by scientific specialization, including York in biology and space science, Waterloo in COMPUTER SCIENCE and engineering, and Victoria in physics.

The relative lack of interest in science as a profession in French Canada meant that the move to modern laboratory-oriented science was slower in Québec. Laval created a FORESTRY school in 1910, followed a decade later with its École supérieure de chimie (1920); at the same time, Université de Montréal became independent of Laval and inaugurated its faculty of sciences. The École polytechnique de Montréal, founded on a small scale by U.E. Archambault in 1873, became linked to the new university as its faculty of engineering. Real expansion in the sciences, in terms of facilities, faculty and student numbers, did not occur until the 1960s. Even by the late 1960s, McGill was producing nearly twice as many PhDs and first degrees in science as Laval and Montréal together.

Scientific Organizations The pattern of growth of Canada's scientific organizations, institutions and publications is unique, because of the nature of Canadian government, education, population mixture and distribution and economic patterns. Professional societies were late in emerging; their predecessors were strongly oriented towards amateurs and those for whom science was a cultural outlet or entertainment. The first of these societies, the LITERARY AND HISTORICAL SOCIETY OF QUEBEC (1824), enrolled amateurs and a small band of military men of the Québec garrison with a penchant for geology or exploration. The Natural History Society of Montreal (1827) was dominated by amateurs until after mid-century when William Dawson, together with his scientific colleagues at McGill, raised the level of professionalism. The Geological Survey's paleontologist, Elkanah BILLINGS, founded in 1856 Canada's first scientific journal, the *Canadian Naturalist and Geologist*, which became the official organ of the society. It remained the most important outlet for papers on geology, botany and zoology until the turn of the century. No francophone scientific society of any size emerged before the 20th century, although Abbé Léon Provancher published the *Naturaliste canadien* from 1868.

In the Maritimes, Saint John geologists Charles Hartt and G.F. Matthew created the Natural History Society of New Brunswick (est 1863) and published its *Transactions*, while a group centered on Dalhousie University directed the Nova Scotian Institute of Science (est 1862) and produced its *Transactions*. In Ontario, the Canadian Institute was formed by engineers and university scientists in 1849, launching the *Canadian Journal* in 1852, the primary outlet for Toronto science until the end of the century. Smaller organizations, some devoted to natural history, others to more general scientific and cultural ends, appeared in Fredericton; Kingston, Ottawa, Belleville, Hamilton and London, Ont; and Winnipeg.

By the time of Confederation, the first societies devoted to one science appeared: the Toronto Astronomical Club (1868), which evolved into the Royal Astronomical Society of Canada, and the Entomological Society of Ontario. None of these societies were for professionals, still too few in number, and many faded and disappeared in the early years of the 20th century. The marquess of LORNE was instrumental

in founding the first organization for distinguished scientists, the ROYAL SOCIETY OF CANADA, in 1882. The Royal Society, with so few specialists in any one field, failed to provide the institutional basis for professional scientists. It has never found a clearly defined role and its journal, the *Proceedings and Transactions*, already marginal in the 19th century, ceased to be of much value for the scientific community in the 20th. The 20th century brought the rise of professional, disciplinary organizations and the demise of most of the amateur and general societies. The largest single discipline, chemistry, has been served by a series of organizations dating from the mid-19th century; in 1920, the nationwide Canadian Institute of Chemistry was formed, which evolved into the Chemical Institute of Canada in 1945, launching *Chemistry in Canada* 4 years later. With more than 10 000 members, the CIC, with its subdisciplinary and regional branches, represents the scientific area most closely allied with the Canadian economy. Other large disciplines followed: the Geological Association of Canada, 1947; Canadian Association of Physicists, 1946, sponsor of the journal *Physics in Canada* from 1949; and several smaller groups in the life sciences which formed the Canadian Federation of Biological Societies in 1957. A number of newer specialties have become foci of societies and journals, mostly dating from the late 1950s to the present. The first truly international journal in Canada, the *Canadian Journal of Research*, established by the NRC in 1929, was successively split into NRC-edited specialist journals, as the quantity of papers in new disciplines grew.

The style and aims of scientific organizations differed in French Canada during the 20th century. Attempts to form scientific societies for Francophones late in the 19th century had mostly failed but, by 1923, several professional groups began to emerge, particularly the Association canadienne-française pour l'avancement des sciences (ACFAS), which affiliated local and specialist societies. ACFAS, like its British, French and American counterparts, successfully grouped scientists from all disciplines and took special pains to popularize science in Québec. No anglophone organization has ever seriously attempted either function; consequently, the association's popular journal, *Québec Science*, has no English-language equivalent. The defunct *Science Forum* appealed more narrowly to those with SCIENCE POLICY interests. The need for a voice in government circles led to the formation by Canadian scientific and engineering societies of SCITEC (Association of Scientific, Engineering and Technical Community of Canada) in 1970 but, as an organization of organizations rather than of individuals, it has primarily restricted its activities to lobbying.

Before the 1960s, popular interest in science had few outlets, besides scientific collections in federal or provincial museums. The great stimulus of space exploration has, as in the US, added new dimensions to popular awareness of science. Most major cities possess planetariums or science-oriented museums such as Ottawa's National Museum of Science and Technology, Toronto's ONTARIO SCIENCE CENTRE and Winnipeg's Manitoba Museum of Man and Nature, attracting millions of visitors annually (*see* SCIENCE CENTRES). The Canadian media have been more conservative in their attempts to popularize science (*see* SCIENCE AND SOCIETY). Amateur societies and clubs for geology and natural history exist across the country, while astronomy, perhaps the most popular amateur science, is represented by the 3000-strong Royal Astronomical Society of Canada.

The outstanding feature of 20th-century Canadian science is specialization. In the last century, Canadian contributions to areas other than the earth sciences were few, but a sign of matur-

ity of science is its broadening into new areas, followed by a steady stream of results. The Canadian population has been small in relation to that of world scientific leaders and its scientific manpower numbers only a few thousand; therefore, excellence is possible only in a few areas. The earth sciences have continued to grow in strength, not only in practical work but also in the theoretical, as J.T. WILSON's contributions to PLATE TECTONICS shows. The demands for mining and energy sustain the importance of applied research. Chemistry, too, despite fundamental research in the universities and the NRC, has retained its strong practical orientation because of our essentially resource-based economy. Forestry research centres at Laval and Toronto, and the Pulp and Paper Research Institute of Canada at McGill are internationally known; research in METALLURGY by International Nickel (INCO LTD), Falconbridge, DOMINION FOUNDRIES AND STEEL, LTD and STELCO is necessary to maintain a competitive place in the metals markets; PHARMACEUTICAL chemistry in Montréal and biomedical and GENETIC research in centres in Toronto, Montréal, London and Saskatoon have placed Canada in the vanguard of life science research. AGRICULTURAL RESEARCH has a long and illustrious history, dating from the production of Marquis WHEAT by Saunders. Researches on new grains, such as TRITICALE or new uses for older plants such as rapeseed (CANOLA), pest control methods and widespread work on plant breeding and ANIMAL BREEDING in government laboratories, research councils and universities, especially Saskatchewan, Guelph and Manitoba, have created a pool of expertise and products employed throughout the world.

As a result of the small communities of researchers and the lack of financial resources, the glamour areas of contemporary science, such as astrophysics, radio astronomy, nuclear particle research, solid state physics, recombinant DNA research and theoretical work in general, are cultivated on a much more modest scale in Canada than in the US, the USSR or Britain. Canadian scientists in these specialties have built up relationships with colleagues in other English- and French-speaking nations, which have allowed them access to facilities impossible to obtain at home. These links ensure that Canadian scientists will not be restricted to practical, economically oriented research but, in small numbers, can share in the excitement at the cutting edge of modern research.

The concepts and methods of science are universal but its social relations, politics and structure are unique to each nation. In a country as large as Canada, these aspects of science also have a regional flavour. Canadian science has strong similarities to American science but has its special properties: the strong and central role of the NRC in its laboratories and funding; the federal-provincial division of science funding and policy making; the specialization of science strengths in areas tied closely to the economy. The "big science" element in American science, ie, large financial resources and extensive facilities, are lacking in Canada, where no substantial industrial research effort is undertaken and where a small defence establishment has not required large-scale projects of science-based technology. Nonetheless, Canadian science has made significant contributions to knowledge and, during the 20th century, has become an integral part of the international scientific effort.   RICHARD A. JARRELL

Reading: Richard A. Jarrell and N.R. Ball, eds, *Science, Technology and Canadian History* (1980); T.H. Levere and R.A. Jarrell, eds, *A Curious Field-Book: Science and Society in Canadian History* (1974); G.F.G. Stanley, *Pioneers of Canadian Science* (1966).

Science and Society Most Canadians are unaware of the profound effect SCIENCE has on their daily lives. While politicians, labour leaders and business people take actions which influence our lives, most of these actions pale in significance when compared to the long-term effects of experiments going on in laboratories around the world. Consider the impact of a few of the discoveries that have occurred in a single generation: polio vaccine, kidney and heart transplants, transistors, jet planes, space travel, nuclear weapons, GENETIC ENGINEERING, cloning, antibiotics, tranquillizers, microwave heating, computers, LASERS, PLASTICS, TELEVISION, contraceptives, test-tube babies and the extinction of smallpox.

N American society exhibits a puzzling dichotomy: we have the highest level of LITERACY, the most widely available higher EDUCATION and the broadest exposure to information (via print and electronic media) in history, yet there is a remarkable ignorance of science and TECHNOLOGY. Only a handful of NEWSPAPERS and MAGAZINES employ full-time science or medical reporters, while primetime television is virtually devoid of science. Tabloids that publish sensational stories of monsters, UFO landings and miracle cancer cures are much more widely circulated than are science magazines. In fact, Canada lacks a national science magazine of interest to the general reader. Québec is the exception, with the popular *Québec Science*. This broad ignorance of science and technology is reflected in our elected representatives: over 80% of all Members of Parliament come from the law or business — 2 professions whose members are notoriously ignorant of science. Yet these leaders daily make decisions in which a considerable amount of scientific and technical expertise is required. Our society readily accepts the products of scientific innovation but remains virtually ignorant of their source. In order to understand how this situation has arisen, we must look back to our evolutionary roots.

Human Evolution Our prehistoric, proto-human ancestors were not gifted with the survival attributes of many of their mammalian contemporaries (speed, strength, size, armour, fangs, camouflage or claws). Their genetically dictated survival strategy rested primarily on a complex brain which, with its capacity to remember, imagine and think in abstract terms, freed early humans from the tight constraints of instinct and gave them choice. Nevertheless, there were numerous situations in which the rational, analytical functions of the brain were too slow and the capacity to react instantly, without conscious thought, had an important survival value. The imprint of both evolutionary developments remains with us as we struggle with the duality of human personality: the rational, analytical side that often conflicts with the emotional, nonrational, visceral impulse. The power of the human brain was unprecedented in the history of life on the planet. *Homo sapiens* evolved language and the ability to transmit knowledge from generation to generation. Not only did this ability compensate for the lack of other physical attributes but it also enabled human beings to develop CULTURE. Cultural evolution was thousands of times more rapid than biological evolution.

In their attempts to impose order on the apparent chaos of events, early humans began with the recognizable regularities in the world: day and night, the seasons, TIDES, plant succession, animal MIGRATION. Their explanations of these regularities and other, more unusual events were embodied in mythologies and usually referred to divine forces as the ultimate cause. World views had to be all-embracing and, therefore, were vulnerable to disruption by events which simply could not be explained.

Our complex brain has been a spectacularly "successful" survival strategy, based on the numbers of our species and the territory we occupy. However, while we as a species have transcend-

ed the constraints of day-to-day survival, we nevertheless behave as if that remains our dominant priority. We are still compelled to reproduce, accumulate material goods and fight rivals as if we lived under the same conditions that existed tens of thousands of years back. In the Western world, the ultimate expression of the human brain, its technological inventions, has become so powerful and fast, that they now exceed the brain's ability to control them.

Evolution of Science In the 17th century, Francis Bacon recognized that "knowledge [*scientia*] is power." Through science, Bacon thought, we could come to understand how God works and, armed with these insights, could carry out the biblical injunction to dominate and subdue nature. Bacon saw science in the service of God and foresaw no conflict with the established church. Early scientists perceived that nature reflects an overall design, obeys recognizable principles and laws, and follows a wonderful regularity — all of which pointed to the divine work of God. Thus, understanding nature only increased one's sense of the greatness of God. The scientific method admits to the impossibility of making sense of the entire cosmos with a single, all-inclusive explanation. Instead, science concentrates on a very small part of nature, isolating it as fully as possible from everything else. The power of this way of knowing soon became apparent as astronomers, such as Copernicus, Kepler and Galileo, began to question cosmic dogma. Their work led to the heliocentric theory of planetary movement, which clashed with the notion of Earth as the centre of the universe. In the 19th century, geologist Charles Lyell countered church estimates of Earth's age by proposing that the planet might be tens of millions, if not billions, of years old. In 19th-century Canada, the descriptive approach of natural history provided an ideal activity for the deeply religious English communities. There was no history of experimental investigation in this young country but there was a strong sense of colonial status. However, N America was a new frontier with untold and untapped "resources." Science was valued insofar as it could aid directly in the exploitation of these resources; eg, by identifying the locations of ore deposits, geological surveys provided valuable information for a mining industry, just as descriptions of plants and animals became an inventory of potentially useful biological organisms. The thrust of Canadian "science" thus was highly descriptive and based on the conviction that by meticulous cataloguing of God's works, unexpected insights would be obtained.

Charles Darwin then shook the Christian notion of man's special place on Earth with the proposal that, like all other life forms, humans had evolved from ancestral species. In each instance (the heliocentric theory, geological age, evolution, etc) the battle which took place between church dogma and scientific theory ended with the confirmation of the validity of scientific insights, while having a secondary effect of reducing the church's sphere of influence. Science came to be freed not only from the constricting bonds of dogma but also from considerations of morality.

In Canada, one of the leading opponents of Darwin's ideas was Sir J.W. DAWSON, an eminent geologist and principal of McGill University. Dawson vigorously attacked Darwin's key proposal that evolution proceeded by the gradual accumulation of genetic change over long periods of time. Dawson argued that the fossil record did not support this notion — the changes in fossils seemed to occur suddenly. Ironically, Dawson's arguments lost to the forces of Darwinism, yet today, his very evidence is accepted and used to support a modern theory that evolution does occur suddenly in

major jumps, rather than by slow incremental change.

The scientific method, of necessity, is "reductionist" in that its power comes from focusing on a small part of nature. The success of this approach suggested that the whole could be inferred from the sum of its parts. For example, researchers in PHYSICS were driven by Newton's faith that, as the layers of complexity in nature were stripped away, we would ultimately arrive at the fundamental particle of which all matter is made, and from that elementary entity, the entire cosmos would eventually be comprehensible. But early in the 20th century, physics underwent a profound philosophical upheaval when Albert Einstein introduced the "Alice-in-Wonderland" concept of relativity, where mass and energy are interchangeable, and a universe in which what we see depends on our point of view. Werner Karl Heisenberg further clouded the Newtonian dream by pointing out that, in studying nature, the investigator intrudes in a way that alters the phenomenon under observation; ie, we alter even subatomic particles in the attempt to measure them. Niels Bohr's new theory of the atom altered the picture of electrons orbiting nuclei like planets around a sun, to one of clouds of electrons in which the density of the cloud reflected the probability that an electron would be found in that region. Thus, the behaviour of subatomic particles is neither absolute nor fixed. Furthermore, at each increase in complexity of matter, new properties emerge which could not have been predicted from the properties of the constituent parts. Thus, while a great deal is known about the atomic properties of oxygen and hydrogen, very little of that information is useful for predicting what their properties will be when combined in a water molecule.

Clearly a reductionist approach cannot provide adequate information about the structure or properties of matter; still less does it allow for the control of natural phenomena. Unfortunately, these philosophical insights have not percolated from physics to the other natural sciences. Much of BIOLOGY, both cellular and ecological, is still predicated on the principle of understanding the whole by studying its isolated parts. The limitations of the reductionism of science become apparent when the theory is applied. The untenable notion that we can "manage" SALMON or FORESTS, as if they were cows or tomatoes, is an expression of faith in the reductionism of science, yet the results of our attempts put the lie to that faith.

Modern Science The most important aspect of modern science has been its close association with industrial and military activities; the primary stimuli for its growth and support have been global crises. This pattern is especially true in Canada where, as we have already noted, "science" had been concerned primarily with cataloguing the wondrous storehouse of nature. While most technology was imported, there were exceptions, such as the breeding of Marquis WHEAT at the turn of the century. As Omond SOLANDT has noted, modern Canadian INDUSTRIAL RESEARCH, innovations and development were closely tied to the needs of the Allies in WWII. The growth of HIGH TECHNOLOGY industries in nuclear power, telecommunications, computers and aerospace was possible because of the support of military interests through the Defence Research Board.

From its origins as an indulgence by aristocrats or pure curiosity of university scholars, science has become the source of ideas for technology and INDUSTRY, a multi-billion-dollar activity spewing forth a cornucopia of weapons and consumer items. The enormous proliferation of the scientific profession in the latter part of this century is illustrated by the fact that "of all scientists who ever lived, 90% are still alive and publishing today." Before this century, the interval between a discovery and its application was usually measured in decades; that interval has now been reduced practically to zero. The rapidity with which innovations such as chemically modified female hormones (eg, ESTROGEN) for oral consumption, lasers and transistors have been adapted for use attests to the speed of application of new ideas. In some cases, systems for using phenomena precede their actual discovery. For example, while BLACK HOLES have been extensively discussed by theoretical physicists and none has yet been proved to exist, already a proposal has been made to harness them to produce energy. Because of the intricate relationship between industry, jobs and the economy, it is often found that upon detection of a potential hazard (such as an environmental carcinogen or occupational risk), the burden of proof rests with the potential victim. Usually this means that there must be a convincing body of proof before corrective action is taken. Canada's difficulty in stimulating action on US-caused ACID RAIN illustrates the problems of taking political action, even when the data are very clear.

In society, the impact of television, birth-control pills or computers ripples far beyond the immediate value of the technology itself. In this century, science and technology are creating problems for which there are no precedents and which are altering our very concepts of society and humanity. For example, in MEDICINE, the major health problems of malnutrition, infection and sepsis have been effectively controlled in N America. Medical research, therefore, is turning to the treatment of non-life-threatening problems (psychiatric disorders, herpes, cosmetic surgery, etc) and the consequences of effective medical treatment (eg, retinal detachment in diabetics, congenital defects, diseases of old age). Hearts were transplanted before there was an accepted definition of DEATH, while sophisticated life-support technologies raise the dilemma of quality of life, medical priorities and euthanasia. The ability to recover human eggs, fertilize them *in vitro* and implant the embryos into a recipient womb now by-passes all biological constraints to parenthood and introduces hitherto undreamed-of legal and moral questions.

Our ability to escape the pull of Earth's gravity has brought outer space within human reach. To whom does this new frontier belong? Can we claim new bodies, such as asteroids or the MOON, in the same way that explorers claimed new continents, by setting foot or capsule and planting a flag? Is outer space a zone to be fought over and in which any nation can park industrial debris or establish new generations of weapons?

The explorations of astrophysicists, eg, the debate over whether the universe is closed or open, are full of philosophical implications for humanity as well. In a closed universe, there is sufficient mass to bring expansion of the universe to a halt 30 billion years after a big bang and to induce its collapse back in another 30 billion. Thus, our present universe would be only the latest in a series of explosions and contractions extending back forever. In an open universe the big bang could only have occurred once, so the universe will continue to expand forever. Of equal philosophical importance is the search for signals indicating the existence of intelligent life elsewhere in the universe. SETI, the Search for Extra-Terrestrial Intelligence, has been prompted by speculations on the probability that, given the number of planets in the universe with conditions comparable to those in the early history of Earth, the evolution of life is highly probable. But demonstration of intelligent life elsewhere will have enormous repercussions for those who accept that human

Debates over the nature of the universe are full of philosophical implications for humanity. The concept of black holes has challenged the long-standing theories of gravitation and quantum mechanics — and may provide the long-sought link between the two (*artist's conception by Helmut K. Wimmer*).

beings were specially created in the image of God and to our notions of uniqueness.

Given the limited view provided by scientific insights, we should have learned to be extremely cautious when applying new knowledge to manipulate nature. In this half of the century this caution is becoming especially necessary in the field of GENETICS. We have come to identify DNA as the actual chemical material of heredity, the blueprint that dictates the hereditary properties of all organisms. The structure of DNA has been discovered and the principles whereby it stores and transmits information delineated. Molecular biologists have developed tools to isolate specific sequences of DNA, read the information contained in them, synthesize identical replicas and insert them into virtually any living organism. Genetic engineering, the ability to manipulate the very stuff that determines our special qualities, is now a reality, fraught with potential benefits and hazards.

Perhaps no greater challenge exists than in the creation, by humans, of a technology that could conceivably exceed the intelligence of its creators. Computers with ARTIFICIAL INTELLIGENCE (AI) are now accepted as a real possibility by computer scientists. With the arrival of genuine thinking machines, we will reach a new stage in evolution — from biological to cultural to machine intelligence. For, just as human intellect produced an acceleration in cultural evolution, AI will accelerate information processing because of its enormous storage capacity and speed. Human neurons transmit signals at about 100 m/s; computer commands travel at the speed of light. Human performance is disrupted by fatigue, sleep, illness, memory loss, emotional upset and hunger; computers can perform continuously 24 hours a day. Humans must begin each new generation with a prolonged period of education and training; computers will be able to transfer all of their accumulated knowledge to improved machines at the speed of light. The long-term implications of AI become staggering for it will be a technology that will rapidly evolve and soon exceed our comprehension.

Nothing illustrates more the terrible dilemma of human inventiveness than nuclear weapons. The release of vast amounts of energy by splitting the atom was an exciting corroboration of the predictions of fundamental physics. The controlled release of energy by atomic fission was a dramatic demonstration of the potential of basic research to contribute to society in a

practical way. However, the Allied effort in harnessing the atom was motivated by the fear that German physicists would use it to produce a bomb. Canada played a major role in the development of the first atomic bomb as a full partner with Britain and the US (many British scientists worked with Canadian colleagues at Chalk River, Ont, and after the war became part of the daring venture to develop the CANDU reactor). The successful detonation of the first atomic bomb at Alamogordo, New Mexico, 16 July 1945, ushered in a new era of destruction that depended on the inventive abilities of scientists and engineers.

Today the nuclear arsenal contains weapons that operate on the same principle that allows the sun to burn (NUCLEAR FUSION). Now, the nuclear arsenal contains enough explosive potential to destroy every human being on the planet. The arms race has been "rationalized" by military planners with an appropriate acronym, MAD (Mutual Assured Destruction). Yet, the reality of nuclear weapons is that if even a small proportion perform as expected and hit their targets, neither side will be able to claim a victory as an electromagnetic surge knocks out most electrical systems to create chaos, while the resulting debris will so blacken the atmosphere that the surface temperature of the planet will plummet (thus creating a so-called "nuclear winter").

What becomes clear is that, while the scientific analytical part of the brain has created terrible weapons, we are impelled to use them by more primitive impulses of self-defence, territoriality and emotion. Each leader of a country, however articulate and reasonable normally, is ultimately a complex individual whose biases, fears and areas of ignorance will affect the way the weapons are used. Modern technology, the crowning achievement of the human brain, has reached a scale of size and speed that is literally out of human control. Thus, nuclear-tipped missiles can now hit targets anywhere on the planet within 10-15 minutes. Even with a perfect defence system that detects and identifies an enemy missile within seconds of its launch, the problems of human reaction time, complex emotional responses to the event, and the need to assimilate the information and formulate a response at several levels of command preclude a rational, considered decision in the response time allowed by the weapons. Thus, as US President Ronald Reagan admitted in Apr 1984, weapons such as his proposed "star-wars" machines in outer space act too fast for human control and will have to be trusted to computers. As the technology increases in speed and complexity, not only do we lose control, but the probability of an accidental firing of a weapon through human or machine error increases proportionately. Nuclear weapons graphically illustrate the dilemma of modern technology — once invented and used, there is no going back; the situation is irreversible. Profound consequences usually become apparent only much later.

Science and Morality How, then, are we to deal with science and its applications in a way that will maximize the quality of our lives, while minimizing detrimental effects on the environment and other people? Victory on any specific issue, such as acid rain, nuclear weapons or PCBs (polychlorinated biphenyls), will not have affected the primary factor generating the problem in the first place. There must be a fundamental shift in perspective that will come from a recognition that as long as we see ourselves as separate from nature, superior to all other beings, compelled to use every "resource" and capable of understanding and controlling all of nature through science and technology, we will never escape the cycle of harmful or destructive results. Scientific research provides powerful insights that lead to the capacity to interfere with and control a part of nature. But the necessity of seeing nature in bits and pieces precludes any ability to evaluate the effect of a manipulation on the rest of nature. Science is a way of knowing, but there are many others (music, art, literature, etc). Science is not in the business of finding absolute truth; instead, it is constantly disproving or modifying its current theories. The assumption of human control that is not ultimately subject to unpredictable or uncontrollable natural forces or human fallibility dooms us.

All technological designs and plans are predicated on the notion that human beings will respond rationally in all predictable situations. Yet anyone who has participated in a debate over ABORTION, nuclear power, political ideology or religion realizes that rationality plays a small role in shaping our actions. Technologies cannot be "foolproof" unless they eliminate the "fool" who, as HAL the computer in the movie *2001* realized, is any fallible human being. People get sick, emotionally disturbed, intoxicated, tired; in short, we are distractable and no one can predict the foolish behaviour that may result. Unless technology is designed with that insight, it will remain prone to breakdown. It is not clear how that can be done; however, without a shift in perspective before examination of the challenge, it will not be possible.

The way to change profoundly thinking about science and technology must come from a broad public understanding of the foundations of the scientific enterprise, its basic methodology and its limitations, and of the social context within which it is used. As long as science is effectively removed from the social reality of most people, that change will not take place. As long as society continues to fragment its activities into spheres of expertise distinguished by special knowledge and jargon, we are effectively barred from affecting those activities. Science must not continue to remain in the jurisdiction of experts and people with vested interests, for theirs is a severely restricted perspective. Just as military leaders must, in a democracy, submit to the dictates of the popularly elected government, so those who apply science should come under the control of our political representatives who, in turn, must be capable of understanding the scientific and technical counsel of experts. The process of making science a political priority comes from the bottom up, impressed on candidates for office by an informed and concerned electorate.

Science Education Canada's educational system pays little attention to the need to educate future lay citizens as well as prospective science students in science and technology. In the first national survey of science education in Canada, the SCIENCE COUNCIL OF CANADA documented serious deficits from elementary to high schools. The study pointed to problems in both teaching personnel and facilities. Across Canada, over half of all early (grades 1-6) schoolteachers have had no university level MATHEMATICS courses, while three-quarters had no science. In the middle years (grades 7-9), one-third of all teachers have had no math or science since high school. In the senior years, while 95% of teachers have had some university level science, over one-third had taken their last course over a decade ago. In science, experimental observation is a critical part of the activity, yet in elementary schools, fewer than one in 5 teachers even have occasional access to a science room. In consequence, science is taught sporadically, often varying from school to school. These conditions are in striking contrast to the Japanese school system, in which science is a priority subject from primary school on. In Canadian high schools, science courses are designed for the small percentage of graduates who will go on to

enrol in science programs in universities and technical schools. There is considerable emphasis on mathematics as a prerequisite for doing science, with the result that students who have difficulty with math often conclude that science is simply beyond their grasp. Eventually, being unable to do math leads to the conclusion that science does not affect one in daily life.

The results of the above deficiencies and others, such as inadequate textbooks, lab equipment, etc, are that science is rarely taught adequately (if at all) in elementary schools across Canada; students who are high achievers and science enthusiasts are not challenged by science courses; very little is taught about the interactions among science, technology and society; Canadian students are taught very little about scientific and technological advances made in this country; from an early age, girls are turned away from science and do not see career opportunities in science and technology. This situation has led the Science Council to endorse a concept of science for all, stated by the US National Science Teachers Association: "Every child shall study science every day of every year." In order to achieve a scientifically literate society, the Science Council warns of the hazards of the current situation and strongly urges the adoption of 46 recommendations which would radically change the teaching of science without requiring major overhauling of the educational system. The lack of scientific literacy reflects itself in the priorities of upper management in the electronic and print media as well as in politicians. If a society is to consider seriously the place of science and technology, then it must have an aware public.

Science education should not be restricted to knowing the definition of terms, principles and the latest theories. The greatest lesson from science for all aspects of culture is its skepticism, its demand for a rigorous presentation and analysis of data. Canadians today consume information at an astonishing rate. By the criteria of hours of television watched, newspapers, books and magazines purchased and years of schooling, we have access to information to an unprecedented degree, although most of this information will ultimately be judged wrong, trivial or unimportant. Scientific skepticism demands more than repeating an anecdote or referring to something "I saw on TV" or "I read." Science does not accept as truth a statement based simply on a television program or a printed source. The profound thrust of science education must be to inculcate this rigour and skepticism in the INFORMATION AGE. *See* ASTRONOMY; BIOCHEMISTRY; BIOETHICS; ELECTRONICS; GALAXY; IMMUNOLOGY; INVENTORS AND INNOVATION; MEDICAL ETHICS; MOLECULAR BIOLOGY; NUCLEAR SAFETY; PHILOSOPHY; POLLUTION; ROBOTICS; SCIENCE POLICY; SCIENTIFIC RESEARCH AND DEVELOPMENT. DAVID T. SUZUKI

Reading: Carl Berger, *Science, God and Nature in Victorian Canada* (1983); Science Council of Canada, *Science Education in Canada*, 3 vols (1984).

Science Centre, establishment devoted to the popular exposition of science by means of participatory exhibits. For example, an elementary PHYSICS gallery might invite visitors to push handles to test the effects of leverage, swing on merry-go-rounds to experience changes in moments of inertia, pump air or water to demonstrate the principles of fluid dynamics and crank handles to generate electricity. While science museums, with static displays of scientific and technological objects, have existed for many years, science centres are a contemporary phenomenon aimed at making science subjects more accessible to the general public. The movement to popularize science has been fueled in many Western societies by the perceived economic threat of newly industrialized nations such as Japan. Japan's success in producing quality manufactured goods at lower prices is

partly attributed to better scientific and technological education.

Most physical-science subjects are difficult to display. The first to succeed in building participatory exhibits were German industrialists at the Deutsches Museum in Munich in 1906. Later, other museums of the history of science (eg, in London, Chicago, Philadelphia, Boston) added some working exhibits to their historical artifacts. Only after 1960 did the Philips Company in Amsterdam, Frank Oppenheimer in San Francisco and the Ontario government in Toronto establish museums devoted predominantly to experiments in modern science rather than to the display of historical objects.

The ONTARIO SCIENCE CENTRE, designed by Toronto architect Raymond MORIYAMA, is the oldest in Canada and opened in Toronto in 1969. The Ontario government founded it as a museum of the history of technology but, when it was discovered that historical exhibits of the highest quality were almost unobtainable, the Cabinet ordered the centre to abandon its traditional objectives and to build working exhibits. It has 400 "hands-on" exhibits, more than any other institution. The centre caters to organized groups of students (as many as 3000 students and teachers in a single day) and to the general public (over 16 000 people on the busiest days). The average annual attendance is equal to 65% of the population of Metro Toronto. In 1982 the 1 610 000 visitors approximately equalled the combined audiences of the province's 5 most popular arts attractions (the festivals at Stratford and Niagara, and Toronto's opera, ballet and symphony).

In 1982, in collaboration with the Chinese, the OSC staged an exhibition on Chinese science that attracted visitors who paid over $3 million in fees. It was the largest temporary exhibition of a cultural nature ever held in Canada and toured the US. On 20 Sept 1983 the OSC opened a return exhibition in Beijing. Copies of OSC exhibits were sold to the Chinese by Ontario industry for $400 000. On 8 Oct 1983 the centre opened a tour in Japan; the Japanese paid $780 000 for the Canadian-made exhibits. Delegates from the UK, the US and France have also visited Canada to investigate science centres and purchase exhibits.

Today, Canada is fortunate in having more science centres, in various stages of development, than any other country, except perhaps the US. These developments are the result of local initiatives across the country. In Vancouver a group of volunteers raised funds and opened the Vancouver Arts, Science and Technology Centre. The centre eventually expects to move to new quarters being built for the Vancouver World Exhibition (1986). In Alberta, contributions from the provincial government ($5 million), city of Edmonton ($5 million) and private and corporate donors have allowed construction of the Edmonton Space Sciences Centre. The striking building was designed by D.J. CARDINAL. Zeiss Jena produced the star projector for the planetarium (Margaret Ziedler Star Theatre) and Imax, the curved-screen film projector for the Devonian Theatre. The centre has 2 large galleries to be devoted to largely participatory exhibits. Edmonton also boasts a smaller centre, devoted to ENERGY and natural science, which has many computer exhibits. In Regina volunteers have acquired the shell of an abandoned power plant in Wascana Park in the city centre for a science centre. In Sudbury INCO, Falconbridge Mines, the Ontario government and many citizens made possible the renovation of a working mine and built a pavilion for a science centre, Science North, at a cost of $15 million. The centre, designed by Raymond Moriyama, was due to open in May 1984. In London, Ont, the London Regional Children's Museum is now operating in a downtown school. The museum has participatory experiments and programs, which enable students to dig and reassemble the casts of dinosaur bones, dress up and re-enact the past, or perform scientific experiments on their own. In Niagara Falls, Ont, work has begun on converting the powerhouse above the falls into the Engineerium. The building, the finest conspicuous example of architecture in the region, was opened in 1983 for 2 months as a science centre and museum. On 13 Nov 1983 Premier René Lévesque announced that Québec intends to build a science centre on Île Ste Hélène, Montréal, on the 1967 world's fair site. Other centres are planned for Calgary, Winnipeg and the Atlantic provinces.   J. TUZO WILSON

Science Council of Canada, organization created by federal statute in 1966 to advise the government on SCIENCE and TECHNOLOGY policy. The original membership was 25 appointed scientists and senior federal civil servants, later altered to 30 appointed scientists, from the natural and SOCIAL SCIENCES, and no civil servants. While the statute provided that the council would undertake specific studies at ministerial request, its practice has been to determine its own study program, with virtual autonomy from ministerial direction. The council's published work consists primarily of signed background studies expressing the views of the authors, but certified by council for reliability and methodology; and formal council reports, expressing the consensus of members, and usually recommending actions to governments and other parties. The council's judgements derive their legitimacy from the fact that its members are broadly representative of the Canadian scientific community, in both the academic and private sectors.

Over the first 17 years of its work, the council has held different perceptions of its primary role, depending on the beliefs of its various chairmen and members. It has most often seen itself as a national adviser, transcending purely federal considerations. It has also assumed an early warning function, to alert governments and society to emerging opportunities and problems. It has championed university research, especially basic research, against government predispositions to cut budgets. Occasionally, it has essayed an international role. Although its statute was specifically amended to give it responsibility for enhancing public awareness of science and technology policy, the council's published output was, until recently, extremely scanty in this area. It has, however, undertaken a public discussion role through stimulating or organizing conferences and other meetings aimed at professionals.

Probably its most enduring preoccupation and greatest contribution has been in advocating a national industrial strategy. The council has argued against the mainstream of advice from other agencies, public and private, and against the apparent inclinations of federal ministers. By 1983 it seemed to have begun to turn the tide, at least in general terms. Indeed, the council's recommendations have more often been effective in helping to create a policy climate than in providing specific blueprints for government action. Since its inception, the council's chairmen have been Omond SOLANDT, Roger Gaudry, Joseph Kates, Claude Fortier and Stuart L. Smith.   LESLIE MILLIN

Science Policy, term which came into use in the 1960s to denote the co-ordinated measures that should be taken by governments to promote the development of scientific and technological research and, especially, to guide the exploitation of research results to further national economic growth and welfare. State patronage of SCIENCE and TECHNOLOGY was not new; indeed it has a long history. What was new was the growing sense, among the public and political leaders, of the central importance of science and

technology in the modern world and of the need for more systematic action by governments to direct and control their use. A 1963 Organization for Economic Cooperation and Development report stated: "To say that a government needs an articulated science policy is simply to note that there has devolved upon that government a major and continuing responsibility to make choices about issues that involve science." Science had become a "national asset" (*see* INVENTORS AND INNOVATION).

The need for national science policy was widely promoted in the 1960s and early 1970s by international agencies (eg, OECD) and by a multiplicity of official and unofficial bodies in many countries; however, there were serious disagreements about the precise form science policy should take and the appropriate governmental institutions for making it. The most important institutional developments in Canada were the creation of a Science Secretariat (1964) in the PRIVY COUNCIL OFFICE, establishment of the SCIENCE COUNCIL OF CANADA (1966), and creation of the Ministry of State for Science and Technology (1971). The most important documents to emerge in the debate were reports by the Science Council, especially its 4th report, *Towards a National Science Policy in Canada* (Oct 1968), the *Review of Science Policy, Canada* by OECD (1969), and the 3 comprehensive reports from the Senate Special Committee on Science Policy (the Lamontagne Committee), which was set up in 1967 and sat for more than 5 years.

Science policy can be said to have 2 complementary aspects: policy for promoting science, ie, the provision by governments of an environment that fosters growth of scientific and technological knowledge; and policy for using science, ie, the exploitation of this knowledge in development and innovation. The former might be taken to mean a collection of policies that are pursued, more or less independently, by government agencies to sponsor research relating solely to their specific functional responsibilities. In this sense, most "advanced" nations (and certainly Canada) could be said to have had a policy for promoting science for more than a century. However, more than this minimal definition is intended: namely, a comprehensive and coherent policy for government support of science and technology generally. This point was made by the Glassco Commission (*see* GOVERNMENT ORGANIZATION, ROYAL COMMISSION ON) in a report published in 1962. The commission was strongly critical of the unco-ordinated and policyless expansion of science and technology in Canada after WWII and this criticism led directly to the establishment of the Science Secretariat. Moreover, in an era in which advances in scientific knowledge were creating many more opportunities for exploitation than could be satisfied with the resources that were available, there was need for establishment of priorities.

In a "small-science" country like Canada, especially, there were severe limits on what kinds of science and technology could be supported. Thus, it was argued that a policy for promoting science must be based on carefully specified "criteria for scientific choice"; ie, on principles for deciding how much support in the form of public money and other resources (eg, trained personnel) should go to the nation's science and technology as a whole; how this "pool" should then be distributed sector by sector (ie, among university research, "in-house" research done by government agencies, and research done by industry); and, lastly, how each of these sectoral allocations should be distributed among the various scientific and technological disciplines. The implementation of these criteria would have an indirect effect on the rate of growth and the direction taken by the various sciences and technologies, and a direct effect on the balance between basic science, applied science and de-

velopment through technological innovation. The Science Council, OECD and the Lamontagne Committee all argued strongly that the promotion of Canadian science had been too heavily weighted towards basic research and that both basic and applied research were too far removed from the point where development could take place (namely INDUSTRY). Much has been done since the 1970s to correct this imbalance, although problems persist, since so much Canadian industry is "branch-plant industry," for which the research and development is done in the laboratories of parent companies in the US.

A government could pursue a coherent policy for promoting basic and applied science using criteria that make little or no reference to the relevance of the research to specific social needs or national priorities. Such a policy could support those areas of research that seem to promise the most important results from a scientific point of view, and those scientists who were demonstrably the most competent and productive. Indeed, this policy was pursued for many years by the NATIONAL RESEARCH COUNCIL, the objective of which was to build a viable "science base" in Canada and to create a body of competent scientists who could take their place in the international science community. If, however, science policy is also to relate directly to the use of science, criteria of social "relevance" must necessarily be invoked. There are then 3 possibilities. In deciding how government support is to be allocated, public agencies responsible for supporting projects may simply be given a directive to ensure that priority is given to those projects that can demonstrate a direct relevance to specific social needs or to the solution of important social problems. Canadian science policy eventually took this route.

The second possibility, explored by the Science Council in its 4th report, requires that at least a major portion of the nation's scientific and technological effort should be pursued through very large "mission-oriented" projects involving government science agencies, universities and industry. The prototype scientific "mission" was the Manhattan Project in WWII, which produced the first atomic bombs. Postwar examples are the Canadian NUCLEAR-ENERGY program that developed the CANDU reactor, and the American and Soviet space programs. The Science Council recommended "that most new undertakings in Canadian science be organised as large, multi-disciplinary, mission-oriented projects having as a goal the solution of some important economic or social problem in which all the sectors of the scientific community . . . must participate on an equal footing." These "major programs" would each contain components of basic and applied research, development and innovation. The council foresaw future basic research as being done principally in fields allied to these programs, but stressed that it should also be supported as a possible source of new theoretical discoveries and as a means of providing the necessary body of expertise for understanding and absorbing advances made in other countries (notably the US). The council suggested several broad areas in which "missions" would be appropriate, including upper atmosphere and SPACE, WATER resources, TRANSPORTATION, the URBAN environment, and development of the Canadian NORTH and of new ENERGY sources. These proposals were not entirely without effect on the subsequent progress of government support for science and technology in Canada, but the basic idea of a series of major multidisciplinary missions has never been implemented.

The third possibility for structuring policy for the use of science was hinted at, perhaps unwittingly, in the 1963 OECD report which suggested that science policy should lead to "national decisions about where and how fast science will go, and about the national goals to which it will contribute." Implicit in this statement is the idea of the comprehensive planning of science, according to state-prescribed objectives, such as is supposed to occur in the USSR. The pursuit of science policy within a framework of national goals was given some attention by the Science Council in its 4th report, but there was little apparent relationship between the very general goals it suggested (national prosperity, personal freedom, etc) and the programs it actually prescribed. The notion that science can be comprehensively planned in a free society has now been abandoned by all countries that may have contemplated it, even by France with its long tradition of *dirigisme* and its (post-WWII) adoption of *planification*. In a totalitarian state like the USSR the central planning of science is in principle possible (although in practice it is frequently attended by unfortunate consequences), but in highly pluralistic and decentralized democracies, such as Canada, the idea is now recognized as unattainable, except, perhaps, in the highly unlikely circumstance of a future conventional world war. This situation does not solely, or even primarily, arise from inadequacies in governmental machinery; rather, it results from the fact that it is impossible, in Western democracies, to establish by fiat broad societal objectives towards which scientific and technological progress must be directed.

In the course of the international debate about science policy, 3 major options emerge respecting the governmental machinery that might be adopted. The first was the creation of a minister for science, with executive responsibilities, who would head a department for running at least the major government scientific establishments, for funding and other support of the nation's scientific and technological research and development, and (through the minister) for advising on science policy (in the case of parliamentary, cabinet systems of government like Britain and Canada, directly to the Cabinet). The second option was creation of a minister of scientific affairs or minister for science policy (possibly heading a department or assisted by an appropriately sized ministerial staff), who would have no executive functions but would serve in an advisory capacity to other departments and agencies and to the Cabinet, and might also be given certain co-ordinating functions (eg, chairmanship of a Cabinet science-policy committee). The third option was to establish a nonministerial advisory agency in the central core of government (ie, in the Cabinet office or, possibly, in the department responsible for authorizing all government spending). Such an agency would be responsible for advising on the science policy aspects of all government policies and programs, and might be headed by a chief scientific adviser to the government, with direct access to the chief executive (in a parliamentary cabinet system, to the prime minister).

The minister for science option was rejected for Canada, chiefly on the grounds that a minister with direct responsibilities for the performance of research in agencies of his own department would not be an impartial adviser on government science policy in general and that the concentration of so many science functions in "one place" would create an overcentralized and unwieldy administration. The idea was particularly disliked by scientists, who have traditionally been jealous of their autonomy, preferring to operate within a decentralized and pluralistic system. The advisory agency option was adopted, at least in part, by the creation of a Science Secretariat within the Privy Council Office in 1964, and the appointment in 1968 of its director as principal science adviser to the Cabinet. This promising move was abandoned in 1971 when the government shifted to the second

option and set up the Ministry of State for Science and Technology. This option has proved to be weak, given the political realities of the Canadian Cabinet and bureaucratic system, and there has been a succession of short-lived incumbents of the office of minister of state, none of whom has been particularly effective. In this system, a minister without executive responsibilities tends to have little influence in Cabinet (and, hence, in relation to the operating departments) and this lack of influence means that the office is usually filled either by a prominent political figure for whom the office is simply a temporary stepping-stone to more important posts, or by a lesser figure who is unlikely to advance much farther. On the other hand, if the post is filled by a minister who is given a second (executive) portfolio (as has happened on several occasions), the duties of this portfolio tend to take precedence, to the neglect of the science policy advisory functions.   J.W. GROVE

Reading: G.B. Doern, *Science and Politics in Canada* (1972); N.H. Lithwick, *Canada's Science Policy and the Economy* (1969); Science Council of Canada Background Study No 31, *Knowledge, Power and Public Policy* (1974); Senate Special Committee on Science Policy, *A Science Policy for Canada* 3 vols (1970, 1972, 1973).

Scientific Research and Development The history of scientific research and development ("R & D") in Canada has barely been examined. Some studies have been devoted to federal government activities, in particular those of the NATIONAL RESEARCH COUNCIL; however, much less work has been done on university research, and practically none on industrial R & D. Nevertheless the general historical outlines may still be sketched. The Canadian government established scientific agencies in the 19th century to deal with primary industries such as MINING, agriculture, FORESTRY and FISHERIES. The support and organization of scientific and industrial research in Canada gained momentum in the early decades of the 20th century, when a movement arose promoting such research. The movement was both a reaction to similar efforts in other industrialized countries, in particular following the outbreak of WWI, and a response to developments within Canada. Many Canadian universities attempted to improve and expand on their science and ENGINEERING programs, to foster graduate studies and promote the ideal of research. The federal government founded the NRC in 1916 to encourage R & D in Canada. The ALBERTA RESEARCH COUNCIL was formed in 1921; the ONTARIO RESEARCH FOUNDATION in 1928; and other provincial RESEARCH organizations followed, especially after WWII.

In Canadian industry, the turn of the century witnessed a trend towards industrial concentration, specialization and the growing dominance of large corporations, all of which fostered the emergence of industrial R & D. The CANADIAN MANUFACTURERS' ASSOCIATION was an important advocate of increased R & D in Canada. The amount of industrial R & D expanded very rapidly following WWI: approximately 37 Canadian firms had research laboratories in 1917-18, by 1939 there were 998 industrial laboratories. The exponential rate of growth of gross expenditures on R & D after WWII reflects the rapid development of R & D activities in Canada. Accompanying this increase in the late 1960s and 1970s was a widespread concern about the lack of an explicit SCIENCE POLICY and about the performance of industrial innovation in Canada. As a result, the federal government created a number of study and advisory groups, among them the SCIENCE COUNCIL OF CANADA (est 1966) and the Ministry of State for Science and Technology (1971).

According to Statistics Canada, in 1982 an estimated $4.39 billion was spent on scientific R & D in Canada (approximately another $425 million was spent on R & D in the human sciences).

Of the $4.39 billion, the federal government funded 35.1%; the provincial governments, 5.6%; business, 44.5%; higher education, 9.6%; private nonprofit organizations, 2%; and foreign sources, 3.2%. The federal government spent 63.4% of its R & D funds on its own programs; 13.6% was contributed to business; 22.7% to higher education.

Of the R & D performed by business, 84% was funded by business; 9.1%, by the federal government; 1.3%, by provincial governments; 5.6%, by foreign sources. As in other countries, industrial R & D in Canada is concentrated in manufacturing, mostly in electrical products, PETROLEUM products, MACHINERY, chemicals and chemical products, transportation equipment (aerospace), primary metals, and paper and allied products. For R & D performed by higher education, the federal government contributed 38.2%; provincial governments, 8.3%; business, 0.2%; private nonprofit organizations, 6.7%; higher education, 45.7%; foreign sources, 0.9%. Regionally, in 1980, 51% of R & D was performed in Ontario; 23%, in the western provinces; 21%, in Québec; 5%, in the Atlantic provinces. Employment of scientists, engineers, technicians and support staff in R & D in Canada stood at 53 870 full-time equivalents (not persons) in 1980. Full-time equivalent scientists and engineers composed 43.4% of this figure. The federal government employed 28.3% of the 53 870; provincial governments, 3.8%; provincial research organizations, 1.8%; business, 48.9%; higher education, 16.1%; private nonprofit organizations, 1.2%.

Gross expenditure on R & D (GERD) in Canada was an estimated 1.32% of the gross domestic product in 1982. By comparison, the percentage for the US in the same year, one of the highest, was 2.62%. There is no theoretical basis for determining the optimum ratio of GERD/GDP and this ratio must be interpreted in the light of the individual country's economic and scientific structures. Thus, while Canada's GERD/GDP has consistently been one of the lowest among major industrialized countries, Canada is classified by the Organization for Economic Cooperation and Development as a medium R & D country along with others which have higher ratios. Nonetheless the level of funding for R & D in Canada has long been thought to be too low. In 1978 the federal government responded by establishing a target for R & D expenditures of 1.5% of the GROSS NATIONAL PRODUCT. This goal was to be reached in 1983 and was later postponed to 1985. One-third of the total was to be the federal government's share, one-half was to come from industry; the balance was to be financed by other funders. Despite a significant rise after 1978, GERD/GNP did not realize its target in 1985.

The major concern about the state of R & D in Canada, aside from its level of funding, has been its distribution and, here, the dominant problem has been industrial R & D. Critics have argued that in the past the federal government overemphasized basic research to the detriment of development and spent too much of its R & D funds intramurally. Universities have also been criticized for being too insulated from the needs of business. In the late 1960s, and especially in the 1970s, the federal government began to take some steps towards contracting out R & D, supporting R & D performed by industry, and establishing links to foster the transfer of ideas and technology from government and university to industry. Industry's funding and performance of R & D has also been a source of considerable unease. Both are held to be too low and, thus, to affect the Canadian economy adversely. There has been much debate over the role of FOREIGN INVESTMENT in truncating industrial R & D in Canada. Foreign subsidiaries are said to decrease the amount of research in Canada and to increase reliance on foreign technology; however, it seems unlikely that Canada would have been able to achieve the growth rates it did without subsidiaries and, through them, Canada gains invisible inflows of technology. The evidence for either of these views is mixed and, although it does now appear that Canadian-owned firms are more research intensive than their foreign-owned counterparts, it is still not known if this situation is the result of ownership or of other factors, such as structural differences within industries. PHILIP C. ENROS

Reading: G.B. Doern, *Science and Politics in Canada* (1972); C. Freeman, *The Economics of Industrial Innovation* (1974); K. Green and C. Morphet, *Research and Technology as Economic Activities* (1977).

Scorpion, carnivorous arthropod of class ARACHNIDA, order Scorpiones. Known from fossils 400 million years old, scorpions are among the oldest terrestrial animals. They have front appendages modified into claws for catching and holding prey, 7-segmented preabdomen, and 5-segmented posterior with a tail ending in a stinger. Ventrally, they have 2 comblike appendages, thought to be sensory organs. Although they have up to 12 eyes, scorpions can only distinguish dark from light. The largest living species are about 15 cm long. About 1000 species are found worldwide, throughout tropical and warmer desert regions; only one species occurs in Canada (southern Sask, Alta and BC). It is about 5 cm long and has a 2-year life cycle. Although many scorpions have poisonous stings for defence or killing prey, most are harmless to humans. The effect of the sting is like that of a bee. Scorpions are nocturnal, living under logs, bark or rocks. The young are usually born alive; shortly after birth, they crawl onto the mother's back for protection. ROBIN LEECH

Scorpionfish, or rockfish (Scorpaenidae), family of bottom-dwelling, marine FISHES with large heads, mouths and eyes, stout bodies and large pectoral fins. Over 300 species are distributed worldwide, in temperate and tropical waters. The greatest variety of forms is found in the Indo-Australian region, where several bizarrely shaped, deceptively coloured and often venomous species exist. The highly venomous lionfish and turkeyfish can inflict painful injuries. Like SCULPINS, scorpionfish belong to the "mail-cheeked fishes," characterized by a bony stay or splint extending from the eye to the cheekbone. The head and fins exhibit many spines, and the body frequently has cirri and skin flaps, thought to help in camouflage. Many forms have internal fertilization and bear live young, but a few egg-laying species are known. The family has been divided into several subgroups, based on various criteria. In Canadian waters, it is represented by over 30 forms on the Pacific coast; fewer than 5 on the Atlantic. Many are important, commercial food fishes, eg, Pacific ocean perch and rockfish, and Atlantic redfish — all members of genus *Sebastes*. Rockfishes range in size from about 15 cm in dwarf forms to almost 100 cm in some Alaskan representatives. Depending upon the species, young are born from winter to late spring. Young rockfish drift with and feed upon PLANKTON. After several weeks they settle, becoming bottom dwellers. The mechanism triggering settling is unknown. Many young rockfish are brightly coloured and differently coloured from adults of the same species. Recent analyses indicate that rockfish are among the longest-lived marine fishes, frequently surviving for 80-90 years. Scorpionfishes occur from subtidal waters to depths of over 500 m. Some live close inshore, among rocks and kelp, in small groups or associations. Others, including the commercially important species, live in massive schools in offshore waters at mid-depths. Offshore populations undergo diurnal and seasonal movements. They

are generally fished by trawl, and are competed for by several nations on both Canadian coasts. NORMAN J. WILIMOVSKY

Scotian Shelf A 700 km section of the continental shelf off Nova Scotia. Bounded by the Laurentian Channel on the NE, and Northeast Channel and the Gulf of Maine on the SW, it varies in width from 120 to 240 km; the average depth is 90 m. Deep basins and channels, separating shallow offshore banks (dry land during the ice age), characterize its irregular bathymetry. Only SABLE I, the notorious "graveyard of the Atlantic," remains above water today. Circulation over the inner shelf is dominated by a southwesterly longshore current that varies seasonally with freshwater runoff from the Gulf of ST LAWRENCE. Over the banks the circulation is weaker and more variable, under the influence of storms, tides and the Gulf Stream several hundred km S. Strong tidal streams around southwestern NS produce vertical mixing and enrichment of the herring and lobster fisheries; offshore an international fleet annually removes around half a million tonnes of fish and squid. Recent discoveries of natural gas near Sable I have stimulated further hydrocarbon explorations, creating potential conflict between renewable and nonrenewable resources on the shelf. P.C. SMITH AND R.J. CONOVER

Scots Although often considered Anglo-Canadians, the Scots have always regarded themselves as a separate people. The connection between Scotland and Canada dates to the 17th century. The Scots have been immigrating in steady and substantial numbers for nearly 200 years. In 1961, the last census for which the category was recorded, 1 894 000 Canadians, or 10.4% of the population, listed themselves as of Scottish origin.

The kingdom of Scotland established one of the earliest colonies in Canada in 1621, when Sir William Alexander was granted a charter for New Scotland, now Nova Scotia. Alexander established small settlements on Cape Breton and on the Bay of FUNDY, but they did not flourish and Scottish claims were surrendered to France in 1632. A few Scots immigrated to NEW FRANCE, but the major early movement of Scots to Canada was a small flow of men from Orkney — beginning about 1720 — recruited by the HUDSON'S BAY COMPANY for service in the West. Soldiers from the Highlands of Scotland comprised the crack regiments of the British army that defeated the French in the SEVEN YEARS' WAR. Many soldiers remained in N America, and Scots merchants moved on to Québec after 1759 where they dominated commercial life and the fur trade.

Between 1770 and 1815 some 15 000 Highland Scots came to Canada, settling mainly in PEI, NS (*see* HECTOR) and Upper Canada. Most of these immigrants came from the western Highlands and the islands of Scotland. They were almost exclusively Gaelic speaking and many were Roman Catholics. They congregated in agrarian communities in the new land and, in the early years of the 19th century, Gaelic was the third most common European language spoken in Canada. A few Highlanders were brought to the RED RIVER COLONY by the earl of SELKIRK, and other Scots from the fur trade moved with their Indian families to Red River after 1821. In all these communities Highland traditions were preserved and for many years they remained distinctive ethnic enclaves.

After 1815 Scottish immigration increased in numbers, and the pattern altered. Scots from the Lowlands area, encouraged by the British government, joined Highlanders in coming to Canada. Some 170 000 Scots crossed the Atlantic between 1815 and 1870, roughly 14% of the total British migration of this period. By the 1850s most of the newcomers were settling in United

Canada rather than in the Maritime colonies. According to the 1871 census, 157 of every 1000 Canadians were of Scottish origin, ranging from 4.1% in Québec to 33.7% in NS. The immigrants of this period represented a cross section of the Scottish population. Most were farmers and artisans, although large numbers of business and professional people were included, especially teachers and clergymen. Most of the newcomers were Presbyterians and most spoke English. They tended to live and fraternize together and were particularly active in establishing schools (eg, the St John's College in Red River) that emphasized training for the talented.

Scots were highly visible in politics and business; men such as James Glenie and John Neilsen often led the criticism of elitist political structures, although other Scots such as John STRACHAN were members of the ELITE. The first 2 Canadian prime ministers — John A. MACDONALD and Alexander MACKENZIE — were born in Scotland. Scots dominated the fur trade, the timber trade, banking and railway management; nearly 50% of the nation's industrial leaders in the 1880s had recent Scottish origins. Scots in Canada increasingly found themselves in an ambivalent position, both part of the dominant British culture and yet insistent on maintaining their own identity. It was largely because of their influence that the preponderant culture in Canada was British, rather than ENGLISH, and distinctive Scottish patterns can be discerned in Canadian education and moral attitudes, eg, Sabbath observance and TEMPERANCE. Scottish moral philosophers strongly influenced philosophical teaching in Canada.

Since 1870 patterns of Scottish immigration and settlement have altered significantly, reflecting shifts in both Scotland and Canada. When population pressures in the Highland region lessened, Highlanders no longer emigrated to Canada in substantial numbers. In the Scottish Lowlands, urbanization and industrialization reduced the agricultural component of the population and the percentage of farmers among immigrants to Canada fell correspondingly. Meanwhile, in Canada burgeoning factories and cities were attracting Scottish immigrants, although many made their way to the last great agricultural frontier in western Canada. The flow of people from Scotland to Canada continued unabated, however. From 1871 to 1901, 80 000 Scots entered Canada seeking a better future: 240 000 arrived in the first years of the century before WWI, 200 000 more between 1919 and 1930 and another 147 000 between 1946 and 1960.

Like most immigrant groups, the Scots since 1870 have shunned the Atlantic region and Québec in favour of Ontario and the West. A substantial population of Scottish origin in the Maritime provinces is native-born. Newfoundland, like Québec, has never had a significant Scottish population. Scots are widely distributed across the remaining provinces and territories in both urban and rural communites. Like most ethnic groups in Canada, the Scots have become increasingly assimilated into Canadian society, although still retaining an awareness of their distinctive heritage. Like other ethnic groups as well, the Scots have tended to focus on a few highly visible symbols of their origins, such as clans, tartans and Highland dancing. The number of Gaelic speakers has declined in Canada as in Scotland itself, and only a few thousand people, mainly in Cape Breton, keep the language alive in Canada.

Scots have been involved in every aspect of Canada's development as explorers, educators, businessmen, politicians, writers, artists, etc. A few of many well-known Canadians of Scottish descent include Sir A.T. GALT, Lord ELGIN, Donald SMITH (Lord Strathcona), William Lyon MACKENZIE, Harold INNIS, Sir William MACKENZIE, Maxwell AITKEN (Lord Beaverbrook), W.L. MORTON, Blair Fraser, Norman BETHUNE, Farley MOWAT, Douglas CAMPBELL and Norman MCLAREN.

The history and culture of Scots developed quite differently from that of other groups from the British Isles and Scots have always regarded themselves as distinctive from — indeed superior to — their English, WELSH and IRISH cousins. Their pattern of immigration to and development in Canada is clearly quite unlike that of most other ethnic peoples, for it has been protracted over several centuries rather than chronologically or regionally specific. Scots have never been sufficiently numerous to dominate, nor sufficiently lacking in numbers to vanish. Their Scottish background has on the whole served them well as successful Canadian settlers. Sufficiently close culturally to the English to become part of the dominant society, their Scottish background has provided them with skills and aspirations well suited to a developing country. 　　　　　　　　　　　J.M. BUMSTED

Reading: R. Connor, *Glengarry School Days* (1902); J.K. Galbraith, *The Scotch* (1964); M. Laurence, *The Diviners* (1974); Sir A. MacPhail, *The Master's Wife* (1939); F.J. Niven, *The Flying Years* (1953) and *The Transplanted* (1944); W. S. Reid, *The Scottish Tradition in Canada* (1976).

Scott, Anthony Dalton, professor of economics (b at Vancouver 2 Aug 1923). Scott is perhaps best known for his pioneering contributions to the economics of natural resource use and management. His thesis, published as *Natural Resources: The Economics of Conservation* (1955, repr 1973), is considered a classic in the field, as is his book with Francis Christy, *The Commonwealth in Ocean Fisheries* (1965). He is also noted for work on human capital flows (the "brain drain") and for work on the economics of FEDERALISM. He has served with several government bodies and many professional associations. He was a commissioner on the INTERNATIONAL JOINT COMMISSION 1968-72.

Scott, Barbara Ann, figure skater (b at Ottawa 9 May 1929). One of Canada's best-remembered athletes, Scott endeared herself to Canadians in winning the 1948 St Moritz Olympics figure-skating title. At age 9, she had begun a daily 7-hour training routine; a year later, she became the youngest Canadian to earn a gold medal for figures. She was Canadian senior women's champion 1944-48, N American champion 1945-48, and European and world champion 1947-48. Her capture of the coveted Olympic gold medal made her a celebrity; in Ottawa she was honoured by adoring crowds and showered with gifts; she was the object of endless media attention. Scott received the LOU MARSH TROPHY as Canada's athlete of the year in 1945, 1947 and 1948. She toured in an ice show as a professional 1949-54. On retirement, she began training show horses, and in her mid-40s was rated among the top equestrians in the US.
　　　　　　　　　　　BARBARA SCHRODT

Barbara Ann Scott's gold medal in figure skating at the 1948 St Moritz winter Olympics made her a celebrity (*courtesy Canada's Sports Hall of Fame*).

Duncan Campbell Scott's poetry, with its precise imagery and flexible form, has weathered well the transition from traditional to modern poetry (*courtesy Public Archives of Canada/C-3187*).

Scott, Duncan Campbell, poet, short-story writer, civil servant (b at Ottawa 2 Aug 1862; d there 19 Dec 1947). Scott's ambition was to become a doctor, but family finances were precarious and in 1879 he joined the federal Dept of Indian Affairs. He became its deputy superintendent in 1913, a post he held until retirement in 1932. Scott is commonly placed with the "poets of the Confederation," but although the exact contemporary of Archibald LAMPMAN, Bliss CARMAN and C.G.D. ROBERTS he was personally close only to Lampman, who in the 1880s had sparked him to try poetry. By the late 1880s he was a regular contributor to *Scribner's Magazine.* In 1893 he published his first volume of poetry, *The Magic House and Other Poems.* This was followed in 1896 by *In the Village of Viger,* a collection of delicate sketches of French Canadian life. Two later collections, *The Witching of Elspie* (1923) and *The Circle of Affection* (1947), contained many fine short stories about Indians and traders in wilderness settings. But as a spare-time writer Scott found the pursuit of poetry more manageable than fiction. Seven collections of poems followed: *The Magic House: Labor and the Angel* (1898), *New World Lyrics and Ballads* (1905), *Via Borealis* (1906), *Lundy's Lane and Other Poems* (1916), *Beauty and Life* (1921), *The Poems of Duncan Campbell Scott* (1926) and *The Green Cloister* (1935). *The Circle of Affection,* chiefly a collection of prose, included a number of poems not previously published.

Although Scott complained of critical neglect, his literary reputation has never been in doubt. He has been well represented in virtually all major anthologies of Canadian poetry published since 1900. His "Indian" poems, in which he drew on his experiences in the field, have been widely recognized and valued. There is some conflict here between Scott's views as an administrator committed to an assimilation policy, and his sensibilities as a poet saddened by the waning of an ancient culture. Precise in imagery, intense yet disciplined, flexible in metre and form, Scott's poems weathered well the transition from traditional to modern poetry in Canada.

Scott valued music even above poetry and was an accomplished pianist. Murray ADASKIN was a friend, as were painters Homer WATSON and

Edmund Morris and later Lawren HARRIS and Clarence GAGNON. Scott was a prime mover in the establishment of the Ottawa Little Theatre and the Dominion Drama Festival. A one-act play, *Pierre,* was first performed at the Ottawa Little Theatre in 1923 and subsequently published in *Canadian Plays from Hart House Theatre* (1926).

There is ample evidence of Scott's engagement as a writer. He contributed (with Lampman and Wilfred CAMPBELL) informal essays to the Toronto *Globe* in 1892-93, published as *At the Mermaid Inn* (1979). He wrote a novel which did not go to press until it was brought out in 1979 as *The Untitled Novel.* For the Makers of Canada series, which he directed with Pelham Edgar, he wrote a biography of John Graves SIMCOE (1905). In 1947 he published a book on Walter J. PHILLIPS. Perhaps most impressive was Scott's lifelong concern for Lampman's literary reputation. This loyalty to his good friend was expressed mainly by Scott's editions of Lampman's poems (1900-47). 　　　　　　R.L. McDOUGALL

Scott, Ephraim, Presbyterian minister, editor (b in Hants County, NS 29 Jan 1845; d at Montréal 7 Aug 1931). After graduating from Dalhousie Coll in 1872, he studied at Pine Hill Coll and in Edinburgh, Scotland, until 1875 when he was called to Milford and Gays R, NS. In 1878 he moved to New Glasgow, NS, serving there until his appointment as editor of *The Presbyterian Record* in Montréal in 1891. From this position he provided active leadership for the entire church until his retirement in 1926. Scott is best remembered for his staunch opposition to union with the Congregational and Methodist churches. In 1925 he was elected moderator of the Presbyterians remaining apart from the newly formed United Church and maintained a keen and active leadership in the church's affairs until his death. 　　　　　　　　　NEIL SEMPLE

Scott, Francis Reginald, poet, professor of constitutional law, founding member of the socialist movement in Canada (b at Québec City 1 Aug 1899; d at Montréal 30 Jan 1985). As a man of letters and social commitment, Scott profoundly influenced the evolution of modern Canada's artistic and political culture. He was the sixth of 7 children of Amy and Canon Frederick George Scott, an Anglican priest, minor poet and staunch advocate of the civilizing tradition of imperial Britain, who instilled in his son a commitment to serve mankind, a love for the regenerative balance of the Laurentian landscape and a firm respect for the social order. His mother's quiet presence figures in various of his poems. Scott passed a peaceful childhood and adolescence in Québec, his pastoral upbringing disturbed only slightly by WWI, though the war claimed the life of an older brother and took Canon Scott to Europe as pastor to the Canadian troops. Scott was first exposed to social disorder through the CONSCRIPTION riots in Québec. The carnage and social upheaval brought by WWI did not affect him until the mid-1920s when he began reading modern poetry. After graduating from Québec High School and Bishop's Coll (1919), Scott went as a Rhodes scholar to Magdalen Coll, Oxford, and as a member of the Student Christian Movement began to explore socialist theory through the works of R.H. Tawney.

He returned to Canada in 1923, largely ignorant of his own country. Montréal seemed to him singularly ugly, bereft of the ancient beauty of Europe. Scott settled down to teach at Lower Canada Coll and write poetry. In 1924 he enrolled in the McGill law faculty, where H.A. Smith was to spark his interest in constitutional law. In 1924-25, as a contributor to the *McGill Daily Literary Supplement,* he met the poet/critic A.J.M. SMITH, who became a lifelong friend; they later founded the *McGill Fortnightly Review.* Under Smith's influence Scott began to introduce to his poetry a more contemporary diction, leading eventually to poetic portraits of the austere Laurentian landscape — an inspiration comparable to the antiquity of Europe. His progress into such landscapes matched his intellectual movement away from a self-regarding universe and towards the social environment. In 1927-28 he undertook a year's legal practice, joined McGill's law faculty as a professor, and married Montréal painter Marian Dale SCOTT. He also continued to participate in "The Group," an informal, socially aware discussion group composed of Oxford graduates. By the end of the 1920s, as illustrated by *The Canadian Mercury*, which he helped to found, Scott was chastising his fellow Canadians for genuflecting to the cultural values of imperial Britain.

The onset of the Depression led him to probe the economic causes of the ugliness and social deprivation that surrounded him. Inspired by J.S. WOODSWORTH, Scott and historian Frank UNDERHILL founded the LEAGUE FOR SOCIAL RECONSTRUCTION (LSR) in 1931-32, a socialist study group that drafted national economic and social policies to combat the misery caused by the Depression, and became the brain trust for the new CO-OPERATIVE COMMONWEALTH FEDERATION. Scott helped to frame the now-famous Regina Manifesto of the CCF and to write *Social Planning for Canada* (1935). Over the years he was a stalwart of the CCF, both nationally and in Québec. The goal of the LSR and the CCF to create a more egalitarian society was to shape the satiric poetry and the constitutional and socialist essays that Scott published during the Depression, often in the *Canadian Forum*, of which he was an editor. During the late 1930s he was consumed by such issues as the Spanish Civil War and campaigned for Canadian neutrality in the face of the threatening war, a position that earned him much criticism.

WWII, seeming to prove that collective man could not peacefully resolve problems, profoundly disturbed Scott. In his poems of the period, he swings from deep anxiety to a reawakened faith in mankind. He finally convinced himself that collective man could prosper in the postwar era. In such magazines as *Preview* and *Northern Review*, in the philanthropic Canada Foundation, and in artists' organizations, Scott urged artists to cultivate a socially critical intelligence and abandon narrow regional and artistic perspectives in favour of a democratic national culture. As national chairman of the CCF (1942-50), his renewed interest in socialism brought him into conflict with McGill authorities who refused to appoint him dean of the law faculty.

In 1950-51 Scott cofounded Recherches sociales, a study group concerned with the relationship between English and French Canada. He also became an active translator of French Canadian poets such as Anne HÉBERT and Saint-Denys GARNEAU. In 1952 he went to Burma as a UN technical assistant to help build a co-operative, socialist state. In the mid-1950s he successfully completed 2 landmark legal cases before the Supreme Court, the PADLOCK ACT and RONCARELLI V DUPLESSIS, in which he battled autocratic Québec Premier Maurice DUPLESSIS. Scott's poetry of the 1950s shows a singularly critical eye turned to his national society and to man in general.

In 1962, with the CCF having transformed itself into the NEW DEMOCRATIC PARTY, a process in which Scott participated actively, he retired from partisan politics. McGill appointed him dean of law (1961-64), and he began to devote increasing attention to the survival of Canadian Confederation. He was a member of the Royal Commission on BILINGUALISM AND BICULTURALISM and an ardent defender of the civil order of Confederation, supporting the invocation of the War Measures Act in 1970.

In later years Scott produced a retrospective series of largely summary volumes, including *Poems of French Canada* (1977), which won the Canada Council's translation prize; *Essays on the Constitution* (1977), which won the Gov Gen's Award for nonfiction; and *Collected Poems* (1981), which won the Gov Gen's Award for poetry. Scott worked to help develop Canada into an international model of co-operation. His social vision sought to realize the best of both the individual and the community, though his loyalty to the social whole might limit the freedom to be enjoyed by the individual. His political commitments and his poetry illustrated the continuing tension between the needs of the individual and those of the potentially homogeneous society.   KEITH RICHARDSON
Reading: David Lewis and F.R. Scott, *Make This "Your" Canada: A Review of C.C.F. History and Policy* (1943).

Scott, Marian Mildred Dale, painter (b at Montréal 26 June 1906). For 50 years Scott has experimented with fresh art forms, reaching for symmetry, often through repetition of small abstract forms. After study at the Ecole des beaux-arts, Montréal, and the Slade School of Art, London, she painted landscapes, later plant life, buds and pods, organized geometrically. A series of human faces, influenced by Modigliani, show strong linear forms set ambiguously in a background of heavy black paint. During the Depression years, Scott depicted the people of urban Montréal, up against machines, bureaucracy and hard times, showing them in pictures like *Tenants* and *Escalator*. She taught 1935-38 with Fritz BRANDTNER at the Children's Art Centre set up by Norman BETHUNE, and joined the Contemporary Arts Soc in 1939. She was married to poet and lawyer F.R. SCOTT.
ANNE MCDOUGALL

Scott, Robert Balgarnie Young, biblical scholar (b at Toronto 16 July 1899). After serving in the RCN Volunteer Reserve in WWI, he studied Greek and Hebrew at U of T (PhD 1928). He spent a year studying in Britain and Palestine, was appointed professor of Old Testament studies at Union Coll, Vancouver, in 1928 and at United Theological Coll, Montréal, in 1931, becoming in 1948 first dean of the McGill Faculty of Divinity. From 1955 until retirement in 1968 he taught at Princeton, being annual professor at the American School of Oriental Research in Jerusalem in 1962-63. A prolific writer, Scott published 5 books on the Old Testament, innumerable articles, book chapters and reference works, as well as lyrics for 10 hymns. He was a founder and first secretary-treasurer of the Canadian Soc of Biblical Studies and its president in 1972. He has received 5 honorary degrees for his biblical scholarship.   JOHN S. MOIR
Reading: John S. Moir, *A History of Biblical Studies in Canada* (1982).

Scott, Thomas, adventurer (b at Clandeboye, Ire *c*1842; d at Red River Colony, Man 4 Mar 1870). Immigrating to Canada in 1863, Scott was "a violent and boisterous" individual with Protestant and Orange sympathies. He drifted to the RED RIVER COLONY in 1869. Captured and imprisoned several times by the Métis, he was court-martialed and executed with Louis RIEL's approval; he became an anglophone-Protestant martyr and his execution a symbol of Métis hostility to Ontario.   J.M. BUMSTED

Scott, Thomas Seaton, architect (b at Birkenhead, Eng 16 July 1826; d at Ottawa 15 June 1895). Scott immigrated to Montréal in the mid-1850s, and became best known for his work in the Gothic style, which included churches in Ontario and Québec and an 1874 design for the MacKenzie Tower on the W block of the PARLIAMENT BUILDINGS. From 1871 until 1881 he was the first chief architect of the federal Dept of Public Works. He directed the post-Confedera-

tion building program, which produced some of Canada's finest examples of public building in the Second Empire style.   JANET WRIGHT

Scott, Thomas Walter, politician, journalist, printer, premier of Saskatchewan (b at London Twp, Ont 27 Oct 1867; d at Guelph, Ont 23 Mar 1938). As the first premier of Saskatchewan, he played a key role in the province's early development. Scott went to PORTAGE LA PRAIRIE in 1885 and apprenticed as a printer. He moved to REGINA in 1886 and by 1896 had become an influential journalist and owner of the Regina *Leader* and the Moose Jaw *Times*. As the Liberal member for Assiniboia West in 1900 and 1904, he participated in the autonomy debates. In 1905 he was chosen leader of the Saskatchewan Liberal Party and asked to form the first provincial government. Under his leadership, the party won the elections of 1905, 1908 and 1912. Ill health forced him to resign in Oct 1916 and he retired from public life.   D.H. BOCKING

Scouine, La, by Albert LABERGE (1918), a series of discrete, interlocking sketches forming a novel, is French Canada's first example of naturalism. Demythologizing the romantic portrait of 19th-century peasant life promoted by the church, it blends close descriptive detail, local speech and humour and a pessimistic attitude toward human nature. Paulima, the daughter of Urgèle and Maco Deschamps, is nicknamed "La Scouine" because of her strong, unpleasant odour; the sobriquet reflects her character as an avaricious, gossipy spinster. Traditional scenes such as harvest, the fall fair and the pastoral visit are introduced with Christian imagery which is immediately undermined by the peasant's unsavoury earthiness. The publication of excerpts in 1903 resulted in censorship and a private edition (1918) of only 60 copies. Gérard Bessette's anthology of Laberge's writing led to a facsimile edition (1968), which was withdrawn from circulation at the insistence of Laberge's son. Finally published in 1972, the underground classic *La Scouine* was then translated by C. Dion as *Bitter Bread* (1977).   MICHÈLE LACOMBE

Sculpin, one of many common names given to the FISH family Cottidae and its close relatives. The group, comprising over 400 species, is one of the dominant faunal components of the N Pacific Ocean, where it is believed to have evolved. Sculpins also occur in the Arctic and N Atlantic oceans; a few have penetrated to the SW Pacific, S American and southern African waters. Freshwater forms occur in temperate and arctic waters of N America, Europe and Asia. Sculpins and related families (eg, stonefish, SCORPIONFISH) are characterized by a bony stay extending from below the eye to the cheekbone. This brace, often armoured with spines, gave rise to the name "mail-cheeked fishes." Sculpins are generally small (5-20 cm), although some species approach 100 cm. Marine sculpins are found from intertidal waters to depths of several hundred metres; most inhabit relatively shallow waters (100 m or less). Freshwater forms generally live in shallow water. Most sculpins are bottom living; a few occupy pelagic or mid-water habitats. About 50 species occur in Canadian marine wa-

Arctic staghorn sculpin (*courtesy National Museums of Canada/National Museum of Natural Sciences*).

ters, mostly on the West Coast; a few in rivers and lakes throughout the country. Sculpins are generally scaleless; a few groups have a narrow band of scales down the upper back. Others exhibit platelike structures on the body; still others have extensive patches of small cirri covering the skin, giving them a furry appearance. Spines and other "armour" on head and body make them spectacular objects. Reproduction varies: most exhibit external fertilization, laying eggs in masses or clumps under or among rocks; others show internal fertilization; some bear live young. Sculpins are found singly or in small groups, although "schooling" has been reported in at least one species. Some intertidal forms exhibit restricted ranges and "home" to their resident pool. Sculpins, important as food for other fishes, are not generally eaten by humans.

NORMAN J. WILIMOVSKY

Sculpture The first sculpture in NEW FRANCE was in wood and was the work of craftsmen who were imported from France. In 1671 Intendant Jean TALON asked the French government to send him sculptors to do the decorative work on a merchant vessel he had commissioned. Religious communities and local leading citizens imported sculpture from Europe, though a tabernacle ordered for the Hôtel Dieu in Québec in 1704 took 12 years to arrive. In 1675 the SÉMINAIRE DE QUÉBEC brought the 2 sculptors Samuel Genner and Michel Fauchois from France, who, during their 4-year stay, did the ornamentation for the séminaire's various chapels. Thereafter a steady stream of sculptors immigrated to New France. The best known are Denis Mallet from Alençon, Charles Chabouilé from St-Rémi de Troyes and Jan Jacques Bloem from Brussels. This first group of sculptors met the colony's needs and, by establishing an apprenticeship system, trained the first local sculptors (see ART EDUCATION).

Other sculptors arrived during the 18th century: Gilles Bolvin from St-Nicolas d'Avennes in Flanders, François Guernon *dit* Belleville from Paris and Philippe Liébert from Nemours. Local sculptors emerged as well. In 1651 the brothers Levasseur settled as carpenters in New France; their grandsons Noël and Pierre-Noël became sculptors; they were the first of several generations of indigenous sculptors prominent in New France, who also had cordial contacts with new arrivals in their trade such as Chabouilé and Bloem. Little remains from that century, either in religious or secular sculpture. The splendid baldachin (ornamental canopy) in the choir of the church of Neuville near Québec City is the oldest sculpture ensemble in Canada. Created between 1690 and 1700 for the chapel of the episcopal palace of Mgr de St-Vallier, this baldachin is a scaled-down copy of one in the chapel of Val-de-Grâce in Paris and shows the importance of European models to the colony (see ARCHITECTURE; ART; PAINTING). In 1712 Bloem, a protégé of Noël Levasseur, created the reredos (screen located behind an altar) of the chapel of the Recollet convent in Montréal, now in the choir of the church of St-Grégoire-de-Nicolet opposite Trois-Rivières. The reredos in the Ursuline Chapel in Québec City, created by Noël Levasseur between 1732 and 1737, recalls a triumphal arch; even though mostly in relief, it creates a 3-dimensional illusion, heightened by the play of white decorated surfaces, black columns and gilded narrative panels, and statues in the round. In complexity, monumentality and latent baroque style it echoes favourably French prototypes (see RELIGIOUS BUILDING).

Sculptors of the French regime did not limit themselves to religious work. Around 1749 one of the Levasseurs was commissioned to carve the royal arms to be placed over doors of official buildings in the colony. The example preserved in the Musée du Québec is the oldest surviving

nonreligious sculpture in Canada. In 1700 Denis Mallet carved a ship's figurehead of a lion for Sieur Brouve; in 1704 a captain from Québec, Louis Prat, commissioned an anonymous sculptor to carve a figurehead of St-Michel l'Archange in armour for the bow of his ship, the *Joybert*, and a VOTIVE PAINTING preserved in Ste-Anne-de-Beaupré shows us this figure. This same Prat in 1715 hired Noël Levasseur to sculpt the decorations for his new ship, the *Raudot*.

The establishment of a royal shipyard in the colony encouraged naval sculpture. Noël, Pierre and Jean-Baptiste Levasseur won handsome contracts to decorate the vessels of the French navy. The frigate *Castor* was decorated with a figurehead of a beaver on a shield of the arms of France. The rear escutcheon of the supply ship *Caribou* was given a bas-relief of this native Canadian animal. The different Amerindian tribes were also honoured; the *Algonquin* was launched in 1753, the *Abénaquise* in 1756, the *Iroquoise* and the *Outaouaise* in 1759. Unfortunately, no examples survive, and we know of their existence only through archival records. An agent responsible for the royal shipyards frequently complained about the poor quality of local sculptors; it was probably he who sent Pierre-Noël Levasseur to the sculpture workshop of the French arsenal in Rochefort in 1743, though the apprentice chose not to return.

While the wood sculptors of New France acknowledged the fashions prevalent in 17th-century France, from the few surviving examples it can be assumed that stylistically sculpture in the colony was somewhat different. The rich, round forms of the French baroque were usually subdued by a robustness which makes them essentially Canadian. This robustness was to linger on in the sculpture of French Canada until well into the 19th century; it was probably also tied to the qualities and limitations of the material used by the sculptors of New France, that is, wood. In contrast to France, sculptors in New France almost never worked in stone.

The change in administration in 1763, the poor economy exacerbated by wartime destruction, and the departure of French officials ushered in a lean time for sculptors in the colony. With the American War of Independence, warships were constructed in St-Jean-sur-Richelieu in 1775, some of which, the schooner *Maria* and the frigate the *Royal George*, were given figureheads.

The economic situation improved in Canada in the last quarter of the century and steady population growth forced ecclesiastical authorities to open new parishes. The resulting wave of church construction was a boon to sculptors. A new dynasty arose, the BAILLAIRGÉ family. François Baillairgé studied in France, 1778-81, visited London, and on his return introduced a fusion of 2 great artistic traditions and many new trends to the colony. He sculptured a huge baldachin against the choir walls and a high altar for Notre-Dame-de-Québec. In 1815 he created his finest work in the little church of St-Joachim near Ste-Anne-de-Beaupré: the placing and embellishment of the 4 monumental columns were inspired by the theoretician Jacques-François Blondel. Baillairgé was also involved with secular sculpture, including more than one-third of all ship figureheads made in Québec. He became sculptor of the king's shipyards in St-Jean-sur-Richelieu and in Kingston. His plans for 2 military vessels have been preserved: the *Royal Edward* and the *Earl of Moira*. He also sculpted signboards for Québec merchants, and the mace of Lower Canada's legislative assembly.

This was the time when Philippe Liébert rose to the height of his career. Around 1790 he made his reputation by carving the high altar for the chapel of the Grey Nuns in Montréal. Soon after, other parishes in the area (Sault-au-

Recollet, Ste-Rose, Vaudreuil) commissioned similar work from Liébert. Louis QUÉVILLON became the most important sculptor of the Montréal region in the early 19th century; and his models came from Liébert. In almost all the churches built between 1800 and 1825 works can be found by Quévillon and his associates, including Joseph Pépin, René St-James, Paul Rollin and many apprentices. In order to keep up with demand, Quévillon standardized his works, and his altars systematically followed the Liébert model. The best-preserved example of work by the Quévillon group is in the little church of St-Mathias, near Chambly.

Secular works continued to be important in the early 19th century. England needed ships for its merchant marine, which had suffered heavy losses in the Napoleonic Wars. The shipyards of British North America now included Québec City, and Yarmouth, Lunenberg and Halifax in NS, various yards in the Saint John Valley and on the Miramichi R in NB, and Bath (near Kingston) and Niagara-on-the-Lake in Upper Canada. Of the 2112 ships built in Québec City during the period from 1762 to 1897, 1651 were embellished with figureheads. Probably 10 000 figureheads were sculpted in Canada during the 19th century, and almost all of the sculptors in the country were involved, including Louis-Xavier Leprohons, Louis-Thomas Berlinguet, André Giroux and Jean-Baptiste Côté. Scotsmen like John Rogerson worked out of NB. Many carvers of ship ornamentations in wood were anonymous. Figureheads in the bows of ships were modelled on historic personages, local notables, Amerindians and members of the shipowner's family. There were also generalized images, such as women, animals (especially native creatures such as the bear, caribou, beaver) or simple scrolls. The sterns of ships were also ornamented, mostly with coats of arms or shields with armorial bearings, often amplified with other types of decorative devices. But it was the end of the age of traditional shipbuilding; as of the mid-19th century, sails were replaced by the steam engine, and metal plates gradually replaced the old wooden hull. New decorative solutions made obsolete the once lucrative business of ship decorators (see SAILING SHIPS; FOLK ART).

Sculptors were also involved in the woodworking business. FURNITURE such as chair backs were often ornamented with sculpture, and merchants, especially tobacconists, tavern keepers and sellers of navigation instruments, sometimes called on sculptors to make their shop signs (see FOLK ART).

The second half of the 19th century saw the appearance of a phenomenon that was to shatter the traditional wood-sculptor's market — plaster statuary. In 1824 the Italian Donati made a copy in plaster of François Baillairgé's carvings on the panelled vaults of the cathedral of Québec. Sculpture became the reason for the mold. Thirty years earlier Liébert had already used molds to make decorative elements for his altars; Quévillon also did so, probably using some molds that had belonged to Liébert. In 1846 Mgr Bourget, on his return from a trip to Italy, introduced Hector Vacca to the Montréal market. Carlo Catteli arrived at the same time and made plaster statues for Montréal churches. Around 1855, 2 French sculptors, G.H. Sohier and Alexis Michelot, set up an "Académie des beaux-arts" which, though it lasted less than a year, heralded the arrival of academic sculpture, made in plaster, in Canada.

Wood sculptors reacted slowly; they failed to see the extent of the change taking place or the impact of new techniques. As the industrial revolution took hold of Canada, wood sculptors gradually became obsolete. One of the most important wood sculptors of the time, Jean-Baptiste Côté, summed up the situation in a sentence: "My time is over." By scrounging whatever commissions they could, a few sculptors managed to survive.

Louis JOBIN, a sculptor who had trained in the workshop of François-Xavier Berlinguet, had to go to New York to complete his studies. He then worked for 5 years in Montréal and in 1876 moved to Québec City. He carved the neogothic statues of the church of St-Henri in Lévis and in 1880 worked on the allegorical floats for the St-Jean-Baptiste parade; the agriculture float is preserved in the Musée du Québec. He was among the original carvers of ice sculptures at the early Québec winter carnivals. At the end of the century Jobin was forced to leave Québec City for Ste-Anne-de-Beaupré, the last bastion of religious wood sculpture, where he tried to imitate in wood what a new generation of sculptors was doing in other materials such as bronze. His death in 1928 was also the death of traditional wood sculpture. On a much smaller scale, often created with a deep feeling for a lost past and mostly attractive to tourists, aspects of the wood-carving tradition in Québec have survived, particularly in the town of St-Jean-Port-Joli; however, these carvings have little in common with the monumental art forms in wood which once embellished the churches and ships of the New World. JEAN BÉLISLE

Sculpture 1880-1950

It was fashionable for critics considering Canadian sculpture between 1880 and 1950 to mourn the demise of traditional wooden sculpture and the invasion of plaster and bronze, as though wood possessed certain authentic virtues missing in the other 2 materials. However, it was because of the limits of wood that the sculptors of the period, inspired by the needs of a new realism, often preferred bronze. Wood, like stone, sculpture is referred to as a subtractive method; also it is difficult to dissociate the finished sculpture from the tree trunk. The preparations for a bronze object are called additive sculpture; a model is built in flexible material, such as clay, from which a mold is made into which molten bronze is cast. This technique provided much greater flexibility, offering sculptors almost unlimited opportunities for expression. Since there were no specific facilities in Canada to cast bronze art objects until the 1960s, sculptures, especially large monuments, had to be cast in the US or Europe and shipped back to Canada.

Stylistically the sculpture of this period may be considered under 3 headings, each corresponding to similar European movements of the period: realism, art nouveau, art deco. Canadian sculpture did not develop in isolation, and yet it showed a certain originality.

Realism In Québec realism is represented by Napoléon BOURASSA (a multitalented artist who distinguished himself in architecture and painting as well as in sculpture) and by Anatole Partnenais and Louis-Philippe HÉBERT. Hébert was the most important, and it is thought he learned his art from Bourassa when they collaborated around 1870 on the Notre-Dame-de-Lourdes chapel in Montréal. The dominating ideology of this period in Québec attempted to define the people of French Canada in terms of their French Catholic origins; this too was important for Hébert. In sculpture he created memorable examples of his countrymen's history. He was also influenced by the French realist tradition which he combined with his robust talent; when he finally received commissions, he was ready to meet the challenge. These included a number of bronze sculptures of Indians (including the famous *Pêcheur à la nigogue* beside a fountain) which he produced for the legislative building in Québec City; the statue of *Maisonneuve* at Place d'Armes in Montréal; and his proud monument *Madeleine de Verchères*, located

in the middle of the Québec village of Verchères. Those of his works devoted to English rulers (*Queen Victoria* in Ottawa) or to contemporary personages are less inspired. Historical subjects stimulated his imagination, and it is here that he produced his best work (see PUBLIC ART). Hamilton MacCarthy is also known for his historical monuments, in particular his *Sieur de Monts* at ANNAPOLIS ROYAL (1904). The historical works of Henri BEAU and Charles HUOT have been largely forgotten.

The late 19th century was a period of expansion which saw the settlement of the Canadian West. It is therefore not surprising that many N American artists, English Canadian sculptors as well, concentrated with deep, often romantic feelings on Indians and subjects involving Indians. Emmanuel Otto Hahn, a German sculptor who immigrated to Canada early in his life and married the sculptor Elizabeth WYN WOOD, is noted for his Indian subjects; Alexander Phimister Proctor, although known primarily for his animals, also included Indians in his sculptures. These "noble savages" were nostalgically perceived as the descendants of a vanishing race whose characteristics had to be captured before they disappeared under the wheel of civilization. Realism was the preferred style.

WWI greatly stimulated sculpture in the 1920s, as everywhere there was a call for monuments to commemorate Canada's participation in the war. Walter Seymour Allward was commissioned to create a memorial on site in France to the Canadians who died at Vimy Ridge; Alfred Howell was responsible for monuments in Saint John, NB, and Guelph, Ont; Frances Norma LORING for a memorial in Galt, Ont, and R. Tait MCKENZIE for works in the US, England and Scotland. Each contract afforded the opportunity to illustrate the courage of Canadian troops and to express pride in the achievements of the country's sons. Loring dealt with women's participation in the war effort on the "home front" in *Girls with a Rail*, which is part of a series preserved at the Canadian War Memorial in Ottawa.

Art Nouveau Canadian sculptors did not escape the influence of art nouveau. The works of Alfred LALIBERTÉ illustrate the problems raised by applying to sculpture a style initially conceived to decorate flat surfaces. He broke away from the French academic influence of Gabriel-Jules Thomas and Antoine Injalbert to explore new avenues, and explored the possibilities of art nouveau's fluid line when, ceasing to be merely decorative, it animates interior space and sets it in wave-shaped relief. His romantic imagination may be seen in his 1920 monument *Dollard des Ormeaux* in Lafontaine Park, Montréal. His works also display a late 19th-century sensuality, and portray women as figures to be both feared and exalted. Muse and source of the artist's inspiration, woman is also seductress! Laliberté worked in a variety of subjects, from the historical monument (*Louis Hébert* in Québec and *Tomb of Sir Wilfrid Laurier* in Ottawa) to jewels of the purest art-nouveau style, to self-portraits and folk scenes. The Musée de la province de Québec has 215 of his sculptures on the trades, customs and legends of French Canada.

Other Canadian sculptors were influenced by art nouveau. Marc-Aurèle de Foy SUZOR-COTÉ, whose sculpture cannot be neglected even though he is better known as a painter, was touched by it. His *Indiennes de Caughnawaga* appears to be sculpted by the wind which the figures in their large coats are fighting. The wind theme of *The Storm* enabled Allward to drape the human anatomy of his figure, thus creating freer and more fluid forms. In *Sun Worshipper* by academic sculptor Florence WYLE, the figure is bent backward, its arm extended beyond the limit of the sculpture.

Art Deco The influence of art deco appeared

in the work of a number of sculptors in the 1930s, artists such as Elizabeth Wyn Wood of Toronto (whose bas-relief, *Passing Rain,* is famous) and Sylvia Daoust of Montréal. Two prolific sculptors of lesser talent were Émile Brunet, who produced the bas-reliefs and ornamental façade of the Musée de la province in Québec City, and Marius Plamondon.

The influence of art deco on sculpture may be seen in the elimination of surface detail and in giving space a more massive presence, making joints more defined and replacing the spiral art-nouveau line with straight or curved lines. It may be seen in the work of Phyllis Jacobine Jones, who produced the bronze doors of the Bank of Canada in Ottawa in 1938; in Orson Wheeler's works; in some of the later works of Florence Wyle; and in the larger-than-life-sized *Chemin de Croix,* sculpted by Louis-Joseph Parent in 1959 for the Oratoire St-Joseph in Montréal.

In Europe during this period, modernism was to lead from cubism to constructivism. Canadian sculpture was awakened to modern styles only later. It was not until the work of Louis ARCHAMBAULT and Anne KAHANE in the early 1950s that the influence of Julio Gonzalez, Pablo Picasso and Jacques Lipchitz began to be felt in Canadian sculpture. FRANÇOIS-MARC GAGNON

Contemporary Sculpture

Some of the most inventive art made in Canada since WWII is in the realm of sculpture. The period exposed sculptors to a great variety of new materials, and they responded with new kinds of constructions, multimedia works, installations and site-specific inventions, along with more traditional freestanding objects (see ART, CONTEMPORARY TRENDS).

The new vigour of sculpture in Canada is part of a widespread cultural coming of age, owing something to improved communications and transportation. Artists today have far more experience of works of art than their predecessors, because of colour photography, ease of travel and the frequency of touring exhibitions. The CANADA COUNCIL and related provincial agencies support artists and assist their travel, and encourage the growth and programs of galleries and museums across the country. There is no simple explanation for the recent burgeoning of Canadian sculpture. A new climate of experiment at art schools and universities has been both a cause and an effect. Particular exhibitions, teachers and critics, symposia and major purchases have stimulated sculptors of various regions. For some, reaction against influences has been as important as response to them. Whatever the reasons, the proliferation of serious sculptors is a new phenomenon (see ARTISTS' ORGANIZATIONS).

In Canada, as in Europe, the development of advanced sculpture lagged behind that of advanced painting. For centuries, sculpture had meant carved or modelled figurative sculptures, usually upright on pedestals or part of an architectural complex, and made of wood, stone or bronze. Gradually, as in other art forms, sculpture also challenged traditional notions of form, content and technique, sharing in the aesthetic revolution known as "modernism."

At first, even the most adventurous Canadian sculptors (who were largely removed from the mainstream of innovative art) joined this revolution cautiously. While undoubtedly modernists, Québecois sculptors such as Louis Archambault and Charles DAUDELIN used more or less traditional techniques to make nontraditional images in the 1940s. By the 1950s these pioneers had been joined by others, but much of the most successful modernist sculpture retained a strong preference for the figure. John Ivor Smith, Anne Kahane, George Wallace and William McElcheran all used the figure as a starting point, but simplified and stylized it, smoothing or elaborating its surfaces. Kahane worked in many materials, while the others preferred bronze.

In the late 1950s and early 1960s relatively traditional techniques still prevailed, even among those who departed from literal figurative reference. The use of smooth, carved or cast masses suggests an awareness of Henry Moore, as in the meticulously finished marbles of Hans Schleeh. Even among those interested in alternatives, there was a conservative quality related to British and European sculpture of the time. Robert ROUSSIL's works seem to amalgamate both Moore and a spiky expressionism. David Partridge developed an idiosyncratic type of relief made by driving nails of various sizes into wood. Ulysse COMTOIS, known for his brilliant, optically active paintings, also made elegantly crafted sculpture with geometric movable parts. Armand VAILLANCOURT attracted attention for aggressively textured abstract castings. A peculiarly self-contained movement, structurism, has flourished since the 1950s, particularly on the Prairies, under the influence of Eli BORNSTEIN. Structurists such as Gino Lorcini and Ron Kostyniuk explore geometric permutations in shallow, elegantly crafted reliefs.

Since there were no indigenous models for advanced sculpture, it is not surprising that Canadians should have looked to Europe, especially to England, for inspiration. Many had studied in England or with British artists in Canadian art schools, but more importantly, Henry Moore was internationally acclaimed by the 1950s. His amalgam of natural and invented forms seemed a pattern for carrying the great tradition of sculpture into the 20th century. But another "new tradition," dating from the late 1920s, was becoming just as powerful: drawinglike, abstract sculpture constructed out of iron, steel and found objects. This radical rethinking of what sculpture could be, begun by Pablo Picasso and Julio Gonzalez in France, was being continued in New York, as were equally radical notions about painting. By the late 1950s and the 1960s it was obvious that the centre of important innovative art had shifted from Europe to N America, and adventurous Canadians, like everyone else, began to find great stimulation on their own continent.

Art of the late 1960s was characterized by a new openness, a willingness to accept new ideas, new materials and techniques, and we see these expanded possibilities clearly reflected in Canadian art. A new generation of Canadian sculptors came to maturity in the 1960s, with far more adventurous ideas than their predecessors. Some, such as Les Levine and Michael SNOW, were painters as well as multimedia artists, but their 3-dimensional work established their reputations. Levine's vacuum-formed plastic modules introduced a generation of Canadians to the then most modish kind of environmental sculpture, and the thick stainless-steel versions of Snow's "cookie cutter" walking-woman image were greeted with enthusiasm. Others, such as Gord SMITH, were exclusively sculptors. Smith, Yves TRUDEAU, Gerald Gladstone and Vaillancourt were all testing the possibilities of welded-steel construction.

Modernist sculpture gradually gained adherents across the country. If an earlier generation of Canadians responded most to Henry Moore's example, many sculptors of the 1960s and 1970s looked to the work of the American sculptor in steel, David Smith, and his younger British colleague, Anthony Caro. Otto ROGERS in Saskatoon has continued to work with equal facility as a painter of landscape-derived abstractions and as a sculptor of vigorous, linear steel pieces. John Nugent in Regina was an early admirer of David Smith and an ambitious sculptor in steel. In Calgary, Katie Von Der Ohe exhibited complex pilings of interlocking forms. In Toronto, Ted Bieler received numerous public commissions

Kosso Eloul, *Time* (1973), aluminum, 6.4 x 38.1 m (*courtesy Kosso Eloul*).

and Sorel ETROG became known for a signature style of "knotted" bronze which owed a great deal to the later work of the French Cubist Jacques Lipchitz. In Québec, Françoise Sullivan, a modern dancer, choreographer and visual artist, abandoned her other activities to make painted steel constructions. Robert MURRAY is probably the most significant Canadian sculptor of his generation, internationally recognized for his severe metal constructions. He works with fabricators to produce large-scale structures of inflected planes, richly coloured with industrial finishes.

The most exciting aspect of Canadian sculpture in the 1970s and 1980s is its diversity. Approaches vary from "orthodox" object making to a stretching of the limits of the discipline. The object makers range from Kosso ELOUL, whose modular constructions of rectangular solids can be seen on many public sites, to Roland Poulin and Peter Kolisnyk, whose works are the sparest possible indicators of sculptural notions, threatening to disappear into pure idea.

The "new tradition" of constructed sculpture in various materials is especially strong on the Prairies, although it has gifted practitioners elsewhere, such as Ontario's André FAUTEUX and Louis Stokes. In the West, Douglas BENTHAM, Alan REYNOLDS and Peter HIDE have all developed intensely personal, potent ways of working in welded metal. Each is a distinct individual, but collectively they seem less interested in sculpture as "drawing in space" and more concerned with finding new ways of appropriating the mass and volume of the traditional monolith for abstract construction. Michael Bigger, Tommie Gallie, Haydn Davies, Patrick Thibert

Walter Redinger, *Spermatogenesis II* (1968), fibreglass and wood (*courtesy Art Gallery of Ontario*).

and Henry Saxe testify to the range of the tradition across Canada, from Gallie's piled timbers to Thibert's suggestive "tables." Saxe has worked in both orthodox steel construction and complex multisection works. David RABINOWITCH further extends the range with inquiries into the expressive possibilities of the weight and mass of steel, while Royden RABINOWITCH explores horizontality and layering. In Toronto, John McEwen comments on the new tradition of sculpture in steel with naturalistic images, flame cut from massive metal slabs. In Québec, Claude Mongrain and Jean-Serge Champagne have evolved variations on the ideas of construction, incorporating unexpected combinations of materials. Catharine Burgess, Don Foulds, John McKinnon, Anthony Massett and Delio Fonseca belong to an even younger generation of constructors in steel.

Many recent sculptors have been fascinated by new technology and media: Michael Hayden has used neon tubing in both static and kinetic works; Walter Redinger and Ed Zelenak use fiberglass; Don Proch uses molded fiberglass, often covered with drawing, along with elements in other media. Mark Prent's nightmare images depend upon combinations of made and recycled objects in technical *tours de forces*. Richard Prince's delicate, improbable machines are intimate kinetic constructions. For other sculptors, the single discrete object seems too restrictive. They make structures which respond to particular settings and sites, often on a scale which demands that we enter or move through the work. Like architecture, these sculptures depend upon physical participation as well as upon visual perception, but unlike architecture, they are without specific function. George TRAKAS and Melvin CHARNEY make arresting, often poetic, parodies of man-made structures. Robert Bowers and Mark Gomes also use everyday, often banal, objects as points of departure in more self-contained works. Roland Brener expands this notion, employing stock materials in systematic ways; angle iron and industrial scaffolding have been used with equal success.

While these sculptors explore challenging new ideas, they are still makers of objects, albeit unconventional ones. Other artists are more interested in process than in result, and their "sculptures" are often simply the by-product of an event or the symbol of an idea. Documentation of the event can become part of the final structure, as in Colette WHITEN's works. Mowry Baden's environmental constructions exist more for the physical sensations they create in the "viewer" who moves through them than for

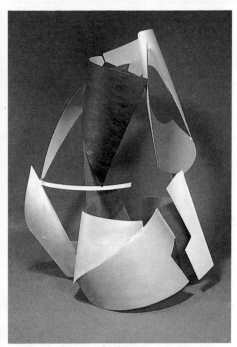

Douglas Bentham, *Saraband* (1984), steel paint (*courtesy Douglas Bentham*).

their appearance. The size and shape of Robin Peck's objects are dictated by the proportions of their settings. For others, ephemeral moments or phenomena take precedence over the object. The work of these artists can incorporate film projections, sound, temporary or perishable structures, and the passage of time itself. While their works often involve a great deal of 3-dimensional equipment, and for this reason often get termed "sculpture," they seem to have little to do with sculptural notions; they belong to some other category, closer to literature or theatre, to the "happenings" of the 1960s.

Relatively traditional sculpture continues to have adherents. While not very large, because of the constraints of the medium, the best work of ceramic artists such as Victor Cikansky and Joe FAFARD recalls the tradition of portrait sculpture. Among the younger generation, Evan Penny's haunting nudes and torsos are noteworthy. Ric Gomez's abstract bronzes are elegant, precious objects.

In the 1980s just about anything can be considered sculpture. There is no "official" approach, no single method or medium which guarantees success or seriousness. The antithesis of the traditional academy has been reached, with its preconceived standards of excellence and measurable levels of achievement. Recent Canadian sculpture is a history of individuals who speak an international sculptural language, probably with a Canadian accent. It is difficult to isolate their Canadianness easily. The bewildering variety of contemporary Canadian sculpture may be a sign of health and strength. *See also* INDIAN ART; INUIT ART; NORTHWEST COAST INDIAN ART.   KAREN WILKIN

Reading: Artmagazine, Sculpture Issue (May/June 1978); Dalhousie Art Gallery, *Sculpture '81* (1981); D. Burnett and M. Schiff, *Contemporary Canadian Art* (1983); The Guildhall, *Contemporary Outdoor Sculpture at The Guild* (1982); N. Karczmar, ed, *Canadian Sculpture Expo '67* (1967); Musée d'art contemporain, *Panorama de la sculpture au Québec, 1945-1970* (1970); Musée du Québec, *Profil de la sculpture québecoise: XVIIe-XIXe siècle* (1969).

Sea Ice, any ICE formed by the freezing of seawater. As it varies widely in thickness, strength, behaviour and appearance, it is classified in several ways. In bays, inlets and shallow COASTAL WATERS, one usually encounters fast ice, a smooth, even layer from 30-40 cm to 2-3 m

thick. Fast ice remains where formed until spring thaw, or until melting or the action of wind and current causes it to break up and become pack ice. Each winter, fast ice covers most of the waterways of the ARCTIC ARCHIPELAGO and significant coastal areas of BAFFIN BAY, HUDSON BAY and the Labrador Sea.

Pack ice is found in oceanic areas and broad expanses like the Gulf of ST LAWRENCE, BEAUFORT SEA, FOXE BASIN and Hudson Bay. It is in more or less continuous motion as a result of ocean currents, WINDS or TIDES and is composed of floes ranging from a few metres up to 10 km or more. Its thickness varies from 5-30 cm in the case of new and young ice, up to 30-200 cm for first-year ice and 2-4 m for old ice. First-year ice is formed in winter, having grown progressively from the young stage. In summer it becomes covered with puddles of melted snow and ice and, in temperate areas, eventually melts completely. In the Arctic, complete melting may not occur and, once summer ends, the ice floes "graduate" to become second-year or eventually multiyear ice, collectively called old ice. These terms related to thickness and age can be applied to either pack or fast ice. Because they are formed from seawater, young and first-year ice contain a small percentage of salt. During the melting process, this brine drains out of the floes and, if melting is not complete, the resulting old floes are much fresher and stronger than in their first year. They then become an increased hindrance to mariners. Old ice predominates in the northernmost passages of the QUEEN ELIZABETH IS, the Arctic Ocean and the western part of PARRY CHANNEL. First-year ice prevails in southern Beaufort Sea, from Amundsen Gulf to Boothia Pen, from LANCASTER SOUND and Baffin Bay to Foxe Basin, Hudson Bay and HUDSON STR, and to the Gulf of St Lawrence and the northern GRAND BANKS E of Newfoundland. Because first-year ice predominates, it follows that all sea ice clears from this vast area every summer. In old ice areas, clearing is unusual, if it occurs at all.

Pack ice is continually deformed by its motion, in some cases merely by having one floe bump into another, but more often by wind and current forcing floes together to form pressure ridges and hummocks. These mounds of deformed ice fragments rise 1-5 m above level surfaces and can occur every 100 m. Below each pressure ridge there is an ice keel extending downward 4-5 times as far as the ridge projects upward. This mass of ice is needed to provide the buoyancy to support the ridge. It is these underwater features that cause most of the problems for ship operation through pack ice. Keels under ridges of old ice are even more of a hindrance than those under first-year ice. In Canada, an ice information and forecasting service is provided by the Atmospheric Environment Service, Environment Canada. Terminology and chart symbols used were developed by the World Meteorological Organization. Canada participated in developing and establishing these procedures. *See* ICEBERG.   WILLIAM E. MARKHAM

Sea Lion The northern sea lion (*Eumetopias jubata*), the largest eared SEAL, occurs on the N Pacific coast from Japan to California. There are 2 large breeding colonies on the BC coast. In winter sea lions migrate southward and inshore. Bulls average 3 m long and weigh up to 900 kg; cows are less than half that weight. The short, coarse pelage lacks underfur. There is a blubber layer. Both sexes are reddish brown, the bulls with buff upperparts. Cows are slender and streamlined but adult bulls have massive necks and foreparts. The flippers are large and hairless; those of the forelimbs are used for propulsion. The hind flippers are turned forward on land and permit the animal to move at a hobbling run. Sea lions are powerful and graceful swimmers. Food is a wide variety of fish

and invertebrates. Breeding is polygamous; the harem master bulls defend 5-20 cows. Pups arrive in May-June and cows mate again in about a week. The gestation period is about 51 weeks. Some fishermen accuse sea lions of stealing salmon from lines and nets and urge control of their numbers.   IAN McTAGGART COWAN

Sea Otter (*Enhydra lutris*), largest and most marine WEASEL, lives exclusively in shallow seas of the N Pacific, formerly from Japan to California. Ruthless hunting for their valuable pelts almost exterminated sea otters before 1900. A few survived in Alaska and California. Protection has permitted them to increase and reoccupy some former range. Transplants to SE Alaska and BC have been successful. Males reach 1.6 m in length and 36 kg in weight; females about 3/4 of this. The body is long; tail and legs short. Forefeet are padlike and have sharp claws; hindfeet are flippers and fully furred. The head is broad, flattish with small ears. The animal is dark brown, frequently with a whitish face. Fur so dense that water cannot penetrate provides insulation; there is no blubber. Food, mainly sea urchins, molluscs and fish obtained during dives to 80 m, is consumed at the surface. The sea otter is known to use a stone as a hammer to break shells. Although concentrated in June, some breeding occurs in all months; most births occur in summer. The single pup may be born ashore (Alaska) or at sea (California) and is nursed about 11 months. Pups are carried on the female's chest as she swims belly up. They are groomed frequently to maintain waterproofing. Females breed in alternate years. *See* ENDANGERED ANIMALS; FUR TRADE.
                    IAN McTAGGART COWAN

Sea Urchin, radially symmetrical marine INVERTEBRATE. Sea urchins and near relatives, the sand dollars and heart urchins, belong to class Echinoidea of phylum ECHINODERMATA; about 900 species are known worldwide. A characteristic external covering of movable spines serves for protection and locomotion. In some tropical forms, spines can be 30 cm long and, being poisonous, can inflict painful wounds on swimmers. The body wall contains an internal skeleton that gives characteristic shapes: sea urchins, spherical; heart urchins, heart-shaped; sand dollars, flattened discs. Sea urchins have the mouth on the undersurface and anus directed upwards. Usually, 5 double rows of tube feet encircle the body. These are the principal means of locomotion and attachment. Like other echinoderms, sea urchins have a water-vascular system to operate tube feet. Pedicellariae, small, pincerlike appendages, cover the body surface at the base of spines. These often have a poison sac with a hypodermiclike fang, used to deter predators. Sea urchins are common in Canada, intertidally and subtidally. They are usually associated with rocky bottoms. They feed on algae. In some countries they are harvested for eggs, eaten like caviar.   R.D. BURKE

Seabird, BIRD that spends a large proportion of its life at sea. Primary seabirds (AUKS, GULLS, GANNETS, SHEARWATERS, FULMARS, etc) belong to families of which all members are adapted to life at sea; secondary seabirds (eg, eider DUCKS, PHALAROPES) belong to families that otherwise live in terrestrial habitats. The more specialized species have a long life expectancy and adolescent period, and lay only one egg. These can adjust only with difficulty to additional mortality, eg, from HUNTING and oil POLLUTION, and their populations have recently declined sharply. One Canadian seabird, the GREAT AUK, is extinct. Forty-five primary seabird species breed in Canada today, including 16 gulls and 11 auks. They number well over 4 million pairs with the largest colonies in Hudson Str and SE Nfld. The best-known site is the northern gannet (*Sula bas-*

sanus) colony on Bonaventure I, Qué, a federal migratory BIRD SANCTUARY, PROVINCIAL PARK and major tourist attraction. R.G.B. BROWN

Seaborn, James Blair, public servant (b at Toronto 18 Mar 1924). Seaborn joined the Dept of External Affairs in 1948. In 1964-65, while the Canadian member of the International Commission for Supervision and Control (Vietnam), he visited Hanoi 5 times in an effort by Ottawa to establish communications between the US and North Vietnam. The "Seaborn Mission," undertaken with the active involvement of the US, was one of the most controversial aspects of Canadian diplomacy during the Vietnam War. Seaborn was subsequently assistant deputy minister of consumer and corporate affairs 1970-74 and deputy minister of Environment Canada 1975-82. He was appointed Canadian chairman of the INTERNATIONAL JOINT COMMISSION in 1982 and in 1985 became a senior adviser to the Privy Council Office on intelligence and security coordination. NORMAN HILLMER

Seafarers' International Union In 1949, supported by the federal government and some union leaders and shipping executives, an unsavoury ex-convict was allowed into Canada to destroy the powerful, communist-dominated Canadian Seamen's Union. Within a few months, Hal BANKS and the "goons" he brought with him, through beatings, threats and even murder, had replaced the CSU with the American Seafarers' International Union. Although the union was expelled from the CANADIAN CONGRESS OF LABOUR, its practices condemned by a royal commission, and Banks arrested and forced to flee the country, the SIU remains Canada's dominant seamen's union. IRVING ABELLA

Seagram, Joseph Emm, distiller, turfman, politician (b at Fisher Mills [near Cambridge], Ont 15 Apr 1841; d at Waterloo, Ont 18 Aug 1919). Founder of the world's largest producers and marketers of distilled spirits and wines, owner and breeder of an unprecedented 15 QUEEN'S/KING'S PLATE horse-race winners, and Conservative MP for Waterloo North 1896-1908, Seagram was one of Canada's most prominent gentleman entrepreneurs. He realized the market potential of high-quality, brand-name products. In 1883 he became sole owner of a Waterloo distillery and created Seagram's '83, which became one of Canada's most popular whiskies. Seagram's V.O., first blended in 1907, is now the largest-selling Canadian whisky worldwide. The Seagram commitment to product excellence permitted the BRONFMAN FAMILY, which acquired controlling interest in 1928, to mold the company into a corporate empire. Noted for his physical likeness to King Edward VII, Seagram was a racing enthusiast. The Seagram Stables, begun in 1888, won 8 consecutive Queen's Plates 1891-98. Seagram was president of the Ontario Jockey Club 1906-17 and a founder of the Canadian Racing Assn in 1908. DON SPENCER

Reading: P.C. Newman, *Bronfman Dynasty: The Rothschilds of the New World* (1978); W.F. Rannie, *Canadian Whisky* (1976).

Seagram Company Limited is a producer of distilled spirits and wines, with head offices in Montréal. The company was incorporated in 1928 as Distillers Corporation-Seagrams Limited as a holding company to acquire the capital stocks of Distillers Corporation Limited and Joseph E. Seagram & Sons Limited, and adopted its present name in 1975. It gained a certain notoriety in the PROHIBITION era and enjoyed a certain celebrity thanks to the colourful nature of its owner, Samuel Bronfman (*see* BRONFMAN FAMILY). The company has continued to expand in the liquor business and in other areas, although in 1980 it sold its oil, gas and related properties in the US to Sun Company, Inc. Today, its principal business and products are the manufacture and marketing of distilled spirits and wines through its subsidiaries and affiliates in 29 countries on 6 continents. As of July 1982, it had annual sales or operating revenue of $2.2 billion (ranking 39th in Canada), assets of $6.6 billion (ranking 13th) and 14 000 employees. Bronfman family trusts own 39%. *See* DISTILLING INDUSTRY. DEBORAH C. SAWYER

Seal, carnivorous, marine MAMMAL with streamlined body, limbs developed into flippers, eyes adapted for vision under and out of water, and valved nostrils. The respiratory, circulatory and excretory systems are adapted to diving and to life without fresh water. Nine species, classified in 3 families, occur in Canadian seas: elephant seals and northern fur seals (*Mirounga angustirostris, Callorhinus ursinus,* respectively) are Pacific; ribbon, bearded and ringed seals (*Phoca fasciata, Erignathus barbatus, P. hispida),* exclusively Arctic; harp, hooded and grey seals (*P. groenlandica, Cystophora cristata, Halichoerus grypus*), N Atlantic; common or harbour seal (*P. vitulina*), all 3 oceans and a few lakes. All are fish, crustacean or squid eaters. Eared seals (eg, northern fur seal) can run on land using fore and hind limbs and swim with the large fore flippers. They breed on the Pribilof Is, Alaska, and migrate to winter off BC. The young are helpless with a long nursing period. Elephant seal are winter visitors from the south. The 7 species of earless seals (family Phocidae) move on land by undulating, swim with the hind flippers and have precocious young that nurse for a few weeks only. Best known is the harp seal. Many thousands of its newborn, white-furred young are taken each year off Québec and Labrador for the FUR INDUSTRY. *See* SEALING. IAN McTAGGART COWAN

Sealing Fourteen species of SEALS, SEA LIONS and WALRUS inhabit the waters surrounding continental N America. Most of these may be found within Canadian boundaries for at least part of each year. Seals are taken by Canadian native people in subsistence hunts for food and clothing. Coastal Inuit communities in the Canadian Arctic have long relied on ringed seals (*Phoca hispida*) for food, clothing and fuel. Pelts may also be sold directly to processors.

The plush pelt of the northern fur seal (*Callorhinus ursinus*) has been the object of a commercial hunt since discovery of the species's Pribilof Is breeding grounds in the late 18th century. By 1910, there were concerns that the herds had been seriously depleted by intensive pelagic (high-seas) sealing. Representatives from the US, Russia, Japan and Great Britain (on behalf of Canada) met and signed the North Pacific Fur Seal Convention (1911). Under the terms of this treaty, pelagic hunting of fur seals ceased and a regulated land hunt was maintained. Canada and the other member countries signed a revised treaty in 1957. Together, these countries form the North Pacific Fur Seal Commission, which co-ordinates fur-seal management and research. While Canada takes no active part in the hunt, profits from the sale of pelts are shared by the 4 nations. In spite of active management programs, there are indications that this herd may be decreasing.

Each spring a large-scale commercial hunt takes place off Canada's East Coast and in the Gulf of ST LAWRENCE. Two species are hunted: harp seals (*Phoca groenlandica*) and hooded seals (*Cystophora cristata*). In the past 2 decades, this commercial hunt has come under considerable public scrutiny. Consequently, although seals are commercially hunted in other countries, when they hear of sealing many people think first of the annual Canadian hunt.

Seals have long provided man with food and clothing. Bones unearthed in archaeological digs show that Stone-Age men caught harp seals off the coasts of Western Europe 10 000 years ago. The indigenous peoples of N America hunted seals long before the arrival of Europeans. When the first European colonists arrived in Newfoundland in the late 16th century, they evidently caught seals in nets placed under water; the Inuit had long used this method. In the mid to late 1700s, the European demand for oil and skins led to the development of a commercial seal fishery, based in Newfoundland. Seal oil produced an almost smokeless light, particularly useful in miners' headlamps. At first, an offshore hunt was carried out from small boats, and wooden sailing ships first left St John's harbour in 1794 in search of seals. The industry grew, bringing foreign investment and employing not only sealers but shipbuilders, carpenters, sailmasters and refiners who extracted the prized oil from seal blubber. Between 1800 and 1840, more people from more ports worked in the sealing industry than at any other time. This era culminated in 1831 when 300 ships are reported to have returned from the hunt with over 680 000 pelts. Only the celebrated cod fishery was more important to the colonial economy. Wooden sailing ships gradually gave way to those powered by steam (1863) and made of steel (1906). The advantage of heavier vessels lay in their speed and ease of handling and also in their ability to force a passage through ice.

By the late 19th century, production of PETROLEUM had cut the demand for seal oil. The industry continued to decline through the world wars

Nine species of seal occur in Canadian waters. The young of the harp seal (*Phoca groenlandica*) was long hunted for its white fur (*photo by Norman R. Lightfoot*).

(when sealing ships were claimed for other pursuits) and the Depression. Markets reopened after WWII, when the hunt again became profitable, primarily because of demands for fur and leather. Norway, Québec and NS joined the offshore hunt. Between 1949 and 1961 an average of 310 000 seals were taken annually off the East Coast. More than 400 000 seals were caught in 1951. The NW Atlantic harp seal population declined by up to 50% between 1952 and the early 1970s.

Today, sealing is part of a national Canadian FISHERIES industry, under the jurisdiction of the Department of Fisheries and Oceans. The Seal Protection Regulations (first established in 1966 and amended annually) set down rules governing issuance of sealing permits, annual seal quotas and opening and closing dates of the hunt (first introduced in 1961). Only those holding a valid permit may hunt.

Seals often migrate great distances; therefore, their pursuit must be governed by international agreements. Outside Canada's 200-nautical-mile (370 km) territorial zone, sealing comes under the jurisdiction of the Northwest Atlantic Fisheries Organization (NAFO), which includes countries using major aquatic resources of the region. The Canadian Atlantic Fisheries Scientific Advisory Committee (CAFSAC) advises on matters concerning fisheries within the 370 km zone, as does the independent Committee on Seals and Sealing (COSS), established by the federal government in 1971 to monitor the hunt and advise on sealing policy. The quota of seals that may be caught in the NW Atlantic each year is established initially by the Canadian government. Subsequently, negotiations take place with other sealing nations, particularly Norway and the European Economic Community (EEC), which represents Denmark (Greenland).

The commercial hunt is divided between those who travel to the hunt on foot or in boats under 20 m (landsmen) and those hunting from vessels longer than 20 m (large vessel hunt). Recently, the landsmen's catch has exceeded the large-vessel catch, particularly in the Gulf of St Lawrence. Sealers in the Gulf may not take hooded seals. Farther east sealers sail from ports in Newfoundland and NS to hunt amid the ice floes off the NE coast of Newfoundland-Labrador (the Front). On the ice, sealers carry a hardwood club (bat), curved knife and sharpening steel. Those hunting from large vessels may carry a long-handled iron weapon (hakapik) with a curved head. Fisheries officers, members of COSS and other observers travel to the hunt to ensure that it is carried out humanely and according to regulations. The pelt from a newborn (whitecoat) or fully molted harp seal pup (beater) is of great economic value to the sealer, although that of a young hooded seal (blueback) is more highly prized.

Canada imposed a partial quota on its sealers in the Gulf in 1965; quotas limiting catch at the Gulf and the Front were introduced by the federal government in 1971. In 1982 hunters were permitted to take up to 186 000 harp and 15 000 hooded seals in Canadian waters. Approximately 164 000 harp and 10 000 hooded seals were caught. In 1983, the total allowable catch was not met; in 1984 only 30 000 harp and 250 hooded seals were taken because of the failure of the commercial market.

Pelts are graded and sold to processors directly or through an agent. While initial pelt processing (eg, removal of blubber and oil) is done in Canada, final processing and sale of skins usually takes place abroad. Seal oil is still sold for use in tanneries and in food. Seal meat is popular in Newfoundland-Labrador; the flippers are an eagerly awaited delicacy.

Since the early 1960s, intense opposition to the commercial hunt has arisen from both national and international groups. This is countered by the equally fierce desire of the sealers and their supporters to preserve not only a source of income but what they regard as their heritage. There are estimated to be 1-2 million harp seals and 300 000 hooded seals in the NW Atlantic. The harp seal is not an ENDANGERED ANIMAL; the hooded seal's status is still curiously unknown. These marine mammals may be potentially more threatened by environmental changes (eg, biochemical contamination and the search for and transportation of fossil fuels) than by a regulated commercial hunt. Although harp and hooded seals travel great distances and theoretically could avoid highly contaminated areas, an oil spill could have disastrous consequences, particularly at breeding or whelping grounds or in northern waters, where biodegradation is slow and cleanup difficult. Man is also placing considerable pressure on fish stocks, including species on which seals depend. Clearly the management of any species must owe a greater debt to reason, caution and sound scientific knowledge than to emotionalism or human overconfidence in our ability to predict the future.　　　K. RONALD AND J.L. DOUGAN

Seashell Shell is a hard covering made primarily of calcium carbonate, secreted by INVERTEBRATE animals (eg, MOLLUSCS, BRACHIOPODS, BARNACLES, SEA URCHINS). Some shells grow with the animal; others are shed and replaced periodically. The shell provides protection, a site for muscle insertion and, in a few cases, buoyancy. In most molluscs it consists of 3 layers secreted by the mantle and its marginal lobes. The outer layer (periostracum) consists of an organic material, conchiolin. It may be thin and glossy or coarse, flaky or spiny. The underlying prismatic layer, usually the thickest part of the shell, consists of calcium carbonate crystals laid down in an organic matrix, obliquely or at right angles to the periostracum. The inner layer is of similar composition but is laid down as flat plates. This often iridescent, nacreous layer is called mother of pearl because if a sand grain or a parasite becomes trapped between mantle and shell, nacreous material secreted around it forms a pearl. Many bivalves, including common freshwater MUSSELS (*Lampsilis* and *Anodonta*) and bay mussel (*Mytilus*), can make pearls; the valuable forms are secreted by members of tropical genera of pearl OYSTERS (*Pinctada* and *Pteria*).

The 3 forms of crystalline calcium carbonate forming the shell are calcite, aragonite and vaterite. Calcium is less abundant in fresh water than in the ocean; consequently, pond snails have thin, fragile shells, which can be partly regenerated following injury.

The study of shells, conchology, dates to the 17th century when merchants and explorers brought back tropical shells for the "curiosity cabinets" of the wealthy. Until Linnaeus's system of taxonomy was accepted in the late 18th century, conchology was relatively unscientific. It flourished during the Victorian era when popular interest in natural history was fuelled by such voyages of discovery as the CHALLENGER EXPEDITION (1872-76). This great oceanographic enterprise, which visited Halifax briefly, pioneered deep-sea dredging for marine organisms, including molluscs. Modern conchologists place as much emphasis on the BIOLOGY and ecology of the organism as on the structure of its shell.

Beach specimens may be collected as souvenirs. Although sometimes worn or damaged, they indicate which species may be found alive in the vicinity. If a collection is intended to have scientific or commercial value, the animals should be collected live at low tide or by diving and dredging. The collector must make sure in advance that harvesting is permitted (some countries have strict conservation programs and ban export of rare species). Joining a malacological or shell club, through which shells are exchanged or bought, allows collectors to acquire exotic species such as beautifully shaped and coloured cones, cowries, tuns, conches, strombids and olives. Satisfactory examples of these are often found in souvenir shops at museums and aquaria, or through dealers and catalogues. Shells may be conical, planispiral, spiral cones, dome shaped, plain or sculptured. Shells have been collected since prehistoric times for use in adornment and mosaics, as fertility symbols, money, dishes, trumpets, sources of mortar, and adzes for constructing dugout canoes. Crusaders and pilgrims wore scallops or "coquilles St Jacques." FOSSIL shells are used as a means of determining the age of SEDIMENTARY ROCKS. The shells most likely to be found on beaches belong to one of the 5 classes of the phylum Mollusca described below.

Gastropoda, including snails, whelks, limpets, cone shells, cowries and conches, are the most numerous class. Some species bear a horny or shelly covering on the foot (operculum), which can seal the opening for protection against predators or desiccation.

Amphineura, the chitons, have cradle or coat-of-mail shells, divided into 8 overlapping, butterfly-shaped plates.

Bivalvia, the clams, cockles, oysters and mussels, have 2 convex valves joined dorsally by an elastic hinge ligament. Hinge teeth help lock the valves along the hinge line. Concentric lines in the shell sculpture may be "growth checks," so-called since they result from variations in growth rate. Sculpturing may consist of spines, plates, knobs or corrugations.

Scaphopoda, the tusk or tooth shells, have a conical, tubular shell open at both ends. They were used as currency by Northwest Coast Indians.

Cephalopoda In octopus, cuttlefish and squid, the shell is lost or much reduced, except in *Nautilus, Spirula* and *Argonauta* (paper nautilus). *Nautilus* is an Indo-Pacific genus; its large, white, coiled shell, decorated with russet stripes, is common in collections. *Spirula* has a white, coiled shell that is washed up on Atlantic beaches as far N as Cape Cod; its shell, like that of *Nautilus,* is known as a chambered cone. The female *Argonauta* secretes a delicate, frilled pseudo-shell to protect her eggs.　　　A.M. REID AND R.G.B. REID
Reading: Tucker R. Abbott, *Seashells of North America* (1968); Peter S. Dance, *Sea Shells* (1973).

Seaweed, Willie, or the formal address Hiamas, meaning "right maker," or more commonly Kwaxitola, meaning "smoky-top," Northwest Coast artist, singer, dancer (b at Nugent Sound, BC *c* 1873; d at Blunden Harbour, BC 1967). Seaweed participated in the development of southern Kwakiutl art from the "restrained" style of the 19th century to what Bill Holm describes as the "baroque period which reached its culmination in the cannibal bird masks of the 1940s and 1950s." The years during which Seaweed practised his art were times of great change. Most of his carving was done for traditional uses. One of his best-known works is a memorial Dzoonokwa and Thunderbird pole, in the graveyard at Alert Bay. The work was executed with a contemporary of Seaweed, Mungo MARTIN, in 1931. Seaweed never signed his work, but it remains identifiable because of his consistent use of 3 circles placed within one another with evenly spaced centres and black and white paint.　　　GERALD R. McMASTER

Seaweeds are multicellular marine ALGAE, visible to the naked eye. They extend from the uppermost reaches of sea spray on the shore to the lower limits of light beneath the surface of the water. They fringe all ocean coastlines, with few species found below 30-40 m depth. Seaweeds are most abundant in lower intertidal and shallower subtidal zones. Some are small filaments, barely visible; others are large and complex in structure. There are reports of giant kelp (*Macrocystis*) attaining 100 m in length, and single plants of bull kelp (*Durvillaea*, genus of Southern Hemisphere) weighing more than 100 kg. Seaweeds, as algae, are classified as "greens," "browns" and "reds." Most seaweeds belong to the red or brown algae, most green algae occurring as planktonic or freshwater forms (*see* PLANKTON). Many species of seaweeds occur along Canadian coasts: about 175 are reported for the Arctic; 350 in the Atlantic; nearly 500 in the Pacific.

The use of seaweed as food is largely restricted to the Orient. The Japanese include many species in their diet, the most noteworthy being nori (*Porphyra*), which is "farmed," the annual crop valued at about $1 billion. The Chinese still consume kelp (*Laminaria*) to prevent goitre. In the West, only purple laver (*Porphyra*), IRISH MOSS (*Chondrus crispus*) and dulse (*Palmaria palmata*) are eaten routinely, the latter 2 in Atlantic Canada. Seaweeds are included in animal rations and used as soil conditioners and fertilizers. Hydrocolloids (water-soluble gums) are employed in industry, particularly food and textile sectors. These include agar and carrageenan from "reds" and algin from "browns." Irish moss is harvested in the Maritime provinces and exported for processing of carrageenan. In NS, knotted wrack (*Ascophyllum nodosun*) is harvested for alginate. Seaweeds are little used in BC. Some species, especially "reds," are beautiful and have been collected and mounted.   J. McLACHLAN

Sechelt Peninsula, approximately 35 000 ha, pop 5500 (1981 est), is part of a coastal area known as the "Sunshine Coast," isolated from nearby VANCOUVER, BC, by both Howe Sound and the COAST MTS. The name, meaning "place of shelter from the sea," is that of an Indian village and band. Settlement by Europeans began in 1870. Now linked by ferries with Saltery Bay and Horseshoe Bay, the peninsula still attracts settlers and is a popular cottage, tourist and yachting area.   PETER GRANT

Second-Language Instruction The language that children first acquire naturally in the home is known as a first language (also as "mother tongue" and "native language"); any language learned after the first language has been acquired is a second language. Most children appear to learn their first language without any special instruction or formal teaching. Some linguists have attributed this facility to an innate, specific language-learning capacity; others believe it to be attributable to general cognitive capacities. Even in the first language, however, reading and writing must be taught, and thus first-language and second-language teaching and learning have much in common.

Languages in Canada

There are 3 major classes of languages in Canada: official or "charter" languages (French and English) which are recognized under the federal OFFICIAL LANGUAGES ACT (under provincial legislation, however, only in Québec and New Brunswick is French an official language); immigrant languages, which enjoy no official status in Canada but which are spoken as national or regional languages elsewhere; and ancestral languages of native peoples, which are not protected legally at the federal level (*see* NATIVE PEOPLE, LANGUAGES). The language issues of particular significance in Canada include the learning of French as a second language (FSL) by English-speaking Canadians and by immigrants to Québec; the learning of English (ESL) as a second language by Francophones in Québec, by native people and by immigrants to English-speaking Canada; and the maintenance of other ethnic languages, ie, languages of immigrants and of native people.

French as a Second Language

The great importance attached to the teaching of French reflects changes in the long history of FRANCOPHONE-ANGLOPHONE RELATIONS. Until recently, because economic power was largely in the hands of the English, the French language did not enjoy the same status in Canada as English, despite the historical significance of French, its demographic significance, and the fact that French is one of the world's major languages. This was true even in Québec, where the vast majority of the population speaks French. In response to the discontent of francophone Quebeckers with this situation, successive Québec governments since the 1960s have taken measures to protect the French language, culminating in legislation such as BILL 101, which was passed to promote the use of the French language. In the early 1960s some members of the English community of St Lambert, Qué (the St Lambert Bilingual School Study Group) reacted to the evolving importance of French and to the isolation of the French and English communities from each other by questioning methods of FSL instruction in English schools. Searching for better methods, this group consulted Wallace Lambert of McGill University, who had studied the sociopsychological and cognitive aspects of BILINGUALISM, and Wilder PENFIELD of the Montreal Neurological Institute, who had studied brain mechanisms underlying language functions. At this parents' initiative, an experimental kindergarten French immersion program was established in St Lambert in 1965. In the program, participating children received the same type of education they would receive in the regular English program, except that the material was all taught in French. The teachers have generally been native speakers of French who understood English, and children were generally treated as though they too were native speakers. By 1983 over 100 000 anglophone students were enrolled in French immersion programs in over 600 schools across Canada. There are now 3 main types of programs in existence.

Early Total Immersion Programs are divided into a monolingual phase (usually kindergarten to grade 2 or 3) when all curriculum materials are presented in the second language but children may speak among themselves or to the teacher in English; a bilingual phase (usually grade 2 or 3 to grade 6) when English and French are used equally for instruction; and a maintenance phase (usually from grade 7 to the end of secondary school) when 3 to 5 subjects are offered in French.

Delayed Immersion Programs are those in which the use of French as a major medium of instruction is delayed until the middle elementary grades.

Late Immersion Programs postpone intensive use of FSL until the end of primary school or the beginning of secondary school.

Immersion education, pioneered in Canada, is internationally recognized as one of the few successful experiments in second-language instruction. A distinguishing feature of this movement has been the active involvement of parents' groups across Canada. In 1977 a national association, Canadian Parents for French (CPF), was created to promote increased opportunities for FSL of all types. CPF has become a powerful lobby group at all levels of government.

Although immersion is a widespread and popular option across Canada, the majority of English-speaking students in elementary and secondary schools still learn French as a second language in classes where French is taught as a subject (so-called "core" French) and is not the medium of instruction. Because of the success of immersion, core French is less popular and is regarded as a less successful "Cinderella" language course and improvements in core French instruction are widely demanded.

English as a Second Language

If French LANGUAGE POLICIES raise questions about Canadian unity and francophone-anglophone relations, the debate over English as a second language (ESL) has been less political. For immigrants to English-speaking Canada, for example, learning English is a necessary prerequisite for economic survival. It was not until after WWII that provincial governments created language and citizenship programs for adult newcomers, that school boards established language classes for immigrant children, and that the growth of community colleges led to the development of post-secondary ESL programs. By the early 1970s teachers of ESL had founded a number of provincial ESL associations, and in 1978, TESL Canada, a nationwide federation of associations involved in teaching ESL, was created.

No coherent national strategy concerned with the problems of immigrant adaptation has yet been formulated, and immigrant services are still provided by a complex network of school boards, universities and community colleges, and by agencies of the federal and provincial governments. A wide variety of approaches has been developed to meet the needs of ESL students, but the field is beset by problems (which also beset FSL), such as insufficient numbers of teachers and consultants, inadequate teacher training, a paucity of appropriate curricula and materials, and the lack of clear goals. In the late 1970s, with the wave of refugees from Southeast Asia, the inadequacies of the language-training system and of settlement services became apparent. In 1981, after a national symposium on the problems of adult refugees, the TESL Canada Action Committee urged the development of a national policy of refugee settlement. The committee recommended a 2-stage approach in which a basic 3-month program would be followed by a variety of vocational options, with special provision being made for literacy training, for English in the workplace and English as a second dialect, and for special groups such as young adults, senior citizens, women and people in remote areas.

Language-Training Program

Because any federal public service must be available in either official language, many federal public servants must be bilingual. The federal public service has established its own language-training program. Since the early 1970s, over 2000 public servants annually have received language training in French or English in language centres across Canada.

Teaching Methods

A century ago, the most popular method of second-language instruction was *grammar translation*, ie, the teaching and practice of grammar rules through translation exercises. Around 1900, the moderately successful *direct method* was created. It involved teaching without translation and dispensing with the mother tongue completely in class. In the 1960s, the *audiolingual method* (ie, speaking and listening in rapid drills) was popular. Since then, a number of new methods have been advocated. One of these emphasized the training of listening abilities through actions (*total physical response*); another the use of psychological relaxation (*suggestopedia*); and a third the use of techniques based on group therapy (*counselling learning*). In the 1970s other second-language instruction reformers suggested that more emphasis be paid to the curriculum and to the practical needs and specific purposes of language learners. There has been an accompanying attempt to ground second-language instruction more thoroughly in the language sciences, eg, linguistics, psycholinguistics, sociolinguistics and applied linguistics. The most widely used method of language teaching in the 1980s is *communicative language teaching,* ie, teachers involve students as much as possible in realistic language use. New technologies have also been recruited in the search for better instructional techniques. In the 1950s, the language laboratory was created; in the 1980s microcomputers and videocassette recorders are increasingly used as teaching resources. None of these innovations, however, has resulted in a radical breakthrough in second-language instruction.

Maintenance of Nonofficial Languages

The 1963 Royal Commission on BILINGUALISM AND BICULTURALISM took the view that linguistic diversity is an important personal and social resource. In 1977 Ontario initiated its Heritage Languages Program, which provided funds for the teaching of "heritage" languages, ie, languages other than English or French. Similar programs have been started in Québec, Manitoba, Alberta, BC and the NWT.

Native Indian Languages Linguists generally recognize 11 major groups of Canadian native languages, some of which contain a number of languages and dialects. Some native peoples (particularly in the North) have strongly retained their languages, but the medium of instruction in northern native schools is usually French or English (which most students must learn as a second language) and recently there has been a growing interest in developing ESL and FSL curriculum materials for native students and in conducting research into the conditions under which these students learn second languages. However, few teachers of native children have had second-language training, and appropriate methods of second-language instruction are not yet widely employed. Some bilingual education programs have been designed to maintain ancestral languages while allowing native children to acquire a knowledge of French or English. Here, as in other areas of second-language instruction, much still remains to be done to provide satisfactory programs.   H.H. STERN

Secondary School Originally established as schools offering a narrow, classical curriculum to the sons of gentlemen, secondary schools became coeducational, offering a widened variety of programs and courses to all children who had completed the elementary school program.

In English-speaking Canada the first secondary schools, modelled after the English grammar schools, were usually operated by comparatively well-educated Church of England clergy. The ruling group considered these training schools for future leaders to be of greater importance to the colony than schools for the children of the common people, an "official" view reflected in the earlier provision for the establishment and generous public support of secondary schools for the few. These schools, however, were forced to offer elementary instruction as well because many of their students were not prepared to undertake secondary-school work. When publicly supported elementary schools were established, there were then 2 types of schools offering elementary instruction, a "necessary" duplication at a time when few aristocrats were prepared to send their children to the common schools.

Despite the financial advantage enjoyed by the grammar schools, they did not prosper, largely because they were unsuited to a sparsely populated region that was to become socially democratized at an early date. Proving more acceptable to a growing number of people were the later academies, coeducational institutions offering a more varied program to a wider segment of society. These academies flourished because they offered what an increasing number of parents demanded for their children, namely less emphasis on the classics and more emphasis on commercial and work-related studies.

In Ontario, Egerton RYERSON, superintendent of public instruction during an important period (1844-76) in Canada's development, concentrated his attention on setting up a system of common (elementary) schools before turning to the problems of the secondary schools. Noting that the grammar-school enrolment had remained low and that many of the smaller grammar schools were concerned more about ways of obtaining increased government grants than on ways of improving instruction, Ryerson introduced central control of these schools. As a part of this centralization, he established a system of regular inspection and a short-lived system of "payment by results," under which the government grant was, in part, based on the examination results obtained by students. Through the introduction of an entrance examination to secondary schools, Ryerson removed the problem of duplication of programs in common (elementary) and secondary schools, the elementary school becoming the first division of the school system extending from the earliest grade to university.

Even after the elementary and secondary schools were made into a single public system within each province, there was much controversy about the role to be played by the secondary school. To those who considered it an upward extension of the elementary school, it was obvious that the secondary school's program should not be primarily university-oriented. As the compulsory school attendance age was raised over the years, the need to offer a variety of programs in addition to the academic, university-oriented program became evident, especially when it was noted that a high proportion of the students entering high school were not completing their program or moving on to university studies.

The curriculum of the secondary school and the methods of instruction used therein have tended to reflect the university orientation. For example, when provincial secondary-school graduation examinations were in general use, these were prepared by subject committees usually dominated by university professors. The great importance attached to these examinations by both the educational authorities and the public helped to increase the universities' role in determining the secondary-school curriculum, largely as a result of the schools' "teaching to the exams," a widespread practice that has been of decreasing importance in recent years. Another result of this close association of secondary schools with the universities has been the long-delayed provision for the professional training of secondary-school teachers. Because university instructors were ready to support the widely held view that the secondary-school teacher did not need training in methods of teaching but only intensive preparation in his specific subject area, provision for the training of secondary-school teacher candidates tended to come much later than that for elementary teachers.

As a result of the higher academic qualifications required of secondary teachers, salary scales for secondary teachers have generally been considerably higher than those for elementary teachers, thereby tending to create barriers between the 2 groups.

Among the recent developments that have affected secondary schools in Canada has been the attempt by provincial authorities to tear down the long-standing wall between elementary and secondary schools. Significant progress toward this objective has been made by placing within university faculties of education the teacher education programs for all teachers, a noteworthy change from the earlier arrangement whereby elementary teachers were trained in normal schools (or teachers' colleges) while secondary teachers were enrolled in university faculties of education. This change, together

with the move requiring all teachers to hold a university degree, will undoubtedly lead to a lessening of the old distinctions, academic and financial.

One of the most serious problems in secondary education in Canada has been that of providing equal educational opportunities in rural and urban areas. Because the cost of providing the academic program is less than the cost of programs requiring expensive shop equipment, the smaller rural secondary schools found themselves unable to offer the more expensive work-related programs and, as a result, tended to offer academic programs and to be taken by a relatively small proportion of students. This problem has usually been dealt with by enlarging the secondary-school unit of administration to permit the offering of a variety of programs and courses to a larger pool of secondary students.

In western Canada, for example, the high schools established in rural areas before the advent of large school units in the 1940s were often one-room, one-teacher schools, offering a limited curriculum, largely academic. The creation of large units of school administration, however, made possible the establishment of large regional secondary schools offering programs to accommodate students who wished to enter university as well as those with vocational interests. In this, as in other areas of development, the western provinces showed greater readiness than did the eastern provinces to introduce change.

Another means of making secondary education more readily available to students in smaller communities was legislation that enabled common (or elementary) schools to add secondary grades in a combination known in some provinces (eg, Ontario) as a continuation school. In certain regions, especially in the Atlantic provinces, one-room rural schools often conducted classes from grades 1 to 10, with larger communities adding grades 11 and 12 to their offerings.

Although education is constitutionally a provincial responsibility (there are exceptions; *see* NATIVE PEOPLE: CONTEMPORARY SOCIETY; NATIVE PEOPLE, EDUCATION), there have been periods in Canada's history when the federal government has poured large amounts of money into education, especially in areas considered to be of national importance (eg, agricultural education, vocational and technical training). Such infusions have tended to occur during national crises.

Marked differences characterize secondary education in Québec, notably in the early estab-

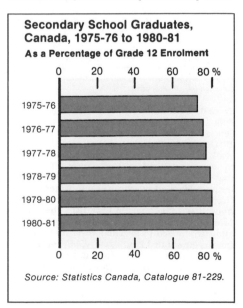

Secondary School Graduates, Canada, 1975-76 to 1980-81

As a Percentage of Grade 12 Enrolment

Source: Statistics Canada, Catalogue 81-229.

lishment of *collèges classiques*, which combined secondary and college education in an 8-year program. Affiliated with the French-language universities, these institutions were for males only during the greater part of their existence. Unlike the English-style grammar schools, the classical colleges admitted boys from all social levels and had a notable impact on all sectors of French Canadian society.

During Québec's QUIET REVOLUTION the reform of secondary education moved that province from the position of having one of the lowest secondary-school retention rates in Canada to having one of the highest. No longer was the classical college practically the only avenue open to the French-language universities and no longer were students to pay fees in public secondary schools.

In all Canadian provinces, secondary education aims to prepare students for tertiary-level education at university or community college and to prepare them to live and work in society.

Because the teaching of citizenship has long been one of the objectives of Canadian secondary schools, A.B. Hodgetts's widely discussed analysis of the shortcomings of the civic-education programs in Canada received careful attention from curriculum planners, administrators and teachers at the elementary- and secondary-school levels. Among the shortcomings noted by Hodgetts were the lack of any contemporary meaning in the courses of study in Canadian history, the narrowness of the program ("confined to constitutional and political history"), the lack of controversy ("a bland, unrealistic consensus version of our past") and the use of uninspiring teaching methods. The report of this inquiry, *What Culture? What Heritage?* (1968), caused nationwide soul-searching that led to the creation in 1970 of the Canada Studies Foundation, an independent, nonprofit organization designed to find ways of improving the quality of Canadian studies in both elementary and secondary schools.

For a variety of reasons, a number of students have found the traditional secondary-school program unsuited to their interests. In some instances, this has led to the "dropout problem" which received much public attention at various periods, particularly during the late 1950s and 1960s. Largely in response to this problem, certain kinds of alternative education were established, usually for secondary-school students in urban areas who were seeking an approach to teaching and learning different from that normally found in the larger, more traditional, schools. The fact that these alternative schools have been publicly supported for several years indicates that they have been accepted as filling an important need in Canadian education.

WILLARD BREHAUT

Reading: F.H. Johnson, *A Brief History of Canadian Education* (1968); R.M. Stamp, *The Schools of Ontario 1876-1976* (1982); J.D. Wilson, R.M. Stamp, L.P. Audet, *Canadian Education: A History* (1970).

Secord, Laura, née Ingersoll, heroine of the WAR OF 1812 (b at Great Barrington, Mass 13 Sept 1775; d at Chippawa (Niagara Falls), Ont 17 Oct 1868). During the War of 1812, Laura walked 30 km from Queenston to Beaver Dams to warn the British officer, James FitzGibbon, that the Americans were planning to attack his outpost. She had overheard some American officers discussing their plan while dining at her house. Two days later, 24 June 1813, the Americans were ambushed by Indians at Beaver Dams and surrendered to FitzGibbon. Years later, historians questioned Laura's story, but found confirmation of it in 3 testimonials by FitzGibbon. Monuments to Laura Secord stand in Lundy's Lane, Niagara Falls and on Queenston Heights.

RUTH MCKENZIE

Reading: Ruth McKenzie, *Laura Secord* (1971).

Secret Societies are sometimes seen as religious, philosophical or spiritual sects that confer upon their initiates a certain mystery; the mystery is patiently and meticulously maintained and gradually made accessible, in succeeding stages, through the performance of secret rites designed to purify the fortunate elect. At other times, secret societies are seen as seditious political organizations, clandestine economic associations, criminal groups, ideological movements with revolutionary intentions, or occult interest groups. They may also be viewed as agencies for mutual aid, support, brotherhood, charity or good works.

In order to attract the attention of the curious or the spiritualistic, a group generally need only indulge in clandestine activities (eg, the Freemasons), have an unusual series of rites and customs (many social clubs), or maintain a certain secrecy around initiation ceremonies (some native groups). Myth-makers capitalize on man's interest in the immaterial and supernatural to maintain in initiates and aspirants the superrational element necessary for any lasting socialization.

Historically, all secret societies, whether brotherhoods, trade-guilds, mystery societies, initiating associations and spiritualist societies or, more simply, closed associations with specific economic, political or religious purpose, have or have had their own oaths, rituals, customs and secret languages to promote and maintain necessary group solidarity. All have adopted signs of recognition and passwords, rhythmic chants and other ways of reminding one another of their society's moral conditions of behaviour. All have developed and followed successive stages to the attainment of secret knowledge or power, periods of apprenticeship and trial, and an often intricate hierarchy. All have evolved internal ceremonies capable of separating the neophyte from the member of long standing, the profane from the chosen. All have identified themselves with certain moral principles and beliefs that distinguish them from that which surrounds them and which is therefore foreign or subordinate to them. All have given a sacred significance to their existence.

It is therefore not very helpful to attempt to differentiate between secret societies and other organizations on the basis of distinctions of place (primitive societies, Western societies), culture (Caribbean, Germanic, Slavic or American Protestant societies), religion (ORDRE DE JACQUES-CARTIER, ORANGE ORDER), nationality (Amerindian, Spanish, Italian, Irish or French) or sex (witches and high priests).

Secret societies have been in existence at least since the date of the earliest known writings. Some have served utilitarian ends, others speculative; some have been visible, others invisible, except to government information services, which have always been aware of their existence. Each has based its existence on a secret, the secret of its mystery, purpose, direction, ritual or, more generally, its organization. Ultimately, what has at all times and in all places distinguished secret societies from other associations is that the former are organized in a manner parallel to, but often above, official forms of government, whatever those forms may be.

In Canada, secret societies were often founded by ethnic groups, particularly the Irish; the Whiteboys and the United Irishmen were active before 1812 and the FENIANS (Irish Republican Brotherhood) during the Confederation period. Farm and labour organizations like the Grange and KNIGHTS OF LABOR began as secret societies. Today, the best-known societies are the Freemasons, Orange Order, Ordre de Jacques-Cartier, Opus Dei and, at certain periods, the KU KLUX KLAN. *See also* NEW RELIGIOUS MOVEMENTS.

G.-RAYMOND LALIBERTÉ

Secretary of State, Department of One of the oldest departments of the federal government, it was established in 1867 as the official channel of communication between the Dominion of Canada and the imperial government. Its diverse responsibilities have at times included Indian affairs, crown lands, the RCMP, the civil service and government printing and stationery. It has had a continuous responsibility for state and ceremonial occasions. Present responsibilities include encouraging the use of the 2 official languages of Canada, programs for the achievement of national arts and cultural objectives, state protocol and ceremonies and events, education policies, translation services, promotion of a Canadian identity and the granting of Canadian citizenship. The department reports to Parliament for the PUBLIC SERVICE COMMISSION's Advisory Council on the Status of Women, and Public Service Commission. The Multicultural Directorate is part of the administrative apparatus of the department. The 1984-85 budget for the department was \$2.7 million.

Sedge, grasslike PLANT common throughout temperate and cold regions. The genus name, *Carex* (family *Cyperaceae*), is probably derived from *keiro* [Gk, "to cut"], referring to the sharp leaf margins. Worldwide this taxonomically involved complex is represented by some 2000 species; in Canada by about 270, plus others of subspecific rank and several hybrids. Sedges are readily distinguished from GRASSES by their 3-sided, solid stems and by leaves with 3 ranks instead of 2. Within the spike, the minute individual flowers are solitary in the axils of scales. Male flowers normally have 3 stamens; female flowers (enclosed in a sac, the perigynium) have 2 or 3 stigmas. The seed, surrounded by the persistent perigynium, may be lens shaped or three angled. Flower spikes and mature seeds are needed for accurate identification to specific or lower rank. The position of male and female spikes on the plant is another important identification characteristic. In milder climates *C. pendula*, grown as a garden ORNAMENTAL (usually near water), is prized for its bold effect (up to 1.5 m tall) and long, drooping spikes. Also grown is Japanese sedge grass (*C. morrowii* var *expallida*), which has leaves striped white. The hardier *C. plantaginea*, found wild in

Sedge (*artwork by Claire Tremblay*).

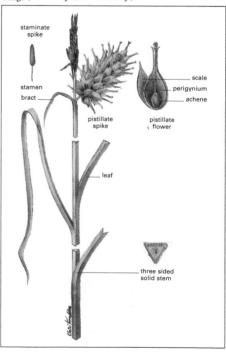

staminate spike

stamen

bract

pistillate spike

scale

perigynium

achene

pistillate flower

leaf

three sided solid stem

deciduous woods from NB to Manitoba (and south), is conspicuous with its broad evergreen leaves and purple sheaths. While sedges are of limited garden value, they are sometimes planted for erosion control. The ancient Egyptians cultivated *Cyperus papyrus* to provide the earliest form of paper. Today the value of sedge is most evident in its native habitat, bordering sloughs and other wet places, where it provides cover and food for waterfowl. ROGER VICK

Sedgewick, Robert, lawyer, jurist (b at Aberdeen, Scot 10 May 1848; d at Chester, NS 4 Aug 1906). Sedgewick was the prime mover in the establishment of Dalhousie Law School in 1883, the first common-law institution of its kind in Canada. He was appointed municipal judge for Halifax in 1883 and also lectured in equity jurisprudence at Dalhousie. In 1886 he was appointed deputy minister of justice for Canada. In 1890 he drafted both the Bills of Exchange Act, the first codified legislation in Canada, and with Judge BURBIDGE, the Canadian CRIMINAL CODE, the first legislation of its kind in the British Empire. With Sir John THOMPSON, he planned the strategy whereby the bill became law in 1892. In 1893 he was appointed to the bench of the Supreme Court of Canada. D.H. BROWN

Sedimentary Rock, one of the 3 major classes of ROCK comprising the Earth's crust (the others being IGNEOUS and metamorphic), is made up of loose, unconsolidated sediment that has been transformed into rock (ie, lithified) during GEOLOGICAL HISTORY. Only about 5% of the Earth's crust is composed of sedimentary rocks, but they cover 70-75% of the exposed surface and contain many economically important MINERALS, COAL and PETROLEUM. As exposed at the surface, the most important types by volume are shale 50%, sandstone 30% and limestone 20%. Calculations suggest that total surface plus subsurface proportions may be shale 79%, sandstone 13% and limestone 8%.

Seed Plants, the most abundant and familiar component of Earth's VEGETATION, comprise an estimated 250 000-300 000 species. They outnumber all other PLANT groups, dominate the land, thrive in bodies of fresh water and are found to a limited extent in the oceans. They include the largest (giant sequoia) and oldest (bristlecone pine) living things, and encompass tiny water-meal scarcely 1 mm long and ephemeral annuals that survive only a few weeks. Seed plants share with other vascular plants (plants with woody conducting systems) basic organs (root, stem and leaf), cell types and tissues. In response to different environments, they have evolved many forms. The common feature uniting them is the "seed habit," a unique method of sexual reproduction. In all vascular plants, the conspicuous plant is a spore producer (sporophyte) that alternates, in the life cycle, with a sexual phase (gametophyte). In seed plants, the spore that produces the female gametophyte is not shed to initiate an independent plant, but is retained in the sporangium (reproductive structure), which is surrounded by a protective covering (integument). This is the immature seed or ovule. Spores that produce male gametophytes are released as the gametophytes begin to develop. These are the pollen grains, which are transferred to the ovules where fertilization is completed, resulting in seed development. The EVOLUTION of this method of reproduction, more than 350 million years ago, was one of the most significant steps in the adaptation of plants to life on land. MOSSES and lower vascular plants (eg, FERNS), like their aquatic ancestors, release sperm that must swim through water to effect fertilization. Seed plants are freed from this dependence on water.

Seed plants fall into 2 major groups, gymnosperms and angiosperms. Gymnosperms, the more ancient group, include CONIFERS, cycads and the maidenhair tree (*Ginkgo*). Although there are only about 700 living species, gymnosperms are important in the flora of many areas (eg, boreal forest). The FOSSIL record shows that they were much more important in the past, and included several now-extinct forms (eg, seed ferns). Pollen and ovules are produced in separate cones. Pollen grains are transferred directly to ovules, ultimately being drawn inside through an opening in the integument. Thus the ovules are exposed at the time of POLLINATION (gymnosperm means "naked seed"), although usually enclosed later by growth of the cone scales. In the mature seed, the embryo is embedded in a nutritive tissue that is actually the female gametophyte.

The angiosperms, flowering plants, have dominated Earth's vegetation since the Cretaceous period (between 140 and 65 million years ago). Their distinctive reproductive structure, the flower, occurs in diverse forms related to different methods of pollination. Pollen and ovules may be found in the same or separate flowers. Pollen is produced in stamens. Ovules are formed inside the pistil; they are not exposed at the time of pollination (angiosperm means "vessel seed"). Pollen is transferred to a receptive surface on the pistil where it germinates; sperm are carried into the ovule by growth of the pollen tube. Seeds mature inside the pistil, which becomes the fruit. Some one-seeded fruits (eg, cereal grains) are often confused with seeds. The nutritive tissue of the angiosperm seed is a new tissue, endosperm, which with the embryo results from the fertilization process. The endosperm frequently is absorbed by the embryo before the seed is mature. There are 2 major evolutionary lines of angiosperms: monocotyledons, with flower parts usually in threes, major leaf veins parallel and only one cotyledon (embryo leaf); and dicotyledons, with flower parts usually in fours or fives, net-veined leaves and 2 cotyledons.

The economic significance of seed plants cannot be overemphasized. Angiosperms provide most of our important food CROPS (*see* GRASS) and produce spices, drugs, fibres, timber and industrial raw materials. Gymnosperms (conifers) are major sources of wood products; seeds of a few (eg, pinyon pine) are minor food sources. T.A. STEEVES

Seeman, Mary Violette, clinical psychiatrist, psychopharmacologist (b at Łódź, Poland). She was educated at McGill, the Sorbonne, the Adolf Meyer Psychiatric Hospital (New York) and Columbia U. Psychopharmacological research begun in 1965 in New York was expanded during periods at Fulbourn Hospital at Cambridge, at Toronto Western Hospital (1967-75), and at the dept of psychiatry, U of T, after 1975. Seeman was also co-ordinator of studies in schizophrenia at the Clarke Institute of Psychiatry, Toronto. Her clinical research on schizophrenia has resulted in a clearer understanding of its physiological, biochemical, cellular and psychohormonal basis and she has published widely on its molecular basis and treatment. Seeman and co-workers have summarized the current state of research on the scientific and clinical basis of schizophrenia and its management in a book for the layperson, *Living and Working with Schizophrenia* (1982). ROSE SHEININ

Seeman, Philip, molecular neuropharmacologist, educator (b at Winnipeg 8 Feb 1934). Educated at McGill and Rockefeller U he has studied the structure and function of the plasma membrane at the surface of animal cells. His special interest is in neurologically active compounds, their interaction with receptors on the periphery of nerve cells, and their effect on human behaviour and mood. Seeman's major scientific discoveries concern the nerve-cell receptor for the neurohormone L-dopamine, whose aberrant function is manifest in one or more forms of Parkinsonism. The studies of Seeman and coworkers of the interaction of L-dopamine, its analogues and its antagonists with nerve cell membranes have brought a rational basis to the understanding and treatment of Parkinson's Disease and other illnesses that derive from faulty neurohormone function. In 1977 Seeman became head of the dept of pharmacology, U of T. His publications include the text *Principles of Medical Pharmacology* (1976). ROSE SHEININ

Sefton, Lawrence Frederick, Larry, labour leader (b at Iroquois Falls, Ont 31 Mar 1917; d at Toronto 9 May 1973). A firm believer in international unions and political action, he was secretary of the mine, mill and smelter workers in KIRKLAND LK and helped lead the historic 1941 strike for union recognition. Blacklisted after the strike collapsed, he moved to Toronto and became an organizer on the steelworkers' union staff. He led the 1946 Stelco strike in Hamilton, becoming senior union representative in the Hamilton-Niagara area. In 1953 he was elected director of District 6 of the steelworkers, which covered Canada west of Québec. From 1958 he was an active VP of the Canadian Labour Congress; his greatest contribution internationally was as an initiator of the 1971 World Nickel Conference of unions. A CCF candidate for Parliament in 1949, he served on the party provincial council. LAUREL SEFTON MACDOWELL

Seigneurial System, an institutional form of land distribution and occupation established in NEW FRANCE in 1627 and officially abolished in 1854. It was inspired by the feudal system, which involved the personal dependency of *censitaires* (tenants) on the seigneur; in New France the similarities ended with occupation of land and payment of certain dues, and the *censitaire* was normally referred to as a HABITANT. The COMPAGNIE DES CENT-ASSOCIÉS, which in 1627 was granted ownership and legal and seigneurial rights over New France, also obtained the rights to allocate the land to its best advantage. The land was therefore granted as fiefs and seigneuries to the most influential colonists who, in turn, granted tenancies.

This politically determined system of land distribution was regulated by law and had many advantages. Its purpose was to promote settlement in a systematic way. Seigneuries, which were usually 1 x 3 leagues (5 x 15 km) in size, were generally divided into river lots (*rangs*), a survey system based on the French experience in Normandy. The long, rectangular strips were particularly well adapted to the local terrain, since they facilitated interaction between neighbours and provided multiple points of access to the river, the principal communication route. Individual holdings were large enough (usually about 3 x 30 ARPENTS) to provide a reasonable living to farmers. Finally, the seigneurial system established between the seigneur and the tenant a well-defined individual relationship.

The state established regulations to govern the operation of this system and the relationship between the seigneurs and their tenants. The principal one was that the state granted to a person, who thus became seigneur, a parcel of land which he was to put into production, either directly or through concession to habitants who requested land; portions of the seigneur's land were usually leased on the basis of a duly notarized contract. These acts of concession set out the rights and obligations of each party. The seigneur had both onerous and honorary rights. He could establish a court of law, operate a mill and organize a commune. He received from the habitants various forms of rent: the *cens*, a small tithe dating from the feudal period, which reaffirmed the tenant's theoretical subjection to the seigneur; the *rente* in cash or kind; and the *banalités*, taxes levied on grain, which the tenant had to grind at his seigneur's mill. He also usually granted hunting, fishing and woodcutting licences. In the early 18th century, seigneurs began to insist that their tenants work for them a certain number of days annually (*see* CORVÉE).

The seigneurial system was central to France's colonization policy and came to play a major role in traditional Québec society. Despite the attractions of city life and the fur trade, 75-80% of the population lived on seigneurial land until the mid-19th century. The roughly 200 seigneuries granted during the French regime covered virtually all the inhabited areas on both banks of the St Lawrence R between Montréal and Québec, and the Chaudière and Richelieu valleys, and they extended to the Gaspé. Seigneuries were granted to the nobility, religious institutions (in return for education and hospital services), military officers and civil administrators. Other institutional organizations such as parishes, municipalities and the militia held land bordering on these seigneuries.

This method of land settlement left its mark on both the countryside and the Québec mentality. The land of the habitant was a kind of economic unit essential for survival. Everyone hoped to be the sole tenant, producing most of what he required in order to live. The system of land tenure, which placed rural inhabitants close to one another, and — in the early 19th century — the village, were the foundation upon which the family, neighbour relations and community spirit developed. The closeness of this agricultural society to the soil led naturally to a feeling that land was included in one's patrimony, to be passed from generation to generation.

After Canada was ceded to Britain in 1763, new British laws respected the private agreements and the property rights of francophone society, and the seigneurial system was maintained. But as new land was opened for colonization, the township system developed. As time went on, the seigneural system increasingly appeared to favour the privileged and to hinder economic development. After much political agitation it was abolished in 1854 by a law that permitted tenants to claim rights to their land. The last vestiges of this institution, which many historians believe profoundly influenced traditional Québec society, did not disappear until a century later. JACQUES MATHIEU

Reading: R.C. Harris, *The Seigneurial System in Early Canada* (1968); Marcel Trudel, *The Seigneurial Regime* (1956).

Sekani, "people of the rocks or mountains," were first contacted by Samuel BLACK in 1824. They consisted of several family groups or bands, each of 30-40 persons, who hunted and traded along the Finlay and Parsnip tributaries of the PEACE R. Since the band rather than the tribe was the primary unit of affiliation, identification of some bands with the Sekani is arbitrary. Sekani speak a form of the Beaver-Sarcee-Sekani branch of Athapaskan and appear to have diverged from the BEAVER only late in the 18th century.

Traditional Sekani subsistence was based primarily on hunting moose, caribou, mountain sheep, bears and, prior to the time they were excluded from the prairies, bison and wapiti. Whitefish were caught but salmon were inaccessible prior to Sekani expansion westward after contact. Most aspects of Sekani technology, including tools, shelters and food preparation, were similar to those of other western Subarctic Athapaskans. However, dogs were not used either for traction or for packing. Toboggans were adopted only in the 20th century and the dugout canoe was copied from others, although aboriginally the Sekani made spruce-bark canoes.

The Sekani had trading alliances with the SLAVEY and Beaver to the E, and the TAHLTAN and

the CARRIER to the W. Their trade goods were furs and high-quality tanned skin goods. Several bands were said to have wintered at their trade locations, often in the territory of other peoples, where salmon and bison or caribou were available. Early in the 19th century, however, they were driven out of the eastern foothills of the Rocky Mts by the Beaver. They also fought with their southern neighbours into whose territory they tried to intrude.

Trading posts were established in or near Sekani territory in 1826-27, beginning with Bear Lake Post, but they continued to obtain European goods from the coast through carrier and TSIMSHIAN middlemen. After intermarriage with these 2 groups, the bilateral Sekani adopted many elements of matrilineal West Coast social organization, including clan crests and potlatching, but their attempts to take on the tripartite clan system failed.

During the Omineca gold rush in 1861, Bear Lk (Pacific drainage) became their permanent wintering quarters. Many Sekani followed fortune seekers northward to the next major gold rush in the Cassiar area and, around the turn of the century, settled at Ft Ware; other Sekani attached themselves to Ft Grahame and Ft McLeod. Further relocation to Ingenika and nearby Mackenzie occurred in the 1960s when the Bennett Dam caused Ft Grahame to be flooded. By 1982 the Sekani numbered approximately 600, a threefold increase in population since the early 20th century. *See also* NATIVE PEOPLE: SUBARCTIC and general articles under NATIVE PEOPLE.

Reading: J. Helm, ed, *Handbook of North American Indians, 6: Subarctic* (1981); D. Jenness, *The Sekani Indians of British Columbia* (1937).

Selkirk, Man, Town, pop 10 037 (1981c), inc 1882, is located on the W bank of the RED R, 29 km N of Winnipeg. In the mid-1800s the area was an Indian agricultural settlement. Land speculation and frenzied building began 1875 with proposals to route the CPR across the Red R here. Winnipeg gained the rail crossing, but Selkirk went on to become a river port and centre for shipbuilding, lumber, fish exports and agricultural services. Manitoba Rolling Mills (Canada) Ltd, producer of steel products and the town's major employer, was established here in 1913. Steel, light manufacturing, the service sector and government administration are key parts of Selkirk's economy today. The town has an industrial park, a shipyard, a regional mental health centre, and one of 2 companies in Canada producing high-grade silica sand for glass manufacturing. It has its own radio station and a regional secondary school. Selkirk — named for Lord SELKIRK — is near Lower Fort Garry National Historic Park and the St Andrews Locks on the Red R. The town has a marine museum and celebrates its Scottish heritage in July with the Manitoba Highland Gathering. D.M. LYON

Reading: B. Potyondi, *Selkirk: The First Hundred Years* (1981).

Selkirk, Thomas Douglas, 5th Earl of, colonizer (b St Mary's Isle, Scot 20 June 1771; d at Pau, France 8 Apr 1820). The youngest son in a large family, he unexpectedly became next in line to the title and upon his father's death (1799) sought to make his mark in the world. He found his place in the sponsorship of displaced Highlanders to settlements in BNA. In 1803 he settled 800 Highlanders on land he had purchased in PEI, and in 1804 he established a settlement at BALDOON, UC. Selkirk's motives were a complex mixture of humanitarianism, land improvement and personal ambition. In 1806 he was elected to the House of Lords and in 1807 was appointed lord lieutenant of Kirkcudbright. Less than successful in politics and public life, Selkirk resumed his interest in settlement and in 1811 — he and his family having bought into

Thomas Douglas, earl of Selkirk. His motives in founding colonies in PEI, Upper Canada and at Red R were a complex mixture of humanitarianism and personal ambition (*courtesy Public Archives of Canada/C-1346*).

the HUDSON'S BAY COMPANY — received from the company a large land grant of ASSINIBOIA, in what is now Manitoba. An advance party, sent under Miles MACDONELL in 1811, established RED RIVER COLONY in 1812. Conflict with the NORTH WEST COMPANY and local mixed bloods led to the colony's dispersal in 1815, and Selkirk arrived in Canada to supervise in person. On his way to Red River in 1816 with a party of disbanded Swiss soldiers, Selkirk learned of the deaths of Governor Robert Semple and a number of colonists at SEVEN OAKS; accordingly he occupied the NWC depot at Ft William. Embroiled in complex litigation with the NWC and Canadian opponents of his colony, Selkirk visited Red River in 1817 before returning to Canada to battle his opponents in the courts. Selkirk regarded as a stain upon his honour his inability to convince either the Canadian authorities or the British government that the western disputes resulted from a conspiracy against him and the HBC. Ill with consumption, he departed for Britain in 1818. Deteriorating health inhibited his efforts at vindication and he died in France, on his way to a more congenial climate. Although his ventures were expensive failures in his lifetime, Selkirk is best remembered as an earnest and articulate advocate of the right of cultural minorities to preserve their way of life through resettlement in BNA, and as an early opponent of efforts by the British government to restrict emigration as a way of improving living standards. J.M. BUMSTED

Selkirk Communications Limited is among Canada's largest broadcasting group owners, with 14 radio stations (Vancouver, Calgary, Edmonton, Blairmore, Lethbridge, Grand Prairie, Elkford and Vernon), television stations (CFAC-TV in Calgary-Lethbridge, CHCH-TV in Hamilton, and partial owner of CHEK-TV, CHAN-TV and CHBC-TV in BC), a half interest in CABLE-TELEVISION systems serving Winnipeg and Ottawa, and a 15% interest in Canadian Satellite Communications Inc (CANCOM). Selkirk's international holdings include interests in radio stations and cable television in the UK; cable television in the US; the manufacture and sale of security systems in Canada and the US; the marketing of broadcasting advertising in Canada, the US and the UK; and radio news services in Canada and the UK. Selkirk also owns Quality Records, a manufacturer and distributor of phonograph records and audiotapes in Canada and the US. In 1983, total assets of Selkirk were $194 million, with revenues of $149 million.

PETER S. ANDERSON

Selkirk Mountains are ranges in southeastern BC between the COLUMBIA R on the W and the valley of KOOTENAY LK. Around ROGERS PASS in Glacier National Park and N to the ROCKY MOUNTAIN TRENCH are many impressive peaks (to 3593 m) with spectacular relief. The more accessible southern ranges were settled in the 1880s, when mining activity drew prospectors from the northwestern US. Small silver mines are still operating in the Slocan Valley. Successive waves of settlers in the Kootenay and Slocan valleys have included religious groups like the DOUKHOBORS. TRAIL is the industrial centre of the Kootenay region; NELSON and CASTLEGAR are forest-products manufacturing centres. PETER GRANT

Sellar, Robert Watson, politician (b at Huntingdon, Qué 6 Aug 1894; d at Ottawa 4 Jan 1965). Born into a prominent publishing family, Sellar tried various careers before securing a berth in Ottawa as private secretary. He became assistant deputy minister of finance in 1930 and then was treasury comptroller 1932-40. Appointed auditor general in 1940, Sellar reorganized the office, employing a system of personal cajolery and private reproaches. Retiring in 1959, Sellar became royal commissioner examining problems of government organization.

ROBERT BOTHWELL

Selwyn, Alfred Richard Cecil, geologist (b at Kilmington, Eng 28 July 1824; d at Vancouver 19 Oct 1902). A natural interest in GEOLOGY was encouraged by Selwyn's education in Switzerland. In 1845 he was assistant geologist with the Geological Survey of Great Britain, in 1852 director of the Geological Survey of Victoria, Australia, and in 1869 succeeded Sir W.E. LOGAN as director of the GEOLOGICAL SURVEY OF CANADA. Selwyn's directorship coincided with Canada's territorial expansion to the Pacific, necessitating a complex expansion of the GSC as a bureaucratic and scientific institution. In addition, Selwyn carried out much fieldwork himself, surveying southern BC in 1871 and helping establish a route for the CPR in 1875. He also made studies of the eastern Canadian goldfields. As an outsider replacing a man of Logan's stature during a crucial period in Canadian history, Selwyn was in a difficult position, but he ably supervised the GSC's enormous growth and solved some of its theoretical problems. SUZANNE ZELLER

Reading: Morris Zaslow, *Reading the Rocks* (1975).

Selwyn Mountains straddle the Yukon-NWT border, trending northwestward. They comprise chains of glaciated mountain peaks, ridges, plateaus and U-shaped valleys, and are composed of faulted, folded and intruded sedimentary rocks. Named for A.R.C. SELWYN, director of the Geological Survey of Canada 1869-95, their peaks range in altitude from 2130 to 2740 m. The highest mountain is Keele Peake 2972 m. Major ice fields cover Keele Peake, the Itsi Range and the Ragged Range. The Selwyns were virtually unexplored and unmapped until after WWII. LIONEL E. JACKSON, JR

Selye, Hans, endocrinologist, world-famous pioneer and popularizer of research on "biological stress" in human individuals and groups (b at Vienna, Austria 26 Jan 1907; d at Montréal 16 Oct 1982). Educated in Prague, Paris and Rome, he joined the staff of McGill in 1932. He became the first director of the Institute of Experimental Medicine and Surgery at U de M (1945) and guided its activities until his 1976 retirement. In 1977 he founded the International Institute of Stress, based in his own home.

His theorizing about a General Adaptation Syndrome based on much experimentation on rats, provoked much controversy. Briefly put, his model suggests that all stimuli are "stressors" which produce a general response of "stress" in the affected person. (Selye later claimed that he was hampered by his inadequate English and "should have called my syndrome the 'strain syndrome.'") For Selye, "stress plays some role in the development of every disease" and is "the non-specific response of the body to any demand made upon it." This process, which he called the General Adaptation Syndrome, has 3 phases: alarm, resistance and exhaustion. Failure to "cope adequately" with stressors results in and is displayed by "diseases of adaptation" (eg, high blood pressure, gastric and duodenal ulcers, various mental disorders). Later, Selye spoke of 2 major types of "stress": "pleasant or curative stress" ("eustress") and "unpleasant or disease-producing stress" ("distress"). He also had earlier flirted with the idea that an entire "nation" could experience a General Adaptation Syndrome, whereby, in a situation of mass "frustration" and insecurity, "the incidence of all stress diseases will increase."

A prolific author and lecturer, he strove to make his ideas accessible to the general public in writings such as *The Stress of Life* (1956; rev ed 1976); *Stress without Distress* (1974), and his autobiography, *The Stress of My Life* (1977; 2nd ed 1979). Although he received many honours including some 20 honorary degrees and was a companion of the Order of Canada, he never received a Nobel Prize, an honour he may have deserved for his pioneering work. Selye's overly "biological" focus ignored or underestimated the role played by the person's psychology and culture in shaping and affecting the body's physiology, and his theoretical model has now been superseded by the "cognitive" models of stress and coping put forward by psychologist Richard Lazarus (U of Calif, Berkeley) and others. Nevertheless, Selye's pioneering influences on the study of stress cannot be forgotten.

D. PAUL LUMSDEN

Semaines sociales du Canada, annual conferences started in 1920 by Jesuit Fr Joseph-Papin Archambault and organizers from the Ecole sociale populaire. The goal was to train an elite who would spread a Christian spirit and the church's SOCIAL DOCTRINE throughout Québec's mores, institutions and laws. Participating intellectuals applied the teachings of papal encyclicals — especially *Rerum Novarum,* the basis of Action sociale — to the social questions of trade unionism, the family, rural life, education, etc. Like the Roman Catholic Church with which it was linked, the semaines sociales were much more popular before WWII than after, although meetings continued until 1962. FERNANDE ROY

Séminaire de Québec, an educational institution consisting of the Grand Séminaire and the Petit Séminaire. The former, fd 26 Mar 1663 by Mgr François de LAVAL, was to train priests and guarantee parish ministries and evangelization throughout the diocese. In 1665 it was affiliated with the Séminaire des Missions Étrangères de Paris. The Petit Séminaire opened Oct 1668, accepting Indian and French students who were going to study at the Collège des Jésuites. In 1692 the Séminaire de Québec was forced to give up control of parish ministries and become merely a centre for the training of priests, under the ultimate control of the bishop. The CONQUEST (1760) ended its control of the presbytery of Québec and of the missions in Illinois; in 1768 affiliation with the Séminaire des Missions Étrangères de Québec also ended. Three years earlier the Petit Séminaire had become a college, teaching the *cours classique* (liberal arts) along

Le Séminaire de Québec (*photo © Hartill Art Associates*).

Jesuit lines and accepting students who did not intend to become priests. In 1852 the Séminaire de Québec was asked to found UNIVERSITÉ LAVAL and provide its first officials; it became the centre of the Faculty of Arts, with which all seminaries and colleges in the province had to be affiliated. In 1964 the liberal-arts course was divided into a secondary section and a college section (the final 3 classes). When the Québec government took over control of the entire educational system, the Séminaire de Québec remained a private institution. It was recognized as being of public interest in 1969, and its students in the college section took the public program of general education in preparation for all university faculties. Since 1971 women have also been accepted into the college section.

Architecture The Séminaire's buildings are laid out according to 17th-century planning principals, with wings or pavilions arranged around interior courtyards reached through a covered carriageway. The principal quadrilateral, though composed of buildings ranging in age from the 17th to early 20th centuries, displays features characteristic of French regime public architecture: rubble masonry covered with stucco, or *crépi,* casement windows with small panes of glass, steep roofs with dormers, and massive chimneys set in raised firewalls. Of particular note are the Bursar's wing, designed from 1678 to 1681 by architect Claude BAILLIFF and restored in 1866 after a fire, which conserves intact its vaulted kitchen, and Mgr Briand's chapel with its delicate alterpiece carved in 1785-86 by joiner Pierre Emond.

NIVE VOISINE AND CHRISTINA CAMERON

Semlin, Charles Augustus, prospector, schoolteacher, rancher, premier of BC (b at Barrie, UC Oct 1836; d at Ashcroft, BC 3 Nov 1927). After teaching in Barrie, Semlin came to BC in 1862, buying the Dominion Ranch in 1869. Elected Conservative MLA for Yale in 1871, he was defeated in 1875. Re-elected in 1882 he became leader of the Opposition in 1894 and premier in Aug 1898, but his government was defeated in 1900. Semlin himself was defeated in the ensuing election but regained his seat in a by-election in 1903. When MCBRIDE called an election shortly after, Semlin retired to his Cariboo ranch, where he remained active in ranching and stockbreeding associations. SYDNEY W. JACKMAN

Semple, Robert, governor of HBC territories (b at Boston, Mass 26 Feb 1777; d at RED RIVER COLONY 19 June 1816). The son of Loyalists, he went into business and travelled widely. He wrote numerous books describing his experiences, including *Walks and Sketches at the Cape of Good Hope* (1803), *Observations on a Journey through Spain and Italy to Naples, and thence to Smyrna and Constantinople* (1807) and *Sketch of the Present State of Caracas* (1812). Through Lord SELKIRK's influence, Semple succeeded Miles MACDONELL in 1815 as governor of the HBC, at a time of great rivalry with the North West Co. In March 1816 he destroyed the Nor'Westers' fort at Red River settlement. On 19 June, he and his party were killed by Nor'Westers at SEVEN OAKS. D. EVANS

Senate Upper House of PARLIAMENT, appointed by the GOVERNOR GENERAL on the advice of the PRIME MINISTER. It has 104 members; 24 from the Maritimes (NS and NB 10 each, PEI 4), 24 from Quebec, 24 from Ontario, 24 from the western provinces (6 each), 6 from Newfoundland, one from the Yukon, and one from the NWT. There is also a provision, never used, for 4 or 8 extra senators, drawn equally from the first 4 divisions. Until 1965 appointments were for life, but are now until age 75.

Senators must be subjects of the Queen, at least 30 years old, hold unencumbered real property worth at least $4000, reside in the designated area, and in Quebec (divided into 24 senatorial divisions) reside or have their real property in the division for which they are appointed. Senators lose their seats if they become aliens; become bankrupt, insolvent or public defaulters; are attainted or convicted of felony or any infamous crime; lose their residence or property qualification; or are absent for 2 consecutive sessions of Parliament. They receive a sessional indemnity of $48 600 (1984) and a tax-free expense allowance of $7900 (both partially indexed for increases in the cost of living), mail privileges, free coach-class rail transportation, and a limited amount of free air transportation.

Created under the CONSTITUTION ACT, 1867, to provide what George-Etienne CARTIER called a "power of resistance to oppose the democratic element" (on the Senate chamber walls still hangs a quote from Cicero, "It is the duty of the nobles to oppose the fickleness of the multitudes"), the Senate was designed to protect regional interests. The HOUSE OF COMMONS was to be elected on the basis of representation by population. In 1867 Ontario was the most populous, fastest-growing province, but Quebec and the Maritimes were more important to the national economy than their population suggested, and their interests were by no means identical with Ontario's. They dared not leave matters such as tariffs, taxation and railways to the mercy of an Ontario-dominated Commons, and they insisted on equal regional representation in the Upper House, without which there would have been NO CONFEDERATION. The Senate was not set up to represent provincial governments or legislatures, or to protect them against federal invasion of their powers. The protection of provincial interests in matters under federal jurisdiction soon fell mainly to the ministers from each province in the federal CABINET.

The first Cabinet had 5 ministers in the Senate out of a total of 13. From 1911 to 1979, there were seldom more than 2, often only one. From 1979 until their electoral success in 1984, however, the Conservatives have had to eke out their Quebec and French Canadian representation for the Cabinet, and the Liberals their western representation, by choosing ministers from the Senate.

The Senate was intended also to provide "sober second thought" on legislation (though the Commons has passed very few bills that even the Senate could consider radical) and to protect minorities, but although the Senate was responsible for establishing official BILINGUALISM in the original North-West Territories, it has not been very effective in this role, partly because the Commons has done the job so effectively.

The Senate has legal powers almost equal to those of the House of Commons, but it cannot initiate or raise amounts in money bills (supply and revenue) and has only a 180-day veto on constitutional amendments. It must pass, amend or defeat Commons' bills. It has not in fact vetoed a bill for more than 40 years and has been restrained in its lawmaking and surveillance, preferring not to excite the periodic agitation for Senate abolition or reform. It did kill a bill on customs-tariff legislation in 1961 by insisting on an amendment the Commons

View of the Senate Chamber in the Parliament Buildings, Ottawa (*courtesy National Film Board/Photothèque*).

refused to accept. It has also dropped 3 bills: one to remove the governor of the BANK OF CANADA (who removed himself by resigning), one because the proposed legislation was beyond the powers of the federal Parliament, and one because it would have legalized a marriage which was already legal. The amendments the Senate makes now are almost always those to clarify, simplify and tidy proposed legislation. Its COMMITTEES have also produced careful studies on UNEMPLOYMENT, LAND USE, SCIENCE POLICY, POVERTY, AGING, the mass media (*see* COMMUNICATIONS) and INDIAN AFFAIRS. It is usually less partisan in its operations than the House of Commons, but in certain areas, eg, tax reform, the heavy representation of lawyers and businessmen, many of whom hold positions with private companies, is reflected in its reactions. The Senate's legally absolute veto was expected to be really no more than a delaying veto because, until the late 1860s, governments were usually short-lived, and none, it seemed, would be able to build up a large enough majority in the Senate to block a successor government of the opposition party. But most Canadian governments since then have been long-lived, and as appointments are almost invariably partisan, the Senate has often had a large opposition majority, and for the last 20 years a heavy preponderance of Liberals.

A traditional objection to the Senate is that PATRONAGE appointees have no right to a position of authority in a democracy. Proposals to make the Senate more representative of regional interests were introduced by the Liberal government in 1978 but received little support. Some provinces have proposed that Senate appointments be a provincial responsibility (*see* Task Force on CANADIAN UNITY). Senators could act as provincial delegates, although critics charge that such a system would run counter to the principles of FEDERALISM. The powers of the Senate, the method of selecting senators and the proportionate representation of the provinces cannot be altered except by constitutional amendment approved by Parliament and by the legislatures of at least 7 provinces representing at least 50% of the country's population. EUGENE A. FORSEY

Seneca, the farthest west and most populous member of the IROQUOIS Confederacy, played a major role in the dispersal of the HURON, PETUN and NEUTRAL in the mid-17th century. Much of southern Ontario then became Seneca hunting territory, until OJIBWA expansion into this region confined Seneca influence to S of the Great Lakes. Periodically at war with New France, all Seneca villages were burned by Gov DENONVILLE in 1687. Revenge was extracted through the destruction of Lachine, outside Montréal, 2 years later (*see* IROQUOIS WARS). After construction of the French post at Niagara in the 1720s, the western Seneca frequently sided with the French in conflicts with the English. With the expulsion of French power from the Great Lakes, these same western Seneca in 1763 joined PONTIAC and his followers against the English, who had taken possession of the region. During the AMERICAN REVOLUTION, the full weight of Seneca arms supported the royal cause, but the Seneca, except for a small segment, chose not to follow Joseph BRANT after the war to a new homeland in Canada. They negotiated peace with the Americans, and still reside on reservations in the US guaranteed at that time. In 1799 HANDSOME LAKE experienced a vision which led to a regeneration of traditional Iroquois religion. *See* NATIVE PEOPLE: EASTERN WOODLANDS and general articles under NATIVE PEOPLE.   THOMAS S. ABLER

Reading: B.G. Trigger, ed, *Handbook of North American Indians*, vol 15: *Northeast* (1978); A.F.C. Wallace, *Death and Rebirth of the Seneca* (1969).

Senécal, Louis-Adélard, businessman, politician (b at Varennes, LC 10 July 1829; d at Montréal 11 Oct 1887). A colourful and controversial public figure, Senécal was considered by some contemporaries as the symbol of French Canada's economic awakening and by others as dishonesty incarnate with both hands in the public purse. Beginning in the regional grain trade of the Richelieu valley, he took advantage of opportunities offered by the 1854 Reciprocity Treaty with the US to establish himself in shipping, sawmilling and real-estate speculation. In 1867 his annual volume of business was estimated at $3 million. A Liberal, he sat as a Québec MLA 1867-71 and federal MP 1867-72. Financial difficulties, however, occupied most of his time during these years. He turned his attention to railway construction in the early 1870s. With the Liberals in opposition in Québec, he changed his allegiance to the provincial Bleus in 1874, and his assistance in returning the Bleus to power in 1879 earned for him the position of superintendent of the government-owned Quebec, Montreal, Ottawa and Occidental Railway 1880-82. In 1884 Senécal failed to gain the British and French financial support he sought for 3 multimillion-dollar projects, including a transatlantic cable, because of doubts circulated by the Canadian press as to his business ethics. He then turned to the Richelieu and Ontario Navigation Co, having replaced Sir Hugh ALLAN as president in 1882. He was named to the Senate on 25 Jan 1887.   JOHN KEYES

Senneterre, Qué, Town, pop 4339 (1981c), is located 130 km E of Rouyn-Noranda in Québec's Abitibi region. It was founded around 1914 with the arrival of the Transcontinental Railway. At that time, it was called Nottaway, after the river that flowed alongside the railway, one of the largest rivers in the Abitibi region. Senneterre became a township municipality in 1919 and a town in 1959. Located in the eastern part of the Abitibi region, it has grown because of its sawmills and CNR station. The town took its name from Henri de Senneterre, duc de la Ferté, a commander in Montcalm's army.

BENOÎT-BEAUDRY GOURD

Separate School In both the US and Canada parents are free to choose to send their children to the state-run public SCHOOL SYSTEM or to a variety of private fee-paying schools. In Canada, several provinces, through systems of public separate schools or public support of PRIVATE SCHOOLS, allow families greater choice, usually on the basis of denominationalism. A strict interpretation of the doctrine of the separation of church and state in the US, however, restricts choice somewhat. For parents there, education ceases to be free if they decline to exercise their prior right to send their children to the public schools. In contrast to US constitutionalism, under which state aid is denied to separate schools, Canadians have used constitutional provisions to guarantee state aid to such schools.

The basic framework for Canada's use of public monies for separate and denominational schools and, more generally, for the relation between the state and schooling was established in the 19th century. Fundamental to the creation of a system of free and universal education was the notion, then common, that education and religion were inseparable and that the state had a responsibility to foster, wherever possible, a harmonious relationship between them. Religion in education was important, even essential, to both Protestants and Catholics.

Many residents of the British N American colonies became convinced that it was essential to organize truly public common schools for all children to attend. This conviction was spurred by the fear of both denominational fractionalism and US republican influence, but nondenominational public schools were also seen as an effective nation-building instrument. In Nova Scotia and New Brunswick, for example, separate denominational schools were regarded as socially divisive. In contrast, in Upper and Lower Canada the trend was to accept dissentient and separate schools as a way to maintain some publicly controlled uniformity while also recognizing the validity of certain minority rights. This pattern was duplicated elsewhere later, eg, in Saskatchewan and Alberta, with the result that the Canadian practice generally became one of subsidizing the education of some religious minorities in confessional, separate and dissentient schools. The accommodation of these minorities was made for educational, not religious reasons, reflecting a consensus that the parent is an important agent of education and that schools should be responsive to parental demands in matters relating to moral and religious education.

The situation in early and mid-19th-century Canada was strikingly different from that in the US, primarily because of the great political power of those associated with the dominant Church of England in the early days of UPPER CANADA and because of the existence of a French Catholic majority in LOWER CANADA. These 2 conditions and the tensions they engendered, with non-Anglican Protestant and Catholics fighting for their legitimate rights in Upper Canada and Anglo-Protestants seeking security against French Catholic domination in Lower Canada, impelled the state to avoid establishing a nondenominational common school system and moved it instead to assume legal protection and support for denominationally based schooling. These arrangements were enshrined in the CONSTITUTION ACT, 1867, and despite a growing secularization and increased homogenization among Protestant denominations in the 20th century, the responsibility of the state to support denominational schools in some form has remained intact in most provinces. The concept that church and state are partners, not hostile and incompatible forces that must be kept at a distance, has made it possible for educational authorities in Canada to subsidize Jewish schools in Québec and Hutterite schools on the Prairies, to condone Amish schools in Ontario, and to permit the Salvation Army to develop its own public schools in Newfoundland.

By 1867 each of the 4 colonies of British N America that formed the Dominion of Canada had its own system of common schools. After Confederation, by the provisions of section 93 of the Constitution Act, 1867, each province maintained exclusive jurisdiction over its own educational structure. The effect of subsection 1 of s93 was to give all legally established existing denominational schools at the time of Confederation perpetual rights to public funds. What was left unsaid, however, was that denominational schools established by custom but not by law were not guaranteed the same right to existence.

In the wake of the Constitution Act, 1867, the provinces were free to forge their own education statutes, subject to the guarantees for denominational schools already legally established. Five different administrative arrangements emerged. In Québec a dual confessional public school system developed, composed of 2 separate and independent streams, Catholic and Protestant, representing the 2 confessions of Western Christianity. In each school district, the confessional schools of the minority were known as dissentient schools, but like the majority's public common schools, they controlled their own curriculum, teacher training and inspection through their confessional section of the Council of Public Instruction (now Ministry of Education). After the establishment of a provincial ministry of education in 1964, however, confessional autonomy was considerably reduced to the point where the 2 branches now essentially share a common curriculum.

Ontario, Saskatchewan and Alberta established a separate school system, normally Protestant or Catholic segregated confessional systems, along with the common nonsectarian public schools. Both the separate schools and the nonsectarian public schools were and are administered by either a department or ministry of education with control over curriculum, teacher training and certification, special programs and inspection. Nova Scotia, New Brunswick, PEI and Manitoba adopted informal arrangements for funding denominational schools. (Between 1871 and 1890 Manitoba had the dual confessional system, ie, Catholic and Protestant, similar to that of Québec. From then until the late 1960s it granted no aid to any religious group.) Officially, in these provinces, there are single nonsectarian public school systems. In practice, however, political compromises and administrative leeway over the years allowed Catholic schools to receive state funds with varying degrees of state supervision attached. Thus a separate school system has virtually come into being in all but name.

Newfoundland and BC until quite recently, have represented the poles of Canadian funding patterns. Before the late 1960s, Newfoundland provided support exclusively for denominational schools; thus a truly denominational public school system was in operation. Then, in March 1969 the Anglican Church, United Church and Salvation Army signed a Document of Integration, which the Presbyterian Church later accepted. Each church thereby relinquished its right to operate its own schools, but retained an executive secretary to advise the provincial department of education on denominational questions. The other denominations — Roman Catholic, Pentecostal Assemblies and Seventh Day Adventist — also appointed executive secretaries to the Denominational Education Commission operating outside the department but advisory to it. Until 1977, BC alone among the provinces funded no religiously based schools. The first school legislation enacted by the new province's legislature in 1872 established free nonsectarian public schools, thereby invoking the doctrine of the separation of church and state. The public system remains intact but, with the passage of Bill 33 in 1977, BC now provides funding to private denominational and nondenominational schools.

The organizational structure, assumptions and practices that emerged a century ago have been contested, often bitterly, and occasionally modified, but on the whole there was little substantive administrative change between the end of the century and the 1960s. Over the years Canadian courts have established that denominational rights with respect to schooling are based on religion, not language, and that the religion of the parent is the decisive factor. However, parents do not always have a free choice as to which school, public or separate, their children may attend, nor for which they shall be taxed. In Ontario, for example, a Catholic parent may elect the school system to which his or her taxes go; the children will then attend the system to which such taxes are paid. Although a Catholic may choose to be a public school supporter, however, a non-Catholic may not elect to support a Catholic separate school. In Saskatchewan, if a separate school exists in a district the taxpayer has no choice but to support the school operated by members of his or her denomination. In Alberta, once a Roman Catholic separate school district is established, all Catholic residents are separate school supporters and all non-Catholic residents are public school supporters. In Edmonton, Calgary and Saskatoon the school boards have arranged that non-Catholic children may attend Catholic separate schools and Catholic children may attend public schools at no cost. But it is not clear whether non-Catholics can be separate school supporters even if they declare themselves Catholic for tax purposes. In Alberta and Saskatchewan there was equal provision of corporation taxes, larger units and secondary schools to both streams. In Ontario, however, not only were non-Catholic parents denied the right to choose Catholic schooling for their children, but equal public support for both systems soon disappeared and funding for separate schools was not extended beyond grade 10 until Sept 1985. In June 1984 Prem William DAVIS announced, amid considerable controversy, that his government would extend public funding of separate schools beyond the previous limit of grade 10 through to grade 13.

Despite these striking differences among the provinces, certain factors remain common: the property tax remains the basic source of all school revenue; public schools, whether separate or common, are on the whole tuition-free; a centralized administrative structure (though varying in power) is in place in each province and normally exercises a similar supervisory role over both public and separate schools; until the 1960s all provinces insisted upon religious instruction in all public schools and religious exercises (the Lord's Prayer, Bible reading from selected passages) to open the day; and funding arrangements are quite similar in a number of provinces.

In the past 20 years a number of significant changes have occurred and political controversy over separate school funding has intensified. The changes result from several developments. The growing importance of education as a means of access to the labour market, manifest in the conversion of the secondary school into a mass institution and the rapid expansion of post-secondary schooling, increased the financial costs of providing separate schools and raised questions about the adequacy of the secular instruction available within them. In both cases, separate school advocates had a larger stake in gaining more public funds. The consolidation of small school districts into larger units often meant that ethnically or denominationally homogeneous schools were converted into more heterogeneous institutions, complicating or eliminating the monolithic basis of the original schools. This was particularly true in Atlantic Canada. The centralization of funding at the provincial level replaced the previous dominance of locally based financing and usually coincided with larger funding. Simultaneously, however, centralization tended to increase state supervisory powers and led to a diminution of autonomy among schools accepting provincial funds. The expansion of provincial involvement in schools and the growing importance of schooling itself affected separate school funding and church-state relations in every province.

Atlantic Canada presents a typical picture of how efforts to modernize the public schools reduced both the informal and formal authority and autonomy previously held by the Catholic denominational schools. In Nova Scotia, New Brunswick and PEI informal agreements continue to link church and state in education, allowing, for example, teachers in public schools in Catholic areas to wear religious dress, but the effort by provincial governments to improve educational services through more efficient and economic organizational structures, by centralizing and consolidating funding so as to distribute public money more equitably and by increasing supervisory control over all schools, seriously challenged the denominational basis of schooling. Likewise, although denominationalism remained in Newfoundland, it is now confined to an advisory rather than a policy-making role.

The politics of separate-school funding in Ontario is in many ways unique. Thanks to recent large-scale immigration from Catholic Europe (from countries such as Italy and Portugal), 37% of Ontario's population is Catholic and about 30% of elementary school pupils are in separate schools. Of the 177 elementary school boards, 60 are Catholic and only one is Protestant. Public funding for separate schools is 95% of that provided public schools on a per pupil basis. For Francophones in some regions of the province, there was (until Sept 1985) another way to receive public funds for Catholic students in grades 11 to 13: they attended public French secondary schools. Significantly, this required a shift in emphasis from religion to ethnicity and language.

The extraordinary growth in the past 2 decades of enrolments in separate and nonpublic denominational schools and the increased political power of denominational groups attest to the importance parents attach to schooling as a means of preserving religio-cultural values and improving economic position. Other groupings of parents with language, ethnocultural or educational interests not currently served in public or grant-aided private schools are likely to emerge and demand support in a version of Canadian educational pluralism unmatched since the pre-public-school era of the mid-19th century. By the mid-1980s denominationalism had gained an educational prominence few would have predicted 20 years ago. J. DONALD WILSON

Separatism, the advocacy of separation or secession by a group or people of a particular subunit or section from a larger political unit to which it belongs. In modern times, separatism is frequently identified with a desire for freedom from perceived colonial oppression. It is a term commonly associated with various movements in Québec in the 1960s. Some of these movements merged to form the PARTI QUÉBÉCOIS, which abandoned the term separatism for "independence" and for the more complex SOVEREIGNTY-ASSOCIATION.

The first full-fledged secessionist movement in Canada emerged in Nova Scotia shortly after Confederation in response to economic grievances, but it was quickly defeated. No other serious separatist force appeared in an English-speaking province for another century. In Québec the Manifesto of the PATRIOTES in the REBELLIONS OF 1837 included a declaration that the province secede from Canada. After the defeat of

that rebellion, separatism no longer existed as a genuine component of the conservative FRENCH CANADIAN NATIONALISM which emerged and which was dominant for over a century in Québec. There were, however, isolated advocates of the doctrine of separatism, eg, the journalist Jules-Paul TARDIVEL, and occasional flirtations with it in the early 1920s and mid-1930s by strong nationalists such as Abbé Lionel GROULX and his followers.

The separatist movement reemerged as a political force in modern Québec in the late 1950s and the 1960s, a time of great socioeconomic change and nationalist ferment in that province. The earliest organizational signs of this rejuvenation were the right-wing secessionist Alliance laurentienne (1957), the left-wing Action socialiste pour l'indépendance du Québec (1960) and, most important, the centre-left Rassemblement pour l'indépendance nationale (RIN) in the 1960s. The RIN first competed electorally in 1966, and together with its right-of-centre offshoot, the Ralliement national, garnered over 9% of the Québec vote. Some violent radical fringe movements committed to independence also operated in the province during this decade, most notably the FRONT DE LIBÉRATION DU QUÉBEC (FLQ), which attained notoriety in the OCTOBER CRISIS of 1970.

Popular support for separatism in Québec and for the organizations which represented it rapidly increased in the province in the late 1960s and the 1970s, particularly after the Parti Québécois was formed in 1968. The party was able to rally most of the province's political groups to its program of political independence coupled with economic association ("sovereignty-association") with English-speaking Canada. Founded and led by the dynamic René LÉVESQUE, in 1970 the PQ gained 23% of the popular vote in Québec and won 7 seats. In 1973 it increased its support to 30% of the vote and, despite its reduction to 6 seats, became the official Opposition. On 15 Nov 1976 it swept to power, with 41% of the popular vote and 71 seats, on a promise to delay any move toward independence until after the people of Québec had been consulted in a referendum, which was to be held before the end of its electoral mandate. During the next 3 years Lévesque's government attempted to flesh out its separatist option, which it published in the form of a White Paper on Sovereignty-Association in 1979. The White Paper envisaged full exercise of sovereignty for Québec and a few institutions in common with Canada, eg, a community council, secretariat, monetary authority and court. The QUÉBEC REFERENDUM campaign was launched shortly afterwards. The people of Québec were asked for a mandate to negotiate sovereignty-association with the rest of Canada. Although this was only a mild expression of the independence option, it was decisively rejected on 20 May 1980 by about 60% of the Québec electorate, including a majority of the French-speaking population. Despite the referendum defeat, which constituted a severe setback for the separatist cause, the PQ was re-elected in 1981 on a program that included a promise to defer the independence question for at least another full term of office. Polls taken from 1981 to 1985 showed a declining interest in the independence issue among Quebeckers as well as plummetting support for the PQ. In Jan 1985 the PQ Party voted to shelve the independence option in the next provincial election. Although this resulted in the defection of many prominent Cabinet ministers, it did cause an improvement in the popularity of the PQ among voters.

The modern form of separatism in Québec has been particularly popular among the new middle classes, especially those linked to state structures and with aspirations for upward mobility in other expanding bureaucratic sectors of soci-

ety. The principal adherents of the Parti Québécois, both within the rank and file and the leadership, have been certain liberal professionals (eg, teachers, administrators and media specialists), white-collar workers and students. There has also been considerable support from trade-union members. There is relatively poor support from the business sector and from the traditional liberal professions such as law and medicine. This is not surprising, since both the ideology of independence and the social-democratic orientation of the PQ appeal to those favouring an expanding state apparatus and the strengthening of French-language institutions in Québec. Francophone businessmen and traditional professionals are more sympathetic to pan-Canadian political appeals, which are more in tune with their national economic interests.

In English Canada, recent disaffection with the policies of the federal government has helped spawn some separatist activity as well. The DENE people of the Mackenzie District of the NWT attracted some attention by invoking the right of self-determination in their testimony to the Berger Commission on the MACKENZIE VALLEY PIPELINE in 1976. Since that time, however, the Dene have made it clear that they are only seeking a greater measure of political autonomy within the NWT, not outright political independence or secession from Canada (see NORTH).

After the failure of the negotiations on constitutional revision in Sept 1980, and the announcement of the federal government's National Energy Policy the following month, separatist sentiment rose dramatically in Alberta and moderately in BC, although it actually declined slightly in Saskatchewan and Manitoba. It was widely viewed as a more extreme manifestation of historically deep-rooted western attitudes of alienation and protest against central Canada and the federal government. Separatism was embodied in the Western Canada Concept Party, an amalgam of 2 earlier provincial political organizations. Its objectives were to rectify perceived injustices in western Canada concerning such matters as freight rates, tariff barriers, oil pricing, bilingualism and western representation in the federal governing party and, failing that, to secede from Canada. It was difficult to characterize those predisposed to western separatism by the usual indicators, eg, age, education, income or occupation. The major differences of opinion occurred among the 4 provinces and among supporters of the national political parties. Polls conducted Mar 1981 found that 79% of the Progressive Conservative respondents felt that the West "might as well go it alone." The figure for the NDP was 46% and for the Liberals only 28%. In that poll, 11% of Albertans supported outright western independence. In Feb 1982 a separatist candidate succeeded in gaining a seat in a by-election for the Alberta legislature though he was defeated in the following provincial election. Internal wrangling and splits in the separatist party and some improvement in the climate of Ottawa-western Canada relations have since resulted in a decline in the separatist party's popularity.

MICHAEL STEIN

Reading: R. Lévesque, *An Option* for Québec (1968); M. Rioux, *Québec in Question* (1978); M. Watkins, ed, *Dene Nation* (1977).

Sept-Îles, Qué, City, pop 29 262 (1981c), inc 1951, metropolis of the North Shore region and centre of its mining industry, is located on the ST LAWRENCE R, 230 km NE of Baie-Comeau. It is one of Canada's most important seaports. The site, visited by MONTAGNAIS-NASKAPI tribes, was known to BASQUE fishermen long before 1535, when Jacques CARTIER named it — after the 7 islands that protect access to the bay. The first permanent European settlement dates from 1651: the Ange-Gardien mission founded by Father Jean de Quen. A trading and fishing post set up

there in 1676 by Louis JOLLIET was ceded in the 19th century to the HUDSON'S BAY CO. At the start of the 20th century, Sept-Îles had only 200 inhabitants, mostly ACADIANS by birth, living from fishing, plus 600 Montagnais on the reserve. In 1908 development of the pulp industry at Clarke City caused an influx of new workers. The exploitation of the mining resources of the hinterland, starting in the 1950s, led to rapid expansion of the city and it became the nerve centre of activities related to the exploitation of the mineral and IRON ORE deposits of Nouvelle Québec and Labrador. Its port was improved in 1954 and 1970 to receive the massive cargo of ore brought down the QUEBEC, NORTH SHORE AND LABRADOR RY from SCHEFFERVILLE. Sept-Îles has a mineral processing plant. The Vieux-Poste, restored after archaeological digs, houses the Sept-Îles museum. CLAUDINE PIERRE-DESCHÊNES

Serbs are South Slavs. It is commonly believed that they migrated to the Balkans during the 6th and 7th centuries, where they constituted an independent South Slav state until the Turks invaded the Balkans. From 1804, when the Serbs initiated their struggle for national independence, to 1918 the princedom (later the kingdom) of Serbia evolved into a constitutional and democratic state. In 1918 Serbia, Montenegro and other lands united to form the kingdom of Serbs, Croats and Slovenes, which became Yugoslavia in 1929.

Today, Serbia is one of the 6 constituent republics comprising Yugoslavia and accounts for 41.5% of its population. Before 1900 immigrant Serbs were classified in the Canadian census as Austrians, Hungarians or Turks. In 1901 the term "Serbian" appeared in the census, although in succeeding years this group was again unlisted, reappearing eventually in official statistics as Serbo-Croats or Yugoslavs. Today, over 60 000 Canadians (of the quarter of a million Canadians of Yugoslavian ancestry) claim Serbian descent.

Migration and Settlement In the 1850s the first Serbs to immigrate to Canada (probably from Boka Kotorska on the southern Adriatic coast) settled in BC along the Fraser R and in Vancouver. Most of them were young, single men who worked in the mining and forest industries. The second wave arrived in the 1870s. In 1900 Serbs began to migrate to other provinces, particularly Saskatchewan; the Serbian community in Regina dates from this time. Between 1907 and 1908 many Serbs migrated to Canada from the US, working in coal mines around Lethbridge, Alta, building roads and working on the railway. Before WWI, Serbian communities were founded in Toronto, Hamilton and Niagara Falls, Ont. The third wave of immigration occurred between the wars, particularly 1924-29 and 1934-39. Most of these immigrants settled in industrial centres of Ontario. Of the fourth wave of immigrants (1947-1953), many were highly educated. Of the fifth group (generally university educated), after 1955, many were sponsored by family or friends.

Social and Cultural Life Serbian voluntary associations and organizations were established to ease the economic hardships of new immigrants and to help them adjust to Canadian society. Serbian organizations in Canada today

include the Serbian Brother's Help; Serbian National Shield Society of Canada; the Serbian National Defence; the Serbian National Heritage Academy; and the Serbian National Federation. Serbian cultural organizations include the Culture and Historical societies, "Njegos" and "Karadjordje," and several folklore organizations and youth groups, eg, the Strazhilova Choir of Toronto and Hajduk Veljko Dance Group. The first Serbian newspaper in Canada (1916) *Kanadski Glasnik* (*Canada Herald*) was followed by *Serbian Herald* and several others.

The first Serbian Day was held in Canada on 23 June 1946, and annual festivals, featuring singers and dancers, are sponsored by Serbian and other Yugoslav organizations. Several Serbian and Yugoslav radio programs are available to Serbians. In sports, they are known for their success in organizing soccer clubs.

Seventy percent of Serbs have maintained knowledge of the Serbian tongue, although there is some variation by occupation and group. Almost all Serbs adhere to the Orthodox Church. They have built some 15 churches and cultural centres across Canada. Those in Toronto, Windsor, Niagara Falls and Sudbury, Ont, are noteworthy for their Byzantine architectural design. VLADISLAV A. TOMOVIĆ

Reading: H.W.V. Temperley, *History of Serbia* (1969).

Serpent Mound, situated on a bluff overlooking Rice Lk in southern Ontario, is the only known effigy mound in Canada. It is a sinuous earthen structure, some 60 m long and 2 m high; excavation indicates that it was an accretion mound, gradually built up between 128 and 302 AD. Serpent Mound was a sacred place, visited periodically for religious ceremonies. Although grave furniture was sparse, distribution shows it was restricted to individuals of high status within the community, who were buried either at the base of the mound or in shallow, submound pits. Commoners were scattered throughout the mound fill. W.A. KENYON

Service, Robert William, poet, novelist (b at Preston, Eng 16 Jan 1874; d at Lancieux, France 11 Sept 1958). Educated in Scotland, Service worked in a bank after he left school. In 1894 he immigrated to Canada, where, after wandering from California to BC, he joined the Canadian Bank of Commerce. He was stationed throughout BC and eventually at Whitehorse and Dawson City. In 1907 he published his first collection of poems, *Songs of a Sourdough*; an immediate success, it was followed by *Ballads of a Cheechako* (1909) and *Rhymes of a Rolling Stone* (1912). Poems such as "The Shooting of Dan McGrew" assured Service of lasting fame and gave rise to his nicknames: "the Canadian Kipling" and "the Poet of the Yukon." During WWI he was an ambulance driver, and after the war he travelled throughout Europe but lived mostly in France. His later works include *Ballads of a Bohemian* (1921), *Rhymes of a Roughneck* (1950) and his autobiographical works: *Ploughman of the Moon* (1945) and *Harper of Heaven* (1948). DAVID EVANS

Service Industry The Canadian ECONOMY has 2 main components, the goods-producing sector and the service sector. The former includes agriculture, forestry, mining, fishing, construction and manufacturing. The latter includes noncommercial activities, such as health and welfare, EDUCATION, religion and charity; commercial services, such as restaurants, recreation, amusement, personal care, etc; trade including wholesale and retail; TRANSPORTATION, COMMUNICATIONS and utilities; and financial and legal, including INSURANCE, REAL ESTATE, BANKING and investment.

As Canada's population has grown and its economy has expanded, and as the goods-producing sector has increased its efficiency and productivity, there has been a steady growth in

the share of the working population employed in the service sector. In 1911 about 66% of the working population were employed directly in the goods-producing sector and 33% in the service sector; by 1981 these ratios had been reversed. As the farm population has declined the number of people employed in service activities has increased. At Confederation, 50% of the workforce was employed in agriculture, but by 1980 this had dropped to less than 5%.

From Confederation, 1867, to WWII there was steady but slow growth in the service sector but after WWII, as Canada exported more of its resource products and manufactured goods, more services could be afforded and employment in this area (particularly in education and health and welfare) mushroomed.

In addition to expansion of such personal services there has been significant growth in services provided to the goods-producing sector. This growth has resulted from increased output of that sector as well from new services that have become available through new technology. As the output of the goods sector increased it expanded the work of providing services for transporting goods, warehousing, ACCOUNTING, communications and other supporting activities. Certain service industries now provide functions previously performed internally by companies themselves, such as data processing and other computer services, professional consulting, industrial design and maintenance.

Commencing with the first industrial computer installation in Canada in 1957, new technology has vastly expanded the activities of the service sector by creating new functions, eg, the provision of "on-line" information to subscribers for financial and stock market data, weather reports and general news, or by increasing the efficiency of conducting existing functions, eg, automatic tellers in banking, vastly improved productivity in worldwide transactions through the use of computers and communication satellites. In the medical field new technologies have made it possible to provide new and better services for detection, prevention and correction of ailments.

Many organizations in the service sector are owned or regulated by governments, although in the 1970s and 1980s there has been some movement toward freer competition and less regulation arising to some extent from competitive pressures from the US, where a policy of deregulation was pursued during the early 1980s.

During the 1970s and early 1980s, Canadian industry faced increased competition from many countries. Initially, this had little direct effect on the service sector, but with the increasing intensity of the worldwide competition in the 1980s, the service industries have felt the pressure of foreign competition not only di-

Employment by Sector (000s) (Source: Historical Statistics of Canada, 2nd ed, 1982)				
	1911	1951	1971	1981
Total work force	2 725	5 286	8 627	12 005
Goods producing	1 720	2 773	2 995	3 800
Public administration and unspecified	188	389	1 295	1 293
Service industries				
– transportation	192	450	671	936
– retail and wholesale trade	260	746	1 269	1 956
– finance, insurance, real estate	37	144	358	621
– education	47	153	569)	
– health and welfare	34	174	513)	
– food and lodging	56	155	331)	3 399
– personal and recreation	138	187	253)	
– other services	53	115	373)	
Total service industries	817	2 124	4 337	6 912

rectly in activities such as data processing, banking and tourism, but also indirectly in activities such as communications and utilities.

In the 1960s and 1970s it was predicted by many that computers and other technological advancements would replace people and destroy jobs, but new products and services have also created jobs that were not available previously. The fastest-growing occupations since the advent of computers have been the secretarial, clerical, sales and other service-industry occupations. It is expected they will continue to be the fastest-growing occupations through the remainder of the 20th century. R.A. PHILLIPS

Seton, Ernest Thompson, author, naturalist, artist (b at S Shields, Eng 14 Aug 1860; d at Seton Village, Santa Fe, New Mex 23 Oct 1946). Educated at the Ontario College of Art, he continued his studies in London, Paris and New York. Settling in Manitoba, he began his lifetime study of wildlife. He published *The Birds of Manitoba* (1891) and was appointed Manitoba government naturalist. Moving to the US in 1896, he founded a youth group, the Woodcraft League 1902, and acted as chief of the Boy Scouts of America organization 1910-15. He spent his later years at his New Mexico institute of wildlife and woodcraft (est 1930). A prolific writer, and precursor of Kipling in the development of the anthropomorphic animal story, he wrote *Wild Animals I Have Known* (1898), *Lives of the Hunted* (1901), *The Arctic Prairies* (1911) and his autobiography, *Trail of an Artist-Naturalist* (1940). DAVID EVANS

Ernest Thompson Seton, naturalist whose prolific writings anticipated Kipling in the development of the anthropomorphic animal story (*courtesy Public Archives of Canada/C-9485*).

Seul, Lac, 1658 km², elev 357 m, 55 m deep, located in northwestern Ontario, 50 km N of Dryden, drains W via the English and WINNIPEG rivers to Lk WINNIPEG. It appears as "Lake Alone" — a literal translation of its present French name — on Peter POND's map of 1784. The Cree, who inhabited the area until the mid-18th century, were gradually displaced by the Ojibwa. Descendants of the latter now occupy the Lac Seul Reserve adjacent to the towns of Hudson and Sioux Lookout. Although the lake was off the main fur-trade routes, both the HBC and NWC were active in the area, and the former continues to be represented at Lac Seul Post. The lake supports a small commercial fishery, but present resource development is concentrated in

the forest industry. The unspoiled environment, with its abundant fish and wildlife, also makes this one of the prime outdoor recreation areas in northwestern Ontario. The natural capacity of Lac Seul is augmented by the diversion of water from the ALBANY R watershed, allowing hydroelectric stations at Ear Falls, where the English R leaves the lake, and Manitou Falls, 30 km downstream, to generate 90 600 kW of electricity. DAVID D. KEMP

Seven Oaks Incident, a violent encounter on 19 June 1816 at Seven Oaks, near the HBC's Ft Douglas in the RED RIVER COLONY, a manifestation of the struggle between the NWC and the HBC for control of the Northwest. In spring 1816 the HBC destroyed the NWC's Ft Gibraltar at the junction of the Red and Assiniboine rivers, just as pemmican was being moved down the Assiniboine to supply Nor'Westers returning from the annual council at FORT WILLIAM. The HBC then denied passage on the Red R both to the Nor'-Westers and to their Métis provisioners. Brandon House, an HBC post on the upper Assiniboine, was captured on June 1 by Métis under Cuthbert GRANT, who organized an escort to secure the pemmican supplies. Grant and his men, striking NE across the plain to meet the Nor'Westers, were intercepted by the HBC colony's governor, Robert SEMPLE, who with some 25 men had unwisely ventured out of Ft Douglas. Although the clash was not premeditated, the Métis quickly enveloped Semple's party and he and 20 of his men were killed. The Métis suffered only one casualty. The Seven Oaks "massacre" provoked Lord SELKIRK's retaliation on Ft William that winter. Lawsuits and countersuits ensued. Only Selkirk's death in 1820 cleared the way for an end to the rivalry; the companies merged in 1821. J.E. REA

Seven Years' War, 1756-63, was the first global war. The protagonists were Britain, Prussia and Hanover against France, Austria, Sweden, Saxony, Russia and eventually Spain. Britain declined to commit its main forces on the continent, where it depended on the Prussians and German mercenaries to defend George II's Electorate of Hanover. Britain's war aims were to destroy the French navy and merchant fleet, seize its colonies, and eliminate France as a commercial rival. France found itself committed to fighting in Europe to defend Austria, which could do nothing to aid France overseas.

Hostilities began in 1754 in America's Ohio

Valley when a Virginian major of militia, George Washington, ambushed a small French detachment. He was subsequently forced to accept humiliating terms dictated by the commander of the French force sent to bring him to account. The British then ordered 2 regiments, commanded by Maj-Gen Edward Braddock, to America. Other regiments were to be raised in the colonies, and a 4-pronged attack was to be launched against the French at FORT BEAUSÉJOUR on the border of NS, against their forts on Lk Champlain, and at Niagara, and against Ft Duquesne on the Ohio R.

On learning of these movements the French ordered 6 battalions under Baron Armand Dieskau to be sent to reinforce LOUISBOURG and Canada. Vice-Adm Edward Boscawen was then ordered to sail with his squadron to intercept and capture the French convoy, although war had not been declared. He captured only 2 ships. The British had even less success on land. The army advancing on Lk Champlain was stopped by the French near Lk George but Dieskau was wounded and taken prisoner. The proposed assault on Niagara collapsed through military ineptitude, and Braddock's 1500-man army was destroyed by a small detachment of French and Indians. Only in ACADIA did the British enjoy success. Ft Beauséjour with its small garrison was captured. The Acadian settlers were subsequently rounded up by the New England forces and deported.

In Apr 1756 more French troops and a new commander, the marquis de MONTCALM, arrived in Canada, and the next month Britain declared war. The strategy of the commander in chief and governor general, the marquis de VAUDREUIL, was to keep the British on the defensive and as far from Canadian settlements as possible. He captured the British forts at Oswego on Lk Ontario and thereby gained control of the Great Lakes. At the same time Canadian and Indian war parties ravaged the American frontier settlements. The Americans could not cope with these attacks and Britain was forced to send over 23 000 troops to the colonies and commit most of its navy to blockading the French ports. The French aim was to tie down these large British forces with a small army and the Canadians and Indian allies, thereby sparing more valuable colonies from attack.

Contemporary plan of the St Lawrence R and Québec, showing British action during the siege of Québec, 1759 (*courtesy Public Archives of Canada/NMC-2716*).

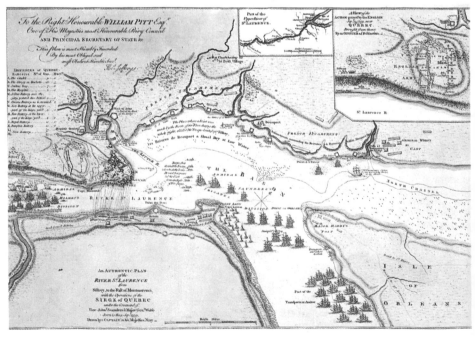

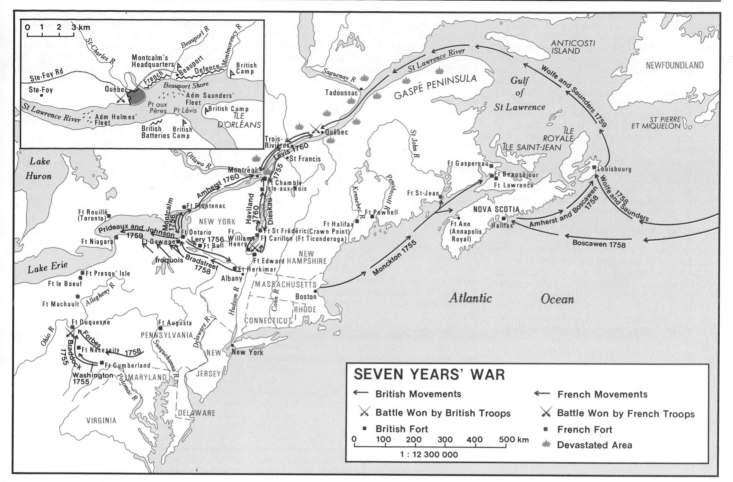

SEVEN YEARS' WAR

← British Movements   ← French Movements

✕ Battle Won by British Troops   ✕ Battle Won by French Troops

▪ British Fort   ▪ French Fort

0   100   200   300   400   500 km   Devastated Area

1 : 12 300 000

In Aug 1757 the French captured Ft William Henry on Lk George. The next year Maj-Gen James Abercromby, with an army of over 15 000 British and American troops, suffered a crushing defeat at Ft Carillon (Ticonderoga) at the hands of Montcalm and 3500 men. The tide of war now turned against the French. On Lk Ontario, FT FRONTENAC [Kingston, Ont] was destroyed in Aug 1758 with its stock of supplies for the western posts. Elsewhere Louisbourg and Guadeloupe were taken by the British. The following year France's Indian allies in the Ohio region concluded a separate peace with the British, forcing the French to abandon Ft Duquesne. Supply ships reached Québec every year but the French refused to send more than token troop reinforcements. They pinned their hopes on an invasion of Britain to force the British to come to terms.

In 1759, 2 British armies advanced on Canada while a third captured Niagara. The Royal Navy brought Maj-Gen James WOLFE with 9000 men to Québec and Gen Jeffery AMHERST advanced up Lk Champlain only to halt at Crown Point. After maneuvering fruitlessly all summer Wolfe induced Montcalm to give battle on Sept 13 outside Québec, and inflicted a shattering defeat in the BATTLE OF THE PLAINS OF ABRAHAM. The city surrendered a few days later. The Chevalier de LÉVIS took over command of the French army and the following Apr soundly defeated the British on the same battlefield (see BATTLE OF STE-FOY). On May 16 he had to raise the siege of the city when British frigates arrived to dash all hope of French reinforcements. Retiring to Montréal, the French army was forced to capitulate to Amherst on 8 Sept 1760 (see CONQUEST), freeing the British forces for service elsewhere. In 1762 Martinique was taken and only the intervention of Spain that year saved the other French islands in the W Indies.

France and Spain had organized a major expe-

dition for the invasion of England, but the British naval victories at Jagos, Portugal, in Aug and Quiberon Bay, France, in Nov 1759 had ended that. The British, however, were now war weary and staggering under a colossal national debt. The war minister, William Pitt, was driv-

The Death of General Wolfe by American artist Benjamin West, oil on canvas, 1770. Though the content of the painting was largely apocryphal, its romantic symbolism made it one of the most famous images of its time (*courtesy National Gallery of Canada / Gift of the duke of Westminster, 1918*).

en out of office in 1761 by the new king, George III, and peace negotiations began. The first minister in the French government, the duc de Choiseul, was determined to regain Martinique and Guadeloupe and to retain a base for the Grand Banks fisheries. He also wanted CAPE BRETON, but had to settle for St-Pierre and Miquelon. He left Canada to Britain, convinced that the American colonies, no longer needing British military protection, would soon strike out for independence. The loss to France of Canada would be

as nothing compared to the loss to Britain of her American colonies. To force the stubborn Spanish king to agree to peace terms, France ceded the vast Louisiana territory as compensation for the loss of Florida. Despite some opposition in Britain from those who foresaw what Choiseul privately predicted, Guadeloupe rather than Canada was returned to France by the TREATY OF PARIS (1763). Twelve years later the American colonies rose in revolt against Britain. Ironically, it was only with the military aid of the French that they finally gained their independence. W.J. ECCLES

Reading: Sir J.S. Corbett, *England in the Seven Years' War,* 2 vols (1918); W.L. Dorn, *Competition for Empire, 1740-1763* (1940); L.H. Gipson, *The British Empire Before the American Revolution,* vols IV-VIII (1936-64); G. Frégault, *Canada: The War of the Conquest,* trans M.M. Cameron (1969); L. Kennett, *The French Armies in the Seven Years' War* (1967); G.F.G. Stanley, *New France* (1968); R. Waddington, *La Guerre de Sept Ans,* 5 vols (1899-1914).

Seventh-Day Adventists are heirs of the American Millerite Adventist movement of the 1840s. When Christ failed to come in 1844 as William Miller's followers expected, it was explained that He had had to cleanse the "heavenly sanctuary rather than the earthly one." This idea was confirmed by Ellen White, who became a founder and prophet of the Seventh-Day Adventists.

Primary doctrines of the denomination are broadly EVANGELICAL. They include the imminent return (advent) of Christ, the observance of Saturday as the sabbath (seventh day), baptism by single immersion and a fundamentalist-literalist interpretation of the Bible. The immortality of human beings is contingent on their acceptance of Christ as saviour. Many members are vegetarians and all are enjoined to abstain from alcohol and the use of tobacco. Seventh-Day Adventists are noted for high moral standards, a commitment to human rights and the promotion of medical missions in many lands. Recently they have experienced some turmoil within their ranks over the question of whether White's writings should be treated as the works of a true prophet.

Congregations are administered partly on a PRESBYTERIAN pattern, but ministers are assigned by conferences. Groups of local conferences form union conferences, which in turn are members of the General Conference, the worldwide administrative body of the church. With headquarters in Washington, DC, the SDA has become a worldwide movement with millions of members. Although Seventh-Day Adventists have been in Canada since the establishment of their church about 1860, they are not numerous. In 1981 there were 41 605 Adventists in the country, most of them Seventh-Day Adventists. M. JAMES PENTON

Reading: Don F. Neufeld, ed, *Seventh-Day Adventist Encyclopedia* (1976).

Severn River, 982 km long, rises in the wooded SHIELD country of NW Ontario and flows NE through Severn Lk to HUDSON BAY. Part of the territory inhabited by the Woodland CREE, it was discovered for Europeans in 1631 by Thomas JAMES while searching the bay for a NORTHWEST PASSAGE. Later in the 17th century the HBC erected a trading post at its mouth. The river was used by fur traders travelling between the bay and Lk WINNIPEG. It was named after the Severn R in England. DANIEL FRANCIS

Sévigny, Joseph-Pierre-Albert, contractor, politician (b at Québec C 17 Sept 1917). Son of a prominent politician and judge, Pierre Sévigny was an early Québec supporter of John DIEFENBAKER. A Conservative candidate in a Québec dominated federally by the Liberals, he was defeated several times before his election to the House in 1958. A good speaker and strong Canadian nationalist, Sévigny was appointed deputy

Speaker in May 1958 and associate minister of defence in Aug 1959. Dissatisfied with Diefenbaker's politics, particularly those relating to defence, he resigned in Feb 1963 and was defeated in the 1963 general election. He was again in the spotlight during the MUNSINGER AFFAIR. PATRICIA WILLIAMS

Sévilla, Jean-Paul, pianist (b at Oran, Algeria 26 Mar 1934). A graduate of the Paris Conservatoire, he won the Geneva International Competition in 1959). He first appeared in Canada as a teacher at the JEUNESSES MUSICALES DU CANADA camp at Mount Orford, Qué, in 1961; in 1970 he began to teach at U of O. He tours frequently in the Americas and Europe and has given many premieres, including *Complémentarité,* a work dedicated to him by composer Jean PAPINEAU-COUTURE. His vast repertoire includes the complete works by Ravel; an amazing sightreader, he also has a wide knowledge of the vocal and chamber music literature. A Canada Council grant (1978-79) enabled him to begin a critical study of the piano works of Fauré. The Canadian government has sponsored him in concerts and master classes in S America, and he frequently judges national and international competitions. DOUGLAS VOICE

Sewell, Jonathan, judge, politician (bap at Cambridge, Mass 29 June 1766; d at Québec 11 Nov 1839). Chief justice of Lower Canada 1808-38, he was also an influential political leader of those opposing Louis-Joseph PAPINEAU's Patriote Party. The son of a Loyalist, Sewell's political views were determined by the AMERICAN REVOLUTION. He sat in the LC Assembly 1796-1808, and was president of the Executive Council 1808-29 and Speaker of the Legislative Council 1809-39. He favoured a strong imperial and executive authority, anglicization of Canadian children through the schools, eliminating the French legal code, replacing the seigneurial system by freehold tenure, and reducing the position of the Roman Catholic Church. While he shared many of the political goals of the British officeholder clique, he was more conciliatory than his colleagues and was subtle of mind. An intellectual of many talents, he was the first president of the Literary and Historical Soc of Quebec and wrote on history, literature and law. Harvard honoured him with an LLD degree in 1832. JAMES H. LAMBERT

Sexton, Frederic Henry, educator, mining engineer (b at New Boston, NH 9 June 1879; d at Wolfville, NS 12 Jan 1955). After serving as an assistant in metallurgy at the Massachusetts Institute of Technology 1901-02, he worked for the General Electric Company as a research chemist and metallurgist. Subsequently, he

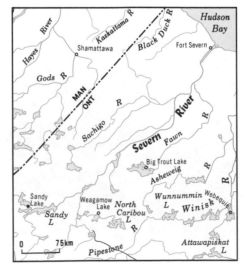

taught mining engineering and metallurgy at Dalhousie from 1904. When the TECHNICAL UNIVERSITY OF NS was founded in 1907, he became its first principal and remained in that position until his retirement in 1947. Created CBE in 1944, he was the author of many articles and monographs on technical and industrial education as well as on mining. PHYLLIS ROSE

Sexual Abuse of Children has been defined in Ontario as abuse that includes "any sexual intercourse, sexual molestation, exhibitionism or sexual exploitation involving a child that could be a violation of the Criminal Code or render the child in need of protection under the Child Welfare Act. This includes incidents between family members and between those who are not related." More simply, child sexual abuse is the exploitation of children to meet the sexual needs of adults. For true consent to occur, 2 conditions must prevail: a person must know what it is that he or she is consenting to, and a person must be free to say yes or no. By this definition, children cannot give informed consent to sex.

The Criminal Code of Canada states that "everyone commits incest who, knowing that another person is by blood relationship his or her parent, brother, sister, grandparent or grandchild, as the case may be, has sexual intercourse with that person." Father-daughter incest is most reported, although brother-sister incest is apparently 5 times more frequent. Incestuous activity is not only a criminal offence but can be a symptom of serious family problems. It causes fear and humiliation for the victims and creates secrecy and shame in the family. A child experiences fear and guilt that "telling" may send a parent to prison. A wife fears that exposure will destroy a marriage and leave her family without support. These factors strongly hinder discovery and correction of the problem. If the criminal conduct is prosecuted through the judicial system, those same emotional responses are devastating to a child who must testify in court to incestuous acts with a parent.

It is estimated that about 20-30% of all sexual abuse is committed by nonfamily members and that most victims are girls. The vast majority of abusers are male. The methods of sexual abuse include indecent exposure and genital contact of the children by fondling. Sexual intercourse is rarely committed and violence is seldom used. Abusers generally use threats or coercion in the form of bribes, toys, candy, money or affection. On the basis of limited evidence, some authorities believe that the actual incidence of sexual abuse is unknown but that it may be as common as one in 4 for females and one in 10 for males, if all forms of inappropriate sexual behaviour towards children from birth to 16 years are included.

As a result of changing public attitudes it is now possible to acknowledge publicly and clinically the existence of child sexual abuse in Canadian society, but more objective research is needed to examine the multifaceted issues arising from this problem. B. SCHLESINGER

Reading: B. Schlesinger, *Sexual Abuse of Children* (1982).

Sexually Transmitted Disease (STD) is the name now used to describe a group of infections previously referred to as venereal disease or VD. Primarily affecting the genital organs of the body, the organisms or germs causing these diseases are transmitted through "skin to skin" contact, ie, sexual intercourse or other intimate physical contact. Until recently only syphilis and gonorrhea were regarded as significant sexually transmitted diseases, but it is now known that at least 20 different conditions may be communicated this way, many exclusively, others only occasionally. The most common sexually transmitted diseases in Canada include syphilis, gonorrhea, nongonococcal urethritis, genital herpes, certain types of vaginal infections, venereal warts and infestations of pubic lice (also known as "crabs") and scabies.

Each STD is caused by a specific germ or organism. Although different in nature, most organisms can only survive in the environment of the areas of the body lined with mucous tissue, eg, the mouth or the vagina. Warmth and moisture must be present as well, to allow the organisms to multiply and produce an infection. Most germs rapidly die when removed from this environment; subsequently, they can only be transmitted when there is direct contact between an uninfected susceptible tissue and an infected one. The most common sites of infection are the cervix and vagina in women and the urethra in the male. In certain circumstances or as the result of some sexual practices, the throat, rectum and conjunctiva (eye) can also be affected.

Sexually transmitted diseases can affect anyone, regardless of age, sex, race or socioeconomic background, though the highest incidence is among sexually active individuals from their middle teens to late twenties.

The signs and symptoms of sexually transmitted diseases usually appear in or around the genital area. Although each disease produces a particular symptom, the same symptom may occur with different diseases or may resemble symptoms produced by nonsexually transmitted infections. In a sexually active person a discharge of pus from the urinary opening, vagina or rectum, burning pain on urination, the appearance of blisters, growths or sores on or around the genital organs, or itching of the genital or pubic areas may signal infection. Several STDs, however, can cause an infection without producing symptoms. This is frequently the case with women in particular, in whom signs of infection are often hidden and go unnoticed. Depending upon the disease, this can lead to the development of serious complications of the reproductive organs that can result in pelvic inflammatory disease, tubal pregnancy, sterility and chronic pelvic pain. Unborn infants or infants at the time of delivery can also be affected by STDs.

All sexually transmitted diseases can be detected and differentiated by laboratory testing utilizing either cultures or blood tests. With the exception of genital herpes, which is caused by a virus, each of the common STDs can be treated by appropriate medications (usually antibiotics), although this therapy, while curing the infection, may not reverse the damage produced by complications. However, none of these diseases will produce immunity against future infection should re-exposure occur.

The real incidence of STD in Canada is difficult to determine. Of the common infections, only cases of syphilis and gonorrhea must be reported, under federal and provincial law, to the health authorities. Available statistics indicate that the incidence of STD is exceedingly high; in 1981 they comprised more than 70% of all notifiable diseases reported in Canada. Over the past 70 years the number of reported cases has varied, rising after each of the world wars and declining during the beginning of the antibiotic era in the early 1950s. However, since 1970 the incidence of gonorrhea has steadily climbed to a point where health authorities consider the disease to be epidemic. The occurrence of the non-reportable STDs can only be estimated, but it is felt that cases of these common infections, may equal or exceed those of gonorrhea.

The high incidence of STD in Canada can be attributed both to biological and social factors. The diseases have the ability to become more resistant to the treatment drugs and in many cases asymptomatic infections prevent early detection. Although changes in attitudes towards acceptance of more permissive sexual behaviour have favoured the increase of opportunities for disease transmission, this openness has not been accompanied by similar attitudes toward diseases that may be acquired through sexual activity. This stigma attached to STD results in widespread ignorance and fear and interferes with both medical and public recognition of the problems.

Each province has jurisdictional authority to establish public-health programs for the control of the notifiable STDs. Most programs make provisions for diagnostic and treatment centres and clinics, for statistical data collection and for the promotion of education programs for the medical community and the public.

The concern about STD is international, and research is being conducted worldwide to gain a better understanding of the diseases and the organisms causing them, to examine and identify patterns of incidence within given populations, to develop and explore the potential of new therapies, and to devise preventive measures such as vaccines. Scientists in Canada are conducting or participating with other countries in numerous studies examining all these issues. Continued surveillance is essential to determine changes in patterns of STD incidence, to apply new knowledge and technology, and to be alert to the emergence of new diseases, eg, acquired immunodeficiency syndrome (AIDS). This disease, to which homosexual and bisexual men, intravenous-drug abusers, hemophiliacs and Haitians are at high risk, was first recognized in 1981 and is characterized by unusual infections resulting from failure of the body's immune system to function properly.

The existence of disease undermines the physical and emotional health and productivity of a nation. Sexually transmitted disease can only be controlled through the combined efforts of government, health-care professionals and the Canadian public. B. ROMANOWSKI AND M. STAYNER
Reading: R. Lumiere and S. Cook, *Healthy Sex and Keeping It That Way* (1983); A.S. Meltzer, *Sexually Transmitted Diseases* (1981).

Seymour, Frederick, colonial administrator, governor of BC (b at Belfast, Ire 6 Sept 1820; d at Bella Coola, BC 10 June 1869). Seymour obtained an appointment in the colonial service of Van Diemen's Land [Tasmania] in 1842, and in 1848 he was sent to the West Indies, where he spent the next 16 years in various senior administrative posts. He was appointed governor of mainland BC in 1864 but he left the following year for consultations with the Colonial Office in England. He returned in 1866 as governor of the united colony of BC under an Act of union that incorporated many of his recommendations. Despite his achievements within the colony, Seymour treated the issue of CONFEDERATION with Canada with indifference. He died suddenly while returning from successful treaty talks with the Tsimshian.   DAVID EVANS

Seymour, Horace Llewellyn, urban planner (b at Burford, Ont 1882; d at Ottawa 21 Apr 1940). One of the founders of modern Canadian URBAN AND REGIONAL PLANNING, Seymour was a leading exponent of the scientific approach to planning and of zoning as the best means of achieving efficient cities. Seymour worked as a land surveyor before joining the town-planning section of the Commission of Conservation in 1914. His broad experience over the next quarter of a century included the reconstruction of Halifax (1918-21) and a plan for Vancouver (1926-29). He also served as a consultant to the governments of NB and NS and to many municipal governments, chiefly in Ontario. Seymour was director of town and rural planning for Alberta 1929-32, and his planning system for Alberta set a model that other provinces eventually followed.   P.J. SMITH

Seymour, Lynn, née Springbett, dancer, choreographer (b at Wainwright, Alta 8 Mar 1939). One of the greatest dramatic ballerinas of the century, Seymour studied at the Rosemary Deveson School and with Nicolai Svetlanoff in Vancouver before entering the Sadler's Wells School in England (1954). By 1959 she was a principal dancer with the Royal Ballet. Famed for her fluent, impetuous movement, extraordinary musicality and intense dramatic power, Seymour is best known in works created for her by Sir Frederick Ashton (*The Two Pigeons, A Month in the Country, Five Waltzes in the Manner of Isadora Duncan*) and by Sir Kenneth MacMillan (*The Burrow, The Invitation, Romeo and Juliet, Anastasia, Mayerling*). Ballerina of the Deutsche Oper Ballet (Berlin, 1966-69) and director of the Bavarian State Opera Ballet (Munich, 1978-79), Seymour is also a talented choreographer. She has appeared in Canada with the Royal Ballet, Western Dance Theatre and the NATIONAL BALLET OF CANADA.   PENELOPE DOOB
Reading: R. Austin, *Lynn Seymour: An Authorized Biography* (1980).

Shadbolt, Douglas, architect, teacher (b at Victoria 18 Apr 1925). Educated at Victoria Coll, UBC and McGill, Shadbolt finished his architectural studies (while also teaching and working for various architectural firms) at U of Oregon between 1955 and 1957. In 1958 he began teaching at McGill and in 1961 organized a new architecture program at Nova Scotia Technical Coll, the first Canadian program alternating periods of study with periods of training in architectural offices. In 1968 Shadbolt became head of a new architecture program at Carleton U. In 1979 he returned to Vancouver to head the UBC school. *See* ARCHITECTURAL PRACTICE.
MICHAEL McMORDIE

Shadbolt, Jack Leonard, artist, teacher, author, poet (b at Shoeburyness, Eng 4 Feb 1909). Best known as a painter and draftsman, he has written 3 books and many articles and has through his teaching profoundly influenced art and artists in BC and across Canada. He has lived in BC since 1912. He studied at the Art Students' League in New York C (1928, 1948), and in London (1937) and Paris (1938). After teaching art to children in BC between 1929 and 1937, he joined the Vancouver School of Art. He served in WWII 1942-45, including 1944-45 as a Canadian war artist, and then returned to the school where he was head of painting and drawing until 1966. He has been an influential teacher and adviser across Canada and the US, having conducted workshops (he was the first artist to do so at Emma Lake in 1955) and juried exhibitions throughout N America. Over 50 solo exhibitions of his work have been mounted and his many major international exhibitions include the Venice Biennale, XXVIII.

An extraordinarily prolific artist, he works in large series (or suites), which derive from his personal experiences of nature and native art in BC; his many travels in Europe; his recognition of calligraphy and OP-art; in paint slashes and in incisive lines, in butterflies and totem poles, in insect life and ritual brides, in poetry and architecture. Everything is transformed by his emotions as much as by his intellect. As well as painting many murals, he has done stage, ballet and costume designs and theatre posters. His books are *In Search of Form* (1968), *Mind's I* (1973) and *Act of Art* (1981).   GEORGE SWINTON

Shaganappi [Algonquian, "flayed cord"], thongs or cord made of rawhide. During the settlement of the West, one use of shaganappi was to bind together the parts of RED RIVER CARTS. The word also means "inexperienced" or "inferior," as in "shaganappi pony," a pony that is untrained or undersized.   JOHN ROBERT COLOMBO

Shaker Religion originated in the mid-18th-century religious tension among Indians of the American West that also produced the Smohalla

Cult, the Ghost Dance and many prophets. In 1881 a Skokomish, John Slocum, was being prepared for burial when he "came back to life," claiming to have "been to heaven" and to have new spiritual and moral teaching for the Indians. He preached the imminent millennium of Christ. In 1882 Slocum again became ill, but his wife Mary "received the gift of healing" accompanied by trembling and shaking and cured him. This gave the name to the new religion. It is composed of Protestant, Roman Catholic and traditional Indian elements of doctrine, belief and ritual. "Getting the shake" is said to confer enlightenment, powers of healing and divination, and "second sight." Sunday worship, healing services, public confession and baptism are the main ceremonies. Not every adherent has the power of "shaking" and healing. Shakerism has extended to tribal groups in NW California, Oregon, Washington state and southern BC. Traditionally, it was indifferent, even hostile, to conventional Christian churches and traditional Indian religions, especially in its healing rituals (*see* SHAMAN). In recent years, however, in NW Washington and BC, the Shakers have accommodated to both Christian and Indian religions, and many spirit dancers are also members of the Shaker congregations. There is no direct connection with the American Shakers (The United Society of Believers). *See also* NATIVE PEOPLE, RELIGION.   DEREK G. SMITH

Reading: H.G. Barnett, *Indian Shakers* (1957).

Shaking Tent rite was widespread among the OJIBWA, MONTAGNAIS-NASKAPI, CREE, Penobscot and ABENAKI and involved the shamanistic use of a special cylindrical lodge or tent. A SHAMAN, paid by a client, would construct his tent and enter it at dark. Singing and drumming summoned the shaman's spirit helpers, whose arrival was signified by animal cries and the shaking tent. These spirit helpers were used in curing and in antisorcery. *See also* NATIVE PEOPLE, RELIGION.
                                      RENÉ R. GADACZ

Shaman is a religious or mystical expert (male or female) who in Indian and Inuit societies undergoes initiation experiences in altered states of consciousness (trance or possession). Initiates have frequently reported experiences of death, followed by a rebirth and total healing. The healed shaman is believed to become a bringer of health and prosperity, as a power-filled guide and technician in religion, and in magical, prophetic and mythic dramas. Some are thought to possess evil powers. Translations such as "witch doctor" are pejorative.   DEREK G. SMITH

Shandro, Alta, UP, is located 70 km NE of Edmonton. It is named for Nikon Shandro

Shaman's drum (*courtesy National Museums of Canada/ National Museum of Man/S77-264*).

(1886-1942), its first settler and, as MLA for Whitford, Alta (1913-21), the first UKRAINIAN elected to a legislature in Canada. The Historical Living Village and Pioneer Museum recreates the pioneer life of early Ukrainian settlers. It contains Shandro's thatched log home, a granary, blacksmith shop, a gristmill, a replica of a *boorday* and one of the province's oldest Orthodox churches, St Mary's, completed in 1904.   ERIC J. HOLMGREN

Shanly, Francis (Frank), engineer, railway builder (b at Stradbally, Ire 29 Oct 1820; d near Brockville, Ont 13 Sept 1882). Encouraged by H.H. KILLALY, he followed his brother Walter SHANLY into railway building. Both were employed on the Ogdensburg and Lk Champlain Railroad. Frank was responsible for building part of the GRAND TRUNK and Northern railways in Canada. With his brother in 1869 he undertook completion of the Hoosac Tunnel in Massachusetts, still the longest railway tunnel E of the Mississippi. They completed it in 1875. Shanly had just been appointed chief engineer of the INTERCOLONIAL RY when he died in a train between Kingston and Brockville.   R.F. LEGGET

Shanly, Walter, civil and consulting engineer and builder (b at Stradbally, Ire 11 Oct 1817; d at Montréal 17 Dec 1899). Encouraged by H.H. KILLALY, he started work in 1840 on canal construction but moved to railways in 1848. With his brother Francis SHANLY, he worked on the Ogdensburg and Lk Champlain Railroad. He then became chief engineer of the Bytown and Prescott Ry. For 4 critical years (1858-62) he was general manager of the GRAND TRUNK RY. After completing the Hoosac Tunnel in Massachusetts with his brother in 1875, he became increasingly famous as a consulting engineer and advised on many major engineering works. In 1863 he was elected to the Legislative Assembly of the Province of Canada and, in 1867, to the House of Commons, where he remained a member until 1891. A confidant of Sir John A. MACDONALD, the last letter written by Macdonald was to Shanly.   R.F. LEGGET

Shannon, Kathleen, film director, producer (b at Vancouver 11 Nov 1935). She joined the NFB as an editor in 1956. Seven years and about 115 films later, she became interested in film editing. In 1970 she participated in the celebrated Challenge for Change, a production program that dealt with social and economic change in Canada. Shannon then directed *I Don't Think It's Meant for Us* (1971), followed by *Working Mothers* (1974-75), a series of 11 films about women's work. Since 1974 she has been executive producer of Studio D, an NFB production unit primarily staffed by women, whose principal function has been to examine the role of women in society.   PIERRE VÉRONNEAU

Shanty, winter lumber camp. Early camps were simple, made of notched pine or spruce logs with a flat roof of rough shingles or bark and poles. By the 1840s larger "camboose" shanties could accommodate over 40 men in their 110 or 140 m²; the central fire with its large open chimney for light and ventilation did not yield to the stove until late in the century. Men slept fully clothed in bunk beds of hay or boughs; cooking facilities, the foreman's office, barrels of wash water and grindstones occupied much of the remaining space. *See* TIMBER TRADE HISTORY.
                                      GRAEME WYNN

Shark, marine FISH with cartilaginous skeleton belonging to subclass Elasmobranchii, class Chondrichthyes, order Pleurotremata. Modern shark ancestry dates back at least 150 million years. About 340 species in 90 genera are found worldwide from arctic to antarctic waters, including ocean depths. The greatest abundance

Twenty-five species of shark are found in Canada's coastal and offshore waters, including the Greenland shark (*Somniosus microcephalus*) (*courtesy National Museums of Canada/National Museum of Natural Sciences*).

and diversity occurs in tropical and warm temperate regions. A few species invade tropical fresh waters. Twenty-five species occur in Canada's coastal and offshore waters including thresher, great white, porbeagle, mako, basking, blue, hammerhead and dogfish. A few species occur off both coasts throughout the year, especially in deep water; the large, predacious forms appear mainly during summer and fall. Sharks range from 15 cm and a few grams (*Squaliolus laticaudas*) to over 18 m and many tonnes (whale shark, *Rhincodon typus*, the world's largest fish). They are typically elongate, cylindrical fishes with one or 2 dorsal fins, large pectoral and moderate to small pelvic fins and, usually, an anal fin and the characteristic tail fin with its enlarged upper lobe. The crescent-shaped mouth is normally ventral. The jaws have multiple rows of teeth, continuously replaced from inside the mouth. The skin is covered with pointed, toothlike denticles. Male sharks have copulatory organs (claspers) on the pelvic fins for internal fertilization. Most species are live bearers (ovoviviparous) but a few deposit eggs in horny capsules (oviparous). The gestation period for the dogfish shark (*Squalus acanthias*), 20-22 months, is one of the longest for a vertebrate.

Sharks of family Lamnidae (eg, mako, great white) have heat-regulating mechanisms allowing maintenance of a warm body temperature and, thus, increasing swimming and predation efficiency. The large liver stores food reserves allowing survival during prolonged fasting. Small species of sharks eat planktonic crustaceans and other invertebrates; large predaceous species prey on marine fishes, cephalopods, marine mammals and other vertebrates. The largest sharks (eg, basking and whale) are plankton feeders. Shark fisheries are conducted in many countries by longlines, gill nets and purse seines for food, fishmeal and leather. Shark meat is marketed fresh, frozen, salted and dried. Dogfish sharks are used extensively in biomedical research. Most sharks are harmless, but about 10% are a hazard to humans and another 10% a potential hazard. The danger of shark attack is greatly exaggerated.   W.B. SCOTT

Sharp, Francis Peabody, orchardist, horticulturalist (b at Northampton, NB 1823; d at Upper Woodstock, NB 1903). When Sharp moved to Upper Woodstock in 1844, he established the first of many family orchards that developed into the major New Brunswick fruit industry. Apples and plums were exported widely to other parts of Canada and the US. At his first orchard, he imported fruit and nursery stock from England and the US. He was one of the first 2 people in N America to hybridize apple and pear varieties scientifically and was the first horticulturalist in Canada. He developed his first new apple variety, "New Brunswick," in 1853, and several followed, most notably "Early Scarlet," later known as "Crimson Beauty," produced about 1880.   MARTIN K. MCNICHOLL

Sharp, Frederick Ralph, military officer (b at Moosomin, Sask 8 Dec 1915). Sharp joined the RCAF in 1938, receiving a DFC in 1944. He returned to Canada in 1945 and served variously at Ottawa, Trenton, North Bay and with NORAD. He was largely responsible for implementing the ARMED FORCES unification policy. Appointed deputy commander in chief NORAD HQ, Jan 1969, he returned to Ottawa as chief of the defence staff in Sept with the rank of general, retiring in 1972.   JEAN PARISEAU

Sharp, Mitchell William, public servant, politician (b at Winnipeg 11 May 1911). He joined the Dept of Finance in 1942 and attracted the attention of C.D. HOWE, who had him transferred to the Dept of Trade and Commerce in 1951. As associate deputy minister and then deputy minister, Sharp worked closely with Howe, providing economic analysis and writing speeches. It was made plain that the new Conservative government did not want him, and Sharp entered private business, 1958-63. Elected to Parliament for Eglinton, 1963-74, Sharp became PM PEARSON's minister of trade and commerce and then of finance, and was known as the leading antinationalist in the Cabinet, as well as a reformer of federal-provincial financial relations. After running unsuccessfully for the Liberal leadership, he became PM TRUDEAU's minister of external affairs, 1968-74, then president of the Privy Council. He retired from politics in 1978 and became commissioner for the Northern Pipeline Agency.   ROBERT BOTHWELL

Shatford, Sidney Smith, business executive (b at Hubbards, NS 1 Dec 1864; d at Halifax 8 June 1956). In partnership with his brother, he founded NS's first oil business. He started work as a hardware clerk in Halifax, and in 1885 he and his brother established an oil-importing and wholesale business with $4000 borrowed from their father. Shatford Brothers Ltd imported kerosene and lubricating oil from New York and distributed it throughout most of NS, PEI and Newfoundland. In 1894 the business was merged with competitor Joseph Bullock of Saint John under the name of Eastern Oil Co, which was purchased by Imperial Oil 1898. Sidney Shatford then headed Imperial's operations in NS until retirement in 1930.   EARLE GRAY

Shaughnessy, Thomas George, first Baron Shaughnessy, railway executive (b at Milwaukee, Wis 6 Oct 1853; d at Montréal 10 Dec 1923). In 1869 Shaughnessy joined the Milwaukee Road as a clerk. On becoming manager in 1880, W.C. VAN HORNE promoted Shaughnessy storekeeper, and in 1882 persuaded him to join the CANADIAN PACIFIC RY as general purchasing agent in Montréal. Shaughnessy helped save the CPR from bankruptcy in 1884-85 by placating creditors, became vice-president in 1891 and president in 1899. Under Shaughnessy's leadership, the CPR became a large and profitable transportation corporation. From 1899 to 1913 its trackage in Canada increased from 11 200 km to 18 000 km and 70% of the Prairie main line was double-tracked. Shaughnessy launched the Atlantic steamship service and made the CPR a major world shipowner. Under his direction, Consolidated Mining and Smelting (now Cominco) became an important producer of lead and zinc. He retired as president in 1918 but remained chairman until his death.   JOHN A. EAGLE

Shaw, Walter Russell, farmer, politician, premier of PEI (b at West River, PEI 20 Dec 1887; d at Charlottetown 29 May 1981). Elected late in 1957, Shaw led the Conservatives to victory in 1959. Under Shaw, the civil service was enlarged and modernized and in 1963 the Island's electoral system was reformed. Despite the alarms over the "farm crisis" raised by Shaw when in Opposition, the number of family farms and persons engaged in farming continued to decline throughout his tenure. His government concentrated on the problems of Island development but was unable to establish resource-based secondary industry. Defeated by the Liberals under Alex CAMPBELL in 1966, he

remained leader of the Opposition until 1970. Eloquent, witty and personable, Shaw remained a highly respected public figure after he retired from politics.   DAVID A. MILNE

Shaw Festival (Niagara-on-the-Lake, Ont) was founded in 1962 by lawyer/playwright/producer Brian Doherty and is the only festival in the world devoted to the production of plays by George Bernard Shaw. After an initial season of 8 amateur performances, directed by Maynard Burgess, the festival went professional. Radio producer Andrew ALLAN was appointed artistic director with Sean Mulcahy between 1963 and 1965. In 1966 Barry Morse transformed the festival into a major event, and in the decade 1967-77 Paxton Whitehead consolidated its international reputation. He broadened the repertoire to include any play falling within the long span of Shaw's life and introduced musical events and mime. Several of the productions went on tour. Housed for 11 years in the historic courthouse, this popular tourist attraction achieved permanent status when a handsome new 860-seat theatre designed by architect Ron THOM was inaugurated by Her Majesty Queen Elizabeth II on 28 June 1973. Tony Van Bridge was artistic director in 1975 during Whitehead's sabbatical. The festival faltered in 1977 with the departure of Whitehead. After interim managements by Richard Kirschner (1978) and Leslie Yeo (1979), Christopher Newton became artistic director in 1980.

Newton continued the eclectic policy begun by Whitehead, skillfully juxtaposing European farces with *Saint Joan, Camille* and even plays by Bertolt Brecht. His refreshingly offbeat seasons included revues and Edwardian musical comedies at a third festival playhouse, the Royal George, as well as unfamiliar Shavian one-act plays for lunchtime audiences. In 1982-83 the Shaw Festival enjoyed a great artistic success with Derek Goldby's production of *Cyrano de Bergerac* featuring Heath Lamberts in the title role, a Canadian actor brought to stardom by the festival. In 1983 the festival began a policy of mounting productions in Toronto during the winter season. The extensive archives of the Shaw Festival are housed at University of Guelph. *See also* THEATRE, ENGLISH-LANGUAGE.

DAVID GARDNER

Shawinigan, Qué, City, pop 23 011 (1981c), inc 1921, home of the Québec chemical industry, is located 30 km NW of TROIS-RIVIÈRES on the shores of the Rivière ST-MAURICE. The name derives from the Indian word *ashawenikam,* referring to the "angular portages" used to avoid the area's major waterfalls.

History After 1825 the government of Lower Canada had the territory of the Mauricie region surveyed. The first concessions were given out in 1831. Shawinigan was first the site of a waterslide (1852), built so that log booms could be sent downstream to Trois-Rivières. From 1843 to 1883 the region's very sparse population spread a little S of Shawinigan to the Grès sawmill. Shawinigan was born of the desire to exploit the hydroelectric potential of the falls. In 1899, after an extension of the Great North Ry line, Shawinigan Water & Power (SWP) built a dam and organized the development of the set-

The hydroelectric potential of Shawinigan Falls, on the Rivière St-Maurice, led to the founding of nearby Shawinigan (*photo by John deVisser*).

tlement, which then grew rapidly. Several industries, attracted by the available electricity, moved there: in 1900 Belgo-Canadian Pulp (since 1967, Consolidated Bathurst), in 1901 Pittsburg Reduction (Alcan), and in 1903 the Carbure Co of Shawinigan (Shawinigan Chemicals).

Economy SWP began providing electricity for Montréal in 1903, but the power soon stimulated Shawinigan's own growth. The great industrial development of the early 20th century, based on paper, aluminum and chemicals, continued with the arrival of Prest-O-Lite in 1907, Shawinigan Cotton in 1909 and CIL in 1931. The pace slowed with the Depression of the 1930s and began picking up again in 1940. However, there has been a marked decline since the 1960s: the old industries have reduced or ceased activity and no significant new employer has arrived. In 1963 HYDRO-QUÉBEC took over the SWP installations.   CLAUDINE PIERRE-DESCHÊNES

Shawinigan, Lac, 3.2 km², 6.3 km long, 80 m deep, lies on Québec's Laurentian Plateau, 70 km N of Lac St-Pierre on the St Lawrence R. This lake of glacial gouging is prolonged to the E by Little Shawinigan Lk, Bernard Lk and Lac en Croix. The Shawinigan R runs out of this last lake to meet the ST-MAURICE R at Baie-de-Shawinigan. In Algonquin, *Ashawenikan* means "portage on the crest."   SERGE OCCHIETTI

Shawnandithit, also Nance April or Nancy, the last BEOTHUK (b c1801; d at St John's 6 June 1829). A member of one of the small and dwindling family groups of native Red Indians, Shawnandithit was the niece of DEMASDUWIT. In Mar 1823 she, her mother and her sister, all starving, were captured by English furriers at Badger Bay and taken to St John's. The authorities determined to return them, laden with presents, to their people, but no contact could be made. The other 2 women died of pulmonary consumption and Shawnandithit was taken into the household of planter John Peyton at Exploits-Burnt Is. In 1828 she was brought to the Beothuk Institution at St John's and from her its president, W.E. CORMACK, recorded valuable information about the language and customs of her unfortunate people during their last melancholy years; her deftness with pencil and

sketchbook was especially useful. She too died of consumption and was buried in the military and naval cemetery. G.M. STORY

Sheaffe, Sir Roger Hale, army officer (b at Boston, Mass 15 July 1763; d at Edinburgh, Scot 17 July 1851). Commissioned in the British army in 1778, Sheaffe was posted to Canada 1787-97, 1802-11 and 1812-13. At the Battle of Queenston Heights, 13 Oct 1812, he led the regular and militia forces to victory after Sir Isaac BROCK's death. In Apr 1813, as president and administrator of Upper Canada, he unsuccessfully defended York against an American raid (*see* WAR OF 1812). CARL A. CHRISTIE

Shearer, John George, Presbyterian minister, social reformer (b at Bright, Canada W 9 Aug 1859; d at Toronto 27 Mar 1925). Shearer left parish work in 1900 to become secretary of the LORD'S DAY ALLIANCE, editor of the *Lord's Day Advocate* and architect of the 1906 Lord's Day Act. In 1907 he became the permanent secretary of the new Committee on Temperance and Other Moral Reforms (organized in 1909 as the Board of Temperance and Reform and renamed in 1911 the Board of Social Service and Evangelism) of the Presbyterian Church of Canada. From 1918 until his death he was the full-time secretary of the Social Service Council of Canada, which he helped to establish. For his speeches and articles against unsafe housing and working conditions, abuse of women and children, alcoholism, venereal disease, prostitution and political corruption, Shearer was called the mouthpiece of the social conscience of Canadian Christianity. JOHN S. MOIR

Shearwater (order Procellariiformes, family Procellariidae), medium-sized SEABIRD (up to 50 cm long) related to the albatross and FULMAR. Shearwaters are all dark or dark above and white below. They breed in large colonies which they visit only at night, and lay their single, white eggs in burrows. Only the Manx shearwater (*Puffinus puffinus*) breeds in Canada, in a small colony in Nfld. However, large numbers of Southern Hemisphere shearwaters visit Canadian waters in summer. Short-tailed shearwaters (*P. tenuirostris*) from Tasmania and sooty shearwaters (*P. griseus*) from New Zealand and Tierra del Fuego occur off BC. Some sooties and the world population of greater shearwaters (*P. gravis*) from Tristan da Cunha come up to Nfld waters; these migrants probably outnumber the local breeding population of seabirds. Shearwaters feed on squid, capelin, herring and swarms of crustaceans, and scavenge from fishing boats. R.G.B. BROWN

Shebib, Donald, filmmaker (b at Toronto 17 Jan 1938). Shebib's *Goin' Down the Road* (1970) — perhaps the single most important film in English Canada — proved that Canadians could make feature films about English Canada that audiences would want to see. He studied cinema in California and returned to Canada in 1963 to direct several documentaries for the CBC. *Goin' Down the Road* built on these documentary roots as it followed the vicissitudes of 2 Maritimers in Toronto. *Between Friends* (1973) established Shebib as a major filmmaker but did poorly at the box office. He has subsequently made more commercially accessible films: *Second Wind* (1976), *Fish Hawk* (1979) and *Heartaches* (1981). PIERS HANDLING

Shediac, NB, Town, pop 4285 (1981c), inc 1903, is located on Northumberland Str, 20 km E of MONCTON. Its name derives from a Micmac word meaning "running far back," a reference to its location on Shediac Bay at the mouth of the Scoudouc R. Although first settled by ACADIANS in the mid-1700s, it received English immigrants after 1785. Nineteenth-century prosperity was based on the export of square timber and

sawn lumber to Britain, as well as shipbuilding. Construction of a railway link with Saint John (1860) made Shediac a centre for freight and passenger traffic to and from PEI until WWI. Tourism is now the major industry in this popular summer resort, which has some of the province's finest beaches. Fishing, particularly for lobster, remains a mainstay for many residents. Each July the Shediac Lobster Festival, held annually since 1948, attracts thousands to the "lobster capital of the world." DEAN JOBB

Sheep Farming Sheep (genus *Ovis,* primarily *Ovis aries*) are ruminant MAMMALS now raised in Canada primarily for their meat and milk. The French brought the first sheep to what is now Canada when they established the first permanent settlement in 1604. In 1677 there were 85 sheep in NEW FRANCE; in 1698, nearly 1000; by the mid-18th century, just over 28 000. To the early settlers, sheep were important not only for their meat and milk but also as a source of wool for CLOTHING and TEXTILES. Today, wool production is minimal and consumption of lamb and mutton vary according to the consumer's ethnic origin, the region and season.

According to Statistics Canada, Canada's 1984 sheep and lamb population was 790 800 head, a decrease of -2.2% from 1983, and a decrease from a 1965 high of over one million head. Although sheep can be raised in most settled parts of the country, Canada's sheep production is so small that the demand for lamb and wool is met largely by imports. There are 3 major categories of lamb on the market: new crop lamb (about 15 kg), light lamb (about 25 kg) and heavy lamb (40 kg). Producers deal directly with consumers or sell live animals to the MEAT-PROCESSING INDUSTRY through slaughterhouses, auctions or public markets. Canadian annual per capita consumption of lamb is 0.85 kg. The promotion of fresh lamb, demand for which has risen over the past decade, should bring per capita consumption to 1.5 kg by 1985-90.

The breeds of sheep are categorized according to appearance, adaptation and use. Factors influencing choice of breed include type of farming operation, personal taste, availability of breeding animals, precocity, hardiness, breeding capabilities, meat quality, maternal qualities and milk production. The major breeds are grouped into 2 classes. Breeds that pass on useful characteristics for breeder ewes (eg, climatic adaptability, maternal instinct, fertility, milk production capacity) are the so-called maternal breeds and may be used for cross-breeding purposes. Breeds that pass on useful qualities for meat-producing animals (eg, daily weight gain, food conversion, meat quality) are the paternal breeds and are also used in terminal cross-breeding with hybrid females to produce animals for meat. Some of the principal breeds in Canada are as follows.

Border Cheviot, developed in the mountainous border area between England and Scotland, is a small, cold-hardy breed, capable of surviving on poor pasture. Desirable characteristics include good mothering, good-quality meat and soft, lightweight fleece.

Dorset, developed in the English counties of Dorset and Somerset, is a prolific breed (ewes often lamb twice annually). The fleece is particularly white; ewes have a high milk-production capacity.

Hampshire, developed in England's Hampshire County, is known for its good food conversion and high daily weight gain. Hampshires are chunky sheep with a dark brown face and ears, and fine fleece.

North Country Cheviot, a cold-hardy, dark sheep with a white face, ears and legs, is native to northern Scotland. The breed yields good meat, but its fleece contains wiry fibres making it less valuable.

Oxford, a heavy breed originating in England's Oxford County, is characterized by a light body fleece and grey face, ears and legs. Ewes have good milk-production capacity.

Suffolk, a large, hardy breed originating in England's Suffolk County, is characterized by good milk production. Lambs mature early and yield high-quality meat. Head and legs have fine black hair, instead of wool.

The goal of every sheep-farming operation is to produce meat, wool and milk. Key technical factors influencing effective production are selection, diet and management. Generally, a breed may be improved by working on heredity or on environmental factors influencing heredity. Breeders at Agriculture Canada's RESEARCH STATION at Lennoxville, Qué, have been cross-breeding Dorsets, Leicesters and Suffolks for the past 15 years to produce a unique Canadian breed (the DLS breed). The Russian Romanov breed was imported in 1981 to increase lamb production in the DLS breed. The Finnish Landrace or Finnsheep is also popular in crosses because of its proneness to multiple births; litters of 3-5 lambs are not uncommon. Experiments are also taking place at the Lethbridge, Alta, research station. *See* ANIMAL AGRICULTURE; COMMODITY INSPECTION AND GRADING.

JEAN-PAUL LEMAY

Shelburne, NS, pop 2303 (1981c), seat of Shelburne County, inc 1907, located on Shelburne harbour, lies 208 km SW of Halifax. At the close of the American Revolution some 16 000 LOYALISTS, including 2000 black Loyalists, found temporary refuge here, drawn by the magnificent harbour. Today, many 18th-century buildings remain, fishing is the mainstay of the economy and 70% of citizens trace their ancestry back to the Loyalist refugees. The historic complex on Dock Street includes 4 Loyalist houses and the John C. Williams Dory Shop built by the grandson of Loyalist Amos Williams. Shelburne was named for Lord Shelburne, prime minister of England during the American Revolution. Donald Mckay, the famous designer and builder of clipper ships, was born in Jordan Falls, 11 km NE. MARY ARCHIBALD

Shell Canada Limited is an integrated energy resource company with head offices in Toronto. Active in Canada since 1911 (Dominion incorporation, 1925), the company is involved in natural gas and petroleum, petrochemicals and refined oil products, and alternative fuels research. Shell is the second-largest producer of natural gas and the largest producer of sulphur in Canada. The company is also working with oil sands and is constructing the first refinery in the world designed to process only synthetic crude oil; it opened in 1984. In 1982 the company had sales or operating revenue of $5.3 billion (ranking 10th in Canada), assets of $5.2 billion (ranking 15th) and 7975 employees. Shell Investments Limited (Netherlands/Britain) is the major shareholder, and foreign ownership stands at 79%. DEBORAH C. SAWYER

Shepherd, Francis John, anatomist, surgeon, dermatologist, medical administrator, art connoisseur and critic (b at Como, Qué 25 Nov 1851; d at Montréal 18 Jan 1929). Shepherd revolutionized the teaching of anatomy at McGill. In his time it was a common saying that McGill medical graduates "knew their anatomy." His diagnostic power, surgical judgement, technical skill and knowledge of anatomy made him one of the most successful and reliable surgeons of his generation. He was also a pioneer dermatologist. As a medical administrator, he served McGill as dean of medicine. As an art connoisseur and critic, he commanded sufficient respect to be president of the Montréal Art Assn and chairman of the board of trustees of the National Gallery at Ottawa. EDWARD H. BENSLEY

Sherbrooke, Qué, City, pop 74 075 (1981c), inc 1875, located 160 km E of Montréal, is the principal city of the EASTERN TOWNSHIPS. Situated in the heart of a region of lakes and mountains near Orford Provincial Park, it was for many years a commercial, industrial and railway centre. As of the 1960s, it also became a service centre. A Catholic archdiocese and headquarters of the judicial district of St-François, Sherbrooke is also the administrative centre of Québec's Region No 5.

Settlement and Development Located on ABENAKI land, Sherbrooke was initially known as Ktinékétolékouac or Grandes Fourches ("The Forks"), and was the site of a portage at the foot of the falls of the Magog R. The first permanent settlement was established in 1802 when American pioneers from Vermont built several mills. The village took the name of Gov Gen John Coape SHERBROOKE in 1818. The city owes its initial urban growth to industrialization, which occurred in waves from the 1840s. It became a textile centre with the establishment of Canada's first cotton manufacturing plant in 1844 and a large wool plant in 1867. The town owed its success in the 19th century as much to its dynamic anglophone businessmen, who established a regional bank and promoted railways and new industries, as to its francophone population, which supplied much of the industrial manpower. The development of agriculture and mining in the region also enhanced Sherbrooke's role as a wholesale trade and services centre. Since the 1950s, the city has had difficulty attracting new industry and has experienced a decline in its textile and clothing industries. The founding of UNIVERSITÉ DE SHERBROOKE in 1954 and the decentralization of the province's administration have helped restore much of the city's dynamism.

Cityscape Located at the confluence of the Magog and ST-FRANÇOIS rivers, Sherbrooke resembles a basin, the curved sides of which have become residential areas. After 1950 the urban community expanded along an E-W axis under the polarizing influence of the university and the outlying commercial centres. The city centre, the traditional commercial area, took on a new vitality in the 1970s. Several residential areas near the centre contain predominantly wooden buildings that display 19th-century Victorian and American architecture. The city's many open spaces, a lake located right in town and a mountain offering ski trails provide an abundant source of outdoor recreation for its citizens.

Population and Economy Because of its fluctuating industrial activity, the city's demographic growth was slow in the 19th century. It had 3000 inhabitants in 1852, 10 000 in 1891 and over 50 000 in 1951. Since 1971 (80 700) the population has declined, many people having moved to the Fleurimont, Ascot and Rock Forest suburbs. The percentage of Francophones has risen from 50% in 1871 to almost 94% today. There are 4500 Anglophones in the community.

Sherbrooke's industrial base is still dependent upon the textile and machinery industries and the food sector. Since the 1960s, however, most of the work force has been involved in the tertiary sectors of commerce, teaching, health services and regional administration.

Government and Transportation Incorporated as a city since 1952, Sherbrooke has been governed by a mayor and councillors representing 4 areas. From 1890 to 1952 the mayors were alter-

Sherbrooke, Qué, owed its initial growth to industrialization after the 1840s; it became a textile centre with the establishment of Canada's first cotton plant (*courtesy City of Sherbrooke*).

nately francophone and anglophone. Municipal policies are now rarely the object of vehement debate and concentrate on providing sound administration and attracting new industries. Since 1908 the city has had its own electrical system, supplied by several hydroelectric dams.

For nearly a century, Sherbrooke has been a major intersection for railway lines radiating towards Montréal, Québec City, Halifax, and Portland, Maine and Boston, Mass. Passenger service, which had been offered since 1852 with the ST LAWRENCE AND ATLANTIC RAILROAD, ceased in 1981. The city is now at the intersection of the Trans-Québec Autoroute, running N towards TROIS-RIVIÈRES and S to the US, and of the Eastern Township Autoroute to Montréal. Tramways were the predominant form of urban transportation from 1897 to 1931, when they were replaced by buses.

Cultural Life In the heart of a region that attracts many artists, Sherbrooke has an active cultural life, with the university's cultural centre, a symphony orchestra and several theatre groups. It also has a Musée des beaux-arts (1982) and Musée de sciences naturelles (1879). The city has 2 TV and 4 radio stations (one of which is English) and 2 daily newspapers, the *Tribune* (French) and the *Record* (English).

JEAN-PIERRE KESTEMAN

Sherbrooke, Sir John Coape, soldier, administrator, governor-in-chief of British N America (b in Eng 1764; d at Calverton, Eng 14 Feb 1830). A British army officer, Sherbrooke was stationed in Nova Scotia in 1784-85. He then saw active service in the Netherlands (1794), India (1799) and throughout the Mediterranean (1805-09). He distinguished himself while serving under Wellington in the Peninsular War (1809-10). Plagued by recurring illness, which had begun in India, Sherbrooke returned to England. In 1811 he was appointed lieutenant-governor of NS and vigourously defended the colony during the WAR OF 1812. Despite poor health, he led military campaigns, in particular an expedition up the Penobscot R through Maine which compensated partly for Sir George PREVOST's defeat at Plattsburgh in 1814. Succeeding Prevost as governor-in-chief in 1816, Sherbrooke handled his short term with competence. By 1818, however, his illness — exacerbated by a paralytic stroke — forced his retirement to England.

DAVID EVANS

Sheriff In each county and judicial district in Canada sheriffs, appointed by the lieutenant-governor-in council, serve processes (eg, writs of summonses); attend upon supreme and county court judges and maintain order in the courts (performed by constables); execute judgements, eg, seizing the judgement debtor's goods (performed by BAILIFFS); summon and supervise JURIES, and take custody of noncriminal prisoners.

K.G. McSHANE

Sherman, Frank Albert, industrialist (b at Crown Point, NY 19 May 1887; d at Surfside, Fla 27 Jan 1967). Sherman worked in the steel industry at Pittsburgh, Pa, and in 1914 moved to Hamilton, Ont, to work in his brother Clifton's Dominion Foundry and Steel Co (DOFASCO), eventually becoming president and chairman. By matching salaries at the rival Stelco plant and by profit sharing, Sherman achieved labour peace and kept his plant free of unions. An active Liberal, Sherman helped raise election funds for C.D. HOWE; he was also a president of the HAMILTON TIGER-CATS.   ROBERT BOTHWELL

Shickluna, Louis (Lewis), shipbuilder (b at Senglea, Malta 16 June 1808; d at St Catharines, Ont 24 Apr 1880). By 1835 he was engaged in ship construction at Youngstown, NY. He later moved to St Catharines and purchased a shipyard on the WELLAND CANAL. His expanding operations contributed significantly to the region's commercial prosperity. Between 1838 and 1880 he directed the construction of some 140 schooners, barkentines, steamers and other vessels designed for service on the Great Lakes. In 1871 he was presented with a Scroll of Honour by the people of St Catharines, where he had also served as a councillor.   GEORGE BONAVIA

Shield, or Precambrian Shield, extensive structural unit of the Earth's continental crust composed of exposed Precambrian ROCKS (basement rocks 600 million years old or older). Shields have been unaffected by mountain-building activity since Precambrian times and, because their original mountain belts have been almost completely eroded, are slightly convex, flat, low-lying areas. The best-known examples are the Canadian Shield and the Baltic Shield exposed in Scandinavia.

Canadian Shield The Canadian Shield covers about 4.6 million km² and extends from the arctic islands around Hudson Bay, S to the US to form the Adirondack Mts and E across Labrador. Repeated advances and retreats of ice sheets have scoured its surface and left it strewn with countless lakes, rivers, streams and ponds. Along its edge lie many of the great lakes and waterways of Canada: the eastern shores of GREAT BEAR LK, GREAT SLAVE LK, Lk ATHABASCA and Lk WINNIPEG; the northern shores of LAKE OF THE WOODS, Lk SUPERIOR and Lk HURON; and the N shore of the ST LAWRENCE R.

The origin and age of the shield were among the great mysteries of Canadian GEOLOGY. The shield's southern limits were traced by Alexander Murray, who examined the country below Gananoque, Bytown [Ottawa], the St Lawrence and Ottawa rivers and the perimeter from Kingston to Lk Superior in 1851-52. A.C. LAWSON made an important contribution by working out the Precambrian succession in the 1880s, but a more current time scale was not developed until the 1950s, when geologists such as C.H. Stockwell had seismic and gravity measures at their disposal (see GEOLOGICAL HISTORY). Stockwell divided the shield into 3 great provinces — Superior, Churchill and Grenville — and 23 subprovinces. It is now considered to fall into 9 provinces (see GEOLOGICAL REGIONS).

The shield has had a profound effect on Canadian history, settlement and economic development. In pre-European times it was the home of Algonquian nomadic hunters, who developed the birchbark CANOE to travel its myriad waterways. Similar canoes were used by the COUREURS DE BOIS, VOYAGEURS and explorers to penetrate the continent. The abundant fur-bearing animals were the basis of the colonial economy until about 1810. The hegemony of MONTRÉAL was thus extended far into the wilderness, via the Ottawa R and connecting waterways into the northwest, forming the precedent for future Canadian sovereignty.

Aerial view near Killarney, Ont, showing typical Shield landforms (*photo by Karl Sommerer*).

The bare rock, thin soils, MUSKEG and insects of the shield have presented a barrier to settlement; the agricultural frontier of eastern Canada ends abruptly at its perimeter. The railway link to the West had literally to be blasted through its rock, coincidentally exposing the shield's great treasures: GOLD, SILVER, NICKEL, COBALT, ZINC, COPPER and IRON ORE. Its coniferous forests and hydroelectric power support a large PULP AND PAPER industry. Gigantic power developments at CHURCHILL FALLS, Lab; JAMES BAY, Qué; Kettle Rapids, Man; and elsewhere feed electricity to the urban south. The shield's stark and rugged beauty has attracted Canadian artists, writers, tourists and cottagers and has become almost synonymous with Canada itself.
JAMES MARSH

Shields, Thomas Todhunter, clergyman (b at Bristol, Eng 1 Nov 1873; d at Toronto 4 Apr 1955). A self-educated man and pastor of Jarvis Street Baptist Church, Toronto, for 45 years where he edited the *Gospel Witness*, Dr Shields championed BAPTIST Christianity and British imperialism against liberal Protestantism and Roman Catholicism. He verbally abused the leaders of Catholic Québec for "slacking" in 2 world wars and was expelled from the Baptist Convention of Ontario and Québec for his intolerant, personal attacks on professors at McMaster. In response he founded his own denomination and seminary.
TOM SINCLAIR-FAULKNER

Shilling, Arthur, artist (b at Rama IR, Orillia, Ont 19 Apr 1941). Shilling attended the Mohawk Institute Residential School (Brantford, Ont) and the Ontario College of Art. He won national acclaim at his first solo show in Ottawa in 1967. Using oil on canvas, he depicts life on the Rama Reserve, where he has built an art gallery to encourage local talent. His specialty is portraits in a broad impressionist style. In May 1983 Shilling was one of 7 Canadian artists invited by Gov Gen SCHREYER to show at RIDEAU HALL, Ottawa. The NFB's *The Beauty of My People* (1978) documents his life.
MARY E. SOUTHCOTT

Shilo, CFB, is located on the western boundary of Manitoba's Spruce Woods Provincial Forest, 195 km W of Winnipeg and 25 km E of Brandon. Most of the forest is leased to the federal government for the Shilo military reserve. Assiniboine Indians inhabited the region when the first Europeans arrived to set up trading posts along the Assiniboine R. Homesteaders followed in the 1880s but found the land unsuited to farming. Spruce Woods was created as an experimental forestry reserve 1895. Military planners soon became interested in the site and by 1910 had established Camp Sewell (later Camp Hughes) to the NE of present-day Shilo. A busy training area during WWI, it later became a military summer camp and by 1932 a relief camp for the unemployed who began building permanent structures for a new base at Shilo. During WWII Shilo expanded into a permanent, year-round facility. It became the home station of the Royal Regiment of Canadian Artillery and a summer militia camp in the postwar years. Since 1974 West German troops have received tank and artillery training here under a NATO agreement. A federal-provincial monitoring committee was formed to safeguard the forest's Bald Head Hills, a rare area of sand dunes, evergreen stands and grassy plains. Military activity dominates the Shilo economy. The base site includes recreational and cultural facilities, a shopping centre, a hotel and a military museum.
D.M. LYON

Shiners' Wars, 1837 to 1845, were a period of violent outbreaks between IRISH and French Canadian lumbermen in the Ottawa Valley. After construction of the RIDEAU CANAL was completed the Irish moved to the Bytown [Ottawa] area and began displacing the French in the timber trade. Violence, primarily in the form of brawling, peaked in 1837, at the time of the highest annual Irish immigration to date, a financial crisis, rising prices, and increased unemployment in the lumber camps. Bytown's outraged citizens formed "The Association of the Preservation of the Public Peace in Bytown," but terrorism continued until the late 1840s. The term "Shiners" may have come from the French word, *cheneur* ("oakman"); from the shiny hats worn by newcomers to the region; or from the kind of coins paid to the lumbermen.

Shinguacöuse, or Little Pine, Indian leader (b c1773; d at Garden R, Canada W 1854). Son of an OJIBWA woman and possibly Lavoine Barthe, a trader, Shinguacöuse became a warrior, orator and medicine man. He joined the British during the WAR OF 1812, but afterward promoted harmony between the Ojibwa and the American government, which drew acclaim from H.R. Schoolcraft. In 1832 he requested that Lt-Gov COLBORNE help establish a native settlement near Sault Ste Marie. With Allan McDonnell, a mine shareholder, Shinguacöuse devised a plan in 1849 whereby Indians might benefit, under government protection, from revenues and employment opportunities arising from mining on unsurrendered Indian territory. When the government failed to respond, Shinguacöuse, accompanied mainly by Métis and Indians, forcibly took possession of mining operations at Mica Bay that fall. Although prominent in Robinson Treaty negotiations in 1850, Shinguacöuse failed to gain recognition for his plan, since prevailing policy viewed Indians as wards, not participants, in the developing nation. JANET CHUTE

Shinplasters, 25-cent Dominion government notes that were first issued in 1870 as a temporary measure to counteract the effects of an excess of American silver coinage circulating in Canada. Shinplasters were popular and were reissued in 1900 and 1923. Over 5 million were in circulation in 1929, but in 1935 the new BANK OF CANADA began recalling them. The term may have been used initially in American revolutionary times by soldiers who used similar bills to pad their shoes.

Ship Harbour, NS, UP, pop 175 (1981c), is located 67 km E of Dartmouth. Three communities, East Ship Harbour, Head Ship Harbour and Lower Ship Harbour, share this name. Called *Tedumunaboowek* ("waterworn rock") by the Micmac, its present name is derived from a cliff in the harbour that resembled a ship under full sail. LOYALISTS from S Carolina founded the settlement in 1783. The early years were trying, owing to a shortage of supplies and the difficulty of growing crops. Fishing and lumbering became the chief industries, and they remain so today. Seasonal lobster fishing is also carried on.
JEAN PETERSON

Shipbuilding and Ship Repair are among Canada's oldest industries. The long inland waterways and coastlines, rich timber supplies, fisheries and offshore oil, together with the need to export natural resources, have generated a demand for ships. Though Canadians have demonstrated high-quality workmanship in both enterprises, and at times innovation on a world scale, success has been cyclical.

The first SAILING SHIPS built in what is now Canada were 2 small craft launched at PORT-ROYAL, Acadia, by François Gravé Du Pont in 1606. The first recorded seagoing vessel, *Galiote*, was built in NEW FRANCE in 1663. Some building continued at Québec City and a brisk industry was recorded in 1715 despite the mercantilist system which discouraged industry in the colony. As a result of encouragement by French Minister of Marine de Maurepus, Intendant Hocquart gave the industry a real impetus with the establishment of a shipyard in 1732 on the R St-Charles. The 10 merchant vessels built there that year may be termed the true start of the industry as a commercial enterprise in Canada. These merchant ships impressed French authorities and warships were also ordered for the French navy, including a ship-of-the-line mounting 70 guns built in 1750.

In 1677-78 Cavelier de LA SALLE presaged the development of a transportation system on the lakes with the building on Lk Ontario of a single-decked barque of 10 tons, *Frontenac*, and 3 other vessels. This achievement was eclipsed by the construction in 1679 at Cayuga Creek on the Niagara R of the ill-fated GRIFFON, 20 m overall, perhaps 60 tons burden, to further fur-trade interests on the upper Great Lakes. Between 1732 and 1745 a number of vessels were built, 6 for Lk Ontario and one for Lk Superior. In the Seven Years' War, the French war fleet on Lk Ontario consisted of 4 vessels, 2 rated as corsairs, *Marquise de Vaudreuil* of 14 guns and *La Hurault* of 12 guns, launched in 1756 and 1755, respectively.

The ready supply of timber for shipbuilding attracted artisans and shipwrights to the colonies after the Conquest. George HERIOT in his travels (1807) stated that vessels "from fifty to a thousand tons burthen" were constructed at Québec City and commercial vessels at Kingston.

The WAR OF 1812 generated a flurry of shipbuilding. The *St Lawrence*, built in Kingston in 1814, was a 3-decker mounting 102 guns, and was larger than Nelson's *Victory*.

The early years of the 19th century saw rapid growth of ship construction in the British colonies. Vessels were built on creeks, rivers and coves in every colony of British N America — at Alma, on the Bay of FUNDY; at the Ellis-Yeo property in PEI, now a historical restoration; and at shipyards extending for 20 km on both sides of the Miramichi R in NB.

The expansion of the timber trade in the early 19th century stimulated a rapid expansion of shipbuilding. The *Columbus* and *Baron of Renfrew* built in 1824 and 1825, respectively, were built of heavy timbers near Québec, sailed to England to be broken up and sold as timber in order to evade a British tax. Though freak vessels at over 90 m length, they could claim to be the largest sailing ships in the world at the time and for 30 years after. Many conventional vessels were also built, and Lévis to Lauzon in Québec became a vast timber yard and shipyard. The timber droghers of this period are celebrated in Canadian folk songs and chanteys.

The construction of fishing vessels was more of a cottage industry than a commercial enterprise. A natural response to demand throughout the colonies, these vessels were built of a size and type suited to the fishery, whether inshore or offshore. Among them was *Jenny*, built in Newfoundland in 1783, the first recorded tern (3-masted) schooner in the world.

The most colourful and profitable days of Canadian shipbuilding were from 1849 to 1895, when many famous full-rigged ships and barques were built. In 1853 some 80 ships of between 1000 and 2000 tons each were launched in the Canadas and the Maritimes. In 1858, of the 100 sailing ships of 1200 tons or more that cleared Liverpool, Eng, for Australia, 64 were Canadian built. The Shipping Register of Liverpool showed that more than 85% of the ships over 500 tons were built in British N America. In 1875, the peak year, nearly 500 ships were built in Canadian shipyards. A prominent vessel of that glorious period was MARCO POLO, built at Saint John in 1851. She was big, 1625 tons, strong, and for a time "the fastest ship in the world." Another was W.D. LAWRENCE, 2459 tons, built in 1874 at Maitland, NS, the largest Canadian-built full-rigged ship afloat. The Canadian merchant fleet in 1878 numbered 7196 vessels, of 1 333 015 aggregate tonnage, making Canada the fourth shipowning nation in the world, a position that has been regained on 2 occasions since, in 1918 and in 1944. The industry gave employment to craftsmen and lumbermen, provided bottoms for transport of goods and immigrants and, perhaps the greatest commercial advantage, had favourable influence on the balance of payments; at times ships were the most valuable exports of the colonies. Between 1786 and 1920, over 4000 wooden sailing ships exceeding 500 tons were built in eastern Canada. The fast passages made by Canadian-built ships, their great size and innovative design made them popular among British owners and contributed to Britain's commercial conquest of the seas.

As iron- and steel-hulled sailing ships and steamships built in Britain, Germany and Denmark replaced wooden square-riggers, Canada found it harder and harder to compete. By 1895 the Canadian builders were out of the big-ship business, although construction of fishing schooners and coasters continued for many years. Tens of thousands of men skilled in marine ironworking, sail making, wood shaping, etc, were put out of work.

In 1809 the first Canadian steam vessel, ACCOMMODATION, was built and launched in Montréal by John MOLSON adjacent to his brewery.

The vessel was 26 m in length and carried passengers between Montréal and Québec City. Steam engines of greater strength were rapidly developed. The 100-hp engine of the Montréal tug *Hercules* (1823) was at the time the largest in the world. The paddle steamer ROYAL WILLIAM was built at Wolfe's Cove, Qué, in 1831, with a 200-hp engine made in Montréal. In 1833 she was the first merchant vessel to make a transatlantic voyage (from Pictou to Cowes) largely under steam. One of her owners was Samuel CUNARD of Halifax, founder of the CUNARD COMPANY. As well as pioneering the building of marine steam engines, Canada produced the first compound steam engine. The St John R steamboat *Reindeer* had a 43-hp compound engine installed in 1846 and built in Fredericton, NB.

Collingwood Shipyards (1902), the first Canadian steel shipbuilding yard on the upper lakes, and Canadian Vickers Ltd at Montréal (1912) are examples of enterprises still in existence. The shipyard at Pt Arthur [Thunder Bay] was built in 1912, and next year produced the passenger steamer NORONIC. By then, 1980 steamers aggregating 415 089 grt were registered in Québec and Ontario ports compared with only 598 steamers totalling 89 079 grt registered in the Maritime ports.

The Canadian shipyards of this period exhibited a versatility that remains their strength to this day, in the construction of vessels of many diverse types and special purpose including bulk grain, coal and ore LAKE CARRIERS, passenger ships, coasters, FERRIES, ICEBREAKERS and government patrol vessels. Tugs, dredges and hopper barges, many still in service, were also built in the prewar years. The dimensions of the vessels for the St Lawrence canal system and the upper lakes were controlled by the size of the locks. As such, they were long, slender vessels efficient for that trade but unsuitable for open sea, although many of these ships did ply the N Atlantic during WWI and WWII.

The need for bottoms to transport supplies overseas during WWI led the IMPERIAL MUNITIONS BOARD to place many orders for ships in Canadian yards. In 1917-18 approximately 60 steel cargo steamers of 1700-5800 grt were built, as well as submarine chasers, tugs, drifters and minesweeping trawlers. Because of urgency of demand, wooden shipbuilding was revived as well. In BC alone, 134 vessels comprising 20 wooden schooners, 69 wooden steamers and 45 steel steamers were built by West Coast shipyards. Wooden steamers were also built in Montréal, Trois-Rivières, Québec and Saint John. Some steel vessels built on the lakes were constructed in halves, in order to pass through the St Lawrence canals, and then joined together at Montréal.

At the end of WWI the Canadian Government Merchant Marine Ltd was incorporated in an effort to maintain shipyard employment and to continue Canada's position in ocean shipping. As the vessels became obsolete they were not replaced, and were sold off during the GREAT DEPRESSION. By 1936 the fleet ceased to exist. From 1930 to 1939 the Canadian shipyards built only 14 steamers exceeding 46 m in length, but in the same period many vessels for the lakes and canal trade were imported from Britain.

Canada's response to the Allies' need for ships at the outbreak of WWII was immediate, effective, and on a much larger scale than that of WWI. This quick expansion under the direction of the Dept of Munitions and Supply was managed by a cadre of resident Canadian shipbuilders and naval architects, a delegation of shipbuilders sent by the British Admiralty, and experienced managers from other Canadian industries recruited for the duration. War production peaked in 1943 and, though for a time building barely kept pace with sinkings, a stage was reached where construction had to be

phased down because of a surplus of ships. At peak there were 7 shipyards building 10 000 tonners, 3 producing 4700 tonners, 10 engaged in naval work, and 62 producing tugs, lighters and landing craft. In total, 398 merchant ships and 393 naval vessels were built. The naval vessels were primarily corvettes, minesweepers, frigates, and eventually destroyers. The cargo vessels were operated by the Park Steamship Co, a crown corporation. They were sold off after the war, many to Canadian shipowners in an attempt to maintain a Canadian merchant fleet; if resold the proceeds went into escrow for the construction of new Canadian registered vessels. Most went to foreign owners (*see* SHIPPING INDUSTRY).

Since 1945 the Canadian shipbuilding industry has been much reduced in scale. Various subsidy programs, accelerated depreciation allowances, export development grants, and import duties helped the industry, but not sufficiently to meet the competition from abroad assisted by more generous subsidies, foreign-exchange rates, and lower labour wage scales.

Canadian shipyards of necessity cannot concentrate on multiple production of vessels of standard design or on a limited range of special service vessels, but must be capable of adapting to a very wide range of vessel types, many of them prototypes. They specialize in high-quality construction for inland and coastal trade and in government service and naval vessels. They are pre-eminent in ice-capable vessels, from the icebreaking car ferry *Abegweit*, built in 1947 for the Northumberland Strait, which established design standards for welded steel icebreakers with diesel-electric propulsion and multiple propellers, to the 23 200-hp icebreaking supply vessel *Terry Fox*, built in 1983 to support oil exploration in the Beaufort Sea. Other examples of Canadian innovation are the thorough design effort devoted to the Arctic Pilot Project; the proposed 395 m, 140 000 m³ class, 10 Arctic LNG carrier; vessels for oceanographic, hydrographic and fisheries research which are of world class; the development of tug-and-barge operations on the West Coast and, in particular, self-dumping log barges. The development of hydrofoil craft, begun in Canada with the early experiments of Alexander Graham BELL in Cape Breton, was brought to success with *Bras d'Or* in 1964, a prototype of advanced design despite metallurgical faults in the foils material. Canadian shipyards have also been active in the construction of offshore oil exploration platforms, from semisubmersible rigs built by Victoria Machinery Depot Ltd in the late 1960s to jack-up rigs built at Davie Shipbuilding Co Ltd. In the 1970s Halifax Shipyards Ltd and in the early 1980s Saint John Drydock and Shipbuilding were active in semisubmersible vessel construction.

Naval construction since the war has been maintained to a degree. Canada's NATO role of submarine hunting and escort tasks has been met by a series of destroyer construction pro-

The Halifax shipyards, showing construction of a stern "dragger" (*photo by Barrett and MacKay/Masterfile*).

grams. From the *Tribal* class of the end of the war to the Canadian-designed *St Laurent* class of the 1950s was a quantum leap in design and production to provide an escort vessel that was the envy of other navies. *MacKenzie* class of the 1960s followed, then the new Tribal class and the CPF (Canadian Patrol Frigate) currently being built. A variety of service vessels ranging from wood-and-aluminum minesweepers to replenishment vessels such as *Provider* have also been built.

Canadian Shipbuilding and Ship Repairing Assn Shipyards, 1938-83

Year	Workers Employed	Year	Workers Employed
1938	3 372	1963	12 797
1943	50 529	1968	9 913
1948	14 787	1973	10 654
1953	19 456	1978	10 574
1958	13 076	1983	6 821

Ship Repairing is a necessary service wherever ships ply and, as an exporting nation, Canada must provide such facilities. Naval strategic requirements have a bearing on the location of drydocks and repair shops on Canada's coasts; repair installations also provide employment for essential shipbuilding technical staff, managers and tradesmen during slack times between new building contracts.

On the Great Lakes are large drydocks at Pt Arthur, Collingwood and Pt Weller, all associated with shipyards and capable of docking large lake carriers. Docks at Kingston, and the St Lawrence Dry Dock and Cantin Dry Dock at Montréal for the 245-ft canalers are now gone. The major drydocks on the West Coast are at Esquimalt adjacent to Yarrows Ltd and the Burrard Dry Dock in Vancouver harbour. On the East Coast is a floating dock of 36 000-ton capacity at Halifax, and the Saint John Drydock, which when built in 1914, and for 40 years after, was the largest in the world. Lauzon has a large dock, and Montréal a floating dock similar to that at Halifax. The Newfoundland Dockyard, located virtually in the middle of the N Atlantic shipping lanes, was built of wood in 1884, and later replaced by a stone graving dock. A new ship-lift system at the same location, for the repair of deep-sea factory trawlers and offshore supply vessels, is capable of lifting 4000-ton vessels into 3 berths. Many other Canadian harbours have marine railways, ship lifts and small drydocks for repair of floating equipment and vessels. A few of these are a legacy of the wartime installations for the maintenance of frigates and corvettes and the repair of war-damaged merchant ships, but many have been built or improved since then for commercial or fishery vessel repair.

The Canadian Shipbuilding and Ship Repair Assn was formed in 1944 to ensure the continuance of a viable industry after the war and to prevent the repetition of the gradual dissolution of the dearly won industry in the early 1920s. It also serves to encourage technical-information exchange within an industry where technology transfer is vital to survival. The CSSRA member shipyards currently account for 97% of all ship construction in Canada of vessels in excess of 30 m length. Although total shipyard employment in recent "good" years is down from the peak years of 1952 and 1953, current manufacturing capacity is higher than at any time since WWII. An estimated 400 000 dwt tons of standard shipping could be built annually. W.J. MILNE

Reading: Canadian Shipbuilding and Ship Repairing Assn *Annual Reports;* K. Matthews and G. Panting, eds, *Ships and Shipbuilding in the North Atlantic Region* (1977); F.W. Wallace, *The Story of Shipbuilding in Canada* (1944) and *Wooden Ships and Iron Men* (1924, repr 1973).

Shipman, Ernest G., "Ten Percent Ernie," film producer, promoter (b at either Hull, Qué, or Ottawa 16 Dec 1871; d at New York C 7 Aug 1931). The most successful FILM producer during the expansive period 1914-22, he was responsible for 7 feature films, all adaptations of Canadian stories and filmed on location. Educated at Ryerson, he established the Canadian Entertainment Bureau in Toronto and later became a successful promoter of theatrical stock companies in New York. Following a move to California in 1912, he became increasingly active in films as publicist, agent and then promoter. A 1918 contract for the film rights of James Oliver Curwood's stories led to the establishment in Calgary of a company to film *Back to God's Country* (1919), a major success. He then created production companies in Winnipeg, Ottawa, Sault Ste Marie and Saint John. Five of the films made were modest successes, but the last, *Blue Water* (1923), was not released. He left Canada, attempted to promote production elsewhere, but died in relative obscurity. PETER MORRIS

Reading: Peter Morris, *Embattled Shadows* (1978).

Shipping, Maritime, *see* MARITIME SHIPPING HISTORY TO 1900.

Shipping Industry As one of the world's oldest transport modes, shipping, or carriage of goods by water, has played a significant role in the development of human society over the centuries. Shipping has been a crucial link by which commercial relationships have been established between widely separated parts of the world.

There are 2 major types of shipping services: shipload services, which move goods in bulk for one or 2 shippers; and liner services, which carry relatively small shipments of general cargo on a regular schedule for many shippers. Some ships are owned by firms engaged in the production or processing of goods in bulk. Examples are tankers owned by petroleum companies, and bulk carriers owned by steel companies. Most ships, however, are owned by firms whose prime business is shipping. These owners make their vessels available to importers/exporters through a highly efficient international network of shipping brokers.

History and Development Shipping is often the least expensive way of moving large quantities of goods over long distances. The existence of reliable water transportation has been a key to the economic and political well-being of most nations throughout history. For example, the merchant fleet of Great Britain during the Industrial Revolution was instrumental in the growth of that nation as a world power. Shipping services have always been an economic lifeline for Canadians. For the first settlers, ships were the source of essential supplies from the Old World, and provided the means by which fur, agricultural, forestry and mining products could be marketed. In eastern Canada, especially in the Maritimes, a tradition based on SHIPBUILDING, fishing and trade flourished.

In 1840 Samuel CUNARD of Halifax established a transoceanic service that developed into the world-famous CUNARD CO, and by 1878 Canada ranked fourth among the shipowning nations of the world. However, in the last decades of the century, Canadian participation in shipbuilding and shipping diminished, as steel and engineering skills, which Canada lacked, became prerequisites for a successful shipbuilding industry. The 2 world wars caused temporary booms in shipping under the Canadian flag, but since 1949, when the Canadian government decided to sell off its Canadian-registered fleet, the vast majority of Canadian overseas trade has been carried in ships registered in other countries. Most Canadian-registered ships now operate on domestic routes, such as the ST LAWRENCE SEAWAY, the Great Lakes and the coastlines.

Economic Significance Shipping is especially important to Canada because of the high proportion of the GROSS NATIONAL PRODUCT that is derived from exports (23.3% in 1983), the high proportion of imports in final domestic consumption of goods and services (19.8% in 1983), and the importance of water transport in facilitating this export and import trade. In 1981, 31.8% of exports and 22.0% of imports (both figures by value) were transported by water, more than half of this by liner vessels. By weight, however, the quantity of goods carried by shipload services greatly exceeds that carried by liners.

Although the Canadian-registered deep-sea fleet is small, officers and crews are needed to operate vessels on domestic routes. Vessels arriving from abroad require a variety of services, including Canadian pilots and tugs to bring them into port, as well as repair facilities and supply services in port. The movement of the cargoes themselves also creates considerable employment. For example, longshoremen help load and unload cargoes on the docks, and many persons, such as customs and insurance agents, look after documentary and other related requirements. Shipping agents, located in many Canadian cities, strive to sell their company's shipping services to prospective customers.

Domestic and Transborder Routes Domestic shipping can be divided into 3 main categories. East Coast traffic consists primarily of fuel, pulpwood and general cargo shipments to Newfoundland and along the coastlines of the Maritime provinces and into the St Lawrence. The St Lawrence-Great Lakes traffic is by far the most important route. The main commodity movements are grain from the Lakehead to the St Lawrence ports, and IRON ORE from Canada to the US (*see also* CANALS AND INLAND WATERWAYS). West Coast shipping services include the movement of forest products and other natural resources, often by tug and barge operations. On both the East and West coasts there is an extensive network of ferry services (*see* FERRIES). Other shipping services include occasional intercoastal movements of bulk commodities, barge services on the MACKENZIE R AND supply services to arctic communities. Shipping is a key to the development of Canada's North, a means by which natural resources can be reached (*see* TRANSPORTATION IN THE NORTH). The supply lines to many remote northern communities are maintained as the weather permits. In 1969 the American tanker SS *Manhattan* successfully navigated the NORTHWEST PASSAGE with the aid of a Canadian Coast Guard vessel, thereby proving that mineral and petroleum resources in remote northern areas could be reached by water (*see* ICEBREAKERS).

Overseas Shipping Canada's most important overseas trading partners are Japan, Great Britain and other western European nations, so that the busiest shipping routes are the N Atlantic and the N Pacific. One-third of Canada's trade with the US moves by water. Significant ties are maintained with all regions of the world, and bulk shipping services are available as needed. Canada's trade is carried in vessels registered in many different countries. Many of these deep-sea vessels are registered in so-called flag-of-convenience nations, such as Liberia and Singapore, where favourable tax and legal environments permit lower-cost operations.

Ships and Harbour Facilities are efficiently serving Canadian trade. Specially designed ships and harbours have been built to accommodate particular commodities. In eastern Canada, for example, ships called LAKE CARRIERS are built to the maximum allowable seaway dimensions. Maximum-sized lakers can carry about 29 000 tonnes (28 000 cargo capacity, 1000 fuel etc). On the West Coast, the self-dumping barge has been developed for use in the forest industry. Roberts Bank, BC, is the site of a large coal superport, specially designed to handle the large volume of coal which arrives by rail for export overseas.

Canadian Shipping Today Few Canadian-flag ships operate deep-sea routes. However, some Canadian-incorporated companies operate foreign-registered ships. The major Canadian companies owning deep-sea fleets are CP Ships Ltd, Cast North America Ltd, Papachristidis Maritime Inc and Fednav Ltd. Owing to government regulations that give preference in coastal waters to Canadian-flag vessels, all ships operating domestic routes are registered in Canada, unless a foreign-flag vessel is granted a waiver.

As of 30 June 1982 the Canadian-flag fleet of vessels over 100 gross registered tons (grt) was 3.2 million grt. By comparison, the Liberian fleet at 70.7 million grt was the largest, the British fleet at 22.5 million grt was sixth and the US fleet at 19.1 million grt was eighth (Lloyds Register of Shipping). Most Canadian-registered merchant vessels operate on domestic routes, although recent technological development has seen the introduction of several vessels constructed for the Great Lakes-St Lawrence Seaway traffic which are also capable of transoceanic voyages.

The present lack of a Canadian-flag deep-sea fleet is a source of frequent debate. Some importers and exporters argue that foreign-flag operations permit lower-cost operations and thereby help to keep Canadian trade competitive. This view is opposed by others, who feel that selective employment of Canadian-registered and manned vessels could be efficient if the government would provide tax concessions comparable, for example, to those of Great Britain. A Canadian fleet, they argue, would increase employment and would also safeguard against intervention by foreign governments.

Regulation Most shipping is by nature international — the carriage of goods between countries and across international waters. A ship may be owned, financed, registered, insured, and managed, each in a different country. When a ship is registered in any given country, it becomes subject to the laws of that country at all times. Each country has the right to establish its own shipping laws. International shipping conventions have been reached by a number of intergovernmental organizations, such as the International Labour Organization (ILO), the United Nations Conference on Trade and Development (UNCTAD), and the International Maritime Organization (IMO). Many of the conventions have been ratified by Canada (*see* INTERNATIONAL LAW; LAW OF THE SEA).

In Canada, shipping falls under the jurisdiction of the federal Department of TRANSPORT. The Canada Shipping Act sets out the basic rules for ships flying the Canadian flag or operating in Canadian waters. The CANADIAN COAST GUARD ensures that ships meet the requirements of the Shipping Act and follow pollution-prevention procedures. The Water Transport Committee of the Canadian Transport Commission is responsible for economic regulation: for example, shipping conferences must file their rates with the committee. Ports Canada administers the major ports in Canada.

Recent Developments Since 1958 the United Nations Conference on the Law of the Sea has met 3 times in an attempt to codify international maritime law. Many of these discussions have been of interest to shipowners and shippers, for they have dealt with areas such as environmental-protection laws and rules for defining international maritime boundaries. UNCTAD has tried to help developing nations participate in international shipping. The Code of Conduct for Liner Conferences was drawn up under the auspices of UNCTAD. It allows countries to reserve 40% of their liner cargo to national carriers.

Significant technological advances have oc-

curred in shipping. Large specialized ships are used for bulk cargoes; general cargo is carried by liners in containers. In Canada, improvements have included the development of the self-unloading carrier for use particularly in the Great Lakes — St Lawrence Seaway trade. Liquefied-natural-gas (LNG) carriers will transport western natural gas to Japan. Special vessels are being discussed for the movement of petroleum and mineral resources from arctic areas. Petroleum may eventually be carried by specially strengthened vessels or even by submarine tankers. The development of trade will be linked, as always, to cost-reducing technologies in shipping. *See also* MARITIME SHIPPING HISTORY.

TREVOR D. HEAVER

Reading: J. Bird, *Seaports and Seaport Terminals* (1971); A.E. Branch, *The Elements of Shipping* (1977); E. Gold, *Maritime Transport, The Evolution of International Marine Policy and Shipping Law* (1981); G.K. Sletmo and E.W. Williams, *Liner Conferences in the Container Age* (1981).

Shoes and Shoemaking, *see* FOOTWEAR INDUSTRY; LEATHERWORKING.

Shooting As Canada was developing as a nation, the sport of shooting played an integral role in the life-style of its early settlers, both as a means for survival and for amusement and enjoyment as a recreational pastime. Firearms could be found in every home and as the nation developed so did the sport of shooting. Today, it is one of the fastest-growing sports in the world, offering the widest appeal to both men and women, young and old, and to the recreational or more competitive participant. Shooting can truly be called a lifetime sporting activity.

Shooting is a diversified sport that can be practised in a variety of forms and with an array of firearms. The 3 main types of arms are the rifle, pistol and shotgun. During the 1860s, rifle associations were formed in Canada to accommodate the growing interest in shooting sports. The first record of a Canadian team representing Canada abroad was in 1871 when a fullbore team shot at Wimbledon, Eng. By 1890, shooting clubs had developed in most provinces.

Rifle shooting is divided into 3 basic categories based on the type of rifle used: smallbore, fullbore and air rifle. Further subdivisions in competitive shooting are based on the type of shooting position: prone, kneeling and standing. The average weight of a rifle is between 5 and 8 kg. Targets range in distance from 10 to 300 m. The rifle events included in the Olympics are, for men, air rifle, prone smallbore, 3-position smallbore and running game target, and for women, standard rifle and air rifle.

The pistol, designed to be light in weight, was invented by an Italian, Caminello Vitelli, in 1540 and its name derives from his home town of Pistola. Competitive pistol shooting is growing rapidly in Canada and is as popular as other forms of shooting. Some of the most common pistols used today are the rim fire, air, and centre-fire pistols. In competitive pistol shooting the targets range from 10 to 50 m, depending on the event. In the Olympics there are 3 pistol events: rapid fire and free for men and match pistol for women.

The third category of firearms, the shotgun, is used in clay pigeon shooting, where saucerlike clay targets are released into the air at various angles. There are 2 types of clay pigeon shooting — trapshooting and skeet. Trapshooting dates from the early 19th century in England. Because the supply of birds had been severely exhausted throughout the 1880s, marksmen had to find a substitute. In 1880 George Ligowsky of Cincinnati, Ohio, developed the first clay pigeon, which was made of finely ground clay mixed with water and baked. The first record of a trapshooting competition in Canada was the Canadian Clay-Pigeon Championships held in Jan 1886 at Carlton Place, Ont. Trapshooting clubs

were established throughout the country in the late 1880s and early 1890s.

There are 2 types of trapshooting in Canada: International Clay Pigeon shooting (also known as Olympic Trap) and ATA (Amateur Trapshooting Assn) trapshooting. A 12-gauge shotgun is used in both. In International Clay Pigeon shooting there are 15 machines that throw the target at various angles between 0° and 45° horizontal and different heights for a distance of 70 to 80 m. Competitors are allowed 2 shots at each clay pigeon. In ATA trapshooting one machine is used to throw the clay pigeon 50 m at various angles between 0° and 22°. Only one shot is taken by competitors. International Clay Pigeon shooting was first introduced into the Olympics in 1900.

Skeet shooting was started in the US in 1926. Intended as a way to help shooters improve their field shooting, it is now an intensely competitive and popular sport. There are 2 types of skeet shooting in Canada: International Skeet and NSSA (National Skeet Shooting Assn) or American skeet. The 3 significant differences in International and American skeet are the starting position of the gun, the variable-time release system for throwing the target, and the distance to which targets are thrown — 71 yards versus 55 to 60 yards. Skeet shooting was introduced into the Olympics in 1968 in Mexico City.

Shooting has been a recognized Olympic sport since the revival of the modern Olympics in 1896 and the founder, Baron Pierre de Coubertin, was a renowned French pistol champion. The International Shooting Union (ISU) was formed in 1907 to oversee and implement the rules, regulations and safe conduct of shooting competitions. Canada applied for membership in the ISU in 1908, and that same year sent a shooting team for the first time to the Olympics. Walter EWING, a trapshooter, was Canada's lone gold medalist.

A national organization was formed in Canada in 1932 under the name of the Canadian Small Bore Rifle Assn. In 1949 it became the Canadian Civilian Assn of Marksmen. The present name, the Shooting Federation of Canada (SFC) was authorized in 1964 when the trap and skeet associations affiliated to form one umbrella organization. The SFC is responsible for the coordination and administration of all programs regarding Olympic-style shooting sports in Canada. *See also* G. GENEREAUX; B. HARTMAN; G. OUELLETE and S. NATTRASS.   SUSAN M. NATTRASS

Shooting Star (genus *Dodecatheon*), perennial herbaceous PLANT of Primulaceae family (primrose). Most of the 13 known species are native to western N America; 6 to Canada. *D. hendersonii* and *D. jeffreyi* occur in coastal BC; *D. dentatum* in southern BC; *D. frigidum* in northern BC, coastal YT and Mackenzie R delta. These 4 species grow on damp meadows, heaths and streambanks, in low to high elevations. *D. conjugens* ranges from southeastern BC to southwestern Saskatchewan in seepage areas in sagebrush plains and up to alpine meadows. *D. pauciflorum*, the most widespread, is found from the Mackenzie R delta to southern Manitoba, in meadows, open woods, moist slopes and saline places. One to several flowers are borne on a long, leafless stalk arising from a rosette of leaves on the ground. White to purple petals are turned inside out like a wind-blown umbrella, exposing stamens and pistil. Most flower Mar-June. The fruit, a capsule, opens by valves to release seeds.

Shoppers Drug Mart was started in 1952 by Murray Koffler, who pioneered the chain drugstore concept in Canada. There are now 440 franchised and company-owned Shoppers Drug Marts in the US and Canada. In 1983 the company had sales or operating revenue of over $1 billion, ranking sixth among all drugstore chains in N America.   DEBORAH C. SAWYER

Shopping Centres, *see* RETAIL TRADE.

Shore, Edward William, hockey player (b at Ft Qu'Appelle, Sask 25 Nov 1902; d at Springfield, Mass 16 Mar 1985). He played semiprofessional hockey in Edmonton and joined Boston Bruins in 1926. Called the "Iceman," Shore was aloof and aggressive, a fearless rushing defenceman and brutal checker. He was a brilliant and exciting player, but combative as well, and his career was marred by controversy. In Dec 1934 he almost killed "Ace" Bailey with a vicious check, and he himself suffered numerous serious injuries as a result of violent play. He was the greatest defenceman of his day, and was awarded the HART TROPHY 4 times. Tales of his eccentric, even bizarre behaviour as owner of the AHL Springfield Indians, which he purchased in 1939, have become part of hockey folklore, but he had an astute understanding of the sport's fundamentals.   JAMES MARSH

Shorebird (order Charadriiformes), long-legged BIRD, usually with long, thin bill. Shorebirds are found beside seashores, by lake and river margins, and in marshy areas. Most take their prey on the surface of the water or probe for it in soft ground. They lay clutches of 4 camouflaged eggs in scrapes in the ground and often distract predators from them by feigning a broken wing. Forty-eight species regularly breed in Canada, mainly in the Arctic. These range from least SANDPIPERS (about 13 cm long) to long-billed curlews (about 65 cm). Millions of semipalmated sandpipers and red-necked PHALAROPES visit the Bay of FUNDY in autumn. By contrast, piping PLOVERS are rare and endangered by man's use of their habitat of sandy beaches; Eskimo curlews, hunted to excess, are almost extinct. SNIPE and WOODCOCK, popular GAME BIRDS, are the only shorebirds legally hunted in Canada today.   R.G.B. BROWN

Short Fiction in English encompasses a wide range of forms, including ESSAY, sketch and short story; and elements of all these forms may blend in individual works, as in "The Village Inside" and "Predictions of Ice" from Hugh HOOD's *Around the Mountain: Scenes from Montreal Life* (1967). Questions of form tantalize writers and readers. Hugh MACLENNAN, for example, has composed nearly 400 essays and only one short story ("An Orange from Portugal," which he later called an essay) yet has remarked that "The secret of writing a successful personal essay...is to turn it into a short story."

There are other ways of classifying short fiction — the most time-honoured category, in which Canadian writers like Ernest Thompson SETON and Charles G.D. ROBERTS have made major contributions, being the animal story. Another category, in which Gregory Clark, Morley CALLAGHAN, Hugh HOOD, Mordecai RICHLER, W.P. Kinsella and George BOWERING have excelled, is the sports story. A third category is the writer's story, in which authors momentarily unmask themselves as they examine their lives as writers, and sometimes even question the purposes of their fiction. The number of such subgenres is great, and includes initiation stories, war stories, mystery, science-fiction and adventure stories, humorous stories, ethnic stories, etc.

Canadian short fiction has always maintained close associations with the popular markets provided by newspapers and magazines (*see* LITERARY MAGAZINES). A pattern of first publication in periodicals and subsequent collection in book form was established in the 19th century, and has continued to the present day. It began with Thomas MCCULLOCH, whose "Letters of Mephibosheth Stepsure" was first published in the *Acadian Recorder,* 1821-23, but was not collected in book form until 1862. Satirist Thomas Chandler HALIBURTON's "The Clockmaker" was first published in Joseph HOWE's *Novascotian* in 1835-36,

then expanded into book form in 1836, with sequels in 1838 and 1840. In total, Haliburton published 10 collections of sketches. Portions of Susanna MOODIE's ROUGHING IT IN THE BUSH were first published in *The Literary Garland* before appearing in book form in 1852. Stephen LEACOCK published SUNSHINE SKETCHES OF A LITTLE TOWN in *The Montreal Daily Star* (Feb-June 1912), then as a book later the same year.

Since the 1920s the connections between short fiction and newspapers or magazines have remained strong, as seen in the publication of work by Raymond Knister, Morley Callaghan, Gregory Clark, Mavis GALLANT, Alice MUNRO, Hugh Hood, Jack HODGINS and Leon Rooke in periodicals as diverse as *Star Weekly, The TAMARACK REVIEW, Journal of Canadian Fiction, Canadian Fiction Magazine* and *The New Yorker*. Several writers have also edited newspapers, magazines or anthologies.

Sketches Carole Gerson and Kathy Mezei define the sketch as "an apparently personal anecdote or memoir which focusses on one particular place, person, or experience, and is usually intended for magazine publication." Its colloquial tone and informal structure relate it to the epistolary form employed in several early Canadian works. One common kind is the humorous or satirical sketch, as found in the works of McCulloch, Haliburton and Leacock. A second kind is the autobiographical, descriptive or travel sketch, as practised by Howe, William "Tiger" DUNLOP, Catharine Parr TRAILL, Anna Jameson, Archibald LAMPMAN, William Wilfred CAMPBELL, Duncan Campbell SCOTT, Sara Jeannette DUNCAN and Frederick Philip GROVE. Raymond Knister's country sketches about Corncob Corners represent a third kind of sketch. The sketch had slipped into the shadow of the short story by the late 1920s, although it has continued in the works of several humorists, including Paul Hiebert (*Sarah Binks,* 1947), Robertson DAVIES (*The Diary of Samuel Marchbanks,* 1947, *The Table Talk of Samuel Marchbanks,* 1949, and *Samuel Marchbanks' Almanack,* 1967) and Earle BIRNEY (*Big Bird in the Bush,* 1978), as well as in such AUTOBIOGRAPHICAL WRITING as Emily CARR's KLEE WYCK (1941) and Mordecai Richler's *The Street* (1969). Hood's *Around the Mountain* is an important late 20th-century contribution to the history of the sketch in Canada.

Animal Stories The most distinctive early contribution by Canadians to short fiction was the animal stories of Seton and Roberts. According to Alec Lucas, Seton's first book, WILD ANIMALS I HAVE KNOWN (1898), "established . . . the realistic animal story." Seton saw his own development of the animal story as an evolution from "the archaic method, making the animals talk" to "the more scientific method." But it is important to recognize that Seton's realistic stories, like later realistic stories by such writers as Howard O'HAGAN and W.D. Valgardson, are decidedly fictions, regardless of their basis in real life. Moreover, Seton's avowedly moral purpose and characteristic romanticism shaped all his stories and made them something other than strictly realistic.

Romantic elements are also evident in the numerous books of animal stories by Roberts, whose first full collection was *The Kindred of the Wild* (1902). In its preface, Roberts defines the animal story at "its highest point of development" as "a psychological romance constructed on a framework of natural science." Although the romantic animal story's popularity has declined, the Canadian tradition of the animal story has continued to thrive, not only in the nonfictional and fictional prose writing of naturalists and storytellers Roderick HAIG-BROWN, Fred BODSWORTH, Sheila Burnford and Farley MOWAT, but also in the highly literary, formally conceived short fiction of Dave GODFREY (*Death Goes Better with Coca-Cola,* 1967).

Scott, Callaghan, Wilson, Gallant and Their Successors In the introduction to his pioneer anthology *Canadian Short Stories* (1928), Raymond Knister writes of the "unobtrusive influence" of D.C. Scott's story cycle *In the Village of Viger* (1896) and praises it as "a perfect flowering of art." Subsequent critics, such as Stan Dragland, have supported Knister's view. *In the Village of Viger* was followed by *The Witching of Elspie* (1923) and *The Circle of Affection* (1947). Scott's work looks back to 19th-century American gothic and romantic and local-colour writing, yet its ironic tone connects it with mid-20th-century writing, and his use of imagery anticipates the poetically conceived short stories written later in the century. Moreover, as a unit, *In the Village of Viger* is a foundation stone in the Canadian tradition of the story cycle.

In Robert Weaver's view, Morley Callaghan was "the first and most important of the modern short-story writers in Canada." Callaghan was also a significant influence on writers such as Norman Levine, whose first book of stories, *One Way Ticket,* was published in 1961, and Hugh Hood, whose first book of stories, *Flying a Red Kite,* appeared in 1962. Callaghan's early books of short fiction were *A Native Argosy* (1929), the novella *No Man's Meat* (1931) and *Now That April's Here and Other Stories* (1936). Most of these stories were collected, with a number of more recent ones, in *Morley Callaghan's Stories* (1959); *No Man's Meat & the Enchanted Pimp* (1978) contains a slightly revised version of his 1931 novella and a new novella. Callaghan's stories were important for his choices of subject and situation; his modern, urban, even international outlook; his understanding of the importance and the difficulty of writing about everyday life; and the intimately human moral complexities that he explored. Furthermore, as Margaret AVISON has observed, they created a strong feeling of immediacy because of his special and new way of using words plainly. Even more important to the succeeding generation of writers was the reputation that Callaghan had made for himself.

Callaghan did not establish a standard of stylistic elegance. That achievement belonged to Ethel Wilson. Two novellas by Wilson, "Tuesday and Wednesday" and "Lilly's Story," were published as *The Equations of Love* (1952); and some of her short stories, first published in magazines, appeared in *Mrs. Golightly and Other Stories* (1961). Wilson's fiction — novels, novellas and short stories — significantly influenced Canadian writers from the late 1940s to the early 1960s, including Margaret LAURENCE and Alice Munro, both major contributors to the history of short fiction in Canada. Laurence's first book of stories, *The Tomorrow-Tamer and Other Stories,* was published in 1963. Her story cycle *A Bird in the House* (1970) stands with Scott's *In the Village of*

The strength of Alice Munro's fiction lies in its vivid sense of place, as well as in Munro's sense of the narrator as the intelligence through which the world is articulated (*photo by Larry Dillon*).

Viger, Leacock's *Sunshine Sketches of a Little Town* and Hood's *Around the Mountain* as major benchmarks for subsequent creators of story cycles (or sketchbooks) in Canada. Munro's first book of stories, *Dance of the Happy Shades* (1968), contained the best of her work from nearly 2 decades. By the early 1980s, Munro had the best popular and international reputation of Canadian short story writers. She emerged as the writer most often identified with the rebirth of the Canadian short story, and as the writer most prominently concerned with trying to shape short stories into coherent books or storycycles — most notably in *Who Do You Think You Are?* (1978).

The most truly international of Canadian short-story writers, however, are Mavis Gallant and Clark BLAISE. Gallant's *The Other Paris* (1956), *My Heart Is Broken* (1964), *The Pegnitz Junction* (1973), *The End of the World and Other Stories* (1974), *From the Fifteenth District* (1979) and *Home Truths* (1981) brought a more intricate internationalism, a richly textured political awareness and exquisite craft to Canadian short fiction. This combination appeared also in the work of Blaise, in *A North American Education* (1973) and *Tribal Justice* (1974).

Leon Rooke and Hugh Hood Leon Rooke published *Last One Home Sleeps in the Yellow Bed* (1968) in the US before moving to Canada, and numerous books of his fiction have subsequently appeared in both countries. His achievement, as Blaise and John METCALF have recognized, lies in his mastery of voices, tones and especially language — from Rooke's native American South back to Renaissance England and ahead to contemporary times. This mastery, amply demonstrated in *Sing Me No Love Songs I'll Say You No Prayers* (1984), sets Rooke in a class almost by himself — with the exception of Hugh Hood.

Hood's subtle explorations of the possibilities of language and form began with the publication of *Flying a Red Kite* and continued in *Around the Mountain*. In *None Genuine Without This Signature* (1980), Hood's fifth collection of new work, the stories "Gone Three Days" and "God Has Manifested Himself Unto Us as Canadian Tire" are astonishing examples of the union of language, feeling and form. "The Woodcutter's Third Son" is a quietly dazzling treatment of the conflicting implications for human character of magical folklore and sacred scripture.

Experimental Writing A number of writers of short fiction have created works that, in the words of W.H. New, "strive for the expression of a total linguistic gesture: the restructuring of the world in the mind of the writer/reader." As examples New cites Ray Smith's audacious collection, *Cape Breton is the Thought Control Centre of Canada* (1969), Malcolm LOWRY's *Hear Us O Lord from Heaven Thy Dwelling Place* (1961), George Elliott's *The Kissing Man* (1962), Godfrey's *Death Goes Better with Coca-Cola* and Blaise's *A North American Education*. Smith's *Cape Breton* was followed by an even more verbally and structurally and psychologically exciting volume, the story cycle *Lord Nelson Tavern* (1974). Other interesting experimental works published between the late 1960s and the early 1980s include Lawrence Garber's *Garber's Tales from the Quarter* (1969) and *Circuit* (1970); Matt COHEN's *Columbus and the Fat Lady and Other Stories* (1972), *Night Flights* (1978), *The Expatriate* (1982) and *Café Le Dog* (1983); Andreas Schroeder's *The Late Man* (1972); Gwendolyn MACEWEN's *Noman* (1972); Terence Heath's *the truth & other stories* (1972); John GLASSCO's *The Fatal Woman* (1974); Rudy WIEBE's *Where Is the Voice Coming From?* (1974), *Alberta: A Celebration* (1979) and *The Angel of the Tar Sands and Other Stories* (1982); bp NICHOL's *Craft Dinner* (1978); Sheila Watson's *Four Stories* (1979); Margaret ATWOOD's *Murder in the Dark* (1983); and Phyllis GOTLIEB's *Son of the Morning and Other Stories* (1983).

Continuing Concerns and Evolving Forms Short fiction has many forms and purposes, yet trends exist. Jack Hodgins writes, in part, to challenge "a reader's concept of reality"; he, like Ernest BUCKLER (*Ox Bells and Fireflies*, 1968), Hood and Rooke, believes that writers must recognize the moral implications of their work. Nevertheless, there are major differences between these writers and earlier moral realists such as Callaghan, Grove, Sinclair ROSS, Hugh Garner and W.O. MITCHELL. As John Metcalf states in "Editing the Best" (*Kicking Against the Pricks*, 1982), "Where twenty years ago Canadian stories stressed content — what a story was *about* — the main emphasis now is on the story as verbal and rhetorical *performance*." These differences can be perceived in the evolution of some individual writers' conceptions of the short story. Alice Munro's stories, for example, move from her early narrative style towards a freer, more open, more dreamlike form. This movement is true also of the development of Canadian short-story writing in general.

New Directions Hood's "The Woodcutter's Third Son," Rooke's "The Birth Control King of the Upper Volta" and Metcalf's "Gentle as Flowers Make the Stones" represent 3 important directions that late 20th-century Canadian short fiction is taking: towards allegory of the human spirit, fantasy and poetic expression. The allegorical quality of Hood's writing is also evident, to varying degrees, in works by Rooke, Hodgins, Blaise and Peter Behrens. The fantastic character of Rooke's stories can be found as well, again to varying degrees, in the writing of Hood, H.R. Percy, Elliott, Schroeder, Wiebe, Seán Virgo, Hodgins, Margaret Gibson and Atwood. The poetic quality which is a mark of Metcalf's writing is apparent also in the structural and emblematic keys to stories by many of Metcalf's finest contemporaries. All 3 directions are represented in the opening paragraph of W.P. Kinsella's elegy for Janis Joplin, "First Names and Empty Pockets."

Reputations Canadian writers of short fiction, like authors in other genres, are subject to fluctuations in popularity. As personal likes shift back and forth between plain style and verbal play or between realism and fantasy, individual writers' reputations rise and fall accordingly — regardless of their work's quality. Furthermore, attention is rarely given to a writer's literary development, to a writer's changing views of the form of the short story. The most unfairly neglected authors are the border crossers: the new Canadians (including Elizabeth Spencer, Eugene MacNamara, Leon Rooke, Jane RULE, Audrey THOMAS, Kent Thompson, John Metcalf and Daphne Marlatt) and the so-called expatriates (including Wallace Stegner, Mavis Gallant, for many years Norman Levine, and now Clark Blaise) — writers who have made significant contributions to Canada's literary traditions but are generally regarded as not fully belonging to them. However, several deserving authors of recently published collections are gaining fine reputations; these writers include Keath Fraser, Terence Byrnes and Guy Vanderhaeghe. It is to be hoped that they, together with newcomers whose work is as yet uncollected, will have the breadth of vision, the determination, the energy and the good fortune to contribute significantly to the tradition of short fiction in Canada. *See* LITERATURE IN ENGLISH. J.R. (TIM) STRUTHERS

Short Fiction in French Tales (*contes*) and POETRY lie at the origin of Québec literature, perhaps by chance, perhaps as a necessary stage in the evolution of literary genres. Whatever the reason, the specific context of the beginnings of Canadian LITERATURE IN FRENCH seems in itself to justify the preponderance of short texts. Institutional theory has it that in the 19th century, books were rare and publishers essentially operated printing houses involved in everything but literature. Authors could often publish only in journals and LITERARY PERIODICALS, and this encouraged the production of short texts. Another possible explanation is aesthetic: the influence of romanticism made a fashion of FOLKLORE, popular traditions and local colour. The third possible explanation is ideological: at a time when the novel was viewed as pernicious because of the passions it revealed (17th-century THEATRE fell into similar disrepute), the short story seemed morally less offensive.

The short story proliferated, and appeared in the form of narratives embedded in the first NOVEL published in Québec, INFLUENCE D'UN LIVRE by Philippe AUBERT DE GASPÉ, JR. It became a permanent feature of literary journals and daily newspapers and emerged as an important genre in James Huston's *Répertoire national* (1848-50). The genre encompasses various types of short narratives, including summaries, novellae, exempla, short stories, anecdotes, portraits and various types of picturesque descriptions. These texts were both naive and detailed, often containing pompous rhetoric or a heavily didactic message. Of some 1100 works published in 19th-century periodicals, roughly 200, identified as tales and legends, have been published in collections. From a literary viewpoint, these tales and legends constitute the period's most interesting production of short narrative texts.

Many imaginative tales were drawn from legends. Major recurring themes included stories about the devil in which a character who has defied or ignored religious teaching is guided back to righteousness by some exemplary punishment. But this triadic organization (prohibition, transgression, punishment) is an oversimplification of the scope of these texts throughout which the transgression described has the glamour of a voluntary action. Of the devil's various acts (seduction, pact, possession), the first 2 appear most frequently. The character coming into contact with Satan is usually not a victim, but a person in search of his own destiny. Rose LATULIPPE deliberately dances on Ash Wednesday with her "handsome devil dancer," despite the alarmed looks of those close to her. In the CHASSE-GALERIE, 8 lumberjacks risk their lives and souls to see their girl friends on New Year's Eve. Werewolves, rough and ready characters who ignore the priest's orders, are somewhat aware of having caused their own possession. The devil himself, the unmistakable protagonist, is cowardly and impotent, his power limited by those of the priest and of sacred objects: he flees at the sight of a few drops of holy water.

To consider these texts an attempt by triumphant 19th-century ULTRAMONTANISM to reassert its influence on literature would be to ignore the internal tensions and contradictions contained in the many levels of meaning. The content of the written tale cannot be divorced from the form it usually took in early Québec literature. A substitute for oral communication, it frequently reproduces the signs of ORAL LITERATURE by including the festive character of the story in a 2-level narrative. The tale's introductions (prologue, preface or first narrative) proceed from a masterly description of the setting in which the relationship between storyteller and story is defined and the nature of the narrative pact established according to the form of dialogue chosen. This pact varies from one author to the next. Louis-Honoré FRÉCHETTE (*Contes I* and *II*) is more ironic, playful and free-thinking than his fellow writers, taking pleasure in demystifying the supernatural and presenting as his main character Jos Violon, an unrepentant storyteller of a popular culture with which he maintains a tacit complicity. Marie-Louis-Honoré Beaugrand (*La Chasse-*

galerie, 1900) is closer to myth and to the archetypal figures of the imagination, whereas Léon-Pamphile Lemay (*Contes vrais*, 1899) is at the same time more literary (craftily playing with oral/written ambiguity, truth and falsehood), digressive and moralizing. His texts cover a variety of significant themes, historical, legendary and commonplace. Others, such as Joseph-Charles Taché or N.H.E. Faucher de St-Maurice wrote documentary or moral texts. Despite these differences, the 19th-century literary tale had a certain uniformity that displayed basic characteristics: the predominance of a set exemplary narrative, explicit references to oral expression, presentation of a narrator who is also a character in the story, and a view consistent with the Christian idea of the supernatural, which in many cases precludes the possibility of the fantastic.

The short texts of the 20th century are fewer and more diverse. The relative importance of the tale has diminished. A number of writers have tried their hand at short stories before writing novels; others, such as Jean-Aubert LORANGER, Jacques FERRON and Roch CARRIER, periodically return to this genre, choosing to make it the leitmotif of their literary production. This gives rise to various types of texts. Lionel GROULX and Brother MARIE-VICTORIN wrote tales of the land, whereas Michel TREMBLAY writes fantasy; Loranger's and Ferron's tales are philosophical and ironic, and those of Félix LECLERC, Carrier, Gilles VIGNEAULT, Yves THÉRIAULT and Réal Benoît are poetic, tragic and playful. The works of Marius BARBEAU, Luc Lacourcière, Félix-Antoine SAVARD, Jean-Claude Dupont and other specialists in folklore and ethnology present transcriptions of oral narratives. Social scientists have now taken upon themselves the task of preserving this literature, something formerly the preserve of writers of the romantic generation.

The novella is more discreet than the tale. It appeared mainly as a collective expression in the 1960s when writers such as Jacques RENAUD and André MAJOR used it as a vehicle for literary and social ideas. It is making a vigorous comeback in the 1980s among authors who, after Gabrielle ROY, Madeleine Ferron, Louise MAHEUX-FORCIER and Claire Martin, are seeking to reveal the immediacy and harmonies of a situation. Suzanne Jacob, Marilu Mallet and Gaétan Brulotte represent this "post-modernist" generation of writers. The tale, although it may seem to have disappeared, has nevertheless found its way into the 20th-century novel (Yves BEAUCHEMIN's *Le Matou*, 1981, and Louis Caron's narratives), in which techniques and themes are very similar to those used by 19th-century storytellers.

A study of Québec literature through the history of its forms shows that the tale — paradoxically because of its fixed or permanent elements — lends itself to a broader range of modulations and reveals the literary profile of a period perhaps even more than the novel or the short story. If every tale is a "chasse-galerie," the adventure is made all the more fascinating by the fact that it transports the reader to another world full of reminders of the past, of everyday existence and, inevitably, of culture. LISE GAUVIN

Shoyama, Thomas Kunit, economist, public servant (b at Kamloops, BC 24 Sept 1916). Shoyama was prominent among the young civil servants who set up the machinery for new social programs in Saskatchewan under T.C. DOUGLAS. He was economic adviser to the premier when he left in 1964 to become a senior economist with the ECONOMIC COUNCIL OF CANADA. He held many senior positions with the federal government, including deputy minister of energy, mines and resources, deputy minister of finance and special adviser to the Privy Council on the Constitution. In 1980 he was appointed a

visiting professor at U of Victoria and he was a member of the ROYAL COMMISSION ON CANADA'S ECONOMIC PROSPECTS. BILL CAMERON

Shrew (Soricidae), family of small insectivores represented today by approximately 250 species worldwide, 16 in Canada. Shrews are small (35-180 mm long), and have short legs; a well-developed tail; long, pointed snout; small eyes; and ears usually partially hidden in soft, often velvetlike fur. The long, narrow, somewhat conical skull lacks zygomatic arches (bone arches in skull extending beneath the eye sockets). The unique dental structure has hooklike upper incisors that, with the elongated, horizontally projecting, lower incisors, form a tweezerlike organ with shearing tips, perfectly adapted for grasping and cutting insects. The molars are suited to piercing the tough external skeleton of insects and shredding food. Shrews are continually active and, to maintain their high metabolic rate, daily may consume their own weight in insects, other small animals and vegetable matter. If deprived of food, they die quickly. Shrews occur throughout Canada except in the arctic islands. Most species live in leaf litter and dense ground cover of woods and in open grassland and tundra. Short-tailed and least shrews (*Blarina brevicauda, Cryptotis parva*) dig well and spend much time underground. Gaspé and rock shrews (*Sorex gaspensis, S. dispar*) are largely restricted to talus slopes. Water shrews (*S. palustris, S. bendirii*) are semiaquatic. C.G. VAN ZYLL DE JONG

Shrike, common name for the family Laniidae of singing BIRDS. The family, which includes 74 species, ranges widely in Africa, Europe, Asia and N America. The only 2 species found in Canada, loggerhead and northern shrike (*Lanius ludovicianus* and *L. excubitor*), are both migratory. Shrikes range from 15 to 37 cm in length. Plumage is mainly grey or brown above; white or light coloured below. Wings are black; the long tail is black and white. Both Canadian species have a bold black mask across the eyes. The black bill is strong, hooked, and toothed in many species (as in BIRDS OF PREY). Legs and feet are strong with sharp claws. Shrikes are solitary except during nesting season. Both parents cooperate in building a deep, bulky nest, usually in trees or bushes. The eggs (2-8) are incubated by the female, with assistance from the male in some species. Young are fed by both parents. Shrikes are perching songbirds, with a great variety of notes; Canadian species have a melodious song. They are predators, feeding on insects, small reptiles, birds and mammals. They watch for prey from exposed perches and are bold and aggressive, attacking swiftly. They carry their prey away, often impaling it on thornbushes before eating. HENRI OUELLET

Shrimp, decapod ("10-footed") CRUSTACEAN, differing from other decapods (CRABS, CRAYFISH, LOBSTERS) in being adapted for swimming, a fact reflected in the large, laterally compressed abdomen and well-developed pleopods (pairs of swimming legs). All shrimp native to Canada are marine, although the large, freshwater Malaysian prawn (*Macrobrachium*) has been reared experimentally. In Canadian waters, there are more than 100 species of shrimp, of which 85 have been recorded off the Pacific coast. These vary considerably in size, ranging from less than 20 mm to well over 200 mm in length. Females are almost always larger than males; some species are protandric, ie, grow up and mature as males, then change into females for the balance of their reproductive lives. The most valuable commercial species in Canada are the prawn (*Pandalus platyceros*) on the Pacific coast, and the pink shrimp (*Pandalus borealis*) on the Atlantic coast. Although the terms "shrimp" and "prawn" are used interchangeably in N America,

a culinary distinction may be made between small shrimp and large prawns. D.E. AIKEN

Shrum, Gordon Merritt, physicist (b at Smithville, Ont 14 Jan 1896). After service in WWI, Shrum took a PhD under J.C. MCLENNAN at U of T, where he discovered in 1925 the "green line" in the spectrum of the aurora. He joined UBC that year and eventually became dean of graduate studies. Shrum's personality, and membership in such bodies as the NATIONAL RESEARCH COUNCIL and Defence Research Board, gave his influence national scope. He was the apostle of research in BC (a prime promoter of the BC Research Council, created in 1944) and of the competence of scientists as public servants. After retiring from UBC at age 65, he became chairman of BC Hydro for 12 years and chancellor of SFU; at age 80 he began work as chairman of the Robson Square redevelopment project in Vancouver. DONALD J.C. PHILLIPSON

Sicamous, BC, UP, pop 1057 (1981c), is located at the eastern end of Shuswap Lk in S-central BC, 550 km E of Vancouver and 140 km E of Kamloops. It lies at the western end of the EAGLE PASS through the Monashee Mt Range, on a narrow strip of land between Shuswap and Mara lakes. Its name derives from an Indian word meaning "in the middle." Sicamous is on the CPR main line and is at the junction of the TRANS-CANADA HWY and Hwy 97, which leads S to the Okanagan Valley. Tourism and the beaches and resorts on the lakes are mainstays of the local economy, along with some lumbering and agriculture. Attractions in the area are primitive rock paintings along the shores of the lakes, and CRAIGELLACHIE station, 25 km E, where the "last spike" of the CPR was driven. JOHN R. STEWART

Sicotte, Louis-Victor, lawyer, politician, judge (b at Boucherville, LC 6 Nov 1812; d at St-Hyacinthe, Qué 5 Sept 1889). He was a fervent Patriote and is considered a co-founder of the ST-JEAN-BAPTISTE SOCIETY of Montréal. He was not convinced of the wisdom of the REBELLIONS OF 1837 and opposed the Patriotes' border forays because he feared they would bring reprisals. First elected to the Assembly for St-Hyacinthe in 1851, he identified with the dissident Reformers whose position lay somewhere between LAFONTAINE's supporters and the PARTI ROUGE. In 1854 he was named Speaker over the government's candidate, George-Étienne CARTIER. Commissioner of crown lands 1857-10 Jan 1859, he resigned to become leader of the opposition from Canada East. In May 1862, Sicotte formed a new government with John Sandfield MACDONALD, but having had to lead the country in a period of deep economic and political trouble, the ministry was defeated in the Assembly on 8 May 1863. Sicotte refused a Cabinet position in the new Sandfield Macdonald-Dorion government and was named a puisne judge of the Superior Court for St-Hyacinthe on 5 Sept 1863, a post he held until 7 Nov 1887. ANDRÉE DÉSILETS

Sidbec-Dosco Limitée Sidbec (Siderurgie du Québec) was established by the Québec government in 1964 so that the province would have an integrated steelmaking facility. In May 1972 the company's name became Sidbec-Dosco Limitée. Sidbec does not use conventional iron and steelmaking technology. Its plant at Contrecoeur, E of Montréal, produces sponge iron using the Midrex process, in which IRON ORE pellets are directly reduced by reformed natural gas in a shaft furnace. The sponge iron is melted with scrap steel in an electric-arc furnace to make steel. The first Midrex unit became operational in Apr 1973, the world's second plant making tonnage high-quality flat-rolled products by electric-furnace steelmaking. Power is supplied by Hydro-Québec; natural gas by Gaz-Metropolitain. The Contrecoeur plant has 2 Midrex furnaces, 4 large electric melting furnaces and continuous casting facilities. The annual raw-steel capacity is about 1.5 million t, most of it processed into bars and rods. JOHN G. PEACEY

Sidney, BC, Town, pop 7946 (1981c), inc 1967, is located on the E side of the Saanich Pen on Vancouver I, 30 km N of VICTORIA, facing Haro Str. It is the business hub of the northern part of the Saanich Pen and the gateway to Vancouver I, with 2 official ports of entry: the Anacortes Ferry from the US and the international airport, 1.6 km W of the town. Eight km to the N is the Swartz B terminal of the BC Ferry system, which connects with the mainland. Salish first inhabited the area, and permanent settlement began only in the late 1880s, when agriculture developed. Nearby Sidney I was named 1859 for F.W. Sidney of the Royal Navy. In 1895 the Victoria-Sidney Ry opened, and by the early 1900s local industries included a roofing factory, a cannery and a large sawmill. During the 1920s a major fire and competition from the mainland destroyed Sidney's early industries. They have since been replaced by service functions, boat building, fishing and tourism. The area is popular for sailing and has a well-used racing track. ALAN F.J. ARTIBISE

Siemens, Jacob John, farmer, teacher, farm organizer (b at Altona, Man 23 May 1896). After attending the Manitoba Normal School, he taught school 1918-29, but then assumed management of the family farm and started to reorganize his liberal Mennonite community. His organizational skills were soon transferred to co-operatives, and he established the Rhineland Consumers Co-operative Ltd, probably Manitoba's first, in 1930 or 1931. He eventually helped promote and establish 32 other co-operatives which he organized into the Federation of Southern Manitoba Co-operatives. Convinced that economic and community stability depended on diversification he promoted new crops, serving as the first president of Co-operative Vegetable Oils Ltd (1946), the first plant in N America to extract oil from sunflower seeds, and as VP of the Manitoba Sugar Beet Growers Association (1947). MARTIN K. McNICHOLL

Sifton, Arthur Lewis, judge, politician, premier of Alberta (b at St Johns, Canada W 26 Oct 1858; d at Ottawa 21 Jan 1921). Firm, stoical and politically astute, Sifton was one of the most outstanding figures in the political life of the early West. He practised law in Brandon, Man, 1883-85 (with his brother Clifford), in Prince Albert in the North-West Territories 1885-88, and in Calgary after 1889. In 1899 he was elected to the territorial legislature for Banff and from 1901 served on HAULTAIN's Executive Council. He was an early and strong advocate of provincial status. In 1903 LAURIER appointed him territorial chief justice, and in 1907 he became the first chief justice of Alberta. As a trial judge he was excellent; he said little and gave short, sound and prompt judgement. In 1910 he resigned and became Liberal premier of Alberta, succeeding A.C. RUTHERFORD. Sifton held together a divided party and was an effective premier, a strong leader and skilled administrator. He pressed for the transfer of natural resources, finally accomplished by J.E. BROWNLEE in 1930. In 1916 women were given the vote and 2 were made magistrates. During the CONSCRIPTION crisis of 1917, PM BORDEN invited leading Liberals, including Sifton, to join a Union government. Though not conspicuous in the Commons, Sifton was valuable in Cabinet and as a delegate to the Paris Peace Conference. In 1919 he became minister of public works and secretary of state, and in 1920 was named an imperial privy councillor. W.F. BOWKER

Reading: L.G. Thomas, *The Liberal Party in Alberta* (1959).

Sir Clifford Sifton (c1900), aggressive promoter of immigrant settlement in the West (*courtesy Public Archives of Canada/PA-27943*).

Sifton, Sir Clifford, lawyer, politician, businessman (b near Arva, Canada W 10 Mar 1861; d at New York C, NY 17 Apr 1929) and brother of A.L. SIFTON. One of the ablest politicians of his time, he is best known for his aggressive promotion of immigration to settle the PRAIRIE WEST.

Sifton moved to Manitoba in 1875, graduated from Victoria College (Cobourg, Ont) in 1880, and was called to the Manitoba Bar in 1882. He was first elected as a Liberal MLA for Brandon North in 1888, and on 14 May 1891 became attorney general in the government of Thomas GREENWAY. His brilliant defence of the national school system (est 1890) brought him to prominence. After the Laurier-Greenway compromise on the MANITOBA SCHOOLS QUESTION in 1896, Sifton became federal minister of the interior and superintendent general of Indian affairs in LAURIER's government Nov 17.

Sifton's energy, mastery of political organization and incisive analytical capacity, his dynamic view of the role of government in stimulating development, and his broad grasp of Canada's material and economic problems all set him apart. He was the principal negotiator of the CROW'S NEST PASS AGREEMENT with the CPR. He was responsible for the administration of the Yukon during the gold rush; controversial among his policies was the endeavour to shift from individual placer-mining operations to large-scale mechanized mining for gold. He was agent in charge of presenting Canada's case to the Alaska Boundary Tribunal in 1903.

His promotion of immigration was an immense success. Taking advantage of a strong economic recovery that made farming in the West more attractive, he established a vigorous organization to seek out settlers in the US, Britain and — most controversially — east-central Europe. Against attacks by nativists, he defended the "stalwart peasants in sheep-skin coats" who were turning some of the most difficult areas of the West into productive farms.

Sifton resigned on 27 Feb 1905 following a dispute with Laurier over school policy for Alberta and Saskatchewan. He never acquired a broad view of the compromises necessary to protect minority rights in Canada. In 1911 he broke with the Liberal Party on RECIPROCITY with the US, supporting the Conservatives, though he

did not run for Parliament again. He was chairman of the Canadian COMMISSION OF CONSERVATION 1909-18, promoting a wide spectrum of conservation measures. He was knighted 1 Jan 1915. Instrumental in the formation of Union Government in 1917, he subsequently preferred the PROGRESSIVES, and then the Liberals under Mackenzie KING. He left an estate valued at nearly $10 million, but was highly secretive about his private and business affairs. His most important acquistion was the *Manitoba Free Press*; its editor, J.W. DAFOE, became his closest confidant and eventual biographer. Sifton was a man of unusual achievement despite the deafness that afflicted him most of his life. He considered the settlement of the West a sufficient monument to his endeavours. DAVID J. HALL

Reading: J.W. Dafoe, *Clifford Sifton in Relation to His Times* (1931); David J. Hall, *Clifford Sifton,* 2 vols (1981, 1984).

Signal Hill, overlooking the harbour of ST JOHN'S, Nfld, was for many years the centre of the town's defences. A signal cannon was placed here in the late 16th century, and stone fortifications were built in the late 18th century during the Napoleonic Wars. By that time a system of flags flown from the hill warned ships of weather and sea hazards. Cabot Tower was built 1897-98 to commemorate the 400th anniversary of John CABOT's landing. Italian inventor Guglielmo Marconi chose this site to conduct an experiment to prove that electrical signals could be transmitted without wires, and on 12 Dec 1901 he received the world's first radio transmission, sent in Morse code from Cornwall, Eng. Signal Hill was declared a national historic park in 1958, and an interpretive centre has been developed. *See* HISTORIC SITE. C.J. TAYLOR

Sigogne, Jean-Mandé, Roman Catholic missionary (b at Beaulieu-lès-Loches, France 6 Apr 1763; d at Sainte-Marie [Church Point], NS 9 Nov 1844). Forced in 1792 to flee persecution in revolutionary France, he came by way of England to southwestern NS in 1799 as missionary to the Acadians of 2 widely separated missions. He was authoritarian by temperament and a moral rigorist, and this, coupled with his being the only man among them both learned and fluent in English, gave Sigogne an ascendancy over temporal and spiritual affairs. His most substantive legacy was the survival of the French and Catholic traditions among the Acadians of Digby and Yarmouth counties, to whom he ministered for 45 years. BERNARD POTHIER

Sikhism, a major world religion, arose through the teachings of Guru Nanak (1469-1538) in Punjab, India. Its adherents call themselves Sikhs (disciples), and like JEWS they are distinguished both as a religion and as an ethnic group. Though in principle universalistic and open to converts regardless of race, Sikhism has been identified primarily with Punjabi people, events and culture. Guru Nanak travelled widely and incorporated many ideas from the HINDU Sant (saint) tradition, some from the Hindu Bhakti (devotional) tradition and, indirectly, some from the Muslim Sufis (*see* ISLAM) into his own distinctive theology. He believed in monotheism and rejected Hindu notions of caste, idol worship and bodily mortification, as well as the belief in salvation through ascetic isolation from worldly affairs. Nanak claimed that salvation was accessible to all through devotion to God and the maintenance of a moral, responsible and selfless everyday life. Nanak's ideas were elaborated by 9 subsequent gurus. Guru Angad (1504-52) had Nanak's teachings written in Punjabi. He also strengthened the unique Sikh practice of *Guru ka langar*, in which Sikhs repudiate caste by eating together. Guru Amar Das (1479-1574) further organized the church, fought against *purdah* (seclusion of women) and *sati* (widow burning); Guru Ram

Das (1534-81) founded Amritsar, Punjab, now the centre of the Sikh faith. Guru Arjun (1563-1606) collected Sikh scriptures into a single volume, later termed the *Adi Granth*, which became the main scriptural base of Sikhism.

Oppression by the Moguls and unsettled conditions in Punjab gave rise to increasing ethnic consciousness and militancy among Sikhs. The tenth and last Guru, Gobind Singh (1666-1708), both a spiritual and a military leader, in 1699 brought Sikh theology to its final development by creating the Khalsa (the pure), the community of believers who receive *amrit* (ritual baptism). Men who did so took the name "Singh" (lion), while women took "Kaur" (princess). Men of the Khalsa were directed to observe the five *kakas* ("Ks"): to keep their hair and beard uncut (*kes*), and to wear a comb (*kangha*) symbolizing neatness, a steel bracelet (*kara*), soldier's breeches (*kach*) and a dagger (*kirpan*). While some Sikhs (Sahijdharis) have not accepted these conventions, among those who did (Keshadharis) are an overwhelming proportion of Canadian Sikhs.

Seeing death impending, Guru Gobind Singh passed on the spiritual leadership of the faith to the *Adi Granth*, naming it the *Guru Granth Sahib*. After his death, Sikhs continued to have a turbulent history. As the Mogul empire weakened, military and political conflict in Punjab escalated, only to be subdued by the rise to power of the Sikh, Ranjit Singh (1780-1839), who consolidated much of Punjab and Kashmir. Sikh converts increased dramatically during this period, as they did after Punjab was conquered by the British in 1846. Sikh men soon were an important part of the British Indian army, and thus migrated in small numbers throughout the British Empire.

Sikhism in Canada Some 68 000 Canadian Sikhs (1981 c), practising one of Canada's best-represented non-Christian religions, form this country's largest SOUTH ASIAN ethnic group. The first Sikhs came to Canada in 1902 as part of a Hong Kong military contingent travelling to the coronation of Edward VII. Some soon returned to Canada, establishing themselves in BC. More than 5000 South Asians, over 90% of them Sikhs, came to BC before their IMMIGRATION was banned in 1908. This population was soon reduced to about 2000 through out-migration, almost all by Sikhs. Despite profound racial discrimination (*see* KOMAGATA MARU), Sikhs quickly established their religious institutions in BC. The Vancouver Khalsa Diwan Society was created in 1907. Through its leadership Sikhs built their first permanent *gurdwara* (temple) the following year. By 1920, other gurdwaras had been established in New Westminster, Victoria, Nanaimo, Golden, Abbotsford, Fraser Mills and Paldi. Each was controlled by an independent, elected executive board.

From the beginning, gurdwaras were the central community institutions of Canadian Sikhs. Through them, Sikhs provided extensive aid

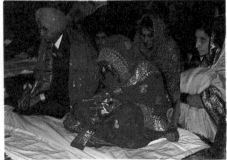

The Sikh "Ceremony of Bliss." The couple sits in the presence of a copy of the *Guru Granth Sahib* during a marriage ceremony in the Sikh community, Calgary (*courtesy Provincial Museum of Alberta/Folk Life Program*).

to community members in need. The dramatic fight to have the immigration ban rescinded was also centered on the temples. By 1920 Vancouver Sikhs alone had contributed $300 000 to charitable causes in India and to the defence of Sikhs in Canada. Temples were also the focus of much anti-British revolutionary activity. Canadian Sikh religious institutions reached another stage of development in the 1920s, when wives and children of legal Sikh residents were allowed entry to the country. In accord with the teachings of the gurus, men, women and children participated fully in temple observances. Sikh religion provided the basis for a strong collective identity between the world wars, so that virtually no Sikhs renounced the faith or married outside it. The only significant religious revision was a tendency among second-generation men to cut their hair and beards to conform to Canadian dress.

Sikhism in Canada began to change its character in the 1950s as immigration resumed. Many postwar immigrants were more urbane, educated, westernized and religiously untraditional than those already here. The democratic basis of control over temples soon reflected this division in the establishment of alternative, more orthodox temples in Vancouver and Victoria. In the 1960s and 1970s skilled Sikhs, some highly educated, settled across Canada, especially in the urban corridor from Toronto to Windsor. As their numbers grew, Sikhs established temporary gurdwaras in every major city eastward to Montréal. These have been followed in many instances by permanent gurdwaras and Sikh centres. Some cities now have several gurdwaras, each reflecting a different shade of religious, social or political opinion. As before, they are the central community institutions. Through them Sikhs now have access to a full set of public observances. Central among these are Sunday prayer services followed by langar. Services are open to anyone who obeys the conventions for entering a temple: that one do so shoeless with the head covered, and refrain from smoking or drinking. Temple observances are also held to celebrate the various gurus and such traditional Sikh calendrical celebrations as Baisakhi Day. The temples are also used for marriages and funeral services.

Perhaps the most important aspects of Sikh religion in Canada are personal and devotional. A daily routine would include rising early for a bath and prayers. Many Sikh families have a copy of the *Guru Granth Sahib* in their homes and in the morning select a passage from it for inspiration. A hymn is read at sunset, and a hymn and prayer at night. Sikhs are expected to abstain from tobacco and alcohol, stealing, adultery and gambling. They are not to make caste distinctions, worship idols or acknowledge any living religious teachers as gurus. Sikhism emphasizes the importance of family life, philanthropy, service and defence of the faith. Sikh philanthropy has been extensive, especially in support of local gurdwaras. Service has been interpreted chiefly as service to the religion and the community. Save for a possible resident *gyanji* (priest), volunteers take on all the affairs of local gurdwaras, from administration to cooking food at the weekly langar.

Sikhs have gone to great lengths to teach their children their culture and religion. Many temples support classes to teach religious precepts and the written language to children; most second-generation Sikhs speak Punjabi, but must be taught the unique Sikh *gurmukhi* written script in order to read from the *Guru Granth Sahib*. There have been several attempts to develop a national Sikh organization, but by 1984 this objective had not been achieved. National and regional conferences held to discuss Sikh issues have been held in several cities, and informal contacts between various regional temple organizations are usually maintained. The primary organizational basis of Canadian Sikhism remains, however, the local temple association. Sikh Canadians maintain strong religious ties with India. A continual stream of theologians and teachers visit Canada, and Indian religious texts are in wide circulation. Sikh Canadians visiting India often go on PILGRIMAGE to the famous Sikh shrines, especially the Darbar Sahib (commonly called the Golden Temple) in Amritsar. Canadian Sikhs are also strongly affected by events concerning Sikhs and Sikhism in India, where the central issue in recent years has been the rise of a vocal movement in Punjab for an independent Sikh state, Khalistan. Many Canadian Sikhs have supported this movement financially, especially after the Indian army's attack on the extremist Sikh independence sect led by Jarnial Singh Bhindranwali, which had established itself on the grounds of the Golden Temple. This attack in 1984 left Bhindranwali and more than 1000 others dead, and seriously damaged the Sikh's most sacred shrine. In Canada the consequences were militant demonstrations against the Indian government by Sikhs and Hindus. Canadian Hindu-Sikh relations were further strained when Indian PM Indira Gandhi was assassinated by 2 of her Sikh security guards 31 Oct 1984; in India, over 2500 Sikhs were killed in the rioting and looting that followed.

With its strong community institutions and group consciousness, Sikhism has found fertile ground in Canada, where many other sects and religions have fallen prey to assimilationist pressures. With continued immigration and the rise of a large second generation, Canadian Sikhs could number 250 000 by 2000 AD. *See also* PREJUDICE AND DISCRIMINATION.   NORMAN BUCHIGNANI

Reading: N. Buchignani and D. Indra, *Continuous Journey: A Social History of South Asians in Canada* (1985); W.O. Cole and P. Singh Sambhi, *The Sikhs* (1978); C.H. Loehlin, *The Sikhs and Their Scriptures* (1964); W.H. McLeod, *Guru Nanak and the Sikh Religion* (1968); H. Singh, *The Heritage of the Sikhs* (1964); K. Singh, *A History of the Sikhs*, 2 vols (1977).

Silica, or silicon dioxide (SiO$_2$), occurs as the MINERAL quartz and is the most abundant rock-forming compound, making up approximately 60% of the Earth's crust. Quartz forms hexagonal crystals, will change form slightly when heated and melts at 1723°C. It is extremely resistant to weathering. Pure quartz is colourless, but GEMSTONES such as amethyst, rose quartz, cairngorm (smoky quartz) and jasper result from impurities. The term silica is used whether the silica is found as loose, unconsolidated quartz grains (eg, beach sand), sandstone, quartzite, vein quartz or pegmatitic quartz. Silica is used in the manufacture of optical glass, glass containers, tableware, window and automotive glass; as a metallurgical flux (to promote fluidity) in the base-metal industry; as glass fibre; as an ore in the manufacture of silicon metal, ferrosilicon and silicon carbide; as foundry sand for metal castings; for sandblasting and other abrasives; as filler material in tile, asbestos pipe, concrete and bricks. Very high-purity silicon is used to produce transistors and computer chips. Silica deposits occur throughout Canada. To be economically viable, a deposit should be 95-99% pure, easily mined from open pits and close to a market or transportation. A cheap power source is a consideration in beneficiation (ie, treatment to improve properties). The above factors may make it advantageous for a Canadian company to import silica from a nearby foreign source. Similarly, Canada is able to export silica to nearby US markets. *See* MINING.   HELEN R. WEBSTER

Sillery, first Canadian INDIAN RESERVE, was established 1637 near Québec City. It was funded by a French nobleman, Noël Brûlart de Sillery, who answered Fr Paul Le Jeune's call in the JESUIT

RELATIONS to draw together in a suitable place the wandering Indians in order to convert them. It was granted as a seigneury to Christian Indians under Jesuit supervision. Alcoholism, EPIDEMICS and the difficulties of adapting to sedentary life depopulated the settlement by the 1680s. The Jesuits long maintained Sillery's celebrated house, now a museum. DALE MIQUELON

Silver (Ag), metallic element with brilliant white lustre and melting point of 962°C. It has the highest electrical and thermal conductivities of all metals and, although tarnished by sulphur, is relatively corrosion resistant. Silver is second to GOLD in malleability and ductility, being easily rolled or beaten into foil or drawn into fine wire. Its use for ornaments and utensils predates recorded history. Silver has been an important medium of exchange since very early times. Mines in the eastern Mediterranean and Spain were early sources, but the centre of production had moved to the Western Hemisphere by the 16th century. Important producing countries now are Mexico, the USSR, Peru, the US, Canada, Australia and Poland. Photographic films and papers account for about 40% of silver consumption, but silver also has applications in the electrical and ELECTRONICS INDUSTRIES for contacts, conductors and batteries. Silver is widely used in silverware, jewellery and works of art, as sterling silver (92.5% silver, 7.5% copper) and for silver plating. Other uses are in brazing and soldering, in alloys, mirrors and catalysts, and in medicine. The use of silver in coinage is now largely confined to numismatic coins and medallions (see MINTING; COINAGE). Some silver is recovered from ores mined principally for the silver content, eg, around Cobalt, Ont; Great Bear Lk, NWT; Coeur d'Alene, Idaho; and Mexico; however, about 80% of supply is a by-product of lead-zinc-copper ores. The main producing areas in Canada are Ontario, BC, NB and the YT. In 1981 Canadian production was 1.2 million kg, over 14% of the world total. Ores at primary silver mines are concentrated by gravity and flotation, and the silver recovered by cyanidation or pyrometallurgy (see METALLURGY). Silver occurring in base-metal ores follows these metals in concentrating and smelting processes, ends up in residues and is recovered by electrolysis. J.J. HOGAN

Silver, Church A large proportion of the silver objects surviving from Canada's colonial years were made for ecclesiastical use. This important legacy of church silver results from the early establishment of the Catholic Church in NEW FRANCE. Laws of the church required that chalices and patens used in the celebration of the mass be made of a noble metal. As gold was too expensive, SILVER was used for these sacred vessels and for as many other religious objects as possible. Works of art were encouraged as outward expressions of faith and their beauty was regarded as inspirational.

In the 17th century, religious silver was brought to the colonies by missionaries, or sent from patrons in France. The Huron of Lorette, Qué, have an important French reliquary presented to the mission in 1679 and a monstrance of 1664 that originally belonged to the Jesuits. The Jesuits also passed on a Parisian monstrance to the Iroquois at Caughnawaga, Qué, and dispersed other, early French-made works to various parishes and institutions. Colonial churches sometimes commissioned silver objects from makers in Paris. About 1700, as new parishes appeared and prospered, and the demand for silver works increased, French-trained silversmiths began to emigrate to New France. They taught others the skills of their trade through an APPRENTICESHIP system and passed on their coveted tools. Soon it became faster, safer and cheaper to entrust a local maker with a church commission than to order from

Monstrance, by Laurent Amiot. The monstrance displays the Host at the top of its long stem in a small glass lunette surrounded by radiating rays (*courtesy Royal Ontario Museum*).

abroad. The scarcity of silver was a constant problem and coins or worn-out objects were saved to be melted down and fashioned into new vessels. Much Catholic silver is preserved in early Québec parishes and religious institutions. It is also exhibited at the Québec Museum, the Montreal Museum of Fine Arts, the ROYAL ONTARIO MUSEUM, the NATIONAL GALLERY OF CANADA and other art galleries and museums.

The most sacred of the vessels are the chalice, a goblet that contains the wine for the mass, and the paten or plate, used for the blessed wafer or "host." Although these objects are made of silver, the interior surfaces that come in contact with the sacraments are usually gilt. Other church objects were often made of PEWTER, COPPER or brass; these were replaced with silver ones as soon as the parish could afford it. Important pieces include the ciborium, a goblet-shaped, lidded vessel used to hold the host, and the monstrance that displays the host at the top of its long stem in a small glass lunette surrounded by radiating rays. Other large works in silver are processional crosses, holy-water pails (stoups), sanctuary lamps, candlesticks and ewers. Small birdlike burettes or cruets on trays hold wine and water; censers on chains hold burning incense and navettes store it. Baptismal ewers are tiny, as are lidded containers (ampullae) for holy oils; these articles are often set into boxes for carrying on visitations. Other items are the pyx (a portable ciborium), crucifixes, reliquary crosses and cases. The pax, now dated, is a little plaque formerly kissed by the clergy and congregation during the mass.

The most important silversmiths during the French regime, eg, Paul Lambert, Jean-François Landron and Jacques Pagé, worked in Québec City. Roland Paradis and Ignace-François Delezenne produced religious silver for both the Québec City and Montréal areas. Early makers followed traditional Louis XIV provincial styles, perhaps using local treasures from France for inspiration, but producing their own less

elaborate interpretations. Favourite motifs included simple bands of stylized leaves, beads or gadroons, usually offset by smooth surfaces. Decoration was created by embossing, chasing and engraving and sometimes by applying details that had been cast. Rounded shapes were raised with the hammer from flattened sheets of silver and soldered to bases. The stems of chalices and ciboria were made in sections, cast and raised, and screwed together with threaded rods.

Québec City remained the centre of church silver production after the British CONQUEST (1759-60). Here the exceptional Ignace François Ranvoyzé created many religious works in a free and decorative style. Among these are 4 gold objects, made for the parish at L'Islet between 1810 and 1812. Laurent Amiot, who returned to Québec in 1787 after studying in Paris, introduced neoclassical elements, reflecting France's newly popular Louis XVI style. Elegant, elongated shapes are decorated with simple reeding, fluting and circular motifs. Smooth surfaces are sometimes engraved with gentle designs; often they are left completely free of decoration. Large sheets of flat silver, introduced about this time, enabled the silversmith to cut and seam hollow parts, instead of raising and hammering them.

There is less early silver from Protestant churches and few of these works are exhibited. Eighteenth-century Anglican churches obtained silver from patrons in England, including royalty. Queen Anne sent plainly elegant chalices, patens, tankard-shaped flagons and alms basins. A communion set she gave to ANNAPOLIS ROYAL is now at St Paul's Church in Halifax. Another set went to the Mohawk in New York; it was later brought to Ontario and is preserved on the Six Nations Reserve near Brantford. George III sent silver to Saint John and Québec City; some of the Québec pieces are in the cathedral there, but 2 are at the St Armand parish in the Eastern Townships. Many forms used in the Anglican Church are similar to Catholic ones, but they tend to be simple in decoration and follow British stylistic traditions. Silver was used in other early Protestant churches but to a lesser degree. Works in the Presbyterian and Methodist churches are very plain and often resemble domestic forms. Communion plate came primarily from Great Britain and the US.

The various churches in the Maritimes received most of their silver from France and Britain, but some was made locally. An early Acadian piece is the pyx in Moncton Cathedral, made by Jean Ferment of Québec about 1751. In 1835 John Munro made a pair of silver patens for St Andrews Presbyterian Church in Saint John, NB. In Halifax, Peter Nordbeck and others made beautiful works for NS churches from 1820 into the middle of the century.

As the rest of the country was settled and churches were established, most religious silver was imported. By the middle of the 19th century new manufacturing and silver-plating techniques resulted in cheaper wares from abroad. Although Montréal's Robert Hendery and François Sasseville of Québec City made a great deal of church silver, it was increasingly difficult for the individual craftsman to compete. This is still true today, when only a small amount is Canadian made. Protestant churches rely primarily on British and American imports; Catholic churches buy silver from various parts of the world. HONOR DE PENCIER

Silver, Domestic, has existed in Canada since colonial times. The ruling classes of the French regime owned substantial quantities of SILVER objects, which they brought with them or imported from France. The earliest known works actually made in NEW FRANCE, dating from the first quarter of the 18th century, were produced by French-trained craftsmen who passed on their skills through an APPRENTICESHIP system. Among the important silversmiths active in Québec City and Montréal during the French regime were Paul Lambert, Roland Paradis, Jacques Pagé and Jean-François Landron.

As little domestic silver has survived, it is difficult to determine how much was made in the colony. Silver, obtained by melting coins or existing silver articles, was always in short supply. Some locally made works no doubt were lost in refashioning, were converted into cash, destroyed in fires or taken back to France. Early surviving flatware indicates that tablespoons were the most numerous items made, along with forks and long-handled *ragout* spoons. Examples are of considerable weight and follow the plain, handsome 18th-century French style, with handle tips turned up. It was customary to lay spoons and forks facedown on the table and variations occur in such details as the engraved decorative drop on the back of the spoon bowl. Owner's initials are often engraved on the back near the maker's marks.

In hollowware, many small tumbler cups bear the marks of Québec silversmiths. Another popular French form is the 2-handled dish or *écuelle*, for stews or soups. Plates, wine tasters, candlesticks and salt cellars are less common, although enough exist to indicate they were made locally, as were snuffboxes and buckles. These colonial domestic works, although unoriginal in form, reflect a restrained style, competently executed. Decoration consists of simple raised or engraved bands, small details such as a shell or leaf motif and, sometimes, a coat of arms or the owner's name as an integral part of the piece.

After the establishment of British rule, silversmiths continued to make domestic silver in the traditional French forms. As the colony was cut off from French sources of supply, resident craftsmen occasionally received important commissions such as soup tureens or ewers. Remaining works confirm the excellent workmanship of such smiths as Ignace-François Delezenne, Jacques Varin and Ignace François Ranvoyzé (one of Québec's greatest silversmiths).

Gradually, the influence of British and European immigrants and imports changed the colony's style of living and the silver that reflects it. With the introduction of sheet silver, a new method for making hollowware emerged: the silversmith cut and joined separate parts into cylindrical forms, instead of raising a vessel into shape by hand. From the 1780s to 1840s, Canadian silversmiths, inspired by the new techniques, produced teapots, sugar bowls, creamers, beakers and mugs in fashionable neoclassical styles from Britain and the Continent. They also created small articles such as pepper and spice casters, nutmeg graters, wine strainers, mustard pots, snuffboxes, vinaigrettes, buckles and buttons. In flatware, tablespoons and forks, as well as soup, sauce and toddy ladles, appear in the "Old English" and "Fiddle" styles, with handle tips turning down. A few spoons are decorated with a shell motif or bright-cut engraving; more often they are plain. Some have owner's initials in script on the front of the handle end. Other utensils used include teaspoons, sugar-sifting spoons and tongs; salt, mustard and marrow spoons; meat skewers and fish servers. These forms changed little until the Victorian era, when more decorative styles became fashionable.

In Québec City, Laurent Amiot became the leading silversmith, after Ranvoyzé; they were followed by a line of excellent craftsmen. However, Montréal emerged as the centre for domestic silver, spurred on by a growing population and the economic success of the FUR TRADE. Important silversmiths from Britain were Robert Cruickshank, James Hanna and, later, George Savage. Among the Europeans were the Arnoldis, Schindlers and Bohles. Canadian makers

Domestic silver teapot, sugar bowl and creamer by Salomon Marion (*courtesy National Gallery of Canada/gift of the Henry Birks Coll of Canadian Silver, 1979*).

followed, notably Salomon Marion and Paul Morand, both apprentices of the distinguished workshop of Pierre Huguet *dit* Latour, another locally born silversmith.

Halifax was the third major silversmithing centre in pre-Confederation Canada. By 1800 British and German immigrants and American LOYALISTS had established a tradition of the craft in NS. Their works closely echo those being made in Québec at the time, although their flatware is often more decorative. Rare pieces of early hollowware include an epergne, an inkstand and a silvergilt clock. Among the NS silversmiths, of whom Peter Nordbeck was perhaps the most skilled, are James Langford, William Veith and, later, Julius Cornelius and Michael Septimus Brown. Many are also known for their JEWELLERY, into which they incorporated local gold, stones and shells. Among NB Loyalists included were silver craftsmen who also advertised as jewellers and watchmakers. Their table silver consists primarily of flatware. Imports remained the prime source of domestic silver in all the Atlantic provinces. In Newfoundland and PEI, advertisers only occasionally mentioned making their own silverware.

Ontario produced little handmade silver before the transition to manufactured wares. The first local work may be by Loyalist Jordan Post, who settled in York [Toronto] in 1787. Early 19th-century flatware bears the marks of makers in Niagara, Kingston and Toronto. Known hollowware is scarce, although large presentation cups were made by William Stennett (1829) and Henry Jackson (1838).

By the 1850s technical discoveries in England and the US had further affected the silversmith's role. New manufacturing techniques and the introduction of silver electroplating on to base-metal forms resulted in the mass production of inexpensive tableware. Imports increased and local manufacture of silver became concentrated in the hands of a few craftsmen who supplied dealers and were known as "makers to the trade." The firm of Robert Hendery, later Hendery and Leslie, became the leading manufacturer in Montréal. Their marks consist of a lion rampant in an oval and a sovereign head in a square with clipped corners. These marks appear on most Canadian silver from the last half of the 19th century, usually accompanied by the name or initials of the dealer for whom the piece was made. Over 100 dealers, including one in BC, ordered silver from the Hendery firm. In 1899 Henry BIRKS and Sons took over Hendery and Leslie and expanded across Canada to become the country's largest silversmithing firm.

Individually created sterling presentation pieces are the most unique silver made in Canada during the era of mass production and plated wares. Cups, medals, trowels, ewers and trays were specially ordered to celebrate a victory, occasion or particular skill. Their engraved inscriptions date and identify the item and often name the donor and recipient. Many of these pieces and other small souvenir items were intended for display rather than use, a fact that

has helped preserve them. Some examples bear decorative motifs in the form of maple leaves and beavers.

By the mid-20th century, silver craftsmen were once again producing handmade works in Canada, usually for special commissions. These orders were placed in an individual's studio and meant that the public was renewing contact with the individual silversmith. Large manufacturing firms and dealers dominate the industry, but a growing interest continues in the craftsmen who combine traditional techniques and styles to form unique designs.

No guild or official rules governed the marking or quality of silver used in Canada until the 20th century. During the French regime, silversmiths used a typical punchmark showing their initials, with a fleur de lis or crown above and a star or crescent-type motif below, all enclosed in an irregular-shaped cartouche. Towards the end of the 18th century, Québec makers tended to place their initials, in block capitals or script, in a rectangular or rounded cartouche. Sometimes they added a punch indicating their city. This practice was repeated in the Maritimes but with additional marks of a sovereign's head, a lion and perhaps an anchor. Similar British-type symbols were also loosely used by silversmiths in Québec from 1820 and in Ontario slightly later.   HONOR DE PENCIER

Silver, Indian Trade Silver JEWELLERY was traded to the Indians by European fur traders from the mid-17th to early 19th centuries. From the earliest exchanges (between seasonal fishermen and the Indians) SILVER played an important role. The first pieces of silver were medals and military gorgets (ie, crescent-shaped pendants symbolizing rank), presented by the French, British, Dutch and Spanish to their respective Indian allies. Then came a number of other designs, based on European fashions and traditions, such as crosses and Luckenbooth hearts, a love token popular in Scotland in the 18th century. Circular brooches of varying sizes, sometimes decorated with engravings or cutout geometric designs, were very common. Eventually, Indian designs were fashioned in silver as well, to produce such items as concave, round brooches that copied similar adornments made from shell in precontact times. Earrings, bracelets, headbands, square brooches and animal effigies were also worked in silver for the FUR TRADE.

Trade silver was made by silversmiths in Québec City, Montréal, London and various American cities, including New York, Philadelphia and Detroit. Because of the high demand between 1780 and 1820, it became a mainstay of the silversmiths' trade. Major Canadian makers included Robert Cruickshank, Charles Arnoldi, Pierre Huguet *dit* Latour, Joseph Schindler and Narcisse Roy. At times, such masters would employ up to 30 other silversmiths to help meet the demands of fur traders. Larger pieces bore the mark of the silversmith; smaller pieces usually did not. Fashioned from coin silver, usually melted down and shaped or hammered into thin sheets, trade silver was produced in large quantities (*see* COINAGE). The most important requirement from the trader's point of view was that the pieces be thin, both to reduce cost and to make the silver light for transportation into the interior.

Silver became a symbol of friendship and alliance and was first used in military alliances during the colonial wars. Later, fur traders presented gifts of silver to the chiefs of tribes with whom they wanted to trade. Viewed not as a bribe but as a token of goodwill, the practice followed an Indian tradition most commonly associated with WAMPUM exchange, and symbolized an agreement between equals. Eventually, fur traders realized that silver could be a lucrative trade item: small, easy to transport, locally made and much sought after by the Indians. An Indian hunter might as easily trade 3 beaver pelts for a silver brooch as for a blanket or iron knife blade. In the fierce competition between the HUDSON'S BAY COMPANY and the NORTH WEST COMPANY, the British-based HBC tried to avoid introducing silver into its trade because it was a fairly expensive item. However, the NOR'WESTERS were so successful that the British were forced to introduce trade silver in 1796. In 1821, when they took over control of the Montréal-based NWC, the first item dropped from the trading lists was silver.

In the mid-19th century, Indian silversmiths began to rework some of the larger pieces into smaller items. Eventually, they also fashioned pieces from new silver. Although there was a hiatus during the early part of the 20th century, the period since 1960 has brought a revival of interest in traditional designs. Today, Indian silversmiths in eastern Canada are once again producing trade-silver designs for Indian and non-native customers. SANDRA GIBB

Silver Dart, the first powered, heavier-than-air machine to fly in Canada; designed and built by the Aerial Experiment Assn (Oct 1907-Mar 1909) under Alexander Graham BELL, a flight enthusiast since boyhood. After several successful flights at Hammondsport, NY, early in 1909 the *Silver Dart* was dismantled, crated and brought to Baddeck the Bells' Canadian home. The "aerodrome" (Bell's preferred term) had a 14.9 m wingspan and an all-up weight of 390 kg, pilot included. J.A.D. MCCURDY was the principal designer and pilot; Glenn H. Curtiss developed the water-cooled engine, an advance on the association's earlier experiments. Pulled on to the ice of Baddeck Bay by horsedrawn sleigh on Feb 23, the silver-winged machine rose on its second attempt after travelling about 30 m, flying at an elevation from 3 to 9 m at roughly 65 km for 0.8 km. Over 100 of Bell's neighbours witnessed the first flight of a British subject anywhere in the Empire. The *Silver Dart* flew more than 200 times before being damaged beyond repair upon landing in the soft sand of Petawawa, Ont, during military trials in early Aug 1909. The engine was later retrieved and restored and is now on display at the National Museum of Science and Technology in Ottawa. A full-scale model of the *Silver Dart* may be found in Ottawa's National Aeronautical Collection. NORMAN HILLMER

J.A.D. McCurdy pilots the *Silver Dart* over Baddeck Bay, NS, in the first airplane flight in Canada, 23 Feb 1909 (*courtesy Library of Congress*).

Silver Islet lies off the tip of Sibley Pen, across the harbour from THUNDER BAY, Ont. In 1868 prospectors found nuggets of pure SILVER, and from 1869 to 1884 shafts were sunk deep beneath the rock, which rose only 2.5 m above the water, and \$3.2 million in silver was taken. A virtual town was erected on the rock, which is only 24 m in diameter, along with massive docks and a lighthouse. The mine shut down in 1884; its shafts are now flooded and its buildings in ruin. JAMES MARSH

Silverheels, Jay, professional name of Harry (Harold Jay) Smith, later legally changed to Jay Smith Silverheels, actor (b on the Six Nations Indian Reserve, Ont 26 May 1919; d at Woodland Hills, Calif 5 Mar 1980). A leading athlete on his reserve as a youth, he was a top lacrosse player and boxer. He was spotted by comedian Joe E. Brown during a Hollywood tour with a lacrosse team in 1938. Joining the Actor's Guild with Brown's help, he worked his way up from extra to starring roles in over 30 films, including *Broken Arrow* (1950), *Saskatchewan* (1954), *The Man Who Loved Cat Dancing* (1973) and of course the *Lone Ranger* films (1956, 1958), based on the TV series (1949-57) in which he immortalized the role of Tonto. He assisted many budding actors personally and through the Indian Actors Workshop which he founded in Hollywood in 1963. He was active in sports, especially harness racing, throughout his life. ROY WRIGHT

Silviculture, the branch of FORESTRY that deals with establishing, caring for and reproducing stands of timber, usually with the aim of a sustained yield of forest products. It requires a knowledge of how various TREE species will grow under particular conditions of SOIL, CLIMATE and spacing. The way in which a forest is harvested influences how it is regenerated. Some systems leave it to nature to provide new seedlings; others require seeding or planting by man. When seeding or planting is required, silviculturists must decide the species and tree spacing most suited to the particular area. They must also be able to predict how a stand of timber will grow and how much wood may be harvested from it.

Until recently, seedlings were grown from ordinary tree seed, but silviculturists are increasingly using seed from genetically superior trees in order to establish healthier and faster-growing forests. Ordinary seed comes directly from the forests, but genetically improved seed is grown in "seed orchards" where special trees are cultivated just to produce seed crops. Seedlings are grown in nurseries before being planted out, usually in spring or fall, on the land where they

are needed. Sometimes it is necessary to clear brush or surface litter from an area before the seedlings can be planted. This site preparation may be done mechanically, with fire or with chemicals.

Once the trees are planted, several other steps may be taken to tend the stand. At all stages of growth a FOREST is vulnerable to damage by fire, INSECT PESTS or PLANT DISEASE. It is an important step in silviculture to protect timber stands from these enemies. Since young seedlings may be suffocated by weeds and brush, it is also sometimes necessary to weed or "brush" a recently regenerated area. As the young trees get taller, reaching perhaps 3 or 4 m in height, they may overcrowd each other, and the stand will stagnate. In this case, it is desirable to thin them out, either mechanically or with chemicals, in an operation known as "juvenile spacing" or "precommercial thinning." Later on, when the trees are big enough to be used commercially, the stand may be thinned out one or more times before the final harvest. Other silvicultural practices that may be used include pruning to reduce the number of knots in the lumber, fertilizing to increase growth, and sometimes "sanitation spacing" to remove diseased or undesirable trees.

Silviculture is roughly divided into "basic," comprising REFORESTATION and protection (the minimum requirements of good forest management), and "intensive," comprising the other operations that improve growth and yield. Although silviculture is practised intensively in Europe, other forested countries, including Canada, have not yet progressed as far in this field. In 1980, 17% of the area logged in Canada was planted, but intensive silviculture was practised on only 0.03% of the nation's productive forest area. *See* MYCORRHIZAE. M.F. PAINTER

Simcoe, Ont, Town, seat of Norfolk County, pop 14 326 (1981c), inc 1878, located on the Lynn R, 10 km N of Lk Erie. It was named after John Graves SIMCOE, first lt-gov of Upper Canada (1791 to 1796), who visited here 1795. He granted milling privileges to Aaron Culver, a Loyalist settler, whose mill became the centre of a small hamlet. It was destroyed by American soldiers during the WAR OF 1812, but a new village was laid out 1819-23. It serves the surrounding agricultural area, in particular the flue-cured tobacco industry, a major regional enterprise. DANIEL FRANCIS

Simcoe, Elizabeth Posthuma, née Gwillim, diarist, artist (b at Whitchurch, Herefordshire, Eng Nov 1766 [she invented the date and may have invented the place of her birth — she was bap 22 Sept 1762 at Aldwickle Church, Northamptonshire]; d at Wolford Lodge, Devon, Eng 17 Jan 1850). Orphaned, she was raised by her mother's sister, receiving an education in languages, drawing and music. She married John Graves SIMCOE in 1782 and came to UC when he was appointed the first lieutenant-governor in 1791. She left a diary of her stay in Newark [Niagara-on-the-Lake] and York [Toronto], and her line and watercolour sketches of the Canadian landscape are of topographical and historical interest. JAMES MARSH

Simcoe, John Graves, army officer, lt-gov of Upper Canada (b at Cotterstock, Eng 25 Feb 1752; d at Exeter, Eng 26 Oct 1806). Commander of the Queen's Rangers in the AMERICAN REVOLUTION, he became in 1791 the first lt-gov of UPPER CANADA, where he arrived in 1792. He began the policy of granting land to American settlers, confident that they would become loyal settlers and aware that they were the main hope for rapid economic growth. He saw the southwestern peninsula as the future centre not only of the province but of trade with the interior of the continent. He founded York [TORONTO], intending it to be a temporary capital, and laid the foundation of a road system. He wanted to make the colony an example of the superiority of British institutions, and he appointed lieutenants of counties, introduced a court of king's bench and had slavery declared illegal. He also effectively defeated attempts to set up elected town meetings on the New England model. He proposed municipal councils, urged a university with preparatory schools and sought the full endowment of the Church of England. He had few critics in the province but could not persuade the imperial government to finance his projects or to exempt him from the military authority of Guy CARLETON, Lord Dorchester at Québec. Concerned about defence and in ill health, he left the colony in 1796. He was then governor of Santo Domingo [Haiti] and later commander of the Western District in England. Appointed commander in chief for India in 1806, he died before he could take up the position.   S.R. MEALING

Readings: S.R. Mealing, "The Enthusiasms of John Graves Simcoe," *Canadian Historical Assn, Report* (1958) and "John Graves Simcoe" in R.L. McDougall, ed, *Our Living Tradition, Fourth Series* (1962).

Simcoe, Lake, 743 km², elev 219 m, is situated in southern Ontario between Georgian Bay and Lk Ontario, 65 km N of Toronto. In the N, Atherley narrows divides it from Lk Couchiching at ORILLIA, and both lakes drain NW via the Severn R to Georgian Bay. On the S, it touches a fertile marshland that has developed into an extensive market-gardening area. BARRIE lies at the head of the lake's deep western arm, Kempenfelt Bay. Long frequented by Indians who hunted its shores and fished its waters, the lake was visited in 1615 by Samuel de CHAMPLAIN who was recruiting Huron allies for a campaign against the Iroquois. During the French regime it was part of a fur-trade portage route linking Georgian Bay to Lk Ontario. Originally known by the French as Lac Aux Claies, it was named by Lt-Gov John Graves SIMCOE after his father. During the latter half of the 19th century, loggers proceeded N around Lk Simcoe and the area attracted summer vacationers from the growing cities of southern Ontario. The lake is part of the Trent-Severn navigation system and a centre for recreational boating. Fishing for trout, whitefish and muskellunge has always been popular, today especially during the winter through the ice.   DANIEL FRANCIS

Siminovitch, Louis, molecular biologist (b at Montréal 15 May 1920). He received his undergraduate and graduate education in chemistry from McGill and he trained at the Institut Pasteur, where he shared in the discovery of bacteriophage lysogeny. Returning to U of T, Siminovitch participated in the formation of the dept of medical biophysics, founded the dept of medical cell biology (now medical genetics) as its first chairman, established the dept of genetics at the Hospital for Sick Children as geneticist in chief, and in 1984 was appointed scientific director of the Mount Sinai Research Institute. In his unofficial capacity as Canada's chief biologist, he has served nationally and provincially on various bodies, as editor of the scientific journals *Virology* and *Molecular and Cellular Biology* and was a founding member of the Canadian science journal *Science Forum*. He has had a major influence on the careers of numerous Canadian molecular biologists. His research has centered on somatic cell genetics, as a founder of the field, and on the MOLECULAR BIOLOGY of mammalian cells. Some 170 publications in books and leading scientific journals have come from his work. Among numerous awards are the Centennial Medal, Gairdner Fdn Award, Flavelle Gold Medal and membership in the Royal Society (London).   JAMES D. FRIESEN

Simon Fraser University, Burnaby, BC, was founded in 1963 as one of Canada's instant universities, built to meet the anticipated need

Enrolment: Simon Fraser University, 1982-83
(Source: Statistics Canada)

Full-time Undergrad	Full-time Graduate	Part-time Undergrad	Part-time Graduate
4 606	985	5 562	477

for higher education in BC's lower mainland. Situated on top of Burnaby Mt, the award-winning campus designed by architects Arthur ERICKSON and Geoffrey Massey includes a central mall bordered by 5 main buildings. SFU's academic programs emphasize an interdisciplinary approach to traditional and newer disciplines, and the university operates all year round on a trimester system. There are 6 faculties: arts, business administration, education, engineering science, interdisciplinary studies and science, offering a wide range of courses and programs. In addition there are co-operative education programs in accounting (CA, CGA and RIA), biological sciences, chemistry/biochemistry, computing science, engineering science, kinesiology, management and systems science, mathematics and physics. SFU also offers correspondence courses enabling students to complete credit courses entirely by mail. Graduate studies at the master's and doctoral levels are offered in all faculties except engineering science, and SFU is enriched by many research institutes and centres.   B. BEATON

Simonds, Guy Granville, army officer (b at Bury St Edmunds, Eng 23 Apr 1903; d at Toronto 15 May 1974). Much favoured by Field Marshal Montgomery for his ruthlessness and offensive spirit, Simonds commanded the 1st Canadian Infantry Division and 5th Canadian Armoured Division in Italy before taking over the 2nd Canadian Corps in NW Europe in 1944. Credited with developing armoured personnel-carrier tactics during the NORMANDY INVASION, he also commanded the First Canadian Army while General CRERAR was ill, leading it through the Scheldt battle (Oct-Nov 1944). Chief instructor at Britain's Imperial Defence College 1946-49 (a signal honour for a Canadian), Simonds was later commandant of Canada's National Defence College (1949-51) and chief of the general staff (1951-55). He advocated peacetime conscription and close ties with Britain, criticizing the government for seeking a closer military relationship with the US.   STEPHEN HARRIS

Simoneau, Léopold, tenor, teacher, administrator (b at St-Flavien, near Québec City 3 May 1918). He was widely regarded as the most elegant Mozart tenor of his time, noted for his clear and precise tone, but he was praised for performances of other parts of the lyric tenor's repertoire as well. In 1941, while studying with Salvator Issaurel, he made his debut with the Variétés lyriques. In 1943 he first interpreted a role in a Mozart opera, Basilio in *Le Nozze di Figaro*. On various occasions (the last being in 1970), he sang with his wife, Pierrette ALARIE. Named assistant to the office of Québec's Ministry of Cultural Affairs, he prepared the report that led to the creation of the Opéra du Québec in 1971; that year as well he was made an officer of the Order of Canada. He and his wife were also teachers of music, notably at the BANFF CENTRE SCHOOL OF FINE ARTS.   HÉLÈNE PLOUFFE

Simons, Beverley, née Rosen, playwright (b at Flin Flon, Man 31 Mar 1938). Simons's dramatic works, highly condensed and symbolic, have encountered production difficulties and audience resistance. Best known and most widely produced is *Crabdance*, a ritualistic treatment of women as elders which premiered in Seattle, Wash, in 1969. Other successful stage plays — *Green Lawn Rest Home* (produced 1969, pub 1973), a study of life in a retirement home; *Preparing*

(1962, 1969), a monodrama; *Crusader* (produced 1976, pub 1975) and *Triangle* (produced 1976, pub 1975), based on oriental theatrical models — show the influence of her early musical education and performance. Simons dramatized her Jewish background in "My Torah, My Tree" (written 1956) and "The Elephant and the Jewish Question" (produced 1968). She regards *Leela Means to Play* (produced 1978, pub 1976), an orientally inspired process drama, as her most serious exploration of the contemporary human condition. The importance of her work was recognized by a special issue of *Canadian Theatre Review* (1976).   ROTA HERZBERG LISTER

Simpson, Sir George, governor of the HUDSON'S BAY COMPANY (b at Lochbroom, Scot about 1787; d at Lachine, Canada E 7 Sept 1860). Simpson's knowledge of the FUR TRADE and fur traders was never before equalled. An able administrator and indefatigable traveller, he was imperious when it suited his purposes and loyal to those whose interest paralleled his. Simpson was sent by the HBC from London to N America in 1820 to take charge should the company's governor, William Williams, be arrested by the NWC. He spent his first winter on Lk Athabasca in uneasy competition with the Nor'Westers. When the 2 companies amalgamated in 1821, Simpson was made governor of the large Northern Department, and 5 years later governor of the company's trading territories in British N America. He held this position until his death. Many of his voluminous reports and correspondence have survived in the HBC Archives.

From 1833 Simpson made his headquarters at Lachine, outside Montréal, where he courted politicians, entertained lavishly and invested his money in banks and transportation projects. He was a director of the North Shore Railway Co, Montréal, and of the Champlain Railroad, and he was on the Montréal board of the Bank of British North America. He published his ghostwritten travels, *Narrative of a Journey Round the World, During the Years 1841 and 1842*, and was knighted in 1841 for his contribution to arctic discoveries. In 1830 he married his cousin Frances Ramsey Simpson. They had 2 sons and 3 daughters. Simpson, who was himself illegitimate, also had at least 5 illegitimate children.   SHIRLEE ANNE SMITH

Reading: J.S. Galbraith, *The Little Emperor-Governor Simpson of the Hudson's Bay Company* (1976).

Sir George Simpson, able governor of the Hudson's Bay Co, 1821-60, and indefatigable traveller (*courtesy Public Archives of Canada/C-44702*).

Simpson, James, printer, journalist, trade unionist (b at Lindal-in-Furness, Eng 14 Dec 1873; d at Toronto 24 Sept 1938). In the 1890s Simpson rose quickly from printer's "devil" to a career as a journalist for the Toronto *Star*. At the turn of the century he moved into prominence as a leader in his own printers' union, as vice-president of the Toronto and District Trades and Labor Council, and later as manager of the Labor Temple. He served 3 terms as vice-president of the TRADES AND LABOR CONGRESS OF CANADA (1904-9, 1916-17, 1924-36). He was on a federal royal commission on technical education in 1910 and was a delegate to the International Labour Organization in the 1920s and 1930s. A committed socialist, he stood as a candidate for early socialist organizations and contributed to the socialist press as writer and editor. He served as a Toronto school-board trustee (1905-1910) and controller (1914 and 1930-34) and as Toronto's first labour mayor (1935). For more than 30 years he remained one of Canada's best-known labour radicals. CRAIG HERON

Simpson, Robert, merchant, founder of the Robert Simpson Co (b at Morayshire, Scot 16 Sept 1834; d at Toronto 14 Dec 1897). After his apprenticeship, he arrived in Canada in 1854 and found employment as a clerk in a store in Newmarket, Ont. The following year he opened his own dry-goods store there. In 1872, seeking greater opportunities, he opened a small store in Toronto and by 1894 had erected a new 6-storey building which became a longtime competitor of T. Eaton Co across Queen St. Though a fire completely destroyed the new building in March 1895, Simpson set up in temporary quarters and in early 1896 opened another building utilizing every new fire-prevention measure. It had nearly 500 employees and 35 departments. His sudden death at age 63 resulted in the sale of the store for $135 000 to a syndicate of 3 Toronto businessmen, A.E. Ames, J.W. FLAVELLE and H.H. Fudger. JOY L. SANTINK

Reading: J.W. Ferry, *A History of the Department Store* (1960).

Simpsons, Limited, with head offices in Toronto, is the present-day successor to the dry-goods store opened in 1872 by Robert SIMPSON in Toronto. Originally averse to the idea of running a "departmental store," Simpson eventually added shoe and specialty-food departments and a mail-order business. Catalogues were published regularly after 1894. That year a large new store was built which, because of its impressive architecture, became known as "the most copied store" on the continent. Fire destroyed it in 1895 and soon after a new building (built in the same style) opened. In 1897 Simpson died and the store was bought by a group of financiers. Over the next several decades, Simpsons expanded into a cross-Canada enterprise. In 1953 the mail-order business was acquired by Sears, Roebuck and Co of the US (*see* SIMPSONS-SEARS). In 1978 Simpsons was acquired by the HUDSON'S BAY COMPANY, and in 1983 it had sales or operating revenue of $750 million and about 14 000 employees. DEBORAH C. SAWYER

Simpsons-Sears Ltd, headquartered in Toronto, is a Canadian retailer incorporated in 1952. In 1953 it acquired the mail-order agency and order office of SIMPSONS, LIMITED and its subsidiaries, and today operates 1263 catalogue sales units, 4 catalogue centres and 72 retail stores. As of Feb 1983 it had sales or operating revenue of $3.1 billion (ranking 26th in Canada), assets of $1.8 billion (ranking 48th) and 58 000 employees. Sears Roebuck and Co of Chicago and the HUDSON'S BAY COMPANY each own 36% of the shares; total foreign ownership stands at 40%. DEBORAH C. SAWYER

Sinclair, Robert William, painter (b at Saltcoats, Sask 9 Feb 1939). Sinclair continued his art studies at the universities of Manitoba and Iowa and began teaching art at U of A in 1965. He has developed a unique and distinctly western Canadian theme in his landscape paintings and sculpture. He uses the symbol of a highway as a familiar shape to draw the eye into a simplified 2-dimensional composition. The painted road device gives an immediate illusion of space, yet this is counterbalanced by strongly drawn linear elements and paradoxical unpainted areas that flatten the space. Sinclair's landscapes portray connections between 2 observed states or combinations of elements such as sky, hills and mountain peaks. Drawing dominates all of his work — watercolours, canvases and his hand-formed plexiglas landscape sculptures. KATHLEEN LAVERTY

Singing is the production of musical tones by the human voice. Singing has been a vital part of the life of people in all societies and cultures. The Indians and Inuit, original inhabitants of Canada, used singing to communicate with supernatural powers and in aspects of their work, rituals, dances and recreation. The European settlers who came to Canada brought their own wealth of folk songs (13 000 texts of French-language folk songs were collected by Marius BARBEAU) as well as sacred or secular songs. As songs and masses could be sung without instrumental accompaniment, singing was a very important part of recreation and religious ceremonies. Concert programs in the late 18th century included the singing of art songs and songs with instrumental accompaniment, as well as oratorio or opera selections with instrumental or orchestral accompaniment. The chamber opera *Colas et Colinette* (1788) by Joseph QUESNEL premiered in Montréal in 1790.

Mother de St Joseph, an Ursuline who came to Canada in the mid-1630s, was one of the first to train young singers. From about 1776 to 1900 singing schools were established in various locations, usually for brief periods, by itinerant teachers from the US who stressed music reading and on-pitch singing. Many fine singers came as immigrants to Canada and taught singing, and Canadian singers went abroad to study in various centres in Italy, Germany, France and England. Travelling theatrical companies visiting Canada from the US and Europe provided opportunities to hear singers.

Voice training entails developing the human body into a musical instrument and depends on posture, breath control, producing pure vowels, focusing tone and building resonance. Notable Canadian teachers of singing over the last 150 years include Achille Fortier, Rolande Dion, Guillaume COUTURE, Bernard Diamant, Irene Jessner, Emile Larochelle, Dorothy Allan Park, George Lambert, May Lawson, Helen Davies Sherry and Ernesto Vinci. As a result of the varied backgrounds of singing teachers, Canadian singers have been able to perform in various styles and in several languages. Emma ALBANI (about 1847-1930) became one of the world's foremost sopranos and travelled the world taking leading opera roles and performing in concerts in major centres. She made 2 trans-Canada tours. Singers of popular songs are usually identified by name and term alone (eg, Alan Mills, folksinger). Those who sing opera, oratorio and art songs are identified by name and voice range, as indicated by Albani's designation: coloratura soprano. Among Canadian singers who have gained international fame are Lois MARSHALL, lyric soprano; Teresa STRATAS, lyric soprano; Mary MORRISON, soprano; Pauline DONALDA, soprano; Jeanne Dusseau, soprano; Phyllis Mailing, mezzo-soprano; Eva Gauthier, mezzo-soprano; Maureen FORRESTER, contralto; Jon VICKERS, dramatic tenor; Edward JOHNSON, tenor; Raoul JOBIN, tenor; Léopold SIMONEAU, lyric tenor; John Boyden, baritone; Louis QUILICO, baritone; Morley Meredith, baritone; James

Milligan, baritone; Donald Bell, bass-baritone; Claude Corbeil, lyric bass; Joseph Rouleau, bass. *See also* POPULAR MUSIC. ISABELLE MILLS

Sinnisiak (d c1930) and **Uluksuk** (d 1924), Inuit hunters from the Coppermine region of the NWT, were the first Inuit to be tried for murder under Canadian law. In 1913 they had been hired by 2 Oblate missionaries, Jean-Baptiste Rouvière and Guillaume Le Roux, to act as guides and sled drivers NE of Great Bear Lk. When Le Roux threatened and struck Sinnisiak, the 2 Inuit killed both priests, ate part of Le Roux's liver, and took some of their goods. A mounted police expedition headed by Inspector Charles Dearing La Nauze arrested both men in 1916. They were tried in Edmonton in Aug 1917 for the murder of Rouvière but were acquitted; later that month they were convicted in Calgary of murdering Le Roux. The death sentences were commuted to life imprisonment at Ft Resolution, NWT, and after 2 years they were released. W.R. MORRISON

Reading: R.G. Moyles, *British Law and Arctic Men* (1979).

Sioux, see DAKOTA.

Sioux Narrows, Ont, Village, pop 394 (1981c), centre of Improvement Dist, inc 1944, located on eastern shore of LAKE OF THE WOODS, 80 km SE of KENORA; traditionally considered the site of an Ojibwa victory over the Sioux. Pictographs in Sioux Narrows Provincial Park indicate early Indian occupation of the area. Some 500 Ojibwa currently live on the nearby Whitefish Bay Reserve. European settlement dates from the late 1920s, although previously there were numerous lumber camps in the area. The present economy depends on tourism and related services provided for a summer population of as many as 5000 vacationers. DAVID D. KEMP

Sise, Charles Fleetford, businessman (b at Portsmouth, NH 27 Sept 1834; d at Montréal 9 Apr 1918). Before coming to Canada, Sise had careers as a sea captain, owner of shipping businesses and insurance executive. In 1880 he was appointed special agent in Canada of the National Bell Telephone Co of Boston, Mass, and promptly organized its Canadian subsidiary: The Bell Telephone Company of Canada. He became VP in 1880 and was its second president 1890-1915. Sise directed Bell's emergence into a powerful business entity, molding its very structure: he oversaw its victorious battles with independent telephone companies, its sale of territory in the Maritimes (1887-89) and on the Prairies (1908-09), and its incorporation of an equipment manufacturing subsidiary in 1895 (today known as Northern Telecom). perhaps most importantly, he defended the company before the 1905 parliamentary Select Committee on Telephone Systems, chaired by Sir William MULOCK, deflecting popular and political agitation for nationalization of Bell into regulatory supervision by the Board of Railway Commissioners for Canada. ROBERT E. BABE

Reading: R.C. Fetherstonaugh, *Charles Fleetford Sise: 1834-1918* (1944).

Sissons, John Howard, "Jack," lawyer, judge (b at Orillia, Ont 14 July 1892; d at Edmonton 11 July 1969). As first judge of the Territorial Court of the Northwest Territories (est 1955), he took "justice to every man's door" by aircraft and dogsled. Sissons practised law in the Peace R country from 1921 and was Liberal MP for that area 1940-45. He was named a district court judge in southern Alberta in 1946 and was chief judge 1950-55. From Yellowknife he travelled 64 000 km in twice-yearly circuits, holding trials in remote communities. Several of his decisions relating to hunting rights and to native marriage and adoption practices became legal landmarks. His views were not always popular with the bureaucracy, but he became a legend to the native people and was called *Ekoktoegee*, "the one who listens to things," by the Inuit. He retired in 1966 and wrote his memoirs, *Judge of the Far North* (1968). LEE GIBSON

Sisterhood of St John the Divine, *see* CHRISTIAN RELIGIOUS COMMUNITIES.

Sitting Bull, Ta-tanka I-yotank, Sioux chief (b somewhere in the buffalo country about 1834; d at Standing Rock, N Dak 5 Dec 1890). For a decade after the Battle of the Little Bighorn in Montana on 25 June 1876, in which the Sioux (DAKOTA) destroyed Lt-Col Custer's force, Sitting Bull was the best-known and most-feared native warrior on the continent. For 4 of those years, he and 5000 of his people were unwanted guests in Canada, in the Wood Mountain area of southern Saskatchewan.

American and Canadian authorities were unhappy with this turn of events and the Canadian government, fearful that his presence would incite intertribal or racial warfare, refused Sitting Bull's request for a reservation. The task of surveillance was assigned to Major James Morrow WALSH of the NWMP who came to sympathize with and admire the chief. But the government stood firm in refusing reservation and food, and gradually the hungry Sioux began returning to accept American promises of rations. Among the last to surrender to the threat of starvation was the old chief who was finally settled at Standing Rock Reserve in N Dakota. GRANT MACEWAN

Sivuarapik, Charlie (Sheeguapik), sculptor (b near Povungnituk, Qué about 1911; d 26 Sept 1968 of tuberculosis). Prohibited by ill health from participating in the hunting economy, he was rescued from abject poverty by his carving skill, but he benefited only briefly from the escalation in INUIT ART prices during the 1960s. A perfectionist, he studied his own anatomy and produced powerful, elegantly realistic hunters with their prey. He was the first Inuk member of the Sculptors Soc of Canada, and was a founding member and first president (1958-67) of the Povungnituk Co-operative Soc. MARY M. CRAIG

Six Nations, *see* IROQUOIS.

Skate, *see* RAY.

Skeena River, 580 km long, rises in the northern interior of BC and flows generally SW, draining about 54 000 km², to meet the Pacific Ocean at Chatham Sound S of PRINCE RUPERT. The second-largest river (after the FRASER) entirely within BC, its main tributaries are the Bulkley and Babine rivers. It was called *K-shian* ("water of the clouds") by the Tsimshian ("people at the mouth of the K-shian") and Gitskan ("people who live up the K-shian"), and has always played an important role in the lives of the native people.

Non-Indian influence is relatively recent. Because of strong native control of the lower river, the first non-Indian penetration of the Skeena watershed was from the E, when the HBC established posts on Babine and Bear lakes (1822, 1826). In 1859 a reconnaissance for a transcontinental railway was made up the Skeena as

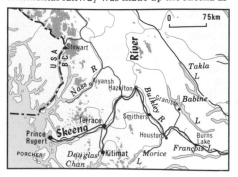

far as the Bulkley R. 1871 saw a gold rush up the Skeena to the Omineca goldfields; some good strikes were made on the Skeena itself. With the establishment of Port Essington near the mouth, and Hazelton at the head of navigation at the Bulkley confluence, freight traffic on the Skeena developed rapidly. From 1880 the HBC used the Skeena route to supply its inland posts. Salmon fishing became an important activity, as it is today. By the 1890s there were 7 canneries in the Skeena estuary. Interest in the agricultural potential of the Skeena below Hazelton grew next, and the provincial government encouraged settlement.

The Skeena provides Canada's only practical alternative rail and road outlet to the Pacific besides the Fraser. In 1914 the GRAND TRUNK PACIFIC RY (now CN) was completed from Hazelton to the coast, terminating at Prince Rupert. Following WWII the valley was reached by the Yellowhead Highway. The town of TERRACE is a regional centre today for the lumber industry. ROSEMARY J. FOX

Reading: R.G. Large, *Skeena, River of Destiny* (1981).

Skelton, Oscar Douglas, academic, public servant (b at Orangeville, Ont 13 July 1878; d at Ottawa 28 Jan 1941). After a brilliant student career in classics at Queen's, Skelton graduated in 1908 from the U of Chicago with a PhD in political economy. He returned to Queen's, where he was John A. Macdonald Professor of Political Science and Economics, 1909-25, and dean of arts, 1919-25. Skelton was a dedicated, popular teacher and he published widely on economics and history as well as current affairs. A liberal democrat and an uncompromising nationalist who believed Canada must take control of its own affairs, he worked for the LIBERAL PARTY as early as the election of 1911 and was close to Sir Wilfrid LAURIER in his last years. Mackenzie KING engaged him as a foreign-policy consultant after winning the election of 1921, and appointed him undersecretary of state for external affairs in 1925. He held the position until his death, serving King and also Conservative PM R.B. BENNETT. Although unassuming and unaffected and not a strong administrator, Skelton was the leading civil servant of his time, with a finger in every bureaucratic pie: a key adviser on domestic as well as foreign policy, the founder of the modern Department of EXTERNAL AFFAIRS, and an architect of the Canadian public service. His major publications were *Socialism: A Critical Analysis* (1911), *Life and Times of Sir Alexander Tilloch Galt* (1920), *Life and Letters of Sir Wilfrid Laurier* (2 vols, 1921) and *Our Generation, Its Gains and Losses* (1938). NORMAN HILLMER

Ski Jumping Although informal ski jumping had taken place for decades, the first officially measured jump (30.5 m) was made by Sondre Nordheim in Norway in 1860. About 20 years later, Scandinavian miners and lumbermen brought the sport to western Canada, where it flourished. In 1891 local Scandinavians formed a ski club in Revelstoke, BC, to promote ski-jumping competition. Although it lasted only a few years, it provided excellent jumping meets in its rivalry with neighbouring Rossland, BC. The Rossland winter carnival of 1898, for example, attracted thousands to watch the local hero Olaus Jeldness win Canada's first ski-jumping championship. Over the next 25 years ski jumping was one of Canada's most popular winter spectator sports. Large crowds watched jumpers hurtle down mountainsides in the Rockies, large wooden trestles on the Prairies, Mont Royal in the heart of Montréal, and the "cliffs" of Rockliffe Park in Ottawa.

In 1919 Ted Devlin set up the Cliffside Ski Club in Ottawa to challenge Sigurd Lockeberg's Ottawa Ski Club. During several years of intense but friendly competition, jumping reached its

all-time peak of popularity. Almost 10 000 spectators gathered at the Fairy Lake jump (near Hull, Qué), designed by Gunnar Sjelderup, to watch an international field compete in a meet presided over by the governor general. Somersaults over the jump, and even a tandem somersault performed by 2 Dartmouth University students, added a spectacular element, anticipating today's freestyle skiing.

Although the newly formed Canadian Amateur Ski Association held its first national championships in Montréal in 1921 (won by E. Sundberg), the centre of Canadian jumping soon shifted back west. Resurrected in 1914, the Revelstoke Ski Club became internationally famous through the efforts of its founder, Sigurd Halverson, and Nels Nelson, a young local athlete. After many years of near misses, Nelson set a world amateur record of 224 feet in 1925 and went on to coach several other world-famous Canadian-born jumpers, including Bob Lymbourne, who jumped a world record 287 feet in 1933.

From 1933 to the 1970s, ski jumping assumed a much lower profile, as alpine SKIING captured most of the public attention. Strong local programs persisted across the country, however, and suddenly pushed the sport back into prominence in 1979 when Ottawa's Horst BULAU won the world junior championship, followed closely by Thunder Bay's Steve COLLINS in 1980. Since then, the 2 have gone on to many world cup wins and have rekindled Canadian public interest in the sport. MURRAY SHAW

Skiing It is probable that the first skiers in Canada were the NORSE, who established several East Coast settlements about 1000 AD. Although no direct proof has been found, it would be remarkable if they had not brought their then 4000-year-old tradition of winter travel on long wooden sticks ("skath") with them. The birth of modern skiing in N America, nearly 1000 years later, can be credited to their direct descendants. Scandinavian prospectors and miners participating in the 1849 gold rush used wooden "snowshoes" or "gliding shoes" up to 12 feet long as a means of travel as well as for highly competitive professional downhill racing competitions. From 1856 to 1869, the Norwegian John "Snowshoe" Thomson provided the only winter overland mail route from the East to California. He was famous throughout the West for his 300 km round trips, accomplished in 5 days with up to 50 kg of mail. Many of Canada's Scandinavian prospectors and railway builders were probably inspired by Thomson to polish the skiing skills developed in their homelands.

While westerners were out skiing unobserved in the wilderness, the first recorded Canadian ski outing was a trip by "Mr. A. Birch, a Norwegian gentleman of Montreal," who skied from Montréal to Québec in 1879 on a 9-foot pair of "patent Norwegian snowshoes" using a single pole. In 1883 the Montréal *Daily Star* published a major article, "New Winter Sport in Norway," describing in detail the use of 8-foot wooden "snowskates" plus a single 5-foot staff. In 1887 Frederick Hamilton, the governor general's aide-de-camp, introduced skiing to Ottawa "amidst universal derision." In Montréal, however, skis were being adopted by the most adventurous members of the many large snowshoe clubs popular at that time. As skis slowly supplanted snowshoes for social winter sporting excursions in eastern Canada (*see* SNOWSHOEING), major ski clubs sprang up in Montréal (1904), Québec and Toronto (1908) and Ottawa (1910).

Initially the popularity of the sport was largely based on SKI JUMPING competitions, featuring such famous Scandinavian immigrants as Olaus Jeldness (Rossland, BC), Andy Ohlgren (the Lakehead) and Sigurd Lockeberg (Ottawa). The large crowds attracted to these meets financed a wide variety of social activities for many fledgling ski clubs. The supremacy of jumping lasted right up to the mid-1930s in western Canada, where world ski-jumping distance records were set on the giant Revelstoke jump from 1925 (Nels Nelson, 224 feet) to 1933 (Bob Lymbourne, 287 feet). In the East, the emphasis shifted from nordic (jumping and cross-country) to alpine (downhill, giant slalom and slalom) disciplines during the 1920s. Open hills in the vicinity of most major cities were frequented by skiers who packed the snow by climbing the hill sideways in the morning and then spent the day practicing Telemark and Christiania turns developed in Norway.

The first professional instructor in Canada, Emile Cochand, was brought to the LAURENTIANS from Switzerland in 1911. By 1917 he had built the first Canadian ski resort, Chalet Cochand, in Ste-Marguerite, Que. During the 1920s and early 1930s the Laurentians, the Gatineau hills and the Collingwood area of Ontario began attracting trainloads of skiers for weekend excursions to large hills. Normal equipment in those days comprised wooden skis with adjustable steel toeplates and leather heel straps, plus a pair of short bamboo poles with large baskets. When worn with flexible leather boots, this gear was also suited to ski touring on the miles of trails being blazed by "Jackrabbit" JOHANNSEN all across the Laurentians.

In 1932 a number of events combined to change the face of the sport completely. The Redbirds of McGill hosted an Oxford-Cambridge ski team at the first major Canadian slalom race at Ste-Marguerite. The victorious British team introduced steel edges (invented in Austria by Rudolf Lettner about 1930) and the Arlberg turning technique developed in the Austrian ski schools established by Hannes Schneider during the 1920s. A few miles away in Shawbridge, Qué, Alex Foster jacked up an old 4-cylinder Dodge to power the world's first rope tow. For 25 cents a half day, "Foster's Folly" enabled Canadian skiers to concentrate on the new downhill techniques without spending time and effort climbing back up. Within a few years, rope tows and downhill ski runs were found all over N America.

The 1932 Lake Placid Winter OLYMPIC GAMES marked the last time that international ski competition was restricted to nordic events, since increased resort skiing was causing a worldwide surge of interest in the alpine events. The end of old-time ski touring came with the introduction of the cable binding in 1935. The new "Kandahar" bindings, by fastening the skiers' heels down, gave them dramatically improved downhill performances, but made ski touring and hill climbing unacceptably awkward. Fortunately, many ski pioneers were building just the sort of resorts the new generation required, eg, Mike Dehouck at Mont Ste-Anne, Joe Ryan at Mont Tremblant, John Clifford at Camp Fortune, Cliff White in Banff and Rudolph Verne on the West Coast. The resorts to which the new generation of skiers now flocked offered a wide variety of ski lifts and groomed slopes, as well as ski schools run by professional instructors, mostly Swiss and Austrian but including a few well-known Canadians such as Harvey Clifford, Louis Cochand and Ernie McCulloch.

Canada's international competition began rather modestly. In 1933 the McGill team took what they had learned from the British back to Europe to win the international intercollegiate relay championship. On the same trip, George Jost also won the first individual Canadian overseas title, the Roberts of Kandahar downhill. For the next 15 years, Canadian skiers remained largely unnoticed at major world competitions.

WWII had an important impact on Canadian skiing in 2 areas: it provided ski training for a number of soldiers, and it produced large quantities of solid dependable equipment which subsequently became available at very low prices as war surplus. Large heavy skis, metal-framed khaki rucksacks and bulky canvas parkas gave the sport a decidedly utilitarian air well into the 1950s but offered many young postwar families an inexpensive start. The beginning of skiing's mass popularity in Canada, however, coincided roughly with the introduction in 1955 of stretch pants, buckle boots, polyethylene bases and brightly coloured metal skis. Skiing at a rapidly increasing number of resorts became a fashionable way to spend an exciting and healthy winter weekend.

The glamour of the sport was sharply enhanced in 1958, when Lucile WHEELER unexpectedly won the world championship titles in both downhill and giant slalom. These wins attracted great public interest to the sport in Canada and inspired the country to send a national team to Europe the following year. A tradition of internationally competitive female skiers has been maintained ever since, featuring world champions or Olympic gold medalists Anne HEGGTVEIT (1960), Nancy GREENE (1967, 1968), Betsy CLIFFORD (1970) and Kathy KREINER (1976). The 1984 team, starring Laurie Graham and Gerry Sorenson, continued to provide strong international competition. The international stature of Canadian male skiers was slower to develop. "Jungle Jim" Hunter's alpine combined Olympic bronze medal in Sapporo, Japan, in 1972 was a remarkable individual achievement for such an inexperienced national team. In the early 1970s a decision was made to concentrate the team's resources on downhill, the international glamour event. In 1975-76 the success of the strategy became obvious. Hunter, in his last year, placed in the top 10 in 4 World Cup races, but was overshadowed by the new team of Dave Irwin, Dave Murray, Steve PODBORSKI and Ken READ. They burst into prominence with Read's season-opening win at Val D'Isere, followed only a few weeks later by a win by Irwin at Schladming. Famous for their daring assaults on the toughest, iciest courses, the "Crazy Canucks" took the international press by storm. During careers lasting well into the 1980s, these 4 skiers provided consistent excitement with 14 World Cup victories and dozens of top 10 placings. Their successors, headed by Todd BROOKER, remain a major power in downhill skiing.

In 1984 over 2 million Canadians own alpine ski equipment. About 860 000 ski once a week or more, providing 70% of the activity at roughly 650 ski areas, staffed by about 6000 certified instructors and 6000 ski patrollers. Their equipment normally consists of fibreglass skis rigidly fastened to stiff synthetic boots by safety-release bindings. The skis have become shorter over the last decade, to enable recreational skiers to manoeuvre more easily. Use of shorter skis by competitive skiers soon led to the creation of freestyle skiing, an acrobatic branch of the sport highlighting performances in 3 new disciplines: aerial, ballet and moguls. Canadian athletes such as Marie-Claude Asselin, Peter Judge, Bill Keenan and Yves Laroche have dominated international competition through the early 1980s.

The popularity of alpine skiing has not been achieved at the expense of the original nordic disciplines. Although ski jumping does not involve great numbers of participants, it has attracted a great deal of public attention during the early 1980s through the unprecedented international victories of Horst BULAU and Steve COLLINS. Over the last decade, the most significant trend in Canadian skiing has been the tremendous growth in CROSS-COUNTRY SKIING. In 1984 over 3.5 million Canadians owned cross-country equipment, of whom almost 2 million ski once a week or more. After 50 years of increasing specialization of equipment and technique, it is interesting to observe a strong movement afoot today to return to all-purpose touring skis, flexible leather boots and bindings that leave the heels free. Using such equipment and the Telemark turning techniques of the early 1900s, skiers are again able to enjoy both the challenge and exhilaration of downhill and the healthy exercise and serenity of cross-country.
MURRAY SHAW

Skink, *see* LIZARD.

Skinner, Frank Leith, farmer, horticulturalist (b at Rosehearty, Scot 5 May 1882; d at Dropmore, Man 27 Aug 1967). After schooling in Aberdeen, he immigrated to Dropmore in 1895 and ran a large grain and stock farm with his brother. In a search for hardy varieties able to withstand the harsh climate, he pioneered horticulture on the Canadian prairie. Skinner introduced many economically important fruits and shrubs, at first as a hobby, but after 1924, as part of a nursery business. He wrote widely in popular and scientific literature and served as president of the Manitoba Horticultural Soc.
MARTIN K. McNICHOLL

Skinners Pond, PEI, UP, pop 132 (1981c), 135 km NW of Charlottetown, is a fishing port on the western coast of Prince County. There are 2 suggestions for the community's distinctive name: the bay could have been the site of pelting operations or it might have been named after a shipwrecked sea captain. The ACADIANS were the first settlers to establish a permanent community, to be joined by IRISH immigrants around the mid-19th century. Thanks to the sheltered, navigable harbour, fishing has been the community's economic backbone. Beginning in the 1940s, the fishermen have supplemented their incomes by raking IRISH MOSS from the harbour beaches, from which a gelatinous substance called carrageen is extracted for use in pharmaceutical and certain food products. As in the other small communities on the Island's northwestern peninsula, the people of Skinners Pond are commercially tied to the centrally located town of Tignish. A recent addition to the community is a museum dedicated to the career of Canadian country-music star and former resident Stompin' Tom CONNORS. W.S. KEIZER

Skunk, carnivorous, cat-sized member of the WEASEL family, black in colour with conspicuous white stripes or spots. Two genera occur in Canada. Skunks are notorious for a foul-smelling secretion (mercaptan) produced in a pair of anal glands. Used in self-defence, it can be projected a distance of 3-4 m. The horned OWL is one of the skunk's few natural predators. The striped skunk (*Mephitis mephitis*) occurs in every province except Newfoundland. Adults average 54 cm long and weigh 1.6 kg. Skunks are nocturnal, passing the day in burrows. They hibernate through the coldest months, frequently several animals together. Insects, vegetation, fruit, birds' eggs and small mammals are major

The striped skunk (*Mephitis mephitis*) occurs in every province except Nfld (*artwork by Claire Tremblay*).

foods. Males are polygamous and the female alone cares for young. Litters, averaging 5-6 young, are born after a 62-day gestation. Young grow rapidly and at 2 months are fully weaned and have operational scent glands. They usually stay with the mother through the winter. The smaller spotted skunk (*Spilogale putorius*) occurs in southwestern BC, and ranges south to the western US and Mexico. IAN McTAGGART COWAN

Škvorecký, Josef, novelist, editor, teacher (b in Nachod, Czech 1924). In Prague he studied medicine briefly and received a PhD in philosophy in 1951. He was active in the cultural efflorescence of postwar Czechoslovakia as a teacher, translator, editor, scriptwriter and novelist. His first novel *Zbabělci* (1958, trans *The Cowards*, 1970) was banned. He lost his editorial post as part of a purge of intellectuals and emigrated with his wife, the writer-actress Zdena Salivarova, after the Soviet invasion in 1968. He joined the U of T English dept and in 1971 he and his wife established the publishing firm Sixty Eight, through which he has published his own recent novels in Czech, the writings of other exiled Czech writers and manuscripts ferreted out of Czechoslovakia.

Škvorecký's novels and stories, which include *The Bass Saxophone* (1963, tr 1977), *The Mournful Demeanor of Lieutenant Borukva* (1966, tr 1974), *Miss Silver's Past* (1968, tr 1975), *The Swell Season* (1975, tr 1982) and *The Engineer of Human Souls* (1983), deal powerfully with the themes of the fate of man and the function of art in society. The writers and musicians of his fiction celebrate the dignity of human life and freedom. His work has a fervent underground following in his native land, while English translations have been widely acclaimed. He has also written literary criticism and what he calls "a personal history of the Czechoslovakian cinema," *All the Bright Young Men and Women* (1972). He was awarded the Neustadt International Prize for Literature and a Guggenheim Fellowship in 1980.
HALLVARD DAHLIE

Reading: World Literature Today (Autumn, 1980), issue devoted to Škvorecký's work; "The Mark of the Exile," *Books in Canada* (Oct 1981).

Slave River, 434 km, connects the PEACE R and the drainage from Lks CLAIRE and ATHABASCA to GREAT SLAVE LK, forming the short upper reaches of the Slave-MACKENZIE R system in the NWT. It has a sinuous, often multichannelled, course traversing the flat, extensively glaciated Archean granitic terrain of the Canadian SHIELD and is currently used almost entirely as a transportation waterway and an important habitat for wildlife. The Alberta government is evaluating the possible construction of a major (2000 MW) hydroelectric-power dam at the Pelican Rapids near FORT SMITH. This controversial project may destroy nesting grounds of the white pelican, endanger breeding areas of the rare whooping crane and cause flooding in the Peace-Athabasca Delta. IAN A. CAMPBELL

Slavery in what is now Canada was practised by a number of Indian tribes, notably those on the Northwest Coast. As practised by Europeans it may have begun with the Portuguese explorer Gaspar CORTE-REAL, who enslaved 50 Indian men and women in 1501 in Newfoundland. Black slaves were introduced by the French as early as 1608. The first slave transported directly from Africa was sold in 1629. Slavery received a legal foundation in NEW FRANCE, 1689-1709, and by 1759 there were 3604 recorded slaves, of whom 1132 were black. Whereas the French preferred *panis* (Indians, so called after the often docile Pawnee), the English settlers brought in African slaves. Slavery expanded rapidly after 1783, as American LOYALISTS brought their slaves with them. The total was never high, however, as slavery was generally unsuited to Canadian ag-

riculture or commerce, and most of the BLACKS who settled in Nova Scotia immediately following the AMERICAN REVOLUTION were free. Slavery technically remained legal in most of Canada until it was abolished for the entire British Empire in 1834, though slavery as an institution declined steadily after 1793, when John Graves SIMCOE challenged the legality of slavery for Upper Canada. Upper Canada's Act to abolish slavery freed no slaves, however, since it proposed only gradual emancipation.

In Canada slaves generally worked as personal servants or on the wharves. A few settlers had many slaves, but more than 20 was considered unusual. This made the attack on slavery far simpler than it was in plantation economies, where their labour was more important. The most effective and sustained attack on slavery came in New Brunswick in 1800, when Ward CHIPMAN prepared an especially thorough legal, historical and moral statement against slavery. Generally, slavery was physically benign, and especially so in PEI, though there were recorded instances of harsh punishment and many advertisements for the return of runaway slaves. The UNDERGROUND RAILROAD assisted fugitive American slaves to reach Canada prior to the abolition of slavery in the US during the AMERICAN CIVIL WAR. The last surviving former slave died in Cornwall, Ont, in 1871. ROBIN W. WINKS

Reading: Robin W. Winks, *The Blacks in Canada* (1971).

Slavey (Slave) are a major group of Athapaskan-speaking (or DENE) people living in the boreal forest region of the western Canadian Subarctic. Although there is no equivalent in Dene languages, the term has been adopted by many Dene as a collective term of self-designation when speaking English. The Slavey inhabit an area dominated by lakes, mountains and river systems, which extends along the Slave, Athabasca and Mackenzie drainages S from Ft Nelson, BC, on the W and from the Hay Lakes region of Alberta on the E, N to a region near Ft Norman and the S shore of Great Bear Lk in the NWT. They are closely related linguistically and culturally to the HARE, KUTCHIN, DOGRIB, BEAVER and CHIPEWYAN. The Slavey, according to a 1978 census, number about 4000, of whom 2500 live in the NWT. The term Slavey may be a translation of the Cree word meaning captive or, as Father Petitot suggested in the 19th century, the term may indicate timidity.

Archaeological evidence suggests that the Slavey region has been inhabited from at least 3000 BC (*see* PREHISTORY). During the late precontact period, the Slavey economy was based on the harvesting of fish, small game, moose, caribou and berries. In winter the Slavey camped in groups or local bands of some 10-30 kin-related individuals. In summer these groups came together briefly near the shores of a major lake to form a regional BAND of perhaps 200 persons.

Initial European contact occurred with Alexander MACKENZIE's expedition in 1789. Soon after, trading posts were established throughout the area. After 1821 the HBC made Ft Simpson its major terminus for the Mackenzie region and in 1858 Anglican and Roman Catholic missions were established. Slavey in Alberta, BC and some parts of the NWT were incorporated into Treaty No 8 between 1900 and 1911; those in the rest of the NWT into Treaty No 11 in 1921-22 (*see* INDIAN TREATIES). Despite the influx of many non-Dene, evidence indicates that the Slavey, between contact and the end of WWII, still lived for most of the year in small, kin-based communities, harvested traditional foods, spoke their own languages, and continued to raise children in the manner of their parents.

After WWII new government programs intended to extend benefits including health care and schooling to the Slavey, together with economic conditions which resulted in a collapse of

the fur trade, brought about a major transformation in the life-style of the Slavey, as people moved into town and sent their children to school. However, recent studies show that subsistence obtained through traditional harvesting has remained a significant activity. *See also* NATIVE PEOPLE: SUBARCTIC and general articles under NATIVE PEOPLE. MICHAEL I. ASCH

Reading: J. Helm, ed, *Handbook of North American Indians*, vol 6: *Subarctic* (1981) and *The Lynx People: The Dynamics of a Northern Athapaskan Band* (1961); J.J. Honigmann, *Ethnography and Acculturation of the Fort Nelson Slave* (1946).

Slemon, Charles Roy, air marshal (b at Winnipeg 7 Nov 1904). One of the first group of provisional pilot officers trained in the RCAF after its creation in 1924, Slemon spent much of the following decade as a "bush pilot in uniform" flying aerial photography operations over the North. He was senior staff officer and then commander of western air command 1938-41, and in 1942 was posted overseas. He served as senior air staff officer of No 6 (Canadian) Bomber Group 1942-44, and was deputy air officer commanding in chief of the RCAF overseas in 1945. A fine administrator, he was appointed chief of the air staff 1953-57, leaving to become the first deputy commander in chief of NORAD. He retired to live in Colorado Springs, Colo, in 1964. NORMAN HILLMER

Slemon Park, PEI, is the site of CFB Summerside's permanent married quarters. Situated in St Eleanors near the air base, the village is 60 km NW of Charlottetown. The residential community was opened in 1951 by its namesake Air Vice-Marshal Roy SLEMON. The community is today home for about 120 families. W.S. KEIZER

Slocan, BC, Village, pop 351 (1981c), inc 1901, is located 27 km S of Silverton and 70 km by road NW of Nelson, at the S end of Slocan Lk. It was founded to service the Springer and Lemon Creek galena mining boom, and began as a transportation centre at the foot of the lake in 1895. However, it declined rapidly with the demise of Slocan Mines. It revived during WWII when 4800 JAPANESE were relocated at Lemon Cr. Today, logging and sawmilling are Slocan's main enterprises. Creation of Valhalla Park to the NW (1982) gives the area a future as a tourist centre. WILLIAM A. SLOAN

Slovaks The first known Slovak immigrant to Canada was Joseph Bellon, who landed in 1878 in Toronto and started a wireworks factory. The majority of the early immigrants were manual workers from the US. According to the 1981 census, only 43 070 Canadians declared their ethnic origin as Slovak (0.00017% of Canada's population) but in fact it can be assumed that there are about 100 000 Canadians of Slovak origin. Slovaks are generally a deeply religious people; they are proud of their origin and are therefore quick to correct those who refer to them as CZECHS.

Migration and Settlement There have been 4 main waves of Slovak immigrants, inspired mainly by economic and political conditions in their homeland. Immigrants of the first wave (1885-1914) settled on farmland in the West. Later groups went to work in Alberta and BC mines, and for the CPR. The second wave, estimated at 30 000, took place during the interwar years. Many were young skilled workers who emigrated to earn good wages in order to buy land in Slovakia. Others, however, sent for their families and went either to farming settlements in the West or to Ontario and Québec mining towns. The declaration of Slovakia's independence in 1939 created divisions in the community; those supporting it were denounced by Czechoslovak diplomats in Canada. The third wave (some 20 000) began after WWII and included war refugees as well as those fleeing the communist takeover of 1948. Many were government officials who gave new impetus to Slovak organizations and periodicals; most settled in the major urban centres.

The fourth wave was sparked by the Warsaw Pact invasion of Czechoslovakia in 1968. These refugees (some 13 000) were among the best educated to leave their homeland. Settling in urban centres, they contributed to the growth of Slovak organizations and found their place in the Canadian economic, political and cultural life.

Social and Cultural Life Social stratification among Slovak Canadians today is determined by date of arrival in Canada, the position held in Slovakia, the success achieved in Canada and the willingness to participate actively in Slovak organizations. Catholic and Protestant clergy have played an important role as spiritual and community leaders, and Slovak parishioners of all denominations have helped immigrants to overcome linguistic and cultural differences. Slovak newspapers have played an equally important role in assisting immigrants, and they have also reflected the political and economic divisions in the community. The early immigrants created benefit societies because of difficult economic conditions and lack of state-supported welfare measures. Today the Canadian Slovak League is the most important Slovak organization. It publishes *Kanadský Slovák (The Canadian Slovak)*, and helps to maintain Slovak traditions. Literary works are fostered through a network of Slovak publications in the Western world and by the Slovak World Congress, headquartered in Toronto.

Group Maintenance The political fate of the Slovaks in their homeland has been the main factor in preserving the group's consciousness and cohesion in Canada. Despite political divisions mirroring those in Slovakia, most Slovak Canadians today support freedom for Slovakia. Parish life, especially for the first 3 waves, and Slovak organizations have helped to foster the Slovak language and enhance family cohesion.

STANISLAV J. KIRSCHBAUM

Reading: Joseph M. Kirschbaum, *Slovaks in Canada* (1967); Anthony X. Sutherland, *The Canadian Slovak League 1932-1982, A History* (1984).

Slovenes are inhabitants of Slovenia, a republic of Yugoslavia. Until the 1971 census, Canadian statistics included immigrant Slovenes among Hungarians, Italians, Yugoslavs or Austrians, and some (those who had settled in France first) as French. By 1981 there were 7000 persons of Slovene origin in Canada.

Migration and Settlement In 1830 Reverend Frederick Baraga, a Slovenian missionary, later the first bishop of Sault Ste Marie and Marquette, came to work among the Indians around Lk Superior. He learned the language of the Ottawa and Chippewa and published *A Theoretical and Practical Grammar of the Otchipwe Language* (for which he is known as "Father of Indian Literature") and a dictionary of the Ojibwa language (1853). Large numbers of Slovenes, attracted partly by Father Baraga's reports, began to immigrate to N America 1875-1900. Those who settled in Canada worked primarily in mines, in road construction around Timmins and Kirkland Lake, and farming in the Niagara Peninsula. At Beamsville, they established the Slovenian Farmers' Co-operative and Slovenian Farmers' Home. Others settled in centres such as Nanaimo, Port Alberni, Vancouver, Rossland, Penticton and Cassidy in BC; Canmore, Bankhead, Banff and Evergreen in Alberta; Quill Lake, Sask; New Waterford and Caledonia Mines, NS; and in Montréal.

Between 1921 and 1936 (according to Yugoslav statistics) only 4281 Slovenes immigrated to Canada, primarily for economic reasons, but after 1948 large numbers immigrated (many of whom settled in Toronto) following the establishment of the communist regime in Yugoslavia. Some Slovenes also immigrated to Canada (1956-58) after the Hungarian uprising.

Social and Cultural Life Early settlers organized mutual benefit societies which also served as social and cultural centres. Cultural activities increased with the settlement of post-WWII political refugees. Slovenes are predominantly Roman Catholic and Slovene parishes such as those in Toronto, Hamilton, Montréal and Winnipeg are major centres of religious, social, cultural and recreational activities, including Slovene language classes for children, choirs, drama societies and religious organizations.

In Toronto a religious monthly, *Božja beseda (God's Word)*, is published. The Slovenian National Federation, established in 1952 to promote the idea of a noncommunist and democratic Slovenia, publishes the monthly *Slovenska država (Slovenian State)*. Slovenes in the Toronto area are served by 2 Slovenian credit unions.

RUDOLPH ČUJEŠ

Slug, common name for several terrestrial pulmonate and numerous marine gilled species of gastropod MOLLUSCS conspicuous by the lack of an exposed shell. Terrestrial slugs have rudimentary shells, embedded in the body tissue. The mantle encapsulates a lung sack which communicates with the outside atmosphere through a single breathing pore; gills are absent. The head bears sensory tentacles and encloses a rasping feeding organ, the radula. Land slugs possess a muscular foot which employs peristaltic muscle waves, aided by mucous secretions, to creep over the substratum. Canada's introduced greyish brown European slug (*Limax maximus*) grows to about 15 cm, but most land slugs are much smaller. The most destructive slug is the black slug (*Arion ater*). Most slugs are herbivorous but *Arion ater* will, in addition, feed voraciously upon animal flesh and feces. Fortunately, this species is easily attracted to slug baits.

The sea slug (*Melibe leonina*), a predacious, semipelagic opisthobranch gastropod, inhabits open, quiet channels, eelgrass beds and kelp forests from BC to California. The genus name *Melibe* ("honeylike") refers to the resin-sweet odour that it imparts to anything touching it. This sea slug can attain 10 cm in length and resembles a diaphanous, truncated soupspoon, with several inflated, ovoid leaves on its handle. Delicate in appearance, it is often mistaken for a strange jellyfish. *Melibe* usually comes in translucent shades of yellow, brown, grey and lavender, but can be colourless. A convincing swimmer of the thrashing-twisting school, the sea slug can also trap air in its oral hood for buoyancy. The large, basket-shaped hood is fringed with a mane of slender tentacles which are used as strainers for retaining minute ZOOPLANKTON as water is forced out of the oral basket. Reproduction is a gregarious affair with hundreds of animals collecting at one site for mating. The broad, spiral ribbons of eggs are laid in summer. PETER V. FANKBONER

Small Business is a term difficult to define, but generally it refers to the many business firms that are small compared to the relatively few giant firms (characterized by multi-locational operation, large numbers of hired employees, ownership by publicly traded stocks and management by professionally trained salaried managers) dominating most sectors of industry and trade. Economic activity has become concentrated in the frequently conglomerate, usually foreign-owned MULTINATIONAL CORPORATIONS, the wealth and power of which sometimes exceeds that of most nation-states. By contrast, small businesses are typically local operations owned privately by a family or by a small number of shareholders, some of whom also manage the operation, and staffed by a small number of hired workers (if any) in addition to the owner-

Small Business as a % of Total Business in Four Major Sectors, Canada, 1978		
	% of number of firms	% of business sales
Manufacturing	87.0	7.5
Construction	98.1	52.2
Trade	95.2	27.6
Services	99.0	56.4
Total	96.8	22.2

managers. By any criterion some 90% of all businesses are small, but a further distinction can be made between small and medium-sized businesses. Generally, it is accepted that a firm ceases to be small when it employs more than about 20 employees. In certain sectors, eg, construction business, personal services, that do not lend themselves to standardization and centralized management, small businesses are still responsible for a large part of economic activity.

Role in the Economy If a small business is defined arbitrarily as a firm with sales of up to $2 million per year (excluding both the agricultural sector, where most of the 300 000 farms are small businesses, and businesses with sales of less than $10 000, as these are generally not full-time commercial businesses), then some 700 000 (96.8% of the total number) small businesses exist in Canada. Their sales amount to about 22% of total business sales.

Small businesses produce goods for which there is no mass market — specialty items, high-quality and hand-crafted items, custom-made goods and components that require detailed design and production. Small business does much of the wholesaling and retailing where the sales and service requirements (owing to the nature of the goods or to the absence of high-volume customer traffic) are high, and in certain cases, particularly construction, services and agriculture, where individual application is at a premium, small business continues to hold its own. The most important nonstandardized types of goods and services are those that are new and innovative; despite the commercial technological successes of gigantic, concentrated research and development efforts, a large number of the most fundamental advances have been developed by individuals working alone or in small firms.

The indispensable role of small business in providing "high-care" goods and services and in contributing new ideas, products and methods will probably expand in the future. For example, with the long-term decline in some major industries, Canada will be turning more to innovative small businesses to create new international markets for specialized goods and services.

Characteristics of Small Business Small businesses vary greatly from one another in size, lines of business and type of organization. Most businesses begin as small firms. The difficulties and myriad details of setting up require all the attention of the entrepreneur and securing adequate financing is usually a difficulty. It is variously estimated that about 50% of all new businesses fail within 5 years of their creation and do so most often as a result of limited capital. Because smaller businesses are undercapitalized they rely heavily on banks for financing, which leaves them peculiarly vulnerable to recessions and management error. Ironically, large firms like DOME PETROLEUM or MASSEY-FERGUSON, may lose millions of dollars and still survive. Nevertheless, it is vitally important to the economy that new firms are formed regularly because frequently new ideas or processes can only realize development in a new firm.

Small business has had to overcome the general feeling by both the public and the government that large businesses are more efficient and progressive. Only in the 1970s has it developed a national voice to represent its concerns before government and the general public. The Canadian Federation of Independent Business, formed in 1971, grew to 64 000 members within 10 years. Various studies have shown that small business has been growing more rapidly in numbers of employed than larger businesses since the late 1960s or early 1970s in the US, Canada and other industrial countries. Larger business will reduce numbers of employees throughout the 1980s as a result of fierce international competition; consequently, governments are introducing policies more favourable to entrepreneurship and small business.

PATRICIA C. JOHNSTON

Small Claims Court, the common name of courts established by provincial legislation for civil matters involving small sums of money. In Québec, the upper limit of the small claims court is $10 000, but in the other provinces it is $1000, $2000 or $3000. The procedure in these courts is less formal than in higher courts and it is usually possible for individuals to conduct their cases without a lawyer. In Québec, lawyers are barred from appearing on behalf of clients. Most provinces have created a small claims or civil division of the provincial court, but PEI has established a small claims section of the General Division of the Supreme Court of PEI, just as in NB small claims are handled by a section of the Court of Queen's Bench. In NS, the Municipal Court in Halifax is responsible for claims of less than $500. In the Yukon Territory, claims of less than $500 can be dealt with by a small-debt official of the territorial court and a magistrate can deal with claims of less than $1000. In the NWT, the territorial court deals with actions for less than $5000.   P.K. DOODY AND T.B. SMITH

Small Presses, publishing companies operating on a small scale, have appeared in Canada almost entirely since WWII. More than larger, commercial publishers they tend to be oriented towards furthering, by publication of appropriate material, the peculiar views and interests of their founders. Their function is largely critical and educational. In an era of social and technological change and the consequent fragmentation of life-styles, they attempt to offer modes of thought, behaviour and expression which are alternatives to those normally encountered by readers of commercial publications. Many small presses originated as direct offshoots of little magazines (*see* LITERARY MAGAZINES), others as writers' co-operatives. Some presses specialize in genre publication; others limit themselves to promoting a certain aesthetic within genres. Some promote political causes; others try to preserve the essential flavour of a region. A few attempt a limited commercialism through the use of fine paper, hand-set printing and numbered, limited editions (*see* PRIVATE PRESSES).

This fringe industry requires for its survival adequate financing, an educated audience and a means of reaching that audience. The postwar proliferation of universities and community colleges and a growing disillusionment with the products of mass circulation have done much to supply a potential readership. At the same time, the development of offset and computerized printing has made possible the production of relatively low-cost, attractively designed books. The establishment of the CANADA COUNCIL in 1957 prepared the way for government funding, of which small-press proprietors were quick to take advantage. Coincidentally, a postwar expansion into Canada by multinational book companies created a backlash among authors, educationalists, the Canadian public and the relatively few Canadian publishers. The Independent Publishers Association, organized in 1969, was made up largely of representatives of the small presses; it lobbied so successfully for an indigenous industry that within a decade most

larger, more commercial Canadian houses joined it to form the Association of Canadian Publishers. In this organization the interests of the small presses are served by a special subdivision, the Literary Press Group.

Small presses are now scattered from coast to coast. Serving writers and audiences in the Atlantic region are Breakwater Books of St John's, Ragweed of Charlottetown, Lancelot Press of Windsor, NS, and Fiddlehead Poetry Books of Fredericton. In Montréal Tundra Books has gained international renown for its CHILDREN'S LITERATURE, whereas Véhicule Press has branched out from local authors to national and American authors. Tecumseh Press of Ottawa and ECW Press of Toronto concentrate on academic and bibliographical publications. In Toronto are Coach House, distinguished for its handsome graphics and experimental poetry; the House of Anansi, which publishes fiction and criticism; and Playwrights Canada, which issues plays that have been professionally produced. Penumbra Press of Moonbeam, Ont, is devoted to publications on the North, and Potlatch of Hamilton issues the *Canadian Children's Annual.* Turnstone of Winnipeg, Thistledown of Saskatoon and Longspoon of Edmonton concentrate on Prairie poets. On the West Coast, which has the liveliest publishing trade outside Toronto, are Talonbooks of Vancouver, best known for its plays, Sono Nis Press of Victoria, which focuses on avant-garde poetry, and Theytus Books, which publishes works by and about native peoples.

Traditionally the little presses have published new poets or noncommercial writers, as did such early ones as First Statement, CONTACT and Quarry, but more recently they have attracted many major and commercial writers such as Hugh HOOD, Robert KROETSCH, Carol BOLT and Northrop FRYE. Several firms, notably Hurtig (Edmonton), Oberon (Ottawa) and Lester, Orpen & Denys (Toronto), have enlarged their businesses to move beyond the designation "little press."

The circumstances governing library purchases and the bookstore trade in Canada have made the distribution and sale of small-press books difficult compared to that by the mass-market commercial publishers. However, the small presses have largely avoided the high costs of national distribution by concentrating on regional and local markets. A number of small publishers have gained access to national and foreign markets through participation in the *Literary Press Group Catalogue,* published since 1975 with the financial assistance of the Ontario Arts Council. Such subsidies, from both provincial and federal governments, are needed to maintain the small-press industry. Despite their precarious financial circumstances, however, the regional publishers awakened a new interest in regional literature, and by the 1980s had demonstrated the vigour of publishing outside Toronto. *See also* BOOK PUBLISHING; REGIONALISM IN LITERATURE.   FRED COGSWELL AND GEORGE L. PARKER

Smallboy, Johnny Bob, (also Robert), or Apitchitchiw, community leader (b on Peigan Reserve, SW of Ft Macleod, Alta 7 Nov 1898, d at Smallboy Camp near Nordegg, Alta, 8 July 1984). Chief Smallboy focused national attention on urban and reserve Indian problems when he "returned to the land" with followers from troubled Indian settlements. Born of a traditional Cree family who were among the last to settle on their allotted reserve at Hobbema in central Alberta, Smallboy became a hunter, trapper, farmer, and eventually chief of the Ermineskin Band from 1959 to 1969. In 1968, to escape deteriorating social and political conditions on the reserve, he moved to a bush camp on the Kootenay Plains, accompanied by some 125 people, or over a third of his band. Despite

factional splits, the return of many residents to Hobbema, and the group's failure to obtain permanent land tenure, Smallboy Camp persisted into the 1980s as a working community used as a retreat by Plains and Woodlands Indians from western Canada and the US.   BENNETT McCARDLE

Smallpox, *see* EPIDEMIC.

Smallwood, Charles, physician, professor of meteorology, founder of the McGill Observatory (b at Birmingham, Eng 1812; d at Montréal 22 Dec 1873). Arriving in Montréal in 1833, he later set up medical practice in St-Martin. There he kept a weather notebook and built an observatory for astronomy and meteorology. The astronomy had practical application: for "time from the stars," the observatory was connected by the Montréal telegraph with major US cities. Smallwood examined and photographed snow crystals through a microscope, surely one of the first to do so. Fifteen of his scientific articles and 11 weather reviews appeared in the *Canadian Naturalist* between 1857 and 1872. In 1856 McGill granted him an honorary LLD and appointed him professor of meteorology (without salary). The work of this pioneering Victorian scientist foreshadowed modern CLOUD physics.   J.S. MARSHALL

Smallwood, Joseph Roberts, journalist, politician, premier of Newfoundland 1949-72 (b at Gambo, Nfld 24 Dec 1900). As a bright young man, he became a journalist and covered the 1919 transatlantic flights. In New York, 1921 to 1925, he worked for a left-wing daily and campaigned for the Progressive Party; ever since, he has called himself a "socialist." Back in Newfoundland, he became a union organizer, radio broadcaster, an unsuccessful candidate in the 1932 election, and during WWII he ran a piggery at the air base at GANDER. His chance came when Britain's new Labour government announced that Newfoundlanders, then ruled by an appointed COMMISSION OF GOVERNMENT, could elect representatives to a convention which was to advise the government on the choice to be put to the electorate in a referendum about their political future. Smallwood, who favoured CONFEDERATION with Canada, was elected to the Convention in 1946. For the next 3 years, he demonstrated the willpower, courage, ruthlessness and mastery of populist propaganda that made him one of the most remarkable of contemporary politicians. Despite opposition from in-

Pen-and-ink drawing entitled *Joey Smallwood* (1969), by Nickolay Sabolotny (*courtesy Public Archives of Canada/ C-45054*).

fluential St John's merchants who accused him of betraying Newfoundland for arguing that it should not retain its independence, he dominated the convention debates, there delivering his finest speech in which he told Newfoundlanders the bitter truth: "We are not a nation. We are a medium-sized municipality . . . left far behind the march of time." With the bait of family allowances, welcome hard cash for many Newfoundlanders, he won the second of 2 hardfought and close referenda on 22 July 1948. He was appointed premier of the interim government 1 Apr 1949, elected leader of the Liberal Party, and he won the first provincial election in May 1949. He was not seriously challenged for decades.

Smallwood's early years in power alternated between farce and tragedy. An attempt at forced industrialization ended in bankruptcy for most of his manufacturing plants and in the imprisonment for embezzlement of his economic adviser, the mysterious Latvian Alfred A. Valdmanis. The tragedy happened in Mar 1959 in the small town of Badger where striking loggers clashed with police officers; in the melee, one member of the Newfoundland constabulary was clubbed and later died. Smallwood, who had opposed the strike and decertified the union a few days before, made him into a martyr. No longer a socialist, except in his rhetoric, Smallwood from then on consorted with corporate tycoons such as John C. DOYLE and John Shaheen and devoted himself to large industrial endeavours like the CHURCHILL FALLS power project, at the same time encouraging Newfoundlanders to leave isolated outports for new "resettlement" communities. He retained power through the 1960s because he, and Newfoundlanders, benefited from lavish new federal spending schemes. The progress proved his undoing as a new, educated and relatively affluent generation of Newfoundlanders came of age. He survived his first challenge, by disaffected Cabinet minister John CROSBIE, at the 1969 Liberal leadership convention. But in the Oct 1971 election, the Conservatives led by Frank MOORES won 21 seats, Smallwood 20, and the New Labrador Party one. He resigned 18 Jan 1972 after 3 tense and intrigue-ridden months. Characteristically, Smallwood refused to give up. He tried to win back the Liberal leadership in 1974 and to form a new party, the Liberal Reform Party. Only after both attempts failed did he give up politics. He resigned his seat in 1977 to take on a new role as elder statesman and return to writing, most notably in his planned, 4-vol *Encyclopedia of Newfoundland* (1981-). RICHARD J. GWYN

Reading: Richard J. Gwyn, *Smallwood: the Unlikely Revolutionary* (1968).

Smallwood Reservoir, 6527 km², elev 472 m, tenth-largest freshwater body in Canada, is situated on the remote Labrador Plateau, near the Québec border. It was created in the 1960s for hydroelectric-power production by damming the CHURCHILL R at CHURCHILL FALLS and diking other rivers. The water level varies by 8.7 m, giving a usable water reserve of 28 billion m³. MICHIKAMAU and Lobstick lakes were the largest of hundreds of lakes that now make up the reservoir, named for Joseph R. SMALLWOOD, first premier of Newfoundland. Originally inhabited by Naskapi, the area was first visited by Europeans John MCLEAN and Erland Erlandson in 1839. The area was first mapped by the Oblate missionary Father Babel, and later, in detail, by Albert LOW of the Dominion Geological Survey (1895). IAN MacCALLUM

Smart, Elizabeth, novelist, poet (b at Ottawa 27 Dec 1913). Smart was educated at Hartfield House, a private school in Cobourg, Ont. At the age of 19, she travelled to London, Eng, to study piano. She returned to Canada to work briefly for the *Ottawa Journal*, writing society news. During the 1930s, Smart travelled extensively and through contact with Lawrence Durrell she met George Barker, the British poet who was to become the father of her 4 children. She worked at the British Embassy in Washington during WWII and moved to England in 1943 where she worked to support herself and her family for the next 2 decades writing advertising copy and working for *Vogue* (as literary editor) and *House and Garden*.

Smart's first work, *By Grand Central Station I Sat Down and Wept* (1945), immediately established a cult following. Republished in 1966, 1975, 1977 and in Canada in 1982, it has been critically hailed as a masterpiece of poetic prose and a homage to love unique in its style and sensibility. In 1977, following 32 years of silence, 2 new works appeared: *A Bonus,* a collection of sharp and witty poems, and *The Assumption of Rogues and Rascals,* a prose-poem that is both a continuation of and a comment on her early work. In 1984 a collection of unpublished poetry and prose, *In The Mean Time,* further established her literary reputation. ALICE VAN WART

Smellie, Elizabeth Lawrie, nurse (b at Port Arthur, Ont 22 Mar 1884; d at Toronto 5 Mar 1968), first woman promoted colonel in the Canadian Army (1944). A graduate of Johns Hopkins Training School for Nurses, she joined the Canadian Army Nursing Service in WWI, served in France and Britain (mentioned in dispatches, 1916; awarded Royal Red Cross, 1917), and on her return to Canada was appointed assistant matron in chief (1918-20). During the following years she helped build the VICTORIAN ORDER OF NURSES into a thriving nationwide organization and was its chief superintendent in Canada 1923-47. Taking leave of absence from the VON during WWII, she served as matron in chief in Canada of the Royal Canadian Army Medical Corps (1940-44) and in 1941 laid the foundations of the Canadian Women's Army Corps. CARLOTTA HACKER

Smelt (Osmeridae), family of small, iridescent FISHES of class Osteichthyes, found in coastal seas, streams and lakes of the Northern Hemisphere. Worldwide, 6 genera, 11 named and 2 unnamed species are known; in Canada, 6 genera and 9 species. Rainbow smelt and capelin occur on all 3 coasts; pond smelt on the Arctic Coast and drainage; pygmy smelt in Québec and NB lakes; the others on the Pacific coast and drainage. Some smelts are marine fishes; some live in fresh water; others live in the sea but spawn in fresh water (anadromous). The family name derives from their characteristic, cucumberlike odour. Their shape and fins are much like those of a slender SALMON, but they lack the tiny, triangular structure found just above the pelvic fins on the abdomen of salmonids. Like salmon, they have a small, tablike, adipose (fleshy) fin on the back, just in front of the tail fin. Smelts seldom exceed 41 cm. At spawning time, the male develops granulations on the scales and fins to help maintain contact with the female while fertilizing eggs on sand or gravel. The egg membrane peels back, sticking the egg to the bottom. Spawning occurs in spring or summer; the eggs are left unguarded. Smelts are excellent to eat and are sought by fishermen angling through ice or dip netting, seining or gill netting during spawning, and by commercial trawlers. They are also an important food for many animals, including Atlantic cod, beluga whales and aquatic birds. The famed eulachon (candlefish) was and is used by native Canadians for food, especially for its nutritious oil. Formerly, it was also burned like a candle. Most young smelts eat PLANKTON; adults of some species (eg, rainbow smelt) eat small fishes and shrimp. D.E. McALLISTER

Smith, Sir Albert James, lawyer, politician, premier of NB (b at Shediac, NB 12 Mar 1822; d at Dorchester, NB 30 June 1883). Smith was the anti-Confederation leader of NB who almost wrecked the movement in 1865. Entering politics as a radical in 1852 and a member of the reform government that took office 1854, he was appointed attorney general in 1861 when S.L. TILLEY became premier. The 2 divided over government railway policies in 1862 and battled over CONFEDERATION, which Smith regarded as a devious scheme from the "oily brains of Canadian politicians." The "antis" trounced the Confederation forces in the 1865 election. Smith failed to suppress the unionists as premier 1865-66 and was eventually driven from office by an arbitrary lieutenant-governor. After Confederation, Smith went to Ottawa, becoming minister of fisheries under PM Alexander MACKENZIE. In 1877 he was the "ruling spirit throughout" the Halifax Fisheries Commission which awarded Canada $5.5 million, the first diplomatic victory over the US. For his efforts Smith became the first native-born New Brunswicker to be knighted, an ironic twist not lost on those who supported Confederation.

CARL M. WALLACE

Reading: P.B. Waite, *The Life and Times of Confederation* (1962).

Smith, Andrew, veterinarian, educator (b at Dalrymple, Scot 12 July 1834; d at Toronto 15 Aug 1910). A graduate of Edinburgh Veterinary Coll in 1861, he came to Canada that year. In 1862 he started lectures on veterinary science leading to the founding of the Upper Canada Veterinary School (later Ontario Veterinary Coll), the oldest such college in N America. He graduated over 3000 veterinarians during his 40-year tenure as principal. A pioneer of VETERINARY MEDICINE and education in N America, Smith was a great promoter of his profession. He was first president of the Ontario Veterinary Assn and a prime mover for its organization (1874) and incorporation (1879). He was a founder of what is now the CANADIAN NATIONAL EXHIBITION. R.G. THOMSON

Smith, Arnold Cantwell, diplomat (b at Toronto 18 Jan 1915). He was a Rhodes scholar and joined the Dept of External Affairs in 1943. Already fiercely anti-Soviet and convinced that aggression must be met by determined response, he was posted to Russia, 1943-45, and he acted as secretary to the Kellock-Taschereau Royal Commission (*see* GOUZENKO). His subsequent service included stints in Brussels, New York, Cambodia and London, and culminated in terms as ambassador to Cairo, 1958-61, and to Moscow, 1961-63. From 1965 to 1975 he was an enthusiastic, creative, deeply committed first secretary-general of the COMMONWEALTH, a period he recalls in *Stitches in Time* (1981). NORMAN HILLMER

Smith, Arthur James Marshall, poet, critic, anthologist (b at Montréal 8 Nov 1902; d at East Lansing, Mich 21 Nov 1980). A.J.M. Smith was educated at McGill and U of Edinburgh. In 1925, while a graduate student in Montréal, he founded and edited the *McGill Fortnightly Review* with F.R. SCOTT, the first journal to publish modernist poetry and critical opinion in Canada. This began a period of significant activities for the staid provincialism of contemporary Canadian letters. In 1936 he coedited *New Provinces,* followed in 1943 by publication of both Smith's own first collection, *News of the Phoenix* (Gov Gen's Award) and *A Book of Canadian Poetry,* in which he distinguished a separate national voice. He continued to edit numerous anthologies and produce his own poetry and, in 1973, published a collection of critical essays, *Towards a View of Canadian Letters.*

Early in his career Smith moved to Lansing, Mich, to teach at Michigan State U although he spent most of his summers near Magog, Qué. In 1966 the RSC awarded him the Lorne Pierce Medal. In 1972 Smith retired and the university created the A.J.M. Smith Award, given annually for a noteworthy volume by a Canadian poet. MARLENE ALT

Smith, David Laurence Thomson, veterinarian, teacher (b at Regina 18 Apr 1914; d at Saskatoon 15 Nov 1983). After serving in the Royal Canadian Army Medical Corps in WWII, he joined the faculty of the Ontario Veterinary College in 1946, and was head of pathology and bacteriology there 1955-63. Smith is best known as the founder of the Western College of Veterinary Medicine at U of Sask, where he was dean 1963-74 and professor of pathology 1974-81. Highly regarded in the profession for his leadership and integrity, he was president of the Canadian Veterinary Medical Assn in 1980-81. After retirement, he was heavily involved in CANADIAN INTERNATIONAL DEVELOPMENT AGENCY projects related to veterinary colleges in Uganda, Malaysia and Somalia. R.G. THOMSON

Smith, Donald Alexander, 1st Baron Strathcona and Mount Royal, fur trader, railroad financier, diplomat (b at Forres, Scot 6 Aug 1820; d at London, Eng 21 Jan 1914). The son of a tradesman, Smith joined the HUDSON'S BAY COMPANY in 1838 and worked his way through the ranks from apprentice clerk to chief commissioner in 1871. By 1883 he was a director of the company and, through careful investments, its largest shareholder. In 1889 he was chosen governor, or chief executive officer, of the company. Smith came to public attention in 1869 when sent to Ft Garry to assist in settling the terms of union between Louis RIEL's provisional government and Canada. The mission was successful and Smith began a political career, representing Winnipeg-St John in the Manitoba legislature 1870-74 and Selkirk in the House of Commons 1871-78. In 1874, when dual representation was abolished, he elected to sit in the Dominion Parliament. A Conservative, he voted against the Macdonald government in the PACIFIC SCANDAL, and thereafter relations between Macdonald and Smith were cool. After a 9-year absence Smith returned to Parliament, representing Montréal W 1887-96. In 1873-74 Smith joined his cousin George STEPHEN, J.J. HILL and others in acquiring the depreciated bonds of the St Paul, Minneapolis and Manitoba Ry, a line running through Minnesota to the Canadian border. He was an enthusiastic supporter of the CANADIAN PACIFIC RY, and his financial backing was essential to its progress. He was therefore invited to drive the last spike when the railroad was completed in 1885. Smith was a principal shareholder and, in 1887, president of the BANK OF MONTREAL, which was closely associated with the CPR. In April 1896 Sir Mackenzie BOWELL appointed Smith high commissioner for Canada in the UK, a post he held, along with the HBC governorship, until his death. He became prominent in British public affairs and spokesman in London for the self-governing colonies. During the SOUTH AFRICAN WAR he personally maintained Strathcona's Horse, a regiment of over 500 mounted riflemen. He was elevated to the peerage in 1897 and served as chancellor of McGill, where he founded Royal Victoria College for women in 1896. D.M.L. FARR

Smith, Donald Graham, swimmer (b at Edmonton, Alta 9 May 1958). A breaststroke specialist, Graham Smith became the youngest Canadian male to win 2 national titles in one meet, winning both the 100 m and 200 m breaststroke events in 1974. At the 1976 Montréal Olympics, he was on the 2nd-place 400 m medley relay team, and in 1977 and 1978 he set world records in the 200 m individual medley over the 25 m course. At the 1978 Common-

Donald Smith's financial backing was essential to the completion of the CPR, and he was given the honour of driving the "last spike" (courtesy Public Archives of Canada / C-3841).

wealth Games, Smith won an unprecedented 6 gold medals — in the 100 m and 200 m breaststroke, the 200 m and 400 m individual medley, and the 400 m freestyle and medley relays. Later that year he won the 200 m individual medley at the World Aquatic Games. Smith received the LOU MARSH TROPHY as Canada's outstanding athlete for 1978 and was honoured with the Order of Canada that same year. BARBARA SCHRODT

Smith, Ernest John, architect (b at Winnipeg 17 Dec 1919). A founding member of Smith Carter Partners (1972), Smith studied architecture at U Man and MIT. Smith, Carter, Parkin was founded in 1947 with Dennis Carter and John C. PARKIN, co-principals. The firm's work included major projects, public and private in Manitoba, the Prairies and later abroad. Many of the projects Smith directed changed the urban character of Winnipeg; these included Winnipeg Square and the underground concourse at Portage and Main, the Woodsworth Bldg on Broadway and the Monarch Life Insurance Bldg. Major international work under Smith's direction includes the Warsaw Chancery. WILLIAM P. THOMPSON

Smith, George Isaac, lawyer, politician, premier of NS (b at Stewiacke, NS 6 Apr 1909; d at Truro, NS 19 Dec 1982). He began his career as a lawyer and served with the army in WWII. He then became politically involved, helping to recruit R.L. STANFIELD as Progressive Conservative Party leader in NS in 1948. Smith entered the legislature in 1949 and occupied various strategic Cabinet posts, until 1967 when he replaced Stanfield as premier. He supported regional equalization and federal-provincial conferences, and was praised for decisiveness in the government takeover of Sydney Steel in 1968. After his administration was defeated in 1970, he resigned as party leader in 1971. He remained an MLA until 1974 and was appointed a senator in 1975. LOIS KERNAGHAN

Smith, Goldwin, "Annexation" to his opponents, historian, journalist (b at Reading, Eng 13 Aug 1823; d at Toronto 7 June 1910). An acknowledged historian and journalist when he settled permanently in Canada in 1871, Smith became best known to Canadians as the advo-

cate of union with the US as a prerequisite to moral unification of the Anglo-Saxon race. Smith was educated at Eton and Oxford, where his liberal stand against the conservative Tractarian movement led to his appointment to 2 royal commissions on the university. He befriended Richard Cobden and John Bright of the Manchester School, who taught that abolition of tariffs and introduction of free trade between nations would lead to interdependence and make war impossible. Smith supported this creed, derived from Adam Smith, in contributions to the *Morning Chronicle, Daily News* and *Saturday Review.* In 1858 he was appointed Regius Professor of Modern History at Oxford, and in his *Lectures on Modern History* (1861) preached the gospel of the "invisible hand": man as an economic being wresting a living from nature is in an unfallen world which, naturally harmonious, should be left unregulated.

In 1866 Smith resigned to nurse his ailing father. After his death, Smith moved to the US to teach at Cornell. He settled in Toronto in 1871 to be near relatives. In 1875 he married Henry Boulton's widow and moved into The Grange, where as a self-declared bystander he wrote extensively on Canadian and international affairs. Initially he supported the CANADA FIRST movement but its collapse convinced him Canada was not viable as a nation — a view he expressed in *Canada and the Canadian Question* (1891). As a journalist Smith wrote for the *Liberal,* the *Nation, The Canadian Monthly and National Review,* the *Week,* which he founded in 1883 with Charles G.D. ROBERTS as literary editor, *The Bystander* and the *Weekly Sun.* He opposed Canadian participation in the SOUTH AFRICAN WAR and the imperial federation movement. His *Reminiscences* and a selected *Correspondence* were published after his death. TOM MIDDLEBRO'

Reading: E. Wallace, *Goldwin Smith* (1957).

Smith, Gordon Appelbe, painter, teacher (b at Hove, Eng 18 June 1919). In 1934 Smith immigrated to Winnipeg where he studied under L.L. FITZGERALD. Wounded during WWII, he moved to Vancouver in 1944, where he joined his wife and completed his studies at the Vancouver School of Art. He taught at the VSA 1946-56, and at the Faculty of Education, UBC, as professor of fine arts 1956-82. Smith attracted national attention for his award-winning *Structure with Red Sun* at the First Biennial of Canadian Painting in 1955. His work is a form of Romantic lyric abstraction that balances the pervasive influence of the West Coast landscape with a gestural, nonobjective manner of painting. In 1976 the Vancouver Art Gallery mounted a 30-year retrospective of his work. PETER MALKIN

Smith, Harold Greville, industrialist (b at Sheffield, Eng 25 Jan 1902; d at Montréal 19 Feb 1974). After graduating from Oxford, Smith was hired by a chemical firm later absorbed by Imperial Chemical Industries. ICI sent Smith to Canada in 1932 to direct chemical development in Canadian Industries Limited (CIL). In 1939 he became a VP of CIL and VP and general manager of Defence Industries Ltd, a CIL subsidiary (and not, as is commonly believed, a crown corporation) engaged in defence work for the government. In 1951 he became president of CIL and was confronted by an antitrust judgement against its 2 parent companies, ICI and DuPont. With the agreement of C.D. HOWE, Smith supervised division of the company into CIL (ICI) and DuPont of Canada. He was president of CIL until 1958; he was chairman and chief executive officer of Brinco 1960-63. ROBERT BOTHWELL

Smith, Irving Norman, journalist, author (b at Ottawa 28 Oct 1909). He was a newspaperman for more than 40 years, mostly with the Ottawa *Journal,* where he began 1928. In the 1960s, following his father, E. Norman Smith, he became editor, then president, of the paper and did much to make it more than the party organ it had been. Also interested in the North, Smith served for a time on the NWT Council and edited *The Unbelievable Land*, a collection of essays about the Arctic.

Reading: I.N. Smith, *The Journal Men* (1974).

Smith, Joseph Leopold, Leo, composer, cellist, writer, teacher (b at Birmingham, Eng 26 Nov 1881; d at Toronto 18 Apr 1952). At a crucial period in Canada's musical development, Smith influenced many of the country's future leaders in performance, composition, writing and teaching. A child prodigy in England, he later played cello in the Halle and Covent Garden orchestras before coming to Canada in 1910. He joined the Toronto Symphony and was its principal cellist 1917-18 and 1932-40. He taught at the Toronto Conservatory from 1911 and was a professor of music at U of T 1938-50. Smith wrote 3 widely used textbooks: *Musical Rudiments* (1920), *Music of the 17th and 18th Centuries* (1931) and *Elementary Part-Writing* (1939). His compositions, sensitive impressionistic works, included Québec folk material, West Coast Indian songs and settings of verse by Canadian poets.
BARCLAY McMILLAN

Smith, Lois, ballet dancer (b at Vancouver 8 Oct 1929). Dancing with the NATIONAL BALLET OF CANADA 1951-69, she was Canada's first prima ballerina. She began her formal ballet training in Vancouver at age 15 and her early performance experience was in musicals and light opera. Celia FRANCA, recognizing her potential, invited her to join the National Ballet at its inception in 1951 as principal dancer. Smith performed in a wide range of ballets, from comedy to drama, but was most acclaimed for her roles in the great classic ballets. After an injury forced her retirement in 1969, she opened her own school in Toronto.
JILLIAN M. OFFICER

Smith, Mary Ellen, née Spear, politician (b at Tavistock, Eng 11 Oct 1863; d at Vancouver 3 May 1933). Smith was the first woman member of BC's Legislative Assembly and the first woman Cabinet minister in the British Empire. As an independent, she won a Jan 1918 Vancouver by-election called after the death of her husband Ralph Smith, finance minister in the BC Liberal government. Re-elected as a Liberal in 1920 and 1924, she served as minister without portfolio from Mar to Nov 1921. She was an advocate of BC's first Mothers' Pensions and Female Minimum Wage Acts.
DIANE CROSSLEY

Smith, Sidney Earle, lawyer, professor, politician (b at Port Hood, NS 9 Mar 1897; d at Ottawa 17 Mar 1959). He lectured at Dalhousie and Osgoode Hall before becoming dean of the Dalhousie Law School in 1929. In 1934 he began a successful tenure as president of U of Man and in 1945 was appointed president of U of T, where he was a strong supporter of liberal-arts education. In Sept 1957 he was sworn in as John DIEFENBAKER's minister of external affairs. After an initial period of adjustment, Smith was gaining respect in the international community and had just hit his stride as minister when he died suddenly.
PATRICIA WILLIAMS

Smith, Titus, naturalist, surveyor, traveller, agriculturist (b at Granby, Mass 4 Sept 1768; d at Dutch Village near Halifax 4 Jan 1850). To his innate interest in all natural studies, Smith brought a mind well schooled in botany and a keen interest in the conservation of animal and plant life. He became well known to his contemporaries first through his one-man expedition around NS reporting to Gov WENTWORTH on the colony's resources. Later he acclimatized seeds and sold improved varieties that he introduced into British N America. Smith testified before the DURHAM Commission in 1839 concern-

ing conditions in NS, and served 1841-50 as secretary to the Central Board of Agriculture. With his writings in the press and his lectures to the Mechanics' Institute, his name became a household word and his advice was sought on diverse subjects. Smith advocated careful use of resources and a commonsense approach to problems of agriculture and forest management.
TERRENCE M. PUNCH

Smith, William, fourth chief justice of Quebec (b at New York C 18 June 1728; d at Québec C 6 Dec 1793). Smith, a Yale graduate (1745), succeeded his father as a judge in New York (1767) and was subsequently chief justice there (1780). He remained loyal to the British Crown during the American Revolution. He was a friend of Governor Guy CARLETON and was named chief justice of Quebec (1786). He is now remembered for his interpretation of the QUEBEC ACT (1774) and his view that English or French law applied according to whether the litigants were of French or English expression. That position is now seen as having been motivated by political considerations. Smith is also known as an historian of NY state.
JOHN E.C. BRIERLEY

Smith-Shortt, Elizabeth, née Smith, physician, feminist (b at Winona, Canada W 18 Jan 1859; d at Ottawa 14 Jan 1949). She belonged to the prosperous LOYALIST family that founded the E.D. Smith preserves company. After teaching for a short time she almost single-handedly stimulated Queen's to introduce medical coeducation. After Elizabeth and others were forced out of medical school by jealous male students, the first Canadian Women's Medical Coll was established by Kingston's leading citizens on 9 June 1883. Next year 3 women graduated and Dr Elizabeth Smith entered general practice in Hamilton, Ont. In 1886 she married Queen's professor Adam Shortt and returned to Kingston as a lecturer in medical jurisprudence in the Women's Coll. Thereafter she became an enthusiastic champion of women's rights. When her husband became Canada's first civil service commissioner in Ottawa, Elizabeth battled unsuccessfully for numerous women's causes which led to her election as VP of the National Council of Women.
A.A. TRAVILL

Smithe, William, politician, premier of BC (b at Matfen, Eng 30 June 1842; d at Victoria, 28 Mar 1887). In 1862 Smithe settled as a farmer in southern Vancouver I. Elected in 1871 to BC's first provincial legislature, he had by 1875 become leader of the loosely organized opposition to G.A. WALKEM's government, a post he gave up to A.C. ELLIOTT. Smithe was a Cabinet minister in the Elliott government of 1876-78 and then again led the Opposition until he replaced BEAVEN as premier in 1883. Smithe remained in office until his death, initiating the "Great Potlatch" era, during which successive administrations made generous grants of crown-owned resources to entrepreneurs. By settling with Ottawa intergovernmental issues outstanding from the construction of the CPR, Smithe cleared the way for the development boom.
H. KEITH RALSTON

Smiths Falls, Ont, Town, pop 8831 (1981c), inc 1882, located on the Rideau R, 60 km SW of Ottawa. The site was granted to Major Thomas Smyth, a LOYALIST, and named for him, but

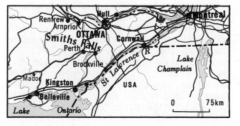

active settlement awaited Abel Russel Ward (1826), and was much expanded with the building of the RIDEAU CANAL. The town is an important lockport on the waterway. The falls provided power for early industries, such as farm implements. Now sheet metal, electrical implements, chocolate and textiles are the main products. The town is a CPR divisional point, tourist centre for the RIDEAU LAKES, and houses the Rideau Regional Centre for Retarded Children. Smiths Falls was among the first municipalities in Ontario to have an official plan for development.
K.L. MORRISON

Smokehouse Fish, especially PACIFIC SALMON, was a vital food supply for the SALISH, HAIDA, KWAKIUTL and TSIMSHIAN of the Northwest Coast. To ensure a steady supply throughout the year, fish was preserved by drying and smoking. Smokehouses, built of cedar planks over a post and beam frame, often had 2 stories. Smoke drifted upward from low fires to open holes in the roof, and circulated around the fish arranged on racks and pegs. When smoked, fish became hard and had to be cooked to be made edible. *See also* NATIVE PEOPLE.
RENÉ R. GADACZ

Reading: H. Stewart, *Indian Fishing: Early Methods on the Northwest Coast* (1977).

Smoking is a universal health hazard. All forms of TOBACCO smoking are potentially risky, depending on the amount of smoke inhaled and the duration of the habit. About 35% of Canadians over 15 years of age and 23% of those under 15 smoke cigarettes regularly. Many individuals who do not smoke breathe "secondhand" smoke and may suffer respiratory damage as a result. This is particularly true of children whose parents smoke and of persons with allergies or asthma.

Cigarette smoke contains more than 3000 substances, many of which have a deleterious effect on biological systems. The immediate consequences of smoke inhalation include constriction of the airways of the lung, an increase in heart rate, constriction of blood vessels and an elevation of blood pressure. Carbon monoxide in the blood of smokers deprives tissues of oxygen, a fact of potential critical importance for individuals with severe HEART DISEASE. Chronic elevation of blood carbon monoxide contributes to the gradual narrowing of arteries (arteriosclerosis). The inhalation of cigarette smoke by pregnant women subjects the circulation of the fetus to the same stresses as the smoker, which leads to a higher rate of certain obstetrical complications, perinatal mortality and the birth of slightly smaller, less mature infants.

In addition to vascular diseases, there are 2 other serious long-term effects from smoking. The first is emphysema (commonly found in older smokers), a disease in which the air sacs of the lung break down. This disease (and chronic bronchitis) account for the symptoms of cough, sputum production and shortness of breath in most long-term smokers. The second is lung CANCER, the major cause of death from smoking. Lung cancer is difficult to detect in an early stage and only a small minority of cases are curable. The incidence of lung cancer in Canada has been increasing steadily and has reached about 70 per 100 000 in males and 18 per 100 000 in females annually. The increase has been greater in women, as the proportion of smokers who are female increases. Cancers of the tongue, pharynx, larynx, esophagus and even remote organs such as the bladder are all more common among smokers than nonsmokers. The hazards of exposure to carcinogenic substances, such as asbestos, uranium and certain industrial products, are enormously increased for smokers.

Most smokers have developed a strong habit, but many may be helped to stop by various methods, eg, medical education programs, hypnosis or prescription medications. So-called

"mild" brands of cigarettes have no medically proven benefits (*see* TOBACCO).　ALEC HERBERT
Reading: W.J. Millar, *Smoking Behaviour of Canadians* (1981).

Smuggling, clandestine transportation of goods or persons across a boundary in such a way as to evade the payment of CUSTOMS duties or internal taxes, or to evade a prohibition on import or export. In Canada, smuggling has always been of considerable importance because of the long land frontier with the US, and because the Atlantic and Pacific seacoasts are extensive and poorly policed. Traditionally, smuggling in Canada was a business: it is at least as old as white settlement, and occasionally in coastal communities it has been almost a way of life.

Most smuggling is international, but there can be interprovincial smuggling because the provinces tax goods at different rates and apply differing markups within their liquor monopolies. Every nation, including Canada, attempts to stop smugglers. The provinces, however, do not, so interprovincial smuggling cannot be prevented. International smugglers have always been especially interested in valuable commodities that are not bulky and that government tends to tax heavily — liquor, tobacco products, wine and jewels. In the 1920s and 1930s, because of the American prohibition on the import or consumption of alcoholic drinks, a great deal of liquor was smuggled from Canada into the US, allowing some large fortunes to be made. Professional smugglers now concern themselves chiefly with prohibited drugs or druglike substances — heroin, cocaine, marijuana and various chemicals. More recently, because the Canadian government controls the exports of arms and other strategic materials, there have been more or less successful attempts to smuggle such goods out of Canada. In addition, a new kind of smuggling has developed, in which importers or exporters attach fictitiously low values to the goods they are trading so that customs duties will be lower than they should be.

The smuggling of traditional products by amateurs has obviously become much more tempting insofar as many more Canadians than previously are travelling between countries and provinces. However, because the costs of travel are high in comparison with the amount that can be saved, amateur smuggling rarely makes economic sense unless one is travelling for some other reason. There are no reliable statistics on the volume or value of smuggled goods, but the practice produces an understatement of the volume and value of Canada's INTERNATIONAL TRADE and a loss of government customs revenue.
　IAN M. DRUMMOND

Smyth, Sir Edward Selby, military officer (b at Belfast, Ire 31 Mar 1819; d in Eng 22 Sept 1896). He was adjutant general and general officer commanding the Canadian militia, 1874-80, an appointment capping a British service career in India, Africa, Ireland and Mauritius. Economic depression and decreased militia expenditures forced Selby Smyth to concentrate on the survival of the militia as an institution. Although many of his proposals were rejected by the government, his relations with his Canadian political masters were better than those of his successors. In 1875 Selby Smyth undertook an 11 000-mile tour through the Canadian West to inspect NWMP and militia units. His timely arrival in Batoche with 50 policemen forestalled declaration of a Métis republic.
　O.A. COOKE

Smythe, Constantine Falkland Cary, "Conn," sports entrepreneur (b at Toronto 1 Feb 1895; d there 18 Nov 1980). He was awarded the Military Cross in WWI, and was severely injured by shrapnel in WWII. His reputation for hockey acumen derived from his success coach-

ing U of T Varsity Grads to the Allan Cup (1927), and from the success of the original New York Ranger team, which he assembled in 1926. In 1927 he and associates raised $160 000 and bought Toronto St Pats, changing their name to TORONTO MAPLE LEAFS. Maple Leaf Gardens was built largely owing to his efforts (1931). He sold his controlling interest in the Gardens and the team in 1961 to his son Stafford and others. His autobiography, *Conn Smythe: If you can't beat 'em in the alley,* with Scott Young, appeared in 1981.
　JAMES MARSH

Snag, YT, UP, is located at the mouth of Snag Cr, 465 km NW of Whitehorse. The creek was so named in 1898 by members of the US Geological Survey, possibly because it was choked with dead trees. In 1942 the federal Dept of Transport established an emergency-landing strip and weather station, which were maintained until 1966. On 3 Feb 1947 the station recorded a temperature of -63°C, the lowest official temperature ever measured in Canada. This small Indian village is accessible by road from Snag Junction at kilometre 1895 of the ALASKA HIGHWAY.
　H. GUEST

Snail, common name for members of several groups of gastropod MOLLUSCS. Snails inhabit all moist habitats, but most forms are marine. Typically, snails possess a protective spiral shell secreted by the mantle, a muscular foot for locomotion, a definable head region, housing both sensory structures, and a rasping ribbon of minute, chitinous teeth (the radula) for feeding. Gills are present in most snails (orders Prosobranchia and Opisthobranchia), but in the lung-breathing forms (Pulmonata), the mantle cavity forms the respiratory exchange surface. The common terrestrial snail (genus *Helix*) is edible. When prepared with seasoned garlic butter, this pulmonate is more familiar as the escargot of French cuisine. Other edible snails include the ABALONE and the conch. Freshwater snails are especially abundant in the Great Lakes region; in the temperature extremes of the more northern latitudes, species' numbers are reduced. Gastropod feeding processes range from filter feeding and grazing to predation on organisms much larger than themselves (eg, sea slugs feed upon coelenterate anemones). The sexes are often separate, but snails such as the slipper limpet (genus *Crepidula*) may change from male to male-female to female in the course of a lifetime.
　PETER V. FANKBONER

Snake, long, slender REPTILE of suborder Serpentes, order Squamata (which also includes LIZARDS). Snakes are limbless; however, primitive forms have a pelvic girdle and spurs, which are vestiges of hind limbs (eg, Canadian rubber boa). As with other reptiles, the body is covered by large scales which help reduce water loss in dry environments and provide mechanical protection. This epidermis is shed, usually as a single piece, a few times a year. About 2267 species occur worldwide, mostly in the tropics. One species reaches N of the Arctic Circle (to 68° N) in Scandinavia; another reaches 50° S in S America. In Canada, 25 species, classified in 3 families, are native: Boidae (1), Viperidae (3) and Colubridae (21). Boids and viperids feed mainly on warm-blooded prey. Canadian colubrids are harmless, although larger species can give painful bites. Larger colubrids prey on small mammals; medium-sized species take amphibians and fish; smaller species eat insects, invertebrates and smaller amphibians. Most occur in southern Canada, but the common garter snake reaches about 60° N near Fort Smith, NWT. Although some tropical snakes attain great lengths (eg, reticulated python and anaconda, at 10 m the longest snakes known), Canadian species range from about 40 cm (northern redbelly snake) to over 180 cm (black rat snake and bullsnake). Snakes live in various ways and include

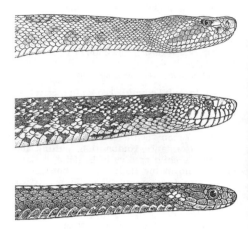

Western rattlesnake, top (*Crotalus viridis*), which may produce a brood only every 2 years or more; bullsnake, centre (*Pituophis melanoleucus*), which grows to lengths of more than 180 cm; and redbelly snake, bottom (*Storeria occipitomaculata*), a smaller snake of only *c*40 cm (*courtesy National Museums of Canada/National Museum of Natural Sciences/Charles Douglas*).

burrowing, tree-dwelling, freshwater and marine forms; most Canadian species are terrestrial ground dwellers but some are semiaquatic or aquatic, mainly in fresh water.

Although limbless, snakes can move in different ways. In the most common method, lateral undulation, the body is formed into a series of horizontal curves, the back of each curve pressing against irregularities in the ground; this technique is also used in swimming. Heavy-bodied snakes can also exhibit rectilinear (straight line) locomotion, propulsion being provided by the forward movement and anchoring of the relatively loose skin, followed by the body within. Concertina movement is used by some species in confined spaces; the snake anchors its posterior end by a few horizontal curves, extends and reanchors its anterior end, then brings the posterior part forward. The most specialized form of locomotion, sidewinding, is used on soft (and hot) substrates such as desert sands, and is not practised regularly by any Canadian species.

All snakes are carnivores; most species are adapted to swallowing large prey whole. The many joints between bones of the skull and the elastic ligament joining the 2 lower jaw bones allow the various parts of skull and lower jaws to move independently. While back-curved teeth hold prey, snakes "walk" the 4 quadrants of the jaws over their prey when swallowing. Elastic skin and a windpipe opening in the mouth are also adaptations to the often lengthy process of swallowing large food whole. Most species detect prey visually and chemically. Snakes' main chemosensory organ is Jacobson's organ, in the roof of the mouth; molecules are delivered to this organ by the forked tongue, which is continually flicked out of the mouth when the snake examines potential prey. Pit vipers (eg, rattlesnakes) feed mainly on warm-blooded animals and can accurately locate prey even in darkness via the thermosensory pit below the eye; many boas and pythons have thermosensory organs along the lips. Although snakes can detect earthborne vibrations, their hearing is poorly developed and is probably of no importance to predation.

Many species simply grab prey and swallow it live, usually head first; however, the risk of injury is relatively high with some prey. More specialized modes involve killing before eating. Constrictors coil around prey, preventing it from breathing but rarely crushing it. Although the boas and pythons are the most famous constrictors, constriction is practised by many other species, eg, bullsnake and black rat snake in Canada. The most effective and least risky means of handling prey is by envenomation. Venomous snakes have a venom gland above the upper jaw, connected by a duct to a tubular fang at the front of the mouth. Injected venom kills prey and begins its digestion while the snake waits for it to die. In vipers and pit vipers, the fang is so long that it is hinged back along the roof of the mouth when not in use. The 3 rattlesnakes native to Canada are pit vipers. Other highly venomous snakes have shorter, permanently erect fangs. The most primitive have grooved teeth at the rear of the jaw and "chew" venom into prey. The only Canadian rear-fanged snake is the secretive night snake, recently found to reach its northern limit in BC.

Like other reptiles, snakes are ectotherms (having body temperature governed mainly by external conditions) and can regulate body temperature to some extent by moving in and out of shade. While northern snakes are generally more cold tolerant than tropical species, the extreme seasonality of north temperate regions means that they are regularly faced with conditions too cold for continued activity or survival.

Snakes of Canada

Common Name	Scientific Name	Range
Family Viperidae:		
timber rattlesnake	Crotalus horridus	southwestern Ont; possibly extirpated in Canada
western rattlesnake	C. viridis	southern Sask, Alta, BC
massasauga rattlesnake	Sistrurus catenatus	southwestern Ont
Family Boidae:		
rubber boa	Charina bottae	southern BC
Family Colubridae:		
(black) rat snake	Elaphe obsoleta	southern Ont
fox snake	E. vulpina	southwestern Ont
bull (gopher) snake	Pituophis melanoleucus	southern BC, Alta, Sask
milk snake	Lampropeltis triangulum	southern Ont, Qué
eastern hognose snake	Heterodon platyrhinos	southern Ont
western hognose snake	H. nasicus	southern Prairies
common garter snake	Thamnophis sirtalis	coast to coast, except Nfld, N to Fort Smith, NWT
Butler's garter snake	T. butleri	southwestern Ont
eastern ribbon snake	T. sauritus	southern Ont, southwestern NS
plains garter snake	T. radix	Alta, Sask, Man
western terrestrial garter snake	T. elegans	central Sask to BC
northwestern garter snake	T. ordinoides	Vancouver I and southwestern mainland
northern water snake	Nerodia sipedon	southern Ont, Qué
queen snake	Regina septemvittata	southwestern Ont
redbelly snake	Storeria occipitomaculata	Sask to Maritimes
brown snake	S. dekayi	southern Ont, Qué
racer snake	Coluber constrictor	southern BC, Sask, Ont
ringneck snake	Diadophis punctatus	southern Ont to Maritimes
smooth green snake	Opheodrys vernalis	central southern Sask to Maritimes
sharptail snake	Contia tenuis	Vancouver I, Gulf Is, Chase, BC
night snake	Hypsiglena torquata	extreme southcentral BC

Snakes in Canada must therefore hibernate below the frost line. In areas with very cold winters, sites which allow snakes to go deep enough to avoid subfreezing temperatures may be scarce and available sites are used by many snakes. Communal hibernation is demonstrated particularly well in western Canada by the western rattlesnake and the common garter snake; hibernating groups of the latter may number in the thousands. Because overwintering sites are often concentrated in particular areas, communal hibernation is sometimes accompanied by migrations of several kilometres between hibernating site and summer habitat.

In Canada, most species of snakes mate in spring shortly after hibernation. Western rattlesnakes, however, mate in late summer or fall and the female retains sperm over winter; fertilization occurs the following spring. Fertilization in snakes is always internal and sperm are transferred into the female by a copulatory organ. Each male has 2 such organs (hemipenes) housed in the base of the tail. Snakes include egg-laying and live-bearing species. While egg-laying species are more numerous worldwide, the proportion of live-bearing species is higher in cooler environments (eg, 14 of the 25 species in Canada are live-bearers). Live bearing is, presumably, a useful adaptation where summers are short because the female can better regulate the temperature at which the young develop than if eggs were simply laid in the ground. Females may give birth late in summer and be unable to feed enough before hibernation to reproduce again the following summer. Consequently, females of live-bearing species at high altitudes or latitudes may produce a brood only every 2 or more years (eg, the western rattlesnake). In Canada, as elsewhere, litters or clutches usually include 3-16 young, although some species occasionally produce broods of 50 or more.   PATRICK T. GREGORY

Snipe, name given to 16 species of small to medium-sized SHOREBIRDS (254-406 mm) of the SANDPIPER family. Like WOODCOCKS, snipes have long bills with flexible tips and eyes set well back on the skull, allowing almost all-round vision. They are renowned for courtship and territorial displays known as winnowing — birds circle over their territory and dive with a loud "bleating" noise caused by air rushing past the extended outer tail feathers. Hence, they are sometimes called "goat of the bogs." The common or Wilson's snipe (*Gallinago gallinago*) nests from Alaska to California, E across Canada and the northern US to Newfoundland, and winters S to Venezuela and Colombia.   A.J. BAKER

Snooker, *see* BILLIARDS.

Snow, *see* ICE.

Snow, Clarence Eugene, "Hank," singer, songwriter, guitarist (b at Liverpool, NS 9 May 1914), one of the fathers of Canadian COUNTRY AND WESTERN MUSIC. His singing style, with its clear enunciation, influenced scores of artists in Canada and the US. He ran away to sea to escape his home and was soon entertaining crew members with his singing. By 1929 he was singing professionally and by 1935 had a radio show in Halifax. In 1936 he signed with RCA Victor and recorded his first hits. He tried to break into the US market in the late 1940s, but with slight success. In 1950 RCA released "I'm Movin' On," the song that established his career in the US, and Snow became one of the top stars of country music in the 1950s. He eventually moved to Nashville and became an American citizen, though he still appeared in Canada regularly. He was selected for the Country Music Hall of Fame in 1976 and the Juno (Awards) Hall of Fame in 1979.   RICHARD GREEN

Snow, John, or *Îtebijan°Mârî,* meaning "Walking Seal," Indian spokesman, philosopher,

statesman, spiritual leader (b at Morley, Alta 31 Jan 1933). Snow was the first Stoney Indian ordained in the United Church of Canada (1963). After serving parishes in Saskatchewan and Alberta, he returned to his home reserve at Morley (1968). In 1969 he became chief of the Wesley band. When the government tabled the 1969 Indian assimilationist policy, "The White Paper," Snow in 1970 presented the Alberta chiefs' response, "The Red Paper," asserting aboriginal and treaty rights (*see* NATIVE PEOPLE, GOVERNMENT POLICY). In 1975 Snow was named chairman of the Indian Ecumenical Conference, a continent-wide gathering of Indian traditional elders, youth and church leaders concerned about their spiritual heritage. His 1977 book, *These Mountains Are Our Sacred Places,* presents his philosophy on Indian culture and spirituality.   IAN A.L. GETTY

Snow, Michael James Aleck, painter, sculptor, photographer, filmmaker, musician (b at Toronto 10 Dec 1929). After study at the Ontario Coll of Art (1948-52) and a visit to Europe (1953-54), he worked for a small Toronto film company until 1956, during which time he produced his first independent film. In 1956 Snow held his first solo exhibition at Avrom Isaacs's Greenwich Gallery in Toronto. Following extended stays in New York (1962-64), he settled there in 1964, returning to Toronto in 1972. Between 1961 and 1967 his work in all media was based on the silhouette of a young woman. This important series of works, titled the *Walking Woman Works,* culminated in an 11-part sculpture for the Ontario Pavillion at EXPO 67. In 1970 Snow represented Canada at the Venice Biennale and was also given a retrospective exhibition of his work at the Art Gallery of Ontario. In 1979 a comprehensive survey of his work was shown in Lucerne, Bonn and Munich. The same year, he received a sculptural commission, *Flight Stop,* for Toronto's EATON CENTRE.

Venus Simultaneous (1962), oil on canvas and wood, by Michael Snow (*courtesy Art Gallery of Ontario/Purchase, 1964/Photo by James Chambers*).

Film has occupied a major place in his work from the mid-1960s with works such as *Wavelength* (1967), *La Région centrale* (1971), *Rameau's Nephew by Diderot (Thanx to Dennis Young) by Wilma Schoen* (1974) and *Presents* (1981). Snow has received critical acclaim in the US and Europe as an experimental filmmaker. His work has been continuously concerned with defining and redefining the relationships between media themselves, the acts and interpretations of perception and the complex of sound, language and meaning. He is also an accomplished pianist and trumpet player. He played professionally, was a member of the Artists' Jazz Band in Toronto and founder of the Canadian Creative Music Collective.   DAVID BURNETT
Reading: R. Cornwell, *Snow Seen* (1980); L. Dompierre, *Walking Woman Works, 1961-1967* (1983).

Snowbirds, successors to the Canadian Armed Forces' aerobatics teams of the 1950s and 1960s, the Golden Hawks and the Centennaires, were formed in 1971 by Col O.B. Philp, base commander at CFB Moose Jaw. Later known as 431 Air Demonstration Squadron, Snowbirds, they

are the only 9-plane aerobatic flight demonstration team outside Europe. The team performs annually to over 5 million people at 65 airshows in the US and Canada. The 21 man team of pilots and technical crew changes half of its members each year, so that the entire team revolves every 2 years. Flying the Canadian-designed and built Canadair CL-41 Tutor jet painted red, white and blue, they have become the pride of the CAF.
ROBERT M. MUMMERY

Reading: Robert M. Mummery, Snowbirds (1983).

Snowmobile, automotive vehicle for travel on snow. As with most technical innovations, the development of the snowmobile is obscure. Joseph-Armand BOMBARDIER, a mechanic from Valcourt, Qué, developed the first of many over-snow vehicles — a propeller-driven sled — in 1922. A moderately successful motor toboggan was developed in Wisconsin in 1927, but it was Bombardier who incorporated the motive sprocket wheel and double, endless track that made the vehicle practical. In 1937 he sold 50 of his B-7 model as buses and medical transport, and he designed vehicles used in WWII; by 1948 about 1000 B-12s had been produced. Bombardier patented many other improvements to suspension, transmission and braking systems to make the snowmobile more reliable, and in the mid-1950s the introduction of the air-cooled, 2-stroke engine made possible the small sport models common today. From sales of 225 recreational snowmobiles in 1959, about 250 000 were being absorbed per year in N America by the 1970s. Today, there are about one million households in Canada with at least one snowmobile, ranging from 1.7% of households in BC to 7.5% in Ontario, 9.2% in Saskatchewan, 9.7% in Québec and 10.5% in NB. In 1970 there were 129 manufacturers in N America, 26 in Canada — of which 20 were in Québec. Bombardier never yielded its lead, and after the number of companies shrank by the 1980s to a half dozen, it remained the world's largest.

Most innovations in transportation have been adapted to recreation, eg, the bicycle, boat and car, and widespread use of the snowmobile was a logical development in Canada. Over snow-covered ground it provides transportation previously impossible except on skis, snowshoes or dogsled. It has provided a means for Canadians to enjoy winter in an unprecedented way and enabled year-round use of recreational facilities such as cottages. Unlike other recreation equipment, ownership of snowmobiles is more heavily rural than urban, since the vehicle is very useful in farm work. A small number of vehicles are used for racing, but the main attraction seems to be enjoyment of the outdoors and socializing; there are an estimated 10 000 clubs in N America.

The explosion of snowmobiling brought serious concerns, particularly in the early years, about noise disturbance, ecological damage and safety (100 deaths in 1970). The snowmobile was misused for vandalism, habitat destruction and chasing game. By 1972 all provinces except

J.-A. Bombardier's use of a motive sprocket wheel and double, endless track created the snowmobile industry in 1937. By the 1980s, Bombardier Inc was the world's largest producer *(courtesy Bombardier Inc)*.

PEI had legislation governing and restricting the use of snowmobiles. The provision of extensive trails, notably in Québec, overcame many of the objections. Although other forms of winter recreation, such as CROSS-COUNTRY SKIING, gained in popularity in the late 1970s and early 1980s, snowmobiling remains popular in N America. In the North the snowmobile has changed the hunting, herding and trapping patterns of the Inuit, although dogsleds continue to be used in extreme conditions.
CHRIS DEBRESSON

Snowshoeing is a form of physical activity that utilizes 2 wooden-frame "shoes," each strung together with interlaced webbing, to walk or run over snow. A common form of transport, and probably of sport, among native peoples prior to European settlement in N America, the "encumbrance" was first embraced by fur trappers. Twelve English-speaking men from Montréal met regularly around 1840 to tramp or hike on snowshoes on Saturday afternoons. In 1843, these men, some of whom were Montréal's most prominent businessmen, formed the Montreal Snow Shoe Club (MSSC) — the first of its kind in the world. Nicholas "Evergreen" Hughes was a key figure in organizing the club and in the growth of snowshoeing itself.

Long-distance "tramps" were the most common form of the activity for almost 20 years. Men from the MSSC and a handful of other clubs would rendezvous near McGill College to tramp 19 km or more, following the club's senior officer in single file. At the rear of the line was the "whipper-in," an accomplished snowshoer whose job was to keep the pack together. Halfway through, or after these tramps, the snowshoers rested their feet at a local chophouse or tavern in the city or atop Mount Royal. Meals were eaten, songs such as "Rise, Ye Sons of Canada" and "Partant pour la Syrie" were sung, poems were recited and cotillions were danced. Race meetings were held as early as 1843 and featured dashes, 2-mi (3.2 km) events and hurdles over 4-ft (1.2 m)-high barriers. There is good evidence that the hurdle race in snowshoeing preceded its summer counterpart by almost a decade. (Similarly, the word "jogged" was used to describe the slow, chugging motion of trampers during the early 1870s.) Prior to WWII, track athletes used the snowshoe as a winter training device.

By the late 1860s, the number of snowshoe clubs and race meetings in Montréal had proliferated. The increased interest in competition was also reflected in prestigious trophies such as the Tecumseh Cup; in new events such as the mountain steeplechase; in the appearance of outstanding competitors, especially the fleet-footed Keraronwe and W.L. Maltby; in improved times in all events (1.6 km in 6 min became common); in the introduction of the 1.5-pound (0.68 kg) racing shoe that replaced the old regulation "four-pounder"; in the birth of competitive clubs in Ottawa, Toronto and Québec City; in the snowshoe races featured by skating rinks as their premier event at annual races; and in the development of a snowshoe-racing vocabulary, for example, the "brush," connoting a successful acceleration of one racer past another. By the early 1880s, snowshoeing was clearly the most popular winter amusement. Clubs were in evidence from Winnipeg to Terra Nova, Nfld. The MSSC was instrumental in forming the multi-sport Montreal Amateur Athletic Assn in 1881 and, along with other Montréal snowshoe clubs, organized, promoted and staged the world-famous, week-long winter Mardi Gras or carnival from 1883 to 1889. Snowshoers also gave concerts, engaged in campaigns to raise charity funds and organized pedestrian clubs in the summer. In facing the rigours of long tramps, frostbite, bleeding toes and the ever-present side stitch, snowshoers dis-

Man Strapping on Snow Shoes (1884), watercolour and gouache over pencil by R.W. Rutherford *(courtesy Public Archives of Canada/C-98974).*

played a particularly Canadian example of the 19th-century sporting phenomenon called "muscular Christianity."

A skating resurgence in the 1890s and fanatical interest in a new winter sport, ICE HOCKEY, halted and reversed the growth and development of snowshoeing. Winnipeg became the centre of the sport during the early 20th century, and the Canadian Snowshoe Union, the current governing body for the sport's 70 modern clubs, was formed in 1907.
DON MORROW

Snowshoes for winter travel were almost universal among native people in Canada outside the Pacific and Arctic coasts. The Athapaskans of the West and Algonquians of the northeast made the most sophisticated snowshoes. Frames were generally made of durable, flexible ash wood, and lacing from deer, caribou and moose hide. The toe and tail sections of the shoe were laced with a light BABICHE and the central body with a heavy babiche for better weight suspension. The Indian-style MOCCASIN is the traditional snowshoe footwear. Much Indian FOLKLORE centered on the snowshoe. The OJIBWA, for example, celebrated the first snowfall of the winter with a snowshoe dance. During the early historic period the snowshoe was as important as the canoe, wagon or railway in opening up the country. *See* SNOWSHOEING. RENÉ R. GADACZ

Soapstone, a metamorphic rock composed essentially of talc with varying amounts of mineral impurities, including mica, chlorite, pyroxene, amphibole, serpentine, quartz, calcite and iron oxides. The rock may be massive or schistose (ie, strongly foliated and capable of being split into thinner sheets). In commercial usage the term refers to the primary product, block soapstone, and talc refers to the processed (ground) product. Colour varies from white to greenish grey and dark green. It is soft (1-2 on the Mohs scale), with a specific gravity of 2.2-2.8, but these properties vary with type and amount of impurities. Soapstone has a greasy feel (hence the name), can be ground to a powder or carved, has a high fusion point, low electrical and thermal conductivity, superior heat retention and high lubricating power. It is chemically inert.

Soapstone's use dates back to antiquity: early Egyptians carved it into scarabs and seals; in China and India it was used for ornaments, implements and domestic utensils. It was similarly used at various times over the past 7500 years by Indians, Inuit and Norse in Canada (*see* INUIT ART). In recent years, soapstone has been used to produce purely decorative, rather than functional, objects. The term soapstone carving is often used for sculptures carved from other soft, compact carving mediums, including serpentine and the talclike mineral pyrophyllite. Block soapstone is used as refractory material, for metalworkers' crayons, sculpture and the recently revived griddle plates. It was used infrequently as a building stone. The ground material talc is used mainly as a filler in paper, plastic, rubber and paint industries and for cosmetics and pharmaceuticals.

Soapstone occurs in Québec, Ontario, BC, Alberta, Saskatchewan and NS. Canada's first production was in 1871 from a deposit in the Eastern Townships, Qué. The 1982 Canadian production of soapstone, talc and pyrophyllite of 47 592 t came from underground and open-pit mines in Québec (Broughton and South Bolton) and Ontario (Madoc and Timmins). Canada is a minor producer, far behind the world leaders, Japan and the US. Block soapstone for the northern carving industry is quarried from deposits at Markham Bay, Baffin, Broughton (near Frobisher) and scattered localities in the North. Annual production of 500-1000 t is supplemented by sculpture-grade soapstone from Québec producers who also supply hobby shops and sculptors in southern regions.   ANN P. SABINA

Soaring, or gliding, is the sport of flying a motorless aircraft, or glider, by utilizing currents of rising air. The term "gliding," although still in common use, does not correctly describe the sport, as it refers to being towed to a height and then gradually losing altitude. In soaring, the craft also gains altitude by using rising air currents. Gliders are launched by air-tow, winch or car-tow. Gliders were first successfully flown in the late 19th century. The Wright brothers built gliders, installed the first practical aero engine and thus invented the airplane. Soaring was developed as a sport by the Germans after WWI; prohibited by the Treaty of Versailles from making airplanes, they built and flew gliders. The first successful international contest was held in England in 1922. International proficiency badges are awarded for duration, distance and height of flights. The first Canadians to qualify for these awards were Evelyn Fletcher and Arthur Larsen of Saskatchewan in 1939.

The focus of early gliding in Canada was Alberta, where Norman Bruce of Medicine Hat organized gliding clubs in the 1920s. In 1935, he formed the Canadian Gliding Boosters, a group that toured the Prairies, giving exhibitions of glider flights. Clubs were formed in other parts of Canada during the 1930s, and in 1945 the Soaring Assn of Canada was established. National championships have been held since 1949 in distance and altitude events. In 1970 Wolf Mix of Toronto placed fourth in the world championships, and in 1978 J. Carpenter, also of Toronto, placed sixth.   BARBARA SCHRODT

Sobey, William Macdonald, executive (b at New Glasgow, NS 9 June 1927). As chairman of the board of Sobeys Stores Ltd, he continues the family control of the Nova Scotia-based chain of food stores founded in 1907 by his grandfather, John William Sobey. The retail and wholesale company owns numerous supermarkets and has a market that extends beyond the Atlantic provinces into the Gaspé and southern Ontario. Sobey was mayor of Stellarton, NS, for 5 years. His directorships include the Bank of Montreal, Eastern Provincial Airways, and Empire Co Ltd, the holding company controlled by his family.   MARY HALLORAN

Soccer (Association Football) is a sport played by 2 teams of 11 players each, using a round ball, usually on a grass field called the "pitch." Only the 2 goalkeepers may intentionally handle the ball, which is moved from player to player by kicking, and a goal may be scored either by kicking or heading the ball into the opponent's goal. Association Football, the traditional name of the game, has now been shortened to "football," while the term "soccer" is derived from the second syllable of the word "association." In Canada and the US the game is usually referred to as soccer to distinguish it from other forms of FOOTBALL.

Soccer in Canada was played under a variety of rules from the early years of the 19th century. The first game played as we would play it today

seems to have taken place in Toronto in Oct 1876 between 2 local clubs. From 1876 on, the game grew and spread across the country. The Dominion Football Assn was organized in Montréal in 1878 and operated a loosely arranged cup competition largely involving college teams from southern Ontario. The Western Football Assn of Ontario was formed in Jan 1880 in Berlin (Kitchener) and had 19 clubs in membership by April of that year. Its formation led to the first international soccer match in N America, with Canada defeating the US 1-0 in Nov 1885 in Newark, NJ; the following year, Canada lost 3-2. On the Canadian side in both games was David Forsyth, a teacher at Berlin High School, who was instrumental in founding the WFA, playing the first internationals and organizing a tour to Britain in 1888. In Britain the Canadian touring team won 9 games, tied 5 and lost 9 against some of the finest opposition of the day. A similar tour took place in 1891; the touring party this time was made up of both Canadian and American players, with disastrous results.

Represented by the Galt Football Club, Canada entered Olympic competition for the first time in 1904 and came away with the gold medal at the Olympic Games in St Louis, Mo. Faced with 2 American teams in a competition abbreviated because of travel problems, Canada won its first game 7-0 and the second 4-0. By 1912, when the Dominion of Canada Football Assn (forerunner of today's national governing body, the Canadian Soccer Assn) was formed, there were leagues and associations across the country. In 1914 Canada gained full membership in the Fédération internationale de football association (FIFA), the governing body of world soccer. A national championship came into being in 1913 when the Connaught Cup (presented by the duke of CONNAUGHT) was offered for competition. The first winners were the Norwood Wanderers of Winnipeg. In 1926 the Connaught Cup was succeeded by a new trophy, donated by the Football Assn of England and still played for today. The most successful national champions have been the New Westminster Royals, who have appeared in 10 finals, winning 8 times. A Canadian national team toured Australia in 1924 and New Zealand in 1927, while in the 1920s and 1930s numerous teams from Britain toured Canada. One member of the Canadian team in New Zealand was Dave TURNER; another notable player of this era, Joe Kennaway, played for Canada and Scotland, and in his day was one of the finest goalkeepers in the world.

The influx of immigrants from around the world following WWII changed the face of Canadian soccer. In the prewar years the influence had been largely British, but it rapidly became international, particularly in the 1950s and 1960s. As the immigrants were assimilated into Canadian life, the accent began to shift to the development of Canadian players. As a result, Canada's status as a soccer power is steadily improving, and Canada has regularly fielded teams in World Cup (world professional championship), Olympic, Pan-American and youth competition. A number of players have distinguished themselves, notably Sam and Bobby Lenarduzzi, Buzz Parsons, Jimmy Douglas, Robert Iarusci and Bruce Wilson. Canada first entered the World Cup in 1957, but did not pass beyond the first preliminary round until 1978, when the team narrowly missed qualifying for the final rounds. Similarly, in 1982 only one goal prevented the team from playing in the world finals for the first time. In the 1976 Montréal Olympics, Canada played in the final rounds, losing narrowly to the Soviet Union and North Korea. In the final, East Germany defeated Poland 3-1 before a Canadian record crowd of 71 619 in Montréal's Olympic Stadium. Canada's national youth team made the world finals in 1979 in Japan, beating Portugal

3-1 before being narrowly defeated 1-0 by South Korea and outclassed 3-0 by Paraguay.

Most of the players who represent Canada in World Cup competition today are full-time professionals playing for clubs in the North America Soccer League. Prior to the NASL's formation in 1968, there were few Canadians playing professionally, and even those leagues classed as professional, such as the National Soccer League, employed few full-time professionals. The first attempt to form a professional league in Canada came in 1913 and was short-lived. Other attempts have been made, with the NSL (formed in 1926) being the longest running. The advent of the NASL gave Canadians the chance to play alongside some of the world's top players. In 1976 Toronto Metros-Croatia won the NASL championship, a feat duplicated by the Vancouver Whitecaps in 1979. In contrast to Canadian and American football, soccer has spread to virtually every nation of the world, and FIFA boasts a larger membership than the UN. Despite its failures as a professional sport in Canada — Montreal Manic was disbanded in 1983, Vancouver in 1984 and Toronto Blizzard and the entire NASL in 1985 — soccer continues to grow in popularity and ranks second to hockey as a team sport.   COLIN JOSE

Reading: R. Henshaw, *The Encyclopedia of World Soccer* (1979); Colin Jose and B. Rannie, *The Story of Soccer in Canada* (1982); Desmond Morris, *The Soccer Tribe* (1981).

Social and Welfare Services There is a general division, in Canada, between SOCIAL SECURITY programs and social and welfare services. Social security programs, which are the responsibility of all levels of government, provide direct economic assistance in one form or another to individuals or families. Included in this category are programs such as FAMILY ALLOWANCES, OLD AGE PENSIONS and provincial and municipal social-assistance programs. Social and welfare service programs, on the other hand, have been developed in an attempt to respond to personal, social and emotional needs. Included are the services for the residential care of people in government-run or private residences, care of people in their own homes, and a wide range of community-based services such as DAY CARE, home-delivered meals and counselling. These services are now often referred to as the "personal" social services and have been developed and expanded primarily during the 20th century, particularly during the last 2 decades.

In the past, the family was expected to care for its members with assistance from the church, private charity and work-place associations when the family's own resources were insufficient. With INDUSTRIALIZATION, there was a shift in emphasis from farm labour to industrial labour. As MANUFACTURING expanded the cities attracted more wage earners, which resulted in congested living conditions and also created new social needs. The state responded initially by financing the expansion of private and church charities but then began to administer social and welfare services itself.

There are still many residential services provided for people in need, but in addition a great variety of noninstitutional social and welfare services have been developed. The growth of state-run services has not eliminated the role of the more informal sources of help, such as the family and the church, but it has shifted the primary responsibility for financing, administration and direct provision of services to the 3 levels of government. In some provinces various private social-service organizations, funded in part by government and in part by United Way campaigns, also exist, as do a number of alternative services that function outside both government and established private organizations.

Purpose and Range of Services Social and welfare services are organized primarily around the populations they serve, eg, children and families, youth, the elderly, the physically handicapped and the developmentally handicapped. However, no matter what population they serve, these services exist for a number of different purposes. Some provide daily, 24-hour care; others support the family (particularly mothers, who are in most cases responsible for meeting the social and emotional needs of the family); others provide protection for those in jeopardy, eg, neglected or abused children. For children who may require temporary or permanent removal from their own family, a range of foster homes, group homes and residential services are provided. Included in the general child-welfare system are services for ADOPTION of children. For children with psychological problems, counselling services are available and MENTAL HEALTH centres for residental care have been established. A limited number of day-care services have been established in each jurisdiction, primarily for preschool children. There are very few spaces for children of school age and for children with special needs; indeed the availability of day-care spaces of any kind falls short of the actual need.

There are a number of smaller, and in some cases, more recent programs designed to support the family, including homemaker services, which provide help in the home; parent-education programs; and respite services that allow mothers a break from the daily demands of caring for young children. Family-planning programs across the country provide information and counselling to families. There are also a small number of alternate services for women, established at the initiation of local groups of women in the absence of state activity. The services include local women's centres which provide information, advice, counselling and referral; rape crisis centres; and a number of interval or transitional houses for battered women and their children. These services, while they respond to pressing needs, suffer from inadequate and insecure funding.

To meet the needs of the elderly, residential homes, including large centres for long-term care and an expanding network of smaller community-based nursing homes, have been established. In some areas community-based services for the elderly include drop-in centres, home-delivered meal services and homemaker services. A network of services including large-scale institutions and smaller, community-based residential services such as foster homes and group homes, has been developed for the physically and mentally handicapped (see DISABILITIES). Some jurisdictions have established sheltered workshops to provide training to facilitate the integration of the handicapped person into the community. Local associations for the mentally retarded, which advocate on behalf of the developmentally handicapped and also provide some services in their local communities, have been founded in many parts of Canada.

Services for the mentally ill have been set up outside the general health system (see PSYCHIATRY). In some areas there are community-based rehabilitation programs for the mentally ill who have been institutionalized that help to integrate them back into the community; in others, emergency housing facilities and drop-in services are provided to assist people recently released from hospital.

Jurisdiction Under the Canadian CONSTITUTION, the responsibility for social and welfare services rests with the provincial and territorial governments. The services are operated primarily under provincial and territorial legislation. Each province and territory has established its own variety of services. Some provinces delegate partial responsibility for the administration of social and welfare services to the local or municipal level of government and in some instances

the municipal governments also contribute to the financing of some of these services.

The federal government, through its cost-sharing agreements with the provinces and territories, is also involved in social and welfare services. For example, through the federal Canada Assistance Plan, the cost for many services is split on a 50-50 basis with the provinces.

A small percentage of social and welfare services are under the jurisdiction of private or church organizations. In many cases these organizations receive some financing from the government bodies and the remainder is solicited through private donations, including the annual campaigns of United Way appeals. In some jurisdictions the private agencies have essentially been taken over by the government; in others these agencies (essentially semipublic organizations) have been maintained, although they operate primarily on government funding and frequently under mandates legislated by the provincial government.

Regional Variation During the past 20 years most jurisdictions in Canada have reviewed their pattern of social services. For example, Alberta initiated a preventive social service program in 1966; Québec launched an enquiry into health and social welfare services in 1966; Manitoba began some integration of health and welfare services in 1968; New Brunswick established a task force on social development in 1970; BC began a review of social services in 1972; and Ontario established a task force on social services in 1979. In most provinces these developments have resulted in an increase in the control of the provincial government over social and welfare services. The now terminated experience with community resource boards in BC represented a move towards decentralization of decision making. Québec, Manitoba and Alberta have chosen to integrate health and welfare services while Ontario has maintained a separation of health and welfare services in different ministries. Generally the reorganization of services has bypassed the local level of government.

Over this period some provinces, eg, Québec and BC, have assumed wide control over private agencies, while others, eg, Ontario, have continued to support some private agencies. Most of the jurisdictions have established some form of decentralization of responsibility for the actual administration of services, while maintaining central government control of policy and financing. Québec, for example, has established regional bodies, community-service centres, and local neighbourhood organizations called "local community service centres." Alberta and Québec have both established regional offices and in some cases local area offices for their provincial social and welfare services. Newfoundland's regionalized services reflect the geography of the country and the number of isolated communities. Newfoundland's Resettlement Program of the early 1960s, however, disrupted family and community life by forcing the closure of small industries in an attempt to centralize economic activity. This resulted in a shift of population to the larger centres and a concentration of social and welfare services.

The provision of social and welfare services for native people is complicated by a debate over jurisdiction (see NATIVE PEOPLE, HEALTH). The federal government has overall responsibility for native people and their lands under the Constitution Act, 1867, in general, and under the Indian Act in particular. Certain services, such as child welfare, have been delegated to the provincial governments but not all provinces have willingly assumed this responsibility. In other areas of social and welfare services it is not clear who is responsible. Indian organizations, eg, band councils, have sometimes taken on responsibility for the actual administration of child-

welfare services. In addition, native people are demanding more direct control over the development and administration of their social and welfare services. In 1982, under an agreement signed by the federal government, the Manitoba government and the Four Nations Confederacy, child-welfare services were to be administered by native organizations, but in other regions there has been little such direct participation in administration.

Recent Developments One of the most important developments affecting social and welfare services is the general cutback in state expenditure on these services by both the federal and provincial governments. For welfare recipients, this has exacerbated the problem of the erosion of real purchasing power which they have suffered since about 1975 and which worsened in the economic recession of the early 1980s.

In addition to curtailing any needed expansion and actually cutting back on the amount of money spent on social services, a number of additional strategies have been developed. The first is de-institutionalization, which involves both the removal of people from institutions and the prevention of institutionalization in the first place. This is resulting in the closing of some large institutions across the country, eg, institutions for the handicapped, the mentally ill, the elderly, and children. Related to this is the second strategy of community care, ie, an emphasis on caring for people in their own community and in many cases in their own family. Part of this strategy is focused on receiving people back into the community from institutional settings; part is focused on trying to provide some services in the community so that people will not have to be institutionalized. It appears that considerable emphasis in this strategy is on having women take care of children, handicapped persons and old people in their own homes. At present serious problems exist as a result of a lack of adequate community facilities and services in response to the de-institutionalization of a great many people across the country. A third strategy of transferring the responsibility for the administration of social services to the private sector has been more pronounced in some parts of the country than others. It is particularly conspicuous in the development of profit-making nursing homes for the elderly. JIM ALBERT

Reading: A. Armitage, *Social Welfare in Canada* (1975).

Social Class refers to persistent social inequalities. Two distinct types of social inequality have been identified by researchers working with 2 different sociological theories. One theory is derived from the work of Karl Marx, the other from writings by Max Weber, which are somewhat critical of Marx's work. The Weberian approach became popular in Canadian and American sociology in the 1940s to 1960s but currently the Marxian approach is in ascendancy.

In the Marxian approach, social classes, which are defined by ownership of the means of production and labour power (see also ECONOMICS, RADICAL) exist in all capitalist societies. Means of production include the machines, buildings, land and materials used in the production of goods and services. Labour power (the physical and mental capacity of people to work) is bought and sold for wages (or salary) by the owners of the means of production or by their agents. Marxists identify 3 main classes: the *petite bourgeoisie*, who own businesses (the means of production), work for themselves, and do not employ others; the *proletariat* or working class, who do not own the means of production and who sell their labour power for wages; and the *bourgeoisie* or capitalist class, owners of the means of production, who purchase labour power and acquire a living and accumulate wealth from surplus value provided through workers' labour. (The theory of surplus value is based on the premise that part of the value of goods or services that people produce is determined by the labour power that goes into them.) Surplus value is the total value of commodities when production is complete minus the value of labour power and the value of the means of production. The rate of surplus value is surplus value divided by total wages. This rate is used by Marxist researchers as an indicator of the rate of class exploitation, ie, the rate at which wealth is being extracted from the labour power of the working class by the bourgeoisie.

The Marxian social class distinctions do not refer to types of occupation or levels of income. For example, a plumber could be a member of the working class (because he sells labour power and does not own a business), or he could be a small capitalist who owns a company and purchases the labour of several plumbers, or a member of the petite bourgeoisie. Also, members of different classes may have similar, or overlapping, incomes. An owner of a small engineering firm with a few employees may in one year earn less than a worker, eg, a successful engineer working for a large firm. However, capitalists generally have more power than workers to determine the distribution of wealth, because capitalists own and control the means of production and because the working class is not fully organized in opposition (eg, in unions or political organizations). Marxists believe that a conflict of interests (eg, wage disputes, and opposition by capitalists to the formation of unions) between capitalists and the working class is an inherent feature of capitalism. Capitalists try to keep wages low and productivity high to maximize their proportion in the distribution of wealth; workers attempts to increase their share of wealth through higher wages and to improve their working conditions.

The non-Marxists claim that social classes can be defined through inequalities in income, educational attainment, power and occupational prestige, and they often study these forms of social inequality to the neglect of social class in the Marxian sense. They have identified different kinds of social classes depending, for example, on which of the other dimensions of social inequality has been selected for study. People are categorized and given ranks according to their income, occupational prestige, power or education, the difficulty being that the same people may fall into different ranks according to different dimensions of social class. For example, the very rich, the middle class and the poor can be easily distinguished from one another by using standards of income and wealth, but those in the middle-income category, eg, white-collar and blue-collar workers, will be accorded quite different degrees of prestige for their different jobs. By the same token, although white-collar jobs usually carry more prestige and income, this is not always the case. The same is true of differences in educational levels. Those with secondary-school diplomas more often have white-collar jobs and higher incomes than those with less education, but some skilled blue-collar workers, such as electricians, earn comparatively high wages without high-school training. Finally the respective amounts of power attached to different jobs, incomes and educational credentials are difficult to discern.

The non-Marxists emphasize the distribution patterns of scarce rewards, ie, the numbers and social backgrounds of the people who acquire university educations or high prestige jobs, while the Marxists emphasize the social activities and interactions of the classes, eg, who purchases labour power from whom and what is the rate of exploitation of one class by another. The non-Marxists are concerned with explaining the patterns of social inequality, while

the Marxists study the way class relations explain social change. Because of the attention to change, Marxist research generally has a historical dimension.

Marxist-oriented researchers in Canada have studied the development and consequences of Canada's branch-plant ECONOMY, the process of "de-industrialization" (see INDUSTRIAL STRATEGY), the heavy investment of both foreign multinationals and Canadian-owned corporations in the Third World (see CANADA-THIRD WORLD RELATIONS) and the exploitation, in Canada, of staple raw materials for export, which incurred a dependence on export markets beyond the control of local capitalists and workers. Other research of this kind indicates that there has been a long-term trend in industrialized countries of a rise in the rate of surplus value, and that owners in various industries have stood together to try to enforce low wages. Studies have also shown that Canada's *petite bourgeoisie* has declined to a small proportion of the labour force (eg, from 12% in 1951 to about 7% in 1981), that the working class has remained fairly stable over recent years (approx 86% in 1951 and 81% in 1981), and that the capitalist class has grown (2% in 1951 and about 6% in 1981). There is also evidence that the capitalist class has evolved into a class of investment capitalists, with stock ownership but limited managerial control. At the same time, a large category of top-level managers has been formed.

Non-Marxist researchers have discovered that, by the occupational criterion, Canada has a large and growing middle class of white-collar workers (eg, 25% of workers in 1921, 52% in 1981); a smaller and rather stable blue-collar sector (eg, 31% in 1921, 40% in 1981); and fewer workers in the primary sector (fishing, logging and mining) and in agriculture (the number of workers in agriculture declined from 33% in 1921 to 6% in 1981). As far as education is concerned, the middle category of those with some secondary-school education is the largest (58% for males and 60% for females in 1981). The category of those with some university training had grown to 18% for males and 17% for females in 1981. Studies of income distribution reveal that the top 20% of individual income earners receive about 50% of all earned income while the bottom 20% receive only about 3% of all income (see INCOME DISTRIBUTION). Further studies have shown that the attainment of income, education and occupational prestige are related to the social class of parents and to region and ethnic origin. Also, it has been found that people with better occupations, income and education have better life expectancies, better health, use medical facilities more, belong to more clubs and organizations, vote more frequently, and have fewer children.

A synthesis of Marxist and non-Marxist ap-

proaches to social class may eventually emerge because researchers from each tradition are now beginning to study, too, the types of inequality emphasized by the other. This should result, fortunately, in different terms being used for the categories identified in each approach. "Social class" or "class" is increasingly being reserved for the types of distinction described by Marx, while the term "socioeconomic status" will likely apply to differences in income and occupational prestige.   JAMES E. CURTIS

Reading: C.J. Cuneo, "Class, Stratification and Mobility," in R. Hagedorn, ed, *Sociology* (1980); James E. Curtis and W.G. Scott, eds, *Social Stratification: Canada* (1979); D. Forcese, *The Canadian Class Structure* (1980); A.A. Hunter, *Class Tells: On Social Inequality in Canada* (1981).

Social Credit is an economic doctrine that for a time in Canada was influential as the touchstone of a significant political party. Its principles were formulated by an English engineer, Maj C.H. Douglas (1879-1952), who argued that economic hardships resulted from an inefficient capitalist economy which failed to provide people with sufficient purchasing power for them to enjoy the fruits of a well-developed productive capacity. He advocated the distribution of money, or "social credit," so that people might purchase the goods and services readily produced by capitalist enterprise. He believed the total wages paid individuals who produced goods (which he called "A") would always be less than total costs of production ("B"). This meant that, without social credit, there would be insufficient money in the community for the purchase of all goods and services produced. This was known as the "A plus B theorem."

Douglas's doctrine had little political impact elsewhere in the world and likely would have remained relatively unknown in Canada, except that in 1932 Alberta evangelist William ABERHART became converted to it. He used his radio program to encourage other Albertans to adopt social credit as the means of rescuing the province and Canada from the drastic effects of the GREAT DEPRESSION. In 1935 Aberhart led the new Social Credit Party to victory in Alberta, capturing 56 of 63 seats with 54% of the popular vote. Social Credit, first under Aberhart, and then, after his death in 1943, under Ernest C. MANNING, won 9 successive elections and governed the province until 1971. This remarkable success was purchased in part by the replacement of social credit fundamentalism with conservative financial and social policies which even bankers could applaud. Success was also purchased by judicious use of massive oil revenues which flowed to provincial coffers after 1947.

In 1952 a Social Credit government under

Prosperity certificate issued by the Alberta Social Credit government in 1936 (*courtesy Glenbow Archives*).

THE GOVERNMENT OF THE PROVINCE OF ALBERTA

PROSPERITY CERTIFICATE

DATE OF ISSUE
AUGUST 5, 1936   A   96158

THE PROVINCIAL TREASURER WILL PAY TO THE BEARER THE SUM OF ONE DOLLAR ON THE EXPIRATION OF TWO YEARS FROM DATE OF ISSUE HEREOF UPON PRESENTATION HEREOF PROVIDED THERE ARE THEN ATTACHED TO THE BACK HEREOF ONE HUNDRED AND FOUR ONE CENT CERTIFICATE STAMPS

ONE DOLLAR

William Aberhart
PREMIER

C. Cockroft
PROVINCIAL TREASURER

WESTERN PRINTING & LITHOGRAPHING CO LTD CALGARY

W.A.C. BENNETT was elected in British Columbia. Bennett paid no attention to social credit doctrine but combined a mixture of conservative financial policies with aggressive development schemes. He ruled BC in the name of Social Credit for 20 years, and his son, William R. BENNETT, became premier in 1975. During the 1950s and early 1960s the party was successful also in sending a few members to the Saskatchewan and Manitoba legislatures.

In 1935 the federal Social Credit Party won 17 seats in the House of Commons — 15 from Alberta, where it received 46.6% of the popular vote. The federal party's support gradually declined in Alberta until 1968, when it became insignificant. During the 1950s and early 1960s the party won a handful of federal seats in BC. In Québec, under the leadership of Réal CAOUETTE, the federal Social Credit Party (and later a breakaway group under Caouette called the Ralliement des CRÉDITISTES) won 26 federal seats in 1962. Under the leadership of Robert THOMPSON the party held the balance of power, along with the NDP, in Parliament during John Diefenbaker's minority government, 1962-63. It continued to have representation in Parliament until 1980.

Social Credit had disappeared as a viable political force by the early 1980s, voting to disband as a party in Alberta. The BC government continued to use the name, but had severed its links with "Socreds" in the rest of the country and remained a relatively mainstream conservative government.   T.J. MORLEY

Social Darwinism generally refers to the extension of Charles Darwin's theories of natural selection in EVOLUTION, as used in his *Origin of Species* (1859), into the realm of social relations. Darwin had not intended his theories to be extended by analogy into the examination of racial groups, societies or nations. But certain British and American social theorists, notably Herbert Spencer and William Graham Sumner, made the analogy. The result was a social theory that provided late Victorians with a "scientific" explanation and social justification of racial inequality, cultural exploitation and laissez-faire capitalist activity. Canada produced few such extreme social theorists during the Darwinian revolution. The critic William Dawson LESUEUR sought to explain the theories of both Darwin and Spencer to Canadians in the *Canadian Monthly and National Review* during the 1870s and 1880s, but he consistently rejected the metaphoric extension of Darwin's phrase into the study of society. The logic of Darwin's notion of competition within and between species led instead, he argued, to the necessity of mutual aid and co-operation. Other Canadian observers agreed, with the exception of Goldwin SMITH, whose social views were more akin to those of Spencer. The dependent nature of Canadian economic and political life pointed most Canadian commentators toward ideas similar to those of Peter Kropotkin in *Mutual Aid, a Factor of Evolution* (1902).   A. BRIAN McKILLOP

Social Democracy, historically, is a term that has been used by individuals on both the far and moderate left to describe their beliefs, but in recent years the latter have embraced the term almost exclusively (indeed radical left-wing critics often use the term disparagingly). For many adherents, the term "social democracy" is interchangeable with the term "democratic socialism."

By the beginning of the 20th century, workers in many industrial countries had acquired the vote and the right to organize into unions and parties. Many socialists were thus led to believe that the working class, the largest group in modern society, could increasingly direct the STATE towards abolishing POVERTY, inequality and

class exploitation, ie, capitalism could be transformed through legislation. The German socialist Eduard Bernstein (1850-1932) pioneered the idea that all-out class struggle was not inevitable and that a peaceful, nonrevolutionary road to socialism was both possible and desirable (*see also* MARXISM).

The Russian Revolution of 1917 and the founding of the Communist International (Comintern) in 1919 precipitated an irrevocable split in socialist ranks between the revolutionary and evolutionary wings — with the former emerging as communist parties and the latter as social democratic parties. After this date, social democracy could be defined not only by its opposition to capitalism but also to communism. Social democrats are resolute in their defence of individual rights, constitutional methods, and in their repudiation of the Marxist concept of the dictatorship of the proletariat. They also argue that political democracy (eg, equal right to vote) needs to be expanded to include social and economic democracy (ie, equal right to an education, medical care, pensions, employment and safe working conditions). Believing in the power of education and persuasion, and the potentially benevolent power of the state to redistribute wealth, social democrats have encouraged the emergence of an activist, interventionist state that provides extensive SOCIAL SECURITY assistance to the less privileged.

In Canada, one of the earliest exponents of reformism was the Social Democratic Party of Canada, founded in 1911 out of frustration with the more doctrinaire and revolutionary Socialist Party of Canada, established in 1904. Later, the LEAGUE FOR SOCIAL RECONSTRUCTION (1932-42), closely patterned after Britain's Fabian Society, provided the most visible intellectual expression in Canada of democratic socialism. Through the journal the *Canadian Forum* and the book *Social Planning for Canada*, individuals such as F.R. SCOTT, Frank UNDERHILL, Eugene FORSEY, Leonard MARSH and Harry Cassidy communicated their ideas on social democracy. The CO-OPERATIVE COMMONWEALTH FEDERATION (CCF) and its successor, the NEW DEMOCRATIC PARTY (NDP), have most consistently among political parties expressed a social democratic vision. Accordingly, the NDP belongs to the Socialist International, a confederation of social democratic parties. Several CCF-NDP manifestos provide detailed illustrations of the social democratic philosophy: the Regina Manifesto (1933), the Winnipeg Declaration (1956), the New Party Declaration (1961) and the New Regina Manifesto (1983). Leading political practitioners of social democracy have included J.S. WOODSWORTH, T.C. DOUGLAS, "M.J." COLDWELL, Stanley KNOWLES, David LEWIS, Ed BROADBENT and Allan BLAKENEY. The PARTI QUÉBÉCOIS, in addition to being nationalist and separatist, also lays claim to being a social democratic party and has sought and received observer status in the Socialist International.

Social democratic thought in Canada inspired legislation such as WORKERS' COMPENSATION, MINIMUM WAGE, OLD AGE PENSION, UNEMPLOYMENT INSURANCE, FAMILY ALLOWANCE, subsidized housing (Canada Mortgage and Housing Corporation) and medicare (*see* HEALTH POLICY). The WELFARE STATE has largely been the product of joint action by social democrats and reform-minded liberals. Certainly the birth of the CCF in 1932 and its rapid growth in the early 1940s induced the LIBERAL PARTY to shift to the left lest it be displaced like its counterpart in England. However, social democracy appears to have had its greatest impact in the provincial governments formed by the CCF-NDP in BC, Saskatchewan and Manitoba. Most notable was the Douglas regime in Saskatchewan, N America's first socialist government, which pioneered medicare. While the party has never formed the government federally, it has had considerable influence on the

policy of MINORITY GOVERNMENTS. Internationally, social democracy's greatest advances occurred in the postwar era of the late 1940s and 1950s when it seemed to offer a moderate alternative to the extremes of capitalism and communism.

However, as socialists came to power, the practical problems of governing led many to question important socialist assumptions about methods employed. Unlike the communists, social democrats do not believe that wholesale nationalization of the means of production is a panacea to the ills of capitalism. Instead, they propose selected expansion of PUBLIC OWNERSHIP (eg, co-operatives, CROWN CORPORATIONS and state enterprises) in a mixed economy. In the past, social democrats have favoured the creation of public enterprises such as the Canadian Broadcasting Corporation and Air Canada and state institutions such as the Bank of Canada. With the emergence of KEYNESIAN ECONOMICS, social democrats had begun to argue that government FISCAL POLICY and MONETARY POLICY (eg, TAXATION rates, government expenditure, regulation of the money supply) could regulate the market economy in a socially beneficial manner; for example, through a combination of government planning and legislation, public enterprises and use of the market mechanism, full employment, greater equality and economic growth could be achieved.

Social democrats have not only advocated the lessening of inequalities between SOCIAL CLASSES, but also between regions (see REGIONALISM). They have thus supported government actions to redistribute wealth from the richer to the poorer provinces, and encouraged Canadianization of the economy through greater public ownership (eg, PETRO-CANADA) and state regulation (eg, FOREIGN INVESTMENT REVIEW AGENCY) which would lessen Canada's dependency on other countries, particularly the US (see CANADA-US ECONOMIC RELATIONS).

In recent years, social democratic doctrine has come under increasing criticism from both the left and the right. The more radical and revolutionary left charges that social democratic reforms are too eclectic and produce only cosmetic changes, making capitalism appear more humane and workable and delaying needed structural change. These critics claim that social democrats have nationalized too few and mostly unprofitable industries and question whether social democracy can ever lead to socialism. They cite detailed statistical analyses of Canadian society that reveal that the welfare state has not altered class inequality to the degree expected and that poverty is more firmly entrenched than the optimistic social reformers suspected. The welfare state is also under attack by neo-conservatives. Critical of large increases in government expenditure and the size of the civil service, conservatives question both the desirability of increasing state power and the growing cost of that power. They note that economic growth, a premise of Keynesian economics and past social democratic thought, is now slowing down. STAGFLATION raises the spectre of reduced funds with which to finance social programs, and the universality of some programs (eg, pensions and medicare) has been challenged.

Several additional problems have arisen as well. Social democratic theory has long had a predisposition towards central government planning, and in a country such as Canada with strong concerns about provincial rights, particularly in Québec, such centralizing policies have hindered the spread of social democratic thought. Indeed, there is a significant gulf between the social democratic forces in English and French Canada, represented by the NDP and the PQ respectively.

In the mid 1980s many social democratic parties seem to be faltering electorally. In Canada, the NDP appears stalled federally as a third party; critics have suggested a need to reformulate its social democratic doctrine. Social democrats seem less certain today than in the 1950s about the most effective means to pursue their goals. To survive, any ideology must be an evolving doctrine that provides more effective answers to problems. As Canada moves into the postindustrial era, social democrats will need to deal with the growing concern about ecology, the danger of nuclear war, the changing composition of the workforce, technical innovation in the workplace, the decline in the economic growth rate, high levels of unemployment, the plight of the Third World, the growing power of the state and the quest for greater industrial democracy.   ALAN WHITEHORN

Social Doctrine of the Roman Catholic Church, defined particularly in 2 papal encyclicals: *Rerum Novarum,* by Leo XIII (1891), and *Quadragesimo Anno,* by Pius XI (1931). The church wished to show its preoccupation with the fate of the working classes, often victims of unbridled capitalism. Both documents preached a Christian humanism, decried the insufficiencies of capitalism and warned against the evils inherent in socialism and in the doctrine of class struggle. The church clarified its teachings concerning employers' responsibilities and workers' rights, as well as related duties of the state. Leo XIII wrote that workers had a right to fair wages, and that they could form Catholic unions whose existence should be protected by governments.

Through various organizations, study sessions and publications, the Catholic Church, in Canada as elsewhere, publicized and applied pontifical doctrine. In Québec, however, a conservative clergy rooted in rural society was ill-prepared to confront urban problems. Catholic trade unions were slow to be established and it was 1921 before the Canadian Catholic Confederation of Labour emerged (*see* CONFEDERATION OF NATIONAL TRADE UNIONS). The École sociale populaire, a Jesuit organization charged with interpreting the church's social doctrine and with preparing an elite to put it into practice, was founded in 1911, 20 years after *Rerum Novarum.* The group proved particularly influential in the 1930s with the "Programme de restauration sociale" that became the basis of the radical electoral platforms of the ACTION LIBÉRALE NATIONALE and the UNION NATIONALE 1934-36. After WWII the social doctrine underwent considerable modernization, thanks in part to the work of the Sacerdotal Commission on Social Studies which in 1950 published a pastoral letter on social conditions. During the 1950s, however, with the increasing secularization of QUÉBEC SOCIETY, the church's social role declined markedly. *See* CATHOLICISM; SOCIAL GOSPEL.   RICHARD JONES

Social Gospel, an attempt to apply Christianity to the collective ills of an industrializing society, and a major force in Canadian religious, social and political life from the 1890s through the 1930s. It drew its unusual strength from the remarkable expansion of Protestant, especially EVANGELICAL, churches in the latter part of the 19th century. For several decades the prevalent expression of evangelical nationalism, the social gospel was equally a secularizing force in its readiness to adopt such contemporary ideas as liberal progressivism, reform Darwinism, biblical criticism and philosophical idealism as vehicles for its message of social salvation. It developed, however, a distinctive spirituality elevating social involvement to a religious significance expressed in prayers, hymns, poems and novels of "social awakening." Its central belief was that God was at work in social change, creating moral order and social justice. It held an optimistic view of human nature and enter-

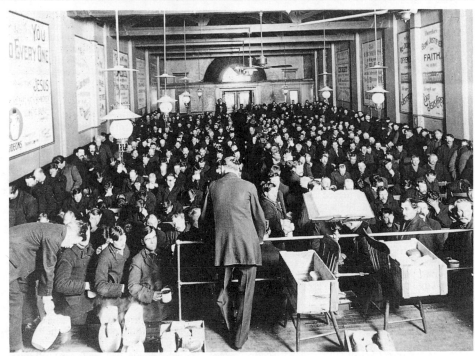
Social Gospel meeting, Yonge Street Mission, *c*1915 (*courtesy City of Toronto Archives/James 1964*).

tained high prospects for social reform. Leaders reworked such traditional Christian doctrines as sin, atonement, salvation and the Kingdom of God to emphasize a social content relevant to an increasingly collective society. The social gospel at large gave birth to the new academic discipline of social ethics, and in Canada contributed most of the impetus to the first sociology programs.

It appeared in Canada in the 1880s, a decade of materialism, political corruption, economic distress and a growing sense of urban disorder. Moved by the difficulties of the time, by Protestant negativism and otherworldliness, and enthused by such social prophets as Carlyle, Ruskin, Tolstoy and Henry George, young Protestants such as J.W. BENGOUGH and Salem BLAND, together with idealist philosophers such as John WATSON at Queen's U, precipitated a movement that by the mid-1890s had become the stuff of church journalism, ministerial institutes, college alumni conferences and youth movements. Early evidence of the church's expanding role came with the founding of city missions and institutional churches such as the St Andrew's Institute (Toronto, 1890) and the Fred Victor Mission (Toronto, 1894), followed by a chain of church settlement houses (1901-19). Whereas METHODISM probably fielded the social gospel most easily, between 1894 and 1910 all the major Protestant denominations created board structures to handle its mushrooming concerns. Older moral causes — TEMPERANCE, sabbath observance and social purity (against prostitution) —were reinterpreted, reinvigorated and incorporated into the progressive reforms. Joined nationally and provincially in 1908 under Presbyterian J.G. SHEARER in the Moral and Social Reform Council, the churches readily aligned these concerns with others: the child, health, housing, urban reform. In 1912 the council was reorganized as the Social Service Council of Canada, and the churches began sponsoring comprehensive surveys of urban conditions. In 1914 the council sponsored the first national congress on social problems. With notable exceptions, the male leadership did not give a high place to WOMEN'S SUFFRAGE, but many women of the National Council of Women, the WOMAN'S CHRISTIAN TEMPERANCE UNION and the suffrage organizations

found in the social gospel a convenient vehicle for articulating reforms based on their maternal feminist creed.

Although the social gospel is often categorized as an urban middle-class phenomenon, it did attract agrarian and labour reformers. W.C. GOOD of the UNITED FARMERS OF ONTARIO, R.C. Henders of the Manitoba GRAIN GROWERS' ASSOCIATION, E.A. PARTRIDGE of the Saskatchewan Grain Growers' Association and H.W. WOOD of the UNITED FARMERS OF ALBERTA were all enthusiasts, as were labour leaders, including James Simpson in Ontario, A.W. PUTTEE in Manitoba and Elmer Roper in Alberta. By WWI it had become a primary informing principle of social reform. The increase in social purpose occasioned by the war brought the movement to a height of influence as reforms it espoused — direct legislation, prohibition, women's suffrage, civil service reform, bureaus of social research, expansion of cooperatives, the decline of party government and, for some, state direction of the economy for national efficiency — all made immense strides.

Postwar unrest gave the social gospel further prominence through association with the WINNIPEG GENERAL STRIKE of 1919 and the PROGRESSIVE PARTY campaign, 1919-21. Radical social gospellers such as J.S. WOODSWORTH and and William IRVINE became increasingly alienated from the church-based social gospel. In turn, its hopes and accomplishments were compromised by economic decline, the secularizing of social work and the backlash against PROHIBITION, while labour and agrarian factional strife undermined the basis of radical social-gospel action. The formation of the UNITED CHURCH in 1925, itself in part a product of the social gospel, did not stem the growing crises in the movement, whose fortunes plummeted.

The reasons for decline in the 1920s were manifold: the accomplishment of many reforms; a delayed disillusionment with the war, a weariness with doing good and a general abandonment of moral earnestness for a new hedonism; the decline of idealism as a reigning philosophy. The social gospel, ideologically bound to the primacy of reason in a being vitally attuned to a benevolent God, could hardly survive in a world apparently animated by power and unreason on the one hand and frivolity on the other. However, under the impact of the GREAT DEPRESSION, a younger generation combined the insights of Alfred North White-head, Reinhold Niebuhr and Karl Marx to fashion what some termed a new social gospel, others a "radical Christianity," which recognized the need for personal as well as social renewal, accepted the importance of class struggle and sought a society of "mutuality."

Associated in the Fellowship for a Christian Social Order (later complemented by the Anglican Fellowship for Social Action), most of this younger leadership (J.W.A. Nicholson in the Maritimes, King GORDON and Eugene FORSEY in central Canada, T.C. DOUGLAS and J.H. Horricks on the Prairies and Harold Allen in BC) contributed to the creation of the CO-OPERATIVE COMMONWEALTH FEDERATION (1933). A broadly diffused older social gospel played a less obvious role in the creation of the SOCIAL CREDIT and Reconstruction parties and in the Depression attempts to transform the Conservative and Liberal parties. After WWII the social gospel could be given much credit for public readiness to maintain Canada's new welfare state and its international posture as a PEACEKEEPING nation. Sons and daughters of the social gospel could be found critically placed throughout both enterprises. That an almost apocalyptic age of the later 1960s and 1970s has overtaken the grandly progressive, if somewhat vaguely entertained, social hopes of a residual social gospel is evident in the limited objectives of church-based coalitions on native rights, corporate responsibility and the environment. Nonetheless, Third-World Christianity, Marxist-Christian dialogue and Catholic liberation theology have had some effect in regenerating a body of Canadian Christian social thought and action reminiscent of the radical social gospel (see ECUMENICAL SOCIAL ACTION).   A. RICHARD ALLEN

Reading: Richard Allen, *The Social Passion* (1971).

Social History is a way of looking at how a society organizes itself and how that organization changes over time. It is an approach, not a subject. The ultimate goal of social historians is to write the complete history of social relations, but that goal is unlikely ever to be achieved. Nevertheless the goal serves as a constant reminder to historians that aspects of history cannot be considered in isolation, and that social history is an integrative study concerned with building towards a global picture of society. Any aspect of society can usefully be studied, but what is important is that it be studied within its relationships to other social institutions.

Social history began as the garbage collector of the discipline. With some notable exceptions, social history, as practised earlier in the 20th century, was usually seen as what was left over after political and ECONOMIC HISTORY had been written. The result was purely descriptive accounts of "daily life in pioneer days" or administrative histories of welfare agencies and the like. This began to change after about 1960, as the influence of new approaches, developed in France and Britain, rippled across the historical world. A group of French scholars, dubbed the *Annales* school for the journal in which their work appeared, showed the potential of truly integrative approaches. They brought together insights from the social sciences, "quantitative" or statistical studies, at times an extravagantly literary style, and an interest in "material culture" — the objects of everyday life — in their attempt to write complete history. Equally influential has been the "new social history" from Britain, which is in large part an attempt to view the working class as a group with its own dynamics, distinctive customs and ideologies.

Canada presents some particular problems for the social historian, since it is a complex mosaic of ethnic groups, cultures, traditions and institutions. In Canada's history the French and English cultural backgrounds made themselves felt in political institutions, in the "established" Anglican and Roman Catholic churches and in elite cultural activities; but at the popular level of entertainment, architectural styles, marriage customs, etc, the social forms and institutions have come from the US, Ireland, Ukraine and elsewhere. Once imported, these diverse forms have sunk roots into the different regions of Canada, there to develop in ways that have been sometimes markedly, sometimes subtly, different.

Geography thus influenced social development through the sharply regionalized character of Canada (*see* REGIONALISM). It did so in other ways as well. The relationship between geography and government was very different from that in the US. Americans have often explained their social and political uniqueness by the impact of the "frontier," that meeting point between civilization and the wilderness that moved W across the US as settlement advanced; at the frontier Americans were cast upon their own resources and learned to be independent and inventive. However well the FRONTIER THESIS applies to American development, Canada had a very different experience, although the theory was popular during the interwar years among Canadian historians such as A.R.M. LOWER and Frank UNDERHILL. Whereas a frontier line moved W across the American colonies and the US for over 250 years, making the frontier experience a pervasive one, Canada had such a continuous frontier only during the French regime, before 1763. Thereafter the wilderness was quickly pushed back in eastern Canada, the arable land rapidly occupied. The frontier experience lapsed, to be renewed 2 generations later on the PRAIRIE WEST, where a similarly rapid settlement process occurred. For most Canadians the frontier was transitory; for most, in fact, the American-style frontier never existed. Canadians were rarely far from authority and from social institutions, rarely divorced from social solutions to problems. Government moved out onto the frontier with, sometimes before, the population, in the form of the British military, colonial officials and later the NORTH-WEST MOUNTED POLICE.

Theories of Canadian social development involve disciplines other than geography. The STAPLE THESIS, formulated in the 1920s by economic historians H.A. INNIS and W.A. MacIntosh asserted that Canada's export of staples influenced its social and political systems. The LAURENTIAN THESIS, expounded from the 1930s to 1950s, argued in favour of the influence of the St Lawrence Valley on the Canadian development; its most sophisticated presentation was in D.G. CREIGHTON's *The* COMMERCIAL EMPIRE OF THE ST. LAWRENCE. Since the 1950s the METROPOLITAN-HINTERLAND THESIS, presented by historians such as J.M.S. CARELESS, has been used to explain the development of Canada's economy and regional tensions.

Government has helped to give shape to Canadian social structure. NEW FRANCE has been called an "aristocratic welfare state," with a tiny population protected by the French military, supported by enlightened laws and sustained by government expenditures. After the CONQUEST, 1759-60, British aristocratic pretensions were imported into Canada with the structure of colonial government, which created such local elites as Upper Canada's FAMILY COMPACT. Government initiative helped launch the CANADIAN PACIFIC RAILWAY and western settlement; immigration policy determined the Prairies' ethnic mix.

Social history is concerned with how all of these influences shape social structure. It shares many interests and some methodology with other SOCIAL SCIENCES, especially historical SOCIOLOGY. In fact, if anyone could claim to be the parent of Canadian social history it is sociologist S.D. CLARK, in his many works, beginning with *The Social Development of Canada* (1942). Clark assessed the impact of the frontier, social movements and Canadian economic activities on our society and demonstrated the possibilities of an integrated social approach. Even where sociology and history overlap in content and concern, however, differences are apparent. Traditional historians are more concerned with chronology and tend to be less comfortable with general theories that approximate "laws" of development; they are likely to be conscious of the individual and the idiosyncratic, even when they generalize to groups. Nevertheless, sociology continues to influence and to stimulate social history. Beginning in the 1970s, as Canadian scholars drew on the example of British historian E.P. Thompson and "cultural history," ANTHROPOLOGY also began to influence historians. A good example of disciplinary cross-fertilization is *Modern Canada, 1930-1980* (1984), vol V of Readings in Social History, ed M.S. Cross and G. Kealey: the authors include 5 historians, 2 sociologists, 2 economists and a political scientist.

Two ongoing series of books in social history give some sense of the interests of Canadian historians working in the field. The Social History of Canada series (University of Toronto Press) and the Canadian Social History series (McClelland and Stewart) were both launched in the early 1970s. The M&S collection has presented studies of poverty in Montréal, the ideology of 19th-century businessmen, attitudes towards immigrants, educational reform, working-class history, and the history of childhood, of medicine and of women. The UTP series was begun to reprint important books and documents, such as Mackenzie KING's 1918 musings on industrial relations, *Industry and Humanity* (1973), and H.B. AMES's pioneering sociological study of working-class Montréal, *The City Below the Hill* (1897; repr 1972). In the 1980s the series began to publish original monographs, including Geoffrey Bilson's *A Darkened House* (1980) on cholera epidemics and Judith Fingard's study of the life of 19th-century sailors, *Jack in Port* (1982).

In the first generation of Canadian social history some long neglected areas came to prominence. One was the history of women. A natural interest for those pursuing an integrated history of society, the study of women was given additional impetus by the growth of feminism and by the entry of increasing numbers of women into the academic world. Themes from WOMEN'S SUFFRAGE to the ideology of reproduction to women's work were explored in early collections on women's history such as *Women at Work: Ontario, 1850-1930* (1974) and *The Neglected Majority* (1977), ed by S.M. Trofimenkoff and A. Prentice. The history of CHILDHOOD has been studied in works such as Joy Parr, ed, *Childhood and Family in Canadian History* (1982). Other previously neglected areas drawing new attention were the immigrant experience (*see* IMMIGRATION), ethnic groups, COMMUNICATIONS, urban history (*see* URBAN STUDIES), NATIVE PEOPLE and the history of VIOLENCE in Canada.

Since the 1960s some of the most significant social history has been written in Québec on a wide variety of topics by historians such as Fernand OUELLET (*Histoire économique et sociale du Québec, 1760-1850,* 1966; trans *Economic and Social History of Quebec, 1760-1850,* 1980), Jean Hamelin (ed, *Histoire du Québec,* 1976), Louise Dechêne (*Habitants et marchands de Montréal au XVII siècle,* 1974) and Jean-Pierre Wallot. S.M. Trofimenkoff's *The Dream of Nation* (1983) is a major contribution to Québec social history.

More than any other area, WORKING-CLASS HISTORY prospered both in Québec and in the rest of Canada. The study of unions already had a strong tradition and it waxed further in the work of labour historians such as Irving Abella, David Bercuson (*Confrontation at Winnipeg,* 1974) and Jacques Rouillard (*Les Syndicats nationaux au Québec de 1900 à 1930,* 1979). More of a departure were the forays into working-class life and culture by historians such as Gregory Kealey, (*Toronto Workers Respond to Industrial Capitalism*, 1980), and Bryan Palmer, whose works include *Working-Class Experience* (1983); both were strongly influenced by E.P. Thompson.

Historical Outline Geography, economy, class, sex, ethnicity and institutions are the major themes of the new social history. They can be seen interplaying in Canadian history, with particular clarity at the beginning of European penetration. The aboriginal population was divided into hundreds of tribal units. Regional splintering made impossible any unified response to European threats; instead, it created intertribal animosities (such as that between the HURON of central Ontario and the IROQUOIS of northern New York) which could be exploited by whites seeking to use native peoples in European struggles for supremacy (*see* IROQUOIS WARS). These struggles, in turn, sprang from both political rivalries and the needs of the European economies for American resources. Marked differences in the institutional structures of Indian and European societies contributed to the eventual outcome of their contact. Native concepts of citizenship and ownership were usually flexible and accommodating, and their religious beliefs were tolerant. As a result most native groups accepted French visitors, and they were prepared to share land and resources with the newcomers and to consider French religious and social practices sympathetically. In contrast, the whites tended to have rigid, proselytizing religious beliefs, which they were anxious to impose on the aborigines, and exclusive concepts of ownership and of appropriate social behaviour to which all had to conform.

The flexibility of Indian societies was indicated by the skill with which some natives learned to conduct the FUR TRADE with Europeans and with other tribes. Ultimately, however, native societies buckled under the combined pressure of European economic demands, constant warfare, and the European diseases that swept through Indian communities. By the time of the British Conquest, the Indians of eastern Canada had been so reduced in numbers and power that they were no longer a key factor in either the economy or politics.

As native power waned, it was replaced by that of the French and British, whose empires had competed for dominance from the beginning of the 17th century until the fall of Québec in 1759. Each had reached out to the New World with its own imperial forms and its peculiar institutions. Economic motivations were primary and, as a result, the initial form of social organization was essentially that of a business. Until 1663 the control of New France was granted to a series of private companies, each charged with developing the fur trade and settling the colony. The English, for their part, rested their imperial hopes in Canada on the HUDSON'S BAY COMPANY (chartered 1670). The French pursued an intrusive fur-trade policy, sending traders into native villages to conduct their business, whereas the English company required natives to come to its posts on Hudson Bay to trade. One consequence of this difference was that French traders more often established marriages with native women "in the style of the country," a practice that the HBC actively discouraged. In addition, relations between the many traders in the West and native women created a whole new society, the MÉTIS. After the Conquest removed France from competition in the fur trade, rivalries arose between the HBC and other traders of British background, particularly those who formed the Montréal-based NORTH WEST COMPANY. Alcohol and violence were used more frequently to gain furs, with profound effects on the cohesion of native social organization.

New France had been a controlled society, at least in design. The basic institution of the colony was the SEIGNEURIAL SYSTEM, a quasi-feudal form of landholding in which large lots were granted to lords or seigneurs, who in turn provided farms to peasants. But few lower-class French migrated to Canada (no more than 10 000 in the entire history of the colony). These few always had alternatives to seigneurial farming, particularly in the fur trade. The government needed to keep its people on the farms in the St Lawrence Valley to supply food for the army and to help defend New France, but it had difficulty coercing the people into giving up the fur trade, and had to make seigneurial life attractive. Strict limits were placed on the dues and taxes that seigneurs could levy, and a state legal system (*see* CIVIL CODE) protected the peasants against feudal oppression. As a result, the Canadian peasant retained far more of the product of his labour than did the European peasant, and he was far freer. A symbol of this was that the farmers in New France rejected the traditional appellation *paysan* and instead called themselves HABITANTS.

This unique evolution of New France was within limits defined by the nature of the originating society of France, the economy of the colony and the character of the population. It is easy enough to see the pattern in a society so small, around 70 000 people by the time of the Conquest. The British N America that succeeded New France grew quickly and its social patterns became more complex. Although the patterns became more difficult to discern, as in New France the social structure emerged from the interplay of institutions, geography, economy, ethnicity and class. The most obvious elements were geography and its adjunct, climate. BNA existed on a large continent which, after the AMERICAN REVOLUTION, it shared with an aggressive rival, the US. That geographical fact helped to give contradictory conservative and progressive casts to Canadian society. Many of the LOYALIST refugees who resettled in BNA carried with them a powerful bitterness against the US, republicanism and democracy. The WAR OF 1812 reinforced TORY belief in the duplicity, irrationality and menace of the US and in the need to protect Canada from "infection" by American ideas. The colonial form of government imported from Britain was a suitably conservative instrument for the purpose. So were institutions such as the Church of England (*see* ANGLICANISM) and a highly stratified class system. Elites emerged to implement this Tory ethos, groups such as the Family Compact in Upper Canada [Ontario], the CHÂTEAU CLIQUE in Lower Canada [Québec] and the COUNCIL OF TWELVE in NS.

At the same time, American ideas and practices were permeating Canada despite the best Tory efforts. Many Americans who came to BNA before 1812 were not Loyalists, but were simply landseekers with no political motivation. Even the Loyalists were as much American as British; Britain found them as likely as non-Loyalists to cling to American concepts of local self-government. The Canadian colonial period was marked by a conscious rejection of the political hegemony of the US but, equally, by an instinctive refusal to become a facsimile of Britain. The American phase of settlement had passed by 1812, and after 1818 a new wave of British migration broke over Canada. The values and customs of the British settlers intermixed with those of the Americans to produce the essential compromise that was "English" Canada. Geography continued to be a powerful influence, so that the economic assumptions, business forms and TECHNOLOGY of Canada remained predominantly American, and the economic success of the US was the brass ring pursued by English Canadians. Social institutions, however, were often a blend of the 2 cultures. American individualism influenced Canadians, but it was coloured by a British sense of group and class

solidarities and a more explicit class system. Characteristically, Canada did not definitively abolish titles of HONOUR until 1936.

French Canada, too, was influenced by American and British migration. In some respects, however, that influence would work to emphasize the unique characteristics of French Canadian society. Again geography played a major role. The Conquest left French Canada surrounded by the "English." By the early 19th century the growing population was already bursting the seams of the seigneuries, producing overcrowding and overcultivated farms, with a resultant decline in the standard of living. The seigneurial system was finally abolished in 1854, but that was too late to solve the problem of Québec agriculture or to prevent the economic retardation of French Canada. The end of seigneurialism put even greater emphasis on 2 other institutions which helped French Canadians to retain their distinctiveness: the Roman Catholic Church (*see* CATHOLICISM) and the FRENCH LANGUAGE. The church remained central in the Québecois identity until the 1960s. Its decline then under the force of modern secularism left language as the key mark of distinctiveness. The often fervid attempts by successive Québec governments in the 1960s, 1970s and 1980s to compel the use of French in schools and workplaces and on public signs demonstrated the significance of this last great distinction in an increasingly homogenous N American continent.

In Canada's cultural mix, ETHNICITY and RELIGION assumed special importance, for English as well as French Canadians. From the 1830s, for example, the ORANGE ORDER played a major, bloody role in the life of Ontario, Québec and New Brunswick. Militantly Protestant and ostentatiously loyal to the British Crown, the order was a focus of identity and reassurance for many immigrants, especially Protestant Irishmen (*see* SHINERS' WAR). Unhappily for social peace, Orangemen expressed their identity in verbal abuse of Catholics (and often French Canadians), provocative parades and frequent riots with Catholic opponents. The result could be violent, but the Orange Order was an important institution of social adjustment for hundreds of thousands of Protestant immigrants. To some degree, ethnic and religious bonding papered over class differences in Canada, obscuring socioeconomic conflicts that might have been even more productive of social conflict.

The transition to an industrial society (*see* INDUSTRIALIZATION) altered many social patterns. Mechanized industry began to emerge in Canada in the 1840s; it was dominant by the 1890s and produced widespread concentration of economic power before WWI. The old elites, created by British economic and political needs, gave way to elites of industrialists and financiers who were represented politically by professional men, especially lawyers. Industrialism also created a working class and an organized response — trade unionism — to the new economic order. Unions sprang up in the 1870s and were a permanent feature of the social environment by the end of the 19th century. As with the economic system itself, unions were heavily influenced by American ideology and example. By 1902 "international" unions with headquarters in the US had become dominant in the Canadian labour movement. Their espousal of moderate, apolitical approaches helped to prevent class conflicts in industrial Canada. Exceptional conditions could cast light on class differences, which were given sharper outlines by the gulf between capital and labour in an industrial setting. The unrest that grew out of WWI produced the labour upheaval of 1919, focused on the WINNIPEG GENERAL STRIKE (much as Québec's QUIET REVOLUTION would trigger unprecedented labour militancy in that province in the 1960s and 1970s). For the most part, however, Canadian labour remained moderate, committed to peaceful collective bargaining. The American example, N American ideology and the influence of institutions, such as schools and the mass media, which cut across class lines and inculcated a classless ideology, minimized social group conflict (*see* SOCIAL CLASS; CLASS AND POLITICS).

Industrialism had a homogenizing effect. Mass markets were created for mass-produced products, railways sped goods and ideas across the country, and NEWSPAPERS (later radio and TV) helped to reduce regional differences. Geography continued to resist these tendencies, however. Confederation was, in many ways, a logical political response to the needs of the railway, or industrial, age (*see* RAILWAY HISTORY). It erected a larger political and economic structure, which could press forward with grander economic programs. But the continuing reality of regional economic and social communities required that Confederation, like Canada itself, be a compromise. It was a federal, not a unitary state; it was a parliamentary system on the British model, but one operated by political parties whose style was more American than British (*see* FEDERALISM).

Industrialism also demanded a larger labour force. After 1897 a booming Canadian economy supplemented its familiar American and British sources of immigrants with large numbers of continental Europeans. Canadians who in the 19th century had defined theirs as either an American or a British society — but certainly an Anglo-Saxon-dominated one — in the 20th century had to deal with a cultural mosaic. What is striking is how little the basic social institutions had to adjust to ethnic diversity. Political and economic forms continued to evolve within the same broadly Anglo-American patterns, and leadership continued to be exercised by those of British stock. Geographic proximity to the US, the maintenance of a modified free-enterprise economy and the inertia of social institutions allowed Canadian society to absorb and assimilate immigrants.

Québec, the most rapidly modernizing part of Canada after 1960, was also the most troubled by the social implications of a mass N American society. Among other groups, as well, there were somewhat paradoxical reactions. If institutions such as the media helped inculcate a stabilizing common ideology, it also became clear to some disadvantaged elements that they were not receiving an equitable share of the bounty promised by those institutions. NATIVE PEOPLE began to demand, especially after 1960, compensation for economic and social losses they had suffered. More influential were the demands of women, who formed a majority of the population. As in Québec and among the native peoples, women began during the 1960s to insist on the removal of some of their disabilities. The economic system had delivered the promised improvement in wages and working conditions to male workers, and the media had become pervasive and pervasively successful in publicizing the triumphs of the society. Women began to demand a place in the mainstream, and social institutions slowly responded. A royal commission on the STATUS OF WOMEN was appointed in 1967; divorce reform was introduced in 1968; traditionally all-male professions began to open to women. However, the basic institutions of society were resilient enough to survive the adjustment with little disruption.

The pace of 20th-century change seemed very great. A predominantly rural country until about 1940, Canada became thereafter an overwhelmingly urban one (*see* RURAL SOCIETY). In 1941, for example, 41% of Québec Francophones lived on farms, in 1971 only 6%; the Quiet Revolution was stimulated in significant measure by the upheaval produced by this shift.

The family, always the rhetorical focus of social ideology, seemed to be challenged. Canadian divorce rates soared after WWII, especially after the divorce law reform of 1968, while birth rates, especially in Québec, declined. Yet the patterns remained remarkably stable. Although many more women worked outside the home in the 1980s, the gap between male and female wages had not narrowed. Far more marriages ended in divorce, but most Canadians still chose to marry. Although agricultural employment was replaced by urban employment, the distribution of wealth in Canada changed little.

Geography remained a solid anchor for society, sheltering regional and economic differences. Social classes and institutions evolved, and growing importance was attached to the educated professionals who serviced more complicated social needs. Yet studies such as John PORTER'S *The* VERTICAL MOSAIC (1965) and Wallace Clement's *The Canadian Corporate Elite* (1975) suggested a remarkable continuity in the groups that wielded social and economic power in Canada. The relative influence of organized religion in Canadian life declined, again most dramatically in Québec. Fraternal groups and SECRET SOCIETIES lost prominence after WWII as the religious and imperial causes they espoused became less significant. The visit of a pope to Canada in 1900 would have set off religious riots; in 1984 it produced celebrations in a country whose population was by then almost half Roman Catholic. Part of the reason for the decreasing influence of voluntary organizations, as well, was the WELFARE STATE, in which government assumed responsibility for charity, job placement and training, education, social adjustment and a myriad other social roles once filled by voluntary organizations and religious and ethnic communities. Still, the social and institutional patterns in which these changes were worked out were those of the Anglo-American compromise that was at the base of Canadian society.

For a treatment of specific themes in social history, *see* CHILDHOOD, HISTORY OF; DISEASES, HUMAN; EPIDEMIC; GREAT DEPRESSION; IMMIGRATION; POLITICAL PROTEST; SOCIAL DOCTRINE OF THE ROMAN CATHOLIC CHURCH; SOCIAL GOSPEL; TEMPERANCE.

MICHAEL S. CROSS

Social Impact Assessment (SIA), a set of procedures designed to identify social changes likely to occur because of a major project or new program. In Canada a social impact assessment is usually conducted as part of an environmental impact assessment. In 1973 a federal Cabinet decision established the Environmental Assessment and Review Process to ensure that both biophysical and social consequences are considered in the planning of major projects and programs. Most provinces have similar legislation or regulations, and Canada is a signatory of a 1972 international declaration on the human environment. Federal procedures involve several steps. Initial screening and evaluation predicts potentially significant effects. If any are identified, a panel is formed, guidelines are established for an EIA and its SIA component, studies are conducted to produce environmental and social impact statements, a public review is held, and the panel makes recommendations to the federal minister of the environment. The review panel may recommend and the minister may decide that the project proceed as proposed, proceed with modifications to mitigate undesirable effects, be postponed or be cancelled. The environmental assessment and review process is similar to a judicial process, considering testimony and direct evidence, including social impact assessment research reports and opinions and information provided through public participation.

ROY T. BOWLES

Reading: Roy T. Bowles, *Social Impact Assessment in Small Communities* (1981); K. Finsterbusch, *Understanding Social Impacts* (1980).

Social Insurance Number (SIN) Almost every Canadian who pays money to, or receives benefits from, the federal government has a 9-digit Social Insurance Number (SIN). The numbers are used in addition to names and addresses so that computers may more easily keep unique records of certain transactions between Canadians and their federal and provincial governments.

The Unemployment Insurance Commission (UIC) invented the SIN in 1964. The UIC, created under the Unemployment Insurance Act (1940), began in 1942 to issue numbered cards to both insured and uninsured persons. Twenty years later the UIC master index contained information on 7.5 million persons holding UIC cards. However, a new numbering system was needed to promote accuracy in computer processing of data and because adequate combinations of numbers and letters could no longer be generated under the old numbering system. Two additional factors contributed to the adoption of the SIN. In 1962 the report of the Royal Commission on GOVERNMENT ORGANIZATION (the Glassco Commission) concluded that a unique personal identifier was necessary to increase administrative efficiency in federal government services as large computers came into widespread use. In 1963, the Canadian Pension Plan (CPP) was proposed. About 80% of those who would be covered by the pension plan were already registered with the UIC. Thus, it seemed logical that a single number should be used for both purposes.

Although the use of SINs is a source of continuing political controversy, Parliament has never been given the opportunity to vote on the issue. The regulations governing the issuance of SINs were authorized by an order-in-council and took effect in April 1964. Employers were required at the time to ensure that their employees and any employees subsequently hired had SINs. By June 1964, 6.3 million SINs had been issued. In the 20 years thereafter more than 22 million numbers were issued; virtually every adult residing in Canada, and many children, have a SIN.

The use of the SIN was initially restricted in practice to the UIC and CPP. Anyone with insurable employment or anyone over the age of 18 and making CPP contributions was required to obtain a number. But since there were no restrictions placed on further uses of the SIN, it gradually came into service as a unique personal identifier in all sectors of society and is now used, for example, on income tax returns, family allowances, school records and even on permits for wheat farming. Anyone filing an income tax return must provide a SIN on the return. Similarly a parent applying for a family allowance must furnish his or her SIN. Basically, most financial and service program transactions between governments and Canadian citizens are controlled by means of a SIN.

It seems reasonable to suggest that at least nongovernmental use of the SIN is improper, though it is not illegal. It is arguable that to request a SIN as identification to cash a cheque is an example of abuse. Similar examples of abuse include requiring a SIN to obtain a telephone or burial permit, or to rent an apartment. In addition, both provincial and municipal governments use SINs to establish and record the identity of individuals involved in their programs. A person choosing not to furnish their SIN on demand risks denial of services.

Another aspect of abuse of SINs involves data linkage or record matching. If all interactions with the federal government are recorded using an individual's SIN, then checking government data banks for information associated with that number can reveal all available information on that person, such as whether a family allowance was declared on an income tax return. Clearly, it is useful to have controlled access to such information. On the other hand, indiscriminate use of this technique is obviously an invasion of PRIVACY, and many people fear that personal information in government data banks can and will be used for social control. The federal Privacy Act (1982) is silent on the uses of SINs, even though these numbers are the most frequent source of complaint to the federal privacy commissioner.

Abuse of the SIN is less likely to occur if those with a number make sure that they only use the number when they are required to do so by law. Moreover the use of SINs may decline as sophisticated new computers become able to identify persons and link their records without relying on such numbers.   D. FLAHERTY AND P. HARTE

Social Mobility, the movement of individuals, families and groups from one social position to another. The theory of social mobility attempts to explain the frequency of these movements, but the study of social mobility is also a study of how people became distributed into various social positions (social selection). Scholars were first attracted to the study of social mobility by the regularity with which people end up in roughly the same social position as their parents. Despite some intergenerational movement up and down the social ladder, it is clear that people born into wealthy and important families are likely to live their lives as wealthy and important people, while those born into the working class are not. This regularity is the consequence of inherited wealth, useful social contacts and education — not superior intelligence, strength and judgement. Societies have been characterized as "open" or "closed" according to the degree to which the fortune of children is independent of or dependent upon that of the parents. Late 18th- and 19th-century writers, in their critiques of their societies, were concerned with the institutional and personal factors affecting mobility. They advocated a society in which merit and talent were rewarded and opportunities for their development and application were freely available. Contemporary writers have been more inclined to substitute summary statistical indices of the frequency of mobility for critical analysis of the entire society. Sociologists usually distinguish structural mobility (all people are doing better than they used to, or better than their parents did) from exchange mobility (some people are changing their positions relative to others). In the 20th century, structural mobility in Canada, the US, Britain and other industrialized countries has increased, but exchange mobility has changed very little.

Changes in Structural Mobility With INDUSTRIALIZATION, agricultural labour declined and labour in factories and offices increased. As certain jobs become more common, the opportunity to enter these jobs (as compared to other jobs) increases. Thus mobility into growing sectors of the economy outstrips mobility into declining sectors. This is one kind of structural mobility. At the same time, the opportunity to enter a job is greatest when competition for the job is least; mobility into highly competitive sectors of the economy is less than mobility into equally growing but less competitive sectors. This is the other kind of structural mobility. Rates of structural mobility are thus determined by both the number of jobs and the number of competitors for these jobs. When the economy booms, UNEMPLOYMENT declines, new jobs are created and old jobs are often improved. Higher salaries and benefits are paid to attract the best workers. In times of economic stagnation few new jobs are available, upgrading is less frequent and mobility decelerates. This boom-and-bust cycle is particularly relevant to Canada. Because the economy is largely owned by foreign investors (*see* FOREIGN INVESTMENT) and dominated by the export of raw resources to foreign

consumers, Canada is particularly susceptible to fluctuations in foreign economies. Economic growth and technological change are also largely determined by outside forces.

Generally, the size of the LABOUR FORCE and competition for jobs within it is determined by natural population growth, the migration of workers and change in the rates of adult participation. During the GREAT DEPRESSION birthrates fell dramatically, but afterward, particularly between 1946 and 1962, birthrates rose to very high levels. The BABY BOOM generation crowded schools in the 1950s, universities in the 1960s and the market for entry-level jobs during the 1970s. Since the Baby Boom, birthrates have fallen once again, although some observers believe 40-year cycles of strong and weak competition will result from future demographic booms and busts.

Since the Depression, IMMIGRATION into Canada has remained consistently high, but because the Canadian government has generally encouraged the immigration of workers who will accept jobs that native-born Canadians will not or cannot do, a rise in immigration rates does not necessarily indicate increased competition for all jobs. Nevertheless, in the mid-1960s the altered immigration laws favoured those with more education, resulting in an increase of urban, educated migrants who competed successfully for white-collar jobs. Canadians also drifted westward for over a century, particularly during the economic expansion in Alberta and BC in the 1970s and early 1980s. Economic expansion in the Atlantic provinces, especially NS, has also attracted interprovincial and international migrants, although in smaller numbers. As migrants arrive, competition for jobs intensifies and rates of mobility may decline.

Participation rates, particularly those of women, also influence the numbers of competitors for positions. Public education, urbanization, the development of office work and economic need have all resulted in increasing numbers of entrants to the labour force. More young women are planning careers, having fewer children and returning to work shortly after childbearing.

Other kinds of social mobility are apparently less affected by changes in the size and composition of the work force. For example, the social characteristics of the Canadian elite have changed little in the last half century or more, despite changes in the general population. Members of the elite still tend to be male, white, Anglo-Saxon Protestants born into upper- or upper-middle-class families, although there is some variation from one part of Canada to another. More francophone Catholics would be found in the Québec BUSINESS ELITE or the federal political elite than in the Ontario business or political elite. Otherwise excluded social groups enter the elite and the upper class in growing areas of the economy, eg, Italians and Jews in real estate and construction. Multinational corporations also seem more likely to provide opportunities for upward mobility than indigenous Canadian corporations. In general, however, social characteristics that hinder entry into the elite — characteristics such as gender, race, religion and class of origin — also appear to limit the extent and rate of occupational mobility.

Forms of Unequal Opportunity Rates of mobility are also affected by the type of recruitment characterizing positions and by social barriers that stand between positions. Average individuals are most able to enter positions with agencies that recruit outsiders and are committed to impartial recruitment, such as the federal civil service. Elite positions are generally filled by the children of elite parents; positions in medical schools are disproportionately filled by the children of doctors, while even in many skilled

trades and small businesses the right or opportunity to enter is passed from parent to child. Parental social class largely determines early educational opportunities and choices that are important to later mobility. By and large, people do not make radical changes in their occupational or social position after entering the work force; they advance beyond their parents right away or not at all. Once they have started on a particular job ladder, they advance largely by seniority, so they can hardly change their position relative to their workmates. The labour market is also split into many segments, eg, jobs entered by means of credentials, jobs entered by means of union membership and jobs entered by anyone. People starting out in a certain kind of work will never actually compete with people doing a very different kind of work. Casual labourers will rarely have occasion to compete with licensed skilled workers or accredited professionals.

Outside of structural mobility, and because little exchange mobility exists in the truest sense, Canadians do not enjoy equal opportunity to advance. They compete unequally for power because Canadian society protects power in various ways. Family power is preserved in wealth. Many occupations and positions of authority are closed to people without credentials, eg, university degrees, and those who can obtain such credentials are drawn disproportionately from the middle and upper classes.

Attempts to Equalize Opportunity The attempt to redistribute wealth through TAXATION and TRANSFER PAYMENTS has failed to reduce inequality of wealth significantly, but antidiscrimination laws or affirmative-action efforts are especially valuable for traditionally excluded groups, such as women and racial minorities, and evidence suggests these efforts are beginning to affect occupational mobility. The widening of educational opportunity — more universities, increased admittance of students, the provision of more scholarships — has weakened the original value of the credentials and has led to demands by employers for rarer credentials. Higher education has helped many children of poorer families to obtain better jobs than they might have otherwise, but has not increased the rate of exchange mobility because it is still largely restricted to the already advantaged. Collective mobility, however, has been a very effective means of equalizing opportunity. Increasingly, groups of people with a common goal, eg, unions or associations of professionals, or a common disability have co-operated to advance themselves. But other, less obvious groups have also mobilized collectively, including ethnic groups, such as the Toronto Italian community, language groups, such as Canadian Francophones, regional or provincial groups, and networks comprising personal acquaintances, friends or family. In many instances collective mobilization has advanced both group and individual interests. Yet the collective mobilization of everyone would ensure a new stalemate — an indirect, inefficient way of eliminating social inequality.

Trends in Canadian Research and Writing Summarizing the state of mobility research in Canada, one observer commented that "Canadian studies have led to a fuller understanding of the origins of elite groups than has been achieved in the US." However, although valuable census data have been available, they have not been fully exploited and Canadians have not been responsible for much innovation in quantitative methodology. Canadian research continues to emulate American mobility research based on occupational and status attainment. Research initiated by John PORTER and his colleagues at Carleton University, Ottawa, set out to replicate in Canada the studies of P. Blau and O.D. Duncan. Partial results suggest a continuing importance of gender and a declining importance of ethnicity and language group in status attainment. The limited mobility of women is also documented in other studies, using other data. Other research on the experience of immigrant and nonimmigrant, non-Anglo-Saxons confirms that Porter's image of Canada as a VERTICAL MOSAIC (1965) of ethnic groups is less valid now and that social mobility in Canada more closely resembles mobility in the US and other modern industrial nations. Class origin or parental occupation strongly influences the level of education a person attains, but although education determines occupational-status attainment, it is not as likely to equalize opportunity as people once believed.

Recent research on social mobility is following fairly traditional lines, with a few modifications. Research on the mobility of women pays increasing attention to economic theories of labour-market segmentation and to effects of the introduction of new technologies. Research on the mobility of language and ethnic groups is focusing on actual work settings and the centre of control in these settings. Research on elites has tended to examine national and international networks of interlocking directorships.
L. TEPPERMAN

Reading: John Porter, *Vertical Mosaic* (1965); Wallace Clement, *Canadian Corporate Elite* (1974).

Social Science, in general, has come to refer to the specialized teaching and research conducted in disciplines characterized by their concern with human beings, their culture and their economic, political and social relationship with the environment. Academicians generally categorize knowledge into 4 main areas: physical sciences, biological sciences (or natural sciences), humanities and social sciences, although others recognize only 2 categories — natural sciences and social sciences. Social sciences are included in various disciplines in different universities and there is no clear demarcation between a number of the member disciplines within these areas. Generally, the social sciences include ANTHROPOLOGY, ECONOMICS, POLITICAL SCIENCE, PSYCHOLOGY and SOCIOLOGY and sometimes also CRIMINOLOGY, EDUCATION, GEOGRAPHY, LAW, PSYCHIATRY, PHILOSOPHY, RELIGION and history.

The beginnings of modern social science can be traced to the 18th-century Enlightenment. The rise of capitalist society and attendant phenomena inspired social inquiry. In France, through the work of the physiocrats, economics was launched as an empirical science. Moral philosophy also made substantial advances, laying the foundations for modern sociology, psychology and anthropology. During the 19th century, social science became diversified, but some thinkers (Comte, Marx) in an opposing trend tried to construct a synthesis. Five changes characterize the 20th-century advances in the social sciences. First, the development of modest theorizing and high standards of empirical testing; second, the recognition of the interdependence of social, political and economic forces; third, the rise of several branches of psychology important to the analysis of social behaviour; fourth, the improvement of quantitative methods; and fifth, the incorporation of social sciences into society.

In the 1950s the term "behavioural sciences" came into widespread use, usually in reference to anthropology, sociology and psychology. As an attempt to emphasize the method of scientific process, behavioural science concentrates on those aspects of the social sciences that can be explored, recorded and interpreted. Social scientists generally, however, are as much concerned with method as with results. English economist John Maynard Keynes, speaking of economics, described all social sciences when he said that "it is a method rather than a doctrine,

an apparatus of the mind, a technique of thinking, which helps its possessor to draw correct conclusions." However, unlike much natural-science research, only a very small part of research in social science is conducted in controlled, laboratory settings.

Social Sciences in Canada The changes in higher education in Canada from 1663 to 1960 and the retarded development of social-science subjects relative to those closely connected with the humanities and natural sciences have been documented, but each of the social-science disciplines has its own history, its own periods of gestation, birth and growth to adulthood as a distinctive profession. Some, eg, history, economics, political science and psychology, were approaching adulthood while others, eg, geography, anthropology and sociology, were still in their infancy. These latecomers were not firmly established until the 1950s.

Growth in the social sciences was encouraged by the recognized need to resolve or understand the many problems associated with the increasing size and complexity of Canada and its institutions. Outside of Québec, much of the growth during the first 40 years of this century was promoted by spokesmen who argued that universities should provide training for the expanding public service, as well as for institutions in the private sector. In contrast, the first Québec social-science programs in the 1930s were sponsored by the Roman Catholic Church in an attempt to shape the changing society according to the social doctrines set forth in the papal encyclicals; the orientation stressed social service in the interest of French Canadian society as a whole. The social sciences helped prepare the way for the formation of co-operatives, credit unions, workers' syndicates and other institutions. The social sciences in Québec have since been secularized but remain strongly committed to participation in the shaping of Québec society.

From 1945 to the early 1960s, earlier gains made by the social sciences throughout Canada were consolidated. Many new departments in universities were founded and older ones expanded at a steady rate. Unfortunately, in most of the social sciences, graduate study programs were only feebly developed so that it was impossible to meet from within Canada the surge in demand for professional social scientists that occurred in the 1960s. Many prospective social scientists had to leave Canada to earn their professional degrees elsewhere, particularly in the US.

The tidal wave of students that engulfed the universities in the 1960s and early 1970s had an enormous impact on the social sciences. There was also a growing demand for the teaching of social-science subjects in community colleges and high schools. Within many universities the growing strength of social-science disciplines was accompanied by their fusion into divisions or, in some universities, into faculties of social science. The increasing importance of social science is reflected as well in the application, both directly and indirectly, of its perspectives and methods to many areas in society. Although a large number of social scientists teach in universities, thousands work in the private sector and in government and in their jobs apply social-science knowledge and methods of research. Furthermore, social-science theories and findings are applied by many who do not have advanced social-science degrees, eg, those employed in such fields as administration, commerce, education, health, leisure, social work, etc.

Social scientists are primarily concerned with research, although it is true that social-science research does not have the impact, prestige or the same degree of financial support as does research in the natural sciences. As well, the findings of social-science research do not reach a

very wide audience and are often difficult to understand because they are couched in jargon. Those it does reach may be disappointed and frustrated with the contradictory and biased analyses, and lack of certainty in the predictions, which often reflect the difficulties and uncertainties of human life itself, and not the failure of the discipline.

Some social-science research is conducted for corporations, school boards, government agencies and other institutions; in such cases the client poses the questions. At the other extreme, research is generated by the scholars themselves, by universities, private foundations, or by a government-sponsored body like the SOCIAL SCIENCE AND HUMANITIES RESEARCH COUNCIL OF CANADA.

Contributions of social science to public policy are channeled through a number of streams, eg, the ECONOMIC COUNCIL OF CANADA and the Institute for Research on Public Policy. Social scientists of many specialties have played an important part on scores of task forces, committees of inquiry and royal commissions. For example, the Royal Commission on BILINGUALISM AND BICULTURALISM involved both English- and French-speaking demographers, economists, historians, linguists, political scientists and sociologists.

The spectacular growth in the social sciences in Canada is reflected in the number of national and regional associations and journals established since 1950, before which time fewer than 10 associations and no more than 7 journals existed. By 1980 there were 37 associations and 29 journals catering entirely or partly to the social-science community.

Individual social-science disciplines have developed an impressive capacity to organize, but less impressive has been the capacity for the social sciences to create and sustain a strong collective organization that transcends the boundaries of the disciplines. The first attempt to bring together the various social sciences under an umbrella organization was the founding (1940) of the Social Science Research Council (later changed to Social Science Federation of Canada). This voluntary association was organized by a small group of distinguished scholars to promote research, the training of social scientists, the publication of studies and the holding of conferences. Almost all of the funding for these activities derived from American sources — the Carnegie, Ford and Rockefeller foundations. The council was able to function on only a small scale without government support. With the establishment of the CANADA COUNCIL in 1957, government support for the social sciences as well as the humanities was instituted, although on a more modest scale than for the natural sciences. In 1978 the functions of the Canada Council relating to the social sciences were taken over by the Social Science and Humanities Research Council, a federal agency. Its role is to promote the interests of the social-science community vis-à-vis the public and the state.
FRANK G. VALLEE

Social Sciences and Humanities Research Council of Canada (SSHRC), created 29 June 1977 by an Act of Parliament. It began operations 1 Apr 1978, taking over the programs previously administered by the CANADA COUNCIL's humanities and social sciences division. With the Medical Research Council and the Natural Sciences and Engineering Research Council, SSHRC administers federal funds for university-based research. It is governed by a 22-member appointed council selected from the academic community and other groups.

SSHRC's mandate, defined in section 5 of the Government Organization (Scientific Activities) Act, 1976, is to assist research and scholarship in the social sciences and humanities and to advise the minister on matters referred to it by the minister. SSHRC enhances the advancement of knowledge by assisting research; advises on maintaining and developing the national capacity for research; facilitates the dissemination of research results; and increases Canada's international presence and recognition in the social sciences and humanities.

SSHRC has a staff of 100, based in Ottawa. Its annual budget (voted by Parliament) is approximately $60 million. The type of research funded ranges from proposals of individual scholars to major national projects such as the *Canadian Historical Atlas* and the DICTIONARY OF CANADIAN BIOGRAPHY.   JEFFREY HOLMES

Social Security denotes public programs intended to maintain, protect and raise basic living standards. Specifically the term covers publicly financed and administered programs that replace income lost because of pregnancy, illness, accident, disability, the death or absence of a family's breadwinner, unemployment, old age or retirement, or other factors. Since WWII social security in Canada has been expanded to protect the adequacy of individual and family incomes threatened by the costs of medical and hospital care, of family size or of shelter (although Canada, unlike many western European countries, provides only limited help to ensure a disproportionate share of people's income is not spent on shelter). Governments have also introduced MINIMUM WAGE legislation and provided help for workers to upgrade job skills or to relocate. Federal and provincial governments have recently been experimenting with programs to supplement the incomes of working people when their earned income falls below a level considered adequate.

The history of social security in Canada can be divided into the colonial era (from the arrival of the first European settlers in the 17th century to 1867); from Confederation to WWI; 1919-39; and the post-WWII era. The settlers who colonized NEW FRANCE introduced the 17th-century French practice of assigning the care of the elderly, sick and orphaned to the Catholic Church and its institutions. The British who established Halifax in the mid-18th century introduced the English poor law enacted by the English Parliament in 1598, which assigned the care of the poor to the smallest unit of government, the parish, financed by property taxes raised there. The British legislation introduced the idea of public responsibility for the care of the destitute, replacing a much older tradition of licensed begging and reliance on voluntary donations. The English poor-law model was also imported into the American colonies and from there to what is now NB by the LOYALISTS. In 1763 NS enacted legislation modelled on the English poor law, as did NB in 1786. Money raised locally was supplemented occasionally by a provincial grant to meet an extraordinary emergency, eg, serious fire or an outbreak of typhoid fever. But PEI had only one or 2 towns of any size and all emergency help was dispensed from there; in Newfoundland (where the Colonial Office in London had actively discouraged settlement and the development of municipal institutions), charity organizations, friends and family were the principal sources of help. UPPER CANADA failed to enact a poor law in 1792 when the main body of English civil law was introduced into the new province; one result was the encouragement of voluntary charities. LOWER CANADA, with its French traditions, relied upon voluntary charitable collections to finance the welfare work of the Catholic Church. English Protestants settling in Lower Canada formed their own charitable agencies to take care of English-speaking poor.

In the colonial era, people who lived primarily in small, rural communities were more self-sufficient than Canadians today, not only from

necessity but because it was more feasible. They produced most of their own food on small family farms and obtained many other necessities through barter; in emergencies neighbours helped each other. However, for those without friends and family, the only recourse was charity, considered proof of personal failure in many instances. In French Canada even asking for help from the churches was resisted. The help offered by charitable agencies was often paternalistic and meagre, and frequently administered in a harsh and demeaning manner. The classic example of this was the municipal poorhouse, a poor-law institution found in larger towns and cities. It housed the destitute of all ages, the sick, the senile, the mentally ill, the unemployed, children and infants. Its reputation was so fearsome that only those facing starvation would seek such help. In NB some of the smaller communities that could not afford the cost auctioned off the care of the poor to local families, an utterly demeaning practice which continued until the latter part of the 19th century.

Under the BRITISH NORTH AMERICA ACT the relatively minor roles of government were assigned to the provinces, among them the exclusive right to legislate regarding "the establishment, maintenance and management of hospitals, asylums, charities and charitable institutions," a succinct description of existing organizations. The implicit judgement was that health and welfare were matters of purely local interest and control and the provinces should reassign much of the responsibility to the municipalities or voluntary charities. Provincial governments, however, became increasingly involved in a range of health and welfare programs, particularly in western provinces, where municipal organizations were rudimentary or nonexistent.

After 1867, industrialization drew people to the towns and cities. In search of greater economic opportunity, many discovered they had traded the relative security of the family farm for the insecurity of a factory job. People were now dependent upon a regular cash income, and any event which interrupted it gravely threatened their livelihood. In the years following Confederation, peoples' attitudes toward the appropriate government role regarding the economic security of the individual were still shaped by the pioneer values of independence and individualism, reflected in furious public debates about the necessity for, and value of, public schools, public-health measures and government regulation of working conditions. Poor relief was still delivered in a stigmatizing manner, and POVERTY, which was still related in the public mind to individual failure, was commonly blamed on excessive drinking. To avoid dependence on charity, 19th-century workers organized fraternal societies, each member contributing a small, regular amount to a special fund from which he could draw if sickness or accident prevented him from working. Trade unions, which also originated at this time, struggled to raise standards of living and to provide income protection against the risk of wage loss, but these limited protections were available only to a minority of the work force. With the increasing industrialization of the late 19th century the number of work accidents rose. Trade unions and other groups made this a public issue, and the result in 1914 was the first modern social-security program, the Workmen's Compensation Act of Ontario. Injured workers could now claim a regular cash income as a right. Ontario's example was soon copied by other provinces.

Social insurance, based on the assumption that risks to income security are a normal aspect of life in an urban-industrial society and not the result of individual shortcomings, was pioneered in Germany in the 1880s. Britain intro-

Christmas food and clothing hampers presented to a poor Winnipeg family (*courtesy United Church Archives*).

duced the world's first UNEMPLOYMENT INSURANCE scheme in 1911. Nearly all workers contributed to a fund from which all could draw; employers were also asked to contribute, and government could contribute toward administration costs. Workers' contributions provided a sense of entitlement to help that the old poor law never did.

WWI accelerated the processes of urbanization and industrialization and led to increased agitation for OLD-AGE PENSIONS and allowances for civilian widows, deserted wives and their children. In 1916 Manitoba was the first province to pass a Mothers' Pensions Act to provide a small but assured income to widows and divorced or deserted wives with children to support. Within 5 years, all provinces from Ontario west had passed similar legislation. Called public assistance, the help was based on a means test and constituted a modern version of the English poor law. In 1919 the Liberal Party pledged to pass legislation on health insurance, contributory old-age pensions and unemployment insurance. To circumvent the BNA Act, the federal government devised the conditional grant, which enabled them to initiate programs by offering to share the cost of provincially administered social-security programs, provided they met certain federal guidelines (*see* INTERGOVERNMENTAL FINANCE). The first old-age pension program was introduced in 1927. In its first major entry into the social-security field, the federal government paid 50% of a $20 monthly pension to needy citizens age 70 and over. The pension was subject, however, to a strict and often humiliating means test — proof that poor-law attitudes still influenced Canadian political leaders in the 1920s.

The GREAT DEPRESSION seared Canadian society. Thousands of formerly independent Canadians joined the public-welfare rolls. The federal government was compelled to become involved in the massive problem of unemployment relief, previously a purely local concern. The 1930 programs to relieve poverty and destitution were essentially left over from the 19th-century poor-relief systems of municipal aid supplemented by voluntary charitable agencies. Rather than cash, assistance was granted in the form of grocery, fuel and clothing orders. Single, unemployed men were herded into military-style camps, reminiscent of the 19th-century poorhouse (*see* UNEMPLOYMENT RELIEF CAMPS). In Alberta nonstatus Indians and Métis could only collect welfare on "halfbreed" agricultural colonies. By 1939 a majority of Canadians realized that it was the economic and social systems that had failed and not the individuals.

WWII temporarily solved the unemployment problem, but Canadians demanded more economic security and an end to stigmatizing health and welfare programs. In 1940 the federal government introduced the Unemployment Insurance Act; in 1943, as part of its envisaged postwar planning, it published the *Report on Social Security for Canada*, by Leonard C. MARSH, which created a public sensation and provided a blueprint for a comprehensive social-security system. It emphasized the use of contributory social insurance and a universal system of family allowances and health care. Although the report had caught the imagination of the country, the federal government selected only some of its ideas and ignored its central advice — the need for comprehensive, co-ordinated planning. In 1944 the government introduced the Family Allowances Act, under which, without a means test, all Canadian mothers, on behalf of their children under the age of 16, would receive an allowance. The gross cost of the program, estimated at $250 million for the first year, was until then the largest expenditure on a social-security program. In 1945 the federal government offered a social-security plan to the provinces involving a cost-shared medical and hospital insurance scheme, federal assumption of old-age pensions for Canadians over the age of 70 and a cost-shared plan for pensions for people 65 to 69, plus federal responsibility for the unemployed, but in a squabble over revenue sharing the 2 levels of government abandoned the plan. In 1951 a universal old-age pension system was instituted. All Canadians, at the age of 70, were now entitled to receive a pension, an acknowledgement that upon retirement the majority of Canadians had little or no income or savings.

Canadians were also aware that access to health care was blocked for many by their inability to afford it and that public-health insurance offered a solution. Saskatchewan's highly successful hospital insurance plan, which covered every Saskatchewan resident, was launched in 1945. It prompted residents in other provinces to seek similar protection. In 1957 the federal government agreed to share in the cost of provincial hospital insurance programs, and by 1961 all 10 provinces had provided them. The charity ward of hospitals vanished overnight, but doctors' bills were still beyond the means of many people. The Saskatchewan government, again a pioneer, introduced a universal, tax-supported, publicly administered medical-care insurance plan, the first province or state in N America to do so. In 1966 the federal government passed the Medical Care Insurance Act, according to which it would contribute to provincial medical-care insurance plans provided that benefits should include general practitioner and specialist services; that they cover residents of a province on uniform terms and conditions; that they were publicly administered; and that the benefits were portable (*see* HEALTH POLICY). By 1971 all provinces were participating under these terms.

Earlier, in 1965, the federal government had passed the CANADA PENSION PLAN, which provided social-insurance protection for retirement, disability and the provision of survivors' benefits. The plan, designed to improve the adequacy of old-age pensions, was also an acknowledgement that a majority of workers were not protected by an occupational pension plan. A national program (with the exception of Québec, which legislated the equivalent QUÉBEC PENSION PLAN), it meant that workers did not lose their membership when changing jobs or moving to another province. The compulsory plan covers almost the entire labour force. It was also the first Canadian social-security program to provide for automatic increases in benefits in accordance with increases in the cost of living.

A Senate inquiry (1969) revealed that 1 in 4 Canadians lived below the poverty line and that close to 2 million of these were working poor — people whose income from employment was insufficient to lift them out of poverty. Saskatchewan (1974), Québec (1979) and Manitoba (1980) began to supplement the income of working-poor families. A 1975 federal proposal, the result of a 3-year, federal-provincial,

Percentage of Old Age Security Pensioners Receiving the Guaranteed Income Supplement, Canada

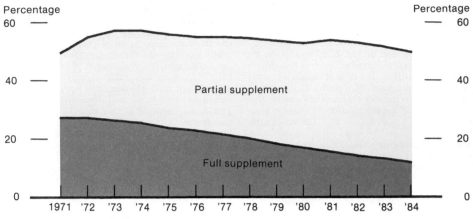

Source: Statistics Canada, Catalogue 86-201.

social-security review, offered to share the cost of an income-supplement scheme for working-poor families, but it was rejected by the provinces as being too expensive. In 1967 the Guaranteed Income Supplement program provided an income-tested supplement to pensioners with little or no income other than their universal old-age-security pension. In 1975 the federal government also introduced the Spouses' Allowance, paid to old-age pensioners' spouses aged 60 to 64 when other income is less than adequate. Family allowances were raised in 1973, and in 1978 the federal government introduced a child tax credit that paid $200 for each child under 18 to families where total family income did not exceed $18 000 annually, but this credit was raised by reducing family allowances. Under the Canada Assistance Plan (1966), another federal cost-sharing program, the federal government supports provincial social-assistance programs which provide both financial and other services. During the 1970s the provinces also began providing supplements to their most needy pensioners and offering tax credits for housing costs.

From the prospect of the 1980s, Canadians can look back to 1874 when the bill for education and public welfare for all of Canada was a scant $4 million. In 1985, federal expenditures in the "social affairs" envelope is projected at $41 billion. This figure reflects not only the increase in social security coverage, but also the impact of the recent inflationary period, the recession of 1981-82 with its record high unemployment, the increase in the population generally and the rise in the number of Canadians over the age of 65 specifically. Some 4 million Canadians still live below the poverty line. Families headed by women are particularly vulnerable, as are minority groups such as the disabled and native people. The social-security system now provides a measure of protection for the majority of Canadians (as the recession of 1981-82 proved), but a residue of the old poor law remains in the administration of provincial social-assistance programs jointly financed by the federal government through the Canada Assistance Plan. These programs, according to their critics, continue to stigmatize clients and rob them of their dignity. Some authorities suggest that the concept of a guaranteed annual income is the next stage of social-security development and may someday eliminate all trace of poor-law practice from Canada.   DENNIS GUEST

Reading: K.G. Banting, The Welfare State and Canadian Federalism (1982); Dennis Guest, The Emergence of Social Security in Canada (1980); L.D. Marsh, Report on Social Security for Canada (1975); M.G. Taylor, Health Insurance and Canadian Public Policy (1978).

Social Work is intended to assist individuals, families and communities in understanding and solving their personal and social problems. Historically social work was associated with charities and volunteer assistance to the needy. The professionalization of social work was a consequence of industrialization and the conviction that rational solutions to social problems were possible.

Prior to 1860 social work in Canada meant, as it did in England and the US, relief of the poor, whose situation was generally believed to result from weakness of character, exemplified in a publication of the London Charity Organization Society: "If the head of the family makes no provision in case of his death part of the responsibility falls on his wife and it is doubtful whether the widow ought to be relieved of the consequences by charitable aid."

The Associated Charities, part of a movement originating in England in 1869, was established in Canada in 1881. It differed from similar organizations of the time in stressing the importance of systematic investigation rather than the simple provision of relief. By 1912 the Associated Charities were being replaced by municipal social-service commissions; simultaneously the social casework method of investigation was being popularized in Canada by followers of Mary Richmond, one of America's social-work pioneers. In 1914 a training program for social workers was established at University of Toronto, followed (1918) by a similar program at McGill. In 1926 the Canadian Association of Social Workers was formed. The first charter members were drawn principally from child and family welfare agencies, municipal departments and settlement houses. Social work grew slowly during the 1920s and 1930s. The GREAT DEPRESSION years placed heavy demands on social-work agencies, but governments were reluctant to promote the advancement of trained social workers in universities. Only 2 new training programs opened during this period — one at UBC (1928) and the other at U de Montréal (1939). After WWII the profession expanded, along with the development of medicare, hospital insurance, old-age PENSIONS, SOCIAL SECURITY, homes for the aged and special services for the handicapped; many agencies supplying these services employed social workers. In 1941 the census reported 1767 social workers in Canada; by 1981 there were over 27 590.

Some of Canada's principal social reformers have been associated with the social-work profession, including J.S. WOODSWORTH, founder of the CCF; Charlotte WHITTON, child-welfare activist and mayor of Ottawa; Leonard MARSH, author of an influential report on social security; and

Harry Cassidy, writer and director of University of Toronto School of Social Work for many years.

Training and Specialization At the undergraduate level (BSW), courses include human behaviour and social development, social services, social security, and social intervention (eg, counselling, group work, community organizations, administration, etc). At the graduate level (MSW, DSW or PhD), students specialize in various fields of study (eg, family and child welfare, mental health, corrections, etc). Masters' programs in social work are offered at Carleton, UBC, U of Manitoba, Dalhousie, McGill, Memorial, U of Regina, U of T, Wilfrid Laurier, U of Windsor; and doctoral programs are offered at McGill and U of T. New specialties of social work develop in response to personal and social problems created by changes in society. Across Canada, at least 4 specializations are recognized: counselling, group work, community development and social administration, although they share a common body of theory and practice integral to the profession as a whole. As counsellors, social workers work with individuals and families suffering difficulties from problems such as marital breakdown, parenting inadequacies, CHILD ABUSE, ALCOHOLISM and drug abuse, as well as those that may arise in schools or in the workplace. Group work generally refers to programs in which participants are not necessarily closely related. Sometimes the groups are organized around social-recreational programs, eg, senior-citizen centres or day care; sometimes they are formed to deal with personal problems or simply share common experiences. Community development refers to activities aimed at improving social conditions, co-ordinating services or promoting public-policy changes. Emphasis is on the development of community leaders and self-help initiatives.

Finally, with the growth of public and voluntary services, social workers are increasingly required to specialize in social administration, ie, the management of a wide range of services and the direction of large bureaucracies.

Field of Practice Many social workers are employed in public social services contributing to the care and rehabilitation of the physically and mentally ill, youth, the aged, the mentally handicapped or the disabled. SCHOOL BOARDS engage social workers to counsel students with emotional and social problems. Settlement houses, community centres, senior-citizen centres and hostels hire social workers to work with groups. Some social workers are employed in industry to assist employees with personal problems. In the corrections field, social workers counsel offenders, prisoners and parolees. Some are employed as organizers in social-planning agencies, community organizations and trade unions, while others work as administrators for government or voluntary associations. Some teach in universities and community colleges. A few are self-employed as private practitioners.

Institutions, Societies and Journals The Canadian Assn of Social Workers (CASW), a national, professional organization, is a federation of provincial and territorial associations representing about 8500 members; 66% of members are female, 33% are male, reflecting the fact that social work has traditionally been a female occupation. The CASW establishes a code of ethics, issues guidelines for practice and publishes books on social-work/social-welfare systems. The federal and provincial associations have been active in helping to develop social-service and social-security programs in Canada. The Canadian Assn of Schools of Social Work (CASSW) is the accreditation body for schools of social work. It promotes research and scholarly publications. A bachelor's degree (BSW) is a prerequisite for professional practice. Principal professional journals in Canada include *The Social Worker, Canadian Social Work Review, Service Social* and *Intervention.*

Future of Social Work Despite the significant changes in the discipline over the last 80 years, and its evolution from a residual function in early industrial society to an institutional function in advanced industrial society, controversy still prevails within the profession, as within the larger society, about the extent to which welfare services should be institutionally integrated into society. Some social workers, for example, believe social services should be universally available to all Canadians as a right, while others believe that programs should be offered selectively. Some social workers are persuaded that social security helps to safeguard the dignity of the individual, others believe that there is too much government intrusion into the daily lives of people. The resolution of these debates will inevitably affect the future development of social work in Canada.   GLENN DROVER

Socialism, a political doctrine focusing on the economic order in society and on the broad differences in the people's circumstances produced by economic factors. It proposes STATE intervention to lessen inequality of conditions in society, with social and economic planning as the key. Socialism has enjoyed such a wide expression in so many countries by so many parties and governments that many politicians today eschew the term to avoid confusion. What was "socialism" in 1940 is now "SOCIAL DEMOCRACY" or, among the bolder, "democratic socialism." Socialism did not originate with Karl Marx and not all socialism is MARXISM. Marx, however, gave the idea its most forceful and elaborate expression, postulating not only that a revolution of the workers was necessary, but that it was historically inevitable. Many interpreters have elaborated and reinterpreted Marx's ideas. A socialist today would believe in the active involvement of the state to ensure an equitable society — one in which the major means of production, distribution and supply are either owned or closely controlled by the state. Socialism places more emphasis on the goals of the community than on those of the individual. Obviously, this is a broad definition with which many socialists would disagree, but such diversity is the nature of modern socialism. In Canada the most important socialist political party began in 1933 as the CO-OPERATIVE COMMONWEALTH FEDERATION, which in 1961 became the NEW DEMOCRATIC PARTY. The first socialist government in N America was Saskatchewan's CCF government, formed in 1944 by T.C. DOUGLAS.
       WALTER D. YOUNG

Socialist Party of Canada (SPC) emerged in 1904 when the Socialist Party of British Columbia, a group of Marxists influential in BC mining camps and among BC trade unionists, merged with the Canadian Socialist League. By 1910 it had spread from coast to coast. Members of the SPC held the revolutionary view (known as "impossiblism") that attempts to reform the capitalist system were useless, and that militant political action was necessary in order to destroy the wage system and usher in the co-operative commonwealth. The party's support waned after the collapse of the general strikes of 1919 when most workers adopted a reformist stance and their organizations a gradualist strategy. Many of the activists in the SPC who continued to reject reformism and labourism later joined the COMMUNIST PARTY OF CANADA.   J.T. MORLEY

Society of Friends, *see* QUAKERS.

Sociology is the study of human relationships, of the rules and norms that guide them, and of the development of institutions and movements that conserve and change society. Sociological methodology includes the analysis of data obtained through questionnaires and surveys, the analysis of official statistics, the observation of human interaction and the study of historical records. Theories developed from the analysis of such data are subjected to testing, modification and further verification by continuing research. Within the discipline of sociology there are numerous specializations and subspecializations. Sociology of the FAMILY, of WORK and the professions, of education, and of political, economic and labour organizations are among the major specializations in the discipline today. Others include CRIMINOLOGY, statistics, social DEMOGRAPHY, and sociology of religion, of ETHNIC AND RACE RELATIONS, of sport, of sex roles, of AGING and of knowledge.

Between 1940 and 1960, when sociology was being established in N America as an academic discipline, the drive toward scientific status led to the separation of sociology from the humanistic disciplines and the greater internal specialization of fields within the discipline, although since its emergence sociology has been closely allied for some purposes with social PSYCHOLOGY and social ANTHROPOLOGY. The 1970s witnessed a strong interdisciplinary movement, a broadening of the scope of sociological inquiry toward the inclusion of historical, economic and political aspects of human relationships. Hence the work of many sociologists has overlapped with that of scholars outside their discipline. Sociologists now study the historical development of class relations and its relationship to economic, political and ideological processes.

Origins of the Discipline and Historical Development in Canada The intellectual origins of sociology are numerous, but as a special science it originated in France. Auguste Comte gave the name "sociology" to the new discipline and outlined a philosophy (positivism) that shaped its development. Positivism holds that only actual phenomena and facts constitute knowledge. Emile Durkheim contributed most to the emergence of sociology in France, by combining empirical research and theories in the development of a general set of propositions about social relations. The 2 other traditions that have significantly shaped modern sociology are grounded in the works of the German sociologists Max Weber and Karl Marx. The common problem that Durkheim, Weber and Marx confronted was the historical transition from feudalism to capitalism and its effects on social integration, the organization of power and SOCIAL CLASS relations. Coincident with this transition were the rapid and profound changes, often involving individual and social disorganization, that resulted from the Industrial Revolution.

In N America, the first academic course in sociology was introduced at Yale in 1876; University of Chicago was the first to offer a doctorate in sociology in 1893. Sociology had not made an appearance in Canada as an academic discipline in the 1890s, but by 1920 courses in sociology were being offered in a number of disciplines and were included in theology curricula. The Canadian Political Science Association, formed in 1913, accepted sociologists as members. The association was inactive during WWI and was not reactivated until 1929. The first academic appointment in sociology in Canada was that of Carl A. Dawson in 1922 at McGill. Honours programs were established at McGill in 1926 and at U of T in 1932. Still, in 1941, Harold INNIS, one of the founding figures in Canadian social science, described sociology as the "Cinderella of the social sciences." The work of S.D. CLARK at U of T at this time was important to the subsequent recognition of sociology as a legitimate field of study, despite opposition from the entrenched disciplines. Significant SOCIAL SCIENCE research had been underway from the late 1880s to the late 1930s. This included the work of Marius BARBEAU, Carl Dawson, Léon GÉRIN, Diamond JENNESS and Everett Hughes on Canada's indigenous peoples; the human ecological approach to urban growth and planning; and studies of ethnic groups in the West, education and Québec's rural population, and ethnic relations (particularly FRANCOPHONE-ANGLOPHONE RELATIONS). By 1940 a substantial body of material on Canadian economic, political and social development existed.

While the social problems of the times were common to all parts of Canada, sociology developed differently in the anglophone and francophone academic communities. Francophone sociology in Québec originally took its inspiration from the encyclical *Rerum Novarum* (1891). The Roman Catholic Church defined the limits and content of early francophone sociology, and the Catholic Action Movement became the vehicle for a Catholic sociology in Québec. By the early 1930s, Catholic sociology was taught at Laval and U de M. From the outset sociology was viewed as an instrument for "national" development in Québec and helped foster ideological self-awareness and critical debate.

During the 1940s, Father Georges-Henri Lévesque of Laval was a leading force in a movement to establish a secularized sociology in Québec. He encouraged a greater scientific sophistication, and directed the attention of francophone sociologists away from "la survivance" of French Canadian traditions and to the aim of aiding the INDUSTRIALIZATION and modernization of the Québec economy and society. This secularized view of sociology and its role in Québec reinforced a profederalist ideology. In the 1960s a new nationalism appeared in Québec sociology in support of an ideology of self-determination and sovereignty for Québec society. With the growth of the state bureaucracy in Québec during the 1960s and 1970s, sociologists became directly involved in the programming and administration of the new society.

Both anglophone and francophone sociology share stylistic similarities, but certain traditions are more influential in one than the other. For instance, in Québec, perspectives from Europe (and from France in particular) are more evident than they are elsewhere in Canada, where American influence is relatively stronger.

Beginning in the 1960s, sociology underwent a spectacular expansion everywhere in Canada. In 1960 to 1961 there were 61 sociologists in Canadian universities, no doctorates were awarded in sociology and only 2 had been awarded up to that date. During the next 2 decades, sociology was established in virtually every academic institution; in 1981, 41 doctorates and 136 masters degrees in sociology were conferred by Canadian universities. In 1960 sociology had been organized at the departmental level in only 4 universities in Canada: Carleton, McMaster, Saskatchewan and U de M. In 1981 there were 34 departments of sociology, and 13 departments in which sociology and anthropology were combined. Five of these departments of sociology were francophone and 2 were bilingual.

Applications Sociological knowledge is used indirectly in teaching and in everyday work of many kinds, and is applied directly to policy issues either through research conducted during the course of officially sponsored inquiries or through independent research. Sociology is taught primarily at the university level, although since the 1970s sociological content has permeated courses at the community-college and high-school levels. In teaching, research is used not so much as an end in itself but as a means of conveying the perspectives of sociology. Indirectly, sociological research also informs the everyday activities of people in certain jobs, eg, those employed in administration, education, marketing, recreation, SOCIAL WORK and other sectors — although it is impossible to gauge the extent of such practical applications.

It is easier to determine how sociological re-

search feeds directly into the deliberations of those responsible for shaping social policy. For example, the recommendations of the Royal Commission on Health Services (1961-63) were strongly influenced by sociological research (4 studies and numerous submissions) conducted on behalf of the commission. The reports of this commission helped shape Canadian HEALTH POLICY. Of similar importance, in the shaping of LANGUAGE POLICIES and cultural policies, were the recommendations of the Royal Commission on BILINGUALISM AND BICULTURALISM (1963-67). Sociologists contributed to the Royal Commission on the STATUS OF WOMEN IN CANADA (1967-69); some of the recommendations have been accepted as public policy. Research by sociologists was significant in developing the recommendations of La Commission d'enquête sur l'enseignement au Québec (1964-66), often referred to as the Parent Commission after its chairman. The educational reforms based on these recommendations drastically altered Québec's educational system. Sociological research in the early 1970s helped shape many of the recommendations of the Gendron Commission (Commission d'enquête sur la situation de la langue française au Québec), the policy implications of which have been profound.

Other public inquiries to which sociologists have made significant contributions include the Senate committees on poverty and on aging, and institutional research under independent and quasi-governmental sponsorship. In this latter category are the projects undertaken by the former Saskatchewan Centre for Community Studies at U of Sask; by the Institute of Social and Economic Research at Memorial U; and by the Bureau d'aménagement de l'est du Québec at Laval.

As these examples show, much social research and planning in Canada has been conducted collectively under the auspices of government and university research institutes. Canada has also been the subject of significant research and writing by independent scholars. On the relationship between culture and environment and their effects on social and economic life in Québec, 2 pioneer studies were particularly important: Léon Gérin's *Le Type economique et social des canadiens* (1937); and Everett C. Hughes's *French Canada in Transition* (1943). French sociologist Marcel Giraud's *Le Métis canadien* (1947) remains the most comprehensive study of the Métis. S.D. Clark's *Church and Sect in Canada* (1948) was a major study of religious and political movements in the West. American sociologist S.M. Lipset's *Agrarian Socialism* (1950) was a definitive study of the rise of the socialist movement and the rise of the CO-OPERATIVE COMMONWEALTH FEDERATION. John PORTER's *The Vertical Mosaic* (1965) challenged the conventional view of Canada as an egalitarian society. More than any other scholar of his time, Porter influenced the theoretical, empirical and critical directions of modern Canadian sociology. Many contemporary scholars have turned their attention to the effects of a resource-based economy on national and regional social organization. Rex Lucas's *Minetown, Milltown, Railtown* (1971) has influenced the direction of many of these studies.

Fields of Work Most of the professional sociologists in Canada have masters or doctoral degrees in that subject. Of course, not all who have taken advanced degrees in sociology are professional sociologists; many are employed as administrators, executives, entrepreneurs and in other capacities. Because precise figures are lacking, it is impossible to say how many people in Canada are working as professional sociologists, but it is safe to assume that the majority who do so are full-time university teachers. According to one report, the number of full-time university teachers of sociology in Canada for the 1979 to 1980 academic year was 962. Perhaps scores of

others teach full-time at the community-college level. The number of professional sociologists working in research in government and other public and private agencies has been estimated at about 400.

Until 1956, when the Sociology-Anthropology Chapter of the Canadian Political Science Association was formed, there was no national organization that brought sociologists together. A decade later, this chapter was transformed into an officially bilingual independent organization, the Canadian Sociology and Anthropology Association. Several affiliated regional associations represent sociologists in western Canada, Ontario, Québec and the Atlantic provinces. One of these, l'Association canadienne des sociologues et anthropologues de la langue française, caters especially to Francophones.

Sociologists in Canada publish their scholarly work within and outside of Canada. Within Canada their articles are published primarily in 4 journals: the *Canadian Journal of Sociology; Canadian Review of Sociology and Anthropology; Récherches sociographiques;* and *Sociologie et sociétés.* Besides these outlets, the publications of sociologists often appear in such journals as *Cahiers québécois de démographie; Canadian Ethnic Studies; Canadian Journal of Criminology; Canadian Studies in Population; Canadian Women's Studies;* and *Studies in Political Economy,* to mention a few.

DONALD R. WHYTE AND FRANK G. VALLEE

Reading: Donald Whyte, "Sociology and the Nationalist Challenge in Canada," *Journal of Canadian Studies* 19, 4 (1984-85).

Sod Houses, built primarily before WWI in the PRAIRIE WEST, where sod was the only construction material at hand. Sod buildings were inexpensive ($4 or $5), the only cost being for windows, hinges and perhaps boards for a door and framing. First, long, straight furrows generally 30-40 cm wide were ploughed, preferably in dry sloughs since fibrous grass roots there prevented soil from crumbling. Sods, some 10 cm deep, were cut into 60-80 cm lengths. Placed grass-side down they were used like bricks, usually with 2 courses side by side making thick, tight walls. Spaces were left for the door and windows. For the roof, boards or light poplar poles, extending from the side walls to a ridge pole, were covered with hay, then with a layer of thinner sod. The average house was 18' by 24' (5.5 by 7.3 m), the minimum size required under HOMESTEADING law. The interior walls might be covered by paper or cloth, or plastered with a clay mixture and whitewashed. Houses were often partitioned with blankets or poles; many women, by using curtains and other touches, made their sod houses attractive and homey. Unfortunately, sod roofs leaked; one day's rain outside resulted in 2 inside. However, sod houses were warm in winter and cool in summer, and served their purpose well.

SHEILAGH S. JAMESON

Sod houses were common first dwellings on the prairies prior to WWI. The house shown is at the Steinbach Mennonite Museum, Steinbach, Man (*photo by John deVisser/Masterfile*).

Soft-Drink Industry comprises companies that manufacture nonalcoholic beverages and carbonated mineral waters or concentrates and syrups for the manufacture of carbonated beverages. Naturally occurring bubbling or sparkling mineral waters have been popular for thousands of years: the ancient Greeks believed that such waters had medicinal properties and bathed in them regularly; the Romans established resorts around mineral springs throughout Europe. In the 1500s the village of Spa in Belgium became famous for its waters, which by the early 1600s were sold, in bottles, as far away as London.

Development of the first man-made sparkling or carbonated water is credited to Joseph Priestley, the British scientist who discovered oxygen. In 1772 he invented a method of "pushing" carbon dioxide into water by dissolving it under pressure, thus creating fairly long-lasting bubbles. The technique led to development of the soft-drink industry. By the beginning of the 19th century, carbonated water was being made commercially in France and N America; shortly thereafter, flavours (normally fruit concentrates) were added to enliven the taste. In the 1820s, small carbonated bottling operations were established in Canada, producing carbonated drinks in refillable bottles which were merchandised as medicinal elixirs or tonics. Most soft drinks are still carbonated to give drinks a "tangy bite" and stimulate the tongue. Furthermore, because scent is an important part of taste, the flavours carried as vapours in the bubbles enhance taste.

The principle of "pushing" carbon dioxide is still used, but now the water is first purified in a process known as "polishing." Cooled carbon dioxide is then injected at pressures of 275-550 kilopascals. Some of the early drinks bottled in Canada were called Birch Beer, Ginger Beer, Sarsaparilla, Sour Lemon, None-Such Soda Water and Cream Soda. The first carbonated beverage or "pop" bottles were sealed with corks held tightly in place with a wire binding. Because they had to be stored neck down so the cork would not dry and allow the carbonation to leak away, they were manufactured with rounded bottoms. By the mid-1800s, soft drinks sold in Canada were packaged in 8-ounce round-bottom bottles for about 25 cents a dozen, except ginger beer, which was sold in draught form from wooden kegs. Wired cork closures were used until about 1884 with Codd's Patented Globe Stoppers (25 types in all). Such closures were replaced by the Hutcheson Spring Stopper. The crown cap was introduced around 1905 and improved versions are still widely used, although they are gradually being replaced, especially on larger containers, with reclosable screw caps.

Other packaging innovations since the mid-1960s include canned carbonated beverages, nonreturnable glass bottles and containers made from rigid plastics. However, an effort is being made, often through provincial legislation, to increase the use of returnable glass containers to reduce waste.

In the industry's early years the number of carbonated-beverage plants increased steadily, most serving small regional markets. In 1929 the industry was made up of 345 production plants and the value of shipments reached $12.3 million. By 1960 the number of plants had increased to 502 and the value of sales to $172.7 million. Subsequently, consolidation began, prompted by improved production, packaging and distribution facilities. By 1973, 337 plants were in production and the value of shipments was $484 million. In 1982, with sales of about $1.3 billion, the industry had 203 plants in production: Nfld had 3; PEI, 1; NS, 8; NB, 7; Qué, 75; Ont, 64; Man, 8; Sask, 10; Alta, 14; BC, 13. Production volume has also increased dramatically:

in 1939, soft-drink bottlers produced about 162 million litres of carbonated beverages; by 1967, production passed 758 million litres; in 1982, shipments were estimated at over 1.4 billion litres.

The industry is regulated by both federal and provincial agencies, 3 of the most important being Consumer and Corporate Affairs (responsible for the Consumer Packaging and Labelling Act), Health and Welfare Canada (which administers the Food and Drug Act) and Environment Canada (which focuses on environmental matters). The industry is represented by the Canadian Soft Drink Association in Toronto and by several provincial associations.

The recent introduction of diet carbonated beverages is changing the industry's profile. Several years ago, in response to increasing consumer diet consciousness, the industry introduced the first successful sugar-free diet drinks using the artificial sweetener cyclamate. But questions were raised about the safety of this additive and, based on existing scientific data, Health and Welfare Canada banned its use in Canadian commercial FOODS AND BEVERAGES. This decision, estimated to have cost the industry more than $15 million, was a setback to diet-drink development. The industry turned to saccharin, but this too was eventually banned. Now, a new sugar-free additive, aspartame, has been approved for use in diet soft drinks, and the cyclamate/saccharin situation is not expected to recur because aspartame consists of amino acids, which occur naturally. Aspartame-sweetened diet drinks have had a dramatic effect on the Canadian carbonated-beverage industry. Just before the saccharin ban in 1977, diet drinks accounted for about 10% of the soft-drink market; following the ban the diet share dropped to about 2%, consisting of beverages partially sweetened with small amounts of sugar. In 1982, the first full year that aspartame was used in Canada, diet drinks increased by 15.2% of total soft-drink sales, while the total soft-drink industry grew 8%. This single development has encouraged strong growth in the industry and carbonated beverages will continue to see steady growth in coming years.
ROBERT F. BARRATT

Softball, *see* BASEBALL.

Soil, upper, unconsolidated, usually weathered layer of planet Earth. Seldom more than a metre thick, soils constitute a skin on Earth resembling, in relative thickness, a paper cover on a beach ball. Soils influence air and water quality and are the basis for most food and fibre production. Linking cycles of nutrients with the hydrologic cycle, soils are central to all terrestrial ecosystems. Unlike other parts of the solid Earth, soil is characterized by life: most energy trapped in terrestrial ecosystems is dissipated by organisms forming part of soil. Soils change with time, forming over many centuries and often being destroyed in decades.

Soil Classification Classification involves arranging individual units with similar characteristics into groups. Soil classification contributes to organizing and communicating information about soils and to showing relationships among soils and environments. It also provides a means for showing on maps the kinds of soils in the landscape.

The land area of Canada (excluding inland waters) is approximately 9 180 000 km², of which about 1 375 000 km² (15%) is rock land. The remainder is classified according to the Canadian system of soil classification, which groups soils into sets of classes at 5 levels or categories, ie, from most general to most specific, order, great group, subgroup, family, series. There are 9 orders, several thousand series. Thus the system makes it possible to consider soils in different degrees of detail. The classes are defined

as specifically as possible to permit uniformity of classification. Limits between classes are arbitrary as there are few sharp divisions of the soil continuum in nature. The classification system will change as soils knowledge grows through soil mapping and research in Canada and elsewhere. It is hoped that ultimately all national systems will give way to an international one.

Order The 9 classes in this category are based on properties of the pedon reflecting major soil environment factors (especially climatic factors) and dominant soil-forming processes.

Great Group classes are formed by subdividing order classes on the basis of soil properties that reflect differences in soil-forming processes (eg, kinds and amounts of organic matter in surface soil horizons).

Subgroup classes are formed by subdividing great group classes according to the kinds of horizons present in the pedon, and their arrangement.

Family classes are formed by subdividing subgroup classes on the basis of parent material characteristics (eg, proportions of SAND and CLAY) and soil temperature and moisture regimes.

Series classes are formed by subdividing family classes according to detailed properties of the pedon (eg, horizon thickness and structure).

Orders and Great Groups

The orders are discussed according to the sequence followed in classifying a pedon.

Cryosolic Order includes soils having PERMAFROST (permanently frozen material) within one metre of the surface (2 m if the soil is strongly cryoturbated, ie, disturbed by frost action). As permafrost is a barrier to roots and water, the active layer (seasonally thawed material) above it may become a saturated, semifluid material in spring. Commonly the permafrost layer near the surface contains abundant ICE. Melting of ice and frozen materials, resulting from disturbance of the surface vegetation (boreal forest or TUNDRA), may cause slumping of the soil and disruption of roads, pipelines and buildings. Cryosolic soils, occupying about 3 672 000 km² (about 40%) of Canada's land area, are dominant in much of the YT and the NWT and occur in northern areas of all but the Atlantic provinces.

The order, containing 3 great groups, was defined in 1973, after soil and terrain surveys in the Mackenzie Valley yielded new knowledge about the properties, genesis and significance of these soils. Turbic Cryosols have a patterned surface (hummocks, stone nets, etc) and mixed horizons or other evidence of cryoturbation (*see* PERIGLACIAL LANDFORMS). Static Cryosols lack marked evidence of cryoturbation; they are associated with sandy or gravelly materials. Organic Cryosols are composed dominantly of organic materials (eg, PEAT). Because organic material acts as an insulator, Organic Cryosols occur further S than the boundary of continuous permafrost.

Organic Order soils are composed predominantly of organic matter in the upper half metre (over 30% organic matter by weight) and do not have permafrost near the surface. They are the major soils of peatlands (eg, SWAMP, bog, fen). Most organic soils develop from the accumulation of plant materials from species that grow well in areas usually saturated with water. Some organic soils are composed largely of plant materials deposited in lakes; others, mainly of forest leaf litter on rocky slopes in areas of high rainfall. Organic soils cover almost 374 000 km² (4.1%) of Canada's land area: large areas occur in Manitoba, Ontario and northern Alberta, smaller areas in humid regions of Canada.

Organic soils are subdivided into 4 great groups. Fibrisols, common in Canada, consist predominantly of relatively undecomposed organic material with clearly visible plant fragments; resistant fibres account for over 40%

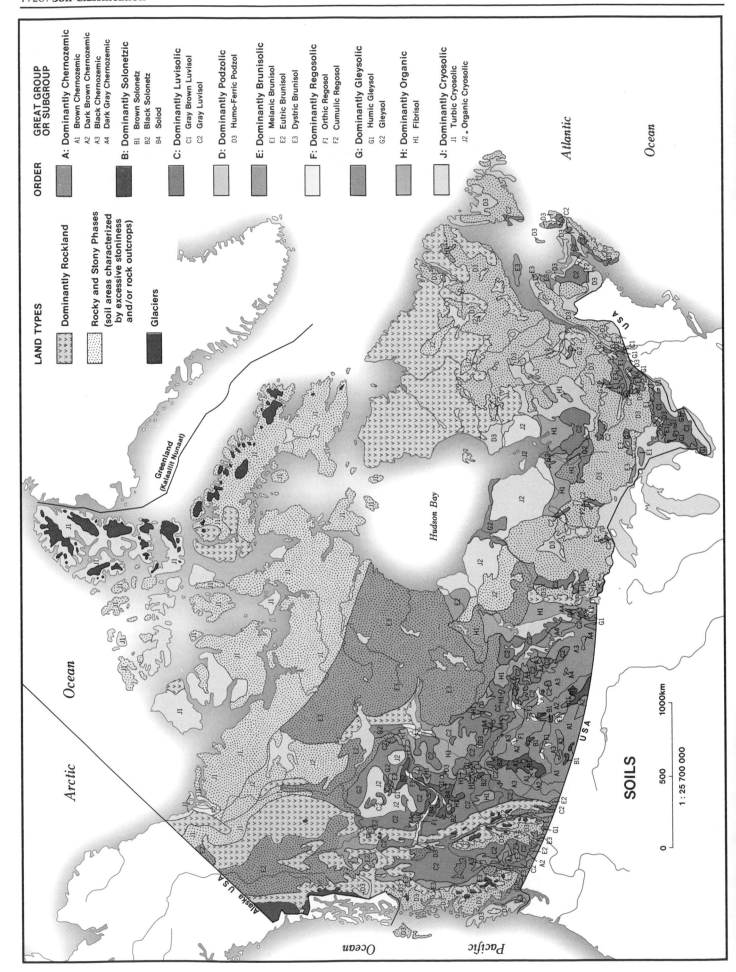

by volume. Most soils derived from *Sphagnum* mosses are Fibrisols. Mesisols are more highly decomposed and contain less fibrous material than Fibrisols (10-40% by volume). Humisols consist mainly of humified organic materials and may contain up to 10% fibre by volume. Folisols consist mainly of thick deposits of forest litter overlying bedrock or fractured bedrock. They occur commonly in wet mountainous areas of coastal BC.

Podzolic Order soils have a B horizon containing accumulations of amorphous materials composed of humified organic matter associated with aluminum and iron. They develop most commonly in sandy materials in areas of cold, humid climate under forest or shrub vegetation. Water moving downward through the relatively porous material leaches out basic elements (eg, calcium), and acidic conditions develop. Soluble organic substances formed by decomposition of the forest litter attack soil minerals in surface horizons, and much of the iron and aluminum released combines with this organic material. When the proportion of aluminum and iron to organic matter reaches a certain level, the organic complexes become insoluble and are deposited in the B horizon. Silicon-aluminum complexes and iron oxides also occur. An Ae (light grey, strongly leached) horizon usually overlies the podzolic B horizon.

Podzolic soils occupy about 1 429 000 km² (15.6%) of Canada's land area and are dominant in vast areas of the humid Appalachian and Canadian Shield regions and in the humid coastal region of BC. They are divided among 3 great groups on the basis of the kind of podzolic B horizon. Humic Podzols have a dark B horizon with a low iron content. They occur mainly in wet sites under humid climates and are much less common than other Podzolic soils. Ferro-Humic Podzols have a dark reddish brown or black B horizon containing at least 5% organic carbon and appreciable amounts (often 2% or more) of aluminum and iron in organic complexes. They occur commonly in the more humid parts of the area of Podzolic soils, eg, coastal BC and parts of Newfoundland and southern Québec. Humo-Ferric Podzols, the most common Podzolic soils in Canada, have a reddish brown B horizon containing less than 5% organic carbon associated with aluminum and iron complexes.

Gleysolic Order soils are periodically or permanently saturated with water and depleted of oxygen. They occur commonly in shallow depressions and level areas of subhumid and humid climate in association with other classes of soil on slopes and hills. After snowmelt or heavy rains, depressions in the landscape may be flooded. If flooding occurs when the soil temperature is above approximately 5°C, microbial activity results in depletion of oxygen within a few days. Under such conditions, oxidized soil components (eg, nitrate, ferric oxide) are reduced. Depletion of ferric oxide removes the brownish colour of many soils, leaving them grey. As the soil dries and oxygen re-enters, the reduced iron may be oxidized locally to bright yellow-brown spots (mottles). Thus, Gleysolic soils are usually identified by their poor drainage and drab grey colour, sometimes accompanied by brown mottles. Gleysolic soils cover about 117 000 km² (1.3%) of Canada's land area.

Three great groups of Gleysolic soils are defined. Humic Gleysols have a dark A horizon enriched in organic matter. Gleysols lack such a horizon. Luvic Gleysols have a leached (Ae) horizon underlain by a B horizon in which clay has accumulated; they may have a dark surface horizon.

Solonetzic Order soils have B horizons that are very hard when dry, swelling to a sticky, compact mass when wet. They usually develop in saline parent materials in semiarid and sub-

humid regions. Properties of the B horizons are associated with sodium ions that cause the clay to disperse readily and swell on wetting, thus closing the large pores and preventing water flow. Solonetzic soils cover almost 73 000 km² (0.7%) of Canada's land area; most occur in southern Alberta, because of the large areas of saline parent material and semiarid climate.

The 3 great groups of Solonetzic soils are based on properties reflecting the degree of leaching. Solonetz have an Ah (dark, organically enriched) horizon overlying the solonetzic B, which occurs usually at a depth of 20 cm or less. The Ae (grey, leached) horizon is very thin or absent. Solodized Solonetz have a distinct Ae horizon between the Ah and the solonetzic B. Solods have a transitional AB or BA horizon formed by degradation of the upper part of the solonetzic B horizon. The developmental sequence of Solonetzic soils is from saline parent material to Solonetz, Solodized Solonetz and Solod. As leaching progresses, the salts and sodium ions may be translocated downward. If leaching proceeds for long enough and salts are removed completely, the solonetzic B may disintegrate completely. The soil would then be classified in another order.

Chernozemic Order soils have an A horizon darkened by the addition of organic matter, usually from the decay of grass roots. The A horizon is neutral to slightly acid and is well supplied with bases such as calcium. The C horizon usually contains calcium carbonate (lime); it may contain salts. Chernozemic soils have mean annual soil temperatures above 0°C and occur in regions of semiarid and subhumid climates. Covering about 468 000 km² (5.1%) of Canada's land area, they are the major class of soils in the southern Interior Plains, where grass was the major type of native vegetation.

The 4 great groups of Chernozemic soils are based upon surface horizon colour, associated with the relative dryness of the soil. Brown soils have brownish A horizons and occur in the driest area of the Chernozemic region. Dark Brown soils have a darker A horizon than Brown soils, reflecting a somewhat higher precipitation and associated higher organic-matter content. Black soils, associated with subhumid climates and tall-grass native vegetation, have a black A horizon which is usually thicker than that of Brown or Dark Brown soils. Dark Gray soils are transitional between grassland Chernozemic soils and the more strongly leached soils of forested regions.

Luvisolic Order soils have eluvial horizons (ie, from which clay has been leached after snowmelt or heavy rains) and illuvial horizons (ie, in which clay has been deposited), designated Ae and Bt, respectively. In saline or calcareous materials clay translocation is preceded by leaching of salts and carbonates. Luvisolic soils occur typically in forested areas of subhumid to humid climate where the parent materials contain appreciable clay. Luvisolic soils cover about 809 000 km² (8.8%) of Canada's land area; large areas occur in the central to northern Interior Plains; smaller areas in all regions S of the permafrost zone.

The 2 great groups of Luvisolic soils are distinguished mainly on the basis of soil temperature. Gray Brown Luvisols have an Ah horizon in which organic matter has been mixed with the mineral material (commonly by earthworm activity), an eluvial (Ae) horizon and an illuvial (Bt) horizon. The mean annual soil temperature is 8°C or higher. The major area of Gray Brown Luvisols is found in the southern part of the Great Lakes-St Lawrence Lowlands. Gray Luvisols have eluvial and illuvial horizons and may have an Ah horizon if the mean annual soil temperature is below 8°C. Vast areas of Gray Luvisols in the Boreal Forest Zone of the Interior Plains have thick, light grey eluvial horizons

underlying the forest litter and thick Bt horizons with clay coating the surface of aggregates.

Brunisolic Order soils include all soils that have developed B horizons but do not conform to any of the orders described previously. Many Brunisolic soils have brownish B horizons without much evidence of clay accumulation, as in Luvisolic soils, or of amorphous materials, as in Podzolic soils. With time and stable environmental conditions, some Brunisolic soils will evolve to Luvisolic soils; others, to Podzolic soils. Covering almost 790 000 km² (8.6%) of Canada's land area, Brunisolic soils occur in association with other soils in all regions S of the permafrost zone.

Four great groups are distinguished on the basis of organic matter enrichment in the A horizon and acidity. Melanic Brunisols have an Ah horizon at least 10 cm thick; they are not strongly acidic, their pH being above 5.5. They occur commonly in southern Ontario and Québec. Eutric Brunisols have the same basic properties as Melanic Brunisols, but do not have an Ah horizon 10 cm thick. Sombric Brunisols have an Ah horizon at least 10 cm thick and are acid, with pH below 5.5. Dystric Brunisols are acidic and do not have an Ah horizon 10 cm thick.

Regosolic Order soils are too weakly developed to meet the limits of any other order. The absence or weak development of genetic horizons may result from a lack of time for development or from instability of material. The properties of Regosolic soils are essentially those of the parent material. Two great groups are defined. Regosols consist essentially of C horizons; they may have an Ah horizon less than 10 cm thick. Humic Regosols have an Ah horizon at least 10 cm thick. Regosolic soils cover about 73 000 km² (0.8%) of Canada's land area.

Subgroups, Families and Series

Subgroups are based on the sequence of horizons; many subgroups intergrade to other soil orders. For example, the Gray Luvisol great group includes at least 7 subgroups, of which the Orthic Gray Luvisol is most typical, the others being defined by additional features. Transitional Gray Luvisols are also defined, eg, Gleyed Gray Luvisol, with rusty mottles indicating an intergrade to Gleysolic soils.

Families Subgroups are divided into families according to parent material properties and soil climate. For example, the Orthic Gray Luvisol subgroup includes soils of a wide range of texture (gravelly sandy loam to clay), different mineralogy and different temperature and water regimes. The soil family designation is much more specific, eg, Orthic Gray Luvisol, clayey, mixed (mineralogy), cold, subhumid.

Series have a vast array of properties (eg, horizon thickness and colour, gravel content, structure) that fall within narrow ranges. Thus, for example, the series name Breton implies all the basic properties of the Luvisolic order, the Gray Luvisol great group, the Orthic Gray Luvisol subgroup and the clayey, mixed, cold, subhumid family of that subgroup as well as series-specific properties. A series name implies so much specific information about soil properties that a wide range of interpretations can be made on the probable suitability of the soil for various uses.
                                    J.A. McKeague

Soil Conservation Soil is Canada's basic RESOURCE: finite, immobile and diverse in quality. Clearly, soil's principal use is in agriculture. AGRICULTURE (including production, marketing, transportation, etc) accounts for one-sixth of Canada's GROSS NATIONAL PRODUCT, and the farmgate value of agricultural products in 1982 was about $20 billion. Technology now available would permit management of soils so that their economic productivity would be sustained and, in many cases, improved. Unfortunately, soils are often managed so that rapid, often irreversible deterioration, or actual removal from agricultural use, occurs.

A major problem of cropland CONSERVATION in Canada is the alienation of land to non-agricultural uses. The greatest concern is for soils which are relatively free of severe physical limitations and capable of supporting field CROPS on a sustained basis. These soils form Canada's prime agricultural land base and total 45 million ha (70% in the Great Plains region). The average rate of transfer from agriculture to urban and related uses (eg, access highways, recreational development, etc) is approximately 20 000 ha per year. The highest rate of urban takeover is occurring in southern Ontario — the area with climate and soil most favourable for agriculture. The rising demand for land for urban development and for rural, nonfarm dwellings is translated into a price which is much higher than the land's true agricultural value. BC and Québec have legislated province-wide agricultural zoning that has reduced drastically the loss of high-quality soil to urban development. Curiously, in Ontario where such losses are the most rapid of any province, there has been little legislation to prevent the loss of agricultural land to urbanization (see URBAN AND REGIONAL PLANNING). The other provinces have left the major responsibility for land-use planning to municipal or regional governments. In general, planners are only now recognizing that agricultural land is more than a resource to be tapped for urban expansion.

Soil quality is a measure of a soil's capability for sustained, profitable production of high-quality food. Major causes of deterioration are water and wind EROSION, depletion of soil organic matter and the spread of salts. Throughout Canada erosion of fertile topsoil and, in some cases, subsoils is accelerating. In the semiarid Great Plains, salinization of the more productive soils has effectively reduced crop yields by over 50% on some 1.5 million ha in Saskatchewan alone. The main reason for the spread of salinity is the very low efficiency of water use for food-crop production (1 cm of water required to produce 23 kg grain per hectare) under the traditional crop-fallow farming system. Cropping practices that depend on continuous cultivation of a single crop (ie, monoculture systems) have also precipitated rapid soil degradation throughout Canada.

Soil Erosion across Canada

Northern Alberta and British Columbia Erosion, primarily by water, in the PEACE R area is a serious problem. It is most severe where erodible, fine-textured soils predominate; long, gentle slopes encourage accumulation of large volumes of runoff water; and impermeable strata restrict downward movement of water. Agronomic factors also contribute, eg, extensive use of summer fallowing and removal of crop residues in autumn.

Prairie Provinces Over large portions of the prairies, external drainage is poorly developed on the dominant glacial landforms; thus, material eroded by water is primarily moved to lower elevations within a field and external losses are not large. A recent study shows a loss of around 15 t/ha per year on the knolls, versus a gain of 40 t/ha per year on the footslopes. Studies conducted in Saskatchewan show that for each 2.5 cm of topsoil lost yields are reduced by about 200 kg/ha. LANDSLIDES and earthflows present problems along all the major prairie rivers.

Ontario and Québec Water erosion, always a serious problem in agriculturally developed areas, has become increasingly significant. A major contributing factor is the popularity of row-cropping systems (potatoes, horticultural crops, corn, soybeans). Soil losses of up to 50 t/ha per year are not uncommon in southern On-

tario. An inventory of several agricultural watersheds in Ontario shows erosion on 37% of the banks, rotational slumping on 25%. Cropping land too close to municipal drains and local streams contributes to accelerated bank erosion. Major earthflows and landslides have occurred on the Leda clays of the Ottawa Valley, and similar earthflows have been reported in Québec (see CHAMPLAIN SEA).

In Québec the reduction in soil quality also results from the conversion of dairy farm soils (cropped one year in CEREALS, 4 years in hay) to continuous cropping of CORN. This practice has resulted in a large drop in soil organic matter content and an accompanying drop in productivity which cannot be corrected with heavy use of fertilizer. In some cases a decrease of up to 55% in organic matter has resulted from intensive tillage associated with row crops.

Nova Scotia Soil loss by sheet, rill and gully erosion has affected all upland cultivated soil. Areas most seriously affected are those used primarily for silage corn, VEGETABLE and potato crops, where annual losses typically range from 20 to 80 t/ha. Increases in silage corn acreages will probably further accelerate the severity of the problem. Stream-bank erosion has affected adversely some 48 000 ha of prime alluvial farmland. Stream-channel improvements are needed to control further deterioration. Shoreline erosion is also a problem, particularly adjacent to the Bay of Fundy and Northumberland Str. The estimated loss of exposed uplands is about 0.6 ha/100 m of shoreline every 100 years.

New Brunswick Monoculture potato production has led to soil compaction, precipitating rates of water erosion 5 times greater than those in a rotation system including potatoes once every 2 years. Stone removal, essential for mechanical potato harvesting, has further accelerated water erosion.

Prince Edward Island While less serious than in other Maritime provinces, water erosion is closely associated with potato production in PEI. Losses on the Charlottetown soil series have been measured at about 20 t/ha per year. In general, maximum water erosion occurs in spring.

Newfoundland Newfoundland, because it has little agricultural land, is the only province which has not reported serious erosion problems.

Soil Conservation Technology

Most of the impressive gains in soil conservation technology have occurred in the area of land management. Preliminary information suggests that it is now technically possible to improve most Canadian agricultural land through cropping systems uniquely adapted to local conditions and through fertilization, timely cultivation, use of improved tillage practices and equipment, terracing, land levelling, drainage, etc. Soil erosion can be held to acceptable levels or, in some cases, reduced to zero. These practices may even lead to an improvement in soil quality.

The obstacles that impede adoption of "conservation farming" are not restricted to a lack of capital. Extensive educational programs are required to enable farmers to benefit from new tools and techniques, and enable agricultural policymakers to establish a socioeconomic environment offering incentives for efficient production. For example, in western Canada, newer, water-efficient soil-conserving farming systems will lead to levels of production ranging from 75% to 100% or more above present levels.

Conservation Legislation

There are many Acts and regulations relating to soil and water conservation in Canada, but few directly address the loss of soil or productivity through erosion or degradation. Those that impinge directly on soil erosion were developed primarily to support farm planning, conservation districts, land use, water resources, con-

servation and development, watersheds, drainage, irrigation, water rights and agricultural zoning. Federal Acts such as the Agricultural Land Rural Development Act and the Prairie Farm Rehabilitation Act address some aspects of soil conservation, particularly on the prairies. However, only the provinces can directly legislate the management or disposition of provincial land resources within their boundaries. Thus in Alberta the control and prevention of erosion and land degradation is embodied in the Soil Conservation Act and the Agricultural Services Board Act. Other provinces have similar legislation which encourages adoption of soil conservation practices and addresses the loss of soil and soil productivity through negligence and misuse. Many, but not all, such Acts embody the principal of ownership responsibility. In general, the major responsibility for land-use planning, particularly as it pertains to soil conservation, is left to the local (municipal) authority.

In Canada soil conservation has traditionally been subject to a laissez-faire policy from governments. All levels of government are responsible, but provincial governments undoubtedly bear the greatest responsibility. In many instances (eg, the Lift Program, 1970), government intervention encouraged practices leading to accelerated erosion, salinity and organic matter loss. While Canada is perhaps unique among developed nations in having no clearly defined soil conservation legislation, this deficiency cannot be criticized unduly since legislation inevitably is a reaction to the problem of soil degradation after it has become serious, rather than a means of addressing prevention before degradation occurs. Thus society's increasing concern for conservation of soils can best be met by providing research, extension education and financial incentive programs which will encourage, but not legislate, conservation farming.

See ACID RAIN; ENVIRONMENTAL LAW; HAZARDOUS WASTES; PRAIRIE FARM REHABILITATION ADMINISTRATION.   D.A. RENNIE

Soil Science, the SCIENCE that deals with soils as a natural RESOURCE. It studies soil formation, classification and mapping, and the physical, chemical and biological properties and fertility of soils as such and in relation to their management for CROP production. This definition, adopted by the Canadian Society of Soil Science, is somewhat dated. In the last 20 years, soil science has expanded to include the study of soil resources in relation to ecology, FORESTRY, Quaternary GEOLOGY, HYDROLOGY, watershed management, ENGINEERING, ARCHAEOLOGY, renewable RESOURCE MANAGEMENT and land-use planning. Biometeorology and REMOTE SENSING are very closely allied to soil science.

Soil has been studied scientifically for approximately 2 centuries. The major concepts were developed over the past 100 years, following the contributions of V.V. Dokuchaiev and others in Russia. These scientists demonstrated that soils are natural bodies, developing as a result of environmental factors. Two important concepts have emerged: pedology considers soil as a natural body, placing less emphasis on its immediate use; edaphology studies soil from the standpoint of higher plants. Pedologists study and classify soil as it occurs in the natural environment; edaphologists consider soil properties as they relate to food and fibre production.

History In Canada soil has been studied systematically for approximately 100 years. The first work, written by Dominion Chemist F.T. Shutt and published in 1893, originated from the Experimental Farms Service of the federal Department of Agriculture. During this early period, work on soils was begun at the Ontario Agricultural College (department of agricultural chemistry) and at Macdonald College, Mc-

Gill (department of agricultural physics). Soil surveying was initiated in 1914 by A.J. Galbraith of the OAC. F.A. Wyatt began soil-survey work in Alberta in 1920; R. Hansen in Saskatchewan 1921. Surveys began in BC in 1931; Qué and NS, 1934; NB, 1938; PEI, 1943; NWT, 1944; Nfld, following its entry into Confederation, 1949. The earliest surveys, financed by provincial governments, were conducted under co-operative programs among the federal and provincial departments of agriculture and the universities.

Many individuals contributed to the development of soil science in Canada, but its founders were professors F.A. Wyatt (Alta), A.H. Joel and R. Hansen (Sask), J.H. Ellis (Man) and G.N. Ruhnke (Ont). E.S. Archibald, former director of the Dominion Experimental Farms Service, played an important role in reviving the soil survey in the 1930s.

Training Professional education is offered mainly through departments of soil science at the universities of BC, Alberta, Saskatchewan, Manitoba and Laval. In Ontario, U of Guelph offers the degree from the dept of land resources science. In Québec, professional education is given at Macdonald College, McGill, by the dept of renewable resources. In addition, universities which do not have departments specializing in soil science often have professors of soil science in departments of GEOGRAPHY.

Most universities offering soil-science programs award bachelor's, master's and doctoral degrees. Although there is some variation in the designation of specialization, some of the major areas of study include soil BIOLOGY, chemistry, physics and fertility; soil classification, genesis, mineralogy and conservation; land classification; and FOREST soils. Often specialization occurs only at the postgraduate level. Students require a background in biology, chemistry, mathematics and physics, and also study agronomy, botany, computer science, ecology, economics, Engish, geology, geomorphology, hydrology, land-use planning, meteorology, microbiology, mineralogy, photogrammetry, remote sensing, resource management, etc. Soil-science education is useful to botanists, plant scientists and civil and agricultural engineers.

Research Research is carried out by various federal agencies, notably Agriculture Canada (through Land Resource Research Institute), ENVIRONMENT Canada, NATIONAL RESEARCH COUNCIL and Canadian Forestry Service. Some provincial departments of agriculture, notably those in Alberta and Ontario, also conduct research. In some provinces (eg, BC) departments of forestry are beginning to do research. University departments conduct research along with teaching. Private companies are supporting work in such areas as forestry, MINING and PETROLEUM resources. Mining and petroleum research focuses on land reclamation.

Research concerned with SURVEYING, mapping and classification remains a joint effort of federal and provincial governments and universities. Several universities (eg, Alberta, Saskatchewan, Guelph, Laval) have established institutes of pedology to co-ordinate these activities. Much of the research conducted in Canada has international applications.

The early work carried out by the dept of soil science, UBC, on organic matter decomposition led the country in soil microbiology. The U of Alberta's dept of soil science carried out innovative research on the management and genesis of Gray Wooded (Gray Luvisol) soils. The use of radioactive isotopes in relation to soil fertility and phosphorus was pioneered at U of Saskatchewan. Study of the effects of application of sewage sludge to soil was initiated at Guelph. Fundamental research on soil properties relating them to the physical behaviour of soils (eg, correlation of shear strength with the electro-chemical properties of clays and forces involved in clay swelling) was carried out at Macdonald College. Researchers from Agriculture Canada have taken a leading role in understanding the reclamation and management of solonetzic soils, and have pioneered studies of soil organic matter, its properties, characteristics and functions in the soil system. The Canada Soil Survey Committee, composed of federal and provincial scientists and university professors, has developed a soil-classification system and unique approaches to soil-survey and soil-information data banks. Québec researchers were in the forefront of farm drainage for intensive agriculture. Soil scientists from Atlantic Canada have developed management techniques for the important potato industry.

Agencies involved in soil research have developed testing procedures for better crop growth on Canadian soils. This process is endless as new varieties of crops, with different requirements, are steadily being developed or introduced into Canada. Research efforts focus on soil EROSION, salinity and conservation and make use of remote sensing and computer-assisted laboratory and field techniques, computer-assisted information systems and automatic graphic and cartographic displays.

Application Most soil research is applied to agriculture, especially to improving crop yields. Thus, much research has focused on the nutrients and trace elements essential for plant growth. Knowledge of soil properties has helped to develop irrigation and drainage projects, promote proper use of fertilizers and PESTICIDES and explain the effect that soil management has on the resource. The availability of soil surveys for much of the country allows planners to make choices, depending on the capability of soils, among agriculture, forestry, recreation and wildlife uses. Highway engineers are beginning to use soil surveys for siting roadways. Other engineers and planners use soil information for locating septic tank disposal fields, effluent irrigation, urban subdivisions, PIPELINE and TRANSPORTATION corridors and for regulating and predicting water supply. Regional planners make use of soil science in developing plans for municipalities and counties. Land appraisers must know soil productivity to make fair assessments of value. Soil properties and genesis are important in understanding terrestrial ecology and groundwater flow. Knowledge of soil genesis aids better understanding of the events that have taken place during the Quaternary, and soils hold the record of facts important in archaeology. Rangeland managers must take into account the productive potential of soil so that range deterioration will not accelerate. Increasingly, agencies involved with land restoration (eg, mining and petroleum exploration companies) are making use of soil-science principles. Soil scientists are employed by federal and provincial governments and consulting firms, forest companies, mining and petroleum companies, banks, real-estate firms and large corporate farms.

Societies and Institutions In Canada the recognized society fostering soil science is the Canadian Society of Soil Science. The CSSS was founded in 1955 from an earlier organization, the Soils Group, which had been formed in 1932 and was closely affiliated with the Canadian Society of Technical Agriculturalists. Today the society has about 384 members. The CSSS is affiliated with the Agricultural Institute of Canada (AIC), the Canadian Geoscience Council and the International Society of Soil Science. In 1978 the society hosted the XI International Society of Soil Science Congress in Edmonton. There were approximately 1125 registered participants from more than 50 countries. The CSSS holds annual meetings and technical sessions and publishes the quarterly *Canadian Journal of Soil Science*. The CSSS honours distinguished soil scientists by bestowing fellowships in the society. Over 30 fellowships have been awarded since 1962, when the program was initiated.   L.M. LAVKULICH

Sointula, BC, pop 567 (1981c), UP, is situated on the S shore of Malcolm I between Vancouver I and the BC mainland, in the Regional Dist of Mt Waddington. Sointula was started at the turn of the century as a utopian community by Finnish political refugee Mattii Kirikka (1862-1915). Sointula means "a place of harmony." The colony was to be an independent enterprise based on logging, fishing and agriculture. By 1902 there were 127 inhabitants, and a sawmill was in operation. But prosperity did not materialize and by 1905 the colony was liquidated. A community remained but its socialistic ideals were discontinued. Today, only a few descendants of the original settlers still live there. Once a totally Finnish-speaking community, Sointula is now mainly English speaking. A few buildings date back to the original settlement, including the "Finnish Order" hall, a firehall and a school. Since 1905 the majority of the population has engaged in fishing. A few small businesses exist on Malcolm I. Many artists also reside here.   ALAN F.J. ARTIBISE

Soirées canadiennes, Les, magazine fd 1861 by H.R. CASGRAIN, A. GÉRIN-LAJOIE, F.A.H. LaRue and J.C. Taché, which published assorted "collection[s] of national literature" in monthly instalments. *Les Soirées canadiennes* followed the spirit of James Huston's *Répertoire national* (1848-50) and welcomed all original writing as long as it was Canadien: legends, poetry, studies of society, novels (which were serialized), travel accounts, historical sketches, biographies, topographies, etc. It attracted such writers as P.J.O. CHAUVEAU, Octave CRÉMAZIE, J.B.A. Ferland, Louis-Honoré FRÉCHETTE, François-Xavier GARNEAU and Étienne PARENT. Five volumes appeared, 1861-65. A dispute with the printers in late 1862 provoked a break between Taché and the others, who quit *Les Soirées* to found an equivalent publication, *Le Foyer canadien*. It appeared until 1866, publishing 4 annual collections, 4 bonus volumes for subscribers and 5 other works, including *Les Anciens Canadiens* and *Les Mémoires* by Philippe AUBERT DE GASPÉ. The so-called "Literary Movement of 1860" revolved around *Soirées* and *Foyer*.   RÉJEAN ROBIDOUX

Solandt, Omond McKillop, research director (b at Winnipeg 2 Sept 1909). He studied at Toronto and began a research career in physiology under C.H. BEST before winning a scholarship to England for advanced training in 1939. When running a London blood bank in 1940 Solandt was asked to investigate why army tank crews were fainting in action. It turned out to be because, when the gun fired, its gases went back into the tank rather than outside. His success led to his becoming one of the chief British army advisers on scientific methods, and he became superintendent of the British Army Operational Research Group, with the rank of colonel.

In 1946 Solandt was recruited by the Canadian government to plan postwar military research, and he became in 1947 the founding chairman of the DEFENCE RESEARCH board. He later was VP for research and development at CANADIAN NATIONAL RAILWAYS, 1956-63, at DE HAVILLAND AIRCRAFT, 1963-66, and he was chancellor of U of T, 1965-71. From 1966 to 1972, Solandt was chairman of the SCIENCE COUNCIL OF CANADA, and thus one of the most influential voices in the SCIENCE POLICY debate of those years. His last annual report as chairman proposed the foundations of the CONSERVER SOCIETY movement. In retirement, Solandt remained active as a company director and consultant, specializing in agricultural research in developing countries.   DONALD J.C. PHILLIPSON

Solar Energy is electromagnetic radiation (including infrared, visible and ultraviolet light) released by thermonuclear reactions in the core of the sun. With a few exceptions (eg, NUCLEAR ENERGY; GEOTHERMAL ENERGY), solar energy is the source of all ENERGY used by mankind. Indirect forms include HYDROELECTRICITY, ocean thermal energy, TIDAL ENERGY and WIND ENERGY; the sun also powers the process of photosynthesis that is the original source of the energy contained in BIOMASS, PEAT, COAL and PETROLEUM. Usually, however, the term solar energy refers to the portion of the sun's radiant energy harnessed for a specific purpose by man-made devices. A further distinction is often made between "active" and "passive" solar systems: active systems capture energy by mechanical means (eg, rooftop collectors, focusing mirrors); passive systems incorporate solar principles into the design of buildings (eg, south-facing windows), without any special mechanical systems. Most energy statistics refer only to active solar-energy systems, thus vastly understating the importance of solar energy. Active solar energy accounts for only a tiny fraction of Canada's energy use, but some studies have indicated that it could meet as much as 5% of the country's energy needs by the year 2025.

Low intensity and high variability have limited the use of active solar energy in Canada. Most purposes demand that the energy be concentrated into useful quantitites and require either a storage system or a supplemental energy source for nighttime and cloudy days. Technologies have been developed for these purposes, but until recently most of them have been too expensive and too untried for widespread use. The main applications of solar-energy technology in Canada have been for space heating, domestic hot water and drying crops and lumber. Photovoltaic cells are used in some remote areas of Canada to power radio transmitters and navigational aids but have been too expensive for widespread use. Other countries have developed solar systems that produce steam to run conventional electrical generators but this work has not been pursued in Canada. At northern latitudes, the solar resource is too seasonally variable for exploitation of many energy applications developed elsewhere. North of the ARCTIC CIRCLE, there are periods during the winter when the sun remains below the horizon.

The Future The sun delivers solar energy to all parts of Canada. Direct use of this ambient energy minimizes the need for expensive and inefficient transmission and delivery systems. The remote expanses of Canada, where costs of conventional nonrenewable energy are high, offer opportunities for developing and using many cost-effective solar technologies. Although the continuing supply of solar energy is free, the capital cost of capture hardware can be expensive; however, simple passive-heating systems may only increase the cost of buildings by 1-5%. Active systems usually require several years of operation to recover the initial cost of operation in fuel savings. Until economic support structures match those for conventional energy sources, solar energy will have difficulty competing in all but remote or small applications. However, once the system is in place, delivery energy costs are stable and immune to market fluctuations that affect conventional nonrenewable energy resources. The Solar Energy Soc of Canada is the national technical organization that promotes education and information dissemination on all aspects of solar-energy use. It is affiliated with the International Solar Energy Soc. The Canadian Solar Industries Assn is a manufacturers' organization promoting industrial development. RICHARD KADULSKI

Reading: J.F. Kreider and F. Kreith, *Solar Energy Handbook* (1979).

Soldiers of Fortune, a term used to describe those ready to serve under any state or person. Often confused with mercenaries who are motivated chiefly by gain, monetary or otherwise, soldiers of fortune seek adventure or serve from idealism and have existed since the earliest times. Columbus was a Genoese in the Spanish Navy, Hessians served the British in the American Revolution and the French and Spanish Foreign Legions attracted soldiers of fortune as did International Brigade units in the Spanish Civil War, and "Chinese" Gordon's Ever-Victorious Army in 19th-century China. Canadian soldiers of fortune often have been professional soldiers or entrepreneurs who have become adventurers by chance as, for example, William WILLIAMS of NS, commander of a Turkish army against the Russians, and Torontonian Alex DUNN who won a VC at Sevastopol during the same war. In other wars Jim Cornwall ran guns to Venezuela, Bill STAIRS seized Katanga (Shaba) for the Belgians, Morris COHEN commanded a Chinese army, and Frank Worthington (founder of the Canadian Armoured Corps) and Jan van den Berg served in the Mexican Revolution. Canadians have served in the Russian Civil War (Ray COLLISHAW, Klondike Joe BOYLE, Jack LECKIE and Walter Sussan), Nicaragua, the Spanish Civil War, the Israeli War of Independence and African wars of the 1960s and 1970s. ALLAN LEVINE

Soleil, Le, a French daily newspaper published in Québec City, was founded as *L'Electeur* in July 1880 by a group of moderate Liberals including Wilfrid LAURIER. Ernest Pacaud, editor for the first 2 decades, is regarded as the true founder, and in Dec 1896 he changed the name to *Le Soleil*. With the advent of Maurice DUPLESSIS in 1936, *Le Soleil* abandoned its Liberal stance and adopted the policy of "reporting only news." In 1974 the paper was bought by UNIMEDIA. Daily circulation was 3000 in 1881, 22 000 in 1907, 49 000 in 1932, 160 000 in 1971 and 150 000 in 1984. Once a national newspaper with reporters across Canada, *Le Soleil* has become a regional newspaper of fluctuating quality. Its principal reporting focuses on the politics, economics and social life of Québec City, with only 5% allotted to international news. *Le Soleil* has always responded to technological change. In 1984 it became a morning newspaper, including a Sunday edition, with a special tabloid sport section. *See also* NEWSPAPERS. ANDRÉ DONNEUR AND ONNIG BEYLERIAN

Solicitor, a lawyer who advises on legal problems, and whose work — contracts of sale, real-estate transactions, wills and trusts — normally does not require court appearance. The term has a distinct legal definition in England, but in Canada's common-law provinces, lawyers are called to the bar (*see* BARRISTER) and admitted as solicitors simultaneously. There is no exact corresponding designation under Québec civil law, where the legal profession is divided into *notaires* (*see* NOTARIES) and *avocats*. K.G. McSHANE

Solicitor General The office of the solicitor general has its historic roots in England. In Canada the office varies substantially from jurisdiction to jurisdiction. In some provinces the office of the solicitor general is subsumed under one or more different portfolios, but in most it is separate and distinct. In the former situation, functions of the solicitor general are likely to be assumed by the office of the ATTORNEY GENERAL. Federally the office of the solicitor general is separate and distinct from other Cabinet portfolios.

Generally speaking, a provincial solicitor general is responsible for matters relating to POLICING in the province, corrections, motor vehicles and liquor licensing. However, the functions assigned to the solicitor general's office differ from province to province. Federally the solicitor general of Canada is responsible for the

Canadian Correctional Service, the Royal Canadian Mounted Police and the National Parole Board. As of July 1984 the federal solicitor general was made responsible for the new Canadian Security Intelligence Service now established separate and apart from the RCMP; however, one of the controversies concerning the enactment of the new security legislation relates to considerable independence of the service from the responsible minister.

Federally, there is a close working relationship between the offices of the attorney general and the solicitor general as their functions somewhat overlap. G. GALL

Solicitor General, Department of Before 1936, the department was either a Cabinet post or ministerial post outside Cabinet. Between 1936 and 1945, the solicitor general's responsibilities were handled by the attorney general. The Solicitor General Act of 1945 reestablished the Cabinet post and in 1966 the department was created, making the solicitor general responsible for federal prisons and penitentiaries, (eg, Correctional Services of Canada), parole and remissions, law enforcement (eg, the ROYAL CANADIAN MOUNTED POLICE). The solicitor general reports to Parliament for the National Parole Board.

Solid Waste, general term for all discarded materials other than fluids. Solid wastes, including some HAZARDOUS WASTES, are by-products of industrial, MINING and agricultural operations as well as the garbage and sewage produced by society. The first 3 categories of wastes involve special disposal techniques which are, or should be, integral parts of the operation that produces them. The by-products of human activities become more and more a problem as concentrations of population increase; in Canada, they are largely the responsibility of the municipalities. Municipalities must cope with 2 general categories of solid waste: garbage and sewage sludge.

Garbage Most Canadian communities probably produce domestic, commercial and urban industrial waste at a rate near the N American average of 2.5 kg per person per day, with considerable seasonal variation. This high rate is attributed to N American affluence, a preoccupation with exploitation of virgin RESOURCES and a high level of subsidization of garbage disposal. The disposal of this volume of garbage is expensive; costs are estimated to average $25 per person per year. Traditional open garbage dumps are now generally illegal because they attract large mammals, rodents and birds which may be hazards to health and safety. If properly operated, sanitary landfills reduce POLLUTION problems (air and groundwater contamination, odour, litter). Garbage collection and disposal is generally a local government responsibility, whether carried out by municipal employees or by private contractors. Federal and provincial laws relate to health, clean air and water supply.

Solid-waste management should adhere to 3 priorities: to reduce the volume of waste generated, through control of packaging and emphasis on durability and repairability as design criteria for products; to direct the recycling of materials through separation at source (business or home), where volumes of garbage and population densities allow; to provide economic incentives to reduce waste and to encourage recycling and use of recycled products.

Sewage Any concentration of humans will eventually encounter problems with disposal of human wastes. On average, each human adult produces approximately 0.5 L of urine per day and 115 g of feces. Safe return of body wastes to the ecosystem maintains the natural cycles of nutrients and moisture. However, population concentrations soon create problems which lead to disease, pollution of natural systems and a generally offensive environment. The development of sewage handling and treatment technologies has reduced or eliminated sewage-related diseases and made our cities much more pleasant places to live (*see* WATER TREATMENT; WATER-BORNE DISEASE). Most communities dump their treated or untreated sewage into bodies of water, creating special WATER POLLUTION problems, including the incorporation of toxic materials and disease-causing organisms, and the accelerated growth of unwanted vegetation and algae. Many towns now use sewage lagoons, large-scale equivalents of the septic tanks in less densely populated areas. Composting toilets are a dry alternative to septic tanks.

Another solution to water pollution problems from sewage is land disposal where soil conditions are suitable. This practice is followed throughout the world, especially in countries which cannot afford the loss of the valuable nutrients. In Canada some ecologists advocate using sewage for fertilizer. Where soils are suitable, especially on the prairies, use of liquid effluent in farm IRRIGATION eliminates the water pollution problem and provides water and nutrients for crops. In 1983 the number of land-application sites for treatment of municipal wastewater was as follows: NWT, one; BC, 31; Alta, 26; Sask, 12; Man, 4; Ont, 3; Qué, one; Nfld, one. In addition, there were 20 industrial wastewater irrigation projects. A large city such as Calgary would require about 50 000 ha of land to dispose of its effluent. DIXON THOMPSON

Solitaire, common name for 11 species of New World THRUSHES, one of which occurs in Canada. Ornithologists also use the term for 2 species belonging to an extinct family related to the dodo and the modern pigeon family. Townsend's solitaire (*Myadestes townsendi*) summers in open mountain forests N to YT, and winters at lower elevations N to southern BC. Males and females are similar in appearance, being brownish grey overall with longish tails and short bills. They nest on or near the ground or in rock crevices and lay dull white eggs, spotted with brown. In summer, solitaires feed on insects; in winter, as much as half their diet is fruit. Their clear, sweet, loud warbling notes are among the most beautiful of BIRD SONGS. R.D. JAMES

Solomon's Seal (genus *Polygonatum*), herbaceous PLANT of lily family (Liliaceae). About 50 species occur in the Northern Hemisphere. Two are found in Canada, *P. biflorum* and *P. pubescens*, in moist woods and thickets from southeastern Saskatchewan to the Maritimes. Stems, up to 1 m high, have greenish white, pendant flowers and alternate leaves. Berries are blue to blueblack. Both native species were a source of food, cosmetics and medicines (eg, for bruises, headaches) for Indian peoples. Both native and introduced species are good garden plants (easily propagated by division). Introduced species have flowers and habit of growth similar to native species, except for *P. hookeri*, a good alpine garden plant, 2 cm high, with small, lilac flowers in leaf axils. Common name refers to marks on the rhizomes (underground stems) which resemble seals used on legal documents. *Smilacina*, false Solomon's seal, also a member of lily family, may be confused with *Polygonatum*.
PATRICK SEYMOUR

Somers, Harry Stewart, composer (b at Toronto 11 Sept 1925). Somers began studying piano and classical guitar, but working first with John WEINZWEIG and then with Darius Milhaud in Paris led to his career as a composer. He supported himself by ushering, driving a taxi and copying music, acquiring his meticulous handwriting in the process. By 1960, after further study in Paris, he was able to live on his commission fees. He is one of Canada's most productive and original composers and a keen promoter of contemporary Canadian music; he was a founding member in 1951 of the Canadian League of Composers. Concerned about the teaching and performance of Canadian music in schools, he became involved in 1963 in the John Adaskin Project to introduce Canadian composers and hosted several youth concerts on CBC. A grant from the Canadian Cultural Institute in Rome permitted him to study there (1969 to 1971), completing works that reveal his interest in new vocal techniques. Eastern music and philosophy have also influenced him considerably. Somers's music is internationally respected and is performed throughout the Western world. He has received major commissions from most of Canada's musical and theatrical organizations. His opera *Louis Riel* was commissioned for Canada's Centennial by the Floyd S. CHALMERS Foundation and was subsequently performed in Washington, DC, for the US Bicentennial. Always associated with intense feeling, his work is simple, eloquent and forceful, often employing dramatic juxtaposition of styles, dramatic silences and sharp fluctuations in volume, which he calls "dramatic unrest." Somers in 1972 became a companion of the Order of Canada. MABEL H. LAINE

Somerset Island, 24 786 km², ninth-largest island in the ARCTIC ARCHIPELAGO. Its western part is on Precambrian bedrock, reaching an elevation of 503 m, but the larger part is an elevated plateau of sedimentary rocks. Vegetation is scant, except in some depressions and lowlands where Peary caribou are common. Muskoxen are making a comeback after having been decimated by whalers around the turn of the century. Hundreds of thousands of birds nest on the sheer cliffs of Prince Leopold I, off the NE tip of Somerset. The island was named after the county in England by Lt W.E. PARRY, who discovered it in 1819. S.C. ZOLTAI

Sonar (*so*und *n*avigation *a*nd *r*anging), method for locating objects by the reflection of sound waves. It is used naturally by such animals as BATS and DOLPHINS to locate food and obstacles. Sonar was first developed — as a practical method of detecting underwater hazards (eg, submarines, icebergs) and for measuring water depths by Constantin Chilowsky and Paul Langevin in France during WWI, with the collaboration of the Canadian R.W. BOYLE. During WWII the Royal Canadian Navy, specializing in convoy escort and in antisubmarine activities, called on Canadian oceanographers to assess water-stratification conditions and study the behaviour of sound under water. J.P. TULLY and W.M. CAMERON worked with G.S. Field of the NATIONAL RESEARCH COUNCIL on ways of improving sonar detection of submarines. Sonar has since been further developed for civilian and scientific as well as military uses.

Because sonar techniques can be used to locate and map changes in the medium through which sound waves travel, they can be used to determine variations in the sedimentary structure of the Earth beneath the sea, through a method known as seismic reflection, and to map the seafloor surface. Seafloor sediments absorb normal high-sonar frequencies very rapidly, so that early application of seismic-reflection techniques at sea used repeated detonation of explosives as a low-frequency sound source (*see* SURVEYING).

Seismic Deeptow In marine seismic exploration the acoustic sound source and receiver are normally towed behind the survey vessel at a shallow depth below the sea surface. In Canada, 2 deep-towed seismic systems have been developed to provide the high resolution required for mapping unconsolidated seabed sediments. In both systems the sound source and receiving hydrophones are on or towed from a hydrodynamically designed "fish," itself towed at depths of 200-600 m and at speeds up to 6-8 knots by a survey vessel. The Nova Scotia Research Foundation (NSRF) system uses a 1.2 m V-fin underwater vehicle as the deep-towed stable platform to house the source and receiver. The Deep Tow Seismic System was developed by Huntec '70 Ltd in Toronto as part of the joint Government/Industry Seabed Project (1975-80) and uses a specially designed hydrodynamic tow body to house power supplies and transducers. The Seabed Project brought together the scientists and engineers required to develop the technology to quantify the acoustic response of marine sediments and to apply seismic deep-tow techniques to the mapping of the surficial sediments over the Canadian Continental Shelf. DAVID I. ROSS

Songs and Songwriting Song may be described as a tonal vocalization of words and emotions. It can be fragmentary or extended, and range from simple, unaffected statement to highly complex linear and harmonic structure. What determines its character is the situation which elicits the music, the text being treated (or the emotion being expressed) and the vocal and instrumental resources used. Song is usually thought of as text set to music, and it is frequently the nature and purpose of the words that form the basis for categorizing song types; thus, there are such familiar divisions as folksong, religious song, patriotic song, children's song or art song. Music can heighten the meaning of words, and the combination of text and tone can enhance the emotional statement. The presence of peoples from many lands and cultural backgrounds has contributed to the growth of Canadian songwriting. In addition, technology now makes available music from around the world. Artistic influences are no longer simply those from native traditions, patterns of privileged travel or emigration. Influences are as varied as international touring, broadcasting and recording allow.

Predating and contemporary with immigration of people from Western Europe were the songs of the native people, conveyed by oral tradition and often associated with dance. In this century indigenous music has been the subject of extensive study and has also been a source of material for composers working within the Western tradition. The early French Canadian settlers brought with them their own melodic and stylistic material, dependent on oral tradition, and subsequently evolved forms, such as rhythmical paddling songs, that were often related to the occupation of the singer. The Anglo-Canadian folksong tradition was equally vigorous, and examples of both musical streams have been collected and preserved and have formed the basis of new works (*see* FOLK MUSIC). Every national group of any size represented in Canada's population has brought its own tradition.

Like the paddling songs of the voyageurs and fur traders, the shanties were sailors' work songs and served to provide not only a lifting of the spirit but a measured pulse for the task. Most of the shanties and sea songs of Canadian heritage or adoption come from the East Coast, mainly from NS and Newfoundland, and to a lesser degree from the Great Lakes region. W. Roy Mackenzie, the first to collect Anglo-Canadian songs, gathered work songs from old Nova Scotia seamen, including shanties such as "Santy Anna," "Sally Brown" and "We're Homeward Bound." There were other sea songs with texts describing activities, events and superstitions; the vocal narratives of such ballads tell of sealing and fishing trips and voyages ("The Ferryland Sealer," "The *Greenland* Disaster"). Even the dance songs reflect the Maritimers' dependence on the sea, as in "I'se the B'y That Builds the Boat" and "The Feller from Fortune." The land itself also offered opportunities for work-related song. The lumber camps of NB and

Ontario, agricultural areas from the Maritimes to the Prairies and, to a lesser degree, the mining regions of both coasts and Ontario have contributed songs ("Cobalt Song," "The Scarborough Settler's Lament"). Though tunes were at times shared between regions or even occupations, texts often possessed a local focus; thus the tune of "The Lumbercamp Song," patterned after an English ditty, is found, with various texts, among East Coast fishermen as well as loggers. Hardships endured by the workers are recounted in songs such as "Canaday-I-O" or "The Rock Island Line." Ballads describing death in the woods or on the rivers are numerous ("Peter Amberley," "The Haggertys and Young Mulvanny"). In the West both homesteaders and cowboys borrowed songs from the US. Cowboys were often hired from the US and brought with them popular songs like "The Streets of Laredo" and "Bury Me Not on the Lone Prairie." "Dakota Land" and other parodies of the old hymn "Beulah Land" were rewritten in Canada as "Prairie Land," "Alberta Land" and "Saskatchewan." It is easy to dismiss such material as unsophisticated and unimportant, but the texts provide insight into Canada's history. The nature and use of melody can reveal much about taste, the transmission of artistic ideas and the movement of people across the country and across borders.

Together with occupational songs may be categorized the limited number of trade-union and political songs. The body of material is small and some of it is adaptive in nature, making use of existing tunes, and much of it is related to specific events. Political or labour songs have sometimes suffered the same fate as many clever political cartoons — the particular relevance is lost, though the principle involved may be taken up at another time. A similar fate might have overtaken the shanties after the demise of sail, but the larger body of material and the effects of nostalgia and romantic notions have served to sustain their popularity. Examples of political songs survive in the form of 18th-century satirical material from Québec ("Chanson sur les élections") and songs stemming from 19th-century crises and elections. In this century, world wars and other events and issues such as working conditions in mining and lumbering ("Hard, Hard Times," "The Loggers' Plight") and the aspirations of the Acadians and the Québecois have given rise to protest songs.

The distinction between songs which are political and those which are patriotic often depends on the views and emotions of one group or another. Nevertheless, Canada has a considerable list of songs which display national sentiment. These works often owe their creation and popularity to an event, eg, Confederation, or to an idea such as the preservation of the entity and spirit of a region, culture and language. Hence, in Québec we find "Canada, terre d'esperance," "O Canada! beau pays, ma patrie," along with "À la claire fontaine" and "Vive la canadienne"; in NB and NS, "Un Acadien errant"; and in English Canada, works like "The Maple Leaf for Ever," "Canada for Ever," and "O Canada, Dear Canada." LAVALLÉE's "O Canada, terre de nos aieux" (original text by A.-B. Routhier) is the country's national anthem.

Children have their own songs. Here again, pieces are handed from one generation to another, and like occupational songs are often associated with particular activities such as bridge games ("Trois fois passera"), ring games ("The Farmer in the Dell") or skipping ("On yonder mountain stands a lady"). Camp and campfire songs are popular with some adults, and children frequently share these, for example, rounds like "Row, Row, Row Your Boat," parodies like "Found a Peanut" (sung to the "Clementine" melody) and others. Once more, there is a universality to such material; we can hear many of these songs in NS or BC; some of them

have their origin outside Canada or outside our range of history ("Three Blind Mice" was printed by Thomas Ravenscroft in *Deuteromelia,* 1609). Among Canadian composers, Lionel Daunais has written at least 30 chansons, popular pieces and songs for children.

There is a considerable wealth of Canadian songs, though most are relatively neglected and unknown beyond circles of devotees and concert and recital goers. The chansons of Québec have an interesting history and again reflect the merging of imported cultural influences and, more recently, folksong and modern trends in popular music and developments in audio electronics. English Canadian POPULAR MUSIC has lately followed the same path, though it is not as concerned with the stimulation and preservation of a linguistic and cultural heritage. The works of Ernest Whyte, Clarence Lucas and W.O. Forsyth have rested, until the mid-1980s, in undeserved shade, along with those of Achille Fortier and Calixa Lavallée. Some mid-20th-century composers who have contributed to Canadian song are Violet ARCHER, Michael Baker, John BECKWITH, Jean Coulthard, Lionel Daunais, Kelsey Jones, Ernest MACMILLAN, Oskar MORAWETZ, Jean PAPINEAU-COUTURE, Barbara PENTLAND, Clermont Pépin, André Prévost, Leo Smith, Healey WILLAN and Charles Wilson. Notable is the extent to which vocal music has attracted Canadian composers over the years (*see also* CHORAL MUSIC). The output often reflects broad trends in technique and style in serious music, but also bears the mark of individual character and taste. Composers have frequently found inspiration in words by Canadian writers, a tendency which is likely to continue as both arts flourish. Further, many Canadian composers (MacMillan and Willan, for example) have written some remarkable and unique arrangements of existing songs, some of which have origins in other lands. Such arrangements, like original works, form a proper part of Canadian music.

If there is a problem for the Canadian writer of serious songs it lies not in a lack of something to say but in the difficulty of getting the musical statement to the potential audience in Canada. Recitals are still too few, and though radio, especially the CBC, has offered many opportunities to composers, TV has not used the wealth of available material. Both radio and TV have assisted popular song, but though Canadian-content requirements offer a measure of comfort, more must be done. In evaluating songs and songwriting, it is not enough to reflect on melody and harmony: the texts will tell us about our life and our land as well. Any art must also be considered in a larger context — against trends and styles in other arts, political and social movements, economic conditions, geography, climate and other factors, both within the country and internationally. *See also* MUSIC HISTORY; SINGING.   BRYAN N.S. GOOCH

Reading: Encyclopedia of Music in Canada (1981).

Soper, Joseph Dewey, naturalist, explorer, writer (b near Guelph, Ont 5 May 1893; d at Edmonton 2 Nov 1982). Soper exemplified the quiet, unpretentious men who, surveying for the Dominion government, established the outline and substance of Canada. The wilderness of western Canada attracted him before WWI. After the war, he opened new territory in the eastern Arctic (1923-31) and discovered the breeding grounds of the blue goose. Later he contributed important knowledge about bison in Wood Buffalo National Pk. He also ranged the prairies, (especially along the international boundary), the Rocky Mt parks, the NWT and the Yukon. His more than 100 scientific and popular articles and books were illustrated often with his own pen sketches and watercolours. The names of several mammals (eg, Soper's ringed seal) and

geographical features on Baffin I (eg, Soper R) testify to his work. In 1960 he received an LLD from U of A.   J.R. NURSALL

Sorel, Qué, City, pop 20 347 (1981c), inc 1889, is located on the S shore of the St Lawrence R, at the mouth of the Rivière RICHELIEU, 76 km NE of Montréal. Pierre de Saurel, a captain in the CARIGNAN-SALIÈRES REGIMENT, gave his name to the seigneury granted in 1672. In 1781 Sir Frederick HALDIMAND, the governor of Québec, built a manor on the Richelieu (later used as a summer residence for governors general of Canada) and made plans to build a town he hoped would be populated by Loyalists. However, few such settlers came to the area. Until 1787 the town was called William Henry, after the Prince of Wales. It was renamed Sorel in 1845, with a slightly changed spelling. In 1784 the first Anglican mission was established.

In the mid-19th century, the rapidly growing town was a terminal for river shipping originating in Lac CHAMPLAIN and profited from the trade between Montréal and Québec City. The lumber industry and shipyards also prospered. In the 20th century, Sorel has remained a busy year-round seaport, and is the commercial centre for agriculture in the Richelieu Valley. In WWII, as a centre for wartime industry, it employed 20 000 workers. Today, shipbuilding and heavy industry are its principal activities. It also has textile plants, clothing, plastics, concrete and light manufacturing industries.

SYLVIE TASCHEREAU

Souris, Man, Town, pop 1731 (1981c), inc 1903, is located at the junction of Plum Cr and the SOURIS R, 45 km by road SW of Brandon. Souris is known for its semiprecious agate stones, used in costume jewellery, and one of the longest (177 m) suspension footbridges in Canada. The Souris area has seen Indian warfare, fur-trading rivalries, Red River brigade buffalo hunts, and feudallike settlements under English and French landowners. The townsite's first permanent settlers arrived 1880, followed in 1881 by a group of Ontarians. Souris, then called Plum Creek, was soon a developing agricultural centre. During WWII the town had a large Commonwealth air school. Souris services the surrounding agricultural region (grain production, dairying, purebred stock breeding) and has a few small industries.   D.M. LYON

Souris, PEI, Town, pop 1413 (1981c), is a port located 80 km NE of Charlottetown. The town is likely named, after the French word for mouse, for the plagues of mice that appeared in the area around 1750, devouring the Acadians' crops. With the demise of the Island's shipbuilding industry in the late 19th century, the seaport's economy was buoyed by the harvests of land and sea. Today Souris remains one of the province's main ports; its harbour is not only the site of the Magdalene Islands ferry terminal, but provides shelter for both inshore and offshore fishing fleets. It is also noted for its lobster industry and fine beach on NORTHUMBERLAND STR. The town is the commercial centre of northeastern Kings County.   W.S. KEIZER

Souris River, about 720 km long, rises in the Yellow Grass marshes N of Weyburn, Sask, flows SE past ESTEVAN and wanders S across the N Dakota border before entering Manitoba. Near the town of Souris it swirls through a series of deep gorges, then makes an abrupt NE turn to join the ASSINIBOINE R. Much of its drainage basin is fertile silt and clay deposited by former glacial Lk Souris, and much of the river's course follows the cut of the lake's outfall. The river's name, French for mouse, aptly describes its meandering course, which from a distant vantage resembles the track of a mouse. The river was an ancillary route of the fur trade, and at least 7 posts were built along its gentle banks between

1785 and 1832. It is still a popular canoe route, but the dominant feature around it now is wheat. JAMES MARSH

Sourkes, Theodore Lionel, biochemist, neuropsychopharmacologist (b at Montréal 21 Feb 1919). One of Canada's great scholars, he became professor of PSYCHIATRY at McGill in 1965 and director of the neurochemistry laboratory at the Allan Memorial Inst of Psychiatry; in 1970 he was appointed professor of biochemistry as well. He has been a prime mover in the establishment of biochemical psychiatry as an accurate discipline. He is a brilliant scientist, internationally known as a pioneer in nutrition, particularly the role of vitamins in the nervous system and the metabolism of brain neurotransmitters. He was one of the originators of the studies that led to the use of L-DOPA in the treatment of Parkinson's disease, and his introduction of α-methylDOPA into the pharmacological literature resulted in its widespread use to combat hypertension. He received the senior award of the Parkinson's Disease Foundation 1963-66, became a fellow of the Royal Soc of Canada in 1971 and was honoured with the first Heinz-Lehmann Award in neuropsychopharmacology in 1982. Esteemed by students and colleagues, he is the author of more than 300 publications, among them a landmark study of the biochemistry of mental disease (1962) and an account of the Nobel Prize winners in medicine and physiology. LEONHARD S. WOLFE

Souster, Raymond, poet, editor (b at Toronto 15 Jan 1921). Souster has spent all his life in Toronto except for service in the RCAF in the Maritimes 1941-45. His published works include over 12 books of poetry, beginning with *When We Are Young* (1946), and including his collected poems, *The Colour of The Times* (1964), which received the Gov Gen's Award. In his poems Souster celebrates man's ability to sing in the face of despair. He draws his images from the immediate environment and his view of the poet's function is as a recorder of the human condition. Souster exhibits a distaste for the genteel forms of poetic tradition as well as a preference for natural speech rhythms over controlled metrics. He has been much influenced by the American poets Ezra Pound and William Carlos Williams.

Souster has enriched the literature of Canada from behind the scenes as well. In 1943 he helped found the magazine *Direction;* went on to found and edit *Contact* (1952-54), instrumental in experimental poetry in the 1950s, and *Combustion* (1957-60). He has also edited a number of influential peotry anthologies. MARLENE ALT

South African War (Boer War), 11 Oct 1899 to 31 May 1902 between Britain and the 2 Afrikaner republics of South Africa (SAR, or Transvaal) and the Orange Free State. When war began, Canadian opinion was already sharply divided on the question of sending troops to aid the British. French Canadians led by Henri BOURASSA, seeing growing British imperialism as a threat to their survival, sympathized with the Afrikaners, whereas English Canadians, with some notable exceptions, rallied to the British cause. Under intense public pressure, Wilfrid Laurier's government reluctantly authorized recruitment of a token 1000 infantrymen, designated the 2nd (Special Service) Battalion, Royal Canadian Regiment, commanded by Lt-Col William D. OTTER. They sailed Oct 30 from Québec. With British reverses and mounting casualties Canada had no difficulty procuring 6000 more volunteers, all mounted men, including 3 batteries of field artillery which accompanied Canada's 2nd contingent, the 1st Regiment, Canadian Mounted Rifles; another 1000 men, the 3rd Battalion, RCR, were raised to relieve regular British troops garrisoned at Halifax, NS. Only the 1st, 2nd and Halifax con-

Durban Camp in South Africa, 1902 (*courtesy Public Archives of Canada/PA-16431*).

tingents, 12 instructional officers, 6 chaplains, 8 nurses and 22 artificers (mostly blacksmiths) were recruited under the authority of the Canadian MILITIA ACT and organized, clothed, equipped, transported and partially paid by the Canadian government, at a cost of $2 830 965. The 3rd contingent, Strathcona's Horse, was funded entirely by Lord Strathcona (Donald SMITH), Canada's wealthy high commissioner to the UK. The rest, the South African Constabulary, the 2nd, 3rd, 4th, 5th and 6th Regiments of CMR and the 10th Canadian Field Hospital, were recruited and paid by Britain. All men agreed to serve for up to one year, except in the Constabulary, which insisted on 3 years' service. Canadians also served in imperial, irregular units, such as the Canadian Scouts and Brabant's Horse.

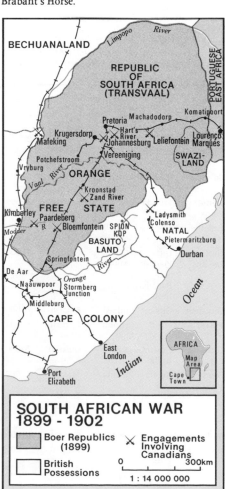

SOUTH AFRICAN WAR 1899 - 1902

Boer Republics (1899)

British Possessions

× Engagements Involving Canadians

0   300km

1 : 14 000 000

The war can be divided into 3 phases. Euphoria marked the start of hostilities and ended in Britain's "Black Week" of mid-Dec 1899. This first period, characterized by British blunders and defeats, startled Canadians as the Afrikaners, highly mobile and armed with modern weapons and the determination to defend their homeland, confounded the British. The second phase, Feb-Aug 1900, reversed the trend. During this period the British reorganized and reinforced, and under new leadership began their steady march to Bloemfontein and Pretoria, the capitals of the OFS and the SAR. After Paul Kruger, SAR president, fled to Europe following Pretoria's fall, the war continued another 2 years. But it had become dull, dirty guerrilla warfare, with the British resorting to blockhouses, farm burning and concentration camps to subdue the "bitter-enders."

Only the 1st and 2nd contingents, Lord Strathcona's Horse and the Constabulary saw active service; the rest arrived around the Peace of Vereeniging, signed 31 May 1902. In battles at Paardeberg, Bloemfontein, Mafeking, LELIEFONTEIN and elsewhere, Canadian troops had distinguished themselves. Their tenacity, stamina and initiative seemed especially suited to the Afrikaners' unorthodox, guerrilla tactics. Four Canadians received the VICTORIA CROSS, 19 the Distinguished Service Order and 17 the Distinguished Conduct Medal; 117 were mentioned in dispatches, and Canada's senior nursing sister, Georgina Pope, was awarded the Royal Red Cross.

Canadians at home viewed their soldiers' martial success with pride and marked their victories by massive parades and demonstrations lasting several days. They insured their lives upon their enlistment, showered them with gifts upon their departure and during their service, and feted them upon their return. They formed a Patriotic Fund and a Canadian branch of the Soldiers' Wives' League to care for their dependants and a Canadian South African Memorial Association to mark the graves of the 244 Canadian casualties, over half of them victims of diseases, principally enteric fever. After the war they erected monuments to the men who fought. The wounded, men such as the celebrated trooper L.W. Mulloy, who had been blinded, remained for years a living testimony to the war's human cost.

The success of Canada's soldiers and their criticism of British leadership and social values fed a new sense of Canadian self-confidence, which loosened rather than cemented the ties of empire. The war also damaged relations between French and English Canadians. Once during the war the bitterness created by the conflict erupted into a 3-day riot in Montréal. Consequently, although the war undoubtedly sharpened English Canada's identity, it left distrust and resentment in its wake. CARMAN MILLER

Reading: Thomas Pakenham, *The Boer War* (1979).

South Asians Those people referred to as South Asians or East Indians are easily the most diverse ethnocultural population in Canada. They trace their origins to South Asia, which encompasses India, Pakistan, Bangladesh and Sri Lanka (formerly Ceylon). Most South Asian Canadians are immigrants or descendants of immigrants from these countries, but about 40% are from South Asian communities established during British colonial times in East and South Africa, the Caribbean, Fiji and Mauritius. Others come from Britain, the US and Europe. There are now over 300 000 South Asians in Canada, comprising 1.2% of the total population.

People who are called "South Asian" view the term in the way that those from European countries might view the label "European." While they acknowledge that South Asians share cultural and historical characteristics, their basic identification is with more specific ethnocultural roots. In cities such as Toronto, over 20 distinct ethnic groups can be identified within the large South Asian population.

Origins The ethnic diversity of South Asian Canadians reflects the enormous cultural variability of South Asia's 800 million people. About 40-50% of South Asian Canadians come from India, where 14 major languages are spoken and where there are hundreds of discrete ethnic groups. This pluralism extends to religion, for though 83% of Indians are Hindus, over 50 million are Muslims, and many others are Sikh, Christian or Jain. Islam is the predominant religion in Pakistan and Bangladesh, yet both countries are culturally diverse. A third major world religion (BUDDHISM) is practised by most Sri Lankans, but large Hindu, Christian and Muslim religious minority groups exist there as well. Those communities outside South Asia are much more homogeneous, but in each community people have developed a unique identity and way of life which is distinct from any in South Asia.

Migration The first South Asian migrants to Canada arrived in Vancouver in 1903. The great majority of them were Sikhs who had heard of Canada from British Indian troops in Hong Kong, who had travelled through Canada the previous year on their way to the coronation celebrations of Edward VII. Attracted by high Canadian wages, they soon found work. Immigration increased quickly and reached 5209 by the end of 1908; all of these immigrants were men who had temporarily left their families to find employment in Canada. Virtually all of them remained in BC.

The BC government quickly limited South Asian rights and privileges. In 1907 South Asians were provincially disenfranchised, which denied them the federal vote and access to political office, jury duty, the professions, public-service jobs, and labour on public works. In the following year the federal government enacted an immigration regulation which specified that immigrants had to travel to Canada with continuous ticketing arrangements from their country of origin. There were no such arrangements between India and Canada and, as was its intent, the continuous-passage provision consequently precluded further South Asian immigration. This separated men from their families and made further growth of the community impossible. Vigorous court challenges of the regulations proved ineffective and in 1913 frustration with government treatment culminated in support of the Ghadar Party, an organization which aimed at the overthrow of British rule in India. The immigration ban was directly challenged in 1914, when the freighter KOMAGATA MARU from Hong Kong sailed to Canada with 376 prospective South Asian immigrants. The ship remained isolated in Vancouver harbour for 2 months until it was forced to return to Asia. Revolutionary sentiment thereafter reached a high pitch, and many men returned to India to work for Ghadar.

The federal government's continuous-journey provision remained law until 1947, as did most BC anti-South Asian legislation. In 1919, because of community pressure and representations by the government of India, Canada allowed the wives and dependent children of South Asian Canadian residents to immigrate, and by the mid-1920s a small flow of wives and children had been established. This did not counter the effect of migration by South Asian Canadians to India and the US, which by the mid-1920s had reduced the South Asian population in Canada to about 1300.

During the 1920s South Asian economic security increased, primarily through work in the lumber industry and the sale of wood and sawdust as home heating fuel. In addition, a number of lumber mills were acquired by South Asians, 2 of which employed over 300 people. The effects of the GREAT DEPRESSION on the community were severe, but were mitigated by extensive mutual aid. By WWII South Asians in BC had gained much local support in their drive to secure the vote, especially from the CO-OPERATIVE COMMONWEALTH FEDERATION. In 1947 the ban against voting and other restrictions were removed. Faced with the coming independence of India, the federal government removed the continuous-passage regulation in the same year, replacing it in 1951 by an annual immigration quota for India (150 a year), Pakistan (100) and Ceylon (50). There were then only 2148 South Asians in Canada, 1937 of them in BC. Moderate expansion of immigration increased the Canadian total to 6774 in 1961.

As racial and national restrictions were removed from the immigration regulations in the 1960s, South Asian immigration mushroomed. It also became much more culturally diverse; a high proportion of immigrants in the 1950s were Sikh, while the 1960s saw sharp increases in immigration from other parts of India and from Pakistan. By the early 1960s, 66% of South Asian immigrant men were professionals — teachers, doctors, university professors and scientists. Nondiscriminatory immigration regulations enacted in 1967 resulted in a further increase in South Asian immigration.

In 1972 all South Asians were expelled from Uganda. Canada accepted 7000 of them (many of whom were Ismailis) as political REFUGEES. Thereafter a steady flow of South Asians have come to Canada from Kenya, Tanzania and Zaire, either directly or via Britain. Since 1975 a weak Canadian economy has significantly reduced South Asian immigration, but it will likely remain above 10 000 a year for the foreseeable future.

Settlement Patterns Virtually all South Asians lived in BC until the late 1950s, when professional South Asian immigrants began to settle across the country. The South Asian population of the urban corridor from Metro Toronto to Windsor grew dramatically to a present total of about 100 000. BC's South Asian population is now some 70 000, most of which is concentrated in the Vancouver area. Calgary, Edmonton and Montréal each have a South Asian population of about 15 000. Most of the other South Asian Canadians also live in cities or industrial areas; few live in rural areas. In addition, some ethnic South Asian populations are quite localized, primarily as the result of chain migration. For example, Sikhs are heavily represented in Vancouver and Toronto; South Asians from Fiji in Vancouver; those from Guyana and Trinidad in Toronto; and Ismailis in Vancouver, Edmonton and Calgary.

Economic Life The first Sikhs living in BC were almost entirely involved in the lumber industry. They are still involved in this industry, both as workers and millowners. Skilled South Asian professionals who arrived between 1960 and 1975 are now well established.

The occupational distribution began to broaden in the 1970s with the arrival of South Asian blue- and white-collar workers. Many more recent immigrants from South Asian countries now have similar backgrounds. The exodus of Ugandan South Asians brought many business people to Canada, and a number have taken up entrepreneurial activities ranging from the ownership of taxis to the control of corporations. The participation of other South Asians in businesses has also been high. South Asian Canadian women have been active participants in the economy in a variety of blue- and white-collar jobs. South Asians have also been involved in farming, especially in BC.

Social Life and Community South Asian Canadians have such widely varying backgrounds that few generalities can be made about their social and community life; but they all come from places where extended families, kinship and community relations are extremely important. Immigrants from South Asia quickly accept most Canadian cultural practices, but they have tried to maintain some continuity in the area of family and community. Parents frequently attempt, often unsuccessfully, to deal with their children along paternalistic South Asian lines. Husband-wife relations are also changing, especially as wives acquire access to economic and social resources. Future family changes are likely, particularly in regard to intermarriage, as the second generation matures. Among the social and economic difficulties experienced by South Asians, racial prejudice is also significant.

As a rule, informal social links between individuals of similar backgrounds are strong. South Asians do not form geographically concentrated communities, and relationships are supported chiefly by continual visiting. In contrast, links between South Asian communities are extremely weak and are chiefly restricted to contacts among leaders. As a consequence, it is inaccurate to speak of "the" South Asian community of a given place, for there are likely to be

Basic South Asian Canadian Ethno-cultural Categories			
Group	Primary place of origin	Majority religion	Major languages	Number
Sikhs	Punjab, India	Sikh	Punjabi	120 000
Pakistanis	Pakistan	Sunni Muslim	Urdu	22-25 000
Trinidadians	Trinidad	Christian Hindu	English	23 000
Ismailis	East Africa	Ismaili Muslim	Gujarati	20 000
Northern Indians	Uttar Pradesh and Punjab, India	Hindu Muslim	Hindi Punjabi	20 000
Guyanese	Guyana	mixed	English	20 000
Fijians	Fiji	Hindu	English Hindi	12 000
Gujaratis	Gujarat, India	Hindu	Gujarati	20 000
Southern Indians	Kerala and Madras, India	Hindu	Malayalam Tamil Telugu	5 000
Sinhalese	Sri Lanka	Buddhist	Sinhala	4 000
Bengalis	Bengal, India	Hindu	Bengali	2 000
Bangladeshis	Bangladesh	Sunni Muslim	Bengali	1 000

many. Contacts between communities most frequently arise when communities are small or where culture, language or religion are shared.

Religious and Cultural Life South Asian communities vary widely in the emphasis they place on cultural events. As a rule, groups with high ethnic consciousness, eg, Sikhs, maintain a full round of these activities, whereas groups such as Fijians and Guyanese, and South Asians of the professional classes do not. A similar degree of variability exists in regard to religious institutions. Sikhs are numerically large, their identity is both ethnic and religious, and their religious institutions have been in place since the first Canadian Sikh temple was founded in 1908. They have consequently been very successful in preserving their religion. Ismaili Muslims, whose spiritual leader is the Aga Khan, are also both an ethnic and religious group, and have founded strong religious institutions wherever they have gone. Sunni Muslims have generally allied themselves with other Sunnis in support of pan-ethnic mosques, and they too seem to be effectively transmitting their religion to their children. In Hindu populations of sufficient size, people have banded together to establish Hindu temples, which are used for prayer, for the presentation of annual ceremonies, and for important rituals linked to marriage and death.

Most communities support a variety of other activities and institutions. Nominally religious organizations frequently support language classes for children and cultural activities such as South Asian music and dance. In addition, there are now over 250 South Asian sociocultural associations in Canada, most of which have been formed in the past 10 years. Folk and classical music and dance traditions are popular. In addition, South Asian Canadians now support a number of newspapers and newsletters. South Asian programming on radio and cable television is expanding rapidly, especially in major centres (*see* HINDUISM; ISLAM; SIKHISM).

Politics Until 1965, South Asian politics were devoted primarily to lobbying for elimination of the legal restrictions enacted by the BC legislature and to changing immigration laws. Over the past 10 years, South Asians have become increasingly involved on several political fronts. Their sociocultural associations now actively lobby for government support for cultural programs, for greater access to immigration, and for government action to reduce PREJUDICE AND DISCRIMINATION. South Asians have frequently held local level offices, but their participation has not yet been extensive at higher levels.

Group Maintenance Most South Asian Canadians are immigrants whose children are only now approaching adulthood. Only the Sikhs have been in Canada long enough to have demonstrated a clear pattern of group maintenance. Strong group consciousness and minority-group status resulted in high rates of cultural retention among BC Sikhs prior to 1960. Virtually all of the second generation are knowledgeable in the ways of Sikh culture and language.

Other groups, eg, Ismailis, Pakistanis and other Sunni Muslims, have stressed religious above cultural and linguistic maintenance. For most South Asian groups, however, acculturation in the second generation will be extensive. Whether social integration will be equally thorough will depend chiefly on the future development of relations between South Asians and others. Few South Asians lived anywhere in Canada outside BC until the 1960s, and even there they were not numerous. Increases in South Asian immigration were met by some racial prejudice in the mid-1970s, especially in Toronto and Vancouver. This reached a peak in 1977-78 and has since decreased. *See also* SOUTHEAST ASIANS. NORMAN BUCHIGNANI

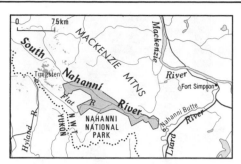

South Nahanni River, 563 km long, flows SE out of the Ragged Range of the Selwyn Mts, cuts across successive spines of the Mackenzie Mts and empties into the LIARD R. In 1972 the federal government formed NAHANNI NATIONAL PK to enclose the lower two-thirds of the S Nahanni and the lower half of its main tributary, the Flat R. The area's geological diversity is unexcelled: hot springs, glaciers, KARST landscape with bottomless sinkhole lakes, marshes, desertscapes, tundra plateaus, towering hoodoos and thick forests. Through it plunges the river called *Nahadeh* by the SLAVEY, "powerful river," with its whirlpool rapids, waterfalls and the 3 most spectacular river canyons in Canada. The name "Nahanni" is Athapaskan for "people of the west," referring to the NAHANI. The gorges of Five Mile Canyon, Figure of Eight Canyon and Hell's Gate have been cut by the river through the spine of the Mackenzie Mts and remain sharp and narrow because this is one of the few spots in Canada that escaped the gouging of the last continental ice sheets. About 150 km from the confluence with the Liard, the river constricts to one-fifth its previous width, forms a jet called the Chutes and flares out into a waterfall — half again as high as Niagara — called Virginia Falls for the daughter of Fenley Hunter, who first measured it in 1928. NAHANNI BUTTE (pop 85), an Indian village, is practically the only settlement in the area. The first whites to see the river were passing traders on their way to the Klondike. JAMES MARSH

The South Nahanni River flows through canyons of unexcelled natural beauty. Gate Pulpit Rock is shown *(courtesy Parks Canada/Prairie Region)*.

South Porcupine, Ont, subdivision of the city of TIMMINS, located about 300 km NW of Sudbury. Although traces of gold in the Porcupine district had been discovered earlier, serious prospecting began 1906 and culminated in the rush of 1909. South Porcupine, inc 1911, and named for an island in a local river reportedly shaped like the animal, stood on the S shore of Porcupine Lk at a point intersecting a branch line of the Temiskaming and Northern Ont Ry, then under construction. This position, along with the town's accessibility to a major producer, Dome mine, gave it an initial advantage over rivals such as Golden City. In June 1911, however, the town was destroyed by fire and Noah TIMMINS, owner of the Hollinger mine, established a new townsite, also on the railway, that was closer to his own property. Though rebuilt, South Porcupine lost its advantage and thereafter Timmins emerged as the chief urban centre, as acknowledged by the town's 1973 incorporation into Timmins. MATT BRAY

South Sea Company, chartered in 1711 by the British Parliament, with a monopoly over the W coast of the Americas to a distance of 300 leagues out to sea. In 1720 it assumed a large part of the British national debt and almost collapsed that year in a stock market crash known as the South Sea Bubble. However, until 1833 British vessels trading on the NORTHWEST COAST were obliged to carry licences from the company, as well as from the EAST INDIA COMPANY. BARRY M. GOUGH

Southam, William, newspaper publisher (b near Montréal 23 Aug 1843; d at Hamilton 27 Feb 1932). He was a typical 19th-century printer-publisher who lived to see a modern newspaper chain bearing the name he shared with the 6 sons who were the instruments of his dream. Southam had spent years on the London *Free Press* when, in 1877, he and a partner took over the ailing Hamilton *Spectator,* hoping a return to Conservative government in Ottawa would improve its health; it did. Despite comparatively low start-up costs, he continued to buy existing dailies rather than begin his own, acquiring the Ottawa *Citizen,* Calgary *Herald,* Edmonton *Journal,* Windsor *Star* and Montréal *Gazette.* Subsequent diversification into broadcasting, magazines and business publications has not prevented Southam Inc, still family controlled, from retaining a high-quality and devoutly Conservative flavour traceable to its founder's influence. DOUG FETHERLING
Reading: C. Bruce, *News and the Southams* (1968).

Southam Inc is one of the oldest and largest cross-media group owners in Canada. With 16 newspapers and 27% of the country's aggregate weekly circulation in 1982, Southam is also the largest Canadian NEWSPAPER-chain owner. According to the Kent Commission, Southam in 1980 controlled 65.8% of circulation in BC, 65.1% in Alberta, 22.2% in Ontario and 19% in Québec. Total daily circulation in 1983 was 1 616 000. Southam also publishes *TV Guide* and *TV Hebdo,* 50 business publications, and 16 annuals and directories. It operates Coles Book Stores Ltd and is involved in trade shows and exhibitions, data and special information services, commercial printing and, through SELKIRK COMMUNICATIONS, broadcasting. Southam holds a major interest, along with TORSTAR CORPORATION, in Infomart, an electronic publishing firm involved in the development of TELIDON-based videotex services. Assets for Southam Inc totalled $209 million in 1983, with revenues of $898 million. *See* MEDIA OWNERSHIP.
PETER S. ANDERSON

Southampton Island, 41 214 km², is situated between FOXE BASIN and HUDSON BAY. It combines the 2 basic regional relief types. Its N and NE consist of undulating highlands of Precambrian

SHIELD rocks, reaching elevations of 400 m and terminating in steep cliffs on Foxe Channel. In complete contrast, its S and SW are made up of gently sloping flat-lying Paleozoic rocks, forming limestone plains and plateaus of low relief (less than 200 m). Frost-shattered boulders and clayey gravels give the surface a desertlike appearance. Exposures of ancient reefs hint at the possible presence of hydrocarbons, but economically significant accumulations more likely lie offshore. The island was named for the earl of Southampton (1573-1624).   DOUG FINLAYSON

Southeast Asians Southeast Asia includes Indonesia, Brunei, Singapore, the Philippines, Burma, Malaysia, Thailand, Vietnam, Kampuchea and Laos. The major ethnocultural groups of Southeast Asians in Canada are the Vietnamese (estimated population 43 725), Vietnamese Chinese (30 000), Lao (9000) and Khmer or Kampucheans (5000).

Migration and Settlement Southeast Asians have come to Canada in 3 waves. Some who arrived as students during the 1950s and 1960s remained, so that by 1970 there were about 1200 Vietnamese and a few hundred Lao and Khmer living in Canada, chiefly in Québec. The American defeat in Vietnam and the fall of the Thieu regime in early 1975 led to a mass flight of Vietnamese, about 6500 of whom were admitted to Canada as political REFUGEES. Because this flow was later augmented by relatives, there were 10 000 Southeast Asians in Canada by 1978, primarily in Montréal and Toronto. Almost all of them were Vietnamese, and most of the men were professionals, bureaucrats, military personnel or students. In late 1978 the exodus of "boat people" from Vietnam (Vietnamese political refugees and Vietnamese Chinese), fleeing Vietnam for economic and political reasons, increased dramatically. Canada accepted 604 refugees from the freighter *Hai Hong* in Nov 1978. The situation of the boat people and of Lao, Khmer and Vietnamese "land people" who fled to Thailand grew increasingly severe, and Canada took in 70 000 more, 1979-81. Over 32 000 of these refugees were sponsored by 7000 private groups or churches. This sponsorship process resulted in the dispersal of Southeast Asians across the country. Thereafter, many have migrated to the cities, especially to Toronto, Montréal, Edmonton, Calgary, Vancouver and Victoria.

Economic Life The primarily Vietnamese refugees of the 1975-76 exodus were well educated and many were fluent in English or French. Despite some downward social mobility, they were quickly integrated into the Canadian economy. The Southeast Asians who arrived 1977-78 were more heterogeneous in every respect and included, among the ethnic Vietnamese, blue-collar workers and soldiers, and individuals with no previous occupation. A high proportion of Vietnamese Chinese had been involved in small-scale businesses but few knew English or French. The Lao and Khmer were also quite heterogeneous; Canadian immigration officials apparently limited the number of farmers accepted into Canada but did accept many ex-government workers.

The post-1976 refugees found it more difficult to adapt to new economic circumstances, although there was some variation among provinces. For example, most refugees were able (1977-80) to find some sort of job in Alberta, but not necessarily in Ontario or Québec. The subsequent recession (1981-84) had a negative effect on refugee economic adaptation, for it threw many people out of work.

Social and Cultural Life Southeast Asians emigrated under traumatic circumstances, and their efforts have been directed primarily towards employment, English- and French-language training, family unification, and coping with a host of refugee-related personal and

Vietnamese family arriving in Montréal in 1978, following a long trip from Vietnam as part of the "boat people" migration (*courtesy Canapress*).

familial difficulties. Although for some, many problems remain, community life is already well developed. In larger communities, formal associations put on a variety of annual celebrations (most importantly to mark the New Year) as well as sports and cultural events. Each group has an impressive cultural tradition, and these are now being supported by the re-establishment of religious and life-cycle customs and through dance, music, periodicals and newsletters. *See also* BUDDHISM; SOUTH ASIANS.
    DOREEN MARIE INDRA

Southern Indian Lake, 2248 km², elev 255 m, max length 146 km, is located in N-central Manitoba, 40 km NE of Leaf Rapids and 94 km E of Lynn Lake. Together with its eastern neighbour, the much smaller Northern Indian Lk, Southern Indian Lk is an expansion of the CHURCHILL R, which drains it in a northeasterly direction and eventually empties into the W side of HUDSON BAY. The lake has an irregular shape and a heavily indented shoreline. It is dotted with many small islands. An HBC post was established at South Indian Lk, a settlement on the S shore, as the river and the lakes it joined became one of the most important arteries in the FUR TRADE. The community was flooded in 1980 when the lake was dammed by Manitoba Hydro. The lake appears on Peter FIDLER's map (1814) and is probably named after the "southern Indians" or Cree.   DAVID EVANS

Sovereign, the head of STATE who reigns by hereditary right, as opposed to the elected head of GOVERNMENT. In Canada, a constitutional monarchy, the sovereign is one of the 3 components of Parliament. Since the 16th century some 32 French and British kings and queens have reigned over Canada. In 1867 the FATHERS OF CONFEDERATION vested executive authority and

Sovereigns Who Have Reigned Over Canadian Territory

British Isles

(1485)-1509	Henry VII	1702-1714	Anne
1509 -1547	Henry VIII	1714-1727	George I
1547 -1553	Edward VI	1727-1760	George II
1553 -1558	Mary I	1760-1820	George III
1558 -1603	Elizabeth I	1820-1830	George IV
1603 -1625	James I	1830-1837	William IV
1625 -1649	Charles I	1837-1901	Victoria
1649 -1660	(Republic)	1901-1910	Edward VII
1660 -1685	Charles II	1910-1936	George V
1685 -1688	James II	1936	Edward VIII
1689 -1702	William III	1936-1952	George VI
1689 -1694	and Mary II	1952-	Elizabeth II

France

(1515)-1547	François I	1589-1610	Henri IV
1547 -1559	Henri II	1610-1643	Louis XIII
1559 -1560	François II	1643-1715	Louis XIV
1560 -1574	Charles IX	1715-(1775)	Louis XV
1574 -1589	Henri III		

many statutory responsibilities in Queen Victoria, her heirs and successors. In 1947, under Letters Patent issued by George VI, all of the sovereign's powers and authorities in Canada were delegated to the GOVERNOR GENERAL. Contrary to popular belief, the sovereign's presence in Canada does not supersede this delegation except when the sovereign is actually asked to perform specific royal functions, eg, the opening of Parliament. George VI was the first reigning sovereign to visit Canada. In the spring of 1939 he toured with his consort, Elizabeth (now the Queen Mother), and on May 19 gave royal assent to several Canadian Bills in the Senate Chamber.

On 6 Feb 1952 Elizabeth II became sovereign, and in 1953 the Canadian Royal Style and Titles Act officially entitled her Queen of Canada. Her full title is "Elizabeth II, by the Grace of God, of the United Kingdom, Canada, and her other Realms and Territories Queen, Head of the Commonwealth, Defender of the Faith." In 1957 she was the first sovereign to open Parliament. She opened Parliament again for her Silver Jubilee in 1977, and on 17 Apr 1982 she proclaimed the Canadian CONSTITUTION. *See* CROWN; ROYAL TOURS.
    JACQUES MONET S.J.

Sovereign Council In early NEW FRANCE a governing council was created, comprising the GOUVERNEUR, the bishop and representatives ("syndics") of Québec, Trois-Rivières and Montréal. In 1663 Louis XIV equipped the colony with a complete administrative system modelled on those used to govern French provinces. The Sovereign Council, which in 1703 became the Superior Council, was comparable to the *parlements* of those provinces. The council initially comprised the governor, the bishop, the INTENDANT and 5 councillors. In 1703 membership grew to 12, to which 4 associated judges were added in 1742. Members, usually recruited from the French gentry, were nominated initially by the governor and the bishop and later by the king.

The council acted also as a court of appeal for civil and criminal matters originating in the lower courts. Its decisions could be reversed only by the King's Council, under which a judicial structure was established in each government of the colony: the provost marshal of Québec City (1663), the royal courts of Trois-Rivières (1665) and Montréal (1693), and the Admiralty (1717). The council also played an administrative role in regulating trade and public order, in registering the king's edicts, ordinances and commissions, and in promulgating them in the colony. After the CONQUEST of 1760 its appeal-court functions were taken over by a board of British military officers.   JACQUES MATHIEU

Sovereignty-Association First used as a slogan by one of the main precursors of the PARTI QUÉBÉCOIS, sovereignty-association (Mouvement souveraineté-association), has been used by the PQ to describe the restructuring of Québec's relationship with Canada and has become the main objective of the party. As defined in a 1979 Québec government White Paper titled *Québec-Canada: A New Deal*, sovereignty-association would involve the sharing (between Canada and Québec) of a common currency, but reorganization of central bank functions into community institutions with a joint central monetary board; a free-trade zone with a common external tariff, with each community free internally to protect agriculture; and freedom of movement of citizens between Canada and Québec, with special arrangements regarding jobs and immigration. Differences between the 2 nations would be referred to the Québec-Canada Council of Ministers. Québec and Canada would be linked constitutionally by a treaty establishing 4 community agencies, with the council acting as the central institution. The council would be served by the monetary board, by a commission of experts, and by a court of justice with equal representation of the 2 states which would adjudicate on differences arising from the treaty and Acts of association. Sovereignty-association, according to the White Paper, is not an end in itself but a means of enabling Québec to manage all its affairs freely. Québec would retain the economic advantages of the federal union but would also have the benefits of political independence. In the 1980 QUÉBEC REFERENDUM, a majority of Québecois rejected sovereignty-association as the basis for negotiation with the rest of Canada. In early 1985 sovereignty-association was dropped from the PQ's platform, causing dissension within the party. *See also* FRENCH CANADIAN NATIONALISM.

CLINTON ARCHIBALD

Soybean (*Glycine max*), herbaceous annual belonging to the legume family, grown as an OIL-SEED CROP in Canada. The soybean, among the oldest of cultivated crops, probably originated in East Asia. Introduced into the US as a hay crop about 1800, it was not recognized as a valuable source of edible oil until the early 1900s. During and immediately after WWII, soybean production expanded rapidly, with the US, China and Brazil accounting for over 90% of world production. In processing, the seed is crushed and the oil extracted. The oil, a high-quality cooking oil, is used in the production of margarine, shortening and salad oils. The meal remaining after the oil is extracted is a high-protein livestock and poultry feed. As a legume, the soybean plant can fix atmospheric nitrogen in its root nodules. The nodules are formed early in the growth of the plant, as a result of an interaction between the roots and a soilborne bacterium, *Rhizobium jabonicum*. Soybeans are a warm-season crop, requiring a mean summer temperature of 21°C and a frost-free period of 120-150 days for optimum production; therefore, most of Canada's annual production (*c* 600 000 t) is grown in southern Ontario.

E.N. LARTER

Space Technology Canada's entry into the Space Age was prompted by an interest, which increased markedly during WWII, in the investigation of the properties of Earth's upper atmosphere and, in particular, the ionosphere, ie, the layer of charged particles which reflects shortwave radio signals. An agreement signed with the US National Aeronautics and Space Administration (NASA) led to the launching of a series of 4 Canadian SATELLITES, beginning with Alouette 1 (on 29 Sept 1962) from the Western Test Range in Vandenburg, California, by a Thor-Agena rocket. Alouette 1 carried 2 Canadian-developed spacecraft antennae with tip-to-tip lengths of 23 and 45 m, respectively, which were deployed after the satellite was in orbit. Alouette 1 was followed by Alouette 2 (1965) and by ISIS (International Satellites for Ionospheric Studies) 1 (1969) and 2 (1971). These satellites were designed and built at the Defence Research Telecommunications Establishment in Ottawa, which had previous experience in using rockets for upper-atmosphere research. Each was increasingly complex in design and measurement capability and each involved greater participation by the then developing Canadian AEROSPACE INDUSTRY. Other Canadian and foreign organizations contributed equipment and experiments to the program and studies were carried out using the results from the satellite investigations in conjunction with ground-based measurements in various countries. In its time, Alouette 1 established a longevity record for operation of a complex satellite. Alouette 1 and ISIS 2 were launched into near-circular orbits, at about 1000 km and 1400 km above Earth, respectively; Alouette 2 and ISIS 1 were launched into elliptical orbits with perigees of about 500 km and apogees of 3000 and 3500 km, respec-

tively. ISIS 1 and 2 were still in operation, providing data for nearly 3 hours per day in 1984.

Canada's attention soon turned to applying space technology to serve the unique requirements imposed by the country's widely dispersed population, its vast distances, harsh terrain and severe CLIMATE. In 1964 Canada joined with several other nations in establishing an international system (Intelsat) for the exchange of commercial international telecommunications traffic. Following a 1968 White Paper on the possibility of establishing a domestic SATELLITE COMMUNICATIONS system, the Telesat Canada Corp was established by Act of Parliament in 1969. The corporation is owned jointly by the federal government and Canadian telecommunications carriers. With the launch of the first of Telesat's 3 Anik A satellites in late 1972, Canada became the first country to implement a commercial domestic satellite system operating in geostationary orbit (35 700 km above the equator). The satellites were stabilized in orbit by the technique known as spin-stabilization, in which the communications antenna and associated platform are despun so that the antenna points continually towards Earth. This series was built by a US prime contractor but involved major participation by Canadian industry. These satellites transmitted at frequencies of 4 GHz (billion Hertz) and received at 6 GHz and were located at 104°W, 109°W and 114°W longitude.

Anik B, which followed in late 1978, was somewhat higher powered and was 3-axis stabilized to maintain a precisely controlled fixed orientation in space. The Anik D series replaced the capacity of the now failing Anik A and aging Anik B satellites. Anik D1, launched in Aug 1982, was the first commercial satellite built by a Canadian prime contractor, Spar Aerospace Limited. The first of the Anik C satellites, which operate in the higher 12 and 14 GHz frequency bands, was one of 2 satellites launched to inaugurate the operational use of the US Space Shuttle in Nov 1982. Another in the Anik C series was launched in June 1983.

In 1971 Canada entered into an agreement with NASA for the development and launch of an experimental Communications Technology Satellite (CTS). CTS, known as Hermes in Canada, was launched on 17 Jan 1976. Hermes had several objectives: to develop and flight-test a high-power, high-efficiency travelling-wave-tube amplifier (wide band power amplifier such as those used in RADAR or communications transmitters) operating at 12 GHz; to develop and flight-test a 3-axis stabilization system to maintain accurate antenna pointing; and to conduct communications experiments in the newly allocated 12 and 14 GHz frequency bands using small, transportable Earth stations. The satellite was designed and built in Canada at the Communications Research Centre (CRC) of the Dept of Communications by a joint government/industry team of scientists and engineers. Use of the satellite permitted investigation of a number of innovative approaches to the delivery of new communications services and extension of existing services to remote and rural regions. Hermes was the first satellite capable of broadcasting television and radio programs directly to inexpensive home receivers and was equipped with spot-beam antennae which could be directed to any point on Earth that was visible from the satellite. Hermes was built to last 2 years but operated for nearly 4.

To test various subsystems of the satellite in a simulated space environment, the federal government established the satellite assembly, integration and test facilities of the David Florida Laboratory at CRC. These were later expanded to permit testing of complete spacecraft of a shuttle class in the simulated thermal, vacuum, vibration and electromagnetic environment of space. Techniques for computer simulation and

analysis of spacecraft motions were also developed.

Because of the success of the Hermes program and under an arrangement between Telesat and the federal government, Anik B was equipped with 4 transponders operating at 12 and 14 GHz, in addition to transponders at the 4 and 6 GHz frequencies used by the earlier Anik A satellites. A transponder is an electronic device which receives a signal and retransmits it at a different frequency. Anik B thus became the world's first satellite to operate simultaneously in both of these pairs of frequency bands.

In 1975 Canada signed an agreement with the US to participate in the Space Transportation System (Shuttle) by providing a unique remote-manipulator system, later named the CANADARM, to be mounted on the shuttle to move payloads in and out of the shuttle bay. This work was carried out by a Canadian industry team led by Spar Aerospace under contract to the NATIONAL RESEARCH COUNCIL OF CANADA. A general-purpose simulation facility (called SIMFAC) was designed, using mathematical modelling techniques, to verify Canadarm's operability in a zero-gravity environment and to train ASTRONAUTS to operate the Canadarm in space. While the arm cannot support its own weight on Earth, it is capable of manipulating a payload of nearly 30 000 kg in space, maneuvering it at 3 cm/s and placing it in any position with an accuracy of about 5 cm. The Canadarm was declared operational in Nov 1982, after having been flown successfully on the second, third and fourth shuttle launches, and having been used in maneuvering and handling exercises.

Another area in which Canadian space and related technology has also pioneered is in the application of space techniques to assist in search and rescue. All aircraft in Canada are equipped with emergency locator transmitters (ELTs) which may be turned on manually or are activated automatically on impact. A concept was developed to use satellites in low orbits highly inclined to the equator to detect aircraft and ships in distress. Canada joined with France and the US and several other countries to demonstrate the operational use of the concept through the SARSAT (Search and Rescue Satellite Aided Tracking) Project. Canada supplied the satellite transponders operating at frequencies of 121.5, 243 and 406 MHz, and designed and built the ground station for reception of the satellite-relayed signals. France provided the on-board signal processor and the US contributed the spacecraft antennae and tested, integrated and launched the SARSAT space hardware on board the NOAA series of meteorological satellites. First launch of a SARSAT-equipped spacecraft was in Feb 1983. To allow more frequent coverage of Earth's surface, an arrangement was concluded with the USSR for the launch of a compatible system, called COS-PAS. The first satellite equipped with the COS-PAS system was launched in June 1982.

Canada has also been involved in applications of satellite technology to REMOTE SENSING of the Earth's surface. Readout stations are used for the reception of signals from various US satellites and for ground-based processing of sensor data. In addition, design studies are carried out in preparation for the possible implementation by Canada of a remote-sensing satellite equipped with synthetic aperture radar to provide all-weather information on ice coverage in the Canadian Arctic, and to assist in surveillance of oceans and land resources. Other sensors are being considered for inclusion on Radarsat. Canadian industry will supply part of the radar and ground-based data-processing systems for the European Space Agency's European Remote Sensing Satellite, to be launched in 1988. The satellite will provide information on ice and ocean conditions. The use of large spacecraft to provide data communications to terminals on board ships and aircraft and on land, as well as improved service to mobile radio and radio telephones, is also being investigated. Such a system would use highly efficient narrow-bandwidth voice and data transmissions.

Based on capabilities developed over 20 years in space, Canadian industry is participating in the L-SAT program of the European Space Agency which involves the design and development of a large spacecraft platform to carry various payloads, eg, direct television broadcasting. Canada is contributing the critical extendible solar array subsystem and certain payload elements, and will have major responsibilities in the final integration and test of the spacecraft. Spar Aerospace is currently building, as prime contractor, a domestic communications satellite for Brazil for launch in 1985.

Space-science activities are co-ordinated by the Canada Centre for Space Science of the NRC. The major element of the current activity is a co-operative program with NASA to place a number of instruments in the shuttle, primarily to study plasmas in space. The program will include a network of ground stations to obtain complementary information and a data-processing system. In a co-operative program with Sweden, Canada provided an ultraviolet imager for the Swedish Viking satellite, launched in 1984, to obtain images of the Aurora to support studies of the magnetosphere (*see* NORTHERN LIGHTS; PHYSICS).

In 1984 the space industry employed over 3200 people and, as a result of further investment promised by the federal government, was expected to involve 3700 people by 1987. Canada's exports of space technology represent over 70% of total sales. In fact, industry sales generate more money than does goverment investment, a situation unique in the world. In recognition of Canada's contributions to the US space program, NASA has made places available to Canadian astronauts on various shuttle flights, and Canadian scientists are studying the feasibility of participating in the US Space Station Program. *See* John Herbert CHAPMAN.   B.C. BLEVIS

Spanish Canada's relations with Spain date back several centuries to the voyages of the BASQUE fishermen to the Atlantic coast and to Spanish exploration of the Pacific coast. Basque expeditions are recalled in names such as Channel-Port aux Basques and Île aux Basques. Archaeologists have uncovered traces of a 16th-century Basque whaling station at RED BAY, Labrador. The numerous Spanish explorations on the Pacific Coast of Canada between 1542 and 1792 are recalled in names such as Alberni, Laredo Strait, Carmelo Strait, Mazaredo Sound, Mount Bodega, Quadra Rocks and Narvaez Bay. At one time Vancouver I was called Quadra I and Vancouver I to commemorate the friendship between the Spanish navigator BODEGA Y QUADRA and English Captain George VANCOUVER.

Migration and Settlement Significant Spanish settlement did not occur in Canada until the 20th century. Between 1913 and 1914 about 2000 Spaniards arrived in Canada. A small trickle immigrated during the interwar period. Just over 1000 had immigrated 1946-55, but the figure rose to 11 000, 1956-67, and to 5000 in the years 1970 to 1977.

Spanish-speaking people have immigrated to Canada from Spain and from several S American countries. They have immigrated for a number of reasons, including a desire for greater economic opportunities and a desire to escape political oppression. Because of improvements in Spain's economic and political climate, emigration has decreased dramatically. In 1981, 68% of the estimated total of 53 540 people of Spanish origin in Canada resided in Québec and in Ontario; Alberta and BC had 9% each. The balance was sparsely scattered across the country. In Canada the Spanish have overwhelmingly settled in cities, particularly Montréal, Toronto and Vancouver.

Social and Cultural Life Many Spanish immigrants are skilled workers, eg, welders, technicians, professionals; some are farmers who immigrated to Canada in 1957 under an agreement between Canada and Spain; others are labourers. Most Spanish immigrants are Roman Catholic, but there is also a very small group of active Protestants. Religion is one important basis of social organization. In areas of Spanish concentration there are recreational and social organizations to help immigrants adjust to Canadian life and to provide language instruction.

Several Spanish newspapers are published in Toronto and Montréal. In the smaller settlements the Spanish and Latin Americans are involved in joint publishing ventures. Dance groups, especially of the flamboyant flamenco variety, flourish in several centres and soccer is a popular sport.

Group Maintenance Spanish immigrants tend to maintain their former regional allegiances. The Basques openly express their desire for the independence of their homeland from Spain. Other areas of Spain are distinguished by regional languages, eg, the Gallegos from Galicia in the NW and the people from Valencia in the SE of Spain each speak their separate, though related, languages. Many northerners are of Gaelic ancestry, whereas some of the southerners are of Moorish background. Small settlements of Sephardic Jews from Spain in both Toronto and Montréal form separate enclaves.

Spanish is generally not spoken past the second generation, although Spanish-language classes are frequently available. The immigrants assimilate readily in French communities, with whom they identify more easily than with English-speaking areas.   GRACE M. ANDERSON

Reading: Grace M. Anderson, "Spanish- and Portugese-speaking Immigrants in Canada," in *Two Nations, Many Cultures: Ethnic Groups in Canada* (1979).

Spanish Exploration Following the global circumnavigation of Magellan's expedition, 1519-1522, Holy Roman Emperor Charles V wished to locate a N American strait into Asian waters. The Spaniards possessed information on the Newfoundland and Labrador coasts from Portuguese voyages and from BASQUE fishermen and whalers. In 1523 Spain, which had previously focused on Central and S America, dispatched Esteban GÓMEZ to explore the New England coast. On the Pacific, the California and Oregon coasts were explored from Mexican ports in the 1540s, but Spain's claim to the entire Pacific littoral of America was not based upon actual exploration. To confuse the situation, apocryphal voyages such as those of Juan de FUCA, Lorenzo FERRER MALDONADO and Bartholomew de Fonte caused cartographers to place imaginary passages and inland seas in present-day Canada.

During the 1770s reports of Russian expansion from Kamchatka into N America forced Spanish exploration of the NORTHWEST COAST. Within Spanish administrative structure the viceroyalty of Mexico was responsible for Pacific operations north of San Blas. In 1774 Juan PÉREZ HERNANDEZ sailed north from Mexico, reaching the Queen Charlotte Is, where the HAIDA paddled out in their canoes to trade. Fearful of shipwreck, Pérez did not land to take possession, although he did anchor off Nootka Sd, Vancouver I. The inconclusive results caused the Mexican viceroy to dispatch another expedition. In 1775 Juan Francisco de la BODEGA Y QUADRA reached Alaska with 2 ships at about 58°30'N. He took possession and located excellent ports in Prince of Wales I. The Spaniards were impressed by the civilization of NW Coast Indians. Their maritime, artistic, commercial, architectural and military capabilities had not been anticipated by Spanish observers familiar with northern Mexico and California.

When reports reached Madrid about James COOK's third Pacific voyage (1776-79), King Charles III of Spain, concerned with imperial expansion and scientific discovery, ordered new efforts to counter the foreign challenge. Short of ships and personnel, the Spaniards missed Cook entirely. In 1779 Ignacio de Arteaga and Bodega y Quadra sailed to Bucareli Bay and explored as far as Cook Inlet. The expedition produced scientific charts and ethnological data, but Spain did not publish the results. Cook's journal became the handbook for those who would pursue exploration or commerce in the N Pacific.

In 1788 the controversial Esteban José MARTÍNEZ led an expedition back to Alaska and as far west as Unalaska I. He visited Russian posts and returned to Mexico with information that in 1789 Russian traders planned to occupy Nootka Sd. Unaware that British and American FUR TRADERS were active in the sea-otter trade along the NW Coast, the Mexican viceroy ordered Martínez to occupy Nootka Sd. The resulting clash produced the NOOTKA SOUND CONTROVERSY with Britain. In 1791 the scientific expedition of Alejandro Malaspina (see MALASPINA EXPEDITION) was diverted into the N Pacific to search for a NORTHWEST PASSAGE. Other Spanish expeditions were dispatched from Yuquot (Friendly Cove) at Nootka Sd and from Mexico. Bodega y Quadra and other explorers, including Francisco de Eliza, Jacinto Caamaño, Manuel Quimper, Dionisio Alcalá-Galiano and Cayetano Valdés, explored the coast from Alaska to California. With the final settlement of the Nootka Sd issues in 1795, Spain withdrew from the N Pacific. See SUTIL AND MEXICANA.   CHRISTON I. ARCHER

Reading: W. L. Cook, *Flood Tide of Empire* (1973); Iris H.W. Engstrand, *Spanish Scientists in the New World* (1981).

Spar Aerospace Limited, *see* ELECTRONICS INDUSTRY.

Sparling, Gordon, filmmaker (b at Toronto 13 Aug 1900) pioneer director, writer and producer of some 200 films, especially the Canadian Cameo series of short films (1932-55). These were Canada's first major films with sound and in the 1930s represented virtually the only reflection of Canada on its own and the world's screens. Sparling graduated from U of T and joined the Ontario Motion Picture Bureau in 1924. After a brief period as assistant director on the feature *Carry on Sergeant!* (1928) and with the federal Motion Picture Bureau, he moved to New York in 1929. He returned to Canada in 1931 to make sponsored films for Associated Screen News in Montréal on condition that he could also produce short films for theatrical release. During the war, he supervised newsreels and training films for the Canadian Army, rejoining ASN in 1946 and remaining until its production department closed in 1957. He later worked for the NFB.   PETER MORRIS

Sparrow, name given to several unrelated groups of BIRDS. Sparrows are classified in 3 families: Emberizidae, which includes New World sparrows; Estrildidae; and Passeridae, which includes the familiar HOUSE SPARROW. About 34 species of the subfamily Emberizinae occur in Canada. They are primarily ground feeders, eating mostly seeds, although insects are eaten in summer. Adults of most species feed insects to young. They are small to medium-sized, ranging in length from LeConte's sparrow (*Ammodramus leconteii*), as small as 11 cm, to the rufous-sided towhee (*Pipilo erythrophthalmus*), up to 22 cm. Generally, sparrows have dull plumage with distinctive head markings; the exceptions are the brightly coloured towhees and the sharply patterned juncos and longspurs. Males and females of most species are similar in size and plumage; eg, male and female song sparrows (*Melospiza melodia*), widespread in Canada, are virtually indistinguishable by plumage alone. Usually, only males sing; thus a singing song sparrow is almost certainly male. Songs differ considerably among species. Lark sparrows (*Chondestes grammacus*), of dry fields with scattered bushes and trees, sing long, melodious songs containing many trills. White-throated sparrows (*Zonotrichia albicollis*), of coniferous and mixed forests, utter songs of pure tone; one rendition, paraphrased as "Oh sweet Canada Canada Canada," has given them the local name Canada bird. Grasshopper sparrows (*A. savannarum*), of grassy fields in the extreme southern prairies and Ontario, give tuneless, insectlike reelings. Henslow's sparrow (*A. henslowii*), of weedy fields of southern Ontario, gives one of the poorest vocal efforts of any bird, a hiccoughing "tsi-lick." All species of sparrows in Canada are migratory to some extent. American tree sparrows (*Spizella arborea*) nest in scrub willow of the Subarctic and winter in southern Canada and northern US. Clay-coloured sparrows (*S. pallida*), of brush-covered prairies, winter in Mexico. The Ipswich sparrow (*Passerculus s. princeps*), a well-marked subspecies of the widely distributed savannah sparrow (*P. sandwichensis*), breeds only on SABLE I and winters on the Atlantic seaboard. RICHARD W. KNAPTON

Sparwood, BC, District Municipality, pop 4167 (1981c), inc 1966, is located 30 km NE of Fernie in the Elk R Valley. The local timber was considered "suitable for spars" by early railway builders. Recently developed after the historic mining towns of Michel, Natal and Middletown were levelled, Sparwood is a residential centre for coal mining and processing, as well as for outdoor recreation. It has experienced rapid growth in the 1970s, with the development of the Line Creek Mine and the nearby Byron Creek Collieries. WILLIAM A. SLOAN

Speaker, the presiding officer of the HOUSE OF COMMONS, chosen from its membership after each general election for that Parliament's duration. The choice of Speaker is made by the prime minister, seconded by the leader of the Opposition and finalized by acclamation. The Speaker represents the House and speaks for it. At the opening of each Parliament the Speaker requests confirmation of the privileges of the Commons and, at royal assent presents appropriation bills on its behalf. To be disrespectful of the Speaker is to be disrespectful of the House. The Speaker, who is responsible, as chairman, umpire and manager, for House proceedings, is expected to be fair, patient and understanding, but also to prevent obstructive members from frustrating the House. With the 4 other Commissioners of Internal Economy, the Speaker applies to the CROWN for money to pay the indemnities of members, expenses for summoned witnesses, and salaries for pages, cooks and secretaries. He or she appoints HANSARD staff, constables, etc. After being forced to the Chair — nominees feign resistance out of modesty — the Speaker severs party ties. In 1963 PM John Diefenbaker appointed the Hon Marcel Lambert, the 1962-63 Speaker, to the Cabinet, and in 1980 PM Pierre Trudeau moved the Hon Jeanne SAUVÉ from the Cabinet to the Chair — 2 moves criticized by those favouring a strong, independent Speaker. All recent Speakers have been bilingual.

Under the CONSTITUTION ACT, 1867, Speakers vote only to break a tie and then not according to their views, but so as to leave the substance of the question to be decided later by the House. In Britain, the House of Lords has no Speaker, and a minister, the Lord Chancellor, presides, but at Ottawa the Senate has a "speaker" (the post is not mentioned in the BNA Act), appointed by the Crown and permitted to vote. The Speakers of provincial assemblies follow the pattern of the Commons Speaker. JOHN B. STEWART

Speck, Frank Gouldsmith, anthropologist (b at Brooklyn, NY 8 Nov 1881; d at Philadelphia, Pa 6 Feb 1950). He pioneered study of the Algonquian peoples of eastern Canada and New England. After studying under Franz BOAS at Columbia, he taught at University of Pennsylvania from 1909 and began a lifelong project of recording the changing cultures of the Algonquians and their neighbours. He collected Algonquian artifacts for the National Museum of Canada, recorded their myths and customs and mapped their hunting territories. His maps of individual and band hunting territories documented Algonquian land rights. Research of this kind has become crucial to native LAND CLAIMS, as Speck predicted. BRUCE COX
Reading: F. Speck, "The Family Hunting Band as the Basis of Algonquian Social Organization," *Cultural Ecology,* ed Bruce Cox (1973); and *Naskapi* (1935, repr 1977).

Spectroscopy is the field of study that examines, measures and interprets the electromagnetic spectra produced when radiant energy is emitted or absorbed by a substance. Spectroscopic methods are important in performing chemical analyses of substances and are used in astronomical studies (*see* CHEMISTRY; ASTRONOMY; PHYSICS). Spectroscopy started in 1666 when Sir Isaac Newton passed rays of light from the SUN through a glass prism and observed the colours of the visible spectrum. Light is composed of electromagnetic waves, each colour corresponding to a different wavelength. The separation of light into the individual wavelengths by means of a device, such as a prism or a diffraction grating, forms the basis of optical spectroscopy. However, the visible segment comprises only a small fraction of the complete electromagnetic spectrum. The ultraviolet region begins at wavelengths shorter than the violet and extends eventually into the X-ray region; the infrared portion starts at wavelengths longer than the red and extends into the microwave and radio regions. In these regions it is more usual to characterize the radiation by its frequency rather than its wavelength, although the 2 are interconnected by the relation: wavelength times frequency equals velocity of light (299 792 458 m/s).

All substances emit or absorb radiation at their own characteristic frequencies or wavelengths; therefore the spectrum of a substance provides a "fingerprint" by which it can be identified. When light from a star is spread out according to colour, many fine details, called spectral lines, can be seen. A study of the frequencies and intensities of these lines gives information on the amounts of the various substances present and about the temperature, pressure and radiation within the emitting gas. An early example of this research involved Joseph von Fraunhofer's observation of dark absorption lines in the visible spectrum of the sun, caused by the presence of sodium, calcium and other elements in the solar atmosphere. Helium was discovered in the spectrum of the sun before it was found on Earth.

A detailed understanding of the spectra of atoms and molecules originated with the introduction of the quantum theory by Max Planck in 1900. According to this theory, energy is emitted or absorbed in discrete units called quanta. In 1913 Niels Bohr was able to give a detailed explanation of the spectrum of the hydrogen atom by postulating that the atom can exist in a series of discrete energy levels and that emission or absorption of radiation only occurs when there is a change from one energy level to another. The introduction of quantum mechanics by Werner Heisenberg and Erwin Schrödinger in 1925-26 was another important development. Spectra associated with a change of the rotational quantum numbers of a molecule are normally studied in the microwave and adjoining regions of the spectrum; those associated with a change in the vibrational quantum numbers occur in the infrared region. Electronic spectra are usually studied in the visible and ultraviolet regions. In 1925 S.A. Goudsmit and G.E. Uhlenbeck postulated that the electron possesses an intrinsic angular momentum (or spin) with which is associated a magnetic moment. This idea was introduced to explain some groups of lines found in the spectra of the alkali and alkaline earth metals. A similar multiplicity of lines is found in the spectra of molecules containing one or more unpaired electron spins. Such species are often called free radicals. Similarly, many nuclei have magnetic moments the energies of which depend on their orientation in a magnetic field. The study of nuclear magnetic resonance (NMR) spectroscopy has yielded valuable information on the structures of molecules.

Since the advent of LASERS in 1950 many new forms of spectroscopy have evolved. With fixed-frequency lasers, molecules and free radicals can be tuned into resonance by applying electrical or magnetic fields. With tunable lasers many types of high-resolution spectroscopy have been developed. All these techniques yield very precise measurements of the properties of atoms and molecules. Lasers have also extended the use of Raman spectroscopy, in which molecules are excited by strong monochromatic radiation and the scattered radiation is found to contain extra frequencies which are characteristic of the molecule excited.

Spectroscopy has numerous applications. Atomic emission and absorption spectroscopy is used to identify elements present in MINERALS or to determine traces of impurities of the order of one part per million or even one part per billion. Nuclear magnetic resonance spectroscopy and infrared spectroscopy are used routinely by chemists to identify materials and to monitor reactions. Various forms of spectroscopy are used to measure the concentrations of pollutants in the atmosphere. Optical spectroscopy has identified many molecules present in the atmospheres of the stars and planets, while microwave spectroscopy has identified over 50 molecular species in the interstellar medium.

In Canada research in spectroscopy has taken place at the NATIONAL RESEARCH COUNCIL; in university departments of chemistry, physics and astronomy; and at observatories across the country. The spectroscopy section of NRC's Physics Division received world recognition through the work of Gerhard HERZBERG and his many colleagues. At University of Toronto H.L. WELSH has done significant work on the Raman spectra of molecules. Early workers at the Dominion Astrophysical Observatory include J.S. PLASKETT, J.A. PEARCE, A. MCKELLAR and C.S. BEALS.
D.A. RAMSAY

Speech From The Throne reveals to the SENATE and the HOUSE OF COMMONS the work the ministers propose for the session of Parliament then beginning. Historically, in England, the speech sometimes explained why Parliament had been called into session when many years had elapsed between sessions. Now, with Parliament doing very much the same kinds of business year after year and in session almost constantly, few speeches arouse great curiosity. The speech contains comments on the state of the nation and outlines the measures on which the government will seek parliamentary action. Although delivered by the queen or her representative (usually the GOVERNOR GENERAL) the speech is entirely the work of ministers; consequently the opposition parties feel obliged to dismiss the speech as vacuous or misconceived. Normally the first business of the House of Commons —

and of the Senate — is to authorize a response to the speech. This is the "Address in Reply to the Speech from the Throne." A government back-bencher moves for a thankful Address; then members in opposition move amendments lamenting the content of the speech and usually declaring their nonconfidence in the ministers. In the House of Commons the debate on the Address is limited to 8 days. Given the very general nature of the motions, a member can speak on almost any subject and remain relevant. To demonstrate that the House can initiate business other than what has been proposed in the speech the first bill introduced in a session always deals with a matter not mentioned in the speech.

JOHN B. STEWART

Speed Skating races are held for men and women both indoors and outdoors. In Olympic and world-championship events, these races are held on open-air oval tracks 400 m in length. Two competitors race against each other and the clock in separate lanes, changing lanes on each lap so that both skaters go the same distance. For men, there are races of 500, 1500, 5000 and 10 000 m. Women race distances of 500, 1000, 1500 and 3000 m. This is commonly regarded as the European style of speed skating; in N America, mass races, where more than 2 compete, and indoor racing have always been popular.

Although there is evidence of the appearance of ICE SKATING in 1250, the first organized race was not recorded until 1763 in England. The first race in Canada is believed to have taken place in 1854, and the first organized competitions were held at the Victoria Rink in Saint John, NB, in 1883. Four years later, the Amateur Skating Assn of Canada was formed and held its first official Canadian championships. In 1894 the ASAC joined the International Skating Union, bringing Canadian skating on to the international scene. In those formative years, speed skating and FIGURE SKATING were both under the auspices of one organization, with the concerns of the speed skaters predominating. Figure skaters did not form their own association until 1939.

Speed skating, at the world level, has largely been the preserve of Dutch and Scandinavian skaters. The Russians and Americans have also enjoyed considerable success; the most notable of the Americans, Eric Heiden, won 5 gold medals at the 1980 Winter Olympics. Canada, however, has also produced many outstanding speed skaters. In 1897 Jack McCulloch of Winnipeg won the world championships held in Montréal. Fred Robson, Gladys Robinson and Lela BROOKS, all of Toronto, were prominent in N American skating competitions and set a number of world records in the first 3 decades of this century. Another prominent skater of that time was Charlie GORMAN of Saint John. Jean WILSON of Toronto won gold and silver medals at the 1932 Olympics, where women's speed skating was a demonstration event.

From then until the 1970s, Canada's main

The greatest speedskater in Canada's history is Gaétan Boucher, who captured 2 gold medals at the Sarajevo Olympics in 1984 (*courtesy Canapress*).

speed-skating achievement was Gordon Audley's bronze medal in the 500 m event at the 1952 Olympics. Twenty-four years later, Cathy Priestner won a silver medal in Innsbruck, Austria. In 1973 Sylvia Burka became the unofficial world junior ladies' champion and won the women's world championship in 1976. The following year she won the world sprint championship. For men, Gaétan BOUCHER of Québec was second only to Heiden in world competition in 1980, and set a world record for the 1000 m event. In the 1984 Olympics at Sarajevo, Boucher stimulated interest in speed skating with 2 gold medals and one silver.   J. THOMAS WEST

Reading: J. Hurdis, *Speed Skating in Canada — 1854-1981: A Chronological History* (1981).

Spence Bay, NWT, UP, pop 431 (1981c), is located in a narrow inlet on the W side of the BOOTHIA PENINSULA, 1231 air km NE of YELLOWKNIFE. Inuit settled at the site in 1947 after the HBC had taken a group of them from an inappropriate location to another. Spence Bay was the location of a well-known legal case in 1966, when 2 Inuit were tried after executing an insane woman. The execution had been carried out according to traditional custom. The outcome of the trial blended Western law with Inuit tradition, with one man acquitted and the other receiving a suspended sentence. Most of the Inuit residents still subsist today on trapping, hunting and fishing.   ANNELIES POOL

Spence-Sales, Harold, urban planner (b at Lahore, India 22 Oct 1907). Professor of architecture at McGill 1947-70, he led the first Canadian university program in town planning and in the later 1940s and the 1950s frequently advised governments on policy measures for land use and planning legislation. His more notable works relate to the planning of new towns (eg, Oromocto, NB, and Préville, Qué) and to master-plan schemes for Moncton, NB; Charlottetown; Sudbury, Ont; Prince Albert, Sask; and other towns. His teaching and consulting work emphasized not only the aesthetics of urban planning but sensitivity to the environment, treating town planning as both an art form and a social mission. His writings include *How to Subdivide* (1949), *A Guide to Urban Dispersal* (1956) and *Beautifying Towns* (1967). Two generations of Canadian planners have been influenced by his original thought and imaginative style of planning.

WILLIAM T. PERKS

Spencer, David, merchant (b at St Athan, Wales 9 Aug 1837; d at Victoria 2 Mar 1920). A farmer's son, he was apprenticed to a dry-goods merchant in Wales and came to Victoria in 1862. After operating a book and stationery business, in 1873 he bought a dry-goods store from which developed the department store which bore his name. Branches were established in Nanaimo in 1889, Vancouver in 1907 and other BC centres. Spencer, a local preacher for the Methodist Church, was cofounder of the first TEMPERANCE society on Vancouver I and a benefactor of Victoria's Protestant Orphanage and other philanthropies. His eldest child, Christopher (1868-1953), was active in the firm until it was sold to the T. Eaton Co in 1948.

PATRICIA E. ROY

Sphagnum, *see* MOSS; PEAT; SWAMP, MARSH AND BOG.

Spider, carnivorous arthropod (segmented, jointed-limbed animal) of class ARACHNIDA, order Araneae. About 30 000 species are known of an estimated 50 000 world total. Spiders occur throughout the world excluding Antarctica, inhabiting terrestrial and aquatic environments. Almost 1300 species are known from Canada, including 9 species of tarantulas from Ontario and BC. Thirteen species of spiders occur on Ellesmere I, the northernmost point in Canada. Spiders have 8 legs and 2 body parts, abdomen

The black widow spider (with its distinctive hour-glass pattern) is among the most poisonous of all creatures. Its venom is 200 times as poisonous as that of a rattlesnake (*photo by Stephen J. Krasemann/DRK Photo*).

and cephalothorax (fused head and thorax). Spinnerets on the abdomen produce silk, used for making webs and draglines, wrapping prey and protecting eggs. Some spiders build a new web daily, eating the old one and recycling the silk. Although most species have 8 eyes, they can only distinguish light and dark. Jumping and wolf spiders have good, binocular vision for about 15-20 cm. Most spiders in Canada produce young annually, or once in 2 years. Dwarf spiders may lay only 8-10 eggs; black widow spiders, 1000 or more. The smallest adults are about 0.4 mm long; the largest, about 25 cm (total leg span). In grassy fields, spider populations may reach over 2 million per hectare. Some spiders have amazing powers of dispersal. Large spiders may crawl only a few metres per day, but small ones "balloon" through the air 50 km or more in a day.

Spiders can ingest only liquids. After catching prey, they suck its blood. Then they exude enzymes into and on to prey, converting its tissues to a soup, which is then sucked up. All spiders are poisonous to some degree, even those few species that have poison glands partly modified into glue-spitting glands. Black widow spiders, which are among the most poisonous of animals, are found in southern Ontario, Saskatchewan, Alberta and BC. Their venom is about 200 times as poisonous as that of a rattlesnake. Spiders are important predators, eating many destructive insects, and helping to control INSECT PESTS.   ROBIN LEECH

Spinach (*Spinacia oleracea*), leafy, cool-season VEGETABLE belonging to the Chenopodiaceae family. First cultivated in Persia over 2000 years ago, spinach was introduced to Europe in the 12th century. The plant consists of a leafy rosette formed around a crown (compressed stem). One variety, with smooth leaves, is used in the processing industry; another, with wrinkled foliage, is used solely for the fresh market. First sown in early spring, spinach requires only 40 days to mature and will produce several crops if sowing is staggered. The crop is usually harvested mechanically. Spinach is susceptible to VIRUS diseases, mildew and attacks by burrowing insects. It is rich in iron and contains vitamins A and C. Traditionally used in salads, spinach is now used increasingly in various food products (eg, purées). In Canada only a few hundred hectares are devoted to commercial production; however, spinach is popular in home gardens. PIERRE SAURIOL

Spinks, John William Tranter, chemist, educator (b in Norfolk, Eng 1 Jan 1908). He moved to Canada in 1930 to join the staff of U Sask and has since earned an international reputation as a teacher and researcher. While on leave in Germany in 1933 he worked with Gerhard HERZBERG, and he was instrumental in bringing him to Canada. During WWII Spinks developed search-and-rescue operations for the RCAF and took part in the early work on atomic energy. Later he pioneered the use of radioactive isotopes in research, coauthored with R.J. Woods the first textbook on the chemical effects of high-energy radiation, and represented Canada at meetings on the peaceful uses of atomic energy. Appointed dean of graduate studies at U Sask in 1949 and president in 1959, he has been a member of many national and international groups concerned with university education. He is the author of more than 250 scientific and other works and has been honoured by universities and governments alike. He is companion of the Order of Canada. R.J. WOODS
Reading: John Spinks, Two Blades of Grass: An Autobiography (1980).

Spiraea (*Spiraea*) is a genus of small shrubs of the family Rosaceae (rose). The genus consists of some 70-80 species, as well as many horticultural varieties of garden origin that have resulted from hybridization. Probably the most noteworthy of these hybrids is *S. vanhouttei* (bridal wreath spiraea), derived from 2 Asiatic species, *S. trilobata* and *S. cantoniensis,* which is widely cultivated in Canada and elsewhere for its spectacular spring blossoms. Spiraeas are deciduous, with simple leaves and generally dense clusters of small, white, pink or purple flowers. They are native to the N temperate zones of Eurasia and N America, generally growing on moist, wooded slopes and meadows. Canada has 7 native species, none of which is found all across the country. The most widespread, *S. alba,* occurs from Alberta to Newfoundland. One species, the western *S. beauverdiana,* extends northward to the Arctic Ocean.

Spiritualism, *see* NEW RELIGIOUS MOVEMENTS.

Spitsbergen, a bleak Norwegian island group only 965 km from the North Pole, became strategically significant in WWII when Germany attacked the USSR in June 1941. Weather reports broadcast from the island were useful to the Germans in N USSR, and a German occupation would have threatened the USSR's vital arctic supply route. Consequently, some 600 Canadian troops were sent from Britain to evacuate the 2800 inhabitants and lay waste the island's 4 settlements. Between 25 Aug and 3 Sept 1941 that was done, leaving Spitsbergen deserted and devastated. However, both German and Anglo-Norwegian weather stations were subsequently established there. BRERETON GREENHOUS

Spohr, Arnold Theodore, dancer, choreographer, teacher, director (b at Rhein, Sask 26 Dec 1927). One of the most respected figures in Canadian BALLET, Spohr was responsible for leading the ROYAL WINNIPEG BALLET to its position as an internationally acclaimed troupe. Spohr trained in London (Eng), New York C and Hollywood. He danced with the then Winnipeg Ballet, 1945-54, becoming a principal dancer. In London he partnered the famous ballerina Alicia Markova. Interim director of the Royal Winnipeg Ballet in 1957, Spohr was officially appointed artistic director in 1958. He set about restoring the company's vitality following a period of crisis after its premises were destroyed

by fire in 1954. Through frequent travel at home and abroad Spohr sought choreographers to construct skillfully blended programs that would show off the dancers to advantage and please audiences. Under Spohr, the company has undertaken many successful foreign tours and has become arguably the most popular ballet troupe in Canada. Spohr's concern for the training of dancers led him in 1970 to establish a professional division of the Royal Winnipeg Ballet School. For many years he helped direct the ballet summer school of the BANFF CENTRE SCHOOL OF FINE ARTS. Among Spohr's honours are the MOLSON PRIZE (1970), the Dance Magazine Award (1982) and the Dîplome d'honneur of the Canadian Conference of the Arts (1983).
MICHAEL CRABB

Sponge (Porifera), phylum of bottom-dwelling, attached, aquatic organisms which, as adults, generate vigorous water currents through their porous bodies by action of internal fields of microscopic flagella (whiplike structures). Sponges are the most primitive multicelled ANIMALS. The 5000-10 000 known species are distributed worldwide in marine and freshwater habitats (98% and 2% of species, respectively). They are common in Canadian waters, but a thorough inventory has not been made. The phylum is usually divided into 4 classes (Hexactinellida, Calcarea, Demospongiae and Sclerospongiae), according to the form and chemical nature of the skeleton. Living tissues of common, shallow-water sponges consist of loosely organized cells. Deep-sea hexactinellids (glass sponges) are syncytial, ie, lack division of living tissues into separate cells. In both types, water pulled into small surface pores and distributed through internal canals provides oxygen, food (caught by filtration), waste removal (by water leaving the larger body pores) and distribution of sperm and eggs. Sponges are important in the bath sponge industry, as boring organisms damaging oysters and limestone coastlines, as sources of bioactive compounds in the PHARMACEUTICALS INDUSTRY, and in studies of cell specialization and intercommunication. H.M. REISWIG

Sportfishing The presence of anglers shown in 5000-year-old Egyptian drawings suggests that fishing for pleasure emerged when time became available for activities other than the acquisition of food and shelter. In Canada, sportfishing ranks among the most popular and enduring forms of outdoor recreation and dates back to the first Europeans, who brought with them well-established sportfishing interests and traditions, and laws relating to FISHERIES. Species such as salmon played an important role in the life and culture of coastal Indians, but the enjoyment of Indian and Inuit youths in emulating the fisheries exploits of elders is shared by youths the world over. Succeeding settlers and visiting writers sent back reports of unlimited abundance of fish, thus laying the foundation for Canada's international image as a sportfishing mecca.

The appeal of sportfishing is universal, although it has always had a special attraction for the very young and old. A national survey in 1980 showed that 6 million anglers fished for pleasure in Canada, about 20% of them under 16 years of age. About 5 million were Canadians, 20% of the total population. The other million were visitors (primarily from the US). Catches ranged from MINNOW, SMELT and other smaller fishes sometimes counted by the bucket, to bluefin TUNA, weighing up to 460 kg, found off North Lk, PEI. Total weight provides one measure of the angler's overall catch. Results from an earlier survey show that in 1975 a conservatively estimated 77 000 t were landed by anglers. This represented about 8% of the weight of Canada's total combined commercial and sport catch of finfish for the year.

For anglers, however, the sport centres on the fish and the experience. Traditionally, anglers use lure, bait and fly, but gear and methods vary by species, season, place and preference, ranging from the most primitive gear to boats outfitted with the most modern electronic equipment and conveniences. Among the 100 or so species that are sought, many rank the SALMON, on both coasts, supreme. Atlantic salmon, historically, has been esteemed the king of gamefish. Rivers such as the MIRAMICHI in NB, and the RESTIGOUCHE, shared by Québec and NB, are known to fly-fishermen worldwide. Canada's 5 species of Pacific salmon are far more numerous, with 2 (coho and chinook), weighing up to 40 kg, providing the main focus for BC ocean sport fisheries. Thousands of anglers are drawn to YT and NWT in search of wilderness solitude and opportunities to fish for trophy-sized lake TROUT, northern PIKE, arctic CHAR and arctic GRAYLING. Elsewhere, anglers enjoy wide choice. Northern pike, WALLEYE and lake trout are widely distributed. However, there are major regional differences and preferences: brook trout are favoured in Newfoundland; lake trout and northern pike are main attractions for fly-in fishing in northern Sask, Man, Ont and Qué. In overall landings, however, 4 species, yellow PERCH, walleye, brook trout and northern pike, head the list. Winter adds another dimension to the sport, when anglers go ice fishing.

Responsibility for protection and management is shared by the federal and provincial governments. Tidal fisheries are exclusively under federal jurisdiction. In inland fresh waters, there is an overlap based on court interpretations of provisions of the BNA Act (1867). All laws for fisheries regulation, as such, are federally enacted. Provinces, however, possess and exercise proprietary rights over fresh waters, largely through setting and collecting licence fees. While there is a mosaic of federal-provincial arrangements for the administration of fisheries laws, there is a further anomaly regarding public access. Two provinces, NB and Québec, have retained riparian ownership in their fresh waters and the exclusive right to fish can be privately owned. All tidal fisheries are common property and, with a few exceptions, so are freshwater fisheries of the territories and the other 8 provinces.

Governments face increasingly complex fisheries problems. Much of Canada's treasure of relatively unfished northern waters is in areas vulnerable to ACID RAIN. POLLUTION, in the form of industrial and natural contaminants (eg, mercury), does not necessarily kill fish, as does acid rain, but these and an ever-increasing list of man-made compounds tend to become concentrated in larger, predator gamefish and, in certain instances, are a health threat to all who eat them. Some fish stocks, like the salmons, are depleted and overfished, and with the prospect of ever-growing numbers of anglers, there is intensified competition with other users of fish and the habitat, as well as problems of funding fisheries restoration and enhancement.

Sportfishing on the Miramichi River. A 1980 survey showed that some 6 million people fish for pleasure each year in Canada (*courtesy New Brunswick Tourism*).

Support for the role and welfare of sport fisheries comes from many sources. Organized anglers are Canada's prototypal consumer advocates. Some Atlantic salmon clubs were organized over a century ago, and organized anglers in nationally affiliated provincial fish and game federations are in the forefront of endeavours to protect and enhance sport fisheries. According to the 1980 survey, anglers spent and invested $1.7 billion in sportfishing in Canada. Thanks to the $300 million spent the same year by visiting anglers, Canada leads the world in foreign exchange earnings from sportfishing. From an environmental viewpoint, the continuing natural abundance of gamefish is regarded by many as a key measure of the quality of the aquatic habitat.

With 20% of the population fishing every year, the extent of public goodwill and support for sportfishing is not surprising. However, Canada has also been blessed by the contributions made to sportfishing literature by individuals such as Roderick HAIG-BROWN, the Izaak Walton of this era.   A.L.W. TUOMI

Reading: D.E. McAllister and E.J. Crossman, *Guide to the Freshwater Sport Fishes of Canada* (1973).

Sporting-Goods Industry The Canadian sporting-goods industry has grown and diversified a great deal in the past 50 years, as a result of the increasing amount of leisure time available to Canadians. As early as 1929, 30 manufacturers, employing 1212 people, produced goods (eg, skates, lacrosse equipment, snowshoes) worth $4.8 million. The GREAT DEPRESSION of the 1930s severely curtailed the infant industry, and by the beginning of WWII production had declined by over 50%. The war years spurred recovery and output increased from $5 million in 1940 to $8.6 million in 1945. The industry reacted positively to the buoyant economy of the 1950s and to the first signs of changes in living patterns that favoured active and outdoor life-styles. Shipments increased from $9.4 million to $31.6 million during the 1950s; the number of manufacturers grew from 70 to 107. Throughout the 1960s, the industry grew steadily, as nonwork activities took on even greater importance for Canadians and as family outdoor recreation and physical fitness activities became more attractive. Industry shipments increased during the 1960s from $31.6 million to $81.7 million and employment in the industry rose by 45% to 5463 persons.

The greatest period of growth occurred in the 1970s, when significant export markets opened up for ice HOCKEY and CAMPING equipment, and for sports goods ranging from swimming pools to fitness and gymnasium equipment. Domestic shipments increased about 400% in this decade, from $81.7 million to $321.3 million. Exports rose over the same period from $22 million to $96 million. The number of manufacturers grew from 123 to 189 and employment increased 24% to 6798. By 1981 employment reached almost 7400 and there were 195 manufacturers, of which 90 were in Ontario and 66 in Québec. Most of the rest were in BC, Alberta and Manitoba. Manufacturers are equally divided between large-city and small-town locations. Most (67%) are small operations, employing less than 20 workers and usually specializing in one product area. They account for only 6% of total sales and only 7% of employment.

Pressure from trading nations in Asia, Europe and the US has resulted in increasing rationalization of the Canadian industry in the past 20 years, and several large manufacturers (more than 100 employees) have emerged. They represent only 9% of establishments, but they produce 65% of all shipments and employ 81% of workers. Most Canadian sporting-goods firms are domestically controlled; Statistics Canada

data show that, in 1976, 87.6% were Canadian owned and they accounted for 77.5% of shipments and 79% of employment.

The main sectors of the industry (according to 1979 total domestic shipments) are as follows: ice sports, 36.6%; bicycles, 17.7%; swimming pools, 17.0%; SKIING equipment, 6.5%; gym equipment, 5.7%; GOLF equipment, 5.7%; playground equipment, 2.6%; FISHING equipment, 2.6%; BASEBALL equipment, 2.1%; billiards equipment, 1.5%; HUNTING equipment, 1.0%; and CURLING equipment, 1.0%. In addition, there are more than 30 domestic manufacturers of skiwear and other sports clothing in Alberta, BC, Ontario and Québec. There are more than a dozen manufacturers of athletic FOOTWEAR, ranging from high-tech running shoes to alpine ski boots.

Canada exports about 24% of total domestic shipments. While 75% went to the US in the early 1970s, significant new markets have been developed in Japan and Europe in the past decade. Total exports grew from $22 million in 1970 to $95.7 million in 1980, with shipments to the US declining from approximately 75% of all exports in the early 1970s to 63% by 1982. The market for sporting-goods equipment grew 183% in Canada in the first half of the 1970s. Domestic suppliers could not meet the demand for more and newer products; therefore, imports increased 200% from 1970 to 1975, while domestic production increased 133%. By 1975, imports represented $146 million in shipments, while domestic production represented $190 million. In the latter 1970s, the total market increased by 68%, as did imports, and domestic shipments increased by 94%, reflecting increased export activity by domestic manufacturers. Recently, several European suppliers of equipment such as hockey sticks and cross-country skis have established plants in Canada to serve growing US and Japanese as well as Canadian markets. Some Canadian ski-industry companies have acquired plants in Italy and France to serve world markets.   A.J. RENNIE

Sports History Canadian sport is indebted to the Indian for the TOBOGGAN, snowshoe, lacrosse stick and CANOE. The COUREURS DE BOIS and the VOYAGEURS, through their close contact with the Indians, helped introduce into European settlements the activities that resulted from the use of these pieces of equipment. Many Indian games had utilitarian purposes related to survival (eg, wrestling, jousting, archery, spear throwing and foot and canoe racing), while activities such as dancing and baggataway (*see* LACROSSE) had religious significance. The Indians also developed a great variety of games, such as awl games, ring and pole, snow snake, cat's cradle, dice and birchbark cards, partly for the sheer love of play and sometimes for the purpose of gambling. The games of the Inuit were similarly related to preparing youth for co-operative existence in a harsh environment where one also needed to know one's tolerance limits. Blanket toss, tug-of-war, dogsled races, drum dances, spear throwing and ball games, as well as self-testing games such as arm-pull, hand-wrestling and finger-pull, helped to fulfil this purpose. Gambling was common and even useful, as it served to redistribute surplus goods.

In the pioneer settlements of the Europeans, play was relatively unimportant compared with the serious work of survival, yet social and recreational activities were necessary and did occur. From France, the French Canadian inherited his love of social gatherings, and N America's first social club, the ORDRE DE BON TEMPS, was formed at PORT-ROYAL in 1606. Social gatherings in pioneer societies, in the form of "bees" (husking, quilting and barn raising), also had a utilitarian basis, as participants could benefit from co-operative labours. Such gatherings usually

Lord Hawke's cricket team and the Eastern Canada Eleven in a match played at Ottawa, 22-24 Oct 1891 (*courtesy Public Archives of Canada/C-3127*).

offered music and dancing, wrestling and horse racing, and in French Canada provided opportunity for the "strong man" tradition to develop, exemplified later in Louis CYR. Where pioneer settlements consolidated into rural communities, a more organized form of recreation developed, largely from British migration in the 19th century. The formation of agricultural societies within these communities provided the administrative structure for regular competitions in ploughing and horse racing. Rural regattas followed in which settlers plied their skills against voyageur and Indian, since, even to the farmer, the canoe often provided the swiftest and easiest method of transportation.

The ubiquitous SCOTS played a major role in transporting British sporting traditions to N America. GOLF was played by some of Gen Wolfe's Scottish officers, though it did not become an established sport before Confederation. CURLING, by contrast, after its introduction under similar circumstances, thrived in Canada; the first sporting club, founded in 1807, was the Montreal Curling Club. In 1865 curling became one of the select group of sports to enter international competition. Golf's initial failure and curling's success serve to demonstrate the relationship between sport and society. In the early period, the large tracts of land required to maintain a small number of golfers were an unaffordable luxury, whereas in the Canadian winter ice was plentiful and accessible to all. Also, scattered throughout the provinces after 1760 were the British military garrisons whose soldiers perpetuated 2 traditional loves, CRICKET and EQUESTRIAN SPORTS.

Games introduced by Scotsmen or Englishmen soon found adherents among the mixture of cultures developing in the colony. In addition, sports that owed little traditional allegiance to a particular ethnic origin were emerging and growing in popularity. These ranged from simple and useful sports such as tobogganing, sleighing, ICE SKATING and sailing, through individual sports advocated for their general health values (GYMNASTICS, TRACK AND FIELD, and swimming), to such highly complex sports as ROWING, where the skill of the rowers was combined with the science of the boat builders. In 1867 a Saint John crew won the world rowing championship at the Paris Exposition in France. In the early 19th century, the majority of the active sportsmen were gentlemen players from the merchant or upper strata of society and officers of the garrison. Not only did these officers re-establish in their new environment the sporting traditions of their homeland, but they were also eager to adopt and sponsor new activities. Their love of horse racing, along with their leisured existence, gave impetus to such allied sports as hunting, trotting and steeplechasing. They also added colour to the skating rink, the toboggan slide, the sleigh ride and the ballroom. Their all-encompassing interest and enthusiasm, allied with their managerial expertise, resulted in a broad spectrum of sport being established within the communities.

In theory, skating, SNOWSHOEING, cricket, FOOTBALL and similar activities were available for the workingman, but he lacked time and organizational experience. Those for whom Sunday provided the only leisure time were deterred from sporting activities on that day by religious groups, and by the law after the Lord's Day Act was passed in 1845. It was not until early closing hours for shop and factory became more widespread in the mid-1860s that the workingman's participation in sport became possible. In this context, the advent of lacrosse and BASEBALL was timely, although even these sports tended to exclude members of the lower class, or "rowdies" as they were called, from organized teams. Where an activity was dependent upon organization, it still remained largely the prerogative of the affluent members of society.

Most pioneer women were far too busy to enjoy much leisure, but even when the opportunity presented itself, the conventions of the time prevented their active participation in most of the outdoor recreational activities followed by men. In the cities, their passive involvement was always encouraged through attendance at horse races, regattas, cricket matches and other spectator sports. It was permissible for them to be passengers in carrioles, iceboats and yachts; the more fortunate and independent were allowed to ride horses, skate or play croquet. The 1850s witnessed a change in attitude towards women engaging in sport that was also aided by changes in sporting attire. Female participation in fox hunting, the Ladies' Prince of Wales Snowshoe Club (1861), the Montreal Ladies' Archery Club (1858), rowing regattas, FIGURE SKATING championships and foot races at social picnics was evidence of growing emancipation.

Probably the greatest role sporting competition played prior to 1867 was as social gathering and mixing ground. City and country dwellers could meet at the agricultural-social events; voyageurs could compete with Indians and settlers at canoe regattas; Indians could engage townsfolk in lacrosse. Race meetings were very popular and attracted thousands of spectators in the large urban centres. Horse racing provided a social as well as sporting environment for the townsfolk and was the setting for the greatest social mingling of 19th-century society. The upper classes tended to resist this mingling, however, and made unsuccessful efforts to preserve horse races for themselves by erecting fences around the courses and charging admission. This exclusion policy may also be seen in the appearance of events for "gentlemen amateurs" in regattas and horse races, ensuring that the practised fisherman rower or the skilled farmhand could not compete with the social elite.

The greatest impact upon sports came from advances in TECHNOLOGY. The steamboat, railway locomotive and steam-powered printing press made it possible for sport to be brought before the public. Steamboats carried sporting teams and spectators on excursions that had previously been highly impractical by stagecoach. They even followed the boats and yachts during regattas. The rapid expansion of railways during the 1860s made the one-day excursion for match play feasible (*see* RAILWAY HISTORY). More widely represented team meetings and bonspiels could be arranged, provincial associations formed and rules of play made more uniform. The larger newspapers, made possible by steam-powered printing presses, carried greater sports coverage, and the invention of the telegraph brought quicker reporting of results.

Sport, by Confederation, 1867, was approaching a new era. Old activities such as cricket, rowing and horse racing continued to be important, while the emergence of new ones, such as lacrosse and baseball, were the mark of a country with expanding sporting interests. Urbanization advanced liberal attitudes among civic leaders towards the population's need for healthy diversion and exercise. As these 2 forces gathered strength and allied with advancing technology, increased organization of sporting activities was the natural result. Of even more importance was an emerging Canadian identity in sport. Sport played an integral part in the development of national feeling, at least among English-speaking Canadians. This trend is clearly seen in the phenomenal growth of lacrosse from 6 to 80 clubs during the summer of 1867, as George BEERS urged — unsuccessfully, despite popular support — that this sport be proclaimed Canada's national game. The unifying force of sport was also clearly shown when all of Canada basked in the glory achieved by the Saint John crew in Paris. Sport had given Confederation a deeper significance.   PETER L. LINDSAY

Sport from 1867 to 1900

On 26 Sept 1867, at a convention in Kingston, Ont, the National Lacrosse Assn was formed — the first of many such SPORTS ORGANIZATIONS to be established in Canada before the turn of the century. During the last 3 decades of the 19th century, sport in Canada matured and established the foundations that would carry it through much of the 20th century. It came under the influence of men who sought to rationalize and codify their games as they brought form and order to their sporting pursuits. Moreover, sport became a means for Canadians to express their feelings of pride in their new nation, aggressively searching for international competition and finding considerable success on the playing fields of the world.

This was a time when sport was intensely creative and exciting. Canadians were at the forefront of the development and popularization of 3 sports: lacrosse, HOCKEY and BASKETBALL. In football, Canadians introduced to their American neighbours the oval ball and the rules of RUGBY. Lacrosse was so popular in the 1880s that the myth grew that it had been declared, by Act of Parliament, to be the national game. By the 1880s the game had been introduced to England and was spreading to western Canada. Eventually baseball would challenge lacrosse for public support and interest as a summer sport. The Canadian Baseball Assn was formed in 1876 and the first baseball leagues shortly thereafter. Much of baseball's early success occurred in southwestern Ontario, where the proximity of the US was enhanced by railway links.

Football, too, had a rapid evolution. The year 1874 marked the beginning of a series of annual matches between McGill and Harvard universities. As a result, the Americans shifted away from association football, called SOCCER today in N America, and adopted the oval ball and scrum of rugby. The links of the game to the universities and colleges of both countries, well established during this time, contributed to its long-standing success. In 1884 the first national championship for this largely Ontario- and Québec-based sport was held. By the turn of the century, through numerous rule changes, play had evolved away from rugger to the unique game of Canadian football. Both rugby and lacrosse contributed to hockey's evolution from an ill-defined version of British stick and ball games. Many of its practices, including the face-off, its regulations concerning offsides, and the use of goals to score points owe a debt to one or other of the former games.

Montréal was the cradle for most of these dynamic developments of the late 19th century in Canada. The Montreal Amateur Athletic Assn (est 1881) was the first club of its kind, and acted as an umbrella for many sports clubs in that city. It was a social as well as a sports centre, with a large building providing reading and meeting rooms, a gymnasium and, eventually, a swimming pool. This club was the driving force behind the formation of the Amateur Athletic Assn of Canada, the first attempt to unify and regulate all sport in the country.

It is clear that the thrust behind the organization of sports in Canada's cities at this time came from members of the professional and business classes, who had the contacts, organizational skills and time to devote to this development. Faith in a scientific approach to all matters in life helped shape their attitudes to sport. One result of this approach, besides the development of sports organizations, was a fervent belief in amateurism and amateur codes. At the beginning of the 19th century, sport was largely controlled by the upper classes, and restrictive codes were established to segregate undesirables; the earliest forms were often racially based, restricting Indians and blacks from competing with whites. Eventually, as the working classes gained more free time, there arose the need to restrict them too. Having the time to develop strength and skills became a determinant, but eventually it was money, which released one from having to find other means of livelihood, that separated the amateurs from the professionals. The Amateur Athletic Union of Canada, in 1895, defined an amateur as "one who has never pursued or assisted in the practice of manly exercise as a means of obtaining a livelihood."

There was more than social exclusivity behind the development of amateur codes. The desire for order moved Canadian sportsmen of the period to end a system of sporadic challenge matches which had open gambling and paid, imported athletes. Professionals were highly suspect and held in very low regard. The man who contributed most to changing these attitudes was Toronto's great Ned HANLAN, the world's professional sculling champion 1880-84. Thousands travelled great distances on special excursions arranged by railway promoters to watch him row against the world's

Parkdale Baseball Club, Toronto, 1888 (*courtesy Public Archives of Canada/PA-60605/John Boyd*).

Members of McGill's first hockey team in 1881 (*courtesy Public Archives of Canada/C-81739*).

Members of the Grand Trunk Ry Amateur Athletic Association "Wheelmen" Toronto, Sept 1898 (*courtesy Public Archives of Canada/PA-60593/John Boyd*).

best. He became the focus of a growing national spirit and helped create a broad public acceptance, indeed adulation, for those who possessed great athletic skills. Deriving commercial benefit from his talent was simple affirmation of his ability.

Those who continued in the amateur tradition included Louis RUBENSTEIN and George ORTON. Rubenstein won the unofficial world championship in figure skating in 1890 and eventually became a pillar in the development of that sport, and in others like cycling. Orton became the first Canadian champion in the modern OLYMPIC GAMES, the great forum for the amateur athletic ideal. Canada sent no representative to the first Olympics, held in Greece in 1896, but Orton won the 1500 m steeplechase event as a member of the US team at the second Olympics in 1900.

As Canada entered the 20th century, it had regionally and nationally based structures for the governing of sports that provided the means of athletic competition. The amateur ethic was strong and would remain the basis for much athletic participation, but the door was open for professional sports where public interest made it commercially viable. Moreover, Canadians had found success and pride in challenging athletes from other parts of the world. It is little wonder that historians have regarded the years from Confederation to the turn of the century as the golden age of sport in Canada.   J. THOMAS WEST

Sport from 1900 to the Present

The twin processes of urbanization and industrialization, which had helped sow the seeds of modern sport in the 19th century, continued into the 20th century with even greater impact. One result was the full maturing of professional sports into great commercial spectator attractions. A second development, as the world was made smaller by air travel, was a growth of competitive opportunities for Canadians against athletes from around the world. As success in international events became of increasing importance, with sport taking on a geopolitical role as an expression of national pride, it came to be seen as part of the "national interest" to support athletes with government assistance.

By the turn of the century, hockey's roots were firmly planted in Canada and it was rapidly replacing lacrosse as the "national game." By 1908 it epitomized the divergent trends of sports towards amateurism and professionalism. The STANLEY CUP became emblematic of the professional championship and the Allen Cup and Memorial Cup of the amateur championships. After WWII, first through Foster HEWITT's radio broadcasts and later through television, professional hockey gained an almost mesmerized national audience. At the same time, small communities across the country were linked through the Allen Cup, the symbol of the national senior amateur title. Until 1952 Canada could count on its amateur champions to win

the world title, but that changed after 1952 with the emergence of the Soviet Union as a hockey power (*see* CANADIAN OLYMPIC HOCKEY TEAM).

The belief that hockey's professionals were the world's best was shattered through various competitions in the 1970s (*see* CANADA-SOVIET HOCKEY SERIES). Nevertheless, professional hockey continued to be Canada's most popular sport and the sport most associated with the national identity. Lacrosse, in contrast, had dropped from being by far the most popular sport of the first decade, in number of spectators and press attention, into a state of serious decline by the 1920s. The press of the day was critical of the recurring violence in lacrosse matches. The game failed to develop a system of minor leagues that could produce future talent. Furthermore, it was a summer sport and the arrival of the automobile enabled people to escape the hot cities for other forms of recreation. Finally the media lost interest in lacrosse, turning their attention to baseball, with its "big league" glamour.

Despite baseball's popularity as a summer sport, however, it took nearly 70 years before a major league franchise was established in the country, although Montréal and Toronto had teams in the "Triple A" International League. There were several variations of the game played throughout the country. As well as hardball, softball in fast-pitch and slow-pitch versions have been popular. The Toronto Tip Tops claimed the world softball championship in 1949 and the Richmond Hill Dynes repeated this feat in 1972. With the formation of the MONTRÉAL EXPOS in 1969 and the TORONTO BLUE JAYS in 1977, 2 Canadian cities had franchises in the American-based professional major leagues of baseball. However, only a few Canadians have starred in professional baseball since WWII.

Football was another sport that experienced healthy growth in the 20th century, evolving from a game with a large amateur base into one that was played by professionals in a highly commercialized milieu. Although Canadians actually introduced the game in its earliest variation to their American neighbours in 1874, football evolved in Canada under strong American influences. Until the 1920s the game was played and watched by a small but relatively well-educated and wealthy group of Canadians. It was based mainly in the country's large eastern universities and it used these roots to ensure its long-term survival. In the 1920s western teams began to use American players, and in 1936 the Canadian Rugby Union passed its first "residency" rule to curb such practices. Still, the pattern had been set so that, by the late 1960s, most of the key playing and coaching positions were held by Americans, with Canadians playing supporting roles. (Since the retirement of Russ JACKSON no Canadian has played quarterback regularly for a CFL team.) Nevertheless, Canadian football has retained its unique flavour and enjoys, in its own season, a status equal to hockey as a major commercial endeavour capable of drawing widespread public interest. One of the reasons for this is the East versus West rivalry that the game has generated. This began in

1921, when the EDMONTON ESKIMOS first provided a western challenge for the GREY CUP. In 1935 Winnipeg won the national championship, a first for a western team. In 1948, the antics of Calgary fans in Toronto started the idea for a full-blown festival associated with the Grey Cup Game — perhaps the closest thing to a national sports celebration Canada has.

While certain team sports enjoyed growing popularity and professionalization, the sector of Canadian sport that is broadly regarded as amateur survived and grew slowly, first under the broad umbrella of the Olympic movement and finally with government support. Canada has entered an official team at the Olympic Games since 1908 (except for the boycott of the 1980 Moscow games). Hamilton, Ont, was the host for the first British Empire Games (later the COMMONWEALTH GAMES) in 1930 and the PAN-AMERICAN GAMES were started in 1955. All 3 multi-sport festivals provide a highly visible international stage for amateur athletes to focus their training programs and aspirations for success. In the 1920s Canada produced some of the world's finest amateur boxers, oarsmen and track and field competitors. However, by 1936, when Canada's gold medal success at the Olympics was limited to Frank Amyot's victory in canoeing, it was apparent that the world was beginning to leave Canadians behind, and a long period of feelings of national failure in athletics set in. Since the arrival of a strong Soviet team at the 1952 Olympic Games, the world of international sport has become increasingly the focus of political and national rivalries. Athletes have come to be seen as national spear carriers, increasingly under pressure to perform well in order to defend their country's honour. These pressures weighed heavily on nations such as Canada, which in 1960 returned from the Rome Olympics with but one silver medal.

As in other nations that come to consider sports to be wrapped up in the "national interest," Canadian sport sought the aid of the federal government. In 1961 the Fitness and Amateur Sport Act was passed. It was intended to provide $5 million annually to amateur sport and fitness-related activities. Growth was slow, however, and it was only after the stimulation provided by the findings of the Task Force on Sport for Canadians in 1969 that the federal government took a more aggressive approach to funding amateur sport. By the 1980s, the annual budget of the Fitness and Amateur Sport Programme exceeded $50 million. One result of this government support was the growing bureaucratization of sport. Most of the affairs of national and regional sports organizations became the responsibility of paid administrators instead of long-time volunteers. However, another result has been increasing international success. Since 1980 Canadians have won world championships or held world records in alpine skiing, speed skating, figure skating, yachting, track and field, equestrianism, swimming, trap shooting, boxing, wrestling and modern pentathlon. In Sarajevo in 1984, Canada produced its most successful winter Olympian in speedskater Gaétan BOUCHER, who won 3 medals: 2 gold and a bronze. In sharp contrast to the 1976 Montréal games in which Canadians won 11 medals, none of them gold, in the 1984 Los Angeles Olympics Canadians won 44 medals, including 10 gold. The 1984 triumph included 2 gold medals and Olympic records in swimming by Alex BAUMANN; the first woman in history to win an Olympic shooting gold medal (Linda THOM); the first Canadian woman swimmer to win a gold medal (Anne OTTENBRITE); and the first Canadian diver to take an Olympic gold (Sylvie BERNIER). Although the medal count was somewhat inflated by the boycott of Soviet bloc nations, Canada still placed a surprising fourth among the 140 nations that did attend.

Elite sport is not the only area enjoying growth and success in Canada. Under the urgings of the government-funded organization, ParticipAction, more and more Canadians are pursuing FITNESS and finding enjoyment through sports activities. Golf and curling always had widespread popularity as participation sports for Canadians of all ages. Cycling enjoyed a great boom in the 1970s. Joggers number in the hundreds of thousands. Events such as the Ottawa Capital Marathon annually attract thousands of competitors, most of whom took up running for their personal fitness and are trying to meet the challenge of finishing the 26 mile distance. The development of Canadian sport in the 8 decades of this century has given it a vital place in the Canadian cultural mosaic. *See also* entries under individual sports. J. THOMAS WEST

Reading: F. Cosentino, "A History of the Concept of Professionalism in Canadian Sport," *Canadian Journal of History of Sport and Physical Education* VI, 2 (1975); D. Fisher and S.F. Wise, *Canada's Sporting Heroes* (1974); T. Frayne and P. Gzowski, *Great Canadian Sport Stories* (1965); H. Roxborough, *One Hundred — Not Out: The Story of Nineteenth-Century Canadian Sport* (1966); B. Schrodt, G. Redmond, R. Baka, *Sport Canadiana* (1980).

Sports Medicine and sports sciences are terms used by physiologists, physicians, psychologists, physiotherapists, trainers, coaches and physical educators, all of whom are interested in the sociological, psychological and physiological aspects of sports, the prevention of injury to athletes and the treatment of injured athletes, and the needs of average Canadians (particularly young children, adolescents, women, the handicapped and the elderly) who participate in some form of active pastime. Only a few hundred physicians and specialists in Canada, however, are fully qualified in all aspects of sports medicine and sports science.

Sports medicine practitioners help serious athletes plan preseason training and testing, provide early treatment for injuries, identify groups that may be susceptible to risk, and record frequencies in patterns of injuries. The study of safety equipment and modification of rules to preclude injuries have also become integral to sports medicine.

The evolution of sports medicine in Canada was somewhat haphazard until 1965, when a joint subcommittee of the Canadian Medical Association and the Canadian Association of Health, Physical Education and Recreation was established to investigate problems relating to sports medicine and national fitness. This led to the formation of the Canadian Association of Sports Sciences in 1967.

Groups specializing in motor learning and the sociology, physiology and psychology of sport have also emerged. Since the early 1970s the Medical Committee of the Canadian Olympic Association, the Canadian Academy of Sports Medicine, the Sports Medicine Division of the Canadian Physiotherapy Association and the Canadian Athletic Therapists Association have helped develop a system to aid top Canadian athletes. In 1978 the Sports Medicine Council was founded to advance the development of medical, paramedical and scientific services and their provision to Canadian amateur athletes, and specifically to establish policies to safeguard high-quality care; to promote education and research in the fields of sports science and sports medicine; to develop an information bank on epidemiology and management of sports injuries and illnesses; and to stimulate and provide for applied research related to the training, treatment and evaluation of athletes. The council is associated with the Sports Information and Resource Centre, a documentation centre headquartered in Ottawa for sports, physical education, recreation and sports sciences.

The major sports-medicine clinics are in universities across Canada, in contrast to the US, where many of the largest sports medicine clinics are private enterprises.

Sports and Drugs According to most sports-governing bodies, the performance of athletes should reflect their inborn ability, training techniques, perseverance, dedication and skill. Unfortunately, success for athletes has become synonymous with the success of a training system, a country and even an ideology (*see* CANADA-SOVIET HOCKEY SERIES); pressure on international athletes is enormous and the use of drugs common. Canada is not exempt from these practices. Many of these drugs are dangerous during their immediate use and because of their long-term side effects. They can be broadly divided into anabolic substances capable of enhancing body bulk and mass; stimulants that alter states of alertness and awareness; and drugs that alter the body's metabolism, allowing more rapid recovery of oxygen or enhancing its delivery to muscles. At present, more money is spent policing drug abuse than is spent on injured athletes, and it is really only the athletes who bear the punishment for drug abuse. DAVID C. REID

Reading: D.H. O'Donoghue, *Treatment of Injuries to Athletes* (1976).

Sports Organization, Amateur The earliest athletic body organized to administer sport was the Montreal Amateur Athletic Assn (MAAA). Formed in 1881, it comprised clubs for lacrosse, swimming and bicycling. The first national organization was the Amateur Athlete Assn of Canada, founded in 1884. It was to establish the standards for an amateur code and mediate disputes among its participants. It was later named the Canadian Amateur Athletic Union. In 1907 the MAAA formed its own group, the Amateur Athletic Federation of Canada. In 1909, the Amateur Athletic Union of Canada was formed, comprising the MAAA and the CAAU. This group encouraged the entry of individual sports groups and became the common thread from which Canadian sport organizations grew. Dr A.S. Lamb of McGill was later to have a strong role in its development.

The Canadian Olympic Committee emerged in 1909 from an earlier 1907 Central Olympic Committee. This committee was empowered to select teams and secure finances for travel to the Olympic Games, and was part of the larger AAUC organization. Sir John Handbury Williams was appointed Canada's first representative to the International Olympic Committee. In 1913 the COC became the Canadian Olympic Assn, a member of the AAUC. Finally, in 1949, the Canadian Olympic Assn was formed, independent of the AAUC. C.A. Sydney Davis, of Montréal, was its first chairman.

The AAUC controlled amateur sport in Canada throughout the first half of the 20th century. On 1 Oct 1943 the Canada National Physical Fitness Act (NPFA) was passed. Although it did not compete with the AAUC, it recognized the importance of physical fitness for Canadians through physical education, sports and athletics. Most significantly, it brought the federal government into the sphere of amateur sport. In 1951, the NPFA brought into being the Canadian Sports Advisory Council, later to become the Sports Federation of Canada, which became the official lobbyist for national sport-governing bodies in Ottawa. Bill C-131, An Act to Encourage Fitness and Amateur Sport, was passed on 29 Sept 1961, to promote and develop fitness and amateur sport in Canada. For the first time, sport was to be actively supported by the federal government; the Fitness and Amateur Sport Directorate was formed as the administrative body.

A significant year for amateur sport in Canada was 1969. The Task Force on Sport for Canadians made numerous recommendations to the federal government, many of which were implemented. The most important consequence for amateur sport organizations was that in 1970 the Centre for Sport and Recreation became a reality, incorporated in 1974 as the National Sport and Recreation Centre. In return for locating in Ottawa, the federal government offered to amateur sport groups financial support for technical, executive and program staff, office expenses and secretarial help, and use of the centre's services at a reduced cost. There followed the creation of a print shop, translation services, mail and shipping help, graphic design, promotion of elite athletes and many other services. Today, 58 amateur sport groups reside in Ottawa; another 22 organizations are affiliated as nonresident sports.

Associations receive contributions for their annual budgets from Sport Canada based upon their needs, popularity and status in the international competitive arena. The COA, Canadian Federation of Sports, Coaching Assn of Canada, Game Plan, Sport Canada and Fitness Canada work together with organizations to provide one of the most comprehensive systems in the world. The growth of public support for amateur sport associations in Canada has been acknowledged by the creation of a federal ministry for Fitness and Amateur Sport.

LORNE SAWULA

Spremo, Boris, press photographer (b at Susak, Yugoslavia 20 Oct 1935). A graduate of Belgrade's Cinematographic Institute, Spremo immigrated to Canada in 1957. He began his career in newspaper PHOTOGRAPHY in Toronto 5 years later when he joined the *Globe and Mail*. In 1966 he switched to the *Toronto Star*. In addition to photographing many politicians, entertainers and sports personalities, Spremo has covered the FLQ crisis in Québec, drought and famine in central Africa, and the end of the war in Vietnam, when he spent a month with Canadian peacekeeping troops. His photographs have appeared in magazines such as *Maclean's* and his books include *Twenty Years of Photojournalism* (1983). LOUISE ABBOTT

Spring, a point of natural, concentrated GROUNDWATER discharge from SOIL or ROCK. Some springs are located in RIVER or LAKE beds (subaqueous springs) or below mean sea level along the coast (submarine springs), but many are found some distance from surface water bodies. Springs with water temperatures near the local mean-annual air temperature are commonly called cold springs. Springs with higher temperatures are known as thermal springs: warm springs have temperatures up to 37°C; hot springs between 37°C and the boiling temperature of water at the spring location (often well below 100°C at higher elevations in mountainous areas); boiling springs have a temperature equal to the boiling temperature. Intermittent hot springs that eject columns of hot water and steam into the air, at more or less regular intervals, are called geysers (after Stora Geysir, Iceland). All spring waters contain dissolved MINERALS, derived from slow dissolution of rocks which the groundwater contacts during its movement to the spring. Freshwater springs produce water with under 1 g dissolved mineral content per litre. Mineral springs have dissolved mineral contents of 1-35 g/L (the approximate salt concentration in seawater). Brine springs have concentrations ranging to over 300 g/L. The minerals dissolved in spring waters include mainly carbonates, sulphates, chlorides and sulphides (of calcium, magnesium, sodium, potassium and iron). Spring waters also generally contain small quantities of common gases, including carbon dioxide, nitrogen, oxygen and methane, and minute quantities of helium, radon, neon, argon, krypton and xenon.

All thermal springs known in Canada occur in the western mountain region of Alberta, BC,

the YT and the NWT, where high relief permits deep circulation of RAIN and snowmelt, leading to GEOTHERMAL heating of the water. Some of these springs are only warm (eg, Cave and Basin Springs in BANFF NATIONAL PARK, Alta; Rabbitkettle Hot Springs in NAHANNI NATIONAL PARK, NWT). Many are true hot springs (eg, Upper Hot Spring in Banff; Fairmont Hot Springs and Harrison Hot Springs, BC; Takhini Hot Spring, YT). These hot springs are also mineral springs. The notable exception is the McArthur Hot Springs, YT, with a dissolved mineral content of under 0.2 g/L. Cold mineral springs are found in other parts of Canada. Cold brine springs occur in areas with marine SEDIMENTARY ROCKS (eg, limestone, dolomite, gypsum, rock salt) near the eastern edge of the Interior Plains in Alberta and Manitoba, and in sedimentary basins in the St Lawrence Lowland and Appalachian regions in Québec, NB and NS. Some thermal and mineral springs produce spring deposits at or near their outlets through precipitation of part of their mineral content. The mineral composition of a spring deposit reflects the chemical composition of the spring water. For example, the Cave and Basin Springs deposit mainly calcium-carbonate, through loss of CO_2 and evaporation; the McArthur Hot Springs produce small amounts of silica, through cooling and evaporation; the Paint Pots, in KOOTENAY NATIONAL PARK, BC, produce iron sulphates and iron oxyhydroxides, through evaporation, oxidation and hydrolysis; and the cold Fly-by Springs in the Mackenzie Mts deposit barium sulphate. The most spectacular spring deposit in Canada is the terraced calcium-carbonate cone of Rabbitkettle Hot Springs in Nahanni National Park.
R.O. VAN EVERDINGEN

Springfield, Man, Rural Municipality, pop 8986 (1981c), was formed when the communities of Springfield and Sunnyside (Dugald) jointly incorporated 1873. It covers 105 866 ha immediately E of Winnipeg, with Birds Hill Provincial Park in the NW, and Agassiz and Sandilands provincial forests to the E. Its largest communities are the villages of Oakbank, Dugald and Anola. Though governed by a reeve and 6 councillors, about one-fifth of its area is under the planning jurisdiction of the city of Winnipeg. Large-scale settlement by Ontario, British and American farmers occurred in the area in the early 1870s. Subsequent settlers included French Canadians, German, Ukrainian, Polish, Belgian and Danish immigrants, and more recently Hutterites. Mixed farming and gravel extraction have dominated Springfield's economy. Since the 1960s the area has experienced migration from Winnipeg of families wishing to combine urban employment with a country life-style.
D.M. LYON

Springhill, NS, Town, pop 4896 (1981c), inc 1889, located in the heart of Cumberland County on the Chignecto Isthmus, is so named because the hill on which it is situated once contained numerous springs. Once noted for its coalfields, Springhill is now famous as the hometown of pop singer Anne MURRAY. The town was first settled about 1820 by LOYALISTS. Coal was soon discovered and a small mine opened in 1834. Mining began on a large scale in 1872 when the Springhill and Parrsboro Coal and Ry Co Ltd sank shafts and opened a rail line. Several mining DISASTERS have plagued the town, the worst occurring in 1958 when 74 men

died in the deepest mine in N America. After this, the DOSCO-owned mines were shut down. Small coal seams have been mined only intermittently since then. There is high unemployment and little secondary industry here. The Springhill Miners Museum, opened in 1972, and the Springhill Medium Security Institution (1960) provide some employment for residents.
HEATHER MACDONALD

Sproatt and Rolph, architectural firm (est 1899) of Henry Sproatt (b at Toronto 14 June 1866; d there 4 Oct 1934), and Ernest Ross Rolph (b at Toronto 21 Jan 1871; d there 4 May 1958). Sproatt, an authority on Gothic architecture, served as the principal designer. He was trained in New York C 1886-89 and commenced architectural practice in Toronto in 1890. He was in partnership with Frank Darling in the 1890s. Rolph, the pragmatic designer and builder, trained with David Roberts, an early Toronto architect (Gooderham Mansion, York Club), and then worked as an architect and engineer for the Canadian Pacific Ry in BC. The firm Sproatt and Rolph was responsible for numerous institutional, commercial and residential buildings in Toronto, including Hart House and the Memorial Tower at U of T (American Inst of Architects Gold Medal, 1926); Bishop Strachan School, Manufacturer's Life Building, Ontario Club and National Club. Both men were widely recognized as patrons on the arts and were elected fellows of the Royal Inst of British Architects.
ANDREA KRISTOF

White, or "Canadian," spruce (*Picea glauca*), with female flowers, male flowers and cones, bottom right (*artwork by Claire Tremblay*).

Spruce, evergreen CONIFER (genus *Picea*) of PINE family (Pinaceae). About 40 species occur worldwide, in circumpolar distribution in the Northern Hemisphere; 5 are native to Canada. White spruce (*P. glauca*) and black spruce (*P. mariana*) are found nearly from coast to coast in the boreal forest; Sitka spruce (*P. sitchensis*) in a narrow band along the West Coast; Engelmann spruce (*P. engelmannii*) in interior BC; red spruce (*P. rubens*) in the Great Lakes–St Lawrence and Acadian forest regions. Norway spruce (*P. abies*) and blue spruce (*P. pungens*) have been introduced. Trunks are long and straight; crowns dense and narrow. Evergreen leaves are needlelike, usually 4-sided, often sharply pointed and borne on woody pegs or stalks. Seed cones are 2-10 cm long, nonwoody with rounded scales and small bracts. POLLINATION occurs in spring. Winged seeds are shed in fall. Spruces, used for pulp, paper and lumber, are the most important commercial conifers.
JOHN N. OWENS

Spruce Grove, Alta, Town, pop 10 326 (1981c), inc 1971, is located 30 km W of Edmonton.

Named for the spruce trees once common in the area, the town grew up around a station on the Grand Trunk Pacific Ry. It serves an agricultural district, and since the 1960s many residents commute to Edmonton.
ERIC J. HOLMGREN

Spry, Graham, journalist, diplomat, international business executive, political organizer, advocate of public broadcasting (b at St Thomas, Ont 20 Feb 1900; d at Ottawa 24 Nov 1983). As cofounder with Alan PLAUNT in 1930 of the Canadian Radio League he was instrumental in mobilizing popular and political support for public broadcasting in Canada. A Rhodes scholar in history at Oxford, Spry began his career as a reporter and editorial writer for the *Manitoba Free Press* (1920-22). He was chairman of the Canadian Radio League 1930-34 (and years later of the Canadian Broadcasting League 1968-73). The CRL campaigned for the general recommendation of the 1929 royal commission on broadcasting — the establishment and support of a national system operated as a public undertaking. Spry's famous 1932 aphorism, "The State or the United States," is apt even today (*see* CANADIAN BROADCASTING CORPORATION).

A political activist, he published the *Farmers' Sun,* renamed the *New Commonwealth* (1932-34); was coauthor of *Social Planning for Canada,* published by the LEAGUE FOR SOCIAL RECONSTRUCTION (1935); and was chairman of the Ontario Co-operative Commonwealth Federation (1934 to 1936). He then joined Standard Oil of California, becoming director (1940-46) of UK-based subsidiaries engaged in Arabian and other operations. At the same time he was personal assistant to Sir Stafford Cripps of the British War Cabinet (1942-45), accompanying him on his mission to India, and served in the Home Guard. As agent general for Saskatchewan in the UK, Europe and the Near East (1946-68), among other duties he recruited doctors, nurses and other skilled personnel. He was instrumental in neutralizing the 1962 doctors' strike against medicare. In Canada 1968-83, he continued to work for public broadcasting until the end of his life.
ROBERT E. BABE

Spying, *see* TREASON.

Squamish, BC, District Municipality, pop 10 272 (1981c), inc 1964, is located 70 km N of Vancouver at the head of Howe Sound. It is the service centre for a richly endowed recreational area, with road, rail and water access to Vancouver. Some of BC's best skiing is available at nearby Whistler Mt, and Garibaldi Park, alpine meadows, waterfalls and glacier-fed lakes are close by. The area was originally inhabited by the Squohomish tribes, and Squamish is the Indian word for "strong wind." The first Europeans settled in the Squamish Valley about 1873. Though their settlement was known for a while as Newport, the older name was eventually restored. In the early years, hop farming was the valley's main industry, and Squamish hops were some of the finest shipped to England. The primary industries in the area are logging, milling, and chemical and pulp production. BC Railway has 500 employees in its main shops in Squamish. The municipality is governed by a mayor and 6 aldermen.
ALAN F.J. ARTIBISE

Squash (genus *Cucurbita*), annual PLANT belonging to the Cucurbitaceae family and native to the New World. Squash may have been domesticated as early as 7000 to 5000 BC in the Tehuacan Valley in Mexico; evidence suggests that it was cultivated in present-day Ontario by the HURON and related groups by about 1400 AD. Both running and bush types occur. Squashes have large yellow flowers which attract bees; each plant carries male and female flowers. Squashes are classifed as either summer or winter varieties, depending on when they are harvested. Summer squashes (mainly *C. pepo*) are harvested before maturity, when they are still small and tender; common varieties are zucchini and yellow crookneck. Winter squashes (mainly *C. maxima*, but also *C. pepo, C. moschata* or *C. mixta*) are harvested at full maturity (3-4 months after planting), when the rind is hard; common varieties are acorn squash and butternut squash. Winter squashes have a higher carbohydrate content and are more nutritious. Squash grows rapidly, producing abundant foliage and a well-developed but rather superficial root system. Summer squash is normally seeded directly in the field, as is winter squash if the growing season is long enough. Winter squash can be stored at about 10°C, under dry, well-ventilated conditions. Squash species crossbreed readily; numerous cultivars vary enormously in shape, colour, size and texture. Squash has a low commercial value, although found in most family gardens and is grown by a few specialized growers. *See* PUMPKIN. ROGER BÉDARD

Squash Racquets is played with a long-handled, small-headed racquet in an enclosed court that resembles a giant, lidded shoebox. Each player (or pair in doubles) takes turns hitting the ball to the front wall — rather like lawn TENNIS but with both players on one side of the net. The game is an offshoot of racquets, but is played with a soft, "squashy" ball, hence the name. The international game, also called "softball," is played throughout the world, including N America, where it has made great inroads recently; the N American version is played almost solely in Canada and the US. Southern BC, Toronto, Hamilton and Montréal have always been the major centres, although squash has flourished in such places as Québec City, Winnipeg and Saint John, and is burgeoning in many others. Although courts may have existed in Vancouver as early as the 1880s, it was the Montreal Racquet Club, Toronto Racquet Club and Hamilton Squash Racquets Club that formed the Canadian Squash Racquets Assn (CSRA) in 1913 — the world's first national squash organization.

Canadians who have excelled at the game include Ernest Howard of Toronto, who was the first Canadian to win the US singles championship (1953); Colin Adair of Montréal, the only Canadian to win the US title twice; Michael Desaulniers, who won the US championship in 1978; and S. McElhinney of Toronto, winner of the N American women's open. The residence in Toronto of the world's premier player, Sharif Khan, and of former Australian Heather McKay has helped to develop the game in Canada.

Until the 1970s most squash courts in Canada were privately owned, or found in social clubs, sports clubs, universities or private schools. As many new commercial courts are being constructed with large galleries and facilities for televising games, a business approach has opened the game to numerous spectators and participants, particularly women. Although facing stiff competition in some centres from RACQUETBALL, the intense competition and high levels of skill and fitness demanded by the game guarantee its popularity. BRIAN T.P. MUTIMER

Squid, decapod ("10-footed") MOLLUSC of class Cephalopoda. Squid are usually of the order Teuthoidea, but only an expert could distinguish a slow squid from a fast CUTTLEFISH (order Sepioidea). Generally the term is applied to fast-swimming, streamlined forms in which a powerful jet-propulsion system provides the "squirt" by which the squid moves. Squid are the only INVERTEBRATE competitors of pelagic (open sea) fish; some are even capable of brief, jet-powered flight. Thirty teuthids occur in Canadian waters including *Gonatus fabricii*, found on all 3 coasts, and the giant squid *Architeuthis dux*. The former has commercial potential. The largest fishery is for Atlantic squid (*Illex illecebrosus*).

These squid migrate hundreds of km to warm waters to spawn and die after growing to 500 g in 9 to 12 months. Their schools have some social structure and they communicate by changing colour patterns. The flying squid (*Ommastrephes bartramii*) of the Pacific is taken by Japanese fishermen using drift-net sets up to 45 km long. There is a potential fishery for this squid off the BC coast. R.K. O'DOR

Squires, Sir Richard Anderson, lawyer, politician, prime minister of Newfoundland 1919-1923 and 1928-32 (b at Harbour Grace, Nfld 18 Jan 1880; d at St John's 26 Mar 1940). Squires entered the Newfoundland Assembly in 1909. Defeated in 1913, he was appointed to the Legislative Council and the Cabinet by Sir Edward MORRIS as a reward for his electoral battle against the Fishermen's Protective Union. He lost his Cabinet post when Sir William LLOYD formed the second National Government in 1918. On its 1919 collapse, Squires founded the Liberal Reform Party, which, in alliance with the FPU, won the election that year and had to face postwar chaos in the fishing industry. In July 1923 Squires resigned in the face of corruption charges, later substantiated. He rebounded to win the 1928 election, but his government proved virtually helpless as the economic crisis of the period deepened. Corruption charges were levelled against him again in 1932, sparking a riot in St John's in Apr. In the June election his party was decimated. A Tory government was elected to preside over the end of responsible government in 1934, a debacle to which Squires contributed. *See* COMMISSION OF GOVERNMENT. J.K. HILLER

Squirrel, common name for family (Sciuridae) of RODENTS, comprising 261 species, found in N and S America, Eurasia and Africa. Twenty-two species occur in Canada: 6 are tree species (*Scurius carolinensis, S. niger, Tamiascurius hudsonicus, T. douglasii, Glaucomys volans, G. sabrinus*), the latter 2 flying squirrels; and 16 are ground-dwelling species, of which 6 are ground squirrels (*Spermophilus richardsonii, S. columbianus, S. parryii, S. tridecemlineatus, S. franklinii, S. lateralis*), 5 are CHIPMUNKS, 4 are MARMOTS and one a PRAIRIE DOG. Squirrels have 4 toes on forefeet; 5 on hindfeet. Tree squirrels have bushy tails and small, agile feet; ground squirrels have less bushy tails and more robust forefeet. Ground squirrels and chipmunks carry food in cheek pouches. The flying squirrel has a skin fold along its flanks and attached to its feet that enables it to glide. There is great variation in size: the largest Canadian squirrel, the hoary marmot, is 80 cm long and weighs 6 kg; the smallest, the least chipmunk, 22 cm and 50 g. In Canada, most species reproduce once annually. Mating occurs in spring; gestation lasts 24-44 days and litters average 3-8 young, depending on species. At birth, young are hairless and poorly developed; growth is rapid. All Canadian species, except flying squirrels, are diurnal. While most ground squirrels hibernate, tree squirrels are active year round. Certain species are found throughout Canada; others only inhabit specific areas. Preferred habitats are varied, including forests, prairies, mountains and arctic regions. Primarily herbivorous, squirrels sometimes eat insects, eggs and even small birds. Some are gregarious; others, solitary. Tree squirrels generally build nests; ground-dwelling species dig burrows. Squirrels can damage cereal crops, maple-tapping equipment and telephone wires; burrows and hillocks can harm livestock and agricultural machinery. JEAN FERRON

Stabilization refers to government MONETARY POLICY, FISCAL POLICY, or other actions taken with the goal of minimizing BUSINESS CYCLE fluctuations in important economy-wide variables — especially employment, output and INFLATION. For example, a cyclical decline in output might be cushioned by fiscal initiatives such as tax cuts

or increased government expenditures, or by a monetary policy generating lower INTEREST rates to stimulate investment expenditures. The reverse of these policies, accompanied by the introduction of WAGE AND PRICE CONTROLS, may be adopted to forestall any acceleration of inflation.

The development of the modern idea of stabilization policy can be attributed to the British economist John Maynard Keynes. During the GREAT DEPRESSION, Keynes argued forcefully that cyclical fluctuations were not sufficiently self-correcting, and that active government intervention might be needed to prevent a repetition of such a severe and prolonged economic downturn. Although this principle is now generally well accepted, critics assert that the effectiveness of stabilization policy is limited by conflicts among objectives (eg, actions to reduce inflation may increase unemployment) and by inconsistencies between short-term and long-term effects — especially when the pressures of political expediency are considered. These issues continue to be debated both at theoretical and practical levels. RONALD G. WIRICK

Stacey, Charles Perry, historian (b at Toronto 30 July 1906). Stacey was a Princeton PhD and taught there 1934-40. He had been a committed part-time soldier since his student days at U of T and Oxford, and he served as the Canadian Army's historical officer in London 1940-45 and chief army historian 1945-59. A lively teacher possessed of a mischievous wit, he was a professor at U of T, 1959-76, briefly returning to preside over National Defence's newly unified triservice directorate of history 1965-66. A fine historical craftsman, superb researcher and easy stylist, Stacey has written, among other books, *Canada and the British Army, 1846-71* (1936); *The Military Problems of Canada* (1940); *The Canadian Army, 1939-45* (1948); *Six Years of War* (1955); *Quebec, 1759* (1959); *The Victory Campaign* (1960); *Arms, Men and Governments* (1970); *A Very Double Life* (1976); *Canada and the Age of Conflict* (2 vols, 1977-81); and his memoirs, *A Date with History* (1983). *See* EXTERNAL AFFAIRS. NORMAN HILLMER

Stadacona, IROQUOIS village located at the present site of QUÉBEC CITY, had an estimated population of about 500. Jacques CARTIER was led to the village on his second voyage in 1535 and wintered the distance, across the St Charles R. In midwinter more than 50 Stadaconans died, likely of European diseases to which they had no immunity, and 25 French died of scurvy before the Indians provided them with a cure — a potion made from fronds of white cedar. Cartier unwittingly offended the Stadaconans by establishing a base without their permission and by travelling upriver to HOCHELAGA. He kidnapped DONNACONA, his 2 sons and 7 others and returned to France, but all except a young girl perished before Cartier returned to Stadacona in 1541. He established a second base at Cap Rouge, upstream from Stadacona, but increasing hostility and his belief that he had found gold and diamonds prompted his retreat. Jean-François ROBERVAL arrived at Stadacona shortly after and though relations with the Indians improved, he abandoned the fledgling colony. By the time the French returned to the site in 1603, the Stadaconans and the St Lawrence Iroquois had vanished. Various theories about their fate have been put forward: that they were driven out by the Montagnais and ALGONQUIN; that they suffered poor harvests brought on by climatic changes; that they succumbed to European diseases; that they were dispersed by the southern Iroquois, eg, the Mohawk. There is some evidence that refugees from Stadacona and Hochelaga were adopted by the HURON. By Samuel de CHAMPLAIN's time, the St Lawrence Valley was a no-man's-land travelled only by war parties of the Montagnais and Iroquois. JAMES MARSH

Stage and Costume Design in Canada reflect the practices and standards of London and New York. The American influence is absorbed through visits to NY, contact with theatre departments in American universities, and touring productions. British standards were introduced by talented individuals who visited or chose to live here. Until the 1950s there were no true stage designers; there was minimal recognition of scenic and costume design as an art. At the Dominion Drama Festival, the amateur competition held annually from 1932 to 1970, there was no travel allowance for designers and initially no design award was made. Though this was later rectified with an award honouring Martha Jamieson, the producing group and not the designer's name went onto the plaque. Established amateur companies copied sets of the original productions or asked local artists to provide them. In the 1920s and 1930s some well-known painters, particularly the GROUP OF SEVEN, designed sets and costumes for Hart House Theatre and the Arts and Letters Club in Toronto. Firms which rented formal wear introduced costume departments; Mallabar's, now an international concern, began this way. The costumes were the work of anonymous sewers and pattern drafters, not designers.

As professional theatre, ballet and opera companies were established and the CBC began TV broadcasting in the 1950s, opportunities for designers were suddenly provided, though there were few designers and fewer technicians (*see* BROADCASTING; TELEVISION PROGRAMMING). Initially many of the CBC set designers were European. But it was the STRATFORD FESTIVAL, and Tanya Moiseiwitsch, who designed its stage and first productions, that made Canadian artists aware of the possibilities in theatrical design. Young Canadians, many still at art schools and universities, were employed as technicians, and with their Stratford training became the core of the designers working at the regional and festival theatres established in the 1960s and 1970s.

Moiseiwitsch continued to work at Stratford for the next 30 years. Other British designers followed. Leslie Hurry contributed important designs to the festival: some of his best work was done in Canada. His vision was singular and painterly but capable of rendering a fine barbarism, as in *Pericles*. Desmond Heeley's spare yet exotic designs have made their mark on this country. Robert Prevost, Daphne Dare and Susan Benson have been prominent designers for the festival in recent seasons.

By the 1970s theatrical design was an established profession in Canada. The Associated Designers of Canada, founded in 1965, now has some 120 members employed at most of the theatres in the country. Outstanding practitioners include Murray Laufer, whose architectural settings established the house style of the St Lawrence Centre in Toronto; Suzanne Mess, prominent as a costume designer for grand opera in N America; François Barbeau, preeminent in Montréal; Philip Silver, the pioneer designer at the Citadel in Edmonton; Jack King, whose designs for new Canadian works with the NATIONAL BALLET have been notable; and Cameron Porteous, who has done impressive work as head of design at both the SHAW FESTIVAL and the VANCOUVER PLAYHOUSE.

Stratford's influence was felt beyond Canada. Tyrone GUTHRIE's demonstration of the effectiveness of the thrust stage was widely imitated. A style of design consisting of carefully lit and detailed costumes and properties on an elaborate scale against a plain background offered an exciting alternative to proscenium-arch settings.

Nationwide there are now about 60 schools, in addition to the National Theatre School, offering training for the theatre, and over 100 professional companies producing plays. The regional and institutional theatres provide varied employment, and the small alternative theatres encourage experimentation. Designers are no longer restricted to individual productions, but are actively involved with architects in the design of new buildings and restoration of old structures. Canada is recognized for the ingenuity with which its architectural and theatrical designers transform 19th-century industrial and public buildings to new use in the 20th century. In less than 30 years Canadian theatrical design has begun to earn international recognition.

Canadian designers now work outside Canada, and at the Prague Quadrennial, the juried exhibition of the best in theatrical design from around the world, the Canadian exhibition has received an honourable mention in every competition since 1975. Two Canadian designers, Murray Laufer in 1975 and Ray Robilschek in 1983, received special commendations. *See also* TELEVISION DRAMA; LITTLE THEATRE MOVEMENT; THEATRE FOR YOUNG AUDIENCES.　MARTHA MANN

Stagflation, the combination of high unemployment and high rates of INFLATION. Prior to the late 1960s, variations in economic activity were caused primarily by "demand shocks" (fluctuations in aggregate demand or total expenditure). Increases in aggregate demand led to increased output, employment and prices, while reductions resulted in reduced output, higher unemployment and lower inflation. Stagflation in the 1970s and 1980s has been caused partly by "supply shocks" (increases in price). If governments respond to a large supply shock by maintaining total expenditure, a severe RECESSION will result because the increased expenditure on energy or food means reduced expenditure on other goods and services, and therefore reduced output and employment. If governments increase total expenditure, inflation will result. Most Western governments have chosen a policy in between these 2 extremes, creating both higher inflation and unemployment. Expectations can also affect stagflation. If people expect inflation to continue, they set wages and prices accordingly, giving inflation a momentum that cannot quickly be halted.　W.C. RIDDELL

Stairs, John Fitz-William, merchant, shipper, politician (b at Halifax 19 Jan 1848; d there 24 Sept 1904). Eldest son of William Stairs, MLA and a leading merchant, Stairs studied at Dalhousie. Elected to the NS Legislative Assembly in 1879, he resigned in 1882. From 1883 until 1896 he sat as a Conservative in the House of Commons. President of many companies, including Nova Scotia Steel, Eastern Trust, Trivodad Electric and Royal Securities, Stairs was also director of the Dartmouth and Halifax Steamboat Co, Nova Scotia Sugar Refining, the Union Bank of Halifax, Consumer Cordage, and dominated the financial elite of the Maritimes during the last 15 years of his life. He also employed Max AITKEN (Lord Beaverbrook) at the beginning of Aitken's business career, hiring him in 1902 when he set up Royal Securities, the first investment firm in eastern Canada.　JORGE NIOSI

Stairs, William Grant, explorer, soldier (b at Halifax 28 Feb 1863; d at Chinde, Mozambique 9 June 1892). He was discoverer of one source of the Nile, the Semliki R, and the first non-African to climb Mt Ruwenzori. Stairs was educated in Halifax, Edinburgh and RMC and was a civil engineer in New Zealand 1882-85. He was then commissioned Captain, Royal Engineers and achieved distinction as a military commander in the Emin Pasha Rescue Expedition, 1886-89. He became a fellow of the Royal Scottish Geographical Soc in 1890. After accepting a commission in the Royal Welsh Regiment, he was appointed by King Leopold to command the force that seized the Katanga (Shaba) copper lands for Belgium. Shortly afterward he died of fever.　ALLAN LEVINE

Stamp Collecting Almost immediately after their issue in 1840, POSTAGE STAMPS became a collectible item. The first stamp catalogues were published in Europe as early as 1861 (Potiquet, Paris). The first magazine devoted to stamp collecting in N America was published in 1864 in Montréal (*Stamp Collectors Record*, S. Allan Taylor). Stamp collecting, or philately, is a truly international hobby with its own local, national and international organizations. At the local level clubs exist where collectors may meet to exchange or exhibit stamps, and there are national and international conventions held each year. Canada's national society is the Royal Philatelic Society of Canada, based in Ottawa. The Canadian Post Office (now CANADA POST CORPORATION) has also had a special philatelic service since 1932.

The variety of themes and colours of stamps is endless and stamps often give a miniature pictorial history of a country, its culture and its development, and even its flora and fauna. Collectors may form basic collections by country, by series, by period or by specialty, such as airmail stamps, first-day covers, postmarks or plate numbers. Some people collect stamps because they are rare; others collect a particular subject such as Canadian ships. The "50-cent Bluenose" of 1929 is said to be the world's most beautifully engraved stamp. A 1933 stamp commemorated the ROYAL WILLIAM, the first ship to cross the Atlantic entirely under steam. One of the scarcest Canadian stamps is the 1851 "Twelve-Pence Black" showing Queen Victoria at the age of 19. It was, along with the "Three-Pence Beaver" (designed by Sandford FLEMING) and the Six Pence Prince Consort, which carried a portrait of Prince Albert, Canada's first issue.

Twelve-Pence Black of 1851, one of the first 3 stamps issued in Canada; "50-cent Bluenose" of 1929, which is said to be the world's most beautifully engraved stamp.

Canada issues 2 kinds of stamps: definitive, which are printed for up to 5 years, and commemorative, which recognize specific subjects or events. Shown above are airmail (top) and special delivery stamps, issued in 1942.

Totem pole pictorial, issued 2 Feb 1953.

David Thompson commemorative, issued June 1957 (all stamps courtesy Canada Post Corporation).

Stamp commemorating the Canadian Centennial, issued 5 June 1967.

Garden stamp, issued 1980.

Modern stamp commemorating the "Tall Ships," issued 1984.

Canada's first stamp following Confederation was a profile of Queen Victoria issued in 1868.

Canada issues 2 kinds of stamps. Definitive or regular stamp issues are printed from the same plates for 3 to 5 years. Commemoratives, or special issues, recognize specific subjects or events each year; when the issue is run off the plates are destroyed.   KENNETH ROWE AND H. GRIFFIN

Reading: Cimon Morin, Canadian Philately, Bibliography and Index (1979); Supplement (1983).

Standard of Living, a measure of economic welfare. It generally refers to the availability of scarce goods and services, usually measured by per capita income or per capita consumption, calculated in constant dollars, to satisfy wants rather than needs. Because the well-being that living standards are supposed to measure is an individual matter, per capita availability of goods and services in a country is a measure of general welfare only if the goods and services are distributed fairly evenly among people. If income distribution is very uneven, then despite high per capita availability of commodities, large numbers of persons may have a very low standard of living and others a very high standard — valid comparisons can be made only among reasonably homogeneous groups. Improvement in standard of living can result from improvements in economic factors such as productivity or per capita real economic growth, income distribution and availability of public services, and noneconomic factors, eg, protection against unsafe working conditions, clean environment, low crime rate, etc.

GNP per capita is a commonly used measure of the standard of living, but not necessarily an accurate one because, among other reasons, it does not distinguish between consumer and capital goods; it does not take income distribution into account; it does not take account of differences in the economic goods and services that are not measured in GNP at all; it is subject to the vagaries of translating income measures into a common currency (see NATIONAL INCOME) and it fails to take into account differences of tastes among nations. According to the World Bank, Canada's 1983 GNP per capita (measured in $US) was about $13 600 compared with about $14 000 for the US and about $8000 each for Sweden and the UK. See also GROSS NATIONAL PRODUCT.   M.C. URQUHART

Stanfield, Robert Lorne, lawyer, politician, premier of NS (b at Truro, NS 11 Apr 1914). Member of a family that had long contributed to the industrial and political life of NS and Canada, Stanfield began the rehabilitation of the provincial Conservative Party in 1946 during the only period in which it held no assembly seats. Becoming its leader 2 years later, he improved its position in the next 2 elections and became premier in 1956, the first of his party since Confederation to do so under noncrisis conditions. In the 3 subsequent elections he became the undisputed political master of the province. A man of moderation, common sense and genuine humility, he sought to create a self-reliant NS.

On becoming national Conservative leader in 1967, he tried to build a party with national appeal. He sought to have official bilingualism fully accepted by his party and was prepared, at least in moderation, to grant special arrangements to Québec. But he found it difficult to project across Canada the image that had led to his success in NS or to win seats in Québec against PM Pierre TRUDEAU. After 3 successive defeats he gave up the leadership in 1976. Eschewing highly doctrinaire politics, his conservatism, which caused him to be called a "pink" if not a RED TORY, was above all a compassionate conservatism with a genuine concern for the disadvantaged. He ranks as one of the outstanding premiers of NS since Confederation.

J. MURRAY BECK

Stanier, Roger Yate, microbiologist, professor (b at Victoria 22 Oct 1916; d at Paris, France 29 Jan 1982). Stanier was a major influence in the development of modern microbiology and correlated biochemical, physiological, ecological, and taxonomic studies to provide a remarkably coherent view of the bacteria. He studied at UBC, U of Calif (Los Angeles) and Stanford. His re-

Robert Stanfield (right). As premier of NS, he sought to make the province more self-reliant. He was national Conservative leader 1967-76 but failed in 3 elections to become PM (*courtesy Canapress*).

search included oxidative degradation and the adaptation of enzyme pathways, bacterial carotenoids and photosynthesis, and the biology and taxonomy of many groups including photosynthetic bacteria, pseudomonads, cytophagas and cyanobacteria, among other studies. Stanier was professor of microbiology at U of Calif, Berkeley 1947-71. An accomplished interpreter of the biology and taxonomy of bacteria, he expressed his understanding in major essays and reviews (1941-79) and in a remarkable textbook, *The Microbial World* (1975). The last decade of his life was spent as a professor at the Institut Pasteur, Paris, initiating a study of pure cultures of cyanobacteria (BLUE-GREEN ALGAE). His accomplishments were recognized by awards such as the Légion d'Honneur (France) and by election as a foreign member of the Royal Soc, the French Academy of Sciences and of the National Academy of Sciences (US) and as honorary member of the American Soc for Microbiology. He worked abroad for most of his life, but retained Canadian citizenship. R.G.E. MURRAY

Stanley, Frederick Arthur, Baron Stanley of Preston, 16th Earl of Derby, governor general of Canada 1888-93 (b at London, Eng 15 Jan 1841; d at Holwood, Eng 14 June 1908). His father was 3 times British PM, and Stanley himself was an MP 1865-86, and then sat in the House of Lords. He was a member of the government 1874-80 and 1885-88, including a short stint as secretary of state for the colonies. Although a strong advocate of closer ties between Great Britain and dominions such as Canada, he was a publicly shy and politically careful governor general. He is primarily remembered for his donation in 1893 of the STANLEY CUP, designed to determine a Canadian hockey champion in a fair and uniform manner. NORMAN HILLMER

Stanley, George Francis Gillman, historian, educator (b at Calgary 6 July 1907). Educated at U of A and Oxford, Stanley was a professor and administrator at Mount Allison 1936-40 and 1969-75, UBC 1947-49 and RMC 1949-69. He served in WWII, becoming an invaluable aide to C.P. STACEY and retiring in 1946 as deputy director of the army's historical section. His first book, *The Birth of Western Canada* (1936), combined his passion for the West with an appreciation of the importance of military factors; later he wrote a biography of Louis RIEL (1963). Other major works are *Canada's Soldiers* (1954), *New France: The Last Phase* (1968), *Canada Invaded 1775-1776* (1973) and *The War of 1812: Land Operations* (1983). He proposed the basic design of Canada's flag in 1965; in 1982 he was appointed lieutenant-governor of New Brunswick. NORMAN HILLMER

Stanley, Robert Crooks, mine executive, metallurgist, (b at Little Falls, NY 1 Aug 1876; d at Dongan Hills, Staten Island, NY 12 Feb 1951). Stanley joined International Nickel in 1902 and was president 1922-49. He was responsible for the development of Monel Metal, a nickel-copper alloy, and promoted peacetime commer-

cial applications for Inco's NICKEL, which prior to 1919 had been used primarily in armament production. In the late 1920s he played a major role in the merger of Inco and the Mond Nickel Company. J. LINDSEY

Stanley Cup, the oldest trophy competed for by professional athletes in N America. Donated by Gov Gen Lord STANLEY in 1893 for presentation to the amateur HOCKEY champions of Canada, it was first awarded to Montreal A.A.A. (1892-93) and except for 1918-19 (owing to an influenza epidemic) it has been presented every year since. Before professional hockey concentrated the sport in a few large urban centres, the cup was contested under a variety of formats and was captured by such far-flung teams as Winnipeg Victorias (1895-96, 1900-01), Ottawa Silver Seven (1902-03, 1903-04, 1904-05), Kenora Thistles (1906-07), the Vancouver Millionaires (1914-15), Seattle Metropolitans (1916-17) and Victoria Cougars (1924-25). A professional team (Ottawa Senators) first won the cup in 1909 and in 1926 it came under the exclusive control of the NATIONAL HOCKEY LEAGUE. The MONTREAL CANADIENS, with 22 victories (including 5 straight 1956-60), have been by far the most successful team in Stanley Cup history, followed by TORONTO MAPLE LEAFS with 11 wins. The New York Islanders' string of 4 consecutive victories was ended by the EDMONTON OILERS in 1984.

The cup itself has had a colourful history. It has been lost, misplaced and stolen (once from its home in the HOCKEY HALL OF FAME and Museum). The original silver bowl is now on permanent display at the Hockey Hall of Fame and a replica sits on top of the existing structure. The names of all the players on winning teams since 1930 are engraved on the base. JAMES MARSH

Staple Thesis, a theory asserting that the export of natural resources, or staples, from Canada to more advanced economies has a pervasive impact on the economy as well as on the social and political systems. Furthermore, different staples (fur, fish, timber, grain, oil, etc) have differing impacts on rates of settlement, federal-provincial conflicts, etc. The thesis was formulated in

the 1920s by economic historians Harold A. INNIS and W.A. Mackintosh. Agreeing that Canada had been born with a staple economy, they differed insofar as Mackintosh saw a continuing evolution toward a mature industrialized economy based on staple production, whereas Innis saw a tendency for Canada to become permanently locked into dependency as a resource hinterland. Contemporary proponents of the thesis argue that Innis's version more accurately describes the Canadian situation to the present. The thesis may be the most important single contribution to scholarship by Canadian social scientists and historians; it has also had some influence internationally, notably in the analysis of a comparable country such as Australia (*see* CANADA AND AUSTRALIA). MEL WATKINS

Reading: W.T. Easterbrook and Mel H. Watkins, eds, *Approaches to Canadian Economic History* (1967).

Star, Alta, UP, pop 24 (1981c), is located 60 km NE of Edmonton. It is the oldest Ukrainian Catholic parish in Canada, founded 1897 by UKRAINIAN immigrants who settled in the area 1892-94. The impressive parish church — the third — was built in 1926-27. ERIC J. HOLMGREN

Star Weekly began publication in Apr 1910 in Toronto. Founded by J.E. Atkinson, the publisher of the TORONTO STAR, *Toronto Star Weekly* was an attempt to create a Canadian counterpart to the popular British type of Sunday newspapers. Initially the *Weekly* was a grab-bag of features, articles by the daily paper's reporters, ADVERTISING and pieces purchased cheaply from syndicates. Before long, however, the *Weekly* had comic strips, good illustrations and cartoons, and by 1920 it was lavishly using colour. Eventually, able writers were recruited as freelances or put on staff, a list that included at various times Morley CALLAGHAN, Ernest Hemingway and Gregory Clark; artists found in the *Star Weekly*'s pages included Arthur LISMER, Fred VARLEY, C.W. JEFFERYS, and in the cartoons, Jimmy Frise's "Birdseye Centre." The *Weekly* had a national audience, and after 1938 the "Toronto" identification was dropped from the masthead. Like the MONTREAL STANDARD, the *Star Weekly* fell

Stanley Cup Champions 1892-1984

Season	Club	Season	Club	Season	Club
1892-93	Montreal AAA	1923-24	Montreal Canadiens	1954-55	Detroit Red Wings
1894-95	Montreal Victorias	1924-25	Victoria Cougars	1955-56	Montreal Canadiens
1895-96	Winnipeg Victorias	1925-26	Montreal Maroons	1956-57	Montreal Canadiens
1896-97	Montreal Victorias	1926-27	Ottawa Senators	1957-58	Montreal Canadiens
1897-98	Montreal Victorias	1927-28	New York Rangers	1958-59	Montreal Canadiens
1898-99	Montreal Shamrocks	1928-29	Boston Bruins	1959-60	Montreal Canadiens
1899-1900	Montreal Shamrocks	1929-30	Montreal Canadiens	1960-61	Chicago Black Hawks
1900-01	Winnipeg Victorias	1930-31	Montreal Canadiens	1961-62	Toronto Maple Leafs
1901-02	Montreal AAA	1931-32	Toronto Maple Leafs	1962-63	Toronto Maple Leafs
1902-03	Ottawa Silver Seven	1932-33	New York Rangers	1963-64	Toronto Maple Leafs
1903-04	Ottawa Silver Seven	1933-34	Chicago Black Hawks	1964-65	Montreal Canadiens
1904-05	Ottawa Silver Seven	1934-35	Montreal Maroons	1965-66	Montreal Canadiens
1905-06	Montreal Wanderers	1935-36	Detroit Red Wings	1966-67	Toronto Maple Leafs
1906-07	Kenora Thistles (Jan)[1]	1936-37	Detroit Red Wings	1967-68	Montreal Canadiens
1906-07	Montreal Wanderers (Mar)[1]	1937-38	Chicago Black Hawks	1968-69	Montreal Canadiens
1907-08	Montreal Wanderers	1938-39	Boston Bruins	1969-70	Boston Bruins
1908-09	Ottawa Senators	1939-40	New York Rangers	1970-71	Montreal Canadiens
1909-10	Montreal Wanderers	1940-41	Boston Bruins	1971-72	Boston Bruins
1910-11	Ottawa Senators	1941-42	Toronto Maple Leafs	1972-73	Montreal Canadiens
1911-12	Quebec Bulldogs	1942-43	Detroit Red Wings	1973-74	Philadelphia Flyers
1912-13	Quebec Bulldogs[2]	1943-44	Montreal Canadiens	1974-75	Philadelphia Flyers
1913-14	Toronto Blue Shirts	1944-45	Toronto Maple Leafs	1975-76	Montreal Canadiens
1914-15	Vancouver Millionaires	1945-46	Montreal Canadiens	1976-77	Montreal Canadiens
1915-16	Montreal Canadiens	1946-47	Toronto Maple Leafs	1977-78	Montreal Canadiens
1916-17	Seattle Metropolitans	1947-48	Toronto Maple Leafs	1978-79	Montreal Canadiens
1917-18	Toronto Arenas	1948-49	Toronto Maple Leafs	1979-80	New York Islanders
1918-19	No champion[3]	1949-50	Detroit Red Wings	1980-81	New York Islanders
1919-20	Ottawa Senators	1950-51	Toronto Maple Leafs	1981-82	New York Islanders
1920-21	Ottawa Senators	1951-52	Detroit Red Wings	1982-83	New York Islanders
1921-22	Toronto St Pats	1952-53	Montreal Canadiens	1983-84	Edmonton Oilers
1922-23	Ottawa Senators	1953-54	Detroit Red Wings		

[1] split season

[2] Victoria defeated Quebec in challenge series. No official recognition

[3] series called off by the local department of health because of influenza epidemic

victim to television and the NEWSPAPERS' weekend supplements, and it ceased publication in 1973. *See also* MAGAZINES. J.L. GRANATSTEIN

Reading: R. Harkness, *J.E. Atkinson of the Star* (1963).

Stare Decisis [Lat, "let the decision stand"] refers to the doctrine of precedent, according to which the rules formulated by judges in earlier decisions are to be similarly applied in later cases. The reason for the doctrine is that similar cases should be treated alike so as to ensure consistency and certainty in the law. It evolved in the primarily "judge-made" COMMON-LAW system of the law and attained its most formal expression in late 19th-century England.

In practice today the doctrine means only that prior decisions of higher courts are binding on lower courts of the same jurisdiction, for neither the Supreme Court of Canada nor many of the provincial courts of appeal consider themselves bound by their own previous decisions. Lower courts are also free to analyse the reasons (*ratio decidendi*) given by the higher court and to decide, in light of the facts of the actual dispute before them, whether to apply the precedent or to distinguish the rule contained on the basis of factual differences in the 2 cases. The doctrine, within these same limits, also applies in the interpretation of statutes. Its role in Québec civil law is of less importance and is a matter of debate. JOHN E.C. BRIERLEY

Starfish, or sea star, common marine ANIMAL found from seashore to ocean depths; 1600 species are known worldwide. They belong to the INVERTEBRATE phylum ECHINODERMATA. Starfish are usually radially symmetrical, often with 5 radiating arms joined to a central disc. The mouth is located on the underside and anus on the upper surface of the disc. Another important characteristic is the water-vascular system, an arrangement of canals and tubes that operates the starfish's tube feet by hydraulic pressure. Tube feet occur on undersurface of arms and are the principal means of locomotion and attachment. Although feeding habits are varied, starfish are often formidable predators which generate frantic escape behaviour in snails and bivalve prey. There are many species on Canada's coasts, ranging in size from tiny (50 mm) *Leptasterias hexactis* to giant *Pycnopodia helianthoides*, up to 1 m in diameter and with as many as 24 arms. R.D. BURKE

Starling, common name for Old World family (Sturnidae) of BIRDS, comprising 111 principally tropical species. Two introduced species occur in Canada: European starling (*Sturnus vulgaris*) and crested myna (*Acridotheres cristatellus*). In fall the European starling has buff-coloured spots resembling stars at tips of fresh feathers, hence its name. These disappear as feathers wear, leaving a glossy, iridescent plumage in spring. This bird, introduced worldwide, seems to owe its colonizing success to its omnivorous diet and ability to live with man. The European starlings in N America are derived from 2 introductions in New York City: 60 birds, 1890; 40 birds, 1891. In 90 years, they have spread to the US Pacific coast and up into central Canada. The crested myna, introduced to Vancouver from SE Asia about 1900, has not spread successfully. A.J. BAKER

Starnes, John Kennett, public servant (b at Montréal 5 Feb 1918). A WWII veteran, Starnes was with the Dept of External Affairs 1944-70. He was ambassador to Germany 1962-66 and to the United Arab Republic and Sudan 1966-67, when he oversaw the withdrawal of the Canadian contingent of the UN Emergency Force after the SUEZ CRISIS. The first civilian director-general of the RCMP Security Service in the eventful years 1970-73, Starnes was criticized by the McDonald Commission (INQUIRY INTO CERTAIN ACTIVITIES OF THE ROYAL CANADIAN MOUNTED POLICE) for his acquiescence in unlawful undercover

operations. He has written a fictional espionage trilogy, *Deep Sleepers* (1981), *Scarab* (1982) and *Orion's Belt* (1983). ANNE HILLMER

Starowicz, Mark, radio and TV producer (b at Worksop, Eng 8 Sept 1946). The son of Polish émigrés, he lived in England and Argentina before coming to Montréal at age 7. He was educated at McGill where he edited the *McGill Daily* and he worked for the Montréal *Gazette*. He covered Québec politics for the Toronto *Star*, and in 1969 moved to that city. In 1970 he began to produce national programs for CBC Radio. After improving "As It Happens" (1973-76), he created the popular 3-hour "Sunday Morning" current-affairs show, serving as its executive producer 1976-80 and winning a number of ACTRA awards. After a study of CBC-TV programming, he conceived "The Journal" to follow the CBC evening news (1982). Although his 3 programs have been panned as well as praised by critics, they have been the most influential news programs in Canada since 1970. ALLAN M. GOULD

Staryk, Steven, violinist, teacher (b at Toronto 28 Apr 1932). He is widely considered to be the leading Canadian-born virtuoso of his generation. Beginning as a Toronto orchestral violinist in 1950, also competing successfully in international competitions, Staryk soon became concertmaster of 3 prestigious orchestras: London Philharmonic (1956), Amsterdam Concertgebouw (1960) and Chicago Symphony (1963-67). In 1969 he formed a duo with pianist John Perry, which performed extensively in major Canadian and US cities. He became concertmaster of the Toronto Symphony in 1982. Staryk's gifted teaching at institutions in Canada and abroad has helped launch many successful violinists. Several Canadian composers have dedicated compositions to him. Performances of some of these are included among Staryk's many recordings of solo and orchestral works. BARCLAY McMILLAN

State, a broad concept that includes government as the seat of legitimate authority in a territory but also includes bureaucracy, judiciary, the ARMED FORCES and internal POLICE, subcentral structures of legislative assemblies and administration, public corporations, regulatory boards, and ideological apparatuses such as the education establishment and publicly owned media. The distinguishing characteristic of the state is its monopoly over the use of force in a given territory.

The state as a concept in political research was for a long time unfashionable in Western SOCIAL SCIENCE, largely because of the pluralist notion, dominant for some 2 decades after WWII, that the key questions traditionally asked about it — especially those concerning the state as an apparatus of power over society — were resolved in Western democracies. It was assumed that power in society was now competitive, fragmented, and diffused among virtually all social groups and that the "political system" represented a neutral and evenhanded mechanism for fulfilling or harmonizing conflicting demands.

The state has now re-emerged as a central concept of social science in Canada and elsewhere. The increasing size and scope of the state in advanced capitalist countries, the failure of elected social democratic parties to effect fundamental changes in society, and the emergence of many new Third World states which have all the formal attributes of sovereignty but preside over economies dependent on foreign capital (a subject particularly relevant to Canada) have helped revive the question of the state in social science.

In medieval Europe, the term "state" was associated with the rank and status of royalty and nobility. The state was seen as embodying power and sovereignty, but not in a way that

was distinctive from the hierarchical ordering of feudal society itself. As capitalism developed, "state" took on a more distinctly political meaning. The class relations in society between owners and nonowners were no longer formally codified in the state, which instead presented itself as the sole political community and the guarantor of the legal equality of individuals. Sovereignty and power now became exclusively political notions, and a generalized and formal disjuncture developed between the public and the private.

In the growing awareness of this disjuncture from the 17th to the 19th centuries modern social science sunk its roots, turning the old question of political philosophy, "What is the art of politics?" into, "What is the nature of the state in relation to society?" Different philosophical traditions continued to provide different answers. The conservative tradition (particularly strong in Canada) maintained the medieval notion of the state as embodying the mutual rights and obligations of hierarchically arranged social orders. The liberal tradition oscillated between characterizing the state as a necessary evil designed for defence against external enemies and for the internal expression of unbridled individual self-interest, and seeing it as the foremost human community designed to develop the potential of the individual in market society. In the socialist tradition (and particularly in its intellectual bedrock, MARXISM) the state was perceived as the product of class division in society, playing the role of reproducing class relations and moderating or repressing class conflict (*see* SOCIAL CLASS). In the anarchist view, the state was the prime source of human inequality and alienation.

Recent work on the theory of the state has attempted to uncover the development and dynamics of particular types of state in relation to particular types of society. Most advance has been made in work dealing with the liberal democratic states of advanced capitalist societies. The growth of the state in the 20th century is seen not in some vague sense as "creeping socialism," but as an ineluctable aspect of the development of capitalism. By absorbing many of the private risks and social costs of production, the state facilitated capital accumulation and regulated class conflict. The connections between state and class structure have also been examined, in an attempt to understand the link between the formal political equality of liberal democracy and the socioeconomic inequality of capitalist society. In this respect, the concept of the "relative autonomy of the state" has been used to amend the classical Marxist notion of the state as "the executive committee of the bourgeoisie," so as to invite investigation of the full range of social forces represented in the state as well as of the political compromises that dominant classes undertake to maintain their hegemonic position.

One of the virtues of Canadian social science is that it has long recognized that the large role of the state in the Canadian economy has not been antithetical to Canadian society; it has been part of the nature of that society. The Canadian POLITICAL ECONOMY tradition has emphasized that in a dependent, staples-oriented economy such as Canada's, the state has provided, partly out of economic necessity, partly out of close ties with the capitalist class, much of the necessary technical infrastructure and economic regulation necessary to keep capitalism viable. The state has attempted to provide a favourable fiscal and monetary climate for economic growth; it has underwritten the private risks of production at public expense through grants, subsidies and depreciation allowances; it has played a crucial role, via land and immigration policies, in developing the labour market and, more recently, in absorbing the social costs of production through sanitation services, medicare, unemployment insurance, educational facilities, etc; and it has often directly provided the infrastructures for economic development (canals, railways, airports, utilities) when this was too risky or costly for private capital. Research that has uncovered the close ties between state personnel and private capitalists in Canada has also demonstrated that while these ties may inhibit innovative WELFARE STATE activities, they hardly preclude active state involvement in sustaining the capitalist economy. The Canadian state is distinctive, however, because it tends to be equally active in this role at the provincial and federal levels, reflecting the binational character of Canadian society and the geographic and cultural diversity as well as the unevenly developed economies of the various regions. It also reflects the limited relative autonomy of the state from the capitalist class, in that regional fractions of this class have been able to use the provincial state to represent their interests to the federal government and to other regional capitalists. *See also* PRESSURE GROUP; ELITES. LEO PANITCH

Reading: H.A. Innis, *Political Economy in the Modern State* (1946); Leo Panitch, *The Canadian State: Political Economy and Political Power* (1977).

Station PAPA Ocean Weather Station "P" is commonly called Station PAPA after the code word for the letter P in the phonetic alphabet used by radio operators. Station PAPA is located in the N Pacific Ocean (50° N, 145° W) and has a water depth of 4200 m. Weather ships, stationed there from 1949 through 1981, were intended primarily to support aviation by providing surface and upper air weather observations and navigational assistance as well as potential rescue for downed aircraft. They also provided search and rescue services for mariners and were used to collect a wide variety of scientific data for oceanographic and meteorological research and for WEATHER FORECASTING. Several international scientific experiments were conducted near Station PAPA to take advantage of the presence of the weather ships and the large base of existing information from the site.

Initially the ships stationed at OWS "P" were provided by the US Coast Guard. Canadian occupation of the station began in 1950 using converted frigates (CCGS *St. Catherines* and CCGS *Stonetown*) operated by the Canadian Coast Guard. These ships were replaced in 1967 by the CCGS *Quadra* and CCGS *Vancouver*, built and equipped specially for the task. OWS "P" was continually occupied; each weather ship spent 6 weeks on station and one travelling to and from its home port of Esquimalt, BC. Required to remain within 100 km of the station position, the ships normally drifted while on station, occasionally steaming upwind to remain within the grid. The ships were withdrawn in 1981 as an economy measure. JOHN GARRETT

Statistics, the SCIENCE concerned with the collection and analysis of numerical information in order to answer questions wisely. The term also refers to the numerical information that has been collected. Humorist Stephen LEACOCK wrote: "In earlier times, they had no statistics, and so they had to fall back on lies. Hence the huge exaggerations of primitive literaturegiants or miracles or wonders! They did it with lies and we do it with statistics; but it is all the same." Thomas Chandler HALIBURTON's picaresque character, Sam Slick, stated: "Figures are the representatives of numbers, and not things." It is usual to think of statistics as collections of numbers, ie, data or facts in numerical form (eg, birthrates, death rates, amounts of rainfall, oil reserves, hockey records). However, numbers alone have little significance; to be meaningful, they must be placed in context. Statisticians work with numbers, but their goals are ambitious: insight, discovery, exploitations, confirmation, explanation, prediction, control and decision.

Statistical Concepts

Statistics depend on certain basic concepts:

Sample is a collection of objects or individuals meant to represent a larger collection (eg, the population). The innovation of statisticians was the recognition that, if objects were selected randomly from a population of interest, then those selected (the sample) would be representative of that population and that measures of the error resulting from the use of the sample (ie, rather that the population) might be computed.

Stratification is the operation of grouping objects into collections of similar objects, before selecting a sample or experimenting on the objects, For example, students at school might be grouped by grade and then separate samples selected for each grade.

Randomization is the scientific breakthrough of 20th-century British statistician R.A. Fisher. For example, to discover which of 2 methods of language instruction is better, an educator might use a randomized experiment, involving obtaining a group of similar students and randomly choosing half to experience the first method of instruction. Those remaining experience the second method. At the end of the experiment, test scores for those experiencing methods one and 2 would be compared. The random division of the students would make it most unlikely that the brighter students would all be taught by inst one method, thereby biasing the results.

Replication is the act of repeating a measurement of interest, eg, in the instructional experiment just referred to, repeating the study for a number of groups of students. Replication allows improved estimation of quantities of interest and facilitates computation of the error of the estimates.

Stochastic Model is a simplified description of a circumstance in mathematical language (eg, equations) that includes some element of randomness. Stochastic models lead to effective summarization and analysis of complex circumstances.

The statistical history of Canada began many years ago. The first systematic census (ie, complete enumeration of a population) was carried out in NEW FRANCE in 1666 for Louis XIV by Intendant Jean TALON. The documents he prepared are in the Public Archives, Ottawa. The first nationwide census took place in 1871. The census is now the responsibility of STATISTICS CANADA, formerly the Dominion Bureau of Statistics (est 1918). Some Canadian universities have separate statistics departments (eg, Alberta, British Columbia, Manitoba, Toronto, Waterloo, Western Ontario); others have joint departments or have kept statistics within mathematics departments. Statistics often forms part of the curriculum of the subjects that make use of quantitative techniques (eg, economics departments, schools of business and commerce, various physical, social and biological sciences). The Canadian statistics profession is represented by the Statistical Society of Canada (est 1978), which publishes *The Canadian Journal of Statistics*. DAVID R. BRILLINGER

Reading: David Freedman, Robert Pisani and Roger Purves, *Statistics* (1978); Ronald J. Wonnacott and Thomas H. Wonnacott, *Statistics, Discovering its Power* (1982).

Statistics Canada, est in 1918 as the Dominion Bureau of Statistics, is the nation's central statistical agency. Under the 1971 Statistics Act, it has the responsibility to "collect, compile, analyse, abstract and publish statistical information relating to the commercial, industrial, financial, social, economic and general activities and condition of the people of Canada." The agency collaborates with government departments in the development of integrated social and economic statistics for Canada and the provinces. In addition, Statistics Canada is a scientific research organization responsible for leadership in the development of statistical methodologies and techniques. The agency, which is subject to the budgetary control of Parliament, is committed to meeting the statistical needs of all levels of government and the private sector for research, policy formulation, decision making and general information purposes. Some of its major programs are the Census of Population, the Labour Force Survey, the Consumer Price Index, the Gross National Product and the International Balance of Payments.

Statistics Canada issues about 500 titles a year. The *Canada Handbook*, the monthly *Canadian Statistical Review*, the *Statistics Canada Daily*, vehicle of first release for agency data, and *Infomat*, a weekly summary of statistical highlights, are among the agency's most widely used publications. Statistics Canada also makes its information available on microfiche, microfilm, computer tape, and through the agency's extensive machine-readable data base CANSIM. Regional offices in St John's, Halifax, Montréal, Sturgeon Falls (Ont), Toronto, Winnipeg, Regina, Edmonton and Vancouver conduct survey and census operations and also offer reference and consultative services to statistical users.

Status of Women The first European expeditions that came to Canada to explore and trade for furs did not include women. Early records of fur-trading companies suggest it was common for both French and English traders to enter into marriage with Indian women *à la façon du pays*, — by a mix of European and Indian customs.

The Indian women who married fur traders provided an important link between the 2 cultures: the trader secured the trade of his wife's band or tribe and he learned from her survival skills, native customs and languages. Some Indian women acted as unpaid interpreters for fur-trading companies and achieved a good deal of importance. Such marital arrangements continued until missionaries and fur-trading companies actively discouraged them in the 19th century. In the early days of the FUR TRADE an Indian woman whose husband had left her would return to the tribe, but as the economic base of Indian life deteriorated, it became difficult for tribes to reabsorb women and their children. Their vulnerability was confirmed with the passage of the INDIAN ACT in 1876. Indian women who married non-Indian men immediately lost their status and relinquished the right to live on reserves. Such discrimination, since native men marrying whites were not affected, was the source of great distress and ultimately political protest for native women.

French Colonization A few French women arrived in NEW FRANCE beginning in the 1630s. Their numbers remained small until 1663 when young women of marriageable age, known as FILLES DU ROI, were given free passage to New France and provided with a dowry. The majority of women in the colony, including widows, were quickly married. They were expected to bear and raise children for the colony, to care for their homes, cook, sew and garden. Early French Canadian records also indicate that it was not unusual for women to own property, run inns, keep books and generally manage the family business (*see* COMMUNAUTÉ DES BIENS). The resourcefulness and fortitude of these pioneers was exemplified by Agathe de Saint-Père, who took over the raising of 10 brothers and sisters when she was only 15 and continued her own business career after marrying at age 28. She had weaving looms installed in houses throughout Montréal and ran the cloth industry for 8 years until she retired and devoted herself to work at a Québec hospital.

Women in religious orders played a significant role in developing the early institutions of New France. Marguerite BOURGEOYS founded the

Congrégation de Notre-Dame, which opened its first school in 1658, and was active in the establishment of many more schools, including la Providence, an industrial school for girls. In 1753 Marie d'YOUVILLE was granted a Royal Charter for the Grey Nuns, Sisters of Charity. The Grey Nuns ran the Hôpital général in Québec and became the most active order of nursing sisters in the hospital field (*see* CHRISTIAN RELIGIOUS COMMUNITIES).

The British Period, 1713-1914 The predominantly rural nature of Canada before 1850 had implications for the position of women in society. Settlement was characterized by small independent landholdings and the labour of women was crucial to the survival of the economic unit (*see* HOMESTEADING). Census figures for the 19th century indicate that more than 90% of female children born in any decade between 1810 and 1870 eventually married. Married women and their children worked as a production unit on the farm in the area immediately surrounding the house and outbuildings. Although by 1800 few farms were entirely self-sufficient, women produced a great deal of the goods that their families required. They tended livestock, managed the garden, preserved fruit and vegetables, spun yarn, wove cloth and sewed clothing. Accounts of 19th-century writers like Susanna MOODIE and Catharine Parr TRAILL describe some of the work of women during this century (*see* PIONEER LIFE).

As the century progressed a number of trends converged to alter the traditional position of women in society. The agricultural unit was increasingly drawn into the money economy as demand increased for cash crops and as agricultural technology improved. Many necessities that had been produced on the farm were replaced by purchased goods. The mixed production characteristic of early landholdings gave way to more specialized agricultural production. As there was less for children to do on farms and as urbanization progressed, children spent less time in productive work and more time at school. The tendency of these changes was also to diminish the involvement of women in agricultural and domestic production and to emphasize their role as one of service towards family members as they related to the larger society. More than city women, however, rural women found themselves still bound, albeit in fewer ways, to the pace and needs of production.

The rapid growth of WOMEN'S ORGANIZATIONS by the end of the 19th century reflected the increasing politicization of women. Women's missionary societies were formed in most Canadian churches in the 1870s and 1880s; the first Canadian YOUNG WOMEN'S CHRISTIAN ASSOCIATION was founded in 1870; the WOMAN'S CHRISTIAN TEMPERANCE UNION in 1874 (*see* TEMPERANCE MOVEMENT); the Dominion Order of King's Daughters in 1886; and women's organizations in Ontario and Manitoba formed the first suffrage associations in the 1880s and 1890s (*see* WOMEN'S SUFFRAGE). By the end of the century a number of women's associations had achieved national stature and a federation of women's groups, the NATIONAL COUNCIL OF WOMEN OF CANADA, was formed in 1893. The women who agitated for the vote went through those who had gone through a period of "apprenticeship" for political action in organizations that preceded the suffrage movement.

Despite vigorous debate on the advisability of educating female children, the percentage of girls attending school rose from 23.1% in 1842 to 75.6% in 1881 (*see* WOMEN AND EDUCATION). Female students who went on for training in normal schools could enter the paid labour force as teachers, the first of the so-called "female professions." By the final quarter of the century, women occupied the majority of teaching posi-

tions in Canada. Religious orders had provided nursing care for centuries, as they had played a significant role in teaching. Women had acted in a voluntary capacity as midwives in rural communities (*see* BIRTHING PRACTICES), and the establishment of training schools for lay nurses after 1874 permitted graduates to find work as paid nurses. In 1875 Grace Annie LOCKHART became the first woman to earn a university degree in Canada, at Mt Allison U. Emily STOWE, Canada's pioneering woman doctor, began to practise in 1867, although she had been obliged to take her medical training in the US. Clara Brett Martin became the first Canadian woman lawyer in 1899.

INDUSTRIALIZATION was given a boost in Canada after Sir John A. MACDONALD introduced his NATIONAL POLICY of protective tariffs in 1879. Girls and women moved to the towns and cities looking for work and many found jobs in sweatshops and factories. Garment and textile industries, in particular, hired large numbers to labour in factories or to do piecework in small shops or at home (*see* WOMEN IN THE LABOUR FORCE). Though poorly paid, factory work did provide women with more freedom than traditional work in DOMESTIC SERVICE and on farms.

The demand for household servants continued throughout the 19th century and IMMIGRATION policies encouraged women to come to Canada in domestic service. By 1891 census figures reflected the entrance of women into the economy as paid workers. Almost 196 000 women had jobs and they represented 11.07% of the labour force. The jobs they held were predominantly in low-paying "female" occupations: domestic service (41%), dressmaking, teaching, sewing, tailoring, housekeeping, laundering, millinery and salesclerking.

Canada remained a predominantly rural nation until after WWI, but the manufacturing sector was growing in importance, and with it the service-producing sector whose operation required large numbers of office workers. Between 1901 and 1911 the female labour force increased by 50%, particularly in occupations such as clerk, typist and salesclerk. Female pay was regularly 50-60% of male pay and in 1907 the National Council of Women adopted a resolution calling for "equal pay for equal work." Owing to the prevailing ideology of separate spheres for men and women, of the male breadwinner and of woman's place in the home, it was mostly single women who held jobs in the prewar years; other women who took paid work were considered "unfortunates" — widows, divorcées, deserted or separated women, or wives of the unemployed.

1914 to 1945 During WWI women were brought into the labour force as new jobs were created and as men left their jobs to join the armed forces. Most found familiar jobs as secretaries, clerks, typists and factory workers. For the first time, however, many women worked in heavy industry, particularly the munitions industry where by 1917 there were 35 000 women employed in munitions factories in Ontario and Montréal. Most of the women who worked during the war were unmarried. Although their wages increased during the war years, they never equalled men's; in the munitions factories women's wages were 50-80% of those paid men. Despite the movement of women into a few new areas of the economy, domestic service remained the most common female occupation.

The war effort increased women's political visibility. Women's organizations had supported the war effort by recruiting women to replace men in the domestic labour force and by collecting massive amounts of comforts for Canadian troops. A Women's War Conference was called by the federal government in 1918 to discuss the continuing role of women, who took the opportunity to raise a number of political is-

sues, including suffrage. Suffrage movements had been gaining strength since the turn of the century, particularly in the West, and in 1916 Manitoba, Saskatchewan and Alberta had given women the provincial vote, Ontario and BC followed in 1917. On 24 May 1918 the Parliament of Canada bestowed the federal franchise on women, and by 1922 women had the provincial vote in all provinces except Québec and Newfoundland (where they were only partially enfranchised provincially). In the early 1920s the WOMEN'S INTERNATIONAL LEAGUE FOR PEACE AND FREEDOM was formed in Canada to work for peace and disarmament.

In 1919 women were granted the right to hold political office in Parliament, and in 1921 Agnes MACPHAIL was the first woman to be elected as a federal member. In 1929, 5 Alberta women led by Judge Emily MURPHY successfully brought the PERSONS CASE before the King's Privy Council in England with the result that women in Canada became eligible for senatorial appointment.

Cutbacks and layoffs of women took place in the years immediately following the war, but by the 1920s women had reestablished their wartime levels of labour-force involvement. Some new "female" professions, such as library work, social work (*see* Charlotte WHITTON) and physiotherapy were emerging, but the most rapidly growing occupations were clerical. Domestic service remained the most common paid occupation of women, but for the first time in the century the percentage of women working as domestics fell below 20%. Women were entering universities in large numbers and, by 1930, 23% of all undergraduates and 35% of all graduate students were female. The GREAT DEPRESSION reversed this trend and in the 1930s many women were forced back into domestic service. Federal employment figures show that even in the garment industry, a longtime employer of women, they were being laid off at a higher rate than men.

Canada entered WWII with a high level of unemployment, but by 1942 the government was facing a labour shortage. With the help of 21 national women's organizations, a federal National Selective Service program was launched to recruit women into the industrial labour force. The program first sought to register only single women for employment, but continuing labour shortages forced it to recruit childless married women and finally married women with children. As an enabling measure, federal-provincial child-care agreements were drawn up, eventually leading to the establishment of 28 day nurseries in Ontario and 5 in Québec. Large numbers of married women joined the paid work force for the first time, and by 1945, 33.2% of all women were employed (*see also* CANADIAN WOMEN'S ARMY CORPS).

1945 to the Present After WWII women were expected and, in the case of federal government employees, required to relinquish their jobs to returning servicemen. The day nurseries were closed, many women returned to the home, often to have children, and by 1946 the rate of women's participation in the labour force had dropped to Depression levels. The patterns of married employment had been established, however, and married women began entering the labour force in such numbers that by the 1960s they made up one-third of the labour force and represented 55% of the labour-force growth. Despite their numbers, the earnings of working women continued to be significantly lower than those of men: in 1961 earnings of women employed full-time, year-round, were 59% of the earnings of men in the same categories; when part-time workers were added, women's wages dropped to 54% of men's.

This phenomenon could be partially attributed to limitations in federal legislation governing equal pay and to a lack of enforcement of its provisions because women were paid less than men on the average even when they did the same work. Full-time female clerical workers earned 74% of the wage of male clerical workers in 1961. The situation was more clearly attributable to the different occupational structures for men and women: men were more likely to work in unionized occupations, to be employed in highly paid professions, and they held 89.7% of all proprietorial and managerial positions. Women remained locked into "female" occupations, predominantly clerical. Over 20% of the female labour force still worked in personal service jobs as maids and baby-sitters and those women in professions tended to be dieticians and librarians rather than doctors and lawyers.

Women in the 1960s remained underrepresented in political institutions, faced the quota system in some universities, and were generally subject to a range of discriminatory policies and legislation in both the public and private sectors. By the end of the decade the burgeoning WOMEN'S MOVEMENT voiced protest in the form of women's centres, consciousness-raising groups and rape crisis centres.

As a response to the issue of equality for women, a Royal Commission on the STATUS OF WOMEN was established in 1967. In 1970 the commission presented its report, making 167 recommendations on such matters as employment, educational opportunities and family law. The publication of the report, the continued proliferation of women's organizations, and the establishment of the NATIONAL ACTION COMMITTEE ON THE STATUS OF WOMEN as a lobby group ensured that the political visibility of women's issues continued into the 1970s.

The federal government responded by creating new offices and procedures to deal with women's rights: a portfolio for the status of women in the federal Cabinet (1971); an Office of the Co-ordinator of the Status of Women to monitor the progress of all federal ministries in implementing the RCSW's recommendations (1971); an Office of Equal Opportunities in the Public Service Commission (1972); and an Advisory Council on the Status of Women (1973). Certain federal statutes were amended to remove sections that were discriminatory to women, in particular the Canada Labour Code (1971); sections of the Criminal Code pertaining to jury duty (1972); the Public Service Superannuation Act (1975); a Federal Omnibus Bill on the Status of Women containing amendments to 11 statutes (1975); the Citizenship Act (1975); and an Omnibus Bill to amend the Labour Code (1978).

In 1978 the Canadian Human Rights Act came into effect prohibiting discrimination on the basis of sex (among other things) in the case of employees under federal jurisdiction. The Act contains provisions to ensure "equal pay for work of equal value," specifying that "value" should be determined with reference to skill, effort, responsibility and working conditions. A Woman's Program was established within the Secretary of State and began to make money available for special projects of women's centres, rape crisis centres, women's research programs and professional associations, and transition houses for physically abused women.

By the early 1980s women in Canada still did not have equality. Full-time female employees earned 62% of that earned by men, two-thirds of all minimum-wage earners were women, and only 5% of women were employed in managerial or administrative positions. Only 20% of working women were unionized and almost three-quarters of all part-time workers were women — a situation which allowed women to be excluded from employee and pension benefits. Since work-related pensions are based on earnings, women on average receive significantly lower amounts; unlike the Québec Pen-

sion Plan, the Canada Pension Plan has not implemented a "child-care drop-out" provision to protect pension entitlements of mothers who leave the labour market to raise children; when a man dies, his widow usually receives drastically reduced Canada/Québec Pension Plan benefits and nothing at all from the husband's employer-sponsored pension plan. As a result, 70% of widows and single women over 70 live in poverty. In 1978 an estimated one-half million Canadian women were battered by the men they lived with and, in 1982, 3633 rapes were reported to the police, though these figures represented only a fraction of the sexual assaults committed against women. Women's groups fought hard to ensure that the Charter of Rights and Freedoms in the Canadian Constitution (1982) enshrined equality for both sexes, but many controversial issues affecting the status of women — ABORTION, PORNOGRAPHY, equal pay, PENSIONS — remain unresolved. *See also* CHILDHOOD, HISTORY OF; FAMILY; HOUSEWORK; SOCIAL HISTORY. DORIS ANDERSON

Reading: J. Acton and B. Shepard, eds, *Women at Work* (1974); P. and H. Armstrong, *The Double Ghetto* (1978); P. Connelly, *Last Hired, First Fired: Women and the Canadian Work Force* (1978); G. Matheson, ed, *Women in the Canadian Mosaic* (1976); *Report of the Royal Commission on the Status of Women in Canada* (1970); Status of Women, Canada, *Towards Equality for Women* (1979); M. Stephenson, ed, *Women in Canada* (1977); S.M. Trofimenkoff and A. Prentice, eds, *The Neglected Majority* (1977); S. Van Kirk, *Many Tender Ties: Women in Fur Trade Society 1670-1870* (1980).

Status of Women in Canada, Royal Commission on the, instituted by PM Lester B. PEARSON on 16 Feb 1967 in response to a campaign mounted by a coalition of 32 women's voluntary groups. The campaign lasted 6 months and was led by Ontario activist Laura Sabia. It was a direct response to the WOMEN'S MOVEMENT and similar initiatives by other governments in the 1960s. Florence BIRD, an Ottawa journalist and broadcaster, was appointed as chairwoman. The other commissioners were Jacques Henripin, professor of demography, Montréal; John Humphrey, professor of law, Montréal; Lola Lange, farmer and community activist, Claresholm, Alta; Jeanne Lapointe, professor of literature, Québec City; Elsie Gregory MacGill, aeronautical engineer, Toronto; and Doris Ogilvie, judge, Fredericton, NB. The RCSW, the first Canadian commission headed by a woman, was given a mandate to investigate and report on all matters pertaining to the status of women, and to make specific recommendations for improving the condition of women in those areas which fell within the jurisdiction of the federal government.

The commission's public investigation began in the spring of 1968, and for 6 months public hearings were held across Canada, including the Far North. This commission attracted extensive public interest, hearing 468 briefs and additional testimony, all of which attested to widespread problems experienced by women in all walks of Canadian society.

The RCSW produced a 488-page report containing 167 recommendations on such matters as equal pay for work of equal value, maternity leave, DAY CARE, BIRTH CONTROL, FAMILY LAW, the INDIAN ACT, educational opportunities, access of women to managerial positions, part-time work and PENSIONS. The recommendations were based on fundamental principles which assumed that equality of opportunity for Canadian men and women was possible, desirable and ethically necessary. The *Report of the Royal Commission on the Status of Women in Canada* was tabled in the House of Commons on 7 Dec 1970. The RCSW played a major role in defining the status of women as a legitimate social problem. It focused attention on women's grievances, recommended changes to eliminate sexual inequality by means of

social policy, and mobilized a constituency of women's groups to press for implementation of the commission's recommendations.

By the early 1980s most of the 167 recommendations in the RCSW report had been partially implemented and many had been fully implemented. Several controversial recommendations, however, had not been acted upon by the federal government. *See also* STATUS OF WOMEN. CERISE MORRIS

Reading: Advisory Council on the Status of Women, *Ten Years Later* (1979); N. Griffiths, *Penelope's Web* (1976); *Report of the Royal Commission on the Status of Women in Canada* (1970).

Statute of Westminster, 11 Dec 1931, a British law clarifying the powers of Canada's Parliament and those of the other Dominions, and granting the former colonies full legal freedom except in those areas where they chose to remain subordinate. Until this time the British government had certain ill-defined powers, and ultimately overriding authority, over Dominion legislation. The Imperial Conference of 1926 began to give legal substance to the BALFOUR REPORT declaration that Britain and the Dominions were constitutionally "equal in status." The 1929 Conference on the Operation of Dominion Legislation and the Imperial Conference of 1930 continued to work towards agreement on fundamental changes in the COMMONWEALTH's complex legal system. Finally, at the request and with the consent of the Dominions, the Statute of Westminster was passed by the British Parliament. After consultation between Canada's federal and provincial governments, the repeal, amendment or alteration of the BRITISH NORTH AMERICA ACTS, 1867-1930, was specifically excepted from the terms of the statute: the amendment of the Canadian Constitution remained exclusively the preserve of the British Parliament until passage of the CONSTITUTION ACT, 1982. Nor did Canada immediately take up all of its new powers under the statute. Not until 1949, for instance, did the JUDICIAL COMMITTEE OF THE PRIVY COUNCIL cease to be a final court of appeal for Canadians. NORMAN HILLMER

Stavert, Reuben Ewart, mine executive (b at Kingston, Jamaica 3 Oct 1893; d at Montréal 19 Nov 1981). Stavert graduated from McGill in 1914 and served in the CEF in WWI. He worked at Canadian General Electric 1919-22, when he joined the British Metal Corp of Canada, of which he was president 1931-34. He then became assistant to the president of Consolidated Mining and Smelting. Appointed VP in 1941 and president in 1945, Stavert played a major role in Cominco's postwar expansion, which included the development of Pine Point Mines at Great Slave Lk, the construction of an ammonium-phosphate plant in Kimberley, BC, and the formation of Cominco Products Inc. He retired as president in 1959 and as chairman in 1964. He was a governor of U de M and a director of several large corporations. J. LINDSEY

Steacie, Edgar William Richard, physical chemist, scientist-statesman (b at Westmount, Qué 25 Dec 1900; d at Ottawa 8 Aug 1962). Steacie was an internationally acclaimed research authority in free radical kinetics and, as a senior administrator at the NATIONAL RESEARCH COUNCIL, was influential in increasing Canada's capabilities in scientific research in both government and the universities. Steacie took his PhD in 1926 at McGill, remaining there as a research fellow in physical chemistry. In 1930 he became assistant professor and began his pioneering research studies in free radical kinetics, the measurement of the rates of chemical reactions and the determination of the mechanisms of such processes. In 1939 he was appointed director of the Chemistry Division of NRC, which under his leadership became an international centre for chemical research. By 1944 Steacie was an obvious choice for deputy director under Sir John Cockcroft of the joint British-Canadian Atomic Energy Project. Steacie continued to maintain his fundamental program and in addition published his major treatise, *Atomic and Free Radical Reactions* (1946), which rapidly became the essential reference in its field.

He was appointed vice-president (scientific) of NRC in 1950 and became president in 1952. Through his efforts, many distinguished scientists were appointed to the NRC staff, including Gerhard HERZBERG. Steacie also persuaded the federal government to provide more support to universities for scientific research. Instrumental in upgrading industrial research as well, he obtained special tax concessions to assist companies in financing research, and through his efforts a new program of federal research grants was initiated to support innovative industrial research. Steacie not only laid the foundation for the development of Canadian science but also pioneered the government support structure necessary to promote those research industries that represent the growth points of modern industrial technology.   HARRY E. GUNNING

Steamboats and Paddle Wheelers Steamboat refers to the flat-bottomed, shallow-draft, steam-powered vessels, generally associated with inland navigation, as opposed to the deep-keeled, oceangoing and Great Lakes steamships. As invented in 1685 by French physicist Denis Papin, the paddle wheel (driven by compressed steam from wood- or coal-fired boilers) was affixed to the boat hull either laterally (side-wheeler) or at the rear of the boat (stern-wheeler) and provided forward and reverse propulsion.

Demonstrated in France on the Saône R in 1783, the paddle-wheel steamboat first appeared in N America for use on the Delaware R in 1787. After inauguration at New Orleans in 1811 by Robert Fulton, hundreds of boats worked the Mississippi R system between 1830 and 1870. The first paddle steamer in Canadian waters, the ACCOMMODATION, was a side-wheeler launched for a 36-hour maiden voyage from Montréal to Québec in 1809. Other paddle-wheel steamboat firsts in Canada include the *Frontenac* on Lk Ontario (1817); the *General Stacey Smyth* on the Saint John R (1816); the *Union* on the upper reaches of the Ottawa R (1819); the *Richard Smith* visiting PEI (1830); the ROYAL WILLIAM steaming from Québec to Halifax (1831); the seagoing BEAVER, which first plied waters off BC (1836); the *Spitfire*, first steamboat into St John's harbour (1840); and the ANSON NORTHUP, first paddle wheeler to cross the international boundary on the Red R (1859).

Paddle steamers figure significantly in Canadian history. The *Accommodation* moved troops on the St Lawrence during the War of 1812. The *Royal William*, built at Québec, was the first vessel to cross the Atlantic almost entirely under the power of steam in 1833. BC steamers ferried thousands of gold seekers into the Fraser (1858), Cariboo (1862) and Yukon (1898) river valleys (300 steamboats worked BC and Yukon waterways between 1836 and 1957). The Red R steamer *International* was commandeered by the forces of Louis Riel at Fort Garry in 1870; and the Saskatchewan R stern-wheeler NORTHCOTE engaged Gabriel Dumont's Métis at the Battle of BATOCHE.

Paddle steamers carried the first wheat exported from Manitoba, precipitated a sophisticated inland canal and lock system in Ontario, freighted the first locomotive to Winnipeg for the CPR, brought the first mail to the Klondike and ferried the first fresh fruits and missionaries into the Far North. The utilitarian steamboat was also a social force. Staterooms, grand pianos and fine wines came with first-class passage aboard even the frontier steamers, and cabin

Stern-wheelers at Whitehorse, YT, c 1900 (*courtesy Public Archives of Canada/PA-122784*).

and boiler decks below had fiddle playing, folk dances and card games. After 1900, when railways replaced steamboats as the major means of freight transport, hunting and picnic excursions and moonlight cruises were commonplace aboard steamboats. The last fully operational stern-wheeler, the *Samson V* (built in 1936 for use on the Fraser R), was taken out of service in 1981.   TED BARRIS

Reading: Ted Barris, *Fire Canoe: Prairie Steamboat Days Revisited* (1977); Peter Charlebois, *Sternwheelers & Sidewheelers, The Romance of Steamdriven Paddleboats in Canada* (1978); Art Downs, *Paddlewheels on the Frontier: The Story of British Columbia and Yukon Sternwheel Steamers* (1972).

Stedman, Donald Frank, scientist (b at Tunbridge Wells, Eng 4 Apr 1900; d at Ottawa 2 May 1967). Primarily a chemist, he was one of the earliest staffers of the NATIONAL RESEARCH COUNCIL (1930). As a youngster in BC, Donald began his higher education by correspondence courses, gained a BSc from UBC and a doctorate in physical chemistry from U of London. Returning to Canada in 1924, he was engaged in industry and academia before joining the NRC. There he was soon involved in the exploitation of the Turner Valley, Alta, gas deposits. One outcome was his invention of the Stedman fractionating column, which was to become widely used by industry. His work in Ottawa diversified, as he studied, among other things, windshield rain repellents, forest-fire hazard indicators, the physics of time and the classification of the chemical elements. He also invented a wondrous "sea-walker suit" to facilitate lifesaving in marine accidents. An eccentric loner, not all Stedman's ideas fulfilled their early promise, however, and he had to abandon a search for "new heavy inert gases" on account of sabotage by supernatural forces.   N.T. GRIDGEMAN

Stedman, Ernest Walter, aircraft engineer (b at Malling, Eng 21 July 1888; d at Ottawa 27 Mar 1957). Stedman trained as an engineer and ended his WWI service as a lt-col in the RAF. He then joined the Handley-Page aircraft company and came to N America with the firm's (unsuccessful) entry in the 1919 race to fly the Atlantic (won by J.N.W. Alcock and A.W. Brown). He liked Canada and immigrated in 1920, planning to manufacture aircraft parts, but took the post of director of the technical branch of the newly appointed Canadian Air Board. Thus, he was from 30 Oct 1920 the government's chief aeronautical engineer, under various titles, until his retirement in 1946 as an air vice-marshal, director general of air research of the RCAF. His work involved every aspect of aviation in Canada, including the W.R. TURNBULL propellor,

J.H. PARKIN's research at U of T and the NATIONAL RESEARCH COUNCIL, the R-100 airship flight to Canada in 1930, practical work on winter flying (eg, starting cold engines and landing on snow), the foundation of TRANS-CANADA AIRLINES, buying and building aircraft for WWII, and jet-engine design in 1944. After retirement he was a Canadian witness at the Bikini atomic bomb test of 1946 and founded the engineering faculty of Carleton. His *From Boxkite to Jet: the Memoirs of an Aeronautical Engineer* was published posthumously in 1963.   DONALD J.C. PHILLIPSON

Steel, *see* IRON AND STEEL INDUSTRY.

Steel, William Arthur, radio pioneer (b 3 Nov 1890; d at Ottawa 28 Nov 1968). Steel was chief wireless officer in the Canadian Corps in France at the end of WWI and chief radio engineer of the Canadian Army Signals Corps throughout the 1920s, when he organized the Northwest Territories radio system and, together with A.G.L. MCNAUGHTON, invented the Cathode Ray Direction Finder, an early form of RADAR. He organized the NATIONAL RESEARCH COUNCIL's radio laboratory 1931-32 and was commissioner in charge of engineering operations of the Canadian Radio Broadcasting Commission 1933-36. He retired from the army with the rank of lt-col in 1936 and had a brief excursion in politics, in W.D. HERRIDGE's New Democracy Party. He thereafter worked in Ottawa as a consulting engineer in radio and radar, notably aircraft navigation aids and the construction of the DEW Line radar system.   DONALD J.C. PHILLIPSON

Steele, Mount, elev 5073 m, is located among Canada's highest mountains in the St Elias Range of the YT. It is joined to Mt LUCANIA by a high snow saddle; their summits are 13 km apart. Together, they form a huge snow and ice massif covering over 90 km² and spawning many glaciers, the 2 largest being Walsh and Chitina. Mt Steele's triangular, ice-covered NE face helps feed Steele Glacier, which flows NE. The mountain was named after Sam STEELE, former NWMP commander stationed in the Yukon during the gold rush. Its first ascent was made Aug 1935 by W. Wood, H. Wood, J. Fobes and H. Fuhrer via the E ridge.   GLEN BOLES

Steele, Sir Samuel Benfield, mounted policeman, soldier (b at Purbrook, Canada W 5 Jan 1849; d at London, Eng 30 Jan 1919). Steele joined the militia in 1866 during the FENIAN troubles, was a private in the Red River expedition, joined the Permanent Force Artillery in 1871 and, in 1873, became a sergeant major in the newly created NWMP. A man of enormous physical strength and endurance, Steele managed to be where the action was hottest. He achieved commissioned rank in 1878, acquired

Sam Steele, a man of enormous strength and endurance, managed through his eventful career to be where the action was hottest (*courtesy Public Archives of Canada/PA-28146*).

his first command at Ft Qu'Appelle in 1879, where he was in charge of police detachments supervising the building of the CPR, and was promoted superintendent in 1885. In 1898 he helped establish the authority of the Canadian government during the KLONDIKE GOLD RUSH. Steele was given command of Lord Strathcona's Horse in the SOUTH AFRICAN WAR, and in 1915 he commanded the second Canadian contingent to be sent overseas. In 1916 he was appointed general officer commanding the Shorncliffe area in England, a post he held until the end of the war and his retirement in 1918.   R.C. MACLEOD

Reading: S. Garrod, *Sam Steele* (1979); S.B. Steele, *Forty Years in Canada* (1915); R. Stewart, *Sam Steele* (1979).

Stefansson, Baldur Rosmund, plant breeder (b at Vestfold, Man 26 Apr 1917). Stefansson has been a leader in development of rapeseed from an unadapted crop producing modest amounts of industrial oil to an adapted food and feed crop (CANOLA) rivalling wheat in acreage and value. He is an internationally acclaimed plant breeder, best known for suggesting elimination of erucic from rapeseed oil and for production of the oil's first low erucic, low glucosinolate varieties. He is also recognized for subsequent significant genetic alterations to the food value of the oil, industrial quality of the oil, and feed value of meal produced from the seed. Most recently, Stefansson has been active in studies relating to production of hybrid rape. In recognition of his achievements he has earned many awards, including the Manitoba Institute of Agrologists' Distinguished Agrologist Award 1981. Stefansson has been associated with the department of plant science at U Man since 1952.
ANNA K. STORGAARD

Stefansson, Vilhjalmur, arctic explorer, ethnologist, lecturer, writer (b at Arnes, Man 3 Nov 1879; d at Hanover, NH 26 Aug 1962). One of Canada's most renowned arctic explorers and winner of a host of international awards, Stefansson was no stranger to controversy and created more interest in the Arctic among Canadians than any other individual of his time. The son of ICELANDERS who moved to the Dakotas in 1880, educated at the universities of Iowa, N Dakota and Harvard, Stefansson made 3 forays into the Arctic between 1906 and 1918, travel-

ling more than 32 000 km² of arctic territory. In 1910 he discovered the "Blond Eskimos" (COPPER INUIT) of Victoria Land and, as commander of the Canadian Arctic Expedition (1913-18), which was fraught with internal dissension, he discovered some of the world's last major landmasses — Lougheed, Borden, Meighen and Brock islands, while drifting dangerously, but deliberately, on ice floes. A prolific writer, his most famous book being *The Friendly Arctic* (1921), Stefansson had a simple message regarding Canada's NORTH: the Arctic was not a bleak, frozen waste but a habitable region that must be developed. The over-the-pole routes of today's airlines, nuclear submarines surfacing at the N Pole, and the possibility of using gigantic submarine tankers, all had their origin in Stefansson's vision of a strategic and commercial polar Mediterranean which, if controlled and exploited by Canada (and the British Empire), could make the Dominion one of the great powers of the 20th century. To some he was the "prophet of the North"; to others he was an arrogant charlatan. He left Canada under a cloud, partly because he had made enemies during the Canadian Arctic Expedition, but also because the projects he later undertook to prove his theories failed. His poorly planned scheme for the domestication of reindeer in northern Canada (1921-25) ended in chaos; his unauthorized claiming of Wrangel I, N of Siberia, for Canada generated an international incident (1921-24) that upset the USSR and the US and embarrassed Great Britain. The Canadian government was infuriated, seeing his action as high-handed and undercutting Canada's claims to its ARCTIC ARCHIPELAGO. Also, all 4 members of the Wrangel I expedition, including a young Canadian student, died tragically and, some say, unnecessarily. Stefansson, who had not gone on this expedition, was now perceived as a troublemaker whose ideas and presence in Canada were unwelcome. From the mid-1920s on, most of his time was spent in the US, where he was regarded as one of the world's foremost arctic experts. *See* ARCTIC EXPLORATION.   RICHARD J. DIUBALDO

Stefansson Island, 4463 km², elev 256 m, in the ARCTIC ARCHIPELAGO, is a low, gently rolling, lake-strewn plain. Being largely barren, with continuous vegetation only in wet lowlands, it supports few muskoxen and Peary caribou. It was discovered in 1917 by members of V. STEFANSSON's expedition.   S.C. ZOLTAI

Steinbach, Man, Town, pop 6676 (1981c), inc 1946, is located 48 km SE of Winnipeg. Eighteen Kleine Gemeinde families developed a traditional MENNONITE agricultural village at the Steinbach site in 1874. They were among several thousand Mennonites from southern Russia who emigrated in the 1870s to 2 reserves established for them in Manitoba. Despite the absence of rail links, Steinbach developed as an agricultural centre and later as a commercial, industrial and administrative centre. Located in a mixed-farming region, the town serves a trade-area population of 30 000. Its economic activities include farm-products processing, concrete products, trucking, millworking and boat manufacturing. Steinbach also has a Bible institute. Its heritage is celebrated during annual Pioneer Days in August and by the Mennonite Village Museum, a reconstruction of the original settlement.   D.M. LYON

Steinberg, Samuel, grocer (b in Hungary 1905; d at Montréal 24 May 1978). In 1909 the Steinberg family immigrated to Canada and established a small grocery store in Montréal. Samuel and his 4 brothers began working in it in 1917 and turned it into one of Canada's largest supermarket chains. In 1934, under Samuel's management, Steinberg's opened Québec's first self-service store in Montréal. Five years later

Samuel opened a branch at Arvida, Qué. In 1959 Steinberg's bought the 38 Ontario stores of Grand Union Ltd. When Steinberg died, the company was grossing over $1 billion a year from its Steinberg and Miracle Mart stores and other enterprises. At that time it was the largest supermarket chain in Québec and was owned completely by the family. Steinberg was also a director of Petrofina, Ivanhoe and Pharmaprix.
JORGE NIOSI

Steinberg Inc is a diversified Canadian retailing organization with head offices in Montréal. It was incorporated in 1930 as Steinberg's Limited, and adopted its present name in 1978. Between 1958 and 1981 the company expanded by acquiring other enterprises, including the entire chain of Grand Union stores in Ontario. Today, it has several wholly owned subsidiaries, including Steinberg Foods Limited. It is engaged in food retailing and manufacturing, general merchandise retailing and real estate. Among other enterprises, it or its subsidiaries operate 312 supermarkets and grocery stores, 32 department stores and 196 restaurants. As of July 1983, it had annual sales or operating revenue of $3.35 billion (ranking 25th in Canada), assets of $998 million (ranking 86th) and 32 400 employees. It is 100% owned by Steinberg family trusts.
DEBORAH C. SAWYER

Steinhauer, Henry Bird, Shahwahnegezhik (Ojibwa) or Sowengisik (Cree), meaning "Southern Skies," Methodist minister, native leader (b at Rama Indian settlement, Lk Simcoe, UC *c*1818; d at Whitefish Lake, Alta 29 Dec 1884). After an American benefactor named Steinhauer in Philadelphia provided his foster name and funds, he attended Cazenovia College, NY, and Upper Canada Academy, Cobourg, UC. He accompanied James EVANS to the Hudson's Bay territories in 1840. Appointed to Oxford House in 1850, he was ordained by the Canada Conference (Methodist) in 1855 and sent to Lac La Biche, Alta. In 1858 he moved to Whitefish Lake, Alta, to found a native Christian community.   GERALD M. HUTCHINSON

Steinhauer, Ralph Garvin, farmer, Indian leader, lt-gov of Alberta (b at Morley, Alta 8 June 1905). The first native person to serve as lieutenant-governor, he was educated at Brandon Indian Residential School and farmed at Saddle Lk, Alta. He founded the Indian Assn of Alta and was president of the Alberta Indian Development Corp. In 1963 he ran as a Liberal candidate in the federal election. On 2 July 1974 he was sworn in as lt-gov of Alberta and served until 1979. He was made a companion of the Order of Canada.   ERIC J. HOLMGREN

Steinhouse, Tobie Thelma, née Davis, printmaker, painter (b at Montréal 1 Apr 1925). Her intricate abstractions gleam through effects of prism-coloured glass, fish nets or cobwebs, reflecting the soft haze of Paris, where she lived 1948-57, and revealing her continuing search for light. She was strongly influenced by Montréal painter and teacher Anne SAVAGE. Steinhouse studied graphics and painting at Montréal, New York and Paris, where she had a solo exhibition in 1957. Returning to Montréal she has worked at the Atelier libre de recherches graphiques since 1965. Frosted glass and snow storms are Canadian motifs now forming part of her muted, restrained style. ANNE McDOUGALL

Stelco Inc, with headquarters in Toronto, is Canada's largest steel producer. Incorporated in 1910 as The Steel Company of Canada, Limited, the company consolidated existing companies engaged in the production of iron, steel and related products: Montreal Rolling Mills Company, The Hamilton Steel and Iron Company, Canada Screw Company, Canada Bolt & Nut Company, and Dominion Wire Manufacturing

Company. The company grew steadily through acquisitions, and in 1969 amalgamated with Page-Hersey Tubes Ltd, Premier Steel Mills Ltd and The Canadian Drawn Steel Co Ltd. The present name was adopted in 1980.

Stelco produces a wide range of flat-rolled and coated steels, bars, rods, wire and wire products as well as pipe and tubing, fasteners and forgings. Its annual raw steel production capacity is over 7 million t and it operates 20 plants in Ont, Qué, Alta and Sask. It annually produces almost 35% of Canada's steel. Stelco also has interests in coal, iron-ore and limestone properties in Canada and the US, either directly or through its subsidiaries. Since 1971 it has been involved in a joint venture with THE T. EATON COMPANY LTD and TRW Inc of Cleveland, Ohio, in the Canada Systems Group (EST) Ltd, which applies computer technology, data processing and systems technology to environmental problems. In 1983 it had sales or operating revenue of $2 billion (ranking 42nd in Canada), assets of $2.8 billion (ranking 30th) and 19 519 employees. Its shares are widely held.   DEBORAH C. SAWYER

Stephansson, Stephán Gudmundsson, Stefán Gudmundur Gudmundsson, poet, pioneer farmer (b at Kirkjuhóll, Skagafjördur, Iceland 3 Oct 1853; d at Markerville, Alta 10 Aug 1927). Known as "the poet of the Rocky Mountains," Stephansson became the foremost west-Icelandic poet in Canada and one of Iceland's major poets. Although he wrote in Icelandic, his poetry reflects his love for Alberta, concern with contemporary political issues and awareness of 20th-century thought as well as his Icelandic heritage. He lived at Kirkjuhóll until 1862, at Vídimýrarsel until 1870 and at Mýri in Bárdardalur until he was 20. In 1873 he emigrated with his parents to Wisconsin and worked as a day labourer. Later he claimed land in Shawano County and worked as a farmer and logger. He moved to N Dakota in 1880 and to Canada in 1889, homesteading and farming near Markerville, Alta, until his death. Largely self-educated, Stephansson took an active part in the social and cultural life of Icelandic Canadians, as well as writing prolifically and carrying on a large correspondence. He was a romantic realist and satirist, known for his pacifism and interest in women's rights. His poems were published in west-Icelandic magazines continuously after 1890. His published books are *Úti a Vídavangi* (poems, 1894); *A Ferd og Flugi* (poems, 1900); his collected poems *Andvökur* I-VI (1909-38); *Kolbeinslag* (poetry, 1914); *Heimleidis* (poems from his 1917 visit to Iceland); *Vígslódi* (antiwar poem, 1920) and his collected letters and essays, *Bréf og Ritgerdir* I-IV (1938-48). His own essays are an excellent source of information on his life and writing.   KRISTJANA GUNNARS

Stephen, George, 1st Baron Mount Stephen, banker, railway president (b at Dufftown, Scot 5 June 1829; d at Hatfield, Eng 29 Nov 1921). Stephen has been described as the person most responsible for the success of the CANADIAN PACIFIC RY. He immigrated to Montréal at 21 to join a relative's draper establishment and by 1860 was the sole proprietor. His energy and capital, however, were increasingly directed to banking and railways. He became a director of the Bank of Montreal in 1873 and was president 1876-81. In 1873-74 he participated along with his cousin Donald SMITH and J.J. HILL in the syndicate which bought the ailing St Paul, Minneapolis and Manitoba Ry. It became a favoured route for settlers and made its owners wealthy. In a reorganization of the revived railway in 1879, Stephen was named president. A much larger project, the Pacific railway, engaged his attention after 1880. One of its original promoters, Stephen was the first president of the CPR, 1880-88. His wealth and standing in the Montréal business community were of inestimable

benefit in gaining the investors' confidence, but his personal contribution to the line was enormous. Resourceful and cool, he never lost faith in the project nor in the future of the West. Stephen moved to England in 1888. Created a baronet in 1886, he was raised to the peerage as Baron Mount Stephen in 1891. He was a generous philanthropist in Montréal and England and is said to have given away over $1 000 000 during his life. The Royal Victoria Hospital, Montréal, and hospitals in England benefited from his wealth.   D.M.L. FARR

Reading: Heather Gilbert, *Awakening Continent* (1965), and *The End of the Road* (1977).

Stephenson, Sir William Samuel, inventor, businessman, master spy (b at Winnipeg 11 Jan 1896). Stephenson flew as a fighter pilot in WWI, winning several medals for bravery. While a student at U Man he invented the wire-photo and then a radio facsimile method of transmitting pictures without need of telephone or telegraph wires. He moved to Britain in 1921 to develop and market this invention to newspapers and rapidly earned a fortune and an entrée to influential political circles in London. Thus, for example, he served on a royal commission in the 1930s to plan the development of India's natural resources.

At the beginning of WWII, Stephenson was placed in charge of British Security Co-ordination (counterespionage) in the Western Hemisphere, with headquarters in New York C (where the telegraphic address was INTREPID — later popularized as Stephenson's code name). His organization's activities ranged from censoring transatlantic mail, breaking letter codes (which exposed at least one German spy in the US) and forging diplomatic documents, to obtaining Vichy French and Italian military codes, protection against sabotage of American factories producing munitions for Britain, and training (at Camp X, near Oshawa, Ont) allied agents for surreptitious entry into Nazi-occupied Europe.

Although Stephenson was knighted by King George VI and awarded the US Medal for Merit, not much was known about his war services until the publication of H. Montgomery Hyde's *The Quiet Canadian* (1962). William Stevenson (no relative to Stephenson) later published 2 books about him, *A Man Called Intrepid* (1977) and *Intrepid's Last Case* (1983). The claims made regarding Stephenson's career have been treated with reserve by professional historians and experts on intelligence. Stephenson lived in the W Indies after WWII, becoming chairman of the Caribbean Development Corp, and eventually retired to Bermuda.   DONALD J.C. PHILLIPSON

Stephenville, Nfld, Town, pop 8876 (1981c), inc 1952, is located on the N shore of St George's Bay in southwestern Newfoundland. Named for Acadian pioneer Stephen Le Blanc, it was settled as a fishing/farming site around 1845. On the great circle air route between the US and Europe, it was chosen as the site for the American-built-and-maintained Ernest Harmon Air Force Base, which opened in 1941, causing the small town to grow rapidly. The base closed in 1966 with severe economic consequences for the region, but the Harmon Field airport was converted to a

commercial air facility run by the Canadian Dept of Transport; the base passed to the provincial government and was administered by the Crown's Harmon Corp, formed in 1967 to attract new industry. In 1972 a $140-million linerboard mill went into production, but closed 1977. In 1979 the world's largest producer of newsprint, Abitibi-Price, purchased the mill and converted it for newsprint. It opened 1981, providing significant employment for the town, now an established regional service centre with a unique annual "Festival of the Arts."
                    JANET E.M. PITT AND ROBERT D. PITT

Steppenwolf, Los Angeles-based blues-rock band (fl1967-72), had its genesis in the Toronto quintet Sparrow (fl1964-67). Popular for its blustery recordings "Born to be Wild" and "Magic Carpet Ride," the group initially included 3 musicians from Sparrow: singer John Kay, drummer Jerry Edmonton and organist Goldy McJohn. Kay's attempts to revive Steppenwolf after 1972 had mixed success.   MARK MILLER

Sternberg, Charles Mortram, paleontologist (b at Lawrence, Kansas 18 Sept 1885; d at Ottawa 8 Sept 1981). From a family of famous American fossil collectors, Sternberg worked for some years in the western US before the family came to Canada to exploit the rich fossil fields of the Red Deer R valley in Alberta for the GEOLOGICAL SURVEY OF CANADA. Charles stayed in Canada and after 1919 progressively took over the scientific description of fossil vertebrates for the Geological Survey. But his field collecting continued, mainly in Alberta, but also in Saskatchewan, northeastern BC and NS. He published 47 papers on fossil vertebrates, mostly dinosaurs, many based on his own remarkable discoveries. He retired as assistant biologist, National Museum of Canada, in 1950. Later he helped set up DINOSAUR PROVINCIAL PARK in Alberta. He was elected a fellow of the Royal Soc of Canada in 1949 and was granted honorary degrees by U of Calgary and Carleton.   L.S. RUSSELL

Reading: L.S Russell, *Dinosaur Hunting in Western Canada* (1966); C.H. Sternberg, *Hunting Dinosaurs in the Bad Lands of the Red Deer River, Alberta, Canada* (1917).

Stevens, Dorothy, portrait and figure painter (b at Toronto 2 Sept 1888; d there 5 June 1966). Entering the Slade School of Art, London, at age 15, she studied under Wilson Steer and Henry Tonks. She subsequently studied in Paris and travelled on the continent before returning to Canada. Her early etchings were highly regarded; she was elected a member of the Chicago Soc of Etchers 1912 and awarded the silver medal for etching at the 1915 Panama Pacific Exposition at San Francisco. In later years she was highly regarded as a painter of oil and pastel portraits of women and children in Toronto, Mexico and the West Indies. She taught children's art classes for 15 years at the Women's Art Assn in Toronto and later served as that organization's president. Described as "loud, raucous, profane [and] amusing," with a "voice like Tallulah Bankhead," she is reputed to have thrown the best parties in the city. Unfortunately, her sensitive etchings and figure paintings have not yet benefited from the revival of interest in women Canadian painters. CHRISTOPHER VARLEY

Stevens, Henry Herbert, politician, businessman (b at Bristol, Eng 8 Dec 1878; d at Vancouver 14 June 1973). An MP for nearly 30 years, he was one of the most controversial figures in Canadian politics in the 1930s. First elected to Parliament in 1911 as the Conservative member for Vancouver City, he was a minister in the MEIGHEN governments (1921, 1926) and minister of trade and commerce (1930-34) in R.B. BENNETT's government (as member for E Kootenay). In 1934 he was made chairman of a royal commission on price spreads after an inquiry he had headed exposed serious abuses by

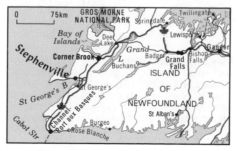

big business. Stevens embarrassed Bennett by attacking large-business interests and calling for drastic reform, and later resigned from Cabinet and the commission chairmanship. He formed the Reconstruction Party in 1935, hoping to protect the "little man" against economic abuse and the GREAT DEPRESSION. Though his party took nearly 10% of the popular vote in the 1935 election, Stevens was its only successful candidate. He returned to the Conservative caucus in 1939. After 3 election defeats and an unsuccessful bid to become the Tory leader in 1942, Stevens turned to full-time business interests in Vancouver. BILL CAMERON

Stevens, Sinclair McKnight, politician (b in Esquesing Twp, near Milton, Ont 11 Feb 1927). A graduate of Western and Osgoode Law School, Stevens was called to the Ontario Bar in 1955. He practised law and established his own business before being elected a Conservative MP in the 1972 election. He ran for the leadership of the PC Party in 1976, finishing 7th on the first ballot and throwing his support to the eventual winner, Joe CLARK. Stevens was a highly visible and somewhat controversial (in part because of his advocacy of big cuts in the public service) president of the Treasury Board in the Clark government 1979-80. A believer in free enterprise, a strong defence and closer ties with the US, he was a prominent supporter of Brian MULRONEY for the Conservative leadership in 1983. Stevens was appointed minister of regional industrial expansion and chairman of the committee on economic and regional development in the Mulroney government in 1984. NORMAN HILLMER

Stewart, Charles, farmer, politician, premier of Alberta 1917-21 (b at Strabane, Ont 26 Aug 1868; d at Ottawa 6 Dec 1946). Stewart brought his family to the Killam area of central Alberta in 1906. He represented Sedgewick in the Legislative Assembly 1909-21 and entered the Executive Council in 1912, holding first the municipal affairs and later the public works portfolios. On the resignation of Premier A.L. SIFTON, Stewart was sworn in as premier and minister of railways and telephones on 13 Oct 1917, but his effectiveness as government leader at the head of a party divided by railway scandals and the federal CONSCRIPTION crisis was constantly in question. The entry of the UNITED FARMERS OF ALBERTA into politics in the 1921 election ended the Liberal administration. Stewart accepted PM KING's invitation to enter the federal Cabinet and served as minister of the interior, minister of mines and superintendent general of Indian affairs 1921-30, except for a brief interlude in 1926. CARL BETKE

Stewart, Charles James, second Anglican bishop of Québec (b at London, Eng 13 Apr 1775; d there 13 July 1837). A man of independent means, a former fellow of All Souls, Oxford, closely related to men and women prominent in social and political life and in the British army and navy, Charles Stewart was an unusual recruit for pioneer missionary service in the diocese of Québec. But from 1807, when he came to Canada as a missionary under the Soc for the Propagation of the Gospel and began working in mission stations in the Eastern Townships, through his 7 years as travelling missionary in Lower and Upper Canada, and in his 11-year episcopate from 1826 to 1837, he created a record for unremitting toil and devotion to duty. He raised money for the building of 40 churches and was instrumental in the opening of 25 missions, in creating a body of lay catechists, in maintaining clergy stipends at a critical time, and in raising the level of education from Sunday school and elementary school to university. Though he was said to have been somewhat ungainly and at times lacking in political and

business sense, his deep religious faith, asceticism, generosity of spirit and purse, and his genuine care for the spiritual interests of pioneer immigrants and native Indians earned the bachelor bishop the affection of his clergy and people, and a secure place among the builders of the church in Canada. T.R. MILLMAN

Stewart, Frances, née Browne, diarist, letter writer (b at Dublin, Ire 24 May 1794; d near Peterborough, Ont 24 Feb 1872). One of the first white settlers in Douro Township, Upper Canada, Stewart's lively letters and journals describe pioneer life and nearby friends — the Stricklands, Traills and Langtons — providing the earliest account of settlement around Peterborough. Frances was raised and educated by her cousin, author Harriet Beaufort. Married to Thomas Alexander Stewart, 17 Dec 1816, she immigrated with him and 3 infant daughters to unsurveyed bush in 1822, overcoming isolation and initial privations to become an established settler. For 50 years Frances wrote regularly to Irish relatives describing her experiences. A proposal by Maria Edgeworth to publish some of these letters was withdrawn, but after Frances's death her daughter, E.S. Dunlop, published a heavily edited collection entitled *Our Forest Home* (1889). A second edition was published at Montréal in 1902. JOYCE C. LEWIS

Stewart, George Lawrence, business executive (b at Winnipeg 2 Dec 1890; d at Toronto 21 Mar 1985). Graduating in engineering from McGill in 1914, he served on McGill's engineering faculty for 2 years before joining Imperial Oil at its Sarnia, Ont, refinery as a draughtsman. Four months later he rejoined McGill for another year, then returned to Imperial. In 1918 he was in charge of constructing its refinery at Dartmouth, NS, and after working at Regina and Toronto, returned to Sarnia to become superintendent of the company's largest refinery in 1931. In 1934 he was appointed general manager of overall refining operations. Appointed a director of the company in 1944, he was chairman of the board 1947-49, president 1949-53 and again chairman 1953-55. EARLE GRAY

Stewart, Herbert Leslie, philosopher (b in County Antrim, Ire 31 Mar 1882; d at Halifax 19 Sept 1953). He arrived in Halifax to teach philosophy in 1913, having written his first book, *Questions of the Day in Philosophy and Psychology* (1912). In Canada his commitment shifted from realism to idealism. Realist causal explanations for WWI seemed insufficient, and Stewart looked to the history and continuity (or fragmentation) of ideas common to all people. In his later years he made national CBC broadcasts on public affairs, commenting on the evils of communism and supporting militarism and capital punishment in his campaign against the incursion of destructive ideas. His books on religion, *Modernism Past and Present* (1932) and *A Century of Anglo-Catholicism* (1929), rounded out his successful career. He founded the DALHOUSIE REVIEW in 1921 and served as editor for 26 years. ELIZABETH A. TROTT

Stewart, James David, lawyer, politician, premier of PEI (b at Lower Montague, PEI 15 Jan 1874; d at Charlottetown 10 Oct 1933). Stewart was premier of PEI 1923-27 and from 1931 until his death. The defeat of his Conservative government in 1927 resulted primarily from his promise to end total PROHIBITION in the province. H.T. HOLMAN

Stewart, Nelson Robert, Nels, "Old Poison," hockey player (b at Montréal 29 Dec 1902; d at Toronto 21 Aug 1957). He was the first player to score 300 goals and his record of 324 goals held until broken by Maurice RICHARD. A big, rugged player with a deadly shot, he performed many of his scoring feats on a line with Hooley Smith and Babe Siebert. He played for Montreal Ma-

roons (1925-32), Boston Bruins (1932-35), New York Americans (1935-36), the Bruins again in 1936-37, and New York again from 1937 to 1940. He won the HART TROPHY in 1926 and 1930 and still holds the record for the fastest 2 goals — 4 seconds. The story that he spat tobacco juice in the eyes of opposing goalies may be apocryphal but apparently is in keeping with his temperament on the ice. JAMES MARSH

Stewart, Robert Meldrum, astronomer (b at Gladstone, Man 15 Dec 1878; d at Ottawa 2 Sept 1954). Astronomer at the Dominion Observatory, Ottawa, 1902-24 and director 1924-46, Stewart supervised the scientifically complex installation of the Meridian Circle telescope at the observatory between 1907 and 1911, using it to improve the catalogue positions of stars used in the survey of western Canada. Subsequently, he added thousands of observations to improve the international star catalogue, established a time service within the government offices in Ottawa which ultimately became the source of correct time for Canada, used wireless time signals for longitude determination, approved Canada's participation in 2 world longitude campaigns (1926, 1933), using international wireless time signals, and devised an ingenious mechanical method for producing mean time from a sidereal primary standard.

MALCOLM THOMSON

Stewart, Robert William, scientist (b at Smoky Lk, Alta 21 Aug 1923). Stewart is known internationally for original work in turbulence, oceanography and meteorology and is a recognized authority on exchange processes between ocean and atmosphere. He has held visiting professorships at universities in N America, the UK and at the Institute of Atmospheric Physics, USSR. Stewart was one of the first to recognize the importance of studying the oceans and atmosphere as a combined system. During his career, he has been a scientist with the Defence Research Board 1950-61; professor of physics and oceanography at UBC 1960-70; director general, Institute of Ocean Sciences, Sidney, BC, 1970-79; and was appointed deputy minister of universities, science and communications in 1980. Stewart received the Patterson Medal of the Canadian Meteorological Soc and the Sverdrup Medal of the American Meteorological Soc.

C.R. MANN

Stewart, Wilson Nichols, paleobotanist, educator (b at Madison, Wis 7 Dec 1917). An imaginative and creative scientist, Stewart strongly influenced the field of BOTANY during his tenure at U of Alberta. Following completion of a PhD at U of Wisconsin (1947), Stewart established a sound reputation at U of Illinois, Urbana, for work with Isoetales and their fossil relatives and with pteridosperms. He became a professor at U of A in 1966 and was chairman of its botany department until 1971. Following retirement in 1978, Stewart undertook the writing of a comprehensive and finely illustrated textbook, *Paleobotany and the Evolution of Plants* (1983), a lasting contribution. JAMES F. BASINGER

Stickleback (Gasterosteidae), family of FISHES found in freshwater lakes, streams and along northern coastlines of the Northern Hemisphere. There are 5 genera and about 8 species worldwide; 4 genera and 5 species in Canada. Canadian sticklebacks are most common in the Maritimes but occur in all provinces and much of the NWT. Brook and ninespine sticklebacks are common from the prairies to Québec. Threespine sticklebacks, well known in Europe, occur along the Pacific and Atlantic coasts; some populations enter the ocean, while others live only in fresh water a short distance inland. The other 2 species are confined to the East Coast. Sticklebacks derive their common name from a row of spines along the back and their scientific

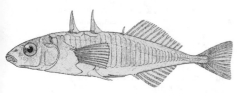

Three-spine sticklebacks show a wide diversity of forms and range in colour from green to black, with silver underbelly (*courtesy National Museums of Canada/ National Museum of Natural Sciences*).

name from a bony plate beneath the stomach area which supports 2 pelvic spines. In a few areas of their range (particularly in western Canada), some sticklebacks fail to develop pelvic spines. Three-spine sticklebacks show a wide diversity of forms. In some lakes and streams of BC different forms occur in the same or adjacent areas, which suggests that there is actually more than one species. Sticklebacks rarely exceed 8 cm in length and range in colour from green to black, with a silver underbelly. Most males of three-spine sticklebacks at mating time are distinguished by bright red underparts. Stickleback males are territorial when mating. They build nests of aquatic material in which females lay eggs. Males fertilize eggs, fan them and guard the nest. Despite their spines, which in some situations function to deter predators, sticklebacks can be important in the diet of other fish and birds. They feed on small crustaceans and insects. Well known as subjects of studies on behaviour, physiology and EVOLUTION, they can be used to test for WATER POLLUTION. JOSEPH S. NELSON

Stikine River, 539 km long, rises in Spatsizi Wilderness Park in northwest BC, and flows in a wide arc N and W out of the Stikine Plateau uplands, then S through the spectacular COAST MTS Range to meet the Pacific Ocean near Wrangell, Alaska. It drains about 50 000 km², its largest tributary being the Iskut R. Separating the upper and lower sections of the river is the 90 km unnavigable Grand Canyon, where a precipitous narrow gorge has been cut through volcanic rock to a depth of 450 m. Stikine, meaning "the (great) river," is the name given by the powerful TLINGIT, who came upriver regularly to collect berries and catch and dry salmon in the arid climate E of the Coast Mts, and also to trade with the Tahltan of the upper Stikine watershed.

In 1824 Samuel Black of the HBC crossed the headwater drainage of the Stikine. In 1838 Robert Campbell was sent by the HBC to open communication with its posts and shipping on the coast from the Mackenzie R, and was led by Indian guides to their great trading rendezvous at the Stikine-Tahltan confluence. Shortly afterwards the HBC acquired the Russian Fort Dionysius (now Wrangell) near the mouth of the Stikine. The discovery of gold near present-day Telegraph Creek in 1861 led to a minor gold rush and the establishment of a river steamer service. For the next 100 years the Stikine was an important transportation route for penetration of the interior by non-Indians. Traffic reached its peak in 1898, when thousands used the Stikine to reach the Klondike goldfields.

Since the advent of airplane and highway access to the North, the Stikine is no longer a major route. The people of Telegraph Creek, the only town on the river, who are mostly Tahltans, and the people of Wrangell rely heavily on the salmon that ascend as far as the Grand Canyon. Although development of minerals and timber resources around the river and a potential massive hydroelectric scheme in the canyon could at any time change the river drastically, it remains essentially a scenic wilderness waterway increasingly used for recreation. ROSEMARY J. FOX

Reading: R.M. Patterson, *Trail to the Interior* (1966).

Stikine Territory Between 1839 and the 1867 American purchase of Alaska, the HUDSON'S BAY COMPANY leased the continental portion of the Alaska Panhandle from the Russian American Fur Co. In 1861 gold was found on the Stikine R in British territory contiguous to the leased area; the region was removed from HBC authority and organized as Stikine (or Stickeen) Territory on 19 July 1862. The boundaries were, on the west, Alaska; on the south, the colony of BRITISH COLUMBIA; on the east, 125° W long; and on the north, 62° N lat. BC's governor was territorial administrator, with the power to appoint officials; the BC Supreme Court was responsible for civil and criminal matters, and English law was in force. Thus, Britain ensured British authority in a region with a potential GOLD RUSH. Stikine Territory had a short existence: in July 1863 most of it was absorbed into an enlarged BC. *See also* TERRITORIAL EVOLUTION. J.W. SHELEST

Reading: M.A. Ormsby, *British Columbia* (1958).

Stirling, David, architect (b at Galashiels, Scot 6 Dec 1822; d at Charlottetown 13 Apr 1887). Stirling immigrated to St John's in 1847 and worked on the rebuilding of the town after the great fire of 1846. He established practices in Charlottetown and Halifax, designing and supervising the construction of all kinds of buildings in a career spanning 35 years. In 1872 Stirling was appointed Dominion architect for federal works in NS and in 1880 was made an associate architect of the Royal Canadian Academy of Arts. His buildings include the Pictou County Court House (1855), the Halifax Club, and, with W.C. HARRIS in 1877, Hensley Chapel, King's College, Windsor, NS, and the Kirk of St James, Charlottetown.

GRANT WANZEL AND KAREN KALLWEIT

Stock and Bond Markets are created by associations of brokers and dealers to trade company shares. Shares represent ownership of companies and their prices depend largely on the companies' expected profits. They represent only the right, under certain conditions, to receive payments in the future. Ultimately, no security is worth more than it will fetch in the marketplace. Companies can issue new shares to raise funds. Firms of investment dealers underwrite these new issues, buying them from the companies directly and reselling them to the public through sales offices across the country and abroad. Although issues are usually marketed through groups of dealers, occasionally a single dealer may place an entire issue. After shares are issued they may be listed on various stock exchanges and bought or sold through brokerage firms. Shares may be listed on a stock exchange if the companies have the size, stability and financial strength and are willing to report publicly on their operations. Not all shares are listed on stock exchanges; some are traded in the over-the-counter (OTC) market which is a securities market made up of dealers who may or may not be members of a stock exchange, and the types of securities traded are ones not listed on any recognized stock exchange, as well as bonds and debentures. The OTC market is also called the "unlisted market," the "street market" or the "between-dealer market."

While shares represent ownership, bonds represent only a borrower's promise to make certain payments of interest and repayment of principal. Companies and governments are major issuers of bonds. Probably the best-known bonds in Canada are CANADA SAVINGS BONDS, issued by the federal government; they can be redeemed for their face value at any time. Most other bonds fluctuate daily in price because each one entitles its owner to receive a specific series of interest payments — rise in interest rates is equivalent to a fall in bond prices, as the given series of payments will only represent a higher rate of interest if the cost of purchasing the bonds falls. Bonds may be protected if the issuing company mortgages specific assets against bankruptcy or other default. Shares and bonds are underwritten by investment dealers and can be bought and sold through brokerage firms. Government of Canada bonds can be purchased through banks or other financial institutions and, in the case of savings bonds, through popular employer payroll-deduction plans.

Shares are either "preferred" or "common." When a company cannot pay regular dividends on all its shares, holders of preferred shares are ranked ahead of those holding common shares in receiving whatever dividends are available (these provisions may be overridden in the case of bankruptcy). Shares may or may not carry the right to vote at shareholders' meetings and to elect the company's board of directors. An investor wanting to buy or sell bonds or shares contacts a brokerage firm and opens an account. The sales representative ("broker") of a firm advises on the relative merits of available investments and might permit an investor (with sufficient collateral) to buy or sell "on margin" — eg, the firm would lend the investor a considerable percentage of the funds required (against the investor's collateral security in case the price went to his disadvantage), charging interest on the borrowed funds. If they expect the price to drop quickly, investors can even "sell short" bonds or shares they do not own, so that they can buy them back cheaply and make a speculative profit. In such cases the firm would borrow the shares and sell them for the investor's account.

Brokers can provide a wide range of specialized services, such as the "stop order," an order to buy or sell shares only if the price touches a certain level. Investors can place a "stop sell" order at a price slightly below the current price so that if prices decline the shares would automatically be sold out at a small loss. Brokers can also sell "options," which give the right to buy or sell certain shares at preset prices at any time up to a prespecified future date, but the value of these options can fluctuate dramatically, creating a risk for the investor.

The Board of Stock and Produce Brokers was set up in Montréal in 1842 and the Montreal Stock Exchange (MSE) in 1874. The MSE listed 63 securities, including stock in banks, gas utilities, railroads and mining companies and government debentures. The Toronto Stock Exchange (TSE) was established in 1852 by a group of Toronto businessmen who formed an association of brokers to create a market in industrial securities. At first they met informally in each other's offices but by 1871 they had a common meeting place and formal rules and regulations.

Expansive mining activity led to the establishment of the Standard Stock and Mining Exchange (SSME) in 1899. After the discovery of important silver and gold deposits in northern Ontario in the first decade of the 20th century, transactions on the SSME expanded dramatically and in 1934 the TSE merged with the SSME, keeping the name Toronto Stock Exchange. The Montreal Curb Market, which started on the curb outside the MSE as a place to trade shares in ventures too small or risky to meet listing requirements of the latter exchange, became the Canadian Stock Exchange but then joined the MSE in a merger in 1974. Canada's 3 western stock exchanges are in Vancouver, Winnipeg and Calgary. They have provided local trading facilities primarily for shares in small, new ventures. By 1984 the dollar value of shares traded on the Toronto, Montréal, Vancouver, Alberta and Winnipeg stock exchanges was $36.1 billion, of which 73.8% was transacted on the TSE. The quoted market value of all Canadian-based firms' shares listed on the TSE at the end of 1984 was $177.8 billion.

Although the exchanges are regulated by provincial securities commissions, they are essentially self-regulating. The public's risk is minimized because brokers and dealers must be adequately capitalized against default. Public issues of new corporate bonds or shares must be cleared for distribution by the securities commissions of the provinces in which they are offered, and printed prospectuses outlining and updating important facts on the new securities must be provided to potential buyers. Because public information about the economy or companies' prospects is quickly reflected in the prices of the securities, it is difficult even for professional investors (such as managers of pension funds) to earn consistently higher rates of return than those provided by the market as a whole. However, because "insiders" with privileged information about company affairs have been able to trade profitably on such information, the law requires public disclosure of, or may even outlaw, their trading. There have been many instances of promotional fraud and manipulation of the prices of shares, but such abuses are now illegal and severely penalized. No security is worth more than it will fetch in the marketplace. Security prices are ultimately dependent on expectations, since they represent only the right, under certain conditions, to receive payments in the future. Securities markets uniquely blend risk, uncertainty, potential profit and potential loss; by doing so, they provide a cornerstone of the modern capitalist economy. JOHN GRANT

Stoicheff, Boris Peter, physics professor (b at Bitola, Yugoslavia 1 June 1924). A specialist in SPECTROSCOPY, LASER physics and nonlinear optics, he is known for his innovative use of lasers. After receiving a PhD from U of T in 1950 he joined the National Research Council of Canada in 1951. In 1960 he joined the physics department at U of T and was chairman of engineering science 1972-77. He was president of the Optical Society of America in 1976, a member of the council of the NRC 1977-80 and 1981-83, and president of the Canadian Association of Physicists 1983-84. Fellow of the Royal Society of Canada, honorary fellow of the Indian Academy of Sciences and fellow of the Royal Society, London, he has received the Ives Medal of the Optical Society of America and the Gold Medal of the Canadian Association of Physicists. His 130 articles in scientific journals discuss light, spectroscopy, molecular structures and lasers in relation to physics. J. KNELMAN

Stone Angel, The, by Margaret LAURENCE (Toronto, London and New York, 1964), is the first of Laurence's "Manawaka" novels. Hagar Shipley relives her life by narrating memories as she battles to come to terms with herself before she dies. Hagar at 90 is a proud, powerful, tyrannical woman suffering the indignities of old age. *The Stone Angel* is shaped by the alternating rhythms of Hagar's voice, searching through her past and returning to her present condition; her widely ranging tones reveal the labyrinths of her pride. Hagar's character and voice are justly praised as Laurence's most inspired creations. As she tells her story, Hagar also looks back to Manawaka (a fictionalized small town that Laurence has placed in Manitoba), recalling and recreating the effects of the town's constricting mores and her own family's position in the rigid hierarchy of Manawaka's deeply puritan society. Many readers find Hagar to be a rich fictional composite of actual women's lives in small towns on the Prairies. *The Stone Angel* has been translated into French, as *L'Ange de pierre* (Montréal, 1976), and German. NEIL BESNER

Stonefly, common name for small to medium-sized, usually brown, aquatic INSECTS of order Plecoptera [Gk, "folded wings"]. About 2000 species are known worldwide, almost 300 in Canada. Because the aquatic larvae normally cannot live in warm or polluted water, stoneflies are more common in mountainous areas of Canada. Eggs are deposited in cool, clean, running water. The larval stage lasts 1-3 years, depending on species. Larvae are generally elongate, with a pair of long antennae at the front of the body, and a pair of thin appendages (cerci) at the rear. Most feed on plant material; others are predators, feeding on MAYFLY or midge larvae. Larvae crawl out of the water before transformation to the adult stage. Although most adults have wings, they tend to walk rather than fly. Some do not feed as adults; others feed on algae and lichens and may live 3-4 weeks. Before mating, adults often communicate by drumming with the end of their abdomen. G. PRITCHARD

Stoney (Stone) or *îyârhe Nakodabi,* "Rocky Mountain Sioux," are culturally and linguistically allied to the Plains ASSINIBOINE, but in Saskatchewan and Montana are characterized by differences in language and culture. They speak the N dialect of the Dakota language. Stoney oral tradition asserts that their forefathers resided along the Rocky Mt foothills from time immemorial. The first recorded story (cited in the JESUIT RELATIONS) was that the Stoney-Assiniboine separated from the Sioux nation sometime before 1640 and then migrated westward with the CREE as the FUR TRADE moved W along the Saskatchewan R trade routes. HUDSON'S BAY COMPANY trader Anthony HENDAY met Stoney-Assiniboine camps on his journey to Alberta in 1754; Father de Smet reported in 1840 that the Rocky Mt Stoney separated from the Plains Assiniboine about 1790, though he might have been referring to groups such as the Bearspaw band who have by oral accounts had a tradition of fleeing westward to escape devastating smallpox epidemics.

The Stoney bands, commonly composed of extended families, lived along Alberta's Rocky Mt foothills from the headwaters of the Athabasca R south to Chief Mt in Montana. These forest and foothill people hunted bison and other big game animals. With the establishment of Edmonton House (1795) and ROCKY MOUNTAIN HOUSE (1799), they traded furs, hides and fresh meat, and were invaluable guides to traders, explorers (Lord Southesk, John PALLISER, James HECTOR), surveyors (CANADIAN PACIFIC RAILWAY; GEOLOGICAL SURVEY OF CANADA) and missionaries. They were introduced to Christianity by Methodist missionaries after 1840.

The Stoney, led by Chiefs Jacob Bearspaw, John Chiniki (also Chiniquay) and Jacob Goodstoney, signed Treaty No 7 at Blackfoot Crossing in Sept 1877. The original reserve of 109 square miles was surveyed at Morleyville mission in 1879. The Bearspaw and Wesley bands later claimed additional reserve land to the south and north. After years of petitions and negotiations, both the Bighorn reserve (west of Nordegg) and the Eden Valley reserve (west of Longview) were established in 1948. Stoney people also live on the Alexis and Paul reserves west of Edmonton, which were set aside under the provisions of Treaty No 6 (1876).

The economic base of the Stoney includes trapping, big-game hunting, guiding, ranching, lumbering, handicrafts, labouring, and various professions. The bands at Morley enjoy a high standard of living based on natural gas royalties and operate several commercial enterprises (such as stores, restaurants, service stations and tourist facilities). Their social life centres on family and cultural activities — the POWWOWS, TREATY DAYS, RODEO, stampede, and camp meeting. Band membership at Morley, Bighorn and Eden Valley numbers over 2400 (1984); at Alexis reserve, over 600; and at Paul band, over 700 (1980). *See also* NATIVE PEOPLE, PLAINS and general articles under NATIVE PEOPLE. IAN A.L. GETTY

Reading: H.A. Dempsey, *Indian Tribes of Alberta* (1978); J.G. MacEwan, *Tatanga Mani-Walking Buffalo of the Stonies* (1969); Chief John Snow, *These Mountains are our Sacred Places* (1977).

Storey, Frederick Lewis, curler (b at Empress, Alta 3 Mar 1932). He won Canadian and world curling championships in 1966, 1968 and 1969, playing lead for Ron NORTHCOTT, and was selected all-star lead at several briers. He participated in 10 Alberta provincial curling championships and 7 Canadian curling championships (briers). He has won numerous provincial and national titles, including the Canadian curling championship Edmonton Carspiel in 1965, Evergreen Tournament of Champions (Vancouver) in 1971 and 1973, Edmonton Tournament of Champions in 1961, CBC Cross Canada in 1964 and Ontario Invitational in 1968. PAULINE McGREGOR

Storm-petrel (order Procellariiformes, family Hydrobatidae), small SEABIRD (14-25 cm long) related to albatrosses and like them having nostrils encased in a tube. Storm-petrels are usually blackish with a white rump. The name petrel derives from the habit of fluttering low over the waves and seeming to "walk on water," like St Peter. Superstitious seamen, believing they warned of coming storms, called them Mother Carey's chickens, the birds which Mater Cara (Virgin Mary) sent to protect them. Petrels nest in burrows on offshore islands, visiting these only at night. Introduced cats and rats have caused havoc in many colonies. The fork-tailed storm-petrel (*Oceanodroma furcata*) and Leach's storm-petrel (*O. leucorhoa*) breed in BC. Leach's also breeds in Atlantic Canada; its enormous colonies in SE Newfoundland contain most of the N Atlantic population. Large numbers of Wilson's storm-petrel (*Oceanites oceanicus*) from Antarctica and Tierra del Fuego occur off NS in summer. R.G.B. BROWN

Stowe, Emily Howard, née Jennings, physician (b at Norwich, UC 1 May 1831; d at Toronto 30 Apr 1903). A lifelong champion of women's rights, Emily Stowe taught school in Brantford and Mount Pleasant, Canada W, and in 1856 married John Stowe, whose illness from tuberculosis inspired her to seek a career in medicine. No Canadian college would accept a woman student, so she enrolled at the New York Medical College for Women and on her graduation in 1867 set up a practice in Toronto. She was the first Canadian woman to practise medicine in Canada, although she was not licensed until 1880. Emily Stowe's struggle to enter the medical profession caused her to organize the Woman's Medical College, Toronto, in 1883. In 1876 she had founded the Toronto Women's Literary Club, Canada's first suffrage group, and she was principal founder and first president of the Dominion Women's Enfranchisement Assn (1889). CARLOTTA HACKER

Emily Stowe was the first Canadian woman to practise medicine in Canada (*courtesy Public Archives of Canada/C-9480*).

Stowe-Gullen, Ann Augusta, née Stowe, physician (b at Mount Pleasant, Canada W 27 July 1857; d at Toronto 25 Sept 1943), daughter of Emily STOWE. She was the first woman to gain a medical degree in Canada, graduating from Victoria Coll, Cobourg, Ont, in 1883, having studied at Toronto School of Medicine. On graduation she married Dr John B. Gullen, who was a founder in 1896 of Toronto Western Hospital, with which she was associated for many years. Meanwhile, she taught at the Ontario Medical Coll for Women (known 1883-94 as the Woman's Medical Coll, Toronto) and was on U of T Senate 1910-22. A leading figure in the suffrage movement, she succeeded her mother as president of the Dominion Women's Enfranchisement Assn in 1903.   CARLOTTA HACKER

Strachan, John, Anglican bishop, educator (b at Aberdeen, Scot 12 Apr 1778; d at Toronto 1 Nov 1867). One of 6 children of a quarryman, Strachan was sent to grammar school to fulfil his mother's hope that one son would become a minister, but his father's early accidental death forced him into teaching. He studied divinity part-time at St Andrews U and in 1799 came to Kingston, UC, to tutor the children of Loyalist Richard Cartwright. Strachan was ordained by Bishop Jacob MOUNTAIN in 1803 and became a government-paid missionary in Cornwall, UC. There he opened an excellent school and in 1807 married Ann Wood, widow of fur trader Andrew McGill. In 1812 Strachan accepted the rectorship of York (Toronto) after Sir Isaac BROCK added to it the garrison and legislative council chaplaincies.

For Strachan the WAR OF 1812 proved another turning point. When the Americans occupied York in Apr 1813, he assumed leadership of the town to protect lives and property. Convinced that his destiny was to keep Upper Canada British, he tried after the war to exclude democratic and American influences. Many former pupils now had senior posts in government, and Strachan himself was made executive councillor in 1817 and legislative councillor in 1820. To promote loyalty he began a school system, capped with the charter of King's College (U of T) in 1827. He sought special status for the Church of England and became the centre of politico-religious controversy as he defended Anglican monopoly of the CLERGY RESERVES and Anglican dominance in politics and education. Strachan was removed from the Executive Council in 1835 by Lt-Gov Sir John COLBORNE, and his political decline was completed when the 1841 union of Upper Canada and Lower Canada destroyed the conservative FAMILY COM-

PACT that had dominated Upper Canada for a quarter century.

Strachan's religious influence, however, was rising. In 1839 he became bishop of Toronto, ruling the Anglican Church in Upper Canada. The Reformers secularized King's College in 1849 and the Clergy Reserves in 1854, but Strachan responded by opening Trinity College (Anglican) in 1852 and by including laymen in church government as early as 1851. In 1857 he formed a self-governing synod of clergy and laity and began dividing his large diocese by holding synodic elections for new bishops. Strachan proposed a convention of all Anglican bishops, which took shape as the Lambeth Conference in 1867, but was too frail to attend.   JOHN S. MOIR

Strait of Anian, part of the legendary NORTHWEST PASSAGE linking the Atlantic and Pacific oceans, likely Bering Strait The name probably originated with Ania, a Chinese province mentioned in a 1559 edition of Marco Polo's book; it first appears on a map issued by Italian cartographer Giacomo Gastaldi about 1562. Five years later Bolognini Zaltieri issued a map showing a narrow and crooked Strait of Anian separating Asia from America. The strait grew in European imagination as an easy sea-lane linking Europe with the residence of the Great Khan in Cathay (northern China). Voyages by John CABOT, CORTE-REAL, Jacques CARTIER and Sir Humphrey GILBERT were motivated by its supposed existence, and cartographers and seamen tried to demonstrate its reality. Sir Francis DRAKE sought the western entrance in 1579. The Greek pilot Juan de FUCA claimed he had sailed the strait from the Pacific to the North Sea and back in 1592. The Spaniard Bartholomew de Fonte (who, some scholars have stated, was fictitious) claimed to have sailed from Hudson Bay to the Pacific via the strait in 1640. James COOK dispelled rumours of its existence in 1778 during his third Pacific voyage. The myth was finally destroyed by George VANCOUVER 1792-94, and by Alexander MACKENZIE in his voyages to the Arctic and Pacific oceans in 1789 and 1793, respectively.   BARRY M. GOUGH

Strange, Thomas Bland, army officer (b at Meerut, India 15 Sept 1831; d at Camberley, Eng 9 July 1925). After active service with the artillery in India, including service during the Indian Mutiny (1857), Strange became inspector of artillery and warlike stores in the Canadian Militia, where he laid the essential groundwork for the development of the Canadian artillery and commanded one of its founding permanent units, 1871-82. Too eccentric and controversial for more senior command, he retired to ranch in Alberta, but on the outbreak of the NORTH-WEST REBELLION, he commanded the improvised Alberta Field Force and led it in action at Frenchman's Butte. He published his lively memoirs, *Gunner Jingo's Jubilee,* in 1894.   ROGER SARTY

Stratas, Teresa, née Anastasia Stratakis, soprano (b at Toronto 26 May 1938). Daughter of Greek immigrant restaurateurs, Stratas began as a singer of Greek pop songs and had ambitions of becoming a nightclub singer. She made her operatic debut as Mimi in *La Bohème* at the Toronto Opera Festival (1958) and was co-winner of the Metropolitan Opera auditions in Mar 1959. Since her debut at the Met in 1959 Stratas has sung more than 25 roles there. She appeared at Vancouver's International Festival in 1960 and sang Desdemona in *Otello* at EXPO 67. She has sung at La Scala, the Bolshoi Opera, Vienna State Opera, Covent Garden, the Deutsche Oper Berlin, Bavarian State Opera, San Francisco Opera and the Salzburg Festival. At the Paris Opera, May 1979, she sang the title role in the first performance of the complete version of Alban Berg's *Lulu.* Stratas has appeared in Norman CAMPBELL's CBC television production of *La Rondine* (1972)

and in numerous opera films, including Franco Zeffirelli's *La Traviata* (1983). Her recordings include Berg's *Lulu,* Mozart's *Cosi fan tutte,* Verdi's *Otello* and the widely acclaimed *The Unknown Kurt Weill.* Her performances combine a strong stage personality with an instinctive sense of drama, and, despite an earthy sense of comedy, her interpretations are profoundly emotional and rich in subtlety and intelligence. She was named artist of the year by the Canadian Music Council in 1980.   MABEL H. LAINE

Strate, Grant, dancer, choreographer, educator (b at Cardston, Alta 7 Dec 1927). A graduate of U of A, Strate was a charter member of the NATIONAL BALLET OF CANADA as dancer in 1951 and was resident choreographer 1964-70. Among his more than 50 ballets for many companies are *Ballad* and *The House of Atreus* (music by Harry SOMERS), *Bird Life* and *Cyclus.* Strate has continued to foster artistic experimentation and the development of DANCE EDUCATION as founder of York's dance dept (1970) and of Dance in Canada Assn (1974), organizer of National Choreographic Seminars (1978, 1980), and director, Centre for the Arts, Simon Fraser (1980).

PENELOPE DOOB

Stratford, Ont, City, pop 26 262 (1981c), inc 1886, the highest city in Ontario (elev 364 m), is located 143 km W of Toronto and 52 km NE of London. Settlement began in the 1830s after the townsite, beside the Avon R, had been selected and named by the CANADA CO as a focal point for peopling the million-acre Huron Tract. The ethnic mix of immigrants to the Stratford area was about 40% Irish, 30% German, 20% Scottish and 10% English. The blend has changed little, except for Dutch and German immigration since 1945. Urban growth was slow until the railway-building boom of the 1850s. Stratford businessmen lobbied for the forming in 1853 of the County of Perth, with Stratford as the county seat, and the county at once voted bonuses to railway companies. Stratford became the intersection point of 3 railways, which successively became bankrupt and were merged with the CNR. For 80 years railways were the principal employer in divisional offices and motive-power shops for repair of steam engines. When diesels replaced steam and Stratford ceased to be a divisional point in the 1950s, the city lost 2000 jobs, which have since been replaced by diversified industry. Thirty-two manufacturing firms employ 25 or more people each; 11 employ 100 or more. Civic policy has kept industry on the perimeter and prevented encroachment on the 70 ha park in the city's middle, adjacent to the commercial core. World-class theatre is provided by the STRATFORD FESTIVAL, founded in 1953, which has a 27-week season in the 2262-seat Festival Theatre and 410-seat Third Stage, both on parkland, and the 1102-seat Avon Theatre downtown. The Festival has 130 employees year-round and 900 in season. Yearly paid attendance is about 500 000, with 30% of box-office revenue coming from US visitors.

STAFFORD JOHNSTON

Stratford Festival In 1951 Stratford businessman Tom Patterson formed a local committee to explore the prospects for an annual drama festival. The following year Tyrone GUTHRIE, a leading British director, agreed to be artistic director and to present a Shakespeare festival in a tent theatre. The festival opened in July 1953 for a 6-week season, and presented *Richard III,* with Alec Guinness playing the lead, and *All's Well That Ends Well.* The 1954 season ran for 9 weeks and contained a non-Shakespearean play, *Oedipus Rex.* Musical programs, including jazz and pop concerts, symphony concerts, opera, comic opera and solo performances, were introduced in 1955, and in 1957 the tent theatre was replaced by the Festival Theatre, designed by Canadian architect Robert Fairfield, at a cost of

The patriarchal Bishop John Strachan, who was convinced that it was his destiny to keep Upper Canada British and free of American 'democratic' influences (*courtesy Public Archives of Canada/C-7432*).

Stratford Festival Theatre (*courtesy Stratford Festival*).

over $2 million. Guthrie was succeeded by Michael Langham (1956-67), followed by Jean GASCON (1968-74), Robin Phillips (1975-80) and John HIRSCH (1981-85). John Neville is scheduled to become artistic director in late 1985. In 30 years, the Stratford Festival has developed such actors as William HUTT, Tony Van Bridge, Douglas CAMPBELL, Richard Monette, Martha Henry, Frances Hyland, Douglas Raine, Kate REID, John Colicos and Christopher PLUMMER, and has made a great contribution to the training of Canadian actors, designers, technicians and directors (*see* STAGE AND COSTUME DESIGN).

The stage of the main theatre, designed by Tanya Moiseiwitsch with Guthrie, was revolutionary for its time. Guthrie wanted a return to the open stage of the Elizabethans, but not an antiquarian copy. The amphitheatre is steeply sloped, with a 220-degree sweep around the stage. Although the auditorium seats 2262, on 3 sides of the stage, no spectator is more than 19.8 m from the stage. The festival later acquired 2 more stages. The Avon Theatre (seating 1102) in downtown Stratford was purchased in 1963 and redesigned by Moiseiwitsch. It has a conventional proscenium stage. Since 1971 the festival has also presented drama and music at the Third Stage, a small, modestly equipped theatre suited for workshops, experimental work and the training of young actors.

The Stratford Festival is an internationally acclaimed drama festival. It offers a program of classical and modern plays, and musical productions. Including school previews, the season ran for 27 weeks in 1984. The festival has a permanent administration and requires an acting corps of around 100. Though the festival is supported by the CANADA COUNCIL and the Ontario provincial government, most income is generated from box-office receipts and private contributions. The theatre possesses a major archive, which maintains records of all productions. Foreign tours to the US, Australia and Europe have consolidated its reputation as the leading classical theatre in N America. *See also* THEATRE, ENGLISH-LANGUAGE.   RALPH BERRY

Reading: R. Davies et al, *Renown at Stratford* (1953), *Twice Have the Trumpets Sounded* (1954) and *Thrice the Brinded Cat Hath Mew'd* (1955); P. Raby, *The Stratford Scene* (1968) and *Stratford Festival Story 1953-1982* (1982); G. Shaw, *Stratford under Cover* (1977); R. Stuart, "The Stratford Festival and Canadian Theatre," in L.W. Conolly, ed, *Theatrical Touring and Founding in North America* (1982).

Strathcona Provincial Park includes some 2310 km² of mountain wilderness in central VANCOUVER ISLAND, 9 km E of Gold R and 26 km W of CAMPBELL RIVER. The park includes numerous peaks, valleys and lakes; elevations range from sea level at Herbert Inlet to 2200 m at GOLDEN HINDE, the island's highest peak. Small GLACIERS, remnants of an ice sheet that sculp-

tured the area thousands of years ago, cling to a few peaks in the S. Small, swift streams and waterfalls in the centre of the park drain into Buttle Lk. Vegetation and wildlife distribution reflect the marked variations in altitude, aspect and climate. Vegetation at lower elevations is dominated by western red cedar, various firs and western hemlock; subalpine fir, mountain hemlock and creeping juniper are found higher up. Between the TREELINE and the glaciers are extensive alpine meadows offering spectacular displays of WILDFLOWERS (eg, paintbrush) in the short summer. The island's isolation has limited the area's fauna but wildlife includes deer (common), Roosevelt elk, wolves and cougars. Birdlife includes kinglets, gray jays, grouse and white-tailed ptarmigan. Trout are common in such areas as Buttle Lk. The area was explored in the mid-1800s. When designated BC's first provincial park in 1911, it was named after Donald SMITH, 1st Baron Strathcona and Mount Royal. Logging, mining and reservoir development have influenced the park and aroused debate and opposition by CONSERVATION groups. The Forbidden Plateau, on the park's E side, was added to the park later. Recently, 3 roadless tracts, comprising 122 500 ha, have been designated Nature Conservancy Areas to protect the environment. Facilities include campgrounds, backpacking and cross-country skiing trails, and downhill ski resorts. Strathcona Park Lodge, on Campbell Lk, is a popular centre for wilderness courses and outdoor education.
                    JOHN S. MARSH

Strawberry, *see* BERRIES, CULTIVATED; BERRIES, WILD.

Street Railways (also known as streetcars or trams) began operation in Canada during the era of horse-powered local TRANSPORTATION, expanded rapidly with electrification, shrank with a public policy switch in favour of rubber-tired vehicles, and recently re-emerged as light rail transit. With a simple, robust technology, street railways have had a profound impact on our society, not only as a transportation mode but also in the development of the electric-power industry and on the shaping of our cities.

Technology The low rolling resistance of steel wheels on steel rails, plus the simple guidance mechanism offered by flanges, has made railbound transport attractive for a variety of applications. Montréal and Toronto were the first cities with horse-drawn tramcars in Canada, using systems incorporated in 1861 by Alexander Easton of Philadelphia. In spite of the need to substitute sleighs for the cars in winter, both operations did well. Toronto had 109 km of track, 361 trams and 100 sleighs at its peak. The Montréal network extended over 40 km, using 150 trams, 104 sleighs and 49 horse omnibuses. Other cities to establish such services included Hamilton, Winnipeg, Halifax and Saint John.

Railway lines between cities developed rapidly, moving to steam power and long trains. As cities grew, so did urban railways, which were characterized by smaller vehicles more appropriate for mingling with pedestrians and other street traffic. Steam and later cable traction systems were applied in some US cities but never caught on in Canada. The major breakthrough came with electric power in the 1880s, and here Canada was a leader. In 1884 the Toronto Agricultural Fair (now CANADIAN NATIONAL EXHIBITION) offered electric-car rides, devised by American engineer J. Gaboury and Belgian inventor Charles J. Van Depoele. As the technology matured, the typical system had tracks mounted flush with the pavement, current collection by trolley, and overhead wire supported by poles, often also used for lighting. Costs for both installation and operation were low, and streetcar services spread rapidly. St Catharines, Ont, installed the first electric tram system in 1887. Vancouver followed in 1890, Winnipeg in 1891,

Montréal, Hamilton and Toronto in 1892, Edmonton in 1908, Calgary in 1909 and Regina in 1911. By WWI, 48 Canadian cities and towns boasted streetcar systems.

The first intercity application of electric street railway technology was also at St Catharines in 1887, with a line to Thorold, Ont, followed by construction of a 13-mile (20 km) interurban system between New Westminster and Vancouver in 1891. Some of these interurban lines were later overtaken by urban expansion and became part of city streetcar lines (eg, the Long Branch line in Toronto); others provided a right-of-way for eventual rapid transit construction (eg, Vancouver to New Westminster).

In the 1930s the street railway industry responded to increased competition from automotive transport by developing lightweight, high-performance cars, best typified by the (US) Street Railway Presidents' Conference Car. Licensed for manufacture in Canada, these popular, comfortable machines were used in Vancouver, Montréal and Toronto. Toronto still uses them, but in other cities they gave way to the motorbus and trolleybus, which can operate on roads built at public expense, rather than requiring track provided by the transit system itself.

Technological changes came into play again during the 1970s and 1980s, with the use of trains of modern articulated cars (having several body sectors joined together by flexible joints) to provide transit service that has many of the characteristics of conventional "heavy" rapid transit with lower costs. Capable of running on city streets, Light Rail Transit services are reinstating the street railway. Edmonton opened the first all-new LRT service in N America in 1978, using a combination of subway and freight railway alignments. In 1981 Calgary followed, combining a new streetcar operation downtown, with short tunnel sections, roadside alignments and a freight railway line. A second line, opening in 1985, makes extensive use of central medians of major roadways. The success of these installations has inspired plans for LRT lines in Toronto and Vancouver and in a number of western US cities.

Social and Economic Impact Transit systems were the first major consumer of electricity and promoted the use of electricity for other purposes, such as lighting. Many electric-power companies began life as streetcar companies, eg, those of Winnipeg, Montréal, Québec City, Saint John, Halifax, Victoria and Vancouver. Some power companies operated transit systems into the 1970s: Nova Scotia Light and Power ran motorbuses and trolleybuses until 1969, and BC Hydro in Vancouver and Victoria until 1978.

Electric street railways produced a revolution in social and political life. The low price and widespread availability of streetcar service meant that for the first time people could gather *en masse* from all over a city, with a major impact, in an era preceding radio or widespread telephones, on political responsiveness and institutions. Streetcars also had a major impact on the shape of cities. "Streetcar suburbs" offered an entirely new way of life for Canadians, providing access to urban amenities while at the same time permitting relatively low-density housing, yet avoiding the major sprawl often associated with later auto-dominated suburbs.

The "streetcar strip," a linear development of retail and professional service establishments outside of downtown, remains to this day even where streetcars have disappeared, in Vancouver's Broadway, Calgary's 17th Ave, Edmonton's 124th St, Ottawa's Bank St, Toronto's Eglinton Ave and Montréal's St Laurent St. Wherever 2 or more lines met or crossed, surrounding land became particularly attractive for retail, office or apartment construction. *See* URBAN TRANSPORTATION; SUBWAYS AND LIGHT RAPID TRANSIT.   BRIAN E. SULLIVAN

Streit, Marlene Stewart, golfer (b at Cereal, Alta 9 Mar 1934). Streit played junior golf in Fonthill, Ont. She was a powerful competitor, her game marked by fierce pride and will to win. She won the Canadian Ladies' Open Amateur title 11 times between 1951 and 1973, the Ontario Ladies' Amateur Championship 11 times, the Ladies' British Open Amateur in 1953, the US Women's Amateur in 1956 and the Australian Women's Amateur in 1963. Streit was voted Canada's athlete of the year in 1951 and 1956. LORNE RUBENSTEIN

Stress was originally viewed as an overpowering external force acting upon individuals or objects. The mechanical engineer still uses the word in this sense, but human biologists have been less consistent in their terminology. Some retain classical usage, whereas others regard stress as the physiological and psychological reaction to adverse circumstances, or as a subjective response to any situation that the individual regards as unfavourable. Any factor threatening the constancy of the stable internal environment which the body's mechanisms are designed to preserve may be viewed as a "stressor," whether self-imposed (eg, by excessive physical or mental work) or external (eg, a hot and humid environment).

Much of the early investigation of stress was undertaken by Dr Hans SELYE, of the Institute of Experimental Medicine and Surgery at Université de Montréal, who defined stress as the state manifested by a specific syndrome that consists of all nonspecifically induced changes within a biological system. He postulated a general 3-phase reaction of the body to any stressor. First, an acute alarm reaction was associated with the discharge of hormones from the adrenal glands, a decrease in the size of the thymus, a decrease in one type of white blood cell (eosinophils) and a propensity to gastric ulcers. In the second phase, resistance or adaptation to the stressor was manifested by a hypertrophy (exaggerated growth) of the adrenal glands. If the exposure continued, exhaustion resulted; in animals, damage to the outer part (cortex) of the adrenal glands might result, and in humans there was indirect evidence of parallel changes. Based on this research, Selye postulated a condition of "eustress," an ideal amount of stress that maintains individuals in the phase of adaptation.

In popular thought stress is defined mainly in psychological terms (although hard physical work or a hot and noisy environment also increase the stress imposed by a mental task). Stress usually results if the pace of work is too fast, if the consequences of error are grave or if there is inadequate definition of the task to be performed. However, researcher David Coburn (then working at U of Victoria) suggested that boring, monotonous and repetitive work also imposes stress on a worker. It may be that in such circumstances much effort must be devoted to sustaining the necessary vigilance to avoid accidents and maintain quality production. Psychologists describe an inverted U-shaped relationship between task difficulty and performance — moderately demanding work ensures the best performance and imposes the least stress upon the employee.

Attempts to relate poor health to stress exposure have been unsatisfactory because "stressful" work is often associated with adverse habits such as inadequate physical exercise and heavy cigarette smoking. However, occasional reports have linked stressful employment, eg, air-traffic control, with an increased incidence of heart attacks and gastric ulcers. It has been hard to prove, through research, that exercise helps to counter either psychological stress or the resultant strain. If a task is boring, exercise can certainly provide a countermeasure, increasing the total stress on the body to the "eustress" level. Ex-

ercise also offers a pleasant relaxation to the overstressed individual, although exercise may be no more effective than some other type of respite from an overdemanding task.

According to observers, humans have always encountered stress, but modern automation of the workplace has both increased the proportion of "mindless" tasks and provided supervisors with the tools to monitor employee performance ever more closely. Moderate amounts of stress may be essential to both worthwhile effort and a resultant sense of achievement, but happiness and health depend upon a careful matching of the demands of work with the skills of the employee. R.J. SHEPHARD
Reading: H. Selye, *The Stress of Life* (1976).

Strickland, Edgar Harold, entomologist, soldier (b at Erith, Eng 29 May 1889; d at Victoria 31 May 1962). After studies in England 1909-11, Strickland attended Harvard 1911-13. In 1913 he was "loaned" to Canada to obtain field experience for proposed research on sleeping sickness in Africa. He was entomology officer for Alberta 1913-21, operating an entomological field station at Lethbridge. He founded and headed U of A's entomology dept 1922-54 (the sole member for 24 years). Strickland's 60 entomological papers range through history, ecology, life cycles, taxonomy and adverse effects of DDT, with pest control a major concern of his careeer. His academic endeavours were paralleled by military activity, in the Canadian Machine Gun Corps during WWI, as CO of U of Alta COTC 1935-40 and the Canadian Army Base at Wetaskiwin, Alta, 1942-44, and as aide-de-camp to the lieutenant-governor of Alberta 1936-39. Honours included the King's Jubilee Medal (1935) and the Coronation Medal (1937). MARTIN K. McNICHOLL

Strickland, John Douglas Hipwell, biological oceanographer (b at London, Eng 3 Aug 1920; d at La Jolla, Calif 12 Nov 1970; naturalized Canadian). Strickland was a senior scientist with the Pacific Oceanographic Group of the Fisheries Research Board, Nanaimo, BC, 1956-66 and head of the Marine Food Chain Group at the Institute of Marine Resources, La Jolla, after 1966. He initiated biological oceanographic studies as part of the West Coast research effort of the FRB. A scientist of international acclaim, Strickland started many new studies on the ecology of the oceans, which later gave rise to a new generation of biological oceanographers. He is best remembered for his analytical work on micronutrients and his initiation of marine mesocosm experiments in Departure Bay, BC, during the early 1960s. A research vessel of U of Victoria and part of the Marine Ecology Laboratory at Bedford Institute of Oceanography, Dartmouth, NS, are named after him. T.R. PARSONS

Strikes and Lockouts A strike is a work stoppage decided on by the employees in a bargaining unit in order to compel an employer to agree to or to modify certain working conditions. Generally, strikes are only legal after a collective agreement has expired and certain conditions (eg, a bargaining period, a strike vote, conciliation effort and a lapse of time) have been met. A lockout is a labour dispute in which an employer shuts down his business temporarily or refuses to continue employing a number of his employees to compel them to agree to certain terms or conditions of employment. Like strikes they can occur only after certain steps have been taken. Lockouts were very uncommon until the 1960s and are still much less frequent than strikes. Most statistics count them together as work stoppages.

The right to strike was implicitly granted in Canada in 1872 by the Trade Union Act. Picketing remained a criminal offence until the Criminal Code was amended in 1934 in order to

allow information picketing. Since the 1970s BC has forbidden the use of professional strike-breakers and Québec has forbidden subcontracting of struck operations as well as the use of any employee (except local management personnel) to continue production during a legal strike. A strike can be professional, economic or political, positive or defensive, for one's own demands or in solidarity with other workers. It can be authorized or "wildcat," legal or illegal. Characterized by its tactics, it can be rotating, hit-and-run, sit down, or work to rule. It can also be partial, plant wide, company wide, industry wide or general. And it can be very short (a symbolic strike) or very long. In the 19th and early 20th centuries, most strikes, such as the WINNIPEG GENERAL STRIKE, were waged for union recognition. After recognition was legally confirmed through the certification system (1944) strikes were initiated primarily for better working conditions. In the late 1960s and the 1970s, strikes were increasingly directed at levels of governments as employers or as legislators.

Strike activity can be measured by the number of strikes per month or year, the number of workers involved and the total number of person-days lost by all workers affected. One ratio devised calculates the percentage of time lost in relation to total estimated time worked during one year in a country. In Canada and the US this ratio hovers around 0.1% and 0.2%. In 1919, 1946 and 1976 it reached 0.6%. These 3 peaks fall into 3 periods (1910-19, 1945-47 and 1965-81), when Canada experienced waves of labour conflicts. The first 2 waves, during or following WWI and WWII, resulted from the drive of trade unions to catch up with economic conditions. The third wave was caused by a variety of factors.

The causes of greater strike activity have never been definitively established, although workers are less likely to strike when unemployment is high and more likely to strike in periods of increasing or high economic activity. The long crest of the third wave (1965-81) has taken place in a period of relative prosperity and rising inflation. The growth of public-sector unions is another factor. Each negotiation in this sector tends to involve more employees than in most private sector cases, causing a greater loss of person-days and influencing greatly the general picture of work stoppages in the 1970s. Conflicts in the 1970s have been more violent and involved more illegal activities than before. Wildcat strikes and political strikes have also become more important, an example of the latter being the Day of Protest, launched by the Canadian Labour Congress, on 14 Oct 1976, against anti-inflation legislation; that day alone accounted for close to one million person-days lost. *See also* COLLECTIVE BARGAINING; LABOUR RELATIONS; LABOUR ORGANIZATIONS. GÉRARD HÉBERT

		Strikes and Lockouts in Canada: Selected years 1901-1983		
	Work stoppages	Workers involved	Person-days lost	% of estimated working time
1901	99	24 089	737 808	–
1911	100	29 285	1 821 084	–
1919	336	148 915	3 400 942	0.60
1921	168	28 257	1 048 914	0.22
1931	88	10 738	204 238	0.04
1941	231	87 091	433 914	0.06
1946	226	138 914	4 515 030	0.54
1951	258	102 793	901 620	0.09
1961	287	97 959	1 335 080	0.11
1966	617	411 459	5 178 170	0.34
1969	595	306 799	7 751 880	0.46
1971	539	211 493	2 714 560	0.16
1972	567	686 129	7 423 140	0.41
1976	1 039	1 570 940	11 609 890	0.55
1981	1 048	338 548	8 878 490	0.37
1983	645	329 309	4 443 960	0.19

Stringer, Arthur John Arbuthnott, popular novelist and expatriate bohemian (b at Chatham, Ont 26 Feb 1874; d at Mountain Lakes, NJ 14 Sept 1950). Despite his trilogy of novels about the Canadian Prairies — *Prairie Wife* (1915), *Prairie Mother* (1920) and *Prairie Child* (1921) — Stringer was not in any recognizable stream of Canadian writing but rather was a prolific American hack-fiction writer of the David Graham Phillips strain, able to satisfy, by his facile and compromising pen, the demands of the popular magazine press for sentimental tales. The fact that he lived most of his life in the US, however, did not prevent him from frequently inventing Canadian characters and sometimes, starting with *Empty Hands* (1924), setting them in the Far North, a region he misunderstood lavishly, thereby contributing to foreign stereotyping of Canada.   DOUG FETHERLING

Strom, Harry Edwin, farmer, politician, premier of Alberta (b at Burdett, Alta 7 July 1914; d at Edmonton 2 Oct 1984). He served as municipal counsellor, school trustee and chairman of the local Rural Electrification Assn and was also interested in water conservation. First elected to the Alberta legislature in 1955, he was re-elected in 1959, 1963, 1967 and 1971 as a Social Credit member. He served as minister of agriculture 1962-68 and minister of municipal affairs July-Dec 1968 in the administration of E.C. MANNING. In Dec 1968 he became premier on the retirement of Manning but in Sept 1971 the Social Credit government was defeated by the Progressive Conservatives under Peter LOUGHEED. From 1971 to 1973 he was leader of the Opposition and following the provincial election of 1975 he retired from politics. He was the first Alberta-born premier.   ERIC J. HOLMGREN

Strong, Maurice Frederick, business administrator, environmentalist, statesman (b at Oak Lk, Man 29 Apr 1929). Strong began a business career as a trading-post employee for the HUDSON'S BAY CO in the Arctic in 1944. His business talents developed as he quickly moved from being accountant for a mining group in Toronto (1945) through a series of management and investment positions with various energy and financial corporations (1948-66). In 1966 he shifted to international and later environmental affairs. He headed the CANADIAN INTERNATIONAL DEVELOPMENT AGENCY until 1970, then was secretary-general of the UN Conference on the Human Environment and also undersecretary-general of the UN Switzerland office (1970-72) and executive director of the UN Environment Program in Nairobi, Kenya (1973-75). Strong returned to business as head of PETRO-CANADA (1976-78), after which he became chairman of the International Energy Development Corp (1980-84).

Numerous volunteer activities have included positions with the International Union for Conservation of Nature and Natural Resources; the World Wildlife Fund; the World Council of Churches; the Soc for Development, Justice, and Peace (the Vatican); and the North-South Inst. His numerous conservation and humanity awards include the Freedom Festival Award (1975) and the first Pahlavi Environment Prize (1976).   MARTIN K. McNICHOLL

Stuart, Kenneth, army officer (b at Trois-Rivières, Qué 9 Sept 1891; d at Ottawa 3 Nov 1945). Stuart graduated from RMC in 1911 and served with the Royal Canadian Engineers overseas 1915-18. Editor of the *Canadian Defence Quarterly* while at headquarters in the 1930s, he was appointed chief of the general staff in Dec 1941 and chief of staff, Canadian Military Headquarters, London, from Dec 1943 to Nov 1944. Instrumental in removing Gen A.G.L. MCNAUGHTON as commander, 1st Canadian Army, Stuart was sacked by McNaughton when the latter became defence minister in Nov 1944. Stuart's miscalculations in forecasting infantry casual-

ties helped force the government to impose CONSCRIPTION in Nov 1944.   STEPHEN HARRIS

Student Rights There are basically 2 sorts of rights that apply to students: substantive rights, ie, the actual rights that students should enjoy, and procedural rights, ie, methods by which students claim their rights. This article is concerned with students in public institutions, although those in private schools can claim rights under the common law and provincial education Acts.

Provincial governments affirm the basic right to an education when they approve financing for primary and secondary schools. Governments also extend the right to an education by underwriting part of the expenses for colleges and universities. When education budgets are debated, arguments occasionally surface to augment this principle, eg, to make small class sizes a moral right or to guarantee that all qualified high-school graduates may have access to post-secondary education. Courts are usually reluctant to enter this debate, not wishing to define "good" teaching or to rule on government spending.

A second substantive right, particularly important for minority groups, guarantees equal EDUCATIONAL OPPORTUNITY. In the spirit of this provision, which mirrors the value that governments should treat persons equally, provincial policymakers have attempted to reduce imbalances between schools and regions. For example, elaborate funding mechanisms exist to ensure that public treasuries treat school boards in different parts of the same province equally. Students occasionally vie for influence in the allocation of equitable resources, eg, female pupils have argued that budgets should be revised so that their PHYSICAL EDUCATION programs are as well funded as those of male students.

Legislatures also require teachers to institute special education programs for students limited by handicaps and learning disabilities. Parents and advocates for children try to ensure that students' rights are not abridged through malpractice, inadequate diagnosis or faulty placements in remedial groupings. Separate or demonstrably substandard education for handicapped children may be challenged in courts under the CANADIAN CHARTER OF RIGHTS AND FREEDOMS.

Administrators typically have the legal power to punish students for serious disruptions in schools. Offences may include persistent opposition to authority, habitual neglect of duty, use of profane or improper language, and conduct "injurious" to a moral tone. A number of schools and major post-secondary institutions now extend to students the right of due process, according to which administrators must immediately state reasons for suspensions or expulsions; within days, students and their parents can appeal these administrative actions, and authorities thereafter can reverse or modify punishments that are unjust or arbitrary. In post-secondary school, students can turn to ombudsmen or directors of student services for help in redressing such problems as sexual harassment, undeclared grading practices and too-restricted access to records about themselves.

The Canadian Charter of Rights and Freedoms has generated due process procedures in schools. Schools are refining their codes of conduct so that students may confront accusers, contest the evidence, cross-examine witnesses, appeal beyond immediate supervisors, participate in hearings where each side makes cases in the presence of the other, and have controversies settled by rules that are known to all in advance.

Elementary Schools In academic and political matters, students in primary and junior high schools enjoy the least latitude. Teachers in these institutions are empowered to exercise the discipline of a kind, firm and judicious parent.

This empowerment, *in loco parentis* ("in place of the parent"), stems from the European practice of wealthy parents voluntarily and individually contracting with tutors for their children's training. The idea of teacher as substitute parent has been so absorbed into the compulsory and mass education systems of N America that school boards and governing bodies for private schools are slow to question constraints that elementary educators may impose on learners' expression, association, opinion and assembly.

Deriving their authority from COMMON LAW, teachers in the past have administered corporal punishment. In recent years, officials in ministries of education have disapproved of the strap, but its use has not been forbidden in all provinces. In restraining a child, teachers have to stay within limits set by their boards. "Drawing blood" is generally considered going too far.

Secondary Schools Adolescents are more likely to use the provocative language of "demanding" their rights. During the 1960s, students wore armbands, picketed and clashed with officials, seeking the unqualified exercise of speech, press and assembly for which university students were clamouring. In the process, Canada's secondary students did gain some control over matters such as hair length, aspects of dress and cigarette smoking within designated areas. In the wake of that turmoil, conflicts over students' academic and political freedoms have not been as widespread or as intense.

Regulation of student life has increased in the 1980s. High schools have adopted codes of behaviour that spell out requirements for attendance, access to school areas, punctuality, and respect for others. A few boards of education have disallowed the practice by students of gathering names on petitions for politicians.

Secondary-school educators generally believe that students should have little or no involvement in determining curricular activities, but critics of this point of view argue that students should have greater share in the policymaking process affecting rule changes, noting that such involvement would provide training in democracy. In response, many educators claim that the student body has such unequal standing in relation to themselves that an equal voice in school government would be inappropriate.

Legal precedent is gradually emerging over PRIVACY freedoms in Canadian high schools. Although guaranteed by the Charter of Rights, a student's privilege to be secure from unreasonable search and seizure must be balanced with the educators' long-standing responsibilities to maintain order and to protect pupils from enticement into illegal behaviour. Accordingly, if a teacher has a reasonable suspicion that contraband materials, such as drugs or weapons, may be secreted in a student's desk or locker, that teacher may have the right to search the desk or locker without a warrant and without prior consent from the student. Educators are expected to proceed, however, only after weighing the suspect's age, history, record in school, and the immediate seriousness of the situation.

Post-secondary Institutions Students in colleges and universities have made the greatest strides in acquiring privacy rights. Typically, searches (of lockers, rooms, etc) are sanctioned (and conducted warily) only in cases of emergency or with high-level authorization. University students have also won the right of freedom of association. As a result of the protests of the 1960s and early 1970s, post-secondary students are relatively free from regulations that guide their lives outside class. On some campuses, undergraduates can operate their own pubs. University students sit on department committees and at intermediate levels of their institutions' governing councils but few students actually participate in governing. In some provinces graduate students, employed as part-time teaching assistants, have won the right to bargain collectively for better wages, and improved working conditions.   RICHARD G. TOWNSEND

Students, Financial Aid to, Some form of financial support to needy post-secondary students has always been available in Canada. Until 1939 this primarily took the form of privately funded assistance from universities and colleges to students with high scholastic achievement.

The foundation of a national co-ordinated policy for student assistance began in a modest way with the federal government's passage of the Dominion-Provincial Student Aid Program (DSAP) in 1939. All provinces had joined the plan by 1944. The CONSTITUTION ACT, 1867, granted the provincial legislatures the exclusive right to "make laws in and for each province" in relation to education, but the federal initiation of a national aid program was legitimized on the grounds that it related to activities in areas under federal jurisdiction, eg, economic growth, labour training and labour mobility. Thus, DSAP formed a part of the Youth Training Act, which was part of a national economic policy.

Under DSAP the federal government contributed funds to each participating province and the province was expected to provide an equal amount of assistance. Some provinces provided only loans, others only grants. It has been estimated that overall the federal government contributed less than $5 million to DSAP, and that fewer than an average of 3000 students a year received support under the program.

The implementation of the DSAP affected financial aid to students in 3 major ways. First, provincial responsibility for administrating aid regardless of source of funding stimulated a diversity in provincial programs. Second, merit alone became less of a criterion for determining eligibility for aid than need, ie, aid shifted from scholarships to bursaries. Third, the role of the federal government in financing and co-ordinating aid increased in importance. Québec opted out of the joint arrangement in 1954, citing constitutional reasons of provincial primacy and autonomy in higher education.

The 1960s witnessed rapid growth in post-secondary education and a consequent need for reformed student aid plans. The Canada Student Loan Plan (CSLP) established in 1964, superseded the DSAP, which was discontinued in 1967. Under the CSLP, the federal government guarantees loans to all full-time students who demonstrate financial need to a provincial or territorial government on the understanding that the money will be repaid over a period not exceeding 9.5 years at a rate of interest set annually beginning 6 months after studies are terminated. The federal government guarantees the loan with a designated lender, such as a chartered bank or credit union, and pays the annual interest before repayment is made.

In seeking assistance, students first apply to a province or territory for aid, providing information about their financial resources and needs. The province or territory then determines the amount of aid for which the student is eligible, either in the form of a nonrepayable grant or bursary, or as an authorization for a guaranteed loan, or a mix of both. The student negotiates the loan at a bank or other commercial lending institution.

In Feb 1980 the Federal-Provincial Task Force on Student Assistance was created. Its report was tabled Dec 1980, and in 1983 the CSL Act was amended according to the task force's recommendations. The maximum loan was increased from $56.25 to $100 a week for full-time students. The amendments also permitted loans for part-time students (up to $2500 at any one time), interest relief for unemployed borrowers, and cancellation of debt for certain borrowers. Nei-

ther these amendments nor the provincial systems of aid are intended to supplement the student's available resources. Each province administers the program under jointly agreed-upon administrative criteria. Under the CSLP, each province must establish an appeals process for students who are denied loans.

In all provinces except Québec, student assistance programs include a mix of aid provided from the CSLP and from supplementary provincial funds for loans, bursaries and special grants (money granted to students as a result of a special government policy or program, often to encourage students to follow specified careers after graduation). Students cannot apply directly to the federal government for a CSLP loan. Québec elected to remain outside the formal joint financing and administrative arrangements, choosing to make its own financial arrangements with Ottawa.

Provincial systems of aid under the CSLP differ. While all provinces use administrative criteria developed annually for CSLP by federal, provincial and territorial officials and approved by their respective governments, differences occur because national criteria set only maximum allowances. Individual provinces can set tighter criteria and offer less than the maximum loans and have established methods of calculating the total amount of assistance to each student. Loans and bursaries are issued by the province where the student resides and not where he or she studies. Each province designates the post-secondary institutions, inside or outside the province, to which students may take their loans and grants. As part of general fiscal restraint, in the 1980s most provinces adopted much more stringent criteria for loan eligibility.

CSLP has been criticized on a number of counts, including the following.

Loan-Bursary Balance The Canadian Federation of Students, which represents close to 500 000 post-secondary students, contends that the debt loan held by students after graduation represents a heavy burden. Although a few provinces are introducing a loan rebate program to ease this burden, the trend seems to be towards giving more loans than grants. Several provinces have also raised loan requirements.

Neglected Groups Critics maintain that many of the disadvantaged, eg, native people, single parents, children of lower-income families, are not served well by the existing student aid programs. They argue that financial pressures, the reluctance of low-income families to assume loan commitments, and inadequate information combine to restrict aid accessibility for certain groups of Canadians.

Loose Criteria Critics have also charged that financial aid is more readily available for some student applicants than others, eg, that the test used by provinces to decide the amount each student receives favours members of groups such as the self-employed.

The federal government has paid increasing sums of money into student aid. In 1982-83 it authorized $308 million in bank loans, a figure that jumped to close to almost $500 million in 1984, after loan limits were raised. In the early 1980s about 33% of Canadian post-secondary students received some form of government aid.

One of the difficulties behind financial assistance programs is that they seek to meet diverse goals, ie, to ensure access to post-secondary education to students in financial need and to provide indirect support to post-secondary institutions which are under the financial control of the provinces.

Supplementary aid schemes are available in most provinces for groups such as the handicapped, native people and single parents on welfare. New Brunswick and Alberta offer different kinds of loan remissions to graduates. In Québec, interest-free loans are available for

study at certain post-secondary institutions. A work-study program is available for exceptionally needy students in Ontario. Loans are available in Saskatchewan for applicants studying in some courses where the entrance requirements do not meet CSLP criteria.

Education of registered Indians and Inuit is the constitutional responsibility of the federal government. Eligible Indian and Inuit people may attend provincial universities and colleges; the Department of Indian Affairs and Northern Development provides financial and other assistance. Certain provinces also provide special programs of assistance.

Various priorities deemed in the national interest have prompted the implementation of other significant federal programs. The Veterans Rehabilitation Act, 1945, provided financial aid to returning veterans. An extensive scholarship program in the arts, humanities and social sciences was supported by the Canada Council, 1957-67, and 10 years later the Social Sciences and Humanities Research Council and the Engineering Research Council became responsible for the grant and scholarship programs of the Canada Council. The National Training Act, 1983, authorizes the Canada Employment and Immigration Commission to operate adult vocational programs that support the training and upgrading of workers needed in a wide variety of occupations. Student youth-employment programs encourage summer employment as well as co-operative programs that enable students to alternate university study with periods of employment. These programs overshadow early federal initiatives (1919) in providing loans to disabled veterans and grants and fellowships (est 1916) from the National Research Council.   LIONEL ORLIKOW

Studhorse Man, The, novel by Robert KROETSCH (Toronto, London and New York, 1969). The story of Hazard Lepage, Kroetsch's studhorse man, is told by Demeter Proudfoot, a madman in a bathtub. Lepage undertakes an Albertan odyssey in quest of a mare for his virgin stallion, the noble Poseidon; the stallion and Lepage's adventures acquire mythological dimensions in a text that comments on the nature of sexuality, history, time and the western Canadian character. *The Studhorse Man* exemplifies Kroetsch's powers as an explorer of western Canadian mythology, and demonstrates his exuberant use of language.   NEIL BESNER

Stump, Sarain, native name Sock-a-jaw wu, meaning "the one who pulls the boat," painter, poet (b at Fremont, Wyo 1945; d by drowning near Mexico City, Mexico 20 Dec 1974). He had little formal education and was encouraged to learn from his Shoshone-Cree elders. Moving to an Alberta ranch 1964, he began the poems and drawings for *There Is My People Sleeping* (1969). Stump promoted traditional Indian values and sought to help young Indians gain pride in their heritage while coping with the modern world. He was the Indian art program co-ordinator at the Saskatchewan Indian Cultural College 1972-74. As a painter he was influenced by the traditional art of the Plains Indian; as well he was interested in searching for what he called his Aztecan roots, since the Shoshone tribe is related by language to the Uto-Aztecan family.   GERALD R. McMASTER

Stupart, Sir Robert Frederic, meteorologist (b at Aurora, Canada W 24 Oct 1857; d at Toronto 27 Sept 1940). A pioneer in METEOROLOGY, Stupart's career spanned 6 decades. He was first Canadian-born director of the national meteorological service 1894-1929 and led the expansion of the service throughout the West and into the North as telegraph and radio communication became available for transmitting weather data and forecasts. Employed by the service when he was 15, Stupart learned meteorology on the job and prepared the first public weather forecasts in 1876. As director, he was the first Canadian to participate in the activities of the International Meteorological Organization. A fellow of the RSC, he was knighted in 1916. MORLEY THOMAS

Sturgeon, large, primitive, bony FISH of class Osteichthyes, family Acipenseridae. The 4 genera and 23 species live in fresh and coastal waters of the Northern Hemisphere. In Canada, 5 species, all of genus *Acipenser,* occur: white and green sturgeons in Pacific coastal waters and rivers; lake sturgeon in fresh waters E of the Rockies; and Atlantic and shortnose sturgeons in Atlantic coastal waters and rivers. At least some populations of each Canadian species venture, at times, into brackish or salt water. Sturgeons are characterized by a long snout with 4 barbels (hairlike appendages) underneath, a toothless mouth, and 5 rows of shieldlike, bony plates on the body. The upper lobe of the tail fin is longer and more slender than the lower lobe. Sturgeons are an ancient group; fossils are known that date back to the Upper Cretaceous, about 65 million years ago.

Sturgeons typically grow slowly, but they may attain a great size. A white sturgeon weighing 629 kg was caught in the Fraser R at New Westminster in 1897, and an Atlantic sturgeon caught in the St Lawrence weighed 160 kg and was 267 cm long and 60 years old. Female Atlantic sturgeon must be at least 10 years old before spawning, and they usually spawn in rivers where the current is rapid. They grow to 22 cm in one year, 49 cm in 5 years and 90 cm in 10 years. Sturgeon usually feed on bottom invertebrates (eg, insect larvae, amphipods, molluscs, marine worms), but some also eat fishes. They feed on the bottom, using their protruding, sucking lips. They probably locate food with their barbels.

Sturgeons are valuable commercial fish; perhaps 150 000 t are caught annually. The flesh, delicious fresh or smoked, fetches a high price; the caviar is worth several dollars per kilogram. Each year, 9000-14 000 kg of white sturgeon is taken by anglers in the Fraser R. Anglers also seek lake sturgeon. Populations have declined drastically. In 1845, 800 000 kg of lake sturgeon were caught in Lake of the Woods, Ont. By 1957 the catch was only 0.005% of the maximum catch. Pollution, impassable dams and overfishing, combined with late maturity, have all taken their toll. The shortnose sturgeon is classified as rare by the Committee on the Status of Endangered Wildlife in Canada and is an endangered species in the US. Other sturgeons in Canada, eg, lake sturgeon, are declining in parts of their ranges. D.E. McALLISTER

The lake sturgeon (*Acipenser fulvescens*) dates back at least 65 million years. It is a highly valued commercial and sport fish (*courtesy National Museums of Canada/ National Museum of Natural Sciences*).

Sturgeon Falls, Ont, Town, pop 6045 (1981c), inc 1895, located 5 km up the Sturgeon R from Lk Nipissing. Long a site of Indian activity, and known to European fur traders since the 17th century, town growth awaited the arrival of the CPR in 1881. Earliest to arrive were English Canadians from Simcoe and Muskoka; their numbers were engulfed by lumber and pulp-and-paper workers, the latter industry beginning 1884. Closure of the Abitibi Power and Paper, Ltd, plant in 1912 caused a considerable English exodus; the town became 75-80% French speaking, an early voice for French-language rights and culture in Ontario. Paper, tourism, outdoor recreation and local agricul-

tural supply provide economic sustenance in the still largely francophone (75%) and Roman Catholic (87%) community. PETER KRATS

Submersible, small vehicle designed to operate under water, to carry out such tasks as research, equipment recovery and seabed surveys. A submersible must be supported by a surface vessel or platform; hence, it differs from a submarine, which is an independent, self-supporting vessel.

Manned submersibles are used worldwide. Several classes have been designed and manufactured in Canada, eg, Pisces, a one-atmosphere vehicle, and SDL, a lock-out vehicle, both operated by branches of the Canadian government. Manned submersibles have depth capabilities exceeding 6000 m, but generally operate at depths less than 2200 m. Remotely operated vehicles (ROVs) are also operational worldwide and are manufactured by several nations, Canada being a major contributor. ROVs designed and manufactured in Canada include the Dart, Trec and Trov classes of free-swimming vehicles. F.J. CHAMBERS

Substantive Law, body of law concerned with rights and obligations, as opposed to PROCEDURAL LAW which concerns how to enforce and defend such rights and obligations. For example, murder is a criminal offence (substantive law) while the rules to be followed in prosecuting an offender of that law are referred to as procedural law. K.G. McSHANE

Subways and Light Rapid Transit Subways, sometimes referred to as heavy-rail transit, are urban, electric, rapid-transit lines capable of carrying large numbers of people: between 20 000-40 000 passengers per hour in each direction. No other traffic is permitted to interfere with the separate rights-of-way of subway trains. Most subways are underground, hence the name, but portions can be at grade (ground level) with suitable fences or barriers, depressed in a cut without covering, or even elevated. Power is supplied to the trains by means of a "third rail," although overhead wire is sometimes also used. Station platforms are built at the same level as the floor of the subway car, eliminating steps for entry and exit. Fare collection occurs in stations rather than on vehicles, and a full signal system is used for operation to ensure safety. Light rail transit is simpler and less costly than a subway, but also has less capacity, between 8000-20 000 passengers per hour in each direction. The vehicles are lighter than subway cars, and are essentially streetcars. The right-of-way may be only partially separated, with grade crossings and portions of a line operating in mixed traffic on the street. Power collection is from overhead wires; passenger loading may use platforms or steps or both, and fare collection can be either on board or at the stations. Light rail systems are usually, but not always, signalized (*see* STREET RAILWAYS).

Canada has 2 subway systems, in Toronto and Montréal. Toronto had the first system, with the Yonge St line (7.4 km in length) opening in Mar 1954. The Toronto system was expanded in stages; in 1982 it was 56.9 km long and had 59 stations on 2 major lines. The Montréal system opened its initial portion in 1966, with 3 lines, 26 stations and a total length of 22 km. In 1982 it was 38.4 km long and had 46 stations; by 1984 another 4.5 km and 4 stations were being added. Further expansion was planned. The Toronto subway cars are 3.15 m in width, with steel wheels running on rails. The Montréal cars are 2.5 m in width, and use rubber tires.

There were 2 Light Rapid Transit systems in Canada in 1982. The Edmonton LRT line, 10.5 km in length, was opened in 1978 and extensions were opened in 1981 and 1983. It has 8 stations, 4 of them underground. The capacity is 6000 passengers per hour on a fully separate right-of-way. The Calgary LRT line, opened in

1981, is 13 km in length, totally at grade, using at-grade crossings at road intersections and with railway-type signals and lights giving the LRT vehicles priority. Line capacity is 4800, and a 9.7 km extension was scheduled to open Apr 1985. The design capacity of the Edmonton and Calgary lines is much higher than present usage. Both the Edmonton and Calgary systems use 2-section, 23 m articulated LRT vehicles designed and built in West Germany. Ontario's Urban Transportation Development Corporation has designed an advanced LRT technology using automated train control, lightweight cars and linear-induction motors with steerable trucks to reduce noise levels. Apart from the technology, the major difference of this system is its capacity, which is between those of LRT and subway. A 21.4 km line using the ALRT technology will open in 1986 in Vancouver, and a similar line of some 6.5 km in length was scheduled to open in Toronto in early 1985. JURI PILL

Such Is My Beloved, novel by Morley CALLAGHAN (Toronto and New York, 1934) is, on the surface, the story of an idealistic young Catholic priest's failure to help 2 prostitutes he befriends. Stephen Dowling's relationship with the prostitutes is condemned by his rich, sanctimonious parishioners and his bishop; Dowling's anguish over the girls' fate drives him mad, and the novel closes on his realization of the purely Christian love he bears for them and for humanity. But the novel's apparent simplicity becomes the means to a symbolic exploration of Dowling's faith, as set against the various secular, socioeconomic and political creeds of the time. *Such Is My Beloved* has been translated into French as *Telle est ma bien-aimée* (Montréal, 1974). NEIL BESNER

Sucker, freshwater FISH of the family Catostomidae, closely related to MINNOWS. There are about 65 species of suckers; most occur in N America but one extends into eastern Siberia and another occurs in China. There are 7 genera and 17 species in Canada; none are found in Newfoundland or Vancouver I. Longnose and white suckers have the largest distribution, in lakes and rivers from the Maritimes to BC. The longnose sucker even extends N to near the arctic coastline. The family also includes quillbacks (carplike fish) and redhorses (which can have reddish fins). Very few suckers exceed 40 cm in length. Most species have a ventral mouth (located on lower body surface) with large lips covered with papillae (small, nipple-shaped protuberances). Most species feed primarily on small, bottom-dwelling organisms which are sucked up (giving rise to the common name). Spawning usually occurs in spring or early summer. Breeding males, especially, may have nuptial tubercles (small, white, horny projections) on parts of the body and certain fins. Suckers are usually drably coloured, but a spawning male longnose sucker can have a bright red stripe along its side. Suckers, usually regarded as coarse fish, are rarely fished commercially or recreationally in Canada, although they occur in large numbers and can be readily taken. Although bony, they are eaten occasionally (sometimes marketed as "mullet") and are used for dog food. Suckers are important in the diets of many other fish. They may compete with salmonids, but the extent of this is not well known and probably exaggerated. JOSEPH S. NELSON

Sudbury, Ont, City, judicial seat for Dist of Sudbury in NE Ontario, is located on Lk Ramsey near the Sudbury Basin, a geological structure likely formed by meteorite impact. Situated 390 km N of Toronto on the TRANS-CANADA HWY, it serves as a gateway to northern Ontario. Its population (1981c) is 91 388 (1981c, 91 829; met area pop 149 923).

Settlement and Development The area was

Population: 91 829 (1981c); 149 923 (CMA)

Rate of Increase (1971-81): City 1.4%; CMA -3.5%

Rank in Canada: Twentieth (by CMA)

Date of Incorporation: Town 1893; City 1930

Land Area: 262.7 km²; 2381.1 km² (CMA)

Elevation: 250-300 m

Climate: Average daily temp, July 19°C, Jan -13°C; Yearly precip 835 mm; Hours of sunshine 2110 per year.

originally inhabited by Ojibwa belonging to the Algonquian group of Indians. Though HBC trading posts had operated in the area earlier in the century, the construction of the CPR main line in 1883, which included a station at this location, marked Sudbury's beginning. James Worthington, superintendent of construction, gave the site the name of his wife's birthplace in England. The discovery of NICKEL and COPPER during digging for the railway provided the impetus for growth. The Canadian Copper Co was formed 1886 and smelting operations were started 1888. In 1902 Canadian Copper merged with Orford Refining Co to form International Nickel (INCO LTD). Falconbridge Nickel Mines was formed in 1928. After 1960 the significance of the mining sector declined in relation to employment in health care (4 major hospitals), telecommunications (Bell Canada), government (Revenue Canada), tourism (Science North) and education (LAURENTIAN U and Cambrian College).

Cityscape Sudbury's development was constrained by railway lines and the topography. The community was also hindered by the lack of a solid property-tax base, receiving no taxes from the mining industry. It gradually expanded outwards along the major roads divided by rocky ridges into the adjoining townships and the "valley" within the Sudbury Basin, the centre of which forms an extensive plain. Plan-

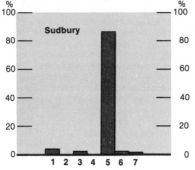

Distribution of Industrial Activity* by Industry Grouping within Census Metropolitan Areas, 1980

Industry groupings

1. Food and beverage and tobacco products industries
2. Leather, textile, knitting mills and clothing industries
3. Wood, furniture and fixtures, paper and allied and printing, publishing and allied industries
4. Machinery, transportation equipment and electrical products industries
5. Primary metal and metal fabricating industries
6. Rubber and plastic products, petroleum and coal products and chemical products industries
7. Non-metallic mineral products and miscellaneous manufacturing industries

* Industry activity based on the average of percentage shares of the value shipments of goods of own manufacture, total value added and total number of employees for each of the selected metropolitan areas.

Source: Figure II, Catalogue 31-209, Statistics Canada.

ning in the 1950s led to numerous projects, including one of Canada's most successful urban renewal schemes and an outstanding civic centre. The mining industry created some barren landscapes, but the area has been the site of one of the world's largest urban land-reclamation schemes.

Population Sudbury's population was 2027 in 1901 and doubled in each census decade up to 1931; as a result of a major amalgamation and annexation (1960) it rose to 80 120 by 1961. In 1971 the city and metropolitan area totalled 90 535 and 155 424, respectively. With another expansion in 1973, the city reached 91 829 by 1981 and the metropolitan area fell to 149 923. The ethnic makeup is bicultural, with the British and French each constituting at least 30% of the population. More than 60% is Roman Catholic.

Economy and Labour Force Sudbury is Canada's most important mining community. In 1951 more than 40% of the population was engaged in mining, though by 1981 that sector employed less than 25% of the community. The area remains the largest single source of nickel in the world and is Canada's largest copper producer. IRON-ORE pellets, acid and precious metals are also produced. Employment in services and public administration has grown considerably, along with wholesaling and distribution operations. With uncertain long-term prospects for mining, Sudbury will capitalize on its location and political importance for new employment opportunities. The labour force has contributed significantly to Canada's union movement.

Transportation After 1883 rail connections were established with Sault Ste Marie (1887) and Toronto (1908). Highway links with North Bay and Sault Ste Marie were initiated in 1912. In 1956 Hwy 69 S to Gravenhurst was opened. The first connection with Timmins, via Hwy 144, began in 1970. Air service has been provided

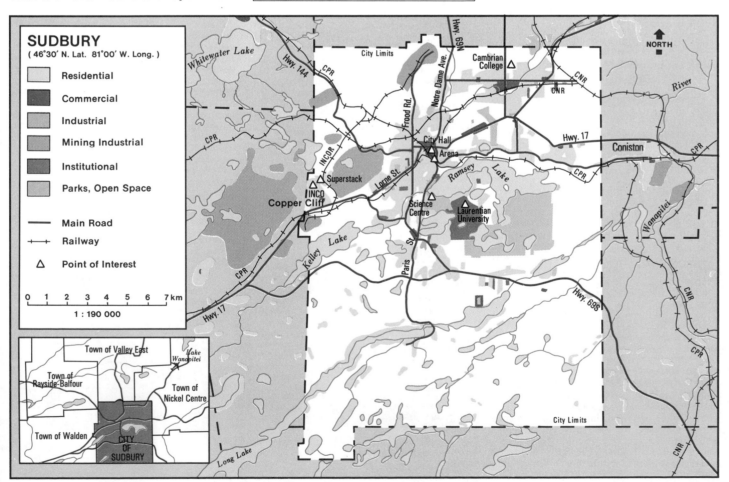

by the Sudbury Municipal Airport from 1954. Since 1971, Norontair, a provincially owned airline, has offered an important connective service.

Government and Politics Town and city status were acquired in 1893 and 1930, respectively. In 1973 the city became part of the Regional Municipality of Sudbury, which includes as well the towns Capreol, Nickel Centre, Onaping Falls, Rayside-Balfour, Valley East and Walden. The major political issue concerns the need to diversify the economy.

Cultural Life The cultural scene has been enhanced by the establishment of Laurentian U (1960) and Cambrian College (1966). An increasing francophone influence is evidenced by the organization La Slague and the opening of Place St Joseph. Sudbury has 3 main museums: Laurentian Museum and Arts Centre, Flour Mill Museum and Copper Cliff Museum. Professional theatre is performed by the Sudbury Theatre Centre and Le Théâtre du Nouvel-Ontario. The Philharmonic Society (1957) was reconstituted in 1975 as the Sudbury Symphony Orchestra. Other musical groups include the Karl Pukara Accordian Orchestra, the singing group CANO and several ethnic choirs. The Northern Lights Folk Festival is a popular event. Local newspapers include the Sudbury *Daily Star*, *Northern Life*, *Le Voyageur* and *Northern Ontario Business*. Sudbury Wolves are a popular junior hockey team.   O.W. SAARINEN

Reading: Laurentian University, *Centennial History of Sudbury* (1983).

Suez Crisis On 26 July 1956 Egyptian President Nasser seized the predominantly Anglo-French Suez Canal Co, which had operated the canal since 1869. Nasser's takeover of the canal, connecting the Mediterranean and Red seas, was a blow to Western pride and commerce. Diplomacy failed, and Britain, France and Israel secretly agreed to move against Egypt. Israel attacked Oct 29, advancing in a single day to within 42 km of the canal. As planned with Israel beforehand, Britain and France ordered Israel and Egypt to withdraw from the immediate area of the canal. Nasser refused. On Oct 31 Britain and France intervened directly, bombing the Canal Zone.

Privately the Canadian government was angry at an action that split the COMMONWEALTH and alienated the US. Publicly the Canadian role was that of conciliator. L.B. PEARSON, secretary of state for external affairs, and his colleagues at the UNITED NATIONS won overwhelming General Assembly support Nov 4 for an international force "to secure and supervise the cessation of hostilities." Canadian Gen E.L.M. BURNS was immediately named commander of the UN Emergency Force (UNEF). The British and French, however, ignored the UN resolution and landed paratroopers in the Canal Zone late on Nov 4. After pressure, largely American, was placed on British PM Sir Anthony Eden, a cease-fire was achieved Nov 6. Pearson fought successfully to have Canadian soldiers included in UNEF; advance units of the force arrived in mid-Nov. Although Pearson was awarded the 1957 Nobel Peace Prize for his peacemaking efforts at the UN, there were many in Britain and Canada who were dismayed by Ottawa's apparent lack of support for Britain. Such sentiment was probably a factor in the Liberal government's defeat in the general election of 1957. *See* PEACEKEEPING.   NORMAN HILLMER

Sugar Industry, a sector of Canada's FOOD AND BEVERAGE INDUSTRIES composed of companies that make cane, beet and invert sugars, sucrose syrup, molasses and beet pulp. The Canadian sugar-refining industry (excluding the MAPLE-SUGAR segment) began in the early 1850s with the establishment of a cane sugar-refining company in Montréal. By the early 1900s there were

refining operations in Halifax, NS; Saint John, NB; Toronto, Ont; and Vancouver, BC. All of these operations produced refined sugar from imported raw sugar, extracted from tropical sugarcane plants. Another important source of Canadian sugar has been domestically grown sugar beets. The first refinery designed to extract sugar from beets, La Compagnie de sucre de betterave de Québec, was established in Farnham, Qué, in 1881. Two more Québec-based beet refineries started in the same year. By 1902 there were 4 sugar-beet manufacturing plants in operation in Ontario; in 1903 the Knight Sugar Company was established in Alberta. At present, no beet sugar is produced in Ontario; all Canadian production comes from plants in Québec, Manitoba and Alberta.

The latest sweetening agent, high-fructose corn syrup or sweetener (HFCS), is increasingly important. This product is already used in SOFT-DRINK production and some CONFECTIONERY products and many more food products will use it in future. Two large HFCS production facilities were in operation in Ontario in 1982; a third began production in 1983. By 1982 HFCS was supplying 14-16% of sweetener demand in Canada; by 1983-84 it supplied about 25%, reducing dependence on imported raw cane sugar.

The traditional profile of the sweetener industry was also changed in 1982 when the Health Protection Branch of Health and Welfare Canada approved the use of "aspartame" in Canadian foods. This artificial sweetener, which adds no calories, was immediately used for diet soft drinks and, within a year, appeared in at least 8% of the industry's total beverage output. Industry executives feel that aspartame will eventually be used in some 20% of Canadian soft-drink production and, increasingly, in diet or low-calorie food products (eg, processed fruits, fruit fillings, etc).

Most countries that produce or use sugar, including Canada, are signatories to the International Sugar Agreement (ISA), which aims to prevent extremes in world sugar prices, and thus to protect the interests of both cane-producing countries and consumers of raw sugar. In Canada the industry is regulated by several federal agencies including Agriculture Canada and Consumer and Corporate Affairs. The industry is represented by the Canadian Sugar Institute in Toronto; members include all Canadian refining companies.

In recent years, annual production of refined sugar from raw sugarcane has averaged about 0.9-1.0 billion kg and production of refined sugar from Canadian-grown sugar beets has fluctuated between 90-135 million kg. Thirteen sugar-refining establishments now operate in Canada (excluding HFCS facilities): NB has 1; Qué, 6; Ont, 3; Man, 1; Alta, 1; and BC, 1. This number will remain fairly static.

The sugar-refining industry employs 1800-1900 people and spends $350 to $650 million for materials and supplies annually. The extremely volatile nature of international raw-sugar prices accounts for the radical cost fluctuation. The international situation also drastically influences the annual value of the refining industry's shipments, which in recent years ranged from $443 to $777 million.   ROBERT F. BARRATT

Suicide is the act of voluntary and intentional self-destruction. In Western societies suicide has nearly always been interpreted as voluntary self-destruction and many philosophers have taken it as a starting point for reflection on human existence. Suicide was decriminalized in Canada in 1972; someone who now attempts suicide is not liable to sanction under the Criminal Code. However, anyone found guilty of counselling another to take his or her own life or of aiding a suicide is liable to imprisonment of up to 14 years, whether or not the suicide is successful. A peace officer or a physician may order involuntary detention of any person judged a danger to himself or herself.

Suicide statistics are described in Statistics Canada records as "deaths reported by coroners and medical examiners of official death registrations as having been due or 'probably due' to suicide, following the usual postmortem inquiry, investigation, or inquest as required by law." Official statistics on suicide in most countries are inadequate because of poor record keeping, insufficient information, and tendencies on the part of medical personnel and other officials to mislabel or hide suicides, or refrain from investigations of suspicious deaths to protect the survivors of the victim. However, suicide statistics from many nations do indicate trends between years, differences among countries, and differences among specific groups within a country. Canada's rates of 12-15 suicides per year per 100 000 people places it between nations with rates of over 20 suicides per 100 000,

Deaths — Suicides, Canada, 1982

Age specific rates per 100,000 population

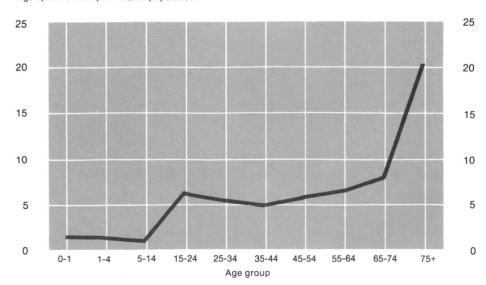

Source: Statistics Canada Catalogue 84-206 Annual

eg, Hungary, Czechoslovakia and Sweden, and those with rates of approximately 5 or under, eg, Mexico, Ireland and Israel. Emile Durkheim's observation in *Suicide* (1897) on the suicide rates of nations is still true: a given nation has a characteristic suicide rate that fluctuates very little from year to year and which generally remains relative to the rates of other nations. In 1982, 3523 suicides were recorded in Canada, 2726 by males, 797 by females. Suicide is among the top 10 causes of death in Canada, and is second to accidents as the leading cause of death for people under 35. Males are more likely to employ more violent and certain methods, eg, firearms, explosives, hanging, while females are more likely to use drugs.

There is substantial provincial variation across Canada, ie, suicide rates rise from east to west. Newfoundland has the lowest rate of all the provinces and the territories; the Yukon has the highest rate. Generally, in Canada the incidence of suicide is low among youth, increases until the middle years and declines after the age of 55 except among single males, for whom it increases until approximately 75 years of age. However, there has been a recent increase in rates among younger people, especially younger males. Married people are less likely to commit suicide than are single, widowed or divorced people, the exception being widowed women over 75, who have a low rate of suicide. Proportionately, native people and prison inmates also have a far higher incidence of suicide than does the general Canadian population.

While it has been established that climate and heredity bear no relationship to the incidence of suicide, a considerable array of social and psychological characteristics have been linked with self-destruction. Students of suicide agree that some personality types seem to be more vulnerable to suicidal behaviour. The major psychological theory of suicide, deriving from Freud, links suicide with hostile impulses turned back upon the self. Karl Menninger has suggested every suicide reflects the wish to kill, the wish to be killed, and the wish to die. Immediate difficulties, eg, loss of a loved one, or of a career, despair, loneliness or an unhappy home life may also precipitate self-destruction.

Programs aimed at preventing suicide range from those that attempt to identify potential suicides to those that provide effective first-aid and follow-up for suicide attempters. Restricting the availability of firearms, erecting barriers on bridges and other "attractive hazards" and reducing the toxicity of gas have reduced suicide rates in some locations. Recently the growth of crisis or distress centres, which provide the opportunity for people to telephone trained volunteers and discuss problems anonymously have been regarded as hopeful developments in suicide prevention. F.K. ANDREWS

Suicide (Male-Female Ratios): Totals and per 100 000 for Canada and Provinces and Territories, 1982
(Source: Statistics Canada)

	Total number of suicides		Per 100 000 of population	
	Male	Female	Male	Female
Canada	2726	797	20.2	5.8
Nfld	32	2	11.3	0.8
PEI	10	1	15.6	1.7
NS	82	22	17.7	4.9
NB	78	12	20.7	3.4
Qué	811	260	22.5	6.9
Ont	832	279	17.5	5.6
Man	109	30	19.4	5.1
Sask	146	25	27.4	4.9
Alta	291	68	23.1	5.7
BC	324	94	20.5	5.8
Yukon	6	1	47.9	14.6
NWT	5	3	15.3	10.7

Sullivan, Sir William Wilfred, journalist, lawyer, politician, premier of PEI, judge (b at Hope River, PEI 6 Dec 1843; d at Memramcook, NB 30 Sept 1920). Appointed assistant editor of the *Charlottetown Herald* 1864, Sullivan was elected, initially as a Liberal, to the PEI Legislative Assembly in 1872 and thereafter until he resigned in 1889. Elected leader of the Opposition in 1877, Sullivan, a Catholic, formed a Conservative government in 1879. Premier for over 10 years, a strong advocate of the Island's rights, Sullivan was appointed chief justice in 1889 and created a knight bachelor in 1914, 3 years before he retired from the bench. NICOLAS J. DE JONG

Sulphur (S), bright yellow to yellowish brown, brittle, nonmetallic element which melts at 119°C. Sulphur is widely distributed: in elemental form, especially associated with gypsum and limestone in SEDIMENTARY ROCKS of Tertiary age; and in combined form, in most rock types of all ages. Sulphur has been used since antiquity; today it is employed in production of almost everything we eat, wear or use. In Canada sulphur is obtained from metallic sulphides and hydrocarbons. The processing of metallic sulphides for their sulphur content began in 1866. Early operations involved roasting pyrite (an iron ore, FeS_2) for sulphuric acid (H_2SO_4). In the 1920s use of base-metal smelter gases for the manufacture of by-product sulphuric acid began near Sudbury, Ont, and at Trail, BC. Effluent gas from smelting sulphide ores contains 1-12% sulphur dioxide (SO_2). Recovered SO_2 is used directly to manufacture sulphuric acid. The largest H_2SO_4 plant in Canada is that of INCO Metals Company at Copper Cliff, Ont. Pyrite and pyrrhotite concentrates produced as a by-product of base-metal mining operations are sometimes marketed for their sulphur content.

Before the first sour-gas recovery plant was built in 1951, almost all Canadian sulphur production was from metallic sulphides. Highly toxic and corrosive hydrogen sulphide (H_2S), the dominant sulphur compound in sour natural gas, is at present the most important source of sulphur. There are plants in Alberta, BC and Saskatchewan. Most producing sour-gas fields contain 1-20% sulphur by weight, which is recovered by the modified Claus Process. The H_2S is extracted by means of a chemical reaction and fed to a furnace. Gas from the furnace is then passed through a condenser-converter series and liquid sulphur is removed until 95% or more of the original sulphur has been drawn off. The liquid sulphur is pumped to outside blocks where it solidifies, to storage tanks for direct shipping in liquid form, or to slating or prilling plants. Declining production has led to the development of sulphur melters to reclaim sulphur from block storage. A minor amount of sulphur is recovered from domestic and imported crude oils and tar sands. Some crude oils contain as much as 5% sulphur; domestic crudes generally have less sulphur than imported ones. Recovery techniques are similar to those used in sour gas. As yet almost no sulphur is recovered from COAL.

World production of all forms of sulphur was about 51 million t in 1983. Shipments by Canadian producers reached a record level in 1981 of 9 million t, valued at $727 million, over 2% of the total value of Canadian mineral production. Canada ranks third in world production (after the US and the USSR) and has been the world's largest exporter of elemental sulphur. The principal export markets are Africa, Asia and the US, each accounting for about 21% of exports. Canadian consumption of sulphur in all forms was almost 1.5 million t in 1983. The principal users are the fertilizer (55%), pulp and paper (20%) and metal-refining (10%) industries. *See* ACID RAIN; CHEMICAL INDUSTRIES; METALLURGY; PETROCHEMICAL INDUSTRY. J.Y. TREMBLAY

Staghorn sumac (*Rhus typhina*) (*artwork by Claire Tremblay*).

Sumac, shrub of genus *Rhus* of family Anacardiaceae. Family includes cashew, smoke tree, mango, pistachio, POISON IVY and several cultivated tropical ornamentals. In eastern Canada, the most familiar variation is staghorn sumac (named because hairy twigs resemble stags' horns), a large, nonpoisonous, clone-forming shrub bearing scarlet leaves in autumn, used as an ORNAMENTAL. Red, hairy fruits can be made into pink "lemonade" by bruising them, straining the acid water and adding sugar. Fragrant sumac (*R. aromatica*) is a small, nonpoisonous, thicket-forming shrub about 1 m tall. Poison sumac (*R. vernix*), a 5 m tall shrub, is extremely poisonous; contact results in the dermatitis associated with poison ivy. Smooth sumac (*R. glabra*) is most common in BC and extends to Ontario. It resembles staghorn sumac, but has smooth twigs. *See* PLANTS, NATIVE USES; POISONOUS PLANTS. J.M. GILLETT

Summerside, PEI, Town, pop 7828 (1981c), inc 1877, is located near the head of Bedeque Bay on the province's southern shore, 60 km W of Charlottetown. Until the Loyalist arrival in Prince County, the first settlers in the area had been MICMAC and then ACADIANS. Around 1800 the tiny village was known as Green's Shore, after Daniel Green, the tract's former owner. It was likely named after Summerside House, a licensed inn (est 1840). The village was launched as a shipbuilding centre when inadequate draught at his shipyard in Bedeque compelled Joseph Pope to rebuild his company in deeper water across the bay. Later in the same decade the village was renamed following a public comment on its favourable weather. After the late 19th-century collapse of shipbuilding, trade with the county's farming community sustained Summerside's economy.

Beginning around 1910, the town experienced renewed prosperity as a fur-trading centre, stimulated by Sir Charles Dalton and Robert T. Oulton's successful breeding of silver foxes in captivity. In 1920 Summerside was established as the headquarters of the Canadian National Silver Fox Breeders' Assn. Owing to overproduction, changing women's fashions and innovative dyeing techniques, this highly profitable enterprise collapsed around 1945. However, economic decline was offset by the 1941 construction of an air force base in nearby St Eleanors. As the Island's principal port for potato shipments,

and with the development of a number of small manufacturing businesses, as well as the trade with CFB Summerside and the county's farmers and fisherman, Summerside is today a thriving community.   W.S. KEIZER

Sun, a typical star, is an incandescent gaseous globe, 1.39 million km in diameter, with a mass of 2×10^{30} kg, an effective temperature of approximately 5800 K and surface radiant power of 4×10^{20} megawatts (MW). Earth intercepts only 17×10^{10} MW, mostly as visible light and infrared radiation; for comparison, the total generating capacity of Canadian electrical plants is under 10^5 MW. The current theory, called solar nucleosynthesis, states that the sun's power originates in nuclear reactions occurring in a hot (15 million K) core which contains half the solar mass in only 1.5% of its volume. Geological and astronomical evidence suggests that the reactions were triggered 5 billion years ago when the temperature and density at the centre of a condensing cloud of primordial interstellar gas rose to levels where hydrogen atoms fused into helium atoms. The heat released by this NUCLEAR FUSION creates enough internal pressure to counterbalance gravitational contraction. This equilibrium will last for billions of years before the sun's outflow of energy is drastically altered. The theory of solar nucleosynthesis is being challenged because observational tests have failed, so far, to detect the predicted flux of neutrinos, ie, highly penetrating particles which should be emitted abundantly from the sun's nuclear furnace.

Because the sun's visible surface (photosphere) is opaque, the nature of its interior must be deduced by applying fundamental laws of PHYSICS to the measured surface properties. The application of seismic methods to "sunquakes" (ie, vibrations of the entire sun) can fix the location and motions of internal disturbances and reveals that convective turbulence extends to a depth of 200 000 km. Such knowledge is vital to explain sunspot formation. The cool (about 3700 K), strongly magnetic spots are believed to emerge from below the photosphere. They range in size from pores of 1000 km to elongated, irregular clusters of spots spanning 200 000 km. A typical spot, 30 000 km across, emerges in a day or 2, accompanied by smaller companions of opposite magnetic polarity; the group disintegrates in under 2 weeks. Intense magnetic fields exist outside of sunspots as clusters of elements, each element being no more than 300 km across. An active region consists of a sunspot group embedded in irregular, dense aggregates of magnetic elements. The sun moves about its axis by differential rotation: the solar equator rotates in 25 days, a solar parallel of latitude at 60°, in 29 days. This rotation causes churning of the gaseous fluid in the sun's shell, thus generating the magnetic patterns characteristic of sunspot activity. The average number of spots grows and fades in an 11-year cycle. Successive cycles can vary greatly in amplitude; however, extremely low activity can last for almost a century (eg, the "Maunder Minimum," 1645-1715 AD). Solar activity may influence CLIMATE CHANGE on Earth but no direct, physical link has yet been demonstrated.

The sun's rarefied outer atmosphere (chromosphere and corona) is too faint to be visible to the unaided eye, except when the moon blocks the photosphere during a total solar eclipse. The chromosphere then appears as a highly irregular, pink-red band, a few thousand kilometres thick, surrounded by the silvery corona that extends in jagged streamers for millions of kilometres. Magnetic fields shape both regions. A temperature inversion begins 300 km above the photosphere: the top of the chromosphere is 15 000 K hotter than its base; the corona is at 1.5 million K. The explanation of the high tem-

peratures is disputed. The corona is too hot to be restrained by the sun's gravity; it expands as a supersonic solar wind consisting chiefly of electrons, protons and helium atoms and having a speed, near Earth, of 300-800 km/s. The rate of mass loss, millions of tonnes per second, is only 3×10^{-14} solar masses annually.

Explosions called solar flares erupt when stresses stored in magnetically confined structures are suddenly released. Terrestrial side effects of large flares include geomagnetic storms, enhanced NORTHERN LIGHTS and other ionospheric disturbances. In addition, high-speed streams in the solar wind, unrelated to flares or sunspots, strongly agitate the Earth's magnetosphere. These streams originate in "coronal holes," vast spaces of reduced temperature and density, where coronal magnetic field lines are open to interplanetary space.

Canadian research in solar physics dates from the construction in 1905 of spectrographic apparatus at the Dominion Observatory, Ottawa, for application to solar eclipses and to the measurement of the sun's differential rotation. Solar radio ASTRONOMY in Canada began in 1946 at the Radio and Electrical Engineering Division of the NATIONAL RESEARCH COUNCIL, Ottawa. Since then, NRC laboratories have daily monitored the flux of microwaves emitted by the sun at 2800 MHz, a measurement used worldwide as an index of solar activity. NRC's Ottawa River Solar Observatory (est 1970) records and analyses fine chromospheric structures related to sunspot activity and flares. Observations of the sun's far infrared spectrum are made by U of C from stratospheric BALLOONS and high-altitude aircraft. *See also* SOLAR ENERGY.   V. GAIZAUSKAS

Sun, Vancouver's largest daily newspaper (1983 average daily circulation: 228 185), first appeared as the *Vancouver Sun,* 12 Feb 1912, "to consistently advocate the principles of Liberalism." Under publisher Robert Cromie and his sons, notably Donald Cromie, the *Sun* tended to support the Liberals but was often critical of them. The *Sun* expanded by buying out other NEWSPAPERS. With its 1917 purchase of the *Daily News-Advertiser* (est 1886), it claimed to be the city's oldest newspaper; with its 1924 acquisition of the *Evening World* (est 1888), it became undisputedly the city's second most important newspaper. Not until its chief rival, the *Vancouver Daily Province,* suffered a prolonged labour dispute (1946-49) did the *Sun* emerge as the leading journal of the city and province. The majority of Cromie family holdings in Sun Publishing Co were sold to FP Publications Ltd in 1963 and in 1980 SOUTHAM INC bought the newspaper. The *Sun* has been politically independent for many years.   PATRICIA E. ROY

Sun Dance, an annual Plains Indian culture ceremony given at midsummer when bands and tribes congregated at a predetermined location. The Sun Dance was forbidden under the Indian Act of 1885, but this ban was generally ignored and was dropped from the Indian Act of 1951. The ceremony was arranged by an individual either as a request for supernatural aid or in response to a vision. Among the BLACKFOOT and SARCEE, women took the initiative. Following 4 days of preliminary ritual, the Sun Dance lasted another 4 days and focused on erecting the sacred dance pole and the sacred lodge. On the final day a number of dances took place. The Sun-Gaze Dances symbolized capture, torture, captivity and escape, and involved self-torture. Successful dancers enjoyed prestige from that time on. The Sun Dance was an emotional experience for participants and an opportunity to renew kinship ties, arrange marriages and exchange property. *See also* NATIVE PEOPLE, RELIGION; NATIVE PEOPLE: PLAINS.   RENÉ R. GADACZ

Sunday, John, or Shah-wun-dais, meaning "sultry heat," Mississauga (Ojibwa) Chief, Meth-

John Sunday as a young man. Engraving by J. Thomson of a painting by W. Gush, which appeared in the March 1839 issue of *Wesleyan-Methodist Magazine (courtesy Methodist Archives and Research Centre, Manchester, England).*

odist missionary (b at New York C, 1795; d at Alderville, Ont 14 Dec 1875). This hardened warrior, a veteran of the WAR OF 1812, only knew 3 words of English before his conversion to Christianity: "pint," "quart" and "whiskey." After he joined the Methodists in 1826 he immediately stopped drinking and won back his self-respect and the respect of his tribe. An eloquent speaker in Ojibwa, he was a travelling missionary in the Lk Superior region and later in 1836 was ordained a regular minister. Elected chief of his band, the Ojibwa of the Belleville and Kingston area, he presented their LAND CLAIMS to the government of Upper Canada. After his return from a missionary tour of Britain in 1837 he served for 20 years at missions at Alderville, Rice Lk and Muncey. Among his Methodist brethren Shah-wun-dais was in constant demand as a speaker at church gatherings.   DONALD B. SMITH

Sunday Schools, fd 1780 in Gloucester, Eng, by newspaper publisher Robert Raikes, to take labouring children off the streets on Sundays. Religious instruction, later the principal curriculum, was at first secondary to teaching reading and writing. Religious education has been an element in the Roman Catholic Church for some 2000 years, primarily through catechism classes. However, Sunday schools have been limited almost exclusively to the Reformed or Protestant traditions, largely as a legacy of John Calvin's stress on rational learning. Raikes's innovation, quickly copied in Britain, was brought to Canada mainly by the PRESBYTERIAN and CONGREGATIONAL churches.

The date and location of Canada's first Sunday school are unclear. The Church of England (*see* ANGLICANS) had one in Halifax in 1783. A Congregational minister, Rev Francis Dick, may have organized the first Sunday school in the Canadas, in Québec in 1801. The first documented inauguration was by Secessionist Presbyterian minister Rev William Smart, who arrived in Brockville, Ont, 7 Oct 1811 and opened a Sunday school the following Sunday. The movement grew rapidly. The Montréal-based Sunday School Union of Canada was founded probably in 1822, and in 1836 its apparent successor, the Canada Sunday School Union, was formed to promote development in new regions. In 1865 a nationwide convention of teachers and leaders resulted in the new Sunday Schools Association of Canada.

Initially the Bible was the sole curriculum, with much emphasis placed on memorization of scripture. Gradually supplementary curricula were developed locally, and in 1874 the International Uniform Lessons series was introduced, based on current pedagogical methods. In 1908 a graded curriculum became available and refinements followed. The first curriculum developed entirely in Canada was the UNITED CHURCH's "New Curriculum" of 1963. It was attacked in the media by conservative denominations for being too "liberal" in its theology and ended several decades of curriculum co-operation between the United and BAPTIST churches. Though widely praised by educators and theologians and copied in varying degrees by other denominations, the New Curriculum had the misfortune to be introduced just when Sunday school populations began to plummet in all denominations. United Church registration declined from 757 338 in 1961 to 231 535 in 1981; during the same period some 1400 Sunday schools were closed.

Other denominations experienced similar losses. Sociologist Reginald Bibby notes that 2 out of 3 Canadian adults claim to have attended religious services regularly as children, but only one in 3 now exposes children to religious education in the churches. Since the Protestant churches have traditionally depended on Sunday schools as the source of adult memberships, Bibby forecasts church attendance declining to one in 6 by the turn of the century.   C.J. TAYLOR

Sunflower (genus *Helianthus*), common name for annual or perennial herbaceous PLANTS native to the Western Hemisphere and belonging to the family Compositae. Some N American Indians grew a species of sunflower, later brought to Europe by Spanish explorers. It evolved into an important crop (*H. annuus* var. *macrocarpa*) in Russia in the 18th century and was introduced to Canada in 1875. Modern cultivars (commercial varieties) are mainly single cross or three-way hybrids. Sunflowers grow 1.25-1.75 m tall and mature in 90-120 days. The more important or OILSEED type has dark, thin-hulled seeds, with 40-50% oil content. The confectionery type has larger, lighter-coloured seeds, with thicker hulls and lower oil content. Sunflowers grow in soils ranging from sand to clay, but prefer well-drained soils. Intertillage and herbicides control weeds. PLANT DISEASE is controlled by resistant cultivars and rotations with crops not attacked by the several pathogens of sunflowers. Natural parasites, insecticides and cultural practices combat INSECT PESTS. The highly polyunsaturated oil, popular for cooking, is also used in margarine and mayonnaise. The high-protein meal remaining after the oil is extracted is formulated into livestock feeds. Confectionery seed is sold whole, roasted and salted, or dehulled. Significant Canadian seed production started with 2000 ha in 1943. Recent plantings, over 90% being of the oilseed type, have ranged up to 155 000 ha, mostly in Manitoba.   ERIC D. PUTT

Sunshine Sketches of a Little Town, by Stephen LEACOCK (Toronto, New York, London, 1912), is a series of vignettes dramatizing the comedy of day-to-day life in Mariposa, bustling and big-time small town on the shores of the magnificent Lake Wissanotti. Thrumming with self-importance, endowed with a solemnly quirky populace, Mariposa is modeled on ORILLIA, Ont; for generations of readers, it has also been the centre of Leacock's fondest and most amusing portrait of small-town life. Leacock's humour depends on his gift for creating a straight-faced storyteller, an earnestly deadpan narrator who cannot imagine what his readers are laughing about. Nowhere is this gift more apparent than in Leacock's warm but gently mocking scrutiny of the foibles and pretensions of his Mariposan Canadians.   NEIL BESNER

Superior, Lake, area 82 103 km², of which 28 749 km² lies in Canada; elev 183 m. It is 563 km long, 257 km wide and 406 m at its greatest depth. The lake is fed by some 200 rivers, including the Nipigon, St Louis (formerly Pigeon), Pic, White, Michipicoten and Kaministikwia, and it discharges via the St Mary's R into Lk Huron. Being the most northwesterly of the GREAT LAKES, it was called Lac Supérieur by the French, a name that is appropriate in English as well — Superior is the largest freshwater lake in the world. It has 2 large islands: Isle Royale, which is a US national park, and Michipicoten in Canadian waters, which is being considered for an Ontario provincial park.

Vast, remote, deep and cold, with sheer rock cliffs rising on the N shore, the lake's austere beauty has become part of the Canadian imagination. The tale of billions of years of GEOLOGICAL HISTORY is exposed in its rocks. Stromatolites, the oldest fossils found anywhere, have been found in the rocks along Whitefish R — evidence of life 1.8 billion years ago. At AGAWA BAY, volcanic action has created one of the finest pebble beaches in the world. The rocks around Superior also contain valuable mineral deposits, especially IRON ORE in the great Mesabi Range in Minnesota. Silver was taken from beneath the lake at SILVER ISLET and copper was mined by the Indians long before the arrival of Europeans. Gold has recently been discovered at Hemlo, some 30 km E of Marathon.

Etienne BRÛLÉ was likely the first European to see the lake (1622). Hugues Randin was in the SAULT STE MARIE area around 1670, and Sieur DULHUT laid formal claim to the area around the lake in 1679. For 100 years the voyageurs braved the storms of Superior and carried furs along the N shore to GRAND PORTAGE and later FORT WILLIAM. Ft Michipicoten, at the eastern end of the lake, was established in 1725 and operated until 1904. After 1855 a ship canal was completed at Sault Ste Marie, and steamers passed in increasing numbers as huge quantities of grain and iron ore were carried to the lower lakes. Today, THUNDER BAY is the second-largest port by volume in Canada. LAKE SUPERIOR PROVINCIAL PARK fronts on the lake between the Montréal and Michipicoten rivers and PUKASKWA NATIONAL PARK between the Pukaskwa and White rivers. The parks preserve a rugged environment of ancient mountains scoured in the last ICE AGE.
JAMES MARSH

Supply and Services, Department of, is the purchasing and accounting arm of the federal government. It was established in 1969 through the merger of the departments of defence production and public printing and stationery (Queen's Printer), the shipbuilding branch of the transport department, the office of the comptroller of the treasury, the central data-processing service bureau of the Treasury Board and the bureau of management consulting services from the Public Service Commission. The 2 branches (*Supply* and *Services*) operate under their own deputy ministers. The supply administration is responsible for purchasing, printing, publishing, traffic management, security, equipment maintenance and repair for the federal public service. It offers its services to customers on a cost-recovery basis. The services administration provides payment or cheque-issuing services for all federal departments and accounting, auditing and computer services for federal departments and agencies. The minister of supply and services acts as the receiver general for Canada and reports to Parliament for Crown Assets Disposal Corporation, the Royal Canadian Mint and STATISTICS CANADA. The department's 1984-85 budget was $233 million.

Supreme Court of Canada has been the highest court for all legal issues of federal and provincial jurisdiction since 1949, when appeals to the JUDICIAL COMMITTEE OF THE PRIVY COUNCIL OF THE UK were abolished. In 1875 Parliament passed a statute of the CONSTITUTION ACT, 1867 (s101), establishing a General Court of Appeal for Canada and an Exchequer Court (now FEDERAL COURT OF CANADA). The creation of the Supreme Court had caused sharp debate among the FATHERS OF CONFEDERATION. In 1865 John A. MACDONALD argued that the Constitution did not anticipate the creation of such a court, and attempts by his Conservative government in 1867 and 1870 to set up a general court of appeal suffered overwhelming defeat. Many Liberal and Conservative MPs opposed the project, fearing the possible consequences for provincial rights. By establishing a supreme court, Parliament would be providing itself with a constitutional interpreter, and some MPs questioned the impartiality of such an arbiter because the federal government would appoint its members and determine the court's field of competency. The Liberal government of Alexander MACKENZIE finally persuaded Parliament to vote for a supreme court, arguing that it was needed to standardize Canadian law and provide constitutional interpretations on issues that would affect the evolution of the new federation.

A chief justice and 8 puisne (junior) justices, appointed by the governor-in-council, comprise the Supreme Court. Members may be selected from among provincial superior court judges, or from among those barristers and advocates who have belonged to a provincial bar for at

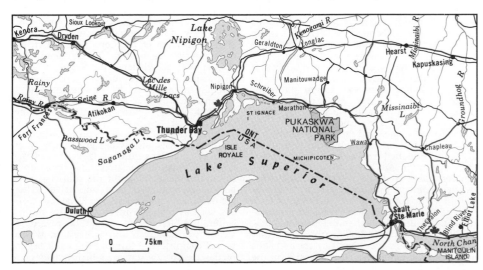

least 10 years (see JUDICIARY). The Supreme Court Act stipulates that at least 3 of the judges be appointed from Québec; they can be judges of the Court of Queen's Bench (appeal court), the Superior Court or lawyers. Traditionally, 3 other judges from Ontario, one from the Maritimes and 2 from the western provinces are appointed. The judges may not hold any other salaried position while sitting on the Supreme Court Bench. The Supreme Court meets in Jan, Apr and Oct. Five justices constitute a quorum, but for constitutional cases the justices normally sit as a full court. Under the Supreme Court Act (s55), the court not only pronounces judgement but also advises the federal and provincial governments on important questions of law or fact concerning the interpretation of the constitution, or the constitutionality or interpretation of federal or provincial legislation, or the powers of Parliament and the provincial legislatures. The most famous and perhaps most important of these opinions is that of 28 Sept 1981 on the constitutionality of the patriation of the constitution.

The Supreme Court is also a general court of appeal for criminal cases. In theory any citizen may come before the Supreme Court to plead his own case, but such instances are rare. In criminal cases the court will hear appeals if an acquittal has been set aside or if there has been a dissenting judgement in a provincial Court of Appeal on a point of law. A guilty verdict in a case of first-degree murder may automatically be appealed to the Supreme Court. If it first grants leave to appeal, the court may also hear appeals on questions of law arising from summary convictions or indictable offences. In civil cases appeals may only be presented with the prior permission of the court; such permission is granted when the court believes that the case raises a question of public importance or an important issue of law or of mixed law and fact that ought to be decided by the court in the national interest. The DRYBONES and MURDOCH cases are 2 famous examples. The limitation on appeals was included in the 1975 modifications to the Supreme Court Act. However, the number of appeals on constitutional or administrative issues has increased.

In about 75% of its cases, the court explains its reasoning along with its decision. In about 66% of these cases, it has upheld the decision of the lower court. Normally the justices go into conference immediately after the argument of a case, review its elements and compare their opinions. One of the justices drafts the court's judgement. If, after receiving and reading this judgement, his colleagues disagree with it, there may be further work sessions. In principle, the court tries to hand down unanimous verdicts, but frequently this cannot be done, and the justices who disagree with the majority opinion write a dissenting judgement which is published along with the other. These dissensions are very important because they permit jurists to see the tendencies at work within the court. The rules of procedure ensure that the parties provide the court with a dossier of everything that happened in the court of first instance and in appeal, including all transcripts and main procedural documents. As well, parties must present a factum containing a summary of the case facts, the points in dispute, the reasons the case is being pursued and their conclusions.

After Confederation the Judicial Committee of the Privy Council was the major interpreter of the Constitution Act. With difficulty the Judicial Committee established a certain balance between federal and provincial legislative responsibilities. The committee had to interpret texts which in a number of ways were more appropriate to a unitary state than to a federated one. In 1949 the important question arose of whether the Supreme Court was bound by the decisions of the Judicial Committee. It is essential for the

functioning of Canada's judicial system — which is based primarily on common law, on precedent as an authority and on respect for the rule of STARE DECISIS — that courts of appeal ensure uniform application of law. This principle of upholding judgements, which means the decision of a superior court is binding on lower courts, is the very heart of the judicial system. The principle also means that the courts are to some extent bound by their own judgements. Although the Judicial Committee of the Privy Council did not respect this rule rigorously, generally it took its own previous decisions into account. Until 1949 the Supreme Court had to respect the judgement of the Judicial Committee on appeals of its decisions. Even though it now seems the court is no longer legally bound to follow decisions of the Judicial Committee and reserves for itself the right to examine and review those decisions, as well as its own, it frequently refers to Judicial Committee judgements and always feels the need to explain carefully any decision it may take which appears to run contrary to them. This is a fortunate development because it allows the court greater creativity, but it can be dangerous in constitutional matters, given the problems that may arise from disregard for the federalist principles that were firmly established by the Judicial Committee.

The few Supreme Court decisions overturned by the Judicial Committee were not in fact significant. The Supreme Court had tended to interpret the Constitution Act very literally, whereas the Judicial Committee had taken sociopolitical considerations into account in its decision making. It is usually said that the Judicial Committee favoured the provinces but that the Supreme Court was and still is centralist in nature, an oversimplified view of Canada's JURISPRUDENCE. In fact, the difference between these 2 great interpreters is essentially one of approach. The Judicial Committee was frequently more political than juridical, whereas the Supreme Court, until recently, stuck to strictly legal interpretations. It is also true that some of the Judicial Committee judgements that most favoured the provinces seemed to amount to legal sleight-of-hand. The English high court had managed to give a federalist character to the Canadian constitution that had not necessarily been implied in the Constitution Act. Moreover, all Judicial Committee judgements are publicly unanimous, precluding more balanced thought within the committee and encouraging the domination of some committee members by others. It would probably be more accurate to arrive at the history of the Judicial Committee's constitutional interpretation by studying the lords who have sat on its bench than by studying their decisions. The controversial question of whether courts must interpret the law and the constitution in a literal, textual sense or consider as well the social, political and economic context is now more important than ever, because of the patriation of the Constitution with its CANADIAN CHARTER OF RIGHTS AND FREEDOMS. The Charter will be whatever the Supreme Court chooses to make it, because only a constitutional amendment approved by Parliament and 7 provinces totalling at least 50% of the population of all the provinces may alter a Supreme Court decision.

The new role of the court, with its social and political dimensions, will significantly alter the way Canadians think of it. Reform of the method of appointing justices and of the composition and methodology of the court has also become important. The court must try to reflect the dominant characteristics of Canadian society, such as regionalism, dualism and multiculturalism. Its reform should be part of a second phase of constitutional reform which would complete and improve the work begun by the CONSTITUTION ACT, 1982, which provides for

the necessity of the unanimous consent of the provinces for any modification of the Supreme Court's composition and the necessity of an amendment by general procedure for its other elements. GIL RÉMILLARD

Reading: Articles commemorating the 100th anniversary of the Supreme Court of Canada appear in special editions of the *Alberta Law Review* 14 (1976) and *Canadian Bar Review* 53 (1975). Also see Paul Weiler, *In the Last Resort* (1974).

Surfacing, novel by Margaret ATWOOD (Toronto, 1972; New York and London, 1973). *Surfacing* takes its title from its central metaphor, dramatizing a woman's passage from a precarious sense of self through madness towards a fuller identity. The novel is a powerfully poetic and political exploration of Canadian consciousness, personal and social, defined against a metaphorically "American" state of mind. To be "American" is to be violently depersonalized, disembodied, without a language, a past or a relation with nature. The woman and 3 friends go to her father's isolated cottage in northern Québec where, after a few days, relationships deteriorate and sexuality becomes a currency to bargain with. The woman's search for her missing father ends with the discovery of his drowned body, precipitating her descent into temporary, healing madness before she surfaces with a less "American," saner vision. The novel has been translated into French as *Faire Surface* (Montréal, 1978). NEIL BESNER

Surrey, BC, District Municipality, pop 147 138 (1981c), area 36 039 ha, inc 1879, is the second-largest municipality in BC, after Vancouver. Part of the Greater Vancouver Regional Dist, it is bounded by the FRASER R on the N and the state of Washington on the S. The municipalities of Langley and Delta lie to the E and W. The residential development of Surrey is spread along 3 upland areas of glacial till extending into N Delta, Langley and White Rock. Intervening lowland areas of peat and other deltaic materials are primarily agricultural, and the floodplains of the Fraser R are used for industry.

Surrey grew slowly in the beginning, with lumbering and agriculture as the main industries. A double-span bridge across the Fraser (1904) provided Surrey's only access to New Westminster and Vancouver until the Pattullo Bridge was built in 1937. Railways and roads brought steady industrial and commercial growth, which was furthered by an influx of people from the drought-stricken Prairies in the 1930s. Political unrest led to the secession in 1957 of Ward 7, which became the municipality of White Rock. In 1960 the opening of the Port Mann Bridge and subsequent freeway development brought further growth and change. A 5-town concept emerged, with Whalley, Guildford, Newton, Cloverdale, and South Surrey developing around shopping malls, recreation facilities, housing, green belts, industrial lands and farms.

Key features of the economy are manufacturing (sawmilling and metal fabrication), wholesaling, agriculture and commerce (especially in Guildford Town Centre and Surrey Place Mall). Surrey is governed by a mayor and 8 aldermen and has a full range of educational and recreational facilities. ALAN F.J. ARTIBISE

Surrey, Philip Henry, painter (b at Calgary 8 Oct 1910). He studied at the Winnipeg School of Art (1926-27), with Fred VARLEY in Vancouver, and at the Art Students League, New York (1936). Surrey was a member of the Eastern Group of Painters and a founding member of the Contemporary Arts Soc (1939). The surrealistic tendencies in his work melded well with the society's goal of promoting modern art movements in a Canadian context. His cityscapes have dreamlike groupings of figures taking part in familiar activities, often in juxtaposition, conveying more than one level of reality (eg, *La Procession* 1940). The aim of Surrey's type of illusion is to caution the viewer to question perceptions of reality and to address the problems of city life.   KATHLEEN LAVERTY

Survenant, Le (1945), a novel by Germaine GUÈVREMONT — the first in a projected trilogy — depicts the life of the HABITANT with a blend of sympathy and sophistication new to French Canadian fiction. Set in Le Chenal du Moine, near Sorel, Qué, it employs local speech and folklore to portray the daily and seasonal rhythms of a passing era. A figure of mythical proportions, the "survenant" (mysterious stranger) doubles as the heroic son whom Didace Beauchemin has failed to produce and the romantic suitor whom Angélina Desmarais has secretly desired. For a year, Venant unsuccessfully fights the wanderlust setting him apart from his neighbours. Revisiting the romantic myth of MARIA CHAPDELAINE and the naturalistic tragedy of TRENTE ARPENTS, Guèvremont's novel survived as a popular radio and television serial. *The Outlander* (1950; published in England as *Monk's Reach*), Eric Sutton's translation of the novel and its sequel, *Marie-Didace* (1947), won the Governor General's Award.   MICHÈLE LACOMBE

Surveying is the scientific measurement of natural or man-made features of the Earth's surface. On any area of land to be measured, it is always possible to choose 2 points and measure the distance between them, thus creating a line which can be drawn to scale on a map, plan or section (*see* CARTOGRAPHY). Other points can be located, relative to the line, by taking 2 other measurements, which can also be drawn to scale. These measurements may be 2 angles, one measured line and one angle, or 2 measured lines. From these measurements, a map can be built up with the features accurately located with reference to each other. Surveying is used to make maps of all kinds, accurately locate buildings and engineering works (eg, dams, bridges, tunnels), establish property lines, chart waterways, and position such devices as SATELLITES and oceangoing oil-drilling platforms.

Location of points is made through operations which deal with the 2 dimensions of the horizontal plane and those which locate the vertical or levelling plane. Plane surveys of small areas treat the surveyed area as a horizontal plane, perpendicular to the direction of gravity as defined by a plumb bob (ie, a suspended weight which, when hanging freely, points to the Earth's centre). Plane surveys are limited to an area of about 250 km². In larger areas, the discrepancy between the horizontal plane and the curvature of the Earth's surface becomes too great. Geodetic surveys correct for the curvature by establishing a network of precisely located "control points" on the surface. They are used to locate the position of parallels of latitude and meridians of longitude and to build up a grid to serve as a control for other types of survey work. Cadastral or land surveying determines property lines and other legal boundaries. Hydrographic surveys chart the features of waterways, determining the shape of coastlines, currents, underwater terrain and the position of shoals and other hazards to navigation (*see* HYDROGRAPHY).

Until very recently, manually controlled instruments were used to take distance and angular measurements. The surveyor's chain, introduced in 1620, was 66 feet (about 20 m) long, composed of 100 links. The chain was used as a standard measurement in many Canadian surveys, eg, the Dominion Lands Survey, until replaced by steel tapes. Distance could also be determined though the use of telescopic sighting devices (eg, transit) and optical devices (eg, range finder). Angular measurements were made with the theodolite and the transit, telescopic measuring devices that permitted precise de-

termination of angles between 2 sighted targets. Astronomical observations and magnetic compass readings were used to determine location and magnetic bearings, while levels and barometers were used for vertical measurement.

On larger projects electronic instruments, which use radio, RADAR or LASER frequencies to determine distance very precisely, are employed. Signals may be bounced off a reflector target and received by the instrument again; or signals may be sent out to a repeating transmitter which rebroadcasts them immediately back to the transmitter. In both cases, the elapsed time is measured, allowing precise determination of distance. Many of these electronic distance meters provide a simultaneous printout of measurements being made. Location through the satellite method involves triangulation from a point on Earth to the position of 2 satellites and is exact to millionths of a metre. Calculations can be made and co-ordinated through computers, which can also be used as an aid in plotting maps and sections.

Photogrammetry, the method of determining the shapes and sizes of objects and their relative positions using photographs, has been in use since the 1860s. Aerial photogrammetric techniques (ie, aerial surveys) have been developing in Canada since about 1920. REMOTE SENSING is a more recent technology which uses information or images from orbiting satellites, such as the Landsat satellite, to build up comprehensive data on features of Earth's surface.

Canada has a land area of nearly 10 million km²; hence, survey work has developed as a major public enterprise. After Confederation, 1867, a vigorous period of BOUNDARIES surveying began, with the determination of the FORTY-NINTH PARALLEL between the Rocky Mts and Lake of the Woods completed in 1874. By 1925 the joint Canadian-American INTERNATIONAL BOUNDARY COMMISSION had completed work on about 8000 km of border between the YT and Alaska, western Canada and the US and through the Great Lakes and eastern Canada to the Bay of FUNDY.

The Dominion Lands Survey of the Dominion Lands Branch was established in 1871 to survey the western territories of the HUDSON'S BAY COMPANY, which had become part of Canada (*see* RUPERT'S LAND; DOMINION LANDS POLICY). Under J.S. Dennis from the office of the surveyor general, work began to divide the newly acquired lands into 6 mile square (10 km by 10 km) townships, containing 36 sections of 640 acres (about 259 ha) and, thus, open the lands for settlement. The areas surveyed were record breaking. In 1883 about 11 million ha were surveyed in connection with land grants to the CANADIAN PACIFIC RY, along its western route.

The GEOLOGICAL SURVEY OF CANADA was founded in 1842 under Sir William LOGAN. Throughout the 19th and early 20th century, exploratory and geological surveys were performed in remote regions of the country by adventurous surveyors such as A.P. LOW, G.M. DAWSON, D.B. Dowling, R.G. MCCONNELL and J.L. Charles. In the same period, hydrographic and topographic surveying intensified. Edouard DEVILLE introduced photogrammetric techniques into surveying, while the work of Otto Klotz and W.F. KING in extending longitude meridians to the Pacific led to the founding of the Dominion Observatory for ASTRONOMY in Ottawa.

Canadian surveying techniques have undergone continuous refinement in the 20th century and precise maps have now been made for all parts of the country. The accuracy of present-day surveying is an important factor in sophisticated transportation networks, major hydro-electric installations, communications networks and other facilities where safety and success depend upon exact location. Surveying is an important field within CIVIL ENGINEERING and students can receive training at schools or faculties

of engineering or other educational establishments (eg, RYERSON POLYTECHNICAL INSTITUTE). Graduates may complete articling programs to become eligible to take the Canada Land Surveyor examinations.   CLAUDE LAJEUNESSE

Reading: D.W. Thomson, *Men and Meridians,* 3 vols (1966, 1967, 1969).

Survival: A Thematic Guide to Canadian Literature, by Margaret ATWOOD (Toronto, 1972), has enjoyed a controversial, sometimes heated reception. Readers who disagree with Atwood find her thesis — that most Canadian literature deals with victims of various types, and that "grim survival" is its central theme — forced, and argue that she has selected works which will support her argument. But those who see more merit in Atwood's thesis find the book challenging and exciting. In either case, *Survival* is written with intelligence, candour and wit and has had a powerful influence on readers of Canadian literature.   NEIL BESNER

Sutherland, Donald, actor (b at Saint John 17 July 1934). His tall, earnest and diffident image is a familiar one throughout the world: he is now probably Canada's best-known film actor. After studying at U of T, he trained in the UK and appeared on the London stage before beginning his prolific movie career. Although most of his work has been for Hollywood, he has been seen in some Canadian movies, such as *Act of the Heart* (1970), *Murder by Decree* (1979) and *Threshold* (1981), where, apart from his gifts as an actor, his high visibility has attracted investment dollars and his nationality has satisfied Canadian-content requirements. He has made notable appearances in *The Dirty Dozen* (1967), *M*A*S*H* (1970), *Klute* (1971), *Don't Look Now* (1973), *Day of the Locust* (1975), *Invasion of the Body Snatchers* (1978), *Ordinary People* (1980) and *Eye of the Needle* (1981) and also in the CBC television drama *Bethune* (1977). His reputation for seriousness, his evident distaste for the Hollywood glitz-parade, and his unique physical appearance prompted Bertolucci to cast him in *1900* (1976) and Fellini to give him the title role in *Casanova* (1976): together the epitome of his "gargoyle phase." Unlike many internationally successful Canadians, he is affectionately regarded in his own country.   WILLIAM BEARD

Sutherland, John, writer, editor (b at Liverpool, NS 21 Feb 1919; d at Toronto 1 Sept 1956). Sutherland's formal studies (Queen's 1936-37 and McGill 1941-42) were interrupted by ill health which dogged him all his life. He brought critical insight and energy to his editorship of the important literary journal, *First Statement* (1943-45). This journal eventually merged with another, *Preview,* to become NORTHERN REVIEW, first appearing in 1946. Through his fervent, Marxist-slanted criticism and editing, he championed the emergence of modern Canadian literature. Poetry became his dominant interest at the end of his life, at which time he was a convert to Catholicism. This religious conversion informed his book on the poetry of E.J. PRATT. A collection of his writing is *John Sutherland: Essays, Controversies and Poems,* ed by Miriam Waddington (1972).   PETER STEVENS

Sutil and Mexicana In 1792, after exploratory voyages by Spaniards Manuel Quimper (1790) and Francisco de Eliza (1791), the extent of JUAN DE FUCA STR remained a mystery. Some still believed the strait held the entry to the fabled NORTHWEST PASSAGE. Moreover, pressures caused by the NOOTKA SOUND CONTROVERSY suggested the strait as a possible boundary between Spanish and British territories.

Alejandro Malaspina, who had completed his own voyage to the NORTHWEST COAST in 1791 (*see* MALASPINA EXPEDITION), recommended Dionisio Alcalá-Galiano and Cayetano Valdés to command the small schooners *Sutil* and *Mexicana.*

They were to survey the strait and the coast S to San Francisco. In early June 1792 they visited the Spanish post of Nuñez Gaona [Neah Bay, Wash] and, guided by Indian chief Tetacu, they crossed to Vancouver I. After charting many of the Gulf Is, on June 21 the Spaniards sighted George VANCOUVER's *Discovery* and *Chatham* near present-day Vancouver. Each side was mortified to discover its major competitor, but relations were amicable. The 2 groups shared provisions and information before continuing separately to circumnavigate Vancouver I. The 4-month Spanish expedition produced a wealth of geographical and ethnological information, but no evidence of usable resources. The voyage became better known than other Spanish expeditions since the government permitted publication of the journal in 1802. *See* SPANISH EXPLORATION.

CHRISTON I. ARCHER

Suttles, Duncan, chess grandmaster (b at San Francisco, Calif 21 Dec 1945). He moved to Vancouver as a child and became Canada's second grandmaster in 1972. He played on 6 Canadian national teams in the World Olympiads beginning at Tel Aviv (1964), and represented Canada in the Interzonal tournaments of 1967 and 1970. He won the Canadian Closed Championship in 1969 and the Canadian Open in Ottawa in 1973. In 1975 he retired from tournaments to concentrate on stock analysis and correspondence chess. In 1981 he received the title of correspondence grandmaster and returned to over-the-board play to share first place in international competition in Vancouver. Suttles is a pioneer of modern chess strategy, particularly the King's Fianchetto Defence. LAWRENCE DAY

Sutton, Catherine, née Sonego, or Nahne bahwequay, or "upright woman", Mississauga (Ojibwa) spokesperson (b on the Credit R flats, UC 1824; d in Sarawak Township, Canada W 26 Sept 1865); niece of Peter JONES. She grew up on the Credit R Mission, but because of her marriage to Englishman William Sutton she eventually lost the Indian annuity money owing her and her children. Annoyed by the Indian dept's treatment of both her family and Indians in general the determined Mrs Sutton went to England in 1860, even obtaining a private audience with Queen Victoria. Little changed, however, and 2 years later she wrote bitterly that the whites' "ideas of justice [were] that might is right." DONALD B. SMITH

Suzor-Coté, Marc-Aurèle De Foy, painter, sculptor, church decorator (b at Arthabaska, Qué 5 Apr 1869; d at Daytona Beach, Fla 27 Jan 1937). Suzor-Coté's highly successful career was the result of his sure talent, extroverted personality and favorable circumstances. In secondary school, his talent for drawing attracted attention and in 1887 he became involved in the church decoration projects of the Joseph Rousseau company of St-Hyacinthe. Through family connections, he met Wilfrid LAURIER from whom he secured numerous commissions. He led a cosmopolitan existence between 1891 and 1912, travelling constantly between Canada, the US and Europe. He studied in France (1891-94, 1897-1901) where he acquired sound training from Bonnat at the École des beaux-arts, and later from Harpignies, and in the open studios of Julian and Colarossi. From 1892 on, he attracted attention at exhibitions of the Art Assn of Montreal (he won the Jessie Dow award for *Les fumées, port de Montréal* in 1912), at the Salons of the Société des artistes français in Paris as early as 1894, and at Royal Canadian Academy of Arts exhibitions. In 1901, William Scott and Son of Montréal became his dealer, spreading his popularity. Further travels between 1904-07 and 1911-12 firmly established his reputation. As his fame grew, however, so did his desire for a more private life. After 1912 he worked

in the Arthabaska studio he had built in 1895 and in his Montréal studio. He mastered pastels as well as oils, and in 1911 began developing his talent for sculpting, in which he excelled after 1918. In this medium he returned to the rural subjects of his canvases and, inspired by his surroundings or by literary works such as *Maria Chapdelaine,* he gave them new life. An historical painter, he was able to capture famous historical events as well as depicted winter scenes in which he translated the essence of his subject with subtle use of colour and disciplined execution. A master artist, he had to abandon all his activity after becoming paralysed in 1927.

LAURIER LACROIX

Suzuki, Aiko, fibre artist (b at Vancouver 1937). Although not a weaver or tapestry designer in the traditional sense, she is one of a growing number of Canadian artists who use fibres and textile techniques as a medium for expressing abstract concepts. She began her artistic career as a painter, but her involvement with the TORONTO DANCE THEATRE in the late 1960s as a free-form set designer opened unexpected possibilities for her creativity. She worked with strands of fibre to explore 3-dimensional spatial forms of dramatic, emotional impact. Her suspended fibre sculpture, *Lyra,* was installed in the Toronto Public Library in 1981. REBECCA SISLER

Suzuki, David Takayoshi, geneticist, broadcaster (b at Vancouver 24 Mar 1936). Of Japanese parentage (he was interned with his family in WWII), Suzuki joined UBC after study at the universities of Amherst and Chicago (PhD 1961) and in 1969 won a Steacie Memorial Fellowship as the best young Canadian scientist. He specialized in meiosis, the early division of living cells where differentiation begins (eg, between reproductive and other cells), and the study of mutations caused by changes in temperature. The TV series "Suzuki on Science" began to make him a public figure in 1971. While continuing his university teaching and research in GENETICS, he wrote widely on science and SCIENCE POLICY, created the radio series "Quirks and Quarks" in 1976, and served on the SCIENCE COUNCIL. Some academic colleagues criticized Suzuki's broadcasting as a waste of his talents, but Suzuki was convinced that public awareness of science would contribute to both better science policies and an enriched culture. His rare combination of personal charm and scientific ability, as displayed for 10 years in the CBC-TV series "The Nature of Things," have made Suzuki a unique figure in English-speaking Canada.

DONALD J.C. PHILLIPSON

Sverdrup, Otto Neumann, arctic explorer (b at Bindal, Norway 31 Oct 1854; d at Oslo 26 Nov 1930). An experienced sailor and outdoorsman, he was introduced to arctic travel by Fridtjof Nansen, who invited him in 1888 to ski across Greenland's interior. From 1893 to 1896 Sverdrup was captain of Nansen's ship *Fram* when it made its celebrated drift across the top of the world. Sverdrup is known chiefly for his expedition to the ELLESMERE I area between 1898 and 1902. During 4 winters in the ice he discovered several islands W of Ellesmere and mapped large portions of the High Arctic. Eventually Canada claimed this territory and purchased Sverdrup's maps. DANIEL FRANCIS

Sverdrup Islands, located in the High Arctic, comprise a large island, AXEL HEIBERG, and 2 smaller ones, ELLEF RINGNES and AMUND RINGNES. Their geological history began as an area of subsidence and sedimentation on a landmass margin. Deformation occurred, followed by a second episode of uplift. In the early Tertiary, after a long period of sedimentation, the basin sediments were folded and faulted and the present land surface was uplifted and mountains formed. Today, glaciers occupy a large

proportion of the mountainous area — some reaching the sea. A narrow coastal strip of thin sediments was laid down in the early Pleistocene along the arctic shore. The discovery of these islands by the Second Norwegian Polar Expedition (1902), under the command of Otto SVERDRUP, led to a sovereignty dispute, settled in Canada's favour only in 1931. DOUG FINLAYSON

Swallow (Hirundinidae), small family of BIRDS including 80 species worldwide, of which 7 breed in Canada, including the PURPLE MARTIN. All feed mainly on flying insects, spending much time in flight. Their long wings give the impression of a larger bird, but they are actually small. Many are colonial, build nests in enclosed situations, and lay 4-6 eggs. In Canada most swallows rear one brood annually; in the West, barn swallows raise 2. Several species nest around settlements. Native swallows fall into 3 groups. The brown-backed species, bank swallow (*Riparia riparia*), and northern roughwinged swallow (*Stelgidopteryx serripennis*), nest in burrows in sea cliffs or riverbanks and in crevices in rock cliffs, respectively. Both range across the continent. Bank swallows are found far into the North and in Europe. Northern rough-winged swallows enter Canada only in the south, ranging down to S America. Tree swallows (*Tachycineta bicolor*) and violet-green swallows (*T. thalassina*) are early migrants, harbingers of spring. Both are iridescent bluegreen above and white below. They nest in treeholes or nest boxes. Tree swallows range across Canada, N to TREELINE; violet-green swallows are strictly western. Cliff swallows (*Hirundo pyrrhonota*) and barn swallows (*H. rustica*) are metallic blue above and rusty brown below. Both construct nests from clay pellets in situations sheltered from rain and runoff water. The enclosed, gourd-shaped nests of cliff swallows are under cliff overhangs or eaves. Originally, barn swallows nested in caves or under cliff overhangs; now, they almost always nest under eaves of or inside buildings. Canadian swallows do not sing but all have distinctive call notes. They are accomplished, graceful fliers. In late summer, they mass in flocks on roadside wires, often several species together. Within a few weeks they have gone S, not returning to Canada for 7-8 months. A.J. ERSKINE

Seven species of swallow breed in Canada, including the tree swallow (*Tachycineta bicolor*), an early migrant and harbinger of spring (*photo by Tim Fitzharris*).

Swamp, Marsh and Bog, the most common wetland habitats, are similar in having the WATER table at, near or above the soil surface or root layer of plants. The most important factors influencing development and maintenance of these wetlands are CLIMATE, mineral nutrient availability, water levels and water flow. Their most obvious distinguishing features are the plant species characteristically found in each and the amount of standing water present.

Swamp, wetland characterized by the presence of TREES growing on silty to organic muck soils, usually occurring along river floodplains and in poorly drained basins. Swamps are often inundated seasonally, or remain continuously flooded (as do saltwater mangrove swamps of tropical coastlines). Most swamps in N America are found in the southeastern US and in the GREAT LAKES region, where common deciduous swamp trees include red maple, black ash, white elm and silver maple. Eastern white cedar, a conifer, is commonly found throughout and forms dense swamp forests on shallow, wet soils where limestone bedrock is near the surface.

Marsh, treeless wetland where lush growths of herbaceous plants (eg, GRASSES, SEDGES, reeds and CATTAILS) predominate. Marshes usually form in quiet shallows of ponds, lakes and rivers, and along sheltered coastlines where mineral nutrients are available. Freshwater marshes are abundant and widely scattered across N America. A particularly important concentration, found in the prairie pothole region stretching from the south-central Prairie provinces and northern Montana to the Dakotas and western Minnesota, is the most important WATERFOWL nesting area on the continent. Saltwater marshes are restricted to temperate regions. In N America, they are found mainly along the southern and eastern coastlines from the Gulf of Mexico states to the Maritime provinces. In western N America, numerous inland saltwater marshes fringe the shores of saltwater lakes (the remnants of ancient seas) and alkali ponds. Marshes are highly productive ecosystems, teeming with life.

Bog, poorly drained, peat-filled depression dominated by *Sphagnum* mosses, evergreen shrubs of the heather family and CONIFERS. The water table, at or near the surface of the living moss layer, may be visible as open pools of water. The extensive cover of sphagnum mosses makes bog waters acidic, preventing the growth of many micro-organisms. Because of lack of adequate water movement for aeration, water is low in oxygen, and because of the insulating effect of the surface blanket of moss, it is also relatively cold. As a result, little decay occurs in the accumulating layers of organic debris which build up as peat. Bogs are only one of several kinds of wetlands, called "peatlands," that develop in cool, moist, previously glaciated regions of the Northern Hemisphere. In countries such as Ireland, dried peat has traditionally been used as fuel. Peat moss is also used extensively as a soil conditioner. *See* BIOMASS ENERGY; GROUNDWATER. ERICH HABER

Reading: P.D. Moore and D.J. Bellamy, *Peatlands* (1974); W.A. Niering, *The Life of the Marsh* (1966).

Swamp Angel, Ethel Wilson's finest novel (Toronto, 1954), follows Maggie Vardoe's movement from an unhappy marriage toward the vision she gains by re-establishing her own identity. Maggie's flight from Vancouver into the BC interior symbolizes her return to the natural world of time, change and mortality. Through serene passages of natural description and quiet evocations of Maggie's strength, Wilson makes her character's transformation seem to arise naturally but also dramatically out of her circumstances; like its protagonist, *Swamp Angel* moves quietly but with assurance toward its realization. NEIL BESNER

Swan, large WATERFOWL with elongated neck and narrow patch of naked skin in front of the eye. Swans (genus *Cygnus*), the largest members of family Anatidae, are found in N and S temperate and arctic zones, including Australia and S America. Swans have longer necks with more vertebrae (23-25), shorter legs and larger feet than do geese, which they superficially resemble (*see* GOOSE). There is some dispute as to the number of genera. Five species of true swans are recognized. The 3 Northern Hemisphere species are pure white; the S American, white with black neck; the Australian, black with white primaries. All young swans (cygnets) are unpatterned,

Only 2 species of swan are native to Canada, the whistling swan and the trumpeter swan (*Cygnus buccinator*), shown here, which breeds in the YT, the Grande Prairie region of Alberta, and the Cypress Hills (*photo by Tim Fitzharris*).

white, grey or black. Whistling and trumpeter swans (*Cygnus columbianus* and *C. buccinator*) are native to Canada; the mute swan (*C. olor*), native to Eurasia, has become established as a breeding bird in Canada. The whistling swan breeds in the lower arctic islands, Mackenzie Delta, northern Hudson Bay and NE Manitoba. The trumpeter swan breeds in the YT, the Grande Prairie region of Alberta and the CYPRESS HILLS. It has been reintroduced at Swan Lake, near Vernon, BC, and winters in western BC. The whistling swan, the most numerous species in N America, has a population of 200 000; the 'trumpeter swan, now greatly reduced, fewer than 15 000; the mute swan, perhaps 5000 feral (wild) individuals in N America. F.G. COOCH

Swan, Anna Haining, giantess (b at Mill Brook, NS 7 Aug 1846; d at Seville, Ohio 5 Aug 1888). In 1862 she joined P.T. Barnum's American Museum in New York, attracted by the monthly salary of $1000 and by the opportunity to further her education through private tutoring. She became one of Barnum's star attractions. Promoted as being 246 cm (8'1") tall, Anna was in reality 228 cm (7'6"), and at age 22 weighed 160 kg (352 lbs). When the museum burned in 1865, it took 18 men with a block and tackle to rescue her. In 1871, during an overseas tour, Anna met and married Martin Van Buren Bates, a Kentucky giant. They were presented to Queen Victoria, travelled throughout Europe, and then settled on an Ohio farm; summers were spent touring with the W.W. Cole circus. Before her death from tuberculosis, Anna had 2 children; both were abnormally large and died within hours of birth. LOIS KERNAGHAN

Sweat Lodge, used by most N American Indian tribes, was significant in certain purification rites. There were 2 sweating techniques, reflected in lodge construction. The system of direct exposure to fire within the confines of a small, often semisubterranean, structure was prevalent in northern Alaska, California and parts of Mesoamerica. The common system was to heat stones in a fire, place them inside a small domed structure and pour water on them to produce steam. Direct fire sweathouses doubled as men's houses, but steam lodges were often used by a single person. RENÉ R. GADACZ

Swedes Three Swedish names appeared among Lord Selkirk's group of settlers in the Red River Valley of Manitoba, the first evidence of Swedish settlers in Canada. After the American Civil War, land opportunities in the US began to attract Swedes in huge numbers, but as farmland became scarce and costly in the American West, Swedes in the US began to migrate to the Canadian West. From 1868 to 1914, more than one million Swedes moved to the US and Canada. By 1971 there were 101 870 people of Swedish Canadian origin; the 1981 census included Swedes with other Scandinavian groups.

Origins In the early years of the 19th century, Sweden experienced a rapid growth in population. A very large segment of the agrarian population became landless and social divisions between the propertied and unpropertied classes hardened. Many Swedish farmers sought new opportunities elsewhere. A series of crop failures (1866-68) brought starvation and economic hardship to many parts of Sweden and provided an added impetus to emigration.

Migration and Settlement The greatest proportion of the more than one million Swedish emigrants were landless labourers and the sons and daughters of small landholders and crofters. The state Lutheran Church in Sweden actively encouraged destitutes to emigrate. Labour organizers blacklisted by their employers in Sweden also left, and as women became more economically emancipated, many found their way overseas. Emigration promoters from the US and Canada worked actively in Sweden to attract settlers.

Swedish immigration to Canada began on a small scale in the late 1860s. Until 1914, most Swedish immigrants arrived in Canada by way of the US, primarily from Minnesota and North Dakota. Between 1921 and 1930, over 20 000 Swedes (many of them industrial workers) migrated directly to Canada. By 1930 Sweden had developed a large industrial base and since 1945 Swedish migration to Canada has been primarily on an individual basis.

In the early 1870s, some Swedes travelled by boat along the Red River to Winnipeg. With the completion of the CPR, many Swedes took advantage of the Canadian government policy offering inexpensive Prairie farmland (*see also* IMMIGRATION POLICY). Winnipeg attracted many Swedish immigrants and for years it was the main centre for most nationwide Swedish organizations. Swedes in Manitoba settled as well in Scandinavia, Erickson, Teulon, Mulvihill and Eriksdale. Saskatchewan also attracted Swedish settlers; one of every 4 Swedes listed in the 1931 census lived in that province, particularly in the Qu'Appelle Valley communities of Stockholm and Dubuc. Swedes settled in Alberta before it became a province, and Swedish communities still exist in Edmonton and Calgary. During WWII many Swedes moved to the Pacific because of the milder climate and the job opportunities. Today, BC has the largest number of Swedish Canadians.

Many early Swedish immigrants settled in northwestern Ontario as farmers and lumber workers, particularly around Kenora; after WWII a large number of Swedish immigrants settled in Toronto.

Economic Life The great majority of the early Swedish immigrants to Canada were attracted by the opportunity of owning farmland. Around the turn of the century, skilled and unskilled workers immigrated to the urban-industrial areas of Canada. After 1945 Swedish immigrants included engineers, businessmen and representatives of Swedish export industries. Over the years, large numbers of Swedish Canadians moved from farms into industry, business and the professions.

Social Life and Community Swedish settlers, especially in western Canada, established a number of social clubs and organizations. Temperance societies established in a number of communities were among the first Swedish-language clubs. In 1901 the Norden Society was organized as a benefit society.

The Vasa Order of America, now a social and cultural organization, was founded in 1896 in the US and in 1913 in Canada as a mutual-benefit society; it maintains lodges throughout the US and Canada.

Religion and Cultural Life Much of the religious and cultural life of the early Swedish communities in Canada centered around churches, which became bastions of the Swedish language and provided a cultural link between Swedish immigrants and their Canadian-born children. For many immigrants, religious dissension in the homeland had been a major factor for leaving Sweden and it affected their choice of religious denomination in N America.

The Lutheran Church has been the strongest church organization in N America among Swedes. In 1860 the Swedish Lutheran congregations in the US established the Augustana Synod which, for over a century, guided Swedish Lutheran activities throughout Canada and the US before becoming the Lutheran Church in America. The Canada Conference of the Augustana Evangelical Lutheran Church was located in Winnipeg.

Canada-Tidningen (est in Winnipeg, in 1892), was the longest-running and most influential Swedish-language newspaper in Canada. In 1970 it amalgamated with the *Swedish-American Tribune* of Chicago. A number of other Swedish-language periodicals have been published, in Winnipeg, Vancouver and Toronto.

Education The children of the early Swedish settlers adapted readily to the Canadian educational system and to the English language. The 1981 census recorded less than 8000 residents whose mother tongue was Swedish.

Politics Many Swedish Canadians actively participated in community activities, eg, co-operatives, credit unions and wheat pools of the Prairie provinces, and in the early BC trade-union movement. Many Swedes supported populist movements such as the CO-OPERATIVE COMMONWEALTH FEDERATION in Saskatchewan and SOCIAL CREDIT in Alberta. Harry STROM, former Social Credit premier of Alberta (1968-71), was of Swedish origin. LENNARD SILLANPAA

Sweezey, Robert Oliver, engineer, promoter (b at Trois-Rivières, Qué 8 Dec 1883; d at Montréal 13 May 1968). Sweezey was the promoter and president of the massive Beauharnois Light, Heat and Power Corp and of other hydroelectric, forestry and transportation endeavours. The Beauharnois project was designed not only to divert and harness the flow of the St Lawrence R, but also as part of the ST LAWRENCE SEAWAY. As an engineering project it was a great success, but Sweezey and other company officals became implicated in a monumental political scandal. As a result the Sweezey interests were removed and control passed to the rival Montreal Light, Heat and Power Consolidated. Thereafter, Sweezey was involved in several mining and power schemes, mainly in western Canada. A graduate of Queen's, Sweezey was an important benefactor, fund raiser and trustee of that institution for many years. T.D. REGEHR

Swift, common name for about 80 species of BIRDS in 2 closely related families (Apodidae, Hemiprocnidae), sometimes grouped with HUMMINGBIRDS. Swifts occur almost worldwide, wherever their flying-insect prey is sufficiently abundant. Four species breed in Canada. Long, slender, pointed wings and cylindrical bodies make possible the rapid, acrobatic flight for which these most aerial of birds are named. Family name, Apodidae [Gk, "footless"], is derived from the tiny feet, with strong claws on 4 toes all projecting forward in adults but not in nestlings. Swifts are mostly dull coloured. Most species nest colonially in caves or hollow trees; others under waterfalls, in sandbanks, in old swallow nests and even on palm leaves. The saliva that glues together most nests is the sole component of nests of some oriental species — which are used for bird's-nest soup! Chimney swifts (*Chaetura pelagica*), which breed across S Canada from E Saskatchewan to the Maritimes, and sometimes Vaux's swift (*C. vauxi*) of southern BC may attach nests inside chimneys and building walls. Two cliff-dwelling species nest

in western Canada, the large black swift (*Cypseloides niger*) through much of BC and locally in Alberta, and the white-throated swift (*Aeronautes saxatalis*) generally restricted to the Okanagan, but occasionally wandering to coastal sites. MARTIN K. McNICHOLL

Swift Current, Sask, City, pop 14 747 (1981c), inc 1914, is situated in southwestern Saskatchewan, 245 km W of Regina. The city took its name from a creek that flows through it and eventually empties into the S SASKATCHEWAN R. Since this particular creek bore the same name as the S Saskatchewan in the 1860s, fur traders avoided confusion by referring to it as Swift Current, the English derivative of the word "Saskatchewan." In 1882 the CPR bridged the creek and established a depot at the present site. Swift Current began to adopt the persona of a community in 1883 with the appearance of a dam, water tank, freight sheds, roadhouse and dining room. For many years it has served a large ranching, mixed-farming and grain-farming area. Oil, natural-gas, sodium-sulphate and helium production have diversified the expanding economy of the city. DON HERPERGER

Swimming, Speed Competition is recognized for 4 swimming styles — freestyle (usually the crawl), breaststroke, backstroke and butterfly — over various distances up to 1500 m. In medley events, the swimmer uses all 4 strokes, in a prescribed order. Freestyle and medley relay races are also staged, usually with 4 swimmers per relay team. Most top-level competitions are held in 50 m pools, but some are raced over 25 m lengths, and records are maintained for both distances. Long-distance, or MARATHON, swimming is organized separately from speed swimming.

Swimming was considered to be an important survival skill by the ancient Egyptians, Greeks and Romans, but was not contested as a sport. The first country to organize swimming on a national scale was Japan; an imperial decree of 1603 ordered swimming to be included in the country's educational program. Swimming meets were held in Japan for over 300 years; however, no impact was made on other countries because Japan was closed to the outside world until 1867. Competitive swimming in Great Britain started in the 1830s, and the first international competition was held in Melbourne, Australia, in 1858. The first European championships were held in 1889, and swimming for men was included in the 1896 Olympic Games. Women began participating in Olympic events in 1912. The governing body for international competition, the Fédération Internationale de Natation Amateur (FINA), was formed in 1908 and is responsible for all amateur aquatic sports: speed swimming, diving, synchronized swimming and water polo. Its first world championships were held in 1973.

In Canada, speed swimming is controlled by the Canadian Amateur Swimming Assn (CASA), formed in 1909. Prior to then, swimming had been organized by a committee of the Amateur Athletic Union of Canada. The CASA remained the dominant aquatic-sports organization in Canada, and assumed control of diving, water polo and synchronized swimming. By 1969, this arrangement was no longer

satisfactory to diving and water polo (synchronized swimming had withdrawn in 1950), and the Aquatic Federation of Canada was created as an umbrella organization. All 4 aquatic sports are members of the federation, which in turn serves as the Canadian affiliate to FINA.

Swimming clubs in Canada began to organize meets in the 1870s. The Dolphin Club of Toronto, formed in 1875, and the Montreal Swimming Club, established one year later, were influential in the development of competition, and the 1876 meet of the Montréal club was the first such event in Canada. But lack of facilities hampered the spread of the sport in most parts of the country. Races were often held in open waters, over courses marked by floats and booms. Long-distance swimming was very popular. The outstanding Canadian swimmer in the early days of competition was George HODGSON, who swam with the Montreal Amateur Athletic Assn. In 1911, he won the mile race at the Festival of Empire Games in London, and the next year thrilled Canadians by winning the 400 m and 150 m events at the Olympics. He set world records at these distances that stood until 1924. At the 1920 Olympics, George Vernot, also of Montréal, was 2nd in the 1500 m race and 3rd at the 400 m distance.

With the inauguration of the British Empire Games in 1930, Canadian swimmers began to excel at shorter distances. The outstanding swimmer of the pre-WWII era was Phyllis DEWAR, of Moose Jaw and Vancouver. At the 1934 Games she won 4 events; her 5th win in 1938 set a record for gold medals won by a Canadian that stood until 1978. After the war, BC swimmers coached by Percy Norman of the Vancouver Amateur Swim Club and George Gate of the Ocean Falls Swim Club began to dominate Canadian speed swimming. It was during the 1950s and early 1960s that swimmers such as Lenora Fisher, Jack Kelso, Dick Pound, Peter Salmon, Helen Stewart, Mary Stewart and Beth Whittall started to establish Canada's status as a world power in speed swimming.

In 1966, Elaine TANNER, coached by Howard Firby of Vancouver's Dolphin Swim Club, set world records and won a number of British Commonwealth and Pan-American Games events, as well as 2 silver and one bronze medal in the 1968 Olympic Games. Other outstanding swimmers emerged at this time, and during the 1960s and 1970s Canada gradually rose to a position close to 3rd in the world, 2nd in the Pan-American Games and 1st in the Commonwealth. Bruce Robertson, of Vancouver, won the 100 m butterfly at the 1973 world championships, the first world title for Canada since George Hodgson's 1912 achievements. Leslie Cliff (Vancouver), Nancy GARAPICK (Halifax) and Donna-Marie Gurr (Vancouver) were the leaders of a remarkably strong group of women swimmers; and Graham SMITH, of Edmonton, with 6 gold medals, led the 1978 team that com-

Anne Ottenbrite in action at the 1984 Los Angeles Olympics, at which she won gold and silver medals (*courtesy Athlete Information Bureau/Service Information-Athlètes*).

pletely dominated the Commonwealth Games. Later that year, Smith won the 200 m individual medley race at the World Aquatic Championships. Other outstanding swimmers during this period were Wendy Cook, Angela Coughlin, Cheryl Gibson, Ralph Hutton, Ron Jacks, Marion Lay, Becky Smith, Shannon Smith, Patti Stenhouse and Judith Wright. The postwar improvement of Canadian swimmers can be measured by the achievements of its Commonwealth Games teams: 1 gold and 2 silver medals in 1950; 2 gold, 3 silver and 6 bronze in 1962; and 15 gold, 7 silver and 9 bronze in 1978. At the 1984 Los Angeles Olympics Canadian swimmers won 4 gold medals, 3 silver and 3 bronze, contributing greatly to Canada's most successful Olympic competition. The medal winners were as follows: Alex BAUMANN (gold in the 200 m IM, world record, and the 400 m IM, world record); Victor DAVIS (gold in the 200 m breaststroke, world record, and silver in the 100 m breaststroke); Anne OTTENBRITE (gold in the 200 m breaststroke and silver in the 100 m breaststroke); Davis, Sandy Goss, Tom Ponting and Mike West (silver in the 400 m medley relay); West (bronze in the 100 m backstroke); Cam Henning (bronze in the 200 m backstroke); Ottenbrite, Reema Abdo, Michelle MacPherson and Pamela Rai (bronze in the 400 m medley relay).

Competitive swimming in Canada has traditionally been organized through swimming clubs. The Toronto Dolphin Club was one of the leading clubs during the 1930s, and the Vancouver Amateur Swim Club dominated Canadian swimming during the 1940s and 1950s. The Ocean Falls, BC, club produced outstanding swimmers far out of proportion to the size of that small, isolated coastal community; its swimmers were featured in Canadian meets, record books and teams during the 1950s and 1960s. The Montreal Amateur Athletic Assn team re-emerged as a strong club during the 1950s, with coaches Ed Healey and George Gate. The successor to the Vancouver Club has been that city's Dolphin Swim Club, coached by Howard Firby and then Derek Snelling. In 1964 George Gate moved to the Pointe Clair Club near Montréal, and the strength of that club was demonstrated through the 1970s. Other important clubs of the 1970s and early 1980s were the Thunder Bay Thunderbolts, under Don Talbot; the Etobicoke Club of Toronto, coached by Derek Snelling; the New Westminster Hyack Swim Club, with Ron Jacks; and the Keyano Club of Edmonton, coached by Tom and Dave Johnson. At the start of the 1980s, efforts to build Canada's university swim teams began to bear fruit, and the trend of Canadian swimmers training at universities and colleges in the US was reversed as Canadian programs became more attractive.

Competitive swimming is one of the most popular and successful sports in Canada, with age-group and summer swim meets supplementing the regular program of regional, national and international championships.

BARBARA SCHRODT

Swiss In 1604 reference was made to the military quarters of Swiss soldiers at St Croix I in Acadia, soldiers who were followed in 1643 by 5 young Swiss who served under the lieutenant-governor of Acadia and by (1721-45) a small contingent of the Karrer Regiment, which reinforced the LOUISBOURG garrison for the French king. By 1881, 4588 people of Swiss origin had settled in Canada. By 1981 the figure was 29 805.

One of the first Swiss to settle in Canada was Pierre Miville (1602-69). He and his son were granted lands on the seigneury of Lauzon on the S shore of the St Lawrence R across from the Plains of Abraham. Records also show the Miville family were granted lands in 1665 by de Tracy, who named the land "Canton des Suisses

fribourgeois." Jacques Bizard (1642-92), who accompanied Count Frontenac to New France, became seigneur of l'Ile de Bonaventure, now known as Ile Bizard. Lawrence Ermatinger was one of the founders of the NORTH WEST COMPANY; Sir Frederick HALDIMAND became governor general of Québec in 1778 and Sir George PREVOST (born in the US but of Swiss origin) was governor general of Canada between 1812 and 1816. Prevost's armies, which helped defend Canada during the WAR OF 1812, included the Swiss de Watteville and DE MEURON regiments.

Many of the approximately 2000 German-speaking Mennonites who emigrated to Upper Canada from Pennsylvania (1786 to 1820) were of Swiss origin. After the War of 1812 and the disbanding of the de Watteville and de Meuron regiments, a small number of Swiss officers and civilians established themselves in Perth (Ont), and near Drummondville in Lower Canada. Another 30 or so Swiss from these regiments joined expeditionary forces with Lord SELKIRK, who was organizing relief for the RED RIVER COLONY.

Swiss-born Sebastian Fryfogel (1791-1873) was credited with opening the Huron Tract E of Lk Huron. Later in the 19th century and early in the 20th century other Swiss communities were founded in Blumenau, Alta, and Zurich, Ont. A small group of Swiss alpinists helped open the Rockies to tourism and the first western painter, Peter RINDISBACHER, was Swiss.

Despite their small numbers in Canada, the Swiss support several associations and clubs, eg, the Swiss National Society, est 1874; the Swiss Club, est 1918; the Matterhorn Young Swiss Club; and various periodicals. Nevertheless, Swiss settlers never felt the need to unite as a group. They became immersed in the well-organized German and French community groups and associations. Swiss-born Canadians have made outstanding contributions in many fields, eg, hotel and restaurant business, dairy farming, music, arts, education and sports.

ROXROY WEST

Swiss Chard, see BEET.

Sydenham, Charles Edward Poulett Thomson, 1st Baron, politician, colonial administrator (b at Wimbledon, London, Eng 13 Sept 1799; d at Kingston, Canada W 19 Sept 1841). Son of a prominent merchant, he entered the family firm at age 16. An outspoken free trader, he was first elected to the House of Commons in 1826, and became vice-president (1830) then president (1834) of the Board of Trade. Appointed governor general of British N America in 1839, he persuaded the legislature of Upper Canada to consent to a union with Lower Canada and framed the constitution of the united province. Although he opposed the principle of RESPONSIBLE GOVERNMENT and acted as his own prime minister, he turned the Executive Council into a Cabinet composed of heads of departments who sat in the legislature. He also established a variant of this system in NS in 1840. It could work only so long as the proponents of complete responsible government did not control the Assembly, and in Canada he interfered flagrantly in the 1841 election to prevent a Reform victory. His policy of anglicization won him the support of the anglophone majority in the colony but the undying hatred of the French Canadians. His system was already beginning to collapse when he died in 1841. P.A. BUCKNER

Reading: Adam Shortt, *Lord Sydenham* (1926); J.M.S. Careless, *The Union of the Canadas* (1967).

Sydney, NS, City, pop 29 444 (1981c), inc 1900, is located near the eastern extremity of CAPE BRETON ISLAND. It is the principal city of Cape Breton and centre of the second-largest urban complex in NOVA SCOTIA. Its fine harbour, known as Spanish Bay in colonial times, is ringed by the richest coalfield in eastern Canada. Since 1900 it has been noted for its huge steel mill, the largest and most modern in Canada at its construction. The industrial core around the mill has been in decline since the end of WWII as the coal mines of the surrounding communities became less pro-

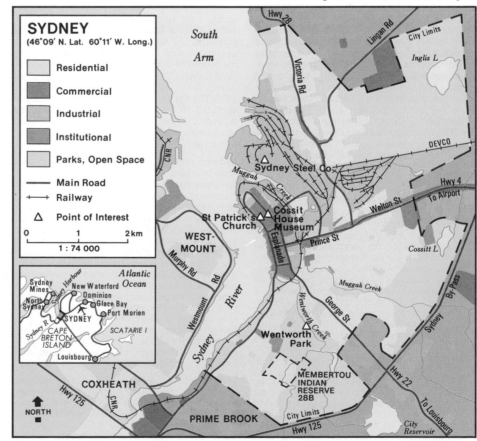

SYDNEY
(46°09' N. Lat. 60°11' W. Long.)

Residential
Commercial
Industrial
Institutional
Parks, Open Space
Main Road
Railway
Point of Interest

0   1   2 km
1 : 74 000

Sydney, NS, on the eastern extremity of Cape Breton Island, is ringed by the richest coalfield in eastern Canada (*courtesy City of Sydney*).

ductive and the obsolete steel mill less competitive with central Canadian producers.

History When Cape Breton was separated from NS in 1784 as a refuge for LOYALISTS, Sydney was chosen as its capital. A townsite was developed under the direction of Gov J.F.W. DESBARRES and named for Lord Sydney, then colonial secretary. Less successful as a separate colony than New Brunswick, Cape Breton was rejoined to NS in 1820 after nearly 4 decades of maladministration, political intrigue and general underdevelopment. Sydney, still a tiny outpost of a few hundred residents, but with the pretensions of a colonial capital, was reduced to being shiretown to Cape Breton County, which then included the entire island. Generally underdeveloped throughout the 19th century, it remained the administrative centre of the island.

Economy Sydney's fate has been inextricably linked to the mining of coal. Sea coal had been taken by the French during the occupation of LOUISBOURG in the 18th century, but only came under intensive development towards the middle of the 19th century, responding to increased demand first in the US and later in central Canada. Sydney provided services and shipping facilities for surrounding coal towns. The location of steelmaking there in 1899 transformed Sydney. The Dominion Iron and Steel Co (later Dominion Steel Corp) occupied prime waterfront property and invested several hundred million dollars in plant and land. The town's population doubled and redoubled several times over the next decade, drawing migrants from the exhausted farms of the island and large numbers of Europeans as well, giving the city the most polyglot population in the region. Thereafter the steel mill, based on local coal resources, limestone from nearby quarries and iron ore from BELL ISLAND, Nfld, formed the city's core. Hospitals, government services, cultural and educational institutions all centered here. The island's commercial life radiated from the core of merchants along Sydney's waterfront. Connection to central Canada by rail in the 1880s solidified its commercial dominance. Yet, like most similar communities in Canada, it has risen and fallen with the development of its hinterland region. Sydney's has been in decline for some time.

Townscape Sydney's oldest portions were established along the waterfront, much like all seaport towns in the Atlantic provinces. Bisected by the steel mill, which occupies most of the S side of the outer harbour, it spread out to encroach on a series of hills behind. The mill is surrounded by rings of drab company-built frame houses that house one of the most militant work forces in Canada. The steelworkers of Sydney struggled from the beginning to establish their right to collective bargaining. They did not succeed until WWII when the United Steelworkers of America finally gained recognition as bargainers for the steelworkers. Sydney has a fine central park and several large institutional buildings, including UNIVERSITY COLLEGE OF CAPE BRETON (1979), located on the outskirts of the city.

D.A. MUISE

Reading: P. MacEwan, *Miners and Steelworkers* (1976).

Sydney Mines, NS, Town, pop 8501 (1981c), inc 1889, is located on N side of Sydney Harbour, 19 km from SYDNEY. The presence of coal was noted by Nicholas DENYS in 1672 and strip-mined coal was shipped out as early as 1724. Large-scale operations began in 1826 when the General Mining Assn took over the mines. Shafts were sunk, ironworks established and railway tracks laid. The NS Steel and Coal Co succeeded the GMA in 1900, later expanding operations and building blast furnaces. The town enjoyed a period of prosperity and expansion until 1920 when the blast furnaces shut down. The last mine, Princess Colliery, closed in 1975. There is no other industry, and unemployment is high. The "Princess" was once a museum where visitors could descend in a mine that at one time operated as far as 8 km out below the ocean floor.   HEATHER MACDONALD

Sydney Steel Corporation (Sysco) Steel has been produced in SYDNEY, NS, since 1899, when the Dominion Iron and Steel Co established a steelworks to exploit Cape Breton COAL and Newfoundland IRON ORE. Production of railway rails began in 1905. Several changes in ownership took place until Hawker-Siddeley took over and ran the plant in the 1960s. The steelworks has been operated by the NS government since 1967. The government, faced with a socially unacceptable shutdown, formed a CROWN CORPORATION to keep the industry alive. The plant consists of 2 small blast furnaces and several basic open-hearth furnaces, with an annual raw-steel capacity of about one million tonnes. The low productivity of the plant and the poor demand and prices for its products (mainly rails and semifinished steel) make Sysco's future as a steel producer uncertain.   JOHN G. PEACEY

Symbols of Authority One of the earliest signs of authority (the right to enforce obedience) was probably a wooden club, in which symbolism grew directly out of practical application: the humble club became both an instrument by which power was exercised and (consequently) a symbol of authority. Today, long dignified by the name "mace," the caveman's club, which evolved into the steely weapon of medieval knightly combat and then into a symbol of kingly power, still serves as the symbol of authority in Canada's Parliament and in the provincial legislative assemblies. It is part of Canada's British heritage. Until the mace has been placed on the table before the Speaker's chair, the legislators have no authority under which to make or repeal laws. They are, in effect, without power, for they have no authority to wield it: although Parliament has the power to govern, it has that power only under the authority of the CROWN.

Within the COMMONWEALTH, the Crown is the supreme symbol of unity and authority; and all laws are enacted and carried out in the name of the Crown. Its supremacy in Canada is evident from the representation of this symbol of authority at the upper end of the mace, substituting for the deadly bulge of the caveman's club and the spiked ball of the medieval warrior's mace. Here is evidence of the fine line that developed between authority and power. Centuries ago the Crown appeared in small replica, capping what was then the handle of the king's mace. Grasped by the hand of authority, the power was in the hitting end. But the need for brute force receded and the royal mace ceased to be an instrument for exercising power directly on the battlefield. It became a symbol of authority under which legislation could take place. Today the configuration of the mace is reversed, a large crown, the symbol of authority, now dominating the mace's onetime hitting end.

The Crown, an ancient symbol of monarchy, is easily recognized, appearing as it does ensigning the coat of arms of Canada (*see* EMBLEMS OF CANADA) and displayed in many other ways to indicate governmental, judicial and military authority. We also speak of the Crown as the prosecutor in courts of law, as the possessor of government-owned lands, and with respect to governmental agencies such as crown assets and various CROWN CORPORATIONS. In fact, "Crown" is used as the general term expressing the legal personality of the executive of government. Executive power, originally in the monarch's own hands, has come, through constitutional evolution, to be entrusted to bodies of legislators — who still exercise it in the sovereign's name. One place where the authority of the Crown is still in evidence is the giving of royal assent. No bill can become law until it has been read the appropriate number of times and passed in both Houses of Parliament. This having been done, it automatically receives royal assent, the symbolic agreement of the supreme authority, and becomes law.

The symbolism of the Crown is deeply entrenched in the entire process of British democracy, to which Canada has fallen heir. Authority is vested in the Crown, but in practice the Crown acts only on the advice of those members of the PRIVY COUNCIL who make up the Cabinet of the day. Since Cabinet ministers are also members of Parliament, they are, as members, responsible to the electorate, so that the people are in fact sovereign. The Crown therefore becomes the symbol of the sovereignty (or authority) of the people. The Crown is also a symbol of political unity, for the Government and Her Majesty's Loyal Opposition are still united under the Crown for the betterment of the country, although pursuing different policies in an effort to achieve that betterment.

Coats of arms were developed during the Crusades as aids to the identification of warriors on the battlefield. These soon became symbols of authority when the designs on the warriors' surcoats, banners and shields were transferred to the wax seals which served as signatures in those days, when even the most authoritative in the land was likely to be illiterate. The first recorded use of a coat of arms to proclaim supreme authority in Canada was on 24 July 1534, when French explorer Jacques CARTIER erected a cross at the entrance to the Baie de Gaspé. "Under the crosspiece we put a coat of arms with 3 fleurs de lys in relief and over this was a wooden placard engraved with large letters that read *Vive Le Roi de France*." Three conventionalized golden lilies on a blue shield were the armorial bearings of François Iᵉʳ; his arms raised by Cartier identified him as the possessor of the new land and were the symbol of his authority over it.

Since armorial bearings are found not only upon shields but also upon banners, it is not surprising that the symbol of authority which John CABOT set up on Newfoundland soil in 1497, when he claimed that territory for Henry VII of England, was "the royal banner." A banner is either a square or an oblong flag. In the age of imperialism no greater symbol of authority existed than the flag of any nation establishing or claiming authority over some distant undeveloped territory. Numerous imperial flags — notably British, French and Spanish — have flown over what is now Canadian soil. In addition, flags such as those of the HUDSON'S BAY COMPANY and the NORTH WEST COMPANY have been used to indicate claims of territory by corporate interests.

Authority, no matter what its source, becomes embodied in either a person or an office. In Canada each of these embodiments has its own seal, by means of which every conferment of authority is marked. The Great Seal of Canada is the official seal. It gives formal expression to the traditional and legal authority of the state to make provisions for the well-being of the nation. The seal depicts Elizabeth II on the Coronation throne, wearing St Edward's Crown and holding other symbols of royal authority in her hands. Before the queen are the armorial bearings of Canada. This seal is used to sanction the commissions issued to persons appointed to the most important offices of state. It also used to confer approval upon various kinds of documents, such as letters patent constituting the office of governor general, proclamations, land grants by the Crown and election writs.

The Governor General's Privy Seal, which is a personal seal, depicts the personal arms of the incumbent. Among the commissions issued under the Privy Seal are those of the officers of the ARMED FORCES, of which the governor general is commander in chief. This particular application of the Privy Seal testifies to an important feature of our Constitution: that the legal use of military force in Canada is ultimately dependent on the personal authority of the monarch's representative. It is not dependent on the power of the leader of the government, even though, since the beginning of RESPONSIBLE GOVERNMENT, he has had access to the official seal.

When a party leader takes the oath of office and receives the commission as PRIME MINISTER, power, coming from the people, and authority, coming from the Crown, are joined. Thus the party leader who forms the government becomes, during his period in office, the most powerful person in the country. Yet no one, according to the German sociologist Max Weber, has greater authority than the monarch, for his or her authority rests on all 3 bases of authority that we have accepted as legitimate: charisma, tradition and law.

Not only nations, but religious communities, public and secret societies and countless other organizations around the world possess symbols of authority under which their citizens, adherents or members respond to the laws and regulations that govern and sustain them. Symbols of authority come in many forms. Crowns, maces, coats of arms, seals, flags — even the "tin star" worn by gun-slinging US lawmen of fact and fiction — are symbols of authority under which people are governed. In Canada's history perhaps no symbol of authority has been more quickly and universally recognized than the scarlet jacket of the NORTH-WEST MOUNTED POLICE and their successors, the ROYAL CANADIAN MOUNTED POLICE. STROME GALLOWAY

Reading: A.B. Beddoe, *Beddoe's Canadian Heraldry* (ed Strome Galloway, 1981); C. Swan, *Symbols of Sovereignty* (1977).

Symington, Herbert James, lawyer, executive (b at Sarnia, Ont 22 Nov 1881; d at Montréal 28 Sept 1965). Symington, admitted to the Manitoba Bar in 1905, became a prominent corporation lawyer and a notable figure in Winnipeg public affairs. A Liberal, he was a member of the informal "Sanhedrin" around J.W. DAFOE and T.A. CRERAR, and he was put on the board of the CNR in 1936. During WWII he controlled the allocation of supplies of electrical power, and from 1941 to 1947 he was president of TRANS-CANADA AIRLINES. He helped found the International Civil Aviation Organization and later became chairman of the board of Price Brothers. ROBERT BOTHWELL

Symonds, Norman, composer (b near Nelson, BC 23 Dec 1920). Symonds came to the forefront of the Canadian third-stream movement under Gordon Delamont in Toronto. His major compositions, combining elements of jazz (improvisation, colour) and classical music (structure, orchestration), include *Concerto Grosso* for jazz quintet and symphony orchestra (1957), *Autumn Nocturne* (1960), *The Nameless Hour* (1966) and *The Democratic Concerto* (1967). Symonds has composed works for TV (*Black Hallelujah*) and stage (*Lady in the Night*), as well as such expressionist pieces as *Big Lonely* (1975) and *The Gift of Thanksgiving* (1980), both inspired by Canada's natural beauty. Later works explore electronic and choral idioms; Symonds has also composed works for student audiences. Some of his concert pieces have been recorded by the CBC and National Youth orchestras and by Ron COLLIER; some of his stage works have been produced by the CBC and by the CANADIAN OPERA CO. MARK MILLER

Symons, Thomas H.B., teacher, historian, university president, author (b at Toronto 30 May 1929). He was educated at U of T, Oxford and the Sorbonne. As an academic and administrator he has played many roles. He was founding president of TRENT UNIVERSITY (1960-72), and founding vice-president of the Social Sciences and Humanities Research Council of Canada (1978-84). He is perhaps best known as chairman of the Commission on Canadian Studies (1972-84). As author of *To Know Ourselves: The Report of the Commission on Canadian Studies* (1976), he alerted Canadians and Canadian universities to the importance of teaching and research about Canada, its prospects, problems and circumstances. That report, and the challenges contained in it, are balanced by Symons's concern that Canadians participate in the wider scholarly world, both through contributions about Canada and by a willingness to learn about, and be open to, the perspectives of others. His view of the importance of a Canadian presence on the wider international academic stage is demonstrated by international service, which has included work with the Commonwealth Standing Committee on Student Mobility (1982-), chairmanship of the Int Board of United World Colleges (1980-), and chairmanship of the Assn of Commonwealth Universities (1971-72).

Not only a theoretician, but a practitioner, Symons has advised the provincial government of Ontario as the chairman of the Ontario Human Rights Commission (1975-78), for example, and the federal government as a member of the Federal Cultural Policy Review Committee (1979-82). He was also chairman of the Policy Advisory Committee to R.L. STANFIELD (1968-75). His publications, articles, reviews and monographs on a host of topics, include *Life Together: A Report on Human Rights in Ontario* (1977), with Rosalie Abella et al, and *Some Questions of Balance: Human Resources, Higher Education and Canadian Studies* (1984), with James E. Page. Symons is a fellow of the Royal Soc of Canada, holder of the Queen's Silver Jubilee Medal and of the Canadian Centennial medal, as well as many other honours. *See* CANADIAN STUDIES. JAMES E. PAGE

Synchronized Swimming is the performance in water of a series of movements in time to music. It is a popular activity for many in N America and increasingly so around the world. Canada has developed an excellent recreational program for all ages and skill levels called the "Star" program, and has a highly developed competitive program as well as programs for training officials and coaches.

The basic skills of synchronized swimming are strokes and figures, which were originally part of the Royal Life Saving Society program. In 1924, the first competition in strokes and figures in Canada was held at the YWCA in Montréal. In the following 2 years, swimmers in Ontario and Québec became more interested in this kind of competition, and the first Dominion championship in strokes and figures was held at the Montreal Amateur Athletic Assn in 1926. Margaret Shearer (Mrs Peg Seller) became the first Canadian champion, winning the Frances C. Gale Trophy. The rules for this competition changed slightly over the years, but the trophy has been in continuous competition to the present time. By 1954, Canadian synchronized-swimming championships included competitions in solo, duet and team, and Canadian synchronized swimmers have competed around the world. The 1979 Canadian Female Athlete of the Year, Helen Vanderburg, won gold medals in Canadian, Pan-American, Pan-Pacific, FINA Cup and World Aquatic championships in 1978 and 1979. Synchronized swimming was in the Olympics for the first time at the 1984 Los Angeles Games; Canada's duet and solo entries placed 2nd behind the US. GLADYS BEAN

Szilasi, Gabor, photographer, teacher (b at Budapest, Hungary 3 Feb 1928). He immigrated to Canada in 1957. Both as a teacher (Collège du Vieux Montréal 1970-79 and Concordia 1979-) and as a photographer he has influenced a generation with his carefully considered approach to photographing people. He has recorded people within their environments, particularly in Québec regions such as Charlevoix County (Ile-aux-COUDRES), Beauce County, Abitibi, Lac SAINT-JEAN and Lotbinière. His large format and panoramic photographs of Québec architecture demonstrate his interest in the built environment. He was associated with the Groupe d'action photographique in Montréal 1970-72 and, as a participant in "A Photographic Project: Alberta 1980," documented Falher, a small town in northwestern Alberta. ANN W. THOMAS

Photographer Gabor Szilasi has influenced a generation with his careful approach to photographing people (*courtesy National Film Board/Photothèque*).

Taber, Alta, Town, pop 5988 (1981c), inc 1907, is located 50 km E of Lethbridge. Taber was settled by MORMONS in the first decade of the 20th century, and the name is said to come from the first part of the word "tabernacle," although the first post office (1904) was called "Tabor," presumably after Mt Tabor, Palestine. The local economy at first depended upon beef cattle and wheat but, with the development of irrigation, the cultivation of sugar beets became important and a processing plant was built in the town.

ERIC J. HOLMGREN

Table Tennis is played by 2 (singles) or 4 (doubles) players, normally indoors. Opponents face each other and hit the ball with a racquet, alternately, over a 6-inch (15.25 cm) net stretched midway across an 9- x 5-ft (274 cm x 152.5 cm) table. The celluloid ball makes a hollow sound that led to "ping-pong" as a common name for the game. It first appeared in the late 19th century as an attempt to miniaturize tennis for play indoors. The pimpled-rubber racquet covering was developed in 1903, allowing for the development of spin on strokes. World championships have been held since 1926 and dominated by players from Japan and China.

The Canadian Table Tennis Assn was formed in 1929, with Québec as the founding provincial member, Ontario joining 5 years later. A long association with the Canadian National Exhibition began in 1936, when the first Canadian Table Tennis Championships were staged there. The CTTA operates a computerized rating system that allows any competitive player to be ranked, both provincially and nationally. Canada's table-tennis stars of the 1930s were Paul Chapdelaine and J.J. Desjardins of Montréal, winners of the international championship men's doubles in 1939 and 1940. In the 1970s, Violette Neskaitis, of Toronto, emerged as a strong international player. Winner of 4 N American open championships, she travelled to China in 1971 on a Canadian team, the first table-tennis team to be invited to that country. In 1973 she was ranked 3rd among Commonwealth women players. At the 1979 Pan-American Games, Ed Lo won the men's singles event.

BARBARA SCHRODT

Taché, Alexandre-Antonin, missionary, Roman Catholic priest, archbishop (b at Rivière-du-Loup, Qué 23 July 1823; d at St-Boniface, Man 22 June 1894). He entered the Oblates of Mary Immaculate in 1844, went to the RED RIVER COLONY in 1845 and was ordained priest on 12 Oct 1845 by Bishop Norbert Provencher. After studying the Sault language in St-Boniface, he left for the immense territory of the Île-à-la-Crosse mission in 1846. He was named coadjutor to Provencher in 1850. He founded many new missions and helped the large number of settlers who flooded into the region. The bishop was severely tested by the RED RIVER REBELLION. At a Vatican Council when problems began, he was called back to Canada by government authorities and helped restore order. His promises to the Métis in so doing, however, were controversial. He fought just as vigorously for French and Catholic schools (see MANITOBA SCHOOLS QUESTION). The bishop left behind him important accomplishments in the country. A devoted missionary and enlightened patriot, he was one of the great Catholic bishops of Canada.

GASTON CARRIÈRE, OMI, CR

Taché, Sir Étienne-Paschal, doctor, politician (b at St-Thomas [Montmagny], Qué 5 Sept 1795; d there 30 July 1865). He began studying medicine while serving as an officer in the WAR OF 1812. After completing his studies in Philadelphia, he practised medicine in Montmagny for 22 years, 1819-41. Though he did not participate in the REBELLIONS OF 1837, he was an ardent PATRIOTE. After the union of the Canadas, along with

his compatriots A.N. MORIN, L.H. LAFONTAINE, and G.E. CARTIER, Taché became more willing to compromise. He was first elected to the new Assembly in 1841. In 1846 he resigned to become deputy adjutant general of the Canada East militia, and was responsible for its reorganization. In 1848 he became an executive councillor, commissioner of public works and then legislative councillor, and was a member of every government until 1857. He replaced Morin as leader of Canada E and formed a ministry with A.N. MAC-NAB 27 Jan 1855. After MacNab resigned in May 1856, Taché joined John A. MACDONALD in a ministry that sealed the alliance of Upper Canadian Conservatives and Canadien Liberals in a unified party. The Taché-Macdonald government manoeuvred well under difficult circumstances, but Taché resigned in 1857, though he remained a legislative councillor. He returned to active politics in 1864 amidst yet another political crisis. At Governor MONCK's request, he formed a coalition government with J.A. Macdonald, an entirely Conservative administration which lasted only one month — the third government to fall in 2 years. On 22 June 1864 Taché subsequently formed the coalition ministry that was to give birth to the CONFEDERATION he so passionately promoted. Before his death, he presided over the QUEBEC CONFERENCE and defended the 72 Resolutions determining the shape of Confederation.

ANDRÉE DÉSILETS

Taconis, Kryn, photographer (b at Rotterdam, Holland 7 May 1918; d at Toronto 12 July 1979). In the 1960s and 1970s, he became one of Canada's leading photojournalists, known for his integrity and compassion. The outbreak of WWII shaped his career in still photography. He joined the Dutch resistance movement and clandestinely recorded the appalling suffering resulting from acute food shortages. In 1950 he became a member of the free-lance photo agency Magnum. He travelled throughout Europe, the Middle East, Africa and Australia, and his work appeared in the great picture magazines of the day, including *Life* and *Paris-Match*. In 1959 Taconis and his wife moved to Toronto, where he began to free-lance for publications such as the *Star Weekly*. He also worked for the National Film Board for 3 years. Among his best-known Canadian work is a photo-essay of HUTTERITE communities in the West.

LOUISE ABBOTT

Tadoussac, Qué, Village, pop 900 (1981c), inc 1899, is located at the confluence of the SAGUE-

NAY and ST LAWRENCE rivers, 210 km NE of Québec City. In the Montagnais language, its name means "nipples" or "breasts," from the rounded hills found here. When Europeans arrived, Tadoussac was already an important trading centre for tribes of the N and S shores of the St Lawrence. This activity drew European traffickers by the mid-16th century. Pierre Chauvin tried in vain to establish a colony here in 1600, and it was here that Samuel de CHAMPLAIN concluded a first treaty between Europeans and Indians (1603). A major fur-trading centre from the 17th century on, Tadoussac gained a new and lasting role in the 19th century — forestry and tourism. Chauvin's habitation has been reconstructed. One of the oldest wooden chapels in N America (1647) is found here as well.

MARC ST-HILAIRE

Tagish, numbering between 100 and 150, live in northern BC and the southern Yukon Territory around a series of lakes that are part of the Yukon R headwaters. The high Coast Mts prevent the nearby Pacific Ocean from ameliorating the harsh climate of the plateau. Until the 20th century the Tagish camped at the junction of Tagish and Marsh lakes, but did not stay year round because of their seminomadic subsistence cycle. After 1900, most began to live permanently in Carcross.

The traditional subsistence economy was that of boreal forest hunters, fishers and trappers later augmented by fur trading with surrounding Athapaskans. The near extinction of the coastal sea otter by about 1800 led to a demand for fine land-animal furs from the subarctic Cordillera. The Tagish acted as middlemen between Indians farther inland and the Coast TLINGIT, for until shortly before the KLONDIKE GOLD RUSH of 1898-99 the Tlingit prevented the Tagish from crossing the passes to trade directly with white fur traders. The gold discovery was made by George Carmack, a white man prospecting in HAN country with a party of Tagish.

The Tagish originally spoke a dialect of Tagish-Tahltan-Kaska, but became Tlingit speakers and adapted Tlingit social organization because of extensive trade and intermarriage with Coast Tlingit. The 2 Tagish matrilineal clans belong to the Wolf (Eagle) and Crow (Raven) moieties, respectively, and each clan built a coast-style HOUSE embellished with clan crests. Concepts of rank associated with a fixed pool of personal names, renewed each generation through reincarnation, and elaborate memorial potlatches were incorporated into Tagish life (*see* NATIVE PEOPLE: NORTHWEST COAST; POTLATCH). A rich repertoire of oral literature, singing and dancing reflected concerns with living harmoniously with powerful spirits of the natural world, and with social etiquette and morals. There were rigorous puberty observances for both boys and girls.

In the 20th century, Tagish have become successful big-game guides. Some Tagish leaders have taken the initiative in efforts to settle native LAND CLAIMS and to ensure adequate social services for both status and nonstatus Indians (*see* INDIAN). Since the 1970s they have actively promoted many earlier Tagish traditions. *See also* NATIVE PEOPLE: SUBARCTIC and general articles under NATIVE PEOPLE.

CATHARINE McCLELLAN

Tahltan inhabit the STIKINE R drainage, a dry, rugged plateau between the Coast Mts and the Rocky Mts in northern BC. They now number about 800. The Tahltan, TAGISH and neighbouring KASKA speak dialects of an Athapaskan language. The Tahltan frequently visited, traded and intermarried with the Kaska and the Stikine TLINGIT. Relations were often hostile with the Taku R Basin Tlingit and Athapaskan speakers to the N and the Nass R TSIMSHIAN.

The Tahltan ancestors infiltrated the Stikine Valley from the E about 300 years ago. The large, dependable salmon runs and excellent drying conditions on the Stikine R provided a year-round food supply larger and more reliable than that E of the Rockies. A more settled and prosperous life developed, enhanced by elements derived from the Tlingit at the Stikine R mouth. Such characteristics as mortuary houses and posts, wooden boxes, matrilineal clans and moieties, POTLATCH ceremonies, inherited titles and RAVEN myths were incorporated into Tahltan culture (see NATIVE PEOPLE: NORTHWEST COAST). While the earliest records report that the Tahltan organized into bands, each with a territory, gradually the BAND organization was superseded in social importance by matrilineal clans, some bearing Tlingit names. One clan chief, holding the title Nan-nok, was regarded as chief of the Tahltan.

In the early 1800s the Tahltan monopolized trade along the Stikine "grease trail" (so-called because of the importance of fish oil in the trade) between the Tlingit and groups further into the interior. Eulachon (candlefish) oil, dentalium shells and Tlingit and European artifacts were exchanged for furs, tanned hides and other interior products. The monopoly and the relative isolation of the Tahltan were ended by the GOLD RUSHES to the Cassiar (1872-80) and the Yukon (1898-99). With the onslaught of new diseases, the Tahltan dwindled and concentrated at a single site, Tahltan Village, which was subsequently abandoned in favour of Telegraph Creek, the head of navigation on the Stikine R and the local seat of Canadian government and commerce. In the 1920s the Tahltan were joined at Telegraph Creek by a group of SEKANI, who were incorporated into the officially recognized Tahltan Band. The Sekani left 40 years later and were constituted a distinct Iskut Band. Many modern Tahltan work in government jobs, sport hunting, prospecting and mining, though hunting, fishing and gardening are also important. See also NATIVE PEOPLE: SUBARCTIC and general articles under NATIVE PEOPLE.

BRUCE B. MacLACHLAN

Taiga, see VEGETATION REGIONS.

Tailfeathers, Gerald, artist (b at Stand Off, Alta 13 or 14 Feb 1925; d at Blood IR, Alta 3 Apr 1975). One of the first native Canadians to become a professional artist, he came to prominence in the 1950s. His art had several influences: study in the Summer Art School in Glacier National Park (Montana) with New York portrait painters Winold Reiss and Carl Linck, the cowboy school of painting led by Charles Russell, the Oklahoma school of Indian painting, the Banff Centre School of Fine Arts, and the Provincial School of Technology and Art in Calgary. In the main, his work exhibits a romantic and nostalgic vision of his BLOOD people's life in the late 19th century. Thus, it features warriors in their traditional activities of warfare, hunting and ceremonial life. Tailfeathers later began experimenting with cast-bronze sculpture that depicted themes inspired by cowboy art, which he studied on a 1969 visit to the Arizona studio of George Phippin.

JOHN ANSON WARNER

Sundance Scene, Blood Reserve, 1906 (1956), watercolour by Gerald Tailfeathers, typical of the artist's nostalgic vision of his people (*courtesy Glenbow Museum*).

The eccentric Thomas Talbot successfully settled large tracts of land extending over present-day southwestern Ontario (*courtesy McIntosh Art Gallery/University of Western Ontario*).

Taillon, Sir Louis-Olivier, lawyer, premier of Québec (b at Terrebonne, Qué 26 Sept 1840; d at Montréal 25 Apr 1923). Known for his ultra-conservative stance, especially on educational issues, he was first elected Conservative MNA in Montréal-Est (1875). He resigned in 1884, only to return a few months later. Premier for 4 days in Jan 1887, he had to yield to Honoré MERCIER, who then attacked him for his support of the federal Conservative government in its actions towards Louis RIEL. Again premier from Dec 1892 to Apr 1896, he headed an extremely conservative administration. After his resignation he briefly served as federal postmaster general.

DANIEL LATOUCHE

Takakkaw Falls, situated just W of the Continental Divide in YOHO NATIONAL PARK, is Canada's highest waterfall and the sixteenth highest in the world. Not as panoramic or as extensive as Niagara Falls, but having a spectacular vertical drop of 380 m, the falls cascade into the Yoho R below. One of the park's most prominent attractions, the falls are fed by snow and ice melt that originate in Daly Glacier in the Rocky Mts and then course through a U-shaped hanging valley.

DAVID EVANS

Takijuq Lake, 1080 km², elev 381 m, max length 60 km, is located in the NWT almost on the Arctic Circle, 173 km S of Coppermine, NWT. The lake is fed by a tributary of the COPPERMINE R and drains NE to Bathurst Inlet via the Hood R. It was discovered by Samuel HEARNE (May 1771) and appears on his map as *Thaye Chuckgyed* Lake and in his narrative as *Thoy-noy-kyed* Lake. Mackenzie referred to it as *Theye Check* Lake, which appears to have evolved into the present name.

DAVID EVANS

Talbot, Thomas, soldier, settlement promoter, colonial official (b at Malahide, Ire 19 July 1771; d at London, Canada W 5 Feb 1853). A member of the Anglo-Irish aristocracy, Talbot spent 50 years developing the Talbot Settlement in Upper Canada. He was educated in Malahide and Manchester, Eng, and at age 11 received his first commission in the British army. In the turbulent period of Anglo-French conflict during the late 18th century, Talbot saw duty in Europe and N America. He was private secretary to Gov SIMCOE of Upper Canada 1791-94. Not only did he visit many parts of the Great Lks area but he cultivated the friendship of Simcoe, which later proved invaluable. In 1801 Talbot sold his commission and emigrated to UPPER CANADA. There he became an official promoter of settlement in

the London Dist and within 10 years had developed 3 principal routes — the Talbot streets — as well as a dozen separate townships. His ability to acquire personal property as well as successfully settle extensive tracts of land made Talbot unique. By 1836 he had settled portions of 29 townships extending over a huge area of present-day southwestern Ontario along the N shore of Lk Erie, with a population of over 30 000. Success resulted, in large part, from Talbot's insistence on actual settlement on the land, including clearance and house construction. Full, legal possession was withheld until these conditions were met.

After 1825, Talbot's power began to decline for reasons that included a popular spirit of reform, increasing bureaucracy and Talbot's eccentricity. Socially intolerant and exclusive, he lived alone and isolated in his Pt Talbot "castle." On his death he bequeathed his considerable estate largely to his personal servants.

A.G. BRUNGER

Talon, Jean, INTENDANT of New France (bap at Châlons-sur-Marne, France 8 Jan 1625/26; d in France 24 Nov 1694). As "Intendant of Justice, Public order and Finances in . . . Canada, Acadia and Newfoundland" 1665-68 and 1669-72, Talon was a determined, energetic and imaginative servant of the king and his minister, Jean-Baptiste Colbert. This first intendant of NEW FRANCE was to convert a small, weak, fur-trading and missionary outpost under company rule into a profitable, well-populated royal province, capable of defending itself. To diversify the economy, Talon had the mineral and timber resources evaluated, encouraged commercial farming, domestic crafts, shipbuilding and the fishery, established a brewery and fostered trade with the French West Indies. Almost 2000 immigrants and disbanded soldiers were settled on the land. It was assumed that the population would increase through intermarriage with Indians instructed in the religion and ways of the French, but few natives abandoned their culture. Talon relied on penalties against bachelors and rewards for early marriage and large families among the French for population growth. When his dream of a territorial empire conflicted with Colbert's desire for a compact, defensible colony, Talon obediently encouraged continuous settlement in the St Lawrence Valley and founded 3 villages. Talon had accepted the post in Canada as a route to promotion, and in 1671 asked the king's permission to return to France in view of "my obedience in leaving Eu-

Jean Talon, imaginative and energetic intendant of New France (1665-68 and 1669-72), who sought to develop New France into a viable, profitable royal province (*courtesy Public Archives of Canada/C-7100*).

rope for America, exposing my life to the different perils of sea and sickness . . . and my labours in a land as rough as this was in its beginnings." He returned in 1672 and was appointed secretary to the king, member of the royal household and was named Count d'Orsainville. In New France, Talon's industries, commercial agriculture and trade with the West Indies failed; for 3 years there was no intendant and the Crown would no longer invest large sums of money in colonial development. Talon is remembered as an industrial entrepreneur and originator of the family allowance, but his enduring legacy was the centralized, royal administrative and legal framework. PETER N. MOOGK

Tamarack, *see* LARCH.

Tamarack Review (1956-82), a literary magazine founded at an especially bleak time for Canadian literary reviews. John SUTHERLAND'S NORTHERN REVIEW had ceased publication, and for some years *Tamarack Review* had the field virtually to itself. It filled the space with distinction until it ceased publication. Robert Weaver was the leading spirit in the founding of *Tamarack* and remained its most active editor to the end, although William Toye and John Robert COLOMBO also played considerable roles. *Tamarack Review* covered all literary genres, publishing fiction, poetry, travel memoirs, autobiography, criticism and even drama. The early work of many distinguished Canadian writers, including Timothy FINDLEY, Jay MACPHERSON, Hugh HOOD, Alice MUNRO and Mordecai RICHLER, appeared in its pages. It set the standard by which later Canadian literary magazines have been judged. GEORGE WOODCOCK

Tanabe, Takao, artist, painter (b at Prince Rupert, BC 16 Oct 1926). His art studies included the Winnipeg School of Art (1946-49), Hans Hofmann (1951), Central School of Arts and Crafts, London, Eng (1954), and Tokyo U of Fine Arts (1959-61), where he combined painting and calligraphy with travel in Japan. He worked in Vancouver as a graphic designer (1956-59) and established Periwinkle Press (1963). He began teaching at the Vancouver School of Art in 1962. He regularly exhibited his paintings throughout Canada and did murals on commission. In 1968 he left for Philadelphia and he painted in New York 1969 to 1973. He was head of the art department at the BANFF CENTRE SCHOOL OF FINE ARTS 1973-80. His mature paintings, from this period, reveal a gradual synthesis of earlier influences, including Japanese art and the hard-edge style of New York. Dominated by a strong horizontal sweep, his progressively more simple and dramatic compositions examine the nature of space and light. Series such as *The Land,* though influenced by his experience of the Prairies, allude to a larger and metaphysical experience of space. JOYCE ZEMANS

Tanager (Thraupinae), subfamily comprising about 240 species of small songbirds of the family Emberizidae. The subfamily is sometimes given family rank. Tanagers are found only in the Americas, largely in tropical regions. They are not noted as singers. Many are brightly coloured, often in boldly contrasting, solid patches. Bills are typically short and conical with a notch or "tooth" on the upper jaw. Tanagers are mainly nonmigratory, arboreal birds which eat insects, fruit and flowers. Only 2 migratory species (genus *Piranga*) breed in southern Canada (a third, summer tanager, *P. rubra,* occurs occasionally in southern Ontario and as an accidental in Manitoba). The bright red, yellow and black western tanagers (*P. ludoviciana*) breed in coniferous woods from BC to Saskatchewan; the red and black scarlet tanagers (*P. olivacea*) prefer deciduous forests from Manitoba to NB. Females of both species are olive green. Nests are loosely constructed of small twigs and are placed 3-30

m high in trees. The pale blue, brown-spotted eggs are incubated by the female for about 2 weeks. Males assist with rearing young. Tanagers' songs are robinlike, but hoarser. Scarlet tanagers, the most migratory of the family, are the only species known to undergo pronounced seasonal molt, with males also becoming olive green in winter. R.D. JAMES

Tanner, Elaine, "Mighty Mouse," swimmer (b at Vancouver 22 Feb 1951). Tanner's career in international competition was brief but outstanding, and she is considered Canada's best female swimmer. Her specialties were the backstroke, butterfly and individual medley; she also swam on winning freestyle relay teams. In 1966 she set world records in the 220-yard individual medley and 220-yard butterfly and, at the Commonwealth Games, won 4 gold and 3 silver medals — the most successful woman swimmer at those Games. She received the LOU MARSH TROPHY as Canada's outstanding athlete that year at age 15 — the youngest ever to receive the award. She won 2 gold and 2 silver medals at the 1967 Pan-American Games, and 2 silver and 2 bronze at the 1968 Mexico City Olympics. In 1969 she received the Order of Canada. BARBARA SCHRODT

Tanner, John, "The Falcon," scout, interpreter, amateur ethnologist (b in Virginia *c*1780; d at Sault Ste Marie, Ont 1846?). Son of a clergyman who migrated to Kentucky, Tanner was captured by Shawnee about 1789 and sold to the OTTAWA. He grew up as an Indian in the area W of Lk Superior, participating in wars against the Sioux. Later he showed up at the settlement founded by Lord SELKIRK, remembering little English and hardly his name. Here he was employed as a guide and scout, while Selkirk helped him contact his relatives in Kentucky. A marginal man who drifted between white and Indian societies, Tanner settled at Sault Ste Marie. In 1830, with the aid of Dr Edwin James, Tanner wrote his *Narrative,* an account of 30 years with Indians together with the first detailed descriptions of the Saulteaux and Cree. He spent his remaining years in trying circumstances and disappeared under suspicion, charged with murder. GEORGE A. SCHULTZ

Tantalum (Ta), grey, heavy, very hard metal with a high melting point (2996°C). When pure, it is ductile and can be easily fabricated. Tantalum has good rectifying properties (ie, converts alternating to direct current) and dielectric properties (ie, does not conduct direct current). Alloyed with other metals it imparts strength, ductility and a high melting point. The principal industrial use is in electric capacitors and cemented carbide cutting tools. Because of its high resistance to corrosion by most acids, tantalum is used increasingly by petroleum and chemical plants. It occurs principally in the mineral columbite-tantalite. Tantalum ores are found in Canada, Australia, Brazil, Zaire and China. In Thailand and Malaysia, tantalum is recovered mainly from tin slags. Tantalum Mining Co of Canada, Ltd (TANCO), located in Bernic Lake, Man, produced 135 t of tantalite (Ta_2O_5) in concentrates — about 12% of world output in 1981. TANCO, Canada's only producer, is the world's largest single producer of tantalite. D.G. FONG

Tantramar Marsh is one of 4 saltwater tidal marshes covering 20 230 ha on the narrow Chignecto Isthmus that connects New Brunswick and Nova Scotia. Its complex system of bogs, rivers, lakes and marshes once provided a habitat for thousands of waterfowl. However, the building of dikes to reclaim the land for farming, which the ACADIANS began in the 1670s, drained more than 90% of the Chignecto marshes by the early 1900s. At that time the nutrient-rich silt deposited by Bay of FUNDY tides supported a lucrative haying industry and the

region came to be called "the world's largest hayfield." With the subsequent growth of the automobile industry, however, the hay market declined and the dikeland gradually fell into disrepair. In recent years, hundreds of hectares of marshland are being reclaimed for waterfowl by federal, provincial and private concerns. The largest project, conducted by the Canadian Wildlife Service, involves restoration of a suitable wildlife habitat on 1740 ha in the Tintamarre National Wildlife Reserve on the upper reaches of the Tantramar R. The present-day marshes are among the densest breeding grounds in the world for some species, such as the marsh hawk, and support small industries in muskrat and wild rice. The name derives from the French *tintamarre* ("din"), referring to the noise of the rushing tide in the river or of flocks of wild geese in the marshes. *See* SWAMP, MARSH AND BOG. P.C. SMITH

Tardif, Jean-Paul, financier (b at Québec City 15 May 1923). After graduating from Laval, Tardif began work in 1947 with his father's investment company, Savings and Investment Corp, first as treasurer and then as managing director. In 1951 he became chief executive officer and in 1959, president. In the 1960s and 1970s several subsidiaries were created and the company became a conglomerate. The companies within the group include Savings and Investment Trust, Aeterna-Life and La St-Maurice (assurance company), Savings and Investment Fund, and Savings and Investment American Fund Ltd. With assets in 1981 of $1.3 billion, the Savings and Investment Group is one of the major conglomerates under francophone control. Tardif is also a member of the board of the Donohue Co Ltd. JORGE NIOSI

Tardivel, Jules-Paul, journalist, novelist (b at Covington, Ky 2 Sept 1851; d at Québec C 24 Apr 1905). Tardivel came to Québec in 1868 to study French. After working for *Le Courrier* in St-Hyacinthe in 1873, *La Minerve* in Montréal 1873 to 1874 and *Le Canadien* in Québec 1874 to 1881, he founded in 1881 his own weekly paper, *La Vérité,* in Québec. Until his death he devoted himself to this newspaper, concentrating on 2 lifelong obsessions: ULTRAMONTANISM and nationalism. Tardivel was a strong proponent of the ultramontane, conservative doctrine that dominated Québec in the second half of the 19th century. A ferocious adversary of liberalism, socialism, democracy and freemasonry, he relentlessly promoted his plan for a rural, agricultural, hierarchical society controlled by the Roman Catholic Church. After CONFEDERATION Tardivel was the first Québecois to envision Québec's separation from Canada and to recommend creation of an independent French Canadian republic. In 1895 he published *Pour la patrie,* a futuristic novel in which he synthesized separatist thinking, a position that he first outlined in 1885 but received little support during his lifetime. RÉAL BÉLANGER

Tarragon Theatre in Toronto was founded in 1971 by Bill GLASSCO as a showcase for new Canadian plays interpreted by Canadian theatre artists. Glassco remained artistic director until 1982, when he was succeeded by Urjo Kareda. From its first production, *Creeps,* by David Freeman, the Tarragon established itself as a primary source for the Canadian dramatic repertoire. Works premiered at the Tarragon (and subsequently presented elsewhere) include plays by David French (*Leaving Home; Of the Fields, Lately; Jitters*); James REANEY (*The Donnellys* trilogy); Joanna M. Glass (*Artichoke*); Carol BOLT (*One Night Stand*); Tom Walmsley (*White Boys*); Steve Petch (*Sight Unseen; Cousins*); Mavis GALLANT (*What Is To Be Done?*); Judith Thompson (*White Biting Dog*); and the first productions in English by Québec playwrights Michel TREMBLAY (*Ho-*

sanna; *Forever Yours, Marie-Lou; Bonjour, là, bonjour*) and Roland Lepage (*Le Temps d'une vie*). The 230-seat theatre occupies a former warehouse. In 1980 the Tarragon opened the Maggie Bassett Studio as an additional space for professional training classes, workshops and rehearsals; in 1983 the Extra Space — a second performing facility, seating 100 — was added to the complex. The Tarragon maintains extensive ongoing programs for script analysis and development, ensuring a continuum of playwriting energy. *See also* THEATRE, ENGLISH-LANGUAGE.   URJO KAREDA

Tarte, Joseph-Israël, journalist, politician (b at Lanoraie, Canada E 11 Jan 1848; d at Montréal 18 Dec 1907). A brilliant, caustic and often impulsive polemicist, Tarte owned and edited several newspapers in the course of his career, including *Le Canadien, L'Événement, La Patrie* and the *Quebec Daily Mercury.* He used these newspapers to serve a variety of causes and political factions.

As a Liberal-Conservative in the early 1870s, Tarte opposed the *Programme catholique;* in 1876, however, he shifted to ULTRAMONTANISM and for 7 years was one of its chief exponents. (He sat in the Québec Assembly 1877-81.) When Rome resolved the issue of clerical interference in politics, Tarte returned to a more moderate position. Undoubtedly his greatest moment came in 1890-91 when, first in the pages of *Le Canadien,* then on the floor of the House of Commons to which he was elected in 1891, he exposed the McGreevy-Langevin scandal. This affair discredited the Conservative Party, forced Sir Hector LANGEVIN's resignation from the Cabinet and eventually brought Tarte into the Liberal fold. The MANITOBA SCHOOLS QUESTION cemented this alliance, and Tarte contributed greatly to LAURIER's triumph in Québec in the 1896 election.

As minister of public works in the Laurier Cabinet, Tarte distributed patronage, strengthened Liberal links with the Montréal business community and oversaw the development of the Port of Montréal. He was most notorious, however, for his outspoken and often contradictory views on controversial issues. In 1899 he vigorously opposed sending Canadian troops to South Africa; in 1900 his speeches on Canadian independence drew bitter condemnation from the Conservative press in Ontario; and finally, in 1902, his campaign in favour of imperial economic unity and a higher level of tariff protection led to his dismissal by Laurier and to the end his political career.   RICHARD JONES

Taschereau, Elzéar-Alexandre, Roman Catholic archbishop of Québec C and first Canadian cardinal (b at Ste-Marie de la Beauce, LC 17 Feb 1820; d at Québec C 12 Apr 1898). His father Jean-Thomas, a descendant of the leading seigneurial family of the Beauce, distinguished himself as a politician and through his articles for *Le Canadien* opposing Gov James CRAIG. His mother, Marie Panet, was niece of Bishop Bernard-Claude Panet of Québec. After precocious and brilliant studies at the SÉMINAIRE DE QUÉBEC (1826-36, 1837-42), which he capped with a doctorate in canon law obtained in Rome (1856), Taschereau had a dual career in teaching and the episcopacy. At the Séminaire de Québec, he was a teacher, director, prefect of studies and superior; he helped found Laval U in 1852 and served as its second rector (1860-66, 1869-71); he made several trips to Rome to defend the institution.

Adviser to archbishops Pierre-Flavien Turgeon and Charles-François Baillargeon, theologian for the latter to the First Vatican Council and vicar-general from 1862, Taschereau became archbishop of Québec in Dec 1870 and was consecrated 19 Mar 1871. He quickly showed his intention to reaffirm the prerogatives of his position and willingness to oppose the determined ULTRAMONTANES. As leader of a diverse group of

suffragan bishops, he brought a moderate approach to the resolution of the great debates on Catholic liberalism, excessive clerical influence in politics, reform of the civil code and church-state relations. At the same time he unswervingly defended Québec C's university monopoly against Montréal's claims and the efforts of Laval U's opponents, notably bishops Ignace BOURGET and Louis-François LAFLÈCHE. Because of his energy and a network of friends in Rome created by the archbishopric's representative, Benjamin Pâquet, the Holy See backed him unconditionally, despite contrary opinions of 2 apostolic delegates, George Conroy (1877-78) and Dom Henri Smeulders (1883-84). At the urging of, among others, the Canadian government, on 7 June 1886 Pope Leo XIII created Taschereau cardinal, an honour that gave him unequalled prestige throughout the country. He could not long enjoy it, for illness soon forced him first to reduce and then abandon his workload to a coadjutor, Louis-Mazaire Bégin, named in 1891.

A man of great culture and ability, though taciturn, Cardinal Taschereau strongly influenced the Catholic Church (*see* CATHOLICISM) in Québec and helped it avoid confrontation with the state, even as he strengthened its religious vitality and political power.   NIVE VOISINE

Taschereau, Louis-Alexandre, lawyer, politician, premier of Québec (b at Québec City, 5 Mar 1867; d there 6 July 1952), son and father of Supreme Court justices. The *bête noire* of Québec nationalists, he welcomed the surge of American investment in the 1920s and resisted calls for social and economic reform in the 1930s.

Destined to continue his family's brilliant legal tradition, Taschereau rose slowly and somewhat unexpectedly to the premiership. He believed that industrial development in Québec was critical and that it could be achieved only with the help of outside capital and expertise. In his early years as premier, he was accused of anticlericalism for attempting reforms in education and social service, and of sacrificing agriculture to industry for rapid development of Québec's natural resources. As premier, Taschereau championed provincial autonomy but defended Sir Wilfrid LAURIER's moderate approach to the problem of Canadian unity, condemning both the tactics of Henri BOURASSA and the intolerance of English Canadian nationalists.

His downfall came with the Depression. Though he worked to protect major industries and municipalities from bankruptcy, his refusal to establish permanent social-security measures or nationalize hydroelectric power created the impression that he was "a tool of the Trusts," an image reinforced by his links with major financial institutions. In 1934 young rebels in his own party formed the ACTION LIBÉRALE NATIONALE and, in alliance with the Conservatives, nearly defeated him in 1935. Taschereau was further humiliated and driven from office by scandalous revelations about his brother and several high government officials.   BERNARD L. VIGOD

Taschereau Legal Dynasty Spanning 3 centuries and 2 legal cultures, the Taschereau family perpetuated itself, along with several other groups, as a core constituent in Québec's law-making institutions. The patriarch of the family, Gabriel-Elzéar Taschereau, member of the Legislative Council of Lower Canada, seigneur and judge (b at Québec C 27 Mar 1745; d at Ste-Marie de la Beauce, LC 18 Sept 1809), was twice married, and a distinct and distinguished legal lineage arose from each marriage.

As a result of his marriage to Marie-Louise-Elisabeth Bazin in 1773 he became the father of Jean-Thomas, MLA, judge, and publisher (b at Ste-Marie de la Beauce, 26 Nov 1778; d at Québec C 14 June 1832), and the grandfather of Jean-Thomas, puisne justice of the Supreme Court of

Canada (b at Québec C 12 Dec 1814; d there 9 Nov 1893). The younger Jean-Thomas was the father of Sir Henri-Thomas, chief justice of the Court of King's Bench of Québec (b in Québec C 6 Oct 1841; d at Montmorency, France 11 Oct 1909), and of Louis-Alexandre TASCHEREAU, lawyer and premier of Québec and grandfather of Robert, chief justice of the Supreme Court of Canada (b at Québec C 10 Sept 1896; d at Montréal 26 July 1970).

Gabriel-Elzéar was also, through his second marriage to Louise-Françoise Juchereau Duchesnay (d 1841) in 1789, grandfather of Joseph-André, solicitor general of Lower Canada (b at Ste-Marie de la Beauce, 30 Nov 1806; d at Kamouraska, Canada E 30 Mar 1867); and great-grandfather of Sir Henri-Elzéar, chief justice of the Supreme Court of Canada (b at Ste-Marie de la Beauce, 7 Oct 1836; d at Ottawa 14 Apr 1911).

This powerful seigneurial family was also related through marriage to members of other prominent Québec legal families. Although many Canadian families constituted legal dynasties, the continuing presence on the Bench of one family is rare.   G. BLAINE BAKER

Task Force, established, like a ROYAL COMMISSION, under the Inquiries Act. Members are appointed by the governor-in-council. The subject matter of a task force is generally less important than that of a royal commission. Investigation is less formal and extensive, and with smaller budgets the reports are not as lengthy. Less impartial and authoritative, the reports are usually more closely identified with the government and need not be made public. The government is not bound to follow the advice of a task force or even to comment on its report. Like the Task Force on CANADIAN UNITY, which was established in 1977 and reported in 1979, a task force is often one voice in a debate. The weakness of interest groups and their inability to represent adequately all members of society means that, unlike their Swedish counterparts, Canadian task forces cannot be used to gain the consent of the general public through that of their spokesmen. Recently the House of Commons has established some small special COMMITTEES to investigate topics such as North-South relations. These are not to be confused with task forces established under the Inquiries Act, nor with the interdepartmental short-term project committees of civil servants, also called task forces, which are dependent, internal creatures of the government.   C.E.S. FRANKS

Task Force on Foreign Ownership (the Gray Report) was established (1970) under Herb GRAY to analyse the impact of the high degree of foreign control on Canadian development and its effect on the capacity of Canadians to control their national economic environment; and to examine policies that would enable Canadians to exercise greater control over their economy and to retain and increase Canadian ownership of business where feasible or desirable for economic, social, cultural or other reasons. In the 1960s, foreign control reached nearly 60% of total Canadian manufacturing, and 90% of industries such as rubber and petroleum.

The task force concluded (1972) that, in a highly qualified way, FOREIGN INVESTMENT had had a moderately favourable effect overall but that problems did exist, eg, "truncated firms" which performed only a narrow range of activities in Canada and were dependent on foreign technology and management. It suggested that some problems could be handled through general economic policies, eg, tariffs, taxes and patents, but that others would be better solved through flexible administrative intervention on all new foreign investment, case by case. It rejected a major policy shift, such as a "buy-back" strategy, towards increased Canadian ownership.   C.E.S. FRANKS

Tata, Sam, photojournalist, portrait photographer (b at Shanghai, China 30 Sept 1911). He immigrated to Canada in 1956. An unobtrusive but lively personality permitted him to witness discreetly the events surrounding the 1949 Chinese Revolution. His extraordinary work recorded life on the streets and in the courts of Shanghai. In 1948, in India, he had seen the photographs of Henri Cartier-Bresson and found his approach to photography radically altered. Tata's portraits of Canadian artists, writers, poets and photographers, taken over a 20-year period, are an important contribution to Canadian history and photography. ANN W. THOMAS
Reading: Canadian Fiction Magazine 29 (1979).

Tatamagouche, NS, UP, pop 600 (1981c), located on NORTHUMBERLAND STR, 50 km NW of NEW GLASGOW, takes its name from the MICMAC *Takamegoochk* ("barred across the entrance with sand"). ACADIANS may have settled here as early as 1710, mining a deposit of copper ore. In the Expulsion of 1755 the village of 12 buildings was burned by the English. In 1770 Joseph Frederick DESBARRES, a Swiss, settled 18 Lunenburg families on a grant of 8100 ha in a futile attempt to manage a manor estate like an English landlord. In 1790 a shipbuilding industry began, enduring until 1917. In 1958 the Atlantic Christian Training Centre, owned and operated by the United Church, was built. Today, agriculture is the chief industry, with fishing, farming, lumbering and service industries also important. Recreational facilities and a 19 ha park along the scenic Northumberland shore draw tourists and campers. JANICE MILTON

Taverner, Percy Algernon, ornithologist (b at Guelph, Ont 10 June 1875; d at Ottawa 9 May 1947). Taverner first earned a living as an architectural draughtsman while studying birds in his spare time. In 1911 he was appointed ornithologist at the National Museum of Canada, where he developed a unique system of distributional maps linked to card indexes on individual species containing up-to-date information on bird distribution in Canada. Taverner played an important part in Canadian ornithology and in wildlife conservation, such as the designation of Point Pelee as a national park (1918) and the protection of Bonaventure I and Percé Rock in the Gulf of ST LAWRENCE as bird sanctuaries (1919). His ornithological writings culminated in *Birds of Canada* (1934). Comprehensive in content, readable in style, with coloured illustrations by Allan Brooks, it helped popularize bird study. J.L. CRANMER-BYNG

Tax Court of Canada, est 1983, is an independent body under the federal minister of justice. Its objective is to provide an easily accessible tribunal for the disposition of disputes between taxpayers and the minister of national revenue. Known previously as the Tax Review Board (1958-83) and the Tax Appeal Board (1946-58), it has the powers, rights and privileges of a superior court of Canada. The board consists of up to 7 members who must be former judges or barristers of not less than 10 years standing at a provincial bar. At any time, either the chairman or assistant chairman must have been a judge of the Superior Court of Québec or a member of the bar of that province.

Taxation Taxes are compulsory payments by individuals and corporations to government, levied to finance government services, redistribute income and influence the behaviour of consumers and investors. Of the various methods available for financing government activities, only taxation payments are compulsory. Taxes are imposed on individuals, business firms and property to finance public services or enable governments to redistribute resources, allowing governments to increase expenditures without causing inflation of prices, because private spending is reduced by an equivalent amount.

The CONSTITUTION ACT, 1867 (formerly BNA Act), gave Parliament unlimited taxing powers and limited those of the provinces to direct taxation (*see* DISTRIBUTION OF POWERS). The federal government was responsible for national defence and economic development, the provinces for education, health, social welfare and local matters which then involved only modest expenditures. The provinces needed access to direct taxation mainly to enable their municipalities to levy property taxes. For more than 50 years customs and excise duties provided the bulk of Dominion revenues; by 1913 they constituted over 90% of the total. Provincial revenue derived primarily from licences and permits, public domain and sales of commodities and services; in addition, the provinces received substantial federal subsidies. They hesitated to impose direct taxes, but by the late 1800s were taxing business profits and successions. Taxes on real and personal property were the bulwark of local government finance, and by 1930 total municipal revenues surpassed those of the Dominion.

The GREAT DEPRESSION bankrupted some municipalities and severely damaged provincial credit. Customs and excise duties declined by 65% 1929 to 1934. Parliament resorted more to personal and corporate taxation and raised sales taxes dramatically. To finance WWI, Parliament had introduced personal income tax (1917), corporate taxes and, in 1920, manufacturers' sales tax and other sales taxes. Before the Depression was over, all provinces were taxing corporate income; all but 2 levied personal income taxes, and 2 had retail sales taxes.

The Canadian tax structure changed profoundly during WWII. To distribute the enormous financial burden of the war equitably, to raise funds efficiently and to minimize the impact of inflation, the major tax sources were gathered under a central fiscal authority. In 1941 the provinces agreed to surrender the personal and corporate income-tax fields to the federal government for the duration of the war and for one year thereafter; in exchange they received fixed annual payments. In 1941 the federal government introduced succession duties; an excess-profits tax was imposed, and other federal taxes increased drastically. By 1946 direct taxes accounted for more than 56% of federal revenue. The provinces received grants, and the yields from gasoline and sales taxes increased substantially. The financial position of the municipalities improved with higher property-tax yields. In 1947, contrary to the 1942 plan, federal control was extended to include succession duties as well, but Ontario and Québec opted out, choosing to operate their own corporate income-tax procedures. There was public pressure for federal action in many areas, and the White Paper on EMPLOYMENT AND INCOME advocated federal responsibility for employment and income. As a result, direct taxes became a permanent feature of federal finance. But the provinces also have a constitutional right to these taxes and there is a growing demand for services under provincial jurisdiction, such as health, education and social welfare. The difficulties of reconciling the legitimate claims of both levels of government to income taxation have since dominated federal-provincial negotiations (*see* INTERGOVERNMENTAL FINANCE).

From 1947 to 1962 the provinces, with mounting reluctance, accepted federal grants as a substitute for levying their own direct taxes. In 1962, however, the federal government reduced its own personal and corporate income-tax rates to make tax room available to the provinces. Because taxpayers would pay the same total amount, provincial tax rates would not be risky politically. Further federal concessions between 1962 and 1977 have raised the provincial share of income-tax revenues significantly. To taxpayers' advantage, provincial income taxes are integrated with federal taxes; all provinces except Québec use the federal definition of taxable income (Québec has operated its own income tax since 1954), while provincial tax rates, which now differ considerably among the provinces, are simply applied to basic federal tax. For all provinces except Québec the federal government collects personal income taxes; it also collects and administers the corporate income tax for all provinces except Ontario and Québec, which administer their own, and Alberta. In 1983, provincial personal income-tax rates, as a percentage of basic federal tax, ranged from 38.5% (Alberta) to 60% (Newfoundland). The federal government allows an abatement equal to 10% of corporate taxable income earned in the province; lower provincial tax rates apply to small businesses rather than to large ones in all provinces.

Principles of Taxation The criteria by which a tax system is judged include equity, efficiency, economic growth, stabilization and ease of administration and compliance. According to one view, taxes, to be fair, should be paid in accordance with the benefits received, but the difficulty of assigning the benefits of certain government expenditures, eg, defence, restricts the application of this principle. Provincial motor-fuel taxes are one instance of the benefit principle. According to another view, individuals should be taxed on the basis of their ability to pay (typically indicated by income). The personal income tax is in part a reflection of this principle. Horizontal equity (individuals with equal taxpaying ability should be treated equally) is not easily achieved because income alone is an imperfect measure of an individual's ability to pay. Vertical equity (higher incomes should be taxed accordingly) has been opposed by business and those with higher incomes, who claim that progressive tax rates discourage initiative and investment, although with the progressive tax, tax deductions benefit those with high taxable incomes. Taxes can affect the rate of economic growth as well. Income taxes limit capital accumulation, and corporate taxes, it is claimed, reduce capital investment. Business so strongly opposed the royal commission's recommendations for full inclusion of corporate gains as taxable income that only 50% of capital gains in Canada are taxable — the lowest rate of any Western industrialized country. The cost of taxpayer compliance increased in 1971, although the broadened and complicated income-tax base did introduce more equity.

Tax Shifting and Incidence Taxes levied on some persons but paid ultimately by others are "shifted" forward to consumers wholly or partly by higher prices or backward on workers if wages are lowered to compensate for the tax. Some part of corporate income taxes, federal sales and excise taxes and local property taxes is shifted, altering and obscuring the final distribution of the tax burden.

Revenue Elasticity The more elasticity (the percentage change in tax revenue resulting from a change in national income) a tax has, the greater its contribution to economic-stabilization policy. Income taxes with fixed monetary exemptions and rate brackets have an automatic stabilization effect because tax collections will grow faster than income in times of economic growth and will fall more sharply than income in recession. In Canada, the revenue elasticity of personal income tax is attenuated by indexing; since 1974 both personal exemptions and tax brackets have been adjusted according to changes in the CONSUMER PRICE INDEX. But sales taxes have less revenue elasticity because consumption changes less rapidly in response to changes in income, and these taxes are not progressive in relation to consumption.

While property-tax yields do not grow automatically with rising NATIONAL INCOME, they exhibit some revenue elasticity.

Current Tax System

Taxes levied by all governments in Canada represented 76% ($104.7 million) of total government revenues in the 1982-83 fiscal year. The remaining percentage was derived from a wide variety of charges and profits of public enterprises, and for provinces and municipalities from intergovernmental transfers. Personal income taxes alone raised nearly 43% of total tax revenues, followed by sales taxes (13.8%), property taxes (10.4%) and corporate income taxes (10.0%). The remaining percentage derived from sources ranging from federal customs duties and excise taxes, provincial health-insurance premiums and motor-fuel taxes to the relatively minor municipal business taxes.

Tax Revenues of all Levels of Government by Major Source, 1982/83

Income taxation:	Millions$	% distribution
Personal	44 609	42.6
Corporate	10 463	10.0
Sales tax	14 475	13.8
Excise taxes & duties	3 632	3.5
Customs duties	2 831	2.7
Property taxes	10 841	10.4
Subtotal	86 851	
Other taxes	17 891	17.1
Total tax revenue	104 742	100.0

Federal Tax Revenues

Tax receipts, particularly from income taxation, including the withholding tax on interest and dividends earned by nonresidents, accounted for about 90% of total federal revenues in fiscal year 1982-83; personal, corporation and nonresident tax collections combined comprised 63% of federal budgetary revenues. Compared with the manufacturers' sales tax (10.7% of total revenue), the other federal sources of revenue are modest. Personal income tax applies to all sources of income of residents in Canada, with the exception of gifts and inheritance and some other specific exemptions (see UNDERGROUND ECONOMY). Tax reforms (1972) significantly broadened the tax base, especially by the inclusion of 50% of capital gains realized after that date. Single taxpayers are allowed a basic personal exemption; larger exemptions apply to married persons and to taxpayers over the age of 65. Deductions are also permitted for certain expenses, eg, child-care expenses, unemployment-insurance premiums, Canada or Québec Pension Plan contributions and the employment-expense deduction. Since 1974 personal exemptions and tax brackets have been increased annually to take account of INFLATION.

The manufacturers' sales tax applies to all

Federal Tax Revenues, 1982/83
(Source: Canadian Tax Foundation,
The National Finances, 1983/84, p 63)

Income taxation:	Millions$	% distribution
Personal	26 330	47.8
Corporate	7 139	13.0
Nonresident	998	1.8
Sales tax	5 894	10.7
Customs duties	2 831	5.1
Excise taxes and duties	3 632	6.6
Oil export charge	2 352	4.3
Other	132	0.2
Total taxes	49 308	89.5
Nontax revenue	5 816	10.5
Total budgetary revenue	55 124	100.0

goods produced in Canada or imported into the country unless specifically exempted, eg, foodstuffs, electricity and fuels, drugs, clothing and footwear, materials incorporated into manufactured goods, farming and mining machinery, pollution-control equipment and construction equipment. The tax on goods manufactured in Canada is applied to the manufacturer's selling price, exclusive of all other excise taxes, but inclusive of import duties; for imported goods, the tax is levied on the duty-paid value. The sales tax is difficult to administer and widely criticized for several reasons, including the unequal burden it places on different consumer purchases. In 1966 the Royal Commission on TAXATION recommended its replacement by a retail sales tax; in 1984 the federal Liberal government withdrew its intention to shift the sales tax to the wholesale level.

Provincial Tax Revenues

In 1982-83, taxation constituted 54% of provincial revenues, 18% of which were attributable to federal transfers and nearly 28% of which were classified as nontax revenues, including motor-vehicle user charges, natural-resource levies and liquor-store profits. Seventy percent of provincial tax revenues derive from personal and corporate income taxes and general retail sales taxes. Succession duties have disappeared in every province except Québec following the introduction of the capital-gains tax. Retail sales taxes are imposed by all provinces except Alberta. All provinces exempt certain categories of consumer goods from these taxes (usually food, fuel, prescription drugs and medical appliances, most books and children's clothing), but the treatment of others varies widely. Most provinces tax hotel rooms and restaurant meals above a specified minimum, but typically at differential rates. These exemptions are designed to reduce the regressivity of these taxes, which bear more heavily on lower-income families.

Provincial Tax Revenues, 1982/83
(Source: Canadian Tax Foundation,
Provincial and Municipal Finances, 1983, p 97)

Income taxation:	Millions$	% distribution
Personal	18 279	23.0
Corporate	3 324	4.2
General sales tax	8 581	10.8
Motor fuel taxes	3 347	4.2
Health insurance premiums	3 248	4.1
Social insurance levies	2 071	2.6
Quebec pension plan levies	1 096	1.4
Tobacco taxes	1 125	1.4
Other	2 002	2.5
Total taxes	43 073	54.2
Nontax revenue	21 806	27.5
Transfers from other governments	14 557	18.3
Total gross general revenue	79 436	100.0

Municipal Tax Revenues

The municipalities derive the smallest proportion of their revenues from taxation. Over 46% of total municipal revenues were transfers from the other levels of government, particularly the provinces. The property tax provided nearly 85% of municipal tax revenue, but only 31% of gross municipal revenue. The property tax in all provinces is levied on real property (land and buildings). Personal property tax still applies in several provinces to machinery and fixtures that provide services to buildings. In the 1960s, property-tax laws were extensively reviewed in all provinces except Newfoundland and BC, and further studies were conducted

in several provinces and municipalities in the 1970s. The property tax has been criticized for, among other things, imposing regressive burdens on low-income families, for its indifference towards people's financial status and because it is unfairly administered. Ontario and Manitoba introduced reforms allowing a property-tax credit against provincial income tax, and BC and Alberta allow rental tax credits to reduce the tax burden for low-income persons. NB, PEI, Ontario and NS set property-tax rates and collect the tax for their municipalities. General reforms have included broadening the tax base by reducing or eliminating a number of exemptions and implementing equalized assessment.

Municipal Tax Revenues, 1982
(Source: Canadian Tax Foundation,
Provincial and Municipal Finances, 1983, p 97)

	Millions$	% distribution
Real property taxes	10 460	31.0
Special assessments	381	1.1
Business taxes	1 237	3.7
Other	283	0.8
Total taxes	12 361	36.6
Grants in lieu of taxes	945	2.8
Nontax revenue	4 833	14.3
Transfers from other governments	15 608	46.3
Total gross general revenue	33 747	100.0

Federal-Provincial Fiscal Arrangements

Income-tax sharing, federal financing of specific provincial programs, EQUALIZATION PAYMENTS and special tax abatements to Québec characterize federal-provincial fiscal arrangements. In time, the revenues of one level of government will no longer meet expenditure needs, while the opposite situation will develop at the other level. As it is, public policies now often require joint federal-provincial action. Technological change in transportation, communications and methods of production, population growth and urbanization have increased interdependence and population mobility. Consequently, government programs legitimately combining national and provincial interests have greatly expanded.

Federal conditional grants and shared-cost programs have enabled the provinces to expand the provision or improve the quality of a remarkable number of provincial services, but the grants are now politically unpopular. Québec in particular regards them as federal intrusions into areas of provincial jurisdiction. Since 1965 Québec has been allowed to opt out of the important programs, receiving compensatory assistance in the form of federal abatements of the personal income tax. In 1977 hospital insurance, medical care and post-secondary education were consolidated under the Established Programs Financing (EPF) arrangement. The provinces have gained flexibility over the use of the funds. Federal EPF cash transfers and remaining conditional grants, eg, the Canada Assistance Plan and the program for promoting bilingualism in education, amounted to almost $10 billion in 1982-83.

Equalization grants, which originated in 1957, enable provincial governments in poorer provinces to provide services at levels comparable to those of other provinces. Since 1982-83 federal grants have gone to each province whose per capita yields from specified provincial and local revenue sources would fall below the weighted per capita average of 5 "representative" provinces. In 1984-85 all provinces except Ontario, Saskatchewan, Alberta and BC will receive equalization grants, expected to reach about $5.4 billion.

GEORGE E. CARTER

Taxation, Royal Commission on, under Kenneth Carter, appointed (1962) by PM John Diefenbaker to examine and to recommend improvements to the entire federal TAXATION system. The 6-volume report (1967) declared fairness should be the foremost objective of the taxation system; the existing system was not only too complicated and inefficient, but under it the poor paid more than their fair share while the wealthy avoided taxes through various loopholes. The commissioners proposed that the same tax be levied on increases in economic power of the same amount however acquired, for as Carter reputedly said, "a buck is a buck." If its recommendations were implemented, the commission estimated, nearly 50% of taxpayers would have their taxes reduced by more than 15%; 10% would face increased tax liabilities of more than 15%, and the remaining taxpayers would notice little change. The wealthy, paying more taxes, would nevertheless share in the benefits of an efficient taxation system. A White Paper was released (1969) proposing implementation of some recommendations. Opposition, however, especially from several provincial governments, oil and mining companies and small business groups, was so vociferous, as it had been to the report, that the Trudeau government retreated from any major reform. The new Income Tax Act contained many special exemptions and incentives the commission had found objectionable and removed the federal Estate Tax Act, which had been a significant obstacle to the increasing concentration of wealth. Nevertheless, while the post-1972 federal taxation system bears little resemblance to that advocated in the Carter report, the report's influence is reflected in the partial taxation of capital gains and changes in tax administration.
LES MACDONALD

Taylor, Charles, philosopher, political theorist (b at Montréal 5 Nov 1931). He was educated at McGill and Oxford. In *Explanation of Behaviour* (1964), Taylor maintained that explanations of human actions involve reference to purposes and an element of interpretation. As a result he saw the SOCIAL SCIENCES as different in method from the physical sciences. After teaching philosophy and political science at McGill, he became Chichele Professor of political and social theory at Oxford (1976); he returned to the political science department at McGill in 1982, was VP of the federal NEW DEMOCRATIC PARTY and president of the Québec NDP. In addition to his well-known *Pattern of Politics* (1970), he produced a noteworthy philosophical commentary, *Hegel* (1975), and in 1979 published *Hegel and Modern Society*.
THOMAS MATHIEN

Taylor, Edward Plunkett, "E.P.," businessman (b at Ottawa 29 Jan 1901). Educated at McGill, Taylor joined the stockbroking firm McLeod, Young, Weir and Co in Ottawa in 1923, moving to Toronto in 1928 and becoming a director in 1929. In 1930, through a series of mergers, Taylor formed the Brewing Corp of Canada Ltd (later Canadian Breweries) and, by 1935, could indulge in his hobby of horses and horse racing. In 1940 C.D. HOWE placed Taylor on the executive committee of the Dept of Munitions and Supply. In 1941 he was moved to the US to handle the exchange of supplies between Canada and the US. He was appointed president and vice-chairman of the British Supply Council in N America and in Jan 1942 became head of the British Purchasing Commission as well. Exhaustion forced his resignation from the latter in Sept 1942, but he continued as Howe's deputy on the Anglo-American-Canadian Combined Production and Resources Board. After the war Taylor formed an "investment company," ARGUS CORPORATION with Wallace McCutcheon and Eric PHILLIPS. Taylor was president until 1969 and chairman 1969-71. In later years he concen-

By 1935 industrialist E.P. Taylor was rich enough to indulge in his hobby of horse breeding. He is shown here with the famed Northern Dancer in the 1960s (*courtesy Canada's Sports Hall of Fame*).

trated on land development in the Bahamas and on his racing interests. A director of the Ontario Jockey Club, he helped expand it in the 1950s. His thoroughbred operation, Windfields Farms, grew to be among the most successful in N America, NORTHERN DANCER and NIJINSKY being 2 of its famous horses.
ROBERT BOTHWELL

Taylor, Frederick Wellington, "Cyclone," hockey's first great star (b at Tara, Ont 23 June 1883; d at Vancouver 9 June 1979). He played in Listowel, Ont, and Portage la Prairie, Man, and joined hockey's first professional team in Houghton, Mich (1906). A swift, agile skater, Taylor attracted crowds and commanded high salaries. He played for Ottawa in 1908, Renfrew Millionaires 1910-11 and Vancouver Millionaires 1913-21, scoring 194 goals in 186 games. His fame as the outstanding player of hockey's formative years spread even to the Soviet Union, which he visited twice.
JAMES MARSH

Taylor, George William, clergyman, entomologist, conchologist (b at Derby, Eng 1854; d 22 Aug 1912, buried at Nanaimo, BC). After emigrating to Victoria, BC, in 1882, he studied theology and was ordained an Anglican priest in 1886. With the exception of 2 years in Ottawa (1888-90), he served his entire ministry in BC. Always an avid INSECT collector, he compiled the first list of insects, mainly moths and butterflies, native to the province. He was appointed the first provincial entomologist (honorary) of BC in 1887 in recognition of his expertise. Many new species of Lepidoptera were described by him in the *Canadian Entomologist* and the *Ottawa Naturalist*. He had, in addition to his collection of insects, the most comprehensive collection of marine shells in Canada, was a recognized authority on conchology, and published often on the MOLLUSCS of BC in *Nautilus*. In 1907 he was appointed curator of the Marine Biological Station on Departure Bay, a station that would be built under his direction.
P.W. RIEGERT

Taylor, Kenneth Douglas, diplomat, businessman (b at Calgary, Alta 5 Oct 1934). Joining the Trade Commissioner Service in 1959, Taylor became ambassador to Iran in 1977 and was catapulted to prominence by engineering the "Canadian Caper." For over 2 months, he and immigration officer John Sheardown and their wives hid 6 Americans after the US Embassy had been seized by Iranian revolutionaries and 66 hostages taken. On 28 Jan 1980 the 6 Americans, with Taylor not far behind, escaped the country using Canadian passports. Coming at a low point in America's self-esteem, the news was sensational, and the stylish, gregarious, unorthodox Taylor became an instant celebrity. He was Canadian consul general in New York, 1981-84, and then left the public service, remaining in the US in business.
NORMAN HILLMER

Taylor, Roy Lewis, botanist (b at Olds, Alta 12 Apr 1932). A taxonomist and cytologist, Taylor was involved in the first major study of the QUEEN CHARLOTTE IS flora (1957-65), culminating in *Flora of the Queen Charlotte Islands* (1968). From 1965 to 1968 he was head of the taxonomy and economic botany section of the Dept of Agriculture, Ottawa. In 1968 he became director of the botanical garden and professor of botany and plant science at UBC. Taylor's major research interest is development of BC's cytological flora. Author, coauthor or editor of over 120 publications (1963-), he has received many awards and honours, such as the Queen's Silver Jubilee Medal and membership in the Linnean Soc of London.
SYLVIA TAYLOR

Taylor, Thomas Griffith, geographer, educator, explorer (b at Walthamstow, Eng 1 Dec 1880; d at Sydney, Australia 4 Nov 1963). A dynamic personality who did research on every continent, Taylor founded the first Canadian department of geography at U of T (1935). He was educated as a geologist at U of Sydney, Australia, and at Emmanuel College, Cambridge. He was chosen chief geologist for the 1910-12 Scott Antarctic Expedition and did the first mapping of that continent. A glacier and a dry valley are named for him. Taylor also founded the first department of geography in Australia in 1920 at U of Sydney, then moved to U of Chicago's dept of geography (1927). It was on the initiative of economist Harold INNIS that Taylor was invited to U of T in 1935. He remained there until 1951 during which time the department achieved an international reputation. An outstanding teacher, Taylor was the author of some 20 books and 200 scientific articles.
MARIE SANDERSON

Teacher's Cove is one of the largest of nearly 100 prehistoric sites discovered in southern NB's PASSAMAQUODDY BAY region. An extensive shell-midden deposit represents over 2000 years of human habitation. The site was inhabited at different times in the past, both on a year-round basis and as a seasonal camp. A distinctive feature first found at this site was the use of semi-subterranean house dwellings of about 2000 years ago. In later times, the WIGWAM became the major house type. The site was most intensively occupied about 1000 years ago. Shellfish, deer, moose, bear and beaver provided the major food sources as well as raw materials for clothing and tools. These ancient people were probably the ancestors of the MICMAC—MALISEET natives now living in the Maritimes.
DAVID L. KEENLYSIDE

Teaching Profession, broadly defined, includes all those offering instruction in public or private institutions or independently. As defined here, the teaching profession includes only those who are licensed by the provincial and territorial authorities to provide instruction to elementary and secondary students in publicly supported schools.

The gradual development of publicly supported SCHOOL SYSTEMS in the early 1800s was the critical factor in the creation of Canada's teaching profession. The ideals of free and universal education accorded well with the aspirations of many pioneers who had emigrated to Canada to seek a better life (*see* EDUCATION, HISTORY OF). Initially, communities hired almost anyone who was willing to teach. By the mid-1800s, however, the colonial governments had begun to express more interest in public education and to provide more financial support; at the same time, various superintendents of education were fighting to establish schools for the training of teachers (normal school) and a certification system that would ensure minimal teacher qualifications.

Formation of Teachers' Associations The advances in education in the 1800s were accompanied by repeated attempts by teachers to form local associations. In the early days teachers' organizations were dominated by Department of Education officials, inspectors, clergymen and influential laymen. As a result, association meetings tended to be devoted principally to inspirational addresses or discussions of teaching methods and rarely to teachers' concerns about their living and working conditions, which in the early 1900s were very poor. In 1910 annual salaries for women elementary-school teachers in urban schools were in the $300-$1000 range, while those for men ranged from $600 to $1400. In the secondary schools, salaries ranged from $800 to $1800 for women and $1000 to $2100 for men. Job security was virtually nonexistent. Conditions were particularly harsh in rural areas, where poorly paid teachers were assigned to spartan, ill-equipped, one-room schools and were often obliged to function as janitors and to accept primitive and isolated accommodation.

Teacher dissatisfaction finally came to a head in the years during and immediately after WWI. Teachers' salaries had remained static, but the cost of living had nearly doubled. In one area after another, teachers formed provincial associations to fight for improvements in salary, tenure and pensions. A national body, the Canadian Teachers' Federation (CTF), was founded in 1920, by which date there was at least one association in every province. Much of this organizational activity took place in secret because of the general hostility towards labour unions at that time. Although a majority of the modern teacher associations existed by 1920, the profession was not in fact completely organized in the provinces and territories until 1955. In 1983 the 14 provincial and territorial associations which are members of the CTF represented more than 220 000 teachers.

In Québec the first provincial organization of French-speaking teachers was a federation of rural female teachers formed in 1937. In 1946 this group and 2 others, representing rural male teachers and urban teachers, became federated as la Corporation générale des instituteurs et institutrices catholiques de la province du Québec. In 1967 the name was changed to la Corporation des enseignants du Québec. A fundamental organizational change occurred in 1974 when the corporation became the Centrale de l'enseignement du Québec and made membership available to groups representing all persons working in Québec schools. Neither CEQ nor any of its predecessors have ever been members of the CTF.

The fledgling teacher associations sought, first of all, to improve salaries and procure TENURE protection and pensions, and to attain professional status and advances in education. In 1919 a group of 178 teachers in Victoria, BC, staged a 2-day strike over salaries — the first teacher strike in the British Empire. The BC Department of Education succeeded in mediating an amicable settlement. The government subsequently took the first step toward establishing an arbitration procedure for salary disputes. Further strikes and resignations occurred in the western provinces during the 1920s. A particularly bitter incident occurred in Brandon, Man, in 1922, when 80 teachers resigned in protest against the board's request that they accept a 25% reduction in salary.

The early economic goals of the teacher associations were not met quickly. Although the delegates to the 1920 CTF convention adopted the slogan "Double the 1914 basis" as part of a Canada-wide campaign, the average annual salary ($1600) to which they aspired was not achieved until after WWII. On the other hand, pension protection was more easily achieved. In 1920 only Québec (since 1856), NB, Newfoundland and Ontario had pension plans for teachers. In the next 20 years plans were established in Man (1925), NS (1928), BC (1929), Sask (1930), PEI (1931) and Alta (1939).

During the GREAT DEPRESSION, teaching salaries were cut and competition for employment increased. Although economic conditions improved generally, the federal government's order-in-council of 1942-43 froze teachers in their jobs and severely limited their salary increases. The postwar period of prosperity and rapidly expanding population brought a critical shortage of teachers that continued until the early 1970s. The number of teachers rose from 38 000 in 1910, to 76 000 in 1940, to 249 000 in 1970 and to a peak of 270 000 in 1978. Although the number of full-time teachers has dropped, the size of the teaching force has continued to grow as a result of the increasing employment of part-time teachers. The percentage of teachers employed part-time rose from 2% in 1973 to more than 7% in 1983.

Collective Bargaining Rights The Alberta Teachers' Association was, in 1941, the first association to acquire full bargaining rights, including the right to strike. The Manitoba Teachers' Society acquired similar rights in 1948. However, in 1956, negotiation procedures substituting binding arbitration for strike rights were written into the Manitoba Public Schools Act. Saskatchewan teachers also gained the right to bargain in the 1940s. Teachers in the other provinces continued to bargain informally and to obtain improvements in salaries and benefits without resorting to sanctions. There were only 5 or 6 minor strikes in the 1950s, but in the 1960s there were 6 mass resignations and 42 strikes in 5 provinces. The majority of the strikes occurred in Québec. Strike action by teacher associations that still had no formal bargaining rights continued in the 1970s.

Professional Concerns Founders of the various teachers' associations sought not only economic security but the establishment of teaching as a profession that was equal in status to LAW and MEDICINE. In particular, teachers fought for compulsory membership in their association, a code of ethics, the power to discipline members who did not abide by the code, and ultimately for control over standards of entrance to the profession.

The legislatures of Saskatchewan (1935) and Alberta (1936) enacted teaching profession Acts making membership in teachers' professional organizations mandatory for all teachers employed in the public schools. By 1960 membership in all provincial associations was automatic or compulsory and most associations had acquired some disciplinary powers. All of the teacher associations outside Québec have adopted professional codes of ethics that serve as guides to teacher conduct.

Teacher Education and Certification Although the provincial departments of education reserve the power to issue teaching certificates, teachers have nevertheless campaigned for higher standards of certification. Initially the goal was to ensure that all teachers completed high school before entering normal school, a goal that had not been achieved by 1939. After WWII it was agreed that all teachers should hold degrees and that all teacher preparation should take place under university auspices. In 1950 only about 10% of teachers held degrees and most teachers were still trained in teachers' colleges; by 1980, 73% of the teaching force held degrees. Eight provinces currently require all or most new teachers to hold a degree. The transfer of teacher training to the universities was not completed until the late 1970s.

Self-Regulatory Powers Teachers' associations have not yet assumed complete responsibility for the certification, decertification, competence and continuing education of their members. In the early 1980s, however, Ontario and Alberta proposed to the teachers' associations that they adopt a full self-governing role on the condition that the teachers agree to split their organiza-

tions into 2 groups — a professional college in which membership would be compulsory, and a voluntary-membership association responsible for collective bargaining. Teachers rejected the proposal, preferring to maintain single united associations.

Educational and Social Concerns Canadian teachers have long argued for the reorganization of the school system into larger units of administration in order to ensure the availability of schools with better facilities and broader course offerings. They have also consistently pressed for adequate financing for the school system.

Evaluation of students has been a source of persistent concern among teachers. For example, the need for external examinations for secondary-school students has been debated within educational circles for decades. Teachers have generally maintained that evaluation of student progress should be the responsibility of the school in which the student is enrolled. Teachers have also participated actively in revisions of provincial curriculum guidelines (*see* CURRICULUM DEVELOPMENT) and in developing local modifications of curriculum and units of work in CANADIAN STUDIES. The maintenance of discipline in the classroom and school appears to be an increasing problem. Studies reveal that, although violence is rare in Canadian schools, verbal abuse of teachers is fairly common.

Teachers have consistently supported equal rights and opportunities for women (who now comprise only 56% of the teaching force, compared to 81% in 1910). Nevertheless, although sex discrimination in salary schedules has disappeared and no overt barriers to promotion exist, the proportion of principalships and vice-principalships held by women has declined dramatically, from 34% in 1960 to 14% in 1980.

International Development In 1962 CTF initiated a program of assistance through which Canadian teachers devote their vacation periods to providing in-service programs for teachers in various countries. Since 1962 over 900 volunteer Canadian teachers have provided academic and professional upgrading for over 22 000 overseas teachers.   GERALDINE GILLISS

Reading: S. McCurdy, *The Legal Status of the Canadian Teacher* (1968); C.E. Phillis, *The Development of Education in Canada* (1957).

Team Handball is also known as European or Olympic handball. The object is to score goals by passing and throwing a ball (about the size of a soccer ball) into the opponents' goal. It is played indoors on a court similar in size to that for basketball, with teams of 7 players. The game was introduced in Germany in the 1890s but did not become popular until after WWI, when it adopted many rules from SOCCER. At first played outdoors with teams of 11 players, the indoor version became the standard form in 1952. It has been an Olympic Games event since 1972. Team handball is widely played in Europe, where its popularity is second only to that of soccer. In Canada, the game was originally called "Borden Ball" because a simplified version was introduced during WWII by European prisoners of war detained at Camp Borden, Ont. During the 1950s, team handball became an organized competitive sport, and the Canadian Team Handball Federation was formed in 1962.
                                    BARBARA SCHRODT

Technical University of Nova Scotia, Halifax, was founded in 1907. It provides 3 years of professional engineering after the preliminary 2-year courses offered by other Maritime universities. The university's charter was amended in 1947 to permit curriculum expansion and research. Programs are available in most branches of modern engineering and in specialties such as architecture, planning, food science and computer science. The university has major research centres in fisheries technology, energy studies, water resources, applied microelectronics, CAD/CAM (*see* ROBOTICS), materials science and biomedical engineering. The community is served by extension facilities, including several of the academic departments and research centres and the Atlantic Region Management Training Centre. LOIS KERNAGHAN

Technology Definitions of technology have ranged from "everything we learn" to "the application of science to the solution of industrial problems." A more useful definition might be "technology is the skills, tools and machines used by members of a society to convert material objects [eg, natural RESOURCES] into products useful to themselves." Technologies affect and are affected by the society that uses them, and the importance of a technological development can only be evaluated after consideration of a variety of social and technical factors. Technological developments depend upon necessary pre-existing technology as well as a favourable political or economic climate.

The technologies by which the native people adapted to the regions of Canada, from the Great Lakes to the Far North, depended greatly on geographical conditions and local resources. Notable achievements include the birchbark CANOE, the SNOWSHOE, the TIPI, the IGLOO and the KAYAK. Long after European settlement, Canada still had a relatively sparse population, and because of its colonial status was primarily a source of raw materials and an importer of manufactured goods and technology (*see* MERCANTILISM). MANUFACTURING remained proportionally smaller in Canada than in Europe or the US until WWI, and most ENGINEERING achievements to that time involved the solution of special problems associated with settlement in a cold climate, TRANSPORTATION over long distances and to remote areas, or extraction of natural resources.

The Pioneer Period (1600-1850)

The first period, extending from the arrival of the first Europeans to the beginning of the RAILWAY age, covers the settlement of Canada as a European colony. Generally the technologies practised were transplanted directly from Europe and with minor changes were those in use since the medieval period. Houses were built using timber frames; canal locks had mitre gates and cut-stone chambers; and mines were developed with brute force and black powder. Such modifications as were made reflected the efforts of settlers to adjust to Canadian GEOGRAPHY, climate and natural resources, and to native technologies. They paralleled political and social adjustments experienced by the young colony.

Fisheries The earliest significant technology was associated with the FISHERIES. The international rivalry for the GRAND BANKS cod resource resulted in the first English and French settlements in Newfoundland and NS. These settlements were directly affected by existing fishing technology. The French and Portuguese salted their catch immediately and sailed for home without much contact with land (ie, the "green" fishery). English fishermen, on the other hand, did not have cheap supplies of salt and were forced to establish shore stations to dry their catch to preserve it for transportation to market (ie, the "dry" fishery). During the period, this basic technology changed very little, but undoubtedly shaped the character of the people and led to establishment of the SHIPBUILDING industry for which Maritimers became world famous in the 1860s and 1870s.

Construction The major technical problem facing all settlers was shelter. In the first urban areas, construction directly copied European methods; in rural areas it illustrated adaptations to local materials and conditions. Western European timber-frame construction, familiar to most colonists, was first used and adapted by the HABITANTS and ACADIANS. Wood, rather than masonry, was used to fill in walls. LOYALISTS, settling in the Maritimes and in Upper Canada, built HOUSES of logs fastened together at the corners, an excellent way of using the abundant timber resource (*see* LOG HOUSES). Settlers on the treeless prairies near the Red R used heavy prairie sod (see SOD HOUSES) for their first shelters.

Agriculture All pioneers practised some form of AGRICULTURE, which involved probably the most universal technology. Often Canadian agriculture was quite different from that practised in Europe. Agricultural technology, more than any other, is profoundly affected by local conditions of weather, soil, water and pests, and by land-tenure systems. The Canadian farmer did not inherit a farm, he created one: Acadian farmers had to build dikes to protect their fields in the Fundy marshes; habitants or Loyalists in the St Lawrence Valley had to clear thick stands of huge trees with primitive tools and inadequate labour. Each group of 5 Loyalist families received a set of tools. Every 2 families received a crosscut saw and a whipsaw. The axes that were issued to the settlers were short-handled ship axes, rather than felling axes, and were almost useless because they would not hold an edge (*see* TOOLS, CARPENTRY). It often took many years for these pioneer farmers to clear a few acres, while building shelters, cultivating crops and looking after animals.

Early farmers were fortunate in being able to learn from the Indians how to use indigenous animals, birds, fish and plants (*see* PLANTS, NATIVE USES). The culture of CORN, BEANS and SQUASH, a legacy of the HURON, was invaluable. Gradually, subsistence mixed farming was established. Heavy plows, called "French" plows, similar to the medieval 2-wheeled plow drawn by oxen, were first used by the Acadians and habitants. A smaller, rugged implement called the bull plow, with no wheels or coulter, was developed for maneuvering around stumps and rocks. Gradually, iron was substituted for wood, and frequently an all-iron "Scotch" plow was imported to Canada. Plows continued to be refined in shape and size until the steel-bladed plow was designed for the heavy sod of the prairies in the 1880s. Wherever farmers had access to markets, they sold surpluses and improved their farms with the proceeds. In the early 19th century, horse-drawn mowers were brought in from the US; local blacksmiths adopted the design and the Canadian AGRICULTURAL IMPLEMENTS INDUSTRY was born.

Mills The 2 greatest chores facing settlers were grinding grain and sawing lumber. Champlain built a gristmill in 1607, probably the first mill of any kind in N America, at PORT-ROYAL on the Bay of Fundy. It was the right and responsibility of the seigneur in NEW FRANCE to build gristmills and SAWMILLS, although they were seldom built as often as they were needed. Many early mills had simple saws and a run of stones using the same waterwheel. The arrival of the Loyalists in

Philemon Wright's mill at the Chaudière Falls on the Ottawa R in 1823. Early industrial development depended largely on wind, water or animal power (*courtesy Public Archives of Canada/C-608*).

Upper Canada brought an immediate need for additional mills. Gristmills and sawmills were established in Kingston Mills on the Cataraqui R in 1783-84 and on the Napanee R at Napanee in 1797. Both operations, which had been mechanized during the Middle Ages in Europe, could be fairly easily adapted to Canadian conditions. Most areas of eastern Canada had waterpower to drive mills; some relied on wind or tide. Eventually, mills were established to produce TEXTILES and to work iron. Mills were the nuclei of many small villages and introduced mechanical engineering to Canada.

Transportation has been the greatest challenge facing Canadian engineers. The rough country, scattered settlements and difficult climate posed problems seldom encountered in western Europe. The first solutions involved the importation from Europe of various forms of water transport which varied from full-rigged ships to smaller boats (oar and sail) that were normally carried on the larger ships. The French were quick to adopt the Indian birchbark CANOE for travel on the inland waterways of the Canadian SHIELD. The Hudson's Bay Co developed the YORK BOAT for the journey inland from Hudson Bay. Early settlement was restricted to water routes and, as it spread westward along the St Lawrence past the Lachine rapids, these routes were improved by construction of CANALS, varying from tiny ditches transporting bateaux, to complex waterways, eg, the RIDEAU CANAL.

Shipbuilding began in the 17th century but was generally retarded by colonial restrictions until the mid-19th century, when shipyards in the Atlantic provinces and Québec City began to turn out larger and larger ships. Steamship technology, developed by Robert Fulton in the US, was quickly borrowed by engineers and businessmen on the St Lawrence and Great Lakes. John MOLSON financed the construction of the ACCOMMODATION in Montréal in 1809 to service the busy route to Québec City, using a locally made steam engine. In 1816 the FRONTENAC, a comparatively large ship with a Boulton and Watt engine imported from England, was the first steamship to operate on the Great Lakes. These simple, low-pressure steam engines were not very powerful and used large quantities of fuel wood. In the second period of technology, the development of the compound engine, which burned coal, increased the efficiency of these vessels so much that they virtually eliminated sailing ships.

Early land-vehicle transportation was limited almost exclusively to urban areas. Initially, construction of roads over the long distances between settlements was prohibitively expensive, even for dirt trails. By the end of the pioneer period some arterial roads were completed. Cedar logs were used to build "corduroy" sections in swampy locations and gravel surfaces were laid where traffic was heaviest. In the 1840s Canadians even experimented with plank roads, using cheap forest products, but the winter ice and spring thaw left most of these roads a shambles. Only urban roads were paved, usually with crude cobblestones. The RED RIVER CART, drawn by oxen or horses, was used in the reasonably level and treeless prairies.

Lumbering The TIMBER TRADE began along the major rivers of NB and spread to the St Lawrence and Ottawa rivers in the early 19th century. The single-bitted axes for felling, broad axes for squaring, and sleighs for hauling to water were borrowed almost unchanged from similar operations in eastern Baltic countries.

Mining The first loads of ore hauled back to Europe by CARTIER and FROBISHER proved worthless and it was not until the discovery of gold in BC and the KLONDIKE, and of silver and gold in the Canadian Shield in the late 19th century, that the great MINERAL RESOURCES of Canada were successfully exploited. COAL was mined sporadically in Cape Breton from the early 18th century. Bog IRON ORE was mined, smelted and processed at FORGES SAINT-MAURICE near Trois-Rivières from 1733 and at Normandale in Upper Canada. The GEOLOGICAL SURVEY OF CANADA (est 1842) played an enormous part in developing Canada's MINERAL wealth as field parties meticulously examined the country's rock outcroppings, interpreted their significance and plotted their results on maps, which led many prospectors to new deposits of economic minerals.

Summary The pioneer period is characterized by the struggle to survive in a new and often hostile climate. Pioneers brought familiar technologies from Europe and the US, and skillfully adapted them to local conditions. Examples of such adaptations include the infilling of timber-frame houses by logs, rather than masonry; the use of local woods such as tamarack for shipbuilding; and the positioning of waterwheels inside mills to protect them from snow and ice. During this period, Canada was a water oriented society, dependent on water for agriculture, fish, transportation and power.

Many of the engineers who were to play a vital role in Canada's development received their first training on transportation projects. Although they were practical people with little theoretical education, they successfully undertook very large construction projects. Thomas KEEFER started his career on the Erie Canal and the WELLAND CANAL and went on to build railways, bridges and aqueducts. Sandford FLEMING worked as an engineer on the INTERCOLONIAL RY and later developed Standard TIME.

Developmental Period (1850-1900)

Sweeping changes in machines, materials and power moved engineering from the Middle Ages to the Machine Age in these 50 years. In the 1850s, political as well as economic forces promoted the growth of railways, while steam engines and new MACHINERY began to transform mill and farm. In 1867 Confederation brought about the Intercolonial Ry, and eventually the NATIONAL POLICY, the Patent Act, the CANADIAN PACIFIC RAILWAY and the opening of the PRAIRIE WEST. The Atlantic provinces saw the end of the sailing ship and the fishing industry was expanded by refrigeration and use of the steamship. Domestic manufacturing became established on a modest scale, encouraged by the National Policy.

Transportation The advantages of railways for Canada were obvious: they were far more flexible than canals and did not freeze up in winter. When the GUARANTEE ACT (1849) offered financial help, many local railways were started in Upper and Lower Canada and the Atlantic provinces. While most of the expertise and rolling stock came originally from England, Canadian engineers did much of the construction. Canadian shops, which began by making spikes and rolling rails, moved on to building locomotives. By 1860 most major communities in the Canadas were connected by the GRAND TRUNK RY, while the ST LAWRENCE AND ATLANTIC ROAD joined Montréal with Portland, Maine. Completion of the Intercolonial Ry in 1876 fulfilled a condition of Confederation by joining central Canada and NS and NB. Construction of the CPR through the incredibly difficult rock and muskeg of the Precambrian Shield, across the prairies and through the Rockies became one of Canada's greatest engineering feats. This task brought the highest levels of railway technology to Canada from the US (Canadian innovations were negligible), opened the vast grainfields of the prairies, encouraged immigration and literally tied the country together. Railway technology also had an effect on BRIDGE building. The tubular construction of the Victoria Bridge at Montréal (completed Dec 1859) was an engineering marvel of the day. Some of the world's first cantilever bridges were constructed over the

Grand Trunk Railway locomotive No 162 (c1860). Development of steam technology had a profound influence on transportation and industrial development (courtesy National Gallery of Canada).

Niagara and Fraser rivers in 1883 and over the Saint John R in 1884.

Canals were recognized as efficient carriers of bulk cargo, and as shipping increased on the Great Lakes improvements were needed. The Welland Canal was rerouted and deepened, from 3 m to 4.6 m, in 1883. A canal was built at Sault Ste Marie in 1895; the Soulange Canal was opened in 1899. In NS the long-awaited Shubenacadie Canal, connecting the Bay of Fundy and Dartmouth, was opened in 1861. More construction was undertaken on the TRENT CANAL to provide another route to the upper Great Lakes.

In Atlantic Canada, the shipbuilding industry began to mature, and, as Canadian sailing ships, such as the MARCO POLO, began to acquire a world reputation, dozens of yards in Québec, NS, NB and PEI entered a period of great activity. Ships built in Canada for Britain traded all over the Empire. Meanwhile, steamboat technology matured and wooden hulls with crude engines were replaced by high-pressure compound engines, contained in iron and steel hulls. The changing technology had a devastating effect on the Maritime shipbuilding industry.

In the 1880s, Canada's cities began to grow beyond the size where everyone could walk to work and public transportation was needed. Horse-drawn omnibuses were followed by horse-drawn streetcars on rails, and when the electric street car was developed, Toronto (1885) and Windsor (1886) had some of the earliest lines in N America. The safety bicycle appeared in the 1890s, radically transforming the common person's transportation.

Agriculture Eastern Canada lost its preferential markets in Britain for wheat and gradually adopted DAIRY FARMING. The concept of CHEESE factories was brought to Ontario from New York in the 1860s; factories produced a more uniform cheese of higher quality suitable for sale in the cities. Farm machinery took over many tasks. Massey, Harris, Hamilton, Shantz, Frost and Wood, and other companies developed a full line of farm machinery for most operations. Various kinds of food processing, meat packing and eventually refrigeration greatly extended produce markets. In western Canada, new strains of early-maturing WHEAT permitted the cultivation of more areas, and by 1900 most of the problems of adjusting to the climate and creating marketing procedures had been solved. Steam tractors, steel plows, efficient binders and threshing machines transformed the grasslands into a granary. Although many traction engines and implements were imported from the US and Britain, the Massey and Harris mowers and binders were world famous for efficiency and reliability.

Fishing By the 1860s Atlantic fishing technology had been changed by the introduction of the longline or "bultow." Refrigeration and railroads increased the fresh-fish market. The growth of the live lobster trade and the rapid spread of the lobster-canning industry occurred towards the end of the period, as the New England lobster beds were depleted.

Lumbering continued in eastern Canada as huge sawmills were built to supply the growing cities of New England. By the late 1860s, wood pulp was being incorporated into the papermaking process in Canada, and pulpwood cutters began to harvest bush areas that had previously been thought valueless. The railways brought large-scale lumbering to BC, where some of the greatest stands of trees began to fall for lumber and PULP AND PAPER. Technology differed somewhat in eastern and western Canada: the western mountains did not have convenient river systems to float out the huge logs; more mechanization was needed and sawmills were therefore on a larger scale.

Mining started dramatically in BC with the Fraser R gold rush of the late 1850s. Of more lasting technical implication was the discovery of base-metal deposits in southeastern BC. These deposits, such as the Sullivan Mine (COMINCO), which are still being worked, launched one of Canada's first large-scale mining camps. The huge nickel-copper deposits in the Sudbury Basin were originally uncovered in a CPR rock cut. Metallurgical techniques were often the final key to unlocking the wealth of these mines. The Orford process was used to separate the copper-nickel ores of the Sudbury Basin; differential flotation was used to extract the complex ores, containing mostly lead and zinc, at the Trail smelter in BC. While pools of tar and PETROLEUM were known and used by the Indians for medicine for generations, the first commercial development occurred in 1858 at Oil Springs, Ont, when a small well was dug with ordinary water-well equipment. A refinery was built at nearby Sarnia where the oil was taken by a pipeline. Although the field was depleted in a few decades, the tremendously important OIL AND NATURAL GAS industries started in Canada. The ASBESTOS mines in the Eastern Townships of Québec went into production in this period. The KLONDIKE GOLD RUSH (1898) attracted world attention and forced the establishment of new transportation routes. One of the main routes was forged through the WHITE PASS to Whitehorse by the narrow-gauge WHITE PASS AND YUKON RAILWAY. The Canadian engineer's first confrontation with PERMAFROST occurred in the gold diggings, where it was penetrated by wood fires and then steam thawing hoses. The real challenge for engineers came later when they had to redesign dredges to withstand the increased wear caused by the rock-hard permafrost.

Power Steam engines transformed transportation and, when applied to INDUSTRY and agriculture, gave a much more flexible power source. Steam power was only gradually applied to industry. Mills or factories would often add steam as a backup or would use steam if expanding. Steam power permitted new plants to locate near suppliers or markets because they were not tied to waterpower sites. Finally, ELECTRIC POWER made its Canadian debut in the 1880s. Many waterpower sites were developed to exploit this new, flexible and adaptable ENERGY source. Some of the earliest sites were developed to provide electric lighting for big commercial mills (where open flames were a fire hazard), such as at Young's sawmill, Ottawa, in 1882, and at the Canada Cotton Co in Cornwall, Ont, in 1883. The harnessing of the awesome power of NIAGARA FALLS (1895) heralded a new age.

Manufacturing The farm machinery industry grew dramatically, employing new sources of power, manufacture and assembly; the railway made possible wider distribution and greater concentration. Engine and tool companies were established to provide machinery to the railway and forestry industries, eg, the Victoria Foundry and Machine Shops (1854), Ottawa, which manufactured steam engines, boilers and sawmill machinery; the Canadian Locomotive Co started as Tutton and Duncans Foundry in Kingston, Ont (1854), which made locomotives and mining machinery; and Goldie-McCulloch (1859), Galt, Ont, which manufactured boilers, engines, pumps and flour-mill equipment. Flour milling was radically changed by the introduction of rolling mills, which processed hard western wheat more quickly. One of the first to try the new roller mills was the E.W.B. Snider mill at St Jacobs, Ont, in the 1870s. The Ogilvie Flour Milling Co, founded in 1801, built a huge new plant in Montréal in 1886, incorporating the latest reduction roller mills. Bessemer patented his method of producing steel in 1856, but it was nearly the end of the century before steel was available in large quantities for bridge and building construction in Canada. Most of the early steel imported to Canada was used by the railways for rails. The changeover from iron rails to steel started in the early 1870s. However, it took many years for metallurgists to improve the quality of steel so that it could withstand the varied strains of a structure such as a bridge. One of the first all-steel bridges in Canada was the cantilever railway bridge built at Saint John, NB, in 1884. Like steel, CEMENT had been used for centuries, but reliable, cheap, hydraulic cement was not available in Canada until the 1890s. The first plant to manufacture true hydraulic or "Portland" cement was likely the Napanee Cement Co at Strathcona, Ont, in 1891.

Wood continued to be a basic material in construction; the advent of commercial sawmills made standard-sized lumber available. The balloon frame, built up from the common "two-by-four" (about 5 cm by 10 cm), began to replace timber-frame construction. Wire nails became cheap and universally available. In composite buildings, cast-iron columns and wrought-iron beams gradually gave way to steel by 1900. The federal PARLIAMENT BUILDINGS in Ottawa, constructed in the 1860s, were among the first buildings in N America to have an interior iron frame. Brick construction became much more common as beehive and downdraft kilns and brick-forming machines were introduced. Concrete began to be used more frequently in floors and foundations and, when reinforced with steel, eventually took over, transforming the CONSTRUCTION INDUSTRY. By the end of the period, multistoreyed urban buildings and factories had central heating, electric light, elevators, and water and sewer services.

Communication technology advanced rapidly with the electric TELEGRAPH, ushered in as a companion to the railways in the 1850s. Bell's TELEPHONE appeared in the 1870s and, by the 1880s and 1890s, exchanges were common in most larger cities. The first telephone exchange in Canada was installed in 1878 in Hamilton and by the end of the year it had 40 telephones.

Water and Sanitation Urban areas require large supplies of WATER for domestic and industrial use and fire protection and a corresponding system to handle WASTE. By the 1870s the water supplies of most large cities were pumped by steam, and by 1900 some were using sand filters or hypochlorite of lime for WATER TREATMENT. Toronto and Kingston had pumping stations by 1841 and 1850, respectively. Halifax and Saint John had gravity systems even earlier (1848 and 1838, respectively). Many cities had drainage systems designed to handle surface water from heavy rain and snow, but not sewage.

Technical Education began in this period in the workshops of railways, factories and schools. Formal engineering education began slowly with CIVIL ENGINEERING at King's College, Fredericton (1854); McGill (1871); School of Practical Science, Toronto (1873); École Polytechnique, Montréal (1873); Royal Military College, Kingston, Ont (1876), and the School of Mining and Agriculture, Queen's University, Kingston (1893). Most of these universities offered courses in civil, MINING and MECHANICAL ENGINEERING, and quickly added ELECTRICAL and CHEMICAL ENGINEERING programs. The engineering profession had grown rapidly since the great canal and railway building days. Engineers of the time included Thomas Keefer and his brother Samuel, Sir Casimir GZOWSKI, Sir John KENNEDY and the SHANLY brothers.

Early Modern Period (1900-1940)

The first decade of the century brought unparalleled agricultural development and prosperity, and appeared to mark the maturation of the national economy. The harnessing of Niagara (1895) began a new industrial revolution based largely on electricity and related CHEMICAL INDUSTRIES. WWI was a proving ground for the internal combustion engine in wheeled vehicles and aircraft. WWI developments, applied to BUSH FLYING, helped open the Canadian North. The gasoline engine found many uses after the war, and the diesel engine became popular in public transportation. Finally, RADIO, TELEVISION and aircraft allowed Canadians to communicate more effectively.

Agriculture Mechanization of the prairie farm continued through the boom of 1901 to 1911. The gasoline tractor replaced the steam tractor during WWI and power takeoff, pneumatic tires and hydraulic-lifting equipment were developed in the 1920s. Many cultivating and harvesting machines were developed, eg, row cultivators for tobacco and corn crops and the Sylvester auto-thresher that appeared in western Canada. New strains of early maturing wheat (eg, Marquis, Garnet, Reward) permitted farming farther N on the prairies. The new technologies of pasteurization, refrigeration and the commercial canning of meat, vegetables and fruit, as well as condensed milk and processed cheese, helped provide food to growing urban areas after the war. In 1900 farming was still mainly traditional, but by the end of WWII it was becoming a highly mechanized industry.

Fishing in the Maritime provinces underwent great changes. Corporate amalgamations provided more capital for technological development and, by 1908, many steamships were converted to trawlers, as were naval minesweepers after WWI. The traditional schooner began to disappear. Improved refrigeration, transportation and communication provided better facilities for handling fresh fish. Freezing of bait fish had been introduced in the 1890s, but the freezing of fresh fish was developed in the Great Lakes fisheries at the turn of the century. The practice was adopted on both the Atlantic and Pacific coasts, although the process gave only short-term preservation. In 1929 the American Clarence Birdseye demonstrated that quick-freezing produced a better product and the greater use of freezers by retailers greatly changed marketing procedures. Finally the introduction of the internal combustion engine to small craft gave fishermen increased mobility.

Transportation The success of the CPR encouraged 2 competitors, the GRAND TRUNK PACIFIC and the CANADIAN NORTHERN, to build transcontinental lines. The Temiskaming and Northern Ontario Railway (ONTARIO NORTHLAND) was constructed from North Bay, Ont, to James Bay (1901-31). The HUDSON BAY RY (1906-32) was built to open another saltwater port, at Churchill, Man, to prairie grain. Many branch lines were started into the PEACE RIVER LOWLAND.

Canals on the St Lawrence at Cornwall and Williamsburg, Ont, and Beauharnois, Qué were enlarged (1900-03). A final effort was made to complete the Trent Canal between 1895 and 1920, when the various sections were linked together. The PETERBOROUGH lift lock, designed by R.B. Rogers, was the largest of its kind in the world and an outstanding engineering achievement. In 1910 Manitoba's only canal lock was completed on the Red R at St Andrews. The increased size and number of ships on the Great Lakes made the New Welland Canal obsolete and a larger, more direct canal, called the Welland Ship Canal, was started in 1913, interrupted by the war and finished in 1932.

Cars and trucks passed from being curiosities to necessities. In the 1920s, provincial departments of highways were given authority to take over major trunk roads and to plan and supervise road planning and construction at all levels within the province. The building of highways was facilitated by a new generation of trucks and trawler tractors, adapted for road construction. Public transport was vital to the growing cities: horse-drawn buses had been replaced by electric streetcars in 46 Canadian cities by the 1920s (see URBAN TRANSPORTATION). The first motor buses were also appearing; a diesel bus was used in Montréal as early as 1932.

The flight of the SILVER DART (at Baddeck, NS, in 1909) was the first in the British Empire. Canadian pilots made major contributions to the war effort in WWI and returned home eager to fly. Surplus military aircraft were quickly adapted to peacetime tasks, often associated with lumbering and mining in northern areas. In 1919 a federal government agency, the Associate Air Research Committee, was established to foster aeronautical research in Canada. In 1925 W.R. TURNBULL perfected the electrically operated variable-pitch propeller, which was adopted around the world. The most famous of a new generation of bush planes was the NOORDUYN NORSEMAN, which was designed by Robert Noorduyn after he consulted with a large number of active pilots in 1935. During the GREAT DEPRESSION, one of the government's most successful, innovative, make-work programs involved building a string of AIRPORTS across the country (see AVIATION).

Mining The building of the Ontario Northland Ry led prospectors to the huge deposits of silver at Cobalt, then gold at Timmins and Kirkland Lk. These mines financed and encouraged other ventures, eg, the mines at Rouyn, Qué, and Flin Flon, Man. They also pioneered many of the underground hard-rock mining practices used throughout the rest of Canada. The Precambrian Shield was thoroughly examined by geologists and prospectors, who discovered many other precious and base-metal deposits. The BC coalfields expanded with the railways and deposits of natural gas were tapped in southern Alberta.

Metallurgists were forced to keep up with this expansion. New processes, varying from mine to mine, were needed for the extraction and refinement of ore. In 1903 Bett's electrolytic process was installed at the refinery in Trail, BC, to refine the lead content of the ore. In 1911 the first basic lined converters in Canada were used to smelt copper matte at Copper Cliff. International Nickel built a new electrolytic refining plant at Port Colborne, Ont, in 1916 to take advantage of the cheap electrical power available. Part of the solution to the problem in the Flin Flon smelter was the introduction of a suspended magnesite furnace arc in 1930. Electricity was fundamental to many of these processes. For example, in 1901, the manufacture of ALUMINUM and aluminum products began at Shawinigan Falls, Qué. This valuable industry advanced rapidly almost from coast to coast because, although the ore was imported and many of the finished products were exported, the processing required huge amounts of electricity, available at several locations in Canada.

Power Many sites in Québec on Canadian rivers were tapped primarily to serve new mines and pulp and paper mills, eg, at Grand Falls, NB (1928), pulp and paper; Shawinigan Falls (1902 on), pulp and paper, aluminum, industry; Saguenay Power at Isle Maligne, Qué (1925), pulp and paper, aluminum; Quinze R, western Qué (1923), mining; Abitibi Canyon, northern Ont (1929-33), mining, pulp and paper; Island Falls, Churchill R, Sask (1930), mining; West Kootenay Power (1897 on), Bonnington Falls, BC, mining. Industries which had used steam or waterpower converted to electricity whenever feasible, especially when the technology of transmitting electricity over long distances developed. The first long-distance transmission of electricity in Canada, and perhaps the British Empire, was carried out between the Batiscan R and Trois-Rivières, Qué, in 1897. The line was about 29 km long and carried 11 000 volts.

Another new source of power, the internal-combustion engine, found many uses as a stationary power source for running pumps, saws, generating equipment, etc.

Manufacturing The AUTOMOBILE INDUSTRY was added to the established and expanding industries related to railways and resource extraction. While dozens of cars were designed and built across Canada, only the McLaughlin really achieved success. Gordon McGregor, manager of the Walkerville Wagons Works, in Windsor, Ont, established the FORD MOTOR COMPANY OF CANADA in 1904. Production began almost immediately using Ford's famous assembly-line process, probably the first use in Canada. TEXTILE production, primarily woolens, continued in eastern Ontario and southern Québec, mostly using imported technology and raw material. Most new factories began employing the latest machine tools and electrical equipment, particularly during the serious labour shortages of the war.

US investment in Canada increased steadily after the American Civil War and by WWI had eclipsed British investment. As American investment was mostly equity investment, American ownership of Canadian companies rose from approximately 100 companies in 1900 to 1350 companies in 1934. Most advanced technology was imported directly from the US and many large manufacturers were subsidiaries of US companies (*see* FOREIGN INVESTMENT).

Forestry Starting in the early 20th century, steam "donkey" engines powered winches that dragged the huge logs out of the BC forests in a system called "ground leading." Eventually, "high leading" replaced the process because of greater efficiency. The first power saws appeared in 1939, but were so heavy and unreliable that they had to be operated by 2 men. The one-man light chain saw appeared after WWII.

Construction The skyscraper was pioneered in Chicago and New York, but tall buildings with steel skeletons soon appeared in Winnipeg (1904) and Toronto (1914), and when the federal Parliament Buildings were rebuilt (1916) a structural steel frame was used. Longer-span bridges were built, culminating in the Québec bridge (1917). Toronto's Governor's Bridge (1923) is said to be the world's first welded-steel bridge. In the 1920s reinforced concrete was used extensively in bridges in Peterborough, Calgary and Saskatoon. These bridges are among the most beautiful in Canada.

Industrial Chemistry The rapid expansion of electrochemistry in the 20th century permitted the economical production of many chemicals. A Canadian, Thomas WILLSON, developed the first successful commercial process for manufacturing calcium carbide. The first plant was established at Shawinigan, Qué, in 1904. The first contract sulphuric acid plant was established at Sulphide, Ont, in 1908. The SALT deposits at Windsor, Ont, were used to produce a number of sodium and chlorine compounds, such as the electrolytic production of sodium carbonate in 1919. Liquid and gaseous chlorine was produced at Sandwich, Ont, in 1911 for water purification, bleaching of pulp, and many other purposes. The electrolytic cell, used for many of these processes, was patented in Canada in 1908 by A.E. Gibbs. Another important technology was the manufacture of artificial fibres. The production of viscose rayon in Canada was started by the British firm Courtaulds in Cornwall, Ont, in 1925. The process used cellulose from wood pulp. In 1928 Canadian Celanese Ltd started to manufacture cellulose acetate rayon at Drummondville, Qué. Canadian Industries Ltd (CIL) began to manufacture transparent cellulose film at Shawinigan Falls in 1931.

Sanitation services improved as better sand filters cleansed city drinking water, but sewage treatment advanced slowly. Methods of decomposing sewage in tanks were adopted after 1910, and by 1916 the activated sludge process had been adopted by many cities. Some large cities disposed of garbage by incineration in high-temperature furnaces.

Communications The early telephone was improved with better cable sheathing and instruments; the improved loading coil appeared in 1916. Vacuum-tube telephone repeaters (installed in 1917) improved long-distance telephony, making possible the TRANSCANADA TELEPHONE SYSTEM (inaugurated in 1932). Dial telephones were first installed in Edmonton (1905), and during the 1920s and 1930s most urban areas of Ontario and Québec were converted.

Marconi established long-range, wireless telegraphy across the Atlantic in 1901, and in the 1920s the development of shortwave transmission vastly improved the signal. The first "wireless" (radio) broadcast was sent by a Canadian, Reginald FESSENDEN, in 1906 from a station in the US. In 1920 Marconi followed with the first broadcast in Canada, from Montréal. Commercial broadcasting progressed slowly as receiving sets became available, first in kit form, then preassembled. By 1927 Canadians could telephone Europe via the US, and by 1931 direct connections were possible. In 1925 a rudimentary form of telephotography (television) was established.

Technical Education Engineering colleges were established at the western universities (1906 to 1913). The engineering profession increased in numbers and prestige, and separate provincially chartered professional organizations were established in all provinces, except PEI, by 1923. Provincial associations were given the right to control entry into the profession, thus ensuring that only legally qualified engineers could practise in the provinces.

This period witnessed the foundation of most of Canada's modern primary and secondary industries. A basic network of transportation existed across the country and the conquest of the Canadian Shield was almost complete. The interdependence of technologies became more apparent as, for example, mining, electrical power, machine-tool factories, metallurgical and chemical industries were interconnected. Much of the impetus built up during and after WWI was lost during the Great Depression but revived in the next period.

Modern Period (1940-present)

The modern period of technology was ushered in by WWII. Canada's participation placed enormous demands on primary and secondary industries, transport and manpower. By 1945 farms, mines, shipyards and factories were highly mechanized and as efficient as any in the world. The war accelerated the development of young industries (eg, aluminum products) and brought about entirely new industries (eg, those centered around uranium).

Manufacturing During WWII Canadian industry expanded rapidly to produce munitions. This expansion stimulated the manufacture of tools, electrical apparatus, and chemicals and materials (eg, synthetic rubber). Heavy industries, eg, ship and aircraft manufacture, were vital to the war effort. The creation of atomic weapons by the US ushered in the field of NUCLEAR POWER, which stimulated Canada's uranium mining. By the end of the war, Canada had truly become industrialized: more people worked in secondary (ie, manufacturing) industry than on the farms or in the forests, and the output of secondary industry exceeded that of primary industry by any system of measurement. The postwar challenge was to convert this manufacturing potential to consumer goods, eg, in the buildup of the Canadian automotive industry (mainly as a subsidiary of giant US corporations), and the rapid expansion of mining and agricultural equipment manufacture.

Power A further challenge was to provide the energy necessary to sustain industry and to fuel public and private transportation. More hydroelectric sites were developed in BC, Ontario, Québec and Manitoba. Thermoelectric stations were built in the Maritimes and the Prairie provinces. Ontario opened the first nuclear-powered thermal station, at Rolphton in 1962. Natural-gas exploration continued in Alberta and Saskatchewan; the huge LEDUC oil field was discovered in 1947. The oil industry became very complex, producing gasoline, diesel and heating fuels, heavy oils for lubrication, and developing the huge PETROCHEMICAL INDUSTRY with its hundreds of by-products. Sarnia and Montréal became centres of the petrochemical industries, although gradually some industry shifted closer to the oil fields.

Mining and Metallurgy Chemical technology helped solve the metallurgical problems of the expanding mining industry. Plants producing war explosives were altered to produce mining and construction explosives. Mining technology was also in great demand after the war. Oil exploration revealed one of the world's largest deposits of POTASH in Saskatchewan. The extraction of this deep-lying mineral was a great challenge. The need to develop new sources of iron became urgent as US mines began to be depleted. Huge projects at Steep Rock, Ont, and in Labrador required the most modern, large-scale, earth-moving equipment, as well as hydroelectric power to bring the ore to steel mills in Hamilton and the US. The gold-mining industry that had supported Canada through 2 world wars was waning and the major postwar effort was directed to base metals and coal.

Transportation One of the largest engineering projects in Canada was the construction of the ST LAWRENCE SEAWAY, undertaken in conjunction with the US. This enterprise opened the up-

The Avro Arrow was one of the most advanced aircraft designs in the world. Its abrupt cancellation and replacement by American weapons was to many a symbol of Canada's unwillingness to develop its technology (*courtesy The Arrow Heads/Boston Mills Press*).

per Great Lakes to foreign and domestic saltwater ships, and also facilitated shipment of iron ore from Labrador to steel mills on the shores of Lks Ontario and Erie, as well as providing additional hydroelectric supplies.

Canada's wartime aircraft industry would have disappeared in competition with industries in other nations. Its demise was almost assured when the federal government cancelled the AVRO ARROW project. The cancellation of the most advanced military aircraft of its kind has been considered a great setback to the development of technology in Canada, although the Canadian aircraft industry continued to develop innovative STOL *(short-take-off-and-landing)* aircraft, such as the DE HAVILLAND OTTER and DE HAVILLAND DASH-7.

Postwar shipbuilding dwindled until only a few LAKE CARRIERS and saltwater fishing boats were produced. Canadian shipyards have already produced some of the most advanced ICE-BREAKERS and, with increased exploration for oil, gas and minerals in the Arctic, this technology has great potential.

Agriculture and Forestry Powerful and sophisticated machinery and new chemicals have made Canadian farmers among the most productive in the world. New, large-scale technologies of cutting and hauling were introduced into forestry, particularly in BC, as loggers pushed farther into the mountains. Canadian paper mills now possess new, high-speed machinery that supplies much of the world's newsprint.

Canada has long depended on imported technology to fuel its economic development and Canadian INVENTORS AND INVENTION have seldom received the kind of support necessary for long-term developments. Canada's widely dispersed population, its dependence on foreign investment and resource exploitation and its tradition of regional political independence have made the task of formulating a coherent industrial strategy very difficult. Although Canadian engineers lead the world in the use of computers for communication, and although dramatic advances in COMMUNICATIONS IN THE NORTH have taken place, Canada cannot compete with foreign producers of ELECTRONIC and domestic electrical equipment. Without reliable access to HIGH TECHNOLOGY there is the danger that secondary industries will not be competitive and that Canada may revert to its traditional role as supplier of raw materials.   W.G. RICHARDSON

Tecumseh, Shawnee war chief (b in the Ohio Valley c 1768; d at what is now Thamesville, Ont 5 Oct 1813). Tecumseh attempted, like other native leaders including Joseph BRANT, to form an alliance of tribes to combat US territorial ambitions more effectively.

Tecumseh participated in the futile Indian struggle to preserve the Ohio Valley and was present at the battle of Fallen Timbers in Aug 1794. Along with his half-brother, The Prophet, who preached a return to native religion and traditional values, he tried to rally the tribes in a

common defence against the Americans, and visited the southern nations in 1811 to try to induce them to join. He allied his forces with those of the British and Canadians during the WAR OF 1812, and his active participation was crucial during the critical summer months of 1812. He was present at Detroit (16 Aug 1812) and won a decisive victory against the Americans in the woods at Ft Meigs (May 1813). Following the defeat of the British fleet at the battle of PUT-IN-BAY, the British retreated from the Detroit front, and at the follow-up battle of Moraviantown (5 Oct 1813), Tecumseh was killed fighting with his people after the British had broken and fled. Tecumseh's death virtually marked the end of Indian resistance S of the Great Lakes. Tecumseh, as a heroic and tragic figure, has captured the imagination of writers over the years, including John RICHARDSON and Charles MAIR.   ROBERT S. ALLEN

Teit, James Alexander, ethnographer (b in Shetland Is, Scot 1864; d at Spence's Bridge, BC 30 Oct 1922). Much of our knowledge of traditional Salish cultures of Interior BC is based on Teit's meticulous descriptions and artifact collections for major museums in Ottawa, New York and Chicago (*see* SALISH, INTERIOR). Teit's wife was from a Thompson Indian village near his home at Spence's Bridge, and he became conversant with Thompson language and culture, as well as the Shuswap and Lillooet languages. His enthnographic work was stimulated in 1895 when he met anthropologist Franz BOAS, who was on a field trip to BC; they collaborated periodically for the rest of Teit's life. Teit published not only on Interior Salish culture and mythology, but also on the traditions of several DENE groups farther N. With his deep interest in native affairs, Teit helped form and served as secretary for the Allied Tribes of BC organization, working until his death for the protection of Indian land and other rights.   KATHLEEN MOONEY

Tekakwitha, Kateri (Catherine), known as the Lily of the Mohawks, first N American Indian candidate for sainthood (b at Ossernenon [near Auriesville [NY], 1656; d at the St-François-Xavier Mission [Caughnawaga], Qué 17 Apr 1680). Her rejection of several marriage offers and desire for a life of virginity put her at odds with Mohawk life even before she became a Christian. Her baptism in 1676 led to persecution, and a year later she left home for the St-François-Xavier Mission. There she became known for her sanctity and was given permission by the Jesuits in 1679 to make a private vow of chastity. Her death the next year from a prolonged illness was perhaps partly brought on by her penitential life-style. Her relics are preserved in a shrine at Caughnawaga, and numerous miracles have since been reported there. She was beatified 22 June 1980.   JOHN RASMUSSEN

Telecommunications is the transmission of signals over long distances. The earliest form was visual signalling with smoke, flags or lamps. Today, electronic telecommunication systems transmit messages to many locations throughout Canada and the world. The first method used to send messages by electricity was the TELEGRAPH. On 24 May 1844 Samuel Morse sent the first telegraph message, "What hath God wrought!" between Washington, DC, and Baltimore, Md. Over the next 50 years systems of wires were constructed across the US, Canada and other countries, bringing a revolution in the speed of communication over distance.

On 10 Mar 1876 Alexander Graham BELL spoke the first words over a telephone, "Mr Watson, come here. I want you," at his laboratory in Boston. In Aug 1876 he received the first one-way long-distance call over a 13 km line he had built between Brantford and Paris, Ont. Construction soon began on systems of telephone wires and cables within cities and towns, and

switchboards to provide interconnections of TELEPHONES in a network organization.

Early telephone systems could only carry intelligible voice signals for several miles, but continuing research and development led to technical improvements that kept extending the distance over which calls could be made. Hard-drawn copper wire was stronger than ordinary copper wire and a better conductor of electricity than steel wire. Dry-core cables and 2-wire circuits improved transmission so that by 1900 long-distance circuits had been extended as far as 1900 km (1200 miles). The loading coil doubled this distance by reducing signal distortion and the repeater provided a means of amplifying the signal. By 1920 coast-to-coast transmission was possible, and thereafter most local telephone systems were upgraded to long-distance standards, which in turn have been continuously improved over time.

Sending signals across the ocean proved more difficult. The working lives of repeaters were short and in a submarine cable they could not be replaced. Shortwave radio was used beginning in 1926, but an undersea cable awaited the development of the higher capacity coaxial cable and the vacuum-tube amplifier with an expected working life of 20 years. The first ocean cables were laid in 1956 between Scotland and Newfoundland with a capacity of 60 telephone circuits. This has been followed with many additional cables of substantially increased capacity connecting many locations throughout the world. Satellites became available for international service in 1964 and domestically in Canada in 1973. Distance has been conquered.

System Characteristics The basic functional components of the telecommunication system are (1) the communication terminal, which today could be a telephone, a teletypewriter, a facsimile machine, a personal computer or a large computer central processor; (2) the local loop, ie, the network of wires, cable, poles and related equipment that connects terminals to a local central office; (3) switching equipment in the central office that provides the necessary connections when calls are made; (4) larger capacity trunk cables that connect central offices, eg, a local end office with a long-distance toll office; (5) transmission equipment that sends and receives signals over long distances, including higher capacity cable, microwave radio and satellites. For signals to be communicated effectively over this system, there must be technical compatibility among all functional components, and each component must be capable of handling the signals of the highest quality service that will be provided over it. When the system was upgraded to meet the requirements of national and international long distance, it involved not only the transmission function but others as well, including the telephone instrument.

The telecommunication system is used to provide a variety of different communication services. Each service provides connections within a network of potential users, employing a particular type or quality of communication signal. Local telephone service provides public access to telephones in the local area at voice-grade technical standards. The local telecommunication facilities also provide private connections for voice, telegraph, video and data signals that are separate from the local public telephone network, such as private communication lines connecting only a few locations, or local data networks. Some services require 4-wire loop connections for higher quality service rather than the 2-wire loop required for voice telephone. The local facilities also provide access to the public long-distance network and, if the particular facilities have been upgraded, to national networks for video or data signals, eg, airline reservation systems.

The telecommunication system has been designed to meet the standards of voice communication. It employs the analogue transmission method which uses signals that are exact reproductions of the pattern of sound waves being transmitted. But this restricts the speed with which digital data signals can be transmitted. In addition, signal distortions which do not significantly affect the quality of voice communication create errors in data transmission. A major thrust of research and development is a search for new techniques that will improve error performance in data communications.

Telephone companies now are converting their signal standards from analogue to digital and upgrading the system to the standards of digital computers. Progress has been most rapid for the transmission function, and digital terminals are widely available. The conversions of local switching and loops are more costly and are being implemented more slowly. POTS (the plain old telephone system) is being converted to an ISDN (integrated services digital network), a sophisticated multipurpose network used to provide a wide variety of communication and information services (see COMPUTER COMMUNICATIONS; COMMUNICATIONS TECHNOLOGY).

The Canadian Industry and its Regulation

The installation of telephone wires and cables required use of city streets and public rights-of-way. Thus the approval of government authorities was required. Although there was some experience with competitive telephone companies in some cities, generally it was concluded that the public interest would be served better by a single local company, and competitive companies were not licensed. For most of its history, the telecommunication system has been operated as a monopoly either subject to government regulation, government ownership, or both.

Telephone companies in Canada range in size from BELL CANADA ENTERPRISES INC, the largest (a transnational corporation serving two-thirds of Canadian telephones in Ontario, Québec and the eastern NWT), to small town private companies and municipal operators. The Maritime provinces are served primarily by subsidiaries of Bell Canada subject to provincial regulation. In the Prairie provinces the systems are publicly owned. British Columbia Telephone (a subsidiary of the US General Telephone Co) and Bell Canada are regulated by the federal CANADIAN RADIO-TELEVISION AND TELECOMMUNICATIONS COMMISSION, as is Telesat Canada (a quasi-public/private corporation), the monopoly supplier of domestic satellite service. Telesat and the larger companies that provide long-distance services in their respective provinces are members of Telecom Canada, through which they provide nationwide services. Teleglobe Canada is a crown corporation that provides international satellite and cable services in conjunction with other countries and international agencies.

CNCP Telecommunications provides an alternative long-distance network. It grew from telecommunication facilities initially established by the CANADIAN NATIONAL RAILWAYS and CANADIAN PACIFIC RAILWAY to control their rail operations. Now it competes with Telecom Canada for a small portion of business long-distance private-line and data services. Subsidiaries of CN serve the Yukon and the western NWT and part of Newfoundland. Within this larger framework, many small companies, of which Edmonton Telephones is the largest, provide only local facilities and service.

Traditionally, telecommunication services have been supplied under the concept of end-to-end service by a monopoly supplier. The telephone companies owned all the equipment, including the terminals, purchasing the great majority of it from affiliated manufacturing companies. The attachment of other equipment, or the interconnection of other systems, has been prohibited. Services to the public have been pro-

Control room of Telesat Canada, Ottawa (*photo by Jim Merrithew*).

vided at rates approved by government regulatory agencies. The agencies have attempted to limit the profit of the telephone companies to a reasonable level, although great flexibility has been allowed in setting individual rates.

Since the early 1970s this end-to-end service concept has come under increasing criticism, stemming primarily from the growing use of the telecommunication system by the computer industry. Other manufacturers of equipment and other potential suppliers of service have claimed that they could provide improvements to the system that would benefit consumers. As of 1984, the CRTC and some provincial regulatory agencies have ordered the telephone companies under their respective jurisdictions to unbundle their services, separating the terminal and network components of service so that subscribers can choose to purchase their own terminals from any supplier and plug them in like electrical appliances. Businesses such as hotels may purchase their entire internal communications systems from alternative suppliers if they choose.

In the fall of 1984 the CRTC held hearings on an application by CNCP to provide long-distance telephone service to the public in competition with Telecom Canada. To do this service, CNCP must be able to obtain, at a reasonable price, the necessary interconnections to the local facilities of the telephone companies, which are resisting.

The telephone companies claim that competition for long-distance service will mean that they no longer will be able to subsidize local service, local rates will have to increase dramatically, and the near-universal telephone service in Canada will be threatened. By the term "subsidy," they mean revenue contributions from long-distance services to cover a share of the local facility costs used in common for both local and long-distance services. Local companies claim that this contribution is not enough and that local service subsidizes long-distance services. CRTC regulatory policies will be instrumental in determining whether Canada will follow the US in permitting competition in public long-distance services, or whether it will attempt to retain the monopoly approach to as great a degree as possible.

Of even greater significance for the future is determining which services will be assigned the massive costs of the system upgrading to computer standards. Under current industry accounting and regulatory practices, the great majority of these costs will be allocated to local telephone service and could require dramatic local rate increases, thereby threatening universal service. More detailed accounting and rate regulatory standards will have to be adopted by the regulatory authorities if these costs are to be assigned to the services responsible for the system upgrading. The CRTC (and its predecessor, the Canadian Transport Commission) have been engaged in a telecommunication cost inquiry since 1972, attempting to address these issues, but little progress has been made.

One possible scenario for future telecommunication service pricing is a flat monthly charge for the right of access to the system and usage charges for all services actually used, including local telephone service. This approach is favoured by industry, but consumer groups feel that high access charges and local measured service may force low-income people to disconnect from the system, losing basic telephone service. These issues will be actively debated for some time. The task of the CRTC and the provincial regulatory agencies of fashioning effective policy, in an environment of rapid technological change and increasing competitive market forces, will be formidable. *See also* COMMUNICATIONS; INFORMATION SOCIETY; SATELLITE COMMUNICATIONS.   WILLIAM H. MELODY

Reading: R.J. Buchan et al, *Telecommunications Regulation and the Constitution* (1982); Canada, Telecommunications and Canada, *Report of the Consultive Committee on the Implications of Telecommunications for Canadian Sovereignty* (1979); Dept of Communications, *Instant World: A Report on Telecommunications in Canada* (1971); Dept of Consumer and Corporate Affairs, *Telecommunications in Canada*, 3 vols (1981-83); P.S. Grant, ed, *Telephone Operation and Development in Canada, 1921-1971* (1974); J.E. Kingsbury, *The Telephone and Telephone Exchanges* (1915).

Telefilm Canada, *see* CANADIAN FILM DEVELOPMENT CORPORATION.

Telegraph, originally conceived by Samuel Morse, is a means of electrically transmitting encoded messages through the systematic opening and closing of electric circuits. In Canada, the first telegraph company, the Toronto, Hamilton and Niagara Electro-Magnetic Telegraph Co, was formed in 1846. Among the major companies in Canada during the early years of the industry was the Montreal Telegraph Co, controlled by Hugh ALLAN (founded in 1847); it connected such centres as Sackville (NB), Detroit, Montréal, Ottawa, Buffalo and Portland. In 1868 the Montreal Telegraph Co began facing direct competition from the newly established Dominion Telegraph Co (subsequently acquired by Western Union Telegraph Co of the US); these 2 rivals entered into price wars. In 1880 the Great North Western Telegraph Co was established to connect Ontario and Manitoba. In 1881 Erastus Wiman and Western Union took control of the Montreal Telegraph Co; as a result, they briefly controlled most of Canadian telegraphy.

Canadian Pacific Railway Telegraphs commenced service in 1883 and interchanged traffic with non-Western Union companies in the US (principally the Postal Telegraph and Cable Co). Perhaps attributable to this new competition, the Great North Western Telegraph Co faced bankruptcy in 1915, and was taken over by the telegraph subsidiary of Canadian Northern Railway Co. The railway itself was in financial difficulty, however, and was soon purchased by the federal government, subsequently forming a component of Canadian National Railways Co. In this way Great North Western Telegraph Co became Canadian National Telegraph Co.

By the 1930s CN and CP railway companies had established themselves as the principal providers of telegraph service in Canada, the latter interchanging traffic with Postal Telegraph and the former with Western Union. They continued to operate competitively until 1967, when agreement was reached for reciprocal office abandonment. Today, CNCP Telecommunications is jointly owned by Canadian National (owned by the federal government) and Canadian Pacific (a private enterprise). CNCP Telecommunications offers a wide range of business-telecommunications services in competition with members of the TRANSCANADA TELEPHONE SYSTEM. In 1979, by order of the CANADIAN RADIO-TELEVISION AND TELECOMMUNICATIONS COMMISSION, CNCP Telecommunications was authorized nondiscriminatory access to Bell Canada's switched telephone network for the purpose of offering competitive data-transmission services.

A major principle of provisioning TELECOMMUNICATIONS facilities, namely the separation of control of the content of messages from control over transmission, was established in 1910 by the Board of Railway Commissioners for Canada. During the first decade of the century, news gathering was controlled by the major telegraph companies, which had established contractual links with the major news agencies in New York City and themselves condensed and selected news items for distribution to Canadian newspapers. Canadian telegraph operators were the principal collectors of Canadian news. In 1907, Canadian Pacific Telegraphs attempted to quadruple prices charged for its news service to 3 Winnipeg newspapers which, in opposition, joined to form an independent news service, the Western Associated Press (WAP). Subsequently, Canadian Pacific cut off its news service to the Nelson, BC, *News,* an action attributable to publication of articles critical of CP. In 1910 WAP challenged Canadian Pacific rates in proceedings before the railway commissioners; the board found CP rates to be discriminatory and the company abandoned the field of news gathering and selection. Today, there is general recognition that telecommunications companies should operate as common carriers only, by accepting for transmission all messages without interference, upon payment of lawful rates.

ROBERT E. BABE

Telephones The inventions of the TELEGRAPH (1837) by Samuel Morse and the telephone (1876) by Alexander Graham BELL were milestones in the quest to communicate over great distances with reliability, accuracy and speed. Previously, communication over distance necessarily entailed encoding human thought through such means as drum and smoke signals, semaphores and trumpets or physically transporting written messages by carrier pigeons and human travel.

Telegraph and telephone both encode messages electrically at their origin; consequently, they may be transmitted literally at the speed of light over various types of transmission facilities such as copper wire, coaxial cable, fibre optics and through space to their destinations, where they are decoded into original form. The telegraph [Gk, *tele graphos,* meaning "writing at a distance"] encodes each letter of the alphabet into a combination of long and short bursts of electric current through a circuit by the systematic depression of a key which thereby completes an electric circuit. The telephone [Gk, *tele phone,* meaning "distant voice"] encodes variations in sound waves (that is, changes in the density of air which we perceive as sound) into variations of electrical waves through vibrations of a diaphragm in the mouthpiece of the telephone instrument.

The telephone, as compared to the telegraph, encodes messages directly for transmission, thereby permitting greater individual autonomy in sending messages. Moreover the telephone allows instantaneous routing of messages to the receiver through complex switching devices, whereas the public telegraph service routes messages to a central terminal and thereafter requires delivery of the message to the addressee. The telephone permits simultaneity in message exchanges, whereas the telegraph transmits complete messages unidirectionally.

The basic configuration of the telephone network comprises the terminal device (which may be, but is no longer limited to, the telephone instrument); a "local loop," a pair of copper wires or fibre-optic cables connecting the terminal to a local switching centre; trunk cables connecting switching centres or exchanges within a community; toll switching centres, which route

long-distance messages; and long-line facilities (cables, fibre optics, microwave towers, communications satellites), which provide electrical interconnection between communities.

In 1876 the world's first definitive tests of the telephone occurred in Brantford, Ont. These were one-way transmissions. The era of the telephone in Canada was inaugurated in 1877 when its inventor transferred, for 1 dollar, 75% interest in the telephone patent for Canada to his father, Alexander Melville Bell. A.M. Bell hired agents to solicit subscribers for "private lines" (that is, unswitched or point-to-point service), and in 1879 the Dominion Telegraph Co secured a licence to operate the Bell patent for Canada for 5 years. Subsequently, however, the Dominion Telegraph Co was unable to raise $100 000 asked by Bell for outright purchase of the patent, and Canadian patent rights were sold in 1879 to the National Bell Telephone Co of Boston (today, American Telephone and Telegraph Co). Rival service was offered until 1880 by the Montreal Telegraph Co, using disputed patents of Elisha Gray, Thomas A. Edison and others.

In 1880 the National Bell Telephone Co had incorporated, through an Act of Parliament, the Bell Telephone Company of Canada (today also known as BELL CANADA), which was thereby authorized to construct telephone lines over and along all public property and rights-of-way. In Nov 1880 agreement was reached with rival companies (principally Western Union Telegraph Co and its Canadian affiliates) to surrender their patents, and by 1881 the Bell Telephone Co of Canada had acquired all other existing telephone interests in Canada.

In 1885, however, the Bell patents were voided by the government of Canada, and independent telephone companies were now entitled to offer service, even in direct competition with Bell. Several hundred independent companies later came into existence.

The rise of competing companies in Nova Scotia, New Brunswick and PEI may have been instrumental in causing Bell Telephone to withdraw from these provinces, thereby enabling Bell to pursue consolidation of its operations in its remaining territory. In 1885 the Telephone Co of Prince Edward Island was formed, and in 1888 it purchased Bell rights and property in PEI. In 1888 Bell sold its facilities in NB and NS to the newly formed Nova Scotia Telephone Co, although at the time the latter was still controlled by Bell. Later in 1888 the New Brunswick Telephone Co was incorporated by legislative Act and was given an exclusive franchise to provide long-distance service in the province; in the following year it acquired the provincial facilities of the NS Telephone Co. In 1910 Maritime Telegraph and Telephone Co (MT and T) was incorporated, and in 1911 it acquired the Telephone Co of PEI and the NS Telephone Co. In 1966 Bell Canada procured majority interest in both MT and T and NB Telephone.

Newfoundland's principal telephone company was incorporated in 1919 as the Avalon Telephone Co, which was operated on a private basis by the Murphy family. The company's controlling interest was acquired by a group of Newfoundland and Montréal businessmen in 1954. In 1962 Bell Canada became the major shareholder. On 1 Jan 1970 the Avalon Telephone Co became Newfoundland Telephone Co Ltd, and in 1976 public shares were issued, making Newfoundland Telephone a widely held company with Bell Canada holding majority ownership. Today, Newfoundland Telephone is regulated provincially and provides a wide range of telecommunications services to approximately 75% of the 550 000 people of Newfoundland and Labrador.

In other regions of the country, however, Bell Telephone met the emerging competition more aggressively. Two policies developed at the turn

of the century — pricing and interconnection practices — are of particular interest, since they have remained controversial to the present. Bell's pricing was alleged to be noncompensatory and hence detrimental to competition in instances where direct or potential competition existed; indeed, telephone service was for a time offered free in some communities (Peterborough, Ft William, Pt Arthur). Moreover, Bell Telephone did not interconnect rivals to its local or long-distance network, thereby disadvantaging subscribers to independent companies. Nonetheless the independent telephone industry in Ontario and Québec continued to grow, especially through the period 1906-25. By 1915 independent telephone companies in Ontario accounted for 79 000 telephones, or one-third of the provincial total. However, during the 1950s and 1960s Bell acquired most of these independents, with the result that in Ontario at present non-Bell telephone companies account for under 5% of the province's telephones.

In the years before 1906 there was much dissatisfaction with rates and with the reluctance of Bell to extend service to less lucrative rural areas. Consequently, PM Sir Wilfrid Laurier formed a select committee of the House of Commons in 1905, chaired by Post Master Gen William MULOCK, to investigate the telephone industry in Canada and make recommendations. The committee published verbatim proceedings which provide a valuable history.

In 1906, through revisions to the Railway Act, certain aspects of the operations of the Bell Telephone Co of Canada were brought within the jurisdiction of the Board of Railway Commissioners for Canada. Henceforth, all telephone tolls charged to the public by the company were subject to the prior approval of the board; the board was also empowered to order interconnection between Bell and other telephone companies. Regulatory jurisdiction over Bell Telephone was transferred to the CANADIAN TRANSPORT COMMISSION in 1967 and to the CANADIAN RADIO-TELEVISION AND TELECOMMUNICATIONS COMMISSION in 1976. The major responsibilities of these regulatory tribunals are to ensure that the tolls charged are reasonable and just, and not unduly preferential or discriminatory; furthermore, terms and conditions of interconnection with other companies must be authorized by the regulator. Long, complex public hearings are frequently held to ascertain the ramifications of applications put forth by Bell.

The retention of Bell Canada under private ownership after 1906 was in opposition to policies advocated by certain municipal and provincial governments and led to further dramatic changes in the structure of the Canadian telephone industry. In 1908 and 1909 Bell Telephone operations in Manitoba, Alberta and Saskatchewan were purchased by the provincial governments and are operated today as provincially owned utilities.

The Canadian telephone industry in 1980 consisted of 183 companies, comprising 16.5 million telephones and employing more than 100 000 workers. Canadians placed 26.8 billion telephone calls in 1980, representing 1114 calls per capita. The Canadian telecommunications industry, comprising both telephone companies and other common carriers (including CNCP Telecommunications, Teleglobe Canada and Telesat Canada) in 1980 received revenues of $6.3 billion, had net fixed assets of $14.5 billion and paid wages and salaries of $2.3 billion.

Next to Bell Canada the largest telephone company in Canada is the British Columbia Telephone Co (BC Tel), serving all of BC apart from the city of Prince Rupert, which is served by a municipally owned system. BC Tel is controlled by General Telephone and Electronics Corporation of the US. BC Tel in turn controls AEL Microtel, an unregulated manufacturer of

TELECOMMUNICATIONS equipment from which BC Tel procures the largest portion of its equipment. BC Tel is about 20% the size of Bell and, like the latter company, is regulated by the CRTC.

Manitoba Telephone System (MTS), owned by the provincial government and regulated by the Public Utilities Board, is the sole provider of telephone service in Manitoba. It is about 40% as large as BC Tel. Saskatchewan Telecommunications (Sask Tel) is a provincially owned telephone utility which, together with numerous co-operatively owned systems, serves Saskatchewan. The Public Utilities Review Commission supervises Sask Tel. Sask Tel is about the same size as MTS. The third provincially owned telephone system in Canada is Alberta Government Telephones (AGT). AGT and a municipally owned system in Edmonton (Edmonton Telephones) are the exclusive suppliers of telephone service in Alberta. AGT, which is about 75% the size of BC Tel, is regulated by the Alberta Public Utilities Board, and Edmonton Telephones is supervised by the city council. Other municipally owned systems in Canada are located in Thunder Bay and Kenora.

Telesat and 9 major telephone companies in Canada participate in an association, the TRANS-CANADA TELEPHONE SYSTEM (TCTS), renamed Telecom Canada in 1983, for national co-ordination of telephone service. Though telephone service is provided primarily on the basis of monopoly in each area, federal regulatory initiatives in recent years have reopened competition in selective services. In 1979, for example, the CRTC ordered Bell Canada to grant CNCP Telecommunications access to Bell's local switching network for purposes of offering business-communications services in competition with Bell Canada. In 1977 the CRTC ruled that Bell Canada must afford cable TV companies access to its poles and ducts, without restriction to the services sold by such companies. In 1979 the CRTC required Bell Canada to afford access to its switching facilities to a mobile-telephone company. These new pockets of competition again bring into question the issue of compensatory pricing. Following a 1982 CRTC decision, changes have been effected regarding subscriber ownership of terminal equipment. Single-line residence and business subscribers, with or without extension telephones, will be able to own or lease their telephones. However, the inside wiring remains the property of the telephone company.

Western societies are entering the information age, or post-industrial society, and telecommunications companies are of great significance in this transition. It has been estimated that up to 50% of the labour force is now engaged in information production or distribution. At the same time, technology is transforming hitherto distinct information industries into a highly complex, interrelated system. Microelectronic circuitry, communications satellites, broadband cable and fibre optics brought into the home appear to be eradicating previously distinct industry boundaries. Also, online word processors allow office-to-office transfer of messages. Virtually all forms of information that were defined by their singular mode of material encapsulation (film, newsprint, books, computer printouts and so forth) can now be encoded and diffused electrically over vast geographic areas at low cost. There is increased interdependence between telephone companies and newspapers, banks and financial institutions, computer companies and others. The future may well bring increased competition for telephone companies from cable TV systems and SATELLITE COMMUNICATIONS firms. ROBERT E. BABE

Television Drama, English-Language, is fictional narrative material ranging from short illustrative sketches to original, full-length scripts. The term covers various forms, though situation comedies, mysteries, soap operas, serials, miniseries, family adventures, revues, docudramas and topical dramas are most popular. Throughout the history of Canadian television drama, the anthology has survived. Under titles such as "Folio," "Festival," "First Performance," "Q for Quest," "To See Ourselves" and "For the Record," self-contained teleplays revealed a mixture of experiment, sentiment, history, comedy, tragedy and adaptations of the best of foreign and domestic, classic and contemporary storytelling. Since 1952 Toronto and Montréal have been the major national production centres for drama, with Vancouver, Winnipeg, Halifax, St John's and Regina producing fine regional drama during some periods.

Kinescopes (8 mm films made from the image on a monitor) were made of early live productions and shipped to remote locations for transmission. When recordings on reusable videotape replaced kinescopes, fewer copies were made and those were sometimes erased for reuse. Nevertheless, a collection of drama scripts, kinescopes and tapes from the CANADIAN BROADCASTING CORPORATION's first 3 decades of television has survived.

The CTV network, established in 1960, has bought from independent Canadian producers only a handful of situation comedies and police and animal shows. These programs were indistinguishable from their American prototypes despite the conditions attached to the licence by the Board of Broadcast Governors and its successor, the CANADIAN RADIO-TELEVISION AND TELECOMMUNICATIONS COMMISSION. Up to 1985 the history of Canadian TV drama has been primarily a history of CBC drama or CBC collaborations with independent producers.

During the past 30 years, many of the forms of TV drama have become more complex while others, like the Western, simply disappeared. The CBC has both created distinctive variants on many familiar forms and pioneered others: eg, from 1960 to 1967 "Cariboo Country" was a completely distinctive contemporary Western; "Wojeck," 1967-69, was innovative in both visual style and content. Over the years a daily ration of TV drama has become a habit for most people. Yet in 1982 only 3% of TV drama shown in Canada was Canadian in origin. However, well over one million Canadians will watch a particular CBC drama special.

A variety of broadcasting Acts have evolved a mandate for the CBC to meet the changing needs of the country and the rapidly changing technology. In the early 1980s the CBC was expected to educate, inform and entertain people of different ages, interests and tastes; to present a balance of views on controversial issues over the whole range of programming; to serve as a patron of the arts; to promote Canadian unity, provide for continuing expression of regional diversity, and reflect the Canadian identity. CBC drama has responded with fictional characters as diverse as Charlie Farquharson, Bob and Doug McKenzie, Ada, Nick Adonidas and Relic, "The King" of Kensington, Wojeck, Maria, Louie Ciccone, Ol' Antoine and others in "Cariboo Country," Katie, and real-life folk heroes like Sir John A. MACDONALD, Norman BETHUNE, Louis RIEL, Emily CARR, Stephen LEACOCK and Emily MURPHY.

At its worst, Canadian TV drama is derivative, bland, sometimes incoherent, and self-indulgent — ranging from "Radisson" (an inept riposte to the Davy Crockett phenomenon of the 1950s) to plays which reinforce society's unthinking stereotypes. The CBC has never developed a consistent focus on unions, small towns or the political process at the municipal or provincial levels. However, TV is a 2-way mirror reflecting its audience, and audience attitudes have changed in 3 decades. As always, TV drama can stimulate discussion about controversial issues or widen an audience's perceptions through innovative and imaginative scripts in the hands of talented producers, directors and actors. "Flight into Danger" thrilled its audience; "The Open Grave," a "direct cinema" version of the Resurrection, raised questions in Parliament; "Anne of Green Gables" went on to become a stage hit; "Tar Sands" provoked Prem LOUGHEED of Alberta into a successful lawsuit.

In the mid-1950s and 1960s there were few Canadian playwrights and stage companies. CBC TV drama took over from CBC radio as our national theatre, providing training and work for actors, designers, producers, directors, technicians and composers. Zoom lenses, more mobile cameras and sound equipment, videotape and the introduction of colour freed some kinds of drama from the confines of studios. Live television drama disappeared. Yet from the very beginning, the limitations of the technology and the dramatic conventions were transformed into art, a very few examples being "Ward Number Six" (1959), "Kim" (1963), "Pale Horse, Pale Rider" (1964), "The Paper People" (1967), "Bird in the House" (1973), "The Freedom of the City" (1975) and "Blind Faith" (1980). When taste shifted from anthology drama to series drama which focuses on one set of characters, the CBC produced "Wojeck," the forerunner of topical series drama; "McQueen"; "Quentin Durgens MP"; and later, when teams of characters or families became popular, "The Manipulators," "The Collaborators," "Sidestreet," "A Gift to Last" and "Home Fires." In the 1980s "Seeing Things" and "Hangin' In" continue the pattern of blurring television genres with swiftly changing tones and a wide variety of topical issues.

Characteristics which have distinguished the best of Canadian TV drama are a tolerance of moral ambivalence, open-ended narrative structures, a willingness to experiment with the medium itself and an ironic vision of authoritarian values. When Canadian series function well they retain many of the characteristics of anthology drama. From the early days, distinctively Canadian TV dramas have been sold in large numbers all over the world. The CBC has also shown some of the best of contemporary Canadian theatre, adapted with varying success for television: "Ten Lost Years," "The Farm Show," "On the Job," "Paper Wheat," "Leaving Home," "Les Belles Soeurs," "La Sagouine," "Billy Bishop Goes to War," as well as adaptations of the finest international and classical drama.

Television drama performs many important functions. We stay in touch with one another by caring about the PLOUFFES or the Sturgesses, by arguing about Riel or laughing at "The King." We tell our children stories about themselves through an excellent children's TV service. We educate ourselves about issues, recapture history, debunk old myths and create new ones (*see* TELEVISION PROGRAMMING). MARY JANE MILLER
Reading: Canadian Drama 9 (Spring 1983), an issue directed to articles on Canadian radio and TV drama; Mary Jane Miller, "Canadian Television Drama, 1952-1970," *Theatre History Journal* 5 (Spring 1984).

Television Drama, French-Language Television has greatly enriched Québec drama. Since 1952, writers and actors originally drawn to RADIO DRAMA have helped produce a body of television drama which, after 30 years, has reached impressive proportions: more than 800 television plays, 80 televised novels, 100 works of children's drama and, since 1980, a growing number of miniseries.

The most prestigious form of television drama is televised theatre, most of it produced by Radio-Canada (more precisely, by CBFT in Montréal). The first evening that Radio-Canada was on the air, 6 Sept 1952, the station broadcast

Cocteau's *Oedipe-Roi*. Between 1952 and 1958 television theatre had pride of place in Radio-Canada's programming. In those days of live broadcasting, and despite the difficulties and costs involved, CBFT offered one or even 2 plays a week, peaking in 1958 with almost 100 hours of televised theatre. Production then declined and from 1965 to 1983 averaged about 20 hours a year, or one play each month.

At first both classic and contemporary plays were selected, running 30-120 minutes. Novels and short stories were then adapted, followed by texts written specifically for the small screen. Between 1952 and 1977, 80% of the theatrical works televised were the original work of, or were translated or adapted by, Canadian (especially Québecois) authors. Although foreign plays left their mark on viewers' memories, Québec playwrights made the strongest impression. Marcel DUBÉ, Hubert AQUIN, Françoise Loranger, Pierre Dagenais, Jacques LANGUIRAND and Michel TREMBLAY, in particular, provided high-quality television drama and innovated in ways that expanded the televisual vocabulary. Since 1952, plays by more than 150 Québec writers have been produced on television.

Most of Radio-Canada's theatrical presentations have been part of series such as "Théâtre d'été" (1954, 1955, 1958 and 1961), "En Première" (1958-60), "Théâtre du dimanche" (1960-61), "Jeudi Théâtre" (1961-62) and "Théâtre d'une heure" (1963-66). The 2 most important series were "Le Téléthéâtre de Radio-Canada" (which, 1953-66, offered more than 160 works) and "Théâtre populaire" (which, 1956-58, presented more than 100). However, since 1966 television theatre has only appeared as an increasingly rare offering on the program "Les Beaux Dimanches."

Critics have generally applauded the televised plays, but the greatest public acclaim has gone to televised novels. Ever since the 1953 debut of the first Québec serial ("La Famille Plouffe" by Roger LEMELIN), these weekly instalments have known immediate and lasting success. Televised serials, broadcast in 30-minute episodes in peak hours, usually from September to May, generally run 2-3 years. Two, however, have lasted much longer: "Les Belles Histoires des pays d'en haut" (14 years) by Claude-Henri GRIGNON and "Rue des Pignons" (11 years) by Louis Morisset and Mia Riddez.

The first televised serials were usually adapted from novels or radio serials, their success being guaranteed by previous popular acclaim and their quality by the calibre of their authors. In the 1960s original serials were more contemporary in topic and structure, and the majority were serious in tone and in subject.

Until 1965, public television broadcast the most popular series, among them "Quatorze, rue de Galais" (1954-57) by André GIROUX, "Le Survenant" (1954-57, 1959-60) by Germaine GUÈVREMONT, "Cap-aux-sorciers" (1955-58) by Guy Dufresne, "La Pension Velder" (1957-61) by Robert Choquette, "La Côte de sable" and "De 9 à 5" (1960-62, 1963-66) by Marcel Dubé, "Sous le signe du lion" (1961) by Françoise Loranger, and "Septième nord" (1963-67) by Guy Dufresne. Although Télé-Métropole produced a daily serial from 13 Mar to 19 May 1961 ("Ma femme et moi" by Pierre Dagenais), private television only began competing with Radio-Canada with the 1965-70 production of "Cré Basile" (written by Marcel Gamache, starring comedian Olivier Guimond).

The comic nature of "Cré Basile" was a turning point for television drama, and Télé-Métropole went on to schedule burlesques ("Lecoq et fils," "Symphorien," "Les Brillant") and situation comedies ("Chère Isabelle," "Dominique," "Peau de banane"). Radio-Canada (through CBFT) met the competition after 1966 with comedy series ("Moi et l'autre," "La P'tite Semaine," "Du tac au tac,"

"Jamais deux sans toi," "Poivre et sel") or, at least, with lighter productions than those of the early 1960s. Thereafter, Radio-Canada and Télé-Métropole competed fiercely for audience favour. When the private network produced its celebrated "Berger" series in 1970, competition moved to the level of family "sagas" as well. The public could enjoy "Rue des Pignons," "Grandpapa," "Terre humaine" or "Le Temps d'une paix" on Radio-Canada, and "Les Berger," "Le Clan Beaulieu," "Marisol" or "Les Moineaux et les pinsons" on Télé-Métropole. Finally, after 1980, Radio-Québec produced the occasional serial.

Television serials, whether humorous or dramatic, historical or contemporary, are strongly and specifically Québecois, despite the inevitable influence of American and European series. Their success has not been limited to French Canada: several series ("Quelle famille!," "La P'tite Semaine," "Le Temps d'une paix") have been sold abroad.

Since 1952, children's drama has kept a young public glued to the screen. Also, in the early 1980s several miniseries, "Les Plouffes," "Duplessis" and "Bonheur d'occasion," proved very popular. CHRISTINE EDDIE

Reading: G. Laurence, "La Rencontre du théâtre et de la télévision au Québec (1952-1957)," *Études littéraires* 14 (août 1982); R. Legris and P. Pagé, "Le Théâtre à la radio et à la télévision au Québec," in Archives des lettres canadiennes, vol 5, *Le Théâtre canadien-français* (1976) and *Répertoire des dramatiques québecoises à la télévision, 1952-1977* (1977); Relations publiques services français Société Radio-Canada, *Vingt-cinq ans de dramatiques à la télévision de Radio-Canada, 1952-1977* (1978).

Television Programming Television must provide information and entertainment suited to the tastes and needs of a very large public. This cultural fact dictates that television programming will come in many different forms: newscasts and news magazines or documentaries, talk shows, sports broadcasts, games and quizzes, variety shows, children's programs, as well as a range of dramatic entertainment. The same fact helps to explain why this programming appears repetitive, even hackneyed, for familiarity breeds popularity; why it is expensive, since success requires stars and high production values; and why it commonly employs the format of storytelling, because no other mode of explanation or diversion is so universally accepted.

What has been called the golden age of Canadian programming occurred during the first decade of television (1952-62), when the publicly owned CANADIAN BROADCASTING CORPORATION enjoyed a monopoly of network broadcasting. The CBC organized separate French- and English-language networks (which reached over 85% of Canadian homes by 1962), beginning its schedule at first in the evening for family viewing but slowly extending that schedule into the afternoon for women, children and teenagers. Producers created a mix of programming, representative of all the major forms of television and derived from their past experience with radio, as well as from lessons learned from British and American initiatives. It proved to be a time of excitement and experiment.

The CBC was determined to inform the public about life and affairs. Regular newscasts commenced in the spring of 1954 on both networks. Much air time was devoted to major, and sometimes controversial, public affairs shows, notably "Point de mire" (1956-59) hosted by René LÉVESQUE and "Close-Up" (1957-63) produced by Ross McLean. There were talk shows, interview series such as Toronto's popular "Tabloid," specializing in personalities, and sports roundups such as the "Jim Coleman Show."

Even greater effort went into entertainment, reflecting the special importance of television as the main source of mass diversion. Highbrows

could enjoy the quiz show "Fighting Words," regular concert hours and, more infrequently, ballets, operas and sophisticated drama. Sports fans were better served with weekend broadcasts of hockey and football — the telecast of National Hockey League games began in 1952. Montréal producers developed a host of games and quizzes with titles like "Le nez de Cléopâtre" and "La clé de champs," although it was their Toronto counterparts who fashioned the long-lasting "Front Page Challenge" in the summer of 1957. The English-language service worked hard to foster variety favourites: the comedy team of Johnny Wayne and Frank Shuster (*see* WAYNE AND SHUSTER), that enduring singing star JULIETTE (Sysak), and assorted country-music groups such as those led by Gordie Tapp, King Ganam, Tommy Common, Tommy HUNTER and Don MESSER. Both networks boasted a number of dramatic anthologies — "Télétéâtre," "General Motors Presents," "En Première" and "Festival" — which specialized in original plays. Only Radio-Canada, the French-language network, succeeded in the realm of popular drama with a series of *téléromans* such as "La Famille Plouffe," "La Pension Velder" and "Marie Didace," each drawing upon the history and culture of Québec (*see* TELEVISION DRAMA, FRENCH-LANGUAGE).

Many of these programs proved successful. French Canadian television, in particular, won enormous audiences, earning the title of a tribal medium because it seemed to reflect the "soul" of old and new Québec. Yet there were signs of trouble ahead. In the 1950s the CBC was unable to manufacture an appealing brand of popular English Canadian drama, although it tried with "The Plouffe Family" (1954-59), with a prime-time historical adventure series for children called "Radisson" (1957-58), and with a big-budget crime drama entitled "RCMP" (1959-60) (*see* TELEVISION DRAMA). To its evening schedule, the network added American situation comedies and action/adventure series such as "I Love Lucy" and "Have Gun, Will Travel." Even Radio-Canada began to air translations of American shows like "The Naked City" (a crime drama) and "The Donna Reed Show" (a situation comedy). Furthermore the CBC soon discovered that imported variety, such as "The Ed Sullivan Show" or "The Perry Como Show," was usually judged more pleasing by English Canadian audiences than the homegrown equivalent. In competitive markets such as Toronto and Vancouver, where viewers could easily pick up American stations, the CBC lost large chunks of its audience at peak times when Canadian shows were aired. Indeed, across the country, public pressure had increased for greater choice, an end to the CBC monopoly, and a more popular style of television entertainment modelled on the American experience.

One myth of the times was that commercial interests would somehow fashion a television service which could act as an agency for made-in-Canada popular culture. Moreover, in 1959, the Board of Broadcast Governors had issued a series of Canadian-content regulations which were supposed to ensure the persistence of indigenous programming on all stations. These served to justify the introduction of a new era of competition, which changed the shape of Canadian television by the mid-1970s. Acting first through the BBG and later through the CANADIAN RADIO-TELEVISION AND TELECOMMUNICATIONS COMMISSION, the state licensed competing stations across the land, authorized the operations of private networks (the English-language Canadian Television Network, or CTV, in 1961, Télé-Diffuseurs Associés or TVA in Québec in 1971 and Global in Ontario in 1974), and allowed the extension of CABLE TELEVISION to over 40% of Canadian households by 1975.

The language and culture of French Canada ensured the survival of local programming in Québec. Yet there were changes. The dramatic anthologies of the 1950s virtually disappeared, because French-language programmers, especially those on the independent station CFTM-Montréal, turned to movies to win peak-time audiences. The amount of American programming did rise, particularly on the non-CBC stations. Yet from the beginning CFTM-Montréal originated variety programs to showcase Québec's comedians and singers. Nor did popular drama suffer. The homegrown situation comedy, Radio-Canada's "Moi et l'autre," running 9:00-9:30 PM on Tuesdays (1966-71), purportedly attracted around 2 million viewers a week in the early 1970s. The private challenger, TVA, had to respond with its own series. And Radio-Canada strove to improve the quality of its information programming by moving the newscast "Téléjournal" to 10:30 PM (1971-72), by adding a popular late-night talk show on Fridays with Lise Payette entitled "Appelez-moi Lise," and by broadening the scope of its public-affairs and feature programming. A survey of programming 1974-75 showed that Radio-Canada offered a more balanced schedule of quality performances in the realm of drama, music and dance (5%), information (32%) and light entertainment (63%), while TVA was emphatically popular, emphasizing light entertainment (82%) and a limited quantity of information (18%). The rival networks shared almost equally the French Canadian audience.

Events took a very different course in English Canada. The only route to quick popularity open to the newcomers was to schedule as many Hollywood-produced shows during prime-time as could be allowed under what proved to be the very loose regulations about Canadian content. So CTV's evening schedule 1966-67 offered the American favourites "The FBI," "Bewitched," "Dean Martin," "Mission Impossible," "Run for your Life" and "The Jackie Gleason Show." Global's schedule was similarly peppered with imports a decade later. What might seem more puzzling was that the same could be said of the CBC. One explanation was financial: a typical 1974-75 import cost $2000 a half hour (the actual production cost being roughly $125 000) and yet it could generate a profit of between $20 000 and $24 000 in advertising revenue on the CBC or CTV. Contrast this with domestic production: a half-hour show cost about $30 000 (meaning its production values were inferior to American shows) and realized a profit of $55 on CTV and a loss of $2050 on the CBC. The scheduling of a Canadian show, moreover, usually meant a loss of audiences and revenues in that time slot, since viewers could change channels to find an import that was more appealing. True the networks did offer variety and game shows where the costs could be kept down. On the CBC, "Front Page Challenge" continued, Tommy Hunter became a regular with his own show and "The Irish Rovers" rose to fame; CTV boasted such imitations as "Headline Hunters," "The Ian Tyson Show" and "Pig & Whistle." CTV actually had a Canadian situation comedy, "Excuse My French" (1974-75), on which it was losing about $14 000 an episode. And both networks offered a wide sports coverage. In effect, however, the networks had given up the notion of competing effectively with Hollywood for the mass audience.

Where the CBC and eventually CTV did work hard was in the fields of news and public affairs, genres which capitalized on viewers' interest in their collective or public life. Early on, the CBC aired one smash hit in the field of public affairs, "This Hour Has Seven Days" (1964-66), a news magazine which boasted an eclectic mix of showbiz techniques, hard reporting and interviewing, and much editorializing to win a huge audience of excited viewers. "Seven Days" was a highly dramatic show, a

Television production of "Romeo and Juliet," performed by the Royal Winnipeg Ballet in Toronto, 1983 (*CBC Photo / Fred Phipps*).

collection of sensational stories, which sparked too much controversy to survive on an increasingly cautious network. This said, the network did carry excellent documentaries, did offer a range of features and public-affairs shows like "Telescope," "Man Alive," "Take 30," and "Fifth Estate," and did improve "The National," its nightly newscast. Though less active, CTV aired an equivalent national newscast, a major news magazine called "W5," and a news documentary series entitled "Maclear." Indeed the record of English Canadian television was better than that of its American counterpart.

Competition had brought English Canadians a breathtaking range of choice. The CBC remained the most balanced network, giving viewers a diversity of program types, while CTV and Global were clearly more restricted and popular in their offerings. Cable brought in several American channels. Ratings data showed that the CBC had lost heavily in the competition for viewers. In 1968 the English-language CBC could claim just over one-third of the total Canadian (English and French) audience; by 1980 it could claim slightly under one-fifth. By comparison, American channels had increased their share from 24% to 32%, and CTV had grown from 25% to 30%. Put another way, during a typical week in 1979 and 1980 the national English audience watched foreign-produced programs three-quarters of the time. In 1982 this figure remained about the same.

These facts have provoked a series of agonizing reappraisals of the whole television scene. Even so, the situation has not changed dramatically since the mid-1970s, except perhaps to worsen. News, public affairs, sports, and in Québec the téléromans, remain the best and most popular forms of Canadian television. In English Canada, the CBC has attempted to bring about a renaissance, increasing the amount of Canadian content in prime time and returning to the field of light entertainment. This resulted in the highly successful family program "The Beachcombers," a hit situation comedy "The

King of Kensington," an assortment of variety specials, the serial "Home Fires," and above all "The National/Journal," a combination of news and views on weekdays from 10:00 to 11:00 PM. The private networks have not followed the CBC's lead, perhaps because competition has raised the costs of acquiring foreign programs and threatened their profit margins. The CRTC's efforts to coerce more Canadian drama out of the CTV, and by implication out of all private stations, have been fiercely resisted. The government's plans to foster more Canadian production through the licensing of PAY TELEVISION, a willingness to subsidize independent producers, and the revamping of Canadian content regulations have not yet borne fruit.

Everywhere in Canada, American imports and stations have slowly increased their audiences. The audience share of the most Canadian network, the CBC, has continued to deteriorate, even in Québec, where after 1977 TVA gained a clear dominance. Indeed, statistics show a growing preference among younger French Canadian viewers for American shows, whether in English or French, which in time could jeopardize Québec's own programming. Hollywood movies, prime-time soap operas such as "Dallas," children's shows such as "The Wonderful World of Disney," and situation comedies such as "M*A*S*H" typically dominate the rankings of top-10 programs in any given week, which suggests that prime time is a N American cultural phenomenon. *See also* BROADCASTING, RADIO AND TELEVISION; COMMUNICATIONS IN THE NORTH; COMMUNICATIONS IN QUÉBEC; MUSIC BROADCASTING.

PAUL RUTHERFORD

Reading: P. Audley, *Canada's Cultural Industries: Broadcasting, Publishing, Records and Film* (1983); R.E. Babe, *Canadian Television Broadcasting Structure, Performance and Regulation* (1979); A. Barris, *Front Page Challenge* (1981) and *The Pierce-Arrow Showroom Is Leaking: An Insider's View of the CBC* (1969); P. Hindley, G. Martin and J. McNulty, *The Tangled Net: Basic Issues in Canadian Communications* (1977); P. Trueman, *Smoke & Mirrors: The Inside Story of Television News in Canada* (1980).

Telidon, a combination of the Greek words meaning "to know at a distance," is a relatively new form of technology, developed by researchers in the federal Department of COMMUNICATIONS in Ottawa in the late 1970s. This technology combines aspects of television, the TELEPHONE and the computer to produce a new medium of communication and information processing. From television comes the ability to display letters and images on a screen; from the telephone, the ability to communicate over a distance; from the computer, the ability to manipulate, store and retrieve information quickly and inexpensively. The federal government hoped that this combination of capabilities into a new medium of communication would stimulate the development of high-technology industries and help Canada take a position of leadership in the developing field of information technology.

There are 3 major ways to implement Telidon systems: videotex, teletext and as stand-alone systems; and there are significant differences in the capabilities of the resultant systems.

Videotex systems allow the user to receive information from and send information back to a computer located in a different place. These systems might use telephone lines, coaxial cable, optical fibre, laser or radio-communication links to connect the user to the computer. The 2-way capability enables users to exchange messages and perform such interactive tasks as information retrieval, banking and shopping. The Grassroots system, for example, provides agricultural information and services to farmers and ranchers in Manitoba.

Teletext systems are not interactive in the same way as are videotex systems. The information is broadcast in the unused portion of a regular television signal called the "vertical blanking interval" and is decoded by a device attached to the television set. Teletext is a one-way system that neither requires nor permits communication from the user back to the computer. The information to be displayed is simply cycled again and again. Most teletext systems display a menu or index page on the screen when the decoder is first turned on. The user decides which topic is of interest and enters the number on a keypad attached to the unit. When the page the user wants comes around, the "frame grabber" on top of the TV set "grabs" it, stores it in its memory, decodes and displays it on the screen until the user requests the next frame. A major limitation is the amount of information — the number of "pages" or "frames" — that can be kept cycling around.

Stand-alone systems differ from videotex and teletext systems mostly in the way they connect the computer with the user. Because these units may have everything combined into a single box, they are sometimes called "electronic slide projectors." They can be programmed to run a fixed cycle, or may be connected to keypads or other kinds of input devices that allow the user to select the desired pages or to use various "action pages" that have a wide range of response possibilities.

How Telidon Codes Information In addition to the hardware items already mentioned — the television set, the telecommunications link, the computer — a decoder is also required to accept the coded instruction from the computer and generate an electronic signal that creates the display on the screen. The heart of any Telidon system is the Picture Description Instruction — the special code that instructs the decoder what to draw on the display screen. The PDI coding scheme, which was selected to be the N American standard, uses a system whereby different kinds of geometric shapes — lines, points, arcs, polygons — are specified in concise form. In this "alpha-geometric method," images may be created and manipulated with comparative ease; only a small amount of information is required to specify an image; and the quality of the final image is dependent mainly on the ability of the display device to resolve fine detail. Telidon, claim its developers, will thus not be made obsolete by technological advances.

Information in a Telidon system is currently accessed by one of 2 methods. In the first, the user is greeted by a master menu when the system is turned on, selects the topic that is of interest and enters a command on a keypad. This causes the next menu, which is more detailed, to come up on the screen. The user continues in this manner until the desired page of information is displayed. The second method requires the user to type a simple command that includes a keyword or set of keywords that are used as an index to the content of the pages.

The Dept of Communications has been attempting to stimulate the development of applications of Telidon in educational, industrial, commercial and public settings. These efforts have included establishing an Industry Investment Stimulation Program, in which the government paid part of the cost of any application of Telidon technology; creating a $1-million Public Initiatives Program; funding a $6.7-million program to assist the CBC in developing Telidon applications; developing and supporting groups to conduct research into the social implications and uses of Telidon and other videotex technologies; developing policies to deal with the legal and regulatory issues arising from videotex services; and attempting to sell Telidon in other countries. By Jan 1984 the government had spent $67 million and industry $200 million in attempts to develop and market Telidon applications.

Initial press releases regarding Telidon were optimistic, promising a rapidly growing new

industry that would revolutionize life in Canada and save the electronics industry. Since 1980 stories in the press have promised the imminent birth of this burgeoning industry, but these promises have all been followed by long delays and periods of silence, as the economic and technical problems resist easy and fast solution. Recent government reports indicate that no large short-term market can be expected for Telidon, but rather that the market will grow slowly, over the course of several years. *See also* COMPUTER COMMUNICATIONS; INFORMATION SOCIETY; OFFICE AUTOMATION. WILLIAM RICHARDS

Reading: P.J. Booth, *The Social Impacts of Telidon* (1984); Department of Communications, *Telidon Behavioural Research Series*; D. Godfrey and D. Parkhill, eds, *Gutenberg Two* (1979); Godfrey and E. Chang, eds, *The Telidon Book* (1983); *Microelectronics*, A Scientific American Book (1977); B. Raphael, *The Thinking Computer* (1976); J. Weizenbaum, *Computer Power and Human Reason* (1976).

Temagami, Ont, Town, pop 1224 (1981c), inc 1968, located on NE arm of Lk Temagami, 100 km N of North Bay. Temagami originated in the 1890s as a tourist centre, when campers from southern Ontario first discovered the natural beauty of the area, celebrated in a well-known poem by Archibald LAMPMAN. It had previously been an Indian settlement dependent on fur trading. With construction of the Temiskaming and Northern Ontario Ry, 1903 (later ONTARIO NORTHLAND), a trickle of summer visitors became a flood. One of them was Archie BELANEY, better known as "Grey Owl," who lived in Temagami 1906-10. For most of this century tourism has been the town's raison d'être, with periodic developments in lumbering and iron mining since the 1920s. MATT BRAY

Témiscaming, Qué, Town, pop 2097 (1981c), is located at the southern end of Lac Témiscamingue (spelled TIMISKAMING in Ont) near the rapids that link the lake with the Ottawa R. It was established in 1917 by the Riordon Pulp and Paper Co, which built it to house the employees of its Kipawa Mills paper mill. Since 1896, the hamlet of South Témiscaming had been the CPR terminal for the area and the steamship port for goods destined for the new communities to the N of Lac Témiscamingue. The name is derived from an Algonquin expression meaning "deep water," a reference to the lake. Témiscaming was for many years a COMPANY TOWN. Originally owned by the Riordan Co (1917-25), it was then directly administered by the Canadian International Paper Co until the end of the 1960s. CIP had bought the town as well as the Kipawa Mills plant. Témiscaming's economy is still based on its paper mill, which is now owned by Tembec, a Québec crown corporation.

BENOÎT-BEAUDRY GOURD

Temperance Movement, a movement to control alcohol consumption, arising early in the 19th century, when social aid was negligible and when a majority of Canadians were self-employed as farmers, fishermen or small businessmen. From the belief that self-discipline was essential to economic success and that alcohol was an obstacle to self-discipline followed the decision to be temperate in the use of alcohol or to abstain entirely. Many concluded that the urban poverty developing with the growth of cities in the mid-19th century was caused by drink. Accordingly, there was a shift of emphasis from temperance as an individual decision to legal PROHIBITION as a social one. Religious belief and concern about crime were sec-

ondary incentives, though disorders arising from drinking among railway construction workers in the Prairie West provided a powerful motive. By 1900 prohibitionists also argued that prohibition would force European immigrants to conform to what the prohibitionists perceived to be Canadian standards of behaviour.

The first temperance societies in Canada appeared about 1827 in Pictou County, NS, and Montréal. These tolerated moderate use of beer and wine, an attitude which was to persist in Québec but soon gave way elsewhere to abstinence or prohibition of all alcoholic beverages. Despite the shift from temperance to prohibition, temperance, abstinence and prohibition groups were all commonly called temperance groups. About 1848 the Sons of Temperance lodge, a fraternal and prohibitionist society modelled on the Odd Fellows, reached Canada from the US. Other such lodges were the Royal Templars of Temperance and the International Order of Good Templars. Though popular for many years, the temperance lodges declined sharply after 1890. The most important temperance society for women was the WOMAN'S CHRISTIAN TEMPERANCE UNION, an American movement whose Canadian counterpart was founded 1875 by Letitia YOUMANS of Picton, Ont, as one of the few organizations through which women could play a political role. In 1875 the hundreds of societies, lodges and church groups committed to prohibition convened at Montréal to form a federation named the Dominion Prohibitory Council. Renamed in 1876 the Dominion Alliance for the Total Suppression of the Liquor Traffic, it became the major organizing force for prohibition campaigns. A decisive figure for much of its history was its secretary, Francis Stephens Spence of Toronto. The predominantly English and Protestant Dominion Alliance discouraged francophone and Catholic participation. Furthermore, Catholics, particularly francophone Catholics, regarded prohibition as an extreme measure. When La Ligue anti-alcoolique was formed 1906 as a counterpart of the Dominion Alliance, it supported legal restriction of the liquor trade, but not full prohibition.

Jurisdiction over the trade was shared by governments, since the provinces could prohibit retail sale, whereas the federal government could prohibit the manufacture and retail, wholesale and interprovincial trade of alcohol. However, neither level was enthusiastic about prohibition, since it would cause losses of tax revenue and party support. Both often put forward compromise legislation known as local option, eg, the Canada Temperance Act of 1878, which gave local governments the right to prohibit by popular vote the retail sale of alcohol (*see* RUSSELL CASE). The referendum was also frequently used as a delaying tactic or to shift responsibility for legislation from governments to voters. A side effect was to give prohibitionists political experience, through organizing local-option and referendum campaigns, which led to a major success when in 1900 the PEI government prohibited retail sale of alcohol.

When WWI broke out, the movement was close to its peak. Alcohol consumption, though beginning to rise after a half century of decline, was relatively low; organization and funding for the movement were substantial; and local option was widely accepted. Finally the Dominion Alliance campaigned for prohibition as a patriotic measure. Such an appeal made further opposition almost impossible; in 1915 and 1916 all provinces but Québec prohibited retail sale of alcohol. Québec prohibited retail sale of distilled liquor in 1919, but only briefly. Prohibition was short-lived. Though the federal government prohibited manufacture, importation and sale of alcohol by orders-in-council in 1918, these expired shortly after the war. Most provincial legislation was abandoned during

Reverse side of St John's Total Abstinence Society medal, struck in England in 1840 (*courtesy Public Archives of Canada*).

the 1920s in favour of government sale. PEI followed in 1948. Meanwhile, Canadian liquor interests found a large, illegal market in the US, under prohibition until 1933. There has been a substantial Canadian presence in that market ever since. The assertion that prohibition was ended because it failed is unconvincing. The laws were in effect so briefly and were so inconsistently enforced that their effectiveness must remain a question. As to the claim that prohibition encouraged drinking, the steady rise of alcohol consumption under conditions of legal sale must raise further questions. More likely, changes in Canadian society and within the movement doomed prohibition.

Those self-employed Canadians who saw temperance as an aid to economic success were a diminishing proportion of the population, displaced by urban workers to whom self-betterment seemed a remote possibility. Hence the decline of the prohibition vote in the 1920s. Within the movement, prohibitionism had provided an opportunity for close study of urban problems, leading many to conclude that those problems had more to do with the political and economic system than with alcohol. Many left the movement for other forms of activism. It had been thought that the extension of the franchise to women would sustain prohibition, since it was commonly believed that women were sympathetic to it. However, referenda of the 1920s, in which women had the vote, showed a consistent decline of support. The temperance movement was the creature of a society that was already fading when its prohibition victories were won. However, as a means by which Canadians came to grips with social problems and formulated responses, the movement was valuable. GRAEME DECARIE

Reading: M.G. Decarie, "Something Old, Something New," in Donald Swainson, ed, *Oliver Mowat's Ontario* (1972); *The Facts of the Case: a summary of the most important evidence and argument presented in the Report of the Royal Commission on the Liquor Traffic* (1973); James H. Gray, *Booze* (1972); R.E. Spence, *Prohibition in Canada* (1919).

Temple, Sir Thomas, governor of Nova Scotia (b at Stowe, Eng Jan 1615; d at Ealing, Eng 27 Mar 1674). One of 3 partners obtaining rights of trade and government in NS following the English conquest of 1654, Temple emerged as sole governor by 1662, but was forced to restore the colony to France in 1670. JOHN G. REID

Templeton, Charles Bradley, evangelist, journalist, broadcaster, editor, author (b at Toronto 7 Oct 1915). Templeton began a career in journalism as a sports cartoonist. In 1936 he turned to religion but, although he became a renowned evangelist, introducing the "Youth for Christ" movement to Canada in 1945 and then to Europe and Japan, he later became an agnostic. He

achieved new prominence as senior editor of the *Toronto Star* and *Maclean's* and news public-affairs director of CTV, and narrowly missed becoming leader of the Ontario Liberal Party in 1964. He has written 3 best-sellers — his nonfictional *Jesus* (1971) and 2 thrillers, *The Kidnapping of the President* (1974) and *Act of God* (1977) — an apparently semiautobiographical novel, *The Third Temptation* (1980), and his autobiography, *Charles Templeton: An Anecdotal Memoir* (1983). GERALD J. RUBIO

Tenant League, popular name for the Tenant Union of Prince Edward Island, a militant agrarian movement fd 19 May 1864 in Charlottetown, PEI. The organization opposed payment of rent by tenant farmers and advocated sale of lands by estate owners to the farmers in actual occupation (*see* LAND QUESTION, PEI). Members who were tenants were pledged to pay no further rent, and all members were expected to support tenants who refused payment, even in open defiance of law officers. Crowds of members and supporters numbering as many as 200, alerted by the blowing of tin trumpets, would surround and harass a sheriff and his assistants, with the result that by mid-1865 the authorities found it impossible to enforce the law between landlord and tenant by ordinary means, particularly in Queens County. The Conservative government of James Colledge POPE summoned troops from Halifax in August, and in the autumn used them to assist the sheriff in 2 lengthy forays into the countryside. The tenant organization seemed to collapse in the face of this pressure, and by mid-1866 it was apparently defunct. Nonetheless, pro-Tenant Union sentiment remained alive, and several Liberals openly sympathetic to the movement were elected to the legislature in 1866 and 1867. The disorders of 1865 marked a crucial turning point in undermining the leasehold system of land tenure in PEI, and the use of troops against the tenantry was a major factor in the defeat of the Conservative government on 26 Feb 1867.

IAN ROSS ROBERTSON

Tennant, Veronica, ballet dancer (b at London, Eng 15 Jan 1946). As ballerina with the NATIONAL BALLET OF CANADA, she has achieved international recognition for her dramatic intensity and superb technique. Trained at the NATIONAL BALLET SCHOOL, she made her debut with the company as principal in 1965, dancing Juliet in John Cranko's *Romeo and Juliet*. Leading roles in *The Nutcracker* and *Swan Lake* during her second season marked an unusually rapid establishment in the top rank of the company. Since then she has performed in a wide range of ballets and has been partnered by most of the world's great male dancers, including Nureyev, Baryshnikov, Dowell and Schaufuss. She has also appeared internationally as a guest artist and in the Emmy-award-winning CBC productions of "Cinderella" (1968) and "Sleeping Beauty" (1972). Tennant is the author of a children's book, *On Stage, Please* (1977). JILLIAN M. OFFICER

Tennis Lawn tennis is a game played on a rectangular court (23.7 m long and 8.2 m wide for singles play, divided into equal halves by a net 0.914 m high at the centre and 1.07 m high at the posts) by 2 players (or 4 in doubles) whose objective is to hit the cloth-covered rubber ball with their racquets into their opponent's side of the court so that it cannot be returned. Top-class players demonstrate superb fitness and psychomotor skills; the action may be rapid and heated or fluidly graceful. Matches usually last one to 2 hours, but often continue for longer; a recent Canadian Davis Cup match was contested for more than 6 hours. Emotions are intense in such contests, and successful players must demonstrate exceptional concentration and mental control.

Modern tennis almost certainly originated in

The 1892 Port Sandfield lawn tennis champions, Muskoka Lakes, Ont (*courtesy Public Archives of Canada/PA-68320/F.W. Micklethwaite*).

France in the 11th century as a form of handball called *le jeu de paume*. The game, also called "court tennis" or "real tennis," was played on an indoor court — originally in a monastery — with a ball, and by 1500 a racquet was introduced. The word "tennis" likely derived from the French *tenez* — "hold" or "take heed," perhaps called before service. The unusual scoring came from the medieval use of 60 as a base number (as we use 100 today), and the term "love" for zero perhaps came from French *l'oeuf* ("egg," implying "zero") or from English usage, in which love is the equal of nothing ("love or money"). Lawn tennis developed as an outdoor game in England during the mid-19th century. An early popularizer was Major W.C. Wingfield, who devised a set of rules and a court in the shape of an hourglass, with a net 1.5 m high. Wingfield conducted the first game at a garden party in Wales in 1873. In the next few years, the game was improved as the court was made rectangular and the server was moved to the baseline. When the first Wimbledon championship was held in 1877, the game was basically in the form it is played today.

Lawn tennis began to develop and spread in Canada soon after its popularization in England. J.F. Helmuth formed a club in Toronto that is believed to be the forerunner of the Toronto Lawn Tennis Club (fd 1875). The first Canadian tournament was held at the Montreal Cricket Club in 1878 and the first indoor tournament took place in Ottawa in 1881. The 1880s saw clubs formed in Winnipeg; London, Ottawa, Niagara and Kingston, Ont; Fredericton and Saint John, NB; Halifax, NS; Victoria and Vancouver, BC; Regina, Sask; Lethbridge and Edmonton, Alta (1891). In 1890 the Canadian Lawn Tennis Assn was formed and the first Canadian championships were held in Toronto. Today, in addition to the national governing body (called Tennis Canada since 1977), each province has an autonomous association. Co-operatively the associations organize extensive programs, championships and team competitions for juniors, elite players and seniors. It is estimated that over 2 million people play tennis in Canada, making it the third most popular sport activity after swimming and ice skating.

Since 1968 the annual national championships have been divided into open and closed competitions. The commercially sponsored Canadian Open Men's Championships, which are held in Toronto, now have prize money exceeding $200 000 and the tournament results count towards a larger, year-long international grand prix circuit. Similarly the Montréal-staged Women's Open Championships are a segment of the major women's commercially sponsored annual international tour. Since 1982 the revamped Canadian Nationals (closed) have been held in Ottawa; a commercial sponsor donates $25 000 in prize money. Among the lead-up tournaments to the national championships are a variety of commercially sponsored regional tournaments and circuits as well as the various provincial championships.

The Davis Cup international competition for men was first held in 1900; the Federation Cup for women was inaugurated in 1963. The International Lawn Tennis Federation (ILTF, now ITF) was founded in 1913; open competition between amateurs and professionals received ILTF sanction in 1968. Canada entered the worldwide Davis Cup competition for the first time in 1913, losing to the US in the final played at Wimbledon. The team was led by R.B. Powell and included B.P. Schwengers, H.G. Mayers and J.F. Foulkes, with G.H. Meldrum acting as nonplaying team captain. In the years since, Canada has continued to participate in international competitions but has had no major individual or team successes. The most successful Canadian player since 1981 has been Carling BASSETT, who was placed 19th in the 1983 Women's Tennis Association computer ranking. She was the 30th ranked money winner in 1983 with $75 568 and *Tennis* magazine named her "Women's Rookie of the Year." The Canadian male player ranked highest by the Association of Tennis Professionals in 1983 was Glen Michibata who was placed 78th; however, he was beaten in the Canadian Nationals by Derek Segal. The harsh winter climate is often blamed for Canada's lack of success in tennis competition, although there are fine indoor facilities, good coaching programs and many Canadian players on tennis scholarships in the US.   JOHN J. JACKSON

Tenure, generally, is the holding of a secure position within an educational institution or system, although it can also refer to an individual's length of service in a particular position or system. Usually associated with appointments of university or college faculty members, the granting of tenure by the institution signifies that the individual so classified has an ongoing appointment that may be terminated only through resignation, retirement, or dismissal for good reasons as established by a proper hearing.

University and college professors consider tenure essential because it enables the holder to exercise free but responsible criticism of his institution and all aspects of society without fear of dismissal. Among the more widely publicized tenure cases in Canada has been that of Frank UNDERHILL, a history professor at University of Toronto, whose resignation was demanded by the university's board of governors in 1941 because of his "ill-considered" statements about Canada's changing relationships with Britain and the US. Despite considerable controversy, Underhill remained, signalling to the Canadian academic community and the public that academic tenure continued to be in effect, even in wartime. Despite the strong arguments set forth by academics in defence of a system of tenure, however, it has on occasion offered refuge to those who have ceased to meet the high standards of scholarship expected of them by colleagues and by the public. The effects of such a tenure policy are not likely to be as deleterious in a period when universities and colleges are expanding in number and size (eg, in the 1960s in Canada) as in a period of limited growth or retrenchment (1970s and 1980s). To counter these effects, some people have supported the elimination of tenured positions and the introduction of 3- or 5-year contracts open for free competition, charging that because of the scarcity of academic jobs and the overabundance of qualified candidates, the standards required of

new academics have steadily escalated and tenure is denying them the right to compete for jobs on the basis of equality. It should be noted that in times of financial crises in universities and colleges, even tenured academic positions may disappear.   W. BREHAUT

Tepee, *see* TIPI.

Termite, term referring to nearly 2000 species of mostly tropical and subtropical INSECTS generally placed in order Isoptera, but closely related to COCKROACHES (Dictuoptera). Often called "white ants," termites are unrelated to true ANTS. In Canada, 3 native species are known (from BC and western Alberta); another dubiously native species occurs in southern Ontario. The latter and other introduced species may establish themselves indoors. The earliest known termite was discovered recently in 120-million-year-old deposits in England; previously the 100-million-year-old *Cretatermes carpenteri,* from Labrador, held this distinction. Living species resemble these forms. Termites, typically, are pale, and about 5-15 mm long; swollen, egg-laying queens may be much larger. They have short legs and antennae. Reproductive forms have 4 long wings, of similar shape, shed after the nuptial flight. Eyes are reduced or absent. Like other fully social insects, colony members are divisible into castes: reproductive males and females, and sterile workers and soldiers. Unlike ants, wasps and BEES, sterile termites are of either sex, not females alone, and the reproductive female (queen) retains the services of the king. Complexity of social organization and size of colonies vary among species. Termites are sophisticated architects, having invented effective air conditioning and concrete. Sanitation is perfect; the dead are consumed and excrement recycled for building materials. Some exotic species are excellent fungus-gardeners. Their habitations are often shared by other animals, mostly arthropods. Termites feed on cellulosic substances (especially in wood or vegetable-fibre products), digested by intestinal microorganisms — usually bacteria, but protozoa in 2 species. Termites may be divided into categories: dry-wood termites living in seasoned wood; damp-wood termites living in decaying wood in contact with the ground; mound-building termites, plant-feeders that construct conspicuous "termitaria" on the ground or on trees but are most active beneath soil surface; and "subterranean" termites, humus-feeders, nesting entirely underground. Termites frequently destroy structural and other timber and may damage crops. Canadian species may do significant structural damage.   D.K. McE. KEVAN

Tern, medium-sized BIRD of the GULL family. Terns are usually grey and white; in spring and summer most species have a black cap. Similar to gulls in appearance, terns differ in having more pointed wings and usually a noticeably forked tail. Terns are more streamlined than gulls and fly more buoyantly. When feeding, most species dive into the water, which gulls rarely do. Approximately 40 tern species occur worldwide, most in the Pacific Ocean. In Canada 12 species occur, 6 as breeders. Of the latter, Caspian, common, roseate and usually arctic terns (*Sterna caspia, S. hirundo, S. dougallii, S. paradisaea,* respectively) nest on grass, sand or small pebble substrates, usually on low-lying islands or peninsulas. Nests usually consist of a small scrape or depression in the ground. Black and Forster's terns (*Chlidonias niger, S. forsteri*) sometimes build their nests over water, attached to emergent vegetation or a structure in the water. Terns usually lay 2-3 eggs. Their breeding cycle is shorter and their young develop more quickly than those of gulls. In Canada, arctic terns generally nest above TREELINE. They migrate down the eastern N American coast, over to southern

The arctic tern (*Sterna paradisaea*) nests above the treeline and migrates to southern S America via Europe and Africa (*photo by G.J. Harris*).

Europe, partway down the African coast, and over to southern S America, a round trip of over 16 000 km and one of the longest bird MIGRATIONS.   D.V. WESELOH

Terra Nova National Park (est 1957, 396 km²), Canada's most easterly national park, is located on BONAVISTA BAY, Nfld. The park's rocky headlands, drumlins, till deposits and numerous ponds show the influence of glacial activity on the landscape. Island-sprinkled bays and deep fjords indent the coastline. Inland, the boreal forest, composed mainly of black spruce and balsam fir, is home for native species, including beaver, meadow vole, black bear, otter and lynx, and introduced species such as common shrew, snowshoe hare, mink and moose. Numerous PEAT bogs provide an ideal environment for orchids and pitcher plants, while the rocky shoreline supports colonies of arctic tern, herring gulls and crevice-nesting black guillemots. The park shows evidence of Paleo-Eskimo, DORSET, Maritime Archaic and BEOTHUK cultures; all are now extinct. Lumbering and fishing began in the park area in the late 1700s, after colonization, and evidence of these activities still can be found.   LILLIAN STEWART

Terrace, BC, District Municipality, pop 10 914 (1981c), area 2143 ha, inc 1927, is located on the SKEENA R, 60 km by road N of Kitimat and 160 km E of Prince Rupert. Its name describes the terraces formed by the Skeena's banks. A member of the Kitimat-Stikine Regional Dist, Terrace is governed by a mayor and 6 aldermen. The site was originally a TSIMSHIAN village. Laid out in 1910 by the Grand Trunk Pacific Ry, Terrace was a sawmill town until the 1950s, when it began to serve as a distribution centre for the new town of Kitimat. Its economy today is based primarily on forest industries. Terrace is also an important transshipment point for rail and truck freight. Nearby Lakelse Lake Provincial Park and Kleanza Provincial Park offer spectacular alpine scenery, and future growth of Terrace may depend on increased tourism in the area. Terrace is the gateway to the Stewart-Cassiar Hwy.   ALAN F.J. ARTIBISE

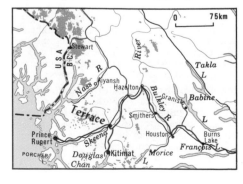

Territorial Evolution The evolution of CANADA as a political entity began with the arrival of French and English colonists at the beginning of the 17th century, and the establishment of the HUDSON'S BAY COMPANY in 1670. By the TREATY OF PARIS in 1763 all of eastern N America except St Pierre and Miquelon became British. Britain established governments for NOVA SCOTIA (including the present NB and PEI), NEWFOUNDLAND (which included Labrador, Anticosti I and the Magdalen Is) and the PROVINCE OF QUEBEC (lower St Lawrence watershed). All other territory was assigned to the Crown or to the HBC. In 1769 St John's Island (PRINCE EDWARD ISLAND) was administratively separated from Nova Scotia, and in 1774 Québec was enlarged to include Anticosti I, the Magdalen Is and the land SW between the Ohio and Mississippi rivers. After the US became independent, Québec was confined to the area N of the Great Lakes, and in 1784 NEW BRUNSWICK was created as a home for LOYALISTS. From 1784 to 1820 CAPE BRETON was also administered as a separate colony. After the US acquired Louisiana from France in 1803, it became necessary to determine its boundary with British territory W of the Great Lakes. This was established as essentially the 49TH PARALLEL to the Rocky Mts by the Convention of 1818; the area W of the Rockies was occupied by both Britain and the US. The limits between British territory and Russian Alaska were described in 1825. The area under joint British-American occupation was divided by the OREGON TREATY of 1846. The 1842 ASHBURTON-WEBSTER TREATY settled the NB-Maine boundary, and described the boundary between BNA and the US from Lk Huron to Lake of the Woods. In the far West, the British colonies, Vancouver's I, est 1849, and British Columbia, est 1858, were united in 1866. In 1867, 3 provinces of BRITISH NORTH AMERICA, Canada, Nova Scotia and New Brunswick, were united in CONFEDERATION, the former PROVINCE OF CANADA being divided into Ontario and Québec.

In 1870 RUPERT'S LAND and the North-West Territory, purchased 1869-70 by the federal government from the HBC, were officially transferred to Canada, and from them a small province of Manitoba was created to accommodate agricultural colonies established after 1811 (*see* RED RIVER COLONY). The next year BC joined the federation, and PEI followed in 1873. In 1876 the District of Keewatin was created from part of the North-West Territories to deal with the administrative problems arising from settlement N of Manitoba. The Territories were enlarged in 1880, when British rights to the arctic islands passed to Canada, but were reduced again when Manitoba, Ontario and Québec were enlarged in 1881, 1889 and 1898. The remainder of the North-West Territories was divided into provisional districts for administrative and postal purposes, beginning with Athabaska, Alberta, Saskatchewan and Assiniboia in 1882, and then Yukon, Mackenzie, Franklin and Ungava in 1895 (in 1898 Yukon District became a separate territory in order to provide proper government for gold seekers moving into the region (*see* KLONDIKE GOLD RUSH). In 1905, as agricultural settlement spread into the Prairies, the provinces of Alberta and Saskatchewan were created. Their expansion north to the 60th parallel gave rise to requests from Manitoba, Ontario and Québec for northern extensions. In 1912 those provinces attained their present limits, and the NWT districts disappeared except for Mackenzie, Keewatin and Franklin. The final addition of territory came when Newfoundland joined Confederation in 1949 with the area determined by the Imperial Privy Council in 1927. *See also* LABRADOR BOUNDARY DISPUTE.

N.L. NICHOLSON

Reading: Energy, Mines and Resources Canada, *Canada Then and Now* (1982); N.L. Nicholson, *The Boundaries of the Canadian Confederation* (1979).

Territorial Government Canada's 2 territories, the NORTHWEST TERRITORIES and the YUKON TERRITORY, are governed by the federal government and by territorial governments which may legislate where the former has delegated the necessary authority. The government of the NWT holds its legislative powers under the NWT Act; the powers of the Yukon Territory's government are set out in the Yukon Act. The government of each territory is headed by a federally appointed commissioner and an elected body, known in the NWT as the Territorial Council and in the Yukon as the Legislative Assembly. The commissioner reports directly to the federal minister of Indian affairs and northern development. In the NWT the commissioner chairs the executive committee, which comprises the commissioner and members of the Territorial Council. The commissioner is not required to act on the advice of the executive committee or that of the Council (which has 24 elected members), but does so by tradition.

In 1979 the federal Conservative government transferred executive power in the Yukon from the commissioner to an Executive Council, or Cabinet, comprising members from the 12-member Legislative Assembly. The commissioner does not sit on the Executive Council and has been specifically instructed by the federal minister to follow its decisions, except in matters of special concern to Ottawa. In contrast to the NWT, candidates for seats in the Yukon Territorial Legislative Assembly are affiliated with political parties. In both territories the legislative responsibilities of the commissioners-in-council are roughly analogous to those allocated to the provinces under the Constitution Act, 1867. The federal government retains control over lands, natural resources, taxation and claims of native rights. In April 1982, 56% of voters in a NWT plebiscite endorsed the division of the NWT. The then minister of Indian affairs and northern development indicated the territories would be divided when residents agreed on a boundary between the eastern and western territories and when outstanding native land claims were settled. *See* NORTH-WEST TERRITORIES ACT.

KATHERINE A. GRAHAM

Terrorism, as the term is frequently used today, denotes the use of VIOLENCE or threats of violence to attain a political objective. The waves of violence that occurred in Québec between 1963 and 1971, for which the FRONT DE LIBÉRATION DU QUÉBEC claimed responsibility, were the most important outbreak of terrorism in Canada. As in other countries, this type of terrorism was justified and rationalized with various arguments. The FLQ defended its actions by claiming that Francophones in Canada suffered economic discrimination; that the constitutional system was unjust; and that democratic channels to change were blocked.

The terrorist acts of the FLQ increased in intensity from 1963 to 1971. Bombs became increasingly sophisticated and powerful, and selective kidnappings forced the governments of the day to enter into negotiations. Although its activists generally attempted to issue a warning by telephone before each explosion, the FLQ caused 7 violent deaths.

Terrorism is generally not the term used to describe the violence on the part of public authorities because of the legal monopoly the state enjoys over certain forms of power. However, implementation of the WAR MEASURES ACT in 1970, the army's occupation of Québec, and above all the arrest, without formal proceedings, of more than 450 persons, have been challenged as a disproportionate response to FLQ actions.

MARC LAURENDEAU

Tessier, François-Xavier, doctor, politician (b at Québec C 15 Sept 1799; d there 1835). Tessier studied in Québec City and New York and was

admitted to the practice of medicine in 1823. He is known primarily for founding the first medical newspaper in Canada, *Le Journal de médecine de Québec* (Jan 1826-Oct 1827). Despite his short life, his exceptional qualities brought him several important positions in the Québec region. He was named apothecary of the Emigrant Hospital in 1823; health officer for the port of Québec and administrator of the Pointe-Lévy Fever Hospital in 1830; and doctor of the Marine and Emigrant Hospital in 1834. He represented Saguenay in the Assembly of Lower Canada from 1833 until his death. JACQUES BERNIER

Texaco Canada Inc, an oil company that is involved in all aspects of petroleum exploration, development and marketing, with head offices in Toronto. Incorporated in 1927 as McColl-Frontenac Oil Co Ltd, the company became Texaco Canada Ltd in 1959. It adopted its present name in 1978 as a result of its merger with Texaco Explorations Canada Ltd. The company refines and distributes petroleum products throughout Canada and is directly and indirectly engaged in exploration for oil and gas fields in western Canada. Texaco operates 5 refineries and numerous retail outlets. In 1983 it had sales or operating revenue of $5.65 billion (ranking 8th in Canada), assets of $3.1 billion (ranking 23rd) and 3904 employees. Foreign ownership stands at 90%, with Texaco Inc owning 68% and Texaco International in New York 22%. DEBORAH C. SAWYER

Texada Island, 28 700 ha, pop 1146 (1981c), lies in the Str of GEORGIA near POWELL RIVER, BC. The island was named by Spanish explorer Jose Maria Narvaez (1791). In 1883 American capital started the first of several iron and copper-gold mines around Vananda. Mining was a mainstay until the 1920s and from WWII to 1976. A local smelter (1898) concentrated copper by-products; both ore and concentrates were shipped from deep-sea berths. Since about 1895 limestone quarries and lime kilns on the island's end have furnished material for cement, stucco, Kraft pulp and other off-island manufactures. Texada I now produces most of BC's limestone. The island's timber has been intensively logged since the 1940s. PETER GRANT

Textile Industry includes establishments that convert man-made and natural fibres into yarn, cloth, felt, etc, for use in MANUFACTURING clothing, upholstery, household linens, etc. The textile and CLOTHING INDUSTRIES together are among Canada's largest manufacturing-sector employers. Total employment averages about 150 000, broken down as follows: primary textiles, 58 000; knitting mills, 17 000; clothing factories, 80 000. Textile-mill shipments average about $5 billion annually.

History Records show that as long ago as 1671 pioneer settlers were making wool materials for clothing and furnishings. Eventually, there were hundreds of custom carding and cloth-fulling mills scattered in communities throughout Upper and Lower Canada and the Maritimes. The first complete factory system of woolen cloth manufacture started in 1826 when Mahlon Willett established a mill at l'Acadie in Lower Canada. The earliest record of a knitting factory with powered knitting machines is that of a mill at Ancaster, Ont, in 1859. It is believed that the first cotton mill was the Lybster Mills, established in Merritton, Ont, in 1860. The first silk-manufacturing concern was established in Montréal by Belding Paul & Co in 1876.

The age of synthetics began in 1925 when Courtaulds (Canada) Ltd built a plant in Cornwall, Ont, to make the then new viscose rayon, often called artificial silk. Courtaulds was quickly followed in 1926 by Celanese Canada, which erected a plant in Drummondville, Qué, to make acetate yarn. In 1942 the first nylon yarn was produced in Canada by Du Pont. At the time, the height of WWII, nylon remained a well-kept secret; the first production was 45 denier yarn for weaving into parachute cloth. The first product made after the war was nylon hosiery yarn.

Polyester was introduced to Canada in the 1950s by ICI Ltd. Later, Du Pont and Celanese became important manufacturers of this synthetic fibre, with the trade name "Dacron" used by Du Pont and "Fortrel" by Celanese. Another major producer of nylon fibre in Canada is Badische Canada, of Arnprior, Ont. Its product is used mainly in carpets. Polypropylene, a most versatile synthetic fibre made by Celanese, is widely used for indoor-outdoor carpeting and for types of nonwoven textiles.

There are about 1000 textile-manufacturing plants in Canada, most of them located in Québec and Ontario. The Canadian clothing or apparel industry is the largest single consumer of textiles, using about 45% of the industry's output (fibre-weight equivalent). The ability of the textile industry to supply its home furnishings and industrial customers depends, in large part, on the continued existence of the clothing industry. Without the economies of scale made possible by the total market, almost every subsector of the textile industry would be threatened. Thus, textiles and clothing, while separate industries, are indivisible from the standpoint of industrial survival. They are also only 2 links in a long chain that starts with the consumer, goes back through retailers to apparel manufacturers, dyers and finishers, weavers and knitters, fibre producers, the PETROCHEMICAL INDUSTRY (from which the raw materials for synthetic fibres come), and finally to the oil and gas wells. The disappearance of any link would weaken, perhaps fatally, the rest of the chain.

The employment links are also important. The weighted average employment multiplier for the textile and clothing industries has been estimated to be 1.65; ie, each job in textiles and clothing supports 1.65 jobs elsewhere in the economy. By this measure, the industries' 150 000 jobs support 247 500 additional jobs in other sectors.

Canada remains a relatively open market for textile and clothing imports from developed and developing nations. Canada's consumption of textiles and clothing by volume is about 2% of the world's total, and Canadian mills now supply less than 50% of this amount. The largest proportion of textile imports comes from developed countries; the largest proportion of clothing imports from developing countries. Despite substantial import-restraint legislation, Canada accepts 9 times more per capita in textiles from developed countries than the US and 3 times as much as the European Economic Community. Steps by the Canadian government, assuring the textile industry of the continuation of special protection measures, have created a fairly stable climate of confidence and have stimulated investment. Another step has been taken by the creation of the Canadian Industrial Renewal Board, a government agency that will provide funds for modernization of those plants judged to have a viable future.

The Canadian textile industry is internationally competitive with other developed countries in price, quality and product variety. The primary industry is as technologically efficient and productive as any in the world. Major technological advances have been introduced to accompany the shift from natural to man-made fibres and blends, including the adoption of advanced spinning, weaving, knitting, nonwoven and finishing machinery, electronic and computerized control equipment and methods of reducing energy consumption. Canada was a pioneer in introducing a new open-end type of yarn spinning and is a leader in the use of shuttleless weaving machines. Canada rates with the leaders in the production and technical development of nonwoven fabrics, particularly in their use in geotextiles (eg, ASBESTOS fibres). Computers and microprocessors are widely used in manufacturing operations.

Today the industry consists of the survivors of an extended and rigorous period of rationalization. The remaining firms are efficient, cost conscious and adaptable to the changing marketplace. Dominion Textile Inc is by far the largest textile manufacturer in Canada, with annual sales of about $800 million (about 20% of Canadian production). The company has 40 manufacturing facilities, 26 located in Canada, 7 in the US, 6 in Europe and one in Hong Kong. Of the Canadian plants, 17 are in Québec, 8 in Ontario and one in NS. Total employment is in excess of 12 000.

The textile industry continues to spend large sums on new machinery and modernization of facilities. For example, spending on capital equipment and repairs during the 1970s amounted to $1.8 billion, and it is likely that about $1.2 billion will be spent in the 1980s. The industry has improved its export performance without imposing sacrifices on its domestic customers. To be successful in the export of commodities, such as textiles, a secure domestic base must underpin the higher risks, costs and lower net returns inherent in export marketing. The industry now operates in a more confident climate, which has encouraged a strong flow of investment into efficient, highly productive textile processes. W.A.B. DAVIDSON

Textiles, Woven Canada has a rich history of weaving stretching back to the precontact native peoples and enriched by each succeeding wave of immigrants. The working together of lengths of fibre (threads) to make a fabric can be done in simple and universal forms by the fingers alone to produce braiding and basketry constructions. Netted and knitted fabrics can be made with very simple tools. To produce a woven textile, 2 sets of threads must be interlaced: one set, the warp, is held by some kind of support; the other, the weft, is worked over and under the warp threads to hold them together in a firm but flexible form. With simple weaving equipment every movement is done by hand; however, over a long period of time, technological advances meant that more work was done by the loom and less by the weaver. The key development that turned the weaving frame into a true loom was the heddle which, in its simplest form, is made up of a pair of rods with attached string loops through which the warp threads pass. These rods can be manipulated to make an opening (a shed) through the warp threads for an easy passage of the weft. From these simple beginnings looms have become more and more complex with increasingly automatic action. Many forms of weaving devices, from very simple to quite complex, have been used by local craftspeople in Canada.

The native peoples produced beautiful weaving without benefit of a shed-making device. Therefore, although their weaving was skillful and of high quality, it was very time consuming. Skins were used for utilitarian purposes; woven textiles were reserved for prestige items such as the magnificent ceremonial blankets used on the West Coast (see CHILKAT BLANKET; NORTHWEST COAST INDIAN ART), MEDICINE BUNDLES, WAMPUM, bands and exquisite ornaments woven with porcupine quills. The weave used was a special technique (weft-twined weave), which developed from the making of baskets. In weft twining, 2 weft threads enclose each warp or group of warps in turn and then twist around each other before moving on to the next warp. From early times, this technique was used in many parts of the country with wide variations of texture, material and design. As trade goods became available, they supplanted the native weaving, but for some purposes the skills were maintained and are still practised today.

The first migrants to come from Europe were the French, who settled in Québec and parts of the Atlantic region in the early 17th century. At that time France was famous for tapestry weaving, but the settlers brought with them the simple country skills, home spinning of yarn and weaving of cloth for utilitarian clothing and bed coverings. At first, few textiles were produced but, as time went on, home production of textiles became important; girls were taught to spin, and farmhouses contained looms on which household goods and some material for barter were produced. The loom used in New France was very simple; the cloth woven, very plain. For bed coverings, 2 simple hand-patterning techniques were used: à la planche, in which a narrow board was used to open a pattern shed for a coloured weft to form simple block designs; and boutonné, in which multicoloured wefts were pulled up in loops to make motifs (eg, stars, pine trees). There was also a considerable production of heavy lengths of material with a weft of old cloth torn into rag strips. In the early days these catalogne lengths were used for bed coverings; in more recent and affluent times, for floor coverings.

LOYALISTS who moved N to the Atlantic region and the future provinces of Québec and Ontario were from a variety of ethnic backgrounds, many of them British. Most of the women could spin and some could weave. As soon as possible, flax was grown to provide fibre for linen and sheep were raised for wool. Household linens and blankets and warm lengths for clothing were made in many homes, but among the settlers there were a number of trained, professional handweavers, usually men, who could operate complex pattern looms. These craftsmen wove fancy linens and ornamental bed coverings, often the pride of a bride's trousseau. The coverlets were usually in either summer and winter weave or double cloth, both of which produced striking geometric patterns and were usually of dark blue wool and white linen or cotton.

Of the many European immigrants who followed the Loyalists, those who had the most impact on Canadian weaving traditions were the SCOTS, IRISH and GERMANS. Trained craftsmen had been thrown out of work during the Industrial Revolution by the mechanization of the weaving industry in Scotland and Germany, and many of the out-of-work weavers came to Canada. They expected to farm but found they could again practise their profession profitably. One or more of these experienced weavers could be found in most areas in the older parts of English-speaking Canada. Housewives usually prepared the yarns, but much of the weaving was done by the professionals. Imported materials could be purchased in settled areas of Canada from the early 19th century on, but many of the blankets, carpets, linens and clothing materials were locally produced by handweavers, both home and professional, until quite late in the century, when it ceased to be profitable.

Ornamental bed coverings, or coverlets, were an especially popular production of the local professional weavers. In the Scottish-Irish areas the usual weave was one called overshot, ie, an extra weft shoots over and under a plain ground, forming quite complex and striking geometric patterns and making a very warm covering. The patterns were usually in wool, dark blue or plain, bright red, sometimes banded. The ground was almost always white cotton. In German areas the weaves used for ornamental coverlets and decorative horse blankets required very complex handlooms for elaborate twill interlacings and a type of patterning that had rows of stars alternating with diamonds.

The complex Jacquard loom, in which the opening of the pattern sheds is controlled by a series of punched cards, was introduced in the 1830s. The loom was used by a comparatively small number of local professional hand-weavers in Ontario. The patterns that were possible with this new loom were semirealistic with flowers and birds and other motifs that were beyond the capabilities of earlier looms. A Jacquard coverlet was a much-treasured possession and often survives from a wedding trousseau.

Spinning and weaving are crafts that go with pioneering and, just as the skills were falling into disuse in eastern Canada (around 1900), the West was opening up. Store-bought goods were available by mail-order catalogue, but many textiles were produced locally. Pioneers from eastern Canada or Britain had, for the most part, lost their textile-making skills a generation or 2 before. Those from Scandinavia, Germany or eastern Europe were accustomed to spinning yarn from their own home-grown wool, flax and hemp. Many spinning wheels used on the prairies have survived, but the hand-spun yarn was knitted into warm garments that have worn out. Fewer looms have survived; most of the weaving was for perishable things like rag RUGS, few of which still exist. UKRAINIANS and DOUKHOBORS did more ornamental weaving, some of which has been preserved. Ukrainians furnished their homes with handsome, woven bench covers of linen, hemp and wool banded in colour, and gave their rooms a warm brightness with tapestry-woven woollen wall hangings in bright geometric patterns. The Doukhobors produced coarse tapestry weave in very bright colours and rugs with a thick woollen pile knotted into a plain firm ground (in the same way that oriental carpets are made). These 2 patterning techniques, typical of their earlier homes in the Caucasus, have been quite widely used since the Doukhobors settled in Saskatchewan and BC. Canada's weaving traditions reflect the nation's fascinating cultural diversity. Some of the older traditions have blended together; those that came later still stand uniquely on their own.   DOROTHY K. BURNHAM

Reading: Harold B. Burnham and Dorothy K. Burnham, *'Keep me warm one night': Early Handweaving in Eastern Canada* (1972); Dorothy K. Burnham, *The Comfortable Arts; Traditional Spinning and Weaving in Canada* (1981).

Thacker, Herbert Cyril, army officer (b at Poona, India 16 Sept 1870; d at Victoria 2 June 1953). Thacker, briefly chief of the general staff in 1927-28, was commissioned in the Royal Canadian Artillery in 1891. He fought in the SOUTH AFRICAN WAR and accompanied the Japanese army as military attaché during the Russo-Japanese War 1904-05, the first appointment of its kind for a Canadian officer. Thacker commanded divisional artilleries of the CANADIAN EXPEDITIONARY FORCE, 1915-19. He took the position of chief of the general staff reluctantly and despite ill health.   NORMAN HILLMER

Thanksgiving Day Proclaimed as "a day of General Thanksgiving to Almighty God for the bountiful harvest with which Canada has been blessed," Thanksgiving draws upon 3 traditions: harvest celebrations in European peasant societies for which the symbol was the cornucopia (horn of plenty); formal observances, such as that celebrated by Martin FROBISHER in the eastern Arctic in 1578 — the first North American Thanksgiving; and the Pilgrims' celebration of their first harvest in Massachusetts (1621) involving the uniquely American turkey, squash and pumpkin. The celebration was brought to Nova Scotia in the 1750s and the citizens of Halifax commemorated the end of the SEVEN YEARS' WAR (1763) with a day of Thanksgiving. Loyalists brought the celebration to other parts of the country.

In 1879 the Canadian Parliament declared Nov 6 as a day of Thanksgiving; it was celebrated as a national rather than a religious holiday. Later and earlier dates were observed, the most popular being the third Monday in October. After WWI, Thanksgiving and Armistice (later Remembrance) Day were celebrated in the same week. It was not until 31 Jan 1957 that Parliament proclaimed the observance of Thanksgiving on the second Monday in October. E.C. DRURY, the former "Farmer-Premier" of Ontario lamented later that "the farmers' own holiday has been stolen by the towns" to give them a long weekend when the weather was better.   DAVID MILLS

Thatcher, Wilbert Ross, premier of Saskatchewan (b at Neville, Sask 24 May 1917; d at Regina 23 July 1971). Educated locally and at Queen's U, Thatcher was a businessman. After holding aldermanic office, he was elected CCF member of Parliament in 1945, 1949 and 1953, but left his party in 1955, sitting first as an Independent and then as a Liberal. He ran unsuccessfully in the 1957 and 1958 federal elections. Critical of CCF administration, he termed Saskatchewan's crown corporations a dismal failure, a charge which led to the Mossbank debate (May 1957) with CCF premier T.C. DOUGLAS and established him as the anti-CCF standard bearer. In Sept 1959 Thatcher defeated 3 other challengers for the provincial Liberal leadership. Under him Saskatchewan Liberals became identified with free-enterprise rhetoric but pragmatic policies and won the provincial election in 1964 — the first time in 20 years a provincial Liberal government had ruled west of Québec. His devotion to economic development led to friction with federal Liberals whose priorities differed: social welfare under Lester PEARSON and constitutional reform under Pierre TRUDEAU. Intra-party organizational disputes so fractured Saskatchewan Liberals that Thatcher entered the 1971 provincial election beleaguered by partisan allies and partisan foes alike, losing 20 of 35 seats to the NDP under Allan BLAKENEY. He died one month later.   DAVID E. SMITH

Reading: David E. Smith, *Prairie Liberalism* (1975); J. Wearing, *The L-Shaped Party* (1981).

The Imperialist, novel by Sara Jeannette DUNCAN (Toronto, 1904), is set in Elgin, Ont (modeled on Duncan's native BRANTFORD). *The Imperialist* conducts its exploration of Canadian attitudes toward the mother country through the development of 2 romances. One involves Lorne Murchison, a fervent imperialist, with the pretty but shallow Dora Milburn, who eventually marries an asinine Englishman; the other pairs Lorne's sister Advena with Rev Hugh Finlay, who was already engaged to an older woman before he emigrated to Canada, but submits to New World imperatives and his love for Advena. The novel is at once a delightful comedy of manners and a thoroughgoing analysis of Canadian society as it looks back to England, south to the US and into its own evolving idea of itself.   NEIL BESNER

The Pas, Man, Town, pop 6390 (1981c), inc 1912, is located on the S bank of the SASKATCHEWAN R, about 50 km N of where the river enters CEDAR LK. At first an Indian encampment, The

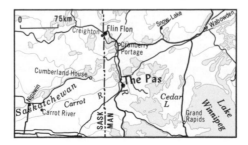

Pas site was visited by early explorers Henry KELSEY, the LA VÉRENDRYE sons and Sir John FRANKLIN. It became a FUR-TRADE centre, beginning with the French Ft Paskoyac (also spelled Pasquia and Paskoya) in the mid-1700s. Members of a rescue expedition sent to search for the missing Franklin helped create a new Anglican mission while wintering at The Pas in 1847. A Roman Catholic mission established in 1887 played a significant role in the development of various institutions, including the hospital. The origin of the name is uncertain, but may derive from a Cree word meaning "a narrow place" (in the river). The townsite was obtained in 1906 from the Cree, who subsequently moved to the N bank of the Saskatchewan. In the early 1900s mining and commercial fishing in the N, lumbering and development of a railway divisional point enhanced the town's importance as an economic and administrative centre. Mixed farming became more viable W of the town following completion of a major drainage project in 1960. The Pas is an important link between the mining, fishing and trapping areas of the Canadian SHIELD and the mainly agricultural lands of southern Manitoba. Its principal employer is Manitoba Forestry Resources Ltd, an integrated sawmill and pulp and paper complex owned by the Manitoba government. Among facilities at The Pas is Keewatin Community College.   D.M. LYON

Reading: S. Wilton, *The Pas . . . A History: Adventure and Romance* (1970).

The T. Eaton Company Limited, with head offices in Toronto, is a major Canadian retailer founded in Toronto in 1869 by Timothy EATON. Eaton revolutionized the commercial practice of the day by selling items for cash at a fixed price and offering satisfaction or money refunded. His store became one of the largest department stores in N America. Eaton's son John Craig EATON assumed the presidency on the death of his father in 1907; he was later knighted. His cousin, Robert Young Eaton, took over in 1922, followed by Sir John's son, John David Eaton, in 1942. The current president, Fredrik S. EATON, is Timothy Eaton's great-grandson.

A cornerstone of the Eaton empire was its catalogue business, established in 1884 along with mail-order facilities to reach pioneer farm communities. The discontinuation of this business in 1976 spurred internal reorganization and revitalization. Other early innovations are still thriving: the Product Research Bureau was established in 1916 by John Craig Eaton, who was inspired by his father's insistence that customers should always know what was in their merchandise; it was the first developed in Canada by a retailer. Eaton's is still the only retailer in the country with its own complete research facilities. The company's sales revenues and assets are undisclosed, in 1984 it had an estimated 35 000 employees and some 110 outlets. All shares are held by the Eaton family.

DEBORAH C. SAWYER

Theatre, English-Language It is a common misconception that theatre on the N American continent began with the arrival of Spanish and French explorers and settlers. Indian and Inuit ceremonials and rituals evidenced a highly sophisticated sense of mimetic art, and occupied a central place in the social and religious activities of their peoples (*see* NATIVE PEOPLE, RELIGION). When Sir Humphrey GILBERT took his expedition to Newfoundland in 1583, he was equipped with "toyes . . . Hobby horsse, and Maylike conceits to delight the Savage people," which suggests some kind of rudimentary theatrics. The first significant theatrical event organized by European explorers, however, was a masque, or *réception*, written by a French lawyer, Marc LESCARBOT, for performance at PORT-ROYAL in 1606 in honour of the return of his commander, Sieur de Poutrincourt, from a voyage along what is now the coast of New England: *Le Théâtre de Neptune* was performed in the Annapolis Basin by a cast of Europeans before an audience which included some Amerindians.

The Jesuits in 17th-century New France soon began to exert a strong influence on the development of theatre. Evidence from the JESUIT RELATIONS indicates that morality plays and allegories were staged by the Jesuits for the edification of their students as well as for indoctrinating the Indians. Original works were also written and performed by the Jesuits: *La Réception de Monseigneur le Vicomte d'Argenson par toutes les nations du païs de Canada à son entrée au gouvernement de la Nouvelle-France* in 1658 is one example. Contemporary plays were also produced. Jesuit records reveal that members of the colony's administration stationed in Québec entertained themselves and the resident population with productions of plays such as Racine's *Mithridate* and Corneille's *Nicomède,* both performed in the winter of 1693-94.

Towards the end of the 17th century a rift developed between church and civil authorities over the control of theatrical productions. A proposed performance of Molière's *Tartuffe* in 1694 led Bishop SAINT-VALLIER to issue a forceful pastoral letter condemning plays of this type for their evil influence, thereby beginning a long history of conflict between the church and the theatre in Québec. As a result of church opposition to the theatre and its alleged immoral influence, Québec enjoyed little public theatrical entertainment again until after the 1763 CONQUEST. Subsequently the British garrison in Montréal revived theatre with, ironically, productions of Molière, and was soon emulated by local francophone groups. Popular English plays were also performed by the garrisons of Montréal and Québec City; amateur thespian societies were formed, and Jesuit students once more began staging plays in their colleges.

This new theatrical impetus in late 18th-century Québec was matched by developments in Atlantic Canada. Performing in makeshift theatres in taverns and other public buildings, at first with all-male casts, the officers and men of the British garrisons promoted theatre. The Halifax garrison built the New Grand Theatre, fitted with boxes and 2 pits, which opened on 26 Feb 1789 with a production of *The Merchant of Venice.* Charlottetown built its first theatre in 1800, and by 1809 Saint John had its own Drury Lane Theatre. Thus a lively garrison and amateur theatrical tradition emerged in the Maritimes, hampered sometimes by puritanical attacks ("a Christian cannot with a safer Conscience enter into the Play-House than into a Brothel," declared a writer in the *Nova Scotia Chronicle* in Jan 1770), but confident enough to mount full-length productions from the classical and contemporary English repertoire, as well as new Canadian works. Among these was a romantic comedy called *Acadius; or, Love in a Calm,* the first recorded English Canadian play, performed in Halifax in 1774.

Theatrical activity in Québec and the Maritimes in the 18th century was predominantly amateur, but the growing population in both regions began to attract professional companies from the US. The first resident professional company in Canada was the American Company of Comedians, believed to have performed at the Pontac Inn, Halifax, in the summer and fall of 1768. Another group of actors, headed by an Englishman, Edward Allen, arrived in Montréal from Albany, NY, in March 1786 for a 4-month season, then moved on to Québec City. Other professional entertainment was provided by the American circus of John B. Ricketts, whose company performed in Montréal and Québec City in 1797 and 1798.

By the end of the 18th century Canadian theatre was poised for rapid growth, and the 19th century provided a rich mosaic of theatrical development in all regions of the country. Elaborate theatres were constructed in the Maritimes and Québec. Montréal's THEATRE ROYAL, built by a group of investors headed by John MOLSON, Sr, in 1825 to seat an audience of 1000, cost $30 000, and featured a Doric portico, 2 tiers of boxes, a pit and a gallery, comfortable backstage facilities and lavish decorations. The Theatre Royal at Spring Gardens, Halifax, opened in 1846 and had boxes to accommodate over 160 patrons. By this time theatre had also firmly established itself in Upper Canada, again encouraged by amateur groups and enthusiastic garrisons in settlements on the sites of such present-day cities as Toronto, Ottawa, London and Kingston. As early as 1809 there was a performance at York [Toronto] by New York actors of *The School for Scandal,* but it was not until 1834 that Toronto had its first real theatre, a converted Wesleyan church. Others followed, including the Royal Lyceum (1848) and the Grand Opera House, which opened in 1874 and burned down in a spectacular fire 5 years later. London's Grand Opera House (1881) was also destroyed by fire, but, like its Toronto counterpart, was replaced (*see* GRAND THEATRE). Numerous smaller towns across the country boasted opera houses of various sizes and longevity.

When the West began to be accessible to touring companies, theatres were among the first priorities of new communities. The Royal Engineers built a rudimentary theatre in New Westminster in 1858, and Victoria's Colonial Theatre opened in Feb 1860, following some years of theatrical productions performed by sailors on British ships anchored in Esquimalt Harbour. By 1891 Vancouver had a 1200-seat Opera House, and adequate theatres also existed in prairie cities. Winnipeg's Walker Theatre (1907) was especially impressive, with seating for close to 2000 and a liberal supply of ivory and marble in its fittings.

Audiences that regularly filled Canadian theatres in the 19th century were, with some notorious exceptions, mostly polite, attentive and self-disciplined. Ontario audiences were more inhibited than their Québec counterparts, whether the latter were Anglo-Canadians vigorously assaulting American visitors with sticks and canes for not removing their hats during the playing of the national anthem in a Montréal theatre in 1811, or French Canadian students rapturously welcoming Sarah Bernhardt to Montréal in 1880. Torontonians gave Adelaide Neilson a standing ovation after her Canadian farewell performance in 1880, but the most volatile audiences in 19th-century Canada were to be found in the West. A serious race riot occurred in the Colonial Theatre, Victoria, in Nov 1860, when black members of the audience forced their way into areas reserved for whites; Winnipeg audiences in the 1880s were enlivened by the presence of boisterous youths and uninhibited prostitutes; Klondike theatres were often uproarious; and a performance of *The Cowboy's Romance* in High River, Alta, in May 1902 ended with the director of the Great Bostock Theatrical Co wielding a club against the egg-flinging audience.

The social, cultural and educational benefits of theatre were stressed by many apologists, but the Catholic Church and some Protestants (especially Methodists) continued their strong moral opposition, holding theatrical entertainment responsible for debauchery, dissipation and sundry other ungodly habits. Bishop BOURGET of Montréal issued condemnations of the theatre in pastoral letters in 1859 and 1872, and in 1880 Bishop Fabre forbade his parishioners to attend performances by the visiting French actress Sarah Bernhardt.

Despite these handicaps, and the necessity of competing with foreign plays and players, Canadian playwrights, actors and managers began to achieve some prominence. In Québec the comedies of Félix-Gabriel MARCHAND (premier of the province, 1897-1900) were performed, as were the plays of Louis-Honoré FRÉCHETTE. Professional companies in theatres such as the Nouveau Théâtre empire (1893), the Monument national (1894) and especially the Théâtre des variétés (1898) fostered the career of Québec actresses Blanche de la Sablonnière and Juliette Béliveau. In English Canada the turgid poetic dramas of Charles HEAVYSEGE, Charles MAIR and Wilfred CAMPBELL received little attention, but lively farces and political satires by Nicholas Flood DAVIN, J.N. McIlwraith and W.H. Fuller found audiences, as did conventional melodramas by McKee Rankin and the historical romances of W.A. Tremayne. Rankin also achieved recognition as an actor, both in Canada and abroad; and Tremayne wrote for Robert Mantell, a popular star in Canada. Many Canadian actors spent much of their time performing in the US and Britain: Julia Arthur worked with Henry Irving in London, and later founded an American touring company; Margaret ANGLIN who, it was said, could wring emotion from a keg of nails, was renowned for her productions of Greek plays in Berkeley, Calif; Franklin McLeay spent 5 years of his brief career with Wilson Barrett's company in London; Marie Dressler made her name in American vaudeville; and Henry Miller, who began his career in Toronto in 1878, became well-known as an actor-manager in New York. There were, however, Canadian actors who made their livelihood primarily in Canada. Charlotte Morrison ran a successful stock company in Toronto in the 1870s, and Ida Van Cortland (with her husband, Albert Tavernier) toured her company from Winnipeg to St John's in the 1880s. The 7 companies of the famous Marks Brothers toured small-town Canada regularly from 1879 to 1922, making a great deal of money in the process. At the turn of the century Harold Nelson, one of the country's first acting teachers, began a remarkable career producing Shakespeare, melodrama and comedy across the western provinces.

Throughout the 19th century, and well into the 20th, Canadian producers, actors and playwrights faced overwhelming competition from foreign touring stars and companies. This competition seriously retarded the development of indigenous professional theatre. In 1911 critic Bernard K. Sandwell bemoaned the annexation of the Canadian stage by US theatre magnates such as Charles Frohman, the Shubert Brothers and the powerful New York Theatrical Syndicate formed in 1896. The British Canadian Theatrical Organization Society (1912) attempted to balance American influence by organizing tours of British actors. The result was that British and US managements, by acquiring controlling interests in Canadian theatres, held a commercial and cultural stranglehold on the country's theatrical growth. The Trans-Canada Theatre Society (1915) was Canadian owned, but its purpose was to organize tours by foreign companies.

The process had begun, haphazardly, a century before, first with the arrival of minor actors from the US, then with major stars from America and Europe. Virtually every leading actor from Edmund Kean onwards performed in Canada. Kean acted in Montréal and Québec City in 1826, and scores of actors followed: W.C. Macready, the Kembles, E.A. Sothern, Charles and Ellen Kean, Charles Fechter, Edwin Booth, Joseph Jefferson, Sarah Bernhardt, Coquelin, Helena Modjeska, Tommaso Salvini, Laurence Barrett, Julia Marlowe, Henry Irving, Ellen Terry, John Martin-Harvey, Mrs Fiske, Mrs Campbell, Robert Mantell, the Kendals, Ben Greet and Johnston Forbes-Robertson, as well as distinguished companies from Dublin's Abbey Theatre and England's Stratford. As dedicated professionals, these performers brought good acting and, sometimes, good plays, but most saw Canada as a theatrical appendage to the US, with some commercial potential. WWI interrupted the touring circuits. Escalating costs, competition from film and radio and the Depression then combined to end touring companies. Foreign touring stars and companies helped create and sustain a tradition of theatregoing, and they gave impetus to the building of many excellent theatres. But when the touring era ended, Canada, having failed to nurture its own professionals, was left with negligible professional theatre.

Visiting companies still appeared in Canadian theatres, and resident foreign repertory companies performing popular Broadway and London plays sometimes established themselves. One example is Vaughan Glaser's company in Toronto (1921-27). There were also intermittently successful Canadian professional and semiprofessional companies working throughout Canada. The John Holden Players performed in Bala, Ont, and Winnipeg in the late 1930s. Sidney Risk's Everyman Theatre Co, which originated in Saskatchewan as a student touring company, opened in Vancouver in 1946 and performed a classical repertoire throughout the West for many years. Toronto's Jupiter Theatre started in 1951, and in Ottawa the Canadian Repertory Theatre, with actress and director Amelia Hall, was prominent in the early 1950s. Several companies were founded in Québec between the wars: the Barry-Duquesne Co at Montréal's Théâtre Stella (opened 1930), Émile Legault's amateur Compagnons de Saint-Laurent (1937), Pierre Dagenais's Équipe (1943), together with Fridolinons, the popular annual stage reviews by Gratien GÉLINAS (*see* MUSICAL THEATRE). Shortly after WWII the THÉÂTRE DU RIDEAU-VERT opened in Montréal, followed in 1951 by the THÉÂTRE DU NOUVEAU MONDE. Companies at both theatres have had a major impact on French-language drama, in Canada and abroad.

Toronto's New Play Society, though benefiting throughout its history from volunteer help, operated for some years on a professional basis. Founded by Dora Mavor MOORE (1946), the NPS succeeded in developing Canadian talent in all areas of theatre. Plays by Morley CALLAGHAN, Harry BOYLE, John COULTER, Mavor MOORE, Lister Sinclair and Andrew ALLAN were produced in the theatre of the ROYAL ONTARIO MUSEUM. NPS also originated the famous annual touring revue *Spring Thaw*. Dora Mavor Moore was a major force in the creation of the STRATFORD FESTIVAL and many NPS actors appeared there.

Nevertheless, Canadian theatrical activity in the first half of the 20th century was predominantly amateur: Having relied heavily on imported theatre for a century or more, Canada had no established professional base on which to build when the imports declined. When a growing national self-consciousness demanded theatrical expression, it was largely amateurs who were available to provide it. The need for theatrical self-expression was enunciated by Gov Gen Earl Grey in 1907 when he created the Earl Grey Musical and Dramatic Competition for the encouragement of dramatic arts throughout the Dominion. The competition was held annually until 1911, and was by invitation. Unlike the later Dominion Drama Festival, there was no regional screening process, and Canadian judges were used. The Earl Grey Competition was short-lived and had only a minimal effect on Canadian theatre, but vice-regal approval of theatrical endeavour was a welcome change from puritanical opposition by church authorities.

Grey's initiative coincided with important developments elsewhere in amateur theatre. In 1905 the Arts and Letters Players of Toronto was formed. Dedicated to serious noncommercial theatre, and performing in cramped quarters in the Old Court House on Adelaide St, the company was at the forefront of the LITTLE THEATRE MOVEMENT. Led by Roy Mitchell, the Arts and Letters Players demonstrated the value of innovative and experimental theatre with productions of plays by Maeterlinck, Yeats, Tagore, Synge and Lady Gregory. When U of Toronto's Hart House Theatre opened in 1919, it absorbed the ideals and energies of the Arts and Letters Players, and Mitchell became the new theatre's first director. Hart House Theatre fostered the distinguished careers of many directors, actors and playwrights, among them Bertram Forsyth, Raymond MASSEY, Carroll Aikins, Dora Mavor Moore, Edgar Stone, Merrill DENISON, Herman VOADEN, Jane Mallet, Andrew Allan, Robert GILL, Kate REID, Barbara Chilcott and Elizabeth Stirling Haynes. Other Little Theatres emerged and sometimes flourished — the Ottawa Drama League by 1913 and the Montreal Repertory Theatre by 1930, for example. At the Sarnia Drama League (1927), Voaden experimented with "symphonic expressionism" and generally challenged theatrical norms. By the 1930s all major cities, as well as many smaller communities, had an established amateur theatre.

In an attempt to co-ordinate and give some focus to amateur theatre activity in the country, the Dominion Drama Festival was formed in 1932. Initiated by Gov Gen Lord Bessborough, and relying heavily on the influence and expertise of Vincent MASSEY, the DDF organized bilingual competitions and regional drama festivals from which the best productions were selected to compete in the annual final, held in a different city each year. In 1970 the DDF succeeded by Theatre Canada, which survived until 1978. The DDF outlived its purpose, as amateur enthusiasm, however skilled, was overtaken by professional expertise. Yet the DDF can justifiably claim a major contribution to 20th-century theatre. By providing incentives and opportunities for actors, playwrights, designers, directors and technicians, and by building and maintaining audiences across the country, the DDF helped create the circumstances that made possible a fully professional theatre.

Other early 20th-century amateur activity of note occurred in the universities. The lead was taken by western Canada, particularly at U of Saskatchewan, where the first chair of drama in the British Commonwealth was founded in 1945; U of Alberta established a department of fine arts in 1946 and the BANFF CENTRE SCHOOL OF FINE ARTS produced the early works of Gwen Pharis RINGWOOD and other Canadian playwrights. Drama and theatre programs, the majority of them established in the 1960s, are now found at universities and colleges in every province. In many instances the universities, unfettered by commercial considerations or social convention, have premiered deserving plays by Canadian and foreign playwrights. The universities have also provided a vital educational and training service in all aspects of theatre production, history and criticism (*see* THEATRE EDUCATION). Another form of amateur drama emerged and briefly flourished in the Depression years. The Progressive Arts Club was formed in Toronto in 1932 for the development of a militant working-class art and literature. From PAC developed the Workers' Experimental Theatre, consisting largely of groups of unemployed workers who performed short plays and political skits on topical issues wherever they could find a space, which was frequently outdoors and often on picket lines. The most celebrated production of the Workers' Theatre was *Eight Men Speak* (1933), a full-length play based on the trial and imprisonment of 8 Canadian communists. The play was later banned in Toronto and

Winnipeg. The Workers' Theatre, with its international political and cultural links, had a unique excitement and inventiveness, but faded after the Depression and left no lasting mark on subsequent developments in Canadian theatre.

A vital impetus to continued progress of professional theatre came from the 1951 Report of the Royal Commission on NATIONAL DEVELOPMENT IN THE ARTS, LETTERS AND SCIENCES. Chaired by Vincent Massey, the commission made recommendations which led to the formation of the CANADA COUNCIL in 1957.

The transition from a predominantly amateur to a predominantly professional theatre began with the founding of the Stratford Festival in 1953. Thereafter, professional theatre rapidly began to consolidate itself. The Crest Theatre opened in Toronto in 1954, and the Canadian Players, an offshoot of the Stratford company, undertook tours throughout the US and Canada. The founding of major regional theatres and government acceptance of a responsibility to fund the arts revitalized professional theatre. Unlike the professional theatre of the 19th century, however, the new professionalism had national as well as international interests, and the early 1960s opened a phase of advancement in Canadian theatrical arts of greater scope and intensity than anything previously witnessed in its 350-year history. L.W. CONOLLY

Contemporary

One serious attempt at an early "national" theatre was Gratien Gélinas's Comédie-Canadienne, 1958-69, which set out to produce original plays in both French and English. The last gasp of this kind of nationalism was the founding in 1960 of the colingual National Theatre School, which was originally to be located in Stratford as well as in Montréal. However, in the early 1960s francophone theatre was destined to go its own way, and soon the West too would free itself from eastern domination. This decentralization (or "democratization," as it was called in Canada) was championed by Peter Dwyer, arts supervisor of the Canada Council.

The "Regional Theatre Movement" was defined, and summer festivals and winter stock companies sprouted up across the country to serve the principal municipalities and, by touring, their immediate environs. Toronto's Crest Theatre (1954-66) under Donald and Murray Davis had evolved out of amateur beginnings at Hart House Theatre, but did not become the regional model. This honour went to Winnipeg and the MANITOBA THEATRE CENTRE, one of the earliest recipients of a Canada Council grant. Founded by John HIRSCH and Tom HENDRY in 1958 out of a merger of 2 amateur groups, MTC attained full professionalism within 4 years, thereby demonstrating the value of government support for the arts. By 1966 the pioneering Crest Theatre and the Canadian Players were allowed to collapse, causing shock waves in Toronto, the nominal English-language centre. The SHAW FESTIVAL joined the Vancouver International Festival (1958 to 1968) in 1962; NEPTUNE THEATRE (Halifax) and the VANCOUVER PLAYHOUSE were added to the national chain in 1963. Others followed in rapid succession: the Charlottetown Festival, home of the Canadian musical (1964); the CITADEL in Edmonton (1965); the GLOBE in Regina (1966); the Saidye Bronfman Centre in Montréal (1967); Theatre New Brunswick in Fredericton and Theatre Calgary (1968); Ottawa's NATIONAL ARTS CENTRE and Montréal's CENTAUR THEATRE (1969); and Toronto Arts Productions (now CentreStage) at the St Lawrence Centre (1970). Theatre London (now the GRAND THEATRE Co), Sudbury Theatre, Theatre North-West (Thunder Bay) and Victoria's Bastion Theatre went professional in 1971, leaving Newfoundland as the only province without a regional theatre.

Provincial and civic arts councils mushroomed to broaden the base of private and governmental support, until Canada's nonprofit theatre was subsidized sometimes to the extent of 50%. Concurrent with the nationwide establishment of professional acting companies was a rash of theatre construction, the first such in 40 years. Civic centres, opera houses and huge multipurpose auditoriums were erected, usually to help celebrate various provincial anniversaries or Canada's impending 100th birthday as a nation in 1967. Regrettably, most of these spaces were unsuitable for the new Canadian troupes burgeoning around them. However, the era of ballet and opera in hockey arenas was over, and the new buildings reopened the touring circuits for American musicals and palladium-type entertainments that had not flourished since the 1920s. Small pocket theatres (*théâtres de poche*) began to appear in the late 1950s, primarily in Montréal and Toronto, and produced some of the first cabaret revues and original plays of the postwar period. *Up Tempo* (1956-65) ran for over 8 years in Montréal, and Toronto's *Clap Hands* revue was a successful export to London, 1961-63. Among the dramas, Len PETERSON's *The Great Hunger* (1960) stood out, as did *Hey, Rube!* (1961), one of the initial "collective creations" produced by George LUSCOMBE's Toronto Workshop Productions (1959-).

Tom Patterson's dream of a Yukon festival in Dawson City evaporated in 1962. A year later Montréal lost a beloved roadhouse, Her Majesty's, while in Toronto Ed Mirvish rescued the Royal Alexandra from the wreckers, just as he would buy and refurbish London's famed Old Vic Theatre 20 years later. Stratford successfully toured Gilbert and Sullivan to London in the early 1960s, and took Shakespeare and Molière to Chichester in 1964 (Chichester had copied the Stratford, Ont, stage). Canadian input to New York was less happily received. Robertson DAVIES's *Love and Libel* (1960) and Eric NICOL's *Like Father, Like Fun* (1966-67, retitled *A Minor Adjustment*) were unfortunate failures. In 1967 John Herbert's *Fortune and Men's Eyes* cracked the off-Broadway jinx. Centennial year marked a watershed for Canadian nationalism. The Canadian Theatre Centre hosted the international theatre Colloquium '67 in Montréal, and there were important new plays: George RYGA's *The Ecstasy of Rita Joe*, Ann Henry's *Lulu Street*, James REANEY's *Colours in the Dark* and a cross-country tour of the 1965 musical version of Lucy Maud MONTGOMERY's enduring hit *Anne of Green Gables*. In 1968-69 Theatre Toronto made a bid for world-class status. While its production of Rolf Hochhuth's *Soldiers* caused a stir in New York and London, the company itself lasted only 2 seasons.

Although Canada had produced a first generation of postwar dramatists, writers such as Davies, Herbert, Nicol, Peterson and Ryga, as well as John Coulter, Patricia Joudry, W.O. MITCHELL, Arthur Murphy, Lister Sinclair and Wilfred WATSON, Canadian plays were seldom seen on regional stages. The winter stock companies and summer festivals were labelled "dinosaurs" producing only imported or "museum" theatre, and they became targets for a jingoistic fervour. A flurry of small groups rose to provide an alternative to the established companies, ensembles like Toronto's Passe Muraille (1968-) and Canadian Place Theatre at Stratford (1969). At first, the alternate theatres produced American "hippie" dramas that utilized the new-found freedoms of language and nudity to make political protest. Passe Muraille's *Futz* (1969) and the year-long run of *Hair* at the Royal Alexandra (1970) were symbols of the times. A 1970 Canadian Festival of Underground Theatre (FUT) in Toronto was also important. Meanwhile, Ken Gass's Factory Theatre Lab (1970-) and Bill GLASSCO's TARRAGON THEATRE (1971-) shifted the emphasis dramatically to original plays, providing the "alternates" with a Canadian cause.

Clashes over indigenous works occurred at the regional theatres between certain artistic directors and their boards of governors. In the summer of 1971 the Canada Council, at the instigation of theatre officer David Gardner, convened a historic think tank in the Gaspé on "The Dilemma of Canadian Playwriting." It produced the catalytic recommendation that 50% subsidy should entail at least 50% Canadian content. This conference was followed by a larger and more public gathering at Niagara-on-the-Lake, which led to the formation of Playwrights Co-op (now Playwrights Canada) to foster the publishing of new works, a field already opened up by Talonbooks in 1969 on the West Coast. The 1970s saw hundreds of new plays printed and produced, an exciting turnaround as Canada's professional theatre became more truly Canadian. Noteworthy among the second wave of writers were Carol BOLT, Peter Colley, Michael Cook, Rex Deverell, David Fennario, David Freeman, David French, Joanna Glass, John Gray, Cam Hubert (also known as B.A. Cameron), John Murrell, Sharon Pollock, James Reaney, Erika Ritter, Rick Salutin, Bernard Slade, George F. Walker and Tom Walmsley. Even the regional theatres clambered on the bandwagon, picking up the new hits produced by the "alternates" and giving them major mainstage productions.

Between 1971 and 1974, 2 federal make-work schemes, Local Initiatives Programs and Opportunities for Youth, provided funds for another spate of instant theatre companies to flower overnight. Many of these survived to swell the alternate ranks: groups such as Vancouver's Tamahnous (1971-), BC's horse-drawn Caravan Stage Co (1970-), Edmonton's Theatre 3 (1970-81), Toronto Free Theatre (1972-) and the Famous People Players (1974-), a blacklight puppet troupe employing young mentally handicapped adults. Another yardstick of the times was a summer festival at Lennoxville, Qué (1972-82), devoted to repeat showings of lesser-known English Canadian plays. Unlike Ontario's BLYTH FESTIVAL (1975-), FESTIVAL LENNOXVILLE originated no dramas of its own.

In 1972 a statistical survey of leisure activities revealed that over 2 million Canadians, or about 10% of the population, attended live theatre annually, if not regularly, and that participation in arts activities exceeded that in sports, a radical reversal of traditional patterns. New companies continued to multiply. Some of the most interesting were Vancouver's reorganized Arts Club Theatre (1971-) and New Play Centre (1970-); Calgary's Alberta Theatre Projects (1972-); Saskatoon's 25TH STREET THEATRE (1972-); Ottawa's Great Canadian Theatre Company (1974-); and in Toronto, Open Circle (1972-82), Toronto Truck (1971-), Theatre Plus (1973-) and N America's renowned satiric ensemble, the Second City comedy cabaret (1973-). With approximately 40 theatre companies in Toronto, it was inevitable that groups with special identities would emerge, companies dedicated to women's theatre, senior citizens, stand-up comics, medieval drama, French-language theatre, 2 groups for blacks and, since 1975, an annual multicultural festival (*see* THEATRE, MULTICULTURAL). Newfoundland made up for lost time with its zany Codco Company (1973-78) and its comic successors, WNOBS (1979) and the Wonderful Grand Band (1977-). The Mummers Troupe (1972-82) revived the 19th-century tradition of MUMMING plays at Christmas and brought "collective creations" to the outports. A splinter group, Rising Tide Theatre, appeared in 1978, and in 1979 a training project at Stephenville developed into Theatre Newfoundland and Labrador.

There were further forays into New York, though to little acclaim: Tarragon's *Hosanna* in 1974 and, in 1976, Charlottetown's *Kronborg: 1582* (renamed *Rockabye Hamlet*), a pop-rock musical treatment of Shakespeare's masterpiece. But success or failure on Broadway seemed to matter less as Canadians found pride in their differences and realized that Toronto could become second only to New York as a N American theatre capital. The West gained 3 important companies: Vancouver's Westcoast Actors' Society and Saskatoon's Persephone in 1974, and Victoria's Belfry in 1975. An undoubted peak of the 1970s was Tarragon's presentation of James Reaney's Donnellys trilogy (1973-75) and its autumn 1975 national tour under the banner of the NDWT company (1975-82).

By mid-decade the first flush of excitement was over and a slump set in. Many of the "alternatives" were now part of the establishment and the spotlight swung back to the larger theatres. Vancouver's Playhouse added a theatre school in 1974; the Robin Phillips era began at Stratford in 1975; and on 13 Nov 1976 the new Citadel Theatre complex opened in Edmonton. The importation of British directors like Phillips for Stratford and Peter Coe for the Citadel provoked controversy and the imposition of protectionist policies. In 1980 a crisis over leadership at Stratford rocked the nation's cultural community and threatened the very existence of the renowned festival. In 1976 the "Cultural Olympics," a poorly organized performing-arts festival, accompanied the Montréal athletics. The games themselves proved a popular theme for several "collective creations," although some critics were finding that since Passe Muraille's *Farm Show* (1972) this distinctive Canadian style was wearing thin. Owing to financial losses, Neptune had to close its doors during 1976 for 8 months. It survived, however, and the following year the Mulgrave Road Co-op began, another in the intermittent attempts to root a sturdy second theatre in Halifax. In response to the election of the Parti Québécois in Nov 1976, federal monies were made available for 1977-78 "unity" tours of Canada by National Arts Centre companies in both languages. More to the point were Rick Salutin's *Les Canadiens* (1977) and David Fennario's bilingual *Balconville* (1979), both at Centaur.

Also significant in 1977 were the first signs of an extended economic recession that would change the tone and direction of the youthful Canadian professional theatre once more. Financial cutbacks necessitated smaller-cast plays and a more commercial approach. Comedies, musicals and thrillers began to dominate the playbills, works like *Jitters* (1979), *Automatic Pilot* (1980), *Nurse Jane Goes to Hawaii* (1980), *18 Wheels* (1977), *Eight to the Bar* (1978), *Rock 'n Roll* (1981), *One Night Stand* (1977) and *I'll Be Back for You before Midnight* (1979). The carefully balanced subscription seasons started to give way to open-ended runs and a scramble for transfer houses. Corporate sponsorship of individual productions became a pattern, and for the first time some independent entrepreneurs eschewed subsidy and mounted shows for profit. There were also more coproductions and co-operative exchanges between companies so that seasons would not be shortened. A stunning, Bunraku-inspired puppet production of Strindberg's *A Dream Play* (1977), for instance, was sponsored by 4 different theatres. Cross-country touring also extended the life of productions. There were several triumphs: *Ten Lost Years* from the East (1974-75); *Cruel Tears* (1977) and *Paper Wheat* (1977-78) from the West. Of course, extended runs of a year or more were no longer a surprise. *The Mousetrap*, London's perpetual success, has continued unbroken at Toronto Truck since 1977; Regina's *The Trial of Louis Riel* has played every summer since 1967 and Charlottetown's *Anne of Green Gables* since 1965. The record, however, still belongs to *Spring Thaw*, the New Play Society's comedy revue, which appeared annually for 25 years, 1948-73, and was reincarnated in 1980.

In the search for new solutions to the economic problems, the medieval idea of combining spiritual and bodily refreshment was revived. Cabaret was already well established, but lunch and dinner theatres were a relatively new twist in Canada. Lunchtime theatre had been tried by Montréal's *Instantheatre* between 1965 and 1971. In the 1970s and 1980s the chief exponents were Citystage in Vancouver (1972-), Lunchbox Theatre in Calgary (1975-), Northern Light in Edmonton (1975-) and Solar Stage in Toronto (1978-). One of the most ambitious and successful dinner-theatre concepts was Stage West, an eventual quartet of supper clubs in Edmonton (1975-), Regina (1978-83), Winnipeg (1980-) and Calgary (1981-), with prospects of more in Vancouver and Palm Springs, California. All-nude revues were money-makers in Toronto in the 1980s. *O! Calcutta* ran for over a year and *Let My People Come* for more than 3 years. But Passe Muraille's *I Love You Baby Blue* had provided far more erotic sparks in 1975, before the police closed it after 12 weeks. The other money-saving phenomenon of the late 1970s and early 1980s was the one-person show. It had been essayed as early as 1970 by Paddy Crean (*The Sun Never Sets*) and Tony Van Bridge as G.K. Chesterton. In the years that followed they were joined by at least 30 others, with Eric Peterson's *Billy Bishop Goes to War* (1978-81), Linda Griffiths's *Maggie and Pierre* (1979-81) and Viola Léger's *La Sagouine* (1979 in English) probably the most famous exponents. Many of the new productions were seen on television, and the Stratford Festival, London's Grand Theatre and Edmonton's Catalyst Theatre (1977-) turned winning productions of the 1980s into films and videotapes for the lucrative TV market.

For all the advantages wrung from the tight money situation, there were a disturbing number of small and middle-range companies that went bankrupt or closed shop in the early 1980s: the Mummers Troupe in Newfoundland; Open Circle, NDWT and Phoenix in Toronto; Theatre 3 in Edmonton; Westcoast Actors in Vancouver; Festival Lennoxville; the English-language theatre at the Saidye Bronfman Centre in Montréal; and Theatre 2000 and the National Arts Centre's theatre program in Ottawa were a few of the nearly 30 casualties. Ironically, the curtailment of production at the NAC was one of the few theatre recommendations made by the Applebaum-Hébert Report in Nov 1982. Publishing too was threatened. The magazine *Scene Changes* (1973-81) disappeared; Talonbooks (1967-) and the *Canadian Theatre Review* (1974-) were in trouble. However, the Assn for Canadian Theatre History, founded in 1976 to encourage research and publication in the history of Canadian theatre, organized annual conferences and helped to establish the scholarly journal *Theatre History in Canada* (1980-). Two other journals, *Performing Arts in Canada* (1961-) and *Canadian Drama* (1975-) were also survivors. Histories of 19th-century theatre in Saint John, Edmonton and BC appeared, and larger regional surveys for Québec, Ontario and the Prairies were in the works. There was even talk in 1985 of a series of theatre museums, and a *World Encyclopedia of Contemporary Theatre* to be edited and published in Canada.

As the population of Canada approached 25 million, the preservation and restoration of theatres like the Imperial-Capitol in Saint John, Kings Playhouse in Georgetown, PEI, Victoria Hall in Cobourg, Ont, and the Winter Garden in Toronto proved important. New architecture was also in the wind. The Sudbury Theatre Centre opened in Sept 1982, the St Lawrence Centre in Toronto was renovated in 1983, and the NWT

opened its first Northern Arts and Culture Centre in Yellowknife, 17 May 1984. A third playhouse for the Citadel was completed in 1984 and a new home for Theatre Calgary and Alberta Theatre Projects were also underway. If theatre buildings cost too much in the 1980s, there was a trend for populist theatre out-of-doors in the parks of Vancouver, Edmonton and Toronto; Winnipeg's thriving Rainbow Stage (1954-) survived by covering its musicals with a triodetic dome after Vancouver's "Theatre under the Stars" (1940-63) was rained out of existence.

The 1980s saw a trend towards internationalism at home and abroad. Plays and companies travelled frequently to Europe and the US. Performers such as Len Cariou, Hume CRONYN, Roberta Maxwell, Kate Nelligan, Christopher PLUMMER and Kate REID were stars either on Broadway or in the West End. Canada also hosted a veritable parade of international events: Onstage '81 in Toronto; 2 festivals of mime (1978, 1983) in which 25 Canadian troupes participated; festivals of clowning (Dartmouth, NS, 1982); indigenous theatre (native peoples, 1981, 1982); World Theatre Mosaic, a congress of amateur theatre at Calgary in 1983; and a major International Theatre Institute World Congress scheduled for Montréal and Toronto in June 1985. Since 1978 an International Festival of Children's Theatre has played each spring in Vancouver, Calgary, Toronto and Montréal (*see* THEATRE FOR YOUNG AUDIENCES). The work of Canadian set and costume designers was also exhibited abroad and won recognition at the Prague Quadrennial.

Now that the battle to perform Canadian plays has been won, experimentation is surfacing among many avant-garde fringe groups. Mention must be made, too, of the network of summer stock theatres stretching from coast to coast, and of new organizations like PACT (Professional Association of Canadian Theatres), the Association of Canadian Designers, the Canadian Theatre Critics Association, and even the Council for Business and the Arts. The 1980s saw the introduction of the Dora Mavor Moore Awards in Toronto (1981-) and the Jessie Richardson Theatre Awards in Vancouver (1983-) to honour achievement in Canadian theatre, a welcome addition to the Clifford E. Lee (1971 to 1981) and Floyd S. Chalmers awards (1973-) for play writing. A third wave of dramatists has already put its stamp on the 1980s: Anne Chislett, James DeFelice, Warren Graves, Paul Gross, Lawrence Jeffery, Rick Shiomi, Sherman Snukal, Allan Stratton, Judith Thompson and Charles Tidler. In 1982 Manitoba Theatre Centre and the Canada Council proudly celebrated their 25th anniversaries. That year the council helped fund 184 professional theatre companies in Canada. To this number should be added another 30 to 50 independent organizations. From its minimal postwar beginnings, and conveniently framed between the Massey Commission and the Applebaum-Hébert Report, Canada's professional theatre has been transformed within a generation. *See also* THEATRE, FRENCH-LANGUAGE; RADIO DRAMA; TELEVISION DRAMA; DRAMA IN ENGLISH; DRAMA IN FRENCH.

DAVID GARDNER

Reading: J. Ball and R. Plant, comps, *A Bibliography of Canadian Theatre History 1583-1975* (1976; *Supplement*, 1979); L.W. Conolly, ed, *Theatrical Touring and Founding in North America* (1982); M. Edwards, *A Stage in Our Past: English-Language Theatre in Eastern Canada from the 1790s to 1914* (1968); C. Evans, *Frontier Theatre* (1983); F. Graham, *Histrionic Montreal* (1902); B. Lee, *Love and Whisky: The Story of the Dominion Drama Festival* (1973); H. McCallum, comp, *Research Collections in Canadian Libraries: Theatre Resources* (1973); J. Orrell, *Fallen Empires: The Lost Theatres of Edmonton* (1981); T. Ryan, *Stage Left: Canadian Theatre in the Thirties* (1981); M.E. Smith, *Too Soon the Curtain Fell: A History of Theatre in Saint John 1789-1900* (1981); A. Wagner, ed, *Canada's Lost Plays*, 4 vols (1978) and *The Brock Bibliography of Published Canadian Plays in English* (1980).

Theatre, French-Language Only 3 dramatic texts composed in Canada during the French regime survive, all belonging to a genre called *réceptions*, written and performed in celebration of the visit or return of an important religious or civil dignitary: Marc LESCARBOT's *Le Théâtre de Neptune*, enacted at Port-Royal in 1606; the anonymous *Réception de monseigneur le vicomte d'Argenson* (1658); and the untitled work composed by the Jesuit Pierre de La Chasse and performed by female students in 1727 for Bishop Saint-Vallier of Québec. Despite its tiny, scattered population, NEW FRANCE seems to have known periods of regular theatrical activity, particularly during the middle years of the 17th century. Most plays were imported, however, for demography and the increasingly overt opposition of the church, as crystallized in the famous *Affaire Tartuffe* 1693-94, militated against the development of a native tradition. It was only after the TREATY OF PARIS (1763), when printing presses were established and true urban communities began to form, that an indigenous theatre began to take root, a process that would take more than a century to mature.

Initially, there was a continuing reliance upon imported plays, especially those of Molière, but the beginnings of a true native dramaturgy were soon perceptible, particularly in newspapers and in institutions of secondary education. Theatre composed in French Canada before WWII was of 4 kinds: religious, pedagogic, political and "social," the latter being theatre intended for the entertainment, as opposed to the edification, instruction or politicization, of its audience. Religious/pedagogic theatre, predominant in New France, reappeared soon after 1763 and was cultivated in the expanding system of collèges classiques during the 19th century, exemplified by Antoine GÉRIN-LAJOIE's *Le Jeune Latour* (1844), Hospice-Anselme Verreau's *Stanislas de Kostka* (1855) and Jean-Baptiste Proulx's *Le Mal du jour de l'an ou scènes de la vie écolière* (1870). Inspired and often composed by clergy, drama of this kind could develop without economic stress or fear of church intervention. Political theatre is the most original genre to develop in French Canada. Dramatized dialogues in early newspapers in the 1760s soon evolved into full-length satirical plays directed against political opponents, eg, the 5 *Status Quo Comedies* published in 1834. Every major political confrontation during the remaining years elicited a fresh spate of playlets, the years 1848 to 1868 being particularly active. These political dramas ranged from the sober prose of the first 18th-century examples to rollicking song and verse, and from "paratheatre" (plays not intended for performance) to works enacted with considerable public success. Elzéar Labelle's delightful operetta *La Conversion d'un pêcheur de la Nouvelle-Ecosse*, a satire of both sides in the CONFEDERATION debate, was performed frequently in Montréal between 1868 and 1899. These plays are clear predecessors of the satirical revues (fleshed out with song and dance and stuffed with references to current events) that dominated Montréal repertory in the 1890s and continued well into the 20th century.

"Social" theatre, which elsewhere constituted the mainstream of theatrical activity, remained a backwater in Québec. French-born Joseph QUESNEL composed a successful operetta, *Colas et Colinette*, which was first performed in Montréal in 1790 and was revived occasionally thereafter, most recently in 1968. Pierre Petitclair was the first native-born author of this type of drama, for though his 1837 publication *Griphon, ou la vengeance d'un valet* was apparently never performed, 2 later plays were staged in Québec City with considerable success, *La Donation* in 1842 and *Une Partie de campagne* in 1856. Louis-Honoré FRÉCHETTE adapted *Félix Poutré* from the memoirs of a self-proclaimed Patriote hero. First performed in 1862, it became a great success, particularly with amateur groups; its strong nationalistic fervour emerged as the most salient characteristic of Québec drama for the rest of the century. A good selection of such plays is included in Etienne F. Duval's *Anthologie thématique du théâtre québécois au XIXe siècle* (1978).

By the middle of the 19th century, Montréal had become the dominant centre of theatrical and economic activity. It thus also became a regular stop for professional touring companies from the US, Britain and France. The years after 1880 in particular saw glittering tours of Parisian troupes, the most spectacular of them being those of Sarah Bernhardt. The style and repertory of touring French companies were soon emulated by local troupes and playwrights, evidenced in the theatre of Félix-Gabriel MARCHAND, Régis Roy and Fréchette. In the 1890s the first local, professional French-language companies were established, performing in professionally appointed theatres and, in conjunction with the many English-language troupes then active, creating what has been called the first Golden Age of theatre in Montréal, described by J.M. Larrue in his *Le Théâtre à Montréal à la fin du XIXe siècle* (1981).

Unfortunately, these foundations were laid at a precarious time for live theatre — just as its most serious competitor, cinema, began to make its appearance. After a decade of struggle, exacerbated by the economic effects of WWI, stage arts in Québec underwent a long period of decline, the clearest symptom of which is visible in repertory which dominated the 1920s and 1930s. Satirical revues, monologues and burlesque prevailed, interspersed with populist melodramas of little aesthetic quality, such as *Aurore l'enfant martyre* by L. Petitjean and H. Rollin, which would continue to attract huge audiences for 30 years. It was the advent of radio that led indirectly to a rekindled interest in theatre, for the new medium made it possible for authors and actors to ensure their immediate livelihood, allowing them to channel remaining energies back into the more precarious live stage (*see* RADIO DRAMA, FRENCH-LANGUAGE).

Although opposition by the Roman Catholic Church to the public performance of theatre had been one of the principal obstacles to its development in French Canada, it was generally the clergy who, by their encouragement of drama as a pedagogic tool, had also inculcated the knowledge and appreciation of dramatic forms which are prerequisite to the success of a public stage. The birth of contemporary drama in Québec can thus be traced in large part to the clergy, for it was the dedication of dynamic priests such as Émile LEGAULT, Georges-Henri d'Auteuil and Gustave LAMARCHE that helped rescue theatre from stagnation in the 1930s; the first 2 as catalysts and impresarios for student troupes in the colleges of Saint-Laurent and Sainte-Marie, and the third as author/director of some 50 religious and pedagogic plays that caught the attention of students and eventually of Québec's population at large, despite intense continuing competition from radio and cinema. Legault's contribution is more visible, because of his formation 1937-38 of a small company of dedicated amateurs, the Compagnons de Saint-Laurent, and his aim of restoring to drama its freshness and magic. He and his group set out to free the stage, to poetize, refine and Christianize it. In this he was directly influenced by attempts at revitalizing theatre then current in Europe, where he went to study 1938-39, and in particular by the work of Henri Ghéon and by the new theories of stagecraft espoused in France by Jacques Copeau and the famous "Cartel" which shared his aims. The most important role of Legault and d'Auteuil was that of inspiring and training the future leaders in the renewal of stage arts in French Canada, Jean GASCON, Jean-

Louis ROUX, Pierre Dagenais, Guy Hoffman and many others. Some went on to found their own professional companies such as Dagenais's l'Équipe (1943) and Roux and Gascon's THÉÂTRE DU NOUVEAU MONDE (1952). The TNM succeeded l'Équipe on the stage of le Gésu and set professional standards in acting and in stage, set and costume design for a generation, remaining the most stable theatrical company in Québec.

By the time they disbanded in 1952, the Compagnons had succeeded in forming a large, sensitive and demanding audience, capable of appreciating genuine professional skills and talent. In conjunction with the emergence of Montréal as a true metropolis and the burgeoning self-awareness of the province of Québec, this enthusiasm would lead to the vigorous theatrical activity which characterized the 1960s and 1970s. The influence of d'Auteuil and Legault had done much to elevate and modernize repertory, staging and interpretation, but had achieved little for native dramaturgy. Playwrights felt more secure writing for radio, and some of them, such as Robert Choquette, constructed highly successful careers writing mainly or exclusively for that medium. An important milestone in the evolution of contemporary theatre was the 1948 premiere of Gratien GÉLINAS's full-length play *Tit-Coq*, which was performed at least 200 times in Montréal alone over the next few years. Gélinas too had written for radio and was well known for his humorous monologues, collectively entitled *Fridolinades* from their fictive author, Fridolin. Gélinas would add 2 more plays to Canadian repertory, *Bousille et les justes* (1959) and *Hier, les enfants dansaient* (1966) — all 3 translated into English and frequently performed. *Tit-Coq*'s success was soon emulated by other Québec writers, just as television, a formidable competitor to live theatre, was inaugurated by Radio-Canada in 1952. Television's influence has been pervasive, and sometimes nefarious, but in enabling playwrights to earn a living writing through the performing arts, it encouraged Canada's first professional dramatists (*see also* TELEVISION DRAMA, FRENCH-LANGUAGE; TELEVISION PROGRAMMING).

The playwright most successful in adapting his craft to the new medium was Marcel DUBÉ, whose prolific career has spanned 25 years and produced more than 2 dozen plays, many of them now considered classics, such as *Zone* (1953), *Un Simple Soldat* (1958) and *Au Retour des oies blanches* (1966). It was partially to counterbalance television's perceived threat to live theatre that the first 2 public agencies financing cultural activity, the CANADA COUNCIL and Montréal's Regional Arts Council, were created in 1957, followed in 1961 by Québec's provincial Ministry of Cultural Affairs. Their conjoined influence has profoundly affected the development of dramatic arts, through their diverse strategies of subsidizing theatrical companies. While there has been an impressive increase in the number of companies, sometimes at the expense of quality, a theatre "establishment" has tended to receive most of the subsidies. This imbalance has encouraged a "counter establishment" that has proven exceptionally rich and productive.

By 1960 there were enough traditional playwrights of considerable merit (Eloi de Grammont, Yves THÉRIAULT, Paul Toupin, Pierre PERRAULT) to represent, along with Gélinas and Dubé, an establishment in dramaturgy as well, which in turn has fostered successive waves of "new" (antiestablishment) theatre. The first wave of *nouveau théâtre* had been prefigured in the works of Jacques FERRON (*Les Grands Soleils* 1958) and Jacques Languirand (*Les Insolites* 1956), the latter strongly influenced by European Theatre of the Absurd. By the mid-1960s, "new" theatre rapidly became identified with political commitment. Politics is the primary fo-

cus of works such as Claude Levac and Françoise Loranger's *Le Chemin du roy*, an incisive parody, in the guise of a hockey game between Québec and Ottawa, of the confrontation caused by France's President de Gaulle's eventful visit in centennial year. Robert Gurik's *Hamlet, prince du Québec* (1968) is a savage satire of the individuals and institutions embroiled in the ongoing federal-provincial struggle, while Loranger's *Medium saignant* (1970) is more intense but more local, focusing on the exacerbated problem of language rights in the embattled Montréal suburb of Saint-Léonard. The most blatantly political theatre has been written, or rather improvised, by Le Théâtre euh!, created in the heady atmosphere of Europe's "Student Spring" of 1968 and ending with the group's deliberate self-destruction 10 years later. Euh! was not only antiestablishment and antitheatre: it soon became deeply committed to populist causes and Marxist ideology, performing throughout the province and improvising its "nontexts," such as its version of Léandre Bergeron's *Histoire du Québec* (1972) and *A bas le plan Trudeau!* (1978).

For the general evolution of theatre in Québec in the 1960s, the most important event was the performance in 1968 of Michel TREMBLAY's *Les Belles-Soeurs*. Blending stark realism with an almost lyrical compassion, this play portrays the frustration of a whole generation of women in working-class Montréal. Here, for the first time, the diction and the unalloyed accent of popular Québecois speech are faithfully reproduced, the language itself becoming a symbol of the characters' frustrations and a powerful tool for the author's purposes. Tremblay's excursion into JOUAL, the language of the semiliterate working class, has been followed by many others, most notably Jean BARBEAU (*Ben-Ur, Manon Lastcall* and *Joualez-moi d'amour* 1970), Jean-Claude GERMAIN (*Diguidi, diguidi, ha! ha! ha!* 1969), Victor-Lévy BEAULIEU (*En attendant Trudot* 1974) and Michel Garneau (*La Chanson d'amour du cul* 1974). This linguistic democratization has not escaped strenuous protest from French Canada's intellectual and cultural elite, a protest sometimes evidenced in the decisions of municipal and provincial funding agencies not to allocate funds for such works (eg, for the performance of *Les Belles-Soeurs* in France).

Les Belles-Soeurs is important also for its innovations in structure and staging, its stylized chorus and chants, its imaginative use of spotlighted monologues, all within the classical unities of time, place and action. The play itself had first been read and approved in 1965 by an antiestablishment group, the Centre d'essai des jeunes auteurs dramatiques, created to fill the gap left by the discontinuation of the Dominion Drama Festival and followed a few years later by the more durable Assn Québecoise du jeune théâtre (AQJT), increasingly committed to experimentalism on stage. Best known in this area is Jean-Claude Germain, one of the founders in 1969 of Montréal's Théâtre du même nom (TMN), a mocking anagram of that most established of theatrical companies, the Théâtre du nouveau monde (TNM). The TMN has specialized in mordant social satire, such as *Un Pays dont la devise est je m'oublie* (1976), and its healthy iconoclasm has been much abetted by the Théâtre expérimental de Montréal and the Ligue nationale d'improvisation, founded in the mid-1970s. But perhaps the most influential of the experimentalist-collectivist troupes was Le Grand Cirque ordinaire (1969), whose early successes such as *T'es pas tannée, Jeanne d'Arc?* (1969) encouraged other such undertakings in Montréal (Théâtre de l'Eskable) and elsewhere (Le Théâtre Parminou in Victoriaville, Les Gens d'en bas in Rimouski).

These organizations have catalysed and channeled the most dynamic forces at work in Québec's theatre, from Tremblay's polished, masterful innovations (*A toi pour toujours, ta Marie-Lou* 1971; *Hosanna* 1973; *Sainte Carmen de la main* 1976) to the improvised "happenings" of experimental troupes, all those forces who reject identification with what they perceive as the "corporate" stage. In a natural, ironic progression, Tremblay soon became identified with the corporate "haves" as well, and therefore a target for the next wave of "have-nots." As these groups increased in number in the 1970s, the allocation of public subsidies became a more and more critical problem, exacerbated by the deteriorating economic conditions of the province and of the nation. By 1980 a clear demarcation had appeared between the 11 "established" companies (8 in Montréal, 2 in Québec, with one semiofficial touring company, the Théâtre populaire du Québec) and the 100 or so "new" amateur or experimental troupes, most of which operated in the Montréal area and many of which were condemned to a brief and difficult existence. By 1983 there were more theatrical troupes in Québec than in all other provinces combined. The heady years of the 1960s, when Québec's dramatists, directors and actors seemed to take the lead in expressing their society's cultural and political aspirations, have given way to sober reassessment and a certain retrenchment in the 1980s.

Since the Parti Québécois victory in 1976 there has also been considerable movement away from narrow propagandistic works, which sometimes did disservice to the stage, and towards a healthy preoccupation with broader issues. More distance has been particularly beneficial for comedy, as demonstrated in the later works of Tremblay (*L'Impromptu d'Outremont* 1980) and the brilliant collaborations of Louis Saia and Claude Meunier (*Broue* 1983). But it is the feminist awakening that has brought perhaps the most promising new direction for Québec's playwrights since the late 1970s, following the creation of women's troupes such as Montréal's Théâtre expérimental des femmes. A few of their early productions appear to have been too narrowly committed to endure, but feminist concerns have been strikingly portrayed by Jovette Marchessault (*Le Saga des poules mouillées* 1981), Marie Laberge (*C'était avant la guerre à l'Anse à Gilles* 1981), Louisette Dussault (*Moman* 1981), and especially by Denise Boucher, the performance of whose *Les Fées ont soif* in the spring of 1978 led to the play's temporary censorship and to a resonant legal battle that was decided by the Supreme Court only in 1980.

In the course of 2 generations, theatre has progressed from being the "weak sister" among the arts to its current status as an inseparable part of the rich fabric of French Canadian culture. Not surprisingly, in the past decade the stage arts have attracted more, and generally more competent, attention from critics and historians than in their entire previous history.

The Maritimes After the performance of Lescarbot's *Théâtre de Neptune* in 1606, some 260 years passed before dramatic activity in French returned to ACADIA. Soon after the foundation in 1864 of the Collège St-Joseph in Memramcook, NB, a literary and dramatic society was established and theatre became a regular occurrence. From their foundation in the 1890s, the Collège Ste-Anne in NS and the Collège du Sacré-Coeur in NB also introduced plays performed by students as a central part of the academic year's activities. Choice of plays ranged from "expurgated" classics to plays written by clerics in France for college theatre, but there are references as well to works written specifically for these occasions by members of the faculty.

First of these to survive is the verse drama *Subercase*, by French-born Father Alexandre Braud, performed at Ste-Anne in 1902. Acadian patriotism and loyalty to French origins are the inspiration of this play (Daniel d'Auger de Subercase was the last French governor of Acadia), as they

were to be for Father Jean-Baptiste Jégo, also a native of Brittany and an instructor at Ste-Anne. Jégo's *Le Drame du peuple acadien* was performed at the college with great success in 1930, awarded a prize by the Académie Française and published in Paris (1932). Less didactic but equally patriotic were the works of another priest, James Branch, the first native Acadian dramatist whose works have survived. His 3 best-known plays were written and performed before his ordination, while he was still a student at Bathurst's Collège du Sacré-Coeur: *L'Emigrant acadien* (1929), *Jusqu'à la mort! . . . pour nos écoles* (1929) and *Vivent nos écoles catholiques! ou la Résistance de Caraquet* (1932). All 3 are intensely nationalistic, with a degree of political commitment rare in his time.

Theatre continued to thrive in Acadian colleges throughout the 1940s and 1950s, frequently enriched by touring companies from Québec. In the 1950s, formal courses in drama were instituted, and Acadian troupes began to compete regularly in the Dominion Drama Festival. But the further development of native dramaturgy had to await Antonine MAILLET, the region's outstanding writer in French, whose first play, *Entr'acte* (unpublished), was performed in 1957. With the founding in 1963 of U de Moncton, amalgamating NB's francophone colleges, a second Acadian Renaissance began, its dynamism reflected in poetry, fiction, history and theatre. Its highwater mark was probably Maillet's *La Sagouine* (1971), a dramatic monologue by an illiterate but philosophic Acadian charwoman, first written for a Moncton radio station, performed with great success in Montréal, and highly popular with television viewers across Canada in its French and English versions. Maillet has added half a dozen other plays, notably *Evangéline deusse* (1975), in which an 80-year-old Acadian exile in Montréal expresses eloquently the sorrows and aspirations of her nation. The preoccupation with past sorrows and their distillation into present struggles is the central theme of Maillet's theatre, as it has become for Laval Goupil, the only other Acadian playwright to have attracted attention outside the Maritimes. His *Tête d'eau* (1974) was followed by the more committed *Le Djibou* (1975), dealing with regional concerns. Huguette Légaré (*Les Criquets sous la neige* 1974) and Germaine Comeau (*Les Pêcheurs déportés* 1974) continue this preoccupation, the latter work depicting the forced emigration, for economic reasons, of so many contemporary young Acadians.

Ontario Ottawa-Hull was the birthplace of French-language theatre in Ontario, whose genesis has been well documented by Edgar Boutet in his *85 Ans de théâtre à Hull* (1969). The first theatre was constructed under the auspices of the Oblate order in 1884, and theatrical activity has continued with little interruption. Encouraged by the clergy and by U of Ottawa, amateur activity has been constant, its repertory generally modelled on that of Québec, with little attempt at creating any regional tradition of composition. Dedicated directors and managers of local troupes (Wilfrid Sanche, Léonard Beaulne, Ernest Saint-Jean, René Provost) assured the survival of a theatrical tradition through the worst years of the 1920s and 1930s until, with the foundation of Provost's School of Dramatic Arts in Hull in 1945, a nucleus was provided for rekindled interest in the stage. The organization, by Guy Beaulne, of the Assn canadienne du théâtre d'amateurs in 1958 was significant for regional French-language troupes across the country, and the opening in 1969 of the NATIONAL ARTS CENTRE in Ottawa has provided a stable centrepiece as well as glittering inspiration for local theatrical activity.

But if the National Capital Region has long been the principal focus of Franco-Ontarian theatre, it has not been the only one: there were (in

1980) some 25 French-language troupes active in the province, including the Troupe oxygène in Cornwall, Pourquoi pas? in Rockland, Les Franco-Fous in Sudbury, and the Théâtre du p'tit bonheur in Toronto. This strong and relatively long tradition of theatrical performance has not, however, been accompanied by a tradition of dramatic composition. The 1960s saw the publication of Jacqueline Martin's *Trois Pièces en un acte* (1966), but it is only in the next decade that sustained writing is observed: Claude Belcourt's *Les Communords* (1974); the collective text *La Parole et la loi* by Vanier's troupe, La Corvée, performed several times with great success before its publication in 1980; and in particular the collected plays of Ontario's most significant French-language dramatist to date, André Paiment (1978). Paiment's theatre, like that of the others mentioned, focuses heavily on the explication and defence of Franco-Ontarian causes. *La Vie et les temps de Médéric Boileau*, written in 1974, explores the harsh life of forest workers with great sensitivity, but his best-known work, first performed in 1975, is *Lavalléville*, a description of violence and greed in a small, fictional Ontario village governed by a dictatorial family.

Manitoba Unlike French-language theatre elsewhere outside Québec, Manitoba theatre has had a detailed, scholarly monograph devoted to it, Annette St-Pierre's *Le Rideau se lève au Manitoba* (1980). The history of stage arts began in the 1870s, again under the auspices and supervision of the teaching clergy, in this case the Grey Nuns in their boarding school at Saint-Boniface. Many of the plays performed in educational institutions were written by members of the local clergy, in particular by Sister Malvina Collette, one of whose plays, *Un Souvenir de la patrie*, performed in 1870, has been published in *Chapeau bas: Réminiscences de la vie théâtrale et musicale du Manitoba français* (1980), edited by the Société historique de St-Boniface. As the population grew and the school system with it, amateur theatre became a central part of local cultural activity. When, after 1885, the Jesuits were entrusted with the Collège de St-Boniface, their predilection for college theatre came to the fore, with well-advertised programs that attracted spectators from all the little settlements along the Red R. The formation of amateur theatrical societies independent of schools was the next step, as enthusiastic local troupes sprang up in nearly every settlement during the Golden Age, 1914 to 1939. There were parish groups, organizations based on national origin (le Club belge, les Dames auxiliaires des vétérans français, Les Canadiens de naissance), troupes founded by religious societies (les Enfants de Marie, la Ligue des institutrices catholiques de l'ouest) and politico-social groups (le Cercle ouvrier, les Amis de Riel, l'Union nationale métisse). But perhaps the most significant, certainly the most enduring, was the Cercle Molière, founded in 1925 and still vigorous 60 years later. Under the leadership of André Castelein de la Lande, Arthur and Pauline Boutal and their talented successors, this organization has attracted to it virtually all those interested in the performing arts in Manitoba. Despite its title, its repertory has covered everything from the French classics to light, modern theatre from Paris and Montréal.

An impressive number of plays has been composed in Manitoba as well, although relatively few have as yet been published. Auguste-Henri de Trémaudan, a Québécois by birth, but educated in France, was the author of 5 published plays, such as the melodrama *De fil en aiguille* (1925) and the historical drama *Quand même* (1928) which played with considerable local success. André Castelein de la Lande, a Belgian immigrant, composed some 50 popular plays, 4 of them published in Montréal, nearly all dealing with general, noncontroversial topics. Roger Auger, a native Franco-Manitoban, is the author of *Les Eléphants de tante Louise* (1972) and *Je m'en vais à Régina* (1976), portraying the problems encountered by a family of Francophones. *Les Manigances d'une bru* (1980) by Roger Legal and Paul Ruest deals with this theme also, whereas Rosemarie Bissonnette's *La Bagarre* (1977) portrays Manitoba's painful history for those of French origin. Other works by provincial playwrights have been performed, sometimes with great success, such as Claude Dorge's *Le Roitelet,* concerning the execution of Louis Riel, performed by the Cercle Molière in 1976. Theatre is the most visible and most vigorous of Manitoba's cultural manifestations in French. *See also* DRAMA IN FRENCH.

LEONARD E. DOUCETTE

Reading: Archives des lettres canadiennes, vol 5: *Le Théâtre canadien-français* (1976); E. Boutet, *85 Ans de théâtre à Hull* (1969); B. Burger, *L'Activité théâtrale au Québec, 1765-1825* (1974); *Dictionnaire des oeuvres littéraires du Québec* (1978-); Leonard E. Doucette, *Theatre in French Canada 1606-1867* (1984); P. Gobin, *Le Fou et ses doubles* (1978); J.C. Godin and L. Mailhot, *Théâtre québecois,* 2 vols (1970, 1980); A. Gruslin, *Le Théâtre et l'état au Québec* (1981); J. Laflamme and R. Tourangeau, *L'Église et le théâtre au Québec* (1979); E.G. Rinfret, *Théâtre canadien d'expression française,* 4 vols (1975-78); A. Saint-Pierre, *Le Rideau se lève au Manitoba* (1980).

Theatre, Multicultural, may be defined in Canada as mainly European-style theatre by groups other than that of English or French origin. Performance may be in either official language or in the native tongue of the particular ethnic group. Although examples of multicultural theatre can be found in the 19th century, it was not until the years following WWII that ethnic theatre was firmly established. Two major factors contributed to this growth: the concentration in a single area of a minority group large enough to support theatre; and the arrival of a substantial number of immigrants who had been artists in their own countries but could not practise professionally on English stages because of language difficulties. At the same time, children of immigrants, who were well educated and more financially secure than their parents, sought creative outlets to preserve their culture.

Many of the ethnic theatre companies formed in the 1950s are still thriving today. Toronto's Hungarian Art Theatre, whose dynamic founder, Sandor Kertész, emigrated in 1957 after 30 years of acting and directing in Budapest theatre companies, produces impressive large-scale musicals as well as comedies and dramas. The Ukrainian Dramatic Ensemble, the New Czech Theatre and the Estonian National Theatre, all of Toronto, have earned faithful audiences for their consistently high-calibre work. Though Yiddish theatre was performed frequently in Toronto in the late 1920s and early 1930s with guest artists from the US, later efforts to produce Yiddish theatre regularly were unsuccessful. The Yiddish Drama Group of the Saidye Bronfman Centre in Montréal is the exception. Founded in 1956 by Dora Wasserman, a graduate of the famed Moscow Yiddish Art Theatre, the company performs many plays from the classic Yiddish repertoire as well as original musicals and dramas. The Leah Posluns Theatre, a branch of the Jewish Community Centre of Toronto, and its resident company, Art Theatre Production Co, produces in English 5 plays each season which reflect a Jewish conciousness. The company has featured Canadian premieres of leading writers including Henry Denker, Isaac Bashevis Singer and William Gibson.

Although most ethnic or multicultural theatre remains amateur in status, many of the companies have subscription series, go on tour, and represent their regions in national and international festivals. The Winnipeg Mennonite Theatre is known for its outstanding opera productions in German; and Ukrainian theatre is well represented in the West with 3 notable

groups: Edmonton's Story Théatre for children, which performs throughout the school system with adaptations of Ukrainian legends; the Ukrainian Children's Theatre in Winnipeg; and the spectacular Ukrainian Shumka Dancers, a 25-year-old amateur troupe that has performed for heads of state and at professional theatres across the country. The Spanish Language Theatre, based at U of Calgary, fills an educational void for the community at large in depicting the life and people of Spain and Latin America, and the Alianza Cultural Hispano-Canadiense of U of T represents the cultural interests of the entire Spanish-speaking community, offering concerts, folk dancing, art shows and live theatre productions in Spanish. Calgary's Shamrock Players began as a reading group of theatre people of Irish-Scottish ancestry to preserve the Gaelic heritage. The Irish Newfoundland Society in St John's mounts an annual Irish play to promote an appreciation of the Irish cultural heritage. Montréal's Black Theatre Workshop began in 1965 as the Trinidad and Tobago Assn Drama Committee with play and poetry readings, workshops, and eventually original productions such as Lorris Elliott's *How Now Black Man.* When the workshop incorporated in 1972 it drew upon all the black communities in Montréal. The now professional company presents 3 plays a year, including contemporary works and new Canadian plays, all of which retain elements of the black community's root culture. In Toronto the professional Black Theatre Canada is dedicated to representing black people's contribution to the country's cultural development; besides its playbill of new and established productions, the company also performs in schools, gives workshops and holds conferences. La Compagnie dei Giovani of Toronto performs everything from classical to contemporary Italian plays and translates Canadian plays into Italian.

While the majority of multicultural theatre companies in the country perform Western-style drama, the Chinese United Dramatic Society of Toronto has been performing Cantonese opera in the city since 1933. The elaborate productions which are presented twice yearly feature lavish costumes designed and made in Hong Kong and professional actors brought in from the US and Hong Kong to augment the mainly amateur but highly skilled cast. The society's 800 members and the Chinese community support the Cantonese operas, many of which are over 1000 years old. Other Chinese opera societies exist in Toronto, Montréal and Vancouver.

Native theatre, historically ceremonial dance and ritual, has undergone some dramatic changes over the last decade as native Indian groups have begun to write and perform Western-style drama. In the past, productions such as George RYGA's *The Ecstasy of Rita Joe* and Michael Cook's *On the Rim of the Curve* used native themes and performers. However, Winnipeg's Manitou Theatre, Vancouver's Tillicum Theatre and the 1977 production of George Kenney's *October Stranger* by the Assn for Native Development in the Performing and Visual Arts have introduced native playwrights as well. ANDPVA has been instrumental in promoting training in the performing arts. In 1974 it founded a native theatre school, now situated in Owen Sound, Ont, where young people are given intensive training by professional teachers. ANDPVA's founder, James Buller, also helped to initiate the first annual Indigenous Theatre Celebration, held in Toronto in 1980, which brought together artists from all over the world demonstrating native people's non-European concept of theatre. Other native Canadian theatre groups of note are KSAN in BC, which presents colourful ritual potlatches; Northern Delight from Sioux Lookout; Native

Theatre Productions from Winnipeg; Heyoka (formerly Rama Reserve Theatre Group) in Orillia, Ont; and the annual Six Nations Pageant held on the Six Nations Reserve in Brantford, Ont. In Toronto the newly formed Native Earth is a professional touring company which travels to native communities and combines traditional and contemporary performance techniques through collective creations.

The rapidly growing multicultural theatre movement in the 1970s, enhanced by the multiculturalism policy of the federal government, prompted the formation of the National Multicultural Theatre Assn (NMTA) in 1975, to foster a better understanding and a mutual appreciation of the multitude of cultures that form Canada's diverse lingual and racial theatrical mosaic. The NMTA serves as a liaison between the provincial associations and stages the National Multicultural Theatre Festival, which is held each year in a different province and city. Total membership in the NMTA approximates 350 theatre groups, of which only half perform exclusively in minority languages. In 1979 the NMTA was appointed by the International Amateur Theatre Assn as the national centre for Canada's community theatres. JENIVA BERGER

Reading: M. Kovacs, ed, *Ethnic Canadians Culture and Education* (1978); S.A. Reddoch, *Our Cultural Heritage* (1979); K. Sandor, *Curtain at Eight* (1981).

Theatre Ballet of Canada is a small chamber troupe based in Ottawa. Much of its repertoire consists of works by artistic director Lawrence Gradus, who favours a neoclassical style of choreography. The company was established in 1980 from 2 separate companies, Ballet Ys (Toronto) and Entre-Six Dance Company (Montréal), which had been founded by Gradus and Jacqueline Lemieux in 1974. Both companies faced a variety of financial and administrative problems, and an amalgamation was arranged. The new company made its debut at the National Arts Centre in Feb 1981, and has since toured Canada and abroad. MICHAEL CRABB

Théâtre du nouveau monde (TNM), was founded by Georges GROULX, Jean GASCON, Jean-Louis ROUX and Guy Hoffmann in 1951 as a repertory theatre with emphasis on Molière. A period of experimentation (1956-66) with eclectic programming proved to be a difficult time for the theatre: artistic director Roux left in 1963 and Gascon in 1966. After Roux returned in 1966, the TNM became a theatre for the Québec public. In the 1972-73 season the TNM was established in the former home of the COMÉDIE-CANADIENNE. Under the current direction of Olivier Reichenbach, the TNM is a successful "establishment theatre" with a repertory drawn from popular international and Québec playwrights. MARILYN BASZCZYNSKI

Reading: *Les Vingt-cinq ans du TNM* (1976).

Théâtre du rideau vert, founded in 1949 by Yvette Brind'Amour (still artistic director in 1984) at the Théâtre des compagnons, ceased activity shortly thereafter and resumed in the 1955-56 season. The Rideau vert preferred "boulevard" theatre and light comedies, its repertory was popular Parisian classics as well as modern authors such as Lorca, Sartre, Montherlant and Bernanos. In the mid-1960s an effort was made to create and present Québecois theatre, including Michel Tremblay's *Les Belles Soeurs* and Antonine Maillet's *La Sagouine.* Between 1968 and 1979 André Cailloux ran a successful program for young children. Since 1968 the Rideau vert has been housed in the Stella in Montréal, and presents a repertory of classic and modern authors (Shakespeare, Molière, Ibsen, Giraudoux), some boulevard theatre (Feydeau, Labiche) and Québecois works (Françoise LORANGER, Antonine MAILLET, Marcel DUBÉ and Michel TREMBLAY).

MARILYN BASZCZYNSKI

Theatre Education All theatre activity connected with schools and teaching could be termed educational theatre; however, the accepted designation is confined to universities and private theatre schools. Theatre education has expanded rapidly since WWII. Statistics in the Black Report on Theatre Training in Canada (1977) suggest that educational theatre in colleges and universities is now the largest single theatre enterprise in Canada. This does not take into account the immense growth recorded in secondary-school and recreational theatre.

In Québec, a 1694 ban of the proposed production of Molière's *Tartuffe* loosed a deluge of church disapproval, and French-speaking theatre languished for almost 150 years (*see* THEATRE). However, the Jesuit practice of presenting intramural productions of the classics and morality plays in their colleges continued into the 20th century. Formal training in theatre arts in Québec began only in the 1950s, and people wishing to work in theatre before that time took courses at the Lasalle Conservatory (1907-) or from private teachers, joined existing theatre companies, or studied in France. The dynamic priest, Father Émile LEGAULT, who founded the influential Compagnons de Saint-Laurent in 1937, added a short-lived theatre school of good reputation 10 years later.

The THÉÂTRE DU NOUVEAU MONDE opened an acting school in 1951, and in 1954 the Conservatoire d'art dramatique was established in Montréal, followed by a sister conservatory in Québec City in 1958. The National Theatre School of Montréal was founded in 1960 on the artistic principles of adviser Michel Saint-Denis. Still regarded as a major acting and design school, it offered separate training in French and English. By the end of the 1960s 2 schools at the CEGEPs of Ste-Thérèse and St-Hyacinthe were offering training to actors, technicians and designers. In the 1970s the French-speaking universities began drama divisions, most notably Ottawa, UQAM and Sherbrooke.

In the 19th century, universities in English Canada included almost no formal theatre courses. Students wishing to enter the minuscule professional theatre learned their art as apprentices in the existing professional or semi-professional companies. Their training was often supplemented by tutoring in private academies, almost all of which were short-lived. The birth of a vital Canadian professional theatre in the second half of the 20th century was greatly aided by the amateur theatre (educational and community) that preceded it (*see* LITTLE THEATRE MOVEMENT). Actors, directors and designers had their training in amateur productions.

Until the early 1960s there was no thorough training in the theatre arts at the college level. Most universities followed the English tradition of offering credit courses in dramatic literature and criticism, while regarding practical work as an extracurricular activity best left to student drama societies, departments of extension, and intercollegiate festivals. There were early signs of campus drama activity. The University Dramatic Club of Montréal, using mainly McGill personnel and alumni, staged Shaw's *Arms and the Man* for the first Earl Grey Musical and Dramatic Competition (Ottawa, 1907). During the winter of 1914-15 the dept of extension at U of Alberta distributed plays and dispensed production advice to Alberta communities. The UBC Players Club (1915-58) was the first all-student drama society. Hart House, at U of T, was established in 1919 with a mandate to encourage and develop amateur drama activities on the campus. Within a decade almost all universities had a student drama society. By 1930 McGill's dept of English was presenting plays for children. In central and eastern Canada it was often the English department that

first offered academic respectability to courses in drama. However, it was not until 1941 that a few theatre courses were tentatively offered by the McGill department. In 1957 Canada's most successful college musical, *My Fur Lady*, was presented by McGill students.

Growth was much faster in the western universities. Following the American pattern of offering degree programs that included some practical courses, U of Saskatchewan founded Canada's first dept of drama in 1945, offering a BA in drama. U of Alberta followed with a drama division in 1947. The BANFF CENTRE SCHOOL OF FINE ARTS began as the Banff School of Theatre Arts in 1933, and has since offered a wide spectrum of practical courses. The U of Alberta was the first to offer professional training programs: the BFA in acting and in design (1966), and the MFA in design and in directing (1968). In 1966 the Graduate Centre for the Study of Drama was founded at U of T, offering the first PhD in drama.

The Black Report notes only 2 private schools having minimum requirements for acting training; the National Theatre School of Montréal and the VANCOUVER PLAYHOUSE Acting School (1975-). While several regional professional theatres, such as Edmonton's CITADEL THEATRE and the MANITOBA THEATRE CENTRE, have teaching programs, the majority cater to hobbyists. The STRATFORD FESTIVAL's long awaited and often promised academy of classical acting has yet to materialize.

By the 1980s Canadian-trained drama faculty fill six-tenths of the university and college teaching positions compared to one-tenth in the 1960s. Graduates of university drama training programs are found in all professional theatre companies, and many others make their mark in London and New York.

Campus drama organizations have traditionally offered opportunities to the beginning playwright when none were available from the profession. Campus support for young playwrights began with the Hart House production of Merrill DENISON's first play, *Brothers in Arms* (1919). The Banff School began instruction in playwriting in 1935. Gwendolyn Pharis RINGWOOD was a student in the first classes and is the program's most famous graduate. UBC's dept of English and the Alberta and Saskatchewan drama departments now have strongly supported playwriting programs.

In 1955 there were 8 full-time instructors teaching in fledgling drama programs at 4 universities. In 1977, 22 institutions offered professional or preprofessional training, and another 15 offered programs with some form of drama specialization. In 1984 more than 300 faculty, 50 programs and over 10 000 enrolments make up the educational theatre establishment in Canada. GORDON PEACOCK

Reading: E. Crampton, comp, *Drama Canada: Trends in Drama in Education during the Past 25 Years* (1972); *Directory of Canadian Theatre Schools* (1982); *Report of the Committee of Inquiry into Theatre Training in Canada* (Black Report) (1977).

Theatre for Young Audiences is a 20th-century phenomenon, invented in Russia shortly before the revolution by actress Natalia Sats. In 1953 Joy Coghill and Myra Benson founded Holiday Theatre, making Vancouver the first Canadian city to enjoy specialized theatre for children. Other early companies were Theatre Hour in Toronto and Jeunes Comédiens in Montréal. Repertoire performed by these pioneer troupes was dominated initially by influences from the US, England and France. Holiday Theatre produced many American adaptations of fairy tales, and Theatre Hour and Jeunes Comédiens chose English and French theatre classics for their high-school audiences. As they matured, these companies commissioned Canadian works.

Three companies formed in the 1960s eventually encouraged local writers, but began with foreign fare. Nouvelle Compagnie théâtrale (Montréal) began performing classics for adolescents in 1964 and after 1968 added recent Québec plays and winners of an annual playwriting contest. In the late 1960s Regina's GLOBE THEATRE toured Saskatchewan schools with plays of British playwright Brian Way. His technique of participation — asking audiences to advance the plot and help the hero by contributing noises, ideas and imaginary objects — became popular and influential throughout Canada. In the 1970s the Globe hired Rex Deverell, Canada's first playwright-in-residence assigned to write children's plays. Young People's Theatre in Toronto has an eclectic approach to repertoire, but always includes some new Canadian works. In 1977 it became the first Canadian company to have its own building devoted exclusively to entertainment for young audiences. Alberta Theatre Projects, established in 1972 "to bring history to life" for schoolchildren, also brought its audience to a special theatre, the historic Canmore Opera House in Calgary's Heritage Park. Despite an excellent record of success with adventurous scripts, the company has shifted its energies and priorities to its adult season.

In the 1970s Simon and Pierre, Talonbooks and the Playwrights Co-op (later Playwrights Canada) began to publish plays for young people. In the decade 1971-81 the number of groups producing theatre for young audiences increased from 19 to 70, and included Mermaid Theatre in Nova Scotia; Theatre New Brunswick's Young Co; Theatre Five, Carousel Players, Hexagone and l'Hexagone, and The Great Canadian Theatre Co in Ontario; Théâtre des pissenlits, Marmaille, Théâtre soleil, Cannerie, Bebelle, Théâtre de carton, Théâtre de l'oeil, Grosse Valise, Théâtre des confettis, Amis de chiffon, and Youtheatre in Québec; Manitoba Theatre Workshop; Citadel-on-Wheels and Theatre Calgary's Stage-Coach Players in Alberta; and Green Thumb, Axis Mime, Carousel Theatre and Kaleidoscope in BC. Since 1978 an International Festival of Children's Theatre has played each spring in Vancouver, Edmonton, Calgary, Toronto and Montréal.

Most companies consider school tours a vital part of their mandate and bring live theatre to a cross-section of young Canadians. The economy of means imposed by touring sometimes leads to ingenious solutions to problems of small casts, 45-minute plays, and rudimentary technical resources. Long runs in original plays encourage neophyte actors to develop skills in creating and then sustaining characterizations for dozens, sometimes hundreds, of repeat performances. Close connections with schools also present problems: educational content is implied, if not dictated; budgets often strike first at live theatre; artists feel isolated and miss media and peer feedback; and touring one-act plays for months of one-day stands is gruelling and exhausting.

Innovative influences sometimes enter the mainstream of Canadian drama through work developed for children. Because many young professionals find their first work in theatre for the young, they often bring fresh thinking to old problems. In particular, collaboration between playwrights, directors and designers produces striking and memorable effects. Improvisation, mime, mask work, collective creation and puppetry enrich our theatrical vocabulary and expand the boundaries of style. James REANEY, poet, playwright and teacher, has often conducted workshops with children to allow their energy, grace and open attitude toward myth and metaphor to contribute to his plays. Other authors and companies have followed his example and, in this way, contemporary concerns have taken their place beside archetypes, history and legend in the repertoire. Distinctive Canadian styles of writing and production have developed and there has been an increase in support for live performances that speak directly to the dreams of Canada's young people in compelling theatrical forms.   JOYCE DOOLITTLE

Theatre Royal When in the early 1800s Montréal failed to attract talented artists for lack of a decent hall, John MOLSON transformed the Belmont Hall into the 1500-seat Theatre Royal. The 71-member company opened in 1825 and presented a varied but repetitive repertory of Shakespeare, and comedies and farces by Knowles, Cowley and Sheridan. Until 1840 the theatrical seasons were irregular, and during the winter the playhouse was often used for concerts and sometimes circuses. The theatre contributed greatly to the cultural development of the city: it attracted touring British and American celebrities (Edmund Kean, John Reeve and Charles Dickens) and many amateur groups, including the Garrison Amateurs. Under the mismanagement of Frederick Brown, the company went bankrupt in 1844, and the playhouse was sold and demolished to make way for the Bonsecours Market.   MARILYN BASZCZYNSKI

Thelon River, 904 km long, issues from Lynx Lk, E of Great Slave Lk, NWT. It has a DRAINAGE BASIN of 142 000 km² — third among rivers flowing into Hudson Bay — and a mean discharge of 804 m³/s. It flows N and then E across the Barren Lands through Beverly, ABERDEEN, Schultz and Baker lakes and empties into CHESTERFIELD INLET, on Hudson Bay. Its main tributaries are the DUBAWNT R, flowing N from DUBAWNT LK, and the KAZAN R, draining numerous lakes to the SW. The area was once the haunt of the CARIBOU INUIT, until the herds were depleted. J.W. and J.B. TYRRELL examined the river in 1893-94. The Thelon Game Sanctuary (38 850 km²) was established in 1927 to protect the endangered MUSKOX.   JAMES MARSH

Theosophy, philosophical system based on a belief in a universal, eternal principle fundamental to all life. The mystical overtones of its proposition of the fundamental identity of all "Souls with the Universal Soul" are similar to the doctrines of Buddhism and Hinduism. The Theosophical Society was founded in New York in 1875 by Helena Petrova Blavatsky and others, "to form the nucleus of a universal brotherhood of humanity, without distinction of race, creed, sex, caste or colour." The society has also sought to encourage study of comparative religion, philosophy and science.

The first Canadian branch of the society was formed in Toronto in 1891 by Algernon Blackwood, Dr Emily STOWE, Dr Augusta STOWE-GULLEN and newspaper editor Albert Smythe (father of Conn SMYTHE, who was also a lifelong member). In 1919, an autonomous Canadian section, The Theosophical Society in Canada, was formed. Albert Smythe was its head and first editor of its journal, *The Canadian Theosophist,* which has published continuously ever since. The society was closely associated with the GROUP OF SEVEN, notably Lawren HARRIS. Among other prominent members were critic William Arthur DEACON and Roy Mitchell, first director of Hart House Theatre.

Related organizations in Canada include the Canadian Federation of the Theosophical Society, La Société theosophique du Québec and the United Lodge of Theosophists. Active lodges are in Montréal, Toronto, Hamilton, Edmonton, Calgary, Vancouver and Victoria.

Thériault, Gérard-Charles-Édouard, military officer (b at Gaspé, Qué 5 June 1932). The son of an RCMP officer who left the force to begin a small aviation company, Thériault as a youth wished to fly, and, after earning an economics degree at Sir George Williams U [Concordia], he joined the RCAF in 1951. He was a squadron

commander by 1966 and moved to the Collège militaire royal, St-Jean, Qué, as vice-commandant 1967-70 and commandant 1970-71. He was commander of 1 Canadian Air Group in Germany 1973-75, and he was promoted deputy chief of defence staff in 1978, vice chief in 1980, and chief in 1983 — the third airman and third Francophone to hold the top job in the Canadian Forces. Thériault was inevitably more the military manager and immediately emphasized the smooth operation of headquarters. Indeed, he made it clear that Canada's defence depended on the maintenance of international stability, a political not military problem.   NORMAN HILLMER

Thériault, Yves, writer (b at Québec C 28 Nov 1915; d 20 Oct 1983). The originality, diversity and importance of his work make Thériault one of Québec's most popular writers, both in Canada and abroad. Son of a carpenter, he tried various occupations before earning his living from writing. The 1944 publication of his first book, *Contes pour un homme seul,* attracted great public attention, but it was his novel *Agaguk,* published in 1958 and translated into more than 10 languages, which made him famous. He wrote in many different genres for many different audiences. The expression of insistent sexuality, of an often savage and unconquerable nature, of characters seeking the absolute, torn between their desire for power and their need for tenderness, and the effectiveness of his writing style, which alternates between the oral and the written, testify to the evocative power of his imaginary universe.   MAURICE EMOND

Thetford-Mines, Qué, the largest asbestos production centre in the Western world. The streets of the town are built between the mines and the asbestos tailings (*photo by John deVisser*).

Thetford-Mines, Qué, City, pop 19 965 (1981c), inc 1892, is located on the Rivière Bécancour in the Appalachians, 107 km S of Québec City. It was named in 1905 after the town of Thetford in Norfolk, Eng. In 1876 Joseph Fecteau scraped some fibres from a greenish rock with his fingernail; without realizing it, he discovered ASBESTOS. The first mining rights were bought in 1877, and in 1879 the arrival of the railway made it possible to transport the mineral in larger quantities and more quickly to LÉVIS, Qué. The town grew rapidly as the mines attracted people from other areas. Today, both underground and open-face mines are in operation, and the streets of the town are built between the mines and the asbestos tailings. Called the "Asbestos Capital" and the "City of White Gold," it is the largest production centre for this fibre in the Western world. The town has also developed

other sectors such as trailer, snowmobile and mining-equipment factories. It has a famous mineralogy and mining museum.
                    JEAN-MARIE DUBOIS AND PIERRE MAILHOT

Third Option, a 1972 pronouncement by Mitchell SHARP, secretary of state for external affairs, calling for a lessening of US economic and cultural influence on Canada. Sharp's paper, "Canada-U.S. Relations: Options for the Future" (*International Perspectives,* 1972), was the final and most important part of a detailed review of Canadian foreign policy undertaken by the Trudeau government after it took power in 1968. Noting an increasing nationalism on both sides of the border, Sharp addressed the question of how to live "distinct from, but in harmony with" the US. He rejected 2 options, status quo and a deliberate policy of "closer integration with the United States." Instead, he argued for a "third option" which would "develop and strengthen the Canadian economy and other aspects of its national life and in the process reduce the present Canadian vulnerability." This was to be achieved through trade diversification abroad and an industrial strategy at home that emphasized specialization and Canadian ownership and, as a consequence, increased self-sufficiency. In the cultural sphere, he believed policies involving government subsidies and Canadian content regulations should be extended. The third option, Sharp insisted, was not anti-American; a stronger, more self-confident Canada would be a better neighbour.

Although the third option was easier to applaud than to implement, official Ottawa regarded it very seriously, particularly in the period 1972-76, when the FOREIGN INVESTMENT REVIEW AGENCY and PETRO-CANADA were established and Canadian businesses were discouraged from advertising on American radio and television stations. A "contractual link" was signed with the European Economic Community in 1976, but this and other efforts at trade diversification have not been notably successful. Ten years after the third option, exports to the US remained over 70% of Canada's total, while the percentage of US imports had actually increased. See CANADIAN-AMERICAN RELATIONS.   NORMAN HILLMER

Thistle (Carduaceae tribe, family Compositae or Asteraceae), spiny herbaceous PLANT with white to purple flowers. There are 800 species worldwide, 46 in Canada (15 native). Native species (none serious WEEDS) are mainly "true" or "plumed" thistles of genus *Cirsium.* The remainder are nonspiny arctic or alpine herbs of genus *Saussurea.* Naturalized species are mainly common weeds. Common burdock (*Arctium minus*) has burs which attach themselves to clothing or skin. A chemical irritant in the bur can cause a rash similar to that caused by poison ivy. Canada thistle (*Cirsium arvense*) is not native but is found in agricultural areas of all provinces. It is variable in appearance and spreads in pastures and grasslands by root fragments. Bull thistle (*C. vulgare*), a common weed of Québec, Ontario and southern BC, is biennial and spreads by seeds only. Several species of knapweed are regarded as pernicious weeds in the BC Interior. Diffuse knapweed (*Centaurea diffusa*) and spotted knapweed (*C. maculosa*) are subjects of major efforts in biological weed control.   PAUL B. CAVERS

Thode, Henry George, scientist, university administrator (b at Dundurn, Sask 10 Sept 1910). He graduated from U of Sask, earned his doctorate from Chicago in 1934 and was appointed to McMaster in 1939. His WWII research in atomic energy was sponsored by the NRC. He served as McMaster's vice-president 1957-61 and president 1961-72. He was the moving force behind the university's developing science, engineering and health-sciences faculties and its research and graduate programs. A brilliant nuclear scientist, Thode's work led to the construction at

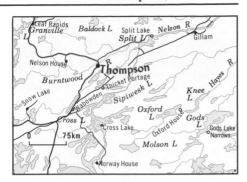

McMaster in 1957 of the first nuclear-research reactor at a Commonwealth university. A fellow of the RSC (and its president 1959-60), the Chemical Institute of Canada and the Royal Society of London, he was named an MBE in 1946 and was the first scientist appointed companion of the Order of Canada in 1967. Author of over 150 articles and professor emeritus at McMaster since 1979, his current research focuses on isotopes and fission products, including isotopic abundances in terrestrial, meteoritic and lunar materials. MANUEL ZACK

Thom, Linda, shooter (b at Hamilton, Ont 30 Dec 1943). She won the ladies match national pistol championship in 1982 and 1983 and the national ladies air pistol championships in 1983. She finished first in the Swiss International pistol tournament and third in the West German international in 1984, and then won a gold medal in the ladies sport pistol at the 1984 Los Angeles Olympics.

Thom, Ronald James, architect (b at Penticton, BC 15 May 1923). He first became known nationally as the designer of MASSEY COLLEGE, Toronto (1963) while still a partner of Thompson, Berwick and Pratt, Vancouver. His own Toronto-based practice, the Thom Partnership, was established in 1963. Earlier, he had designed a distinguished series of private houses and many other BC buildings. From Toronto he planned the campus and designed colleges and the main library for TRENT UNIVERSITY, Peterborough, Ont (1963-79), as well as thoughtful alterations and additions to existing buildings in town for the university's use. The SHAW FESTIVAL Theatre in Niagara-on-the-Lake, Ont (1973), was also a sensitive addition to an historic environment. A more utilitarian project is the Atria North office complex (Toronto, 1980), an energy-efficient commercial office development.

Thom was trained as a painter at the Vancouver School of Art, and his interest in architecture was awakened there by painter B.E. BINNING. His work had been notable for his ability to include richness of colour and detail within projects that encompass many buildings on large sites. His buildings manifest a clear sense of coherence without geometric rigidity.
MICHAEL MCMORDIE

Thomas, Alexander, writer, native leader (b at Port Alberni, BC 25 Dec 1891; d there 28 July 1971). Chief Alex Thomas, while living by traditional hunting and fishing, was the first NOOTKA to write down and translate texts on the culture and history of his people. Working as translator for his grandfather, a field consultant of Edward SAPIR 1910-14, Alex learned to write the standard alphabet developed by Sapir and his teacher Franz BOAS. From 1914 on he gave his people a literature of thousands of pages, still today only partly published, as in E. Sapir and M. Swadesh, *Nootka Texts* (1939) and *Native Accounts of Nootka Ethnography* (1955) and in A. Thomas and E. Arima, *t'a:t'a:qsapa. A Practical Orthography for Nootka* (1970). ROY WRIGHT

Thomas, Audrey Grace, née Callahan, writer (b at Binghampton, NY 17 Nov 1935). Thomas is a novelist and short story writer whose forte is analysis of the minutiae of women's lives. She was educated at Smith College, Mass, and St Andrews U, Scot, and then taught in England for a year. In 1959 she moved to Canada and in 1963 earned an MA at UBC. From 1964 to 1966 she lived in Ghana, and much of her subsequent fiction concerns her African experience. Thomas's novels include *Mrs Blood* (1970), *Munchmeyer and Prospero on the Island* (1971), *Songs My Mother Taught Me* (1973), *Blown Figures* (1974) and *Latakia* (1979). As well, she has written several collections of short stories: *Ten Green Bottles* (1967), *Ladies and Escorts* (1977) and *Real Mothers* (1981).
JEAN WILSON

Thomas, William, architect, engineer, surveyor (b in Suffolk, Eng 1799; d at Toronto 26 Dec 1860). Thomas is considered a founder of the Canadian architectural profession both for his contribution to ARCHITECTURAL DEVELOPMENT and for the quality and scope of his work. The elder brother of sculptor John Thomas, he established an extensive practice in Birmingham and Leamington Spa, Warwickshire, before immigrating to Toronto in 1843. Eventually with offices also in Hamilton and Halifax, his firm was one of the largest in British N America, and his works included at least 15 substantial public buildings and 15 churches, as well as numerous residences, commercial buildings and schools. Undoubtedly the best-known of his works is ST LAWRENCE HALL, Toronto. His most ambitious religious building was St Michael's Cathedral — the largest church in Toronto at the time.
NEIL EINARSON

Thomas, William Tutin, architect (b at Toronto 1828; d at Montréal 26 June 1892). A member of a distinguished family of architects (son of William THOMAS and nephew of English architect and sculptor John Thomas), he served his apprenticeship under his father and came to Montréal in 1864. He began in partnership with his brother, Cyrus Pole Thomas, then continued to practise architecture alone in Montréal when Cyrus emigrated to Chicago, Ill, in the 1870s. Stylistically eclectic, his work was characterized by a masterly proportioning. JULIA GERSOVITZ

Thompson, Man, City, pop 14 288 (1981c), inc 1970, is located on the S side of the Burntwood R, 740 km N of Winnipeg. In 1956 significant NICKEL deposits were found 32 km SW of Moak Lk. INCO and the provincial government reached agreement on development of Thompson, and by winter 1957 construction was underway. A rail link with the CNR's Hudson Bay line and a fully serviced new town, named for John F. Thompson, Inco's chairman, had to be built. Production began in 1961 at what was the first integrated nickel-mining, smelting, concentrating and refining complex in the Western world. Copper, cobalt and precious metal byproducts were produced as well. During the 1960s new mines were opened and the population topped 20 000, even though the townsite was designed for 8000 to 12 000.

Thompson's economy is highly dependent on the export demand for nickel. Inco's world position has been challenged in recent years by mines in developing countries and the prospect of deep-sea mining. Unfavourable markets led to reduced operations and decline in Thompson's population in the 1970s. Despite being a retail and service centre, the city has had a limited ability to attract secondary industry.

To avoid the unplanned growth seen in other new RESOURCE TOWNS, Thompson was created in an orderly manner, with full health, education, water and protection services. D.M. LYON

Thompson, Arthur, Nuu-chah-nulth artist (b at Whyac Village, Vancouver I 1948). An innovative and prolific printmaker, Thompson is best known for his introduction of unconventional and original subject matter and colours to the silkscreen medium in contemporary NORTHWEST COAST INDIAN ART. Equally competent in woodcarving and silver engraving, he is also fluent in his native Westcoast language and is known for his dancing and singing talents in traditional ceremonial settings. He is active as a silkscreen designer and one of his finest works is an octagonal drum design titled "A Tribute To My Grandmother." CAROL SHEEHAN

Thompson, Berwick, Pratt and Partners, architects, Vancouver, BC. Founded in 1908 as Sharp and Thompson by Englishmen G.L.T. Sharp and Charles J. Thompson, this firm has played a major role in Vancouver and Canadian architecture through the century. Its founders first designed medieval and classically inspired commercial, institutional and residential buildings in BC, especially on UNIVERSITY OF BRITISH COLUMBIA campus whose plan they produced in 1913. In 1937 they were joined by recent U of T graduates Robert A.D. Berwick and Charles Edward Pratt, committed to developing a regional architecture inspired by the principles of European modernism. Through the 1950s and 1960s the firm received international attention for such projects as the BC Electric Building (1957). A succession of major Canadian architects worked within the firm before pursuing independent careers, including Barry DOWNS, Arthur ERICKSON and Ron THOM. MICHAEL MCMORDIE

Thompson, David, fur trader, explorer, surveyor, mapmaker (b at London, Eng 30 Apr 1770; d

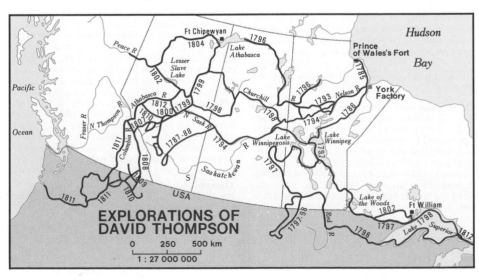

EXPLORATIONS OF DAVID THOMPSON

0   250   500 km

1 : 27 000 000

at Longueuil, Canada E 10 Feb 1857). Apprenticed to the HUDSON'S BAY CO in 1784, Thompson devoted most of his life to the study of geography and the practice of mapmaking. The maps, based primarily on his own explorations and observations, were the first to provide a comprehensive view of the vast western territories that became part of Canada in 1869 (see CARTOGRAPHY).

As an apprentice to the HBC, Thompson rapidly acquired the knowledge needed to be a successful trader. While recovering from a broken leg in 1790, he studied surveying and mapmaking with Philip Turnor, the HBC's official surveyor. His new skills were recognized in 1792 when he was assigned to seek a more direct route from Hudson Bay to Lk Athabasca. Frustrated by faltering support for his surveys, he left to join the NORTH WEST CO in 1797 to locate and map their posts and the waterways connecting them. Within 2 years he had completed most of this assignment, including the first accurate delineation of those parts of the West most affected by the expansion of American authority under the terms of JAY'S TREATY — the upper Red River valley, the Mandan villages on the Missouri R, the sources of the Mississippi R, and the Fond du Lac and Rainy R regions W of Lk Superior. In 1799 Thompson was given additional duty as a trader and for the next 7 years he pursued his surveys whenever his other responsibilities permitted, as he rose from clerk to partner. During these years he completed mapping the fur-trading territories E of the Rocky Mts.

In 1806 Thompson set out to open a trade with the Indians W of the Rockies. Over the next 5 years he explored the passes W from the Saskatchewan and Athabasca rivers, building posts and mapping the hitherto uncharted COLUMBIA R basin from its source to the Pacific, which he reached on 15 July 1811, a few weeks after the American Astorian expedition. His failure to reach the mouth of the river before the Americans could establish a claim to it has resulted in some debate among historians about his instructions. Most now agree that Thompson was not aware that an agreement between the NWC and Jacob Astor to support jointly the proposed voyage to the mouth of the Columbia had fallen through, and that he had not been ordered to reach the mouth first in order to forestall them.

In 1812 Thompson retired to Canada with his wife and family. After settling in Williamstown, UC, Thompson pursued his career as a surveyor and mapmaker, his most notable achievement being the completion of maps of his western explorations and the charting of the official boundary between the US and Canada from the St Lawrence R to Lake of the Woods. Business failures left him penniless, and in later life he turned to writing the narrative of his explorations in western Canada, regarded by many as his greatest legacy. See EXPLORATION.

JOHN S. NICKS

Reading: J.B. Tyrrell, ed, *David Thompson's Narrative* (1916; repr 1968).

Thompson, Ian Maclaren, anatomist (b at Harbour Grace, Nfld 13 Sept 1896; d at Winnipeg 26 Dec 1981). His education at Edinburgh was interrupted by service in WWI, during which he was wounded and mentioned in dispatches. He taught anatomy at McGill 1920-27, U of Calif (Berkeley) 1927-36 and U of Man, where he was head of the department 1937-65. He is remembered for his emphasis on the study of the living body and the importance of anatomical clinics and for his neuroanatomical research. A fellow of the Royal Soc of Canada (1947) and the Royal Soc of Edinburgh (1952), he was founding president of the Canadian Assn of Anatomists.

T.V.N. PERSAUD

Sir John Sparrow Thompson, 4th prime minister of Canada, 1892-94. He was a capable leader whose main contribution was the Canadian Criminal Code (*courtesy Public Archives of Canada/C-698*).

Thompson, Sir John Sparrow David, lawyer, judge, politician, prime minister (b at Halifax 10 Nov 1845 [not 1844 as often cited]; d at Windsor Castle, Eng 12 Dec 1894). He was admitted to the NS Bar in 1865 and elected alderman for Halifax in 1871, a position he held for 6 years. Although raised a Methodist, he converted to Roman Catholicism in 1871. In 1877 he was elected to the NS Assembly as member for Antigonish, a Scottish Catholic constituency, and was attorney general in the Conservative regime of Simon Holmes, 1878-82. On Holmes's retirement, he was briefly premier, but he and his government were defeated in the 1882 election. He was then appointed judge of the Supreme Court of NS.

In 1885 Thompson was persuaded to return to political life, this time at Ottawa. He was sworn in as minister of justice in Sir John A. MACDONALD's government in Sept 1885 and was elected MP for Antigonish, positions he held for the rest of his life. Confident, courteous and always master of his subject, Thompson soon became important in Cabinet. When Macdonald died in June 1891, he was the logical successor, but J.J.C. ABBOTT reluctantly took office to avoid the acrimony that would have been caused by Thompson's religion. Nevertheless, Thompson acted as House Leader and, when Abbott retired, became prime minister 24 Nov 1892, when he was 48 years old. He was a capable leader, though without Macdonald's ability to soothe his party's divisions. His main contribution was the Canadian CRIMINAL CODE of 1892. He died only an hour or so after being sworn in as a member of the Imperial Privy Council by Queen Victoria. His funeral took place in Halifax 3 Jan 1895. His estate, which amounted to $20 000, was a measure of his probity in public office, but it left his family, which included a crippled daughter, hard up. A public subscription was launched. Thompson's death left the Conservative Party bereft of moral courage and force.

P.B. WAITE

Thompson, Margaret Anne Wilson, geneticist (b at Northwich, Eng 7 Jan 1920). She obtained a BA in 1943 from U Sask and a PhD in 1948 from U of T where she studied under the pioneering human geneticist Norma Ford Walker. She contributed to human genetics through research on a variety of genetic disorders, particularly muscular dystrophy. She also

taught at Western (1948-50), U of A (1950-63) and U of T (1963-85), where she supervised many graduate students and taught genetics to medical students. In addition to numerous scientific articles, she has written a widely used text, *Genetics in Medicine* (1966), coauthored with her husband James Scott Thompson. She founded a genetic counselling service at U of A Hospital in 1956 and she joined the staff of Toronto's Hospital for Sick Children in 1963. DIANE WILSON COX

Thompson, Paul, director, producer, playwright (b at Charlottetown 4 May 1940). Influenced by his work with Roger Planchon's socially and politically committed theatre in France (1965-67), he emerged as an important figure in the Canadian alternative theatre movement as artistic director of Toronto's Theatre Passe Muraille (1971-82). Thompson pioneered the development of the "collective creation" process in which actors, a director and writer develop a script through acting improvisations. His productions were characterized by their Canadian subject matter and the exploration and creation of Canadian myths. They include *Doukhobors* (1971), *The Farm Show* (1972), *1837: The Farmers' Revolt* (1972), *I Love You, Baby Blue* (1975), *Far As the Eye Can See* (1977) and *Maggie and Pierre* (1980). ANTON WAGNER

Thompson, Robert Norman, politician, teacher (b at Duluth, Minn 17 May 1914). He came to Canada in 1918, was educated in Alberta, taught school, practised chiropractic and served in the RCAF (1941-43). His prominence in Canadian politics began in 1960 when he was elected president of the SOCIAL CREDIT Assn of Canada. In 1961 he became national leader of the Social Credit Party. He was elected to Parliament in 1962 for Red Deer, Alta, and returned in 1963 and 1965. In these elections the Social Credit Party, with Réal CAOUETTE as deputy leader, had enough success to help prevent the Conservatives or Liberals from winning a majority. Thompson resigned as Social Credit leader in Mar 1967, citing lack of support from provincial party organizations. In 1960 he joined the Progressive Conservative Party and retained his Red Deer seat in Parliament. He left politics in 1982 to teach political science at Trinity Western Coll, Langley, BC. In 1984 he was chairman of the board, Fraser Academy, Langley, a school for students with dyslexia; chairman of a foundation set up by his family to raise and distribute funds for charity; and president of Vanguard Institute, which researches political aspects of Canadian economics. BILL CAMERON

Thompson, Thomas Phillips, journalist, socialist intellectual (b at Newcastle upon Tyne, Eng 25 Nov 1843; d at Oakville, Ont 20 May 1933). Under the pseudonym "Jimuel Briggs," Thompson wrote political satire for the St Catharines and Toronto press, and in 1874 he launched *The National,* a weekly paper of political commentary. After some years in the US, he returned in 1879 to editorial work on Toronto newspapers, notably the lively *News.* During the 1880s, he promoted radical challenges to the emergent industrial capitalist society and became a spokesman for the KNIGHTS OF LABOR. In 1887 he produced the labour movement's most articulate critique, *The Politics of Labor* (repr 1975). The short life of his new radical weekly, *Labor Advocate* (1890-91), did not discourage this pioneering voice of Canadian socialism; he continued to speak and write for the new socialist movement until the 1920s. CRAIG HERON

Thompson, Walter Palmer, plant geneticist, university administrator (b near Decewsville, Ont 3 Apr 1889; d at Saskatoon 30 Mar 1970). Raised on a farm in Haldimand County, Ont, Thompson graduated from U of T in 1910 and received his PhD from Harvard in 1914. He began his career at U Sask as head of biology in

1913, became dean of arts and science in 1939 and was president 1949-59. He became famous for his work on the genetics of cereal grains, studying chromosome numbers and breeding the first new strains of rust-resistant wheat. President of the RSC in 1947, he received their Flavelle Medal in 1949, was president of the Int Botanical Congress in 1959 and received honorary doctorates from 7 Canadian universities. He was chairman of Saskatchewan's Advisory Planning Committee on Medical Care; its recommendations in 1962 formed the basis for medicare in Saskatchewan.   C. STUART HOUSTON

Thompson River, 489 km long, rises in the Cariboo district of the Rocky Mts and flows S as the North Thompson R. It is joined at KAMLOOPS by the South Thompson R from Shuswap Lk, and the 2 flow united, carrying their blue-green waters into the FRASER R at LYTTON. The banks of the lower course are hilly and almost barren, except for sagebrush, and many of the spectacular terraces are used for cattle grazing and fodder crops. Both the CPR and CNR transcontinental lines follow the river from Kamloops to Lytton. Simon FRASER mistakenly believed that David THOMPSON had found the river, and named it for him.   JAMES MARSH

Thomson, Andrew, meteorologist (b at Dobbinton, Ont 18 May 1893; d at Toronto 17 Oct 1974). Following graduation from U of T in 1916, Thomson studied and worked in the US, Samoa, New Zealand and Europe before returning in 1932 to the national meteorological service. He planned Canada's participation in the 1932-33 International Polar Year and was instrumental in establishing the first graduate program in meteorology at U of T. Thomson assisted John PATTERSON in planning for and administering a program of meteorological services for continental and transatlantic civil aviation in the 1930s and for military aviation during WWII. He led the postwar expansion and development of METEOROLOGY in Canada and was one of a small group who reconstructed international meteorology after 1945. As director of the national meteorological service 1946-59 he reorganized and expanded the service for peacetime. He travelled the world as a member of the executive committee of the World Meteorological Organization. A fellow of the RSC, he was created OBE in 1946 and awarded the Patterson Medal in 1965.   MORLEY THOMAS

Thomson, Kenneth, businessman, financier (b at Toronto 1 Sept 1923). Although in 1976 he succeeded his father, Roy THOMSON, as Baron Thomson of Fleet (a title he uses only in Britain), he waited several more years before becoming — reluctantly, one senses — a figure familiar to the Canadian public. In 1979 he purchased the HUDSON'S BAY CO and in 1980 the FP Publications newspaper chain, both after protracted takeover battles. By the time of his decision in 1981 to sell *The Times* of London, he was already one of Canada's wealthiest citizens, through newspaper properties in Canada, Britain and the US and through North Sea oil. In other circles he is renowned as an enthusiastic collector of art.

Thomson, Roy Herbert, Baron Thomson of Fleet, newspaper tycoon (b at Toronto 5 June 1894; d at London, Eng 4 Aug 1976). The son of a Toronto barber, Thomson showed little potential to become wealthy and notable until middle age, when he emerged as the owner of small radio stations and newspapers in northern Ontario. He went on to control hundreds of newspapers in the US, Canada and the Commonwealth, including the *Scotsman* of Edinburgh (his first large prize) and *The Times* and *Sunday Times* of London. He seemed to care little for the romance, tradition and democratic importance of newspapers, running them with the same tightfistedness and quality control he applied

Tom Thomson's *Autumn Foliage,* oil on panel, is one of the brilliant sketches made on his trips to Algonquin Park *(courtesy Art Gallery of Ontario/gift from The Reuben and Kate Leonard Canadian Fund, 1927).*

to his other businesses (magazines, travel agencies, TV) and for which he was notorious. Quite unburnished and American in manner and deportment, he was nonetheless a child of the British Empire in outlook, coveting influence in Britain; at the same time he limited his Canadian holdings to smaller newspapers free of both competition and prestige. By international standards, he was already very wealthy when, late in his career, he diversified into oil exploration. He was created a peer in 1963.

Reading: R. Braddon, *Roy Thomson of Fleet Street* (1965); R.H. Thomson, *After I Was Sixty* (1975).

Thomson, Thomas John, painter (b at Claremont, Ont 4 Aug 1877; d at Canoe Lk, Ont 8 July 1917). Tom Thomson grew up on a farm near Leith, Ont, sixth of 10 children in a family much concerned with music and literature, a background that balanced his passion for hunting and fishing. During his twenties, Thomson apprenticed as a machinist, enrolled in business college and then spent a few years in Seattle, working as an engraver. He returned to Canada in 1904 and worked for several photoengraving houses in Toronto, including Grip Ltd. Within 5 years Thomson had acquired a reputation as a designer-illustrator.

In 1906 he took art lessons and first used oil paint. His work of this period is tentative, unpromising and rough. After joining Grip in 1907 he came alive to his own creative possibilities and was influenced by fellow artists J.E.H. MACDONALD, Albert Robson, William Broadhead and Rowley Murphy, and later by Fred VARLEY, Arthur LISMER, Franz JOHNSTON, and Franklin CARMICHAEL. This group worked past the restrictions of their commercial lives by sketching on the Don and Humber rivers and Lk Scugog. The subdued and tidy landscape these trips offered encouraged an appetite for rougher terrain.

The year 1912 was pivotal in Thomson's career. That spring he sketched in ALGONQUIN PARK for 2 weeks and from late July to Sept he made a long trip with Broadhead along the Spanish R to the Mississagi Forest Reserve. On his return, Robson and others inspired Thomson to scale *Northern Lake* into a full-sized canvas, which was purchased by Ontario for $250. At the time this

was a huge sum (Thomson was then earning 75 cents an hour), and he spent the next summer and fall sketching in Algonquin.

In Toronto in Oct 1913 Thomson met his future patron Dr James MacCallum and his creative mentor, A.Y. JACKSON. MacCallum offered them a year's expenses if they would devote themselves to painting. Jackson and Thomson moved in Jan 1914 into a studio and made another trip to Algonquin Park in late Feb. During that spring and fall Thomson painted with Varley, Lismer and Jackson in the park and in the early spring of 1915 returned to Canoe Lk. Bolstered by the $500 sale of *Northern River* to the National Gallery, his work now had the smash and stab of passion flying before thought.

The Arts and Letters Club in Toronto gave Thomson an exhibition in 1915 and he passed the winter productively in his studio. Employed as a fire ranger in Algonquin Park in the summer of 1916, Thomson managed to complete many sketches in the bravura style of his late period, his loaded brush producing images of surprising plasticity. In Apr 1917, determined to spend more time painting, he bought a guide's licence and returned to the park, where it is said he completed 62 sketches depicting the daily unfolding spring.

Near noon on 8 July 1917, Tom Thomson paddled past Wapomeo Island ostensibly to fish. His upturned canoe was discovered later that day and his body was recovered on July 16. The mystery surrounding Thomson's tragic death separated the man from the passion of his work, and his accomplishments have been obscured by endless conjecture over his death. Though middle-aged, Thomson burst free from an ordinary past, painting with heat that went to the edge separating the figurative from the abstract. The small sketch panels and even the larger canvasses could no longer contain his joy and power and needed a larger format to subsume his vision of rock, tree and sky. In the last years he had complete control of the picture plane and seemed to know instinctively what colours recede. His colour arrangements were closing in on simultaneous vibration within hue. With his instinctive technical command of the medium, fueled by an intense love of the North, Thomson, at the time of his death, had all the elements necessary to become a great painter. Time will dull the mystery of his death and can only enhance the lovely intense work of his last years. HAROLD TOWN

Reading: Harold Town and David B. Silcox, *Tom Thomson* (1977).

Thomson Group, one of the largest publishing empires in the world, is owned and controlled by the Thomson family. In 1983 the family, headed by Kenneth THOMSON, controlled 83 newspapers in the US, 71 in Britain and 54 daily and weekly NEWSPAPERS in Canada, including the *Globe and Mail.* The Canadian chain is Canada's largest in number of newspapers sold and is second to SOUTHAM INC in daily circulation (1 171 000 in 1983). Other international interests include magazines and book publishing, wholesaling and retailing, real estate, oil and gas, travel, financial and management services, trucking and fur trading. Holdings in Canada include the HUDSON'S BAY CO, Zeller's, Fields and SIMPSONS. The Thomson Group's total assets in 1983 exceeded $6 billion, with revenues of $7 billion. PETER S. ANDERSON

Thorburn, Clifford Charles Devlin, snooker player (b at Victoria 16 Jan 1948). Since leaving school after grade 10, Cliff Thorburn has played snooker and pool virtually full-time. In 1971 he won the N American Snooker championship and since 1973 has played in nearly all snooker-playing countries in the world. In 1980 he became the first player from outside the UK to win the world professional championship. He has been N American champion twice, Canadian champion 5 times, Australian Masters, Canadian professional and world mixed pairs champion each once. In addition he holds the world's record of 19 perfect games (147 runs) at snooker. GRAHAM DUNCAN

Thorburn, Robert, merchant, politician (b at Juniper Banks, Scot 28 Mar 1836; d at St John's 12 Apr 1906). Thorburn went to Newfoundland in 1852. For most of his political life (1870-85, 1893-1906) he was an Upper House member who championed the cause of governing the colony along "strict commercial" lines. Economic, social and political conditions had combined by 1882 to install in office a Liberal Party based on government-sponsored diversification and industrialization. When sectarian riots precipitated a political crisis in 1884, Thorburn's class exploited the resulting denominational bitterness by forming a "Protestant Rights" Party and attracted sufficient Protestant support to defeat the Liberals in 1885. The resulting Thorburn-led administration unsuccessfully tried to develop the colony along "fishery" lines. Thorburn was forced by circumstance to fall back on a belated program of public works, but then was swept from power in 1889. JOHN GREENE

Thorlakson, Paul H.T., surgeon (b at Park River, N Dak 5 Oct 1895). In 1900 the Thorlakson family moved to Selkirk, Man, and in 1919 Thorlakson graduated in medicine from Manitoba Medical College. After postgraduate study in Europe, he and Dr Neil John Maclean formed the Maclean-Thorlakson Surgical Clinic in 1926, and in 1942 he founded the Winnipeg Clinic. A pioneer in encouraging the development of medical research, Thorlakson was responsible for the formation of the Winnipeg Clinic Research Institute to advance medical education and research. Thorlakson served on innumerable committees and as chancellor of U of Winnipeg 1969-78. He has been honoured by U of Man and the universities of Winnipeg, Brandon and Iceland. On the medical faculty for many years, in 1984 he was professor emeritus of surgery at U of Man. He was appointed a Companion of the Order of Canada in 1970. In his honour, his friends and colleagues established the Paul H.T. Thorlakson Research Foundation in 1980. HARRY MEDOVY

Thornton, Sir Henry Worth, railway official (b at Logansport, Ind 6 Nov 1871; d at New York C 14 March 1933). After graduating from U of Pennsylvania in 1894, Thornton joined the engineering department of the Pennsylvania Railroad. In 1914 he went to Britain as general manager of the Great Eastern Ry. He was knighted in 1919 for his wartime service as director general of railways behind the battle lines in France. In 1922 he was appointed by the Liberals as president of CANADIAN NATIONAL RY, and under him the varied railways under government control were unified. During the 1920s there was intense rivalry between the CNR and the CANADIAN PACIFIC RY. When the Conservatives came to power in 1930, Thornton was attacked as a Liberal partisan, and feeling that he had lost the support of the government, he resigned in 1932. JOHN A. EAGLE

Thorold, Ont, City, pop 15 412 (1981c), inc 1975 (city), situated in the Niagara Peninsula. Though physically linked to ST CATHARINES, its large neighbour directly to the N, Thorold is independent. The area was settled in the 1780s and named after British MP Sir John Thorold. Its growth is linked with the development of the 4 courses of the WELLAND CANAL. At the canal's commencement (1829) a townsite was laid out, and Thorold attracted various marine services and industries, such as limestone quarrying, flour milling, wood products and Canada's first cotton mill, many using the canal for transportation or water power. The advent of cheap hydroelectric power from nearby NIAGARA FALLS after 1900 led many heavy industries such as pulp and paper, abrasives and metal goods to locate here. Since 1945 the long-standing Anglo-Saxon and Irish flavour of this industrial community has been changed by sizable Italian immigration. A monument at Battle of Beaver Dams Park recalls the famous encounter of the War of 1812. H.J. GAYLER

Thoroughbred Racing is the racing of a special breed of horse over courses which, in N America, range from less than 1 mile to 1½ miles in length (1.6-2.4 km). In Canada and the US, flat races on grass or dirt are the rule. In Europe, both flat and steeplechase races (in which the horse and rider are also required to clear a number of obstacles, such as fences or hedges) are carried out. All thoroughbred horses are descended from the Arabian, Turkish and Barbary horses imported into England in the 1600s. In fact, most thoroughbreds trace their lineage to one of three horses — Byerly Turk, the Godolphin Arabian and the Darley Arabian.

On the one hand, horse racing is viewed as a sport of the wealthy, based on the traditions of a long and valued history. At the same time, it also has its shady side, associated with gambling and complemented by the rich subculture of its citizens on the back stretch. From its earliest days in Canada, it has reflected this dichotomy. There is ample evidence that it has always been a popular sport, particularly in a pioneer society where the horse was a vital means of transportation. Still, in 1771 horse racing was banned by Halifax authorities because they believed it turned the local citizenry into idle, immoral gamblers. Nevertheless, in 1825 the Halifax Turf Club was formed and held its first meeting. Ownership of a horse — even at the expense of economic hardship — was a potent status symbol among French Canadians, and horse racing enjoyed great popularity in Lower Canada [Québec] in the late 18th and 19th centuries — to the extent that sporting reports in newspapers of the time show a concentration on racing equal to that of almost all other sports combined. The Québec Turf Club was formed in 1789, and in 1836 the King's Plate, a race for a purse of 100 guineas, was first held in Trois-Rivières. Initially, it was restricted to horses bred in LC, but in 1859 horses from Upper Canada were admitted. The next year the QUEEN'S PLATE was held in Toronto for the first time; it has been run continuously since then, making it the oldest continuing stakes race in N America — 15 years older than the Kentucky Derby. The winner of that 1860 race was a horse named Don Juan, owned by the James White Stable of Bronte and Milton, Ont. Small breeders with limited means could hope to win the race at that time. This was also a period when the quality of the horses was questionable and the practices of many owners suspect. In 1865 the judges disqualified 3 horses before declaring a winner of the Queen's Plate. Ten years later, the winner of Canada's most prestigious race was a previously unsuccessful 8 year old named Trumpeter. In August 1881, Colonel Casimir GZOWSKI held a meeting in Toronto with some of that city's most respected citizens to form the Ontario Jockey Club in order "to lift horse racing out of the mire." As the club's first chairman, Gzowski sought to bring the sport to respectability by ridding it of its bad reputation and improving the quality of Canadian thoroughbreds. A major step towards these aims occurred 2 years later when the club was successful in getting the governor general, the marquis of Lorne, and his wife, the Princess Louise, 4th daughter of Queen Victoria, to attend the Queen's Plate. Not only did this result in the race being held permanently in Toronto, it also helped attract the interest of the richer classes of Canadian society. In 1891 a horse named Terror Colt, owned by Joseph Seagram, a wealthy distiller from Waterloo, Ont, won the first of 20 Plate victories for the Seagram Stables. The era of the wealthy owner was established.

The sport has also been sustained by the 2-dollar bettor, whose interest over the years helped ensure that racing would continue to draw a large share of space in the print media. At the turn of the century, the activities of bookmakers were enough to scare away even the most courageous of patrons. Odds were shortened in their favour; they ran their horses under others' names and fixed races. Finally, in 1910, the Canadian Parliament, by one vote, banned bookmakers. Next year, the establishment of pari-mutuel betting at tracks in Toronto, Winnipeg and Calgary brought more honesty to betting and helped save the sport. It got an important boost in Canada's West from R.L. "Jim" Speers, a feed and grain entrepreneur who had moved from Toronto to Winnipeg and ultimately became the dean of the sport there. In 1922 he bought his first racetrack, and by 1925 owned 3 more. He eventually came to control tracks or meetings in Winnipeg, Regina, Saskatoon, Calgary and Edmonton. Realizing the difficulty in obtaining quality horses that would provide attractive racing meetings, he set up his own breeding farm in Winnipeg, which by the mid-1930s had become the country's largest.

Economic difficulties experienced throughout Canada in the 1930s affected racetrack operations, heightening many of the abuses associated with the sport. Through the efforts of governments and racing operators, however, a clean up was accomplished by the late 1940s. The sport was evolving into a business, and one of the main forces behind this transformation was E.P. TAYLOR. President of the Ontario Jockey Club 1953-73, Taylor was responsible for making horse racing more efficient by closing down several old, unprofitable tracks and using their charters to organize racing days at the rebuilt Fort Erie track and Woodbine, a large new facility in NW Toronto. The longer racing seasons that resulted saw greater attendance, higher purses and better horses. Taylor had also, in 1949, bought Parkwood Stables from R.S. McLaughlin, the Canadian automobile pioneer and one of the top racehorse breeders in the 1930s and 1940s. Renamed the National Stud Farm, it produced 15 Queen's Plate winners, including the legendary NORTHERN DANCER. The result of a long-term breeding plan instituted by Taylor, this chunky little horse displayed a tremendous will to win, and in 1964 became the first Canadian-bred horse to win the Kentucky Derby. He also won the Preakness, thus taking two jewels in the American triple crown. Retired to stud by a leg injury that same year, his winnings in purses totalled $580 000. In his second year at stud, he sired the magnificent NIJINSKY, which had a brilliant career in Europe, winning the Epsom Derby, the Irish Derby and several other major-stakes races. Another of his progeny, the Minstrel, won $2 million in prizes in 1977. It has been said that Northern Dancer has influenced the bloodlines of all the top N American thoroughbreds.

Other Canadians fared well in 1973. New Brunswick's Ron TURCOTTE rode Secretariat to victory in the American triple crown. Turcotte's career ended 5 years later in a spill that left him paralyzed from the waist down, but not before he had established himself as one of N America's best jockeys. 1973 also saw Sandy HAWLEY, of Mississauga, Ont, ride 515 winners, becoming the first jockey to surpass the 500 mark in one year. Ten years later Sunny's Halo won the Kentucky Derby. By September 1980, Hawley, at the age of 31, had rode his 4000th career winner, becoming one of only 10 men to reach that goal. Earlier, Johnny LONGDEN rode 6032 winners between 1927 and 1966. His contemporary, George Woolf, was known as "the Iceman" because of his coolness in the saddle. He rode many major-stakes winners, including Seabiscuit during his great victory over War Admiral in a 1938 match race. Woolf was killed in 1946 in a racing accident. Another top jockey of that era was Newfoundland's Nick Wall, who rode Stagehand to win the 1938 Santa Anita Derby. Avelino Gomez, rider of 4078 winners, led all N American jockeys in victories in 1966. He was killed in an accident at Woodbine during the Canadian Oaks race in June 1980. Woolf, Longden and Gomez have been honoured by the US Racing Hall of Fame.   J. THOMAS WEST

Reading: J. Coleman, *Hoofprints on My Heart* (1971); T. Frayne, *The Queen's Plate: The First 100 Years* (1959).

Thorvaldson, Thorbergur, "TT," cement chemist (b in Iceland 24 Aug 1883; d at Saskatoon 4 Oct 1965). Settling with his parents near Gimli, Man, he went on to attend U Man and Harvard (MSc, PhD). In 1919 he became head of the dept of chemistry at U Sask, and in 1945 the first dean of graduate studies. He was made a Knight in the Icelandic Order of the Falcon in 1939 and was president of the Canadian Inst of Chemistry in 1941. His research on the chemistry of cement and the development of cements resistant to deterioration through chemical attack won him international recognition and many honours. Thorvaldson Lake in northeastern Saskatchewan was named after him in 1966 — a rare honour for a chemist.   GORDON R. FREEMAN

Thousand Islands (Ontario part) An 80 km long section of the ST LAWRENCE R, extending downstream from Lk Ontario between KINGSTON and BROCKVILLE and containing over 1000 rocky, wooded islands ranging from several square kilometres to barely emergent rocks and shoals.

This scenic landscape of varied islands and labyrinth passages owes its origin to a projection of Canada's Precambrian SHIELD extending from eastern Ontario across the St Lawrence, where it underlies the Adirondack Mts in New York

The scenic landscape of varied islands and labyrinth channels of the Thousand Islands owes its origins to a projection of the Canadian Shield across the St Lawrence R (*photo by Barbara K. Deans/Masterfile*).

state. This old (over 900 million years), complex rock, composed largely of hard granites and gneisses, was scoured and sculpted by glacial erosion into a "knob and hollow" surface. In the altered landscape after continental glaciation, the GREAT LAKES system found a new drainage route E from Lk Ontario, forming the present St Lawrence R. The hollows flooded and the rocky knobs became islands.

This section of the great St Lawrence corridor into Canada is rich in flora and fauna, beauty and history. Waterfowl are abundant. As this area is on the southern limit of the Great Lakes-St Lawrence forest region, there is forest diversity: southern species such as shagbark hickory, American basswood and pitch pine mingle with the familiar southern Ontario deciduous and coniferous species. The varied bottom contours of the St Lawrence offer diverse fish habitats — some 38 species have been identified, of which northern pike, muskellunge, large and smallmouth bass, and yellow perch have long attracted fishermen.

A favourite camping ground of the IROQUOIS before European exploration, this part of the great river highway to the interior was traversed by explorers, missionaries, fur traders and soldiers. Colonial military conflict between England and France (SEVEN YEARS' WAR), and later between England and the US (WAR OF 1812), was responsible for many place-names, such as the Navy, Admiralty and Lake Fleet islands. Endymion, Camelot and Mermaid islands are named after gunboats; others such as Gordon and Stovin were named after military commanders.

Immigrants travelling to Upper Canada in the late 1700s and early 1800s and romantic writers of that period spread knowledge of the area's beauty. Accessibility to a prospering urban society in both Canada and the adjacent US also led to early recreational use. Fishing and boating were popular. Hotels, often palatial, were built primarily for fishermen from the 1850s to 1870s. Church camping grounds, such as the Methodist Thousand Island Park on Wellesly I (1875), proliferated on the islands, and frequently evolved to cottage communities. Increased railway access on both sides of the river helped expand affluent tourism. Luxury hotels and steamboat excursions became popular, and elaborate summer homes began to appear, even before Confederation, 1867. In 1914 ST LAWRENCE ISLANDS NATIONAL PARK was established through acquisition of several dispersed islands from the

Mississauga Indians. Twenty-three islands and many smaller islets, with a mainland base at Mallorytown Landing, now constitute the park.

From the early 1800s, tourism has been an important economic contributor. Apart from some national and provincial campsites, the islands and shoreline today are largely privately owned, and are dominated by summer vacation homes. Along the St Lawrence shoreline, cottages are interspersed with small hotels and marinas. The Thousand Islands International Bridge (1938) crosses the St Lawrence at Hill I, linking Ontario and New York state highways, and has given rise to many tourist facilities on that island. Ontario's Macdonald-Cartier Freeway (Hwy 401) greatly increased metropolitan access after WWII and the scenic Thousand Island Parkway skirts the wooded coves and bays of the St Lawrence shore from GANANOQUE to Brockville. Tourist services also serve an important economic function for the adjacent communities of Kingston, Brockville, Rockport, Ivy Lea and Gananoque. The Thousand Islands landscape and its history have preserved what FRONTENAC described in 1673 as "the most delightful country in the world."   D.M. ANDERSON

Thrasher (Mimidae), small family of slender, long-tailed, medium-sized, insectivorous and frugivorous BIRDS with loud, musical, repetitive songs. Some species mimic songs of other birds. The family comprises 32 species. Four breed in Canada, including thrashers, brownish above with whitish, brown-spotted or plain breasts; MOCKINGBIRDS, blue or grey above and whitish below; and catbirds, grey or black overall. This family, which is restricted to the New World, apparently evolved in the American tropics and is most closely related to DIPPERS and WRENS. The widespread but rare northern mockingbird is a permanent resident in Canada. The migratory gray catbird (*Dumetella carolinensis*) summers from southern BC to Cape Breton I. The brown thrasher (*Toxostoma rufum*), also migratory, occurs from southeastern Alberta to southwestern Quebec. Both species frequent scrub and woodland edges. The migratory sage thrasher (*Oreoscoptes montanus*) is a local summer resident in sagebrush grassland in southern BC and, rarely, SE Saskatchewan. Mimids breed May-July, building bulky nests of twigs and grasses placed low (under 6 m) in shrubs or trees or on the ground (eg, sage thrasher). They lay 4-5 eggs per clutch. Mimids are territorially aggressive. They are parasitized, rarely, by brown-headed cowbirds (*Molothrus ater*).   J.C. BARLOW

Thrips, order Thysanoptera, are among the smallest INSECTS, being slender and usually less than 2 mm long. About 4500 species have been described, but only 104 of a probable 250 species are known from Canada. Thrips are most closely related to BUGS (order Hemiptera) and are adapted to life in confined spaces (eg, in flowers, under bark or in leaf litter). They are widely distributed across southern Canada but few species occur in the Arctic and Subarctic. They have asymmetric, "punch and suck" mouthparts (right mandible is absent) and feed on fungi, pollen, leaves or small animals. Adults generally have 4 long, straplike wings fringed with long hairs, but some are wingless or vary in wing length. Metamorphosis is intermediate between complete and incomplete. Two active, feeding, larval stages are followed by 2-3 sluggish, nonfeeding, "pupal" stages. Males usually develop from unfertilized and females from fertilized eggs, but only females are known in some species. Thirty species are crop pests; 11 occur in Canada, including onion thrips (*Thrips tabaci*), which transmits tomato spotted wilt virus and is of major importance. B.S. HEMING

Thrush (Muscicapidae), very large family comprising about 1400 species of small passerines (perching BIRDS) ranging from 11 to 33 cm in length. Because of its diversity, the family has been divided into 13 subfamilies, including the Turdinae (309 species), which is devoted to thrushes alone. Thrushes have almost worldwide distribution. Twelve species regularly occur in Canada: northern wheatear (*Oenanthe oenanthe*), eastern, western and mountain BLUEBIRDS (*Sialia sialis, S. mexicana, S. currucoides,* respectively), Townsend's SOLITAIRE (*Myadestes townsendi*), veery (*Catharus fuscescens*), gray-cheeked, Swainson's, hermit, wood, and varied thrushes (*C. minima, C. ustulata, C. guttata, Hylocichla mustelina, Ixoreus naevius*) and American ROBIN. All of the above are largely migratory. Plumage can be very glossy in some species. Combinations of browns, greys, olives, black, white, chestnut and blue are often blended or contrasted in adults. Males are often more brightly coloured than females. Plumage of immature birds is almost always spotted. Bill varies in length but is usually short, straight and slender; it may curve downward at the tip and have a small notch on the mandible. The short tail can be square or slightly rounded. Wings are long and pointed, with 10 primary feathers. In most species, the feet are strong and stout and the front of the leg is covered with an undivided sheath. Thrushes, with their extremely varied voices and highly developed songs, are considered by many to be the best singers among birds. The hermit thrush is judged by some to have the most melodious song of all Canadian birds. Thrushes can be arboreal or terrestrial. They are usually solitary or in pairs, although they flock readily during the nonbreeding season and during MIGRATIONS. Insects and other small invertebrates are main food, but small fruits and berries are eaten in season. For nesting, thrushes construct an open cup, often reinforced with a rim of mud, lined with grass or leaves. It is placed on the ground or in a bush or tree. Thrushes lay 2-6 eggs, which may be white, greenish to bluish white or olive green. Eggs may be speckled. Both parents incubate eggs and take care of young until they leave the nest. HENRI OUELLET

Thule Culture, 1000-1600 AD, represents the expansion of Alaskan Eskimos across arctic Canada about 1000 AD and the gradual displacement of the DORSET Paleoeskimos who occupied the area previously. Thule people brought with them a sophisticated sea-hunting technology that had been developed in the Bering Sea area. They hunted animals as large as bowhead whales and were able to store sufficient food to allow winter occupation of permanent villages composed of houses built from stone, whalebones and turf. Most Thule artifacts were made from bone, antler, ivory and wood; they used

few stone tools, preferring cutting edges of metal obtained either from natural deposits or from Greenlandic Norse. Thule economy declined with deteriorating climatic conditions after about 1600 AD, but the people continued to occupy arctic Canada and are directly ancestral to the historic INUIT. ROBERT MCGHEE

Reading: Robert McGhee, *Canadian Arctic Prehistory* (1978).

Thunder Bay, Ont, pop 112 468 (1981c), created in 1970 by the amalgamation of the cities of Fort William and Port Arthur and the adjacent townships of Neebing and McIntyre, is located in the NW part of the province on the W shore of the LAKE SUPERIOR bay of the same name. Its physical and economic hinterland is dominated

by the rocks, lakes and forests of the Canadian SHIELD.

Settlement The area has been inhabited for 10 000 years, originally by Paleo-Indian hunters and at the time of the first European contact by OJIBWA. The bay's name refers to the thunderbird of Indian folklore. DULHUT built Ft Caministigoyan beside the Kaministikwia R in 1679, and the fort was used by French traders until the route was abandoned in favour of the GRAND PORTAGE. Permanent settlement on Thunder Bay was established only in 1803 with the construction of the North West Co's FORT WILLIAM.

Development Between 1805 and 1821, Ft William was the most important settlement in the interior of N America as the centre of the NWC

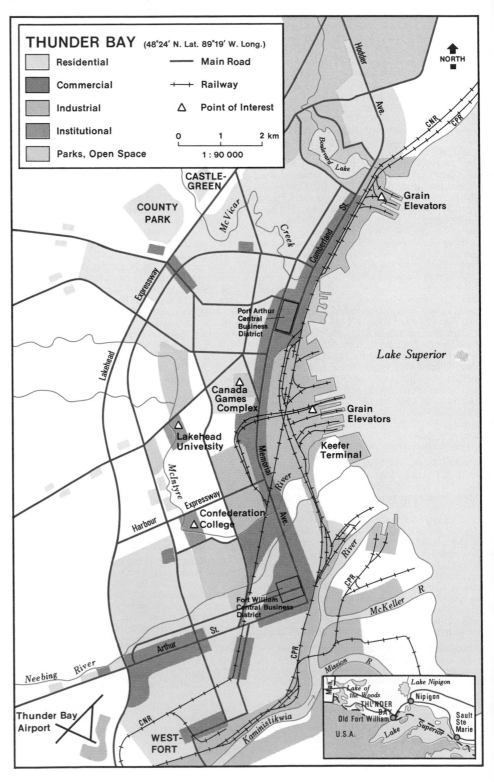

THUNDER BAY (48°24' N. Lat. 89°19' W. Long.)

Residential		Main Road
Commercial		Railway
Industrial		△ Point of Interest
Institutional		
Parks, Open Space		

0   1   2 km
1 : 90 000

Population: 112 486 (1981c); 121 379 (CMA)

Rate of Increase (1971-81): (City) 3.75%; (CMA) 5.83%

Rank in Canada: Twenty-second (by CMA)

Date of Incorporation: Thunder Bay, 1970;
Port Arthur, 1907;
Fort William, 1907

Land Area: 323.5 km²

Elevation: 183 m (harbour); 488 m (Mt McKay)

Climate: Average daily temp, July 17.5°C, Jan -14.8°C;
Yearly precip 738 mm; Hours of sunshine 2161
per year

fur-trading empire. Its importance declined, but settlement persisted until in 1870 it was joined by Prince Arthur's Landing several km NE, at the E end of the Dawson Road. Better docking facilities and the discovery of silver allowed the landing to outpace its older neighbour, but in 1875 new life was injected into the latter when the construction of the transcontinental railway commenced at Fort William. The mutual hostility and suspicion engendered by that event continued for nearly a century. The landing was incorporated as the town of Port Arthur in 1884, Ft William in 1892, and both settlements were granted civic charters in 1907. The 2 cities developed similarly but separately until 1970 when under pressure from the provincial government they were incorporated as the city of Thunder Bay.

Cityscape Thunder Bay occupies the floodplains of the lower Kaministikwia, Neebing and McIntyre rivers, the former shorelines of Lk Superior to the NE and the higher ground of the Port Arthur Hills. To the S rises Mt McKay, and E, across the bay, stands the impressive rock formation of Nanibijou, the Sleeping Giant. Amalgamation produced a city with 2 downtown core areas, each with its adjacent older residential districts, but both continue to suffer economically in competition with suburban malls. Since the 1960s, the city has spread W into the 2 incorporated rural townships. Industrial land is concentrated along the waterfront and the Westfort and Intercity areas, with Balmoral Industrial Park created in the mid-1970s to encourage the establishment of new light industries.

Population In keeping with the frontier nature of the economy, the late 19th-century pioneer population of the Lakehead communities fluctuated wildly in response to changing employment opportunities in railway construction, shipping and silver mining. From about

Thunder Bay, Ont (*photo by Con Stefurak*).

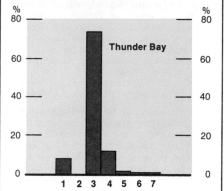

Distribution of Industrial Activity* by Industry Grouping within Census Metropolitan Areas, 1980

Thunder Bay

Industry groupings
1. Food and beverage and tobacco products industries
2. Leather, textile, knitting mills and clothing industries
3. Wood, furniture and fixtures, paper and allied and printing, publishing and allied industries
4. Machinery, transportation equipment and electrical products industries
5. Primary metal and metal fabricating industries
6. Rubber and plastic products, petroleum and coal products and chemical products industries
7. Non-metallic mineral products and miscellaneous manufacturing industries.

* Industry activity based on the average of percentage shares of the value shipments of goods of own manufacture, total value added and total number of employees for each of the selected metropolitan areas.

Source: Figure II, Catalogue 31-209, Statistics Canada.

3000 inhabitants each in the late 1890s, the 2 cities grew rapidly up to 1914, with Ft William in the lead. At amalgamation, each had close to 50 000 inhabitants and since then growth has been slow. Early settlement was essentially Anglo-Saxon and that group controlled the city's economic and political establishment until WWII. Major concentrations of Ukrainians and Italians occur in Ft William, whereas in Port Arthur and adjacent McIntyre the main immi-

grant group is Finnish. Polish, Scandinavian, Slovakian, Greek, German and Dutch groups also have strong cultural identities. Since the 1960s, there has been little direct immigration from Europe, but Chinese and East Indians moved into the community in increasing numbers in the 1970s.

Economy and Labour Force The economy of Thunder Bay continues to be based on natural-resource extraction, processing and transportation. The forest industry, with woodlands operations, pulp-and-paper mills, and wood-processing plants, is the largest industrial employer. Forest products, coal, iron ore, potash and sulphur are exported through Thunder Bay harbour, but grain predominates in the world's largest grain-handling facility, with its 15 terminal elevators capable of cleaning and storing 2.2 million t of grain. Secondary industries include railcar construction, brewing and the manufacture of bricks and clothing. Administrative and service functions employ a large proportion of the labour force, and the tourist industry caters to as many as 250 000 summer visitors, with others drawn in winter to the 7 ski areas around the city. This diversity and the city's dominant position in the grain trade maintain a certain buoyancy during periodic fluctuations in the resource industries.

Transportation Ft William was the very hub of the fur-trade route to the NW. It gained new importance in 1885 when the CANADIAN PACIFIC RY was completed, and a steadily increasing flow of western grain came into the Lakehead for shipment E. With the completion of the CANADIAN NORTHERN RY (1902), Thunder Bay became one of the world's largest grain ports. Lakehead harbour benefited from the opening of the ST LAWRENCE SEAWAY (1959) and the Keefer Terminal, a lake and ocean freight-handling dock (1962); despite the disruption of the freeze up, it remains the third-busiest port in Canada. CP, CN and Via Rail link Thunder Bay to the national rail network and the Trans-Canada Hwy offers first-class road communication. Air Canada, Nordair, Norontair and Austin Airways provide national and regional air services.

Government and Politics The present municipal government is headed by a city council elected every 2 years, consisting of a mayor (elected at large) and 12 aldermen (from 7 wards). Council policies are administered by 27 departments, including the second-largest independent telephone system in Canada. The city also participates in the Lakehead Region Conservation Authority. The public and separate school boards have their administrative offices in the city with jurisdiction extending into the adjacent rural municipalities.

Cultural Life Post-secondary education is provided by Confederation College of Applied Arts and Technology and LAKEHEAD UNIVERSITY. Various ethnic groups promote an annual multicultural festival and support a variety of cultural organizations. The Thunder Bay Symphony Orchestra and Chorus and the Fort William Male Choir, along with local amateur and professional theatre groups, provide regular music and drama. Local history is kept alive at the Thunder Bay Historical Museum and at Old Fort William. There are 2 daily and 2 weekly newspapers (one in Finnish).

City teams have won national titles in hockey and curling, and the city has hosted the Ontario Winter Games (1976), the Canadian Figure Skating Championships (1980), several World Cup ski-jumping meets and, in 1981, the Canada Summer Games, which left the city a $7.5-million multi-sport complex. DAVID D. KEMP

Thunderbird, a supernatural creature prominent in Northwest Coast Indian myths. Thunder and lightning are attributed to the thunderbird, which produces thunder by flapping its wings and lightning by opening and closing its eyes. The thunderbird is said to hunt whales, using its wings to shoot arrows. Among some Plains Indians, thunderstorms are a contest between the thunderbird and a huge rattlesnake. Individuals who had been struck by lightning and survived often became SHAMANS, for they had received the power of the monster bird.   RENÉ R. GADACZ

Thunderstorm, a towering CLOUD system that moves across the countryside accompanied by LIGHTNING, thunder activity and usually RAIN showers, together with gusty WINDS near the Earth's surface. Other possible components of the storm system are HAIL, occasionally, and TORNADOES, rarely. Thunderstorms typically occur on summer afternoons. While a thunderstorm typically affects a given locality for only an hour or so during its passage overhead, the entire lifetime may be as long as 6-10 hours, along a pathway of several hundred kilometres.

While single thunderstorms may be produced on any reasonably warm, sunny day, the more intense ones frequently occur as a line of such storms (squall line) associated with the passage of a cold front (*see* METEOROLOGY). When particularly intense, one or more tornadoes may be formed along the thunderstorm squall line. Thunderstorms occur most frequently in late afternoon but they have been observed at all hours of the day and night. They are prevalent from late May to early Sept, peaking in July, and are rare in Dec to Mar. The settled parts of southern Canada have some 10-25 thunderstorm days per year, with the greatest frequency averaging 30-35 in Ontario. Thunderstorms are rare on the West Coast and in Newfoundland, under 5 per year; their frequency also falls off rapidly north of 55° N to only 2-3 per year over most of the NWT.   J. MAYBANK

Thurston, Frank Russel, aircraft engineer (b at Chicago, Ill 5 Dec 1914). Thurston's British parents took him at age one to England, where he worked from 1937 at the National Physical Laboratory. He was recruited by the NATIONAL RESEARCH COUNCIL in 1947, one of hundreds of British engineers brought to Canada to develop the postwar aircraft industry. He became head of the NRC's Structures Laboratory and in 1959 director of the National Aeronautical Establishment, charged with finding a new industrial role for the NAE, after the cancellation of the AVRO ARROW project. This was done by developing new installations for low-speed aerodynamics, useful in fields from short takeoff and landing aircraft to urban planning. Before retirement in 1979, Thurston was chairman of the NATO Advisory Group for Aerospace Research and Development and organized development of the CANADARM used by US space shuttles.   DONALD J.C. PHILLIPSON

Tibetans Following a Chinese invasion in 1959, the Dalai Lama and 100 000 of his followers fled Tibet. In 1962 the Tibetan Refugee Aid Society (TRAS) was founded in Vancouver. Devoted first to relief and then to rehabilitation, TRAS (with the aid of CIDA from 1970 onwards) collaborated with European agencies in the resettlement of thousands of Tibetans in craft communities in the Himalayas and large agricultural settlements in Mysore. In 1971-72, 228 Tibetan refugees emigrated to Canada under a special arrangement between the Canadian government and the Dalai Lama. Since 1973 very few Tibetans have emigrated. Tibetans settled across Canada, but primarily in Ontario, Québec and BC. They have worked on farms, in factories, grocery stores, the construction industry, and as school janitors. In Toronto they have joined forces with the Asian community, but have also established their own societies in Toronto and Montréal and published a newsletter. While largely assimilated into Canadian society,

they retain their language and pledge their religious adherence to the Dalai Lama, who paid a pastoral visit to Canada in 1980. In a less direct way, Tibetan influence has spread in Canada through the establishment of meditation centres and other institutions in various centres, from Victoria to Montréal, devoted to spreading Mahayanist Buddhist doctrines as taught by Tibetan lamas. Two of the most important of these leaders, Karmapa (head of the Kargyupa sect) and Sakya Trizin (head of the Sakya sect) have visited Canada to further the spread of Buddhist *dharma* in this country.   GEORGE WOODCOCK

Tick, common name for bloodsucking parasites of vertebrates (mainly of terrestrial mammals and birds) belonging to class ARACHNIDA, order Acari. About 800 species are known worldwide; the 35 species in Canada are found in all areas S of TREELINE. Among the largest of Acari, ticks are 1-5 mm long when unfed, up to 30 mm when fully gorged. Ticks are distinguished by their highly modified mouthparts, used in piercing and attaching to hosts, and by a specialized sensory structure (Haller's organ) near the tip of each first leg, used in locating hosts. In Canada, ticks are important pests of humans, livestock and game animals. Members of genus *Dermacentor* sometimes cause serious loss of cattle from tick paralysis, a condition the ticks cause by feeding on the cattle, not by transmitting disease. Ticks may transmit Rocky Mountain spotted fever, tularemia and several viruses, but fortunately, the strains in Canada are usually not of serious medical or veterinary importance.   EVERT E. LINDQUIST

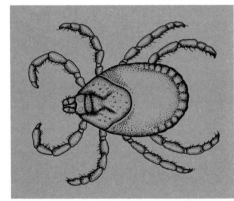

Female Rocky Mountain wood tick (*Dermacentor andersoni*) (*artwork by Shirley Stacey*).

Tidal Energy is a largely untapped, renewable ENERGY source based on lunar gravitation rather than solar radiation. The potential of tidal HYDROELECTRICITY has long been recognized. However, compared to river dams, tidal-power projects are very expensive, since massive structures must be built in a difficult saltwater environment. The relatively low head of water above the turbines restricts the capacity of individual generators to about 25-50 megawatts (MW = 10^6 watts); therefore, many machines are needed to produce a significant block of power. The machinery also has to withstand the rigours of saltwater operation. For all this investment, the average ELECTRIC POWER output is severely limited by the twice-daily ebb and flow of tides: average output of tidal electricity is less than 40% of the installed generating capacity; production of power from river dams typically averages 70-100% of installed capacity. Finally the lunar cycle of 24 hours 50 minutes means the raw production of tidal energy moves in and out of phase with the normal, solar-oriented daily pattern of electrical consumption. Unlike the energy from river dams, the daily, monthly and annual availability of tidal energy is fully predictable, but it must be either stored or inte-

grated with other sources of generation that can be adjusted to accommodate the fluctuations of tidal generation.

There are relatively few coastal locations in the world where the tidal range (ie, the difference between high and low tides) is large enough to justify exploitation of the available tidal energy. Not only must there exist a sufficiently high tidal range (at least 5 m) for construction of an economically feasible plant, but the site should also include a natural bay which can store a large volume of seawater at high tide and be so situated within the estuary that the operation of the plant will not change significantly the tidal resonant system (*see* TIDE). The location of the plant could reduce the tidal range (lowering the potential head of water available for actuating the turbines), and therefore its electrical-energy output, or the location could increase the tidal range.

The world's most powerful tides occur in the upper reaches of the Bay of FUNDY, where they may attain a range of up to 17 m. UNGAVA BAY and estuaries along the coast of BC also exhibit fairly high tides. The coasts of Argentina, NW Australia, Brazil, France, India, Korea, the UK, the USSR and the American states of California, Maine and Alaska possess coastal configurations and sufficiently large tidal ranges to provide sites at which potentially large sources of tidal energy may be exploited. Current estimates of the total capacity of all potential tidal-power sites in the world are about one billion kilowatts, with an expected electrical-energy output of 2-3 trillion kilowatt-hours annually, ie, 10 times Canada's present combined electrical output.

The idea of exploiting the energy of the tides is not new. Tidal mills were built in Britain, France and Spain as early as the 12th century. A mill powered partially by tidal energy was built at PORT-ROYAL, NS, in 1607. These early mills extracted only the equivalent of 20-75 kW, or less than the power available in modern compact cars. As industrial-scale power-generation technology concentrated on river hydro power and fossil-fueled conversions to electricity, tidal mills became obsolete. A few of the early mills are now preserved as historic sites.

Canadian Installations Detailed studies of the Bay of Fundy tidal-power resource concluded that the most efficient scheme of development would be one that would generate power for a period of about 4 hours, twice daily, on the ebb tide. The most cost-effective project was found to be a site in Cobequid Bay at the upper end of the Bay of Fundy. This development would have a capacity in excess of 4800 MW, an amount equal to the entire 1980 installed generating capacity of the Maritime power systems. The cost of the development was estimated in 1982 at $22-25 billion on the basis of coming into service in 1995. Such a project would be very difficult to finance. The more modest alternative project, at a site in Cumberland Basin through which the NB-NS border passes, has been projected at approximately 1150 MW, one-quarter the capacity of the larger site, but one-third the capital cost. While it is forecast that the local Maritime power systems would be able to absorb its output, the huge capital investment required for even this smaller project makes the financial considerations discouraging. However, a small, 20 MW, single-unit power station has been constructed by the NS Power Commission on a tidal reach of the Annapolis R, near ANNAPOLIS, NS. This project was undertaken primarily to demonstrate the application of a particular type of turbine generator (trade-name Straflo) for tidal and other low-head hydro applications. At the estimated cost of $48 million, this development would not have been an economically viable component of the NSPC power system without a $25-million federal grant in

Annapolis tidal power plant, officially opened Aug 1984, is the first in the Western Hemisphere to transform tidal energy into electrical energy; photo taken at the completion of construction, with dredge and erection crane still in position (*courtesy Tidal Power Corp*).

support of its demonstration aspect, including Canadian manufacture of the turbine-generator equipment. The Straflo machine differs from the conventional hydroelectric turbine-generator set up in that the turbine and generator are integral rather than separate units. The average tidal range in Annapolis Basin is only about 6.4 m, but the plant, in which only one large turbine (7.6 m diameter) is installed, will produce about 50 million kW-hours annually for the electrical-utility system of NS.

Technology River hydro power and tidal power have many characteristics in common, but forces involved are fundamentally different: terrestrial gravitation causes water to flow downward on the Earth's surface, while the upward-acting lunar gravitation causes water to oscillate in estuaries. There is often a tendency to ignore this dissimilarity and to treat tidal-electric developments simply as low-head hydroelectric developments with added complications. The most practical scheme for harnessing tidal energy is still the old tidal-mill concept, closing off an estuary or tidal basin from the sea with a structure composed of a powerhouse, a sluiceway section and a solid embankment section. The sluiceways are closed at high tide and the ebbing sea level causes a head differential between the basin level and the sea. When this differential becomes large enough, flow is permitted through the turbo-generators until the difference in levels becomes too low to drive the turbines. When the tide begins to turn and the sea level to rise, the sluiceways are then opened once more, so that the tidal basin can be filled for the next cycle of electrical generation. These cycles take place about twice a day (2 flood tides and 2 ebb tides during each lunar day). This simple, single-basin setup with generation from the basin to the sea is known as single-effect operation. Using new technology, turbines can be built to generate electricity in both directions and also to operate as pumps in both directions, a flexibility that is extremely useful in tidal-power developments. Now a single-basin tidal-power station can be designed to generate electricity not only on the ebb tide but on the flood tide as well. It is obvious that the output from a single-basin plant is intermittent, but in the latter case it would produce 4 "slugs" of energy daily rather than the 2 slugs produced by a single-effect station. Modern large power systems can readily absorb the intermittent output of a tidal plant. The output from conventional fossil-fueled generating stations can be reduced when the tidal plant begins generation and it can be brought back into the system during the few hours that a tidal plant must remain idle. In this way, large savings in coal and oil can result and pollutants from such fuels be substantially reduced.

The NS government expects that tidal power will, in the long run, provide useful energy for the province and for export. However, because of uncertainties about the costs and the markets

for this power, only the Annapolis Royal pilot project is included in the NS electric-generation expansion program. Tidal power has also been considered by both the NB and BC governments, but is not included in either province's planning. The National Energy Board did not include tidal power in its 1981 estimates of Canadian energy supply and demand for the years 1980-2000 because it considered that the case for early development of tidal power in Canada has not yet been established.   R.H. CLARK
Reading: R.H. Charlier, *Tidal Energy* (1982).

Tide Although tides exist in the atmosphere and the solid earth as well as in the OCEAN, only the ocean tide reveals itself in everyday experience. It is seen as a regular oscillation in WATER levels and in speed and direction of ocean currents. Tides originate with the gravitational forces of the MOON and SUN (*see* ASTRONOMY). Earth is actually not in orbit around the sun, but around the centre of mass of the Earth-sun system. Since all parts of the Earth move in the same orbit, they experience the same acceleration, but only at the Earth's centre is this acceleration exactly balanced by the sun's gravitation. On the side near the sun, gravitation is greater; thus things (eg, water) tend to move toward the sun and away from the Earth's centre. On the side away from the sun, gravitation is less and things tend to move away from the sun and away from the Earth's centre. The unbalanced portion of the gravitation causes level surfaces to bulge outward on the sides of the Earth toward and away from the sun, and these 2 bulges pass around the Earth once each day as the Earth rotates on its axis. Earth is also in orbit around the centre of mass of the Earth-moon system; consequently, tidal bulges also occur on the sides of the Earth toward and away from the moon. Because the sun is farther away, its tidal effect is only 0.46 that of the moon. When the sun or moon are off the equator, one bulge will be N and one S of the equator, and the 2 will not be experienced equally, except on the equator. This imbalance causes the diurnal inequality in the semidiurnal tides. At new and full moons, the lunar and solar bulges nearly coincide, causing tides of large range, called spring tides. At the moon's first and last quarters, the lunar bulges fall near the solar hollows, causing tides of small range, called neap tides. Tides also tend to have greater range when the moon is closest to Earth (perigean tides).

The range of a tide is the vertical distance between high water and the succeeding low water. Flood is horizontal flow in the landward (upstream) direction; ebb is flow in the seaward (downstream) direction. Slack water is the short period of rest as the flow reverses from flood to ebb, or vice versa. The interval between slack water and high water or low water may vary from place to place, but in most coastal regions slack waters occur near the times of high water and low water. A tide is semidiurnal when it exhibits 2 high waters and 2 low waters in a lunar day (about 25 solar hours), diurnal when it exhibits only one of each. Most tides are intermediate, with 2 daily tides differing from each other in height and range, the difference being called the diurnal inequality. A tidal bore, a tumbling wall of water moving upriver with the advancing tide, is sometimes formed when the tide rises rapidly at the entrance to a shallow, gently sloping river. Bores occur in several rivers off the Bay of FUNDY, the best known being that in the Petitcodiac R, NB. A tide race is a rapid flow of water through a narrow passage, driven by the rising or falling tide at one end. The Reversing Falls at Saint John, NB, is a tide race, flowing in on the rising and out on the falling tide (*see* WATERFALL). A tide rip is a patch of rough water formed when wind-generated ocean waves run up against a tidal flow in the

opposite direction. The waves pile up on each other, steepen and break in what can be violent turmoil.

While tidal forces originate in the gravitational influences of heavenly bodies, the tides themselves propagate as long waves, experiencing reflection and amplification or attenuation along their paths. Thus the character of the tide may differ from that of the tidal forces at the same location. The large ranges in the eastern Arctic result from tidal energy propagated in from the Atlantic Ocean, and the large Bay of Fundy tide is the result of resonance in the Bay of Fundy-Gulf of Maine system. The latter tidal range, reaching over 17 m, is the most remarkable in Canada and probably the world. The tide at Victoria, BC, is seen to have more diurnal inequality than that at Halifax, NS, although both locations have nearly the same latitude and thus experience almost the same tidal forces. Because of these differences, tides can be predicted for a site only after sufficient observations have been obtained to define the local tidal character in astronomical terms. Small tides (about 5 cm) occur in the Great Lakes, and a tidal flow of up to one knot has been observed in Little Current Channel, Lk Huron. The study of tides in Canada began in 1893, when the Canadian Tidal Survey was established. Its first director, W.B. DAWSON, was responsible for setting up a network of tidal stations on the Atlantic Coast and in the Gulf of ST LAWRENCE, and for prompting tidal studies on the East and West coasts. The tidal-station network has continued to expand and is now maintained by the Dept of Fisheries and Oceans. *See* TIDAL ENERGY.   W.D. FORRESTER
Reading: W.D. Forrester, *The Canadian Tidal Manual* (1983); G. Godin, *The Analysis of Tides* (1972).

Tidnish, NS, UP, pop 165 (1981c), is located on Northumberland Str about 25 km NE of AMHERST, near the NB border. The name, derived from a Micmac word, probably means "a paddle." The community was to have been the eastern terminus of the Chignecto ship railway begun in the 1890s. The railway was never completed, and Tidnish missed out on the population and economic boost it would have experienced. The picturesque stone bridge of the ship railway still stands, a landmark of Cumberland County. Tidnish used to support a flourishing if relatively small fishery, a small shipyard on the NB side of the community at Tidnish Bridge and several sawmills. All of these industries have since failed. Some small farms remain, but today Tidnish is principally a cottage area.   JANICE MILTON

Tiktak, John, sculptor (b at Kareak, a small camp between Eskimo Point and Whale Cove, NWT 1916; d at Rankin Inlet, NWT 1981). At first a hunter, he moved to Rankin Inlet in 1958 to work at the nickel mine. The mine closed in 1962, and he took up carving "professionally" in 1963, having previously carved "small sculptures representing Eskimo faces" that he sold as souvenirs. His work, dating back to 1961, is in every museum and major private collection of INUIT ART. His personal style, with its rounded shapes and hollows, has definite affinity with Henry Moore, who admired Tiktak's work greatly. Like Moore, he is an icon maker, producing form and symbols rather than subject matter. He was elected to the Royal Canadian Academy of Arts in 1973.   GEORGE SWINTON

Tilley, Leonard Percy de Wolfe, lawyer, premier of NB (b at Ottawa 21 May 1870; d at Saint John 28 Dec 1947). Tilley, son of Sir Samuel Leonard TILLEY, began his career as a lawyer in Saint John and served as an MLA for 9 years before being appointed minister without portfolio in 1925 and president of the Executive Council under J.B.M. BAXTER. In 1931 he was appointed minister of lands and mines and 2 years later became premier. His government was defeated in 1935 and he was appointed exchequer court judge and judge of the county court, a position he held for 10 years. Unlike his esteemed father, Tilley is remembered for little more than holding office during the Depression and leading his party to defeat in 1935.   ARTHUR T. DOYLE

Tilley, Sir Samuel Leonard, politician (b at Gagetown, NB 8 May 1818; d at Saint John 25 June 1896). Tilley got his start in a Saint John drugstore, and eventually went into partnership with his mother's relations in that business. He sat in the NB Assembly in 1850-51, 1854-56, 1857-65, 1866-67. A lifelong temperance advocate, he was provincial secretary in the Charles FISHER regime. Its members were called the "Smashers" after having tried unsuccessfully to bring prohibition in NB in 1851-52 and 1855-56. Tilley actively promoted railway development and CONFEDERATION. A delegate to the Charlottetown and Québec conferences, he and his government were defeated on Confederation in NB in 1865, but were returned to power in 1866 after what amounted to a coup d'état by the lieutenant-governor, Arthur Gordon. In 1867 Tilley became minister of customs in Sir John A. MACDONALD's first government. With the fall of Macdonald, 5 Nov 1873, Tilley was appointed, that same day, lieutenant-governor of NB. With Macdonald's return to office in 1878, Tilley became minister of finance, and as such brought in the NATIONAL POLICY tariff in 1879. In 1885, unwell, he retired to Government House, Fredericton, staying on as lieutenant-governor until 1893. Clever and adroit, he was always a sensitive political barometer, and he advised Macdonald in 1868 to pacify NS. Tilley was uneasy about the government's commitments to the CPR in the 1880s, and doubtless would have pulled the plug had he been allowed to do so. Almost the last letter he wrote (sent to Sir Charles TUPPER) was a remarkably shrewd assessment of the 1896 election.   P.B. WAITE

Reading: W.S. MacNutt, *New Brunswick* (1967); P.B. Waite, *The Life and Times of Confederation* (1962); and *Canada 1874-1896: Arduous Destiny* (1971).

Timber Axe Two basic types of axe were used in the early 19th-century eastern forest industry. The more common poll axe had a single, fanshaped cutting edge, a narrow head weighing 1.5-2.5 kg, and a hickory or maple handle. It was used for felling, scoring and lopping branches off fallen trees. The large, distinctive broadaxe was used for hewing masts and square timber. Its 5 kg, 25 cm wide bevelled blade resembled a large chisel. The hewer cut down diagonally across the grain of the roughly squared baulk to leave a smooth, even surface. On the West Coast, larger double-bitted axes were used, their narrow 25 cm blades and long handles designed to fell the enormous trees of the Pacific slope. Smaller double-bitted axes were used in eastern pulpwood operations; they were also common in the square timber trade: one bit was used for felling and the other for clearing out stumps and roots on skid roads. By the late 19th century the crosscut saw had largely replaced the axe for felling trees. *See* TIMBER TRADE HISTORY; FORESTRY; TOOLS, CARPENTRY.   GRAEME WYNN

Timber Duties First imposed in the 18th century to provide revenue, Britain's tariffs on imported wood were an integral component of the 19th-century British North American TIMBER TRADE. As duties increased 1803-11, in order to replenish depleted treasury coffers and in response to Napoleon's Continental Blockade, Britain established a protected market for colonial producers. With Napoleon's defeat in 1815, colonial preference was attacked by Baltic timber interests and a growing free-trade lobby. Committees in 1820 and 1821 reduced the foreign-colonial differentials without removing the

after-freight advantage they gave colonial wood. During the 1830s economic uncertainty increased the instability of the colonial trade. After Britain moved toward free trade in 1842, the colonial timber preference was halved within 2 years. Imports of wood from BNA lost ground to Baltic shipments after 1850, but despite the gloomy forebodings of colonial timber interests, the transatlantic trade was not eliminated by these changes. By 1860 foreign and colonial wood paid the same low rate and in 1866 Britain abolished the duties. Although the preference may have been essential to the establishment of N American trade, its continued high level through the 1830s probably inflated the price of wood in Britain.   GRAEME WYNN

Timber Slide, water-filled chute or runway built to carry RAFTS of timber around rapids and falls; similar devices for individual pieces of wood were called "flumes." Ruggles Wright of Hull claimed to have built the first Canadian slide in 1829. Built of wood and designed to spread the river's fall over a kilometre or more, slides quickened the drive, lessened chances of a jam and reduced damage. Most common in the Ottawa Valley, slides were originally private toll-levying facilities. By 1846 public slides were operating as far up the Ottawa as Calumet Lk, and by 1870 the Canadian government maintained many public slides to facilitate the Ottawa valley TIMBER TRADE. In 1860 the Prince of Wales (later Edward VII) rode down a timber slide during his visit to BNA.   GRAEME WYNN

Timber Trade History Wood was the great staple of Canadian trade for much of the 19th century. Founded upon European demand, the timber trade brought investment and immigration to eastern Canada; it fostered economic development; and it transformed the regional environment far more radically than did the earlier exploitation of fish and fur (*see* FISHERIES HISTORY; FUR TRADE). It encouraged the building of towns and villages, the opening of roads and EXPLORATION. It also contributed at times to economic instability. BUSINESS-CYCLE swings produced wide fluctuations in the demand for, and the price of, wood; and weather conditions, commercial uncertainties and imperfect market intelligence magnified these difficulties.

Wood entered 19th-century trade in many forms. Large masts, cut for the Royal Navy from the finest trees of the mixed forest that swept through the Maritimes and the St Lawrence Valley, were the most valuable commercial product of British North American forests, which also produced shingles, barrel staves, box shooks and, later, spoolwood for textile factories. But sawn lumber and square timber were the major wood staples. Lumber, the product of SAWMILLS, was prepared mostly as deals (rough pieces of wood at least 12' long, 7" wide and 2½" thick, or about 366 x 18 x 6 cm), planks and boards. Square timber, known in the Maritimes as "ton timber," were baulks or "sticks" of wood hewn square with axes and shipped to England,

where they were often resawn. Strict specifications governed the market; a "wane" (bevel) and slight taper were allowed, but they varied according to the stick's dimensions and changed with time. Waste was considerable: 25-30% of each tree was discarded.

The naval mast trade, always limited by its specialized and high quality requirements, shifted from the Saint John to the St Lawrence Valley early in the 19th century when contractors sought oak, as well as pine, from the deciduous forests of the southern Great Lakes area. The square timber industry developed rapidly to meet the enormous demand from Britain, which was at war with Napoleonic France and was also undergoing industrialization. The transatlantic timber trade, fostered by economic and strategic imperatives, was quickly sheltered by TIMBER DUTIES when Napoleon's 1806 blockade of Britain's traditional supply areas in northern Europe drove domestic prices up some 300% in 2 years. On average, 9000 loads (almost 1.5 m³ each) of colonial timber entered Britain annually between 1802 and 1805; in 1807 the total was 27 000, 2 years later 90 000, over 500 000 in 1840 and 750 000 in 1846. Thereafter imports fluctuated for 20 years around 600 000 loads and then declined until WWI.

The pattern of the lumber trade is less easily summarized, since international markets were widely separated. Beginning in the 1830s, increasing quantities of lumber were shipped to Britain, there was a growing trade between the Canadas and the US, and many mixed cargoes of lumber and small wood products left the Maritimes for the West Indies. During the period of RECIPROCITY with the US and the construction of railways and canals, the importance of the American market grew; 400 million board feet of BNA lumber passed through Oswego, NY, 1864-66, and wood exports to the US from the PROVINCE OF CANADA were worth almost $7 million in 1866-67. But until the 1880s combined lumber and timber sales to Britain were more valuable than those to the US. Not until 1905, with imports of some $18 million, did the US account for more than half of Canadian forest-product exports.

Although small quantities of BIRCH, white OAK, rock ELM, ASH, basswood and butternut were squared, some CEDAR was cut, and SPRUCE and HEMLOCK lumber increased in importance after mid-century, PINE was the industry's major species. Its exploitation rapidly encompassed a wide area. By 1810 only the fringes of New Brunswick's pine forests had been cut, and the Ottawa-Gatineau confluence marked the inland limit of lumbering in BNA. By 1835 barely a tributary of the Miramichi, Saint John and Ottawa rivers remained unexploited. By 1850 much of the pine had been harvested from the more accessible reaches of these river systems, and trade from many small ports and coastal inlets had ceased. Railways broke the industry's dependence on water courses for the movement of wood to markets and opened the backcountry of lakes Ontario and Erie to the trade. Exports from the Peterborough area increased fivefold when the railway arrived in 1854; between 1851 and 1861, Simcoe County rose from insignificance to pre-eminence among lumber producers in Canada West. Mills proliferated along railways pushing northward into the Canadian SHIELD.

This onslaught on the forest only slowly came under government control. Initially BNA forests were ineffectively protected by the imperial "broad arrow" system, implemented in N America early in the 18th century to reserve valuable trees for the Royal Navy. As demand rose after 1806, crown reserves were violated; surveyors appointed to protect them profited from the administrative confusion. In 1824 in New Brunswick and 1826 in Upper and Lower Canada, a

Lumbermen's shanty, Upper Ottawa River, in 1871 (*courtesy Notman Photographic Archives*).

coherent regulatory system was established. In BNA provinces except Nova Scotia, the sale of licences conferred a temporary right to cut trees and returned revenue to the government. Periodic amendments attempted to limit the illegal cutting and trespassing that vexed administrators intent on maximizing revenues, but the basic principles of crown ownership and leasehold tenure of the resource were upheld. In marked contrast to the American pattern, present-day Canadian (with the exception of NS) forest law — shaped by the interplay of tradition, self-interest, and the limitations of a vast and hostile environment — has preserved something of the 18th-century conservative idea of how the state should serve the common good.

Logging was essentially a wintertime occupation, beginning with the first snowfall. In the fall loggers would build camps (see SHANTY) and clear rough roads for hauling hay and provisions and for moving logs or timber to the streams. The industry depended heavily on the muscles of men and beasts. Trees were normally felled with various types of TIMBER AXES (until the 1870s, when the crosscut saw became more common), and "bucked" to stick length with a crosscut saw. Timber was squared by axemen: the log was "lined" along 2 sides to mark the dimensions of the desired square; "scorers" then removed the unwanted outside wood in rough slabs, and the sides of the log were rough-hewn and then smooth-hewn with broad-axes. The log was rolled through 90° and lined, scored and hewn on the remaining 2 sides of the square. Before transportation the ends of the stick were trimmed to a pyramid shape. A snow road eased the hauling of logs and baulks to riverbanks by oxen and later horses. With the coming of the thaw, the timber drive began. Men equipped with "jam dogs" (iron hooks), canthooks or PEAVEYS, and often immersed in chilly water, engaged in the hectic and dangerous task of floating the cut out on the freshet. When more open water was reached, or where falls and rapids could be bypassed by TIMBER SLIDES, logs and timber were assembled into RAFTS to continue downstream to mills or rivermouth booms (especially at Québec, Saint John and the mouth of the Miramichi R), where they were shipped abroad. As steampower replaced water power in sawmills, it increased mill capacity and extended the season of mill operation, but did not break the pattern of winter logging. Although railways reduced the industry's dependence on rivers to transport timber to the mills, their initial importance was in carrying lumber from mill to market; by the end of the century, specialized logging railways still made only a slight impact on eastern Canadian operations.

Before 1825 most BNA timber was produced by small-scale independent operators, many of them farmers who were attracted to the work in their off-season. Good timber was readily available and little capital was required to enter the trade. By 1850, however, as lumbering moved into more remote areas, expenditure on the clearing of boulder-strewn streams became necessary, regulation of the crown domain tightened, more capital was invested and the declining trade intensified competition among operators, and entrepreneurs were seeking to make their positions secure. Large, diversified, integrated operations emerged, although smaller enterprises persisted on the settlement frontiers. Generally the skilled, the well capitalized and the well connected dominated the trade by acquiring licences, employing lumbering gangs under contract, building large, efficient sawmills and operating their own vessels or railways. For example, in the 1840s Joseph CUNARD and 3 branch houses of the great Scottish firm of Pollok, Gilmour and Co virtually controlled the trade of northeastern New Brunswick by these

Sinclair's Mill, Newcastle, NB c1900. The timber trade was of enormous importance to NE New Brunswick in the second half of the 19th century (courtesy Provincial Archives of New Brunswick).

means. Subsidiaries of the latter concern were also important in the St Lawrence Valley. William PRICE, "le père du Saguenay," was said to employ 1000 men in the 1830s; by 1842 he had sawmills at Chicoutimi and a steam tug to take ships up from the St Lawrence. In the Ottawa country, J.R. BOOTH's firm produced over 30 million board feet of pine lumber in the 1870s; in the next decade it built the Canada Atlantic Ry to bring out the cut from its Parry Sound licences. In Canada West the firms of Mossom Boyd and D.D. Calvin experienced similarly spectacular successes. The early diffuse and informal trade gave way to an industry dominated by relatively few well-capitalized family firms and partnerships. Thus the chronic instability of the early trade was somewhat reduced. In the 20th century, as pulp and paper production grew, capital requirements increased further. Many firms amalgamated, and joint-stock financing began to shape the patterns of corporate dominance that mark the forest industry today. Technological changes accompanied developments; long persistent patterns and practices of forest exploitation yielded to mechanization after 1875, but generally innovations gained acceptance more slowly in the forests of eastern Canada than in the rugged, newly opened areas of BC. Working and living conditions improved as city industries and West Coast logging camps competed for labour. By the end of the century, the locus of Canadian wood production had shifted westward with the opening of the CPR and the Panama Canal, the exhaustion of eastern forests and the attractions of the Cariboo GOLD RUSH.

Although James COOK's men had cut logs for masts on Vancouver I in 1778, lumbering in BC did not begin seriously until the 1850s, when former prospectors turned to BC's vast timber stands for profit. The trees were huge, some over 60 m high, and varied: DOUGLAS FIR, red cedar, Sitka spruce, hemlock and balsam fir. The construction of the CPR in the 1880s created a demand for BC wood and provided transportation to eastern markets; soon it was popular worldwide. Lumbering on the West Coast required considerable adaptation of eastern techniques: 3 times as many oxen were required; snowroads were impossible in the milder coastal climate, so skid roads had to be built of logs; cuts were made higher on the huge trunks, and a springboard was required for each of the 2 axemen to stand on; and heavy, double-bitted axes were developed. Manual logging techniques were used until about 1912; horses had replaced bulls by the 1890s, and were used until the 1920s. By far the most important innovation was the steam-powered donkey engine, introduced about 1897 from the US, which could drag logs up to 150 m. The "donkey" allowed coastal loggers to compete with those in the interior, where smaller trees and general conditions more closely resembled those of eastern Canada. An-

other innovation was the "high lead system," in which a line high over the skids pulled or lifted the log over obstacles. In 1910 BC production surpassed Québec's; in 1917 it surpassed the production of every other province; and by the late 1920s BC was producing half of Canada's annual cut of timber. As in the East, railways as well as waterways brought timber to mills or ports; now both use primarily trucks. FORESTRY is still a vital part of Canada's export base. See also FOREST ECONOMICS.
GRAEME WYNN

Reading: E. Gould, Logging (1976); M. Allerdale Grainger, Woodsmen of the West (1964); A.R.M. Lower, The North American Assault on the Canadian Forest (1938); D. MacKay, The Lumberjacks (1978); Graeme Wynn, Timber Colony (1981).

Time Precise timekeeping in Canada began in the middle of the 19th century as an aid to navigation on the high seas, a control for the railways and a vital assistance to WEATHER reporting. OBSERVATORIES were commissioned in Québec City, Saint John, Montréal, Toronto and Victoria. The Meteorological Service in Toronto ultimately became responsible for co-ordinating correct time. CONFEDERATION and the survey of western Canada saw the development of a new time service centered in Ottawa and the inauguration in 1905 of the Dominion Observatory. By order-in-council in 1941, the observatory was named the source of time for official purposes. In 1970 the standards of time and frequency were amalgamated under the NATIONAL RESEARCH COUNCIL OF CANADA (NRC), which then became the custodian of official time in Canada.

Enormous strides have been made in the art of timekeeping during the past few decades. Today, as a result of exploiting the properties of atoms (particularly those of cesium and hydrogen) the second can be represented with an accuracy of one part in 10^{13} or one-10-billionth of a second per day. By contrast, the most precise pendulum CLOCKS, used until the middle of the century, could be relied upon to only about 0.01 of a second per day (one part in 10 million). Time was determined by measuring the Earth's rotation, as indicated by transit observations of the stars. The primary pendulum therefore indicated sidereal or star time, which was readily translated into mean solar time for the general public. After observations with a transit telescope, the error of the clock was known with an accuracy of about 0.05 of a second. Several nights' work was required to determine the behaviour of the primary clock to within a few milliseconds (0.001 sec). Mean solar time was the best available and was assumed to be entirely uniform; hence the second was defined as 1/86 400 of the mean solar day.

Developments in ELECTRONICS and PHYSICS during the 1920s and 1930s led to the use of the piezo-electric properties of the quartz crystal to develop the quartz clock, which in 1951 replaced the pendulum at the Dominion Observatory. Concurrently the visual transit telescope gave way to the photographic zenith tube (PZT). Timed by the quartz clock, the PZT was programmed to photograph certain time stars each clear night. This new method proved to be 10 times more exact and the quartz clock ultimately became about 1000 times more precise than the pendulum. The star images produced in the PZT also yield a very precise measure of the instrument's latitude, which provides valuable information to the geophysicist as well as the time keeper. Two Canadian PZTs are in operation, in Ottawa and Calgary.

Solar Time Mean solar time suffers irregularities from 4 causes: a shift in the Earth's crust with respect to the direction of the axis of rotation, resulting in polar wander and measured as a variation in latitude; seasonal variation, a slight slowing down in late spring and a speeding up in fall; a gradual slowing, about a millisecond per century, in the Earth's rotation; random changes in the rate of the Earth's rotation. The first 2 causes are small, measurable and can be accounted for; the third is too small to be of concern; the fourth is quite unpredictable. By the 1960s Earth's rotation had slowed so that the mean solar day was 3 milliseconds longer than the average during the previous 2 centuries; hence the unit of time was not uniform.

Ephemeris time (ET) was the average solar time during the 18th and 19th centuries. Observations accumulated then formed the basis of equations of motion for members of the solar system. ET can be determined by observing the position of the MOON against the background of stars, but many observations must be combined to achieve a precision of a millisecond. In 1956 the Int Committee on Weights and Measures defined the second as 1/31 556 925.9747 of the tropical year 1900, Jan 0, 12 hours ET (ie, 12 midnight between 31/12/1899 and 1/1/1900). By this definition the second is a constant.

Cesium Clock By 1955 the first cesium frequency standard had been built at the National Physical Laboratory (NPL) in England. Such a standard is similar to a clock except that it is intended to run for brief intervals only, during which the performance of a continuously running ensemble of quartz clocks can be precisely determined and their rates adjusted. A 3-year experiment between NPL and the US Naval Observatory demonstrated that the second of ET was equal to the duration of 9 192 631 770 periods of the radiation corresponding to the transition between the 2 levels of the ground state of the cesium-133 atom. The second cesium standard, called CsI, was built at NRC in 1957, and in 1958 became the frequency reference for the quartz clocks at NRC and in the time laboratory at the Dominion Observatory. The passage of years vindicated the evaluation of the atomic second, which in 1967 was adopted by the General Committee on Weights and Measures as the official unit of time in the international system (SI) of units (*see* WEIGHTS AND MEASURES).

Further NRC research into the properties of cesium frequency standards resulted in the development of CsIII (1965), CsV (1970) and 3 CsVI clocks (1976). CsI and CsIII are frequency standards; the others are real clocks operating continuously with an accuracy of about 1 x 10^{-13} and a stability of few parts in 10^{14}. CsV, which in 1975 started operating as the world's first primary clock, is the official basis for time in Canada and an important contributor to the exact determination of international atomic time. Research into a more compact design resulted in CsVI, half the size of CsV. The only similar primary clock in operation is at the Physikalisch-Technische Bundesanstalt in West Germany.

Two atomic hydrogen masers have also been built at NRC. They have very good short-term stability of a few parts in 10^{15} for periods of up to an hour, although they deteriorate to several parts in 10^{14} over several days, and to parts in 10^{13} over a year. They are not used as clocks but are valuable short-term frequency references.

Precise observations of the mean solar day, using several PZTs located in different parts of the world, indicate that the Earth is continuing to run slow, ie, the cesium clock is gaining on mean solar time. In order to maintain an approximate synchronization between atomic time and solar time, the atomic time-scale rates were adjusted by as much as 3 parts in 10^8 to lose 3 milliseconds a day. The SI second was thus not transmitted to the public. In Jan 1972 it was decided to remove the rate offset and to insert a leap second into the time of the cesium clock at zero hours on either Jan 1 or July 1, so that at no time would atomic time differ from mean solar time by more than 0.8 second. Provision was also made for deleting a second if the rotation of the Earth should speed up. Since that time, the SI second has been available to everyone.

Time Distribution The distribution of precise time in Canada is performed by NRC radio station CHU at frequencies of 3330, 7335 and 14670 kHz. Seconds pulses (0.3 sec long) are accompanied by a bilingual announcement of Eastern Standard Time each minute. Every 10 seconds, the time is available by telephone: (613) 745-1576, English; (613) 745-9426, French. A highly accurate digital time signal, giving the date, hour, minute and second to 0.1 millisecond accuracy, is also available by telephone and via CHU. Decoding is by specially designed synchronizable clocks. The most familiar time signal is the one sent each weekday at 1:00 PM Ottawa time over the CBC network. Noon or 9:00 PM time guns or other signals may still be heard in some cities. Radio time signals, via WWV and WWVH of the National Bureau of Standards, US, are available throughout Canada.

Canadian time and frequency are compared with those of other national time laboratories by the reception of Loran-C radio signals, the use of portable cesium clocks, the monitoring of TV signals and the direct exchange of time signals via SATELLITE. The records are co-ordinated by the Bureau international de l'heure in Paris, France, which is responsible for establishing the international atomic time scale and the derived scale, Universal Co-ordinated Time.

Standard Time The development in the 19th century of rapid railway and telegraph communication was followed by the establishment of standard time zones. The American, Charles Ferdinand Dowd, encouraged the US railways to recognize uniform zones and the Canadian, Sir Sandford FLEMING, advocated using the principle on the international scale. The Washington Conference in 1884 recommended that the world be divided into 24 zones, each 15° wide, the first centered on the Greenwich meridian. Within each zone, time would be the same and the boundary would mark the place where time would change abruptly by one hour. Canada and the US had adopted standard time on 18 Nov 1883. In practice, time-zone boundaries now tend to conform to more convenient national or geographical divisions so that zones differ in size, shape and amount of change (eg, the Newfoundland time zone differs by only half an hour).

Time zones E of Greenwich are later hour by hour until, at the 180th meridian, the time is 12 hours later. It takes 12 hours for the sun to travel from the antimeridian to the Greenwich meridian. Similarly, to the W, the time is earlier hour by hour until again at the 180th meridian the time is 12 hours earlier. Thus, there is a difference of a whole day at the point directly opposite Greenwich, the International Date Line. Fortunately the date line is located, for the most part, in the Pacific Ocean. In order that it may not pass through settled lands, the date line is deflected eastward through the Bering Str, westward to include the Aleutian Is, then eastward again to include Chatham I and the Tonga Is. The practical consequence of the date line is that when crossing it going westward, a day is dropped from the calendar; in the opposite direction, eg, from Hong Kong to Honolulu, a day is added.

Canada extends E and W almost 90°. Originally there were 7 time zones but, with the Yukon Territory electing to use Pacific time, there are now only 6.

Newfoundland Standard Time (NST), near St John's, Nfld, 52½° W, 3½ hours earlier than Greenwich Mean Time, is used throughout the island.

Atlantic Standard Time (ATS), near Sydney, NS, 60° W, 4 hours, is used throughout NS, PEI, NB, the coast of Labrador and those parts of Québec E of the 63rd meridian and the NWT E of the 68th meridian.

Eastern Standard Time (EST), near Cornwall,

Ont, 75° W, 5 hours, is used in Québec W of the 63rd meridian, in Ontario E of the 90th meridian and in the NWT between the 68th and 85th meridians.

Central Standard Time (CST), near Thunder Bay, Ont, 90° W, 6 hours, is used in Ontario W of the 90th meridian, in Manitoba, in eastern and most of southern Saskatchewan and in the NWT between the 85th and 102nd meridians.

Mountain Standard Time (MTS), near Regina, Sask, 105° W, 7 hours, is used in western Saskatchewan, Alberta, parts of eastern BC, and in that part of the NWT west of the 102nd meridian.

Pacific Standard Time (PST), near Kamloops, BC, 120° W, 8 hours, is used throughout most of BC and the YT.

Yukon Standard Time (YST), near Whitehorse, YT, 135° W, 9 hours, is used only in a portion of the Alaska Panhandle.

The use of daylight-saving time, in which clocks are advanced by one hour during summer, has been encouraged since early in the century. Federal legislation establishing it was limited to a portion of both world wars. Several provinces have legislation controlling the provincial or municipal adoption of daylight saving; elsewhere, it is necessary to refer to individual municipalities to determine adoption in any particular year. In recent years, mainly because of the impact of radio and television (and perhaps influenced by legislation in the US), it has become an established custom in those parts of Canada where daylight saving is observed to advance clocks for the 6-month interval from the last Sunday in April to the last Sunday in October.   MALCOLM M. THOMSON

Reading: Derek Howse, Greenwich Time and the Discovery of Longitude (1980); Malcolm M. Thomson, The Beginning of the Long Dash, A History of Time-keeping in Canada (1978).

Timiskaming, Lake, 313 km², 128 km long, elev 180 m, located on the Ontario/Québec border in the SW corner of Québec; in Québec the name is spelled Témiscamingue. Varying from a few hundred metres to 8 km in width, Lk Timiskaming straddles the boundary, half in Ontario and half in Québec. Its physical character is well summarized in its name, an Indian word meaning "at the place of the deep, dry water." The lake is deep — the mean depth is 122 m — except for the clay flats in the NE corner, which are dry at low water. Along its E and SE shores are steep cliffs, a part of the LAURENTIAN HIGHLANDS, that until the 19th century were covered by pine forests. On the SW shore this same topography prevails, but N of the Montréal R, where the lake widens, the hills give way to gentler slopes. Geologically, Lk Timiskaming is a remnant of Lk Barlow, a glacial lake dating from about 10 000 years ago.

Before European intrusion into the area, Algonquian Indians occupied lands to the NE of the lake, OJIBWA to the S and CREE to the NW. All were drawn into the FUR TRADE in the early 1670s, and from then until the beginning of the 19th century, when the trade shifted northwestward, Lk Timiskaming was mainly a transportation route for a succession of fur companies and their traders. In the 1830s and 1840s, however, missionary fervour brought first the Sulpicians and then the Oblates into the area. In these same years, lumbermen acquired cutting rights along the eastern shore of the lake in the Kipawa region. By the 1870s, lumbermen had fanned northward and crossed the lake to the western shore. In the 1880s, permanent settlement began around Lk Temiskaming, on the Québec side thanks to the efforts of missionary colonizers such as Father Paradis at VILLE-MARIE, and in Ontario through the work of such men as C.C. Farr, founder of HAILEYBURY. The first commercial steamer appeared on the lake in 1882; 14 were in operation in 1900. By then, however, railways had begun to take over the lake's transportation role. The CPR branch line, the Temiskaming Colonization Railroad, running northward in Québec from Mattawa, reached TÉMIS-CAMING in 1894 and Ville-Marie in 1925. The Ontario government began construction of its own colonization railway, the Temiskaming and Northern Ontario, in 1902. By 1905 the T & NO had reached NEW LISKEARD, the farming village at the mouth of Wabi Creek on Lk Timiskaming, and 3 years later it connected with the National Transcontinental Ry at COCHRANE in the Great Clay Belt. As a developmental instrument the T & NO proved to be immensely successful, making possible the establishment of a host of silver (COBALT) and gold (TIMMINS, KIRKLAND LAKE) mining towns to the W and NW of the lake. Because of these railways and the highways constructed into the area from NORTH BAY and Mattawa in the 1920s, after WWI Lk Timiskaming declined as a commercial transportation route, but became important for tourism and recreational purposes. MATT BRAY

Timlin, Mabel Frances, "Timmie," economist, professor (b at Wisconsin Rapids, Wis 6 Dec 1891; d at Saskatoon 19 Oct 1976). In 1917 Mabel Timlin immigrated to Saskatchewan and in 1921 joined U Sask as a secretary, at the same time taking classes. She graduated in 1929 and continued her studies, completing her PhD at U Wash in 1940, and in 1950 was appointed full professor at U Sask. She applied her considerable analytical talents to theoretical and policy issues, in particular a critique of postwar monetary policy. Best known for her *Keynesian Economics* (1942, repr 1976) — a pioneering interpretation of Keynes's *General Theory* — she also published *Does Canada Need More People?* (1951) and, with Albert Faucher, *The Social Sciences in Canada: Two Studies* (1968). She was elected to the Royal Soc of Canada in 1951 and made a member of the Order of Canada in 1976. PAUL PHILLIPS

Timmins, Ont, City, pop 46 114 (1981c), located 298 km NW of Sudbury. Prospecting in the region began in 1906, with the first large GOLD discoveries made in 1909 by Benjamin Hollinger, Sandy Mcintyre and others. The main population centre was SOUTH PORCUPINE until 1911, when it was destroyed by fire. Noah TIMMINS, a Mattawa merchant who first made a fortune in the COBALT silver rush and then moved N, gave his name to a new town that was officially inc on 1 Jan 1912. For the first half-century of its existence, the town's population and prosperity fluctuated with the fortunes of the various gold mines — Hollinger, McIntyre, Dome. Since the 1960s its economic base has been diversified, with the addition of copper mining (Kidd Creek Mines) and waferboard production. Through regional amalgamation 1971, Timmins achieved city status and now claims the distinction of being, geographically (3212 km²), the second-largest city in N America. MATT BRAY

Timmins, Noah Anthony, mining executive (b at Mattawa, Canada W 31 Mar 1867; d at Palm Beach, Fla 23 Jan 1936). In association with his brother Henry, David DUNLAP and John and Duncan McMartin, Timmins acquired the LaRose silver mine at COBALT and, in 1909, properties in the Porcupine district that formed the basis of Hollinger Consolidated Gold Mines, of which he was president. During the 1920s and 1930s he continued to play a major role in Cana-

dian mining development, most notably by bringing together the principals of the Hollinger and Noranda mining companies to finance the start-up costs of Noranda's copper operations in northern Québec. The town of TIMMINS, Ont, is named after him. JOSEPH LINDSEY

Reading: D.M. LeBourdais, *Metals and Men: The Story of Canadian Mining* (1957).

Tipi, a conical skin house, was an easily moved yet substantial dwelling used by Indians dependent upon the buffalo. The Plains Indian tipi, used by a nomadic nuclear family throughout the year, was 4-6 m in diameter at the base, tapered upward to form a smokehole at the top, and was draped with a cover made of 8-12 buffalo skins sewn together and arranged over about 20 poles, which averaged 7-8 m in height. Doorways commonly faced east, and buffalo robes and blankets were distributed around the central fireplace. Outside the plains, smaller variants of the tipi were covered with bark or caribou skin. RENÉ R. GADACZ

Reading: R. and G. Laubin, *The Indian Tipi* (1977).

Titanium (Ti), metallic element estimated to form about 0.5% of the rocks of the Canadian SHIELD. Titanium minerals of commercial importance include rutile (TiO_2), anatase (TiO_2) and ilmenite ($FeTiO_3$). About 90% of titanium mineral production is used to make titanium dioxide pigments, some 60% of which are used in the PAINT INDUSTRY. Most titanium pigments are obtained through the sulphate process, in which finely crushed and concentrated ilmenite is dissolved by sulphuric acid. The product is then clarified, filtered and dried before bagging. Another process involves reacting rutile with gaseous chlorine, then reacting the product with oxygen. Most new plants use this chlorine process. In Canada, the industry is restricted to Québec. QIT-Fer et Titane Inc mines ilmenite at Havre St-Pierre and smelts it in electric furnaces at Sorel. The smelted product, sorelslag, contains 80% TiO_2 in 1983; some 750 000 t are produced annually, of which 700 000 t are exported, mainly to US and Europe. The remainder is sold to Canadian producers of titanium pigments. Titanium metal and its alloys are light and have very high tensile strength, even at high temperatures. Utilized in aircraft and spacecraft construction, titanium is not yet produced in Canada, though both the titanium minerals and the inexpensive electricity required are readily available. M.A. BOUCHER

Tlingit, Inland centered in Atlin in northernmost BC and Teslin in the adjacent Yukon Territory, exploit the boreal forest around the large lakes forming the headwaters of the YUKON R. In the 19th century their ancestors lived on the upper reaches of the Taku R that flows into the Pacific near Juneau, Alaska. The move across the height of land to the Yukon was prompted first by its rich fur resources, then by the KLONDIKE GOLD RUSH of 1897-98. In each homeland the Inland Tlingit intermarried with Athapaskans. While in the Taku basin, some Tlingit had married TAHLTAN, but they also feuded with them over rights to control the flow of fine furs from the interior to the coast. Both groups coveted the fur of the Liard R KASKA, but were themselves dominated by Coast Tlingit who monopolized access to white fur traders.

Nineteenth-century Inland Tlingit depended on annual salmon runs in the Taku drainage, but also hunted caribou, moose, sheep and goats, as well as small game, birds and freshwater fish. This seminomadic subsistence pattern was equally adapted to the Yukon, where fur bearers were more numerous but salmon resources were poorer. Tlingit technology was like that of neighbouring Athapaskans (*see* TUTCHONE), well suited to the hard conditions of the subarctic Cordillera. Social organization, however, was modelled on that of the Coast Tlingit. Their 6

matrilineal clans, grouped into the exogamous Wolf (or Eagle) and Crow (Raven) moieties, structured rank, marriage and naming practices. Because a headman's authority was limited to his own clan segment, there were no BAND chiefs until after WWII when the Dept of Indian Affairs instituted elected band chiefs and councils. Social relations rested on reciprocal obligations between members of clans in opposite moieties, the most important being associated with death and the memorial feasts or potlatches that followed a year or so afterwards (*see* POTLATCH.)

Although increasingly acculturated to white society following the gold rushes and the building of the ALASKA HIGHWAY in 1942, the present population of about 400 Inland Tlingit has renewed their interest in traditional arts. Teslin have also set up commercial enterprises such as CANOE and SNOWSHOE manufacturing. Since they have signed no INDIAN TREATIES, the Inland Tlingit are pursuing LAND CLAIMS settlements in both the US and Canada. *See also* NATIVE PEOPLE: SUBARCTIC and general articles under NATIVE PEOPLE. CATHARINE McCLELLAN

Reading: J. Helm, ed, *Handbook of North American Indians,* vol 6: *Subarctic* (1981).

Toad, common name for certain members of the AMPHIBIAN order Anura, the FROGS. The distinction is not firm, but the word toad is generally applied to frogs with relatively short legs and thick bodies, dry skin and reduced webbing between the toes. Toads live in drier habitats than other frogs. Most toads belong to the family Bufonidae (17 genera), which occurs worldwide, except in Antarctica. In Canada 4 species of genus *Bufo* are known: western toad (*B. boreas*), Great Plains toad (*B. cognatus*), American toad (*B. americanus*) and Fowler's toad (*B. fowleri*). Two so-called "spadefoot toads," belonging to family Pelobatidae, are known in Canada. These are the Plains spadefoot (*Scaphiopus bombifrons*) and the Great Basin spadefoot (*S. intermontanus*). G.M. SANDERS

Tobacco (*Nicotiana tabacum*), annual (potentially perennial) herbaceous plant of the NIGHTSHADE family. It evolved in Central America from a natural crossing between *N. sylvestris* and *N. tomentosiformis*. The plant has a fibrous root system and a cylindrical stem which terminates in a cluster of over 150 funnel-shaped, pink flowers with 5 petals. The fruit is a capsule with 2 or 4 compartments; each capsule may produce 4000-8000 seeds. The commercially important part of the plant, the leaves, are arranged in a spiral on the stalk, and are oval with a pointed apex. Leaves average 23-30 cm wide and 55-60 cm long. Canada ranks among the top 12 tobacco-producing countries and produces 5 major types: flue cured, ie, heat cured; and burley, cigar, dark and pipe, which are air cured. Tobacco is primarily smoked as cigarettes or cigars; chewing and snuff products constitute a small proportion of the consumer market.

Tobacco was cultivated by the PETUN, NEUTRAL and HURON of southwestern Ontario and was an important item of trade. Commercial tobacco cultivation in Canada began in the early 1800s and, until 1920, was mainly restricted to the burley type. Flue-cured tobacco was was introduced to Ontario around 1900, and it is now the major tobacco type (95-98%) grown in Canada; 90% is produced in southwestern Ontario. Flue-cured tobacco was introduced to Québec, NS, PEI and NB in 1930, 1958, 1959 and 1963, respectively. Tobacco seeds are sown in sterile muck in greenhouses during the first week of Apr, and seedlings are transplanted into the field in late May and early June. Plants require approximately 220-250 mm of rainfall, 115-120 frost-free days, and mean monthly temperatures of 19-23°C. Pests and other problems include cutworms, hornworms, aphids, damping-off, black root rot, blue mold, NEMATODES and WEEDS.

Plants are topped at a height of 16-19 marketable leaves, generally in late July. Leaves start maturing from the bottom and are harvested in batches of 2-3 leaves per harvesting or priming, a week apart. Harvested leaves are cured in a curing barn or kiln. High-temperature drying arrests the natural chemical processes and turns the leaves a golden colour. Air-cured tobaccos are usually stalk cut, hung on sticks and allowed to dry naturally in a barn. The final product is brown. *See* SMOKING.   P.W. JOHNSON

Tobacco-Products Industry Although Canada's TOBACCO industry has developed largely during this century, tobacco growing goes back to early colonial days, when settlers around the St Lawrence R adopted the SMOKING customs of native peoples. French settlers began by copying the primitive agricultural model set by the Indians. Some years later, a French colonial ordinance forbade retail sale of tobacco in Québec, leaving the settlers without an incentive to improve crop quality or yields. Consequently, they grew only enough for their own use, curing it naturally in the open air. This simple method of preparation produced a unique tobacco, *tabac canadien*. The French colonists began trading tobacco in 1652, but the French government did not encourage tobacco growing in Canada until 1735, after which the crop was cultivated regularly. Two varieties were native to Québec, *petit canadien* and *Rose Quesnel*. In Ontario the tobacco-growing industry was founded around Kent and Essex counties by LOYALISTS who came from the southern US during the American Revolution and brought tobacco seeds with them.

When tobacco growing expanded commercially in the late 19th century, the principal type cultivated in Québec and Ontario was burley (with some additional varieties of pipe tobacco in Québec). At this time, Québec led production: the yield in Canada in 1870-71 was 723 589 kg, of which 181 381 kg were produced in Ontario and 542 208 kg in Québec. Production in the 2 provinces expanded rapidly, reaching 7 938 000 kg by 1910, with Québec still the leader.

At the start of the 20th century, important changes took place in the industry. During WWI the popularity of chewing and pipe tobaccos declined and the demand for cigarettes grew rapidly. At the same time, a new curing method, flue curing, produced a type of tobacco (Virginia) better suited for cigarettes. This development revolutionized the Canadian tobacco industry. William T. Gregory and his brother Francis were primarily responsible for developing flue-cured tobacco in Canada. William came to Canada from N Carolina in 1900 to work for the Empire Tobacco Co (then a subsidiary of the American Tobacco Co, later taken over by the Imperial Tobacco Co of Canada). He arrived in Leamington, Ont, when only burley tobacco was being grown, and decided to plant Virginia tobacco. Francis came to Canada in 1901 to supervise these experiments. The company encouraged the brothers, hoping to replace expensive US imports with Canadian-grown, flue-cured tobacco. William chose the Leamington district as the initial growing area because of its desirable soil type and its claim to a longer frost-free period than any other area in Ontario. The results were encouraging and skilled US growers were brought to Canada to teach farmers growing and curing methods. By 1920, 3.6 million kg of flue-cured tobacco were being produced around Leamington. In 1922 further experimentation with flue-cured tobacco was done in the Lk Erie area, which had large tracts of sandy soil suited for the plant. The first successful crop was grown in 1925, beginning a new era in the history of Canadian tobacco.

With the development of this new growing belt, the industry eventually spread to 12 other areas in the province. Ontario is now the major

tobacco producer in Canada. The major growing areas in Québec are N of Montréal, in Montcalm and Joliette counties. Production of flue-cured tobacco in the province started in 1930 and, by 1933, 2 curing kilns had been built, one in each county. Today a flue-cured tobacco industry exists in the Maritime provinces; major production is in PEI, followed by NS and NB.

The Modern Industry Today, Canada ranks in the top 12 of the 100 tobacco-growing countries, producing 100 million kg annually. In 1983 most of the crop was sold locally for use in domestic products, but some 27.2 million kg, worth over $100 million, were exported, mainly to European Economic Community countries, the US and the Middle East. Tobacco growing permanently employs some 10 000 Canadians and creates another 40 000 seasonal jobs.

Six plants (5 in Ontario, 1 in Québec) process all tobacco for domestic manufacture and for export. More than 1630 people are employed in this sector. Nine cigarette-manufacturing plants (6 in Québec, 3 in Ontario) produced 63 billion units in 1983. Four cigar factories produced 342 million cigars. In addition, tobacco-products-manufacturing plants produced 6.2 million kg of fine-cut tobacco, 140 400 kg of pipe tobacco and some 132 700 kg of plug, chewing and snuff tobacco. In 1983 the 4 major manufacturers employed 7700 workers. Sales of domestically produced cigarettes totalled $62.7 billion. In addition, some 752 million cigarettes were imported in 1983, mostly from the US. Domestic cigar sales totalled 344 million units and 17.8 million were imported. Domestic sales of fine-cut tobacco totalled 6.0 million kg in 1983, up by 8.2% from the 1982 total. Sales of domestic pipe tobacco were 156 000 kg; imported pipe tobacco was some 838 000 kg. Sales of chewing, plug and twist tobacco and snuff produced domestically were 134 700 kg in 1983.

Sales were made through a network of 550 wholesalers and some 90 000 retailers and 30 000 vending machines. Employment in this sector is estimated at 22 000. Federal and provincial governments now receive almost 62% of the retail price of a package of cigarettes. In 1983 the federal government alone received an estimated $1.27 billion from the sale of tobacco products (that is $144 970 an hour, every hour of the year). The provinces collected almost $1.4 billion in taxes. In addition, major tobacco companies paid more than $105 million in corporate income tax. Of the 4 major manufacturers, 2 are 100% American-owned and 2 are publicly held companies in Canada.   C.M. SEYMOUR

Toboggan, a common form of transportation throughout the Subarctic. Toboggans were constructed of 2 thin boards of larch or birch wood, secured to one another by crossbars, with the boards turned up at the front. The wood was bent while still green or wet, then held in position by lashing until the wood dried. Among the Inland TLINGIT, the planks were steamed. Toboggans were well adapted to light, powdery snow but, useless in wet snow, were replaced during spring thaw by canoe-sleds. They were dragged by dogs, or people, with cords across their chests. Among the CHIPEWYAN, toboggans were pulled by women.   RENÉ R. GADACZ

Todd, Robert Clow, artist, decorative painter (b at Berwick-upon-Tweed, Eng *c*1809; d at Toronto 7 May 1866). Todd left a lively record of Québec winter life in a series of horse-and-sleigh paintings reminiscent of British artist Stubbs, whose work Todd may have admired while decorating carriages in Edinburgh and London before coming to Québec C in 1834. In Québec, sportsmen and officers commissioned him to paint pictures of their favourite horses; he also did summer views of MONTMORENCY FALLS and the Québec docks. He moved to Toronto in 1853, advertising as "banner, herald, sign and

ornamental painter," but business was poor. He is best remembered for the crisp linear finesse and feeling for the local scene in paintings such as *The Ice Cone, Montmorency Falls* (*c*1845). He taught at both the SÉMINAIRE DE QUÉBEC and Loretto Abbey, Toronto.   ANNE McDOUGALL

Tolmie, Simon Fraser, veterinarian, farmer, politician, premier of BC (b at Victoria 25 Jan 1867; d there 13 Oct 1937), son of William Fraser TOLMIE. After graduating from the Ontario Veterinary College in 1891 and working in a professional capacity in both the provincial and federal agricultural departments, he became chief inspector of livestock for the Dominion. He also operated a successful farm in suburban Victoria. Elected as the Unionist (Conservative) MP for Victoria in 1917, he served as minister of agriculture, 1919-21 and in 1926. Although elected provincial Conservative leader in 1926 he remained until 1928 when he resigned to contest the provincial election. Personally elected in Saanich, he became premier and minister of railways on 21 Aug 1928. His lacklustre administration gradually disintegrated under the pressure of the Depression and internal squabbles, and was soundly defeated by the Liberals under T.D. PATTULLO in 1933. Tolmie won the Victoria federal by-election in June 1936 and died in office.   PATRICIA E. ROY

Tolmie, William Fraser, surgeon, fur trader, politician (b at Inverness, Scot 3 Feb 1812; d at Victoria 8 Dec 1886). Tolmie came to the North-West in 1833 in the service of the HBC. After serving at posts on the northern coast, he was given charge of trading and farming operations at Ft Nisqually on Puget Sound, 1843-57. His fair dealing won the Indians' respect but aroused the suspicions of American immigrants. In 1859 he moved to Victoria and was on the board of management of the HBC 1861-70. He was a member of the House of Assembly of Vancouver I 1860-66 and of the Legislative Assembly of BC 1874-78. His works include *Comparative Vocabularies of the Indian Tribes of British Columbia* (1884). For his diaries 1830-43, see *The Journals of William Fraser Tolmie* (1963).   W. KAYE LAMB

Tomahawk is a name commonly given to axes used by Indians. Soon after European contact, aboriginal stone axes were replaced by trade tomahawks with metal heads made of iron or steel, and sometimes of brass, bronze or copper. While used as a woodworking tool, the tomahawk was also a weapon of war. The handles were decorated with carvings and sometimes with feathers, fur, beads and ribbons, and heads were often elaborate, often incorporating a pipe bowl. Many tomahawks saw no use in either the woods or war, but served only as symbols of status. Highly ornate and decorated pieces were presented to noted warriors by the French and British.   RENÉ R. GADACZ

Reading: H.L. Peterson, *American Indian Tomahawks* (1971).

Tomato (*Lycopersicon esculentum*), herbaceous perennial which, in Canada, is grown as an annual because of early frost. Fruits range from a few grams to over 450 gm. Tomatoes are usually red or orange, but may be pink (colourless skin) or yellow. Tomatoes contain vitamin A, thiamine, riboflavin, niacin and ascorbic acid. Worldwide, 2 species are cultivated, *L. esculentum* (including common, cherry, pear, upright and large-leaf varieties) and *L. pimpinellifolium*. The tomato originated in Peru and was used by the Indians of South and Central America in precontact times. Introduced into Europe in the 16th century, the tomato was viewed with suspicion as a member of the NIGHTSHADE family. There was no known commercial production before the early 1800s.

Outdoor production is limited in Canada by the coolness and shortness of the summer season. Tomatoes must be started by seeding and transplanting in a greenhouse. When frost danger is over, they can be transplanted to the field, where cloches or other forms of shelter can bring on an earlier start. If night temperatures fall below 14°C, many tomato varieties fail to set fruit. For good production about 70-90 days of temperatures in the mid to high 20s°C are required. Crowding of tomato plants results in earlier maturity. Most Canadian soils must be irrigated to supplement rainfall. Tomatoes are subject to blossom-end rot (in erratic water regimes), all forms of PLANT DISEASE and INSECT damage. Warm-season plants, tomatoes are grown commercially, predominantly in southern Ontario. Tomatoes are grown in Canadian home gardens, season permitting. Greenhouse production occurs across Canada. I.L. NONNECKE

Tombstones, upright markers or monuments placed at gravesites, are of 2 general types — the stele, an upright slab or pillar; and the 3-dimensional sculptural type, sometimes referred to as Victorian. The Victorian monuments were most common in Canada in the 19th and early 20th centuries. Materials for the stele are commonly stone, slate or marble; for the Victorian the range includes marble, granite in a variety of colours and finishes, stone and cast iron. The stele tombstone pattern consists, generally, of an upper panel of bas relief sculpture — angel's or death's head with wings, hourglass, willow tree or other symbols suggesting death or grief. Lettering takes up the space below and includes factual records of birth, death, marriage and usually an epitaph. The best examples of this delicate sculpture are seen in the Maritimes, but this work is very vulnerable to harsh winter weather and the growth of lichens.

The visitor to Canadian cemeteries will find, in addition to the stele, such sculpture as a grieving woman resting against a structure or the "Old Rugged Cross." Carrara marble from Italy was a favourite material. Unfortunately, alternate freezings and thawings have caused angels to lose their wing tips and noses, and male cherubs have suffered their particular indignities. Many cemeteries started as parks to which the public was invited for picnicking. The specimen trees that have grown up now form a cool and leafy forest for the historian or tombstone enthusiast. *See* CEMETERIES. ERIC ARTHUR

Tompkins, James John, Jimmy, priest, university administrator, pioneer in ADULT EDUCATION (b at Margaree, NS 7 Sept 1870; d at Antigonish, NS 5 May 1953). A visionary, communicator and propagandist, Tompkins's most lasting contribution was his transformation of a university from an elitist institution to one open to all. After studying at St Francis Xavier in Halifax and Urban College, Rome, Tompkins was ordained in 1902 and returned to St Francis Xavier as an administrator at a time of great social change. Determined to help the "common man," in 1920 Tompkins published *Knowledge for the People* (1920), a blueprint for adult education, and in 1921 founded the People's School at the university. Banished to Canso, NS, in 1922 for supporting a plan to federate Maritime universities, Tompkins began his pastoral career. He publicized the plight of Maritime fishermen so effectively that a royal commission was established to investigate their situation. Later, in Reserve Mines, NS, he introduced a credit union, inspired the first co-operative housing project (Tompkinsville) and established one of the first regional libraries. He may justly be called the father of the ANTIGONISH MOVEMENT of adult education. Both Dalhousie (1919) and Harvard (1941) conferred honorary degrees on him. DOUGLAS F. CAMPBELL

Tonnancour, Jacques Godefroy de, painter (b at Montréal 1917). His early influences ranged from the GROUP OF SEVEN and Goodridge ROBERTS

in his landscapes to Picasso in figure painting. Seventeen months (1945-46) in Brazil produced a formal brilliance and truthfulness in his landscapes. Back in Canada he temporarily abandoned landscapes 1946-50, and, influenced by Picasso and Matisse, created his most accomplished still life and figurative paintings. He was a member of the 1948-49 Prisme d'yeux group which opposed the AUTOMATISTES. By 1960, Tonnancour had produced his best-known simplified landscapes, as in *Paysage de juin*. The early 1960s saw a further simplification and abstraction of his landscapes, and his subsequent experimentation with collage and foreign material, resulting in work which approaches pure abstraction. He has taught at the Montreal Museum of Fine Arts and the Ecole des beaux-arts, Montréal. ERIK J. PETERS

Tonquin, a ship of 269 tons built in New York in 1807 and purchased 23 Aug 1810 by New York fur merchant and entrepreneur John Jacob Astor. She sailed from New York on 6 Sept 1810, bound for the mouth of the COLUMBIA R, where Astor's PACIFIC FUR COMPANY intended to found a post and develop trade in opposition to the NORTH WEST COMPANY. The *Tonquin*'s captain, Jonathan Thorn, was a brutal disciplinarian and had little use for Astor's traders. Clerk Gabriel Franchère's journal describes the captain's tyranny and disregard for human life, especially evident when the ship arrived on 22 Mar 1811 at the Columbia R mouth, where 8 sailors drowned attempting to take soundings.

On June 5 the *Tonquin* sailed on a trading cruise from the new fort, Astoria. About June 15, evidently near Echatchet village, Templar Channel, Clayoquot Sound, Vancouver I, she was blown up, perhaps by Thorn to prevent her from falling into the hands of local Indians, who were attacking the ship. The tremendous explosion sank the *Tonquin,* and with her went Thorn and Astor's hopes for dominance in the NORTHWEST COAST trade. BARRY M. GOUGH

Tonty, Henri de, explorer, VOYAGEUR (b 1649 or 50; d at Ft Louis-de-la-Louisiane Sept 1704). He was the son of Lorenzo de Tonty, inventor of the "tontine" system of life annuity. He served in the French army and navy and had his right hand blown away by a grenade. In 1678 he travelled to New France as lieutenant to LA SALLE and supervised construction of Ft Conti and the bark GRIFFON (1679) on the Niagara R. He led a party to the Illinois R, helping to build Ft Miami and then Ft Crèvecoeur (1680), but while he was absent from Crèvecoeur, his men mutinied, destroying the buildings. Tonty also survived an Iroquois attack, a canoe wreck near Green Bay and near starvation. In 1681 he led an advance party to Chicago portage and was rejoined by his commander La Salle; the expedition reached the Gulf of Mexico 7 Apr 1682. In 1686 he helped DENONVILLE in his campaign against the Iroquois by organizing the Illinois in a rearguard action, and in 1690 he was granted the fur-trading concession after La Salle's murder. In 1698 Tonty returned to the Mississippi, under IBERVILLE's command, working to expand trade, but he died of yellow fever. The Indians called him *bras de fer* as much for his tenacity and courage as for his hook-shaped artificial arm. JAMES MARSH

Tookoolito, "Hannah" (b near Cumberland Sound, NWT 1838; d at Groton, Conn 1876), and **Ebierbing,** "Joe" (b near Cumberland Sound, NWT; d on Baffin I, NWT *fl* 1851-79), Inuit guides. In 1851 Tookoolito (sister of EENOOLOOA-PIK) and her husband Ebierbing were taken to England for 2 years by a whaling captain. There they caused a sensation and were received by Queen Victoria. After their return to Baffin I they met explorer C.F. Hall, who was amazed to find Tookoolito, fluent in English, knitting woollen socks and drinking tea. Ebierbing enabled him to confirm the site of Sir Martin

FROBISHER's historic landfall in Frobisher Bay. They accompanied Hall back to the US and on his second expedition to Repulse Bay, searching for clues to the fate of Sir John FRANKLIN. In 1872 they joined Hall's attempt to reach the North Pole and that fall they and a group of seamen were marooned on an ice floe in Smith Sound. The castaways drifted 2080 km S and, having survived the 6-month ordeal thanks to the hunting skill of Ebierbing and another Inuk, were rescued off Labrador by a sealer. After Tookoolito's death, Ebierbing accompanied the British *Pandora* expedition as Schwatka's interpreter on his 1878 search for Franklin. JOHN BENNETT

Tools, Carpentry The craft of carpentry involves the shaping of wood for architectural, utilitarian or ornamental purposes. European colonists who settled what is now Canada brought with them a rich heritage of CRAFTS and craft tools. In N America the highly trained and experienced craftsmen worked mainly in the cities and towns; settlers and farmers, in urgent need of dwellings and furnishings, often had to be their own carpenters. Government immigration pamphlets encouraged settlers to bring a "good box with tools." These implements were used to fell trees, build shelters, FURNITURE and vehicles, and make a range of objects for the home and farm (ie, WOODENWARE). Industrialization, accompanied by machine TECHNOLOGY, made such craftsmanship redundant and the older tools are collected today as reminders of our pioneer past. The following is a short list of selected woodworking tools.

Axe Of all the woodworking tools brought from Europe, the axe was the most widely used and most urgently needed, for it was the tool that cleared the land and provided wood for construction and fuel. The European axe was not well suited to pioneer conditions, and in the course of settlement British colonists developed the American axe. The blade of this implement is moderately flared and the socket for the handle is long; the head is extended above the socket as a narrow, hammerlike poll. The handle (helve) is also distinctive, having an S-curve, which allows for a more natural sliding movement of the right hand during the stroke.

The pioneer dwelling, the LOG HOUSE, was constructed by placing logs one above the other to form 4 walls, the corners being secured by some form of joint. The logs were usually squared, ie, the convexities on all 4 sides were chopped away to form a roughly squared cross section. Squaring was done with a broad axe, in which the cutting edge was long and the blade flat on one side, concave on the other. In use, the hewer stood near the log and swung the axe in a vertical arc, working his way along the log and leaving a neatly defined flat side. A variety of small axes (hatchets) were developed for special applications. In the adze, used for fine trimming of timbers, the blade is at right angles to the socket and handle and slopes or curves slightly toward the user.

Saw, next to the axe the most basic woodworking tool, is a flat metal blade, with one serrated edge. In most saws the teeth are "set," ie, bent a little, alternately, to one side or the other, to produce a cut (kerf) wider than the blade, thus avoiding binding. The saw was used primarily to produce boards. A pit saw, ie, a long blade with large teeth and a handle at each end, was employed. It was operated by 2 men; the log was propped up at one end or extended over a pit. When boards were available, the handsaw was the most important tool for cutting. There are 2 kinds of handsaw: the crosscut saw, a smaller saw, with finer, pointed teeth, intended for cutting across the grain of the wood; and the ripsaw, which has larger teeth with chisellike points, for cutting with the grain.

The keyhole saw, used for cutting circular

openings or curved edges, has a very narrow tapering blade. The tenon saw, a short wide blade with the upper edge reinforced with a metal bar, is used for making fine cuts at various angles. Framed saws have narrow flexible blades, kept rigid by a springy bow (bucksaw) or a twisted rope stretched between extensions of the handle (bow saw). Fine carpentry requires a variety of small saws, mostly miniature framed saws (eg, coping saw, fretsaw). Fitted to a foot-powered mechanism, the flexible blade became a jigsaw.

Chisel Various carpentry tools employ a cutting edge: in the drawknife, the blade is mounted between 2 handles and pulled by the operator to shave off slices of wood; in the chisel, the long narrow blade with the cutting edge at the far end is pushed or hammered to cut grooves or holes. The gouge is a chisel with a trough-shaped blade and a curved edge, used for cutting depressions and rounded grooves.

Plane The most variable slicing tool is the plane, in which a chisellike blade is mounted at an angle in a wooden block or metal frame, the cutting edge protruding forward through an opening in the base of the tool. The plane is pushed along the wood and the cutting edge peels off a layer (ie, shaving). Planing smooths an edge or a surface. Specially shaped cutting edges and blocks enable the plane to cut grooves, channels, steps (rabbets) and moldings. Planes vary in size from the long jack plane for smoothing to tiny cabinetmaker's planes for delicate trimming.

Boring Tools The awl has a narrow blade with pointed or chisel-shaped end and is pushed or hammered into wood to make a hole. The auger is like a miniature gouge and is used with a twisting motion. The spiral drill is screwlike, with cutting edges at the lower end. It is used in a mount, usually a brace, which is a sort of hand crank, permitting rotation and application of pressure at the same time.

File is a steel blade with transverse grooves on one or both sides. When pushed across a surface, the sharp edges of the grooves cut into and remove material. The rasp has small projections instead of grooves and cuts more quickly but more roughly than the file. Both are used for minor smoothing and shaping.

Nail Pieces of wood can be held together by joints, pegs or glue, but the usual device for this purpose is the nail, a slender piece of metal (usually IRON) pointed at one end and expanded into a head at the other. Nails were originally shaped individually in a small forge on a miniature anvil. Later they were made by cutting oblique strips from a sheet of metal. Modern nails are formed from extruded, wirelike steel rods.

Hammer The carpenter's hammer or claw hammer, used to drive nails, has a head with the upper end drawn into a pair of curved claws. The tapered slot between the claws is used to grasp a protruding nail, which can then be extracted by pulling on the handle. The mallet has a wooden head and is used to drive chisels.

A special kind of woodworking is the manufacture of barrels (cooperage), which employs modified forms of hatchet, adze, drawknife and plane to form the curved, tapered staves and the circular bottom and lid. The importance of barrels, kegs, tubs and pails at one time made cooperage a widely practised craft. LORIS S. RUSSELL

Topley, William James, photographer (b at Montréal 13 Feb 1845; d at Vancouver 16 Nov 1930). He learned photography as a boy from his mother. In 1864 he joined the studio of William NOTMAN in Montréal. Three years later he opened Notman's new Ottawa studio and purchased the business in 1872. For the next 50 years the studio produced views from across the country and portraits of all Canadian political leaders, providing an invaluable source for Canadian social history. In 1924 Topley retired and his studio closed 2 years later. ANDREW BIRRELL

Topographic Painters Topographic studies grew out of 16th-century Europe's interest in specific views of places and their details. Precision was important, either for reasons of pride and record taking, for strategic purposes, or for evocation of poetic views which opened new vistas to the viewer's imagination (*see* ART; PAINTING). In Canada topographic views in paintings can be seen in some rare examples of church paintings and portraits from as early as late 17th-century New France, or from the recent 20th century, when portions of the St Lawrence R were recorded before they became the Seaway. However, the richest period was the late 18th and 19th centuries, a period when the art of draftsmanship and painting in watercolour flourished, particularly in Great Britain, and was pursued by professional and amateur alike. Among the British soldiers and civilians stationed in Canada during this period, many were topographic painters who left a rich heritage of early views of the country and its people.

Topography was a subject taught at the Woolwich Royal Military Academy by artists such as Paul Sandby, who achieved his fame with ornamental landscapes that combined the precision of topography with a flexible and poetic visual technique. Among those influenced by such teachers were soldier-topographers such as Hervey Smyth, who depicted the size of the English military force which captured France's strongholds; Richard Short, whose drawings of Québec City after the siege show the strength of the British fleet as well as the architectural richness of the town and its good-natured inhabitants; Thomas Davies, who preferred watercolours which show scenes in which man and nature live in harmony; George HERIOT, whose illustrated *Travels Through the Canadas* enjoyed a large readership in Europe and N America; and James Pattison Cockburn, who produced a large collection of watercolours of Québec City and its environs.

Topographic artists portrayed an idealized and often spectacular landscape. MONTMORENCY FALLS was a favourite subject with many of them. As others of their age, Davies and Heriot believed that all of nature could be drawn for man's pleasure like a large parkland in the British style, far removed from the more serious concerns of living; in their landscapes, habitants and American Indians tended to be exotic and picturesque and colonial administrators genteel and well dressed. There were also less idealistic views, as for example those of John Webber, a crew member on the ship of James Cook when he explored the Pacific Ocean. Since such paintings or drawings were sometimes produced as engravings in Europe or the US, topographical painters helped to spread interest elsewhere in British N America, later Canada.

The techniques and approaches continued to be used by others, by explorers such as George BACK, adventurers such as William HIND, wives of administrators, such as Lady Dufferin and Elizabeth SIMCOE, wives of churchmen, such as Henrietta Cartwright, or engineers such as William ARMSTRONG. Topographic painters helped, through their records, to enliven aspects of Canadian history not visually accessible otherwise, and also allowed some scope for the imagination. PIERRE DOYON

Reading: M. Bell, *Painters in a New Land* (1973); J. Russell Harper, *Painting in Canada* (1977) and *Early Painters and Engravers in Canada* (1970); G. Heriot, *Travels Through the Canadas* (1807, repr 1971); D. Reid, *A Concise History of Canadian Painting* (1973).

Tornado, an intense rotary storm of small diameter (tens or hundreds of metres), characterized by at least one vortex reaching the Earth's surface. The vortex is usually visible as a funnel cloud associated with a THUNDERSTORM, although on occasions it is invisible. In either case, damage results at ground level. A tornado may be composed of a single funnel, several funnels occurring simultaneously, one or more funnels reforming one after the other, or various combinations of these states. A tornado's life cycle typically consists of 3 stages. It starts when a funnel-shaped protuberance (tuba) develops beneath a rotating section of the SW flank of a thunderstorm. The tuba elongates downwards from the cloud and is enveloped by a rotating sleeve (annulus) which develops upwards from the ground. The full merging of the 2 constitutes the mature tornado vortex. This stage is followed by the third or degenerating phase, when the tuba rises back towards the cloud base and disappears. Cases where the tuba alone develops are called "funnels aloft" and are not tornadoes. The rotation of tornadoes is almost always cyclonic (clockwise in the Northern Hemisphere, anticlockwise in the Southern Hemisphere, when the circling clouds are viewed from below). Tornadoes occur in all parts of Canada except those with an arctic CLIMATE. They are relatively frequent in the interior, from NB to the Rocky Mts, and are most common in southern Ontario (which experiences an average of 21 per season), followed by southern Manitoba. In Canada, the tornado season begins as early as Mar and ends as late as Oct, generally lasting 107 days in the interior and about 60 days elsewhere. Activity peaks in late June and early July. The average tornado causes a damage swath with median values of 6.2 km in length, 83 m in width and 0.6 km^2 in area. A tornado is most likely to occur in the afternoon, 3-7 PM local standard time, and approach from the W or SW. Tornadoes range in intensity from very weak (winds from 64 km/h) to devastating (winds up to 509 km/h), on a scale of zero to 5 devised by T.T. Fujita. Over 90% of Canadian tornadoes can be categorized as weak, FO to F1 on the Fujita scale. The most severe so far known, the Regina tornado of 30 June 1912, which killed 28, injured hundreds and demolished much of the downtown area, is rated as F4 (winds of 330-416 km/h). Less than 1% of all tornadoes fall into the F4 category; none of F5 intensity are known to have occurred in Canada. MICHAEL J. NEWARK

Torngat Mountains extend 200 km S from Cape Chidley, Labrador, to Hebron Fjord. The Torngat (Inuktitut, "home of spirits") rise to 1738 m at Mt Caubvick, crown of the Selamiut ("Aurora") Range and highest peak in Newfoundland and Québec. Other high summits such as Torngarsuak ("great spirit"), Cirque Mt, Razorback and Mt Tetragona lie entirely within Newfoundland, E of the UNGAVA BAY-LABRADOR SEA drainage divide. The mountains are part of the Precambrian SHIELD; Archean gneissic rocks at Saglek are the oldest known in N America (3.6 billion years). Proterozoic structures which govern much of the N to S trend in relief were forged around 2 billion years ago. Proterozoic sedimentary rocks in the Sorviluk Range con-

The Torngat Mountains of Labrador have deep fjords which attract Inuit from Nain for summer char fishing (*photo by John Foster/Masterfile*).

tain chalcedony, much used in prehistoric northeastern America.

Deep FJORDS and finger lakes, bound by spectacular rock walls, cut sharply across the high ranges; they are the legacy of glaciation. The Laurentide Ice Sheet, centered far to the W, covered all but the highest summits at least once, although during the last glaciation ice cover was limited and many NUNATAKS provided refuge for arctic and alpine flora and fauna. Over 70 small, active glaciers survive in the Torngat, shaded in deep cirques and sustained by the southernmost extension of arctic climate. Vegetation is sparse TUNDRA, with willow thickets in low, sheltered valleys, and rock desert above 300 m. Wildlife is arctic, with caribou numerous.

Tent rings and stone structures remain from over 6000 years of Maritime Archaic, Dorset, Thule and more recent Inuit settlement. In 1763 over 500 Inuit inhabited the fjords; in 1935 fewer than 50; now none. Trading posts at Saglek and Nachvak and Moravian missions at Hebron and Ramah are abandoned. The closest settlements are NAIN, 200 km S, and Port-Nouveau-Québec, 100 km W. Inuit from Nain visit the fjords for the summer char fishery. An airstrip at Saglek is used in offshore oil and gas exploration. *R.J. ROGERSON*

Toronto, capital city of Ontario, is situated on the southern margin of the province, fronting Lake ONTARIO. Metropolitan Toronto, Canada's largest city by population, comprises the cities of Toronto, North York, Scarborough, York and Etobicoke, and the borough of East York. Its economic hinterland lies basically in Ontario, but in financial terms extends across Canada. The city is well placed to control the populous industrial and agricultural region of southern Ontario and, being located on the neck of the Ontario peninsula that juts into the Great Lakes system, has ready access both to the Upper Lakes basin and to American territory S of the Lower Lakes. The city has been able to spread its influence through the Canadian Great Lakes area and far beyond. Toronto's physical features include a natural harbour sheltered by sandy islands (originally one long peninsula), backed by gently rolling, well-watered, fertile country. The area has a fairly mild and humid average climate, by Canadian standards, though with some changeable extremes.

Settlement Toronto's Indian-derived name has several possible meanings. Of these, "place of meeting" seems most apt, since long before settlement, native peoples came there to follow a trail and canoe route that gave a shortcut overland between lakes Ontario and HURON. The Toronto Passage, used as early as 1615 by Etienne BRÛLÉ, became well known to French fur traders. They set a small store by its entry (1720-30), and a larger, fortified post in 1750-51. This Ft Rouillé, whose remains have been excavated in Toronto's present Exhibition Grounds, was burned in 1759 by its French garrison retreating from British forces. Following the British CONQUEST, the Toronto site again saw only minor traders and Mississauga Indian encampments. The outcome of the AMERICAN REVOLUTION sent LOYALISTS northward to remaining British territory. Their settlements along the Upper St Lawrence and Lower Lakes led to the creation of the province

Population: 2 998 947 (1981c; CMA)

Rate of Increase (1971-81): (CMA) 2.6%

Rank in Canada: First (by CMA)

Date of Incorporation: City 1834; Metro 1953

Land Area: 632 km²

Elevation: 111 m (U of T station)

Climate: Average daily temp, July 22°C, Jan -5°C; Yearly precip 800.5 mm; Hours of sunshine 2045.4 per year

Toronto, Ont, from the air. The Royal York Hotel is seen lower right, with the dark towers of the Toronto-Dominion Centre to its left, the triangular Royal Bank complex to its right and the taller Canadian Imperial Bank of Commerce and Bank of Montreal buildings beyond. Roy Thomson Hall is lower left (*photo by Tibor Bognàr*).

of UPPER CANADA (1791), and to plans for a town at centrally located Toronto, which were effected by Upper Canada's first governor, John Graves SIMCOE. He viewed the site mainly as a commanding position for a naval and garrison base to guard a troubled American boundary. But in 1793 he had a little town laid out by the harbour, naming it York; then made it his capital, erecting parliament buildings and cutting roads inland. York's officialdom and garrison attracted merchants, craftsmen and labourers, while spreading rural settlement beyond made it a local market centre. By 1812 this frontier village still had only 700 residents; yet its governing role, harbour and rough roads inward gave it initial advantage in the Lk Ontario area.

Development During the WAR OF 1812, York was twice raided and pillaged by US forces (1813), leaving a British-minded populace with keen anti-American memories. Afterwards, it felt the rising wave of British immigration to Upper Canada. Its hinterland trade mounted with expanding farm frontiers as its merchants supplied country dealers as wholesalers; and it became the province's banking centre. By 1834 the fast-building town of over 9000 inhabitants was incorporated as the city of Toronto, with an elected civic government led by William Lyon MACKENZIE as first mayor. This prominent Reform journalist and politician tried to seize the city by force in the Upper Canadian REBELLIONS OF 1837; but his attempt collapsed more in confusion than bloodshed, strengthening Toronto's conservative tendencies. In the 1840s Toronto increased its commercial lead, as busy steamboat port activity and gaslit, sewered main streets marked its urban rise. In the 1850s railway building brought the city a radiating web of tracks connecting it to New York and Montréal, the Upper Lakes at Georgian B, and across western Upper Canada to Detroit and Chicago. Hence its own regional grasp was widely extended; wholesaling, banking and railway entrepreneurship grew accordingly. The city was made capital of the new province of Ontario at CONFEDERATION in 1867, and by the 1870s it was becoming industrialized. Hart MASSEY's agricultural machinery firm, clothing factories, publishing plants, and metal foundries grew large

in the 1880s. A city of 30 000 in 1851 was over 5 times bigger by 1891, aided by industrial tariff protection after 1879 and the promotional drive of leaders such as railway builder Casimir GZOWSKI and department-store builder Timothy EATON.

From the later 1890s into a booming early 20th century, the settlement of the Canadian West and the tapping of northern Ontario's forests and mines opened further markets and resources to Toronto. Commerce with the North and West flowed into the city, while it dealt with either Montréal or New York as outlets or suppliers. Major firms such as Eaton's spread their mail-order business into the West. Hydroelectric power from NIAGARA FALLS (1911) gave cheap energy for more factory growth. Above all, the city's banks, investment and insurance companies invaded regions well beyond Ontario. By 1914, although older, larger Montréal still held the lead, Toronto's financial head offices, factories and stores had made it a second national metropolis. WWI expanded its investment and manufacturing scope, the latter ranging from large-scale meat processing to munitions, both forwarded by businessman Sir Joseph FLAVELLE.

In the prosperous 1920s development continued, as new suburban municipalities rose around an overflowing city of some half a million. It was checked by the GREAT DEPRESSION of the 1930s, yet Toronto was proportionately less hard hit than many other Canadian centres. Its well-developed, more varied hinterland sustained business better than regions heavily dependent on staples such as wheat or lumber. WWII revived growth, shaping electronic, aircraft and precision-machine industries. And in the postwar era Toronto boomed with Canada, as a ravaged Europe renewed its material stock. Population swelled further, to over a million in the Greater Toronto area by 1951.

The service needs of this urban complex and inadequate revenue in its suburbs led to a metropolitan-area government. Set up in 1953 under a vigorous first chairman, Frederick GARDINER, the Metropolitan Toronto Authority handled area-wide requirements. The subway system begun by the city in 1949 was built up, parks and drainage projects effected, and arterial through roads constructed. In 1967 small suburbs were amalgamated, leaving a Metro structure of the city of Toronto and 5 boroughs, of which all but East York had also become cities by 1984, as their numbers soared. In recent

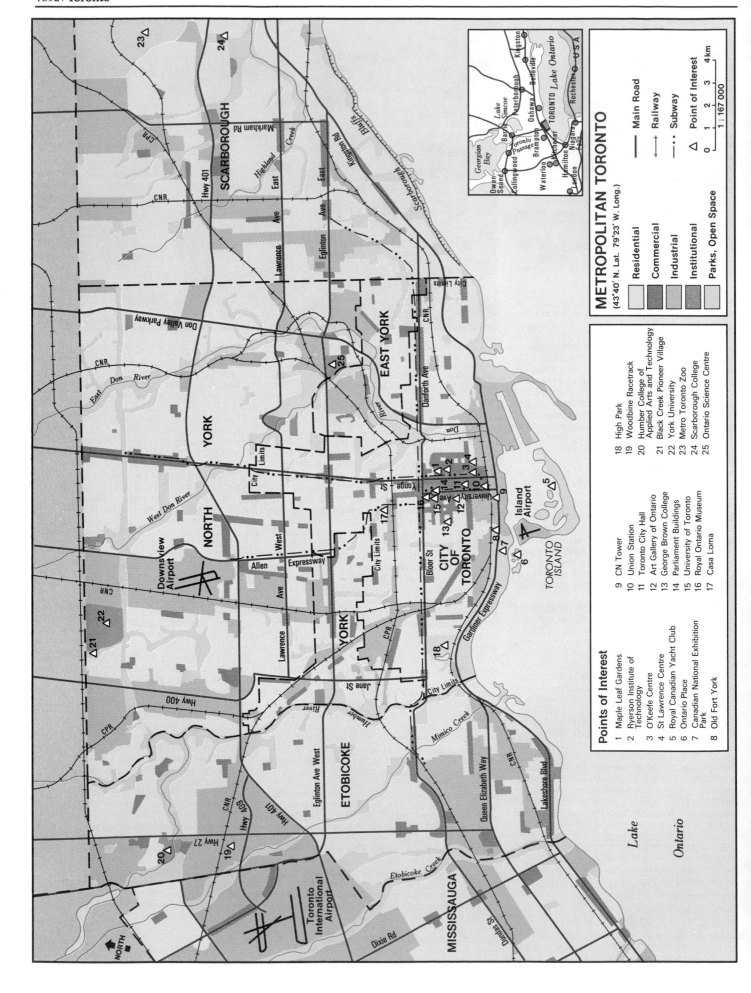

METROPOLITAN TORONTO

(43°40' N. Lat. 79°23' W. Long.)

1 : 167 000

Residential
Commercial
Industrial
Institutional
Parks, Open Space

Main Road
Railway
Subway
△ Point of Interest

0 1 2 3 4km

Points of Interest

1 Maple Leaf Gardens
2 Ryerson Institute of Technology
3 O'Keefe Centre
4 St Lawrence Centre
5 Royal Canadian Yacht Club
6 Ontario Place
7 Canadian National Exhibition Park
8 Old Fort York
9 CN Tower
10 Union Station
11 Toronto City Hall
12 George Brown College
13 Art Gallery of Ontario
14 Parliament Buildings
15 University of Toronto
16 Royal Ontario Museum
17 Casa Loma
18 High Park
19 Woodbine Racetrack
20 Humber College of Applied Arts and Technology
21 Black Creek Pioneer Village
22 York University
23 Metro Toronto Zoo
24 Scarborough College
25 Ontario Science Centre

SCARBOROUGH

EAST YORK

YORK

NORTH YORK

CITY OF TORONTO

ETOBICOKE

MISSISSAUGA

TORONTO ISLAND

Island Airport

Downsview Airport

Toronto International Airport

Lake Ontario

Don Valley Parkway

Allen Expressway

Gardiner Expressway

Queen Elizabeth Way

Hwy 401

Hwy 400

Hwy 27

Hwy 409

Lakeshore Blvd

Eglinton Ave West

Markham Rd

Kingston Rd

Danforth Ave

Bloor St

Yonge St

University Ave

Dixie Rd

Dundas St

Jane St

Lawrence Ave

Eglinton Ave

East Don River
West Don River
Don River
Humber River
Highland Creek
Etobicoke Creek
Mimico Creek

City Limits

CNR
CPR

NORTH

years, Toronto has gained priority over Montréal as a national (and international) financial focus, and leads Canada in its concentration of specialized services, including professional facilities, advertising and has a major hold on information media, especially press and TV.

Cityscape Toronto emerged on the shore plain beside its harbour, beyond which, some 4 km inland, a fairly abrupt rise led to higher plains, then to rounded lines of hills. The courses of rivers and creek ravines offered ways up from the plain even for fur canoes, and practicable grades for later roads and railways. Though the low-lying waterside area gave early York dank marshes and mud-filled streets, and the rise impeded road lines, these were not long-term barriers to the steady spread of the cityscape. Today, Toronto extends far E and W of the harbour stretch, and to Metro limits well inland (632 km²). The present Toronto-region conurbation of around 3 million reaches to near-suburban Richmond Hill on the N, E to Oshawa, and W approximately to Oakville — from where the urbanized "Golden Horseshoe" still runs on through Hamilton to the Niagara Peninsula.

The shore plain by the harbour has remained Toronto's downtown core, first shaped by its waterfront relationship. Gov Simcoe's layout of 1793 was a small-town plot with a plain grid of straight streets along the eastern end of the harbour, with a military reserve for a garrison post westward to its entry. As the town grew, the basic straight-line grid pattern was essentially extended; but under municipal self-government from 1834, planning was replaced by uncoordinated private developments. Nevertheless the cityscape began to sort itself out. King St was a main commercial E-W artery by the 1840s, Yonge St a N-S axis, leading to the northern highway into the hinterland. As railways arrived on the waterfront in the 1850s, they built up a transport zone between the city and the lake. Thereafter, industrial areas emerged at either end of the harbour along rail lines, and to the N, close-built, working-class districts. Larger residences spread more above the central downtown, and homes of the wealthy on the rise behind the shore plain.

Streetcars advanced the sorting out. Horse-drawn cars in the 1860s and electric in the 1890s fostered middle-class movement to roomier suburban fringes and promoted annexations of suburban communities, beginning with Yorkville 1883 and ending with N Toronto 1912. In another fashion, electric elevators, larger iron-framed buildings and telephones from the 1880s facilitated greater business concentration on expensive downtown property. During the early 1900s steel skyscrapers climbed in this central district, which had further sorted out in land use: wholesaling around Yonge below King, major retailing along Yonge near Queen and finance down Bay and along King. From WWI the massing inward and spreading outward continued, aided by the automobile, until depression and a second war intervened. Since the late 1940s it has surged on, with only short downturns. Public planning revived in the 1940s, but its fuller impact grew from the 1950s and with Metro; still further with the onset of environmental reformers (or conservers) in the 1960s and 1970s. The balance between the "move traffic" and "save life quality" kinds of planning remains a shifting one. The high rise now dominates Toronto — in the central business district, in residential apartment masses and in office towers around main intersections and subway stations.

Despite its modest natural setting and largely plain street layout, Toronto has an interesting building stock and some noteworthy heritage structures. These include the Grange, a gentry mansion of about 1819, ST LAWRENCE HALL (1850),

Finnish architect Viljo Revell's bold design for Toronto City Hall was chosen through an international competition (*photo by Tibor Bognàr*).

Osgoode Hall (rebuilt 1857), UNIVERSITY COLLEGE (1859), the Ontario Parliament Buildings (1892), the City Hall of 1899, the Royal Alexandra Theatre (1907) and UNION STATION (1927) — a prime N American survivor of classical railway grandeur. Later eras have largely produced more and bigger office buildings, hotels and shopping centres, though the new City Hall (1965) is striking in design and setting. Boldly original, too, is Roy Thomson Music Hall (1982). The central city skyline soars in mass and height, topped by the 72-floor Bank of Montreal (1978) and the even taller CN TOWER (1975), a 550 m telecommunications spire. While the building systems have chiefly been imported throughout, Toronto designers have set their stamps on them. The lines of high-peaked Victorian brick homes in the older city have a distinctive Toronto character only lately appreciated.

Population From its start as a seat of colonial officialdom, Toronto had a markedly British population compared to the far more American rural society of early Upper Canada. British immigrants after the 1820s increased this predominance, also bringing a large strain of Protestant Ulster Irish. Late in the 1840s the outrush from famine-stricken Ireland added a sizable Catholic Irish minority as well, leading to religious discord in the city. The Ulstermen's ORANGE ORDER became guardians of British Protestant ascendancy, wielding power in civic politics. In the latter 19th century, British immi-grants, largely English, continued arriving, though Canadian-born (of British stock) were a majority by 1871. Toronto stayed remarkably homogeneous, strong on church life, Sunday observance and morality.

Movement from the countryside to an expanding industrial city became a mounting factor from the 1870s, as did natural increase, especially as public-health measures improved. Immigration rose again by the 1900s and increasingly brought continental Europeans as well, including Jews, Italians and Ukrainians. Clustering first in poor inner-city areas, the new ethnic elements were a small (13%) but compact segment in an Anglo-Celtic, mainly Protestant, community by 1920. Their influx continued over the next decade. After depression and war, another far bigger inflow developed, to continue with minor fluctuations to the 1980s. British newcomers still led at first, but Italians became a chief component by the 1960s (11.6%), while Germans, Poles, Hungarians, Balkan Slavs, Greeks and Portuguese steadily widened the non-Anglo-Celtic segment (1961, 44%; 1971, 50%). In the 1970s W Indian, S Asian and E Asian migrants added "visible minorities" to Toronto increasingly. Older "Anglo" elements continued sizeably in Metro's suburban units; and still dominate its business elite and chief social institutions. Yet in the original city, a powerful ethnic press and politics, expanded Catholicism, many languages and cultures, racial concerns and, above all, a much livelier, multifaceted community indicate how greatly Toronto's population patterns have changed.

Economy and Labour Force In order, though with overlapping and continuance, Toronto grew through the stages of commercial lake port, railway and industrial focus, financial nexus and high-level service and information centre. At present, its port and commercial functions remain important, though relatively less so, apart from heavy retail activity; its railway role persists, modified by air and automotive transport; its industry has lost ground to foreign competition and Canadian decentralization, but remains high in value; while its financial power continues to increase and its office-service sector stays pre-eminent in Canada. Advanced technology will likely reinforce its service and industrial sectors, while Toronto's money market keeps a national role and the city becomes more reliant on its regional Ontario domain.

Banking head offices in Toronto include the CANADIAN IMPERIAL BANK OF COMMERCE and the

Population Growth in Toronto and Suburbs 1951-81				
	1951	1961	1971	1981
City of Toronto	675 754	672 407	712 785	599 217
East York	64 616	90 988	101 963	101 974
Etobicoke	53 779	156 035	282 690	298 713
North York	85 897	269 959	504 150	559 521
Scarborough	56 292	217 286	334 310	443 353
York	101 582	129 645	147 305	134 617
Totals	1 037 920*	1 536 320**	2 083 203	2 137 395

* Excludes Long Branch, New Toronto, Mimico, Swansea, Weston, Forest Hill and Leaside, totaling 79 550

** Excludes Long Branch, New Toronto, Mimico, Swansea, Weston, Forest Hill and Leaside, totaling 101 046. In 1967 Long Branch, New Toronto and Mimico were annexed to Etobicoke; Swansea and Forest Hill to the city of Toronto; Weston to York; and Leaside to East York

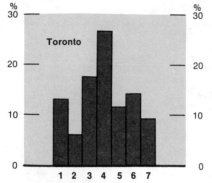

Distribution of Industrial Activity* by Industry Grouping within Census Metropolitan Areas, 1980

Industry groupings
1. Food and beverage and tobacco products industries
2. Leather, textile, knitting mills and clothing industries
3. Wood, furniture and fixtures, paper and allied and printing, publishing and allied industries
4. Machinery, transportation equipment and electrical products industries
5. Primary metal and metal fabricating industries
6. Rubber and plastic products, petroleum and coal products and chemical products industries
7. Non-metallic mineral products and miscellaneous manufacturing industries.

* Industry activity based on the average of percentage shares of the value shipments of goods of own manufacture, total value added and total number of employees for each of the selected metropolitan areas.

Source: Figure II, Catalogue 31-209, Statistics Canada.

TORONTO-DOMINION BANK. Principal Canadian insurance and investment companies centre in the city. The Toronto Stock Exchange is one of the leaders in N America outside New York. Toronto is also headquarters for national newspaper chains such as SOUTHAM and the THOMSON Press: the latter's Toronto *Globe and Mail* maintains regional editions across the country. The MACLEAN HUNTER magazine empire and English-language TV and radio similarly have main Toronto bases, as does English-Canadian book publishing and film. There is a close concentration of Canadian head offices of industrial, resource and retail corporations and of American or multinational giants — from Abitibi through Eaton's to Xerox.

The city's labour force by now is chiefly massed in office, manufacturing and retail work, in that order (1981). It is widely unionized in public sectors, large private enterprises and skilled trades. From the York Printer's Union of 1832, Toronto has been a centre of labour organization, though it did not become broadly based until the growth of industrialism from the 1870s. By the close of WWI union movement was firmly emplaced, and though its fortunes have varied, as in the grim 1930s, from WWII organized labour has been an influential economic and political factor in the city. To the present, Toronto labour has been largely stable and fairly conservative in character compared with western cities.

Transportation Water traffic, once Toronto's vital link outward, still brings bulk goods by lake and direct overseas shipments. From 1911, under the Toronto Harbour Commission, port facilities have been repeatedly improved, notably after the ST LAWRENCE SEAWAY (1959) opened it to ocean shipping. Docks for ocean

vessels, new harbour areas behind man-made islands and large recreational and residential waterside developments mark the port today. Though ice closes navigation each winter, Toronto benefits by having both water and land transportation systems. On land, the railway net supplies the city and distributes its products by both CN and CP Rail, while Government of Ontario "GO" trains provide essential commuter services. Bus, truck and car traffic use a similar main road net, especially Highway 401, a many-laned crosstown throughway, and Highway 400, now the prime route N. By air, Toronto's Lester Pearson Airport (Canada's busiest), though congested, offers national and world communications, while the small Island Airport by the harbour is being redeveloped for short-leg business airflights.

This substantial external transport is complemented by good internal transit. Though automobile routes such as the Gardiner Expressway along the southern edge of the downtown, or the Don Valley Parkway running northward, bear heavy loads, the city has successfully maintained its public streetcar, bus and subway systems. Amid all the metropolitan intensity, there are bicycle paths and quiet walking routes through wooded ravine parklands.

Government and Politics At civic incorporation (1834), Toronto had a mayor and a city council elected by wards. The mayor, originally chosen from and by council, became directly elected by the voters in the 1870s; a board of control was added in the 1890s, arising from an URBAN REFORM wave for "clean," efficient government, but was abolished in the 1960s. Sizeable civic departments grew for services such as roads, water, police and health, while the separately elected board of education became a powerful municipal body in its own right. Canada's first METROPOLITAN GOVERNMENT was formed in Toronto in 1953, when 13 municipalities, including the city of Toronto, were reorganized to form the Municipality of Metropolitan Toronto. The Metro Council, under a chairman, had prime responsibility for overall concerns such as finance, education, transport, welfare and water supply, to which police and housing were later added. The city proper and member boroughs kept more local service tasks. Yet clearly, the bigger duties and expenditures now lay with Metro. As the populations of the surrounding boroughs mounted, the Metro chairman elected by his council came to replace Toronto's mayor as the chief figure in municipal operations.

Civic politics have ostensibly not operated on party lines, though Conservative partisans have usually been dominant (backed through the 19th century by the influential Orange Order). The radical first mayor, William Lyon MACKENZIE, was a scarce exception, as was the moral reformer, Mayor William Mowland, in the 1880s. Far more typical were respectably cautious guardians who gave fairly competent government but took few chances. Some pragmatic mayors also lasted as sympathetically popular, like Tommy Church through WWI and after, or Nathan Phillips from the 1950s into the 1960s, who did lead in promoting the new City Hall. Still, some others were more associated with change, such as Horatio Mocken, who faced the needs of expanding city services before WWI, or David CROMBIE and John Sewell in the 1970s, who worked with a newer breed of civic reformers to save the quality of city life from uncontrolled development. Now, however, Metro chairmen have top political significance. Moreover, the Metro entity, so populous and financially demanding, inevitably bulks large for the Ontario govenment also, while federally, Toronto's major "clout" certainly affects national election and cabinet-making strategies.

Cultural Life Toronto is the main urban cultural focus in English Canada. It is the home of

the big UNIVERSITY OF TORONTO (1827), more recent YORK U and RYERSON POLYTECHNICAL INSTITUTE; the Ontario Art Gallery and Ontario College of Art, the world-renowned ROYAL ONTARIO MUSEUM and the innovative ONTARIO SCIENCE CENTRE; the TORONTO SYMPHONY and the NATIONAL BALLET OF CANADA. Other nationally eminent artistic, musical and library institutions are found here along with top Canadian centres of medical and scientific research, and a world-class Metro Zoo. Toronto is English Canada's leading theatre town; and now its rich multicultural variety is reflected in the performing arts, as well as in ethnic journals and restaurants. The city has long been a potent factor in Anglo-Canadian literature as a national base for literary periodicals, publishing houses, and successions of noted authors from Goldwin SMITH and Sir Charles G.D. ROBERTS to E.J. PRATT, Morley CALLAGHAN, Marshall MCLUHAN, Margaret ATWOOD and Robertson DAVIES. Similarly in art, it has been the base for Paul KANE, the GROUP OF SEVEN and numerous contemporary painters such as Harold TOWN, as well as musicians such as Glenn GOULD.

In popular culture, the city's top-circulation Toronto *Star*, tabloid *Sun* and *Globe and Mail* have a massive readership. In TV, the CBC, private stations and readily available trans-border American ones, provide a wide choice. Popular concerts attract large crowds, notably at Ontario Place, a lakeside recreational area, or the CANADIAN NATIONAL EXHIBITION, Canada's largest annual exposition. Other leading public draws include hilly High Park, Fort York (restored to 1812 days), Casa Loma (the grandiose castle home of a 1900s financial magnate), the CN Tower and Toronto Island, a harbour park preserve. In professional sports, Toronto displays the TORONTO MAPLE LEAFS (hockey), TORONTO BLUE JAYS (baseball), TORONTO ARGONAUTS (football) and Toronto Blizzard (soccer, disbanded 1985). Amateur sports range from yachting to curling, Olympic-level skating, swimming and rowing. Soccer is keenly popular among the immigrant community. Facilities from Maple Leaf Gardens to local rinks, the O'Keefe Centre and Thomson Hall to community dramatic and music stages, public swimming pools to park athletic fields, serve a recreation-minded citizenry year-round.

J.M.S. CARELESS

Reading: E. Arthur, No Mean City (1964); J.M.S. Careless, Toronto to 1918 (1984); G.P. Glazebrook, The Story of Toronto (1971); W. Kilbourn and R. Christl, Toronto in Words and Pictures (1977); J.T. Lemon, Toronto, The English-Speaking Metropolis since 1918 (1984); H. Scadding, Toronto of Old (F.H. Armstrong, ed, 1966).

Toronto, a raunchy, loud rock band with a large Canadian following after 4 albums, is led by vocalist Holly Woods and keyboard player Scott Kreyer. Founding members Sheron Alton and Brian Allen quit in 1983. JOHN GEIGER

Toronto Argonauts, football team. In 1873 members of Toronto's Argonaut Rowing Club formed a rugby team, choosing as their colours the double blue of the English universities of Oxford and Cambridge. They lost to U of T in their first of 16 GREY CUP appearances (1911), winning their first of 11 Grey Cups against the same club in 1914. Led by the great all-round athlete Lionel CONACHER, they defeated the EDMONTON ESKIMOS in the first East-West Grey Cup (1921) and won 8 more national championships in the ensuing 31 years (1933, 1937, 1938, 1945, 1946, 1947, 1950 and 1952), with such distinguished Canadian players as Joe KROL. Quarterback Joe Theismann took them to a 1971 championship loss to Calgary, and under coach Bob O'Billovich they lost to the Edmonton Eskimos in the 1982 Grey Cup game. The team ended 31 years of frustration with a victory in 1983 over the BC LIONS. In 1959 they moved from Varsity Stadium to Canadian National Exhibition Stadium, which now seats 54 533.

DEREK DRAGER

Toronto Blue Jays The first Canadian team admitted to baseball's American League, the franchise was awarded to a group consisting of Imperial Trust Ltd, Labatt's Breweries, and the Canadian Imperial Bank of Commerce after a bid in 1976 to purchase and move the National League Giants to Toronto was thwarted by a San Francisco court. Peter Bavasi was appointed to oversee BASEBALL operations and the Blue Jays began play in 1977 at Exhibition Stadium on Toronto's Lakeshore Blvd. They achieved their first winning season in 1983 with a record of 89-73 for a fourth-place finish. Memorable moments in the team's history include their first place standing at the All-Star break in 1983, Dave Stieb's winning pitching assignment in the 1983 All-Star game, and Alfredo Griffin's consecutive playing streak of 391 games which ended in May 1984. In 1983 Lloyd Moseby became the first Jay to score 100 runs and Willie Upshaw the first to drive in 100 runs in a single season.   WILLIAM HUMBER

Toronto City Hall (architects Viljo Revell and John B. PARKIN Associates, 1965) is the product of a highly successful international competition (1957-58) which attracted 532 entries from around the world and was won by Finnish architect Revell. A minority report suggested that the 2-tower arrangement was functionally impractical, but the building has been a great popular success. The curved towers and circular council chamber created instantly recognizable shapes, unlikely to be lost among the rectangular commercial office buildings of the downtown. The elevated walkway around Phillips Square in front of the building clearly defined that space, at the expense of interrupted views inward and outward. As picturesque in its way as E.J. Lennox's sandstone and terracotta old City Hall (1886-99), Revell's buildings is a fitting neighbour and successor.   MICHAEL MCMORDIE

Toronto Dance Theatre is a modern-dance company. In recent years it has numbered about 10 in membership. It was founded in 1968 when Patricia BEATTY, who already had her own school and company, the New Dance Group of Canada, joined forces with the young dancer-choreographers David EARLE and Peter RANDAZZO. The 3, who had all been trained in the technique of the American modern-dance pioneer Martha Graham, continued to direct the company co-operatively until 1983, when Kenny Pearl became sole artistic director. The company is distinguished for its commitment to originality and creativity. Beatty, Earle and Randazzo have together choreographed more than 60 works for the company, half of which have used commissioned scores by Canadian composers. Since 1980, the works of resident choreographer Christopher House have also occupied an important place in the company's repertoire. The company has toured across Canada as well as in the US and Europe. During the early 1980s the company was plagued with financial problems, in part the result of its ambitious move into a new home — a large renovated church building with accommodation for both the company and its associated school. A number of dancers developed within the company have joined some of the world's leading modern-dance groups.   MICHAEL CRABB

Toronto-Dominion Bank, with head offices in Toronto, is a Canadian bank chartered in 1955 upon the amalgamation of the Bank of Toronto (incorporated 1855) and the Dominion Bank (incorporated 1869). The Toronto-Dominion Bank has grown steadily. In 1960 it formed T-D Realty Co Limited, and in 1968, in partnership with the ROYAL BANK OF CANADA, CANADIAN IMPERIAL BANK OF COMMERCE and the Banque canadienne nationale, formed Chargex Ltd (now VISA). Other ventures undertaken by the T-D Bank, as it is popularly called, include

Tordom Investments Ltd, formed in partnership with Leamor Holdings Ltd, a registered loan corporation, which subsequently became Tordom Corporation International. In 1973, in partnership with the BANK OF NOVA SCOTIA, the bank formed Scotia-Toronto Dominion Leasing Limited, which leases equipment to Canadian industry. With 1000 branches located throughout Canada and around the world, the Toronto-Dominion Bank offers a full range of banking services. As of Oct 1983, it had revenues of $4.8 billion (ranking 5th among banks and financial institutions in Canada), assets of $42.8 billion (ranking 5th) and 17 571 employees.
DEBORAH C. SAWYER

Toronto Islands, 332 ha, are an archipelago of 15 islands in Lk Ontario about 1.6 km S of downtown TORONTO. Known to the Mississauga as "the place of trees standing out of the water," this car-free area was originally a peninsula made up of eroded sand and gravel carried W from the Scarborough Bluffs. The islands were separated from the mainland in 1858 by a violent storm. From an area of 145 km in 1870, they have more than doubled in size. Winds, currents, dredging and landfill operations have helped shape the islands, curving them into an 8 km hook broken on the inside into tiny lagoons and islets. The 8 largest islands are Centre, Muggs, Donut, Forestry, Olympic, South, Snake and Algonquin. Centre I, with its amusement park, beaches and gardens, attracts one million visitors a year. Toronto Island Airport, forming the NW area of Hanlan's Point, is one of Canada's busiest, with an average 100 000 takeoffs and landings per year.

Lt-Gov SIMCOE, who picnicked, hiked and went horseback riding on the islands in 1793, decided in 1794 to make Toronto the naval and military centre of Upper Canada, with Gibraltar Point (now Hanlan's Pt) guarding Toronto harbour. In 1813, however, American soldiers landed and destroyed fortifications on the islands. A residential community for over 150 years, Ward's I, at the eastern edge of the archipelago, was named after fisherman David Ward who settled there with his family in 1834. The Ward's I community is linked by bridge to that on Algonquin I, and together they have a residential population of around 650 people occupying 250 homes, owned by islanders on land leased from Metro Toronto. In the early 1950s, 8000 people lived on Centre I, but its elegant summer resort hotels, theatres and stores were demolished in the late 1950s and 1960s to make room for parkland. Since 1956 the remaining residents have struggled to save their homes. In 1981 the Government of Ontario passed legislation ensuring that the community will continue to exist at least until 2005.   ROBERT SWARD

Reading: Robert Sward, *The Toronto Islands* (1983).

Toronto Maple Leafs, hockey team, was formed in 1927 when Conn SMYTHE purchased and renamed the Toronto St Pats. A veteran of WWI and an outspoken patriot, Smythe chose the maple leaf symbol in the hope of giving his team broader appeal. In the depths of the Depression he was able to arrange financing for a new arena, and Maple Leaf Gardens was built in 5 months in 1931. Meanwhile, the flamboyant owner purchased "King" CLANCY from Ottawa Senators for the unprecedented sum of $35 000 and 2 players, and the team won its first STANLEY CUP in 1931-32. In their most successful years the Maple Leafs were known as a gutsy, hardworking team, exemplifying Smythe's (perhaps apocryphal, but apt) dictum "if you can't beat them in the alley, you can't beat them on the ice." The team has won few individual awards: the last Maple Leaf to win the scoring title was Gord Drillon in 1938, and only 2 Leafs have won the HART TROPHY — Babe Pratt (1944) and Ted KENNEDY (1955). Nevertheless the team has won

the Stanley Cup 11 times and enjoyed 2 eras of dominance, winning in 1944-45 and, after a dramatic trade of 5 players for Max BENTLEY, again in 1946-47, 1947-48, 1948-49 and 1950-51. "Punch" Imlach rebuilt the team with an infusion of aging or lesser-known players such as Bert Olmstead, Johnny Bower and Red KELLY, along with brilliant young players such as Dave Keon, Carl Brewer and Frank MAHOVLICH. The team won the trophy in 1961-62, 1962-63, 1963-64 and 1966-67. Smythe relinquished control in 1961 to his son Stafford, Harold Ballard and John Bassett, and Ballard gained complete control after Stafford's death in 1971. The team deteriorated after its unexpected triumph in 1967 and has failed to reach the Stanley Cup finals since then.   JAMES MARSH

Toronto Mendelssohn Choir, fd 1894 by Augustus Stephen VOGT as an extension of his Jarvis St Baptist Church choir, presented its first concert in MASSEY HALL 15 Jan 1895. After 3 successful years Vogt disbanded the choir, only to resume again with 200 voices in 1900. Succeeding conductors have been Herbert Austin Fricker, 1917-42, who collaborated with various US orchestras; Sir Ernest MACMILLAN, 1942-57, who merged the Toronto Conservatory of Music Choir with the TMC and established annual performances of Handel's *Messiah* at Christmas and Bach's *St Matthew Passion* at Easter; Frederick Silvester, 1957-60; Walter Susskind, 1960-63; and Elmer ISELER, 1964- , who brought in his FESTIVAL SINGERS OF CANADA as the professional nucleus of the choir, 1968-79, when that group was succeeded by the Elmer Iseler Singers. Each conductor has introduced new repertoire, including Canadian compositions and the Canadian premiere of major European works. The choir has made frequent appearances in the US and toured Europe in 1972 and 1980. It has performed at many major festivals in Europe including the Edinburgh Festival, the Lucerne International Festival, the Festival Estival in Paris, the Flanders Festival and the Henry Wood Promenade Concerts in London's Royal Albert Hall. In 1977 a Toronto Mendelssohn Youth Choir was formed. This choir of high-school-aged singers, at present under the leadership of Robert Cooper, participates in educational workshops and presents annual Christmas and spring concerts.
ISABELLE MARGARET MILLS

Toronto Star, Canada's largest newspaper, was established in 1892. In 1899 its Liberal proprietors hired Joseph E. Atkinson to run the paper; by 1913 he had become the majority shareholder. Until Atkinson's death in 1948, the *Star* reflected the highly personal style of JOURNALISM he preferred. Stressing human interest and local issues over broader coverage, Atkinson made his paper dominant in the Toronto area, and then across the S-central portion of Ontario. At the same time, he maintained a liberal attitude to public affairs, and used his newspaper to advocate a left-of-centre point of view. In 1910 he established the *Toronto* STAR WEEKLY, which plugged the gap left by the absence of Sunday newspapers from the Canadian scene.

Writing at the *Star* was determinedly lively. In the 1920s and 1930s writers included Morley CALLAGHAN, Ernest Hemingway, Gordon Sinclair and Gregory Clark. The *Star's* political stand earned it the enmity of Ontario's Conservative government during the 1940s, and after Atkinson's death there was a spectacular battle between the Government of Ontario and the Atkinson Foundation. Under Harry Hindmarsh, Atkinson's son-in-law, the *Star* became more partisan and was closely identified with the federal Liberal Party. After Hindmarsh's death in 1956 the paper recovered some of its independence, although it continued to favour the nationalist wing of the Liberal Party and particularly its spokesman, Walter GORDON. The 1960s

and 1970s brought expansion and prosperity to the *Star*, which dominated the Toronto-evening newspaper field after the demise of its longtime rival, the *Toronto Telegram*, in 1971. A Sunday edition and finally a morning edition appeared. Despite its dominance and success, the *Star* remains a local, Toronto paper and has not attempted to attain the national standing of its morning rival, the GLOBE AND MAIL. The circulation of the *Star* (Sept 1983) was 497 909 (Mon-Fri), 799 038 (Sat) and 488 680 (Sun). It is published by TORSTAR CORPORATION. *See also* NEWSPAPERS.   ROBERT BOTHWELL
Reading: R. Harkness, *J.E. Atkinson of the Star* (1963).

Toronto Symphony was founded in 1906 as the Toronto Conservatory Symphony Orchestra. Under conductor Luigi von Kunits, 1922-31, the orchestra gave its first concert in MASSEY HALL on 23 Apr 1923. Sir Ernest MACMILLAN was music director, 1931-56, and was succeeded by Walter Susskind, 1956-65, who led the orchestra in its successful Carnegie Hall debut on 3 Dec 1963. Seiji Ozawa, 1965-69, introduced new repertoire and attracted public enthusiasm and he took the orchestra on tour to Britain, France and Japan. The experienced European conductor Karel Ančerl led the orchestra, 1969-73, to artistic and financial success and began the popular summer concerts at Ontario Place Forum. Under Andrew Davis since 1975, the orchestra has expanded its repertoire, toured China, Japan, Europe and the US, and performed annually at Carnegie Hall in New York. In Sept 1982 the orchestra moved to Roy Thomson Hall where, in its first season, it performed over 150 concerts for nearly half a million people.

Since 1961 the orchestra's general manager has been Walter Homburger, one of Canada's most experienced arts administrators. The orchestra began recording under MacMillan, and has since recorded extensively for RCA, CBC and CBS Masterworks. In 1974 the Toronto Symphony (the word Orchestra was dropped from the name in 1964) organized the Toronto Symphony Youth Orchestra with Victor FELDBRILL as its first conductor.   BARBARA NOVAK

Torstar Corporation, a broadly based information and entertainment communications company, publishes the TORONTO STAR, Canada's largest newspaper (1983 Mon-Fri circulation 497 909). Other newspaper publishing interests include Metroland Printing and Publishing, commercial printers and publishers of 20 midweek and 5 weekend publications reaching over 1.5 million readers in the Toronto area. Torstar's subsidiary, Harlequin Enterprises, the world's largest publisher of romance fiction, sold over 200 million books and published 4000 different editions in 13 languages in 1983. Torstar, with SOUTHAM INC, owns Infomart, which operates Grassroots, Teleguide, Information Management Service, Contel and other electronic publishing services in Canada and the US. The company's only nonpublishing interest is Miles Kimball, a US gift and home-products catalogue business. Torstar's assets in 1983 totalled $445 million, with revenues of $563 million.
                        PETER S. ANDERSON

Torts [Med Latin, *tortum*, "wrong," "injustice"], a large area of private law concerned with compensating those who have been injured by the wrongdoing of others. Unlike criminal law, tort law involves only 2 parties, one of whom, the plaintiff, claims damages from the other, the defendant. Unlike contract law, where 2 parties agree to their respective rights and obligations, in tort law it is the society, through its judicial and legislative systems, that imposes obligations on everyone to act in consideration of the rights of others. The law of torts is mainly judge-made law; courts over the centuries have defined people's rights and obligations with respect to their fellows. These are constantly in flux and change

to meet new technological and social concerns. Some tort law, however, originates in statutes, which vary from province to province.

The purpose of tort law is not to punish wrongdoers but to provide damages to victims as compensation for their losses. For example, monetary settlements are used, as best as possible, to restore the lives of accident victims to their condition before the accident. Intentional torts are the most serious, as they involve acts undertaken with the deliberate intention of injuring others. A battery is the intentional application of force to another; an assault is to place another in fear for his safety; a false imprisonment is to prevent unjustifiably another from going where he pleases. For these torts, not only may compensatory damages be awarded, but a court may award extra or punitive damages to punish the wrongdoer, although this rarely happens. Instead recovery is often through victim compensation funds established by statute in 8 provinces and the territories and maintained under cost-sharing agreements with the federal government. People who commit an intentional tort may plead they had a valid defence, such as the victim's consent, self-defence, defence of property, necessity or lawful authority. If any of these defences are accepted by the court, the action will be dismissed. Intentional torts may also occur against property. To enter a person's house or land without permission is to commit a trespass; to interfere with another's goods is a conversion; to refuse to return something which belongs to another is a detinue.

People are usually injured because of the carelessness, rather than the deliberate acts of others. This is the tort of negligence, the most important of the modern torts. The famous English case of *Donoghue* v *Stevenson*, in which a manufacturer of a soft drink carelessly allowed a snail to crawl into a bottle of drink, established the principle that everyone is under a legal obligation to take reasonable care to ensure that others will not be injured because of careless conduct. Everyone must live up to the standards of the "reasonable man," an important concept of the negligence tort. Based on objective guidelines and built on precedence, the standard allows the court to adapt to the changing circumstances of what might be considered "reasonable." Similarly, if persons by their own fault cause or contribute to their own injuries, they will be held at least partly responsible for their damages. If found liable, wrongdoers must compensate victims in full for losses. Compensation will not only include medical bills, lost income and the costs of future care, but also an award for pain and suffering and the loss of the enjoyment of life, because if a tort causes death, the estate and dependants are entitled to seek compensation from the tortfeasor (person guilty of tort) for their losses. Certain activities are so fraught with risk that compensation to those injured is awarded without the need to establish the defendant's fault. These are strict liability torts. According to the English case of *Rylands* v *Fletcher*, anyone who brings something on to his land which is not naturally there is strictly liable if the thing escapes and injures someone. People are strictly liable for injuries caused by wild animals they keep or by fires they have started.

There are other, less familiar, torts. People who unreasonably interfere with another's use and enjoyment of his land will be liable to him for a private nuisance. Under the law of occupier's liability, everyone who occupies a building owes a duty of care to those who visit and who are injured on the premises. Manufacturers are responsible under the law of products' liability to those who are injured by defective products. Under the rules of vicarious liability, employers are responsible for the torts committed by their employees in the course of their employment. By virtue of the economic torts, persons will be

held liable if they wrongfully prevent others from earning a living or making expected profits. It is tortious to encourage someone to break a contract which the latter has entered into with someone else. It is also wrongful to intimidate someone by threats of unlawful acts to force him to do something which is to his economic disadvantage.

Of course, many injuries result from pure accident, and if the victim cannot prove that the person who caused the accident acted wrongfully, he will not be entitled to any compensation, despite his own innocence. This has been strongly condemned by critics of negligence law, who consider it unfair that persons who cannot prove that their injuries resulted from someone else's negligence are left to bear their losses on their own. Most accidents occur either at work or on the road. Because of their frequency and tort law's inability to compensate adequately all those injured at work, every province has WORKERS' COMPENSATION legislation, allowing workers to receive compensation without the need to establish fault. Many Canadian provinces have enacted similar legislation for highway traffic accidents and have replaced tort law by "no fault" compensation schemes. There is a lively debate about the extent to which these schemes ought to be enlarged at the expense of the traditional tort-law process.

Recently new torts have emerged. Invasion of privacy has gained in importance. Older torts, such as negligence, are applied increasingly to professional groups, such as doctors and lawyers, to force them to live up to higher standards of competence when serving the public. People are held accountable not only for their negligent acts but for misleading advice which may cause loss to others. Even government officials and agencies are being held liable in tort for damages they cause the public in carrying out their functions. Those who support tort law have applauded these developments, arguing the civil remedy in tort has been and can continue to be valuable to citizens fighting against more powerful elements of our society.   LEWIS N. KLAR

Tory [Irish *tóraidhe*, "pursuer"], name applied to members of the CONSERVATIVE PARTY and its antecedents. The name originated as an epithet for dispossessed Irish "papists" who plundered English settlers and soldiers in Ireland. It was applied 1679-80 to supporters of the succession of the duke of York (later James II, a Roman Catholic) to the English throne. From 1689 it was the name of the political party associated with conservative beliefs and later closely identified with the Church of England. The term survived as a nickname for the British Conservative Party and was applied by analogy to the Conservative Party that emerged in Canada in the 19th century. "Tory" is still the American term for supporters of Britain during the American Revolution; those who are called LOYALISTS in Canadian parlance.   JAMES MARSH

Tory, Henry Marshall, educator (b at Port Shoreham, NS 11 Jan 1864; d at Ottawa 6 Feb 1947). Awarded one of McGill's earliest doctoral degrees in science, Tory did not himself become a researcher but was the principal founder of several universities — UBC, U of A and Carleton — and of the ALBERTA RESEARCH COUNCIL and the National Research Council Laboratories.

Son of a Methodist minister, Tory trained for the ministry but was offered a teaching post at McGill after graduation by J.W. DAWSON. In 1905, when professor of mathematics, he was sent to BC to advise on the future of McGill's affiliated Vancouver and Victoria colleges, leading to the 1908 UBC Act. His tour of the West led to his appointment in 1908 as founding president of U of A, which he built into a lively institution, with both services (eg, a travelling rural library and radio station) and high standards of teaching and research. In 1917 he organized the "Khaki University" for Canadian soldiers in England, and in 1919 was instrumental in creating the organization that in 1921 became the Alberta Research Council.

Appointed in 1923 to the NATIONAL RESEARCH COUNCIL, Tory became its chairman within 6 months, apparently because no other member had faith in its political future. His first priority was persuading the government to build the national laboratories planned in 1919 but vetoed in 1921 through procedural confusion in Parliament. He succeeded in 1927 and the following year moved to Ottawa as the NRC's first full-time president. Tory was then 64 years old.

Depression conditions frustrated Tory's ambition of making the NRC as vigorous an influence in Canada as the university had been in Alberta, but the laboratories were completed and staffed between 1928 and 1932 with about 50 scientists, the essential nucleus for the NRC's expansion in WWII. Though embittered by the manner of his 1935 retirement, Tory regarded the NRC Laboratories as his supreme achievement. At age 77 he headed the committee that opened Carleton College in 1942, serving as unpaid president and lecturer until his death.

Throughout his life, Tory's main characteristic was enthusiasm. The promotion of science was his central theme, but his interests ranged from the League of Nations to populating the Canadian Prairies. The most famous educator of his day, he was a controversial and proud man: but he had much to be proud of.

DONALD J.C. PHILLIPSON

Totem Pole, the signboard, genealogical record and memorial of Northwest Coast Indian tribes. Crests carved on poles were lineage property and reflected the history of the lineage. Animals represented on the crests were helping spirits, and included the beaver, bear, wolf, shark, whale, raven, eagle, frog and mosquito. There were 6 principal types of poles: memorial or heraldic poles, grave figures, house posts, house-front or portal poles, welcoming poles and mortuary poles. They varied in size, but house-front poles could be over 1 m in width at the base, reaching a height of over 15 m. HAIDA erected sturdy

Totem pole "Hole in the Sky," Kitwancool, BC (*photo by Karl Sommerer*).

poles, and those of the TSIMSHIAN and particularly the KWAKIUTL were more slender. *See also* NORTHWEST COAST INDIAN ART.   RENÉ R. GADACZ

Touch-me-not, or Jewelweed, common names for family of herbaceous PLANTS (Balsaminaceae) of which *Impatiens* is the principal genus. Genus name derives from the fact that a ripe seed capsule, when touched, explodes violently, projecting seed some distance. Between 600 and 700 species occur worldwide, primarily in Eurasia and Africa. There are 4 native species in Canada (*I. ecalcarata,* southeastern BC; *I. capensis,* southern BC and Alberta; *I. noli-tangere,* the YT and BC to Manitoba; *I. pallida,* Ontario to Atlantic provinces) and 2 introduced. Flowers vary from bright orange to reddish or pale yellow. Native plants are annuals, prefer moist environments, have delicate appearance and vary in height (up to 1.5 m). The introduced perennial *I. glandulifera* is much taller, has more flowers and tends to become a WEED. The introduced perennial *I. sultani* (patience plant or busy Lizzie) is a common houseplant or bedding plant. Multicoloured introduced annual *I. balsamina* (garden balsam) is a useful bedding plant. Recently, many new species have been introduced to cultivation and hybridized, producing new strains. *I. capensis* and *I. pallida* were used medicinally by Indians and settlers, especially for poison ivy and as dye.

PATRICK SEYMOUR

Toupin, Paul, dramatist, essayist, educator (b at Montréal 7 Dec 1918). His plays, classical in language and structure and universal in theme, have been more appreciated by critics than by audiences in Québec. *Brutus* (1952) is one of the few tragedies ever composed in French Canada, and was televised in 1953. *Le Mensonge* (1960) and *Chacun son amour* (1961) were performed for television only, and Toupin turned thereafter to essays, such as *L'Écrivain et son théâtre* (1964), and autobiographical memoirs. His *Souvenirs pour demain* (1960) was awarded the prize for best foreign publication in French from the Académie française in 1960. Since 1970 Toupin has been living in Spain.   L.E. DOUCETTE

Tourism, a complete and naturally related collection of services with a single unifying purpose: to provide TRANSPORTATION, accommodation, food and beverage services, recreation and entertainment to Canadians or foreigners travelling in Canada for any purpose. It is an important and fast-growing industry. At the close of 1982 Canada's tourism industry earned over $17.7 billion, contributing over 5% to the GNP, representing over 1.3 million Canadian jobs and more than 10% of the labour force. By the year 2000 it could be one of the most important single economic activities in Canada. Money spent on tourism products has a great impact on employment, both directly and indirectly, that is at least equal to, and in many cases more than, spending in the nation's leading 40 industries.

Visitors from outside Canada spent $3.8 billion in 1983, up from $3.7 billion a year earlier, making tourism Canada's fifth-largest earner of foreign exchange after motor vehicles, auto parts, natural gas, newsprint and wood pulp. The bulk of Canada's tourism comes from Canadians travelling in and exploring their own country; the $13.9 billion domestic tourism of 1982 far exceeded the $2.4 billion contributed by US visitors and the $1.3 billion from offshore visitors. On the international travel account, Canada has a falling share of the international market and a $2.1-billion deficit: Canadians spent $5.9 billion outside Canada. Catering to tourists in Canada involves many large companies and about 100 000 small and medium-sized businesses, including almost 300 000 hotel and motel rooms, more than 45 000 eating places and 4000 travel agencies. These businesses serve over 34 million visitors a year. Every 100 000 visitors to a community can mean $9 million in revenue.

At the federal level, until the Sept 1984 election of the Conservative government, tourism was the responsibility of the minister of small business and tourism through Tourism Canada in the Dept of Regional Industrial Expansion. In Sept 1984 a minister of state for tourism was appointed. The promotion and development of tourism through a designated federal agency dates from 1934. The recognized national industry association is the Ottawa-based Tourism Industry Assn of Canada (TIAC). It is an umbrella organization representing private sector companies, organizations, institutions and individuals engaged in tourism in Canada and working in partnership with provincial and territorial tourism-industry associations. TIAC has represented the Canadian tourism industry for 53 years and exists to lobby government, communicate with industry, and increase public awareness of the importance of tourism and the need for public support.

In 1983 a Tourism Advisory Council was appointed by David Smith, then minister for small business and tourism. The 32-member body is to advise the minister on tourism issues but in no way replaces TIAC's mandate as the organization representing the Canadian tourism industry to the federal government. William Pattison, a former TIAC chairman, was named chairman of the new Tourism Advisory Council.

Tourism dates back to the early history of Canada. Writings by the early explorers and traders contributed to the growing knowledge of the Canadian landscape, still the primary attraction of Canada's tourism industry (*see* EXPLORATION AND TRAVEL LITERATURE). From the mid-18th to the early 19th century TOPOGRAPHIC PAINTERS recorded an idealized landscape, scenes that were often reproduced as engravings in travel books published in Europe. The CANADIAN PACIFIC RAILWAY, through its rail and steamship services, its hotels and publicity campaigns, attracted affluent European and American tourists to Canada. Modern travel and the opportunity for mass travel came with the jet airplane. Business travel illustrates the degree of change: travel and related expenses are the third-largest expenditure of Canadian business, after payroll and data-processing expenditures. Canadian companies are reported to have spent $7 billion on business travel in 1982.

The Canadian tourism industry requires sophisticated marketing, delivering value and service to offset continuing negative effects in the world economic, social and political environment. The main negative factors affecting travel to Canada include slow recovery from economic recession, the high cost of gasoline and other items such as liquor, continuing high unemployment in most industrialized countries, relatively weak currencies in comparison to American and Canadian dollars in most countries, aging European populations, and the related drop in the friends-and-relatives markets. The best potential source for travellers to Canada is likely in the Pacific. Arrivals from Japan show a modest decline but Hong Kong is expected to show an increase, continuing an upward trend that started in 1979. Australia remains stable. No major changes are expected in the flow of travel from the US to Canada, unless costs are reduced. Traditional European markets, including the UK, France, W Germany and the Netherlands, are seen as remaining at 1983 levels with little prospect of growth.

Contemporary Canadian tourist attractions are often the same as those extolled by early travel writers — the fjorded coast of BC, the majestic grandeur of the Canadian Rockies, the wide open spaces of the Prairies, the lakes, forests and rivers of central Canada, the Atlantic coast in its infinite variety of bays, coves, beaches and scenic vistas, the arctic environment and people, and, of course, such old favourites as NIAGARA FALLS. The works of man have been added to these natural assets through the development of modern and sophisticated cities, galleries and museums, performing arts, historic sites, FESTIVALS and events such as EXPO 67, the CALGARY STAMPEDE and winter OLYMPIC GAMES. To most of the world Canada is known as a tourist destination through its scenery, space and environment.

F.G. BRANDER

Tousignant, Claude, painter (b at Montréal 23 Dec 1932). Tousignant studied at the School of Design, Montreal Museum of Fine Arts, with Jacques de TONNANCOUR and Gordon Webber (1948-52). From his earliest works his intention was to make purely abstract paintings in which nothing interfered with the viewer's sensation of colour. He chose a circular format in which sequences of colour produce a dynamic optical effect. Recent works, still nonobjective, are composed of a single colour and built to stand away from the wall on which they are hung. Tousignant was a member of the Association des artistes non-figuratifs de Montréal and, with MOLINARI and LEDUC, was a major force in the continuing development of abstraction in Montréal.

MARILYN BURNETT

Tousignant, Serge, camera artist (b at Montréal 28 May 1942). His early work, after study at the École des beaux-arts, Montréal (1950-62), was as a painter and sculptor. His concern was the relationship between abstract structures and illusion, later broadened to include direct images of the natural world. He stopped painting after 1967 and by the early 1970s was working exclusively with photographic images. In 1978 he began the photographic series *Geometrisation solaire,* based on arrangements of sticks and the shadows they cast. The apparently arbitrary placement of the sticks is resolved by the consistent geometric figures formed by their shadows.

DAVID BURNETT

Reading: David Burnett, *Serge Tousignant, geometrisations* (1981).

Towers, Graham Ford, banker, public servant (b at Montréal 29 Sept 1897; d at Ottawa 4 Dec 1975). Towers served in WWI and graduated from McGill in 1919. Although originally intending to study law, he entered the service of the ROYAL BANK OF CANADA. Towers rose rapidly, becoming assistant general manager in 1933. In 1934 PM BENNETT summoned Towers to Ottawa, making him first governor of the BANK OF CANADA, a post he occupied until 1954. Under the governments of Mackenzie KING and Louis ST. LAURENT, Towers had immense influence over economic policy and was instrumental in, for example, the appointment of the Rowell-Sirois commission in 1937. After his retirement, Towers held a number of directorships in private business.

ROBERT BOTHWELL

Town, Harold Barling, artist (b at Toronto 13 June 1924). Educated in art at Western Technical School and at the Ontario College of Art, Town was first recognized as a skilful illustrator for such magazines as MACLEAN's and *Mayfair.* His reputation in the art galleries began with a 1954 exhibition at the Picture Loan Society in Toronto of his "single autographic prints." He was a central figure in PAINTERS ELEVEN, a radical group which exhibited from 1954 to 1960. Town at certain moments has shown the influence of other artists (Picasso in his early drawings, New York abstractionists in his nonobjective paintings of the 1950s and 1960s), but quite early in his career he emerged as a unique figure, the most diversely talented artist of his time and perhaps in Canadian history. He has painted murals and portraits, made drawings and sculpture, produced *collages* and prints, illustrated books and articles — all on a high level of accomplishment. He has written books on Tom THOMSON (with David P. Silcox) and Albert

Spengler Writing "The Decline of the West" at his Desk on top of the Kitchen Table (1980), oil on canvas, by Harold Town (*courtesy Harold Town*).

FRANCK, as well as many contentious articles and catalogue notes. From the late 1950s to the late 1960s, he was the most widely publicized visual artist in English Canada, a symbol of the then-dominant abstractionists. But certain elements in his work — for example, his devotion to ancient mythology and his continuing commitment to portraiture — have set him outside the mainstream of Canadian art. During 3 decades as a professional artist, he has created a body of work remarkable for its demonstration of protean talent and its consistent visual energy.

ROBERT FULFORD

Townsend, William, sculptor (b at London, Eng 23 Feb 1909; d at Banff, Alta 4 July 1973). He studied at the Slade School of Fine Art, London (1926-30) and then worked in England as a painter and book illustrator. He came to Canada in 1951 to teach at the Banff Centre School of Fine Art and returned regularly to teach there and at U of A until his death. He set up the Leverhulme Scholarship for Canadian artists to study abroad and edited *Canadian Art Today.* Of his many paintings produced in Alberta, his *Cascade* series (1966-68), based on one of the mountains that overlooks Banff, is considered the most accomplished of his career. The paintings and related drawings utilize abstract shapes indicating proportion, light and a sense of the atmosphere. These highly refined paintings connote a response to a vast scale. He transferred what he knew from the British tradition to this new environment, addressing the daunting nature of the landscape. He kept detailed diaries throughout his life, which he donated to University Coll, London, and *The Townsend Journals,* edited by Andrew Forge (1976), cover the period 1928-51.

KARYN ELIZABETH ALLEN

Township, introduced into Canada in the late 1700s, is the basic land-survey division of land. Townships of varying sizes were laid out in Nova Scotia and New Brunswick, but they were essentially superseded by the COUNTY structure. In large parts of Québec and Ontario the township was laid out in a general checkerboard pattern; a typical township has about 16 km on each side and is divided into lots and concessions. The basic unit of the township in Québec is a farm of 105 acres (42 ha), whereas the sizes in Ontario vary from 10 acres (4 ha) to 200 acres (81 ha).

The municipal township in Québec is the first order of administration. Each of the EASTERN TOWNSHIPS (now called Estrie) forms the principal network of LOCAL GOVERNMENT of one of the

14 regional county municipalities (MRCs) in the Sherbrooke area of Québec. The township in Ontario is also the first tier of government administration; groups of townships are united with villages and towns to form a county. Populations of the municipal townships in Ontario vary widely, from less than 200 for Brougham in Renfrew County to over 24 000 for Flamborough in Hamilton-Wentworth regional municipality. Hundreds of named townships in both Ontario and Québec are unpopulated and are not municipally organized.

In western Canada, the township describes a square land unit with 10 km a side. Each township has 36 sections, with the basic unit, a quarter section, being 160 acres (64 ha). Townships are numbered north from the 49th parallel. An example of a full land description is Northwest Quarter Section 15, Township 5, Range 6, West of the Third Meridian (NW¼ Sec 15, Tp 5, R 6, W3). Each township in the western provinces does not itself have municipal or administrative structure.

ALAN RAYBURN

Reading: C.R. Tindal, *Local Government in Canada* (1979).

Toys and Games In the 19th century, Canadians shared current Victorian ideas on child-raising, which saw children as a special group needing play and recreation, along with a firm and religious upbringing. The view coincided with introduction of mass-production methods. Toy manufacturers in England, France, Germany and, after 1850, the US, supplied their own markets but also exported to Canada. Between 1860 and 1915 some 20 Canadian manufacturers also made toys for Canadian children.

Canadian toys were made almost entirely of wood, a plentiful and cheap material. Then, as now, part of play was preparation for the adult world, and toys reflected that world in miniature. Toy furniture, vehicles and horses were the basic wooden toys made by early manufacturers. In addition, cabinetmakers might, on special order, make toy tables, chairs, beds, cradles, chests of drawers, dish cupboards and sideboards. In the 1860s, chairmakers, carriage-, wagon- and sleigh-makers began to advertise child-sized versions of their products; some also offered toys. From 1880 to 1890 the C.T. Brandon Co, Toronto, included Indian clubs, toy wagons, carts and washboards in their list of WOODENWARES. In 1890, the Gendron manufacturing Co, Toronto, one of the longest-lived Canadian toy producers (1890-1970s), began making children's carriages, wooden toys, carts and wheelbarrows. Children's carriages followed the latest fashion, as did toy carriages. By the 1890s they were produced in rattan as well as wood. Two potteries advertised toys. In 1851 James Bailey, Bowmanville, Ont, offered molded toys. By the 1880s, the St Johns Stone Chinaware Co, St Johns, Qué, made doll sets in blue or white clay.

In this early period, only 2 craftsmen made toys as their sole product. In 1876 Edouard Alfred Martineau, Montréal, began making wooden toys; he continued until 1914, supplementing his toy making with a retail business. By 1881, Mositz Lindner, Berlin [Kitchener], Ont, was making rocking horses and toys. Cosgrove and Co (1890-91) and the Berlin Novelty Works (1899), both in Berlin, made hobby or rocking horses, perhaps as a sideline. These toymakers probably also made other popular horse toys, eg, stationary-platform rocking horses, small horse-on-platform pull toys, and, for very young children, the shoofly, 2 boards cut in the shape of a horse, mounted on rockers and joined by a flat seat.

Games played in the late 19th century included CHESS, checkers, cribbage, backgammon, dominoes, Parcheesi and dissected maps and pictures (jigsaw puzzles). In Québec, where checkers were particularly popular, many boards were homemade. Croquet, an American fad of the 1860s, was much played in Canada. In 1871, 2 Toronto woodturning firms, Hastings and Peterkin, and Leslie and Garden, made croquet sets for the lawn or parlour. They may also have made chessmen, checkers or backgammon men.

Although many toys were available, it is unlikely that any one child would have had many toys. For some children economic necessity meant that play was a rare luxury. Farm children were expected to help with lighter chores and, until 1880, children as young as 10 worked 9-hour days in some city factories. For them, toys would be improvised or homemade from available materials.

WWI curtailed German and English toy production and spurred the Canadian industry. Crokinole boards, toy battleships and building blocks were added to the staple wooden toys. Between 1915 and 1920, 80 individuals or companies made toys: some lasted only one year; others failed as a result of renewed postwar competition. A wider range of companies making more general lines of wares also made a toy line, using brass, tin, iron, lead and rubber. Some, like the Dominion Toy Manufacturing Co, Toronto (1911-34), made dolls and stuffed animals. A flourishing cottage industry produced many varieties of rag doll. Some firms, like the Toy Soldier Novelty Co, Kitchener, Ont, and the Beaver Toy Manufacturing Co, Toronto, made toy soldiers; the Incandescent Light Co, Toronto, made toy bugles and trumpets. The Consolidated Rubber Co, Toronto, made rubber balls, hockey pucks, rattles and animals. The Ideal Bedding Co, Toronto, made a line of toy brass furniture. Thomas Davidson Manufacturing Co, Montréal, made enamelware dishes and toy trunks. The Macdonald Manufacturing Co, Toronto, which made a line of decorated tinware from 1917 to 1942, also made tin toy pails, shovels, cups, plates and banks. The Coleman Fare Box Co, Toronto, made banks; the Belleville Hardware and Lock Manufacturing Co made cast-iron toys. In Toronto, the Manual Construction Co and Reliance Toy Co made steel construction sets. Canadian Toys Ltd, Hamilton, Ont, from 1920 to 1929, made metal humming and dancing tops, and steel construction toys.

From 1920 to 1980 the industry expanded. Production of wooden toys continued; some were made in new variations (eg, swan shoofly, beaver platform pull toy). Vehicles included kiddie and pedal cars, scooters, automobiles, trucks, tractors, metal pull trains and trucks, and model airplanes. The Canadian Buffalo Sled Co and Werlich Manufacturing Co, both of Preston, Ont, concentrated on children's vehicles and toys. Dolls were the major product of Dee and Cee Toy Co, Regal Toy Ltd, Reliable Toy Ltd and York Toy Novelty Co, all of Toronto. The Canadian toy industry was not a large one. By 1928 only 10 firms specialized in toy production. The industry, concentrated in Ontario and Québec, employed 129 people. Value of toys made (excluding toy vehicles and dolls) was $465 424 ($320 986 for wooden toys). Toy vehicle production was worth $394 754; doll production, $281 393.

In the 1940s PLASTIC was introduced for rattles and later for beach toys, tractors, wagons, trucks and construction sets. Cheerio Toys and Games, Toronto, made plastic miniature furniture and gym sets. Aluminum and fibreglass were used to make flying saucers. Toy sets for all purposes made their appearance: tools (garden, carpenter, mechanic), archery, printing, construction and road racing sets, embroidery, sewing, tea, coffee and cooking sets, brushes and cleaning sets, ironing boards and irons, table and chair sets. By 1942, 17 firms (4 in Montréal, 13 in Toronto), employing 604 people, were exclusively devoted to toy making. In 1960, although 126 firms were making toys in Canada, only about 20 special-

ized in toy making. In the 1960s and 1970s several multinational firms began making toys in Canada (Louis Marx, Mattel, Tonka, Coleco). While the industry remained concentrated in central Canada, this period saw the renewal of a CRAFT industry, in NB, PEI and BC, making perennial favourites in wood.   JANET HOLMES

Toys and Games Industry The Canadian toy and game MANUFACTURING industry numbers more than 85 firms, which have annual sales volumes varying from under $250 000 to over $40 million. In total, Canadian toy and game manufacturers produced more than $400 million worth of toys and games in 1984 (manufacturers' selling prices). An additional $340-million worth of toys are imported annually. Much of the import market is controlled in Canada by Canadian manufacturers through licensing or other agreements. Retail sales of toys and games rose from $152.6 million in 1970 to almost $1 billion in 1984. Of that total, Ontario accounts for 38.1%; Québec 24.7%; and BC 11.8%.

Through their trade association, the Canadian Toy Manufacturers Assn, manufacturers have been instrumental in improving the safety of toys; collaboration among the industry, government agencies and articulate consumer groups has resulted in the establishment of stringent SAFETY STANDARDS.

Lead times involved in manufacturing toys may be as much as 2-3 years, but no matter how much effort is put into design, manufacture and marketing, the product must be able to pass scrutiny by the ultimate consumers and most critical judges — children. Impulse buying does play a significant role in toy buying, but most purchases are planned and occur mainly during the last quarter of the year in preparation for Christmas. More than 60% of all toys are sold in the Oct-Dec period. Over 16 000 Canadian children have birthdays each day of the year, and Easter, Halloween and other holidays are gaining in importance as gift-giving occasions. These celebrations help the toy industry over seasonal peaks and valleys.

The marketing of toys is critical for the toy manufacturer. Nearly $20 million is spent annually to advertise toy products, 75% on television ADVERTISING. More than 40 000 different toys are on the market at any given time, and 6000-10 000 products are introduced each year. Although often criticized, television advertising provides a medium for the demonstration of the special features of new toys. To ensure accuracy in advertising, the Canadian toy industry has worked with other interested groups to develop a set of industry-imposed, self-regulated standards: the Broadcast Code for Advertising to Children. Strict adherence is mandatory.   HENRY WITTENBERG

Rocking horse of butternut and maple, from Québec, late 19th century (*courtesy Royal Ontario Museum*).

Tracadie, NB, Town, pop 2452 (1981c), inc 1966, is situated on the Gulf of ST LAWRENCE, 83 km SE of BATHURST. Known by the Indians as *Telakadik*, meaning "a place to camp," the area was used by them for temporary camping while fishing the Little and Big Tracadie rivers. There is evidence of Indian occupation here around 1000 years ago. The location was first settled in

1784 by ACADIANS who had either avoided the deportation or who had since returned, followed shortly thereafter by English settlers. In 1849 the provincial government established a lazaretto (hospital for contagious disease) at Tracadie, the first such institution in Canada. During the 19th century, economic activity in the area centered primarily on the wood industry. Both the Big and Little Tracadie rivers were used to carry timber to Tracadie mill sites or to the shipyards of the Miramichi. The present-day economy is based chiefly on tourism, farming and fishing. Tracadie also serves as a commercial centre for the many neighbouring villages.   ALLEN DOIRON

Track and Field, or athletics as it is sometimes called, is a composite sport encompassing discrete competitions in walking, running, hurdling, jumping (high jump, pole vault, long jump, triple jump), throwing (javelin, discus, shot, hammer) and multiple events (eg, decathalon, heptathalon). At the OLYMPIC GAMES, the sport's best-known competition, there are 41 events, 24 for men and 17 for women. More national communities compete at the Olympics in track and field than in any other sport.

A major goal of participation is the achievement of measurable improvement, the *"citius, altius, fortius"* of the Olympic motto. Competitors train and compete not only to surpass each other but to attain personal and group best-ever performances, or "records," which are given special status by the governing bodies in the sport, the International Amateur Athletic Federation and its Canadian affiliate, the Canadian Track and Field Assn. Organizers, athletes and followers have thus imbued track and field with a purpose significantly different from that of its classical antecedent, the athletics of the ancient Olympics. Although the ancient Greeks had the technology to measure times and distances, these results were unimportant to them — they were preoccupied by the contest — and they did not record them. It is felt by many that the heady pursuit of records in activities common to most of the world's cultures is what gives track and field its widespread fascination, for it dramatizes the modern quest for scientific progress.

While Canadians have long known about classical athletics — in 1844 a group of Montréalers staged a 2-day event they called "the Olympics" — the origins of Canadian track and field are to be found much closer to home, in the running and throwing competitions of the native peoples, the colonial athletics of British officers and civil servants, the Caledonian Games of Scottish immigrants, and the tests of strength at rural "bees" and fairs. By Confederation, 1867, highly competitive meets and match races were a regular part of the sporting scene. Perhaps the most popular event was the professional pedestrian or "go-as-you-please" race, in which competitors ran or walked to achieve a maximum distance within a fixed time, often 6 days. In 1884, to bring some order to these various competitions, the Montreal Amateur Athletic Assn worked to create a national governing body, the Amateur Athletic Union. Although briefly challenged by the more liberal Amateur Athletic Federation and a professional running circuit early in the 20th century, the AAU and the CTFA, formed in 1969, have controlled the most competitive levels of the sport ever since.

With AAU control came strict amateurism — the belief in the moral superiority of participation for its own sake, without any material reward, enforced through a list of prohibitions governing eligibility — which effectively limited participation to those individuals who enjoyed the leisure and the financial means to pursue the sport on their own and those educational and social institutions (the universities, YMCAs and police athletic associations) that accepted the accompanying ideology of self-improvement. The sport's social base was restricted by gender as well. Until the 1920s, the men who controlled the sport, aided by the physicians and moralists who sought to guard female health and virtue in a patriarchal society, were successful in keeping women out on the dubious grounds that vigorous physical activity would damage their reproductive organs and was "unseemly." In the 1920s pressure from women forced the AAU to create a women's committee and the IAAF to include women's events in the Olympic Games, but the new opportunities were never equal to those enjoyed by men.

Canadians have competed in every aspect of the sport with flair and distinction. Almost every generation has produced its fine sprinters. Early in the century, Hamilton's Robert KERR used his blazing start to dominate Canadian, American and British Empire competitions. He won gold and bronze medals at the 1908 Olympics in London. Perhaps the greatest era of Canadian sprinting began at the 1928 Olympics at Amsterdam, when Vancouver's diminutive Percy WILLIAMS won both the 100 and 200 metre sprints with his spectacular leaping finish, and Fanny ROSENFELD, Florence Bell, Ethel Smith and Myrtle Cook combined to capture the first-ever 4 x 100 metre women's relay. In the next decade, Canadian sprinters won another 6 Olympic medals and 22 in the British Empire Games. These feats were not equalled until the 1960s when Vancouver's Harry JEROME tied the world record for 100 metres and won Commonwealth and Pan-American championships and an Olympic bronze medal.

Canadian middle-distance runners have also excelled. Before he won Canada's first Olympic gold medal in the 2500 metre steeplechase at the Paris Games of 1900, Toronto miler George ORTON had compiled a long string of championships and records; in the interwar period, Montréal's Phil Edwards and Toronto's Alex Wilson brought back 7 medals from 3 Olympics; Toronto's Bill Crothers, one of the most graceful runners of all time, continued that tradition during the 1960s, winning a silver medal at the 1964 Olympics in Tokyo and dominating the 1000-yard event on the N American indoor track circuit for many years. Canadian distance runners have generally fared better on the road than on the track. They have won Olympic (Bill Sherring in the now unrecognized 1906 Athens Games), British Empire (Harold Webster in London in 1934) and Pan-American (Andy Boychuk in Winnipeg in 1967) marathon titles and the prestigious Boston Marathon 16 times. Some of these Boston champions, such as Onondaga Tom LONGBOAT (1907), Sydney's John Miles (1926 and 1929), St-Hyacinthe's Gerard Côté (1940, 1943, 1944 and 1948), Toronto's Jerome Drayton (1977) and Montréal's Jacqueline Gareau (1980) have become legendary figures in the sport. Toronto's Rich Ferguson placed third in what was likely the most famous race of all time — the confrontation between Britain's Roger Bannister and Australia's John Landy at the 1954 COMMONWEALTH GAMES at Vancouver — won by Bannister in a time of 3:58.8.

More than half the medals Canadians have won in international competition have come in the less popular field events. The strongest tradition has been in the high jump, where Ethel CATHERWOOD (1928), Duncan MCNAUGHTON and Eva Dawes (1932) and Greg Joy (1976) have won Olympic medals; and Debbie Brill (1970 and 1982), one of the pioneers of the now almost-universal back-layout technique, Claude Ferrange (1978) and Milt Ottey (1982) have won Commonwealth titles. Other outstanding Canadian champions include Montréal's Étienne DESMARTEAU, who won Canada's first field event Olympic gold medal at the 1904 St Louis Games in the 56-pound weight toss, throwers Ed Coy,

Dave Steen, George Puce, Jane Haist and Boris Chambul; vaulters Ed Archibald, William Happeny and Bruce Simpson; and horizontal jumpers Garfield McDonald, Cliff Bricker and Hal and Wally Brown.

In the last 20 years, the structure of Canadian track and field has been radically changed, as the rapid growth of federal and provincial programs initiated by the Fitness and Amateur Sport Act of 1961 has brought about the professionalization of coaching and administration and the recruitment of the medical and scientific communities to the goals of high performance. Previously the sport was conducted almost entirely by volunteers, who often combined the roles of coaching, officiating and administration, using their homes as offices and financing much of the activity out of their own pockets. Now the sport exhibits a formal division of labour among coaching, officiating and administration. The heavily subsidized CTFA and its provincial affiliates enjoy permanent offices, full-time staffs and a network of paid coaches who direct and monitor athletes' training. The top athletes are no longer "amateur," as most receive state grants for living and training expenses (permitted by IAAF rules since 1974) and are eligible for money prizes and endorsement fees (permitted since 1982). Many pursue the sport full-time. These changes have meant significantly improved training and competitive opportunities and longer careers. As a result, the overall quality of Canadian performances is higher than ever before. In 1964 only 14 Canadians met the IAAF Olympic qualifying standard; in 1984, 71 did so.

Canada's poor medal showing at the 1968 Mexico City Olympics (no medals in track and field) gave rise to demands for further action. In 1972 the Canadian Olympic Assn (COA) and Sport Canada initiated "Game Plan," a funding partnership of the federal and provincial governments and the national sports-governing bodies, with the objective of lifting Canada into the top 10 nations by the 1976 Montréal Olympics. Game Plan would fund competition tours (such as the first Canada-US dual track meet for women in 1972) and training camps (eg, at Toronto's Fitness Institute and the National Athletic Training Camp, a converted Canadair hangar in Montréal). At the same time others, including former middle-distance runner Abigail HOFFMAN lobbied Canada's Olympic committee to allow amateurs to train more than the prescribed 60 days every 4 years, and to be legally compensated for training expenses. Athlete assistance programs under a "carding" system, based on performance and world ranking, were initiated and between May 1975 and the 1976 Olympics, some $2.3 million was distributed to about 600 Canadian athletes for training and living expenses. This kind of investment demanded a high return, and a dispute between the COA and the CTFA over standards (distances, heights and times required to earn positions on the national team) came to head at the Olympic track and field trials prior to the 1972 Munich Games. Consequently, 9 of Canada's best track and field athletes were cut from the team. Pole vaulter Bruce Simpson's fifth-place finish was the best by a Canadian track and field athlete at Munich.

As work got underway in Montréal for 1976, the CTFA invited Polish sprint specialist Gerard Mach to conduct clinics in 1973; soon after, he became Canada's first professional track and field coach. The CTFA then organized its own "game plan" around a technical director, Lynn Davies, and 4 national coaches: Derek Boosey (jumps and multiple events), Jean-Paul Baert (throws), Paul Poce (distance running) and Mach (sprints, hurdles and relays). Of 56 track and field athletes at the Montréal Olympics for Canada, 9 women and 5 men achieved Olympic

qualifying standard, and 4 individuals, plus 3 of the 4 relay teams, achieved personal bests and Canadian records during the games. Greg Joy's high-jump silver was the only medal in track and field, and Canada placed eleventh in overall team standings.

The fruits of Game Plan '76 were harvested at the 1978 Commonwealth Games in Edmonton, as Canadian athletes placed first overall. In athletics, gold medals were won by Boris Chambul (discus), Claude Ferrange (high jump), Carmen Ionesco (discus), Diane JONES KONIHOWSKI (pentathlon), Phil Olsen (javelin) and Bruce Simpson (pole vault); the track and field team also won 8 silver medals and 9 bronze. The harvest continued at the Pan-American Games in San Juan, Puerto Rico, where Canada placed third in team standings overall, with track and field athletes bringing home 18 medals.

In spite of the setback of the boycott of the 1980 Moscow Games, the CTFA's philosophy of separating athletic events, begun with Game Plan, continued in the form of "event training centres" where recognized coaches could work with emerging talent: a Toronto sprint centre under coach Charlie Francis; distance-running centres under coaches Ron Bowker in Victoria and Alphonse Bernard in Winnipeg; and multiple-event centres in Saskatoon under coach-athlete Diane Jones Konihowski and in Toronto under coach Andy Higgins. Trust funds, pioneered in athletics by the CTFA and approved by the IAAF at its 1982 congress, cleared the way for amateur track and field competitors to earn and spend money legally (from corporate sponsorship, commercial endorsement or government grant) for living and training expenses, without losing amateur status.

By staging the first-ever World Track and Field Championships in 1983 at Helsinki, Finland, the IAAF signalled the return of athletics to their ancient Olympic Games prominence; for the first time since the 1972 Munich Olympics (because of the African boycott at Montréal and the American boycott at Moscow), the world's track and field best competed in 41 events. Canadians won no medals at the IAAF championships but placed seventh in the world (setting one Commonwealth and 3 Canadian records) — Canada's best-ever track and field team showing to that date. In the 1984 Los Angeles Olympics Ben Johnson won a bronze in the 100 m and Lynn Williams a bronze in the 3000 m. The men's relay team won a silver in the 4 x 100 m and the women's a bronze in the 4 x 400 m.

Canadians will no doubt continue to pursue and take pleasure from track and field for many years to come, but future opportunities for world-class performance are now contingent upon state support. The cost of training and competition — which includes facility rentals, coaching fees, scientific consulting, specialized medical treatment, travel and living expenses — are well beyond the resources of all but a few. Other public agencies, notably schools and the universities, bear some of these costs. The CTFA and a few clubs have been able to generate some revenue by fund raising and marketing — selling the goodwill outstanding athletes enjoy for use in advertisements. But these contributions have not proved sufficient in themselves. As much as the leaders of the sport would like to regain the autonomy of the old AAU, they remain dependent upon state funds and services and subject to government direction and control. To date, there has been a widespread consensus that the provision of high-performance opportunities in the Olympic sports such as track and field should be a public undertaking, but ultimately, as Abigail Hoffman, now director of the federal agency Sport Canada, has stressed, "It's very much a political decision." That is the most significant measure of the transformation of the sport in Canada. BRUCE KIDD AND TED BARRIS

Trade Mark, a manufacturer's or merchant's registered name, emblem or design used to identify the business or its goods or services. Some successful trade marks, eg, "Coke," are known worldwide. In the common law, trade marks were introduced to prevent goods or services being "passed off" in a way that confused the public about the source or quality of the product. A trader could complain that a mark similar to his own was being used and that the goodwill in his mark was being prejudiced.

Special remedies are provided in Canada for the breach of trade marks or names that are registered under the federal Trade Marks Act. Such marks, if registered after examination by the Trade Marks Office and passed without objection after advertising for public comment, give the trade-mark owner exclusive right to the use of the mark throughout Canada. Certain marks are prohibited, including any that suggest sanction by the Crown, or association with the International Red Cross. Other marks may be disallowed if they are the name of a living or recently dead person, if they describe the goods or services in connection with the way in which they are used, or if they might be confused with already existing marks.

The use of the mark must be such that at all times there is one controlling entity for the product or services identified by the mark. However, other persons may be allowed to use the trade mark if they become registered users with the permission of the owner and the recording of the registered user (entry of a notice) in the Register of Trade Marks. If a mark is not actively used it may be considered to have been abandoned. It may also be so commonly used that it ceases to describe the owner's products and becomes part of the general language to describe the product (eg, "Thermos," to describe a vacuum bottle).

Certification marks are owned by associations not actually involved in trade and are used to indicate that products have met certain standards. Thus, "CSA" is used on all electrical goods to show that the goods have met the minimum standards prescribed by the Canadian Standards Association. PETER J.M. LOWN

Trade Unions, see WORKING-CLASS HISTORY; UNION CENTRALS.

Trades and Labor Congress of Canada, the second Canadian central labour organization, was founded in 1883 on the initiative of the Toronto Trades and Labor Council. A successor to the Canadian Labor Union (1873-77), it first met in Toronto as the Canadian Labor Congress, but changed its name to TLC at its second convention in 1886. Largely controlled by the KNIGHTS OF LABOR, the TLC initially brought together trade unionists from Ontario, but by 1900 the organization had become national in character. In 1902 at the Berlin [Kitchener], Ont, convention, however, its expulsion of all unions which were also American Federation of Labor chartered bodies ended its near hegemony of the Canadian labour movement. Thereafter the movement was splintered by national unions, overtly socialist and syndicalist bodies, and the rise of INDUSTRIAL UNIONISM.

In 1919 political tensions within the TLC reached crisis level, and socialist and industrial unionists bolted to form the ONE BIG UNION. After the defeats suffered by industrial unionists during the massive 1919 strike wave, the TLC re-emerged as the major central body. Its next challenge came with the renewed drive for industrial unionism led by the Workers' Unity League and later by the Committee for Industrial Organization. Again splits in the US between AFL and CIO supporters led to a reluctant 1939 expulsion of Canadian industrial unionists from the TLC. The renegades founded the CANADIAN CONGRESS OF LABOUR in 1940. Rapid growth of industrial unionism during and immediately after WWII left the CCL as the major labour power.

After a hysterical witch-hunt against communists in both labour centrals in the late 1940s and early 1950s and the merger of the AFL and the CIO in the US in 1955 (see AFL-CIO), the CCL and the TLC united in 1956 to create the CANADIAN LABOUR CONGRESS. GREGORY S. KEALEY

Traffic Law The regulation of traffic on highways and roads is one of the greatest legal challenges of the 20th century. Not only do 3 levels of government — federal, provincial and municipal — make traffic laws, but common-law rules still play an important role in this area as well. The federal involvement derives primarily from criminal law. The Canadian Criminal Code provides for numerous serious offences, including dangerous driving, criminal negligence in the operation of a motor vehicle, criminal negligence causing death, and impaired driving. Each province is responsible for maintaining the highways which run through it and for governing the conduct of drivers. The provincial highway-traffic Acts control all matters pertaining to the use of the roads, including licensing of drivers, registration of vehicles, safety and condition of motor vehicles and rules of the road, which in turn include speed limits, the observation of traffic signals, and rights of way at intersections. Failure to obey these rules may lead to fines, the suspension of the right to drive and even imprisonment. Municipalities also have jurisdiction, delegated to them by their provincial governments, to control highway traffic and maintain the roads within their control. Traffic rules of municipalities are created by bylaws. Municipalities are also responsible for the safe condition of their roads and can be held civilly liable to persons who are injured while on a dangerous road.

In addition to the control and regulation of traffic and roads, traffic law includes the huge area of civil liability arising from the thousands of annual traffic accidents. In most provinces, this area of law is still governed by normal negligence principles, modified somewhat by highway-traffic Acts (see TORTS). In some provinces civil actions have been replaced by compulsory no-fault schemes which compensate victims of motor-vehicle accidents without litigation and without regard to fault. The most extensive scheme, which has abolished civil action in all motor-vehicle cases, is in Québec. All provinces, even those that maintain fault law, have compulsory liability-insurance laws which provide for at least some compensation to motor-vehicle accident victims without the need for costly litigation. LEWIS N. KLAR

Trail, BC, City, pop 9599 (1981c), inc 1901, is located on the COLUMBIA R at the mouth of Trail Cr, just N of the international boundary, 630 km by road E of Vancouver. Settlement in the area began at ROSSLAND, with its proximity to the rich ore of Red Mt. Development at Trail (after the Dewdney Trail) came with the realization that shipping ore to American smelters was too costly. American F.A. Heinze built the original foundry 1895, then a narrow-gauge railway to

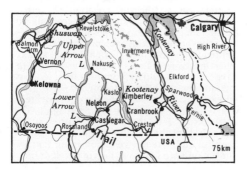

Rossland 1896. With the CPR's decision to build lines through CROWSNEST PASS and the Kettle Valley, American interests were soon bought out, and the mines came under CPR ownership through its subsidiary, Consolidated Mining and Smelting Co (Cominco). A move to electricity brought extensive hydro development on the Kootenay R. Trail's smelter rapidly expanded (by 1910, 40-50% of BC's output came from the Kootenays) and in time it grew to be the largest smelter in the British Empire. Long-term development was ensured by the ready access to cheap, bountiful hydroelectric power on the Kootenay and Pend-d'Oreille rivers.

Trail continues to be dominated by Cominco's activities. Silver, lead and zinc ores from the Kootenay, Alberta, the NWT and the US are smelted and refined here, yielding refined metals, chemicals and fertilizers. Trail also acts as a commercial centre for the adjoining towns of Fruitvale, Montrose and Warfield. Trail Smoke Eaters were, in 1961, the last Canadian hockey team to win the world championships.

WILLIAM A. SLOAN

Trail of '98, a reference to the CHILKOOT TRAIL and other northern trails scaled by prospectors during the KLONDIKE GOLD RUSH, which began in 1898. Robert W. SERVICE tells the story of these prospectors in his first novel, *The Trail of '98* (1910). JOHN ROBERT COLOMBO

Traill, Catharine Parr, née Strickland, pioneer writer, botanist (b at London, Eng 9 Jan 1802; d at Lakefield, Ont 29 Aug 1899). In 1832 Catharine immigrated to Canada with her husband, half-pay Lt Thomas Traill, and settled on the Otonabee R near Peterborough, next door to her sister Susanna MOODIE. There Mrs Traill wrote her most famous book, *The Backwoods of Canada* (1836), a factual and scientific account of her first 3 years in the bush, a pragmatic and optimistic work stressing the kind of realistic detail that has become a tradition in Canadian literature in such writers as Farley MOWAT and Pierre BERTON. Her published works include juvenile fiction, a housekeeping manual, *The Female Emigrant's Guide* (1854), and treatises on Canadian botany, *Canadian Wildflowers* (1868) and *Studies of Plant Life in Canada* (1885). MARIAN FOWLER
Reading: Marian Fowler, *The Embroidered Tent* (1982).

Trakas, George, sculptor (b at Québec C 11 May 1944). After a year at Sir George Williams, Trakas continued his studies in New York, and he has remained in the US. His work belongs in the context of environmental art in that his quasi-architectural structures are inextricably integrated into the gallery interiors or landscape settings that he uses as sites. He strives for multi-levelled inclusiveness, and his work is potent with symbolic and metaphoric meaning. Central to his sculpture is the idea that our perspective on the world is not only a function of vision but of the whole body. To experience a sculpture by Trakas in its entirety requires that we walk, climb and otherwise physically negotiate it. Most of his work has been commissioned for specific projects or exhibitions, such as *Rock River Union* (for the Artpark, Lewiston, NY, 1976), *Union Pass* (Documenta 6, Germany, 1977) and *Structures for Behavior* (Art Gallery of Ontario, 1978). Since 1972 Trakas has been working on a large landscape project on Cap Trinité, Baie d'Éternité, Qué. ROALD NASGAARD

Trans-Canada Airlines was created 10 April 1937 by Act of Paliament as a subsidiary of CANADIAN NATIONAL RAILWAYS to provide air service to all regions of Canada. TCA began with 2 passenger aircraft and a small bi-plane, which was used to survey new routes. Passenger service began between Vancouver and Montréal 1 Apr 1939, and 2 years later TCA provided scheduled flights across the Atlantic Ocean. By 1947 the line linked major centres in Canada and operated services to the US; in 1948 service began to Bermuda, the Caribbean, Florida, Shannon (Ire), London, Paris and Düsseldorf. Although it rejected the Canadian designed AVRO JETLINER, the line converted to turbines in the 1950s, with Super Constellations and Vickers Viscounts. Polar flights to Europe were introduced and TCA was the first N American airline to have direct service to Moscow. The name was changed to AIR CANADA in 1965.   JAMES MARSH

Trans-Canada Highway Public agitation for a national road began as early as 1910, but more than half a century elapsed before it was completed.The 7821 km Trans-Canada Hwy was formally opened at ROGERS PASS on 30 July 1962. Canadians could now drive, using ferry services on both coasts, from St John's, Nfld, to Victoria, BC, but more than 3000 km were still unpaved. Work started in the summer of 1950 with an infusion of $150 million of federal funds (half the estimated cost) provided for in the Trans-Canada Highway Act (1949). Cost-sharing plans, revised twice, increased the federal contribution to $825 million. Standards called for pavement widths of 6.7 m and 7.3 m; ample shoulder width, bridge clearances and sight distances; low gradients and curvature; elimination of railway grade crossings wherever possible; and a maximum load-bearing capacity of 9.1 t per axle. Construction was supervised by the provinces. The target date for completion was Dec 1956, but the job was more difficult and more expensive than anticipated. For example, the route between Golden and Revelstoke, BC, passes through Rogers Pass, where snowfall reaches 15.2 m per year and presents tremendous avalanche hazards. Snowsheds, earth mounds and other devices for avalanche control had to be provided. In Québec, the tunnel under the St Lawrence R at Boucherville Islands, which is part of the entranceway to Montréal, was a difficult project costing approximately $75 million and covering little more than one km of the highway. Finished in 1970, the highway had cost over $1 billion. It is the longest national highway in the world.   C.W. GILCHRIST

TransCanada PipeLines Ltd, a natural gas transmission company with head offices in Calgary. First incorporated by Act of Parliament on 21 Mar 1951, TransCanada owns and operates a high pressure natural PIPELINE system extending from Alberta into parts of Québec and into the

The Trans-Canada Highway, shown winding its way through Rogers Pass, BC (*photo by Doug Leighton*).

US. The company is also engaged in the search for, and production of, crude oil and natural gas, and sells natural gas to Canadian and US customers. In 1983 it had sales or operating revenue of $3.5 billion (ranking 22nd in Canada), assets of $5.0 billion (ranking 17th) and 1915 employees. Bell Canada Enterprises Inc owned 42% of the shares. *See* PIPELINE DEBATE.
DEBORAH C. SAWYER

TransCanada Telephone System (TCTS) is a voluntary association of 9 telephone companies and Telesat Canada, and was first formed (1931) to integrate national telephone service. Prior to the formation of TCTS, Canada had relied on transmission facilities in the US for most of its cross-Canada requirements. In 1972 the Computer Communications group was formed within TCTS to improve the service for data transmission by computer communications. Membership of TCTS comprises British Columbia Telephone Co, Alberta Government Telephones, Saskatchewan Telecommunications, Manitoba Telephone System, Bell Canada, New Brunswick Telephone Co, The Island Telephone Co, Maritime Telegraph and Telephone Co, Newfoundland Telephone Co and Telesat Canada. The system is directed by a board of management composed of directors from all member companies; unanimous agreement among the directors is required before policies are implemented. The board is supported by inter-member operational and administrative committees.

In addition to integrating and co-ordinating technical factors, TCTS also arranges the apportionment of revenues among members that may be attributed to that portion of interprovincial telephone traffic using the facilities of 3 or more members. Its members negotiate separately on other interprovincial traffic. Until recently there was little regulatory supervision of interprovincial toll rates but, since assuming jurisdiction over BC Tel, Bell Canada, Telesat Canada and CNCP Telecommunications in 1976, the CANADIAN RADIO-TELEVISION AND TELECOMMUNICATIONS COMMISSION has been reviewing the policies of TCTS with greater thoroughness. ROBERT E. BABE

Reading: E.B. Ogle, *Long Distance Please: The Story of the TransCanada Telephone System* (1979).

Transfer Payments, direct payments from governments to other governments or to individuals, a mechanism for providing social security, income support and for alleviating regional disparities. Federal transfer payments to individuals include family allowances, old-age pensions and unemployment insurance; in 1983, they represented $22.6 billion. Federal transfer payments to provinces, including equalization payments ($5.4 billion in 1983), cash payments for medicare and post-secondary education under the Established Programs Financing Act ($7.6 billion in 1983) and other, smaller programs, represent about 20% of federal spending and a large proportion of provincial revenue: about 60% in PEI and 10% in Alberta (1983-84). Transfer payments from provincial governments to local governments, school boards, universities and hospitals are part of provincial PUBLIC FINANCE.   RICHARD SIMEON

Translation is "the interpretation of verbal signs by some other language," according to Russian linguist Roman Jakobson. It is most often thought of as the presentation of works written in one language to a public that speaks other languages, but its original use seems to have been to facilitate administration within the ancient multilingual empires. The first known religious translation, that of the Hebrew Old Testament into Greek (the Septuagint version), occurred in the first 2 centuries BC, at about the time that the Roman authors Plautus, Caecilius and Terence were pioneering literary translation with Latin versions of Greek drama.

Another major field that has long relied heavily on translation is that of trade and commerce.

For centuries translation was considered part of the art of rhetoric, and rightly so, for it is a language art that draws on sciences such as contrastive grammar and lexicology (the study of word derivations and meanings). Although theories of translation techniques were proposed as early as Roman times, it was only in the late 18th century that the issues were fully articulated. Still central to the debate is the question of whether to attempt to translate word for word (ie, literal translation) or "sense for sense" (free translation). A number of factors influence the choice of method, such as the degree of similarity between the languages and cultures involved, the genre of the text (eg, poetry, literary or technical prose) and the medium (oral, written or sign language). In Canada translation between French and English (both oral and written) predominates, although considerably more works written in French have been translated into English than the reverse. There is also a good deal of translation of other languages spoken and written here, such as Italian, German and Ukrainian. Since the QUIET REVOLUTION of the 1960s and the work of the Royal Commission on BILINGUALISM AND BICULTURALISM, changes in the political balance between French and English have caused work from French to English to increase.

The first translators in Canada were Indians. In 1534 Jacques CARTIER took 2 Indians, Taignoagny and Domagaya, back to France, had them taught French, and in 1535 used them as interpreters in negotiations with the natives at STADACONA. Until the SEVEN YEARS' WAR most translation and interpretation work was in the hands of missionaries, who produced many glossaries, dictionaries and grammars of Indian languages. After the defeat of the French in 1759-60 the major weight of translation moved to French-English and the predominant mode from oral to written. The arrival of immigrants speaking other languages necessitated translation to and from those languages, most of it unofficial.

Despite the need for translation in government, from 1760 until the late 19th century its occurence was only ad hoc. It was finally given official status by the language provisions of the BNA Act of 1867, which required that both languages be official in Parliament and in Québec; in 1870 this provision was extended to Manitoba. Early in the 20th century the translation offices of individual government departments were absorbed into the federal Bureau of Translations, which came under the control of the secretary of state. In the early 1980s both Québec and New Brunswick had translation bureaus, that of Québec also having close links with l'Office de la langue française, which possesses a terminology bank. Canadian commercial life has also depended on translation, and commercial and technical translation firms have existed in Canada since the early 20th century. Literary translation flourishes. *Bibliography of Canadian Books in Translation* (2nd ed, 1981) was compiled by Philip Stratford for the Humanities Research Council of Canada, and it is regularly updated.

The major translation association in Canada is the Council of Translators and Interpreters of Canada. Only PEI, Newfoundland and Nova Scotia do not have professional associations affiliated with CTIC. Entry to the provincial associations is by examination. Other associations are the Literary Translators' Assn and the Assn of Legal Court Interpreters and Translators. The major professional journal is *Meta*, published by U de Montréal. Several universities have translation components in their language degrees, but the major translation schools are at U de M, U of Ottawa, Laurentian U, Laval and U de Moncton. Canadian work on translation theory, through linguistics at these schools and literature elsewhere, is internationally recognized. Translators into Indian and Inuit languages draw on work done at the Summer Institute of Linguistics (Dallas, Tex), which specializes in descriptions of, and translation from and into, languages so far unknown outside their own area.

A recent development in translation is the use of computers. Extensive research in ARTIFICIAL INTELLIGENCE is taking place in Canada and elsewhere in the hope that fast, high-quality machine translation will one day be possible. At the present time, however, computers play a limited role in translation. *See* BILINGUALISM; DICTIONARY.   LOUIS G. KELLY

Reading: "Histoire de la traduction au Canada," *Meta* 22,1 (1977; special issue).

Transport Canada is the federal government department responsible for the regulation and administration of transportation policy in Canada. It was established in 1936 as a consolidation of the Department of Railways and Canals, Department of Marine, and the Civil Aviation Branch of the Department of National Defence. It is now a corporate structure that includes crown corporations with varying degrees of autonomy and groups responsible for various departmental activities. The administration for air transport provides and operates much of the public air-transportation system including air terminals, air-traffic control and licensing of aviation personnel and aircraft. The marine transport adminstration co-ordinates the CANADIAN COAST GUARD, the NATIONAL HARBOURS BOARD, the St Lawrence Seaway Authority and 4 pilotage authorities. The land transport administration is responsible for federal activity in railway, highways, ferries and motor vehicle safety. AIR CANADA, CANADIAN NATIONAL RAILWAYS and VIA RAIL report to Parliament through the minister of transport. The CANADIAN TRANSPORT COMMISSION, Aircraft Accident Review Board and Canadian Aviation Safety Board are autonomous agencies reporting to Parliament through the minister. The department's 1984-85 budget was $3 billion.

Transportation Since the earliest days of recorded history, transportation has been important to mankind. Transportation vehicles and transport systems facilitate the movement of people and goods from one place to another. Transportation is of particular importance to Canada because of the country's vast size and because there are great distances between its mines, farms, forests and population centres.

Efficient transport systems are of particular significance to trading nations such as Canada. This country exports about one-third of all that it produces, and earnings from these exports are exceedingly important to the Canadian ECONOMY. Many of Canada's exports, such as grain, coal, minerals and timber, must compete with similar products from other exporting nations. Since some of these competitors are much closer to major export markets in Japan, Europe and Asia, Canada's transport system must be efficient. Managers of Canada's transport systems seek to make them more efficient through improvements in transport technology and organization. In recent years larger, faster and more efficient transport vehicles have improved transport productivity. In future years, transport productivity may be increased by making better use of computers, by communications systems which provide more timely information, and by various devices, such as radar, which can improve transport technology.

History of Transportation Canada's history is a history of transportation and its development. In the early days, European settlers ventured only into those areas that were accessible by water and boats, and canoes were the primary

Illustration from a travel book published in 1799, showing stagecoach travel in the early Canadas (*courtesy National Library of Canada/Rare Book Div*).

mode of transportation. The first settlers made use of the nation's lakes and rivers; later they constructed CANALS. After the steam engine was invented, railways were built. Settlement in much of Canada followed the construction of railway lines. As ROADS AND HIGHWAYS were built and cars and trucks became available, regions of Canada that had not been served by railways were developed. Today, transport by air makes it possible for Canadians to live, work and vacation in any area of the nation, regardless of how remote it may be (*see* TRANSPORTATION IN THE NORTH).

RAILWAYS have always played an important role in Canada. They were built to open new areas to settlement, to make profits for the railway builders, and for defence and political reasons. Canadians have an enormous investment in their railways. A century ago Canadian taxpayers helped finance railway construction, and since that time they have paid taxes to support passenger trains and uneconomic branch lines. When privately owned railways faced bankruptcy and were taken over by the government, their debts were assumed by the taxpayers. Since that time citizens groups, politicians and local communities have been concerned with the costs of the nation's railways and the services they provide. Each time a railway has sought to abandon an uneconomic branch line, local groups have protested. When VIA RAIL CANADA reduced passenger services on which it was losing money, many people protested. The most contentious issue of all was the CROWSNEST PASS AGREEMENT governing grain rates. For years the railways contended that these statutory rates were so low that they caused enormous losses, but it was not until 1983, after much bitter debate, that the rates were changed.

The first railway line in Canada was built in 1836, some 10 years after England built her first steam railway line. In the 1850s railway construction began in earnest with the GRAND TRUNK RAILWAY from Sarnia through Toronto and Montréal to Portland, Maine. In 1854 the GREAT WESTERN RAILWAY built a line between the Niagara and the Detroit rivers via Hamilton. It

Hudson's Bay Co ox train at Fort Smith, NWT, in 1875 (*courtesy Provincial Archives of Alberta/E. Brown Coll*).

connected with US railways in New York and Michigan. Much of this early railway construction resulted from a speculative boom in which some promoters sought to make quick profits. As a result many railways were poorly planned and constructed. Much early construction was financed by British capitalists, Canadian merchants and landowners, and by municipalities. Some construction was financed by bonds. The INTERCOLONIAL RAILWAY was the largest system of all. Completed in the 1870s, it was built for national defence and unity, in fulfillment of the terms of CONFEDERATION, and was never expected to make a profit. Many of Canada's rail lines had financial problems. When it appeared that a number of them might collapse, they were amalgamated into the CANADIAN NATIONAL RAILWAYS system and taken over by the federal government. Many financial problems were thus inherited by that crown corporation.

The railways have been responsible, in part, for some of the provinces joining the Canadian confederation. It was not until the central government agreed to build a railway to the Pacific Ocean that BC agreed to join, an agreement that led eventually to construction of the western sections of the CANADIAN PACIFIC RAILWAY. Transportation also played an essential role in the history of PEI, which was at first unenthusiastic about confederation; the severe financial problems of its railway paid a large part in the decision to join Canada in 1873. Part of the confederation arrangement provided that the federal government would assume the railway's enormous debt. Newfoundland, the last of the provinces to join Canada, also received guarantees from the central government that it would be provided with various transport services.

Contemporary Transportation Canada has an excellent system of transportation, with each mode serving particular needs. But the system has interrelated parts, some of which serve certain areas of the country or a particular segment of the economy. As a service industry, the quality of transportation depends in large measure on the calibre of its employees and management. Since about half of every revenue dollar received by a transportation company is used for employee salaries, wages and benefits, transportation is labour intensive. Transportation provides more jobs for Canadians than any other activity. It uses more energy than any other industry, and is one of the largest purchasers of cement, steel, aluminum and other commodities. It enables Canadians to enjoy an enormous variety of products from all parts of the world and to sell great quantities of grain, coal, lumber, automotive products and other goods to customers in every continent.

In most areas of transportation there is competition and in some areas that competition is intense. Large shippers often have several transport alternatives available to them: rail, water or truck. Air transportation is available to most Canadians, and the shippers of petroleum, chemicals and other products in liquid or gaseous form may sometimes ship by pipeline. Pas-

sengers usually have available several transport alternatives. Because of competition, there is a continuing need for research to improve transport technology.

Transportation Modes There are 5 modes of transportation: water, rail, motor carrier, air and pipeline. In Canada water transportation is generally used for the movement of bulk commodities of relatively low value per tonne, such as coal, ore, grain, gravel and salt. Rail transportation is used principally for the movement of such bulk commodities as grain, coal, ore, lumber and chemicals, for the movement of containers, and for other types of merchandise freight. Trucks are used in a variety of ways. Small trucks are used as delivery vehicles in cities and towns. In the North, trucks transport logs, petroleum, consumer goods and a great variety of industrial products. Air transportation is used to move both large and small items when speed is important. PIPELINES are used for the transportation of petroleum, petroleum products, gas and certain chemicals. All modes of transportation, except pipeline, are used for the transportation of passengers.

Water Transportation may be separated into 3 general categories: ocean transportation, inland water transportation and coastal transportation. Ocean transportation is important to Canada, because about one-third of all that Canada produces is exported. Much of this export traffic moves by ship to customers overseas, carried by large, oceangoing vessels which serve Canada's major ports. About one-third of all of the exports which go by sea move through Vancouver, the largest port (in tonnage) on the west coast of the Americas. Substantial export tonnages also move through the ports of Churchill, Montréal, Québec City, Halifax and Saint John (*see* SHIPPING INDUSTRY).

The GREAT LAKES and the St Lawrence R system provide inland water transportation to the heartland of Canada. Great quantities of grain, coal, iron ore and other commodities are moved by vessels called lakers. About half of these commodities are moved by US carriers, and about half by Canadian companies. Most of the Canadian operators are represented by the Dominion Marine Assn. In recent years, more tonnes have been moved by vessels operating on the Great Lakes than have been moved by either of Canada's transcontinental railways. Much of Canada's iron ore moves via the Great Lakes-ST LAWRENCE SEAWAY system to steel mills in the US. On the return journey, many of these vessels carry coal from US mines (*see* LAKE CARRIERS).

Coastal water transportation is also important. Great quantities of logs, wood chips, lumber, chemicals and other bulk commodities are moved by barge in BC's coastal waters. Sometimes logs are gathered together to form a log boom, then pulled by tug from northern coastal areas to Vancouver for processing into lumber, plywood, wood pulp and paper. Other logs are moved by large self-loading barges that are able to dump themselves when they reach their destination. Barge movements on Canada's East Coast are on a much smaller scale, but are nonetheless significant. Canada's barge operators have been responsible for many improvements in barge technology. Barge transportation is slow but relatively cheap.

Rail Transportation Canada has 2 major railways and several smaller ones. The major railways are approximately equal in size and revenues. In 1984 the CPR operated some 34 000 km of railway, utilizing about 1200 LOCOMOTIVES. Its annual revenues are about $2 billion and it is owned by stockholders. The CNR is a federal crown corporation. The railway operates under legislation passed by Parliament which relates specifically to the CNR, and it reports to the government through the minister of transport. In 1984 the CNR operated some 51 000 km of track,

using over 2000 locomotives. The BRITISH COLUMBIA RAILWAY, third largest, is owned by the BC government. Approximately 60% of the revenues of the BCR come from forest products in 1982. The BCR operates some 2655 km, largely in mountainous terrain, using 126 locomotives.

Each year Canada's railways move millions of tonnes of bulk commodities, such as coal, potash, grain and sulphur. Much coal is moved by "unit trains." These trains often consist of 100 cars or more, which can carry as much as 100 tonnes each. Railways are able to transport large quantities of bulk materials over long distances and at relatively low cost, thus enabling the products of Canada's mines, fields and forests to compete effectively in world markets.

For many years passenger trains represented an important part of the railway business. In major cities the railway station was a hub of activity. Today, railway passenger trains face intense competition from other forms of transport. The resultant loss of patronage, coupled with rising costs, has caused them to lose millions of dollars each year. For a time direct subsidies were given to the railways to compensate them for part of these losses. The government then decided to handle the matter in a different way and created a new CROWN CORPORATION, VIA Rail Canada, which is now responsible for most of the passenger train operations. It contracts with the 2 major railways for the operation and maintenance of trains. Although it has tried to make passenger trains more attractive and to increase their patronage, VIA Rail Canada's losses amounted to about $500 million in 1982. In order to reduce those losses, VIA discontinued service on several unprofitable lines; some of these lines are scheduled to reopen in 1985.

Motor Carrier Transportation Possibly the greatest virtue of motor carrier transportation is its flexibility. Trucks do not require an airport, a waterway or a track on which to operate. They can move wherever there is a highway, a road, a street — or even a relatively flat, hard surface. They are flexible also in size. Giant trucks may move logs, coal, construction machinery or other bulky items. Tiny delivery vehicles are available that are highly fuel efficient and can maneuver in crowded city areas. In the North, enormous off-road vehicles transport tremendous tonnages of coal, logs and minerals for short distances. Throughout Canada trucks transport fruit, vegetables and manufactured products over long distances. Within our cities trucks of various sizes, shapes and design transport mail, parcels and thousands of other items. Virtually everything that we eat or wear has made at least some of its journey to us by truck (*see* TRUCKING INDUSTRY).

A number of large companies operate trucks. Both of Canada's major railways have trucking divisions. There are several other large trucking companies, owned by a single individual or family, or by a group of stockholders. There are thousands of small truck operations, some consisting of a single truck driven by its owner.

Air Transportation Canada has 2 major transcontinental airlines, 4 regional carriers, several charter operators, and some 600 smaller operators, including specialized air services and HELICOPTER operators. Most communities have some type of air transportation service available, whether by floatplane, helicopter or conventional aircraft. For long-distance travel, far more Canadians use air transportation than train or bus (*see* AIRPORTS and AVIATION).

Canada's largest airline, AIR CANADA, is a crown corporation. In Sept 1984 Air Canada had an operational fleet of 111 planes and had an average of 21 600 employees. Air Canada's overseas routes extend to Europe and the Caribbean. Within Canada the airline serves every major population centre, every provincial capital and many smaller communities. CP Air, a sub-

STOL airport, Ottawa. The development of short-takeoff-and-landing technology has been an important contribution to Canadian transportation (*photo by Roland Weber/Masterfile*).

sidiary of Canadian Pacific Ltd, operates international routes to Europe, Asia, Australia and S America, in addition to serving all of the major cities in Canada and a number of smaller communities in BC and the Yukon. It also serves Los Angeles, San Francisco and Honolulu. In 1982 CP Air operated 31 planes and had some 7200 employees. PACIFIC WESTERN AIRLINES, Canada's third-largest carrier, is now 14% owned by the province of Alberta. It had 2650 employees in 1984 and flew 24 aircraft. Other Canadian airlines include QUEBECAIR, Eastern Provincial Airways, Nordair (owned by, but separate from, CP Air), and Canada's largest all-charter operator, WARDAIR. Okanagan Helicopters, one of the world's largest helicopter companies, operated about 110 helicopters in 1983. Smaller operators served many small, remote communities, providing them with milk, fresh fruits and vegetables, and also carrying mail.

Pipeline Transportation Pipelines, the unseen carrier, transport enormous quantities of petroleum, gasoline, chemicals and other products — sometimes for long distances. As pipeline transportation requires little labour and is relatively trouble free, it is able to provide reliable, low-cost transportation. However, pipeline transportation has 2 principal drawbacks: pipelines require an enormous amount of capital, and they are seldom efficient unless large quantities are moved from a single point of origin to a single destination over a long period of time. Pipelines have also been used for the transportation of coal (in slurry form) in the US and elsewhere, but their potential as transporters of coal and other bulk commodities has not yet been fully exploited in Canada.

Intermodal Transportation Except for items moved by truck, virtually all other movements utilize 2 or more transport modes. "Piggyback" transportation is an example. Goods may be loaded into trucks or trailers and hauled to some point on a railway where the truck or trailer is loaded on a railroad flatcar. The goods then move by rail, sometimes over a relatively long distance. At the end of their rail journey, the trailers or containers are again moved by truck to their final destination. There are other ways in which the various transport modes can cooperate to provide more efficient intermodal transportation. Trucks can be carried on board ferries or ships. This is sometimes called "fishy-back" transportation or Ro/Ro (roll on-roll off) transportation. In recent years, Canada Steamship Lines has experimented with the transfer of coal directly from self-unloading bulk carriers to oceangoing ships without the use of a port or other terminal facilities.

Canada's "land bridge" is also based on intermodal operations. Shipments from Japan and Hong Kong destined for Europe can move by ship via the Panama Canal. Or, by using Canada as a land bridge, they can move by water to Vancouver or other western ports, then by rail to one of Canada's eastern ports, and again by water to their European destinations, saving a significant amount of time.

Types of Carriers In legal terms there are 3 types of carriers: common carriers, contract carriers and private carriers. A common carrier transports the goods of any shipper wishing to make use of its services. Most shippers in Canada have available the services of some common carrier, and sometimes many of them.

A contract carrier makes agreements with one or more shippers to haul goods, sometimes over specific routes, and usually for a given period of time. The possible variations in such contractual arrangements are limited only by the needs of the respective parties and their ingenuity in drawing up a contract. Many large shippers in Canada use contract carriers.

A private carrier is one that transports its own goods. Many farmers transport their own grain and other products to a local elevator or to market. Logging companies ordinarily transport their own logs, at least for a short distance. Many manufacturing companies transport some of their raw materials and semifinished products. Many retail stores, including the large grocery chains, have private carrier operations. The large forest-products companies and steel, oil and chemical companies often have private carrier operations. Some operate their own trucks, barges and ships as private carriers, and they may also operate their own railroad.

General Carriers and Specialized Carriers A carrier's rate schedule gives the prices charged for hauling various types of freight between various points, and its tariff describes in detail the services which the carrier undertakes to provide and the extent of its liability. For instance, the tariff may stipulate that the carrier will deliver shipments but that the consignee must unload them. It may state that the carrier is not responsible for damage to perishable commodities, for delays in shipment, or for any damage resulting from strikes, floods or so-called "acts of God." The tariff of a general freight carrier may state that it carries all types of package freight up to a given maximum size and weight, but that it does not carry liquids, explosives or live animals. Specialized carriers provide service to particular types of shippers, or for particular types of shipments. Some specialized carriers haul only bulk petroleum. Others carry only shipments of pharmaceuticals from wholesalers or retail drugstores. Some carry only live animals; others handle only refrigerated cargo. In recent years there has been a substantial growth in the number and variety of specialized carriers. For instance, some carriers specialize in carrying money, cheques, bonds and other high-value items for banks and other financial institutions. Others carry small parcels between Canada and the US and between communities in Ontario, and other carriers specialize in carrying items when next-day delivery is important, and serve much of the US and many large Canadian cities. There are hundreds of messenger and courier services in Canada, and their number appears to be growing.

Facilitators, Consolidators and Expeditors There are many organizations that provide services that are ancillary to transportation. Some deal with customs formalities and other paperwork. Some select carriers and monitor shipments, relieving industrial firms of much paperwork and detail. Some expedite shipments or take advantage of volume rates. Many facilitators and expeditors are called freight forwarders. Domestic freight forwarders normally have trucks which pick up shipments from their customers and consolidate them with the shipments of other customers into full loads (either truck or rail). Once the full carloads reach their destination, the freight forwarder then "breaks bulk," ie, unloads the car and delivers the various shipments to the respective consignees. A foreign freight forwarder arranges for ocean shipping and for inland transportation at the foreign destination. He may also arrange for insurance, and may handle customs formalities. Sometimes the work of a freight forwarder is performed by a shippers' co-operative. Canada has several shippers' co-operatives. Canada's leading department stores operate their own freight-forwarding organization. This enables them to pool their shipments and use the lower freight rates given to volume shippers.

Transport Infrastructure Every mode of transportation has 2 essential parts: the transport vehicle itself and the road, track or way on which it operates. When 2 modes of transportation are co-ordinated, there may be a junction or terminal at which the transfer is made. Some of the transport infrastructure is natural, but much of it is man-made. A canoe, for instance, may operate quite well on a natural lake or stream, but a large, oceangoing vessel needs some man-made facilities if it is to operate well, as does a train, a plane or a truck.

Most of the man-made infrastructure for water transportation in Canada has been provided by the federal government. Hundreds of millions of dollars have been spent for ports, docks and other devices designed to facilitate water transportation. The St Lawrence Seaway system was paid for by both Canadian and US taxpayers. The rail infrastructure consists of the bridges, tunnels, tracks, roadbed and other structures necessary for the operation of a railway. Although much of the early railway infrastructure was financed by the federal government through direct grants, the gift of land and other means, in more recent years infrastructure has been financed by the transcontinental railways themselves through retained earnings.

Virtually all of the infrastructure for aviation has been financed by the federal goverment. The federal Dept of Transport (now called TRANSPORT CANADA) has built most of Canada's airports, as well as the airways and the radio and navigation systems. Most of these facilities are maintained and operated by Transport Canada.

Roads, highways and streets are the infrastructure for motor carrier transportation. Most of Canada's roads and highways have been built by provincial governments — the major exceptions being highways in national parks and INDIAN RESERVES, the ALASKA HIGHWAY and the TRANS-CANADA HIGHWAY. Most streets have been built by cities and have been financed in a variety of ways.

In recent years the federal goverment has announced a "user pay" philosophy (those using the transport infrastructure should bear the cost of such facilities). Users of airports, seaway locks and port facilities, for instance, pay landing fees, lockage fees and port duties to compensate in part for the taxpayers' investment.

Passenger Transportation includes many modes of travel, including planes, trains, boats and BUSES. Millions travel by AUTOMOBILE, taxi or limousine, others by bicycle, horse or dogsled. The automobile accounts for the greatest percentage of passenger travel in Canada today.

Urban Transportation Most of Canada's urban areas have some form of public transportation. Both Montréal and Toronto are served by commuter railway systems. Some cities have subways; others are served by buses, streetcars, electric trolley cars, or a mixture of vehicle types. Some URBAN TRANSPORTATION systems are operated by the cities themselves, some by regional districts and some by special transit authorities. Cities can minimize the downtown congestion caused by automobile traffic by providing comfortable, convenient and relatively inexpensive urban transportation. Some cities provide special transport services for handicapped persons, and others utilize "dial-a-bus" services for that purpose. Under this system a patron may telephone to have a bus stop for a pickup; the route the bus follows on any particular trip will depend on the locations of the persons who have telephoned.

Most Canadian cities have taxi service. In some cities a licence is required to operate a taxi, and a limited number of licences are issued. Some taxi companies enjoy a monopoly. One or more companies may be given the exclusive right to pick up passengers at airports, RAILWAY STATIONS or other areas where passengers originate.

Ferry Transportation The largest ferry system in Canada is operated by the BC Ferry Corp, providing service between the Vancouver area and the cities of Victoria and Nanaimo on Vancouver I. The BC Ferry Corp also provides service to many of the GULF IS and to some remote, northern communities. Other ferry service in BC is provided by the provincial Highways Dept. There are FERRIES on Canada's East Coast and on some of its lakes and inland waterways. Ferry service is provided from NB to PEI. CN Marine operates ferry services between Newfoundland and the Canadian mainland and between NS and Portland, Maine.

Some ferries carry passengers only; others carry passengers, trucks and automobiles. Some ferries carry only railcars; others sometimes carry dangerous commodities (such as dynamite). Most ferries operate at a loss, and a subsidy is often paid by federal or provincial taxpayers. Some ferries make no charge for transporting cars and passengers and are fully subsidized.

Other Transport Devices Many other devices are used for transportation. Bicycles are used for personal transportation and for the movement of letters and some small parcels. Dogsleds, motorized sleds and SNOWMOBILES are used in northern areas in the winter. Wheelchairs (motorized or human powered) are used to transport many handicapped persons. Moving sidewalks and "endless belts" transport persons in airport terminal buildings, shopping centres and elsewhere. Ski lifts and similar devices transport people in mountainous areas, and particularly in scenic areas or ski resorts. Elevators provide vertical transportation, literally moving hundreds of millions of passengers and millions of tonnes of freight each year. Horse-drawn vehicles are still used for transportation in some areas, although their numbers have decreased in the last century.

Technological Change, Productivity and Trends New inventions, technological change and human ingenuity have resulted in many changes in Canada's transport. Most changes have meant greater speed, lower cost or increased productivity. Some have made possible the development of entirely new industries.

Recent advances in water transportation have resulted in greatly increased productivity. Some improvements have come through the development of larger ships. Today a large oceangoing vessel can haul 2 or 3 times more oil, coal or other commodity than a vessel could carry a decade ago. As large ships seldom require more crew members than smaller ships, crew productivity has increased, and shipping costs have been reduced. There have been advances in navigation, ship design and ship propulsion. Research has been done on the use in ships of powdered coal and other petroleum extenders and substitutes for fueling ships. Still other increases in productivity have resulted from the use of containers. Today, enormous cranes at a modern port may load a large oceangoing liner with containerized freight in half a day. It would have taken 3 or 4 days to load that freight before the shift from manual loading of freight to the mechanical loading of containers. Much of the savings stem from ships spending less time in port. This makes it possible for them to move more cargo each year, since they can spend a greater portion of their time at sea.

Railway productivity has also increased in recent years through the use of more efficient railway cars, some of which were specially designed to carry a particular product (such as grain or coal). Other increases in productivity have come from the use of longer trains, robot locomotives and better train scheduling. Robot locomotives, placed near the middle of trains, make it possible to use longer trains. The train engineer can effectively handle 5 or 6 diesel locomotives and control a train more than a kilometre long, even in mountainous areas. Better communications and electronic signals systems make it possible to operate far more trains over a track than was possible with more primitive manual signals. Less space is required between trains, and especially between trains going in opposite directions on a single railway track. With a modern control system the railway dispatcher can determine the location and speed of every train quickly and electronically. He is able to plan train movements carefully and to shunt approaching trains into railway sidings so that other trains may pass. This makes it possible for more trains to use the track and thus increases railway productivity. Other improvements have come from more efficient use of railway cars, locomotives and other expensive equipment. Much research has focused on the linear induction motor which is highly efficient and which should enable trains to accelerate and decelerate more rapidly. These motors will be used in the LRC (light, rapid and convenient) trains being developed by the Urban Transport Development Corporation for urban transit. In some cities the cost of urban transit has been reduced by the introduction of articulated buses (2 passenger units pulled by a single engine). Such buses have been used in European cities for some time.

Aviation technology has changed radically in recent decades. Today's planes are much larger than the planes they replaced. Modern jets are twice as fast as propeller-driven planes, and engines are quieter and more fuel efficient. Aviation technology is changing in other areas too. Modern conveyor belts handle passengers' baggage faster and more efficiently. Photoelectric cells and other devices "read" baggage labels, and robots direct baggage and freight to specific bins and carts so that they can be quickly loaded on aircraft. Better radar and other electronic devices have been developed to enable planes to operate in bad weather with a high degree of reliability. These advances make for more efficient use of aircraft and personnel and promise lower operating costs. Aviation technology is also changing on the ground. Airlines are experimenting with better systems for reservations and ticketing. One day Canadians may be able to order their tickets by telephone and have them issued by their own personal computer and charged to their credit card, all of this being done electronically and within minutes.

There have been significant increases in productivity in the motor carrier industry. Some increases have resulted from the use of trucks and trailers which are longer, wider and higher. Other productivity increases have come from utilizing more of the available space and in scheduling vehicles more efficiently. Some provinces permit a truck (or tractor) to pull more than one trailer. As a truck requires little more fuel to pull 2 trailers than one (and only one driver is required), trucks which pull 2 trailers can be more efficient. Motor carrier productivity has also increased because of the development of more fuel-efficient engines and because of experimentation with the use of lower grade fuel.

In pipeline transportation, productivity increases have come through the use of larger pipes and faster speeds. This has been made possible because of technological improvements in valves, compressors and friction-reducing agents.

As much of transportation is labour intensive, increases in productivity in the next decade will depend to a large degree on the effective utilization of personnel. While there have been enormous increases in transport productivity in recent years because of improvements in vehicle technology, fewer such increases can be expected in the next decade. Take for instance the productivity increases in aviation. In the 1940s when the airlines flew the DC-3, one plane could produce about 3500 passenger/miles per hour. In the 1980s one Boeing 747 could produce about 200 000 passenger/miles per hour — an increase of some 5700%. Unless the airlines use supersonic planes, they cannot increase their speed. At the present time Canadian markets cannot efficiently utilize large planes, so there is little prospect for improved productivity from new planes themselves.

Interrelationship with Communications The transportation and communications industries have always been related. When good COMMUNICATIONS are established with another country, trade will often follow. Certainly, there cannot be much trade without good communications. Some system has to be available for the transmission of orders and the movement of shipping documents and other shipping details. In these areas transportation and communication are complementary. In other areas they may compete. A salesman may fly or drive to meet with a customer; on the other hand, he may simply call the customer by telephone. Thousands of dollars in cash may be shipped by armoured car; or a banking transfer may be made by telex. Valuable documents may be sent by air courier, or a facsimile may be transmitted via SATELLITE.

As transport costs increase and better communications systems are developed, transportation and communications will compete increasingly in certain areas (see COMPUTER COMMUNICATIONS; TELECOMMUNICATIONS). Should COMMUNICATIONS TECHNOLOGY develop in ways that some experts envisage, much that the postal service handles at present could be transmitted electronically, perhaps using satellites for transmission and cathode ray tubes (TV screens) or home teletype printers for reception. The handwritten letter could become obsolete.

Transportation and Travel About 80% of all air travel is for business reasons, although each year more Canadians travel for pleasure. The availability of comfortable, convenient and relatively low-cost transportation (by air, train and bus or automobile) has encouraged the development of the travel industry — one of the fastest-growing segments of the Canadian economy (see TOURISM). Much of this growth results from cooperative arrangements between transportation companies, travel agents and the operators of hotels, car rental agencies and other such facilities. Tour packages that include hotels, meals, guides and other items are frequently arranged by a tour operator (sometimes called a wholesaler) and marketed by travel agents. A number of these operators are subsidiaries of airlines.

Government Role in Transportation Since the first Europeans set foot in N America, governments have played some role in transportation. That role has taken several forms: promotion, regulation, subsidization and operation. The Canadian government began the promotion of transportation more than a century ago when it encouraged the construction of the railways. It promoted railway development through loans, grants and guarantees. After the railways were built, they had enormous power over users of their services. Governments then introduced and began to regulate the rates charged by the railways to ensure the fair treatment of all shippers and a fair return to the transportation companies (see TRANSPORTATION REGULATION).

Governments have subsidized every form of transportation in Canada at one time or another. Transportation subsidies may be divided into 2 general categories: direct subsidies and indirect subsidies. As mentioned, enormous construction subsidies were given to the railways. Substantial operating subsidies have been given to VIA Rail Canada and to other carriers. Most urban transportation systems are subsidized. Governments have also given indirect subsidies of many kinds. Sometimes a government has permitted the use of government-constructed facilities at less than the cost of providing these facilities, thus providing an indirect subsidy to the users of the facilities. For many years the railways have carried export grain at far less than it cost them to haul it. Additional indirect subsidies result when a government agency provides transport infrastructures (such as an airport, highway or port facilities) and does not charge sufficient user fees to recover the cost of providing these facilities (see TRANSPORTATION AGENCIES).

Governments also operate transportation companies, usually in the form of crown corporations. Today the federal government owns railways, airlines, steamship companies and ferries, and has a financial interest in pipeline operations. Provincial governments own airlines, trucking companies, ferries, bus companies and railways. Sometimes these operations compete with stockholder-owned companies.

In Canada the federal government has generally assumed responsibility for water transportation. Through Transport Canada and Ports Canada (formerly the National Harbours Board) the federal government builds, maintains and operates ports. Through the St Lawrence Seaway Authority (in co-operation with the US) it promotes, maintains and operates the St Lawrence Seaway. During WWII the government operated a large fleet of oceangoing vessels, but these were disposed of during the late 1940s.

The federal government, through Transport Canada, regulates and promotes air transportation, and builds, maintains and operates all of Canada's major airports, and most smaller airports too. In the early 1980s Canada was starting to move towards less regulation although by early 1985, the new Conservative government of Brian Mulroney had not announced specific plans for deregulation.

Roads and highways generally fall within the purview of provincial governments. Large provincial departments build and maintain most of the other roads and highways. The provinces regulate truck and bus operations, and they regulate motor vehicle safety.

Transportation Research Because of the importance of transportation to Canada, transportation research is uncommonly important. The federal government sponsors transportation research in several ways. The SCIENCE COUNCIL encourages research dealing with transportation devices and engineering. Transport Canada encourages research dealing with the management of transportation enterprises and the ways in which their operation can be made more efficient. Many of the major transport companies have research departments. Some of these work with vehicle and equipment manufacturers in the development and adaptation of new technology; some engage in market research, and some make contributions to more basic research. But since much of this research is of a proprietary nature, there are no good statistics concerning its extent.

Some research is conducted by consulting organizations, other research is conducted by transport institutes and universities. Five such institutes are funded by Transport Canada. These are the Centre for Transportation Studies at UBC in Vancouver; the Transportation Centre at U of Manitoba in Winnipeg; the York-Toronto Joint Program in Transportation in Toronto; the Canadian Institute of Guided Ground Transportation at Queen's U in Kingston; and the Transportation Centre at U de Montréal.

Employment Opportunities in Transportation Since transportation is vital to so many sectors of the economy, it provides many good job opportunities. These vary from entry level jobs as a clerk, a truck driver or a maintenance apprentice to high-level jobs as the manager of an airport, a steamship company or a transportation conglomerate. Some transportation jobs require personnel who are interested in accounting, finance or marketing; others require personnel skilled in labour relations, production management or computer systems. As transportation technology changes and as greater demands are made on Canada's transport systems, job opportunities will increase, particularly for trained, hardworking and innovative personnel.

KARL M. RUPPENTHAL

Reading: N.C. Bonsor, Transportation Economics; Theory and Canadian Policy (1984); H.L. Purdy, Transport Competition and Public Policy in Canada (1975); Karl M. Ruppenthal, Canada's Ports and Waterborne Trade (1983).

Transportation, Royal Commission on (Mac-Pherson Commission), appointed by the federal government (1959) to investigate transportation policy, particularly freight-rate inequities. In their 3-volume report (1961) the commissioners, under chairman M. MacPherson, recommended that railways be allowed more freedom to eliminate uneconomic passenger service and branch lines and that they receive extra subsidies for grain-handling responsibilities imposed by Parliament. A new National Transportation Act was consequently passed. Its principles, eg, the value of competition between different forms of transportation, the need to reduce regulatory control (which led to the establishment of the CANADIAN TRANSPORT COMMISSION as the one overseeing agency), and payment of reasonable charges by transportation operators for facilities provided by government, reflected the commission's influence. JOHN R. BALDWIN

Transportation Agencies (Government) The 2 major categories of government activities in transportation are administration and development of public policies, which includes the regulation of transport activities and the investment and operation of transport services and facilities. These responsibilities are allocated directly to the Department of Transport as well as to specialized government agencies and autonomous bodies.

Federal Agencies The Department of Transport (TRANSPORT CANADA) was created (1936) by amalgamation of the Department of Railways and Canals, the Marine Department and the civil aviation branch of the Department of National Defence. The department advises the federal government on transportation policy and provides and operates specific elements of the national transportation system. Furthermore the department has technical and safety regulation functions. Transport Canada is headed by the minister of transportation. The deputy minister is responsible for policy advice and the overall administration of the department. Transport Canada crown corporations (AIR CANADA, CANADIAN NATIONAL RAILWAYS, VIA RAIL, Northern Transportation Co Ltd, ST LAWRENCE SEAWAY Authority, 4 pilotage authorities and the Canadian Transport Commission) report to Parliament through the minister. There are 3 "modal" administrations, Canadian Air Transportation Administration (CATA), Canadian Marine Transportation Administration (CMTA) and Canadian Surface Transportation Administration (CSTA). CATA provides, operates and maintains approximately 160 airports, provides en route and airport air-navigation and air-traffic-control facilities and services and is responsible for the technical regulation of aircraft and flight personnel. CMTA is responsible for the management of the CANADIAN COAST GUARD, the Harbours and Ports Directorate, the Canada Ports Corporation, the St Lawrence Seaway Authority and 4 pilotage authorities. Through these organizations, CMTA provides marine services and facilities and develops and implements regulations for the safety of ships, navigation and the prevention of water pollution. The Canada Ports Corporation, a federal crown corporation established in 1983 (replacing the NATIONAL HARBOURS BOARD), has charge of 15 major Canadian ports. Other public ports are managed by the Harbours and Ports Directorate and 11 harbour commissions. The St Lawrence Seaway Authority was established (1951) to construct, maintain and operate, in conjunction with the St Lawrence Seaway Development Corporation of the US, a deep waterway allowing the passage of large vessels from the Port of Montréal and Lake Erie. The Canadian Surface Administration is responsible for the support of major ferry services, for rail-freight and passenger services, including grain transportation, for motor-vehicle safety regulations and defect investigations, for highway transportation and railway relocation and grade crossings.

Provincial Agencies With the exceptions of BC and Ontario, which have operated provincial railways, initially provincial involvement in transportation was restricted to the construction and maintenance of highways and highway-traffic regulation. Subsequently the range of provincial interests and activities has expanded and the highway departments have been reorganized as transport departments or ministries (often with added responsibilities for communications). At present, provincial transport departments have both the policy administration and co-ordination role as well as direct-investment, operating and regulatory functions. They are also involved in the planning and financing of urban transport. Economic regulations of transport activities under provincial jurisdiction (road transport) are administered by quasi-judicial regulatory commissions or boards. The comprehensiveness of regulations varies greatly between the provinces.

Special intergovernmental committees have been created that operate both at the ministerial and the official (ie, civil-service) levels to deal with provincial and federal transport policies and activities. They perform consultative and information-exchange roles. In general, such committees are organized regionally, and at present there exists no national structure.

K. STUDNICKI-GIZBERT

Transportation in the North If Canada as a whole represents the triumph of TRANSPORTATION over geography, the same is doubly true of the Canadian NORTH. Organized settlement in the North depends to an extraordinary degree on the development of transportation systems, whether by land, air, rail or water.

Water transport was the first means of penetrating the North. Explorers came from the E, by sea, fur traders from the S, via the MACKENZIE R, and, much later, whalers from the W, around Alaska. The first organized transport in the North was connected with the FUR TRADE, either in HUDSON'S BAY COMPANY ships in the eastern Arctic or in canoes and other small craft in the West (see CANOE, BIRCHBARK). The line of settlement was so far to the S that road transport was prohibitively expensive and, while it was occasionally proposed to link the North with the S by railway, the schemes for doing so verged on the fatuous. Population and economic development N of the 60th parallel did not justify the expense, and so the North continued to be served by water, which meant that for between 7 and 9 months of the year transportation was blocked by ice. Along the Mackenzie, virtually continu-

James Wolkie with his dog team, Paulatuk, NWT. Largely replaced by the snowmobile, the dog team still finds a use in the North (*photo by Karl-Heinz Raach*).

ous water transport was possible from the railhead at Waterways (now FT MCMURRAY, Alta), in northern Alberta, all the way to the Arctic Ocean. There was one major portage, on the Slave R near Ft Smith, and shipments depended to a high degree on water levels in the southerly parts of the system. The HBC dominated the traffic, and maintained a small fleet of steamships to carry it.

Transportation was revolutionized by the appearance of the airplane. Bush pilots, often air-force veterans from WWI, could take their small craft where no boat could go (see BUSH FLYING). Better still, an airplane was virtually an all-season craft. The North's winter isolation was finally broken. Using airplanes, prospectors could work more efficiently. A PROSPECTING boom was followed by mining development, particularly at YELLOWKNIFE and at GREAT BEAR LK. Mining development raised traffic volume along the Mackenzie, and created a demand for competition to lower the rates charged by the HBC. Several companies arose, of which the most enduring was Northern Transportation Co Ltd, which became a subsidiary of Eldorado Gold Mines Ltd (now Eldorado Nuclear Ltd), a uranium- and radium-producing company. Meanwhile the bush pilots' operations were being amalgamated into larger entities, particularly Canadian Pacific Airlines, a CPR subsidiary.

WWII brought further changes. The ALASKA HIGHWAY was built from northern BC through the southern Yukon, opening the North to road traffic for the first time, as well as demonstrating that an all-weather road was possible. The US army developed airfields and an oil PIPELINE in the Mackenzie Valley, again augmenting traffic volumes in that area. Wartime saw the appearance of new and bigger airplanes, especially the DC3 and DC4, making air cargo something more than a luxury for the first time. Just after the war, the HBC abandoned its riverboat business, leaving the field to Northern Transportation Co Ltd, which by then had become a federal crown company. Northern Transportation greatly expanded its operations, particularly after the construction of the DEW Line in the mid-1950s. It operated as a common carrier down the Mackenzie and into the Arctic Ocean — W to Alaska and E to the Arctic Archipelago. In 1975 it set up a branch at CHURCHILL, Man, to service Hudson Bay.

Airports were improved to handle the larger aircraft of the postwar period. The WHITE PASS AND YUKON RAILWAY had been built between Whitehorse and Skagway, Alaska, at the turn of the century; in 1960 another was completed linking Alberta with Great Slave Lk. A regular highway was built linking Yellowknife with northern Alberta. The Dempster Hwy, from Dawson to Inuvik, is Canada's northernmost highway. Ice roads, connecting such places as Great Bear Lk with Yellowknife, could also be established and kept open during the long winter. Air service increased, as did expenditure on airports. In 1981 the CANADIAN COAST GUARD stationed 8 ICEBREAKERS in northern waters, and

114 vessels were recorded in Canada's Arctic waters. By the early 1980s maritime traffic was expanding in the Northeast, servicing the usual customers — the government and the native population — as well as mining developments (eg, at Nanisivik). ROBERT BOTHWELL
Reading: Dept of Indian and Northern Affairs, *Government Activities in the North, 1981.*

Transportation Policy *see* CANADIAN TRANSPORT COMMISSION; CROW'S NEST PASS AGREEMENT; RAILWAY HISTORY; TRAFFIC LAW; TRANSPORTATION; TRANSPORTATION AGENCIES; TRANSPORTATION REGULATION.

Transportation Regulation is administered by all levels of government (federal, provincial, municipal) and covers prices, conditions and levels of service, and the operating authority of transport units. The purpose of regulation is to assure that transportation services are provided adequately and that users of these services are protected from excessive prices or unfair practices. Regulation can also be used to assist certain regions, industries or user groups.

Canadian transport regulation began with the establishment of a Railway Committee of the Privy Council in 1868. In 1903 the regulatory powers of the committee were transferred to the Board of Railway Commissioners, an independent, quasi-judiciary regulatory agency. Subsequently the board was given jurisdiction over express, telegraph and telephone companies (1908); government-owned railways (1923); international bridges and tunnels (1929); abandonment of railway lines (1933); Hudson Bay Railway (1948); and Newfoundland Railways. The Transport Act of 1938 changed the name of the board to the Board of Transport Commissioners for Canada and gave it regulatory powers over transportation by air and water. In 1944 regulation of civil aviation was transferred to the Air Transport Board. The National Transportation Act (1967) created the CANADIAN TRANSPORT COMMISSION (CTC).

Railway Rates Regulation The railways have occupied a prominent position in Canadian transportation. Basic geographical considerations of distance and population density, combined with economical and political disparities, have created a complex transport situation for regulation policy. Establishing fair and reasonable rate levels that are nondiscriminatory has been difficult because of variations in financial structure and resources among railways, the degree of direct or indirect competition, the commodities being transported, alternative routings and the permissible rates of return. These variations have been further complicated by political and regional policy considerations.

An important class of railway rates, grain export, were outside regulatory jurisdiction until 1983. These rates were originally established by the CROW'S NEST PASS AGREEMENT (1897) between the Dominion government and Canadian Pacific, and were redefined by legislation in 1922.

Following WWII and the growth of road transport, railway regulators were faced with additional problems. A continual increase in costs led to periodic demands by the railways to increase rates, and the growth of competition led to competitive rate applications and to special contract rates. But the increase in road transport meant that the general rate increases applied to a diminishing part of the transport market. Furthermore, competition had uneven effects in different regions of the country. The political implications resulted in intervention by the Diefenbaker government which imposed a rollback of railway freight rates and their subsequent freeze (Freight Rates Reduction Act, 1960). At the same time a ROYAL COMMISSION on transportation was appointed. The recommendations of the MacPherson Royal Commission (1961) were based on recognition of competition and the benefits of such competition in trans-

port. The commission proposed that railways be compensated for providing uneconomic services that were imposed by government in the public interest, and that they be free to compete in the transport market. It also proposed reliance on market forces to the fullest extent possible, protection of captive shippers (shippers with no practical alternative means of transport), and prevention of predatory pricing through the requirement that rates be compensatory, ie, that they cover the variable costs of transport.

Air Transport The main concerns of air-transport regulation have been the structure of the industry and of the route network. The problems of price regulation, which at first were largely restricted to the maintenance of price stability, became more complex and important in the 1970s with the growth of charter carriers and the advent of "seat sales" and other marketing devices by scheduled airlines. In the immediate postwar period air-transport regulations had been based on the principle of route monopolies; major intercity routes were allocated to TRANS-CANADA AIRLINES (TCA, later renamed AIR CANADA), and regional and local routes were assigned to Canadian Pacific Air Lines (CPA, later renamed CP Air) and to independent airlines. An increased degree of competition was gradually introduced, starting with a deregulation experiment in the small aircraft charter field and with the granting to CPA of limited access to the transcontinental market in 1958. The regulation of air transport was administered initially by the Board of Transport Commissioners (1938-44). In 1944, when the Aeronautics Act transferred regulatory powers to the Air Transport Board, the government was given considerable powers of policy intervention.

Canadian Transport Commission Federal transport regulations entered a new phase with the passing of the National Transportation Act in 1967. This legislation concentrated transport regulation in a new agency, Canadian Transport Commission (CTC), replacing the Board of Transport Commissioners, Air Transport Board and Canadian Maritime Commission. The CTC has also been granted regulatory powers over commodity pipelines, and the sectors of highway transport placed under federal control. Initially the CTC also had regulatory powers over TELECOMMUNICATIONS, but these were transferred to the CANADIAN RADIO-TELEVISION AND TELECOMMUNICATIONS COMMISSION in 1976.

The CTC is organized by transport modes (eg, Railway Transport Committee, Air Transport Committee, Water Transport Committee) and operates with the status of a quasi-judicial body. The regulatory decisions of CTC committees can be appealed to the Review Committee of the Commission, to the governor-in-council (the Cabinet) and, in the case of decisions by Air Transport, Water Transport and Commodity Pipelines Committees, to the minister of transport. Judicial review is provided for by appeals to the Federal Court of Canada.

The present structure of railway rate regulations follows the principles proposed by the MacPherson Commission: protection of the "captive shipper" and prohibition of noncompensatory rates. The CTC also deals with specific cases where the rates impose a burden on the shippers or regions that is not justified by the existence of specific cost factors. A large part of the regulatory activities of CTC in the railway field has been related to branch lines abandonment and passenger services.

In air transport the regulatory activities of CTC largely reflected government policies which have brought about a gradual increase of competition by granting competing carriers operating authority over major scheduled routes and by permitting a substantial increase of competition by nonscheduled (charter) airlines in the discretionary travel market.

Highway Transport Regulation is divided between the federal and provincial governments; the provinces have the right to regulate transport undertakings operating within the provinces, but interprovincial undertakings are subject to federal jurisdiction. However, federal regulatory authority has been delegated to the provincial boards (Motor Vehicle Transport Act, 1954). The National Transportation Act provides for the reassumption of federal regulatory powers over interprovincial road-transport undertakings, and provides certain authorities over some aspects of road-transport operations (mergers, Sunday operations). For all practical purposes the highway transport industry is provincially regulated. The scope of licensing and rate regulation of the TRUCKING industry varies from province to province, from virtually no regulation in Alberta to comprehensive regulation in Québec. BUS routes are regulated by exclusive franchises, or route monopolies. Municipalities regulate courier and taxicab services.

Deregulation Debate Until the 1970s the existence and the advisability of regulation in transport had been unquestioned in N America. In the US the regulatory authorities (Interstate Commerce Commission, Federal Maritime Board and Civil Aeronautics Board) were generally stricter than similar agencies in Canada, until the late 1970s when major regulatory reforms were instituted in the US, along with deregulation of transport. The case for transport deregulation has been argued by economists on the grounds of efficiency and the achievement of more flexible and efficient pricing systems. It has also been argued that functional regulation (general legal protection against monopolistic abuses and consumer protection) would be better than industry-specific regulation.

The opposite arguments are based on the assertion that the nature of transport markets and the national interest in transport make government intervention unavoidable, and thus the problem is not whether to regulate or not but how to improve the functioning of a system of pragmatic regulation. K. STUDNICKI-GIZBERT

Transportation Research Centres Recognizing the need for Canada to have specialists competent in the various facets of TRANSPORTATION, in 1971 the CANADIAN TRANSPORT COMMISSION established transportation centres at universities in each region of Canada. The administration of the centres was later transferred to TRANSPORT CANADA. These centres serve as focal points for research, bringing together qualified professionals who can address problems that are important to government and to industry. Basic financing in support of the centres is provided by Transport Canada. Additional funds come from research contracts, seminars, publications and gifts. The universities at which they are located also provide some support. Transport Canada provides base support for centres located at Dalhousie, U de Montréal, Queen's, U of Manitoba and UBC. It also supports the York-Toronto joint centre. Additionally, Transport Canada supports research activities at UNB, Carleton, McMaster, Waterloo, U of Saskatchewan and U of Calgary through research grants and contracts.

Each of the transport centres specializes in at least one area. The Canadian Marine Transportation Centre at Dalhousie specializes in marine transportation. The Centre de recherche sur les transports at Montréal focuses on the application of computers and management science to transportation problems. The Canadian Institute of Guided Ground Transportation at Queen's is mostly concerned with railway problems — present and future. The York-Toronto Joint Program concentrates on URBAN TRANSPORTATION; Manitoba is largely concerned with the transportation of agricultural products. The Centre for Transportation Studies at UBC has associated with it experts in every mode of transportation. Its research focuses on managerial problems, industry-government relations and aspects of transportation economics.

There is much transportation research that is not university based. Transport Canada's Transport Development Centre promotes and manages various types of research and demonstration projects. It has participated in the development of the ALRT system that was designed for Vancouver's International Exposition Expo 86. Many transportation companies undertake various kinds of research, as do transportation equipment manufacturers. The CANADIAN NATIONAL RAILWAYS, for example, does research on various mechanical, technical and economic problems of interest to railways, as does the CANADIAN PACIFIC RAILWAY. All of the major airlines engage in research dealing with various types of aviation problems — often in co-operation with aircraft manufacturers. Various trade associations and several government agencies undertake research, and some finance research. The NATIONAL RESEARCH COUNCIL is involved in engineering research. The Canadian Transport Commission does work on problems relating to transportation economics. Some of the provincial ministries of transport sponsor research in areas of interest to their province, while others have research staff of their own.

KARL M. RUPPENTHAL

Traquair, Ramsay, architect (b at Edinburgh, Scot 29 Mar 1874; d at Guysborough, NS 26 Aug 1952). Traquair's pioneer studies in the history of French Canadian building styles, culminating in *The Old Architecture of Quebec* (1947), helped awaken interest in the province's distinctive architectural heritage. Traquair studied in Edinburgh under architects S.H. CAPPER and Robert Lorimer and conducted important research on Byzantine architecture before succeeding Percy NOBBS as third Macdonald Professor of Architecture at McGill, 1914-38. He published papers on Québec's old houses, churches and woodcarvings; he also wrote *The Old Silver of Quebec* (1940). SUSAN WAGG

Travels and Adventures in Canada and the Indian Territories between the Years 1760 and 1776 (New York, 1809; Toronto, 1901), was written by Alexander HENRY (the elder), one of the first Britons to venture into western Indian territory after the defeat of the French at Québec. Henry describes his experiences among the Indians and Canadiens in sharp, clean prose. Particularly memorable is his eyewitness account of the capture of Fort Michilimackinac; the OTTAWA slaughtered the British garrison after entering the fort on the pretext of chasing a lacrosse ball, and Henry narrowly escaped with his life. Henry's comprehensive, detailed and occasionally blood-chilling narrative is among the most engaging and best written of the fur traders' records. NEIL BESNER

Travois, a device for transportation among Plains Indians, consisted of 2 long poles, each lashed to the sides of the dog (and later horse) pulling it. The poles dragged behind and a framework at the rear carried household baggage, including the TIPI cover. The webbed willow frame attached to the ASSINIBOINE travois was circular, and the BLACKFOOT constructed both round and rectangular frames. The dog travois of pre-European times was small, capable of pulling not more than 20 to 30 kg. When dogs were replaced by horses, the greater pulling power allowed tipis to increase in size and household goods to multiply. RENÉ R. GADACZ

Treason is probably the oldest and most serious offence in political society, with the possible exception of murder. The earliest English treason legislation, which dates from 1351, is the basis of all treason legislation in the English-speaking world. Originally, treason meant an attack upon the person or life of the monarch, but as the state became more important than its sovereign, treason came to indicate any act directed at the overthrow of the government or against the security of the state. Anyone participating in a rebellion or an unsuccessful revolution is technically guilty of treason, although only the leaders tend to be prosecuted. Conversely, it is not uncommon for the leaders of a successful revolution to try former politicians for treason. In Canada, it would be treason for a province to break away from the confederation without the consent of the federal government, expressed in an Act of Parliament.

For individual offenders, treason is defined in the Canadian Criminal Code (s46) as the wounding, imprisoning, restraining or killing of the sovereign. It is treason for anyone in Canada and therefore under the protection of Canadian law (although treason can be committed outside the country as well) to raise a rebellion — in legal terminology, to wage or levy war against Canada — or to assist any enemy of Canada or to participate in a conflict with Canadian forces, even if no war (in the strict sense of the term) is being waged. The Code condemns as traitors those who use force or violence to overthrow the government, or who provide information prejudicial to Canadian security to any agent of a foreign state, or who form a CONSPIRACY, that is to say, an agreement to commit any treasonable act. It is also treasonous to intend to commit any act of treason, provided intention is manifested by some overt act. Life imprisonment has replaced CAPITAL PUNISHMENT as the penalty for treason. L.C. GREEN

Treasury Board, the only statutory committee of CABINET (thus formally a PRIVY COUNCIL committee), was created in 1867. The president of Treasury Board (ministerial portfolio) chairs a board which comprises the finance minister and 4 other ministers appointed by the governor-in-council. Its extensive staff is called the Secretariat. The board is responsible for recommendations to Cabinet on the selection of programs and appropriate allocation of funds; administrative policy for financial management in the public administration and for matters related to personnel, office space, supply and contracts for service; and government negotiations in COLLECTIVE BARGAINING arrangements with PUBLIC SERVICE unions and associations. In 1978 the addition of the office of comptroller general, with special responsibility for upgrading the quality of financial administration and program evaluation within departments, enlarged the board's role as controller of the expenditure budget.

J.E. HODGETTS

Treaty Day, the annual meeting at which treaty annuities were distributed by representatives of the Dept of Indian Affairs to members of particular bands under the numbered INDIAN TREATIES. These meetings were often attended by hundreds of Indians and their families. Along with the distribution of treaty monies, food, ammunition and hunting or fishing equipment were also given out. Government officials were often accompanied by doctors and officers of the law to help Indians in any way they could. Although treaty is now often paid by cheque, treaty-day meetings still occur in many areas, particularly in the western provinces.

RENÉ R. GADACZ

Reading: R. Fumoleau, *As Long as This Land Shall Last* (1973).

Treaty-Making Power describes any and all types of international agreements governed by international law which are concluded between and among states and international organizations. Terms such as "convention," "protocol" and "declaration" are sometimes used to describe such agreements. Treaties may be either bilateral, ie, between 2 parties, or multilateral, ie, between more than 2 parties. Informal agreements or understandings between states that are not intended to create legal obligations are not regarded as treaties. Most treaties that have entered into force for Canada are published in the Canada Treaty Series and the UN Treaty Series.

Only states and international organizations possessing an international personality, such as the UNITED NATIONS, have the capacity to conclude treaties. Before Canada became an independent sovereign state, a process that occurred over a number of years, Canada's EXTERNAL RELATIONS were controlled by Britain, which negotiated, signed and ratified treaties on behalf of the British Empire, which included Canada. The first multilateral treaty to be signed by Canada in its own right was the TREATY OF VERSAILLES (1919). The first bilateral treaty negotiated and signed by Canada was the Halibut Fisheries Convention of 1923 with the US. In Canada treaty-making power remains part of the royal prerogative, the residue of authority left in the CROWN. The delegation of the prerogative powers to Canada was an evolutionary process completed with the issuance of the Letters Patent of 1947, by which the governor general was authorized to exercise all the powers of the sovereign in respect of Canada. In practice the treaty-making power is exercised on the basis of policy approval from Cabinet or the ministers most directly concerned, coupled with an executive authority in the form of an ORDER-IN-COUNCIL issued by the governor-in-council. The secretary of state for external affairs, as the minister responsible for foreign relations, advises and recommends on treaty action to be taken by Canada.

Canada is bound by the terms of treaties that it enters into and breach thereof may give rise to international claims. However, in Canada treaties are not self-executing; they do not constitute part of the law of the land merely by virtue of their conclusion. If domestic law must be changed in order to carry out treaty obligations, implementing legislation is required. It follows that if the existing laws of Canada do not give the Government of Canada the capacity to discharge treaty obligations, then it will be necessary for the appropriate legislative body, federal or provincial, or a combination of both, to enact implementing legislation. This is the effect of the LABOUR CONVENTIONS Case of 1937.

Although competent to conclude treaties, the federal government can only enact legislation in relation to those treaties whose subject matter falls within the federal field of competence. If the treaty concerns matters within provincial legislative competence, the provincial legislatures must adopt the necessary implementing legislation. As a general practice, the federal government carries out prior consultation with those provinces that may be called upon to implement a treaty. The modern form of federal state clause enables Canada to become a party to international conventions such as the 1980 Hague Convention on International Child Abduction and designate the provinces to which the convention applies; in practice this means the provinces that have adopted the required implementing legislation. The wording of the clause enables Canada to file subsequent declarations extending the application of the convention to other provinces as soon as they pass implementing legislation.

A general rule of international law is that only a central government can bind a state in a treaty. Thus the Canadian government alone can bind Canada internationally, but its legislative limitations restrict its implementation powers. On the other hand, the provinces cannot bind Canada internationally even in those subject matters in which they enjoy legislative competence. In recent years the provinces have entered into a variety of arrangements or understandings with foreign governments that are not considered binding in international law. For example, Ontario and Québec have signed a number of educational and cultural arrangements with foreign governments.

In spite of what is regarded by some as an unsatisfactory system of treaty making and treaty implementation, Canada is among the most active treaty-making nations in the world. Much of the INTERNATIONAL LAW governing treaties is incorporated in the Vienna Convention on the Law of Treaties to which Canada acceded in 1970. EMILY F. CARASCO

Treaty of Breda, agreements signed 21 July 1667 at Breda, Netherlands, between England and the Netherlands and between England and France, ending the second Anglo-Dutch War. The former treaty recognized the English conquest of Nieuw Amsterdam (New York) in 1664. The latter provided for French restoration of the English part of the island of St Christopher's, West Indies, in exchange for ACADIA, captured from the French in 1654 by Britain's New England forces while France and England were allies. The actual handover of territory was delayed until 1670. STUART R.J. SUTHERLAND

Treaty of Ghent, signed in Ghent, Belgium, on Christmas Eve 1814 by Great Britain and the US to end the WAR OF 1812. The military situation was so balanced that neither side had achieved its war aims. Consequently, none of the issues over which the nations fought was included in the treaty. It was simply agreed to return to the *status quo ante bellum:* there was nothing on neutral rights or IMPRESSMENT, no mention of the question of Indian lands in the Midwest, and all captured territory was returned. Because communications were slow, a major battle — the American victory at New Orleans — took place 2 weeks after the signing. Issues not covered by the treaty, such as disputed boundaries between the US and parts of what is now Canada, were later decided by JOINT COMMISSIONS, and since then Britain and the US have settled their differences peacefully. CARL A. CHRISTIE

Treaty of Paris (1763), signed 10 Feb 1763 by France, Britain and Spain after 3 years of negotiations, ended the SEVEN YEARS' WAR. Britain obtained Île Royale [Cape Breton I] and Canada, including the Great Lakes Basin and east bank of the Mississippi R, from France, and Florida from Spain. France retained fishing rights in Newfoundland and the Gulf of ST LAWRENCE, acquired Saint Pierre and Miquelon as an unfortified fishing station and had her lucrative West Indian possessions, trading centres in India and slaving station in Goré (in present-day Chad) restored. In accordance with the conditional capitulation of 1760, Britain guaranteed Canadians limited freedom of worship. Provisions were made for exchange of prisoners; Canadians were given 18 months to emigrate if they wished; and government archives were preserved. Britain had acquired a large empire and France was still able to challenge British naval supremacy, but Spain achieved none of her war aims. *See* PROCLAMATION OF 1763. CORNELIUS J. JAENEN

Treaty of Paris (1783) concluded the AMERICAN REVOLUTION. On 20 Sept 1783 Britain acknowledged American independence and recognized a boundary along the centre of the 4 northerly Great Lakes and from Lake of the Woods "due west" to the imagined location of the Mississippi's headwaters, then S along the Mississippi R. This gave the US Niagara, Detroit and Michilimackinac, and valuable lands reserved to Indians by the PROCLAMATION OF 1763. The Americans, negotiating through the French comte de Vergennes, obtained fishing rights off Newfoundland and access to the E banks of the Mississippi;

in turn they promised restitution and compensation to British LOYALISTS. The treaty was ineffective. Britain retained its western posts until after JAY'S TREATY (1794), and denied the US free navigation of the St Lawrence. The Americans largely ignored their promises to the Loyalists, many of whom settled in Canada. Nevertheless, Britain soon resumed trade with and investment in the new republic. CORNELIUS J. JAENEN

Treaty of Ryswick, concluded 20 July-30 Oct 1697 between England, the Netherlands, Spain and the Holy Roman Empire on the one side and by France on the other, ending the War of the Grand Alliance (King William's War) and recognizing William III as king of England. The agreement between England and France provided for restoration of all territorial conquests (principally HUDSON'S BAY COMPANY posts seized by Pierre le Moyne d'IBERVILLE between 1686 and 1697) and the establishment of a commission to determine the status of 3 disputed forts in the Hudson Bay region. STUART R.J. SUTHERLAND

Treaty of Utrecht, concluded 11 Apr 1713 at Utrecht, Netherlands, between Britain and France as one of a series of treaties ending the WAR OF THE SPANISH SUCCESSION. In N America, France agreed to restore the entire drainage basin of Hudson Bay to Britain and to compensate the HUDSON'S BAY COMPANY for wartime losses. France ceded all claims to Newfoundland, although French fishermen retained certain rights on its coasts. ACADIA passed to Britain, although France still possessed part of the territory (modern NB) because of differences in interpreting Acadia's size. France retained CAPE BRETON I, where it began to construct LOUISBOURG, and Île Saint-Jean (PEI). STUART R.J. SUTHERLAND

Treaty of Versailles, 28 June 1919, the peace settlement imposed on Germany after WORLD WAR I, drawn up at the Paris Peace Conference and signed near the French capital at Versailles. The treaty broke up and redistributed the German Empire and required substantial reparation payments from it. Canadian PM Sir Robert BORDEN publicly characterized the terms as severe, and justly so. Canada had little impact on the final shape of the treaty, but Borden led a successful fight for separate Dominion representation at the conference and separate signatures on the treaty. He believed passionately that Canada, with 60 000 war dead, had paid the price of such recognition. In addition to representation in its own right, and along with the other Dominions and India, Canada was represented on the British Empire delegation, a fact that increased Canada's prestige and the opportunities for making its views known. However, when it came to signing the treaty, the British PM did so for the entire Empire, the Dominions included, thus reducing the importance of their hard-won individual signatures. Canada's involvement reflected the ambiguity of its position in the world. Canada remained subordinate to Britain, in fact and in the perception of other nations, but her emerging international personality had been recognized. The treaty also made provision for a LEAGUE OF NATIONS, providing another vehicle for the advancement of Canada's national status. NORMAN HILLMER

Treaty of Washington, negotiated in 1871, came into effect in 1873. Canadian PM Sir John A. MACDONALD was one of 5 commissioners chosen to represent British interests, but held little power during the deliberations. The issues were the American claim for losses stemming from the ALABAMA's depredations; the American desire to resume use of Canadian and Newfoundland inshore fisheries, denied 1818-54 and after the 1866 lapse of the RECIPROCITY Treaty; ownership of the San Juan Is in the Str of Georgia; and restitution to Canada for FENIAN raids, 1866-70. The Americans refused to have

the last item on the agenda. Some Americans hoped Britain would cede Canada in the negotiations. However, the treaty was settled in a series of arbitrations: the *Alabama* claims were settled in 1872 in Geneva for $15.5 million; the San Juan Is question was resolved by Germany, which gave them to the US; and the US was admitted to the Canadian inshore fishery for 12 years, in return for free entry to the American market for Canadian fish and $5.5 million. Britain eventually compensated Canada for the Fenian raids, with a $2.5-million loan guarantee. P.B. WAITE

Treeline marks the limit of TREES latitudinally on continental plains and altitudinally on highlands and mountains (where it is sometimes called timberline). Tree species still occur beyond this limit, but in shrub form, extending to the "tree-species line." The treeline is controlled by CLIMATE in interaction with SOIL. In the North, it is correlated generally with the modal (most common) position of the southern edge of the arctic front in summer, and with such temperature indices as the July 10°C isotherm. But wherever soils are deeper and warmer than normal, as in river valleys (eg, the THELON) or on upland, sandy ESKERS, ribbons of trees extend the treeline far into the tundra. Characteristic treeline species are alpine fir, whitebark pine and alpine larch in the Rocky Mts; in Alaska and northern Canada, coexisting black spruce, white spruce and tamarack (larch). Similar species of spruce and larch, with pine and birch, continue the circumpolar treeline across Eurasia. The pollen record (*see* PALYNOLOGY) and preserved wood show that treelines on this continent have fluctuated greatly in the past, advancing hundreds of kilometres during warm phases and retreating southward when the climate has deteriorated. Such movements take hundreds of years. Slight climatic changes can cause major shifts in the treeline, because seed production and survival of seedlings is precarious near the limit of trees. The conifers are also susceptible to fire during dry cycles, and this and cutting by man make today's treeline a diffuse and unstable boundary. The dotted lines and the label "Approximate Limit of Trees" that indicate the treeline on northern National Topographic Survey maps are appropriately vague. J. STAN ROWE

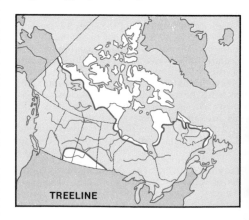

TREELINE

Trees are single-stemmed, perennial, woody PLANTS taller than 3 m and exceeding 8 cm in diameter at breast height; shrubs are multistemmed and smaller. These definitions are somewhat arbitrary, since many species (eg, willow, alder, cherry, maple) can grow as trees or shrubs, depending on environment. Counting the 30-odd shrubs that assume tree form under favourable conditions, there are about 140 native Canadian trees. The largest and oldest grow in the Pacific temperate rain FOREST. Douglas fir is an imposing example and, although it does not reach the size of redwoods or the age of bristlecone pines, specimens 90 m tall, 5 m in basal diameter and older than 1000 years have been reported.

Trees have always impressed by their massiveness and majesty, by the sound of wind in their branches, and by their visual beauty. Legend and folklore suggest attitudes of awe and reverence: yews, symbols of eternity; birches, holy trees; larches, guardians against enchantment. The Greeks populated trees with spirits (dryads), attributing religious significance to them, as did the druids, who conferred on forest groves and oak woods a sacred, precommercial value now, unfortunately, lost. Today, trees are valued for their products: pulpwood, sawtimber, poles, plywood, particle board, paper, cork, rubber, gums, tannin, pharmaceuticals, fruits, nuts, syrups. Indirect benefits include soil stabilization and prevention of EROSION, windbreaks, sound barriers and air purification.

Apart from a few large, single-stemmed FERNS, trees are classified as gymnosperms (with naked seeds in cones) and angiosperms (with seeds enclosed in ovaries of flowers). Gymnosperms (CONIFERS), with scalelike or needlelike leaves, appear first in the FOSSIL record (Carboniferous period, 345-280 million years ago) and, by early Mesozoic times (225-190 million years ago), dominated the earth's vegetation. Later, during the Cretaceous period (140-65 million years ago), broadleaf angiosperms evolved to become the more important group, perhaps profiting from their close relationships with insect pollinators (see POLLINATION) and with larger animals which spread their fruits. Angiosperms also developed the ability to reproduce vegetatively by sprouting, an advantage shared by few conifers.

Softwoods, the conifers, tend to concentrate growth in a central trunk from which many small branches are offset, producing a conical crown. They are usually evergreen, an adaptation fitting them for difficult environments by allowing internal recycling of nutrients from old to new foliage. Hardwoods, the broadleaf trees, tend to have rounded crowns because side branches grow just as well as main stems, which may fork repeatedly. They are typically deciduous, and grow on more fertile soils and in more moderate climates. There are numerous exceptions: some conifers (eg, larches, cypresses, dawn redwood) are deciduous; some pines have relatively hard wood; some broadleaf trees (eg, poplars) have soft wood; others are evergreen, especially in subtropical and tropical climates. The only native Canadian broadleaf evergreen is the red-barked arbutus of southwestern BC.

Tree roots perform both anchoring and absorbing functions. Like the tops, they are distinctive according to species and environment. They may penetrate deeply (taproots of pine) or spread horizontally just below the surface (platelike system of spruce). Buttress roots, thickened vertically, characterize wet sites, particularly in the tropics, although they are sometimes seen on elm. Adventitious roots, sprouting from the lower trunk (as on spruce and poplar), are a response to burial by accumulations of peat, silt on river floodplains, or windblown sand.

In climates that vary seasonally, the "growth ring" is a characteristic anatomical feature of trees. Regenerative, meristematic cells (cambium and cork cambium) sheathe the living trunk, branches and roots just under the bark, annually forming layers of phloem and corky cells to the outside (bark) and xylem cells to the inside (wood). Both bark and wood thicken with age. Products of photosynthesis and various other biochemicals are transported by phloem; water is transported chiefly by active xylem in sapwood surrounding older, darker, nonfunctional heartwood. The water-conducting efficiency of xylem cells is a function of their size, controlled by growth regulators released from the tree's growing tips. When shoot growth begins in spring, cambium produces large-diameter cells.

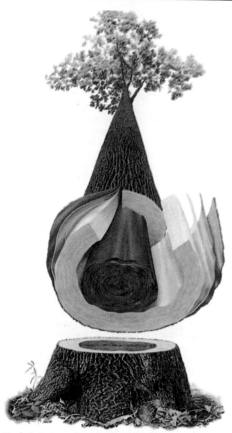

Exploded view of trunk of white ash (*Fraxinus americana*), showing heartwood, sapwood, cambial zone, the inner bark and the outer bark (*courtesy National Museums of Canada/National Museum of Natural Sciences*).

Later, in summer, as growth slows and stops, wood-cell diameters decrease. Therefore a cross section of trunk, root or branch shows concentric "growth rings" outlined by the contrast between small, dense, latewood cells of one year and larger, lighter earlywood cells of the next. An uncritical count of a tree's growth rings may overestimate its true age, since extra flushes of growth in a year can be triggered by weather changes or defoliation, forming false annual rings. Ring size reflects growing conditions. Where precipitation is the limiting factor, sensitive trees record wet and dry years in wide and narrow rings. Where heat is limiting, ring sizes mirror sequences of warm and cold summers.

Trees were eliminated by ice-age GLACIERS which covered most of Canada. Deglaciation began about 17 000 years ago, allowing immigration of plants to newly exposed soils. Species with small, winged seeds travelled fastest and farthest, and the boreal zone was filled by spruce, pine, larch, fir, poplar and birch. Trees that migrated more slowly or were less stress tolerant came later, and they now characterize more favourable environments: southern BC, with numerous conifers; and southern Ontario, with an even greater variety of broadleaf deciduous trees. Altitudinal and latitudinal distributions are in part related to wood anatomy: small-diameter xylem cells of boreal species (spruce, fir, aspen, alder, willow, birch) are less prone to freezing damage than larger cells of "ring porous" southern hardwoods (oak, hickory, walnut). Each wide-ranging tree species includes locally adapted varieties. Although they seem similar, white spruces from the Territories, Newfoundland and southern Manitoba are genetically different, and respond differently when planted together. Successful planting is best accomplished, therefore, by using seed from trees native to the area. This variation within species means that preservation of native trees, as well

as other plants and animals, in all their genetic diversity, requires the protection of many large, widely distributed, natural areas as ecological preserves. *See* individual tree entries; MYCORRHIZAE.
J. STANLEY ROWE

Reading: R.C. Hosie, *Native Trees of Canada* (1979).

Tremblay, Gilles, composer, pianist, sound specialist (b at Arvida [Jonquière], Qué 6 Sept 1932). His research into the field of sound is reflected in all his work by the use of instruments at the limits of their sound possibilities. He studied with Jean PAPINEAU-COUTURE, Claude CHAMPAGNE, Germaine Malépart and Jean VALLERAND in Canada; with Yvonne Loriod, Olivier Messiaen, Maurice Martenot and Andrée Vaurabourg-Honegger in Paris, where he also studied with the Groupe de recherches musicales of the ORTF; and with Karlheinz Stockhausen, Pierre Boulez and Henri Pousseur in Darmstadt. His magnificent *Sonorisation du Pavillon du Québec,* electroacoustic music written for EXPO 67, won him the 1968 Prix de musique Calixa-Lavallée. His commissions include one from the Société de musique contemporaine du Québec for *Souffles (Champs II),* 1968, and one from the Montréal Symphony Orchestra for *Fleuves,* 1976. His major works also include *Kékoba, Oralléluiants* and *Envoi.* In 1973 he received the medal of the Canadian Music Council, which also proclaimed him "composer of the year" for 1977. Tremblay teaches at the Montreal Conservatory of Music and is chairman of the Société de musique contemporaine du Québec. He has also taught at the Conservatoire de musique de Québec.
HÉLÈNE PLOUFFE

Tremblay, Marc-Adélard, professor of anthropology (b at Les Éboulements, Qué 24 Apr 1922). After completing his PhD at Cornell U (1954), he held leading academic and administrative positions at Laval, in professional and research organizations and in national academies. For his contributions to the study of Québec society and cultural life, he earned the Québec Literary Competition (1965), Innis-Gérin medal (1979) and Centenary Medal of the Royal Society of Canada (1982). His well over 100 articles and books include *Les Comportements économiques de la famille salariée* (1964), *Initiation à la recherche dans les sciences humaines* (1968), *Famille et parenté en Acadie* (1971), *Communities and Culture in French Canada* (1973) and *L'Identité québecoise en péril* (1983).
RENÉ R. GADACZ

Tremblay, Michel, writer (b at Montréal 25 June 1942). In 1959 Tremblay entered the Institut des arts graphiques and wrote his first play, *Le Train.* He worked as a linotype operator 1963-66. In 1964 *Le Train* won first prize in the Concours des jeunes auteurs sponsored by Radio-Canada; it was broadcast on 7 June 1964. This was the beginning of a long career devoted primarily to theatrical works. The novelist side of Michel Tremblay first appeared with his *Contes pour buveurs attardés* (1966).

Le Train was produced again, at the Théâtre de la Place Ville-Marie between 1965 and 1968. The Mouvement contemporain presented excerpts from *Contes pour buveurs attardés* and le Patriote mounted *Cinq* (original version of *En pièces détachées*) in Dec 1966. In 1968 Tremblay went to Mexico on a Canada Council grant and wrote *La Cité dans l'oeuf,* a fantasy novel, and *La Duchesse de Langeais,* a one-character play about the loves and disillusionments of an old transvestite. After a public reading of *Les Belles-Soeurs* on 4 Mar 1968 by the Centre d'essai des auteurs dramatiques, the play was produced on 28 Aug 1968 by André Brassard, who has continued to stage virtually all productions and revivals of Tremblay's work. *Les Belles-Soeurs,* written in the Montréal street language JOUAL, offered a transformed vision of the working-class neighbourhood where the author was born. Critics have included him in the theatre of realism, but his frequent use of antirealistic devices (chorus, flashback) and of fringe characters show he is not following predecessors Gratien GÉLINAS, Marcel DUBÉ, Françoise LORANGER and Jacques LANGUIRAND.

Tremblay has also written musical comedies, has translated and adapted many American and other authors and is a scriptwriter and songwriter. His many outstanding plays include *A toi, pour toujours, ta Marie-Lou*, 1972 winner of the Chalmers Award. He is now concentrating on fiction. The first 3 novels have appeared in his Plateau Mont-Royal series, which brings to life the same world as his plays. Tremblay has won many prizes and distinctions, including the Prix Victor-Morin in 1974. In Aug 1978 he was named the most remarkable Montréaler of the last 2 decades in theatre. PIERRE LAVOIE

Trent Affair, the most serious diplomatic crisis between Britain and the US federal government during the AMERICAN CIVIL WAR. On 8 Nov 1861 Capt Charles Wilkes of the Northern navy stopped the *Trent*, a British merchantman and mail packet, in neutral waters between Havana, Cuba, and London, to take captive 2 Confederate emissaries to London and Paris. In both Britain and British North America news of the seizure (and violation of British neutrality) was greeted by demands for apologies from the US and for its surrender of the diplomats. War appeared possible between Britain and the North, with Canada bound to be a battleground, and colonial and provincial officials conferred about how best to defend Canada. When British troops, sent to reinforce the meagre border garrisons, had to cross through Maine to reach Canada, Canadian leaders recognized Canada's vulnerability. The crisis passed. The North returned the Confederate commissioners, but without apology, on Dec 26. ROBIN W. WINKS

Trent Canal system links Lk Ontario (at Trenton) with Lk Huron (at Port Severn on Georgian Bay). The water route (388 km long) utilizes the Trent R to Rice Lk, the Otonabee R, the Kawartha Lks, man-made channels to Lk Simcoe and Lk Couchiching and the Severn R to Georgian Bay, as well as 2 marine railways (at Big Chute). Locks overcome a rise of 181 m to the summit at Balsam Lk and then a drop of 79 m to Lk Huron. Two of the locks, at Peterborough and Kirkfield, are hydraulic-lift locks, unique in N America. Early settlers constructed simple connections between some lakes to facilitate the floating of timber cut from nearby forests. Logging, milling, steamboating, grain handling and recreation were all linked to the development of the waterway. Work was sporadic and covered 87 years. Under the control of Ontario until 1892, the system was taken over and completed for the federal government by the Department of Railways and Canals. Now under Parks Canada, the waterway is used every summer for leisure boating. It also plays a role in providing water for municipal supplies, hydroelectric-power generation, wildlife-habitat protection and flood control. ROBERT LEGGET

Trent University, Peterborough, Ont, was founded in Apr 1963 by Act of the Ontario legislature. Trent embodies the academic objectives of its founding president, Prof Thomas H.B. SYMONS. Five residential colleges provide excellent small-group teaching in the traditional arts and science disciplines and in a number of interdisciplinary programs, including admin-

istrative and policy studies, Canadian studies, computer science, cultural studies, environmental and resource studies, comparative development studies and native studies. Teacher education is carried out in co-operation with QUEEN'S UNIVERSITY. Graduate programs in specialized areas include anthropology, freshwater science, Canadian heritage and development, and watershed ecosystems. ROBERT D. CHAMBERS

Trente Arpents (1938), a novel that breaks with the tradition of the regional idyll by portraying the Canadien farmer as a tragic rather than a romantic figure, presents Québec rural life as subject at once to the vagaries of climate and the impact of URBANIZATION. Under the pseudonym "Ringuet," author Philippe PANNETON dramatizes Euchariste Moisan's fall from youthful prosperity, married to his farm, to impoverished old age, trapped in an American factory town. Conflicts between generations are equally pervasive in the country and the city; rural life before WWI is only marginally better than city life. Claiming to write realism rather than naturalism, Panneton employs the seasons as a symbolic and structuring device in order to reveal the frailty of human hopes compared to the indifferent but powerful forces of nature and time. The novel was awarded prizes in both France and Québec; Felix and Dorothea Walter's translation, *Thirty Acres*, won the GOVERNOR GENERAL'S LITERARY AWARD in 1940. It has also been translated into German. MICHÈLE LACOMBE

Trenton, Canadian Forces Base, is 167 km E of Toronto on Lk Ontario's Bay of Quinte. Begun 1929 on 384 ha of flat farmland adjacent to the town of Trenton, it replaced Camp BORDEN's inadequate airforce facilities. Constructed during the Great Depression as a relief project, it became the centre for the RCAF's sea and land operations and training in the 1930s. During WWII it was the hub of the BRITISH COMMONWEALTH AIR TRAINING PLAN. Renamed CFB Trenton upon unification (1968), the base at various times has housed units of air operations, training and support, their activities including air-traffic control and communications, transport and air movement, civil and military search and rescue, weather forecasting and air maintenance and training systems for the Canadian Forces and the UN. Trenton is Canada's primary air base. With its 3500 military and civilian employees, 8600 dependants and modern urban facilities, it has an operating budget of $104 million. As such, it is a prime economic influence on the nearby cities of BELLEVILLE and Trenton and the surrounding district. R.G. HAYCOCK

Trigger, Bruce Graham, anthropologist, archaeologist (b at Preston, Ont 18 June 1937). He has received the Queen's Silver Jubilee Medal and the Cornplanter Medal for Iroquois Research, and is a fellow of the RSC. Staff archaeologist at the Oriental Institute, Trigger conducted research in the Sudan and Egypt before joining McGill in 1964. Author of articles on Egyptian and Sudanese archaeology, ethnohistory of eastern Canada and archaeological theory, Trigger is best known for *History and Settlement in Lower Nubia* (1965) and his outstanding 2 volume history of the HURON, *The Children of Aataentsic* (1976). RENÉ R. GADACZ

Trillium, common and generic name of a perennial PLANT of the Trilliaceae family (sometimes classified as a subfamily of the LILY family). The name derives from the arrangement of leaves, petals and sepals in groups of 3. The plant grows in clusters. It has a short, tuberlike rootstock and a fleshy stalk bearing a whorl of 3 leaves near the top. A single flower is produced in spring. The fruit is a red berry. Of the 40 species known worldwide, about 30 are American, the remainder Asiatic. Five species are native to Canada. *Trillium grandiflorum* (white tril-

Five species of trillium are native to Canada, including the white trillium (*Trillium grandiflorum*), the floral emblem of Ontario (*photo by Mary W. Ferguson*).

lium, white lily, wakerobin) flowers Apr-May in the hardwood forests of western and central Québec and in the lower Ottawa Valley, Ont. It is illegal to pick trillium in Ontario, where it has been the PROVINCIAL FLORAL EMBLEM since 1937. The roots were valued for their astringent and antiseptic properties. CÉLINE ARSENEAULT

Trilobite, extinct marine arthropod of the Paleozoic era (570-240 million years ago). Its closest modern relative is the horseshoe crab. Trilobites had 2 eyes on top of the head, antennae projecting from beneath the head and, in some, from under the tail, and 2 rows of paired limbs. Each paired limb consisted of 2 branches joined near the base: a comblike gill branch (exite) for breathing and swimming, and a jointed walking leg. After hatching, each trilobite secreted a shell, composed of calcite and organic material. The shell consisted of head and tail pieces (cephalon and pygidium, respectively) separated by several articulated segments (thorax). Adults ranged from less than 1 cm long (eg, genus *Scharyia*) to over 60 cm (eg, *Terataspis* of Ontario).

Some trilobites were pelagic, floating near the surface of ancient oceans. Most were benthic, crawling on or ploughing through seafloor mud, extracting organic particles from mud or filtering them from seawater through their comblike exites. Predatory trilobites apparently used sharp spikes on the undersides of their walking legs to clasp prey. Some could swim by using their exites as oars. Trilobites of genus *Illaenus* had smooth, hemispherical heads and lived in burrows, their heads acting as caps to the burrows if predators threatened. Seafloor dwellers left characteristic, grooved trail or trilobite-shaped resting burrows.

Trilobites appeared early in the Cambrian period. They increased in numbers and diversity and are used to date Cambrian rocks (575-500 million years old). A second period of adaptive radiation, early in the Ordovician (500-425 million years ago), produced all major post-Cambrian groups. Their number and variety dwindled until extinction at the end of the Paleozoic era. They probably died out because they were unable to compete with or escape from active, aggressive FISH. Trilobites were also preyed on by starfish, cephalopods, coelenterates, etc.

Trilobite FOSSILS are abundant from western Newfoundland to the Rocky Mts, and from the 49th parallel to the High Arctic. Their most spec-

Enrolment: Trent University, 1982-83 (Source: Statistics Canada)			
Full-time Undergrad	Full-time Graduate	Part-time Undergrad	Part-time Graduate
2 407	37	1 223	4

tacular occurrence is probably the BURGESS SHALE near Field, BC (a World Heritage Site). Here, soft parts of trilobites and related arthropods are preserved: hence, the site has provided information on the relationships of trilobites to other arthropod groups. Specimens from the Canadian Shield are often beautifully preserved. Complete skeletons of *Triarthrus eatoni* and *Pseudogygites latimarginatus* from Collingwood, and of *Phacops rana* from southern Ontario, are particularly well known and are prized by collectors. Specimens of giant *Terataspis grandis* and *Isotelus maximus* are also known from Ontario. The Mackenzie Mts, NWT, contain a unique sequence of trilobite faunas, in which quartz has replaced the skeletons. These fossils, which range from 350 to 520 million years of age, are used to study trilobite evolution, ecology and geographic distributions. BRIAN CHATTERTON

Trinity, Nfld, Community, pop 375 (1981c), inc 1969, is located on TRINITY BAY in NE Newfoundland. The first recorded English reference to the sizable, 3-armed harbour was in 1580 by Richard Whitbourne who, in 1615, held there the first court of admiralty in the New World. Though the nascent fishing outport was periodically raided by the French 1696-1713, Trinity grew as a major fortified fishing and trading centre. In the 1720s local magistrates were appointed, and in 1730 a small church was erected, among the first such events in Newfoundland. In 1762 inhabitants yielded the town and fortifications to French Admiral de Ternay in exchange for a guarantee of safety. A strong, resident merchant class, mainly from Poole, Eng, a prosperous fishery, and extensive trade ensured Trinity's growth, and by the late 1700s it was one of the few settlements with benefit of clergy, magistrates and a surgeon. In 1800 John Clinch, resident surgeon-clergyman, became the first in N America to inoculate against smallpox, using vaccine sent him by his boyhood friend, Edward Jenner. Clinch also compiled a BEOTHUK vocabulary, the only linguistic record of Newfoundland's now extinct indigenous people. In 1833 the Roman Catholic Church of St John the Baptist was built; it remains one of the oldest standing buildings and the oldest Roman Catholic church in Newfoundland. The

Trinity, Nfld, preserves the look and flavour of a 19th-century town through its historic buildings (*photo by Freeman Patterson/Masterfile*).

withdrawal of the great merchant firms after 1850 led to Trinity's decline as a major fishing centre. Because of its considerable past, the preservation of many of its historic buildings and records, and the restoration of some merchant premises, Trinity retains much of the look and flavour of a 19th-century town. JANET E.M. PITT

Trinity Bay, reputedly named by Gaspar CORTE-REAL on Trinity Sunday, in 1500, is entered between Grates Pt on the N side of Newfoundland's AVALON PENINSULA on the N tip of the Bonavista Pen, 60 km NW, which forms the bay's western shore. The bay stretches S nearly 110 km to Chapel Arm and has steep headlands to the NE and NW that rise over 85 m. The bay shelters superb fishing grounds and is indented with numerous coves and harbours, the largest being at TRINITY on the NW shore. English West Country merchants began settlement at Trinity in the 1600s and settlers spread across the bay to the SE and SW to RANDOM I, a large island occupying a deep pocket in the bay's W coast. At HEART'S CONTENT, a fish-processing centre on the SE coast, the first successful transatlantic cable was landed in 1866. Clarenville, W of Random I, has become a major transportation and commercial centre as the importance of Trinity has declined. Communities such as Catalina and Old Perlican, near the mouth of the bay, are today principal fishing centres. JANET E.M. PITT

Triticale (*Triticosecale* Wittmack), the first man-made CROP species, is initially produced by crossing wheat (genus *Triticum*) with rye (*Secale*), and resembles wheat. Treatment with the chemical, colchicine, restores fertility to the otherwise sterile hybrid. The development of triticale as a CEREAL CROP in Canada first began in 1954 at University of Manitoba, Winnipeg. Triticale is still a minor crop in Canada, grown on about 10 000 ha; however, production is gradually increasing as better cultivars (commercial varieties) are developed. Triticale grain is used either as a human food (bread and pastry products and in the BREWING INDUSTRY) or as a livestock feed. Relative to wheat, triticale grain is high in lysine, a component of protein required by humans and most other animals for normal growth and development. Hence, triticale is expected to assume an increasingly important role as a food grain in regions in which cereal crops already constitute the main dietary source of protein. E.N. LARTER

Trois-Pistoles, Qué, Town, pop 4445 (1981c), inc 1916, is located 250 km NE of Québec City on the S shore of the ST LAWRENCE R, between Rivière-du-Loup and Rimouski. According to legend, the name was given to the river at whose mouth the town is located because sailors once lost a silver goblet worth 3 gold *pistoles* in the river. BASQUE fishermen and whale hunters sailed to the river's estuary before N America was discovered. The remains of several ovens used to melt whale oil have been found on the island opposite the town, appropriately named Ile-aux-Basques. The seigneury of Trois-Pistoles was granted to Denis de Vitré in 1687. The mission was served by priests from Kamouraska until 1783 and by missionaries 1783-1806, at which time the first resident priest arrived. The municipality's major economic activities were agriculture and forest resources. Trois-Pistoles is now a small service-industry town where tourism (whale observation) is growing in importance as a result of the summer ferry link with the N shore. ANTONIO LECHASSEUR

Trois-Rivières, Qué, City, pop 50 466 (1981c), inc 1857, the regional capital of Québec's Mauricie region, is located on the E shore of the mouth of the ST-MAURICE R, midway between Québec C and Montréal. Its name derives from the 3-armed delta formed by the river's islands at its mouth.

Population:	50 465 (1981c); 111 453 (CMA)
Rate of Increase (1971-81):	(City) -9.8%
Rank in Canada:	Twenty-fourth (by CMA)
Date of Incorporation:	City 1857
Land Area:	77.9 km²
Elevation:	55 m
Climate:	Average daily temp, July 19°C, Jan -12°C; Yearly precip rain 763 mm, snow 26 cm; Hours of sunshine 1922 per year

Settlement The fortified settlement built at CHAMPLAIN's request in 1634 replaced the stockade abandoned earlier by the Algonquin, who had likely fled the hostile IROQUOIS. The former lived for a long time in or near the small French village, whose major function was to organize the FUR TRADE in the interior. After 1663 Trois-Rivières became the seat of local government, with a governor, king's lieutenant, major, court of royal jurisdiction and vicar general. In 1760 the town had 586 inhabitants.

Development The St-Maurice R played a major role in Trois-Rivières's history, being first used to transport furs from the northern forests. With the boom in forestry operations in the early 1850s, Trois-Rivières became an administrative centre, with several large sawmills and a major port for exporting timber. Then, with the development of hydroelectric power, the river's energy potential stimulated the development of the PULP AND PAPER INDUSTRY and made Trois-Rivières the world's capital for paper products around 1930. The pace of urbanization in the early 20th century was dramatic.

Cityscape Built on a sandy terrace overlooking the St Lawrence R, the early village was concentrated around the governor's manor, the Ursuline monastery and the Recollets' church. In the mid-19th century, industry began to spring up around the town, first along the shores of the St-Maurice and the St Lawrence rivers, then along the railway that skirted Trois-Rivières to the N. The Chemin du Roi, leading to Montréal, parallel to the St Lawrence R, was renamed rue Notre-Dame. Rue des Forges, running N to S, led to the FORGES ST-MAURICE (1735-1883), an iron and steel works about 12 km to the N. In the early 20th century, working-class districts developed near the pulp and paper and textile factories. Postwar prosperity and the automobile encouraged the population to live farther from the centre. Urban expansion to the N annexed St-Michel-des-Vieilles-Forges in 1961. With the population spread and the construction of shopping centres on the edge of the city, the downtown core declined commercially. This area is now under renovation. The terrible fire that ravaged Trois-Rivières in 1908 destroyed much of the old city, sparing only a dozen buildings from the French regime, among them the Ursuline monastery and the Tonnancour manor. A few beautiful early 19th-century buildings, including the old prison (1816) and the cathedral (1856), also survived. Trois-Rivières has nonetheless long been a modern city, with an avant-garde city hall (1967) and several high buildings that tower above the cathedral. .

Population With the establishment of sawmills and the development of commercial and port activities 1850-60, the population of Trois-Rivières doubled. The population grew rapidly again in the early 20th century, with the opening of paper and textile mills and an influx of people from neighbouring parishes. So many people moved to the suburbs during the 1960s that in 1976 the city's population began to decline. The population has always been predominantly francophone (nearly 95% in 1981).

Economy When manufacturing became more diversified, especially into foodstuffs, clothing, metals and electrical appliances, the dominant

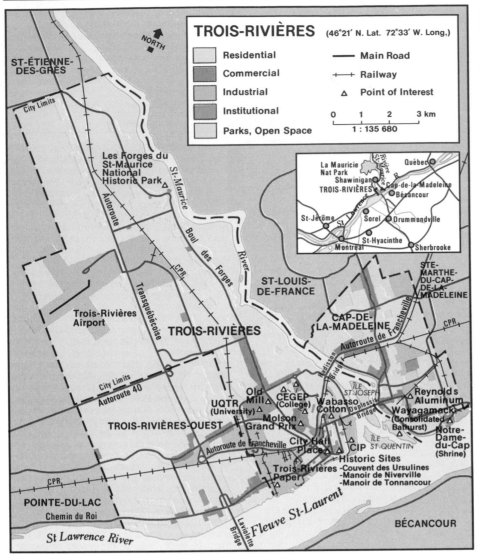

TROIS-RIVIÈRES (46°21' N. Lat. 72°33' W. Long.)

- Residential
- Commercial
- Industrial
- Institutional
- Parks, Open Space
- Main Road
- Railway
- △ Point of Interest

0   1   2   3 km
1 : 135 680

pulp and paper and textile industries declined, and by 1961 provided slightly less than half the total manufacturing jobs. The tertiary sector has grown steadily, mainly through the establishment of government offices serving the regional population and the creation of UNIVERSITÉ DU QUÉBEC à Trois-Rivières in 1969.

Transportation As the major route penetrating the continent, the river continued to be the only link with the rest of the colony until construction of the Chemin du Roi was completed along the N shore in 1737. By the mid-19th century, a road network linked Trois-Rivières to the region's new parishes. In the late 1870s, the North Shore Railway linked the city directly to Québec C and Montréal. The port came under the control of the National Harbours Board in 1882. Its grain silos were erected in 1936. In 1968 Trois-Rivières was linked to the S shore by Laviolette bridge. The city has had a local airport since 1961.

Cultural Life The major cultural centre for the Mauricie region, the city has entertainment centres, art galleries, museums, a cultural centre and a municipal library. Visitors are attracted to its historic buildings, and the site of the forges has been developed by Parks Canada. The Québec National Archives has a regional branch here. The city has been a Catholic diocesan centre since 1852. Its role as an episcopal seat attracted several religious communities which took charge of education and hospital care before these responsibilities were assumed by the state in the 1960s. Trois-Rivières has one daily

paper, *Le Nouvelliste* (1920), as well as 3 TV and 4 radio stations. It has hosted a major agricultural exhibition for nearly a century. A Grand Prix automobile race is held every year in the city's streets, and international canoeing races on the St-Maurice R finish at Trois-Rivières.

CLAIRE-ANDRÉE FORTIN, RENÉ HARDY, NORMAND SÉGUIN

Trotteur, Alexis Le French Canadian designation of Alexis Lapointe, called le Trotteur because of his fantastic running ability. He lived in the Murray Bay-Lk St-John region of Québec. He could run over 240 km in a day and ran races with horses and even with trains. His stride was supposed to be 6 m long. Some said he had the legs of a horse, and an autopsy supposedly revealed that he had double joints and bones and muscles like a horse. He died around the beginning of the 20th century. NANCY SCHMITZ

Trotting, *see* HARNESS RACING.

Troupes de la Marine (also known as independent companies of the navy, or colonial regulars), about 80 companies of 100 men each, established Dec 1690 as infantry for France and its colonies. About 30 companies were usually stationed in Canada and up to 20 at LOUISBOURG. The former gradually developed into the first permanent "Canadian" force. Initially composed entirely of Frenchmen, the companies came to be officered largely by Canadians. In the 18th century they became highly proficient in bush warfare, usually operating in small groups with

militia (*see* ARMED FORCES) and with friendly Indians in attacks on British forts and settlements. In 1758, during the SEVEN YEARS' WAR, the Louisbourg companies were taken prisoner by the British with the fall of that fortress. After the CONQUEST of 1760, many men settled in Canada, and many others repatriated to France went reluctantly. STUART R.J. SUTHERLAND

Trout, freshwater FISHES, genus *Salmo*, of the SALMON family (Salmonidae). Worldwide, there are 6-7 species. In Canada, 3 species, the rainbow (*S. gairdneri*) and cutthroat (*S. clarki*) trouts, and the ATLANTIC SALMON (*S. salar*), are native; 2 others, the brown and golden trouts (*S. trutta, S. aquabonita,* respectively) have been introduced. Trouts are distinguished from other salmonids by black spots on the head and body and 7-12 anal fin rays. Trouts have both sea-run and freshwater forms, except golden trout, a California species, restricted in Canada to small, high-altitude lakes in western Alberta. All trouts spawn in streams. While some spend their lives in streams, young of most species migrate to lakes or to the sea, returning as adults to spawn in the natal stream.

Rainbow trout is native to western N America (northern Mexico to Alaska) and has been successfully introduced in temperate zones worldwide. It is one of 2 fish species considered domesticated (the other being common carp), and is the trout most commonly AQUACULTURED, with stock having spent at least 30 generations in captivity available. Trout have an excellent growth rate, take well to crowding in ponds or tanks, are fairly disease resistant and are in great public demand. They are popular sport fish because of fighting and jumping characteristics and because they readily take a shallow-water lure. Where sea-run populations called steelhead exist, they are most sought after in rivers when returning to spawn. Steelhead are large, up to 18 kg, and very strong.

Cutthroat trout, in Canada, is restricted to BC and southwestern Alberta. There are 2 subspecies: coastal cutthroat, with sea-run and freshwater forms, and freshwater Yellowstone or mountain cutthroat. Coastal cutthroat ranges throughout coastal BC and is larger (up to 8 kg) than Yellowstone cutthroat. In Canada, Yellowstone cutthroat is restricted to southeastern BC and southwestern Alberta. Both subspecies are important sport fish, and stocking programs exist to assist in maintaining populations.

Brown trout, introduced to N America from Europe (1883), is now most common in Alberta and the 5 eastern provinces, although populations exist throughout southern Canada. It was the first salmonid species to be cultured (Germany, 1741). Brown trout has sea-run and freshwater populations and until the mid-1900s was heavily cultured and used to stock lakes and streams. However, domestic rainbow stocks have replaced brown trout in most areas as the prime sportfishing trout. E.D. LANE

Rainbow trout (*Salmo gairdneri*), one of only 2 fish species which have been domesticated (*courtesy National Museums of Canada/National Museum of Natural Sciences*).

Trout, Jennie (Jenny) Kidd, née Gowanlock, physician (b at Kelso, Scot 21 Apr 1841; d at Los Angeles, Calif 10 Nov 1921). She grew up near Stratford, Ont, and after her marriage in 1865 to Toronto publisher Edward Trout decided to become a doctor. As no Canadian medical school admitted women, she enrolled at the Woman's Medical College of Pennsylvania, graduating in 1875. That same year, on passing the Ontario registration exam, Dr Trout became the first Canadian woman licensed to practise medicine in Canada. A fervent promoter of women in medicine, she helped endow the Women's Medical College, Kingston, Ont, in 1883.

CARLOTTA HACKER

Reading: Carlotta Hacker, *The Indomitable Lady Doctors* (1974).

Troyes, Pierre de, soldier (d at Niagara 8 May 1688). He arrived at Québec in Aug 1685 with reinforcements for the beleaguered colony. Departing on 20 Mar 1686, de Troyes led a force of 30 colonial regular French troops and 60 militia from Montréal overland to James Bay. Using the skills of the VOYAGEURS, the audacious expedition ascended the Ottawa R, portaged via Lks Timiskaming and Abitibi to the Abitibi R and descended on the astonished English at Moose Fort, which quickly succumbed on June 20. De Troyes next occupied Rupert House (Ft Charles) July 3 and with the captured English ship *Craven* took Ft Albany (July 26) before leaving Pierre Le Moyne d'IBERVILLE in charge and sailing back to Québec. In June 1687 de Troyes commanded one of the French companies led by Gov DENONVILLE into Iroquois territory (*see* IROQUOIS WARS). He was left in command at Niagara where he died of scurvy.

JAMES MARSH

Trucking Industry consists of persons and firms engaged in the business of owning and operating motor trucks to transport goods. The industry is composed mainly of 3 elements: contract, private and common carriage. A contract carrier transports goods for one or a limited number of consignors, according to contractual agreements specifying rates of compensation and other terms. A private carrier transports his own goods by his own motor vehicle, eg, raw materials to processing, finished products to market. It is estimated that private carriage is at least as large as common carriage in tonnage moved. The common-carrier (or for-hire) industry is composed of individuals and establishments that own and operate for-hire motor trucks for the transportation, by road, of any and all goods. Thus, unlike the private or contract carrier, the common carrier serves the general-shipping public. The common-carrier industry provides shippers with full-service, door-to-door delivery, with an enforceable legal obligation to provide service at a published rate to even the smallest hamlet in Canada or the US.

History The Canadian war effort provided a major impetus to commercial trucking. The enormous demand for raw resources, manufactured goods, ships, aircraft and vehicles placed a great burden on Canada's total transportation system. A major labour shortage in the trucking industry developed and the federal government complied with a request from carriers that the industry be declared essential to the war effort, gaining recognition for the industry as a flexible and effective means of commercial transportation. In 1950 the nation's first mass railway strike occurred presenting an opportunity to demonstrate the potential of the truck. Round-the-clock mobilization of 45 000 trucks in the Toronto area alone allowed businesses to remain open and the city to obtain food and essential supplies. This, and the expansion and improvement of the highway system, made it possible for the trucking industry to become a vital part of Canada's transportation network.

Regulation and Operation Provincial governments determine most of the operating conditions and the regulatory economic environment for intraprovincial carriers, eg, driver qualifications, fuel taxes, vehicle weights, vehicle dimensions, rules of the road, vehicle inspection, securement of loads, vehicle licensing and mandated safety equipment. The authority of

the federal government to regulate trucking was established (1954) by a Privy Council decision which stated that such jurisdiction applied to the entire operation of the journey when it crossed provincial or international boundaries. However, since no federal-government regulatory mechanism was in place, jurisdiction was delegated back to the provinces. The only guideline was that each province apply its laws equally to intraprovincial and extraprovincial traffic. As a result of this nonspecific mandate, economic regulation has developed with wide disparities among provinces. When companies or individuals use for-hire trucks to cross a provincial or international boundary, certain federal regulations supersede provincial laws. The federal government also regulates safety standards.

The common-carrier industry provides service among Canada's 72 metropolitan areas, with a population of 50 000 or more, and 4250 smaller centres. All of these points, plus cities in the US with a population of over 47 000, are accessible to shippers either by direct service provided by one carrier or by transferring from one carrier to another until final delivery. The shipper or consignee pays the total freight charges, and the carrier collecting these funds distributes them to each of the participating carriers. The annual operating revenue of the common-carrier segment of the industry is about $5.7 billion. The 5 commodities most commonly carried by for-hire trucks in Canada are transportation equipment, primary metal products, pulp and paper, fabricated metal products and food products — constituting almost 50% of total tonnage. Although the average distance for an intercity truck haul in Canada is about 482 km, the reliance on trucks to carry perishable goods over much longer distances has been increasing. Some carriers, specializing in long-distance movements, advertise that shipments leaving Toronto are scheduled for arrival in Vancouver less than 70 hours later.

In 1983 the 4209 for-hire establishments that grossed revenues for the year in excess of $100 000 operated 133 178 pieces of revenue equipment. These units travelled almost 3 billion km and used over 1½ billion litres of fuel, of which nearly 90% was diesel. The rapid and continuing increase of fuel prices, beginning in 1973, with a concomitant rise in fuel taxes, has brought expenditures for fuel to unprecedented levels. On average, 11% of gross carrier revenue is now spent on fuel; in 1983 for-hire carriers spent over $621 million on diesel fuel and gasoline. As countermeasures, truck suppliers have been providing carriers with fuel-efficient vehicles and suppliers of truck components have been producing air-drag reduction devices, radial tires, synthetic lubricants and modulated fans. Equally important are training programs for drivers, emphasizing conservation. The trucking industry is labour intensive: in 1983 common carriers paid their 80 500 employees nearly $2 billion.

Although provincial transport officials are responsible for their own highways, decisions concerning the establishment of specific regulations are often made only after consultation with regulators in other provinces. This is done through a permanent secretariat known as the Canadian Conference of Motor Transport Administrators. Although CCMTA's concerns are not confined to trucking, a great deal of work has been done to rationalize truck regulation in bonding requirements for drivers, cargo insurance, vehicle inspections, transportation of dangerous goods, and driver licensing. Probably the most significant accomplishment of the CCMTA is the introduction of a pro rata type vehicle-licensing system, under which carriers pay each jurisdiction a percentage based on the distance driven in that jurisdiction. Though there are

significant provincial differences in the maximum axle and gross weights permitted, a 5-axle unit, the workhorse of the industry, may legally operate anywhere on designated Canadian highways with a gross of 36 400 kg.

It is estimated that 70% of manufactured goods moving between Canada and the US are carried by truck. Canadian carriers engaging in this international movement must, among other requirements, apply for US authorization and satisfy the requirements of both US and Canadian customs regulations.

CANADIAN TRUCKING ASSOCIATION

Trudeau, Pierre Elliott, politician, writer, constitutional lawyer, prime minister of Canada 1968-79 and 1980-84 (b at Montréal 18 Oct 1919). Trudeau was born into a wealthy Montréal family, the son of a successful French Canadian businessman and a mother of Scottish ancestry. Educated at the Jesuit Collège Jean-de-Brébeuf, U de M, Harvard and London School of Economics, he also travelled extensively in his youth. Upon his return to Québec from a year's travels in 1949, he supported the unions in the bitter ASBESTOS STRIKE, a formative event in postwar Québec society. In 1956 he edited a book on the strike, to which he contributed an introduction and conclusion criticizing the province's dominant social, economic and political values.

After serving briefly in Ottawa as an adviser to the Privy Council Office in 1950-51, Trudeau returned to Montréal and devoted his energies to opposing the Union Nationale government of Maurice DUPLESSIS and agitating for social and political change. With other young intellectuals he founded the review CITÉ LIBRE. In this and other forums, Trudeau sought to rouse opposition to what he believed were reactionary and inward-looking elites. In the process, he picked up a reputation as a radical and a socialist, although the values he espoused were closer to those of liberalism and democracy.

After the Liberals' victory in the 1960 provincial election, the QUIET REVOLUTION fulfilled some of Trudeau's hopes for change. At the same time, it revealed a deep rift between Trudeau and many of his former colleagues who were moving toward the idea of an independent Québec. A law professor at U de M by the 1960s, Trudeau became a sharp critic of the contemporary Québec nationalism and argued for a Canadian FEDERALISM in which English and French Canada would find a new equality.

In 1965 Trudeau, with union leader Jean MARCHAND and journalist Gérard PELLETIER, joined the federal LIBERAL PARTY and were elected to Parliament. Trudeau was later appointed a parliamentary secretary to PM Lester PEARSON, and was named minister of justice in 1967. In the latter post, he gained national attention for his introduction of divorce law reform and Criminal Code amendments liberalizing the laws on abortion, homosexuality, and public lotteries. He also established a reputation as a defender of a strong federal government against the nationalist demands of Québec.

He was persuaded to contest the Liberal leadership in 1968 and was elected on the fourth ballot; on 19 Apr 1968 he was sworn in as Canada's fifteenth prime minister. In the ensuing general election — which was dominated by "Trudeaumania" — his government won a majority, and thus he began a period in office which was to last longer than that of any other prime minister, save Mackenzie KING and Sir John A. MACDONALD.

The most dramatic event of his first government was the OCTOBER CRISIS of 1970, precipitated by the kidnapping of British diplomat James Cross and the kidnapping and later murder of Québec Cabinet minister Pierre LAPORTE by the terrorist FRONT DE LIBÉRATION DU QUÉBEC (FLQ).

In response, Trudeau invoked the WAR MEASURES ACT, with its extraordinary powers of arrest, detention and censorship. Controversy over the appropriateness of these emergency measures and their effect on liberal democracy in Canada and Québec has continued to the present. Less dramatic, but of lasting significance, was the OFFICIAL LANGUAGES ACT, a central feature of Trudeau's new federalism. At the same time, he began to improve the position of Francophones in Ottawa. A growing antibilingual backlash in English Canada, however, was one result of these policies. Western Canada's growing alienation against a perceived lack of interest in western economic problems and in western perspectives on national issues also began in his first term. An important initiative in government brought about under Trudeau's direction was the attempt to centralize and nationalize decision-making under nondirect control of the PRIME MINISTER'S OFFICE and by CENTRAL AGENCIES such as the PRIVY COUNCIL OFFICE and TREASURY BOARD. Although very much along the lines of administrative reorganization in Washington and in other Western capitals, these changes proved controversial, leading critics to charge inefficiency and the undermining of the role of Parliament and Cabinet. In the 1972 election, Trudeau came close to losing office and was forced to form a MINORITY GOVERNMENT with the support of the NDP.

In 1971 Trudeau, hitherto a bachelor, married Margaret Sinclair, daughter of a former Liberal Cabinet minister. Their tempestuous marriage, beset by many well-publicized differences, finally ended in separation in 1977 and divorce in 1984, with Trudeau retaining custody of their 3 sons, Justin, Sasha and Michel.

After restoring a Liberal majority in 1974, Trudeau faced the effects of inflation. In an atmosphere of economic crisis, various expedients were tried, including mandatory WAGE AND PRICE CONTROLS in 1975. This economic crisis was compounded in 1976 when the PARTI QUÉBÉCOIS under René LÉVESQUE was elected to office, dedicated to Québec independence. In 1979 Trudeau and the Liberals suffered a narrow defeat at the polls. A few months later he announced his intention to resign as Liberal leader and retire from public life. Three weeks after this announcement, the Progressive Conservative government of Joe CLARK was defeated in the Commons and a new general election was called. Trudeau was persuaded by the Liberal caucus to remain as leader and on 8 Feb 1980 — less than 3 months after his retirement — he was returned once again as prime minister with a parliamentary majority, thus accomplishing a remarkable resurrection.

Trudeau's last period in office as prime minister was eventful. His personal intervention in the 1980 QUÉBEC REFERENDUM campaign on SOVEREIGNTY-ASSOCIATION was significant. The defeat of the Parti Québécois's proposition was a milestone in his crusade against Québec separatism. In the wake of that victory, Trudeau pushed strongly for an accord on a new Canadian constitution. Unable to gain provincial agreement, he introduced into Parliament a unilateral federal initiative to "patriate" the BNA Act to Canada with an amending formula and an entrenched CANADIAN CHARTER OF RIGHTS AND FREEDOMS. There followed one of the epic federal-provincial battles of Canadian history, culminating in the final compromise and the proclamation of the CONSTITUTION ACT, 1982, on 1 July 1982. With the inclusion of entrenched minority language and education rights, and a charter of individual rights, Trudeau had thus fulfilled a goal he had set himself upon entering public life (see CONSTITUTION, PATRIATION OF).

In other areas, his 1980-84 government was less successful. Continued inflation and high levels of unemployment, along with huge fed-

Pierre Elliott Trudeau, prime minister of Canada 1968-79 and 1980-84, shown at Edmonton City Hall during "Trudeaumania" of 1968 (*courtesy Provincial Archives of Alberta/Edmonton Journal Coll*).

eral deficits, cut deeply into his popular support. His government's National Energy Program, one of the major government interventions in the economy since WWII, further alienated the energy-producing regions in western Canada. A continuing problem that plagued his entire tenure of office was that of CANADIAN-AMERICAN RELATIONS. Trudeau often played an ambiguous role with regard to the US, but in his last period in office he moved towards a more nationalist position in economic relations with the US, and began to criticize its foreign and defence policies more freely than in the past. At the same time the policies of US Pres Reagan's administration were becoming more damaging to many of Canada's economic interests. In these years Trudeau devoted more and more time to the international stage, first to encouraging a "North-South" dialogue between the wealthy industrial nations and the underdeveloped countries, and then in 1983-84 to a personal peace initiative in which he visited leaders in several countries in both the eastern and western blocs to persuade them to negotiate the reduction of nuclear weapons and to lower the level of tension in the Cold War. These activities led to his being awarded the Albert Einstein Peace Prize. At the same time, his government was responsible for the decision to allow US testings of the Cruise missile, which roused widespread opposition from Canadians concerned about the worsening nuclear arms race. Public opinion in Canada remained hostile to Trudeau and the Liberals from 1981 on. His personal style — sometimes charismatic, sometimes contemptuous of opposition, often mercurial and unpredictable — seemed to have become less of an electoral asset in difficult economic times. On 29 Feb 1984, Trudeau announced his intention to retire; on June 30 he left office, and his successor, John TURNER, was sworn in.

Trudeau's career as prime minister was one of electoral success, matched in this century only by Mackenzie King. Moreover, he served longer than every other contemporary leader in the Western world, becoming the elder statesman of the West. His achievements include the 1980 defeat of Québec separatism, official bilingualism, the patriated Constitution and the Charter of Rights. He was unable, however, to alleviate the alienation of western Canada or end the conflict between federal and provincial governments. He left office much as he had entered it: a controversial figure with strong supporters and equally strong critics. That he was one of the dominant figures in 20th-century Canada is not in dispute.   REG WHITAKER

Reading: R. Gwyn, *The Northern Magus* (1980); C. McCall-Newman, *Grits* (1983); G. Radwanski, *Trudeau* (1978). Trudeau's writings are collected in *Federalism and the French Canadians* (1968), *Approaches to Politics* (1970) and *The Asbestos Strike* (1974).

Trudeau, Yves, sculptor (b at Montréal 3 Dec 1930). He studied at the École des beaux-arts in Montréal. Moving from stylized bronze spiral figures in the late 1950s, Trudeau's "iron and wood" creations of the 1960s became highly charged with symbolism. Sometimes anthropomorphic, sometimes of organic shapes, the works in this series demonstrate his progressive abandonment of figurative representation (*L'homme-révolté*, 1961). In the geometrical and abstract series "Murs fermés et ouverts" of the 1970s, compositions circumscribe space: wooden triangles appear on an uninterrupted surface, broken by a bend or a straight line, sometimes by a flat curve. These works, painted white to capture light and shadow, sometimes contain social or political graffiti.   LOUISE BEAUDRY

Truro, NS, Town, pop 12 552 (1981c), inc 1875, is located 80 km NE of Halifax on Cobequid Bay, MINAS BASIN. A land grant including the area was awarded in 1689 by Louis XIV, and ACADIANS were present as early as 1701, finally leaving in 1755 in the turbulent year of the expulsion. The town received its name in 1759 from New England settlers and likely honours Truro in Cornwall, Eng. Transports of settlers arrived in the 1760s and further development of the town began. A major railway centre since the days of the INTERCOLONIAL RY, Truro is a terminus for people travelling to most parts of NS. Metal foundries, machinery, printing and lumbering have bolstered the economy. The Brookfield Dairy Co, located here since 1920, is a major employer. Stanfield's Textile Mills, established 1868, still operates. Always a thriving farming area, Truro is home to an agricultural college and the NS Teachers Coll.   JANICE MILTON

Trust, an equitable obligation binding a person (trustee) to hold or manage property for the benefit of others (beneficiaries). The trust originated in the Middle Ages; by conveying property to one person "to the use" or for the benefit of another, a landowner could avoid the prohibition (until the 16th century) that land could not be conveyed by will, and could avoid payment of feudal dues. The Crown became the feudal lord to whom dues were payable and King Henry VIII of England, attempting to abolish the use, persuaded Parliament to enact the Statutes of Uses (1535), but the courts decided these statutes did not affect uses of personal property. The surviving uses in common law became known as trusts. No directly comparable concept exists in the Québec system of civil law.

The person who creates the trust is the settlor. The beneficiaries may include the settlor, and any of the beneficiaries may enforce the equitable obligations imposed upon the trustee, who must account to the beneficiaries for the management of the trust. A trustee may neither purchase trust property nor sell or lease his own property to the trust. The trustee must select suitable investments. Unless the trust deed provides otherwise, many Canadian provinces limit the trustee to investments contained in the "legal list," which favours fixed-interest securities and reflects the concept of the conservation of wealth in its nominal dollar value, but these provinces will probably follow the example of New Brunswick in abolishing the list and permitting trustees to invest in any asset prudently selected. Since the 17th century, the trustee has been excluded from receiving remuneration, but the trust can provide for payment to the trustee and the Trustee Acts of all the common-law provinces and the territories now enable the courts to award "fair and reasonable" compensation.

Trusts can be classified according to the way in which they were created, the most important type being the "express trust," which arises when a settlor (either living or through a will, which must comply with the Wills Act and be in written form) has explicitly stated an intention to create a trust. It may be either *inter vivos* (created by a living person) or testamentary (created by the will of a deceased person). Trusts created by a living person are usually also declared in writing, but those of personal property may be made orally, excepting those for land. Another type is the constructive trust, which is imposed by the court as a remedial device (eg, in *Pettkus* v *Becker* the Supreme Court of Canada, in 1980, awarded one-half interest in property legally owned by a common-law husband to his common-law wife).

For an express trust to be valid, the "three certainties" — of word, of subject matter and of object — must exist. If the validity of an express trust is disputed, the court must be convinced that the testator or settlor intended to create a trust. There must also be certainty about the property subject to the trust and certainty of object or beneficiaries. A trust is said to be completely constituted when the 3 certainties exist and the property has been transferred to the trustee. A trust may also come into existence by the owner declaring himself to be trustee of the particular property for the specified beneficiaries. In this case the settlor is also the trustee and no transfer of property is required for a trust to be fully constituted trust. Such a trust is irrevocable in the sense that the settlor cannot get the trust property back unless, in the trust settlement, he or she has reserved a power of revocation.

The trust has been used primarily for the administration of personal wealth, eg, trusts are often used for postponing or reducing income-tax liability, by splitting income tax. Also, a testator might by will establish a trust of all his property, giving to the surviving spouse all the income for life with the capital to be distributed to the children equally on the death of the surviving spouse. The will might also provide a power to encroach on capital in case the income was not sufficient to maintain the spouse. Today, where the trust property is substantial, an incorporated trustee (a trust company) will often administer the property. It is also possible to select one or more individuals to be trustees, together with a trust company. The trust is now being used in business and commerce as a security device for preincorporation financial holding and for administering large pension funds.

Trusts are also the vehicle for the creation of most future interests in property, giving rise to a dilemma of balancing the rights of present and future generations. The compromise evolved by the courts and modified by many provincial legislatures is called the Rule Against Perpetuities.   GORDON BALE

Trust Company, a corporation that functions as a trustee, as well as providing regular BANKING services; they are the only corporations in Canada with the power to conduct fiduciary [Lat, *fiducia,* trust] business, eg, to act as executors, trustees and administrators of wills. The first Canadian trust company opened in 1872; by 1900 there were 14. Spawned by entrepreneurs, and encouraged by the government in an attempt to separate commercial banking and trust services in order to avoid CONFLICTS OF INTEREST, they prospered with the nation as a whole. In 1982 Canada's 101 trust companies (which, whether incorporated under provincial or federal charter, are regulated by the Department of

Insurance in Ottawa or by comparable provincial bodies) had over 900 branches, 500 real-estate offices, 35 000 employees and $120 billion in assets. Trusts, unlike banks with whom they are in competition for expanded commercial lending power, are usually closely held and sometimes entirely private affairs; most big banks are required to limit ownership by one shareholder to 10%, but no such laws exist for trusts. Although the trust companies were at some disadvantage for years by not having direct access to the Bank of Canada clearing system, this has now changed with the Canadian Payments System, and where retail deposits are concerned they are virtually on an equal footing with banks. Customer deposits are protected (to a certain maximum) by the Canada Deposit Insurance Corporation. Banks control 56% of the finance industry's total assets, while trust companies hold 50% of the total mortgage market. The failures in the early 1980s of Astra Trust Co, Re-Mar Investment Management Corp and Argosy Financial Group of Canada, Ltd, as well as the government seizure of 3 Ontario trust firms, have raised concern about the issue of ownership and about the amount of trust-company funds that should be devoted to commercial lending. Various trust companies pioneered new product features: daily-interest chequing accounts, on-line inter-branch banking, variable-rate mortgages and longer hours. They provide alternatives to the consumer and are an ongoing market challenge to the banks.
                                        ERIC W. DALY

Tsetsaut were probably named from a TSIMSHIAN word used by the Gitksan for various Athapaskans in the interior of northern BC. There is scant information on their language, history and traditions, though there is some evidence that they were most closely related to the KASKA. For unknown reasons the Tsetsaut left the Plateau, moving W across the southern waters of the Stikine R and the northern headwaters of the Nass R as far as the Pacific coast. The main area they inhabited was in the vicinity of the Portland Canal. The Tsetsaut economy was based on inland game hunting and apparently they never adapted fully to the environment of the river systems or to the coast. The Tsetsaut were harassed and raided by their neighbours, particularly the TAHLTAN, and survivors were assimilated into the Nishga. When Franz BOAS visited them in 1894, their total number was 12, reduced from an estimated population of 500 just 60 years earlier. Today, there are no persons identified as Tsetsaut. The last speaker of the Tsetsaut language died around 1935. *See also* NATIVE PEOPLE: SUBARTIC and general articles under NATIVE PEOPLE.   BERYL C. GILLESPIE
Reading: F. Boas, "Fifth Report on the Indians of British Columbia," *British Assn for the Advancement of Sciences, Annual Report* (1895); J. Helm, ed, *Handbook of North American Indians,* vol 6: *Subarctic* (1981).

Tsimshian ("People of the Skeena") is a linguistic grouping that includes 3 languages: Coast Tsimshian, Southern Tsimshian and Nass/Gitksan. The Tsimshian communities are situated along the NASS and SKEENA rivers of northern BC and adjacent coastal areas south to Milbanke Sound. Also, Tsimshians live in the settlement of New Metlakatla near Ketchikan, Alaska, founded in 1887 when a group of 825 Tsimshian, following missionary William DUNCAN emigrated to that site. Total BAND membership in Canada is about 9000 (with another 3000 in Alaska), and many nonstatus natives are recognized as being of Tsimshian descent.

Tsimshians can claim one of the oldest continuous cultural heritages in the Americas (*see* PREHISTORY). Archaeological excavations in the harbour at Prince Rupert indicate continual habitation for 5000 years. Although aboriginal cultural patterns are being replaced, these peo-

ples take pride in their heritage and many families maintain traditional ceremonies at community feasts (*see* POTLATCH). Originally, descent was reckoned through the female line and each Tsimshian belonged to a family CLAN group and to one of 4 divisions or phratries: Frog or Raven, Wolf, Eagle, and Killer Whale or Fireweed. Each person was expected to marry into a different phratry.

Although few Tsimshians trap for a living today, fishing remains an important subsistence activity, and the diets of many families also include meat from hunting and berries seasonally picked at traditional grounds. The Nishga still harvest the eulachon (candlefish), and render the pungent oil, which is eagerly traded between Tsimshian groups. Elders, and in a few villages the middle-aged, continue to speak Coast Tsimshian, Nass (Nishga) and Gitksan, but most others now know and use English exclusively. Native languages are taught as a subject in many schools of the area, but trends suggest increasing replacement of these native tongues by English. In the 1970s the establishment of KSAN, a reconstructed Gitksan village and carving school in Hazelton, resulted in a revival of traditional artistic skills (*see* NORTHWEST COAST INDIAN ART; MASKS; TOTEM POLE). Hereditary titles are still maintained by both men and women for ceremonial purposes, but elected band and tribal councils now administer social services. Band projects provide most employment on reserves. The Nishga were the first native group to initiate a legally constituted LAND CLAIMS action against the federal government (1912), and claims from other Tsimshian are pending. *See also* NATIVE PEOPLE: NORTHWEST COAST and general articles under NATIVE PEOPLE.   J.V. POWELL and V. JENSEN
Reading: J. Adams, *The Gitksan Potlatch* (1973); F. Boas, *Tsimshian Mythology* (1916); V. Garfield and P. Wingert, *The Tsimshian Indians and their Arts* (1966).

Tuktoyaktuk, NWT, Hamlet, pop 772 (1981c), is located on the BEAUFORT SEA coast, E of the MACKENZIE R delta, 1135 air km NW of YELLOWKNIFE. The area is the traditional home of the whale-hunting Karngmalit Inuit, who diminished owing to a series of epidemics in the late 1800s. The Inuit who settled at the site after it was established as a port of choice (Port Bralsant) in 1934 were from other parts of the North. It was given its present name (Inuktituk for "looks like caribou") in 1950. Today the community has a mostly wage-based economy, as it has grown to be a transportation, government and DEW Line maintenance centre and a base for oil and gas exploration.   ANNELIES POOL

Tully, John Patrick, oceanographer (b at Brandon, Man 29 Nov 1906). As oceanographer in charge of the Pacific Oceanographic Group, Nanaimo, BC (1946-65), Tully influenced the entire growth of West Coast oceanographic research, including studies in physical, chemical and biological oceanography. He is best known for his research in descriptive oceanography and in his practical application of oceanography to contemporary military and industrial problems. His published works on estuarine mechanisms and physico-chemical processes in the oceans earned him particular distinction. He is an MBE, has received the Commemorative Medal of Albert I of Monaco and other medals, and in 1964 was made a fellow of the RSC.   T.R. PARSONS

Tully, Kivas, architect, civil engineer, politician (b at Garrarucum, Queen's County, Ire 1820; d at Toronto 24 Apr 1905). Architect of prominent early institutional buildings in Ontario, he also served as councillor and alderman for the City of Toronto, was a founding member and officer of the (Royal) Canadian Institute, and a mason. Tully emigrated to Canada in 1844, established a practice and, in 1868, was appointed architect and engineer of the Dept of

Public Works of Ontario. Among his important works are the Customs House, Trinity Coll on Queen St and the Bank of Montreal at Yonge and Front streets, all in Toronto, the Welland County Courthouse, asylums in London, Hamilton and Brockville, and engineering proposals for the Toronto and Georgian Bay Ship Canal and the Toronto Harbour Front and Railways.

ANDREA KRISTOF

Tumpline [Algonquian *tump*, "pack strap"], a long leather strap or sling, broad at the middle and tapered at both ends, which crosses the chest or forehead and attaches to a pack or other load. It was used to PORTAGE loads of fur-trade goods.

JOHN ROBERT COLOMBO

Tuna, swift, elegant marine FISHES of class Osteichthyes, family Scombridae (MACKEREL). There are about 48 species in the family, including kingfishes, mackerels, tunas and bonitos. Strictly speaking, tunas are restricted to the tribe Thunnini which includes 3-9 genera, depending on the authority. For present purposes, 13 species of tuna in 3 genera (*Auxis, Euthynnus* and *Thunnus*) are recognized. Genus *Thunnus* contains 7 species: *T. alalunga* (albacore), *T. albacares* (yellowfin tuna), *T. atlanticus* (blackfin tuna), *T. maccoyi* (southern bluefin tuna), *T. obesus* (bigeye tuna), *T. thynnus* (bluefin tuna) and *T. tonggol* (longtail tuna). Tunas are wide-ranging, pelagic (open sea) fishes, inhabiting tropical and temperate waters worldwide. In Canada, 4 species occur in Pacific waters, 6 in Atlantic. Small species weigh under 9 kg but larger species may grow to weights of 45-450 kg. All tunas have hydrodynamically efficient, streamlined bodies and widely forked tails. Behind the second dorsal fin and the anal fin are a series of small finlets. Individual species are strikingly colourful. True tunas are unusual among fishes because they are warmblooded and can maintain a body temperature of up to 10°C above surrounding waters through retention of heat from muscle contractions. Tunas are exceedingly active, ranging widely over the oceans and travelling thousands of kilometres on extensive MIGRATIONS. They consume large quantities of crustaceans, squids and fishes (up to 25% of their body weight daily) to meet their energy requirements. Commercial fisheries employ purse seines, trapnets, longlines and angling. Tuna are canned or sold fresh. Bluefin tuna are trapped on Canada's East Coast, retained alive and fattened for shipment to Japan, where they are sold fresh for the sashimi market. The world's record rod-caught bluefin (560.19 kg) was caught off PEI in 1978.

W.B. SCOTT

Landing tuna at Hubbards, NS, early 20th century (*courtesy Public Archives of Canada/PA-41868*).

Tundra [Finnish, *tunturi*], also called "barren land," large region of the Northern Hemisphere lacking trees and possessing abundant rock outcrops. In Canada, the southern boundary extends from the Mackenzie Delta to southern Hudson Bay and NE to Labrador. Many CLIMATE variables combine to determine the position of this boundary. The tundra environment is characterized by the general presence of PERMAFROST

(except beneath some lakes and rivers); short summers with almost continuous daylight; long winters and arctic "nights"; low annual precipitation (hence the name polar desert); strong winds and winter blizzards; discontinuous vegetation; unstable, wet SOIL conditions resulting from permafrost and frost action. Tundra plants have developed many adaptations for survival. Their low stature exploits the more favourable microclimate near the ground; small, leathery, hairy leaves prevent desiccation by evaporation. Perennial life habit, vegetative propagation, short reproductive cycle and effective seed dispersal by wind are common among tundra plants (eg, LICHENS, MOSSES, GRASSES, low shrubs). Many birds and some animals live in the tundra in summer, migrating in autumn (*see* ARCTIC ANIMALS). Tundra environments present many impediments to human activities. Buildings, PIPELINES, roads and airports must be so constructed that they can cope with cold climate and permafrost, and proper advance planning must precede RESOURCE development and WASTE DISPOSAL to avoid damage to ecosystems. The term "alpine tundra" has been used for areas above the TREELINE in mountains. Although alpine tundra resembles arctic tundra proper in some respects, the differences are substantial and significant. *See* PHYSIOGRAPHIC REGIONS.

J. TERASMAE

Reading: J.D. Ives and R.G. Barry, eds, *Arctic and Alpine Environments* (1974).

Tungsten, or wolfram (W), silver-grey metallic element with the highest melting point of any metal (3410°C). Tungsten has a high density, high strength at elevated temperatures and extreme hardness. Its first important use, during the mid-1800s, was in the manufacture of high-speed steel. Tungsten steel is important in industry because it retains its hardness and strength at high temperatures. Sintered tungsten-carbide tools, developed in the 1920s, have become the most important use. Limited amounts of metallic tungsten are used in the ELECTRONICS INDUSTRY, particularly for light-bulb filaments. There are 4 important ore minerals of tungsten: scheelite, wolframite, ferberite and huebnerite, the first 2 being far more abundant than the others. Canada is the largest producer of scheelite in the Western world and will probably remain so as new deposits are brought into production. The largest tungsten deposits are located in the YT and the NWT (where there is a community named for the metal); smaller deposits are dispersed across the country. Wolframite is produced in NB. Most Canadian tungsten production is exported to the US, Japan and western Europe. There is also a relatively large, domestic, cemented tungsten-carbide tool industry based on imported tungsten. The MINING, metalworking and petroleum industries are the major users of tungsten-carbide tools. Canadian tungsten production is relatively low in volume.

DON LAW-WEST

Tungsten, NWT, UP, pop 320 (1981c), is located in the SELWYN MTS, 700 air km W of YELLOWKNIFE. The name comes from 2 Swedish words meaning "heavy" and "stone." It is the site of Canada's largest TUNGSTEN-producing mine. The plant was built in 1962 and went into production later that year. Operations were suspended from Aug 1963 until July 1964 because of the low price of tungsten, but since then, this unique mining community has grown rapidly.

ANNELIES POOL

Tunnels Unlike other mountainous countries such as Switzerland, and despite its size, Canada is not distinguished by well-known tunnels. It is possible to travel from sea to sea, from Halifax to Vancouver, by CANADIAN NATIONAL RAILWAYS, without going through any major tunnels, merely a few short ones west of Thunder Bay. There are, however, some notable tunnels in Canada, and some that are unique. Tunnels for coal mining in Cape Breton extend far out under

the sea; the Granduc Mine in BC can only be reached by a 16.5 km tunnel under 3 glaciers. At NORTH BAY, the Canadian headquarters of NORAD are housed in an unusual set of great tunnels excavated in Precambrian bedrock, complete even to an underground powerhouse, approached through 2 ordinary access tunnels large enough to accommodate passenger buses.

Canada's oldest tunnel is at BROCKVILLE, Ont; it runs from the waterfront, under the City Hall, below Market St. When the Brockville and Ottawa Railroad was built in the 1850s, the British contractors took the view that a railway, to be complete, had to have a tunnel. It was used first on 31 Dec 1860 and last in 1970, and is still there, with its great oak doors at each end.

No tunnels were required when the main line of the GRAND TRUNK RY was built from Montréal to Toronto in the 1850s, and only one very short tunnel was needed in the entire length of the INTERCOLONIAL RY (Halifax to Montréal) completed in 1876. But between 1889 and 1891, the first underwater railway tunnel in N America was built under the ST CLAIR R, linking the Grand Trunk Ry at SARNIA with the Grand Trunk Western Ry at Port Huron, to complete a through line between Toronto and Chicago. The tunnel was over 1800 m long between portals and was the first tunnel in N America to be built under compressed air, the first to be built with shields and only the second tunnel to be lined with cast-iron segments. When the CANADIAN PACIFIC RY was built 10 years later, a series of short tunnels along the N shore of Lk Superior could not be avoided, but the route through the mountains of the West was achieved without resort to tunnelling. The resulting grades (up to 4%) made operation difficult and uneconomic as traffic increased, and so the Spiral Tunnels between Hector and Field were opened for use in 1909, reducing the maximum grade in that section to 2.3%. In 1916 the 5-mile (8 km) Connaught Tunnel was opened under ROGERS PASS to reduce grades and eliminate trouble from avalanches. In 1984 preparations were in hand at Rogers Pass for what would be the longest railway tunnel in N America, duplicating the Connaught Tunnel to reduce grades for west-bound traffic.

Shorter tunnels, to give access to terminal facilities, were built in later years, such as the CNR tunnel under Capital Hill, Vancouver; the CPR access tunnel to Wolfe's Cove terminal at Québec; and the 4.8 km Mount Royal Tunnel, Montréal. Originally constructed to give the CANADIAN NORTHERN RY access to downtown Montréal, the Mount Royal Tunnel is now a part of the CNR, incorporated into the efficient complex of Montréal's Central Station.

Just as railway building in Canada passed its peak, new waterpower plants increased in number and size, often requiring tunnels for transferring water from impounding RESERVOIRS to penstocks and powerhouses. The twin 15.2 m diameter tunnels that convey water under the city of NIAGARA FALLS (90 m below the surface) for supplying the Sir Adam Beck powerhouse at Queenston are of special interest, as is the tunnel of the Kemano power plant of the Aluminum Co of Canada in BC which serves the smelter plant at KITIMAT. This tunnel conveys water from a new reservoir in the headwaters of the Fraser R through the mountains of the Coast Range, to a precipitate drop almost to sea level at the powerhouse (*see also* ELECTRIC-POWER GENERATION).

One little-known but important tunnel in the West runs below the seabed of the First Narrows at Vancouver, conveying fresh water under pressure from reservoirs in the foothills of the Coast Range to supply the city of Vancouver. Tunnels for water supply and sewage disposal are to be found beneath the streets of all major Canadian cities. Beneath the streets of Ottawa, for example, are at least 160 km of such tunnels. One sewage collector tunnel along the N shore of the Island of Montréal is 48 km long. These are the "major" tunnels of Canada, unseen and generally unknown, but providing vital civic services. Underground railways necessitate large tunnels, also beneath city streets, the first section of the Toronto subway, almost all in tunnel, having been opened in 1954 (*see* SUBWAYS AND LIGHT RAPID TRANSIT).

Canadian tunnelling expertise, largely gained in the tunnels required for metal-ore mining, was called upon in WWII when the Canadian Army was responsible for extending the labyrinth of tunnels that form a honeycomb beneath the Rock of Gibraltar. Completion of the major part of what is still the longest railway tunnel east of the Mississippi R, the Hoosac Tunnel in Massachusetts, was the successful work of 2 pioneer Canadian engineers, Walter and Francis SHANLY, in 1874.   ROBERT F. LEGGET

Tupper, Sir Charles, politician, diplomat, prime minister (b at Amherst, NS 2 July 1821; d at Bexleyheath, Eng 30 Oct 1915). He was the last survivor of the original FATHERS OF CONFEDERATION. Educated at Horton Academy (Acadia) and Edinburgh, Tupper returned to Amherst in 1843 to follow a successful medical career. (He was the first president of the Canadian Medical Assn, 1867-70.) In 1855 he sought a seat in the NS Assembly as a Conservative, dramatically winning Cumberland County from the popular Reform politician, Joseph HOWE. He soon entered the administration, serving as provincial secretary, 1857-60 and 1863-67. In May 1864 he became premier, championing Maritime or British N American union, which he did not feel to be incompatible goals. He was a delegate at the Charlottetown, Québec and London conferences but was unable to win approval for the Quebec Resolutions in the NS Assembly.

In 1867 he left provincial politics and won a federal seat as the only supporter of CONFEDERATION from NS. Although his claim for a Cabinet post was strong, he stood aside to allow others from NS to enter the ministry. He helped bring about the "better terms" settlement which led Howe into the Cabinet in 1869. In 1870 Tupper began his long ministerial career. He was successively president of the Privy Council (1870-72), minister of inland revenue (1872-73), and minister of customs (1873) in the first John A.MACDONALD government. When the Conservatives returned to office, Tupper served as minister of public works (1878-79) and minister of railways and canals (1879-84) during the critical period of Pacific railway construction. He became high commissioner to the UK in 1884, but returned to Ottawa to serve as minister of finance (1887-88). Resuming his duties in London, he became known as an outspoken advocate of imperial federation and preferential tariffs. Macdonald was not pleased with Tupper's views but his political standing allowed him immunity from censure.

In Jan 1896 Tupper was recalled to Ottawa to serve as secretary of state in the failing government of Sir Mackenzie BOWELL. Passed over for the party leadership in favour of J.J.C. ABBOTT, J.S.D. THOMPSON and Bowell, Tupper finally became prime minister 1 May 1896. In a desperate attempt to stave off defeat in the House, Tupper and his colleagues had introduced remedial legislation to protect the educational rights of the French-speaking minority in Manitoba. Blocked in the Commons, Tupper and the Conservatives suffered a stunning general election defeat in June, as Québec's returns were decisive. He resigned on 8 July, having served only 10 weeks as prime minister. He continued in Parliament as leader of the Opposition but was defeated in the election of 1900. On retirement he lived in Vancouver before moving to England in 1913. Tupper was a decisive figure

After a long career as a champion of Confederation, Sir Charles Tupper finally became prime minister in 1896, but he served only 10 weeks (*courtesy Public Archives of Canada/C-10109*).

in Canadian political life. As one of Macdonald's principal lieutenants, he had a real capacity for administration as well as a reputation for parliamentary bluff and bullying.   D.M.L. FARR
Reading: C. Tupper, *Recollections* (1914) and *Political Reminiscences* (1914).

Turcotte, Ron, jockey (b at Drummond, NB 22 July 1941). Once a lumberjack in his native New Brunswick, he became the first jockey in 70 years to ride Kentucky Derby-winning horses in consecutive years and, in 1973, rode the great Secretariat to N American horse racing's Triple Crown. One of 11 children, Turcotte was always a strong jockey because of his early years as a lumberjack. Unemployment in 1959 sent him to Toronto where he obtained a job as a hot-walker at E.P. TAYLOR's Windfield Farms. He recorded his first win in 1962 and was named Canada's top jockey that year and in 1963. In 1972 he rode Riva Ridge to victories in the Kentucky Derby and the Belmont Stakes. The following year, he was aboard Secretariat, the first Triple Crown winner in 25 years. His career ended on 13 July 1979 when he broke his back after falling from his horse in an accident at the Belmont track. Now confined to a wheelchair, he operates a restaurant and trains horses in NB. J. THOMAS WEST

Turks Turkey is a republic of southeastern Europe and Asia Minor. Turkey in Europe is separated from Turkey in Asia (Anatolia) by the Bosporus, the Sea of Marmara and the Dardanelles which link the Black Sea to the Mediterranean. It is predominantly a Moslem country, with minorities of Kurds, ARMENIANS, GREEKS and Jews.

The earliest Turkish immigrants to Canada are believed to have arrived in the 1880s; by 1981 the Turkish Canadian population was estimated to be about 4000 (not including Armenians or Greeks). The main immigrations were in 1900-04 (156), 1906-14 (3922), 1915-55 (1262) and 1956-75 (5710). Of the last group, 43% settled in Québec, 43.5% in Ontario, 4.6% in BC, 4% in Alberta and 4% in other provinces.

Social and Cultural Life Almost all Turks celebrate the Islamic religious holidays. The Turkish community is served by the periodical *Sesimiz* ("The Voice") established in 1964. Through their Cultural Association of Montréal, Turks enjoy a number of activities, eg, folk dancing, sports, social evenings, conferences and a weekend school for their language, culture and heritage. Many other clubs and organizations exist as well.   FOUAD E. SHAKER

Turmel, Antoine, businessman (b at Thetford-Mines, Qué 25 Apr 1918). In 1945 Turmel joined Compagnie Denault Ltée as sales manager and later took over control of the company. In 1969 he negotiated the merger of 3 independent food companies (Denault Ltée, Couvrette et Provost, and Lamontagne Ltée) and formed Provigo Inc, one of the largest food chains in Canada. Turmel is one of the principal shareholders of Provigo and also sits on the boards of the National Bank of Canada, Canadian General Electric, Noranda Mines, Provident Assurance Co, Québec-Téléphone, Shell Canada and UAP Inc. He holds an honorary doctorate in administration from Sherbrooke (1970).   JORGE NIOSI

Turnbull, Wallace Rupert, aeronautical engineer (b at Saint John 16 Oct 1870; d there 26 Nov 1954). From a wealthy family, he studied science at Cornell and in Germany to age 25 and worked at the Edison Lamp Works, Harrison, NJ, for 6 years. In 1902 he built the first wind tunnel in Canada at his private laboratory in Rothesay, NB, where he worked for the rest of his life, geographically remote, but collaborating with aviation pioneers such as Alexander Graham BELL and J.H. PARKIN. Turnbull's research was recognized early — he won a medal from the Royal Aeronautical Soc in 1909 — but his greatest achievement was the variable-pitch propellor, tested in flight in 1927. This device adjusts the angle at which propellor blades cut the air and became as essential to aviation as the gearbox to the automobile. It provides for safety and efficiency at all engine speeds, for example maximum power on takeoff and landings and economical cruising for long distances. It was independently perfected in several countries, so that Turnbull's work has been overlooked by most historians, perhaps because he licensed its manufacture and went on with other inventions. But his variable-pitch propellor (now in the National Aviation Museum, Ottawa) appears to have been the first to fly successfully.
DONALD J.C. PHILLIPSON

Turnbull, Walter James, public servant (b at Toronto 16 Sept 1896). As deputy postmaster general Turnbull directed the Post Office Dept with exceptional efficiency from 1945 to 1957 during a period of traumatic change in the transportation, volume and makeup of mail in Canada. He introduced "all-up" airmail service in 1948, making Canada the first country in the world to transport mail by air efficiently at regular postal rates. He computerized the money-order system and pioneered the development of mechanized mail sorting at Canada Post. He was the first public relations director of CANADA POST and from 1946 he led Canada Post's participation in the Universal Postal Union, culminating in his being, in 1957, the host and chairman of the only congress of that union to be held in Canada. Turnbull was also active in the Postal Union of the Americas and Spain in the late 1940s.   HERBERT L. GRIFFIN

Turner, David, soccer player (b at Edinburgh, Scot 11 Oct 1903). Turner came to Canada at age 11 and played junior soccer in Edmonton. A powerful player with an excellent shot and heading ability, he was one of Canada's top players in the 1920s and 1930s. At age 19 he moved west, playing for Vancouver St Andrews and Cumberland United. After one season as a professional in the US, he played for Toronto Ulster United, before enjoying his greatest success with the New Westminster Royals — Canadian champion in 1928, 1930, 1931 and 1936. Turner also played for Canada in 3 internationals against New Zealand in 1927.   COLIN JOSE

Turner, John Herbert, businessman, politician, premier of BC (b at Claydon, Eng 7 May 1834; d at Richmond, Eng 9 Dec 1923). A merchant in Halifax and Charlottetown, Turner moved in 1862 to Victoria, where in 1865 he established the firm of Turner, Beeton and Co. He was successively alderman and mayor of Victoria (1876-81); was elected to the BC legislature (1886); served as finance minister (1887-95), premier (1895-98), finance minister again (1900) and BC's agent general in London (1901-15). In both his business and political life, Turner epitomized the role of Victoria in late 19th-century BC; his firm was typically engaged in a wide variety of operations — salmon canning, importing, wholesaling, finance and insurance. Turner's premiership marked the final flowering of the Victoria business class in BC politics.

H. KEITH RALSTON AND MAIRI DONALDSON

Turner, John Napier, politician, lawyer, prime minister (b at Richmond, Eng 7 June 1929). Following the death of his father, Turner accompanied his Canadian-born mother to Canada in 1932. Educated in Ottawa private schools, Turner went west with his mother and stepfather, Frank Ross, at the end of WWII. After studies at UBC, Oxford and U of Paris, Turner joined a Montréal law firm, qualifying as a lawyer in Québec in 1954. Recruited by Lester PEARSON as a Liberal candidate in Montréal, Turner was elected to the Commons in 1962 (reelected 1963, 1965). When redistribution abolished his seat, he moved in 1968 to an Ottawa constituency. He first entered the Cabinet as part of a post-election shuffle by Pearson in Dec 1965 and served in minor offices until becoming minister of consumer and corporate affairs in Dec 1967. In 1968 Turner ran for the Liberal leadership, won by Pierre TRUDEAU, making a respectable showing as an "anti-establishment" candidate and as the most prominent younger English-language minister. Trudeau appointed him minister of justice in July 1968, a position he held until Jan 1972. In this capacity Turner sponsored criminal code reform and special legislation that followed the 1970 OCTOBER CRISIS.

In 1972 Trudeau transferred Turner to the dept of finance. When the Trudeau government lost its majority in Nov 1972 Turner found it necessary to tailor policy to the demands of popularity, and tax reductions and pension increases followed. The government still ran a surplus, both in 1973 and 1974, but the overall effect of its policy was to stimulate inflation. Once the Trudeau government regained its majority in an election caused by the defeat of Turner's May 1974 budget in the Commons, Turner concentrated on restraining inflation, but policies had not yet been decided when, in Sept 1975, he suddenly resigned from Cabinet without expla-

nation, quitting politics altogether in Feb 1976 to join a large Toronto law firm. He declined to contest the Liberal leadership in 1979 (a contest which was never held) after Trudeau's first resignation, but with Trudeau's departure in Feb 1984 Turner decided to try for the leadership, which he won on the second ballot on 16 June 1984. Becoming PM on June 30, Turner dissolved parliament on July 9. In the election that followed, Turner directed a disorganized campaign which failed to recoup the Liberals' already massive unpopularity and they suffered a disastrous defeat, winning only 40 seats in the Commons. Turner, who was not able to convince voters that he represented innovation or decisive leadership, won his own seat in Vancouver Quadra and became leader of the Opposition in the new Parliament. ROBERT BOTHWELL

Turner, Philip John, architect (b at Stowmarket, Eng 21 Mar 1876; d at Montréal 13 Aug 1943). Turner studied at the Architectural Assn in London, setting up his own practice in Montréal in 1907. He designed many branches in Québec and Ontario for the Molsons Bank. Notable Montréal works include houses in Westmount, the Crown Trust building (1924) and St Philip's Church (1929). From 1908 to 1942 he taught at the McGill School of Architecture, specializing in building construction and professional practice. He wrote and lectured extensively on library planning, English churches and Canadian architecture. SUSAN WAGG

Turner Valley, Alta, Town, pop 1311 (1981c), inc 1930, located 40 km S of Calgary in the wide valley of the same name. It is named for the first settlers in the area, James and Robert Turner. The presence of oil was apparent through seepage, but it was not until May 1914 that Dingman No 1 came in — heralding the discovery of the first major gas and oil field in Alberta. Wells soon dotted the valley, and the petroleum activity was a bright spot in the otherwise bleak economy of Alberta in the 1930s. The field was depleted by the time the focus shifted N to LEDUC after WWII. Today, there is little oil production in the area. ERIC J. HOLMGREN

Turnip (*Brassica rapa*, Rapifera Group), biennial VEGETABLE belonging to the Cruciferae family and grown in all provinces as a ROOT CROP. Native to Siberia, the turnip was introduced to England around 1550 and brought to America by the first settlers. The turnip is closely related to RUTABAGA but has a smaller, round, flat root, green downy leaves and white or yellow flesh. Various cultivars (commercial varieties) of white-fleshed and yellow-fleshed turnips are grown. A temperate-climate vegetable cultivated in spring or fall, the turnip has a growing season of approximately 60 days. The turnip is prone to clubroot and black rot (fungus diseases) and is attacked by such parasites as the plant louse, flea beetle and cabbage fly. Served like spinach, the leaf is an excellent source of calcium, iron and vitamins A, B and C. The root contains calcium, potassium, sodium, and vitamins A and C. HUGUES LEBLANC

Turtle (order Testudines or Chelonia), egg-laying, toothless REPTILE with limb girdles roofed over by a wide rib cage and fused to bony plates in the skin. The outer skin covering consists of horny, epidermal scales of keratin (sulphur-containing, fibrous protein). This basic body plan, a 3-layered box of ribs, skin-bones and hornlike scales, has remained unchanged over 200 million years and, with minor modifications, has been adapted for life in oceans, rivers, lakes, bogs, forests, grasslands and deserts. When Canada was ice covered and without reptiles, the greatest diversity of N American turtles was probably centered in the SE corner of the continent, where about 16 species occur today. After the ICE AGES, the major chelonian invasion

The snapping turtle (*Chelydra serpentina*), which ranges from NS to Saskatchewan, weighs up to 18 kg. It preys on anything, dead or alive (*photo by Bill Ivy*).

of Canada was via the aquatic avenue of the Mississippi and Ohio rivers to southern Ontario. Subsequently a few species migrated into Québec and some even to chilly NS. Others ventured westward but were deterred by the cold, dry Prairies. On both coasts, migration northward involved crossing many rivers; only one species spread northwestward to BC and 4 species advanced eastward or northward to NB and NS. Over the past 3000-4000 years, a progressive, continental cooling has forced reptiles to move southward or become restricted to a single river valley, lake, bog or pond, where conditions suitable for survival still prevail. Thus, turtles have a tenuous toehold on the southern fringes of Canada, and locating these isolated pockets challenges both professional herpetologists and amateur naturalists.

The 8 native Canadian freshwater turtle species all occur in southern Ontario. The only non-Ontario species reported, the 14 cm northwestern pond turtle (*Clemmys marmorata*), is limited to BC and was probably introduced there. The other BC turtle is the 23 cm common western painted turtle (*Chrysemys picta belli*), an invader from the Prairies. This subspecies ranges from BC, across the southern Prairies into western Ontario. The species is represented by the midland painted turtle (*C. p. marginata*) in southern Ontario and Québec, and by the 18 cm eastern painted turtle (*C. p. picta*) in NB and NS. Most major categories of organisms contain one or 2 species that can adapt to almost any natural or unnatural condition. Such is the painted turtle; the 43 cm snapping turtle (*Chelydra serpentina*) runs a close second, ranging from NS to Saskatchewan. These species not only occupy every natural body of water from lake to marsh, but even take over stagnant ditches, dams, fish ponds and farm water holes.

A floating log studded with basking, shiny black painted turtles is a common sight in many localities in southern Canada, except in turtleless Newfoundland and PEI. Snapping turtles, in contrast, are secretive. These sinister, 18 kg monsters prey on anything, dead or alive. Their population densities can be astounding, as professional hunters have demonstrated; this big, muscular turtle is commercial restaurant fare.

The terrestrial eastern box turtle (*Terrapene carolina carolina*), probably introduced in Canada, and the semiterrestrial wood turtle (*Clemmys insculpta*) can be poisonous if they have recently fed on toxic mushrooms, and should not be eaten. In Canada the 15 cm eastern box turtle, limited to Ontario's POINT PELEE, may be either a relict population or a recent introduction. The 20 cm wood turtle is a truly northern species, ranging from Lk Superior to the Bay of FUNDY. Haunting riverbanks, grassy meadows and floodplain forests, it is partial to wild berries and earthworms. Painted turtles shed old scales as they grow. Wood turtles retain and add annual growth rings to each scale, and their age can be determined, much like that of a tree, by counting the rings.

The remaining species are limited to extreme southern Ontario, with a few adjacent Québec records. Turtles are best located through binoculars when they are basking or when just their

John Turner at the Liberal leadership convention, June 1984 (*photo by Richard Vroom/Miller Services Ltd*).

heads project out of the water. The most distinctive head and neck is the 2-toned black (upper) and yellow (lower) of the 25 cm Blanding's turtle (*Emydoidea blandingi*). Partial to weedy bays, bogs and marshes, it eats fish, tadpoles, insects and crayfish. East of the Ontario-Québec boundary, it is limited to a thriving, very isolated, relict population in southern NS, centered in KEJIMKUJIK NATIONAL PARK.

Two small turtles, the 10 cm stinkpot or musk (*Sternotherus odoratus*) and the 13 cm spotted turtle (*Clemmys guttata*), have a scattered distribution over southern Ontario and, in the latter case, southern Québec. Both are easily overlooked. The dark brown musk turtle wanders about at the bottom of lakes, bogs and marsh pools searching for live or decomposing animal matter. It rarely basks and consequently becomes covered in algae and is very inconspicuous. The spotted turtle is a gregarious basker in spring but extremely shy. It frequents areas of swampy grass in woodlands and pools in marshes and bogs.

In larger lakes and rivers of southern Ontario, 2 large, rather specialized turtles occur, map turtle (*Graptemys geographica*) and eastern spiny softshell turtle (*Trionyx spiniferus spiniferus*). The pattern of maplike lines on the shell accounts for the map turtle's name. It has powerful jaws for crushing clams, etc. The softshell turtle frequents soft bottom areas where, befitting its flatfish shape, it lies in wait, half buried, ready to strike out at fish and crayfish. It has the typical bony casement but the outer skin is a thick, rubbery pancake extending beyond the flattened body. Nostrils are peculiarly extended into a long, tubular snorkel which allows the turtle to remain buried, yet reach the surface to breathe occasionally.

Four of the world's 6 species of sea turtles have been recorded in Canada, but these basically tropical and subtropical reptiles never nest on Canadian beaches. Reports over the past 100 years include 2 dead Pacific green turtles (*Chelonia mydas agassizi*), one washed ashore in BC, one in Alaska; 4 Atlantic ridley turtles (*Lepidochelys kempi*) washed up in NS; and a few Atlantic loggerhead turtles (*Caretta caretta caretta*) seen off the East Coast. Of an entirely different nature are regular reports of leatherback turtles (*Dermochelys coriacea*) near the Queen Charlotte Is and Vancouver I, along Labrador and Newfoundland coasts, and tangled in fishing nets off PEI, NB and NS. One of the largest living reptiles, it is nearly 2.5 m from snout to tail and sometimes weighs over 550 kg. In summer, it regularly haunts the cold Atlantic and Pacific coasts of Canada (also Scotland, Norway, Alaska and the USSR) hunting for its favourite food — giant lion's mane jellyfish. That it has a body temperature near 28°C (18° above the surrounding seawater) was discovered near Halifax in 1971. The leatherlike, oil-saturated, thick (5-7 cm) skin provides a sort of blubber layer that retains heat generated by muscular contractions.

J. SHERMAN BLEAKNEY

Tutchone of the southern Yukon Territory, who speak an Athapaskan language, numbered about 1000 in the 1980s. Traditionally, they exploited the vast plateau dissected by the YUKON R headwaters and flanked SW by the Coastal and St Elias mountains and NE by the Ogilvie and Selwyn ranges. They hunted caribou, moose, sheep and smaller game and also took various birds and freshwater fish. Some bands depended heavily on annual salmon runs. The fluctuating fauna and subarctic climate, characterized by warm summers and very cold winters, required a seminomadic way of life. Families gathered in spring and summer fish camps, at autumn meat camps, and tried to cluster for part of the winter near dried food supplies and at good fish lakes. By late winter, however, they had to scatter to find game and sometimes they starved (eg, RAB-BIT starvation). The 19th-century FUR TRADE also encouraged winter trapping. A few Tutchone, influenced by the Coast Tlingit, had plank dwellings, but most lived in double lean-tos of brush or domed skin tents. Since dog traction came only with white contact, belongings were limited to those which could be easily carried or made on the spot, such as the snares used to catch animals of all sizes. Some Tutchone had raw copper for making knives or arrowheads; the majority used bone and antler. Women made excellent birchbark containers and tailored skin clothing. People expressed themselves in singing, dancing, oratory and a rich store of oral traditions. Dietary and other observances marked birth, puberty and death. Both sexes learned how to maintain harmony with the powerful spirits of animals and other phenomena on whose good will the welfare of humans depended. SHAMANS enlisted spirit powers to locate game and cure illness.

Descent was reckoned matrilineally and lineages were grouped into exogamous moieties. There was no formal political organization, although wealth-based rank began to develop in the 19th century as the result of trading and intermarriage with Tlingit, who were intermediaries between white coastal traders and interior Indians. Tutchone nearest the coast were incorporated into clans bearing Tlingit names.

The influx of whites during the KLONDIKE GOLD RUSH of 1898 and building of the ALASKA HIGHWAY in 1942 drastically altered Tutchone culture. The Indians have shifted to a dual economy based on wage labour as well as hunting, fishing and trapping. They have never signed a treaty (*see* INDIAN TREATIES) and, since 1970, have actively tried to clarify their legal status and settle LAND CLAIMS with the federal government. *See also* NATIVE PEOPLE: SUBARCTIC and general articles under NATIVE PEOPLE. CATHARINE MCCLELLAN

Tweedie, Lemuel John, lawyer, politician, premier of NB (b at Chatham, NB 30 Nov 1849; d there 15 July 1917). After developing an extensive law practice Tweedie served as surveyor general and provincial secretary before becoming premier in 1900. One of the most popular men ever to hold office as premier, his outgoing personality and entertaining oratory made him an institution on the Miramichi at the turn of the century. At the same time he was a shrewd and opportunistic political operator and an exceptionally able lawyer. After 7 years in office he was appointed lieutenant-governor, a post he held until 1912. ARTHUR T. DOYLE

Tweedsmuir, John Buchan, 1st Baron, *see* BUCHAN.

25th Street Theatre of Saskatoon was founded in 1972 by U of Sask drama students, notably Andras Tahn, artistic director until 1983. The theatre developed primarily as a populist grassroots company, producing plays and collective creations on prairie subjects, but also as a venue for new plays from other regions. It is best known for *Paper Wheat* (1977), a collective documentary collage on the history of the SASKATCHEWAN WHEAT POOL, nationally toured in 1978 and 1979. Other premieres include Layne Coleman's *Queen's Cowboy* (1979); Andras Tahn's *Jacob Kepp* (1979); Jim Garrard's *Cold Comfort* (1981); Maria Campbell, Linda Griffiths and Paul Thompson's *Jessica* (1982); and Thelma Oliver's *Diefenbaker* (1983). DIANE BESSAI

Twillingate, Nfld, Town, pop 1506 (1981c), inc 1962, is located on Twillingate Islands, NOTRE DAME BAY in NE Newfoundland. It was a summer base for hunting and fishing for the BEOTHUK as it had been for an earlier aboriginal people, the Dorset Eskimos. Twillingate, from the Breton place-name *Toulinguet*, was a French fishing station until the TREATY OF UTRECHT, 1713. It became England's most northerly fishing settlement in the 1730s and was settled principally by migratory fishermen brought by merchants based in Poole, Eng, in particular the firm of John Slade. A strong resident merchant class developed a local fishery and in the 19th century Twillingate became one of Newfoundland's largest centres for the Labrador cod and seal fisheries. The modern town, now linked by causeway to insular Newfoundland, is a fish-processing and regional centre for smaller communities in the area.

JANET E.M. PITT AND ROBERT D. PITT

Two Solitudes, by Hugh MACLENNAN (Toronto, New York and Des Moines, 1945), is a novel whose title has become emblematic of Canada's most troubling legacy: the relations between English and French Canadians. Using historical settings within a mythological framework, MacLennan explores the tensions in these relations from WWI to 1939. The French Canadian realities are set in the parish of Saint-Marc-des-Érables, which is dominated by its priest, Father Beaubien, and by Athanase Tallard, a powerful but tragic figure ostracized by his church for trying to industrialize the village. Montréal, on the other hand, is dominated by characters such as Huntley McQueen, a Presbyterian businessman from Ontario. Tallard's son Paul, at home in both languages but alienated from both cultures, embarks on an Odyssean quest for his own identity and for a vision of Canada as he struggles to write a novel which will define his own Canadian experience. MacLennan's novel has been translated into French, as *Deux solitudes* (Paris, 1963), Spanish, Swedish, Czech, Dutch and Estonian. NEIL BESNER

Typhus, *see* EPIDEMIC.

Tyrrell, James William, explorer, mine promoter (b at Weston, Canada W 10 May 1863; d at Bartonville, Ont 16 Jan 1945), brother of Joseph Burr TYRRELL. James was educated in civil engineering. He practised in Hamilton until 1893 when he embarked with his brother on a canoe trip across the interior of the Keewatin Dist from Lk Athabasca to Hudson Bay via the DUBAWNT R. His book describing the expedition, *Across the Sub-Arctics of Canada* (1897), is a classic of northern travel writing. In 1900 Tyrrell led a Dominion Lands Survey expedition through the Keewatin. He was later among the pioneer mine promoters in the Red Lk area of northern Ontario and became president of Tyrrell Red Lake Mines. DANIEL FRANCIS

Tyrrell, Joseph Burr, geologist, explorer, historian (b at Weston, Canada W 1 Nov 1858; d in Toronto 26 Aug 1957). Tyrrell explored the vast areas of western and northern Canada, consolidating information gathered by earlier explorers and filling in blank spots on the maps, especially in the NWT, while working for 17 years for the GEOLOGICAL SURVEY OF CANADA (1881-98). He explored the DUBAWNT and THELON rivers to CHESTERFIELD INLET under considerable hardship, discovered the rich dinosaur beds of southern Alberta and important coal beds at Drumheller, Alta, and Fernie, BC, and added knowledge to the geography, botany, entomology, mammalogy and ornithology of many regions. He later became a mining consultant, and then a miner in the Klondike and northern Ontario, eventually acquiring considerable wealth. Highly regarded both in the field and by government officials in Ottawa and Toronto, he was also involved in several historical publications, most notably in editing the diaries of Samuel HEARNE and David THOMPSON. He was president of the CHAMPLAIN SOCIETY and received many honours, including the RSC's Flavelle Gold Medal. A mountain and lake bear his name. MARTIN K. MCNICHOLL

Tyson, Ian and Tyson, Sylvia Fricker, *see* IAN AND SYLVIA.

U-boat Landings German submarines (*Untersee-boote*) landed men in Québec and Labrador twice during WORLD WAR II. On the night of 8-9 Nov 1942 the spy Werner Janowski came ashore from U-518 near New Carlisle, Qué, and was almost immediately captured. On 22 and 23 Oct 1943 the crew of U-537 landed an automatic weather station at Martin Bay, 32 km S of Cape Chidley, Labrador. The station transmitted data for about 3 months. Although sighted by casual visitors it was not properly identified until July 1981. Other landings may have taken place, especially in the Gulf of ST LAWRENCE, but they are not documented.   W.A.B. DOUGLAS

Ucluelet, BC, Village, pop 1593 (1983c), inc 1952, is located on the W side of Vancouver I, 175 km NW of Victoria, at the western entrance to Barkle Sound. Nearby geographic features include Broken Islands, Long Beach and Florencia Bay (part of PACIFIC RIM NATIONAL PARK) and Amphitrite Point, the site of a famous lighthouse. Ucluelet's main industries are lumbering, fishing, tourism and government services. The third-largest fish-landing port in BC, it has a fine natural harbour.   ALAN F.J. ARTIBISE

Ukrainian Writing in Canada began in the 1890s with the first major wave of UKRAINIANS. The first story was written in 1897 by Nestor Dmytriw while he was visiting Calgary, and the first poem in 1898 by Ivan Zbura near Edmonton. From modest beginnings this literature developed and flourished in the genres of poetry, stories, novels and plays. After WWII, books of literary scholarship appeared.

The first period of Ukrainian writing, 1897 to 1920, was permeated with folklore. Zbura, Teodor Fedyk and Daria Mohylianka epitomized the pioneer poetry, which could hardly be distinguished from folklore. However, prose fiction by Sava Chernetskyj, Myroslav Stechyshyn, Pavlo Krat and Vasyl Kudryk had a higher level of creative achievement. These authors and others not only depicted hardships of pioneering but expressed the revolutionary flavour of struggles for a better life.

In the second period (1920-50) the Ukrainian writing in Canada broadened thematically and became more artistic. Ivan Danylchuk, born in Saskatchewan, published sophisticated poetry and Onufrij Ivakh (Honore Ewach) tried to philosophize in his works, paying attention to aesthetic expression, while Myroslav Ichnianskyj (Ivan Kmeta) poured out strong, impressionistic lyricism. In prose fiction, Illia Kyrijak (Elias Kiriak) distinguished himself with his realistic trilogy *Syny zemli* (1939-45; tr and abridged as *Sons of the Soil*, 1959), a panorama of the life of settlers on the prairies. Oleksander Luhovyj also depicted Canadian life in his novel *Bezkhatnyj* (*Homeless*, 1946) and plays. Semen Kowbel was active in drama.

The third period opened with the arrival of political immigrants after WWII. In contrast to the previous realism, there appeared various literary trends and styles, including modernism. Mykyta Mandryka produced poetry with original images and the versified narrative *Kanada* (1961; tr Watson Kirkconnell as *Canada*, 1971). Canadian themes were prominent also in Ulas Samchuk's novel *Na tverdij zemli* (*On the Hard Soil*, 1967). Yar Slavutych, in his poems *Zavojovnyky prerij* (1968; tr R.H. Morrison as *The Conquerors of the Prairies*, 1974), pictured his impressions of settlers' life and the severity of the North. He has also written the long versified narrative "Moja doba" ("My Epoch," in *Zirani tvory*, 1978).

Since the 1960s there has been a revival in Ukrainian literature in Canada. Among the active authors have been lyrical poets Borys Oleksandriv (pseudonym of Borys Hrybinsky), Bohdan Mazepa, Vira Vorsklo and Teodor Matvijenko; patriotic bards Levko Romen, Dan Mur and Oleksa Hay-Holowko; the thinker in poetry

Volodymyr Skorupskyj; the woman poet with preoccupations in ancient Ukrainian mythology, Larysa Murovych; and modernists Iryna Makaryk, Marco Carynnyk and Danylo Struk. In prose fiction, Fedir Odrach, Ivan Bodnarchuk and Oleksander Smotrych have been extensively published. Mykola Kovshun has written drama and Oleh Zujewskyj has been very active in translating, besides writing symbolistic poetry. Orysia Prokopiw has translated much Ukrainian poetry into English.

Ukrainian authors in Canada formed their own literary society, which has published 7 volumes of the almanac *Slovo* (1970-83) and the *Antolohija ukrajins'koji poeziji v Kanadi, 1898 to 1973* (1975). Another almanac, with Canadian overtones, was *Pivnichne siajvo* (*Northern Lights*, 5 vols, 1964-71). Despite the great variety of themes and significant ideas in Ukrainian writing, there are only some 15 Ukrainian Canadian authors whose artistic accomplishments place their literature on a level equal to that in Ukraine. *See* ETHNIC LITERATURE.   YAR SLAVUTYCH
Reading: C.H. Andrusyshen and W. Kirkconnell, eds, *The Ukrainian Poets, 1189-1962* (1963).

Ukrainians In the 19th century, the Russian Empire ruled 80% of Ukraine; the rest lay in the Austro-Hungarian provinces of Galicia, Bukovina and Transcarpathia. Serfs in Austria-Hungary until 1848 and in the Russian Empire until 1861, Ukrainians suffered from economic and national oppression. When attempts to establish an independent Ukrainian state from 1917 to 1921 collapsed, the greater portion of Ukraine became a republic in the USSR, while Poland, Romania and Czechoslovakia divided the remainder. Following WWII the western Ukrainian territories were annexed by the Ukrainian Soviet Socialist Republic. The Ukrainians constitute, after the Russians, the largest Slavic nation in Europe.

Migration and Settlement In 1981 there were 530 000 persons of Ukrainian origin living in Canada. (All figures in this entry derived from the 1981 census are based on single-origin responses and do not include multiple origins.) Isolated individuals of Ukrainian background may have come to Canada during the WAR OF 1812 as mercenaries in the DE MEURON and de Watteville regiments. It is possible that others participated in Russian exploration and colonization on the West Coast, came with MENNONITE and other German immigrants in the 1870s, or entered Canada from the US. The first major immigration (170 000 peasants, primarily from Galicia and Bukovina) occurred between 1891 and 1914. Initiated by Ivan Pylypiw and Wasyl Eleniak, the movement grew after 1896 when Canada solicited agricultural immigrants from eastern Europe.

With the outbreak of WWI, immigration virtually ceased and Ukrainians were classified as "enemy aliens" by the Canadian government, although over 10 000 Ukrainians enlisted in the armed forces. Between the 2 world wars some 70 000 Ukrainians immigrated to Canada for political and economic reasons. They included war veterans, intellectuals and professionals, as well as peasants. Between 1947 and 1954 some 34 000 Ukrainians, displaced by WWII, arrived in Canada. Representing all Ukrainian territories, they were the most complex socioeconomic group. While the Prairie provinces absorbed the bulk of the first 2 immigrations, the newcomers settled mainly in Ontario. Between 1955 and 1960 only 2768 Ukrainians immigrated to Canada, and approximately 500 per year have entered the country since. Today, over 80% of Ukrainian Canadians are native born.

By 1914 the Prairie provinces were marked by Ukrainian block settlements, extending from the original Edna [STAR] colony in Alberta through the Rosthern and Yorkton districts of Saskatchewan to the Dauphin, Interlake and Stuartburn regions of Manitoba. Later immigrants and migrants from the rural blocks developed modest Ukrainian urban communities that began around 1900. In 1981 the largest Ukrainian urban concentrations were in Edmonton (63 000), Winnipeg (59 000), and Toronto (51 000). By 1981, 59% of Ukrainian Canadians resided in the Prairie provinces and 25.3% lived in Ontario.

Economic Life Ukrainians homesteaded initially with limited capital, outdated peasant technology and no experience with large-scale agriculture. High wheat prices during WWI led to expansion based on wheat, but during the 1930s mixed farming came to prevail. Mechanization, scientific agriculture and outmigration in the Ukrainian blocks paralleled developments elsewhere in rural western Canada. Ukrainian male wage earners worked initially as city labourers, miners and railway and forestry workers, while women worked as domestics and as restaurant and hotel help. Discrimination and exploitation radicalized many Ukrainian labourers, who benefited from occupational diversification and specialization only after the 1920s.

By 1971 the proportion of Ukrainian Canadians in agriculture had decreased to 11.2%, slightly above the Canadian average, and unskilled workers to 3.5% of the Ukrainian male labour force. Compared with all Canadians, Ukrainians were overrepresented in manufacturing, construction and related occupations and underrepresented in semiprofessional and professional categories.

Social Life and Community The first Ukrainian block settlements and urban enclaves cushioned immigrant adjustment but could not prevent all problems of dislocation. Local cultural-educational associations, fashioned after Galician and Bukovinan models, combined interest in the homeland with instruction about Canada. Ukrainian Canadians assisted Ukrainian war victims and interwar immigrants; 3 pioneer charitable societies still function.

National organizations emerged in the interwar years. The procommunist Ukrainian Labour-Farmer Temple Association (est 1924) attracted the unemployed in the 1930s. The Ukrainian Self-Reliance League (est 1927) and the Ukrainian Catholic Brotherhood (est 1932) represented Orthodox and Catholic laity, respectively. Organizations introduced by the second immigration reflected Ukrainian revolutionary trends in Europe. The small conservative, monarchical United Hetman Organization (est 1934) was counterbalanced by the influential nationalistic, republican Ukrainian National Federation (est 1932). Despite tensions, all groups publicized Polish pacification and Stalinist terror in Ukraine in the 1930s; only the Ukrainian Labour-Farmer Temple Association condoned the Soviet purges and the artificial famine of 1932-33 that killed 6 million people; its successor, the Association of United Ukrainian Canadians (est 1946), has declined steadily. In 1940, to unite Ukrainian Canadians behind the war effort, noncommunist organizations formed the Ukrainian Canadian Committee. It became a permanent co-ordinating superstructure with such political objectives as the admission of Ukrainian REFUGEES after 1945 and MULTI-CULTURALISM.

The major organizations introduced by the third immigration were the intensely nationalistic Canadian League for Ukraine's Liberation (est 1949) and the scouting Plast (est 1948). In the 1970s the Ukrainian Canadian Professional and Business Federation (est 1965) was politically significant, able to secure public benefits for the Ukrainian community.

Women's groups have traditionally emphasized education, culture, handicrafts, museums and child rearing. Youth affiliates have had both ideological and social dimensions. Only 10-15% of Ukrainian Canadians belong to the organized community; others identify with its cultural but not its national-political goals.

Ukrainian Canadians have published nearly 600 newspapers and periodicals, most of which espouse a particular religious or political philosophy. English and bilingual publications partly compensate for the decline in Ukrainian-language readers, but many Ukrainian Canadians no longer find the press relevant.

Religion and Cultural Life While Ukrainians from Galicia were Eastern-rite Catholic (*see* CATHOLICISM), those from Bukovina were ORTHODOX. No priests immigrated initially, and other denominations tried to fill the religious and social vacuum. Until 1912, when they acquired an independent hierarchy, Ukrainian Catholics were under Roman Catholic jurisdiction. The Russian Orthodox Church worked among Orthodox immigrants but rapidly lost popularity after 1917. In 1918 Ukrainians who were opposed to centralization and latinization in the Ukrainian Catholic Church founded the Ukrainian Greek Orthodox Church of Canada. It has been a metropolitanate since 1951, the Ukrainian Catholic Church since 1956. Once central in preserving the language, culture and identity of Ukrainian Canadians, the 2 churches have seen their religious dominance, moral authority and social influence undermined by assimilation. In 1981 only 30.0% and 18.6% of Ukrainian Canadians belonged to the Ukrainian Catholic and Ukrainian Orthodox churches, respectively; 16.8% were Roman Catholic and 13.3% United Church adherents.

Most agricultural pagan-Christian rituals of Ukrainian peasant life were discarded with urbanization and secularization. Embroidery, Easter egg ornamentation, dance, music and foods have won appreciation outside the Ukrainian Canadian group. Community archives, museums and libraries preserve the Ukrainian Canadian heritage, and they have recently been supplemented by public professional institutions.

Certain art forms have remained static, while others have evolved. Dance ensembles have experimented with Ukrainian Canadian themes; Ukrainian Canadian country music has combined Ukrainian folk and Canadian western elements; and church architecture has skilfully integrated traditional Ukrainian with contemporary N American designs. The paintings of William KURELEK, inspired by his Ukrainian prairie pioneer experience, have been widely recognized. Numerous Ukrainian-language poets and prose writers have described Ukrainian life in Canada; George RYGA is one of few English-language writers of Ukrainian origin to achieve national stature. In the 1970s several films critically interpreted the Ukrainian Canadian experiences.

Ukrainian farm at Fraserwood, Man (known as Kreuzburg until 1918), *c*1918 (*courtesy Provincial Archives of Manitoba*).

Education After 1897 Ukrainians in Manitoba took advantage of opportunities for bilingual instruction under specially trained Ukrainian teachers. Bilingual schools operated unofficially in Saskatchewan until 1918 but not in Alberta. Criticized for retarding assimilation, they were abolished in Manitoba in 1916 despite Ukrainian opposition.

Vernacular schools expanded rapidly after 1916 to preserve the Ukrainian language and culture. Today, they reach only a fraction of youth; most schools exist in urban areas at the elementary level. Pioneer residential institutes provided Ukrainian surroundings for rural students pursuing their education and produced many community leaders. Four of 5 surviving institutes serve as Ukrainian Orthodox community centres and university residences.

Russification in Soviet Ukraine has spurred Ukrainian Canadians to seek public support for their language and culture. They have obtained Ukrainian-content university courses and degree programs, recognition of Ukrainian as a language of study and subsequently of instruction in Prairie schools, and a Canadian Institute of Ukrainian Studies (est 1976) at University of Alberta. Ukrainian and Ukrainian Canadian studies have developed since the early 1950s.

Illiteracy, once prevalent, has almost disappeared. Ukrainian women have traditionally been disadvantaged compared with Ukrainian men and Canadian women, and fewer Ukrainians have been to university than Canadians in more privileged groups. Today, educational levels generally reflect Canadian norms.

Politics Ukrainians originally entered municipal politics, and where they were numerically dominant they came to control elected and administrative organs. William Hawrelak in Edmonton and Stephen Juba in Winnipeg have been prominent mayors. The first Ukrainian elected to a provincial legislature was Andrew Shandro, a Liberal, in Alberta in 1913. In 1926 Michael Luchkovich of the United Farmers of Alberta became the first Ukrainian in the House of Commons. Since then 200 Ukrainian candidatures have been successful provincially and over 60 federally, almost all on the Prairies. By 1980, 22 federal and provincial Cabinet appointments had been made, most of them recent. There have been 5 senators of Ukrainian origin. In 1970 Stephen Worobetz became lieutenant-governor of Saskatchewan.

During WWI approximately 6000 Ukrainians were interned as enemy aliens and those naturalized less than 15 years were disenfranchised. Ukrainians initially tended to vote Liberal, but their low socioeconomic status also drew them to protest parties, and many approved the anti-communism of the Diefenbaker Conservatives. Increasingly, voting patterns have reflected those of their economic class or region.

Group Maintenance Ukrainian Canadians form a mature ethnocultural group with little new infusion. Low organizational membership, decline in traditional religion, intermarriage and language loss have reduced the identifiable

Ukrainian Canadian community. Overt discrimination has largely disappeared, and many Canadians of Ukrainian origin retain a few distinctive ethnic values. Oppression in Ukraine has sustained Ukrainian community goals and group ties in Canada. Since the 1960s the Canadian born have countered assimilation by reviving interest in their heritage, aided by multiculturalism policies.   FRANCES A. SWYRIPA

Reading: J. Kolasky, The Shattered Illusion: The History of Ukrainian Pro-Communist Organizations in Canada (1979); M. Kostash, All of Baba's Children (1977); M.R. Lupul, ed, A Heritage in Transition: Essays in the History of the Ukrainians in Canada (1982); M.H. Marunchak, The Ukrainian Canadians: A History (2nd ed, 1983); W.R. Petryshyn, ed, Changing Realities: Social Trends among Ukrainian Canadians (1980); H. Potrebenko, No Streets of Gold: A Social History of Ukrainians in Alberta (1977).

Ultra Vires-Intra Vires Ultra vires [Lat, "beyond the powers"] is used in CONSTITUTIONAL LAW by the courts who must decide the respective competences of Parliament and provincial legislatures. If one or the other, in enacting a law, goes beyond the jurisdiction allotted to it by the constitution, the court will declare that measure ultra vires. If not, the court will declare it intra vires [Lat, "within the powers"]. These 2 expressions also apply to ADMINISTRATIVE LAW, the law of local collectivities, corporate law, etc. Many bodies, eg, municipalities, school boards and corporations, have powers delegated to them by Parliament or provincial legislatures. These delegated bodies may, within their established limits, adopt regulations which, to be valid, must not exceed the limits prescribed by law.

GÉRALD-A. BEAUDOIN

Ultramontanism in Canada, as in Europe where it began during the French Revolution, was the theory of those who rejected any compromise by CATHOLICISM with modern thought, and demanded the supremacy of religious over civil society. Its central tenet was an attachment to the person of the pope and belief in the doctrine of his infallibility.

Ultramontanism took root 1820-30, first in Séminaire de Saint-Hyacinthe, strongly influenced by the ideas of Félicité de Lamennais, and in Montréal under the influence of its first Catholic bishop, Jean-Jacques Lartigue. This bishop opposed GALLICAN ideas and fought for freedom of the church and religious supremacy in education. His successor, Mgr Ignace BOURGET, led ultramontane ideas to triumph in every field (theology, education, church-state relations, etc) and not only in Montréal but throughout most of Catholic Canada. Ultramontanism, very strong in the 1860s, split into 2 groups. The extreme ultramontanes fought for the immediate application of ultramontane principles in the control of education, the reform of laws in conformity with canon law, and the surveillance of civil legislation by the episcopate, etc. The moderate ultramontanes, whom the extremists called "Catholic liberals," wanted a more prudent application of the principles, with compromise where necessary. The extremists, led first by Mgr Bourget and later by Mgr Louis-François LA-FLÈCHE, mobilized journalists and conservative politicians, who recommended a *programme catholique* which would have guaranteed the supremacy of the church in political life. In following years, the extremists and the "programmists" led an antiliberal crusade, which had, as one consequence, the birth of the CASTORS in 1882. Despite the belief of ultramontanes in the state, ultramontanism became closely linked with those ideals within FRENCH CANADIAN NATIONALISM that pointed towards a church-dominated, self-contained society.

Direct intervention by extreme ultramontanists in politics was a failure, but ultramontane thought, with only the slightest modifications, pervaded philosophic and theological instruction in the *petits* and *grands* seminaries, the SOCIAL DOCTRINE of the Canadian Catholic Church and many of the episcopal directives from the second half of the 19th century until the 1950s. It took the QUIET REVOLUTION and the council of Vatican II to dismantle this ideological edifice.　　　　　　NIVE VOISINE

Umiak Until recent times the chief means of summer water transport for coastal INUIT, the umiak was used for moving family and possessions to seasonal hunting areas and for whaling expeditions. The craft could hold more than 20 people, and was 6-10 m in length and more than 1.5 m wide at the centre. Ownership was sometimes shared by 2 or more families. The frame was constructed of salvage driftwood or whalebone, and hide lashings on pegs of antler, ivory or wood held the boat together. Hides of bearded seal, sewn together with waterproof seams, were stretched to dry tightly around the frame. The umiak dates to THULE times (1000 AD) in the central Arctic, and appeared in Greenland, Baffin I, Labrador, the Mackenzie Delta, Alaska and eastern Siberia.　RENÉ R. GADACZ

Underground Economy refers to economic transactions among individuals which are designed to escape detection — also referred to as the irregular economy. Technically, it includes all illegal transactions, eg, PROSTITUTION and drug transactions as well as evasions of TAXATION on otherwise legal activities. For example, a homeowner may hire someone to repair a roof. This is a legal transaction and is routinely reported when the person doing the repair declares the payment as income. However, the labourer may ask for and receive cash payment in which case the income is not declared in order to evade tax. Individuals in various lines of work can potentially underreport income if payment is received in cash.

Law enforcement and taxation officials readily admit that there is a large underground economy but cannot agree on its size. Because of its very nature the size of the irregular economy is difficult to measure, but there is evidence to indicate that in Canada and elsewhere it has grown recently. Underground activities do not enter the official statistics on GROSS NATIONAL PRODUCT (GNP). Those employed in the underground economy may be counted as unemployed in the official LABOUR FORCE statistics. If they hold a regular job and also work in the irregular economy, then the total quantity of labour input is incorrectly measured. Because current estimates suggest the irregular economy may account for as much as 20-25% of reported GNP, and because the irregular economy is growing at a faster rate than GNP, these effects may be serious.

Because a large fraction of transactions in the underground economy appears to be in cash, measuring cash holdings is one method of estimating the extent of the transactions. Basically, this involves estimating the cash needed for regular transactions and then determining the differences between this amount and actual cash used. This method has been used to estimate the size of the underground economy in Canada, the US and other countries. These estimates explain the apparent paradox in the published data on cash holdings. Although it has been widely predicted that the growth in the use of CREDIT CARDS and electronic fund transfers would lead to a cashless society or one in which cash is less important, currency holdings have not declined. Economists assert that this results from the diversion of increasing quantities of cash for use in the irregular economy.

There are frequent references to the sale of drugs and other controlled commodities on "the black market," a term that aptly describes the illegal component of the underground economy. Officially, such transactions are unreported. However, there is another meaning to the expression black market. If a particular commodity is the subject of legal price controls, eg, food during wartime, then transactions at illegal prices are usually referred to as black-market transactions. An official report, if it is made, will indicate that the transaction took place at the legal rather than the actual price.

Legal activities conducted underground to escape taxation appear to be the fastest-growing component of the irregular economy, largely because of our tax system. The potential gains from illegal tax evasion are greater at high tax rates. If rising incomes push more people into higher tax brackets, and if there are no changes in the penalties or the degree of enforcement of tax laws, an increase in unreported income can be expected; this is exactly what has happened so far. The growth of the irregular economy has important implications for the Canadian tax system, which relies on self-assessment and involves relatively little direct scrutiny of individual tax returns by taxation officials. Continuing growth in unreported income will almost surely lead to changes in this system. If increasing amounts of taxation are being avoided through the irregular economy, the tax burden on reported activities will be higher. Taxation officials correctly worry that as taxpayers observe the growth of unreported income in the irregular economy more of them will be tempted to try to conceal income.

It has been observed that the growth of the underground economy has paralleled the growth of INFLATION after the mid-1960s, although there is no concrete evidence to support this point. Inflation is an unlegislated tax which many economists regard as an important factor in reducing social cohesion. It may well be that this unlegislated tax rather than high rates of taxation explains the increase in failures to report income.

Even if estimates of the size of the underground economy are twice as high as the actual figure, it is clear that it is of greater importance in our economy than are most major industries. Unfortunately the growth of the underground economy also reflects a growth in disrespect for the law. This problem can be dealt with by auditing more tax returns and by increasing the penalties for nonreporting and other forms of tax evasion. The alternative would be to lower tax rates, thereby reducing the incentive to evade taxation.　　　　　　D.A. SMITH

Underground Railroad, an informal network of safe houses and people who helped fugitive slaves pass from slave states in the US to free states or to Canada. It has been the object of much mythmaking, for not nearly so many fugitives passed along it, nor were there nearly so many whites involved, as is generally said. Although most fugitive slaves remained in the free states of the American North, perhaps 30 000 reached Canada. The "railroad," in operation roughly 1840 to 1860, was most effective after the passage of the US Fugitive Slave Act in 1850, which empowered slave hunters to pursue fugitives onto free soil. This Act resulted in several efforts to kidnap fugitives who were in Canada to return them to Southern owners. *See* SLAVERY.　　　　　　ROBIN W. WINKS

Underhill, Barbara Ann, figure skater (b at Toronto 24 June 1963). She began pair FIGURE SKATING with Paul MARTINI in 1978 and they won the Junior world championships that year. They were Canadian champions 1979-83 and though they finished a disappointing 7th in the 1984 Sarajevo Olympics, they rebounded to become World gold medalists at Ottawa a month later.　　　　　　TERESA MOORE

Underhill, Frank Hawkins, historian, political thinker (b at Stouffville [Whitchurch-Stouffville], Ont 26 Nov 1889; d at Ottawa 16 Sept 1971). Describing himself as being born a

"North York Presbyterian Grit," and thus an enemy of the establishment, he achieved his greatest fame as a commentator on the political events and controversies of his times. After studying at U of T and Oxford and serving as an officer in WWI, he taught history at U of Sask until 1927 and then at U of T until 1955. An influential commentator on public affairs as well as a popular teacher, he wrote extensively for *Canadian Forum*. He was the first president of the LEAGUE FOR SOCIAL RECONSTRUCTION and the principal author of the CO-OPERATIVE COMMONWEALTH FEDERATION's Regina Manifesto of 1933. His public activities caused friction with U of T administration, and in 1940 he came close to being dismissed after openly predicting that Canada's ties with the UK would weaken as its ties with the US grew stronger (*see* TENURE). Always more of a liberal than a socialist, an admirer of the US and a strong supporter of the Cold War, he was propelled towards the Liberal Party in the 1940s. In 1955 he was appointed curator of Laurier House, Ottawa, by the Liberal government, and he dedicated a volume of essays to L.B. PEARSON. In his last years he was associated with Carleton U.　　　　　　GARTH STEVENSON

Reading: F.H. Underhill, *In Search of Canadian Liberalism* (1960).

Unemployment literally refers to being without work, or the lack of a paying job at the minimum wage or higher. In social or economic discussions it is more specifically defined; Statistics Canada defines the unemployed as those who did not work in the LABOUR MARKET during the survey reference week (but may have done housework, etc), were available for work and had actively looked for work in the past 4 weeks, were on temporary layoff for 26 weeks or less and expected to be recalled by their employer, or were waiting for a new job to begin within 4 weeks or less. The LABOUR FORCE comprises the unemployed and the much larger number of those who are employed, on their own account or by an employer, and whose absence from work because of illness, strikes, bad weather, etc, would only be temporary.

Unemployment has risen on average since the mid-1960s, both in absolute numbers and as a percentage of the labour force or unemployment rate. The unemployment rate has not fallen below 6.9% since 1975, although it was consistently below that level earlier in the postwar period. Annual average rates of 3-5% were common before 1958 and between 1964 and 1969. Between 1958 and 1963 and in the early 1970s, a 5-7% rate prevailed. From 1975 to 1981 rates of employment grew, but the labour force grew even more rapidly so that the number and fraction that were unemployed rose. Between 1969 and 1978, the labour force increased by 2.7 million persons. The number of women increased by 55%, of men by 22%. Since August 1981, to the end of 1982, employment has been declining, as has labour-force participation, and the fraction of the working-age population (those 15 years of age and over) employed. In 1983 and 1984, these indicators again showed some growth. The unemployment rate rose steadily over this period reaching over 12.8% (seasonally adjusted) at the end of 1982, probably the highest since the 1930s. Unemployment has also increased in many other countries over this period. In Canada unemployment declined to 11.1% by Dec 1983 and to 10.8% by Dec 1984. Further slow declines are forecast.

The annual averages, presented above, for the labour force as a whole conceal large variations within years, between regions and among different groups of people. Regular within-year variation or seasonality occurs as a result of a periodic influx of certain groups into the labour force, eg, students during vacation, and of marked seasonal patterns in certain industries, eg, agriculture, forestry, fishing, construction

Regional Unemployment Rates

Source: Catalogue F1-21/1982E Department of Finance Canada.

and tourism, which combine to produce regular seasonal fluctuations in the levels of unemployment and employment. For Canada as a whole, unemployment is typically at about the yearly average in May, falls gradually to some 90% of the average level in October and then rises to about 130% of it in March. Seasonal patterns for particular regions and demographic groups differ considerably. The numbers or rates are often seasonally adjusted to eliminate these regular fluctuations and to give a clearer picture of other month-to-month changes.

Regions and demographic (age-sex) groups differ also in their typical levels (rates) of unemployment. Traditionally, Québec and the Atlantic provinces have had higher rates than Ontario and the Prairies, but recently, while this general pattern persists, there has been an even more marked difference between East and West (excluding BC) and between Manitoba and Saskatchewan and the rest of the country. Women over 25 also have higher unemployment rates than men in that age bracket, and higher unemployment rates for young people have been persistent. The absolute differences, but probably not the percentage differences, have increased lately. Women's unemployment rates became higher in the 1970s as more women participated regularly in the labour force. (Exact comparisons of detailed and pre- and post-1975 data are difficult because of substantial revisions in survey methods and definitions.) Some of the increase in overall unemployment rates in the 1970s might be attributable to the increasing number of young people and women in the labour force.

Similar differences in the incidence of unemployment exist between groups classified by occupation, marital and family status, educational attainment, etc, and each of these classifications can be delineated more sharply (as are the age and geographic groupings), and 2 or more of them can be combined into various cross classifications. Some of this detail is published regularly. The unemployed can also be classified by the duration of their employ-

ment up to the survey week, their reasons for leaving their last jobs, job search, type of work sought and activity immediately prior to looking for work.

Causes of Unemployment While specific occurrences of unemployment will be caused by a multitude of factors some progress can be made with classifying the general phenomenom according to cause and possible remedy. The general increase in unemployment in 1981-82 and similar episodes in the past are instances of cyclical unemployment resulting from a general decline in production and economic activity, a consequence of the business cycle. FISCAL POLICY and MONETARY POLICY can be designed to alleviate cyclical unemployment by stimulating consumption in the economy. Frictional unemployment, however, covers those in the midst of changing jobs and those just entering the labour force. If there were as many jobs as workers some frictional unemployment would still exist. There is some evidence that the normal or average level of frictional unemployment has increased in the 1960s and 1970s, not only because of demographic changes, but also because of changes in social legislation. Some researchers claim that increases in UNEMPLOYMENT INSURANCE have made looking for work less financially burdensome, thus encouraging longer and less intensive searches, greater readiness to change jobs and more seasonal and otherwise intermittent work. The minimum wage, it is claimed, discourages employers from hiring unskilled workers who may need on-the-job training. This supposedly has a marked effect on new entrants to the labour market, particularly the young who were already having trouble finding work because so many more new, inexperienced workers entered the labour force during the 1960s and 1970s than the economy could easily absorb. Some observers blamed the relative rise in youth unemployment rates in this period on schooling, which did not provide sufficient preparation for work, and on the scarce opportunities for on-the-job training. In consequence, much of the work available to

young people without special training was monotonous and without a future. Employment instability and frequent unemployment resulted. Governments usually respond to frictional unemployment with LABOUR POLICIES designed to provide information about job markets and employment services, to ease the transition from school to work, to change educational and social policies, and to remove barriers to entry into particular occupations (*see* LABOUR RELATIONS). Seasonal unemployment is sometimes included in frictional unemployment, but for farm workers looking for work in winter the difficulty results not from a mismatching of skills but from a predictable lack of demand for certain kinds of labour during parts of the year. Tourism, fishing, logging, construction work and trapping are all affected by seasons.

Structural unemployment results from changes in the demand for labour as technological change or shifting product demands displace workers whose skills are rendered obsolete. Sometimes structural unemployment is exacerbated by a decline in a regional industry, eg, that of the textile industry in the EASTERN TOWNSHIPS of Québec. Attempts to remedy structural unemployment include manpower training programs and subsidized employment. Since 1952 Statistics Canada has conducted a monthly survey of the civilian labour force. The unemployment rate is calculated from a survey of representative households (30 000 from 1952 to 1977, now about 56 000). The territories, Indian reserves, full-time members of the armed forces and residents of mental institutions and prisons are not included in this survey.   S.F. KALISKI

Reading: M. Gunderson, *Labour Market Economics, Theory, Evidence and Policy in Canada* (1980); S. Ostry and M.A. Zaidi, *Labour Economics in Canada* (1979).

Unemployment Insurance, government benefit payments during a period of UNEMPLOYMENT. In Canada, the unemployment insurance system is financed by premiums paid by employers and employees and by federal government contributions. As early as 1919 the Royal Commission on Industrial Relations had recommended a national program of unemployment insurance, but when the R.B. BENNETT government tried to introduce the Employment and Social Insurance Act in 1935, the Supreme Court of Canada and the Privy Council of Great Britain declared the Act unconstitutional on the grounds that it was an infringement of provincial authority. The first compulsory national unemployment insurance program was instituted in 1940 after a constitutional amendment giving the federal government legislative power over unemployment insurance. Unemployment rates in Canada reached levels of about 20% during the GREAT DEPRESSION and hastened the adoption of unemployment insurance, as did the mobilization effort of WWII. To aid the organization of the work force for war, employment bureaus were expanded and used to help administer the unemployment insurance system.

To qualify for unemployment insurance benefits, applicants must show that they were previously employed for 10-20 weeks, according to regional and other criteria. To receive benefits, they must file a claim stating that they are without work, are willing to work and are registered at the Canada Employment Centre. Following a waiting period of 2 weeks (new claims only), individuals are eligible to receive 60% of average weekly insured earnings up to a maximum in 1985 of $267 per week. The number of weeks for which benefits can be claimed varies, depending on the length of previous employment, and the national and regional unemployment rate.

The unemployment insurance system is an important component of the economic safety net provided by government and there is little disagreement, in principle, that it has provided greater income security for Canadians. Among economists, however, there is substantial concern that specific features of the existing system may create unemployment. For example, it has been argued that the relatively short qualifying period may encourage individuals who would not choose to work, were it not for the prospect of also collecting benefits, to enter the labour force; and that unemployment is higher than it should be among those employed in seasonal industries because it may be easier to collect benefits than to look for other work during the off-season. *See also* SOCIAL SECURITY; DISTRIBUTION OF POWERS; TRANSFER PAYMENTS.   D.A. SMITH

Unemployment Relief Camps In Oct 1932, at the end of the third year of the GREAT DEPRESSION, and on the recommendation of Maj-Gen A.G.L. MCNAUGHTON, chief of the general staff, PM BENNETT sanctioned the creation of a nationwide system of camps to house and provide work for single, unemployed, homeless Canadian males. The camps were placed under the Department of NATIONAL DEFENCE in consultation with the Department of Labour, with civilian staffs. Occupants voluntarily entered the camps through the Employment Service of Canada and were free to leave at any time. In return for bunkhouse residence, 3 meals a day, work clothes, medical care and 20¢ a day, the "Royal Twenty Centers" worked 44-hr weeks clearing bush, building roads, planting trees and constructing public buildings. Critics argued that the federal government had established the camps in lieu of a reasonable program of work and wages. The most dramatic demonstration of this resentment occurred in Apr 1935, when 1500 men from BC camps went on strike and after 2 months' agitation in Vancouver set forth on the abortive ON TO OTTAWA TREK. By the time the camps were closed in June 1936, they had been home for 170 248 men who had been provided 10 201 103 man-days of relief. *See also* SOCIAL HISTORY; WORKING-CLASS HISTORY.   VICTOR HOWARD

Ungava Bay is a large, funnel-shaped bay that deeply indents the northern coast of Québec adjacent to LABRADOR. At its mouth, about 265 km wide, it opens into HUDSON STR. Leaf Basin at its SW extremity is noted for its high tidal range and its swift and dangerous tidal currents. Akpatok I in the bay's NW sector is remarkable for its forbidding coastal cliffs and extensive marine-abrasion platform, composed mainly of limestone, and its spectacular suite of raised beaches. Ice covers Ungava Bay from Nov until June, and its near-freezing waters are home to seal and arctic char, which are hunted and fished by the local Inuit population. Polar bear and walrus migrate from Hudson Str down the W coast on ice floes and may be seen in considerable numbers on Akpatok I in the summer.
     J.T. GRAY

Ungava Inuit (New Québec Inuit) live along the shores of Ungava Bay, on the S shore of HUDSON STRAIT and on the eastern coast of HUDSON BAY. They exploit the resources of the vast area N of the treeline, especially sea mammals in the coastal waters, and also move inland to hunt caribou and at times penetrate the traditional CREE and MONTAGNAIS-NASKAPI lands S of the treeline.

The term Ungava, meaning "towards the open water," was used to designate the Inuit band established at the mouth of the Arnaud (Payne) R. The Moravian Brothers, who established missions among LABRADOR INUIT, called the Inuit lands located to the west "Ungava"; the HUDSON'S BAY CO used the name widely in the 19th century, and the federal government then created the federal district of Ungava in 1885. Previously, these Inuit had no generic terms for themselves. Culturally close to the Inuit SE of Baffin I and to the Labrador Inuit, they nevertheless differ from these tribes in a number of linguistic and technological respects and in their social and religious customs. These distinctions have been accentuated by the acculturation and evolution of these Inuit as a result of the administrative division of their lands.

The Inuit of the northern part of Ungava, from Cape Smith to Killinek Is (Port Burwell), hunted large sea mammals (arctic whale, walrus, belugas, bearded seals), had good transportation (UMIAK, kayak, dog teams), and lived in large warm IGLOOs built of snow; they had access to all coastal and inland resources; those in the southern reaches of Ungava lived on fish and small marine or land mammals. Archaeological remains and their oral history show that some bands lived permanently on the shores of the larger inland lakes (eg, Payne, Klotz and Nantais lakes) or on the coastal islands and archipelagos (Ottawa, Sleeper, Mansel and Nottingham Is).

Among the first Inuit in Canada to establish permanent contacts with Europeans, the Ungava were also the first to take charge of the administration and management of their development through INUIT CO-OPERATIVES and the JAMES BAY AGREEMENT; they also became renowned for the fine quality and abundance of their contemporary art (*see* INUIT ART). Though influenced by a strong SHAMAN tradition, they were Christianized by Wesleyan, Anglican and later Roman Catholic missionaries. A number of syncretic and messianic movements also marked their development. During the 1970s a dissident political movement opposed to the James Bay Agreement grew in the northwestern Ungava region. Two writers, Mitiarjuk de Kangirsujuaq (Wakeham Bay), author of the novel *Sanaaq*, and Thomassie Qumak de Povungnituk, author of an encyclopedia and an Inuit dictionary, have been instrumental in spreading Inuit culture through the written word. *See also* INUIT MYTH AND LEGEND; NATIVE PEOPLE: ARCTIC; general articles under NATIVE PEOPLE.   B. SALADIN-D'ANGLURE

Reading: N. Graburn, *Eskimo without Igloos* (1969); L. Turner, *The Ethnology of the Ungava District* (1894, new ed 1979); M. Vézinet, *Les Nunamiut: Inuit au coeur des terres* (1980).

Ungava Peninsula, a large peninsula approximately 350 000 km² in area, washed by the waters of HUDSON BAY, HUDSON STRAIT and UNGAVA BAY, respectively. Peopled along the coastal fringe for centuries by Inuit communities, the interior is a vast, unpopulated, treeless plateau, which attains altitudes of 300 to 600 m. It is underlain by continuous PERMAFROST which attains thicknesses of 200 to 600 m. Rich mineral wealth, mainly asbestos, nickel, copper, uranium and iron ores, has been discovered by recent geological exploration. This wealth remains largely untapped at present, however, because of the high costs of extraction and a poor world market.   J.T. GRAY

Uniacke, James Boyle, lawyer, politician (b probably 1799, bap at Halifax 19 Jan 1800; d there 26 Mar 1858). As the son of Richard John UNIACKE, he enjoyed favoured status in NS politics and society. He became a lawyer and then entered the Assembly, representing Cape Breton County 1832-48, Halifax Township 1848-51 and Richmond County 1851-54, initially as a Conservative, but after 1840 as a Reformer (Liberal). He was appointed to the Executive Council in 1838 and served intermittently in several important offices during the struggle for RESPONSIBLE GOVERNMENT, which culminated in 1848 with Uniacke serving as attorney general and nominal premier. He retired in 1854 to become commissioner of crown lands and surveyor general.
     LOIS KERNAGHAN

Uniacke, Richard John, lawyer, politician (b at Castletown, Ire 22 Nov 1753; d at Mount Uniacke, NS 11 Oct 1830). After a turbulent early career in the Cumberland district of NS as a trader and a sympathizer with the American rebels, he returned to Ireland where he was admitted as an attorney. In 1781 he was named solicitor general of NS. By 1800 his was the province's largest legal practice; combined with his appointment (1784) as advocate general of the Vice-Admiralty Court, it secured his personal fortune. He also sat in the legislature (1783-93, 1798-1805) and served as Speaker (1789-93, 1799-1805). Named attorney general in 1797 he was appointed to the Council 1808, but his great ambition, the office of chief justice, eluded him. His forceful, conservative influence on contemporary politics, education and religion undoubtedly prolonged social dissension in NS, but his vision of colonial union and commercial independence for BNA marked him as a man ahead of his time.   LOIS KERNAGHAN

Reading: B. Cuthbertson, *The Old Attorney General, a Biography of Richard John Uniacke* (1980).

Uniforms, garments of a similar ("uniform") pattern worn by a group of individuals to indicate their identity and function. Uniform clothing was used in ancient times and has been especially popular with the military since the emergence of standing armies in western Europe during the 17th century. Colonels of REGIMENTS found it convenient to require their troops to wear uniforms on which they could realize a profit from pay deductions, a system that lasted into the 1850s in the British army. Uniform colours varied greatly at first. In Canada, the first large body of uniformed men appeared in 1665 with the CARIGNAN-SALIÈRES REGIMENT dressed in brown coats lined with white and grey, black hats and buff and black ribbons. Nations soon standardized the basic coat colours, though there were many exceptions. The colonial infantry companies that garrisoned NEW FRANCE from 1683 to 1760 had grey-white coats, the French infantry colour, with blue linings and cuffs. From 1716, the buttons were brass, the vest, breeches and stockings were blue, and a gold-laced tricorn was worn. The army regiments sent to Canada from 1755 until the CONQUEST of 1760 had the same basic dress with differences in colours, eg, the La Sarre Regiment had a red vest, with grey-white coat linings and grey-white breeches.

The distinctively coloured cuffs, collars, linings and lapels became known as "facings" in the red-coated British infantry, and most units also had lace patterns that were peculiar to each regiment. Shades of yellow, green, blue or buff were the usual facing colours. The impression that the whole British army was in red coats should be dismissed: artillery wore blue with red facings, as did some support services. Green was also adopted by some light infantry and rifle corps from the end of the 18th century, notably by the Queen's Rangers (1791 to 1802) who served in Upper Canada.

Soldier of the Troupes de la Marine, *c*1750 (left) uniform of the 58th Foot, 1759 (centre), and officer of the 4th Canadian Hussars, *c*1890 (right) (*courtesy Parks Canada*).

Infantryman of the 2nd Battalion, Canadian Expeditionary Force, 1916 (left), RCAF bomber crew, Europe, 1944-45 (centre), and RCN officer during the Battle of the Atlantic, 1943-44 (*courtesy Canadian War Museum/NMM/NMC*).

In 1984 new separate uniforms were introduced to replace the single "CF Green." Shown above are navy winter (2 on left), navy summer (3rd from left), air force (centre), army summer — parachute training (3rd from right) — and army winter (2 on right) (*courtesy Canapress*).

The militia of New France had no official uniform. Only the officers were expected to wear gorgets and swords. When the Americans besieged Québec in 1775, the town's militia provided itself with green coats with buff waistcoats and breeches, the first instance that a sizable body of Canadian militiamen took to wearing a uniform. During the WAR OF 1812 and the REBELLIONS OF 1837, militiamen wore what they could get until proper uniforms arrived from England. Apart from the British army and the militia, some units were raised in Canada and dressed as regular troops. Until the 1850s a few units composed of wealthy militiamen uniformed themselves splendidly at their own cost. Canadians feared hostilities during the AMERICAN CIVIL WAR, and in response to government encouragement, formed hundreds of companies. Rifle units usually wore green, artillery and cavalry blue in central Canada. On the Atlantic coast, the variety also extended to grey in many units. During the 1860s infantry units adopted scarlet with blue facings, rifle units green with red facings, artillery blue with red facings, and cavalry blue with buff facings. These are still the colours of the full-dress uniforms of most Canadian units. From the 1880s white pith helmets were popular. Highland dress also became established in several units. The SOUTH AFRICAN WAR brought khaki uniforms to the Canadian contingents, but tradition died hard and some newly raised western cavalry regiments could be seen in scarlet around 1910. With WWI and WWII, khaki and steel helmets (from 1916) became universal because the greatly increased accuracy of weapons made easy targets of brightly coloured uniforms. The Canadians usually adopted patterns similar to the British.

Royal Canadian Navy uniforms resembled those of the British Royal Navy from 1910 (the year the RCN was born), the distinction being "HMCS" instead of "HMS" on the caps. The Canadian Air Force first had dark blue dress in 1920 but adopted the British Royal Air Force's blue-grey in 1924. "RCAF" (Royal Canadian Air Force) replaced "RAF" on the uniforms, and all 3 services had "Canada" on the upper sleeve. With ARMED FORCES unification in 1968 came the "CF Green" uniform which was the subject of controversy until the Mulroney government announced in 1984 a reversion to separate uniforms.

Associated with smartness and efficiency in the 19th century, uniforms became the fashion in certain civilian occupations. Post office, customs, marine service, railway, steamship and hotel employees, prison guards and even milkmen were often dressed in dark blue. Nurses wore only white until recently. Policemen in Canada have usually worn dark blue, except for the famous scarlet of the ROYAL CANADIAN MOUNTED POLICE. The basic styling was of British inspiration, although American influence has lately been considerable. RENÉ CHARTRAND

Reading: W.Y. Carman, *British Military Uniforms* (1957); D. Ross, *Military Uniforms from the Collections of the New Brunswick Museum* (1980).

UniMédia Inc, controlled by Jacques Francoeur through Société générale de publications Inc, publishes 2 daily and 13 weekly NEWSPAPERS in Québec, including *Le Soleil* in Québec City and *Le Droit* in Ottawa-Hull. One of the 3 largest French-language newspaper chains in Québec, UniMédia controlled 12.5% of French-language circulation in 1980. UniMédia's other interests include newspaper and periodical distribution, printing and car rentals. PETER S. ANDERSON

Union Centrals, District and Regional, organizations which unite trade unions from different industries and occupations in the same city, province or region; usually formed in periods of intensifying industrial conflict, notably 1870 to

1890, 1910 to 1920 and 1935 to 1950. The first and most persistent form of inter-union co-operation was the city-based labour council. In 1863 Hamilton's craft unions launched Canada's first trades assembly. The Toronto Trades Assembly followed in 1871, and eventually most large municipalities had such organizations, usually known as Trades and Labour Councils. Before WWII these were important, since they met frequently and could act promptly on workers' concerns. They were usually responsible for initiatives to create larger, regional labour federations or labour parties. By 1900 another form of city-based organization was appearing: councils of skilled workers in allied trades in the same industry, especially printing, construction and metalwork.

Regional labour organizations were generally of 2 types. The first were provincial federations of unions in the same industry. Coal miners formed the Miners' Mutual Protective Society in BC in 1877 and the Provincial Workmen's Association in NS 2 years later. Beginning in the 1880s, other groups of workers created similar regional bodies within the structure of their international unions, in an effort to establish common terms of employment. These declined or disappeared after WWI.

The other common form of regional labour organization was the provincial federation, which united various local and district bodies within one province. Administered by an executive board and typically with few or no full-time staff, it would meet annually to discuss wage earners' concerns and to plan common programs of action, including independent electoral campaigns. It would also make regular representations to provincial governments for labour legislation.

The first labour organization claiming national jurisdiction, the Canadian Labor Union, was actually regional having no affiliates outside central Canada. Similarly the TRADES AND LABOR CONGRESS OF CANADA, which first met 1883, had no representation from outside Ontario and Québec until 1890, and it continued to be dominated by central Canada. At each TLC convention, provincial executives were elected to present the concerns of organized labour to their respective provincial governments.

The first distinct provincial federations were outside the TLC, and occasionally in opposition to its policies. BC's first provincial organizations were short-lived — the Workingmen's Protective Association, 1878-82, and the Federated Labor Congress, 1890-91. The Nova Scotia Provincial Workmen's Association (PWA) first expanded beyond the coalfields in 1881, reaching its broadest representation of workers 1899 to 1904. During the late 19th century the PWA published the *Trades Journal*, edited by Secretary Robert Drummond. After 1904 the association once again became purely a miners' union and in 1917 merged with the United Mine Workers of America.

The Labour Educational Association of Ontario, formed in 1903 outside the TLC structure, was a loosely knit body which promoted labour interests in southern Ontario, especially through the *Industrial Banner* edited by Secretary Joseph T. Marks. The association's fervent commitment to reform sometimes upset more narrow-minded Ontario trade unionists, and the TLC's provincial executive committee continued to assert its right to represent labour interests before the provincial government. The association had nonetheless assumed most of the functions of a provincial federation by WWI, and it organized the founding convention of the Independent Labor Party of Ontario in 1917.

Provincial federations chartered by the TLC were formed in BC in 1910, Alberta in 1911, New Brunswick in 1913 and Nova Scotia for the period 1919-21. The 2 western organizations

quickly became focal points of opposition to the TLC's dominant policies, particularly in their open support of radical socialism and industrial unionism. The BC labour paper, the *BC Federationist*, edited by R.P. Pettipiece, led this radical sentiment. After WWI the 2 bodies supported the ONE BIG UNION, which eventually dissolved the BC federation in 1920.

No new provincial federations appeared until 1935, when the TLC's rival, the All-Canadian Congress of Labour, chartered the NB Council of Labour. During the next 15 years, as the labour movement expanded dramatically and industrial unions were consolidated, provincial federations emerged in most provinces. Until 1956, however, there were separate provincial affiliates of the craft-unionist TLC and the industrial-unionist CANADIAN CONGRESS OF LABOUR: the TLC's Alberta and New Brunswick organizations were joined by parallel bodies in Québec in 1938, Ontario in 1946, Newfoundland in 1949, BC and Saskatchewan in 1953 and Nova Scotia and Manitoba in 1954; the CCL affiliates appeared in Nova Scotia in 1942, Ontario in 1943, BC in 1944, Saskatchewan in 1945, Alberta in 1948 and Québec in 1953. After the 1956 merger of the 2 national organizations, the separate provincial federations in each province amalgamated into a single labour body. The role of district and regional union centrals is now primarily political, representing workers' common interests to provincial governments, which hold most constitutional authority for LABOUR RELATIONS.   CRAIG HERON

Union Centrals, National (NUCs), organizations representing groups of trade unionists. Many 19th-century workers disliked being treated like commodities, and protested the long hours, low wages, dangerous conditions and heightened insecurity of factory work. They formed local trade unions to protect themselves and to compete with employers for control over increasingly mechanized workplaces. In the 1870s and 1880s, when Canadian federal and provincial governments introduced laws affecting relations between workers and employers, trade unionists joined American NUCs or established their own to express their political interests. NUC conventions were called to advocate new labour laws, to discuss ways to exert political influence, and to impress public officials. Revenue came from members through dues based on each union's Canadian membership. NUCs helped organize workers into new unions, resolved disputes between dissident locals and often published labour journals. Annual conventions followed traditional rules of order and familiarized workers with bureaucratic procedures. Over the years a cadre of Canadian WORKING-CLASS leaders emerged from NUC conventions.

The first NUC, the Canadian Labor Union (1873-77), was largely responsible for the 1874 election to the Ontario legislature of D.J. O'DONOGHUE, the "father" of Canadian trade unionism. The most successful of the early NUCs, the TRADES AND LABOR CONGRESS of Canada (1883-1956) organized by O'Donoghue and others, demanded an 8-hour day, universal manhood suffrage, factory Acts, employers' liability laws, and arbitration of industrial disputes. By 1900 some Canadians wished the TLC to become an independent national labour body, but in 1902 an overwhelming majority of its members, responding to American leaders, joined the American Federation of Labor. Thereafter, it generally reflected the policies of its larger American associate.

The National Trades and Labour Congress (1902-09), the CANADIAN FEDERATION OF LABOUR (1909-27) and the All-Canadian Congress of Labour (1927-40) were NUCs composed largely of organizations expelled from or hostile to AFL-

TLC affiliates. Lacking the TLC's resources, these NUCs won the adherence of relatively few Canadian workers. The Workers' Unity League, directed 1930-35 by the Communist Party of Canada, attracted over 40 000 members and provided a cadre of militant labour leaders during the Depression. Québec's Catholic Church rejected AFL-affiliated unions, and in 1921 established a church-controlled NUC. As clerical influence receded after WWII, that NUC's successor, the CONFEDERATION OF NATIONAL TRADE UNIONS (est 1960), began to resemble other NUCs. The CANADIAN CONGRESS OF LABOUR (1940-56) was launched by the American-based industrial unions with Canadian locals in steel, auto, electrical and other mass-production industries. These latter unions had been expelled from the TLC in 1939 upon AFL orders; their leaders generally supported the left-wing CO-OPERATIVE COMMONWEALTH FEDERATION.

During WWII NUC membership spiralled, aided by rapid INDUSTRIALIZATION, favourable government policies and Communist Party activists. Postwar difficulties, however, persuaded the American AFL and CIO to federate in 1955. A year later their Canadian affiliates, the TLC and CCL, merged into a new CANADIAN LABOUR CONGRESS. Promised complete freedom by the new American group, CLC leaders joined with the CCF in 1961 to form the NEW DEMOCRATIC PARTY to represent organized labour's interests in Canada. Canadian NUCs are vastly stronger (2.4 million members in the CLC; 210 000 in the CNTU) and more unified than a century ago. Canadian workers now toil under a panoply of protective laws. But NUC strength still varies greatly from province to province, well over half the work force is not yet enrolled in trade unions, and the NDP usually garners only a portion of the labour vote.   ROBERT H. BABCOCK

Union Centrals, Québec Québec has 4 groups of labour unions: the CONFEDERATION OF NATIONAL TRADE UNIONS (CNTU), fd 1921 as the Canadian Catholic Federation of Labour; the Québec Federation of Labour (QFL), which includes international unions and national affiliates of the CANADIAN LABOUR CONGRESS; the Québec Teachers' Corporation (QTC); and the Confederation of Democratic Unions (CDU), formed in a June 1972 break-away from the CNTU.

The most important association in Québec is the QFL, the CLC's Québec wing, with about 350 000 members (1981). Its member unions belong either to international unions affiliated with the AFL-CIO and headquartered in the US, or to Canadian unions such as the CANADIAN UNION OF PUBLIC EMPLOYEES or the Canadian Union of Postal Workers. The QFL provides union information and education, and represents workers affiliated with the CLC to other intermediary bodies and to the Québec government.

The QFL was the result of the 1957 merger of the Provincial Federation of Labour of Québec (PFLQ) and the Federation of Industrial Trade Unions of Québec (FITQ). This merger followed the 1955 example of the union between the American giants, the AFL and the CIO, and of their Canadian counterparts, the TRADES AND LABOR CONGRESS and the Canadian Congress of Labour, into the CLC. The orientation of the new QFL was more strongly influenced by the INDUSTRIAL UNIONS of the FITQ than by the CRAFT UNIONS of the PFLQ. The federation kept its distance from the DUPLESSIS government, supported the NDP and took some militant stands (eg, the 1957 MURDOCHVILLE STRIKE).

The QFL changed significantly 1964 to 1965, when Louis LABERGE became president and the position of permanent secretary-general was created. Threatened by the CNTU (in both membership and influence), the QFL toughened its criticism of the capitalist system and of governmental action, publishing such manifestos as

L'État, rouage de notre exploitation (1971) and *Le combat inévitable* (1973). It participated in major strikes, including that at *La Presse* in 1971, the United Aircraft strike and the strikes of the public sector common front. It accepted Québec nationalism and publicly supported the PARTI QUÉBÉCOIS in 1976 and 1981. This nationalism has led it to seek greater independence from the CLC and to conduct itself at times as if it were a purely Québec federation.   JACQUES ROUILLARD

Union Government In early 1917, during WORLD WAR I, recruitment for the CANADIAN EXPEDITIONARY FORCE fell to a very low level. PM Sir Robert BORDEN, opposed to any reduction in Canada's commitment to the war effort, announced on 18 May 1917 that the government would introduce CONSCRIPTION to Canada. On May 25 he proposed to Liberal leader Sir Wilfrid LAURIER that the Liberals and Conservatives form a COALITION GOVERNMENT to carry through the measure. After Laurier rejected the proposal on June 6, Borden tried to strengthen his government by bringing in individual Liberals and prominent political independents. His early efforts met with little success. In late summer, however, the WARTIME ELECTIONS ACT and the Military Voters' Act appeared to increase the political prospects for a government supporting conscription. These Acts, together with strong pro-conscription sentiment in the English press and personal convictions that overrode party boundaries, made several Liberals and independents decide to accept Borden's suggestion. On Oct 12 Borden announced the formation of a Union government made up of 12 Conservatives, 9 Liberals or independents, and one labour representative. A general election in Dec 1917 gave the Unionists a large majority.

After its election victory, the Union government began to weaken. The end of the war in Nov 1918 destroyed the reason for unionism in the minds of many adherents. Many Unionists returned to the Liberal Party or joined the new PROGRESSIVE PARTY. Although the Union government was a coalition of varied political interests, many Canadians of non-British background still blamed Borden and the Conservative Party for conscription. The results of Unionist policies included an enduring Conservative weakness among French Canadians and many others of non-British descent — a weakness that contrasted with renewed Liberal strength in French Canada under Laurier's successor as Liberal leader, Mackenzie KING. With Borden's retirement in July 1920, Union government ended.   JOHN ENGLISH

Union Nationale, originally a coalition of the Conservative Party and the ACTION LIBÉRALE NATIONALE, formed to contest the 1935 provincial election in Québec. The coalition's leaders were Maurice DUPLESSIS of the Conservative Party and Paul Gouin of the ALN. Narrowly defeated in 1935, the Union Nationale became a single party under Duplessis's leadership, and easily won the 1936 provincial election. Born during the GREAT DEPRESSION, the Union Nationale at first preached social, economic and political reform. It was defeated by the Liberal Party in 1939, after a campaign in which federal Liberals in Québec argued that they were the ones to protect French Canadians from CONSCRIPTION. The Union Nationale under Duplessis was elected again in 1944, having accused the Liberals, provincial and federal, of betraying Québec's rights. This nationalistic emphasis was to be characteristic of the party thereafter. The Union Nationale was completely dominated by Duplessis until his death in Sept 1959; it was then led by Paul SAUVÉ until his death less than 4 months later. It lost the 1960 election and has held power only once since then (1966-70). The death in 1968 of its leader, Daniel JOHNSON, was a heavy blow, and the government of the new leader J-Jacques

BERTRAND was defeated by a resurgent Liberal Party under Robert BOURASSA in 1970. Supplanted by the PARTI QUÉBÉCOIS as the nationalist party, the UN has never won more than 20% of the vote in subsequent elections.

The Union Nationale won its major support from rural voters, small- and medium-scale businessmen and unorganized labour. Anglophone voters distrusted the party and it had greater success in Québec City than in Montréal. During the 1940s and 1950s, the size of its electoral funding, most of it donated by business, gave it a significant advantage over the Liberal opposition. This advantage disappeared after the party's defeat in 1960 and the reform of electoral practices in Québec. *See* FRENCH CANADIAN NATIONALISM.   VINCENT LEMIEUX

Reading: Herbert F. Quinn, *The Union Nationale* (1970).

Union Station, Toronto, was designed by architects Ross and Macdonald, Hugh G. JONES and John M. LYLE for the GRAND TRUNK RAILWAY OF CANADA and CANADIAN PACIFIC RAILWAY. Construction began in 1915 and continued until 1920. The design and interior details of the building show the influence of the beaux-arts style, which greatly marked N American public architecture of the early 20th century. The building's long facade is divided into 7 sections, and the central portion is distinguished by a long Doric colonnade framed by 2 small projecting porticos. The facade ends in 2 slightly jutting sections with inset pilasters. The ground floor, designed by Lyle, includes a vast hall that contains the ticket windows and various services; it is notable for its huge proportions, vaulted ceiling, materials and colours, and the Canadian inspiration of its decoration.
     NATHALIE CLERK

Reading: R. Bédout, *The Open Gate: Toronto Union Station* (1982).

Unions, *see* CRAFT UNIONISM; INDUSTRIAL UNIONISM; LABOUR ORGANIZATIONS; LABOUR RELATIONS; REVOLUTIONARY INDUSTRIAL UNIONISM; UNION CENTRALS; WORKING-CLASS HISTORY; and articles on individual unions.

Unitarians, adherents to a religious movement which originated in 16th-century Europe and whose members profess a holistic approach to religion. This has been theologically expressed in an emphasis upon the undivided unity of God, though many Unitarians now prefer to use nontheological language. The movement began within CHRISTIANITY but now brings together people from various religious traditions in a spirit of unity in diversity. Individual responsibility for faith and action is stressed, as are reason and personal experience as guides. Most early Unitarians in Canada came from Britain, though New Englanders constituted a strong influence in Montréal, where the first congregation was established in 1832. Throughout the 19th century this remained Canada's leading congregation, including in its membership such prominent persons as Sir Francis HINCKS, John YOUNG, Adam Ferrie and Luther Holton. Joseph WORKMAN, Canadian pioneer in psychiatry, was one founder of the Toronto congregation in 1845. Later a Unitarian movement developed among Icelandic settlers in Manitoba. The tradition of progressive leadership in social and cultural life continued in the 20th century, so that Unitarian influence on politics and society grew more rapidly than membership. Each of the 46 local societies is autonomous and democratically organized, but in 1961 the Canadian Unitarian Council was formed to supplement denominational ties with the American and British movements. Worldwide links are maintained through the International Association for Religious Freedom. The 1981 census showed 14 500 Unitarians in Canada.   PHILLIP HEWETT

United Church of Canada, formed 10 June 1925 by union of the PRESBYTERIAN Church in

Canada, the METHODIST Church (Canada, Nfld and Bermuda), the CONGREGATIONAL CHURCHES of Canada, and the General Council of Local Union Churches. This last represented a group of congregations, mainly in Saskatchewan, that had come together in anticipation of the larger union. A few Congregational churches and roughly one-third of the Presbyterians voted to stay out of the union. In 1968 the United Church was joined by the (eastern) Canada Conference of the Evangelical United Brethren Church (which originated in Methodist-style revivalism among German-speaking settlers in the US in the late 18th century), while the Western Canada Conference remained out. The United is Canada's largest Protestant church, with a confirmed membership of approximately 900 000 and a total constituency of 3 758 000 (1981c); since the mid-1960s membership has declined substantially. The most self-consciously Canadian of all churches, in principle it includes all ethnic groups. The bulk of its members are of British descent, however, and about 10 times as many live in Ontario as in Québec.

United Church policy, declared in its Basis of Union and reaffirmed 1935, is to be "not merely a united, but a uniting Church." Conversations looking to union with the Anglican Church (*see* ANGLICANISM) of Canada began in 1944 and were broadened in 1969 to include the CHRISTIAN CHURCH (DISCIPLES OF CHRIST). Discussions broke down with the former body in 1975, but continue with the latter. Another joint committee is exploring closer relations with Roman CATHOLICS. The United Church has been committed to ecumenism from the outset and has been active in the CANADIAN COUNCIL OF CHURCHES and the World Council of Churches since their formation. It also participates in the World Alliance of Reformed Churches and the World Methodist Council.

The section on doctrine in the Basis of Union, with which candidates for ordination must express "essential agreement," is couched in the traditional language of EVANGELICAL Protestantism. In 1940 the church published an unofficial statement of faith that placed more emphasis on personal and less on legal relations with God. In 1969 it issued, as supplementary to more traditional statements, a creed intended to express the Christian faith in terms both ecumenically acceptable and readily understandable today. In practice the United Church embraces a wide spectrum of belief. "Liberal" views have tended to predominate, but recent years have seen a resurgence of conservative evangelicalism. CHARISMATIC RENEWAL is also influential, and in some segments of the church there is a heightened appreciation of sacramental worship.

Church government is conciliar, consisting of legislative bodies or "courts" in ascending sequence from 2391 pastoral charges through 92 presbyteries and 12 conferences to a biennial general council. Congregations elect their own officers, elders for spiritual affairs and stewards for financial matters. Regional and national bodies consist of laypersons and members of the order of ministry in approximately equal numbers. Although the higher courts determine church policy and legislate on matters of more than local concern, congregations are largely self-governing. By contrast, administration has been highly centralized in Toronto. The present trend is to decentralization; each conference now has its own staff and determines its financial priorities. Some members of the order of ministry are ordained, others commissioned to educational or other forms of service. Congregations normally choose their own ministers, although the church has some voice in appointments. Women may hold any office, including since 1936 the ordained ministry. There are now more than 400 ordained women, and in 1980 Dr Lois M. Wilson was elected the first woman moderator. Dr Robert B. MCCLURE, for many years a medical missionary in China, the Middle East and India, has been the only lay moderator.

Voluntary organizations have always been most successful among women. In 1962 the long-established Woman's Missionary Society combined with the Woman's Association, which had specialized in local fund raising, to form United Church Women. At the time of its founding this was the largest women's organization in Canada, but dislike of sexual segregation has seriously eroded its appeal. The most successful program for men has been AOTS ("As one that serves"), a semiofficial Christian service club. United Church Men, an organization more closely tied to the church, has not caught on to the same extent.

Theological education is carried out at 6 centres, usually in close association with other denominations. Other institutions help to equip lay persons for leadership or provide continuing education for ministers. The United Church inherited, chiefly from the Methodists, a tradition of involvement in secular education. Today, it has official relations of some kind with 4 universities, 4 university-based colleges, and 7 secondary schools. Another Methodist legacy was RYERSON PRESS, which for many years under the editorship of Lorne PIERCE encouraged the development of Canadian literature, both religious and secular.

The United Church was brought into being largely by the conviction that only a strong, broad fellowship could meet the needs of Canada's scattered and diverse population. Accordingly, it has always accepted challenges that seemed to belong specifically to no other denomination, maintaining rescue homes, port chaplaincies, mission boats, hospitals in isolated areas, and ministries among various ethnic groups including native peoples, as well as aiding financially an unusually high proportion of isolated rural congregations. Overseas, the former pattern of mission fields supplied and directed from Canada has been replaced by one of partnership with indigenous churches, none of which represents precisely the same blend of denominational backgrounds as the United Church. Missionaries serve in various countries as need arises, always at the request and under the supervision of the receiving church.

The United Church is probably best known by most Canadians for its outspokenness on moral and social issues, often at the cost of alienating members. Dr James R. Mutchmor, secretary for evangelism and social service 1938-63, attracted much publicity by his denunciations of liquor, gambling and pornography, but also guided the church to progressive stands on such issues as LABOUR RELATIONS and the treatment of prisoners. Since his time there has been a shift from personal morality to social justice, which is now usually promoted in collaboration with other denominations. One of the United Church's persistent problems has been in holding together evangelism and social service, to each of which it is historically committed. On the whole it has been more effective in developing a prophetic critique of society than in inspiring the formulation of constructive theology, although there are signs of renewed interest in the resources inherent in its traditions. *See also* SOCIAL GOSPEL.

JOHN WEBSTER GRANT

United Farmers of Alberta, a farmers' organization established Jan 1909 in Edmonton as an amalgamation of the Canadian Society of Equity and the Alberta Farmers' Association. The UFA was interested in rural economic, social and political issues. In 1913 it prompted the provincial Liberal government to organize the Alberta Farmers' Co-operative Elevator Co, which in 1917 joined with the Grain Growers' Grain Co to form United Grain Growers. In 1915

it organized the United Farm Women of Alberta, which energetically campaigned for WOMEN'S SUFFRAGE (gained in Alberta in 1916) and struggled to secure better education and health services in rural Alberta. In 1916 the American NON-PARTISAN LEAGUE came to the province and encouraged direct political action by farmers. Close ties developed between the league and the UFA, which entered politics amid postwar unrest. The UFA was elected in 1921 and remained in office until 1935. It formed a cautious, pragmatic government which advanced educational and health services and attempted to meet the financial and marketing needs of farmers, but did not cope well with the GREAT DEPRESSION.

The most powerful early force in the UFA was Henry Wise WOOD, a charismatic farmer from Carstairs. He supported group government, but refused to lead the UFA when it was elected. UFA premier 1921 to 1925 was Herbert GREENFIELD, followed by John BROWNLEE (1925 to 1934) and R.G. REID; Reid held office until the 1935 victory of SOCIAL CREDIT. After 1935 the UFA avoided direct political involvement but continued to provide supplies to members through local co-operatives. In 1948 it became the United Farmers of Alberta Co-operative Ltd, today one of the strongest farmer-owned organizations in Alberta.   IAN MACPHERSON

United Farmers of Canada, a militant farmers' organization est 1926 as the United Farmers of Canada (Saskatchewan Section). It combined the radical Farmers' Union of Canada and the more conservative Saskatchewan GRAIN GROWERS' ASSOCIATION. During the late 1920s it led the unsuccessful but intense campaign for "the 100% pool," a system in which governments would market all grain. The UFC maintained strong educational programs for rural people, championed the cause of orderly marketing, and called for extensive reform of the educational and medical systems. During the 1930s the UFC(SS) became dominated by radicals who favoured political action. In 1931 it entered politics on a moderate SOCIALIST platform and in 1932, along with the Independent Labour Party, formed the Farmer-Labour Group. In 1934 the Farmer-Labour Group became the Saskatchewan Section of the CO-OPERATIVE COMMONWEALTH FEDERATION. In 1938 the UFC (Alberta Section) was formed by radical members of the declining UNITED FARMERS OF ALBERTA. In 1943 the Alberta association, in an effort to gain broader support, reorganized as the Alberta Farmers' Union. The UFC(SS) was a powerful force until re-organization in 1949 as the Saskatchewan Farmers' Union. In 1960, along with farmers' unions from other provinces, it helped form the NATIONAL FARMERS UNION, in which the provincial unions held membership. In 1969 the provincial unions (except Alberta) dissolved and the NFU became a national direct-membership organization.   IAN MACPHERSON

United Farmers of Manitoba, fd 1920, an inclusive farmers' organization which replaced the Manitoba Grain Growers' Assn. It supported farmer candidates in the 1920 provincial election and in 1922 succeeded in installing John BRACKEN's government (1922-43). In 1921 the UFM supported 12 successful candidates of the PROGRESSIVE PARTY, but withdrew direct backing in 1924. It was financed by members and by occasional grants from farmers' companies. UFM membership varied from 15 700 in 1923 to 3700 in 1931. Responding to an emphasis upon co-operative marketing bodies, by 1928 it had absorbed the Farmers' Union of Canada (Manitoba Section) and rejected political affiliations. The UFM successfully upheld co-operative marketing, government intervention in transportation and a central bank, but failed to alter the tariff structure, Cabinet government or party politics. In 1939 it became the Manitoba Federation of

Agriculture, now the Manitoba Farm Bureau. *See* GRAIN GROWERS' ASSOCIATIONS.   G.E. PANTING

United Farmers of Ontario, a farmers' educational, social and political organization formed Mar 1914 in Toronto. The UFO united several small Ontario co-operatives, the Grange and the Farmers' Association. Immediately after the founding of the UFO, the same farmers organized a "twin" company, the United Farmers' Co-operative, to buy supplies and sell produce for Ontario farmers. The UFO grew slowly until late in WWI, when labour shortages, inflated costs and a general dissatisfaction with existing political parties led to a rapid growth in membership. Auxiliary organizations, the United Farm Women and the United Farm Young People, helped to mobilize rural areas.

In 1919, with over 50 000 members, the UFO entered politics and won a plurality in the provincial election. E.C. DRURY, a Barrie farmer and longtime rural leader, was chosen premier. The UFO-labour coalition formed an honest and efficient, if unimaginative, administration that significantly improved rural education, transportation and hydroelectric services. After its defeat in 1923 the UFO declined steadily. Maintaining the enthusiasms of the early period proved difficult; many effective farm leaders were drawn to work with the United Farmers Co-operative, and the destruction of the federal PROGRESSIVE PARTY was disheartening. During the 1930s, under the idealistic leadership of Agnes MACPHAIL, H.H. Hannam and Leonard Harman, the UFO organized folk schools and supported the *Farmer's Sun* and the *Rural Co-operator*, and promoted orderly marketing. It briefly supported the CO-OPERATIVE COMMONWEALTH FEDERATION. In 1944 the UFO joined with other farm groups to form the Ontario Federation of Agriculture. In 1948 the United Farmers' Co-operative became the United Co-operatives of Ontario, today one of the largest farmer-owned companies in Canada.   IAN MACPHERSON

United Farmers of Quebec (Fermiers unis du Québec) PM Borden's decision to conscript farm youths caused a huge farmers' demonstration in Ottawa on 15 May 1918 and gave Québec farmers their first contact with the United Farmers movement in English Canada. By July some 20 local associations had sprung up in western Québec. In Sept the Interprovincial Union of Farmers was established as an umbrella for the local organizations. In Jan 1920, 300 farmers voted in Montréal to transform the union into the United Farmers of Quebec. In 1921 the United Farmers had some 5000 members in over 20 counties. That year they joined with the Union des cultivateurs du Québec (fd in 1919) to form the Parti fermier-progressiste du Québec (Progressive Farmers of Québec). They had the support of Joseph-Noé Ponton and his *Bulletin des agriculteurs*. Their detailed program followed the main lines of the progressive movement, but also incorporated elements of Henri BOURASSA's nationalist movement.

The PFQ supported 21 candidates in the federal election of Dec 1921, but none was elected. The Liberals called them Conservatives in disguise, tools of that shameful symbol of CONSCRIPTION, Arthur MEIGHEN. Liberals swept the province; the farmers won a meagre 42 000 votes (11%). They never recovered from this defeat. The apolitical Catholic Union of Farmers (fd in 1924) became the dominant farmers' association and marked the end of the Progressive Farmers.

RENÉ DUROCHER

United Nations, a loosely co-ordinated international system of deliberatory bodies, functional agencies, and temporary and permanent commissions with headquarters in New York, Geneva, and elsewhere. In structure it resembles the LEAGUE OF NATIONS but with a more nearly universal membership. The term was first used

1 Jan 1942 when 26 nations pledged to continue fighting the Axis powers. The UN Charter was drawn up by 50 countries, including Canada, in San Francisco in the spring of 1945. By that time powerful functional agencies such as the International Monetary Fund, the International Civil Aviation Organization, and the Food and Agriculture Organization were already being established, linked to the UN system but with considerable autonomy. For this reason and because the smaller powers resisted the great powers' intention to direct the organization, the UN has proved its adaptability to changing circumstances.

The main organs are the General Assembly of all 156 member states (1982), each having one vote; the Security Council of 15 members, in which 5 great powers have permanent seats and the power of veto; and the Economic and Social Council of 27 members. Although the Security Council was assumed to be stronger than the other organs, which only recommend, the power of any UN bodies to enforce decisions is limited by the need for consensus among members and their willingness to impose military or economic sanctions. The secretary general is bound by decisions of the constituent organs. After one effort to enforce its will in the KOREAN WAR, the Security Council has concentrated on peaceful settlement, including the provision of PEACEKEEPING forces, in which Canadians have played a major role.

Although security was the founders' major consideration, economic and social questions now prevail. The increasing membership of developing countries has directed the attention of most UN bodies to programs of aid and development and recently to devising a "New International Economic Order." Much effort also goes into formulating, negotiating, and extending international conventions and law. The International Court of Justice at The Hague, Netherlands, is an autonomous organ of the UN, settling international cases referred to it. Slow progress in the more complex issues of peace and prosperity has concealed the very considerable success of the UN agencies in laying an infrastructure of rules for communication, travel, commerce, space law, etc.

The UN is essentially a network of institutions for multilateral diplomacy rather than world government. Techniques and patterns of international bargaining have been developed which circumvent the stalemates of formal voting in the main organs, although negotiation is frustrating and perpetual. The principal purpose of the system is to maintain contact between nations, and to avoid the renunciation of the centuries-old effort to create a world order.

Canada was active as a MIDDLE POWER in the founding of the UN organs and has served frequently on the Security Council, ECOSOC, and other bodies. In the first decade it had notable successes in mediatory diplomacy culminating in a solution to the SUEZ CRISIS of 1956 for which L.B. PEARSON won a Nobel Prize. Its influence has inevitably been diluted as the membership grows, but the Canadian contribution has remained effective, if less spectacular, in the kind of multilateral diplomacy which has come to preoccupy the UN, particularly in such matters as commerce, space, coastal waters, and multinational corporations, in which it has special interest and experience. JOHN W. HOLMES

Reading: D. Roche, *United Nations: Divided World* (1984).

United Nations Conference on Trade and Development (UNCTAD), est in 1964 as a permanent organ of the UN General Assembly to promote international trade, with an emphasis on speeding the economic development of developing nations. Total membership (1982) was 166 nation states, including Canada. It has attempted to secure remunerative, equitable and stable prices for primary commodities on which developing countries depend heavily for export earnings; to expand and diversify exports of manufactured products of developing countries; to establish equitable principles for control of restrictive business practices; to improve terms of aid and reduce debt problems of developing countries; and to reach an International Code on the Transfer of Technology. The permanent machinery of UNCTAD consists of the Trade & Development Board which has 6 main committees. The UNCTAD permanent secretariat, located in Geneva, is headed by a secretary-general.
GREGORY WIRICK

Université de Moncton was founded 19 June 1963 by the New Brunswick legislature in accordance with the recommendations of a royal commission. U de Moncton began with the amalgamation of 3 institutions, which agreed to suspend their charters in order to become affiliated colleges: Saint-Joseph (fd 1864), Sacré-Coeur (1899) and Saint-Louis (1946). As amended in 1977, the university's charter authorized campuses in each of New Brunswick's 3 francophone regions, in Moncton, Edmundston and Shippegan. Its academic programs are divided among 5 faculties (arts, science and engineering, administration, education and postgraduate studies) and 4 schools (law, social sciences, nutrition and family studies, and nursing). CLEMENT CORMIER

Enrolment: Université de Moncton, 1982-83
(Source: Statistics Canada)

Full-time Undergrad	Full-time Graduate	Part-time Undergrad	Part-time Graduate
3 288	212	2 000	124

Université de Montréal, Montréal, Qué, was founded in 1876 and opened in 1878 as a branch of UNIVERSITÉ LAVAL of Québec. Its 4 schools were law, medicine, theology and arts. In 1920 the Montréal institution became a full and independent university known as Université de Montréal. For almost a century, U de M was a private, denominational university governed by the Roman Catholic Church. In 1967 the Québec government passed a bill making it a nondenominational university with a public character. Today, U de M is the largest Québec university, with 13 faculties, 60 departments, schools or institutes and affiliated schools of commerce (Ecole des hautes études commerciales) and engineering (Ecole polytechnique). It offers a wide range of undergraduate and graduate programs in all disciplines except agriculture and forestry. Research activities are being carried on in all academic units and in 20 specialized centres or groups; in 1982-83, the value of research grants made to the university and its affiliated institutions was close to $60 million. Every year, U de M awards over 4500 bachelor's degrees, 1500 master's degrees or graduate studies certificates and 150 PhD degrees. RÉJEAN PLAMONDON

The Université de Montréal, founded in 1876, is now the largest university in Québec, with 13 faculties and 60 departments, institutes and affiliated schools *(photo by Derek Caron/Masterfile).*

Enrolment: Université de Montréal and Affiliates, 1982-83
(Source: Statistics Canada)

Full-time Undergrad	Full-time Graduate	Part-time Undergrad	Part-time Graduate
	Université de Montréal		
11 480	3 065*	17 738	4 071
	École polytechnique		
2 696	216	839	617
	École hautes études commerciales		
1 561	174	5 478	923

* Includes medical interns and residents

Université de Sherbrooke, Sherbrooke, Qué, is a French-language institution fd in 1954. Formed from the Séminaire St-Charles Borromée, the university expanded from its initial 3-faculty core (arts, law and science) in order to meet university education needs in the Eastern Townships. Today, it has 9 faculties (administration, arts, law, education, physical education and sports, medicine, theology, science and applied science), one branch (continuing education) and a school of music. The university offers bachelor's, master's and doctoral programs in social sciences, humanities, physical sciences and health sciences. Its broad range of programs, which focus on specific professional training and more general studies, attracts students from across Québec. It was the first university in Québec and the second in Canada to adopt a cooperative teaching system, now offered to over 2000 students. It ranks second among Québec universities and among the top 10 Canadian universities in research expenditures (proportionate to size). The university has 2 campuses and offers a complete range of cultural and sports facilities. MARC BERNIER

Enrolment: Université de Sherbrooke, 1982-83
(Source: Statistics Canada)

Full-time Undergrad	Full-time Graduate	Part-time Undergrad	Part-time Graduate
6 027	1 558*	3 214	—

* Includes medical interns and residents

Université du Québec, a multi-campus university, was founded on 18 Dec 1968 as Québec's first public university, its ninth institution of higher learning and its sixth in the French language. U du Québec was conceived as a vital element in the reform of Québec's educational system which has seen, over a period of 10 years, a reorganization of the elementary, secondary and post-secondary (collegiate) levels. U du Québec can have, according to the law, 3 major types of units: constituent universities, research institutes and superior schools. Each constituent bears a general responsibility for carrying out teaching and research activities with programs leading to the bachelor's, master's and doctoral degrees in most areas of the applied and pure sciences, business administration, the social sciences, the humanities and the arts. The superior schools and research institutes were devised as instruments of development for Québec academic and scientific communities, not only within U du Québec, but for the general public and other universities as well.

The U du Québec system includes 6 constituent universities, in Montréal, Trois-Rivières, Chicoutimi, Rimouski, Hull and Rouyn; 2 research institutes, the Institut national de la recherche scientifique, with research centres throughout the province, and the INSTITUT ARMAND-FRAPPIER in Ville de Laval; and 2 superior schools, Ecole nationale d'administration publique in Québec City and, specializing in the training and development of public administrators, Ecole de technologie supérieure in Montréal. Also considered a unit of U du Québec is the Télé-université, which offers study programs enabling students throughout Québec to study without having to go to a university campus (*see* DISTANCE LEARNING). These institutions now have a combined enrolment of more than 70 000 students. By 1984 U du Québec had given over 80 000 diplomas and that year had an operating budget of $320 million.   GILLES BOULET

Enrolment: Université du Québec (total)
and Constituents, 1982-83
(Source: Statistics Canada)

Full-time Undergrad	Full-time Graduate	Part-time Undergrad	Part-time Graduate
*Université du Québec**			
20 319	1 379	37 495	2 292
à Chicoutimi			
2 292	87	4 022	143
à Hull			
902	10	2 892	200
à Montréal			
10 833	864	13 825	1 043
à Rimouski			
1 497	63	2 725	112
à Trois-Rivières			
3 946	209	4 097	376
à Rouyn			
380	11	1 796	12
École de technologie supérieure			
469	—	536	—
École nationale d'administration publique			
—	74	—	350
Institut Armand-Frappier			
—	10	4	29
Institut national de la recherche scientifique			
—	51	—	27
Télé-université			
—	—	7 598	—

* Figures show totals of all constituent parts

Université Laval, the first francophone Roman Catholic university in N America, was founded 8 Dec 1852 in Québec City by priests of the SÉMINAIRE DE QUÉBEC, who named the institution after their founder, Mgr François de LAVAL. A century later the university gradually relocated to the present campus in Ste-Foy, a Québec City suburb. In 1983 the university had 12 faculties, 9 schools and 15 research centres.

The university originally consisted of the faculties of theology, medicine, law and arts, and served not only the area around Québec City, but also the rest of the province. In 1876 the university established a satellite campus in Montréal with similar faculties. In 1919 this satellite became an independent university (*see* UNIVERSITÉ DE MONTRÉAL), the civil status of which was recognized 14 Feb 1920.

From 1852 to 1935, Laval administered education through its faculties. Québec's *collèges classiques* were affiliated with the Faculty of Arts. The bachelor of arts degree, which was awarded upon completion of college studies, was a prerequisite for admission to the faculties of theology, medicine and law. Beginning in 1907, the Faculty of Arts established a number of schools, some of which were subsequently recognized as faculties.

The Faculty of Theology drew students from Québec's Grand Séminaire, and based its teachings on the directives of the Roman Congregation of Seminaries and Universities. Its professors, most of whom were graduates of the Roman universities, believed it their duty to espouse the most rigorously orthodox Roman Catholic Church doctrine in their teaching. Some professors of law and medicine had also received part of their education abroad, usually in Paris. It was not until the end of WWII that young doctors and law graduates planning a career in university teaching preferred instead to go to the US or London, and the university's law and medicine programs consequently became more closely associated with American and English programs than with those of France.

The graduate schools, which had links with the Faculty of Arts, were created in the early 20th century. In 1935 the graduate school of philosophy became the Faculty of Philosophy. Between then and 1965, 7 other schools left the Faculty of Arts to become separate faculties: science, literature, agriculture, social sciences, forestry, commerce and education.

In late 1968 a reform commission was established to enable the university better to meet the needs of society, the requirements of university teaching and the aspirations of the student body. This commission drew up a new charter, which was adopted by the Government of Québec on 8 Dec 1970, but the charter could not be given force of law until complemented by new statutes. On 1 Sept 1971 the first statutes were laid out and the new charter promulgated, thus bringing into being the new Université Laval. The new university corporation was characterized by a democratic system at all levels, and emphasis was placed on the participation of all parties in planning and decision making. Undergraduate students are encouraged to play a role in deciding the shape of their education; postgraduate research students see the fruits of these efforts in well-organized seminars and laboratories.

Université Laval has resolutely committed itself to the quest for excellence and progressive thinking through the participation of students and professors, liberalized study regulations and the thrust given to research.   PHILIPPE SYLVAIN

Enrolment: Université Laval, 1982-83
(Source: Statistics Canada)

Full-time Undergrad	Full-time Graduate	Part-time Undergrad	Part-time Graduate
15 801	3 097*	5 193	2 061

* Includes medical interns and residents

Université Sainte-Anne, Church Point, NS, was founded in 1890 by the Eudist Fathers. Instruction is in French and English. The only francophone university in Nova Scotia, Université Sainte-Anne is a liberal arts institution offering BA degrees with majors in French, English, history, psychology, sociology, commerce and Canadian studies; a BEd in French education; a bachelor of business administration with a specialization in small business management; the first 2 years of the BSc degree; diplomas in secretarial sciences, community development, business and computing science. The university is well known for its immersion programs. It has special research and teaching programs in Acadian language, culture and history, Maritime studies, and scientific programs of regional interest. The university became nondenominational in 1971. The university had 178 full-time and 141 part-time students in 1982-83.

University Universities are post-secondary institutions invested with degree-granting power. Canada's earliest universities had strong religious affiliations and were generally modelled on European institutions. The 3 King's Colleges (est at Windsor, NS, 1789; York [Toronto], 1827; and Fredericton, NB, 1828) were efforts to bring the ideals of the older English universities to Canada. They were residential, tutorial and Anglican. The more democratic ideals of the Scottish universities were evident in varying degrees in DALHOUSIE UNIVERSITY (Halifax, 1818), QUEEN'S UNIVERSITY (Kingston, 1841) and MCGILL UNIVERSITY (Montréal, 1821). The Methodist (Victoria College, Cobourg, Ont, 1841; MOUNT ALLISON UNIVERSITY, Sackville, NB, 1839) and Baptist (ACADIA UNIVERSITY, Wolfville, NS, 1838) institutions were designed to prepare men for the ministry and to supply education for lay members. Bishop's College which later became BISHOP'S UNIVERSITY was established by the Anglicans in 1843. Roman Catholics maintained their own ethos at the English-language SAINT FRANCIS XAVIER, established at Antigonish, NS, in 1866. Laval was established in 1852 by the SÉMINAIRE DE QUÉBEC, a college founded by Bishop LAVAL in 1663. Laval established a branch in Montréal in 1876, which became UNIVERSITÉ DE MONTRÉAL in 1920.

At the time of Confederation, 1867, 17 degree-granting institutions existed in the founding provinces. Four had a nondenominational basis (Dalhousie, McGill, New Brunswick, UNIVERSITY OF TORONTO); the remaining 13 were church related and controlled. Thirteen of the 17 had enrolments of about 100 students. One way of strengthening this multiplicity of small and financially insecure institutions was by consolidation. In 1868 the Ontario government, by withdrawing financial support, pressured its denominational universities to consider co-operation with the public sector. The 3 church universities that federated with U of T (Victoria College and St Michael's College in 1890; Trinity College in 1904) maintained university status and autonomy in instruction and staffing, but agreed to restrict their offerings to the sensitive and less costly liberal arts subjects (eg, classics, philosophy, English literature, history, modern languages, mathematics, science and theology); responsibility for instruction in all other areas and for the granting of degrees (except in theology) rested with the public university. The federative model, adopted by other Canadian universities in the course of their development, represents a Canadian solution to the problem of reconciling religiosity and secularism, diversity and economic pragmatism.

The western provinces adopted a policy of controlled university development from the beginning. In Manitoba this took the form of combining 3 existing church colleges — St Boniface (Roman Catholic), St John's (Anglican) and Manitoba College (Presbyterian) — under one umbrella. Eleven years after the founding of UNIVERSITY OF MANITOBA (1877) a fourth college, Wesley College (Methodist), was affiliated. In each of the other 3 western provinces a single, public provincial university was created (*see* UNIVERSITY OF ALBERTA, 1906, UNIVERSITY OF SASKATCHEWAN, 1907 and UNIVERSITY OF BRITISH COLUMBIA, 1908). The 3 western provinces adopted as their model the American state university, with its emphasis on extension work and applied research.

The growth of public higher EDUCATION raised the issue of university protection against government interference (*see* ACADEMIC FREEDOM). The pattern of university-government relationships adopted throughout much of Canada was influenced by the provincial University of Toronto Act of 1906, which established a bicameral system of university government consisting of a senate (faculty), responsible for academic policy, and a board of governors (citizens) exercising exclusive control over financial policy and having formal authority in all other matters. The role of the president, appointed by the board, was to provide a link between the 2 bodies and to furnish active institutional leadership. Other important developments in the early part of this century were the expansion of professional education beyond the traditional fields of theology, law and medicine and, to a more limited extent, the introduction of graduate training based on the German-inspired American model of specialized course work and the completion of a research thesis.

By 1939 the number of degree-granting universities in Canada had increased to 28, varying in size from U of T, with full-time enrolment of 7000, to those with fewer than 1000 students. There were 40 000 students, representing 5% of the population between ages 18 and 24. Most universities were regional institutions; only McGill and Toronto had attained an international reputation for research. There was no systematic policy concerning higher education and funding was established year by year. Except for the natural sciences, there was no federal or provincial grant agency providing regular support for graduate work and research. A few LEARNED SOCIETIES and academic journals had been established.

WWII marked the slow beginning of a new era in Canadian higher education. The war effort generated a high demand for scientific research and highly trained personnel (many of whom were imported into Canada) and this brought appreciation for the vital importance to the nation of the university sector. In the immediate postwar period the federal government began to provide some financial assistance to the universities to help them deal with the influx of veterans. As a result of a veterans' rehabilitation program, 53 000 veterans entered university between 1944 and 1951. When the expected return to much lower student enrolments failed to occur, the federal government, following the advice of the Massey Commission, became involved in 1951 in the regular provision of financial support to higher education (*see* NATIONAL DEVELOPMENT IN THE ARTS, LETTERS AND SCIENCES, ROYAL COMMISSION ON).

By the early 1950s the size of the university student population was twice that of 1940 and by 1963 another doubling had taken place. With much larger increases projected as a result of the BABY BOOM, provincial governments abandoned their initial strategy of trying to meet these increases by expanding existing institutions. The single-university policy in the West was changed as existing colleges of the provincial universities gained autonomy as universities: UNIVERSITY OF VICTORIA (1963), UNIVERSITY OF CALGARY (1966), UNIVERSITY OF WINNIPEG (1967) and UNIVERSITY OF REGINA (1974). New universities were created at CARLETON UNIVERSITY (Ottawa, 1957), YORK UNIVERSITY (Toronto, 1959), UNIVERSITY OF WATERLOO (1959), TRENT UNIVERSITY (Peterborough, 1963) and elsewhere. Full-time undergraduate enrolments tripled and part-time undergraduate and full-time graduate enrolments experienced close to a sixfold increase. Some 23 261 additional full-time university teachers were recruited. Because Canadian graduate programs had just started to expand, many university instructors recruited during the 1960s and the 1970s had received their graduate training abroad, particularly in the US and Britain. The costs of operating this expanded university system increased even more dramatically.

The ambitious policy of university education initiated in the 1960s was not just a response to the pressure of numbers. It was motivated by the belief, borrowed from the US and endorsed by economists, that higher education was a key to economic productivity and would yield higher rates of economic returns for both individuals and society. Social justice provided the second rationale. Improving EDUCATIONAL OPPORTUNITY was seen as a major means of accommodating rising social aspirations and of improving the social prospects of disadvantaged social, cultural and regional groups. Financial aid programs aimed at removing financial barriers to university education were introduced at both the federal and provincial levels. In 1980-81, 128 290 students received financial assistance under the Canada Student Loans Plan (*see* STUDENTS, FINANCIAL AID TO).

The Canadian higher-education systems of today are both similar to and different from those

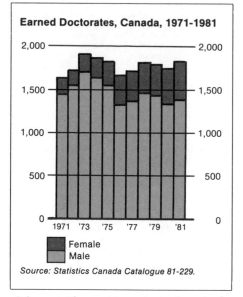

Earned Doctorates, Canada, 1971-1981

■ Female
■ Male

Source: Statistics Canada Catalogue 81-229.

of the past. The most important reform in the organizational framework of higher education was undertaken in Québec with the introduction of the COLLÈGE D'ENSEIGNEMENT GÉNÉRAL ET PROFESSIONNEL (CEGEP) but in other provinces as well higher education had to come to terms with the rapid emergence of the COMMUNITY COLLEGE sector of post-secondary education. In some provinces systematic transfer arrangements between the 2 sectors (university and community college) have been established; in other provinces the 2 sectors operate as separate streams.

Today, Canada has 65 public degree-granting universities, 12 of which are in federation with another university. Canadian higher education has become a public-sector enterprise. Escalating costs have forced denominational universities, eg, Waterloo Lutheran University (which became WILFRID LAURIER UNIVERSITY) and Assumption University (which became UNIVERSITY OF WINDSOR), to sever their religious connections in order to qualify for public support. Another important development has been the provincialization of the system of higher education. While both the federal and provincial govern-

University Enrolment, Degrees Granted, Teachers and Expenditures
(Source: Various Statistics Canada sources)

	1962-63	1981-82
Full-time undergraduate enrolment		
Total	132 700	354 503
% Female	27.8	46.7
Part-time undergraduate enrolment		
Total	38 600	219 461
% Female	41.2	59.9
Full-time graduate enrolment		
Total	8 400	47 159
% Female	15.1	37.3
Bachelor's and first professional degrees		
Total	24 939	84 927
% Female	27.8	50.4
Master's degree		
Total	2 755	12 943
% Female	18.1	39.2
Earned doctorates		
Total	421	1 820
% Female	8.1	23.0
Full-time university teachers		
Total	9 983	33 244
% Female	11.5	15.0
Expenditures on university education (Millions$)	356	4 989

ments provide financial support, university policy is shaped by the provincial governments, particularly since 1966, when the federal government's program of direct grants to universities, begun in 1951, was replaced by a shared-cost contribution to the provincial governments. Other changes, introduced in 1977, reduced the direct financial role of the federal government even more and increased the discretionary power of the provincial governments in the allocation of federal support money.

The governance structure of most Canadian universities is still based on a 2-tier system, except in the case of Laval, U of T and ATHABASCA UNIVERSITY, where systems incorporating the powers of board and senate have been introduced. At most universities, however, the composition of the 2 governing bodies has changed. Although faculty still hold the majority of seats on the academic faculty councils and senates, membership now may include students, alumni and representatives of professional bodies. Similarly, faculty and students are often represented on boards of governors. One important power of the board has been taken away: until the 1950s, TENURE at most universities was held at the pleasure of the board, but this faculty right is now more firmly entrenched.

The contemporary Canadian university is a multipurpose organization striving to achieve a number of objectives simultaneously: teaching — the provision of a "liberal education" or general education; training — the transmission of expert knowledge required for high-level jobs; research — the creation of knowledge through basic scientific research and scholarship; public service — the provision of practical knowledge and science to society; and equalization of opportunity — the removal of all barriers that inhibit the motivated and academically capable person from receiving a university education.

Canadian universities in the 1980s are beset by various "crises" and their position is now under challenge. Higher education began to lose its institutional prominence in the 1970s. High costs in a poor economic climate and loss of confidence in the validity of the assumptions guiding expansion have been contributing factors. Various studies, for example, have revealed substantial increases in UNEMPLOYMENT and underemployment among those earning a bachelor of arts degree.

Although the personal "rate of return" on investment in a university education has fallen in recent years, it does not necessarily follow that universities are failing to achieve their training objectives. Data from all sources confirm that unemployment rates for university graduates are substantially lower than for high-school graduates. If anything, the increase in the number of university graduates most adversely affects the job prospects and careers of those without these credentials insofar as they are forced to compete with more educated peers in a tight job market.

Another problem faced by Canadian universities involves accessibility. Canadian participation rates have fared very well compared with other nations; only the US and Sweden can claim higher participation rates for their 18-24-year-old age groups. Canadian data reveal, however, that educational expansion has not brought about a more equal representation by social class at university. P. ANISEF AND J. LENNARDS

University College, U of T (architects Frederick W. CUMBERLAND and William G. Storm, 1856-59), picturesque in its variety of silhouettes, colours, textures and carved details, eclectic in its rich amalgam of Norman, Romanesque, Anglo-French and Venetian forms, epitomizes the flamboyance and strength of the high-Victorian Gothic style. The architects, aided by their amateur colleague Gov Gen Sir Edmund HEAD, drew inspiration from the work of the Irish firm of Deane and Woodward, especially the contemporary Oxford University Museum. The erection of this vast college building 1856-59 signalled the achievement of a major 19th-century aspiration for a nondenominational institution of higher learning supported by government.

CHRISTINA CAMERON

University College of Cape Breton, Sydney, NS, was founded in 1974 by the amalgamation of the Sydney campus of SAINT FRANCIS XAVIER UNIVERSITY (est 1951) with the Nova Scotia Eastern Institute of Technology (fd 1968). Degree-granting status was obtained in 1982. The university works with the community, and is committed to fostering both technology and theoretical learning. Liberal arts degrees, extensive continuing education programs and diplomas in engineering, applied arts and technology are offered. The university had 925 full-time and 896 part-time students in 1982-83.

LOIS KERNAGHAN

University Magazine, The (1907-20). A Montréal quarterly edited by Sir Andrew MACPHAIL, it succeeded the semiannual *McGill University Magazine* (1901-06). Notable for paying its contributors, the magazine was financially guaranteed by Macphail himself. Under his rigorous editorial direction it set a standard of excellence in English-speaking Canada while attaining a circulation of nearly 6000, a level no comparable Canadian quarterly has subsequently matched. The editor himself contributed 43 pieces of political comment and social criticism (without payment) and for him the magazine was a vehicle to advance "correct thought," by which he meant a Canada that was rural, traditional and, aside from Québec, overwhelmingly British. When these ideals seemed to be in irreversible decline and when at the same time he faced financial pressures, failing eyesight and a drastic decline in circulation owing to his 4-year absence during WWI, he discontinued the magazine. *See* LITERARY MAGAZINES.

IAN ROSS ROBERTSON

University of Alberta, Edmonton, Alta; fd in 1906 through the initiative of Prem A.C. RUTHERFORD in Alberta's first legislature. The U of A opened in 1908 with Henry Marshall TORY as president, and grew steadily until WWI. Development resumed after the war and by 1928, when Tory left, degree programs were available in many areas, while a broad program was carried on by the extension department, with its splendid library service, to outlying parts of Alberta. Affiliation was provided with St Stephen's College (UNITED CHURCH) and St Joseph's College (Roman CATHOLIC), and in 1931 with Calgary's Mount Royal College. Enrolment increased very slowly during the depression, although extension education continued to grow at full pace. In 1933 the extension department conducted a summer theatre program in Banff which was the forerunner of the BANFF CENTRE SCHOOL OF FINE ARTS.

After WWII the university assumed responsibility for all teacher training in the province. Through the 1960s it underwent its greatest surge in enrolment, from under 5000 in 1959 to over 15 000 in 1969. Affiliation was provided with the French-language Collège St-Jean (now a faculty) and junior colleges across Alberta. The university's divisions in Calgary and Lethbridge have become universities in their own right. In 1983 graduate students comprised over 10% of the student body, and the library contained over 2 million volumes and a wide variety of research materials. In addition to the main campus the university owns about 600 ha of land and leases over 3200 more, mainly for AGRICULTURAL RESEARCH.

The university has been a leader in teacher training and physical education (hosting Uni-

Enrolment: University of Alberta, 1982-83
(Source: Statistics Canada)

Full-time Undergrad	Full-time Graduate	Part-time Undergrad	Part-time Graduate
17 992	2 771*	2 808	1 199

* Does not include over 400 medical interns and residents

versiade, the WORLD UNIVERSITY GAMES, in 1983), and has achieved prominence in areas such as in plant breeding, animal and poultry breeding and nutrition. Scientific achievements include pioneer work in extracting oil from BITUMEN, the contribution of J.B. COLLIP to the development of INSULIN and the synthesis of sucrose by R. LEMIEUX. Laser welding, computer-assisted instruction, immunology research and microelectronic engineering are a few examples of the university's current research. The University of Alberta Press, est in 1969, had published some 60 books by 1984. The university was also home base of *The Canadian Encyclopedia* and the Riel project.

WALTER H. JOHNS

Reading: Walter H. Johns, *A History of the University of Alberta, 1908-1969* (1981).

University of British Columbia, Vancouver, was founded in 1908. Before UBC opened, higher education in BC was provided by colleges affiliated with the universities of Toronto and McGill. In 1910 a site at Point Grey was selected for the UBC campus. The outbreak of WWI delayed construction and UBC began operations at Fairview in 1915. Through its association with McGill, the university was provided with the nucleus of its first staff and basic curriculum in arts and science. In 1919, the Faculty of Agriculture was established and nursing and health programs began. In 1920 honours courses, extension services and summer sessions were introduced, and Victoria College in Victoria became an affiliate of the university. In 1925 UBC moved to its permanent site on Point Grey. Expansion of the campus was virtually at a standstill during the late 1920s and 1930s. Academic expansion during this period included establishment of a university extension department (1936) and the further development of work in forestry and commerce.

Military training was a feature of campus life during WWI and WWII. Many faculty members served in the armed forces or were involved in scientific research to aid the war effort. UBC enrolment rose dramatically following WWII from 3058 in 1944-45 to 9374 in 1947-48. Surplus army and air force camps provided temporary classrooms as well as faculty and student housing. In the postwar era several new buildings were erected. Four new faculties were established: law (1945), graduate studies (1948), pharmacy (1949) and medicine (1950); 2 established departments were elevated to faculty status: forestry (1951) and commerce (1957); and the provincial normal school was incorporated into the university as the Faculty of Education (1956).

Growth since the 1960s has made UBC one of Canada's largest anglophone universities. It has a campus of some 420 buildings. The UBC library, one of the largest in Canada, houses 2.5 million volumes, and UBC's computing facilities are among the most extensive in the country. During this period the university added the Faculty of Dentistry (1964), and schools of librarianship, rehabilitation medicine, and audiology and speech sciences. Expansion has also taken place in all of UBC's 12 faculties, 9 schools and 11 institutes and research centres, with special emphasis on forestry, Asian studies, the fine and performing arts, environmental and ecological studies, computer science, molecular genetics, microelectronics and mineral process engineering. Beginning in 1961, the university undertook construction of an extensive health sciences centre which now comprises teaching

and research buildings as well as an affiliated hospital complex for psychiatric, extended and acute care.

A museum of anthropology, completed in 1976 and housing one of the world's leading collections of NORTHWEST COAST INDIAN ART and artifacts, and a 44 ha botanical garden are public facilities as well as teaching and research centres. UBC and other western Canadian universities co-operate in the operation of the TRIUMF cyclotron project, which produces high-intensity meson beams for basic physics research and cancer therapy, and the Bamfield Marine Station on Vancouver I, a major teaching and research centre in marine biology. UBC operates a 5157 ha research and teaching forest at Haney in the Fraser Valley and an AGRICULTURAL RESEARCH farm at Oyster River on Vancouver I.

The university has formal affiliation agreements with 3 theological colleges: Vancouver School of Theology (an amalgamation of Anglican and United Church colleges), St Mark's College (Roman Catholic) and Regent College. St Andrew's Hall (Presbyterian) offers residential accommodation, as does Carey Hall (Baptist), which also provides internship training and continuing education programs.

Enrolment: University of British Columbia, 1982-83
(Source: Statistics Canada)

Full-time Undergrad	Full-time Graduate	Part-time Undergrad	Part-time Graduate
17 603	3 087	5 168	1 170

University of Calgary, Calgary, Alta, was founded in 1966. U of C began in 1945 when Calgary Normal School became a branch of the Faculty of Education of the Edmonton-based UNIVERSITY OF ALBERTA. Gradually, introductory courses were offered in arts, science, commerce and engineering under the respective Edmonton faculties. Known as University of Alberta, Calgary Branch, it moved to its present campus in 1960. In 1963 department heads were established for the faculties of arts and science, education and physical education, and for a division of engineering. The university became fully autonomous in 1966. Subsequently, faculties of medicine, nursing, law, environmental design and social welfare, fine arts, general studies, humanities, management and social sciences have been added. Mount Royal College and Medicine Hat College have been affiliated with U of C since 1966.

B. BEATON

Enrolment: University of Calgary, 1982-83
(Source: Statistics Canada)

Full-time Undergrad	Full-time Graduate	Part-time Undergrad	Part-time Graduate
11 971	1 460	3 969	790

University of Guelph, Guelph, Ont, was founded in 1964. It has 7 academic colleges: arts, biological science, family and consumer studies (fd in 1903 as Macdonald Institute), physical science, social science, Ontario Agricultural College (fd 1874) and Ontario Veterinary College (fd 1862); and 2 university schools: rural planning and development, and part-time studies and continuing education. In addition to its traditional strengths in agriculture and VETERINARY MEDICINE the university now has excellent programs in the basic disciplines in the humanities, the social sciences and the physical and biological sciences; special programs include agricultural and biological engineering, human kinetics, hotel and food administration and landscape architecture. The campus was established in 1874 when the Ontario School of Agriculture opened near Guelph on a 202 ha farm provided by the Ontario government. In 1880 it became Ontario Veterinary College and Experimental Farm. Ontario Veterinary College, founded by Andrew SMITH in Toronto, was acquired by the government and moved to Guelph in 1922. The Macdonald Institute, established as the Division of Home Economics at OAC, was financed by Sir William MACDONALD (founder of Macdonald College, Ste-Anne-de-Bellevue, Qué) as part of a movement led by Adelaide HOODLESS to promote domestic science in rural Canada. From 1887 until 1964 OAC was affiliated academically with UNIVERSITY OF TORONTO, as were OVC and Macdonald Institute from 1919. The University of Guelph was established in 1964 on the basis of the founding colleges.   B. BEATON

Enrolment: University of Guelph, 1982-83
(Source: Statistics Canada)

Full-time Undergrad	Full-time Graduate	Part-time Undergrad	Part-time Graduate
9 541	816	1 426	152

University of King's College, Halifax, is Canada's oldest university. It was founded in 1789 by the Anglican Church at WINDSOR, NS, as an embodiment of LOYALIST political and religious principles. Degree-conferring status dates from 1802. King's remained classically oriented until 1920, when a disastrous fire forced realignment of educational approaches. King's, financially supported during this period by the Carnegie Foundation, moved to Halifax, where it has maintained joint faculties of arts and science with DALHOUSIE UNIVERSITY since 1923. With the exception of its journalism program, all degrees are awarded in conjunction with either Dalhousie or the Atlantic School of Theology. King's emphasizes a modern humanistic education within the tradition of ANGLICANISM. It had 450 full-time undergraduate students in 1982-83.   LOIS KERNAGHAN

University of Lethbridge, Lethbridge, Alta, was founded in 1967. The university offers a liberal education leading to undergraduate degrees in arts and science, education, fine arts, management, music and nursing; a master's degree in education is also available. The continuing education division provides public-interest and credit courses at times and locations convenient to students across southern Alberta. In 1971 the university, which grew out of the University Section of Lethbridge Junior College (an affiliate of UNIVERSITY OF ALBERTA), moved to a new 185 ha campus designed by architect Arthur ERICKSON. A recent addition is the Performing Arts Centre, which has outstanding facilities for fine arts, drama and music. The university had 2191 full-time and 479 part-time undergraduate students in 1982-83.

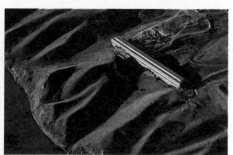

Dramatic view of U of Lethbridge, designed by architect Arthur Erickson (*photo by J.A. Kraulis*).

University of Manitoba, Winnipeg, was founded in 1877, the first institution of higher education to be established in western Canada. At first it acted only as a degree-granting body for its 3 founding denominational colleges: St Boniface College (Roman Catholic), St John's College (Anglican), and Manitoba College (Presbyterian). Wesley College (Methodist) affiliated with the university in 1888, following by 6 years the privately founded Manitoba Medical College. In 1900 the university became a teaching institution by an Act of the provincial legislature. Thereafter, other colleges also received affiliated status: Manitoba College of Pharmacy (1902); Manitoba Agricultural College (1906); St Paul's College (Roman Catholic) and Brandon College (1938). Other forms of affiliation have continued to the present. In 1963 the nondenominational University College, the creation of historian W.L. MORTON, was completed; and in 1964 St Andrew's College, intended to train clergy for the Ukrainian Greek Orthodox Church, became an associated college. It was granted special affiliation status in 1981. In addition, the university recognizes the Canadian Mennonite Bible College and the Canadian Nazarene College, both in the Greater Winnipeg area, as "approved teaching centres." Altogether the system of affiliated colleges provides an accurate replication of the ethnic and religious diversity of Manitoba in the setting of higher education.

The university grew slowly after WWI, but expanded greatly during the 1960s and early 1970s; it now offers programs in 20 faculties and schools. Especially noteworthy among its various contributions to knowledge have been the discovery of a treatment for, and control of, Rh disease and the genetic research that made possible the development of the hybrid cereal grain, TRITICALE.   A. BRIAN McKILLOP

Enrolment: University of Manitoba, 1982-83
(Source: Statistics Canada)

Full-time Undergrad	Full-time Graduate	Part-time Undergrad	Part-time Graduate
12 749	2 233*	5 837	1 619

* Includes medical interns and residents

University of New Brunswick, Fredericton, was founded in 1785 as the Provincial Academy of Arts and Sciences. It is a multidisciplinary institution noted particularly for engineering, forestry, science and the liberal arts. Modelled on the Tory and Anglican ideals of King's College, New York, the academy was tempered by its LOYALIST and wilderness beginnings. It was an early rival to King's College, Windsor, NS, and although enjoying provincial government support, it did not receive a charter until 1800, when it became the College of New Brunswick. In 1828 it received a royal charter as King's College and in 1859 was reconstituted as University of New Brunswick. Religious qualifications were abolished in 1846 and women were admitted in 1885. The early curriculum stressed a classical education, but by the mid-19th century progressive educators such as William Brydone JACK were introducing the newest scientific disciplines. Although financially limited, the institution was regarded as second in quality only to UNIVERSITY OF TORONTO during the late 1800s.

Highlights of expansion included the introduction of forestry science in 1908 and, more recently, business administration, nursing and computer science. St Thomas U, a small liberal-arts university, has shared the Fredericton cam-

---

**Enrolment: University of New Brunswick
and St Thomas University, 1982-83**
(Source: Statistics Canada)

Full-time Undergrad	Full-time Graduate	Part-time Undergrad	Part-time Graduate
University of New Brunswick			
6 607	428	1 825	402
St Thomas University			
1 011	—	199	—

---

pus since its relocation from Chatham, NB, in 1964. A campus opened in Saint John in 1964 and has almost 1000 students and selected degree programs. In 1973 the provincial Teachers' College was incorporated into the university. Prominent alumni include Bliss CARMAN, Sir Charles G.D. ROBERTS, Lord Beaverbrook (*see* Max AITKEN) and Anne MURRAY.   LOIS KERNAGHAN

University of Ottawa, Ottawa, Ont, was founded in 1848. It offers instruction in English and French. U of O began as the College of Bytown, est 1848 by the Missionary Oblates of Mary Immaculate, and in 1861 it became the College of Ottawa. Granted university powers in 1866, the college offered degrees in arts, medicine and law. In 1889 the university received a pontifical charter granting it the status of a Roman Catholic university. In 1933 a revised civil charter gave U of O full university powers in Canada. Its medical faculty was established in 1945 and its science and law faculties in 1953. During the university's expansion in the 1960s, faculties of education, administration, social sciences and graduate studies were started. In 1965 the university became nondenominational, with the Oblates transferring control to a new lay board of governors. The university federated with St Paul U in 1965 to offer degree programs in theology and canon law.   B. BEATON

Enrolment: University of Ottawa, 1982-83
(Source: Statistics Canada)

Full-time Undergrad	Full-time Graduate	Part-time Undergrad	Part-time Graduate
10 366	1 890*	6 435	1 587

* Includes medical interns and residents

University of Prince Edward Island, Charlottetown, was established in Apr 1969 by the Legislature of PEI. UPEI is a public nondenominational institution created·by the merger of 2 venerable institutions of higher learning, Prince of Wales College (est 1834), and St Dunstan's University (fd 1855). UPEI has undergraduate faculties of arts, science and education, and a school of business administration. It offers degrees in arts, science, business administration, education and music. It also offers a diploma in engineering and preparatory courses for agriculture, architecture, dentistry, law, medicine and veterinary medicine. A doctoral program in veterinary medicine will be offered in 1986. Enrolment has been fairly constant since UPEI's foundation. Ninety percent of the student population is normally drawn from PEI, with 8.5% from other provinces and 1.5% from foreign countries. One-quarter of the students live in residence. The comparatively small number of students, and a satisfactory faculty-student ratio, enable the university to implement its central objective, the maintenance of personal and scholarly instruction. Over the years UPEI has preserved a close relationship with its principal constituency, the Island community. The university had 1596 full-time and 663 part-time students in 1982-83.

FRANCIS W.P. BOLGER

University of Regina, Regina, was founded in 1911 as Regina College by the METHODIST Church. In 1925 the college became affiliated with UNIVERSITY OF SASKATCHEWAN and began offering courses in arts and science. In 1934 it was transferred from UNITED CHURCH control to U Sask; degrees were granted after 1961. In 1965 the college moved to southeastern Regina, and university status was granted 1 July 1974. U of R offers degrees in arts, sciences, music, journalism, administration, engineering, education, social work and graduate studies, and programs in Canadian Plains studies, bilingual studies, human justice and co-operative work. Feder-

ated colleges include Campion College, Luther College and Saskatchewan Indian Federated College; affiliated institutes include Canadian Theological College and the Gabriel Dumont Institute of Native Studies and Applied Research.
NANCY BROWN FOULDS

Enrolment: University of Regina, 1982-83 (Source: Statistics Canada)			
Full-time Undergrad	*Full-time Graduate*	*Part-time Undergrad*	*Part-time Graduate*
3 787	84	4 068	269

University of Saskatchewan, Saskatoon, was founded in 1907. In 1879 the Church of England (*see* ANGLICANISM) established Emmanuel College in Prince Albert to train "native helpers" in theology, classics and native languages. In 1883 it became known as "University of Saskatchewan." In 1907 the new province of Saskatchewan chartered U Sask as a nondenominational, coeducational institution. A 1032 ha tract, comprising a 146 ha campus, a university farm and experimental plots, was set aside in Saskatoon. In 1909 courses in arts and science were offered; Emmanuel College moved from Prince Albert to Saskatoon as an affiliate, and Rugby School in England donated a chapel for the new theological school. From 1912 to 1938 the university expanded, adding faculties of agriculture, engineering, law, pharmacy, commerce, medicine, education, home economics and nursing; graduate studies was added in 1946 and dentistry in 1965. In an effort to promote post-secondary education, several junior colleges were authorized to give university credit courses. Of these, Regina College, affiliated in 1934, had the most significant impact on the university's development: in 1959 it was given degree-granting status, becoming U Sask's second campus. Degrees were granted after 1961. It became autonomous in 1974 as UNIVERSITY OF REGINA. U Sask's program in agriculture has grown to include VETERINARY MEDICINE and 3 additional experimental farms totalling 1740 ha in area. Indian education and studies continue to be a particular interest of the university.
B. BEATON

Enrolment: University of Saskatchewan, 1982-83 (Source: Statistics Canada)			
Full-time Undergrad	*Full-time Graduate*	*Part-time Undergrad*	*Part-time Graduate*
10 528	754	3 816	420

University of Sudbury, *see* LAURENTIAN UNIVERSITY.

University of Toronto, Toronto, Canada's largest university, has a long and complex history. It was founded as King's College by royal charter in 1827 and was initially controlled by the colonial establishment and the Church of England. The church affiliation made it unpopular, and on 31 Dec 1849 the institution was secularized, becoming on 1 Jan 1850 the nondenominational University of Toronto. The Anglicans responded by creating Trinity College at Toronto in 1851. In 1853 U of T was reorganized, and UNIVERSITY COLLEGE was created as its teaching arm. Structural changes encouraged other colleges to federate with U of T; Victoria College (Methodist, fd 1841 in Cobourg, Ont) and St Michael's College (Roman Catholic, fd 1852 in Toronto by the Basilian Order) joined in 1890 and Trinity College in 1904, each of them retaining university status in order to continue granting degrees in theology. During this period some of Toronto's theological colleges also federated with the university. Knox College (fd 1844), a Presbyterian seminary, affiliated with the university in 1885 and federated in 1890. Wycliffe

Hart House, built 1911-19 in the collegiate Gothic style, is the social, cultural and recreational centre of U of T (*photo © 1984 Hartill Art Associates*).

College (Anglican, fd 1877) became a federated college in 1889. Emmanuel College (Methodist, fd 1836) became affiliated with the university as a UNITED CHURCH OF CANADA seminary in 1925, the year the United Church came into existence. In 1969 Toronto School of Theology was created as an independent federation of 7 schools of theology, including the divinity faculties of Victoria (Emmanuel), St Michael's and Trinity universities and Knox and Wycliffe colleges. Within its own federation, U of T granted all but theology or divinity degrees, but since 1978, by virtue of a change made in U of T's charter, the university has granted theology degrees conjointly with TST's member institutions.

The 1853 reorganization of U of T had resulted in the abolishment of the faculties of law and medicine, but these were restored in 1887. The Royal College of Dental Surgeons (fd 1875) was affiliated with the university from 1888 until 1925, when it became the Faculty of Dentistry. Engineering students attended the School of Practical Science which was affiliated with the university from its inception in 1878 until 1887, when it amalgamated. The Conservatory of Music became an affiliate in 1896.

After the turn of the century the university expanded rapidly. New faculties included home economics (1906), education (1907), forestry (1907), social work (1914), nursing (1920), graduate studies (1922), hygiene (1926) and the School of Architecture (1948). Affiliate research institutions such as the ROYAL ONTARIO MUSEUM (1914), Connaught Medical Laboratories (1914) and the David Dunlap Observatory (1935) played an important role in the development of the university. The building program during this period included Hart House, a social, cultural and recreational centre which was built between 1911 and 1919 and given to the university in 1919 by Vincent MASSEY.

Canada's evolution was reflected in the growth and diversification of the university. The University of Toronto Press was in place on a modest basis by 1911, and it became a full-scale academic publishing house after 1945. Graduate institutes in various areas of specialization were developed, the first being the Institute of Business Administration (1958). The Ontario Institute for Studies in Education (OISE) was founded in 1965 as a research and development institute

Enrolment: University of Toronto and Ontario Institute for Studies in Education, 1982-83* (Source: Statistics Canada)			
Full-time Undergrad	*Full-time Graduate*	*Part-time Undergrad*	*Part-time Graduate*
University of Toronto			
27 430	5 958	11 702	2 107
Ontario Institute for Studies in Education			
—	634	13	1 551

* Figures do not include "full-time equivalent" enrolment at constituent universities (Victoria, Trinity, St Michael's)

and as a graduate school of education. In this latter capacity it serves as the dept of educational theory in U of T's School of Graduate Studies. By 1984, 19 graduate centres and institutes had come into existence to deal with subject areas as diverse as biomedical engineering, comparative literature, criminology, industrial relations and transportation. MASSEY COLLEGE, the only graduate college in U of T, was built and furnished by the Massey Foundation and opened in 1963 with Robertson DAVIES as master. The need to decentralize the university to meet the needs of metropolitan Toronto's growing population led to the development of 2 suburban campuses, Scarborough College (1964) and Erindale College (1966). The undergraduate college system was expanded at the central campus to include New College (1962) and Innis College (1964). YORK UNIVERSITY was affiliated with U of T from its creation in 1959 until it became fully independent in 1965.

The U of T has made important contributions in many areas of scholarship and research. The discovery of INSULIN and the development of Pablum, liquid helium, an artificial pancreas and the laser-beam image recorder took place at the university. The U of T is the home of many research projects in the arts and humanities, including the DICTIONARY OF CANADIAN BIOGRAPHY, Records of Early English Drama, the Dictionary of Old English and the editing of the works of John Stuart Mill.

University of Toronto Quarterly began publication in Oct 1931 (though an undergraduate magazine of the same name appeared 1895-96). Its first editor, philosopher G.S. BRETT, wrote in an introductory foreword that it was "intended to be neither vocational nor technical"; it would, however, serve "scholarship and academic interests." Between 1935 and 1947 it was edited by A.S.P. WOODHOUSE, who firmly established its reputation as a leading international journal devoted to the humanities. For over 50 years *UTQ* has emphasized sound scholarship and the publication of Canadian scholars alongside international authorities. Perhaps its most distinctive feature is "Letters in Canada," an annual review of the previous year's publications in the arts and humanities, which first appeared in 1936. Since 1937 this has included French Canadian works, and it constitutes the longest continuous survey of francophone literature and scholarship. *See* LITERARY PERIODICALS. W.J. KEITH

University of Victoria, Victoria, was founded in 1903 as Victoria College and affiliated with MCGILL UNIVERSITY, offering first- and second-year arts and science courses towards a McGill degree. The opening of UNIVERSITY OF BRITISH COLUMBIA in 1915 resulted in the suspension of Victoria's university program. Five years later local pressure brought the college back into being, again as a 2-year institution but affiliated with UBC and offering the first 2 years of a BA at that university. Through the 1950s the college expanded its curriculum to a full degree program in basic arts and science. In 1961 it awarded its first bachelor's degree — a UBC degree but completed entirely in Victoria. Two years later it became independent, and soon afterwards moved to its present 115 ha campus. The university offers degrees in arts, science, education, law, engineering, nursing, fine arts, music and social work. Many of these programs include work at the master's and doctoral levels.
WALTER D. YOUNG

Enrolment: University of Victoria, 1982-83 (Source: Statistics Canada)			
Full-time Undergrad	*Full-time Graduate*	*Part-time Undergrad*	*Part-time Graduate*
6 158	565	3 604	465

University of Waterloo, Waterloo, Ont, was founded in 1957 and received its Ontario charter in 1959. U of Waterloo began as a nondenominational engineering faculty associated with UNIVERSITY OF WESTERN ONTARIO in 1957, offering Canada's first co-operative education program, in which students spent alternating 4-month terms on campus (for academic studies) and at work in industry (for practical experience), on a year-round basis. Waterloo's "co-op" enrolment (8500 in 1983-84) is second largest in the world. Waterloo's early association with local arts colleges, Waterloo College (Lutheran) and St Jerome's College (Roman Catholic), ceased in 1960 when University of St Jerome College became federated with U of Waterloo and Waterloo College became Waterloo Lutheran Univerity (now WILFRID LAURIER U), a separate institution. Three other on-campus colleges are affiliated with Waterloo: Conrad Grebel (Mennonite), Renison (Anglican) and St Paul's (United). Waterloo acquired its campus in 1958 and expanded it in 1963 to a total of 405 ha. Waterloo now has undergraduate, graduate and research programs in 42 academic departments and schools, administered through 6 faculties: arts, engineering, environmental studies, human kinetics and leisure studies, mathematics and science. Waterloo enjoys an international reputation for COMPUTER SCIENCE research; its mathematics enrolment (4200 in 1983-84) is probably the largest in the world.

Enrolment: University of Waterloo, 1982-83
(Source: Statistics Canada)

Full-time Undergrad	Full-time Graduate	Part-time Undergrad	Part-time Graduate
14 974	1 326	6 313	471

University of Western Ontario, London, Ont, was founded in 1878 as Western University of London. Huron College, established in 1863 as an ANGLICAN theological school, provided the basis for the new university. In 1881 the first arts courses were given. In 1882 a group of London doctors formed a medical school which was affiliated with Western. A similar attempt in 1885 by London lawyers to organize a law school failed because the Law Society of Upper Canada had a monopoly on legal education in the province. After Western became nondenominational in 1908, it expanded steadily. The Institute for Public Health opened under university management in 1912 and became affiliated in 1917. The medical school became an integrated faculty in 1913. Extension and summer courses started in 1918, and Western opened one of the first French immersion courses in the summer of 1933. As the university grew, new faculties were added: music, graduate studies, business administration, nursing, law, engineering, education, dentistry, library and information science, physical education and journalism. New buildings were designed to complement the original modern Gothic architecture.

In 1919 the Ursuline Sisters had established Brescia College as a Roman Catholic affiliate, and that year Assumption College in Windsor affiliated with the university; it later evolved into UNIVERSITY OF WINDSOR. Similarly, Waterloo College of Arts became affiliated with Western in 1925; today, it is WILFRID LAURIER UNIVERSITY and its science faculty has become UNIVERSITY OF

Enrolment: University of Western Ontario, 1982-83
(Source: Statistics Canada)

Full-time Undergrad	Full-time Graduate	Part-time Undergrad	Part-time Graduate
1 485	2 233*	6 180	756

* Includes medical interns and residents

WATERLOO. St Peter's College seminary of London affiliated with Western in 1939; it eventually became an arts faculty, King's College. Huron and Brescia colleges form part of Western's campus.
B. BEATON

University of Windsor, Windsor, Ont, was founded in 1962. The university began as Assumption College, fd in 1857 by Rev Pierre Point, pastor of Assumption Parish, to provide a liberal education. In 1858 it received its charter. It was directed by various Catholic religious orders until 1919. It was then affiliated with London's Western University (UNIVERSITY OF WESTERN ONTARIO), 1919-53. In 1956 it became Assumption University. Holy Names College for women became affiliated with Assumption in 1934 and merged with it in 1962. Essex College (nondenominational) was incorporated in 1954 to provide courses in science, mathematics, physics, geology and business administration. In 1962 University of Windsor was incorporated by the province. In 1963 and 1964 affiliation agreements were made with Holy Redeemer College, Canterbury College (Anglican) and Iona College (United Church).
B. BEATON

Enrolment: University of Windsor, 1982-83
(Source: Statistics Canada)

Full-time Undergrad	Full-time Graduate	Part-time Undergrad	Part-time Graduate
7 636	664	3 813	428

University of Winnipeg, Winnipeg, was established in 1967 from the former United College, then a member college of UNIVERSITY OF MANITOBA and affiliated with the UNITED CHURCH OF CANADA. United College was founded in 1938 through the amalgamation of Manitoba College (fd in 1871 by the PRESBYTERIAN CHURCH) and Wesley College (fd in 1888 by the METHODIST Church). The University of Winnipeg is a liberal arts and science institution offering a full undergraduate degree program in arts, science and education, a graduate degree program in theology and a unique high-school program taught in a university environment by its Collegiate Division. More than two-thirds of its students study part-time in extensive continuing education programs, which offer both credit and noncredit courses both on and off campus. The campus is located downtown and the city-oriented university provides a variety of educational, recreational and cultural services to the community, as well as action-oriented urban research and education activities through its nationally renowned Institute of Urban Studies.
TOM W. ROBSON

Enrolment: University of Winnipeg, 1982-83
(Source: Statistics Canada)

Full-time Undergrad	Full-time Graduate	Part-time Undergrad	Part-time Graduate
2 760	32	4 391	59

Upper Canada, the predecessor of modern ONTARIO, came into existence when the British Parliament passed the CONSTITUTIONAL ACT, 1791, dividing the old PROVINCE OF QUEBEC into LOWER CANADA in the E and Upper Canada in the W along the present-day Ontario-Québec BOUNDARY. The Act also established a government that would largely determine the colony's political nature and in practice strongly influenced its social and economic character. The area that would become Upper Canada was populated originally by Indians (eg, HURON, NEUTRAL, PETUN, ALGONQUIN). Samuel de CHAMPLAIN visited the region in the early 17th century, and was followed by other French explorers. Missionaries were particularly active in HURONIA, E and S of Georgian Bay. Through the FUR TRADE, the

French were established in the area by the 18th century. Commerce and war provided the substantiation to the French claim. Permanent European settlement was scarcely a feature of the occupation, although the nuclei of modern TORONTO, WINDSOR, NIAGARA and KINGSTON were established.

During the SEVEN YEARS' WAR (1756-63) the French abandoned most of the region to the British, and upon the surrender of Montréal in Sept 1760, Britain effectively took over the territory which would later become Upper Canada. After the TREATY OF PARIS (1763), borders of Britain's new Province of Quebec 1763-91, were extended S into the Ohio Valley. When the AMERICAN REVOLUTION began, the permanent European population of western Quebec consisted of a few French-speaking settlers around Detroit. By 1783 — the end of the American revolt — what had been a trickle of wartime LOYALIST refugees became a stream; 5000-6000 set a tone and fashioned an ideology that would influence much of Upper Canada's future.

The 2-century-old Loyalist myth has these sturdy people overcoming hardship and deprivation but, in fact, few refugees anywhere have been so privileged. Gov Sir Frederick HALDIMAND began Loyalist settlement initiatives, establishing disbanded army regiments in ranges of quickly surveyed townships stretched along the American frontier; in the event of war these veterans were intended to form a defensive barrier. Three main areas were selected: along the St Lawrence, around Kingston and the Bay of Quinte, and in the NIAGARA PENINSULA. A fourth, near Detroit, was considered but its scheduled surrender to the US postponed development. Land was granted in lots, with heads of families receiving 100 acres (40.5 ha) and field officers up to and eventually more than 1000 acres (405 ha). Clothing, tools and provisions were supplied for 3 years. Although there were difficulties, these favoured displaced persons did well, and many disgruntled Americans — some simply "land-hungry" — moved N to join them. By 1790 western Quebec had a population of nearly 10 000.

The Loyalists who came to Upper Canada, mostly American frontiersmen, were well able to cope with the rigours of new settlements; moreover, they were not politically docile. Many had been in the forefront of political protest in the old American colonies, and although they had not been ready to take up arms for colonial rights, they were prepared to use every legal and constitutional means at their disposal to better their lives. It was their constitutional complaints that caused Britain in 1791 to modify the inadequate QUEBEC ACT of 1774.

The Constitutional Act was a clear response by London to the American Revolution. The excess of democracy that had permeated the southern colonies would not be allowed in the 2 new provinces of Upper and Lower Canada. A lieutenant-governor was established in each province, with an executive council to advise him, a legislative council to act as an upper house, and a representative assembly. Policy was to be directed by the executive, which was responsible not to the assembly but to the Crown. The Church of England (see ANGLICANISM) was to tie the colonies more firmly to Britain: in Upper Canada, a permanent appropriation of funds "for the Support and Maintenance of a Protestant clergy" was formally guaranteed by the establishment of one-seventh of all lands in the province as reserves, with the proceeds from sale or rental going to the church (see CLERGY RESERVES). Subsequent instructions established crown reserves, another seventh of the land, the revenue from which would be used to pay the costs of the provincial administration. Land ownership, the question that concerned most settlers, was to be on the British pattern of freehold tenure. The SEIGNEURIAL SYSTEM was per-

View of Kingston from Fort Henry, coloured aquatint by J. Gleadah, 1828 (*courtesy Public Archives of Canada/C-2041*).

manently eradicated in the upper province. The franchise was fairly wide, and the assembly numbered no fewer than 16 members while the Legislative Council was made up of 7.

The first leader of this new wilderness society was Lt-Gov John Graves SIMCOE, whose avowed purpose was to create in Upper Canada a "superior, more happy, and more polished form of government," not merely to attract immigrants, but to renew the empire and by example to win Americans back into the British camp. Governmental institutions were established, first at Newark [Niagara-on-the-Lake] and then at the new capital at York [Toronto]. Simcoe used troops to build a series of primary roads, got the land boards and land distribution underway, established the judiciary, grandly abolished SLAVERY and showed a keen interest in promoting Anglican affairs. When he left the province in 1796 he could take pride in his achievements, although he had failed to convert Americans from republicanism and to persuade Britain to turn Upper Canada into a military centre. To Britain, Canada still meant Québec, and Simcoe's elaborate plans for the defence of a western appendage beyond the sea-lanes were unrealistic.

Upper Canada did not flourish under Simcoe's followers, the timid Peter Russell, the busy martinet Gen Peter Hunter, the scarcely busy Alexander Grant and the lacklustre Francis GORE. It was still a remote frontier of fragmented settlement; and land, the only real source of prosperity, had been carelessly carved up in huge grants by lax administrators. Politics began to emerge in provincial life, bearing the mark of the Constitutional Act, which, by its very nature, had created a party of favourites. Lieutenant-governors chose their executive and legislative councils from among men they could trust and understand, who shared their solid, conservative values: Loyalists or newly arrived Britons. These men (later called the FAMILY COMPACT) quickly became a kind of Tory faction permanently in power. They could not conceive any brand of loyalty to the Crown apart from their own; when opposition arose, as it did frequently over money bills, those advocating extension of the shackled assembly's powers were branded, in exchanges of fiery rhetoric, as Yankee Republicans. But the influence of political critics such as Robert Thorpe, Joseph Willcocks and William Weekes, who were not merely "smoke-makers" but true parliamentary whigs, was to be washed away in the vortex of the WAR OF 1812.

During the war, Upper Canada, whose inhabitants were predominantly American in origin, was invaded, violated and in parts occupied. American forces were repulsed by British regulars assisted by Canadian militia. The war strengthened the British link, rendered loyalism a hallowed creed, fashioned martyr-heroes Sir Isaac BROCK and TECUMSEH, brought a certain prosperity, and appeared to legitimize the political status quo. Later commentators would find in it a touchstone for Canadian NATIONALISM and the explanation for much of Canada's persistent public, if not personal, anti-Americanism.

The war ended Upper Canada's isolation. American immigration was formally halted, but Upper Canada received an increased number of British newcomers — some with capital. The economy continued to be tied to Britain's declining MERCANTILISM and the wheat trade gained primacy among Upper Canadian farmers. Still, the province remained capital-poor: for example, the Welland Canal Co, a public works venture, had to look abroad for investors. The expense of administering the growing colony increased substantially in the early 1820s. Schemes to reunite Upper Canada with Lower Canada were occasionally considered. In 1822 an effort was made to adjust the customs duties shared with Lower Canada to provide the upper province, which had no ocean port, with a larger share of revenue.

Revenues remained inadequate and the province plunged into debt, unable to pay the interest on its own badly received debentures without further borrowings. The establishment of the BANK OF UPPER CANADA (1821) and other banks failed to bring real fiscal stability, and neither did the contributions of the massive British-based colonization venture, the CANADA COMPANY. In fact, Canada Co payments were used to defray the salaries of government officials (the civil list) and thus the assembly was sidestepped in its desire to control government revenues.

The War of 1812 consolidated the political control of the province's ruling oligarchy, whose leading light was Anglican Archdeacon (later bishop of Toronto) John STRACHAN. Many commentators have labelled the Family Compact corrupt, although recent evidence suggests that the group was rigorous and methodical in its administration and thorough in its investigation of irregularities. It had a strong sense of duty to development, as shown by its unswerving support of public works such as the WELLAND CANAL. But an oligarchy, enlightened or not, was an anachronism in an age in which democracy was becoming the fashion.

By 1820 opposition in the province was becoming sophisticated but had not yet taken the form of disciplined parties. Some agitators such as Robert GOURLAY, the celebrated "Banished Briton," had earlier dramatized popular grievances in martyrlike fashion. Until the mid-1830s the major impulse of opposition was frequently conducted by more moderate and whiggish politicians such as Dr William BALDWIN, Robert BALDWIN and Rev Egerton RYERSON. Reformer William Lyon MACKENZIE sometimes wanted Upper Canada to be a kind of Jeffersonian dream and envisaged a province composed of yeomen-farmers wedded to the soil, firmly patriotic and ready to become British-American minutemen. At the same time he never failed to

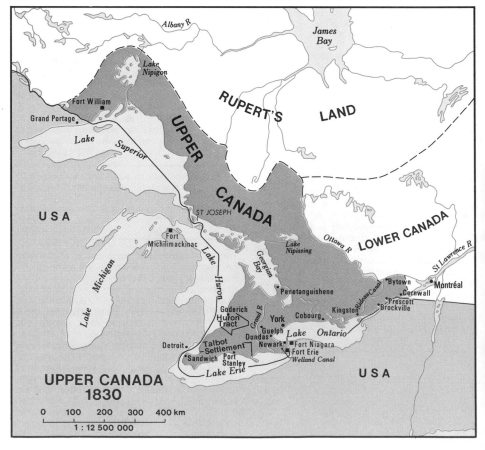

UPPER CANADA
1830

0   100   200   300   400 km
1 : 12 500 000

laud technological advances. He, like the compact he so vigorously opposed, was actually a stranger to the forces and values that eventually dominated the 19th century: moderate liberalism and increasing industrialism. His REBELLION OF 1837 misfired because, like so many politicians after him, he failed to understand the basic, moderate political posture of Upper Canadians. The rebellion marked the nadir of Upper Canada's never-buoyant fortunes. Political chaos was accompanied by economic disaster as the panic of 1837 swept Anglo-American finance and the province found itself over a million pounds in debt.

Mackenzie's violent posturing and his poorly supported rebellion turned out to be unnecessary, since gradual reforms were already underway in both the colony and Britain. The inadequacies of the rigid Constitutional Act were by now apparent. For battered post-rebellion Upper Canada the impetus for real political change could only come from Westminster, although it might be accelerated by advocates in the province, as was later shown by the brief but powerful government of Robert Baldwin and Louis LAFONTAINE. Some immediate change came through the efforts of the earl of DURHAM in 1838. As governor general he spent only a few days in Upper Canada, but he found time for a short, formal visit to Toronto and an interview with Baldwin. He also received sound counsel from his advisers, especially Charles Buller, all of which he placed in his report (*see* DURHAM REPORT).

Durham set in motion a scheme that had long been considered: the reunification of Upper and Lower Canada. By 1838 Upper Canada had a diverse population of more than 400 000 and stretched W from the Ottawa R to the head of the Great Lakes. It was still a rough-hewn and somewhat amorphous community, poorly equipped with schools, hospitals or local government. Durham, from his lofty imperial perch, argued that a reunion of the provinces would swamp the French of Lower Canada in an English sea and, more important, that the economic potential of both colonies would be enhanced and they would thus be less burdensome to Britain. All this Durham insisted would easily be advanced under RESPONSIBLE GOVERNMENT, whereby the Cabinet is rendered responsible to the assembly rather than to the Crown. The errors of the Constitutional Act could be exorcised and unruly politics temporized without fear of further revolts. Britain approved the union, although the granting of responsible government would take almost a decade more. On 10 Feb 1841 Upper Canada's short, unhappy history came to an end. The relationship with its French-speaking counterpart would remain to be worked out under the new legislative union. Meanwhile, Upper Canadians could make some claim to having a collective past and, with the prospects of rapidly increasing population and improving agricultural opportunities, a collective future. *See* PROVINCE OF CANADA. ROGER HALL

Reading: G.M. Craig, *Upper Canada* (1963).

Upper Canada Village, developed during the 1950s and 1960s near Morrisburg, Ont, a replica of a 19th-century community that might have existed along the St Lawrence R. It includes a pioneer farm, general store, doctor's house, tavern, blacksmith shop, school, sawmill, cheese factory and woollen mill. Many original buildings have been moved to the site from nearby, eg, Crysler's Hall, restored to 1846, and Cook's

Church at Upper Canada Village, Morrisburg, Ont (*photo by Malak, Ottawa*).

Tavern, restored to 1835. The buildings are authentically furnished and demonstrate to the visitor various aspects of early life in UPPER CANADA. Guides in period costumes explain the history and demonstrate the way of life of the region's original inhabitants.

The ST LAWRENCE SEAWAY project, beginning in 1954, called for the flooding of a large portion of the old river "front," one of the first areas to be settled in Ontario. To save some of this heritage and develop the new riverbank area, in 1955 the Ontario government established the Ontario-St Lawrence Development Commission. This sponsored the creation of Upper Canada Village to preserve representative buildings and memorialize life as it was along the front. The commission also developed 800 ha of adjacent parkland and relocated the old monument commemorating the 1813 battle of CRYSLER'S FARM.
C.J. TAYLOR

Uranium (U), the heaviest of naturally occurring elements, is metallic and radioactive. It is a hard, dense, malleable, silver-white metal which is never found in nature in its metallic state; it always occurs in combination with oxygen as oxides or silicates. Uranium oxide was first identified in 1789 by M.H. Klaproth in the MINERAL pitchblende, but its distinctive property of radioactivity was discovered much later (1896) by Henri Becquerel. The subsequent discovery in 1898 of the elements polonium and RADIUM led to the development of the radium industry. Uranium was recovered as a by-product of radium until 1939 but found little use except as a ceramic colouring agent. Important developments in nuclear PHYSICS led to the realization that uranium atoms could be split to release large amounts of energy. It was soon recognized that this energy could be harnessed to produce ELECTRIC POWER and nuclear weapons. Demand for uranium began with the initiation in 1942 of an Allied nuclear-weapons program, the Manhattan Project. Major uranium-producing industries were developed in the early 1950s, principally in the US, Canada and South Africa. Peak levels of production were attained by 1959. Production declined precipitously during the early 1960s, and its anticipated revival, based on the demand for uranium for NUCLEAR-POWER generation, was slow to materialize. It was not until the mid-1970s that price levels and market activity were sufficient to prompt significant expansion of exploration and development, and by the late 1970s the industry had been firmly re-established. The US, Canada and South Africa account for some 80% of the Western world's total production to 1980. Other important producing countries have been Australia, France, Zaire and, more recently, Niger and Gabon. Most of Canada's production has come from deposits in the ELLIOT LK area of Ontario and from the URANIUM CITY and Rabbit Lk areas of northern Saskatchewan. It is ex-

pected that Elliot Lk, together with several new developments in northern Saskatchewan, will remain the principal sources of Canadian production to at least the turn of the century. About 85% of Canada's production is exported to the US, Japan and western Europe. R.M. WILLIAMS

Uranium City, Sask, UP, pop 2507 (1984 est), is located 50 km S of the provincial boundary with the NWT and 75 km E of the Saskatchewan-Alberta border. The FUR TRADE was the dominant economic activity until the 1930s when gold was discovered in the Beaverlodge Lk area. From 1938 until the mid-1940s gold was mined in the area. In 1946 URANIUM exploration was initiated and Eldorado Mining and Refining Ltd began production in 1953. In 1952 a townsite named Uranium City was established and in 1956 a special local government jurisdiction was created. A thriving mining community developed and continued in existence until Eldorado announced that it was closing its operations in 1981. DON HERPERGER

Urban and Regional Planning In broadest terms, urban and regional planning is the process by which communities attempt to control change and development in their physical environments. It has been practised under many names: town planning, civic design, urban and rural planning, city planning, community planning, land use planning, and physical planning. The object of planning is the "physical environment," which is taken to mean land and all its uses, along with everything that has tangible existence on or beneath the land surface. Planning also includes the manner and style by which buildings are laid out in a city, and the design of public places (*see* URBAN DESIGN).

Physical environments are partly natural and partly man-made. A satisfying man-made or "built" environment, as it is usually known, is the ultimate goal of planning, but relations between natural and built environments, and interactions between people and their environments, are also of vital concern. It is now understood that human activities can have negative impacts upon the natural environment, just as certain natural conditions are hazardous to human well-being. In the case of polluted air or water, the hazard is caused by human activities; when people build in flood zones or on eroding slopes they have exposed themselves to natural dangers. Planners are equally concerned to protect natural environments from the adverse effects of human use, and to protect people from "risk" environments.

To plan the physical environment means to impose some deliberate order or organization upon it, with the aim of achieving a desired standard of environmental quality. This idea of environmental quality is the heart of planning practice, although there is no universal agreement about the characteristics of a good or well-ordered environment. Different cultures have tended to value environmental qualities differently and to organize their environments in different ways. Many factors influence the choice of qualities that are most desired at a particular time and place. Each community, through social and political processes, must set its own standards of a "good" physical environment. Also, people's needs, tastes and circumstances change. One of the more important ideas in contemporary planning theory is that planning policies and environmental standards should be monitored to alert the community to any change in their effectiveness or appropriateness.

A great variety of issues fall within the scope of urban and regional planning in Canada today, depending partly on the geographical scale of the planning area. Regional planners will be concerned with such matters as the protection of farmland or other valued resource sites (eg, forests, mineral deposits, seashores, lakeshores); the preservation of unique natural or historical features; the locations of highways and other transport facilities, such as PIPELINES or airports; and the growth prospects of communities spread throughout the region. If the region is organized around a large city, the planners must also take account of the problems caused by the city's expansion, and its impact upon the surrounding countryside and nearby towns. It may even be necessary to set up a separate metropolitan planning agency to give these communities a means of working together.

At the city scale, planning issues are of 2 general kinds. First there is a need to think ahead to accommodate the city's growth — deciding which lands should be built on and when, and whether they should be used for residential development, industry or another specialized function, such as a shopping centre or playing fields. Eventually, more detailed plans will also be required to determine the layout of every piece of land. The street network has to be designed; sites have to be reserved for schools and parks, shops, public buildings and religious institutions; provision has to be made for transit services and utilities; and development standards have to be set and design ideas tested to ensure that the desired environmental quality is achieved.

The second group of issues at the city scale concerns those parts of the community that are already developed. Planners will distinguish between areas where change is not desired and those where change is either unavoidable or judged to be needed. In the former case, the concern is for maintaining the built environment at its existing quality, regardless of pressures for change. This applies particularly to inner city neighbourhoods which face pressures for apartment redevelopment or for streets to be widened to permit through traffic. In the latter case, the problem is to facilitate the changes that are considered most desirable. In one situation this may mean that a deteriorating area has to be upgraded; in another it may mean that buildings have to be demolished to allow their sites to be used in a new and different way. The problems of rapidly changing downtowns, of outdated industrial and warehousing districts, and of inner city neighbourhoods experiencing a complex mix of social and physical changes all have to be dealt with by planners and public authorities. So, too, must special issues like HERITAGE CONSERVATION, the relocation of railway tracks, the provision of rapid-transit facilities, and the special housing needs of different groups of people.

Even under conditions of little or no growth, such as many Canadian cities are experiencing in the 1980s, urban environments go on changing. As cities age, it becomes more difficult and more expensive to maintain environmental quality. People's needs and desires change as well, and the environment must be constantly adapted. Special restoration or revitalization programs may be undertaken to try to draw business back to declining shopping districts and stimulate the local economy. Yet investment funds, both public and private, are in shorter supply than in times of economic growth. For Canadian planners, coping with the special problems of slow growth is one of the new issues of the 1980s.

Social and Political Foundations Like all types of planning (eg, REGIONAL DEVELOPMENT PLANNING; NATIONAL CAPITAL COMMISSION), planning cities and regions finds its rationale in the belief that a controllable future offers more promise than an uncontrolled one, and that a planned environment provides better opportunities for all people to enjoy life in their community setting. In this context, urban and regional planning is one of the many approaches adopted by society for the security and long-

term betterment of its members. This does not mean that all plans are prepared by governments, or that all planners are public servants, but it does mean that planning systems are usually designed to ensure that the needs of the entire community are properly considered. Plans come from many sources — from individuals, private corporations and public agencies — all of which have special ends or interests to pursue. In the "planned" community a higher level of forethought and public control is imposed, not to prevent these individual plans from being realized but to ensure they do not conflict with one another or with the overall needs of the community.

Unfortunately, it is rarely possible to demonstrate that an action taken in anticipation of the future will benefit an entire community. It is also difficult to show that a single public interest can be served. More commonly, planning is a matter of trying to decide which of many competing interests is more deserving, while also trying to treat everyone in a fair and reasonable manner. Should city council allow a shopping centre to be built in a residential area? An apparently straightforward issue like this raises large questions about personal rights and freedoms, and about the powers and obligations of public authorities. Hence the ultimate planning decisions must be political decisions, since politics is society's way of settling the conflicts that arise within a community.

Planning then is a way by which communities determine how they would like their environment to be. What kinds of benefits can they then look forward to? Official definitions in Canada have generally responded to this question by describing planning as a type of CONSERVATION. It is aimed at the wise use and management of community resources, the most critical of which is land. The idea that land is both a private commodity and community resource is controversial, but there is a legitimate community interest in the development of any land. Large amounts of public money have to be spent on such things as transport facilities, water treatment plants, schools and parks. The community must also assume most of the responsibility for ensuring that land is developed in a way that will allow these public services to function efficiently. In general, this is taken to mean that the development and use of land should yield the greatest possible public benefit for the lowest possible public cost. Yet the measurement of benefits and costs is no easy matter. For example, deciding upon the "best" use of land on the outskirts of a city depends on knowing how much value to attach to such benefits as an increase in the supply of new houses or an attractive residential environment, and how to weigh these benefits against a different set of costs, such as long journeys to work or the loss of prime agricultural land.

Origins of Planning in Canada The close connection between conservation and urban and regional planning began with the COMMISSION OF CONSERVATION in the years before WWI. At this time, Canada was caught up in a wave of reform enthusiasm that drew its inspiration from several international sources — from the British town planning movement, at last gaining popular support after a slow advance from the "health of towns" crisis of the 1830s; from the progressive reform movement in the US, with its attacks on political corruption and public mismanagement of all kinds; from the housing reform movements in both countries; and from the City Beautiful movement, which offered the ideal of well-ordered cities, with handsome buildings and public spaces, as a symbol of the progress of industrial civilization. All across Canada, groups of citizens organized themselves into "city planning commissions" and "civic improvement leagues" in their quest for a better

approach to the management of the urban environment and urban life (*see* URBAN REFORM). Yet it was not until the Commission of Conservation developed an interest in PUBLIC HEALTH that these local concerns were given national prominence. The commission took the view that the health of the people was the greatest of all resources. Town planning, as it was then called, was thought to be one way of ensuring a healthy and productive population. The first British planning statute of 1909, and the Garden City ideals advanced in the UK by Ebenezer Howard, were seen as the model for encouraging the development of healthy, attractive suburban communities in Canada.

The person chiefly responsible for drawing out the importance of the British example was Dr Charles HODGETTS, adviser to the Commission of Conservation's public-health committee from 1909 to 1915 and the medical health officer for Ontario. Hodgetts was keenly aware of the unhealthiness of the houses in which many working-class families lived in Toronto and other industrial cities. He believed that better standards of city layout and housing design would eliminate these problems. He was familiar with the planning movement and had organized an international city planning conference in Toronto in 1914. That same year he secured the appointment of Thomas ADAMS, one of the most eminent British planners of the day, as the commission's town planning adviser.

Adams was fully in tune with the mandate of the Commission of Conservation. He regarded planning as a combination of art and scientific procedure, requiring the most rigorous analysis of human needs and problems and the natural conditions of an area before a development plan could be proposed. He agreed with Hodgetts about the importance of healthy living conditions and better design standards, but his conception of a well-planned environment went beyond that. Adams represented the "city-efficient" or "city-functional" school of planning. Different parts of the city should be designed to suit their special functions: residential areas provided with all the amenities and services that go with healthy community life; industrial areas well served by railways and other transport facilities; business areas and civic centres designed to satisfy all the commercial and public needs of a modern community; and the whole city arranged to allow communications to be carried out safely and conveniently. In addition, land should always be allocated to its "best" use and never wasted; the special characteristics of each site should be incorporated into detailed development plans; public facilities, such as community centres or hospitals, should always be accessibly located for the people who have to use them; and private land development and public works programs should be carefully co-ordinated and scheduled to economize on public expenditures and to prevent costly mistakes. These principles persist in Canadian planning to this day.

Adams travelled repeatedly across Canada, carrying out planning studies, analysing land use and settlement problems, writing reports, and, above all, acting as spokesman for the planning cause. In 1919 he founded the Town Planning Institute of Canada to give Canadian planners their own professional organization. Interested persons from any profession were admitted as members. Initially, they were mostly civil engineers or land surveyors, along with some landscape architects and municipal officials. Under its charter, the institute sought to promote research, disseminate new knowledge and the results of planning experiences, and generally to advance planning ideas and set a high standard of planning practice. It was also hoped that the subject of planning would be introduced into university programs.

The GREAT DEPRESSION brought an end to most planning activity in Canada. The Town Planning Institute was disbanded in 1932, and was not revived until some 20 years later. Among the notable planning practitioners of this early period were Noulan CAUCHON, Frederic Todd, Horace SEYMOUR and Howard Dunington-Grubb. Many towns and cities drew up master plans, among them Ottawa, Vancouver, Calgary, Saint John, Halifax; and many interesting Garden City suburbs and new towns were planned.

Planning Law and Administration Another of Adams's contributions was his "model planning legislation," which he spent much time urging provincial governments to adopt. Good planning law was important to Adams because it establishes the framework within which individual communities can act on matters affecting their physical environments. He also believed that rural communities were as much in need of planning as urban ones. Not only did they have grave environmental and fiscal problems of their own, but town and country were so closely dependent on each other that they could not be separated for planning purposes. This marked the beginning of regional planning in Canada, and much of the early legislation made some provision for adjoining municipalities to work together when preparing their official plans.

In 1914 only 3 provinces had planning statutes: NS, NB and Alberta. By 1925 every province except Québec had a statute of some kind, although professional planners thought they were all inadequate. For one thing, the Acts did not make it mandatory that municipalities should prepare plans; for another, they did not provide for provincial governments to take an active part in planning. Municipal governments also tended to be critical, because they were mainly interested in having stronger powers to regulate construction and land development. The new American technique of ZONING looked particularly attractive, and the city of Kitchener adopted Canada's first zoning bylaw in 1924. First, however, it was necessary to persuade the Government of Ontario to pass an amendment to its Municipal Act. Not until 1925, when BC adopted its first planning statute, was zoning recognized in planning law. Other provinces followed suit, but the most complete statute of this early period was Alberta's Town and Rural Planning Act of 1929. Canadian planning law has evolved continually since then, and the modern administrative systems of urban and regional planning are far larger and more complex than anyone could have foreseen in 1929. Still, the Alberta Act was the first to provide all the basic elements of a modern planning system. The pattern that it set can be seen in the statutes now in effect, all of which date from the late 1970s and early 1980s.

The essential purposes of all provincial and territorial planning Acts are to secure the orderly, coherent growth and development of municipalities based on sound forethought and considerations of public interest; to bring about, and conserve, physical environments, including buildings and other works, which are satisfying to human needs and community concerns; to regulate how private and public lands may be used; and to allow for public participation in planning decisions. In addition to their planning Acts, each province provides for other types of planning and environmental or land use regulation not conferred specifically on the municipalities — in energy, environment, forestry, heritage and parks enactments. The province of Québec, for example, has an Act to protect agricultural lands (La Loi sur la protection du territoire agricole); Alberta has a Special Areas Board to plan for and administer over one million ha of public lands in agricultural use; the PEI Development Corporation undertakes

comprehensive land planning with powers to acquire, sell and lease lands for several kinds of purposes; Manitoba operates an Interdepartmental Planning Board for the planning and management of the province's crown lands. The federal government performs planning functions for Canadian crown lands through many statutes and a number of Cabinet policies, such as the Federal Policy on Land Use and the Federal Environmental Assessment and Review Process. Thus, in an overall sense, regional land use plans in Canada come about through the co-ordinated administration of many laws within a province, through co-ordination between provincial and federal laws, and by co-ordinative policies among and between pairs of neighbouring jurisdictions. These and municipal planning activities are all supported by modern information systems, such as the computerized mapping and data analysis operation, Canada Land Use Monitoring Program, and Statistics Canada's census data on populations, housing and business activity. All municipalities maintain some kind of data monitoring system to aid both long-range forecasting and planning policy decisions. The larger cities in Canada use computerized operations for the planning of TRANSPORTATION systems and for monitoring certain environmental changes such as AIR POLLUTION.

Provincial planning Acts spell out what municipalities or regional authorities must and may do. Generally speaking, an Act provides for 5 basic measures. First the municipality is to prepare a "general plan," sometimes called the "official plan" or the "plan d'urbanism." This plan sets down the policies that will govern where and when developments on land can take place. It usually includes statements on the community's social, economic and quality-of-life goals, and the fiscal management of the public works (eg, sewers, roads) that will be required. The plan describes by maps, drawings and written texts the various communities and land use districts, and the guidelines concerning building development in the districts. A second set of plans, in more detail, may also be prepared for special areas, such as plans for heritage conservation or redevelopment of inner city neighbourhoods, or for industrial parks. The remaining 3 measures are legal and administrative instruments for implementing a general plan: a "land use" or "zoning" bylaw, subdivision controls, and a building permit process. Before a building permit is issued, the plot of land must first be part of an approved subdivision of land, while specified rules for the type and amount of building space allowed and the requirements of architectural features must be adhered to. Subdivision control governs the process of converting raw land into building plots of adequate size and shape, while zoning establishes the detailed range and limitations of use to which a plot can be put.

Planning laws have the effect of limiting an owner's rights in private property in order to secure benefits for the community as a whole. These benefits include such things as the safety and health of persons; convenience, amenities and agreeable environments for the public; acceptable standards of private and public living and work places; and reasonable burdens of public expenditures that have to be incurred when land is developed. Planning law in some provinces also allows municipalities or the provincial government to prevent the destruction of heritage properties and natural environments, or to force property owners to undertake measures that enhance the architectural, aesthetic, landscaping features, or the convenience to users of any buildings proposed for construction. The balance struck between freedom to use one's land and requirements imposed by public authority depends on the prevailing social val-

ues of the community of the day. Moreover, all planning statutes in Canada now require that citizens be heard before major land planning decisions are made, and there is always a right of appeal by the property owner on any regulatory decision taken.

In Canadian statutes, the province confers responsibility upon urban municipalities to carry out planning in their areas. Rural areas and towns are frequently organized for regional planning around a "regional district" created by decree of the provincial government. In some jurisdictions, the municipalities of selected metropolitan areas have been grouped together, by statute, in order to create a special, "second tier" planning administration (eg, Québec City and Montréal, Toronto, Greater Vancouver, Winnipeg). In the latter cases, the metropolitan administration performs broad policy planning and the co-ordination of major public services and works; detailed plans and development regulation are left to the constituent municipalities.

The foregoing planning arrangements apply essentially to the whole of Canada's privately owned lands. These constitute, however, only some 10% of the Canadian landmass; or, on a provincial basis, as much as 75% (NS) or as little as 6% (BC) of the land. The planning and environmental management of provincial and federal crown lands falls to the various departments and agencies of the governments. In most provinces, and for the federal government, special "integrative" administrative mechanisms have been established to further a comprehensive approach to planning the use of crown lands and the wise development and conservation of resources underneath or upon them. A special aspect of crown lands planning is the settling of native LAND CLAIMS.

New Towns is a specialized aspect of planning of considerable significance to Canadians. It refers to the comprehensive planning, zoning and land subdivision of a community, executed before the arrival of any residents. Typically, one-industry resource-development towns of small size (fewer than 5000 people), Canada's new towns are mainly located in remote areas (eg, KITIMAT, BC, Matagami, Qué, THOMPSON, Man, and URANIUM CITY, Sask). In 1984 there were nearly 200 new towns in Canada, with a population of 700 000. Most of the early examples (1900-20) were not laid out by planners and did not benefit from imaginative site planning. Adams and others began applying the ideas of Garden City, master plans and zoning to new resource towns in the 1920s (eg, TÉMISKAMING, Qué, KAPUSKASING, Ont, Arvida, Qué, CORNER BROOK, Nfld, Port Alice, BC). In the post-WWII period, planners of RESOURCE TOWNS began to pay attention to the acute social and leisure activity problems associated with small, isolated and "closed" communities. Further advancements were made in devising new forms for town layout and housing, making these fundamental components of a new town plan more adapted to the rugged site conditions and cold climate environments. The most notable recent example of progressive new town planning is Fermont, Qué, designed by Norbert Schoenauer and built by the Iron Ore Co of Canada. The overall plan is compact and both the street layout and housing construction serve as screens against the harsh Labrador winter winds. Many of the single-family houses are oriented for passive solar heating. The town's commercial and entertainment centre is fully enclosed within an extensive building complex that also includes apartment dwellings.

Community Planning and Social Policy In its development as a branch of public administration since the 1940s, urban and regional planning has gained a degree of acceptability that Adams could scarcely have hoped for. Yet arguments persist about the appropriate role and purposes of planning as a social institution. It is not that the basic goals of efficiency and orderly development are under challenge; a well-managed environment is obviously of benefit to everyone. The real question is whether order and efficiency should be the only goals, or even the most important ones. In its beginnings in Canada, and in the early American and European reform movements, town planning had offered the promise of something altogether more radical. It was to be part of the antidote to the enormous social costs of the Industrial Revolution, a sweeping movement of social reform in which the building of better cities would contribute to the building of a better civilization. At a more practical humanitarian level, this meant that each community should assume some obligation to care for the victims of economic development and the progress of urban industrial areas.

The main impact of these ideas in Canada began to be felt in the 1950s, although there were earlier signs of concern. Prominent social reformers, such as J.S. WOODSWORTH in Winnipeg and Claire Casgrain in Montréal, made no small contribution to the progressive advancement of the Canadian planning movement. It took the Great Depression of the 1930s, followed by the desire for national reconstruction after WWII, however, for housing reform and physical planning to be linked effectively as instruments of social policy.

One of the first indications of this trend appeared in 1935, in the chapter on housing in *Social Planning for Canada* compiled by the LEAGUE FOR SOCIAL RECONSTRUCTION. The author was a young British-born architect, Humphrey CARVER, who was to become one of the most distinguished Canadian planners of the modern period. Carver argued that all Canadians had a right to live in safe, healthful, comfortable houses and neighbourhoods, even if they could not afford them, and that the state had a responsibility to ensure that good housing conditions were available to everyone. He argued, as Hodgetts and Adams had done, that it was necessary to build better communities to create a physical and social environment conducive to a decent way of life. Carver's argument was developed further in "Housing and Community Planning," a study released in 1944 as part of the final report of the Advisory Committee on Reconstruction, set up by the federal government in 1941. This study is largely the work of 2 men, C.A. Curtis, an economist who chaired the housing subcommittee, and Leonard MARSH, the committee's research adviser. In a manner reminiscent of Adams's most famous report, *Rural Planning and Development*, Curtis and Marsh described the ills of uncontrolled urbanization. They showed that slum conditions were widespread in Canadian cities, and drew attention to the extensive occurrence of wasteful, uncoordinated and unsightly suburban developments. They urged the government of Canada to embark upon a comprehensive national program for social betterment and community development, in which housing, planning and public education would figure prominently.

In 1944 the government made sweeping changes to the National Housing Act to promote the construction of new houses, the repair and modernization of existing houses, and the general improvement of community environments. In 1945 the Central Mortgage and Housing Corporation (now CANADA MORTGAGE AND HOUSING CORPORATION) was created to implement the new national housing policy. That policy was subjected to further refinement over the next 20 years or so, through a series of amendments to the National Housing Act (NHA), which provided a major spur to urban planning activity in the postwar period. For the first time there was

a national planning agency with strong regulatory and financial power. Through its role as an insurer of residential mortgages, particularly in the 1950s and 1960s, CMHC exerted a great deal of control over the design of Canadian suburbs (*see* DEVELOPMENT INDUSTRY). Through its direct grants for housing for low-income families and other disadvantaged groups, CMHC has influenced the social geography of Canadian cities. And through its various urban renewal programs, from the massive slum clearance and redevelopment schemes of the 1950s and 1960s to the neighbourhood rehabilitation projects of the 1970s, CMHC has been a major force of environmental change in inner Canadian city areas.

CMHC's policies and programs have generated their own share of controversy over the years, but the NHA has always been inspired by a clear social objective. As a matter of basic right, of social justice, all Canadians should have access to a decent standard of housing. The "decent standard" must be defined by society, but the more important point is that the community at large assumes the cost of raising everyone's environment to an acceptable condition. The state has intervened to distribute equitably the benefits and costs of life in a modern urban society. That principle is well accepted in Canada today, and underlies numerous social programs of federal and provincial governments alike. Yet the question arises: is physical planning (and land use regulation) a proper instrument for redistributive purposes? On the one hand, the provincial planning statutes largely ignore the issue; their statements of purpose are usually limited to "the economical and orderly development of land," or some like phrase. On the other hand, in the actual planning decisions that are taken, day in and day out, questions of rights and justice are constantly in the forefront, and many Canadian communities have adopted physical planning policies that indeed serve redistributive ends. In general, though, Canadian planners are still struggling to reconcile the social reform ideals that were such a powerful force in the international planning movement with the simpler notion of "proper" use of land.

Planning Profession and Education With the growth of cities after 1945, the Canadian planning profession was revitalized and developed quickly. It is not just that planners were needed in greater numbers than before; the specialized tasks performed in modern planning agencies became far more diverse. In addition to the traditional principles of city layout, land subdivision and architectural arts, planners had to learn about urban sociology and human behaviour, management sciences, data analysis and forecasting, municipal and planning law, and environmental sciences. Educational programs were established after 1947, for which the federal government and CMHC provided invaluable assistance. In 1944, as revisions to the NHA were being drafted, Marsh and others suggested to the deputy minister of finance, W.C. Clark, that provision be made to fund research, professional training and public education. Clark inserted a Part V into the Act, entitled "Housing Research and Community Planning." Parliament authorized $5 million to begin implementing Part V, and has continued its support ever since.

Over the years CMHC has funded much scientific research and conducted numerous practical planning studies in partnership with provincial or municipal governments or the universities. It has awarded hundreds of scholarships for Canadian students to learn urban and regional planning, either in one of the accredited planning schools or in graduate programs in fields closely related to housing and planning. CMHC has also sponsored a variety of informative magazines (eg, *Community Planning Review, Habitat, Living Places*), and Part V funds

made possible the establishment of the Community Planning Assn of Canada in 1946. The CPAC is a nongovernment organization that seeks to increase citizen awareness and understanding of community planning and community involvement in planning matters.

NHA Part V funds were also used to help introduce degree-granting planning programs in the universities, partly by direct grants to the first planning schools: McGill (1947), Manitoba (1949), British Columbia (1950) and Toronto (1951). A French-language program was commenced at U de Montréal in 1961. Several other universities introduced planning programs in the 1960s and 1970s, and a total of 13 were accredited by the Canadian Institute of Planners (CIP) in 1984. A number of the later programs were titled "Environmental Design" or "Environmental Studies," an indication of the expanding breadth and multidisciplinary nature of modern planning profession. U of Waterloo and Ryerson Polytechnical Institute offer 4-year undergraduate degrees, while other approved programs are at the graduate level (which means that students must first obtain an undergraduate degree in a field related to planning). Initially, when urban or civic design was emphasized in the planning curriculum, architects and engineers made up the majority of planning students. This pattern changed as university programs underwent transformations in social outlook and professional scope. By the late 1950s a training in one of the social sciences (eg, geography, sociology or economics) became an equally common route into planning, and this background was further expanded to include the managerial and environmental sciences in the 1960s and 1970s. Today, more than half the practising planners in Canada came to the profession by studying first in the liberal arts or social sciences.

In 1949, 45 persons practised planning in Canada. In 1984 the Canadian Institute of Planners counted some 3500 members. They serve in many roles encompassed by private consultancies, various departments of the provincial and federal governments, municipal and regional authorities, crown corporations, resource industries, and the land development industry. Two years of supervised work experience after obtaining a planning degree are required for admission into the profession. The CIP is a national affiliation of institutes, one in each of the provinces and territories. Besides regulating the professional conduct of its members and supervising standards of practice and admission to membership, the institute carries out programs of public education, and occasionally advises governments on planning matters, legislation and environmental issues. Approximately one-third of the institute's financial resources go to support the publication of *Plan Canada* and *CIP Forum ICU*. The former publishes new knowledge and studies of planning practice; the latter reports on current events in urban and regional affairs across Canada and abroad.

Unlike the architecture and engineering professions, where professional practice and the use of titles are strictly regulated by provincial legislation, planning is generally not regulated. In 2 provinces only, BC and Saskatchewan, provincial enactments reserve the title of "planner" to those persons accredited by the provincial affiliate of CIP. Even here, and in all other provinces and territories except Québec, any person or private company may practise planning, whether or not they are members of the institute. Québec restricts the right to practise planning to persons granted a licence through the Corporation des urbanistes du Québec, an affiliate of CIP. Over the years, institute members in virtually all provinces have endeavoured to persuade governments to accord their profession an exclusive right to practise planning. Yet opinion within

CIP is divided about the desirability of legislation that would have to prescribe, in a finite manner, where a privileged practice of planning should begin and end in relation to other licensed professions, such as architecture and engineering. This doubt is explained by the fact that planning cannot be yet described as a discipline founded upon a discrete body of knowledge and skills. Indeed, as planning has attached itself to an increasingly broad range of urban, regional and environmental management affairs, it has become an "interdisciplinary" profession that embraces highly qualified people from many disciplines.

WILLIAM T. PERKS AND P.J. SMITH

Reading: T. Adams, *Rural Planning and Development* (1917); A.F.J. Artibise and G.A. Stelter, eds, *The Usable Urban Past: Planning and Politics in the Modern Canadian City* (1979), and *Shaping the Urban Landscape: Aspects of the Canadian City-Building Process* (1982); Canada, Dept of Environment, *Report of the Interdepartmental Task Force on Land Use Policy* (1980); H. Carver, *Compassionate Landscape* (1975); L.O. Gertler, *Regional Planning in Canada* (1972); Gertler and R. Crowley, *Changing Canadian Cities: The Next 25 Years* (1977); Gertler, ed, *Planning the Canadian Environment* (1968); S.M. Makuch, *Canadian Municipal and Planning Law* (1983); National Capital Commission, *A Capital in the Making* (1982); William T. Perks and I.M. Robinson, eds, *Urban and Regional Planning in a Federal State: The Canadian Experience* (1979); P. Rutherford, *Saving the Canadian City* (1974).

Urban Citizen Movements are community groups, usually organized because of concern about land use and the way planning decisions are made in local government. "Protect our neighbourhood" and "Open up city hall" are the most familiar demands of citizen movements in Canada. Community groups have been a feature of urban politics since MUNICIPAL GOVERNMENT began in Canada over a century ago. They are usually organized when a neighbourhood, often an older inner-city area, is threatened by a development proposal, particularly for an expressway or high-density building. When high-density office or apartment high-rise development is proposed, the property development company, city council and the city staff (especially the planning department) become targets for protest. The developer and city hall are also the focus of community groups' activities when expressways or other major roadworks are planned. Because most provinces provide a legal procedure for appealing municipal planning decisions, community groups often take their cases to provincial bodies such as the Alberta Local Authorities Board and the Ontario Municipal Board. Sometimes community groups appeal decisions made by such bodies, making their appeal to provincial Cabinets or courts. Citizen movement activity peaked in Canada during the late 1960s and the 1970s when community groups multiplied throughout the country because of the buoyant economy and the resulting development pressures (*see* CITY). Citizens became concerned with broader policy issues; the question of whether an expressway should be built or not was transformed into the problem of automobile traffic versus public transit. Environmental pollution, day-care facilities, racial discrimination and recreational open spaces are other concerns of citizen groups; having experienced difficulty with city hall because relevant information was inaccessible or because decisions were made at private meetings of city staff and council, many citizen groups have called for more open decision-making processes. Those that encountered resistance from city hall have sometimes become involved in civic elections by running their own candidates, transforming the councils of the larger Canadian cities. The citizen movement in Canada continues its efforts to stabilize threatened neighbourhoods and change the composition of city councils and the ways decisions are made. DONALD HIGGINS

Urban Design can be applied to the whole city (as in KITIMAT), to well-defined units of the city (as in Don Mills in Toronto) and to individual streets and clusters of buildings. The earliest extant examples of urban design in Canada are designs for the whole city. Québec City is a compact, fortified city, paying respect in its design to church and state, and acknowledging its existence to the St Lawrence R. Old Montréal, despite considerable demolition and building, preserves the form of the 18th-century street pattern, crowned by Place d'Armes on the height of land at its centre. Halifax derives its visual character from a generous orthogonal grid of streets laid out by British military engineers.

Since the rapid growth of cities at the end of the 19th century, cities have been be planned rather than designed and the term urban design is applied to parts of a city in which there has been particular emphasis on the visual aspect of the streets and open spaces. Ottawa is perhaps the only Canadian city in which, during the 20th century, design of the urban fabric was considered on a large scale. However, in every town, civic pride was important. The visual focus in every new city in the West was on the city hall and legislative buildings (*see* GOVERNMENT BUILDINGS). The street was an important urban-design element; most towns had their Main St, and Sherbrooke St in Montréal and University Ave in Toronto were grand avenues.

After WWII, when cities grew rapidly, there was less concern for the design of the urban environment than for the design of individual buildings. However, in the new, extensive residential areas there were notable attempts to design the whole environment. Don Mills exemplified these new communities, with curved, treed streets and widely spaced buildings. Later, Flemingdon Park in Toronto answered a demand for higher density with tighter massing of buildings and a harder edge to its streets and paths (*see* DEVELOPMENT INDUSTRY; URBAN AND REGIONAL PLANNING; ZONING).

The design of the metropolitan downtown entered a new era with the building from 1956 to 1965 of PLACE VILLE MARIE in Montréal. The project combined retail stores with corporate office space and a major banking hall; introduced the idea of a building complex in which public circulation and access are designed 3-dimensionally, so that entrances are at several levels; made pedestrian connections underground with the public transportation system; and created a plaza for public use. Contrary to fears that business would be diverted from the traditional downtown shopping streets, Place Ville Marie has competed with suburban centres and helped revitalize the downtown core.

The paved civic space had not been an important element in Canadian cities, except in the old French cities of Québec. In the early 1960s both private and public projects began to recognize their function, which is quite distinct from park use. For lunch breaks or for public gatherings, celebrations, exhibitions and protests, these plazas or squares created new views in the city and displayed buildings in their entirety as objects. At the same time, a populist movement emerged in the cities, with a demand for paths exclusive to pedestrians and the closing of some streets to automobiles, as on Sparks St Mall in Ottawa.

Many commercial projects have now been built with a plaza on the street or enclosed by buildings. The Toronto-Dominion Bank complex in Toronto exemplifies the straight-sided group of towers set in a paved plaza. Commerce Court, Toronto, is a skilful grouping of new buildings that complement the ornate 1931 bank headquarters and enclose a serene courtyard. It introduced another element to contemporary urban design: the plaza which is only glimpsed from the street and provides a pedestrian route through the city block. The TORONTO

CITY HALL, on Nathan Phillips Square, and Robson Square in Vancouver are examples of public buildings which created squares and plazas in the city.

The year 1967 was important for urban design in Canada; the celebration of the Canadian Centennial prompted expressions of national and civic pride in new community buildings and parks and also focused attention on a frequently neglected architectural heritage (*see* HERITAGE CONSERVATION; PUBLIC ART; THEATRE). EXPO 67 also played a significant role as a demonstration of urban-design elements, of elegant street furniture, and of the total composition of paths, spaces and buildings to create a memorable image. In 1971, when the Vincent Massey Awards for Excellence in the Urban Environment were instituted, the entries were many and varied: tree planting programs, housing enclaves, historic street preservation, promenades.

Designing the city at different levels (on street, below and above ground level) was a response both to a harsh climate and to the demands of circulation in the downtown core. Besides enclosed pedestrian ways between buildings, it produced large-scale indoor gathering places or atria. The extensive underground pedestrian ways in Montréal and Toronto link atria, in much the same way that streets link squares. Place Desjardins in Montréal was similarly designed for public gatherings. The HUB block at U of Alberta is essentially an elevated indoor street, lined with service outlets and stores on the first-floor level and with student housing above and below. One of the largest and most acclaimed of these indoor urban designs is EATON CENTRE in Toronto, a multilevel street lined with stores and services, connected to the subway and to other city blocks under a great vaulted glass roof. Atria add another dimension to the design of cities, particularly when the connection to the street is generous. The weather-protected city changes the views of the city, besides affecting its appearance. In Calgary the system of glazed bridges crossing the streets between buildings (known as Plus 15) becomes a feature in the design of the street and also offers a new vantage point from which to view the streets.

In the wake of skyscrapers, megaprojects, plazas and atria came a growing concern for the older fabric of the city, for the preservation of historic buildings and for housing. Consequently an increasing number of projects were designed on a modest scale, rehabilitating and preserving the heritage of familiar streets. From the steep, picturesque streets of St John's, Nfld, to Bastion Square in Victoria, in many cities and towns and along innumerable main streets, there has been greater recognition of the worth of the urban image. *See also* LANDSCAPE ARCHITECTURE. BLANCHE LEMCO VAN GINKEL

Reading: H. Carver, *Cities in the Suburbs* (1962); R.W. Collier, *Contemporary Cathedrals: Large-Scale Development in Canadian Cities* (1974); L.O. Gertler, ed, *Planning the Canadian Environment* (1968); G. LePape, ed, *Land Use and Development/Développement et aménagement du territoire* (1975); H. Spence-Sales, *Beautifying Towns/L'embellissement urbain* (1966).

Urban Effect on Climate is one of the best examples of unintentional modification of the atmosphere by humans (*see* CLIMATOLOGY). The construction of every building, road and parking lot creates a new, local microclimate. Taken together with the AIR POLLUTION resulting from human activities, these changes constitute the local effect of a settlement upon its CLIMATE. In Canada such effects have been observed in villages with as few as a thousand inhabitants, as well as in metropolitan areas, and in all climatic regions. Both land surface and air are altered by urbanization. Buildings change the geometric arrangement of the land surface, creating a rigid, rough system of blocks and street "canyons," especially in the centre of cities. This changes the airflow over the city and creates traps for incoming and outgoing radiant energy. Construction materials alter the rate of heat and the rate of water uptake and loss by the surface. Changes in the composition of the air are produced by the release of heat, water vapour and pollutants from combustion of fuels and other activities. Pollutants may alter both the transfer of radiation and the growth of CLOUD droplets.

All of the climatic elements (sunshine, temperature, humidity, wind, etc) are affected by the presence of the city. The impact is discernible on an annual basis and over a period of years as a city grows, but it is usually best displayed on individual days during fine weather (clear skies and light winds). For example, pollution decreases the amount of solar energy in Montréal by about 9% annually, but on individual days the decrease may be as great as 25%. A "heat island" often exists in a city centre because it is warmer than the surrounding countryside. In most large cities in Canada the annual heat-island effect is 1-2°C, but on occasion it is much larger. On clear, calm summer evenings the heat island can be as large as 5-6°C in Brandon, 6-7°C in St-Hyacinthe, 9-10°C in Hamilton, 10-11°C in Vancouver and 11-12°C in Winnipeg, Edmonton and Montréal. The latter values are some of the largest in the world. Even during arctic nights, towns such as Inuvik have a heat island. The relative humidity is almost always lower in a city (because of the warmth), but the actual amount of moisture is often greater, especially at night and in winter. In Prairie centres such as Edmonton, the winter release of water vapour from the combustion of natural gas used for heating gives greater humidity and the possibility of ice FOG at temperatures below about -30°C. Ice fog is also an unpleasant feature of high-latitude settlements such as Inuvik. Winds are generally reduced in the city except around tall buildings where "jetting" may be a problem. Cities also induce their own breeze circulations. Little is known about the effects of Canadian cities on precipitation. Foreign research would suggest that cities enhance summer precipitation, but the heat island may melt some of the snowfall before it is registered.   T.R. OKE

Urban Reform, a loosely knit set of municipal government and citizen group initiatives, from the late 1890s to the end of WWI and from the late 1960s to the mid-1970s, aimed at improving city life. The first reforms showed a political emphasis that favoured vesting authority in the hands of supposedly apolitical experts. A distrust of local democracy, a feeling that government had to be made secure for people of proven talent, underlay structural reform in local government. Occasionally, preference for rule by "the best men" led to new local government bodies of appointed, rather than elected, members. Reformers equated proven ability with business success or — as professions such as urban planning, accounting and public health expanded — with appropriate training.

New MUNICIPAL GOVERNMENT bodies seldom usurped the mayor and council, but a modest tampering with the tradition of civic government by council and its standing committees came with the 1896 introduction of the Toronto Board of Control. It was eventually elected by a city-wide vote, thereby evading ward politics, and had special authority in fiscal matters. Among the cities adopting it were Winnipeg (1906), Ottawa (1907), Montréal (1909), Hamilton (1910) and London (1914). A more extreme change teamed a city manager with a mayor at the head of municipal administration. In 1904 Edmonton hired a "city commissioner," the equivalent of a city manager. Similar arrangements were made in Saint John, NB (1908), and

Little Champlain St, Québec City, *c* 1900-1910 (*courtesy Public Archives of Canada/PA-43301/Notman*).

Regina, Saskatoon and Prince Albert, Sask (1911 to 1912). Long after the reform period, the city manager scheme was adopted in many Québec municipalities, and in Halifax and Victoria.

The real devolution of power by elected representatives to civic bureaucrats occurred in the administration of new civic services, as increased PUBLIC OWNERSHIP led to the management of transit systems and electric-power distribution by appointed commissions; other commissions were established for parks and urban planning. Municipal ownership was not a novel concept. From the 1850s to the 1870s, Canadian cities had either sponsored publicly owned waterworks or assumed control from private companies. Streetcar lines in the 1870s and 1880s and electric-generating and distributing firms in the 1890s had entered into franchise contracts with cities to operate on municipal rights-of-way. But the reputation of this private franchise approach was tarnished by consumer grievances about fares, rates and levels of service. In many Prairie cities municipal ownership accompanied booster campaigns. By 1914 Edmonton's progressive image was enhanced by municipal ownership of a full range of urban services: electricity, streetcars and telephones. In Montréal local businessmen ran private utilities that withstood reform criticism; in Vancouver the streetcars and power network of the British Columbia Electric Railway were British owned. Although municipal ownership was a reform cause across Canada, its outcome confirmed the nation's regional identities.

PUBLIC-HEALTH concerns before the early reform period had taken the form of *ad hoc* reactions to sporadic EPIDEMICS. The advance of the germ theory of disease in the 1880s, and the concurrent growth of government collection of vital statistics, helped foster vigorous public-health campaigns. Most cities relied upon voluntary agencies and a modest public-health budget until the late 1920s. In some communities medical health officers asserted the considerable authority placed in their hands by provincial health Acts and city bylaws passed between 1900 and 1920, working to eliminate outdoor privies, overcrowded dwellings, adulterated food and contaminated water supplies. Other reformers were keenly patriotic and religiously inspired to do good works (*see* SOCIAL GOSPEL); playground movements arose to instill British character, virtue and cleanliness among foreign children. Settlement houses run by pioneering social workers (including Winnipeg's All People's Mission, run for a time by J.S. WOODSWORTH) similarly sought to "improve" immigrants. If such social programs were condescending, they nevertheless served practical ends: a playground was safer than a street, and the settlement houses held classes in conversational English.

Owing to the great population growth of ur-

ban Canada from 1900 to 1920, housing became a reform concern. Recognizing a need to remedy inadequate housing, many groups discussed the feasibility of forming philanthropic housing companies. Most plans were shelved in the 1913 depression, and the frail philanthropic impulse was swept aside in WWI.

Urban planning also began in the first era of urban reform, originating from a concern about shabby streets and a lack of civic grandeur. City governments or citizens' groups commissioned planners to draft sketches of a "city beautiful," with neoclassical civic buildings, park boulevards, broad avenues and realigned railways. But the war dampened optimism; transition towards an interest in health, housing and the efficient layout of services occurred toward the end of the reform era. Thomas ADAMS, hired in 1914 as planning adviser to the COMMISSION OF CONSERVATION (1909), campaigned for provincial planning Acts to bolster the authority of municipal planning agencies; he also supervised reconstruction after the 1917 HALIFAX EXPLOSION.

Political changes during this complex reform era increased the authority of civic experts, but it is doubtful whether this upgraded civic affairs; politicians and administrators clashed and citizens became confused by the array of agencies. Despite improvements effected by health officers, urban planners and social workers, these challenges to neighbourhood or ward-level political decisions did not entirely extirpate old practices. Moreover, although many successful ideas from the US and England influenced Canadian action, Canada experienced modest reform achievements.

The second reform period had a similarly international dimension, in this instance the widespread reaction in Western democracies against centralized and bureaucratic authority, and rejection of the tenet that "bigger is better." In Canadian cities, neighbourhood groups mobilized to halt expressways, demolition and renewal projects and high-rise invasions of the urban core. *City Magazine* was a major voice of the movement in the 1970s. Political style was another feature. Toronto Mayor John Sewell (1978-80) had all the elements of a reformer: identification with community activism and a distrust of nonelected agents of civic authority. There were crusades to save neighbourhoods and defeat drastic land-use changes; some utilized self-interest for a defence of property values. In many cities, action came too late to save remarkable older structures or venerable residential areas. Nevertheless the second and short-lived reform movement affected the way politicians, planners and the middle class perceived the city. Restoration rather than demolition became fashionable; the domination of urban planning by the requirements of the automobile was challenged. *See* HERITAGE CANADA FOUNDATION; HISTORIC SITE; URBAN AND REGIONAL PLANNING.

JOHN WEAVER

Reading: P. Rutherford, ed, *Saving the Canadian City* (1974) and "Urban Reform," *Urban History Review* 2, 76 (1976); John Weaver, *Shaping the Canadian City* (1977); A.F.J. Artibise and G.A. Stelter, eds, *The Usable Urban Past* (1979); H. Kaplan, *Reform, Planning and City Politics* (1982).

Urban Studies, the study of Canada's urban development in all its diverse aspects, including the evolution of communities (urban history); city-building processes (urban geography, urban economics, planning, architecture); urban politics and government (urban political science); and urban society (urban sociology and anthropology, urban demography).

Before the 1960s urban studies were dominated by geographers. In Québec, Raoul Blanchard and his students published numerous urban studies in the 1930s, 1940s and 1950s, while Jacob Spelt, Donald Kerr, J. Wreford Watson and others examined urban development in Ontario. Most studies concentrated on individual communities or regions, and adopted one of 2 approaches: studies that singled out the urban aspects of the man-environment system, resulting in systematic studies of individual phenomena (urban-economic geography); and synthetic studies that attempted to achieve a holistic appreciation of the many interrelated phenomena that evolved over time to give a unique, urban character to the landscape (historical urban geography).

By the early 1970s many other disciplines had become involved in urban studies, and distinct subdisciplines emerged rapidly. This trend was marked by the establishment, for example, of the Centre for Urban and Community Studies at U of Toronto, the Institute of Urban Studies at U of Winnipeg, and the Institut national de la recherche scientifique (INRS) — urbanisation in the U du Québec system. Activity in universities was not restricted to research centres; it also included the introduction or expansion of urban studies courses and teaching programs, and substantial growth in schools of URBAN AND REGIONAL PLANNING.

In government, distinct ministries of urban affairs at the provincial level were formed or expanded, and the federal Ministry of State for Urban Affairs was established (1971). These departments supported research and added to the well-established research programs of such bodies as the CANADA MORTGAGE AND HOUSING CORPORATION (CMHC) and the Canadian Council on Urban and Regional Research (CCURR). Several important projects were undertaken during the 1970s, including the publication of the Urban Profiles Series (1974-75) and the Urban Prospects Series (1975-76).

The urban studies environment was bolstered as well by the appearance of a variety of new journals, newsletters and magazines, including *Urban Focus* (1972), published by the Institute of Local Government; *Urban History Review/Revue d'histoire urbaine* (1972), published by the National Museum of Man; *Urban Reader* (1973), published by the city of Vancouver; *Urban Forum* (1975), published by CCURR; and *City Magazine* (1974), a commercial venture undertaken by Toronto publisher James Lorimer. In 1977 Micromedia of Toronto began to produce a quarterly index of publications in the urban studies field entitled *Urban Canada/Canada urbain*.

The increasing concern over urban issues was also evident at the municipal level. The Federation of Canadian Municipalities either undertook or sponsored urban research, while individual communities organized formal city archives. Preservation of the built urban heritage was another characteristic of the 1970s as many communities established committees and departments and passed by-laws dealing with preservation and conservation (*see* HERITAGE CONSERVATION; HERITAGE CANADA FOUNDATION).

Despite all this activity, no dominant theoretical or interpretative trends emerged in urban studies in the 1970s or early 1980s. Hundreds of books and articles were published, particularly at the community and regional levels. Books included N.H. Lithwick, *Urban Canada: Problems and Prospects* (1970); J. and R. Simmons, *Urban Canada* (1974); G. Nader, *Cities of Canada,* (2 vols, 1975-76); J.N. Jackson, *The Canadian City: Space, Form, Quality* (1973); L. Stone, *Urban Development in Canada* (1967); D.J.H. Higgins, *Urban Canada: Its Government and Politics* (1977); J. Lorimer and E. Ross, *The City Book* (2 vols, 1976-77); L.O. Gertler, *Planning the Canadian Environment* (1968); G.A. Stelter and A.F.J. Artibise, eds, *The Canadian City* (1977) and *Canada's Urban Past* (1981).

By the early 1980s the attention devoted to urban issues was beginning to wane as a result of the recession and because many of the earlier initiatives had not — in the minds of poli-ticians, at least — fulfilled their early promise. Thus the federal urban ministry was disbanded in 1979, several provincial urban ministries were reduced, urban research institutes foundered, and several urban studies journals and newsletters died. But although there was a notable decline in interest in urban studies, there remained a solid core of specialists. *See* CITY; URBAN DESIGN; URBAN REFORM; URBANIZATION.

A.F.J. ARTIBISE AND G.A. STELTER

Urban Transportation With the spread of INDUSTRIALIZATION and the growing size of cities, it was no longer possible for many city dwellers to live within walking distance of work. Urban transportation has become increasingly important as our cities continue to grow.

Early attempts to solve the urban transportation problem were made in other countries. In 1819, for example, Paris benefited from the operation of a system of horse-drawn stagecoaches. In the next decade, omnibuses began operating in New York City and in London, England. The development of railways for intercity passenger transportation in the 1820s and 1830s was quickly followed by their adaptation for use in cities. Steam locomotives were unsuitable for urban use as they scared horses and were dirty, so most of the early street railways used horses or mules for propulsion. Toronto had horse-drawn trams in operation by 1845, Montréal by the 1860s, and soon after other Canadian cities introduced these vehicles.

Horse-drawn trams were a vast improvement, but they were far from ideal transportation. Heavy loads could not be hauled, and horses were expensive and required frequent rest periods; they also polluted the streets. Numerous attempts were made to substitute mechanical power for muscle power: the invention of the first successful electric railway in 1879 by Dr E.W. von Siemens in Germany led to a revolution in transportation. German, US and British inventors were soon busy perfecting the electric streetcar. One of the first full-scale examples of the new technology was built at the Toronto Industrial Exposition of 1885. This short line introduced another important invention, the trolley pole, which permitted the efficient and safe collection of electric power from overhead wires. Commercial use followed, and Canada was one of the first countries to exploit fully the technological advances. The first electric railway line in Canada was established in Windsor, Ont, and opened 28 May 1886 using 1½ miles (2.4 km) of track. Another electric streetcar system was opened the following year in St Catharines, Ont, with several systems following in the

Early streetcar, St Catherine St, Montréal (*courtesy Notman Photographic Archives/McCord Museum*).

next few years. Ultimately, most Canadian cities and their adjoining suburbs, located in every province except PEI, had STREET RAILWAYS.

Although the streetcar provided an effective service when there was no alternative, its era was over almost as soon as it began. The development of the AUTOMOBILE eventually resulted in most Canadians having access to cheap and convenient TRANSPORTATION. The motor vehicle also revolutionized public transportation, as BUSES came into use. Although slower and less comfortable than streetcars, motorbuses provided street railway companies with the means of facing competition from the automobile.

To combine the good features of both streetcars and motorbuses, experiments were made with trolleybuses, which ran on rubber tires but drew their power from overhead lines. Windsor, again, was the first Canadian city to try the new mode, with the Lincoln Road route being opened on 5 May 1922. Toronto also experimented with trolleybuses, opening a route in June 1922. Both of these experiments were abandoned by 1926, but the trolleybus replaced many streetcars after WWII.

The automobile continued to divert traffic from the street railway monopolies throughout the 1920s. The Depression of the 1930s brought further reductions in traffic, and many street railways were abandoned during this period, as the rolling stock deteriorated. With little capital available, bus manufacturers persuaded some street railways to opt for motorbuses. Transit systems in the largest cities, particularly Toronto, Montréal and Vancouver, purchased new streetcars and modernized their equipment.

WWII saw a dramatic resurgence of all forms of public transportation, as supplies of gasoline, tires and spare parts, as well as new cars, were severely restricted. By 1945 most public transit systems in Canada were worn out and required extensive new investment. The return to peace permitted more automobiles to be purchased, and the end of wartime emergencies saw a general decline in the demand for public transport. The decision was made in most cities to abandon all streetcar services, replacing them with modern trolleybuses and motorbuses. After the 1959 closure of the Montréal and Ottawa systems, only Toronto operated streetcars.

An important addition to Canadian urban transportation was the opening of Toronto's Yonge St subway in 1954. SUBWAYS provide high passenger capacities, as their trains operate on protected rights-of-way totally separated from interference by other traffic.

Significant improvements to private transportation were also made possible in the 1950s through the construction of expressways. The dramatic postwar increase in automobile ownership put pressure on conventional street systems, and the average time required to make a particular journey by either automobile or public transit actually increased. Expressways are intended to remove motor vehicles from local streets, placing them on separate rights-of-way, avoiding other traffic. As with subways, traffic on expressways moves at high speeds, permitting greater capacity. Both subways and expressways have severe disadvantages, and cannot be universally applied as solutions to transportation problems. One disadvantage shared by subways and expressways is the extremely high cost of construction. Both forms consume large amounts of scarce land, although land used by subways can be built over once the subway is completed.

Despite the number of expressways constructed, traffic congestion continued to grow in Canadian cities in the 1960s and 1970s. A dramatic increase in the price of oil, as well as increases in parking and other costs, started a return to public transit. Many systems were rejuvenated with new equipment, and passengers once again be-

Aerial view of the Decarie Metropolitain Blvd interchange in Ville St-Laurent, Qué (*courtesy National Film Board/Photothèque*).

gan to use public transportation. Most transit expansion in this era depended on motorbuses and conventional rail-based systems. As the subway systems in Toronto and Montréal were extended, other cities looked for cheaper solutions to their transportation problems. Light Rapid Transit provides most of the advantages of subways at less cost, and LRT lines were opened in Edmonton (1978) and Calgary (1981). Another LRT line, using Canadian-developed driverless trains, is scheduled to open in Vancouver in 1986.

Administration, Planning and Finance No less dramatic than the change in technology has been the change in the administrative, financial and planning structures of urban transportation. Careful planning and scheduling of manpower and equipment are required to provide services at the times passengers wish to travel. Vehicles must be maintained; supervisors must ensure that the vehicles adhere to predetermined schedules and that every passenger pays the fare. These activities are co-ordinated by transportation management. In the early days of public transportation, these organizations were usually privately owned concerns which operated in the expectation of profit. Fares collected were expected to cover all costs and to provide a reasonable return on invested capital. Many cities even charged the private companies a franchise fee for the privilege of using their streets, and imposed other requirements on the transit systems. Other cities had a more direct involvement in the provision of transportation. In some cases, no suitable private company could be found to construct a streetcar system, and in other cities local residents were reluctant to give a private company a profitable monopoly.

In 1909 municipally owned streetcars began to operate in Calgary, and in 1911 the first streetcars in Saskatchewan, also municipally owned, commenced service in Regina. In 1921 the newly created Toronto Transportation Commission took over and extended the networks of both privately and municipally owned street railway companies. Private ownership remained important in other cities, however, with Halifax, Winnipeg and Vancouver, among others, being served by privately owned companies until the 1950s or later.

Whether ownership was private or public, all early transportation systems were operated with the expectation of profit, or at least with the aim of meeting expenses. Within a few years, some systems found it difficult to achieve this goal.

Streetcar services had to be provided not only throughout the day, but on weekends and evenings when there were relatively few riders available. Large amounts of equipment and manpower had to be reserved for the journeys to and from work.

As riders started to drift away from public transportation to private automobiles, the financial problems of the transit systems accelerated. Fewer riders meant that higher fares had to be charged to cover operating costs. Higher fares resulted in even fewer riders. Attempts to cut costs were not totally effective, particularly as transit-system operating costs started to rise dramatically. In 1960 the average Canadian transit passenger brought a profit of 1.7¢ per trip, but by 1971 this profit had disappeared with an average net cost per passenger of 0.7¢. Losses increased through the 1970s so that the average cost per passenger on transit systems was 38.1¢ in 1980.

This reversal of the profitability of urban transportation systems caused planners to revise their thinking. The problems encountered by freeway systems in meeting urban transportation needs made it obvious that support of public transit systems was a viable, less costly alternative. By deliberately deferring or cancelling roadway construction projects and by introducing measures to support transit systems, automobile travel in our cities was made relatively unattractive in comparison to public transit. Innovative traffic management measures, such as "bus-only" lanes and streets, and transit-operated traffic signals, provided cheap ways of accelerating transit schedules. Buses required no downtown parking spaces and, per passenger, consumed less roadway space than that required by automobiles. There was virtual unanimity across the country in the 1970s that public transportation should receive some form of subsidy to attract more passengers and to allow public transit to compete on a fair basis with the private car. Many of the traffic management measures undertaken specifically to aid buses in their travels through city streets have also assisted automobiles, as conflict between buses and other vehicles slows the speed of all traffic.

Having made the commitment to support public transit services, urban planners found that direct control over the type and quality of services enabled them to achieve innovations in the actual design and layout of cities and suburbs. The provision of transit service to a particular area was an added amenity which attracted development. If the transit service was permanent, such as a subway, LRT or trolleybus line, the attraction would be even stronger than that of a motorbus route which could be easily moved to another location without warning. Subway lines in Toronto and Montréal, although underground, can be readily identified from the air by the high-density developments around many stations. Residential areas can be made more attractive if there is a commitment to provide an alternative, reliable, permanent transit service. The development of the False Creek community in Vancouver saved thousands of dollars per housing unit by restricting garage space and by providing a frequent bus service as an alternative to second and third family cars. Even in remote suburbs, which are often difficult to serve effectively by public transit, steps are now being taken to provide walkways at the ends of cul-de-sacs, thereby bringing public transit within easy walking distance of all houses in the subdivision.

The trend towards public transportation was reinforced in the 1970s when automobile fuel and parking costs in major cities rose dramatically. Many Canadians turned to public transit for the first time in their lives as a result of the energy crisis; others moved to individual means of transportation, by foot, bicycle or mo-

Toronto Transit Commission streetcar (*photo by Bill Ivy*).

torcycle. Some transit companies experimented with special bus services to enable handicapped people to use public transport. Although the automobile still has a major role in urban transportation, it is unlikely that it will ever regain its popularity of the 1950s and 1960s.

In 1983 the 73 members of the Canadian Urban Transit Assn operated 10 396 motorbuses, 1435 subway cars, 649 trolleybuses, 392 light rail vehicles and streetcars, and 184 commuter train coaches. Among them, these vehicles operated 685 million revenue km, carried 1.4 billion paying passengers, and earned $788 million in revenue. They consumed 325 million L of diesel fuel, 2.8 million L of gasoline and 636 million kWh (1980) of electricity. Nearly 35 000 persons were employed in the industry.   JOHN M. DAY

Reading: H.W. Blake, *The Era of Streetcars and Interurbans in Winnipeg* (1974); Canadian Urban Transit Assn, *Transit Fact Book, 1981* (1982); J.F. Due, *The Intercity Electric Railway Industry in Canada* (1966); C.K. Hatcher, *Saskatchewan's Pioneer Streetcars* (1971) and *Stampede City Streetcars* (1975).

Urbanization, a complex process in which a country's organized communities become larger, more specialized and more interdependent. Urbanization is the result of many variables — economic, technological, demographic, political, etc — and it is inevitably accompanied by other changes in society. More than 75% of Canada's population lives in urban areas (1981). In this respect it ranks 16th in the world, behind such countries as Belgium, Australia, Israel, the UK and Japan, but far ahead of the USSR, Pakistan, India and China.

Canada became an urban nation relatively early in its history, and the urbanization process has passed through 4 major phases. The earliest began with the founding of Québec in 1608. Urban development was mercantile or colonial in nature and was characterized by imperial (French and British) control over location, function and growth. Functionally, urban places — notably Québec City, Montréal, Halifax and St John's — tended to be administrative or military centres. Economically, they were entrepôts, collection agencies for colonial staples and distribution centres of manufactured goods from the mother country. The second phase began in the early 1800s and was marked by the increasing control of commercial interests over urban development. Interregional trade increased, as did small-scale manufacturing related to the commercial role of urban places. The third phase, which began with the industrial era in the 1870s and lasted until the 1920s, saw the development of a national urban system that tended to concentrate power in major central Canadian cities, notably Montréal and Toronto.

The results of this movement lasted until the mid-1970s, when Canada seems to have entered a new era sometimes referred to as "post-urbanization." Along with other industrialized countries, Canada experienced in the 1970s — for the first decade in its history — a faster rate of growth in rural areas than in urban areas.

A.F.J. ARTIBISE AND G.A. STELTER

Reading: G. Nader, *Cities of Canada* (2 vols, 1975-76); J. and R. Simmons, *Urban Canada* (1974); G.A. Stelter and A.F.J. Artibise, eds, *The Canadian City* (1977); L. Stone, *Urban Development in Canada* (1967).

Percentage of Canadians in Urban Centres, 1851-1981					
Year	*%*	*Year*	*%*	*Year*	*%*
1851	13.1	1901	34.9	1951	62.4
1861	15.8	1911	41.8	1961	69.7
1871	18.3	1921	47.4	1971	76.1
1881	23.3	1931	52.5	1981	75.7
1891	29.8	1941	55.7		

Urgent Ethnology involves recording on sound tapes, films, photographs and in writing the rapidly vanishing languages and cultures of the Inuit, Indian and Métis peoples of Canada. Recent decades have seen a dramatic increase in the pace of social and cultural change, and the traditional cultures of Canada's original inhabitants are closer to extinction than at any other period in our history. Research priority is given to those aspects of language and culture that are undergoing the most rapid change and require immediate documentation to prevent their being lost. This knowledge is of special importance to people of native ancestry who wish to maintain their cultural identity. Such knowledge is also essential for a complete understanding of Canadian history and PREHISTORY.

Contract research conducted by the NATIONAL MUSEUM OF MAN was given a higher profile after 1960 by the Ethnology Division, which initiated the Urgent Ethnology Program in 1972. Research projects cover all cultural regions of Canada including the Prairies, northeastern woodlands and the Subarctic. Fieldwork stresses ethnomedicine, ethnobotany (*see* PLANTS, NATIVE USES), material culture and mythology. There have also been projects in art, cultural ecology, music, individual life histories and genealogy. A major emphasis has been on ethnolinguistics. Nowhere is the infringement of acculturation felt more than in oral tradition, including language itself. As nearly as can be determined, 53 native languages survive in Canada, though only 3 have more than 5000 speakers (*see* NATIVE PEOPLE, LANGUAGES). Of the remainder, two-thirds are spoken by fewer than 1000 speakers and may disappear in less than 2 generations. Some are represented by fewer than 10 speakers and must now be regarded as extinct.

An urgent ethnology program requires not only actual ethnographic fieldwork, but also the contributions of a knowledgeable archival and technical staff. The program of the National Museum of Man has included preservation of the voluminous correspondence and archival collection of Edward SAPIR and Diamond JENNESS, early Canadian ethnologists. At the technical level, scientific work includes the preservation and restoration of quickly deteriorating film, such as movies of Copper Eskimo life, shot between 1913 and 1918 by the Canadian Arctic Expedition. As more natives move to large modern communities, as the number of camps on the land dwindle each year and as the number of men and women knowledgeable in the old ways diminish, the importance of urgent ethnology increases.   RENÉ R. GADACZ

Reading: J.G. Taylor, *A National Programme for Urgent Ethnology* (1977).

Urquhart, Anthony Morse, "Tony," painter, sculptor (b at Niagara Falls, Ont 9 Apr 1934). He studied art at the Albright Art School and U of Buffalo. In 1961 he joined a group of London, Ont, artists including Greg CURNOE and Jack CHAMBERS, who advocated a regional approach to art. Drawing from his own experiences, Urquhart works in a style that makes explicit reference to the underlying complexities and paradoxes he sees in the local landscape. In his boxed landscape sculptures of the 1960s he achieved a surreal juxtaposition of savage and primordial relationships with the actual and familiar. The constructions become at once a personal interior space and a universal collective landscape.   KATHLEEN LAVERTY

Ursuline Convent, Québec City. First occupying this site in 1642 under the leadership of MARIE DE L'INCARNATION, the Ursuline Sisters gradually (1686-1902) erected this complex of buildings dedicated to the education of young girls. The St-Augustin, Ste-Famille and kitchen wings, the largest surviving pre-1700 structures in Canada, have features characteristic of this early period, such as the steep medieval roofs with 2 rows of dormers, massive chimneys, rubble masonry protected by stucco, or *crépi*, and segmentally arched windows with small-paned casements. Although the original church was destroyed by fire, the Ursulines managed to save the magnificent altarpiece and pulpit carved by members of the Levasseur dynasty, 1732-36, a masterpiece that attests to the highly skilled craftsmanship available in NEW FRANCE.

CHRISTINA CAMERON

Ursulines, *see* CHRISTIAN RELIGIOUS COMMUNITIES.

Utilities, often described as businesses so "affected with the public interest" that they must be regulated by government regarding entry into (and exit from) the market, regarding prices or rates charges to customers, rate of return allowed to owners, and the requirement to serve all customers within their area of operation (*see* REGULATORY PROCESS). Businesses engaged in the production and distribution of electricity, distribution of natural gas, distribution of water, telecommunications (particularly telephone service) and pipelines (gas, oil, commodities) are considered public utilities. Cable-television service is also described by some as a utility.

Utilities may be owned by private investors or by governments through, for example, CROWN CORPORATIONS. In earlier times, railways, grain elevators, ferries and privately owned bridges were considered public utilities. Distribution of electricity is provided by provincial crown corporations in most provinces, while that of natural gas to businesses, households and pipelines is almost entirely privately controlled. Telephone services in the 3 Prairie provinces are provided by crown corporations, but in the rest of Canada by privately owned firms (subject to federal and provincial regulation).

Rationale for Government Intervention The most common argument for regulating public utilities is that such businesses are subject to very important economies of scale; that is, the unit cost of supplying a product or service declines as output over time increases. Because a large enterprise can more easily spread these costs over many customers to lower the per unit cost, natural monopolies are created. While a monopoly may result in greater efficiency, its power may be used to exploit consumers (businesses and households) in at least 2 ways. First, prices may be set well above the total costs of production, allowing the utility owner to earn excess profits. Second, the utility may engage in discriminatory pricing, eg, charging different customer groups different prices when the cost of serving each group is the same. In response to these potential problems, government regulators often control entry to the extent of granting a monopoly franchise for a specific market area to one firm, but the regulators are responsible for ensuring that rates charged by the utility are "just and reasonable" and "not unduly discriminatory or unfair" to different classes of customers.

It is also argued that since public utilities supply essential services to industries and households, all those willing to pay the price must have access to such services. Regulation is therefore necessary to ensure the maintenance of essential services. Moreover, utilities are capital intensive, ie, the value of their assets is several times their annual revenues and the incremental costs of serving additional customers (up to a point) are small once the utility's network is in place. The 3 largest electric utilities in Canada (which are among the 5 largest nonfinancial enterprises in Canada measured by assets) control assets of 5 to 6 times their annual revenues. The ratio for telephone companies is much lower (3 to 1) while the ratio of total assets to annual revenues for natural-gas distributors and pipelines is about 2 to 1.

In most cases, utilities provide a nonstorable commodity or service which must be available to the customer on demand. For example, electricity must flow into the house when the lights are turned on; otherwise it has little value. Customers cannot store the product to accommodate fluctuations in demand or supply. Moreover, most utility customers cannot obtain alternative sources of supply. While large-scale industrial buyers can, in time, find alternative sources of supply, households have less opportunity to switch if prices are too high or service is poor.

The rationale for regulating utilities is not constant, and a utility's status may evolve over time. For example, railways, until the growth of truck and airline transport just before WWII, were considered public utilities. Rapid technological change has severely undermined the argument for the monopoly-supply of another utility — long-distance telecommunications services. While entry of competitors into the market in Canada has been limited to nonvoice services, federal regulators in the US have permitted competition in the supply of long-distance voice services. Even the status of local-exchange telephone service, considered a classic natural monopoly, is threatened by cellular radio and by direct transmission to satellites that bypass the local exchange.

Alternative Forms of Intervention Government intervention takes 2 forms. First, governments can assume public ownership of the means of production through the creation of crown corporations. As owners, governments can establish the firm's prices directly and determine the conditions of service. Public ownership, however, does not allow control over entry. Second, governments can leave ownership of utilities in private hands while establishing a regulatory agency (commission or board) to monitor and control the utilities' activities. Public ownership is chosen more on practical than ideological grounds and has often been adopted after private ownership has prevailed for years. For instance, the fact that provincial crown corporations paid no federal corporate income taxes was a major determinant in the nationalization of electricity in both BC and Québec in the early 1960s.

It is important to note that public ownership has not been used as a substitute for government regulation. With very few exceptions (Saskatchewan Telephone, HYDRO-QUÉBEC), government regulation has been imposed on both publicly and privately owned utilities.

Regulation of Public Utilities Governments regulate utilities through specialized agencies (eg, CANADIAN RADIO-TELEVISION AND TELECOMMUNICATIONS COMMISSION, the National Energy Board and the various provincial public utilities commissions), which receive their mandates directly from government through statutes specifying many of the rules by which they operate. Most regulatory agencies operate in a quasi-judicial fashion (*see* ADMINISTRATIVE TRIBUNAL); their most important task being to decide impartially matters such as the level of rates or tariffs, the allowed rate of return the owners may earn and entry into the relevant markets. The decisions of such agencies are usually subject to appeal to the Cabinet. The agencies themselves are less independent than their American counterparts, and their role in policymaking is usually more restricted.

First, an agency decides who is allowed to operate in a given market, such as the extension of a pipeline into a new territory; when the decision was taken to build the gas pipeline from Montréal to Halifax, the NEB chose Trans-Québec and Maritimes Pipelines from among various candidates. Second, the agency must decide to whom the service is available upon demand, the implication being that utilities are not free to withdraw the service once it is established without the regulator's approval. Most of the work of utility regulators, however, involves determining the prices a utility is allowed to charge for its services. In establishing "just and reasonable" rates the agency must determine the total amount of revenue that the enterprise may receive and how much the various classes of customers must pay for a service. Through public hearings the agency seeks to determine the normal costs incurred by the utility in providing the required level of services, in particular, what level of capital expenditure; and, is deemed appropriate and what should be the allowed rate of return on the company's "rate base" (usually the depreciated value of plant and equipment used to provide the commodity or service). In this respect, the agency must regulate monopoly profits while ensuring that the rate of return is sufficient to attract and retain capital in the enterprise. Once the overall level of revenues has been determined, the agency must ensure that no class of customers is treated unfairly, eg, in the case of telephone regulation, a perennial question is how much businesses (as opposed to households) should pay per month for local-exchange service.

Problems with Utilities and Their Regulation The regulation of utilities by quasi-independent agencies is a time-consuming process subject to considerable criticism. First, because utilities appear able to pass higher costs on to their customers, they are not forced to be as efficient as enterprises that have to contend with competition. Second, some classes of customers may pay rates that are lower than the real costs of the services they receive while other classes bear the difference; there is evidence that such cross-subsidization is part of the design of telephone regulation in Canada. Third, it is frequently argued that consumer interests are not well represented before utility regulators and are insufficiently taken into account in the regulators' decisions. Fourth, technological change provides opportunities either to substitute the discipline of the competitive market for the regulation of utilities or to make greater use of competition in some degree to ensure that such firms are as efficient as possible and are responsive to changing economic conditions, yet regulators are reluctant to make greater use of competition. Fifth, utility regulators are accused of devoting too much time to establishing the allowed rate of return rather than to determining whether the utility's actual production costs are the lowest attainable (which involves the difficult task of judging whether the utility has adopted the most appropriate new technology). Sixth, in establishing the prices that utilities may charge, regulators usually focus on historical average cost of "embedded capital" (ie, many hydro dams were built 30 years ago) rather than on the current level of incremental costs. *See* ELECTRIC UTILITIES.
                                                    J.-T. BERNARD

Uxbridge, Ont, Township, pop 11 210 (1981c), is located 68 km NW of Toronto on Hwy 42. Its first settler in 1804 was S.S. Wilmot, but most date settlement from 1806 with the arrival of Dr Christopher Beswick. Both Quakers, they were soon joined by Scots, Germans and Pennsylvania Dutch. Incorporated as a town in 1885, its principal economic activity in the 19th century was as a service centre for local agriculture. The municipality was reputedly one of the first in Ontario to own its own waterworks. The town of Uxbridge was amalgamated in 1974 with the townships of Scott and Uxbridge to form a new township in the regional municipality of Durham. Residents of note include local manufacturer Joseph Gould, an ally of William Lyon MACKENZIE, who named the settlement after Uxbridge, Eng. Lucy Maude MONTGOMERY, author of the "Anne" series, wrote more than half her published works while residing in Leaksdale, a hamlet just N of the town.   GERALD STORTZ

Vadeboncoeur, Pierre, essayist (b at Strathmore, near Montréal, 1920). A man of thought and action who became a full-time writer fairly late in life, Vadeboncoeur has in the last 20 years contributed several major works to the literature of ideas. After studying law and economics, he worked in business, freelance journalism and translation. During the 1949 ASBESTOS STRIKE he allied himself with Jean MARCHAND, P.E. TRUDEAU, and Gérard PELLETIER and, especially, the workers. He became an employee of the Catholic trade union association which in 1960 became the Confédération des syndicats nationaux (CSN).

A contributor to magazines CITÉ LIBRE, LIBERTÉ, *Socialisme* and PARTI PRIS, Vadeboncoeur's first important article was "La Ligne du risque," about Paul-Emile BORDUAS and the creative artist as a prophet of liberty. The essay gave both title and tone to a somewhat disparate collection published in 1963. The tone of the collection *Lettres et colères* (1969) echoed that of the great French Catholic pamphleteers. He also brought together polemical articles about Québec nationalism, *Un Génocide en douce* (1976) and *Chaque jour, l'indépendance* (1978). *Indépendances* (1972), however, is not a political thesis but a cultural essay about youth and youth movements after Marcuse and the events of May 1968 in Paris. *Les Deux Royaumes* (1978) explores the limits inherent in any system, attacks reason for its authoritarianism, and defends intuition, meditation and spirituality. Other books by Vadeboncoeur are *L'Autorité du peuple* (1965), *Un Amour libre* (1970) and *La* DERNIÈRE HEURE ET LA PREMIÈRE (1970).   LAURENT MAILHOT

Vaillancourt, Armand, sculptor (b at Black Lake, Qué 4 Sept 1932). He studied at the École des beaux-arts in Montréal. An inventor of new techniques, he uses modern materials such as welded metal. He sees himself as a sculptor and social activist, committed to the battle to free Québec's political prisoners. The symbolic figurative elements in some of his work stems from this conviction: a hand outstretched to the sky is a sign of despair, an expression of social injustice. The intensity of his symbolism lies in the interaction of the formal tensions of his works, and is reinforced by their gigantic form. In wood or bronze, the play between his triangular, tubular or cubic geometric forms reflects strength and compression, mass and dynamism. Vaillancourt has produced many sculptures for particular settings, including *Je me souviens,* a fountain sculpture (1969-71), Embarcadero Plaza, San Francisco; *Justice!* (1983), Palais de Justice de Québec, Québec. More recently he has progressed towards a smaller scale in an effort to harmonize sculpture with nature.
                                  LOUISE BEAUDRY

Val-d'Or, Qué, Town, pop 21 371 (1981c), inc 1968, is located 95 km SE of Rouyn-Noranda in Québec's Abitibi region, near the source of the Rivière Harricana, one of the major rivers flowing N to James Bay. The name is linked to the gold rush, second only to the Klondike, which took the area by storm in the mid-1930s. The town was originally made up of 2 separate municipalities. The first, Bourlamaque, founded in 1934 by the Lamaque Mining Co, was a COMPANY TOWN for many years. The other, Val-d'Or, was incorporated a village in 1935 and a town 2 years later, began as a bustling gold-rush town. For many years, the twin centres were known as Val-d'Or-Bourlamaque. After amalgamation Val-d'Or became the largest municipality in the Abitibi-Témiscamingue region.

Val-d'Or prospered from the dozens of gold mines discovered in the vicinity. Despite several mine closures, its economy is based largely on 2 of the richest gold-bearing mines in Québec, (Sigma and Lamaque), located within the town's

limits, which have been in production for almost 50 years. The first group of log cabins built beside the Lemaque mine in 1934 are still in their original state. In 1978 this section of the town was designated a historic site. The Bourlamaque Miners' Village commemorates the gold rush that brough Val-d'Or into existence.
                                  BENOÎT-BEAUDRY GOURD

Valdes Island is one of a range of islands on the outer edge of the GULF ISLANDS in the Str of GEORGIA, off the SE coast of Vancouver I, BC. The long, narrow island is heavily wooded and has a few farms. An Indian reserve occupies a third of it and there are several native burial grounds. In the 1920s it provided a refuge for the cult leader Brother Twelve, who is supposed to have built a temple with vaults of gold hidden beneath the floor. The name refers to a Spanish mariner who explored the area in the 1790s.
                                  DANIEL FRANCIS

Vallerand, Jean, composer, critic, administrator, teacher, violinist (b at Montréal 24 Dec 1915). His career as a critic began on *Le Canada* in 1941, followed by *Montréal-Matin, Le* DEVOIR, *Le Nouveau Journal* and *La* PRESSE. During the 1940s and 1950s, he composed incidental music for more than 50 radio dramas on the CBC, where he later became head of musical broadcasts. His opera *Le Magicien* was performed over 100 times across the country during the JEUNESSES MUSICALES DU CANADA 1961-62 tour. Secretary general and teacher at the Conservatoire de musique de Montréal 1942-63, Vallerand also taught at U de M 1950-66. Other positions he has held include cultural attaché for Québec in Paris, director of the Service des arts d'interprétation of the Québec Ministère des affaires culturelles and director of the Conservatoire de musique et d'art dramatique du Québec.   HÉLÈNE PLOUFFE

Valleyfield, Qué, City (official name: Salaberry-de-Valleyfield), pop 29 574 (1981c); inc 1904, is located on the S shore of the ST LAWRENCE R, at the NE extremity of Lac St-François. The townsite was part of the seigneurial land granted to Charles de BEAUHARNOIS, governor of New France from 1726 to 1747. Construction of the Beauharnois Canal (1842-54) attracted many immigrants to the town. A sawmill and a large paper mill were established in the 1850s. A cotton mill (the future Montreal Cotton Co) opened 1875 and dominated the activity and growth of this small industrial town until WWII.

Valleyfield draws its labour force from the local population and its history is marked by often violent labour disputes. Originally (1874), it was called Salaberry, in honour of Charles d'Irumberry de SALABERRY. Through popular usage, the name "Valleyfield" was added by the economically elite anglophone minority (in memory, it is said, of a Scottish paper mill). Served by railway since 1885, Valleyfield be-

came an episcopal seat in 1892. An important commercial and industrial centre, its activities today are diversified: ocean shipping, hydroelectric production, rubber manufacturing, zinc refining, chemical products, textiles and foodstuffs. Each summer it hosts N America's biggest speedboat regatta.   SYLVIE TASCHEREAU

Van den Bergh, Sidney, astronomer, cosmologist (b at Wassenaar, Netherlands 20 May 1929). After completing studies at Princeton (1950), Ohio State U (1952) and U of Göttingen (1956), Van den Bergh assumed a faculty position at Ohio (1956-58) before moving to Toronto (1958). At the David Dunlap Observatory, U of T, he played a key role in expanding the facilities, developing computer techniques, multicolour photometry and other innovations. Although he has contributed to lunar studies and studies of other aspects of our own solar system, his real forte is with extragalactic studies on which he has published original findings and major reviews on nebulae, star clusters, variable stars, supernovae and recently a revision to the perceived age of the universe (*see* COSMOLOGY). In 1977 he was appointed director of the Dominion Astrophysical Observatory, Victoria, taking office in 1978. Since 1982 he has also served as president and chairman of the board of the Canada-France-Hawaii Telescope Corp in Hawaii. A COMET he discovered in 1974 bears his name.   MARTIN K. MCNICHOLL

Van Ginkel, H.P. Daniel, "Sandy" (b at Amsterdam, Netherlands 10 Feb 1920) and **van Ginkel, Blanche,** née Lemco (b at London, England 14 Dec 1923), architects and planners of van Ginkel Associates, Toronto. The firm is distinguished for the first rehabilitation plan for Old Montréal, urban design and transportation planning for such cities as New York, Montréal and Calgary, and numerous studies for development in the Canadian Arctic. Well established as an architect in Europe, Sandy van Ginkel emigrated to Canada in 1957 and established a practice with his wife in Montréal; he has served as chief planner for Stockholm and for EXPO 67 in Montréal and has taught at several universities. Blanche van Ginkel, educated at McGill and Harvard, worked at the Atelier Le Corbusier, Paris (1948), and was dean of architecture at U of T (1977-82).   ANDREA KRISTOF

Van Horne, Sir William Cornelius, railway official (b at Chelsea, Ill 3 Feb 1843; d at Montréal 11 Sept 1915). Van Horne's formal education ended at age 14, when he began his railway career as a telegrapher with the Illinois Central Railroad in 1857. He worked for several American railways and by 1880 was general superintendent of the Milwaukee Road. Van Horne was appointed general manager of the CANADIAN PACIFIC RAILWAY in Jan 1882, and he used his excellent managerial skills to improve the organization of construction on the prairie section, which was completed from Winnipeg to Calgary in Aug 1883. Van Horne's drive and determination were responsible for the rapid completion of the main line between Montréal and Port Moody (*see* RAILWAY HISTORY).

Van Horne succeeded George STEPHEN as president of the CPR in 1888. He regarded the Canadian Pacific as a transportation and communications system. At his insistence, the company developed a telegraph service and entered the express business. He launched the famous Empress line of Pacific steamships in 1891 — fast, luxurious vessels which ran between Vancouver and Hong Kong, carried mail for the British government and increased tourist and freight traffic between Canada and the Orient. Van Horne was also the founder of CP Hotels; as an amateur architect he helped plan the Banff Springs and Château Frontenac hotels. He negotiated the famous CROW'S NEST PASS AGREEMENT,

Sir William Van Horne, brilliant railway manager whose drive and determination were largely responsible for the rapid completion of the CPR (*courtesy Public Archives of Canada/C-8549*).

which substantially reduced freight rates on Prairie grain and flour. After his retirement from the presidency in 1899, he promoted the building of a railway in Cuba. Van Horne was a complex personality: a brilliant railway manager, a gourmet and a man with tremendous intellectual curiosity. He was awarded an honorary knighthood in 1894.   JOHN A. EAGLE

Reading: P. Berton, *The Last Spike* (1971); W. Vaughan, *The Life and Work of Sir William Van Horne* (1920).

Vancouver, the largest city in British Columbia and third largest in Canada, lies on a peninsula in the SW corner of the province's mainland. The surrounding waterways — Burrard Inlet, the Str of GEORGIA and the FRASER R respectively — provide an excellent, sheltered deep-sea port, convenient access to the Pacific Ocean, and an easy route to the rich agricultural lands of the Fraser Valley and the interior.

Settlement Archaeological evidence indicates that coastal Indians settled at Locarno Beach by 500 BC and at Marpole about 400 BC. The English sailor Capt George VANCOUVER and the Spaniard BODEGA Y QUADRA met off Point Grey in 1792 but Europeans paid little attention to the area until the 1860s when 3 Englishmen pre-empted land and built an unsuccessful brickyard. In the 1870s several entrepreneurs established logging camps, sawmills and 3 small settlements on the shores of Burrard Inlet.

Development, Economy and Transportation Vancouver began when CPR VP, William VAN HORNE, announced that the company would extend its line 20 km westward from the statutory terminus, Port Moody, in order to take advantage of a better harbour and terminal site. The provincial government gave the CPR over 2500 ha of crown land at the new terminus and private owners donated land. On 6 Apr 1886 the provincial legislature incorporated the city of

Population: 414 281 (1981c); 1 268 183 (CMA)

Rate of Increase (1971-81): (CMA) 1.1%

Rank in Canada: Third (by CMA)

Date of Incorporation: City 1886

Land Area: 113 km²

Elevation: 4.25 m (CPR station)

Climate: Average daily temp, July 17.2°C, Jan 2.8°C; Yearly precip 1017.8 mm; Hours of sunshine 1925 per year

Vancouver, a name that Van Horne had suggested, in honour of the English explorer. Ratepayers elected M.A. MacLean, a real-estate dealer, as the first mayor. Then on June 13 a clearing fire blew out of control, claimed at least 11 lives, destroyed ramshackle buildings and drew invaluable publicity when residents rebuilt immediately. The CPR, the largest single landowner, recognizing the value of orderly growth, did not "boom" its land. Private real-estate developers such as David Oppenheimer (mayor, 1888-91) advertised the city and, through cash bonuses and tax concessions, attracted new industries such as the BC Sugar Refinery (1891).

The continent-wide depression of the mid-1890s temporarily checked growth, but during the 1897-98 KLONDIKE GOLD RUSH excitement, prosperity returned to Vancouver. By the turn of the century it had displaced Victoria, the provincial capital, as the leading commercial centre on Canada's West Coast. Transpacific ships, including CP Steamship's Empress liners, called regularly; coastal steamship companies, including CP Navigation and Union Steamships, made Vancouver their headquarters; and eastern businesses established their Pacific coast branches in Vancouver. The prewar economic boom expanded markets for such BC products as fish, minerals and lumber. Most lumber was sold on the Prairies. Nevertheless, Vancouver wholesalers complained that the lack of direct rail connections and discriminatory freight rates put them at a disadvantage relative to Calgary and Winnipeg in securing the trade of BC's interior. In response, the provincial government offered aid to new railways, including the Pacific Great Eastern (now BC Railway).

The beginning of worldwide economic

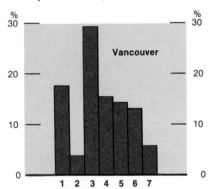

Distribution of Industrial Activity* by Industry Grouping within Census Metropolitan Areas, 1980

Vancouver

Industry groupings

1. Food and beverage and tobacco products industries

2. Leather, textile, knitting mills and clothing industries

3. Wood, furniture and fixtures, paper and allied and printing, publishing and allied industries

4. Machinery, transportation equipment and electrical products industries

5. Primary metal and metal fabricating industries

6. Rubber and plastic products, petroleum and coal products and chemical products industries

7. Non-metallic mineral products and miscellaneous manufacturing industries.

* Industry activity based on the average of percentage shares of the value shipments of goods of own manufacture, total value added and total number of employees for each of the selected metropolitan areas.

Source: Figure II, Catalogue 31-209, Statistics Canada.

depression in 1913 and of war in 1914 severely reduced trade, retarded railway development and, coupled with declining resources, ended much of the mining boom in the Kootenay and Boundary districts. Nevertheless the Vancouver Stock Exchange (1907) survived and remains active in financing BC and Alberta developments, especially of the more speculative kind. During the 1920s growth resumed and Vancouver replaced Winnipeg as the leading city in western Canada. Cheap ocean transport through the Panama Canal opened new markets for BC lumber on the American E coast and made Europe more accessible. The province's successful campaign for freight-rate reduction enabled Vancouver to become a grain-exporting port. The port itself expanded greatly and came under the jurisdiction of a federal agency, the National Harbours Board, in 1936. The export grain trade held up remarkably well during the GREAT DEPRESSION of the 1930s, but the city suffered extensive unemployment, especially since the unemployed of western Canada regarded Vancouver, with its mild climate, as a "mecca." Unrest among the unemployed caused several incidents, including the reading of the Riot Act by Mayor G.G. McGeer in 1935 (*see also* ON TO OTTAWA TREK). The outbreak of WWII and the development of war industries, particularly shipbuilding, ended unemployment but sharply reduced the grain trade.

Trade grew once shipping became available again after the war, especially after Canada began selling large quantities of wheat to China in 1961. By 1963 Vancouver ranked first among Canadian ports in tonnage. Demand around the Pacific Rim for other western Canadian products, notably lumber, potash and coal, has led to the construction of specialized port facilities and the extension of the port as far E as Port Moody and S to the Roberts Bank coal terminal (1970). Because of the importance of the Pacific Rim, CP Air had established its headquarters in the city in 1949 and, along with other international and domestic carriers, uses the Vancouver International Airport, which the federal government expanded significantly after buying it from the city in 1961. Vancouver also expanded its role as the head office centre for such provincial corporations as BC Forest Products, Cominco and MACMILLAN BLOEDEL; a variety of smaller firms; the major provincial labour unions; and the regional offices for national enterprises such as the chartered banks. The BANK OF BRITISH COLUMBIA (chartered 1966) has its head office there.

Cityscape The backdrop of mountains, the proximity of the sea and the presence within the city limits of such wilderness areas as Stanley Park long lulled Vancouver residents into a feeling that none of their doings could seriously impair the city's natural beauty. The original surveyors, many of them CPR employees, showed little imagination as they generally laid out streets according to a grid pattern that made few allowances for such natural features as steep slopes. Apart from establishing fire limits and attempting to keep noisome industries on the outskirts, the city made few efforts to direct land use until the late 1920s when it commissioned the American firm, Harland Bartholomew and Associates, to draw up a town plan. The city adopted some of its suggestions, such as a comprehensive zoning regulation, but could not really enforce these rules until after WWII. Nevertheless, clear land-use patterns emerged. More affluent residents, for example, have always tended to live W of Cambie Street where developers subdivided land into large lots; the less affluent lived to the E, where lots had sometimes as little as 7.5 m frontages.

Since the 1960s the city's older core has undergone a considerable transformation. City planners studied land-use proposals; civic politicians debated and redesigned some of them; and

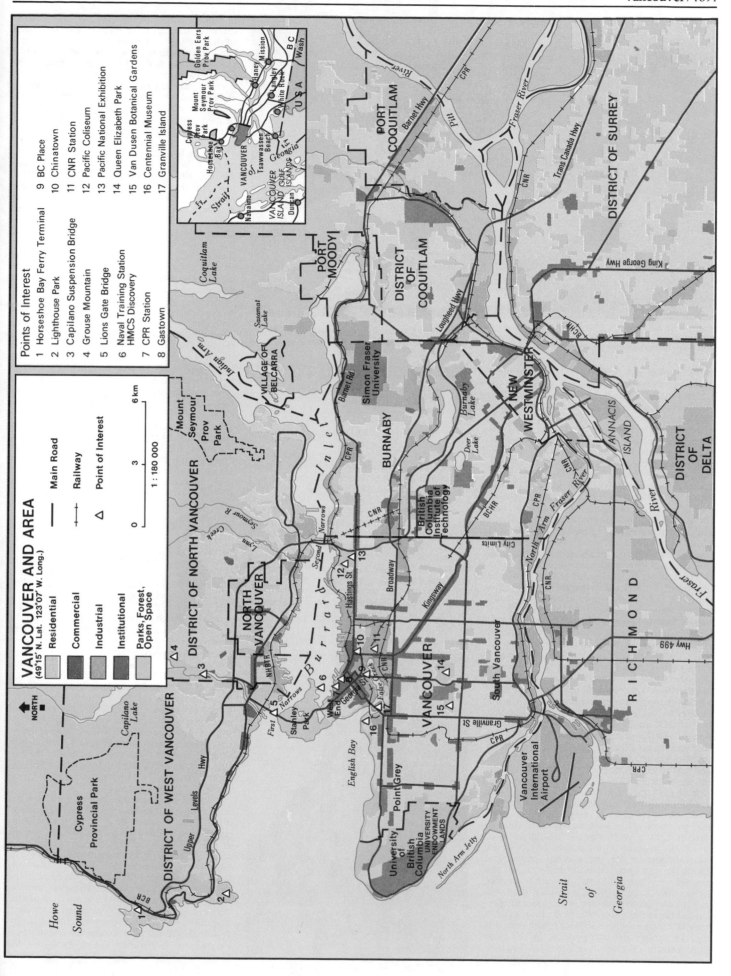

VANCOUVER AND AREA
(49°15' N. Lat. 123°07' W. Long.)

	Residential
	Commercial
	Industrial
	Institutional
	Parks, Forest, Open Space

——	Main Road
—+—	Railway
△	Point of Interest

0   3   6 km

1 : 180 000

NORTH

Points of Interest

1 Horseshoe Bay Ferry Terminal
2 Lighthouse Park
3 Capilano Suspension Bridge
4 Grouse Mountain
5 Lions Gate Bridge
6 Naval Training Station HMCS Discovery
7 CPR Station
8 Gastown
9 BC Place
10 Chinatown
11 CNR Station
12 Pacific Coliseum
13 Pacific National Exhibition
14 Queen Elizabeth Park
15 Van Dusen Botanical Gardens
16 Centennial Museum
17 Granville Island

Vancouver, BC, Canada's 3rd-largest city and its major port on the Pacific. The 60 000-seat BC Place stadium was built in 1983 (*courtesy BC Place*).

private developers financed much of the new building. Downtown, a forest of 20- to 40-storey-high office and hotel towers, including such clusters as the Bentall, Royal, Pacific and Vancouver centres, have replaced the 2- and 3-storey retail blocks of pre-WWI vintage. Architecturally the most interesting new buildings are the Provincial Court House and Robson Square Conference Centre.

A dramatic indication of the city's post-industrial status is False Creek, off English Bay. From the city's earliest days this area, with its easy access to trackage and water transport, was the site of rail yards, sawmills, machine shops and related industries. Indeed, Vancouver was unique among N American cities of comparable size for the importance of first-stage resource processing in its economy. By the 1950s, changing technology in the lumber industry and the obsolescence of old plants turned False Cr into a decaying industrial centre. After much study and controversy, the city decided to develop False Cr town houses and apartments in 1976. Nearby Granville I — created as an industrial site in 1915 when the eastern part of False Cr was filled to provide land for the terminus and yards of the Canadian Northern Ry (now CN) and the Great Northern Ry (now Burlington Northern) — has become home to a public market, art school, theatres and restaurants. On the N side of the creek, on land formerly occupied by the CPR yards, the provincial government opened a 60 000-seat sports stadium in 1983, the first stage in the BC Place development, planned to include stores, office towers, recreational space and up to 19 000 residential units; it will also be the site of Expo 86.

Whereas the downtown and False Cr are being almost completely redeveloped, the city's oldest residential neighbourhood, east-end Strathcona, has been largely rehabilitated. Traditionally a working-class neighbourhood, it is home to many ethnic groups, of whom the most important are the CHINESE. In the late 1950s the city began demolishing some of the poorest dwellings and replacing them with public-housing projects. After a successful protest against a proposed freeway, local residents persuaded the senior governments to provide funds to rehabilitate existing facilities rather than undertake further renewal projects. In the West End, private developers, encouraged by new zoning regulations, began in the 1960s to build high-rise apartment blocks in place of the apartment and rooming houses that had been carved out of the large homes of the city's early well-to-do residents. By 1971 the West End was noted for the density of its population. Paradoxically, Vancouver had once prided itself as a city of owner-occupied, single-family detached homes. Most homes (and this is still true of most neighbourhoods outside the West End) were of wood-frame construction, often influenced by California architectural style (*see* HOUSE).

Population Vancouver's most significant growth spurts occurred during its first 5 years and in the decade before WWI, resulting primarily from immigration from the British Isles and Ontario. The expansion of the 1920s, which saw Vancouver attain its status as the third-largest city in Canada, is explained by the annexation of the adjacent bedroom municipalities of Point Grey and S Vancouver in 1929, natural increase, renewed immigration from Britain and the beginning of significant migration from the Prairies. After a brief wartime and postwar spurt, the rate of population growth tapered off. The 1976 census recorded an absolute decline in the city proper while the population

Gastown, Vancouver (*photo by Jerg Kroener/Reflexion*).

of Greater Vancouver passed the one million mark for the first time. High real-estate values in the city led young families to live in suburban municipalities, especially BURNABY, COQUITLAM, DELTA, North Vancouver City and Dist, RICHMOND and SURREY.

From 1901 (the first year for which statistics are available) to 1951, people of British ethnic origin — many of them Canadian born — formed three-quarters of the population and dominated the elite. After WWII new immigrants made Vancouver more cosmopolitan. In 1979 the school board reported that nearly 40% of the children in elementary school did not speak English as a first language. Pupils of Chinese, Italian and East Indian background were most numerous. Until after WWII, the largest and least popular non-British ethnic group were Asians, mainly Chinese and JAPANESE. An anti-Chinese riot in 1887, an anti-Asian riot in 1907, the tension surrounding the KOMAGATA MARU incident of 1914, and the 1942 decision of the federal government to evacuate all Japanese, including about 8600 city residents, from the coast demonstrates the hostility that Vancouver residents, like other British Columbians, felt towards Asians. With the postwar easing of immigration barriers, an increasing number of ethnic Chinese have come to Vancouver. Although Chinatown flourishes, Chinese reside throughout the city and participate fully in its life. Those Japanese who returned to the coast have blended into the city. Immigrants of East Indian ethnic origin have experienced a mixed reception.

Government and Politics Vancouver is unique among BC municipalities in having its own charter, but it remains very much a creature of the provincial legislature, which must approve every charter amendment. Until 1935 the city was governed by a mayor and aldermen chosen from various wards. When the province abolished the ward system, only the aldermen seriously objected. Taking advantage of the at-large system, the CO-OPERATIVE COMMONWEALTH FEDERATION in 1936 ran a slate of aldermanic candidates and elected 3. The existence of party politics at city hall was confirmed in 1937 with the formation of the Non-Partisan Association (NPA), a loose amalgam of Conservatives and Liberals. The NPA has been dominant in civic politics although it was challenged in 1972 by The Electors Action Movement (TEAM) and recently by several left-wing groups, of which the most important is the Committee of Progressive Electors (COPE).

Vancouver's first experience with METROPOLITAN GOVERNMENT occurred in 1913 with the formation of the Vancouver and Dist Joint Sewerage and Drainage Board. Metropolitan agencies concerned with water, public health and regional planning appeared later. The growth of suburban municipalities encouraged the provincial government to create an elected body, the Greater Vancouver Regional Dist (1967), which has taken over most functions of the earlier agencies and added such responsibilities as capital finance, building regulations, housing and air-pollution control.

Cultural Life Vancouver has long enjoyed a variety of cultural activities. The Art, Historical and Scientific Assn (one of the first groups organized) established a museum 1894. In honour of the 1958 BC centennial, the city built a new museum, a Maritime Museum and, with funds from lumberman H.R. MACMILLAN, a planetarium. As soon as the CPR opened an opera house in 1891, Vancouver became a regular stop for touring concert artists and theatrical companies. As well as supporting local amateur musical and dramatic groups, the city also has such professional bodies as the VANCOUVER SYMPHONY ORCHESTRA, the Vancouver Opera Assn and the Playhouse Theatre Centre. The last was one of many professional theatrical companies that mushroomed in the 1960s and 1970s. All 3 used the Queen Elizabeth Theatre, a civic auditorium opened in 1959, but the symphony now plays in the restored Orpheum Theatre. Since Oct 1983 the Vancouver Art Gallery (est 1931) has been located at the Old Courthouse, a larger site than its previous home and redesigned by architect Arthur ERICKSON.

Institutions of higher learning have also stimulated the arts. The Vancouver area has 2 public universities, UNIVERSITY OF BRITISH COLUMBIA (fd 1908) and SIMON FRASER U (fd 1965); several regional colleges, including Vancouver Community College (1965); and the BC Institute of Technology (1964). Two daily newspapers, the *Vancouver Sun* and the *Province*, a number of specialized newspapers and journals, a host of radio stations, 4 TV stations and easy access to American TV via cable provide information and entertainment.

The Vancouver area offers many opportunities for outdoor recreation, including skiing and boating. Within the city are 138 parks of which the largest and most important is Stanley Park. Amateur teams participate in most sports and the BRITISH COLUMBIA LIONS football team (1964) and the VANCOUVER CANUCKS hockey team (1970) play in major professional leagues. The Lions play their home games at BC Place, where the 1983 Grey Cup between the Lions and the Toronto Argonauts was played. The Canucks use the Pacific Coliseum, on the Pacific National Exhibition grounds.   PATRICIA E. ROY

Reading: Patricia E. Roy, *Vancouver: An Illustrated History* (1980); C. Davis, *The Vancouver Book* (1976); L.J. Evenden, ed, *Vancouver: Western Metropolis* (1978); H. Kalman, *Exploring Vancouver 2* (1978).

Vancouver, George, naval officer, explorer (b at King's Lynn, Eng 22 June 1757; d at Petersham, London, Eng 12 May 1798). Vancouver was with James COOK on his second expedition to the South Seas (1772-75) and on his third to the NORTHWEST COAST (1776-80). In 1790 an expedition was planned to explore that coast. Preparations were delayed by news that the Spaniards had seized British property at NOOTKA SOUND but were resumed, under Vancouver's command, after a convention had been signed with Spain in Oct. Vancouver was charged with 2 missions: to receive back the properties alleged to have been seized at Nootka and to explore the coast from California to Cook Inlet, Alaska. He reached the coast in Apr 1792. In Aug he met the Spanish commissioner BODEGA Y QUADRA at Nootka; negotiations were friendly but futile, and the matter of the seized properties had to be referred to London and Madrid. Three summers were spent exploring the coast, with the intervening winters passed in the Sandwich Is [Hawaii]. Vancouver returned to Eng in Sept 1795 and soon set about revising his journal, published in 1798 as *A Voyage of Discovery to the North Pacific Ocean and Round the World*. In it he claimed with justice that his survey, one of the greatest of the kind, had removed "every doubt" about the existence of a NORTHWEST PASSAGE to the Atlantic "within the limits of our researches."

W. KAYE LAMB

Reading: B. Anderson, *Surveyor of the Sea: The Life and Voyages of Captain George Vancouver* (1960).

Vancouver, Mount, elev 4828 m, situated in the YT's St Elias Range, rises SE of Mt LOGAN between 2 immense glacier systems, Hubbard and Seward. A large massif, it supports 4 summits and measures 24 km from NW to SE at its base. Its SE summit, 4792 m, is a boundary peak between Canada and Alaska, only 32 km from the sea. The highest (NW) peak was first climbed June 1949 by N. Odell, W. Hainsworth, R. McCarter and A. Bruce Robertson. The SE summit, the highest unclimbed summit left in Canada by 1967, was climbed by a joint US-Canadian team

to commemorate the Alaskan and Canadian centennials. It was renamed Good Neighbour Peak.   GLEN BOLES

Vancouver Canucks, HOCKEY team. The Vancouver Canucks had been members of the Western Hockey League since 1948. For a price of $6 million, they joined the NATIONAL HOCKEY LEAGUE on 22 May 1970. They played their first home game on 9 Oct 1970 in the 3-year-old, 15 555-seat Pacific Coliseum, and went on to accumulate 56 points for a sixth-place finish in the 7-team East Division under Coach Hal Laycoe and General Manager Bud Poile. In 1974 team ownership was transferred from the Medicor Corporation of Minneapolis to a group of Vancouver businessmen headed by Frank Griffiths. The Canucks best regular-season performance to date occurred in 1974-75, when they finished atop the Smythe Division with 86 points in 80 games. In 1982 they made a surprising advance through the playoffs but lost in 4 straight games to the New York Islanders in the STANLEY CUP final.   DEREK DRAGER

Vancouver Island, BC, 31 284 km^2, the largest island on the W Coast of N America, is about 460 km long and 50-80 km wide and stretches parallel to the BC mainland. It is separated from Canada by the GEORGIA, Queen Charlotte and Johnstone straits and from the US by JUAN DE FUCA STR. With the QUEEN CHARLOTTE IS, it forms part of a partially submerged chain of the Cordillera and is a continuation of the US coastal mountains. Its coastline is very rugged, especially on the W where there are several fjordlike inlets — the longest being Alberni Inlet and Muchalat Inlet — that cut into a heavily forested, mountainous interior, with mountains averaging 600-1000 m. Higher peaks include GOLDEN HINDE (2200 m), Elkhorn Mt (2194 m) and Mt Colonel Foster (2133 m). In contrast to this mountainous core are the coastal lowlands, which form an almost encircling belt. They are most pronounced in the N and E where the Nahwitti and Nanaimo lowlands form part of a coastal trough stretching from SE Alaska to the Puget Depression in Washington state. The Island has numerous freshwater lakes, the largest being Nimpkish, Cowichan, Buttle, Sproat, Great Central and Campbell. Its climate is damp but mild, with precipitation ranging from 3.8 m in the western flanks of the mountains to less than 0.8 m in the SE Nanaimo Lowland. Much of the precipitation returns to the Pacific through a series of rapid-flowing, deeply incised, relatively short rivers, such as the Nanaimo and Campbell. The Island is most heavily populated in the SE, where the city of VICTORIA is located.

Although the archaeological record is still incomplete, it is clear that Indians have occupied the Island for several thousand years. A tribal, village society evolved, with an economy based on fishing, collecting and hunting. The abundant marine and forest resources along the coasts supported a culture rich in oral tradition and artistic expression. Two main linguistic families, Salishan and Wakashan, developed and continue to exist. Traditionally, villages

comprised stoutly constructed cedar longhouses and were usually situated in sheltered coves or a short distance upriver from the ocean. During the hunting season tribes migrated through well-defined territories. In the early 19th century the native population was about 15 000. Owing to disease, it declined to about 5600 in 1881, fluctuated around 5000 until the 1950s, but increased to more than 7000 by the 1970s.

Spanish, Russian, French, British and American explorers and traders began penetrating the waters of the NE Pacific in the 18th century. Britain gradually ousted the others, however, through the activities of its trading companies, the Royal Navy's presence, and negotiation and threat in Europe. The voyage of James COOK and George VANCOUVER's circumnavigation and hydrographic survey of the Island 1792-94 provided the basis for increased British penetration. The diversity of PLACE-NAMES with which the Island and its surrounding islands and waters abound are a permanent record of this exploratory period. In 1843 the HBC sent James DOUGLAS to the Island to select a site for a fort, and a small settlement at the southern tip developed around Fort Victoria. The Treaty of Washington (1846; *see* OREGON TREATY) established the Island as British territory; it was made a British crown colony in 1849. It united with the mainland BC colony in 1866 and the united colony entered the Dominion of Canada as the province of BRITISH COLUMBIA in 1871.

The European population grew slowly until the 1860s, when the discovery of gold on the mainland and coal on the Island led to a significant increase. Some of those disappointed in the goldfields turned to farming and coal mining and joined a growing trickle of settlers carving out homesteads on the narrow eastern lowlands. Besides Victoria, early settlement centered on the Duncan area of the Cowichan R valley and the COURTENAY-Comox region, both attractive and fertile valleys. Although the forest was an obstacle to the pioneer farmer, its sheer quantity and high quality stimulated the growth of lumber mills at points accessible to tidewater, such as PORT ALBERNI (1861) and Chemainus (1862). The Esquimalt and Nanaimo Ry (1886) provided the basis for expanding the Island's lumber and mining industries. By 1900 the population had grown to around 51 000, with nearly 90% concentrated in the Victoria-NANAIMO region. After 1900 the pace of development increased rapidly as immigration continued and the mining and lumbering industries developed. Nanaimo expanded and new coal mines were opened at CUMBERLAND, LADYSMITH and Union Bay. Population growth slowed between 1921 and 1941, as little suitable land for agricultural development remained; the exhaustion of the best coal deposits left further development to the expansion of the forest industry. The potential for tourism was also becoming apparent as transportation facilities improved, and as the attraction of the Island as a retirement area grew.

The postwar era saw a new surge of growth associated with the increased activity of the forest-products industry, with new or expanded mills at Port Alberni, Crofton, CAMPBELL RIVER and Gold River. The province also became more actively involved in developing and managing the economy, and Victoria, the capital, benefited from expanded government functions. Recent elements of growth have been highway and hydroelectric-power construction, modernization of the ferry system, expansion of military bases and the continued growth of tourism.

The majority of the Island's residents live in Greater Victoria, DUNCAN, Nanaimo, Port Alberni, Courtenay, Campbell River and numerous small towns and villages. Most urban settlements owe their origins and early growth to resource extraction or processing. Since about 1900, those centres possessing both accessibility,

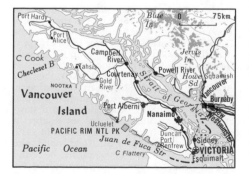

as ports or railway stations, and more than one resource continued to grow, and gradually made the transition from single-enterprise company towns. Victoria's early lead was lost with the growth of Vancouver, which had the advantage of a rail connection to the east. Others stagnated or became ghost towns. Throughout the first half of the 20th century over 77% of the Island's population was of British origin. The CHINESE formed the largest ethnic minority, followed by Scandinavians, JAPANESE and NATIVE PEOPLE. Since WWII the Island's ethnic composition has changed dramatically with an influx of Europeans.   ALAN F.J. ARTIBISE

Reading: C.N. Forward, ed, *Vancouver Island: Land of Contrasts* (1979); M.A. Ormsby, *British Columbia: A History* (1958).

Vancouver Playhouse, completed in 1962 with 647 seats and owned by the city of Vancouver, adjoins the large Queen Elizabeth Theatre. It is viewed as the city's "regional theatre," though the Arts Club Theatre is equally popular. The Playhouse Theatre Co began its first season in 1963, and the next year began a tradition of commissioning original works. Five to 7 plays have been presented annually in a September-to-April season, and sometimes an additional 3 or 4 plays are staged elsewhere. George RYGA's *The Ecstasy of Rita Joe* (1967) was the Playhouse's greatest success. The artistic directors have been Michael Johnston (1963), Malcolm Black (1964-67), Joy Coghill (1967-69), David Gardner (1969-71), Paxton Whitehead (1971-73), Christopher Newton (1973-79), Roger Hodgman (1979-82) and Walter Learning (1982-). *See also* THEATRE, ENGLISH-LANGUAGE.   MALCOLM PAGE

Vancouver Symphony Orchestra has been in continuous existence since 1930, when an earlier Vancouver orchestra was revived. During its inaugural season, the VSO gave 4 concerts, all under conductor Allard de Ridder, 1930-40. A series of guest conductors led the orchestra until Jacques Singer was appointed music director, 1947-52. Under Irwin Hoffman, 1952-64, a protégé of Serge Koussevitzky, the orchestra moved from its home in the Orpheum Theatre to the new Queen Elizabeth Theatre in 1960. Meredeth Davies, 1964-70, revitalized and rejuvenated the orchestra, and Kazuyoshi Akiyama was appointed music director, 1972-85. The orchestra toured Japan in 1974, Canada in 1976 and the US in 1978. In 1977 it moved back to the renovated Orpheum Theatre. By 1984-85, with a season of some 43 weeks and nearly 190 concerts, the VSO was regarded as one of Canada's major orchestras and has almost 40 000 subscribers.
                                    BARBARA NOVAK

Vanderpant, John, photographer (b Jan van der Pant at Alkmaar, Netherlands 11 Jan 1884; d at Vancouver 24 July 1939). A major influence on Canadian photography in the 1920s and 1930s, he established a distinctive style that emphasized light and form and generally shunned popular manipulative processes. After being a photojournalist for a Dutch magazine, he came to Canada in 1911. He opened a studio in Okotoks, Alta, and after WWI moved to BC, eventually settling in Vancouver, where he set up a commercial portrait studio. He began exhibiting in international salons, quickly achieving acclaim and winning awards around the world; his solo exhibitions toured the US, Great Britain and Europe. A fellow of the Royal Photographic Soc of Great Britain, he also wrote and lectured widely. His Robson St gallery, opened in 1926 with Harold Mortimer-Lamb, was a centre for music, poetry and painting. JOAN M. SCHWARTZ

Vanier, Georges-Philéas, governor general 1959-67 (b at Montréal 23 Apr 1888; d at Ottawa 5 Mar 1967). Educated at Loyola and Laval, he was called to the Québec Bar in 1911. He enlisted in 1915 and after winning the Military Cross

Governor General Georges Vanier and Her Excellency Mrs Vanier during a sports event at Camp Fortune (*courtesy Public Archives of Canada/C-75936*).

and DSO he became a founding officer of the Royal 22e Reg, of which he later became commanding officer (1926-28). After WWI he entered the diplomatic service and represented Canada at the League of Nations, in London, and at many international conferences. In 1939 he became Canadian minister to France, and in 1943 minister to all allied governments in exile in London. He returned to France in 1944 as ambassador and served there with great distinction until his retirement in 1953.

Maj-Gen Vanier was installed as governor general on 15 Sept 1959. His years in office were turbulent ones because of a difficult economic situation, a succession of minority governments and the rise of violence and SEPARATISM in Québec. But he won the affection and admiration of Canadians by his concern, manifested in his inspiring public addresses and wide travels across the country, for the poor and the humble, for youth and for the family. A tall, impressive man who moved with great dignity and composure, he was profoundly religious and brought a spiritual and moral dimension to his office. His wife Pauline (née Archer) won equal respect and contributed much to the success of his term.
                                    JACQUES MONET, SJ

Reading: R. Speaight, *Vanier: Soldier, Diplomat, and Governor General* (1970).

Vanier, Jean, spiritual leader, worker with the handicapped (b at Geneva, Swit 28 Sept 1928). The son of Georges VANIER, governor general of Canada, and Pauline Vanier (née Archer), he served in the British and Canadian navies 1945-50. He studied and taught philosophy and theology in France, and then in 1964 established a home for handicapped men living with him in Trosly-Breuil, France. Called L'Arche (the ark), it was the first of many; by 1982 there were 9 in France, 17 in Canada, 6 in the US and numerous others around the world. Vanier is widely esteemed for his leadership of spiritual retreats and for several books, including *Tears of Silence* (1970), *Eruption to Hope* (1971), *Followers of Jesus* (1976) and *Community and Growth* (1979). His writings and way of life challenge people to share life with the disadvantaged, in the belief that each person has a unique value as a human being.   MAC FREEMAN

Varley, Frederick Horsman, painter (b at Sheffield, Eng 2 Jan 1881; d at Toronto 8 Sept 1969). In early life he spent much time in the English countryside and became intensely spiritual, finding God in nature, not in the church. He received a solid art education, first at the Sheffield School of Art (1892-1900), then the Académie royale des beaux-arts in Antwerp, Belgium (1900-02) where he studied original paintings by Rubens. After unsuccessful starts at careers as an illustrator and art teacher in England, Varley immigrated to Canada in 1912. Through Arthur LISMER, a Sheffield friend who had moved to Canada a year earlier, he found employment as a commercial illustrator in To-

ronto and befriended Tom THOMSON and Frank CARMICHAEL.

In 1918 Canadian War Records commissioned Varley to illustrate the war in Europe. He painted several portraits in England and made 2 trips to France. The 4 large war scenes that resulted were critically acclaimed and brought him to the forefront of painters in Canada. In May 1920 Varley became a founding member of the GROUP OF SEVEN. He did not share the Group's enthusiasm for the Ontario landscape, however, and during the early 1920s attempted to make a living as a portraitist. The family of Vincent MASSEY commissioned several, but Varley made little money and in 1926 began to teach at the Vancouver School of Decorative and Applied Arts. During the next 10 years he painted hundreds of landscapes in oil and watercolour, marked by fine draftsmanship, exotic colour, unusual vantage points, and after 1933 by metamorphosis of forms. In 1933, he and J.W.G. MACDONALD opened their own school, the BC College of Arts. Though it was well attended, it closed after 2 years, a victim of the Depression. By 1936 Varley was broke, and moved to Ottawa to try to resume his career as a portraitist. During the next 9 years he drifted between Ottawa and Montréal, making few paintings, except in 1938 when he travelled to the Arctic on the government supply ship *Nascopie*. In 1944 he returned to Toronto and, in 1948-49, taught at the Doon Summer School of Fine Arts near Kitchener. In 1955 he made a sketching trip to Cape Breton, and in 1957 the first of several more painting trips to BC. Romantic and independent, Varley was known as the "gypsy" of the Group of Seven. His gifts as a colourist, draftsman and intimate observer of life are best displayed in his drawings and small watercolours.
                                    CHRISTOPHER VARLEY

Reading: Christopher Varley, *F.H. Varley* (1981).

Vaudreuil, Philippe de Rigaud de Vaudreuil, Marquis de, governor general of NEW FRANCE (b probably near Revel, France *c*1643; d at Québec C 10 Oct 1725). Vaudreuil served in the French army with the Mousquetaires from 1672 and distinguished himself in campaigns in Flanders. He was appointed commander of the troops in Canada in 1687 and took part in campaigns against the Iroquois (*see* IROQUOIS WARS). He followed CALLIÈRE in the governorship of Montréal 1698-1703 and then as governor of New France in 1703. When Vaudreuil took over, the colony was at war with its southern neighbour and her Indian alliances were threatened because of the collapse of the beaver trade and the French withdrawal from the western posts. In his conduct of the war, Vaudreuil tried to preserve the 1701 peace with the Iroquois while encouraging the Abenakis to harass the eastern New England settlements. After the TREATY OF UTRECHT, 1713, he worked through a network of highly effective Indian agents to reassert New France's control of the western FUR TRADE by establishing posts in Iroquois territory, and around the Great Lakes and upper Mississippi drainage area. He continued to exploit the Abenaki alliance to contain the spread of Massachusetts. He was a popular governor who through tenacious work and sometimes ruthless tactics guided New France through a critical era. His success was due in part to the lobbying of his Canadian-born wife at the French court.
                                    MARY McDOUGALL MAUDE

Vaudreuil, Pierre de Rigaud de Vaudreuil de Cavagnial, Marquis de (sometimes Vaudreuil-Cavagnial), officer, last governor general of NEW FRANCE (b at Québec C 22 Nov 1698; d at Paris, France 4 Aug 1778), son of Philippe de Rigaud de VAUDREUIL. He followed his father into the TROUPES DE LA MARINE and the colonial service. After rising through the ranks, he was governor of Trois-Rivières 1733-42. He then succeeded BIENVILLE as governor of Louisiana 1742-53, where his governship brought a degree of economic stability to the colony. In 1755 he was appointed to succeed DUQUESNE as governor general of New France — the only Canadian-born to hold that position. His overall responsibility for military affairs during the SEVEN YEARS' WAR was complicated by the decision to reinforce the Marine troops and militia in New France with 6 regular army infantry battalions, commanded in succession by Baron Dieskau, MONTCALM and LÉVIS. This split command seriously impeded French efforts to pursue the war: Vaudreuil advocated Canadian-style guerilla warfare on the frontiers while Montcalm preferred a defensive stance concentrating on the centre of the colony and the European-style battle. After Montcalm's defeat in the BATTLE OF THE PLAINS OF ABRAHAM, Vaudreuil left instructions with J.B.N.R. de RAMEZAY to surrender the town under certain conditions, orders he was later unable to countermand in time to stop the action. Vaudreuil planned the 1760 operations with Lévis, but despite the latter's successful defeat of the British at the BATTLE OF STE-FOY, the arrival of the English fleet in the spring forced withdrawal again to Montréal. Unable to see any alternative that would not bring suffering to the population, Vaudreuil surrendered the colony at Montréal on Sept 8 after negotiating terms that protected the Canadians in their property, laws and religion but did not allow the troops the honours of war. He was strongly criticized for his action by the French military and the court. He was arrested a few months after Intendant François BIGOT and tried in the famous *affaire du Canada*, but was completely exonerated in Dec 1763. MARY McDOUGALL MAUDE

Vaughan, Robert Charles, railway executive (b at Toronto 1 Dec 1883; d at Montréal 5 Jan 1966). Vaughan joined the CPR as messenger in 1898. He moved on to the GRAND TRUNK RY and to the CANADIAN NORTHERN RY in 1902, rising rapidly to become VP of CANADIAN NATIONAL RYS during the 1920s and 1930s and president 1941-50. Chairman of the Defence Purchasing Board in WWII, Vaughan was created CMG in 1946. He was governor of Montréal General Hospital, president and chairman of Commonwealth International Corp and Commonwealth International Leverage Fund Ltd, and a director of several others. J. LINDSEY

Vaughan, Sir William, colonial promoter, author (b at Carmarthen, Wales 1575; d at Llangyndeyrn, Wales Aug 1641). Vaughan was one of the earliest advocates of Newfoundland as a practical and economically suitable place for English settlement. In 1616 he purchased the southern Avalon Peninsula from the London and Bristol Co and the next year sent out WELSH colonists to Renews. This colony, and further attempts at Trepassey in the 1620s and 1630s, met with failure. Vaughan also wrote 2 of the earliest promotional works about Newfoundland's value to Great Britain, *The Golden Fleece* (1626) and *The Newlanders Cure* (1630). BERT RIGGS

V-E Day Riots, 7-8 May 1945 in Halifax and Dartmouth, NS, began as a poorly co-ordinated celebration of the WORLD WAR II Victory in Europe. This rapidly declined into a rampage by several thousand servicemen (predominantly naval), merchant seamen and civilians, who drank, smashed and looted their way through downtown Halifax. Dartmouth suffered on a smaller scale. Although a subsequent federal inquiry expediently blamed lax naval authority, the true causes lay in bureaucratic confusion, insufficient policing and antipathy between the military and civilians, fueled by the presence of 25 000 servicemen who had strained Halifax wartime resources to the limit. LOIS KERNAGHAN

Vegetable, herbaceous PLANT of which all or a part is eaten, raw or cooked. Vegetables are a valuable source of protein, vitamins, minerals, trace elements and fibre. All vegetables are high in carbohydrates, which contribute to their unique taste. They are most prized when eaten shortly after harvest, either fresh or cooked.

In Canada, at least 53 species or botanical varieties of vegetables are grown: one is a MUSHROOM; 52 are SEED PLANTS (listed below according to family grouping).

Gramineae (GRASS family): *Zea mays* var. *praecox*, popcorn; *Z. mays* var. *rugosa*, SWEET CORN.

Liliaceae (LILY family): *Asparagus officinalis*, ASPARAGUS.

Amaryllidaceae (amaryllis family): *Allium cepa*, ONION; *A. cepa* (Aggregatum Group), shallot; *A. ampeloprasum*, leek; *A. sativum*, garlic; *A. fistulosum*, Welsh onion; *A. schoenoprasum*, chive.

Polygonaceae (BUCKWHEAT family): *Rheum rhabarbarum*, RHUBARB.

Chenopodiaceae (goosefoot family): *Beta vulgaris*, BEET; *B. vulgaris* (Cicla Group), chard; *Spinacia oleracea*, SPINACH.

Cruciferae (mustard family): *Brassica oleracea* (Acephala Group), KALE and collards; *B. oleracea* (Gemmifera Group), BRUSSELS SPROUTS; *B. oleracea* (Capitata Group), CABBAGE; *B. oleracea* (Botrytis Group), BROCCOLI, CAULIFLOWER; *B. oleracea* (Gongylodes Group), KOHLRABI; *B. napus* (Napobrassica Group), RUTABAGA or swede; *B. juncea*, mustard greens; *B. rapa* (Rapifera Group), TURNIP; *B. rapa* (Pekinensis Group), pe-tsai Chinese cabbage; *B. rapa* (Chinensis Group), pakchoi Chinese cabbage; *Nasturtium officinale*, watercress; *Amoracia rusticana*, horseradish; *Raphanus sativus*, RADISH.

Leguminosae (PEA or PULSE family): *Pisum sativum*, garden pea; *P. sativum* var. *arvense*, field pea; *P. sativum* var. *macrocarpon*, edible-podded pea; *Vicia faba*, broad or FABA BEAN; *Phaseolus vulgaris*, green BEAN; *P. coccineus*, scarlet runner bean; *P. limensis*, Lima bean; *Vigna radiata*, mung bean.

Umbelliferae (parsley family): *Daucus carota* var. *sativus*, CARROT; *Foeniculum vulgare*, fennel; *Petroselinum crispum*, parsley; *Apium graveolens* var. *dulce*, CELERY; *A. graveolens* var. *rapaceum*, celeriac; *Pastinaca sativa*, PARSNIP.

Solanaceae (NIGHTSHADE family): *Solanum tuberosum*, POTATO; *S. melongena*, EGGPLANT; *Lycopersicon esculentum*, TOMATO; *Capsicum annuum annuum* (Cerasiforme Group), PEPPER.

Cucurbitaceae (gourd family): *Cucurbita pepo* var. *pepo*, PUMPKIN, acorn SQUASH; *C. pepo* var. *melopepo*, bush summer squash; *C. maxima*, winter squash; *C. moschata*, winter crookneck squash; *Citrullus lanatus*, watermelon; *Cucumis sativus*, CUCUMBER; *Cucumis melo* var. *cantalupensis*, cantaloupe; *Cucumis melo* (Reticulatus Group), muskmelon.

Compositae (composite family): *Cichorium intybus*, witloof, chicory; *C. endivia*, ENDIVE; *Tragopogon porrifolius*, salsify; *Lactuca sativa*, LETTUCE; *Helianthus tuberosus*, Jerusalem artichoke; *Taraxacum officinale*, DANDELION.

Only about 15 of the species listed are widely grown in Canada; 5 or 6 species account for the bulk of all vegetables produced. Vegetables are sometimes classified as cool-season and warm-season types or by their edible parts: for example, flowers — cauliflower, broccoli; leaves — cabbage, lettuce, spinach; shoots — asparagus; leaf stalk (petiole) — rhubarb, chard; roots — beet, carrot, potato, onion; fruit — tomato, pepper, squash.

Cultivation

Vegetable production ranges from highly intensive row cropping to very extensive types of production. Although good soil is beneficial, the grower often finds it more important to use light sandy soils in order to get an early start on the season. Vegetable crops recover from seasonal or short-period DROUGHTS less efficiently

than do most other horticultural crops; thus, a source of water for irrigation during dry spells is necessary. All vegetable-growing operations, from precision seeding to ultimate harvest, handling and packaging, are rapidly becoming fully mechanized. Every mechanical or chemical WEED-control method is used. INSECTS and PLANT DISEASES are closely monitored, and crop losses are minimized by use of chemical PESTICIDES. Many growers have built storage facilities for long-term storage of crops such as potatoes, onions, carrots and cabbages. Canada's long winter season makes it imperative that all vegetables capable of storage in the living state be stored in prime condition.

Areas and Yields The potato is the most widely cultivated vegetable in Canada. Excluding potatoes, Ontario ranks first in vegetable production, both in yield and area; Québec comes second, followed by BC, the Atlantic region and the Prairie region. Ontario also has the greatest potential for increasing production. When potato production is included, Ontario is still in front, but the Atlantic region is second, followed by Québec, the Prairie region and BC. Relatively few sites in Canada have the moderate, reasonably long growing season necessary for vegetable production. Moving from W to E these areas are the lower Fraser Valley, BC; the irrigated area of southern Alberta; the Red and Assiniboine river valleys of Manitoba; the southern Great Lakes rim area of Ontario; the St Lawrence Valley and the muck areas of SW Québec; the St John River Valley, NB; the Annapolis Valley, NS; and most of PEI.

Canadian yields of vegetable crops are comparable to those of similar crops grown in the US or Europe. However, unlike our southern neighbours, we grow only a single vegetable crop on the same land in a year; therefore, total yields usually reflect only one harvest. We compensate by growing vegetables in greenhouses, where our yields of tomatoes and cucumbers are as high as those anywhere in the world. In Canada, maximum yields of carrots, onions, cabbage, celery and lettuce are obtained from muck or organic soils, where adequate summer heat prevails. Upland soils for similar crops are slightly less productive, because the water supply is not usually as constant as on muck. Examples of good yields of major vegetable crops would range as follows: potatoes, 15-20 t; tomatoes, 15-20 t; canning peas, 1-2 t; sweet corn, 3-5 t; carrots and onions, 18-22 t.

Value and Processing Vegetables grown in Canada contribute about 9% of the total agricultural value at the farm gate. Unlike many other agricultural products, their value increases 5-7 fold as the farm-gate value is increased by grading, washing, packaging, transportation, wholesaling and eventual retailing. Whenever vegetables are not immediately consumed, they should be rapidly cooled to retard loss of quality. If summer or field heat is not quickly reduced, vegetables soon lose their desirability. To retain maximum taste and food value, vegetables can be hydrocooled, vacuum cooled, covered with ice, canned or processed, quick-frozen after a brief blanching period and stored, freeze-dried to remove all water in the tissue, or dehydrated under high temperatures. In addition, vegetables handled by any of these means can also be converted to soups, chips, condiments or flakes. Managers of produce departments of modern supermarkets recognize that well-handled, attractively displayed produce carries the greatest unit profit in the store. *See* FRUIT AND VEGETABLE INDUSTRY. I.L. NONNECKE

Vegetable Oil Industry is made up of companies that manufacture oils and their by-products, such as linseed, SOYBEAN and CANOLA oil cake and meal. This industry, the youngest sector of Canada's FOOD AND BEVERAGE INDUSTRIES, did not exist before the early 1940s, as most of Canada's edible oil needs were met by imports. WWII provided the impetus for development, as most of the Allied nations, facing a critical shortage of imported fats, particularly vegetable oils, increased efforts to fill their needs domestically. Soybeans were grown for the first time in southern Ontario; commercial SUNFLOWER production began in Manitoba and Saskatchewan, and a new seed, Black Argentine rapeseed, was planted for the first time. The initial reason for growing rapeseed was to provide desperately needed high-quality marine lubricants for the Allied fleets. After the war, interest in OILSEEDS (especially rapeseed) almost disappeared. In the case of rapeseed, existing varieties were not well suited for producing oil for human consumption or meal for animal feed. The seeds contained high levels of 2 undesirable components, erucic acid (associated with heart lesions in laboratory animals) and glucosinolate (which causes enlarged thyroid glands and poor feed conversion in livestock). However, Canadian agricultural and food scientists, working for the federal Dept of Agriculture and several Canadian universities, began an intense research program, and their accomplishments were remarkable. By 1956 the first improved rapeseed oil for human consumption was being manufactured; by the early 1960s erucic acid had been almost completely removed; and by the early 1970s the glucosinolate content had been dramatically reduced. The new rapeseed varieties, now called canola, were fully accepted in the world's oilseed markets. The achievement was one of Canada's most spectacular AGRICULTURAL RESEARCH success stories. Canola oil and meal have achieved international recognition as an excellent source of human food and livestock feed; canola now provides over 50% of the vegetable oil consumed in Canada. Export sales are now worth about $500 million a year and will unquestionably increase substantially in future. Similar research, which is being done on soybeans to develop varieties that can be grown in cooler areas of Canada, has resulted in a steady increase in Canadian soybean production. Research has begun on reducing the erucic acid and glucosinolate content of mustard seed to create a new oilseed crop, and on using mustard meal as livestock feed.

Statistics Canada figures indicate that, in 1982, 12 oilseed crushing plants were in production: Ont had 3 plants; Man, 2; Sask, 2; and Alta, 5. In 1983 Canada Packers Inc of Toronto started a new $20-million crushing plant in Hamilton, Ont, one of the most advanced in the world. The industry produced 179 316 t of soybean oil and 379 500 t of canola oil in the 1982-83 crop year. The industry had a 1982-83 crop-year output of 1.2 million t of soybean meal and 533 200 of canola meal. The value of factory shipments in 1982 was $722.5 million, up dramatically from $62.8 million in 1961. Cost of materials and supplies in 1982 amounted to $651.8 million.

The industry is represented by the Institute of Edible Oil Foods in Toronto and is also involved with the producer organization, the Canola Council of Canada in Winnipeg. The industry must comply with regulations administered by Agriculture Canada, Health and Welfare Canada and Consumer and Corporate Affairs Canada. *See* FLAX.   ROBERT F. BARRATT

Vegetarianism describes the diet (eg, roots, green vegetables, cereals, seeds, fruit and nuts, and perhaps eggs and dairy products) of those who abstain from animal food, particularly that obtained by killing animals. Many Canadians have chosen a vegetarian diet for economic or religious reasons or because of its legendary benefits.

Semivegetarians are those who have eliminated only red meat from their diet and may substitute for it poultry, fish, milk or eggs. Those who eat no meat are called "lacto-ovo" (milk and eggs) vegetarians. Both milk and eggs provide the necessary protein, plus B vitamins and minerals. For those who cannot tolerate lactose, cheese and fermented milk products can be used. "Lacto vegetarians" have eliminated eggs as well, but a substitute source of iron and other nutrients must be found. Total vegetarians ("vegans") avoid all animal by-products, and some eat only fruit or raw food. Vegetarian diets that exclude all animal by-products can be harmful. For example, diets of "vegans" are low in vitamin B_{12} but contain enough folic acid to mask the early signs of vitamin B_{12} deficiency until irreversible damage to neural tissues in the spinal cord (known as "vegan back") occurs. Protein balance in the vegetarian diet is also a potential problem if the essential amino acids are missing. The Zen macrobiotic diet reflects the risks inherent in all other types of vegetarianism. In the long-term, Zen macrobiotic converts may suffer scurvy, hypoproteinemia, anemia, hypocalcemia and emaciation or starvation with accompanying loss of kidney function. Pregnant and lactating Zen macrobiotics are particularly vulnerable to these nutritional deficiencies. However, vegetarianism generally leads to poor health only in those individuals who completely ignore the need for a balanced diet.
                                        M.T. CLANDININ

Vegetation Regions are geographical areas characterized by distinct PLANT communities. Community composition, determined primarily by CLIMATE (eg, temperature, precipitation, sunlight), may be affected by factors such as GEOLOGY, SOIL composition and EROSION, WATER drainage patterns and human interference. Each vegetation region supports a characteristic animal community which may affect its composition. The principal regions represented in Canada are as follows.

Arctic Tundra

The arctic tundra is the second-largest vegetation region in the country. It covers a greater range of latitude than any other, yet is little understood because of its remoteness and sparse human population. The Arctic is treeless because of its low summer temperatures (a mean of less than 11°C in the warmest month) and short growing season (1.5-3.5 months). The transition from boreal forest to TUNDRA, termed forest-tundra, consists of ribbons or islands of stunted black and white spruce trees in a sea of tundra vegetation. Only a few birch and quaking aspen reach this far North. The major environmental factors which limit plant growth and distribution are cold soils with an active layer in summer of 20-60 cm above the PERMAFROST; varying depth of winter snow; low levels of soil nutrients, especially nitrogen and phosphorus; and soils that can be very dry (on ridges) or very wet (in lowlands) in summer.

The Arctic is often divided into the Low Arctic of the mainland and the High Arctic of the Northern Dist of Keewatin and ARCTIC ARCHIPELAGO. The Low Arctic is characterized by nearly complete plant cover and abundant, low and dwarf woody shrubs. Major plant communities include tall (2-3 m) shrub tundra of alder, scrub birch and willows, along rivers, streams, steep slopes and lake shores; low (30-60 cm) shrub tundra of willow, dwarf birch, dwarf heath shrubs, numerous SEDGES and small herbaceous species and abundant LICHENS and MOSSES, on medium drained slopes; tussock sedge, dwarf heath shrubs, mosses and lichens on poorly drained soils of low rolling hills; and various combinations of sedges, a few GRASSES and herbs, and abundant mosses in poorly drained soils of flatlands. These latter areas are the summer habitat of many waterfowl. Hills of tussock sedge and low shrub tundras are the summer rangelands of barren ground caribou and the year round home of lemming, ptarmigan, fox and wolf.

In the High Arctic, vegetation is sparser and the wildlife it supports is more limited because of colder summers (2-5°C warmest month), shorter growing season (1.5-2.5 months), and low precipitation (100-200 mm). In lowlands, limited areas of sedge-moss tundras occur, decreasing in extent N of 74° N. About 50% of the land consists of scattered clumps of very dwarf shrubs (1-3 cm high) of willow and mountain avens, with small cushion plants (species of draba, saxifrage, chickweed, poppy), and abundant lichens and mosses; or areas of lichens, mosses, scattered clumps of grasses and rushes, and cushion plants. These lands (polar semideserts) can support small scattered herds of muskox and Peary's caribou, with waterfowl in lowland lakes, ponds and sedge meadows.

At higher elevations (above 100 m) in the southern and central islands and at lower elevations in the more northerly islands, the abundance of surface, frost-shattered rock and small pockets of fine soil result in truly barren land (polar DESERTS). Here flowering plants and mosses grow only where large snowbanks provide meltwater. Elsewhere, only tiny scattered flowering plants grow with essentially no lichens or mosses. These lands support rare, small lemming colonies.
                                        L.C. BLISS

Boreal Forest or Taiga

The boreal forest encircles the Northern Hemisphere south of the treeless tundra. This, Canada's largest vegetation region, has FORESTS and woodlands dominated by a relatively few cold-tolerant conifers: species of spruce, fir, pine and larch. Poplars and birches are also common, but more so in the south than in the north. The terrain is characterized by numerous lakes, extensive peatlands, and podzol soils on uplands. The continental climate with short, cool summers and long, cold winters is subarctic. The boreal forest can be traced to near the end of the Miocene (12-15 million years ago) when the trees that today typify the North first appear in the FOSSIL record. Probably they evolved at upper altitudes in the mountains, spread to lowlands as the climate cooled, and eventually replaced the Arcto-Tertiary forest, fragments of which still survive in the southern US, southern Europe and SE Asia.

In N America, the bulk of the boreal forest is in Canada, with extensions into Alaska and the Lake States. The southern subzone has a strong, broadleaf component of aspen and birch which, with jack pine, white spruce and balsam fir, forms upland mixed-wood stands. Associated tall shrubs and herbaceous plants reflect the relatively favourable climate and soils, except on peatlands, where black spruce and larch dominate. In western Canada, mixed woods grade into the grasslands through a belt of aspen parkland; in the East, the transition to the richer forests of the Great Lakes-St Lawrence Region is

Tundra seepage area covered in mosses at Resolute, Cornwallis I, NWT (*courtesy National Museums of Canada/ National Museum of Natural Sciences/E. Haber*).

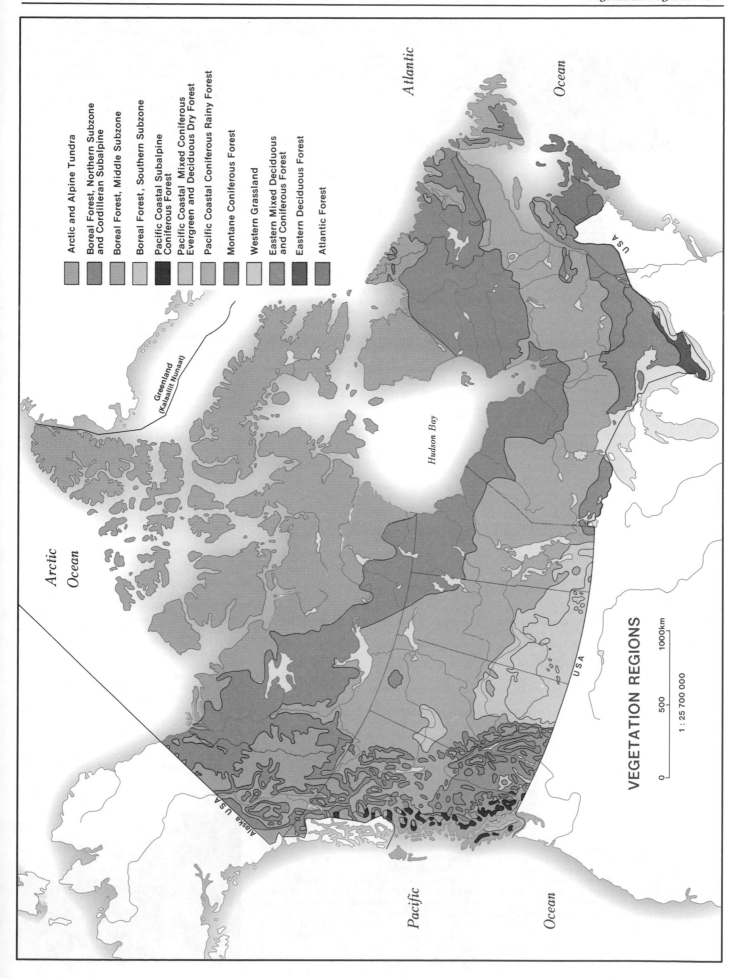

Arctic and Alpine Tundra

Boreal Forest, Northern Subzone and Cordilleran Subalpine

Boreal Forest, Middle Subzone

Boreal Forest, Southern Subzone

Pacific Coastal Subalpine Coniferous Forest

Pacific Coastal Mixed Coniferous Evergreen and Deciduous Dry Forest

Pacific Coastal Coniferous Rainy Forest

Montane Coniferous Forest

Western Grassland

Eastern Mixed Deciduous and Coniferous Forest

Eastern Deciduous Forest

Atlantic Forest

VEGETATION REGIONS

1 : 25 700 000

0   500   1000 km

Atlantic   *Ocean*

Arctic Ocean

Greenland (Kalaallit Nunaat)

Hudson Bay

Pacific   *Ocean*

USA

Alaska U.S.A.

Boreal forest and bog at Heart Lake, NWT (*courtesy Provincial Museum of Alberta*).

marked by a variety of temperate hardwoods and evergreens. The middle boreal subzone is the pulpwood forest par excellence, dominated by dense stands of spruce, pine and fir. On infertile soils, under the closed-crown conifers, feather mosses and small, winter-green herbs are characteristic. Aspen and birch are prominent where soils are richer, especially following logging and fire. The northernmost subzone, the Subarctic, constitutes almost one half of the boreal zone. The Low Subarctic bears extensive lichen woodland: a savannah of spruce or pine scattered through a handsome carpet of lichens. The High Subarctic includes both forest-tundra near the TREELINE, where patches of spruce and larch on low areas alternate with treeless uplands, and the shrub-tundra, extending beyond treeline to the tree-species line.

Throughout the boreal forest, PEAT accumulates in depressions. Fen peat forms along drainageways, its presence being indicated by alder, willow, larch and sedges. Bogs are raised above fens and are identified by acid sphagnum hummocks, dwarf evergreen shrubs (especially Labrador tea) and black spruce. In the Subarctic, all bogs contain permafrost; the larger ones, scarred by thaw pockets, are called peat plateaus. The influence of fire is evident almost everywhere. Burning favours the invasion of sprouters (aspen and balsam poplar), wind-dispersed seeders (birch), and closed-cone conifers (jackpine and black spruce). Such trees flourish in pure or mixed stands when fires are frequent. Areas less subject to burning support forests of white spruce and, the least fire-resistant of boreal trees, balsam fir.   J. STAN ROWE

Pacific Coastal

The Pacific Coastal region, which ranges from nearly 48° N latitude to 55° N, may be divided into 4 distinct growing zones reflecting the great variation in temperature, length of growing season and average precipitation (650-3000 mm per year). Significant rainfall shadows, caused by mountain ranges on Vancouver I and the Queen Charlotte Is, can produce further climatic variation on the eastern flanks of the mountain ranges and in associated, mainland coastal areas.

Vegetation of the outer coasts of island archipelagoes and the exposed coasts of the mainland is predominantly coniferous forest consisting of Douglas fir, western hemlock, yellow cypress, Sitka spruce, shore pine, western red cedar and occasionally western yew. The principal deciduous hardwoods are red alder and Scouler willow. Douglas fir is absent from the Queen Charlotte Is.

The Georgia Strait area on the E coast of Vancouver I and the adjacent mainland has a drier, Mediterranean climate. Here, coastal vegetation must persist through a hot, dry period lasting up to 8 weeks. The vegetation is characterized by a colourful spring flora with several, annual, herbaceous species. Arbutus, western flowering dogwood and Garry oak reach their northern limits in this region. Arbutus is the only native broad-leaved evergreen tree in Canada. Western flowering dogwood is the PROVINCIAL FLORAL EM-

BLEM of BC. Other forest species include Douglas fir, western hemlock, grand fir, bigleaf maple, western red cedar and bitter cherry.

The predominant undergrowth shrubs of the outer-coastal forest are salal, salmonberry, and several species of genus *Vaccinium* (eg, bilberries and huckleberries). These shrubs, notably salal, often form impenetrable thickets on exposed headlands. In the drier, inner-coastal areas, thimbleberry, red elderberry, Nootka rose, ocean spray, snowberry, western sword fern and deer fern are common in the undergrowth. Specialized plant communities are associated with the beaches. Most are cobble or shingle beaches with a prominent driftwood zone containing large logs of the forest tree species. Fine sand beaches occur, most commonly, in the southern portion of the Canadian Pacific coast. Common plants in the driftwood zone are American wild dune grass, beach pea, giant vetch, common cleaver, bluejoint small reed grass, tufted hair grass, Pacific coastal strawberry and sea plantain.

The Pacific coastline is highly dissected by many fjordlike inlets. Salt marsh vegetation is found at the head of such inlets. Common plants of these marshes are various species of alkali grass, seaside arrow grass, pickleweed, springbank clover, salt-marsh starwort, and sedges such as *Carex lyngbyei* and *C. obnupta*. Grasses found in these communities are spike bent grass, red fescue, tufted hair grass and meadow barley. Occasional, but conspicuous, flowering plants include Douglas's aster, western buttercup, entire-leaved gumweed and *Apargidium boreale*. Soft rushes form conspicuous, herbaceous clumps in these marsh lands.

    ROY L. TAYLOR

Cordillera

The Canadian Cordillera can be divided into 12 zones (distinguished by a certain macroclimate, zonal vegetation and soil) which can then be grouped into 7 regions and 4 formations. The variations are staggering: regions represented range from alpine tundra to cool, mesothermal rain forest and include 5 of the 8 major Canadian forest zones.

Alpine Formation contains only the Alpine Region comprising the Alpine Tundra Zone, which extends through YT, Mackenzie Dist, BC and Alberta. Mean temperature of the warmest month is 0°-10°C. Mean total precipitation is 700-3500 mm, 76-80% in snowfall. Vegetation consists of mainly herbaceous plants, mosses, liverworts, lichens and very low shrubs (eg, arctic willow).

Microthermal Coniferous Forest Formation is characterized by cold, forest climates which are meagerly to moderately forest productive. The mean temperature of the coldest months is well below 0°C; the mean of the warmest months, above 10°. Snow covers the ground for more than one month. The formation includes 4 forest regions: Pacific Coastal Subalpine, Interior Cordilleran Subalpine, Boreal Montane and Cordilleran Montane Temperate.

The Pacific Coastal Subalpine Forest Region contains only the Mountain Hemlock Zone which, in Canada, occurs along the Pacific coast. Underneath the snowpack, the ground does not freeze. Mountain hemlock, amabilis fir and Alaska yellow cedar are characteristic tree species. The most characteristic shrubs are mountain juniper, Alaskan, Cascade and oval-leaved blueberries, red mountain heather, copper bush, coastal Douglas fir, Sitka mountain ash, Sitka alder, and deer fern.

The Interior Cordilleran Subalpine Forest Region is characterized by having ground that is often frozen before snowfall. Two zones are recognized. The first, the Engelmann Spruce-Subalpine Fir Zone, occurs in BC and Alberta. Typical tree and shrub species include Engelmann spruce, subalpine fir, lodgepole and whitebark pines, subalpine larch, trembling

aspen, mountain juniper, white-leaved rhododendron, coastal Douglas fir, shrub and water birches, Sitka alder, devil's club, Oregon boxwood, black huckleberry, oval-leaved blueberry, grouseberry, Sitka mountain ash, Utah honeysuckle. The second zone, Spruce-Willow-Birch Zone, occurs in BC, north of 57°10' N latitude and extends to 70° N latitude (YT and Mackenzie Dist). Elevations are: southwest, 950-1550 m; southeast, 1100-1750 m; north, sea level. In northern Alberta, this zone is centered around the Caribou Mts at elevations above 700 m. In the summer, days are long or have pronounced twilight and temperatures remain above freezing. Typical vegetation includes white and black spruces, mountain juniper, shrub birch, green alder, many willows and Northern Labrador tea.

In the Boreal Montane Forest Region, the ground is solidly frozen before snowfall. Mean temperature is above 10°C for 3-4 months, below 0° for 5-7 months. Summer is hot at its peak; winter very severe. Elevations are montane, ie, below subalpine elevations. Two zones occur. The first, the Boreal White-and-Black-Spruce Zone, is found in BC, Alta, YT and NWT, in the latitude of 54-69° N. Elevations range from sea level in the North to 1100 m in BC. In Alberta, growth of trees is poor (except on alluvial soils) because the growing season is short, the winter very severe, and the ground deeply frozen. Permafrost occurs in lenses in central parts and is continuous in the North. Common tree species include white and black spruces, lodgepole and jack pines, larch, subalpine fir, mountain and creeping junipers, trembling aspen, balsam poplar, paper, water, Alaska, shrub and swamp birches, thinleaf and green alders. Common shrubs include dwarf and bog blueberry, mountain cranberry, leatherleaf, etc. High moors are common. In the second zone, the Subboreal Spruce Zone, the mean temperature is below 0°C for 5 months. The zone occurs in BC, between 52°30' and 57°10' N latitudes, and at montane elevations. Compared to the Boreal White-and-Black-Spruce Zone, winter is milder, growth of trees better, especially because low moors are common. High moors are rare and free of permafrost. Tree species are, essentially, as in the Boreal White-and-Black-Spruce Zone, except that Engelmann spruce, black cottonwood and Sitka alder are present; Alaska birch, green alder and creeping juniper are absent. Shrub species include devil's club, black huckleberry, and oval-leaved blueberry.

The final forest region, the Cordilleran Montane Temperate Forest Region, has a mean temperature above 10°C for 4-5 months, below 0° for 3-5 months. Three zones are distinguished. The Cariboo Aspen-Lodgepole Pine Zone occurs only in the central part of interior BC, between 51°10' and 54°15' N latitude, elevation 510-1200 m. The number of conifers is limited by the severe winters and dry, hot summers. Common tree species include lodgepole pine, white spruce, interior variety of Douglas fir, Rocky Mountain and mountain junipers,

Alpine vegetation, Banff National Park, Alta (*photo by Stephen J. Krasemann/DRK Photo*).

trembling aspen, black cottonwood, paper and water birches, thinleaf and Sitka alders. Pine grass is common. The Interior Western Hemlock Zone which, in BC, occurs between 49° and 54°10′ N latitude at elevations of 360-1260 m, is the wettest and most productive temperate forest zone in the BC interior. Vegetation includes the interior variety of Douglas fir, western hemlock, western white and lodgepole pines, western red cedar, western larch, grand fir, Engelmann spruce, mountain juniper, black cottonwood, trembling aspen, paper, water, shrub and swamp birches, Sitka and thinleaf alders, devil's club, Oregon boxwood, Oregon wintergreen, globe and oval-leaved blueberries, black huckleberry, Utah honeysuckle, American skunk cabbage. The Interior Douglas Fir Zone occurs mainly in BC and very little on the eastern slopes of Rocky Mts in Alberta, between 49° and 53°10′ N latitude, at elevations of 300-1350 m. It is the second-warmest interior zone in BC. Vegetation includes interior variety of Douglas fir, ponderosa, lodgepole and western white pines, grand fir, western larch, western red cedar, Rocky Mountain and mountain junipers, creeping juniper, trembling aspen, paper and water birches, redstem and snowbush ceanothus, pine and wheat grasses, and several needle grasses. In Alberta, many of the plant indicators are very rare or lacking.

Semiarid Cold Steppe Formation encompasses dry climates in which evaporation exceeds precipitation and no surplus of water remains to maintain a constant groundwater level. This formation includes only the Cordilleran Cold-Steppe-Savanna Forest Region with only the Ponderosa Pine-Bunchgrass Zone. The mean temperature is above 10°C for 5-7 months, below 0° for 2-3 months. The long frost-free period (207-260 days) allows orchards to develop if artificial irrigation is provided. The zone lies across southern BC between 49-51° N latitude, at elevations of 270-750 m. It includes the Fraser, Thompson, Nicola, Similkameen, Okanagan and Kootenay (most southern part) river valleys. The strongest rain shadow effects in BC are caused by the Western Coast Cordilleras. Limited growth of trees occurs, mainly ponderosa pine in savanna stands. After overgrazing and fires, bluebunch wheat grass, rough fescue, needle grasses and several bluegrass species are replaced by prairie sage brush in cooler, and Big Basin sage brush in warmer areas, and by arrow-leaved balsamroot, 2 prickly pear cactus species, rabbitbrush, several milk vetch species and many other steppe plants. Poison ivy, smooth sumac and tall Oregon grape grow at the bottom of coarse talus slopes.

Mesothermal Forest Formation contains only the Pacific Coastal Mesothermal Forest Region. Winter is mild with Jan mean temperature usually above 0°C. Vegetation includes western hemlock, western red cedar, Sitka spruce, red alder, bitter cherry, black cottonwood, cascara sagrada, salal, evergreen and red huckleberries, western swordfern, deer fern and American skunk cabbage. The region is divided into 2 zones. In the first, the Coastal Douglas Fir Zone, the relative dryness results from the rain shadow effect of insular mountains on Vancouver I. Vegetation includes coastal varieties of Douglas fir, grand fir, western red cedar, Garry oak, arbutus, lodgepole pine, western flowering dogwood, broadleaf and vine maples, Vancouverian variety of trembling aspen, long-leaved Oregon grape, common and trailing snowberry, western trumpet and hairy honeysuckles, and salal. The second zone is the Coastal Western Hemlock Zone, the wettest in BC. In the North, heavy snowfall protects the ground from freezing. Mean temperature is above 10°C for 4-7 months, below 0° for 0-3 months. Sitka spruce, western red cedar, amabilis fir, Alaska yellow cedar and western hemlock have the best

production here. The coastal variety of Douglas and grand firs (both only in the southern parts of the zone) grow best in the drier subzone, where Douglas fir may reach 100 m tall in its best habitats, when 300 years old. Lodgepole pine and Labrador tea are common in sphagnum bogs. Salal forms impenetrable thickets. Among the many, long, hanging epiphytes (plants deriving moisture and nutrients from air and rain) which live on woody plants, *Isothecium stoloniferum* is the most common. *See* BIO-GEOCLIMATIC ZONE.   V.J. KRAJINA

Prairie

Prairie is a natural grassland found in semi-arid to subhumid climates. Plants are perennials, mostly grasses, associated with sedges, forbs (nongrasslike herbaceous plants) and a few dwarf shrubs. Before European settlement, this vegetation occupied valleys of southern interior BC, and much of southern Man, Sask and Alta, from Winnipeg to Calgary and from the US border to Saskatoon and Edmonton. The nature of grassland vegetation depends on climate and soil. Precipitation increases eastward from the Rocky Mts, temperature decreases northward. Both factors are affected by increasing elevation in the foothills of Alberta, on the valley slopes of BC, and in elevated locations across the southern Canadian prairies.

Climatic differences have caused the formation of 3 grassland soil zones. Brown soils of the driest area, southwestern Saskatchewan and southeastern Alberta, are populated by relatively drought-resistant grasses, particularly common spear grass, western wheat grass and blue grama. In the adjacent, dark brown soils (east, north and west), principal species are short-awned porcupine grass and northern wheat grass. These zones comprise the mixed prairie. Fescue prairie occupies black soils in Alta and western Sask, between mixed prairie and northern forest, giving way eastward to the true prairie of southern Man. The principal grass of fescue prairie is rough fescue; in true prairie, bluestems and porcupine grass are most important. In BC, bluebunch wheat grass, occupying semiarid valley floors (lower grassland), changes to a type of vegetation dominated by rough fescue (upper grassland). Usually, 2-3 grass species contribute 70% or more of the vegetation; the number of associated species varies widely, diversity increasing with moistness of habitat. Mixed and true prairie extend southward to Texas, with considerable change in species composition; fescue prairie and BC grassland (palouse prairie) extend only into the adjacent states.

In the black soil zone, forest penetrates prairie where the local climate is moister and cooler than average (north-facing slopes, edges of sloughs, and elevated areas), so that grassland and forest intermingle to form the aspen grove region within fescue and true prairie. In BC, the margin between open grassland and forest is a savanna (grassland with scattered trees) with Douglas fir as the main tree. The character of grassland varies locally with soil texture. In dune sand, various specialized grasses abound (eg, sand grass, sand dropseed and Indian rice grass). In saline flats, salt grass, alkali grass and wild barley dominate. Similarly, the wet slough environment results in a cover of various grass species (eg, slough grass, spangle top, blue-grasses), sedges, bulrushes and cattail.

At the end of the 19th century, rangeland grazing by domesticated livestock was the principal agricultural use made of the prairies. The cultivated area increased rapidly 1900-30; today, about 55% of the area E of the mountains is under crop or summerfallow, representing 65% of cultivated land in Canada. The high fertility of prairie soils is depleted by tillage. It was estimated that, by the early 1980s, 33-50% of organic matter in cultivated prairie soils had

been lost. The large tracts of uncultivated grassland, mostly community pasture or crown land leased by ranchers, are grazed by domesticated livestock. GRASSLANDS NATIONAL PARK, Sask, was established to ensure survival of some native prairie.   ROBERT T. COUPLAND

Eastern Temperate Forests

The most northern expression of the extensive temperate forests of southeastern N America, this region is dominated by deciduous, broadleaved trees. In favourable southern climates, deciduous leaves are most efficient, but they are energy-consuming because they must be renewed annually. A shorter growing season and harsher climate favour replacement by less efficient but less energy-demanding needle-leaved evergreens. Therefore, the zone may be divided into the Southern Deciduous Forests and the more northerly Deciduous-Evergreen Forests.

The summergreen character is most prominent in extreme southern Ontario where 80 different tree species grow naturally (now largely displaced by agriculture). Within this region, many dominance patterns occur because of local variations in soil moisture, soil type and microclimate. In drier environments of the Southern Deciduous Forests, black, red and white oak predominate and shagbark hickory, hop hornbeam, beech, red maple and white pine are strong associates. In mesic (moist) environments sugar maple and beech dominate in association with red elm, black maple, black cherry, white ash and basswood. In wet lowlands and bottomlands, white elm and red and silver maple are major forest components, growing with black walnut, white and green ash, bitternut hickory, cottonwood, pin oak, box elder and black willow. In Canada, many southern species occur only in this region (eg, flowering dogwood, chestnut and Hill's oaks, sweet pignut, pignut and kingnut hickories, sweet chestnut, red mulberry, sassafras, tuliptree, Kentucky coffee tree, hackberry, cucumber magnolia, sycamore, sour gum and honey locust). White pine and pencil cedar are associated evergreens in dry environments; hemlock is the only other significant conifer, in moist forests. Left undisturbed, the trees in these forests grow to great size (40 m) and great age (500 years).

The Deciduous-Evergreen Forests are often referred to as mixed forests; however, pure evergreen or deciduous types are also prevalent. Thus, in the broad triangle from Michipicoten to North Bay, Ont, and Ste-Agathe, Qué, with outliers west of Thunder Bay, at Lac Saint-Jean and in Gaspé, the drier sites support forests of jack pine, red or white pine in association with large-tooth aspen, red oak, beech, paper birch, trembling aspen and hemlock. Moist forests are composed of sugar maple as an almost overriding dominant or in association with beech (south), basswood, hop hornbeam, yellow birch or hemlock. These terminal forests are remarkably similar to those on mesic sites southward. Wet environments support monodominant forests or admixtures of white elm, silver maple

Forests in Ontario's Agawa Valley (*photo by Tom W. Parkin/Pathfinder*).

(southward), red maple (northward), white cedar or black willow. Associated species include green and black ashes and larch.

Northward, evergreen elements are more dominant. Stands of pine, white cedar, tamarack and, occasionally, black spruce become prominent parts of the forest scene. Successional forests are also frequent. Extensive stands, often of a single species (eg, trembling aspen, paper birch, jack, red or white pines), result from frequent fires. Trees are frequently short-lived and vulnerable to wind, disease and fungus attack and, except white and red pine and maple, the forests seldom achieve great age or size.

In summer, deciduous forests are too shady for growth of significant ground cover; however, in spring, flowering plants with short reproductive cycles are abundant. These WILD-FLOWERS provide welcome contrast to the monotony of winter snow and the sombre majesty of the mature forests, but far more spectacular is the brilliant display of colour before leaf-fall. PAUL F. MAYCOCK

Atlantic Coastal Region

The vegetation of this region reflects also the human activity of the area. The island of Newfoundland lies at the eastern limits of the Boreal Forest Region. The Island's forests are dominated by conifers, particularly white and black spruce and balsam fir. Larch and deciduous species such as white birch, trembling aspen and balsam poplar are widespread, but their abundance varies with local conditions. Most of the Maritimes are in the Acadian Forest Region, except for a section of NB adjacent to the Québec border, which is in the Eastern Temperate Forest Region. The maritime forests are intermediate between the conifer-dominated boreal forest and the hardwood deciduous forests common farther south. They are dominated by red and white spruces, balsam fir, yellow birch, beech and sugar maple.

Human activities have decreased the diversity of the original forests. White pine was cut in the 19th century for use as masts for the sailing fleets of England. Land was cleared for farming and fires have taken their toll. A number of tree species have been reduced in abundance by diseases and pests such as white pine blister rust and beech bark disease. Unless they are maintained, the cleared or burnt-over areas are recolonized by stands of white spruce and/or balsam fir. Such relatively pure stands have been plagued by problems common to monoculture situations, such as insect attacks, in this case by the spruce budworm.

Wind, cool temperatures and abundant precipitation are characteristic of the maritime climate. Along sea coasts, forests are usually dwarfed and large areas of peatland and heath occur, particularly in NS and Newfoundland. Peatlands are areas of poor drainage and low productivity, dominated by sphagnum, sedges, heath shrubs, stunted black spruce and larch. Heaths are found along the coasts, on hilltops and in other areas where forests have difficulty becoming established. They are areas of short, shrubby vegetation which are usually dominated by crowberry, bilberries, dwarf birches, junipers and other dwarf or prostrate shrubs. Forest growth improves in inland valleys and in many parts of NB because of better soils and more protected situations. However, the woodland flora is less rich than it is farther south. The growth of blueberries, an important crop of the region, is promoted by controlled burning which reduces competition from other species and keeps the blueberry plants pruned, thus increasing yield. There are some saltmarshes and freshwater marshes, particularly in the Bay of FUNDY area.

The vegetation of the Atlantic Coastal Region has a rugged character with a marked contrast between the sombre coniferous forests and mounds of brightly coloured wildflowers along roadsides during summer and autumn. It is a mosaic of natural, man-altered, and man-made habitats that is a product of glacial history and human colonization. *See* SWAMP, MARSH AND BOG. PETER J. SCOTT

Coastal Marine Flora

A coastal marine flora comprises spermatophytes (flowering plants), and thallophytes (nonvascular, spore-producing plants, eg, algae and lichens) that live in or at the edge of the sea. The highly indented Canadian coastline provides many habitats for marine plants, from sheltered estuaries and lagoons to rocky shores exposed to open ocean. The composition of the flora varies with habitat. Some algae and lichens live just within reach of wave spray; other algae occur as deep as sufficient light for photosynthesis penetrates (about 75 m on the Atlantic coast and slightly less in more turbid Pacific waters). Intertidally, plants are distributed according to resistance to temperature extremes, desiccation, strong illumination, and wave impact, and according to their ability to compete with other species for space. In northern and eastern Canada, the capacity of plants to withstand ice cover and abrasion is a determinant. Paradoxically, confined, shallow coastal waters in Canada may attain summer temperatures of 28°C or higher, and may support more southerly, warm-water species that can tolerate cold winters.

In Canada, marine flowering plants may be dune and beach-dwellers adapted to a dry habitat (eg, sea rocket), saltmarsh species tolerant of periodic flooding by tides (eg, cordgrass), or truly marine and usually submerged sea "grasses" (eg, eelgrass and surf-grass). Marine spore-producing plants are much more numerous, the most conspicuous and diverse being benthic (attached to substratum) algae. They range from microscopic aggregates of a few cells to some of the tallest plants known, and are grouped into 3 main colour classes: red, brown and green. A fourth group, the BLUE-GREEN ALGAE, is widespread and often abundant. It consists chiefly of microscopic forms, poorly documented because of taxonomic difficulties.

The richest Canadian marine algal flora occurs on the Pacific coast, where about 480 species are recognized (66% red, 21% brown, 13% green). This profusion is due to equable ocean temperatures and the upwelling of nutrient-rich water. Diversity is at times spectacular, as in the 16 genera of kelps, cold-water species of which may reach 30 m in length.

In Atlantic Canada, with cold Arctic currents and severe winter conditions, a markedly different and less diverse algal flora of about 345 species occurs (39% red, 37% brown, 24% green). Lesser diversity allows greater density of individual species, and exposed Atlantic shores usually show striking vertical zonation of a few dominant algae. Subtidal kelp forests off NS have an unusually high growth rate compared to many other marine and terrestrial ecosystems; however, much of the subtidal algal flora has been overgrazed by sea urchins, and prospects for recovery are equivocal. About 75 taxa are common to both Atlantic and Pacific shores.

The Canadian Arctic, with low temperatures and limited sunlight, has a meagre algal flora of 170 species (32% red, 38% brown, 30% green). Arctic algae appear to be peculiarly adapted to photosynthesize with minimal light and temperature, although heterotrophy (by absorption and metabolism of organic substances dissolved in sea water) has been suggested as a means of subsistence. Incidence of annual species decreases at higher latitudes, and the intertidal flora is sparse or absent. *See* SEAWEEDS. C.J. BIRD

Veniot, Peter John, "Pierre," journalist, politician, premier of NB (b at Richibucto, NB 4 Oct 1863; d at Bathurst, NB 6 July 1936). First elected MLA for Gloucester in 1894 then resigned in 1900 to become Bathurst collector of customs. Hired in 1912 to reorganize the provincial Liberals, he was re-elected in 1917 and as minister of public works undertook extensive road-building projects. He succeeded W.E. FOSTER as premier in 1923 and supported public ownership of the provincial hydro system and the Maritime Rights Movement. The first Acadian NB premier, he was recognized as the leader of Acadian Liberalism. Following the defeat of his party in 1925, he ran successfully as MP for Gloucester and was appointed postmaster general by PM KING. He sat as an MP until his death. DELLA M.M. STANLEY

Verchères, Marie-Madeleine Jarret de, heroine (b at Verchères, Qué 3 Mar 1678; buried at Ste-Anne-de-la-Pérade 8 Aug 1747). Daughter of an officer and seigneur, François Jarret de Verchères, in 1706 she married another officer and seigneur, Pierre-Thomas Tarieu de La Pérade. By age 21 she was famous for the story of her defence 7 years earlier, in 1692, of the family fort, a story subsequently published by historians Bacqueville de La Potherie and CHARLEVOIX. However, at about age 54, seeking a favour from France after other eyewitnesses had disappeared, the heroine told a new version, one full of exaggerations and lies. (In this one, she did not flee from one Iroquois, she evaded 45 who were firing at her.) This new version, being more dramatic, is the one favoured by most history books. MICHELINE D'ALLAIRE

Verigin, Peter Vasilevich, also Veregin, religious leader (b at Slavyanka, Russia 29 June 1859; d near Grand Forks, BC 29 Oct 1924). He became leader of the pacifist Russian sect of DOUKHOBORS in 1886 and in 1887 was exiled to Siberia. Influenced by the doctrines of the Christian anarchist novelist, Leo Tolstoi, he clandestinely instructed his followers to abandon meat and alcohol and to resume their historic resistance to military service. Persecution resulted, many Doukhobors were exiled in inhumane conditions to Georgia, Russia and, in 1898-99, more than 7000 were admitted to Canada. Verigin followed in 1903. He encouraged his people not to take the oath of allegiance required by the government to secure the land granted to them. When Doukhobor farms were seized, he led his followers, the Christian Community of Universal Brotherhood, to the Kootenay area of BC where, on purchased land, he attempted to create a self-supporting, self-governing commune. An able organizer, he placed the community on a good economic footing, but he struggled with the authorities over such matters as compulsory education. Verigin died in a train explosion of undetermined cause. After his death, the Christian Community fell into financial and organizational disarray. His powerful and imaginative personality had enabled the Doukhobors to weather their difficult first decades in Canada and to retain their special identity as a sect of Christian pacifist communists. GEORGE WOODCOCK

Vermilion Pass, elev 1651 m, is situated between Boom and Storm mountains on the BC-Alberta border, 42 km W of Banff. It takes its name from the mineral springs of iron oxide located along the Vermilion R, 9 km SW of the pass, where Indians gathered material for war paint and decoration. Sir James HECTOR's party of the PALLISER EXPEDITION were the first whites to cross the pass in Aug 1858. GLEN BOLES

Vermilion River, 70 km (from its headstream to its confluence with the Kootenay R), rises in the Continental Ranges on the BC-Alberta border at the N end of KOOTENAY NATIONAL PARK. Fed by Tokumm Cr, it drains in a southerly direction, eventually emptying into the Kootenay R. It takes its name from mineral springs, located 9 km SW of VERMILION PASS, where Indians obtained iron oxide for decorative purposes and body paint. For most of its length, the river is paralleled by the 105 km Banff-Windermere Hwy. Like many mountain rivers, the Vermilion features instances of potholing and abrasion.   DAVID EVANS

Verner, Frederick Arthur, painter (b at Hammondsville [later Sheridan], UC 26 Feb 1836; d at London, Eng 16 May 1928). After study at Heatherly's Art School, London, in 1856, Verner enlisted in the 3rd West York Regiment. On his return to Canada in 1862, he earned his living as a photographer. In time he became a painter of Indians, seeking accuracy in his subjects. He was present with Manitoba's Lt-Gov Alexander Morris in 1873 at the signing of the North West Angle Treaty, Lk of the Woods (Treaty No 3). The sketches he made there were the basis for many of his later paintings. He also carefully studied the buffalo (one sketch, now at the National Gallery of Canada, was made in Buffalo Bill's show in London 1892) and used these sketches for buffalo canvases such as *The Last of the Herd.* His mellow vision conveyed an image of the Canadian West as a secret garden, an oasis of calm and quiet, rather than the tragic battlefield portrayed by many American painters. He moved to London, Eng, in 1880.   JOAN MURRAY

F.A. Verner, *Hudson's Bay Officials Leaving Brûlé Portage* (1876) *(courtesy Glenbow Museum).*

Vernon, BC, City, pop 19 987 (1981c), inc 1892, is located between the N end of Okanagan Lk and Kalamalka Lk. The area was first visited by David Stuart, a fur trader working for the Pacific Fur Co, in 1811, but missionaries built the first settlement in the 1840s. Several large ranches were established in the vicinity in the 1880s and fruit growing started in the 1890s. The townsite was a camp on the fur-trade trail, and the northern terminus for lake steamers was at nearby Okanagan Landing. The town was not connected to the main rail line until the 1890s, when a branch was built to Sicamous, on the CPR. In 1906 a major irrigation canal was built around the Vernon valley. The population swelled with over 10 000 recruits during WWI, as Vernon was the largest military camp in BC. Today, Vernon is a prosperous marketing and distribution centre for the northern OKANAGAN VALLEY; most of the valley's vegetables are grown in the area. Lumber, canning and tourism are important industries, and the military camp is still in operation. The city centre is built on relatively flat land; much of the residential section is on glacial terraces and valley slopes. There is a branch of Okanagan College at nearby Coldstream (DM, pop 6450), on Kalamalka Lk. The Indian name for Vernon was *hun-cul-deep-moose chin,* meaning "jumping over place"; it was named (1887) for George Forbes Vernon, chief commissioner of lands and works for BC, and one of the city's pioneers.   JAMES MARSH

Verrazzano, Giovanni da, explorer (b at or near Florence *c*1485; d in the W Indies *c*1528). Several years before Jacques CARTIER, he established a French claim in N America. A rarity among early explorers, he was of distinguished lineage and was well educated in Florence, then a centre of geographic and navigational science. He moved to Dieppe, France, to pursue a maritime career, and set sail westward from there in 1523 under the French flag. He made landfall around 1 Mar 1524 at or near Cape Fear (33°50' N lat). He sailed S and then N to avoid the Spaniards, coasted N past New York Bay and the coast of Maine and likely departed from the E coast of Newfoundland (about 50° N lat), arriving back at Dieppe 8 July 1524. Although he mistakenly believed that he saw the Pacific Ocean across a narrow peninsula near Cape Hatteras, he was the first to recognize that the coast from Florida to Newfoundland was contiguous and belonged to a New World. On a 2nd voyage in 1528, he rowed ashore to one of the Caribbean islands, likely Guadeloupe, and was slain and eaten by cannibals.   JAMES MARSH

Verrier, Étienne, military engineer (b at Aix-en-Provence, France 4 Jan 1683; d at La Rochelle, France 10 Sept 1747). After 17 years with the engineer corps, Verrier served at LOUISBOURG as chief engineer 1724-45. During these years he planned and revised the layout of the town, completed the bastioned enceinte, with its ornate town gates, the barracks with clock tower and governor's wing, the hospital, the lighthouse, 2 harbour batteries and harbour installations, and designed an unbuilt parish church. Son of a master sculptor, Verrier had a flair for architecture. Militarily he was somewhat less successful. Although his fortifications facilitated a spirited defence against overwhelming odds during the siege of 1745, his advice to abandon the Royal Battery to the enemy is difficult to understand. Verrier's plans and reports, together with archaeological data, have provided the basis for much of today's reconstruction at the Fortress of Louisbourg National Historic Park.   F.J. THORPE

Reading: J. Fortier and O. Fitzgerald, *Fortress of Louisbourg* (1979).

Verrier, Louis-Guillaume, lawyer, teacher, attorney general of the Conseil Supérieur of NEW FRANCE (b at Paris, France 19 Oct 1690; d at Québec C 13 Sept 1758). He is noteworthy for his service as attorney general, the chief law officer for the colony (1728-58), for his survey of notarial deeds (1730-32) and exhaustive register of landed property in the colony (1732-40), and especially for his establishment, in 1733, of Canada's first structured program of LEGAL EDUCATION. Descended from a family of Parisian jurists and himself a lawyer in the *parlement* of Paris, this impecunious bachelor earned the reputation, following his immigration to Québec in 1728, of being a meticulous scholar and compulsive bibliophile. The quality of his law-school graduates moved Louis XV in 1741 to rescind a 1678 ordinance prohibiting lawyers from practising in New France. As a result a literate and active group of schooled advocates emerged who played an important role in the post-Conquest affirmation of SEIGNEURIAL tenure and the COUTUME DE PARIS, and in a 1785 restructuring of Québec's legal profession.   G. BLAINE BAKER

Vertebrate, member of the subphylum Vertebrata of the phylum Chordata. Vertebrates are bilaterally symmetrical ANIMALS with an internal skeleton of bone or cartilage consisting of, at least, a vertebral column and skull. The eyes (if present) and olfactory and feeding structures are always grouped in a distinct head region at the front of the body. At some stage, or throughout life, there is a series of gill slits behind the head, passing from the digestive tract to the outside. These are supported by skeletal bars in their walls. Usually, there are also appendages assisting in movement and manipulation of the environment, ranging from median fins and tails of fishes to the specialized arms and hands of humans. The body covering may range from smooth, mucus-covered skin to a solid shell of bony armour to insulating fur or feathers.

The earliest evidence of vertebrates consists of fragmentary FOSSILS of the external armour of jawless fishes from the late Cambrian period (just over 500 million years ago). Vertebrates apparently remained rare, scattered, and limited to jawless fishes until the appearance of the first jawed fishes in the late Silurian period (almost 100 million years later). In the next 50 million years, during the Devonian period, all major groups of living fishes and the first AMPHIBIANS appeared. The first REPTILES appeared at the beginning of the Pennsylvanian period (about 300 million years ago). The earliest identifiable reptilian ancestors of MAMMALS constitute one of the oldest distinct groups of reptiles, first appearing in the Pennsylvanian period, although mammals themselves date from the late Triassic period (about 200 million years ago). BIRDS, the youngest vertebrate class, apparently arose from small DINOSAUR ancestors during the Jurassic period (180-130 million years ago).

Aquatic, fishlike vertebrates comprise 5 of the 9 classes and about half of the nearly 40 000 living species. This probably reflects the greater age of fishlike groups and the relative stability of marine habitats over long periods, compared to freshwater or terrestrial habitats. Among terrestrial vertebrates, reptiles have shown the widest variety of body plans and adaptations, but birds have the most living species (9000). Mammals have about 4000 and amphibians about 3000 living species.

Vertebrates attain the largest sizes of all animals. They are more capable of efficient, rapid, sustained movements, and have the most complex body organizations. These characteristics are interrelated and derive from the basic vertebrate body plan. The internal skeleton provides the necessary strength to anchor muscles and support the body, and is proportionally lighter than the external skeletons or shells of INVERTEBRATES. It allows for growth without the periodic moulting of a rigid external skeleton, and it increases the mechanical efficiency of muscles. Vertebrates are able to regulate their physiological processes. All (except hagfish, the most primitive vertebrates) regulate the dissolved salt concentrations and water content of their bodies. They also exert some control over their body temperatures, either by selecting environments in which they can gain or lose heat as required (ectothermy), as in FISH, amphibians and reptiles; or by regulating metabolism to produce heat internally (endothermy), as in birds and mammals.

Large size and increased activity has led to the development of systems which allow vertebrates both to take in food, oxygen, water and salts and to excrete metabolic wastes more rapidly than can invertebrates. The gills of aquatic species, or lungs of terrestrial species, have large surface areas through which oxygen can be absorbed and carbon dioxide lost. The kidneys act as filters for removal of metabolic wastes and regulation of water and salt in the body. The digestive system includes mechanisms to increase efficiency of feeding and of breaking up food so that digestion will proceed more rapidly. The intestinal walls have large surface areas through which nutrients can be absorbed. Finally, the closed, high-pressure circulatory system carries substances throughout the body.

All of these must function together to produce the co-ordinated activity required for survival. Co-ordination is supplied by the central nervous system, using information from the surroundings collected by the sensory system. Throughout vertebrate evolutionary history, changes in habitat or activity have been accompanied by changes in the structure and function of body

Classification of the Superclass Gnathostomata
(Numbers refer to living species worldwide and in Canada)

Class	Subclass	Examples	Habitat
Placodermi*		placoderms	mostly marine, open water to bottom feeders (late Silurian to late Devonian)
Chondrichthyes	Elasmobranchii c740; 51	sharks, skates, rays	mostly marine, open water to bottom feeders, coastal to deep sea
	Holocephali c30; 4	chimaeras	marine, bottom feeders, coastal to deep sea
Osteichthyes	Acanthodii*	acanthodians	mostly marine, probably open water (middle Silurian to early Permian)
	Sarcopterygii 7; 0	lobe-finned fishes	mostly freshwater, in shallow, standing water, frequently stagnant and subject to drying
	Actinopterygii c20 800; c880	ray-finned fishes	freshwater and marine, all aquatic habitats
Amphibia	Labyrinthodontia*	labyrinthodonts	freshwater marshes, semiaquatic (late Devonian to late Triassic)
	Lepospondyli*	lepospondyls	freshwater, aquatic to semiaquatic; some were eellike or snakelike (early Mississippian to early Permian)
	Lissamphibia c3 260; 40	living amphibians	freshwater, aquatic to terrestrial, burrowing to tree climbing
Reptilia	Anapsida c220; 12	stem reptiles,* turtles	aquatic, freshwater or marine to terrestrial, some desert dwellers
	Synapsida*	mammallike reptiles	semiaquatic to terrestrial (late Pennsylvanian to early Jurassic)
	Euryapsida*	plesiosaurs and relatives	marine, probably surface dwelling, coastal (Permian to late Cretaceous)
	Ichthyopterygia*	ichthyosaurs	marine, probably open water; some fed on squid
	Archosauria c25; 0	dinosaurs*, flying reptiles*, crocodilians	semiaquatic to terrestrial; crocodilians are semiaquatic, freshwater and marine.
	Lepidosauria c5 575; 30	tuatara, lizards, snakes	mostly terrestrial, burrowing to climbing; few marine forms
Aves	Archaeornithes*	toothed birds	terrestrial (late Jurassic)
	Neornithes c9 000; c420	modern birds	terrestrial to semiaquatic, flying to flightless
Mammalia	Prototheria 3; 0	Mesozoic mammals, monotremes	terrestrial to semiaquatic
	Metatheria c250; 1	marsupials	terrestrial
	Eutheria c3 800; c200	placental mammals	terrestrial in virtually all habitats; some also aquatic, from freshwater to open sea; some fly

* Extinct

systems. An increase in swimming speed in a fish, for example, will cause increased size of muscles and the bones to which they are anchored. However, higher muscle activity also requires a greater flow of nutrients and oxygen, which affects the digestive, respiratory and circulatory systems. The increased production of wastes requires adaptation of the excretory system, and the changing needs of all of these together will affect the sensory and nervous systems, which supply information and coordination for the body as a whole.

The subphylum Vertebrata is divided into 2 superclasses. The first, Agnatha or jawless fishes, includes the lampreys, hagfish and extinct ostracoderms. About 40 species of lampreys occur worldwide (11 in Canada), while there are about 30 species of hagfish (3 in Canada). The second subclass, Gnathostomata, includes all jawed vertebrates. The table summarizes the major classes of jawed vertebrates. The outlines of classification are generally accepted; however, changes may occur as a result of continuing taxonomic studies. K.W. STEWART

Vertical Mosaic, a term used by sociologist John PORTER to convey the concept that Canada is a mosaic of different ethnic, language, regional and religious groupings unequal in status and power. Porter published his book, *Vertical Mosaic: An Analysis of Social Class and Power in Canada,* in 1965. "Mosaic" is often contrasted with the American concept of "melting pot." The Canadian John Murray Gibbon, in his book *The Canadian Mosaic* (1938), disapproved of the American melting-pot policy according to which immigrants and their descendants were discouraged from maintaining close ties with their countries and cultures of origin and instead were encouraged to assimilate into the American way of life. Many Canadians pointed with pride to the alternative Canadian policy of encouraging immigrants and their descendants to maintain important aspects of their ancestral cultures. Porter's view was that in income, occupation and education, this supposedly beneficial policy worked to the advantage of some ethnic groups and to the disadvantage of others.

Porter's book revealed that some groups (eg, those of British origin) have better incomes, educations and health than others (eg, those of eastern and southern European origin). Native Indian and Inuit people were the most disadvantaged. According to Porter, this vertical arrangement also applied to power and to influence in decision making. In the bureaucratic, economic and political spheres, those of British origin are overrepresented among the ELITES.

Since 1965 several studies have shown that the picture sketched by Porter has been modified only slightly, ie, there has been some lessening of the economic gap between ethnic groups and people of French origin are better represented in the political and bureaucratic spheres. The economic elite, still dominated by those of British origin, has changed very little. The book earned Porter the prestigious American Sociological Assn's McIver Award. FRANK G. VALLEE
Reading: W. Clement, *The Canadian Corporate Elite* (1975); J. Heap, *Everybody's Canada* (1974); J. Porter, *The Vertical Mosaic* (1965).

Verville, Alphonse, plumber, socialist, MP, president of the Trades and Labor Congress of Canada (b at Côte-St-Paul [Montréal], Canada E 28 Oct 1864; d 20 June 1930). Verville left Montréal at age 18 to work in Chicago, where he became a member of the International Plumbers' Union. Returning to Montréal in 1893, he actively promoted international unionism there. He then became president of the Plumbers' Union and of the Conseil des métiers et du travail de Montréal, and was president of the TLC (1904-10). A supporter of the political labour movement, Verville was elected federal MP for Maisonneuve under the Parti ouvrier banner in 1906. JACQUES ROUILLARD

Verville, Jean-François Du Verger de, military engineer (b at Paris, France c1670-75; d at Valenciennes or Paris, France 1729). Verville designed the landward front of fortification of the fortress of LOUISBOURG, including the citadel barracks, as well as the Royal and Island batteries; he drew the first plan of the town. Born into a family of architects, Verville served 12 years as a military engineer in Europe prior to his secondment in 1716 to Île Royale [Cape Breton I]. His plan for Louisbourg provided for 3 interdependent batteries and a bastioned front to defend the town against attack, respectively from the harbour and the swampy land to the W. After Verville's recall in 1725 his design, despite evident structural flaws, served as the basis for Etienne VERRIER's Louisbourg. F.J. THORPE

Vesak, Norbert, choreographer (b at Port Moody, BC 22 Oct 1936). Controversial because of his penchant for flashy choreography, trendy subjects and lavish visual effects, Vesak was resident choreographer at Vancouver Playhouse Theatre 1964 before founding Western Dance Theatre (1969-71). He created 2 popular works for the ROYAL WINNIPEG BALLET — *The Ecstasy of Rita Joe* (1971), a multimedia work featuring Dan GEORGE which was commissioned by the Manitoba Indian Brotherhood and based on George RYGA's play, and *What To Do Till the Messiah Comes* (1973), whose "Belong" pas de deux became ballerina Evelyn HART's signature piece and won a gold medal for choreography at the Varna International Ballet Competition 1980. An official choreographer with the Royal Winnipeg for a short time in the 1970s, Vesak later directed the Metropolitan and San Francisco Opera ballets while creating dances for many companies. PENELOPE DOOB

Vetch (genus *Vicia*), semivining, herbaceous PLANT of the legume family, which produces good-quality hay. The 150 species are widely distributed worldwide. Most vetches originated in the Mediterranean region and some species were introduced into Canada by the earliest immigrants. Three species are now grown in Canada: *V. villosa,* hairy vetch; *V. pannonica,* Hungarian vetch; *V. sativa,* common vetch. Vetches have compound leaves, purple, pink or, rarely, white flowers. They form seed pods which explode on ripening. Vetches have tendrils and climb up tall, growing plants or fences. They occur commonly in pasture and in uncultivated fields in moist temperate areas of Canada. When planted early in June, vetches produce a hay crop in the year of seeding. If planted in Sept, they overwinter, producing a crop the following year. Vetch is now of little economic importance and commercial seed is scarce; however, historically, vetches have been used as an emergency FORAGE CROP, alone or with OATS or PEAS. Vetches produce hard seeds and may form dark green patches in uncultivated fields. As legumes, vetches have the ability to fix atmospheric nitrogen in their root nodules and may be used as a green manure crop.   WALTER R. CHILDERS

Veterans Affairs, Department of, est 1944, along with National Health and Welfare, upon division of the Department of Pensions and National Health. Made solely responsible for administering pensions and benefits for Canada's ex-servicemen, it first had to develop a rehabilitation and re-establishment program for those serving in WWII. The Veterans Charter was enacted during the war to deal with hospital treatment, education, insurance, civil-service preference, welfare, allowances and loans, pensions and land settlement. Although some programs have lapsed and the department's general activities have declined, DVA continues to manage special programs providing aging veterans and their dependants with medical care and financial assistance. Pensions and allowances are administered by 4 associated agencies: Canadian Pension Commission, Pension Review Board, War Veterans Allowance Board, and Board of Pension Advocates.   GLENN T. WRIGHT

Veterans' Land Act, passed 20 July 1942, following a Canadian tradition dating from the 17th century of settling ex-soldiers on the land. In 1919 a Soldier Settlement Act had provided returned WWI veterans who wished to farm with loans to purchase land, stock and equipment. Over 25 000 vets took advantage of the scheme, although many had to abandon their farms between the wars because of heavy debts and adverse farming conditions. The VLA, designed to overcome some of the problems inherent in the 1919 plan, gave WWII veterans choices. With only a small down payment, ex-servicemen could purchase land with the help of a government loan; additional funds were available for livestock and equipment. Repayment terms allowed settlers time to re-establish themselves without incurring heavy financial obligations. Veterans were also encouraged to settle small rural or suburban holdings as part-time farmers or to substitute commercial fishing for full-time farming. In 1950 the VLA began to provide loans to veterans who wished to construct their own homes. Under the Veterans' Land Administration, a branch of the Department of VETERANS AFFAIRS, over 140 000 ex-servicemen had sought assistance when new loans were terminated in 1977. GLENN T. WRIGHT

Veterinary Medicine, the SCIENCE dealing with health and disease in VERTEBRATES, has application to 4 broad domains: domestic animals, wildlife, comparative medicine and PUBLIC HEALTH. In Canada in 1982, there were approximately 4000 professionally active veterinarians; this number will rise by 250-300 annually. Veterinarians are distributed in roughly equal numbers in private rural practice, private urban practice and institutional employment. Veterinary education requires at least 2 years of university preveterinary training, followed by 4 years of professional instruction. Postgraduate training in clinical or research programs is undertaken by 10-20% of veterinary graduates. The veterinary curriculum is similar to that of human MEDICINE. The veterinary profession is organized nationally in the Canadian Veterinary Medical Association and in each province as a provincial association.

Clinical veterinary medicine, including food-animal, small-animal and equine practices, or some mixture of these specializations, provides primary health care to an owner's animals. In rural settings, veterinarians deal with all types of animals, most being food animals. In urban centres, many veterinarians practise exclusively on pets or HORSES. Veterinarians practise singly, in partnerships or in corporations, depending on personal preferences. Income derives from fees charged to clients.

Food-Animal Practice involves dairy and beef cattle, pigs, sheep, goats and poultry (*see* ANIMAL AGRICULTURE). Animals are treated on the farm or in a large animal hospital. Food-animal practice may be subsidized by provincial or municipal governments. Subsidies vary from hospital grants, as in Manitoba, to direct assistance in paying professional fees, as in Québec, which has the only "veticare" scheme in N America. In NB all food-animal veterinarians are employed by the province. Veterinarians dealing with poultry disease tend to specialize and are usually employed by government or private industry.

Small-Animal Practice deals most commonly with DOGS and CATS, but can also include rodents (eg, rabbits, mice, gerbils), birds (eg, budgerigars, parrots, finches), fish and more unusual forms (eg, primates, reptiles).

Federal, provincial and municipal governments employ veterinarians to provide services that protect animal and human health. Under the departments of agriculture, health, environment and wildlife, veterinarians conduct laboratory diagnosis, field investigation, food and animal inspection, administration, research and extension education.

University veterinarians teach and do research in veterinary medical science. Most are employed in Canada's colleges of veterinary medicine. A few are also located in faculties of agriculture or medicine or departments of biology and in specialized research institutions such as the Veterinary Infectious Disease Organization (VIDO), U Sask. A few veterinarians find employment in industry, particularly in companies producing or selling PHARMACEUTICAL and BIOLOGICAL PRODUCTS. Their work includes research, sales, administration and extension of advice and information to veterinarians or others in animal-related industries.

The growth of knowledge and technology in veterinary science is motivating some veterinarians to specialize in a branch of veterinary science (eg, internal medicine, pathology, dermatology, microbiology, radiology) or in a class of animal (eg, laboratory animals, food animals, horses, small pets). To specialize, a veterinarian must have appropriate practical experience, undertake formal postgraduate training and pass rigorous examinations. Most specialists are employed by institutions. Many practising veterinarians confine their work to one or a few species, but this limitation is not considered specialization, in the formal sense, by the profession.

Domestic Animals

Food Animals In Canada about one-half of the cash income from farms comes from animals or animal products. The protection of the health of this resource is the responsibility of practising veterinarians and appropriate government agencies. Food-animal practitioners are concerned with the treatment and prevention of indigenous diseases in animals on individual farms. Their primary objective is the economic benefit of the owner; thus, treatment must be economically sensible or imperative because of humane considerations. In food-animal practice, the major emphases are on prevention of disease and reproductive management for optimal productivity (*see* ANIMAL BREEDING). Practitioners must be skilled in diagnosis, surgery, livestock reproduction practices, use of drugs and analysis of production data. Preventive medicine involves monitoring the health of individual animals and of the herd by measuring, recording and analysing production performance.

Agriculture Canada is responsible for major legislation protecting Canada's livestock from diseases identified by law as reportable, and for excluding from Canada exotic diseases such as foot-and-mouth and African swine fever. International travel and transportation of animals is a constant threat because of the risk of introducing exotic, contagious animal diseases. The department's enviable record in controlling such diseases gives Canada's livestock access to world markets. Federal programs also seek to control or eradicate important indigenous diseases, eg, rabies, tuberculosis, brucellosis (contagious abortion). Furthermore, federal veterinarians ensure the quality of food-animal producers, eg, through meat inspection (*see* FOOD LEGISLATION).

Major health problems in livestock include high neonatal mortality from intestinal and respiratory diseases, poor reproductive efficiency and suboptimal production associated with subclinical disease and mismanagement. Veterinary research in food-animal disease and health maintenance is conducted principally by the federal government and the universities. Government research gives priority to detection and control of contagious diseases, especially those reportable by law. An example of an important Canadian contribution to the control of animal disease worldwide is a vaccine against neonatal diarrhea in calves, caused by certain strains of the bacterium *Escherichia coli*. Developed by VIDO, the vaccine was marketed by a Canadian firm (*see* VETERINARY MEDICINES INDUSTRY). New technology in reproduction (eg, embryo transfer, freezing embryos) promises to make livestock production more efficient and to promote more rapid genetic improvement.

Companion Animals or Pets There are several million pets in Canada. Health services are provided almost entirely by private practitioners who must build up their own hospitals or clinics and employ animal-health technicians and other support staff. Facilities accommodating 50-100 animals and providing equipment for surgery, radiology, laboratory diagnosis and various other specialties are common. The capital investment required to establish a hospital is substantial. Small-animal medicine is quite similar to human medicine since pet animals are normally kept for a natural life span and succumb to the infirmities of old age as well as to disease. There are fewer economic constraints on medical treatment of pets in comparison to food animals.

Work and Recreation Animals The health care of domestic animals used in recreation or work is a major field of veterinary medicine. Canadian society is highly mechanized; consequently, animals have a limited role in performing work. In recent years, horses have increased in number: a few are still used as draft animals and for herding cattle, but most are used for recreation and sports (*see* HARNESS RACING; THOROUGHBRED RACING). These athletes of the animal world are prone to injuries and to problems associated with racing or other sports activities. Many veterinarians confine their practice to horses and become skilled at dealing with their special problems, eg, lameness. Dogs are used for various chores: herding sheep, pulling sleds and providing surrogate eyes or ears for handicapped individuals. Their occupational health needs are met by small-animal practitioners.

Fibre and Furs Sheep, the only significant animal fibre producers in Canada, are attended by veterinarians, usually in preventive medical programs. Several other animal species provide woollike fibres that can be used to make clothing. In Canada the native MUSKOXEN produce a high-quality fibre called *qiviut*. In the future, northerners may manage muskoxen in some form of semidomestication to allow the harvesting of *qiviut*. Veterinary researchers are studying the muskox with a view to its more intensive management.

Fur-bearing animals are raised across Canada. Economically important species are MINK and FOX. Disease control is crucial to the success of FUR FARMING, since the relatively close confinement of a large number of animals makes them vulnerable to various highly contagious diseases, eg, distemper, parvovirus intestinal infection. The latter was first described at Fort William and bears this name. Mink have provided an important example of how animals serve as monitors of chemical POLLUTION. The poor reproductive performance developed by ranch mink fed a diet of fish from Lk Michigan was shown to be caused by PCBs (polychlorinated biphenyls) in the fish. This incident was the first indication that PCBs and related compounds were a biological hazard.

Wildlife

In Nature Wildlife, including animals, fish and birds, is an especially rich component of Canada's natural environment. In addition to its intrinsic value, wildlife provides food, clothing and economic benefits, particularly to native people, and is a major source of recreation for naturalists and hunters. Wild animals also act as monitors of environmental problems. Veterinary medicine is among the professions taking an active interest in health and disease in these populations. Wild animals are important in the epidemiology of certain animal and human diseases (eg, rabies, tularemia) because they act as disease reservoirs. For example, tuberculosis and brucellosis are present in BISON in WOOD BUFFALO NATIONAL PARK.

In Captivity The health and reproductive performance of ZOO animals are the principal concerns of zoo veterinary medicine, an emerging practice specialty. High population density and unnatural feeding conditions make zoo animals particularly vulnerable to disease and poor reproductive performance. Canada's many fine zoos and aquariums employ veterinarians full time or part time.

Fish and Aquatic Species Health management of FISH or other marine food sources in nature and in captivity is an emerging concern. Confinement of fish in ponds or by mechanical devices to give high population densities puts them at increased risk from infectious disease. The emergence of fish farming (AQUACULTURE) as an economically viable industry depends on an assured supply of disease-free stock. In Canada various aquatic habitats are adaptable to fish farming, including ocean waters, streams, lakes and prairie sloughs.

Public Health, Laboratory Animals and Comparative Medicine

Public-health veterinarians help ensure a wholesome supply of food of animal origin. This complex government responsibility involves the detection of infectious agents and undesirable chemicals (eg, feed additives, drugs, environmental pollutants) in meat, milk and eggs. Zoonoses are diseases transmissible from animals to humans. Over 200 such diseases may exist in wildlife (eg, rabies, western encephalitis, tularemia, plague) or in domestic animals (eg, tuberculosis, brucellosis). Veterinarians help protect humans from zoonoses, eg, through the immunization of dogs against rabies. The veterinary profession informs the public about other potentially dangerous factors in the relationship between animals and man, eg, the connection between rabies and stray dogs.

Laboratory animals are widely used in medical research and in identification and investigation of hazards to human health. The care

and use of such animals has become an area of specialization. Laboratory animals provide natural and experimental models of human or animal diseases and their study is essential to a better understanding of disease. A primary concern of those working with laboratory animals has been the assurance of high standards of humane care. The Canadian Council on Animal Care has been very successful in working toward this end (*see* ANIMAL ISSUES; HUMANE SOCIETIES).

Comparative medicine studies phenomena that are basic to diseases of all species, through research into natural and experimental disease. Insights gained can be extrapolated to diseases of individual species, including man. Veterinarians and others in the field have recognized many naturally occurring animal diseases that may be used as models for similar or identical conditions in human or other animals. Such model diseases may be numerous because the phenomena of disease causation are similar throughout the animal kingdom. The study of experimental disease in animals has facilitated major advances in medicine, eg, the elucidation of germ theory and the discovery of INSULIN. Comparative medicine is also responsible for the discoveries that arthropods act as vectors of infectious disease and that VIRUSES cause cancer. The transmission by TICKS of a protozoan disease of cattle (Texas fever) was the first demonstration that such a phenomenon was possible, and it led to an understanding of the transmission of malaria and other diseases by MOSQUITOES and other arthropods. That viruses can cause cancer was first demonstrated in chickens and subsequently recognized in many animals. A Canadian contribution to comparative medicine was the discovery of a mycotoxin in 1922 by Francis SCHOFIELD of the Ontario Veterinary College. He found that MOLD growing on damp sweet clover produced a toxin which caused a fatal bleeding disorder in cattle. This toxic material, dicoumarol, a powerful blood anticoagulant, is now used medicinally in humans. Many other mycotoxins have since been described. The discovery of dicoumarol also portended the discovery of other biologically active materials produced by molds, eg, antibiotics.

N.O. NIELSEN

Reading: K. Aspinwall, First Steps in Veterinary Science (1976).

Veterinary Medicine, Education In 1983 there were 3 veterinary colleges in Canada; a fourth will be established at UPEI to serve the Atlantic provinces in 1986. In general, 6 years of training are required to earn a veterinary degree: 2 years of preveterinary courses, which may be taken at a number of institutions of higher learning; and 4 years of specialized professional education at one of the veterinary colleges. Veterinary courses include anatomy, BIOCHEMISTRY, embryology, epidemiology, physiology, microbiology, IMMUNOLOGY, pathology, clinical medicine and surgery. There have been major construction and expansion programs at all 3 colleges in recent years and approximately 260 veterinarians graduate yearly. In 1928 the first woman graduated from a Canadian veterinary college. In 1982 about 50% of graduates were women. Veterinary colleges carry on research on diseases of food-producing and companion animals, and of fish, birds and wildlife.

Ontario Veterinary College (OVC), Guelph, is the oldest in Canada. Until 1965 it was affiliated with the U of T and graduates received their degrees from that university. In 1965 OVC became one of the colleges forming UNIVERSITY OF GUELPH. Until 1963, when the Western College of Veterinary Medicine was founded, OVC was the only veterinary college for English Canada serving students from all provinces. Most students now come from Ontario, although there are generally

a number from Québec and the Atlantic provinces as well. OVC grants Doctor of Veterinary Medicine (DVM), MSc and DVSc degrees. Postgraduate diploma courses are also given. Enrolment in the DVM course is approximately 120 annually.

Faculty of Veterinary Medicine, UNIVERSITÉ DE MONTRÉAL is located in St-Hyacinthe, Qué. Before moving there in 1947, the school was for many years located in OKA, Qué, where it formed part of an agricultural-veterinary educational centre financed by the Québec Dept of Agriculture and operated by the Trappists. With the move to St-Hyacinthe, it became the direct responsibility of the Québec Dept of Agriculture until 1969 when it became a U de M faculty. Considerable development in staff and facilities has taken place. The only French-language veterinary college in N America, it offers the DMV and MSc degrees. Postgraduate diploma courses are also given. About 70 undergraduates register yearly.

Western College of Veterinary Medicine (WCVM) was established at Saskatoon in 1963 as part of U Sask. The first veterinarians graduated in 1969. The second of the English-speaking veterinary colleges in Canada, it serves the 4 western provinces, from which it draws most of its students. Degrees obtainable are the DVM, MSc and PhD. Diploma courses are offered at the postgraduate level. About 70 undergraduates enter annually.

J. FRANK

Veterinary Medicine, History The healing of ANIMAL and human ailments has been a preoccupation of man for centuries. Human MEDICINE became professionalized much before veterinary medicine, which did not become institutionalized until the opening of veterinary schools in France at Lyons (1761) and Alfort (1766). Graduates probably did not come to Canada, immigration from France having been halted by the British CONQUEST in 1760. In England the veterinary art was formally established in 1791, the year in which provision was made to create the colony of UPPER CANADA. Graduates of the Edinburgh Veterinary College, founded in 1823 in Scotland, are the first known veterinary practitioners in Canada with a diploma from a chartered school. Probably the only veterinary surgeon in the colony of NB in 1851 was M.A. Cuming of Saint John, an 1846 graduate of Edinburgh.

Veterinary Education Farriers, without specialized veterinary training, outnumbered trained persons before and long after 1866 — the year in which the graduation of persons in Canada who had received formal training in a diploma course began (*see* BLACKSMITHING). Andrew SMITH, an 1861 graduate of the Edinburgh College, established the first formal course in Toronto (1862). From 1866 to 1908 (when the Ontario Veterinary College was acquired by the provincial government), over 3000 graduates completed the 2-year diploma course. Many of the graduates were from the US and did not remain in Canada; consequently, Canada continued to suffer from a lack of veterinary surgeons. Andrew Smith's college, moved from Toronto in 1921, continues today as the Ontario Veterinary College, UNIVERSITY OF GUELPH.

In 1866, a second private college with high admission standards was established in Montréal by Duncan MCEACHRAN. It eventually became a faculty of McGill University, closing in 1903 from lack of funds. The French-speaking college which arose from this English-speaking one has been in continuous operation since 1886. Founded by V.T. Daubigny it united in 1894 with 2 other Québec schools to form the School of Comparative Medicine and Veterinary Science of Montréal. The school was moved to the Trappist Agricultural Institute of OKA, Qué, in 1928 and taken over by the Québec government and moved to St-Hyacinthe in 1947. It is affiliated with U de Montréal. A college founded in 1895 in association with Queens U, Kingston, Ont, was short-lived, closing in 1899. A fourth college, the Western College of Veterinary Medicine, established at U of Saskatchewan in 1963, admitted its first class in 1965.

Veterinary Associations The advent of the Ontario Veterinary College and its "educated" professionals was followed by a demand that society recognize these qualifications and services in preference to those of the empiric farrier. In 1874 through the aegis of Professor Smith, the Ontario Veterinary Medical Association was founded. It was incorporated as the Ontario Veterinary Association (OVA) in 1879. Veterinary associations were formed in Man (1881), Qué (1902), Alta (1906), BC (1907), Sask (1908-09), NS (1913), NB (1919) and PEI (1920). Each body was autonomous, recognized by provincial legislation established under Section 92, BRITISH NORTH AMERICA ACT, 1867. Each formulated bylaws to govern its membership and especially to decide who should be admitted to practice by virtue of holding a recognized diploma. The 1871 census showed 247 "Farriers and Veterinary Surgeons," most residing in Ontario, the remainder in NS and NB. The Northwest Territories had virtually no veterinary surgeons.

Veterinary medicine thus developed along provincial lines, characterized for many years, and in some instances to the present day, by narrow provincialism. This attitude was probably related to low fees, fear of professional opposition from recent graduates and inability to take a broad view of the profession. It meant that little or no interest developed in a national association. Furthermore the American Veterinary Medical Association, founded in 1863, filled the needs of the affluent who could afford to travel to its annual meetings.

Between 1871 and 1911 the number of veterinary surgeons increased to 1150: Ontario, 50%; western Canada, 30%; the eastern provinces, 20%. Empiricism continued to flourish despite vigorous efforts by provincial associations to confine the treatment of farm animals to their membership. In the early 1890s, veterinary dental schools in Toronto gave instruction to anyone who could attend and pay for the brief instruction and diploma. Instructors were not necessarily veterinary surgeons. In 1896 the Veterinary Science Company of London, Ont, was established and through the London Veterinary Correspondence School ran a course in veterinary medicine and surgery. Besides a home-study course, the school provided a textbook and diploma which it led recipients to believe was sufficient qualification to practise anywhere in Canada. Provincial legislation closed the school in 1921, but before then 77 editions of the text were published and diplomas were issued worldwide. For many years the provincial associations had to cope with the demands of London school "graduates" who unsuccessfully sought membership and practice privileges.

After WWII, the subject of formation of a national veterinary association surfaced in western Canada. The need became evident when the federal government disbanded the Royal Canadian Army Veterinary Corps (RCAVC) without consulting the profession. There was no national group to lobby against disbanding. In addition, displaced veterinarians from Europe were immigrating to Canada and provincial associations were uncertain about their standards. A national association was needed to speak for the profession and to act as an examining body to screen immigrant veterinarians. It was hoped that reciprocity among provincial examining boards could be established through a national association.

In 1912 the British Columbia Veterinary Medical Association (BCVMA) had proposed a national body and by about 1920 most of the provinces were sympathetic. In 1921 a Canadian Veterinary Council was formed with representatives from each provincial association; however, at a conference in Ottawa that year, a draft bill to enact a dominion association faltered on provincial misunderstanding. In 1923 a Canadian National Veterinary Association was founded by individuals attending a national meeting in Montréal but this association died quietly for lack of funds and provincial support. The Western Canadian Veterinary Association (WCVA), formed in the 1930s, became dormant until 1945, mainly because of problems related to reconciling provincial autonomy with national registration. The problem was a draft clause which would give a national association the right to permit recognized graduates to practise anywhere in Canada. A Dominion Veterinary Council formed (1943-44) to try again to organize a viable national association, promoted a dominion body within which provinces would retain the right to set examinations. This council succeeded in starting provincial discussions, but held only one meeting. In 1945 a revived western Canada association proposed a national association and skirted the sensitive areas of national registration and a national examining board. Largely through the efforts of Albertan B.I. Love, as representative of the WCV, the thoughts of presidents of the Eastern Canadian associations began to crystalize and by Apr 1946 plans had been developed for a national body. On 30 June 1948 the Act to incorporate the Canadian Veterinary Medical Association received royal assent.

Mounted Police Veterinarians The mounted police force, enacted by legislation in 1873 to police the North-West Territories, "marched" west from Toronto in June 1874, by train, accompanied by 244 HORSES under the care of John Luke Poett, veterinary surgeon from Stratford, Ont. Poett, an 1860 Edinburgh graduate, had practised in Ontario since 1869, first in London, then in Stratford. One of the first veterinary surgeons in the territories and the first graduate veterinary surgeon of the force, Poett served under a commission 1874-77 and 1884-95, latterly as a staff sergeant.

The NORTH-WEST MOUNTED POLICE (NWMP) became the arm of the federal government responsible for the enforcement of disease control in domestic animals arriving in the Territories with settlers from the US. Initially, control of contagious diseases was mainly related to horses but it soon extended to cattle. In 1884, Poett inspected nearly 2800 imported cattle for evidence of skin diseases and contagious pleuropneumonia. In 1895, 9 other qualified veterinary surgeons belonged to the force. These men were responsible for the health of the horses (782 in 1895) and acted as inspectors of imported animals until the number of veterinarians in the Territories reached a level which permitted their employment in lieu of NWMP veterinarians (about 1896).

Two veterinary surgeons took care of the horses of the government forces suppressing the NORTH-WEST REBELLION. One of these, J. G. RUTHERFORD, an 1879 graduate of OVC, left his newly opened practice in Portage la Prairie to become a commissioned officer in the Winnipeg Field Battery and veterinary surgeon for General Middleton's forces. Subsequently, he practised in Portage, became a politician (provincial and federal government) and then founder of the Health of Animals Branch, Canada Department of Agriculture, with the title Veterinary Director General (1902).

Army Veterinarians Before 1910 no veterinary corps existed in the Canadian Army; veterinary surgeons were noncommissioned officers or regimental officers with mounted and artillery units. In 1910 the Army Veterinary Service (AVS) was established, consisting of qualified veterinary surgeons with commissioned rank, supported by personnel of other ranks. This service, part of the Canadian Militia, consisted of the Canadian Permanent Army Veterinary Corps (CPAVC), veterinary officers gazetted to the corps and NCOs and privates enlisted therein; the Canadian Army Veterinary Corps (CAVC), veterinary officers gazetted to the corps and detailed for duty with mounted corps of the Active Militia; and the short-lived Regimental Veterinary Service (RVS), consisting of officers then on the regimental staff of mounted corps.

The Army Veterinary Service thus had a permanent force and a militia group of officers, each responsible to the quartermaster general of the Canadian Militia. The senior officer of the CPAVC administered the service. Beneath him were the principal veterinary officers of military districts or divisions. There was a Veterinary Remount Establishment and schools for training enlisted men. In 1912 the Militia Council published regulations specifying the duties and functions of all officers, veterinary schools and hospitals, and other facets of the Canadian Army Veterinary Service. When WWI began, the groundwork had been established for the employment of veterinary surgeons, and within 3 months of the outbreak Canadian veterinarians were en route to England with troops and horses. In addition, a Remount Service had begun to purchase horses to supply currently formed units and to replace losses overseas.

Canadian veterinarians enlisted in both Canadian and British Army Veterinary Corps, each corps eventually being awarded the title Royal in recognition of war service. About 300 Canadian veterinarians served varying periods during 1914-18, mainly in Europe but also in India, Egypt, Mesopotamia and Russia. Several received decorations for preserving the lives of horses while under severe enemy attack. Mobile sections removed horse casualties to evacuation stations, which sent severely injured animals to base hospitals for surgical and other treatments. Mange hospitals were essential to control and suppress outbreaks of that debilitating parasite. On the conclusion of hostilities, a few veterinary officers remained in Europe until 1920 in order to aid in the disposal of horses, either as human food or as work animals in Belgium and Italy. In 1915, because of a severe shortage of veterinary officers for the British army, some Canadian veterinary students (final year) had been permitted to forgo final examinations if they enlisted in the British corps as second lieutenants. A few took advantage of this, were graduated in absentia and were in England as fully fledged veterinary officers about 3 weeks after enlisting. The veterinary personnel of the Canadian Expeditionary Force (1914-18), 72 officers and 756 other ranks had cared for 24 000 horses by the time the war ended.

In 1929 the RCAVC establishment was 12 officers and 38 other ranks, in 6 detachments. The CAVC consisted of 100 officers and 55 other ranks, in 11 sections. With replacement of horses by motorized vehicles, a veterinary establishment was no longer needed. In 1940 both corps were disbanded, and during WWII very few veterinarians served in a capacity related to their veterinary qualifications. The majority of those serving belonged to a group concerned with biological warfare; their work remains classified. Technological warfare caused the demise of the army veterinary surgeon in Canada, but not in Britain or the US.   C.A.V. BARKER

Veterinary Medicines Industry Industrial VETERINARY MEDICINE is that sector of the veterinary profession concerned with the research, development, manufacture and marketing of veterinary drugs. The industry is composed of 2

segments: biologicals, ie, drugs derived from living organisms, including vaccines and serums; and PHARMACEUTICALS, ie, other drugs, including antibiotics, steroids, anthelmintics (deworming compounds) and anesthetics. The research, development and application of pharmaceuticals has differed from that of biologicals. With few exceptions, pharmaceuticals have been developed primarily to treat human diseases and their application in veterinary medicine has been a sequel to their use as human drugs. Biologicals are disease specific and species specific drugs, and this exclusivity has resulted in the development of a veterinary biologicals industry discrete from its human counterpart.

Canada has made a number of significant contributions to the veterinary biologicals industry; for example, ERA rabies vaccine, used throughout the world, was developed by CONNAUGHT LABORATORIES Ltd, Toronto. ERA vaccine is a live, attenuated (ie, weakened) vaccine that contains a strain of rabies VIRUS modified so that it will induce immunity in animals for up to 5 years, after a single injection. The vaccine has been conclusively demonstrated to be safe in a wide variety of animal species. In 1979 the Veterinary Infectious Disease Organization (VIDO) in Saskatoon developed a vaccine to protect calves against calfhood diarrhea caused by the bacterium *Escherichia coli*. This vaccine is unique in that it confers protection against all known disease-producing strains of *E. coli* by employing hairlike projections (pilli) on the surface of the cell as the immunizing agent. The antibodies produced by the mother in response to these pilli, which are passed to the calf in the colostrum (precursor of milk) during the first 5 days of life, prevent *E. coli* bacteria from attaching to the inner surface of the intestinal wall, a process which is necessary for the organism to produce disease. The first federally licensed vaccine in N America against Marek's disease, a cancerous complex affecting young chickens, was another Canadian contribution. Other Canadian innovations include an orally administered vaccine to protect swine against erysipelas (St Anthony's Fire), and commercial technique for immunizing young chickens.

The world veterinary drug market is a $5.6 billion industry, of which Canada has a 1.8% share. Drugs used as feed additives constitute 50% of the Canadian market, pharmaceuticals 42%; and biologicals 8%. The $8.0 million biologicals industry is served primarily by 3 Canadian manufacturers (Connaught; Langford Laboratories Ltd, Guelph; Vetrapharm, Woodstock), as well as others based in the US (35), UK (2) and New Zealand (one).   M.J. WALCROFT

Vézina, Georges, hockey player (b at Chicoutimi, Qué Jan 1887; d there 26 Mar 1926). He tended goal for MONTREAL CANADIENS 1910-25 without missing a game. He was noted for his composure under fire, once stopping 78 of 79 shots in a game. He collapsed during a game on 28 Nov 1925 and died 4 months later of tuberculosis. The Canadiens donated the VEZINA TROPHY to the NHL in his honour.   JAMES MARSH

Vezina Trophy is awarded to the goalkeeper voted most valuable to his team. Up until the 1981-82 season, it was awarded annually to the goalkeeper(s) who had played a minimum 25 games for the team that had allowed the fewest goals during the regular NATIONAL HOCKEY LEAGUE season. It was first presented in 1926-27 in memory of Georges VÉZINA. Jacques PLANTE won, or shared, the trophy 7 times, Bill DURNAN 6, Ken Dryden 5 and Terry SAWCHUK 4. The goalie(s) on the team giving up the fewest goals are now awarded the William M. Jennings Award. The Vézina is now awarded to the "most valuable" goalkeeper, who is not necessarily the one who allows the fewest goals.   JAMES MARSH

Via Rail Canada Ltd was established as a CROWN CORPORATION in 1978 after a brief history as a CN subsidiary. Financed by the federal government, it operates all intercity passenger railway services in Canada. The corporation's board of directors reports to TRANSPORT CANADA. In 1981 Via cancelled or reduced numerous routes in an attempt to make passenger service more efficient. A non-confidence vote over the issue in Oct 1981 was won by the government. Many of the services were reinstated by the new Conservative government elected in 1984. With head offices in Montréal, in 1984 Via had operating revenue of $625 million, assets of $652 million and 3475 employees. *See also* RAILWAYS, CONTEMPORARY.

Vickers, Jonathan Stewart, Jon, tenor (b at Prince Albert, Sask 29 Oct 1926). Vickers sang in church choirs and in Gilbert and Sullivan and Victor Herbert operettas, and in 1950 became a scholarship student at the Royal Conservatory of Music, Toronto. His professional career began almost immediately with concert, oratorio and operatic engagements throughout eastern Canada, followed by CBC radio successes. His international career began in 1957 with performances in New York in *Fidelio* and *Medea* and a 3-year contract with the Royal Opera House, Covent Garden, London, Eng. Towering performances at Bayreuth, Dallas, Vienna, Milan and Buenos Aires followed, and Vickers was soon in demand throughout the operatic world. An outstanding performer of the dramatic and Heldentenor repertoire, and in his time the world's greatest interpreter of the role of Siegmund in Wagner's *Die Walküre*, he has made numerous recordings and films, including those in association with Herbert von Karajan in the Salzburg festivals. His approach to his operatic roles includes the study of the composer's philosophy and emotional intent, as seen particularly in his favourite role, Britten's *Peter Grimes*. Vickers has performed infrequently in Canada but he has appeared at EXPO 67, the National Arts Centre, the Guelph Spring Festival, and with the Toronto Symphony and the Opéra du Québec. A Saskatchewan tour in 1977 was climaxed by a concert in Prince Albert in the church where he sang as a boy. Vickers was made companion of the Order of Canada in 1969 and in 1975 received the MOLSON PRIZE.   MABEL H. LAINE

Victoria, capital of British Columbia, is situated on the southern tip of VANCOUVER I, about 100 km S of Vancouver. Occupying a peninsular site, Victorians view the bordering Juan de Fuca and Haro straits, backed by the Olympic Mts of Washington to the S and the Gulf Is to the E, with the majestic, volcanic peak of Mt Baker in the distance. The metropolitan area is characterized by a number of low hills interspersed with relatively flat areas, and is bordered on the W by the fjordlike Saanich Inlet and the richly forested higher elevations of Malahat Ridge and the Vancouver I ranges. Greater Victoria comprises the municipalities of Saanich (pop 78 710, 1981c), Oak Bay (16 990), Esquimalt (15 870), Central Saanich (9890) and North Saanich (6117), and the town of Sidney (7946).

Settlement The site of Victoria was chosen for settlement in 1843 by James DOUGLAS, chief factor of the HBC's Pacific coast headquarters at Ft

---

Population: 64 379 (1981c); 233 481 (CMA)

Rate of Increase (1971-81): (City) 4.2%; (CMA) 19.2%

Rank in Canada: Fifteenth (by CMA)

Date of Incorporation: City 1862

Land Area: 18.8 km²; 438.7 km² (CMA)

Elevation: 15 m

Climate: Average daily temp, July 15.4°C, Jan 4.0°C; Yearly precip 658.6 mm; Hours of sunshine 2190.1 per year

---

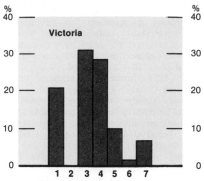

Distribution of Industrial Activity* by Industry Grouping within Census Metropolitan Areas, 1980

Industry groupings

1. Food and beverage and tobacco products industries
2. Leather, textile, knitting mills and clothing industries
3. Wood, furniture and fixtures, paper and allied and printing, publishing and allied industries
4. Machinery, transportation equipment and electrical products industries
5. Primary metal and metal fabricating industries
6. Rubber and plastic products, petroleum and coal products and chemical products industries
7. Non-metallic mineral products and miscellaneous manufacturing industries.

* Industry activity based on the average of percentage shares of the value shipments of goods of own manufacture, total value added and total number of employees for each of the selected metropolitan areas.

Source: Figure II, Catalogue 31-209, Statistics Canada.

Vancouver (Vancouver, Wash), near the mouth of the Columbia R. A boundary settlement between the US and British N America was anticipated, and in the event that the 49th parallel was extended to the Pacific, which did occur in 1846, the HBC wanted an alternative fur-trading headquarters site under development. The smaller harbour of Victoria was chosen over that of Esquimalt for the establishment of Ft Victoria (named after Queen Victoria) because it was bordered by extensive tracts of level to gently sloping land suitable for agriculture.

Development Victoria remained a small community of less than 1000 population until it burgeoned as the supply centre and jumping-off point for the Fraser GOLD RUSH of 1858. It was incorporated as a city in 1862. The commodious ESQUIMALT Harbour nearby was designated as a naval base by the British Admiralty in 1865 and still performs this role today as CFB Esquimalt. Victoria's political capital function remained through the successive stages as capital of the colony of Vancouver I, then of the amalgamated colony and later province of British Columbia (1871). As the dominant urban centre in BC, Victoria was unchallenged until the rise of Vancouver following the arrival of the CPR at Burrard Inlet in 1886. By the turn of the century Vancouver had taken over many of the shipping, commercial and manufacturing functions of Victoria and the capital city gradually settled into its modern role as a government, naval, tourist and retirement centre.

Cityscape The narrow, doglegged Victoria Harbour and its long extension, Gorge Waters, constitute a picturesque, human-scaled focus for the city. The inner harbour, reserved for ferries and pleasure craft, is flanked by the impressive provincial legislative buildings completed in 1898 and CP's Empress Hotel (1908). Recent

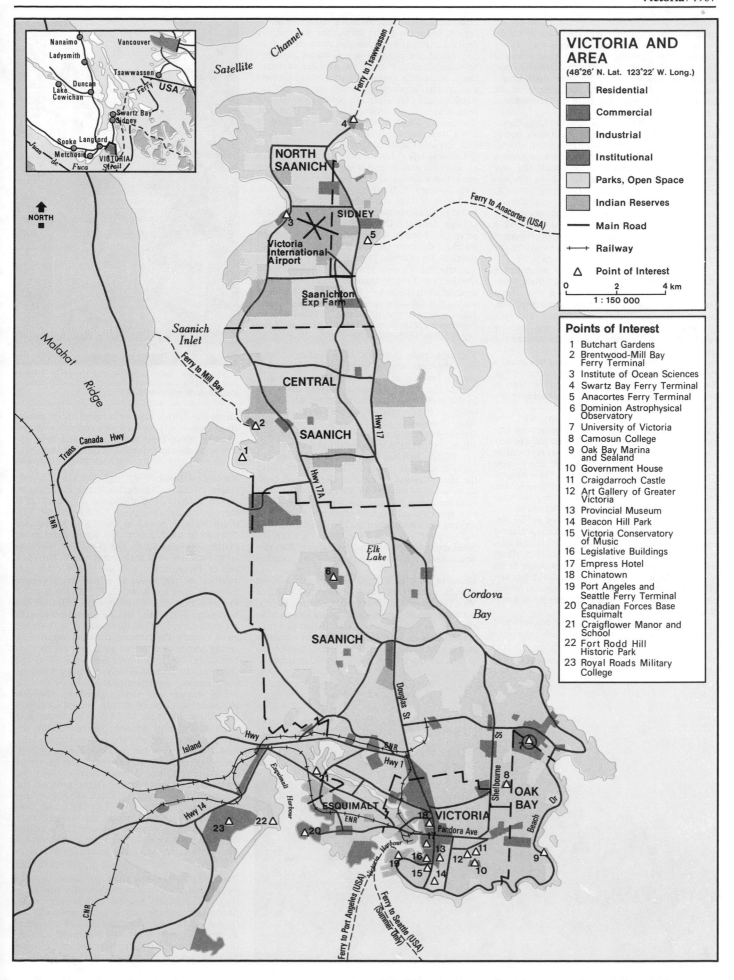

VICTORIA AND AREA
(48°26' N. Lat. 123°22' W. Long.)

Residential
Commercial
Industrial
Institutional
Parks, Open Space
Indian Reserves
Main Road
Railway
Point of Interest

0   2   4 km
1 : 150 000

Points of Interest

1 Butchart Gardens
2 Brentwood-Mill Bay Ferry Terminal
3 Institute of Ocean Sciences
4 Swartz Bay Ferry Terminal
5 Anacortes Ferry Terminal
6 Dominion Astrophysical Observatory
7 University of Victoria
8 Camosun College
9 Oak Bay Marina and Sealand
10 Government House
11 Craigdarroch Castle
12 Art Gallery of Greater Victoria
13 Provincial Museum
14 Beacon Hill Park
15 Victoria Conservatory of Music
16 Legislative Buildings
17 Empress Hotel
18 Chinatown
19 Port Angeles and Seattle Ferry Terminal
20 Canadian Forces Base Esquimalt
21 Craigflower Manor and School
22 Fort Rodd Hill Historic Park
23 Royal Roads Military College

planning developments have capitalized on the unique, old-world charm of this area by establishing an extensive public walkway along much of the harbour front. Another effective planning emphasis has been the rehabilitation of the "old town" area of Victoria, including a redefinition of Chinatown, complete with the colourful and decorative Gate of Harmonious Interest marking its entrance.

Population Compared with other large Canadian cities, Victoria's metropolitan area population is older and more strongly of British origin, despite the infusion of other ethnic groups through postwar immigration. Both the city and metropolitan area had the highest proportion of population 65 and over among their Canadian counterparts, 24% and 15%, respectively, in 1976. Although rates of natural increase are low, the metropolitan population has had a growth rate above the national metropolitan average since the mid-1960s, owing to strong immigration from other parts of Canada.

Economy and Labour Force The prominence of government and tourism in Victoria's economy results in high proportions of the labour force being engaged in public administration, personal services and the retail trade. The lack of well-populated hinterland on the narrow southern tip of Vancouver I has constricted the growth of wholesale trade and Victoria's isolation from major mainland markets has proven to be a strong disadvantage for manufacturing. Some industries have shifted to the mainland in recent years. Sawmilling and shipbuilding are the leading industries that remain.

Transportation Ferry connections with the mainland have always been of the utmost importance to Victorians. The CP Steamships service from Vancouver to Victoria was replaced in 1960 by the provincially owned BC Ferry operating from SIDNEY, N of Victoria, to Tsawwassen, S of Vancouver. Other services include the Washington state ferries from Sidney to Anacortes, Black Ball transport from Victoria to Port Angeles, and the summer service of BC Steamship from Victoria to Seattle. Air transportation especially mitigates the isolation of Island life: Air Canada, CP Air, Pacific Western Airlines and Air BC all have scheduled services from Victoria. As a shipping port, Victoria has declined in importance, and its function as terminus of the Esquimalt and Nanaimo Ry is a minor one.

Government and Politics Recent mayors and city councils have been concerned with the pres-

ervation of Victoria's role as the retail core of the region, but have at the same time successfully resisted attempts by developers to create a highrise downtown in the image of many business-oriented Canadian cities. A number of functions, including regional parks, trunk sewers and hospital services, are carried out by the Capital Regional Dist, although police and fire protection remain under local municipal control. The Greater Victoria Water Dist is controlled by the 4 core municipalities of Victoria, Saanich, Oak Bay and Esquimalt.

Cultural Life Victoria is well endowed with educational and fine-arts institutions. The UNIVERSITY OF VICTORIA (fd 1963), grew out of Victoria College (1902), which was originally affiliated with McGill and subsequently with UBC. Other institutions include Royal Roads Military College, Camosun College and the Victoria Conservatory of Music. The Provincial Museum and Butchart Gardens (20 km NW) are leading attractions for visitors. The Art Gallery of Greater Victoria, the Victoria Symphony Orchestra and the Bastion Theatre have enhanced the city's reputation in the arts.   C.N. FORWARD

Reading: C.N. Forward, ed, *Residential and Neighbourhood Studies in Victoria* (1973); H.D. Foster, ed, *Victoria: Physical Environment and Development* (1976); H. Gregson, *A History of Victoria, 1842-1970* (1970).

Victoria Cross, instituted 1856 by Queen Victoria, is the COMMONWEALTH's premier military decoration for gallantry. It is awarded in recognition of the most exceptional bravery displayed in the presence of the enemy, although in rare instances the decoration has been given to mark other courageous acts. The first recipients saw action in the Crimean War. Among them a Canadian lieutenant, Alexander Roberts DUNN, won the VC for heroism during the charge of the Light Brigade at the Battle of Balaklava. Over the years, Canada's recipients (living and posthumous) have totalled 93, including Canadians who were attached to the forces of other Commonwealth countries and some non-Canadians serving in Canadian units. The decoration is in the form of a bronze cross pattée bearing the royal crest and the words "For Valour." The ribbon is dark crimson. *See* HONOURS.   CARL LOCHNAN

Victoria Day is a legal holiday throughout Canada remembered as "the twenty-fourth of May, the Queen's Birthday." It celebrates, in fact, the birthdays of Queen Victoria and Queen Elizabeth II. Victoria Day was established as a holiday in Canada West in 1845, and as a NATIONAL HOLIDAY by Parliament in 1901. The movement to turn the queen's birthday into an occasion to

Victoria Cross, the Commonwealth's premier decoration for gallantry (*courtesy National Museums of Canada/ National Museum of Man/K71-95*).

salute the British Empire resulted in its association from the 1890s for half a century with EMPIRE DAY. Since 1952 Victoria Day has been observed on the first Monday preceding May 25.   JOHN ROBERT COLOMBO

Victoria Island, NWT, 217 290 km², second-largest island in Canada, lies in the ARCTIC ARCHIPELAGO directly N of the arctic mainland. It is surrounded by Amundsen Gulf to the W, Viscount Melville Sound to the N and M'Clintock Channel in the E. BANKS I lies across the narrow Prince of Wales Str in the NW. The island is largely composed of sedimentary rock. There is a belt of Precambrian rock on the W coast and another on the S coast, veined with copper formerly used by the Inuit. The E side is a flat lowland that rises to prominent cliffs on the Wollaston Pen in the N. The glacial landforms are more complex than those on any of the other arctic islands. The rivers of the lowlands follow gently wandering courses and there are numerous lakes. The rock formations as well as the shape of the S coast closely resemble those of CORONATION GULF immediately S.

The island was first sighted in the SW by John RICHARDSON of the second FRANKLIN Expedition in 1826. In 1839 P.W. Dease and Thomas Simpson named the island for the newly crowned queen. The NW peninsula later took the name of her consort, Prince Albert. John RAE of the HBC examined the shoreline (1851) from Prince Albert Sound to Pelly Pt, travelling by toboggan. The island received the attention of the Canadian Arctic Expedition under V. STEFANSSON in 1915 and 1917, and Diamond JENNESS — for whom the western peninsula is named — made a study of the COPPER INUIT. The HBC established posts at Cambridge Bay, Walker Bay and Holman I in the 1920s.   JAMES MARSH

Victorian Order of Nurses for Canada is a national nonprofit, community-health organization that provides NURSING care in the home, particularly for the elderly and chronically ill. Organized by Lady ABERDEEN in 1897 to commemorate Queen Victoria's Diamond Jubilee, the VON's initial aims were to provide visiting nursing services to districts without access to

Parliament Buildings, Victoria, BC (*photo by M.G. Kingshott/Valan*).

medical facilities and to establish cottage hospitals in isolated areas. The VON established 44 such hospitals, but by 1924 all had been taken over by other authorities and home nursing service became the main focus of VON activities. Within this field, the functions of the VON have evolved in response to changes in Canadian society and new home nursing needs. During 1982, over 1000 VON staff working out of 69 branches made 2 227 540 visits to 108 043 patients. Fees paid through provincial government health-care insurance provide the main source of funding and additional revenue is obtained from local governments and the United Way.

JEAN E. DRYDEN

Victoriaville, Qué, Town, pop 21 838 (1981c), inc 1860, is located on the Rivière Nicolet in the Piedmont Appalachians, 117 km SW of Québec City and 60 km NE of Drummondville. Originally called Demersville after a local businessman (by himself), its name — thought to be too pretentious — was changed in 1861 to honour Queen Victoria. In the early days, the town was only a small train station on the GRAND TRUNK RY line between Québec City and Richmond, Qué. Today, it is renowned for its furniture and clothing industries and has become a major agri-centre for marketing local produce. Its industrial park houses a prosperous group of metal-product machinery plants. Victoriaville's growth and dynamism have made it the focal centre for the surrounding area.

JEAN-MARIE DUBOIS AND PIERRE MAILHOT

Video Art Video is an independent, personal television, created outside commercial channels, using small-format 1/2" or 3/4" magnetic tape (as opposed to the 1" or 2" tape of commercial TV) and simplified recording equipment. In the late 1960s, when the first low-cost portable videotape cameras came onto the market for consumer use, these "portapaks" were taken up by both artists and community organizers as a medium having the qualities of television yet without the costly and restrictive format requirements of commercial systems. Art tapes of the late 1960s and early 1970s related closely to the current art issues and nonproduct emphasis of conceptual art and performance. The first tapes were extremely simple, usually produced by the artist alone for closed-circuit screening in studios or at the artist-run "alternate" galleries then being established with CANADA COUNCIL support.

From the beginning, the major centres for video art — Vancouver, Toronto, Montréal, Halifax — each had a different character. Vancouver turned to video in 1969 to record performances and events associated with Intermedia (1967-71), a group of artists working in different media. By 1973 the artist-run Satellite Video Exchange Society (Video Inn) and Western Front were established as production and viewing centres, growing partly out of the important Matrix International Video conference held that year. Vancouver has continued to see a double purpose for video, in both performance and community collaboration.

Toronto has been oriented to individual expression through video, with artists conscious of international art issues working independently. The first workshops were organized in 1970 at A Space, an artist-run facility. The A Space equipment, now separately incorporated as Charles Street Video, provides editing around-the-clock for 3/4" colour productions, and Trinity Square Video is the source for production equipment, studio recording time, workshops and information on new technologies such as TELIDON.

Many Montréal artists viewed video politically as a tool for social change. The works produced at Vidéographe, which was begun in 1970 in co-operation with the National Film Board's "Challenge for Change" program, developed a video documentary form based somewhat on the film model. *Pea Soup* (1978, 94 minutes) by Pierre Falardeau and Julien Poulin is exemplary, a composite portrait of Québecois street culture, as is *Chaperons rouges* (Little Red Riding Hood, 1979) by Helen Doyle and Hélène Bourgault, an antirape dramatization. Vidéo Véhicule, originating at the artist-run gallery Véhicule Art in the early 1970s and now operating as PRIM (Productions Réalisations Indépendants de Montréal Inc), has generated some individual art pieces, but the co-operative work coming from Coop vidéo de Montréal remains dominant.

Video art began in Halifax in the late 1960s, chiefly structuralist and formal works created at the NOVA SCOTIA COLLEGE OF ART AND DESIGN. NSCAD's tapes by both staff and students reached their peak from 1971 to 1973, a fine example being *Shuffle* by Douglas Waterman. Though production continues at the college, many video artists in eastern Canada have moved to the Centre for Art Tapes, an artist-run exhibition facility established in Halifax in 1978.

Video has changed greatly in its first 15 years, in the 4 main centres and the many smaller cities producing tapes. Toronto, with its emphasis on single-channel works (as distinct from multimonitor pieces or installations) and strong statements by individuals, has also assumed a high profile through sheer volume of production. A significant development in the mid-1970s was the use of narrative, exemplified by Colin Campbell ("The Woman from Malibu" series, 1976) and Lisa Steele (*A Very Personal Story*, 1974). General Idea originated "found-formats," playing ironically on commercial idioms, in their *Pilot* (1977) for TVOntario. Both these threads are seen elsewhere, as in Eric Metcalfe/Dana Atchley's *Crime Time Comix Presents Steel and Flesh* (1980) produced in Vancouver.

Distribution of these noncommercial, independent tapes remains problematic, but the descriptive catalogues and fee schedules developed by Art Metropole (established in Toronto in 1974) may provide a solution. By 1980 the 3/4" colour cassette had become the standard for production and circulation of artists' tapes in Canada, the US and Europe.

The Vancouver Art Gallery, Art Gallery of Ontario, and National Gallery of Canada have substantial videotape collections, and Canadian artists have been included in important exhibitions and festivals around the world, including "Projekt 74" (Cologne, West Germany, 1974), Documenta 6 (Kassel, West Germany, 1979), São Paulo Bienal (Brazil, 1977), Biennale di Venezia (Italy, 1980), "OKanada" (Berlin, East Germany, 1983), and at the Museum of Modern Art in New York. In Canada, artists are considering opportunities for broadcast and other communications options as they are developed, hoping to expand their audiences beyond the museum and artist-run gallery circuit. Canadian video is recognized internationally as having developed a unique visual language and personal communication in both form and content. *See also* ART, CONTEMPORARY TRENDS. PEGGY GALE

Reading: Art Gallery of Ontario, *Videoscape* (1974); J.B. Danzker, ed, *Montréal Tapes: Video as a Community Tool* (1978); A. Duchaine, *Vidéo du Québec* (1982); Peggy Gale, ed, *Video by Artists* (1976).

Vietnamese, *see* SOUTHEAST ASIANS.

Vigneault, Gilles, singer-songwriter, poet, publisher (b at Natashquan, Qué 27 Oct 1928). Like Félix LECLERC, Vigneault revitalized the Québec *chanson* and helped make Québec culture known abroad. After studying at Laval he founded in 1959 Éditions de l'arc to distribute his writings. The next year he began singing his own songs. Despite his hoarse voice and awkward appearance, he could always touch his audience with the poetry, sincerity and youth that

Gilles Vigneault (*courtesy Canapress*).

emanated from his person and his work. His rousing song "Mon Pays" (1965) became virtually an anthem for Québecois and swelled his popularity at home and abroad. He has appeared in various great Canadian halls (several times with the Orchestre symphonique de Montréal at the Montréal Place des Arts, and at the National Arts Centre, Ottawa, as well as Toronto's Massey Hall) and in Europe (France, Switzerland, Poland, Belgium and Luxembourg). He started his own record label, Le Nordet (Editions du vent qui vire). Among his awards are the Prix Denise-Pelletier (1983) and the Prix de l'Académie Charles-Cros (1984). HÉLÈNE PLOUFFE

Ville-Marie, colony fd 17 May 1642 on Montréal I by the Société de Notre-Dame de Montréal, under the governship of MAISONNEUVE, to bring Christianity to the Indians; it was a product of the flowering of French religious life in the early 17th century. Assisted by recruits sent in 1653 and 1659, the little colony sank its roots and withstood Iroquois invasions. In 1663 it was taken over by the Seminary of St Sulpice in Paris, which already supplied its priests. The settlers, from the first preoccupied with the FUR TRADE, lived to see the Roman Catholic ideal of Ville-Marie fade before the realization of a commercial MONTRÉAL. DALE MIQUELON

Ville-Marie, Qué, Town, pop 2651 (1981c), inc 1962, is located on Lk TEMISKAMING near the Québec-Ontario border. It took shape at the end of the 19th century, developing around the Oblate mission settlements and the forestry company posts that had been exploiting the large pine forests of the Lac Témiscaming basin for several decades. The Oblate mission was established in 1836 near Fort Témiscaming, built in 1686 by fur traders. After 1885 settlement of the land around the lake by families from the older regions of Québec led to the establishment of Ville-Marie. The name dates from 1896 and honours the patron of the Oblates of Mary Immaculate, indicating the Oblates' role in the development of the region. Ville-Marie was made a village in 1897. The major town of rural Québec's Témiscamingue region, it has strong ties with the towns of HAILEYBURY and NEW LISKEARD on the Ontario shore of the lake.

BENOÎT-BEAUDRY GOURD

Villeneuve, Gilles, auto racer (b at Berthierville, Qué 18 Jan 1950; d at Zolder, Belgium 9 May 1982). In his brief career Villeneuve was Canada's finest high-speed racer. He first showed his penchant for speed guiding motorized sleds at breakneck speeds, winning the N American championship in 1971, the Québec crown in 1972 and the Canadian title in 1973. Villeneuve used his earnings from snowmobile racing to enter Formula Ford competition, winning the 1973 Québec crown. He progressed to

Formula Atlantic (FA) races in 1974, but broke his leg at his debut at Mosport, Ont. Undaunted, he returned in 1975 to score one victory and rank 5th overall in the standings. In 1976 he dominated Canadian and American FA competition, winning 9 of 10 races. Another Canadian championship followed in 1977 as he entered Can-Am class racing. Villeneuve's success brought an offer to join the Ferrari team on the world circuit. His initial grand prix triumph occurred at Montréal and in 1979 he scored further victories at Kyalami, Long Beach, Calif; and Watkins Glen, NY. He also finished 2nd in the Canadian Grand Prix, and was runner-up to teammate Jody Scheckter as the world's finest grand prix racer. He won 6 of 67 races he drove for Ferrari in Formula One. He was killed in a high-speed qualifying race for the Belgian Grand Prix following a collision with another car at 250 km/h. Montréal's Grand Prix circuit has been named for him.   BOB FERGUSON

Villeneuve, Jean-Marie-Rodrigue, Oblate priest, Roman Catholic archbishop of Québec, cardinal (b at Montréal 2 Nov 1883; d at Alhambra, Calif 17 Jan 1947). After studying philosophy and theology, he began a teaching career and became active in nationalist circles, with Abbé Lionel GROULX. Named first bishop of Gravelbourg (Sask) in 1930, he became the 20th bishop of Québec in 1932, the 10th archbishop, and, in 1933, the fourth Canadian cardinal. While head of the Québec church, Cardinal Villeneuve continued to teach, using his homilies, talks and academic presentations, and spread his ideas through brochures and books. At the same time he also gave new impetus to CATHOLIC ACTION, liturgical renewal and Marist piety; he ran his diocese firmly and was the uncontested leader of Québec and Canadian bishops. Despite his taste for grandeur and a certain stubbornness, he liked to mingle with the crowds that greeted him.

Although his episcopacy faced the serious problems of the GREAT DEPRESSION — strikes, debates about the nature of Catholic Action and relations with public authorities — he skilfully found solutions acceptable to his colleagues. He was less successful with his position on the war. Convinced that "Hitler and Nazism are a catastrophic threat to our Christianity and our rights," he yielded to pressure from federal politicians and was increasingly sympathetic to total war, a position that appalled some bishops, the nationalist circles and a good many French Canadian Catholics. To save unanimity and avoid scandal, he agreed to some concessions. Yet the tensions that remained were indicative of the upheaval beginning to shake Québec.
                                             NIVE VOISINE

Vimy Ridge, battle fought 9-14 Apr 1917 during WORLD WAR I. The long, low ridge formed a key position linking the Germans' new Hindenburg Line to their main trench lines leading N from HILL 70 near Arras, France. Both British and French forces had tried unsuccessfully to take the ridge earlier during the war. In spring 1917 the task was given to the Canadian Corps, commanded by British Lt-Gen Sir J.H.G. BYNG. After careful training and rehearsal, and supported by almost 1000 artillery pieces, the Canadians attacked along a 6.4 km front on 9 Apr 1917. It was the first time the Canadians attacked together, and they achieved a magnificent victory, sweeping the Germans off the ridge. By Apr 14 they had gained more ground, more guns, and more prisoners than had any previous British offensive. Canadian casualties mounted to 10 602, of which 3598 were killed. Nevertheless the sense of achievement and national pride created by this success gave the Canadians a great feeling of self-confidence. The Canadian Corps was to gain recognition as an elite corps.
                                                R.H. ROY

Vinland, see NORSE VOYAGES.

Violence, Political, refers to the use of physical force to achieve or prevent political or economic change. In this specific sense, Canada (as compared to the US) has been a "peaceable kingdom." There has been no bloody revolution or massive civil war and very little of the "lawless West." The incidence of individual crimes of violence has also been very much lower. Nevertheless, Canadian history records a great deal of violence, especially collective violence, eg, that used in war, in the maintenance of "order" (see AID TO (OR OF) THE CIVIL POWER) and as a tool of political method. War and a concern with military defence in the name of "survival" or "protection of national interests" have been instrumental in Canadian history since the founding of NEW FRANCE. Violence characterized the turbulent relations between the settlers and the IROQUOIS, and the response to American attacks and border harrassments in the 1770s, 1812-14, and during the 1830s (see HUNTERS' LODGES) and the 1860s (see FENIANS). Canada was also involved in the SOUTH AFRICAN WAR, WORLD WAR I and WORLD WAR II, the KOREAN WAR (1950-53) and the United Nations PEACEKEEPING activities of the 20th century. Canada's membership in NATO and in NORAD symbolizes its recognition that military strength (however secured) is the chief expression of power in international affairs, although the Canadian government has occasionally rejected requests by her senior allies to contribute military support to what it considered imperial wars. Sir John A. MACDONALD refused to authorize a Canadian contingent to support a British expedition to the Sudan in 1885; similarly, pressure from the US for at least token support for the intervention in Vietnam was resisted in the 1960s. In both cases and in others like them it might be argued that Canada was hypocritical; in the first by accepting the insurance of Pax Britannica and Pax Americana without paying premiums and in the second by profiting from the Defence Production Sharing Agreement in the US. Debates on defence, from the militia bills of the 1860s through the Laurier-Borden struggle over naval contributions to imperial and national defence (see NAVAL AID BILL) to 20th-century CONSCRIPTION crises and the issues resulting from membership in a nuclear-based alliance system, have significantly affected the political process in Canada and the evolution of Canada's Constitution and domestic cultural relations. For example, Mackenzie KING's role in bringing about the BALFOUR REPORT and the STATUTE OF WESTMINSTER, as well as his reliance on Ernest LAPOINTE in all matters concerning Québec, resulted directly from his perception of the impact of military commitments upon domestic politics and upon Canada's international status.

The tortuous and little-examined history of collective violence within Canada reveals a nation that paradoxically combines a national attachment to the notion that only legally constituted government is legitimate (and that it may legitimately use force to maintain order) with an apparent belief that a healthy society must expect political and economic competition to generate violence. The 19th and early 20th centuries were pockmarked with incidents of physical intimidation at the polling booth, and with violence among competing lumber and railway interests and between strikers and militiamen. Political discourse has occasionally been tinged with violence, eg, Joseph HOWE of Nova Scotia once suggested irately that someone would shortly "hire a blackfellow to horsewhip a lieutenant-governor," and some Canadians tend to honour historical leaders of violent political dissent such as W.L. MACKENZIE, L.J. PAPINEAU and Louis RIEL. Religious and cultural antipathies have often sparked violent confrontations; in 1871 a large militia force was re-

quired to ensure the removal of the body of rationalist Joseph GUIBORD from a Protestant to a Catholic cemetery in Montréal. Anti-Asian riots erupted in Vancouver in the early 20th century, and anti-Semitic melées in Toronto and Montréal occurred in the mid-1930s.

In Canada attitudes toward political and cultural violence and those toward individual violence are linked by the perception that social order is an absolute prerequisite of both individual and political liberty. In principal constitutional statements it is declared that "good government" is inseparable from "peace and order," comparatively strict controls on the possession of handguns are maintained and a broad reserve of executive authority is endorsed to prevent or suppress the use of violence as a political method. Retention of the 1914 WAR MEASURES ACT for use in time of "real or apprehended" insurrection allows suspension of habeas corpus by order-in-council. Attempts to replace the Act with more restricted emergency powers legislation have failed — although in early 1985 the new Conservative government in Ottawa indicated a willingness to implement the recommendation of the McDonald Commission for legislation which would provide emergency powers short of those in the War Measures Act. The reaction of Canadians to political trials and collective violence seems to be characterized by a stringent suppression of violence when it occurs or is threatened and lenience towards the instigators once the crisis has been weathered. During the REBELLIONS OF 1837 in UPPER CANADA only 2 rebels were executed; in LOWER CANADA 12 were hanged, and these only after a second attempt on their part in 1838 and because of fears of American intervention. The AMNESTY ACT pardoned the rebels in 1849.

Confidence in the evolving constitutional system has bred tolerance of basic constitutional dissent, allowing political actions which might otherwise be violently suppressed. In 1939 J.S. WOODSWORTH could support his vote in the Commons against the declaration of war with the statement that if any of his sons were "willing to take his stand on this matter, if necessary, face a concentration camp or a firing squad, I shall be more proud of that boy than if he enlisted for war."

Pronouncements of Canadian courts reveal much about Canadian attitudes towards violence. Chief Justice John Beverley ROBINSON of Upper Canada, who had fought under Brock at Detroit and Niagara, explained to Samuel LOUNT and Peter MATTHEWS why, having pleaded guilty, they must be hanged for their part in the 1837 rebellion: "You were not the tenants of rigorous and exacting landlords; you were not burthened with taxes for the State, further than the payment perhaps of a few shillings in the year, to support the common expenses of the district in which you lived . . . regularity and industry would always have ensured you a competency. . . . You lived in a country where every man who obeys the laws is secure in the protection of life, liberty and property. . . . In a country in which you [Lount] have been admitted to the honourable privilege of making laws to bind your fellow subjects, it was due from *you* to set an example of faithful obedience of public authority." (It was also Robinson's view, however, that "some example should be made in the way of capital punishment.")

Stressing the interrelationships of order, liberty and obedience of law, Robinson made clear that violence might be justified only if the avenues of constitutional redress of grievance were demonstrably closed. They appeared to be closed in 1869-70 when Riel's use of force secured provincial status for Manitoba (see RED RIVER REBELLION). Yet when Riel's successful "provisional government" executed the Orangeman Thomas SCOTT this raised an insuperable obstacle to the clemency which would probably have characterized the response to the second Métis rebellion in 1885 (*see* NORTH-WEST REBELLION). Nevertheless the Regina jury recommended Riel to "the mercy of the Crown," apparently attaching weight (as did opponents of the federal government then and later) to Riel's plea that "I have acted reasonably and in self-defence, while the Government, my accuser, being irresponsible and consequently insane, cannot but have acted wrong." Sir John A. Macdonald's decision not to commute Riel's death sentence suggests that prejudice and racism increases the potential for violence. This was certainly the case when fierce anticonscription rioting swept Québec City in the spring of 1918.

The conviction that the state can employ force to suppress the use of violence as a political tool has been exploited by class-biased governments in Canada to impede the protest or organization of workers. In 1935 in Regina police were ordered to break up a large group of unemployed men headed for Ottawa to demand job-creating action by the government and rioting resulted (*see* ON TO OTTAWA TREK). The most dramatic instance of this kind, however, occurred earlier (1919) during the WINNIPEG GENERAL STRIKE. The strike leaders, representing some 30 000 workers who supported demands for union recognition and wage increases to match the sharply rising living costs, had pursued a rigorous policy of nonviolence. Shaken by the ability of the strikers to halt peacefully the city's economic life, business and professional leaders along with civic, provincial and federal authorities pronounced the strike an attempt to overthrow constituted authority and proclaimed that revolutionary violence was imminent. Violence was, in fact, instigated when police and soldiers were ordered to disperse a "silent parade" that had been organized by the strikers and WWI veterans to protest the arrest of their leaders on charges of sedition. When the strike collapsed, 8 leaders were brought to trial; one was acquitted and the others were sentenced to imprisonment for terms ranging from 6 months to 2 years. Perhaps the most interesting aspect of this complicated interaction was the evident opinion of a majority of Winnipeggers that the assumptions of the authorities had been ill-founded. Three convicted strike leaders were elected to the Manitoba legislature in 1920 while still in prison. F.J. Dixon, acquitted on a charge of seditious libel, topped the polls in Winnipeg, while J.S. Woodsworth, similarly charged, was elected MP in 1921. Collective violence by the state was condemned. In the same period the New York state legislature expelled 5 duly-elected members of the Socialist Party of America on the grounds that socialism was "absolutely inimical" to the interests of the state.

The relationship of violence to constituted authority was also at the heart of the 1970 OCTOBER CRISIS in Québec. In Winnipeg and Montréal the governments concerned declared their apprehension of insurrection, in Montréal the FRONT DE LIBÉRATION DU QUÉBEC had actually declared its belief in violence as a means of reconstituting society and it had a record of bombing, murder and kidnapping. When the federal government proclaimed the War Measures Act following the kidnapping of British Trade Commissioner James Cross, and when both the RCMP and the army were given extraordinary powers of search, arrest and detention, many people endorsed the stern measures; after the murder of Québec Labour Minister Pierre LAPORTE and the release of Cross, the emergency orders were withdrawn and any persons who could prove damages resulting from an arbitrary arrest which failed to culminate in legal charges were offered compensation. Charges that the 2 levels of government were motivated largely by perceptions of political advantage led to 2 major investiga-

tions, but the controversy over means and ends that ensued will probably not modify traditional attitudes towards violence and the role of the state.   KENNETH MCNAUGHT

Violet (Violaceae), family of annual or perennial herbaceous PLANTS widely distributed throughout temperate and tropical regions. Tropical species may reach TREE size. Roughly 500 species of genera *Viola* (violets, pansies) and *Hybanthus* (green violets) alone occur worldwide. The 35 species of *Viola* native to Canada are found in abundance in woods, prairies and marshes from the Atlantic to the Pacific and N to the TREELINE. One green violet species (*H. concolor*) occurs in southern Ontario. Some violets produce 2 kinds of flowers. In spring colourful flowers (eg, purple, blue, white) are produced for POLLINATION by insects. Green, petalless, self-pollinating flowers are produced in summer. These are more fruitful and ensure seed set if earlier flowers were affected by cold. Many species are popular as ORNAMENTALS, mainly for rock gardens and shaded areas, where they prefer moist, rich soil. The hooded or purple violet (*V. cucullata*) has a rich purple flower and a rosette of heart-shaped leaves. It has been the PROVINCIAL FLORAL EMBLEM of NB since 1936.

CÉLINE ARSENEAULT

Virden, Man, Town, pop 2940 (1981c), inc 1904, is located 278 km W of Winnipeg on the Trans-Canada Hwy. Large-scale agricultural settlement began in the area in the 1880s, encouraged by construction of the CPR. Virden began as a railway camp on Gopher Creek in 1882, and became a transportation, processing and service centre for surrounding farms started by settlers from Scotland, England, Ontario and Nova Scotia. Evidence concerning the origin of the name is contradictory. It may derive from settlers who were relatives of Lord Mount Stephen, whose home in Scotland had this name, or from the German town of Verden, home of the wife of the duke of Manchester. A BRITISH COMMONWEALTH AIR TRAINING PLAN flying school was located here during WWII. In 1951 the province's first commercially productive oil zone was discovered, leading to development of the Daly field W of Virden. Virden-Roselea and North Virden-Scallion, Manitoba's largest fields, were discovered in 1953. Wells even appeared within the town, where the population doubled in the mid-1950s. Though Manitoba's oil production has declined, the Roselea and Scallion fields contributed 58% of the province's 1982 production (valued at $100.5 million). Agricultural and retail services and a modest manufacturing sector are part of Virden's economy.   D.M. LYON
Reading: I. Clingan, *The Virden Story* (1957).

Vireo (Vireonidae), family of small, basically olive green, insectivorous and partly frugivorous songbirds with repetitive, persistent songs (sometimes musical, often harsh). The 43 known species, restricted to the New World, are related to the cosmopolitan SHRIKE and CROW. Vireos spread northward from the American tropics, 8 species reaching Canada. Seven of these breed here, excluding Bell's vireo (*V. bellii*), which occurs, rarely, in spring at Point Pelée, Ont. The only permanent resident is Hutton's vireo (*V. huttoni*) of broad-leaved coniferous forests in extreme southwestern BC. The thicket-dwelling white-eyed vireo (*V. griseus*) breeds in extreme southern Ont. The yellow-throated vireo (*V. flavifrons*) inhabits mixed forest from SE Qué to SW Ont and occurs locally in SE Man. Solitary vireos (*V. solitarius*) frequent boreal forest transcontinentally N to Fort Simpson, NWT. The abundant red-eyed vireo (*V. olivaceus*), of mixed forests, ranges across Canada to 64° N lat, NWT. The Philadelphia vireo (*V. philadelphicus*), vocally similar to red-eyed vireo, inhabits deciduous woodland from SW Newfoundland to

central BC. The warbling vireo (*V. gilvus*) prefers deciduous woodland from SW Québec to the West Coast. Vireos build distinctive, pensile nests in trees and shrubs, breeding May-July; clutches contain 3-5 eggs.   J.C. BARLOW

Virus, the smallest form of life (20-300 nanometres), is structurally and functionally unique. The size of viruses is such that they do not contain enough GENETIC material to code for the proteins they require for reproduction, nor do they have ribosomes needed to synthesize these proteins. Therefore, being obliged to enter permissive host cells that assist them to reproduce, they are obligate intracellular parasites implicated in DISEASES of humans, other animals and PLANTS.

In Canada, specialists in microbiology, MOLECULAR BIOLOGY, BIOCHEMISTRY, IMMUNOLOGY and other biological sciences are engaged in interdisciplinary research to identify, describe and control disease-causing viruses. Research into human viral disease is carried out primarily in the universities and hospitals, and is funded largely by federal grants, co-ordinated through the MEDICAL RESEARCH COUNCIL OF CANADA. Some research funds are also supplied by provincial agencies. Agriculture Canada and certain of the universities (notably University of Saskatchewan, Saskatoon, through the Veterinary Infectious Disease Organization) operate extensive programs on viral diseases of animals. Work on plant viruses is done in Agriculture Canada RESEARCH STATIONS and in plant pathology laboratories connected to university departments of botany or biology, within science or agriculture faculties throughout the country.

Structure and Function

The mature virus organism (virion) consists of viral genes contained in a protective protein shell (a capsid). Viral genes may be deoxyribonucleic acid (DNA) or ribonucleic acid (RNA); genetic RNA is unique to viruses. RNA viruses include enteroviruses (eg, causing poliomyelitis), rhinoviruses (common cold), rhabdoviruses (rabies), paramyxoviruses (measles), orthomyxoviruses (influenza) and almost all plant viruses. DNA viruses include papavoviruses (warts), adenoviruses (acute respiratory disease), herpesviruses (cold sore, infectious mononucleosis, chicken pox), poxviruses (smallpox, cowpox), hepatitis B, and many viruses infecting bacteria (bacteriophages) and insects. Virions are functionally very limited and serve mainly to protect the viral genetic material (genome) from adverse environmental factors outside the host cell and to facilitate its entry into compatible host cells. Specific types of viruses take advantage of the resources of particular host cells. Bacteriophages (bacteria eaters), named by Canadian virologist Felix d'Herelle in 1917, prey only on bacteria and have specific preferences for particular bacterial species. Similarly, plant-specific viruses (discovered by Russian botanist Dimitri Ivanovsky in 1892) and animal-specific viruses (discovered by Friedrich Loeffler and Paul Frosch in 1898) have preferred host cells. Such preferences may stem from the origins of viruses, which are thought by some theorists to be degenerate, subcellular, self-replicating particles.

Viruses infect cells by fusion, endocytosis or injection. In viruses of a certain structure, the viral envelope fuses with the cell membrane of a host cell and the virus genome it contains is introduced into the cell. In endocytosis the host cell engulfs the virus, engulfment being triggered by contact with a viral particle, and the nucleic material is released from the capsid. Injection, a technique copied in laboratory GENETIC ENGINEERING, is used on bacteria only. The virus attaches itself to the bacterial cell wall and injects its nucleic acid, leaving the capsid outside the wall. Once inside the host cell, the viral nucleic acid and any enzymes participate in replicative activity.

Following "uncoating," the viral DNA or RNA may integrate itself into the genome of the host cell or may immediately initiate replication through a cytolytic (ie, cell-degenerating) infection, depending on the type of virus. In the case of integration, the host cell undergoes changes during which it acquires many of the properties of CANCER cells. The virus genome, being integrated, is conserved and replicated along with the host genome. The virus may, however, initiate a "lytic" infection, ie, replicating the mature virion which is then capable of infecting another host cell. The association between viruses and some tumours in humans is well documented, and viruses are known to cause many cancers in other VERTEBRATE species.

Cells undergoing a lytic virus infection frequently have their own synthetic processes inhibited but produce hundreds of identical copies of the infecting virion. The replicative strategies employed by RNA viruses are diverse and complex, depending upon whether the virus genome can function directly as messenger RNA, which instructs host cell ribosomes (cell organelles through which protein synthesis occurs) to make viral enzymes and proteins, or whether messenger RNA must be synthesized on the viral genetic template, before protein and enzyme synthesis can proceed. Most DNA viruses replicate in the nucleus of the host cell, using host-cell proteins to synthesize messenger RNA on the virus's DNA template.

Assembly of the virus is a complex and still poorly understood process. RNA viruses may assume simple spherical forms, complicated forms with enveloping membranes, and other special structures. DNA viruses may assemble in "factories" in the host-cell cytoplasm or be "budded off" from the host-cell membranes. Viruses that acquire outer membranes from the membrane of the cell's nucleus or cytoplasm incorporate virus-coded glycoproteins into these membranes, before the final assembly of the mature virion.

Viruses cause major diseases in plants and animals, but there are few effective methods for cure. Plant breeding may yield strains resistant to viruses, but this avenue of approach is unavailable to humans. Recently, some antiviral chemicals have shown promise as antibiotics; however, this control technique is of relatively limited application as the life processes of the virus are so intimately bound up with those of the host cell that it is difficult to kill the one without destroying the other. More successful efforts have been directed towards the development of vaccines for preventing viral disease. Properly administered, such vaccines have resulted in the worldwide eradication of smallpox and the virtual disappearance of poliomyelitis, measles and rubella from specific populations. In all Canadian provinces, PUBLIC HEALTH authorities maintain vaccination programs directed especially at small children. It remains to be seen, however, if the elimination of these traditional scourges of man can be maintained. See BIOLOGICAL PRODUCTS INDUSTRY; PHARMACY; VETERINARY MEDICINE. K.R. ROZEE

Voaden, Herman Arthur, playwright, director, educator, editor (b at London, Ont 19 Jan 1903). English Canada's most significant pre-WWII playwright following the departure of Merrill DENISON to the US in 1931, Voaden developed a unique nonrealist, multimedia playwriting and production style, which he termed "symphonic expressionism," 1932-43. Influenced by the paintings and cultural nationalism of the GROUP OF SEVEN, his "symphonic theatre," a fusion of realistic and poetic choral speech, music, dance and nonrealistic lighting and setting, was the primary stylistic alternative to the prevailing realism in Canadian theatre production.

His most important dramatic works include *Rocks* and *Earth Song* (1932), *Hill-land* (1934), *Murder Pattern* (1936), *Ascend As the Sun* (1942) and the realistic *Emily Carr* (1960). Following the suspension of regular theatre production because of WWII, Voaden began a second career as a national arts lobbyist. As first president, Canadian Arts Council (1945-48), national director, Canadian Conference of the Arts (1966-68) and president, Canadian Guild of Crafts (1968-70), he helped to secure government support for the arts in Canada. ANTON WAGNER

Vogt, Augustus Stephen, "A.S.," choral conductor, educator, administrator (b at Washington, Ont 14 Aug 1861; d at Toronto 17 Sept 1926). After studies in Boston and Leipzig, Vogt, a church organist, choirmaster, piano and organ teacher, founded the TORONTO MENDELSSOHN CHOIR in 1894. Soon one of the continent's finest, his choir was renowned for *a cappella* work and for annual festival performances with leading orchestras. Appointed principal of Toronto Conservatory in 1913, he retired from conducting in 1917 to devote all his time to administration. From 1918 until his death he was dean of U of T's music faculty. BARCLAY McMILLAN

Voice of Women, since 1960 a voluntary nonpartisan organization with members in every province of Canada, has opposed violence and war and promoted DISARMAMENT and peace. To this end VOW has organized extensive educational campaigns, lobbied all levels of government, held meetings and conferences including 2 international women's peace conferences, and sent representatives to other countries to consider the mutual concerns of women and promote action. Regular meetings take place in many centres and VOW initiates and supports campaigns with other groups. VOW is a member group of the NATIONAL ACTION COMMITTEE ON THE STATUS OF WOMEN and Project Ploughshares, and has a representative on the federal government's Consultative Group on Disarmament and Arms Controls. See also PEACE MOVEMENT; WOMEN'S INTERNATIONAL LEAGUE FOR PEACE AND FREEDOM.
KAY MACPHERSON

Volcano, an opening in the crust of a planetary body through which liquid, gaseous or solid material is expelled; also the structure formed by eruption of this material. Most terrestrial volcanoes expel magma, a mixture of molten rock and dissolved gases (eg, water vapour, carbon dioxide, sulphur dioxide). The Earth's volcanic belts are located above zones of anomalously high temperature (700-1400°C) where magma is produced by partial melting of solid material in the crust and upper mantle. These areas commonly occur along crustal plate margins at depths of 10-50 km (*see* PLATE TECTONICS). Basalt is the principal magma of diverging plate boundaries such as the oceanic spreading ridges; basalt, andesite, dacite and rhyolite characterize volcanic arcs along converging plate margins. The relatively low density of magma causes it to rise through fractures into regions of lower pressure where dissolved gases expand and propel it toward the surface. Magma trapped in shallow reservoirs may solidify to form subvolcanic intrusions or may undergo chemical change before resuming its ascent. Evacuation of such reservoirs sometimes causes overlying rocks to collapse, leaving steep-walled, circular depressions (calderas). Groundwater heated by magma may discharge as hot mineral SPRINGS, geysers or fumaroles, or steam may escape in explosive bursts (phreatic eruptions) which commonly precede eruptions of magma. Magma reaching the surface may issue as molten lava or as solid, pyroclastic ejecta (bombs, blocks, lapilli, ash).

Eruptive behaviour depends on the magma's temperature, composition and gas content, and on whether the vent is on land (subaerial), under water (subaqueous) or beneath ice (subglacial). Subaerial eruptions of characteristically fluid basalt are usually accompanied by fire fountains of incandescent globules thrown out of the vent by expanding gas. The globules fall back around the vent, building a pyroclastic cone, but most of the magma spreads in the form of thin lava flows which may build broad shields or lava plateaus. Escape of gases is restricted in viscous andesite, dacite and rhyolite magma. The trapped gases may inflate the melt into a porous froth (pumice) or may escape explosively, tearing apart the stiff, enclosing magma and hurling ash and pumice fragments from the vent. In these Plinian eruptions (named for the Roman scholar Pliny the Younger, who witnessed the event), columns of hot gases carry plumes of fine ash high into the atmosphere to be spread for hundreds of kilometres. Dense mixtures of hot gases, ash and pumice sometimes form fluidized flows (eg, ash flows, pyroclastic flows, glowing avalanches) which sweep rapidly down the flanks of an erupting volcano. Lava associated with such eruptions is commonly so viscous that it clings to the slopes in short, thick flows. These alternate with pyroclastic deposits to form steep-sided, composite cones with the classical symmetry of Mt Fuji. Extremely viscous lava, containing little gas, may pile up over its vent into bulbous lava domes or may project from the vent as crumbling spines of incandescent, nearly solid rock. Lava that enters water from a subaqueous vent is quenched, resulting in a glassy rind that may fracture into a pile of fragments or act as a viscous skin enclosing molten lava. In shallow water, magma thrown from a subaqueous vent by expanding gas is quenched to solid ejecta which accumulates as a tuff ring. In contrast, lava from vents on the deep ocean floor issues quietly, its dissolved gas held in solution by enormous hydrostatic pressure. Ejecta from subglacial vents may accumulate on the ice as supraglacial cones which collapse when the ice melts. Alternatively, lava may thaw a hole in the ice and there accumulate to form a steep-sided, flat-topped table mountain (tuya).

The deeply eroded remnants of ancient volcanic belts are found in volcanically inactive regions such as the Canadian Shield. In Canada, geologically young volcanoes are confined to the Western CORDILLERA. The Garibaldi belt of southwestern BC includes many supraglacial and subglacial volcanoes. Lava plateaus and shield volcanoes dotted with pyroclastic cones cover much of central BC; and composite volcanoes, such as Mt Edziza, form a belt extending from northern BC into the southern YT. No historic record of an eruption in Canada exists, but native legends and radiometric dating suggest that the Aiyansh lava flow near Terrace, BC, was extruded about 200 years ago. The explosive eruption in 1980 of Mt St Helens, Washington, left nearly 400 km² of total devastation. Eruption forecasting, based on the detection of precursor events such as seismic activity, tilting and heating of ground and emission of gases, may soon provide a warning to people living in areas threatened by an impending eruption. Volcanoes are not unique to the Earth. The dark maria of the moon are lava plains formed by the eruption of basalt. Olympus Mons, a Martian shield volcano 700 km across and 27 km high, is the largest volcano in the solar system. Io, an inner moon of Jupiter, is the most volcanically active body yet identified in the solar system. Its numerous volcanoes produce a dark lava (probably basalt) and a lighter material believed to be molten sulphur. See GEOLOGICAL REGIONS; GEOTHERMAL ENERGY. J.G. SOUTHER

Reading: M.B. Lambert, *Volcanoes* (1978).

Vole, common name for several RODENTS of family Arvicolidae, found only in the Northern Hemisphere. They have stout bodies, short legs and tails, and ears nearly hidden by moderately long hair. Genus *Microtus* (about 55 species) is most widespread and diverse; 11 *Microtus* species occur in Canada (including woodland, prairie, singing, montane, Townsend's, root, long-tailed, rock, chestnut-cheeked and creeping voles). Meadow voles (*M. pennsylvanicus*), commonly called field mice, occur throughout Canada, in grasslands, forests and low arctic tundra. Red-backed voles (*Clethrionomys*), most abundant in forests, also occur on the prairies and on tundra W of Hudson Bay. Heather voles (*Phenacomys*), found across the boreal forest, are rare; sagebrush voles (*Lagurus curtatus*) are confined to dry grasslands of SW Sask and SE Alta. Voles range in size from 15-20 g (red-backed voles) to 200 g (large Richardson's water vole, *M. richardsoni*). Many make prominent runways and above-ground, grassy nests. They remain active and may breed under the snow cover. Females of many species become fertile immediately after giving birth, bearing litters at close intervals; they may have 2 or more litters in the summer of their own birth. Voles rarely survive more than one winter. Many species undergo cycles of abundance and scarcity, peaking every 3-4 years. They can cause serious losses of hay and cereal crops, and damage fruit trees and ornamental shrubs.   W.A. FULLER

Volkoff, Boris Vladimirovich, dancer, choreographer (b Boris Vladimirovich Baskakoff at Schepotievo, Russia 24 Apr 1900; d at Toronto 11 Mar 1974). Volkoff studied at the Bolshoi dance school, Moscow. He arrived in Toronto via the Soviet Far East, China and the US to become ballet master and dancer at the Uptown Theatre in 1929, and in 1930 he established the Boris Volkoff School of the Dance. Through recitals, performances and lectures Volkoff introduced many to dance and built an audience. In 1936 he and his dancers won a Tanz-Spiele medal at the Berlin Olympics, dancing 2 of his ballets with Canadian themes. By 1939 this group had evolved into the Canadian Ballet. He commissioned and choreographed *The Red Ear of Corn* (1949), a Canadian theme ballet to a score by John WEINZWEIG. In 1951 he donated his studio and dancers to help the nascent NATIONAL BALLET OF CANADA. Volkoff also taught at the Toronto Skating Club and revolutionized choreography for figure skating. He designed the first ice ballet for the club in 1934 and choreographed and produced its ice ballets for 14 seasons. His students include Melissa HAYDEN and Barbara Ann SCOTT.   LILLIAN MITCHELL

Vollenweider, Richard Albert, scientist, limnologist, environmentalist, teacher (b at Zurich, Swit 27 June 1922). He is known for providing a generalized theoretical framework of the relationship between nutrient enrichment and eutrophication (process by which water becomes rich in dissolved nutrients and deficient in oxygen) of freshwaters. In a fundamental reform of the dominant limnological thinking of the time, he provided the first predictions of a lake's trophic (nutritional) state from quantitative data on the lake's nutrient load and hydrology. His work found direct application at the end of the 1960s when the effects of urbanization, industrialization and intensification of agriculture after WWII resulted in excessive nutrient enrichment of runoff and severe problems due to overgrowth of plant life in rivers, lakes and reservoirs. The Organization for Economic Cooperation and Development, Paris, France, appointed Vollenweider chief co-ordinator of a worldwide scientific effort 1966-81. Over this period he was responsible for documenting his approach, directing technical reports on methodology, regional reports of quantitative results, a summary synthesis report and finally a test of all results using information on more than

200 Canadian LAKES. These documents provide a sound basis for water management to alleviate or prevent eutrophication. It was through his involvement in the INTERNATIONAL JOINT COMMISSION that the limit was set for phosphorus loading to the Laurentian Great Lakes as stated in the 1972 Water Quality Agreement Act, thus avoiding severe eutrophication of the world's largest supply of fresh water. Vollenweider has been senior scientist since 1973 at the Canada Centre for Inland Waters, Burlington. He has travelled throughout the world on assignments with UNESCO, FAO, WHO and PAHO and directed major programs for preservation of the Adriatic Sea and Lake Maricaibo.   LORRAINE L. JANUS

Volleyball is a team sport played by 6 players on a side. The playing court, 18 m x 9 m, is divided by a centre line. Above the centre line is an extended net placed 2.43 m high for men, and 2.24 m high for women. The goal of the game is to send the ball, according to the regulations, over the net to the floor of the opposite court. Service, initiated within the service zone by the right back player, puts the ball into play. Each team is entitled to contact the ball 3 times (in addition to the touch on the block) to prevent the ball from touching the floor of its own court. Players, except blockers, are not allowed to contact the ball twice consecutively. The ball remains in play until it touches the floor, walls, ceiling, any other object or until a player commits a fault. Points are scored only by the serving team. The team that scores at least 15 points or more, with an advantage of 2 points over its opponent, wins a set (game). The team that wins 3 sets (games) wins the match.

Volleyball was developed in the US in the last decade of the 19th century. As the game developed from being recreational to a highly competitive sport, skills grew more sophisticated and intricate tactics of attack and defence evolved. It is played competitively around the world and has been an Olympic sport since 1964.

Volleyball was introduced to Canada in 1900 through the YMCA, and intercity competitions began shortly after. The Canadian Volleyball Assn was formed in 1953. Championship tour-

naments were launched in eastern Canada and then nationally. Toronto Central Y' Estonians were men's champions 1953-59; Montreal International Y' Latvians were first women's champions (1953). In international competition, Canadian teams qualified for the 1976 and 1984 Olympics. The Canadian men's team scored impressive wins over the world-leading Soviet team in 1984 and later finished fourth at the 1984 Los Angeles Olympics.   LORNE SAWULA

Voltigeurs, light infantry corps recruited in Lower Canada immediately prior to the WAR OF 1812 and commanded by a Canadian major in the British army, Charles de SALABERRY. In Nov 1812 the Voltigeurs, posted first to the Eastern Townships, helped repel an American army. During Oct-Nov 1813 they helped turn back a 2-pronged American advance on Montréal from the west, participating in the battles of Châteauguay and CRYSLER'S FARM. The following spring they returned to the Eastern Townships, and in Aug participated in a feeble attack on Plattsburg, NY. Although the original corps was disbanded 24 Mar 1815, a REGIMENT in today's ARMED FORCES bears its name.   ROY MACLAREN

Von Gencsy, Eva, dancer, choreographer (b at Budapest, Hungary 11 Mar 1924). She trained and performed as a ballet dancer in Hungary and Austria before immigrating to Canada in 1948. As a principal dancer with the Winnipeg (later ROYAL WINNIPEG) Ballet 1948-53 and Les Ballets Chiriaeff in Montréal 1953-57, Von Gencsy contributed to the beginnings of 2 of Canada's 3 major ballet companies. She then turned to jazz as a medium for personal expression, performing and teaching, and in 1972 founding Les BALLETS JAZZ DE MONTRÉAL with Geneviève Salbaing. Her choreography has a distinctive ballet-jazz style for which she is known internationally.   JILLIAN M. OFFICER

Votive Painting The term "ex voto" comes from the Latin *"ex-voto suscepto"* meaning "in pursuance of a vow." It may be used in reference to a painting, a plaque or any object placed in a

Ex-voto painting, *Mme Riverin and her four children* (1703), by D. de Richeterre (*courtesy Basilique-Ste-Anne-de-Beaupré*).

church or chapel to commemorate a vow or to express thanks for a favour received. This practice, a religious gesture made in the face of death or a simple expression of gratitude to the Divinity, has existed since the beginning of time, and was introduced into NEW FRANCE with the arrival of the French colonists. The STE-ANNE-DE-BEAUPRÉ historical museum (across from Ile d'Orléans) houses Canada's largest collection of votive paintings, dedicated to St Anne, the patron saint of sailors. These paintings date back to the 17th and 18th centuries, each telling a particular story.

Congratulatory ex-votos, offered for a favour received, are the most common. They include the *Ex-voto de Saint-François*, the *Ex-voto du Saint-Esprit de Québec*, the *Ex-voto à sainte Anne et à saint Antoine*, the *Ex-voto des cinq naufragês*, the *Ex-voto d'Iberville*, the *Ex-voto de Monsieur Edouin* (all kept at Ste-Anne-de-Beaupré) and the *Ex-voto de l'Aimable Marthe* kept at Notre-Dame-des-Victoires. To attract the protection of the divine power, the donor may offer a propitiary ex-voto before the event, as in the *Ex-voto de Madame Riverin*. Commemorative ex-votos, such as the *Ex-voto de Louis Prat*, serve as a reminder of a past event. Ex-votos may also be offered out of simple devotion. Usually the saint is depicted in the upper part of the painting and the event for which the ex-voto is offered is shown in the lower part. The artist makes no link between the scene and the sacred person, and the 2 parts are often disproportioned.

In the past, votive paintings were sometimes considered of little artistic value and, having lost their significance for priests in charge of pilgrimage sites, many recorded examples have disappeared, including the *Ex-voto de Saint-François* offered by Antoine Lamorille and Capt Pierre d'Astaritz after their ship was dismasted on 29 Sept 1732. Marble plaques began to appear in Canada in the mid-19th century and gradually replaced the ex-voto artworks. Votive paintings conserved today are important not only to our country's history, but also because few examples dating from the 17th and 18th centuries are found elsewhere. NICOLE CLOUTIER

Reading: Ex-voto marins dans le monde de l'antiquité à nos jours (1981); F.M. Gagnon, *Premiers peintres de la Nouvelle-France* (1976); J.R. Harper, *Painting in Canada* (1977).

Voyageur, an adventurer who journeyed by canoe from Montréal to the interior to trade with Indians for furs. At the close of the 17th century, the term was applied to selected COUREURS DE BOIS, hired by Montréal merchants to arrange and sustain trading alliances with Indian bands. The term later included all FUR-TRADE participants: the merchant (BOURGEOIS), his clerk (*commis*) and contracted servants (*engagés*). Today, "voyageur" suggests the romantic image of men paddling the canoes in the fur brigades which traversed much of the continent, living lives of perilous adventure, gruelling labour and boisterous cameraderie. JOHN E. FOSTER

Vulture, large, long-winged, bald-headed BIRD OF PREY, normally abundant in warmer latitudes. Graceful in flight, it glides and circles for extended periods. The one Canadian representative, turkey vulture (*Cathartes aura*), belongs to the family Cathartidae (New World vultures). It breeds from southernmost Canada to southern S America, inhabiting all but heavily forested terrains. Usually, 2 eggs are laid on the ground, among rocks or in caves. Incubation lasts 30-41 days. As carrion feeders, vultures are threatened in most parts of the world by the general decline in numbers of wandering herds of wild and domestic herbivores and by sanitary practices involving the removal or burning of dead animals. R.W. FYFE

Voyageurs at Dawn (1871), by F.A. Hopkins (*courtesy Public Archives of Canada/C-2773*).

W.D. Lawrence, squared-rigged sailing ship built in 1874 in Maitland, NS. It was designed and built by William Dawson Lawrence, who earned substantial profits from the ship until 1883, when he sold it to a Norwegian. Renamed the *Kommander Sven Foyn,* the windjammer continued in profitable service until 1897, when it was stranded in the English Channel. It finished as a barge in West Africa.　　JAMES MARSH

Wacousta; Or, The Prophecy: A Tale of the Canadas, novel by John RICHARDSON, was published in London and Edinburgh in 1832; and in Montréal in 1868, as *Wacousta; Or the Prophecy. An Indian Tale.* Numerous editions appeared under various titles. Many of them were pirated (eg, Waldie's Select Circulating Library edition, Philadelphia, 1833), and many were abridged. Richardson frames his novel within PONTIAC's 1763 seige of forts Detroit and Michilimackinac, but at the story's centre is the gory and protracted development of Wacousta's revenge upon the British commander, Colonel De Haldimar, who had betrayed Wacousta by marrying his fiancée years earlier in Scotland. Wacousta (formerly a fellow soldier and friend of De Haldimar) is a Herculean savage, made monstrous by his bitterness, who advises Pontiac in his plans to capture the forts. The novel is at once a Gothic romance and a blood-soaked tragedy. *Wacousta's* complex publishing and editing history, and the story of Richardson's tortured life as well, have interested as many critics and bibliographers as has the novel itself. *Wacousta* was translated into German in 1858.　　NEIL BESNER

Waddington, Geoffrey, conductor, administrator (b at Leicester, Eng 23 Sept 1904; d at Toronto 3 Jan 1966). He learned the violin while growing up in Lethbridge, Alta, where he made his conducting debut before age 12. Waddington joined the Toronto Conservatory's faculty in 1922, simultaneously beginning a career as a radio musician. He joined the CBC in 1947, founded the CBC Symphony Orchestra in 1952 and remained its music director until 1964. In this most influential position, he continuously sought out the country's best performing talent for national and international exposure and regularly commissioned new music from Canadian composers.　　BARCLAY MCMILLAN

Waddington, Miriam, née Dworkin (b at Winnipeg 3 Dec 1917). Educated in Ottawa, Toronto and Philadelphia, Waddington joined the faculty at York U in 1964 after many years as a social worker. She has published 11 books of poetry (including *Driving Home,* 1972; *The Visitants,* 1981) and one collection of short fiction (*Summer at Lonely Beach and Other Stories,* 1982). Author of a critical study of A.M. KLEIN (1970) and editor of *The Collected Poems of A.M. Klein* (1974), she has also edited a critical study of John SUTHERLAND. Writing out of her Russian Jewish secular tradition, she has a highly lyrical voice, speaking simply and honestly. Waddington has fought for her place in Canadian letters: she has successfully transferred the 2 strikes against her, being female and Jewish, into powerful, optimistic forces in her poetry and fiction. SHARON DRACHE

Waddington, Mount, elev 3994 m, the highest mountain in BC's COAST MTS, rises near the head of Knight Inlet, 282 km NW of Vancouver. Standing only 39 km from the tidewater, it nourishes at least 5 valley glaciers over 16 km long. Known earlier as Mystery Mt, it was named after English-born industrialist Alfred Waddington, whose dream of a road to the Cariboo goldfields went unrealized. The main summit was climbed 1933 by F. Weissner and W. House.　　GLEN BOLES

Waffle, a group established in 1969 as a caucus within the NEW DEMOCRATIC PARTY. Its members' choice of name was self-consciously ironic. It issued a Manifesto for an Independent Socialist

Canada that demanded that Canadian public ownership replace American private ownership; subsequent Waffle statements called for Québec's right to self-determination and for an independent Canadian labour movement. Its politics were militantly socialist and nationalist, a Canadian manifestation of widespread and diverse political ferment, which included opposition to the war in Vietnam, the support of NEW LEFT politics on the campuses of N America and Europe, and a burgeoning women's movement. University professors Mel Watkins and James Laxer were the Waffle's national leaders; in 1971 Laxer was the runner-up to David LEWIS for the leadership of the federal NDP. The Waffle was also organized provincially, particularly in Ontario and Saskatchewan. Purged from the Ontario NDP in 1972, it became a separate political group. It disintegrated in 1974, except for a surviving remnant in Saskatchewan. Many of its members slowly drifted back into the NDP.　　MEL WATKINS

Wage and Price Controls are comprehensive government restrictions on the maximum rate at which wages and prices may increase during a specified time period. Wage and price controls can be distinguished from other types of government price and wage intervention by 2 characteristics. First, they are adopted for the purpose of controlling overall INFLATION, rather than to achieve some specific economic efficiency or economic equity goal (in contrast, for example, to minimum wage legislation). Second, they affect many sectors of the economy rather than focusing on one particular market, unlike programs such as agricultural price supports. Controls are a type of incomes policy (ie, any government policy that has a direct effect on overall price and wage setting in the economy). Other examples of incomes policy include voluntary wage and price guidelines and tax incentives to encourage lower rates of increase.

Many nations, including Canada, instituted a system of both price controls and rationing during WWII to prevent the profiteering and skyrocketing prices that might otherwise have resulted from wartime shortages (*see* WARTIME PRICES AND TRADE BOARD). These measures were largely abandoned in the postwar era. However, during the 1950s and 1960s a number of European countries experimented with income-policy interventions, including wage and price controls. Controls were primarily used as an attempt to combat inflation, and stimulative monetary and fiscal policies were used to reduce unemployment. The experiences with this type of policy combination were largely unsuccessful. The buoyant demand conditions created by high money-supply growth rates and various government spending and taxation initiatives either made the controls themselves unworkable and ineffective or created substantial latent

inflationary pressure that was manifested when controls were finally lifted. This was also largely the fate of an American trial with controls in the early 1970s.

Subsequently, economists have realized that if controls are to be successful, they must be viewed as a complement to, rather than a substitute for, restrictive monetary and fiscal policy. While high inflation can eventually be controlled by significant lowering of money-supply growth rates, the process may be long and may involve painfully high UNEMPLOYMENT. Controls are seen by some economists as a means of overcoming the strong momentum of high price and wage increases and hence easing the transition to lower inflation.

Canada's only experience in peacetime with controls occurred 1975-78 in response to the exceptionally high inflation rates of 1974-75. The federal Anti-Inflation Act established a 3-year controls system. Wage guidelines were binding on all firms with 500 or more employees, on all federal employees, and (with the agreement of the majority of provincial governments) on most other public-sector employees. Profit-margin controls restricted the price and cost markups of large firms. Although the magnitude of the effect of the legislation is debatable, empirical analysis has generally supported the claim that the controls program did reduce inflation below the level that otherwise would have prevailed.　　R.G. WIRICK

Wagner, Barbara, figure skater (b at Toronto 5 May 1938). Wagner and partner Robert PAUL formed the outstanding Canadian figure skating team that dominated the international pairs event 1957-62. They started skating together in 1952 in Toronto. In their first international experience at the 1956 Cortina Olympics they placed sixth. Following the retirement of Canada's Frances Defoe and Norris Bowden, they won the Canadian, N American and world championships in 1957. They performed flawlessly in winning the 1960 Squaw Valley, Calif, Olympics pairs event; all 7 judges awarded them first place. As professionals, they skated with ice shows until Wagner's marriage in 1964. She became a coach and teacher, serving as principal coach of the Ice Follies.　　BARBARA SCHRODT

Wagner, Claude, lawyer, judge, politician (b at Shawinigan, Qué 4 Apr 1925; d at Montréal 11 July 1979). At first active in legal circles as a crown prosecutor, professor of criminal law and judge in the Sessions Court, he confirmed his reputation as a staunch advocate of "law and order" while serving as minister of justice in Jean LESAGE's administration (1964-66). Elected in a 1964 provincial by-election (Montréal-Verdun), he resigned in 1970 to become again a judge in the Sessions Court. He was elected Progressive Conservative MP for St-Hyacinthe in the federal elections of 1972 and 1974, and ran for the PC leadership in 1976, coming second to Joe CLARK. He resigned his seat in Apr 1978 when named to the Senate.　　DANIEL LATOUCHE

Wainwright, Alta, Town, pop 4266 (1981c), inc 1910, is located 200 km SE of Edmonton. Originally called Denwood, it became a railway divisional point 1908 and was named for William Wainwright, VP of the Grand Trunk Pacific Ry. It developed as the administrative and distributing centre of an extensive farming area. Oil and gas were discovered 1922 and are piped from some 400 wells. In 1909 Buffalo National Pk was established nearby, but the bison were moved elsewhere and the park was converted to CFB Camp Wainwright during WWII. A few bison were returned in 1980. The Wainwright Museum features a reconstructed post office (*c*1900), and an early oil rig is preserved in Petroleum Pk. The weekly newspaper is the Wainwright *Star-Chronicle.*　　ERIC J. HOLMGREN

Walbran, John Thomas, ship's officer, historian, writer (b at Ripon, Eng 23 Mar 1848; d at Victoria 31 Mar 1913). He sailed the seas of the world until 1888, when he joined the coastal service of the Canadian Pacific Navigation Co. Three years later he became captain of the Canadian government steamship *Quadra* and travelled the BC coast, 1891-1903, engaged in fisheries protection and lighthouse supply. Walbran's *British Columbia Coast Names* (1909, repr 1971), as well as a directory of PLACE-NAMES, is a rich store of information on ships, fur traders, explorers and missionaries. ERIC J. HOLMGREN

Walkem, George Anthony, lawyer, judge, politician, premier of BC (b at Newry, Ire 15 Nov 1834; d at Victoria 13 Jan 1908). Educated in the Province of Canada, Walkem moved to BC in 1862, was a member of the colonial Legislative Council (1864-70) and after 1871 sat in the provincial legislature. Associated with Amor DE COSMOS in the Confederation League before BC joined CONFEDERATION, he became attorney general in De Cosmos's Cabinet and succeeded him as premier. The 2 Walkem administrations (1874-76 and 1878-82) were dominated by the struggle with Ottawa over the failure to begin the Pacific railway in the time set out in the terms of union. Walkem led the fight with vigour but with an irascibility that forfeited him community support once construction of the CPR began. He ended his career as a justice of the Supreme Court of British Columbia (1882-1904). H. KEITH RALSTON AND BETTY WILCOX

Walker, Sir Byron Edmund, banker (b in Haldimand County, Canada W 14 Oct 1848; d in Toronto 27 Mar 1924). With little education, Walker took 18 years to rise from a discount clerk to general manager of the Canadian Bank of Commerce in 1886; he was president 1907-24. He showed great organizational talent in developing the first set of written regulations for dividing a bank into the complex array of departments that have come to characterize modern banking. His greatest public notice came in 1911 when, although a Liberal, he opposed the policy of RECIPROCITY with the US announced by the Laurier government, because it would weaken ties with Great Britain. Thus began the surge of IMPERIALISM that led to the defeat of the trade agreement and the government. Walker had helped to found *The Round Table Quarterly* (1910) to promote discussion of imperial issues. A man of wide interests, he was an adviser to the National Gallery, a founder of the CHAMPLAIN SOCIETY, and a fellow of the Royal Society. D.N. SPRAGUE

Walker, David Harry, army officer, novelist (b at Dundee, Scot 9 Feb 1911). Raised in Scotland and England, Walker was aide-de-camp to Canadian Gov Gen John BUCHAN 1938-39, a POW in Europe 1940-45, and comptroller to the viceroy of India 1946-47. A major with an MBE, he retired in 1948 to write full-time in St Andrews, NB. The popular *Geordie* (1950) tells of a small Scottish boy who takes a body-building course and wins an Olympic gold medal. *The Pillar* (Gov Gen's Award 1952) depicts POW life. *Digby* (Gov Gen's Award 1953) tells how a weary N American tycoon is rejuvenated during a Rabelaisian visit to Scotland. *Where the High Winds Blow* (1960) portrays the rise of an entrepreneur in the Canadian North, while NB settings dominate *Mallabec* (1965), *Pirate Rock* (1969) and *Ash* (1976). *Black Dougal* (1973), an adventure thriller, is in part set in Québec, while *The Lord's Pink Ocean* (1972) portrays the survivors of a worldwide biochemical disaster. His 19 books include 5 for children and adolescents. JOHN R. SORFLEET

Walker, Edmund Murton, entomologist (b at Windsor, Ont 5 Oct 1877; d at Toronto 14 Feb 1969). After studies in natural sciences and medicine at Toronto, Walker studied in Berlin, then joined the dept of biology at U of T (1904), retiring in 1948, as head of zoology since 1934. He was largely responsible for the extensive invertebrate collection of the ROYAL ONTARIO MUSEUM, founding the collection in 1914 and serving as assistant director 1918-31 and honorary director 1931-69. His many publications include a 3-vol treatise on the Odonata of Canada and Alaska and editorship of the *Canadian Entomologist* (1910-20). His discovery with T.B. Kurata of "ice-bugs" (*Grylloblatta*) on Sulphur Mt, Alta (1913), resulted in the naming of a new order of insects (*see* ICE-WORM). He served many local and international nature, zoological and entomological associations in various capacities, and was honoured by the RSC's Flavelle Medal (1960). MARTIN K. McNICHOLL

Walker, Hiram, distiller, businessman (b at East Douglas, Mass 4 July 1816; d at Detroit, Mich 12 Jan 1899). Though Walker lived in Canada for only 5 years (1859-64), he built a distillery, a new town and a major railway line. In 1856 he began buying land around what became Walkerville (now part of Windsor, Ont) and in 1859 built the Windsor Distillery and Flouring Mill, which produced high-quality, refined, branded whiskies. By 1910 Walker's Canadian Club Whisky, introduced in 1884, had become Canada's top export whisky. Walker's business interests included wheat and flour trade with the US, hog and cattle fattening and the development of the Lk Erie, Essex and Detroit River Ry, completed in 1885 and providing transportation for Essex County produce and lumber to the American market. DON SPENCER
Reading: William F. Rannie, *Canadian Whisky* (1976).

Walker, Horatio, painter (b at Listowel, Canada W 12 May 1858; d at Ste-Pétronille, Qué 21 Sept 1938). A member of the Canadian Art Club from 1908, Walker painted habitant on Ile d'Orléans, Qué. He received his early training at Toronto's Notman-Fraser photographic studios before moving to the US. By the mid-1880s he was spending his winters in New York and his summers at Ile d'Orléans. His interpretation of Québec farm life is extremely sentimental and reminiscent in style of the French Barbizon painter Jean-François Millet. In a thick, brown impasto, the paintings depict the pious life of toiling peasants, set against glowing skies. This American Barbizon style brought Walker high prices for paintings such as *Oxen Drinking* (1899), many medals and awards, and a reputation during his lifetime as one of Canada's senior painters. DOROTHY FARR

Walker, James, policeman, businessman (b at Carluke, Canada W 14 Apr 1848; d at Calgary 31 Mar 1936). He joined the NWMP in 1874 and was given command of the Battleford (Sask) detachment in 1879. While there he served as Indian agent and was the first civilian justice in the North-West Territories. In 1880 he resigned and in 1883 began a successful sawmill and lumber business in Calgary. He chaired the committee that secured Calgary's incorporation (1884), and served on school and hospital boards. He organized provincial boy scout and cadet corps, and the 238th Forestry Battalion during WWI. At Calgary's centennial (1975), Walker was named "Citizen of the Century" for his outstanding service. ROBERT M. STAMP

Walking Buffalo, Tatânga Mânî, or George McLean, Stoney leader, Indian statesman, philosopher (b in Bow R Valley near Morley, Alta 20 Mar 1871; d at Banff, Alta 26 Dec 1967). Walking Buffalo was present at the signing of Treaty No 7 (1877) and became the most famous protégé of the Methodist missionaries John McDOUGALL and John McLEAN. He witnessed the disappearance of the BISON, the building of the CPR and the evolution of tribal lands into provinces. Educated at the McDougall Orphanage at Morley and in Red Deer and Winnipeg, he worked briefly as a blacksmith and as a scout for the NWMP, then as an interpreter. He was councillor for the Bearspaw band of the Stoney Indians 1907-12 and chief 1912-16. Active in the Banff Indian Days and the CALGARY STAMPEDE, Walking Buffalo was a leader in the Morley United Church. Attracted to the moral rearmament movement in 1934, he was an ambassador for world peace until his death. IAN A.L. GETTY

Wallace, William Stewart, librarian, editor, historian (b at Georgetown, Ont 23 June 1884; d at Toronto 11 Mar 1970). He was educated at Toronto and Oxford and served in WWI as major in the CEF, battalion adjutant and commanding officer of Khaki College, Shorncliffe. He became assistant librarian at U of T in 1920 and was librarian 1923-54. He was general editor of the university program of scholarly publishing 1923-32 and though he served in a number of capacities in library affairs and teaching, he spent the greater part of his time editing and writing. He was the first editor of the CANADIAN HISTORICAL REVIEW (1920-30) and made it the chief vehicle for historians in English Canada. He was editor of the CHAMPLAIN SOCIETY 1923-43 and honorary editor of the Royal Society of Canada 1937-45. His *The Dictionary of Canadian Biography* (1926) was enlarged 1945 and revised under the title *The Macmillan Dictionary of Canadian Biography* (1963). He was general editor and wrote most of the articles for the *Encyclopedia of Canada* (6 vols, 1935-37). These reference works were of inestimable value in Canadian studies. In all, Wallace published more than 30 books and hundreds of articles. After retiring at age 70, he was proprietor of Dora Hood's Book Room. He was distinguished and honoured in both his fields and in his own mind drew no distinction between them. ROBERT H. BLACKBURN

Wallaceburg, Ont, Town, pop 11 506 (1981c), inc 1875 (village), 1896 (town), located on Sydenham R, 53 km S of Sarnia. Settled in the 1830s, it was likely named for Scottish patriot Sir William Wallace. Lumbering was the basis of its early economy. As it was connected by water to the Great Lakes, steamboat building also became important. At the end of the 19th century, logging declined and the town became known for its glass manufacturing and sugar-beet industry. Glass products still highlight the local economy, along with metal goods, plastics and auto accessories. DANIEL FRANCIS

Walleye (*Stizostedion vitreum vitreum*), moderately large, predatory, freshwater FISH of the family Percidae (order Perciformes). Other common names include yellow walleye, pickerel, yellow pickerel, pikeperch, doré or doré jaune. Walleyes should not be confused with true PICKERELS, family Esocidae. Walleyes have a bluntly pointed head, a mouth well armed with teeth, 2 dorsal fins (the first with sharp spines, the second without). Their eyes are specially adapted to low light intensities. Walleyes are bright golden to brownish green, with darker markings; the lower tip of the caudal fin is milk white. They occur in fresh waters from the mouth of the Mackenzie R to near the Gulf of Mexico. In Canada they are found from southern Québec to northeastern BC and N to the mouth of the

Walleye (*Stizostedion vitreum vitreum*), probably the most economically important fish in Canada's inland waters (*courtesy National Museums of Canada/National Museum of Natural Sciences*).

Mackenzie R. Walleyes are adapted to prey on other fishes. This is probably the most economically important species of fish in Canada's inland waters, being prized summer and winter for its delicious white flesh. The closely related sauger (*S. canadense*) is somewhat smaller and has a more restricted range (Québec to Alberta). It is also a popular sport fish.   E.J. CROSSMAN

Walnut (*Juglans*), genus of TREES of the walnut family (Juglandaceae). The roughly 15 known species are widely dispersed through temperate and tropical regions. The 2 species native to Canada (butternut and black walnut) are found only in the East. Walnuts average 20-30 m high and have horizontally spreading branches. The large, compound leaves consist of 15-23 leaflets. The edible kernel, enclosed in a leathery or woody hull, is used as a table nut, for flavouring desserts (eg, ice cream) and for walnut oil. A yellow dye may also be obtained from the fresh bark and from the husk of the fruit itself. Walnuts, usually in scattered stands, may grow in dry areas, but prefer fertile, moist, well-drained soil. They are particularly common in shallow valleys and in alluvial plains bordering waterways. The hard, lustrous dark wood, used primarily for veneer, cabinetmaking, panelling and boat building, was common in pioneer times, but is now rare.   ESTELLE LACOURSIÈRE

Walrus (*Odobenus rosmarus*), massive, seallike MAMMAL with disproportionately small head and huge neck. The feet are flippers, and hind feet can be turned forward for movement ashore. Upper canines project downward as tusks up to 36 cm long. A mass of quill-like whiskers appears on the muzzle. Males average 3 m in length and 900 kgs in weight; females are 9% shorter and 16% lighter. The skin is thick, much folded and creased, with a sparse coat of coarse hair. The colour is cinnamon to grey, with pink in the folds and on the abdomen. There is a thick blubber layer. Walrus, generally associated with the ice edge and arctic seas of 40 m or less in depth, occur from Siberia to Greenland, but in Canada are confined to the eastern Arctic. They feed on invertebrates (primarily bivalves and molluscs). Some males take to killing seals and may scavenge. Breeding is polygamous, occurring Jan-Mar. Gestation is 15-16 months and most births occur from mid-Apr to June; nursing continues for over a year and, at most, pups are produced in alternate years. The killer whale is the only serious predator. European whalers almost exterminated walrus between 1650 and 1850, and there has been only partial recovery. About 500 are taken by Canadian Inuit annually, formerly for dog food, now mainly for ivory. *See* ENDANGERED ANIMALS.
    IAN McTAGGART COWAN

Walsh, James Morrow, police officer, territorial commissioner (b at Prescott, Canada W 1843; d at Brockville, Ont 25 July 1905). As inspector in the North-West Mounted Police 1873-83, he dealt firmly but fairly with SITTING BULL and his followers, who had crossed into Canada in 1876 after the defeat of Custer at Little Bighorn (Montana), and he became friendly with the Sioux chief. In 1883 he established the Dominion Coke, Coal and Transportation Co in Winnipeg. With the onset of the KLONDIKE GOLD RUSH he returned to the force as superintendent and was appointed commissioner of the Yukon District 1897-98.   ERIC J. HOLMGREN

Walter, Arnold Maria, musicologist, educator, administrator (b at Hannsdorf, Moravia 30 Aug 1902; d at Toronto 6 Oct 1973). Immigrating to Canada in 1937, Walter became one of the most farsighted and influential leaders of Canadian MUSIC EDUCATION, effective in establishing programs to develop both musical talent and audiences receptive to it. In 1946 he established an opera school at the Toronto Conservatory. Under

his direction (1952-68), the faculty of music at U of T attained international stature, its research library one of the continent's most comprehensive.   BARCLAY McMILLAN

Walton, Dorothy Louise, née McKenzie, badminton player (b at Swift Current, Sask 7 Aug 1909; d at Toronto 17 Oct 1981). An outstanding all-round athlete at U of Sask, she earned her BA and MA degrees before moving to Ontario in 1932. From 1936 to 1940 she dominated Canadian women's badminton and was never ranked below sixth in tennis. Her career culminated in her winning the All-England Badminton Championship in 1939 and being acclaimed world champion; no other Canadian has won that title.   JOHN J. JACKSON

Wampum, made of white and purple Atlantic coast seashells, had considerable value to Indians in eastern Canada for ornament and ceremony and to non-Indians for currency, particularly in the 17th and 18th centuries. Wampum was threaded on string or woven into belts and sashes. Particular patterns symbolized events, alliances and people, and wampum was used to form relationships, propose marriage, atone for murder or ransom captives. Wampum was closely linked with the FUR TRADE in eastern Canada, where it was used as a trade good. Before Confederation, 1867, some Indian groups indicated their assent to certain INDIAN TREATIES by presenting wampum to crown officials.
    RENÉ R. GADACZ

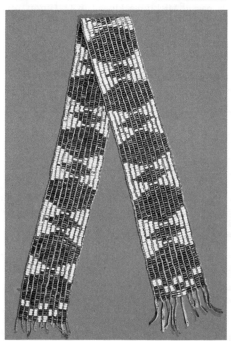

Wampum belt (*courtesy National Museums of Canada/National Museum of Man/S75-620*).

Wangersky, Peter John, oceanographer (b at Woonsocket, RI 26 Aug 1927; naturalized Canadian 1975). Substantial contributions to OCEANOGRAPHY in Canada have come from Wangersky's research and teaching in chemical and biological oceanography. His degree in chemistry and subsequent work at the Scripps Inst, U Calif, and with the US Fish and Wildlife Service equipped Wangersky for further study at Yale. After positions at Miami and Yale, he joined Dalhousie as professor of chemistry in 1965, and then moved to the fledgling Institute of Oceanography in 1968, serving as chairman of the department and director of the institute 1977-80. His major research has illuminated patterns of distribution and dynamics of organic carbon in the sea. A sustained interest in theoretical ecology began with pioneer work on time lags in

population equations and has led to novel analyses of marine communities. His former students are widely placed in universities and government laboratories.   IAN A. McLAREN

Wapiti (*Cervus elaphus*), largest-bodied, most highly evolved Old World DEER, is also known as the American elk. Its name is Shawnee for "white rump." Wapiti came to N America via BERINGIA late in the Ice Ages, but expanded their range and population only after the extinction of the American megafauna about 11 000 years ago. By 1835 they had disappeared from their eastern range (Ont and Qué). Locally (Man to the Peace R district and eastern BC), they remain common and an important game animal. Although valued for its hide by native people, the wapiti was not a favourite food animal and played no great role in aboriginal economics. Wapiti are social, tending towards life in open terrain. Males and females segregate, with females maximizing security from predation and bulls maximizing access to forage. Stags are larger than hinds. In rut, bulls advertise with loud, clear buglings (the most vocal deer in Canada), and by soaking themselves with urine. Females form harems around dominant bulls. The gestation period is relatively long, some 240 days; calves are born in June. Wapiti have been domesticated in Siberia and China where the antlers are used for medicinal purposes.
    VALERIUS GEIST

War Measures Act, statute (1914) conferring emergency powers on the federal Cabinet, allowing it to govern by decree when it perceives the existence of "war, invasion or insurrection, real or apprehended." The Act was proclaimed in force, with detailed regulations limiting the freedom of Canadians, during both world wars. More limited emergency legislation, the offshoot of War Measures, was applied during demobilization after WWII, and during and after the Korean War in the 1950s. The only use of the War Measures Act in a domestic crisis occurred in Oct and Nov 1970 when a state of "apprehended insurrection" was declared to exist in Québec and emergency regulations were proclaimed in response to 2 kidnappings by the terrorist FRONT DE LIBÉRATION DU QUÉBEC (*see* OCTOBER CRISIS). Afterwards PM Pierre Trudeau pledged to refine and limit the application of the Act in internal crises, but by 1984 the emergency powers Act had not been modified (*see* PEACE, ORDER AND GOOD GOVERNMENT).   DENIS SMITH

War of the Austrian Succession, 1739-48, actually 2 wars, one fought in Europe, the other, also known as King George's War, fought in the colonies. Between 1713 and 1739 French overseas trade had increased astronomically, while that of Britain stagnated. Particularly at issue was trade with the Spanish Empire, which France dominated. Britain, determined to oust the French from this vast market, declared war on Spain (the so-called War of Jenkins's Ear) on 19 Oct 1739. War with France would quickly have followed but for the outbreak of hostilities between the continental powers in Europe upon the accession in Oct 1740 of Maria Theresa to the Imperial Habsburg (Austrian) throne.

Britain and France were drawn into this conflict on opposing sides. It proved a disaster for both. A British army was soundly defeated 11 May 1745 at Fontenoy, Flanders (now in Belgium), by the French and driven off the continent. Overseas, French maritime trade was eventually ruined by the Royal Navy, and Canadian war parties ravaged British frontier settlements in NS, NY and New England. A combined British-New England expedition captured LOUISBOURG in June, but the Anglo-American force was no more able to conquer Canada than the Canadians were able to conquer New England. In May-June 1748 the

Treaty of Aix-la-Chapelle (now Aachen, W Germany) ended the war but settled nothing. Britain exchanged Louisbourg for Madras, India, which went to France. The Netherlands were ceded to Austria, and Silesia to Prussia. The powers were all dissatisfied with their respective allies, and so made changes: on the eve of the SEVEN YEARS' WAR Prussia was allied with Britain, Austria with France. W.J. ECCLES

War of the Spanish Succession (Queen Anne's War), 1702-13, was a general European war that also involved the colonies of the major powers. The war was caused by conflicting claims to the Spanish throne after the death of the childless King Charles II. The accession of the grandson of King Louis XIV of France to the Spanish throne as Philip V antagonized England and Holland, which were in growing commercial competition with France, and Holy Roman Emperor Leopold I, who had claimed the succession on behalf of his son.

European war broke out in 1702, with Holland, England and most of the German states aligned against France, Spain, Bavaria, Portugal and Savoy. The conflict spilled over into the N American colonies of France and England, as ACADIA and New England exchanged bloody local raids. French forces destroyed the English settlement at Bonavista, Nfld, in 1704 and captured St John's in 1708. The English gained control of PORT-ROYAL and with it Acadia in 1710, but the following year a British fleet was wrecked in the St Lawrence in an abortive attempt to sail on Québec. The TREATY OF UTRECHT (1713) settled a number of succession disputes between England and France and granted considerable territory to England; France retained Île St-Jean [PEI] and Île Royale [Cape Breton], but ceded Acadia and Newfoundland to the English and restored to them the Hudson Bay drainage basin. The treaty is generally acknowledged as marking the end of French expansion and signalling the rise of the British Empire. JAMES A. OGILVY

War of 1812 On 18 June 1812, at the height of the Napoleonic conflict, the US declared war on Great Britain and struck at the only British possession on the continent: Canada. Most of the battles that followed took place along the international border. The war ended in stalemate. The TREATY OF GHENT, signed 24 Dec 1814, solved nothing, since the reasons for the war — British high-handedness on the high seas, including searching American ships during the Napoleonic blockade and IMPRESSMENT — had been rendered academic by France's defeat. Yet Canada owes its present shape to negotiations that grew out of the peace, while the war itself — or the myths created by the war — gave Canadians their first sense of community.

The British and Canadians were badly outnumbered by the Americans but better prepared for war, thanks to the prescience of Maj-Gen Isaac BROCK, administrator of Upper Canada. If the enemy could move up the traditional Champlain-Richelieu invasion route, seize Montréal and cut the lifeline between Upper and Lower Canada, the war would be as good as over. Brock thought this impossible because his Indian allies, under the Shawnee war chief TECUMSEH, had the American NW frontier in a ferment. The Americans would thus first try to secure their left flank. The bloodless British capture of a key US post at Michilimackinac I in Lk Huron, on July 16, and of Detroit, Aug 6, frustrated that strategy and gave the British control of Michigan territory and the Upper Mississippi. At this point Thomas Jefferson's remark that the capture of Canada was "a mere matter of marching" returned to haunt Washington. Having lost one army at Detroit, the Americans lost another at QUEENSTON Heights, Oct 13, after their militia

stood on its constitutional guarantee and refused to cross into Canada. But Brock was killed — an irreparable loss. A new American army under William Henry Harrison struggled up from Kentucky to try to retake Detroit. One wing was so badly mauled at Frenchtown, 22 Jan 1813, by a force of British, Canadians and Indians under Lt-Col Henry Procter, that further attempts at invasion that winter were abandoned. The only Americans in Canada were prisoners of war.

British strategy was to act defensively and allow the invaders to make mistakes. Gov Sir George Prevost husbanded his thin forces carefully, a sensible precaution given the US's overwhelming numerical superiority. As the campaign of 1813 opened, the invaders determined to seize Kingston to cut the link between the Canadas. But a weakness of resolve diverted the attack to the lesser prize of York [Toronto]. The Americans briefly occupied the town, burning the public buildings and seizing valuable naval supplies destined for Lk Erie; but the British, by burning their half-completed warship, frustrated the enemy's plan to appropriate it and change the balance of naval power on Lk Ontario. Neither side totally controlled that lake for the balance of the war. The Americans abandoned York and on 27 May 1813 their fleet seized Ft George at the mouth of the Niagara R. The British army escaped, however, repulsing the advance of the enemy up the Niagara peninsula by winning the battles of Stoney Creek and Beaver Dams, and driving the Americans back into the enclave of the fort. For all of that season the Niagara peninsula was a no-man's-land of marauding parties. Finally, worn down by sickness, desertion, and the departure of short-term soldiers, the American command evacuated Ft George on Dec 10 and quit Canada. On leaving, the militia burned the town of Newark [NIAGARA-ON-THE LAKE], an act that drove

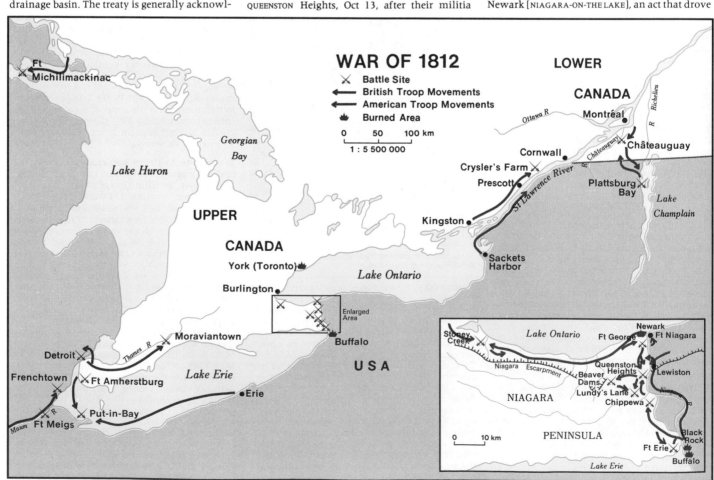

WAR OF 1812

✕ Battle Site
← British Troop Movements
← American Troop Movements
♔ Burned Area

0 50 100 km

1 : 5 500 000

the British to brutal retaliation at Buffalo. These incendiary reprisals continued until Washington itself was burned the following Aug.

The US fared better on the western flank. The British tried and failed to take Harrison's stronghold at Ft Meigs on the Maumee R. A struggle for control of Lk Erie followed. The 2 rival fleets, both built of green lumber on the spot, met Sept 10 at PUT-IN-BAY. The British were hampered by the American seizure of naval supplies at York the previous spring and by the loss, early in the battle, of several senior officers. American commodore Oliver Hazard Perry, a bold seaman, used unorthodox tactics to turn defeat into victory and become the first man in history to capture an entire British fleet. Erie became an American lake, Detroit was abandoned, and the British retreated up the Thames R. At Moraviantown Harrison defeated Procter. Tecumseh died in the battle, an event signalling the end of the northwestern Indian alliance. But Harrison, his lines extended, could not follow up his victory; his Kentuckians were eager to get back to their farms at harvest time.

Meanwhile the US was mounting a 2-pronged attack designed to take Montréal, but this was so halfhearted that it was foredoomed to failure. On the Châteauguay R on Oct 27, a handful of French Canadian VOLTIGEURS under Lt-Col Charles de SALABERRY drove an American army of 4000 back across the border. At CRYSLER'S FARM (near Morrisburg, Ont) on Nov 11, Lt-Col Joseph Wanton Morrison's regulars won a resounding victory over James Wilkinson's superior force, which also quit Canada. Thus the 1813 campaign ended with the Americans in possession of Ft AMHERSTBURG on the Detroit R, and the British holding the 2 American forts, Niagara and Michilimackinac.

The following year the Americans again crossed the Niagara, seized Ft Erie on July 3, and defeated the British at Chippewa on July 5, but failed to retake Ft George. The bitter battle of LUNDY'S LANE followed on July 25 within earshot of the Niagara cataract. Fought in the pitch dark of a sultry night by exhausted troops who could not tell friend from foe, it ended in stalemate. The Americans withdrew to Ft Erie. Here they badly mauled the forces of the new British commander, Lt-Gen Gordon DRUMMOND, when he attempted a night attack (Aug 14-15). With both sides exhausted a 3-month standoff followed. Finally, on Nov 5, the Americans again withdrew. Meanwhile, NS Lt-Gov Sir John SHERBROOKE led a force from Halifax into Maine, capturing Castine on Sept 3. By mid-month British forces held much of Maine, which was returned to the US only with the signing of the peace treaty.

In the west, the Canadian voyageurs took Prairie du Chien on the Upper Mississippi and beat off an American attack on Michilimackinac I, capturing 2 warships on Lk Huron. In the east, the story was different. With Napoleon defeated, the British army now outnumbered the thin American force at Plattsburg on Lk Champlain. Prevost marched S with 11 000 of Wellington's veterans but his hesitancy to attack — he was no Brock — together with the Sept 11 defeat of the hastily built British fleet in Plattsburg Bay by the American commodore, Thomas MacDonough, caused Prevost to abort the ground attack and withdraw. That single action tipped the scales, forcing the British peace negotiators at Ghent to lower their demands and accept the status quo. Had Prevost succeeded, much of upper NY state might be Canadian today. On the other hand, if the Americans had won the battle of Stoney Creek, or taken Montréal, much of Ontario and Québec — perhaps all — might now be under the Stars and Stripes.

Washington had expected the largely American population of Upper Canada to throw off the British yoke as soon as its army crossed the

border. This did not happen. Lured northwards by free land and low taxes, the settlers wanted to be left alone. Nor was it wise after such a bitter war to advocate American political ideals, such as democracy and republicanism. Thus the British and LOYALIST elite were able to set Canadians on a different course from that of their former enemy. And the growing belief that they, the civilian soldiers, and not the Indians and British regulars, had won the war — more mythic than real — helped to germinate the seeds of nationalism in the Canadas. *See* NIAGARA HISTORIC FRONTIER; FORT HENRY.   PIERRE BERTON

Reading: Pierre Berton, *The Invasion of Canada* (1980) and *Flames Across the Border* (1981); G.F.G. Stanley, *The War of 1812* (1983).

Warbler, name applied to several groups of BIRDS, primarily the New World wood warblers (family Emberizidae), and Old World warblers (Muscicapidae) of which only 2 species commonly breed in Canada (*see* KINGLET). About 37 of the approximately 115 species of wood warbler nest in Canada. Many have bright yellow plumage which gives them the name wild canary, a term also applied to American goldfinches (*Carduelis tristis*). In spring males are usually brightly coloured; females have duller plumages, as do males in fall. Warblers are mostly small, active birds. Their sharp, pointed bills are ideal for probing for insect prey, though some species also catch insects by aerial pursuit. Flycatchers often have flatter bills with bristles at the base. Exceptions to the usual cup-shaped nests in shrubs and forks of trees include the dome-shaped ground nest of the ovenbird (*Seiurus aurocapillus*); the hole nest of the prothonotary warbler (*Protonotaria citrea*); and the hanging, lichen-based nest of the northern parula (*Parula americana*). The brown-headed cowbird (*Molothrus ater*), a significant brood parasite of several species, poses a significant threat to the rare Kirtland's warbler (*Dendroica kirtlandii*). Several species have evolved mechanisms which reduce cowbird parasitism, eg, the well-known habit of the yellow warbler (*D. petechia*) of building new nests on top of old. In Canada wood warblers are widespread, breeding virtually everywhere S of the TREELINE and forming spectacular mixed-species flocks during migration, especially in the East. Most Canadian breeding species belong to genus *Dendroica*. Kirtland's warbler, until recently thought to breed only in a restricted area of Michigan, is now believed to nest in Ontario and possibly Québec. Two other widespread genera of several species are *Vermivora* and *Oporornis*, the latter known as "skulkers" of low brush. The creeperlike black-and-white warbler (*Mniotilta varia*), the black-masked, marsh-dwelling common yellowthroat (*Geothlypis trichas*), the flycatching American redstart (*Setophaga ruticilla*), the thrushlike, ground-dwelling ovenbird, the northern waterthrush (*Seiurus noveboracensis*) and 2 species of *Wilsonia* are also widespread. More restricted breeders include Louisiana waterthrush (*Seiurus motacilla*) and prothonotary and hooded warblers (*Wilsonia citrina*) of S Ontario, northern parula of southern Manitoba E through the Maritimes, yellow-breasted chat (*Icteria virens*) of S Ontario and local valleys of southern BC, Alberta and Saskatchewan. Warblers' insectivorous diets make them economically important to humans, especially species which help to control spruce budworm.   MARTIN K. MCNICHOLL

Warburton, Alexander Bannerman, historian, politician, premier of PEI (b at Charlottetown 5 Apr 1852; d there 14 Jan 1929). Warburton practised law in Charlottetown and won election as a Liberal to the provincial legislature in 1891. He was named premier on 27 Oct 1897 but resigned 1 Aug 1898 following his appointment as a judge in June 1898. He held that post until Oct 1904. An MP 1908-11, he returned to

the bench as a judge of probate in 1920 and served until his death. Warburton is best remembered for his 2 landmark histories of PEI.   P.E. RIDER

Ward, Maxwell William, aviator, businessman (b at Edmonton 22 Nov 1921). He joined the RCAF in 1940 and served as a flight instructor during WWII. He worked as a bush pilot after the war and made an outstanding contribution to the service of the northern frontier by air. In 1946 he organized Polaris Charter Co Ltd, based in Yellowknife, NWT, and in 1953 returned to Yellowknife with a newly formed company, Wardair Ltd, which pioneered the air transport of heavy equipment to the Far North. In 1962 he obtained a licence to operate international air charters, changed the company name to Wardair Canada Ltd (now WARDAIR INTERNATIONAL LTD), and moved its head offices to Edmonton. By the mid-1970s Wardair had developed into Canada's largest international air charter carrier. He was awarded the MCKEE TROPHY in 1973 for his contributions to aviation.   JAMES MARSH

Wardair International Ltd, with head offices in Edmonton, is an international and domestic charter airline incorporated in Alberta in 1953 as Wardair Ltd. Initially a bush charter airline based in Yellowknife, NWT, the name was changed in 1962 to Wardair Canada Ltd. It became a public company in 1967. In 1972 the company formed 2 subsidiaries, Canada UK Travel (now Wardair (UK) Ltd) and International Vacations (Intervac), to solicit passengers and operate tour packages. In 1976 the company name was changed to Wardair International Ltd. The company has since expanded and today offers a variety of travel and tour packages in several countries. In 1983 it had sales or operating revenue of $348.3 million (ranking 182nd in Canada) assets of $491.8 million (ranking 156th) and 2215 employees. Its major shareholder is Max WARD, founder of the company.   DEBORAH C. SAWYER

Wardner, BC, UP, pop 119 (1981c), is located at the opening of the KOOTENAY R into Lk Koocanusa. The lake was formed recently, after completion of the Columbia R Treaty Dam at Libby, Montana, and flooding of the original townsite has reduced Wardner to the status of a post office. It was founded in 1897 by an American fortune hunter, James F. Wardner, as a construction camp on the Crow's Nest Pass Ry. A large sawmill operated there, drawing logs from the Kootenay and Bull river drainages. Today, Wardner has limited dairying and ranching on some of the best rangeland in the region, but the farming area has declined 19% because of flooding by Lk Koocanusa. At Kootenay Trout Hatchery, 8 km N, some 8 million trout of various types are bred yearly.   WILLIAM A. SLOAN

Warren, Jack Hamilton, public servant, banker (b in Howard Twp, Ont 10 Apr 1921). Service with the Royal Canadian Navy during WWII and the Dept of External Affairs from 1945 preceded Warren's appointment to the General Agreement on Tariffs and Trade, 1960-64, and to the Dept of Trade and Commerce, where he was deputy minister, 1958-60, 1964-71. He resumed his diplomatic career in 1971, becoming high commissioner to the UK (1971-74) and ambassador to the US 1975-77, spokesman at the Multilateral Trade Negotiations. He became vice-chairman of the Bank of Montreal in 1979.   ANNE HILLMER

Warren, Sir Peter, naval officer (b *c*1703; d at Dublin, Ire 29 July 1752). He commanded the Royal Navy at the 1745 siege of LOUISBOURG, where he was made governor. Warren recommended the deportation of Acadians and the fortification of Chebucto (Halifax) as early as 1739. While serving under Admiral Anson in 1747, his squadron defeated the French off Cape

Ortegal. From the declining Catholic gentry of Ireland, he married into a prominent New York mercantile family and made a great fortune from war, part of which he invested in New England, New York and S Carolina, before buying land and lending money in Ireland and England. He was MP for Westminster 1747-52.

JULIAN GWYN

Warren, Vincent de Paul, dancer, teacher (b at Jacksonville, Fla 31 Aug 1939). During his 18 years with LES GRANDS BALLETS CANADIENS, Warren became one of the most accomplished dancers in the company's history. A fine interpreter of roles from the traditional story-ballets, he also excelled in contemporary works, a number of which were choreographed for him. Warren was trained and began his career in the US. He was a member of Les Grands Ballets Canadiens 1961-79, except for 1970-71 when he performed with the Théâtre français de la danse in Paris and the Cologne Opera Ballet. Since 1979 he has taught ballet and dance history in Montréal, primarily at the school of Les Grands Ballets.

MICHAEL CRABB

Warren, William Robertson, lawyer, politician, judge (b at St John's 9 Oct 1879; d there 31 Dec 1927). He became the sixteenth prime minister of Newfoundland, July 1923-Apr 1924, upon the resignation of Richard SQUIRES. A barrister in St John's at age 21, he was a Liberal member of the Assembly by 1903, Speaker 1909-13 and Squires's minister of justice from 1919. Warren and 3 other ministers quit the Cabinet following the 1923 elections amid accusations of misspending of government funds before the elections. Squires resigned and the party chose Warren as leader and prime minister. Warren immediately determined to investigate the charges and instituted a public enquiry, led by Thomas Hollis Walker. The report, presented Mar 1924, found misconduct in public spending and several arrests followed. In spite of these actions Warren's former supporters moved a motion of no confidence and the government fell. Warren continued in the Assembly until 1926 when he was appointed to the Supreme Court.

ROBERT D. PITT

Wartime Elections Act In 1917 PM Sir Robert Borden's Conservative government feared that CONSCRIPTION, introduced in May to bolster the Canadian fighting forces in WORLD WAR I, was unpopular and that Canadians not of British descent would combine to defeat the government in the upcoming general election. On Sept 20, after an angry debate, Parliament passed the Wartime Elections Act disfranchising citizens of enemy-alien birth naturalized after 31 Mar 1902, except when such citizens had a son, grandson or brother on active duty. It also granted the vote to the wives, mothers and sisters of serving soldiers. The Act undoubtedly increased support for Borden's party, but was not a deciding factor in the 1917 election. In the long run, Conservative popularity among some ethnic groups was affected negatively.

JOHN ENGLISH

Wartime Home Front The 2 world wars of the 20th century were total wars that involved the whole nation, and the "home front" became a critical part of the war effort. In WORLD WAR I farmers broke new land and, with state assistance, began to mechanize their operations; the latter was one attempt to make up for the shortage of farm help caused by enlistment and by the drift of workers to cities in search of employment in war industry. Schemes were devised to send city teenagers into the country to assist with the harvest (a mixed blessing). At the same time the booming war factories were in desperate need of skilled tradesmen, too many of whom had been allowed to enlist before their greater value at home had been recognized. One result was that large numbers of women were brought into war factories, and "aliens," often unacceptable for military service because of their nationality, took factory jobs. Another result of the labour scarcity was that wages rose — although not as much as the cost of living — but because conditions in the plants were often terrible, labour unrest was widespread.

The hothouse atmosphere of war fostered other strange growths. PROHIBITION was a popular measure because it seemed to be a sacrifice that could help the war effort. WOMEN'S SUFFRAGE was widely seen as a reward to Canadian women for their help in the war effort. The IN-COME TAX, an inconceivable measure in 1914, by 1917 had become necessary to help the state finance the staggering costs of total war. Even price controls and controls on coal and steel could be justified on the grounds of necessity.

The war had changed much, not least the attitudes of the public. If prohibition was popular in Canada, it seemed mean-spirited when an attempt was made to apply it to soldiers at the front. But some attitudes died hard. For example, the puritanical morality of the day could scarcely deal with the explosion of venereal disease the war produced. One study attributed the spread of social diseases to the factory girl who saw "women largely predominating in the city" and felt "she must push forward and not miss her chance at romance." As a result of loose behaviour, she became "a disintegrating social force" who spread disease to middle-class men who might in turn infect their wives. The woman, not the man, seemed to be to blame, an attitude that persisted into WWII.

The home front during WORLD WAR II was much better organized than it had been in WWI. In late 1941 the WARTIME PRICES AND TRADE BOARD, est in Sept 1939, was given charge of a sweeping system of WAGE AND PRICE CONTROLS. That made the rising costs of WWI an impossibility and, while not everyone was pleased by controls, the public could see the fairness of the system. That was true also with the use of the nation's manpower. The institution of National Selective Service in early 1942 effectively controlled the destiny of all men and women, told them who could join up and who could not, where they could work, and when they could change jobs. The WPTB also devised major rationing schemes that distributed meat, butter, oil and gas and other scarce goods. Inevitably there was black marketeering, but most people regarded it as a social crime.

The shortage of consumer goods meant that

Parachute Riggers, oil on canvas, by Paraskeva Clark *(courtesy Canadian War Museum/NMM/NMC/14086).*

workers, earning good wages for the first time after 10 years of the GREAT DEPRESSION, had little to buy, and the state acted to acquire as much of the people's savings as possible. In WWI the minister of finance had been astonished at how much money war bond campaigns raised; in WWII the sums were vastly greater as individuals and companies, in addition to paying higher taxes than ever before, put their money at the service of the war effort. Even school children were urged to purchase war savings stamps, each showing a tank or airplane, for 25 cents. Children also did their bit by collecting cooking fat, bones or MILKWEED, all of which were necessary for the war effort, while their parents planted victory gardens on waste patches of land or contributed their old pots and pans for melting down into weaponry.

Opinion surveys demonstrated that by 1944 Canadians had become supporters of a continuation of wartime controls into the peace. That was undoubtedly a reflection of their concern for the future and their fear of renewed depression, but it was also a striking vote of confidence in the fairness of the system the federal government had created. The relatively smooth transition to peace also showed the care with which Ottawa had planned.

J.L. GRANATSTEIN

Reading: M.J. Lennon, *On The Homefront* (1981); D. Read, ed, *The Great War and Canadian Society* (1978).

Wartime Information Board succeeded the Bureau of Public Information, which had been formed early in WWII to issue certain information on the course of the war to the public. By 1942 the government believed that its troubles over CONSCRIPTION derived from inadequate publicity. In Aug, Cabinet approved the creation of a largely autonomous information board. Charles Vining was WIB chairman until Jan 1943, when educator Norman A.M. MacKenzie succeeded him. The real power on the board was held by its general manager, John GRIERSON, who promoted the war as a vehicle for social change. The approach naturally created some political controversy. In 1944 Grierson was succeeded by A. Davidson DUNTON, who followed Grierson's general direction until the end of the war. The board influenced the public's interpretation of the war, and pioneered systematic public-opinion polling in Canada.

JOHN ENGLISH

Wartime Prices and Trade Board, est by the Canadian government immediately after the onset of WORLD WAR II, and initially responsible to the Dept of Labour. Its creation reflected the government's concern that WWI conditions of inflation and social unrest not return. Until Aug 1941 the board's work seemed ineffective in restraining Canadian wartime inflation. It then became the responsibility of the Dept of Finance. On Oct 18 its powers were enormously expanded when PM Mackenzie King announced a price freeze and the "stabilization" of wages and salaries. To manage the large bureaucracy required to supervise the program, the government selected Donald GORDON, a prominent banker. Gordon attracted competent administrators from private industry and quickly built up an effective system in which businessmen administered the industries they knew best. A public-relations campaign urged Canadians to exercise restraint in wage demands and consumer demand. Canadians supported the board's aims until 1943, when labour officials became critical of its arbitrariness, farmers complained about discrimination and business tried to escape price ceilings. The board and the government kept the controls patched together through subsidization, social-security schemes, promises of postwar reforms and strategic political retreats. The board played a major role in postwar decontrol until Gordon resigned in 1947. Although there is much about it that can be criticized, the board's major achievement, a mere 2.8% increase in prices between Oct 1941 and Apr 1945, was a sign of its remarkable overall effectiveness. JOHN ENGLISH

Waskahegan Trail, a 400 km regional hiking trail developed in the Edmonton, Alta, area. It began as a Centennial project to promote hiking opportunities in the Edmonton, WETASKIWIN, CAMROSE, Ft Saskatchewan and ST ALBERT areas. Similar in concept to the BRUCE TRAIL in Ontario, it follows public land as much as possible, but has access across private lands by way of landowner agreements and easements. It connects numerous small communities in the Edmonton region and passes through picturesque Alberta countryside, including ELK ISLAND NATIONAL PK and Miquelon Lake Provincial Pk, highlighting a typical aspen parkland ecosystem. Some overnight camp-shelters are provided. BART DEEG

Wasp, term properly applied to stinging Hymenoptera of the superfamilies Vespoidea, Sphecoidea and Scolioidea. In common usage, a number of parasitic and gall-forming hymenopterans are also referred to as wasps. These INSECTS generally have an abdomen somewhat narrowed at the base, a body covered with simple hairs (contrasting to the branched hairs of BEES) and an ovipositor (egg-laying organ) that may be modified into a sting. Most wasps have 2 pairs of membranous wings; some forms are wingless. Wasps vary in size from tiny parasites less than 1 mm long to large predators 35 mm long. Some 550 species of stinging wasps are found in Canada. If parasitic and gall wasps are included, this number is more than doubled. Wasps are distributed throughout the country.

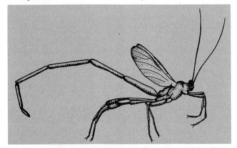

Proctotrupoid wasp (*Pelecinus polyturator*). This shiny black insect, reaching 50 mm in length, is an important control agent of June beetles, whose larvae it parasitizes (*artwork by Shirley Stacey*).

Such a large and diverse insect group exhibits great variation in life-styles and habitats. Gall wasps (family Cynipidae) form characteristic galls on plant leaves and stems, in which their larvae feed and develop. Many wasps are parasites, and place their eggs in or on the bodies of their insect hosts. Velvet ants (Mutillidae) are parasites of ground-nesting wasps and bees. These brightly coloured, hairy wasps have wingless females which can give a very painful sting. Mud daubers (Sphecidae) gather pellets of mud which they fashion into nest cells and provision with spiders as food for their young. Included in the Vespidae are perhaps the best known of this group, the social wasps. The familiar paper nests constructed by these insects house complex societies of from a few dozen to over a thousand individuals. Most wasps are beneficial, being parasites or predators of other insects. Some parasitic forms are reared and released for the biological control of INSECT PESTS. *See* HORNET. M.V. SMITH

Waste Disposal Although the term SOLID WASTE refers to a wide range of discarded materials (from kitchen scraps to mine tailings), the component known as refuse has the greatest potential for environmental contamination. Refuse comprises solid wastes consisting of household garbage and commercial rubbish produced, usually in equal parts, by the residents and merchants of a community. If simply left to decay, refuse can become a serious threat to community health both as a direct source of human illnesses and as an attractant to disease-carrying organisms. Therefore, many Canadian communities collect refuse from its source and deliver it to a waste-disposal site.

Many smaller towns and villages cannot afford a refuse collection service or a proper waste-disposal site. Because small communities are prevalent in Canada, improperly operated dumps outnumber the better-operated facilities used by larger communities. In most provinces the garbage dump is regarded as illegal or unacceptable. As they are on fire most of the time, they are a fire hazard, threatening users of the site, nearby fields, forests and buildings, and resulting in considerable damage each year. Dumps are also an ideal feeding ground for rats and other disease-carrying animals, and attract dangerous mammals as well as flocks of birds, which may pose a hazard to nearby airfields.

Major Canadian cities now use an improved method of waste disposal called sanitary landfilling. At a sanitary landfill, refuse is spread in thin layers, on the ground or in a trench, by a mobile compaction vehicle. Then a layer of clean soil is spread and compacted over the layer of refuse. Hence a series of alternating layers (refuse, soil, refuse) is built up until the trench is filled or a mound created. As cities expand, landfill once on the outskirts is surrounded by housing developments and industrial parks. It may be reclaimed for other uses (eg, in several cities the old dump is now a park).

Incineration is the most common method of refuse treatment in Canada. Some incinerators must handle 200 or more truckloads of refuse daily; hence, units capable of continuous operation are needed. Newer, "starved air" incinerators are so efficient that special air-pollution control devices are not required. Some incinerators are equipped with boilers that use heat from burning garbage to produce hot water or steam, which can be used to heat buildings or operate machinery.

Up to 50% of refuse is said to be reusable; thus, recycling may offer the greatest potential for reducing the growing volumes of waste. Although few recycling experiments have succeeded on a wide scale, Canadians have undergone a measurable change in attitude in favour of more recycling. This shift has been enhanced by the increased awareness that CONSERVATION and RESOURCE self-sufficiency are admirable goals for Canada's future. R.C. MACKENZIE

Wasteneys, Hardolph, professor of biochemistry (b at Richmond, Eng Apr 1881; d at Toronto 1 Feb 1965). As a boy Wasteneys went to Australia and found employment in government laboratories dealing with water purification. He moved to California about 1909 to study this subject further. From 1910 to 1916 he was a technician with Jacques Loeb, famous physiologist at the Rockefeller Inst for Medical Research in NY. His work with Loeb resulted in his only university degree, a PhD from Columbia in 1916. He joined the dept of biochemistry, U of T in 1918 and succeeded Andrew Hunter as head in 1928. He and his students did some pioneering studies on protein synthesis and he encouraged the development of research in his department. His own main interests in later years turned to social service and humanitarian directions. DAVID B. SMITH

Water (H_2O) occurs in the atmosphere and above and below the Earth's surface as a liquid, solid or gas. It is continually changing state (eg, by freezing/thawing, evaporation/condensation) and location (eg, by gaseous, liquid or GLACIER flow). All water is involved in a continuous hydrologic cycle, of which evaporation into the atmosphere from OCEANS, LAKES, RIVERS and LAND surfaces and transpiration through plant leaves may be considered the first phase. This moisture is transported, often great distances, by WINDS and is precipitated, as RAIN or snow, upon water and land surfaces.

Worldwide, over two-thirds of precipitation falling on land surfaces is evaporated and transpired back into the atmosphere. In Canada less than 40% is evaporated and transpired; the remainder, called the water yield, enters into stream flow. In the drier plains, only 10-20 mm of the 300-400 mm of precipitation enters stream flow, largely from drift snowmelt and from heavy rains in some years. In west-facing coastal ranges of the West Coast, where annual precipitation is 3000-7500 mm, approximately 500-600 mm is evaporated and transpired, and 80-95% runs off. In far northern areas where little heat is available, only 100-200 mm is evaporated or transpired and 100-500 mm enters stream flow. The proportion of runoff increases in rocky, paved, fallow and elevated (cooler) areas, where there is little moisture storage, vegetative cover or heat for much evapotranspiration. Small coastal and mountain areas in the West have very high yields; larger areas in the East and in parts of the North have moderately high yields; lower yields occur in the southern plains and in some interior valleys of the western CORDILLERA.

Water use involves withdrawal from rivers, lakes and groundwater supplies and consumptive use of part of these diversions. It may also include nonwithdrawal uses (eg, HYDROELECTRICITY, fishing, navigation, recreation, wildlife habitat), which involve little consumption of water (although some water evaporates from RESERVOIRS and some preserves have high evapotranspiration). Canada is fortunate in having relatively abundant supplies. Withdrawal uses involve only 1.3% of the total; consumptive uses only 0.1%. We are in no danger of running out of water, although there are regional deficiencies and problems of quality. Partly because of these abundant supplies, flooding and drainage problems are relatively large.

Canada's history is closely related to lake and river use. Exploration and development were largely along water TRANSPORTATION routes and the early FUR and TIMBER trades were river oriented. Water transport dominated early commerce. With CANAL development, bulk movement far into the continent became possible, and canal transportation remains very important today. Farm IRRIGATION was and is a major factor in agricultural development in the drier southwestern plains of the Prairie provinces and the southern interior of BC, and supplemental irrigation is expanding into more humid areas. Water power and, later, hydroelectric site developments were major bases for industrial development. Urban and industrial demands have grown rapidly and most cities and industries are river and lake oriented. Commercial and recreational fishing are significant but WATER POLLUTION, dams and other man-made changes have had largely negative effects on these activities. Wildlife and recreational demands are important and have also suffered from human activities. The need for integrated, multiple-use water management is growing but varies greatly from province to province. Environmental enhancement is possible but not widely undertaken, even to compensate for damage done. Water CONSERVATION measures are not yet widely employed, but the growing costs of obtaining high-quality water and avoiding stream POLLUTION are resulting in an increased recycling of water.

Provincial Profiles

Water supply and demand patterns vary greatly from province to province.

British Columbia has the greatest flow, half coming from the one-sixth of the province's area occupied by the Coast and Island ranges. Some interior valleys are very dry, but surpluses from adjoining mountain areas can be used for irrigation and other purposes. For the province as a whole, supply exceeds consumptive use by over 1600 times, but water shortages are present locally. The major conflicts are between non-withdrawal users such as hydroelectric developments and salmon FISHERIES. To protect the salmon industry dam development has not proceeded on some rivers (eg, lower and middle Fraser). Pollution is a growing problem and the costs of control are now a major part of PULP AND PAPER, MINERAL and urban development.

Alberta, with only 2% of the supply, in drier years has over 50% of the consumptive use demand for Canada. Well over half of Canada's irrigated land and most of the secondary recovery of oil and gas (involving pumping of water into the geological formations to replace these fuels) are in Alberta. Substantial expansion of BITUMEN development, involving evaporation of large quantities of water from tailings ponds, might increase Alberta's share of Canadian consumptive demand. The problem is accentuated since almost all of the irrigation, urban and industrial demand and some of the MINING demand is in southern Alberta, while most (87%) of the water supply is in the north (Arctic rather than Hudson Bay or Gulf of Mexico drainage). Moreover, by agreement with Saskatchewan, Manitoba and Canada, one-half of the southern flow is allocated to downstream use. In the near future, dry-year demand may exceed supply and political pressure for massive interbasin transfers is growing.

Saskatchewan, with much less irrigation and oil, is trying to expand with a limited water supply in the S. POTASH mining demands are large and mines and municipalities are served increasingly by canal and pipeline systems. Quality issues in the Qu'Appelle Valley are as acute as anywhere in Canada, largely because there is so little flow to assimilate and dilute wastes. Tertiary treatment of municipal wastes in the southern plains is relatively advanced. Thermal and hydroelectric power alternatives are varied and environmental concerns and multiple-use management are well developed. Prairie sloughs, part of a major migratory WATERFOWL habitat, need protection and enhancement.

Manitoba Hydroelectric power has been dominant in water planning for the province but drainage, flood damage limitation and a significant potential for irrigation development are of strong interest. The supply issue is less critical, partly because of the large amount of water that flows into the province from the W, E and S. Environmental issues are prominent, including some relating to the Garrison Project development in North Dakota and the possible dumping of saline waters or southern fish and other organisms into the province's rivers and lakes.

Ontario had long considered its water resources to be unlimited and indestructible. They are abundant, but by the 1960s it had become widely apparent that river and lake water quality had been severely damaged by industrial, municipal and other pollutants. The GREAT LAKES and connecting rivers had received more pollution from the more populous and highly industrialized American side than from Canadian sources, and joint programs for reducing pollution were instituted. Ontario is coping with the problem through tertiary treatment of most municipal and industrial waste; through the use of multiple-purpose development for withdrawal and on-stream uses and for river control; and through river-basin management, including the institution of conservation measures. Supplemental irrigation in dry periods is becoming more widespread for tobacco fields, orchards and market gardens, where quality control as well as yield increase is important.

Streamflow Originating Within and Passing Through Canada[a]			
	Originating	%	*Passing Through*[b]
YT	140 000	4.2	165 000
NWT	700 000	20.8	890 000
BC	800 000	23.7	870 000
Alta	69 000	2.0	137 000
Sask	56 000	1.7	73 000
Man	94 000	2.8	172 000
Ont	325 000	9.6	500 000
Qué	780 000	23.2	1 060 000
NB	46 000	1.4	67 000
NS	45 000	1.3	45 000
PEI	3 500	0.1	3 500
Nfld	310 000	9.2	310 000
Canada	3 368 500[c]	100.0	4 292 500

[a] Estimates based upon Water Survey of Canada data to 1972 with minor corrections based on later data. Totals for NWT and BC, especially, require upward revision. Measurements are expressed in thousands of decametres^3. One dam^3 = 1000 m^3 or 1 hectare decimetre

[b] The amount originating within the province or territory (the water yield), plus that originating elsewhere and passing through. Because of duplication, totals are less meaningful

[c] Approximately 106 741 m^3/s

Urban and industrial uses are large but most of the water used for washing, cooling and other purposes is returned to streams. Thermal power plant (coal and nuclear based) return flow is potentially damaging to fish, but this heated water can also be a resource. Consumptive use is small and water shortages are not a problem.

Québec has abundant supplies and a long history of water use. Nonwithdrawal uses (eg, hydroelectric power, navigation, fishing, recreation) are very important. Urban and industrial use is large and there has tended to be a greater reliance upon the natural assimilative capacities of streams in WASTE DISPOSAL than there has been in most parts of Canada. Waste treatment is needed and is slowly being instituted. The hydroelectric power potential has been large and, with development in northern basins (eg, Manicouagan and La Grande), over half of it has been realized. Navigation on the St Lawrence is limited by ice in winter, but the shipping season is being extended, especially for downstream ports. Drainage for agricultural development is widespread and some for FOREST site improvement is underway. Flooding is a problem, especially in spring when snowmelt supplies are augmented by heavy rains.

Atlantic Provinces are relatively humid with little need for irrigation. Problems of flooding and drainage relating to seasonal oversupply are more common. Water yields are high and rivers are large, relative to basin areas. Waterpower, followed by hydroelectric power, has long been a basis for industry. Recreational and commercial fishing, navigation (limited by SEA ICE in most winters and most areas) and some withdrawal uses are significant. Pollution is a problem, but streams, TIDES and coastal ocean currents have been used to dilute and assimilate wastes and the problem is not as acute as in some water-short areas.

Territories The measurement data of the last few decades in the YT and the NWT are for much larger rivers than might be expected to be present with the limited precipitation recorded. This may be the result of unrepresentative precipitation records (the settlement stations are in the drier areas); furthermore, gauge undercatch is normal, especially for blowing snow. With low evapotranspiration, the greater part of the precipitation enters stream flow. Many of the problems of water use relate to frost and PERMAFROST and some communities have insulated corridors for water and sewage. River navigation is still very important; actual hydroelectric development represents only a small part of the

potential; withdrawal uses are small. Recreational uses, in fishing-camp development, waterfall viewing and swimming, are growing. Wildlife concerns are of growing importance, partly because fishing and FUR TRAPPING are still important industries.

With increasing competition for limited supplies of pure water, the need for integrated multiple-purpose management and for conservation will grow. Canadian pressure upon supply is much less than in the US where the total supply for the coterminous 48 states is only 40% as large as that of Canada (70% with Alaska); in the US, withdrawal demand in 1975 was 27% of the supply, consumptive demand was 8.5%, and much more of the supply was polluted to varying degrees. Regional shortages are much greater than in Canada, but the demand for interbasin transfers from Canada will continue to be negligible for many decades. There are cheaper alternative supplies in the US; costs of transfer would exceed the value of most products that might be produced; the willingness to subsidize irrigation is declining; and the political, legal, environmental and other problems would be formidable. In the future there could be some transfer, but only if mutually beneficial arrangements, with environmental enhancement at least equalling the minimal damage required, can be worked out. Irrigation is one of the less likely recipients because it is a low-return use, unable to cover the costs of major transfer, and greater increases in agricultural production can be obtained by other cheaper means.   A.H. LAYCOCK

Water-Borne Disease, any illness resulting from ingestion of or contact with water. Like food-borne diseases, water-ingestion illnesses are either infections or intoxications. Organisms responsible for infections are bacteria, eg, SALMONELLA (causing salmonellosis), *Shigella* (shigellosis) and *Vibrio cholerae* (cholera); viruses, eg, rotavirus, Norwalk-type agent and hepatitis A virus; or parasites, eg, *Entamoeba* (causing amebiasis), *Dracunculus* (Guinea worm disease) and *Giardia* (giardiasis). These organisms usually occur in water contaminated with sewage (eg, especially bird and mammal excrement) or by infected persons or animals. Intoxications are invariably chemical in nature (eg, copper, lead, insecticide poisonings) and usually occur as a result of leaching of metal into water (from pipes or containers) and through accidental spillage or seepage of chemicals into water supplies. The illnesses can either be acute or chronic, depending on the contaminating conditions and volume of water consumed. Illnesses acquired through contact with water are caused by bacteria, eg, *Leptospira* (causing leptospirosis), *Chlamydia* (swimming-pool conjunctivitis) and parasites, eg, *Schistosoma* (causing swimmer's itch and bilharziasis).

According to the World Health Organization, most diseases in the world are associated with water. Fortunately, this is not the case in Canada. Documentation of water-borne disease in this country, however, is very limited: only a few outbreaks are reported each year, and it is recognized that many more occur without being investigated. From data available since 1973, typhoid (caused by *Salmonella typhi*) has been associated with water in a camp and a municipal system using inadequately chlorinated water from a lake. Shigellosis and hepatitis were reported mainly from northern rural communities, eg, Indian and Inuit settlements. Giardiasis is becoming more recognized as a cause of severe diarrhea; the parasite is sometimes isolated from tourists travelling abroad, but more often from residents of small communities with no water-filtering systems. Animals such as BEAVER regularly excrete the *Giardia* organism into water. The parasites survive chlorination, but can be filtered out. Occasional intoxications have occurred, eg, through water remaining in newly soldered copper pipes. Water-contact disease is rarely documented and is not considered common in Canada. Swimmer's itch, however, can become a problem with bathers in some lakes, and wounds of swimmers have been invaded by *Vibrio parahaemolyticus* (which can also cause food-borne disease) in the ocean off BC. Concern about WATER POLLUTION (whether the result of toxic chemicals or fecal material) is increasing in Canada. For example, all but 2 beaches in Toronto were closed to swimmers in July 1983 because of the high fecal coliform bacteria count.   EWEN TODD

Water Distribution System, network used to distribute water from a central location to a location of end use. While the most complex distribution systems are those required to supply urban areas, fairly extensive systems are also used in some areas to supply irrigation water to orchards and vegetables and other crops. Elaborate distribution systems may also be required within a major industrial plant (eg, steel mill, PETROLEUM refinery) or commercial complex (eg, large shopping centre, office building).

Nearly 80% of Canada's population is classifed as "urban," and the distribution of water to this group of users is a major task. Most of Canada's larger cities are located on or near a major RIVER system or LAKE, which provides water for distribution. Some cities may obtain their water from a relatively distant but more reliable source (for example, Winnipeg's water comes via aqueduct from Lake of the Woods, 150 km away); groundwater supplies the needs of other cities, notably Kitchener-Waterloo. Canadian cities developed urban water distribution systems quite early: Toronto and Kingston had pumping stations by 1841 and 1850, respectively; gravity systems were operating even earlier in Saint John, NB, and Halifax, NS, in 1838 and 1848. By the 1870s, the water supplies of most large cities were steam pumped. Although the amount of water used for fire protection is small compared to other uses, the high rate of water flow needed in fire fighting is often the most important factor to be considered in designing the system. The system's main components are pumping stations to create and maintain pressure, reservoirs to store water and aid in pressure equalization, and a network of pipes to convey the water to users.

In urban distribution systems, water mains usually are made of iron, steel, cement or asbestos cement. Service pipes may be of copper, brass, lead, cast iron, wrought iron, tin, steel, stainless steel, silicon bronze, other alloys or plastics. Copper tubing is the most widely used material in service pipes, because of its corrosion resistance, flexibility, ease of installation and relatively low resistance to flow. Lead or lead-lined pipes are no longer used in new installations because of health concerns caused by the dissolution of lead into the water supply.

Distribution systems for farm IRRIGATION typically consist of a network of canals or pipes. With pipe systems, pumps are used to maintain sufficient hydraulic head to operate spray irrigation equipment and valves are used to control flow in the pipes. With canal systems, a combination of gravity, pumps, weirs and gates are used to distribute and control the flow of water through the system. In Canada the Prairie provinces have the largest area under irrigation, about 457 000 ha; BC is next with 100 000 ha; the rest of Canada has about 39 000 ha of irrigated land. Irrigation systems may be privately developed or put in place with the assistance of provincial or federal governments (*see* PRAIRIE FARM REHABILITATION ADMINISTRATION).

Three industrial sectors, MANUFACTURING, MINING and thermal power generation accounted for 30% of Canada's total water consumption in

1980. Other industries and commercial establishments are served by urban or rural municipal water distribution systems.   D.W. DRAPER

Water Flea, tiny CRUSTACEAN that swims with jerky movements. The "fleas," found in almost any drop of pond water, use powerful strokes of their antennae for propulsion. These branchiopods belong to the suborder Cladocera, a cosmopolitan, freshwater group of about 400 species. The water flea feeds on phytoplankton and detritus, filtered through bristles on its appendages. Sexes are separate; the female broods eggs in a dorsal chamber. Population sizes are highly seasonal and adverse times are passed in dormant stages. Numerous aspects of cladoceran biology are studied in Canada: there is high commercial potential in their cultivation for fish food.   V. TUNNICLIFFE

Water Lily (Nymphaeaceae), large family of freshwater PLANTS characterized by large, shield-shaped leaves and showy blossoms. They are mostly tropical or subtropical. Four genera and 9 species are native to Canada, of which 3 species are important. *Nuphar advena*, yellow pond lily, cow lily or spatterdock has yellow, globular flowers. It occurs as far N as the YT and is widespread throughout Canada. White or pygmy water lily (*Nymphaea tetragona*) is found in northern Canada. Sweet or fragrant water lily (*Nymphaea odorata*), the most beautiful of the 3, has waxy, white flowers, 10-15 cm across. It is found in ponds and quiet streams from southeastern Canada to Florida. All are edible and were an important emergency food for Indians, the rhizome being boiled, baked or dried, and the seeds roasted and ground into a highly nutritious flour. The root, because of its astringent, antiseptic and demulcent properties, was used externally for healing sores and internally for inflammation and dysentery.   GILLIAN FORD

Water lily (Nymphaeaceae) (*photo by Barbara K. Deans/ Masterfile*).

Water Pollution occurs when discharges of energy or materials degrade water for other users. Population growth and INDUSTRIALIZATION have resulted in POLLUTION of inland and marine waters. Water pollution can be classified according to the nature of pollutants, sources releasing them and water bodies into which they are discharged.

Water pollution is measured by the concentration of pollutants in the water body and their effects on other water uses. Six categories of pollutants are recognized.

Pathogens are disease-causing bacteria, VIRUSES and protozoa, usually from human sewage. As pathogen numbers increase, so does the risk to human health.

Biochemical Oxygen Demand (BOD) is created by organic wastes decaying in the water body. Major sources of BOD are PULP AND PAPER mills and municipal sewage. If dissolved oxygen is depressed to zero, all fish die and anaerobic (ie, without oxygen) decomposition generates noxious gases (eg, hydrogen sulphide).

Nutrients, particularly nitrogen and phosphorus, enrich waters and accelerate the aging of LAKES and streams (eutrophication). The re-

sultant rich plant growth often prohibits recreational activities and PLANKTON blooms depress oxygen levels. Major sources of nutrients are municipal sewage and urban and agricultural runoff.

Toxic Materials can affect the health of aquatic organisms and their consumers, and of those drinking contaminated waters. Toxicants include heavy metals (eg, LEAD, MERCURY), chlorinated hydrocarbons (eg, DDT, PCBs), polycyclic aromatic hydrocarbons (eg, benzopyrene) and phthalates (eg, dibutyl phthalate). They originate from many sources as a result of the large quantities of chemicals used in industries. Mixtures of toxic materials can be toxic even if their individual concentrations are below lethally toxic levels. Oil pollutants are toxic and may also smother aquatic organisms and cause the death of birds, attracted by the appearance of calm water, by destroying the waterproofing properties of their plumage.

Acidification, particularly of lakes, results from precipitation of sulphur and nitrogen oxides emitted by industries and automobiles (*see* ACID RAIN).

Temperature Changes from waste heat discharges (eg, from NUCLEAR POWER PLANT cooling waters) can cause pollution when their elevation reduces dissolved-oxygen levels, accelerates eutrophication, affects ecological processes and blocks migration paths of fishes.

Controls The most cost-effective measure of pollution control depends on the particular pollutant and its source. Pathogens are usually controlled by disinfection (frequently using chlorine) of municipal sewage and domestic water supply (*see* WATER TREATMENT). High costs usually inhibit collecting runoff for disinfection. BOD can be reduced by treating municipal and industrial wastes (eg, in settling and stabilization lagoons and activated sludge plants) to decrease oxygen demand before the effluent is discharged; treatment of runoff is often too costly. Nitrogen and phosphorus are controlled most cost-effectively by regulation of the product (eg, phosphorus-free detergents) and land-use regulations (eg, fertilizer limitations). Specialized treatment processes can remove them from municipal and industrial wastes.

Toxicants cannot be controlled except at great cost at the point of entry into the water but must be regulated earlier in production. Different toxicants present different regulatory possibilities and problems. For example, PCBs (polychlorinated biphenyls) have to be controlled at the point of manufacture to limit dispersal; valuable materials (eg, chromium, lead) can be recycled economically; some toxicants can be replaced by nontoxic substitutes (eg, replacement of cyanide rinses in electroplating). Municipal and industrial treatment processes generally place toxic materials in sludges, which must then be treated or stored. Acidification can be prevented effectively only by controlling discharges of nitrogen and sulphur oxides into the atmosphere. Temperature changes can be prevented only by dissipating heat into the atmosphere by air cooling.

Canada's rich endowment of fresh and marine water is threatened by regional shortages (eg, southern Saskatchewan and Alberta) and serious pollution. Although pollution from pathogens, BOD and waste heat may be relatively easily reversed, eutrophication and oil spills are more difficult, and acidification and toxicity may be irreversible. Thus, control policies at all levels of government are increasingly emphasizing regulation of toxicants and early detection and prevention of pollution.

ANTHONY H.J. DORCEY

Reading: Anthony H.J. Dorcey, ed, *The Uncertain Future of the Lower Fraser* (1976); H.D. Foster and W.R.D. Sewell, *Water: The Emerging Crisis in Canada* (1981).

Water Polo is a game played in water, generally a swimming pool, by 2 teams of 7 players each, with the object of propelling a ball through the opposing goal. The name derives from the original game started in England about 1870, where players rode floating barrels, or "horses," and struck at the ball with a stick. This aspect was soon abandoned and the game became popular in Great Britain, with teams from the north of England dominating. England won the water-polo event at several early Olympic Games 1900-20; then other European teams began to dominate. Starting in the 1920s, the N American Cup was competed for annually. There was prominent representation from Ontario and Québec, along with teams from the New York and Chicago areas. The Canadian Water Polo Assn was formed in 1964. Water polo now enjoys countrywide participation, with Canada ranking in the top 16 national teams in the world.   JACK BODDINGTON

Water Skiing, a sport derived from snow SKI-ING and aquaplaning, was started in the US by Ralph Samuelson in 1922. It is perhaps the fastest-growing, all-family competitive sport. Competition is divided into 3 events — slalom, tricks (figures) and jumping. In Canada, it is also arranged in age categories. Water skiing caused a sensation when it was first introduced in Canada in the 1930s. The sport became more widely known in Canada after an appearance of the Cypress Gardens skiers at the CANADIAN NATIONAL EXHIBITION waterfront shows in 1948. The Canadian Water Ski Assn was founded in 1949, and Canada's first national championship was held that year. Canada has hosted 3 world championships, in 1953, 1967 and 1979. Canada first sent a full team (6 skiers) to the 1958 world championships held at Cypress Gardens, Fla, and has since climbed to second place in the world (1979, Toronto). Canadian world champions include Charlie Blackwell (slalom, 1953); Carol Ann Duthie (overall, jr girls, 1953); George ATHANS, Jr (overall, 1971, 1972 and 1973); Joel McClintock (overall, 1979); and Pat Messner (slalom, 1979).

In the past decade, Canadians have won 3 of a possible 5 world overall titles in the men's division, and the Canadian team has placed no less than fourth in the world and twice finished second. Water skiing has been a participating sport in every Canada Summer Games and was approved as an Olympic category sport in 1981.

Reading: G. Athans, Jr, and C. Ward, *Water Skiing* (1975).

Water Treatment The type and extent of treatment depends on the water's quality and intended use. The *Guidelines for Canadian Drinking Water Quality — 1978* lists approximately 60 physical, microbiological, chemical and radiological criteria for water for human consumption. Recommended acceptable levels and substances are given for pH, colour, total coliform organisms, fluoride, iron, arsenic, copper, PESTICIDES, total dissolved solids, and cesium-137. Concentrations higher than those recommended for drinking water may be tolerable for other uses (eg, industrial cooling). Some industrial uses, however, require concentrations lower than those of drinking water. For example, total dissolved solids in water used for textiles production should be less than 100 mg/L; iron in water used in production of clear plastics, less than 0.02 mg/L.

Several physical and chemical processes are available for water treatment. The most common physical processes are screening, flocculation, sedimentation and filtration. Evaporation and reverse osmosis are used primarily in industrial water treatment. Chemical processes include aeration, coagulation, softening, pH adjustment, adsorption, ion exchange and disinfection. Several processes are usually combined in treating water for any specific end use.

Public water supplies and swimming pools are disinfected to kill pathogenic organisms and to prevent WATER-BORNE DISEASES. Process and cooling waters for industry are also often disinfected to destroy micro-organisms that can cause fouling of pipes and equipment. Disinfection can be accomplished by chlorination, the addition of ozone, heating, exposure to ultraviolet light, the addition of bromine or iodine compounds (for industrial applications), etc. Chlorination is the most common method. An effective germicide, chlorine is also beneficial in colour removal, taste and odour control, suppression of algal growths, precipitation of iron and manganese, etc.   D.W. DRAPER

Reading: M.S. Babbitt et al, *Water Supply Engineering* (1962).

Waterfall, phenomenon which occurs when WATER flowing in a RIVER channel encounters a vertical or near-vertical drop in the channel bed. A cascade occurs when the drop results in a series of small falls; rapids occur where the river is steep and turbulent and the water remains in contact with the bed; and a cataract when a waterfall has a large volume of flow.

Waterfalls can be classified according to nature of origin.

Geological Discordance Falls result from a natural discordance in the river profile caused by geological faulting, GLACIATION, uplift plateaus, SPRINGS emanating from canyon walls, or EARTHQUAKES. Twin Falls near Yoho Glacier, BC, and NIAGARA FALLS, Ont, are examples.

Erosion Falls Cap-rock falls and vertical barrier falls are typical EROSION waterfalls, formed by differential erosion that occurs where erosion-resistant rocks are underlain by or adjoin softer rocks. A cap-rock fall is formed when a surface layer of hard rock rests on a softer layer. Water flowing over the hard rock cap erodes the face of the softer rock underneath, undermining the cap which eventually breaks and tumbles into the river at the foot of the fall or immediately downstream. Over time, a fall of this kind may degenerate to a long cascade. Alexandra Falls on the Hay R, NWT, is a cap-rock fall. When a layer of very hard IGNEOUS rock, extending vertically through great thicknesses of softer rock, lies across a river channel, the erosive force

Horsethief Creek Falls in the Purcell Mts, BC (*photo by Pat Morrow*).

Principal Canadian Waterfalls (over 25m)

Name	Vertical drop (m)	Location
Alexandra Falls	32	Hay R, NWT
Aubrey Falls	33	Mississagi R, Ont
Barrow Falls*	27	Barrow R, NWT
Brandywine Falls*	61	Brandywine Creek, BC
Bridal Veil Falls	122	Bridal Creek, BC
Churchill Falls	75	Churchill R, Nfld
Dog Falls	47	Kaministikwia R, Ont
Elizabeth Falls*	34	Fond du Lac R, Sask
Grand Falls	43	Exploits R, Nfld
Helmcken Falls*	137	Murtle R, BC
Hunlen Falls*	253	Atnarko R, BC
Kakabeka Falls	47	Kaministikwia R, Ont
Marengo Falls*	61	Marengo Creek, NWT
Montmorency, Chute	76	Montmorency R, Qué
Niagara Falls		Niagara R, Ont
Horseshoe Falls	57	
American Falls	59	
Quiatchouane, Chute	79	Quiatchouanish R, Ont
Panther Falls	183	Nigel Creek, Alta
Parry Falls*	40	Lockhart R, NWT
Pigeon Falls*	27	Pigeon R, Ont
Scott Falls	27	Unknown R, Nfld
Shawinigan, Chutes*	46	St-Maurice R, Qué
Takakkaw Falls	380	From Daly Glacier, BC
Thomas Falls	30	Unknown R, Nfld
Twin Falls	274	Twin Falls Creek, BC
Tyrell Falls*	26	Lockhart R, NWT
Virginia Falls*	90	S Nahanni R, NWT
Wawaitin Falls	38	Mattagami R, Ont
Wilberforce Falls*	49	Hood R, NWT

* Not readily accessible

of flowing water will not significantly affect the igneous rock but will wear down the softer rock, especially in the area immediately downstream from the igneous rock. A vertical barrier fall is eventually formed at the face of the vertical layer of hard rock. Little Falls on the Pigeon R, S of Thunder Bay, Ont, is an example.

Tidal Falls are typified by the reversing falls originating from the ebb and flow of ocean tides. A rock shelf across a narrow point where a river empties into the ocean forms a waterfall at low TIDE because the water level in the river above the shelf is then higher than sea level. When sea level rises with the incoming tide to the point where it is higher than the river level upstream from the rock shelf, the seawater forces its way upstream against the flow of the river and through the narrow point in the channel. The resulting rapids, whirlpools and eddies create the impression that the falls have actually reversed. A notable example occurs on the SAINT JOHN R at Saint John, NB, where the very high tides of the Bay of FUNDY create the reversing effect. Other reversing falls in Canada are at Wager Bay, Ford Lk, NWT, and Barrier Inlet, Hudson Str, NWT.

Duration Geologically speaking, all waterfalls are transient because their erosive power makes them self-destructive. This erosion is noticeable within a human lifetime at certain falls, eg, Horseshoe Falls on the Canadian side of the NIAGARA R. The crest of this waterfall has retreated approximately 335 m (roughly one metre per year) since its position was first recorded by Louis HENNEPIN in 1678. Since its beginning with the retreat of the last ice sheet an estimated 12 000 years ago, the Niagara R has eroded a stretch of channel approximately 12 km long, creating the spectacular Niagara gorge. Along the bed of the Niagara R, downstream from the falls, there is evidence of plunge pools, cut during periods when the position of the crest was stable.

When a waterfall undercuts itself and large blocks of rock drop from the scarp (face), the material tends to accumulate at the foot, gradually turning the falls into rapids. The American Falls on the Niagara R are a good example of this process; the relatively rapid erosion is caused largely by the effects of large volumes of water falling from a high plateau. By contrast, there are some very high falls where erosion is much slower because water flow is small and the water is dispersed to a fine mist during its descent. The oldest falls, thought to be many millions of years old, result from water descending from high plateaus. The world's highest waterfall (with a single, vertical drop of 807 m), Angel Falls, Venezuela, is an example.

Height There are various interpretations of what constitutes the height of a waterfall. Most waterfalls start with a series of rapids; the water then goes over the crest and drops vertically or nearly vertically, ending up as a cascade tumbling over accumulated debris. The heights shown in the table refer to the vertical or near-vertical drop from the crest to the top of the debris. The highest waterfall in Canada and sixteenth-highest in the world is Takakkaw Falls (dropping 380 m) which carries snow and ice melt from the Daly Glacier, BC.

Significance Waterways were the highways of Canada's early explorers; waterfalls were obstacles to transportation along these routes and had to be bypassed, usually by overland portages. Townsites were often established near a large falls on a navigable river and they marked the terminus of a portage. Later, CANALS were constructed, eg, the WELLAND CANAL bypassing Niagara Falls. Waterfalls serve as natural barriers that prevent undesirable aquatic life from migrating to upper portions of a watershed. For example, before construction of the Welland Canal, lampreys were unable to move upstream from Lk Ontario. Waterfalls also mark the sites of HYDROELECTRIC-power concentrations; in Canada many have been developed for this purpose. Many Canadian and foreign visitors view these spectacular natural attractions, drawn by the awesome power of falling water and the majestic settings.

P.I. CAMPBELL AND I.A. REID

Waterfowl, general term used for members of the family Anatidae, composed of closely allied species commonly known as DUCKS, geese and SWANS. The group has a worldwide distribution and contains flightless species as well as others capable of long MIGRATIONS. Some species, eg, northern pintail (*Anas acuta*), have very wide distribution; others are restricted to a few ponds on remote islands. Waterfowl range in size from pygmy geese, averaging 300 g when fully grown, to N American trumpeter swans, exceeding 13 kg and having a wingspread of 250 cm. Scientists divide waterfowl into 3 subfamilies, 2 of which are found in N America. The third, the primitive Australian Anseranatinae, contains the magpie geese, which are not true geese. In late summer as many as 80-100 million waterfowl are found in N America. Three species of swan, 7 of geese and 28 of ducks breed in Canada. Unfortunately, one species native to eastern Canada, the Labrador duck, is now extinct. *See also* GOOSE.   F.G. COOCH

Waterton Lakes National Park (est 1895, 525 km²) is situated in Alberta, 276 km SW of Calgary on the Canada-US border. In 1932, this PARK was united with Montana's Glacier National Park to create the world's first international peace park. The setting is spectacular. In less than a kilometre, the dry rolling hills of the prairies soar to icy peaks nearly 3000 m high. The 3 Waterton Lakes, nestling between 2 mountain ranges, are over 150 m deep. Because the park embraces both prairie and mountain, there is a great variety of plant and animal life. Antelope and coyote roam the grasslands; mountain goat, bighorn sheep, grizzly bear and marmot frequent alpine meadows and barren ridgetops. The area, once a Blackfoot stronghold, was discovered by Europeans in the late 1850s during fur-trade expeditions. In the early 1900s

Alta's first oil well was drilled near Cameron Creek. The park provides facilities for tent, recreational-vehicle and primitive winter camping, and has numerous trails.   LILLIAN STEWART

Watkins, John B.C., scholar, diplomat (b at Norval Station, Ont 1903; d at Montréal 12 Oct 1964). A Scandinavian specialist at U of Manitoba, he joined the Dept of External Affairs in 1946. Speaking fluent Russian, he was sent to Moscow as chargé d'affaires, 1948-51. He was minister to Norway, 1952-54, then returned to Moscow as ambassador, 1954-56. He served as assistant undersecretary of state for external affairs and as ambassador to Denmark. Western intelligence suspected him as a security risk because of alleged homosexual contacts in the USSR and, under questioning, he suffered a heart attack and died.   ROBERT BOTHWELL

Watson, Edward A., veterinarian, pathologist, researcher (b in Devon, Eng 2 Jan 1879; d at Victoria 12 Mar 1945). He came to Canada in 1896 and graduated from the Ontario Veterinary College in 1904. In charge of the Lethbridge (Alta) Animal Pathology Laboratory 1906-15, he carried out important research on dourine, a disease of HORSES. He was chief of the pathology division of the federal Dept of Agriculture 1919-42 and established the Animal Diseases Research Inst. Watson was a persistent and dedicated laboratory worker and researcher. His work in dourine is but one example of his many studies on animal diseases. His many ideas, born of an international outlook on science, formed the basis for veterinary research in Canada. *See also* VETERINARY MEDICINE.   J.F. FRANK

Watson, Helen Griffith Wylie, née McArthur, nursing administrator (b at Stettler, Alta 11 July 1911; d at Guelph, Ont 15 Dec 1974). A graduate of University of Alberta, Watson received her first practical experience as a public-health nurse at an isolated settlement in the PEACE RIVER country during the Depression. In 1946 she joined the RED CROSS SOCIETY, eventually becoming national director of nursing services. She served as president of the Canadian Nurses' Assn 1950-54 and was active internationally with the Red Cross. In 1954 she was awarded the Florence Nightingale Award for her work in Korea — the highest award of the International Red Cross. An officer of the Order of Canada, she retired in 1971.   DANIEL FRANCIS

Watson, Homer Ransford, painter (b at Doon, Canada W 14 Jan 1855; d there 30 May 1936). Virtually self-taught, Watson spent 1874-76 in Toronto working with John A. Fraser and Henri Perré and in New York absorbing the influence of George Inness and the Hudson River School. Later in Europe he met Sir George Clausen and Whistler, and admired Millet, the Barbizon painters and Constable. Internationally famous at the peak of his career, Watson developed a landscape style marked by honesty of purpose and a focus on the moods of nature. Many of his canvases depict the countryside

Homer Watson, *Log-Cutting in the Woods* (1894), oil on canvas (*courtesy Montreal Museum of Fine Arts*).

around Kitchener, the trees, fields of grain, grazing cattle — the "Land of Thrift" much prized in pioneer society. He began exhibiting in 1878 but the purchase of his *The Pioneer Mill* for Queen Victoria at the first Royal Canadian Academy of 1880 brought early acclaim. Many significant canvases were completed by the end of the century: *Cornfield* (1883), *The Flood Gate* (1900) and *After the Rain* (1883). His patrons included Lord Strathcona, James Ross, Oscar Wilde and many affluent Canadians. He and Edmund Morris founded the Canadian Art Club in 1907 hoping to replace imported European with Canadian canvases. Watson was president of the Royal Canadian Academy, 1918-21.   J. RUSSELL HARPER

Watson, John, philosopher (b at Glasgow, Scot 25 Feb 1847; d at Kingston, Ont 27 Jan 1939). Canada's foremost early philosopher, he was a charter member of the Royal Soc of Canada and author of 8 books and over 200 articles. He arrived at Queen's in Kingston, Ont, in 1872. Hegelianism influenced much of Watson's writings, which in turn affected the development of religious and political ideas in Canada. He is the only Canadian philosopher ever to be invited to give the prestigious Gifford Lectures in Edinburgh, Scot. These lectures were published in the 2-volume *The Interpretation of Religious Experience* (1910-12) — a landmark in Canadian philosophical history. Watson's main philosophical interest was the metaphysics of religion and he proposed a rational interpretation of Christianity in *Christianity and Idealism* (1896). By focusing on reason he provided a commonality around which people could unite, and thus helped build the intellectual foundations of the UNITED CHURCH OF CANADA (formed during his later years). His first books were about the German philosopher Kant. *Kant and his English Critics* (1881), *The Philosophy of Kant* (1888) and *The Philosophy of Kant Explained* (1908) were classics in the field and are still consulted by Kantian scholars. During those same years Watson wrote texts that introduced hundreds of students to PHILOSOPHY. His clear style and unique commentary contributed to the popularity of his publications. In the aftermath of WWI Watson wrote *The State in Peace and War* (1919), urging world government based on tolerance and multicultural integration. Canada's cultural pluralism and peaceful emergence as a nation influenced his thinking. He advocated fair living conditions for all and rewards for individual effort. His influence on Canada continues today through the many clergy and civil servants who were his students.   ELIZABETH A. TROTT

Watson, Ken, curler (b at Minnedosa, Man 12 Aug 1904). When he skipped his Strathcona Cup (Man) Rink to victory in the 1949 Macdonald Brier, Watson became the first to win the coveted Tankard 3 times (with a career Brier record of 25 and 2). Beginning with 1923 at the Manitoba Bonspiel, he won 32 major bonspiels, including an unprecedented 6 grand aggregates in succession (1942-47). An innovative strategist, he helped develop the sliding delivery and was a supreme exponent of the draw game. Watson also served as an administrator of CURLING at several levels and was a successful author — *Ken Watson on Curling* sold nearly 150 000 copies.   GERALD REDMOND

Watson, Sheila, née Doherty, novelist, critic, teacher (b at New Westminster, BC 24 Oct 1909). Publication of Watson's novel *The* DOUBLE HOOK (1959) marks the start of contemporary writing in Canada. She attended UBC and later completed a PhD at U of T under Marshall MCLUHAN. A distinguished scholar of the early modernist period in Britain, specializing in the works of Wyndham Lewis, Watson taught school in the BC interior and later taught at U of Alberta. She is married to Wilfred WATSON, with whom she retired to Vancouver in 1980. Her *Four Stories* appeared in 1979, and one other story, *And the Four Animals*, in 1980. Her critical articles were collected in a special issue of *Open Letter* (1974). She was the founding editor of the periodical *White Pelican* (1971-75), and a volume of essays in her honour, *Figures in a Ground*, appeared in 1978.

The Double Hook is Watson's only novel; it presents in concise, symbolic terms a drama of social disintegration and redemption, set in an isolated BC community. Watson has said of the novel that it is "about how people are driven, how if they have no art, how if they have no tradition, how if they have no ritual, they are driven in one of 2 ways, either towards violence or towards insensibility — if they have no mediating rituals which manifest themselves in what I suppose we call art forms." These themes are presented in a style which itself balances on a "double hook": it is simultaneously local and universal, realistic and symbolic. Writers such as Robert KROETSCH have seen in the image of the double hook a balancing of opposites that is a fundamental characteristic of Canadian culture. Watson made possible, through her intellectual daring, the sophistication she assumed in her readers and her sceptical care for the nature of language itself, the development of contemporary writing in Canada.   STEPHEN SCOBIE

Watson, Wilfred, poet, playwright, professor of English literature (b at Rochester, Eng 1 May 1911). A highly innovative writer, Watson influenced 1960s theatre in Canada; his number-grid verse is significant to prosody and to poetry performance. His first book, *Friday's Child* (1955) won the British Council and the Governor General's awards for poetry. Its mythological, literary and religious imagery and intense energy persist in his later work. In the 1960s, Watson turned to drama, producing 10 plays, mostly in verse (including *Cockrow and the Gulls*, produced 1962; *O Holy Ghost DIP YOUR FINGER IN THE BLOOD OF CANADA and write, I LOVE YOU,* 1967; *Let's murder Clytemnestra, according to the principles of Marshall McLuhan,* 1969), whose immediate influence was considerable. A close reader of Marshall MCLUHAN (they coauthored *From Cliché to Archetype,* 1970), Watson believes the world of multimedia produces multiconsciousnesses, demanding a theatre of "radical absurdity" in which realistic settings and action are replaced by "multi-environments." Much of his work is political allegory. In the 1970s he returned to poetry: *The Sorrowful Canadians* (1972) counterpoints type fonts, refrains and "voices." With *I Begin with Counting* (1978) and *Mass on Cowback* (1982), he developed number-grid verse, using a vertical grid of 9 numbers with 17 slots for words, syllables or phrases. By stacking the grids, Watson writes a "score" for the performance of multivoice poems, which exist not on the page but in transformations from visual to auditory forms. His 1983 work, *Gramsci x 3,* though partly "docu-drama," is characterized by absurdity, continual experimentation with verse forms, satire alternating with lyricism, and an energy and exaltation that transcends the horrors it depicts.   SHIRLEY NEUMAN

Watson, William, "Whipper Billy," professional wrestler (b at Toronto 25 June 1915). It is claimed that he won 99% of his 6300 matches during a 30-year career. He was popular in the Toronto area and frequently drew capacity crowds. In 1947 he briefly held professional wrestling's world title, and he was the perennial Commonwealth champion. A 1971 automobile accident forced his retirement from the ring. Pursuing a long-standing interest, he began to work full-time on behalf of crippled children. As chairman of fund-raising for the Ontario Soc for Crippled Children, he has raised millions of dollars. He is vice-chairman of Ontario's Advisory Council for the Disabled.   J. THOMAS WEST

Watson Lake, YT, UP, pop 748 (1981c), is located at kilometre 1012 of the ALASKA HIGHWAY, 455 km E of Whitehorse. It is named after Frank Watson, a pioneer trapper and prospector who settled in the area in 1897. During construction of the Alaska Hwy, the townsite was moved 16 km from the lake to a location near the road. Watson Lake became an important communication centre after the construction of a major airport (1943), and is also the centre of the territory's largest logging and lumbering industry. By the highway is a growing "forest" of signs of faraway places begun by homesick soldiers in 1947.   HAL GUEST

Watt, Charlie, Inuk leader (b at Ft Chimo, Qué 29 June 1944). Energetic and dynamic, Watt has helped lead the Inuit through a time of rapidly increasing political sophistication. He founded the Northern Québec Inuit Assn in 1972 and the following year helped establish the Labrador Inuit Assn. He was a negotiator for the JAMES BAY AGREEMENT, signed in 1975, and was founding president of Makivik Corp, the successor to NQI and the first Inuit development corporation. His belief that the Inuit should have a voice in national affairs led him to help create the Inuit Committee on National Issues in 1979, and he worked unsuccessfully toward greater recognition of native rights in the CONSTITUTION ACT, 1982. He was sworn into the Senate in 1984.   JOHN BENNETT

Watters, James C., coal miner, trade unionist, socialist (b at Edinburgh, Scot 1869; d at Victoria 1947). As founding president of the BC Federation of Labour (1910), Watters played an important though ultimately unsuccessful role in labour's 1917 anticonscription coalition. As president of the TRADES AND LABOR CONGRESS, he hoped to rally Québec, ethnic minorities, moderate Liberals and moderate socialists behind the campaign to stop the CONSCRIPTION law of Robert BORDEN's Conservative, later Liberal-Conservative, wartime administration. Socialists and trade unionists, especially in western Canada, did forge a common front with Sir Wilfrid LAURIER during the Dec 1917 national election. No Liberal-Labour candidate, however, was elected and at the 1918 TLC convention Watters lost the presidency he had held since 1911. By 1920 he was reduced to attempting to mediate between conservatives and socialists in the labour movement. When this failed, he drifted into obscurity.   ALLEN SEAGER

Wave Energy is undoubtedly the most visible of the various forms of ENERGY present in the world's water bodies. The sight of waves breaking on a beach or against a cliff at any of Canada's thousands of kilometres of marine or freshwater shoreline appears to give rise in many people to a desire to invent a device to harness this seemingly abundant source of energy. Extensive wave-recording programs have defined the annual average levels of ocean wave energy in deep water, just off the Continental Shelf, at about 80 kW/m (kilowatts per metre) of wave front on Canada's Atlantic coast, and at about 100 kW/m on the Pacific coast. Closer to shore, where it would be more practical to exploit this potential source of renewable energy, the annual averages are substantially lower, about 20 kW/m for both coasts. In the Great Lakes and the Arctic Ocean, levels of wave energy are even lower and, during the winter months, ice eliminates it altogether. The averages for the open-water season in the GREAT LAKES is about 3-5 kW/m. Despite the relatively high averages of wave energy along the E and W coasts, commercial exploitation of this energy source has not been economically practical so far. The actual level of wave energy can vary by up to 3 orders of magnitude during any one year. During most of the summer, the level of

wave energy will be less than 5 kW/m, but during a severe winter storm the level can easily exceed 1000 kW/m. This variance makes it very difficult to design an efficient extractor capable of withstanding winter storms and equally capable of extracting energy at a much reduced level of wave activity — a difficulty which has often been underestimated. Hundreds of patents of wave-energy extractors have been claimed over the last 100 years, but none has reached the commercial development stage. Between 1976 and 1979 Canada joined the UK, US, Ireland and Japan in the Kaimei project, a full-scale wave-energy project off the coast of Japan, under the auspices of the International Energy Agency. The study confirmed a relatively low efficiency of the energy extractor and a high price per kilowatt hour. In Canada, many other sources of renewable energy are available to produce energy at a lower price.   J. PLOEG

Reading: B. Count, ed, *Power from Sea Waves* (1980).

Waxman, Albert Samuel, "Al," TV and movie performer, director (b at Toronto 2 Mar 1935). As title character of CBC TV's situation comedy "King of Kensington" 1975-80, he became one of Canada's most familiar actors. Later roles in TV dramas have brought critical praise. Waxman studied acting in New York in 1959, performed in Hollywood films, and directed short subjects and full-length Canadian movies before his CBC TV role, which earned him an ACTRA award 1976. A stunning performance as an unemployed labourer in "The Winnings of Frankie Walls" won the coveted Earl Grey Award 1981. He has since starred in the American TV series "Cagney and Lacey." Waxman is extremely active in fund raising and charitable activities across Canada.   ALLAN M. GOULD

Waxwing (Bombycillidae), family comprising 8 species, including the true waxwings, the hypocolius of the Middle East and the silky-flycatchers of southwestern US and Central America. True waxwings (3 species) are small passerines (perching BIRDS), 15-19 cm long. They inhabit subarctic and temperate regions of the Northern Hemisphere and are migratory. In Canada, 2 species occur, cedar waxwing (*Bombycilla cedrorum*) and bohemian waxwing (*B. garrulus*). They have very soft plumage dominated by rich fawn or soft grey coloration, with shadings of chestnut. Waxwings have a black throat and band across the eyes. The secondary wing feathers often have waxy, red tips from which the name is derived. Wings and tail are grey. The bill is short, thick, slightly notched and hooked. The crest is prominent. Waxwings are gregarious, particularly during the nonbreeding season. They eat insects which they may catch in flight but, in season, feed primarily on berries, fruits and flowers. They build a bulky nest consisting of an open cup of twigs, moss and grass lined with hair, down or feathers. Clutches, of 3-7 ash grey or bluish eggs, marked with dark brown, are incubated mainly by the female. Young are fed by both parents.   HENRI OUELLET

Wayne and Shuster, comedy team composed of John Louis Wayne (b at Toronto 28 May 1918) and Frank Shuster (b at Toronto 5 Sept 1916). They met at Harbord Collegiate, Toronto, where they performed in annual revues. After receiving BAs in English from U of T, they were both studying for MAs when WWII intervened. After enlisting in the infantry, they were soon reunited, writing and performing for *The Army Show*. Following the war, they returned to Canada and worked together on radio (by 1947 they had their own show on CBC) and later on television. In 1950 they began appearing as guests on various American TV programs, including a record 67 performances on "The Ed Sullivan Show." Although their wide-ranging skits, described as "an amiable mixture of slapstick, pantomime, visual tricks, sheer corn and sometimes ingenious twists on classic situations," have not always met with critical approval, the comedy team has remained popular and has won several international awards. Despite their popularity in the US since the 1950s, Wayne and Shuster have remained based, personally and professionally, in Toronto, repeatedly resisting pressure to pursue greater wealth and fame south of the border.   CHARLES DOUGALL

Weasel, small, long-bodied, carnivorous MAMMAL of family Mustelidae. Three occur in Canada: short-tailed weasel, ermine or stoat (*Mustela erminea*); long-tailed, and least weasels (*M. frenata, M. rixosa,* respectively). Genus *Mustela* also includes MINK, black-footed FERRET and the introduced European ferret. Weasels have dark brown upper-bodies and tails; creamy white underparts. They assume a white winter coat in northern regions. In the FUR INDUSTRY no distinction is made among the coats of the 3 species; all are marketed as ermine. The weasel's head is bluntly pointed; ears, small and rounded. The long, slender body has a thick neck and short feet. Next to WOLVERINES, least weasels, the smallest species, are the rarest mammals in eastern Canada. They occur throughout mainland Canada from interior BC to northern Ontario and Québec. They prefer coniferous forest or tundra but also inhabit marshes, meadows and broken woodlands. Long-tailed weasels, the largest species, occur from S America to about 49° N lat and are found in southern BC, the Prairies, Ontario, Québec and NB. They prefer mixed hardwood forest but also inhabit other forests or open country, always near water. The short-tailed weasel, widespread in the Northern Hemisphere, occurs throughout Canada in habitats including tundra, boreal forest, meadows and riverbanks. All species take small mammals and insects; long-tailed and short-tailed weasels also take young rabbits and larger rodents. Long-tailed weasels breed in July-Aug; 4-9 young are born 205-237 days later. Delayed implantation of the embryo accounts for the long gestation. Short-tailed weasels mate in March; gestation lasts about 30 days; the single litter averages 6 young. Least weasels bear 2-3 litters annually, each of 3-6 young; gestation lasts about 35 days. Males may assist females in hunting food for young. As efficient killers of mice, weasels are useful to farmers, except when they take poultry. They do not make good pets.
                                                C.S. CHURCHER

Weather is defined as the atmospheric conditions prevailing at a specific place and time; CLIMATE is the characteristic weather, including average and extreme conditions, over months, seasons and years. METEOROLOGY is the study of the motions, processes and phenomena of the atmosphere. Although people have always been fascinated and challenged by weather and climate, scientific weather observation and the development of meteorology as a physical science only became possible after the invention of the thermometer and barometer in the 17th century. In the 1980s over 150 national meteorological services collaborate, through the World Meteorological Organization, in exchanging meteorological information several times daily around the globe.

Weather Forecasting attempts to predict the air temperature, humidity, WIND speed and direction, precipitation, CLOUDS, etc, that will occur at a given place or region at a particular time in the future. The atmosphere may be seen as a massive air machine which moves heat and moisture from place to place. Weather is a product of this machine. The workings of the atmosphere follow physical laws, ie, the laws of thermodynamics, motion, conservation of mass and energy, etc, which are very complex to apply (*see* PHYSICS). Since the Earth is almost spherical and

spins on its own axis, the laws of motion cannot be described in simple terms. Some deviations from spherical shape, especially mountains and MOUNTAIN RANGES, create still more problems. In addition, most SOLAR ENERGY reaches the Earth in a band near the equator; the atmosphere plays a major role in distributing this excessive heat northward and southward, and this process further affects the various physical laws. As well, OCEANS have a different effect on the bottom part of the atmosphere than LAND does; and forests, lakes, plains, tundra, cities, etc, all have their own special effects on the atmosphere.

Most modern meteorologists attempt to cope with physical processes by expressing them mathematically, ie, by creating mathematical models of the atmosphere. Powerful computers are then used to solve problems. As computers become more powerful, the models can be made more complex and, often, more accurate. During the 1960s and 1970s, improved atmospheric models permitted useful forecasts projecting much further into the future than had been possible before; by 1980, forecasts extended 5 days into the future. All of the world's weather services are co-operating to push weather predictions out to 2 weeks by the end of the century. Weather forecasting usually involves the following stages: observation of what is now happening at one or many places; analysis of the observations to create a comprehensive picture of what is now happening at various places in the atmosphere; projection of this picture into the future (prognosis); interpretation of that future picture to determine the temperature, humidity, wind, precipitation, etc, to be expected at the time represented by that picture.

Meteorologists who are more interested in a shorter time range (1-2 days) often bypass the mathematical model and use their knowledge of how one weather event follows another. These observations are the basis of much weather lore relating the appearance of the sky, the timing of precipitation, the recent history of the wind or the trend in pressure to predictions of what will happen next. Others observe animal behaviour or consider how people are affected (eg, painful joints, migraine headaches) to make their, often correct, predictions. Severe local storms (eg, showers, damaging windstorms, thunderstorms with HAIL, TORNADOES) are of great interest, but because of their very short life cycles, usually tens of minutes from birth to death, observation by RADAR and extrapolation is usually the only effective approach to prediction.

National or continental boundaries are irrelevant to weather forecasting. This fact has made METEOROLOGY a truly international science. The World Meteorological Organization (WMO), part of the UNITED NATIONS structure, co-ordinates meteorological activities throughout the world. One of the organization's main programs, the World Weather Watch (WWW), attempts to provide the information analysis and exchange required by all national weather services to create weather forecasts. The principal elements of WWW are the Global Observing System, which provides the weather observations required for forecasting; the Global Telecommunications System, which makes the observations available to all countries needing them for weather forecasting; and the Global Data Processing System, which analyses the observations and carries out the prognosis function on behalf of countries lacking these capabilities. All countries benefit from the elements of the WWW; without it Canadian meteorologists could not be reasonably sure that they would get the weather observations required for forecasting, or that weather observations made in Canada would reach other countries needing them.

In Canada weather forecasting is carried out in the same way as in other scientifically ad-

vanced countries. Weather observations from all around the Earth's surface, from balloons released at many locations around the globe, from SATELLITES, radar, aircraft and ships are transmitted freely to all countries over the Global Telecommunications System. These data are analysed in the Canadian Meteorological Centre in Montréal to create a mathematical picture of the present condition of the atmosphere over the Northern Hemisphere. This picture is provided to Canadian meteorologists in the form of a series of weather maps for the surface and various higher levels. (Before 1990 the Canadian model may well cover the whole globe, since what happens in the Southern Hemisphere has an effect over Canada beyond the fourth or fifth day.) Next, the mathematical model is run in a computer in a series of short time steps, some as brief as 6 minutes. New series of charts are provided to meteorologists for specific intervals out to the end of the model run. The results of the model are then translated into weather forecasts. There is a great deal of research under way into using the model to give a direct prediction of the various elements of the weather; but, until that research bears fruit, weather forecasts will continue to be made by forecasters. Many aspects of the forecast are not done well automatically, largely because it is not yet possible to create mathematical models that are as complex as the atmosphere itself.   J.A.W. McCULLOCH

Reading: R.A. Hornstein, *The Weather Book* (1980); J.G. Navarra, *Atmosphere, Weather and Climate* (1979).

Weaving, Contemporary Long before loom weaving was developed, woven and coiled baskets were made from grasses, twigs, root fibres and leaves readily collected from indigenous plants and worked with the hands. Basketry forms have changed little to the present day. Spinning was first used in the production of simple ropes, cords and fishing lines and, later, to create yarns. More complex forms of weaving gradually evolved from basketry and a new tool, the loom, was developed. The loom allowed the interlacing of fibres to make a continuous web (or fabric) composed of 2 sets of threads at right angles to one another: warp threads, stretched under tension down the length, and weft threads, interlaced across the width. In primitive looms the tension on the warp is created by weighting the threads with stones, just as primitive spinning uses a drop spindle under the force of gravity. As the requirements of the loom (stronger threads) brought about changes in yarns (simple and compound) and vice versa, these simple devices developed into modern TEXTILE technology. Tapestry weaving coincided with the invention of loom weaving, but tapestry is worked on a loom of different type. In tapestry the weft threads cover the warp in a discontinuous fashion. Early tapestries often told a story in pictures; modern ones rarely do so.

Early settlers in Canada brought advanced weaving skills with them and their home industry satisfied the community's textile needs. INDUSTRIALIZATION caused a decline in home spinning and weaving but interest has renewed in recent years. In 1982 there were an estimated 7000 or 8000 weavers in Ontario, Québec and BC, and weavers' guilds exist in most large communities in Canada, providing a social outlet, a market and a place to share information and learn new skills. Many weavers belong to more than one guild.

Wool is the most favoured raw material but other natural and man-made fibres are used. Few weavers restrict themselves to one material or technique, and many also spin their own yarns. As a result of the upsurge in CRAFTS in general and weaving in particular, small woollen mills have been established to provide washed and carded wool. Workshops, seminars and competitions are all popular.

Since the 1960s some craftsmen have moved away from traditional weaving into "art fabric," experimenting with traditional techniques but using a wide range of materials in the production of unique works. They usually sell through galleries or their work is commissioned for public places and private homes. Two notable weavers, principally in tapestry, Joanna Staniszkis of BC and Micheline Beauchemin of Québec, have been recipients of the Saidye Bronfman award for excellence in crafts, the most prestigious annual crafts award in Canada.

From PREHISTORY Canadian Indians and Inuit had a knowledge of basketry, a craft, like weaving, usually undertaken by women. The Salishan peoples of the Northwest Coast have had a long history of textile manufacture, using mountain-goat hair, fireweed and woolly dog hair; most famous are the CHILKAT BLANKETS (*see* NORTHWEST COAST INDIAN ART). Native Canadians have revived many of these skills, including basketry, in recent years. The NOOTKA of Vancouver I plait grass, cherry and cedar baskets; the INUIT of Great Whale R make lidded baskets of lime grass, often incorporating soapstone knops; the Micmac, Maliseet and Ontarian Indians customarily use split ash. The Salish weavers of BC are unique in re-establishing a flourishing home industry, using locally grown wool and natural dyes in their own authentic tradition. All this work, and that of many other talented weavers across Canada, is sought after and the economic effect is considerable, although it may only be a supplementary income for many because of the time, care and skill that are still the hallmarks of the dedicated weaver.

DEIRDRE SPENCER

Webb, Phyllis, poet, broadcaster (b at Victoria 8 Apr 1927). Author of several books of poetry and one of broadcast scripts, essays and reviews, Webb is a writer of stature in Canadian letters. Her work is brilliantly crafted, formal in its energies and humane in its concern. In Webb's poetry there is a sadness about the pomposities of human nature, variegated with a visionary sympathy with natural life and landscape and with the human impulse toward freedom. Webb's political activities, her work as a public-affairs broadcaster and her interest in political theory infuse her work with a concern for public life.

Webb attended UBC (BA) and McGill. Her first collection of poems appeared in *Trio* (1954). *Even Your Right Eye* was published in 1956, and in 1957 she won a grant enabling her to study drama and theatre in France. In 1962, *The Sea Is Also a Garden* appeared, followed by *Naked Poems*, a series of intense, haiku-like poems, in 1965. From 1964 to 1969, Webb worked at CBC Toronto, first in public affairs and then, 1967-69, as executive producer of the program "Ideas." Returning to the West Coast in 1969, Webb eventually took up permanent residence on Saltspring I. In 1971, her *Selected Poems 1954-65* was published. *Wilson's Bowl* (1980) is an important collection of poems written during the 1970s. *Talking* (1982) is a collection of some of Webb's reviews, articles and CBC broadcasts, and a new selection of poems, *The Vision Tree*, appeared the same year. She has taught at UBC, U Victoria, U of Alberta and the Banff Centre School of Fine Arts.

SHARON THESEN

Webster, Jack, journalist, broadcaster (b John Edgar Webster at Glasgow, Scot 15 Apr 1918). He is pre-eminent among British Columbia public affairs broadcasters for his knowledge of the province's affairs, his probing and pugnacious approach to his interview subjects, and his ability to make news himself. Late in 1947, he immigrated to Canada and worked on the *Vancouver Sun* to 1953. That year he began a program on CJOR radio called City Mike. During this period his hard-hitting daily reports on a police

scandal in Vancouver created a sensation. In 1963 Webster found his metier in an "open line" radio program. By championing those with grievances against authority, Webster became in effect an ombudsman, helping, for example, to bring about improvements in the care of severely retarded children, to improve the legal aid system, and to better the administration of care for the elderly. In 1978 Webster was planning to retire when he was offered a daily open line show on BCTV. He has repeated his success on television.

CHUCK DAVIS

Webster, Lorne Campbell, financier (b at Montréal 19 Sept 1928). Educated at Lower Canada College and McGill, Webster started his business career with the family fuel-oil company, Canadian Import. In 1968 he founded his own firm, Prenor Group, a holding company with major investments in insurance (through Canadian Provident, Northern Life, Paragon and Personal insurance companies), trust services (with the General Trust of Canada and North America Trust), real estate (through Armand DesRosiers Inc) and investment management (with Bolton Tremblay). Webster is also a director of the Bank of Montreal, Domtar, Murphy Oil, Québecor, Dale-Ross Holdings and several other companies.

JORGE NIOSI

Weeds are PLANTS growing where humans do not want them. Their undesirable qualities are varied: they deprive crop plants of sunlight, water and mineral nutrients; can be poisonous to humans or domestic animals; act as hosts for plant diseases, destructive insects and other pests; contaminate milk or other agricultural products; bear spines or thorns; cause allergies such as hay fever. Weeds are found not just in agricultural areas, but also in forests, lakes, recreational areas, roadsides and all other sites of human activity.

Weeds belong to virtually all plant families. They include algae, primitive vascular plants (eg, field horsetail, *Equisetum arvense,* and bracken fern, *Pteridium aquilinum*), low creeping annuals (eg, purslane, *Portulaca oleracea*), tall coarse herbs (eg, lamb's-quarters, *Chenopodium album*), vines (eg, field bindweed, *Convolvulus arvensis*), parasites (eg, dodder, *Convolvulus*), shrubs (eg, common barberry, *Berberis vulgaris*) and trees (eg, Manitoba maple, *Acer negundo*). Weeds are characterized by the following attributes: rank, vigorous growth; rapid maturation; vigorous regrowth after damage; abundant seed production; intermittent germination of seeds over many years; underground spread of roots or rhizomes. No single weed has all these attributes, but all have several.

In agriculture, weeds are estimated to cause more losses than destructive insects and plant diseases combined. Until the mid 1950s, the principal means of control was cultivation. Increasingly sophisticated cultivators, first horse drawn and then tractor drawn, made the task easier, but much of the labour involved in crop production was for weed control. The development, early in the century, of seed-cleaning plants where weed contaminants were removed from crop seeds, was a major step in weed control. The Canada Seeds Act classifies crop seeds according to weed seed content. Grain exports must have less than a specified minimum content of weed seeds, and seeds of species designated as noxious are subject to the most stringent rules.

Chemical Control of Weeds began around 1950 with widespread use of 2,4-D. At present in Canada, more than 100 chemicals are licensed for sale as herbicides. Millions of dollars are spent on them annually, but this sum is less than would otherwise be spent on weed removal from fields and harvested crops. Federal and provincial legislation is designed to ensure that herbicides are marketed and applied safely.

Modern farmers attempt integrated weed control by a combination of chemical means and tillage. The advent of chemical herbicides has modified, but not eliminated, the weed problem. Across the prairies, infestations of weeds (eg, wild mustard, *Sinapis arvensis*) have been reduced, but species tolerant of common herbicides (eg, green foxtail, *Setaria viridis*) have greatly increased. Similar shifts in weed populations involving various species have occurred in other agricultural regions. In the 1970s, herbicide-resistant forms of several common weeds began to appear. Lamb's-quarters, common groundsel (*Senecio vulgaris*) and redroot pigweed (*Amaranthus retroflexus*) all now have forms that are resistant to the popular triazine herbicides.

Biological Control of Weeds usually involves the introduction of an INSECT or a FUNGUS species to control an introduced weed, and has been attempted in many parts of Canada. In the interior of BC, Saint-John's-wort (*Hypericum perforatum*) has been controlled by beetles. In the same area, the reduction of knapweeds (*Centaurea*) by both insects and fungi is being tried. The targets are usually perennial species in uncultivated land.

Canada's largest and most important agricultural area encompasses the southern part of the Prairie provinces. In cultivated land in Saskatchewan and Manitoba, the most abundant weed (in a 1976-79 survey) was green foxtail; second and third were wild oats (*Avena fatua*) and wild buckwheat (*Polygonum convolvulus*). Other common weeds of Canadian agricultural land are dandelion (*Taraxacum officinale*), Canada thistle (*Cirsium arvense*), common milkweed (*Asclepias syriaca*), leafy spurge (*Euphorbia esula*), pigweeds (*Amaranthus*), sow thistles (*Sonchus*) and ragweeds (*Ambrosia*).

Weeds of other habitats include poison ivy (*Rhusr iradicans*) in woodlands, and common plantain (*Plantago major*) and white clover (*Trifolium repens*) in lawns. The introduced submerged aquatic weed, Eurasian water milfoil (*Myriophyllum spicatum*), poses a multifaceted problem in lakes, canals and streams across southern Canada, much as our native elodea (*Elodea canadensis*) did in Europe in the 1800s. Weeds may have desirable qualities. White clover is a useful pasture plant. Sweet clovers (*Melilotus*) are dangerous roadside weeds because they attract bees near passing cars and obscure road signs, but they are valuable short-term hay and pasture plants and are a source of honey. *See* INSECTS, BENEFICIAL; INSECT PESTS; PESTICIDES.

PAUL B. CAVERS

Reading: G.A. Mulligan, *Common Weeds of Canada* (1976).

Weekend Magazine began publication in Sept 1951, distributed free of charge with 9 daily NEWSPAPERS across the country. *Weekend* offered high-quality colour reproduction to advertisers, good photographs, feature stories and recipes to readers, and a profit-making supplement that boosted circulation for the newspaper publishers. By the 1960s *Weekend Magazine* was carried in 41 newspapers with a circulation over 2 million, and it was the most popular ADVERTISING vehicle in the nation. Colour television and the turn away from general-interest periodicals hurt the magazine, and it got thinner each year. By 1979 it had been merged with *The Canadian*, and in 1982 *Today*, the successor supplement, ceased publication. *See also* MAGAZINES.

J.L. GRANATSTEIN

Weightlifting has been an Olympic sport since the first modern Games in 1896. It also figures in the Commonwealth, Pan-American, Asian, Mediterranean and African Games. Counting 120 nations, the International Weightlifting Federation is one of the largest federations in the world. There are approximately 1200 members of the Canadian Weightlifting Federation.

This spectacular indoor sport is composed of 2

events: the snatch and the clean and jerk. In the snatch, the athlete lifts the bar to arms' length in one continuous motion. In the clean and jerk, he lifts the bar to his shoulders, then jerks it overhead to arms' length. The athlete is allowed a total of 3 attempts in each event. The best snatch is added to the best clean and jerk to give a total result. Medals are awarded in each event, with the overall winner being determined by the total. Competitors are divided into 10 bodyweight categories, ranging from 52 kg to plus 110 kg. In case of a tie, the lighter athlete is declared the winner. Both events, which demand great speed, balance, flexibility and strength, are performed on a 4 m square platform before 3 judges. A team is composed of a maximum of 10 athletes. The apparatus used in competition is standardized by the IWF and all equipment is manufactured to metric specifications.

The legendary figure of early Canadian weightlifting was strong-man Louis CYR, who in competition resulting from his open challenge to any man in the world was undefeated. Among his many outstanding feats were lifting 551 pounds (249 kg) with one finger and lifting (in Boston in 1895) 4337 pounds (1967 kg) on his back — claimed to be the greatest weight ever lifted by one man. In formal competition G. Gratton won a silver medal at the 1952 Helsinki Olympic Games, Doug HEPBURN won the world heavyweight championship in Stockholm 1953 and Jacques Demers won a silver medal (75 kilo class) at the 1984 Los Angeles Olympics.

RICHARD CAMPION

Weights and Measures, terms which traditionally referred to standards of mass (or weight), length and volume. Over the past few thousand years such standards have frequently been introduced throughout the world for trading and tax purposes. However, as measurement is one of the most fundamental aspects of SCIENCE and ENGINEERING, the term now embraces a much wider gamut of units. The development and dissemination of measurement standards has become the science of metrology. To the original basic units of mass and length (volume is a derived unit) have been added other "base units": time, temperature, electric current, luminosity and the somewhat esoteric amount-of-substance unit. These base units and a large number of derived units are rigorously defined in the International System of Units (Système International d'Unités, or SI), a version of the metric system, formulated by and under the aegis of the International Bureau of Weights and Measures (BIPM). First adopted in 1960, the SI is not invariant, but evolves slowly in the interests of greater precision, convenience or internal consistency. Virtually all of the world's scientific work is reported in SI units; construction, engineering and commerce substantially use or will use the system in all major countries except the US and Great Britain, which still largely use the British imperial system.

In 1965 the British government expressed its intention to convert to the SI over a 10-year period; in 1972 the US Senate favoured a voluntary 10-year conversion, but because of a procedural point this suggestion was not endorsed by the House of Representatives. In both countries progress towards metrication has been sporadic and a completion date cannot plausibly be forecast for either. Canada has been converting from the imperial system to SI since 1971; the process is expected to be substantially complete by the end of 1985 (see METRIC CONVERSION).

Canada's former measurement system derived mainly from the imperial system, with some contribution from a French measurement system. The imperial system was codified in its first reasonably "scientific" form in 1838, following a complex history. A number of imperial units (eg, foot, mile) can be traced back to the Roman Empire; however, their magnitude has fluctuated with time and locality. R.E. Zupko's *A Dictionary of English Weights and Measures, from Anglo-Saxon Times to the Nineteenth Century* contains entries for some 3000 measurement units with 25 000 numerical variations. In 1884 the UK (hence Canada, as a colony) became an adherent of the Convention of the Metre, by which the BIPM had been established in 1875. The UK was thus a participant in the first distribution by the BIPM of national prototype metre bars and kilogram masses in 1889. Canada became an adherent to the convention in its own right in 1907. A Canadian, J.C. MacLennan, was a member of the International Committee of Weights and Measures (CIPM) from 1929 to 1935. This committee is charged with the direction and supervision of the BIPM, including its metrological laboratories at Sèvres on the outskirts of Paris. There has been a Canadian member of the CIPM continuously since 1951; one of them, L.E. Howlett, served as CIPM president for the period 1964-68. No country is represented on the CIPM; the 18 members (not more than one per country) are elected in a personal capacity. Their task is to monitor and foster metric-based metrology in all nations adhering to the Convention of the Metre (46 in 1983).

Since 1951 Canadian CIPM members have all been members of the NATIONAL RESEARCH COUNCIL. NRC's Division of Physics maintains or realizes the country's primary standards of measurement and many derived standards. Standards disseminated to laboratories and industries requiring the highest precision are calibrated at NRC. The reference standards for trade (periodically calibrated at NRC) are in the custody of the Dept of CONSUMER AND CORPORATE AFFAIRS and constitute the legal basis for all local standards employed in the application of the Canadian Weights and Measures Act (1971) to commercial or trade transactions (see CONSUMER STANDARDS). In 1982 Canada joined the International Organization of Legal Metrology (OIML, est 1955). The OIML is concerned only with the application of metrology to trade, eg, in establishing uniformity in international trading practices.

All major industrial countries support national standards laboratories equivalent to that of NRC, eg, the National Bureau of Standards in the US and the National Physical Laboratory in the UK. Elaborate control and comparison procedures ensure measurement consistency among national laboratories. For nations such as Canada, measurement standards are now secure and adequate monitoring has reduced fraudulent measure to an incidental problem. This achievement eluded all efforts until well into the 20th century. The reasons for failure were many, but the major one was undoubtedly human cupidity. Today's relatively happy situation is one of the benefits of modern technology coupled with a technological infrastructure so pervasive that we now take it for granted.

International System of Units (SI)

The following descriptions of the 7 SI base units and the 2 SI supplementary units include 1983 estimates of their reproducibilities. These estimates are based on measurements of the highest quality made at various places and times, and are applicable to measurements at unit magnitude. Imprecision will increase at substantially greater or smaller magnitudes; thus, while a mass of one kilogram can be determined to about 2 parts in 10^9, masses of a gram can be determined only to within 3 parts in 10 million (3 in 10^7); those of a tonne, to within one part per million (1 in 10^6).

Length When adopted in 1799, the metre (m) was fixed as one ten-millionth part of a quadrant of the Earth's meridian. In 1983 it was defined as the distance light travels in a vacuum in one 299 792 458th of a second. Units are accurate to 2 parts in 10^{11}.

Mass The unit of mass is the kilogram (kg), not the gram (g). When adopted in 1799, the kilogram was defined as the mass of a cubic decimetre of water. Since 1889 it has been the mass of the international prototype kilogram, a platinum-iridium artifact kept at Sèvres. Unit accuracy is 2 parts in 10^9.

Time The second (s), traditionally one 86 400th of a mean solar day, was established in 1960 as one 31 556 925.9744th of the tropical year 1900. In 1968 it was defined in terms of the frequency radiated from the transition between specified energy levels of the cesium-133 atom. Unit accuracy is 5 parts in 10^{14}.

Electric Current The ampere (A) was defined in 1881 in terms of the force between magnetic poles (a purely theoretical concept); in 1908 as a more reproducible "international ampere" in electrolytic terms. Since 1948 the "absolute ampere" has been defined in terms of the force between parallel, current-carrying conductors. Units are accurate to 2 parts in 10^7.

Temperature (kelvin, K) is the only base unit that is "intensive" rather than "extensive" (ie, 2 temperatures cannot be added together to give their sum). This characteristic presents certain measurement difficulties. The present International Practical Temperature Scale of 1968 evolved from the "hydrogen temperature scale" of 1889 and will probably be superseded between 1987 and 1991. Measurements are accurate to within 0.0002 K at room temperature. Significant celsius equivalents are 273.15 K = 0°C and 373.15 K = 100°C.

Amount of Substance The mole (mol) is a quantity which serves to connect the macroscopic SI units to measurements used in CHEMISTRY and atomic PHYSICS. A 1902 convention using oxygen-16 as a standard was superseded 1960-61 by one using carbon-12; the latter stan-

SI Prefixes					
Factor	Prefix	Symbol	Factor	Prefix	Symbol
10^1	deca	da	10^{-1}	deci	d
10^2	hecto	h	10^{-2}	centi	c
10^3	kilo	k	10^{-3}	milli	m
10^6	mega	M	10^{-6}	micro	μ
10^9	giga	G	10^{-9}	nano	n
10^{12}	tera	T	10^{-12}	pico	p
10^{15}	peta	P	10^{-15}	femto	f
10^{18}	exa	E	10^{-18}	atto	a

Some SI Derived Units with Special Names		
Quantity	*Unit (Symbol)*	*Derivation*
Mechanical		
force	newton (N)	$(m \times kg)/s^2$
pressure	pascal (Pa)	N/m^2
energy, work	joule (J)	$N \times m$
power	watt (W)	J/s
frequency	hertz (Hz)	cycles/s
Electrical		
electrical potential	volt (V)	W/A
electrical resistance	ohm (Ω)	V/A
electric charge	coulomb (C)	$A \times s$
electric capacitance	farad (F)	C/V
magnetic flux	weber (Wb)	$V \times s$
magnetic flux density	tesla (T)	Wb/m^2
inductance	henry (H)	Wb/A
Light		
luminous flux	lumen (lm)	$cd \times sr$
illuminance	lux (lx)	lm/m^2
Nuclear and X-Ray Dosimetry[1]		
activity (of radionuclide)	becquerel (Bq)	disintegrations/s
absorbed dose	gray (Gy)	J/kg
dose equivalent	sievert (Sv)	J/kg

[1] Relations to the earlier curie, rad and rem are as follows: one curie is 3.7×10^{10} Bq; one rad is 0.01 Gy; one rem is 0.01 Sv

dard was incorporated into the SI in 1971. The mole is the amount of substance which contains as many elementary particles (atoms, molecules, ions, etc; the precise ones under consideration must be specified) as there are atoms in 0.012 kg of carbon-12. In some circumstances, relative atomic weights can be determined to one part in

Some non-SI units in use in North America		
Unit (Symbol)	Definition	Approximate SI Value
Length		
parsec (pc)		3.085×10^{16} m
light-year		9.461×10^{15} m
astronomical unit (AU)		1.496×10^{11} m
nautical mile	1.852 km	
mile (mi)	8 furlongs, 1760 yd	1.609 km
furlong	220 yd	201.2 m
arpent	180 Paris feet	58.47 m
yard (yd)	3 ft	0.9144 m
Paris foot	12.789 in	0.3248 m
foot ("ft" or ')	12 in	0.3048 m
inch ("in" or ")		25.4 mm
Area		
acre	(1/640) mi² or 4840 yd²	0.4047 ha
arpent de superficie	32 400 square Paris feet	0.3419 ha
Weight (Mass)		
Avoirdupois		
long ton	2 240 lb	1.016 t
short ton	2 000 lb	0.907 t
long hundred-weight (cwt)	112 lb	50.80 kg
short hundred-weight (cwt)	100 lb	45.36 kg
pound (lb)	0.453 592 37 kg	
ounce (oz)	(1/16) lb	28.35 g
dram (dr)	(1/16) oz	1.772 g
grain (gr)	(1/7 000) lb	64.80 mg
Troy (or Apothecary)		
pound (lb t)	12 oz t	0.3732 kg
ounce (oz t)	20 dwt	31.10 g
pennyweight (dwt)	24 gr	1.555 g
Capacity		
barrel (bbl)	36 gal	163.7 L
barrel [US][1]	42 gal [US]	159.0 L
bushel (bu)	4 pk	36.37 L
bushel [US]	8 gal [US]	30.28 L
peck (pk)	2 gal	9.092 L
gallon (gal)		4.546 L
gallon [US]	231 cu in	3.785 L
quart (qt)	(1/4) gal	1.137 L
pint (pt)	(1/2) qt	568.3 mL
Miscellaneous		
British thermal unit (Btu)[2]		1 005 J
Btu per hour		0.293 kW
calorie[3]		4.184 J
carat		200 mg
fahrenheit (°F)	(t)°F=(9/5) (t)°C +32	
horsepower	550 ft lb/sec	745.7 W
knot	1 nautical mile per hour	0.514 m/s

[1] This is the barrel used by the oil industry

[2] Based on the heat required to heat one pound of water 1°F

[3] Based on the heat required to heat one gram of water 1°C. The "food calorie" used by dieticians is a kilo calorie

10^7. The absolute value of the mole is known to about 5 parts per million (5 in 10^6).

Luminous Intensity The candela (cd) is one of various "standard candles" which have been in use since before 1800. The candela (then called "new candle") was first defined in 1946 in terms of the freezing temperature of platinum. The present definition is a monochromatic (f = 540 x 10¹² Hz) radiant intensity of 1/683 watt per steradian. Unit accuracy is 5 parts per million.

Plane Angle The radian (rad) is the plane angle between 2 radii of a circle that cut off (from its circumference) an arc equal in length to the radius. Thus a full circle (360 arc degrees) is an angle of 2π rad. Units are accurate to 0.0000005 rad or 0.1 arc second.

Solid Angle The steradian (sr) is the solid angle which, having its vertex at the centre of a sphere, cuts off an area of the surface of the sphere equal to that of a square with sides of length equal to the radius of the sphere. Thus the solid angle of an entire sphere is 4π sr, that of a hemisphere 2π sr.

The SI is essentially a decimal system, ie, units are related by factors of 10, expressed in prefixes attached to the unit name.

Many quantities derived from the base units and which could be expressed in terms of those units are more conveniently designated by special names and symbols.

Some non-SI units are used with the SI because they are in worldwide use (eg, hour, knot, nautical mile). Others, eg, the hectare (ha, 10^4 m²), tonne (t, one Mg) and litre (L, one dm³) are not SI units but are used conjointly with the SI for convenience. H. PRESTON-THOMAS

Weinzweig, John Jacob, composer, educator, administrator (b at Toronto 11 Mar 1913). A pioneer of 20th-century composing methods in Canada — the first Canadian to explore 12-tone technique — he created a body of music indispensable to the Canadian repertoire and influenced several generations of young composers who were his students. When he graduated from U of T in 1937, Weinzweig's interest in contemporary composition drew him to the Eastman School of Music in Rochester, NY, for graduate studies. In 1939 he began to teach at the Toronto Conservatory and became composition professor at U of T in 1956, continuing there until his retirement in 1978. Deeply committed to the concerns of career composers, Weinzweig played an important part in the establishment of several support organizations, including the Canadian League of Composers (1951) and the Canadian Music Centre (1959). Weinzweig's ballet suite, *Red Ear of Corn* (1949), is probably his best-known work, though the series of *Divertimenti* (1946-) for various solo instruments and string orchestra offer a more representative view of his music as a whole. In 1974 Weinzweig was made an officer of the Order of Canada.

BARCLAY McMILLAN

Reading: P. Such, "John Weinzweig," *Soundprints* (1972).

John Weinzweig with a student during class at the Faculty of Music, U of T, Feb 1973 (*courtesy Public Archives of Canada/PA-138379/Walter Curtin*).

Weir, Walter C., mortician, politician, premier of Manitoba (b at High Bluff, Man 7 Jan 1929; d at Minnedosa, Man 17 Apr 1985). A Progressive Conservative, Weir was elected to the Manitoba Legislature in 1959. He served consecutively as minister of municipal affairs and then as minister of highways under Duff ROBLIN. Of great personal charm, he was popular among his caucus and Cabinet colleagues and their support enabled him to secure the party leadership in 1967. More conservative than his predecessor, Weir braked the pace of reform established by Roblin. In fact the principal aspects of his brief administration were government restraint, caution about medicare and opposition to federal proposals for constitutional reform and official bilingualism. Misjudging the public mood in 1969, he called an election ahead of schedule and was beaten by the NDP. Widely blamed for the Tory defeat, Weir retired from politics soon after the Manitoba Conservatives set up a process of leadership review in 1970. During the LYON premiership, he served as chairman of a government commission on local taxation.

GEOFFREY LAMBERT

Weldon, Richard Chapman, educator, politician (b at Sussex, NB 19 Jan 1849; d at Dartmouth, NS 26 Nov 1925). His education was unusually broad for his day: BA (1866) and MA (1870) from Mount Allison; he received his doctorate in international law from Yale at age 23. Returning to Mount Allison, he was appointed professor of political economy and mathematics, but after a year took leave to study public law at Heidelberg. Thus equipped he became a pioneer in legal education, being cofounder of Dalhousie Law School in 1883 and its first dean 1884-1914. Dalhousie was the first university law school in the common-law provinces; under Weldon's guidance it offered a systematic and liberal course of instruction, in contrast to the haphazard program of legal apprenticeship then prevalent. A prominent Conservative, he was MP, 1887-96, and a friend of Sir John THOMPSON. D.H. BROWN

Welfare State is a term that was apparently first used in the English language in 1941 in a book written by William Temple, Archbishop of York, England. For many years after, postwar British society was frequently characterized (often pejoratively) as a "welfare state," but by the 1960s the term commonly denoted an industrial capitalist society in which STATE power was "deliberately used (through politics and administration) in an effort to modify the play of market forces." For Asa Briggs, the author of this definition in an article appearing in *The Welfare State* (1967), there are 3 types of welfare state activities: provision of minimum income, provision for the reduction of economic insecurity resulting from such "contingencies" as sickness, old age and unemployment, and provision to all members of society of a range of social services. By this definition, Canada became a welfare state after the passage of the social welfare reforms of the 1960s (*see* SOCIAL SECURITY).

Richard Titmuss, one of the most influential writers on the welfare state, noted in *Essays on the Welfare State* (1959) that the social welfare system may be larger than the welfare state, a distinction of particular importance in Canada, where the social services component of the welfare state is less well developed. In addition to occupational welfare, there is a range of services provided by para-public, trade union, church, and nonprofit institutions. These are often funded by a combination of state and private sources.

Social Welfare and Social Philosophy To some writers, the expansion of the welfare state is a central political focus of SOCIAL DEMOCRACY because of the contribution of welfare state policies and programs to the reduction of inequality, the expansion of freedom, the promotion of fellowship and democracy, and the expression of humanitarianism. In Canada such a view of the welfare state appeared in the LEAGUE FOR SOCIAL RECONSTRUCTION's *Social Planning for Canada* (1935) and in the reports of social reformers, such as Leonard MARSH's classic, *Social Security for Canada* (1943), written for the wartime Advisory Committee on Reconstruction. Politically, this view has been expressed in the platforms of the NEW DEMOCRATIC PARTY (NDP) and its predecessor the CO-OPERATIVE COMMONWEALTH FEDERATION (CCF), and practised most notably by the postwar CCF government in Saskatchewan. However, it is the modern liberal, and not the social democratic, conception of the role of the Canadian state in the provision of social welfare that has been dominant.

In 20th-century liberalism, as practised in Canada and elsewhere, the responsibility for well-being rests with either the individual or the FAMILY, or with both. Simultaneously, there is a clear acceptance that capitalist economies are not self-regulating but require significant levels of state intervention to achieve stability. According to Briggs's definition, there is an emphasis in liberalism on the first 2 of the 3 welfare state activities: minimum income and social insurance. The necessity to develop a more cautious and residual social welfare state has been the theme of a number of major statements and reports by British writers J.M. Keynes and William Beveridge, and of the Canadian *Report of the Royal Commission on Dominion-Provincial Relations* (1940), the postwar *White Paper on Employment and Income* (1945) and the more recent federal *Working Paper on Social Security in Canada* (1973). It is an approach expressed in Mackenzie KING's *Industry and Humanity* (1918), Harry Cassidy's *Social Security and Reconstruction in Canada* (1943), and also in Tom Kent's *Social Policy for Canada* (1962), which presaged the period of high social reform, 1963 to 1968, under the federal minority Liberal government of Lester PEARSON.

The modern conservative conception of the welfare state is guided by the principles of 19th-century liberalism, ie, less government equals more liberty, from which follows the defence of individual pursuit of self-interest and the unleashing of competitive forces operating through private markets (*see* CONSERVATISM). The reduction of inequality, often held to be a goal if not a result of the welfare state, is considered antithetical to the pursuit of freedom and to material progress. Consequently the modern welfare state is criticized from the conservative perspective. In particular, it is often argued that social expenditures have become too heavy a burden for the modern state and that state expenditures on social programs divert resources from private markets, thus hampering economic growth. According to the conservative conception, the welfare state has discouraged people from seeking work and has created a large, centralized, uncontrolled and unproductive bureaucracy. Proponents of this view argue that the welfare state must be cut down and streamlined, and that many of its welfare activities should be turned over to charity and to private corporations.

This view of the welfare state is supported in Britain by the Conservative Party, in the US by the Republican Party, and in Canada by members of the federal Conservative Party and BC's Social Credit Party. The idea of the conservative welfare state had its clearest expression in Charlotte WHITTON's *The Dawn of Ampler Life* (1943) commissioned by John BRACKEN, then Conservative Party leader, to criticize the social democratic views incorporated in Marsh's *Social Security for Canada*; it also appears in the work of the FRASER INSTITUTE and, in Québec, in the publications of the Semaines sociales du Canada.

The re-examination of contemporary capitalist societies begun in the 1960s has produced a Marxist interpretation of the welfare state based on the centrality of the exploitation of labour in societies dominated by private markets and by the drive to acquire ever increasing amounts of private capital. From this point of view, a major role of the modern state is the provision of an appropriately trained, educated, housed and disciplined labour force available to employers when and where necessary. To accomplish this the welfare state becomes involved in the regulation of women, children and the family through laws affecting marriage, divorce, contraception, separation, adoption, and child support, since the family is the institution directly concerned with the preparation of present and future generations of workers and in provisions for employment, education, housing, and public and private health.

Development of a Welfare State in Canada

Social welfare in Canada has passed through roughly 4 phases of development, corresponding to 4 phases of the country's economic, political and domestic development.

The Early Period: 1840-1890 In the early period of capitalist development, the activities of the state, initiated in response to POVERTY and disease, were largely regulatory in nature. Social welfare, considered a matter that was primarily of local and private concern, consisted of the provision of relief, the care of the insane and of handicapped and neglected children (*see* CHILD WELFARE), and the incarceration of lawbreakers. After Confederation, the provision of social welfare services continued to be irregular and piecemeal, depending in part on the philanthropic inclinations and concerns of the upper class — in particular of those upper-class women who viewed charitable activities as an extension of their maternal roles and as an acceptable undertaking in society. Reform of this system was predicated on the notion that the family was the basis of economic security. The institutionalization of the family and the social reproduction of labour, which began with legislation to enforce alimony, to regulate matrimonial property and marriage, and to limit divorce and contraception, was expanded with limitations on hours of work for women and children. Compulsory EDUCATION and PUBLIC HEALTH regulations were developed primarily in response to the spread of disease and fears of social unrest. Provincial governments began to support charitable institutions with regular grants.

The Transitional Phase 1891-1940 Although the primary concern of the Canadian state remained the promotion of profitable capital accumulation, particularly through support of "infrastructural" institutions, the state also came to be associated with the provision of a plentiful supply of appropriately skilled labour through the regulation of the relations of capital and labour, and the maintenance of the family. This was largely achieved by the use of state mechanisms to maintain economic stability in the economic sphere and guarantee family stability in the domestic sphere, and to do both at the least cost and risk to employers. During the same period charity workers and private charity organizations began to consolidate and to battle ideologically, politically and generally unsuccessfully for control of social welfare.

The appearance of legislation compelling children to attend school and providing public authorities with the power to make decisions in relation to "neglected" children was part of a growing number of state interventions to regulate social welfare. INDUSTRIAL RELATIONS legislation was also passed in the first decade of the 20th century, allowing the state to intervene in the relations between labour and capital.

The first piece of compulsory contributory social insurance legislation in Canada, the Workmen's Compensation Act, was passed in Ontario in 1914. During WWI, 2 important events speeded the development of an interventionist welfare state: demands for the support of injured soldiers and demands for the support the families left behind. Both demands led to the establishment of a Dominion scheme of pensions and rehabilitation and, in Manitoba, to the first mothers' allowances legislation (1916). Several provinces followed with mothers' allowance legislation of their own, but by war's end, after the incorporation of many thousands of women workers into the wartime labour force, mothers' allowances were the justification used to remove these same women workers from the labour force and to provide them with only a bare minimum of support. The postwar era also ushered in the first (and brief) Dominion scheme to encourage the construction of housing, but it had died by 1924. While there was considerable debate during the 1920s about whether to establish permanent unemployment, relief and pension schemes, the only result was the passage of the 1927 OLD AGE PENSION legislation, and this was in part the result of the efforts of J.S. WOODSWORTH and a small group of Independent Labour members of Parliament.

It was the traumatic economic conditions of the GREAT DEPRESSION that forced a change in social philosophy and state intervention. In 1930, with hundreds of thousands of Canadians unemployed, the newly elected Conservative government under R.B. BENNETT legislated Dominion Unemployment Relief. By 1935 the Conservative Party's stern resistance to change in the face of an economic catastrophe and Bennett's continuing reliance on the so-called natural "restorative" powers of capitalism were replaced by advocacy of social reform in BENNETT'S NEW DEAL legislation. Although the package was set aside the same year by the returned government of Mackenzie King and although the courts subsequently determined that the federal government did not have the power to pass such legislation, the necessity for major social intervention was reaffirmed in the report of the Royal Commission on Dominion-Provincial Relations, created by King to examine the constitutional and social questions posed by the Depression. In consequence, the Unemployment Insurance Act was passed in 1940 and the Tax Rental Agreement was established in 1941.

The Interventionist Phase 1941-1974 marks the arrival of what is conventionally called the welfare state. By the beginning of WWII, the economic and political lessons of the Depression had been well learned. People increasingly accepted the expanded role of the state in economic and social life and expected this to continue after the war. Nevertheless the postwar Liberal government largely ignored reports on social security, health insurance and public housing; instead, King settled on a political compromise, which at first boiled down to the establishment of family allowances. In all other areas the Liberal government moved to dismantle the apparatus of state intervention that had been constructed during the war. The state was to aid private enterprise rather than providing directly for economic security. During the postwar period, Dominion hospital grants, the provision of old-age pensions and old-age security, the first permanent program for the funding of relief, and permanent programs for the funding of higher education and vocational rehabilitation were introduced.

The Liberal Party was defeated in 1957 but was returned as a reform-minded MINORITY GOVERNMENT under L.B. Pearson in the early 1960s on a cyclical economic upsurge. Influenced by the American "war on poverty" and by the necessity to maintain the political support of the NDP, Pearson's Liberal government presided over the introduction of 3 major pieces of social legislation that constituted the last major building blocks of a welfare state in Canada: Medicare, the Canada Pension Plan and the Canada Assistance Plan. To these were added the Guaranteed Income Supplement, the increase in post-secondary education funding, and the consolidation of hospital, medicare and education grants through the Established Programs Financing Act (*see* INTERGOVERNMENTAL FINANCE). The reorganization of income tax and family allowance, and the expansion of public, co-operative and nonprofit housing, and of unemployment insurance provisions in the early 1970s were additional reform measures. Lastly, there were important reforms in the late 1960s in legislation controlling divorce, ABORTION and the availability of contraceptives, all of which had an important impact on the family.

The Fourth Phase: Erosion and the Future of Welfare, 1975- In the 1970s, state expenditures automatically increased with parallel increases in unemployment, in the AGING of the population, and in the broader use of medical services. The impact of these automatic mechanisms has become increasingly evident since 1975 when the economy began to decline after 10 years of growth. At the same time, revisions to the tax system, eg, indexation and the expansion of corporate tax write-offs, meant a reduction in tax revenue.

In the late 1970s and early 1980s rising inflation and the growing demands of large numbers of newly unionized white-collar workers, particularly public-sector workers, increased demands on expenditure. These conditions ushered in an attack on the state, both as employer and as spender. Corporations and governments advocated cutbacks in expenditures and layoffs of public-sector workers. The resulting unemployment was intended to reduce the power of the labour movement, particularly in the public sector, and help moderate wage increases. Even as inflation dropped in the mid-1980s attacks continued on public expenditure, justified by a need to reduce the public debt.

The attempts to reduce welfare state expenditures have included changing eligibility standards for unemployment insurance, welfare, etc; "privatizing" social programs by contracting out responsibility for social services (particularly those relating to children and the aged); shifting the burden of medical-care financing though the use of premiums and user fees; and decreasing social-program budgets relatively if not absolutely. The election of a new Conservative government in 1984 renewed the debate over "universality"; the minister of health announced a commitment to universal payment of pensions, but proposals were made to alter payment of the baby bonus. There has also been fierce conflict among federal, provincial and municipal governments over which level of government will finance social programs. Provincial reductions in social budgets throw the burden onto municipal governments (in Ontario and Nova Scotia) or onto para-public agencies, or onto the family. Since 1975, as a result of these changes, welfare state structures have eroded. State intervention schemes are still designed to deal with unemployment as a "contingency," an unusual occurrence, and not as the regular feature of economic and social life that it has become. This fact will no doubt exert considerable pressure on future welfare state policy.

ALLAN MOSCOVITCH

Reading: Allan Moscovitch, "The Rise and Decline of the Canadian Welfare State," *Perception* (Nov 1982); Moscovitch et al, *The Welfare State in Canada: A Selected Bibliography 1840-1975* (1983); L. Panitch et al, *The Canadian State: Political Economy and Political Power* (1977).

Welland, Ont, City, pop 45 448 (1981c), inc 1917, located in the Niagara Peninsula, 20 km S of St Catharines. It grew up where the WELLAND CANAL crossed the Welland R, and was the seat of Welland County from 1856 until regional government was established in 1970. Welland experienced industrial growth after 1900 when its canal and railway advantages were supplemented by hydroelectric power from NIAGARA FALLS. Welland is home to the Niagara College of Applied Arts and Technology, and is the centre of French education in the Niagara region. With construction of a bypass channel (1973), inner Welland became surrounded by canal channels, and the abandoned channel became a recreational waterway. The city's present industries include the manufacture of stainless and other steels, agricultural implements and large-diameter pipes. JOHN N. JACKSON

Welland Canal, 43.5 km long, crosses the Niagara Peninsula of SW Ontario, from Port Weller on Lk Ontario to PORT COLBORNE on Lk Erie, overcoming a height difference of 99.4 m between the 2 lakes, and bypassing the turbulent Niagara R and NIAGARA FALLS. A part of the ST LAWRENCE SEAWAY since 1959, the canal has 7 lift locks along its northern length, and one guard lock near the southern entrance. Locks 4, 5, and 6 comprise the world-famous series of twinned flight locks, with a length of almost 1249.7 m and a rise of 42.5 m. The canal has a depth of 8.2 m, a surface width generally of 94.5 m and 152.4 m along the Bypass Channel at Welland. Maximum vessel dimensions are length, 222.5 m; breadth, 23.2 m; draught, 7.9 m; and height above water level, 35.5 m. The canal is crossed by 11 lift-bridges, 3 tunnels, one high-level bridge, and a seasonal pedestrian ferry. Nearly 60 million tonnes of cargo were handled in 1980, principally grain (28.1 million t), iron ore (11.4 million t), coal (7.3 million t), and other bulk cargoes (11.2 million t). Of the 6596 vessel transits, 4968 were in lake vessels and 1628 in seagoing vessels; 70.2% of vessel transits were in Canadian-owned vessels by country of registry.

The Welland Canal bypasses the Niagara R and Niagara Falls, overcoming a height difference of 99.4 m between Lakes Ontario and Erie (*photo by John Reeves/Masterfile*).

A lifeline of trade and commerce into the inland heart of N America, the first Welland Canal opened in 1829, an achievement attributed primarily to a St Catharines businessman, William Hamilton MERRITT. A series of major new construction works have been undertaken at various times, often on different routes. Remnants of the Second Canal (1845-1915) and the Third Canal (1887-1930), and the modern or Fourth Canal (1931-present) with a 13.4 km bypass at Welland (opened in 1973), may be viewed. The Welland Canal created and expanded communities along its length, and has been a primary factor in their urban form and industrial development. JOHN N. JACKSON

Wells, George Anderson, bishop, scholar, lecturer (b at Clarke's Beach, Nfld 18 Nov 1877; d at Toronto 10 Apr 1964). Wells was a fisherman, sealer, labourer and trooper in the SOUTH AFRICAN WAR before continuing his education at various American institutions. Ordained a minister of the Church of England in 1910, he was a chaplain during WWI and chaplain of the fleet during WWII. He was awarded the CMG in 1918. He became bishop of the Cariboo diocese in 1934 and was assistant bishop to the bishop of Toronto 1946-51. J. ROGERS

Welsh If one ignores the improbable voyage of Madoc (the quasi-historical Welsh prince who supposedly discovered N America c1170) but accepts the probability that Welshmen sailed with John CABOT from Bristol on his epic voyage of 1497, a 500-year-old Welsh presence on NEWFOUNDLAND and CAPE BRETON ISLAND can be accepted. Another unsubstantiated view claims that Welsh seafarer John Lloyd (John the Skillful) reached Hudson Bay as early as 1475. In 1612 Sir Thomas BUTTON, a Welsh naval officer in command of the *Resolution,* searched unsuccessfully for the NORTHWEST PASSAGE and for Henry HUDSON. A Welsh settlement was established on the southern Avalon Peninsula in 1617 by Sir William VAUGHAN, an ardent supporter of colonial expansion. Despite the failure of the venture, Vaughan wrote 2 books promoting Newfoundland and thereby provided 2 of the earliest works about English N America. In 1759, at the siege of Québec, a Major Gwillim served under Gen James WOLFE. His daughter (Elizabeth SIMCOE) later married the first lieutenant-governor of Upper Canada. Explorer David THOMPSON, although English-born, was of Welsh descent. In the early 18th-century, eastern coastal waters were plagued by the puritanical Welsh pirate and slaver Bartholomew ROBERTS, and the volatile Acadian population of Nova Scotia was experiencing British rule under the sincere and practical Governor Richard PHILIPPS.

The principality of Wales (incorporated into England by the Act of Union of 1536) has always been overshadowed by England, Ireland and Scotland. One historian has commented that the Welsh "apart from their language, lacked practically every attribute of a nation except for the perverse and persistent belief that they were one." Wales's population (less than 3 million in 1985) has turned to emigration as a means of advancement.

Welshmen serving in the British forces in British N America during the AMERICAN REVOLUTION, the WAR OF 1812 and the REBELLIONS OF 1837 stayed on. There was a specific area of Welsh settlement along Lake Erie that absorbed the immigrants of the 18th and 19th centuries. A second wave of immigration was precipitated by the Cariboo Gold Rush in BC in 1858. Welsh immigration figures for the 20th century are more detailed and, just as for their ENGLISH, IRISH and SCOTS cousins, reflect the ebb and flow of economic depressions and world tensions. After David Lloyd George's visit in 1899, the Canadian West was endorsed as a good prospect for immigrants. In 1902 a third wave of immigrants — the "Patagonian Welsh," so named for their 35-year sojourn as a Welsh colony in Argentina — were relocated in Saskatchewan. The all-time high for Welsh immigration was in 1906, when 5018 settlers arrived. Immigration increased following WWI, and again from 1926 to 1929. Immigration was also high in 1946 (1294) and after the Suez Crisis in 1957 (2629). Overall, from 1900 to 1950, over 50 000 Welsh came to Canada.

Since 1960, Welsh immigration has been slight but steady, representing a small percentage of British immigration. In the 1961 census, 143 942 people claimed Welsh descent. In the 1971 census, this figure was reduced to 74 415 (perhaps because many of Welsh descent were recorded as being English). By 1981, only 46 620 people (0.2%) claimed Welsh descent. The largest grouping of Welsh is in Ontario (17 400), followed by BC (10 950), Alta (8510), Sask (2630), Man (2455), NS (1500), Qué (1170), NB (1055), Nfld (525), PEI (190), the YT (140) and the NWT (105). If at all, they have tended to consolidate in the mining areas of Ontario, BC, Alberta and the Maritimes. Their presence is exemplified in such place-names as Newport, Pontypool and Port Talbot (Ont), Cardiff (Alta) and Bangor (Sask).

Religion (METHODISM, Presbyterianism) and language were important to early Welsh settlers. Some communities developed around a Welsh-speaking nucleus and a Welsh-speaking preacher; however, these characteristics rarely survived the next generation. Most Welsh cultural activities are carried out at the local community level. There has never been a national society for the preservation of Welsh culture. However, although the Welsh are becoming rapidly assimilated into the larger English-speaking group, they do maintain some of their cultural organizations and historic festivals. Most major Canadian cities have a St David's society — named after the patron saint of Wales — and some have Welsh choirs (eg, Montréal, Ottawa, Toronto and Edmonton). St David's Day, March 1, is celebrated by Welsh Canadians, and St David's is the most common name for Welsh churches, eg, Dewi Sant United Church, Toronto. There are also traditional Welsh festivals of *Gymanfa Ganu* and the *eisteddfod*, which celebrate music, song and poetry.

The contribution of Wales to the development of Canada is impressive. Welsh and Welsh Canadians who have left their imprint on Canada, from both past and present, include missionaries Peter JONES and James EVANS; artist Robert HARRIS; scientists Stanley J. HUGHES and George L. PICKARD; writers Sir Charles G.D. ROBERTS and Robertson DAVIES; administrator Leonard W. BROCKINGTON; athlete Diane JONES KONIHOWSKI and cartoonist Yardley Jones.   DAVID EVANS

Wesbrook, Frank Fairchild, physician, educator (b in Brant County, Ont 12 July 1868; d at Vancouver 20 Oct 1918). Having obtained his arts and medical degrees at U of Man 1890, he did postgraduate work in London, Dublin and Marburg, Germany. Elected to a studentship at Cambridge in 1892, he spent 3 heady years amid brilliant fellow students in the laboratory of the eminent physiologist Michael Foster. He was then asked at age 27 to occupy the chair of pathology at U of Minn. Dean of medicine by 1906, he began publishing hard-hitting papers on medical and general university education. With his postgraduate student Moses Barron he was a forerunner of Frederick G. BANTING in the field of DIABETES as it relates to changes in the pancreas. In 1913 Wesbrook was invited to Vancouver to become founding president of UBC. Despite the outbreak of WWI and recurrent illness attributable to Bright's disease, he established the vigorous university that is his legacy.   WILLIAM C. GIBSON

Weslock, Nick, golfer (b at Winnipeg 13 Dec 1917). He is one of the true students of golf, having absorbed lessons from many of the world's great amateurs and professionals in a career that has given him 4 Canadian amateur championships, 7 Ontario open championships and 8 Ontario amateurs championships. Weslock has also been Canadian senior champion 6 times and Ontario senior champion 11 times. He left Winnipeg at age 5 and after living in Windsor and Hamilton, Ont, moved to Detroit, Mich, in 1947. He became a naturalized US citizen in 1956 and returned to Canada as a landed immigrant in 1959. Weslock has represented Ontario in provincial matches 25 times. He has also represented Canada as an Eisenhower world cup team member 5 times and as Commonwealth team member 5 times.   LORNE RUBENSTEIN

Wesson, John Henry, "Jack," farmer, farm leader (b near Sheffield, Eng 24 Aug 1887; d at Regina 13 Nov 1965). Wesson immigrated to Canada in 1907 and homesteaded near Maidstone, Sask. He joined the Saskatchewan Grain Growers' Assn and became well known for his public speaking, musical ability and sense of

humour. An early enthusiast for the pooling movement, he was elected one of the first directors of the SASKATCHEWAN WHEAT POOL (est 1924). He was elected VP of the pool in 1931 and, because of president Louis C. Brouillette's illness, gradually assumed more responsibilities before becoming president in 1937, holding office until 1960. Under his leadership, the pool led campaigns for the CANADIAN WHEAT BOARD, the protection of Canadian agriculture and the expansion of the CO-OPERATIVE MOVEMENT. Wesson served as the first president of the Canadian Federation of Agriculture (1936-40) and was the leader of the 1942 Farmers March on Ottawa protesting low prices for produce. With H.H. HANNAM, Wesson helped organize the first Outlook Conference, a meeting of farm leaders and government officials which became an annual event.   IAN MACPHERSON

West Coast Trail, on W coast of VANCOUVER I, follows the 72 km route of the historic life-saving trail between the communities of Bamfield and Port Renfrew, BC. This trail was constructed by the federal government in the early 1900s so rescuers could assist shipwrecked sailors on this section of coast, known as the "graveyard of the Pacific." The trail today is a challenge for the experienced hiker and can be completed in 6-10 days. Although some sections are wide and easy, following scenic, sandy beaches, the southern portion remains strenuous, requiring hikers to ford fast-moving streams, climb vertical ladders and cross steep gullies. The coastline remains rugged and unspoiled and rich in wildlife.   BART DEEG

West Indians The large and visible presence of West Indians in Canada is a fairly recent phenomenon. A group of 556 Jamaicans arrived in Canada in 1796 after an unsuccessful British attempt to enslave them in Jamaica (*see* BLACKS), but early contacts between Canada and West Indians were few. Large-scale immigration of West Indians really began in the 1960s, and by 1973 accounted for almost 13% of all immigration to Canada. Today the West Indian population of Canada is about 200 000.

English-speaking West Indians are from Antigua, Grenada, Bahamas, Barbados, Jamaica, Trinidad and Tobago, Montserrat, St Lucia, Virgin Islands, St Kitts-Nevis, Dominica, St Vincent; French-speaking West Indians are from Haiti, Martinique and Guadeloupe; and Spanish speakers are from Puerto Rico, Cuba and the Dominican Republic.

There have been 3 major periods of West Indian immigration. From 1900 to 1960, Canada accepted about 21 500 West Indians, only 33% of whom were placed under the ethnic-origin heading of "Black." The slight increase in West Indian immigration from 1945 to 1960 corresponds with postwar economic expansion and the West Indian Domestic Scheme (1955-60). The second period, from 1960 to 1971, corresponds with the "liberalization" of the Canadian Immigration Act. In this period Canada accepted about 64 000 West Indians. The increased migration was part of an international movement in which Canada, in response to slow European emigration, began to depend increasingly on labour from the Third World. The last period, which began in the early 1970s, coincided with the economic recession. Except for 1973 and 1974 (unusual years because of the Addressment of Status Program that helped many persons regularize their status), immigration from the West Indies has generally declined. West Indian immigration fell from 10% of total immigration in 1975 to 6% in 1979.

Before 1960, most immigrants came from the British colonies, especially from Barbados, Jamaica, Trinidad, and Bermuda. From 1973 to 1979, Jamaica provided 48% of the immigration, Trinidad 19% and Haiti 18%.

West Indians are concentrated overwhelmingly in the major urban centres of Québec and Ontario. Between 1973 and 1980, 96% of Haitian immigrants to Canada settled in Québec, particularly in Montréal. Of the English-speaking immigrants in the same period, 80% settled in Ontario, primarily in Toronto, but also in Kitchener, Waterloo and Windsor. Almost 11% from the same group settled in Montréal and 8.6% chose to establish themselves in the West, particularly in Alberta and BC.

Economic Life From the early 1900s, West Indian immigrants have contributed to Canada's economic life by providing cheap labour. Between 1900 and 1945, they were employed primarily on farms or in mines and factories. They also worked as mechanics and domestics or as waiters, porters, clerks, etc.

In the 1960s, thousands of skilled workers came to fill a bludgeoning job market, particularly in education, health services and office work. Between 1962 and 1966, almost 33% of West Indian immigrants sought work in the professional and technical categories. Because of the savings in labour-training costs and the productivity of the new arrivals, Canada was one of the beneficiaries of this Third World "brain drain."

In the late 1970s, there was a marked change in immigration eligibility categories (fewer independents, more sponsored applicants) and in labour qualifications (education and training). At the same time, employers continued to hire temporary workers in agriculture and in the services sector.

West Indian immigrants have included a minority of family entrepreneurs and highly educated and qualified professionals who form a small, separate bourgeoisie, and a majority of taxi drivers, factory workers, building superintendents, domestics, etc, whose working conditions are unstable and difficult.

Social and Cultural Life The West Indian community is not homogeneous. Class distinctions cut across regional differences which stem as much from the identity of the European countries that divided up the West Indies in previous centuries as from each island's individual history. The principal cleavage, however, is linguistic. Haitians moved en masse to Québec (Montréal) whereas anglophone West Indians chose Ontario (Toronto). Where the 2 groups coexist, as in Montréal, they have relatively little contact with each other. Where the language is the same, other differences come into play, eg, religion and social class.

West Indians have fought a number of battles in Canada over school issues. Many associations have instituted transition programs to deal with the problems experienced by young West Indians in adapting to various school programs. These programs are also meant to give children a better knowledge of their origins and to counter prejudice in Canadian society. Courses in Creole have also been established for some Haitian immigrants. Montréal has become one of the main publishing centres for Haitian literature, which deals with both memories of home and the difficulties of immigrant life. Haitian painting and sculpture have also appeared in Québec.

In the West Indian community the nuclear family is part of an extended family group spread over several major N American cities, and ties are often maintained with the country of origin. Aside from the family, the Protestant church plays an important role both in welcoming new arrivals and in helping persons in difficulty. Montréal's Haitians meet in masonic lodges, where they indulge in an original form of spirituality, some of which stems from Haiti's voodoo practices.

Jamaican immigrants introduced Rastafarianism to Canada. Originally (1933) a messianic movement in which Haile Selassie (who before he became emperor was called Ras Tafari) was believed to be the god of the blacks who comes to overthrow the white world (Babylon), Rastafarianism has since had considerable influence on the entire Jamaican society. Jamaicans also introduced "reggae" music, which originated in the ghettos of Kingston, Jamaica. A blend of African musical traditions and rhythm and blues, reggae was born during the 1960s and spread to England and America.

Trinidadians introduced calypso and the carnival. Held each year at the beginning of the summer in Montréal and Toronto, the carnival has become a symbol of identity for the entire Canadian West Indian community.

Politics The political battles of West Indians in Canada have been waged over improved working conditions, pervasive racism in employment, education and accommodation, the right to immigrate, and the right to participate in the political life of their mother country and of Canada. Anglophone West Indians have long fought through what is now the Order of Sleeping Car Porters, and have tried to affiliate this labour organization with the International Brotherhood of Sleeping Car Porters (AFC-CIO).

Since the early 20th century, West Indians have fought on behalf of women's issues through the Coloured Women's Club. The National Congress of Black Women, a more recent organization, includes anglophone and francophone women from Canada, the West Indies and other countries.

To defend the interests of blacks and to fight racism at various levels, a number of organizations were established, uniting blacks of Canadian and West Indian origin. Among these was the Canadian League for the Advancement of Colored People, inspired by the large American organization. Between the 2 wars, the Universal Negro Improvement Association, founded by Marcus Garvey, a Jamaican and one of the great black American leaders, led a different black movement advocating a return to Africa and nonintegration. This association gave rise to a string of satellite organizations in Canada.

At the end of the 1960s, student and youth organizations mobilized against the existing school system. This movement was influenced by the Black Panther movement in the US, the national liberation struggles throughout the world and the incident at Sir George Williams University [CONCORDIA U], Montréal, in 1968-69 when several black students, protesting against the racist grading system of a professor, attacked a computer. The Black United Front has been founded in Nova Scotia.

Haitian organizations in Québec have been active in the fight against the Duvalier regime in Haiti, the deportation of Haitians in 1974 and 1979, and have established information, emergency, literacy and other services. Haitians have also exerted enough pressure on the government so that political refugee status is given more freely to Haitian and Latin American immigrants. M. LABELLE, S. LAROSE, V. PICHÉ

Reading: K. Levitt, *Canada-West Indies Economic Relations* (1967) and *The Canadian Family Tree* (1979); R. Winks, *The Blacks in Canada* (1971).

West Vancouver, BC, District Municipality, pop 35 728 (1981c), area 9893 ha, inc 1912, is located on the N shore of Burrard Inlet, bounded by Howe Sound on the W, North Vancouver on the E and the Hollyburn, Strachan and Black mountains on the N. Until 1912 it was known as the West Capilano region of the Dist of NORTH VANCOUVER. West Vancouver is a mountainside community bisected by 19 major creeks, with rich coastal vegetation and a temperate climate typical of the Lower Mainland. The municipality is governed by an elected council and 6 aldermen.

West Vancouver is primarily a residential suburb, with most of its residents employed in other parts of Metropolitan Vancouver; 80% of the labour force commutes across Lions Gate Bridge each day. It grew slowly after incorporation (pop 700), until the catalyst of British Pacific Properties investments set off a residential boom after WWII. Growth was rapid up to and including the 1960s, but future expansion is greatly limited by topography and very high real-estate prices. Manufacturing exists only on a small scale, but tourism is important. Two scenic highways, the Upper Levels and Marine Drive, traverse the area, whose attractions include exclusive residential districts, Hollyburn Ridge (a year-round alpine recreation area), Lighthouse Park and Horseshoe Bay. The area is noted for its excellent salmon fishing, its rugged coastline and numerous outdoor recreation spots. ALAN F.J. ARTIBISE

Western Dominion Investment Co Ltd, a holding company with interests in bakeries, supermarkets, mining, oil and gas, radio, television, CABLE TELEVISION and NEWSPAPERS, is controlled by the BLACK family, headed by brothers G. Montegu and Conrad. Western's media holdings include Standard Broadcasting Corporation Ltd (SBC); Bushnell Communications Ltd; and Sterling Newspapers, with 15 daily newspapers, the third-largest newspaper chain in Canada in terms of number owned. SBC owns radio stations in St Catharines, Ont, Toronto, Ottawa and Montréal; the CTV affiliate CJOH-TV in Ottawa; a 9.3% interest in CTV; the radio news service Standard Broadcast News; "Music by Muzak" franchises for Québec and the Maritimes; and shares in private radio stations in Great Britain. PETER S. ANDERSON

Western Separatism, *see* SEPARATISM.

Western Settlement, *see* ALBERTA; DOMINION LANDS POLICY; HOMESTEADING; MANITOBA; PIONEER LIFE; PRAIRIE WEST; RED RIVER COLONY; RUPERT'S LAND.

Weston, Willard Garfield, food merchant, manufacturer (b at Toronto 26 Jan 1893; d there 22 Oct 1978). The son of biscuit manufacturer George Weston, he developed the family business into one of the largest food conglomerates in Canada. He became a VP of GEORGE WESTON LTD in 1921, and was elected president and general manager upon his father's death in 1924. By 1928 he had started the international expansion of the firm, first to the US in 1929, then in 1933 to the UK, where he soon became England's largest biscuit manufacturer. He moved to England in 1933 and was elected to the British House of Commons but never gave up his Canadian citizenship. The Weston conglomerate, now run by his sons **W. Gordon Galen** (b Eng 29 Oct 1940) and **Garry** (b 1927), controls retail and food manufacturing companies in the US, Canada, UK, Australia, S Africa, New Zealand, Germany and Ireland. Galen, who heads Canadian operations, used his own funds to build up a chain of supermarkets in Ireland while still in his twenties and became involved in real estate and department stores. After his father's death, Galen reorganized the conglomerate by restructuring the flagging Loblaws and pruning others. His homes include an Irish manor and English castle. JORGE NIOSI

Westport, NS, Village, pop 356 (1981c), inc 1946, is located at the southern tip of Digby Neck, on the eastern side of BRIER I, western NS. Originally known as Brier I Settlement, it was named Westport in 1839 because of its location. Two New Englanders were its sole occupants until the arrival of LOYALISTS in 1783. With the best cod and pollock grounds in the Bay of FUNDY located here, fishing is the principal industry. A cod-liver-oil factory was established in 1880. A memorial plaque in the town commemorates the solo voyage of Capt Joshua Slocum around the world (1895-98) in an 11 m

long sloop. Brier I is becoming quite well-known among bird-watchers for the variety of species of land and seabirds concentrated here during migration. It is also a good place for lapidary enthusiasts to collect agate. JEAN PETERSON

Westville, NS, Town, pop 4522 (1981c), inc 1894, is located near the Middle R, 8 km SW of NEW GLASGOW. Originally called Acadia Village, it was renamed Westville in 1868, 2 years after the Acadian Coal Co discovered coal. In 1868, 3 mines were in operation and a railway was built to join the mines to the INTERCOLONIAL RY. Coal from these mines supplied ironworks in a nearby town or was shipped elsewhere. The town's prosperity peaked in 1910, when coke ovens, a coal washer and a brick plant were also in operation. By 1953 the only mine in operation was the Drummond. Demands for Westville coal declined and by 1969 only a little over 100 men were working. Today, most residents work in the nearby towns of New Glasgow or Stellarton. There is some manufacturing and a small service industry. HEATHER MacDONALD

Wetaskiwin, Alta, City, pop 9597 (1981c), inc 1906, distribution centre and headquarters for the Battle River Regional Planning Commission, is located 70 km S of Edmonton. The town began (1891) as Siding 16 on the Calgary-Edmonton Ry and was a point of departure for early, predominantly Scandinavian, homesteaders. A CPR branch line was built eastward in 1906, and the town grew as wheat farming and cattle ranching prospered in the area. The Reynolds Museum has more than 1000 antique cars, trucks, airplanes and tractors, including a rare Innes car, a 1917 Curtiss JN4D "Jenny" biplane and a rare Canadian-built Menard automobile (1908). The city has 2 weekly newspapers, the Wetaskiwin *Times* and the *News Advertiser,* and also a local radio station and an airstrip. Its name is Cree for "hills (or place) of peace," referring to the nearby Peace Hills, where a peace treaty was concluded between the Cree and Blackfoot in 1867. ERIC J. HOLMGREN

Wetmore, Andrew Rainsford, jurist, politician, premier of NB (b at Fredericton 16 Aug 1820; d there 7 Mar 1892). Born into a distinguished Loyalist family, Wetmore's father, George Ludlow Wetmore, was the last New Brunswicker killed in a formal DUEL (20 Oct 1821). Andrew Wetmore went into law. He joined the anti-Confederationists for the 1865 electoral victory, expecting the attorney generalship. Refused that office, he moved to the Confederationists to be "certain to have been right at least once," even though he was considered a "political weathercock" for his move. The 1867 mass exodus of NB politicians to Ottawa propelled Wetmore to the premiership and the attorney general's office. He was also promised the Supreme Court. Under him provincial affairs were chaotic, and his elevation to the NB Supreme Court (1870) was the occasion for political realignment under firmer leadership. As a judge, Wetmore's talents finally were properly utilized. CARL M. WALLACE

Weyburn, Sask, City, pop 9523 (1981c), inc 1912, is located on the SOURIS R in southeastern Saskatchewan, about 75 km from the international boundary. Weyburn became a village in 1902 as the result of a heavy inflow of AMERICANS. There are 2 versions as to how it received its name. Most people prefer the romantic one, which concerns a party of thirsty Scots working

their way west on a hot summer day. One member was said to have exclaimed "wee burn" upon seeing the Souris R for the first time. The second, and more practical, version contends that the city got its name from a railway construction contractor who named the site after his brother-in-law. In the 1950s the Weyburn oil field was discovered in the area and since then oil has played a very significant role in the city's economy. Agricultural production continues to be its dominant industry.   DON HERPERGER

Whale, common name for large, aquatic or marine MAMMALS of order CETACEA, which inhabit all oceans. Whales range from about 30 kg for some of the smaller dolphins to over 150 t for the blue whale. Whales belong to 2 suborders: Mysticeti, baleen or toothless whales; and Odontoceti, toothed whales (smaller kinds of which are called DOLPHINS or porpoises). Canadian waters are rich in whale fauna (8 species of mysticetes, about 25 species of odontocetes), and the commercial search for these animals was significant in early exploration (*see* WHALING). Because of over-exploitation, several species are rare, eg, bowhead (*Balaena mysticetus*), an arctic mysticete; right whale (*Eubalaena glacialis*), a temperate zone mysticete; humpback (*Megaptera novaeangliae*), known for its haunting "song"; and blue whale (*Balaenoptera musculus*), largest animal ever known. The grey whale (*Eschrichtius robustus*) was extirpated in the N Atlantic and depleted in the N Pacific. Today, however, its migration along the N American Pacific coast is one of the world's great wildlife spectacles. The cosmopolitan sperm whale (*Physeter macrocephalus*), the largest odontocete, preys mainly on squid and usually remains in deep water. Adult bulls seasonally visit high latitudes; females and young remain in temperate or tropical waters. The beaked whales (family Ziphiidae) are rare in coastal areas, but Baird's beaked whale (*Berardius bairdii*) off the BC coast, and the northern bottlenose (*Hyperoodon ampullatus*) off NS, have been hunted by shore-based whalers. Since the 1972 moratorium on commercial whaling in Canada, whale watching has become popular. Several species, especially BELUGA, fin and minke whales (*Delphinapterus leucas, Balaenoptera physalus, B. acutorostrata,* respectively) and blue whales, occur along the N shore of the St Lawrence estuary. Pilot (*Globicephala melaena*), humpback and fin whales are the main attractions off Newfound-

land; right whales in lower Bay of FUNDY; killer whales (*Orcinus orca*) and grey whales off BC. *See* ENDANGERED ANIMALS.
                    R. REEVES AND E.D. MITCHELL

Whaling Over 20 WHALE species occur in Canadian waters, of which about 13 have been commercially significant. The earliest exploited were the relatively easily hunted right, bowhead and grey whales. As the numbers of these species declined, humpback and sperm whales became the preferred prey. Later still, when technological advances made it feasible, the very fast blue, fin and sei whales were taken. The first whalers in Canada were native people, the INUIT of the Far North and the NOOTKA of Vancouver I who hunted for subsistence. As early as the 15th century, BASQUE seamen from France and Spain sailed to the Gulf of ST LAWRENCE, where large numbers of whales congregated each summer to feed. In the 18th century, British and American ships cruised the Atlantic seaboard. In the 19th century, Canadians entered the field, establishing a whaling station in Newfoundland, and taking whales as part of a deep-sea fishery operation from Gaspé. Norwegian whalers entered the area toward the end of the century, establishing stations in Newfoundland, Labrador and the Gulf of St Lawrence. Beginning in the 1830s American whalers cruising N to the Bering Sea hunted whales migrating along the Pacific coast. A local Canadian industry was established for a brief period (1868-72) at harbours on Vancouver I and in the Gulf of Georgia. From 1905 at least one company operated at any given time (excluding the period 1942-47) until 1967 when the last Canadian West Coast whaling company (the Western Canada Whaling Co) ceased whaling.

Whaling began in the DAVIS STR region of the Arctic in the 17th century. Dutch, German, English and Scottish whalers largely confined their efforts to the eastern (Greenland) side until the expeditions of John Ross (1818) and W. Edward PARRY (1819) crossed Baffin Bay and showed the way to LANCASTER SOUND. The northernmost extent of whaling was Ellesmere I. The most important area for autumn whaling was CUMBERLAND SOUND. The peak of whaling activity was from 1820 to 1840, when there were sometimes almost 100 vessels in the Davis Str area; in some years the catch exceeded 1000 whales.

Ordinarily, arctic whaling voyages lasted a single summer; ships arrived in Davis Str in Apr and tried to begin the return journey by Oct. However, on many occasions vessels were trapped by ice and either imprisoned through the winter or sunk.

While British whalers dominated the Davis Str grounds, US ships opened the NW corner of Hudson Bay (1860) and after 1889 pushed past Point Barrow in the BEAUFORT SEA. By the late 1890s vessels had penetrated Amundsen Gulf. Compared to the eastern Arctic, whaling in the Beaufort Sea was of short duration (1889-c1914). These areas were so inaccessible that whalers extended their visits over a year, spending the winter months frozen in sheltered harbours to get an early start in spring. The population of whalers was not large: at most, 500 seamen wintered in the Beaufort Sea and 200 in Hudson Bay. Wintering did not begin on Baffin I until the 1850s and it was not until later in the century that permanent shore stations, such as Kekerton and Blacklead I on Cumberland Sound, were established. However the impact of the whalers on the Inuit was profound. Natives were employed as pilots, hunters, dog drivers, and seamstresses, and were eager to procure European trade goods. Liquor was imported and violence increased. Relations between whalers and Inuit at shore stations inevitably resulted in the spread of alien diseases. Epidemics of measles, typhus and scarlet fever swept through the

native populations. At the beginning of the 20th century an entire people the SADLERMIUT of Southampton I in Hudson Bay, were wiped out. The influx of whalers placed a great strain on arctic resources. Caribou herds were decimated to provide meat for the ships' crews. As supplies of meat and leather dwindled, and as tastes changed, many Inuit came to rely on food and clothing traded from the whalers. Some native people were employed on the ships as hunters or crewmen and increasingly the economic life of the Inuit was changed.

The activities of foreign whalers in the Arctic stimulated the Canadian government to assert sovereignty over the ARCTIC ARCHIPELAGO. Officially, these islands had belonged to Canada since 1880 but no presence had been established and foreign whalers continued to operate in the Arctic without any regulation. By 1900 suspicions were growing that the US planned to annex the area, using the activities of American whalers as a pretext. Detachments of North-West Mounted Police were established (1903) to collect customs, regulate the liquor traffic, impose whaling licences and maintain order.

Whales have been valued for different products at different times. The Inuit used all of the whale: skin, blubber, flesh and internal organs were eaten; baleen and bones were used for buildings, furniture and innumerable smaller items; oil provided heat and light. Europeans were more wasteful. Initially, oil extracted from blubber was used in street lamps and for soap. By the late 19th century, coal gas and petroleum products replaced animal oil as an illuminant, but it continued to be used in margarine, paints and varnishes, and as a lubricant. The waxy spermaceti produced by sperm whales was used for candles, lubricants, cosmetics and shoe polish. In Canadian waters, the most important whale was the bowhead, which supplied baleen (whalebone), a substance which hangs in long, curtainlike strips from the roof of its mouth. A large bowhead might produce over 700 strips. By the end of the 19th century, it became common practice to remove baleen and discard the carcass. This flexible substance was used for a range of products including buggy whips, skirt hoops, umbrellas, carriage wheels, corset stays and fishing rods. It was replaced in the 20th century by spring steel and plastics. Whale meat has been used for human consumption, chiefly in Japan and Norway, and for animal food.

At first commercial whalers armed with hand-held harpoons and lances pursued the animals in small boats. The harpoon was thrust into the whale and the animal was allowed to run out line. "Nantucket sleigh rides" occurred when all the line had run out and the whale was "tethered" to the boat. When the whale was exhausted, the whalers moved in for the kill. New weapons were introduced in the middle of the 19th century. The shoulder gun fired an explosive missile with a time fuse which detonated inside the animal. The harpoon gun, a cannonlike weapon mounted at the bow of the boat, fired a barbed harpoon with an explosive charge attached. Such weapons transformed the hunt from a contest to a slaughter. The steam engine was first applied to whaling ships in the 1850s. By 1870, most of the Davis Str fleet had converted to steam and American whalers in the Beaufort Sea quickly followed suit. The increased speed, power and maneuverability allowed whalers to carry the hunt farther from home ports and reduced dangers of ice and storm.

In the Canadian Arctic, commercial whaling had all but ceased by the outbreak of WWI. Whale stocks were depleted to the point of extinction and the demand for baleen had decreased. Along the BC coast, however, and in Newfoundland and NS, whaling continued from several land-based stations with catcher

Right whale in the Bay of Fundy (*courtesy Bill Brooks/ Masterfile*).

boats pursuing and killing whales and towing the carcasses to land for processing. Whaling entered a new phase internationally in 1925 with the introduction of factory ships. More recently, helicopters and SONAR have been used, especially by the USSR and Japan, to locate whales, which are then chased by catcher boats and processed aboard factory ships. Annual catches rose dramatically: in the late 1930s more than 50 000 whales were taken annually. After formation of the International Whaling Commission (IWC) in 1946, the killing of several species was banned completely and quotas were established to control exploitation of the rest. In 1972, the federal government ordered a halt to all whaling operations based in Canadian ports. The last West Coast company had stopped whaling in 1967; thus the government order affected only 2 shore-based operations in Newfoundland and one in NS. The Inuit are still allowed to take whales. As a result of conservation measures, some whale stocks have shown signs of recovery. In the 1930s, the bowhead was thought to be on the brink of extinction and was declared an ENDANGERED ANIMAL. Recent studies indicate that it has survived and may be recovering slowly in some areas.

Canada was a member of the IWC but withdrew from the organization in 1982. The commission had achieved some significant success; however, because member nations are not bound to conform to its recommendations, the commission can be only as effective as the whaling nations allow. Decisions have often been tempered by the desire to keep nations in the organization, where some control is possible, rather than outside, where their activities would be totally unregulated. For this reason Canada disagreed with efforts in 1980 to declare a moratorium on commercial whaling. Canadian officials also thought the measure unnecessary because the selective quota system was effectively conserving whale stocks. Canada's position on the moratorium issue earned a great deal of criticism from anti-whaling groups. A moratorium to take effect in 1985 was declared in 1982. Although no longer a member of the IWC, Canada continues to ban commercial whaling in its territory. *See* WILDLIFE CONSERVATION AND MANAGEMENT.   DANIEL FRANCIS

Reading: J.N. Tønnessen and A.O. Johnsen, *The History of Modern Whaling* (tr 1982).

Wheat, common name for members of genus *Triticum* of the GRASS family (Gramineae) and for the CEREAL grains produced by these grasses. Wheat is the most important cereal in the world: with rice and maize it accounts for about 73% of world cereal production. Canada is the world's sixth-largest producer and second-largest exporter of wheat, producing annually an average of over 20 billion t and exporting about 14 billion t. Cultivated forms evolved from natural crossings of wild species, followed by domestication and selection by humans. Wheat was domesticated in SW Asia over thousands of years and spread across Asia, Africa and Europe. Introduction to the New World took place in the late 15th and 16th centuries. The most important modern cultivated species (ie, cultivars) are common and durum wheats, usually given the binomial designations *T. aestivum* and *T. turgidum* var. *durum,* respectively.

History In Canada, wheat probably was first grown at PORT-ROYAL in about 1605; the first exports were made in 1654. Although personnel at some HUDSON'S BAY COMPANY posts experimented with wheat, and the settlers at the RED RIVER COLONY had some success in 1815, the early years in western Canada were precarious ones for wheat farmers. Many cultivars from Europe were tried: some were winter wheats that could not survive Canada's severe winters; others were spring wheats that matured too late for the short

Wheat harvesting in Manitoba (*photo by Karl Sommerer*).

growing season. The cultivar Red Fife, developed in Ontario, became very popular because of its good yield and excellent milling and baking qualities. By about 1870 Red Fife was very popular on the prairies but it, too, froze in the fields in years with early frosts. Later investigations have revealed that Red Fife is actually the central European cultivar Galician.

William SAUNDERS, first director of the Dominion Experimental Farms, was interested in plant breeding. His son, Sir Charles SAUNDERS, took over the wheat-breeding work in 1903 and developed the cultivar Marquis from a cross, made some years earlier, between Hard Red Calcutta and Red Fife. Marquis matured earlier than Red Fife and had excellent yield and superior milling and baking qualities. It was distributed in the spring of 1911 and quickly became very popular throughout Canada. Western wheat production was increasing rapidly at this time: 2 million t, 1904; 3.7 million t, 1906; 7.7 million t, 1913. Red Fife and Marquis made Canada famous for its high-quality hard red spring wheat. Marquis was later adopted as the statutory standard of quality for this class of wheat, a position it still holds.

Protection Stem rust (*Puccinia graminis tritici*) is a FUNGUS disease disseminated by spores, which can be carried by wind for thousands of miles. In Canada, epidemics in 1916, 1927 and 1935 caused losses estimated at 3.6, 3.3 and 3.2 million t of grain. The Dominion Rust Research Laboratory was set up in Winnipeg in 1925 to investigate stem rust and develop resistant cultivars. Renown, their first cultivar, distributed in 1936, has been followed by several other important cultivars (eg, Selkirk, Manitou, Neepawa); however, the Thatcher cultivar, developed in Minnesota and licensed in Canada in 1935, became the dominant form for many years. A new physiologic race of stem rust (15B) became epidemic from 1953 to 1955, causing losses of at least 8 million t of grain. Since that time, stem rust has caused little loss, but leaf rust (*P. recondita*) has been a problem because of its rapid changes in virulence. Cultivars resistant to both rusts are available.

In Alberta and western Saskatchewan, rust was rarely a problem, but drought and wheat-stem sawfly (*Cephus cinctus*) were. The sawfly, which occurs mainly in the Swift Current, Sask, to Lethbridge, Alta, area, cuts stems so that the heads fall on the ground and cannot be harvested. Resistance has been obtained by developing cultivars with solid stems, eg, Rescue (licensed 1946). RESEARCH STATIONS in the area have since developed a number of resistant cultivars with better yield and quality. They also work on developing drought-resistant cultivars.

Production Within Canada, wheat is the most important cultivated crop (grown on over

10 million ha). Only one class of durum is grown, amber durum (spring); however, there are several classes of common wheat, based on seed hardness and colour, and on sowing time (autumn or spring). About 20% of Canada's 318 000 farms are classified as wheat farms, and wheat contributes about $2 billion (1%) to Canada's GROSS NATIONAL PRODUCT. Soft white winter wheat is grown on an area of some 200 000 ha, mainly in Ontario; over 675 000 t are produced annually, of which about 60% is exported. The protein content is usually 9-10%, and this class is used for cake and pastry flour and breakfast cereals. The flour, mixed with hard wheat flour, produces an all-purpose flour.

Saskatchewan alone grows about 60% of Canada's wheat. Production on the PRAIRIES usually amounts to about 3 times domestic consumption; therefore, the industry is export oriented. The area devoted to common wheat averaged 9.4 million ha over the 1977-81 period; durum wheat averaged 3 million ha. The protein levels of prairie wheats are usually 12-15%. Durum wheat is used for the production of semolina for pasta products, and hard red spring wheat is used for bread. Wheat contains gluten protein, which forms minute gas cells that hold carbon dioxide during fermentation, allowing dough to rise and resulting in light bread. Importers of Canadian wheat often blend it with weaker wheats before using it for bread. For this reason, much effort goes into maintaining the strength and mixing qualities of Canadian wheat. Maintenance involves controlling cultivars grown and applying a comprehensive grading system. *See* COMMODITY INSPECTION AND GRADING; GRAIN HANDLING AND MARKETING.   A.B. CAMPBELL

Wheeler, Arthur Oliver, surveyor, mountaineer (b at Lyrath, Ire 1 May 1860; d at Banff, Alta 20 Mar 1945). Qualifying in 1881 as Ontario land surveyor and Dominion land surveyor, Wheeler worked on surveys throughout the W with the federal government and privately. He pioneered in photogrammetry, developed by E.G. DEVILLE. A founder of the Alpine Club of Canada in 1906, he was a tireless promoter of the Rockies and Selkirks and participated in many first ascents.   ERIC J. HOLMGREN

Wheeler, Kenneth Vincent John, jazz trumpeter, composer (b at Toronto 14 Jan 1930). After studying music in Toronto, Wheeler moved to London, Eng, in 1952, rising to prominence in Britain in the 1960s, and in the European avante-garde in the 1970s. His association from 1971 to 1976 with American reedman Anthony Braxton brought him back to perform in N America. He is recognized as a major figure in jazz, and his extensive discography includes recordings with John Dankworth, Braxton, Globe Unity, and the co-operative trio Azimuth, as well as several of his own records (*Gnu High, Deer Wan, Around 6*) after 1973.   MARK MILLER

Wheeler, Lucile, alpine skier (b at Montréal 14 Jan 1935). She started skiing at age 2. In 1956, after 5 winters of rigorous training at Kitzbühel, Austria, with coach Pepi Salvenmoser, she won Canada's first Olympic ski medal, a bronze in the downhill. In 1958 she shattered a European monopoly of world ski championships by winning both the downhill and giant slalom titles, thereby inspiring Canada to begin sending a national ski team to Europe the following year. Her honours include Canada's Outstanding Athlete of the Year (1958).   MURRAY SHAW

Wheeler, Seager, plant breeder, farmer (b on the Isle of Wight, Eng 1869; d at Victoria, 15 Dec 1961). After starting work at age 11, Wheeler immigrated to Saskatchewan in 1885, working on farms near Moose Jaw and Saskatoon until 1897, when he bought his own farm near Rosthern. In 1904 he began selective breeding of spring wheat, developing such popular varieties of the time as Early Triumph, Kitchener, Red Bobs and Supreme. He was 5 times the world champion hard spring wheat grower between 1911 and 1918, a fact used by agents of the Canadian government in the US to promote settlement of the Canadian Prairies. He also developed hardy fruits and other crops, winning several awards. Some of his techniques were documented in his 1919 *Wheeler's Book on Profitable Grain Growing.*   MARTIN K. McNICHOLL

Whelan, Edward, journalist, politician (b at Ballina, Ire 1824; d at Charlottetown 10 Dec 1867). In 1831 Whelan immigrated with his mother to Halifax, where he was apprenticed in 1832 in the printing office of Joseph HOWE. After his schooling in Halifax, he arrived in Charlottetown in 1843, already having had editorial experience. He established his own semiweekly Reform newspaper, the *Palladium,* which he discontinued in 1845 for financial reasons. Next year, at age 22, he was elected to the Assembly and in 1847 commenced the weekly *Examiner,* which he continued to publish, with some interruptions, until his death. An exceptionally able writer with a brilliant satiric pen and keen insight into character, Whelan was the leading journalistic spokesman for the Reformers in their struggle for RESPONSIBLE GOVERNMENT and a solution to the LAND QUESTION. In the mid-1860s he strongly supported CONFEDERATION, which was one reason for his first electoral defeat in Apr 1867. He seems not to have recovered from the ensuing bitterness and died that Dec.

IAN ROSS ROBERTSON

Whelk, common name for a carnivorous marine SNAIL which may be included with the Buccinid, Muricid or Purpurid families. Whelks are advanced prosobranch gastropod MOLLUSCS possessing a heavy, spindle-shaped shell with a siphonal groove. Arising from the latter is a sensory siphon that whelks use for detection and tracking of prey. Several muricids are pests on oysters and, because of this, their biology and control have been extensively investigated. The Eastern oyster drill (*Urosalpinx cinerea*) and the Japanese oyster drill (*Ocenebra japonica*) have caused extensive damage to East and West Coast oyster fisheries, respectively. Oyster drills employ an auxiliary boring organ, located in the foot, to perforate the shell of their prey. The organ secretes enzymes that dissolve the organic matrix of the oyster's shell causing it to collapse, a process analogous to the collapse of a brick wall when mortar is removed. The proboscis bears a small, toothed feeding organ, a radula, which is inserted through the shell hole to feed on the victim's flesh. Separate sexes occur and copulation leads to production of lidded egg cases. Cannibalism within the egg cases results in the emergence of a few vigorous snails.

PETER V. FANKBONER

Whitby, Ont, Town, pop 36 698 (1981c), is located on Lk Ontario, 48 km E of Toronto. First called Perry's Corners, it was renamed Whitby, after a Yorkshire town, at the time of incorporation (1855). Whitby is the county town for Ontario County. In 1970, with the formation of Durham regional government, the administrative unit was changed to the township. Utilizing an excellent harbour, the Whitby-Port Perry Ry (1869) and road connections, Whitby's primary 19th-century economic activity was as a transportation centre. By 1871, however, it had been eclipsed by both Oshawa and Toronto. Whitby was in William Lyon MACKENZIE's riding and he held so many pre-1837 meetings in the town square that it became known as "radical corners." Other notables included local editor and Liberal organizer W.H. Higgins, whose letter to Archbishop Lynch of Toronto helped spur Ontario's "No Popery" campaign. A Senior "A" hockey team, the Whitby Dunlops was one of the last Canadian teams to win the world championship (1958).   GERALD STORTZ
Reading: L.A. Johnson, *History of the County of Ontario* (1973).

White-Collar Crime consists of occupational crime and corporate crime. Occupational crime refers to offences committed against legitimate institutions (businesses or government) by those with "respectable" social status. It includes the embezzlement of corporate funds, tax evasion, computer crime and expense-account fraud. Corporate crime refers to offences committed by legitimate institutions to further their own interests and includes conspiring to fix the prices of goods or services, the dumping of pollutants, the payment of kickbacks by manufacturers to retailers, misleading advertising, selling unsafe drugs, etc.

In Canada, most occupational crime is prohibited under the Canadian CRIMINAL CODE, which is enforced by municipal or provincial POLICE, a complicated procedure because the suspects are often employees of the institutions from which they are stealing, and the employers either do not discover the theft quickly or prefer to avoid publicity by not reporting the loss. The culprit may be fired or asked to make restitution. Corporate crimes are prohibited by a wide variety of federal, provincial and municipal laws. Enforcement is the responsibility of government inspectors who generally have fewer powers than police to detain suspects and search for evidence.

The Combines Investigation Act (s36.37) prohibits advertising special sales when prices have not been reduced, making false claims about what a product can accomplish, and selling used cars as new ones. According to the federal Ministry of Consumer and Corporate Affairs, these are common crimes, and the ministry receives more complaints than it can investigate, so it chooses only the most serious and significant for prosecution. Compared to other Western countries, fines are low and enforcement infrequent. Excluding these sections, there have been 89 other prosecutions under the Combines Investigation Act from 1952 to 1975. Of these, 8 were acquitted and 2 were dismissed at a preliminary hearing. Twenty-two defendants (individuals and corporations) were served only with Order of Prohibition (a device whereby judges tell guilty parties not to repeat the offence) while 57 defendents were convicted and were fined amounts ranging from $300 to $50 000 (averaging $7500 per case). Illegal combines can net the offending companies several million dollars per year in profits, so such fines are unlikely to be effective deterrents.

Other laws directed at corporate crime include the Food and Drugs Act (preventing the sale of contaminated food and drugs); Hazardous Products Act (preventing the sale of dangerous items); Weights and Measures Act (preventing dishonest scales); Environmental Protection Acts, both federal and provincial; laws to protect the investor against unscrupulous promoters and brokers; and laws to ensure that workers are not exploited, eg, by being forced to work 18-hour days in unventilated facilities. However, these laws are not always stringently enforced; in general, authorities use persuasion first, and criminal sanctions as a last resort; when cases do go to court, they take longer, are more likely to be appealed by the defendant and to lead to an acquittal or withdrawal by the CROWN, and are less likely to lead to imprisonment than are comparable criminal-code cases; both judges and laymen are uncertain whether individuals and corporations convicted for acts against consumers, employees, rivals or the environment are truly criminals.

Laws against occupational crime do not include ones against computer crime. Breaking computer codes and copying private information or records are not indictable offences, although a possible rewriting of the laws on theft is being studied.

Legal reform is needed to enforce laws against corporate crime. The federal government has been trying since 1969 to reform the Combines Investigation Act. In 1975 the maximum fine for illegal combines price fixing was increased to $1 million, an important if symbolic step, because judges traditionally do not assess fines anywhere near the maximum allowable amount for corporate crimes; it became illegal for professionals to eliminate competition by setting uniform prices for their services; heavier sanctions were prescribed for misleading advertising; and many new deceptive selling practices (bait and switch, pyramid sales) were prohibited. However, laws on merger and monopoly remain unaltered and ineffective because of lobbying efforts by major corporate powers. Attempts to strengthen environmental protection or MINIMUM WAGE laws have frequently been defeated by corporate threats to close up shop, eliminating badly needed jobs; and the public, not realizing the damage caused by corporate crime, has been slow to demand reform.

LAUREEN SNIDER

White Paper, a government document which outlines both government policy on an issue and possible future action, including legislation. It is sometimes a reaction to the report of a ROYAL COMMISSION or TASK FORCE. The Trudeau government, after its experience with the White Paper on Tax Reform, discovered that White Papers provided elites, rather than the public, with access to decision making and publicity. There has often been confusion about whether a White Paper has expressed government intentions or whether its purpose has simply been to raise an issue for discussion, like a GREEN PAPER. White Papers can be withdrawn with less embarrassment than legislation can.   C.E.S. FRANKS

White Pass, elev 889 m, sits on the Alaska-BC boundary, approximately 125 km S of Whitehorse, YT. In 1887 the federal government sent William Ogilvie to survey the 141st meridian national boundary where it crosses the Yukon R; members of his party found the pass. It was named for Thomas White, then minister of the interior. After the KLONDIKE gold strike (1896), thousands crossed White Pass 1897-98 to reach the goldfields at Dawson City. The narrow-gauge WHITE PASS AND YUKON RY, from Skagway to Whitehorse, and a recently completed highway traverse the pass.   GLEN BOLES

White Pass and Yukon Railway, at 175 km long, was the steepest pitched railway in Canada. Work began in 1898, at the height of the KLONDIKE GOLD RUSH, to provide transportation from Skagway, Alaska, to WHITEHORSE, YT. Building of the narrow gauge railway was an extremely difficult ENGINEERING feat, requiring extensive blasting, tunnels and precarious bridging. Thirty-five of the approximately 35 000 who men worked on construction were killed. The summit of WHITE PASS was reached in Feb 1899 and the "last spike" was driven at Carcross on 29 July 1900. The gold was exhausted by the time work was complete, though the line struggled along carrying passengers and freight. The mining boom in the Yukon revived the railway, as lead-zinc was hauled from Faro, Mayo and Clinton Creek. The shutdown of the WP&Y in 1982, as a result of the collapse of the mining boom, deprived Whitehorse of some employment and its rail link to the sea.　JAMES MARSH

White, Robert, labour leader (b at Upper Lands, N Ireland 28 Apr 1935). He came to Canada at age 13. He worked for Hay and Co in Woodstock, Ont, and by 1959 had become president of United Auto Workers Local 636. He was appointed UAW international representative and in 1964 co-ordinator of organizing staff. In 1972 he became assistant to UAW director, Dennis MCDERMOTT. He travelled across Canada to mobilize protests against the federal wage-control program. He led the UAW opposition to corporate demands for wage concessions. Firmly believing that the Canadian wing of the UAW should act primarily in the interest of its 120 000 Canadian workers, White led the Canadian members in a strike and eventually a secession movement from the American UAW.

White Rock, BC, City, pop 13 550 (1981c), inc 1967, when it separated from municipality of SURREY, is 48 km by road SE of Vancouver and is bounded on the N, E and W by Surrey. It began as a recreational resort on the shores of Semiahmoo B. A boulder on the beach was painted white as a navigation mark by sailors. The bay's fine beach was famous for its swimming, fishing and boating. Cottages were built along the waterfront in the early 1900s and slowly a community developed, with a post office and general store, schools, waterworks and a hospital being established. Retail trade and services are its leading sources of employment, but it is primarily a resort and retirement community. White Rock has 2 newspapers, an active summer theatre company and a wide range of community services.　ALAN F.J. ARTIBISE

Whitefish, common name for several freshwater FISHES of class Osteichthyes, family Salmonidae (SALMON), subfamily Coregoninae (sometimes elevated to family rank). Whitefishes are widely distributed throughout the Northern Hemisphere. In Canada, 3 genera and 18 species are found, including 3 species of genus *Prosopium* (round, mountain and pygmy). Genus *Coregonus* includes the whitefishes proper and the ciscos (formerly classified in genus *Leucichthys*). Whitefishes tend to be bottom feeders, with the snout overhanging the lower jaw and a few gill rakers for sifting large food particles. Ciscos feed in midwater, have a lower jaw at least as long as the upper, and many gill rakers for sifting small food items. There is considerable confusion concerning the relationships of species within genus *Coregonus*, but it includes at least 3 species of whitefish and 11 of cisco (5 found only in the Great Lakes). In southern Canada, most species, marketed as "chubs," are confined to lakes. In the North, river and even anadromous (seagoing) populations are common. The latter may undertake long journeys, eg, migrating over 1000 km in the Mackenzie R. The third genus, *Stenodus*, includes a single species, inconnu (*S. leucichthys*), the largest of the whitefishes (up to 150 cm long and over 28 kg). The inconnu preys on other fishes and has a pike-shaped body and a large mouth with a projecting lower jaw. It occurs in large lakes and streams but, in Canada, is confined to the Mackenzie drainage and areas west.

Lake whitefish (*C. clupeaformis*) is Canada's most important commercial freshwater species, although catches have declined over the last 20 years, particularly in the Great Lakes, because of environmental degradation and overfishing. Several species of ciscos were formerly fished commercially in the Great Lakes, but are now much depleted and no longer commercially exploited. Several species of whitefish remain important in native food fisheries. Whitefishes are not important for sport, although angling for mountain whitefish (*P. williamsoni*) is gaining popularity in BC and Alberta.　PETER J. McCART

Whitehorse, capital city of the YUKON TERRITORY, pop 14 814 (1981c), inc 1950, is located at kilometre 1470, just off the ALASKA HIGHWAY, about 105 km N of the BC border. The city lies mainly on the W side of the YUKON R on a 600 m wide river plain backed by a steep scarp with a plateaulike summit 60 m above.

History Located at the head of navigation on the Yukon R, in 1898 Whitehorse became a temporary stopping point — past 2 major obstacles on the river, Miles Canyon and the Whitehorse Rapids — for prospectors during the KLONDIKE GOLD RUSH. In 1900 it became a permanent settlement, based on transportation and services, with the completion of the WHITE PASS AND YUKON RAILWAY from Skagway, Alaska. The community grew around the point where the railway and river met, on the western bank of the river. Since 1900 the White Pass and Yukon Route Corp has helped the city and territory develop by providing services and employment. Apart from its railway, the corporation established the British Yukon Navigation Company, which built riverboats and operated them to DAWSON until 1954.

A short-lived copper boom in the Whitehorse copper belt ended in 1920. Throughout the 1920s and 1930s, the corporation promoted the tourist industry and Whitehorse became an outfitting and takeoff base. In 1935 it established the British Yukon Aviation company to transport mail, freight and passengers from its base in Whitehorse. From an estimated 2000 after the gold rush, Whitehorse's population dropped by 1941 to about 750.

During WWII Whitehorse played a significant role as a key link in the N-S transportation system supporting the war effort. About 30 000 American and Canadian servicemen and civilian workers expanded the facilities of the Northwest Staging Route (a series of airfields

Whitehorse, capital city of the Yukon Territory, originated as a temporary stopping point for prospectors bound for the Klondike (*photo by Fred Breummer*).

across the Northwest), which acted as the air link; built the 2400 km Alaska Hwy, and constructed the Canol pipeline from NORMAN WELLS, NWT, and an oil refinery at Whitehorse. After the war, the Alaska Hwy was opened to civilian traffic and replaced the Yukon R as the dominant transportation route. Whitehorse became the headquarters of the Northwest highway system. In 1953 the territorial capital was moved from Dawson to Whitehorse, adding the government sector to the city's economic base.

Economy In the 1950s the federal government initiated a road-construction and financial-aid program to stimulate the territory's mining economy. As a result silver production expanded at Mayo, and copper and lead-zinc production started at Faro. By the end of the 1950s an integrated ship-train-truck containerized transportation system was moving ore through Whitehorse to external markets.

Improved accessibility also directly affected Whitehorse's economy through the tourist industry. Since 1960 there has been an average annual growth rate of 12%. In 1977 about 300 000 people visited the territory, bringing revenues of around $28 million.

Cityscape Whitehorse's original townsite, surveyed on a conventional grid pattern, evolved into 3 functional zones: commercial and retail located on Main and Front streets, residential N and S of Main Street, and the railway and docking facilities between Front St and the Yukon R. The industrial area, including mining company offices, lies N of the city, while government offices dominate blocks on the edge of the commercial area, located in the city centre. Whitehorse's colourful past is preserved in its restored riverboat *Klondike* and the Anglican log church built in 1900. The shutdown of the lead-zinc mine at Faro in 1982 and the subsequent closing of other mines in the Yukon have had an adverse effect on the city — notably in the closure of the WP&Y rail operations. Nevertheless, optimism for the future prevails, based on government service, transportation and the potential for tourism of the compelling northern landscape.　PAUL M. KOROSCIL

Whiten, Colette, sculptor (b at Birmingham, Eng 7 Feb 1945). In 1972 she graduated from the Ontario College of Art, recipient of the Governor General's Medal, and exhibited her first cast piece, a wooden structure filled with fibreglass molds of her friends' arms and legs, documented by photographs and slides to record the creative process. Her figures are concerned with the nature of human existence, with human interaction (particularly power relationships) and with the process of art. Since 1975 her focus has shifted to an intimate exploration of the nature of identity and the duality inherent in the cast image (*September, 1975*).　JOYCE ZEMANS

Whiteshell Provincial Park (est 1961), 145 km E of WINNIPEG, Man, by the Trans-Canada Highway, is Precambrian SHIELD country. Glaciation acting on the 2.5-billion-year-old rocks, has formed many lakes and granite outcrops. West Hawk Lk, the deepest in Manitoba (111 m), is believed to have been created by a meteorite. Most of the area is forested, with both coniferous and deciduous species; numerous wetland plants occur (eg, lilies, WILD RICE). Mammals include black bears, moose, deer, coyotes, beavers and mink. Bird life is varied, Canada geese being especially abundant at the Alfred Hole Sanctuary. Indian presence can be traced archaeologically to 3000 BC and is revealed in petroglyphs at Bannock Point. In 1773 the LA VÉRENDRYE expedition traversed the area via the Winnipeg R; other explorers (eg, MACKENZIE, THOMPSON, HENRY, KANE) followed. The transcontinental railway was built in the 1880s and sporadic mining, logging and farming occurred. In the 1920s, the area's recreation potential was recognized, cottages were developed and, in 1931, a Forest Reserve was established. The park is accessible by several roads, although the NE section remains a roadless wilderness. Resort facilities are available at Falcon Lk and West Hawk Lk. Activities include motorboating, fishing, swimming, camping, horseback riding and interpretation events and, in winter, downhill and cross-country skiing and snowmobiling. Many canoe routes, day-use or interpretive hiking trails, and the 60 km Mantario wilderness trail are available.   JOHN S. MARSH

Whiteway, Sir William Vallance, lawyer, politician, premier of Newfoundland 1878-85, 1889-94, 1895-97 (b near Totnes, Eng 1 Apr 1828; d at St John's 24 June 1908). Whiteway came to Newfoundland in 1843 and began a legal career in 1852. He entered politics in 1859 and achieved prominence as a leading confederate in the late 1860s. Defeated in the anticonfederate landslide of 1869, he later returned to the Assembly, becoming solicitor general in 1874 and premier in 1878. Ambitious and energetic, Whiteway worked to develop the Newfoundland economy. His instrument was a trans-island railway, begun in 1881. The policy was controversial, and Whiteway found himself maneuvered out of office in 1885 by a mercantile party that favoured more attention for the troubled fishing industry. He was triumphantly re-elected in 1889 and again in 1893 on a platform stressing railway building and economic progress. He was out of power 1894-95 and was defeated in the 1897 election, when he also lost the leadership of the Liberal Party. Whiteway's principal legacy is the railway, though his assertion of colonial rights on the FRENCH SHORE is historically important. He was among the first Newfoundland politicians to cast the political process in class terms.   J.K. HILLER

Whitney, Sir James Pliny, lawyer, politician, premier of Ontario 1905-14 (b in Williamsburg Twp, Canada W 2 Oct 1843; d at Toronto 25 Sept 1914). After breaking a 33-year Liberal hold upon the province, he headed an administration noteworthy for its reforms and its creation of an enduring political machine. Son of a blacksmith, Whitney was a staunch Conservative long before being called to the bar in 1876. He won the provincial riding of Dundas in an 1888 by-election, and never yielded it. Chosen leader of the Ontario party in 1896, he inherited a dispirited body weakened by religious controversy, a shortage of promising men and a poor organization. As Opposition leader, he rebuilt the Tories and healed most of the wounds, while constantly berating the governing Liberals and slowly shaping a party platform.

In office, his administration began Ontario's publicly owned hydroelectric power system, set U of T on a firm financial foundation, passed ground-breaking workmen's compensation legislation, created new bureaucratic forms such as the Ontario Ry and Municipal Board, and enacted tough but fair liquor legislation. On the negative side, his government produced Regulation 17 governing the use of French as a language of instruction in some Ontario schools; this sparked a bitter controversy with Franco-Ontarians that did nothing for national unity as WWI approached (see ONTARIO SCHOOLS QUESTION).
                    CHARLES W. HUMPHRIES

Whitton, Charlotte, social worker, politician, feminist (b at Renfrew, Ont 8 Mar 1896; d at Ottawa 25 Jan 1975). Whitton was one of this century's most colourful and controversial women. Pugnacious and energetic, she is best remembered as Ottawa's flamboyant and outspoken mayor during the 1950s and 1960s. Her more significant accomplishments, however, occurred during her earlier career as the director and driving force behind the Canadian Council

on Child Welfare (later the Canadian Welfare Council and the CANADIAN COUNCIL ON SOCIAL DEVELOPMENT) from 1920 to 1941. Whitton joined the fledgling council after a brilliant academic career at Queen's during WWI. In the 1920s she crusaded relentlessly for professional standards in the care of juvenile immigrants and neglected and dependent children. During the Depression, she became a key adviser on federal unemployment relief policy. An arch social conservative, however, Whitton's opposition to more liberal spending on the unemployed in the 1930s placed her increasingly on the margins of Canadian SOCIAL WORK.

After resigning from the Welfare Council in 1941, Whitton championed women's equality in politics and the workplace. However, her views on women, as on the WELFARE STATE, were contradictory. She opposed more liberal divorce laws and criticized married women who worked. Elected as a controller to Ottawa's municipal council in 1950, Whitton became Canada's first woman mayor in 1951. She was re-elected mayor in 1952, 1954, 1960 and 1962. Defeated in 1964, Whitton continued as an alderman until her retirement from politics in 1972. Her tenure as mayor was notable chiefly for her stormy verbal and, in one celebrated instance, physical battles with hostile male colleagues.   JAMES STRUTHERS

Who Has Seen the Wind (Toronto and Boston, 1947), a novel by W.O. MITCHELL, tells the story of a prairie boy's initiation into the mysteries of life, death, God, and the spirit that moves through everything: the wind. The novel's greatest strengths lie in its sensitive evocations of Brian O'Connal's "feeling," sometimes associated with his various experiences of death, sometimes with a child's fundamental, inarticulate, but insistent curiosity to discover the world within and beyond himself. Brian learns about life and death in town and on the prairie: the town is the setting for social conventions, institutions and hypocrisies; and on the prairie is a natural order throughout which the wind metes out its invisible imperatives, chief among them change and death. Vibrant with the serious comedy of children's dialogue, rich with poetic descriptions of the prairie in all its guises, *Who Has Seen the Wind* articulates a universal theme in a classically western Canadian voice. The novel has been translated into French as *Qui a vu le vent* (Montréal, 1974) and into several other languages; it was also made into a successful movie.   NEIL BESNER

Wholesale Trade Wholesalers either sell goods for resale to retailers (see RETAIL TRADE), to industrial, commercial, governmental, institutional and professional users or to other wholesalers. They also act as agents in connection with such sales. Firms engaged in wholesaling as well as retailing, contracting, service trades, manufacturing, etc, are considered to be primarily wholesalers whenever they derive a larger gross margin (the difference between total sales and the cost of goods sold) from wholesale trade than from any other activity. Wholesalers include primary-product dealers, eg, those engaged in the wholesaling of grain, livestock, fish, leaf tobacco, raw furs and so on; wholesale merchants, who buy and sell goods on their own account (that is, they take legal title to them); agents and brokers, who buy and sell goods for others on commission; manufacturers' sales branches and offices, which are wholesale businesses owned for wholesaling their own goods; and petroleum-bulk tank plants and truck distributors who specialize in the distribution of petroleum products.

Wholesalers perform basic marketing functions for the firms from which they purchase and for the firms to which they sell. They anticipate customers' needs and demands, carry in-

ventories, deliver merchandise, extend credit, provide market information, provide consulting services and purchase merchandise. For manufacturers, the wholesaler may offer to sell and store merchandise, finance the production by purchasing in advance, reduce credit by screening customers and provide marketing information. In order to be successful, the wholesale firm must offer these functions at a lower cost than manufacturers or retailers. In Canada wholesalers are successful because of the great numbers of small and medium-sized manufacturers and retailers who cannot perform such functions as effectively, partly because of the distribution of cities country-wide and partly because of the great distances between manufacturing and intermediate and retail centres.

Types of Wholesalers Merchant wholesalers, agents and brokers, and manufacturers' sales branches are the 3 major types of wholesalers. Specialized wholesalers include co-operative marketing associations, petroleum-bulk plants, terminals, and liquified-petroleum (LP) facilities. There are about 22 000 merchant wholesaling firms in Canada which are either full-service wholesalers who perform all of the marketing functions or limited-line or -service wholesalers. Electrical, hardware and pharmaceutical wholesalers, for example, who sell all of the products in the category are full-service wholesalers. Limited-line wholesalers, in contrast, only carry narrow lines such as paint or electric motors; they also include cash-and-carry firms which do not provide credit or transportation to their customers. Agents and brokers (eg, auction companies, agricultural commission merchants, manufacturing agents, food brokers, selling agents, and export and import agents and brokers) specialize in exchange functions and are organized by product lines; they make their profits by commissions. Manufacturers' sales branches are wholesale businesses established by manufacturers which often sell the products of other suppliers as well — an important type of wholesaling in Canada. All of the types of wholesaler operate in most of the different product categories. For merchant wholesalers the most important lines of trade are food, petroleum products, and machinery and equipment; for agents and brokers, the most important areas are farm products, petroleum products, apparel, and dry goods.

Wholesale trade at the federal level comes under the Combines Investigation Act, which regulates mergers and monopolies, specialization agreements, export agreements, price discrimination, delivered prices (that is, forcing the customer to pay a delivered price regardless of where or how the manufacturer delivers the merchandise), reciprocal buying and resale price maintenance (pressuring customers to sell at a price set by the wholesaler).

Over several decades the dominant position of independent wholesale middlemen in the marketing system has declined because manufacturers and retailers have grown in size. The functions of the wholesaler are now performed either by manufacturers or by customers or retailers largely because, in their attempt to become price competitive, retailers have gone directly to manufacturers to purchase at lower prices. However, wholesalers have also failed to adapt to market conditions. Independent wholesalers will continue to dominate in the sale of industrial goods, machinery and petroleum products sold primarily to agricultural segments. In these areas, they have been able to specialize and adapt to the vast distribution of customers throughout Canada. The independent wholesaler will decline in importance in the marketing of retail goods, especially food items. This is a nationwide phenomenon, especially where wholesalers have been affected by large chain retailers.   RONALD SAVITT

Whoop-up, a shortened form of "whoop it up" which means to celebrate boisterously. It recalls Ft Whoop-up, the fort built in 1869 by American fur traders in what is now southern Alberta. The fort, which was the centre of the illegal exchange with the Indians of whisky for buffalo hides, was abandoned when the NORTH-WEST MOUNTED POLICE came West in 1874.

JOHN ROBERT COLOMBO

Whooping Crane (*Grus americana*), standing almost 1.5 m high, is the tallest N American BIRD. Adults may weigh 7.5 kg and have a 2.2 m wingspan. They are impressive in their pure white plumage with black wing tips, long black legs, black moustachelike markings and red crown. In their first summer and fall, juveniles are predominantly cinnamon and white. After their first birthday, they are almost indistinguishable from adults. Whooping cranes, indigenous to N America, number less than 100 wild birds and are officially classified as ENDANGERED ANIMALS. In 1941 only 15 wild birds remained, and conservation measures and joint management by the Canadian and US Wildlife Services and other organizations were instituted. In 1984, 84 wild birds migrated from their only breeding range, in WOOD BUFFALO NATIONAL PARK, to their winter range in the Aransas National Wildlife Refuge on the Texas coast. Each year, 15-19 pairs nest in Wood Buffalo and are watched by Canadian Wildlife Service biologists. Whoopers nest and raise their young in inaccessible bogs and bulrush marshes. In some years, dry weather destroys nesting and feeding habitat, and wolves may take some young, leaving only a few juveniles to begin the 3900 km MIGRATION with their parents. En route, hazards such as powerlines may endanger them, particularly if the birds are flying low because of poor weather conditions. They spend the winter feeding and resting. During late Mar and early Apr the northward migration begins. They arrive the last week in Apr. Two eggs (rarely one or 3) are laid in a large nest of bulrushes. Eggs are incubated by both parents and reddish brown chicks hatch after 29-30 days. Usually, only one chick survives. Each year since 1975, a small number of excess eggs have been removed and placed in nests of greater sandhill cranes (*G. canadensis tabida*) in Idaho. The foster parents hatch and rear the whooper chicks. It is hoped that these whoopers will mate with their own kind to form a new, self-perpetuating population. At least 13 Idaho-raised whoopers have adopted the migration pathway of their foster-parents, and the 2 species winter together in New Mexico. Two viable, geographically separate populations would greatly reduce the danger of extinction.

E. KUYT

Whooping crane and chick (*courtesy Parks Canada/Prairie Region*).

Wiarton, Ont, Town, pop 2074 (1981c), inc 1893, located at the head of Colpoys B on GEORGIAN BAY, 225 km NW of Toronto. The site of 17th-century French missions, it was first settled 1866, and was named for Wiarton Place, near Maidstone, Eng, birthplace of Sir Edmund HEAD,

governor general when the area was surveyed. Logging predominated until WWI. Nestled at the base of the ruggedly picturesque BRUCE PENINSULA, it is now a service centre for the tourist industry and the site of a large provincial fish hatchery.

DANIEL FRANCIS

WIC (Western International Communications Ltd), controlled by Frank Griffiths and the Owen family, is one of western Canada's largest media companies. Its broadcasting holdings include radio stations in Vancouver, Calgary, Winnipeg and Hamilton, and in television a 59% interest in British Columbia Television Co (BCTV), which owns CHAN-TV, Vancouver, and CHEK-TV, Victoria, stations that provide CTV television service for all of BC. Western, through BCTV, has a 19% interest in Canadian Satellite Communications Inc, which provides television services via satellite to rural and remote regions of Canada (*see* SATELLITE COMMUNICATIONS). Other interests include broadcast commercial production, sales and promotion operations. Total revenues in 1983 were $67 million.

PETER S. ANDERSON

Wickananish, or Wikinanish, meaning "having no one in front of him in the canoe," Nootka chief (*fl* 1788-93). Wickananish was the leading chief at Clayoquot Sound, on the W coast of Vancouver I, during the period of initial European contact. Because trading vessels visited Clayoquot Sound less frequently than Nootka, Wickananish was not as well known as MAQUINNA but he was certainly as wealthy and powerful as his neighbour. Wickananish had achieved prominence in Nootka society according to traditional patterns and then, with the coming of the white man, he was able to consolidate and enhance his position by controlling the local maritime FUR TRADE.

ROBIN FISHER

Wickett, Samuel Morley, political economist, leather-goods manufacturer (b at Brooklin, Ont 17 Oct 1872; d at Toronto 7 Dec 1915). A graduate of U of T (1894), he was one of the first Canadians to pursue advanced studies in economics in Europe (Austria, Germany), where the traditions of state planning so impressed him that he became Canada's foremost advocate of employing professional administrators at all levels of government. A pioneer in urban studies and reform and lecturer in POLITICAL ECONOMY at U of T (1898-1905), he launched a monograph series on Canadian municipal government and helped found the Toronto Bureau of Municipal Research (1913-82). Elected an alderman in 1913, he prepared a transportation committee report recommending the establishment of a Toronto metropolitan region for planning urban services. He went into business in 1905 and led the Canadian Manufacturers Assn in its unsuccessful efforts to secure technical education and a nonpartisan tariff board. Stressing the need for data upon which to base rational decisions, he lobbied for a statistical bureau in Ottawa. Like other Canadian businessmen concerned about urban problems in the period 1895 to 1914, Wickett was an elitist who distrusted popular democracy and opposed extending the franchise. It was exposure to the German ideals of state service and planning based on statistics that made his contributions unique. *See also* URBAN AND REGIONAL PLANNING.

JOHN WEAVER

Wiebe, Rudy Henry, writer (b at Speedwell, near Fairholme, Sask 4 Oct 1934). Wiebe has written impressive novels not only about his own people, the MENNONITES, but about other minority ethnic groups living close to the land. Born in a small Low-German-speaking community in northern Saskatchewan 4 years after his parents emigrated from Russia, Wiebe was the youngest of 7 children and did not learn English until he went to school. He attended high school in Coaldale, Alta, and later U of Alberta. His

Rudy Wiebe has written impressive novels about his own people, the Mennonites, as well as about others who live close to the land (*photo by Jorge Frascara*).

first novel, *Peace Shall Destroy Many* (1962), set in a community similar to that in which he had grown up, began as an exercise for his MA. It is a powerful problem novel concerned with the split between pacifist principles and the urge to violence in the hero and in the congregation in which he lives during WWII. On publication it caused bitter controversy among Mennonites. It was followed by *First and Vital Candle* (1966), set in an Indian community in northern Ontario and dealing didactically with moral and religious issues. In 1970, his first "epic" novel, *The Blue Mountains of China,* presented a saga of the Mennonite people dispersed yet enduring in Russia, Paraguay and Canada.

Wiebe then turned to historical fiction. *The Temptations of Big Bear* (1973) is a long, intricate novel centered on the Plains Cree chief imprisoned after the 1885 Frog Lake incident. It won a Governor Gen's Award. *The Scorched-Wood People* (1977) is set in the same period and offers an interpretation of Louis RIEL from the viewpoint of the Métis. Both books are based on detailed historical research, and each offers a sympathetic but not idealized portrait of a complex and controversial figure. His latest novel, *My Lovely Enemy* (1983), combines his interest in Mennonite and Indian subjects; it is a daring, experimental book involving a radical theology of love. He has also published 3 volumes of short stories, *Where Is the Voice Coming From?* (1974), *Alberta/A Celebration* (1979) and *The Angel of the Tar Sands* (1982); a play, *Far as the Eye Can See,* written in collaboration with Theatre Passe Muraille (1977); and a novella, *The Mad Trapper* (1980), based on the RCMP hunt for Albert Johnson.

Wiebe holds a bachelor of theology degree from the Mennonite Brethren Bible College, Winnipeg (1962), and for 18 months edited the *Mennonite Brethren Herald.* In 1967 he began teaching English and creative writing at U of Alberta. He is remarkable for the ambitious scope of his fiction, his treatment of important moral issues, and a craggy style which, though sometimes ungainly, frequently results in an eloquence that is both appropriate and evocative.

W.J. KEITH

Reading: W.J. Keith, *Epic Fiction* (1981) and, ed, *A Voice in the Land: Essays by and about Rudy Wiebe* (1981).

Wieland, Joyce, artist, filmmaker (b at Toronto 30 June 1931). Wieland studied at Central Technical School, Toronto, and in 1960 held her first exhibition of paintings at the Isaacs Gallery, Toronto, where she showed paintings in an ab-

Joyce Wieland, *The Artist on Fire* (1983), oil on canvas (*courtesy Robert McLaughlin Gallery, Oshawa*).

stract expressionist genre, drawings and cartoons, and later her constructions. From 1962 to 1970 she and her husband, artist Michael SNOW, lived in New York where she became an important figure in the experimental film world with such award-winning films as *Rat Life and Diet in North America* (1968) and *Le Raison avant la passion* (1967-69). She is known for her feature-length film *The Far Shore* (1976). Passionately concerned with the aesthetic perspective of the woman artist Wieland draws inspiration from Canadian history, politics and ecology and she has worked in a variety of media (painting, drawing, construction, quilting, embroidery and film). In 1971 the National Gallery of Canada organized "True Patriot Love," its first retrospective of a living Canadian woman artist. Recently in her paintings she has turned to visionary landscape and figurative imagery. Her commissions include *Barren Ground, Cariboo*, Spadina Subway (Toronto) and *Défende la terre*, National Science Library (Ottawa). JOYCE ZEMANS

Wiens, Clifford Donald, architect (b at Glenn Kerr, Sask 27 Apr 1926). Raised on a Mennonite farm, Wiens studied painting with A.Y. JACKSON at the BANFF CENTRE SCHOOL OF FINE ARTS, agriculture at U of Sask and machine tooling at the Moose Jaw Technical School before graduating from the Rhode Island School of Design in 1954 and founding his own firm in Regina in 1957. Saskatchewan's most respected architect, Wiens has received numerous awards and his distinguished body of work, from rural schools to the 1983 CBC headquarters in Regina, reflects both corporate modern architecture and a broader expressionist movement. TREVOR BODDY

The Central Heating and Cooling Plant at U of Regina, designed by Clifford Wiens (*photo by Henry Kalen*).

Wiesner, Karel, chemist, educator (b at Prague, Czech 1919). Wiesner studied chemical engineering in Prague, receiving his doctorate in 1945 for research in polarography at Bulovka Hospital. He studied in Switzerland before coming to UNB in 1948 where he developed Canada's leading school of natural products chemistry. His former students are found at most of the major chemistry schools in Canada. In 1957

he was elected a fellow of the RSC and in 1963 received the highest honour of the Chemical Institute of Canada. He has authored over 200 papers in organic chemistry, making major contributions in the fields of alkaloids, terpenoids and steroids. W.A. AYER

Wigwam, an Algonquian domed or conical dwelling prevalent in the eastern half of N America. The circular framework of poles was covered with bark or reed mats. A hole in the roof allowed the smoke from the fire to escape. The wigwam was occupied by one or more families. RENÉ R. GADACZ

Wild Animals I Have Known (New York, 1898), Ernest Thompson SETON's most famous collection of animal stories, reprinted numerous times and translated into at least 15 languages, is reputed to be one of the best-selling books of any Canadian writer. Seton was a lifelong naturalist, scientist, painter and illustrator; the first edition of *Wild Animals* appeared with "two hundred drawings by the author." For some critics, Seton is one of the originators of the realistic animal story; to others his stories exemplify the Canadian writer's tendency to depict animals as victims (*see* SURVIVAL). Seton's best-known story, "Lobo, The King of Currumpaw," is representative in its dramatic but meticulous recreation of a particular animal and its notorious exploits, as well as in its presentation of the wolf's tragic end at the hands of man. *Wild Animals I Have Known* established Seton with a wide public as a keen-eyed naturalist and a natural storyteller. NEIL BESNER

Wild Rice, a true GRASS (*Zizania aquatica*, family Gramineae or Poaceae), grows in marshlands and along waterways from Manitoba to the Atlantic Ocean in southern Canada, and over much of the eastern US. Botanists recognize several varieties; some treat these as 3-4 separate species. An annual with stalks up to 3 m high, wild rice bears long, thin grains in loose, drooping clusters. When ripe, grains drop readily, and can be harvested by bending laden stalks into a boat and flailing them. They were and are an important food for Indians, who sow and harvest the crop, particularly in the Great Lakes region. Wild rice, one of the few wild plant foods harvested and marketed in Canada, can be purchased throughout the country. Large quantities are exported annually. The nutty-flavoured grains, an ideal dressing for wild game, are good in casseroles and other dishes. Today, wild rice is increasing in importance as a cash crop. The 2 major growing areas in Canada are Manitoba and Ontario. In 1980 Canada exported 685 t ($1.9 million), mainly to the US. *See* PLANTS, NATIVE USES. NANCY J. TURNER

Reading: William G. Dore, *Wild-Rice* (1969).

Wildflowers include all flowering PLANTS growing without cultivation. In popular use, the term refers mainly to the numerous nonwoody (herbaceous) plants and smaller shrubs with showy flowers. Plants with inconspicuous, petalless flowers, eg, the GRASSES and the superficially similar SEDGES, are not usually recognized as wildflowers. There are approximately 4000 species of flowering plants in Canada, of which about 3000 may be considered wildflowers. About one-quarter of these have been introduced from other regions of the world. These introduced WEEDS differ from most native wildflowers mainly in their ability to spread rapidly into disturbed habitats and agricultural lands. Their prolific growth and often harmful or objectionable properties make many of them unwanted aliens. Some native wildflowers, such as milkweed (*Asclepias*) and locoweed (*Oxytropis*), can also be considered weeds since they commonly grow in fields and pastures in considerable numbers and may cause livestock poisoning. The common names of many wild-

flowers (eg, locoweed) make reference to some property of the plant or its use in native cultures and folk medicine. Names such as may apple (*Podophyllum*), fairy-spuds (*Claytonia*), wild ginger (*Asarum*) and miner's lettuce (*Montia*) refer to the edible nature of the plant or its parts. Others like heal-all (*Prunella*), liverleaf (*Hepatica*) and toothwort (*Dentaria*) refer to a belief in the curative power of the plant, specific to the part of the body recorded in the name.

Distribution Some of the most widespread native wildflowers in Canada are the plants of the coniferous boreal forest. Within this broad belt, extending from Newfoundland to the YT, are found such common wildflowers as twinflower, mitrewort, bunchberry and Labrador tea. Because of the relatively uniform conditions beneath this evergreen canopy throughout the growing season, no obvious displays of seasonal flowering occur. Within the deciduous and mixed deciduous-coniferous forests of the Great Lakes and the St Lawrence R valley, an array of showy, woodland wildflowers heralds the arrival of each new growing season. These perennial herbs, many of which are members of the lily, buttercup and saxifrage families, come to flower and set seed before the unfolding new leaves of the canopy overhead shade the forest floor. As summer progresses, the wildflowers of the forest clearings, meadows, riverbanks and lakes gradually come to flower. In the shortening days of fall, the numerous and sometimes confusing members of the daisy family (Asteraceae or Compositae), such as the asters and goldenrods, carpet the fields and pastures in a final splash of colour. In central Canada, nearly all of the original prairie is now gone, plowed to accommodate expanding agricultural needs. The common grasses and characteristic wildflowers such as the prairie lily, blue-eyed grass and coneflower are now found mainly along roadsides and railway lines, or in coulees and sandy areas. The prairie crocuses, prairie lilies and wild roses have also proved adaptable. The coniferous forests of the western mountains share many wildflowers with the boreal forest. Other flowers, such as Lyall's saxifrage and heartleaf arnica are strictly alpine. Still others, such as the woolly fernweed, are arctic-alpine in distribution, ie, they range widely through the Arctic and extend southward throughout the mountains in suitable habitats. Although both the dry, interior montane forest and the wet, coast forest of BC have distinctive species of wildflowers, perhaps the showiest displays of western wildflowers occur in the alpine meadows. On sheltered slopes and in moist depressions fed by melting snow, lush growths of tall herbs flower in profusion, while on the drier rocky and turfy slopes and exposed ledges dwarfed rosette and cushionlike plants hug the ground and bask in the bright, high altitude sunlight of the brief alpine summer.

Beyond the TREELINE, the number of flowering plants decreases rapidly to as few as about 300 species for all of the arctic islands. The most abundant growths of arctic wildflowers occur in sheltered and moist TUNDRA habitats, where the shallow soil is saturated with meltwater that has been prevented from draining by PERMAFROST not far below the roots of the plants. Among the clumps of tundra grasses and sedges occur such plants as the arctic lupine, Lapland rosebay and arctic white heather. Low year-round precipitation makes most of the high arctic islands into rock deserts. Here, plants with rosette or cushionlike growth (eg, arctic poppy, purple saxifrage, mountain avens and large-flowered wintergreen) flower in seepage areas, boulder fields, and on gravel beds wherever adequate moisture is present. Arctic wildflowers survive in the rigorous climate with its short summer by taking advantage of the nearly continuous daylight of the low arctic sun and

Wildflowers: 1. Milkweed (*Asclepias syriaca L.*), 2. Buttercup (*Ranunculus acris L.*), 3. Bunchberry (*Cornus canadensis L.*), 4. Heal-all (*Prunella vulgaris L.*), 5. Chicory (*Cichorium intybus L.*), 6. Goldenrod (*Solidago*), 7. Blue-eyed grass (*Sisyrinchium L.*), 8. Blue flag (*Iris versicolor L.*) (*artwork by Claire Tremblay*).

the warm air temperatures close to the ground. In spite of this, many plants cannot always produce flowers, and must rely on "vegetative growth," including the formation of bulbils in place of seeds, as in the nodding saxifrage, to ensure their continued survival. *See* individual species entries; VEGETATION REGIONS. ERICH HABER

Wildlife Conservation and Management
Wildlife comprises those forms of ANIMAL life that are not domesticated. Individual members of wild species held tame in captivity are still considered "wildlife" as they are not genetically different from those remaining in a wild state. Wildlife conservation and management is the protection and use of wild-animal populations and of the land necessary to support them to ensure that productivity and ecological balance are maintained in perpetuity, while social benefits are realized. Human activity has become one of the most significant influences on the abundance and well-being of wildlife.

The first European explorers and settlers in N America found wildlife in abundance. This wealth was recognized as having immediate commercial value, with FISHERIES and the FUR TRADE being the first, widespread exploitive activities. As further exploration revealed the vast, sparsely populated expanse of land, it was believed that natural resources were unlimited; hence, there was no apparent need to practise CONSERVATION. Wildlife, fish and timber were free for the taking for personal use, or could be converted into a monetary return. The practical result of this attitude became apparent in the latter half of the 19th century. WAPITI once roamed to their eastern limit in Ontario. Land development and uncontrolled harvest had extirpated them in that area by 1850. Wild turkey disappeared well before 1900, but only with the extinction of the once abundant PASSENGER PIGEON was there sufficient concern to cause the passage of wildlife conservation laws. While concern and consequently protective legislation developed in eastern Canada, western and northern Canada were still held to be boundless frontiers. Wapiti rapidly diminished in what is now Manitoba, Saskatchewan and Alberta so that by 1890 only scattered, remnant populations remained throughout their former western range. In the 1820s BISON teemed in millions, defying counting, across the N American plains. Their numbers remained significant to the late 1870s but, by 1885, they were almost gone.

The people of Canada, however, still believed in the myth of unlimited land and wildlife. Government and people were preoccupied with economic prosperity, transcontinental railways and Confederation. The BRITISH NORTH AMERICA ACT (1867) assigned resource-management responsibilities to governments; wildlife is obvious by its omission, being lumped under "matters of private and local nature." Wildlife enthusiasts of the 1880s solemnly predicted the extinction of most large N American mammals, but the next 2 decades marked a significant turning point in wildlife history in Canada. Following Confederation and the assumption of resource-management control by the original provinces, a move was made to develop wildlife conservation laws. The first national park in Canada, BANFF NATIONAL PARK (est 1885), was not initially created to protect wildlife, although this soon became one of its significant functions. The concept led to the creation of Bison Recovery Park at Wainwright, Alta, and WOOD BUFFALO NATIONAL PARK, Alta and NWT.

International concern for the well-being of migratory birds slowly gained support and led to the signing, between Great Britain (on behalf of Canada) and the US, of the Migratory Birds Convention Treaty (1916). This treaty led to the passage of the Canada Migratory Birds Convention Act in Aug 1917. In 1919 the Canadian government convened the first national wildlife conference among various government representatives. The first BIRD SANCTUARY in N America (and perhaps the Western Hemisphere) was created at Last Mountain Lk [Sask] in 1887; however, the declaration establishing it remained essentially unrecognized until after the signing of the Migratory Birds Convention Treaty. Land and population protection through park and sanctuary creation became a common solution, although not always without heated argument and dispute. Sanctuaries have been created by federal and provincial governments in key locations throughout the country. Some notable coastal island sanctuaries for seabirds have been declared on Bird Rocks, PERCÉ ROCK and Bonaventure I in the Gulf of St Lawrence, while many inland sanctuaries have also been recognized. Initially, these areas were designed to protect against overharvest of populations but, more recently, they have come to reflect protection of original habitats as well.

Between 1900 and 1960 considerable success was achieved in wildlife conservation. The banning of commercial killing of wildlife over vast areas, combined with favourable climatic trends, has allowed for dramatic recovery. Bison were returned from the brink of extinction. The WHOOPING CRANE population was protected from hunting, and its nesting and wintering areas have been safeguarded. Whitetailed DEER now flourish in regrowth forests and in fringe agricultural areas. Wapiti, aided by transplanted populations, have regained strength in the mountain regions and in the localized areas of the prairie that are associated with parks. SEA OTTERS have responded to protection from commercial overharvest. BEAVER have returned from dangerously low levels to become a problem species, causing damage where populations are not controlled. Through protection, northern tundra MUSKOXEN have shown a dramatic recovery, as have prairie grassland PRONGHORN, which once shared their endangered status.

Wildlife Management Wildlife management in Canada is a reflection of legislation which can be divided into that concerning fisheries and marine mammals and that dealing with other forms of wildlife. The Fisheries Act of Canada provides that all fishes and marine mammals in Canadian waters are the responsibility of Canada's Department of Fisheries and Oceans (DFO). The DFO actively protects and manages marine mammals (seals, whales, walrus, etc) and offshore fisheries. Marine fish and mammal populations are viewed primarily as a commercial resource. Legal harvesting seasons and quotas on lobster, salmon and other species reflect the continued monitoring of populations and harvest. Harvest management, together with pollution-control laws, is designed to maintain healthy, viable populations. The industry depends on the sustained yield of a quality product.

To provincial and territorial governments are delegated the active responsibility for inland freshwater fisheries, subject to federal laws. These fisheries are largely managed as a recreation resource for sportfishing but also have significant commercial value. The Great Lakes and the larger lakes of the northern and prairie regions support sizable industries, including the export trade. Fisheries research is conducted by both levels of government, often in concert with various universities.

Birds, land mammals, amphibians, reptiles, etc, make up the second major group. Migratory bird conservation is managed in an unusual manner, being conducted co-operatively by federal and provincial governments under the authority of the Canada Migratory Birds Convention Act. This law also ensures international co-ordination. Migratory birds include WATERFOWL, cranes, SHOREBIRDS, SEABIRDS and birds generally grouped as songbirds and insect eaters.

A wildlife veterinarian works with biologists to weigh a drug-immobilized moose (*courtesy Western College of Veterinary Medicine, University of Saskatchewan*).

Other land-related wildlife is managed and protected primarily by provincial laws, when possible in co-operation with the federal government. Nongovernmental conservation organizations and individuals play an increasingly active role in wildlife management and general wildlife education.

Population surveys are conducted regularly on a wide variety of wildlife to allow management agencies to monitor population trends and distribution. Surveys may be conducted on the ground or from aircraft, often with the aid of photographic techniques. The harvest of wildlife is monitored and recorded for comparison with other population information, in an effort to ensure the maintenance of optimal populations. Less visible forms have defied accurate monitoring techniques. Sample counts, conducted mainly by volunteer conservation organizations, provide some insight into the well-being of these species.

The Canadian native peoples have been granted special-use rights to wildlife through a varied and complex process of treaties and laws (*see* INDIAN ACT, LAND CLAIMS). While the continuance of existing rights have been assured by the CONSTITUTION ACT, 1982, the exact rights of individuals residing in different areas or being of diverse ancestry remains unclear. Supreme Court of Canada rulings have clarified the rights in some areas, but others remain unresolved, thus posing serious limitations to individual resource users and management agencies.

Just as humans and domestic livestock require food, shelter and space in order to survive, so do the various forms of wildlife. Efforts are made by all Canadian wildlife agencies to preserve and protect key wildlife areas on government lands. Government agencies and nongovernmental groups operate programs for the purchase of unique wildlife lands from private individuals. If many species are to be maintained at desirable levels, a means must be found of encouraging the management of all lands in accordance with an awareness of wildlife needs. Government wildlife agencies and public groups have formed the Committee on the Status of Endangered Wildlife in Canada (COSEWIC), which encourages and commissions studies on rare and ENDANGERED ANIMALS or on species of unknown status. Recommen-

dations of the committee encourage increased protection as required. Through its membership in the Convention on International Trade in Endangered Species (1973) (CITES) Canada is involved with most conservation-minded countries of the world in the protection of endangered species. Canada's increasingly urban society moves most people away from direct interaction with wildlife. Thus, there is need for an increasing effort toward wildlife conservation and toward management education, information, and interpretation programs.

Conclusion Recovery of wildlife, primarily from 1920 to 1970, has reflected societal concern which demanded active management programs. Public and nonprofit organizations such as the Canadian Wildlife Federation, Canadian Nature Federation, Ducks Unlimited (Canada), World Wildlife Fund (Canada) and the Nature Conservancy of Canada, at the national level, and their provincially based affiliates, have played a significant role in concert with government conservation agencies (eg, the Canadian Wildlife Service of Environment Canada). However, populations have returned only to those areas that remain suitable for their production. Habitats suitable for population production have been the key ingredients of conservation programs. Populations will not return where land has been modified from its natural state through agriculture or industrial and urban development.

While many forms of wildlife are more abundant in the 1980s than they were in 1870, a number of species have continued to decline to threatened levels or are in danger of extinction. Wetland drainage permanently removes the habitat required by many species. POLLUTION of rivers and estuaries render them unfit for wildlife survival. ACID RAIN from industrial effluent stacks, automobiles and urban areas continues to sterilize vast tracts of the land and waterways of eastern Canada. Marine birds and mammals increasingly face the threat of offshore oil spills and general pollution of the oceans. The direct threat of uncontrolled harvest, so devastating in the 19th century, has been replaced by the indirect, insidious but permanent threats of environmental degradation that are characteristic of the 20th century. If society wishes to maintain wildlife in its variety and abundance, a place for wildlife must be maintained in land-use planning and environmental management.

The uses and value of wildlife to society are varied. Wildlife is one part of the equation which, together with vegetation and the nonliving ENVIRONMENT, constitutes the "balance of nature," ie, the set of complex natural processes on which human survival depends. A country fit for wildlife is a country fit for people. Wildlife is a direct source of food and other products for many Canadians. While this value is most apparent in northern regions, it is also significant in southern Canada. Coastal and inland commercial fishing, based on naturally reproducing populations, is a significant industry. The wild FUR INDUSTRY provides a direct source of income for thousands, representing the highest continuing economic return of any resource in mid-northern regions. These harvest uses not only give direct economic return but, provided their management is biologically sound, also keep populations in balance with their food supply, preventing overpopulation and dramatic losses from starvation and disease.

Wildlife is a basic component of outdoor recreation and part of the national heritage of all Canadians. Wildlife reflects the condition of the environment, and constitutes a "barometer" for measuring environmental change. Throughout Canada, wildlife is the legal property of all Canadians. Its ownership is entrusted in law to the stewardship of the various governments. Sound conservation and management of all wildlife is thus the rightful concern and responsibility of all Canadians. GORDON R. KERR

Reading: J. Foster, *Working for Wildlife: The Beginning of Preservation in Canada* (1978); R. Vontobel, *Man and Wildlife in a Shared Environment* (1982).

Wildlife Preserve, an area of land or water set aside from development or recreational use to protect wildlife and habitats. Wildlife preserves are found, under extremely varied conditions, in virtually every part of the world. In Canada, they are established federally, provincially and privately to protect a rare species from extinction or to provide a sanctuary for species that are important for hunting or tourism. Most of southern Canada is too heavily populated for large, new wildlife preserves to be feasible, but pressure is being put on governments to set aside large preserves in northern Canada, before habitats or species are eliminated. The educational facilities provided by wildlife preserves are in part responsible for the growing awareness of CONSERVATION. For example, the Prairie Wildlife Interpretation Centre, near Swift Current, Sask, combines excellent educational facilities with the opportunity to see native PRAIRIE flora and fauna.

Canadian conservation had its start in the later 1800s, when the extinction or near-extinction of the passenger pigeon, Labrador duck, great auk, wild turkey, elk and bison in the East, and the drastic reduction of large mammals in the West (bison, pronghorn, elk) and North (muskox), caused Canadians to press for wildlife preserves. The first preserves were national parks in the West where land was, as yet, unsettled. These were established primarily for tourism. To save the bison, WOOD BUFFALO NATIONAL PARK was established on the Alberta/NWT border (1922), and bison from Montana were settled there. In Saskatchewan and Alberta, 3 national sanctuaries were established (1914-15) to counteract habitat alteration caused by farming, which was endangering the pronghorn. These were so successful that they were abolished by 1947 because the pronghorn no longer needed protection. Muskoxen were saved, first through game laws, then by the establishment of the Thelon Game Sanctuary, NWT (1927).

Today, wildlife preserves protect many different PLANTS and ANIMALS. For example, Ducks Unlimited (Canada), a private waterfowl conservation organization, has secured and developed over one million hectares of WATERFOWL habitat across Canada, thanks, in part, to Canadian landowners who provide land free of charge. Long Point Provincial Park, Ont, is visited by many kinds of waterfowl, and is home to at least 5 rare or endangered species of REPTILES and AMPHIBIANS. POINT PELÉE NATIONAL PARK, Ont, is a world-renowned stopping point for songbirds during migration. BIRDS OF PREY, rare in much of N America, are relatively common in western and northern Canadian preserves. Several preserves in British Columbia's QUEEN CHARLOTTE ISLANDS are refuges for the peregrine falcon; others, in the East, protect marine birds (eg, cormorants, kittiwakes, gannets and razorbills). A recently developed form of wildlife preserve, and one for which Canada, with its many lakes and extensive coastline has a great potential, is the aquatic preserve, intended to protect aquatic wildlife and habitats. Fathom Five Provincial Park, Tobermory, Ont, is the best Canadian example. Such preserves, even more than terrestrial ones, are prone to recreational overuse. Motorboating, scuba diving and even swimming cause considerable disturbance in aquatic ecosystems, including the habitats of nesting waterfowl.

Preserves are often in jeopardy from human exploitation. If an area is popular for recreation, campers and hikers may trample and degrade vegetation; their campsites sometimes cause FOREST FIRES. There may be pressures to permit logging, use as rangeland, oil exploration and drilling, or mining. Roads through a preserve result in animals being killed by vehicles. POLLUTION from spraying timber with insecticides or pollution from distant industries (eg, acid rain) can affect both plants and animals. Controversy about the rights of native peoples to use land and wildlife resources will have a bearing on the future of preserves (*see* LAND CLAIMS). These problems mean that the establishment of a preserve is only the beginning, and management should ensure that conditions remain suitable for preservation. A.I. DAGG AND S. SLOCOMBE

Reading: A.I. Dagg, *Canadian Wildlife and Man* (1974); J. Foster, *Working for Wildlife: The Beginning of Preservation in Canada* (1978).

Wilfrid Laurier University, Waterloo, Ont, was founded in 1959. The Evangelical Lutheran Seminary of Canada was established in 1911 in Waterloo because most Ontario Lutherans lived in the area and land was available free of charge. To provide post-secondary courses, in 1924 the Lutheran Church founded Waterloo College of Arts, which was affiliated with UNIVERSITY OF WESTERN ONTARIO, 1925-60. In 1959, when UNIVERSITY OF WATERLOO was being incorporated, plans were made for Waterloo College of Arts to become its arts faculty. However, the Lutheran Church did not want the college to lose its denominational character. Instead the college and the Lutheran seminary were chartered as Waterloo Lutheran University in 1960. The Mennonite Brethren College of Arts was affiliated with Waterloo Lutheran, 1961-71. In 1973 the university was transferred to the province, and became Wilfrid Laurier University. Waterloo Lutheran Seminary remains an affiliate of the nondenominational university. WLU Press, established in the mid-1970s to produce moderately priced academic publications, annually publishes a number of books and academic journals. B. BEATON

Enrolment: Wilfrid Laurier University, 1982-83 (Source: Statistics Canada)			
Full-time Undergrad	*Full-time Graduate*	*Part-time Undergrad*	*Part-time Graduate*
4 023	285	2 627	290

Wilgress, Leolyn Dana, public servant (b at Vancouver 20 Oct 1892; d at Ottawa 21 July 1969). Entering the Trade Commissioner Service in 1914, Wilgress served in Russia, Romania, England and Germany 1916-32, when he was appointed director of the Commercial Intelligence Service in Ottawa. He was one of Canada's key trade negotiators in the 1930s, becoming deputy minister of trade and commerce in 1940. An indifferent administrator, he happily returned to the USSR as minister, 1942-44, and ambassador, 1944-46. Even as the COLD WAR took hold, Wilgress remained moderate on East-West issues. Among other postings he was chairman and one of the principal architects of the General Agreement on Tariffs and Trade 1948-51 and 1953-56, high commissioner to the UK 1949-52, undersecretary of state for external affairs 1952-53 and permanent representative to NATO, 1953-55. He published his *Memoirs* in 1967. NORMAN HILLMER

Wilkinson, Anne, née Gibbons, writer (b at Toronto 21 Sept 1910; d there 10 May 1961). A member of the family of William OSLER, Wilkinson grew up in London, Ont, and was educated privately. She is known chiefly for her poetry, which is sensuous and wittily intellectual. She is included in many anthologies and contributed to many small magazines. In 1951 she published her first book, *Counterpoint to Sleep.* A second volume, *The Hangman Ties the Holly,* appeared in 1955. Wilkinson was founding editor (1956) and generous patron of *The Tamarack Review,* in which was published posthumously an auto-biographical fragment about her childhood, "Four Corners of My World," also included in *The Collected Poems* (1968). Besides her poetry, she published *Lions in the Way: A Discursive History of the Oslers* (1956) and *Swann and Daphne* (1960), a modern fairy tale for children. JEAN WILSON

Willan, James Healey, composer, organist, choir director, educator (b at Balham [London], Eng 12 Oct 1880; d at Toronto 16 Feb 1968). A dominant figure in Canadian musical life for over half a century, Willan influenced several generations of composers, organists, choir directors, singers and audiences through his teaching and example. After immigrating to Canada in 1913 he taught at the Toronto Conservatory (1913-36) and U of T (1937-50). From 1921 until his death he was organist-choirmaster of the Anglican Church of St Mary Magdalene. Apparently uninfluenced by musical innovations of the times, Willan's compositions reflect variously the enthusiasms of his boyhood and training — Anglo-Catholic liturgy, choral music of Tudor and contemporary English masters, the rich romanticism of Brahms and Wagner. He composed operas, symphonies, concertos and music for band, piano, organ, choir and solo voice — in all some 800 works. The *Introduction, Passacaglia and Fugue* (1916) for organ and *An Apostrophe to the Heavenly Hosts* (1921) for unaccompanied choir represent Willan's most opulent style, contrasting with the more austere liturgical music most frequently performed. Willan was made a companion of the Order of Canada in 1967. BARCLAY McMILLAN

Reading: F.R.C. Clarke, *Healey Willan: Life and Music* (1983).

Willcocks, Joseph, office holder, journalist, politician, army officer (b at Palmerston, Ire 1773; d at Ft Erie, UC 4 Sept 1814). A keen observer of IRISH and local politics, Willcocks initially eschewed participation in Upper Canada in favour of a "genteel income" as an office holder. In 1807 he was removed from office by reason of "general and notorious bad conduct," whereupon he established the *Upper Canada Guardian; or, Freeman's Journal* (Niagara-on-the-Lake). Elected to the Assembly in 1807, 1808 and 1812 and leader of the coalition of interests that formed the Opposition, he was an 18th-century Whig, concerned to "check the progress of inordinate power, and keep alive the sacred flame of a just and rational liberty." Motivated more by political principle than self-interest, Willcocks, after a period of active loyalty during the WAR OF 1812, joined the Americans in 1813, raising the Company of Canadian Volunteers "to assist in changing the government of this province into a Republic." He was killed in action. ROBERT L. FRASER

Williams, Eleazer, Protestant Episcopalian minister, pretender to the French throne (b at Lk George, NY about 1788; d at St Regis Reservation, NY 28 Aug 1858). Williams was an Iroquois of mixed Indian and white ancestry from the Caughnawaga Reserve near Montréal. The young Mohawk fought on the American side in the WAR OF 1812 and remained in the US. After many years as an Indian missionary, Williams began presenting himself as the lost Bourbon dauphin. J.H. Hanson of New York City published *The Lost Prince* on Williams's behalf in 1854. Shortly before the Caughnawaga Mohawk's death in 1858 his extraordinary claim had been disproven. His biography of his real father, *Life of Te-ho-ra-gwo-ne-gen, alias Thomas Williams,* appeared in 1859. DONALD B. SMITH

Williams, James Miller, manufacturer, politician (b at Camden, NJ 14 Sept 1818; d at Hamilton, Ont 25 Nov 1890). Immigrating to Canada in 1840, he was a successful carriage and railway-car builder at London, Ont, and Hamilton. Engaged in oil production and refining in

Lambton County after 1857, Williams is considered the father of the oil industry in Canada. Claims that Williams drilled the first oil well in N America are shared with E.L. Drake of Pennsylvania. He was a member of the Ontario Legislature 1867-79 and registrar of Wentworth County 1879-90.   EDWARD PHELPS

Williams, Percy Alfred, runner (b at Vancouver, 19 May 1908; d 29 Nov 1982). As a child Williams suffered from rheumatic fever, which left him with a damaged heart. But just a year out of high school, the 59 kg runner became the sensation of the 1928 Amsterdam Olympics, winning gold medals in the 100 and 200 m sprints against the fastest field ever assembled. He had previously tied the world mark of 9.6 seconds over 100 yards and, following the Olympics, clinched his domination of the world's top stars by going unbeaten in a spectacular series of indoor races in New York, Chicago, Boston and Philadelphia. Williams's Olympic double stands as the most brilliant solo achievement by any Canadian in international TRACK AND FIELD competition.   BRIAN S. LEWIS

Williams, Sir William Fenwick, army officer (b at Annapolis Royal, NS 4 Dec 1800; d at London, Eng 26 July 1883). A British officer on loan to the Turkish army, Williams became a hero in 1855 when he led the determined, though unsuccessful, defence of Kars against Russia during the Crimean War. From 1859 to 1865, as commander in chief in BNA, he organized preparations for defence against the US during the AMERICAN CIVIL WAR although the British government doubted his capacity to command should an invasion occur. Valuing his charm and popularity, however, the British made him lieutenant-governor of NS (Nov 1865-Oct 1867) so he could use his influence to counter provincial opposition to CONFEDERATION.   ROGER SARTY

Williams Lake, BC, City, pop 8362 (1981c; 10 200, 1983e), inc 1929, is located in the Cariboo country of central BC, 545 km NE of Vancouver. Williams Lake received its name from the adjacent lake, named in 1860 after Chief William of the Sugar Cane Indian Reserve. The Indian name for the location, "Colunetza," means "the gathering place of the lordly ones." The highway and the railway have been essential in the city's development, especially in recent years. Its economy was long based primarily on agriculture, as the service centre and market for the numerous cattle ranches of the great Cariboo and Chilcotin plateaus. In recent decades forestry, logging and lumbering have overtaken ranching in importance. Mining, tourism, service industries and government offices give a varied economic base for the city. Williams Lake is also the home, every July, of the famous Williams Lake Stampede.   JOHN R. STEWART

Williamson, Curtis Albert, painter (b at Brampton, Ont 2 Jan 1867; d at Toronto 18 Apr 1944). A founding member and secretary of the Canadian Art Club 1908-09 and member of its executive council 1910-15, Williamson brought Dutch subject matter and technique to Toronto in the 1890s. Nicknamed "the Canadian Rembrandt," and known primarily as a portraitist, he also painted genre scenes, interiors and landscapes, typically in a dark tonal style developed after more than 10 years of painting in France and Holland following a brief period of study in Paris (1889). He returned to Toronto in 1904, and that year was awarded a silver medal at the St Louis Universal Exposition. His later work is more loosely painted and in a higher key. Notable among his portraits is that of Frederick BANTING.   CHRISTINE BOYANOSKI

Williamson, John Thoburn, geologist, diamond-mine owner (b at Montfort, Qué 10 Feb 1907; d at Mwadui, Tanganyika, E Africa 7 Jan 1958). After receiving a doctorate in geology from McGill in 1933, he began mining exploration in Northern Rhodesia [Zambia] but soon switched to Tanganyika [Tanzania]. Williamson was one of many N American geologists in SE Africa whose role in the development of mining was fundamental. Six years of prospecting, much of it as an impoverished independent geologist, were finally rewarded by a diamond strike in 1940 near Lk Victoria. Retaining ownership himself, Williamson became a significant force in the world diamond market. A lifelong bachelor, he lived simply at the mine and developed it as a model property, noted for humane labour practices. He became a benefactor of Makerere University, Uganda.   ALAN JEEVES

Willingdon, Freeman Freeman-Thomas, 1st Marquess of, governor general of Canada 1926-31 (b at Ratton, Eng 12 Sept 1866; d at London, Eng 12 Aug 1941). After a period as an MP (1900-10) and terms as governor of the Indian provinces of Bombay (1913-18) and Madras (1919-24). Willingdon was governor general of Canada 1926-31 and viceroy of India 1931-36. The British Conservative government did not favour Willingdon as a suitable candidate to be Canadian governor general, claiming that he had less general ability, knowledge of affairs and public appeal than others. But King George V, whom Willingdon had served both as lord-in-waiting and tennis partner, intervened to request that his name be included on the list sent to Canada, and Canadian PM KING promptly chose Willingdon, a fellow Liberal. Thin and grandfatherly, he brought a sense of humour and air of informality to his duties. He was the first governor general to act solely as the king's agent and the first to visit the US in his capacity as head of state. He initiated the Willingdon Arts Competitions for excellence in music, literature, painting and sculpture, and privately worried about the "peaceful penetration" into Canada of American media and economic influences.   NORMAN HILLMER

Willison, Sir John Stephen, journalist, historian, imperialist, publicist (b at Hills Green, Canada W 9 Nov 1856; d at Toronto 27 May 1927). Willison's extraordinary public career stretched from 1881 until his death. In Toronto he edited the Liberal *Globe* 1890-1902; the independent, then Conservative *News* 1903-17; and *Willison's Monthly* 1925-27. He reported Canada to the British elite in *The Times* 1909-27. In turn he was an intimate adviser of prime ministers LAURIER and BORDEN. His biography of Laurier (1903) and his *Reminiscences* (1919) remain charming and insightful. His conversion to IMPERIALISM was evident in his writings and through his membership in the empire-wide ROUND TABLE MOVEMENT. An early free trader, he became president of the protectionist Canadian Reconstruction Assn 1918-21.   RICHARD T. CLIPPINGDALE

Williston Lake, 1660 km², is the largest freshwater body in BC. Created in 1968 as the reservoir of the W.A.C. Bennett hydroelectric dam on the PEACE R, it was named for Ray Williston, BC minister of lands and forests 1956-72, who encouraged the development of a pulp economy from the unused forest resource in interior BC, coincident with government hydroelectric energy projects. Spruce forests around the lake supply pulp mills and sawmills at the district municipality of MACKENZIE, an "instant town" on the Parsnip Reach of Williston Lk. The lake is used to transport timber to the mills.   PETER GRANT

Willow (*Salix*), genus of TREES and shrubs of willow family (Salicaceae). About 300 species occur worldwide, chiefly in the Northern Hemisphere; in Canada, some 54 native species (7 or 8 reaching tree size) are known, plus numerous forms of subspecific rank. Identification is complicated because plants are dioecious (ie, male

Weeping willow (*Salix babylonica L.*), with male flowers (l) and female flowers (rt) (*artwork by Claire Tremblay*).

and female flowering catkins occur on different plants) and the catkins frequently appear before the leaves. Leaves are simple, alternate and usually long and pointed; flowers are petalless. Distribution is transcontinental; some of the smallest woody plants, eg, dwarf willow (*S. herbacea*), extend the genus range to the High Arctic. Introduced species include the large, popular weeping willow (*S. babylonica*). Willows are widely grown for ornament, shelterbelt plantings and sometimes waterside erosion control. The tough, flexible young branches are wickerwork material (osier). Like the ancient Greeks, Canadian Indians used the bitter inner bark which contains salicylic acid as a painkiller and to reduce fever. Although the wood is soft, it is used by artisans in the weaving and crafting of rustic furniture.   ROGER VICK

Willson, David, religious leader (b in Dutchess County, NY 7 June 1778; d at Sharon, Canada W 16 Jan 1866). Having disagreed with the Quakers in 1812, he formed his own sect, the Children of Peace, promoting peace, love and equality among all people. Like other dissident leaders of his time, he turned a backwoods settlement into a cohesive community, strong in faith, charitable and dedicated to education. Lovers of music, they had a band, a choir and the oldest extant barrel organ built in Upper Canada. Their temple is an architectural gem, rich in symbolism. Willson wrote many hymns and sermons, and some political treatises, especially around the time of the 1837 Rebellion.   JEAN McFALL

Willson, Thomas Leopold, "Carbide," inventor (b 1860; d at New York C 20 Dec 1915). Propelled by curiosity, Willson was a chronic inventor gifted in both recognizing the potential of his discoveries and funding their development. He obtained over 70 patents in Canada. The earliest concern electric dynamos and their application in ALUMINUM production and domestic lighting. He moved to the US, where he discovered a process for the production of bulk calcium carbide and acetylene gas in 1892. Willson then returned to Canada to participate in carbide concerns and promote early hydroelectric development. He also patented several marine devices using acetylene. Finally, intrigued with triple phosphates and their fertilizer and paper product potential, "Carbide" mortgaged his assets to American J.B. Duke to obtain development capital. He lost the gamble, and then died. Willson's carbide discovery laid a basis for development of the electrochemical industry.   MARGARET CARTER

Wilmot, Lemuel Allan, politician, lawyer, judge (b in Sunbury Co, NB 31 Jan 1809; d at Fredericton 20 May 1878). A brilliant, flamboyant orator, Wilmot used his skills in the courtroom, in the NB Assembly and in public speeches, often in support of Methodism. While appearing to be a Reformer in his fights against the privileges of the old system, Wilmot aggressively sought those advantages for himself. Never defeated between 1834 and 1851, he rattled off the catch phrases of RESPONSIBLE GOVERNMENT while never understanding the principle. An effective provocateur, Wilmot was eventually appointed attorney general in 1848 when he abandoned all pretense of support for Reform. He sought and received an appointment to the Supreme Court in 1851, creating a serious crisis in government. A competent if controversial judge, Wilmot was never promoted. His public support of CONFEDERATION was considered unethical, but the success of the movement led to his becoming NB's first native-born lieutenant-governor (23 Jan 1868-15 Nov 1873).

CARL M. WALLACE

Wilmot, Montagu, British army officer, governor of Nova Scotia (d at Halifax 23 May 1766). An officer from 1730, Wilmot served almost exclusively in Nova Scotia 1746-66 and was at the siege of LOUISBOURG in 1758 as a regimental commander. Appointed lieutenant-governor of NS Mar 1763, he was advanced to governor May 1764, both appointments won by patronage. Unfortunately he was plagued by illness and lacked sufficient willpower to govern effectively. During his term the province suffered from a postwar depression, caused in part by sharply reduced British government spending and, in addition, 2.5 to 3.5 million acres (1.0-1.4 million ha) were granted away, often to speculators who did little to improve their acquisitions. Generally regarded as weak, Wilmot died in office.

STUART SUTHERLAND

Wilmot, Samuel, pisciculturist (b at Belmont Farm, Clarke Twp, West Durham, Upper Canada 22 Aug 1822; d at Newcastle, Ont 17 May 1899). Wilmot became interested in the new practice of artificially hatching fish as a means of saving the Lk Ontario salmon and in 1865 established a small hatchery on his farm. Although his effort to save the salmon failed, the hatchery itself succeeded. The government leased his hatchery in 1868 and Wilmot was superintendent of fish culture 1876-95. Active in local government and agriculture as well, in 1879 he was president of the Ontario Agricultural and Arts Assn. Wilmot established 15 hatcheries across Canada. His designs were widely copied in N America and in 1883 a working model of his hatchery won a gold prize at the International Fisheries Exhibition. In 1891 and 1892 he conducted extensive inquires into the fisheries of Ontario and BC. *See* AQUACULTURE.

A.B. McCULLOUGH

Wilson, Alice Evelyn, paleontologist (b at Cobourg, Ont 26 Aug 1881; d Ottawa 15 Apr 1964). Educated at Toronto and Chicago, Alice Wilson spent all her professional career, 1909-46, with the GEOLOGICAL SURVEY OF CANADA, from museum assistant to geologist. She was the recognized authority on the Paleozoic formations of eastern Ontario, which she recorded for distribution, stratigraphy and structure. She described the fossils, mostly of Ordovician age, in numerous papers and monographs. Through lectures, field trips, publications and museum exhibits she brought geology to the general public, especially the children. In 1937 she was elected fellow of the Royal Soc of Canada, the first woman to receive that honour.

LORIS S. RUSSELL

Wilson, Bertha, née Wernham, lawyer, judge (b at Kirkcaldy, Scot 18 Sept 1923), first woman appointed to the SUPREME COURT OF CANADA. Educated at U of Aberdeen she immigrated to Canada with her husband, Presbyterian minister John Wilson. She was admitted to Dalhousie Law School in 1954 and was called to the NS Bar in 1957 and of Ontario in 1959. She practised law 1958-75 with the large Toronto firm Osler, Hoskin and Harcourt where she specialized in legal research and opinion writing on a wide range of subjects for the other lawyers. She was appointed to the Ontario Court of Appeal in Dec 1975 and captured public attention by her imaginative and humane decisions in cases involving human rights, ethnic and sex discrimination, matrimonial property, child custody and the access of citizens to information about themselves collected by government and police. In 1982, after intense feminist pressure to name a woman to the Supreme Court, Wilson was appointed.

JENNIFER STODDART

Wilson, Cairine Reay, née Mackay, Canada's first woman senator, philanthropist (b at Montréal 4 Feb 1885; d at Ottawa 3 Mar 1962). Cairine Wilson was active in the organization of Women's Liberal clubs and youth groups during the 1920s. A member of the Liberal establishment, she was appointed to the Senate on 20 Feb 1930. She was president of the League of Nations Soc of Canada 1936-42 and Canada's first woman delegate to the UN in 1949. As chairman of the Canadian National Committee on Refugees 1938-48, she was outspoken against anti-Semitism in Canada.

HARRIET GORHAM

Wilson, Sir Daniel, scientist, author, educator (b at Edinburgh, Scot 5 Jan 1816; d at Toronto 6 Aug 1892). Wilson was a man of many talents. He was educated at Edinburgh U, studied art briefly with William Turner, wrote essays for *Chambers' Journal*, published a history of Oliver Cromwell, and was fascinated with antiquity during his Scottish years. In 1847, while secretary of the Scottish Antiquarian Soc, he published *Memorials of Edinburgh in the Olden Time* (illustrated by the author); 4 years later appeared *The Archaeology and Prehistoric Annals of Scotland*, in which was coined the word "prehistory."

In 1853 Wilson was appointed professor of history and English at the yet-to-be-constructed University College in U of T. He contributed to the design of the building, was a major defender of the "provincial university" against denominational attack and became president of University College (nondenominational) in 1880. During these years Wilson continued his scientific research, especially in the emerging field of ethnology. He became a major interpreter in Canada of the scientific consequences of the work of Charles Darwin. While he accepted the extension of geological time and the evolution of species, Wilson rejected — as did his colleague J.W. DAWSON at McGill — the notion of natural selection as unproven speculation, and insisted upon innate differences between man and animal, largely on religious grounds. Wilson's 2-vol *Prehistoric Man: Researches into the Origin of Civilisation in the Old and New World* (1862), a masterpiece of 19th-century ethnology and erudition, was meant to disprove natural selection. One of the best-known scholars in Canada, Wilson was president of the ROYAL SOCIETY OF CANADA (which he helped found in 1882) in 1885.

Much of Wilson's energy was taken up with university administration. In the 1880s he sought to preserve the best interests of U of T and University College in the face of a movement to federate denominational colleges with the provincial university. He opposed the notion, but accepted political and economic realities, and became the first president of the University of Toronto under the Federation Act of 1887. His last years were plagued by bitter animosities and professorial bickering within the university community.

A. BRIAN McKILLOP

Wilson, Jean, speed skater (b at Glasgow, Scot 19 July 1910; d at Toronto 3 Sept 1933). After winning international honours, she died of the muscular disease myasthenia gravis. Jean Wilson started SPEED SKATING when she was 15. A strong, natural skater, by 1931 she was able to challenge the sport's reigning queen, Lela BROOKS, and prior to the 1932 Winter Olympics established herself as N American champion. At the Olympics in Lake Placid, she won the 500 m event. Although she set a world record in the 1500 m in her preliminary heat, she was closely beaten by America's Kit Klein in the final. She fell while leading the 1000 m race. Within months of the Olympics, she entered hospital and battled her rare disease for a year before succumbing at age 23.

J. THOMAS WEST

Wilson, John Armistead, civil servant, aviation pioneer (b at Broughty Ferry, Scot 2 Nov 1879; d at Ottawa 10 Oct 1954). Trained as an engineer, he became interested in the potential of aviation while in the Department of Naval Services in WWI. As secretary of the Air Board (1920-22) and later controller of civil aviation (1922-41), Wilson guided the national policies that led to the use of aircraft in the remote regions of Canada, built the Trans-Canada Airlines, formed the flying-club movement, initiated air mail service and promoted transoceanic flying. He was director of the selection, surveying and construction of aerodromes used by the RCAF for the BRITISH COMMONWEALTH AIR TRAINING PLAN and other wartime needs.

W.J. McANDREW

Wilson, John Tuzo, geophysicist (b at Ottawa 24 Oct 1908). After obtaining U of T's first BA in geophysics (1930), Wilson attended Cambridge (1932, 1940) and Princeton (1936), and worked with the GEOLOGICAL SURVEY OF CANADA (1936-39). He was professor of geophysics at U of T 1946-74 and principal of Erindale Coll 1967-74. He is internationally respected for work on glaciers, mountain building, geology of ocean basins, and structure of continents; his greatest contribution lies in his explanation of PLATE TECTONICS. He also pioneered the use of air photos in geological mapping and was responsible for the first glacial map of Canada.

While searching for unknown arctic islands in 1946-47, Wilson became the second Canadian to fly over the North Pole, a site he revisited in 1982. He has served on the NRC (1958-64), the Defence Research Board of Canada (1960-66), and the Science Council of Canada (1977-83). Besides his academic work, Wilson has written for popular audiences, including 2 books on China that helped reopen relations between China and Western countries. In 1935 he became the first person to ascend Mt Hague in Montana, following the example of his mountain-climbing parents. Mt Tuzo in the Rockies bears his mother's name. After "retirement" in 1974, Wilson combined his science and public interests as director general of the ONTARIO SCIENCE CENTRE (1974-), remained at U of T as a distinguished lecturer (1974-77) and was appointed chancellor of York in 1983.

Recognition of his contributions to geophysics has included his election as president of the International Union of Geodesy and Geophysics (1957-60), and medals or awards from the RSC (1955) and various physics, geology and geography organizations. He is a companion of the Order of Canada.

MARTIN K. McNICHOLL

Wilson, Michael Holcombe, politician (b at Toronto 4 Nov 1937). Brought up in Toronto's comfortable Rosedale district, he attended Upper Canada Coll and U of T. In 1961 he joined the investment firm of Harris and Partners Ltd; apart from 2 years in the Dept of Finance, 1964-66, he remained in the Toronto investment business for the next 18 years, becoming executive VP of Dominion Securities, 1973-79. He was elected to the Commons as Conservative MP for Etobicoke Centre in 1979, and was minister of state for international trade in the short-lived CLARK government, winning a reputation for being hardworking and evenhanded. He ran for the PC leadership in 1983; disappointed by his first-ballot showing, he threw his support to Brian MULRONEY. Mulroney named him minister of finance after the 1984 election. NORMAN HILLMER

Wilson, Montgomery, "Bud," figure skater (fl1926-64). Wilson was the first Canadian to place in the top 3 in the world championships, coming 2nd in 1932. He also won the Olympic bronze medal that year. His reign as Canadian men's champion (1929-34, and 1938-39) has not been equalled, and he held the N American championship 1929-39. Competing in pairs (his principal partner, Constance Samuel, became his wife), he won the Canadian championship 6 times between 1926 and 1934. After retiring he appeared in skating club carnivals. He later taught at the Boston Skating Club 1949-63 and, after 1964, at Mich State U. BARBARA SCHRODT

Wilson, Ronald York, painter (b at Toronto 6 Dec 1907; d there 10 Feb 1984). A commercial artist, he first painted portraits of people caught in nervous moments: musicians playing to a table in a nightclub (1944), teenagers at the Saturday night hop (1945), the dressing room of a burlesque house (1946), young telegraph messengers talking to each other (1947) or a ballet class. But with the late 1950s Wilson made the change to abstraction, a move that isolated him from contemporaries such as Carl SCHAEFER but which proved central to his future. Like his early paintings, his abstractions, with their witty shapes, give a general impression of gaiety and constant movement. His colour sense changed for the better: now more gorgeous, it is at its best with blue and black, or as in certain geometrical abstractions, in brown stripes. His landscapes, very large and French in style, convey a sense of scale. Sometimes they seem to brood, recalling certain early abstractions of Paul-Emile BORDUAS. JOAN MURRAY

Wiman, Erastus, journalist, businessman (b at Churchville, UC 21 Apr 1834; d on Staten I, NY 9 Feb 1904). Wiman made his reputation in Toronto as a commercial reporter for the *Globe* and the Board of Trade, as publisher of his own market and trade reviews, and, from 1860, as a reporter and manager for R.G. Dun's Mercantile Agency in Toronto and Montréal. He left Canada in 1866 to become Dun's New York C manager, but he retained a partnership in the Canadian agency, Dun, Wiman and Co, and personal and business ties. In the 1880s Wiman emerged as an enthusiastic advocate of commercial union with the US, writing and speaking on both sides of the border. The story told in his autobiographical *Chances of Success* (1893) ended in the same year with the loss of his fortune, invested in the development of Staten I, and of his position as general manager of the Dun firm, upon Dun's discovery that he had diverted company funds to his own use. WENDY CAMERON

Wind is the motion of air relative to the rotating surface of the Earth. Winds are caused by differences in atmospheric pressure: the greater the difference, the stronger the wind. The horizontal component of a wind is much greater than its vertical component; therefore, winds are usually thought of as moving horizontally. On a nonrotating Earth, air would move directly from areas of high pressure to those of lower pressure, ie, warm air would rise at the equator and flow poleward, as cold polar air sank and flowed towards the equator. However, in Canada as elsewhere in the Northern Hemisphere, winds are deflected to the right of the path of motion by the Coriolis effect, a force resulting from the Earth's rotation. This deflection produces the prevailing westerly winds. In the at-mosphere, between about 1.2 and 1.6 km, winds tend to blow parallel to rather than across the lines of equal pressure (isobars). These winds, known as geostrophic winds [Gk *geo,* "earth," *strophikos,* "turned"], are balanced because they are acted upon equally by the horizontal pressure force and the horizontal Coriolis effect. Gradient winds have the same direction as geostrophic winds, but move more quickly in cyclonically curved, counterclockwise paths (low pressure areas), and more slowly in anti-cyclonically curved, clockwise paths (high pressure areas). Near the ground, friction reduces wind speed and deflects the wind towards lower pressure. Consequently, winds converge and lift in lows. The result is bad weather. In high pressure systems they diverge. The subsidence which accompanies divergence leads to clear weather.

Winds play a major role in the heat and moisture balance of Canada. They pick up moisture from the oceans and lakes and distribute it across the country as precipitation. They transport heat from the oceans and from southerly latitudes into the interior and bring cold air from the Arctic to the rest of the country and beyond. In Canada, wind speed is strongest in the North. Resolution I, NWT, has the greatest average annual wind speed in the country (35.5 km/h). The average in the prairies is about 18 km/h, compared to 14 km/h for the rest of the country. Some of the strongest winds in the country are associated with hurricanes and typhoons. Regional and local winds occur in many parts of the country. Mountain and valley winds (downslope and upslope, respectively) are found in interior BC. In coastal areas and around the Great Lakes, land and sea/lake breezes alternate; land breezes occur at night, sea/lake breezes during the day. CHINOOKS are warm, dry, gusty, foehn-type winds, ie, winds which blow down alpine valleys. They occur in southern Alberta.

Strong winds can cause damage to life and property. For example, on 20 Aug 1970 winds of tornadolike intensity struck Sudbury, Ont. Four persons were killed, 750 were left homeless and damage exceeded $6 million. The cooling effect of winds is familiar to most Canadians. Although this effect is present at all temperatures, it is most strongly felt in the winter. Wind chill results from the transfer of heat, primarily by convection, from the warmer human body to the colder atmosphere. The stronger the wind the greater the heat loss. Wind chill is expressed as the number of watts of energy lost per square metre of surface (W/m^2) or as the still air temperature which would cause the same heat loss (°C). *See* TORNADO. L.C. NKEMDIRIM

Wind Energy is ENERGY obtained from moving air. The motion results from the heating and cooling of the Earth; thus, wind energy is an indirect form of SOLAR ENERGY. It is normally turned into useful energy by the action of WIND currents on moving surfaces such as a the sails of a ship or the blades of a windmill. Wind energy is one of the oldest forms of energy used to supplement human muscle. Windmills and other spinning wind-energy devices — more accurately known as wind turbines — were used for grinding grain by the 7th century AD, and were in wide use for this purpose and for pumping water by the Middle Ages; they were brought by the French to Canada in the 17th century and were commonly used for grinding grain. Ships have used sails for at least 3000-4000 years. Before the advent of rural electrification systems, wind turbines were also used to generate electricity on farms in N America, notably on the Canadian prairies.

The advantage of wind-energy systems is that they tap an inexhaustible energy source that has no competing uses; hence, there is no fuel cost. The disadvantage is that wind conditions are unpredictable: they are subject to gusting and becalming, to daily and seasonal variations in strength, and to interactions with local topographic features. To meet a continuous demand such as a community's lighting and heating, a wind-energy system must either be integrated with other energy sources or include a means of storing energy for use during calm periods. If the demand is not continuous (eg, in agricultural water systems or unscheduled water transportation) wind energy can be employed very usefully. The reawakening of interest in wind-energy conversion systems is the result of increasing energy demands and the relatively high costs of conventional energy sources. New wind-energy conversion equipment uses advanced AERODYNAMIC features, modern structural design and new materials. The revival encompasses not only land-based systems but also commercial marine applications. New sail configurations have been devised to improve ship performance dramatically. However, the greatest effort has been focused on land-based generation of ELECTRIC POWER using high-speed wind turbines.

Applications The areas of Canada with the prime potential for wind-energy applications are those where there is a coincidence of good wind-energy sites with nearby energy users. Such a combination minimizes the size of wind turbine required for a given output, the capital cost of the energy-transmission system required and the associated transmission losses. Areas of maximum wind energy availability in Canada tend to occur on the E and W coasts, in a portion of northern Manitoba and in the southern portions of Alberta and Saskatchewan. The greatest potential appears to be for ELECTRIC-POWER GENERATION to serve nearby population centres and rural communities. Where circumstances permit, the electricity would be fed into existing electrical distribution grids. This is the type of system that utilities such as Newfoundland and Labrador Hydro and Saskatchewan Power Corp are using experimentally. Fairly large-scale water-pumping applications may also be feasible in Alberta and Saskatchewan for irrigation. Special cases where wind energy appears to be particularly attractive occur in very isolated areas that have high conventional energy costs, eg, some northern communities. In these cases wind-turbine generators will almost certainly be combined with, for example, power from internal-combustion engines to provide a continuous and reliable supply. The alternative, using wind-turbine generators to charge batteries, appears to be too costly for large-scale plants. Additional opportunities for Canadian industry may arise from the export of wind-energy systems to other countries.

The most recent developments in wind-energy applications relate to the generation of electrical power. This use arises from the prior

Old windmill on Highway 1 near Tompkins, Sask (*photo by G.J. Harris*).

existence in many areas of electrical-distribution grids, as well as the general convenience and flexibility of electrical power. Direct uses of mechanical energy produced by wind turbines are primarily for water pumping. At present, wind-turbine-driven water pumps are typically small machines, used mostly for watering stock. In the future, larger machines may be produced for IRRIGATION pumping and other applications. One possibility is pumped-storage systems in which water pumped from a low elevation to a reservoir at a higher level is allowed to flow back through a hydroelectric turbine.

Turbine Characteristics Different turbine characteristics are required for each type of application. Most electrical-power generators, or alternators, tend to require a relatively high speed of rotation. Consequently, turbines that run fairly fast, with the tips of the rotor moving 3-10 times the wind speed, are generally preferable to low-speed turbines because less gearing is required between the shaft of the wind turbine and the armature of the generator. A relatively low running speed is generally favoured for wind turbines that are directly coupled to water pumps or other mechanical loads.

A striking feature of wind turbines intended for high-speed operation is the low rotor solidity, that is, the very small blade area in proportion to the turbine rotor's total projected area. Low-speed turbines feature a high solidity (either a small number of relatively broad blades or a large number of narrower ones). All modern high-speed turbines and most of the low-speed units incorporate blades designed on airfoil principles. Some inefficient low-speed machines depend on a drag effect, as does a square-rigged sailing ship. The foregoing remarks apply equally to wind turbines that are arranged with horizontal or vertical axes of rotation.

Typical horizontal-axis high-speed wind turbines have either 2 or 3 blades and resemble aircraft propellors. The blades of these machines are commonly arranged to vary in pitch automatically to optimize performance under conditions of varying wind speed. The most common high-speed vertical-axis turbine is the Darrieus rotor, named for its inventor. This machine is also known as an "egg beater" because of its characteristic appearance.

The most common form of low-speed machine is the horizontal axis, multibladed form often found on farms. The turbine is usually connected, via a crank, to a reciprocating water pump. A related design is the multibladed "bicycle-wheel" turbine, an example of a relatively low-speed turbine used for electrical-power generation. A simple vertical-axis design, often used for water pumping, is the split-cylinder configuration known as the Savonius rotor, after its originator. In this turbine each of the 2 or 3 rotor blades consists of a semi-cylinder offset radially from the axis of rotation. The design relies, in part, on a drag effect for its operation. It is not, therefore, a particularly efficient configuration, but is relatively simple to make.

General advantages of wind turbines are the complete absence of air pollution and a high energy-conversion efficiency. Well-designed wind turbines can recover up to 60-80% of the kinetic energy from the flow passing through their rotors. However, the low energy density available in the wind typically restricts output to a range 0.1 to 0.8 kW/m^2 (kilowatts per square metre) of the rotor's projected area. The result is a large machine size in relation to output; for example, in a machine rated at 5 MW (MW $= 10^6$ W), a high output for a single wind turbine, the rotor diameter can be as large as 100 m. This size problem results in the use of clustered machines, known as wind farms, to extract large power outputs from individual sites. Another problem

with wind-energy systems is the variability of wind strength, which leads to substantial fluctuations in power since output is roughly proportional to the cube of the wind speed. Furthermore, all wind-energy conversion devices incur additional costs because they must be capable of withstanding storms.

In N America the main organization promoting the use of wind energy is the American Wind Energy Assn, Washington. The Solar Energy Society of Canada, Winnipeg, also supports work in the field. The NATIONAL RESEARCH COUNCIL OF CANADA has promoted research into wind energy since the 1960s. In 1984 construction began on the world's largest Darrieus-type wind turbine at Cap-Chat on the Gaspé Pen. Project Eole, a joint HYDRO-QUÉBEC and NRC enterprise, will erect a wind turbine 110 m tall at a cost of $35 million. The turbine will be designed and built by Canadian industries. A predecessor of Eole was the 230 kW wind turbine erected in the Magdalen Is, Qué. It was built by DAF INDAL Ltd, Mississauga, Ont, which has subsequently developed a 500 kW commercial variant of this experimental machine.   J.A.C. KENTFIELD

Reading: J. Park, *The Wind Power Book* (1980).

Windigo, the spirit believed by the Algonquian to take possession of vulnerable persons and cause them to engage in various antisocial behaviours, most notably cannibalism. People are most susceptible when isolated in the woods (akin to being "bushed") for some considerable time. The resultant psychosis is well documented and the subject of medical and psychological research.   CAROLE CARPENTER

Windsor, Ont, Canada's southernmost city, is located on the DETROIT R in the extreme SW corner of the province. Lying directly S of Detroit on the rich agricultural peninsula nestled between lakes ERIE and ST CLAIR, Windsor is an international gateway through which millions of foreign visitors enter the country each year. Metropolitan Windsor has grown from the coalescing of a chain of separate communities along the Detroit R and Lk St Clair and spreading inland, and today includes the towns of Tecumseh, Essex and Belle River; the village of St Clair Beach; and the townships of Sandwich W and S Maidstone, Rochester and Colchester N.

Settlement The area was visited by Jesuit missionaries and French explorers in the 17th century, and permanent settlement followed Cadillac's founding of Detroit. The first land grants for settlement were made in 1749. French settlers were augmented by English-speaking LOYALISTS in the 1780s. By the 1820s the introduction of steamships on Lk Erie, the opening of the Erie Canal and WELLAND CANAL and regular stage service from the E stimulated frontier expansion westward. The ferry connection with Detroit led to the establishment of a small hamlet around the ferry dock. Known variously as the Ferry, Richmond and south Detroit, the community in 1836 agreed upon Windsor with its Loyalist and British associations.

Development With the arrival of the GREAT WESTERN RAILWAY in 1854 the village was incorporated; it reached town status 4 years later. Initially, there were barriers to international commerce and travel, eg, a difference of gauge between US and Canadian railways, but in the

1860s standardized gauges and the development of huge ferries capable of transporting entire trains allowed cargoes and passengers to pass directly across the river. By then Windsor had also become a service centre for the surrounding agricultural area. The railway network was completed in 1910 with the opening of a railway tunnel under the river.

Industrial activity began upriver in Walkerville, a company town (inc 1890) developed by Hiram WALKER around his distillery. In 1904 Ford Motor Co of Canada was established just E of Walker's distillery, creating the industry that would become the area's economic lifeline. Through the early 20th century, Ford, General Motors, Chrysler and a host of long-forgotten auto companies and parts plants helped make the area the "Auto Capital of the British Empire." With hundreds of American firms taking advantage of favourable tariff policies, the area experienced unparalleled prosperity and optimism. The new auto age was capped by the opening of the Ambassador Bridge (1929) — the world's longest international suspension bridge — and the Detroit-Windsor Auto Tunnel (1930) — the only international vehicular tunnel in the world.

Cityscape The French system of land division had encouraged a stringing out of settlement along the Detroit R. Over time communities were established (Sandwich) or sprang up around some function such as the ferry dock (Windsor), a distillery (Walkerville) or an auto maker's plant (Ford City). The transformation of the industrial base by the auto industry attracted rapid population growth and increased demands for administering the metropolitan area

Population: 192 080 (1981c); 246 110 (CMA)

Rate of Increase (1971-81): -5.5%

Rank in Canada: Fourteenth (by CMA)

Date of Incorporation: City 1892

Land Area: 1198 km^2

Elevation: 183 m

Climate: Average daily temp, July 22.3°C, Jan -4.3°C; Yearly precip 835 mm; Hours of sunshine 1995 per year

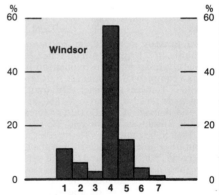

Distribution of Industrial Activity* by Industry Grouping within Census Metropolitan Areas, 1980

Industry groupings
1. Food and beverage and tobacco products industries
2. Leather, textile, knitting mills and clothing industries
3. Wood, furniture and fixtures, paper and allied and printing, publishing and allied industries
4. Machinery, transportation equipment and electrical products industries
5. Primary metal and metal fabricating industries
6. Rubber and plastic products, petroleum and coal products and chemical products industries
7. Non-metallic mineral products and miscellaneous manufacturing industries.

* Industry activity based on the average of percentage shares of the value shipments of goods of own manufacture, total value added and total number of employees for each of the selected metropolitan areas.

Source: Figure II, Catalogue 31-209, Statistics Canada.

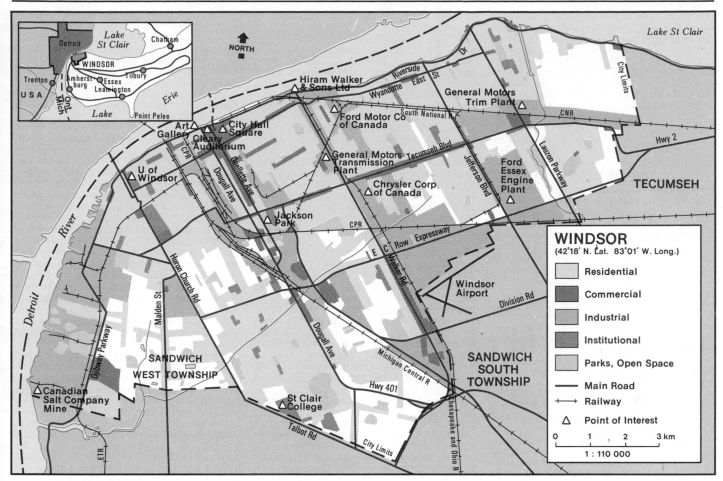

as a single functioning unit. Plans for zoning, waterfront beautification and other urban improvements were lost on those whose priorities were rebuilding the city's tax base and providing new employment. The short-sighted, development-at-all-costs view resulted in a disillusioning experience with riverfront development, but the community learned a lesson. As a result there has been a heightened community commitment to the riverfront and its protection.

Population From 21 000 in 1908, population grew to 105 000 in 1928. This rise was almost entirely due to employment offered in the automobile industry. This industrial work force was young, had a high male to female ratio and a high percentage of foreign born. Another attraction was the opportunity of employment in Detroit; in 1927 over 15 000 Windsor residents held jobs there. During the Depression unemployment reached 30% of the work force, immigration ceased and the area suffered an outmigration. WWII production of war materials and postwar demand for automobiles meant employment and population gains, but from 1953 to 1962 the number of auto workers dropped to nearly half. In the period following the 1966 annexation and the signing of the Autopact, employment was high and there was a continual immigration from many lands. The ITALIANS were the largest postwar group and perhaps the most visible, but the Asian population has grown recently. Slightly more than half of the population is Catholic.

A considerable boost was given to the eroding French culture by official national bilingual and bicultural policies with support from Ontario's educational policies. Designated an official bilingual district, Windsor is served by French-language radio and television and by École secondaire l'Essor.

Economy and Labour Force Windsor is Canada's fifth-largest manufacturing centre. Since its inception the auto industry has set wage and employment patterns for the area. Two billion dollars of new investment at Chrysler, Ford and General Motors augurs well for Windsor's future. Chrysler has head offices in Windsor and is the city's largest employer. Windsor also has significant employment in construction, transportation, trade and service industries. Much of the food and beverage industry consists in processing locally grown farm products. Windsor's best-known processor is Hiram Walker and Sons, Ltd, makers of Canadian Club Whisky. Windsor is also Ontario's fourth-ranked tourist and convention centre.

Transportation Located in the heart of N America, Windsor is a transportation centre and Canada's busiest port of entry. It is served by 5 railways, 4 provincial highways and the Macdonald-Cartier Freeway (401) connecting with Toronto and Montréal. A deepwater port near the centre point of the ST LAWRENCE SEAWAY, the city is also served by the Windsor International Airport.

Government and Politics In the early 20th century, the border community was swept by municipal reform currents from both Canada and the US and experimented with at-large elections, reduction of wards and councillors and commission government.

The entry of labour into municipal politics occurred in 1918 when the local Trades and Labor Congress ran a slate that captured one-third of the council seats. Though labour faltered in the prosperous 1920s, this form of union political action reached its apex in the 1935 election of George Bennett, a trade unionist and CCF member, but it was short-lived. Much of labour's strength was siphoned off in Windsor by 2 remarkable Liberal mayors — David Croll and Arthur Reaume — who dominated local politics from 1930 to 1954. The economic crisis of the 1950s marked the turn to dominance of the

structural reformers who implemented City Manager Government. A very politicized ward system was re-established in 1979 on the assumption that the "city interest" was insensitive to special groups and neighbourhood concerns. Currently there are 5 wards and 10 councillors serving 3-year terms.

Cultural Life Windsor's reputation as a community devoted to the arts is increasingly being recognized. The Art Gallery of Windsor has attained national status; the Cleary Auditorium and Convention Centre is the city's major centre for the performing arts and houses the Windsor Symphony and the Windsor Light Opera. Windsor's stock of interesting and diverse historic architecture includes the Hiram Walker Historical Museum, Mackenzie Hall and Willistead Manor.

Windsor's tradition in higher education began with the establishment in 1857 of Assumption College, which became UNIVERSITY OF WINDSOR, a nondenominational, provincially supported university in 1963. St Clair College of Applied Arts and Technology, fd in 1967, continues a tradition begun early in this century by F.P. Gavin, a pioneer in technical education.

Windsor's special relationship with Detroit is marked by the Windsor-Detroit International Freedom Festival — a week of co-operative activities and events topped off with a gigantic fireworks display on the Detroit R. Windsor has one major newspaper, the *Windsor Star*, owned by the Southam chain.   LARRY L. KULISEK

Reading: E.J. Lajeunesse, *The Windsor Border Region* (1960); N. Morrison, *Garden Gateway to Canada* (1954); T. Price and Larry L. Kulisek, *Windsor: An Illustrated History* (1985).

Windsor, Nfld, Town, pop 5747 (1981c), inc 1942, is located in N-central Newfoundland, adjacent to the pulp and paper town of GRAND FALLS. When a pulp and paper mill was constructed by

1909 on the route of the trans-insular railway at Grand Falls, a new settlement called Grand Falls Station grew up parallel to the railway. In contrast to the Anglo-Newfoundland Development Co town of Grand Falls, Grand Falls Station, renamed Windsor (possibly for the royal house of Windsor), grew without benefit of planning and services. In 1942 it was the second municipality in Newfoundland, after ST JOHN'S, to be incorporated. Municipal and community facilities followed, remedying some of the town's problems caused by rapid settlement and growth. Since the beginning, Windsor has been economically dependent upon Grand Falls.

JANET E.M. PITT AND ROBERT D. PITT

Windsor, NS, Town, pop 3646 (1981c), inc 1878, is located in central NS, at the mouth of the Avon and St Croix rivers. Its short distance from HALIFAX (66 km) has long made Windsor a town of commuters. It was first settled by ACADIANS in 1684 and was called Pisiquid, a name of Micmac origin. The English township of Windsor (after Windsor, Eng) was established 1764, and wealthy Halifax businessmen and politicians were granted land here. During the AMERICAN REVOLUTION, troops were kept at Windsor's Ft Edward to ensure the loyalty of Annapolis Valley residents. Following the war, many LOYALISTS came to the town. They farmed, traded and opened shops, disrupting the pastoral luxury of the big Windsor estates. In 1789 Bishop Charles Inglis established University of King's College, the oldest university in Canada. It is now located in Halifax. Windsor thrived during the 1800s, gaining sawmills, furniture and fertilizer factories, a foundry, tannery, cotton mill and plaster mine. The arrival of the first train to Windsor in 1858 tied the town closer to Halifax. Today, Windsor is mainly residential. Light manufacturing and tourism are the main industries. Visitors may see the remains of Ft Edward and "Clifton," the home of Judge Thomas Chandler HALIBURTON, the famous 19th-century author and creator of Sam Slick. HEATHER MACDONALD

Windsor Strike, 12 Sept–29 Dec 1945, at the WINDSOR, Ont, plant of Ford Motor Co. The walkout of some 17 000 workers was the first and most significant of the many strikes occurring immediately after WWII as Canada's unions attempted to capitalize on their great wartime advances. But most companies were determined to limit organized labour's gains. There was really only one strike issue at Ford: union recognition. The United Automobile Workers demanded it; the company refused to grant it. "Union shop and checkoff" had been the union's slogan for some time. Negotiations had lasted for almost 2 years, and the plant had been subject to many wildcat strikes during the war. The company, with the help of the provincial government, desperately strove to break the strike. Police attempts to break through the picket line were thwarted by strikers who blockaded all the streets in downtown Windsor, surrounding the plant with their cars — parked, locked and abandoned.

On Dec 29 both parties agreed to binding arbitration under Mr Justice Ivan Rand of the Supreme Court of Canada. In his arbitration award, he denied the UAW's demand for a union shop and condemned both the union and the company for their behaviour. Most importantly, he provided for a compulsory check-off of union dues for all employees in the bargaining unit whether they were union members or not. Finally, he developed a system of financial penalties, to be drawn from union dues, which would be levied against the union in the event of a wildcat or illegal strike, based on the duration of the strike. This arbitration ruling, later known as the RAND FORMULA, became widely used in collective bargaining in Canada.

IRVING ABELLA

Wine Industry The cultivation of GRAPES to produce wine occurs in only 2 areas of Canada: southwestern Ontario and the OKANAGAN VALLEY of BC. The 55 km long belt of the NIAGARA PENINSULA, in which 80% of the nation's wine grapes are grown, and the Okanagan, reaching down to the Similkameen vineyard pocket near the US border, are well within the North Temperate Zone, in which the world's major vineyards are located. The number of degree-days (a method of scientifically recording the amount of warmth required to ripen the grape and increase its sugar content) is higher than that of all German vineyards and, in the Niagara Pen, close to that of Bordeaux, France. However, low winter temperatures and the risk of late May frosts that damage blossoms have necessitated the use of exceedingly hardy vines. This factor is the main difference between Canadian viticulture and that of all other parts of the world, except New York state.

In Canada, historically, the basis of wine has been grapes from N American *Vitis labrusca* vines; in Europe *V. vinifera* vines are used. However, there has been a dramatic change in the past decade, and today over half the wine in Canada is made from hybrids of vinifera vines. The presence of wild native labrusca vines spurred the first attempts at wine making; Seneca, Tuscarora and Cayuga used them before European contact, and Le Jeune's *Relation* of 1636 records that early Jesuit missionaries made sacramental wine. The first wine was made for commercial sale in 1811 by a German mercenary, Joseph Schiller, who used vines growing on the banks of the Credit R, 32 km W of present-day Toronto. Forty-six years later, Porter Adams was the first to plant vines. He did so near St David's (in what is now the heart of the Niagara grape-growing region) on land deeded to him by the family to which Laura Secord belonged.

Through the 19th century, wine making was a cottage-industry. Grapes were grown in many areas, eg, Pelée I, Essex County and plots near Brantford. However, in 1873 George Barnes started a larger winery at St Catharines that is still operating. A year later, Thomas Bright and a partner began what is today Canada's largest winery. The wild blue Concord grape accounted for 70% of all production and ensured a predominance of red wines. The wine was invariably "fortified" with spirits to produce port or sherry, a practice that continued until the 1960s.

Two significant developments occurred during the 1920s. First, the BC wine industry was started on Vancouver I to make use of surplus loganberries. The industry then expanded to irrigated lakeside grape plots in the arid Okanagan; however there have never been enough local grapes for winery demands, and a large tonnage is imported annually from the US. Second, the sale of domestic wine was permitted in Ontario during PROHIBITION, leading to creation of a multiplicity of wineries, many producing drink of dubious quality. As a result, when prohibition ended, wine making, marketing and sale came under strict regulation by provincial liquor commissions, beginning in Ontario. In consequence, quality control of both domestic and imported wines is now possibly the highest in the world and Ontario is exploring further improvements in wine standards for 5 categories: varietal, vintage, estate bottled, superior wines and champagne.

A few winemakers, such as the redoubtable Adhemar F. de Chaunac, and crossbreeding specialists, like those at Ontario's Vineland Horticultural Station, realized that improvements in wine could only come from doing more research, from using hybrid or vinifera vines and from aging the wines. However, they worked virtually "in the wilderness" for 3 decades because most Canadians were not wine drinkers

and those who were preferred the cheapest products with high alcohol content. Life-style changes, including concerns about health, the increase in women drinkers and the availability of wine with meals affected the industry radically. Beginning in the 1960s, tastes changed and consumption increased. In 1964 the Canadian per capita wine consumption for all ages was 2.4 L; by 1983 it was 8.8 L. This figure is far below the 95 L and 93 L of France and Italy, respectively, but is above per capita consumption in Britain. Perhaps more important, the proportion of per capita consumption represented by light table wines (under 14% alcohol by volume) increased from 33% in 1968 to 89.3% in 1981.

In the 1980s dry white table wines became extremely popular at home and in restaurants and wine bars in major cities. Canadian products battle imports from 29 countries but are becoming more popular because, after 25 years of experimentation, they have been developed from hybrid grapes (eg, the Siebel group) and high-quality viniferas (Cabernet Sauvignon, Pinot Noir, Gewürztztraminer). Small Ontario and BC "estate" wineries now specialize in these higher-quality wines. The large wineries continue to make sparkling wines, sherries and ports and the so-called "pop" wines of less than 7% alcoholic content, in addition to the traditional reds.

Standards of production (from crushing and pressing to clarification) have also improved. Many wine makers come to Canada after rigorous European oenological training. Grape harvesting by machine to reduce labour costs is common. New cellarage of the highest hygienic standards has been added. Canadian wines in 1983 won more than 35 medals in international competitions. Canadian wine making has become scientific and has spread: wineries now exist in 7 provinces. In 1981 there were 33 wineries in Canada, producing products valued at more than $191 million. Canadian vintners are concerned about the industry's inability to achieve a 50-50 import-domestic market share of liquor-board listings. In 1981 domestic wines made up 43% of liquor-board listings; the figure was 37% in 1983. The industry is represented by the Canadian Wine Institute. PERCY ROWE

Winisk River, 475 km long, rises in Wunnummin Lk in the Kenora Dist of northern Ontario, and flows E and NE into HUDSON BAY. The name is from a Cree word meaning "groundhog" or "woodchuck." The river drains an area of 62 000 km², most of it uninhabited.

DANIEL FRANCIS

Winkler, Man, Town, pop 5046 (1981c), inc 1954, is located in the Pembina Valley region, 115 km SW of Winnipeg and 22 km N of the international boundary. Winkler began in 1892 with the establishment of a CPR siding on land owned by Valentine Winkler, a businessman and politician. Nearby were agricultural villages in the NW part of the West Reserve, one of 2 areas in Manitoba set aside in the 1870s for Mennonite immigrants from southern Russia. Favourable soil and climate, combined with the farming expertise of these religious settlers, helped develop one of Manitoba's richest farming regions. Winkler grew as a trade, service and processing centre for the agricultural sector and, after WWII, as a regional retail and industrial centre. Industrial production includes recreational vehicles, mobile homes, agricultural machinery, metal and plastic products, and manufactured homes. Among the town's facilities are a radio station, municipal airport and museum. D.M. LYON

Reading: F. Brown, *A History of the Town of Winkler, Manitoba* (1973).

Winnipeg, capital and largest city of Manitoba, is located at the confluence of the RED R and AS-

SINIBOINE R. 100 km N of the Minnesota border. Lying midway between the Atlantic and Pacific oceans, it has been called "Bull's Eye of the Dominion," and situated where the Canadian SHIELD gives way to the prairie, "Gateway to the West." The name derives from the Cree name for the lake 65 km N, *win-nipi*, possibly meaning "murky water".

Settlement The area was frequented by Cree hunters, and attracted fur traders as early as 1738, when LA VÉRENDRYE built Ft Rouge at the "forks." The first settlement on the site was established in 1812 around a general store some distance from the future HBC post Upper Fort Garry, built on the Red R 1821-22. Winnipeg was incorporated as a city in 1873, though it numbered only 3700 and was little more than a collection of shacks.

Development Winnipeg's strategic geographical location made it the natural focus for the western extension of the transcontinental railways. With the arrival of the CPR (1885), the city was launched into a period of growth and prosperity unequalled in Canadian urban development. A flood of immigrants, high wheat prices, plentiful capital and improved dry-land farming all contributed to sustained growth. The city became the wholesale, administrative and financial centre of the West. By 1911 Winnipeg ranked 4th in Canada in manufacturing.

This meteoric rise had peaked by 1914, when the city entered recession. The WINNIPEG GENERAL STRIKE (1919) left scars, and the GREAT DEPRESSION plunged business, manufacturing, wholesale trade and the mail-order business into sharp decline. Factories closed and unemployment soared. Not until WWII did the city lift out of its stubborn depression. Conditions improved greatly in the postwar years, but growth was steady, compared to the frenzied pace earlier this century. In the interim, the development of oil, gas, coal and potash shifted economic power westward. Winnipeg's previous monopoly of the marketing of agricultural products and distribution of goods has been challenged by Regina, Saskatoon, Edmonton and Calgary. The city's traditional resources have sustained its commerce and its position as the largest city on the Prairies, but its recent fortunes pale in comparison with its rivals.

Cityscape River lots and fur-trade routes shaped early street patterns, and later the dominant feature was the railway, which physically divided the city in two: the "North End" was the home of most of the city's Slavs and Jews; the prosperous and politically dominant Anglo-Saxons were concentrated in the W and S. Commerce centered at Portage Ave and Main St, and after 1866 industry moved from the riverbanks to the rail lines. Early ARCHITECTURE was in the indigenous form, called "Red River Frame," composed of vertical and horizontal logs. Early public buildings and better houses were built of limestone in imported styles, and after the railway arrived, Winnipeg began to resemble other cities of the time. Prosperity brought greater pretensions, notably the famous "gingerbread" city hall, a picturesque Victorian fantasy. Much of the city had to be rebuilt after the disastrous Red River Flood (1950), and shopping centres began to proliferate. Since 1960 Winnipeg has changed steadily, though not as

Winnipeg, Manitoba's capital and its largest city; view of the Legislative Building (*photo by Douglas J. Fisher/Masterfile*).

---

dramatically as places like Calgary. Nonetheless, almost the entire urban landscape was remade. New industrial parks housed relocated industries. A new city hall, convention centre and a Centennial Centre, including a planetarium, concert hall and museum, were completed. Numerous high-rise hotels, banks and office buildings altered the skyline.

Population Winnipeg changed in several distinct stages, from a small, compact, ethnically homogeneous community to a large, sprawling, cosmopolitan city. With the exception of a sharp increase in the early 1880s, growth was steady and primarily resulted from immigration from Britain and Ontario. These early groups established a dominance that persisted until after 1945, despite the arrival of other "foreigners." In contrast, the growth from 1900 to 1913 was phenomenal, and by 1911 Winnipeg was the third-largest city in Canada. Rapid growth placed strains on the city, which faced serious problems of public health and the provision of services. But the most serious problem was the conflict of values between the charter groups and the immigrants, many of whom were Slavs and Jews who did not fit into the Anglo-Canadian mold, and as a result experienced overt discrimination, ranging from residential segregation to job discrimination and destruction of their property. A deeply prejudiced majority saw the immigrants as a threat, and by 1920 Winnipeg was a city of isolated and frequently bitter ethnic groups. Tensions eased as immigration declined 1920-60, and natural increase played a greater role. The decrease in hostilities was apparent when Stephen Juba, a Ukrainian, was elected mayor in 1956. Juba was joined by increasing numbers of other non-Anglo-Saxons on city council and in other public positions.

After 1960 the population of the city proper actually declined as surrounding municipalities grew. The region was recognized as one city with the creation of Unicity (1972), which also included the large concentration of Francophones from ST-BONIFACE. Winnipeg has become more cosmopolitan with each succeeding decade, with recent increases in Italians, Indians and Métis; young members of these groups have shown renewed interest in their native language and culture. Since 1970, an annual week-long festival, called Folklorama, has celebrated Winnipeg's cosmopolitan character.

Economy Winnipeg dominates Manitoba's economy, containing half the provincial popu-

lation and 68% of its employees, producing 83% of its manufactured goods and accounting for 62% of its retail sales. It is still pre-eminently a transportation centre, and much of its industry is geared to the transportation systems. Secondary manufacturing has traditionally been seen as the key to expansion, and prairie settlement has given impetus to consumer industries. Recently, the large increases in employment have been in the public and private service industries.

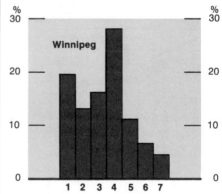

Distribution of Industrial Activity* by Industry Grouping within Census Metropolitan Areas, 1980

Industry groupings

1. Food and beverage and tobacco products industries
2. Leather, textile, knitting mills and clothing industries
3. Wood, furniture and fixtures, paper and allied and printing, publishing and allied industries
4. Machinery, transportation equipment and electrical products industries
5. Primary metal and metal fabricating industries
6. Rubber and plastic products, petroleum and coal products and chemical products industries
7. Non-metallic mineral products and miscellaneous manufacturing industries.

* Industry activity based on the average of percentage shares of the value shipments of goods of own manufacture, total value added and total number of employees for each of the selected metropolitan areas.

Source: Figure II, Catalogue 31-209, Statistics Canada.

Population: 564 473 (1981c); 584 842 (CMA)

Rate of Increase (1971-81): (CMA) 8%

Rank in Canada: Seventh (by CMA)

Date of Incorporation: City 1873; under Unicity 1972

Land Area: 570 km²

Elevation: 231.6 m

Climate: Average daily temp, July 19.7°C, Jan -18.3°C; Yearly precip 535.2 mm; Hours of sunshine 2230 per year

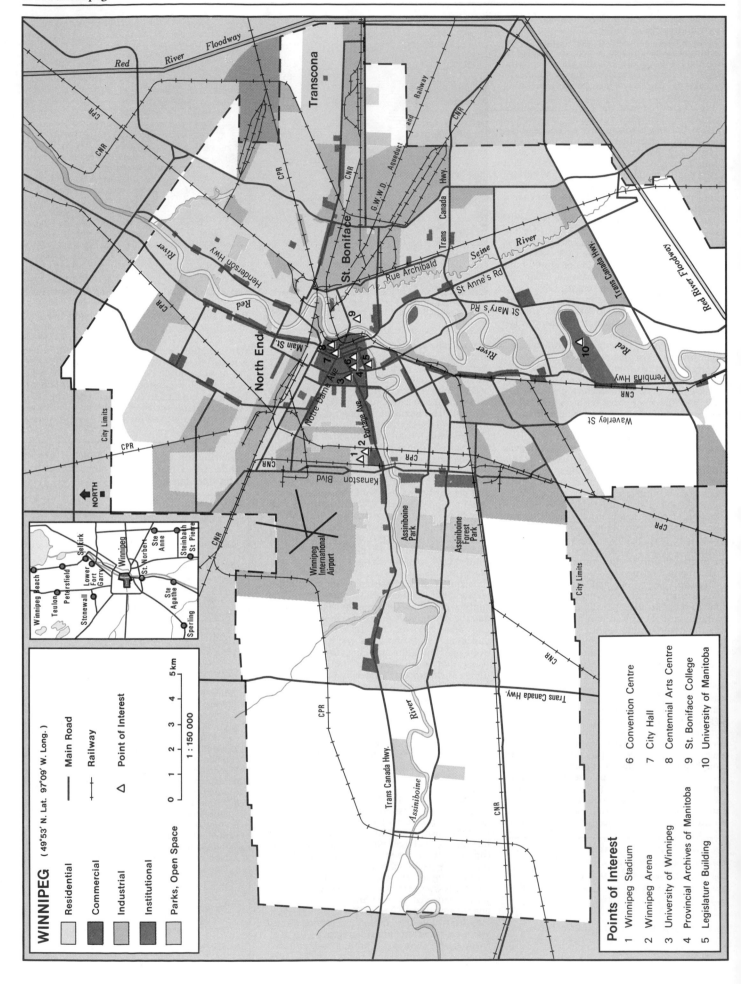

WINNIPEG (49°53' N. Lat. 97°09' W. Long.)

- Residential
- Commercial
- Industrial
- Institutional
- Parks, Open Space

— Main Road
—+— Railway
△ Point of Interest

0 1 2 3 4 5 km

1 : 150 000

Points of Interest

1 Winnipeg Stadium
2 Winnipeg Arena
3 University of Winnipeg
4 Provincial Archives of Manitoba
5 Legislature Building
6 Convention Centre
7 City Hall
8 Centennial Arts Centre
9 St. Boniface College
10 University of Manitoba

The provincial and federal governments support a large public service, and Winnipeg has remained a financial and insurance centre. The city has a long tradition of "boosterism". In 1906 the Winnipeg Development and Industrial Bureau was organized to promote manufacturing and commerce. It became the Industrial Development Board (1925) and operated until 1979, when a new group — Winnipeg Business Development Inc — was formed to attract high-technology industry to the city.

Government and Politics Until 1920 Winnipeg was governed by a mayor and 14 aldermen from 7 wards. In 1920, after the general strike, the ward system was, in effect, gerrymandered by business interests to prevent labour representatives from gaining control of city government. The move worked, for although a few radical mayors and aldermen were elected, the so-called "Citizens' League" retained a majority on council. The powerful Board of Control, created in 1907, was representative of the URBAN-REFORM movement of the time. The mayor and 4 controllers, elected annually, carried out the executive work. The board was disbanded in 1918.

The next attempt at reform did not take place until the 1960s when Winnipeg was moved into the forefront of N American cities by first creating a metropolitan form of government and then moving to a unified, single level of government. Although the division of the region into a number of separate jurisdictions made it difficult to provide services and administer community affairs, it was not until the 1950s that the first step was taken towards REGIONAL GOVERNMENT. In 1960 the Metropolitan Winnipeg Act was passed, creating a new alignment of 7 cities, 5 suburban municipalities and one town. The Metropolitan Corp of Greater Winnipeg was given sole authority over planning, zoning, building, flood control, transportation, etc. Many of the municipalities were unhappy with the format.

In 1972 the provincial government replaced the area municipalities with a 50-member city council that controlled an urban territory with a population of 550 000. With the formation of Unicity, Winnipeg became the first large N American city to move beyond the stage of split-level metropolitan government to a single administration. The original Unicity format has been studied extensively, and in 1977 further reforms were undertaken, reducing the council in size from 50 to 29 members.

Cultural Life Winnipeg is a major cultural centre of the Prairie provinces and has long held a reputation as a thriving community of literature, sport, religion, ethnic organizations, music, education and art. There has been an outpouring of novels either set in Winnipeg or written by novelists who had spent considerable parts of their lives in the city. Works by such noted writers as Jack Ludwig, John Marlyn, Dorothy LIVESAY, Adele WISEMAN, Margaret LAURENCE and Patricia Blondel have some strong link with the city. The city is the home of the acclaimed ROYAL WINNIPEG BALLET, the WINNIPEG SYMPHONY ORCHESTRA, Rainbow Stage, the Winnipeg Art Gallery and the MANITOBA THEATRE CENTRE — one of the most important regional theatres in N America. The Assiniboine Park Zoo, the Manitoba Museum of Man and Nature, the Provincial Archives of Manitoba, the Royal Canadian Mint and LOWER FORT GARRY (a historic restoration located just N of the city) are also major attractions. The Manitoba Music Festival, held each spring in the city, is the largest in Canada.

In sports Winnipeg is noted especially for curling and football. Between 1947 and 1971, Winnipeg rinks won the Canadian curling championship 8 times while the WINNIPEG BLUE BOMBERS have won the GREY CUP 8 times. In 1972 the WINNIPEG JETS joined the World Hockey Assn,

and are now members of the National Hockey League. In 1967 Winnipeg was host to the fifth Pan-American Games, leaving the city with many new sports facilities, including the Olympic-size Pan-Am Swimming Pool (which includes the Aquatic Hall of Fame and Museum of Canada), a cycling velodrome, a high-school stadium, a track facility and a rifle range.

Winnipeg is the location of UNIVERSITY OF MANITOBA (fd 1877), UNIVERSITY OF WINNIPEG (fd 1871), St-Boniface College (fd 1818) and the more recent Red River Community College. There are, as well, numerous private schools and special facilities, such as the Manitoba School for the Deaf. The city has one major newspaper, the *Winnipeg Free Press* (the rival *Winnipeg Tribune* ceased publication 1980), several TV stations and numerous radio stations. A cosmopolitan city of many ethnic and religious groups, Winnipeg has a wide variety of ethnic clubs and organizations, synagogues, cathedrals, religious colleges and institutes.   ALAN F.J. ARTIBISE

Reading: Alan F.J. Artibise, *Winnipeg: An Illustrated History* (1977); Artibise and E.H. Dahl, *Winnipeg in Maps, 1816-1972* (1975); Artibise and G.A. Stelter, *Canada's Urban Past: A Bibliography and Guide to Canadian Urban Studies* (1981); R.C. Bellan, *Winnipeg First Century: An Economic History* (1978); T.J. Kuz, ed, *Winnipeg, 1874-1974: Progress and Prospects* (1974); P.L. Sloane et al, *Winnipeg: A Centennial Bibliography* (1974); T.R. Weir, *Atlas of Winnipeg* (1978).

Winnipeg, Lake, 24 390 km², elev 217 m, estimated maximum depth 18 m, sixth-largest freshwater lake in Canada, is located in central Manitoba. Extending 416 km N-S, it drains approximately 984 200 km² of land by way of the SASKATCHEWAN, RED-ASSINIBOINE and WINNIPEG river systems. This drainage basin extends from the foothills of the Rockies across Alberta, Saskatchewan and Manitoba to the rolling metamorphic uplands of Ontario's Precambrian SHIELD. In the S it extends along the Red R to the headwaters of the Mississippi, including large parts of the states of Minnesota and N Dakota. Lk Winnipeg discharges its waters into the NELSON R, which flows to HUDSON BAY at an average annual rate of 2066 m³/s. Since the construction of a lake-outlet control structure at Jenpeg, Man, the monthly discharge has been maintained between 25 000 m³/s and 183 300 m³/s. The control structure maintains lake levels at about 217 m and assures an adequate supply of water for the numerous hydroelectric generating stations on the Nelson.

The lake lies in a lowland basin that was scoured out of the limestone and shale bedrock by continental glaciers during the ice ages. When the glaciers finally melted, about 12 000 years ago, a large lake, Glacial Lk AGASSIZ, filled the entire basin. It gradually drained and ex-

posed a flat plain that extends from the Manitoba Escarpment in the W to the rocky edge of the Precambrian Shield in the E. Today the glacial lake bottom constitutes the Manitoba Lowlands and is occupied by Lks Winnipeg, WINNIPEGOSIS and MANITOBA.

English explorer Henry KELSEY (1690) may have been the first European to see the "murky waters" (*win-nipi*) and adopted this Cree Indian name for the vast freshwater body. The lake soon became an important transport link between the Hudson Bay port of York Factory and the fur-trade hinterlands of the Red-Assiniboine watershed. In 1812 Lord Selkirk's boats traversed the length of Lk Winnipeg on their way to founding the RED RIVER COLONY at the junction of the Red and Assiniboine rivers. Later the lake gave its name to this community, and in 1871 WINNIPEG became capital of the new province of Manitoba.

On long and relatively narrow lakes such as Lk Winnipeg, interesting wind and wave effects occasionally take place. When prevailing northerly winds blow along the length of Lk Winnipeg, they exert a horizontal stress on its surface. Surface waters move in the direction of the wind and pile up along the windward S shores — a phenomenon known as a setup or wind tide. Setups greater than 1 m above normal lake levels have been recorded along many of southern Lk Winnipeg's recreational beaches, and the associated high waves with their uprush effects have caused considerable storm damage, backshore flooding and shoreline erosion. The highest setups occur in the fall, when the northerly winds are strongest. If the winds die down suddenly, the waters rush northward, then slosh back and forth in a process called seiching.
R.A. MCGINN

Winnipeg Blue Bombers, football team. Winnipeg had been represented in interprovincial play by several different teams since 1911 (the Winnipeg Tigers appearing in the 1925 GREY CUP), but the Winnipeg Rugby Football Club was not established until 1930. They were christened the Blue Bombers in 1935, the year they became the first western team to win the Grey Cup, defeating the Hamilton Tigers 18-12. Led by the great Fritz Hanson, this squad returned to the national final in 1937 and 1938, losing both times but winning in 1939 and 1941. The postwar years saw 5 western championships (1945-47, 1950, 1953) but no Grey Cup victories. In 1957 Winnipeg's golden era under coach Bud Grant began. In 10 seasons (1957-66) he took the Blue Bombers to 6 Grey Cups, winning 4 (1958, 1959, 1961, 1962) and losing 2 (1957, 1965), all against the HAMILTON TIGER-CATS. The next victory did not come until 1984, again against Hamilton. Winnipeg Stadium, the community-owned Bombers' present home, was opened in 1953.
DEREK DRAGER

Winnipeg Commodity Exchange The WCE was established in 1887 by western farmers and grain merchants to provide a marketplace for the expanding agricultural production of the Canadian prairies. For its first 18 years, the WCE operated strictly as a cash market, ie, a marketplace for grains that have already been grown (as distinct from a "futures market" in which contracts are traded for the delivery of grain at a later date). In this capacity, WCE provides meeting rooms, communications facilities and rules of trade for the grain and produce grown in the West.

In 1904 the WCE established a futures market for wheat. Other futures markets were opened later for oats and flaxseed (1904), barley (1913) and rye (1917). Wheat futures trading was discontinued in 1942. Rapeseed (CANOLA) futures trading opened in 1963, gold in 1972, feed wheat for domestic use in 1974; silver, Government of Canada bonds and Treasury bill futures markets opened in 1981. Lumber is also traded.

The WCE is the only agricultural commodities exchange and futures market in Canada. A voluntary, nonprofit, unincorporated association, its 330 members (farmers, elevator companies, grain processors' merchandisers, exporters, overseas importers and the general public) represent virtually every group with an interest in Canadian grains. The CANADIAN WHEAT BOARD is also a member.

The futures markets of the WCE are used by the grain industry for price protection and price discovery. Through the process known as "hedging," producers, handlers and users of grain buy and sell futures contracts to protect themselves against the possibility that prices will change. They trade in an open, competitive auction on the trading floor in Winnipeg, trying to obtain the best price they can for the grain they own or the grain they need to buy later. The market prices established through this process are used throughout the grain industry (*see* GRAIN HANDLING AND MARKETING).

Publications of the WCE include *The Winnipeg Commodity Exchange,* booklets on each of the futures contracts, *Using the Grain Markets, The Winnipeg Gold & Silver Markets* and *The Interest Rate Futures Markets.*   K.S. KEARNS

Winnipeg Free Press Founded as the *Manitoba Free Press* by W.F. Luxton in 1872, the newspaper displayed a distinct Liberal preference from its earliest days. It was purchased in 1898 by Clifford SIFTON, a prominent Liberal politician and Cabinet minister, and thereafter was the organ of the Liberal Party on the Prairies. In 1901 Sifton appointed a young journalist from Montréal, John W. DAFOE, as editor. Even after Sifton's departure from the Laurier Cabinet in 1905, the *Free Press* continued to support Laurier, and in 1911 it opposed its owner's personal preference by championing Laurier and reciprocity with the US. Owner and newspaper were reunited in 1917, when the *Free Press* backed UNION GOVERNMENT and CONSCRIPTION. During the 1920s, however, Dafoe and Sifton returned to the Liberal fold to support Mackenzie King and his government.

During this period the *Free Press* was a generally profitable enterprise and ran a highly successful farm weekly. Dafoe also began to gather together a skilled group of journalists. Employing such men as Grant Dexter and Bruce HUTCHISON, Dafoe's paper was the best-informed in Canada during periods of Liberal government. The *Free Press* was also notable for its coverage of foreign affairs. In 1931 the paper became the *Winnipeg Free Press;* two years earlier, when Sifton died, it had passed into the hands of his children. Dafoe remained the dominant influence at the *Free Press* until his death in 1944. Although the *Free Press* employed some distinguished journalists as editors afterwards, George FERGUSON, Hutchison and Tom KENT, it tended to become less distinctive and more profitable. In 1980 it absorbed its longstanding rival, the *Winnipeg Tribune,* and confirmed its dominance in the Winnipeg newspaper field. *See also* JOURNALISM; NEWSPAPERS.   ROBERT BOTHWELL

Reading: R. Cook, *The Politics of John W. Dafoe and the Free Press* (1963); D. Hall, *Clifford Sifton,* vol 1 (1981).

Winnipeg General Strike, 15 May-25 June 1919, Canada's best-known general strike. Massive unemployment and inflation, the success of the Russian Revolution (1917), a wave of strikes across Canada and rising REVOLUTIONARY INDUSTRIAL UNIONISM all contributed to postwar labour unrest. In Mar 1919 in Calgary western labour leaders met to discuss the creation of ONE BIG UNION. In Winnipeg on May 15, when negotiations broke down between management and labour in the building and metal trades, the Winnipeg Traders and Labor Council called a general strike. At stake were the principle of col-

Great War Veterans' Assn parade lining up on Broadway to march on the Legislative Building, during the Winnipeg General Strike, 4 June 1919 (*courtesy Public Archives of Canada/C-48334/© Brown Brothers, NY*).

lective bargaining, better wages and the improvement of often dreadful working conditions. Within hours almost 30 000 workers had left their jobs. The almost unanimous response by working men and women closed the city's factories, crippled its retail trade and stopped the trains. Public-sector employees such as policemen, firemen, postal workers, telephone operators and employees of waterworks and other utilities joined the workers of private industry in an impressive display of working-class solidarity. The strike was co-ordinated by the Central Strike Committee, composed of delegates elected from each of the unions affiliated with the WTLC. The committee bargained with employers on behalf of the workers and coordinated the provision of essential services.

Opposition to the strike was organized by the Citizens' Committee of 1000, created shortly after the strike began by Winnipeg's most influential manufacturers, bankers and politicians. Rather than giving the strikers' demands any serious consideration, the Citizens' Committee, with the support of Winnipeg's leading newspapers, declared the strike a revolutionary conspiracy led by a small group of "alien scum." The available evidence failed to support its charges that the strike was initiated by European workers and Bolsheviks, but the Citizens' Committee used these unsubstantiated charges to block any conciliation efforts by the workers.

Afraid that the strike would spark confrontations in other cities, the federal government decided to intervene; soon after the strike began, Senator Gideon Robertson, minister of labour, and Arthur MEIGHEN, minister of the interior and acting minister of justice, went to Winnipeg to meet with the Citizens' Committee. They refused requests from the Central Strike Committee for a similar hearing. On their advice, the federal government swiftly supported the employers, and federal employees were ordered to return to work immediately or face dismissal. The Immigration Act was amended so that British-born immigrants could be deported, and the Criminal Code's definition of sedition was broadened. On June 17 the government arrested 10 leaders of the Central Strike Committee and 2 propagandists from the newly formed One Big Union. Four days later, a charge by Royal North-West Mounted Police into a crowd of strikers resulted in 30 casualties, including one death. "Bloody Saturday" ended with federal troops occupying the city's streets. Six of the labour leaders were released, but Fred Dixon and J.S. WOODSWORTH were arrested. Faced with the combined forces of the government and the employers, the strikers decided to return to work on June 25.

The General Strike left a legacy of bitterness and controversy. In a wave of increased unionism and militancy across Canada, sympathetic strikes erupted in centres from Amherst, NS, to Victoria, BC. Seven of the arrested leaders were

unfairly convicted of a conspiracy to overthrow the government and sentenced to jail terms from 6 months to 2 years; the charges against J.S. Woodsworth were dropped. Almost 3 decades passed before Canadian workers secured union recognition and collective bargaining. *See* RAND FORMULA; WORKING-CLASS HISTORY.   J. NOLAN REILLY

Reading: D.J. Bercuson, *Confrontation at Winnipeg* (1974); A.R. McCormack, *Reformers, Rebels and Revolutionaries* (1977).

Winnipeg Jets, HOCKEY team. An original World Hockey Association (WHA) franchise (1972), the Winnipeg Jets brought instant credibility to the league by signing NHL superstar Bobby HULL in their first year. They also pioneered the importation of European hockey players to N America, beginning with the 1974 acquisition of Swedish stars Anders Hedberg and Ulf Nilsson. They won 3 out of the 7 WHA championships, including the final one in 1979. Under majority owner and president Michael Gobuty, their home base, the Winnipeg Arena, was expanded to 15 250 seats upon their 1979 entry into the NHL's Smythe Division, but merger conditions also stripped them of 10 players. They won only 29 games in their first 2 NHL campaigns but rallied under since-departed coach Tom Watt for a second-place finish in 1981-82.   DEREK DRAGER

Winnipeg River, 813 km long (to head of Firesteel R), issues from the N end of LK OF THE WOODS and flows NW to Lk WINNIPEG. The name is from the Cree *win-nipi,* meaning "murky water." After its discovery by Jean-Baptiste de LA VÉRENDRYE (1733) the river was a major link in the FUR-TRADE route between Lks Superior and Winnipeg. Both the NWC and HBC built forts on the river, but traffic dwindled after the merger of the 2 companies in 1821. The river has a heavy, rapid flow and was first used for power by a lumber mill at Pine Falls (1870). Its first hydroelectric power was fed to pulp mills at KENORA, Ont, in 1892, and the first hydroelectric plant on the Manitoba reach began construction at Pinawa, 1902. Today, 6 generating stations harness all but a few metres of the river's 106 m drop. The once turbulent river, with its 26 portages, is now placid, though still frequented by boats and canoes. Since 1965 its water has been used to cool organic coolant in the Whiteshell Nuclear Research Establishment.

JAMES MARSH

Winnipeg Symphony Orchestra gave its first performance on 16 Dec 1948 in the Winnipeg Auditorium under conductor Walter Kaufmann. He was succeeded in 1958 by Victor FELDBRILL who, in the next decade, regularly programmed Canadian works and established the WSO as a full-time symphony orchestra. In 1968 the WSO moved to the Manitoba Centennial Concert Hall and appointed George Cleve as conductor. Piero Gamba was music director, 1971-80, and in 1979 led the WSO in a gala concert at Carnegie Hall. In 1983 Kazuhiro Koizumi became director. In addition to its 34-week, 60-performance season, the WSO is the official orchestra for the Manitoba Opera Assn and the ROYAL WINNIPEG BALLET.   BARBARA NOVAK

Winnipegosis, Lake, 5374.5 km², 195 km long, elev 254 m, maximum depth 12 m, Canada's eleventh-largest lake, is located in W-central Manitoba. It drains approximately 49 825 km² of western Manitoba and eastern Saskatchewan, drawing most of its waters from the Manitoba Escarpment — in particular Riding Mt, Duck Mt, Porcupine Hills and the Pasquia Hills — and discharging them through the Waterhen R at an average annual rate of 80.9 m³/s into Lk MANITOBA, and thence into Lk WINNIPEG. Its interesting name is derived from 2 sources: *win-nipi,* Cree for "murky waters," and the suffix *osis,* meaning "little."   R.A. McGINN

Winnipeg's Contemporary Dancers is a modern dance repertory company which was until 1983 under the artistic direction of its founder, Rachel Browne. First formed in 1964, it became fully professional in 1970. Until the late 1970s it was generally known as Contemporary Dancers. Although Rachel Browne's own choreography, amounting to more than 25 pieces, has been presented by the company throughout its existence, today the WCD offers a repertoire by leading Canadian and foreign choreographers, much of it created originally for the company. The company, consisting generally of about 10 dancers, performs throughout Canada and has made several tours abroad.   MICHAEL CRABB

Wintemberg, William John, archaeologist (b at New Dundee, Ont 18 May 1876; d at Ottawa 25 Apr 1941). Wintemberg worked as a compositor and later a coppersmith before his varied and dedicated antiquarian activities led to an association with the Ontario Provincial Museum. In 1911 he was hired as a part-time field-worker by the Victoria Memorial Museum (later National Museum of Canada) and subsequently as a preparator, assistant archaeologist and finally associate archaeologist (1937) at that institution. Wintemberg's archaeological surveys and excavations ranged from Ontario to Newfoundland despite his delicate health. His prolific and model publications established the foundation for much of the prehistory of eastern Canada, in particular, for knowledge of the prehistoric Iroquoian farmers of Ontario.   J.V. WRIGHT

Reading: N. Swayze, *Canadian Portraits: The Man Hunters* (1960).

Winter, Sir James Spearman, politician (b at Lamaline, Nfld 1 Jan 1845; d at Toronto 6 Oct 1911). Winter began his political career in 1873 and entered Sir William WHITEWAY's Cabinet as solicitor general in 1882. In 1885 Winter, then grand master of the ORANGE ORDER, resigned, expecting to become leader of a new Protestant party. He was disappointed, but became a dominant influence as attorney general in Sir Robert THORBURN's 1885-89 administration. Defeated in 1889, Winter became a Supreme Court judge in 1893. He resigned from the bench to lead the Tory Party to victory in the 1897 election. His administration soon ran into severe problems and was defeated in 1900. In 1909 Winter helped present Newfoundland's case in the N Atlantic fisheries dispute to The Hague tribunal.   J.K. HILLER

Wintergreen is the common name for smooth, low-growing, woodland, herbaceous PLANTS in genus *Pyrola* of the wintergreen family (Pyrolaceae). These plants were known to the Cree as "beaver's ears" because of their small, round, evergreen leaves. Nine of the 12 known species are native to Canada. The name also applies to the closely related genera: *Chimaphila* (pipsissewa), with 3 species in Canada; and *Moneses* (one-flowered wintergreen), with one species in Canada. Also widely known as wintergreen is genus *Gaultheria* of the related heath family (Ericaceae). *Gaultheria* contains about 100 species worldwide, mostly in the Andes, and 5 native to Canada. Of these, the name wintergreen is most frequently used for *G. procumbens,* which has persistent leaves and dainty pink or white, urn-shaped flowers, followed by scarlet, berrylike capsules. This plant's volatile oil contains methyl salicylate (oil of wintergreen) which is used in perfumery; it was once valued in the treatment of rheumatic disorders but is now largely replaced by safer, synthetic formulations.   ROGER VICK

Wintering Partner (also "winterer"), inland trader and shareholder, most notably in the NORTH WEST COMPANY. The wintering partner system evolved in NEW FRANCE, where fur merchants divided their profits with associates conducting the trade. Elected only from among clerks trained as apprentice traders and motivated by profit and participation in corporate decision making, NWC wintering partners were proprietors of the departments they managed. Considered the key to the company's geographic and commercial expansion, this system of management was adapted by such rival firms as the XY COMPANY, the PACIFIC FUR COMPANY and HUDSON'S BAY COMPANY. *See* FUR TRADE.   JEAN MORRISON

Winters, Robert Henry, politician, businessman (b at Lunenburg, NS 18 Aug 1910; d at Monterey, Calif 10 Oct 1969). Educated at Mt Allison U and Massachusetts Inst of Technology, Winters joined Northern Electric in Montréal in 1934. He became a lt-col in the army in WWII. Elected to the House of Commons for Lunenburg 1945 as a Liberal and reelected in 1949 and 1953, he sat in the Cabinet 1948-57. Defeated in the 1957 election, Winters entered private business and was president and chairman of Rio Algom Mines 1963-65. At Lester PEARSON's urging, he re-entered politics. He was elected in the 1965 election (York West) and was rewarded with the post of minister of trade and commerce. Narrowly defeated by Pierre TRUDEAU in the contest for the Liberal leadership after Pearson's resignation, Winters retired from politics. He was president and director of Brazilian Light and Power Ltd in 1968-69.   ROBERT BOTHWELL

Wise, Jack Marlowe, painter (b at Centerville, Iowa 27 April 1928). During his art training at New Orleans, at Washington U and Florida State U, Wise absorbed the prevailing abstract expressionist style of painting. He moved to Mexico and from 1958 to 1961 taught batik in a workshop at San Miguel. In 1963, conscious of a need to restructure his approach to art, he immigrated to Canada and farmed in BC. When he returned to painting it was as a miniaturist dedicated to the microcosmic patterning of archetypal images. Wise's paintings since that time have been essentially icons, with the mandala, the mystic circle, as dominant image. Like many contemporary BC artists, Wise has turned to Asian art traditions. In 1966 he studied with Tibetan painting masters in India, who taught that the ultimate answers lay within oneself. With much virtuosity he combined eastern and western religious symbols in paintings reflecting the great archetypes that dominate the human unconscious. After periods in Vancouver, on Texada I and in Victoria, where he taught at the Victoria College of Art, Wise returned in 1982 to the BC interior.   GEORGE WOODCOCK

Wiseman, Adele, author (b at Winnipeg 21 May 1928). Wiseman's Russian Jewish parents fled Ukraine pogroms in the 1920s. Their escape and subsequent New World adjustment influenced Wiseman's first novel, *The Sacrifice,* for which she won the Gov Gen's Award (1956). Like A.M. KLEIN, Wiseman's fictional search for truth is nurtured by her religious roots: *The Sacrifice* is based on the biblical story of Abraham, as well as murder within the Winnipeg Jewish community, a forbidden topic. Wiseman's second novel, *Crackpot* (1974), deals with another forbidden subject, a Jewish prostitute. She published a play, *Testimonial Dinner* (1978), and *Old Women at Play* (1978), an exploration of the artistic process as seen through her own mother's craft of dollmaking. She has taught at McGill and Sir George Williams.   SHARON DRACHE

Wiseman, Clarence Dexter, general of the SALVATION ARMY (b at Moreton's Harbour, Nfld 19 Jun 1907). Wiseman was commissioned as an officer in the Salvation Army in 1927. During WWII he became the senior SA representative with the Canadian Armed Forces Overseas. He held several positions 1945-67, including chief secretary of Canada and Bermuda, territorial commander of East Africa and principal of the International Training College in London, Eng.

He became territorial commander of Canada and Bermuda (1967) and was elected general of the International Salvation Army (1974). General Wiseman retired in 1977 and published his autobiography, *A Burning in My Bones* (1980) and *The Desert Road to Glory* (1982).   AUBREY VINCENT

Witch Hazel, the common name for a family (Hamamelidaceae) of TREES or shrubs, refers especially to members of the genus *Hamamelis*. Four species of *Hamamelis* are found in E Asia, 2 are native to N America. *H. virginiana* (witch hazel or snapping hazel), a fall-flowering shrub, is native to Canada, growing in woods in Qué, NS, NB and Ont. The plant grows to 5 m, and flowers are bright yellow with 4 long thin petals. Spring-flowering Chinese witch hazel (*H. mollis*), introduced from China in the 1890s, is a popular ORNAMENTAL in milder regions of Canada. Witch hazel may be called "hazel" because the leaf shape resembles that of true hazels (genus *Corylus* of the birch family). "Witch" may come from the use of *Hamamelis* branches for divining rods, although true hazels, not *Hamamelis* plants, were traditionally associated with witches. A leaf and bark extract of *H. virginiana* was a common remedy among N American Indians and was introduced to Europe in 1736. It was used for soothing inflammations and bruises, and for treating hemorrhoids, congestions and tumours; its astringent and soothing properties are still appreciated for external application.   GILLIAN FORD

Southern witch hazel (*Hamamelis virginiana* L.), with flowers and fruits (*artwork by Claire Tremblay*).

Withers, Ramsey Muir, soldier, public servant (b at Toronto 28 July 1930). An engineering graduate of RMC and Queen's, Withers was commissioned in the Signal Corps in 1952 and served with the Royal 22nd Regiment in Korea in 1952-53. An effective, articulate organizer with a crisp manner and open personality, he was promoted brigadier in 1970, the first officer commissioned after WWII to reach that rank, and became the first commander, Northern Region Headquarters (Yellowknife). This was followed by senior management assignments at headquarters, 1973-76, and command of the Canadian Forces in Europe, 1976-77. He was vice chief and then chief of the defence staff, 1977-1983, excelling in the bureaucracy of flowcharts, management systems and political awareness. He was appointed deputy minister of the Dept of Transport (1983).   NORMAN HILLMER

Wix, Edward, Church of England clergyman, missionary (b at Faulkbourne, Eng 1 May 1802; d at Swanmore, Isle of Wight, Eng 24 Nov 1866). Wix graduated from Oxford in 1824 and was ordained in 1825. He first served as a missionary in Nova Scotia, but moved to Newfoundland where he was appointed archdeacon in 1830. He spent the next 8 years travelling around the Island, preaching, raising funds and organizing the Church of England. After a 6-month missionary tour along the S and W coasts of Newfoundland in 1835, he published *Six Months of a*

Newfoundland Missionary's Journal (1836). Wix was the driving force behind fund raising for St Thomas' Church, St John's, which opened in 1836. In Oct 1838 he returned to England. His appeals to church officials in England undoubtedly led to the appointment in 1839 of the first Church of England bishop of Newfoundland, Aubrey George Spencer.   JOHN PARSONS

Wolf, largest wild member of the dog family. Living wolves belong to the species *Canis lupus* (except red wolf, *C. rufus* of the N American Gulf Coast). The grey wolf is largest, weighing 25-45 kg, and has a distinctively massive head with a strong forehead. It resembles a German shepherd dog, usually with a greyish coat (black or almost white individuals exist). Northern forms are the largest in N America. Wolves mate with domestic dogs, producing individuals similar to huskies. Wolves were common in N America in forests, tundra and prairies but are now restricted to wilder northern regions. They live in packs (usually 3-7) with a dominant male and his breeding bitch. Breeding starts at about 2-3 years. Litters of about 7 (4-13) pups are born after 63 days gestation. The bitch whelps in a den, either a burrow or natural shelter. The pack protects and brings food to the nursing mother. Wolves are shy, usually nocturnal and elusive. They hunt deer, caribou, moose, wapiti and, in summer, smaller game. Their only enemy, man, hunts them for sport and to protect livestock, and has extirpated them from the settled parts of N America, where coyotes or feral dogs replace them.   C.S. CHURCHER

Wolf (*Canis lupus*), the largest wild member of the dog family; the grey wolf can weigh 25-45 kg (*photo by Hälle Flygare*).

Wolfe, James; British army officer, commander of the British expedition that took Québec in 1759 (b at Westerham, Eng 2 Jan 1727/28; d at BATTLE OF THE PLAINS OF ABRAHAM 13 Sept 1759). One of the legendary figures of Canadian history, Wolfe has become known as the man whose defeat of MONTCALM in 1759 marked the beginning of British rule in Canada. He saw fighting in both Flanders and Scotland, and gained a notable reputation before going to N America in 1758 as a senior officer in Jeffery AMHERST's expedition against LOUISBOURG. During the siege, Wolfe, a charismatic figure, played a distinguished and active role, which influenced this selection as commander of the expedition against Québec planned for 1759. Yet for most of the 1759 campaign he made little headway, partially because of his vacillation and limited ideas.

Wolfe's assault on the strong MONTMORENCY position of July 31 was a bloody failure, and neither the bombardment of Québec nor the destruction of neighbouring settlements had any real effect. He was ravaged by illness, and his relations with 3 senior officers, Robert MONCKTON, George Townshend and James MURRAY, and with the navy were marked by sharp disagreements. But when in Aug his subordinates proposed landing above Québec he began to

plan an amphibious landing that would cut the enemy's supply lines and force a battle. A midnight passage of the St Lawrence and a series of fortunate strokes saw his force established on the Plains of Abraham on Sept 13 Montcalm's forces attacked, and the smaller but better-trained British army routed the French in a short action. Wolfe himself was mortally wounded but lived long enough to hear of his victory. His reputation in both Britain and Canada survived until this century, when several works questioned the consistently favourable picture hitherto drawn of him.

Reading: C.P. Stacey, *Québec, 1759* (1959).

Wolfville, NS, Town, pop 3235 (1981c), inc 1893, is located on MINAS BASIN, 75 km NW of Halifax. Once part of the Acadian district of Les Mines (Minas), the site was known as *Mtaban* ("mud-cat-fish ground") to the Micmac and Mud Creek to the Connecticut emigrants who settled Horton Township after the deportation of the ACADIANS. The route of the Halifax-Annapolis Road and the natural harbour encouraged settlement at this site. The name was changed to Wolfville in 1830, perhaps in honour of descendants of 3 DeWolfe cousins who were among the original grantees. With the decline of shipbuilding E of the harbour, Wolfville became a quiet New England-style university town. Established as a BAPTIST college in 1829, ACADIA U is now nondenominational. With 34 main buildings and 2500 students, it is the main local employer and the cultural, political and recreational centre for the town and its surrounding agricultural hinterland. Wolfville United Baptist Church has the oldest continuing Baptist congregation in Canada (1763). The easy pace of life in the town has attracted numerous senior citizens and a small counterculture colony. Many descendants of the original New England settlers remain.   DEBRA McNABB

Wollaston Lake, 2681 km², elev 398 m, lies in the wooded SHIELD country of NE Saskatchewan. To the NW it drains via the Fond Du Lac R into Lk ATHABASCA and the MACKENZIE R system; to the NE it drains via the Cochrane R into REINDEER LK and the CHURCHILL R system. Discovered by Peter FIDLER about 1800, it was used by fur traders as a link between the 2 watersheds. It was named in 1821 by Arctic explorer John FRANKLIN after the English chemist William Hyde Wollaston.   DANIEL FRANCIS

Wolseley, Garnet Joseph, Wolseley, 1st Viscount, soldier (b at Golden Bridge House, Ire 4 June 1833; d at Menton, France 25 Mar 1913). Wolseley served with the British army in India, the Crimea and China. In 1861 he was sent to Canada as assistant quartermaster general, becoming deputy quartermaster general in 1865. In 1870 he commanded the expedition to the Red River, where his organizational skills won plaudits. After 1871 he alternated between the War Office and field command and was commander in chief of the British army 1895-1900. His autobiography, *The Story of a Soldier's Life*, appeared in 1903.   J.M. BUMSTED

Wolverine, or carcajou (*Gulo gulo*), largest of the WEASELS, resembles a powerful, miniature bear. Adult males weigh about 14 kg; females, 9 kg. Fur is usually dark brown; head and tail are slightly lighter than the body. Usually, 2 tan stripes run from the neck along the sides, meeting at the tail. Wolverine fur is preferred for trimming parka hoods because outer hairs shed frost without wetting. The wolverine is a rare animal in Canada. They are now absent from the southeast and the prairies, rare in the East, and sparse in western and northern regions. They are known for travelling long distances (up to 112 km in 24 hours). In Alaska adult males have been found to have territories of up to 770 km²; females, 355 km². Wolverines are

normally solitary except when breeding or raising young. Mating occurs May-July; implantation is delayed and the 2-5 young are born Feb-Mar. The wolverine's supposed strength, ferocity, and ability to raid traplines and cabins have become legendary. The powerful teeth and jaws are adapted for crushing frozen meat. Wolverines are better scavengers than hunters. In winter they eat mainly carrion; in summer, berries and vegetation as well. Wolverines do best in sparsely populated areas with abundant ungulate populations. BC provides about one-third of all pelts (300-500) taken in Canada annually. Exploitation by man is the most important external factor influencing abundance and distribution.   STEPHEN HERRERO

Woman's Christian Temperance Union in Canada originated in Ontario in 1875 and by 1886 had spread from coast to coast. Believing that the abuse of alcohol was the cause of unemployment, disease, poverty and immorality, the WCTU campaigned for the legal prohibition of all alcoholic beverages. The organization also promoted reforms such as female suffrage, sex hygiene, antismoking legislation and social-welfare improvements. Prohibition at the national and provincial levels during WWI was a highlight for the WCTU, and its subsequent defeat and the adoption of government control of alcoholic beverages during the 1920s heralded the decline of the organization. In 1982 there were 3787 members in 102 branches. *See also* TEMPERANCE MOVEMENT.   NANCY M. SHEEHAN

Reading: L. Kealey, *A Not Unreasonable Claim: Women and Reform in Canada, 1880s-1920s* (1979).

Women and Education Although women have always been well represented in schools as students and teachers, it is possible, by examining women's participation in schooling, to understand how that participation has both reflected and produced the unequal position of women in society.

Prior to 1850, middle-class families tended to hire governesses and tutors to educate their children at home. Some pioneers ran their own schools; for example Anne Langton (1804-93) ran a small informal school with her brother at Fenelon Falls. By 1871, with the establishment of the free provincial public schools, the number of girls enrolled in Ontario schools approximated that of boys. Most post-secondary education for female students was available only at private colleges, which provided special instruction in the personal, social and domestic proprieties. The curriculum was designed to train women in "the arts and graces of life" and to prepare them to become schoolteachers.

Teaching has always provided employment opportunities for women (*see* TEACHING PROFESSION). In the early 19th century, Canadian women taught children in private domestic settings, in so-called "dame" schools, while men dominated the public schooling. By mid-century, women began to be employed in public schools, and by 1900 elementary school teaching was done almost entirely by women. In 1872 the BC superintendent of education declared that a woman's mission was "predominantly that of an educator," specifically of infants and young children. The change occurred largely because women could be hired at lower wages than men, at a time when the cost of an expanding school system weighed heavily on taxpayers. The change both caused and reflected an increasing acceptance of the participation of middle-class women in work outside the home and an ideology that emphasized women's special abilities to nurture and educate children.

While teaching provided new employment opportunities for many women (many prominent women suffragists entered the work force as teachers) it also reaffirmed the secondary position of women. Women teachers, paid less than men, were kept in the lower ranks where they were supervised by male administrators. They were mainly young women, who left or were let go when they married and who rarely gained any seniority or administrative responsibility.

Women teachers today have generally won equal salaries with men and can no longer be laid off simply because they marry or have children. However, they are seldom in administrative positions and are increasingly underrepresented in teaching at the higher grades. Only 15.5% of university teachers and 4% of full professors are women. According to a 1984 report from the Commission on Canadian Studies, discrimination against women in Canadian universities is still a "national disgrace." The commission's report, called *Some Questions of Balance*, was prepared for the Association of Universities and Colleges of Canada. Commissioners Thomas SYMONS and James Page claim that women are deterred by discriminatory practices and attitudes from participating in many areas of higher education and research. Women university teachers hold lower academic ranks and receive lower pay at every academic rank and in almost every age group. The many (over 32) major university reports commissioned in the 1970s and early 1980s to investigate problems facing women have had virtually no effect, the commission reported, on hiring, promotion, tenure and salary differentials.

Women comprise about 50% of all teachers in the public schools which breaks down to 33% of all teachers in secondary schools, 70% of those in elementary schools and over 95% of those in kindergartens.

Girls and boys enjoy formally equal schooling. Canada's public-school system has always been overwhelmingly coeducational, but for reasons of convenience and cost, rather than a belief in the similar needs of male and female students. Girls have tended to stay in school longer than boys and to do better academically. It was only in 1950 that the number of males in school in the 15-19-year-old age group began to surpass that of females. The number of Canadian women who have graduated from high school still surpasses the number of men. In universities, on the other hand, women comprised 16% of undergraduate enrolment in 1920, almost 20% from 1930 to 1960, 35% by 1970, and almost 50% by 1980. It is anticipated by Statistics Canada that female recipients of bachelor degrees will increasingly outnumber men.

Despite the evidence of women's achievements in schools, the opportunities offered women in the educational system are often circumscribed by the view that women belong in the home, and schools in many ways help to maintain the secondary status of women in society. Analyses of textbooks, teaching materials, films and readers used in schools (*see* CURRICULUM DEVELOPMENT) have consistently revealed that women are underrepresented and are portrayed in traditional ways. While publishers and ministries of education have begun, in the 1980s, to screen new materials for evidence of bias, old materials are still being used, especially since the budget for new materials has been reduced. Women's-studies courses and materials have been increasingly developed to provide a balanced representation of women in the curriculum, but while most universities now offer women's studies as an option, materials conveying the experience of women are rarely available at high-school or elementary-school levels.

Studies of teachers' attitudes toward sex roles and their interactions with students have also revealed that male and female students are treated differently, eg, male students receive both more praise and criticism. Teachers reward traditionally "masculine" behaviour in boys and "feminine" behaviour in girls.

Male and female students often study different courses, particularly in the higher grades. In many high schools HOME ECONOMICS for girls and industrial arts for boys are no longer compulsory, and a more flexible program incorporating both kinds of skills for everyone is offered. In a system of academic electives, girls are more likely to drop out of mathematics, physics and chemistry than boys, and are likely to avoid industrial arts altogether. A 1984 report from the Science Council of Canada has noted the low participation of girls in physical science courses and recommended changes in curriculum, teaching methods, and CAREER COUNSELLING to ensure greater involvement of girls in science and technology education. Girls comprise the majority of students in home economics (especially sewing), business education and languages.

At the community-college level women comprise more than 90% of the student body in household science, nursing, rehabilitative medicine and secretarial science; more than 70% in library and SOCIAL WORK; and more than 60% in education and the fine and applied arts. In universities, they are underrepresented in engineering, forestry, dentistry, architecture, computing science, law, business, science and medicine. These patterns are changing somewhat, especially at the university level, where increasing numbers of women are enrolling in professional faculties dominated by men, but women still represent only 33% of the enrolment in law, medicine and business, and 5% of the enrolment in engineering. These patterns of differential enrolment contribute directly to the maintenance of a sexually segregated work world.

Guidance and career counsellors have also been criticized for their tendency to encourage girls to enter traditional fields. Feminist counsellors urge that more attention be paid to the fact that female students must plan for many years of work outside the home, must learn assertiveness and must examine the issue of sex-role stereotyping.

The discussion and changes in schools generated by a renewed attention to women's place confronts parents, teachers and administrators with new dilemmas. The notion that the school should reflect the community's standards sometimes conflicts with the notion that schools must provide equal opportunities for all students. Those who believe women belong in the home are opposed to those who believe women should have the same education and opportunities as men. JANE GASKELL

Reading: Jane Gaskell, "Equal Educational Opportunity for Women" in *Canadian Education in the '80s* (1981); J. L'Espérance, *The Widening Sphere* (1982).

Women and Health In Canada women are the greatest users of the health-care system, primarily because of their roles as child bearers and child raisers, but also because on average a woman's life expectancy in Canada exceeds a man's by approximately 8 years. Women also occupy over 75% of jobs in the health and medical fields, although they are occupationally segregated into the low-status and low-paying positions. Although the number is rising, in 1981 only 21% of practising physicians and surgeons in Canada were female.

Despite the inferior occupational status of women in the field of health care and the low percentage of female doctors, women have always played an important role in health care. Historically, mothers were the primary health resource of families, and women healers who derived their knowledge from apprenticeship and oral tradition were essential to the development of both native and white settlements. With their knowledge of herbs and medicinal plants, these women were the people most likely to be consulted in medical emergencies. Midwives, who assisted women during pregnancy and childbirth, were important members of early Canadian communities.

Religious sisters from Europe who helped meet the physical and spiritual welfare of Canada's new inhabitants (*see* NURSING) also played a significant role in early Canadian medical history. Canada's first hospital (1639), HÔTEL-DIEU in Québec City, was founded and run by nuns of the nursing order Religieuses Hospitalières. Emily STOWE, the first Canadian woman with a medical degree (1867) to practise medicine in Canada, was forced to study at the New York Medical College for Women, because women were not allowed into medical schools in Canada. Emily Stowe's daughter Augusta was the first woman to graduate in medicine in Canada (1883), having been permitted to study at the Toronto School of Medicine in 1879.

By the mid-19th century, partly as a result of efforts of the male medical profession to convince legislators and the general public that care traditionally provided by women (midwives and lay healers) could be better provided by technically trained doctors, many women, particularly in urban areas, were forced out of their traditional roles as health-care providers. Midwifery was officially outlawed in various provinces. In the contemporary Canadian health-care system, the important positions of power and decision making are held primarily by men, which tends to influence the kind of health care women receive. For example, there has been increased medical intervention in the birth process, reflected in the rising rate (from 8% to 15% in the 1970s) of Caesarean section deliveries. To the concern of many women, this operation, considered a "last resort" procedure some 25 years ago, is now viewed by many obstetricians as a standard measure and is, according to some critics, indiscriminately used.

A recent study by the Addiction Research Foundation revealed that women are twice as likely as men suffering from the same complaints to be prescribed tranquillizers. Doctors tend to send men, but not the women, for additional tests or X rays, which suggests that women's complaints are likely to be taken less seriously than men's.

Women have also attempted to draw attention to the fact that many female health problems result from occupational and environmental factors, and are therefore related to women's status in society. A recent report of the Canadian Advisory Council on the Status of Women focused on some occupational health hazards (chemical, biological, physical and those affecting mental health) to which women in particular were vulnerable. The occupations studied included airline flight attendants (86% female), dental nurses, technicians and assistants (68% female), electronic equipment fabricators (67% female), nurses (96% female), laboratory technicians (73% female), dry-cleaning workers (62% female), switchboard operators (95% female) and textile industry workers (80% female). Some of the health hazards associated with these occupations are fatigue, noise, and exposure to solvents, detergents, mercury, radiation, asbestos, beryllium, lead, trichloroethylene, resins, methylene chloride, silicone, and anesthetic gases. Research has indicated that certain levels of exposure to these health hazards are harmful not only to women but to fetuses.

With the rise of the women's movement in the late 1960s and early 1970s, and as a result of growing dissatisfaction with current medical attitudes and the rise of medical technology, women began to speak out against ABORTION laws, hazardous drugs, BIRTH-CONTROL methods, paternalistic medical care, and the increased medicalization of the BIRTHING PRACTICE. Self-help groups, rape crisis centres, birth-control and venereal disease clinics, and patient advocacy groups have been formed.

A prototype for women's health groups is the Vancouver Women's Health Collective, established in 1972 to provide for women "a critique of, but not a substitute for the traditional health-care system." The group is structured as a collective. It maintains an extensive resource library on women's health, conducts self-help groups, offers birth-control counselling and publishes material on a variety of health issues.

ANNE ROCHON FORD

Women and the Law Traditionally, laws in Canada upheld the STATUS OF WOMEN as dependants. In the 20th century, as women increasingly demanded a new legal position, laws seen as symbols of inferiority became the subject of controversy. In the 1970s many women, like those in the earlier suffrage campaigns, again became aware that the law must be reformed if they were to achieve autonomy and equality within Canadian society (*see* WOMEN'S SUFFRAGE).

Under the French regime, important posts in the army and the government were, by custom, granted only to men. Under the British regime, women were usually excluded by law from holding public office until the beginning of the 20th century. Certain criminal laws applied only to women, such as infanticide, or involved women as victims, such as laws concerning rape or seduction under promise of marriage. Different punishments were meted out, depending on the sex of the offender. In prostitution, for example, punishment inevitably fell upon the prostitute (almost always a woman).

It is in the area of FAMILY LAW that women have been treated most clearly as dependents. In NEW FRANCE, where 25 was the legal age of majority, a woman usually passed from the control of her father to that of her husband when she married. A husband's permission was necessary for a wife to engage in business, or even to administer or sell property which she had owned before marriage. French law, however, provided that half of the common property belonged to the wife and her heirs on marriage dissolution, whereas British law gave a husband wide authority over his wife's property and made no provision for division of assets. Although Married Women's Property Acts were passed in the late 19th century in most common-law provinces, giving women the right to control their own property, the laws made no provision for the equitable division of property held by the spouses in case of marriage breakdown or death. Nor did they improve the economic situation of women (*see* WOMEN IN THE LABOUR FORCE).

By the end of the 19th century, many women and some men were questioning the severe restrictions of rights for female citizens. A loophole in the law allowing some women, particularly in LOWER CANADA, to exercise the franchise had been specifically removed by the 1850s throughout Canada. Feminists argued for a fuller participation of women in public life, on grounds both of moral justice and because "feminine virtues" might help bring about needed reforms. After a lengthy campaign, women in Manitoba, Alberta and Saskatchewan gained the right to vote in 1916, and in Ontario and BC the following year. On the federal level, the vote was first given to relatives of enlisted men in 1917 and then broadened to all women in 1918. The other provinces followed suit by 1922, with the exception of Québec, where women were denied the vote until 1940.

Women recognized that the ability to use or challenge existing laws was one of the keys to raising their status. In 1897 Clara Brett Martin was admitted to the Law Society of Upper Canada. In 1929, 5 women from Alberta successfully challenged the law that excluded female citizens from becoming senators (*see* PERSONS CASE). However, women were slow to enter the legal profession and, by 1980, only about 10% of practising Canadian lawyers were female. In 1982 Bertha WILSON was appointed as the first woman to the SUPREME COURT OF CANADA.

The report of the Royal Commission on the Status of Women in 1970 recommended a new agenda for legal reform that would reflect more accurately the changing reality of women's lives (*see* WOMEN'S MOVEMENT). Homemakers and mothers became increasingly aware that their tasks gave them almost no legal right to financial security. Inequities in matrimonial property laws that did not recognize the wife's contribution to marriage were crystallized in the MURDOCH CASE. By the early 1980s most provinces had rewritten their family law to allow better recognition of women's unpaid contribution to marriage.

By the 1970s approximately one half of Canadian women were in the paid labour force, though, overall, women in 1982 earned 64% of what men earned. In a drive for fairer labour legislation, especially legislation recognizing equal pay for work of equal value, women's groups and unions proposed affirmative action programs to counteract employment policies that were intentionally or inadvertently discriminatory to women. Parental and pregnancy benefits became an important issue as, increasingly, women remained in the paid work force during childbearing years. After 1971 Canada's unemployment insurance scheme provided for limited pregnancy benefits for workers, but the Bliss case (1979) showed how inadequate its provisions were when the Supreme Court of Canada ruled that if a worker, otherwise entitled, was denied benefits because of pregnancy, it was not because she was a woman. In 1983 amendments were made to the Unemployment Insurance Act concerning parental benefits to eliminate this problem.

Sexual harassment on the job was first considered by federal and provincial human rights commissions in the 1970s and, by the early 1980s, unions began to insist that employers enforce policies against it. In 1984 legislation providing redress for victims of sexual harassment was introduced into Canada's Labour Code.

In the 1970s and 1980s the issue of violence claimed public attention, particularly among women. The double sexual standard was mirrored dramatically in the Criminal Code laws on RAPE, which permitted questions as to the victim's, but not the accused's, previous sexual history and encouraged defence counsel to argue that the women had consented. In 1982 major changes to the Criminal Code addressed the situation where the victim of a sexual assault was, in effect, put on trial along with the accused. The legal concept of rape was replaced by one of sexual assault and violence.

Domestic violence, which is almost always against women and children (*see* CHILD ABUSE), has long been considered a private matter in Canada. Although wife beating is a form of assault and punishable under the Criminal Code, social attitudes and prejudices have meant that police were reluctant to intervene in domestic disputes. The courts hesitated to find a husband guilty of beating his wife without a third-party witness. In the late 1970s WOMEN'S ORGANIZATIONS drew public attention to wife and child battering and to the fact that laws on the books were not being applied. Across Canada, law enforcement agencies began to intervene in cases of domestic assault. It soon became evident, however, that simply punishing the offenders was not in itself a long-term solution. In many cases, the woman was economically dependent on the man and feared for the welfare of the family if he was sent to prison. Women's shelters, therapy and public campaigns against family violence were some of the alternate approaches developed.

In the 1970s women became more conscious of their legal rights, or lack of them, than ever before. As courts and lawyers are prohibitively expensive for most women, the recently formed federal and provincial human rights commissions proved to be an alternate and less expensive way of dealing with individual complaints of discrimination. The Bliss case, dealing with pregnancy discrimination, as well as the earlier LAVELL and Bedard cases, dealing with discrimination against female Indians on the basis of their sex, pointed out to Canadian women how inadequate were the existing constitutional guarantees against sexual discrimination. It was cases such as these, as well as a growing consciousness of the need for stronger legal measures against discrimination, which fueled the successful drive by women for better guarantees in the new CANADIAN CHARTER OF RIGHTS AND FREEDOMS (1984). Section 15 of the Charter, which came into force in Apr 1985, attempted to provide the broadest possible definition of equality rights, while specifically allowing affirmative action programs. The Charter, women hoped, would provide a new standard of equality against which laws in Canada could be measured. However, the federal and the provincial governments retained the right to suspend such provisions for a specific time period and it remains to be seen, given the provincial right to "opt out" and resistance to equality generally, whether such optimism is justified. *See also* ABORTION; NATIVE PEOPLE; LAW; PORNOGRAPHY.

JENNIFER STODDART

Reading: A. Bayefsky and M. Eberts, eds, *Equality of Rights in the Canadian Charter of Rights and Freedoms* (1984); A. Doerr and M. Carrier, eds, *Women and the Constitution in Canada* (1981); L. MacLeod, *Wife Battering in Canada* (1980); Royal Commission on the Status of Women in Canada, *Report* (1970).

Women in the Labour Force Women are considered LABOUR FORCE participants only if they work outside the home. Women have been expected to be in the labour force only until they marry; this reflects the historical, idealized notion of a society in which the man is the breadwinner and the woman the homemaker. This notion of the FAMILY has not been a reality in the past and is not so today, since over 50% of all married women work outside the home; but the idea that women belong in the home has had a significant effect on the conditions under which they participate in the labour force (*see* MARRIAGE AND DIVORCE). That participation is characterized by segregation and low pay. The majority of women in the labour force have always been isolated in "female" occupations, called such because they are often extensions of the work women do at home and because the vast majority of the people doing them are women (*see* STATUS OF WOMEN). Some occupations have changed over time and new ones have come into existence, but various occupations are still defined as women's work. Women have always been paid lower wages than men; they are paid less both when their jobs are not the same as those of men but could be seen as equally valuable and when the work is exactly the same (*see also* WORK). Women earned 52.8% of what men earned in 1911 and 58% in 1971.

History of Female Labour At the end of the 19th century the factories replaced families as the main productive unit. Factory work involved long hours, low wages and often brutal working conditions. For example, young girls worked for 60 hours a week for 80 cents, or less than 2 cents per hour. In 1901 women comprised 13% of the total labour force and the female labour-force participation rate (FLFPR, defined as that proportion of working-age female population with jobs or looking for jobs) was 14% (this refers to women who worked for pay; many women worked but were not paid). The majority of women were employed as servants, dressmakers, teachers, seamstresses, tai-

Female Workers over 16 years of age without dependents (Source: Annual Report of the Ontario Bureau of Industries, 1889)	
Average number of hours/week worked	54
Average number of days/year worked	259
Average wages/year from occupation	$216.71
Cost of clothing	$ 67.31
Cost of board and lodging	$126.36
Total cost of living	$214.28
Surplus	$ 2.43

lors, housekeepers, launderers, milliners and saleswomen. During the first half of the 20th century the number of jobs available to women was limited and strong sentiment existed against married women working outside the home. Men feared that the cheap labour of large numbers of women would undercut their wages; employers and moral reformers were concerned that work would impair the femininity and high moral standards of women and distract them from their true calling as wives and mothers. During WWI, women replaced men who had joined the armed services, but the labour shortage was not severe enough to warrant their large-scale employment. Although women did men's jobs, they did not receive men's wages. At the end of the war, women were strongly encouraged to leave the work force and married women employed by government were legislated out of it. By 1921, 65% of all women workers were in clerical, domestic service and professional (mainly teaching and nursing) occupations.

In the early part of the 20th century, women's fight for equality focused on political rights and was characterized by the suffrage movement. The right to the federal vote was finally won in 1918, but it was not until the end of the 1920s that women had won the right to vote in most provinces. In 1929 they were recognized as "persons" eligible to hold a seat in the Canadian Senate (*see also* PERSONS CASE). The expansionary period of the 1920s was cut short by the Great Depression, but production and employment expanded enormously with WWII and once again employers hired single and then married women to do men's jobs, once again for lower wages. Incentives, eg, free government nurseries and income-tax concessions, were provided to attract married women into the labour force. At the end of the war the incentives were withdrawn and married women were again encouraged and in some cases regulated out of the labour force. This time, however, many stayed and found employment in the expanding number of "female" jobs in the service-producing sector of the economy.

The greater numbers of women entering the labour force presented male-dominated trade unions with a dilemma. Trade unionists feared the competition from "unskilled" female labour and were concerned as well with maintaining the traditional role of women. Simultaneously, they were interested in protecting all workers, including women. Women workers, however, with or without the support of the trade-union movement, have traditionally fought for higher wages and better working conditions (*see* WORKING-CLASS HISTORY).

The 1950s were a time of rapid economic expansion. Changes in the productive process, emphasis by government and private industry on construction and on research and development, expansion in health, welfare and educational services, and the need to advertise, sell and finance new products all created new jobs for women. By 1951 women comprised 22% of the total labour force and the FLFPR was 24%. As the economy developed and as labour's productivity increased, consumer goods, cheaper in price, became available to more people. Mass

consumption of these goods was imperative to the economic system. By mid-20th century many families, to be able to afford more goods and to educate their children, needed 2 income earners. Because young people were staying in school longer, married women entered the labour force to help their families raise their STANDARD OF LIVING. Between 1951 and 1981 the FLFPR of married women rose from 11% to 50.5%. Since the 1950s there has been a steady increase in part-time work and by the mid-1970s the number of part-time jobs, which have few benefits and little security, had expanded enormously; 72% of these were filled by women, the majority of whom were married. Women continued to earn lower wages than men and in 1978 the average wage rate for full-time women workers was 58% of that of the average wage rate for men workers. The vast majority of women were still employed in clerical, sales, service, teaching and medicine and health occupations. By 1981 women comprised 41% of the total labour force, the FLFPR had risen to 52% and the average wage rate for full-time women was 64% of that for men workers. Women worked (in order of numbers employed) primarily as secretaries and stenographers, bookkeepers and accounting clerks, saleswomen, tellers and cashiers, waitresses and hostesses, nurses, elementary and kindergarten teachers, general-office clerks, typists and clerk typists, janitors, charworkers and cleaners.

From 1971 to 1981 women organized to demand greater equality in wages and working conditions, and to gain recognition of their social, economic, legal and political position in society. The women's movement of the 1960s had made many women aware of their right to independence and control of their own lives. Women joined unions and other organizations in greater numbers. The women's movement also raised and debated issues such as wages for HOUSEWORK and pensions for housewives. Considerable agreement existed about the prohibition of discrimination in employment policies on the grounds of gender or marital status; affirmative action; equal pay for work of equal value; maternity leave and benefits; adequate day-care facilities; provision for health and safety; and protection against sexual harassment in the workplace.

During the deep recession of the 1980s, real wages and consequently the standard of living has generally been declining, bringing into sharp focus the connection between women's unpaid work in the home and their underpaid work in the labour force. For example, the number of single-parent households headed by women has grown steadily in recent years, but the traditional notion, which has not changed, that there is a male breadwinner to support every household reinforces the occupational segregation and low wages of women in the labour force. As a result many employed, female single parents do not earn enough to live on after child care and other costs of working outside the home are deducted. The percentage of female-headed families (the majority of them single-parent families) with incomes below the poverty line increased from 38% in 1981 to 45% in 1982. An increasing number of elderly women also live in poverty; because most of these women worked all their lives in the home they have no work-related pension of their own. Husbands' pension plans seldom provide adequate protection for their surviving wives. Government restraint has increased unemployment and decreased necessary services in health, welfare and education. Unemployment rates are higher than at any time since the Great Depression and the development of microelectronic technology will likely result in greater unemployment for women and strand many women at home in "high-tech" sweat-

shops — a modern incarnation of the traditional piece-rate work for which little legislation exists. Without adequate government services, the care of the elderly, the disabled and the unemployed will once again fall on the shoulders of women, who are still generally considered responsible for this work. It appears therefore that women's work in the home is expanding, although it is increasingly necessary for women to be income earners, either as sole supporters of single-parent families or as members of 2-parent families.   M.P. CONNELLY

Women's International League for Peace and Freedom, fd 1915 in The Hague, the Netherlands, by women active in the WOMEN'S SUFFRAGE movement in Europe and N America. These women wished to end WWI and seek ways to ensure that no more wars took place. The league came to Canada in the early 1920s on the initiative of socially and politically conscious women such as Dorothy Steeves and Laura Jamieson, founders of the Vancouver branch. Branches were also formed in Toronto, Edmonton and Winnipeg. In Toronto J.S. WOODSWORTH's wife, Lucy, was an active member. Agnes MACPHAIL was probably the best-known member, serving for a number of years as honorary president. In the West, Violet McNaughton, a journalist and ardent supporter of the concerns of both women and farmers, played a key role in promoting the organization and in uniting other groups concerned with peace and disarmament.

In Canada the league was involved in promoting peace education and conducting campaigns for DISARMAMENT and against militarism in general. The protest against CADET training in the schools was one of its most persistent campaigns. WILPF also conducted a study into school textbooks that, members felt, glorified war and paid insufficient attention to the values of co-operation and harmony. In 1931 the international body initiated a petition campaign for universal disarmament; 491 000 signatures were collected in Canada. Just before and during WWII the Toronto branch worked to help REFUGEES settle and learn English. But the league declined during the 1940s and 1950s, in part because of renewed militarism and fear engendered by WWII and the subsequent COLD WAR. Only the Vancouver branch remained after the mid-1950s, and with a greatly reduced membership. However, in the late 1970s a branch was formed in Ottawa and membership again began to grow across the country (*see also* PEACE MOVEMENT).   DEBORAH POWELL

Women's Labour Leagues (WLL) emerged in Canada prior to WWI. Modelled on the British Labour Leagues, auxiliaries to the Independent Labour Party, their purpose was to organize women workers and support the trade-union movement. After a period of limited growth, they were rejuvenated in 1923-24 by the COMMUNIST PARTY OF CANADA. Under the direction of Florence Custance, the leagues grew to number 37 locals in 1927, and the Federation of WLLs published the monthly paper *The Woman Worker*, which discussed women's issues from a Marxist perspective. League members were usually working-class housewives, sometimes wage-earning women, and many were Finnish, Yiddish or Ukrainian speaking. The WLL platform, radical for its time, included demands for equal pay, maternity care and birth control. Although the WLLs were not successful in unionizing women, they did educational work, raised money for the Communist Party and the labour movement, and developed their members' understanding of socialism. In 1930 they were advised to join the Workers Unity League, and subsequently some faded away, although a few functioned until the 1940s.   JOAN SANGSTER

Women's Movement Since the end of the 19th century Canadian women have been organizing to redefine their place in society, to demand equality and justice. Through legal and political means, the women's movement has allowed Canadian women to obtain a certain formal equality. Parallel to this slow conquest of equal rights, the lifestyle of Canadian women, as for women in most other Western countries, has undergone profound changes. Goods and services traditionally produced in the home are now available for purchase by consumers; and these technological developments, together with the growth of the service sector, have facilitated the increasing participation of women in the labour market, so that by the early 1980s the majority of Canadian married women had a paying job. Serious inequalities in the relative position of men and women in society remain, however. The federal government in 1967 set up the Royal Commission on the STATUS OF WOMEN to examine the situation, and in its 1970 report the commission made 167 recommendations for greater equality of women.

The late 1960s in Canada, as throughout the Western world, saw the emergence of a new women's movement. This new feminism rejected all limits to the equality of women's rights and showed that equality in daily life cannot be obtained through simple legal, political or institutional modifications. Women were greatly influenced by books and articles by feminists such as Kate Millett, Germaine Greer, Gloria Steinem, and Shulamith Firestone and by publications such as *Women Unite: An Anthology of the Women's Movement* (1972) and Margaret Anderson's *Mother Was Not a Person* (1973). These writers held that society's major power relationship was one of domination and oppression of women by men. The existing body of social relationships, along with the very functioning of society, was analysed and criticized.

In the late 1960s, discovering that "sisterhood is powerful," women from Vancouver to Halifax began forming groups. The Vancouver Women's Caucus was organized in 1968 and published *The Pedestal* from 1969 to 1973. The Montréal Women's Liberation Movement was founded in 1969, the Front de libération des femmes du Québec published a feminist manifesto in 1970, and the Centre des femmes edited the first French-language radical feminist periodical, *Québécoises deboutte!* (1971-75). At first, some were consciousness-raising groups, but others quickly turned to concrete action, providing abortion services, health centres, feminist magazines, militant theatre, daycare, shelters for battered women, rape-crisis centres, and organizing for equal pay. By the end of the 1960s Canadian society had begun to adjust to the rebirth of a major social movement, the women's movement.

Social Movements, which can be loosely defined as conscious collective efforts to change some aspects of the social order, are difficult to describe with precision. Major social movements contain within themselves many subgroupings which may differ in important ways. The women's movement, for example, includes liberal, radical and Marxist feminists, lesbian separatists, and those who view lesbianism as one life-style among others; although these groupings debate vigorously on a number of issues, they do agree on the basic need to improve the situation of women. The women's movement has been working for social justice for women along many different fronts, including politics, culture, the mass media, law, education, health, the labour force and the home. Organizations of every size, from every region participate. Some concentrate on self-help; some on working for general social change. While in the beginning, in the early 1970s, the movement seemed to consist of smaller radical groups, the movement's base has been gradually expanding to incorporate women of diverse opinions and from all parts of Canadian society, including welfare mothers, professional, business and executive women, native women and immigrant domestic workers. Large, well-established organizations have adopted feminist practices and the women's movement itself has generated a number of autonomous organizations.

The women's movement uses diverse methods to promote its goal of social justice for women. Public events, including lectures, entertainment in various forms and leafletting, are arranged to "raise consciousness" and disseminate information. Protest actions, such as demonstrations, marches, vigils and petitions, are organized. Government, political parties and particular agencies, institutions and employers are lobbied for reform. Action often takes the form of first establishing a committee (caucus, interest group) on the status of women, then documenting existing inequities, formulating proposals for improvement, and finally lobbying for their implementation. In response, the federal and various provincial governments have established consultative councils on the STATUS OF WOMEN, and municipalities and educational and health institutions have set up councils or units specifically for women.

Another important activity of the women's movement centres on publication, ranging from informal flyers to posters to highly academic volumes, and including children's books, self-help manuals and newspaper columns. These contributions are published through mainstream outlets as well as through an emerging network of feminist presses.

The women's movement has been effective in organizing action on particular issues, employing a multitude of means and involving a coalition of groups and individuals. Issues generating mass efforts include, for example, the right to choice in obtaining a legal abortion, the entrenchment of women's rights in the CANADIAN CHARTER OF RIGHTS AND FREEDOMS in 1982, PORNOGRAPHY, and threats to the ENVIRONMENT, CIVIL LIBERTIES and peace (*see* PEACE MOVEMENT).

In sum, women have broken their isolation and have set up groups and organizations across the country, or have joined existent organizations. Since the late 1970s co-operation among the various groups has intensified. Some of the national groups include the NATIONAL ACTION COMMITTEE ON THE STATUS OF WOMEN, Canadian Research Institute for the Advancement of Women, Canadian Congress for Learning Opportunities for Women, Canadian Assn for the Advancement of Women in Sport, Canadian Day Care Advocacy Assn, Charter of Rights Coalition, Fédération des femmes canadiennes-françaises, Indian Rights for Indian Women, Media Watch, National Congress of Black Women, NATIONAL COUNCIL OF WOMEN, VOICE OF WOMEN, Women in Science and Engineering, and many more. Such groups consist mainly of women from the anglophone provinces, for French Canadian women tend to align themselves on linguistic rather than truly "national" lines. Thus, Québec has a whole series of counterpart organizations to the "national" ones mentioned above, eg, Affiliation des femmes du Québec and L'Association feminine d'éducation et d'action sociale. These groups and organizations define to some extent the structure of the feminist movement in Canada. While a majority of Canadian women are in sympathy with the goal of social justice for women, much of the actual work falls to "front-line" feminist organizations, some of which appear to be more or less permanent and others more ad hoc groups which surface only to confront specific tasks.

There is no overall leadership structure for the movement, although there are some individuals who have been highly visible at different times and for different issues. The movement stresses the importance of issues over the personalities involved and rejects the notion that a few women can speak on all issues for all women. The main point is that women desire to speak for themselves, and they may speak from a multitude of theoretical and political orientations. Ideological debates over tactics and theory are ongoing.

Changing the Social Structure Creating a just society for women means the elimination of sexism in all areas and particularly in the legal system, in the organization of social production, in the perception and treatment of women's bodies, and in the arts, sciences, education and the mass media.

Most progress has been achieved in the legal area. Among the earliest targets for action were the various family laws. In 1973 the MURDOCH CASE, in which an Alberta farm wife was denied a half interest in the farm that she and her husband had built up together over a 25-year period because her work was seen simply as the fulfilment of her wifely duties, raised awareness about the injustices of FAMILY LAWS. Since that time, all provinces have reformed their family laws in the direction of greater equality between spouses. Another legal decision in the LAVELL CASE (1973) involved an Indian woman who had lost her Indian status and privileges upon marriage to a non-Indian. The discriminatory aspect of the INDIAN ACT remains a problem in 1984, although an equitable solution may be found under section 28 of the Charter of Rights and Freedoms. The Charter itself is perhaps the most important step towards legal equality of male and female persons in Canada. In addition, immigration laws, sexual assault laws, and human-rights legislation have been generally amended in the direction of equalizing rights and responsibilities (*see* WOMEN AND THE LAW).

One of the primary concerns of the women's movement has been the securing of appropriate rewards for WORK performed by women. In this context, "work" includes both paid and unpaid work, and involves the realization that the 2 are inextricably linked. It was the women's movement that first emphasized that work done within the home is, indeed, work, and should be regarded as such. The Wages for HOUSEWORK movement has been instrumental in focusing attention on this issue. Out of this concern have sprung campaigns for good DAY CARE, maternity and paternity benefits in employment, and some recognition in both the pension system and in case of divorce of work performed by the housewife.

In the paid labour force, concern focused initially on equal pay for equal work. More recently, the demand for equal pay for work of equal value has prompted comparisons of dissimilar jobs in order to establish fair pay scales for jobs requiring similar skills, efforts and responsibilities. A few Affirmative Action programs try to overcome historical discrimination by facilitating the promotion of women into levels and types of occupation from which they have so far been excluded. There has also been a concern to recognize the contribution of wives who work in partnership with their husbands in nonincorporated businesses, so that wages paid to the wife can be rated as such for tax and legal purposes. Under pressure from unionized women, many unions are now including equal pay and other women's issues among their demands (*see* WOMEN IN THE LABOUR FORCE).

The most controversial field of feminist action is the attempt to affirm women's right to control over their bodies, with respect, eg, to fertility, sexual relationships, sexual violence, and medical power over women's health. The most fiery demonstrations have been about the control of ABORTION, a struggle which began in the late 1960s. Dr Henry MORGENTALER, who supported the establishment of free-standing abortion clinics, was at the centre of the debate. After several court trials, he was finally acquitted in Québec, where abortions in family-planning clinics became possible. The abortion question flared again in the 1980s, with the opening by Dr Morgentaler of abortion clinics in Toronto and Winnipeg. Dr Morgentaler was prosecuted and acquitted again. The passionate debate surrounding this issue clearly reveals the competing views of society that are at stake.

The abortion debate has had its corollary in a re-evaluation of medical practices and initiatives in the field of contraception. It includes such questions as: Is it necessary for women alone to carry its burdens? Why are they the only ones to suffer the side-effects of contraceptives? Why has research into male contraception been so slow? Why do doctors so commonly perform hysterectomies on menopausal women? Such questions have led feminists to produce written and visual health "kits," to open self-help health clinics, and to champion alternative medicine and the removal of pregnancy and childbirth from medical structures. Some militant groups in the women's movement concentrate on regaining women's control over childbirth and winning the right for midwives to practise (see WOMEN AND HEALTH).

Male control over women's bodies has also traditionally expressed itself through violence. New halfway houses for battered women have opened in several cities and analyses and reports on this hitherto forbidden topic are published in newspapers and magazines. RAPE, the chief representation of aggression against women, has escaped from the silence which formerly surrounded it. Rape-crisis centres have existed in major cities since 1973; a lobby has been organized to press for changes in the law; each fall urban women parade to demonstrate their right to use the streets safely at night; and every year thousands of Canadian women take courses in self-defence. Violent pornography is strongly denounced and the Canadian Coalition Against Media Pornography is an increasingly active lobby group.

The new feminism has also affected the arts, creative activities, education and the mass media. Discussions about women are analysed, evaluated and dissected, with the result that women are using new languages, images and methods of analysis.

Women's writing in the last few years has seen an unprecedented and revitalizing explosion. Women now talk about what it is to be a woman. They talk about things that were previously private, hidden or mythologized, such as rape, incest and family violence. Some writings focus on the denunciation of oppression; others "celebrate the differences" and talk about maternity, mothers' daily work, children, marriage, the family, the relationship of women to nature and love between women. Female writers such as Nicole BROSSARD, Louky Bersianik, Madeleine Gagnon, Denise Boucher, Margaret ATWOOD, Alice MUNRO, Jane RULE and many others mark a turning-point in Québec and Canadian literature. Theatrical production includes such acclaimed feminist plays as *La Nef des sorcières* (1976), written by a feminist collective, Boucher's *Les Fées ont soif* (1978), and Betty Lambert's *Jenny's Story* (1982). Feminist theatre troupes have existed since the 1970s and feminist plays are now in the repertory of various small or institutional theatres.

In the mass media, feminist journalists and the work of feminist groups have had some effect in generating higher awareness of women as readers and newsmakers. Columnists in several major newspapers and periodicals now write from an explicitly feminist perspective. Nevertheless, the relationship between the women's movement and the mass media remains strained, as the media sometimes misrepresent the movement. As a result, a feminist press has developed, with its own media production and distribution system.

Politically committed humorists, rockers and women performers challenge audiences. Female producers at the NATIONAL FILM BOARD have made several documentaries, including the major series "En tant que femmes" (1973) as well as *Mourir à tue-tête* (1979) and *Not A Love Story* (1981). Video has always been open to women: in 1975, to honour International Women's Year, feminist video production and distribution centres opened in 8 Canadian cities. Some still exist and each year they produce material or fictional work which is distributed through community and educational circles.

A great effort has been put into eliminating sexism in education. WOMEN'S STUDIES are now an accepted part of many curricula. In 1983 the SOCIAL SCIENCES AND HUMANITIES RESEARCH COUNCIL created a committee for facilitating the equal treatment of the sexes in social science and humanities research. In general, integrating women into our thought processes is now widely seen as important and legitimate, although the process of doing so has just begun.

Conclusion In the time since its re-emergence, feminism has had a major impact on our society. Ultimately, creating social justice for women involves a profound restructuring of society and of the way people think and experience the world. By stressing that "the personal is political," the women's movement has made the social inequality of women a public and not merely a private problem. This accomplishment is its single most important contribution. The scope of the task has been defined; its full implementation has yet to be achieved.

MARGRIT EICHLER AND MARIE LAVIGNE

Reading: M. FitzGerald et al, Still Ain't Satisfied: Canadian Feminism Today (1982); L. Gagnon, Vivre avec les hommes: un nouveau partage (1983); P. Kome, The Taking of Twenty-Eight: Women Challenge the Constitution (1983); A. Miles and G. Finn, Feminism in Canada: From Pressure to Politics (1982); V. O'Leary and L. Toupin, Québécoises deboutte!: une anthologie de textes du Front de libération des femmes et du Centre des femmes, 2 vols (1982); Royal Commission on the Status of Women in Canada, Report (1970).

Women's Organizations In the early 19th century affluent women grouped together at the local level for charitable and religious purposes. They set up refuges and orphanages to help needy women and children and worked for their churches through ladies' auxiliaries. By the end of the 19th century this activity had expanded to include a myriad of reform organizations, now increasingly interdenominational and secular, such as the WOMAN'S CHRISTIAN TEMPERANCE UNION, the YOUNG WOMEN'S CHRISTIAN ASSOCIATION and the NATIONAL COUNCIL OF WOMEN. Unlike the earlier groups, these organizations were national in extent and appealed to a much broader segment of Canadian womanhood. They sought to improve society and were willing, in specific instances, to use the power of the state through compulsory legislation to effect reforms. Their focus, however, had not really altered, since these societies also concentrated their efforts on helping needy women and children.

The women who joined such organizations felt a responsibility to become involved in society. For the most part they accepted women's domestic role, but were convinced that their position necessitated a more public stance since increasingly society impinged on family life. This seemed particularly true in urban areas where alcoholism, prostitution, delinquency and disease were prevalent. Rural women anticipated the challenge of urbanization and, in addition, wanted to overcome the problems of isolation and depopulation. Farmers' organizations in the early decades of the 20th century accepted women's auxiliaries and associations as an integral part of the farmers' movement. Women's institutes became so successful that they were established throughout the world (see FEDERATED WOMEN'S INSTITUTES OF CANADA). In addition to the women's organizations which were instrumental in nature, many others existed which were expressive, designed solely for the benefit of their membership. Some, such as reading and musical associations, catered to the woman at home, but others represented the specific needs of professional women such as teachers and nurses (see WOMEN IN THE LABOUR FORCE).

By 1912 it was estimated that one out of every 8 adult women in Canada belonged to a women's group, making the women's organizational movement a significant force in Canadian society. However, it was not a movement which appealed to all women. Joiners were, in the main, middle aged, middle class, English-speaking and Protestant. French-speaking and Roman Catholic women found the Catholic church with its sisterhoods and groups a rich source of organizational life. Not until the early 20th century did these women organize such societies as the Fédération nationale St-Jean-Baptiste, which agitated for change in society, along the same lines as English-speaking and Protestant initiatives. Nevertheless, religious inspiration and influence remained crucial to a greater degree for them than for English-speaking Canadians.

The work of the various organizations, especially the instrumental ones, was impressive. They made the public aware of the needs of working women, the deficiencies of the educational system, the problems of intemperance, the existence of the double standard of morality between men and women, and the abysmally high infant mortality rate in some Canadian cities. Women's participation in these groups helped change the image of Canadian women. By joining together, women experienced the power of collective action and the joys of sisterhood. They also learned how to be administrators and fund raisers. In encountering resistance to reform, they came face to face with their own powerlessness as women. They learned that because they lacked the right to vote, politicians would not listen to them and certainly would not respond to their requests. This encouraged them to support WOMEN'S SUFFRAGE, an issue that brought about a concerted effort on the part of many women's organizations in the second decade of the 20th century.

After women gained the right to vote at the federal level in 1918, there was no longer one issue which joined the various women's groups and they lost some of their visibility and appeal. In the 1920s energies were taken up with church union and the peace movement (see WOMEN'S INTERNATIONAL LEAGUE FOR PEACE AND FREEDOM). Young women were not attracted by the organizational movement, preferring to explore their potential individually. With the emergence of the WOMEN'S MOVEMENT in the late 1960s a new organizational impetus emerged. Added to the older groups were new ones, many of which were self-directed. They concentrated their activities on increasing women's awareness of their subordinate status in society. Out of this awareness developed specific groups for native women, working women, ethnic women and lesbian women. In addition, the NATIONAL ACTION COMMITTEE ON THE STATUS OF WOMEN emerged as a political voice and lobby for Canadian women. Once again public attention was focused on the collective action of women. However, this time their concern has not been the acceptance of one reform but a fundamental shift in the way women are treated and perceived by society.

WENDY MITCHINSON

Reading: E. Collins et al, *Fifty Years of Achievement: Federated Women's Institutes in Ontario* (1948); E. Forbes, *With Enthusiasm and Faith: History of the Canadian Federation of Business and Professional Women's Clubs, 1930-1972* (1974); J.P. Harshaw, *When Women Work Together: A History of Young Women's Christian Association in Canada, 1870-1966* (1966); M.Q. Innis, *Unfold the Years: A History of the Young Women's Christian Association in Canada* (1949); L. Kealy, ed, *A Not Unreasonable Claim* (1979); Wendy Mitchinson, "Women's Missionary Societies in Nineteenth Century Canada," *Atlantis* 2 (spring 1977), and "The YWCA and Reform in the Late Nineteenth Century," *Histoire Sociale* 12 (Nov 1979); V. Strong-Boag, *The Parliament of Women: The National Council of Women of Canada, 1893-1929* (1976).

Women's Studies is a generic term for a diverse and growing field of knowledge, which is sometimes described as feminist studies, nonsexist scholarship or, less often, feminology. Women's studies is characterized by a multitude of subfields (eg, psychology of women, sociology of women) which share 2 basic concerns: that knowledge be generated and taught which is relevant to women; that knowledge generated and taught in the past was often sexist, based on a male perspective of the world. United by a commitment to these central concerns, women's studies also embraces differences which further guarantee the dynamic quality of this new field of study. A sexist bias is reflected even in everyday language, which often utilizes male terms (he, workman's compensation, etc) to express both general as well as sex-specific facts. Sexist biases are also embedded in the most basic assumptions on which science is based; eg, until recently economics has treated housework as nonwork, and rarely has history studied the lives of women with the same attention as it looked at the lives of men.

Women's studies cuts across all disciplines in the social sciences and humanities, and embraces a diversity of perspectives, methodologies and tactics. There is an interdisciplinary flavour to the work, although some of the most important work is done within specific disciplines: anthropology, history, psychology, sociology, political science, theology, economics, linguistics, literature, philosophy and, more recently, the natural sciences.

Women's studies in Canada were started around 1970, usually being developed and taught at the university level. Community support from the WOMEN'S MOVEMENT was at times crucial in establishing and maintaining academic programs. By the 1980s most universities in Canada had some courses in this area, and several offered degree programs with a major in women's studies. Instruction in women's studies now spans the entire educational spectrum, from primary grades to graduate school as well as adult noncredit courses.

People involved in women's studies organized conferences, founded periodicals and organizations devoted to this growing field of study. As a consequence there is now a community of feminist scholars, dispersed all across the country and working in different disciplines. Resistance to women's studies on the part of academics who themselves do sexist research has not yet vanished, but the scholarship generated in the years since women's studies began clearly establishes its validity and significance. In 1984 the secretary of state announced the establishment of 5 chairs in women's studies.

The first Canadian periodical dedicated to the discipline was the *Canadian Newsletter of Research on Women*, later renamed *Resources for Feminist Research*. Founded in 1972, it lists information on current research projects across the country. Three other important journals are *Atlantis, Canadian Woman Studies* and the *International Journal of Women's Studies*. The first 3 journals are bilingual. The most important organizations concerned with some aspect of women's studies are the Canadian Research Institute for the Advancement of Women (1976), Canadian Congress for Learning Opportunities for Women (1976) and the Canadian Women's Studies Association (1982), founded with the specific goal of fostering women's studies in high schools, colleges and universities. MARGRIT EICHLER

Reading: Corrective Collective, *Never Done: Three Centuries of Women's Work in Canada* (1974); Margrit Eichler, *The Double Standard* (1980); L. Rasmussen, L. Rasmussen, C. Savage and A. Wheeler, eds, *A Harvest Yet to Reap* (1976); M. Stephenson, ed, *Women in Canada* (1977); V. Strong-Boag and Beth Light, eds, *True Daughters of the North: Canadian Women's History: An Annotated Bibliography* (1980); S.M. Trofimenkoff and A. Prentice, eds, *The Neglected Majority* (1977).

Women's Suffrage In the 19th century, female property holders could demand municipal voting rights on the principle of "no taxation without representation." Propertied women in Québec voted unchallenged between 1809 and 1849, when the word "male" was inserted into Québec's franchise Act. What Québec women lost, Ontario women soon gained: from 1850, women with property, married or single, could vote for school trustees. By 1900 municipal voting privileges for propertied women were general throughout Canada. But most 19th-century Canadians, women as well as men, believed that the sexes had been assigned to "separate spheres" by natural and divine laws that overrode mere man-made laws, and this stood squarely in the way of achieving votes for all women as a democratic right.

At the provincial level, public debate in Ontario began among members of the Toronto Women's Literary Club, a screen for suffrage activities created 1876 by Dr Emily Howard STOWE, Canada's first woman doctor. She and her daughter, Dr Augusta STOWE-GULLEN, spearheaded Ontario's suffrage campaign for 40 years. In 1883 the club became the Toronto Women's Suffrage Association, then in 1889 the Dominion Women's Enfranchisement Association — a national group in name only. Despite numerous petitions and bills, Ontario's lawmakers, confident that they had public opinion behind them, repeatedly blocked changes. Suffrage groups were thus forced to undertake long years of public education. Valuable support came in the 1890s from the WOMAN'S CHRISTIAN TEMPERANCE UNION, whose leaders saw votes for women as necessary in achieving PROHIBITION. In 1910, the respected and influential National Council of Women spoke out for suffrage.

The WCTU was also active in Manitoba, where women's suffrage had first been proposed in 1870 by the Icelandic community. Among Manitoba's early leaders were Mrs M.J. Benedictssen, Mrs A.V. Thomas, Dr Amelia Yeomans and Mrs J.A. McClung. McClung's daughter-in-law, Nellie MCCLUNG, later became the Prairie movement's dominant figure. Between 1912 and 1915 there was a sharp, concerted campaign. Then on 28 Jan 1916 Manitoba women became the first in Canada to win the rights to vote and to hold provincial office. They were followed by Saskatchewan on Mar 14 and Alberta on Apr 19. BC approved women's suffrage on 5 Apr 1917, and Ontario suffragists, after many years of struggle, celebrated their hard-won victory on Apr 12.

Meanwhile, pressure was mounting on federal politicians. In the controversial WARTIME ELECTIONS ACT of 1917 the federal vote was extended to women in the armed forces, and to female relatives of military men. At the same time thousands of loyal citizens, naturalized after 1902, were disenfranchised. It was not an honourable victory for Canadian women.

On 24 May 1918 all female citizens aged 21 and over became eligible to vote in federal elections, regardless of whether they had yet attained the provincial franchise. In July 1919 they gained the complementary right to stand for the House of Commons, although appointment to the Senate remained out of reach until after the PERSONS CASE of 1929. Throughout the preceding debates, the compelling argument in women's favour was their service, sacrifice and proven competence during WWI — just as Prairie women had gained provincial rights largely on their record in helping to settle and build the country. Although democratic right did have a place in the argument, service was the keynote.

The provincial franchise for Nova Scotia women came on 26 Apr 1918 after a lacklustre campaign. The cause was even less popular in New Brunswick, which approved women's suffrage on 17 Apr 1919. PEI, with practically no popular agitation, changed its franchise Act on 3 May 1922, and Newfoundland women gained the vote on 13 Apr 1925. In NS, PEI and Newfoundland, the right to stand for provincial office accompanied voting rights, but New Brunswick avoided that radical step until 9 Mar 1934. In Québec, under the courageous leadership of Thérèse CASGRAIN, the struggle continued until 25 Apr 1940, when women finally achieved the provincial counterpart to the federal vote they had been exercising for over 20 years.

Compared to the flamboyance and occasional violence of British, French and American suffrage campaigns, Canada's was peaceable and urbane, with humour, reason and quiet persistence. Canadian women have generally remained outside politics, and with the exception of municipal politics, only a small handful have so far been elected to provincial legislatures or to the House of Commons, or appointed to the Senate. In the 1984 federal election, the greatest number of women (28) were elected to the House of Commons and the greatest number (6) subsequently became Cabinet ministers. Canadian women only began to consider careers in politics seriously in the 1970s, having learned in the preceding half century that winning the vote was only a first step in a movement, far from over, for fundamental political and social change. SUSAN JACKEL

Reading: C.L. Bacchi, *Liberation Deferred?* (1983); C.L. Cleverdon, *The Woman Suffrage Movement in Canada* (1950).

Wood, Edward Rogers, financier (b at Peterborough, Canada W 14 May 1866; d at Toronto 16 June 1941). Originally a telegraph operator, Wood joined the Central Canada Loan and Savings Co in 1884. He later became managing director and VP, and was elected president in 1914. Out of Central Canada came Dominion Securities Corp, one of the largest investment houses in Canada, incorporated in 1901 by Senator George A. COX, Henry PELLATT and Wood, who eventually became its president. He was also a VP of National Trust; Brazilian Traction, Light and Power; Canada Life Assurance; and the Canadian Bank of Commerce; and a director of Massey-Harris; Mexican Light and Power; Canadian Barcelona Traction, Light and Power; International Paper; Toronto Savings and Loan; and Canada Northern Power Corp. JORGE NIOSI

Wood, Henry Wise, farmer, farm leader (b on a farm near Monroe City, Mo 31 May 1860; d at Calgary 10 June 1941). A member of a prosperous family with farms in Missouri and Texas, Wood became an expert stockman while a teenager. He belonged to the Campbellite Church, a Christian sect that emphasized the New Testament, the brotherhood of man, a democratic congregational system, and the need for Christian ethics in economic activities. Educated in local schools and Christian College (Canton, Mo), Wood was an earnest student of agrarian reform. He observed the Alliance and Populist movements in Missouri during the 1890s and agreed essentially with their programs for rural economic and social organization, but he disagreed with their attempt to develop into a conventional political party.

In 1904 he visited Alberta, "the Last Best

West," and a year later purchased a wheat farm near Carstairs. He joined the Society of Equity, an early farm association, and in 1909, its successor, the UNITED FARMERS OF ALBERTA. In 1914 Wood became a director of the UFA; in 1915 he was elected vice-president and was president 1916-31.

Wood emerged as one of the most powerful agrarian and political figures in Alberta from 1915 until his death. Devoting nearly all his time to visiting UFA locals, he preached the need for a strong, broadly based farm organization so that rural people could offset the growing power of bankers, industrialists and professionals. He gradually developed a theory of group government, in which occupational groupings would be the framework for political organization. Although originally a Liberal, Wood reluctantly became convinced that direct farmer involvement in politics was needed to protect rural interests. He helped develop the federal PROGRESSIVE PARTY platform as it evolved from the programs of the Canadian Council of Agriculture at the end of WWI. He also played a key role in the entry of the UFA into politics during 1919 and 1920. When the UFA candidates elected a majority in 1921, Wood declined to become premier but continued to play a powerful role in determining the government's policies and programs.

During the early 1920s Wood became increasingly involved in the wheat-marketing question. In 1920 the federal government had ended its control over grain marketing begun in 1917. Western farm organizations, fearing high marketing costs and low prices, frantically sought orderly marketing under provincial or federal government control. Wood was a central figure in these attempts although he personally preferred marketing through farmer-owned co-operatives. When attempts to involve government failed, therefore, Wood became a leader in the wheat pool movement which swept rural Alberta in 1923-24.

Wood's influence among Prairie farmers was based on a widespread respect for his sincerity, religious conviction and devotion to the farmers' cause. A gifted orator with a powerful personality, he was a cautious leader who never embraced new issues prematurely, and he was effective as a conciliator.   IAN MACPHERSON

Reading: W.K. Rolph, *Henry Wise Wood of Alberta* (1950).

Wood, Josiah, businessman, politician (b at Sackville, NB 18 Apr 1843; d there 13 May 1927). A graduate of Mt Allison Coll (MA 1866) and a lawyer, Wood inherited his father's wholesaling, lumbering and shipping firm in 1875. During the 1880s he diversified into manufacturing, directing a sugar refinery, a cotton mill and other industries in nearby Moncton, NB. Wood secured government subsidies for a railway between Sackville and the Northumberland Str. It was completed in 1886, and he served as president until 1913. A Conservative, he was MP for Westmorland, NB, 1882-95 and became a leading advocate of tariff protection for Canadian industry. He was appointed to the Senate in 1895, resigning in 1912 to become lieutenant-governor of NB. He retired in 1917. Wood was a generous benefactor of the Methodist Church and Mt Allison.   DEAN JOBB

Wood, William Burke, actor-manager (b at Montréal 26 May 1779; d at Philadelphia, Pa 23 Sept 1861). He was the first native-born N American to achieve notable success in the theatre; Wood's parents had emigrated to Canada before the American Revolution and returned to NY c1784. At 19, Wood made his acting debut in Annapolis, Md, with Thomas Wignell's company. Over the years he found favour as a polished comedian. Wignell's troupe was based at the Chestnut St Theatre, Philadelphia, which Wood eventually managed for 16 years (1810 to

1826). He introduced many indigenous plays and wrote *Personal Recollections of the Stage* (1855).   DAVID GARDNER

Wood, William John, labourer, artist (b near Ottawa 26 May 1877; d at Midland, Ont 5 Jan 1954). Although isolated from the contemporary artistic centres of his day, and obliged to work as an unskilled labourer for most of his life, Wood nonetheless pursued an intense lifelong interest in art, especially etching, through which he expressed his immediate experience of life in Midland in a bold, personal style. This style, evolved from familiarity with impressionism and the Swedish etcher Anders Zorn, attracted the attention of the GROUP OF SEVEN, with whom he exhibited on several occasions. Wood was a member of the Soc of Canadian Painter-Etchers and Engravers, the Canadian Soc of Graphic Art and a founder member of the Canadian Group of Painters.   CHRISTINE BOYANOSKI

Wood Buffalo National Park (44 840 km²), Canada's largest PARK, was established in 1922 to protect the last herd of wood BISON. Straddling the Alberta/NWT border, it includes 3 major environments: fire-scarred forested uplands; a poorly drained plateau etched with meandering streams and pocked with bogs; and the Peace-Athabasca Delta, a water world of sedge meadows, marshes and shallow lakes. The park provides excellent habitat for a variety of wildlife. The bison herd has grown from fewer than 500 to over 5000. Moose, caribou, wolves and black bear are also plentiful. In the wetlands, muskrat, beaver and mink thrive; in the forests, fox, lynx, ermine and red squirrels. Waterfowl abound in the delta. Over one million ducks, geese and swans pass through on MIGRATION; many remain to nest. The park is famous as the only nesting site for WHOOPING CRANES. The area has been inhabited by humans since the retreat of the glaciers. In recent centuries, nomadic Cree, Chipewyan and Beaver bands were integral to this ecosystem. Their descendants still occupy the park and carry on fishing, hunting and trapping activities.   LILLIAN STEWART

Salt plains in Wood Buffalo National Park, Alta, Canada's largest park (*courtesy Parks Canada/Prairie Region*).

Wood Mountain, elev 1000 m, is located about 135 km SW of MOOSE JAW, Sask, near the FORTY-NINTH PARALLEL. It is underlain by sedimentary rocks that were not eroded by downcutting rivers because of their position between drainage systems. Flat-topped hills, dissected by coulees, rise some 400 m above the surrounding prairie. Métis settled on the slopes of *Montagne de bois* in 1870, building houses from the plentiful poplar trees. In 1871 the HBC trading post at Wood Mt became the prairie depot of the Boundary Commission. Use of the area by whisky runners and horse thieves prompted the NWMP to purchase the depot in 1876 and maintain a post until 1918. Over 5000 Dakota Sioux and their leader, SITTING BULL, took refuge in this area after the Battle of the Little Big Horn in 1876. A provincial historic park was established in 1965. The only known sources of helium in

Canada exist around Wood Mt and SWIFT CURRENT.   DAVID SAUCHYN

Woodchuck, *see* MARMOT.

Woodcock, name given to 4 species of SHORE-BIRDS of the SANDPIPER family (Scolopacidae). Woodcock occur in open woodlands with damp soil. Their characteristic long, straight bills are very flexible at the tip and can be opened below the soil surface to grasp prey (earthworms). The skull is much modified to accommodate the large eyes; hence, the ear openings are located under instead of behind the eyes, as in other birds. American woodcock (*Scolopax minor*), the only species in Canada, breed in eastern N America from southern Canada to southern Texas, and winter in southern US.   A.J. BAKER

Woodcock, George, author, essayist, man of letters (b at Winnipeg 8 May 1912). Although most widely known as a literary journalist and historian, Woodcock has exerted a strong influence on political thinking as well as on cultural matters. He spent virtually all his first 37 years in England, and it was there that he was trained in British literary journalism, whose facility he transferred to the Canadian scene after his repatriation in 1949. Residence in the UK also meant that Woodcock was heir to the British radical tradition with its sense of historical continuity and its feeling that leftward progress is achieved partly by progress in the arts. His political beliefs are based on ANARCHISM, ie, the mutual non-involvement of the state and the individual — an ideology he gave voice to in the 1930s and 1940s through such editorial ventures as the magazines *Now* and *Freedom*. But when in 1962 he sat down to write *Anarchism*, his historical account of the movement, he did so with a sense that he was composing its obituary. The book, however, helped rekindle the principles of anarchism. Since then, Woodcock has been the pre-eminent figure in English-speaking anarchist circles and his book the movement's bible.

He began his writing life as a poet, with such works as *The Centre Cannot Hold* (1943), and has returned to poetry in his later years, but poetry of a very different sort, bearing stylistic traces of Margaret ATWOOD and other Canadian poets whom he has long championed. Over the years he has written many prose books — so many and on so many different subjects that they have tended to obscure his views even while boosting his reputation. Yet most of them can be fitted into various categories which, taken together, show both the breadth and the single-minded dedication of his life's work. First there are the purely political writings, such as his works on anarchists and pacificists, including *The Anarchist Prince: A Biographical Study of Peter Kropotkin* (1950) and *The Doukhobors* (1960) both coauthored with Ivan Avakumovic; *Pierre-Joseph Proudhon* (1956); and *Gandhi* (1971). Closely related are works combining history and travel, such as *Faces of India* (1964), *South Sea Journey* (1976) and *The Canadians* (1979), the latter being aimed at non-Canadians. More important are Woodcock's works of literary criticism, such as the books about his near contemporaries, eg, *Dawn and the Darkest Hour: A Study of Aldous Huxley* (1972) and *Thomas Merton, Monk and Poet* (1978). The best known of such works is *The Crystal Spirit* (1966), about George Orwell, who was Woodcock's cohort or antagonist in a number of early struggles. Also a part of Woodcock's literary criticism are his works on modern Canadian writers, eg, *Hugh MacLennan* (1969), *Mordecai Richler* (1970) and 2 books of literary essays, *Odysseus Ever Returning* (1970) and *The World of Canadian Writing* (1978). Much of such material has its provenance in the quarterly journal, *Canadian Literature*, which Woodcock founded at UBC in 1959 and edited until 1977. *Letters to the Past* (1982) is the first volume of his autobiography.   DOUG FETHERLING

Woodenware, or treen, simple, small objects made entirely of wood, usually by home craftsmen who were their own carpenters, joiners, carvers and turners. Normally, woodenware was made from a single piece of wood (block or plank, rough or milled), cut, hollowed or turned but rarely joined. Treen is always functional and utilitarian, of good form, made with simple techniques and easy to use. Wooden utensils, especially those associated with the preparation, serving and storage of food, are considered to be treen; ornamental objects (eg, carved figures, panels) are not.

In early Canada, treen items replaced costly and often unobtainable domestic objects normally made in Europe of glass, earthenware, stoneware, porcelain, china, silver or pewter. Even a pitchfork could be made of hardwood, the tines formed by making 2 parallel cuts and by using steam to bend the pieces. Wood was used because of its many practical qualities: it was durable, easily worked, recyclable and, most important, always available. The objects, worked one at a time during the long pioneer evenings, were made in the same useful shapes for hundreds of years. The familiar forms were copied from European models that remained unchanged from generation to generation. Great care was taken in selecting wood suitable for the purpose at hand, in order to provide the desired shape, colour, grain, strength or ornament. It was also very important to select the appropriate woodworking technique.

Canadian forests provided a good variety of hardwoods (eg, ash, birch, cherry, walnut, maple) and softwoods (eg, cedar, basswood, spruce, pine, poplar). New-felled timber, cut in planks, was usually left to season for at least one year before being used.

Hardwoods were used for objects in which weight and durability were important. For example, the hard, dense grain of maple, which can be lathe turned, was ideal for ladles, stirrers, breadboards, butter prints, spoons, mashers and rolling pins. Maple was often used in mallets because it could withstand constant pounding. Ash and hickory, exceptionally resilient hardwoods which can be bent without breaking, were steamed into hoops, box and wheel rims, and even bootjacks. The springiness of ash was extremely useful in the handles of mashers, mallets, hammers and axes because it was able to absorb the shock of each blow. Small bundles of fine birch twiglets or smooth hickory rods could be used as an eggbeater.

The bowls were made using a variety of techniques and methods. An adze or chisel could be used to hollow out the shape of a bowl; some bowls had handles carved right into the body of the piece. Bowls might also be made by lathe turning, using well-seasoned wood. Maple and ash were commonly used for turned bowls, but burls, abnormal protruding growths found on many hardwood species, were prized for use for carved or lathe-turned bowls. Although the attractive, erratic, dense grain of the burl was hard to work, it seldom split, and its resistance to water was useful. Their rarity is one reason why burl bowls have survived and are still prized.

Softwoods were employed in lightly used utensils. Pine, a lightweight, odourless and tasteless wood, was often selected for kitchen utensils. Maple sugar molds, introduced in Québec in the 18th century, were sometimes made of pine because its softness allowed it to be carved. A spoon or stirring rod could easily be whittled out of softwood and was easily replaced.

Carving was rarely done because embellished decorating would be secondary to the utilitarian purpose of a treen item, although wood with an unusually figured grain was sometimes selected particularly for its decorative qualities. Pieces such as butter prints or maple sugar molds were exceptions; their carved decoration helped iden-

tify the product and make it more attractive to the user. "Print butter" was much sought after.

It is easy to detect the touch of the maker in a piece of treen. The variety of rolling pins, for example, shows that there was no single style; there would be as many variations of an object as makers. The rough-hewn rolling pin could be as functional as the smoothly sanded lathe-turned rolling pin. Each piece had small individual details; a handle might be grooved around its edge, or the knobs might be of varying shapes. It is easy to see these details as unselfconscious additions, produced quickly by the tool at hand, just before the rolling pin came off the lathe.

The maker of a woodenware object was also its user and the objects often reflect this close relationship. The maker could create an object according to his needs without taking any shortcuts in technique or material. Thus, beauty of form and love of craftmanship were never divided from the utility of an object of treen. The work would express the craftman's pride and reveal his cultural tradition. The object would be used until it was worn out, at which point it would be discarded and a new one made. Surviving examples of treen found today are thus among the most recent made and date only from the later 19th century. Human irreverence for objects of treen is not the only reason there are so few surviving examples. Wood is a vulnerable material which rots and warps, burns readily and wears with use. The use of woodenware began to diminish with the coming of industrialization in the 19th century. It became impractical to produce commonplace objects in wood when these items were so readily and cheaply available in other, hardier materials. CAROL BAUM

Woodhouse, Arthur Sutherland Piggott, teacher, scholar, humanist (b at Port Hope, Ont 27 Sept 1895; d at Toronto 31 Oct 1964). He was educated at U of T and Harvard, taught for 5 years at U of Man and joined the Faculty of English at U of T in 1928. He subsequently became head of the department at University College (1944-64) and head of the graduate dept of English. An advocate of "historical criticism," he demonstrated his scholarship in a long series of essays on the work of John Milton, which led to *The Heavenly Muse* (1972). His contribution to the history of ideas includes studies in the Puritan revolution (*Puritanism and Liberty*, 1938), of nature and grace as intellectual framework in Renaissance literature, and of the evolution of the Romantic doctrine of the imagination. He fostered the growth of the humanities in Canada by writing in their defence, by editing the UNIVERSITY OF TORONTO QUARTERLY, and by administrative action. Three times president of the Humanities Research Council of Canada, he worked effectively for the support of pure research. The clarity, strength and zest of his scholarship were evident in his teaching.
HUGH MACCALLUM

Woodpecker (Picidae), large family of climbing BIRDS comprising 204 species. Thirteen woodpecker species occur in Canada. These are red-bellied, red-headed, Lewis's, hairy, downy, white-headed, three-toed, black-backed and pileated woodpeckers (*Centurus carolinus, Melanerpes erythrocephalus, Asyndesmus lewis, Picoides villosus, P. pubescens, P. albolarvatus, P. tridactylus, P. arcticus* and *Dryocopus pileatus*, respectively); yellow-bellied, red-breasted and Williamson's sapsuckers (*Sphyrapicus varius, S. ruber, S. thyroideus*); and northern flicker (*Colaptes auratus*). Woodpeckers have almost worldwide distribution. Most species are nonmigratory; however, many found in Canada migrate. Their flight is strong, rapid and undulating. These birds vary in length from 8 to 60 cm. Plumage can contain black, white, yellow, red, brown or

Pileated woodpecker (*artwork by Crosby*).

green, in various combinations, and they often have red or yellow on the head. Many species are barred, spotted or streaked, especially on underparts; several have a prominent crest. Woodpeckers are heavy bodied and have moderately long, rather rounded wings, and round or wedge-shaped tails. The chisel-shaped bill is strong and usually straight. Nostrils are hidden under tufts of bristlelike feathers. Usually, legs are short and strong with 2 toes in front and 2 behind. A few species (2 occur in Canada) have 3 toes, 2 in front and one behind. The toes have strong, sharp, downward-curving nails, allowing the birds to cling to vertical tree trunks or to undersides of branches. Stiffened, pointed tail feathers provide support when the birds climb up and down trees. Woodpeckers rarely perch. They are primarily arboreal, although some species such as the northern flicker spend much of their life on the ground. With chisellike bills, woodpeckers dig into tunnels in wood where larvae of wood-boring insects live. Sapsuckers bore series of holes in the bark of deciduous trees to obtain running sap. Certain species (eg, northern flicker) secure ants by a sticky secretion of the salivary glands that covers the long, extensible tongue. In season, most species eat berries; some even snap insects in flight.

Woodpeckers excavate a cavity in a tree trunk or branch, rarely in a bank, for nesting. White eggs (2-8), laid on a layer of wood chips, are incubated by both parents. Young are naked at hatching and remain in the nesting cavity until ready to fly. They are cared for by both adults. Woodpeckers have a loud voice and a variety of call notes. They also drum with the bill, particularly during nesting season and when they have found a particularly resonant surface. They are very useful in destroying wood-boring larvae. Studies show that trees in which they dig holes contain larvae of wood-boring insects, even if they appear insect free. HENRI OUELLET

Woodstock, NB, Town, pop 4649 (1981c), inc 1856, shire town of Carleton County, is located 103 km up the SAINT JOHN R from Fredericton, at the mouth of the Meduxnekeag R. It was named for the community of the same name in Oxfordshire, Eng. The disbanded troops of the 2nd battalion of Delancey's were the initiators of Woodstock's development. Despite its LOYALIST tradition, the ethnic mix of the community rapidly changed and by the mid-19th century the town was the site of a riot between members of the Loyal Orange Order and Roman Catholics. By the beginning of the 20th century Woodstock was the site of sawmills, tanneries, harness shops, carriage factories, woodworking plants, a woolen mill, a canning factory and several foundries. With the development in the 1960s of a head pond for the Mactaquac Power project, much of the town's recreational area, on islands in the Saint John, was destroyed; new facilities have since replaced these. FRED FARRELL

Woodstock, Ont, City, seat of Oxford County, pop 26 603 (1981c), inc 1901, located on the Thames R, 140 km SW of Toronto. The first settler, Zacharias Burtch, arrived in 1800, but extensive development did not take place until the 1830s. Previously known as Oxford, then Town Plot, it was renamed for Woodstock, Eng. British Adm Henry Vansittart was a prominent pioneer settler. At first a farming centre, it attracted such a variety of industry — ironworks, buggy makers, mills and breweries — that at the turn of the century it was known as "The Industrial City." This tradition continues today in textile, auto-parts, machinery and metal-goods manufacturing. Woodstock remains a market town for the surrounding agricultural area. The yellow-brick town hall (built 1851-52) is a national historic site and houses a museum of artifacts from the county. DANIEL FRANCIS

Woodsworth, James Shaver, Methodist minister, social worker, politician (b at Etobicoke, Ont 29 July 1874; d at Vancouver 21 Mar 1942). First leader of the CO-OPERATIVE COMMONWEALTH FEDERATION (CCF), he was the best known of the reform-minded SOCIAL GOSPEL ministers and led many of them into the politics of democratic socialism. Woodsworth moved to Brandon, Man, in 1885 where his father became superintendent of Methodist missions in the Northwest. Ordained in 1896, he spent 2 years as a Methodist circuit rider in Manitoba and a further 2 years studying at Victoria College and Oxford.

Observing the grim results of industrial capitalism in Canada and Britain, Woodsworth concluded that his church's stress upon personal salvation was wrong. Moving from middle-class pulpits to a city mission, All People's, Winnipeg, he worked with immigrant slum dwellers 1904-13. At the same time he wrote extensively, expounding the "social gospel" — a creedless movement calling for establishment of the Kingdom of God "here and now." By 1914 he had become a controversial supporter of trade-union collective bargaining and an ardent democratic socialist — on Fabian and British Labour Party lines. He was also adamantly pacifist, seeing war as a product of capitalist and imperial competition, and he was fired from a governmental social-research position in 1917 for openly opposing CONSCRIPTION. In 1918 he resigned the ministry in protest against church support of the war. To support his young family he joined a longshoremen's union and worked for a year on the Vancouver docks.

In June 1919 Woodsworth was arrested in Winnipeg and charged with seditious libel for editorials written during the WINNIPEG GENERAL STRIKE. Following the arrest of several strike leaders on 13 June and "Bloody Saturday," 21 June, when a nonviolent protest parade was broken up by mounted police and soldiers, Woodsworth had written about "Kaiserism" in Canada. The case was dropped although the charges, including Woodsworth's citing of 2 relevant verses from Isaiah, were never formally withdrawn. His popularity assured by his role in the strike, Woodsworth plunged with renewed zeal into the organizing work of the Manitoba Independent Labour Party. With a platform modelled on that of the British Labour Party, the ILP succeeded in electing Woodsworth to the House of Commons in 1921 for Winnipeg North Centre, with the slogan "Human Needs before Property Rights." While details of organization and policy would change, Woodsworth's principles remained constant as he held Winnipeg North Centre until his death in 1942.

In Parliament Woodsworth moved a resolution each session calling for replacement of capitalism's competitive profit motive with public and co-operative ownership of the means of production and distribution. Knowing his "co-operative commonwealth" would not arrive instantly, he worked tirelessly to promote immediate changes to benefit those who suffered most under the market system. Vigorously

rejecting the shortcut of revolution, and any association with the new Communist Party, Woodsworth became a master of parliamentary procedure, and used the Commons as a public platform. In so doing he helped establish a multiparty political system and his own reputation as the "conscience of Canada." He documented the government's hostility to labour; its timorous approach to the LEAGUE OF NATIONS; its antiquated procedures for parliamentary divorce; its refusal to enact promised social-security measures; and its compliant support of banking and other corporate legislation. In 1926 he demonstrated the worth of the parliamentary process when he bargained his vote (and that of one colleague) in return for a promise from the politically insecure PM Mackenzie KING to enact an old-age pension plan. Introduced in 1927, the plan was the cornerstone of Canada's social-security system.

Woodsworth collaborated in the 1920s with a "GINGER GROUP" of more radical Progressives. When the Depression struck, they joined with various labour and socialist groups to found a federal socialist party. At Regina in 1933 the new party adopted a democratic socialist manifesto and chose Woodsworth as its leader under the banner of Co-operative Commonwealth Federation. By 1935 the CCF had attracted the interest of a number of academics and professionals who joined together in the LEAGUE FOR SOCIAL RECONSTRUCTION and supported both the CCF and the lively political journal *Canadian Forum.* Woodsworth was the spokesman for these people and the unionists and farmers who looked to the CCF. Although the 1935 election sent only 7 CCFers to Ottawa, that little group included such political dynamos as T.C. DOUGLAS, and the party had become the official opposition in BC and Saskatchewan.

For Woodsworth the tragedy of the Depression was increasingly overshadowed by the impending horror of WWII and he gave his attention to Canada's international position. Inside the CCF he faced the growing concern of some of his colleagues that Hitler's threat could only be met by force. Believing that war breeds only war he strove to persuade the government to declare Canada's right to neutrality. He failed, as he did in the CCF National Council in Sept 1939 that gave limited support to a Canadian declaration of war. J.W. COLDWELL stated the official CCF position in the special parliamentary session while Woodsworth was permitted to explain his dissent. Reviewing the interwar period and repeating that war settles nothing, Woodsworth declared: "I rejoice that it is possible to say these things in a Canadian parliament under British institutions. It would not be possible in Germany, I recognize that . . . and I want to maintain the very essence of our British institutions of real liberty. I believe that the only way to do it is by an appeal to the moral forces which are still resident among our people, and not by another resort to brute force." He alone rose to record his opposition to the declaration of war. In 1940 Woodsworth won his last election with a sharply reduced majority. He was already weakened by a stroke and died in the spring of 1942. KENNETH MCNAUGHT

Reading: G. MacInnis, *J.S. Woodsworth, A Man to Remember* (1953); Kenneth McNaught, *A Prophet in Politics* (1959); J.S. Woodsworth, *The Strangers Within Our Gates* (1908, repr 1972) and *My Neighbor* (1910, repr 1972).

Woodward, Charles, merchant, politician (b in Wentworth County, Canada W 19 July 1842; d at Vancouver 2 June 1937). After failing as a farmer and having mixed success as a merchant on Manitoulin I and at Thessalon, Ont, Woodward decided Vancouver offered better opportunities. On 1 Mar 1892 he began selling boots, shoes and groceries. He added other lines and in 1902 incorporated Woodward Department

Stores Ltd. In 1926 he opened a branch in Edmonton, Alta. Woodward always took an interest in public life. In 1924 after he was a millionaire and 2 of his sons had taken on many management responsibilities, Woodward ran as a Liberal candidate in the 1924 provincial election. He became senior member for the city but often clashed with the Liberal government of John OLIVER and J.D. MACLEAN over timber policy, the Pacific Great Eastern Ry and Vancouver's lack of representation in the Cabinet. Today a grandson, **Charles Namby Wynn Woodward** (b at Vancouver 1924), is chairman of the board of Woodward Stores Ltd, which had in 1983 annual sales of $1.1 billion and assets of $558 million. Charles ran the company until 1979 and now devotes much of his time to ranching; he owns Canada's largest ranch (Douglas Lake, BC). PATRICIA E. ROY

Reading: D.E. Harker, *The Woodwards* (1976).

Work At different times in different cultures, work has been thought of as divine punishment, as an activity unworthy of free citizens, as the best possible way to accomplish the will of the Creator, or as the best possible way to earn a living. In modern Canadian society, work as the central activity around which social life revolves has been challenged in recent decades. The reduction in work hours, growing concerns about major changes in TECHNOLOGY and their impact on the form and content of work, and strong signs of dissatisfaction with work indicate that "work" may be on the threshold of a new era.

Until the 20th century Canada was a traditional RURAL SOCIETY in which work was directly related to the production of life's staples but was also important in the individual's social life. The purposes and circumstances of farming activities of production were part of the general organization of society. The independent workers (farmers or artisans) often owned their own means of production, organized their work as they wished and sold their produce themselves.

Despite the independence and the nature of the work (both of which distinguished farmers from shop or factory workers), traditional farmers still did arduous and demanding work with rudimentary tools. The result of their labours depended largely on the caprices of temperature and climate; they were often as bound to local merchants and moneylenders for funds to acquire land, animals, etc, as were workers in town to their employer. Many farmers, to earn money to cover their farming expenses, became seasonal employees.

Work in the other resource industries was no easier. The early FUR TRADE demanded great endurance, and the portages were strewn with the graves of VOYAGEURS who expired under their heavy loads. Forestry work attracted rural youth, peasants and immigrants, but it was seasonal and required great physical endurance (*see* TIMBER TRADE HISTORY). The workers lived in primitive lodgings and worked long days on meagre rations (beans, fresh beef, salted bacon and lard were not introduced to the menu until the 1850s). In the spring, the work was dangerous and demanded great agility. The drivers (raftsmen) worked 16-hour days, often in icy water up to their waists. This was also the age when squared logs were floated in log booms down the Ottawa and St Lawrence rivers to Québec City, a voyage of about 2 months.

Fishing was another seasonal activity with long hours for highly variable results that depended on the whims of climate and the availability of fish. Earnings fluctuated with the market, making it hard for fishermen to survive without supplementary work in agriculture or forestry (*see* FISHERIES HISTORY).

In secondary industry, it was the age of the independent producer of commodities, such as furniture, and of the establishment of carding houses, sawmills, flour mills, breweries and distilleries, tanneries and foundries. The work was usually done in small shops employing 3 or 4 men, eg, the proprietor, a master artisan, one or 2 companions and a few apprentices. Employer-employee relationships were paternalistic, especially in the APPRENTICESHIP system. For 3-10 years, the apprentice was bound by a contract under which his master was virtually his father. The apprentice could not absent himself without his master's permission, could not marry and was sworn to keep the secrets of his master's trade. In return, the master had to provide the apprentice with food, lodging and an acceptable amount and quality of education. However, the apprenticeship system became a form of bonded labour rather than a craft-training program accompanied by moral and educational supervision. As the masters accumulated capital, increased their production demands and took on more apprentices to do the dirty and often unskilled work required in the shop, apprentices experienced only the tyranny of their obligations and resented their masters' inadequate or totally nonexistent compliance with their own responsibilities.

Qualified artisans, who prior to the 20th century comprised about 10% of the urban labour force, formed a well-paid workers' aristocracy whose social status was closer to that of the middle class. A craftsman earned twice as much as a day-labourer, 4 times as much as a domestic servant. WOMEN IN THE LABOUR FORCE and children in the labour force were the most poorly paid, and one worker in 5 lived in extreme poverty.

A working-class culture had already appeared in the FOOTWEAR INDUSTRY and TEXTILE INDUSTRY and among the French Canadian workers who floated the log booms to Québec City and workers (usually IRISH) in the canal-building construction camps. Work conditions were hard, hours long. Monthly salaries were low and were often paid in the form of chits that could only be used in the company store where the price of merchandise was invariably inflated. Entrepreneurs frequently disappeared without paying the labourers, who were generally charged high rents for miserable quarters where the hygiene standards often led to EPIDEMICS of cholera, fever and other illnesses.

Work and the Industrial Revolution In Canada, as in other Western countries, the development of a free-market ECONOMY that accompanied INDUSTRIALIZATION drastically altered the nature of work for most individuals. Work lost its intrinsic value and became a way to earn a living, a commodity to buy and sell like other goods. The evolution of society progressively eliminated the direct relationship between the productive effort of individuals and the consumption of goods and services.

As Canada's rural economy, based on self-sufficiency, changed to an industrial economy characterized by an increasingly more sophisticated and complex system of production and exchange, production enterprises themselves were transformed, the number of occupations increased, work conditions and organization changed, and work took on a new meaning in relationship to the other activities of life.

In the mid-19th century, with the development of means of TRANSPORTATION (CANALS, RAILWAYS) and the appearance of the steam engine, the first factories and large businesses appeared in the major urban centres (Montréal, Hamilton, Toronto) in the tobacco and textile industries, in foundries, and in the railway-supplies business. The demand for unskilled labour (especially for construction gangs) and the numbers of skilled workers (eg, carpenters, bricklayers, tailors, and foundry and leather workers) grew rapidly. At this time the traditional enterprises, eg, small stores, offices, craft and manufacturing shops (businesses in which several craftsmen and apprentices still did handwork), were still very important. These enterprises were still unspecialized; each worker created the product from start to finish. Employer-employee relations were still largely personal, production was still primarily determined by commissions received.

The turning point came in the last third of the 19th century with the introduction of the factory system, in which workers were considered a cost of production. To minimize costs, businesses tried to "rationalize" production by eliminating the freedom of the small workshop, by closely regulating working hours, increasing the work pace and reducing skill levels where possible. The system, which spread everywhere, was based on techniques of co-ordination, supervision and discipline of the work force.

Workers laboured under a harsh system of disciplinary measures (eg, they were forbidden to talk, to leave their posts, be late) and of punitive ones (fines, dismissals, physical abuse), which were later complemented with more sophisticated techniques of persuasion, manipulation and economic incentives. The "sweatshop system" (which still exists), under which maximum labour was extracted from workers for minimum salary and in conditions where the usual rules of health and comfort were ignored, appeared at this time, especially in the textile and food industries. This system was linked with contract and subcontract labour carried out in the workers' homes.

The new system of exploitation was described in the Royal Commission on the Relations of Capital and Labour (1889): meals taken at the work post; lack of job security; poor protection against the belts, pullies and steam engines; lack of compensation for victims of industrial accidents; crowded and unhealthy conditions; authoritarian discipline; widespread child labour; frequent unemployment; and permanent material insecurity.

The processes of concentration, centralization and bureaucratization of businesses accelerated after the turn of the century with the increase in the size of businesses and industries. The work process became even more rationalized and specialized. Companies needed more administrators, managers and intermediaries and clerical help. Furthermore the increasing mechanization, fragmentation and simplification of work created a growing demand for unskilled labour. This heavy demand was met by the use of IMMIGRANT LABOUR for the most unpleasant, dirty, dangerous and ill-paid positions. Many immigrants were (and are) "BUNKHOUSE MEN," the do-anything labourers found in isolated regions, employed in the big construction camps for railways, hydroelectric dams and industrial projects, and in lumber camps.

The COMPANY TOWN appeared along with this rapid development of primary (especially mining) and secondary (textiles, pulp and paper, etc) industries. In these new industrial centres, which sprang up like mushrooms, the employer controlled not only the work but also all the other institutions and material facilities necessary to the life of the population: housing, stores, water and sewage systems, etc. These centres were concentrated in Ont, Qué and BC.

The factory system, which by 1920 had virtually eliminated craft production, underwent at this time a particularly marked refinement of its policies and methods of co-ordination, supervision and work specialization through the introduction of the scientific administration of work and the techniques of mass production. Under this scientific administration, work was characterized by a more complex division of labour based on the increased separation of the conceptualization of work (mental work) and its execution (manual work), by the assignment of a specific task to each worker through very precise selection procedures, by the simplification and compartmentalization of tasks, by the regulation of the rhythm of work; by economic incentives, and by an increase in foremen and managerial cadres.

The objective of this new system was to reduce as much as possible the real control over work processes (methods, standards, pace) which skilled industrial workers had retained despite the new managerial policies. Mass-production techniques (essentially the assembly line introduced by Henry Ford in the AUTOMOTIVE INDUSTRY) reinforced the principles of precision, economy, continuity, speed and repetition.

Workers reacted in a variety of ways to the profound changes in work and working conditions. Individually, they resorted to industrial sabotage, insubordination, absenteeism, occupational mobility, the refusal of work; collectively, they used demonstrations, such as the WINNIPEG GENERAL STRIKE, the ON TO OTTAWA TREK during the GREAT DEPRESSION, pickets, various forms of STRIKE and above all the formation of LABOUR ORGANIZATIONS. A federal law of 1872 had removed workers' associations from the provisions of criminal law but not until almost 30 years were federal laws protecting workers adopted (eg, the 1900 Conciliation Act on voluntary conciliation and ARBITRATION, and the federal Industrial Disputes Investigation Act of 1907 concerning inquiries into industrial disputes). Among the first laws regulating working conditions were the manufacturing laws adopted in 1884 in Ontario and in 1885 in Québec; those concerning work by women and children adopted in Québec in 1910; and those concerning work-related accidents adopted in Québec in 1909 and in Ontario in 1914.

Most of these early protective laws were hard to apply and often inoperative because of highly inadequate and almost toothless inspection services; but once workers' unions were recognized, LABOUR LAW developed into an increasingly complex institutional apparatus and labour laws were progressively improved and broadened. SOCIAL SECURITY legislation also developed considerably in the postwar years.

Work Today

The development of increasingly large and concentrated factories and businesses was marked by extensive mechanization and automation which greatly eased the physical burden of work. However, the physical environment of modern work exposes workers to the risks of poor ventilation, excessive heat and noise, dust and air POLLUTION, exposure to toxic gas, acids and radioactive substances (see OCCUPATIONAL DISEASE). Also, despite its diversity, work is characterized in most cases by repetitive, meaningless, narrow and specialized tasks which require little skill and training and involve little responsibility. Semiskilled workers who may have developed certain skills while learning a specific task in a specific context usually find these skills worthless if they change jobs.

Whatever the workplace — a small business with paternalistic employer-employee relations or a large one where authority is bureaucratic and impersonal — most workers must follow orders and directives telling them the purpose of their work, its methods and pace, and even behaviour patterns that are only indirectly related to the work itself.

Working for oneself (eg, in SMALL BUSINESS) has always been an attractive way to escape the problems associated with wage labour, but the joys of such an escape are generally illusory. For many, the dream ends in bankruptcy; for the successful minority, it takes long hours of hard, stubborn work and many disillusionments.

Almost half of the active and experienced LABOUR FORCE in Canada now belongs to nonmanual occupational groups, known as the tertiary sector, it includes office workers, specialized cadres and technicians, administrators, salespeople and commercial workers. The growth in this sector has been most sustained and impressive among office workers, administrators, and specialized workers and technicians. This growth has been attributed to the increased size of businesses and multinational activities, the growing complexity of financial activities, the increased importance of marketing, and the growth in the creation and processing of information.

Until the 1920s, clerical work was not as mechanized or rationalized as manual labour, but since then and especially since WWII, office and saleswork has been progressively mechanized, specialized, downgraded and simplified. Most of it is now carried on in the impersonal world of the major corporations where a clear gap exists between employees and supervisors. The so-called "professional" nonmanual occupations (administrators, specialized cadres and technicians), which offer the most interesting work and should have retained considerable autonomy, have also been affected. The very idea of the professions has been changed. Because of the prestige associated with those who carry out professional activities in Canada, many nonmanual occupational groups have tried to win social and governmental recognition for their activities (eg, real-estate salespeople, hairdressers). The traditional idea of profession has been so extended that observers speak of the "professionalization" of the labour force. In fact the attributes of professional activities (the knowledge and abilities required to exercise the profession, the nature of the professional activity, the nature of the relationship between the professional and the client, and professional autonomy) have lost much of their specific character or have been transformed.

Traditionally the acquisition of specialized knowledge through lengthy training constituted the essential element of a profession. But the average training level for workers and the training and apprenticeship requirements in many occupations (eg, airline pilots) have risen considerably as a result of industrial and technological progress and their corollaries (eg, rising educational levels in the population, increased job specialization). The idea of service is no longer exclusive to the professions, and because of technological developments, many of these specialized service activities have become as difficult to conduct and evaluate and as weighted with consequence for the eventual clients and for society as the traditional professional activities.

In the past, the typical professional-client relationship (modeled on the medical profession) was based on confidentiality, the total responsibility of the professional, and the unique and specific nature of each professional decision. These elements are no longer part of most professional activities. The client is often not a person but a business, a group or an institution, and the question of confidentiality occurs in a different context. As well, professionals are now often salaried employees and are no longer the only people privy to confidential information or involved in decision making.

Finally the idea of professional autonomy, whereby practitioners work for themselves in private practice (only 10% of those with professional training), has been shattered by the increasing phenomenon of salaried professionals (eg, engineers, doctors and lawyers) and by the appearance of professions composed largely of employees of businesses, establishments or institutions. In these cases, professionals who are in specialized cadres or are technicians are subject to a bureaucratic organization of their work. Their authority and professional autonomy is further reduced by their obedience to the political objectives (in the public sector) or the profit (in the private sector) objectives of their employers. These professionals, whose numbers and central role in production are constantly growing, remain caught between their knowledge and skills on the one hand and, on the other, their narrow sphere of activities and their limited freedom. It is therefore not surprising that some groups, eg, doctors, engineers, teachers, nurses, have virtually abandoned professional objectives (and with them at least part of their control over their labour) and formed their own labour unions.

Employers are caught up in rapid technological change and constant market shifts that require them to adapt rapidly to changes in products and services. As they did in the past, they seek solutions to labour problems through new forms of work organization; however, today these forms include quality-of-life programs designed to give more room to workers' desire for autonomy, responsibility, creativity and conviviality. Tasks have been upgraded and workers' groups have been given greater autonomy, eg, semiautonomous production circles. Some employees have eliminated time clocks, introduced flex-time and shortened hours, and designed programs (eg, suggestion programs, various joint consultative committees on issues such as productivity, welfare, health and job security) to increase the workers' participation and interest in their work. Profit-sharing and other forms of financial participation have also been tried. The goal of all these efforts is to increase the workers' identification with the company, and their motivation and productivity. These new organizational forms have not been widely applied and the advantages for workers are still unclear. Essentially the wage-earning system remains unchanged.

Finally new forms of employment have developed in which the position of workers is generally precarious, eg, part-time, free-lance or contract work, interim work and shared jobs. These kinds of employment use the condition or needs of certain categories of workers (eg, working mothers, students, handicapped and older workers), to meet the needs of businesses (decreased labour costs and more flexible response to production fluctuations) and of the governmental authorities (spreading available employment over more workers).

The present preoccupation with working conditions marks a change in perspective towards various aspects of work, eg, organization of work, interpersonal relations and HEALTH and safety. There is less attention to the purely functional concept of work and more recognition that the quality of a wage earner's working life affects off-the-job quality of life as well.

Youth and Work Between 1953 and 1984, the number of young people (under 25 years) in the labour force grew from 1.3 million to 2.8 million. But, in hard economic times, because of their inexperience and lack of seniority and training they are the first to be laid off. Thus they have a disproportionately high UNEMPLOYMENT rate. They also have the highest rate of job mobility, though it is often involuntary. Those who voluntarily change jobs (the best educated, the unmarried or the young married without children) usually do so for experience. But for many, job changes are an expression of their unhappiness with modern work — both its intrinsic aspects and its material conditions. Many young people, children of a more liberal society, tend to challenge traditional forms of authority in the workplace. Better educated than their elders and accustomed to a higher standard of living, they seek more demanding and more enriching work which will use the capabilities developed by their education.

Work, Education and Training Not so long ago, the (usually limited) training received at school would see people through their professional careers. They entered the work force young, having undergone an apprenticeship which often began in the family and continued on the job. Today, given the social demand for general and diversified education and the need for skilled labour, a diploma is essential. Young people are entering the labour force at a later age all the time.

During the prosperous 1950s and 1960s, a diploma was the passport to the more interesting jobs. Since 1970, and especially in a period of economic crisis, the diploma no longer guarantees a job in a given occupational category. Educational level is often used as a pretext for stricter selection and the assurance of the individuals' ability to adapt to the procedures of the organization of production. Young people now enter the work force in more difficult conditions, and many of them must make do with occasional and part-time work. Moreover, their prior training offers less guarantee of career advancement. Technological progress, office reorganization, the shift toward employment in the tertiary sector, unemployment or its threat, the possibility and the attractions of job mobility, and the search for a higher standard of living are all incentives leading adults in ever greater numbers to seek supplementary training at some stage in their working life.

While this training can be found in educational institutions, businesses (especially the biggest ones) have also begun offering professional training to increase the productivity of their work force. These courses are usually short, focusing on a particular task or job function and dealing with immediate needs. They are largely controlled by the corporation, and usually favour managers and professionals over unskilled labourers.

Women and Work The proportion of women in the labour force has risen from 20% in 1921 to more than 50% in the early 1980s. This rapid growth is mainly due to the rising number of working wives (11% in 1951; 52% in 1981).

The growing number of working women may have a profound long-term effect on the nature and organization of work itself, but so far the repercussions are limited and the structure of female jobs has remained static. Women are usually found in traditionally "female" occupations (eg, office work, sales, teaching, hospital services and light industry). Those who venture into traditionally male strongholds still suffer discrimination. Working conditions in female jobs are usually characterized by longer work hours, unusual shifts, lack of job security, and systematic pay and benefits discrimination in those jobs (which comprise the majority) not covered by collective agreements. Although they are usually better educated than men, women generally hold junior positions and dead-end jobs.

The explosion in part-time work (at the present rate, by the year 2000 more than half of all workers will have part-time jobs) has occurred in such a way that most of the people so employed are women. The concentration of women in precarious jobs and in the tertiary sector largely explains their higher unemployment rate (in 1980, 44.7% of the unemployed though only 40% of the working population) and the fact that they are especially threatened by the technological changes being wrought by the microelectronic revolution.

Various legislative measures (eg, against job discrimination, in favour of maternity leave), passed because of pressure from the women's movement and from trade unions, have improved conditions for women who already work and are an incentive for more women to seek salaried employment. But major improvements are still needed, especially in the application of these laws. The idea of women working outside the home is better accepted today, but traditional attitudes have not disappeared. Recently, a poll revealed that the majority of men and women still feel that a woman's place is in the home.

Work and Retirement Because of the sharp rise in life expectancy, more attention is being paid to the relationship between work and the quality of life in retirement years. The nature and conditions of work and its level of remuneration have a determining influence not only on workers' standard of living during retirement (especially on their income) but also on their state of physical and mental health. These preoccupations have intensified in the last 20 years because of the strong trend toward earlier retirement.

Several factors have caused this trend, eg, the establishment of obligatory retirement at age 65 and universal public PENSION programs and voluntary private ones; the desire for more active lives outside the job; and the rise in incomes that allows more people to retire before age 65. As well, competition in the labour market and the effects of technological change mitigate against employing older workers. Lowering the retirement age has become a popular way of reducing the labour force. Governments and businesses have introduced early-retirement incentive programs, the former to fight unemployment and the latter to reduce the numbers and costs of their labour forces.

Yet for both economic and social reasons, a counter trend has recently developed against obligatory retirement. Social-security measures have failed to assure most workers and their dependents of a satisfactory level of material security. In the mid-1970s, more than half the retired people in Canada needed a guaranteed income supplement to stay above the POVERTY line. Moreover, the rapid AGING of the population raises the problem of insufficient pension funds. From the social point of view, retired workers find themselves socially isolated, marginalized, and insecure. The abolition of obligatory retirement (Québec was the first province to do so) allows staggered retirements that better respect the needs, circumstances and hopes of individual workers.

Work and Technology The applications of information technologies based on microelectronics in communications (ie, the switching and transmission of information) in business through word-processing machines and in manufacturing through robotics has amounted to a technological revolution (*see* COMPUTER COMMUNICATIONS; COMPUTERS AND SOCIETY).

The productivity gains being realized in the quantity and structure of employment will undoubtedly cause a significant reduction in clerical and low-ranking specialized jobs in the tertiary sector, the sector most affected by these changes and the most important sector (accounting for more than 60% of Canada's labour force) in modern economies. These losses will likely be only partially balanced by the creation of new specialized and professional jobs in the industries producing and using the new technologies. Though the professional structure in place since the turn of the century will undergo profound changes, it is very unlikely Canada will be left with only 2 kinds of workers, ie, those who push the buttons and those who invent the programs and technologies. It is more likely that workers in the traditional trades and operators will be replaced by technicians and workers specialized in maintenance, tooling, information technologies and electronics. The move to an information age could therefore lead to greater uniformity of skills (*see* INFORMATION SOCIETY).

The content and organization of work will also be affected. In the past, technological progress had contradictory effects: reduced physical labour and increased salaries versus highly specialized jobs and increased job pace and controls. Today's changes will also have contradictory effects which may well accentuate trends from the past. The new technologies will make it possible to eliminate many repetitive, dangerous manual jobs and to create new tasks connected with the control, supervision and maintenance of automatons. However, the technologies may also increase the compartmentalization and repetitive nature of some tasks which until now could not be simplified and downgraded. It is also possible that there will be tighter controls over workers and a faster job pace, an increased sense of isolation on the job because of reduced interaction, and new health and job-security problems (eg, stress-producing conditions, different types of fatigue and physical ills from radiation exposure). Finally the new technologies could lead to the development of work teams, to job decentralization into smaller work units, work at a distance (eg, working at home), increased use of contract workers, and more flexible and shorter hours.

Future of Work Work is both an instrumental activity (ie, it creates social status and personal independence), and a liberating, creative activity through which individuals may shape and express their own identities. In Canadian society today, work for most people is almost entirely instrumental. Can it also become a free and creative activity? The changes now underway may cause work to lose its exclusively instrumental nature and take on new significance within a socioeconomic balance where the relationships of production, which are based on the private ownership of the means of production, will be replaced by relationships based on principles of codetermination or social self-management.

More probably, however, organized work will remain instrumental in nature. If so, it is possible that the production and consumption cycle will be perpetuated; increased productivity will allow higher wages and increased consumption; and organized work will remain a central activity. On the other hand, organized work may remain instrumental but lose its central position in society. Productivity gains might lead to shorter work hours, leaving more time for other activities, including independent or self-chosen work. This work would consist of the production of goods and services for personal use, or for exchange outside the organized market. People's desire for part-time work is an expression of their desire for greater control over their own time. Further reduction in organized working hours (eg, the 32-hour week) may lead people to pay more attention to their other activities, particularly to work of their own choosing, rather than simply to recreation. *See also* WORKING-CLASS HISTORY.   CAMILLE LEGENDRE

Workers' Compensation, legislation designed to provide benefits, medical care and rehabilitation services to individuals who suffer workplace injuries or contract OCCUPATIONAL DISEASES. Prior to workers' compensation legislation, workplace accidents were dealt with entirely under the common law (*see* TORT). In practice, this meant that workers could sue employers with some probability of success only if they could establish employer negligence. In the absence of a more widespread compensation plan, many trade unions maintained their own accident funds but these covered only a minority of the labour force. In 1889 the Royal Commission on the Relations of Labour and Capital reported the high level of injury among workers and condemned the oppressiveness of working conditions in many industries. It made many important recommendations to improve working conditions, but the federal government claimed that to act upon them would constitute an infringement of provincial authority. The premise of modern workers' compensation legislation is that some level of injury is inevitable and that compensation should be provided without regard to responsibility. The Ontario Workmen's Compensation Act of 1914 was the first Canadian statute to accept this principle. It served as a model for provincial legislation in NS (1915), BC (1916), Alberta (1918) and NB (1918). Workers' compensation Acts now exist in all Canadian jurisdictions and provide medical rehabilitation services as well as financial benefits.

The range of workers covered under compensation varies from province to province. Initially, only workers in hazardous industries were included but now the law applies to almost every industry and 70-90% of workers are covered. In most jurisdictions, however, agricultural labourers, domestic workers, casual workers and outworkers are not covered by the legislation, although in some provinces inclusion can be obtained by application or other special means. Benefit levels are based on previous earnings with the general formula being that 75% of wages are replaced by compensation payments up to a legal maximum. Financing procedures and contribution rates to workmen's compensation funds vary, but in all jurisdictions the fund is financed exclusively by employer contributions. These contributions are calculated on the probability of accident in different industrial groupings. For example, firms in industries with very few accidents and with few employees drawing compensation benefits might pay as little as 25¢ per $100 of payroll, while other firms in industries that record more accidents and more claims on the system might pay $15 per $100 of payroll. The system is, therefore, similar to an insurance policy in which high-risk customers pay higher premiums.

Workers' compensation plays a major role in alleviating hardship caused by injuries or death, but because its major contribution is the provision of compensation to individuals after accidents occur, it is only part of a broader set of policies aimed at reducing accidents and producing a safer work place. *See also* LABOUR POLICY; INDUSTRIAL RELATIONS.   D.A. SMITH

Working-Class History is the story of the changing conditions and actions of all working people. Most adult Canadians today earn their living in the form of wages and salaries and thus share the conditions of dependent employment associated with the definition of "working class." The Canadian worker has been a neglected figure in Canadian history and, although Canadians have always worked, working-class history has received little attention. Until recently, the most common form of working-class history has been the study of the trade union, or labour, movement (unions are organizations formed by workers in order to strengthen their position in dealing with employers and sometimes with governments). Although the development of organized labour provides a convenient focus for the discussion of working-class history, it is important to remember that most working people, past and present, have not belonged to unions: in 1982 only about 3.6 million Canadians, approximately 30% of the LABOUR FORCE, belonged to unions. However, because unions have often pursued goals designed to benefit all workers, the labour movement has won a place in Canadian society. Canadian workers have contributed in many ways to the development of Canadian society, but the history of working people in their families, communities and workplaces is only gradually becoming part of our view of the Canadian past. Canadian historians have often studied the various Canadian cultural and regional identities, but the working-class experience is now proving to be one of the unifying themes in Canadian history (*see* WORK).

English Canada

The working class emerged during the 19th century in English Canada as a result of the spread of industrial capitalism in British North America. At the time most Canadians were self-employed, independent producers who made their living as farmers, fishermen and craftsmen. Entire families contributed to the production of goods (*see* CHILDHOOD, HISTORY OF). The expansion of resource industries (*see* RESOURCE USE), the construction of canals and railways, the growth of cities and the rise of manufacturing all helped create a new kind of work force in which the relationship between employer and employee was governed by a capitalist labour market and where women and children no longer participated to as great an extent. COMPANY TOWNS, based on the production of a single resource such as coal, emerged during the colonial period and provided a reserve of skilled labour for the company and a certain degree of stability for the workers. The workers were often cruelly exploited; when violence erupted, the companies' responses varied from closing the company-owned store to calling in the militia. DOMESTIC SERVICE (servants, housekeepers, etc) emerged as the primary paid employment for women. CHILD LABOUR reached its peak in the late 19th and early 20th centuries, supplemented by immigrant children brought from Britain by various children's aid societies. For any worker job security and assistance in the event of illness, injury or death were almost nonexistent, and when INDUSTRIALIZATION hit Canadian urban centres after the mid-19th century, working conditions often deteriorated.

For most of the 19th century, unions were usually small, local organizations. Often they were illegal: in 1816 the Nova Scotia government prohibited workers from bargaining for better hours or wages and provided prison terms as a penalty. Nevertheless, workers protested their conditions, with or without unions, and sometimes violently. Huge, violent strikes took place on the Welland and Lachine canals in the 1840s. Despite an atmosphere of hostility, by the end of the 1850s local unions had become established in many Canadian centres, particularly among skilled workers such as printers, shoemakers, moulders, tailors, coopers, bakers and other tradesmen. The labour movement gained cohesiveness when unions created local assemblies and forged ties with British and American unions in their trade. In 1872 workers in Ontario industrial towns and in Montréal rallied behind the NINE-HOUR MOVEMENT, which sought to reduce the working day from up to 12 hrs to 9 hrs. Hamilton's James Ryan, Toronto's John HEWITT and Montréal's James Black led the workers. Toronto printers struck against employer George BROWN, and in Hamilton, on 15 May 1872, 1500 workers paraded through the streets. The ambitiously titled Canadian Labor Union, formed in 1873, spoke for unions mainly in southern Ontario. It was succeeded in 1883 by the TRADES AND LABOR CONGRESS OF CANADA, which became a lasting forum for Canadian labour. In Nova Scotia the Provincial Workmen's Association (1879) emerged as the voice of the coal miners and later spoke for other Maritime workers. The most important organization of this era was the KNIGHTS OF LABOR, which organized more than 450 assemblies with more than 20 000 members across the country. The Knights were an INDUSTRIAL UNION which brought together workers regardless of craft, race (excepting Chinese) or sex. Strongest in Ontario, Québec and BC, the Knights were firm believers in economic and social democracy, and were often critical of the developing industrial, capitalist society. Key Knights included A.W. WRIGHT, Thomas Phillips THOMPSON and Daniel J. O'DONOGHUE.

By the late 19th century the "labour question"

Men and women workers in a textile plant, c 1908 (*courtesy City of Toronto Archives / James 137*).

had gained recognition. The Toronto printers' strike of 1872 led PM Sir John A. Macdonald to introduce the Trade Unions Act, which stated that unions were not to be regarded as illegal conspiracies. The Royal Commission on the Relations of Labour and Capital, which reported in 1889, documented the sweeping impact of the industrial revolution in Canada, and the commissioners strongly defended unions as a suitable form of organization for workers: "The man who sells labour should, in selling it, be on an equality with the man who buys it. . . ." Another sign of recognition came in 1894 when the federal government officially adopted LABOUR DAY as a national holiday falling on the first Monday in Sept.

The consolidation of Canadian capitalism in the early 20th century accelerated the growth of the working class. From the countryside, and from Britain and Europe, hundreds of thousands of people moved to Canada's booming cities and tramped through Canada's industrial frontiers (*see* BUNKHOUSE MEN). Most workers remained poor, their lives dominated by a struggle for the economic security of food, clothing and shelter; by the 1920s most workers were in no better financial position than their counterparts had been a generation earlier. Not surprisingly, most strikes of this time concerned wages, but workers also went on strike to protest working conditions, unpopular supervisors and new rules, and to defend workers who were being fired. Skilled workers were particularly alarmed that new machinery and new ideas of management were depriving them of some traditional forms of workplace authority.

Despite growing membership, divisions appeared between unions and that limited their effectiveness. The most aggressive organizers were the CRAFT UNIONS, whose membership was generally restricted to the more skilled workers. Industrial unions were less common, though some, such as the United Mine Workers, were important. The American Federation of Labor (fd 1886, *see* AFL-CIO) unified American craft unions, and under Canadian organizer John FLETT, chartered more than 700 locals in Canada between 1898 and 1902; most were affiliated with the TLC. At the TLC meetings in 1902 the AFL craft unions voted to expel any Canadian unions, including the Knights of Labor, in jurisdictional conflict with the American unions, a step which deepened union divisions in Canada. The attitudes of government were also a source of weakness. Though unions were legal, they had few rights under the law. Employers could fire union members at will, and there was no law requiring employers to recognize a union chosen by their workers. In strikes employers could ask governments to call out the troops and militia in the name of law and order, as happened on more than 30 occasions before 1914 (*see*, for example, FORT WILLIAM FREIGHT HANDLERS STRIKE). With the creation of the Dept of Labour in 1900, the federal government became increasingly involved in dispute settlement. The Industrial Disputes Investigation Act (1907), the

brainchild of William Lyon Mackenzie KING, required that some important groups of workers, including miners and railwaymen, must go through a period of conciliation before they could engage in "legal" strikes. Since employers were still free to ignore the unions, dismiss employees, bring in strikebreakers and call for military aid, unions came to oppose this legislation.

One of the most important developments in the prewar labour movement was the rise of REVOLUTIONARY INDUSTRIAL UNIONISM, an international movement that favoured the unification of all workers into one labour body to overthrow the capitalist system and place workers in control of political and economic life. The INDUSTRIAL WORKERS OF THE WORLD, founded in Chicago in 1905, rapidly gained support among workers in western Canada such as navvies, fishermen, loggers and railway workers. The "Wobblies" attracted nationwide attention in 1912 when 7000 ill-treated immigrant railway workers in the Fraser Canyon struck against the CANADIAN NATIONAL RY. A number of factors, including government suppression, hastened its demise during the war.

WWI had an important influence on the labour movement. While workers bore the weight of the war effort at home and paid a bloody price on the battlefield, many employers prospered. Labour was excluded from wartime planning and protested against CONSCRIPTION and other wartime measures. Many workers joined unions for the first time and union membership grew rapidly, reaching 378 000 in 1919. At the end of the war strike activity increased across the country: there were more than 400 strikes in 1919, most of them in Ontario and Québec. Three general strikes also took place that year, in Amherst, NS, Toronto and Winnipeg. In Winnipeg the arrest of the strike leaders and the violent defeat of the strike revealed that in a labour conflict of this magnitude the government would not remain neutral (*see* WINNIPEG GENERAL STRIKE). In 1919 as well, the radical ONE BIG UNION was founded in Calgary, raised from the ashes of the IWW. It soon claimed 50 000 members in the forestry, mining, transportation and construction industries. Despite the formation of the OBU and the COMMUNIST PARTY OF CANADA, the 1920s remained a period of retreat for organized labour. The exception was the coal miners and steelworkers of Cape Breton I, who, led by J.B. MCLACHLAN and Silby BARRETT, rebelled repeatedly against one of the country's largest corporations (*see* CAPE BRETON STRIKES).

The 1930s marked an important turning point for workers. The biggest problem of the decade was unemployment. In the depths of the GREAT DEPRESSION over one million Canadians were out of work, about one in 4 workers. Emergency relief was inadequate and often provided under humiliating conditions (*see* UNEMPLOYMENT RELIEF CAMPS). Unemployed workers' associations fought evictions and gathered support for UNEMPLOYMENT INSURANCE, a reform finally achieved in 1940. One dramatic protest was the ON TO OTTAWA TREK of 1935, led by the former Wobbly Arthur "Slim" Evans, an organizer for the National Unemployed Workers' Assn. The Depression demonstrated the need for workers' organizations, and by 1949 union membership had exceeded one million workers. Much of the growth in union organization came in the new mass-production industries among workers neglected by craft unions: rubber, electrical, steel, auto and packinghouse workers. The communist-supported Workers' Unity League (1929-36) had pioneered industrial unionism in many of these industries. The OSHAWA STRIKE, (8-23 Aug 1937), when 4000 workers struck against General Motors, was among the most significant in establishing the new industrial unionism in Canada. Linked to the Congress of Industrial Organizations in the

US, many of the new unions were expelled by the TLC and formed the CANADIAN CONGRESS OF LABOUR (CCL) in 1940.

Early in WWII the federal government attempted to limit the power of unions through wage controls and restrictions on the right to strike (*see* WARTIME PRICES AND TRADE BOARD; NATIONAL WAR LABOUR BOARD), but many workers refused to wait until the war was over to win better wages and union recognition. Strikes such as that of the Kirkland Lake gold miners in 1941 persuaded the government to change its policies. In Jan 1944 an emergency order-in-council, PC 1003, protected the workers' right to join a union and required employers to recognize unions chosen by their employees. This long-awaited reform became the cornerstone of Canadian INDUSTRIAL RELATIONS after the war, in the Industrial Relations and Disputes Investigation Act (1948) and in some provincial legislation.

At the end of the war a wave of strikes swept across the country. Workers achieved major improvements in wages and hours, and many contracts incorporated grievance procedures and innovations such as vacation pay. Some industry-wide strikes attempted to challenge regional disparities in wages. The Ford strike in Windsor, Ont, between Sept 12 and 29 Dec 1945, began when 17 000 workers walked off the job. The lengthy, bitter strike resulted in the landmark decision by Justice Ivan C. RAND which granted a compulsory check-off of union dues (*see* RAND FORMULA; WINDSOR STRIKE). The check-off helped give unions financial security, though some critics worried that unions might become more bureaucratic as a result.

By the end of the war Canadian workers also had become more active politically. The labour movement had become involved in politics after 1872 when the first workingman (Hamilton's Henry Buckingham Witton), was elected to Parliament. In 1874 Ottawa printer D.J. O'Donoghue was elected to the Ontario legislature, and in 1888 A.T. Lépine, a Montréal leader of the Knights of Labor, was elected to Parliament. Labour candidates and workers' parties were often backed by local unions. In 1900 A.W. PUTTEE, a LABOUR PARTY founder, and Ralph SMITH, TLC president, were elected to Parliament. The SOCIALIST PARTY OF CANADA appealed to the radical element. During the war, policies such as conscription encouraged unions to increase their political activity at the provincial and federal levels. In the 1921 federal election, labour candidates contested seats in all 9 provinces; OBU general secretary R.B. RUSSELL was defeated, as was Cape Breton's J.B. McLachlan, but Winnipeg's J.S. WOODSWORTH and Calgary's William IRVINE were elected. The social catastrophe of the Great Depression increased the appeal of radical politics; Communist Party support increased, and the CO-OPERATIVE COMMONWEALTH FEDERATION was founded. During the 1940s the CCF became the official opposition in BC, Ontario and Nova Scotia, and in 1944 the first CCF government was elected in Saskatchewan. By the late 1940s the CCF and the Communist Party had a combined membership of 50 000.

The new rights of labour and the rise of the WELFARE STATE were the decisive achievements of the 1930s and 1940s, promising to protect Canadian working people against major economic misfortunes. The position of labour in Canadian society was strengthened by the formation of the CANADIAN LABOUR CONGRESS (1956), which united the AFL and the Canadian Congress of Labour and absorbed the OBU. The CLC was active in the founding of the NEW DEMOCRATIC PARTY, and, despite the emergence of the Confederation of Canadian Unions (1975) and the Canadian Federation of Labour (1982), it continues to represent about 60% of union members. Steady growth in government employment during this period meant that by the 1970s one in 5

workers was a public employee. With the exception of Saskatchewan, which gave provincial employees union rights in 1944, it was not until the mid-1960s, following an illegal national strike by postal workers (*see* POSTAL STRIKES), that public employees gained collective bargaining rights similar to those of other workers. By the early 1980s, 3 of the 4 largest unions in Canada were PUBLIC-SERVICE UNIONS, whose growth has increased the prominence of Canadian over American-based unions in Canada. Another significant change has been the rise in the number of female workers, who in the early 1980s made up over 40% of the work force and 30% of union membership. The change was reflected in the growing prominence of women union leaders and in concern over issues such as maternity leave, sexual harassment and equal pay to women workers for work of equal value.

Despite the achievements of organized labour, the sources of conflict between employers and employees have persisted. Determined employers have been able to resist unions by using strikebreakers and by refusing to reach agreement on first contracts. Workers have continued to exert little direct influence over the investment decisions that govern the distribution of economic activity across the country. In collective agreements such issues as health, safety and technological change have recieved greater attention, but the employer's right to manage property has predominated over the workers' right to control the conditions and purposes of their work. Governments have often acted to restrict union rights: on occasion, as in the 1959 NEWFOUNDLAND LOGGERS' STRIKE, individual unions have been outlawed, and during the 1960s and 1970s governments turned with increasing frequency to the use of legislated settlements, especially in disputes with their own employees. Despite the intervention of the welfare state, many workers have continued to suffer economic insecurity and poverty. The capitalist labour market has failed to provide full employment for Canadian workers, and by the early 1980s more than one million Canadians were regularly reported unemployed; especially in underdeveloped regions such as Atlantic Canada, many workers have continued to depend on part-time, seasonal work. Most working people today are more affluent than their counterparts were in the past, but the distribution of the national income has not changed significantly in favour of working people.   DAVID FRANK

Québec

As in other parts of Canada, the history of working-class Québec has only recently received serious study, and research has concentrated on the trade-union phenomenon. Before the industrialization of Québec (about 1870-80), most businesses were small and crafts-oriented. In 1851 there were only 37 companies employing more than 25 workers. Salaried employees were rare, although there were some in the TIMBER TRADE, construction, and canal and railway earthworks. A few trade unions began a precarious existence after 1827. Montréal craft unions united 3 times in larger associations: in 1834, to win a 10-hour day; in 1867, to form the Grand Association; and in 1872, to win a 9-hour day. But each lasted only a few months and few unions withstood the 1837 economic crisis. Québec workers gave other signs of their presence as well. There were over 80 strikes from 1840 to 1880. The CO-OPERATIVE MOVEMENT, through life and health mutual-assurance funds, expanded rapidly after 1850 among the working class. These early signs of worker consciousness demonstrate the workers' desire to create alliances in response to the insecurities of factory work and urban life, and also the workers' rejection of the capitalist labour market in which they were treated as commodities.

Manufacturing activities overtook commerce around 1880. The industrial bourgeoisie now dominated, and the state adopted the objectives of this new social class. MONTRÉAL's population doubled, 1871-91, as the city became Canada's industrial and financial capital. Workers' solidarity and sense of social class both increased. Trade unionism reached more and more workers, thanks to international unions and the Knights of Labor. The number of unions in Québec jumped from 22 in 1880 to 136 in 1901 and to 491 in 1931. About 12 000 workers belonged to unions in 1901 and some 72 100 (10.3% of all Québec wage earners) in 1931.

Unlike other international unions which stressed the economic betterment of members within their own companies, the Knights proposed a total reform of industrial society, including the abolition of wage-earning and the introduction of co-operatives and small-scale ownership. Their activities helped in the formation of the national TLC and in Québec led to the creation of central workers' councils in Montréal (1886) and Québec City (1890). These organizations gave workers a political voice which, in the period 1886-1930, called for electoral reform, free and compulsory education, social legislation and the nationalization of public services. Their representations, though not revolutionary, reflected a view of society which nevertheless differed greatly from that of the other social classes. Some workers, impatient with government reluctance to adopt pro-worker legislation, moved into party politics, at first within traditional parties and then in the Parti ouvrier (fd 1899). Of 38 candidates, 5 were elected provincially and federally before the Parti joined the CCF in 1933.

The international unions set up their own central council in Montréal in 1897, and a provincial federation in 1937 which became the main union body in Québec. Their greatest challenge came from the Catholic unions. The QUÉBEC SHOE WORKERS' STRIKE (from 23 Oct - 10 Dec 1900), was the first direct intervention in a labour conflict by the clergy, and the first step towards the creation of Catholic unions. The church recognized workers' rights to form unions, but insisted on clerical involvement. The Catholic unions were formed in 1907 in various dioceses under the guidance of the clergy, who feared the "socialist" and anticlerical leanings of the international unions. The Catholic unions established a central in 1921 and gradually adopted many of the methods and principles of international unionism.

As Québec workers became better organized, they increasingly used strikes to gain their objectives. There were 1073 strikes from 1881 to 1940, a wave that peaked with 134 in 1919-20 alone. Thus it was that after 1880 the working class affirmed its existence as it brought its claims to the level of society as a whole. The trade-union movement to which most of the organized workers belonged expressed its claims as part of a larger plan for social reform. The middle class, especially the clergy, tried to control this rising force. Federal and provincial governments met some demands but remained true to liberal capitalism.

In the Great Depression, worker unrest forced governments to reconsider their function. Having been guardians of public order, they now became guardians of economic and social order as well. They tried to stabilize economic growth and adopted some of the social legislation demanded by the unions, including (Québec dates) OLD AGE PENSIONS (1936), MINIMUM WAGE (1937), unemployment insurance (1940), FAMILY ALLOWANCE (1944), hospital insurance (1960) and health insurance (1970).

Pressure from the trade-union movement played a part, as rapid growth gave the unions increasing influence. The population of workers unionized rose from 10.3% in 1931 to 26.5% in 1951 and 37.7% in 1976. Craftsmen, who had formed the bulk of organized workers at the turn of the century, were joined by skilled and semiskilled workers and, in the 1960s, by teachers and employees in the public sector. During this period the Catholic unions (which secularized themselves in 1960; *see* CONFEDERATION OF NATIONAL TRADE UNIONS) accounted for about 30% of union membership, the international unions for about 40%.

The massive unionization of civil servants radicalized the union movement, especially the CNTU and the Québec Teachers Corp, which promoted a socialist view of society and supported Québec independence. The substance of this socialism, which will have a democratic tone, still remains to be fully defined. The establishment of political action committees outside the Québec UNION CENTRALS led to a municipal political party in Montréal in 1970 and, in 1981, to a socialist movement which aspired to become an official provincial party. In Québec the catalyst for partisan political activity was not the Depression but the QUIET REVOLUTION, followed by the ideological transformation of union centrals during the 1960s.

The volatile ideological dimension of Québec unionism produced more militant conflicts. Québec had proportionately fewer strikes than Ontario in the 1950s, but lost twice as many man-days per 100 workers in 1961-79, largely through public-sector strikes. The existence after 1970 of a "common front" (a combined force of labour bodies) for each negotiation with government led to major clashes. There were some spectacular strikes in the private sector, against *La Presse* (1971), United Aircraft (1974-75) and the Commission de Transport de la Communauté urbaine de Montréal (1974), and the general strike protesting WAGE AND PRICE CONTROLS (1976). These followed in the tradition of the great postwar strikes: the ASBESTOS STRIKE (1949) and those at Louiseville (1952) and MURDOCHVILLE (1957).

The Québec labour movement's postwar history divides into 2 phases. The first was dominated by battles against the DUPLESSIS government's reactionary policies (1944-59) and the birth of a vision of society which was to take shape during the 1960s. The second phase, which began with the Quiet Revolution and continued into the 1980s, was marked by a strengthening of progressive forces. By 1983 social policies were more advanced, labour laws gave better protection to workers, the right to organize and to strike was more secure, the minimum wage was higher, and tax rates were more progressive than elsewhere in N America. But the state may threaten these gains at any moment, given the climate of economic crisis prevailing since 1973.   JACQUES ROUILLARD

Historiography

Each period in the recording of Canadian labour history paralleled specific concerns associated with the practical struggles of the time. In 19th- and early 20th-century Canada, workers were not prominent subjects of scholarly production. Royal commissions provided copious evidence of the conditions of work and of labour's attempts to organize, and a few advocates of the working class offered their evaluations of Canadian workers' emergence as a social and political force. But concern with workers was a pragmatic one with explicit political purposes, and when studies were commissioned, as with R.H. Coats's 1915 examination of the cost of living, they were related directly to the perceived needs of the moment.

Between 1929 and 1945 in Britain and the US the study of labour history was channeled into examinations of political activity, the growth and consolidation of unions, and the gradual winning of collective bargaining rights, im-

proved wages and better conditions. In Canada, individuals associated with an emerging social-democratic milieu had similar concerns and were advocates of public ownership, an active state and the preservation of civil liberties. Leading this moderate socialist contingent was historian Frank UNDERHILL, and associated with him were social scientists, economists and researchers at both McGill and the University of Toronto, including Frank SCOTT, Eugene FORSEY and Stuart Jamieson. Forsey eventually produced *Trade Unions in Canada 1812-1902* (1982), an important overview of the institutional development of Canadian unionism in the 19th century, and Jamieson published *Times of Trouble* (1968) on strike activity, 1900-66.

But in the 1930s and 1940s such figures played a more political role, sustaining the LEAGUE FOR SOCIAL RECONSTRUCTION and helping the Co-operative Commonwealth Federation. Often it seemed as though the academic advocates of SOCIALISM regarded labour as the passive recipient of the social reform they sought to stimulate. Those associated with social-democratic thought eased labour into scholarly discourse and defined the character of working-class studies. They regarded the labour movement as one of the forces upon which they could rely for support, but they had little intrinsic interest in labour as a class. The study of labour thus encompassed concern with unions, with labour's political activity and with appropriate and humane leadership and reforms that only the CCF could offer.

After WWII labour history first began to be written in Canada. Often, especially among professional historians, it was a by-product of other concerns. "George Brown, Sir John Macdonald, and the 'Workingman'" in the *Canadian Historical Review* (1943), by Donald CREIGHTON, indicated how concerns with central political figures might provide a footnote to labour's as-yet untold story. D.C. Masters's *The Winnipeg General Strike* (1950) was purportedly part of a projected exploration of SOCIAL CREDIT in Alberta. J.I. Cooper published "The Social Structure of Montréal in the 1850s" in the CANADIAN HISTORICAL ASSOCIATION's *Annual Report* (1956), which took a preliminary step toward the exploration of workers' everyday lives.

Most studies of Canadian workers were not actually done by historians. Political scientist Bernard Ostry wrote on labour and politics of the 1870s and 1880s. The most innovative work came from economist and economic historian H.C. Pentland (*Labour and Capital in Canada (1650-1860)*, 1981), whose studies challenged conventional wisdom, and literary critic Frank Watt. They argued that labour had posed a fundamental criticism, through physical struggles and journalistic attacks on monopoly and political corruption, of 19th- and early 20th-century Canadian society well before the upheaval at Winnipeg and the appearance of the SOCIAL GOSPEL and the CCF. Such studies probably had less force in the universities than among historically minded associates of the Communist Party, who penned histories of early Canada and Canadian workers.

Within the established circles of professional historians Kenneth McNaught exerted a far greater influence. McNaught was a product of the social-democratic movement of the 1940s, and attained significance not so much for what he wrote — which, in labour history, was rather limited — but because he taught a number of graduate students who pushed labour history into prominence in the 1970s. McNaught's work stressed leadership in the experience of Canadian workers, and he was drawn to the institutional approach of labour-economist Harold Logan. Logan had been active in teaching and writing labour economics since the 1920s, and he produced the first adequate overview of Ca-

nadian trade-union development in *Trade Unions in Canada* (1948). His writing in the 1930s and 1940s emphasized the struggle within the Canadian labour movement between CCF followers and associates of the Communist Party. Logan's arguments against communism, together with the practical confrontations of the period, molded social-democratic intellectuals in specific ways: for example, anti-Marxism (equated with opposition to the Stalinist Communist Party) was forever embedded in their approach to Canadian labour. Their horizons seemed bounded by the study of institutions, social reform and the question of proper leadership of the progressive movement and labour itself. McNaught's *A Prophet in Politics* (1959), which was a biography of J.S. WOODSWORTH, father of Canadian social democracy and a central figure in the history of radicalism, was the exemplary study in this genre.

In 1965 Stanley Mealing published "The Concept of Social Class in the Interpretation of Canadian History" (*Canadian Historical Review*, 1965). He concluded that little historical work in Canada had been directed toward workers' experience and that the main interpretive contours of our history would not be dramatically altered by attention to class. Important studies of the Communist Party, the CCF-NDP, early radicalism and labour's general political orientation soon appeared. By the early 1970s studies of such major working-class developments as the rise of the Congress of Industrial Organizations, the consolidation of the AFL before WWI, western labour radicalism and the Winnipeg General Strike were underway or had appeared in print. They were followed by examinations of the One Big Union, the government response to immigrant radicalism and conditions of life and labour in early 20th-century Montréal.

Leading figures in this proliferation of working-class studies were Irving Abella, David Bercuson, Robert Babcock, Ross McCormack and Donald Avery. Their work, in conjunction with labour studies undertaken by social scientists such as Paul Phillips, Martin Robin, Leo Zakuta, Gad Horowitz and Walter Young, as well as historians Desmond Morton and Gerald Caplan, served to establish labour history as a legitimate realm of professional historical inquiry. Their labour histories were written, perhaps unconsciously, out of the social-democratic concerns of the 1940s: leadership, decisive events, conditions demanding reform, the nature of ideology and the evolution of particular kinds of unions. Labour-history courses were taught for the first time, a committee of the Canadian Historical Assn was created, and a journal, *Labour/Le Travailleur*, was launched in 1976. In 1980 Desmond Morton and Terry Copp published *Working People*, an illustrated history of Canadian workers.

After 1975 a new group of historians emerged, uninfluenced by the social democracy of the 1940s and attracted to the MARXISM of the late 1960s and early 1970s. These historians were first struck with the general importance of theory, and looked to a series of debates within Western Marxism after 1917 for the nature of class structure and the character of subordination of the working class in capitalist societies. Second, many drew inspiration from American and British studies (by E.P. Thompson, Eric Hobsbawm, David Montgomery and M.G.Gutman) that appeared in the 1960s and heralded a break with earlier histories of labour. Finally, the emergence of women's history provided a third and complementary influence, which forced consideration of the process through which labour was reproduced in the family and was socialized into a particular relationship to structures of authority and work.

Generally speaking, those who were fashioning labour history in the early 1980s were united in their commitment to write the SOCIAL

HISTORY of the working class. If labour's institutions, political activities and material conditions of life were of essential importance in this broad social history, so too were hitherto-unexplored aspects of the workers' experience: family life, leisure activities, community associations, and work processes and forms of managerial domination affecting both the evolution of unions and the lives of unorganized workers. In all of this work there is a concern with working-class history as an analysis of the place of class in Canadian society. Class is conceived as a reciprocal, if unequal, relationship between those who sell their labour and those who purchase it. Some studies have concentrated on the structural, largely impersonal, dimensions of class experience (the size of working-class families, the numbers of workers associated with particular sectors of the labour market, the rates of wages and levels of unemployment), whereas other works have concentrated on the cultural activities of workers and the conflicts they have waged at the workplace or in the community.

Some published works by this generation of historians — including Joy Parr's *Labouring Children* (1980), an examination of the labouring experiences of pauper immigrant children; Bryan Palmer's *A Culture in Conflict* (1979), a discussion of skilled labour in Hamilton in the late 19th and early 20th centuries; Gregory Kealey's *Toronto Workers Respond to Industrial Capitalism 1867-1892* (1980), a similar study of Toronto workers; and *"Dreaming of What Might Be"* (1982), an examination of the Knights of Labor in Ontario, 1880-1900, by Kealey and Palmer — attempt detailed explorations of working-class experience. A host of articles and postgraduate theses attest to the treatment of subjects that a previous labour history never envisaged: ritualistic forms of resistance, patterns of craft inheritance among shoemakers, the place of the family economy in Montréal in the 1870s and 1880s, the riotous behaviour of early canallers, the significance of the life cycle among Québec cotton workers, 1910-50, the effects of mechanization and skill-dilution upon metalworkers in the WWI era, the nature of life in coal communities, or the role of literacy, housing, tavern life and the oral tradition among specific groups of workers. This work must be placed beside studies of such vital areas of working-class life as unions and labour politics. It is unclear how significantly the developing work will revise the general contours of labour history or, more importantly, how it will affect larger interpretations of Canadian society. BRYAN D. PALMER

Reading: I. Abella and D. Millar, *The Canadian Worker in the Twentieth Century* (1978); M.S. Cross, ed, *The Workingman in the Nineteenth Century* (1974); Eugene Forsey, *Trade Unions in Canada 1812-1902* (1982); Jean Hamelin, ed, *Les Travailleurs québécois 1851-1896* (1973); F. Harvey, ed, *Le Mouvement ouvrier au Québec* (1980); S. Jamieson, *Times of Trouble* (1968); H.A. Logan, *Trade Unions in Canada* (1948); D. Morton with T. Copp, *Working People* (1980); Bryan D. Palmer, *Working-Class Experience* (1983); H.C. Pentland, *A Study of the Social, Economic and Political Background of the Canadian System of Industrial Relations* (1968); J. Rouillard, *Les Syndicats nationaux au Québec de 1900 à 1930* (1979) and *Histoire de la CSN 1921-81* (1981).

Workman, Joseph, psychiatrist, educator (b near Lisburn, Ire 26 May 1805; d at Toronto 15 Apr 1894). He immigrated to Montréal in 1829 and received his MD from McGill in 1835. For a time he ran a successful hardware business in Toronto, but in 1846 he accepted an invitation to teach at Dr John ROLPH's Toronto medical school, lecturing first on midwifery and later on materia medica. After resigning in 1853, he was appointed medical superintendent of the newly opened Provincial Lunatic Asylum in Toronto, a position he retained until his retirement in 1875. Workman was the author of numerous papers on insanity, its etiology and treatment, and he often appeared as an expert witness at

criminal trials. He was undoubtedly Canada's most distinguished and able mid-19th-century alienist, a fact recognized by his colleagues, to whom he was known affectionately as "the Nestor of Canadian alienists." THOMAS E. BROWN

World Hockey Association, professional HOCKEY league established 1972 to challenge the NATIONAL HOCKEY LEAGUE. Canada was well represented in the new league, with teams in Ottawa, Québec City, Edmonton and Winnipeg. The signing of NHL superstar Bobby HULL by the WINNIPEG JETS gave the league credibility and in its second season the Houston Aeros signed Gordie HOWE to play with his sons Mark and Marty. A Canadian division was formed in the WHA's third season, with teams from Québec, Toronto, Winnipeg, Edmonton and Vancouver. In 1975-76 the Jets became the first Canadian-based team to win the championship (Avco World Trophy); the QUEBEC NORDIQUES won it in 1976-79 and the Jets again in 1977-78 and 1978-79. During the league's last 2 seasons, teams from the Soviet Union, Czechoslovakia, Sweden and Finland played games against WHA teams that counted in the standings. The financially troubled league disbanded in June 1979 and Winnipeg, Québec, Hartford and EDMONTON OILERS were taken into the NHL. The long-term effects of the WHL were expansion of professional hockey into Canadian cities previously ignored by the NHL and a dramatic increase in the salaries by the hockey players as a result of competition. FRANK POLNASZEK

World Soundscape Project A research and educational endeavour founded (1969) by Canadian composer R. Murray SCHAFER at Simon Fraser U. The project was concerned with all aspects of sound environments, with emphasis on raising public awareness of sound, documenting environmental sound and its changing character, and establishing the concept and practice of soundscape design as an alternative to noise pollution. Activities have included extensive field recordings made across Canada and Europe, archival and educational work, and the publication of many documents and works on tape. Most important are Schafer's *The Book of Noise* (1970), *The Music of the Environment* (1973), and *The Tuning of the World* (1977), as well as project documents which include *A Survey of Community Noise By-laws in Canada* (1972), *The Vancouver Soundscape* (1974), the radio series *Soundscapes of Canada* (1974), *Five Village Soundscapes* and *European Sound Diary* (1977), and the *Handbook for Acoustic Ecology* (1978). Although the project has not continued as a group effort, courses in acoustic communication and soundscape studies are taught at SFU. Individual composers continue to develop soundscape themes, such as in the "Soundwalking" series of radio programs by H. Westerkamp, and through tape compositions. BARRY D. TRUAX

World University Games were first held in conjunction with the Congress of the International Student's Federation (CIE) in Warsaw, Poland, in 1924. They were the brainchild of Frenchman Jean Petitjean and attracted some 60 students, mainly from Great Britain, Poland and France. Between 1927 and 1939 the Games were held in various European locations: Rome (1927), Paris (1928), Darmstadt, Germany (1930), Turin, Italy (1933), Budapest (1935), Paris (1937) and Monte Carlo (1939). After 1928 the Games began to attract many Olympic competitors and champions. The 1933 Games in Turin had manifest political overtones — the host country's victory seemingly reflecting the strength of its Fascist government — and pushed the Games to the forefront of the athletic world. By 1937 some 26 nations were represented by over 1500 athletes contending for honours in 12 sports.

The CIE organized postwar Games in Paris

(1947) and Budapest (1949) before the International University Sports Federation (FISU), founded in 1948, took over. The Games have since been held in Luxembourg (1951), Dortmund, West Germany (1953), San Sebastian, Spain (1955), Paris (1957), Turin, Italy (1959), Sofia, Bulgaria (1961), Port Allegre, Brazil (1963), Budapest (1965), Tokyo (1967), Moscow (1973), Sofia (1977), Mexico City (1979), Bucharest (1981) and Edmonton, Alta (1983). Since the 1950s, the Games have attracted world-class competitors such as the Press sisters (USSR), Harry JEROME (Canada), David Hemery (Great Britain), Tommie Smith (US) and Alberto Juantorena (Cuba), and have become second only in prestige and importance to the Olympics. At the Edmonton Games, over 3500 athletes from 74 countries competed in 10 sports, the primary focus being track and field, swimming and basketball. The Russians finished as top performers with 115 medals, and Canada completed its most successful appearance at the Games by winning 9 gold medals, including the victory in basketball over the highly favoured Americans. DAVE BROWN

World War I On 4 Aug 1914 Britain's ultimatum to Germany to withdraw from Belgium expired. The British Empire, including Canada, was at war, allied with Serbia, Russia, and France against the German and Austro-Hungarian empires. Prewar Canada had a regular army of only 3000, but 60 000 militia had trained in 1913; most provinces, including Québec, insisted on military training in their schools, and defence spending had risen sixfold since 1897.

The war united Canadians at first. The Liberal opposition urged PM Sir Robert BORDEN's Conservative government to take sweeping powers under the new WAR MEASURES ACT. Minister of Militia Sam HUGHES summoned 25 000 volunteers to train at a new camp at Valcartier near Québec; some 33 000 appeared. On Oct 3 the first contingent sailed for England. Much of Canada's war effort was launched by volunteers. The Canadian Patriotic Fund collected money to support soldiers' families. A Military Hospitals Commission cared for the sick and wounded. Churches, charities, women's organizations and the Red Cross found ways to "do their bit" for the war effort. In patriotic fervour, Canadians demanded that Germans and Austrians be dismissed from their jobs and INTERNED, and pressured Berlin, Ont, to rename itself Kitchener.

At first the war hurt a troubled economy, increasing unemployment and making it hard for Canada's new, debt-ridden transcontinental railways, the Canadian Northern and the Grand Trunk Pacific, to find credit. By 1915, military spending equalled the entire government expenditure of 1913. Minister of Finance Thomas White opposed raising taxes. Since Britain could not afford to lend to Canada, White turned to the US. Also, despite the belief that Canadians would never lend to their own government, White had to take the risk. In 1915 he asked for $50 million; he got $100 million. In 1917 the government's Victory Loan campaign began raising huge sums from ordinary citizens for the first time. Canada's war effort was financed mainly by borrowing. Between 1913 and 1918 the national debt rose from $463 million to $2.46 billion.

Canada's economic burden would have been unbearable without huge exports of wheat, timber, and munitions. A prewar crop failure had been a warning to prairie farmers of future droughts, but a bumper crop in 1915 and soaring prices banished caution. Since many farm labourers had joined the army, farmers began to complain of a labour shortage. It was hoped that factories shut down by the recession would

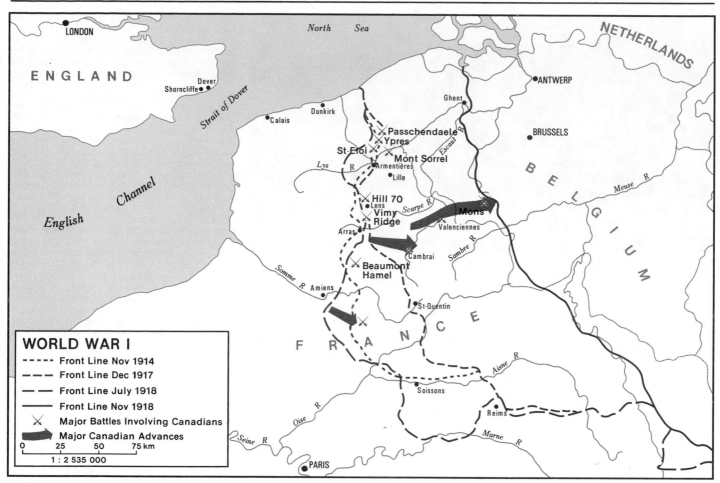

WORLD WAR I

- - - - - Front Line Nov 1914
-- -- -- Front Line Dec 1917
—— —— Front Line July 1918
———— Front Line Nov 1918
✕ Major Battles Involving Canadians
➤ Major Canadian Advances

0   25   50   75 km
1 : 2 535 000

profit from the war. Manufacturers formed a Shell Committee, got contracts to make British artillery ammunition, and created a brand new industry. It was not easy. By summer 1915 the committee had orders worth $170 million but had delivered only $5.5 million in shells. The British government insisted on reorganization. The resulting IMPERIAL MUNITIONS BOARD was a British agency in Canada, though headed by a talented, hard-driving Canadian, Joseph FLA-VELLE. By 1917 Flavelle had made the IMB Canada's biggest business, with 250 000 workers. When the British stopped buying in Canada in 1917, Flavelle negotiated huge new contracts with the Americans, now in the war.

Unemployed workers had flocked to enlist in 1914-15. Recruiting, handled by prewar militia regiments and by civic organizations, cost the government nothing. By the end of 1914 the target for the CANADIAN EXPEDITIONARY FORCE was 50 000; by summer 1915 it was 150 000. During a visit to England that summer, PM Borden was shocked with the magnitude of the struggle. To set even the British an example of earnestness, Borden used his 1916 New Year's message to pledge 500 000 soldiers from a Canadian population of barely 8 million. By then volunteering had virtually dried up. Early contingents had been filled by recent British immigrants; enlistments in 1915 had taken most of the Canadian-born who were willing to go. The total, 330 000, was impressive but insufficient. Recruiting methods became fervid and divisive. Clergy preached Christian duty; women wore badges proclaiming "Knit or Fight"; more and more English Canadians complained that French Canada was not doing its share. This was not surprising: few French Canadians felt deep loyalty to France or Britain. Those few in Borden's government had won election in 1911 by opposing imperialism. Henri BOURASSA, leader and spokesman of Québec's nationalists, ini-

tially approved of the war but soon insisted that French Canada's real enemies were not Germans but "English-Canadian anglicisers, the Ontario intriguers, or Irish priests" who were busy ending French-language education in the English-speaking provinces. In Québec and across Canada, unemployment gave way to high wages and a manpower shortage. There were good economic reasons to stay home.

Canadians in the CEF became part of the British army. As minister of militia, Hughes insisted on choosing the officers and on retaining the Canadian-made Ross rifle. Since the rifle had serious faults and since some of Hughes's choices were incompetent cronies, the Canadian military had serious deficiencies. A recruiting system based on forming hundreds of new battalions meant that most of them arrived in England only to be broken up, leaving a large residue of unhappy senior officers. Hughes believed that Canadians would be natural soldiers; in practice they had many costly lessons to learn. They did so with courage and self-sacrifice. At the second Battle of YPRES, Apr 1915, a raw 1st Canadian Division suffered 6036 casualties, and the Princess Patricia's Canadian Light Infantry a further 678. The troops also shed their defective Ross rifles. At the St Eloi craters in 1916, the 2nd Division suffered a painful setback because its senior commanders failed to locate their men. In June the 3rd Division was shattered at MONT SORREL though the position was recovered by the now battle-hardened 1st Division. The test of battle eliminated inept officers and showed survivors that careful staff work, preparation, and discipline were vital. Canadians were spared the early battles of the Somme in summer 1916, though a separate Newfoundland force, 1st Newfoundland Regiment, was annihilated at Beaumont Hamel on the disastrous first day, July 1. When Canadians entered the battle on Aug 30, their experience helped toward limited

gains, though at high cost. By the end of the battle the Canadian Corps had reached its full strength of 4 divisions.

The embarrassing confusion of Canadian administration in England and Hughes's reluctance to displace his cronies forced Borden's government to establish a separate MINISTRY OF OVERSEAS MILITARY FORCES based in London to control the CEF overseas. Bereft of much power, Hughes resigned in Nov 1916. The Act creating the new ministry established that the CEF was now a Canadian military organization, though its day-to-day relations with the British army did not change immediately. Two ministers, Sir George Perley and then Sir Edward KEMP, gradually reformed overseas administration and expanded effective Canadian control over the CEF.

While most of those forces were with the Canadian Corps or with a separate Canadian cavalry brigade on the Western Front, Canadians could be found almost everywhere in the Allied war effort. Young Canadians had trained (initially at their own expense) to become pilots in the British flying services. In 1917 the ROYAL FLY-ING CORPS opened schools in Canada, and by war's end almost a quarter of the pilots in the Royal Air Force were Canadians. Two of them, Maj William A. BISHOP and Maj Raymond COL-LISHAW, ranked among the top air aces of the war. An independent Canadian air force was authorized in the last months of the war. Canadians also served with the Royal Navy and Canada's own tiny naval service organized a coastal submarine patrol. Thousands of Canadians cut down forests in Scotland and France, and built and operated most of the railways behind the British front. Others ran steamers on the Tigris R, cared for the wounded at Salonika (Thessaloniki), Greece, and fought Bolsheviks at Archangel and Baku (see CANADIAN FORCES IN RUSSIA).

British and French strategists deplored such diversions from the effort on the Western Front.

Canadian troops in France during WWI. Endless shelling created a desolate landscape of mud and death (*courtesy Vancouver City Archives*).

It was there, against the main German forces, that war must be waged. A battle-hardened Canadian Corps was a major instrument in this war of attrition. Its skill and training were tested on Easter weekend, 1917, when all 4 divisions were sent forward to capture a seemingly impregnable VIMY RIDGE. Weeks of rehearsals, stockpiling, and bombardment paid off. In 5 days the ridge was taken. The able British commander of the corps, Lt-Gen Sir Julian BYNG, was promoted; his successor was a Canadian, Lt-Gen Sir Arthur CURRIE, who followed Byng's methods and improved on them. Instead of attacking Lens in the summer of 1917, Currie captured the nearby HILL 70 and used artillery to destroy wave after wave of German counterattacks. As an increasingly independent subordinate, Currie questioned orders, but he could not refuse them. When ordered to finish the disastrous British offensive at PASSCHENDAELE in Oct 1917, Currie warned that it would cost 16 000 of his 20 000 men. Though he insisted on time to prepare, the Canadian victory on the dismal, waterlogged battlefield left a toll of 15 654 dead and wounded.

A year before, even the patriotic leagues had confessed the failure of voluntary recruiting. Business leaders, Protestants, and English-speaking Catholics such as Bishop Michael Fallon grew critical of French Canada. Faced with a growing demand for conscription, the Borden government compromised in Aug 1916 with a program of national registration. A prominent Montréal manufacturer, Arthur Mignault, was put in charge of Québec recruiting and, for the first time, public funds were provided. A final attempt to raise a French Canadian battalion, the 14th out of 258 battalions in the CEF, failed in 1917.

Until 1917 Borden had no more news of the war or Allied strategy than he read in newspapers. He was concerned about British war leadership but he devoted 1916 to improving Canadian military administration and munition production. In Dec 1916 David Lloyd George became head of a new British coalition government pledged wholeheartedly to winning the war. An expatriate Canadian, Max AITKEN, helped engineer the change. Faced by suspicious officials and a failing war effort, Lloyd George summoned premiers of the Dominions to London. They would see for themselves that the Allies needed more men. On Mar 2, when Borden and his fellow premiers met, Russia was collapsing, the French army was close to mutiny, and German submarines had almost cut off supplies to Britain.

Borden was a leader in establishing a voice for the Dominions in policymaking and in gaining a more independent status for them in the postwar world. Visits to Canadian camps and hospitals also persuaded him that the CEF needed more men. The triumph of Vimy Ridge during his visit gave all Canadians pride but it cost 10 602 casualties, 3598 of them fatal. Borden cancelled plans to expand the corps but he returned to Canada committed to conscription. On 18 May 1917 he told Canadians of his government's new policy. The 1914 promise of an all-volunteer contingent had been superseded by events.

Many in English-speaking Canada — farmers, trade union leaders, pacifists — opposed conscription, but they had few outlets for their views. French Canada's opposition was almost unanimous under Henri Bourassa, who argued that Canada had done enough, that Canada's interests were not served by the European conflict, and that men were more needed to grow food and make munitions. Borden felt such arguments were cold and materialistic. Canada owed its support to its young soldiers. The Allied struggle against Prussian militarism was a

Screened Road "A" (unfinished), oil on canvas, by A.Y. Jackson (*courtesy Canadian War Museum/NMM/NMC/ 8188*).

crusade for freedom. There was no bridging the rival points of view. To win conscription, Borden offered Laurier a coalition. The Liberal leader refused, sure that his party could now defeat the Conservatives. He also feared that if he joined Borden, Bourassa's nationalism would sweep Québec. Laurier misjudged his support. Many English-speaking Liberals agreed that the war was a crusade. A mood of reform and sacrifice had led many provinces to grant votes to women and to prohibit the sale or use of liquor (*see* TEMPERANCE). Although they disliked the Conservatives, many reform Liberals like Ontario's Newton Rowell believed that Borden was in earnest about the war and Laurier was not. Borden also gave himself 2 political weapons: in Aug 1917 Parliament gave the franchise to all soldiers, including those overseas; it also gave votes to soldiers' wives, mothers, and sisters and took it away from Canadians of enemy origin who had become citizens since 1902. This added many votes for conscription and removed many certain Liberal voters from the lists. On Oct 6 Parliament was dissolved. Five days later, Borden announced a coalition Union government pledged to conscription, an end to political patronage, and full WOMEN'S SUFFRAGE.

Eight of Canada's 9 provinces endorsed the new government, but Laurier could dominate Québec, and many Liberals across Canada would not forget their allegiance. Borden and his ministers had to promise many exemptions to make conscription acceptable. On Dec 17, Unionists had won 153 seats to Laurier's 82, but without the soldiers' vote, only 100 000 votes separated the parties. Conscription was not applied until 1 Jan 1918. The MILITARY SERVICE ACT had so many opportunities for exemption and appeal, that of 404 395 called 380 510 appealed. The manpower problem continued.

In Mar 1918 disaster struck the Allies. German armies, moved from the Eastern to the Western Front after Russia's collapse in 1917, smashed through British lines. Fifth British Army was destroyed. In Canada, anticonscription riots in Québec on the Easter weekend left 4 dead. Borden's new government cancelled all exemptions. Many who had voted Unionist in the belief that their sons would be exempted felt betrayed.

The war had entered a bitter final phase. On 6

Dec 1917 the HALIFAX EXPLOSION killed over 1600, and it was followed by the worst snowstorm in years. Across Canada, Sir Thomas White's (minister of finance) heavy borrowing finally led to runaway inflation. Workers joined unions and struck for wages. Food and fuel controllers now preached conservation, sought increased production and sent agents to prosecute hoarders. Public pressure to "conscript wealth" forced a reluctant White in Apr 1917 to impose a Business Profits Tax and a War Income Tax. An "anti-loafing" law threatened jail for any man not gainfully employed. Federal police forces were ordered to hunt for sedition. Socialist parties and radical unions were banned. So were newspapers published in the "enemy" languages. Canadians learned to live with unprecedented government controls and involvement in their daily lives. Food and fuel shortages led to "Meatless Fridays" and "Fuelless Sundays."

In other warring countries, exhaustion and despair went far deeper. Defeat now faced the western Allies, but the Canadian Corps escaped the succession of German offensives. Sir Arthur Currie insisted that it be kept together. A 5th Canadian division, held in England since 1916, was finally broken up to provide reinforcements. When Borden went to England in spring 1918, the Canadian Corps was the strongest formation of its size on the British front. Borden was furious at the mismanagement of the war. He condemned the waste of Passchendaele but he agreed that the British army would have to be husbanded and rebuilt for a victory that might have to wait until 1920. He argued that the

Russian front must be revived and was obliged to offer Canadian troops to help Britain in seeking the overthrow of the new Bolshevik government.

To help restore the Allied line, Canadians and Australians attacked near Amiens on 8 Aug 1918. Shock tactics, using airplanes, tanks, and infantry, shattered the German line. When resistance thickened, Currie was among those who advised switching to new lines of attack. In Sept and early Oct the Canadians attacked again and again, suffering heavy casualties but making advances thought unimaginable. The Germans fought with skill and courage all the way to Mons, the little Belgian town where fighting ended for the Canadians at 11 AM (Greenwich time), 11 Nov 1918. More officially, the war ended with the TREATY OF VERSAILLES, signed 28 June 1919.

The CEF lost 60 661 dead. Many more returned from the war mutilated in mind or body. In autumn 1918 almost as many Canadians died from the effects of a worldwide influenza epidemic. Both tolls fell heavily on the young and energetic. The survivors found that almost every facet of Canadian life, from the length of skirts to the value of money, had been transformed by the war years. Governments had assumed responsibilities they would never abandon. The income tax would survive the war. So would government departments later to become the Department of VETERANS AFFAIRS and the Department of Pensions and National Health.

Overseas, Canada's soldiers had struggled to achieve, and had won, a considerable degree of

autonomy from British control. Prewar dreams of imperial federation perished with Borden's own experience in 1917 and 1918. Canada's direct reward for her sacrifices was a modest presence at the Versailles conference and a seat in the new LEAGUE OF NATIONS. However, the deep national divisions between French and English created by the war and especially by the CONSCRIPTION crisis of 1917 made postwar Canada fearful of international responsibilities. Canadians had done great things in the war but they had not done them together.   DESMOND MORTON

Reading: E. Armstrong, *The Crisis of Quebec, 1914-1918* (1974 reprint); W.R. Bird, *Ghosts Have Warm Hands* (1968); M. Bliss, *A Canadian Millionaire* (1978); R.C. Brown, *Robert Laird Borden,* vol II (1980); D.J. Goodspeed, *The Road Past Vimy* (1967); J.L. Granatstein and J.M. Hitsman, *Broken Promises* (1977); Desmond Morton, *A Peculiar Kind of Politics* (1982), and *Canada and War* (1981); G.W.L. Nicholson, *Canadian Expeditionary Force 1914-1919* (1964); J.A. Swettenham, *To Seize the Victory* (1965); J. Thompson, *The Harvests of War* (1978); B. Wilson, *Ontario and the First World War, 1914-1918* (1977); S.F. Wise, *Canadian Airmen and the First World War,* vol I (1980).

World War II Memories of WWI — the tragic loss of life, the heavy burden of debt, and the strain on the country's unity imposed by CONSCRIPTION — made Canadians, including politicians of all parties, loath to contemplate another such experience. The general mood was isolationist. Initially PM Mackenzie KING warmly supported British PM Neville Chamberlain's policy of appeasing German leader Adolf Hitler, and when Chamberlain postponed war

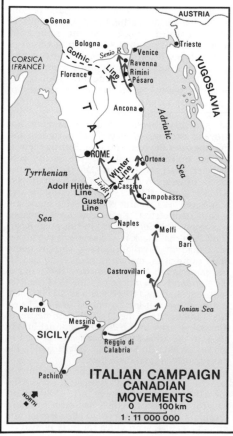

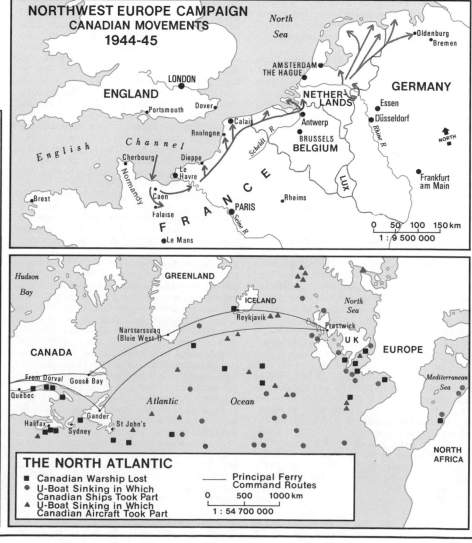

by sacrificing Czechoslovakia in the Munich Crisis of Sept 1938 King thanked him publicly, and Canadians in general certainly agreed. Nevertheless, the shock of this crisis likely turned opinion towards accepting war to check the advance of Nazism. Only gradually did the progress of events, notably Nazi aggression, alter this mood to the point where Canada was prepared to face taking part in another great war. King himself had no doubt that in a great war involving the UK, Canada could not stand aside.

When the German attack on Poland on 1 Sept 1939 finally led Britain and France to declare war on Germany, King summoned Parliament to "decide," as he had pledged. Declaration of war was postponed for a week, during which Canada was formally neutral. The government announced that approval of the address in reply to the speech from the throne, which stated the government's decision to support Britain and France, would constitute approval of a declaration of war. On Sept 9 the address was approved without a recorded vote, and war was declared the following day. The basis for parliamentary unity had in fact been laid in March, when both major parties accepted a program rejecting conscription for overseas service. King clearly envisaged a limited effort, and was lukewarm towards an expeditionary force. Nevertheless, there was enough pressure to lead the Cabinet to dispatch one army division to Europe. The Allies' defeat in France and Belgium in the early summer of 1940, and the collapse of France, frightened Canadians. The idea of limited and economical war went by the board, and thereafter the only effective limitation was the pledge against overseas conscription. The armed forces were rapidly enlarged, conscription was introduced June 1940 for home defence (*See* NATIONAL RESOURCES MOBILIZATION ACT), and expenditure grew enormously.

The army expanded until by late 1942 there were 5 divisions overseas, 2 of them armoured. In Apr of that year FIRST CANADIAN ARMY was formed in England under Lt-Gen A.G.L. MCNAUGHTON. In contrast with WWI, it was a long time before the army saw large-scale action. Until summer 1943 the force in England was engaged only in the unsuccessful raid on DIEPPE (19 Aug 1942), whereas 2 battalions sent from Canada had taken part in the hopeless defence of HONG KONG against the Japanese in Dec 1941. Public opinion in Canada became disturbed by the inaction, and disagreement developed between the government and McNaughton, who wished to reserve the army for a final, decisive campaign. The government arranged with Britain for 1st Canadian Infantry Division to join the attack on Sicily, July 1943, and subsequently insisted upon building its Mediterranean force up to a 2-division corps. This produced a serious clash with McNaughton, just when the British War Office, which considered him unsuited for field command, was influencing the Canadian government against him. At the end of 1943 he was replaced by Lt-Gen H.D.G. CRERAR.

The 1st Division was heavily engaged in the Sicilian campaign as part of the British Eighth Army, and subsequently took part in the Dec 1943 advance up the mainland of Italy, seeing particularly severe fighting in and around Ortona. In the spring of 1944 Canadians under Lt-Gen E.L.M. BURNS played a leading role in breaking the Hitler Line barring the Liri Valley. At the end of Aug the corps broke the Gothic Line in the Adriatic sector and pushed on through the German positions covering Rimini, which fell in Sept. These battles cost Canada its heaviest casualties of the Italian campaign. The final phase of Canadian involvement in Italy found 1st Canadian Corps, now commanded by Lt-Gen Charles Foulkes, fighting its way across the Lombard Plain, hindered by mud and swift-flowing rivers. The corps' advance ended at the

Canadian soldiers in action in *The Hitler Line*, by Charles Comfort (*courtesy Canadian War Museum/NMM/NMC/ 12296*).

Senio R in the first days of 1945. The Canadian government, so eager to get its troops into action in Italy, had soon begun to ask for their return to join the main Canadian force in NW Europe. Allied policy finally made this possible early in 1945, and the 1st Corps came under the First Canadian Army's command in mid-Mar, to the general satisfaction of the men from Italy. All told, 92 757 Canadian soldiers of all ranks had served in Italy, and 5764 had lost their lives.

In the final great campaign in NW Europe, beginning with the NORMANDY INVASION (code name Operation *Overlord*) on 6 June 1944, First Canadian Army under Crerar played an important and costly part. Since the 1st Corps had been sent to Italy, its place had to be filled by British and Allied formations. The army's central kernel, however, was the 2nd Canadian Corps, under Lt-Gen G.G. SIMONDS, who had commanded the 1st Division in Sicily; it was normally composed of the 2nd and 3rd Canadian Infantry Divisions and the 4th Canadian Armoured Division. Throughout, the army was part of the 21st British Army Group commanded by Gen Sir (later Field-Marshal Lord) Bernard Law Montgomery. In the landing phase only the 3rd Division and the 2nd Canadian Armoured Brigade were engaged, fighting under the Second British Army. These formations landed on D Day, experiencing bitter fighting then and subsequently. On July 11 Simonds's corps took over a section of the line near Caen, but Crerar's army did not become operational (on the extreme left of the Allied line, where it remained for the rest of the campaign) until July 23. On the 31st its front was extended to include the Caen sector.

The Canadian formations played a leading part in the breakout from the Normandy bridgehead in Aug, fighting against fierce opposition to reach Falaise and subsequently to close the gap south of it through which the enemy was retiring to avoid being trapped between the British and Canadians coming from the north and the Americans approaching from the south. Falaise was taken on Aug 16 and on the 19th the Allies finally made contact across the gap. The next phase was one of pursuit towards the German frontier. First Canadian Army, with the 1st British Corps under command, cleared the coastal fortresses, taking in turn Le Havre, Boulogne, and Calais. Early in Sept the British took Antwerp, but the enemy still held the banks of the Schelde R between this much-needed port and the sea, and the Canadians fought a bitter battle to open the river through Oct and the first week of Nov.

The first major Canadian operation of 1945, the BATTLE OF THE RHINELAND, was to clear the area between the Maas and the Rhine rivers; it began Feb 8 and ended only Mar 10 when the Germans, pushed back by the Canadians and the converging thrust of the Ninth US Army, withdrew across the Rhine. The final operations in the west began with the Rhine crossing in the British area on Mar 23; thereafter, First Cana-

dian Army, still on the left of the line, liberated E and N Netherlands and advanced across the N German plain. When the Germans surrendered on Field-Marshal Montgomery's front on May 5, the 2nd Canadian Corps had taken Oldenburg, and the 1st Canadian Corps was standing fast on the Grebbe R line while, by arrangement with the Germans, food was sent into the starving W Netherlands. The entire campaign had cost the Canadian Army 11 336 fatal casualties. Some 237 000 men and women of the army had served in NW Europe.

The war effort of the Royal Canadian Air Force was deeply affected by its management of the BRITISH COMMONWEALTH AIR TRAINING PLAN. Great numbers of Canadians served in units of Britain's Royal Air Force, and the growth of a national Canadian air organization overseas was delayed. Nevertheless, by the German surrender 48 RCAF squadrons were overseas, virtually completely manned by Canadian officers and men. A landmark was the formation of No 6 (RCAF) Bomber Group of the RAF Bomber Command on 1 Jan 1943. It grew ultimately to 14 squadrons. It was commanded successively by Air Vice-Marshals G.E. Brookes and C.M. McEwen. Bomber Command's task was the night bombing of Germany, a desperately perilous job calling for sustained fortitude. Almost 10 000 Canadians lost their lives in this command. Canadian airmen served in every theatre, from bases in the UK, N Africa, Italy, NW Europe and SE Asia. Squadrons in N America worked in antisubmarine operations off the Atlantic coast, and co-operated with US air forces against the Japanese in the Aleutian Is. At one time or another 7 RCAF squadrons served in the RAF's Coastal Command over the Atlantic. RCAF aircraft destroyed or had a part in destroying 23 enemy submarines. In the NW Europe campaign of 1944-45, the RCAF deployed 17 squadrons, 15 of them in No 83 Group of the RAF's Second Tactical Air Force. During the war 232 632 men and 17 030 women served in the RCAF, and 17 101 lost their lives.

The Royal Canadian Navy was tiny in 1939, possessing 6 destroyers and 1819 regular personnel. Its expansion during the war was remarkable: it enlisted 99 688 men and some 6500 women, and it manned 471 fighting vessels of various types. Its primary task was convoy, protecting the troop and supply ships across the Atlantic. It carried an increasing proportion of this burden, fighting grim battles sometimes of several days' duration with U-BOAT "wolfpacks." Its vast expansion produced some growing pains; in 1943 measures had to be taken to improve its escort vessels' technical equipment and in some cases the crew training. During the war it sank or shared in sinking 29 enemy submarines. After the Atlantic Convoy Conference in Washington in Mar 1943 the Canadian NW Atlantic Command was set up, covering the area N of New York City and W of the 47th meridian; a Canadian officer, Rear-Adm L.W. MURRAY, was responsible for convoys in this area. Apart from their main task in the BATTLE OF THE ATLANTIC, Canadian naval units took part in many other campaigns, including supporting the Allied landings in N Africa in Nov 1942; and to the Normandy operations of June 1944 the RCN contributed some 110 vessels and 10 000 men. During the war it lost by enemy action 24 vessels, ranging from the "Tribal" class destroyer *Athabaskan*, sunk in the English Channel in Apr 1944, to the armed yacht *Raccoon*, torpedoed in the St Lawrence in Sept 1942. In personnel, the navy had 2024 fatal casualties.

Canada's industrial contribution to victory was considerable, though it began slowly. After the Allied reverses in Europe in 1940 British orders for equipment, which had been a trickle, became a flood. In Apr 1940 the Dept of MUNITIONS AND SUPPLY, provided for in 1939, was established with C.D. HOWE as minister. In Aug 1940 an amended Act gave the minister almost dictatorial powers, and under it the industrial effort expanded vastly. Various CROWN CORPORATIONS were instituted for special tasks. New factories were built, and old ones adapted for war purposes. Whereas in WWI Canadian production had largely been limited to shells (no weapons were made except Ross rifles), now a great variety of guns and small arms was produced. Many ships, notably escort vessels and cargo carriers, were built; there was large production of aircraft, including Lancaster bombers; and the greatest triumph of the program was in the field of military vehicles, of which 815 729 were made. Tanks were produced, chiefly of components imported from the US. More than half the material produced went to Britain. Britain could not possibly pay for all of it; so Canada, in the interest of helping to win the war, and keeping her factories working, financed a high proportion. At the beginning of 1942 a BILLION-DOLLAR GIFT was devoted to this purpose. The next year a program of MUTUAL AID to serve Allied nations generally, but still in practice mainly directed to the UK, was introduced. During the war Canadian financial assistance to Britain amounted to $3 043 000 000.

Canada had a limited role in the development of atomic energy, a fateful business that was revealed when atomic bombs were dropped on Japan in Aug 1945. Canada had an available source of uranium in a mine at Great Bear Lk, which led to Mackenzie King's being taken into the greater Allies' confidence in the matter in 1942. That summer the Canadian government acquired control of the mine. A team of scientists that had been working on the project in England were moved to Canada. Tension developed between Britain and the US, but at the Québec Conference of Sept 1943 an Anglo-American agreement was made that incidentally gave Canada a small share in control. A Canadian policy committee decided in 1944 to construct an atomic reactor at Chalk River, Ont. The first reactor there did not "go critical" until after the Japanese surrender. Canada had no part in producing the bombs used against Japan,

Marshalling of the "Hallies," oil on canvas, by Paul A. Goranson, showing Halifax bombers of No 419 (Moose) Squadron preparing for a raid, at their base in County Durham, Eng, in the spring of 1943 *(courtesy Canadian War Museum/NMM/NMC/11402).*

unless some Canadian uranium was used in them, which seems impossible to determine.

Canada had no effective part in the higher direction of the war. This would have been extremely difficult to obtain, and King never exerted himself strongly to obtain it. It is possible that he anticipated that doing so would have an adverse effect upon his personal relations with British PM Winston Churchill and American Pres Franklin D. Roosevelt which he considered very important to him politically. The western Allies' strategy was decided by the Combined Chiefs of Staff, a purely Anglo-American committee. Its most important decisions were made in periodical conferences with political leaders, 2 of which were held at Québec. Even to these King was a party only as host. Although Canadian forces were employed in accordance with the Combined Chiefs' decisions, it is a curious fact that Canada was never officially informed of the institution of the committee at the end of 1941. Even formal recognition of Canadian sovereignty was minimal; although the directives of the Allied commanders for the war against Japan were issued in the names of the US, Britain, Australia and New Zealand, the directive to Gen Eisenhower, supreme commander in NW Europe, under whom large Canadian forces served, made no mention of Canada.

Canadian relations with the US became notably closer during the war. From the moment King resumed office in 1935 he had cultivated his connection with Roosevelt. During the first months of the war there was little contact, but the fears aroused by early German victories immediately produced a rapprochement. On 18 Aug 1940 King and Roosevelt, meeting at Ogdensburg, NY, announced an agreement (not a formal treaty) to set up a PERMANENT JOINT BOARD ON DEFENCE, which met frequently thereafter to discuss mutual defence problems. In 1941 Canada's balance of payments with the US became serious, largely because of the difficulty of financing imports from the US resulting from Canada's industrial production for Britain. It was solved by the Hyde Park Declaration on Apr 20. Nevertheless, King sometimes worried over what he saw as a danger of the US absorbing Canada. A reaction to American activity in the Canadian North (eg, the building of the ALASKA HIGHWAY in 1942) was the appointment in 1943 of a Special Commissioner for Defence Projects

in the Northwest, to reinforce Canadian control in the region.

The worst political problems that arose in Canada during the war originated in the Conscription question, and King had more difficulties in his own Liberal Party than with the opposition. The election of 26 Mar 1940, before the war reached a critical stage, indicated that the country was happy with a limited war effort and gave King a solid majority. French Canada's lack of enthusiasm for the war and its particular opposition to conscription were as evident as in WWI (voluntary enlistments in Québec amounted to only about 4% of the population, whereas elsewhere the figure was roughly 10%). By 1942 agitation for overseas conscription in the English-speaking parts of the country led King to hold a plebiscite on releasing the government from its pledge. The result was a heavy vote for release in every province but Québec. Nevertheless, there was still little active enthusiasm for conscription in English Canada; when Arthur MEIGHEN returned to the Conservative leadership and advocated overseas conscription he failed to be elected even in a Toronto constituency. But the atmosphere changed after casualties mounted.

After the Normandy campaign in 1944 a shortage of infantry reinforcements arose and Minister of National Defence Col J.L. RALSTON told Cabinet that the time for overseas conscription had come. King, who had apparently convinced himself that there was a conspiracy in the ministry to unseat him and substitute Raiston, dismissed Ralston and replaced him with McNaughton. The latter failed to prevail on any large number of home-defence conscripts to volunteer for overseas service, and King, finding himself faced with resignations of conscriptionist ministers which would have ruined his government, agreed to send a large group of the conscripts overseas. Québec reluctantly accepted the situation, preferring King's to any Conservative administration, and he was safe again until the end of the war.

Canada had little share in making the peace. The great powers, which had kept the direction of the war in their own hands, did the same now. The so-called peace conference held in Paris in the summer of 1946 merely gave the lesser Allies, including Canada, an opportunity of commenting upon arrangements already made. Canada signed treaties only with Italy, Hungary, Romania and Finland. With Germany divided and the eastern part of the country dominated by the USSR, there was never a German treaty. In 1951 Canada, like other Western powers, ended the state of war with Germany by royal proclamation. That year a treaty of peace with Japan, drafted by the US, was signed by most Allied states, including Canada (but not including the communist powers).

The financial cost of the Canadian war effort was astronomical. Expenditure for the fiscal year 1939-40 was a modest $118 291 000. The next year it rose to $752 045 000; in the peak year, 1943-44, it was $4 587 023 000. The total through the fiscal year 1949-50, for the 11 years beginning 1939-40, was $21 786 077 519.12. Other costs due to the war have continued to accumulate. During the war, 1 086 343 Canadian men and women performed full-time duty in the 3 services. The cost in blood was smaller than in WWI, but still tragic: 42 042 lost their lives.

The significance of WWII in Canadian history was great, but probably rather less than that of WWI. National unity between French and English was damaged, though happily not so seriously as in WWI. The economy was strengthened and its manufacturing capacity much diversified. National pride and national confidence were enhanced. The status as an independent country which had been only shakily established in 1919 was beyond doubt after

1945. Canada was a power in her own right, if a modest one. On the other hand, it had been made painfully clear that "status" did not necessarily imply influence. A MIDDLE POWER had to limit its aspirations. Real authority in the world remained with the big battalions, the big populations, and the big money. C.P. STACEY

Reading: J. A. Boutilier, ed, *The RCN in Retrospect 1910-1968* (1982); D.J. Goodspeed, ed, *The Armed Forces of Canada, 1867-1967* (1967); J.L. Granatstein, *Canada's War* (1975); J.W. Pickersgill and D.F. Forster, *The Mackenzie King Record* (1960-70); J. Schull, *The Far Distant Ships* (1950); C.P. Stacey *Arms, Men and Governments* (1970)

Worthington, Edward Dagge, physician (b at Ballinakill, Ire 1 Dec 1820; d at Sherbrooke, Qué 25 Feb 1895). In 1847 Worthington pioneered the use of general anesthesia in Canada. Using an inhalation apparatus he built himself, he performed major operations and assisted at births while his patients were under the influence of first ether and later chloroform. He practised for over 50 years in Sherbrooke, was a military surgeon, a governor of the College of Physicians and Surgeons of Lower Canada, and helped found the Canadian Medical Assn in 1867. He also contributed many articles to contemporary medical journals. In addition to his MD from St Andrews (Scot), Worthington was awarded honorary degrees from Bishop's and McGill. J.T.H. CONNOR

Wren (Troglodytidae), family of small, mainly brown, insectivorous songbirds, characterized by chunky bodies, tails that are often erect, and forceful rather than musical songs. The family, comprising 60 species, apparently originated in the American tropics and spread N to Canada. The northernmost species, winter wren (*Troglodytes troglodytes*), extends into Eurasia. Of the 8 species in Canada, 4 have limited ranges: Bewick's wren (*Thryomanes bewickii*), southwestern BC; canyon wren (*Catherpes mexicanus*), Okanagan Valley; rock wren (*Salpinctes obsoletus*), southern BC to southern Sask and rarely Man; Carolina wren (*Thryothorus ludovicianus*), southern Ont. Winter wrens inhabit boreal and transitional conifer forests across Canada. House wrens (*Troglodytes aedon*), native to more southern, broad-leaved woodland and scrub habitats, penetrate only a short distance N of the US border, except near the Rockies, where they reach 58° N at Ft Nelson, BC. The marsh wren (*Cistothorus palustris*) is found in cattail marshes transcontinentally, reaching its northern limit at Lk Athabasca. Sedge wrens (*C. platensis*) occupy wet sedge meadows. They occur only very locally in eastern N America. In Canada, they are common only in Man but occur locally in Alta. All are migratory, except in southern, coastal BC. All species build enclosed nests. Woodland wrens use tree holes (or nest boxes) and dense brush piles; winter wrens especially favour crannies among upturned roots of fallen trees. Marsh and sedge wrens construct spherical nests of grasses in low, wetland vegetation, often over water. Rock and canyon wrens use cliff crannies and rock piles. Initially, males build several nests, only one of which is used. This occurs especially with marsh and sedge wrens. Clutches average 5-6 eggs (range 4-8). The winter wren's song is one of the longest (5-6 sec) and highest-pitched among Canadian birds. Songs of other species are much shorter and of lower pitch. A.J. ERSKINE

Wrestling is so natural to man and so ancient that its precise origins are impossible to trace. Prehistoric man wrestled first for survival and eventually for sport; in fact, drawings on cave walls portray a form of freestyle wrestling. Wall paintings in Egyptian tombs from about 3400 BC depict matches that show an amazing similarity in moves to those practised today. Homer's *Iliad* describes a wrestling match between Odysseus and Aïas at burial festivities during the Trojan War (*c* 1200 BC), and records show wrestling as one of the original Olympic sports.

In early times there seem to have been as many styles or forms of wrestling as there were villages or towns. Modern competition has brought with it standardized rules and form. Although many folk styles are still practised, there now exist 3 official world-championship styles recognized by the world governing body, FILA (Fédération International de Lutte Amateur): Greco-Roman, with holds above the waist only; freestyle, which allows the wrestlers to use any part of their body in executing their techniques; and Sambo, which incorporates many moves from the martial arts. Wrestling is a sport of strength, speed and the scientific application of both. Thus, there are no points for defence but only for attack — and then only if some degree of command is gained over the opponent. The points scored vary from one to 4 according to the degree to which command over the opponent is established. A wrestling match consists of two 3-minute rounds with a one-minute rest period in between. The match is terminated before the 6-minute term in the event of a fall, a 12-point difference in score, a disqualification or a default.

The most commonly practised style in Canada is freestyle. Since freestyle rules are used in all university and high-school competitions, it is not surprising that Canadians have generally distinguished themselves in this form at the international level. Canadian medallists in OLYMPIC GAMES competition include Jim Trifunov with a bronze and D. Stockton with a silver in 1928; D. McDonald (silver, 1932); and Joe Schleimer (bronze, 1936). World championship medallists for Canada are G. Bertie (bronze, 1973) and C. Davis (silver, 1982). Canadians have excelled at COMMONWEALTH GAMES competitions, notably in 1930 when they won all 7 gold medals. Earl McCready, who in 1930 won every amateur wrestling championship in Canada, the US and British Commonwealth, and Trifunov, a 10-time Canadian champion, have been elected to Canada's Sports Hall of Fame.

Since the first Canadian amateur wrestling championships were held at Toronto's Argonaut Rowing Club in 1901, the sport has grown considerably in Canada. In 1969 the Canadian Amateur Wrestling Assn was formed and amateur wrestling was touted as the fastest-growing sport in the country. Canadian wrestlers now regularly place high in this very competitive sport and Canada has achieved an excellent reputation for the quality of its wrestling officials and administrators. The fact that Canada has hosted the world wrestling championships twice since the inception of the CAWA is a further testament to the high regard in which Canada is held in this sport.

The sport of wrestling is now generally called amateur wrestling to distinguish it from professional wrestling, which is more a spectacle than a sport. WILLIAM F. DOWBIGGIN

Wright, Alexander Whyte, journalist, labour leader, politician (b at Elmira, Ont 17 Dec 1845; d *c*1919). After some business attempts in southwestern Ontario, he became a journalist and newspaper editor in the 1870s. Although a Conservative and prominent advocate of the NATIONAL POLICY, he endorsed currency and labour reform. He believed in the primacy of workers, farmers and productive manufacturers, and in the 1880s became a prominent KNIGHTS OF LABOR leader, first in Toronto and then in the US, becoming secretary of the order and editor of the *Journal of the Knights of Labor,* 1889-93. Returning to Ontario after the order's virtual collapse in 1893, he served as a royal commissioner to investigate sweatshop labour for the Tory federal government (1895). He edited a Toronto Tory labour paper 1909-14 and later was made vice-chairman of the Ontario Workmen's Compensation Board. A talented writer and orator, Wright was both charlatan and reformer and undoubtedly the best Canadian example of a mediator between the working class and the traditional political party. GREGORY S. KEALEY

Wright, Cecil Augustus, "Caesar," educator (b at London, Ont 2 July 1904; d at Toronto 24 Apr 1967). Called Canada's most influential law teacher and the architect of LEGAL EDUCATION in Ontario, Wright taught at Osgoode Hall Law School from 1927, becoming dean in 1948. In 1949, when the Law Society of Upper Canada rejected changes in legal education for which he had been campaigning for years, he and most of the teaching staff at Osgoode Hall resigned. Wright, Bora LASKIN and John Willis then converted the undergraduate law department at U of T into Ontario's first professional university law school, and Wright served as its dean 1949-67. He wrote many articles, edited an important book on tort law, the *Canadian Bar Review* and several law reports, arbitrated labour disputes, provided legal advice to many lawyers, and strove to increase awareness of American legal thought. C. IAN KYER

Wright, Joseph, Sr, oarsman (b at Toronto, Canada W 13 Jan 1864; d there 18 Oct 1950). In 1950 Wright was named Canada's outstanding oarsman of the half-century. In 1885 he stroked a Toronto Argonaut crew to victory at the US Nationals. Twenty years later he led the Argonauts to victory at the Royal Canadian Henley Regatta. In all, he won 137 national titles. One of the most famous rowing coaches in the world, he looked after U of Penn crews 1916-26, and coached his son Joe Jr to victory at the prestigious Diamond Sculls in 1928. Wright was successful at many other sports. He won the Canadian amateur heavyweight wrestling championship at 35, and at 44 played football on the senior Argonaut team. J. THOMAS WEST

Wright, Philemen, lumberman (b at Woburn, Mass 3 Sept 1760; d at Hull, Qué 2 June 1839). The founder of HULL and the man who initiated the Ottawa Valley TIMBER TRADE, Wright came to Canada in 1800 as the leader of a small group from Massachusetts who settled at the present site of Hull. He intended to develop a community of independent farmers, but lack of income

The long-billed marsh wren (*Cistothorus palustris*) is found as far north as Lk Athabasca (*artwork by Claire Tremblay*).

forced him into the timber trade in 1806 in order to provide cash for the settlement and a winter occupation. That year he floated the first raft of square timber from Ottawa to Québec. The growth of the trade ensured Wright continued predominance in the social, economic and political life of Hull. CHRISTOPHER G. CURTIS

Wright, Robert Ramsay, zoologist, educator (b at Alloa, Scot 23 Sept 1852; d at Droitwich Spa, Eng 6 Sept 1933). Educated at Edinburgh U (MA 1871, BSc 1873), Ramsay Wright gave up a position on the CHALLENGER EXPEDITION to become professor of natural history (later biology) at U of T in 1874 and remained there for 38 years. He exerted a tremendous personal influence on the teaching of BIOLOGY in Canada and on a generation of students. He emphasized instruction in the laboratory and developed a large teaching museum in the new Biological Building (1889); his own research ranged from PARASITOLOGY to catfish anatomy. Wright was also a leading figure in the re-establishment of the Faculty of Medicine at U of T in 1887, where his former pupils A. B. MACALLUM and J. P. MCMURRICH later continued his work of applying biology to medicine. Interested in fisheries, he was a member of the Biological Board of Canada (later the Fisheries Research Board) 1901-12, and then retired to Oxford to study classics. SANDRA F. MCRAE

Writers' Union of Canada Prose writing in Canada, especially the writing of fiction, had certain problems associated with it until recently. Readership was small: until the late 1960s, readers shunned most Canadian fiction as second best, and most companies were reluctant to publish it unless an English or American publisher could be involved. Lingering puritanism limited subject matter, and conservatism of taste limited publishing opportunities for avant-garde texts. There were few writers' agents, and writers had either to go to the US or Britain for agents who were unfamiliar with Canada, or to do without. The vast distances between cities meant that writers seldom met, nor was a reading circuit available to them. Prose writers frequently lived isolated lives, receiving scant recognition for their work — if it appeared at all. It was common for writers with serious ambitions to leave the country. Like the other arts, fiction was considered a frill of dubious value by most of Canadian society.

By the 1970s, growing national self-awareness and confidence translated into a larger audience for fiction and nonfiction prose. The indigenous share of the trade book business increased to 25%. Publishing houses established in the 1960s contributed to this new growth, as did a more entrepreneurial and Canadian-centered spirit in older houses such as MCCLELLAND AND STEWART. Soon writers as well as audiences realized they had something of value — and therefore something to lose. Foreign domination was now seen as a threat, and royal commissions were set up by Québec (1971) and Ontario (1973) to investigate the publishing industry.

Out of the Ontario commission hearings grew the idea for a union of Canadian writers. The union initially comprised a small number of authors who felt that writers must work as a unified group if they were to gain any measure of control over the economic conditions influencing them. A planning conference was held in Dec 1972, and the Writers' Union of Canada was officially founded in Nov 1973. Since the League of Canadian Poets (fd 1966) already existed, the union limited itself to prose writers who had published a trade book within the past 7 years, or had a book still in print. It did not, and does not, include journalists and playwrights, who have their own organizations (Periodical Writers' Association of Canada and the Playwrights' Union of Canada). Since 1973 many provincial writers' organizations have

been formed to deal with matters that cannot be well handled by a national organization. The union finances itself through membership dues and fund-raising drives. It receives some federal and provincial grant money, especially for its Annual General Meeting. In 1984 its membership was about 425.

The union has done extensive work on contracts and retains a lawyer to give advice in negotiations; its Grievance Committee helps to resolve problems with publishers; it runs a manuscript-evaluation agency; it gives advice on tax matters; it acts as a clearing house for information and distributes a monthly newsletter. It organizes around particular issues, such as book dumping (the practice of importing from abroad remaindered copies of books by Canadians which are sold at reduced prices while the Canadian edition is still in the stores at full price); through the union's efforts this practice has reached the attention of the public and the government, the latter having announced its commitment to stopping the practice. Union committees work on matters of COPYRIGHT protection, liaison with publishers and librarians, and CENSORSHIP and repression issues. One major objective is the establishment of a "Public Lending Right" fee which would reimburse writers for multiple use of their works through libraries.

But one of the most important achievements of the union is to have fostered a spirit of professionalism and self-respect among writers. This organization, founded by writers for writers, has enabled them to meet and know one another and to take collective responsibility for decisions which affect the ways in which they are seen and treated. Since the 1960s the public's image of the Canadian writer has changed — though the change is incomplete — from defective freak to acceptable member of society, and the union has reflected and fostered that change. *See* LITERATURE AND POLITICS. MARGARET ATWOOD

Wrong, George MacKinnon, historian (b at Grovesend, Elgin County, Canada W 25 June 1860; d at Toronto 29 June 1948). Educated at U of T, Wrong was ordained a priest of the Church of England upon his graduation in 1883. He lectured in ecclesiastical history and liturgics at Wycliffe 1883-92 and in history at U of T 1892-94. From 1894 until his retirement in 1927 he was professor of history and head of the department. He promoted history as a distinct discipline, and Canadian history as a legitimate field of study. In 1896-97 he founded the *Review of Historical Publications Relating to Canada* (since 1920 the *Canadian Historical Review*) and in 1905 he cofounded the CHAMPLAIN SOCIETY. He wrote numerous monographs and texts on Canadian history, the best being *A Canadian Manor and Its Seigneurs* (1908). Formal in habit and something of an Anglophile in taste, Wrong influenced a generation of students. M. BROOK TAYLOR

Wrong, Humphrey Hume, diplomat (b at Toronto, 10 Sept 1894; d at Ottawa 24 Jan 1954). Grandson of Edward BLAKE and son of historian George WRONG, Hume Wrong was raised in privileged circumstances. He attended U of T, was denied enrollment in the Canadian Army because of a blind eye, enlisted in the British Expeditionary Force, and served at the front before being invalided home. He studied history at Oxford and was hired in 1921 to teach history in his father's department at U of T. In 1928, Vincent MASSEY, a family friend, took Wrong to Washington as first secretary in the new Canadian legation, and Wrong spent the next decade there learning the craft of diplomacy. Service at the League of Nations, in London, in Washington once more, and in Ottawa for 3 critical wartime years followed. As Norman ROBERTSON's closest colleague, Wrong devised and honed the idea of functionalism, a principle which argued that in those areas in which Canada had the re-

sources of a great power — food, minerals, air power — she should be treated like a great power. Functionalism became the basis of Canadian wartime policy, and to it must be credited much of the gains in Canadian influence and prestige. Wrong was posted to Washington as ambassador in 1946. There he had great influence, resolved financial problems, and did the actual day-to-day negotiation of the North Atlantic Treaty. In 1953 he returned to Ottawa as undersecretary but died before he could take up the reins. J.L. GRANATSTEIN
Reading: J.L. Granatstein, *The Ottawa Men* (1982).

Wrongful Dismissal, *see* EMPLOYMENT LAW.

Wyle, Florence, sculptor (b at Trenton, Ill 24 Nov 1881; d at Newmarket, Ont 14 Jan 1968). Settling in Canada in 1913, she was considered by contemporaries to be Canada's finest academic sculptor. Reclusive, she was happiest working quietly in her studio in the converted Toronto church that she shared for over 50 years with Frances LORING. Early premedical studies in Chicago had given her the profound respect for anatomical perfection that was evident in her work as a sculptor. Also a poet (*Poems,* 1958), her lyrics reflected her love of nature. As a founding member (1928) of the Sculptors' Soc of Canada, she fought for recognition of Canadian SCULPTURE, and was the first woman sculptor accorded full membership in the Royal Canadian Academy of Arts. While her public commissions were successful, such as the fine memorial in relief to nurse Edith Cavell on the grounds of the Toronto General Hospital, she is best remembered for her smaller, more intimate, studio sculptures, especially her studies of children and animals. REBECCA SISLER

Wyman, Anna, née Roman, dancer, choreographer, teacher and director (b at Graz, Austria). As founder and choreographer of her own Vancouver dance company, Wyman has become a noted figure in Canadian modern dance. She studied ballet and contemporary movement in various European cities and danced in Austria until 1948. Wyman moved to England in 1952 where she taught and opened her own school. Emigrating to Canada, she established the Anna Wyman School of Dance Arts in Vancouver in 1968 and the Anna Wyman Dancers in 1970 (professional debut 1971) which became the ANNA WYMAN DANCE THEATRE in 1973. She has choreographed more than 40 works for her company and has led it on many Canadian and overseas tours. MICHAEL CRABB

Wyn Wood, Elizabeth, sculptor (b at Orillia, Ont 8 Oct 1903; d at Toronto 27 Jan 1966). She made a significant contribution to Canada's cultural life, primarily through her modernist interpretation of the Canadian landscape in sculpture, but also through teaching at Central Technical School, Toronto, and through her involvement with the Federation of Canadian Artists and the Canadian Arts Council (as organizing secretary 1944-45, chairman of the International Relations Committee 1945-48 and VP 1945-48). Just as the GROUP OF SEVEN (several of whom taught her at the Ontario Coll of Art in the 1920s) translated their experience of the Canadian landscape into paint, Wood was innovative in expressing similar artistic concerns through fashioning modern materials (notably tin) into pared-down designs composed of juxtaposed masses in space. Her later work shows a greater social concern as she turned to figural subjects and received a number of important major public commissions in Ontario, such as the Welland-Crowland War Memorial (1934-39), fountains and panels in the Rainbow Bridge Gardens (1940-41), a monument to King George VI (1963) at Niagara Falls, and the Simcoe Memorial at Niagara-on-the-Lake, Ont (1953). CHRISTINE BOYANOSKI

XY Company (New North West Co), was named after the marks used to distinguish its bales of goods from those of the NORTH WEST COMPANY, was a product of conflicts between NWC agents (led by Simon MCTAVISH) and NWC winterers, following the company's reorganization in 1795. In 1797-98, Montréal partners who did not join the 1795 agreement became a focal point for uncommitted or alienated winterers, and in 1798 they fielded an opposition that reached as far as Athabasca. In 1800 Alexander MACKENZIE joined the new concern, which was then popularly known as "Alexander Mackenzie & Co." Rivalry became intense and costly. The use of liquor in the trade rose sharply; more employees were needed and were able to sue for higher wages in both firms. When McTavish's death in July 1804 removed a focus of personal hostilities and disaffection, the NWC and XYC negotiated a coalition. Their agreement of 5 Nov 1804 created a newly powerful and monopolistic NWC of 100 shares, 75 to be held by the old Nor'Westers and 25 by the former XYC partners.
JENNIFER S.H. BROWN

Yachting refers to races of watercraft using sail power only. Competitors are required to complete a prescribed course in the shortest possible time, passing marker buoys in the correct order and on the correct side. It is believed that the sport has Dutch origins. It was introduced to England by Charles II following his exile in Holland and the word itself comes from the Dutch *jaght*. Although the first recorded race took place in 1610, the International Yacht Racing Union, which governs the sport in the world, was not formed until 1906.

Yachting competition takes place with a wide variety of SAILING craft and under quite varied conditions. Races are organized for the smallest of dinghies on lake courses and for oceangoing vessels with substantial crews taking several days to complete the course. Olympic yachting, however, is confined to 6 classes: Tornado, catamarans crewed by 2 people; Flying Dutchman, centre-board dinghies weighing 174 kg with spinnakers and a crew of 2; 470, the same as Flying Dutchman, but the boat weighing 188 kg; soling, a keel yacht with a 3-man crew; Finn, one person sailing a centre-board dinghy; and Tempest, keel yachts with a 2-man crew. There are 7 races in each class and competitors record their 6 best results. The sailor or crew with the lowest number of points is the winner, since a first-place finish earns zero points — points being accumulated on a graduated scale for less favourable placings.

In Canada, yachting traces its origins to Kingston, Halifax and Toronto. The Kingston Boat Club was formed in 1826, but with the establishment of the Royal Nova Scotia Yacht Squadron (later Halifax Yacht Club) in 1837 came the founding of the country's oldest continuous club in the sport. In 1854 the Royal Canadian Yacht Club was formed in Toronto, and by 1892 the sport had spread across Canada with the founding of the Royal Victoria Yacht Club. Three years later, the Canada Cup races were established as a perpetual challenge series between

Yacht Race, Halifax (1850), oil on canvas, by John O'Brien (*courtesy National Gallery of Canada*).

yachts from Canada and the US on the Great Lakes. Although the Canada Cup has generally been won by the Americans, more recent years have brought Canadian domination, starting with the win by *Evergreen* in 1978. One of the most glorious chapters in Canadian yachting was written by the BLUENOSE out of Lunenburg, NS, which dominated the races for the Halifax *Herald's* International Fisherman's Trophy from 1921 until her retirement in 1938.

Besides the *Bluenose*, Canadians have enjoyed many other international successes in yachting. Canadian sailors won Olympic silver and bronze medals in 1936 and a bronze medal in the soling class in 1972. In 1959 Walter Windeyer of Toronto won the world Dragon Class championship. In 1977 and 1979 Glen Dexter of Lunenburg, NS, and his crew of Andreas Josenhans and Sandy Macmillan won the world soling championship. In 1982 Terry Neilson won the world Flying Dutchman championship. Much attention was focused on Canada's unsuccessful challenge (1983) for the prestigious America's Cup for 12 m yachts — a natural interest for a nation bounded by 2 great oceans with thousands of freshwater lakes in between.
J. THOMAS WEST

Yaffe, Leo, educator, nuclear scientist, university administrator (b at Devil's Lake, N Dak 6 July 1916). In 1952 Yaffe established a productive nuclear chemistry research laboratory at McGill. He has contributed richly to measurements of beta radiation, neutron- and proton-induced reactions, nuclear isomer ratios, and analysis of archaeological artifacts, all described in over 150 publications. He was director of Research and Laboratories (1963-65) and International Atomic Energy Agency, Vienna; chairman, dept of chemistry (1965-72) and vice-principal, administration (1974-81) of McGill; and president (1981-82) of the Chemical Inst of Canada. He has been the recipient of many honours. In 1984 he was professor emeritus at McGill.
MARIO ONYSZCHUK

Yahk, BC, UP, pop 172 (1981c), is located on the Moyie R near its passage into Idaho State, 65 km SW of Cranbrook and 40 km E of Creston. In prehistoric times the area was a crossroads, as Interior Salishan people to the S met the Lower Kootenay from the W via Goat R and the Upper Kootenays. The Dewdney Trail was built on the latter 2 trails in 1865. The modern era began with the establishment of the Crowsnest Pass Ry 1898. A large CPR tie-making camp was built close by. In recent years, logging, some sawmilling and post-making have supported the area.
WILLIAM A. SLOAN

Yanofsky, Daniel Abraham chess grandmaster (b at Brody, Poland 26 Mar 1925). He developed a talent for chess at an early age, winning his first tournament at 12. He qualified

for the Canadian Olympiad team for the 1939 world team championships in Buenos Aires, where he received a special prize for best score on Board 2. He played in many European tournaments and in 1953 won the British championship. His career in Canada includes 9 Canadian championships, 1941 to 1979, and 10 appearances on the Canadian national team, most recently in 1980 at Malta. He received the grandmaster title in 1964 for his performance on Board 1 for Canada at the Olympiad in Tel Aviv. Yanofsky is a Winnipeg lawyer and politician.
LAWRENCE DAY

Yarmouth, NS, Town, pop 7475 (1981c), is located at the entrance to Yarmouth harbour at the western tip of NS. Called *Kespoowuit* ("land's end") by the Micmac, and Port Fourchu by CHAMPLAIN, it was settled first by ACADIANS, later by settlers from New England (1761). During the AMERICAN REVOLUTION settlers began to arrive from Massachusetts, the beginning of Loyalist immigration to NS. Settlement in the Chebogue area had by 1810 moved to Yarmouth, which became the administrative and commercial centre. The shipbuilding industry, which began about 1764, had by the 19th century expanded into an impressive merchant fleet. By 1879 Yarmouth reached its peak as a shipbuilding port, being the second-largest port of registry, in tonnage, in Canada. Today the economy of the town is based largely on fishing, fish processing, dairy processing and the production of textiles, knitted goods and wood products. The first township in NS to introduce municipal incorporation (1856), Yarmouth was reincorporated 1890 after repeal in 1858.

As well as being the commercial and industrial centre of southwestern NS, Yarmouth is also its transportation centre, with 2 ferries to Maine. The discovery of a "runic stone," similar to a Norse cemetery stone, near Yarmouth harbour has caused considerable speculation and study suggesting the early presence of Norsemen in the area. Artifacts held by the Yarmouth County Museum serve as reminders of the days when it was a major seaport.
JEAN PETERSON

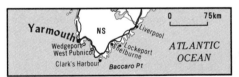

Yarrow, common name for some 200 species of herbaceous PLANTS of genus *Achillea* of the Compositae (Asteraceae) family; 3 species occur in Canada (*Achillea millefolium, A. ptarmica, A. sibirica*). Common yarrow (*A. millefolium* var. *lanulosa*), also known as milfoil, is an erect, aromatic perennial with rhizomes (underground stems). It grows across Canada in grassy places and roadsides from BC to Nfld, N to Great Bear Lk. The genus was named for the Gk hero, Achilles, who was supposed to have used the plant to heal his soldiers' wounds. *Lanulosa* comes from Lat *lana*, "wool." The leaves grow alternately up the densely hairy, 30-100 cm stem, and are finely divided with a feathery appearance [Lat *millefolium*, "thousand leaf"]. Flowers, borne in flat clusters of numerous flowerheads, are composite structures. Yellowish disc florets (3-10) make up the central part, which is surrounded by 5 petal-shaped ray florets. They bloom from May to October. Yarrow has a dry, one-seeded fruit. Throughout the ages, yarrow has been used to stop blood flow, hence one common name, "nosebleed." Blackfoot used it to aid childbirth, for gastroenteritis and liver trouble, as a diuretic, and for sore throat and skin troubles. *A. ptarmica* (sneezeweed) occurs across Canada, from southern BC to PEI. *A. sibirica* is found from the YT to eastern Québec, including central BC. *See* PLANTS, NATIVE USES.
BERYL HALLWORTH

Yeast, group of unicellular fungi with at least 450 known species. Most yeasts are ascomycetes which multiply by budding in various ways or by transverse fission, and may form ascospores in a naked ascus (saclike cell). They may form pseudomycelium or true mycelium. Some yeasts are basidiomycetes (Ustilaginaceae); some of these produce red or yellow carotenoid pigments (*Rhodotorula* spp). All reproduce asexually by budding, and sexually by formation of telio-spores. Classification at genus level is based on the morphology of the spores and vegetative cells and, at species level, by the ability to metabolize different sugars and related compounds. Major genera include *Schizosaccharomyces* (fission yeasts), *Saccharomyces, Kluyveromyces, Hansenula, Pichia, Candida, Rhodotorula* and *Cryptococcus*, the 2 latter being basidiomycetes. Although not as widely distributed as bacteria, yeasts occur in terrestrial and aquatic environments worldwide in association with plants and animals. A few are pathogenic: *Candida tropicalis* and *Cryptococcus neoformans* cause infections in humans; *Candida albicans* causes thrush and vaginitis. Patients treated with immunosuppressants are particularly susceptible to yeast infections. One yeast species is pathogenic for cotton. The best-known yeast is *Saccharomyces cerevisiae* (common bread, brewing and wine yeast), used for leavening and brewing for thousands of years, although its role was unsuspected until the work of Pasteur. It is a source of B vitamins and a valuable research tool for biochemical and genetic investigations. Other species have been used in biotechnological processes: treatment of wood pulp wastes, production of food and fodder yeast (single cell protein), production of SCP from whey and petroleum, production of gums (mannans), polyhydroxy alcohols (glycerol) and glycolipids. Yeasts may act as spoilage agents: *Rhodotorula*, spoiling olives; *Debaryomyces*, preserved meats; and some *Pichia*, mayonnaise and sauerkraut. Sugar-tolerant yeasts can cause explosive bursting of fondant-centered chocolates and spoilage of fruit-flavoured yogurts. *Schizosaccharomyces octosporus* often grows on dried dates, figs and raisins, without impairing their quality. J.F.T. SPENCER

Reading: H.J. Phaff et al, *The Life of Yeasts* (1966).

Yellowhead, William, or Musquakie, Ojibwa chief (d at the Rama Reserve, Lk Simcoe, Canada W 11 Jan 1864). During the WAR OF 1812 Yellowhead, then in his thirties or forties, fought for the British. He had his jaw shattered by a musket ball. Succeeding his father as head chief of the Lk Simcoe Ojibwa in 1817, he participated in the surrender the following year of 1 600 000 acres of their territory. He converted to Methodism in the late 1820s but later became an Anglican. As head chief he kept the great wampum belt which recorded the final peace between the Ojibwa and their hereditary enemies, the Six Nations Iroquois. DONALD B. SMITH

Yellowhead Pass, elev 1133 m, crosses the continental divide between Alberta and BC, 25 km W of JASPER. It was first called Leather Pass, because the HBC obtained moose and caribou hides through the pass 1826-28; it was supposedly later named for a blond Iroquois trapper, Pierre Hatsinaton, nicknamed "Tête Jaune," who hunted and trapped in the area. It provided a route to the Cariboo goldfields 1858 and 1862. The Miette R flows E from the pass to meet the Athabasca R at Jasper. Yellowhead Lk, on the W side, empties into the Fraser R. It was originally proposed by Sandford FLEMING as the route for the CPR, but was rejected. However, early this century both GRAND TRUNK PACIFIC and CANADIAN NORTHERN RY installed trackage over the pass — in some places side by side. Today the CNR and Yellowhead Hwy traverse the pass. GLEN BOLES

Yellowknife (Redknives, Copper) were a BAND of the Athapaskan-speaking CHIPEWYAN associated with the region encompassed by the Coppermine and Yellowknife rivers, the NE shore of Great Slave Lk, and NE into the Barren Grounds. From the first direct contact with European traders in the 17th century until their amalgamation with other Chipewyan and DOGRIB, every account has described them as similar to Chipewyan in language and culture. Their distinctiveness and separate name is largely based on European perception. Early in the 17th century, traders were anxious to make contact with the Indians associated with copper, thus the name Copper Indians. Samuel HEARNE travelled inland to Yellowknife territory, 1770-72, and dispelled the idea of rich copper deposits.

The Yellowknife were the main providers and guides for the Franklin Expedition, 1819-22. Their leader at this time, Akaitcho, acquired respect from the Europeans as a strong and competent leader. To the neighbouring native groups, he was a bullying, cruel leader with a reputation for plundering and killing. In 1823 the Dogrib made·a revenge attack on a Yellowknife camp, killing most of the group. Devastated by European diseases, the Yellowknife soon thereafter ended their raids on INUIT groups, initiating a period of relatively peaceful relations between them and their neighbours.

In 1900 the Yellowknife were still acknowledged as a distinct group (estimated population 200) when they signed Treaty No 8 at Ft Resolution along with other natives of the area (*see* INDIAN TREATIES). Before this date, however, they began to merge with neighbouring Chipewyan and Dogrib. By the 1960s Dogrib and Chipewyan were not aware of any group called Yellowknife, but could recount vivid stories about Akaitcho, whom they both considered to be Chipewyan. *See also* NATIVE PEOPLE: SUBARCTIC. BERYL C. GILLESPIE

Yellowknife, NWT, City, inc 1970, pop 9483 (1981c), is located on the N arm of GREAT SLAVE LK, 966 air km N of Edmonton. Nestled on the jagged rocks of the northern Canadian SHIELD, Yellowknife is the capital and only city of the NWT, headquarters of the territorial government and other territory-wide organizations, and is the base for tours to more remote areas of the North. It is also the home of 2 gold mines. The population is a mix of DENE, INUIT and whites of varied nationalities.

History Named after the YELLOWKNIFE band who moved into the area in the early 1800s, the first settlement was a trading post established in 1789 by Alexander MACKENZIE. But the city's real history is the story of a GOLD rush. Although gold was first discovered in 1896 by miners on their way to the KLONDIKE, the rush only began here in 1934. By 1936 Yellowknife was a boom town and by 1940 had a population of 1000. Development was halted briefly during WWII, but regained momentum after the war. At that time, Giant Gold Mine, still operational today, was established. The second gold rush was aided by the construction of a road from the S. By the end of 1947, gold mines were again producing on a large scale. Creation of a hydroelectric dam on the nearby Snare R in 1948 alleviated the former

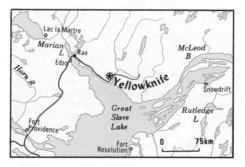

problem of power shortages. The first mayor was elected in 1953. In 1967 Yellowknife was named capital of the NWT and the NWT's commissioner and territorial government offices were established in the city.

Townscape Like many northern communities, Yellowknife boasts an old and a new town. The former, wrapped around Back Bay, is a picturesque collection of old gold-rush buildings and includes a Dene village, called Rainbow Valley for its brightly coloured houses. The new town, with its high-rise office buildings, hotels and apartments, is the most modern of NWT settlements. Each year in March, Yellowknifers enjoy Caribou Carnival, a 3-day festival celebrating the end of winter. The city is also the home of the Prince of Wales Northern Heritage Centre. In May 1984 the 313-seat Globe Theatre of the Northern Arts and Cultural Center officially opened; during its first season, beginning in Sept 1984, it presented a variety of entertainment from the Royal Winnipeg Ballet to local drama. ANNELIES POOL

Yeo, James, shipbuilder and owner, entrepreneur (b at Kilkhampton, Eng 1789; d at Port Hill, PEI 25 Aug 1868). Beginning as an agent for a Devonshire merchant, he established his own transatlantic commercial enterprise between PEI and N Devon, Eng. By 1833 he was the pre-eminent individual in Prince County and, by the mid-1840s, the most powerful businessman in the colony. At mid-century, he was engaged in agriculture, fishing, lumbering, merchandising and shipbuilding, while his son William had established facilities for shipbuilding and repair at Appledore in N Devon. Entering the Legislative Assembly in 1839, Yeo was a powerful member of the government from the late 1850s. GERRY PANTING

Yew is the common name for evergreen CONIFERS, genus *Taxus*, of the yew family (Taxaceae). Yews are unusual conifers in that seeds are not borne in cones but occur singly and are enclosed by a red, fleshy, berrylike structure (aril). Pollen cones and seeds usually occur on different plants. POLLINATION occurs in spring and seeds mature in fall. The flat, needlelike leaves are 2-3 cm long. There are about 10 species of yew, all in the Northern Hemisphere; 2 in Canada. Canada yew or ground hemlock (*T. canadensis*) is a low-spreading shrub which grows from Manitoba eastward. Western yew (*T. brevifolia*) is a shrub or TREE in moist areas of southern and western BC. The hard, reddish wood is prized for wood carving and for making archery bows, but yew has only minor commercial importance in Canada. English and Japanese yew are popular introduced ORNAMENTALS. The leaves, bark and seeds are toxic. *See* PLANTS, NATIVE USES. JOHN N. OWENS

Yoho National Park (est in 1886, 1300 km²). With 28 mountain peaks towering more than 3000 m, it is aptly named after the Cree word meaning "awe." Situated in the ROCKY MOUNTAINS, Yoho has BANFF and KOOTENAY national parks as its eastern and southern boundaries. It is a park of steep, glacier-carved valleys, thundering WATERFALLS (Takakkaw is Canada's highest), turquoise glacial lakes and icy peaks. Crystal caves, natural bridges and HOODOOS add to the spectacular alpine landscape. In the high alpine meadows there are pika, marmot and grizzly bear. Moose, wolverine, marten and elk live lower down in subalpine forests. From the park's many shallow lakes and wetlands to the rocky peaks, a great variety of bird life soars, flits and hops, including golden eagles, white-tailed ptarmigan and Clark's nutcrackers. Yoho was initially discovered in the course of the search for a route to the Pacific. KICKING HORSE PASS provides the route through which trains traverse the Rockies. Services are available in the towns of Field and Golden, BC. LILLIAN STEWART

York Boat, named for the HUDSON'S BAY CO's York Factory; one of 3 types of inland boats (the others being scows and sturgeon-heads) used by the HBC, and the most suitable for lake travel. Boatbuilders recruited from the Orkney Is built the first boat about 1749, for use on the Albany R. In competition inland with the NWC the York boat offered the HBC a distinct advantage, since it carried twice the cargo of a *canot du nord* (*see* CANOE) with the same number of crew; it was less easily damaged by ice and was safer in storms. The typical boat had a 9.1 m keel and an overall length of 12.6 m, beam 2.7 m and inside depth of 0.9 m. It carried 6 to 8 tripmen and a cargo of over 2700 kg. By the late 18th century the HBC had boat-building stations from James Bay to Ft Chipewyan, and in 1795 York boats were first built at Ft Edmonton. In the early 20th century York boats were of 3 sizes, "60 pieces" (2700 kg), "100 pieces" (4535 kg) and "120 pieces" (5440 kg). By the 1920s the York boat had passed from service. JOHN E. FOSTER

The York boat was the basis of the HBC transportation system. It was durable, stable and required less skill than a canoe. It was propelled by oars, as shown here, or a square sail (*courtesy Hudson's Bay Co*).

York Factory, Man, a trading post located on the N bank at the mouth of the HAYES R and permanently established in 1684 by Gov George Geyer of the HUDSON'S BAY COMPANY, is the oldest permanent settlement in the province. Until the British were awarded possession by the TREATY OF UTRECHT in 1713, ownership shifted between France and Britain. Tapping the trade of the entire North-West through the SASKATCHEWAN R system, the factory was the most important of all the company's posts. All goods going into the West and all furs coming out of the interior passed through York Factory. From 1822 to 1834 the governing council of the Northern Department met there. After 1850, when transportation costs through the US became almost two-thirds cheaper, the factory declined rapidly in importance. It was reduced by 1870 to a coastal trading post and was finally closed in 1957. Title was transferred in 1968 to National Historic Sites and until the late 1970s, when it became obvious that rapid erosion would destroy the buildings (parts of which date back to the 18th century), Parks Canada mothballed the site. Archaeologists are studying the site to determine the best method to prevent what appears to be its inevitable destruction. FRITS PANNEKOEK

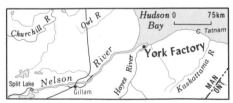

York University, Toronto, was founded in 1959 and took as its name Toronto's early name. Instruction is principally in English, but is bilingual at Glendon College. Founded in response to the rapid growth of Toronto's metropolitan area, York was conceived in the 1950s with support from the North Toronto YMCA, which was interested in the promotion of adult education, and major business and professional establishments. York was originally an affiliate of UNIVERSITY OF TORONTO and maintained that connection 1959 to 1965. In 1961 it moved to the

Enrolment: York University, 1982-83 (Source: Statistics Canada)			
Full-time Undergrad	*Full-time Graduate*	*Part-time Undergrad*	*Part-time Graduate*
13 591	1 429	13 685	1 494

Glendon campus, and the main campus of 243 ha in suburban Downsview opened in 1965. York expanded rapidly in the 1960s, establishing new facilities and programs such as Atkinson College for part-time degree studies, the Centre for Research in Experimental Space Science, the Institute of Behavioural Research and the Faculty of Administrative Studies. Osgoode Hall Law School, est 1862 by the Law Society of Upper Canada, became affiliated with York in 1968, merging an older Toronto institution with a new one. More recently added research units include Joint Centre on Modern East Asia and Joint Program in Transportation (both with U of T); Centre for Research on Latin America and the Caribbean; LaMarsh Research Program on Violence and Conflict Resolution; and Research Program in Strategic Studies. B. BEATON

Yorkton, Sask, City, pop 15 339 (1981c), inc 1928, is located about 175 km NE of Regina. The city acts as a regional service centre for the surrounding rich prairie parkland, known for its good agricultural production, particularly in grain crops. The community's beginnings can be traced back to 1882 with the York Farmers' Colonization Co, a block settlement group from York County, Ont. Originally known as York City, the village was established 4 km NE of its present site and was intended to serve the York colony. In 1884, with the establishment of a post office, the settlement was renamed Yorkton. With the coming of the railway in 1889, the village was moved trackside to its present site. Although the York colony eventually faded, large numbers of immigrants from across Europe settled in the area. Of particular significance were the early UKRAINIANS and DOUKHOBORS who formed a large portion of the population. Today the city performs commercial, transportation and government functions. Points of interest to visitors include a branch of the Western Development Museum, the Godfrey Dean Cultural Centre and the dome paintings of the St Mary's Ukrainian Catholic Church. MARK RASMUSSEN

Reading: Yorkton: York Colony to Treasure Chest City (1982).

Youmans, Letitia, née Creighton, temperance worker (b in Hamilton Twp, UC 3 Jan 1827; d at Toronto 18 July 1896), founder of the WOMAN'S CHRISTIAN TEMPERANCE UNION in Canada. Long interested in Sunday school work and temperance, Youmans attended the CHAUTAUQUA Assembly in 1874 where she met leaders of the American women's temperance crusade. She returned to Canada and formed the second Canadian woman's temperance group at Picton, Ont. Through her efforts, WCTUs spread across the country and in 1885 a national WCTU was formed with Youmans as first president. She continued in this position until 1889 when she was seized with inflammatory rheumatism. An invalid, she remained honorary president until her death. Her autobiography, *Campaign Echoes*, appeared in 1893. WENDY L. MITCHINSON

Young, George Paxton, philosopher, educator (b at Berwick upon Tweed, Eng 9 Nov 1818; d at Toronto 26 Feb 1889). He was educated at Edinburgh U, studying for ordination in the Presbyterian ministry, and was appointed minister of Knox Church, Hamilton, Canada W, in 1850. Subsequently professor of both "Logic, Mental and Moral Philosophy" and "Evidences of Natural and Revealed Religion" at Knox College, Toronto, 1853-64, he resigned from this position, and from the Presbyterian ministry, because of his commitment to reason, rather than theological creed, as the foundation of ethics. From then until 1868 he was inspector of grammar schools for Ontario; his annual reports were instrumental in laying the foundations of the Ontario high school system.

Young spent the remainder of his life as a philosopher and teacher of PHILOSOPHY, first at Knox College, which invited him to return in 1868, and from 1871, as professor of logic, metaphysics and ethics at the nondenominational University College in U of T. Young's influence on University College students was enormous. He had come to advocate a system of idealism similar to that of Thomas Hill Green in England (but antecedent to it), and his ethical system, compatible with, but not dependent upon, Christian revelation, struck a responsive chord in students faced with the intrusion of evolutionary naturalism. A. BRIAN MCKILLOP

Young, John, businessman, journalist, politician (b at Falkirk, Scot 1 Sept 1773; d at Halifax 6 Oct 1837). Young had a brilliant career at Glasgow U and wished to study medicine. His father refused further support so he began a career in business. Immigrating to Halifax in 1814 he established John Young and Company, even selling goods in Castine, Maine, following the British occupation of the town in 1814. Best remembered for a series of essays on agriculture, published under the name "Agricola" in the *Acadian Recorder* (1818-22), he pointed out the need for agricultural reform and his articles led to the formation of the Provincial Agricultural Soc with Young as secretary. He and 2 of his sons later became members of the NS Assembly. Ambitious, he had the ability to reconcile his own goals with the public interest. He believed people to be motivated by self-interest, and his own career suggests that this was so. R.A. MACLEAN

Young, Neil Percival, rock singer, songwriter, guitarist (b at Toronto 12 Nov 1945), son of journalist Scott Young. After early years with Winnipeg and Toronto rock bands (The Squires, Mynah Birds), Young became a founding member 1966-68 of the folk-rock band Buffalo Springfield in Los Angeles, Calif. Thereafter he pursued a solo career while maintaining an informal association (1969-74) with the group Crosby, Stills and Nash. He has released more than 15 albums in as many years; his most popular songs include "Heart of Gold," "Tell Me Why," "Only Love Can Break Your Heart" and "Lotta Love." MARK MILLER

Young, Reynold Kenneth, astronomer, professor (b at Binbrook, Ont 4 Oct 1886; d at Peterborough, Ont 24 Dec 1977). He was astronomer at the Dominion Observatory in Ottawa 1913-18 and at the Dominion Astrophysical Observatory in Victoria, BC, 1918-24, professor at U of T 1924 to 1945 and director of the David Dunlap Observatory in Richmond Hill, Ont, 1935-45. Young's research was primarily in the field of stellar radial velocities, the velocities of stars in the line of sight. His work helped place Canada among the world leaders in radial velocities. His unique contribution was his guidance in the design and construction of the 74-inch telescope at the David Dunlap Observatory, where he planned and developed a far-reaching program of fundamental astrophysics. Copies of the telescope have been mounted in Egypt, South Africa, Japan and Australia. PETER M. MILLMAN

Young, Sir William, lawyer, politician, judge, philanthropist (b at Falkirk, Scot 8 Sept 1799; d at Halifax 8 May 1887). A political opportunist, Young maneuvered his career to achieve 2 goals: the office of premier and that of chief justice. He entered the NS legislature in 1836 as a Reformer (Liberal) and achieved prominence defending Reform journalists in several heated libel cases. He tailored his political climb, hoping to become first premier under RESPONSIBLE GOVERNMENT in 1848, but lost to J.B. UNIACKE, whom he succeeded in 1854. Young's leadership was not outstanding, and was marred by indecision, flagrant patronage and growing religious-political turmoil. In 1860 he resigned to accept the pinnacle of his aspirations — the office of chief justice. His later life was marked by great philanthropy, which brought power and acclaim to a man once described as "so tricky a character that he probably never ate his dinner without a stratagem."   LOIS KERNAGHAN

Young Men's Christian Association, worldwide private voluntary organization that offers a wide range of educational, social and recreational services. Founded in London, Eng, in 1844 by George Williams, it spread rapidly to other cities where groups of young men wished to protect themselves against the temptations of modern urban life. The first N American association appeared in Montréal in 1851 and a Canadian National Council was organized in 1912. The YMCA's original goal was the spiritual improvement of young men and for many years it was closely tied to the Protestant evangelical churches. Today, it serves people of both genders and all ages, walks of life, races and religions. The Canadian YMCA has actively promoted physical education, camping, adult education, youth services, and international development projects. In 1983, 1 400 491 Canadians held memberships to the YMCA. *See also* YOUNG WOMEN'S CHRISTIAN ASSOCIATION.   DIANA PEDERSEN

Young Women's Christian Association co-operates closely with the YOUNG MEN'S CHRISTIAN ASSOCIATION in many Canadian communities, but has retained its distinct identity. Two organizations providing religious fellowship and boardinghouse accommodation to young women were created in England in 1855, amalgamated in 1877. The rapid growth of the YWCA as an international movement was linked to the increasing concentration in cities of large numbers of young unmarried women seeking employment, especially in factories. The first Canadian branch was organized in Saint John, NB, in 1870, and a national body was created in 1895. Sharing the Protestant evangelical orientation of the YMCA, early YWCA programs combined attempts to increase the employment and educational opportunities available to young women with a concern for their physical and moral welfare. The Canadian YWCA today is actively working to improve the social, legal and economic position of all Canadian women. Some half million Canadians annually make use of YWCA facilities in one way or another.
                    DIANA PEDERSEN

Youville, Marie-Marguerite d', née Dufrost de La Jemmerais, founder of the Sisters of Charity of the Hôpital Général of Montréal (b at Varennes, Qué 15 Oct 1701; d at Montréal 23 Dec 1771). Educated by the Ursulines of Québec, in 1722 Marie-Marguerite married François d'Youville of Montréal who died in 1730. She raised 2 children and continued the family business although she had experienced a religious "conversion" and had withdrawn from society in 1727. Ten years later, she and 4 other women formed a lay group dedicated to charity and took simple vows. Called *soeurs grises* (for their grey habit) and also "tipsy sisters" because of the d'Youvilles' alleged profits from brandy traf-

Five Fingers Rapids on the Yukon River, N America's 5th-longest river (*photo by Hans Blohm/Masterfile*).

ficking, in 1747 they were put in charge of the bankrupt Hôpital Général, founded in 1692 by François Charon de La Barre. They reorganized it into a hospice for the aged, foundlings, orphans and "fallen women." In 1750 civil and ecclesiastical authorities decided to unite it with the Hôpital Général of Québec, but the Sulpicians interceded in Paris and, on 3 June 1753, Louis XV gave the community legal status and title to the hospital. The sisters developed various enterprises including farms, an orchard, mill and bakery to finance their work. During the smallpox epidemic of 1755 and the Seven Years' War, their institution truly became a hospital. Mère d'Youville faced disappointments, however; her family returned to France at the Conquest, her hospital burned in 1765, and after years of failing health she died in 1771. Many Montréalers attributed to her prophetic gifts and miraculous healing powers.   CORNELIUS J. JAENEN

Ypres, first major battle fought by Canadian troops during WORLD WAR I. On 22 Apr 1915 a greenish yellow cloud of chlorine gas almost 7 km long was carried by a light NE wind toward the Allied trenches near Ypres (now Ieper), Belgium. It was the first gas attack on the Western Front. Without gas masks, the French and Algerians in the trenches were forced to retreat, choking, gasping, and dying as the chlorine affected their lungs. A wide gap opened to the attacking Germans and 1st Canadian Division, together with British troops, rushed in to halt the enemy's advance. In a week of fierce fighting and bitter counterattacks involving further use of gas, the German thrust was brought to a halt. Although they suffered over 6000 casualties, the Canadians' courage and ability in the face of this new weapon of war won them recognition as first-class troops. *See also* FREZENBERG RIDGE.
                    R.H. ROY

Yukon Field Force (1898-1900), composed of 203 officers and men drawn from all 3 branches (cavalry, artillery and infantry) of the Permanent Force of the Canadian Militia. It was sent to the Yukon, to be based on Ft Selkirk with a detachment at Dawson, as a symbol of Canadian sovereignty and as a support for the civil power in maintaining law and order in the territory during the KLONDIKE GOLD RUSH. Half the force was withdrawn in Sept 1899 and the remainder, restyled the Yukon Garrison, left a year later.
                    BRERETON GREENHOUS

Yukon River, 3185 km long (of which 1149 km lie in Canada), fifth-longest river in N

America, rises in Tagish Lk on the northern BC border, flows N and NW across the YUKON TERRITORY into Alaska, where it flows in a great westward arc to Norton Sound on the Bering Sea. It has a DRAINAGE BASIN of 298 000 km², of which 23 300 km² lie in the US, and a mean discharge of 2360 m³/s where it crosses into Alaska. Four principal tributaries, draining a vast area of the YT, feed the river in Canada. The Teslin R (393 km) rises in Teslin Lk, on the BC border, and joins the Yukon N of Lk Laberge. The Pelly R (608 km) rises in the SELWYN MTS to the E and descends to the Yukon at Fort Selkirk. The White R (320 km) drains the glacial waters of the SW, and the Stewart R (644 km) rises in the mountainous area to the E, in the mining region of Mayo and Keno Hill. In Alaska the major tributaries are the Porcupine R (721 km), which rises in the NW Yukon Territory, the Tanana from the S, and the Koyukuk from the N.

The Yukon is a slow-moving, braided stream, and is shallow except when swollen by spring waters. Its gradient is even and there are few rapids; those at Miles Canyon, which proved so treacherous to the Klondike prospectors, have been drowned by a hydroelectric development. From Fort Selkirk to DAWSON, the river is sprinkled with wooded islands and its long, wide stretches are bordered by mountains. Past Dawson, the valley becomes narrow and then, as it enters Alaska, widens into the broad interior plateau called the "Yukon Flats."

The river mouth was known to Russian fur traders by 1831. The upper reaches were explored by HBC trader Robert Campbell, who explored the Pelly R and established a post at Fort Selkirk on the Yukon in 1848. John BELL of the HBC reached the river via the Porcupine R in 1846. For 3 months of the year, the Yukon is navigable from its mouth to WHITEHORSE (some 2860 km). Steamers plied the river in the 1860s, and there were at least 20 in service in 1900, at the height of the KLONDIKE GOLD RUSH. Today the steamers are antique and the area is served by road and air.

The Yukon basin is believed to be the chief migration route of America's original settlers (*see* PREHISTORY). However, it remains sparsely populated. Several thousand native people maintain their traditional life-style, being at least partly dependent on hunting and trapping. The forest cover of small conifers supplies local needs, but growth is too slow for a viable forestry industry; there is little agriculture. The isolation and scenic beauty of the river attracts tourists. The name Yukon was first applied to the river and is from the Indian word *Yu-kun-ah,* meaning "great river."   JAMES MARSH

Yukon Territory

Capital: Whitehorse
Motto: None
Flower: Fireweed
Largest Urban Centres: Whitehorse, Faro, Watson Lake, Dawson City, Mayo-Elsa
Population: 23 075 (1981c); rank twelfth, 0.09% of Canada; 63.9% urban; 36% rural nonfarm; 0.02% farm; 0.05 per km² density; 5.7% increase from 1976-81; Jan 1984e pop, 21 600
Languages: 96.1% English; 1% French; 2.9% Other
Entered Confederation: 13 June 1898
Government: Territorial — Commissioner, Executive Committee, Legislative Council of 16 members; federal — one senator, one member of the House of Commons; the Minister of Indian Affairs and Northern Development is responsible for directing the Commissioner in the administration of the territory
Area: 482 515 km², including 4481 km² of inland water; 4.9% of Canada
Elevation: Highest point — Mount Logan (5951 m); lowest point — sea level at arctic shore
Gross Domestic Product: $1.2 billion (Yukon and NWT) (1982e)
Value of Mineral Production: $298.2 million (1981); $169 million (1982); $59.3 million (1983 prelim total)
Electric Power Generated: 242 828 MWh (1983)
Sales Tax: None (1984)

Yukon Territory takes its name from the Indian name *Yu-kun-ah* for the "great river" which drains most of its area. Lying in the NW corner of Canada's continental mainland, isolated by rugged mountains, it shares a common border and many characteristics with its American neighbour, Alaska. Historically, it is indelibly associated with the great KLONDIKE GOLD RUSH.

Land and Resources

Geographically the bulk of the Yukon is a subarctic plateau interspersed by mountains. The major exception is the Arctic Coastal Plain, a narrower eastward continuation of the same region in Alaska, which slopes down to the BEAUFORT SEA from the British Mts inland.

Geology The Yukon constitutes the northernmost part of the cordilleran region. It is geologically very complex, but includes 3 parallel sectors oriented NW-SE. In the E, folded sedimentary Paleozoic and Mesozoic formations are set off sharply from the Mackenzie Valley by great faults. The middle sector includes sedimentaries, metamorphics and volcanics ranging from Precambrian to Mesozoic age. Massive plutonic Mesozoic and Tertiary granites make up the core of the western sector.

Surface The geologic structure is reflected in a similar physiographic subdivision into mountain, plateau and mountain regions, all of which continue westwards into Alaska. In detail there are significant variations within each major physiographic region. The high central Yukon Plateau, at an average elevation of 1200 m, is interrupted frequently by local mountain areas and deep valleys — many of the latter strikingly aligned NW-SE, reflecting the structure. The 2400 m Ogilvie Mountains on the N, separate it from the Porcupine Plateau, which is delineated on the N and E by the British and Richardson Mountains, respectively. On the E the Yukon Plateau is bounded by the Selwyn and Mackenzie Mountains. On the S an area of lower terrain near the 60th parallel separates it from the mountainous areas of northern BC. In the SW Yukon the spectacular St Elias and Coast Mountains include Canada's highest mountains, many over 4600 m, with Mt LOGAN (5951 m) the highest in Canada. Many are covered by extensive permanent ice caps — the largest nonpolar icefields in N America — and effectively cut off direct access to the Pacific Ocean despite its relative proximity.

Water Approximately 75% of the territory is drained by the YUKON R system, including the Porcupine R basin N of the Ogilvie Mountains. The two major exceptions are the Peel R, which drains a lesser plateau in the NE, and the LIARD R in the lower-lying plain sector in the SE. These rivers drain into the MACKENZIE R to the E. Included in the Yukon headwaters are magnificant elongated glacial lakes along the eastern edge of the St Elias Mountains. The Yukon includes a large area in the N and NW that was never covered by Pleistocene ice sheets, despite its northern latitude. PERMAFROST is continuous N of the Porcupine R, and discontinuous but widespread through the rest of the territory. As in the NWT, the latter condition results in finely balanced biotic conditions and poses problems for construction and ground transportation.

Vegetation All the Yukon except the Arctic Coastal Plain and the higher mountains lies below the TREELINE but approximately 40% is not treed, and approximately 30% is normally productive forest. The area S of Dawson is fairly well forested, at least in the river valleys, with the best stands in the moist eastern sectors, especially the Liard valley. It forms part of the boreal forest region, including such trees as spruce, pine, aspen, poplar and birch.

Climate The climate of the Yukon is continental, with its mountain ramparts sealing it off from most direct contact with the moderating Pacific Ocean. Winters are very cold most of the time, with the lowest temperature ever recorded in Canada (-63°C) at Snag, NW of Kluane Lk in Feb 1947. At times, Pacific air may edge into the SW sectors resulting in short intervals of milder temperatures. Summers are warm and frequently hot (35°C has been recorded at Dawson) but cooler air from the Arctic can push southward. Precipitation is generally low because the high mountains in the SW seal off access to the moister air; summer dust on unpaved roads is a frequent reminder of this.

Resources Wildlife resources which continue to be important for the native population especially and for sportsmen, trappers, tourists and the general public, include moose, caribou, mountain sheep and goats (largely closed to hunting), bears and furbearers, as well as birds and fish. Pacific salmon ascend the Yukon R and its tributaries from Norton Sound. The isolated northern community of OLD CROW is especially dependent upon these traditional resources. Gold drew the Yukon to the attention of the world in the late 19th century, and though the focus has shifted since, minerals remain the overwhelmingly most important non-renewable resource, present and future, of the territory. Geologically, it has a wide variety of mineral types. Previously its isolation, severe climate and rugged terrain have posed serious problems for development, although the territory has access to tidewater and now has a highly developed road system. It has been estimated that about 13 500 MW of hydro power resources are available in the Yukon, primarily on the Yukon R and its tributaries; however, development would involve flooding many of the valleys in which wildlife resources and population are located.

Conservation The historic and spectacular scenic attractions of the Yukon are important resources for tourism. KLUANE NATIONAL PARK in the SW includes some of the most dramatic mountain and icefield scenery in Canada. Widespread concern has been expressed about the threat of development projects on wilderness areas. Possible oil and gas pipeline construction through the Yukon from Alaska to the southern states gave rise to the Lysyk enquiry. Project costs and unsettled native land claims have delayed action probably more than environmental disruption. The Dempster Highway (1959-79) was pushed through in the northern Yukon with almost no study of its environmental impact. Despite the fact that it cut through the migration route of the (Porcupine) caribou herd on which the northern native largely depend, the highway had less impact on the herd than first feared. Alaska protected the same herd by establishing a wildlife refuge adjacent to the international boundary. In July 1984 the federal government announced creation of the North Yukon National Park from the boundary E to the Babbage R.

People

The first white explorer to reach the Yukon was Sir John FRANKLIN in 1825 when his party followed the Arctic shore. The first lasting contact was made by fur traders of the HBC, in the 1840s, pushing westwards from the Mackenzie R system: Robert Campbell by way of the upper Liard onto the Pelly R, and John BELL onto the Porcupine R. Gold prospecting in the late 19th century, which climaxed in the Klondike Rush, resulted in major white immigration and established the settlement pattern of mining and transportation. The improvements to transportation facilities during WWII shifted the urban focus from Dawson to Whitehorse and had a dramatic impact on the entire Yukon.

Urban Centres Over three-quarters of all Yukoners live in 4 centres, and 2 out of 3 live in WHITEHORSE. Whitehorse (pop 14 800), the territorial capital, is overwhelmingly the transportation, business and service centre for the territory. DAWSON CITY was the original capital, but lost that function to Whitehorse in 1951, and has dwindled to a population of 1251 (1983), based on some continuing gold mining in the area and on tourism. FARO (pop 1000) developed in response to the nearby Anvil zinc-lead mine, and Watson Lk (pop 1348) on the ALASKA HIGHWAY is the service centre for the SE Yukon. Elsa, the company town for the Keno Hill mine has about 500 population. Other communities consist of only 200 or 300 people.

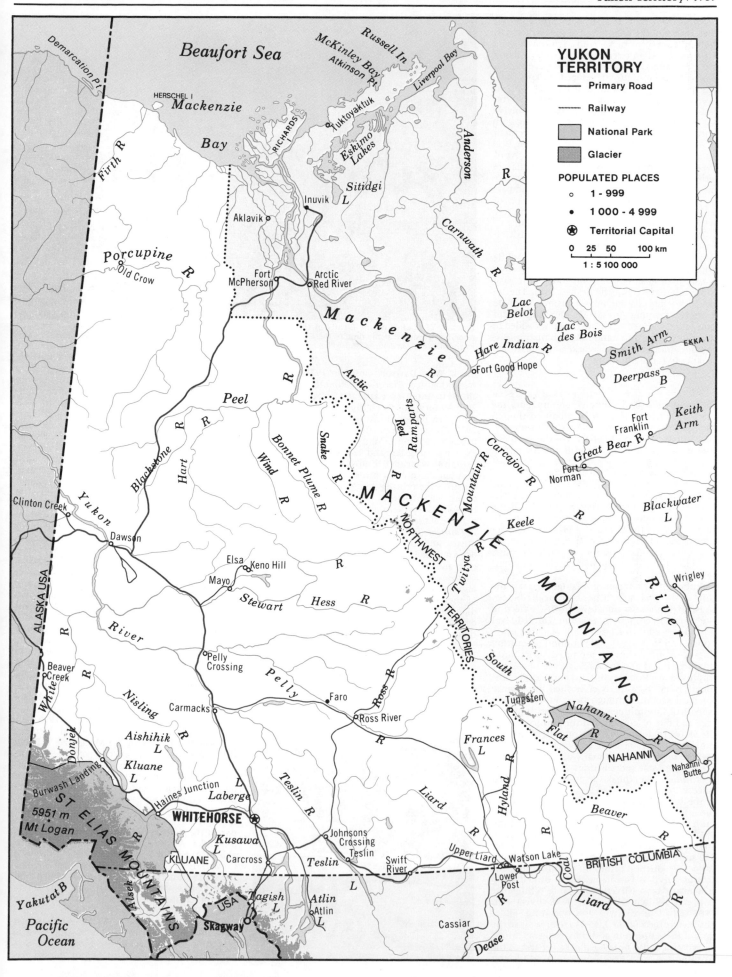

Beaufort Sea

Demarcation Pt

Russell In

McKinley Bay
Atkinson Pt

Liverpool Bay

HERSCHEL I

Mackenzie

Bay

RICHARDS

Tuktoyaktuk

Eskimo
Lakes

Sitidgi
L

Anderson

R

Firth R

Inuvik

Aklavik

Carnwath R

Porcupine R

Old Crow

Fort
McPherson

Arctic
Red River

Lac
Belot

Lac
des Bois

Smith Arm

EKKA I

Deerpass
B

Peel

R

Arctic

Hare Indian R

Fort Good Hope

Fort
Franklin

Keith
Arm

Blackstone R

Hart R

Wind R

Bonnet Plume R

Snake R

Red

Ramparts

Mackenzie R

Mountain R

Carcajou R

Great Bear R

Fort
Norman

Blackwater
L

Clinton Creek

Yukon

R

Keele R

Wrigley

Dawson

Elsa
Mayo

Keno Hill

Stewart

Hess

R

R

MACKENZIE

NORTHWEST

Twitya R

MOUNTAINS

River

Alaska USA

R

Beaver
Creek

White R

Pelly
Crossing

Pelly

Faro

Ross River

Ross R

TERRITORIES

Keele R

South

River

Nisling R

Carmacks

Nahanni

Flat R

Tungsten

Aishihik
L

Frances
L

Hyland R

NAHANNI

Nahanni
Butte

Donjek R

Kluane
L

Haines Junction

Laberge

Teslin R

Liard R

Beaver R

Burwash Landing

ST ELIAS MOUNTAINS

5951 m
Mt Logan

WHITEHORSE

Kusawa
L

KLUANE

Carcross

Johnsons
Crossing
Teslin

Swift
River

Upper Liard

Watson Lake

BRITISH COLUMBIA

Coal R

Yakutat B

Alsek R

USA

Tagish
L

Teslin

L

Lower
Post

R

Liard

R

Pacific
Ocean

Skagway

Atlin
L

Atlin

Cassiar

Dease R

YUKON
TERRITORY
—— Primary Road
----- Railway
National Park
Glacier
POPULATED PLACES
○ 1 - 999
● 1 000 - 4 999
✪ Territorial Capital
0 25 50 100 km
1 : 5 100 000

Ethnicity Yukon Indians comprise approximately 25% of the population of the territory. In 1984, 4747 resided in 12 bands. Although there are 6 small Indian reserves in Yukon only a few are occupied and the Indian Act reserve system has never been highly developed. Yukon Indians live side by side with non-native people in every community in Yukon. Since 1973 Yukon Indians have been negotiating a comprehensive LAND-CLAIM settlement in Yukon involving both status and non-status Indians. The Agreement in Principle for the Yukon Indian Claim was approved by the federal cabinet on 17 April 1984. The proposed settlement has been characterized as "one-government" or co-operative model, under which Yukon Indians would participate as full partners in the mainstream of Yukon society rather than operating separately within the more traditional reserve system.

Transient Population One of the significant problems of both the Yukon and the NWT has been the transient nature of much of the white population. Many workers, attracted by high wages, plan to stay for a short time and return "outside" after saving the desired sum. The labour force usually includes a disproportionate number of young unmarried men and recent immigrants. The constant turnover has added to the costs of operation, and many companies encourage more married workers through assistance in family housing.

Economy

Primary resource extraction has always been the foundation of the Yukon economy. Furs, the original base, continue to be produced though their relative importance has declined greatly. They are especially important for the northern Yukon natives. During a brief but hectic period at the turn of the century an active Arctic WHALING industry was based on Herschel I, the only sheltered harbour along the Yukon's Arctic coast. The economy is vulnerable to reversals in mining, which comprises about 40% of the territory's economic base. The closure of 13 major mines in the Yukon in 1982 because of depressed world markets and depleting resources has resulted in the most serious economic crisis in its history and a consequent decline of population.

Although local farming was significant at the time of the gold rush, it has been negligible because of high costs and low profits, reflecting the poor soil, climatic restrictions, limited level terrain necessary for large-scale machine operations, and improved transportation permitting import of more cheaply produced agricultural products, but is making a resurgence because of improved techniques and favourable government policy. Forestry is of limited importance for local sawmills though most lumber is still imported. Environmental restrictions limit the area and rate of growth, but the Liard valley of the SE is providing the base for a merchantable timber industry. Fish are important as an element in the food base of many of the native people and for some sportfishing.

Mining The emphasis in mining has shifted since WWII from gold to zinc, lead and copper in the 1960s-70s and back to precious metals in the mid-1980s. In 1981, mineral production in the Yukon was valued at $352 million, falling to $200 million in 1982: $75 million from gold, $63 million from zinc, $26 million from lead, $22 million from silver and $14 million from copper. Production came from 3 mines in 1981: Cyprus Anvil at Faro (zinc, lead), United Keno Hill near Mayo (silver, lead), and Whitehorse Copper at Whitehorse (copper, gold, silver) — in 1984 only United Keno was operating. Silver has been mined in the Elso-Mayo area since the turn of the century. In addition, coal was mined at Tantalus Butte near Carmacks for use at the Anvil mine. A former asbestos mine at Clinton

Dawson, YT, located on the E bank of the Yukon R, came into existence at the time of the Klondike Gold Rush (*photo by John deVisser/Masterfile*).

Creek, W of Dawson, closed in 1978 when ore was exhausted. Placer gold from the Yukon declined in importance after the first decade of the 20th century, but much higher gold prices in recent years have resulted in renewed activity. In 1983 all gold production came from placer-mining operations. Many potential new mines exist (eg, tungsten and lead-zinc in the MacMillan Pass area NE of Ross R on the NWT border) but the present mine closures reflect how sensitive the mining and Yukon economies are to outside influences. Mine development costs in isolated northern areas are difficult and expensive at the best of times.

Tourism Tourism is the most important industry since the slump in mining. Visitors are drawn by the Yukon's colourful Gold Rush history and by its scenic and wildlife attractions. Dawson contains many reconstructed buildings and artifacts from its flamboyant era at the turn of the century. Recently, American and Canadian national parks services have co-operated in developing the Klondike Gold Rush International Historical Park, including the Chilkoot Trail through the SW mountains from Skagway, Alaska. Whitehorse puts on an annual winter "Sourdough Rendezvous" and Dawson holds a Discovery Day. The territory also hosts the ARCTIC WINTER GAMES every 6 years. In 1983, 394 000

people visited the Yukon (a large percentage passing through on their way to or from Alaska), with an estimated expenditure of $77 million. Registered outfitters in 22 big game guiding areas provide for hunters while tourist service facilities are available along the Yukon highways. Kluane National Park headquarters is located at Haines Junction. The arts and crafts industry is of increasing importance to the local economy, including that of the native residents.

Transportation Transportation in the Yukon was based upon the Yukon R system until WWII. Shallow-draught, stern-wheeler STEAMBOATS operated seasonally from gold rush days; the main route was between Dawson and Whitehorse where rapids made it the effective head of river navigation. Limited transportation by sleigh or coach was available on winter roads during the closed season. The 177 km narrow gauge WHITE PASS AND YUKON RAILWAY was constructed from tidewater at Skagway, Alaska, through the rugged Coast Mountains to Whitehorse, and was particularly important in exporting minerals from the territory until it was shut down in Oct 1982. The transportation pattern and local population distribution were radically altered during WWII. Construction of the Alaska Highway between Dawson Creek, BC and Fairbanks, Alaska, in 1942 included 1014 km through the Yukon via Watson Lk and Whitehorse. There are now over 4000 km of roads in the territory. In 1978 completion of the Haines Road from Carcross and Whitehorse provided the Yukon with its first road access to the Pacific at Skagway, Alaska. In 1979 the Dempster Highway was completed between Dawson and Inuvik in the Mackenzie R Delta. Originally conceived as part of the government's "roads to resources" program, the Dempster Highway has opened the northern Yukon for potential development. It has also helped reduce prices in the Delta area and encouraged tourism.

New airport facilities were constructed through the southern Yukon during WWII as part of the Northwest Staging Route from the US to Alaska. Airports and airstrips are now available at most Yukon settlements, including Old Crow in the north. That at Whitehorse is by far the most important, providing scheduled and charter links with Alaska, southern Canada (via Vancouver and Edmonton primarily) and the "lower 48" American states.

Pipelines to transport Arctic Alaskan gas overland to the US inevitably would have to cross the Yukon. A 10-year moratorium was placed on the construction of an Alaska gas

Open-pit mines near Faro, YT. Mining suffered difficult times in the 1980s (*photo by Richard Harrington*).

pipeline across the northern Yukon and down the Mackenzie Valley after the hearings of the Berger Commission. In its place the Alaska Highway route was accepted by the Canadian government with the provision that it not prejudice native land claims and that it ensure environmental safeguards. It has since been delayed by political pressures within the US, heavy financial costs and an over-abundance of gas in the world market (*see* MACKENZIE VALLEY PIPELINE).

Energy The Northern Canada Power Commission provides over 90% of all power in Canada's northern territories. In the Yukon its installed capacity is 86 MW, with 58 MW hydro and 30 MW thermal, just the reverse of the relative proportions in the NWT. The major hydro power facilities are at Whitehorse (40 000 kW installed capacity), Aishihik (31 200 kW) and Mayo (5820kW).

Government and Politics

The Yukon moved towards self-government earlier than the NWT, from which it was separated in 1898 by the Yukon Territory Act, but its progress subsequently has been more erratic than the NWT. The original spur to its separation was the large influx of outsiders with the gold rush. The first territorial government consisted of a federally appointed commissioner (James WALSH being the first) and a similarly appointed council. Unlike the condition of the NWT from 1905-67, all these appointed officials were resident in the Yukon from the start. As early as 1899 the Act was amended to provide for 2 elected members of council to be added, and in 1902 3 more. In 1908 a fully elected council of 10 members was established. Dwindling population resulted in the council being abolished in 1918; in the face of local protest it was reinstated, but only as a 3-member elected council in 1919. The office of commissioner disappeared after 1916 as its duties were assumed by the gold commissioner of the territory. Further changes did not occur until after WWII when territorial population began to increase again. In 1948 legal provision was made for the reappointment of a commissioner as chief executive officer of the Yukon, along with the installation of several other appointed territorial officers. In 1951 the council was increased to 5 elected members, and subsequent additions have expanded it to 16. The federally appointed commissioner is the senior executive officer, responsible to Ottawa through the minister of Indian Affairs and Northern Development. From 1970 to 1979 the commissioner chaired an ex-

The Richardson Mts form a boundary between the YT and NWT (*photo by Richard Harrington*).

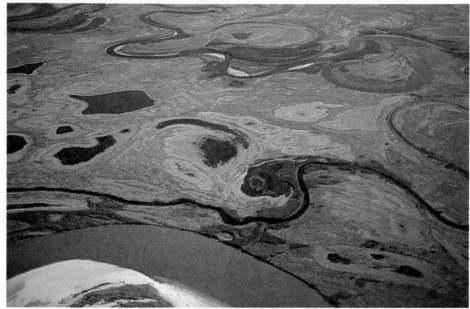

Near Old Crow, YT, 112 km inside the Arctic Circle (*photo by Hans Blohm/Masterfile*).

ecutive committee consisting first of appointed officials and representatives of the legislative assembly (former council) and in its later stages of the deputy commissioner and 5 elected members from the legislative assembly. In 1979 an executive council of 5 elected members functioning as a Cabinet superseded the former executive committee, and reports to the government leader instead of the commissioner. (Party politics were introduced to the Yukon assembly for the first time in 1978.) The territory thus has been moving closer to the format of provincial governments. At present, with different political parties in government in Ottawa and in Whitehorse and with the disastrous economic plight of the Yukon, constitutional change continues to take place, but at a much slower pace. There is an elected "government leader" (but not "premier") and an appointed commissioner.

Judiciary In 1984 the Yukon Territorial Court consisted of a single judge of superior court rank, 2 chief judges and several deputy judges, located in Whitehorse. There are approximately 45 justices of the peace appointed by the commissioner at 15 locations in the territory. The judge of the Supreme Court of the Yukon Territory is ex officio judge in the NWT and vice versa. Permanent courtrooms are located in Whitehorse, Watson Lk and Dawson, while regular court circuits also convene in other communities.

Local government At the local administrative level and following current reorganization, there will be one city in the Yukon (Whitehorse), 3 towns (Dawson, Faro, Watson Lk), and 4 villages (Mayo, Haines Junction, Teslin, and Carmacks). There are other unorganized communities.

Health The territorial government shares with the federal government the responsibility for health service. Modern hospitals are located in Whitehorse, Mayo, Faro, Watson Lk and Dawson, and there is a nursing station at Old Crow. There also are health centres staffed by one or more public health nurses in 11 communities, dental services and a wide range of more specialized medical and social services available.

Politics The 2 major political issues are native land claims and provincial status. The native Indians of the Yukon have never signed treaties with the federal government. Their Council for Yukon Indians continues to prepare its case for a land claims settlement, also with federal government financial assistance. They have threatened to block major development projects (eg, the Alaska Gas Pipeline) unless their claim is settled.

Education

Education is available to university entrance level, based on the BC curriculum, with financial assistance available for those continuing elsewhere. In total, about 5100 students are attending 23 public schools. The Yukon Vocational and Technical Training Centre in Whitehorse offers pre-employment education. Special programs are available in ADULT EDUCATION and to improve the employment opportunities for native residents. In March 1983 Yukon College was established to integrate all post-secondary education and training. It makes available a variety of full-time and part-time programs in several centres.

Cultural Life

Aboriginal native culture in the Yukon has been severely altered by the whaling era at Herschel I, the Klondike Gold Rush, WWII, and modern communications. Pride in native cultural traditions and crafts has been encouraged in recent years by government programs, and by such activities as the Arctic Winter Games with competitors from the Yukon, the NWT and Alaska.

Arts The MacBride Museum in Whitehorse is open part of the year, and the Dawson Museum

and a mining museum in Keno near Mayo are open during the summer. A Yukon Arts Council provides administrative support for cultural organization including the Yukon Contact, an ongoing program bringing together Yukon's performing artists. The Territorial Library and Archives are located in Whitehorse, with library branches in Dawson, Elsa, Faro, Haines Junction, Mayo, Watson Lk and Teslin.

Communications Three newspapers are published in the Yukon Territory, including 2 tri-weekly in Whitehorse. Two radio stations and one TV station are located in Whitehorse, with CBC Radio serving most communities by microwave. Live TV is generally available by means of satellite. Telephone and telex services are available throughout the Yukon (*see* COMMUNICATIONS IN THE NORTH).

Historic Sites Historic sites in the Yukon are particularly associated with the Klondike Gold Rush. The date of the major discovery in the Klondike, Aug 17 (1896), continues to be observed as a holiday ("Discovery Day") in the Yukon. Many historic relics still survive along the route from the Chilkoot and White Passes through the Coast Mountains, through Whitehorse to the culmination in Dawson, with its dramatic old buildings, and up "the creeks" in the vicinity. Other significant earlier sites exist from the FUR TRADE period. The earliest of all are the archaeological discoveries made near Old Crow which have proved to be the earliest known traces of man in Canada.

History

The Yukon Indians all belong to the Athapaskan linguistic family. They included the Nahanni in the E (with Kaska, Goat and Mountain groups), and several groups in the S and W (Teslin, Tutchone, Tagish, etc.). These latter had a greater variety of food sources, including salmon, but were often dominated by the fierce coastal Tlingit, to the extent that some adopted their language. In the central and northern Yukon, the KUTCHIN occupied the basin of the Yukon R downstream from the mouth of the Pelly R, including the Porcupine R area to the N, and also the Peel R basin in the NE.

Exploration Early exploration was associated mainly with the fur trade. By the late 19th century, gold prospectors in growing numbers pushed northwards from the Cassiar and Omineca Mountains of northern BC. Crossing onto the Yukon watershed they worked their way along the various rivers. Others moved inland from the Bering Sea, following up the Yukon R from its mouth by stern-wheeler. Several centres of gold mining developed, often for only a brief period. Fortymile, almost astride the Alaskan boundary, was one. George Carmack's discovery of gold on Bonanza Creek, a tributary of the Klondike R, on 17 Aug 1896, however, marked the beginning of what is often considered the world's greatest gold rush. Thousands of newcomers poured into this hitherto remote corner of Canada, transforming the Yukon permanently. Most of the goldseekers arrived by way of Skagway and the upper Yukon R. Others tried the "Overland Route" from Edmonton, via the Peace or Mackenzie Rs, but few reached their destination. Still others sought an all-American route via Valdez, Alaska, hoping to avoid Canadian government regulations. Dawson came into existence to serve the influx, at the junction of the Klondike and Yukon Rs, with the actual mining up the nearby creeks. In one month, in 1898, it grew into the largest Canadian city W of Winnipeg, developing a complete range of services, including water, sewerage, electricity and telephones. At its peak, the population has been estimated at 40 000. The Yukon was made a separate territory, Dawson named its capital, and a well integrated transportation system was established through much of the territory. White-

horse came into existence as the point where trans-shipping from rail to river took place, but Dawson was the dominant centre. Between 1897 and 1904, it is estimated that over $100 million in gold was recovered from the creek gravels. The population of Dawson began to decline almost immediately. Newcomers seeking easy riches were soon discouraged and lured by reports of other gold discoveries (eg, Nome, Alaska in 1899). By 1906 the most easily worked placer mines were finished and miners left in increasing numbers. They were replaced by large companies, particularly the Yukon Consolidated Gold Corporation, which had the resources to finance the costs of gold dredging. Employees were only there in the summers and Dawson withered to a shell of its former self. Fixed gold prices and rising costs eventually resulted in the closing down of the last gold dredge in 1966. The recent increase in gold prices has resulted in renewed activity in gold mining, but relatively few people are involved since modern equipment reduces the need.

Development The impact of WWII resulted in the population of Whitehorse mushrooming as it became the transportation and service centre for the territory. Transference of the capital from Dawson to Whitehorse (announced in 1951 and completed in 1953) proved yet another blow for the former and added still more residents to its upstart rival. Other mining centres strengthened the economic base of the territory and gave rise to additional communities. The Keno Hill area produced silver and lead as early as 1913 but mainly since 1946, with the mill and townsite at Elsa and Mayo the service centre. Copper has been mined in the Whitehorse area at various times. Asbestos was mined at Clinton Creek W of Dawson between 1958 and 1978. The largest economic development in postwar years in the Yukon was the opening of the giant open-pit Cyprus Anvil mine, to produce zinc and lead primarily for the Japanese market. First concentrates were shipped in 1969, resulting in the creation of an entirely new town, Faro, now the second largest centre in the Yukon. Closings and cut backs of mining operations during the early 1980s, caused by depressed world markets and increased production and transportation costs brings the sensitive nature of the Yukon's economy again into sharp focus.   WILLIAM C. WONDERS

Reading: P. Berton, *Klondike* (1958); L.-E. Hamelin, *Canadian Nordicity: It's Your North Too* (1979); K.M. Lysyk et al, *Alaska Highway Pipeline Inquiry* (1977); W.G. MacLeod, *The Dempster Highway* (1979); D.H. Pimlott et al, eds, *Arctic Alternatives* (1973); K.J. Rea, *The Political Economy of the Canadian North* (1968); William C. Wonders, ed, *The North* (1972); M. Zaslow, *The Opening of the Canadian North, 1870-1914* (1971).

Zeidler, Eberhard Heinrich, architect (b at Braunsdorf, Germany 11 Jan 1926). He is the most successful Canadian exponent of building technology as the central theme for architectural design. Trained at the Bauhaus, Weimar, E Germany and the Technische Hochschule, Karlsruhe, W Germany Zeidler emigrated to Canada in 1951. He joined Blackwell and Craig in Peterborough, Ont and the successor firm, now Toronto based, is Zeidler Roberts Partnership/Architects. The technological themes displayed by Zeidler's work include structural and mechanical services (especially exposed airhandling ducts) and movement and communication systems. McMaster University Health Sciences Centre (1972) combined regular geometric building modules, marked by glazed service and circulation towers, internally exposed steel trusses, ducts and an automated materials delivery system to create a building reminiscent of a child's giant construction set. The display of mechanical efficiency is made more palatable to occupants by colourful interiors, generous greenery and interior court-

yards. Other works include Ontario Place, Toronto (1969), and EATON CENTRE, Toronto (1973, with BREGMAN AND HAMANN), the Walter C. Mackenzie Health Science Centre, Edmonton (1982), Canada Place for Expo 86, Vancouver, and the plan for the $700-million Yerba Buena Gardens in San Francisco.   MICHAEL McMORDIE

Zeisberger, David, Moravian clergyman (b near Ostrava, Czech 11 Apr 1721; d in Ohio 17 Nov 1808). Beginning in the 1740s he carried on Moravian missionary work among the Indians of Pennsylvania and founded a settlement in Ohio. The pacifism of his creed brought him and his converts under suspicion during the AMERICAN REVOLUTION and many were killed. In 1786 he founded New Salem (near Milan, Ohio), but was forced to evacuate in 1791 and moved with his followers to a grant along the Thames R, near present-day Thamesville, Ont. He established a flourishing agricultural colony, called Fairfield in English. However, defections weakened the colony and he reluctantly accepted the encouragement of the Moravian bishop in the US to set up a new colony at Goshen, Ohio. Descendants of Zeisberger's converts still live on the remainder of his Thames R colony, called the Moravian Indian Reserve. He left a valuable legacy of writings on native culture and language.   JAMES MARSH

Zinc (Zn), bluish white metal of low to intermediate hardness, which melts at 419°C and is estimated to comprise about 0.013% of the Earth's crust. Zinc usually occurs as the MINERAL sphalerite. Brass, produced by colouring copper with the zinc mineral calamine, was in use 3000 years ago, but zinc was first identified as a metal in the 16th century. Commercial production began in Europe in the 18th century; and in Canada in 1916 at TRAIL, BC, when Cominco Ltd opened a small electrolytic plant, using ore from the Sullivan Mine. Production was hampered because the complex lead-zinc-iron ore was difficult to treat. In 1920 the differential flotation method was successfully used to separate out lead and zinc concentrates, marking the beginning of substantial zinc production in Canada. In 1982 about 30 mining operations produce about one million tonnes of zinc, in concentrates which are either refined in Canada or exported; the value was just over $1 billion. Zinc mines are located in every province and territory except Alberta, NS and PEI. As well as the original Sullivan Mine, Cominco operates Polaris, the world's northernmost mine.

A total of 671 000 t of refined zinc is produced annually at Trail, BC; VALLEYFIELD, Qué; Hoyle, Ont; and FLIN FLON, Man. Zinc production involves roasting, leaching, electrowinning and melting (*see* METALLURGY). Canada, the world's largest zinc producer, contributes about 25% of the Western world's supply. About 85% of production is exported as refined metal or concentrates; major customers are the US and UK for metal, and Japan, Belgium, the US and Germany for concentrates. Zinc is used principally to galvanize iron and to prepare alloys such as brass and German silver. The next most common use is in die-cast products, eg, small electrical appliances, tools, toys, automobile door and window handles, carburetors, etc. Rolled zinc metal is used in dry-cell batteries and for roofing; zinc oxide is used in paints and as a catalyst in rubber manufacture.   M.J. GAUVIN

Zoning is the term used to describe the control by authority of the use of land, and of the buildings and improvements thereon. Areas of land are divided by appropriate authorities into zones within which various uses are permitted. Any buildings to be constructed thereon are designated for certain uses and their size, location and appearance are regulated. Zoning is thus at the heart of development control by which responsible governments spell out their immediate and long-range land-use goals (*see* URBAN AND REGIONAL PLANNING).

In Canada the control of land and its uses is a provincial responsibility. It is derived from the constitutional authority over "property and civil rights" granted to the provinces under the BNA Act of 1867 and carried forward in the Constitution Act, 1982. The zoning power relates to "real property," or land and the improvements constructed thereon that become part of the land itself (in Québec, "*immeubles*"). Each province has established municipalities and regions empowered to control the use of land within their boundaries. Provision has also been made for control of land use in unorganized areas of the province. In both areas provincial tribunals are the ultimate authority for appeal and review. In Ontario a recent amendment permits the provincial government to affect the exercise of this power in that the official plans must comply with provincial policy statements.

Each municipality may enact bylaws to control the use of land within its boundaries. Plans are made by the municipality and the land area is divided into zones, each zone being set apart from certain defined uses. Plans are based on geographic features and existing development such as harbours, railways, highways, buildings and land use. Bylaws are then enacted to restrict the use of land in the defined areas to those uses established by the planning process.

There are many uses for land: agricultural; forest; highways; parks; industrial (abattoirs, factories, warehousing, etc); commercial (from corner groceries to high-rise office complexes); residential (from single homes to high-rise apartments and to condominiums). Each use ascribed to an area sets the value on the land affected and establishes the profile of a municipality. Their common aim is to allow uses that do not harm one another to be clustered together in the same zone, while keeping "incompatible" uses apart in their separate zones. On the outskirts of cities, by contrast, land may be held under a general zoning category that simply indicates that it is scheduled for development one day. The detailed zoning map cannot be drawn until a detailed development plan has been approved. Some of the outlying land may also be zoned for agricultural use or for a green belt, if it is not needed for urban development in the foreseeable future or if the municipal government wishes to prevent the city from expanding farther onto rural land (*see* NATIONAL CAPITAL COMMISSION). In rural municipalities, zoning is mostly used to protect agricultural land from urban or industrial development.

In addition to separating incompatible uses, the main objective of zoning is to control the intensity with which land is used. In residential districts, eg, there will often be a limit on the number of dwelling units that can be built per acre or hectare. Lot dimensions will also be regulated, and there is an obvious difference in the intensity of development between use zones that permit detached houses on 20 m frontages and those permitting row houses on 5 m frontages. Where the bylaw provides for high-density development, it establishes this density by defining the floor-space index (fsi) that will be permitted on the parcel being dealt with. For example, in a downtown core all land may be zoned commercial with an fsi of 8:1. This means that the office building to be constructed thereon can have 8 times the land area of the parcel as floor space. This could result in an 8-storey building covering the entire lot or, taking into account setbacks from streets or neighbouring buildings, or special designs with patios, etc, even a 16- to 20-storey tower. Many urban municipalities now offer "incentive zoning" or "bonusing" to encourage developers to add features to their buildings. For example, in return for constructing an enclosed garden or an el-

evated walkway to an adjacent building, a developer may be allowed to exceed the fsi for the district (*see* DEVELOPMENT INDUSTRY; URBAN DESIGN).

Power is given to departments of government to "designate" a use of land, or in Québec a line is drawn called a "homologated line," which puts the owner on notice that a special use may be made of some property — a highway, a road widening, a public park — and that nothing can be done on the land so affected until the final decision is made. The value of the land is established as of the date of designation.

Traditional zoning has often been criticized for its inflexibility, but techniques like incentive zoning indicate that municipal governments in Canada are willing to look for more flexible approaches to the regulation of land use. Another example is the transfer of development rights. Under this technique the right to a particular type of development may be transferred to a site that does not have the appropriate zoning, on condition that the use of the original site is not changed. This is especially important if the original site is zoned for more intensive use but is occupied by a building that the city council would like to preserve for historic or architectural reasons (*see* HERITAGE CONSERVATION).

In practice, zoning has been most effective at preventing change in stable, homogeneous districts. It has created the greatest difficulty when applied to areas of mixed land use or to areas where there are great pressures for change. In the former case there have been 2 standard approaches, though both are controversial. The first is "spot zoning," or picking out single sites for a class of use that is incompatible with the surrounding uses. A factory in a residential district would be an extreme example. The alternative approach, which is generally preferred, is to classify the factory as a "nonconforming use." This means that it can remain on condition that there is no change in the industrial use and no alterations to the buildings. Eventually, it is expected that the factory will be closed, allowing the site to be put to a compatible use.

In areas under development pressure, it is difficult to determine in advance the exact zoning that will be required. The needs of communities and of landowners and developers are in constant flux. As a consequence, particularly in rapidly growing cities, there is a continuous demand for amending bylaws, to change the use classifications of particular parcels of land. On one side there is pressure from developers who want sites to be "up-zoned" to permit redevelopment for more intensive use, such as apartments or office towers. On the other, community groups have organized to request "down-zoning" to prevent further redevelopment and to preserve whatever remains of their original neighbourhood.

As can be seen from these examples, zoning is often a contentious political issue that has to be settled by public debate and sometimes by court decisions. The need for land-use controls is now well accepted in Canada, however, and has gained strength from the increasing awareness of the public that land is owned in trust for future generations and not for immediate profit. This is also reflected in the awareness by citizens and public authorities of their respective rights and duties. In many western societies, notably in Europe, there is little freedom for an owner of land to control its use. In Canada too, owners have given up certain rights, or had them taken away, on the ground that the good of the community now and in the future is more important than the individual's rights. Thus, our laws are becoming more stringent and the planning of land use enters the life of every citizen. EILEEN MITCHELL THOMAS

Reading: M.A. Goldberg, Zoning: Its Costs and Relevance for the 1980s (1979); S.M. Makuch, Canadian Municipal and Planning Law (1983).

Zoology is the study of ANIMALS. Zoologists have many interests: some study form (morphology) or function (physiology), from gross to molecular levels; behaviour (ethology); association (ecology); distribution (zoogeography); some specialize in one kind of animal.

Early History People have always been interested in other animals and have needed their company. Among the earliest artifacts are images of animals scratched on bone or stone, or painted on cave walls. Aristotle (384-322 BC) provided the most comprehensive ancient commentaries on nature in his treatises. The understanding of man in nature that pervaded his philosophy dominated Western culture beyond the Renaissance, with the result that zoological knowledge has greatly influenced human behaviour. Following Aristotle, there was a pause in the accumulation of knowledge, lasting nearly 2000 years. Information became codified and dogmatic; argument took the place of experiment. Not until the Renaissance did curiosity and skilled, systematic observation of nature become widespread. Andreas Vesalius (1514-64), relying on his own senses, revivified the study of anatomy; William Harvey (1578-1657) demonstrated blood circulation by experimental means. Skilled dissectors made detailed explorations of animal structure and development. These and other workers made zoology an active science. Perhaps the greatest encyclopedic work of the time was the 44-volume *Histoire naturelle* of Georges de Buffon (1707-88), which provided a basis for the further exploration of nature which followed, literally, as the fleets of Europe set out to discover the world. The culmination of efforts to find relationships among living things and name them in a universally agreed upon manner was reached with the publication (1758) of the 10th edition of *Systema Natura* by Carolus Linnaeus. Thus the ever-growing collections could be systematically stored and catalogued, available for study and synthesis.

Nineteenth Century European science began to take on a clear form in the 19th century. Disciplined empiricism came to be expected of scientists, with the solution of problems leading to the posing of more advanced questions, to more critical and imaginative searching, and to more profound understanding. Comparative morphology, in the broadest sense, dominated zoology in the 19th century. J.B. Lamarck and Georges Cuvier, studying chiefly INVERTEBRATES and VERTEBRATES, respectively, established the pattern of such studies and showed the relationships of FOSSIL to recent forms. Using the microscope, zoologist Theodor Schwann and botanist Matthias Schleiden recognized in 1838-39 that cells occurred in all living things, and so established the first of the great unifying principles of BIOLOGY, the cell theory. This in turn spurred improvements in the microscope and in techniques of microscopy. During the last half of the century, microanatomical studies revealed the nature of egg and sperm and fertilization, the mechanisms (mitosis and meiosis) of cell division and the early progress of embryonic development.

Concurrently, physiology was firmly established as a rigorous experimental science. Great hope was held for the understanding of life on the basis of the laws of physics and chemistry. Among physiologists, Claude Bernard takes preeminence because of his grand generalization that an animal will maintain, as far as possible, a balanced function internally, unaffected by wide fluctuations of its external environment (homeostasis).

Perhaps the most significant event in zoology during the 19th century was the formal expression, in 1858-59, of the theory of EVOLUTION by natural selection by Charles Darwin and A.R. Wallace. Evolution is the second unifying principle of biology. Darwin was the first great ecologist and the greatest synthesizer of the 19th century, equally at home studying animals and plants. Among other things, he recognized that the same forces govern the histories of plants and animals, so closely indeed that many are said to have coevolved.

Twentieth Century The third great unifying principle, that of the mechanism of heredity, ie, the theory of the gene, belongs essentially to the 20th century. The initial statement was made in 1866 by Gregor Mendel, on the basis of his work with plants, but it was not until 1900 that his results were appreciated. Afterward, the development of GENETICS took place rapidly, the study of animals and micro-organisms contributing importantly to its growth. In 1953 James Watson and Francis Crick described the physical nature of the genetic materials, nucleic acids.

It is difficult and, in many respects, quite artificial, to divide biology into zoology and BOTANY. The overwhelming generality of the unifying principles apply equally to all organisms. Together, they lay the foundation for understanding the processes and potentialities of life, the basis of structure, and the external and internal mechanisms of adaptive change.

In the 20th century, zoology has followed several paths. Development, the mysterious process that leads to the final form of an animal, has been the subject of intense research, starting in the 19th century, and culminating, for a time, in the 1920s in the work of Hans Spemann. His demonstration of the phenomenon of embryonic induction and the concept of the organizer (cell masses in the embryo which regulate the development of nearby tissues) provided the basis for most of the work that has followed. A significant part of the work has been biochemical, and that is true in other areas of study, such as physiology (eg, respiration, enzyme kinetics), genetics (eg, nature of gene), evolution (eg, biochemical attributes of species) and ecology (eg, sources of energy). Similarly, biomathematical analysis is becoming increasingly sophisticated and widely used, particularly in a field such as ecology, which more than any other has grown out of natural history, but which is trying to produce hypotheses about environmental associations that are rigorously, quantitatively testable. It too has become an experimental science, simultaneously giving rise to current interest in and concern for the ENVIRONMENT. This influence must be added to the direct effects zoology continues to have on other primary concerns, eg, AGRICULTURE and medical science.

Zoology in Canada Part of the impetus to explore N America came from John Cabot's report (1497) of vast congregations of fish near its E coast. Nicholas DENYS published *Description géographique et historique des costes de l'Amérique septentrionale* (1672), based on experience around the Gulf of ST LAWRENCE. Between 1660 and 1725, first Claude Perreault, then Michel SARRAZIN, dissected and described numerous animals, including beaver, muskrat, wolverine and moose. Later explorers sent back descriptive natural histories which led to the opening of the Northwest for the FUR TRADE. In England, Thomas Pennant published *Arctic Zoology* (1784-87), based on collections made by explorers such as Samuel HEARNE. The best known of the early studies was *Fauna Boreali-Americana* (1829-37) by John RICHARDSON, who was surgeon and naturalist on Franklin's first 2 expeditions (1819-22 and 1825-26) and later commander of the Franklin search expedition of 1848-49. P.H. GOSSE began his career in Newfoundland and the Eastern Townships of Québec; his first work was *The Canadian Naturalist* (1840), written as he sailed home. In 1849, Moses Perley began an analysis of the NB fishery. In 1852, the federal government appointed Pierre FORTIN to control the Gulf of St Lawrence FISHERIES. These were the begin-

nings of fishery science in Canada. Biological stations were established in 1908 at St Andrews, NB, and Nanaimo, BC. The Biological Board of Canada, created in 1912, evolved into the Fisheries Research Board of Canada in 1937. The FRB, synonymous with excellence in fisheries research, was incorporated into the Department of Fisheries and Oceans in 1979.

The universities have been active, both in cooperation with fisheries and marine studies, and in more academic zoology. Natural history, as a separate science department, was established at University of Toronto in 1854, and at McGill and Queen's in 1858. Now, nearly every Canadian university has a zoology or biology department offering graduate study. Almost every field of zoology has outstanding practitioners. These have included Abbé Léon PROVANCHER, whose collections and descriptions provided a basis for the immensely important entomological studies for which Canada is noted; J.P. MCMURRICH, noted for work on subjects ranging from sea anemones to humans; A.G. HUNTSMAN, whose persistent curiosity and immense energy sparked many lines of research in fisheries; E.M. WALKER, one of the most influential entomologists in Canada; R.A. Wardle, godfather to a generation of parasitologists; William ROWAN, whose experiments with birds set the stage for important studies of photoperiodicity as an agent governing animal behaviour; J.B. COLLIP, endocrinologist, of insulin and parahormone fame; J.R. Dymond, influential in initiating systematic fish studies in Canada; W.A. Clemens, who, working both with the FRB and universities, played a vital role in developing zoology on the West Coast; Helen BATTLE, acclaimed teacher and investigator of the physiology, embryology, morphology and ecology of marine organisms; Donald RAWSON whose insights into the structure of lakes continue to excite limnological research; W.E. RICKER, leader in the analysis of fish populations; William Hoar, who set the standard for comparative physiology; C.P. LEBLOND, perhaps Canada's leading practitioner of electron microscopy and cellular analysis; Douglas Pimlott, articulate advocate of environmental concerns. The list represents only a tiny fraction of those who have made important contributions. Today, Canadian zoologists are at the forefront in studies of comparative respiratory and endocrine physiology, neurobiology, population analysis, PARASITOLOGY and vertebrate PALEONTOLOGY.

Extensive collections of organisms are held by the National Museum of Natural History, Ottawa; Royal Ontario Museum, Toronto; and the Entomology Research Institute, Ottawa. Provincial, local and university museums also are important, often especially for local fauna. MOLLUSCS, FISHES, BIRDS and MAMMALS are very well described for Canada, in a number of readily accessible books. The Biological Survey of Canada, supported by the National Museum, is developing descriptions and distributions in Canada of as many more groups of organisms as possible. Under this aegis the Entomological Society of Canada has published *Canada and Its Insect Fauna* (1978) and *Arctic Arthropods* (1981).

Zoology in Canada is served by the Entomological Soc of Canada (founded 1863), the Canadian Soc of Zoologists (founded 1961), and the Canadian Soc of Environmental Biologists, which began in 1959 as the Canadian Soc of Wildlife and Fishery Biologists. There are also provincial and local natural history clubs; groups dealing with special fields, eg, the Soc of Canadian Limnologists; and university activities, eg, the Canadian Committee of University Biology Chairmen; and professional organizations, eg, Assn des biologistes du Québec; the Alberta Soc of Professional Biologists. The Canadian Federation of Biological Societies, which comprises 8 specialist societies, including those

for physiologists, biochemists and cell biologists, provides a bridge between zoology in the broad sense and its medical applications. The Biological Council of Canada includes the Entomological Soc and the Canadian Soc of Zoologists among its constituents. The council and the federation represent the needs of biological sciences to the federal government.

Scientists are cosmopolitan; they communicate with and depend on colleagues from around the world. There are literally thousands of journals specializing in biology; many of these are used by Canadian zoologists. But among the world's leading journals for zoology are the *Canadian Journal of Fisheries and Aquatic Sciences,* which first appeared in 1901 as *Contributions to Canadian Biology,* and the *Canadian Journal of Zoology,* a publication of the NATIONAL RESEARCH COUNCIL, which began as the *Canadian Journal of Research* in 1935; both are published monthly. Other important journals are *Le naturaliste canadien* (from 1868), *The Canadian Entomologist* (from 1868), *The Canadian Field-Naturalist* (from 1887), *Quaestiones Entomologicae* (from 1965) and *Syesis* (from 1968).

Opportunities for careers in zoology continue in Canada as Canadians develop farm and fishery resources, learn to appreciate the environment, advance medical research and contribute generally to an understanding of the history of life.   J.R. NURSALL

Zooplankton, weakly swimming ANIMALS belonging to many phyla (primary divisions of the animal kingdom), which, as larvae or adults, exist wholly suspended within a water body. The marine zooplankton is dominated by copepod CRUSTACEANS, found in great numbers in all oceans. The following organisms appear in lesser quantities in the zooplankton: euphausiid crustaceans (eg, krill), chaetognaths (arrow worms), pteropods (small gastropod MOLLUSCS), tunicates (protochordates), ctenophores (comb jellies) and JELLYFISH. Animals that are planktonic for only part of their lives include clam, crab and barnacle larvae, and fish eggs and larvae. Hundreds of species occur in Canadian waters but few exclusively. Locomotion is by movement of structures resembling oars, wings or fins; by cilia (hairlike appendages); or even by jet propulsion. Zooplankton range from zooflagellates a few micrometres long, to large jellyfish. Most feed on smaller particles, including phytoplankton (microscopic plants), using sievelike devices which may function like flypaper rather than sieves because viscous forces prevail in water at such small scales of motion. Other planktonic animals are omnivores or carnivores. Several steps in the food chain can occur within the PLANKTON if the dominant primary producers are very small (under 1 μm), eg, cyanobacteria (*see* BLUE-GREEN ALGAE). Because energy is lost at each step, the elaborate food webs characteristic of warmer, offshore waters usually do not produce commercially exploitable quantities of fish. Japanese and Russian researchers have tried to improve on the chain by harvesting krill for human consumption. Krill and copepod crustaceans added to the diets of AQUACULTURED salmon, trout, etc, improve flesh colour.

Zooplankton occur everywhere in fresh or salt water, if oxygen is present. Usually, more and larger specimens representing fewer species are found near shore, near the surface and at high latitudes. Fewer, smaller, more diverse plankton occur offshore. Adaptations for pelagic (open sea) existence may include gas-filled floats, but most animals probably adjust their internal ionic composition to regulate buoyancy. Elaborate fans of setae (bristles) or tentacles probably serve for feeding, for flotation and as sensors. Where light penetrates, animals are often transparent to avoid detection by prey or predators.

Near the surface, blue pigment, offering camouflage and protection from ultraviolet light, is common. In the twilight zone animals are darker and frequently possess light-producing organs (photophores) or produce light-emitting (bioluminescent) secretions. Bioluminescence may countershade the animal when seen from below, may confuse predators or serve as an intraspecific recognition signal, but its adaptive role remains in dispute. The daily migrations, often of hundreds of metres, made by many zooplankters are little understood, although reduced predation at night is advantageous to herbivorous forms seeking near-surface phytoplankton concentrations.

Exclusively marine and largely planktonic comb jellies and arrow worms are important zooplankters; comb jellies because of their numbers and predatory impact; arrow worms because of their value as indicators of water quality. Comb jellies, jellyfishlike animals which swim with 8 rows of comb plates, capture food with entangling colloblasts (adhesive cells). Most are bioluminescent. Larvae of most species have tentacles; in some adults, tentacles act as a net to capture other zooplankton. Arrow worms belong to a coelomate phylum of uncertain affinities. Most are transparent ambush-predators, capturing other zooplankton with 8-12 pairs of bony, raptorial spines.　　R.J. CONOVER

Zoos or zoological gardens are facilities exhibiting wild and domesticated ANIMALS for purposes of education, recreation, conservation and research. Zoological gardens can be conventional, dense-occupancy zoos or open animal parks and game farms. They can incorporate aquariums exhibiting FISH and other aquatic life forms. Often, aquariums, oceanariums and sealife parks are independent, specialized, public facilities.

History People have always kept captive wildlife. Nomadic peoples maintained few species, but with the emergence of sedentary societies, animal collections became larger and more commonplace, eg, in Egypt, Assyria and China 3000-1000 BC, and later in Greece and Rome. Augustus Caesar (63 BC-14 AD) maintained a menagerie of over 3500 animals, a collection larger than any Canadian zoo. The famous menagerie of the Aztec ruler Montezuma II (c1480-1520 AD) employed 600 keepers. When monarchies were replaced by parliamentary governments, many private collections became public zoos; eg, the menagerie of Louis XVI, at Versailles, was moved to the Jardin des Plantes (1794). Many zoological gardens have evolved in the last 200 years. The *International Zoo Yearbook* (1981) lists 628 zoological facilities, but is not exhaustive. The roster of *Canadian Zoos, Game Farms and Aquariums 1982*, published by the Canadian Assn of Zoological Gardens and Aquariums (est 1975), notes 61 facilities.

Objectives Private zoos brought prestige to their owners and entertainment to their guests. Early public zoos emphasized recreation, later coming to serve modern objectives of education, CONSERVATION and research. During the first half of the 20th century, zoos commonly attempted to show a wide variety of species in rows of cages, giving animal inventories the character of stamp collections. The concentration of species offered a broad spectrum for taxonomic (systematic classification) study and, by its diver-

sity, considerable entertainment to viewers, but the approach has become outdated, and the zoos have been redesigned to foster a better understanding of animal psychology and behaviour.

The artificial environment of a zoo must accommodate the physical and psychological needs of animals; exhibits must provide seclusion, sight barriers, camouflage, opportunities for hierarchical positioning, and stimulus to prevent boredom and stereotyped behaviour. The reduction of obvious barriers (eg, bars, fences) is important. Many modern exhibits hold animals through their physical and behavioural limitations, using water moats, dry moats, electric fences, light zones, etc. Glass barriers are used to provide an unobstructed view. Many exhibits have off-exhibit facilities (eg, maternity dens, sleeping boxes, treatment enclosures) that are often equipped with closed-circuit television for behavioural monitoring. Urban environments are in sharp contrast to undisturbed natural ecosystems, and zoological gardens serve as a link and catalyst to nature appreciation. Zoos are engaged in various international conservation programs. International studbooks are maintained for many endangered species. The American Assn of Zoological Parks and Aquariums adopted a Species Survival Plan (1981) which has the committed support of participating zoos. Zoos have become wildlife producers, not wildlife users as in former times. Today, few animals are collected from the wild for zoos. Most zoos operate extensive rescue and animal orphanage programs. Rehabilitated specimens are returned to their native habitats, or exhibited and traded with other zoos.

With diminishing wild habitats, countless species of animals become endangered, even extinct. Zoos propagate various species in captivity, and some species now depend on captive management for survival. Relatively few species can be perpetuated in captivity: only about

Janusz Zurakowski, Avro Aircraft's chief test pilot, shown here after the first flight in the Avro Arrow, 25 March 1958 (*courtesy Public Archives of Canada/C-61731*).

350 of 4050 mammal species have had multiple-generation reproductions in captivity.

Zoo Management Zoos have become complex operations. Animal husbandry, research and development, education and interpretation, VETERINARY MEDICINE, public relations, food services, horticulture, facility maintenance, security, marketing, general administration and finance are all important. Many zoos are subsidized by municipal or provincial funding; direct federal funding is less common. Other facilities operate commercially; shareholders receive profits after operating expenses and capital development costs are covered. Commonly, zoos have the support of zoological societies — volunteer, usually tax-exempt, nonprofit organizations; involvement ranges from interested affiliation to managing authority. Major zoos are found in larger cities. The Riverdale Zoo in Toronto (est 1887) was Canada's first. The Metro Toronto Zoo, Canada's largest, opened in 1974; Stanley Park Zoo, Vancouver, 1888; Assiniboine Park Zoo, Winnipeg, 1905; Calgary Zoo, 1917; Moose Jaw Wild Animal Park, 1929; Provincial Wildlife Park, Shubenacadie, NS, 1947; Vancouver Aquarium, 1956; Jardin Zoologique de Montréal, 1957; Valley Zoo, Edmonton, 1959; Aquarium de Québec, 1959; Aquarium de Montréal, 1967; African Lion Safari, Rockton, Ont, 1969; Parc Safari Africain, Hemmingford, Qué, 1972; and Salmonier Nature Park, Holyrood, Nfld, 1978. Canadian zoos range from very modest collections to facilities exhibiting more than 3000 animals of over 400 species. Costly housing requirements during the winter season may limit the number of exotic species. Over 15 million visitors are estimated to visit Canadian zoos annually.

PETER KARSTEN

Zouaves Between Feb 1868 and Sept 1870, 7 contingents of Canadians enrolled in the papal army to help defend Rome from the Italian troops who wanted to bring about Italian unification. The last contingent of 114 recruits left too late and had to turn back, for Rome surrendered on Sept 16. About 390 Canadians served as pontifical troops; well educated in the majority these young men came from most of the Québec parishes. The organizational committee set up by Bishop Ignace BOURGET of Montréal had recruited them for their moral qualities, because the main goal was to create an elite able to oppose the propagation within Québec of liberal ideas formally condemned by the pope. Freedom of speech and conscience, popular sovereignty and the separation of church from state — such were the grand ideals which the zouaves were to combat. Upon their return, they formed an association which still exists and whose objectives gradually adapted to the main concerns of the Roman Catholic Church.　　RENÉ HARDY

Zurakowski, Janusz, aviator (b at Ryzawka, Russia 12 Sept 1914). Raised in Poland, he joined the Polish Air Force in 1937, escaped to England and took part in the Battle of Britain. In 1945 he tested Britain's first jet fighter. In Toronto, he became Avro Aircraft's chief development pilot in 1952. He broke the sound barrier in an AVRO CF-100 — the first Canadian aircraft to reach that speed — and made the first flight of the AVRO ARROW, exceeding 1600 km/h on the seventh flight. He was awarded the MCKEE TROPHY in 1958.　　JAMES MARSH

Addendum

The following entry was inadvertently left out of its alphabetical place during production:

Co-operative Movement, a social and economic movement which emerged in Europe as a reaction to early 19th-century INDUSTRIALIZATION. Co-operative organizations, enterprises owned by and operated for the benefit of their members, follow a set of principles best defined in 1844 by co-operators in Rochdale, England. The most important principles were that members in a co-operative each had one vote regardless of the investments made; anyone could join; surpluses or profits were distributed to members according to their levels of participation; and co-operatives would undertake educational activities for their members. Co-operative marketing organizations began to appear in British North America in the 1840s when British labourers attempted unsuccessfully to start stores similar to those common in Britain. The first stable store, or society, was developed in 1861 in Stellarton, NS. Others appeared briefly in industrial areas from Cape Breton to Victoria. In the 1880s another wave of stores appeared with the KNIGHTS OF LABOR, an early trade union. Most soon closed, the casualties of depression, recession, poor management or member indifference. A number of producer co-operatives, or worker co-partnerships, were also started, but all soon failed. In the 20th century many trade unionists have supported workers' and housing co-operatives, but have generally shown a greater interest in issues of wages and working conditions or in political activity.

Co-operative principles were applied early to community experiments as well. During Canada's settlement period numerous utopian communities were established, but most, such as an Owenite community begun 1813 in Lambton County, UC, and the much later CANNINGTON MANOR in Saskatchewan, did not last long; others, such as the BARR COLONY and Sylvan Lake, Alta, survived, but at the expense of their comprehensive co-operative ideals.

Farmers were the first Canadian group which successfully developed co-operatives. Between 1860 and 1900 farmers in Ontario, Québec and Atlantic Canada developed over 1200 co-operative creameries and cheese factories to meet the needs of the rapidly growing DAIRY INDUSTRY. Mutual-insurance companies were organized to provide inexpensive protection against the ravages of fire, hail and early frost. Prairie farmers led by E.A. PARTRIDGE organized the Grain Growers' Grain Co in 1906 to market directly to millers and European buyers. In 1911 Saskatchewan farmers, aided by the provincial government, organized the Saskatchewan Co-operative Elevator Co. Two years later, Alberta farmers organized the Alberta Farmers' Co-operative Elevator Co. Numerous other Canadian farm groups — fruit growers, livestock producers, tobacco growers — organized smaller but important supply-purchasing and marketing groups before WWI. Meanwhile, workers and farmers in industrial areas formed co-operative stores. A few from Ontario and Nova Scotia met in Hamilton in 1909 to form the Co-operative Union of Canada, a national representative body and educational institution. And in 1900 in Québec, Alphonse DESJARDINS developed co-operative banking in organizing his first CAISSE POPULAIRE.

During WWI co-operative organizations flourished, as more farmers became concerned about marketing, consumers sought cheaper food in an inflationary period, and hard-pressed Canadians explored co-operative ways to save and borrow money. Farm co-operatives expanded rapidly, including the new multipurpose Co-operative Fédérée (est 1910 in Québec), and United Farmers' Co-operative (est 1914 in Ontario).

By 1919 most farmers wished to gain greater control over the marketing of their produce. They were soon drawn to "co-operative pooling," a system whereby members contracted to sell all produce through their co-operative and in return would receive dividends based on the quality of the produce they supplied. In 1923 and 1924 prairie grain growers organized wheat pools according to these principles. Other producers organized similar pools, usually provincially.

Co-operative stores did not develop as rapidly as marketing co-operatives. To secure supplies as inexpensively as possible, to start manufacture of their own goods and to provide assistance to stores needing help, co-operatives in Alberta, Saskatchewan and Manitoba organized wholesales, an important step in creating an integrated co-operative system in the West.

During the GREAT DEPRESSION many co-operatives folded. The wheat pools survived only because of financial assistance from provincial and federal governments. But the movement itself generally found new strength. Surviving co-operatives devoted considerable attention to their memberships and educational programs. The co-operative press, including the *Canadian Co-operator*, the *UFA*, the *Western Producer* and numerous bulletins, flourished. Several co-operatives, particularly the Wheat Pool, also hired organizers to help start co-operatives of all kinds. The most innovative effort was developed by the Extension Dept of ST FRANCIS XAVIER UNIVERSITY in Antigonish, NS. The ANTIGONISH MOVEMENT was particularly effective in developing study clubs which became the basis of CREDIT UNIONS, fishing and housing co-operatives, and co-operative stores. Other forms of co-operatives appearing during the 1930s included handicraft co-operatives in Atlantic Canada, fishing co-operatives on both coasts and on inland lakes, recreation co-operatives, co-operative health facilities, co-operative film clubs, and a petroleum co-operative and a farm-implement co-operative organized by prairie farmers.

During the 1940s, war and postwar prosperity allowed the movement to gain more power and influence. The co-operative financial sector gained significant new dimensions when insurance and TRUST COMPANIES were organized during the late 1940s and early 1950s in Québec, Ontario and Saskatchewan. The wholesales began some manufacturing, and the influence of marketing co-operatives grew steadily. Since the 1950s the co-operative movement has continued to grow. Today, it consists of related organizations with significant influence in the agriculture, finance, insurance, fishing, retail and housing industries. In 1980 there were 12 million memberships. The financial sector controlled \$35 billion in assets; the grain- and dairy-marketing co-operatives dominated their industries; and the retail co-operatives played significant roles on the Prairies and in Atlantic Canada. Since the mid-1970s, co-operatives have become particularly important in Québec — powerful forces in the provincial economy and important for the projected future of the province.

Despite these successes, co-operatives now face many problems. Their strengths lie largely in rural areas where declining populations will ultimately mean reduced total support. There is also a decrease in the number of larger co-operative organizations. As the organizations grow, it is very difficult to maintain the sense of ownership and degree of commitment typical of smaller co-operators. Perhaps most importantly, co-operators are challenged with deciding whether they want to create a distinctly different economic system, operating according to principles and goals different from private or government enterprise, or want merely to own a series of companies operating in those limited areas where, for historical and social reasons, they have happened to emerge. IAN MACPHERSON

Reading: Ian MacPherson, *Each For All* (1979).

INDEX

The reader should look for a subject first among the articles of the encyclopedia. Cross-references within the articles will lead the reader to other articles dealing with the same subject.

The index lists only those subjects that do not have their own articles in the encyclopedia. The index entries are listed alphabetically (in regular type), and are followed by references (in boldface type) to the titles of articles in which information can be found. It is hoped that this system will aid readers in choosing the most appropriate reference.

The reader interested in the computer language Pascal, for example, finding no article on the topic in the encyclopedia, will find the index entry "Pascal: **Computer-Assisted Learning; Computer Science,**" leading to the two articles which deal with Pascal.

A

A. Harris, Son & Co Ltd: **Agricultural Implements; Harris, Alanson; Harris, Lawren S.**

A. Murray MacKay Bridge: **Halifax**

A & P Stores: **Retail Trade**

A.B.L. Engineering Ltd: **Grain Elevators**

A.G. Huntsman award: **Garrett, Christopher John Raymond**

A.J.M. Smith Award: **Purdy, Alfred W.**

A.S. Whiting Co: **Oshawa**

A7 Ranch: **Cross, Alfred Ernest**

A Space: **Art Dealers; Art Writing & Criticism; Video Art**

A.V. Roe (Canada) Ltd: **Aerospace Industry; Avro Arrow; Curtis, Wilfred Austin; Gordon, Crawford; Industrial Research & Development; Zurakowski, Janusz**

Abasand Oils Ltd: **Bitumen**

Abbey, Sask: **Ross, J. Sinclair**

Abbot, Phillip S.: **Mountaineering**

Abbotsfield Airfield: **Automobile Racing**

Abbott, Henry: **Abbotsford**

Abegweit: **Glooscap**

Abegweit: **Ferries; Shipbuilding & Ship Repair**

Abeille canadienne: **Art Writing & Criticism**

Abel, Sid: **Lindsay, R.B. Theodore**

Abella, Irving: **Social History; Working-Class History**

Abella, Rosalie: **Symons, Thomas H.B.**

Abenaki dictionary: **Urgent Ethnology**

Abenaki Motor Inn: **Native People, Economic Conditions**

Abénaquise: **Sculpture**

Aberdeen Hospital: **Fraser, Graham**

Abernathy, Sask: **Motherwell Homestead**

Abitibi Canyon: **Technology**

Abitibi Power & Paper Co Ltd: **Abitibi-Price Inc; Ambridge, Douglas White; Iroquois Falls; Sturgeon Falls**

Abitibi River: **Abitibi, Lake; Fossil Plants; Moose River; Moosonee**

Abitibiwini: **Amos**

Aboriginal Multi-Media Soc of Alberta: **Native People, Communications**

absinthe: **Alcoholism**

Académie canadienne-française: **Charbonneau, Robert; Desrosiers, Léo-Paul; Ethier-Blais, Jean; Guèvremont, Germaine; Laurendeau, J.-E.-André; Panneton, Philippe; Savard, Félix-Antoine**

Académie canadienne Saint Thomas d'Aquin: **Philosophy**

Académie de musique de Québec: **Jehin-Prume, Frantz; Lavallée, Calixa; Music History; Papineau-Couture, Jean**

Académie des lettres et des sciences humaines: **Royal Society of Canada**

Académie française gold medal: **Roy, Camille**

Academy Award (Oscar): **Back, Frederic; Crawley, F.R. "Budge"; Film Animation; Hoedeman, Jacobus**

Academy of Canadian Cinema: **Film Festivals, Prizes**

Academy of Humanities: **Royal Society of Canada**

Academy of Medicine: **Drake, Theodore George Gustavus Harwood**

Academy of Radio Arts: **Greene, Lorne H.**

Academy of Science: **Royal Society of Canada**

Acadia College: **Acadia University; Cramp, John Mockett**

Acadia Village, NS: **Westville**

Acadian Coal Co: **Westville**

Acadian Convention: **Caraquet**

Acadian Entomology Soc: **Entomology**

Acadian Federation of Caisses Populaires: **Caraquet**

Acadian Forest: **Forest Regions**

Acadian Historical Village: **Caraquet**

Acadian Lines: **Bus Transportation; Nova Scotia**

Acadian Orogeny: **Geological Regions; New Brunswick**

Acadian Peninsula: **Pokemouche**

Acadian Recorder: **Literary Magazines in English; Literature in English; McCulloch, Thomas; Young, John**

Acadian studies: **Acadia; Université Sainte-Anne**

Acadian whitefish: **Endangered Animals**

Acadians: **Arsenault, Aubin-Edmond; Bathurst; Belcher, Jonathan; Bougainville, Louis-Antoine de; Brebner, John Bartlet; Buctouche; Campbellton, NB; Charlottetown; Constitutional History; Ethnic Literature; *Evangeline*; Franco-Ontarians; Furniture, Country; Gaspé; Irish; Landry, Pierre-Amand; Le Loutre, Jean-Louis; MacEachern, Angus Bernard; Madeleine, Iles de la; Mascarene, Paul; Meat-Processing Industry; Monckton, Robert; New Glasgow; Perrault, Pierre; Pichon, Thomas; Prince Edward Island; Saint-Pierre & Miquelon; Sept-Îles; Sigogne, Jean-Mandé; Skinners Pond; Stephenville**

Acadiensis: **Historiography; Literary Magazines in English; New Brunswick**

acanthoceplala: **Invertebrate**

Accelerated Christian Education: **Private School**

ACCESS: **Educational Broadcasting**

acetic acid: **Chemical Industries; Farm Silo; Petrochemical Industry**

acetone: **Chemical Industries; Chemistry; Distilling Industry**

acetylene: **Chemical Industries; Chemistry; Lighting; Willson, Thomas L.**

Achard, Eugène: **Children's Literature in French**

acorn: **Flour Milling Industry; Oak; Plants, Native Uses**

acorn squash: **Vegetable**

acoustic guitar: **Musical Instruments**

Act of Settlement of 1700 (Britain): **Constitutional Law**

Action Canada: **Hellyer, Paul T.**

Action canadienne-française: *Action nationale*

Action catholique: **Picard, Gérard**

Action intellectuelle de l'association de la jeunesse canadienne-française: **Literary Prizes in French**

Action nationale: **Germain, Jean-Claude**

Action paroissiale: *Actualité*

Active Pass: **Mayne Island**

Acton Vale, Qué: **Leckie, John E.**

ACTRA Award: **Francks, Don H.; Hutt, William; Pinsent, Gordon E.; Reid, D. Kate; Starowicz, Mark; Waxman, Albert S.**

Actualité économique: **Economics; Parizeau, Gérard**

actuarial science: **Mathematics**

Acworth, W.M.: **Railway History**

Ada: **Computer Science**

Adair, Colin: **Squash Racquets**

Adam, G. Mercer: **Literary Magazines in English; Literature in English - Theory & Criticism; Scadding, Henry**

Adam, Yvan: **Children's Literature in French**

Adams, Ian: **Popular Literature in English**

Adams, Lawrence: **Dance, Modern**

Adams, Levi: **Poetry in English**

Adams, Miriam: **Dance, Modern**

Adams, Porter: **Wine Industry**

Adams Mine: **Iron & Steel Industry**

Addiction Research Foundation: **Women & Health**

Addie, Jack: **Salvation Army**

Addressment of Status Program: **West Indians**

Adelman, Howard: **Lee, Dennis**

ADISQ Gala Award: **Arsenault, Angèle**

administration: **Public Administration**

Administration du droit de reproduction méchanique des auteurs, compositeurs et éditeurs: **Recording Industry**

Administrative Classifications in the Public Service, Royal Commission on: **Gordon, Walter L.**

Administrative Policy & Services Program: **Labour Canada**

Admiralty Inlet: **Baffin Island**

Admiralty Islands: **Thousand Islands**

Admiralty Survey 1819-22: **Georgian Bay**

Adult Occupational Training Act: **Labour Policy**

adulteration: **Distilling Industry; Food Legislation; Pharmaceuticals Industry**

adultery: **Alimony; Conspiracy; Crime; Family Law; Marriage & Divorce, History of**

advance poll: **Electoral Systems**

Advanced Training Opera Centre: **Alarie, Pierrette**

advertising tax: **Magazines**

Advisory Committee on Reconstruction: **Urban & Regional Planning**

Advisory Council on Scientific & Industrial Research: **Macallum, Archibald Byron**

Advisory Panel on Science Policy: **Mackenzie, Chalmers Jack**

Advisory Planning Committee on Medical Care (Sask): **Thompson, Walter Palmer**

adze: **Northwest Coast Indian Art; Tools, Carpentry**

AEL Microtel: **Telephones**

Aerial Experiment Assn: **Armed Forces - Air Force; Bell, Alexander Graham**

aerial spraying: **Manitoba; Pollution**

Aeronautics Act: **Air Law & Space Law; Airport Architecture; Aviation; Safety Standards; Transportation Regulation**

Aeroquay: **Architecture, Development**

aerosol: **Chemical Industries; Pollution**

Aerospace Law: **Air Law & Space Law**

AES Data Ltd: **Electronics Industry**

affidavit: **Commissioner for Oaths; Notary**

Affiliation des femmes du Québec: **Women's Movement**

affirmative action: **Social Mobility; Women & the Law; Women in the Labour Force; Women's Movement**

Affleck, Desbarats, Dimakopoulos, Lebensold, Michaud & Sise: **Place des Arts**

Affleck, Desbarats, Dimakopoulos, Lebensold & Sise: **Affleck, Raymond Tait; Architecture, Development; Bank Architecture; Hotel; Religious Building**

African Orthodox Church: **Orthodox Church**

African swine fever: **Veterinary Medicine**

African violet: **Flowers, Cultivated**

Afrikaners: **Africans; South African War**

Ag-Ex: **Brandon**

agar: **Algae; Seaweeds**

Agassiz, BC: **Research Stations, Agricultural**

Agassiz Provincial Forest: **Springfield**

agate: **Cape Blomidon; Gemstone; Souris, Man; Westport**

age of majority: **Civil Code**

Agence de coopération culturelle et technique: **Léger, Jean-Marc; Québec**

Agent Orange & Agent White: **International Boundary Commission**

Aggeok: **Pitseolak, Peter**

Aging, Special Committee on: **Gerontology**

Agnatha: **Fish; Hagfish; Lamprey**

Agnes Etherington Art Centre: **Biéler, André Charles; Charney, Melvin; Kingston**

Agnes Pépin, Sister: **Île-à-la-Crosse**

agnosticism: **Atheism & Agnosticism**

Agostini, Lucio: **Music History**

Agribition: **Agricultural Exhibitions**

Agricola: **Agriculture History; Young, John**

Agricultural Extension Services: **4-H Clubs**

Agricultural Institute of Canada: **Fredeen, Howard; Soil Science**

agricultural land loss: **British Columbia; Ontario; Penticton**

Agricultural Land Protection Act (Qué): **Québec**

Agricultural Land Rural Development Act: **Soil Conservation**

Agricultural Prices Support Board: **Agriculture & Food Policy**

Agricultural Rehabilitation & Development Agency: **Hamilton, F. Alvin G.**

Agricultural Services Board Act (Alta): **Soil Conservation**

Agricultural Societies Act (Alta): **Corporation Law**

Agricultural Stabilization Board: **Agriculture & Food Policy**

Agriculture, Dept of (Man): **McGilvray, Charles Duncan; Savage, Alfred**

Agriculture, Dept of (Ont): **Roads & Highways**

Agriculture, Dept of (Qué): **Veterinary Medicine, Education**

Agriculture, Dept of (Sask): **McPhail, Alexander James**

Agriculture Canada: **Agricultural Research & Development; Botanical Garden; Crop Insurance; Crop Research; Cuisine; Downey, Richard Keith; Entomology; Flowers, Cultivated; Fruit & Vegetable Industry; Geographical Information Systems; Harness Racing; Herbarium; National Museum of Science & Technology; Pesticide; Plant Disease; Prince Edward Island; Research Stations, Agricultural; Sheep Farming; Soil Science; Virus**

Agriculture Canada Arboretum & Botanic Gardens: **Botanical Garden**

Agriculture Museum: **National Museum of Science & Technology**

Agriculture Rehabilitation & Development Agency: **Geographical Information Systems**

Aguathuna, Nfld: **Port au Port Peninsula**

Ahousat: **Nootka**

AIDS: **Sexually Transmitted Disease**

Aikido: **Breeze, Claude Herbert; Jiu-jitsu**

Aikins, Carroll: **Little Theatre Movement; Theatre, English-Language**

Aims & Objectives of Education, Special Committee on, (Ont): **Education, Alternate**

Air BC: **Victoria**

Air Board: **Biggar, Oliver Mowat; Stedman, Ernest Walter**

Air Cadet League: **Cadets**

Air Canada Silver Broom: **Curling**

Air Council: **Campbell, Hugh Lester; Curtis, Wilfred Austin**

Air Creebec: **Diamond, Billy**

Air Defence Command: **Armed Forces - Unification**

Air Profile Recorder: **Cartography, History of**

Air Reserve: **Reserve Force of Canada**

air rights: **Real Estate**

air taxi: **de Havilland Otter**

air-traffic control: **Airport**

air transport: **Bush Flying; Northwest Territories; Political Campaign; Saskatchewan; Transportation Regulation**

Air Transport Board: **Canadian Transport Commission**

Air Transport Command: **Armed Forces - Unification**

aircraft: **Aerospace Industry; Aviation; Avro Arrow; Avro CF-100 Canuck; Avro Jetliner; Balloon; Bush Flying; Canadair CL-28 Argus; Canadair CL-215; Canadair CL-600 Challenger; de Havilland Beaver; de Havilland Caribou; de Havilland Dash 7; de Havilland Otter; Helicopter; Leaver, Eric William; Military Aviation & Aircraft; Noorduyn Norseman;** *Silver Dart*

Aircraft Accident Review Board: **Transport Canada**

aircraft carrier: **Armed Forces - Unification;** *Bonaventure*

airline industry: **Air Canada; Economic Regulation; Pacific Western Airlines Ltd; Quebecair; Regulatory Process; Trans-Canada Airlines; Wardair International Ltd**

Airline Maintenance Buildings Ltd: **Air Canada**

airmail: **Aviation; Dickins, C.H. "Punch"; Postal System; Turnbull, Walter James; Wilson, John Armistead**

airport security: **Airport; Policing**

Aishihik power project: **Yukon Territory**

Aitken, H.G.J.: **Business History**

Aitken, Kate: **Cuisine**

Aivilik (Repulse Bay): **Sadlermiut Inuit**

Aiyansh lava flow: **Geological Dating; Volcano**

Ajawaan Lake: **Prince Albert National Park**

Ajax, Ont: **Plastics-Processing Industry**

Akaitcho: **Dogrib; Yellowknife (Redknives, Copper)**

Akimiski Island: **James Bay**

Akiyama, Kazuyoshi: **Vancouver Symphony Orchestra**

Akpatok Island: **Ungava Bay**

Alaksen, BC: **Bird Sanctuaries & Reserves**

Alaska birch: **Vegetation Regions - Cordillera**

Alaska Current: **Coastal Waters**

Alaska Gas Pipeline: **Blair, S. Robert; Yukon Territory**

Alaska Pine Co: **Koerner, Leon J.**

Alaska yellow cedar: **Vegetation Regions - Cordillera**

Alaskan blueberry: **Vegetation Regions - Cordillera**

albacore: **Mackerel; Tuna**

Albanel, Charles: **Des Groseilliers, Médard Chouart**

Albarda, Jan: **Musical Instruments**

Alberni, BC: **Port Alberni**

Alberni, Pedro: **Port Alberni**

Alberni Inlet: **Port Alberni; Vancouver Island**

Albert, Prince: **Prince Albert; Stamp Collecting; Victoria Island**

Albert College: **Methodism**

Albert Harbour: **Lancaster Sound**

Alberta, Mont: **Mégantic Hills**

Alberta Achievment Award: **Music Awards & Competitions**

Alberta Agricultural Development Corp: **Alberta Heritage Savings Trust Fund**

Alberta & Great Waterways Railway: **Athabasca; Rutherford, Alexander C.**

Alberta Assn of Municipal Districts: **Greenfield, Herbert**

Alberta Ballet School: **Carse, M. Ruth P.**

Alberta Central Railway: **Red Deer**

Alberta College Music Centre: **Music Education**

Alberta College of Art: **Art, Contemporary Trends**

Alberta Correspondence School: **Distance Learning**

Alberta Farmers' Assn: **United Farmers of Alberta**

Alberta Farmers' Co-operative Elevator Co: **Co-operative Movement (See Addendum, page 1992); Grain Growers' Associations; United Farmers of Alberta**

Alberta Farmers' Union: **United Farmers of Canada**

Alberta Film & Television Awards: **Film Festivals, Prizes**

Alberta Gas Ethylene Co Ltd: **NOVA, An Alberta Corporation**

Alberta Gas Trunk Line Co Ltd: **Blair, S. Robert; Mackenzie Valley Pipeline; NOVA, An Alberta Corporation; Petroleum Industries**

Alberta Government Telephones: **Alberta Heritage Savings Trust Fund; Telephones; TransCanada Telephone System**

Alberta Heritage Foundation for Medical Research: **Immunology; Medical Research**

Alberta Historical Resource Site: **Head-Smashed-In Buffalo Jump**

Alberta Home Mortgage Corp: **Alberta Heritage Savings Trust Fund**

Alberta Housing Corp: **Alberta Heritage Savings Trust Fund**

Alberta Indian Assn: **Native People, Communications**

Alberta Indian Development Corp: **Steinhauer, Ralph G.**

Alberta Legislature Building: **Edmonton; Government Building**

Alberta Liquor Control Board: **Administrative Tribunals**

Alberta Lounge: **Peterson, Oscar E.**

Alberta Microelectronic Centre: **Electronics Industry**

Alberta Motion Picture Industries Assn: **Film Festivals, Prizes**

Alberta Municipal Financing Corp: **Alberta Heritage Savings Trust Fund**

Alberta Native Communications Soc: **Native People, Communications**

Alberta Newstart Inc: **Janvier, Alex S.**

Alberta Nitrogen Products: **Petrochemical Industry**

Alberta Non-Fiction Award: **Literary Prizes in English**

Alberta Oilers: **Edmonton Oilers**

Alberta Opportunity Co: **Alberta Heritage Savings Trust Fund**

Alberta Order of Excellence: **Manning, Ernest C.**

Alberta Petroleum Marketing Commission: **Energy Policy**

Alberta Plain: **Physiographic Regions - Interior Plains**

Alberta Planning Act: **Calgary**

Alberta Plateau: **Physiographic Regions - Interior Plains**

Alberta Playwriting Competition: **Literary Prizes in English**

Alberta Poetry Contest: **Literary Prizes in English**

Alberta Power Ltd: **Coal**

Alberta Provincial Police: **Perry, A. Bowen**

Alberta Regional History Award: **Literary Prizes in English**

Alberta Resources Railway: **Grande Cache**

Alberta Social Credit League: **Aberhart, William**

Alberta Society of Artists: **Artists' Organizations**

Alberta Stock Exchange: **Alberta; Stock & Bond Markets**

Alberta Teachers' Assn: **Teaching Profession**

Alberta Television Playwriting Competition: **Literary Prizes in English**

Alberta Theatre Projects: **Alberta; Theatre, English-Language; Theatre for Young Audiences**

Alberta-Vancouver formula: **Canadian Charter of Rights & Freedoms; Constitutional Law**

Alberta Vocational Centre: **Calgary**

Alberta (western white) spruce: **Biogeography**

Alberta Wilderness Assn: **Beck, Tom**

Alberton, PEI: **Prince Edward Island**

Alberton West Prince: **Prince Edward Island**

Albion Coal Mines: *Samson*

Albion Mines Railway: **Railway History**

albite: **Mineral**

Alcalá-Galiano, Dionisio: **Cartography, History of; Galiano Island; Kwakiutl; Spanish Exploration;** *Sutil & Mexicana*

Alcan Military Highway: **Alaska Highway; Fort St John; Johnson, Byron Ingemar**

Alcock, John: **St John's**

alcohol: **Automobile; Biomass Energy; Chemistry Subdisciplines; Lighting; Petroleum Research & Development; Potato**

Alcoholics Anonymous: **Alcoholism; Mental Health**

Alcoholism Foundation (Man): **Manitoba**

Aldergrove, BC: **Langley**

alderman: **Municipal Government**

Alderson, Sue Ann: **Children's Literature in English**

Alderville, Ont: **Sunday, John**

Alderville Reserve: **Sunday, John**

Aldous, J.E.P.: **Drama in English**

Aldwinkle, Eric: **Graphic Design; Printmaking**

ale: **Brewing Industry; Labatt, John**

Alert, NWT: **Climate; Earthquake; Ellesmere Island; Nordicity**

alewife: **Fisheries Policy; Herring**

Alexander: **Hector**

Alexander, Countess: **Alexander of Tunis, 1st Earl**

Alexander, David: **Painting**

Alexander, Henry: **Linguistics**

Alexander, J.E.: **Exploration & Travel Literature in English**

Alexander, James Lynn: **Poetry in English**

Alexander, Lincoln: **Blacks**

Alexander, William W.: **Printmaking**

Alexander Graham Bell Museum: **Baddeck**

Alexandra Falls: **Waterfall**

Alexandre Fjord: **Ellesmere Island**

Alexis Reserve: **Stoney**

Alfonse, Jean Fonteneau *dit*: **Montmorency Falls**

Alfred Hole Goose Sanctuary: **Rennie**

algebra: **Mathematics**

algin: **Algae**

alginate: **Seaweeds**

ALGOL: **Computer Science**

algology: **Botany History**

Algoma Central Railway: **Jackman, Henry N.R.; Sault Ste Marie**

Algoma College: **Laurentian University**

Algonquian dictionary: **Marie de l'Incarnation**

Algonquian languages: **Kamouraska; Muskellunge; Native People, Languages; Sault Ste Marie**

Algonquian-Wakashan language stock: **Anthropology, Linguistics**

Algonquians: **Abenaki; Algonquin; Beothuk; Blackfoot Nation; Children's Literature in French; Cree; Maliseet; Manitou; Micmac; Montagnais-Naskapi; Nanabozo; Native People - Eastern Woodlands; Ojibwa; Ottawa; Saguenay River; Snowshoes; Speck, Frank G.**

Algonquin: **Sculpture**

Algonquin, Lake: **Holland Marsh; Prehistory**

Algonquin College: **Ottawa, Ont**

Algonquin Hotel: **St Andrews, NB**

Algonquin Island: **Toronto Islands**

Algonquin Radio Observatory: **Observatory**

algorithms: **Computer Science; Computer Systems Applications**

Alianak, Hrant: **Drama in English**

Alianza Cultural Hispano-Canadiense: **Theatre, Multicultural**

Alice, Princess: **Athlone, Earl of**

Alida, Sask: **Danes**

Alien Labour Law: **Labour Policy**

alkali grass: **Vegetation Regions - Pacific Coastal; Vegetation Regions - Prairie**

All-Canadian Congress of Labour: **Canadian Congress of Labour; Canadian Federation of Labour; Cohen, Jacob Laurence; Industrial Unionism; Mosher, Aaron R.; Union Centrals, District & Regional; Union Centrals, National**

All People's Mission: **Gauld, Bella Hall; Urban Reform; Woodsworth, J.S.**

Allaire, Gaston: **Musicology**

Allan, Adam: **Drama in English**

Allan, Alexander: **Allan Line**

Allan, Denis: **Chess**

Allan, George: **Kane, Paul**

Allan, Luke: **Best-Sellers in English**

Allan, M. Martha: **Allan, Hugh Andrew Montagu; Drama in English**

Allan, Ted: **Allan, Andrew E.F.; Festival Lennoxville; Jewish Writing**

Allan, William: **Guelph**

Allan Cup: **Allan, Hugh Andrew Montagu; Smythe, Constantine Falkland Cary; Sports History**

Allan Memorial Institute of Psychiatry: **Biochemistry; Sourkes, Theodore Lionel**

Allanburg, Ont: **Niagara Peninsula**

Allandale, Ont: **Northern Railway of Canada**

allanite: **Mineral**

Allarco Broadcasting: **Allard, Charles A.**

Allarco Developments: **Allard, Charles A.**

Allard, Jean-Louis: **Philosophy**

Allard, Joseph: **Folk Music, Franco-Canadian**

Allard, Lac: **La Mauricie National Park**

Alldrick, A.A.: **Music Criticism**

Allen, A.D.: **Chemistry Subdisciplines**

Allen, Brian: **Toronto**

Allen, Charlotte Vale: **Popular Literature in English**

Allen, Donald: **Poetry in English**

Allen, F.: **Physics**

Allen, Grant: **Popular Literature in English**

Allen, Harold: **Social Gospel**

Allen, Reginald: **Philosophy**

Allen Brothers Theatres: **Film; Nathanson, Nathan Louis**

Allen-Gray, Dorothy: **Cuisine**

Alliance Laurentienne: **Separatism**

Alliance nationale: **Nelligan, Emile**

Allied Tribes of British Columbia: **Kelly, Peter Reginald; Native People, Political Organization & Activism; Native People - Northwest Coast; Paull, Andrew; Teit, James A.**

Allin, Elizabeth J.: **Physics**
Allison, Charles Frederick: **Mount Allison University**
Allison, John Fall: **Allison Pass; Princeton**
Allison, Susanne: **Aubert de Gaspé, Philippe-I.-F.**
Allisons, BC: **Princeton**
Alliston, Ont: **Banting, Frederick G.**
Allouez, Claude-Jean: **Cartography, History of; Nipigon, Lake**
alluvial fan: **Avalanche; Fraser River Lowland; Island; Okanagan Valley; River Landform**
Allward, Walter Seymour: **Public Art; Sculpture**
Allworth, R.H. Christopher: **Musical Instruments**
Alma, NB: **Shipbuilding & Ship Repair**
Alma College: **Methodism**
Almanach du peuple: **Massicotte, Edmond-Joseph**
Almi, A.: **Jewish Writing**
aloe: **Pharmaceuticals Industry**
Aloi, Santa: **Dance, Modern**
Alouette Lake: **Maple Ridge**
Alouette satellites: **Astronaut; Klein, George John; Physics; Satellite, Artificial; Satellite Communications; Space Technology**
alpha particle: **Nuclear Fusion**
Alpha Ridge: **CESAR; Invertebrate**
Alphabet: **Literary Magazines in English**
Alpine Club of Canada: **Mount Assiniboine Provincial Park; Mountaineering**
alpine fir: **Banff National Park; Garibaldi Provincial Park; Glacier National Park; Mount Assiniboine Provincial Park**
alpine larch: **Mount Assiniboine Provincial Park**
alpine meadow: **Kananaskis Country**
alpine sunflower: **Endangered Plants**
alpine tundra: **Physiographic Regions - Cordillera; Tundra**
ALRT system: **New Westminster; Transportation Research Centres**
Alsands consortium: **Bitumen; Megaprojects**
Alsatians: **Printmaking**
alsike clover: **Forage Crops**
alternating current (AC): **Hydroelectricity; Rogers, Edward Samuel**
alternation of generations: **Algae; Club Moss; Conifers; Fern; Horsetail; Irish Moss; Liverwort; Moss; Seed Plants**
Alternative Energy & Oil Substitution, Special Committee on: **Hydrogen; Peat**
Altman, Joshua: **Jewish Writing**
Alton, Ont: **Casson, Alfred Joseph**
Alton, Sheron: **Toronto**
Altona, Man: **Festivals**
alum-root: **Geranium**
Aluminum Co of America: **Alcan Aluminium Ltd; Jonquière**
Aluminum Co of Canada, Ltd: **Agar, Carlyle Clare; Alcan Aluminium Ltd; Arvida Strike; Powell, Ray Edwin**
Alvin Buckwold Centre: **Education, Special**
Alzheimer's disease: **Psychiatry**
Amabile, George: **Italian Writing**
amabilis fir: **Pacific Rim National Park; Vegetation Regions - Cordillera**
Amalgamated Clothing Workers of America: **Clothing Industries; Italians**
Amalgamated Mine Workers of NS: **Barrett, Silby**
Amalgamated Soc of Carpenters & Joiners: **Craft Unionism**
Amalgamated Soc of Engineers: **Bengough, Percy; Craft Unionism**
amalgamation: **Municipal Government**
Amaranth: **Literary Magazines in English**
Amaranth, Man: **Manitoba**
amaryllis: **Ornamentals**
Amateur Athletic Union of Canada: **Ewing, Walter Hamilton; Lacrosse; Sports Organization, Amateur; Swimming, Speed**

amateurism & professionalism: **Sports History; Track & Field**
Amazon: *Mary Celeste*
amazonite: **Gemstone**
Ambacher, Michel: **Philosophy**
Ambassador Bridge: **Windsor, Ont**
Ambedkar Mission: **Buddhism**
amber: **Aphid; Fly; Gemstone; Mineral; Mite**
amber durum: **Wheat**
AMCRO system: **Leaver, Eric William**
amebiasis: **Water-Borne Disease**
Amelia Frances Howard-Gibbon Medal: **Children's Literature in English**
Ameliasburgh, Ont: **Purdy, Alfred W.**
Aménagement rural et développement agricole: **Communications in Québec**
amending formula: **Constitution; Constitution Reference; Constitution, Patriation of; Constitution Act, 1982; Constitutional Law; Federalism**
American basswood: **Thousand Islands**
American beech: **Beech; Rondeau Provincial Park**
American Economic History Assn: **Innis, Harold A.**
American elk: **Wapiti**
American elm: **Biogeography; Elm**
American Falls: **Niagara Falls; Waterfall**
American Federation of Labor: **AFL-CIO; Canadian Federation of Labour; Craft Unionism; Flett, John A.; Hamilton; Labour Relations; One Big Union; Union Centrals, National**
American Hellenic Educational & Progressive Assn: **Greeks**
American Indian Movement: **Native People, Political Organization & Activism**
American League: **Baseball; Toronto Blue Jays**
American Newspaper Guild: **Journalism**
American redstart: **Warbler**
American skunk cabbage: **Vegetation Regions - Cordillera**
American Soc of Human Genetics: **Fraser, F. Clarke**
American wild dune grass: **Vegetation Regions - Pacific Coastal**
Ames, Alfred Ernest: **Simpson, Robert**
Ames, Holden & Co: **Ames, Herbert B.; Rubber Products Industry**
amethyst: **Cape Blomidon; Gemstone; Silica; Thunder Bay**
Amharic language: **Africans**
Amherst Boot & Shoe Manufacturing Co: **Pipes, William Thomas**
Amherst Island: **Fowler, Daniel**
Amherstburg Courier: **Sangster, Charles**
Amherstview, Ont: **Kingston**
amino acids: **Animal Agriculture; Food Additives; Genetics; Insulin; Molecules in Interstellar Space; Vegetarianism**
Amis de chiffon: **Theatre for Young Audiences**
Amis de Riel: **Theatre, French-Language**
Amis d'escoffier: **Cuisine**
Amish: **Anabaptists; Collectivism; Germans; Mennonites; New Hamburg; Separate School**
ammonia: **Chemical Industries; Chemistry; Chemistry Subdisciplines; Hydrogen; Petrochemical Industry**
ammonite: **Gemstone**
ammunition: **Armaments; Bedford Magazine Explosion**
Amnesty International: **Atwood, Margaret E.; Callwood, June; Novel in English**
Amoco Canada Petroleum Co Ltd: **Bitumen**
Amos, Alice: **Amos**
Amos, Bruce: **Chess**
Amos, Janet: **Blyth Festival**
amosite: **Asbestos**
amphetamines: **Drug Use, Non-Medical; Medical Drug Abuse; Non-Medical Use of Drugs, Royal Commission on the**
amphibole: **Soapstone**
amphineura: **Seashell**
amphipod: **Arctic Animals**

Amphitrite Point: **Ucluelet**
Amphitryon: **Drama in French**
Amprimoz, Alexandre: **Ethnic Literature; Italian Writing**
ampulla: **Silver, Church**
Amstel Brewery Canada Ltd: **Brewing Industry**
Amtmann, Willy: **Musicology**
amulet: **Inuit Art; Northwest Coast Indian Art**
Amundsen Gulf: **Holman; Horton River; Land Claims; Prince of Wales Strait; Sea Ice; Victoria Island**
Amyot, John A.: **Amyot, Francis**
Amyot, Laurent: **Art Education; Ste-Anne-de-Beaupré; Silver, Church; Silver, Domestic**
anabolic substance: **Sports Medicine**
Anahareo: **Belaney, Archibald S.**
Anaija: **Inuit Art**
Anakin, Doug: **Emery, John; Olympic Games**
analgesic: **Medical Drug Abuse**
analytical chemistry: **Chemistry Subdisciplines; Harris, Walter E.; Pharmaceuticals Industry**
anaphylactic shock: **Allergies; Black Fly**
anatase: **Titanium**
anatomy: **Altschul, Rudolf; Biology; Grant, John Charles Boileau; Leblond, Charles Philippe; Leeson, Thomas Sydney; McMurrich, James Playfair; Medicine, History of; Moore, Keith Leon; Physical Education; Shepherd, Francis John; Thompson, Ian Maclaren**
Ančerl, Karel: **Toronto Symphony**
Ancaster, Ont: **Hamilton; Textile Industry**
Anchorage Provincial Park: **Heritage Trail**
Ancienne Lorette, Qué: **Québec City**
Anciens Canadiens: **Novel in French**
ancient murrelet: **Endangered Animals**
Ancient Order of Hibernians: **Irish**
Anderson, Anne: **Dictionary**
Anderson, Doris: *Chatelaine*; **Children's Literature in English; Novel in English**
Anderson, Frank: **Chess**
Anderson, Fulton H.: **Philosophy**
Anderson, James: **Anderson River**
Anderson, Jorn: **Rough Trade**
Anderson, Les: **Archery**
Anderson, Margaret: **Women's Movement**
Anderson, Patrick: *Northern Review*; **Poetry in English**
Anderson, R.C.: **Parasitology**
Anderson, Reid: **Dance History**
Anderson, T.G.: **Manitowaning**
Anderson, William Henry: **Music History; Musicology**
Anderson & Co: **Port Alberni**
Anderson Lake: **Lillooet; Salish, Interior**
Anderson Siding, NB: **St-Quentin**
Andover, NB: **Ritchie, Albert Edgar**
André, John: **Odell, Jonathan**
Andrews, Jean: **Kurelek, William**
Andrews, John: **Architecture; Architecture, Development; Art; CN Tower**
anemia: **Alcoholism; Biochemistry; Cancer; Dandelion; Vegetarianism**
anemometer: **Patterson, John**
anesthesia: **Birthing Practices; Medicine, Contemporary; Medicine, History of; Savage, Alfred; Worthington, Edward Dagge**
anesthetic: **Medical Drug Abuse; Veterinary Medicines Industry**
aneurysm: **Medicine, Contemporary**
Anfousse, Ginette: **Children's Literature in French**
Ange-Gardien mission: **Sept-Îles**
Angel, Leonard: **Jewish Writing**
Angel, Roger: **Philosophy**
Angers, François-Réal: **Novel in French**
Anglican Fellowship for Social Action: **Social Gospel**
Anglican-Roman Catholic International Commission: **Anglicanism; Fairweather, Eugene Rathbone**
Anglin, Timothy W.: **Anglin, Margaret**

Anglo-American-Canadian Combined Production & Resources Board: **Taylor, Edward Plunkett**
Anglo-American Copyright Agreement: **Book Publishing, English-Language**
Anglo-American Hotel: **Bronfman Family**
Anglo-American Telegraph Co: **Heart's Content**
Anglo-Boer War: **South African War**
Anglo-French Convention of 1904: **French Shore**
Anglo-Newfoundland Development Co: **Grand Falls, Nfld; Newfoundland Loggers' Strike**
Anglo-Russian Convention: **Boundaries**
Angmarlik Inuit: **Pangnirtung**
Angolans: **Africans**
Angus L. MacDonald Bridge: **Halifax**
anhydrite: **Karst Landform**
ANIK satellites: **Aerospace Industry; Communications in the North; Educational Broadcasting; Satellite Communications; Space Technology**
Animal Diseases Research Institute: **Watson, Edward A.**
animal parks: **Zoos**
Animal Pathology Laboratory: **Watson, Edward A.**
Animal Quarantine Station: **Couture, Joseph-Alphonse**
Anjou: **Drama in French**
ankylosing spondylitis: **Arthritis**
Anna Banana: **Art, Contemporary Trends**
Annacis Island: **Delta, BC; New Westminster**
Annals: **Lawson, George**
Annapolis Basin: **Digby; Port-Royal**
Annapolis River: **Annapolis Lowlands; Annapolis Royal; Coastal Waters; Nova Scotia; Port-Royal**
Annaud, Jean-Jacques: **Héroux, Denis**
Anne: **Amherstburg**
Anne of England: **Annapolis Lowlands; Annapolis Royal; Mohawk; Silver, Church**
annexation: **Municipal Government**
Annual Farm Progress Show: **Agricultural Exhibitions**
annulment: **Family Law**
Anola, Man: **Springfield**
Anse-à-Valleau, Qué: **Gaspé, Qué**
Anse-des-Pilotes, Qué: **Bic, Ile du**
Anson, Frank: **Iroquois Falls**
Ansonville, Ont: **Iroquois Falls**
Antabuse: **Alcoholism**
antenna: **Electronics Industry; Klein, George John**
anthelmintics: **Veterinary Medicines Industry**
anthem: **Religious Music**
anthemis: **Flowers, Cultivated**
anthracite: **Coal**
anthropometry: **Anthropology**
anti-Americanism: **Continentalism; Diefenbaker, John G.; Imperialism; Toronto; Upper Canada**
anti-Asianism: **British Columbia; Japanese; Prejudice & Discrimination; Violence**
antibiotic: **Biology; Birthing Practices; Fungus; Lemieux, Raymond U.; Mold; Pharmaceuticals Industry; Sexually Transmitted Disease; Veterinary Medicine; Veterinary Medicines Industry**
antibodies: **Allergies; Biological Product**
anti-Catholic sentiment: **Canada First; Gavazzi Riots; Prejudice & Discrimination**
anti-Chinese sentiment: **Prejudice & Discrimination**
anti-communism: **Fascism; Ordre de Jacques-Cartier; Ukrainians**
anti-confederation sentiment: **Bennett, Charles James Fox; Parsons, Robert John; Smith, Albert James**
anti-conscription sentiment: **Conscription; Pacifism**
Anticosti Basin: **Petroleum**
anticyclones: **Meteorology**
anti-Darwinism: **Dawson, J. William**
antidepressant: **Medical Drug Abuse**
Anti-Dumping Tribunal: **Finance, Dept of; Footwear Industry**

antigen: **Allergies**
Antigonish harbour: **Antigonish**
anti-histaminics: **Allergies**
Anti-Inflation Act: **Wage & Price Controls**
anti-Japanese sentiment: **Prejudice & Discrimination**
"anti-loafing" law: **World War I**
antinationalism: *Cité libre;* **Economic Nationalism; Nationalism**
anti-nuclear campaign: **Pacifism**
Antiochian Orthodox Church: **Arabs; Orthodox Church**
Antiochian rite: **Catholicism**
anti-Semitism: **Fascism; Jewish Writing; Judaism; Prejudice & Discrimination; Refugees; Violence; Wilson, Cairine R.**
antisepsis: **Medicine, History of**
antisubmarine operations: **Armed Forces - Air Force; Canadair CL-28 Argus; Helicopter; Keys, David Arnold; World War II**
antitank ammunition: **McNaughton, Andrew G.L.**
antivivisection: **Animal Issues; Bengough, John W.**
Antoft, Susan: **Rowing**
Antoine, Patrick: **Drama in French**
Anville, Duc d': **Cartography, History of; Le Loutre, Jean-Louis**
AOTS: **United Church of Canada**
apartment: **Condominium; House**
apatite: **Mineral**
Aperture Synthesis Telescope: **Observatory**
apiculture: **Beekeeping**
APL: **Computer-Assisted Learning; Computer Science**
apocalypticism: **Anabaptists**
Apostles of Infinite Love: **New Religious Movements**
Apostolic Church of Pentecost: **Pentecostal Movement**
Apôtres mission: **Ste Marie Among the Hurons**
Appalachia: **Geological Regions; Lennoxville; Long Range Mountains; Maritime Provinces; Mégantic, Lac; Mégantic Hills; Mineral Resources; Physiographic Regions - Appalachia; Plate Tectonics; Prospecting; St Lawrence River; Spring; Thetford-Mines**
Appalachian geosyncline: **Great Lakes**
appendectomy: **Groves, Abraham**
apple bark borer: **Beetle**
apple maggot: **Crop Research**
apple parer: **Domestic Utensils**
Apple Tree Landing: **Canning**
Appleby College: **Massey, Raymond H.**
Applied Microlectronics Institute: **Nova Scotia Research Foundation Corp**
Apprentis-Sorciers: **Drama in French; Germain, Jean-Claude**
April, Jean-Pierre: **Popular Literature in French**
April Wine: **Popular Music**
aquarium: **Québec City; Zoos**
Aquarius: **Comet**
Aquatic Hall of Fame & Museum of Canada: **Winnipeg**
aquifer: **Esker; Saskatchewan**
Arabic: **Ethnic Languages; Language**
arabis: **Flowers, Cultivated**
aragonite: **Sedimentary Rock**
Aránguiz, Manuel: **Ethnic Literature**
arbor vitae: **Cedar**
Arbos, Fernandez: **La Palme, Béatrice**
Arbour, Roméo: **Literature in French - Scholarship & Teaching**
Arbuthnot, Larry: **Bobsledding**
arbutus: **Forest; Gulf Islands; Trees; Vegetation Regions - Cordillera; Vegetation Regions - Pacific Coastal**
arc lamps: **Electric Power**
Arcand, Adrien: **Internment**
Archaeological Sites Advisory Board (BC): **Duff, Wilson**
archaeology, underwater: *Breadalbane;* **Diving, Underwater**
archaeometry: **Franklin, Ursula Martius**
Archaeopteryx: **Biology; Bird Classification & Evolution**
Archambault, Gilles: **Literary Prizes in French; Music Criticism**
Archambault, J. Sergius: **Autobiographical Writing in French**

Archambault, Joseph-Papin: **Charpentier, Alfred; Semaines sociales du Canada**
Archambault, Richard B.: **Downs, Barry Vance**
Archambault, U.-E.: **Science**
Archambault Commission: **Macphail, Agnes C.**
Archbishop's Palace (Québec City): **Architectural Styles; Architecture, Development**
Archean time: **Geological History; Plate Tectonics**
Archer, S.A.: **Autobiographical Writing in English**
Archer, Thomas: **Music Criticism**
Archibald, Adams G.: **Assiniboia; Boyd, Alfred; Clarke, Henry Joseph; Fathers of Confederation; Manitoba; Métis**
Archibald, Charles: **Archibald, Edith J.**
Archibald, Ed: **Track & Field**
Archibald, Edward Mortimer: **Archibald, Edith J.**
Archibald, W.J.: **Physics**
Architectural Conservancy of Ontario: **Arthur, Eric Ross**
Archives de folklore: **Barbeau, C. Marius; Brassard, François**
Archives nationales du Québec: **Archives; Hull; Trois-Rivières**
Archives of the Rocky Mountains: **Banff**
Arcop Associates: **Affleck, Raymond Tait; Dimakopoulos, Dimitri; Lebensold, Fred David**
ARCQ (association of community radio stations): **Communications in Québec**
Arctic: **Bernier, Joseph-Elzéar**
Arctic Basin: **CESAR; Geological Regions; Petroleum**
Arctic Bay, NWT: **Baffin Island; Inuit Art; Lancaster Sound**
Arctic Biological Station: **Arctic Oceanography**
Arctic Brotherhood Hall: **Dawson**
arctic char: **Arctic Animals; Banks Island; Char; Cuisine; Lancaster Sound; Ungava Bay**
Arctic Co-operatives Ltd: **Inuit Co-operatives**
arctic cod: **Arctic Animals**
arctic fox: **Arctic Animals; Auyuittuq National Park; Banks Island; Fox; Lancaster Sound; Lemming**
arctic grayling: **Cuisine; Dubawnt Lake; Grayling**
arctic hare: **Auyuittuq National Park; Axel Heiberg Island; Banks Island; Brunette Island; Fosheim Peninsula; Gros Morne National Park; Hare**
Arctic Ice Dynamics Joint Experiment: **Arctic Oceanography**
Arctic Institute of North America: **Beck, Tom; Dunbar, Maxwell John; Jenness, Diamond; Logan, Mount**
Arctic International Wildlife Range Soc: **Canadian Nature Federation**
Arctic Pilot Project: **Northwest Territories; Shipbuilding & Ship Repair**
Arctic Platform: **Geological Regions**
arctic poppy: **Auyuittuq National Park**
Arctic Red River: **Mackenzie River**
Arctic Red River, NWT: **Kutchin; Permafrost**
Arctic Shelf: **Geological Regions**
Arctic Small Tool cultures: **Ellesmere Island Archaeological Sites; Microblade Technology; Pre-Dorset**
arctic tern: **Migration; Tern; Terra Nova National Park**
Arctic Vessel & Marine Research Institute: **National Research Council of Canada**
Arctic Waters Pollution Prevention Act: **Environmental Law; Hazardous Wastes; Law of the Sea**
arctic white heather: **Wildflowers**
arctic willow: **Mount Assiniboine Provincial Park; Vegetation Regions - Cordillera**
arctic wintergreen: **Ouimet Canyon**
Arctomys Cave: **Cave**
Ardizzi, Maria: **Italian Writing**

Area Development Agency: **Regional Economics**
Arena Gardens: **Cycling**
Arendaronon: **Huron**
Argall, Samuel: **Privateering**
Argand lamp: **Lighting**
Argent, Lac d': **Disasters**
Argentia Naval Base: **Placentia**
Argentinians: **Ethnic Literature; Latin Americans**
argillite: **Edenshaw, Charlie; Northwest Coast Indian Art**
argon: **Chemistry; Geological Dating; Spring**
Argonaut Rowing Club: **Fear, Alfred Henry; Toronto Argonauts; Wrestling; Wright, Joseph, Sr**
Argosy Financial Group of Canada Ltd: **Trust Company**
Argyle, Man: **Rockwood**
Arian theology: **Jehovah's Witnesses**
Arichat, NS: **Saint Francis Xavier University**
Arima, E.: **Thomas, Alexander**
Arioli, Don: **Film Animation**
Arion Male Voice Choir: **Choral Music; Music History**
Aristotelism: **Philosophy**
arithmetic: **Mathematics**
Ariya Theravada Soc: **Buddhism**
Arles, Henri d': **Literature in French - Criticism & Theory**
Armagh, Qué: **Place-names**
Armand DesRosiers Inc: **Webster, Lorne Campbell**
Armbro Farms: **Harness Racing**
Armdale Chorus: **Choral Music**
Armed Forces Radio & TV: **Canadian Broadcasting Corporation**
Armenian Church of North America: **Canadian Council of Churches; Orthodox Church**
Armenian rite: **Catholicism**
Armington, Caroline: **Printmaking**
Arminianism: **Holiness Churches; Methodism**
Armistice Day: **Remembrance Day**
armoire: **Furniture, French**
armorial bearing: **Heraldry**
Armour, Leslie: **Philosophy**
armoured vehicle: **Armaments**
arms race: **Bloc populaire canadien; Peace Movement; Science & Society**
Armstrong, BC: **Cuisine; Okanagan Valley; Salish, Interior**
Armstrong, Whitworth & Co: **Corner Brook**
Army Cadet League: **Cadets**
army notes: **Banking; Money; Playing-Card Money**
Army Show: **Wayne & Shuster**
Arnakafaluk: **Kalvak, Helen**
Arnaud (Payne) Rivière: **Ungava Inuit**
Arnold, Don: **Rowing**
Arnoldi, Charles: **Silver, Indian Trade**
Arnoldi family: **Pewter; Silver, Domestic**
Aroostook River: **Aroostook War**
Arosaguntacook dialect: **Abenaki**
arrest: **Citizen's Arrest; Jury; War Measures Act**
Arrow: **McTaggart-Cowan, Patrick Duncan**
Arrow Lakes: **Columbia River; Salish, Interior**
arrow-leaved balsamroot: **Vegetation Regions - Cordillera**
arrow worm: **Invertebrate; Zooplankton**
Arrowsmith, Aaron: **Cartography, History of; Grand Lake; Martre, Lac la; Nueltin Lake; Reindeer Lake**
Arrowsmith, Mount: **Port Alberni**
Arsenault, Joseph-Octave: **Arsenault, Aubin-Edmond**
arsenic: **Environmental Law; Hazardous Wastes; Mineral; Pesticide; Pollution**
arson: **Disasters; Inquiry into Certain Activities of the RCMP, Royal Commission of**
Art, Historical & Scientific Assn: **Vancouver**

Art Assn of Montréal: **Art Education; Artists' Organizations; Brymner, William; Contemporary Arts Society; Cullen, Maurice G.; Forster, John Wycliffe Lowes; Franchere, Joseph-Charles; Gagnon, Clarence; Harris, Robert; Holgate, Edwin; Leduc, Ozias; Painting; Printmaking; Suzor-Coté, Marc-Aurèlie de Foy**
Art Bank: **Art; Arts Funding**
Art Gallery of Greater Victoria: **Bell, Alistair Macready; Victoria**
Art Gallery of Nova Scotia: **Nova Scotia**
Art Gallery of Toronto: **Art Education; Art Gallery of Ontario; Bickell, John Paris; Dunlap, David Alexander; Gagnon, Clarence; Group of Seven; Lismer, Arthur; Painting; Pierce, Lorne A.; Printmaking**
Art Metropole: **Artists' Organizations; Video Art**
Art Museum of Toronto: **Art Gallery of Ontario**
Art Theatre Production Co: **Theatre, Multicultural**
Arteaga, Ignacio de: **Spanish Exploration**
arteriosclerosis: **Native People, Health; Psychiatry**
artesian water pressure: **Hydrology**
arthropoda: **Annelida; Arachnida; Centipede; Crustacean; Entomology; Fossil Animals; Insect; Insect Classification; Millipede; Trilobite; Veterinary Medicine**
Arthur, George: **Archaeology**
Arthur, Julia: **Theatre, English-Language**
Arthur, Paul: **Graphic Design**
Arthurs Committee: **Legal Education**
Artibise, A.F.J: **Urban Studies**
articling: **Legal Education**
articulated car: **Street Railways**
artificial gas: **Lighting**
artificial insemination: **Bioethics; Dairy Farming; Family Law; Medical Ethics; Medical Jurisprudence**
artificial joints & limbs: **Arthritis**
artificial pancreas: **University of Toronto**
artillery: **Armaments; Armed Forces - Militia & Army; Bull, Gerald Vincent; Halifax Citadel; Klein, George John**
Artillery Park: **Québec Citadel; Québec City**
Artists' Jazz Band: **Coughtry, Graham; Snow, Michael J.A.**
Arts & Culture Centre: **Affleck, Raymond Tait; St John's**
Arts & Letters Club: **Artists' Organizations; Group of Seven; Musical Theatre; Painting; Stage & Costume Design; Thomson, Thomas J.**
Arts & Letters Players of Toronto: **Theatre, English-Language**
Arts & Water Festival: **Peterborough**
Arts Club of Montréal: **Artists' Organizations; Holgate, Edwin**
Arts Club Theatre: **Theatre, English-Language; Vancouver Playhouse**
Arts Directors Club: **Curtin, Walter A.**
Arts Magazine: **Artists' Organizations**
ArtsAtlantic: **Art Writing & Criticism**
artscanada: **Art Writing & Criticism; Artists' Organizations**
Arvida, Qué: **Jonquière; Saguenay River; Urban & Regional Planning**
Arvida aluminum works: **Chicoutimi**
Arvik, NWT: **Lancaster Sound**
asbestosis: **Asbestos; Pollution**
ascorbic acid: **Carrot; Celery; Tomato**
Ascot, Qué: **Sherbrooke**
Ascot, Rivière: **Lennoxville**
Ash, Joseph: **Cobourg**
Ash, Stuart: **Graphic Design; Logo**
Ashanti language: **Africans**
Ashburham, Ont: **Peterborough**
Ashe, Edward: **Science**
Ashern, Man: **Garson, Stuart Sinclair**
Ashoona: **Pitseolak Ashoona**
Asia: **Hydrography**
Asianadian: **Ethnic Literature**

Asians: **Burbidge, George Wheelock; Chinese; Dunsmuir, Robert; Franchise; Hamilton; Immigration; Japanese; Kingston; New Brunswick; Nova Scotia; Prejudice & Discrimination; Refugees; South Asians; Southeast Asians; Tibetans; Toronto; Vancouver; Windsor, Ont**
Asiatic Exclusion League: **British Columbia**
aspartame: **Soft-Drink Industry; Sugar Industry**
Aspen Beach Provincial Park: **Parks, Provincial**
aspen tortrix: **Manitoba**
asphalt: **Bitumen; Energy in Society; Forestry; Gesner, Abraham; Petroleum; Petroleum Exploration & Production; Petroleum Research & Development; Quarrying Industry**
aspirin: **Arthritis; Chemistry; Pharmaceuticals Industry**
Aspy Valley: **Escarpment**
assault: **Banks, Harold C.; Crime; Prejudice & Discrimination; Robbery; Torts; Women & the Law**
Asselin, Marie-Claude: **Skiing**
Asselin, Olivar: **Franco-Americans; Intellectual History**
Assemblée nationale: **Québec**
Assembly of the Six Counties: **Lower Canada**
assemblyman: **Prince Edward Island**
assessment: **Municipal Finance**
Assignment of Book Debts Act: **Commercial Law**
Assikinack, Jean-Baptiste: **Ottawa**
Assiniboine: **Mainguy, Edmond Rollo**
Assiniboine & Saskatchewan Exploring Expedition: **Hime, Humphrey Lloyd; Hind, Henry Y.; Photography**
Assiniboine Community College: **Manitoba**
Assiniboine Park Zoo: **Manitoba**
Assiniwi, Bernard: **Cuisine**
Associate Committee on the National Building Code of Canada: **Construction Industry**
Associated Board: **Music History**
Associated Designers of Canada: **Stage & Costume Design**
Associated Gospel Churches of Canada: **Evangelical & Fundamentalist Movements**
Associated Screen News: **Film; Film, Documentary; Sparling, Gordon**
Association artistique de Montréal: **Jehin-Prume, Frantz**
Association canadienne des sociologues et anthropologues de la langue française: **Sociology**
Association canadienne du théâtre d'amateurs: **Beaulne, Guy; Theatre, French-Language**
Association canadienne-française de l'Alberta: **Bugnet, Georges-C.-J.**
Association canadienne-française de l'Ontario: **Franco-Ontarians**
Association canadienne-française pour l'avancement des sciences: **Deslongchamps, Pierre; Lévesque, Georges-Henri; Marie-Victorin, Frère; Physics; Religion; Rousseau, Jacques; Science**
Association catholique de la jeunesse canadienne-française: **Catholic Action; Groulx, Lionel-A.; Intellectual History**
Association catholique des études bibliques au Canada: **Religion**
Association catholique des institutrice rurales: **Gaudreault, Laure**
Association coopérative des productions audio-visuelles: **Dansereau, Mireille; Film**
Association des artistes non-figuratifs de Montréal: **Artists' Organizations; Leduc, Fernand; McEwen, Jean; Molinari, Guido; Painting; Tousignant, Claude**
Association des écrivains de langue française: **Literary Prizes in French**
Association des écrivains pour la jeunesse: **Children's Literature in French**
Association des gens de l'air du Québec: **Québec**
Association des graveurs du Québec: **Artists' Organizations**

Association des Métis d'Alberta et des Territoires du Nord Ouest: **Brady, James Patrick; Norris, Malcolm Frederick**
Association des sculpteurs du Québec: **Artists' Organizations**
Association des universités de langue française: **Léger, Jean-Marc**
Association des universités partiellement ou entièrement de langue française: **Francophonie**
Association du disque et de l'industrie du spectacle québécois: **Recording Industry**
Association feminine d'éducation et d'action sociale: **Women's Movement**
Association for Canadian & Québec Literatures: **Literature in English**
Association for Canadian Theatre History: **Learned Societies; Theatre, English-Language**
Association for Native Development in the Performing & Visual Arts: **Theatre, Multicultural**
Association France-Canada: **Literary Prizes in French**
Association of Canadian Archivists: **Archives; Learned Societies**
Association of Canadian Community Colleges: **Canadian Studies; Community College**
Association of Canadian Designers: **Theatre, English-Language**
Association of Canadian Etchers: **Artists' Organizations; Printmaking**
Association of Canadian Orchestras: **Music History**
Association of Canadian Publishers: **Small Presses**
Association of Canadian Television & Radio Artists: **Music, Profession of**
Association of Canadian University Teachers of English: **Literary Periodicals in English**
Association of Clothing Designers: **Fashion Design**
Association of Commonwealth Universities: **Symons, Thomas H.B.**
Association of Dominion Land Surveyors: **Associations**
Association of Legal Court Interpreters & Translators: **Translation**
Association of Métis & Non-Status Indians of Saskatchewan: **Métis**
Association of Professional Engineers of Ontario: **Industrial Quality Control**
Association of Scientific, Engineering & Technical Community of Canada: **Science**
Association of the Preservation of the Public Peace in Bytown: **Shiners' Wars**
Association of United Tahltans: **Land Claims**
Association pour l'advancement des sciences et des techniques de la documentation: **Libraries**
Association professionnelle des industriels: **Dion, Gérard**
Association québécoise du jeune théâtre: **Drama in French; Theatre, French-Language**
Assumption College: **University of Western Ontario; University of Windsor**
Astaritz, Pierre d': **Votive Painting**
asteroid: **Meteor, Meteorite, Impact Crater**
asteroids: **Echinodermata**
asthma: **Air Pollution; Allergies; Climate & Man; Smoking**
Astra Trust Co.: **Trust Company**
Astral lamp: **Lighting**
astrology: **New Religious Movements**
Astronomical & Physical Soc of Toronto: **Associations; Astronomy**
Asturagamicook, Lake: **Manicouagan Réservoir**
asylum: **Bucke, Richard Maurice; Clarke, Charles Kirk; Douglas, James (1800-86); Health Policy; Heritage Conservation; Howard, John George; Lett, Stephen; Lower Fort Garry; Mackieson, John; Mental Health; Nursing; Social Security; Tully, Kivas; Workman, Joseph**
Ataronchronon: **Huron**
Atchealak, Davie: **Inuit Art**
Atchley, Dana: **Video Art**

Atelier libre de recherches graphiques: **Printmaking**
Athabasca, Mount: **Columbia Icefield**
Athabasca Basin: **Geological Regions**
Athabasca Dist: **Dease, Peter W.; Territorial Evolution**
Athabasca fur brigade: **Portage La Loche**
Athabasca Glacier: **Ice Cap; Moraine**
Athabasca Hotel: **Jasper**
Athabasca Landing, North-West Territories: **Cornwall, James K.**
Athabasca tar sands: **Alberta; McConnell, Richard George; Mineral Resources**
athabascaite: **Mineral**
Athabaskan: **World War II**
Athanase Denis house: **Architecture**
Athans, George: **Diving**
Athapaskan languages: **Cree Syllabics; Native People, Languages; Urgent Ethnology**
Athapaskans: **Bearlake; Beaver (Indians); Carrier; Chilcotin; Chipewyan; Dene Nation; Dogrib; Hare (Indians); Indian Art; Kaska; Kutchin; Mountain (Indians); Sarcee; Sekani; Slavey (Slave); Tahltan; Tsetsaut; Tutchone; Yellowknife (Redknives, Copper)**
Athelston, Qué: **Dairy Industry**
Athens, Ont: **Place-names**
Atherley, Ont: **Simcoe, Lake**
atherosclerosis: **Heart Disease**
athlete's foot: **Mold**
Athletic Contests & Events Pool Act: **Lottery**
Atikokan River: **Atikokan**
Atkins, Gordon: **School Facilities**
Atkinson, Joseph E.: **Journalism; Star Weekly**
Atkinson Charitable Foundation: **Educational Foundations & Endowments; Toronto Star**
Atkinson College: **York University**
Atlanta: **Digby**
Atlantic: **Disasters**
Atlantic Advocate: **Magazines; New Brunswick**
Atlantic Canada Studies: **Saint Mary's University**
Atlantic Charter: **Argentia**
Atlantic Christian Training Centre: **Tatamagouche**
Atlantic Convoy Conference: **World War II**
Atlantic Fisheries, Task Force on: **Fisheries History**
Atlantic Geoscience Centre: **Geological Survey of Canada**
Atlantic Groundfish Advisory Committee: **Fisheries Policy**
Atlantic Institute of Education: **Nova Scotia**
Atlantic Neptune: **Cartography, History of**
Atlantic no 3: **Leduc**
Atlantic Oceanography Laboratory: **Mann, Cedric Robert**
Atlantic Provinces Transportation Commission: **New Brunswick**
Atlantic redfish: **Scorpionfish**
Atlantic Region Management Training Centre: **Technical University of Nova Scotia**
Atlantic Research Laboratory: **National Research Council of Canada**
Atlantic School of Theology: **Nova Scotia; University of King's College**
Atlantic Sugar Case: **Competition Policy**
Atlantic Symphony Orchestra: **Nova Scotia**
Atlantic TV: **Advertising; Nova Scotia**
Atlantic Universities Athletic Assn: **Football**
Atlantic Upland: **Nova Scotia**
Atlantic Veterinary College: **Prince Edward Island**
Atlantis: **Literary Magazines in English; Women's Studies**
atlas: **Cartography, History of; DesBarres, Joseph F.W.; Hydrography; Logan, William E.; National Atlas of Canada**
Atleier libre de recherches graphiques: **Steinhouse, Tobie Thelma**
Atlin, BC: **Atlin Lake; Tlingit, Inland**
atmosphere: **Aerospace Industry; Cloud; Drought; Space Technology; Stewart, Robert William; Weather Forecasting**

Atmosphere-Ocean: **Oceanography**
Atmospheric Environment Service: **Climate Information; Forest Fire; Physical Geography; Sea Ice**
atom: **Bell, Alexander Graham; Chemistry Subdisciplines; Electric Power; Foster, John Stuart; Gray, Joseph Alexander; Laser; Mineral; Molecules in Interstellar Space; Nuclear Energy; Nuclear Fusion; Physics; Rutherford, Ernest; Science & Society; Spectroscopy**
atomic bomb: **Disarmament; Early-Warning Radar; Gouzenko, Igor S.; Great Bear Lake; Munitions & Supply, Dept of; Nuclear Energy; Nuclear Safety; Uranium**
Atomic Energy Control Act: **Atomic Energy of Canada Ltd; Energy Policy**
Atomic Energy Control Board: **Air Pollution; Crown Corporation; Electric Power; Laurence, George C.; Mackenzie, Chalmers Jack; McNaughton, Andrew G.L.; Nuclear Energy**
Atoms for Peace Prize: **Lewis, Wilfrid Bennett**
Atrevida: **Malaspina Expedition**
atria: **Architecture, Development; Eaton Centre; Urban Design**
Atria North: **Thom, Ronald J.**
atriplex: **Biogeography**
Attawapiskat, Ont: **Attawapiskat River; James Bay**
Attawapiskat Lake: **Attawapiskat River**
Attignawantan: **Huron**
Attigneenongnahac: **Huron**
Atwater, Qué: **Bull, Gerald Vincent**
Auberge des Gouverneurs: **Gatineau**
Aubert de la Chesnaye, Charles: **Rivière-du-Loup**
Aubigny, Lower Canada: **Lévis**
Aubin, Napoléon: **Essay in French; Printmaking**
aubretia: **Flowers, Cultivated**
Aubry, Claude: **Children's Literature in French**
Aubry, Jérôme: **Couture, Joseph-Alphonse**
Aubut, Lise: **Arsenault, Angèle**
Audit Bureau of Circulations: **Magazines**
auditing: **Accounting**
Audley, Gordon: **Speed Skating**
Aue, Walter: **Chemistry Subdisciplines**
Auerbach, Herbert: **Centaur Theatre**
Augé, Pierre: **Guitar**
auger: **Tools, Carpentry**
Auger, Roger: **Theatre, French-Language**
Augustine burial mound: **Prehistory**
Augustines de la Miséricorde de Jésus: **Christian Religious Communities**
Augustinian Hospitalliers: **Nursing**
auklet: **Auk**
Aulnaies, Rivière des: **Saint-Jean, Lac**
Aulneau, Jean-Pierre: **Lake of the Woods**
Aulneau Peninsula: **Lake of the Woods**
Aurora, Ont: **Northern Railway of Canada; Stupart, Robert Frederic**
Aurora Borealis: **Northern Lights**
aurora char: **Endangered Animals**
Aurore: **Literature in French - Criticism & Theory**
Austin, Horatio T.: **Arctic Exploration; Franklin Search**
Austin Airways: **Thunder Bay**
Australian & New Zealand Assn for Canadian Studies: **Canada & Australia**
Austrians: **Alberta; Croatians; German Writing; Internment; Saskatchewan; Serbs; Skiing; Slovenes**
Austro-Hungarians: **Immigration; Internment; Prejudice & Discrimination**
autogyro: **Helicopter**
Automated Light Rapid Transit: **New Westminster; Transportation Research Centres**
automated tellers: **Banking; Commercial Law**
Automatic Block Signal System: **Railways, Track & Yards**
Automatic Train Control: **Railways, Track & Yards**

Automobile Insurance Act (Qué):
Delict
Autonomous Living Movement:
Disability
autopsy: **Funeral Practices**
Autsosat: **Nootka**
Avakumovic, Ivan: **Woodcock,
George**
Avalon, Isthmus of: **Come By Chance**
Avalon Channel: **Grand Banks**
Avalon Telephone Co: **Telephones**
Avalon Zone: **Geological Regions**
Avco Financial Services: **London**
Avco-World Trophy: **World
Hockey Assn**
aven: **Mountain Avens; Poisonous
Plants**
Avenir: **Dorion, Jean-Baptiste-Eric;
Doutre, Joseph; Institut canadien**
Avery, Donald: **Working-Class
History**
Avery, Lorne: **Molecules in
Interstellar Space**
Avery, Oswald T.: **Molecular Biology;
Moon**
Aviation Hall of Fame: **Fauquier,
John Emilius**
aviation medicine: **Banting,
Frederick G.; Fry, Frederick Ernest
Joseph; Melvill Jones, Geoffrey**
Avis, Walter S.: **Dictionary;
Linguistics**
Avon, Upper Canada: **Stratford**
Avon River (NS): **Windsor, NS**
Avon Theatre: **Stratford Festival**
AWACS: **Armaments; Radar**
awl: **Fur Trade; Northwest Coast
Indian Art; Tools, Carpentry**
axe: **Archaic; Fur Trade; Indian
Trade Goods; Technology;
Timber Axe; Tomahawk; Tools,
Carpentry; Woodenware**
Axis Mime: **Theatre for Young
Audiences**
Axwangayu: **Aqjangajuk Shaa**
Ayee, Howard: **Rough Trade**
Ayerst, McKenna & Harrison Ltd: **Cod
Liver Oil; Estrogen; Genetic
Engineering; Pharmaceuticals
Industry**
Ayerst, W.A.S.: **Cod Liver Oil**
Aylmer, Lac: **St-François, Rivière**
Aylmer, Lady: *Royal William*
Ayot, Pierre: **Printmaking**
Ayoub, Josiane: **Philosophy**
Ayre, Jack: **Dumbells**
Ayre, Robert: **Art Writing &
Criticism**
azalea: **Arboretum; Rhododendron**
Azia, Irfana: **Ethnic Literature**
Aziz, Philip: **London**
azurite: **Mineral**

B

B.F. Goodrich Canada Inc:
**Kitchener-Waterloo; Rubber
Products Industry**
Babb, Cook & Willard: **Architecture,
Development**
Babcock, Robert: **Working-Class
History**
Babcock-Wilcox Canada Ltd:
Machinery & Equipment Industry
Babel, Louis: **Schefferville;
Smallwood Reservoir**
Babel, Mont de: **Island; Manicouagan
Réservoir**
Babine: **Carrier**
Babine Lake: **British Columbia;
Carrier; Skeena River**
Babine River: **Skeena River**
Babkin, Boris P.: **Russians**
baby bonus: **Family Allowance**
baby's breath: **Flowers, Cultivated**
Bacchus, Ile de: **Orléans, Ile d'**
Bach Aria Group: **Forrester, Maureen**
Bach Choir of Montreal: **Choral Music**
Bach-Elgar Choir: **Music History**
Bache Peninsula: **Ellesmere Island**
Bachinski, Walter: **Printmaking**
Bachman, Randy: **BTO; Guess Who;
Guitar**
bacille Calmette-Guérin: **Biological
Product**
Back Bay: **Yellowknife, NWT**
"back to Africa" movement: **Blacks**
"back to the land" projects:
Government
back-to-work legislation: **Labour
Relations; Postal Strikes**

backbencher: **House of Commons**
Backbone Ranges: **Mackenzie
Mountains**
backstaff: **Davis, John**
backswimmer: **Bug**
Bacqueville de la Potherie, C.-C. le
Roy de: **Architecture,
Development; Verchères,
Marie-Madeleine Jarret de**
bacteria: **Animal Agriculture;
Biological Product; Biology;
Biomass Energy; Biotechnology;
Blue-green Algae; Botulism;
Cheese & Cheesemaking; Food &
Beverage Industries; Food
Poisoning; Fossil Plants; Genetics;
Grasshopper; Grosse Ile; Medicine,
Contemporary; Molecular Biology;
Mushroom Cultivation;
Newcombe, Howard Borden;
Parasitology; Plant Disease;
Pollution; Salmonella; Stanier,
Roger Yate; Veterinary Medicine;
Veterinary Medicines Industry;
Virus; Water-Borne Disease;
Water Pollution**
bacterial pneumonia: **Influenza**
bacteriology: **Biology; Frappier,
Armand; Institut
Armand-Frappier**
Badanai, Hubert: **Italians**
Baddeck Bay, NS: *Silver Dart*
Baddeck I: **Aviation**
Baddeley, Frederick: **Science**
Baden, Mowry: **Sculpture**
Badgely, C.R.: **Massey Hall**
Badger, Nfld: **Smallwood, Joseph R.**
Badger Bay: **Shawnandithit**
Baert, Jean-Paul: **Track & Field**
Baffin: **Oceanography**
Baffin Bay Shelf: **Petroleum**
Baffin Current: **Coastal Waters**
Baffin Region Inuit Assn: **Inuit
Tapirisat of Canada**
Baffin Trading Co: **Kiugak Ashoona**
baggataway: **Lacrosse; Sports History**
Bagnall, Samuel: **Furniture, Country**
Bagotville, Qué: **La Baie**
bagpipes: **Highland Games**
Baie-de-Shawinigan, Qué:
Shawinigan, Lac
Baie des Chaleurs Railway: **Baie des
Chaleurs Scandal; Fortin,
Pierre-Etienne**
Baie des Sables recreational complex:
Lac-Mégantic
Baie-Ste-Claire, Qué: **Anticosti, Ile d'**
Baie-St-Paul, Qué: **Aide-Créquy,
Jean-Antoine; Baillairgé Family;
Gagnon, Clarence; Goldhamer,
Charles**
Bailey, "Ace": **Shore, Edward W.**
Bailey, Jacob: **Poetry in English**
Bailey, James: **Toys & Games**
Bailey, Terence: **Musicology**
Baillairgé, Charles: **Baillairgé Family;
Parliament Buildings**
Baillairgé, François: **Baillairgé Family;
Drawing; Ste-Anne-de-Beaupré;
Sculpture**
Baillargeon, Charles-François:
Taschereau, Elzéar-Alexander
Baillargeon, Paule: **Film**
Baillargeon, Pierre: *Amérique française*;
Novel in French
Baillargeon, Samuel: **Literature in
French - Criticism & Theory**
Bain, F.: **Botany History**
Bain, George: *Globe & Mail*
Baird, Elizabeth: **Popular Literature
in English**
Baird, George: **Architecture,
Development**
Baird, Irene: **Literature & Politics;
Literature in English; Novel in
English**
Baird, Spencer: **Archaeology**
Baird, Vaughn L.: **Diving**
Baird, William: **Autobiographical
Writing in English**
bait & switch: **Competition Policy;
White-Collar Crime**
bakeapple: **Cuisine; Festivals;
Newfoundland**
Baker, James: **Cranbrook**
Baker, Michael C.: **Songs &
Songwriting**
Baker, Mount: **Cranbrook**
Baker, Peggy Smith: **Dance, Modern**
Baker, Ray Palmer: *Clockmaker, The*
Baker, Theodore: **Musicology**
Baker Lake case: **Aboriginal Rights**
Baker's Peak: **Random Island**

Bala, Ont: **Theatre, English-Language**
bald eagle: **Broley, Charles Lavelle;
Eagle; Migration**
Bald Head Hills: **Shilo, CFB**
Balding, Al: **Golf**
Baldridge, Mary Humphry: **Drama in
English**
Baldwin, James Mark: **Psychology**
Baldwin, Karen: **Miss Canada**
Baldwin, W.W.: **Bank Architecture;
Osgoode Hall**
Baldy, Mount: **Osoyoos**
baleen: **Cetacea; Karoo Ashevak**
baler: **Agricultural Implements
Industry; Massey-Ferguson Ltd**
Balfour, John: **Printmaking**
Balkind, Alvin: **Art Writing &
Criticism**
Ball, Nelson: **Poetry in English**
ball nettle: **Nightshade**
ballad: **Folk Music, Anglo-Canadian;
Oral Literature in English**
Ballantyne, R.M.: **Children's
Literature in English**
Ballard, Harold: **Hamilton Tiger Cats;
Toronto Maple Leafs**
Ballard, Stephanie: **Dance, Modern**
Ballentine, Leslie: **Philosophy**
Ballet Ys: **Theatre Ballet of Canada**
Ballets Chiriaeff: **Dance History;
Dance on Television & Film;
Paige, Brydon; Von Gencsy, Eva**
Ballets Ruth Sorel: **Orchestral Music**
ballistics: **Defence Research**
Ballon, Ellen: **Music History**
ballot & ballot stuffing: **Electoral
Systems**
Balmoral, Man: **Rockwood**
Balmoral Industrial Park:
Thunder Bay
Baloune: **Popular Literature in French**
Balsam, Phillip: **Lee, Dennis**
balsam fir: **Fir; Laurentian
Highlands; Plants, Native Uses;
Prince Albert National Park;
Terra Nova National Park; Timber
Trade History; Vegetation Regions
- Atlantic Coastal; Vegetation
Regions - Boreal Forest or Taiga**
Balsam Lake: **Kawartha Lakes; Trent
Canal**
balsam poplar: **Cypress Hills; Plants,
Native Uses; Poplar; Vegetation
Regions - Atlantic Coastal;
Vegetation Regions - Cordillera;
Vegetation Regions - Eastern
Temperate Forests**
balsam woolly aphid: **Conservation**
balsamroot: **Plants, Native Uses**
Baltimore, Ont: **Burwash, Nathanael**
Baltzly, Benjamin: **Photography**
bamboo: **Furniture, Country**
Bamfield, BC: **Pacific Rim
National Park; West Coast Trail**
Bamfield Marine Station: **University
of British Columbia**
Bamhara language: **Africans**
"Ban the Bomb" movement: **New Left**
Banbury, Clint: **Equestrian Sports**
Bancroft, Ont: **Gemstone; Milne,
David B.; Ontario**
band-tailed pigeon: **Game Bird;
Pigeon**
bandy: **Hockey, Ice**
Banff Buffalo Days: **Walking Buffalo**
Banff dace: **Endangered Animals**
Banff Festival of Mountain Films: **Film
Festivals, Prizes**
Banff Festival of the Arts: **Festivals**
Banff International Television Festival:
Film Festivals, Prizes
Banff-Jasper Relay: **Long-Distance
Running**
Banff School of Theatre Arts: **Theatre
Education**
Banff Springs Hotel: **Banff; Hotel; Van
Horne, William C.**
Banff-Windermere Parkway:
Kootenay National Park
Bangladeshis: **Prejudice &
Discrimination**
Bangor, Sask: **Welsh**
Bank Act: **Banking; Banking &
Finance, Royal Commission on;
Commercial Law; Consumer Law;
Economic Regulation; Housing &
Housing Policy**
bank clearings: **Business Cycles**
bank notes: **Finance Act**
Bank of British North America:
Simpson, George
Bank of Canada (1858): **Canadian
Imperial Bank of Commerce**

Bank of Canada Building: **Bank
Architecture; Erickson, Arthur C.;
Marani, Ferdinand Herbert;
Ottawa, Ont; Sculpture**
Bank of Hamilton Building: **Bank
Architecture**
Bank of Liverpool: **Liverpool**
Bank of Montreal Building (Toronto):
Tully, Kivas
Bank of New Brunswick: **Banking;
Millidge, Thomas Edward**
Bank of Nova Scotia Building (Calgary):
Architecture, Development
Bank of Ottawa: **Bank of Nova Scotia**
Bank of PEI: **Haviland, Thomas
Heath, Sr**
Bank of Toronto: **Bank Architecture;
Toronto-Dominion Bank**
Bank of Yarmouth: **Killam, Thomas**
Bankhead, Alta: **Slovenes**
Banking & Currency, Royal
Commission on: **Bank of
Canada Act**
Banks, Tommy: **Jazz**
Banks Basin: **Petroleum**
Banner: **Brown, George**
Bannock Point: **Whiteshell
Provincial Park**
Bannon, Paul: **Long-Distance
Running**
Banook, Lake: **Dartmouth Lakes**
Banque canadienne nationale: **French
in the West; National Bank of
Canada; Toronto-Dominion Bank**
Banque d'Hochelaga: **French in
the West**
Banque du Peuple: **Banking; Coinage**
Banque provinciale du Canada: **Caisse
populaire; Lévesque, Jean-Louis;
National Bank of Canada**
Banting Institute: **Biochemistry;
Medical Research**
baptism: **Anabaptists; Catholicism;
Shaker Religion**
baptism of the Holy Spirit:
**Charismatic Renewal; Holiness
Churches; Pentecostal Movement**
Baptist Convention of Manitoba & the
Northwest: **Baptists; Brandon
University**
Baptist Convention of Ont & Qué:
**Baptists; Canadian Council of
Churches; Evangelical &
Fundamentalist Movements**
Baptiste Creek: **Disasters**
Baptiste Lake: **Milne, David B.**
bar mower: **Agricultural Soil
Practices**
Bar of the House: **House of Commons**
Bar of the Province of Québec: **Law
Society**
bar scale: **Flour Milling Industry**
bar steel: **Sidbec-Dosco Limitée**
Bar U Ranch: **Lane, George**
Barachois, Qué: **Percé**
Baraga, Frederick: **Slovenes**
Barbadians: **West Indians**
Barbeau, François: **Stage & Costume
Design**
Barbeau, Mount: **Northwest
Territories**
Barbeau, Victor: **Literature in French
- Criticism & Theory**
Barbeau Committee on Election
Expenses: **Public Opinion**
Barbeau Park: **Ellesmere Island**
Barber, Bruce: **Art, Contemporary
Trends**
Barber, Lloyd: **Land Claims**
barberry: **Crop Research**
barbiturates: **Medical Drug Abuse;
Non-Medical Use of Drugs, Royal
Commission on**
barbotte: **Gambling**
Barbour, Douglas: **Humorous Writing
in English; Literature in English -
Theory & Criticism**
Barcelo, François: **Popular Literature
in French**
Barclay, Robert: **Put-In-Bay**
Barclays Bank (Canada): **Canadian
Imperial Bank of Commerce**
Bareneed, Nfld: **Place-names**
Barford, Ralph: **Electrical Appliances
Industry**
bargeboard: **Architecture,
Development**
Barghoorn, E.S.: **Fossil Plants**
Baribeau et Fils: **Lévis**
barite: **Mineral; Nova Scotia**
Barker, William: **Barkerville**
Barkers Point: **New Brunswick**

Barkley, Charles W.: **Juan de Fuca Strait**
Barkley Sound: **Ucluelet**
Barkway, Michael: *Financial Times*
Barlow Lake (NWT): **Dubawnt River**
Barlow-Ojibway Glacial Lake: **Timiskaming, Lake**
Barnes, Emery: **Blacks**
Barnes, George: **Wine Industry**
Barnes, Joshua N.: **Autobiographical Writing in English**
Barnes, Milton: **Choral Music**
Barnet, Will: **Regina Five**
Barnet Marine Park: **Burnaby**
Barnett, Thomas: **Art Galleries & Museums**
Barnjum, Frederick: **Gymnastics; Physical Education**
Barnum House: **Architecture, Development**
barometer: **Climate Information; Patterson, John; Surveying**
Baron Byng High School: **Savage, Anne Douglas**
Baron Island: **Dundas Island**
Baron of Renfrew: **Orléans, Ile d'; Shipbuilding & Ship Repair**
barque: *Breadalbane*; **Maritime Shipping History to 1900**
Barr, Dave: **Golf**
Barr, Isaac: **Lloydminster**
Barr, Robert: **Literature in English; Novel in English; Popular Literature in English**
Barra lad: **Horse**
Barraud, Cyril J.: **Phillips, Walter J.; Printmaking**
Barré, Raoul: **Popular Literature in French**
Barreau du Québec: **Associations; Legal Education**
barrel organ: **Hymns; Willson, David**
barrel racing: **Rodeo**
barren-ground caribou: **Arctic Animals; Auyuittuq National Park; Caribou; Migration; Vegetation Regions - Arctic Tundra**
Barren Land People: **Montagnais-Naskapi**
Barreto-Rivera, Rafael: **Poetry in English**
Barrett, H.J.: **Children's Literature in French**
Barrette, Jacqueline: **Musical Theatre**
Barriare de Montréal: **Libraries**
Barrie, Robert: **Barrie**
Barriefield, Ont: **Kingston**
Barrier Inlet: **Waterfall**
Barringer, A.R.: **Geochemistry**
Barrington Bay: **Cape Sable Island**
Barristers' Soc of NB: **Associations**
Barrow, John: **Hamilton Tiger Cats**
Barrow Strait: **Arctic Archipelago; Arctic Exploration; Cornwallis Island; Island; Lancaster Sound; Parry Channel; Physiographic Regions - Arctic Lands; St Roch**
Barry, Anne Meredith: **Printmaking**
Barry, Capt: **Barrie**
Barry-Duquesne Company: **Deyglun, Henri; Theatre, English-Language**
Barter Island: **Mackenzie Inuit**
Bartholomew Green 1751 Assn Inc: **Magazines**
Bartlett, N.: **Chemistry Subdisciplines**
Bartlett, William: **Musicology**
Bartocci, Gianni: **Italian Writing**
Barton Myers Associates: **Myers, Barton**
Bartram, Ed: **Printmaking**
Baryshnikov, Mikhail: **Tennant, Veronica**
bas-relief: **Baxter, J. Iain W.; Public Art**
basalt: **Annapolis Lowlands; Geological Regions; Greenstone; Igneous Rock**
Basford, S. Ronald: **Morgentaler, Henry**
BASIC: **Computer-Assisted Learning; Computer Science; Language**
basic oxygen process: **Algoma Steel Corp Ltd; Dominion Foundries & Steel, Ltd; Iron & Steel Industry**
basil: **Condiment Crops**
Basile, Jean: **Literature in French**
Basilian Fathers: **Catholicism; Charbonnel, Armand-F.-M. de; Christian Religious Communities**
Basilian Press: **Catholicism**
Basilian Sisters: **Catholicism**

Basin Head, PEI: **Prince Edward Island**
Basinski, Z.S.: **Physics**
basketry: **Abenaki; Davidson, Florence Edenshaw; Indian Art; Kettle Valley; Maliseet; Masks; Northern Georgia Strait Coast Salish; Northwest Coast Indian Art; Prehistory; Salish, Interior; Weaving, Contemporary**
Basques, Île aux: **Bird Sanctuaries & Reserves; Trois-Pistoles**
bass violin: **Jazz**
Bassano, Alta: **Brooks**
Bassett, David: **Baton Broadcasting Inc**
Bassett, Douglas: **Baton Broadcasting Inc**
Bassett, John: **Toronto Maple Leafs**
Bassin de Chambly: **Chambly**
Basso, Guido: **Jazz**
basswood: **Beekeeping; Furniture, Country; Furniture, French; Plants, Native Uses; Timber Trade History; Vegetation Regions - Eastern Temperate Forests**
Bastien: **Popular Literature in French**
Bastien, Hermas: **Philosophy**
Bastion Square: **Urban Design**
Bastion Theatre: **Victoria**
Bata, Thomas: **Bata, Thomas J.**
Bata Ltd: **Barter; Bata, Thomas J.**
Batawa, Ont: **Bata, Thomas J.**
Batchelor, George: **Dorion, Jean-Baptiste-Eric**
Bates, Bob: **Lucania, Mount**
Bates, Mona: **Music History**
Bath, Ont: **McDowall, Robert**
bathtub race: **Nanaimo**
Bathurst Inlet: **Bush Flying**
Batiscan, Rivière: **St Lawrence Lowland; Technology**
Batstone, Harry: **Football**
battalion: **Regiment**
battered women & children: **Canadian Advisory Council on the Status of Women; Child Abuse; Crime; Foundations; Status of Women; Women & the Law; Women's Movement**
battery: **Antimony; Cadmium; Electronics Industry; Lead; Lighting; Mercury; Silver; Zinc**
Battle Harbour, Nfld: **Grenfell, Wilfred T.; Macpherson, Cluny**
Battle of Beaver Dams: **Secord, Laura; War of 1812**
Battle of Beaver Dams Park: **Thorold**
Battle of Bloody Run: **Pontiac**
Battle of Chippewa: **War of 1812**
Battle of Grand Pré: **Grand Pré**
Battle of Montmorency: **Montmorency Falls**
Battle of Moraviantown: **Moraviantown; Proctor, Henry; Tecumseh**
Battle of Oriskany: **Deserontyon, John**
Battle of Queenston Heights: **Sheaffe, Roger Hale; War of 1812**
Battle of Ridgeway: **Armed Forces - Militia & Army; Fenians; Otter, William D.; Robertson, James**
Battle of St-Denis: **Duel**
Battle of Stoney Creek: **Harvey, John; Niagara Historic Frontier; War of 1812**
Battle of the Grand Coteau: **Falcon, Pierre**
Battle of the Restigouche: **Campbellton, NB; Restigouche**
Battle River: **Battleford; Henday, Anthony**
Battle River Regional Planning Commission: **Wetaskiwin**
Batty Bay: **Kennedy, William**
Baudry, Edouard: **Radio Drama, French-Language**
Bauer, David: **Canadian Olympic Hockey Team**
Bauer, Walter: **German Writing**
Baumé scale: **Maple Sugar Industry**
bauxite: **Aluminum; Quarrying Industry**
Bavasi, Peter: **Toronto Blue Jays**
bawdy house: **Prostitution**
Bawtree, Michael: **Drama in English**
Baxter, Ingrid: **Art, Contemporary Trends; Baxter, J. Iain W.**
Bay Fjord: **Fosheim Peninsula**
bay lynx: **Bobcat**

Bay St George Community College: **Newfoundland**
Bay Street: *Financial Post*; **Ontario; Toronto**
Bayeur family: **Musical Instruments**
Bayfield Laboratory for Marine Science & Surveys: **Canada Centre for Inland Waters**
Bayly, Charles: **Moose Factory**
Bays, Lake of: **Huntsville**
Bayside, NB: **McCain, H. Harrison**
Bazin, Marie-Louise-Elizabeth: **Taschereau Legal Dynasty**
BC Arts Council: **Lowther, Patricia Louise**
BC Cultural Fund: **British Columbia**
BC Electric Building: **Thompson, Berwick, Pratt & Partners**
BC Electric Co: **BC Hydro**
BC Federation of Artists: **Odjig, Daphne**
BC Federation of Labour: **Revolutionary Industrial Unionism; Watters, James C.**
BC Federationist: **Union Centrals, District & Regional**
BC Forest Products: **Vancouver**
BC Heart Foundation: **Friedman, Sydney Murray**
BC Institute of Technology: **Burnaby; Vancouver**
BC Mills Timber & Trading Co: **Bank Architecture**
BC Natural History Soc: **Parks, Provincial**
BC Penitentiary: **New Westminster**
BC Place: **British Columbia Lions; Pattison, James A.; Vancouver**
BC Power Commission: **BC Hydro; Keenleyside, Hugh L.**
BC Pulp & Paper: **Killam, Izaak Walton**
BC Southern Railway: **Fernie, William**
BC Sugar Refinery Ltd: **Vancouver**
BC Timber Pulp Mill & Saw Mill: **Castlegar**
BC Tree Fruits Ltd: **Agriculture History**
BC Winter Games: **Osoyoos**
BC Women's Suffrage League: **Gutteridge, Helena Rose**
BCTV: **Webster, Jack**
BDK: **Popular Literature in French**
Beach, Orm: **Football**
beach flea: **Crustacean**
Beach Grove, BC: **Delta, BC**
beach pea: **Vegetation Regions - Pacific Coastal**
beach seine: **Fisheries History**
Beachville, Ont: **Baseball**
Beacon: **Catholicism**
Beacon Hill Park: **Martin, Mungo**
beacons: **Lighthouses**
beads & beadwork: **Boyd's Cove; Gemstone; Indian Art; Indian Trade Goods; Prehistory; Rainy River Burial Mounds**
Beamsville, Ont: **Baptists; Harris, Alanson; Lincoln; Slovenes**
Bear ceremonial: **Native People, Religion**
Bear Creek: **Disasters**
Bear Lake: **Skeena River**
Bear Lake Post: **Sekani**
Bear Province: **Geological Regions**
bearded seal: **Seal; Umiak**
beargrass: **Northwest Coast Indian Art**
bearskin: **Arctic Animals**
Bearspaw, King: **Lost Lemon Mine**
Bearspaw, King: **Lost Lemon Mine**
Bearspaw band: **Stoney; Walking Buffalo**
Beasley, Richard: **Hamilton**
Beatton River: **Peace River**
Beatty, John W.: **Harris, Lawren S.**
Beatty, Mrs Reginald: **Melfort**
Beatty, Samuel: **Mathematics**
Beatty, William: **Parry Sound**
Beatty, William H.: **Parry Sound**
Beatty scrip: **Parry Sound**
Beau, Paul: **Beau, Henri**
Beaubears Island: **Miramichi River**
Beaubien, P. de Gaspé: **Expo 67**
Beauchamp, Claude: *Affaires*
Beauchemin, Nérée: **Autobiographical Writing in French; *Barre du jour*; Literature in French - Scholarship & Teaching; Poetry in French**
Beauchemin de Montréal: **Book Publishing, French-Language**
Beauchesne, Arthur: **Bourinot's Rules; Parliamentary Procedure**

Beauchesne, Charles: **Arthabaska**
Beaucourt, François: **Drawing**
Beaudoin, Laurent: **Université Sainte-Anne**
Beaufort, Harriet: **Stewart, Frances**
Beaufort Mountains: **Comox, BC**
Beaufort Sea Project: **Arctic Oceanography; Cameron, William Maxwell**
Beaugrand, Honoré: **Exploration & Travel Literature in French; Franco-Americans; Oral Literature in French**
Beaugrand, Marie-L.-H.: **Short Fiction in French**
Beauharnois Canal: **Bridges; Canals & Inland Waterways; St Lawrence River; Valleyfield**
Beauharnois Light, Heat & Power Co: **Christie, Loring C.; Henry, R.A.C., "Red"; Hydro-Québec; Sweezey, Robert Oliver**
Beauharnois seigneury: **Colvile, Eden; Ellice, Edward**
Beaulieu, André: **Literary Bibliography in French; Literature in French - Scholarship & Teaching**
Beaulieu, Jacques: **Laser**
Beaulieu, Michel: **Poetry in French**
Beaulieu, René: **Popular Literature in French**
Beaulieu River: **Great Slave Lake**
Beaulne, Léonard: **Theatre, French-Language**
Beaumont, W.R.: **Medicine, History of**
Beauport, Lac: **Québec City**
Beauport, Qué: **Architecture, Development; Casgrain, Henri-Raymond; Douglas, James (1800-86); Montmorency; Québec City; Religious Building; Riel, Louis**
Beaupré, Georges: **Graphic Design; Logo**
Beaupré, Jean: **Poetry in English**
Beaupré, Qué: **St Lawrence River**
Beauregard, Alphonse: **Poetry in French**
Beauséjour, Man: **Schreyer, Edward R.**
Beausoleil, Claude: **Literary Prizes in French**
Beausoleil Island: **Georgian Bay Islands National Park**
Beaver (magazine): **Ahenakew, Edward**
Beaver Bundle Ceremony: **Sarcee**
Beaver Hall: **Frobisher, Joseph**
Beaver Hall Hill Group: **Art Education; Artists' Organizations; Newton, Lilias; Savage, Anne Douglas**
Beaver Hills: **Elk Island National Park**
Beaver Lake, Man: **Birch-Bark Biting**
Beaver Line: **Canadian Pacific Railway**
beaver motif: **Pewter; Silver, Domestic**
Beaver River (Sask): **Churchill River**
Beaver Toy Manufacturing Co: **Toys & Games**
Beaver Trophy: **Literary Prizes in English**
Beaver Valley: **Bruce Trail**
Beaverbrook, 1st Baron: **Aitken, W. Maxwell**
Beaverbrook Art Gallery: **Forrestall, Thomas De V.; Fredericton**
Beaverlodge, Alta: **Research Stations, Agricultural**
Beaverlodge Lake: **Bennett, William John**
beaver's ears: **Wintergreen**
Bebaminogmat: **Bell, Leland**
Bebelle: **Theatre for Young Audiences**
bebop: **Jazz**
Becaguimec Stream: **Hartland**
Bécancour, Rivière: **St Lawrence Lowland; Thetford-Mines**
Bécancour Reserve: **Abenaki**
Bécart de Granville, Charles: **Drawing**
Becker, Helmut: **Printmaking**
bed: **Furniture, Country; Furniture, English, Scottish & American; Furniture, French; Furniture, German**
Bédard, France: **Children's Literature in French**
Bédard, Pierre: **Journalism**
bedbug: **Parasitology**

Beddoe, Alan B.: **Heraldry Society of Canada**
Bedeque Bay: **Summerside**
Bedford, NS: **Halifax**
Bedford, Qué: **Place-names**
Bedford Basin: **Nova Scotia**
beech bark disease: **Vegetation Regions - Atlantic Coastal**
Beechey, F.W.: **Banks Island**
Beechwood, NB: **Flemming, Hugh John; Saint John River**
Beecroft, Jane: **Beecroft, Norma**
beef: **Animal Agriculture; Insulin; International Trade; Meat-Processing Industry; Ranching History**
beer: **Alcoholism; Brewing Industry; Communications; Cuisine; Film; Labatt, John S.; Nursing; O'Keefe, Eugene**
Beers, Clifford W.: **Mental Health**
Beetz, Jean: *Anti-Inflation Act Reference; McNeil Case*
Bégin, Louis-Nazaire: **Leatherworking; Taschereau, Elzéar-Alexander**
Bégon, Elisabeth: **Literature in French**
Béha, Philippe: **Children's Literature in French**
behaviour modification: **Juvenile Delinquency; Medical Ethics**
behavioural sciences: **Social Science**
Behrens, Peter: **Short Fiction in English**
Beissel, Henry: **German Writing**
Belair, Michel: **Essay in French**
Beland, Luc: **Painting**
Bélanger, Dina: **Saints**
Bélanger, Jeannine: **Poetry in French**
Bélanger, L.: **Leblond, Charles Philippe**
Bélanger Commission: **Bourassa, Robert**
Belcher, James: **Belcher Islands**
Belcourt, Claude: **Theatre, French-Language**
Belding, A.M.: **Maritime Rights**
Belding Paul & Co: **Textile Industry**
Beleoil, Qué: **Richelieu, Rivière**
Belford, Alexander: **Book Publishing, English-Language**
Belford's Monthly: **Literary Magazines in English**
Belfry Theatre: **Theatre, English-Language**
Belgo-Canadian Pulp: **Shawinigan**
Bélil, Michel: **Popular Literature in French**
Bélisle, Louis-Alexandre: **Dictionary**
Béliveau, Juliette: **Theatre, English-Language**
Bell, Andrew: *Histoire du Canada*
Bell, Donald: **Singing**
Bell, Florence: **Track & Field**
Bell, John: **Place-names; Yukon Territory**
Bell, June: **Lawn Bowling**
Bell, Mabel: **Bell, Alexander Graham; Rugs & Rug Making**
Bell, Matthew: **Forges Saint-Maurice**
Bell, R.E.: **Physics**
Bell, Rivière: **Nottaway, Rivière**
Bell Homestead: **Brantford**
Bell-Irving River: **Nass River**
Bell-Northern Research Ltd: **Electronics Industry; Industrial Research & Development; Physics**
Bell Organ Co: **Guelph**
Bell Rock: **Bell Island**
Bell Telephone Co of Canada: **Bell, Alexander Graham; Bell Canada Enterprises Inc; Industrial Quality Control; Manitoba; Roblin, Rodmond P.; Sise, Charles Fleetford; Telephones**
Bella Bella, BC: **Bella Bella**
Bella Coola, BC: **Mackenzie-Grease Trail**
Bella Coola River: **Northwest Coast**
belladonna: **Nightshade**
Belle, Rivière: **Ste-Scholastique**
Belle Isle, Strait of: **Basques; Cartier, Jacques; Coastal Waters; L'Anse Amour Burial Site; Norse Voyages; Physiographic Regions - St Lawrence Lowlands; Red Bay; St Anthony; St Lawrence, Gulf of**
Belle Isle Current: **Sable Island**
Belle River, Ont: **Windsor, Ont**
Belledune, NB: **New Brunswick**
Bellefleur, Léon: **Painting**
Bellerive, Georges: **Art Writing & Criticism**

Bellerose brothers: **Furniture, English, Scottish & American**
Belleville Hardware & Lock Manufacturing Co: **Toys & Games**
Belleville *Intelligence*: **Bowell, Mackenzie**
Belleville Seminary: **Methodism**
Bellevue mansion: **Amherstburg**
Bellin, Jacques-Nicolas: **Cartography, History of**
Bellon, Joseph: **Slovaks**
Bellot, Joseph-René: **Kennedy, William**
Bellot, Paul: **Religious Building; St-Benoit-du-Lac**
Bellot Strait: **Arctic Archipelago; Boothia Peninsula; Franklin Search**
Bell's Corners, Ont: **Coal Gasification; Coal Liquefaction**
Bells Point: **Cape Traverse**
Belly River: **Blood; Grayling; Lethbridge**
Belmont, Ont: **Macallum, Archibald Byron**
Belmont Hall: **Theatre Royal**
Beloeil, Qué: **Marie-Rose, Mother**
Beloeil Bridge: **Grand Trunk Railway of Canada**
Belshaw, Cyril S.: **Anthropology**
"belsnickles": **Mumming**
Belzberg, Hyman: **Belzberg, Samuel**
Belzberg, William: **Belzberg, Samuel**
Belzile, Louis: **Plasticiens**
Beman, Elisha: **Newmarket**
Beman's Corners, Upper Canada: **Newmarket**
Benedict, Ruth: **Literature in English**
Benedictines: **Belgians; Christian Religious Communities; Mission; Religious Building; St-Benoit-du-Lac**
Benedictsen, Mrs M.J.: **Women's Suffrage**
beneficiary: **Trust**
Benevolent Irish Soc: **St John's**
Benjamin, A.D.: **Samuel, Lewis**
Benner, Ron: **Art, Contemporary Trends**
Bennet, John: **Community**
Bennett, BC: **Chilkoot Trail**
Bennett, George: **Brown, George; Davin, Nicholas Flood**
Bennett, George (trade unionist): **Windsor, Ont**
Bennett, Jonathan: **Philosophy**
"Bennett buggy": **Bennett, R.B.**
Bennett Lake: **Carcross**
Benoît, Jehane: **Cuisine; Popular Literature in English**
Benoît, Paul: **Notre Dame de Lourdes**
Benson, Myra: **Theatre for Young Audiences**
Benson, Susan: **Stage & Costume Design**
Benson Building: **Benson, Clara Cynthia**
Bent, Colin: **Architecture, Development**
Bental Centre: **Vancouver**
Bentley, Doug: **Bentley, Maxwell H.L.**
Bentley, John: **Music History**
bentonite: **Clay; Morden**
bentwood: **Furniture, English, Scottish & American**
benzene: **Chemical Industries; Chemistry; Chemistry Subdisciplines**
Beothuk Institute: **Cormack, William E.; Shawnandithit; Trinity**
Beothuk vocabulary: **Demasduwit; Trinity**
Béraud, Jean: **Essay in French**
Bercuson, David: **Social History; Working-Class History**
Berd, Françoise: **Drama in French**
Berg, Richard: **Guitar**
Berg, Roy: **Animal Breeding**
Berg Lake: **Robson, Mount**
Berger, Carl: **Historiography; Philosophy**
Berger, Jean: **Painting**
Berger, Michael: **Musical Theatre**
Berger Inquiry: **Mackenzie Valley Pipeline; Northwest Territories; Separatism; Social Impact Assessment; Yukon Territory**
Bergeron, Elisabeth: **Saints**
Bergeron, Gilles: **Centennial Year**
Bergeron, Léandre: **Dictionary; Theatre, French-Language**
Bergeson, Richard: **New Religious Movements**

Bergman, H. Eric: **Printmaking**
Bergy, Michael: **Hespeler**
Bergytown, Upper Canada: **Hespeler**
Bering Island: **Bering, Vitus J.**
Bering Land Bridge: **Beringia**
Bering Sea: **Prehistory; Yukon Territory**
Bering Strait: **Arctic Exploration; Belcher, Edward; Bering, Vitus J.; Beringia; McClure (M'Clure), Robert J. Le M.; Northwest Coast; Pre-Dorset; Strait of Anian**
Berkeley, Cyril: **Berkeley, Edith Dunington**
Berlin, Ont: **Clocks & Watches; Furniture & Fixture Industry; Germans; Kitchener-Waterloo; Knights of Labor; Soccer; Toys & Games; World War I**
Berlin Novelty Works: **Toys & Games**
Berliner, Emile: **Music History**
Berliner Gramophone Co: **Recording Industry**
Berliner Journal: **German Writing**
Berlinguet, François-Xavier: **Sculpture**
Berlyne, D.E.: **Musicology**
Bermuda lily: **Flowers, Cultivated**
Bermudans: **West Indians**
Bernard, Alphonse: **Track & Field**
Bernard, Hans: **Germans**
Bernard, Harry: **Children's Literature in French; Literature in French - Criticism & Theory**
Bernard, Jean-Paul: **Intellectual History**
Bernard, Lac: **Shawinigan, Lac**
Berne Convention: **Copyright Law**
Bernèche: **Popular Literature in French**
Bernic Lake: **Tantalum**
Bernier, Germain: **Exploration & Travel Literature in French**
Bernier, Jovette: **Poetry in French**
Bernier, R.: **Philosophy**
Berry, George: **Roller Skating**
Bersianik, Louky: **Novel in French; Popular Literature in French; Women's Movement**
Berthelot, François: **Orléans, Ile d'**
Berthiaume, Trefflé: **Journalism; *Presse***
Berthiaume-Du Tremblay family: *Presse*
Berthier-en-Bas, Qué: **Roy, Camille**
Berthier-en-Haut, Qué: **Desrosiers, Léo-Paul**
Berthier-sur-Mer, Qué: **Maguire, Thomas**
Bertie, G.: **Wrestling**
Berton, Laura B.: **Autobiographical Writing in English**
Bertrand, Claude: **Philosophy**
Berwick, Robert A.D.: **Architectural Styles; Thompson, Berwick, Pratt & Partners**
beryl: **Mineral**
Besant, Derek Michael: **Painting**
Bessborough Hotel: **Saskatoon**
Bessborough Trophy: **Coulter, John W.**
Bessemer process: **Algoma Steel Corp Ltd; Iron & Steel Industry**
Best, George: **Cartography, History of**
bestiality: **Pornography**
Beswick, Christopher: **Uxbridge**
Beta Sigma Phi Award: **Literary Prizes in English**
betafite: **Mineral**
betatron: **Physics**
Bethune, Fred A.: **Rugby**
Béthune, Guy: **Rousseau, Jacques**
"Better Farming Trains": **Agricultural Education**
betting: **Gambling; Harness Racing; Thoroughbred Racing**
Betts, Jim: **Musical Theatre**
Betts, Lorne: **Choral Music; Music Criticism**
Bett's electrolytic process: **Technology**
Beveridge, Karl: **Art, Contemporary Trends**
Beverly Lake: **Dubawnt River; Thelon River**
Bhatia, Avadh B.: **Physics**
Bi-Capitol Project: **Saint John**
Bibaud, Michel: **Book Publishing, English-Language; Book Publishing, French-Language; Historiography; Magazines**
Bibby, Reginald: **New Religious Movements; Sunday Schools**
Bible: **Christianity**
Bible Christian Church: **Methodism**

Bible Institute Baptist Church: **Aberhart, William**
Bible Student movement: **Jehovah's Witnesses**
Bibliographical Soc of Canada: **Literature in French - Scholarship & Teaching**
Bibliothèque canadienne: **Literature in French - Criticism & Theory; Magazines**
Bibliothèque nationale du Québec: **Libraries; Literature in French - Scholarship & Teaching**
Biche, Lac la: **Alberta**
Bickerdike, Robert: **Capital Punishment**
Bicket, James: **Curling**
Bidwell, Marshall S.: **Bidwell, Barnabas**
Bieler, Ted: **Sculpture**
Biencourt, Jacques de: **Biencourt de Poutrincourt, Jean de**
Bienfait Coal Co: **Coal**
Bienkowska, Danuta: **Poles**
Bienvenue, Marcella: **Art, Contemporary Trends**
Bierstadt, Albert: **Glenbow Museum**
Bifrost, Man: **Poles**
"Big Bang": **Cosmology; Science & Society**
Big Basin sagebrush: **Vegetation Regions - Cordillera**
Big Bend: **Gold Rushes; Golden; Revelstoke**
"Big Blue Machine": **Davis, William G.; Ontario**
big bluestem: **Biogeography; Grasses**
Big Burnt Bay: **Lewisporte**
Big Child: **Poundmaker**
Big Chute, Ont: **Trent Canal**
Big Country Awards: **Baker, Carroll; Buck, Gary; Country & Western Music**
Big Eddy, BC: **Revelstoke**
big-horned bison: **Paleoindian**
Big Kettle of the Chaudière: **Bridges**
Big Prairie, Alta: **Métis Settlements**
Big Quill Lake: **Quill Lakes**
Big Rideau Lake: **Rideau Lakes**
Big Tracadie River: **Tracadie, NB**
bigamy: **Family Law**
Bigelow, W.G.: **Heart Disease**
Biggar, W.H.: **Biggar**
Bigger, Michael: **Sculpture**
Bighorn Reserve: **Stoney**
bighorn sheep: **Jasper National Park; Kootenay National Park; Mount Assiniboine Provincial Park; Mountain Sheep; Waterton Lakes National Park**
bigleaf maple: **Maple; Vegetation Regions - Pacific Coastal**
Bigras, J.Y.: **Film**
Bigsby, John: **Exploration & Travel Literature in English**
Bigstone Lake: **Island Lake**
Bikkers, Rudolf: **Printmaking**
bilberry: **Berries, Wild; Vegetation Regions - Atlantic Coastal; Vegetation Regions - Pacific Coastal**
bilharziasis: **Water-Borne Disease**
Bilingual District Advisory Board: **Official Languages Act**
Bill 1: **Bill 101**
Bill 16: **Quiet Revolution**
Bill 80: **Conscription**
Bill C-102: **Pharmaceuticals Industry**
Bill C-57: **Rape**
Bill of Rights of 1688 (Britain): **Constitutional Law**
Billes, J.W.: **Canadian Tire Corp, Ltd**
Bills of Exchange Act: **Commercial Law; Consumer Law; Sedgewick, Robert**
Bilson, Geoffrey: **Social History**
binary numbers: **Computer Science**
binder: **Agricultural Implements**
Binder, Otto: **Alikomiak**
Binder Twine Festival: **Kleinburg**
bindery: **Print Industry**
binding arbitration: **Collective Bargaining; Labour Relations; Public Service; Teaching Profession; Windsor Strike**
bindweed: **Morning Glory; Weeds**
Binet, Jocelyne: **Garant, Serge**
Binet-Simon intelligence tests: **Hincks, Clarence M.**
bingo: **Gambling**

Binnie-Clark, Georgina: **Autobiographical Writing in English; Exploration & Travel Literature in English**

binoculars: **Phillips, W. Eric**

Bio Research Laboratories Ltd: **Canada Development Corp**

biogas: **Biomass Energy**

Biological Board of Canada: **Fisheries History; Hachey, Henry Benedict; Macallum, Archibald Byron; McMurrich, James Playfair; Oceanography; Physical Oceanography; Prince, Edward Ernest; Wright, R. Ramsay; Zoology**

biological societies & journals: **Biology; Zoology**

Biological Survey of Canada: **Zoology**

biological warfare: **Veterinary Medicine, History**

bioluminescence: **Crustacean; Zooplankton**

biometeorology: **Soil Science**

biophysics: **Johns, Harold E.; Physics**

Bioscope Co of Canada: **Film**

biosphere: **Conserver Society; Environment; Hydrogen**

Biosphere Reserve: **Mont St-Hilaire Nature Conservation Centre**

biostatistics: **Biology; Goulden, Cyril Harold**

biostratigraphy: **Paleontology**

biosystematics: **Biology**

Biosystematics Research Institute: **Entomology; Herbarium; Research Stations, Agricultural; Savile, Douglas Barton Osborne**

Birch, A.: **Skiing**

Birch Beer: **Soft-Drink Industry**

birch beetle: **Manitoba**

Birch River (Alta): **Claire, Lake**

Birchall, J.R.: **Folk Music, Anglo-Canadian**

Birchy Cove, Nfld: **Corner Brook**

Birchy Lake: **Grand Lake**

Bird, Frederick: **New Religious Movements**

Bird, J.B.: **Geomorphology**

bird banding: **Migration; Miner, John T.; Rowan, William**

bird hatchery: **Nova Scotia**

Bird Rocks: **Wildlife Conservation & Management**

bird's foot trefoil: **Forage Crops**

Birds Hill Provincial Park: **Parks, Provincial; Springfield**

birdseed: **Cereal Crops; Millet**

Birk, Hans D.: **Heraldry**

Birket-Smith, Kaj: **Archaeology**

Birks Building (Montréal): **Birks, Henry; Maxwell, Edward**

Birmingham Bulls: **Mahovlich, Francis W.**

birthing ceremonies: **Native People - Arctic**

birthrate: **Abortion; Baby Boom; Family; Family Allowance; Great Depression; Immigration; Immigration Policy; Ontario; Population; Province of Quebec, 1763-91; Québec; Regional Economics**

Bisby, G.R.: **Botany History**

Bishop, Isabella: **Exploration & Travel Literature in English**

Bishop, R.P.: **Golden Hinde**

Bishop Printing & Engraving Co: **Printmaking**

Bishop Strachan School: **Sproatt and Rolph**

Bishop's College School: **Lennoxville; Ritchie, Octavia Grace**

Bishop's Falls: **Exploits River**

Bishop's Palace: **Québec City**

bismuth: **Lead; Mineral; New Brunswick**

Bison Recovery Park: **Wainwright; Wildlife Conservation & Management**

Bissell, Claude Thomas: **Literature in English - Teaching**

Bissell, Keith: **Choral Music**

Bissell & Holman: **Cardinal, Douglas J.**

Bissett, Man: **Manitoba; Postal System**

Bisson, Laurence-A.: **Literature in French - Scholarship & Teaching**

Bissonnette, Lise: **Essay in French**

Bissonnette, Rosemarie: **Theatre, French-Language**

Bissot, François: **Footwear Industry**

bitter cherry: **Plants, Native Uses; Vegetation Regions - Pacific Coastal**

bittern: **Bird Classification & Evolution; Heron**

bitternut hickory: **Vegetation Regions - Eastern Temperate Forests**

bittersweet: **Nightshade**

bituminous: **Coal; Coal Liquefaction**

bivalvia: **Mollusc; Oyster; Scallop; Seashell**

Bizard, Ile: **Swiss**

Bizard, Jacques: **Swiss**

Black, G. Montegu: **Argus Corp Ltd; Meighen, Maxwell Charles Gordon; Western Dominion Investment Co Ltd**

Black, George: **Black, Martha Louise**

Black, James: **Nine-Hour Movement**

Black, Malcolm: **Vancouver Playhouse**

Black, William: *Racoon*

black alder: **Holly**

Black & Campbell: *Royal William*

Black & Decker Canada Inc: **Industrial Design**

black ash: **Ash; Barachois Pond Provincial Park; Vegetation Regions - Eastern Temperate Forests**

Black Ball ferry line: **Bennett, W.A.C.**

black bass: **Québec**

Black Bay: **Ouimet Canyon**

black bear: **Bear; Garibaldi Provincial Park; Kananaskis Country; Kluane Ranges; Queen Charlotte Islands; Whiteshell Provincial Park**

black brant: **Banks Island**

Black Brant rocket: **Aerospace Industry; Physics**

black-capped chickadee: **Chickadee; Migration**

black cherry: **Poisonous Plants; Vegetation Regions - Eastern Temperate Forests**

Black Clawson-Kennedy Ltd: **Machinery & Equipment Industry**

black cottonwood: **Vegetation Regions - Cordillera**

Black Creek, Ont: **Murray, Alexander**

black guillemot: **Auk; Auyuittuq National Park; Terra Nova National Park**

black gum: **Forest Regions**

black huckleberry: **Vegetation Regions - Cordillera**

Black Island: **Hecla**

Black Lake (Sask): **Cree Lake**

black-legged kittiwake: **Forillon National Park; Gull**

black lung: **Coal Mining; Mining Safety & Health**

black maple: **Maple; Vegetation Regions - Eastern Temperate Forests; Vegetation Regions - Pacific Coastal**

black market: **Underground Economy; Wartime Home Front**

Black Mountain: **West Vancouver**

black oak: **Oak; Vegetation Regions - Eastern Temperate Forests**

black redhorse: **Endangered Animals**

Black Report on Theatre Training in Canada: **Theatre Education**

black spruce: **Forest Fire; Forest Harvesting; Laurentian Highlands; Mistassini, Lac; Pukaskwa National Park; Spruce; Terra Nova National Park; Vegetation Regions**

black-tailed deer: **Deer; Pacific Rim National Park**

black-tailed prairie dog: **Grasslands National Park; Prairie Dog**

Black Theatre Canada: **Theatre, Multicultural**

Black Tusk: **Coast Mountains; Garibaldi Provincial Park**

Black United Front: **West Indians**

black walnut: **Endangered Plants; Furniture, English, Scottish & American; Plants, Native Uses; Vegetation Regions - Eastern Temperate Forests; Walnut**

black willow: **Vegetation Regions - Eastern Temperate Forests**

Blackbeard: **Oak Island**

blackberries: **Berries, Wild**

Blackburn, Maurice: **Music History; Opera**

Blackburn, Robert: **Encyclopedia**

blackcap: **Berries, Wild**

Blackduck culture: **Brockinton; Rainy River Burial Mounds**

Blackfish: **Literary Magazines in English**

Blackfoot Crossing: **Blackfoot; Poundmaker**

Blackfoot-English dictionary: **L'Heureux, Jean-B.**

Blackfoot Reserve: **L'Heureux, Jean-B.**

Blackhead Island: **Baffin Island; Whaling**

"Blackjack": **Lost Lemon Mine**

blackjack: **Gambling**

blackleg: **Animal Agriculture; Beef Cattle Farming**

Black's Harbour, NB: **Resource Towns**

blackspot: **Perch; Pike**

Blackstock, Ont: **Bruce, Herbert Alexander**

Blackstone, Milton: **Hart House String Quartet**

Blackstone Formation: **Sedimentary Rock**

blackstripe top minnow: **Endangered Animals**

Blackwater River (BC): **Carrier; Fraser River**

Blackwell, Charlie: **Water Skiing**

Blackwell & Craig: **Zeidler, Eberhard Heinrich**

Blackwood, Robert: **Furniture, Country**

bladderwort: **Carnivorous Plants**

Blades, Ann: **Children's Literature in English**

Blain, Maurice: *Cité libre*

Blaine Lake, Sask: **Horner, John H.**

Blainville, Qué: **Automotive Industry**

Blainville, Thérèse de: **Place-names**

Blair, Duncan Black: **Ethnic Literature**

Blairmore, Alta: **Czechs; Revolutionary Industrial Unionism; Selkirk Communications Ltd**

Blais, Roger: **Film**

Blake, William Hume (1861-1924): **Essay in English;** *Maria Chapdelaine*

Blakely, Phyllis: **Musicology**

Blakiston, Thomas W.: **Palliser Expedition**

Blanc, Reservoir: **St-Maurice, Rivière**

Blanc-Sablon, Qué: **Labrador**

Blanchard, Raoul: **Geomorphology; Urban Studies**

Blanchet, François-Norbert: **Exploration & Travel Literature in French**

Blanding's turtle: **Kejimkujik National Park; Turtle**

blanket: **Chilkat Blanket; Davidson, Florence Edenshaw; Fur Trade; Indian Art; Indian Trade Goods; Northwest Coast Indian Art; Silver, Indian Trade; Textiles, Woven**

Blanket society: **Kootenay**

blanket toss: **Sports History**

Blankstein, C.M.: **Green, Blankstein, Russell**

Blasco, Steve: *Breadalbane*

Blaskowitz, Karol: **Poles**

blasphemy: **Law & the Press**

blast furnace: **Algoma Steel Corp Ltd; Dominion Foundries & Steel, Ltd; Iron & Steel Industry; Sydney Steel Corp**

Blatchly, William D.: **Printmaking**

Blatter, Robert: **Architectural Styles; Architecture, Development**

Blau, P.: **Social Mobility**

Blaylock Medal: **Convey, John; Murdoch, James Young**

blazon: **Heraldry**

Blennerhasset, Margaret: **Poetry in English**

Bleu, Mont: **Laurentian Highlands**

Blewchamp, Anna: **Dance, Modern**

blewointmentpress: **bissett, bill; Literary Magazines in English**

Bligh, Stanley: **Music Criticism**

Bligh, William: **Canada & Australia**

blight: **Fungus**

"blind pig": **Prohibition**

Bliss case: **Women & the Law**

Bliss, Michael: **Business History**

Bliss Carman Poetry Society: *Fiddlehead*

"block parents": **Police**

Blockhouse Island: **Brockville**

Blodgett, E.D.: **Comparative Literature; Comparative Literature, Canadian; Literature in English - Theory & Criticism**

Bloedel, Stewart & Welch: **MacMillan, H.R.**

Bloem, Jan Jacques: **Sculpture**

Blondin, Marie-Esther: **Christian Religious Communities; Saints**

blood fractions: **Biological Product; Connaught Laboratories Ltd**

Blood Sweat & Tears: **Clayton-Thomas, David**

blood tests: **Family Law; Sexually Transmitted Disease**

blood transfusion: **Biological Product; Birthing Practices; Connaught Laboratories Ltd; Red Cross Society**

blood worm: **Annelida**

bloodroot: **Biogeography; Medicine, History of**

"Bloody Saturday": **Winnipeg General Strike; Woodsworth, J.S.**

Bloom, M.: **Physics**

Bloomfield, Leonard: **Folklore**

blowball: **Dandelion**

blue ash: **Ash; Forest Regions**

Blue Bell Canada Ltd: **Clothing Industries**

Blue Book: **Budgetary Process**

blue camas: **Plants, Native Uses**

Blue Dolphin expedition: **Hamilton Inlet**

blue Douglas Fir: **Forest Regions**

Blue Ensign: **Kean, Abraham (Abram)**

blue-eyed grass: **Wildflowers**

blue flag: **Lily**

blue gas: **Coal Gasification**

blue goose: **Cape Dorset; Soper, J. Dewey**

blue grama: **Biogeography; Vegetation Regions - Prairie**

blue grouse: **Game Bird; Grouse; Migration**

blue jay: **Jay; Migration**

Blue Mountain pottery: **Collingwood; Nepheline Syenite**

Blue Mountains: **Bruce Trail**

blue racer: **Endangered Animals**

blue walleye: **Endangered Animals**

blue whale: **Animal; Crustacean; Saguenay River; Whale**

blueberries: **Berries, Cultivated; Berries, Wild; British Columbia; Crop Research; Cuisine; Mistassini, Lac; Newfoundland; Nova Scotia**

Blueberry Festival: **Mistassini**

bluebunch wheatgrass: **Vegetation Regions - Cordillera; Vegetation Regions - Prairie**

bluefin tuna: **Notre Dame Bay; Prince Edward Island; Tuna**

Bluefish River: **Bluefish Caves**

bluegrass: **Grasses; Vegetation Regions - Cordillera; Vegetation Regions - Prairie**

bluegrass music: **Country & Western Music; Musical Theatre**

Bluejay Dance: **Kootenay**

bluejoint small reed grass: **Vegetation Regions - Pacific Coastal**

bluenose caribou: **Horton Plain**

Bluenose Lake: **Horton Plain**

blueschist: **Geological Regions**

bluestem: **Vegetation Regions - Prairie**

bluetongue: **Midge**

bluff: **Coastal Landform**

Blumenort, Man: **Hanover**

Blumhart, William-Edmond: *Presse*

Blumnau, Alta: **Swiss**

Blythe, Alan: **Popular Music**

BMEWS: **Early-Warning Radar; Radar**

BMI Canada: **Champagne, Claude**

B'nai B'rith: **Jews; Judaism; Manning, Ernest C.**

BNF: **Computer Science**

Boan, Alta: **Romanians**

Board of Broadcast Governors: **Broadcasting, Radio & Television; Canadian Broadcasting Corporation; Canadian Radio-television & Telecommunications Commission**

Board of Health (Ont): **Bryce, Peter Henderson; Hodgetts, Charles A.**

Board of Public Utility Commissioners (NS): **Regulatory Process**

Board of Railway Commissioners: **Canadian Manufacturers' Association; Cauchon, J.-E.-Noulan; Norris, Tobias Crawford; Sise, Charles Fleetford; Telegraph; Telephones; Transportation Regulation**
board of trade: **Chamber of Commerce**
Board of Trade Building (Toronto): **Architecture, Development**
Board of Transport Commissioners: **Canadian Manufacturers' Association; Canadian Transport Commission**
Board of Works: **Crown Corporation**
Boards of Trade Act: **Associations**
"boat people": **Refugees; Southeast Asians**
Bobcat APC: **Armaments**
Bobcaygeon, Ont: **Kawartha Lakes**
Bobet, Jacques: **Comédie-Canadienne**
bobwhite: **Game Bird; Quail**
Bochner, Lloyd: **Allan, Andrew E.F.; Jews**
Bodega, Mount: **Spanish**
Bodkin, R.G.: **Economics**
Bodnarchuk, Ivan: **Ukrainian Writing**
Boeing 747: **Transportation**
Boer War: **South African War**
bog: **Cape Spear; Lake; Mackenzie River; Newfoundland; Niagara Peninsula; Swamp, Marsh & Bog; Vegetation Regions - Boreal Forest or Taiga**
bog blueberry: **Vegetation Regions - Cordillera**
bog iron: **Agricultural Implements; Iron & Steel Industry; St Lawrence Lowland**
Bogaert, Ludo: **Diorama**
Bohatirchuk, Fyodor: **Chess**
Bohdanowicz, Zofia: **Poles**
Bohle family: **Silver, Domestic**
Boiler Code: **Safety Standards**
Boilès, Charles: **Musicology**
boimetry: **Biology**
Bois, Montagne de: **Wood Mountain**
Bois et cuivres du Québec: **Morel, François**
Bois Island: **Bay d'Espoir**
Boisjoli, Charlotte: **Drama in French**
Boissonneault, Fernand-Noël: **Nault, Fernand**
Boîte à clémence: **Deschamps, Yvon**
Boivin, A.: **Physics**
Boivin, Aurélien: **Literary Bibliography in French; Oral Literature in French**
Boldt, George: **Boldt Castle**
Bolduc, David: **Painting**
Bolduc, Jean-Baptiste: **Exploration & Travel Literature in French**
Bolduc, Roch: **Public Administration**
Bolshevism: **Padlock Act; Winnipeg General Strike**
Bolton, Thomas: **Black Hole**
Bolton-Laing survey: **Golden Hinde**
Bolvin, Gilles: **Sculpture**
bombing: **Front de libération du Québec; Violence**
Bompas, Charlotte Selina: **Autobiographical Writing in English**
Bon Echo Provincial Park: **Pictographs & Petroglyphs**
Bonanza Creek: **Klondike Gold Rush**
Bonaventure, Ile de: **Bird Sanctuaries & Reserves; Swiss**
Bonaventure Station: **Montreal & Lachine Railroad**
Bonavista Peninsula: **Bonavista; Cape Bonavista; Trinity Bay**
Bond Head, Ont: **Massey, Daniel; Mulock, William; Osler, William**
Bondar, Roberta: **Astronaut**
bonds: **Banking; Canada Savings Bonds; Canadian Northern Railway; Capital & Wealth; International Trade; Monetary Policy; Mutual Funds; Property Law; Stock & Bond Markets; Transportation**
bone china: **Ceramics**
bone necrosis: **Ocean Industry**
bonemeal: **Animal Agriculture**
Bonet, Jordi: **Public Art**
bonfires: **Lighthouses; Rainmaking**
Bonhomme Carnival: **Festivals**
bonito: **Mackerel; Tuna**
Bonne Bay: **Newfoundland**
Bonne Espérance Harbour: **Music History**

Bonne Renommée: Des Sauvages, ou, Voyage de Samuel Champlain
Bonnechere River: **Renfrew; St Lawrence Lowland**
Bonnes soirées: **Popular Literature in French**
Bonnie Glen oil field: **Petroleum**
Bonnington Falls, BC: **Technology**
Bonnycastle, Henry: **Printmaking**
Bonnycastle, Richard: **Exploration & Travel Literature in English**
Bonsecours Market: **Architecture; Theatre Royal**
Bonsecours seigneury: **L'Islet-sur-Mer**
bonspiel: **Curling**
book dumping: **Writers' Union of Canada**
Book Festival: **Authors & Their Milieu**
Book of Common Prayer: **Anglicanism**
Book of the Year Medal: **Literary Prizes in English**
Book Publishers' Council: *Books in Canada*
Book Publishing, Royal Commission on (Ont): **Book Publishing, English-Language; Magazines**
bookkeeping: **Accounting**
bookmaking: **Gambling; Organized Crime**
Bookman, Max: **Judaism**
Books Canada: **Authors & Their Milieu**
Books in Canada First Novel Award: **Literary Prizes in English**
boom-and-bust cycle: **Agriculture History; Business Cycles; Fisheries History; Resource Towns; Social Mobility**
Boom Mountain: **Vermilion Pass**
Boosey, Derek: **Track & Field**
Boot & Shoe Workers Union: **Québec Shoe Workers' Strike**
Booth, Dudley: **Firearm**
Booth, Felix: **Boothia Peninsula**
Boothia Isthmus: **Arctic Exploration**
bootlegging: **Prohibition**
boots: **Arctic Animals; Leatherworking; Mukluk; Sporting-Goods Industry**
borate: **Mineral**
Borba (The Struggle): **Croatians**
Borcoman, James: **National Gallery of Canada; Photography**
Bordeleau, Leo-Paul: **Philosophy**
Borden, Charles E.: **Archaeology**
Borden, PEI: **Cape Traverse; Northumberland Strait**
Borden Commission: **Energy, Royal Commission on**
Border Line: **Regional Economics**
Border Ranges: **Rocky Mountains**
Boreal Forest: **Dogwood; Forest; Forest Regions; Forestry; Forillon National Park; La Mauricie National Park; Nahanni National Park; Nordicity; Prince Albert National Park; Soil Classification; Terra Nova National Park; Vegetation Regions - Boreal Forest or Taiga**
Borgstrum, Carl: **Carver, Humphrey S.M.**
"born again" conversion: **Evangelism; Great Awakening**
Borson, Roo: **Poetry in English**
Borsos, Phil: **Film, Documentary**
Böschenstein, Hermann: **German Writing**
Boss Brass: **Bickert, Edward Isaac; Jazz; Koffman, M., "Moe"; McConnell, Robert M.G.**
Boss of the River: Menaud maître-draveur
Bossmen: **Clayton-Thomas, David**
Bostock, H.S.: **Geomorphology**
Boston, Stewart: **Drama in English**
Boston Bar, BC: **Cariboo Road; Hell's Gate**
Botanical Institute: **Marie-Victorin, Frère; Rousseau, Jacques**
botanical societies & journals: **Botany; Botany History; Floras & Botanical Journals**
Bote: **Mennonites**
Bothwell, Robert: **Business History**
Bott, E.A.: **Psychology**
Bottenberg, Wolfgang: **Choral Music**
bottle: **Glass; Indian Trade Goods; Plastics-Processing Industry**
Botwood, Nfld: **Newfoundland**
Bouchard, Antoine: **Musicology**
Bouchard, Guy: **Philosophy**

Bouchard, Joseph: **Folk Music, Franco-Canadian**
Bouchard, Laurent: **Children's Literature in French**
Bouchard Report: **Book Publishing, French-Language**
Boucher, Denise: **Drama in French; Theatre, French-Language**
Boucher, Emmanuel: **Archery**
Boucher, Sister: **Ile-à-la-Crosse**
Boucher de Boucherville, P. Georges: **Children's Literature in French; Literature in French**
Boucherville, Qué: **Boucher, Pierre; Quesnel, L.-Joseph-M.**
Boucherville Islands: **Trans-Canada Highway**
Bouchette, Joseph: **Cartography, History of; Exploration & Travel Literature in French; Nordicity**
Bouchette, R. Errol: **Economics; French Canadian Nationalism**
Boularderie Island: **Bras d'Or Lake**
Boulizon, Guy: **Children's Literature in French**
Boullé, Hélène: **Champlain, Samuel de**
Boulton, Charles: **Riel, Louis**
Boulton, D'Arcy, Jr: **Grange, The**
Boulton, J.G.: **Hydrography**
Boundary Bay, BC: **Delta, BC**
Boundary Bay Air Force Station: **Delta, BC**
Boundary Dam Mine: **Coal**
Boundary Demarcation Treaty: **International Boundary Commission**
Boundary Waters Treaty Act: **Environmental Law**
Bourassa-Trépanier, Juliette: **Musicology**
Bourbon Street: **Jazz**
Bourdon, Jean: **Cartography, History of**
Bourgault, Hélène: **Video Art**
Bourgeois, Albéric: **Popular Literature in French**
Bourgeois, Jean-Baptiste-Louis: **Baha'i Faith**
Bourgeois, Joe: **Rossland**
Bourget, Elisabeth: **Drama in French**
Bourlamaque, François-Charles de: **Fort Frontenac**
Bourlamaque, Qué: **Val-d'Or**
Bourlamaque Miners' Village: **Val-d'Or**
Bourne, Adolphus: **Printmaking**
Bourneuf, Roland: **Comparative Literature**
Bourque, Gilles: **Marxism**
Boutal, Arthur: **Theatre, French-Language**
Boutal, Pauline: **Theatre, French-Language**
Boutet, Edgar: **Theatre, French-Language**
Boutet, Martin: **Mathematics**
bow & arrow: **Archery; Armaments; Babiche; Beothuk; Chilcotin**
bow drill: **Inuit Art**
Bow Glacier: **Bow River**
Bow Lake: **Bow River**
Bow Park: **Brown, George**
Bow Pass: **Saskatchewan River**
Bow River Irrigation Project: **Bow River; Prairie Farm Rehabilitation Administration**
Bow Valley Park: **Kananaskis Country**
Bowden, Norris: **Figure Skating; Wagner, Barbara**
Bowdoin Canyon: **Churchill Falls**
Bower, Johnny: **Toronto Maple Leafs**
Bowering, Marilyn: **Literature in English**
Bowers, Robert: **Sculpture**
Bowes, Wayne: **Racquetball**
Bowes Publishers Ltd: **Alberta**
bowhead whale: **Arctic Animals; Baffin Island; Banks Island; Brooman Point Village; Lancaster Sound; Whale**
Bowie, Duncan: **Highland Games**
Bowker, Ron: **Track & Field**
bowl: **Glass; Northern Georgia Strait Coast Salish; Northwest Coast Indian Art; Pewter; Woodenware**
Bowman, Ariel: **Poetry in English**
Bowman, Elaine: **Dance, Modern**
Bowman Arts Centre: **Lethbridge**
Bowmanville, Ont: **Automobile Racing; Macleod, James F.; Maynard, Hannah; Rubber Products Industry; Toys & Games**

Bowmanville Rubber Co: **Rubber Products Industry**
Bowring Brothers Ltd: **Bowring, Benjamin; Jackman, William**
Bowron Lake: **Columbia Mountains**
Bowron Lake Provincial Park: **Quesnel**
Bowsfield, Hartwell: **Hudson's Bay Record Society**
box: **Forestry; Northern Georgia Strait Coast Salish; Northwest Coast Indian Art; Quillwork**
box car: **Locomotives & Rolling Stock; Railways, Contemporary**
box elder: **Ornamentals; Vegetation Regions - Eastern Temperate Forests**
box shooks: **Timber Trade History**
Boy Scouts: **Children's Literature in French; McLaughlin, Robert Samuel**
Boyarsky, Abraham: **Jewish Writing**
Boychuk, Andy: **Track & Field**
Boyd, James: **Printmaking**
Boyd Lake: **Dubawnt River**
Boyden, John: **Singing**
Boys, Beverly: **Diving**
Boys & Girls Clubs: **4-H Clubs**
Boy's Naval Brigade: **Navy League of Canada**
Božja Beseda (God's Word): **Slovenes**
Bozos: **Léveillée, Claude**
BP Resources Canada Ltd (British Petroleum): **Bitumen; Petroleum Industries**
Bracebridge, Ont: **Place-names**
bracken: **Biogeography; Fern; Poisonous Plants**
Braddock, Edward: **Iroquois**
Bradford, Ont: **Holland Marsh; Northern Railway of Canada**
Bradford Mattress Factory: **Holland Marsh**
Bradley, William: **Canada & Australia**
Bradley House: **Architectural Styles**
Bradstreet, John: **Fort Frontenac**
Brady, Alexander: **Political Science**
Bragg Creek Park: **Kananaskis Country**
brain: **Elliott, K. Allan C.; Hebb, Donald Olding; Injury & Prevention; Medical Research; Penfield, Wilder G.; Rossiter, Roger James; Science & Society; Sourkes, Theodore Lionel**
brain-worm disease: **Caribou**
Brainin, Reuben: **Jewish Writing**
brainwashing: **New Religious Movements**
Braithwaite, Leonard: **Blacks**
Bramwell, Barbara: **Children's Literature in English**
Bramwell, Heather: **Children's Literature in English**
Brancato, George: **Ottawa Rough Riders**
Branch, James: **Theatre, French-Language**
Branch, Nfld: **St Mary's Bay**
branch-line abandonment: **Agriculture & Food Policy; Alberta; Buctouche; Lindbergh; Manitoba; Newfoundland; Prince Edward Island; Railway Station; Railways, Contemporary; Transportation**
branchiopoda: **Crustacean**
branchiura: **Crustacean**
Brandon Hills wildlife management area: **Brandon**
Brandon House: **Brandon; Seven Oaks Incident**
Brandon Indian Residential School: **Steinhauer, Ralph G.**
Brandon Sun: **Manitoba**
Brandy Dispute: **Nova Scotia**
brannerite: **Metallurgy**
Brant, Catharine: **Brant, Joseph**
Brantford Co-operative Soc: **Keen, George**
Bras d'Or: **Armaments; Shipbuilding & Ship Repair**
Brascade Resources Ltd: **Noranda Mines Ltd**
brass: **Coinage; Copper; Furniture, English, Scottish & American; Lighting; Made Beaver; Silver, Church; Zinc**
Brassard, Adolphe: **Children's Literature in French**
Brassard, André: **Germain, Jean-Claude; Tremblay, Michel**
Braud, Alexandre: **Theatre, French-Language**

Braun, Victor: **Opera**
Brauneis, Jean-Chrysostome, Jr.: **Choral Music; Music History; Religious Music**
Brauneis, Jean-Chrysostome, Sr.: **Music History**
Brave Mountain: **Labrador Highlands**
Braverman, Harry: **Educational Opportunity**
Braybrooke, David: **Philosophy**
Brayon, NB: **Festivals**
Brazeau Lake: **Rockslide**
Brazilian Traction, Light & Power Co Ltd: **Borden, Henry; Brascan, Ltd; Energy, Royal Commission on; Horne-Payne, Robert Montgomery; Mackenzie, Alexander (1860-1943); Mackenzie, William; Winters, Robert H.; Wood, Edward Rogers**
bread: **Baking Industry; Buckwheat; Canada's Food Guide; Condiment Crops; Rye; Triticale; Wheat**
Breadner, Lloyd S.: **Royal Naval Air Service**
breakfast cereal: **Barley; Buckwheat; Flour Milling Industry; Oats; Rye; Wheat**
breaking & entering: **Juvenile Delinquency; Privacy**
Breakwater Books Ltd: **Book Publishing, English-Language; Children's Literature in English; Regionalism in Literature**
Breault, Gilles: **Birth Control**
Breault, Henri J.: **Pediatrics**
Breault, Rita: **Birth Control**
Brébeuf Park: **Hull**
breech-loading gun: **Firearm; Fortification**
Bregman, Sidney: **Bregman & Hamann**
Bréhant de Galinée, René de: **Port Dover; St Clair, Lake**
Brendt, P.F.: **McPhail, Alexander James**
Brennan, Anthony: **Novel in English**
Brescia College: **University of Western Ontario**
Breslau, Ont: **Musical Instruments**
Brésolles, Lac: **Bienville, Lac**
Bressani, Francesco Giuseppi: **Cartography, History of**
Brest (Labrador): **Religious Music**
Brett, Carl: **Graphic Design**
Brett, Robert George: **Banff**
Brewer, Carl: **Toronto Maple Leafs**
Brewing Corp of Canada Ltd: **Taylor, Edward Plunkett**
Brewster Transport Co Ltd: **Bus Transportation**
Briand, Jean-Olivier: **Séminaire de Québec**
bribery: **Baie des Chaleurs Scandal; Conspiracy; Corruption; Electoral Systems; Pacific Scandal; Political Campaign; Rivard, Lucien**
brick: **Architectural Styles; Architecture; Architecture, Development; Bank Architecture; Clay; La Prairie; Limestone; L'Islet-sur-Mer; Medicine Hat; Newfoundland; Random Island; St Lawrence Lowland; Silica**
Brick, J. Gough: **Peace River, Alta**
Bricker, Cliff: **Track & Field**
bridal wreath: **Spiraea**
Bridge River: **British Columbia**
Bridge River Lillooet News: **Lillooet**
Bridge River Reserve: **Salish, Interior**
Bridgeburg, Ont: **Fort Erie**
Bridgedale, NB: **Riverview**
Bridgeport, Ont: **Baptists**
Bridgetown, NS: **Heritage Canada Foundation**
Bridgeville, Qué: **Percé**
Bridgewater, NS: **LaHave River Estuary; Nova Scotia**
Bridle, Augustus: **Music Criticism; Musical Theatre**
Brier Island Settlement: **Westport**
brig: *Hector*; **Sailing Ships**
Brigade Trail: **Douglas, James (1803-77); Hope; Merritt; Penticton; Prince George; Princeton; Vernon**
Brigden, Frederick H.: **Casson, Alfred Joseph; Drawing; Manly, Charles MacDonald; Printmaking**
Brigden's Ltd: **Printmaking**
Bright, John D.: **Edmonton Eskimos**
Bright, Thomas: **Wine Industry**

Bright's disease: **Wesbrook, Frank Fairchild**
Brill, Debbie: **Track & Field**
Brillinger, David: **Mathematics**
Brinco Ltd: **Gordon, Donald; Reichmann family; Smith, Harold Greville**
Brind'Amour, Yvette: **Théâtre du rideau vert**
brindled madtom: **Endangered Animals**
brine: **Hazardous Wastes; Salt; Saltspring Island**
Brinkman, A.H.: **Botany History**
Brintnell, Leigh: **Bush Flying**
Brion, Île: **Madeleine, Iles de la**
briquettes: **Gesner, Abraham; Peat**
Brisbane, Thomas: **Canada & Australia**
Brisset-Thibaudet, Aliette: **Radio Drama, French-Language**
Brisson, Luc: **Philosophy**
bristletail: **Insect Classification**
Bristol Aerospace Ltd: **Aerospace Industry**
Bristol Bolingbroke aircraft: **Military Aviation & Aircraft**
Britannia: **Cunard, Samuel; Cunard Co**
Britannia Boating Club: **Amyot, Francis**
Britannia Community Services Centre: **Downs, Barry Vance**
Britannia Mine: **Avalanche; Mineral Resources; Mining**
Britannia Settlement, North-West Territories: **Lloydminster**
British: **Alberta; Autobiographical Writing in English; Brandon; British Columbia; Elites; English; Ethnic & Race Relations; Folk Art; Folk Music, Anglo-Canadian; Garson; Guelph; Hamilton; Immigration; Immigration Policy; Iroquois; Kingston; Kitchener-Waterloo; Lincoln; London; Manitoba; Maritime Provinces; Montréal; Moose Jaw; Mountaineering; New Glasgow; North Bay; Nova Scotia; Oak Bay; Ontario; Ottawa, Ont; Population; Prejudice & Discrimination; Prince Albert; Prince Edward Island; Québec City; Rockwood; St Catharines; St-Hyacinthe; St John's; Saskatchewan; Saskatoon; Scots; Springfield; Sudbury; Thorold; Toronto; Urban Reform; Vancouver; Welsh; Winnipeg**
British America Fire & Life Assurance Co: **Allan, William**
British-American Horse Ranch Co: **Cross, Alfred Ernest**
British-American Institute: **Dresden; Henson, Josiah**
British American Oil Co Ltd: **Gulf Canada Ltd; Petroleum Industries**
British & Foreign Bible Society: **Canadian Bible Society; McGregor, James; Orthodox Church**
British & North American Royal Mail Steam Packet Co: **Cunard Co**
British-Canadian Atomic Energy Project: **Steacie, Edgar William Richard**
British Canadian Pathé News: **Ouimet, L.-Ernest**
British Colonist: **De Cosmos, Amor; Drama in English; Printmaking**
British Columbia Act: **Cartier, George-Etienne**
British Columbia Art League: **Artists' Organizations; Fripp, Thomas William**
British Columbia College of Arts: **Macdonald, J.W.G., "Jock"; Varley, Frederick H.**
British Columbia Electric Railway: **Horne-Payne, Robert Montgomery; New Westminster; Urban Reform**
British Columbia Ferry Corp: **Ferries; Hodgson, Stuart M.; Prince Rupert; Sidney**
British Columbia Fruit-Growers' Assn: **Agriculture History**
British Columbia Legislature Building: **Architecture, Development**
British Columbia Medical Society: **Helmcken, John Sebastian**
British Columbia Museums Assn: **Duff, Wilson**

British Columbia Power Corp, Ltd: **Gundy, James Henry**
British Columbia Provincial Museum: **British Columbia; Conservation of Movable Cultural Property; Diorama; Duff, Wilson; Hunt, Henry; Martin, Mungo; Musical Instruments**
British Columbia Soc of Fine Arts: **Fripp, Thomas William**
British Columbia Telephone Co: **Economic Regulation; Lethbridge; Telephones; TransCanada Telephone System**
British Columbia Television Co: **WIC (Western International Communications)**
British Columbia Veterinary Medical Assn: **Veterinary Medicine, History**
British Columbian: **New Westminster; Robson, John**
British Commonwealth Games: **Commonwealth Games; Swimming, Speed**
British Dominions Land Settlement Co: **Harvie, Eric L.**
British Empire: **Architecture; Artists' Organizations; Baddeck; Children's Literature in English; Commonwealth; Constitutional Law; Denison, George T. (3rd); Eddy, Ezra Butler; Grant, George M.; Immigration; Imperial Preference; Imperialism; Labrador Boundary Dispute; Maritime Provinces; Parkin, George R.; Round Table Movement; Slavery; Treaty-Making Power; Upper Canada; Victoria Day**
British Empire & Commonwealth Games: **Commonwealth Games; Hepburn, Douglas**
British Empire Games: **Apps, C.J. Sylvanus; Commonwealth Games; Dewar, Phyllis; Lawn Bowling; McNaughton, Duncan Anderson; Track & Field; Wrestling**
British Empire Motor Club: **Automobile Racing**
British Empire Range: **Innuitian Region**
British Empire Steel Corp: **Cape Breton Strikes, 1920s**
British Indian Dept: **Brant, Joseph; Girty, Simon; Johnson, John; Johnson, William**
British Metal Corp of Canada: **Stavert, Reuben Ewart**
British Mountains: **Old Crow Plain**
British Newfoundland Development Corp: **Churchill Falls**
British North American Exploring Expedition: **Palliser Expedition**
British North American Royal Mail Steam Packet Co: **Cunard, Samuel**
British Pacific Properties: **West Vancouver**
British Preferential System: **International Trade**
British Whig: **Sangster, Charles**
British Yukon Aviation Co: **Whitehorse**
British Yukon Navigation Co: **Whitehorse**
brittle star: **Echinodermata**
Brix scale: **Maple Sugar Industry**
Broad Cove, NS: **Credit Unions**
Broad Cove Coal Co: **Inverness**
Broad Cove (Mines, Shean or Shore), NS: **Inverness**
broadaxe: **Timber Axe**
Broadcast Branch - House of Commons: *Hansard*
Broadcast Code for Advertising to Children: **Toys & Games Industry**
Broadcast News Ltd: **Canadian Press; News Agencies**
Broadcasting Acts: **Broadcasting; Radio & Television; Broadcasting, Royal Commission on; Cable Television; Canadian Broadcasting Corporation; Canadian Radio-television & Telecommunications Commission; Communications Law; LaMarsh, Judy V.**
Broadfoot, Barry: **Manitoba; Oral History**
Broadhead, William: **Thomson, Thomas J.**
Broadhurst, Christopher: **Painting**

Broadland Music: **Buck, Gary**
broadleaf maple: **Vegetation Regions - Cordillera**
broadside: **Burke, Johnny; Folk Music, Anglo-Canadian; Lane, Patrick; Printmaking**
Broadus, Edmund K.: **Essay in English; Literature in English - Teaching**
Broadus, Eleanor H.: **Literature in English - Teaching**
Broadview, Sask: **Place-names**
Brochet, Lac: **Manitoba**
Brochet, Man: **Reindeer Lake**
Brock, Reginald: **Science**
Brock Island: **Arctic Exploration**
Brocket, Alta: **Oldman River**
Brockhouse, B.N.: **Physics**
Brock's Monument: **Historic Site; Hunters' Lodges; Queenston**
Brockville & Ottawa Railway: **Keefer, Samuel; Tunnels**
Brockville Asylum: **Tully, Kivas**
Brodeur, Jean-Paul: **Philosophy**
Brodeur, Toussaint: **Brodeur, Louis-Philippe**
Brodeur Peninsula: **Baffin Island**
Brodie School: **Mather, Bruce**
Broken Islands: **Pacific Rim National Park; Ucluelet**
Brokenhead, Man: **Poles**
Brome, Mont: **Cowansville; St Lawrence Lowland**
bromegrass: **Forage Crops; Grasses; Poisonous Plants**
Bromfield, Bill: **Bowling, Indoor**
bromine: **Mineral**
Bromley, David G.: **New Religious Movements**
bronc riding: **Calgary Stampede; Rodeo**
bronchitis: **Air Pollution; Smoking**
Bronfman, Samuel: **Bronfman Family; Klein, Abraham M.**
Bronfman Family Foundation: **Educational Foundations & Endowments**
Bronson, A.A.: **Art, Contemporary Trends**
Bronson, H.L.: **Physics**
Bronson & Weston Lumber Co: **Bronson, Erskine Henry; Bronson, Henry Franklin**
Bronte, Ont: **Thoroughbred Racing**
Bronte Creek Provincial Park: **Parks, Provincial**
bronze: **Art; Coinage; Copper; Etrog, Sorel; Hébert, L.-Philippe; Laliberté, Alfred (artist); L'Anse aux Meadows; Northwest Coast Indian Art; Pewter; Public Art; Tailfeathers, Gerald; Victoria Cross**
brook trout: **Biogeography; Char**
Brooke, John: **Brooke, Frances**
Brookes, G.E.: **Armed Forces - Air Force; World War II**
Brookfield Dairy Co: **Truro**
Brooks, E.M.: **Brooks**
Brooks, Leonard: **Printmaking**
broom crowberry: **Biogeography**
Broome, Edward: **Choral Music**
Brossard Commission (Qué): *R v Coffin*
Brossard Committee: **Biotechnology**
Brosseau, Alta: **Lacombe, Albert**
Broten, Norm: **Molecules in Interstellar Space**
brothel: **Prostitution**
Brott, Denis: **Orford String Quartet**
Broughton, Qué: **Soapstone**
Broughton Island: **Soapstone**
Brouillan, Jacques-François: **Saint John**
Brouillé, Jean-Louis: *Actualité*
Brouillet, Jean-Baptiste: **Exploration & Travel Literature in French**
Brouillette, Louis C.: **Wesson, John Henry**
Brouve, Sieur: **Sculpture**
Brouwer, Leo: **Guitar**
Brower, Edna Mae: **Diefenbaker, John G.**
Brown, Alan: *Bonheur d'occasion; Salut Galarneau!*
Brown, Alan (1887-1960): **Pediatrics**
Brown, Arthur W.: **St John's**
Brown, Craig: *Canadian Historical Review*
Brown, D.P.: **Painting**
Brown, David K.: **Architectural Styles**

Brown, Donald: **Philosophy**
Brown, Eric: **Art Writing & Criticism; Group of Seven; National Gallery of Canada**
Brown, Frederick: **Theatre Royal**
Brown, G. Baldwin: **Capper, Stewart Henbest**
Brown, George: **Rowing**
Brown, George W.: *Canadian Historical Review; Dictionary of Canadian Biography*
Brown, Gordon: **Harris, Robert**
Brown, Hal: **Track & Field**
Brown, James: **Philosophy**
Brown, Kathryn: **Dance, Modern**
Brown, Michael Septimus: **Art Education; Silver, Domestic**
Brown, Mount: **Douglas, David**
Brown, R.A.: **Calgary**
Brown, Rosemary: **Blacks**
Brown, Thomas: **Art Education**
Brown, Thomas Storrow: **Fils de la Liberté**
Brown, W.E.: **Medicine, History of**
Brown, Wally: **Track & Field**
brown algae: **Algae; Vegetation Regions - Coastal Marine Flora**
Brown & Gilmore: **Almanacs; Brown, William**
brown bullhead: **Catfish**
brown chalcedony: **Linear Mounds**
Brown Corp: **La Tuque**
brown lemming: **Arctic Animals; Lemming**
Brown Report: **Prison**
brown thrasher: **Algonquin Provincial Park; Thrasher**
Browne, Belmore: **Glenbow Museum**
Browne, J.S.L.: **Biochemistry**
Brownites: **Clear Grits; Province of Canada**
Brownridge, George: **Film**
Brownsburg, Qué: **Firearm**
Brownsville, Ont: **Dairy Industry**
Bruce, Charles: **Regionalism in Literature**
Bruce, Harry: **Essay in English**
Bruce, Ian: **Industrial Design**
Bruce, Norman: **Soaring**
Bruce Mines, Ont: **Copper**
Bruce Nuclear Power Development: **Kincardine**
Bruce Park: **Saltspring Island**
Bruce Trail Assn: **Hiking**
brucellosis: **Savage, Alfred; Veterinary Medicine**
Bruchési, Jean: **Exploration & Travel Literature in French**
Brule, Alta: **Company Town**
Brulé, Lac: **Romaine, Rivière**
Brulotte, Gaétan: **Short Fiction in French**
Bruneau, Orphyr: **Daubigny, Victor-Théodule**
Bruneau, Philippe: **Folk Music, Franco-Canadian**
Brunel, Jules: **Marie-Victorin, Frère**
Brunelle, Yves: *Angéline de Montbrun*
Brunet, Berthelot: **Literature in French - Criticism & Theory;** *Relève*
Brunet, Emile: **Sculpture**
Brunet, Michel: **French Canadian Nationalism; Historiography; Intellectual History**
brunisols: **Soil Classification**
Brunswick Mining & Smelting Corp Ltd: **New Brunswick**
brush wolf: **Coyote**
Bruyère, Elisabeth: **Saints**
Bryant, Giles: **Festival Singers of Canada**
Bryant, John M.: **Disasters**
Bryce, George: **Archaeology**
Bryce, George (1844-1931): **Curling; Historiography**
Bryce Commission: **Corporate Concentration, Royal Commission on**
Brydges, Charles John: **Great Western Railway**
Brydone Jack Observatory: **Jack, W. Brydone**
Brymner, Douglas: **Archives; Historiography**
bryology: **Botany History**
bryophyte: **National Museum of Natural Sciences**
Bub, Jeffrey: **Philosophy**
bubble shell: **Mollusc**
bubonic plague: **Flea**
Buchan, David: **Demasduwit**

Buchanan, Donald W.: **Art Education; Art Writing & Criticism**
Buchanan, Isaac: **Great Western Railway**
Buchanan, Peter: **MacNab, Allan N.**
Buck, Robert J.: **Mediterranean Archaeology**
buckboard: **Roads & Highways**
Buckhorn Lake: **Kawartha Lakes**
Buckingham, Qué: **Chemical Industries**
Buckingham, William: **Print Industry**
Buckinghamshire: **Eastern Townships**
Buckley, Helen: **Buckley, Kenneth Arthur Haig**
buckthorn: **Crop Research**
Budden, John: **Krieghoff, Cornelius D.**
budget speech: **Parliamentary Procedure**
Budka, Niceta: **Catholicism**
Buell, John: **Novel in English**
Buell, William: **Brockville**
Buenos Ayrean: **Allan Line**
buffalo: **Bison; Blackfoot; Blackfoot Nation; Blood; Cuisine; Pemmican; Verner, Frederick A.**
Buffalo & Lake Huron Railway: **Port Colborne**
Buffalo Head Hills: **Bitumen**
buffalo hides: **Buffalo Hunt; Peace River; Peace River, Alta**
buffalo ranch: **Métis Settlements**
buffaloberries: **Berries, Wild**
buffet: **Furniture, French**
Buffy's Corners, Upper Canada: **Brampton**
Bugaboos: **Columbia Mountains**
buggy: **Roads & Highways**
Buick automobile: **General Motors of Canada Ltd; McLaughlin, Robert Samuel; Oshawa**
Buissonneau, Paul: **Deschamps, Yvon**
Bukovinians: **Ukrainians**
Bulgarian Eastern Orthodox Church: **Orthodox Church**
Bulgarian Orthodox Church: **Orthodox Church**
Bulgarians: **Internment**
Bulkley River: **Carrier; Ksan; Skeena River**
Bull Back Fat: **Blood**
Bull Head: **Sarcee**
bull riding: **Rodeo**
Bull River: **Wardner**
bull trout: **Char**
bulldogging: **Rodeo**
Buller, A.H.: **Botany History**
Buller, Charles: **Upper Canada**
Buller, James: **Theatre, Multicultural**
Bulletin: **Art Writing & Criticism; Literary Periodicals in English**
Bulletin des agriculteurs: **Popular Literature in French; United Farmers of Québec**
Bulletin paroissial: *Actualité*
Bullmoose Mine: **Coal**
Bullmoose Mountain: **Rocky Mountains**
Bullock, Joseph: **Shatford, Sidney S.**
bulrush: **Cattail; Holland Marsh; Vegetation Regions - Prairie**
bultow: **Fisheries History**
Bunbury, PEI: **Charlottetown**
bunchberry: **Biogeography; Dogwood; Wildflowers**
bunchgrass: **Forage Crops**
Bunge, Mario: **Philosophy**
Bungi: **Ojibwa**
Buntin, Alexander: **Print Industry**
bur oak: **Manitoba; Oak**
Burbank, J.C.: *Anson Northup*
burbot: **Cod; Portage La Loche**
Burdett, Alta: **Strom, Harry Edwin**
burdock: **Thistle**
bureau: **Furniture, English, Scottish & American**
Bureau d'aménagement de l'est du Québec: **Communications in Québec; Sociology**
Bureau des colonies: **Ministère de la Marine**
Bureau des commissaires: **Montréal**
Bureau du ponant: **Ministère de la Marine**
Bureau of Broadcast Measurement: **Advertising**
Bureau of Competition Policy: **Consumer & Corporate Affairs, Dept of**
Bureau of Industries (Ont): **Women in the Labour Force**

Bureau of Intellectual Property: **Consumer & Corporate Affairs, Dept of**
Bureau of Mines (Ont): **Prospecting**
Bureau of Public Information: **Wartime Information Board**
burette: **Silver, Church**
Burgeo Island: **Burgeo**
Burger, Beaudoin: **Essay in French**
Burgess, Catherine: **Sculpture**
Burgess, Maynard: **Shaw Festival**
Burgoyne, W.B.: **St Catharines**
burials: **Archaeology; Archaic; Baffin Island; Gray Burial Site; L'Anse Amour Burial Site; Linear Mounds; Port au Choix; Prehistory; Rainy River Burial Mounds; Serpent Mound; Valdes Island**
buried treasure: **Oak Island**
burin: **Bluefish Caves; Clovis; Microblade Technology**
Burin, Nfld: **Placentia Bay**
Burin Peninsula: **Disasters; Earthquake; Marystown; Placentia Bay**
Burke, Lillian: **Rugs & Rug Making**
Burke, Mount: **Coquitlam**
Burland, Clarissa: **Ami, Henri-Marc**
Burlington, Ont: **Bateman, Robert McL.; Brant, Joseph; Canada Centre for Inland Waters; Folk Art; Hamilton; Hydrography**
Burlington Bay: **Hamilton**
Burlington Beach: **Hamilton**
Burlington Glass Co: **Glass**
Burlington Steel Division of Slater Steels Industries Ltd: **Iron & Steel Industry**
Burlingtons: **Baseball**
Burn, William: **Baldoon**
Burnaby, Robert: **Burnaby**
Burnaby Art Gallery: **Bell, Alistair Macready; Burnaby**
Burnaby Lake: **Burnaby**
Burnaby Mountain: **Burnaby; Simon Fraser University**
Burnaby Print Show: **Printmaking**
Burnett, Brian: **Painting**
Burnford, Sheila: **Children's Literature in English; Short Fiction in English**
Burnham, Asa: **Cobourg**
Burnham, Mark: **Religious Music**
Burns, John: **Meat-Processing Industry**
Burns, Nelson: **Holiness Churches**
Burns Foods Ltd: **Meat-Processing Industry**
Burnside River: **Bathurst Inlet**
Burnt Bay: **Lewisporte**
Burntwood River: **Nelson River; Thompson**
Burrard Dry Dock Co: **North Vancouver**
Burrard Inlet: **Burnaby; Disasters; North Vancouver; Port Moody; Vancouver; West Vancouver**
Burrard Reserve: **George, Dan**
Burridge, K.O.L.: **Anthropology**
Burstall, Sask: **Pipeline Debate**
Burstyn, Varda: **Marxism**
Burtch, Zacharias: **Woodstock, Ont**
Burton, Ian: **Nuclear Safety**
Burwash Bay: **Nettling Lake**
Burwell, John Hood: **Poetry in English**
Bush, Douglas: **Essay in English; Literature in English - Theory & Criticism**
Bush, Thomas: **Drama in English**
bush balsam: **Flowers, Cultivated**
bush summer squash: **Vegetable**
Bushell, John: **Newspapers; Print Industry**
Bushnell Communications Ltd: **Bushnell, Ernest L.; Western Dominion Investment Co Ltd**
bushtit: **Chickadee**
Business Corporations Act (Ont): **Corporation Law**
Business Council on National Issues: **Pressure Group**
business profits tax: **Borden, Robert L.; Taxation; World War I**
Bussières, Johanne: **Children's Literature in French**
Bustamante y Guerra, José: **Malaspina Expedition**
busy Lizzie: **Touch-me-not**
Busy Man's Magazine: **Maclean, John B.; Magazines**
Busza, A.: **Poles**

butane: **Petroleum; Petroleum Exploration & Production**
Butchart Gardens: **Butchart, Robert Pim**
butchering: **Meat-Processing Industry**
Bute Inlet: **Fjord; Northern Georgia Strait Coast Salish**
Butler, Edith: **Music History**
Butler, Hack: **Painting**
Butler, Juan: **Novel in English**
Butler, Leonard H.: **Genetics**
Butler, Peter: **Long-Distance Running**
Butler, Sheila: **Painting**
Butler's Barracks: **Niagara Historic Frontier; Niagara-on-the-Lake**
butter: **Advertising; Agriculture History; Dairy Farming; Dairy Industry**
Butter Pot: **Masterless Men of Newfoundland**
butter print: **Folk Art; Woodenware**
Butterfield, William: **Architectural Styles; Architecture, Development; Christ Church Cathedral; Medley, John**
butterfly weed: **Milkweed**
butternut: **Furniture, English, Scottish & American; Furniture, French; Plants, Native Uses; Timber Trade History; Walnut**
butterwort: **Carnivorous Plants**
Buttle Lake: **Strathcona Provincial Park**
Button Point: **Bylot Island; Lancaster Sound**
Butts, Robert E.: **Philosophy**
Buxton, William: **Electroacoustic Music**
buzzard: **Québec**
by-election: **Double Shuffle; Elections**
Byam Martin Island: **Queen Elizabeth Islands**
Byelorussian Autocephalic Orthodox Church: **Orthodox Church**
Byers, Bettina: **Dance Education**
bylaw: **Censorship; Prostitution; Veterinary Medicine, History**
bylaw enforcement: **Policing**
Bylot, Robert: **Arctic Exploration; Baffin Bay; Bylot Island**
Byng, Viscountess: **Byng of Vimy, Viscount; Lady Byng Trophy**
Byrne, William J.: **Archaeology**
Byrne Commission (NB): **New Brunswick**
Byrnes, Terence: **Short Fiction in English**
Byron Creek Collieries Ltd: **Coal; Sparwood**
byssinosis: **Occupational Disease**
Bystander: **Literary Magazines in English; Smith, Goldwin**
byte: **Computer Science**
Bytown, Upper Canada: **Bridges; Bronson, Henry Franklin; Nursing; Ottawa, Ont; Shiners' Wars**
Bytown & Prescott Railway: **Kemptville; Shanly, Walter**
Bytown *Citizen*: **Billings, Elkanah**
Bytown Museum: **Ottawa, Ont**
Bytown Troubadours: **Music History**
Byward Market: **Ottawa, Ont**
Byzantine Church: **Orthodox Church**
Byzantine rite: **Catholicism**

C

C-Channel: **Pay Television**
C.T. Brandon Co: **Toys & Games**
Caamaño, Jacinto: **Hecate Strait; Spanish Exploration**
cabaret: **Musical Theatre; Theatre, English-Language**
Cabay, Marcel: **Radio Drama, French-Language**
cabbage turnip: **Kohlrabi**
Cabena, Barrie: **Choral Music; Opera**
caber-toss: **Highland Games**
cabinet card: **Photography**
Cabinets de lecture paroissiaux: **Catholicism**
Cablodistribution de l'est: **Cable Television**
caboose: **Locomotives & Rolling Stock**
Cabot Highway: **Bonavista**
Cabot Tower: **St John's**
Caccia, Charles: **Italians**
Caccia, Fulvio: **Italian Writing**

caccine: **Sexually Transmitted Disease**
Cache Creek, BC: **BC Hydro**
CAD/CAM technologies: **Electronics Industry**
cadastral mapping & surveying: **Cartography, History of; Surveying**
cadaver: **Medicine, History of**
Cadbury, Barbara: **Birth Control**
Cadbury, George: **Birth Control**
Cadieux, Leo: **Armed Forces - Unification**
Cadillac Fairview Corp: **Development Industry**
Cadomin, Alta: **Company Town; Prairie West**
Cadran, Qué: **Domestic Utensils**
CAE Electronics Ltd: **Canadarm; Québec**
Caesarean section: **Birthing Practices; Women & Health**
Café St Michèl: **Jazz**
caffeine: **Medical Drug Abuse**
Caffery, Jack: **Long-Distance Running**
Cahiers de la file indienne: **Hénault, Gilles**
Cahiers de Turc: **Literature in French - Criticism & Theory**
Cahiers des Jeunes-Canada: **Essay in French**
Cahiers québécois de démographie: **Demography; Sociology**
Cailloux, André: **Children's Literature in French; Théâtre du rideau vert**
cairngorm: **Silica**
Calanus: **Arctic Oceanography**
calcentine: **Gemstone**
calcite: **Karst Landform; Mineral; Sedimentary Rock; Soapstone**
calcium: **Canada's Food Guide; Dandelion; Geological Dating; Maple Sugar Industry; Soil Classification; Spectroscopy; Spring; Turnip**
calcium carbide: **Chemical Industries; Chemistry; Lighting; Quarrying Industry; Willson, Thomas L.**
calcium carbonate: **Paleontology; Seashell**
calcium cyanamide: **Chemical Industries; Chemistry**
calcium nitrate: **Quarrying Industry**
calcium phosphate: **Paleontology**
calculus: **Mathematics**
Calder, Frank: **Calder Trophy**
Calder, Frank A.: *Calder* **Case**
caldera: **Volcano**
Caldwell, John: **Grand Falls, NB**
Caldwell, William: **Medicine, History of; Nursing**
Caldwell, William G.E.: **Paleontology, History in Canada**
Caldwell's Manor, Qué: **Baptists**
caleche: **Roads & Highways**
Caledon Hills: **Bruce Trail**
Caledonia Mines, NS: **Slovenes**
Caledonian Club of PEI: **Highland Games**
Caledonian Games: **Highland Games**
calendars: **Almanacs; Native People - Plateau; Printmaking**
calf: **Animal Agriculture; Beef Cattle Farming**
calf roping: **Rodeo**
calf scours: **Biological Product; Connaught Laboratories Ltd**
Calgary: **Alberta**
Calgary Altomahs: **Calgary Stampeders**
Calgary & Edmonton Railway: **Leduc; Red Deer; Wetaskiwin**
Calgary Art Club: **Bates, Maxwell**
Calgary Associate Clinic: **Scarlett, Earle P.**
Calgary Brewing & Malting Co: **Cross, Alfred Ernest**
Calgary Bronks: **Calgary Stampeders**
Calgary Canucks: **Calgary Stampeders**
Calgary Centennial Planetarium: **Avro CF-100 Canuck; Calgary**
Calgary Curling Club: **Northcott, Ronald C.**
Calgary-Edmonton trail: **Red Deer**
Calgary Eye Opener: **Edwards, Robert C.**
Calgary Grain Exchange: **Architecture, Development**
Calgary Group: **Artists' Organizations; Bates, Maxwell; Macdonald, J.W.G., "Jock"**
Calgary Herald: **Newspapers; Southam, William**

Calgary International Airport: **Airport; Airport Architecture**
Calgary Municipal Building: **Architecture, Development**
Calgary Normal School: **University of Calgary**
Calgary Philharmonic Orchestra: **Arts Funding; Bernardi, Mario**
Calgary Police Force: **Policing**
Calgary Power Co: **Killam, Izaak Walton**
Calgary Sun: **Maclean Hunter Ltd; Newspapers**
Calgary Tigers: **Calgary Stampeders**
Calgary Trade & Labor Council: **Calgary Stampede**
Calgary Urban Indian Treaty Alliance: **Native People, Political Organization & Activism**
Calgary Zoological Soc: **Harvie, Eric L.**
calico: **Magog**
calisthenics: **Physical Education**
call girls: **Prostitution**
Callaghan, John C.: **Heart Disease**
Callander, Ont: **Canadian Pacific Railway**
Callendar, H.L.: **Physics**
calligraphy: **Gauvreau, Pierre; Germanic Fraktur & Calligraphy**
Callihoo, Louis: **Callihoo, Victoria**
Callihou, James: **Morin, Léo-Pol**
Callihou, Louie: **Grande Prairie**
calomel: **Medicine, History of**
calotype: **Photography**
Calumet Lake: **Timber Slide**
Calvaire, Montagne du: **Oka**
Calvin, D.D.: **Timber Trade History**
calypso: **West Indians**
calypso orchid: **Georgian Bay Islands National Park**
Cambodians: **Southeast Asians**
Cambrian College: **Sudbury**
Cambrian period: **Brachiopoda; Geological History; Innuitian Region; Millipede; Mollusc; Trilobite; Vertebrate**
Cambridge Mills, Upper Canada: **Cambridge**
Camco Ltd: **Electrical Appliances Industry**
Camden East, Ont: **Parker, H. Gilbert G.**
camel: **Clovis**
Camelot Island: **Thousand Islands**
camera: **Photography; Remote Sensing**
Camera Canada: **Patterson, Freeman W.; Photography**
Cameron, A.E.: **Humane Societies**
Cameron, Alex: **Painting**
Cameron, D.R.: **Royal Canadian Mounted Police**
Cameron, Donald: **Banff Centre School of Fine Arts**
Cameron, Dorothy: **Art Dealers; Printmaking**
Cameron, E. Anne: **Literature in English; Theatre, English-Language**
Cameron, Eric: **Art, Contemporary Trends; Painting**
Cameron, Fred: **Long-Distance Running**
Cameron, George Frederick: **Drama in English**
Cameron, John, "Cariboo": **Gold Rushes**
Cameron Creek: **Oil City; Waterton Lakes National Park**
Cameron Lake: **Kawartha Lakes**
CAMMD Award for Medical Achievement: **Medical Devices Industry**
Camosum College: **Victoria**
Camp Aldershot: **Kentville**
Camp Borden: **Borden, CFB; Dextraze, Jacques A.; Team Handball; Trenton, CFB**
Camp Fortune: **Bulau, Horst; Clifford, Betsy; Heggtveit, Anne; Skiing**
Camp Hughes: **Shilo, CFB**
camp meeting: **Evangelism; Horner, Ralph C.**
Camp Niagara: **Niagara-on-the-Lake**
Camp Petawawa: **Italians; Petawawa, CFB**
Camp Sewell: **Shilo, CFB**
Camp Valcartier: **Dextraze, Jacques A.**
Camp Wainwright: **Wainwright**
campaign financing & expenditures: **Baie des Chaleurs Scandal; Corruption; Pacific Scandal; Party Financing; Political Campaign**

Campbell, Archibald: **Garneau, François-Xavier**
Campbell, Colin: **Video Art**
Campbell, Douglas: **Stratford Festival**
Campbell, Elaine: **Campbell, Norman Kenneth**
Campbell, Grace: **Best-Sellers in English**
Campbell, Harry: **Popular Literature in English**
Campbell, Hugh: **Edmonton Eskimos**
Campbell, James: **Book Publishing, English-Language**
Campbell, Ken: **Evangelism**
Campbell, Lydia: **Ethnic Literature**
Campbell, Milton: **Ginger Group**
Campbell, Robert: **Stikine River; Yukon Territory**
Campbell Beach Ridge: **Agassiz, Lake**
Campbell Highway: **Carmacks**
Campbell house (Toronto): **Architecture**
Campbell Lake: **Strathcona Provincial Park**
Campbell River: **Vancouver Island**
Campbell sucker: **Endangered Animals**
Campbellite Church: **Wood, Henry Wise**
Campbellton, Ont: **Pembroke**
Campden, Ont: **Lincoln**
Campeau Construction Co Ltd: **Campeau, Robert**
camphene: **Lighting**
Campion College: **University of Regina**
Camsell Bay: **Nettiling Lake**
Camsell Portage, Sask: **Athabasca, Lake**
Camsell River: **Great Bear Lake**
Camu, Pierre: **Canadian Radio-television & Telecommunications Commission**
Can-Am series: **Automobile Racing; Villeneuve, Gilles**
Can-Amera: **Cambridge**
Can-Dive Services Ltd: *Breadalbane*; **Diving, Underwater; Ocean Industry**
Canada (square-rigger): **Sailing Ships**
Canada (yacht): **Boating**
Canada, Le: **Gill, Charles; Morin, Léo-Pol**
Canada, Rivière de: **Canada**
Canada Act: **Child Abuse; Constitution Act, 1982; Constitutional Law**
Canada & Gulf Terminal Railway: **Mont-Joli**
Canada Assistance Plan: **Day Care; Minority Government; Poverty; Public Finance; Social & Welfare Services; Social Security; Taxation**
Canada Atlantic Railway: **Booth, John Rudolphus; Maxville**
Canada-Australia Literary Prize: **Literary Prizes in English**
Canada Banking Co: **Banking**
Canada Baptist College: **Baptists**
Canada Basin: **Beaufort Sea**
Canada Bolt & Nut Co: **Stelco Inc**
Canada Canners: **Hamilton**
Canada Cement Co Ltd: **Aitken, W. Maxwell; Edwards, William Cameron; Gundy, James Henry**
Canada Cement Lafarge Ltd: **Cement Industry**
Canada Central Railway: **Edwards, William Cameron**
Canada Centre for Mineral & Energy Technology: **Coal Gasification; Coal Liquefaction; Geological Survey of Canada; Mineral Naming**
Canada Centre for Space Science: **Balloon; National Research Council of Canada; Space Technology**
Canada Clock Co: **Clocks & Watches**
Canada Corporations Act: **Corporation Law; Lottery**
Canada Cotton Co: **Technology**
Canada Council Art Bank: **Art Dealers**
Canada Council Children's Literature Prizes: **Children's Literature in English; Little, Jean**
Canada Council Medal: **Champagne, Claude; Karsh, Yousuf; MacMillan, Ernest C.; Pelletier, Wilfrid**
Canada Council Senior Arts Award: **Gaudard, Pierre**
Canada Council's translation prize: **Scott, Francis R.**

Canada Cup: **Yachting**
Canada Cup (hockey): **Eagleson, R. Alan**
Canada Deposit Insurance Corp: **Banking; Trust Company**
Canada East: **Confederation; Province of Canada**
Canada Elections Act: **Constitutional History; Corruption; Electoral Systems; Franchise; Political Campaign**
Canada Employment Centres: **Labour Market; Labour Policy; Unemployment Insurance**
Canada Foundation: **Scott, Francis R.**
Canada-France-Hawaii Telescope: **Astronomy; Observatory; Prus, Victor Marius; Van den Bergh, Sidney**
Canada Gazette: **Communications Law**
Canada Glass Works: **Glass**
Canada goose: **Cape Scott Provincial Park; Coinage; Goose; Hunting; Lake Superior Provincial Park; Mont St-Hilaire Nature Conservation Centre; Whiteshell Provincial Park**
Canada Grain Act: **Grain Handling & Marketing**
Canada (gray) jay: **Garibaldi Provincial Park; Jay; Mount Assiniboine Provincial Park**
Canada Handbook: **Statistics Canada**
Canada Health Act: **Hospitals**
Canada Highways Act: **Roads & Highways**
Canada Institute for Scientific & Technical Information: **Libraries; National Research Council of Canada**
Canada Israel Committee: **Jews**
Canada Labour Code: **Canada Labour Relations Board; Employment Law; Labour Law; Postal Strikes; Postal System; Status of Women; Women & the Law**
Canada Land Use Monitoring Program: **Urban & Regional Planning**
Canada Life Assurance Co: **Cox, George A.; O'Reilly, Gerald; Wood, Edward Rogers**
Canada lily: **Endangered Plants; Lily**
Canada Manpower Training Plan: **Labour Policy**
Canada Medal: **Honours; Medal**
Canada Migratory Birds Convention Act: **Wildlife Conservation & Management**
Canada Mink Breeders Assn: **Fur Farming**
Canada Mortgage Renewal Plan: **Housing & Housing Policy**
Canada Museums Construction Corp: **National Gallery of Canada; National Museums of Canada**
Canada Music Book: **Music History**
Canada News: **Koreans**
Canada Northern Power Corp Ltd: **Wood, Edward Rogers**
Canada Oil & Gas Act: **Resource Rights**
Canada Opera Piccola: **Alarie, Pierrette**
Canada Packers Ltd: **Biochemistry; Canada Packers Inc; Jones, John Walter; McLean, James Stanley**
Canada Ports Corp: **Transportation Agencies (Government)**
Canada Power & Paper Co: **Gundy, James Henry**
Canada Rental Supply Plan: **Housing & Housing Policy**
Canada Safety Council: **Roads & Transportation Association of Canada**
Canada Screw Co: **Birge, Cyrus Albert; Stelco Inc**
Canada Seeds Act: **Weeds**
Canada Shipping Act: **Boating; Canadian Coast Guard; Environmental Law; Safety Standards; Shipping Industry**
Canada Soil Information System: **Geographical Information Systems**
Canada Soil Survey Committee: **Soil Science**
"Canada Standards Sizes": **Consumer Standards**

Canada Student Loans Plan:
**Educational Opportunity;
Students, Financial Aid to;
University**

Canada Summer Games: **Saint John;
St John's; Thunder Bay; Water
Skiing**

Canada Temperance Act: *Russell* **Case;
Temperance Movement**

Canada-Tidningen: **Swedes**

Canada UK Travel: **Wardair
International Ltd**

Canada-US Defence Production Sharing
Agreement: **Aerospace Industry**

Canada-US Environmental Council:
Pimlott, Douglas Humphreys

Canada-US Military Studies Group:
Early-Warning Radar

Canada Water Act:
Environmental Law

Canada West: **Confederation; Gowan,
James Robert; Moberly, Walter;
Province of Canada; Rep by Pop;
Ryerson, A. Egerton; Samuel,
Lewis**

Canada Winter Games: **Brandon**

Canada Wire & Cable Co Ltd: **Physics**

Canada Works: **Labour Policy;
Poverty**

Canada Year Book: **Popular Literature
in English; Statistics Canada**

Canadair Tutor: **Snowbirds**

Canada's Athlete of the Year: **Greene,
Nancy; Heggtveit, Anne; Kreiner,
Kathy; Wheeler, Lucile**

Canadian Academic Centre in Italy:
Mediterranean Archaeology

Canadian Acceptance Corp: **Royal
Bank of Canada**

Canadian Actors' Equity Assn: **Music,
Profession of**

Canadian Advanced Technology Assn:
Electronics Industry

Canadian Aerodrome Co: **Baldwin,
F.W. "Casey"**

Canadian Aeronautics & Space Institute:
**Aerospace Industry; McKee
Trophy**

Canadian Aeroplanes, Ltd (Toronto):
Military Aviation & Aircraft

Canadian Agricultural Services
Co-ordinating Committee:
**Agricultural Research &
Development**

Canadian Air Transportation
Administration: **Airport;
Transportation Agencies
(Government)**

Canadian Airways Ltd: **Aviation;
Bush Flying**

Canadian Alliance of Home Schooling:
Education, Alternate

Canadian Almanac & Directory: **Popular
Literature in English**

Canadian Amateur Athletic Assn:
Gray, George R.

Canadian Amateur Athletic Union:
Sports Organization, Amateur

Canadian Amateur Hockey Assn:
**Hockey Hall of Fame;
International Hockey Hall
of Fame**

Canadian Amateur Musicians: **Music
History**

Canadian Amateur Ski Association: **Ski
Jumping**

Canadian Amateur Softball Assn:
Baseball

Canadian Amateur Swimming Assn:
Diving; Swimming, Speed

Canadian-American Linotype Co Ltd:
Print Industry

Canadian & Dominion Mining:
Company Town

Canadian & Provincial Heart Assn:
Medicine, Contemporary

Canadian Archaeological Assn:
**Archaeology; Emerson, John
Norman**

Canadian Archaeological Institute at
Athens: **Mediterranean
Archaeology**

Canadian Architect: **Art Writing &
Criticism**

Canadian Architecture Collection:
Bland, John

Canadian Arctic Co-operatives
Federation: **Inuit Co-operatives**

Canadian Arctic Expedition:
**Anderson, Rudolph Martin;
Bartlett, Robert Abram; Borden
Island; Coronation Gulf; Jenness,
Diamond; Stefansson, Vilhjalmur;
Urgent Ethnology; Victoria Island**

Canadian Arctic Gas Pipeline Ltd:
**Mackenzie Valley Pipeline;
Megaprojects**

Canadian Arctic Producers: **Inuit
Co-operatives**

Canadian Army: **Armed Forces;
Helicopter; McNaughton,
Andrew G.L.; Stacey, Charles
Perry; Tunnels**

Canadian Arsenals Ltd: **Crown
Corporation; Dominion Arsenal**

Canadian Art: **Art Writing & Criticism;
Artists' Organizations**

Canadian Art Club: **Artists'
Organizations; Brownell, Peleg
Franklin; Cullen, Maurice G.;
Morrice, James Wilson; Painting;
Walker, Horatio; Watson,
Homer R.; Williamson, Curtis
Albert**

Canadian Art Today: **Townsend,
William**

Canadian Arthritis Soc: **Arthritis;
Medicine, Contemporary**

Canadian Artists Representation:
**Artists' Organizations;
Chambers, Jack; Lambeth, Michel**

Canadian Arts Council: **Voaden,
Herman A.; Wyn Wood, Elizabeth**

Canadian Assn for Adult Education:
**Kidd, J. Robbins; Robbins, John
Everett**

Canadian Assn for Health, Physical
Education & Recreation: **Dance
Education; Physical Education;
Sports Medicine**

Canadian Assn for Sport Sciences:
Fitness

Canadian Assn for the Advancement of
Women in Sport: **Women's
Movement**

Canadian Assn for the Mentally
Retarded: **Disability; Education,
Special**

Canadian Assn for the Prevention of
Crime: **Criminology**

Canadian Assn for Underwater Science:
Diving, Underwater

Canadian Assn for University
Continuing Education: **Adult
Education**

Canadian Assn of Anatomists: **Moore,
Keith Leon; Persaud, Trivedi
Vidhya Nandan; Thompson, Ian
Maclaren**

Canadian Assn of Broadcasters:
**Applebaum, Louis; Broadcasting,
Radio & Television; Canadian
Broadcasting Corporation**

Canadian Assn of Children's Librarians:
Literary Prizes in English

Canadian Assn of Equipment
Distributors: **Construction Industry**

Canadian Assn of Law Libraries:
Libraries

Canadian Assn of Physicists: **Gray,
Joseph Alexander; Physics;
Science; Stoicheff, Boris Peter**

Canadian Assn of Professional
Conservators: **Conservation of
Movable Cultural Property**

Canadian Assn of Professional Dance
Organizations: **Dance History**

Canadian Assn of Special Libraries &
Information Services: **Libraries**

Canadian Assn of Sports Sciences:
Sports Medicine

Canadian Assn of University Professors:
Fowke, Vernon Clifford

Canadian Assn of University Schools of
Music: **Music Education**

Canadian Assn of University Teachers:
Academic Freedom

Canadian Associated Press:
Newspapers

Canadian Astronautics Ltd: **Electronics
Industry**

Canadian Athletic Therapists Assn:
Sports Medicine

Canadian Atlantic Fisheries Scientific
Advisory Committee: **Sealing**

Canadian Audubon Soc: **Baillie,
James L.; Canadian Nature
Federation**

Canadian Author & Bookman: **Literary
Magazines in English; Literary
Prizes in English**

Canadian Authors Assn: **Authors &
Their Milieu; Child, Philip Albert;
Children's Literature in English;
Governor General's Literary
Awards; Literary Magazines in
English; Literary Prizes in
English; Literature & Politics;
Literature in English - Teaching;
McClung, Nellie L.; Pierce,
Lorne A.; Poetry in English**

Canadian Automobile Sports Club:
Automobile Racing

Canadian Auxiliary Bible Soc:
McGregor, James

Canadian Aviation League: **MacBrien,
James H.**

Canadian Aviation Safety Board:
Transport Canada

Canadian Ballet: **Carse, M. Ruth P.;
Dance History**

Canadian Ballet Festival: **Dance
History**

Canadian Band Directors' Assn: **Music
History**

Canadian Bank of Commerce:
**Canadian Imperial Bank of
Commerce; Cox, George A.;
Edwards, William Cameron;
Flavelle, Joseph W.; Richardson,
James A., Sr; Service, Robert W.;
Wood, Edward Rogers**

Canadian Bank of Commerce head
office: **Architecture, Development**

Canadian Bar Assn: **Abortion;
Canadian Tax Foundation;
Commercial Law; Doherty, Charles
Joseph; Freedom of Information;
Judiciary; Law Reform; Legal
Education; St Laurent, Louis
Stephen**

Canadian Barcelona Traction, Light &
Power: **Wood, Edward Rogers**

Canadian Bible College & Seminary:
**Evangelical & Fundamentalist
Movements**

Canadian Bibliographical Soc: **Pierce,
Lorne A.**

Canadian Bilingual Dictionary Project:
Dictionary

Canadian Board of Grain
Commissioners: **Howe, C.D.**

Canadian Book Publishing
Development Program: **Authors &
Their Milieu; Book Publishing,
English-Language**

Canadian Book Review Annual: **Literary
Bibliography in English**

Canadian Bookman: **Literary Magazines
in English; Literature in English -
Teaching**

Canadian Books in Print: **Popular
Literature in English**

Canadian Bookseller: **Best-Sellers in
English**

Canadian Booksellers Assn: **Children's
Literature in English; Literary
Prizes in English**

Canadian Botanical Assn: **Cinq-Mars,
Lionel; Hughes, Stanley John**

Canadian Breweries Ltd: **Dawes,
Norman James; O'Keefe, Eugene;
Taylor, Edward Plunket**

Canadian Broadcasting League: **Spry,
Graham**

Canadian Brotherhood of Railway
Employees: **Canadian Congress of
Labour; Mosher, Aaron R.**

Canadian Buffalo Sled Co: **Toys &
Games**

Canadian Campaign for Nuclear
Disarmament: **Pacifism; Peace
Movement**

Canadian Cancer Soc: **Canadian
Medical Association; Medical
Research**

"Canadian Caper": **Taylor, Kenneth
Douglas**

Canadian Centre for Advanced
Instrumentation: **Saskatchewan
Research Council**

Canadian Centre for Folk Culture
Studies: **Folklore; Musicology**

Canadian Centre for Justice Statistics:
Crime

Canadian Centre for Mineral & Energy
Technology: **Convey, John**

Canadian Centre for Occupational
Health & Safety: **Injury &
Prevention**

Canadian Centre for Philanthropy:
Foundations

Canadian Centre for Policy
Alternatives: **Economics, Radical**

Canadian Chamber of Agriculture:
Hannam, Herbert H.

Canadian Chamber of Commerce:
**Adult Education; Chamber of
Commerce**

Canadian Chicken Marketing Agency:
Agriculture & Food Policy

Canadian Children's Annual: **Children's
Literature in English; Small
Presses**

Canadian Choir: **Music History**

Canadian Citizenship Act:
Constitutional History

Canadian Civil Defence College:
Arnprior

Canadian Civil Liberties Assn:
McDermott, Dennis

Canadian Club Whisky: **Walker,
Hiram**

Canadian Clubs: **Biculturalism;
Claxton, B. Brooke**

Canadian Co-operation Project: **Film**

Canadian Coalition Against Media
Pornography: **Pornography;
Women's Movement**

Canadian Coalition on Acid Rain:
Canadian Nature Federation

Canadian Coast Guard College: **Nova
Scotia**

Canadian College of Medical
Geneticists: **Fraser, F. Clarke**

Canadian Commission to UNESCO:
Hicks, Henry Davies

Canadian Committee for Industrial
Organization: **Millard, Charles
Hibbert**

Canadian Committee on Building
Research: **Construction Industry**

Canadian Conference of Catholic
Bishops: **Birth Control; Economics,
Radical**

Canadian Conference of the Arts:
**Alarie, Pierrette; Artists'
Organizations; Voaden,
Herman A.**

Canadian Congress for Learning
Opportunities for Women: **Women's
Studies**

Canadian Congress of Applied
Mechanics: **Mechanical
Engineering**

Canadian Conservation Institute:
**Conservation of Movable Cultural
Property; National Museums of
Canada**

Canadian Consumer Council:
Economic Regulation

Canadian content: **Arts Funding;
Automotive Industry;
Broadcasting, Radio & Television;
Canada-US Automotive Products
Agreement; Canadian
Radio-television &
Telecommunications Commission;
Committee for an Independent
Canada; Country & Western
Music; Economic Regulation;
Music Broadcasting; Radio
Programming; Recording
Industry; Songs & Songwriting;
Television Programming; Theatre,
English-Language; Third Option**

Canadian Copper Co: **Sudbury**

Canadian Council for International
Cooperation: **Kidd, J. Robbins**

Canadian Council of Agriculture:
**Drury, Ernest Charles; Good,
William Charles; Progressive
Party; Wood, Henry Wise**

Canadian Council of Animal Care:
**Rowsell, Harry Cecil; Veterinary
Medicine**

Canadian Council of Industrial
Relations: **Picard, Gérard**

Canadian Council of Professional
Engineers: **Civil Engineering;
Electrical Engineering;
Engineering; Forward, Frank
Arthur**

Canadian Council of Resource &
Environment Ministers:
**Federal-Provincial Relations;
Forestry**

Canadian Council of the Blind:
Education, Special

Canadian Council on Boys & Girls
Clubs: **4-H Clubs**

Canadian Council on Child Welfare:
Whitton, Charlotte

Canadian Countryman: **Hannam,
Herbert H.**

Canadian Crafts Council: **Ceramics,
Contemporary; Crafts**

Canadian Creative Music Collective: **Snow, Michael J.A.**
Canadian Cultural Institute in Rome: **Somers, Harry S.**
Canadian Daily Newspapers Assn: **Journalism**
Canadian Dairy Commission: **Agriculture & Food Policy; Hays, Harry W.**
Canadian Dance Teachers Assn: **Dance Education; Oliphant, Betty**
Canadian Day Care Advocacy Assn: **Women's Movement**
Canadian Defence Quarterly: **Gellner, John; Stuart, Kenneth**
Canadian Development Corp: **Committee for an Independent Canada**
Canadian Dimension: **New Left**
Canadian Directory of Foundations & Granting Agencies: **Educational Foundations & Endowments**
Canadian Drama: **Literary Periodicals in English; Theatre, English-Language**
Canadian Drawn Steel Co Ltd: **Stelco Inc**
Canadian Economics Assn: *Canadian Public Policy*; **Economics**
Canadian Education Assn: **Althouse, John George; Associations; Educational Foundations & Endowments**
Canadian Education Microprocessor Corp: **Computer-Assisted Learning**
Canadian Egg Marketing Agency: **Agriculture & Food Policy**
Canadian Electrical Assn: **Associations; Electric Utilities; Electrical Engineering**
Canadian Electrical Code: **Safety Standards**
Canadian Electrical Contractors Assn: **Construction Industry**
Canadian Engineering Standards Assn: **Kennedy, John**
Canadian Entertainment Bureau: **Shipman, Ernest G.**
Canadian Entomologist: **Bethune, Charles James Stewart; Taylor, George William**
Canadian Environmental Advisory Council: **Beck, Tom**
Canadian Eskimo dog: **Dog**
Canadian Ethnic Studies: **Ethnic Studies; Folklore; Sociology**
Canadian Ethnological Service: **National Museum of Man**
Canadian Ethnology Soc: **Anthropology**
Canadian Farm & Industrial Equipment Institute: **Agricultural Implements Industry**
Canadian Farm Building Code: **Building Codes & Regulations**
Canadian Farm Loan Board: **Farm Credit Corp; MacLean, John Duncan**
Canadian Farmers Survival Assn: **Agriculture & Food Policy**
Canadian Federation of Agriculture: **Pressure Group; Wesson, John Henry**
Canadian Federation of Biological Socs: **Moore, Keith Leon; Science; Thompson, Ian Maclaren**
Canadian Federation of Humane Socs: **Animal Issues; Humane Societies**
Canadian Federation of Independent Business: **Small Business**
Canadian Federation of Music Teachers' Assns: **Music Education; Music History**
Canadian Federation of Students: **Students, Financial Aid to**
Canadian Festival of Underground Theatre: **Theatre, English-Language**
Canadian Field-Naturalist: **Anderson, Rudolph Martin**
Canadian Film Awards: **Brittain, Donald; Crawley, F.R. "Budge"; Elder, Richard Bruce; Film Festivals, Prizes**
Canadian Fisheries Expedition: **Physical Oceanography**
Canadian Fisheries Service: **Fisheries History**
Canadian Flying Clubs Assn: **British Commonwealth Air Training Plan**
Canadian Folk Arts Council: **Folk Dance; Folklore**

Canadian Folk Music Journal: **Fowke, Edith M.; Musicology**
Canadian Folk Music Soc: **Folklore; Fowke, Edith M.**
Canadian Folklore Soc: **Musicology**
Canadian Food & Drug Regulations: **Food Additives**
Canadian Food Processors' Assn: **Fruit & Vegetable Industry**
Canadian Food Products Development Centre: **Manitoba Research Council**
Canadian Forces Decoration: **Medal**
Canadian Forces Headquarters (Washington, DC): **Marani, Ferdinand Herbert**
Canadian Forestry Achievement Award: **Rowe, John Stanley**
Canadian Forestry Advisory Council: **Forestry; Forestry Education; Rowe, John Stanley**
Canadian Forestry Assn: **Edwards, William Cameron; Forest Fire; Forestry Education**
Canadian Forestry Service: **Biomass Energy; Forest Fire; Forestry; Soil Science**
Canadian Foundation for the Advancement of Clinical Pharmacology: **Pharmaceuticals Industry**
Canadian Frozen Food Assn: **Fruit & Vegetable Industry**
Canadian Gemmological Assn: **Jewellery & Silverware Industry**
Canadian General Electric Co Ltd: **Barter; Electrical Appliances Industry; Guelph; Miller, George Martell; Nicholls, Frederic; Pellatt, Henry M.; Peterborough; Stavert, Reuben Ewart; Turmel, Antoine**
Canadian General Investments Ltd: **Meighen, Maxwell Charles Gordon**
Canadian General Standards Board: **Consumer Standards**
Canadian General-Tower Ltd: **Plastics-Processing Industry**
Canadian Geoscience Council: **Soil Science**
Canadian Good Roads Assn: **Roads & Highways; Roads & Transportation Association of Canada**
Canadian Government Motion Picture Bureau: **Film; Film, Documentary; National Film Board; Photography**
Canadian Grain Commission: **Agriculture, Dept of; Grain Handling & Marketing**
Canadian Grand Prix: **Automobile Racing; Montréal; Trois-Rivières; Villeneuve, Gilles**
Canadian Grocer: **Maclean, John B.**
Canadian Group of Painters: **Artists' Organizations; Brandtner, Fritz; Bush, John H.; Carmichael, Franklin; Harris, Lawren S.; Heward, Efa Prudence; McLaughlin, Isabel; Newton, Lilias; Pepper, George Douglas; Savage, Anne Douglas; Wood, William John**
Canadian Guild of Crafts: **Crafts; Voaden, Herman A.**
Canadian Guild of Potters: **Ceramics, Contemporary**
Canadian Handicrafts Guild: **Crafts; Inuit Art**
Canadian Health Industry Development Centre: **Manitoba Research Council**
Canadian Health Libraries Assn: **Libraries**
Canadian Hearing Soc: **Pierce, Lorne A.**
Canadian Home Economics Assn: **Birth Control; Home Economics**
Canadian Home Journal: **Art Writing & Criticism; Magazines**
Canadian Home Market Assn: **Anti-Reciprocity Movement**
Canadian Horological Institute: **Clocks & Watches**
Canadian Horse Shows Assn: **Equestrian Sports; Horse**
Canadian Housing Design Council: **Architectural Competitions**
Canadian Human Rights Act: **Human Rights; Law & the Press; Privacy; Public Service**
Canadian Hunger Foundation: **Agricultural Aid**

Canadian Illustrated News: **Armstrong, William; Cartoons; Desbarats, Georges-Edouard; Drama in English; Julien, O. Henry; Magazines**
Canadian Import Co: **Webster, Lorne Campbell**
Canadian Indian Youth Council: **Native People, Political Organization & Activism**
Canadian Industrial Renewal Board: **Clothing Industries; Textile Industry**
Canadian Industries Ltd: **Art Dealers; Petrochemical Industry; Purvis, Arthur Blaikie; Shawinigan; Smith, Harold Greville; Technology**
Canadian Information Processing Soc: **Computer Science; Electronics Industry**
Canadian Institute: **Art Galleries & Museums; Astronomy; Boyle, David; Croft, Henry Holmes; Hind, Henry Y.; McMurrich, James Playfair; Science**
Canadian Institute for International Peace & Security: **Peace Movement**
Canadian Institute in Egypt: **Classics; Mediterranean Archaeology**
Canadian Institute of Actuaries: **Mathematics**
Canadian Institute of Chartered Accountants: **Accounting; Canadian Tax Foundation**
Canadian Institute of Chemistry: **Chemistry; Science; Thorvaldson, Thorbergur**
Canadian Institute of Child Health: **Injury & Prevention**
Canadian Institute of Economic Policy: **Pharmaceuticals Industry**
Canadian Institute of Guided Ground Transportation: **Transportation Research Centres**
Canadian Institute of Mining & Metallurgy: **Agnew, John Lyons; Associations; Forward, Frank Arthur; Mineral & Mining Engineering**
Canadian Institute of Music: **Mathieu, Rodolphe; Musicology**
Canadian Institute of Planners: **Blumenfeld, Hans; Urban & Regional Planning**
Canadian Institute of Plumbing & Heating: **Construction Industry**
Canadian Institute of Public Real Estate Companies: **Construction Industry**
Canadian Institute of Steel Construction: **Construction Industry**
Canadian Institute of Surveying: **Associations**
Canadian Institute on Public Affairs: **Couchiching Conference**
Canadian Interagency Fire Centre: **Forest Fire**
Canadian Intercollegiate Athletic Union: **Football**
Canadian Intercollegiate Rugby Football Union: **Football**
Canadian Intergovernmental Conference Secretariat: **Federal-Provincial Relations**
Canadian International Paper Co: **La Tuque; Rapson, William Howard; Témiscaming**
Canadian Inventory of Historic Buildings: **Architecture, Development; Heritage Conservation**
Canadian Javelin Ltd: **Doyle, John C.**
Canadian Jewish Chronicle: **Klein, Abraham M.**
Canadian Jewish News: **Plaut, Gunther W.**
Canadian Joint Staff Mission: **Pope, Maurice Arthur**
Canadian Journal: **Astronomy; Hind, Henry Y.; Literary Magazines in English; Literary Periodicals in English; Science**
Canadian Journal of Comparative Medicine & Veterinary Science: **Cameron, Thomas Wright Moir**
Canadian Journal of Criminology: **Criminology; Sociology**
Canadian Journal of Cytology: **Animal Breeding**
Canadian Journal of Economics: *Canadian Journal of Economics & Political Science*; **Economics**

Canadian Journal of Fisheries & Aquatic Sciences: **Oceanography**
Canadian Journal of Genetics & Cytology: **Genetics**
Canadian Journal of Medical Sciences: **Biochemistry**
Canadian Journal of Political Science: *Canadian Journal of Economics & Political Science*
Canadian Journal of Psychiatric Nursing: **Nursing**
Canadian Journal of Religious Thought: **Brett, George S.**
Canadian Journal of Research: **Biochemistry; Chemistry; Marion, Léo Edmond; National Research Council of Canada; Science**
Canadian Journal of Science, Literature & History: **Mathematics**
Canadian Journal of Technology: **Chemistry**
Canadian Journal of Theology: **Fairweather, Eugene Rathbone**
Canadian Judicial Council: **Berger, Thomas R.; Judiciary**
Canadian Kennel Club: **Dog**
Canadian Kidney Foundation: **Medicine, Contemporary**
Canadian Kirkland Mines, Ltd: **Kirkland Lake**
Canadian Labor Protective & Mutual Improvement Assn: **Nine-Hour Movement**
Canadian Labor Union: **Hewitt, John; Nine-Hour Movement; O'Donoghue, Daniel J.; Union Centrals, District & Regional; Union Centrals, National**
Canadian League: **Baseball**
Canadian League for the Advancement of Coloured People: **West Indians**
Canadian Library Assn: **Canadian Association of College & University Libraries; Libraries; Library Science; Robbins, John Everett**
Canadian Linguistics Assn: **Learned Societies; Linguistics**
Canadian Literary Institute: **McMaster, William**
Canadian Literary Magazine: **Art Writing & Criticism**
Canadian Locomotive Co: **Kingston; Technology**
Canadian Lung Assn: **Medicine, Contemporary**
Canadian Lutheran Bible Institute: **Camrose; Norwegians**
Canadian Magazine: **Essay in English; Jones, Alice; Literary Magazines in English; Literature in English; Massey, Hart A.**
Canadian Magazine & Literary Repository: **Literary Magazines in English**
Canadian Malartic Mine: **Malartic**
Canadian Manufacturer: **Nicholls, Frederic**
Canadian Marine Transportation Administration: **Transportation Agencies (Government)**
Canadian Marine Transportation Centre: **Transportation Research Centres**
Canadian Maritime Commission: **Canadian Transport Commission**
Canadian Mechanical Reproduction Rights Agency: **Recording Industry**
Canadian Medical Assn Journal: **Canadian Medical Association; Estrogen; MacPhail, Andrew**
Canadian Mediterranean Institute: **Mediterranean Archaeology**
Canadian Mennonite Bible College: **University of Manitoba**
Canadian Mental Health Assn: **Clarke, Charles Kirk; Hincks, Clarence M.; Psychiatry**
Canadian Mercury: **Kennedy, Leo; Literary Magazines in English; Scott, Francis R.**
Canadian Metal Mining Assn: **Brown, Eldon Leslie**
Canadian Meteorological & Oceanographic Soc: **Oceanography; Stewart, Robert William**
Canadian Meteorological Centre: **Weather Forecasting**
Canadian Microelectronics Corp: **Queen's University**
Canadian Military Colleges: **Military & Staff Colleges**
Canadian Military Headquarters: **Stuart, Kenneth**

Canadian Missionary Society: **Huguenots**

Canadian Monthly & National Review: **Book Publishing, English-Language; Literary Magazines in English; Literary Periodicals in English; Smith, Goldwin; Social Darwinism**

Canadian mosaic: **Culture; Multiculturalism; Vertical Mosaic**

Canadian Motion Picture Distributors Assn: **Film Festivals, Prizes**

Canadian Mountaineering Equipment: **Camping**

Canadian Music Associates: **Canadian League of Composers**

Canadian Music Council: **Campbell, Norman Kenneth; Creighton, M. Helen; Garant, Serge; MacMillan, Ernest C.; Music Awards & Competitions; Music History; Orford String Quartet; Papineau-Couture, Jean; Papineau-Couture, Jean; Pelletier, Wilfrid; Stratas, Teresa; Tremblay, Gilles**

Canadian Music Educators' Assn: **Music Education; Music History**

Canadian Music Publishing Assn: **Recording Industry**

Canadian Musical Heritage Soc: **Musicology**

Canadian National Assn: **Canada First; Foster, William A.**

Canadian National Committee for Mental Hygiene: **Clarke, Charles Kirk; Health Policy; Hincks, Clarence M.; Psychiatry**

Canadian National Committee on Refugees: **Wilson, Cairine R.**

Canadian National League: **Anti-Reciprocity Movement**

Canadian National Livestock Records: **Horse**

Canadian National Physical Fitness Act: **Sports Organization, Amateur**

Canadian National Railways Radio Dept: **Radio Drama, English-Language**

Canadian National Silver Fox Breeders' Assn: **Summerside**

Canadian National Spiritual Assembly: **Baha'i Faith**

Canadian National Telegraph Co: **Telegraph**

Canadian National Veterinary Assn: **Veterinary Medicine, History**

Canadian Native Communications Soc: **Native People, Political Organization & Activism**

Canadian Naturalist: **Smallwood, Charles**

Canadian Naturalist & Geologist: **Billings, Elkanah; Science**

Canadian Nazarene College: **University of Manitoba**

Canadian Newsletter of Research on Women: **Women's Studies**

Canadian North-West Irrigation Co: **Lethbridge**

Canadian Northern Steamships Ltd: **Cunard Co**

Canadian Nurses' Assn: **Girard, Alice M.; Labelle, Huguette; Mussallem, Helen K.; Nursing; Watson, Helen G.W.**

Canadian Oaks Race: **Thoroughbred Racing**

Canadian Oil Co: **Petroleum Industries**

Canadian Olympic Assn: **Sports Medicine; Sports Organization, Amateur; Track & Field**

Canadian One-Act Playwriting Contest: **Literary Prizes in English**

Canadian Operational Research Soc: **Mathematics**

Canadian Ophthalmological Soc: **Ophthalmology**

Canadian Organization for Development Through Education: **Kidd, J. Robbins**

Canadian Pacific Airlines: **Aviation; Beatty, Edward Wentworth; Canadian Pacific Railway; Economic Regulation; McConachie, G.W. Grant; Transportation Regulation; Vancouver**

Canadian Pacific Enterprises Ltd: **Canadian Pacific Railway**

Canadian Pacific Investments Ltd: **Crump, Norris R.; Roblin, Dufferin**

Canadian Pacific Navigation Co: **Vancouver; Walbran, John Thomas**

Canadian Pacific Railway Bill: **Grant, James Alexander**

Canadian Pacific Steamships: **Allan Line; Beatty, Henry; Canadian Pacific Railway; Disasters; Vancouver; Victoria**

Canadian Pacific Telegraphs: **Journalism; Telegraph**

Canadian Packing Co Ltd: **Canada Packers Inc; Meat-Processing Industry**

Canadian Parents for French: **Second-Language Instruction**

Canadian Patent Act: **Biotechnology**

Canadian Patent Office Record: **Desbarats, Georges-Edouard**

Canadian Patriotic Fund: **World War I**

Canadian Patrol Frigate: **Shipbuilding & Ship Repair**

Canadian Payments Assn: **Banking; Credit Card; Trust Company**

Canadian Peace Congress: **Pacifism; Peace Movement**

Canadian Peace Research Institute: **Peace Movement**

Canadian Pediatric Soc: **Medical Ethics; Pediatrics**

Canadian Pension Commission: **Halifax Relief Commission**

Canadian Periodical Index: **Libraries; Literary Bibliography in English**

Canadian Periodical Publishers' Assn: **Magazines**

Canadian Pharmaceutical Manufacturers Assn: **Chemistry**

Canadian Physiological Soc: **Biochemistry**

Canadian Physiotherapy Assn: **Sports Medicine**

Canadian Place Theatre: **Theatre, English-Language**

Canadian Plains Studies: **University of Regina**

Canadian Players: **Theatre, English-Language**

Canadian Plumbing Code: **Building Codes & Regulations**

Canadian Poetry: **Literary Magazines in English; Literary Periodicals in English**

Canadian Poetry Magazine: **Avison, Margaret; Literary Magazines in English; Poetry in English; Pratt, E.J.**

Canadian Poetry Review: **Literary Magazines in English**

Canadian Police College: **Police; Policing; Royal Canadian Mounted Police**

Canadian Police Information Centre: **Police**

Canadian Political Science Assn: **Britnell, George Edwin; *Canadian Journal of Economics & Political Science*; *Canadian Public Policy*; Elliott, George Alexander; Innis, Harold A.; Political Science; Sociology**

Canadian Population Society: **Demography**

Canadian Pork Council: **Hog Farming**

Canadian Portland Cement Assn: **Cement Industry; Construction Industry**

Canadian Postal Employees Assn: **Davidson, Joe; Postal Strikes**

Canadian Power Squadrons: **Boating**

Canadian Provident Gem Inc: **Webster, Lorne Campbell**

Canadian Public Administration: **Public Administration**

Canadian Public Health Assn: **Hastings, Charles John Colwell Orr**

Canadian Pulp & Paper Assn: **Bates, John Seaman; Fowler, Robert MacLaren**

Canadian Racing Assn: **Seagram, Joseph E.**

Canadian Racing Drivers Assn: **Automobile Racing**

Canadian Radio Broadcasting Commission: **Advertising; Aird, John; Broadcasting, Radio & Television; Canadian Broadcasting Corporation; Charlesworth, Hector W.;** *cont...*

Music Broadcasting; **Odlum, Victor W.; Ouimet, J.-Alphonse; Radio Drama, English-Language; Radio Programming; Steel, William Arthur**

Canadian Radio League: **Broadcasting, Radio & Television; Canadian Broadcasting Corporation; Claxton, B. Brooke; Plaunt, Alan Butterworth; Spry, Graham**

Canadian Radio-television & Telecommunications Act: **Communications Law**

Canadian Rand Drill Co: **Business History**

Canadian Rangers: **Reserve Force of Canada**

Canadian Reconstruction Assn: **Willison, John S.**

Canadian Red Cross: **Canadian National Railways; Corporation Law; Gibson, John Morison; Red Cross Society**

Canadian Red Ensign: **Red Ensign**

Canadian Red River (Hind-Dawson) Exploring Expedition: **Hind, Henry Y.; Physical Geography**

Canadian Reformed Churches: **Presbyterian & Reformed Churches**

Canadian Rehabilitation Council for the Disabled: **Education, Special**

Canadian Repertory Theatre: **Hutt, William; Plummer, A. Christopher D.; Theatre, English-Language**

Canadian Research: **Pharmaceuticals Industry**

Canadian Research Institute for the Advancement of Women: **Women's Studies**

Canadian Restaurant & Foodservices Assn: **Cuisine**

Canadian Review: **Poetry in English**

Canadian Review of Sociology & Anthropology: **Sociology**

Canadian Rugby Football Union: **Football; Rugby**

Canadian Rugby Union: **Grey Cup; Hamilton Tiger Cats; Rugby; Sports History**

Canadian Salt Co: **Lindbergh**

Canadian Saltfish Act: **Fisheries**

Canadian Saltfish Corp: **Fisheries History; Fisheries Policy**

Canadian Satellite Communications Inc: **WIC (Western International Communications Ltd)**

Canadian Save the Children Fund: **Marshall, Kenric Rudolphus**

Canadian School Library Assn: **Libraries; Library Science**

Canadian School Trustees Assn: **School Boards**

Canadian Schools Broadcasts & Telecasts: **Educational Broadcasting**

Canadian Seamen's Union: **Banks, Harold C.; Internment; Labour Relations; Seafarers' International Union**

Canadian Section for Philosophy of Law: **Philosophy**

Canadian Seed Growers' Assn: **Newman, Leonard Harold; Robertson, James Wilson**

Canadian Service Colleges: **Royal Military College of Canada**

Canadian Shield: **Shield**

Canadian Soc for Aviation Medicine: **Astronaut**

Canadian Soc of Biblical Studies: **Religion; Scott, Robert Balgarnie Young**

Canadian Soc of Church History: **Religion**

Canadian Soc of Equity: **United Farmers of Alberta**

Canadian Soc of Graphic Art: **Artists' Organizations; Printmaking; Wood, William John**

Canadian Soc of Painters in Water Colour: **Artists' Organizations; Bush, John H.; Carmichael, Franklin**

Canadian Soc of Technical Agriculturists: **Soil Science**

Canadian Soc of Zoologists: **Fry, Frederick Ernest Joseph**

Canadian Social Science Research Council: **Britnell, George Edwin; *National Atlas of Canada***

Canadian Socialist League: **Socialist Party of Canada**

Canadian Sociology & Anthropology Assn: **Sociology**

Canadian Sports Advisory Council: **Sports Organization, Amateur**

Canadian Sports Pool Corp: **Lottery**

Canadian Standardbred Horse Soc: **Harness Racing**

Canadian Standards Assn: **Cement Industry; Industrial Quality Control; Metric Conversion; Safety Standards; Trade Mark**

Canadian Statistical Review: **Mathematics; Statistics Canada**

Canadian Studies, Royal Commission on: **Symons, Thomas H.B.; Women & Education**

Canadian Studies in Population: **Demography; Sociology**

Canadian Suffrage Assn: **Denison, Flora MacDonald**

"Canadian Summer": **Liberation of Holland**

Canadian Surface Transportation Administration: **Transportation Agencies (Government)**

Canadian Systems Group (EST) Ltd: **Stelco Inc**

Canadian Talent Library: **McConnell, Robert M.G.; Music Broadcasting**

Canadian Teachers' Federation: **Lloyd, Woodrow S.; Teaching Profession**

Canadian Textile & Chemical Union: **Parent, Madeleine**

Canadian Theatre Centre: **Hendry, Thomas B.; Roux, Jean-Louis; Theatre, English-Language**

Canadian Theatre Critics Assn: **Theatre, English-Language**

Canadian Theatre Review: **Simons, Beverley; Theatre, English-Language**

Canadian Theological College: **University of Regina**

Canadian Theological Soc: **Religion**

Canadian Toy Manufacturers Assn: **Toys & Games Industry**

Canadian Toys Ltd: **Toys & Games**

Canadian Trade Commissioner Service: **Canadian Manufacturers' Association**

Canadian Trotting Assn: **Harness Racing**

Canadian Turkey Marketing Agency: **Agriculture & Food Policy**

Canadian Union of Postal Workers: **Postal Strikes; Public-Service Unions**

Canadian Union of Students: **New Left**

Canadian Universal & International Exhibition: **Expo 67**

Canadian University Music Soc: **Music Education; Music History; Musicology**

Canadian Uranium Research Foundation: **Forward, Frank Arthur**

Canadian Veterinary Council: **Veterinary Medicine, History**

Canadian Veterinary Medical Assn: **Savage, Alfred; Smith, David Laurence Thomson; Veterinary Medicine; Veterinary Medicine, History**

Canadian Vickers Ltd: **Canadair Ltd; Richardson, James A., Sr; Shipbuilding & Ship Repair**

Canadian Vickers Vedette flying boat: **Armed Forces - Air Force**

Canadian Victor Record Co: **Country & Western Music**

Canadian Volunteer Service Medal: **Medal**

Canadian War Memorials: **Johnston, Francis Hans; Printmaking; Sculpture**

Canadian War Museum: **Medal; National Museum of Man; National Museum of Science & Technology**

Canadian War Records Office: **Jackson, A.Y.; Lismer, Arthur; Photography; Varley, Frederick H.**

Canadian Weightlifting Federation: **Weightlifting**

Canadian Welding Code: **Safety Standards**

Canadian Welfare Council: **Gerontology; Whitton, Charlotte**

Canadian Wheelmen's Assn: **Cycling; Rubenstein, Louis**

Canadian White Water Affiliation: **Canoeing**

Canadian Whitmanite movement: **Denison, Flora MacDonald**
Canadian Who's Who: **Popular Literature in English**
Canadian Wildlife Service: **Bird Sanctuaries & Reserves; Bison; Endangered Animals; Fuller, William Albert; Heritage Trail; Hunting; Tantramar Marsh; Whooping Crane; Wildlife Conservation & Management**
Canadian Woman Studies: **Literary Magazines in English; Sociology; Women's Studies**
Canadian Writers' Foundation: **Pierce, Lorne A.; Robbins, John Everett**
Canadian Yachting Assn: **Boating**
Canadian Youth Congress: **Communist Party of Canada**
Canadian Zionist Federation: **Jews**
Canadiana: **Literary Bibliography in English**
Canadiana collection: **National Library of Canada; Queen's University; Rutherford, Alexander C.**
Canadianization: **Energy Policy; Geopolitics; Literature in English - Teaching; Nationalization**
Canadians of Old: *Anciens Canadiens*
Canadien: **Intellectual History; Journalism; Langevin, Hector-L.; Literature in French; Lower Canada; Newspapers; Parent, Etienne; Parti canadien; Tardivel, Jules-Paul; Tarte, Joseph-Israel; Taschereau, Elzéar-Alexander**
Canadiens de Naissance: **Theatre, French-Language**
Canagigueh River: **Elmira**
Canagrex: **Agriculture & Food Policy**
Canal Lake: **Kawartha Lakes**
canaler: **Lake Carriers**
Cancer Detection Clinic: **Hilliard, Anna Marion**
CANCOM: **Communications in the North; Native People, Communications**
Candelaria, Philip: **Guitar**
candidate: **City Politics; Communications; Election Expenses Act; Electoral Systems; Local Elections; Party System**
candle: **Lighthouses; Lighting**
candle mold: **Pewter**
candleberry: **Biogeography**
candlefish: **Bella Coola; Smelt**
candlestick: **Silver, Church; Silver, Domestic**
CANDU reactor: **Atomic Energy of Canada Ltd; Barter; Bennett, William John; Electric Power; Electric-Power Generation; Industrial Research & Development; Lewis, Wilfrid Bennett; Megaprojects; Nuclear Energy; Nuclear Power Plants; Nuclear Research Establishments; Nuclear Safety; Science & Society; Science Policy**
candy: **Confectionery Industry**
Canerio chart: **Cartography, History of**
CANFARM: **Agriculture & Food**
Caniapiscau, Lac: **Koksoak, Rivière**
Caniapiscau, Rivière: **James Bay Project; Koksoak, Rivière**
Canmore, Alta: **Coal Demethanation; Fossil Plants; Slovenes**
Canmore Opera House: **Theatre for Young Audiences**
cannabis: **Drug Use, Non-Medical**
Cannerie: **Theatre for Young Audiences**
cannibal dance: **Bella Bella**
cannibalism: **Sinnisiak; Windigo**
canning: **Apricot; Corn, Sweet; Fisheries History; Fruit & Vegetable Industry; Glass; Newfoundland; Pea; Pear**
cannon: **Armaments; Bull, Gerald Vincent; Firearm; Forges Saint-Maurice; Fortification; Rainmaking**
Cannon, John: **Automobile Racing**
CANO: **Sudbury**
CANO singers: **Sudbury**
canoe: **Bitumen; Boating; Central Coast Salish; Haida; Native People, Economic Conditions; Nootka; Northern Georgia Strait Coast Salish; Northwest Coast Indian Art; Portage; Sekani; Tlingit, Inland**

canoe brigade: **Athabasca, Lake; Fur Trade; North West Company; Portage La Loche; Red River Colony**
Canoe Lake: **Jackson, A.Y.; Thomson, Thomas J.**
Canol project: **Canadian-American Economic Relations; Fort McMurray; Whitehorse**
Canola Council of Canada: **Vegetable Oil Industry.**
canon & canoness: **Christian Religious Communities**
Cañon Fjord: **Fosheim Peninsula**
Canora, Sask: **Romanians**
Canso aircraft: **Armed Forces - Air Force; Military Aviation & Aircraft**
Canso Causeway: **Canso; Canso, Strait of**
cant-hook: **Timber Trade History**
cantaloupe: **Melon; Vegetable**
Canterbury College: **University of Windsor**
Canterra Energy Ltd: **Canada Development Corp**
cantilevered bridge: **Bridges; Technology**
Cantin, Pierre: **Literary Bibliography in French**
Cantin Dry Dock: **Shipbuilding & Ship Repair**
Cantin Lake: **Island Lake**
Cantino chart: **Cartography, History of**
Cantwell, Frederick F.: **Chemistry Subdisciplines**
Canuck, Janey: **Murphy, Emily**
canyon: **Cave; River Landform**
Canyon City, BC: **Nass River**
Caouette, Mother: **Saints**
Cap-à-l'Aigel, Qué: **La Malbaie**
Cap-aux-Meules, Qué: **Cap aux Meules, Ile du; Madeleine, Iles de la**
Cap-Chat, Qué: **Wind Energy**
Cap de la Hève: **LaHave**
Cap de Nouvelle-France: **Hudson Strait**
Cap-d'Espoir, Qué: **Percé**
Cap-Diamant: **Art; Cartier, Jacques; Disasters; Government Building; Mineral Naming; Québec Citadel; Québec City**
Cap-Eternité: **Saguenay River**
Cap-Luminère, NB: **Northumberland Strait**
Cap-Rouge, Qué: **Provancher, Léon; Québec City**
Cap-Rouge, Rivière du: **Diamonds of Canada; New France**
Cap-Santé, Qué: **Architecture**
Cap-Tourmente, Qué: **Bird Sanctuaries & Reserves; Laurentian Highlands; St Lawrence River**
Cap-Trinité: **Saguenay River; Trakas, George**
CAPAC: **Applebaum, Louis; Pépin, Clermont**
Cape Adelaide: **Boothia Peninsula**
Cape Bathurst: **Mackenzie Inuit**
Cape Breton Colliery League: **Baseball**
Cape Breton Current: **Cape North**
Cape Breton Development Corp: **Coal; Crown Corporation; Glace Bay; Nova Scotia; Regional Economics**
Cape Breton Railway: **Intercolonial Railway**
Cape Cavendish, PEI: *Marco Polo*
Cape Charles, Nfld: **Labrador**
Cape Chidley: **Hudson Strait; Labrador Highlands; Newfoundland; Torngat Mountains**
Cape Columbia: **Arctic Exploration; Ellesmere Island**
Cape Cormorant: **King's Posts**
Cape Croker: **Bruce Peninsula**
Cape Crozier: **Banks Island**
Cape Digges: **Hudson, Henry**
Cape Freels: **Avalon Peninsula; Bonavista Bay**
Cape Gargantua: **Lake Superior Provincial Park**
Cape George, NS: **Northumberland Strait; Nova Scotia**
Cape Henrietta Marie: **James, Thomas; James Bay**
Cape Hopes Advance: **Hudson Strait**
Cape Island boat: **Cape Sable Island; Nova Scotia**
Cape Kellet: **Banks Island**
Cape LaHave Island: **LaHave River Estuary**

Cape M'Clure: **Banks Island**
Cape Mudge Reserve: **Kwakiutl**
Cape Parry: **McClure (M'Clure), Robert J. Le M.**
Cape Pine: **Avalon Peninsula**
Cape Ray: **Cabot Strait; French Shore; Gisborne, Frederick Newton; Long Range Mountains**
Cape St Francis: **Conception Bay**
Cape St George: **Port au Port Peninsula**
Cape St John: **French Shore**
Cape Scott: **Cape Scott Provincial Park; Nootka**
Cape Smith: **Ungava Inuit**
Cape Split: **Cape Blomidon; Fundy, Bay of/Gulf of Maine**
Cape Tormentine, NB: **Northumberland Strait**
Cape Wolstenholme: **Hudson, Henry**
capelin: **Newfoundland; Notre Dame Bay; Saguenay River; Smelt**
Capilano Canyon Park: **North Vancouver**
Capilano College: *Capilano Review*; **Clothing Industries; Morris, Alwyn**
Capilano Lake: **North Vancouver**
Capilano River: **North Vancouver**
Capilano Salmon Hatchery: **North Vancouver**
Capilano Suspension Bridge: **North Vancouver**
capitaines des sauvages: **Métis**
Capital City Park: **Hiking**
Capital Cost Allowance program: **Canadian Film Development Corp; Film**
capital gains: **Foreign Investment; Housing & Housing Policy; Mutual Funds; Taxation**
capitalism: **Bourgeois; Business Elites; Child Welfare; Confederation of National Trade Unions; Corporatism; Corruption; Economics, Radical; Intellectual History; League for Social Reconstruction; New Left; Patriotes; Philosophy; Poverty; Racism; Revolutionary Industrial Unionism; Social Class; Social Doctrine of the Roman Catholic Church; Socialist Party of Canada; State; Welfare State; Working-Class History**
Caplan, Gerald: **Working-Class History**
Caplan, Rupert: **Radio Drama, English-Language; Radio Programming**
Cappello, Luigi: **Leduc, Ozias; Public Art**
Capreol, Ont: **Sudbury**
Capron, H. "King": **Paris**
Captain William Irving House: **New Westminster**
Capuchins: **Christian Religious Communities; Restigouche**
Caraquet, Baie de: **Caraquet**
Caraquet Riots: **New Brunswick School Question**
Caravan: **Festivals; Folklore**
Caravan Stage Co: **Theatre, English-Language**
caraway: **Condiment Crops**
carbohydrate: **Asparagus; Diabetes Mellitus; Forage Crops; Lemieux, Raymond U.; Molecular Biology; Potato; Pulse Crops; Squash**
carbohydrate metabolism: **Baer, Erich; Harding, Victor John**
carbon: **Chemistry Subdisciplines; Coal; Conservation; Iron & Steel Industry; Mineral; Molecules in Interstellar Space**
carbon-arc lamp: **Lighting**
carbon dating: **Geological Dating; Inuit Art; Petroleum**
carbon dioxide: **Automobile; Climatology; Crop Research; Karst Landform; Ocean; Pollution; Quarrying Industry; Soft-Drink Industry; Spring**
carbon monoxide: **Automobile; Coal Gasification; Pollution**
carbonate: **Geological Regions; Karst Landform; Mineral; Spring**
carbonated beverages: **Soft-Drink Industry**
Carbonear Island: **Carbonear**
carbonic acid: **Karst Landform**

Carboniferous period: **Bug; Club Moss; Fern; Forest; Horsetail; New Brunswick; Trees**
Carbotte, J.: **Physics**
Carbotte, Marcel: **Roy, Gabrielle**
Carbure Co of Shawinigan: **Shawinigan**
carcajou: **Wolverine**
Carcajou, Menfrou: **Children's Literature in French**
Card, Charles O.: **Mormon Church**
Cardiff, Alta: **Welsh**
Cardin, Arthur: **Duplessis, Maurice Le Noblet**
Cardin, Lucien: **Munsinger Affair**
cardinal: **Finch**
Cardinal Carter Centre: **Medical Ethics**
Cardinal River Coals Ltd: **Coal**
cardiovascular medicine & surgery: **Heart Disease**
CARE Canada: **Agricultural Aid; MacDonald, Angus Bernard**
Careen Lake: **Clearwater River (Alta/Sask)**
Carey, Bruce: **Music History**
Carey Hall: **University of British Columbia**
Cargill Grain Co: **Baie-Comeau**
cargo: **Air Canada; Commercial Law; Nova Scotia; Shipping Industry**
cargo vessel: **Shipbuilding & Ship Repair**
Carheil, Etienne de: **Métis**
Cariboo Community College: **Kamloops**
Cariboo district: **Thompson River**
Cariboo Gold Quartz: **Barkerville**
Cariboo gold rush: **Brown, J.G., "Kootenai"; Cariboo Road; Chilcotin; Children's Literature in English; Croatians; Dally, Frederick; Fraser River; Germans; Gold; Gold Rushes; Hind, William G.R.; Mining; Photography; Quesnel; Steamboats & Paddlewheelers**
Cariboo Lake: **Gold Rushes**
Cariboo Mountains: **Columbia Mountains**
Cariboo Plateau: **Ranching History; Williams Lake**
Caribou: **Sculpture**
Caribou, NS: **Nova Scotia**
Caribou Carnival: **Yellowknife, NWT**
Caribou Crossing, YT: **Carcross**
Caribou Ferry, NS: **Northumberland Strait**
caribou hide: **Kayak; Mukluk; Parka**
Caribou Hills: **Mackenzie River**
Caribou Island: **Lighthouses**
Caribou Mines, NS: **Musquodoboit Harbour**
Caribou Mountains: **Vegetation Regions - Cordillera**
Caribou Sun: **Print Industry**
carillon: **Price, F. Percival**
Carillon Canal: **Canals & Inland Waterways**
Carillon hydro-electric dam: **Canals & Inland Waterways**
Carion, Louis: **Novel in French**
Cariou, Len: **Manitoba Theatre Centre; Theatre, English-Language**
Carleton, John Louis: **Drama in English**
Carleton, Mount: **Mount Carleton Provincial Park**
Carleton, NS: **Saint John**
Carleton Stakes: **Northern Dancer**
Carli & Petrucci: **Public Art**
Carling, Thomas C.: **Carling, John**
Carling, William: **Carling, John**
Carling Brewing & Malting Co: **Carling, John**
Carling Cup: **Rugby**
Carling O'Keefe Breweries of Canada Ltd: **Brewing Industry; Québec Nordiques**
Carlson, Roy L.: **Archaeology**
Carlton House, Sask: **Drummond, Thomas**
Carluke, Ont: **Walker, James**
Carlyle, Sask: **Place-names**
Carma Developers Ltd: **Allard, Charles A.**
Carmack, George W.: **Carmacks; Klondike Gold Rush**
Carmack, Kate: **Carcross**
Carmelo Strait: **Spanish**
Carmichael, James: **Carmichael, James William**
carnation: **Greenhouse Crops**
Carnaval-Souvenir: **Chicoutimi**

Carnegie Foundation: **Libraries; Music Education; University of King's College**

carnivora: **Badger; Bear; Bobcat; Cat; Cougar; Coyote; Dog; Ferret, Black-footed; Fox; Lynx; Marten; Mink; Otter; Polar Bear; Raccoon; Seal; Skunk; Walrus; Weasel; Wolf; Wolverine**

Caro, Anthony: **Fauteux, André**

Carol Lake: **Iron & Steel Industry; Labrador City**

Carol Mine: **Labrador City**

Caron, Louis: **Short Fiction in French**

Carousel Players: **Theatre for Young Audiences**

Carousel Theatre: **Theatre for Young Audiences**

carp: **Aquaculture; Huron, Lake; Minnow**

Carpé, A.: **Logan, Mount**

Carpenter, Carole Henderson: **Folklore**

Carpenter, Eli: **New Denver**

Carpenter, J.: **Soaring**

Carpenter, W.B.: ***Challenger* Expedition**

carpentry: **Tools, Carpentry**

carpet: **Rugs & Rug Making; Ste-Agathe-des-Monts; Textile Industry**

carrageenin: **Algae; Cook, William Harrison; Irish Moss; Seaweeds**

Carré, L.: **Film**

Carriage by Air Act: **Air Law & Space Law**

Carriage of Goods by Sea Act: **Commercial Law**

Carrier, Louis: **Book Publishing, English-Language**

Carrier, Louis-Georges: **Radio Drama, French-Language**

Carrier, Maurice: **Folklore**

Carrière, Marcel: **Film**

Carrière & Hastings: **Bank Architecture**

Carroll, Joy: **Popular Literature in English**

Carrot River Valley: **Melfort**

Carrothers Commission: **Northwest Territories**

Carson, Ralph: **Diorama**

Carson, William: **Newfoundland Acts; Parsons, Robert John**

"Carspiel": **Curling; Storey, Frederick Lewis**

Carstairs, Alta: **Hays, Harry W.; United Farmers of Alberta; Wood, Henry Wise**

Carte de l'Amérique septentrionale: **Cartography, History of**

carte-de-viste: **Photography**

Carter, Dennis: **Smith, Ernest John**

Carter, Gary: **Montreal Expos**

Carter, Kenneth LeG.: **Taxation, Royal Commission on**

Carter, N.B.: **Physical Oceanography**

Carter Commission: **Taxation, Royal Commission on**

Cartier, Michel: **Feux Follets**

Cartier typeface: **Dair, Carl; Graphic Design**

Cartierville, Qué: **Bethune, H. Norman**

Cartierville airport: **Aerospace Industry**

cartridge: **Firearm**

Cartwright, Ethel Mary: **Physical Education**

Cartwright, Henrietta: **Topographic Painters**

Cartwright, Man: **Drought**

Cartwright, Nfld: **Labrador**

Carver, Jonathan: **Manicouagan Réservoir**

Carver chair: **Furniture, Country**

carving: **Aqjangajuk Shaa; Arluke, George; Brooman Point Village; Davidialuk, Alasua Amittuq; Ellesmere Island Archaeological Sites; Folk Art; Furniture, English, Scottish & American; Furniture, German; Harris, Walter; Inuit Art; Karoo Ashevak; Kavik, John; L'Anse Amour Burial Site; Pangnirtung; Quévillon, Louis-Amable; Sanikiluaq; Seaweed Willie; Sivuarapik, Charlie; Tiktak, John**

Cary, Thomas: **Book Publishing, English-Language; Brown, William; Poetry in English**

Cary, Thomas, Jr.: **Book Publishing, English-Language**

Carynnyk, Marco: **Ukrainian Writing**

Cary's Swan's Nest: **Coats Island**

Casa Loma: **Architecture; Pellatt, Henry M.**

Cascade blueberry: **Vegetation Regions - Cordillera**

Cascades Group: **Cap-de-la-Madeleine**

Cascar: **Kaska**

cascara: **Plants, Native Uses; Vegetation Regions - Cordillera**

case law: **Constitutional Law; Criminal Procedure; Delict; Law; Law Reform; Medical Jurisprudence**

Casgrain, Claire: **Urban & Regional Planning**

Casgrain, Pierre-François: **Casgrain, Thérèse**

Cash, Susan: **Dance, Modern**

Cashman, A.W.: **Alberta**

casino: **Gambling**

Caslan, Alta: **Métis Settlements**

Cass-Beggs, Barbara: **Folklore; Musicology**

Cassel & Co Ltd: **Book Publishing, English-Language**

cassette: **Furniture, Country**

Cassiar, BC: **Cassiar Mountains; Nordicity**

Cassiar asbestos mine: **Gemstone**

Cassiar gold rush: **Gold Rushes; Tahltan**

Cassidy, BC: **Slovenes**

Cassidy, Harry: **Social Democracy; Social Work; Welfare State**

cast iron: **Architecture, Development; Tunnels**

Cast North America, Ltd: **Shipping Industry**

Castelein de la Lande, André: **Theatre, French-Language**

Castle, William Ivor: **Photography**

Castle Frederick, NS: **Astronomy**

Castle Hill National Historic Park: **Newfoundland; Placentia**

Castle Mountain (Alta): **Place-names**

Castleguard Cave: **Cave**

Castleguard River: **Karst Landform**

Castonguay, Charles: **Philosophy**

Castonguay, Claude: **Poverty**

Castor: **Sculpture**

castor bean: **Oilseed Crops; Poisonous Plants**

Casualty Co of Canada: **Jackman, Henry N.R.**

CAT scanner: **Medicine, Contemporary**

Catalina, Nfld: **Trinity Bay**

Catalina aircraft: **Armed Forces - Air Force**

Catalyst Theatre: **Theatre, English-Language**

catalysts: **Mercury; Molybdenum; Platinum; Silver; Zinc**

catalytic converter: **Platinum**

catamaran: **Ferries; Yachting**

cataract: **Waterfall**

cataract surgery: **Ophthalmology**

cataracts: **Blindness & Visual Impairment**

Cataraqui, Ont: **Architecture; Brant, Mary**

Cataraqui River: **Kingston; Rideau Canal**

catbird: **Thrasher**

Catelli, Onorato: **Italians**

Catelli Ltd: **John Labatt Corp; Lethbridge**

caterpillar: **Butterfly; Moth**

Cathedral Grove: **Parksville**

Cathedral Provincial Park: **Cascade Mountains**

Catherine de Saint-Augustin, Mother: **Pommier, Hugues**

Cathode Ray Direction Finder: **Henderson, John Tasker; Steel, William Arthur**

Catholic Emancipation: **MacEachern, Angus Bernard**

Catholic Register: **Essay in English**

Catholic trade union: **André, Brother; Confederation of National Trade Unions; Leatherworking; Québec Shoe Workers' Strike; Social Doctrine of the Roman Catholic Church; Union Centrals, National**

catholic tradition: **Anglicanism**

Caticchio, Tonino: **Italian Writing**

catlinite: **Linear Mounds**

cattalo: **Bison**

Catteli, Carlo: **Sculpture**

cattle: **Agricultural Research & Development; Animal Agriculture; Animal Breeding; Beef Cattle Farming; Dairy Farming; Hays, Harry W.; Ranching History; Salmonella; Veterinary Medicine, History; Veterinary Medicines Industry**

Catton, W.E.: **Bush Flying**

CATV systems: **Cable Television**

Caubvick, Mount: **Torngat Mountains**

Caughnawaga Reserve: **Handsome Lake Religion; Horn, Kahn-Tineta; Iroquois; Lacrosse; Lafitau, Joseph-François; Mohawk; Place-names; Québec Bridge Disasters; Tekakwitha, Kateri**

causation: **Delict**

causeway: **Newfoundland; Prince Edward Island; Random Island**

caustic soda: **Chemical Industries; Chemistry; Salt**

Cavanagh, Beverley: **Musicology**

Cave & Basin Springs: **Fish; Parks, National; Spring**

caveat emptor: **Commercial Law**

Caves, R.E.: **Galbraith, John K.**

caviar: **Cuisine; Sturgeon**

Cawston, BC: **Keremeos**

caysichite: **Mineral Naming**

Cayuga Creek: **Shipbuilding & Ship Repair**

Cazeneuve, Paul: **Little Theatre Movement**

CBA National Book Fair: **Bookselling**

CBC: **Canadian Broadcasting Corporation**

CBC Broadcast Centre, Regina: **Nugent, John C.; Wiens, Clifford D.**

CBC Northern Service: **Canadian Broadcasting Corporation; Communications in the North**

CBC Opera Co: **Marshall, Lois C.**

CBC Radio Competition for Young Composers: **Boudreau, Walter**

CBC Radio Literary Awards: **Literary Prizes in English**

CBC Radio Talent Competition: **Music Awards & Competitions**

CBC Symphony Orchestra: **Gellman, Steven; Music Broadcasting; Neel, L. Boyd; Symonds, Norman; Waddington, Geoffrey**

CBC Talent Festival: **Music Awards & Competitions**

CBC Vancouver Chamber Orchestra: **Avison, John Henry Patrick**

CBC Winnipeg Orchestra: **Brott, Boris**

CBF Montréal: **Deyglun, Henri; Radio Drama, French-Language**

CBFT Montréal: **Television Drama, French-Language**

CCIB Mortgage Investment Corp of Alberta: **Canadian Commercial Bank**

CCIB Realty Ltd: **Canadian Commercial Bank**

Cecil-Smith (Cecilsmith), Edward: **Drama in English; Mackenzie-Papineau Battalion**

cedar bark: **Chilkat Blanket; Davidson, Florence Edenshaw; Longhouse; Native People - Northwest Coast; Northwest Coast Indian Art**

Cedoux, Sask: **Hail**

Celanese Canada Inc: **Kingston; Technology; Textile Industry**

celeriac: **Celery**

celery vase: **Glass**

Celia Award: **Crum, George**

cell: **Biotechnology; Cancer; Genetic Engineering; Genetics**

"Cell 13": **Davey, Keith**

cell structure & function: **Biochemistry**

cell structure & types: **Plant**

Cellar, The: **Jazz**

cello & cello music: **Chamber Music; Eckhardt-Gramatté, S.C. Sonia**

celluloid: **Plastics-Processing Industry**

cellulose fibre: **Biomass Energy; Pulp & Paper Industry**

cellulose film: **Chemical Industries; Technology**

Celtic studies: **Nova Scotia**

cement: **Butchart, Robert Pim; Chemistry; Manitoba; St Lawrence Lowland; Technology; Texada Island; Thorvaldson, Thorbergur**

cemeteries, ancient: **Archaeology; Archaic; Gray Burial Site; Linear Mounds; Rainy River Burial Mounds; Serpent Mound**

Cemetery Companies Act (Alta): **Corporation Law**

cenotaph: **Remembrance Day**

Cenozoic era: **Alberta; Forest; Geological Dating; Geological History; Paleontology**

censer: **Silver, Church**

census: **Statistics**

Census & Statistics Office: **Demographic Data Collection**

CENTAUR: **Northern Lights**

Centennial Auditorium: **Saskatoon**

Centennial Centre: **Winnipeg**

Centennial Flame: **Centennial Year**

Centennial Medal: **Archambault, Louis; Fry, Frederick Ernest Joseph; Lambeth, Michel; Medal; Siminovitch, Louis; Symons, Thomas H.B.; Tremblay, Marc-Adélard**

Centennial Museum: **Peterborough**

Centennial Project, The: **Whiten, Colette**

Centennial projects: **Graphic Design; Ontario Science Centre; Oral History; Steele, Mount; Vancouver, Mount; Waskahegan Trail**

Centennial Train & Caravans: **Centennial Year**

Central Algonquian: **Native People - Eastern Woodlands**

Central British Columbia Airways Ltd: **Pacific Western Airlines Ltd**

Central Canada Exhibition: **Edwards, William Cameron; Ottawa, Ont**

Central Canada Loan & Savings Co: **Cox, George A.; Gundy, James Henry; Wood, Edward Rogers**

Central Canada Railway: **Postal System**

Central Ellesmere Fold Belt: **Ellesmere Island**

Central Experimental Farm: **Agriculture, Dept of; Arboretum; Botanical Garden; Grisdale, Joseph Hiram; National Museum of Science & Technology; Ottawa, Ont; Research Stations, Agricultural**

Central Highlands: **Mount Carleton Provincial Park**

Central Mortgage & Housing Corp: **Canada Mortgage & Housing Corp; Carver, Humphrey S.M.; Housing & Housing Policy**

Central of Democratic Trade Unions: **Confederation of National Trade Unions**

Central Olympic Committee: **Sports Organization, Amateur**

Central Ontario School of Art & Design: **Manly, Charles MacDonald; Reid, George A.**

Central Pentecostal College: **Evangelism**

Central Saanich, BC: **Saanich Peninsula; Victoria**

Central Selling Agency: **McPhail, Alexander James**

Central Station (Montréal): **Railway Station; Tunnels**

Central Strike Committee: **Winnipeg General Strike**

Central Surgical Soc of North America: **Gray, Jessie Catherine**

Central Technical School: **Goldhamer, Charles; Wyn Wood, Elizabeth**

Central Valley: **Cranbrook**

Centrale de l'enseignement du Québec: **Charbonneau, Yvon**

Centrale des syndicats démocratiques: **Construction Industry**

Centralism: **Constitution Act, 1867; Decentralization; Federalism; Government**

Centralized Traffic Control: **Railways, Track & Yards**

Centre culturel Franco-Manitobain: **St-Boniface**

Centre de pédagogie et de psychologie: **Book Publishing, French-Language**

Centre de recherche en civilisation canadienne-française: **Literature in French - Scholarship & Teaching**

Centre des femmes: **Women's Movement**

Centre d'essai des auteurs dramatiques: **Drama in French; Germain, Jean-Claude**
Centre d'essai des jeunes auteurs dramatiques: **Theatre, French-Language**
Centre d'essai des joual: **Theatre, French-Language**
Centre d'études acadiennes: **Acadia; Folk Music, Franco-Canadian**
Centre d'études prospectives du Québec: **Pépin, Clermont**
Centre du théâtre d'aujourd'hui: **Germain, Jean-Claude**
Centre éducatif et culturel: **Book Publishing, French-Language**
Centre for Art Tapes: **Video Art**
Centre for Bioethics: **Bioethics; Jurisprudence; Medical Ethics; Medical Research**
Centre for Broadcasting Studies: **Radio Drama, English-Language**
Centre for Cold Ocean Resources Engineering: **Iceberg; Memorial University of Newfoundland**
Centre for Culture & Technology: **McLuhan, H. Marshall**
Centre for Editing Early Canadian Texts: **Literary Bibliography in English**
Centre for Justice Statistics: **Juvenile Delinquency**
Centre for Medieval Studies: **Dictionary**
Centre for Radio Science: **Physics**
Centre for Research in Experimental Space Science: **Physics; York University**
Centre for Research on Latin America: **York University**
Centre for Spanish-Speaking Peoples: **Latin Americans**
Centre for Sport & Recreation: **Sports Organization, Amateur**
Centre for the Arts: **Strate, Grant**
Centre for the Documentation of Traditional Culture: **Folklore**
Centre for the Performing Arts: **Alberta**
Centre for Urban & Community Studies: **Community; Urban Studies**
Centre franco-ontarien de folklore: **Folk Music, Franco-Canadian**
Centre hospitalier Robert Giffard: **Douglas, James (1800-86)**
Centre-in-the-Square: **Kitchener-Waterloo**
Centre Island: **Toronto Islands**
Centre Le Gyroscope: **Drama in French**
Centre Musquodoboit, NS: **Musquodoboit Harbour**
Centre pédagogigue: **Book Publishing, French-Language**
Centrediscs: **Canadian Music Centre**
Centrefold: **Art Writing & Criticism**
cents: **Coinage**
Century 21: **Hamilton**
cephalocarida: **Crustacean**
cephalopoda: **Cuttlefish; Mollusc; Octopus; Seashell; Squid**
cera: **Mackerel**
Cercle du livre de France: **Book Publishing, French-Language**
Cercle Molière: **Little Theatre Movement; Roy, Gabrielle; St-Boniface; Theatre, French-Language**
Cercle ouvrier: **Theatre, French-Language**
Cercle Saint-Henri: **Little Theatre Movement**
Cercles des jeunes naturalistes: **Marie-Victorin, Frère**
Cerises, Rivière aux: **Mount Orford Park**
Cerp Investments Ltd: **Bronfman Family**
cesium atomic clock: **Henderson, John Tasker; Observatory; Time**
Ceylonese: **Prejudice & Discrimination; South Asians**
CFAC Calgary: **Alberta; Selkirk Communications Ltd**
CFBO Saint John: **Messer, Don, & the Islanders**
CFCF Montréal: **Advertising; Communications in Québec; Music Broadcasting**
CFCN-TV Calgary: **Maclean Hunter Ltd**
CFCW Camrose: **Country & Western Music**

CFCY Charlottetown: **Messer, Don, & the Islanders**
CFQC-TV Saskatoon: **Baton Broadcasting Inc**
CFRB Toronto: **Allan, Andrew E.F.; Bushnell, Ernest L.; Rogers, Edward Samuel**
CFTM Montréal: **Television Programming**
CFTO-TV Toronto: **Baton Broadcasting Inc**
CFTR-AM Toronto: **Rogers Telecommunications Ltd**
Chabanel, Noël: **Ste Marie Among the Hurons**
Chabert, Abbé: **Franchere, Joseph-Charles**
Chabert, Joseph Bernard de: **Astronomy; Cartography, History of**
Chabot, Cécile: **Poetry in French**
Chabot, Jean: **Film**
Chabouilé, Charles: **Sculpture**
Chad Allan & the Expressions: **Guess Who**
Chadwick, Edward Marion: **Genealogy**
Chain of Arrows: **Native People, Religion**
chair: **Furniture, Country; Furniture, English, Scottish & American; Furniture, French; Furniture, German**
chair lift: **Cross-Country Skiing; Mont Ste-Anne; Ste-Agathe-des-Monts**
chalcedony: **Torngat Mountains**
chalcopyrite: **Metallurgy; Mineral**
Chalet Cochand: **Skiing**
Chaleur Area History Museum: **Dalhousie**
chalice: **Silver, Church**
Chalk River Nuclear Laboratories: **Chalk River; Keys, David Arnold; Laurence, George C.; Nuclear Research Establishments**
Chalke, John: **Ceramics, Contemporary**
Challener, Frederick: **Public Art**
Chalmers, J.W.: **Children's Literature in English**
Chalmers, Jean: **Chalmers, Floyd S.**
Chalmers, Robert: **Geomorphology**
Chalmers Award: **Literary Prizes in English; Tremblay, Michel**
Chamber of Notaries: **Law Society**
Chamberlain, Charlie: **Messer, Don, & the Islanders**
Chamberlain, Edson J.: **Edson**
Chamberlains, Nfld: **Conception Bay South**
Chamberland, Albert: **Champagne, Claude**
Chambert, Joseph: **Art Education**
Chambly Canal: **Chambly; Richelieu, Rivière; St-Jean-sur-Richelieu**
Chambul, Boris: **Track & Field**
Chameau: **Coinage**
Chamouchouane, Rivière: **St-Félicien; Saint-Jean, Lac**
Champ-de-Mars station: **Ferron, Marcelle**
champagne: **Wine Industry**
Champagne, Carole: **Laure, Carole**
Champagne, Jean-Serge: **Sculpture**
Champion plough: **Oshawa**
Champlain: **Icebreakers**
Champlain Bridge: **Ahearn, Thomas**
Champlain College: **Bishop's University**
Champlain Street: **Disasters**
Champoux, Roger: *Presse*
Champs de Bataille, Parc des: **Québec City**
CHAN-TV Vancouver: **Selkirk Communications Ltd; WIC (Western International Communications Ltd)**
Chancellery of Canadian Orders & Decorations: **Order of Military Merit**
Chancellory of Honours: **Honours**
Channel, Nfld: **Channel-Port aux Basques**
Chanoines réguliers de l'immaculée-conception: **Notre Dame de Lourdes**
Chanoinesses des cinq plaies du sauveur: **Notre Dame de Lourdes**
Chantry Inlet: **Back River**
Chapais, Qué: **Disasters; St-Félicien**
Chapais, Thomas: **Historiography**
Chapdelaine, Paul: **Table Tennis**
Chapel Arm: **Trinity Bay**

Chapin, Miriam: *Insolences du Frère Untel*
Chapman, Henry Samuel: **Canada & Australia**
Chapman, L.J.: **Geomorphology**
Chapman, William: **Fréchette, Louis-H.; Poetry in French**
Chappell, Benjamin: **Furniture, Country**
Char Lake: **Rigler, Frank Harold**
Charbol, Claude: **Héroux, Denis**
Charboneau, Peter: **Prison**
Charbonneau, Jean: **Essay in French; Poetry in French**
Charbonneau, Joseph: **Léger, Paul-Emile**
Charcoal: **Fort Macleod**
charcoal: **Biomass Energy; Drawing; Goldhamer, Charles; Iron & Steel Industry; Metallurgy; Northwest Coast Indian Art**
Chargex Ltd: **Toronto-Dominion Bank**
charitable donations: **Arts Funding; Business Elites; Canadian Nature Federation; Foundations; Hospitals**
Charitable Irish Soc: **Halifax**
charitable organizations: **Associations; Corporation Law; Foundations; Humane Societies; Social Security**
Charlebois, Ovide: **Saints**
Charles, J.L.: **Surveying**
Charles I of England: **Alexander, William; Emblems, Provincial & Territorial; Newfoundland; Optometry**
Charles II of England: **Horse; Hudson's Bay Company; Rupert's Land**
Charles X of France: **Plamondon, Antoine**
Charles E. Frosst & Co Ltd: **Pharmaceuticals Industry**
Charles Lake: **Dartmouth Lakes**
Charles Street Video: **Video Art**
Charlesbourg, Qué: **Architecture; Chauveau, Pierre-Joseph-Olivier; Québec City**
Charlesbourg-Royal (Cap-Rouge, Qué): **New France; Roberval, Sieur de**
Charlo, NB: **New Brunswick**
Charlotte, Queen: **Charlottetown; Queen Charlotte Islands**
Charlotte Strait: **Balaklava Island**
Charlottetown Examiner: **Whelan, Edward**
Charlottetown Guardian: **Prince Edward Island**
Charlottetown Herald: **Sullivan, William Wilfred**
Charlottetown harbour: **Bayfield, Henry Wolsey; Fort Amherst**
Charlottetown lunatic asylum: **Mackieson, John**
Charlottetown Natal Day: **Festivals**
Charlottetown Patriot: **Prince Edward Island**
Charlottetown Summer Festival: **Campbell, Norman Kenneth; Charlottetown; Festivals; Feux Follets; Lund, Alan; Musical Theatre; Prince Edward Island; Theatre, English-Language**
Charlton Island: **James, Thomas; James Bay**
Charnisay, Charles de Menou, Seigneur D'Aulnay: **Annapolis Royal**
Charon, J.-François: **Le Ber, Pierre; Youville, Marie-Marguerite d'**
Charron, François: **Literary Prizes in French; Poetry in French**
Charron, Ghyslain: **Philosophy**
charter flights: **Air Canada; Aviation; Economic Regulation; Transportation Regulation; Wardair International Ltd**
Charter of Economic Rights & Duties of States: **International Law**
Charter of Rights Coalition: **Women's Movement**
chartered banks: **Bank of British Columbia; Bank of Canada; Bank of Montreal; Bank of Nova Scotia; Bank Rate; Banking; Canadian Commercial Bank; Canadian Imperial Bank of Commerce; Continental Bank of Canada; Mercantile Bank of Canada; National Bank of Canada; Royal Bank of Canada; Toronto-Dominion Bank**
Charters, Michael: **Novel in English**

Chartier, Albert: **Popular Literature in French**
Chartier, Émile: **Essay in French; Literature in French - Scholarship & Teaching**
Chartrand, Joseph-D.: **Autobiographical Writing in French**
Chartrand, Phillipe: **Gymnastics**
Chase, William: **St Catharines**
Chat, Lac du: **Erie, Lake**
Château Champlain: **Architectural Styles**
Château de Chambord: **Comparative Literature, Canadian**
Château de Ramezay: **Historic Site; Medal; Nelligan, Émile; Ramezay, Claude de**
Château de Vaudreuil: **Architectural Styles; Architecture**
Château Frontenac: **Architecture; Canadian Pacific Railway; Hotel; Maxwell, Edward; Van Horne, William C.**
Château Lake Louise: **Lake Louise**
Château Laurier: **Ahearn, Thomas; Architecture; Constitution, Patriation of; Helders, Johan (John) A. J.; Hotel**
Château Menier: **Anticosti, Ile d'**
Château-Richer, Qué: **Guyon, Jean**
Château Saint-Louis: **Château Clique; Government Building; Painting**
Châteauguay, Rivière: **Battle of Châteauguay; Floods & Flood Control; St Lawrence Lowland; War of 1812**
Chater, Man: **Grand Valley**
Chatham: *Sutil & Mexicana*
Chatham Daily News: **Doyle, Richard J.**
Chatham Sound: **Dundas Island; Skeena River**
Chatsworth, Ont: **McClung, Nellie L.**
chattel: **Property Law**
Chattel Mortgages: **Commercial Law**
Chaudière Falls: **Bronson, Erskine Henry; Hull; Ottawa, Ont**
Chaudière portages: **Hull; Ottawa River**
Chaumonot, Joseph Marie: **Neutral**
Chaurette, Normand: **Drama in French**
Chauve, Mont: **Mount Orford Park**
Chauveau Medal: **Charbonneau, Robert; Literary Prizes in English**
Chauvin, Jean: **Art Writing & Criticism**
Chauvin, Pierre: **Huguenots; Monts, Pierre Du Gua de; Tadoussac**
CHBC-TV: **Selkirk Communications Ltd**
CHCH-TV Hamilton: **Messer, Don, & the Islanders; Selkirk Communications Ltd**
Cheadle, Alta: **Physics**
Cheadle, W.B.: **Exploration & Travel Literature in English**
Chebucto, NS: **Halifax; Warren, Peter**
Chedabucto Bay: **Canso; McTaggart-Cowan, Patrick Duncan**
Chee-Choo, Shirley: **Debassige, Blake R.**
Cheerio Toys & Games: **Toys & Games**
Cheese & Wine Festival: **Ingersoll**
CHEK-TV Victoria: **Selkirk Communications Ltd; WIC (Western International Communications Ltd)**
Chekhov Soc: **Russians**
Chellas, Brian: **Philosophy**
Chemainus, BC: **Vancouver Island**
Chemainus River: **MacMillan, H.R.**
Chemical Institute of Canada: **Bates, John Seaman; Chemical Industries; Chemistry; Clark, Howard Charles; Deslongchamps, Pierre; Gunning, Harry E.; Laidler, Keith James; McDowell, Charles Alexander; Manske, Richard Helmuth Frederick; Petrochemical Industry; Schneider, William George; Science; Thode, Henry George; Wiesner, Karel; Yaffe, Leo**
Chemin du Roi: **Trois-Rivières**
Chemistry & Biology Research Institute: **Research Stations, Agricultural**
chemistry journals & societies: **Biochemistry; Chemical Engineering; Chemistry**
Chemong Lake: **Kawartha Lakes; Peterborough**

Chenail Ecarté: **Baldoon**
Chénard, Madeleine: **Children's Literature in French**
Chenaux portage: **Ottawa River**
Chêne, Rivière du: **St-Eustache**
Chénier, Jean-Oliver: **Patriotes**
cheque: **Bank of Canada; Banking; Commercial Law**
cheque forgery: **Crime**
Chercheur de Trésors: Influence d'un livre
Chernetskyj, Sava: **Ukrainian Writing**
Cherney, Brian: **Music History; Musicology**
chernozem: **Soil Classification**
Cherrier, Georges-Hippolyte: **Book Publishing, French-Language**
Cherriman, J.B.: **Mathematics**
cherry bark: **Northwest Coast Indian Art**
Cherry Creek, BC: **Okanagan Valley**
cherry wood: **Furniture, Country; Furniture, English, Scottish & American; Weaving, Contemporary**
chert: **Geological Regions; Neutral**
chervil: **Herbs**
Cheslatta River: **Nechako River**
chest: **Furniture, Country; Furniture, English, Scottish & American; Furniture, French; Furniture, German; Northwest Coast Indian Art**
Chestnut, Thomas Herbert: **Drama in English**
Chestnut Canoes: **Camping**
Cheticamp, NS: **Rugs & Rug Making**
Chevalier, Henri-Emile: **Book Publishing, French-Language; Novel in French**
Chevalier, Leo: **Fashion Design**
Chevrolet, Gaston: **Automobile Racing**
Chevrolet automobile: **McLaughlin, Robert Samuel**
Chevrolet Motor Co of Canada Ltd: **General Motors of Canada Ltd**
chewing gum: **Confectionery Industry**
Cheyne v Cheyne: **Family Law**
CHFI-FM Toronto: **Rogers Telecommunications Ltd**
Chiasson, Anselme: **Folk Music, Franco-Canadian**
Chibougamau, Qué: **Prospecting; St-Félicien**
Chic-Chocs, Monts: **Québec**
Chickadee: **Children's Literature in English**
chicken pox: **Virus**
chickens: **Agricultural Marketing Board; International Trade; Poultry Farming; Veterinary Medicines Industry**
chickweed: **Endangered Plants; Vegetation Regions - Arctic Tundra**
chicory: **Vegetable**
chicots: **Métis**
Chicoutimi, Rivière: **Chicoutimi**
Chief of the Defence Staff: **Armed Forces - Unification; National Defence, Dept of**
Chiefs Point: **Fishing Islands**
Chien d'or/Golden Dog: **Literary Magazines in English**
chigger: **Mite**
Chignecto, NS: **Methodism**
Chignecto Isthmus: **Canals & Inland Waterways; New Brunswick; Nova Scotia 1714-84; Tantramar Marsh**
Chignecto ship railway: **Tidnish**
Chilcotin Plateau: **Ranching History; Williams Lake**
Chilcotin River: **Chilcotin; Fraser River**
Chilcott, Barbara: **Theatre, English-Language**
Child, Francis James: **Folk Music, Anglo-Canadian**
child custody & support: **Courts of Law; Family Court; Family Law**
Child Saving Movement: **Child Welfare**
child tax credit: **Poverty; Social Security**
Child Welfare Acts: **Child Abuse; Child Welfare; Sexual Abuse of Children**
Child Welfare Assn: **Gosling, William Gilbert**
childbirth: **Birthing Practices; Women's Movement**

Children, The: **Cockburn, Bruce**
Children of God: **New Religious Movements**
Children of Peace: **Willson, David**
Children's Aid Soc: **Child Welfare; Gibson, John Morison**
Children's Centre: **Manitoba**
Children's Hospital of Eastern Ontario: **Campeau, Robert**
Children's Law Reform Act (Ont): **Adoption; Family Law**
children's rights: **Canadian Women's Press Club; Family Studies**
Chileans: **Ethnic Literature; Immigration; Latin Americans; Refugees**
Chilkat: **Chilkoot Pass**
Chillas, Robert: **Furniture, Country**
Chillihitza, Chief: **Salish, Interior**
chimney swift: **Migration; Swift**
china: **Ceramics; Nepheline Syenite**
Chinatowns: **Architecture, Development; Chinese; Cumberland; Vancouver; Victoria**
Chinese & Japanese Immigration, Royal Commission on: **Chinese**
Chinese Exclusion Act: **Prejudice & Discrimination**
Chinese Express: **Newspapers**
Chinese Immigration Act: **British Columbia; Chinese**
Chinese National League: **Cohen, Morris (Moishe) Abraham**
Chinese United Dramatic Society: **Theatre, Multicultural**
Chinese Voice: **Newspapers**
Chiniki, John: **Stoney**
Chinook (Indians): **Ogopogo**
Chinook language: **Native People, Communications**
chionodoxa: **Flowers, Cultivated**
Chippewa: **Ojibwa**
Chippewa, Ont: **Niagara Peninsula; War of 1812**
Chiputneticook Lakes: **St Croix River**
Chirikov, Aleksei: **Northwest Coast**
Chisasibi, Qué: **James Bay Project**
chisel: **Northwest Coast Indian Art; Tools, Carpentry**
chiselmouth: **Minnow**
Chisholm, D.A.: **Physics**
Chisholm, William: **Oakville**
Chisholme, Daniel: **Literature in English - Theory & Criticism**
Chislett, Anne: **Blyth Festival; Drama in English; Governor General's Literary Awards; Theatre, English-Language**
chitin: **Paleontology**
Chitina Glacier: **Steele, Mount**
chiton: **Mollusc; Seashell**
Chitty, Elizabeth: **Art, Contemporary Trends**
chives: **Herbs; Vegetable**
chlorargyrite: **Mineral**
chlorastrolite: **Greenstone**
chlorine: **Chemical Industries; Chemistry; Environmental Law; Mineral; Railway Safety; Salt; Water-Borne Disease; Water Pollution; Water Treatment**
chlorite: **Soapstone**
chloroform: **Chemistry; Worthington, Edward Dagge**
CHML Hamilton: **Hunter, Thomas J.**
chocolate: **Confectionery Industry; Salmonella**
Chögyam Trungpa: **Buddhism**
chokecherry: **Berries, Wild; Cuisine; Poisonous Plants**
cholera: **Biological Product; Chinese; Cobourg & Peterborough Railway; Disasters; Epidemic; Grosse Ile; Health Policy; Influenza; Légaré, Joseph; Royal William; Social History; Water-Borne Disease**
chondrichthyes: **Fish**
Chopin, René: **Literature in French; Poetry in French**
Choquette, Ernest: **Leduc, Ozias; Novel in French**
Choquette, Jérôme: **Roy, Fabien**
Choquette, Robert: **Literature in French; Poetry in French; Radio Drama, French-Language; Television Drama, French-Language**
Chorley Park: **Lieutenant-Governor**
chou de Suède: **Rutabaga**
Chouinard, Marie: **Dance, Modern**
Chown, Alice A.: **Home Economics**
Chown, Bruce: **Pediatrics**

Chown, Henry: **Pediatrics**
Chown, Mount: **Chown, Samuel Dwight**
Christian & Missionary Alliance: **Bible Schools; Evangelical & Fundamentalist Movements; Evangelical Fellowship of Canada; Evangelism; Holiness Churches**
Christian Brethren: **Evangelical & Fundamentalist Movements**
Christian Brothers: **Charbonnel, Armand-F.-M. de; French in the West; Saint Mary's University**
Christian Community of Universal Brotherhood: **Verigin, Peter V.**
"Christian Conscience & Poverty": **Ecumenical Social Action**
Christian Guardian: **Ryerson, A. Egerton**
Christian humanism: **Social Doctrine of the Roman Catholic Church**
Christian Labour Assn of Canada: **Construction Industry**
Christian Marxism: **Marxism**
Christian Recorder: **Literary Magazines in English**
Christian Reformed Church: **Alberta; Evangelical Fellowship of Canada; Presbyterian & Reformed Churches**
Christian schools: **Calvinism; Dutch; Education, Alternate; Private School**
Christian trade union: **Calvinism; Construction Industry**
Christie, Robert: **Book Publishing, English-Language**
Christie, Robert (painter): **Painting**
Christmas Day: **National Holidays**
Christmas traditions: **Mumming; Sarcee**
"Christmas tree": **Petroleum Exploration & Production**
Christmas trees: **Forestry; Manitoba; Musquodoboit Harbour; Nova Scotia**
Christopher, Ken: **Painting**
Christy, Francis: **Scott, Anthony D.**
Chromasco: **Metallurgy**
chromate: **Mineral**
chrome tanning: **Leatherworking**
chromosome: **Barr, Murray Llewellyn; Disability; Genetics**
chromosphere: **Sun**
Chronicles of Canada: **Langton, Hugh Hornby**
Chruscicki, E.: **Poles**
chrysanthemum: **Greenhouse Crops**
chrysotile: **Asbestos**
CHSJ-TV Saint John: **Irving Group**
chub: **Huron, Lake; Whitefish**
Chubb Crater: **Québec**
Chuck Stake (Don Mabie): **Art, Contemporary Trends**
chuckwagon races: **Calgary Stampede; Rodeo**
Chudley, Ron: **Drama in English**
chukar: **Game Bird**
Church, A.J.: **Exploration & Travel Literature in English**
Church Action for Emergency Aid: **Ecumenical Social Action**
Church Army: **Evangelism**
Church Council on Justice & Corrections: **Ecumenical Social Action**
Church House, BC: **Northern Georgia Strait Coast Salish**
Church Missionary Soc: **Anglicanism**
Church of Christ: **Bible Schools**
Church of England in Canada: **Anglicanism**
Church of God: **Bible Schools; Holiness Churches**
Church of Jesus Christ Latter Day Saints: **Mormon Church**
Church of Scotland: **Clergy Reserves; Grant, George M.; Presbyterian & Reformed Churches**
Church of the Nazarene: **Holiness Churches**
Church Point: **Nova Scotia**
church-state relations: **Bourget, Ignace; Brown, George; Catholicism; Gallicanism; Intellectual History; Mennonites; Separate School; Zouaves**
Churches & Corporate Responsibility, Task Force on: **Ecumenical Social Action**
Churchill, Edward: **Expo 67**
Churchill Lake: **Churchill River**
Churchill Province: **Geological Regions**

Churchland, Patricia: **Philosophy**
Churchland, Paul: **Philosophy**
Chute à Blondeau: **Canals & Inland Waterways**
Chute à La Savanne: **Saguenay River**
Chute des Passes: **Saguenay River**
Chute du Diable: **Saguenay River**
Chutes, The: **South Nahanni River**
Chuvalo, George: **Boxing**
Ciamaga, Gustav: **Electroacoustic Music**
Ciba Foundation: **Friedman, Sydney Murray**
ciborium: **Silver, Church**
cicada: **Bug**
Ciechomska, M.: **Poles**
cigar: **Tobacco; Tobacco-Products Industry**
cigarette: **Flax; Retail Trade; Tobacco; Tobacco-Products Industry**
Cikansky, Victor: **Sculpture**
Cimon, Henri: **Exploration & Travel Literature in French**
Cinak films: **Lefebvre, Jean-Pierre**
cineraria: **Flowers, Cultivated; Groundsel**
cinnabar: **Mercury**
Cinq-Mars, Alonzo: **Potvin, Damase**
Cinq-Mars, Jacques: **Archaeology**
cinquefoil: **Cypress Hills Provincial Park; Pollination**
CIP Forum: **Urban & Regional Planning**
Cirque Mountain: **Torngat Mountains**
cirripedia: **Crustacean**
cirrus: **Cloud; Ice**
cisco: **Herring; Whitefish**
Citadel-on-Wheels: **Theatre for Young Audiences**
Citizens' Committee of 1000: **Winnipeg General Strike**
Citizen's Forum: **Educational Broadcasting**
Citizenship Act: **Ethnic Studies; Status of Women**
Citizenship & Immigration, Dept of: **Immigration Policy**
Citizenship Day: **Empire Day**
citric acid: **Mold**
CITV Edmonton: **Alberta**
City Bank: **Coinage**
City Beautiful movement: **Lyle, John M.; Urban Reform**
city charter: **Municipal-Provincial Relations; Vancouver**
city commissioner: **Municipal Government; Urban Reform**
City Magazine: **Urban Reform; Urban Studies**
city manager: **Municipal Government; Urban Reform**
City of Toronto: **Sailing Ships**
City of Toronto Book Award: **Literary Prizes in English**
City Savings & Trust Co: **Belzberg, Samuel**
CITY-TV: **CHUM Ltd**
City Woman: **Magazines**
Citystage: **Theatre, English-Language**
Civic Action Party: **Crombie, David**
Civic Improvement League: **Adams, Thomas; Lyle, John M.**
Civic Non-Partisan Assn: **City Politics**
Civic Party: **City Politics**
Civil Action League: **Drapeau, Jean**
Civil Aircraft Agreement: **Aerospace Industry**
Civil Code Revision Office: **Civil Code; Delict**
civil defamation: **Law & the Press**
civil disobedience: **New Left**
civil rights: **Civil Liberties; Company Town; Distribution of Powers; Government; Homosexuality; Prejudice & Discrimination**
civil service: **Distribution of Powers; Douglas, T.C.; Government; Ontario; Public Service; St John's; Secretary of State, Dept of; Social Mobility**
Civil Service Act: **Public Service Commission**
Civil Service Act (NB): **McNair, John B.**
Civil Service Commission: **Heeney, Arnold D.P.; Public Service Commission**
CJBC Toronto: **Music Broadcasting**
CJCB-TV Sydney: **CHUM Ltd**
CJCH-TV Halifax: **CHUM Ltd**
CJOH-TV Ottawa: **Western Dominion Investment Co Ltd**

CJON-TV St John's: **Newfoundland**
CJOR Vancouver: **Webster, Jack**
CJYC Edmonton: **Evangelism**
CKAC Montréal: **Communications in Québec; Desmarais, Paul; Deyglun, Henri; Peterson, Oscar E.; Radio Drama, French-Language**
CKCK Regina: **Armadale Co Ltd**
CKCN Toronto: **Bushnell, Ernest L.**
CKCW-TV Moncton: **CHUM Ltd**
CKLT-TV Saint John: **CHUM Ltd**
CKOC Hamilton: **Armadale Co Ltd**
CKRC Winnipeg: **Armadale Co Ltd**
CKSB St-Boniface: **Manitoba**
CKUA Edmonton: **Educational Broadcasting; Radio Drama, English-Language**
CKVL Montréal: **Deyglun, Henri; Radio Drama, French-Language**
CKVR-TV Barrie: **CHUM Ltd**
CKWG-FM Winnipeg: **Armadale Co Ltd**
CKY-TV Winnipeg: **Moffat Communications Ltd**
Claies, Lac aux: **Simcoe, Lake**
Clair, Frank: **Ottawa Rough Riders**
Clairmont, Donald H.: **Community**
clan: **Koreans; Scots**
Clandebove, Man: **St Andrews, Man**
Clapin, Sylva: **Dictionary**
Clappé, Arthur: **Musical Theatre**
Clapperton, Harry: **Glass**
Clare, John: *Chatelaine*
Claremont, Ont: **Thomson, Thomas J.**
Clarenville, Nfld: **Trinity Bay**
Claresholm, Alta: **Status of Women in Canada, Royal Commission on the**
Clark, A.L.: **Physics**
Clark, Ann: **Painting**
Clark, Catherine Anthony: **Children's Literature in English**
Clark, Donald W.: **Archaeology**
Clark, Gregory: **Essay in English; Short Fiction in English;** *Star Weekly; Toronto Star*
Clark, Philip: **Clark, Paraskeva**
Clark, R.H.: **Hydrology**
Clark, W.C.: **Urban & Regional Planning**
Clarke, F.C.: **Choral Music**
Clarke, Frank: **Mathematics**
Clarke, Hugh A.: **Music History**
Clarke, John: **North West Company**
Clarke, L.G.A.: **Industrial Research & Development**
Clarke, Wayne: **Fashion Design**
Clarke City, Qué: **Sept-Iles**
Clarke Institute of Psychiatry: **Clarke, Charles Kirk; Criminology; Psychiatry; Seeman, Mary Violette**
Clarke Irwin & Co: **Book Publishing, English-Language**
Clarke's Beach, Nfld: **Furniture, Country**
Clark's Harbour, NS: **Cape Sable Island**
Clark's nutcracker: **Migration; Yoho National Park**
Clarkson, Gordon & Co: **Gordon, Walter L.**
Class Actions Act (Qué): **Consumer Law**
class structure: **Business Elites; Central Coast Salish; Elites; English; Ethnic & Race Relations; Lower Canada; Social Class; Social Mobility**
Classics, The: **Chilliwack**
Clatworthy Study: **Native People, Social Conditions**
Claude Aubry Award: **Literary Prizes in English**
Claudet, Francis G.: **Photography**
Claus process: **Sulphur**
Clavius: **Moon**
Clay Brick Assn of Canada: **Construction Industry**
Clayoquot: **Nootka**
Clayoquot Sound: *Tonquin*
Clayoquot Sound Cannery: **Brewster, Harlan Carey**
Clean Air Acts: **Air Pollution; Environmental Law**
Clear Lake: **Kawartha Lakes**
Clear Water Lake: **Claire, Lake**
Clearwater formations: **Bitumen**
Clearwater Lake: **Eau Claire, Lac à l'**
Clearwater River (Alta): **Rocky Mountain House National Historic Park; Saskatchewan River**
Clearwater River (Qué): **Eau Claire, Lac à l'**

Cleary Auditorium & Convention Centre: **Windsor, Ont**
Cleaver, Elizabeth: **Children's Literature in English**
Clément, Beatrice: **Children's Literature in French**
Clement, Wallace: **Business Elites; Business History**
Clench House: **Niagara-on-the-Lake**
cleric: **Christian Religious Communities**
clerical elite: **Elites; French Canadian Nationalism**
Clery, Val: **Books in Canada**
Cleve, George: **Winnipeg Symphony Orchestra**
Cleveland Dam: **North Vancouver**
Cliche Commission: **Mulroney, M. Brian; Québec**
Cliff, Leslie: **Swimming, Speed**
Cliff Street Observatory: **Klotz, Otto Julius**
Clifford, Harvey: **Skiing**
Clifford, John: **Skiing**
Clifford, Wayne: **Poetry in English**
Clifford E. Lee Awards: **Choreography; Dance History; Literary Prizes in English; Marcuse, Judith R.; Pacific Ballet Theatre; Theatre, English-Language**
Clifford E. Lee Foundation: **Choreography**
Cliffside Ski Club: **Ski Jumping**
Clifton, Ont: **Niagara Falls, Ont**
Clifton Bridge: **Keefer, Samuel**
Clifton (house): **Windsor, NS**
Climate Planning Board: **Hare, Frederick Kenneth**
climbing: **Kananaskis Country; Mountaineering**
Clinch, John: **Trinity**
Clinton, Ont: **Blyth Festival; Piano Manufacturing**
Clinton Creek: **Yukon Territory**
clintonia: **Nova Scotia**
clock jack: **Domestic Utensils**
clockwork: **Lighthouses**
Clokie, H. McD.: **Political Science**
closed shop: **Labour Law**
Closse, R. Lambert: **Children's Literature in French; Place-names**
Clothier, Lyman: **Kemptville**
Clothier's Mills: **Kemptville**
Cloutâtre, Jean: **Children's Literature in French**
cloud seeding: **Hail; Rainmaking**
cloudberry: **Berries, Wild; Newfoundland**
Clouston, James: **Exploration**
Cloutier, Eugène: **Exploration & Travel Literature in French; Novel in French**
Cloutier, Réal: **Québec Nordiques**
Cloverdale, BC: **McCowan, Daniel; Surrey**
clowning: **Theatre, English-Language**
Club athlétique canadien: **Montreal Canadiens**
Club belge de St-Boniface: **Belgians; Theatre, French-Language**
Club Coreana: **Koreans**
clubs: **Corporation Law**
Cluett Peabody Canada Inc: **Clothing Industries**
Clutterbuck, W.J.: **Exploration & Travel Literature in English**
Clyde Inlet: **Nunatak**
CN Exploration: **Canadian National Railways**
CN Hotels: **CN Tower**
CN Marine Inc: **Cabot Strait; Cape Traverse; Channel-Port aux Basques; Ferries; Newfoundland; Placentia Bay**
CN Rail: **Canadian National Railways**
CN Real Estate: **Canadian National Railways; Place Ville Marie**
CNCP Telecommunications Ltd: **Canadian Pacific Railway; Economic Regulation; Postal System; Telecommunications; Telegraph; Telephones; TransCanada Telephone System**
coach: **Bus Transportation**
Coach House Press: **Davey, Frank; Poetry in English; Small Presses**
Coaching Assn of Canada: **Sports Organization, Amateur**
Coady International Institute: **Antigonish Movement**
Coal Creek, BC: **Fernie**
Coal Creek Mines: **Fernie**

coal dust: **Mining Work Force**
Coal Mining Research Centre: **Coal Liquefaction**
"coal oil": **Gesner, Abraham**
coal pyrolysis: **Coal Gasification**
Coal Research Centre: **Chemistry; Coal Liquefaction**
Coal Valley, Alta: **Fossil Plants**
Coal Valley Mine: **Coal**
Coalition for Development: **Ecumenical Social Action**
Coast Forest: **Forest Regions**
Coast Microblade: **Prehistory**
Coast Plutonic Complex: **Geological Regions**
Coast Salish: **Bella Coola; Central Coast Salish; Northern Georgia Strait Coast Salish**
Coast Tsimshian: **Metlakatla Pass Sites; Tsimshian**
Coastal Fisheries Protection Act: **Fisheries**
coastal navigation: **Cape Sable; Hydrography; Lighthouses; North Cape**
coastal plains: **Physiographic Regions - Arctic Lands**
coastline: **Coastal Landform; Coastal Waters**
coat of arms: **A Mari usque ad Mare; Coinage; Emblems, Provincial & Territorial; Emblems of Canada; Flag Debate; Heraldry; Heraldry Society of Canada; Nova Scotia; Silver, Domestic; Symbols of Authority**
Coaticook, Rivière: **Lennoxville**
Coats, Robert H.: **Statistics Canada; Working-Class History**
Coats, William: **Coats Island**
coaxial cable: **Cable Television; Telecommunications; Telephones; Telidon**
Cob, Bert: **Film Animation**
Cobalt Mining Museum: **Cobalt, Ont**
cobalt sulphide: **Metallurgy**
cobaltite: **Mineral**
cobbling: **Leatherworking**
Cobequid Bay: **Minas Basin; Tidal Energy; Truro**
Cobequid Mountain: **Nova Scotia**
COBOL: **Computer Science; Language**
Cobourg & Rice Lake Plank Road & Ferry Co: **Cobourg & Peterborough Railway**
Cobourg Car Works: **Railway History**
Cobourg Rail Road Co: **Cobourg & Peterborough Railway**
Coburn, David: **Stress**
Coburn, Kathleen: **Autobiographical Writing in English; Literature in English - Theory & Criticism**
cocaine: **Drug Use, Non-Medical; Medical Drug Abuse; Organized Crime; Smuggling**
coccidia: **Animal Agriculture**
Cochand, Emile: **Skiing**
Cochand, Louis: **Cross-Country Skiing; Skiing**
cochineal: **Insect, Beneficial**
Cochran, William: **Magazines**
Cochrane, Francis: **Cochrane, Ont**
Cochrane, Matthew H.: **Cochrane, Alta; Ranching History**
Cochrane Enterprises Ltd: **Cochrane, Ont**
Cochrane Ranch: **Cochrane, Alta**
Cochrane River: **Reindeer Lake; Wollaston Lake**
Cochrane Times: **Cochrane, Alta**
Cockcroft, John: **Industrial Research & Development**
Cocke, Emmanuel: **Popular Literature in French**
Cocking, George: **Drama in English**
Cocking, Matthew: **Exploration**
cocklebur: **Poisonous Plants**
Cockran, Reverend Mr: **Portage la Prairie**
Cockriell, V.J.R.: *Miller & Cockriell* **Case**
Cockshutt Plow Co: **Agricultural Implements**
Cocktail: **Popular Literature in French**
Codco Company: **Theatre, English-Language**
Codd's Patented Globe Stoppers: **Soft-Drink Industry**
code-breaking: **Stephenson, William Samuel**
Code for Hospital Operating Room Safety: **Safety Standards**

Code Napoléon: **Civil Code; Delict; Law**
codeine: **Medical Drug Abuse**
Coderre, Émile (Jean Narrache): **Poetry in French**
Coderre, Laurent: **Film Animation**
Codification Commission: **Civil Code**
codling moth: **Okanagan Valley**
Codman, Stephen: **Music History**
Codner, Nfld: **Conception Bay South**
Codroy Valley: **Newfoundland**
codtrap: **Fisheries History; Newfoundland**
Cody, BC: **New Denver**
Cody, Betty: **Breau, Lenny**
coffin: **Agricultural Implements; Forestry; Northwest Coast Indian Art**
Coffin, Isaac: **Grande Entrée, Île de; Madeleine, Iles de la**
Coffin, Wilbert: *R v Coffin*
Coffin Island: **Grande Entrée, Île de**
Coghill, Joy: **Theatre for Young Audiences; Vancouver Playhouse**
Cohen, Gerald: **Philosophy**
Cohen, H. Robert: **Musicology**
Cohen, Joseph: **National War Labour Board**
Cohen, Sorel: **Art, Contemporary Trends**
Co-Incidences: **Literature in French - Scholarship & Teaching**
coke: **Bitumen; Chemical Industries; Chemistry; Coal; Energy in Society; Fraser, Graham; Iron & Steel Industry; Metallurgy**
Colborne Lodge: **Architectural Styles; Howard, John George**
cold front: **Thunderstorm**
Cold Mountain Group: **Poetry in English**
cold sore: **Virus**
Coldstream, BC: **Vernon**
Coldwater River: **Merritt**
Coldwell, William: **Print Industry**
cole: **Cabbage; Cauliflower; Kale; Kohlrabi**
Cole, James: **Furniture, Country**
Cole, T.J.: **Flowers, Cultivated**
Cole Harbour, NS: **Furniture, Country**
Colebrook, Colin: **Almighty Voice**
Coleman, A.P.: **Geomorphology; Parks, William Arthur**
Coleman, Jim: **Television Programming**
Coleman, Kathleen (Kit) Blake: **Canadian Women's Press Club; Journalism**
Coleman, Layne: **25th Street Theatre**
Coleman Fare Box Co: **Toys & Games**
Coles Book Stores Ltd: **Authors & Their Milieu; Southam Inc**
Coleson Cove: **New Brunswick**
Colicos, John: **Stratford Festival**
Colinet Harbour: **St Mary's Bay**
Colisée de Québec: **Beliveau, Jean; Québec Nordiques**
Collaborating Centre for Ground & Surface Water Quality: **Canada Centre for Inland Waters**
collards: **Vegetable**
collared lemming: **Arctic Animals; Devon Island; Lemming**
collateral: **Interest; Pawnbroking**
Collectors, The: **Chilliwack**
Collège de Hearst: **Laurentian University**
Collège de Longueil: **Marie-Victorin, Frère**
Collège de Montréal: **School Facilities**
Collège de Nicolet: **Demers, Jérôme; La Flèche, Louis-François**
Collège de Québec: **Charlevoix, Pierre-François-Xavier de; Education, History of; Libraries; Lighting; Philosophy; Québec**
Collège de Saint-Hyacinthe: **Maguire, Thomas**
Collège de St-Laurent: **Legault, Émile**
Collège des Jésuites: **Séminaire de Québec**
Collège des médecins et chirurgiens de la Province de Québec: **Associations**
Collège du Québec: **Classics**
Collège du Sacré-Coeur: **Caraquet; Theatre, French-Language; Université de Moncton**
Collège du Sacré-Coeur (Sudbury): **Laurentian University**
Collège et Grand Séminaire de Montréal: **Marchand, Jean-Omer**
Collège Jean-de-Brébeuf: *Amérique française*

Collège militaire royale: **Military & Staff Colleges**
Collège Notre-Dame: **Automatistes**
College of Bytown: **University of Ottawa**
College of Family & Consumer Studies: **Home Economics**
College of Family Physicians of Canada: **Medical Education; Medicine, General Practice**
College of Fisheries, Navigation, Marine Engineering & Electronics: **St John's**
College of New Brunswick: **University of New Brunswick**
College of Ottawa: **University of Ottawa**
College of Physicians & Surgeons of Lower Canada: **Medicine, History of; Worthington, Edward Dagge**
College of Physicians & Surgeons of Ontario: **Associations; Medicine, History of**
College of Physicians & Surgeons of Québec: **Ophthalmology**
College of Physicians & Surgeons of Upper Canada: **Medicine, History of**
College of Trades & Technology: **Pharmacy; St John's**
Collège St-Anne: **Theatre, French-Language**
Collège Ste-Anne de la Pocatière: **Casgrain, Henri-Raymond**
Collège St-Jean: **University of Alberta**
Collège Saint-Joseph (NB): **Theatre, French-Language; Université de Moncton**
Collège Saint-Joseph (Qué): **Arthabaska**
Collège Saint-Louis: **Edmundston; Université de Moncton**
Collège Sainte-Marie: **Concordia University**
Collège universitaire de St-Boniface: **Manitoba; St-Boniface; Theatre, French-Language; University of Manitoba; Winnipeg**
Collegiate Training, White Paper on (Qué): **Collège d'enseignement général et professionnel**
collembola (springtail & snowflea): **Devon Island; Insect Classification**
Collette, Jean-Yves: *Barre du jour*; **Literary Prizes in French**
Colley, Peter: **Blyth Festival; Theatre, English-Language**
Collier-Macmillan Award: **Literary Prizes in English**
Collin, William Edwin: **Literature in English - Teaching; Poetry in English**
Collingwood Shipyards: **Lake Carriers; Shipbuilding & Ship Repair**
Collingwood skiff: **Mackinaw Boat**
Collins, Henry B.: **Archaeology**
Collins Bay: **Kingston**
Collins Bay penitentiary: **Prison**
Collinson, Richard: **Arctic Exploration; Franklin Search; McClure (M'Clure), Robert J. Le M.**
Colmer, J.G.: **Exploration & Travel Literature in English**
Colonel Foster, Mount: **Vancouver Island**
Colonial Advocate: **Mackenzie, William Lyon; Newspapers**
Colonial & Continental Church Soc: **Anglicanism**
Colonial Building: **Purcell, James**
Colonial Patriot: **McCulloch, Thomas**
Colonial Pearl: **Literary Magazines in English; Photography**
Colonial Standard: **Holmes, Simon Hugh**
Colonial Stock Company: **Moore, Dora Mavor**
Colonial Tavern: **Jazz**
Colonisateur: **Chapleau, J.-Adolphe; Mousseau, Joseph-Alfred**
Colonization & Mines, Dept of (Qué): **Prospecting**
Colonna, Edward: **Railway Station**
Colony Gardens: **Ross, Alexander (1783-1856)**
Coloured Women's Club: **West Indians**
Colpoys Bay: **Bruce Peninsula; Wiarton**
Colter, J.S.: **Biochemistry**
Coltman, Derek: *Saison dans la vie d'Emmanuel*
columbarium: **Cemeteries**

Columbia, Mount: **Columbia Icefield; Saskatchewan River**
Columbia Forest: **Forest Regions**
Columbia Lake: **Columbia River**
Columbia Lake Reserve: **Kootenay**
Columbia Plateau: **Native People - Plateau; Prehistory**
Columbian Orogeny: **Geological Regions**
columbite: **Columbium**
Columbus: **Orléans, Ile d'; Sailing Ships; Shipbuilding & Ship Repair**
Colville, Admiral: **Northumberland Strait**
Colville, Andrew: **Nanaimo**
Colville Lake, NWT: **Hare (Indians)**
Colville Town, BC: **Nanaimo**
comb jelly: **Invertebrate; Zooplankton**
Combat: **Hénault, Gilles**
combine: **Agricultural Implements Industry; Agriculture History; Cereal Crops**
Combined Atlantic Universities Parliament: **Mulroney, M. Brian**
Combined Jewish Appeal: **Judaism**
Combines Investigation Act: **Competition Policy; White-Collar Crime**
combines legislation: **Media Ownership**
Combustion: **Literary Magazines in English; Souster, Raymond**
Comeau, Germaine: **Theatre, French-Language**
Comeau, Napoléon-Alexandre: **Baie-Comeau**
comics: **Foster, Harold; Magazines; Popular Literature in French**
Cominco Ltd: **Canadian Pacific Railway; Castlegar; Chemical Industries; Pine Point; Vancouver; Zinc**
Cominco Products Inc: **Kimberley; Stavert, Reuben Ewart**
Comité catholique de l'instruction publique: **Book Publishing, French-Language**
Commanderies de Bordeaux: **Cuisine**
Commerce Court: **Urban Design**
Commercial Bank of Canada: **Bank Architecture**
Commercial Bank of Kingston: **Galt, Alexander T.**
Commercial Bank of the Midland Dist: **Bank of Upper Canada**
Commercial Block: **Hamilton**
Commercial Graduates Basketball Club: **Edmonton Grads**
Commercial Intelligence Service: **Wilgress, L. Dana**
comminution: **Metallurgy**
Commission de la pièce canadienne: **Drama in French**
Commission de la santé et de la sécurité au travail: **Québec**
Commission de transport de la communauté urbaine de Montréal: **Montréal**
Commission d'enquête sur l'enseignement au Québec: **Sociology**
Commission of Collegiate Instruction: **Collège d'enseignement général et professionnel**
Commission of Indian Lands: **Ethnic & Race Relations**
Commission on Election Contributions & Expenses (Ont): **Party Financing**
Commission on Freedom of Information & Individual Privacy: **Economic Regulation**
Commission sacerdotale d'études sociales: **Catholicism; Dion, Gérard**
commissioner: **Campbell, Hugh Lester; Hodgson, Stuart M.; Northwest Territories; Territorial Government; Yukon Territory**
Commissioner of Official Languages: **Ombudsman**
Commissioners of Internal Economy: **Speaker**
Committee Bay: **Melville Peninsula; Netsilik Inuit**
Committee for Industrial Organization: **Oshawa Strike**
Committee for the Original People's Entitlement: **Inuit Tapirisat of Canada; Land Claims**
Committee of Progressive Electors: **City Politics; Vancouver**
Committee of Trade: **Montréal**
Committee on Mind Abuse: **New Religious Movements**

Committee on the Constitution: **Heraldry Society of Canada**
Committee on the Status of Endangered Wildlife in Canada: **Canadian Nature Federation; Canadian Wildlife Federation; Endangered Animals; Sturgeon**
Committee on Trade & Economic Affairs: **Canadian-American Economic Relations**
Committee's Punch Bowl: **Athabasca Pass**
commode: **Furniture, French**
Common, Tommy: **Television Programming**
common barberry: **Weeds**
common carrier: **Cable Television; Media Ownership; Transportation**
common cleaver: **Vegetation Regions - Pacific Coastal**
Common Front: **Pepin, Marcel**
common-law relationship: **Family Law**
common milkweed: **Botany History; Milkweed**
Common School Acts (Province of Canada): **Education, History of**
Common Schools Act (NB): **Hanington, Daniel Lionel; Hatheway, George Luther; King, George Edwin; New Brunswick; New Brunswick School Question**
common shares: **Corporation Law; Stock & Bond Markets**
common shrew: **Terra Nova National Park**
common snowberry: **Vegetation Regions - Cordillera**
common squid: **Fisheries**
common western painted turtle: **Okanagan Valley; Turtle**
Commonwealth Day: **Empire Day; National Holidays**
Commonwealth International Corp: **Vaughan, Robert Charles**
Commonwealth International Leverage Fund Ltd: **Vaughan, Robert Charles**
Commonwealth Scientific Conference: **Monture, Gilbert C.**
Commonwealth Stadium: **Edmonton**
Commonwealth Eskimos
Commonwealth Standing Committee on Student Mobility: **Symons, Thomas H.B.**
Communauté régionale de l'Outaouais: **Hull**
commune: **Bengough, John W.; Collectivism; Dumont, Gabriel; Hippies; Hutterites; Verigin, Peter V.**
Communication-Jeunesse: **Children's Literature in French**
Communications, Dept of (Qué): **Communications in Québec**
Communications & Electronics Warfare: **Astronaut**
communications museum: **Heart's Content**
Communications Research Centre: **Physics; Space Technology**
Communications Technology Satellite: **Satellite Communications; Space Technology**
communion (Eucharist): **Baptists; Catholicism; Christianity**
communion plate: **Silver, Church**
communism: **Buhay, Rebecca; Labour Organizations; Padlock Act; Rose, Fred**
Community & Cultural Affairs, Dept of (PEI): **Prince Edward Island**
Community Council: **Manitoba**
Community Employment Strategy: **Labour Policy**
Community Folk Art Council: **Manitoba**
Community of the Sisters of the Church: **Christian Religious Communities**
community pasture: **Drought; Prairie Farm Rehabilitation Administration; Vegetation Regions - Prairie**
Community Planning Assn of Canada: **Urban & Regional Planning**
Community Services & Corrections, Dept of (Man): **Manitoba**
commuter train: **Locomotives & Rolling Stock; Railways, Contemporary**
Como, Qué: **Shepherd, Francis John**
Comox: **Courtenay; Northern Georgia Strait Coast Salish**

Comox, CFB: **Comox, BC; Courtenay**
Comox Glacier: **Comox, BC**
Comox harbour: **Comox, BC**
Comox Reserve: **Northern Georgia Strait Coast Salish**
Comox Valley: **Comox, BC**
Compagnie assomption mutuelle d'assurance-vie: **New Brunswick**
Compagnie d'assurances générales: **Lévesque, Jean-Louis**
Compagnie de la colonie: **Beauharnois, François de; Compagnie du Nord**
Compagnie de la Nouvelle France: **L'Orignal; Nova Scotia; Orléans, Ile d'**
Compagnie de pulpe de Chicoutimi: **Chicoutimi**
Compagnie de sucre de betterave de Québec: **Sugar Industry**
Compagnie dei Giovani: **Theatre, Multicultural**
Compagnie Denault Ltée: **Turmel, Antoine**
Compagnie du Masque: **Drama in French**
Compagnie du St-Sacrement: **Lalemant, Charles**
Compagnons de la danse: **Gradus, Lawrence**
Compagnons de Saint-Laurent: **Gascon, Jean; Legault, Emile; Theatre, French-Language; Theatre Education**
Companies Act (Alta): **Corporation Law**
Company of Adventurers to the New Found Land: **English**
Company of Canadian Volunteers: **Willcocks, Joseph**
Company of Young Canadians: **Dunn, William L.; New Left; Poverty**
compensation: **Delict; Gore, Francis; Juvenile Justice Systems; Torts; Violence**
competition: **Cable Television; Competition Policy; Media Ownership**
Composers, Authors & Publishers Assn of Canada: **Music History; Recording Industry**
Comprehensive Development Plan: **Campbell, Alexander Bradshaw; Prince Edward Island**
Compton effect: **Gray, Joseph Alexander**
computer fraud: **Policing**
Computer Innovations Distribution Inc: **Electronics Industry**
computer literacy: **Business Education; Computer Science**
computer music: **Electroacoustic Music**
Computing & Data Processing Assn of Canada: **Computer Science; Gotlieb, C.C., "Kelly"**
Computing Devices of Canada: **Computer Science**
Comtean positivism: **LeSueur, William Dawson**
Comus Music Theatre Foundation of Canada: **Charpentier, Gabriel**
Conan, Laure: **Angers, Félicité**
conch shell: **Linear Mounds; Seashell**
conchology: **Seashell; Taylor, George William**
conciliation: **Collective Bargaining; King, W.L. Mackenzie; Labour Canada; Labour Law; Labour Mediation; Public Service**
Concord grape: **Wine Industry**
Concordia College: **Lutherans**
Concours artistiques du Québec: **Comtois, Ulysse; Daudelin, Charles**
Concours de l'Ile: **Little Theatre Movement**
Concours des jeunes auteurs: **Tremblay, Michel**
Concours d'estampe et de dessin québecois: **Printmaking**
Concours international de musique de Montréal: **Morel, François**
Concours littéraires du Québec: **Bessette, Gerard; Literary Prizes in French**
concrete: **Architecture, Development; Bridges; Cement Industry; Construction Industry, History; Grain Elevators; Quarrying Industry; Roads & Highways**
Condé, Carol: **Art, Contemporary Trends**
conditional discharge: **Criminal Law; Royal Prerogative of Mercy**

Conditional Sales: **Commercial Law**
Cone, William Vernon: **Penfield, Wilder G.**
cone flower: **Wildflowers**
Conefroy, Abbé: **Art; Religious Building**
Conestoga College of Applied Arts & Technology: **Cambridge; Furniture & Fixture Industry; Kitchener-Waterloo**
Conestoga wagon: **Roads & Highways**
Coney, Michael G.: **Popular Literature in English**
Confederacy of Nations: **Assembly of First Nations**
Confederation Centre of the Arts: **Architecture; Charlottetown; Fox, John Richard; Harris, Robert; Prince Edward Island**
Confederation College of Applied Arts & Technology: **Thunder Bay**
Confederation Day: **Canada Day**
Confédération des six-comtés: **St-Charles-sur-Richelieu**
Confédération des syndicats nationaux: **Laberge, Louis; Pepin, Marcel; Picard, Gérard**
Confédération des travailleurs catholiques du Canada: **Charpentier, Alfred; Confederation of National Trade Unions; Corporatism; Dion, Gérard; Marchand, Jean; Murdochville Strike; Pelletier, Gérard; Picard, Gérard; Sauvé, Maurice; Social Doctrine of the Roman Catholic Church**
Confederation Diamond Jubilee Medal: **Medal**
Confederation for Tomorrow Conference: **Ontario**
Confederation League: **Beaven, Robert; Walkem, George Anthony**
Confederation Life Insurance Co: **Insurance**
Confédération mondiale du travail: **Pepin, Marcel**
Confederation of Canadian Unions: **Labour Relations; Parent, Madeleine**
Confederation of Democratic Unions: **Union Centrals, Québec**
Confederation of Free Trade Unions: **Millard, Charles Hibbert**
Confederation Poets: **Literature in English; Oral Literature in English; Poetry in English**
Confederation Square: **National Holidays; Ottawa, Ont; Public Art**
Conference of Canadian Artists: **Biéler, André Charles**
Conference of Eastern British America: **Methodism**
Conference on Quality of Legal Services: **Legal Education**
Conference on the Canadian Novel: **Authors & Their Milieu**
Conference on the Operation of Dominion Legislation: **Statute of Westminster**
confession of sin: **Catholicism; Handsome Lake Religion; Shaker Religion**
Confidence: **Horse**
confidence games: **Crime**
Confidentiality of Health Information, Royal Commission of Inquiry into the (Ont): **Privacy**
conformation shows: **Dog**
Confucianism: **Buddhism; Koreans**
Congdon, H.S.: **Maritime Rights**
congé: **Fur Trade**
congregation: **Christian Religious Communities**
Congrégation de Notre-Dame: **Book Publishing, French-Language; Bourgeoys, Marguerite; Christian Religious Communities; Education, History of; Marchand, Jean-Omer; Pewter**
Congrégation des hospitalières de Saint-Joseph: **Christian Religious Communities**
Congregation of St-Pierre de Solesme: **St-Benoit-du-Lac**
Congregation of the Holy Cross: **André, Brother; Christian Religious Communities**
Congrès de la langue français: **Intellectual History**

Congress of Industrial Organizations: **AFL-CIO; Bedford Magazine Explosion; Canadian Congress of Labour; Communist Party of Canada; Craft Unionism; Hamilton; Hepburn, Mitchell F.; Industrial Unionism; Jackson, Clarence Shirley; Revolutionary Industrial Unionism**
Congress of the International Student's Federation: **World University Games**
Conibear, Frank: **Fur Trapping, Contemporary**
Conjuring society: **Kootenay**
Conjuror Bay: **Great Bear Lake**
Connaught Cup: **Soccer**
Connaught Park Raceway: **Filion, Hervé**
Connaught Tunnel: **Rogers Pass; Tunnels**
Conne River, Nfld: **Bay d'Espoir**
Connell Brothers: **Agricultural Implements**
Connelly, Patricia: **Marxism**
Conners, I.L.: **Newton, Margaret**
Connecticut River: **Boundaries**
Connolly, Amelia: **Douglas, James (1803-77)**
Connolly, Joseph: **Guelph**
Connolly, Thomas L.: **London Conference**
Connolly, William: **Douglas, James (1803-77)**
Connor, Douglas: **Bobsledding**
Connor, Ralph: **Gordon, Charles W.**
Conomos, Dimitri: **Musicology**
Conrad Grebel College: **University of Waterloo**
Conroy, George: **Catholicism**
conscientious objector: **Franchise; Germans; Pacifism**
Conscrits, Mont des: **Laurentian Highlands**
Conseil Attikameg-Montagnais du Québec: **Attikamek; Land Claims; Montagnais-Naskapi**
Conseil central des syndicats nationaux de Montréal: **Chartrand, Michel**
Conseil de la gravure: **Artists' Organizations**
Conseil de la sculpture: **Artists' Organizations**
Conseil des arts et manufactures: **Art Education; Cullen, Maurice G.; Dyonnet, Edmond; Franchere, Joseph-Charles; Hébert, L.-Philippe; Jackson, A.Y.; Laliberté, Alfred (artist); Raphael, William; Saint-Charles, Joseph**
Conseil des métiers et du travail de Montréal: **Francq, Gustave; Laberge, Louis; Verville, Alphonse**
Conseil des ministres: **Québec**
Conseil d'expansion économique: **Québec**
Conseil régional du travail: **Barrette, Antonio J.**
Conseil supérieur de la coopération: **Lévesque, Georges-Henri**
Conseil supérieur du livre: **Book Publishing, French-Language**
Conseil supérieur du travail: **Charpentier, Alfred**
Conservation Assistance Programme: **Conservation of Movable Cultural Property**
Conservatoire d'art dramatique: **Drama in French; Theatre Education**
Conservatoire de musique de l'Outaouais: **Hull**
Conservatoire de musique du Québec: **Music History; Pelletier, Wilfrid; Pépin, Clermont; Prus, Victor Marius; Tremblay, Gilles**
Conservatoire de musique du Québec à Montréal: **Aubut, Françoise; Champagne, Claude**
Conservatoire de musique et d'art dramatique: **Music Education**
Consolidated Bank: **Banking**
Consolidated-Bathurst Inc: **Anticosti, Ile d'; La Baie; New Brunswick; Power Corp of Canada; Sauvé, Maurice; Shawinigan**
Consolidated Computer Inc: **Electronics Industry**
Consolidated Mining & Smelting Co of Canada Ltd: **Kimberley; Nuclear Energy; Shaughnessy, Thomas G.; Stavert, Reuben Ewart; Trail**

Consolidated Revenue Fund: **Farm Credit Corp**
Consolidated Rubber Co: **Toys & Games**
Constantine, Charles: **Gold Rushes**
Constantineau, Gilles: **Poetry in French**
constituency: **Elections; Electoral Systems; House of Commons; Member of Parliament; North-West Territories Act; Political Campaign; Redistribution**
Constitution of Canada, Special Committee on the: **Canadian Charter of Rights & Freedoms**
constitutional amendments: *Constitution* **Reference; Constitution Act, 1982; Distribution of Powers; Forsey, Eugene A.; Provincial Government**
"Constitutional Express": **Native People, Political Organization & Activism**
constitutional monarchy: **Constitutional Law; Monarchism; Sovereign**
Consultative Group on Disarmament: **Voice of Women**
Consumer Packaging & Labelling Act: **Consumer Law; Metric Conversion; Soft-Drink Industry**
consumer protection: **Delict; Economic Regulation**
Consumers Cordage Co Ltd: **Stairs, John Fitz-William**
Consumers' Gas Co of Toronto: **Hiram Walker Resources Ltd**
Consumers Glass Co Ltd: **Glass**
Contact Press: **Layton, Irving P.; Poetry in English; Small Presses**
containerization: **Locomotives & Rolling Stock; Montréal; Nova Scotia; Transportation**
Contant, Alexis: **Chamber Music; Music History; Pelletier, Wilfrid**
Contarini map: **Cartography, History of**
Contel: **Torstar Corp**
Contemporary Quebec Criticism: *Littérature qui se fait*
contempt of court: **Law & the Press**
contempt of Parliament: **House of Commons**
Content: **Journalism**
content tax: **Magazines**
continental drift: **Plate Tectonics**
Continental Ranges: **Vermilion River**
continental shelves: **Arctic Archipelago; Beringia; Brachiopoda; CESAR; Earthquake; Fundy, Bay of/Gulf of Maine; Geological Regions; Geology; Georges Bank; Grand Banks; *Hibernia* Case; Mineral Resources; Ocean; Petroleum Supply & Demand; Scotian Shelf; Wave Energy**
Continuing Committee on Economic & Fiscal Matters: **Federal-Provincial Relations**
continuous-passage regulation: **South Asians**
contraceptives: **Birth Control; Medical Ethics; Safety Standards; Welfare State; Women's Movement**
contract: **Apprenticeship in Early Canada; Calumet; Commercial Law; Insurance; Notary; Seigneurial System; Solicitor; Transportation; Work**
contract killing: **Organized Crime**
contracting-out: **Opting-Out**
Contrecoeur, Qué: **Iron & Steel Industry; Sidbec-Dosco Limitée**
Contrecoeur, Sieur de: **Fort Duquesne**
Control Data Canada Ltd: **Computer-Assisted Learning**
controller: **Municipal Government**
Controller General: **Treasury Board**
Contwoyto Lake: **Back River**
convection: **Lake; Plate Tectonics**
Convention of 1818: **Territorial Evolution**
Convention of Forty: **Boyd, Alfred**
Convention of London: **Forty-ninth Parallel**
Convention of the Metre: **Weights & Measures**
Convention on International Civil Aviation: **Air Law & Space Law**

Convention on International Trade in Endangered Species: **Endangered Animals; Endangered Plants; Wildlife Conservation & Management**
"conventions of the constitution": **Constitution; Constitution, Patriation of; Constitution Act, 1867**
Convergence: **Adult Education**
conversion: **Torts**
conveyor: **Farm Silo; Quarrying Industry; Transportation**
Convocation Hall (U of T): **Hart House String Quartet**
convoy escort: **Armed Forces; World War II**
Conway, NS: **Digby**
cony: **Pika**
Cook, Ephraim: **Mahone Bay**
Cook, F.J. "Bun": **Boucher, Frank; International Hockey Hall of Fame**
Cook, Michael: **Drama in English; Festival Lennoxville; Literature in English; Theatre, English-Language; Theatre, Multicultural**
Cook, Myrtle: **Track & Field**
Cook, Peter: **Business History**
Cook, Ramsay: *Canadian Forum; Canadian Historical Review;* **Historiography; Intellectual History**
Cook, Stanley: **Estrogen**
Cook, Stephen: **Mathematics**
Cook, Wendy: **Swimming, Speed**
cookbooks: **Cuisine; Popular Literature in English**
Cooke, H.C.: **Geomorphology**
cooking oil: **Canola; Oilseed Crops; Soybean; Sunflower**
Cooks Bay: **Holland Marsh**
Cook's Ferry, BC: **Cariboo Road**
Cook's Tavern: **Upper Canada Village**
Coombs store: **Architecture, Development**
Coop vidéo de Montréal: **Video Art**
Cooper, Dorith: **Musicology**
Cooper, J.I.: **Working-Class History**
Cooper, John A.: **Literature in English - Theory & Criticism**
Cooper, Robert: **Toronto Mendelssohn Choir**
Cooper Canada Ltd: **Industrial Design**
cooperage: **Forestry; Tools, Carpentry**
Coopératio: **Film**
Co-operative College of Canada: **Saskatoon**
co-operative federalism: **Dominion-Provincial Relations, Royal Commission on**
Co-operative Fédérée: **Co-operative Movement (See Addendum, page 1992)**
Co-operative government: **Anderson, James Thomas Milton; Saskatchewan**
Co-operative Movement: **See Addendum, page 1992**
Co-operative on Information Technology: **Gotlieb, C.C., "Kelly"**
Co-operative Union of Canada: **Co-operative Movement (See Addendum, page 1992); Good, William Charles; Keen, George; MacDonald, Angus Bernard**
Co-operative Vegetable Oils Ltd: **Siemens, Jacob John**
Coopers Cove: **Cupids**
Cooper's hawk: **Endangered Animals; Hawk**
Coote, G.C.: **Ginger Group**
Cope, E.D.: **Paleontology, History in Canada**
Copeland, Royal: **Krol, Joseph**
copepoda: **Crustacean**
Copers Cove: **Cupids**
Copp, Terry: **Working-Class History**
copper bush: **Vegetation Regions - Cordillera**
Copper Cliff, Ont: **Agnew, John Lyons; Italians; Metallurgy; Resource Towns; Sulphur**
Copper Cliff Museum: **Sudbury**
Copper Indians: **Yellowknife (Redknives, Copper)**
Coptic Orthodox Church: **Arabs; Canadian Council of Churches; Funeral Practices; Orthodox Church**
Coquihalla Canyon: **Hope**
Coquitlam Mountain: **Coquitlam**

Coquitlam River: **Port Coquitlam**
Corbeil, Claude: **Opera; Singing**
Corbeil, Ont: **Dionne Quintuplets**
Corbin Mine: **Coal**
Corcoran, Terence: *Financial Times*
cordgrass: **Vegetation Regions - Coastal Marine Flora**
cordite: **Distilling Industry**
Cordova Bay: **Saanich Peninsula**
corduroy road: **Roads & Highways; Technology**
Corea, Antonio: **Italian Writing**
coriander: **Condiment Crops**
Coriolis effect: **Wind**
cork elm: **Biogeography**
Corkery, J.C.: **Postal System**
Cormier, Bruno: **Automatistes**; *Refus Global*
Cormier, Charlotte: **Musicology**
Cormorant Lake: **Alert Bay**
Cormus Music Theatre: **Opera**
corn borer: **Insect Pests**
corn syrup: **Sugar Industry**
corneal transplant: **Ophthalmology**
Cornelius, Julius: **Silver, Domestic**
Corner Brook Western Star: **Newfoundland**
Cornplanter Medal: **Trigger, Bruce G.**
Cornut, Jacques Philippe: **Floras & Botanical Journals**
Cornwall, Clement: **Ashcroft**
Cornwall, Henry: **Ashcroft**
Cornwall, PEI: **Charlottetown**
Cornwall & York, Duchess of (Queen Mary): **Notman, William McFarlane; Royal Tours**
Cornwall & York, Duke of (George V): **Notman, William McFarlane; Royal Tours**
Cornwall Canal: **Canals & Inland Waterways**
Cornwall *Freeholder*: **Lalonde, É., "Newsy"**
Cornwallis, William: **Cornwallis Island**
Cornwallis Belt: **Mineral Resources**
Cornwallis River: **Annapolis Lowlands; Kentville**
corona: **Sun**
Coronation Futurity: **Northern Dancer**
Coronation Games: **Kerr, Robert**
Coronation Gulf: **Alikomiak**
Coronation Medal: **Strickland, Edgar Harold**
Coronelli, Vincenzo: **Cartography, History of**
corporal punishment: **Student Rights**
corporate crime: **White-Collar Crime**
corporate elite: **Business Elites; Journalism**
corporate income tax: **Equalization Payments; New Brunswick; Nova Scotia; Roblin, Rodmond P.; Utilities**
"corporate welfare bums": **Lewis, David**
corporation: **Advertising; Consumer & Corporate Affairs, Dept of; Farm Law**
Corporation canadienne des sciences religieuses: **Religion**
Corporation de la vieille pulperie: **Chicoutimi**
Corporation des éditions fides: *Anciens Canadiens*; **Book Publishing, French-Language; Children's Literature in French**; *Encyclopedia of Music in Canada*
Corporation des enseignants du Québec: **Teaching Profession**
Corporation des urbanistes du Québec: **Urban & Regional Planning**
Corporation générale des instituteurs et des institutrices catholiques de la Province du Québec: **Gaudreault, Laure; Teaching Profession**
Corporation professionnelle des psychologues du Québec: **Psychology**
Corporations Acts: **Corporation Law; Farm Law**
corpse plant: **Indian Pipe**
Corpus Almanac of Canada: **Popular Literature in English**
correctional centre: **Prison**
Correctional Investigator: **Ombudsman**
Correctional Services of Canada: **Prison; Solicitor General, Dept of**
correspondence schools: **Athabasca University; Distance Learning; Simon Fraser University; Veterinary Medicine, History**

"Corridart": **Art, Contemporary Trends; Charney, Melvin; Public Art**
Corriere Canadese: **Italians**
Corriere Italiano: **Italians**
Corriveau, Hugues: *Barre du jour*
Corriveau, Joseph: *La Corriveau*
Corriveau, Monique: **Children's Literature in French**
Cort, John: **Newcastle**
Corte-Real, Joao Vaz: **Portuguese**
Cortes Island: **Northern Georgia Strait Coast Salish**
cortisone: **Endangered Plants**
cortusa: **Flowers, Cultivated**
corundum: **Mineral**
Corvée: **Theatre, French-Language**
corvette: **Shipbuilding & Ship Repair**
Cosgrove & Co: **Toys & Games**
cosmetics: **Consumer Standards; Soapstone**
cosmic ray: **Physics**
COSPAS satellite: **Space Technology**
cost-price squeeze: **Agriculture & Food Policy**
cost sharing: **Health Policy; Legal Aid; Social & Welfare Services**
Costain, C.C.: **Physics**
Costello Mine: **Coal**
Côté, Cyrille: **Lower Canada; Rebellions of 1837**
Cote, Gerard: **Long-Distance Running**
Côté, J.B.: **Folk Art**
Côté, Maryse: **Children's Literature in French**
Côté, P.M.: **Architectural Styles**
Côte de Beaupré, Qué: **Furniture, French**
Côte-des-Neiges, Qué: **Houde, Camillien; Medicine, History of**
Côte St-Paul, Qué: **Evans, William**
Coteau-du-Lac, Qué: **Engineering; Indian Art**
Cotnam, Jacques: **Essay in French**
Cotnoir, Louise: *Barre du jour*
Cotroni, Frank: **Organized Crime**
Cotroni, Vincenzo: **Organized Crime**
cottage hospital: **Newfoundland; Victorian Order of Nurses**
cotton: **Crafts; Magog; Occupational Disease; Pulp & Paper Industry; Textile Industry; Valleyfield**
Cotton, John: **Printmaking**
cottonwood: **Plants, Native Uses; Poplar; Vegetation Regions - Eastern Temperate Forests**
Couchiching, Lake: **Couchiching Conference; Orillia; Simcoe, Lake; Trent Canal**
Coudari, Camille: **Chess**
Coughlin, Angela: **Swimming, Speed**
Coulonge, Rivière: **Ottawa River**
Coulthard, Jean: **Choral Music; Musicology; Songs & Songwriting**
Council for Business & the Arts: **Music Awards & Competitions; Theatre, English-Language**
Council for Exceptional Children: **Education, Special**
Council for Yukon Indians: **Land Claims; Yukon Territory**
Council of Assiniboia: **McKay, James**
Council of Canadian Filmmakers: **Pearson, Peter**
Council of Colleges: **Collège d'enseignement général et professionnel**
Council of Federal Libraries: **Libraries**
Council of Forest Industries of BC: **Hoffmeister, Bertram Meryl**
Council of Maritime Premiers: **Federal-Provincial Relations; New Brunswick; New Brunswick Research & Productivity Council; Property Law**
Council of Ontario Universities: **Ryerson Polytechnical Institute**
Council of Public Instruction (Qué): **Chauveau, Pierre-Joseph-Olivier; Separate School**
Council of the Guild of Sculptors: **Artists' Organizations**
Council of the North-West Territories: **McKay, James**
Council of Tribes: **Native People, Political Organization & Activism**
Council on Uniform Traffic Control Devices: **Roads & Transportation Association of Canada**

councillor: **City Politics; Prince Edward Island**
counselling: **Career Counselling; Child Welfare; Community College; Distance Learning; Juvenile Delinquency**
counterculture: **Hippies; Literary Periodicals in French; Novel in English; Popular Literature in French; Wolfville**
counterespionage: **Stephenson, William Samuel**
counterfeiting: **Crime**
countertrade: **Barter**
country-born: **Métis; Red River Rebellion**
Country Guide: *Grain Growers' Guide*
Country Harbour: **Piracy**
country marriage: **Métis**
"country party": **Nova Scotia**
county courts: **Courts of Law; New Westminster; Nova Scotia**
County of Strathcona Building: **Janvier, Alex S.**
Courchene, Thomas J.: **Economics**
Courier du Canada: **Langevin, Hector-L.**
Cournoyer, Yvan: **Canada-Soviet Hockey Series, 1972**
Courrier: **Tardivel, Jules-Paul**
Courrier de Sorel: **Guèvremont, Germaine**
Courrier du Bas-Canada: **Literature in French - Criticism & Theory**
court injunction: **Delict**
court martial: *Mackay Case*
Court Martial Appeal Court: **Courts of Law**
court of appeal: **Civil Procedure; Constitution, Patriation of; Courts of Law; Official Secrets Act**
Court of Error & Appeal (Ont): **Draper, William Henry**
Court of King's Bench: **Constitutional History**
Court of Quarter Sessions: **Kingston**
Court of Queen's Bench: **Abortion; Courts of Law; Small Claims Court**
court of sessions: **Nova Scotia 1714-84**
Court of Vice Admiralty: **Privateering**
Courtaulds (Canada) Ltd: **Textile Industry**
Courtenay, George William: **Courtenay**
Courtney Bay: *Marco Polo*; **New Brunswick**
Courtois, Fredette et Cie: **Desmarais, Paul**
courtship: **Folk Dance; Marriage & Divorce, History of**
Couvrette et Provost: **Turmel, Antoine**
Cove Field: **Golf**
Cove Island: **Georgian Bay Islands National Park; Lighthouses**
Coverdale, NB: **Riverview**
covered bridge: **Bridges; Hartland**
cow: **Animal Agriculture; Beef Cattle Farming; Dairy Farming**
Cow Bay: **Coal**
cow-calf enterprise: **Beef Cattle Farming; Forage Crops**
cow lily: **Water Lily**
cow parsnip: **Plants, Native Uses**
Cowan, Ed: **Book Clubs**
Cowan, Peter: **Cowansville**
Cowan Chocolate Co, Ltd: **Confectionery Industry**
cowbird: **Blackbird**
Cowichan: **Duncan; Oral Literature in English**
Cowichan Lake: **Vancouver Island**
Cowichan River: **Duncan; Vancouver Island**
Cowichan sweater: **Northwest Coast Indian Art**
Cowin, Jack: **Printmaking**
Cowley, Reta: **Painting**
cowpox: **Biological Product; Virus**
Cox, Arthur: **Printmaking**
Cox, Kathy: **Parachuting, Sport**
Coxeter, Harold S.M.: **Mathematics**
Coy, Ed: **Track & Field**
Cozzens, John: **Exploration & Travel Literature in English**
CP Air: **Bata, Thomas J.; Canadian Pacific Railway**
CP Hotels Ltd: **Canadian Pacific Railway; Van Horne, William C.**
CP Oil & Gas Ltd: **Canadian Pacific Railway**
CP Rail: **Canadian Pacific Railway**
CP Ships: **Canadian Pacific Railway; Shipping Industry**
CP Transport: **Canadian Pacific Railway**

CPR charter: **Roblin, Rodmond P.**
CPR Folk Festivals: **MacMillan, Ernest C.; Music History**
crabgrass: **Biogeography**
Crackers, The: **Band, The**
Craig, Betty: **Rowing**
Craig, J.A.I.: **Lighting**
Craig, John: **Children's Literature in English**
Craig, Zeidler, Strong: **Architecture**
Craig Harbour: **Ellesmere Island**
Craig Street: **Nursing**
Craigdarroch Castle: **Dunsmuir, Robert**
Cran, Marion: **Exploration & Travel Literature in English**
cranberries: **Berries, Cultivated; Berries, Wild; British Columbia; Cuisine; Native People, Economic Conditions; Nova Scotia**
Cranberry River: **Nass River**
Cranbrook Mountain: **Cranbrook**
Crandall Award for Conservation: **Russell, Andy**
cranesbill: **Geranium**
Cranmer, Douglas: **Northwest Coast Indian Art**
Cranston, Toller: **Figure Skating**
craps: **Gambling**
Crate, Charles: **Dictionary**
crater: **Meteor, Meteorite, Impact Crater**
Crater Lake: **Chilkoot Pass**
craton: **Geological Regions; Shield**
Craven: **Troyes, Pierre de**
crawfish: **Crayfish**
Crawford, Alexander W.: **Literature in English - Teaching**
Crawford, M.F.: **Physics**
Crawford Lake: **Lake**
Crawley, Alan: *Contemporary Verse*
Crawley Films: **Crawley, F.R. "Budge"; Film Animation**
"Crazy Canucks": **Skiing**
Crazy-Dog Society: **Kootenay**
Crazy-Owl Society: **Kootenay**
CRCM: **Radio Drama, French-Language**
cream separator: **Agriculture History**
Cream Soda: **Soft-Drink Industry**
creameries: **Co-operative Movement (See Addendum, page 1992); Dairy Industry**
creamware: **Ceramics**
Crean, Paddy: **Theatre, English-Language**
creation & creationism: **Evolution; McKellar, Andrew; Science & Society**
credit: **Bank of Canada; Banking; Commercial Law; Computer Communications; Consumer Credit; Consumer Law; Farm Credit Corp; International Economics**
Crédit Interprovincial Ltée: **Lévesque, Jean-Louis**
Credit River: **Wine Industry**
Credit River Mission: **Sutton, Catherine**
Cree dialects: **Dictionary; Native People, Languages**
Cree dictionaries: **Ahenakew, Edward; Dictionary; Lacombe, Albert**
Cree Home Guard: **Métis**
Cree Lake, Sask: **Cree Lake**
Cree Regional Authority: **Diamond, Billy**
Cree River: **Cree Lake**
Creed, Samuel: **Furniture, Country**
Creeley, Robert: **Poetry in English**
Creelman, A.R.: **Beatty, Edward Wentworth**
creeping fern: **Biogeography**
creeping juniper: **Juniper; Strathcona Provincial Park; Vegetation Regions - Cordillera**
Crehen, Charles: **Printmaking**
Creighton, J.G.A.: **Hockey, Ice**
Creighton Mine: **Mining**
cremation: **Funeral Practices; Han**
Crémazie, Jacques: **Gallicanism**
Crescent Park: **Moose Jaw**
crest: **Bella Coola; Coppers; Emblems, Provincial & Territorial; Haida; Harris, Walter; Heraldry; Northwest Coast Indian Art; Raven Symbolism; Totem Pole; Victoria Cross**
Crest Theatre: **Drama in English; Gill, Robert**
crested wheatgrass: **Forage Crops; Kirk, Lawrence Eldred**

Creston, Nfld: **Marystown**
Creston Valley Wildlife
  Management Area: **Bird Sanctuaries
  & Reserves; Creston, BC**
Cretaceous period: **Bird Classification
  & Evolution; Bitumen; Dinosaur;
  Fly; Forest; Fossil Plants;
  Marsupialia; Paleontology;
  History in Canada; Petroleum;
  River Landform; Rush; St
  Lawrence Lowland;
  Sedimentary Rock; Trees**
Crevier, Gerald: **Ballet; Dance
  Education**
crib strangulation: **Injury &
  Prevention**
crime control: **Crime; Policing**
crime-detection labs: **Royal Canadian
  Mounted Police**
Crime Victims Compensation Act (Qué):
  Delict
criminal libel: **Journalism;
  Newspapers**
Crimson Beauty apple: **Sharp, Francis
  Peabody**
crimson clover: **Clover; Poisonous
  Plants**
Cringan, Alexander T.: **Music
  Education; Music History;
  Musicology**
crinoids: **Echinodermata**
Crippled Children's Centre: **St
  Catharines**
Cristo, Monte: **Arthabaska**
Critical Trade Skills Training: **Labour
  Policy**
Croc: **Popular Literature in French**
Croche, Rivière: **St-Maurice, Rivière**
crocidolite: **Asbestos**
crocodile: **Fossil Animals**
crocus: **Anemone; Flowers,
  Cultivated; Wildflowers**
Crofton, BC: **Vancouver Island**
Croke, Alexander: **Printmaking**
Cromie, Donald: *Sun*
Cromie, Robert: *Sun*
Cronyn, Margaret: **Blake, Edward**
crop rotation: **Agriculture History;
  Oilseed Crops; Plant Disease**
croquet: **Toys & Games**
Crosbie & Co: **Crosbie, John Chalker**
Cross, James: **Kidnapping; Moore,
  Brian; October Crisis; Royal
  Canadian Mounted Police;
  Violence**
Cross, Michael S.: *Canadian Forum*;
  Social History
cross (crucifix): **Catholicism; Silver,
  Church; Silver, Indian Trade**
Cross Lake: **Hayes River; Manitoba;
  Nelson River**
Cross of Valour: **Decorations for
  Bravery**
crossbill: **Finch; Migration**
Crossley, Hugh T.: **Evangelism**
Croteau, Jacques: **Philosophy**
Crothers, Bill: **Track & Field**
Crouch, R. Weir: **Printmaking**
Crouzet, Jeanne Paul: **Literature in
  French - Scholarship & Teaching**
Crow (Indians): **Cluny Earthlodge
  Village**
crowberry: **Vegetation Regions -
  Atlantic Coastal**
Crowchild, David: **Sarcee**
Crowe, Harry: **Academic Freedom**
crowfoot: **Buttercup**
Crown agency: **Bureaucracy; National
  Capital Commission**
Crown Assets Disposal Corporation:
  Crown Corporation
Crown land: **Company Town; Indian
  Reserve; Manitoba; Métis;
  Montcalm Construction Case; Native
  People, Law; New Brunswick;
  Ontario; Robinson, Peter;
  Saskatchewan; Secretary of State,
  Dept of; Urban & Regional
  Planning; Vegetation Regions -
  Prairie**
Crown Lands, Dept of (Ont): **Parks,
  Provincial**
Crown Mountain: **North Vancouver**
Crown reserves: **Upper Canada**
Crown Trust Co: **Banking; Turner,
  Philip John**
Crow's Nest Pass Coal Co:
  Company Town; Fernie, William
Crow's Nest Pass Railway: **Fernie;
  Nelson; Wardner; Yahk**
Crow's Nest Resources Ltd: **Coal**
Crozier, Francis: **Franklin, John**
Crozier, J.B.: **Musicology**

Crozier, Lief N.F.: **Duck Lake**
crude oil: **Alberta Oil Sands
  Technology & Research
  Authority; Bitumen;
  International Trade; Norman
  Wells; Oil & Natural Gas;
  Petroleum; Petroleum
  Exploration & Production;
  Petroleum Research &
  Development; Sulphur**
cruet: **Silver, Church**
Cruickshank, Robert: **Pewter; Silver,
  Domestic; Silver, Indian Trade**
Cruise missile: **Armaments; Art,
  Contemporary Trends; Peace
  Movement; Trudeau, Pierre E.**
Crusz, Rienzi: **Ethnic Literature**
Crutchfield, Linda: **Bobsledding**
Cry Lake: **Gemstone**
Crysler's Hall: **Upper Canada Village**
Crystal II site: **Archaeology**
Crystal Beach, Ont: **Fort Erie; Niagara
  Peninsula**
Crystal Garden: **Rattenbury,
  Francis M.**
Crystal Glass Co: **Glass**
Crystal Palace: **Canadian National
  Exhibition**
CSL Group Inc: **Canada Steamship
  Lines Inc**
CTV Television Network Ltd:
  **Advertising; Broadcasting, Radio
  & Television; Communications in
  Québec; Television Drama;
  Television Programming;
  Templeton, Charles B.; Western
  Dominion Investment Co Ltd;
  WIC (Western International
  Communications Ltd)**
cuckooflower: **Nova Scotia**
cucumber magnolia: **Vegetation
  Regions - Eastern Temperate
  Forests**
Cugnet, F.J.: **Book Publishing,
  English-Language**
Culham, Gordon: **Landscape
  Architecture**
Cull, David: **Poetry in English**
cult: **New Religious Movements;
  Valdes Island**
Cultural Affairs, Dept of (Qué):
  Beaulne, Guy
Cultural Affairs & Historical Resources,
  Dept of (Man): **Manitoba**
Cultural Assets & Sites Commission
  (Qué): **Lapalme, Georges-Emile**
Cultural Communities & Immigration,
  Dept of (Qué): **Immigration Policy**
cultural exploitation: **Social
  Darwinism**
Cultural Foundation: **Nova Scotia**
Cultural Olympics: **Theatre,
  English-Language**
cultural pluralism: **Ethnic & Race
  Relations; Ethnic Studies;
  Festivals; Germans;
  Multiculturalism**
Cultural Property Export & Import Act:
  Archaeology, Salvage
Culture: **Anthropology; Literary
  Magazines in English**
Culture & Tradition: **Folklore**
Cultus Lake: **Cascade Mountains;
  Chilliwack, BC**
Culver, Aaron: **Simcoe**
Cumberland, F. Barlow: **Rugby**
Cumberland & Storm: **Osgoode Hall**
Cumberland Basin: **Boundaries; Tidal
  Energy**
Cumberland Elementary School: **School
  Facilities**
Cumberland Lake: **Cumberland
  House; Saskatchewan River**
Cumberland Peninsula: **Baffin Island**
Cumberland United Soccer Club:
  Turner, David
Cuming, M.A.: **Veterinary Medicine,
  History**
Cumming, George: **Golf**
Cummings, Burton: **Guess Who**
Cuneo, Carl: **Marxism**
Cunnabell, J.S.: **Magazines**
Cunningham, Frank: **Philosophy**
cupboard: **Furniture, French;
  Furniture, German**
Cupers Cove: **Cupids; Mason, John**
Cupples, Brian: **Philosophy**
Curantul Romanesc (The Romanian Voice):
  Romanians
curare: **Medicine, History of**
Curie, Irène: *Marie Calumet*
curing: **Fisheries; Meat-Processing
  Industry; Tobacco**

curlew: **Bird Distribution & Habitat;
  Sandpiper**
Curling, Nfld: **Corner Brook**
currants: **Berries, Wild; Saxifrage**
Currelly, Charles T.: **Mediterranean
  Archaeology**
currency: **Bank of Canada; Bank of
  Canada Act; Coinage; Distribution
  of Powers; Finance Act; Gold;
  Hincks, Francis; International
  Economics; Minting; Money;
  Playing-Card Money; Seashell;
  Shinplasters;
  Sovereignty-Association;
  Wampum**
Currie, B.W.: **Physics**
curry powder: **Condiment Crops**
Curtis, C.A.: **Urban & Regional
  Planning**
Curtiss, Glenn H.: **Aviation;** *Silver Dart*
Curtiss aircraft: **Bush Flying;
  Disasters; Wetaskiwin**
Curwood, James Oliver:
  **Autobiographical Writing in
  English**
Curzon, Sara Anne: **Drama in English**
Cushing, Eliza Lanesford: **Drama in
  English**
cushion plants: **Flowers, Cultivated;
  Vegetation Regions - Arctic
  Tundra**
cusk: **Cod**
Cusson, Gabriel: **Hétu, Pierre**
Custance, Florence: **Women's Labour
  Leagues**
custom/convention: **Constitutional
  History; International Law; Law;
  Privy Council Office**
Custom House Place Royale:
  Ostell, John
Customs House (Toronto): **Tully, Kivas**
Customs Tariff Act: **Censorship**
customs unions: **International
  Economics**
Cut Knife Hill: **North-West
  Rebellion; Poundmaker**
Cuthbert, James: **Heraldry**
Cutt, W.T.: **Children's Literature in
  English**
CVR-7 Rocket Weapon System:
  Armaments
cybernetics: **Industrial Relations;
  Robotics**
cyclamate: **Soft-Drink Industry**
cyclamen: **Flowers, Cultivated;
  Poisonous Plants**
Cycle of Musical Festivals of the
  Dominion of Canada: **Music History**
cyclone: **Meteorology; Tornado**
Cyclone Mountain: **Red Deer River**
cyclotron: **Physics**
cygnet: **Swan**
Cygnus Corp Ltd: **Hiram Walker
  Resources Ltd**
cylinder press: **Print Industry**
Cyprus Anvil Mining Corp: **Faro**
Cyr, Mary: **Musicology**
cytogenetics: **Barr, Murray Llewellyn;
  Biology**
cytology: **Biology; Plant
  Classification; Taylor, Roy Lewis**
cytotaxonomy: **Botany History**
Czaykowski, B.: **Poles**

D

D. Smillie & Sons: **Printmaking**
D-Day: **Nichols, Jack; Normandy
  Invasion; World War II**
dab: **Flatfish**
Dablon, Claude: **Cartography,
  History of; Marquette, Jacques**
dace: **Minnow**
dacron: **Canadarm; Textile Industry**
Daellenbach, Charles: **Canadian Brass**
DAF INDAL Ltd: **Wind Energy**
daffodil: **Lily**
Dafoe, Edwin: **Dafoe, John W.**
Dafoe, Frances: **Figure Skating**
Dagenais, André: **Philosophy**
Dagenais, Gérard: *Amérique française*
Dagenais, Pierre: **Television Drama,
  French-Language; Theatre,
  English-Language; Theatre,
  French-Language**
Daglish, Peter: **Printmaking**
daguerreotype: **Notman, William;
  Photography**
dahlia: **Flowers, Cultivated**
Daigneault, Pierre: **Popular Literature
  in French**

Daily British Colonist: **Robson, John**
Daily Colonist: **Begg, Alexander**
Daily Ledger: **Newfoundland**
Daily News-Advertiser: *Sun*
Daily Witness: **Newspapers**
daisy: **Prairie; Wildflowers**
Dakelh: **Carrier**
Dalbec: **Folklore**
Dale, Arch: **Cartoons**
Dale-Ross Holdings Ltd: **Webster,
  Lorne Campbell**
D'Alfonso, Antonio: **Italian Writing**
Dalhousie, Countess of: **Botany
  History**
Dalhousie Law School: **Dalhousie
  University; Legal Education;
  Macdonald, Angus L.; Sedgewick,
  Robert; Smith, Sidney E.; Weldon,
  Richard Chapman**
Dalibard, Jacques: **Heritage Canada
  Foundation**
Dall sheep: **Kluane Ranges;
  Mountain Sheep; Nahanni
  National Park**
Dallaire, Michel: **Industrial Design**
d'Allemagne, André: **Essay in French**
D'Almaine, George: **Printmaking**
Dalrymple, Alexander: **East India Co**
Dalton, Charles: **Summerside**
Dalum, Alta: **Danes**
Daly, Dominick: **Metcalfe, Charles
  Theophilus**
Daly, Reginald Alworth: **Moon; Plate
  Tectonics**
Daly Glacier: **Takakkaw Falls**
Daly oil field: **Virden**
damages: **Delict; Jury**
Dames auxiliaires des vétérans français:
  Theatre, French-Language
Damron, Dick: **Country & Western
  Music**
Dance Canada Award: **Farrally, Betty;
  Lloyd, Gweneth**
Dance in Canada Assn: **Dance
  Education; Dance History; Strate,
  Grant**
Dance Interlude: **Carse, M. Ruth P.**
Dance Magazine Award: **Spohr,
  Arnold T.**
Dancemakers: **Dance, Modern**
Dandurand, Albert: **Literature in
  French - Criticism & Theory;
  Literature in French - Scholarship
  & Teaching**
Dandurand, Raoul: **League of Nations**
Danek, Jaromir: **Philosophy**
Daniel, Antoine: **Ste Marie Among
  the Hurons**
Daniel Johnson Dam: **Hydro-Québec;
  Island; Manicouagan Réservoir**
Daniells, Roy: **Dene Nation**
Daniel's Harbour, Nfld:
  Newfoundland
Danish: **Language**
Danko, Rick: **Band, The**
Danse des ombres: *Dance of the Happy
  Shades*
Dansepartout: **Dance, Modern**
Dansereau, Fernand: **Film**
Danseurs de la Rivière Rouge:
  St-Boniface
Danseurs du St-Laurent: **Folk Dance**
Dante Alighieri societies: **Italians**
Dantin, Louis: **Literature in French -
  Criticism & Theory; Novel in
  French; Poetry in French**
Danylchuk, Ivan: **Ukrainian Writing**
Daon Development Corp:
  Development Industry
Daoust, Sylvia: **Sculpture**
Daphne: **Poisonous Plants**
Darbelnet, Jean: **Linguistics**
Darby, John N.: **Evangelical &
  Fundamentalist Movements**
Dare, Daphne: **Stage & Costume
  Design**
Darling, Frank: **Sproatt and Rolph**
Darling & Pearson: **Architecture,
  Development; Pearson, John A.**
Darling & Sproatt: **Pearson, John A.**
Darrah, Phil: **Painting**
Darroch, Murray: **Dance, Modern**
darter: **Perch**
Dartmouth, NS: **Epidemic; Geological
  Survey of Canada; Halifax; Halifax
  Explosion; Hydrography; Mann
  Cedric Robert; Nova Scotia; Nova
  Scotia Research Foundation Corp;
  Stewart, George Lawrence;
  Theatre, English-Language; V-E
  Day Riots**
Dartmouth & Halifax Steamboat Co:
  Stairs, John Fitz-William

Dartmouth Free Press: **Halifax**
Darveau, Louis-Michel: **Literature in French - Scholarship & Teaching**
Das, Urmila: **Chess**
Dassylva, Martial: **Essay in French**
D'Astous & Pothier: **Religious Building**
DATARS Project: **Computer Systems Applications; Industrial Research & Development**
Daughine, Rivière: **Orléans, Ile d'**
Daunais, Lionel: **Choral Music; Songs & Songwriting**
Dauphin Daily Bulletin: **Manitoba**
Dauphin Lake: **Manitoba**
Dauphin River: **Manitoba, Lake**
d'Auteuil, Georges-Henri: **Theatre, French-Language**
d'Auteuil, Marie-Louis: **Children's Literature in French**
Daveluy, Marie-Claire: **Children's Literature in French**
Daveluy, Paule: **Children's Literature in French**
Davenport, S.G.: **Bank Architecture**
Davey Committee: **Magazines; Nova Scotia**
David, Athanase: **Intellectual History; Literary Prizes in French**
David, Barott, Boulva, Dufresne: **Place des Arts**
David, Chief: **Salish, Interior**
David, Hyacinth, Sr: **David, Joe**
David, Jack: **Literary Bibliography in English**
David, Laurent-Olivier: **Literature in French - Scholarship & Teaching**
David Dunlap Observatory: **Astronomy; Dunlap, David Alexander; Hogg, Frank Scott; Observatory; Van den Bergh, Sidney; Young, Reynold Kenneth**
David Florida Laboratory: **Space Technology**
David Mirvish Gallery: **Bush, John H.**
David Thompson University Centre: **Nelson**
Davidson, Alexander: **Hymns**
Davidson, Claude: **Davidson, Florence Edenshaw**
Davidson, John: **Botanical Garden**
Davidson, Reggie: **Davidson, Florence Edenshaw**
Davidson, Robert, Sr.: **Davidson, Florence Edenshaw**
Davidson, "Trump" Jimmy: **Jazz**
Davidson, William: **Newcastle**
Davie Shipbuilding Co Ltd: **Lévis; Ocean Industry; Shipbuilding & Ship Repair**
Davies, Charles: *Canadian Business*
Davies, Haydn: **Sculpture**
Davies, Lynn: **Track & Field**
Davies, Meredeth: **Vancouver Symphony Orchestra**
Davies, William E.: **Meat-Processing Industry**
Davies, William R.: **Davies, Robertson W.**
Davignon, Lise: **Frappier, Armand**
Davis, Andrew: **Toronto Symphony**
Davis, Andrew (tanner): **Leatherworking**
Davis, Arthur Vining: **Jonquière**
Davis, E. Mott: **Archaeology**
Davis, H.F. "Twelve Foot": **Peace River, Alta**
Davis, Sydney: **Sports Organization, Amateur**
Davis, William: **Festival Lennoxville**
Davis, William (miner): **Cape Breton Strikes, 1920s**
Davis House: **Davis, Robert Atkinson**
Davison, Betty: **Printmaking**
Dawes, Andrew: **Orford String Quartet**
Dawes, Eva: **Track & Field**
Dawes, James P.: **Dawes, Norman James**
Dawn, Upper Canada: **Henson, Josiah**
Dawson: **Oceanography**
Dawson, Andre: **Montreal Expos**
Dawson, Carl A.: **Sociology**
Dawson, David: **Poetry in English**
Dawson, J.L.: **Lockhart, Grace Annie**
Dawson, Kenneth C.A.: **Archaeology**
Dawson Museum: **Yukon Territory**
Dawson Point: **Bay d'Espoir**
Dawson Route: **Fort Frances; Thunder Bay**
Day, Angela: **Chess**
Day, Gordon: **Urgent Ethnology**
Day, Lawrence: **Chess**

Day, S.P.: **Exploration & Travel Literature in English**
Day, W.H.: **Holland Marsh**
Day & Ross Ltd: **Hartland**
day lily: **Flowers, Cultivated**
Day of Protest: **Strikes & Lockouts**
day surgery: **Hospitals**
Daziel Barn Museum: **Black Creek Pioneer Village**
Dazois Reservoir: **Ottawa River**
DC 3: **Disasters; Transportation in the North**
DC 4: **Disasters; Transportation in the North**
DC 8F: **Disasters**
DDH280: **Shipbuilding & Ship Repair**
DDT: **Consumers' Association of Canada; Peregrine Falcon; Pesticide; Pollution; Strickland, Edgar Harold**
De Barcelos, Pedro: **Portuguese**
de Boileau, Lambert: **Autobiographical Writing in English**
de Bonnault, Claude: **Intellectual History**
de Brecht, Georg: **German Writing**
de Bussières, Arthur: **Nelligan, Émile; Poetry in French**
de Chaunac, Adhemar F.: **Wine Industry**
de Fehr, William: **German Writing**
de Grandmont, Eloi: **Poetry in French; Theatre, French-Language**
de Grandpré, Pierre: **Literature in French - Criticism & Theory; Literature in French - Scholarship & Teaching**
de Havilland Anson: **Aerospace Industry**
de Havilland Buffalo: **de Havilland Aircraft of Canada Ltd**
de Havilland Chipmunk trainer: **Aerospace Industry; Garratt, Phillip Clarke**
de Havilland Dash 8: **Aerospace Industry; de Havilland Aircraft of Canada Ltd**
de Havilland Mosquito: **Aerospace Industry; Armaments**
de Havilland Tiger Moth: **Aerospace Industry**
de Havilland Twin Otter: **de Havilland Otter; Industrial Research & Development**
de Kresz, Geza: **Hart House String Quartet**
De La Noue, Lac: **Bienville, Lac**
de Lellis, Sylvio: **Musical Instruments**
de Lesseps, Jacques: **Hébert, Henri**
de Montreuil, Gaëtane: *Barre du jour*
De Palma, Ralph: **Automobile Racing**
De Pas, Rivière: **George, Rivière**
De Pasquale, Dominique: **Italian Writing**
de Pencier, Michael: *Canadian Business*; **Magazines; Quill & Quire**
de Ridder, Allard: **Hart House String Quartet; Vancouver Symphony Orchestra**
de Roquebrune, Robert: **Autobiographical Writing in French; Loranger, Jean-Aubert; *Nigog*; Novel in French**
de Smet, Pierre-Jean: **Stoney**
De Teive, Diogo: **Portuguese**
De Verbois seigneury: **Rivière-du-Loup**
de Visser, John: **Photography**
de Wit, Willie: **Boxing**
De Witt, Gerard: **Printmaking**
Deacon, William Arthur: **Essay in English; Humorous Writing in English; Literature in English - Theory & Criticism; Nationalism**
"dead-houses": **Medicine, History of**
deafness: **Auditory Impairment; Bell, Alexander Graham; Bell, Alexander Melville; Medicine, Contemporary**
Dean, Paul: **Loverboy**
Dean Channel: **Bella Coola**
Dearle, R.C.: **Physics**
Dearness, John: **Botany History**
Deas Island Regional Park: **Delta, BC**
Dease Arm: **Great Bear Lake**
Dease Lake: **Gemstone**
Dease River: **Cassiar Mountains**
Dease River Indians: **Kaska**
death camas: **Poisonous Plants**
death certificate: **Funeral Practices**

death rate: **Hastings, Charles John Colwell Orr; Immigration; Population**
debenture: **Corporation Law; Upper Canada**
debit cards: **Commercial Law**
Debydeen, Cyril: **Ethnic Literature**
Debye sphere: **Physics**
Décarie, Vianney: **Philosophy**
Decelles Reservoir: **Ottawa River**
DeCew Falls: **Niagara Peninsula; St Catharines**
Dechêne, Louise: **Historiography**
deciduous conifer: **Larch**
Deciduous Forest: **Forest Regions**
decimal system: **Coinage**
Decker, Franz-Paul: **Haendel, Ida; Orchestre symphonique de Montréal**
Decker, William: **L'Anse aux Meadows**
Declaration of Paris: **Privateering**
Declaration on the New International Economic Order: **International Law**
decompression sickness: **Ocean Industry**
decongestant: **Medical Drug Abuse**
Decouagne, Jean-Baptiste: **Cartography, History of**
Dee & Cee Toy Co: **Toys & Games**
Deed Poll: **Fur Trade; Hudson's Bay Company; North West Company**
deed registration: **Property Law**
Deep Basin gas fields: **Petroleum**
Deep Brook, NS: **Cornwallis**
Deep Cove: **North Vancouver**
Deep River, Ont: **Chalk River**
Deep Tow Seismic System: **Sonar**
deep-well injection: **Hazardous Wastes**
deer fern: **Vegetation Regions - Cordillera; Vegetation Regions - Pacific Coastal**
Deer Lake: **Deer Lake, Nfld; Grand Lake; Humber River**
deerskin: **Moccasin**
Defalco, Martin: **Dunn, William L.**
Defauw, Désiré: **Orchestre symphonique de Montréal**
DeFelice, James: **Theatre, English-Language**
Defence, Dept of: **Gordon, Crawford**
Defence & Civil Institute of Environmental Medicine: **Astronaut; Diving, Underwater**
Defence Industries Ltd: **Smith, Harold Greville**
Defence Industries Productivity Program: **Aerospace Industry**
defence of property: **Criminal Law; Torts**
Defence Production Sharing Agreement: **Violence**
Defence Purchasing Board: **Vaughan, Robert Charles**
Defence Research Board: **Bull, Gerald Vincent; Cameron, William Maxwell; Dunbar, I. Moira; Gordon, Andrew Robertson; Industrial Research & Development; Laser; Maass, Otto; Shrum, Gordon M.; Solandt, Omond McK.; Stewart, Robert William; Wilson, J. Tuzo**
Defence Research Telecommunications Establishment: **Chapman, John Herbert; Computer Science; Industrial Research & Development; Satellite Communications; Space Technology**
Defence Scheme No 1: **Brown, James Sutherland**
defences: **Criminal Law**
defendant: **Civil Procedure; Torts**
Defoe, Frances: **Wagner, Barbara**
Défricheur: **Dorion, Jean-Baptiste-Eric; Laurier, Wilfrid**
Dehem, Roger: **Economics**
Dehouck, Mike: **Skiing**
Deichmann, Erica: **Ceramics, Contemporary**
Deichmann, Kjeld: **Ceramics, Contemporary**
del Vecchio, Rosita: **Jehin-Prume, Frantz**
Delahaye, Guy: **Leduc, Ozias; Poetry in French**
Delamont, Gordon: **McConnell, Robert M.G.; Symonds, Norman**
Delaney, Marshall: *Saturday Night*
Delesalle, Philip: **Gymnastics**
Delezenne, Ignace-François: **Silver, Church; Silver, Domestic**

Delhi, Ont: **Belgians; Research Stations, Agricultural**
Delight: **Gilbert, Humphrey**
Delisle, Guillaume: **Cartography, History of**
Delisle, Jeanne-Mance: **Drama in French**
Della Falls: **Port Alberni**
Delorme, Hyacinthe: **St-Hyacinthe**
delphinium: **Flowers, Cultivated**
Delrue, Denyse: **Art Dealers**
"Delta": **Harvey, Moses**
demand & supply: **Energy Policy; Income Distribution**
Demers, Hector: **Poetry in French**
Demers, Jacques: **Weightlifting**
Demers, Maurice: **Drama in French**
Demers, Modeste: **Exploration & Travel Literature in French**
Demers, P.: **Physics**
Demersville: **Victoriaville**
demijohn: **Glass**
democratic socialism: **Confederation of National Trade Unions; Co-operative Commonwealth Federation; Douglas, T.C.; English; Socialism; Woodsworth, J.S.**
Démons, Île des: **La Rocque, Marguerite de**
demonstration farm: **Mount Pearl**
Demopoulos, William: **Philosophy**
Dempsey, Hugh: **Alberta**
Dempsey, Lotta: *Chatelaine*
Dempster Highway: **Archaeology, Salvage; Arctic Red River, NWT; Permafrost; Transportation in the North; Yukon Territory**
Denault Ltée: **Turmel, Antoine**
Denis, Barbe: **St-Denis**
Denison, William: **Canada & Australia**
Denison Mines Ltd: **Coal; Elliot Lake; Roman, Stephen B.**
Denman naval expedition: **Nootka**
Dennis, John Stoughton: **Lower Fort Garry; Riel, Louis; Surveying**
Dennis, W.H.: **Maritime Rights**
Dennis, William: **Dennis, Agnes**
Dennistoun, Alexander: **Golf**
Denominational Education Commission: **Separate School**
Dent, Nancy Lima: **Dance, Modern**
dentalium: **Kutchin; Linear Mounds**
d'Entremont, Philippe: **Pubnico**
d'Entremont family: **Métis**
Denwood, Alta: **Wainwright**
Denys, Richard: **Denys, Nicolas**
Denys family: **Métis**
department store: **Hudson's Bay Company; Retail Trade; Simpsons, Ltd; Simpsons-Sears Ltd; The T. Eaton Co Ltd**
Departure Bay: **Nanaimo; Strickland, John Douglas Hipwell; Taylor, George William**
Depew, John: **Hamilton**
deportation: **English; Great Depression; Japanese; Labour Policy; Prejudice & Discrimination; Winnipeg General Strike**
depreciation: **Capital Formation; Shipbuilding & Ship Repair**
depression: **Economics; Great Depression; Recession**
depression (mental): **Medical Drug Abuse; Mental Health; Psychiatry**
deprogramming: **New Religious Movements**
Deputy Speaker: **Committees**
Dequen, Jean: **Saint-Jean, Lac**
deregulation: **Regulatory Process; Transportation Regulation**
Dérives: **Literary Periodicals in French**
Derouin, René: **Printmaking**
Déry, Napoleon: **Musical Instruments**
Des Erables portage: **Ottawa River**
Des Groseilliers: **Icebreakers**
Des Joachims portage: **Ottawa River**
Des Plantes, Rivière: **Asbestos**
Des Roches, Roger: **Poetry in French**
desalination: **Bell, Alexander Graham**
Desaulniers, Gonzalve: **Poetry in French**
Desaulniers, Michael: **Squash Racquets**
Desautels, Victor: **Brault, Cédia**
Desbarats, George J.: **Armed Forces - Navy**
Desbarats' printing firm: **Julien, O. Henry**

Desbiens, Jean-Paul: *Insolences du Frère Untel*; **Joual**; *Presse*
Desceliers map: **Cartography, History of**
Deschênes, Lac: **Aylmer**
Deschênes, Qué: **Aylmer**
Deschênes portage: **Ottawa River**
Desclez, Henri: **Popular Literature in French**
Descubierta: **Malaspina Expedition**
Deseronto, Ont: **Deserontyon, John**
desertion: **Alimony; Family Law**
Deshayes, Jean: **Cartography, History of**
design: **Aerospace Industry; Dair, Carl; Fashion Design; Graphic Design; Industrial Design; Interior Design; Urban Design**
Design Canada: **Interior Design**
Designer of the Year Award: **Fashion Design**
Désilets, Alphonse (Jacquelin): **Poetry in French**
Desjardins, Antonio: **Poetry in French**
Desjardins, J.J.: **Table Tennis**
desk: **Furniture, Country; Furniture, French**
Desliens map: **Canada**
Desmarchais, Rex: **Novel in French**
Després, Ronald: **Ethnic Literature**
Desrochers, Clémence: **Claude, Renée; Musical Theatre**
Desrosiers Dance Co: **Desrosiers, Robert Guy**
Desruisseaux-Boisvert, Alice: **Jeunesses musicales du Canada**
Dessaulles, Henriette: **Autobiographical Writing in French**
Dessaulles, L.A.: **Literature in French**
d'Estee, Mimi: **Deyglun, Henri**
Destroismaisons, Léon: **Gagnon, André**
destroyer: **Armaments; Armed Forces - Unification; Shipbuilding & Ship Repair**
destroyer escort: **Armaments**
Destruction, YT: **Kluane National Park**
Destructive Insect & Pest Act: **Hewitt, Charles Gordon**
Detah, NWT: **Dogrib**
detention centre: **Prison**
detinue: **Torts**
Detroit-Windsor Auto Tunnel: **Windsor, Ont**
deuterium: **Hydrogen; Nuclear Energy; Nuclear Fusion; Nuclear Power Plants**
Deuterium of Canada: **Nova Scotia**
Deutz Diesel: **Québec**
Deux Montagnes, Lac des: **Oka; Ottawa River; St Lawrence River**
Devastation Channel: **Kitamaat**
Deveaux, Orpha: **Champagne, Claude**
Deverell, Rex: **Drama in English; Globe Theatre; Theatre for Young Audiences**
Deverell, William: **Novel in English**
Devereux, Helen E.: **Archaeology**
deviance: **Criminology; Juvenile Delinquency; Police; Policing**
devil: **Folklore**
devil fish: **Octopus**
devil's club: **Poisonous Plants; Vegetation Regions - Cordillera**
devil's paintbrush: **Biogeography**
Devlin, Bernard: **Film**
Devlin, E.W.: **Drama in English**
Devlin, Ted: **Ski Jumping**
Devon, Alta: **Alberta Research Council; Coal Liquefaction**
Devon, NB: **Fredericton**
Devonian Botanic Garden: **Botanical Garden**
Devonian Gardens: **Calgary**
Devonian period: **Alberta; Club Moss; Fern; Forest; Fossil Plants; Kindle, Edward Martin; Paleontology, History in Canada; Petroleum; Vertebrate**
DEW Line: **Early-Warning Radar; Happy Valley-Goose Bay; Icebreakers; Inuit Art; Steel, William Arthur**
Dewart, Edward Hartley: **Literature in English - Teaching; Literature in English - Theory & Criticism; Poetry in English**
Dewdney, Christopher: **Literature in English; Poetry in English**
Dewdney, Selwyn: **Agawa Bay**
Dewdney Trail: **Dewdney, Edgar; Trail**

Dewey Soper Bird Sanctuary: **Cape Dorset**
Dexter, Glen: **Yachting**
Dexter, Grant: *Winnipeg Free Press*
Dexter, Walter: **Ceramics, Contemporary**
dhal: **Lentil; Pea, Field**
Dharmacakra Centre: **Buddhism**
d'Herelle, Felix: **Molecular Biology; Virus**
d'Hondt, Walter: **Rowing**
Dhu, Oscar: **Morrison, Donald**
Di Cicco, Pier Giorgio: **Ethnic Literature; Italian Writing**
Di Michele, Mary: **Ethnic Literature; Italian Writing**
diagnostics: **Artificial Intelligence; Connaught Laboratories Ltd; Hospitals; Institut Armand-Frappier; Medical Devices Industry; Medicine, Contemporary**
dialect: **Joual; Language; Native People, Languages**
dialectical materialism: **Marxism**
Diamant, Bernard: **Singing**
diamond: **Mineral**
Diamond & Myers: **Myers, Barton**
"diamond dust": **Ice**
Diamond Flint Glass Co Ltd: **Glass**
Diamond Glass Co (Ltd): **Glass**
Diamond Jenness Peninsula: **Jenness, Diamond**
Diamond Tooth Gertie's Gambling Casino: **Dawson**
Diamonds, The: **Popular Music**
diaries: **Autobiographical Writing in English; Carr, Emily; Climate Information; Drought; Ethnic Literature; Jewitt, John Rodgers; Milne, David B.; Montgomery, Lucy Maud; Perkins, Simeon; Pioneer Life; Ritchie, Charles Stewart Almon; Rowan, William; Simcoe, Elizabeth P.; *Tonquin*; Tyrrell, Joseph B.**
dice: **Gambling**
Dick, Francis: **Sunday Schools**
Dickens, Charles: **Exploration & Travel Literature in English**
Dickey, R.B.: **Fathers of Confederation**
Dickson, Alta: **Danes; Lutherans**
Dickson, Gary A.: **Archaeology**
Dickson, James: **Parks, Provincial**
Dickson, Jennifer: **Printmaking**
Dickson, Lovat: **Autobiographical Writing in English**
Dickson, William: **Galt**
dictionary of classical mythology: **Classics**
Dictionary of Old English: **University of Toronto**
Didsbury, Alta: **Evangelical & Fundamentalist Movements; Notley, W. Grant**
diesel: **Energy in Society; Locomotives & Rolling Stock; Massey-Ferguson Ltd; Petroleum Exploration & Production**
Dieskau, Jean-Armand: **Seven Years' War**
Diestelmeyer, Wallace: **Figure Skating**
diet: **Diabetes Mellitus; Vegetarianism**
diet drinks: **Soft-Drink Industry**
"diet pills": **Medical Drug Abuse**
Dietary Standard: **Canada's Food Guide**
Dietz, William: **Gold Rushes**
Digby, Robert: **Digby**
Digby Cape: **Roads & Highways**
Digby Island: **Metlakatla Pass Sites**
Digby Neck: **Brier Island; Westport**
Digby Scallops: **Cuisine**
Digest éclair: **Germain, Jean-Claude**
Digger House: **Hippies**
Digges Sound: **Razorbill**
dikes: **Cedar Lake Reservoir; Churchill Falls; Creston, BC; Floods & Flood Control; Fraser River Lowland; Grand Pré; Holland Marsh; Hydrology; Tantramar Marsh**
dill: **Condiment Crops; Herbs**
Dille, Lutz: **Photography**
Dimensions: **Germain, Jean-Claude**
Dimić, Milan V.: **Comparative Literature**
Dimson, Theo: **Graphic Design**
dinghy: **Yachting**
Dingman, A.W.: **Calgary**
Dingman no 1: **Turner Valley**

Dinosaur Fossil Museum & Prehistoric Park: **Drumheller**
Dio Cassius project: **Classics**
Dion, Conrad: *Scouine*
Dion, Cyrille: **Billiards**
Dion, Léon: **French Canadian Nationalism**
Dion, Rolande: **Singing**
Dionne, Elzire: **Dionne Quintuplets**
Dionne, François: *Dionne* **Case**
Dionne, Narcisse-Eutrope: **Literature in French - Scholarship & Teaching**
Dionne, Oliva: **Dionne Quintuplets**
Dionne, René: **Literature in French - Scholarship & Teaching**
diphtheria: **Biological Product; Medicine, History of**
diploids: **Genetics**
Diplomat Mine: **Coal**
Diplôme d'honneur: **Bruhn, Erik Belton Evers; Chalmers, Floyd S.; Ljungh, Esse W.; Oliphant, Betty; Pentland, Barbara L.; Spohr, Arnold T.**
diplura: **Insect Classification**
Direct Broadcast Satellites: **Satellite Communications**
direct current (DC): **Fuel Cell; Hydroelectricity**
Direction: **Poetry in English; Souster, Raymond**
Direction des lettres et des arts: **Book Publishing, French-Language**
Directorate of Chemical Warfare & Smoke: **Maass, Otto**
Directors' Guild of Canada: **Pearson, Peter**
dirigible: **Balloon; Military Aviation & Aircraft**
Dirks, Gerald: **Refugees**
Disabilities Removal Act (Nfld): **Greene, Daniel Joseph**
Disciples de Massenet: **Music History**
Disciples of Christ: **Christian Church (Disciples of Christ)**
discipline: **Curriculum Development; Student Rights; Teaching Profession**
Discovery: *Sutil & Mexicana*
Discovery Day: **Dawson; National Holidays**
Discovery Harbour: **Ellesmere Island**
Discovery Passage: **Quadra Island**
discrimination: **Canadian Human Rights Commission; Citizenship; Economic Regulation; Employment Law; Ethnic & Race Relations; Homosexuality; Human Rights; Islam; Jews; Prejudice & Discrimination; Public Service Commission; Winnipeg**
discrimination in law: **Law & Society**
discus throw: **Track & Field**
disease prevention: **Hodgetts, Charles A.**
disorderly person: **Prostitution**
displaced persons: **Immigrant Labour; Latvians; Lithuanians; Mennonites; Refugees**
Displayphone: **Electronics Industry**
dissolution: **Carbonear; King-Byng Affair; Lieutenant-Governor; Parliament**
distemper: **Veterinary Medicine**
Distillers Corp Ltd: **Bronfman Family; Seagram Co Ltd**
distilling: **Metallurgy**
Distinguished Agrologist award: **Stefansson, Baldur Rosmund**
Ditchburn, Anne: **Dance History; Dance on Television & Film; National Ballet of Canada**
Dittmar, William: *Challenger* **Expedition**
dividends: **Co-operative Movement (*See* Addendum, page 1992); Corporation Law; Foreign Investment; Insurance; Regional Economics; Stock & Bond Markets**
Divine Light Mission: **New Religious Movements**
Divinity College: **Acadia University**
division bells: **Allotment of Time; Party Whip**
divorce: **Courts of Law; Family Court; Family Law; Law & Society; Magazines; Marriage & Divorce; Marriage & Divorce, History of**
Divorce Act: **Family; Family Law; *Murdoch* Case**
Dix, Dorothea L.: **Mental Health**
dixieland: **Jazz**

Dixon, Fred J.: **Violence; Winnipeg General Strike**
Dixon, Frederick A.: **Drama in English; Musical Theatre**
Dixon, George: **Dixon Entrance; Haida; King George's Sound Company; Northwest Coast**
Dixon, George (boxer): **Boxing**
Dixon, James: **Queen Charlotte Islands**
Dmytriw, Nestor: **Ukrainian Writing**
DNA: **Biochemistry; Bioethics; Genetics; Khorana, Har Gobind; Molecular Biology; Virus**
Doak, W.A.: **Alikomiak**
Doane, Thomas Coffin: **Photography**
Doat, Jean: **Drama in French; Essay in French**
Dobbs, Arthur: **Cartography, History of**
Dobbs, Kildare: **Essay in English**
documentaries: **Communications in Québec; Film, Documentary; Photography; Radio Drama, English-Language**
dodder: **Morning Glory; Weeds**
Dodge Brothers (Canada): **Chrysler Canada Ltd**
Dodgson, Stephen: **Guitar**
Dodier, Louis: **La Corriveau**
Dofasco Inc: **Dominion Foundries & Steel, Ltd; Hamilton**
DoFor Inc: **Domtar Inc**
dog hair: **Native People - Northwest Coast; Weaving, Contemporary**
dog heartworm: **Mosquito**
dog roundworm: **Nematoda**
dogbane: **Poisonous Plants**
Doherty, Brian: **Shaw Festival**
Doherty, Denny: **Popular Music**
Doherty, Kevin: **Judo**
Doiron, Aubin: **Université Sainte-Anne**
Dolan, John: **Education, Special**
Dolbeau, Jean: **Dolbeau**
Doležel, Lubomír: **Comparative Literature**
Dolin, Samuel: **Gellman, Steven; Orchestral Music**
dollar: **Bank of Canada Act; Banking; Coinage; Exchange Rates; Money**
dollar, American: **Canadian-American Economic Relations; Coinage; Money**
Dollarton, B.C.: **Lowry, C. Malcolm**
dolls: **Inuit Art; Toys & Games; Toys & Games Industry**
Dolly Varden: **Char**
dolomite: **Erie, Lake; Escarpment; Karst Landform; Metallurgy; Mineral; St Lawrence Lowland; Sedimentary Rock; Spring**
Dolphin Swim Club (Toronto): **Swimming, Speed**
Dolphin Swim Club (Vancouver): **Swimming, Speed**
Domagaya: **Translation**
Domaine de l'occident: **Fur Trade**
Domaine du Roy: **King's Posts**
Domanski, Don: **Poetry in English**
Dombrowski, Josée: **Children's Literature in French**
Dome Mines Ltd: **Dome Petroleum Ltd; Gallagher, John P.; South Porcupine; Timmins**
domestic science: **Home Economics; Hoodless, Adelaide**
domestic service: **Housework; Status of Women**
Domglas Inc: **Glass**
Dominicans: **Catholicism; Lachance, Louis; Lévesque, Georges-Henri; Philosophy**
Dominion, NS: **Company Town**
Dominion Alliance for the Total Suppression of the Liquor Traffic: **Temperance Movement**
Dominion & Anglo Investment Corp: **Jackman, Henry N.R.**
Dominion Astrophysical Observatory: **Astronomy; Beals, Carlyle Smith; Harper, William Edmund; Hogg, Helen B.; King, William Frederick; McKellar, Andrew; Molecules in Interstellar Space; Observatory; Pearce, Joseph Algernon; Petrie, Robert Methven; Spectroscopy; Van den Bergh, Sidney; Young, Reynold Kenneth**

Dominion Atlantic Railway: **Halifax; Kentville**
Dominion Bank: **Lyle, John M.; Toronto-Dominion Bank**
Dominion Biologics: **Connaught Laboratories Ltd**
Dominion Botanic Garden & Arboretum: **Arboretum**
Dominion Bureau of Statistics: **Demographic Data Collection; Demography; Ostry, Sylvia; Robbins, John Everett; Statistics Canada**
Dominion (Canadian) Forestry Assn: **Booth, John Rudolphus**
Dominion Cartridge Co: **Firearm**
Dominion Coal Co: **Glace Bay; Ross, James**
Dominion Coin Competition: **Lyle, John M.**
Dominion College of Montréal: **Music History**
Dominion Cotton Mills: **Magog**
Dominion Day: **Canada Day; Parliamentary Procedure**
Dominion Day Games: **Highland Games**
Dominion Drama Festival: **Bessborough, 1st Earl of; Coulter, John W.; Davies, Robertson W.; Languirand, Jacques; Literary Prizes in English; Little Theatre Movement; Scott, Duncan Campbell; Stage & Costume Design; Theatre, French-Language**
Dominion Experimental Farms Service: **Archibald, Edgar Spinney; Mackay, Angus; Saunders, Charles E.; Saunders, William; Soil Science**
Dominion Express Co: **Canadian Pacific Railway**
Dominion Fire Commission: **Public Works, Canada**
Dominion Football Assn: **Soccer**
Dominion Gallery: **Art Dealers; Borduas, Paul-Emile; Hughes, Edward John**
Dominion Glass Co, Ltd: **Glass; Gordon, Charles Blair; Hamilton**
Dominion Grange & Farmers' Alliance: **Drury, Ernest Charles; Good, William Charles**
Dominion Herbarium: **Macoun, John**
Dominion Housing Act: **Cauchon, J.-E.-Noulan; Housing & Housing Policy**
Dominion Illustrated: **Desbarats, Georges-Edouard; Literary Magazines in English**
Dominion Iron & Steel Co: **Fraser, Graham; Ross, James; Sydney; Sydney Steel Corp**
Dominion Lands Act: **Dominion Lands Policy; Germans; Manitoba**
Dominion Lands Survey: **Boundaries; Deville, Edouard Gaston; Forty-ninth Parallel; Meridian, First or Principal; Surveying; Tyrrell, James W.**
Dominion Life Assurance Co: **Gundy, James Henry; Kitchener-Waterloo**
Dominion Magnesium Ltd: **Pidgeon, Lloyd Montgomery**
Dominion Marine Assn: **Transportation**
Dominion Maritime Assn: **Lake Carriers**
Dominion News & Gifts case: **Obscenity**
Dominion notes: **Finance Act**
Dominion Observatory: **Astronomy; Harper, William Edmund; King, William Frederick; Klotz, Otto Julius; Locke, John Lambourne; Millman, Peter MacKenzie; Moon; National Museum of Science & Technology; Plaskett, John Stanley; Spectroscopy; Stewart, Robert Meldrum; Sun; Time; Young, Reynold Kenneth**
Dominion of Canada Football Assn: **Soccer**
Dominion of Canada General Insurance Co: **Jackman, Henry N.R.**
Dominion Order of King's Daughters: **Status of Women**
Dominion Parole Officer: **Salvation Army**
Dominion Police: **North-West Mounted Police; Revolutionary Industrial Unionism; Royal Canadian Mounted Police**

Dominion Prohibitory Council: **Temperance Movement**
Dominion-Provincial Conference: **Demographic Data Collection; Federal-Provincial Relations; Hospitals; Public Health**
Dominion-Provincial Student Aid Program: **Educational Opportunity; Students, Financial Aid to**
Dominion Radio Astrophysical Observatory: **Locke, John Lambourne; Observatory**
Dominion Ranch: **Semlin, Charles A.**
Dominion Rubber Co Ltd: **Manske, Richard Helmuth Frederick; Rubber Products Industry**
Dominion Rust Research Laboratory: **Agricultural Research & Development; Craigie, John Hubert; Goulden, Cyril Harold; Johnson, Thorvaldur; Neatby, Kenneth William; Newton, Margaret**
Dominion Securities Corp Ltd: **Gundy, James Henry; McDougald, John Angus; Wilson, Michael Holcombe; Wood, Edward Rogers**
Dominion Steel & Coal Corp Ltd: **Bell Island; Company Town; Forsyth, Lionel Avard; Gundy, James Henry; Lang, Charles Benjamin; Nova Scotia; Springhill**
Dominion Tar & Chemical Co Ltd: **Domtar Inc**
Dominion Telegraph Co: **Humboldt; Telegraph; Telephones**
Dominion Textile Co Ltd: **Gordon, Charles Blair; Magog; Montmorency; Parent, Madeleine; Textile Industry**
Dominion Toy Manufacturing Co: **Toys & Games**
Dominion Unemployment Relief: **Welfare State**
Dominion Wire Manufacturing Co: **Stelco Inc**
Dominion Women's Enfranchisement Assn: **Stowe, Emily H.; Stowe-Gullen, A. Augusta; Women's Suffrage**
Don Jail: **Architectural Styles**
Don Juan: **Thoroughbred Racing**
Don Mills, Ont: **City; Development Industry; Landscape Architecture; Urban Design**
Don River: **Floods & Flood Control; Ontario Science Centre**
Don Valley Parkway: **Toronto**
Donahue, Jim: **Graphic Design**
Donjek Glacier: **Glaciation**
Donjek River: **Glaciation**
donkey engine: **Timber Trade History**
Donkin, John G.: **Autobiographical Writing in English**
Donlands Dairy Ltd: **George Weston Ltd**
Donnell, David: **Poetry in English**
Donnelly River: **Grayling**
Donner Canadian Foundation: **Educational Foundations & Endowments; North-South Institute**
Donner Lab of Experimental Neurochemistry: **Elliott, K. Allan C.**
Donoghue, Lynn: **Painting**
Donohue Co Ltd: **Amos; St-Félicien; Tardif, Jean-Paul**
Donovan, Peter: **Essay in English**
Donovans, Nfld: **Newfoundland**
Donut Island: **Toronto Islands**
Doolittle, P.E.: **Exploration & Travel Literature in English**
Doon School of Fine Art: **Varley, Frederick H.**
Doppler effect: **Cartography, History of; Observatory; Radar; Spectroscopy**
Dora Hood's Book Room: **Wallace, William Stewart**
Dora Mavor Moore Awards: **Drama in English; Reid, D. Kate; Theatre, English-Language**
Dorchester: **Champlain & St Lawrence Railroad; Locomotives & Rolling Stock**
Dorchester, NS: **Antigonish**
Dorchester penitentiary: **McLachlan, James Bryson; Prison**
Dorchester Street: **Montréal**
doré: **Walleye**
Doré, Fernand: **Drama in French**
Doré et Fils: **Agricultural Implements**

Dorge, Claude: **Theatre, French-Language**
Dorion, Jules: **Exploration & Travel Literature in French**
Dorion Commission: **Favreau, Guy; Gerin-Lajoie, Marie**
Dorn, Peter: **Graphic Design**
Dorothea Klumpke-Roberts Award: **Hogg, Helen B.**
Dorr-Oliver Canada Ltd: **Machinery & Equipment Industry**
Dorrie, Gerhard: **Graphic Design**
Dorset Island: **Cape Dorset**
Dorset Print Making Shop: **Cape Dorset**
Dorval, Qué: **Quebecair; Railway Station**
dory: **Fisheries History; Newfoundland; Nova Scotia**
Dostaler, Yves: **Essay in French**
double-bitted axe: **Timber Axe**
double-crested cormorant: **Cormorant; Forillon National Park; Prince Albert National Park**
Double Diamond Ltd: **Bowling, Indoor**
double predestination: **Calvinism**
double standard of morality: **Prostitution; Women's Organizations**
Doubleday Book Club: **Book Clubs**
Doubleday Canadian Prize Novel: **Literary Prizes in English**
doubloons: **Coinage**
Doucet, Louis-Joseph: **Poetry in French**
Doucet-Saito, Louise: **Ceramics, Contemporary**
Dougall, John: **Magazines**
Douglas, A.E.: **Physics**
Douglas, Alex: **Comet**
Douglas, George Mellis: **Grosse Île**
Douglas, Jimmy: **Soccer**
Douglas, Thomas: **Selkirk, 5th Earl of**
Douglas & McIntyre Ltd: **Book Publishing, English-Language**
Douglas Channel: **Kitamaat; Kitimat**
Douglas Gallery: **Falk, Gathie**
Douglas Gold Medal: **Douglas, Howard**
Douglas Lake: **McLean Gang**
Douglas Lake Cattle Co Ltd: **Merritt; Woodward, Charles**
Douglas Point: **Huron, Lake; Nuclear Safety**
Douglas's aster: **Vegetation Regions - Pacific Coastal**
Douglastown, NB: **Newcastle**
dourine: **Parasitology; Watson, Edward A.**
dovekie: **Auk**
Dow Chemical of Canada Ltd: **Petrochemical Industry**
Dower Acts: **Edwards, Henrietta L.; Family Law; Murphy, Emily**
Dowling, D.B.: **Surveying**
Downes, Wray: **Jazz**
Downie, John: **Children's Literature in English**
Downie, Mary Alice: **Children's Literature in English**
Downs-Archambault Architects: **Downs, Barry Vance**
Doyle, Brian: **Children's Literature in French**
Doyle, Gerald S.: **Musicology**
Doyle, Helen: **Video Art**
draba: **Vegetation Regions - Arctic Tundra**
Drache, D.: **Economics, Radical**
draft animal: **Dog; Horse; Veterinary Medicine**
draft dodger: **Americans; Refugees**
drag racing: **Automobile Racing; Beck, Gary**
draggers: **Nova Scotia**
Dragland, Stan: **MacDonald, Wilson P.; Short Fiction in English**
Dragon: **Nelles, Percy Walker**
Draper, Edward: **Furniture, English, Scottish & American**
Draper, Norman: **Musicology**
Draper, W.A.: **Macdonald, John Sandfield**
Draper site: **Archaeology, Salvage**
drawknife: **Tools, Carpentry**
Dray, William: **Philosophy**
Drayton, Henry: **Railway History**
Drayton, Jerome: **Long-Distance Running**
Drayton Valley, Alta: **Resource Towns**
dredge: **Shipbuilding & Ship Repair**
dressage: **Equestrian Sports; Horse**

dresses: **Clothing; Clothing Industries; Indian Art**
Dressler, Marie: **Theatre, English-Language**
Drew, Andrew: *Caroline*
Drew, Wayland: **Novel in English**
Driedger, K.U.: **Grain Elevators**
Driftpile River: **Lesser Slave Lake**
drill: **Physical Education**
drilling: **Petroleum Exploration & Production; Quarrying Industry**
drilling platform: **Megaprojects; Ocean Industry**
Drillon, Gord: **Toronto Maple Leafs**
drills: **Clovis; Tools, Carpentry**
drogher: **Shipbuilding & Ship Repair**
Droit: **Franco-Ontarians; Literature in French - Criticism & Theory; Ottawa, Ont; UniMédia Inc**
Drolet, Antonio: **Literature in French - Scholarship & Teaching**
Drouillette, Father: **Mégantic, Lac**
Drouin, Mark: **Expo 67**
Drucker, Philip: **Beynon, William**
drug abuse & addiction: **Alcoholism; Family Law; Lett, Stephen; Medical Drug Abuse; Non-Medical Use of Drugs, Royal Commission on the; Sports Medicine**
drug trafficking: *Mackay* Case; **Organized Crime; Smuggling; Underground Economy**
Drumheller, Samuel: **Drumheller**
Drummond, Mount: **Red Deer River**
Drummond Coal Co: **Coal**
Drummond Mine: **Coal; Westville**
Drummondville Moraine: **Physiographic Regions - St Lawrence Lowlands**
drunkenness: **Alcoholism; Crime**
Drury, Charles: **Drury, Ernest Charles**
Drury Commission: **Northwest Territories**
Druzes: **Arabs**
Drybones, J.: *Drybones* Case
Dryden, Kenneth: **Drama in English; Vezina Trophy**
drydock: **Shipbuilding & Ship Repair**
Dryer, Douglas P.: **Philosophy**
drying: **Apricot; Cereal Crops; Fruit & Vegetable Industry; Northern Georgia Strait Coast Salish; Salish, Interior; Smokehouse**
Drysdale, Patrick: **Dictionary**
DSMA Atcon Ltd: **Canadarm**
DSMA International: **Aerodynamics**
Du Creux, François: **Canada; Cartography, History of; Painting**
Du Parc seigneury: **Rivière-du-Loup**
Du Pont, François Gravé: **Champlain, Samuel de; *Des Sauvages, ou, Voyage de Samuel Champlain*; Port-Royal; Shipbuilding & Ship Repair**
Du Pont Canada Inc: **Kingston; Petrochemical Industry; Smith, Harold Greville; Textile Industry**
Dublin, Ont: **Place-names**
Dubois String Quartet: **Chamber Music; Music History**
Dubuc, Sask: **Swedes**
Duchesnay, Alice: **Children's Literature in French**
Duchesnay, Antoine Juchereau: **Maillou House**
Duchesnay, Louis-François Juchereau: **Taschereau Legal Dynasty**
Duchesne, Jacques: **Drama in French**
Duchesneau, François: **Philosophy**
duck, domestic: **Poultry Farming**
Duck Lake, Sask: **Almighty Voice**
Duck Mountain: **Winnipegosis, Lake**
Duck Mountain National Forest: **Dauphin**
Duck Mountain Provincial Park: **Dauphin; Parks, Provincial**
Ducks Unlimited (Canada): **Hunting; Wildlife Conservation & Management; Wildlife Preserve**
Duckworth, H.E.: **Physics**
Ducy, John: **Baseball**
Dudas, Frank: **Industrial Design**
Dufaux, Georges: **Film**
Duff, G.F.: **Mathematics**
Duff, John: **Meat-Processing Industry**
Duff, Mike: **Motorcycle Racing**
Dufferin, Marchioness of: **Exploration & Travel Literature in English; Little Theatre Movement; Topographic Painters**
Dufferin Park: **Highland Games**

Dufferin Terrace: **Dufferin & Ava, 1st Marquess of**
Duffield, Parke & Co: **Pharmaceuticals Industry**
Duffy, James: **Long-Distance Running**
Dufresne, A.: **Religious Building**
Dugald, Man: **Springfield**
Dugas, Marcel: **Autobiographical Writing in French; Essay in French; Literature in French - Criticism & Theory; Poetry in French**
dugout: **Drought; Prairie Farm Rehabilitation Administration; Saskatchewan**
dugout canoes: **Northern Georgia Strait Coast Salish**
Dugré, Adélard: **Leduc, Ozias**
Duguay, Raôul: **Boudreau, Walter; Poetry in French**
Duhamel, Roger: **Bloc populaire canadien; Literature in French; Literature in French - Criticism & Theory; Relève**
Duke Depression: **Kluane Ranges**
Duke Point Industrial Park: **Nanaimo**
Duliani, Mario: **Italian Writing**
dull Oregon grape: **Vegetation Regions - Cordillera**
Dulong, Gaston: **Linguistics**
dulse: **Cuisine; Dark Harbour; Grand Manan Island; Seaweeds**
Dumais, Emile: **Agricultural Education**
dumbcane: **Poisonous Plants**
dumble-dor: **Dandelion**
Dumoine, Lac: **Dumoine, Rivière**
Dumond, Fernand: **Literary Prizes in French**
Dumont, Fernand: **Literature in French; Philosophy; Poetry in French**
Dumont, Isidore: **Dumont, Gabriel**
Dumont, Jean-Baptiste: **Dumont, Gabriel**
Dumoulin, Father: **French in the West**
Dun, Marshall: **Guitar**
Dunbar Point: **Railway History; Samson**
Duncan, Andrew R.: **Maritime Rights; Nova Scotia**
Duncan, Brydone James: **Paige, Brydon**
Duncan, Dorothy: **Exploration & Travel Literature in English**
Duncan, Francis: **Exploration & Travel Literature in English**
Duncan, Kenneth: **Duncan**
Duncan, O.B.: **Social Mobility**
Duncan, Robert: **Poetry in English**
Duncan, William: **Duncan**
Duncan Dam: **BC Hydro; Columbia River**
Duncanson, Robert: **Edson, Aaron Allan**
Dundas, Ont: **Birge, Cyrus Albert; Hamilton; Osler, William**
Dundas Harbour: **Lancaster Sound**
Dundas Street: **Roads & Highways**
Dundas Valley: **Bruce Trail**
Dundela, Ont: **McIntosh, John**
Dundonald, 12th Earl of: **Armed Forces - Militia & Army**
Dundurn Castle: **Hamilton; MacNab, Allan N.**
dune: **Aeolian Landform; Cap aux Meules, Ile du; Cape Sable; Coastal Landform; Desert; Kouchibouguac National Park; Manitoba; Prince Edward Island; Sable Island; Saguenay Provincial Park; St Lawrence Lowland**
Dunham, Qué: **Dairy Industry**
Dunira Island: **Dundas Island**
Dunlap, Jessie Donalda: **Chant, Clarence Augustus**
dunlin: **Sandpiper**
Dunlop, E.S.: **Stewart, Frances**
Dunlop Art Gallery: **Regina**
Dunlop Canada Ltd: **Rubber Products Industry**
Dunlop Trophy Race: **Cycling**
Dunmore, North-West Territories: **Lethbridge**
Dunnage Zone: **Geological Regions**
Dunning, George: **Fruit & Vegetable Industry**
Dunning, George (film): **Film Animation**
Dunnington-Grubb, Laurie: **Landscape Architecture**

Dunnottar, Man: **St Andrews, Man**
Dunnville, Ont: **Niagara Peninsula**
Duparc, Marguerite: **Lefebvre, Jean-Pierre**
Dupas, Île: **La Vérendrye, Pierre**
Duplessis, Nérée Le Noblet: **Duplessis, Maurice Le Noblet**
Dupont, Jean-C.: **Oral Literature in French; Short Fiction in French**
Dupras, Pierre: **Popular Literature in French**
Dupret, H.: **Botany History**
Dupuis, Nathan F.: **Mathematics**
Dupuis Frères: **Lévesque, Jean-Louis**
Dupuis-Maillet, Corine: *Amérique française*
Durán, Claudio: **Ethnic Literature**
Durand, Charles: **Baldwin, William Warren**
Durand, Pierre: **Postal System**
Durell, Philip: **Coudres, Ile aux**
duress: **Criminal Law**
Durham, Ont: **Goat Farming**
Durham Heights: **Banks Island**
Durham Rubber Co: **Rubber Products Industry**
Durocher, Eulalie: **Marie-Rose, Mother**
Dussault, Louisette: **Theatre, French-Language**
Dusseau, Jeanne: **Singing**
"Dust Bowl": **Erosion; Gray, James H.; Kirk, Lawrence Eldred**
Dust over the City: *Poussière sur la ville*
dusty miller: **Groundsel**
Dutch elm disease: **Beetle; Conservation; Manitoba**
Dutch Reformed Church: **McDowall, Robert; Presbyterian & Reformed Churches**
Duthie, Carol Ann: **Water Skiing**
Dutilly, Arthème: **Lepage, Ernest**
Dutoit, Charles: **Orchestre symphonique de Montréal**
Dutton, Paul: **Poetry in English**
Duval, Etienne-F.: **Theatre, French-Language**
Duvernay, Ludger: **St-Jean-Baptiste Society**
Duvivier, François Dupont: **Le Loutre, Jean-Louis**
dwarf birch: **Hudson Bay**
dwarf blueberry: **Vegetation Regions - Cordillera**
dwarf mistletoe: **Forestry**
dwarf willow: **Endangered Plants; Willow**
dwarfism: **Biological Product**
Dwyer, Peter: **Theatre, English-Language**
Dwyer ossuaries: **Archaeology**
Dyck, A.B.: **German Writing**
Dyck, Arnold: **German Writing**
Dyck, Ian G.: **Archaeology**
dye: **Alder; Molybdenum; Petrochemical Industry; Pharmaceuticals Industry; Plants, Native Uses; Quarrying Industry; Quilt; Rugs & Rug Making; Scale Insect; Walnut**
Dyea, BC: **Avalanche**
Dyer, Charles: **Cosmology**
Dylex Ltd: **Clothing Industries**
Dymond, J.R.: **Zoology**
dynamo: **Willson, Thomas L.**
Dyola language: **Africans**
Dyon, Mike: **Long-Distance Running**
Dyott, William: **Concert Halls & Opera Houses**
Dysart, Sask: **Romanians**
dyslexia: **Thompson, Robert N.**
Dyson, Brian: **Art, Contemporary Trends**
Dystonia Medical Research Foundation: **Belzberg, Samuel**
Dzoona & Thunderbird totem pole: **Seaweed Willie**

E

E.G. Prior Co: **Prior, Edward G.**
E-L Financial Corp: **Jackman, Henry N.R.**
E.W.B. Snider mill: **Technology**
E.W.R. Steacie prize: **Deslongchamps, Pierre**
Eager, William: **Printmaking**
Eagle Hills Cree: **Poundmaker**
Eagle Mountain: **Coquitlam**
eagle owl: **Québec**
eagles: **Coinage**

Eaglet: **Hudson's Bay Company; Nonsuch**
Eagling, Wayne: **Dance History**
Ear Falls: **Seul, Lac**
Earl Grey Award: **Waxman, Albert S.**
Earl Grey Music & Dramatic Competition: **Theatre, English-Language; Theatre Education**
Earl Grey Skating Club: **Figure Skating**
Earl of Moira: **Sculpture**
Earlscourt Library: **Public Art**
Early Scarlet apple: **Sharp, Francis Peabody**
Early Triumph wheat: **Wheeler, Seager**
earring: **Silver, Indian Trade**
earspools: **Prehistory**
Earth Day: **Heritage Conservation**
Earth Diver myth: **Native People, Religion**
earthenware: **Ceramics**
earwig: **Insect Classification**
East Africans: **Prejudice & Discrimination**
East-Angus, Qué: **Bourgault, Pierre**
East Indians: **Buddhism; Ethnic Literature; Hinduism; Immigration; Legal Education; Malaysians; Saskatoon; South Asians; Thunder Bay; Vancouver**
East Kootenay coalfield: **Coal Mining**
East Malartic Mine: **Malartic**
East Point, PEI: **Lighthouses**
East Prairie, Alta: **Métis Settlements**
East Prairie River: **Lesser Slave Lake**
East Ship Harbour, NS: **Ship Harbour**
East York, Ont: **Toronto**
Eastend, Sask: **Fossil Plants**
Eastern Algonquian: **Native People - Eastern Woodlands**
Eastern Arctic Marine Environmental Studies: **Oceanography**
Eastern belt: **Geological Regions**
Eastern Canada Hockey Assn: **Hockey, Ice**
eastern cougar: **Endangered Animals; Fundy National Park**
Eastern Extension Railway: **Nova Scotia**
eastern flowering dogwood: **Vegetation Regions - Eastern Temperate Forests**
eastern fox snake: **Georgian Bay Islands National Park**
Eastern Group of Painters: **Artists' Organizations; Lyman, John G.; Roberts, W. Goodridge; Surrey, Philip Henry**
Eastern Irrigation District: **Bow River**
Eastern Oil Co: **Shatford, Sidney S.**
eastern Ontario plain: **Ontario**
Eastern Orthodox Church: **Iranians; Orthodox Church**
Eastern Provincial Airways: **Aviation; Halifax; New Brunswick; Prince Edward Island; Sobey, William Macdonald; Steele, Harold Raymond; Transportation**
eastern red cedar: **Juniper**
Eastern Temperate Forests: **Soil Classification; Vegetation Regions - Eastern Temperate Forests**
Eastern Township Autoroute: **Sherbrooke**
Eastern Trust Co: **Stairs, John Fitz-William**
eastern white cedar: **Cedar; Vegetation Regions - Eastern Temperate Forests**
Eastmain Reserve: **James Bay Project**
Eastman, Qué: **Disasters**
Easton, Florence: **Music History**
Eastwood & Skinner: **Print Industry**
Eaton, George: **Automobile Racing**
Eaton, James: **Eaton, Timothy**
Eaton, Ken: **Finance, Dept of**
Eaton, Richard: **Choral Music**
Eaton, Robert Young: **The T. Eaton Co Ltd**
Eaton Book Club: **Book Clubs**
Eaton Boys & Girls clubs: **Eaton, John C.**
Eaton family: **Baton Broadcasting Inc**
Eaton Operatic Soc: **Ridout, Godfrey**
Eaton Short Story Competition: **Literary Prizes in English**
Eau Claire Lumber Co: **Norwegians**
Eayrs, Hugh: **Book Publishing, English-Language**
Eber, Dorothy H.: **Ethnic Literature; Pitseolak, Peter**

Ebierbing, "Joe": **Tookoolito, "Hannah"**
Éboulements, Mont des: **Laurentian Highlands**
Éboulements seigneury: **King's Posts**
Eby Falls: **Albany River**
Echatchet village: *Tonquin*
Echimamish River: **Hayes River**
Echo Bay: **Great Bear Lake; Mackenzie River**
Echo Centre: **Port Alberni**
echo sounder: **ECOLOG**
Eckankar: **Morrisseau, Norval**
Eckhardt, Ferdinand: **Eckhardt-Gramatté, S.C. Sonia**
Eclipse Sound: **Bylot Island**
École canadienne de préhistoire: **Ami, Henri-Marc**
École de bibliothécaires: **Library Science**
École de plateau: **Gagnon, Clarence**
École de technologie supérieure: **Université du Québec**
École des arts et metiers: **Gill, Charles**
École des beaux-arts: **Art Education; Automatistes; Borduas, Paul-Emile; Dallaire, Jean-Philippe; Daudelin, Charles; Dyonnet, Edmond; Ferron, Marcelle; Holgate, Edwin; Morin, Paul; Mousseau, Jean-Paul Armand; Pellan, Alfred; Printmaking; Saint-Charles, Joseph; Tonnancour, Jacques Godefroy de**
École des hautes études commerciales: **Economics; Parizeau, Gérard; Université de Montréal**
École des sciences sociales: **Economics**
École du meuble: **Art Education; Automatistes; Barbeau, Marcel; Borduas, Paul-Emile; Ferron, Marcelle; Industrial Design**
École littéraire de Montréal: **Gill, Charles; Laberge, Albert; Literary Periodicals in French; Literature & Politics; Literature in French; Loranger, Jean-Aubert; Nelligan, Emile; Poetry in French; Regionalism in Literature**
École moyenne d'agriculture: **Lepage, Ernest**
École nationale d'administration publique: **Morin, Claude; Université du Québec**
École normale du plateau: **Larose, Ludger**
École normale Jacques-Cartier: **Gill, Charles**
École normale Laval: **Gaudreault, Laure**
École normale supérieure: **Roy, Camille**
École polytechnique de Montréal: **Civil Engineering; Mineral & Mining Engineering; Physics; Science; Technology; Université de Montréal**
École québécoise du meuble et du bois ouvré: **Furniture & Fixture Industry**
École secondaire l'Essor: **Windsor, Ont**
École sociale populaire: **Semaines sociales du Canada; Social Doctrine of the Roman Catholic Church**
École supérieure de chimie: **Mathematics**
École supérieure de danse: **Dance Education; Grands Ballets Canadiens**
École Vincent-d'Indy: **Aubut, Françoise**
Ecological Reserves Act (BC): **British Columbia**
Ecology House: **Pollution Probe Foundation**
econometrics: **Economics**
Economic Development & Tourism, Dept of (Man): **Manitoba Research Council**
Economic Development Corp (Sask): **Provincial Government**
economic policy: **Canadian-American Economic Relations; Employment & Income, White Paper on; Howe Research Institute; International Economics; International Monetary Fund; Royal Commission on Canada's Economic Prospects; Students, Financial Aid to**

Economic Union & Development Prospects for Canada, Royal Commission on the: **Macdonald, Donald S.**
Economical Mutual Insurance Co: **Kitchener-Waterloo**
Economists, Sociologists & Statisticians Assn: **Postal System**
Ecouri Romanesti (Romanian Echoes): **Romanians**
Écran: **Popular Literature in French**
Écrits des forges: **Poetry in French**
Ecuadorian-Canadian Soccer League: **Latin Americans**
Ecuadorians: **Latin Americans**
Ecum Secum, NS: **Place-names**
Ecumenical Forum of Canada: **Canadian Council of Churches**
ecumenism: **Burwash, Nathanael; Catholicism; Grant, George M.**
eczema: **Dandelion; Endangered Plants**
Edam, Sask: **Dutch**
edaphology: **Soil Science**
Edel, Leon: **Kennedy, Leo; Klein, Abraham M.; Literature in English - Theory & Criticism; Poetry in English**
Eden Valley Reserve: **Stoney**
Edenshaw, Albert Edward: **Edenshaw, Charlie**
Edenvale, Ont: **Automobile Racing**
Edgar, Pelham: **Literature in English - Theory & Criticism; Scott, Duncan Campbell**
Edgeworth, Maria: **Stewart, Frances**
Edinborough, Arnold: *Saturday Night*
Edison Electric Co: **Peterborough**
Éditions Canada: **Printmaking**
Éditions Clermont-Pépin: **Pépin, Clermont**
Éditions d'Acadie: **Children's Literature in French; Ethnic Literature**
Éditions de l'arbre: **Charbonneau, Robert**
Éditions de l'arc: **Vigneault, Gilles**
Éditions de l'aurore: **Beaulieu, Victor-Levy**
Éditions de l'hexagone: **Book Publishing, French-Language; Ouellette, Fernand; Poetry in French**
Éditions de l'homme: **Book Publishing, French-Language**
Éditions de l'Université d'Ottawa: **Literature in French - Criticism & Theory**
Éditions des plaines: **Children's Literature in French**
Éditions du jour: **Beaulieu, Victor-Levy; Book Publishing, French-Language**
Éditions du noroît: **Poetry in French**
Éditions du pélican: **Book Publishing, French-Language**
Éditions du totem: **Book Publishing, French-Language**
Éditions Erta: **Book Publishing, French-Language; Printmaking**
Éditions Héritage Inc: **Children's Literature in French**
Éditions Hurtubise HMH Ltée: **Book Publishing, French-Language; Literature in French - Criticism & Theory**
Éditions internationales Alain Stanké: **Book Publishing, French-Language**
Éditions jeunesse: **Children's Literature in French**
Éditions La Presse: **Aquin, Hubert; Book Publishing, French-Language**
Éditions Leméac Inc: **Book Publishing, French-Language**
Éditions Mirabel: **Popular Literature in French**
Éditions Orphée: **Book Publishing, French-Language**
Éditions ovale: **Children's Literature in French**
Éditions Parti pris: **Book Publishing, French-Language; *Parti pris***
Éditions pédagogiques: **Book Publishing, French-Language**
Éditions Pierre Tisseyre: **Children's Literature in French**
Éditions prise de parole: **Children's Literature in French**
Éditions Québec-Musique: **Morel, François**

Éditions quinze: **Book Publishing, French-Language; Brossard, Nicole; Literary Prizes in French**
Edmonds, Jack: **Mathematics**
Edmonton: **Alberta**
Edmonton, Dunvegan & British Columbia Railway: **Athabasca; Falher; Grande Prairie; Peace River, Alta; Railway Station**
Edmonton, Jerry: **Steppenwolf**
Edmonton Art Gallery: **Knowles, Dorothy E.**
Edmonton Ballet Co: **Alberta Ballet Company**
Edmonton Buddhist Priory: **Buddhism**
Edmonton Bulletin: **Journalism; Oliver, Frank**
Edmonton Country Club: **Golf**
Edmonton General Hospital: **Allard, Charles A.**
Edmonton House: **Stoney**
Edmonton International Speedway: **Automobile Racing**
Edmonton Journal Awards: **Literary Prizes in English**
Edmonton Mercurys: **Olympic Games**
Edmonton Opera Assn: **Edmonton Symphony Orchestra; Opera**
Edmonton Public School Board: **Ethnic Languages**
Edmonton Sun: **Maclean Hunter Ltd; Newspapers**
Edmonton Telephones: **Telecommunications; Telephones**
Edmund Fitzgerald: **Lake Carriers; Lightfoot, Gordon**
Edmund pianos: **Piano Manufacturing**
Edper Investments Ltd: **Bronfman Family**
Edson Trail: **Edson; Grande Prairie**
education: **Adult Education; Agricultural Education; Art Education; Business Education; Childhood, History of; Computer-Assisted Learning; Curriculum Development; Distance Learning; Forestry Education; Legal Education; Literacy; Mathematics & Society; Medical Education; Music Education; Native People, Education; Native People, Government Programs; Physical Education; Quiet Revolution; Royal Commissions; School Systems; Second-Language Instruction**
Education, Dept of (Alta): **Alberta**
Education, Dept of (BC): **Education, Technical**
Education, Dept of (Man): **Manitoba**
Education, Dept of (Ont): **Currie, Walter; School Facilities**
Education, Dept of (Qué): **Communications in Québec; Québec**
Education, Royal Commission of Inquiry into (Qué): **Collège d'enseignement général et professionnel; Community College; Filion, Gérard; Philosophy**
Education Act (Nfld): **Newfoundland**
education administration: **School Boards; School Trustee**
Educational Planning, Royal Commission on (Alta): **Education, Alternate**
Edvina, Lousie: **Music History**
Edward VII of England: **Coinage; Edwards, William Cameron; Emblems, Provincial & Territorial; Hébert, L.-Philippe; Queen's Plate**
Edward Johnson Music Foundation: **Guelph**
Edward P. Taylor Reference Library: **Art Gallery of Ontario**
Edwards, Caterina: **Italian Writing**
Edwards, Philip: **Lou Marsh Trophy; Track & Field**
Edziza, Mount: **Igneous Rock; Mount Edziza Provincial Park; Volcano**
Edzo: **Dogrib**
Edzo, NWT: **Rae-Edzo**
Eedee Award: **Fashion Design**
eelgrass: **Vegetation Regions - Coastal Marine Flora**
eelworm: **Plant Disease**
EFRB artillery rounds: **Armaments**
eft: **Salamander**
Eganville, Ont: **Gemstone**

eggs: **Agricultural Marketing Board; Agriculture & Food; Agriculture History; Animal Agriculture; Environmental Law; Funk Island; International Trade; Manitoba; Minas Basin; Newfoundland; Poultry Farming; Salmonella; Veterinary Medicine**
Eglinton Island: **Arctic Exploration**
Egoff, Sheila: **Children's Literature in English**
Egrégore: **Drama in French**
egret: **Heron**
Egyptians: **Arabs; Orthodox Church**
Eichler, M.: **Family Studies**
Eid, Nadia: **Intellectual History**
eider: **Baffin Island; Banks Island; Seabird**
Eighteen Mile Island: **French River**
Eikhardt, Shirley: **Country & Western Music**
Einarsson, Magnus: **Folklore**
Eirikr Thorvaldsson: **Eric the Red**
Eisenhower, Mount: **Place-names**
Ekoota: **Inuit Art**
Elberg, Yehuda: **Jewish Writing**
Elbow River: **Calgary**
Elder, Bruce: **Film, Experimental**
Elder, Henry: **Architecture, Development**
Elder, Norman: **Equestrian Sports**
Elderly Persons' Housing: **Manitoba**
Eldorado, BC: **New Denver**
Eldorado, Sask: **Athabasca, Lake**
Eldorado Creek: **Klondike Gold Rush**
Eldorado Gold Mines Ltd: **LaBine, Gilbert; Transportation in the North**
Eldorado Mine: **Mining**
Eldorado Mining & Refining Ltd: **Bennett, William John**
Eldorado Nuclear Ltd: **Energy, Mines & Resources, Dept of**
Electeur: *Soleil*
Election Finances & Contributions Act (Alta): **Corruption**
Electoral Boundaries Readjustment Act: **Electoral Systems; Redistribution**
electoral fraud: **Electoral Systems; Harrington, Gordon Sidney**
Electors Action Movement: **Vancouver**
electric-arc furnace: **Sidbec-Dosco Limitée**
Electric Boat Co: **Aerospace Industry; Canadair Ltd**
electric current: **Weights & Measures**
electric railway: **BC Hydro; Canadian National Exhibition; Railways, Contemporary; Urban Transportation**
electric range: **Ahearn, Thomas; Electrical Appliances Industry**
Electrical Development Co: **Nicholls, Frederic**
electrical discharge: **Lightning; St Elmo's Fire**
electrical wiring: **Aluminum; Copper**
Electricity & Fluid Exportation Act: **Energy Policy**
electrochemistry: **Chemistry Subdisciplines**
electrocution: **Injury & Prevention**
electrodiagnosis: **Optometry**
Electrohome Ltd: **Electronics Industry; Kitchener-Waterloo**
electrolysis: **Chemistry Subdisciplines**
electrolyte solution: **Gordon, Andrew Robertson**
electrolytic cell: **Technology**
electromagnetic radiation: **Chemistry Subdisciplines; Remote Sensing; Spectroscopy**
electron: **Northern Lights; Nuclear Fusion; Physics**
electron microscope: **Burton, Eli Franklin; Medicine, Contemporary**
Electronic Associates Ltd: **Leaver, Eric William**
electronic banking: **Banking; Cable Television; Commercial Law; Underground Economy**
electronic equipment: **International Trade**
electronic music: **Electroacoustic Music**
Electronic Music Studio: **Anhalt, István**
electronic surveillance: **Inquiry into Certain Activities of the RCMP, Royal Commission of; Intelligence Gathering**
electrons: **Gray, Joseph Alexander**

electroplating: **Cadmium; Nickel; Silver, Domestic; Water Pollution**
elementary school: **Education, Alternate; Private School; Public School; Separate School; Student Rights**
Eleniak, Wasyl: **Ukrainians**
elephant ear: **Saxifrage**
elevator: **Grain Elevators**
Elf Oil: **Beck, Tom**
Elfros, Sask: **McPhail, Alexander James**
Elgar Choir of BC: **Choral Music; Music History**
Elgar Choir of Montréal: **Forrester, Maureen**
Elgin, Upper Canada: **Niagara Falls, Ont**
Élie, Man: **Physics**
Élie, Robert: **Novel in French;** *Relève*
Eliza, Francisco de: **Spanish Exploration;** *Sutil & Mexicana*
Elizabeth, Alta: **Métis Settlements**
Elizabeth, Queen Consort: **Queen Elizabeth Way; Queen's Plate; Royal Tours; Sovereign**
Elizabeth I of England: **East India Co; Easton, Peter; English; Gilbert, Humphrey; Place-names**
Elizabeth II of England: **Coinage; *Constitution* Reference; Constitution, Patriation of; Emblems, Provincial & Territorial; Emblems of Canada; Flag Debate; Newton, Lilias; Ouimet, J.-Alphonse; Parliamentary Procedure; Queen Elizabeth Islands; Queen's Plate; Royal Tours; Shaw Festival; Sovereign; Symbols of Authority; Victoria Day**
Elizabeth Fry Society: **Macphail, Agnes C.; Prison; Probation & Parole**
Elizabethtown, Upper Canada: **Brockville**
elk: **Animals in Winter; Banff National Park; Cape Scott Provincial Park; Cuisine; Cypress Hills Provincial Park; Elk Island National Park; Jasper National Park; Kootenay National Park; Prince Albert National Park; Riding Mountain National Park; Wapiti; Wildlife Preserve; Yoho National Park**
Elk River Valley: **Cranbrook; Fernie; Sparwood**
Elkford, BC: **Rocky Mountains; Selkirk Communications Ltd**
Elkhorn Mountain: **Vancouver Island**
Elks, Benevolent Protective Order of: **Chinese**
Ellesmerian Orogeny: **Geological Regions**
Elliot, David: **Painting**
Elliot, Edward: **Fairn, Leslie Raymond**
Elliot, George: **Short Fiction in English**
Elliot, Orville: **Gymnastics**
Elliot brothers: **Bush Flying**
Elliot's Cove, Nfld: **Random Island**
Elliott, J.W.: **Railway History**
Elliott, Lorris: **Theatre, Multicultural**
Elliott, Preston: **Ginger Group**
"Elliott's solution": **Elliott, K. Allan C.**
Ellipse: **Jones, Douglas Gordon; Literary Magazines in English; Literary Periodicals in French**
Ellis, Baie: **Anticosti, Ile d'; Gamache, Louis-Olivier**
Ellis, Eleanor A.: **Cuisine**
Ellis, Frank: **Parachuting, Sport**
Ellis, Henry: **Cartography, History of**
Ellis, J.H.: **Soil Science**
Ellis, John: **Printmaking**
Ellis-Yeo property: **Shipbuilding & Ship Repair**
Ellison & Co: **Photography**
elm bark: **Furniture, Country; Furniture, French; Longhouse**
Elmer Iseler Singers: **Iseler, Elmer W.**
Elmworth, Alta: **Grande Prairie**
Elora Gorge: **Canoeing; Elora**
Elsa, YT: **Yukon Territory**
"Elsie" antipersonnel mines: **Armaments**
ELTs: **Space Technology**
Elvins, Andrew: **Astronomy**
embezzlement: **Cadet, Joseph-Michel; Computers & Society; White-Collar Crime**

emblazonment: **Heraldry**
emblem: **Logo; Provincial Floral Emblems; Trade Mark**
embossing: **Bates, Patricia; Printmaking**
Embro, Ont: **Cody, Henry John**
embroidery: **Bates, Patricia; Indian Art; Ukrainians**
embryo: **Dairy Farming; Family Law; Genetics**
embryology: **Biology; Persaud, Trivedi Vidhya Nandan**
emergency locator transmitters: **Space Technology**
emergency measures: **Floods & Flood Control**
Emergency Planning Canada: **Civil Defence**
Emergency Planning Order: **Internment**
Emergency Powers Act: **Agricultural Products Board**
emergency powers in peace & war: **Distribution of Powers**
Ęmérillon: **Cartier, Jacques**
Emile Nelligan Foundation: **Literary Prizes in French**
Ęmile River: **Great Slave Lake**
Emilie Gamelin, Mother: **Saints**
Emily Carr College of Art & Design: **Community College; Raginsky, Nina**
Emissaries of Divine Light: **New Religious Movements**
Emma Lake Artists' Workshop: **Art Education; Painting; Perehudoff, William; Regina Five**
Emma Lake Artist's Workshop: **Shadbolt, Jack Leonard**
Emmanuel College (Anglican): **Anglicanism; University of Saskatchewan**
Emmanuel College (Methodist): **Grant, John Webster; University of Toronto**
Emmenin: **Estrogen**
Emmy Award: **Campbell, Norman Kenneth; Crum, George; Reid, D. Kate**
Ęmond, Pierre: **Séminaire de Québec**
Emori, Eiko: **Graphic Design**
emphysema: **Air Pollution; Disability; Smoking**
emphyteusis: **Property Law**
Empire Co Ltd: **Sobey, William Macdonald**
Empire Life Insurance Co: **Jackman, Henry N.R.**
Empire Stadium: **British Columbia Lions**
Empire Tobacco Co: **Tobacco-Products Industry**
Empire Valley Ranch: **Ranching History**
Employment & Immigration Canada: **Labour Market**
Employment & Immigration Commission: **Community College; Immigration Policy; Labour Policy; Students, Financial Aid to**
Employment Service of Canada: **Unemployment Relief Camps**
Empress Hotel: **Architecture, Rattenbury, Francis M.; Victoria**
Empress Theatre: **Chaussé, Joseph-Alcide**
Emsdale, Ont: **Christian Religious Communities**
En Croix, Lac: **Shawinigan, Lac**
enamel: **Antimony; Nepheline Syenite**
encephalitis: **Insect Pests; Mosquito; Veterinary Medicine**
Encyclopedia of Newfoundland: **Smallwood, Joseph R.**
Encyclopédie Canadienne: **Magazines**
Endeavour: **Canada & Australia**
Endeavour (research ship): **Oceanography**
Enderby, BC: **Okanagan Valley**
endocrinology: **Cameron, Alexander Thomas; Collip, J. Bertram**
Endymion Island: **Thousand Islands**
enemy aliens: **Internment; Italians; Prejudice & Discrimination; Ukrainians**
Energy & Chemical Workers Union: **Chemical Industries; Petrochemical Industry**
Energy Board (Ont): **Ontario Hydro**
Energy from the Forest Program: **Biomass Energy**

Energy-from-waste projects: **Biomass Energy**
Energy Planning Board (NS): **Nova Scotia**
Energy Pricing Agreement: **Lougheed, E. Peter**
Energy Probe: **Pressure Group**
Energy Research Laboratories: **Petroleum Research & Development**
Energy Resources Conservation Board (Alta): **Petroleum**
Enfants de Chénier: **Germain, Jean-Claude**
Enfants de Marie: **Theatre, French-Language**
Enfield pottery: **Ceramics**
ENFOR program: **Forest Harvesting**
engagé: **Nor'Wester**
Engel, Howard: **Popular Literature in English**
Engelmann spruce: **Banff National Park; Glacier National Park; Mount Assiniboine Provincial Park; Spruce; Vegetation Regions - Cordillera**
engine: **Aerospace Industry; Agricultural Implements Industry; Automobile; Automotive Industry; Folk Art; Foulis, Robert; Gibson, William Wallace; Helicopter; Lake Carriers; Machinery & Equipment Industry; Shipbuilding & Ship Repair**
Engineering Alumni Medal: **Brown, Eldon Leslie**
Engineering & Statistical Research Institute: **Research Stations, Agricultural**
Engineering Institute of Canada: **Associations; Civil Engineering; Mechanical Engineering**
Engineering Research Council: **Students, Financial Aid to**
engineering societies: **Associations; Chemical Industries; Civil Engineering; Electronics Industry; Gzowski, Casimir S.; Keefer, Thomas C.; Mechanical Engineering**
Engineerium: **Science Centre**
Englehart & Co: **Englehart, Jacob Lewis**
English Bay: **Vancouver**
English Language Publishing in Canada Conference: **Authors & Their Milieu**
English Property Corp: **Reichmann family**
English River: **Seul, Lac**
English-Wabigoon river system: **Pollution**
Englishman's River, BC: **Parksville**
Englishtown, NS: **McAskill, Angus**
Ennadai Lake: **Kazan River**
Enterprise: **Poetry in English**
entire-leaved gumweed: **Vegetation Regions - Pacific Coastal**
entomological journals: **Entomology; Zoology**
Entomological Soc of Canada: **Associations; Bethune, Charles James Stewart; Croft, Henry Holmes; Saunders, William; Zoology**
Entomological Soc of Ontario: **Science**
Entomology Research Institute: **Zoology**
entrapment: **Criminal Law**
Entre-Six Dance Company: **Dance on Television & Film; Gradus, Lawrence; Theatre Ballet of Canada**
Entreprises de J. Armand Bombardier Limitée: **Bombardier Inc**
entropy: **Chemistry Subdisciplines**
enumeration: **Electoral Systems; Franchise; Local Elections**
Environment, Dept of the: **Arts Funding; Bedford Institute of Oceanography; Parks, National**
Environment & Land Use Act (BC): **British Columbia**

Environment Canada: **Biomass Energy; Canada Centre for Inland Waters; Diving, Underwater; Drought; Forestry; Geographical Information Systems; Geomorphology; Physical Geography; Sea Ice; Soft-Drink Industry; Wildlife Conservation & Management**
Environmental Assessment & Review Process: **Parks, National; Social Impact Assessment; Urban & Regional Planning**
Environmental Contaminants Act: **Environmental Law; Hazardous Wastes**
Environmental Council of Alberta: **Alberta**
environmental engineering: **Civil Engineering**
environmental protection: **Bedford Institute of Oceanography; Diving, Underwater; Environmental Law; White-Collar Crime**
enzyme: **Arthritis; Biochemistry; Biotechnology; Diabetes Mellitus; Khorana, Har Gobind; Molecular Biology; Stanier, Roger Yate**
eohippus: **Horse**
Eozoon canadense: **Dawson, J. William**
Eparchy of Saints Cyril & Methodius: **Catholicism**
Épaves Bay: **Norse Voyages**
epidemiology: **Institut Armand-Frappier**
epilepsy: **Biochemistry; Disability; Elliott, K. Allan C.; Injury & Prevention; Medical Drug Abuse; Medical Research; Penfield, Wilder G.**
epinephrine: **Insulin**
Episcopal Palace: **Ostell, John**
Episcopalian: **Anglicanism**
epistemology: **Philosophy**
Epp, G.K.: **German Writing**
Epps, Bernard: **Morrison, Donald**
Epworth League: **Evangelism**
equal pay for equal work of equal value: **Employment Law; National Action Committee on the Status of Women; Status of Women; Status of Women in Canada, Royal Commission on the; Women in the Labour Force; Women's Labour Leagues**
equality before the law, principle of: *Lavell Case; Mackay Case*
equality of opportunity: **Educational Opportunity; Public Service**
equality of the sexes: **Baha'i Faith; Citizenship; New Left; Policing; Status of Women in Canada, Royal Commission on the; Women's Movement**
equality rights: **Constitution Act, 1982**
equinox: **Northern Lights**
Equipe: **Theatre, English-Language**
Equitable Life Insurance Co of Canada: **Kitchener-Waterloo**
equity: **Law**
Equity Chambers: **Architecture, Development**
Erdész, Otto: **Musical Instruments**
Erebus: **Franklin, John**
Erebus Bay: **Beechey Island**
ergot: **Fungus; Rye**
Eric Lake: **Cape Scott Provincial Park**
Erickson, Albert: **Erickson**
Erickson, John M.: **Chautauqua**
Erickson, Nola: **Chautauqua**
Erie Creek: **Salmo**
Erie Plain: **Niagara Peninsula**
Eriksdale, Man: **Garson, Stuart Sinclair**
Erin Mountain: **Barachois Pond Provincial Park**
Erindale College: **Botanical Garden; University of Toronto; Wilson, J. Tuzo**
Erlandson, Erland: **George, Rivière; Smallwood Reservoir**
Ermatinger, Charles: **Sault Ste Marie**
Ermatinger, Lawrence: **Swiss**
ermine: **Fur Trapping, Contemporary; Weasel**
Ermineskin Band: **Smallboy, Johnny Bob**
Ernest Harmon Air Force Base: **Stephenville**
Ernest Thompson Seton Award: **Canadian Wildlife Federation**

Erola, Judy: **Finns**
erotica: **Carle, Gilles; Pornography**
Errington, Joseph: **Lindsley, Thayer**
Erskine, John S.: **Archaeology**
ERTS I: **Remote Sensing**
erucic acid: **Vegetable Oil Industry**
erysipelas: **Veterinary Medicines Industry**
escargot: **Snail**
Escheat Party: **Land Question, PEI**
escort service: **Prostitution**
Escuminac, Baie d': **Fossil Plants**
Escuminac, NB: **Disasters**
Esdale, H.: **Remote Sensing**
Eskimo-Aleut language stock: **Anthropology, Linguistics; Eskimo**
Eskimo Dog Research Foundation: **Dog**
Eskimo Point: **Prince of Wales's Fort**
Esler, John K.: **Printmaking**
Espace 55: **Comtois, Ulysse**
Esperanto: **Language**
espionage: **Crime; Intelligence Gathering; Internment**
Esquimalt, CFB: **Esquimalt; Victoria**
Esquimalt & Nanaimo Railway: **Courtenay; Duncan; Dunsmuir, James; Dunsmuir, Robert; Esquimalt; Malahat Pass; Nanaimo; Vancouver Island; Victoria**
Esquimalt harbour: **Theatre, English-Language; Victoria**
Esquires: **Cockburn, Bruce**
Essays on Canadian Writing: **Literary Magazines in English; Literary Periodicals in English; Literature in English - Theory & Criticism**
Essence: **Death & Dying**
Essex, Ont: **Windsor, Ont**
Essex College: **University of Windsor**
Essex Manufacturing Co: **Ford Motor Co of Canada, Ltd**
Essex Packers Ltd: **Meat-Processing Industry**
Esso Resources Canada Ltd: **Bitumen; Imperial Oil Ltd; Libraries; Megaprojects; Petroleum Research & Development**
Essondale, BC: **Horse**
Est, Ile de l': **Madeleine, Iles de la**
Established Programs Financing: **Equalization Payments; Health Policy; Hospitals; Opting-Out; Taxation; Transfer Payments**
"Establishment": **Business Elites**
Estate Tax Act: **Taxation, Royal Commission on**
Esterhazy, Paul O.: **Hungarians**
Estevan Point, BC: **Lighthouses**
Estey, Zebulon: **Hymns**
Estoc: **Drama in French**
Estonian National Theatre: **Theatre, Multicultural**
Estonian Orthodox Church: **Orthodox Church**
Estuaire: **Literary Periodicals in French**
estuarine circulation: **Fjord**
Ętang-du-Nord, Qué: **Cap aux Meules, Ile du**
Etcheverry, Jorge: **Ethnic Literature**
Ętcheverry, Sam: **Montreal Concordes**
Eternité Baie d': **Trakas, George**
ethane: **Petrochemical Industry; Petroleum**
ethanol: **Alcoholism; Biomass Energy**
ether: **Pharmaceuticals Industry; Worthington, Edward Dagge**
ethics: **Anthropology; Artists' Organizations; Bioethics; Contract Law; Engineering; Jurisprudence; Legal Education; Medical Ethics; Medical Jurisprudence; Medical Research; Philosophy; *R v Olson*; Religion; Young, George Paxton**
Ethiopian Orthodox Church: **Orthodox Church**
Ethiopians: **Africans**
ethnic jokes: **Folklore**
ethnobotany: **Plants, Native Uses; Urgent Ethnology**
ethnocentrism: **Ethnic & Race Relations; Racism**
ethnography: **Anthropology; Lafitau, Joseph-François**
ethnohistory: **Association for Canadian Studies**
ethnolinguistics: **Anthropology, Linguistics; Urgent Ethnology**
Ethnological Survey of Canada: **Dawson, George M.**

ethnology: **Anthropology; Barbeau, C. Marius; Jenness, Diamond; McIlwraith, Thomas Forsyth; Urgent Ethnology; Wilson, Daniel**
ethnomedicine: **Aster; Bearberry; Dock; Gentian; Geranium; Groundsel; Hawthorn; Herbs; Holly; Honeysuckle; Indian Pipe; Lady's Slipper; Mint; Mistletoe; Trillium; Urgent Ethnology; Willow**
ethnomusicology: **Folklore; Musicology**
ethology: **Biology**
Ethos: **Literary Magazines in English**
ethyl alcohol: **Alcoholism; Distilling Industry**
Ethylec Inc: **Chemical Industries**
ethylene: **Chemical Industries; Medicine, History of**
Etobicoke, Ont: **Bobsledding; Diving, Underwater; Marathon Swimming; Pay Television; Toronto**
Etobicoke Swim Club: **Swimming, Speed**
Etomami River: **Assiniboine River**
Etter, Philippe: **Purcell String Quartet**
Etudes françaises: **Literary Periodicals in French; Literature in French - Criticism & Theory**
Études littéraires: **Literary Periodicals in French; Literature in French - Criticism & Theory**
EUBEX: **Arctic Oceanography**
Eucharist: **Anglicanism; Catholicism**
Eudist Fathers: **Université Sainte-Anne**
eulachon: **Bella Coola; Nass River; Smelt; Tahltan; Tsimshian**
Eurasian water milfoil: **Weeds**
Eureka, NWT: **Ellesmere Island; Nordicity**
Eureka Sound: **Axel Heiberg Island; Fosheim Peninsula**
Eurekan Orogeny: **Geological Regions**
Eurocan Pulp & Paper Co: **Kitimat**
European spruce sawfly: **Insect, Beneficial**
euthanasia: **Bioethics; Death & Dying; Science & Society**
eutrophication: **Vollenweider, Richard Albert**
Evangelical Lutheran Church of Canada: **Lutherans; Norwegians**
Evangelical Lutheran Seminary of Canada: **Wilfrid Laurier University**
Evangelical Orthodox Church: **Orthodox Church**
Evangelical United Brethren: **Holiness Churches; United Church of Canada**
Evangeline, L': **New Brunswick**
Evans, Arthur, "Slim": **On to Ottawa Trek; Working-Class History**
Evans, Donald: **Philosophy**
Evans, F.S.: **Automobile Racing**
Evans, Richard: **Painting**
Evans Coal Mines Ltd: **Coal**
Evans Research Corp: **Computer Industry; Electronics Industry**
Evanturel, Eudore: **Poetry in French**
evaporation: **Hydrology; Reservoir; Spring; Water Treatment**
evaporite: **Geological Regions; Potash**
Eve, A.S.: **Physics**
Eveleigh, Henry: **Graphic Design**
Evelyn, K.A.: **Biochemistry**
Evelyn Richardson Memorial Award: **Literary Prizes in English**
Événement: **Picard, Gérard; Potvin, Damase; Tarte, Joseph-Israel**
evening grosbeak: **Biogeography; Grosbeak**
evening primrose: **Endangered Plants; Fireweed**
Evening World: **Sun**
Everett, Lemuel C.: **Hymns**
Everett Point: **St Lawrence River**
Evergreen: **Yachting**
Evergreen, Alta: **Slovenes**
evergreen huckleberry: **Vegetation Regions - Cordillera**
Evermon, Bob: **Printmaking**
Everson, Ronald Gilmour: **Poetry in English**
Everyman Theatre Co: **Theatre, English-Language**
evidence: **Criminal Investigation; Examination for Discovery; Law of Evidence; *R v Truscott***
Ewach, Honore: **Ukrainian Writing**

ewer: **Silver, Church; Silver, Domestic**
Ewing Commission: **Métis**
Ex-Mormons for Jesus: **New Religious Movements**
Ex parte Renaud: **New Brunswick School Question**
examinations: **Computer Systems Applications; Curriculum Development**
excess profits tax: **Taxation**
Exchange Bank of Yarmouth: **Lovitt, William Dodge**
Exchange of Service Agreements: **Probation & Parole**
Exchequer Court of Canada: **Burbidge, George Wheelock; Federal Court of Canada; Supreme Court of Canada**
excise tax: **Jewellery & Silverware Industry**
executor: **Trust Company**
Exhibition Park: **Architecture, Development; Canada's Sports Hall of Fame**
Exhibition Stadium: **Toronto Argonauts; Toronto Blue Jays**
exhibitions: **Agricultural Exhibitions; Calgary Stampede; Canadian National Exhibition; Expo 67**
Exide Corp: **Inco Ltd**
existentialism: **Acorn, Milton; Langevin, André; *Parti pris*; Philosophy**
exotists: **Literature in French; Literature in French - Criticism & Theory**
experimental farms: **Agricultural Research & Development; Arboretum; Botanical Garden; Indian Head; Kapuskasing; Research Stations, Agricultural**
exploitation: **Bunkhouse Men; Dionne Quintuplets; Ethnic & Race Relations; Industrial Workers of the World; Pornography; Prostitution; Ukrainians**
Exploits, Bay of: **Exploits River; Notre Dame Bay**
Explorations: **Poetry in English**
Explorer Plate: **Earthquake; Geological Regions**
Explorer Ridge: **Oceanography**
explosion: **Bedford Magazine Explosion; Disasters; Halifax Explosion; Lighting**
explosives: **Armaments; Chemistry; Chemistry Subdisciplines; Defence Research; Distilling Industry**
Expo 70: **Industrial Design**
Expo 86: **Pattison, James A.; Transportation Research Centres**
Expo Theatre: **Niverville, Louis de**
Export Development Corp: **Barter**
export tax: **Energy Policy**
exports: **Aerospace Industry; Agriculture & Food Policy; Agriculture History; Automotive Industry; Balance of Payments; Barley; Barter; Boating; Brewing Industry; Buckwheat; Business Cycles; Business Management; Cadmium; Canadair Ltd; Canadian-American Economic Relations; Canadian Wheat Board; Chemical Industries; Clothing Industries; Computer Industry; Condiment Crops; Conservation; Crops; Dairy Farming; Distilling Industry; Electrical Appliances Industry; Electronics Industry; Energy in Society; Energy Policy; Fisheries; Fisheries History; Flour Milling Industry; Footwear Industry; Foreign Investment; Forestry; Fur Industry; Furniture & Fixture Industry; Great Depression; Hays, Harry W.; Hazardous Wastes; International Economics; International Trade; Iron & Steel Industry; Jewellery & Silverware Industry; Lead; Lumber & Wood Industries; Machinery & Equipment Industry; Manitoba; Manufacturing; Maple Sugar Industry; Meat-Processing Industry; Molybdenum; National Energy Board; Nepheline Syenite; Nickel; *cont...***

Ocean Industry; Pea, Field; Petroleum Supply & Demand; Piano Manufacturing; Prince Edward Island; Print Industry; Pulp & Paper Industry; Québec; Rapson, William Howard; Rye; Salt; Shipping Industry; Sporting-Goods Industry; Staple Thesis; Sulphur; Textile Industry; Third Option; Timber Trade History; Tobacco-Products Industry; Transportation; Uranium; Wheat; Wholesale Trade; Zinc**
Exposition de Québec: **Plamondon, Antoine**
expropriation: **Agricultural Economics; City; Energy Policy; Hecla; Nationalization; Public Works, Canada**
Exshaw, Alta: **Cement Industry**
External Affairs building: **Osuitok Ipeelee**
External Aid Office: **Canadian International Development Agency**
extortion: **Organized Crime**
extra billing: **Health Policy**
Exxon Corp (Canada) Ltd: **Mackenzie Valley Pipeline; Petroleum Industries**
Eyebrow, Sask: **Place-names**

F

F.W. Fearman Co Ltd: **Meat-Processing Industry**
Faber Lake: **Great Bear Lake**
fables: **Folklore**
Fabre, Edouard: **Long-Distance Running**
Fabre, Edouard-Charles: **Theatre, English-Language**
Fabre, Hector: **Literature in French - Scholarship & Teaching**
fabric: **Clothing Industries; Furniture & Fixture Industry; Metric Conversion; Prehistory; Textile Industry; Weaving, Contemporary**
Fabulous Shays: **Clayton-Thomas, David**
faceclock: **Dandelion**
Factory Acts: **Employment Law**
factory ships: **Nova Scotia; Whaling**
Factory Theatre Lab: **Theatre, English-Language**
Faillon, Etienne-Michel: **Historiography**
Fair Wages Commission (Qué): **Duplessis, Maurice Le Noblet**
Fairbairn, A.M.D.: **Drama in English**
Fairfield, Robert: **Stratford Festival**
Fairfield colony: **Zeisberger, David**
Fairford Dam: **Manitoba**
Fairhaven, NB: **Deer Island**
Fairley, Margaret: **Essay in English**
Fairmont Hot Springs: **Invermere; Spring**
Fairview Cove: **Nova Scotia**
Fairway crested wheatgrass: **Kirk, Lawrence Eldred**
Fairweather, Mount: **British Columbia**
Fairy Lake: **Huntsville**
Fairy Lake (Qué): **Ski Jumping**
fairy ring: **Mushroom & Puffball**
fairy-spud: **Wildflowers**
Faith Alive: **Evangelical Fellowship of Canada**
faith healing: **André, Brother; False Face Society; Pilgrimage; Shaking Tent**
Falaise Gap: **World War II**
Falardeau, Jean-Charles: **Literature in French - Scholarship & Teaching**
Falardeau, Pierre: **Video Art**
Falashas ("Black Jews"): **Africans**
Falck, Robert: **Musicology**
Falcon Lake: **Falcon, Pierre; Whiteshell Provincial Park**
Falconbridge, Ont: **Metallurgy**
Falconbridge Ltd: **Lindsley, Thayer; Metallurgy; Nickel; Science Centre; Sudbury**
Falher, C.: **Falher**
Falmouth: **Hector**
Falmouth, NS: **Alline, Henry**
false advertising: **Competition Policy; White-Collar Crime**
false azalea: **Mount Assiniboine Provincial Park; Poisonous Plants**

False Creek: **Urban Transportation; Vancouver**
false cypress: **Cypress**
false embroidery: **Northwest Coast Indian Art**
false enumeration: **Electoral Systems**
false evidence: **Perjury**
false hellebore: **Poisonous Plants**
false imprisonment: **Jury; Torts**
false mitrewort (foam flower): **Saxifrage**
false Solomon's seal: **Biogeography; Solomon's Seal**
Faludy, George: **Ethnic Literature**
Family Allowances Act: **Social Security**
Family Brown, the: **Country & Western Music**
family farm: **Farm Law; Prairie West**
Family Herald: **Authors & Their Milieu; Leprohon, Rosanna E.; Newspapers**
Family Herald & Weekly Star: **Magazines**
Family Law Reform Acts: **Housework**
Family Medicine: **Medicine, General Practice**
family planning: **Birth Control; Child Abuse; Morgentaler, Henry**
family "tree": **Genealogy**
famine: **Hare (Indians); Native People, Health; Ste Marie Among the Hurons**
Famine River: **St-Georges**
Famous People Players: **Theatre, English-Language**
Famous Players Canadian Corp Ltd: **Film; Grand Theatre; Media Ownership; Nathanson, Nathan Louis**
Fanning, Edmund: **Land Question, PEI**
Fanon, Frantz: **Literature in English**
Fanshaw, Hubert V.: **Printmaking**
Far West Mountain Wear: **Camping**
Fardon, George Robinson: **Photography**
Faribault, Marcel: **Deux Nations**
farm accounting & management: **Agricultural Economics; Agricultural Education; Farm Law**
Farm & Ranch Review: **Gray, James H.**
Farm Improvement Loans Act: **Agriculture & Food Policy**
Farm Labour Pool: **Labour Policy**
Farm Machinery, Royal Commission on: **Barber, Clarence L.**
Farm Products Marketing Agencies Act: **Agricultural Marketing Board; Agriculture & Food Policy**
Farm Radio Forum: **Adult Education; Educational Broadcasting; Hannam, Herbert H.**
Farm Syndicate Credit Act: **Farm Credit Corp**
Farmer-Labour Party: **Coldwell, "M.J."; Labour Party; Nova Scotia; United Farmers of Canada**
Farmer Progressive Party: **Jones, John Walter**
Farmers' Assn: **Good, William Charles; United Farmers of Ontario**
Farmers' Elevator Co-op: **Crerar, Thomas A.**
Farmers' Institutes: **Adult Education**
Farmers March on Ottawa: **Wesson, John Henry**
Farmers' Sun: **Plaunt, Alan Butterworth; Spry, Graham; United Farmers of Ontario**
Farmers' Union of Canada: **Agriculture History; Grain Growers' Associations; Partridge, Edward A.; United Farmers of Canada; United Farmers of Manitoba**
Farmersville, Ont: **Place-names**
Farnam, Lynnwood: **Music History**
faro: **Gambling**
Farquharson, Charlie: **Harron, Donald**
Farr, C.C.: **Haileybury**
Farrar, C.B.: **Psychiatry**
farrier: **Blacksmithing, French Canada; Veterinary Medicine, History**
Farrington, Harvey: **Cheese & Cheesemaking**
Farrow, Brad: **Judo**
Farsi: **Language**
Farwell, BC: **Revelstoke**
Fashion-Craft Manufacturers: **Lévesque, Jean-Louis**

fasting: **Childhood, History of; Judaism; Native People, Religion**
Father Lacombe Museum: **St Albert**
Father of Many Children: **Blood**
Fathom Five Provincial Park: **Bruce Peninsula; Wildlife Preserve**
Fathom Oceanology Ltd: **Ocean Industry**
Fatima, Qué: **Cap aux Meules, Île du**
Faucher, Albert: **Economics; Timlin, Mabel F.**
Faucher de Saint-Maurice, Narcisse-H.-E: **Exploration & Travel Literature in French; Oral Literature in French; Short Fiction in French**
Fauchois, Michel: **Sculpture**
Faulkner, Hugh: **Magazines**
Faulknor, Cliff: **Children's Literature in English**
fault: **Delict; Family Law**
faults: **Cumberland Sound; Earthquake; Escarpment; Frobisher Bay; Geological Regions; Kluane Ranges; Melville Peninsula; Physiographic Regions - Arctic Lands; Prince Patrick Island; Rocky Mountain Trench; St Lawrence Lowland; St-Maurice, Rivière; Waterfall; Yukon Territory**
Fauset, Arthur Huff: **Folklore**
Fay, Ferenc: **Ethnic Literature**
Fazakas, Ray: **Donnellys, The**
Fearman, F.W.: **Meat-Processing Industry**
feather mosses: **Biogeography; Vegetation Regions - Boreal Forest or Taiga**
feather star: **Echinodermata**
Fecteau, Joseph: **Thetford-Mines**
Federal Advisory Committee on Election Expenses: **Party Financing**
Federal Building (Vancouver): **Architecture, Development**
Federal Business Development Bank: **Crown Corporation**
Federal Commerce & Navigation Ltd: **Canada Steamship Lines Inc**
Federal Cultural Policy Review Committee: **Applebaum, Louis; Arts Funding; Authors & Their Milieu; Heraldry Society of Canada; Héroux, Denis; Symons, Thomas H.B.; Theatre, English-Language**
Federal Express: **Transportation**
Federal Mediation & Conciliation Program: **Labour Canada**
federal paramountcy: **Constitution Act, 1867**
Federated Labor Congress: **Union Centrals, District & Regional**
Fédération catholique des institutrices rurales: **Gaudreault, Laure**
Fédération de la pulpe et du papier: **Marchand, Jean**
Fédération des co-opératives du Nouveau-Québec: **Inuit Co-operatives**
Fédération des femmes canadiennes-françaises: **Women's Movement**
Fédération des femmes du Québec: **Casgrain, Thérèse**
Fédération des loisirs-danse du Québec: **Folk Dance**
Fédération des travailleurs du Québec: **Laberge, Louis**
Fédération Internationale de Football Association: **Soccer**
Fédération nationale de la métallurgie: **Pepin, Marcel**
Fédération nationale des travailleurs du vêtement: **Chartrand, Michel**
Fédération nationale St-Jean-Baptiste: **Gerin-Lajoie, Marie**
Federation of Canadian Artists: **Biéler, André Charles; Loring, Frances N.; Wyn Wood, Elizabeth**
Federation of Canadian Municipalities: **Municipal-Provincial Relations; Urban Studies**
Federation of Law Socs of Canada: **Legal Education**
Federation of Ontario Naturalists: **Gunn, William Walker Hamilton**
Federation of Saskatchewan Indian Nations: **Deiter, Walter**
Federation of Saskatchewan Indians: **Deiter, Walter; Native People, Political Organization & Activism**

Federation of Silent Sports: **Auditory Impairment**
Federation of Southern Manitoba Co-operatives: **Siemens, Jacob John**
Federation of Women Teachers Assns of Ontario Poetry Award: **Literary Prizes in English**
Fédération provinciale du travail du Québec: **Asbestos Strike; Francq, Gustave**
Fednav Ltd: **Shipping Industry**
Fedyk, Teodor: **Ukrainian Writing**
feed grains: **Agriculture & Food Policy; Canadian Wheat Board**
feedlot: **Beef Cattle Farming**
Feist, Harold: **Painting**
feldspar: **Gemstone; Mineral; Nepheline Syenite; Sedimentary Rock**
Felixstowe flying boats: **Military Aviation & Aircraft**
Feller, Henriette: **Baptists**
Fellowship for a Christian Social Order: **Bland, Salem G.; Gordon, J. King; Social Gospel**
Fellowship of Evangelical Baptist Churches: **Evangelical & Fundamentalist Movements**
Fellowship of Reconciliation: **Pacifism**
felt: **Beaver Pelts; Fur Trade; Textile Industry**
Female Minimum Wage Act (BC): **Smith, M. Ellen**
feminist press: **Folklore; Women's Movement**
fencibles: **Armed Forces - Militia & Army**
fencing: **Organized Crime**
Fenelon Falls, Ont: **Kawartha Lakes; Langton, John**
Fennario, David: **Centaur Theatre; Drama in English; Literature in English; Theatre, English-Language**
fennel: **Condiment Crops; Vegetable**
Fenwick, John: **Musical Theatre**
Fenwick, Kathleen M.: **National Gallery of Canada**
Ferange, Claude: **Track & Field**
ferberite: **Tungsten**
Fergus, Ont: **Groves, Abraham**
Ferguson, Gerald: **Art, Contemporary Trends; Painting**
Ferguson, Harry: **Massey-Ferguson Ltd**
Ferguson, Richard: **Track & Field**
Ferland, Albert: **Literature & Politics; Poetry in French**
Ferland, Jean-Baptiste-Antoine: **Historiography**
Ferland, Jean-Pierre: **Claude, Renée**
Ferment, Jean: **Silver, Church**
Fermiers unis du Québec: **United Farmers of Québec**
Fermont, Qué: **Urban & Regional Planning**
Fernie, Peter: **Fernie, William**
Féron, Jean: **Popular Literature in French**
Ferranti-Packard Ltd: **Computer Industry; Computer Science; Industrial Research & Development**
Ferraté, Juan: **Comparative Literature**
Ferrie, Adam: **Unitarians**
Ferron, Madeleine: **Short Fiction in French**
Ferrona, NS: **Fraser, Graham**
Ferryland Head: **Placentia Bay**
fertility: **Birth Control; Marriage & Divorce; Population**
fertilizer: **Metallurgy**
FERUT: **Computer Science; Industrial Research & Development**
fescues: **Biogeography; Grasses; Vegetation Regions - Cordillera; Vegetation Regions - Prairie**
Festival Canada: **Centennial Year**
Festival des gourmands: **Asbestos, Qué**
Festival du disque: **Charlebois, Robert**
Festival du voyageur: **Manitoba**
Festival Express: **Hippies**
Festival internationale de la bicyclette: **Hull**
Festival of Festivals: **Festivals; Film Festivals, Prizes**
Festival of the Arts: **Stephenville**
Festival of the Empire Games: **Hodgson, George Ritchie**
Festival of the Sound: **Kuerti, Anton E.**

Festival Ottawa: **National Arts Centre; Opera; Orford String Quartet**
Festival Singers: **Canadian Brass**
Festival Theatre: **Stratford Festival**
fetal alcohol syndrome: **Alcoholism**
fetal malformations: **Pharmaceuticals Industry**
Fête Franco-Manitobaine: **Festivals; Manitoba**
Fêtes du Saguenay: **La Baie**
fetus: **Abortion; Birthing Practices**
fiberglass: **Boating; Canadarm; Greenhouse Crops**
fibre optics: **Electronics Industry; Physics; Telephones**
fibrisols: **Soil Classification**
fiction: **Children's Literature in English; Children's Literature in French; Ethnic Literature; *Fiddlehead*; German Writing; Humorous Writing in English; Italian Writing; Jewish Writing; Literature in English; Literature in French; Novel in English; Novel in French; Oral Literature in English; Oral Literature in French; Popular Literature in English; Popular Literature in French; Short Fiction in English; Short Fiction in French; Ukrainian Writing**
fiddle: **Folk Dance; Folk Music, Anglo-Canadian**
Fiddlehead Poetry Books: **Book Publishing, English-Language; Small Presses**
Fidinam affair: **Party Financing**
Fidler, Isaac: **Exploration & Travel Literature in English**
fiefs: **Seigneurial System**
Field, BC: **Trilobite; Tunnels; Yoho National Park**
Field, Cyrus: **Gisborne, Frederick Newton**
Field, G.S.: **Sonar**
Field, Robert: **Printmaking**
Field House: **Niagara-on-the-Lake**
field mouse: **Vole**
Fielding, George: **Piracy**
Fielding, Joy: **Popular Literature in English**
Fields Medal: **Fields, John Charles; Mathematics**
Fields Stores Ltd: **Thomson Group**
15 Dance Lab: **Dance, Modern**
Fifth Thule Expedition: **Archaeology**
fighters: **Armed Forces - Unification; Military Aviation & Aircraft**
Fighting Island: **Detroit River**
Figure of Eight Canyon: **South Nahanni River**
figureheads: **Jobin, Louis; Sculpture**
figurines: **Folk Art; Inuit Art**
Fijians: **South Asians**
file: **Tools, Carpentry**
File: **Art Writing & Criticism**
filiation: **Civil Code; Family Law**
Filiatrault, Jean: **Novel in French**
Filiot, Jean: **Clocks & Watches**
Filles d'aujourd'hui: **Quebecor Inc**
Film Censorship Acts: **Censorship**
Film Design Ltd: **Film Animation**
Filmcraft Industries: **Film**
fin whale: **Fundy, Bay of/Gulf of Maine; Grand Manan Island; Saguenay River; Whale**
Financial Administration Act: **Crown Corporation**
Financial Management & Accountability, Royal Commission on: **Economic Regulation**
Finch, Mary: *Plouffe*
Finch, Robert: **Literature in English; Poetry in English**
Fineberg, Larry: **Beresford-Howe, Constance; Drama in English**
fines & penalties: **Competition Policy; Criminal Law; Food Legislation; Juvenile Justice Systems; Municipal Finance; White-Collar Crime**
Fingard, Judith: **Social History**
finger-pull: **Sports History**
fingerprints: **Criminal Investigation**
Finlay, Hugh: **Postal System**
Finlay & Gregory: **Mackenzie, Alexander (1764-1820)**
Finlay River: **Mackenzie; Peace River**
Finlayson, William D.: **Archaeology**
Finlayson Arm: **Malahat Pass**
Firby, Howard: **Swimming, Speed**

fire: **Architecture, Development; Botany History; Building Codes & Regulations; Canning; Cochrane, Ont; Disasters; Forest Fire; Hull; Montréal Riots; Mount Saint Vincent University; Native People, Social Conditions; *Noronic*; Oral Literature in English; Parliament, Library of; Québec City; Rimouski; Safety Standards; Ste-Anne-de-Beaupré; Saint John; St John's; St-Quentin; Simpsons, Ltd; University of King's College; Waste Disposal; Water Distribution System**
Fire Hall Theatre: **Medicine Hat**
"fire-water": **High Wines**
Fireaway: **Horse**
firebrat: **Insect Classification**
Firestone Canada Inc: **Hamilton; Rubber Products Industry**
firestorm: **Disasters**
first aid: **Nursing; Physical Education**
First Biennial of Canadian Painting: **Smith, Gordon Appelbe**
First Canadian Himalayan Expedition: **Mountaineering**
First Canadian Place: **Bregman & Hamann; Ontario**
First Choice: **Pay Television**
First City Financial Corp Ltd: **Belzberg, Samuel**
First City Trust Co: **Belzberg, Samuel**
First Fruits Ceremony: **Kootenay**
First Ministers' Conferences: **Assembly of First Nations; Federal-Provincial Relations; Native Council of Canada; Quiet Revolution**
First Narrows: *Beaver*; **Tunnels**
First Salmon rite: **Native People, Religion**
First Statement: **Layton, Irving P.; Literary Magazines in English; Poetry in English**
First Statement Press: *Northern Review*
First Western Charter: **Newfoundland**
Firth, Frances: *Fiddlehead*
Firth, Sharon: **Cross-Country Skiing**
Firth, Shirley: **Cross-Country Skiing**
Firth, Wally: **Fort McPherson**
Fischer, Bobby: **Chess**
Fischer, Sarah: **Music History**
Fischer-Baer ester: **Baer, Erich**
Fischer-Tropsch (F-T) process: **Coal Liquefaction**
Fischman, Sheila: *Guerre, Yes Sir*
Fiset, Louis-Joseph-Cyprien: **Poetry in French**
Fisgard, BC: **Lighthouses**
Fish Creek Provincial Park: **Calgary**
fish farming: **Aquaculture; Manitoba; Native People, Economic Conditions; Wilmot, Samuel**
Fish Hawk: **Osprey**
Fish Inspection Act: **Fisheries**
fish ladder: **Hell's Gate**
fish lice: **Crustacean**
fish meal: **Fisheries History**
fish net: **Central Coast Salish; Prehistory**
fish oil: **Bella Coola; Lighthouses; Smelt; Tahltan; Tsimshian**
Fisher, Douglas: **Journalism**
Fisher, Edward: **Royal Conservatory of Music of Toronto**
Fisher, George: **Printmaking**
Fisher, John: **Centennial Year**
Fisher, Lenora: **Swimming, Speed**
Fisher, Orville: **Printmaking**
Fisheries, Dept of: **Fisheries History**
Fisheries Act: **Environmental Law; Fisheries; Fisheries History; Hazardous Wastes; Native People, Law; Wildlife Conservation & Management**
Fisheries & Oceans, Dept of: **Canada Centre for Inland Waters; Diving, Underwater; Endangered Animals; Fisheries; Fisheries History; Hydrography; Invertebrate; Oceanography; Sealing; Tide; Zoology**
Fisheries Exhibition & Fisherman's Reunion: **Lunenburg**
Fisheries Museum of the Atlantic: **Lunenburg**
Fisheries Prices Support Act: **Fisheries; Fisheries Policy**
Fisheries Prices Support Board: **Fisheries History**

Fisheries Research Board of Canada:
**Cameron, Alexander Thomas;
Cameron, William Maxwell;
Dickie, Lloyd Merlin; Hachey,
Henry Benedict; Huntsman,
Archibald Gowanlock; Nordicity;
Oceanography; Parasitology;
Prince, Edward Ernest; Ricker,
William Edwin**
Fishermen's Protective Union: **Coaker,
William F.; Fisheries History;
Fisheries Policy; Squires, Richard
Anderson**
Fishing Lake, Alta: **Métis Settlements**
fishing zone: **Boundaries; Law of
the Sea; Nova Scotia; Saint-Pierre
& Miquelon**
Fishman, Arthur P.: **Interior Design**
"fishyback" transportation:
Transportation
fission: **Cobalt; Nuclear Energy**
Fitness & Amateur Sport Act: **Track &
Field**
Fitness & Amateur Sport Programme:
Sports History
Fitness Canada: **Sports Organization,
Amateur**
Fitness Institute: **Track & Field**
Fitzgerald, John G.: **Connaught
Laboratories Ltd**
Fitzgerald, William: **Canadian
Lacrosse Hall of Fame**
FitzGibbon, James: **Secord, Laura**
Fitzhenry & Whiteside Ltd: **Dictionary**
Fitzhugh, Alta: **Jasper**
Fitzhugh, William W.: **Archaeology**
Fitzroy, Charles: **Canada & Australia**
Five Fingers, NB: **St-Quentin**
Five Mile Canyon: **South Nahanni
River**
Five Nations Confederacy: **Cayuga;
Dekanahwideh; Iroquois;
Mohawk; Native People, Political
Organization & Activism; Oneida;
Onondaga; Seneca**
Fladmark, Knut: **Archaeology**
flag: **Emblems, Provincial &
Territorial; Emblems of Canada;
Heraldry; Red Ensign**
flakes: **Fisheries History**
Flare: **Maclean Hunter Ltd**
Flat River: **Mackenzie River; South
Nahanni River**
flatbed press: **Print Industry**
Flathead River: **Endangered Animals;
Grayling**
flatware: **Jewellery & Silverware
Industry; Pewter; Silver, Domestic**
Flavelle Medal: **Boyle, Robert
William; Huntsman, Archibald
Gowanlock; Person, Clayton O.;
Quastel, Judah Hirsch; Rowan,
William; Siminovitch, Louis;
Thompson, Walter Palmer;
Tyrrell, Joseph B.; Walker,
Edmund Murton**
fleabane: **Endangered Plants**
Fleming, Allan R.: **Graphic Design;
Logo**
Flemingdon Park: **Urban Design**
Flemish: **Belgians**
Fletcher, Cliff: **Calgary Flames**
Fletcher, Evelyn: **Soaring**
Fletcher, Mrs: **Photography**
Fletcher's Field: **Muhlstock, Louis**
Fleur, Rivière la: **Orléans, Ile d'**
Fleurimont, Qué: **Sherbrooke**
Fleury, Claude: **Children's Literature
in French**
flex-time: **Work**
flexography: **Print Industry**
flicker: **Woodpecker**
Flin Flon Curling Club: **Curling**
Flin Flon Daily Reminder: **Manitoba**
Flin Flon Mine: **Mining**
Flin Flon volcanic arc: **Geological
Regions**
flint: **Prehistory; Rock & Mineral
Collecting**
Flintaft, Sask: **Romanians**
flintlock musket: **Firearm; Indian
Trade Goods**
float plane: **Bush Flying; de
Havilland Otter**
floating-heart: **Gentian**
flocculation: **Water Treatment**
floodplain: **Chaudière, Rivière; River
Landform**
Floral, Sask: **Howe, Gordon**
Floralies Internationales: **Montréal**
Florence Nightingale Medal:
**Mussallem, Helen K.; Watson,
Helen G.W.**

Florencia Bay: **Ucluelet**
flounder: **Fisheries History; Flatfish;
Newfoundland; Prince Edward
Island**
flour: **Agriculture History; Barley;
Buckwheat; Cereal Crops; Crow's
Nest Pass Agreement; Foreign Aid; Pea, Field;
Technology; Wheat**
Flour Mill Museum: **Sudbury**
Flowerpot Island: **Georgian Bay
Islands National Park**
Floyd, J. Austin: **Landscape
Architecture**
Floyd, James: **Avro Jetliner**
Floyd S. Chalmers Awards: **Theatre,
English-Language**
Floyd S. Chalmers Foundation:
**Chalmers, Floyd S.; Somers,
Harry S.**
flugelhorn: **Jazz**
fluke: **Animal Agriculture; Mollusc**
fluorine: **Chemistry Subdisciplines;
Mineral**
fluorite: **Mineral**
fluorocarbons: **Chemical Industries**
fluorometer: **Batfish**
fluorspar: **Newfoundland**
flute & flute music: **Aitken, Robert
Morris; Chamber Music**
fluvial landform: **River Landform**
Flyer Industries Ltd: **Bus
Transportation**
flying boats: **Aerospace Industry;
Military Aviation & Aircraft**
flying squirrel: **Kejimkujik
National Park; Squirrel**
Fobes, J.: **Steele, Mount**
fodder: **Beet; Corn, Field; Crops**
Fodi, John: **Orchestral Music**
fog alarm: **Cape Sable; Foulis, Robert;
Lighthouses**
Fogo, Nfld: **Fogo Island**
"Fogo Process": **Fogo Island**
Fogo Shelf: **Fogo Island**
Foire Brayonne: **Festivals**
Folejewski, Zbigniew: **Comparative
Literature**
Folklorama: **Festivals; Folklore**
Folklore & Language Archive:
Musicology
Folkloristes du Québec: **Folk Dance**
Folsom culture: **Paleoindian**
Fond du Lac: **Thompson, David**
Fond du Lac River: **Wollaston Lake**
Fonds de la recherche en sante du
Québec: **Medical Research**
Fonseca, Delio: **Sculpture**
Fontaine, Madeleine: **Madeleine, Iles
de la**
food: **Canada's Food Guide; Cuisine**
Food & Agriculture Organization:
**Environment; Kirk, Lawrence
Eldred; United Nations**
Food & Drug Directorate:
Pharmaceuticals Industry
Food & Drugs Act: **Consumer Law;
Consumer Standards; Distilling
Industry; Flour Milling Industry;
Food Legislation; Medical Drug
Abuse; Pharmaceuticals Industry;
Soft-Drink Industry; White-Collar
Crime**
food locker: **Furniture, French**
food preservation & storage:
**Biochemistry; Crop Research;
Food Additives; Fruit & Vegetable
Industry; Meat-Processing
Industry; Vegetable**
Food Prices Review Board: **Agriculture
& Food Policy; Consumers'
Association of Canada**
Food Research Institute: **Research
Stations, Agricultural**
food science: **Agricultural Education;
Home Economics; Institut
Armand-Frappier; International
Development Research Centre**
fool's gold: **Gold**
Foon, Dennis: **Children's Literature
in English**
foot & mouth disease: **Biological
Product; Veterinary Medicine**
foot racing: **Highland Games; Sports
History; Track & Field**
Foothills Pipe Lines (Yukon) Ltd:
**Mackenzie Valley Pipeline;
NOVA, An Alberta Corporation**
Footner, Hulbert: **Best-Sellers in
English; Popular Literature in
English**
Footner, William: **Architectural
Styles**

Forand, Pierre: **Parachuting, Sport**
Forbes, Elizabeth Armstrong:
Printmaking
Forbes, Francis: **Canada & Australia**
Forbes, John: **Ice Skating**
Forbidden Plateau: **Comox, BC;
Courtenay; Strathcona
Provincial Park**
Forbin-Janson, Msgr de: **Evangelism**
Forbis, Richard G.: **Archaeology**
Ford, Clifford: **Choral Music;
Musicology**
Ford, Leighton: **Evangelism**
Ford, Rivière: **George, Rivière**
Ford, W.: **Oceanography**
Ford City, Upper Canada:
Windsor, Ont
Ford Lake: **Waterfall**
Ford Trimotor aircraft: **Disasters**
Fording Coal Ltd: **Coal**
Fording River Mine: **Coal**
foreign assets: **Banking**
Foreign Claims Commission: **Campbell,
Thane Alexander**
Foreign Enlistment Act:
Mackenzie-Papineau Battalion
foreign exchange: **Balance of
Payments; Bank of Canada;
Chemical Industries; Tourism**
Foreign Exchange Control Board:
Gordon, Donald; Rasminsky, Louis
foreign missions: **Bible Schools;
Catholicism; Christian Religious
Communities; Holiness Churches;
Lutherans; McClure, Robert B.;
Methodism; Presbyterian &
Reformed Churches; Schofield,
Francis William**
foreign service: **External Affairs,
Dept of**
forensic science: **Criminal
Investigation; Palynology; Royal
Canadian Mounted Police**
Forest case: **Constitutional History**
Forest, Ceslas-Marie: **Philosophy**
Forest Engineering Research Institute of
Canada: **Forestry; Pulp & Paper
Industry**
Forest Lake: **Clearwater River
(Alta/Sask)**
forest law: **Timber Trade History**
Forest Pest Management Institute:
Forestry
forest reserve: **Manitoba; Shilo, CFB**
forest tent caterpillar: **Manitoba; Moth**
Forestburg Collieries Ltd: **Coal**
Forestier, Louis: **Charlebois, Robert**
Forestry, Dept of: **Holling, C.S., "Buzz";
Rowe, John Stanley**
Forestry Island: **Toronto Islands**
Forge, Andrew: **Townsend, William**
forgery: **Casson, Alfred Joseph;
Corruption; Inquiry into Certain
Activities of the RCMP, Royal
Commission of; Medical Drug
Abuse**
forges: **Aerospace Industry; Iron &
Steel Industry**
"forgotten school act": **Nova Scotia**
FORINTEK Canada Corp: **Forestry**
fork: **Domestic Utensils; Pewter;
Silver, Domestic**
Forks of the Grand River: **Paris**
Forksdale, BC: **Merritt**
Formation Professionelle: **Legal
Education**
Formolo, Maria: **Dance, Modern**
Formula One Cars: **Automobile
Racing**
fornication: **Conspiracy; Crime**
Forrest Bldg: **Dumaresq, James
Charles Philip**
Forrester, Alexander: **Education,
History of**
Forrester, Ronald W.: **Jiu-Jitsu**
Forsyth, Bertram: **Theatre,
English-Language**
Forsyth, Charles: **Franklin Search**
Forsyth, David: **Soccer**
Forsyth, P.A.: **Physics**
Forsyth, W.O.: **Chamber Music; Music
History**
Forsythe, Richardson, & Co: **North
West Company**
Fort Albany: **Albany River;
Archaeology; James Bay; Troyes,
Pierre de**
Fort Alexander: **Jacobs, Peter**
Fort Amherstburg: **War of 1812**
Fort Anne National Historic Park:
Annapolis Royal; Historic Site
Fort Assiniboine: **Portage; Rundle,
Robert Terrill**

Fort Astoria: **Columbia River; *Isaac
Todd*; Pacific Fur Company;
*Tonquin***
Fort Bourbon: **Radisson, Pierre-Esprit**
Fort Calgary Interpretive Centre:
Calgary
Fort Caministigoyan: **Thunder Bay**
Fort Carillon: **Abercromby, James;
Butler, John; Champlain, Lake;
Lévis, François-Gaston de**
Fort Carlton: **Big Bear; Butler,
William Francis; Diefenbaker,
John G.; Duck Lake; Riel, Louis**
Fort Cataraqui: **Fort Frontenac**
Fort Charles: **Troyes, Pierre de**
Fort Chequamegon: **La Vérendrye,
Louis-Joseph**
Fort-Chimo: **George, Rivière;
Koksoak, Rivière;
Montagnais-Naskapi**
Fort-Chimo Eskimo Co-operative:
Ookpik
Fort Chipewyan: **Janvier, Alex S.;
Libraries; North West Company**
Fort Churchill: **Chipewyan; Churchill
River; Prince of Wales's Fort**
Fort Colville: **Princeton**
Fort Confidence: **Great Bear Lake**
Fort Conti: **Tonty, Henri de**
Fort Cumberland: **American
Revolution; Fort Beauséjour;
Maugerville; Nova Scotia 1714-84**
Fort Dallas: **Lytton**
Fort de la Rivière Tremblante: **Grant,
Cuthbert**
Fort de Lévis: **Prescott**
Fort de Richelieu: **Richelieu, Rivière**
Fort Detroit: **Brock, Isaac; Medal;
Pontiac; *Wacousta***
Fort Douglas: **Manitoba; Red River
Colony; Seven Oaks Incident**
Fort Dufferin: **Emerson**
Fort Dunvegan: **McIntosh, William;
Peace River Lowland**
Fort Edmonton: **Edmonton;
Kane, Paul; Lacombe, Albert;
L'Heureux, Jean-B.; Royal
Canadian Mounted Police;
Rundle, Robert Terrill; York Boat**
Fort Edward: **Windsor, NS**
Fort Ellice: **Assiniboine River; Royal
Canadian Mounted Police**
Fort Erie track: **Thoroughbred Racing**
Fort Fork: **Peace River, Alta**
Fort Frances Pulp & Power Co Ltd: *Fort
Frances Case*
Fort Fraser: **Agriculture History;
Fraser, Simon**
Fort Frederick: **Saint John**
Fort Garry: **Fortification; Horetzky,
Charles G.; Kane, Paul; Nault,
André; Painting; Red River
Rebellion; Riel, Louis; Royal
Canadian Mounted Police**
Fort Garry Hotel: **Architecture**
Fort George: **Niagara Historic
Frontier; Niagara Peninsula; War
of 1812**
Fort-George: **James Bay Project; La
Grande Rivière**
Fort George, Rivière: **La Grande
Rivière**
Fort George (Astoria): **Pacific Fur
Company; *Racoon***
Fort George (Prince George):
Agriculture History; Fraser, Simon
Fort George River: **George, Rivière**
Fort Gibraltar: **Seven Oaks Incident**
Fort Grahame: **Sekani**
Fort Hope: **Princeton**
Fort Howe: **Saint John**
Fort Hughes: **Oromocto**
Fort Kaministiqua: **La Vérendrye,
Louis-Joseph**
Fort Kamloops: **Kamloops; Merritt**
Fort la Reine: **Assiniboine River; La
Vérendrye, Louis-Joseph; La
Vérendrye, Pierre; Portage la
Prairie**
Fort La Tour: **La Tour,
Françoise-Marie Saint-Étienne de;
Saint John**
Fort La Tourette: **Nipigon, Lake**
Fort Lawrence: **Fort Beauséjour;
Pichon, Thomas**
Fort Lennox: **Richelieu, Rivière**
Fort McLaughlin: **Bella Bella**
Fort McLeod: **Carrier; Fraser, Simon;
Sekani**
Fort Macleod Agricultural Fair: **Rodeo**
Fort McMurray Today: **Alberta**
Fort Malden Historical Park:
Amherstburg

Fort Maurepas: **Iberville, Pierre Le Moyne d'; La Vérendrye, Louis-Joseph; Red River**
Fort Miamis (Maumee, Ohio): **Carleton, Guy**
Fort Michilimackinac: **Lacrosse; *Wacousta***
Fort Michipicoten: **La Vérendrye, Louis-Joseph**
Fort Mississauga: **Niagara Historic Frontier**
Fort Mistassini: **King's Posts**
Fort Nelson River: **Liard River; Physiographic Regions - Interior Plains**
Fort Niagara: **Brant, Joseph; Chaussegros de Léry, Gaspard-J.; Johnson, William; Niagara Historic Frontier; Pepperrell, William; Seven Years' War**
Fort Nisqually (Wash): **Tolmie, William Fraser**
Fort Normandeau: **Red Deer**
Fort of the Forks: **Fort Simpson**
Fort Paskova: **The Pas**
Fort Pepperrell: **St John's**
Fort Pitt: **Big Bear**
Fort Pitt (Pittsburg): **Fort Duquesne**
Fort Pontchartrain: **Franco-Ontarians**
Fort Rae: **Dogrib; Great Slave Lake; Nursing**
Fort Richelieu: **Montmagny, Charles Huault de**
Fort Rouge: **Red River; Winnipeg**
Fort Rouillé: **King's Posts; Toronto**
Fort Rupert: **Douglas, James (1803-77); Helmcken, John Sebastian; Kwakiutl**
Fort-Rupert: **James Bay**
Fort St-Charles: **Lake of the Woods**
Fort St-Frédéric: **Butler, John; Champlain, Lake**
Fort St James: **Agriculture History; Carrier; Douglas, James (1803-77); Fraser, Simon**
Fort St-Jean: **American Revolution; Richelieu, Rivière**
Fort St Joseph: **St Joseph Island**
Fort St-Louis: **Fort Chambly**
Fort Ste Marie: **St Mary's River**
Fort Ste Marie II: **Christian Island**
Fort Ste-Thérèse: **Richelieu, Rivière**
Fort Sandoské: **Pontiac**
Fort Saskatchewan: **Alberta; Metallurgy; Waskahegan Trail**
Fort Severn: **Graham, Andrew**
Fort Siveright: **George, Rivière**
Fort Smith, Lab: **Churchill River, Lab**
Fort Stikine: **McLoughlin, John**
Fort Thompson: **Kamloops**
Fort Vancouver (Vancouver, Wash): **Columbia River; Douglas, James (1803-77); Kane, Paul; Victoria**
Fort Vermilion: **Autobiographical Writing in English; McIntosh, William; Peace River; Research Stations, Agricultural**
Fort Victoria: **Craigflower Manor & Schoolhouse; Douglas, James (1803-77); Helmcken, John Sebastian; Victoria**
Fort Ware: **Sekani**
Fort Wellington National Historic Park: **Heritage Trail; Historic Site; Prescott**
Fort White: **Manitoba**
Fort Whoop-up: **Potts, Jerry; Whoop-up**
Fort William, Ont: **Crow's Nest Pass Agreement; Italians; Thunder Bay; Veterinary Medicine**
Fort William Henry: **Lévis, François-Gaston de; Montcalm, Louis-Joseph de; Seven Years' War**
Fort William Male Choir: **Thunder Bay**
Fort York: **Historic Site; Toronto**
Fort Yukon: **Han**
Forteau Bay: **Forteau**
Fortier, Achille: **Singing; Songs & Songwriting**
Fortier, Claude: **Science Council of Canada**
Fortier Danse-Création: **Fortier, Paul-André**
Fortin, André: **Caouette, J.-D.-Réal**
Fortin, Maxime: **Charpentier, Alfred**
FORTRAN: **Computer Science; Language**
Fortrel: **Textile Industry**
Fortune Bay: **Brunette Island**
Forty Mile River: **Forty Mile**

Fosheim, Ivar: **Fosheim Peninsula**
Fossey, John M.: **Mediterranean Archaeology**
Foster, Alex: **Skiing**
Foster, W.W.: **Logan, Mount; Robson, Mount**
Foster Brothers Glass Works: **Glass**
foster care: **Child Welfare; Social & Welfare Services**
Foster Foundation: **Educational Foundations & Endowments**
Foster scanner: **Foster, John Stuart**
Fothergill, Charles: **Almanacs**
Fotheringham, Allan: **Essay in English**
Fouez, Rivière de: **St-Maurice, Rivière**
Foulds, Don: **Sculpture**
Foulkes, J.F.: **Tennis**
foundry: **Aerospace Industry; Agricultural Implements; Agricultural Implements Industry; Dominion Foundries & Steel, Ltd; Forges Saint-Maurice; Iron & Steel Industry; L'Islet-sur-Mer; Mont-Joli; Sackville**
Fountain Reserve: **Salish, Interior**
Fouquet, Father: **Mission**
Four Horsemen: **Nichol, bp; Poetry in English**
Four Lads: **Popular Music**
Four Nations Confederacy: **Social & Welfare Services**
Fourier series: **Mathematics**
Fournier, Claude: **Film**
Fournier, Jules: **Autobiographical Writing in French; Intellectual History; Literature in French - Criticism & Theory; Literature in French - Scholarship & Teaching**
Fournier, Paul: **Painting**
Foursquare Gospel: **New Religious Movements**
fourth estate: **Journalism**
"Fourth World": **Manuel, George**
Fowler, Daniel: **Furniture, Country**
Fowler, W.J.: **Botany History**
Fowler Commission: **Broadcasting, Radio & Television; Broadcasting, Royal Commission on**
Fox Mine: **Brown, Eldon Leslie**
Fox Peninsula: **Baffin Island; Fox (Foxe), Luke**
Fox River: **Hayes River**
fox snake: **Point Pelée National Park; Rondeau Provincial Park**
Foxe Channel: **Baffin Island; Foxe Basin**
Foxe Fold Belt: **Geological Regions**
foxglove: **Poisonous Plants**
foxtail: **Weeds**
Foxtrap, Nfld: **Newfoundland**
Foyer canadien: **Casgrain, Henri-Raymond; Literary Periodicals in French; *Soirées canadiennes***
Foyer de Charité: **Léger, Paul-Émile**
Foyer domestique: **Art Writing & Criticism; *Forestiers et voyageurs***
FP 6000 computer: **Industrial Research & Development**
FP Publications Ltd: *Sun*; **Thomson, Kenneth**
fracture zone: **Ocean Mining**
FRAM: **Arctic Oceanography**
Framfari (The Progress): **Icelanders**
France, Claire: **Novel in French**
France, William: **Choral Music**
Frances C. Gale Trophy: **Synchronized Swimming**
Frances Lake: **Gemstone**
Frances Lake Indians: **Kaska**
Franceschini, Vincent: **Italians**
Franchère, Gabriel: **Exploration & Travel Literature in French; *Tonquin***
Francis case: **Native People, Law**
Francis, Anne: **Bird, Florence B.**
Francis, Charlie: **Track & Field**
Francis, H.: **Drama in English**
Franciscans: **Catholicism; Italians; Laval, François de; Lithuanians; Longpré, Ephrem; Maltese; Philosophy**
Franco-Fous: **Theatre, French-Language**
Franco-Manitoban rights: **French in the West; Lyon, Sterling R.; Manitoba Schools Question**
Francoeur, Jacques: **UniMédia Inc**
Francoeur, Lucien: **Poetry in French**

François I of France: **Cartier, Jacques; Symbols of Authority**
Françoise, Baie: **Fundy, Bay of/Gulf of Maine**
Francophone Confederation of National Trade Unions: **Labour Relations**
Frank Ellis Trophy: **Parachuting, Sport**
Franklin, Benjamin: **Postal System**
Franklin, Lady: **Franklin Search**
Franklin Dist: **Island; Territorial Evolution**
Franklin Mint: **Medal**
Franklin Mountains: **Karst Landform**
Franklin Strait: **Boothia Peninsula**
Franklinian geosyncline: **Innuitian Region**
Frappier, Roger: **Film**
Fraser, D.T.: **Parasitology**
Fraser, Frances: **Children's Literature in English**
Fraser, Ian Forbes: **Literature in French - Scholarship & Teaching**
Fraser, John: **Fraser, Simon**
Fraser, Keath: **Short Fiction in English**
Fraser, Lac: **Mount Orford Park**
Fraser, M.J.: **Biochemistry**
Fraser, Malcolm: **La Malbaie**
Fraser, Mary L.: **Folklore**
Fraser Academy: **Thompson, Robert N.**
Fraser Commission: **Pornography**
Fraser gold rush: **Barkerville; Chinese; Douglas, James (1803-77); Germans; Gold Rushes; Mineral & Mining Engineering; Steamboats & Paddlewheelers; Victoria**
Fraser Lake: **Carrier**
Fraser Mills, BC: **Coquitlam**
Fraser-Nechako Plateau: **River Landform**
Fraser River harbour commission: **New Westminster**
Fraser River Lillooet: **Salish, Interior**
Fraser River Railway Bridge: **New Westminster**
Fraser Valley: **Desert; Libraries**
Fraser Valley College: **Matsqui**
Fraser's Inc: **Edmundston; New Brunswick**
Fraserville, Qué: **Rivière-du-Loup**
Fred Victor Mission: **Massey, Hart A.; Social Gospel**
Frederick Harris Music Co Ltd: **Religious Music; Royal Conservatory of Music of Toronto**
Fredrick Town, NB: **Fredericton**
Fredericton Gleaner: **Irving Group**
Fredericton *Headquarters*: **d'Avray, 2nd Baron**
Free Church: **Caven, William; Forrester, Alexander; Presbyterian & Reformed Churches**
Free Education Act (PEI): **Prince Edward Island**
Free Land Grant Act: **Muskoka Lakes**
Free Presbyterian Church: **Gavazzi Riots**
free radicals: **Chemistry Subdisciplines; LeRoy, Donald James; Spectroscopy; Steacie, Edgar William Richard**
Free Reformed Churches of North America: **Presbyterian & Reformed Churches**
"free schools": **Education, Alternate**
free trade: **Automotive Industry; Canada-US Automotive Products Agreement; Canadian-American Economic Relations; Carmichael, James William; Cartwright, Richard J.; Continentalism; Customs & Excise; Economic Nationalism; Economics; Ontario Economic Council; Progressive Party; Sovereignty-Association**
Freedman, Samuel: **Obscenity**
Freedom Fighter aircraft: **Military Aviation & Aircraft**
freedom of association: **Associations; Intellectual History; Student Rights**
freedom of conscience: **Intellectual History; Zouaves**
freedom of expression: **Pornography**
Freedom of Information Act: **Law & the Press**
freedom of opinion: **Intellectual History**

freedom of speech: **Communications Law; Intellectual History; Parliament; Zouaves**
freedom of the press: **Journalism; Newspapers**
freedom of worship: **Anglicanism**
freehold lands: **Petroleum**
Freeman, David: **Drama in English; Festival Lennoxville; Tarragon Theatre; Theatre, English-Language**
Freeman's Journal: **Willcocks, Joseph**
Freemasons: **Chinese; Secret Societies**
Freer, Mr & Mrs William: **Salvation Army**
Freer, James: **Film**
freezing: **Fisheries History; Fruit & Vegetable Industry; Pea**
Frégault, Guy: **Book Publishing, French-Language; French Canadian Nationalism; Historiography**
freight: **Locomotives & Rolling Stock; Railways, Contemporary; Transportation**
freight rates: **Agriculture & Food Policy; Crow's Nest Pass Agreement; Maritime Shipping History to 1900; Railways, Contemporary; Regional Economics; Separatism**
Freight Rates Reduction Act: **Transportation Regulation**
French, David: **Centaur Theatre; Drama in English; Tarragon Theatre; Theatre, English-Language**
French, Donald Graham: **Literature in English - Teaching**
French-Canadian Education Assn of Ontario: **Ontario Schools Question**
French immersion: **Bilingualism; Education, Alternate; Manitoba; University of Western Ontario**
French Ivory Products: **Plastics-Processing Industry**
French Protestants: **Huguenots; Hymns**
Frenchman River: **Grasslands National Park**
Frenchman's Butte: **North-West Rebellion; Strange, Thomas Bland**
Frenette, Matt: **Loverboy**
frequency standards: **Time**
Frères Charon: **Christian Religious Communities**
Frères de l'instruction chrétienne: **Book Publishing, French-Language; Literature in French - Scholarship & Teaching**
Frères des écoles chrétiennes: **Book Publishing, French-Language; Christian Religious Communities; Marie-Victorin, Frère**
Frères du sacré-coeur: **Book Publishing, French-Language**
Fresh Air Camps: **Salvation Army**
Freshwater Fish Marketing Corp: **Fisheries History; Fisheries Policy; Manitoba**
freshwater seal: **Mistassini, Lac**
freshwater worm: **Annelida**
Freuchen, Peter: **Ittinuar, Peter F.**
Fricker, Herbert A.: **Music History; Toronto Mendelssohn Choir**
"friendly aliens": **Germans**
Friends of the Soviet Union: **Gauld, Bella Hall**
Friesen, Gerhard: **German Writing**
Friesen, Patrick: **German Writing**
frigate: **Armed Forces - Unification; New Brunswick; Sculpture; Shipbuilding & Ship Repair; Station PAPA**
Fripp, E.F.G.: **Exploration & Travel Literature in English**
Frise, Jimmy: *Star Weekly*
Froebe brothers: **Helicopter**
Frog Lake, Alta: **Big Bear; North-West Rebellion**
Frog Portage: **Churchill River**
frogs legs: **Food Legislation; Frog**
Front de libération des femmes du Québec: **Women's Movement**
Frontalières, Montagnes: **Chaudière, Rivière**
Frontenac: **Steamboats & Paddlewheelers**
Frontenac (barque): **Shipbuilding & Ship Repair**
Frontenac Axis: **Rideau Lakes; St Lawrence Islands National Park**

Frontier College: **Adult Education; Bethune, H. Norman; Literacy**
Frood Mine: **Agnew, John Lyons**
Fröschle, Hartmut: **German Writing**
Frosst, Charles E.: **Pharmaceuticals Industry**
frost: **Agricultural Research & Development; Crops; Peace River Lowland; Periglacial Landform**
Frost & Wood Co: **Agricultural Implements**
Frozen Sea Research Group: **Arctic Oceanography**
Fruet, William: **Drama in English**
Fruit Growers' Assn of Ontario: **Saunders, William**
Fruitvale, BC: **Trail**
Fry-Cadbury Ltd: **Confectionery Industry**
Fry medal: **Fry, Frederick Ernest Joseph**
Fryer, Bryant: **Film Animation**
Fryfogel, Sebastian: **Swiss**
fuchsite: **Greenstone**
Fudger, H.H.: **Simpson, Robert**
fuel: **Aviation; Biomass Energy; Coal Gasification; Coal Liquefaction; Forest Harvesting; Hydrogen; Lighting; Native People - Plains; Norman Wells; Nuclear Energy; Nuclear Fusion; Nuclear Power Plants; Oil & Natural Gas; Palynology; Peat; Petroleum; Petroleum Exploration & Production; Petroleum Research & Development; Trucking Industry**
fuel combustion: **Urban Effect on Climate**
fuel gas: **Coal Gasification**
fuel tax: **Alberta; Roads & Highways; Saskatchewan; Taxation**
Fuels Testing Station: **Petroleum Research & Development**
Fugere, Jean-Paul: **Beaulne, Guy**
Fuhrer, H.: **Steele, Mount**
Fujita scale: **Tornado**
Fujiwara, Denise: **Dance, Modern**
Fuller, Chilion: **Parliament Buildings**
Fuller, William H.: **Drama in English; Musical Theatre; Theatre, English-Language**
Fuller & Benecke: **Printmaking**
Fuller & Jones: **Parliament Buildings**
Fulton-Favreau formula: **Constitutional Law; Fulton, E. Davie; Quiet Revolution**
fumarole: **Geochemistry; Volcano**
Funcken, Eugen: **German Writing**
Fund for Rural Economic Development: **Agriculture & Food Policy**
fundamental freedoms: **Associations; Canadian Bill of Rights; Civil Liberties; Constitution Act, 1982; Human Rights**
fundamental research: **Chrétien, Michel; Crop Research; LeRoy, Donald James; Marion, Léo Edmond; Medical Research; Science Council of Canada; Science Policy; University**
fundamentalism: **Evangelical & Fundamentalist Movements**
Fundy Trail: **Acadian Trail**
fungicide: **Oilseed Crops; Pesticide**
funnel cloud: **Tornado**
Funnell, Suzanne: **Painting**
fur: **Clothing; Tahltan**
fur auctions & fairs: **Fur Industry; Fur Trapping, Contemporary; Hudson's Bay Company; North Bay**
Fur Trade Assn of Canada: **Fur Industry**
Furie, Sidney: **Film**
Furniture West Inc: **Furniture & Fixture Industry**
Fury & Hecla Strait: **Arctic Archipelago; Baffin Island; Foxe Basin; Hudson Bay; Melville Peninsula; Rae, John**
Fusion des Arts: **Art, Contemporary Trends; Lacroix, Richard**
Fuster, Geza: **Chess**
futures market: **Winnipeg Commodity Exchange**

G

G.C. Reifel Sanctuary: **Bird Sanctuaries & Reserves**
G.N. Morang publishers: **Book Publishing, English-Language**
G.P. Putnam's Sons: **Coburn, Frederick Simpson**
G.R. Masterson Trophy: **Parachuting, Sport**
Gabarus, NS: **Regan, Gerald A.**
Gaboury, Marie-Anne: **Lagemodière, Jean-Baptiste; Lagemodière, Marie-Anne**
Gabriel Dumont Institute of Native Studies & Applied Research: **University of Regina**
Gabriola Island: **Gulf Islands**
Gaden Chöling: **Buddhism**
gadolinium: **Nuclear Power Plants**
Gadouas, Robert: **Radio Drama, French-Language**
Gaelic College: **McAskill, Angus; St Anns**
Gaelic language: **Bell, Alexander Graham; Calgary; Ethnic Literature; Literature in English; MacEachern, Angus Bernard; McGregor, James; Prince Edward Island; Pugwash; Queen's University; Red River Colony; Scots; Spanish; Theatre, Multicultural**
Gaelic Mod: **St Anns**
Gaëtan Morin Editeur: **Book Publishing, French-Language**
Gage, Chris: **Jazz**
Gage Publishing Ltd: **Authors & Their Milieu; Dictionary**
Gagetown Creek: **Gagetown**
Gaglardi, Philip: **Italians**
Gagne, Jean-Paul: *Affaires*
Gagnier, G.: **Religious Building**
Gagnon, Alain: **Music History**
Gagnon, Cécile: **Children's Literature in French**
Gagnon, François-Marc: **Art Writing & Criticism**
Gagnon, Jean-Louis: **Bilingualism & Biculturalism, Royal Commission on; *Presse***
Gagnon, Louis-Jean: **Children's Literature in French**
Gagnon, Madeleine: **Novel in French; Poetry in French**
Gagnon, Maurice: **Philosophy**
Gagnon, Maurice (art historian): **Barbeau, Marcel**
Gagnon, Maurice (writer): **Novel in French; Popular Literature in French**
Gagnon, Paul-André: **Guitar**
Gagnon, Philéas: **Literature in French - Scholarship & Teaching**
Gaiety Records: **Baker, Carroll**
Gaiety Theatre: **Drama in French**
Gairdner Award: **Quastel, Judah Hirsch; Salter, Robert Bruce; Siminovitch, Louis**
Gaitskell, C.D.: **Art Education**
Gal, Lazlo: **Children's Literature in English**
Gala des Artistes: **Claude, Renée**
Galarneau, Claude: **Intellectual History**
Galaxie Gutenberg: **Gutenberg Galaxy**
Galbraith, A.J.: **Soil Science**
galena: **Lead; Mineral; Slocan**
Galerie 1640: **Printmaking**
Galician wheat: **Fife, David**
Galicians: **Orthodox Church; Ukrainians**
Galinée, René de Bréhant de: **Cartography, History of; Port Dover; St Clair, Lake**
galinsoga: **Biogeography**
Galiote: **Shipbuilding & Ship Repair**
Galissonière, Marquis de la: **Science**
Gall, Hughie: **Football**
gall stones: **Medicine, Contemporary**
Gallant, Melvin: **Children's Literature in French**
Gallendar, Hugh L.: **Barnes, Howard Turner**
Gallie, Tommie: **Sculpture**
Gallion, Aubert: **St-Georges**
Gallop, David: **Philosophy**
Galloway, Jim: **Jazz**
Gallup poll: **Clark, Charles Joseph; Co-operative Commonwealth Federation; Public Opinion**

Galt, Elliot: **Galt, Alexander T.; Lethbridge**
Galt automobile: **Automotive Industry**
Galt Football Club: **Soccer**
Galt *Reformer*: **Pattullo, T. Dufferin**
Gamache, Marcel: **Television Drama, French-Language**
Gamba, Piero: **Winnipeg Symphony Orchestra**
Gamble, Eric: **Painting**
Gambo, Nfld: **Smallwood, Joseph R.**
Gamborg, O.: **Crop Research**
Game-Calling Ceremony: **Kootenay**
game farms: **Zoos**
game management areas: **New Brunswick**
Game Plan: **Sports Organization, Amateur; Track & Field**
game preserve: **Montagnais-Naskapi**
Gamelin, Emilie: **Christian Religious Communities**
gametes: **Genetics**
gamma ray: **Cobalt; Remote Sensing**
Gammon, Donald: *Fiddlehead*
Gammon, George: **Furniture, Country**
Gammon, W.: **Furniture, Country**
Ganam, King: **Television Programming**
Gananoque River: **Gananoque**
Ganaraska River: **Port Hope**
Gandalf Data Ltd: **Electronics Industry**
Gander Bay: **Gander River**
Gander International Airport: **Gander; Lewisporte**
Gander Lake: **Gander; Gander River**
Gander Zone: **Geological Regions**
"Gang of Eight": **Constitution, Patriation of**
Gang Ranch: **Ranching History**
Gangbar, Lynne: **Guitar**
Ganges, BC: **Saltspring Island**
gangue: **Iron & Steel Industry; Metallurgy**
Gannes, Louis de: **St-Denis**
Gannet Island: **Newfoundland**
Gannet Rock: **Lighthouses**
Ganong Brothers Ltd: **Confectionery Industry; St Stephen**
Garand, Edouard: **Popular Literature in French**
garbage: **Biomass Energy; Conserver Society; Pollution; Solid Waste; Waste Disposal**
Garber, Hugh: **Fashion Design**
Garber, Lawrence: **Short Fiction in English**
Garçeau, Raymond: **Film**
Garcia, Gustave: **La Palme, Béatrice**
Garcia, Juan: **Poetry in French**
Gard, Anson: **Exploration & Travel Literature in English**
Garden Court Apartments: **Architectural Styles**
Gardenton, Man: **Orthodox Church**
Gardiner, Robert: **Ginger Group**
Gardiner & Thornton: **Architecture, Development**
Gardiner Expressway: **Toronto**
Gardner, David: **Vancouver Playhouse**
Gardner Canal: **Kitamaat**
Gareau, Jacqueline: **Long-Distance Running**
Gargantua, Cape: **Place-names**
Garibaldi, Lake: **Garibaldi Provincial Park**
Garibaldi, Mount: **Garibaldi Provincial Park; Igneous Rock**
Garibaldi belt: **Volcano**
Garigue, Philippe: **Literature in French - Scholarship & Teaching**
Garland, E.J.: **Ginger Group**
Garland, Iris: **Dance, Modern**
garlic: **Condiment Crops; Vegetable**
Garneau, Alfred: **Garneau, H. de Saint-Denys; Poetry in French**
Garneau, Marc: **Astronaut**
Garneau, Michel: **Drama in French; Poetry in French; Theatre, French-Language**
Garneau, René: **Literature in French**
Garneau, Sylvain: **Poetry in French**
Garneau bookstores: **Book Publishing, French-Language**
Garnier, Charles: **Children's Literature in French; Ste Marie Among the Hurons**
Garrard, Jim: **25th Street Theatre**
Garrett's: **Rugs & Rug Making**
Garrick Club: **Little Theatre Movement**

Garrison Amateurs: **Theatre Royal**
Garry, Nicholas: **Back River**
Garry Lake: **Back River**
Garry oak: **Gulf Islands; Oak; Vegetation Regions - Cordillera; Vegetation Regions - Pacific Coastal**
Garson, William: **Garson**
Gartmore, Man: **Dauphin**
Gartshore beam engine: **Keefer, Thomas C.**
Garvin, J.W.: **Crawford, Isabella Valancy**
gas chromatography: **Chemistry Subdisciplines; Harris, Walter E.**
gas flaring: **Conservation**
gas helmet: **Macpherson, Cluny**
gaslight: **Lighting**
gasohol: **Biomass Energy**
gasoline: **Bitumen; Lead; Oil & Natural Gas; Petroleum; Petroleum Exploration & Production**
Gasparini, Len: **Italian Writing**
Gaspé Bay: **Fossil Plants; Gaspé**
Gaspé Copper Mines: **Murdochville Strike**
Gaspé Current: **Chaleur Bay; St Lawrence, Gulf of**
Gaspé shrew: **Endangered Animals; Mammals; Shrew**
gaspereau: **Miramichi River**
Gaspésie, Parc provincial de la: **Gaspé; Parks, Provincial**
Gass, Ken: **Drama in English**
Gastineau, Nicolas: **Gatineau**
gastroenteritis: **Hospitals; Influenza**
gastropoda: **Abalone; Mollusc; Periwinkle; Seashell; Slug; Snail; Whelk**
Gate, George: **Swimming, Speed**
Gate of Harmonious Interest: **Victoria**
Gathering of the Clans: **Festivals**
Gatineau, Rivière: **Gatineau; Hull; Laurentian Highlands; Ottawa, Ont**
Gatineau Mills, Qué: **Gatineau**
Gatineau Park: **Hull; Kingsmere; Laurentian Highlands; National Capital Commission**
Gatling gun: **Armaments; Batoche; Firearm**
GATT-Fly Project: **Ecumenical Social Action**
Gaudet, Placide: **Genealogy**
Gaudry, Roger: **Science Council of Canada**
Gauthier, Bertrand: **Children's Literature in French**
Gauthier, David: **Philosophy**
Gauthier, Georges E.: **Centennial Year**
Gauthier, Louise: **Krieghoff, Cornelius D.**
Gauthier, Yvon: **Philosophy**
Gauvreau, Marcelle: **Children's Literature in French**
Gavazzi, Alessandro: **Gavazzi Riots**
Gavin, F.P.: **Windsor, Ont**
Gay, Frank: **Musical Instruments**
Gay, Marie-Louise: **Children's Literature in French**
Gay, Michel: *Barre du jour*
Gay, Paul: **Essay in French**
Gayfer, James: **Choral Music**
Gays River, NS: **Nova Scotia; Scott, Ephraim**
Gaz Métropolitain Inc: **Caisse de dépôt et placement du Québec; Sidbec-Dosco Limitée**
Gazeta Katolicka (Catholic Gazette): **Poles**
Gazette littéraire de Montréal: **Literature in French - Criticism & Theory**
gears: **Klein, George John**
Geco Mines Ltd: **Gemstone; Noranda Mines Ltd**
Gedalof, Robin: **Ethnic Literature**
Ge'ez language: **Africans**
Gefin, Kemenes: **Ethnic Literature**
Geiger counter: **Leaver, Eric William; Mineral; Prospecting**
Geiger-Torel, Herman: **Canadian Opera Co**
Geikie, A.C.: **English Language**
Gélinas, Pierre: **Hénault, Gilles; Novel in French**
Gem & Mineral Federation of Canada: **Rock & Mineral Collecting**
Gemini computer: **Industrial Research & Development**
Gemological Institute of America: **Jewellery & Silverware Industry**
Gendron Commission: **Bill 63; Sociology**

Gendron Manufacturing Co: **Toys & Games**
General, Levi: **Deskaheh**
General Steel Wares Ltd: **Copperware**
General Agreement on Tariffs & Trade: **Aerospace Industry; Canada & Australia; Canada-Third World Relations; Canadian-American Economic Relations; Chemical Industries; Furniture & Fixture Industry; Protectionism; Pulp & Paper Industry; Warren, Jack Hamilton**
General & Marine Hospital: **Nursing**
General Bathymetric Chart: **Hydrography**
General Development Agreements: **Regional Economics**
General Dynamics Corp: **Canadair Ltd**
General Foods Inc: **Advertising; Lethbridge**
General Hospital (Toronto): **Dunlap, David Alexander**
General Idea: **Art, Contemporary Trends; Art Writing & Criticism; Artists' Organizations; Video Art**
General Mining Assn: **Sydney Mines**
General Motors Diesel: **Locomotives & Rolling Stock**
General Publishing Co Ltd: **Literary Prizes in French**
General Stacey Smyth: **Steamboats & Paddlewheelers**
General Tire Canada Ltd: **Rubber Products Industry**
General Trust of Canada: **Lévesque, Jean-Louis; Webster, Lorne Campbell**
Genetics Soc of Canada: **Fredeen, Howard; Genetics; Newcombe, Howard Borden**
Geneva Park, Ont: **Couchiching Conference**
Genie Award: **Film Festivals, Prizes; Honours**
genital herpes: **Sexually Transmitted Disease**
Genner, Samuel: **Sculpture**
Gens de mon pays: **Folk Dance**
Genstar Corp: **Canada Permanent Mortgage Corp; Cement Industry**
Gentile, Charles: **Photography**
Gentleman Usher of the Black Rod: **House of Commons; Parliament, Opening of**
Gentlemen's Sparring Club: **Boxing**
Geodetic Survey of Canada: **King, William Frederick**
geoduck: **Clam**
Geographic Board of Canada: **Canadian Permanent Committee on Geographical Names; Golden Hinde**
geographic societies & journals: **Geomorphology; Physical Geography**
geological societies & journals: **Geology; Geomorphology**
Geological Survey of Newfoundland: **Murray, Alexander**
geomagnetic storm: **Sun**
geometry: **Mathematics**
geophysics: **Beals, Carlyle Smith; Geological Survey of Canada; Keys, David Arnold; Petroleum Exploration & Production; Physics; Prospecting; Wilson, J. Tuzo**
George, Graham: **Choral Music**
George, Lake: **Antimony**
George I of England: **Lunenburg; Queen's Plate**
George III of England: **Brantford; Coinage; George, Rivière; Georgetown; Kingston; Literary Prizes in French; Madeleine, Iles de la; New Brunswick; Prince Edward Island; Prince George; Queen's Plate; *Racoon*; Seven Years' War; Silver, Church**
George IV of England: **Coronation Gulf; Georgian Bay**
George V of England: **A Mari usque ad Mare; Coinage; Emblems, Provincial & Territorial; Flag Debate; Willingdon, 1st Marquess of**
George VI of England: **Coinage; George Cross; Governor General; Queen Elizabeth Way; Queen's Plate; Royal Tours; Sovereign; Stephenson, William Samuel; Wyn Wood, Elizabeth**

George Brown College: **Clothing Industries; Fur Industry**
George-Etienne Cartier Centenary Medal: **Medal**
George Lawson Medal: **Hughes, Stanley John**
George Matthews Co Ltd: **Meat-Processing Industry**
George Reed Foundation: **Reed, George R.**
George River caribou herd: **George, Rivière; Hunting; Québec**
Georges Bay: **Tracadie, NS**
George's Island: **Fortification**
George's Spaghetti House: **Jazz; Koffman, M., "Moe"**
Georgetown Seafoods: **Georgetown**
Georgia, Gulf of: **Georgia, Strait of; Prehistory**
Georgia Straight: **Hippies; Literary Magazines in English**
Georgian Bay & Wellington Railway: **Grand Trunk Railway of Canada**
Georgian Bay Survey: **Cartography, History of; Hydrography**
Georgian College of Applied Arts & Technology: **Barrie**
Georgians: **Russians**
geostrategic region: **Geopolitics**
geotextiles: **Textile Industry**
geothite: **Mineral**
Gerald Lampert Memorial Award: **Literary Prizes in English**
geriatrics: **Gerontology; Optometry**
Gerin-Lajoie, Paul: **Education Policy**
Germain, Gaston: **Jeunesses musicales du Canada**
German Pentecostal Church: **Pentecostal Movement**
German silver: **Copper; Zinc**
Gerrard Street: **Franck, Albert Jacques**
Gerrish, Moses: **Grand Manan Island**
Gerrits, Paul: **Guitar**
gerrymandering: **Local Elections**
Gerson, Carole: **Short Fiction in English**
Gertler, L.O.: **Urban Studies**
Gerussi, Bruno: **Italians**
Gesca Ltée: **Newspapers; Power Corp of Canada**
Gesner, Henry: **Gesner, Abraham**
Gésu: **Theatre, French-Language**
Geyer, George: **York Factory**
geyser: **Geothermal Energy; Spring; Volcano**
Ghanans: **Africans**
gherkin: **Cucumber**
Ghost Dance: **Native People, Religion**
Ghost River (Alta): **Fossil Plants**
Ghost River Provincial Park: **Parks, Provincial**
ghost shark: **Chimaera**
ghost town: **Fort Steele; New Denver; Sandon**
ghosts: **La Corriveau; Native People - Northwest Coast**
Giant Angus McAskill Highland Pioneers Museum: **St Anns**
Giant Gold Mine: **Yellowknife, NWT**
giants: **McAskill, Angus; Swan, Anna H.**
giardiasis: **Water-Borne Disease**
Gibbard Co: **Agricultural Implements**
Gibbon, John Murray: **Horse; Music History; Vertical Mosaic**
Gibbons, Alta: **Athabasca Landing Trail**
Gibbons, George C.: **Boundary Waters Treaty**
Gibbs, A.E.: **Technology**
Gibbs, Mifflin: **Blacks**
Gibbs, William T.: **Chemical Industries**
Gibraltar Point: **Lighthouses; Toronto Islands**
Gibson, Alexander, "Boss": **Fredericton**
Gibson, Cheryl: **Swimming, Speed**
Gibson, John: **Literary Magazines in English**
Gibson, John (artist): **Graphic Design**
Gibson, Margaret: **Short Fiction in English**
Gibson, William: **Popular Literature in English**
Gibson First Novel Award: **Literary Prizes in English**
Gibson Merit Award for Literature: **Literary Prizes in English**
Gideons International in Canada: **Canadian Bible Society**
Gift Lake, Alta: **Métis Settlements**
Gilbert, Edward: **Manitoba Theatre Centre**

Gilbert, Gerry: **Art, Contemporary Trends; Poetry in English**
Gilbert, Walter: **Franklin Search**
Gilbert & Sullivan Soc: **Ridout, Godfrey**
Gilchrist, L.: **Physics**
Giles, Robin: **Philosophy**
Gilhooly, David: **Ceramics, Contemporary**
Gilkison, William: **Elora**
Gill, E. Lakshmi: **Poetry in English**
Gill, E.A.: **Autobiographical Writing in English**
Gill, Marie: **Gill, Charles**
gill net: **Babiche; Newfoundland**
Gillanders, David: **Rowing**
Gillespie, Hart & Co: **Hart, John**
Gillespie, John: **Printmaking**
Gillespie, R.J.: **Chemistry Subdisciplines**
Gillis, Margie: **Dance History**
Gillmore, Jack: **Radio Drama, English-Language**
Gilmore, Thomas: **Almanacs; Book Publishing, English-Language; Brown, William; Magazines; Newspapers**
Gilmour, George P.: **McMaster University**
Gilpin, Bernard: **Archaeology**
Gilson, Etienne: **Philosophy**
Ginger Beer: **Soft-Drink Industry**
Gingras, Claude: **Music Criticism**
Gingras, R.: **Governor General's Literary Awards**
Gini ratio: **Capital & Wealth**
Gipps, George: **Canada & Australia**
Giraldeau, Jacques: **Brault, Michel**
Girard, Hélène: **Film**
Girard, Jean: **Music History**
Girard, Rodolphe: **Marie Calumet**
Girardin, maison: **Architecture, Development**
Giraud, Marcel: **Sociology**
Girerd, Jean-Pierre: **Cartoons; Popular Literature in French**
Girling, Oliver: **Painting**
Giroux, André (artist): **Sculpture**
Giroux, André (author): **Novel in French**
Gitanmaax School of Northwest Coast Indian Art: **Davidson, Robert C.; Diesing, Freda; Harris, Walter**
Gitksan: **Beynon, William; Ksan; Skeena River**
Gitksan Carrier Band: **Land Claims**
Gjoa: **Amundsen, Roald; Gjoa Haven**
Glace Bay Gazette: **Cohen, S. Nathan**
Glacier House: **Hotel; Mountaineering**
Glackemeyer, F. Henri: **Germans; Music History**
gladiolus: **Flowers, Cultivated**
Gladstone, Gerald: **Sculpture**
Gladu, André: **Brault, Michel**
Gladu, Roland: **Baseball**
Glaser, Vaughan: **Theatre, English-Language**
Glasgow, Brock & Co: **Book Publishing, English-Language**
Glass, Joanna M.: **Tarragon Theatre; Theatre, English-Language**
glass sponge: **Invertebrate**
Glassburn, NS: **MacDonald, Angus Bernard**
Glassco, J. Grant: **Government Organization, Royal Commission on**
Glassco Commission: **Armed Forces - Unification; Government Organization, Royal Commission on; Mackenzie, Chalmers Jack**
Glasson, Ignace: **Grande Cache**
glaucoma: **Blindness & Visual Impairment; Ophthalmology**
glaucous gull: **Arctic Animals; Auyuittuq National Park**
Glazebrook, Arthur J.: **Round Table Movement**
Glazebrook, G.P. de T.: *Canadian Historical Review*
Glen Warren Productions Ltd: **Baton Broadcasting Inc**
Glenboro, Man: **Icelanders**
Glenbow Foundation: **Archaeology; Harvie, Eric L.**
Glencairn: **Ross, James**
Glendenning's Farm: **Mount Pearl**
Glendon College: **York University**
Glenella, Man: **Poles**
Glengarry Highland Games: **Maxville**
Glenmore Reservoir: **Calgary**

Glenn Kerr, Sask: **Wiens, Clifford D.**
Glenwood, Nfld: **Lewisporte**
gleysols: **Soil Classification**
Glick, Srul Irving: **Choral Music**
gliders & gliding: **Aviation; Soaring**
Global Environmental Monitoring System: **Canada Centre for Inland Waters**
Global Observing System: **Weather Forecasting**
Global TV: **Advertising; Broadcasting, Radio & Television; Evangelism; Television Programming**
Globe Magazine: **Doyle, Richard J.**
Globenski, August F.: **Poles**
glossary: **Dictionary**
glossolalia: **Charismatic Renewal**
Glover, Richard: **Exploration & Travel Literature in English**
Glover Island: **Grand Lake**
gluconic acid: **Mold**
glucose: **Diabetes Mellitus; Insulin**
glucosinolate: **Vegetable Oil Industry**
Gluskabe: **Abenaki**
gluten: **Wheat**
glycerol: **Animal Agriculture; Baer, Erich**
glycine: **Molecules in Interstellar Space**
Glyde, Cyril: **Hart House String Quartet**
Gnarowski, Michael: **Literature in English - Theory & Criticism**
gnat: **Fly**
gneiss: **Geological Regions; Prospecting**
gnosticism: **New Religious Movements**
"go-as-you-please" race: **Track & Field**
GO Transit: **Ontario; Ontario Northland Transportation Commission; Railways, Contemporary**
Goan Indians: **Africans**
Goat (Indians): **Mountain (Indians)**
Goat Island: **Niagara Falls**
Goat River: **Yahk**
goatsucker: **Nighthawk**
Gobuty, Michael: **Winnipeg Jets**
Godard, Barbara: **Literature in English - Theory & Criticism**
Godbout, Réal: **Popular Literature in French**
Goddard, Peter: **Music Criticism**
Godfrey, Ellen: **Godfrey, Dave**
Godfrey, W. Earl: **National Museum of Natural Sciences**
Godfrey Dean Cultural Centre: **Yorkton**
Godin, Gérald: **Poetry in French**
Godin, Jean-Cléo: **Literature in French - Scholarship & Teaching**
God's Lake Gold Mines Ltd: **Brown, Eldon Leslie**
God's Mercy, Bay of: **Place-names**
Gods River: **Hayes River**
Godsell, P.H.: **Autobiographical Writing in English**
godwit: **Sandpiper**
GOES satellite: **Satellite, Artificial**
goethite: **Iron Ore**
Goff, Frank D.: **Holiness Churches**
Goforth, W.W.: **Industrial Research & Development**
Goh Ohn bell: **Moriyama, Raymond**
Gold, Artie: **Poetry in English**
Gold, Gerald Louis: **Community**
gold commissioner: **Douglas, James (1803-77); Fernie, William; Yukon Territory**
Gold Range: **Eagle Pass**
Gold River, BC: **Nootka Sound; Vancouver Island**
Goldberg, Mildred: **Drama in English**
Goldby, Derek: **Shaw Festival**
Golden Ball Building: **Irving, K. C.**
Golden City, BC: **Golden**
Golden City, Ont: **South Porcupine**
golden-crowned sparrow: **Kluane National Park**
golden eagle: **Bathurst Inlet; Eagle; Garibaldi Provincial Park; Jasper National Park; Kluane National Park; Mount Assiniboine Provincial Park; Mount Revelstoke National Park; Nahanni National Park; Yoho National Park**
Golden Ears Provincial Park: **Maple Ridge**
Golden Hawks: **Snowbirds**
Golden Hind: **Gilbert, Humphrey**

golden-mantled ground squirrel: **Mount Revelstoke National Park**
Golden Reel Award: **Film Festivals, Prizes**
golden-seal: **Endangered Plants**
Golden Sheaf Award: **Film Festivals, Prizes**
goldeye: **Claire, Lake; Herring**
goldfinch: **Finch**
goldfish: **Minnow**
Goldie, James: **Guelph**
Goldie, John: **Botany History**
Goldie-McCulloch: **Technology**
Goldkorn, Itzchak: **Jewish Writing**
Goldman, Emma: **Anarchism; Drama in English**
Goldschmidt, Nicholas: **Music History**
Goldsmith, Fred: **Baseball**
Goldsmith, Sidney: **Film Animation**
Goldstein, K.S.: **Folklore**
goldthread: **Plants, Native Uses**
Goldthwait, J.W.: **Geomorphology**
Goletas Channel: **Balaklava Island**
Gomes, Mark: **Sculpture**
Gomez, Avelino: **Thoroughbred Racing**
Gomez, Ric: **Sculpture**
Gonor, A.B.: **Sapp, Allen**
gonorrhea: **Sexually Transmitted Disease**
Good, James: **Locomotives & Rolling Stock**
Good Brothers: **Country & Western Music**
Good Neighbour Peak: **Steele, Mount; Vancouver, Mount**
Goodchild, Frederick: **McClelland & Stewart Ltd**
Goode, Arthur C.: **Printmaking**
Goode, James: **Railway History**
Gooderham, Kent: **Ethnic Literature**
Gooderham & Worts Ltd: **Hiram Walker Resources Ltd**
Gooderham Mansion: **Sproatt and Rolph**
Goodman, Edwin: **Committee for an Independent Canada**
Goodstoney, Jacob: **Stoney**
Goodwin, Albert "Ginger": **Revolutionary Industrial Unionism**
Goodwin, Helen: **Dance, Modern**
Goodwin, Henry: **Physical Education**
Goodyear Canada Inc: **Berkinshaw, Richard Coulton; Medicine Hat; Rubber Products Industry**
Gool, Reshard: **Ethnic Literature**
goose, domestic: **Poultry Farming**
Goose, William: **Nanogak, Agnes**
Goose Bay: **Happy Valley-Goose Bay; Ice; Labrador; Melville, Lake; Newfoundland**
Goose River: **Hamilton Inlet**
gooseberry: **Berries, Wild; Saxifrage**
Gooseberry Lake Provincial Park: **Parks, Provincial**
goosefoot: **Vegetable**
Gopher Creek: **Virden**
Gordon, Arthur: **Tilley, Samuel L.**
Gordon, Bryan H.: **Archaeology**
Gordon, Hortense: **Painters Eleven; Painting**
Gordon, John S.: **Hutchinson, Leonard**
Gordon, Lamont: **Bobsledding**
Gordon, Thomas: **Clocks & Watches**
Gordon Commission: **Economic Nationalism; Royal Commission on Canada's Economic Prospects**
Gordon Head: **McClung, Nellie L.**
Gordon-Ironsides & Fares: **Meat-Processing Industry**
Gordon Island: **Thousand Islands**
Gordon press: **Print Industry**
Gordon V. Thompson Ltd: **Religious Music**
Gore, Arabella Wentworth: **Belleville**
Gore, Charles S.: **Cartier, George-Etienne; St-Denis**
Gore, Samuel: **Cobourg & Peterborough Railway**
Gore Bank: **Canadian Imperial Bank of Commerce**
Gore Bay, Ont: **Manitowaning**
Gore Park: **Hamilton**
Gorge Waters: **Victoria**
Gorman, Harry: **Baseball**
Gorman, Richard: **Painting; Printmaking**
Gospel Band movement: **Evangelism**
Gospel Missionary Assn: **Baptists**
"Gospel" music: **Religious Music**
Gospel Witness: **Shields, Thomas T.**

Gospel Workers Church: **Holiness Churches**
Goss Metroliners: *Edmonton Journal*
Gosselin, Bernard: **Film**
Gossip, William: **Archaeology**
Gotta, Jack: **Ottawa Rough Riders**
Gottlieb, Robert: *Poussière sur la ville*
Gottlieb, Selma: **Helicopter**
Gottschalk, Fritz: **Graphic Design**
Gottschalk & Ash International: **Graphic Design; Logo**
gouge: **Archaic; Northwest Coast Indian Art; Tools, Carpentry**
Gougeon, Helen: **Cuisine**
Gouin, Judy: **Printmaking**
Gouinlock, George W.: **Architecture, Development**
Gould, Joseph: **Uxbridge**
Goulet, Charles: **Music History**
Goupil, Laval: **Theatre, French-Language**
Goupil, René: **Saints**
gourd: **Vegetable**
Government House (Alta): **Edmonton; Lieutenant-Governor**
Government House (NS): **Halifax**
Government-Industry Seabed Project: **Sonar**
Government Insurance Act (Sask): **Saskatchewan**
Government of Canada bonds: **Stock & Bond Markets; Winnipeg Commodity Exchange**
Government of Canada Building: **Whiten, Colette**
Government of Newfoundland & Labrador Arts & Letters Competition: **Literary Prizes in English**
Government Organization Act: **Atlantic Development Council; Communications, Dept of; Energy, Mines & Resources, Dept of; Government Organization, Royal Commission on**
Government Organization (Scientific Activities) Act: **Social Sciences & Humanities Research Council of Canada**
government policies: **Agriculture & Food Policy; Communication Studies; Competition Policy; Dominion Lands Policy; Education Policy; Energy Policy; Fiscal Policy; Fisheries Policy; Health Policy; Housing & Housing Policy; Howe Research Institute; Immigration Policy; Labour Policy; Language Policy; Monetary Policy; National Policy; Public Service; Science Policy**
government printing: *Hansard*; **Secretary of State, Dept of; Supply & Services, Dept of**
Government Purchasing Standards Committee: **Canadian Government Specifications Board**
government secrecy: **Law & the Press; Official Secrets Act**
Governor General's Medal: **Colville, Alexander; Medal; Whiten, Colette**
Governor General's Medal for Architecture: **Architectural Competitions; Moriyama, Raymond**
Governor-General's "Persons Award": **MacInnis, Grace W.**
Governor General's prize: **Curling**
Governor's Bridge: **Technology**
Gowan, Alan: **Art Writing & Criticism**
Gowan, R. Ogle: **Brockville**
Gowans, Kent Glass Co: **Glass**
Gowe, Robert: **Animal Breeding**
GPSS: **Computer Science**
Grace Hospitals: **Fairn, Leslie Raymond; Salvation Army**
Grace Island: **Grosse Ile**
grackle: **Blackbird**
grading: **Crops; Wheat**
"Gradual Reduction System": **Flour Milling Industry**
GRAFF: **Printmaking**
Graff, Oscar: **Guitar**
graft: **Corruption**
Grafton, Ont: **Architecture, Development**
Graham, Billy: **Evangelism**
Graham, Gwethalyn: **Best-Sellers in English; Chaput-Rolland, Solange; Jewish Writing**
Graham, Laurie: **Skiing**
Graham, Roger: **Historiography**

Graham, Victor: **Comparative Literature**
Graham, W.A.G.: **Chemistry Subdisciplines**
Graham Brothers (Canada): **Chrysler Canada Ltd**
Graham Island: **Queen Charlotte Islands**
grain: **Agriculture & Food; Alberta Wheat Pool; Barley; Buckwheat; Canadian-American Economic Relations; Canadian Wheat Board; Corn, Field; Crow's Nest Pass Agreement; Distilling Industry; Lake Carriers; Millet; Oats; Rye; Shipping Industry; Triticale; Wheat**
grain alcohol: **Biomass Energy**
Grain Growers' Grain Co: **Co-operative Movement** (*See* Addendum, page 1992); **Crerar, Thomas A.; Grain Growers' Associations; Partridge, Edward A.; United Farmers of Alberta**
Grain Research Laboratory: **Grain Handling & Marketing**
Grain Transportation Agency: **Horner, John H.**
Grainger, Martin Allerdale: **Literature in English; Novel in English**
Grammy Award: **Mitchell, Joni; Murray, Anne; Peterson, Oscar E.**
granary weevil: **Beetle**
Grand Bank, Nfld: **Hickman, Albert Edgar**
Grand Bay East, Nfld: **Channel-Port aux Basques**
Grand Bay West, Nfld: **Channel-Port aux Basques**
Grand Canyon: **Stikine River**
Grand Cirque Ordinaire: **Theatre, French-Language**
Grand Council of the Cree of Québec: **Diamond, Billy; Land Claims**
Grand Falls Central Railway: **Newfoundland**
Grand Falls Station: **Windsor, Nfld**
grand fir: **Fir; Vegetation Regions - Cordillera; Vegetation Regions - Pacific Coastal**
Grand Forks, BC: **Kettle Valley; Monashee Mountains**
Grand General Indian Council of Ontario: **Native People, Political Organization & Activism**
Grand Harbour, NB: **Grand Manan Island**
grand juries: **Nova Scotia 1714-84**
Grand-Lac-Victoria: **Ottawa River**
Grand Lake (Lab): **Melville, Lake**
Grand Lake (NB): **Coal; New Brunswick**
Grand Lodge of British North America: **Brockville; Irish; Orange Order**
Grand Lodge of Upper Canada of the Ancient Free & Accepted Masons: **Associations**
Grand Medicine Society: **Midewiwin**
Grand-Mère, Qué: **Graham, Stuart; Laurentian Highlands; St-Maurice, Rivière**
Grand Narrows, NS: **Murray, George Henry**
Grand Opera House: **Drama in English; Grand Theatre; Nickinson, John**
Grand Premier Prix: **Aubut, Françoise**
Grand prix littéraire de la ville de Montréal: **Beaulieu, Victor-Levy; Giguère, Roland; Literary Prizes in French**
Grand Rapid of the Saskatchewan: **Cedar Lake Reservoir; McIntosh, William; North West Company; Saskatchewan River**
Grand River (Ont): **Brantford; Elora; Erie, Lake; Galt; Germans; Iroquois; Mohawk; Onondaga; Paris**
Grand Rivière des Algonquins: **Ottawa River**
Grand Séminaire de Québec: **Séminaire de Québec**
Grand Seminary of St Sulpice: **Ostell, John**
Grand Théâtre: **Architecture; Concert Halls & Opera Houses; Prus, Victor Marius; Public Art; Québec City**
Grand Trunk Arrangements Act: **Railway History**
Grand Union Ltd: **Steinberg, Samuel**
Grand Western Canadian Screen Shop: **Printmaking**

Grande Décharge: **Alma**
"Grande Hémorragie": **Franco-Americans**
Grande Hermine: **Cartier, Jacques**
Grande-Ligne Mission: **Baptists; Huguenots**
Grande Prairie *Daily Herald-Tribune*: **Alberta**
Grande République: **Drama in French**
Grande Riding Academy: **Cycling**
Grande rivière de la Baleine: **Bienville, Lac; Northern Lights**
Grande Rivière (Qué): **Electric-Power Generation**
Grandes-Fourches: **Eastern Townships; Sherbrooke**
Grandes-Piles, Qué: **St-Maurice, Rivière**
Grandin, Lac: **Martre, Lac la**
Grandmaison, Éléonore de: **Orléans, Ile d'**
Grand'Maison, Jacques: **Philosophy**
Granduc Mine: **Avalanche; Tunnels**
Grandview Industries Ltd: **Plastics-Processing Industry**
Grandy Island: **Burgeo**
Granet, Lac: **Ottawa River**
Grange, Samuel: **Railway Safety**
granite: **Bank Architecture; Igneous Rock**
Grannan, Mary: **Literature in English**
Granny apple: **McIntosh, John**
Grant, Alexander: **National Ballet of Canada**
Grant, Alexander (1734-1813): **Upper Canada**
Grant, Bud: **Winnipeg Blue Bombers**
Grant, Gordon: **Estrogen**
Grant, William L.: **Grant, George P.**
Grant Land: **Ellesmere Island**
Grant MacEwan Community College: **Clothing Industries; Dance Education**
Granton, NS: **Rubber Products Industry**
Grantown, North-West Territories: **Falcon, Pierre; Grant, Cuthbert**
Granville Falls: **Churchill River**
Granville Island: **Architecture, Development; Vancouver**
Granville Lake: **Manitoba**
Graphex: **Printmaking**
Graphic Arts Club: **Artists' Organizations; Printmaking**
Graphic Associates: **Film Animation**
Graphic Publishers: **Book Publishing, English-Language**
graphite: **Canadarm; Drawing; Mineral; Nuclear Energy; Nuclear Power Plants**
Gras, Lac de: **Coppermine River**
Gras, N.S.B.: **Business History; Metropolitan-Hinterland Thesis**
Grashey, Don: **Baker, Carroll**
Grass River: **Nelson River**
grasslands: **Conservation**
Grassroots system: **Telidon; Torstar Corp**
Grates Point: **Avalon Peninsula; Trinity Bay**
Gratton, G.: **Weightlifting**
Gratton, Hector: **Music History**
Gratton, Olindo: **Bourassa, Napoléon**
grave goods: **Beothuk; Linear Mounds; Neutral; Prehistory; Rainy River Burial Mounds**
grave posts: **Northwest Coast Indian Art**
Gravelbourg, Sask: **Religious Building**
Graves, Thomas: **Labrador Boundary Dispute; Newfoundland**
Graves, Warren: **Theatre, English-Language**
gravimeter: **Petroleum Exploration & Production**
gravity: **Black Hole; Cosmology; Delta; Erosion; Geology; Petroleum Exploration & Production; Shield; Tide**
gravure: **Print Industry**
Gray, Asa: **Floras & Botanical Journals**
Gray, D.F.: **Spectroscopy**
Gray, J.A.: **Physics**
Gray, John: **Drama in English; Governor General's Literary Awards; Humorous Writing in English; Neptune Theatre**
Gray Coach: **Bus Transportation**
gray jay: **Algonquin Provincial Park; Jay; Strathcona Provincial Park**

Gray Report: **Americans; Economic Nationalism; Foreign Ownership, Task Force on**
gray trout: **Mistassini, Lac**
Gray's Publishing Ltd: **Children's Literature in English**
grazing land: **Ranching History**
greasewood: **Biogeography**
Great Bear Belt: **Geological Regions**
Great Bear River: **Bearlake; Great Bear Lake; Mackenzie River**
great blue heron: **Heron**
Great Canadian Oil Sands Ltd: **Alberta; Bitumen; Clark, Karl Adolf; Fort McMurray**
Great Canadian Theatre Co: **Ottawa, Ont; Theatre for Young Audiences**
Great Central Lake: **Port Alberni; Vancouver Island**
Great Clay Belt: **Timiskaming, Lake**
Great Code: Anatomy of Criticism
Great Colinet Island: **St Mary's Bay**
Great Eastern: **Heart's Content**
Great Feather Dance: **Handsome Lake Religion**
great gray owl: **Graham, Andrew; Owl**
Great Lakes Basin: **Environmental Law; Treaty of Paris (1763)**
Great Lakes Fisheries Research Branch: **Canada Centre for Inland Waters**
Great Lakes Power Co Ltd: **Ontario**
Great Lakes-St Lawrence Forest: **Forest Regions**
Great Lakes Shipping Ltd: **Mainguy, Edmond Rollo**
Great North Railway: **Shawinigan**
Great North Western Telegraph Co: **Telegraph**
Great Northern Peninsula: **French Shore; L'Anse aux Meadows; Long Range Mountains; Port au Choix; St Anthony**
Great Northern Railway: **Vancouver**
Great Plain of the Koukdjuak: **Baffin Island; Nettiling Lake**
Great Road: **Kitchener-Waterloo**
Great Seal of Canada: **Constitution Act, 1982; Consumer & Corporate Affairs, Dept of; Emblems of Canada; Royal Commissions; Symbols of Authority**
Great Slave Lake Railway: **Northwest Territories; Railway History; Railways, Contemporary**
Great Slave Plain: **Physiographic Regions - Interior Plains**
Great Southern Railway swindle: **Banking**
Great War Veterans Assn: **Royal Canadian Legion**
Great-West Life Assurance Building (Winnipeg): **Atchison, John D.**
Great-West Life Assurance Co: **Power Corp of Canada; Richardson, James A., Sr**
Great Whale River: **Weaving, Contemporary**
Greater Montreal Arts Council: **Literary Prizes in French**
Greater Winnipeg Floodway: **Barber, Clarence L.; Roblin, Dufferin**
Greatland Mountains: **Innuitian Region**
Gréber, Jacques: **National Capital Commission**
Greco-Gallican tradition: **Anglicanism**
Greek language: **Classics; Language**
Greek Orthodox Church: **Alberta; Byelorussians; Canadian Council of Churches; Greeks; New Brunswick; Orthodox Church; Québec; Regina; Religious Music**
Greely Fjord: **Fosheim Peninsula**
Green, Bartholomew, Jr: **Magazines; Print Industry**
Green, Daniel: **Summerside**
Green, Daniel (cabinetmaker): **Furniture, English, Scottish & American**
Green, Gordon H.: **Essay in English**
Green, J.: **Green, Blankstein, Russell**
Green, Mark: **Furniture, Country**
Green, Terance M.: **Popular Literature in English**
green alder: **Alder; Vegetation Regions - Cordillera**
green algae: **Algae; Biology; Fossil Plants; Vegetation Regions - Coastal Marine Flora**

green ash: **Biomass Energy; Manitoba; Vegetation Regions - Eastern Temperate Forests**
Green Bank: **Grand Banks**
Green Corn Festival: **Handsome Lake Religion**
green feed: **Forage Crops**
green manure: **Beet; Buckwheat; Grape; Vetch**
Green River, Ont: **Burton, Eli Franklin**
Green Thumb: **Theatre for Young Audiences**
Greenaway, K.R.: **Dunbar, I. Moira**
greenbelt: **Ottawa, Ont; Zoning**
Greene, Edward J.H.: **Comparative Literature**
Greene, Henry: **Hudson, Henry**
Greene, Hugh: **Printmaking**
Greene, J.J.: **Roman, Stephen B.**
Greene, Thomas G.: **Graphic Design; Printmaking**
Greenhills Mine: **Coal**
greenhouse effect: **Hare, Frederick Kenneth; Ocean; Oceanography**
Greenidge, Herbert Lawrence: **Greenwich, Sonny**
Greenland right whale: **Arctic Animals**
Greenland shark: **Arctic Animals**
Greenleaf, Elizabeth: **Folk Music, Anglo-Canadian**
greenockite: **Cadmium**
Green's Shore: **Summerside**
Greenspond, Nfld: **Newfoundland**
Greenville, BC: **Nass River**
Greenwich Gallery: **Art Dealers; Snow, Michael J.A.**
Greenwood, BC: **MacLean, John Duncan; Monashee Mountains**
Greenwood, NS: **Canadair CL-28 Argus**
Gregg River Mine: **Coal**
Grégoire, Ernest: **Action libérale nationale**
Gregoire Lake: **Bitumen**
Gregorian calendar: **Orthodox Church; Religious Festivals**
Gregorian chant: **Charpentier, Gabriel; Religious Music**
Gregory, Francis: **Tobacco-Products Industry**
Gregory, Ian: **Graphic Design**
Gregory, Judith: **Graphic Design**
Gregory, McLeod & Co: **Mackenzie, Alexander (1764-1820); North West Company**
Gregory, William T.: **Tobacco-Products Industry**
Grenfell, Anne: **Rugs & Rug Making**
Grenfell Mission: **Forteau; Nain; Rugs & Rug Making; St Anthony**
Grenfell rugs: **Rugs & Rug Making**
Grenville Canal: **Construction Industry, History; Hawkesbury**
Grenville Front: **Geological Regions**
Grenville Province: **Geological Regions**
Grès Falls Co: **Cap-de-la-Madeleine; Shawinigan**
Gretna, Man: **Grain Elevators**
Grey, Francis William: **Novel in English**
grey birch: **Biogeography; Birch**
"Grey Cup smog": **Air Pollution**
grey fox: **Fox; Rondeau Provincial Park**
Grey Goose Corp: **Bus Transportation**
Grey Nuns: **Baillairgé Family; Christian Religious Communities; Fort Resolution; French in the West; Nursing; St-Boniface; Theatre, French-Language; Youville, Marie-Marguerite d'**
Grey Owl: **Belaney, Archibald S.**
grey seal: **Kouchibouguac National Park; Sable Island; Seal**
Grey Sisters of the Immaculate Conception: **Heraldry**
grey sole: **Newfoundland**
grey whale: **Pacific Rim National Park; Whale**
grey wolf: **Hunting; Wolf**
Greyhound Lines of Canada Ltd: **Bus Transportation**
Grierson Film Seminar: **Film Festivals, Prizes**
Griff, Ray: **Country & Western Music**
Griffin, Alfredo: **Toronto Blue Jays**
Griffin, W.H.: **Postal System**
Griffing, Dean: **Calgary Stampeders**
Griffith, Harold: **Medicine, History of**
Griffith, Harry: **Football**
Griffith Mine: **Iron & Steel Industry**

Griffiths, Blair: **Mount Everest Expedition**
Griffiths, Frank: **Vancouver Canucks; WIC (Western International Communications Ltd)**
Griffiths, Linda: **Drama in English; Humorous Writing in English; Theatre, English-Language; 25th Street Theatre**
Grim Reapers: **Organized Crime**
Grimross, NB: **Gagetown**
Grimsby Beach, Ont: **Niagara Peninsula**
Grimshaw, Alta: **Northwest Territories**
grinder: **Domestic Utensils**
Griner, Wendy: **Figure Skating**
Grinke, Frederick: **Music History**
Grinnell Peninsula: **Port Refuge**
Grip: **Bengough, John W.; Cartoons; Jefferys, Charles W.; Print Industry**
Grip Ltd: **Carmichael, Franklin; Johnston, Francis Hans; Lismer, Arthur; MacDonald, James Edward Hervey; Printmaking; Thomson, Thomas J.**
Grip-Sack: **Drama in English**
Grizzly Bear Ceremony: **Kootenay**
Grizzly Bear's Head Reserve: **Assiniboine**
Grohovaz, Gianni: **Italian Writing**
Gros Blanc: **Blackfoot**
Gros Ventre (Atsina): **Blackfoot Nation; Henday, Anthony; Native People - Plains**
Gross, Paul: **Theatre, English-Language**
Gross Domestic Product: **Economic Regulation; Gross National Product; Regional Economics**
Gross Reproduction Rate: **Population**
Grosse Ile: **Madeleine, Iles de la**
Grosse Isle, Man: **Rockwood**
Grosse Valise: **Theatre for Young Audiences**
Groswater Bay: **Labrador**
Groswater culture: **L'Anse aux Meadows**
Grouard, Alta: **Lesser Slave Lake**
Grouard, Emile, J.B.M.: **Grande Prairie**
Groulx, Georges: **Roux, Jean-Louis; Théâtre du nouveau monde**
ground pine: **Club Moss**
ground squirrel: **Animals in Winter; Cypress Hills Provincial Park; Kluane National Park; Mount Assiniboine Provincial Park; Squirrel**
groundfish: **Cape Sable Island; Coastal Waters; Fundy, Bay of/Gulf of Maine; Hecate Strait; Queen Charlotte Islands**
groundhog: **Marmot**
group homes: **Child Welfare; Social & Welfare Services**
group therapy: **Juvenile Delinquency**
Groupe Beaulne: **Beaulne, Guy**
Groupe d'action photographique: **Gaudard, Pierre; Szilasi, Gabor**
Groupe de recherches sociales: **Communications in Québec**
Groupe nouvelle aire: **Fortier, Paul-André**
Grouse Mountain Skyride: **North Vancouver**
Groves Memorial Hospital: **Groves, Abraham**
Grubb, Howard B.: **Landscape Architecture**
Grube, G.M.A.: **Philosophy**
Gruhn, Ruth: **Archaeology**
Grundy, Ernest: **Almighty Voice**
Grunthal, Man: **Hanover**
Gryba, Eugene M.: **Archaeology**
grylloblattid: **Insect Classification**
GSW Inc: **Electrical Appliances Industry**
guano: **Funk Island**
guaranteed annual income: **Income Distribution; Poverty**
Guaranteed Income Supplement: **Aging; Minority Government; Old-Age Pension; Pension; Poverty; Social Security**
Guaranty Trust of Canada: **Campeau, Robert**
guardian: **Family Law**
Guardian of the Game: **Native People, Religion**
Guardian Spirit Quest: **Native People, Religion**

Guay, J.A.: **Disasters**
Guédon, Marie-Françoise: **Folklore**
Guelph-Goderich Road: **Elmira**
Guelph Junction Railway: **Guelph**
Guelph Maple Leafs: **Baseball**
Guelph Spring Festival: **Festivals; Guelph; Opera; Vickers, Jonathan S.**
Guelph-Toronto Centre for Toxicology: **Chant, Donald Alfred**
Guernon, *dit* Belleville, François: **Sculpture**
Guerrero, Alberto: **Gould, Glenn H.; Music History**
Guest, Al: **Film Animation**
Gueudeville, Nicholas: **Lahontan, Baron de**
Guèvremont, Hyacinthe: **Guèvremont, Germaine**
Guèvremont, Lise: *Barre du jour*
Guibord, Henriette: **Guibord Affair**
Guibord, Joseph: **Guibord Affair**
guided missiles: **Military Aviation & Aircraft**
Guideline Instruments Ltd: **Batfish**
Guilbault, Luce: **Film**
Guild of Canadian Musical Theatre Writers: **Musical Theatre**
Guilde graphique: **Lacroix, Richard; Printmaking**
Guildford, BC: **Surrey**
guillemot: **Arctic Animals; Auk; Baffin Island**
Guillon, Jacques: **Industrial Design; Interior Design**
Guimond, Oliver: **Television Drama, French-Language**
Guinea worm disease: **Water-Borne Disease**
guineas: **Coinage; Queen's Plate**
guitarfish: **Ray**
Gujarati language: **Africans; Hinduism**
Gulf Aviation: **Quebecair**
Gulf Canada Square tower: **Energy in Society**
Gulf Oil Canada Ltd: **Gulf Canada Ltd**
Gulf Stream: **Grand Banks; Nova Scotia; Oceanography; Sable Island; Scotian Shelf**
Gull Island: **Hamilton Inlet; Lighthouses; Newfoundland**
Gull Lake (Alta): **Rundle, Robert Terrill**
Gullen, John B.: **Stowe-Gullen, A. Augusta**
Guloien House: **Cardinal, Douglas J.**
"gumbo": **Okra**
gumweed: **Biomass Energy**
Gundy-Clapperton Glass Co: **Glass**
Gunflint chert formation: **Geological Dating; Paleontology; Sedimentary Rock**
Gunnar Mines: **LaBine, Gilbert**
Gunnars, Kristjana: **Ethnic Literature; Literature in English**
Gunnarsson, Sturla: **Film, Documentary**
Gunnery schools: **French, George Arthur; Regiment**
Gunnholme Vu Farm: **Harness Racing**
Gunningsville, NB: **Riverview**
Gunns Ltd: **Canada Packers Inc; Meat-Processing Industry**
gunpowder: **Armaments; Drummondville; Firearm**
Gunshot Treaty: **Indian Treaties**
Gunton, Man: **Rockwood**
Gupta, Anil: **Philosophy**
Gurd, William: **Firearm**
Gurr, Donna-Marie: **Swimming, Speed**
Gury, Paul: **Radio Drama, French-Language**
Gustafson, Ralph: **Literature in English**
Gustin, Lyell: **Music History**
Guthrie, Tyrone: **Moore, Dora Mavor**
Gutteridge, Don: **Regionalism in Literature**
Guttormsson, Guttormur J.: **Ethnic Literature; Icelanders**
Guy, Ray: **Newfoundland**
Guyanese: **Ethnic Literature; South Asians**
Guysborough, NS: **Blacks**
Gwatkin, Willoughby G.: **A Mari usque ad Mare**
Gwen Pharis Ringwood Civic Theatre: **Ringwood, Gwendolyn**
Gwillim, Thomas: **Welsh**
Gwyn, Richard: **Best-Sellers in English**
Gwynne, Horace: **Olympic Games**

gym equipment: **Sporting-Goods Industry**
Gypsumville, Man: **Manitoba**
gyrfalcon: **Falcon; Québec**
gyroplane: **Aviation**
Gzowski, Peter: *Maclean's*
Gzowski & Co: **Grand Trunk Railway of Canada**
Gzowski Medal: **Gzowski, Casimir S.**

H

H.D. Lee of Canada Ltd: **Clothing Industries**
H.J. Heinz Co of Canada: **Leamington**
H.R. MacMillan Export Co: **MacMillan, H.R.**
Ha! Ha!, Baie des: **La Baie; Saguenay Provincial Park**
Habitant Corner: **Canning**
Habitant River: **Canning**
Habitat: **Expo 67; Safdie, Moshe**
Habitat: **Urban & Regional Planning**
hackberry: **Point Pelée National Park; Vegetation Regions - Eastern Temperate Forests**
Hacking, Ian: **Philosophy**
Hackleman, Martin: **Canadian Brass**
Hadashville, Man: **Manitoba**
Hadassah-WIZO: **Judaism**
Haddad, Claire: **Fashion Design**
haddock: **Baffin Bay; Cape Sable Island; Cod; Georges Bank; Grand Banks; Nova Scotia**
Hadwen, Seymour: **Parasitology**
Haeck, Philippe: **Essay in French; Poetry in French**
Haeffely, Claude: **Popular Literature in French**
Hagersville, Ont: **Fossil Animals; Native People, Communications**
Hague Convention on International Child Abduction: **Treaty-Making Power**
Hahn, Emmanuel Otto: **Public Art; Sculpture**
Hahn, Gustav: **Public Art**
Haidasz, Stanley: **Poles**
Hail Galarneau!: **Salut Galarneau!**
Haines, Frederick: **Printmaking**
Haines Highway: **Haines Junction**
Hainsworth, W.: **Vancouver, Mount**
Hairy Hill, Alta: **Place-names**
hairy honeysuckle: **Vegetation Regions - Cordillera**
Haisla language: **Kitamaat**
Haisla Nation: **Land Claims**
Haist, Jane: **Track & Field**
Haitians: **Sexually Transmitted Disease; West Indians**
hakapik: **Sealing**
hake: **Cod; Fisheries Policy; Prince Edward Island**
Hakim, Michael: **Catholicism**
Haldane, James: **Baptists**
Haldane, Robert: **Baptists**
Hale, John: **Maillou House**
Hale, Katherine: **Crawford, Isabella Valancy**
Hales, Charles: **Bellevue House**
Half-Breed Commission: **Métis**
half pennies: **Coinage**
half-tone process: **Print Industry**
halfway houses: **Alcoholism; Probation & Parole; Salvation Army**
Halfway River: **Peace River**
Haliburton, Ont: **Harris, Lawren S.**
Haliburton, Robert G.: **Canada First**
halibut: **Baffin Bay; Cuisine; Flatfish; Grand Banks; Hecate Strait; Hudson Bay; Madeleine, Iles de la**
Halibut Fisheries Convention: **Treaty-Making Power**
halide: **Mineral**
Halifax & Southwestern Railway: **Nova Scotia**
Halifax-Annapolis Road: **Wolfville**
Halifax Banking Co: **Collins, Enos; Cunard, Samuel**
Halifax Board of Trade: **Associations**
Halifax Chess, Pencil & Brush Club: **Artists' Organizations**
Halifax Chronicle: **Connolly, Harold Joseph; Newspapers**
Halifax City Hall: **Fairn, Leslie Raymond**
Halifax Club: **Stirling, David**
Halifax Conservative Women's Auxiliary: **Archibald, Edith J.**

Halifax Conservatory: **Music Education**
Halifax Council of Women: **Archibald, Edith J.; Dennis, Agnes; Leonowens, Anna H.**
Halifax County Court House: **Architectural Styles**
Halifax Daily Star: **Connolly, Harold Joseph**
Halifax Fisheries Commission: **Smith, Albert James**
Halifax Football Club: **Rugby**
Halifax Gazette: **Advertising; Newspapers; Print Industry**
Halifax Grammar School: **School Facilities**
Halifax harbour: **Bayfield, Henry Wolsey; Halifax; Nova Scotia; Piracy**
Halifax Herald: **Bourinot, John George; Dennis, Agnes; Long-Distance Running; Newspapers; Yachting**
Halifax Mail: **Newspapers**
Halifax Monthly Magazine: **Art Writing & Criticism; Magazines**
Halifax *Morning Chronicle*: **Annand, William; Fielding, William S.**
Halifax penitentiary: **Prison**
Halifax Shipyards Ltd: **Gundy, James Henry; Shipbuilding & Ship Repair**
Halifax Star: **Newspapers**
Halifax Theatre Arts Guild: **Little Theatre Movement**
Halifax Turf Club: **Thoroughbred Racing**
Halifax Zeitung: **Germans**
halite: **Mineral; Salt**
Halkomelem: **Central Coast Salish**
Hall, Amelia: **Theatre, English-Language**
Hall, Basil: **Exploration & Travel Literature in English**
Hall, Cecil: **Burton, Eli Franklin**
Hall, Charles F.: **Iglulik Inuit; Tookoolito, "Hannah"**
Hall, Frederick: **Musicology**
Hall, H.: **Logan, Mount**
Hall, Joe: **Lalonde, E., "Newsy"**
Hall, Mary G.: **Printmaking**
Hall, Mary Georgina: **Autobiographical Writing in English**
Hall-Dennis Report: **Education, Alternate**
Hall-Holland, Dorinda: **Equestrian Sports**
Halldorson, Dan: **Golf**
Halley, Comet: **Comet**
Hallowell, Ont: **Picton**
hallucigenia: **Burgess Shale Site**
hallucination: **Alcoholism; Drug Use, Non-Medical; Medical Drug Abuse; Psychiatry**
Halpern, Ida: **Music Criticism**
Halpert, Herbert: **Folklore**
Halter, G. Sydney: **Canadian Football League**
Halverson, Sigurd: **Ski Jumping**
ham: **Hog Farming; Meat-Processing Industry**
Ham, Albert: **Choral Music**
Ham, R.C.: **Green, Blankstein, Russell**
Hamann, George Frederick: **Bregman & Hamann**
Hamatsa dance: **Bella Bella**
Hambleton, Ronald: **Page, Patricia Kathleen**
Hambletonian Stakes: **Harness Racing**
Hambly & Wilson: **Rugs & Rug Making**
Hambourg, Boris: **Hart House String Quartet**
Hambourg Conservatory: **Royal Conservatory of Music of Toronto**
Hambraeus, Bengt: **Music History**
Hamel, Philippe: **Action libérale nationale**
Hamel, Réginald: **Literary Bibliography in French; Literature in French - Scholarship & Teaching**
Hamel, René: **Bloc populaire canadien**
Hamelin, Jean: *Dictionary of Canadian Biography*; **Literary Bibliography in French; Literature in French - Scholarship & Teaching; Social History**
Hamilton: **Diving, Underwater; Ontario, Lake**
Hamilton, Barbara: **Gill, Robert**

Hamilton, Catharine: **St Catharines**
Hamilton, Charles: **Churchill River, Lab; Hamilton Inlet**
Hamilton, Cynthia: **Long-Distance Running**
Hamilton, Frederick: **Skiing**
Hamilton, George: **Hamilton; St Catharines**
Hamilton, Robert: **Hamilton; St Catharines**
Hamilton, Robert M.: **Dictionary**
Hamilton, Ron: **David, Joe**
Hamilton, Ross: **Dumbells**
Hamilton & District Trades & Labor Council: **Mitchell, Humphrey**
Hamilton & North Western Railway: **Northern Railway of Canada**
Hamilton "Around-the-Bay" race: **Long-Distance Running**
Hamilton Art Gallery: **Hutchinson, Leonard**
Hamilton Asylum: **Bucke, Richard Maurice; Clarke, Charles Kirk; Lett, Stephen; Tully, Kivas**
Hamilton Bank: **Coastal Waters; Hamilton Inlet**
Hamilton Birth Control Clinic: **Bagshaw, Elizabeth Catherine**
Hamilton Blast Furnace Co: **Hamilton; Hobson, Robert**
Hamilton College: **McMaster University**
Hamilton Garage & Rubber Co: **Canadian Tire Corp, Ltd**
Hamilton Glass Co: **Glass**
Hamilton harbour: **Canada Centre for Inland Waters; Hamilton; Lake**
Hamilton Herald: **Newspapers**
Hamilton jail: **O'Reilly, Gerald**
Hamilton Philharmonic Orchestra: **Brott, Boris; Canadian Brass; Gellman, Steven; Hamilton**
Hamilton Place: **Concert Halls & Opera Houses; Hamilton**
Hamilton Pumping Station: **Keefer, Thomas C.**
Hamilton River: **Place-names**
Hamilton School of Art: **Hutchinson, Leonard**
Hamilton Sound: **Fogo Island**
Hamilton Spectator: **Hamilton; Southam, William**
Hamilton Steel & Iron Co: **Hobson, Robert; Stelco Inc**
Hamilton Tigers: **Fear, Alfred Henry; Football; Gaudaur, Jacob G., Jr; Hamilton Tiger Cats; Hockey, Ice; Malone, M. Joseph; Winnipeg Blue Bombers**
Hamilton Trades Assembly: **Union Centrals, District & Regional**
Hamilton Wildcats: **Hamilton Tiger Cats; Krol, Joseph**
Hamilton's Players' Guild: **Little Theatre Movement**
hammer: **Tools, Carpentry; Woodenware**
hammer throw: **Track & Field**
Hammond, A.W.: **McLeod, Alan Arnett**
Hammond, John: **Art Education**
Hammond Manufacturing: **Guelph**
Hampton, Ian: **Purcell String Quartet**
Hancock, Geoffrey: **Literary Magazines in English**
Hancock, George: **Furniture, Country**
Hancox, Rich: **Film, Experimental**
hand game: **Beaver (Indians)**
hand-wrestling: **Sports History**
handbill: **Censorship**
Handeles, Ydessa: **Art Dealers**
handicapped: **Building Codes & Regulations; Constitution, Patriation of; Disability; Drama in English; Education, Special; Urban Transportation**
handwriting: **Germanic Fraktur & Calligraphy**
Haney, BC: **Maple Ridge; University of British Columbia**
hanging: **Capital Punishment; La Corriveau; Piracy**
Hanlan's Point: **Toronto Islands**
Hann, Otto: **Science**
Hanna, James: **Silver, Domestic**
Hannaford, E.P.: **Railway Station**
Hannah, Sister: **Christian Religious Communities**
Hannath & Hart Brewery: **O'Keefe, Eugene**
Hanover, Ont: **Heintzman & Co Ltd**
Hansen, Jim: **Printmaking**
Hansen, R.: **Soil Science**

Hansen Lagoon: **Cape Scott Provincial Park**
Hanson, Christilot: **Equestrian Sports**
Hanson, Fritz: **Winnipeg Blue Bombers**
Hantsport, NS: **Nova Scotia**
Hantzsch River: **Baffin Island**
Hanukkah: **Judaism**
Hapkido: **Jiu-Jitsu**
Happeny, William: **Track & Field**
Happy Gang: **Farnon, Robert J.; Niosi, Bert; Radio Programming**
Harbord Collegiate: **Wayne & Shuster**
Harbour Bridge: **Saint John**
Harbour Light centres: **Salvation Army**
Harbour Police: **Police**
harbour porpoise: **Dolphin & Porpoise; Pacific Rim National Park**
harbour seal: **Sable Island; Seal**
Harbour Square: **Bregman & Hamann**
harbours & ports: **Baie-Comeau; Churchill; Corner Brook; Dalhousie; Digby; Esquimalt; Georgetown; Hamilton; Killinek Island; Kitimat; La Baie; Ladysmith; Lévis; Lewisporte; Louisbourg; Marystown; Montréal; Moosonee; Nanaimo; National Harbours Board; New Westminster; Owen Sound; Parry Sound; Port Alberni; Port Dover; Port Hardy; Port Hood; Port Moody; St Anthony; Saint John; Saint John; St John's; Sept-Iles; Ship Harbour; Skinners Pond; Sorel; Toronto; Trois-Rivières; Ucluelet; Vancouver; Victoria; Windsor, Ont; Yarmouth**
Harbours & Ports Directorate: **Transportation Agencies (Government)**
Hard Red Calcutta wheat: **Saunders, Charles E.**
Harder, Hans: **German Writing**
Harder, Rolf: **Graphic Design**
Hardin, Herschel: **Drama in English; Festival Lennoxville**
Hardisty Lake: **Great Bear Lake**
hardwood: **Ash; Botanical Garden; Dogwood; Forest Fire; Forest Harvesting; Forestry; Furniture, Country; Furniture, English, Scottish & American; Furniture, German; Holly; Juniper; Lumber & Wood Industries; Maple; Oak; Pulp & Paper Industry; Walnut; Woodenware**
Hardy, Campbell: **Exploration & Travel Literature in English**
Hare, Alex: **McLean Gang**
Hare, F.G.: **Musicology**
Hare, John: **Intellectual History; Literary Bibliography in French**
Hare Krishna: **New Religious Movements; Religion**
harebell (heatherbell): **Bluebell**
Harel, Pierre: **Film**
Harewood Raceway: **Automobile Racing**
Hargrave, Joseph James: **Historiography**
Harleian world map: **Cartography, History of**
Harlequin Books: **Best-Sellers in English; Literary Prizes in English; Popular Literature in English; Torstar Corp**
Harley, T.H.: **Golf**
Harmac Pulp Mill: **MacMillan, H.R.**
Harman, Leonard: **United Farmers of Ontario**
Harmer Surface Mine: **Coal**
Harmon, Daniel: **Agriculture History**
Harmon Corp: **Stephenville**
Harmon Field: **Stephenville**
harmonica: **Folk Music, Franco-Canadian**
harmonium: **Musical Instruments**
Harms, Dallas: **Country & Western Music**
Harmsworth Trophy: **Boating**
harness: **Leatherworking**
Harney, Robert: **Italian Writing**
Haro Strait: **Oak Bay; Sidney; Victoria**
Harold Moon Trophy: **Garant, Serge**
Harp, Elmer: **Archaeology**
harp seal: **Arctic Animals; Coastal Waters; Labrador Sea; L'Anse Amour Burial Site; Sealing**
Harper, Arthur: **Forty Mile**

Harper, J. Russell: **Art Writing & Criticism; Musicology**
Harper, Lynn: *R v Truscott*
Harper, William: **Philosophy**
harpoon: **Archaeology; Beothuk; Inuit Art; L'Anse Amour Burial Site; Prehistory; Whaling**
harpsichord & harpsichord music: **Gilbert, Kenneth; Musical Instruments**
harquebus: **Armaments**
Harricana, Rivière: **Amos; James Bay; Val-d'Or**
Harrington, E.L.: **Physics**
Harrington, Normand: **Literary Bibliography in French**
Harris, Christie: **Children's Literature in English; Popular Literature in English**
Harris, Cole: **Regionalism in Literature**
Harris, Eric: **Drama in English**
Harris, John: **Bronson, Henry Franklin**
Harris, Lawren P.: **New Brunswick; Pratt, Mary**
Harris, R.W.: **Great Western Railway**
Harris, Thomas M.: **Harris, Lawren S.**
Harris Abattoir Co Ltd: **Canada Packers Inc; McLean, James Stanley; Meat-Processing Industry**
Harris & Partners Ltd: **Wilson, Michael Holcombe**
Harrison, Benjamin: **Harrison River**
Harrison, Charles Yale: **Literature in English**
Harrison, Lance: **Music Broadcasting**
Harrison, Susie F.: **Music History**
Harrison, Ted: **Children's Literature in English**
Harrison, William: **Cod Liver Oil**
Harrison Hot Springs: **Harrison River; Spring**
Harrison Lake: **Harrison River; Lillooet**
harrow: **Agricultural Implements; Agricultural Implements Industry; Agricultural Soil Practices**
Harrow, Ont: **Research Stations, Agricultural**
Harrowby Bay: **Horton River**
Hart, Aaron Philip: **Jews**
Hart, Arthur: **Freedman, Harry**
Hart, Cecil: **Hart Trophy**
Hart, David A.: **Hart Trophy**
Hart, Ezekiel: **Jews**
Hart, Gordon: **Hensley, Sophia Margaretta**
Hart Highway: **Hart, John; Pine Pass**
Hart House: **Coughtry, Graham; Massey, Hart A.; Sproatt and Rolph; Theatre Education; University of Toronto**
Hart House Orchestra: **Neel, L. Boyd**
Hart House Theatre: **Denison, Merrill; Drama in English; Gill, Robert; Hart House String Quartet; Hutt, William; Little Theatre Movement; Massey, Raymond H.; Reid, D. Kate; Stage & Costume Design; Theatre, English-Language**
Hart Jaune, Rivière: **Manicouagan Réservoir**
Hart's Theory of Law: **Jurisprudence**
Hartt, Charles F.: **Bailey, Loring W.; Science**
Harvest House Ltd, Publishers: **Book Publishing, English-Language**
harvester: **Agricultural Implements Industry**
harvestmen: **Arachnida**
Harvey, Florence: **Golf**
Harvey, Pierre: **Cross-Country Skiing**
Hasell, Eva: **Exploration & Travel Literature in English**
hashish: **Drug Use, Non-Medical; Organized Crime**
Hasidic Jews: **Jews**
Haslam Lake: **Powell River**
Hasnain, Arif: **Manitoba Theatre Centre**
Hassam, Jamelie: **Art, Contemporary Trends**
Hastings, NB: **Bennett, W.A.C.**
Hastings & Peterkin: **Toys & Games**
Hastings County Museum: **Belleville**
Hat Creek House: **Hotel**
hatchet: **Tools, Carpentry**
hate propaganda: **Attorney General**
Hatfield, S. Scott: *Canadian Business Review*

Hatfield Industries: **Hatfield, Richard B.**
hats & caps: **Clothing; Clothing Industries; Davidson, Florence Edenshaw; Fur Trade; Northwest Coast Indian Art; Rabbit Farming; St-Denis**
Hatsinatom, Pierre: **Yellowhead Pass**
Hattiangadi, Jagdish: **Philosophy**
Hatzic, BC: **Mission**
Haultain, F.W.G.: **Autonomy Bills**
Haultain, Theodore A.: **Essay in English**
Haure-St-Pierre, Qué: **Titanium**
Haurowitz, Pauline: **Donalda, Pauline**
Hausa language: **Africans**
Havelock, Ont: **Curtis, Wilfred Austin**
Havergal College: **Miller, George Martell**
Havre Aubert, Île du: **Madeleine, Iles de la**
Havre aux Maisons, Île du: **Madeleine, Iles de la**
Havre-St-Pierre, Qué: **French Language; Romaine, Rivière**
Hawes, Jasper: **Jasper National Park**
Hawk: **Feild, Edward**
Hawk Channel: **Cape Sable**
Hawk Inlet: **Cape Sable**
Hawker Hurricane aircraft: **Armed Forces - Air Force; Battle of Britain; Military Aviation & Aircraft**
Hawker Siddeley Canada Inc: **Bell Island; Curtis, Wilfred Austin; de Havilland Aircraft of Canada Ltd; Locomotives & Rolling Stock; Sydney Steel Corp**
Hawkins, John: **Chamber Music**
Hawks, The: **Band, The**
Hawley, William Fitz: **Poetry in English**
Haworth, Frank: **Choral Music**
Hawrelak, William: **Ukrainians**
hay: **Agriculture & Food; Agriculture History; Alfalfa; Animal Agriculture; Annapolis Lowlands; Forage Crops; Hay River; Manitoba; Minas Basin; Occupational Disease; Ontario; Soil Conservation; Soybean; Tantramar Marsh; Vetch**
Hay, G.U.: **Botany History**
Hay, W.: **Botany History**
Hay, William: **Bank Architecture**
hay fever: **Air Pollution; Allergies; Climate & Man; Poisonous Plants**
Hay-Holowko, Oleksa: **Ukrainian Writing**
Haycock, Maurice: *Breadalbane*
Hayes, James: **Hayes River**
Hayes, John F.: **Children's Literature in English**
Hayman, John: **Poetry in English**
Hayman, Lew: **Montreal Concordes**
Hayne, David M.: **Comparative Literature;** *Dictionary of Canadian Biography;* **Literary Bibliography in French**
Haynes, Elizabeth Stirling: **Theatre, English-Language**
Haynes, John Carmichael: **Osoyoos**
Haynes, Tim: **Graphic Design**
hazard: **Insurance**
Hazardous Products Act: **Consumer Law; Consumers' Association of Canada; White-Collar Crime**
hazelnut: **Coudres, Ile aux; Plants, Native Uses**
Hazelton, BC: **Davidson, Robert C.; Ksan; Skeena River**
Hazelton Library Assn: **Ksan**
Hazen, Lake: **Ellesmere Island; Gemstone**
Hazen Plateau: **Ellesmere Island**
Hazen Trough: **Geological Regions**
HD-4 hydrofoil: **Bell, Alexander Graham**
Head, George: **Exploration & Travel Literature in English**
Head Harbour, NB: **Lighthouses**
Head-of-the-Line: **Mackenzie River**
Head Ship Harbour, NS: **Ship Harbour**
head tax: **Chinese; Immigration; Immigration Policy**
heal-all: **Wildflowers**
Healey, Derek: **Choral Music; Opera**
Healey, Ed: **Swimming, Speed**
healing: **Chiropractic; New Religious Movements; Pilgrimage; Shaker Religion**

Health, Dept of: **Heagerty, John Joseph; Influenza; Law & Society; National Health & Welfare, Dept of; Public Health**
Health, Dept of (Man): **Manitoba**
Health, Dept of (NB): **Foster, Walter Edward; New Brunswick**
Health & Welfare Canada: **Advertising; Birth Control; Consumer Standards; Dairy Industry; Day Care; Death & Dying; Labelle, Huguette; Medical Devices Industry; Pharmaceuticals Industry; Safety Standards; Soft-Drink Industry; Vegetable Oil Industry**
health hazards: **Asbestos; Mercury; Smoking**
health insurance: **Alberta; Bloc populaire canadien; Government; Heagerty, John Joseph; Health Policy; King, W.L. Mackenzie; Martin, Paul J.J.; New Brunswick; Pharmaceuticals Industry; Social Security; Taxation; Victorian Order of Nurses**
Health of Animals Branch: **McEachran, Duncan; Parasitology; Veterinary Medicine, History**
Health Protection Branch: **Pharmaceuticals Industry**
Health Resources Fund: **Hospitals; Medicine, Contemporary**
health science: **International Development Research Centre; Medical Research Council; Psychology**
Health Sciences Centre: **Manitoba**
health services: **Aging; Canadian Advisory Council on the Status of Women; Hospitals; Medical Devices Industry; Medical Ethics; Medical Jurisprudence; Medicine, Contemporary; Nursing; Public Health; Women's Movement**
Health Services, Royal Commission on: **Girard, Alice M.; Hospitals; Medical Education; Psychiatry; Sociology**
Health Services & Insurance Commission (NS): **Nova Scotia**
Health Services Tax (NS): **Nova Scotia**
Heard, J.F.: **Spectroscopy**
hearing impairment: **Auditory Impairment; Education, Special**
hearsay evidence: **Law of Evidence;** *R v Coffin*
Hearst, Ont: **Laurentian University**
Heart Island: **Boldt Castle**
heart pacemaker: **Medical Devices Industry; Nuclear Energy**
heart urchin: **Echinodermata; Sea Urchin**
heartleaf arnica: **Wildflowers**
Heart's Delight, Nfld: **Place-names**
Heaslip, R.T.: **Helicopter**
heat island: **Urban Effect on Climate**
heat transfer: **Climatology**
heath: **Dubawnt Lake; Labrador Tea; Mayflower; Mycorrhizae; Nova Scotia**
Heath, Terence: **Short Fiction in English**
Heath-Steele Mine: **Prospecting**
heather: **Garibaldi Provincial Park**
heavy metal: **Agricultural Soil Practices**
heavy water: **Chalk River; Hydrogen; Nova Scotia; Nuclear Energy; Nuclear Power Plants; Nuclear Safety; Physics**
Hebden Mission: **Pentecostal Movement**
Hebert, Chantal: **Essay in French**
Hébert, Jacques: **Authors & Their Milieu**
Hébert, Jean: **Chess**
Hébert, Julien: **Industrial Design**
Hébert, Maurice: **Hébert, Anne; Literature in French - Criticism & Theory**
Hébert, Paul: **Deschamps, Yvon; Drama in French**
Hébert (Sauvageau), Yves: **Drama in French**
Hebrew Benevolent Soc: **Judaism**
Hebrew language: **Ethnic Languages; Ethnic Literature; Jewish Writing; Judaism; Religion**
Hebron, Nfld: **Nain; Torngat Mountains**

Hebron Fjord: **Geological Dating; Torngat Mountains**
Heck, Barbara: **Maitland**
Hecla: **Sabine, Edward**
Hector, BC: **Tunnels**
Hedberg, Anders: **Winnipeg Jets**
heddle: **Textiles, Woven**
Hedley, BC: **Keremeos; Princeton**
Hedrick, Robert: **Painting**
Heeley, Desmond: **Stage & Costume Design**
Heeney, William H.: **Fruit & Vegetable Industry**
Heeney Frosted Foods Ltd: **Fruit & Vegetable Industry**
Heermann's gull: **Migration**
Hefferton Causeway: **Random Island**
Hegelianism: **Watson, John**
Heiden, Eric: **Speed Skating**
heifer: **Animal Agriculture; Beef Cattle Farming; Dairy Farming**
Heiltsuk Cultural Centre: **Bella Bella**
Heiltsuk language: **Bella Bella**
Heimskringla (The World): **Icelanders**
Heinl, George: **Musical Instruments**
Heins, Donald: **Orchestral Music**
Heintzman, Gerhard: **Piano Manufacturing**
Heintzman, Theodore A.: **Heintzman & Co Ltd**
Heinz-Lehmann Award: **Sourkes, Theodore Lionel**
Heinz Unger Award: **Music Awards & Competitions**
Heinze, F.A.: **Trail**
Hélal, Georges: **Philosophy**
Helena, Qué: **Dairy Industry**
helium: **Balloon; Laser; Nuclear Fusion; Nuclear Power Plants; Physics; Spectroscopy; Spring; Sun; University of Toronto; Wood Mountain**
Hell Gate: **Arctic Archipelago**
Hellaby, Charles: **Cosmology**
Hellenikon Vema (Hellenic Tribune): **Greeks**
hellgrammite: **Dobsonfly**
Hells Angels: **Organized Crime**
Hell's Gate: **South Nahanni River**
Helluland: **Baffin Island; Norse Voyages**
Helm, Levon: **Band, The**
Helmer, Terence: **Orford String Quartet**
Helmuth, Izaak: **Poles**
Helmuth, J.F.: **Tennis**
Helwig, David: **Fox, Gail; Novel in English**
hematite: **Beothuk; Iron Ore; Mineral**
hemimorphite: **Mineral**
Hemingway, Ernest: *Star Weekly; Toronto Star*
Hemlo, Ont: **Gold; Mining**
hemlock looper: **Insect Pests**
hemophilia: **Biological Product; Sexually Transmitted Disease**
hemp: **Agriculture History; Crafts; Occupational Disease; Textiles, Woven**
Henders, R.C.: **Social Gospel**
Henderson, Bill: **Chilliwack**
Henderson, Elen: **Fashion Design**
Henderson, G.H.: **Physics**
Henderson, Paul: **Canada-Soviet Hockey Series, 1972**
Henderson, Robert: **Klondike Gold Rush**
Henderson House: **Brantford**
Henderson Lake Park: **Lethbridge**
Hendery, Robert: **Jewellery & Silverware Industry; Silver, Church; Silver, Domestic**
Hendery & Leslie: **Silver, Domestic**
Hendin, Judith: **Danny Grassman Dance Company**
Hendry, William: **Exploration**
Hendy's Candies Ltd: **Confectionery Industry**
Heneker, R.W.: **British American Land Company**
Henrich, Anthon: **Printmaking**
Henripin, Jacques: **Status of Women in Canada, Royal Commission on the**
Henry, Ann: **Festival Lennoxville; Theatre, English-Language**
Henry, Anthony: **Almanacs**
Henry, Martha: **Stratford Festival**
Henry, Mount: **Dundas Island**
Henry IV of France: **Acadia; Biencourt de Poutrincourt, Jean de; Gemstone**

Henry VII of England: **Cabot, John; Symbols of Authority**

Henry Birks & Sons Ltd: **Birks, Henry; Grey Cup; Medal; Silver, Domestic**

Henry Birks Collection: **Jewellery & Silverware Industry**

Henry House Museum: **Luke, Alexandra**

Henry Morgan & Co: **Morgan, Henry**

Henshaw, Don: **Radio Drama, English-Language**

Hensley, Almon: **Hensley, Sophia Margaretta**

Henty, G.A.: **Children's Literature in English**

hepatitis: **Connaught Laboratories Ltd; Virus**

"Hepburn's Hussars": **Hepburn, Mitchell F.; Oshawa Strike**

Hepner, Lee: **Edmonton Symphony Orchestra**

Her Majesty's theatre: **Theatre, English-Language**

Héraly, François: **Pelletier, Wilfrid**

Herbert, Ivor: **Armed Forces - Militia & Army**

Herbert, John: **Drama in English; Theatre, English-Language**

Herbert, Neil: **Guitar**

Herbert Inlet: **Strathcona Provincial Park**

Herbes rouges: **Literary Periodicals in French; Literature in French; Poetry in French**

herbicides: **Agricultural Soil Practices; Environmental Law; Oilseed Crops; Pesticide; Weeds**

Herbier Louis-Marie: **Cinq-Mars, Lionel; Louis-Marie**

Herbier Marie-Victorin: **Herbarium**

Herbinson, Brian: **Equestrian Sports**

Hercules: **Shipbuilding & Ship Repair**

Hercules transport: **Bush Flying**

Here & Now: **Literary Magazines in English**

Here & Now Art Gallery: **Art Dealers**

heredity: **Genetics**

heresy: **Crime; Macdonnell, Daniel James**

heritage buildings: **Conservation; Ontario**

Heritage Day: **National Holidays**

Heritage Festival: **Festivals; Folklore**

Heritage Fund: **Alberta Heritage Savings Trust Fund; Saskatchewan**

Heritage Park: **Calgary; Theatre for Young Audiences**

Heritage Village: **Burnaby**

Herman, Mildred: **Hayden, Melissa**

Hermaniuk, Maxim: **Catholicism**

hermaphrodite: **Hagfish**

hermaphrodite barquentine: **Lake Carriers**

Hermes satellite: **Communications in the North; Satellite Communications; Space Technology**

Hermitage Bay: **Bay d'Espoir**

heroin: **Drug Use, Non-Medical; Medical Drug Abuse; Organized Crime; Smuggling**

Héroux, Omer: **Nationalist League**

Herring Cove, NS: **Rowing**

herring gull: **Forillon National Park; Gull; Terra Nova National Park**

herring roe: **Fisheries; Fisheries History**

Herron, Shaun: **Popular Literature in English**

Herron, W.S.: **Calgary**

Herschel Island: **Alikomiak; Beaufort Sea; Yukon Territory**

Herstein, Israel: **Mathematics**

Hertel, François: *Amérique française*; **Novel in French; Poetry in French**

Hertel, Lac: **Mont St-Hilaire Nature Conservation Centre**

Herzberg Institute of Astrophysics: **Astronomy; Molecules in Interstellar Space; National Research Council of Canada; Observatory**

Herzberg Medal: **Physics**

Herzberger, Hans: **Philosophy**

Hespeler, Jacob: **Hespeler**

Hespeler, William: **Germans**

Hess Mountains: **Fossil Plants**

Hessian fly: **Midge**

hessonite garnet: **Gemstone**

Hester, James J.: **Archaeology**

Hett Gallery: **Art Dealers**

Hétu, Jacques: **Choral Music; Orchestral Music; Papineau-Couture, Jean**

Heureux house: **Architecture**

Hewlett, W.H.: **Hymns**

Hexagone: *Barre du jour*

Heyoka: **Theatre, Multicultural**

Heywood, Carl: **Printmaking**

Heywood, Earl: **Country & Western Music**

Hezeta, Bruno de: **Northwest Coast**

Hiberian Benevolent Soc: **Irish**

hibernation: **Animals in Winter; Snake**

Hibernia oil field: **Atlantic Provinces; Newfoundland**

Hibou: **Children's Literature in French**

Hickey, Clifford: **Archaeology**

Hicklin case: **Obscenity**

hickory: **Huron, Lake; Plants, Native Uses; Timber Axe; Woodenware**

Hickson, Paul: **Cosmology**

Hidatsa: **Cluny Earthlodge Village**

hides: **Beef Cattle Farming; Buffalo Hunt; Cree; Fur Trade; Leatherworking; Masks; Rabbit Farming; Tahltan**

Hiebert, Paul: **Humorous Writing in English;** *Sarah Binks*

Higgins, Andy: **Track & Field**

Higgins, D.J.H.: **Urban Studies**

Higgins, W.H.: **Whitby**

Higgitt, William: **Inquiry into Certain Activities of the RCMP, Royal Commission of**

High Altitude Research Project (HARP): **Bull, Gerald Vincent**

High Bluff, Man: **Scarlett, Earle P.**

high bush cranberry: **Berries, Wild; Medicine, History of**

high jump: **Track & Field**

High Park: **Architectural Styles; Hiking; Howard, John George; Toronto**

High Prairie, Alta: **Cardinal, Harold**

high pressure system: **Drought; Meteorology; Wind**

higher criticism: **Burwash, Nathanael; Carman, Albert; Evangelical & Fundamentalist Movements**

Highland Bell Mines: **Kettle Valley**

highland dancing: **Scots**

Highland Valley: **Mining**

Highvale Mine: **Coal**

highways: **Alaska Highway; Queen Elizabeth Way; Roads & Highways; Trans-Canada Highway**

Highways, Dept of (Ont): **Roads & Highways**

Highways, Dept of (Qué): **Roads & Highways**

Highwood River: **High River**

hijacking: **Airport; Jury**

Hilaire, Mont: **St Lawrence Lowland**

Hill, Charles: **National Gallery of Canada**

Hill, Daniel G.: **New Religious Movements**

Hill, George W.: **Public Art**

Hill, Harry: **Choral Music**

Hill, K.L.: **Children's Literature in English**

Hill, Kay: **Children's Literature in English**

Hill Island: **Thousand Islands**

Hillcrest, Alta: **Disasters**

Hillier, James: **Burton, Eli Franklin**

Hill's oak: **Vegetation Regions - Eastern Temperate Forests**

Hillsborough River: **Charlottetown**

Hilton Canada Ltd: **Lévesque, Jean-Louis**

Hincks, E.P.: **Physics**

Hind-Dawson Expedition: **Physical Geography**

Hinde, G.J.: **Paleontology, History in Canada**

Hindi language: **Hinduism; Language**

Hindmarsh, Harry: *Toronto Star*

Hine, Daryl: **Poetry in English**

Hinton, W.D.: **Hinton**

Hippocratic oath: **Medical Ethics**

Hiram Percy Maxim Award: **Crawley, F.R. "Budge"**

Hiram Walker & Sons, Ltd: **Windsor, Ont**

Hiram Walker Historical Museum: **Windsor, Ont**

histamine: **Allergies**

histology: **Axelrad, Arthur Aaron; Battle, Helen Irene; Biology; Clermont, Yves Wilfrid; Leeson, Thomas Sydney**

Historic Landmarks Assn of Canada: **Canadian Historical Association; Historical Societies**

Historic Properties: **Halifax**

Historic Sites & Advisory Council (NS): **Nova Scotia**

Historic Sites & Monuments Board: **Heritage Conservation; Royal Society of Canada**

Historical & Scientific Soc of Manitoba: **Historiography**

Historical Living Village & Pioneer Museum: **Shandro**

Historical Manuscripts Commission: **Archives**

historical trail: **Chilkoot Trail; Mackenzie-Grease Trail; West Coast Trail**

Hitchcock, H.R.: **Architectural Styles**

Hitchcock Ranch: **Ranching History**

Hjort, Johan: **Murray, John**

Hlady, Walter M.: **Archaeology**

hoarfrost: **Fog**

hoary marmot: **Glacier National Park; Marmot; Mount Revelstoke National Park**

Hobbema, Alta: **Smallboy, Johnny Bob**

hobbies: **Ceramics, Contemporary; Crafts; Genealogy; Quilt; Rock & Mineral Collecting; Weaving, Contemporary**

Hobler, Philip M.: **Archaeology**

Hobo-Québec: **Chamberland, Paul**

Hochelaga Archipelago: **Montréal**

Hochstetter, J.G.: **Printmaking**

hockey, peewee: **Québec City**

"Hockey Night in Canada": **Canadian National Railways**

Hockin, C.H.S.: **Almighty Voice**

Hodges, A.W.: **Bates, Maxwell**

Hodgetts, A.B.: **Canada Studies Foundation; Canadian Studies; Secondary School**

Hodgetts, J.E.: **Public Administration**

Hodgman, Roger: **Vancouver Playhouse**

Hodgson, Tom: **Painting**

Hoffman, Guy: **Roux, Jean-Louis; Theatre, French-Language; Théâtre du nouveau monde**

Hoffman, Irwin: **Vancouver Symphony Orchestra**

Hofsess, John: **Film, Experimental**

Hogg, B.G.: **Physics**

Hogg, Robert: **Poetry in English**

hognose snake: **Georgian Bay Islands National Park**

Hog's Back: **Railway History**

"Hogtown": **Ontario**

Hokan-Siouan language stock: **Anthropology, Linguistics**

Holden & Murdoch: **Murdoch, James Young**

Holderness & Chalton: **Rexton**

Holiday Theatre: **Theatre for Young Audiences**

Holladay, John S., Jr.: **Mediterranean Archaeology**

Holland, S.S.: **Geomorphology**

Holland College School of Visual Arts: **Charlottetown; Clothing Industries; Community College**

Holland House: **Architecture**

Holland River: **Holland Marsh; Newmarket**

Hollinger Consolidated Gold Mines Ltd: **Meighen, Maxwell Charles Gordon; South Porcupine; Timmins; Timmins, Noah A.**

Hollinger North Shore Exploration Co: **Schefferville**

Hollinger Ungava Transport: **Bush Flying**

Hollingsworth, Fred Thornton: **Downs, Barry Vance**

Hollingsworth, Margaret: **Drama in English**

Hollingsworth, Michael: **Drama in English**

hollow ware: **Ceramics; Copperware; Glass; Jewellery & Silverware Industry; Pewter; Silver, Church; Silver, Domestic; Woodenware**

Hollyburn Mountain: **North Vancouver; West Vancouver**

Hollyburn Ridge: **West Vancouver**

hollyhock: **Flowers, Cultivated**

Holm, Bill: **Diesing, Freda; Seaweed Willie**

Holman, Derek: **Choral Music**

Holman, Don: **Printmaking**

Holman, J.R.: **Holman**

Holman English Opera Troupe: **Music History; Opera**

Holman Eskimo Co-operative: **Holman**

Holman Island: **Inuit Art; Northwest Territories; Victoria Island**

Holmes, A.F.: **Botany History**

Holmes, Anne-Marie: **Dance on Television & Film**

Holmes, David: **Dance on Television & Film**

Holmes, Jean: **Geology**

Holmes, Johnny: **Ferguson, Maynard; Peterson, Oscar E.**

Holmes, Robert: **Drawing; Printmaking**

Holocaust: **Jewish Writing; Judaism**

Holocene epoch: **Fisherman Lake**

holography: **Laser; Ontario College of Art**

holothuroids: **Echinodermata**

Holroyd, Robert: **Guitar**

Holt, Simma: **Journalism**

Holton, Luther: **Unitarians**

Holton, R.H.: **Galbraith, John K.**

Holy Blossom Temple: **Plaut, Gunther W.**

Holy Names College: **University of Windsor**

Holy Redeemer College: **University of Windsor**

Holyrood, Nfld: **Conception Bay**

Homalco: **Northern Georgia Strait Coast Salish**

Homathko River: **BC Hydro**

Homburger, Walter: **Toronto Symphony**

Home Oil Co Ltd: **Business History; Gray, James H.; Hiram Walker Resources Ltd; Petroleum Industries**

Home Theatre: **Little Theatre Movement**

Homem, Diogo: **Cartography, History of**

Homem, Lopo: **Cartography, History of**

Homemaker's: **Magazines**

Homestead Act: **Family Law; Manitoba**

Homewood, Man: **Helicopter**

Homewood Retreat: **Lett, Stephen**

Hommy Provincial Park: **Parks, Provincial**

Hone, Jules: **Jehin-Prume, Frantz**

honey locust: **Vegetation Regions - Eastern Temperate Forests**

honey production: **Beekeeping; Buckwheat; Native People, Economic Conditions**

Honeyman, David: *Challenger* **Expedition; Geomorphology**

honeymoon: **Marriage & Divorce, History of**

Honeywell Ltd: **Computer-Assisted Learning**

Honour of Canada: **Wiseman, Clarence Dexter**

Hood River: **Takijuq Lake**

hooded seal: **Coastal Waters; Labrador Sea; Sealing**

Hooker, Clifford: **Philosophy**

Hooker, William J.: **Botany History; Floras & Botanical Journals**

Hooper, Danny: **Country & Western Music**

Hooper, Lou: **Peterson, Oscar E.**

Hoover, Christian L.: **Germanic Fraktur & Calligraphy**

hop: **Agriculture History; Brewing Industry**

hop hornbeam: **New Brunswick; Vegetation Regions - Eastern Temperate Forests**

Hop (Nfld): **Norse Voyages**

Hope, Henry: **Port Hope**

Hope Bay: **Bruce Peninsula**

Hope Iron Works: **Fraser, Graham**

Hope-Princeton Highway: **Allison Pass; Penticton; Princeton**

Hope Slide: **Earthquake; Erosion; Rockslide**

Hopedale, Nfld: **Haven, Jens; Labrador Inuit**

Hôpital de la marine et des emigrés: **Blanchet, François; Douglas, James (1800-86); Tessier, François-Xavier**

Hôpital du sacré-coeur: **Bethune, H. Norman**
Hôpital-général: **Le Ber, Pierre; Luc, Frère; Painting**
Hôpital l'Hôtel-Dieu de Québec: **Hôtel-Dieu**
Hôpital Șt-Charles-Borromée: **Léger, Paul-Emile**
Hôpital Saint-Jean-de-Dieu: **Nelligan, Emile**
Hôpital Saint-Luc: **Frappier, Armand**
Hopkins, Lawford & Nelson: **Architectural Styles**
Hopkins & Wiley: **Bank Architecture**
Hopper, Robin: **Ceramics, Contemporary**
Horić, Alan: **Croatians**
Horizon: **Armenians**
Horlick, Gary: **Chemistry Subdisciplines**
hormone: **Biological Product; Chrétien, Michel; Collip, J. Bertram; Connaught Laboratories Ltd; Dairy Farming; Diabetes Mellitus; Estrogen; Genetic Engineering; Heard, Robert Donald Hoskin; Insulin; Science & Society; Stress**
hormone therapy: **Cancer**
Hornaday River: **Horton Plain**
Hornby, R.A. Phipps: **Hornby Island**
Horne, Adam: **Port Alberni**
horned lark: **Lark; Migration**
horned owl: **Owl; Skunk**
Hornepayne, Ont: **Horne-Payne, Robert Montgomery**
Horner, Frank W.: **Pharmaceuticals Industry**
hornwort: **Liverwort; Moss**
Hornyansky, Nicholas: **Printmaking**
hornyhead chub: **Minnow**
Horowitz, Gad: **Red Tory; Working-Class History**
Horricks, J.H.: **Social Gospel**
horse antitoxins: **Connaught Laboratories Ltd**
horse blanket: **Textiles, Woven**
horse chestnut: **Chestnut**
horse meat: **Horse**
horse nettle: **Nightshade**
horse racing: **Harness Racing; Sports History; Thoroughbred Racing**
Horsefly, BC: **Place-names**
"horsehead": **Petroleum Exploration & Production**
horseradish: **Condiment Crops; Vegetable**
Horseshoe Bay: **West Vancouver**
Horseshoe Falls: **Niagara Falls; Waterfall**
Horseshoe Moraines: **Ontario**
Horton Academy: **Acadia University**
Horton Corner, NS: **Kentville**
Horton Lake: **Horton Plain**
Hosein, E.A.: **Biochemistry**
hosiery: **Clothing Industries; Textile Industry**
"hospice": **Death & Dying**
Hospital for Sick Children: **Dietetics; Drake, Theodore George Gustavus Harwood; Educational Foundations & Endowments; Lowden, John Alexander; Pediatrics; Robertson, John Ross; Salter, Robert Bruce; Siminovitch, Louis; Thompson, Margaret Anne Wilson**
hospital insurance: **Government; Johnson, Byron Ingemar; Medicine, Contemporary; New Brunswick; Nova Scotia; Opting-Out; Psychiatry; Quiet Revolution; St Laurent, Louis Stephen; Saskatchewan; Social Security**
Hospital Insurance Act (BC): **British Columbia**
Hospital Insurance & Diagnostic Services Act: **Health Policy; Hospitals**
host: **Silver, Church**
hot springs: **Algae; Banff National Park; Kootenay National Park; Nahanni National Park; Parks, National; St Catharines; Spring**
Hotel Bonaventure: **Hotel**
Hotel Imperial: **Perth**
Hotel Vancouver: **Canadian Pacific Railway**
Hotson, Norman: **Architecture, Development**
Hottah Lake: **Great Bear Lake**

Houde, Roland: **Philosophy**
Houghton's goldenrod: **Endangered Plants**
Houle, Léopold: **Essay in French**
House, Christopher: **Dance, Modern; Toronto Dance Theatre**
House, W.: **Waddington, Mount**
House of Anansi Press Ltd: **Atwood, Margaret E.; Book Publishing, English-Language; Godfrey, Dave; Lee, Dennis; Patriotes; Poetry in English; Small Presses**
House of Industry: **Miller, George Martell**
House of Providence: **Charbonnel, Armand-F.-M. de**
household appliances: **Electrical Appliances Industry**
Housing & Urban Development, Task Force on: **Hellyer, Paul T.**
Housing & Urban Development Assn of Canada: **Construction Industry**
Housser, Frederick Broughton: **Art Writing & Criticism**
Housser, Yvonne McKague: **McLaughlin, Isabel**
hovercraft: **Dunbar, I. Moira; Ferries; Icebreakers**
Howard, Alfred H.: **Printmaking**
Howard, Arthur L.: **Firearm**
Howard, Ernest: **Squash Racquets**
Howard, Henry: **Ophthalmology**
Howard, Richard: *Menaud maître-draveur*
Howarth, Glen: **Painting**
Howe, John: **Magazines**
Howe, Mark: **World Hockey Assn**
Howe, Marty: **World Hockey Assn**
Howe Sound: **Sechelt Peninsula; Squamish; West Vancouver**
Howell, Alfred: **Sculpture**
Howell Creek: **Endangered Animals**
Howes, Mary: **Humorous Writing in English**
Howie, Al: **Long-Distance Running**
Howison, Alan G.: **Foundations**
Howison, John: **Exploration & Travel Literature in English**
Howland, Henry S.: **Printmaking**
Howland, W.P.: **Fathers of Confederation**
Howlett, L.E.: **Physics; Weights & Measures**
Howorth, E.J.: **Printmaking**
Hoy, Helen: **Literary Bibliography in English**
Hoyle, Ont: **Zinc**
Hoyles, Newman: **Hoyles, Hugh William**
Hrvatski Glas (The Croatian Voice): **Croatians**
Hrvatski Put (The Croatian Way): **Croatians**
Hrybinsky, Borys: **Ukrainian Writing**
HUB Mall: **Myers, Barton; Urban Design**
Hubbard, Robert H.: **Art Writing & Criticism; National Gallery of Canada**
Hubbard, William: **Blacks**
Hubbard Glacier: **Vancouver, Mount**
Hubble Constant: **Cosmology**
Hubert, Cam: **Literature in English; Theatre, English-Language**
Hubert, Yvonne: **Garant, Serge; Music History**
Hubou, Marie: **Nursing**
huckleberry: **Berries, Wild; Cape Scott Provincial Park; Vegetation Regions - Pacific Coastal**
Hudon, Jean-Paul: **Literary Bibliography in French**
Hudson: **Arctic Oceanography**
Hudson, Garth: **Band, The**
Hudson, Ont: **Bush Flying; Seul, Lac**
Hudson, Qué: **Glass**
Hudson-70 expedition: **Oceanography**
Hudson Bay Basin: **Petroleum**
Hudson Bay Fisheries Expedition: **Arctic Oceanography**
Hudson Bay Junction, Sask: **Hudson Bay Railway**
Hudson Bay Lowland: **Coastal Landform; Hudson Bay; Muskeg; Physiographic Regions - Hudson Bay Lowland**
Hudson Bay Mining & Smelting Co: **Flin Flon**
Hudson locomotive: **Locomotives & Rolling Stock**
Hudson Platform: **Geological Regions**
Hudson Point: **Peace River**

Hudsonian Orogeny: **Geological Regions**
Hudson's Bay blanket: **Clothing; Coppers; Northwest Coast Indian Art**
Hudson's Bay coat: **Clothing**
Hudson's Bay Company Archives: **Manitoba**
"Hudson's Bay Company frame": **Log Houses**
"Hudson's Bay offspring": **Métis**
Hudson's Bay Oil & Gas Co Ltd: **Dome Petroleum Ltd; Hudson's Bay Company**
Hudson's Bay tea: **Labrador Tea**
Hudson's Hope, BC: **Peace River**
huebnerite: **Tungsten**
Huel, Georges: **Graphic Design**
Hugh, Everett C.: **Sociology**
Hugh & Andrew Allan (shipping): **Allan, Hugh Andrew Montagu**
Hugh Keenleyside Dam: **BC Hydro; Columbia River**
Hughes, Andrew: **Musicology**
Hughes, Bill: **Football**
Hughes, Everett C.: **Anthropology**
Hughes, Ken: **Graphic Design**
Hughes, Lynn: **Painting**
Huguet *dit* Latour, Pierre: **Silver, Domestic; Silver, Indian Trade**
Hultén, E.: **Botany History**
Human Justice Program: **Criminology**
Human Potential Movement: **New Religious Movements**
Human Rights Charter (Qué): **Delict**
Human Rights Commissions: **Currie, Walter; Racism**
Human Tissue Gift Acts: **Medical Ethics**
Humanities Assn of Canada: **Literary Periodicals in English; Ross, Malcolm**
Humanities Research Council of Canada: **Canadian Federation for the Humanities; Papineau-Couture, Jean; Translation; Woodhouse, Arthur Sutherland Piggott**
Humber Arm: **Corner Brook; Humber River**
Humber College of Applied Arts & Technology: **Collier, Ronald W.; Hydrography**
Humber River (Ont): **Floods & Flood Control; Kleinburg**
Humber Zone: **Geological Regions**
Humbermouth, Nfld: **Corner Brook; Hymns**
Humbert, Stephen: **Religious Music**
Hume, Catherine: **Blake, William Hume**
Humeston, Joy: **Furniture, Country**
humidity: **Climate Information; Urban Effect on Climate; Weather Forecasting**
humisols: **Soil Classification**
humpback whale: **Fundy, Bay of/Gulf of Maine; Grand Manan Island; Saguenay River; Whale; Whaling**
Humphrey, John: **International Law; Status of Women in Canada, Royal Commission on the**
Humphrey & the Dumptrucks: **Musical Theatre**
Humphreys, Sydney: **Purcell String Quartet**
Humpty Dumpty Ltd: **Hartland**
Hungarian Art Theatre: **Theatre, Multicultural**
Hungerford, George: **Olympic Games; Rowing**
Hungry Wolf, Beverly: **Ethnic Literature**
Hunka, Steve: **Computer-Assisted Learning**
Hunt, Don: **Automobile Racing**
Hunt, George: **Huntsville**
Hunt, Richard: **Hunt, Henry; Martin, Mungo**
Hunt, Robert: **Kwakiutl**
Huntec '70 Ltd: **Sonar**
Hunter, Andrew: **Wasteneys, Hardolph**
Hunter, Andrew F.: **Archaeology**
Hunter, Fenley: **South Nahanni River**
Hunter, Horace T.: **Maclean, John B.**
Hunter, John: **Canada & Australia**
Hunter, John E.: **Evangelism**
Hunter, Lynn: **Pine Pass**
Hunter, Peter: **Upper Canada**
Hunter, Robert: **Book Publishing, English-Language**

Hunter, Rose & Co: **Book Publishing, English-Language**
Hunter-Duvar, John: **Drama in English**
Huntington University: **Laurentian University**
Huntsman, W.: **Oceanography**
Huot, Alexandre: **Popular Literature in French**
hurdling: **Snowshoeing; Track & Field**
Hurdman Bridge: **Bridges**
hurdy-gurdy: **Italians**
Huron & Erie Mortgage Corp: **Saunders, William**
"Huron Carol": **Religious Music**
Huron College: **London; University of Western Ontario**
Huron grammar & dictionary: **Brébeuf, Jean de**
Huron Tract: **Canada Company; Stratford; Swiss**
hurricane: **Wind**
Hurricane Hazel: **Disasters**
Hurry, Leslie: **Stage & Costume Design**
Hurst Island: **Balaklava Island**
Hurtig, Mel: **Committee for an Independent Canada**
Hurtig Publishers Ltd: **Book Publishing, English-Language; Small Presses**
Hurtubise, Claude: *Relève*
Husband Transport: **Canadian National Railways**
Hushlak, Gerald: **Painting**
Huskisson, William: **Nova Scotia**
Husky Oil Ltd: **NOVA, An Alberta Corporation**
Hussey, William Penn: **Inverness**
Hustich, S.: **Botany History**
Huston, James: **Book Publishing, French-Language; Literature in French - Scholarship & Teaching; Short Fiction in French;** *Soirées canadiennes*
Hutcheson, Ernest: **Music Education**
Hutcheson Spring Stopper: **Soft-Drink Industry**
Hutchins, Thomas: **Graham, Andrew**
Hutchison & Steele: **Hutchison, Alexander Cowper**
Hutchison & Wood: **Hutchison, Alexander Cowper**
Hutner, Paul: **Painting**
Hutte-Sauvage, Lac de la: **George, Rivière**
Hutton, Maurice: **Essay in English**
Hutton, Ralph: **Swimming, Speed**
hybrid: **Asparagus; Biotechnology; Brussels Sprouts; Corn, Sweet; Grape; Ornamentals; Pear; Plum; Sheep Farming; Triticale**
Hybrid Turkeys Ltd: **Poultry Farming**
Hyde, H. Montgomery: **Stephenson, William Samuel**
Hyde Park Declaration: **Lend-Lease; World War II**
hydra: **Invertebrate**
hydraulic lift: **Technology**
hydraulic mining: **Coal Mining**
Hydro Block: **Diamond, Abel Joseph**
Hydro-Electric Power Commission of Ontario: **Computer Science; Ontario Hydro**
hydrocarbons: **Bitumen; Chemical Industries; Petrochemical Industry; Petroleum; Petroleum Exploration & Production; Petroleum Research & Development; Pollution; Sulphur**
Hydrocéphale Entêté: **Popular Literature in French**
hydrofoil: **Armed Forces - Unification; Baldwin, F.W. "Casey"; Bell, Alexander Graham; Ferries; Shipbuilding & Ship Repair**
hydrogen bomb: **Early-Warning Radar; Nuclear Fusion**
hydrogen sulphide: **Petroleum**
hydroplane: **Boating**
hydroxide: **Mineral**
hygiene: **Cuisine; Hospitals; Nursing; Physical Education; Population**
Hyland, Francis: **Stratford Festival**
Hylo, Alta: **Italians**
Hymas, Alison: **Interior Design**
Hyperion computer: **Electronics Industry**

hypertension (high blood pressure): **Chemistry; Friedman, Sydney Murray; Salt; Sourkes, Theodore Lionel**
hypocalcemia: **Vegetarianism**
hypochondriasis: **Psychiatry**
hypoglycemia: **Diabetes Mellitus**
hypoproteinemia: **Vegetarianism**
Hyslop, Jeff: **Dance on Television & Film**

I

IAC Ltd: **Continental Bank of Canada**
Ianzelo, Tony: **Film, Documentary**
Iapetus Ocean: **Geological Regions**
Iarusci, Robert: **Soccer**
Iberville, Mont: **Québec**
Iberville, Qué: **St-Jean-sur-Richelieu**
IBM Canada Ltd: **Bata, Thomas J.; Computer-Assisted Learning; Computer Science; Hamilton**
IBM Head Office: **Parkin, John B.**
Ibo language: **Africans**
ice bridges & roads: **Bridges; Transportation in the North**
ice core: **Climate Information; Drought**
ice cream: **Dairy Industry**
ice crystal: **Cloud**
ice dancing: **Figure Skating**
ice dating: **Ice Cap**
ice fishing: **Fishing, Ice**
ice floe: **Sea Ice**
ice fog: **Urban Effect on Climate**
Ice Island T-3: **Arctic Oceanography**
ice palace: **Hutchison, Alexander Cowper**
ice polygons: **Old Crow Plain**
ice-worm: **Walker, Edmund Murton**
Icefields Parkway: **Columbia Icefield; Long-Distance Running**
Icelandic: **Ethnic Literature; Language**
Icelandic Reserve: **Fish; Icelanders**
Ichnianskyj, Myroslav: **Ukrainian Writing**
ICI Ltd: **Textile Industry**
Icon computer: **Computer-Assisted Learning**
iconography: **Northwest Coast Indian Art; Public Art; Tiktak, John**
Ideal Bedding Co: **Toys & Games**
Idées: **Literary Periodicals in French**
Idlouk: **Resolute**
idocrase: **Gemstone**
Ignatieff, Alexis: **Russians**
Ignatieff, Nicolas: **Russians**
Ignatieff, Vladimir: **Russians**
Ihnatowicz, J.: **Poles**
Ikseetaryuk: **Inuit Art**
Ile-à-la-Crosse, Lac: **Churchill River; Ile-à-la-Crosse**
Île-Maligne, Qué: **Alma; Technology**
Illecillewaet River: **Rogers Pass**
illegal assembly: **Aid to (or of) the Civil Power**
illegal dumping: **Hazardous Wastes**
illegal transaction: **Underground Economy**
illegitimacy: **Family Law**
illite: **Clay**
Illsley, Percival: **Choral Music**
Illsley, Templeton, Archibald & Larose: **Airport Architecture**
ilmenite: **Mineral; Titanium**
Image Bank: **Art, Contemporary Trends**
Imagine: **Literary Periodicals in French; Popular Literature in French**
Imago: **Bowering, George; Literary Magazines in English**
Imasco Ltd: **Shoppers Drug Mart**
Imax Systems Corp: **Ferguson, Ivan Graeme**
Imlach, "Punch": **Toronto Maple Leafs**
Immigration, Dept of: **Bryce, Peter Henderson; Demographic Data Collection**
Immigration, Green Paper on: **Africans; Prejudice & Discrimination**
Immigration, White Paper on: **Africans**
Immigration Act: **Africans; Blacks; Citizenship; Immigration Policy; Refugees; Winnipeg General Strike**

Immigration & Cultural Communities, Dept of (Qué): **Québec**
Immigration Appeal Board: **Administrative Tribunals; Immigration Policy**
immune response: **Allergies**
immunization: **Nursing; Public Finance; Public Health; Veterinary Medicines Industry**
immunology: **Biochemistry; Frappier, Armand**
Imperial Bank of Canada: **Canadian Imperial Bank of Commerce**
Imperial Conferences: **Balfour Report; Canadian-American Economic Relations; Clark, Clifford; Colonial and Imperial Conferences; Commonwealth; Conscription; Constitutional Law; Halibut Treaty; King, W.L. Mackenzie; Lapointe, Ernest; O'Leary, M. Grattan; Statute of Westminster**
Imperial Federation Movement: **Canada First; Imperialism; McCarthy, D'Alton; Parkin, George R.; Round Table Movement**
Imperial Life Assurance Co of Canada: **Desmarais, Paul**
Imperial Theatre: **Theatre, English-Language**
Imperial Tobacco Co of Canada Ltd: **Guelph; Tobacco-Products Industry**
Imperial Trust Ltd: **Toronto Blue Jays**
imperial units: **Metric Conversion; Weights & Measures**
Imperial War Cabinet: **Commonwealth**
impersonation: **Electoral Systems**
Impertinences of Brother Anonymous: **Insolences du Frère Untel**
import quotas: **International Trade**
imports: **Automotive Industry; Balance of Payments; Barter; Bean, Green; Broccoli; Brussels Sprouts; Business Cycles; Business Management; Canadian-American Economic Relations; Chemical Industries; Clothing Industries; Coal; Computer Industry; Conservation; Crops; Electrical Appliances Industry; Electronics Industry; Energy in Society; Energy Policy; Fisheries; Footwear Industry; Furniture & Fixture Industry; International Economics; International Trade; Iron & Steel Industry; Machinery & Equipment Industry; Petroleum Supply & Demand; Print Industry; Roses, Cultivated; Sheep Farming; Shipping Industry; Sporting-Goods Industry; Third Option; Timber Trade History**
"impossibilism": **Socialist Party of Canada**
Impressions: **Photography**
imputability: **Delict**
Imrie, John M.: **Journalism**
In Flanders Fields: **McCrae, John**
In Review: Canadian Books for Children: **Children's Literature in English**
in situ recovery: **Bitumen**
in vitro fertilization: **Bioethics; Family Law; Medical Ethics; Medical Jurisprudence**
incandescent light bulb: **Lighting**
Incandescent Light Co: **Toys & Games**
incest: **Crime; Native People, Religion; Sexual Abuse of Children; Women's Movement**
Incidences: **Literary Periodicals in French**
incineration: **Hazardous Wastes; Pollution; Waste Disposal**
Income Distributions by Size in Canada: **Statistics Canada**
income tax: **Borden, Robert L.; Credit Unions; Election Expenses Act; Equalization Payments; Federalism; Government; Law & Society; Municipal Finance; Real Estate; Trust; World War I**
Income Tax Act: **Corporation Law; Courts of Law; Energy Policy; Farm Law; Taxation, Royal Commission on**
inconnu: **Fishing, Ice; Whitefish**
indenture: **Child Welfare**
Independancer: **Committee for an Independent Canada**

Independent Citizens' Election Committee: **City Politics**
Independent Labor Party: **Douglas, T.C.; McLachlan, James Bryson; Union Centrals, District & Regional; United Farmers of Canada; Woodsworth, J.S.**
Independent Order of Foresters: **Oronhyatekha**
Independent Publishers Assn: **Small Presses**
Index of forbidden books: **Guibord Affair; Institut canadien**
India pale ale: **Labatt, John**
Indian: **Native People, Communications**
Indian Advisory Board (BC): **Duff, Wilson**
Indian Affairs, Dept of: **Callihoo, John; Erasmus, Peter; Native People, Government Policy; Native People, Political Organization & Activism; Prostitution; Scott, Duncan Campbell; Sutton, Catherine**
Indian & Inuit Affairs Program: **Native People, Government Programs**
Indian Arts & Crafts Soc of BC: **Diesing, Freda**
Indian Assn of Alberta: **Callihoo, John; Cardinal, Harold; Dion, Joseph F.; Gladstone, James; Native People, Political Organization & Activism; Norris, Malcolm Frederick; Steinhauer, Ralph G.**
Indian breadroot: **Plants, Native Uses**
Indian Brotherhood of the Northwest Territories: **Dene Nation**
Indian Claims Commission (Ont): **Land Claims**
Indian consumption plant: **Plants, Native Uses**
Indian Days: **Festivals; Sarcee**
Indian Ecumenical Conference: **Snow, John**
Indian-Eskimo Assn: **Currie, Walter; Monture, Gilbert C.**
Indian Head, The: **Ouimet Canyon**
Indian hemp: **Plants, Native Uses**
Indian Legal Defence Committee: **Horn, Kahn-Tineta**
"Indian liquor": **High Wines**
Indian myth & legend: **Bayefsky, Aba; Children's Literature in English; False Face Society; Glooscap; Kootenay; Maple Sugar Industry; Medicine Bundles; Medicine Hat; Midewiwin; Nanabozo; Native People, Religion; Ogopogo; Raven Symbolism; Sasquatch; Thunderbird; Windigo**
Indian News Media Inc: **Native People, Communications**
Indian paintbrush: **Paintbrush; Plants, Native Uses; Pollination**
Indian Pond, Nfld: **Conception Bay South**
Indian Reserve Act (NB): **Perley, Moses H.**
Indian residential schools: **Bryce, Peter Henderson; Native People, Education; Steinhauer, Ralph G.**
Indian rice grass: **Vegetation Regions - Prairie**
Indian River (YT): **Klondike Gold Rush**
Indian Rivers (Ont): **Muskoka Lakes; Pembroke**
Indian Self-Government, Special Committee on: **Assembly of First Nations; Native People, Government Policy**
Indian tea: **Labrador Tea**
Indians of Québec Assn: **Gros-Louis, Max**
indictable offence: **Courts of Law; Criminal Procedure; Jury; Riot**
Indigenous Theatre Celebration: **Theatre, Multicultural**
Individual Education Plan: **Education, Special**
Indo-European: **Language**
Industrial Acceptance Corp Ltd: **Continental Bank of Canada**
Industrial Banner: **Union Centrals, District & Regional**
Industrial Credit Insurance Co: **Small Business**
Industrial Development Bank: **Bank of Canada Act**

Industrial Disputes Investigation Act: **Collective Bargaining; King, W.L. Mackenzie; Labour Policy; Labour Relations**
Industrial Education Act (Ont): **Education, Technical**
Industrial Estates Ltd: **Nova Scotia**
Industrial Materials Research Institute: **National Research Council of Canada**
Industrial Needle Trades Workers Union: **Buller, Annie**
Industrial Relations, Royal Commission on: **Unemployment Insurance**
Industrial Research Assistance Programme: **Mackenzie, Chalmers Jack**
industrial schools: **Child Welfare; Education, Technical**
Industrial Technology Centre: **Manitoba Research Council**
Industrial Training & Technical Education, Royal Commission on: **Education, Technical; Robertson, James Wilson**
Industry, Trade & Commerce, Dept of: **Agriculture & Food Policy; Flour Milling Industry; Jewellery & Silverware Industry**
Industry Investment Stimulation Program: **Telidon**
Inertial Survey System: **Cartography, History of**
infant mortality: **Childhood, History of; Native People, Health; Native People, Social Conditions; Women's Organizations**
infanticide: **Homicide; Women & the Law**
Infeld, Leopold: **Physics**
influence peddling: **Communications Law; Corruption**
Info Globe: **Newspapers**
Infomart: **Newspapers; Southam Inc; Torstar Corp**
Information Canada: **Graphic Design**
Information Management Service: **Torstar Corp**
information science: **Computer Science; International Development Research Centre; Library Science**
infrared photography: **Physical Geography; Remote Sensing**
infrared radiation: **Meteorology; Observatory; Polanyi, John C.; Remote Sensing; Solar Energy; Spectroscopy; Sun**
Infrasizer: **Haultain, Herbert Edward Terrick**
infrasound: **Acoustics**
Ingenika Mine, BC: **Sekani**
Ingersoll, Charles: **Ingersoll**
Ingersoll, Thomas: **Ingersoll**
Inglefield arctic expedition: **Holman**
Ingleside, Ont: **St Lawrence Seaway**
Inglis, James: **Photography**
Inglis, John: **Bren Gun Scandal**
Inglis, Man: **Romanians**
Ingornachoix Bay: **Basques**
Ingstad, Helge: **L'Anse aux Meadows; Norwegians**
ink: **Print Industry**
inkberry: **Holly**
Inland Revenue, Dept of: **Customs & Excise**
Inland Revenue Act: **Pharmaceuticals Industry**
Inland Waters Directorate: **Canada Centre for Inland Waters; Physical Geography**
Inn on the Park: **Four Seasons Hotels Ltd**
Innes automobile: **Wetaskiwin**
Innis, Mary Quale: **Autobiographical Writing in English**
Innis College: **Diamond, Abel Joseph; University of Toronto**
Innis-Gérin Medal: **Tremblay, Marc-Adélard**
Innisfail, Alta: **Confectionery Industry**
innocence, presumption of: **Criminal Law; Criminal Procedure**
Innotech Aviation Ltd: **Air Canada**
Innovation Place: **Saskatchewan Research Council**
inns: **Hotel; Summerside**
Innuitian Orogen: **Geological Regions**
Innuvialuit: **Aklavik**
inoculation: **Epidemic; Trinity**

inorganic chemistry: **Chemistry Subdisciplines; Clark, Howard Charles; Geochemistry**
Inoucdjouac, Qué: **Inuit Art**
inquest: **Coroner**
Inquiries Act: **Royal Commissions; Task Force**
insanity: **Bucke, Richard Maurice; Criminal Law; Workman, Joseph**
insecticide: **Oilseed Crops; Pesticide; Petroleum Exploration & Production; Quarrying Industry**
insectivora: **Mole; Shrew**
"Inside Passage": **British Columbia**
Instantheatre: **Theatre, English-Language**
Institut agricole: **Agricultural Education; Louis-Marie**
Institut de microbiologie et d'hygiène de Montréal: **Institut Armand-Frappier**
Institut de recherches cliniques de Montréal: **Bioethics; Chrétien, Michel**
Institut des arts appliques: **Industrial Design**
Institut d'histoire de l'Amérique française: **Historiography; Literature in French - Scholarship & Teaching;** *Revue d'histoire de l'Amérique française*
Institut national canadien-français pour la deficience mental: **Education, Special**
Institut national de la recherche scientifique: **Université du Québec**
Institut Nazareth et Louis Braille: **Blindness & Visual Impairment**
Institut québecois de recherche sur la culture: **Philosophy**
Institute for Biotechnology: **National Research Council of Canada**
Institute for Electrochemistry: **National Research Council of Canada**
Institute for Environmental Studies: **Fry, Frederick Ernest Joseph; Hare, Frederick Kenneth**
Institute for Manufacturing Technology: **Manitoba Research Council**
Institute for Materials Research: **Physics**
Institute for Public Health: **University of Western Ontario**
Institute for Research in Human Abilities: **Memorial University of Newfoundland**
Institute for Research on Public Policy: **Economic Regulation; Social Science**
Institute international du théâtre: **Roux, Jean-Louis**
Institute of Aerospace Studies: **Noise**
Institute of Agricultural Technology: **St-Hyacinthe**
Institute of Animal Resource Ecology: **Holling, C.S., "Buzz"; Larkin, Peter Anthony**
Institute of Association Executives: **Pressure Group**
Institute of Behavioural Research: **York University**
Institute of Business Administration: **University of Toronto**
Institute of Canadian Studies: **Dunton, Arnold Davidson; Jewett, Pauline**
Institute of Chartered Accountants: **Business Education; Corporation Law**
Institute of Electrical & Electronics Engineers: **Electrical Engineering; Electronics Industry**
Institute of Environmental Studies: **Nuclear Safety; Solandt, Omond McK.**
Institute of Experimental Medicine & Surgery: **Stress**
Institute of Islamic Studies: **Religion**
Institute of Mediaeval Studies: **Philosophy**
Institute of Ocean Sciences: **Arctic Oceanography; Mann Cedric Robert; Oceanography; Stewart, Robert William**
Institute of Oceanography: **Dunbar, Maxwell John**
Institute of Parasitology: **Cameron, Thomas Wright Moir; Parasitology**
Institute of Public Administration: **Political Science; Public Administration**

Institute of Research on Public Policy: **Ostry, Sylvia**
Institute of Sedimentary & Petroleum Geology: **Geological Survey of Canada**
Institute of Social & Economic Research: **Sociology**
Institute of Space & Atomospheric Studies: **Physics**
Institute of Urban Studies: **Axworthy, N. Lloyd; University of Winnipeg**
Institution nationale: **Art Education**
Instructor in Roadmaking (Ont): **Roads & Highways**
instrumentation: **Electronics Industry**
Insular Belt: **Geological Regions**
Insular Mountains: **British Columbia**
insulin syringes: **Safety Standards**
intaglio: **Print Industry; Printmaking**
Intégrale: **Brossard, Nicole**
integrated circuits: **Microchips & Transistors**
intelligence test: **Education, History of; Education, Special; Psychology**
Intelpost: **Postal System**
Intendant's Palace: **Government Building; Québec City**
Inter-Church Committees: **Ecumenical Social Action**
Inter Pares International Development Service: **Agricultural Aid**
Inter-Varsity Christian Fellowship: **Christianity**
Intercontinental Packers Ltd: **Saskatoon**
Interdepartmental Planning Board (Man): **Urban & Regional Planning**
Interest Act: **Consumer Law**
interest group: **Environment; Municipal-Provincial Relations; Pressure Group; Women's Movement**
interferon: **Genetic Engineering**
Intergovernmental Affairs, Dept of (Qué): **Québec**
Intergovernmental Oceanographic Commission: **Hydrography**
Interior, Dept of the: **Geological Survey of Canada; Henry, R.A.C., "Red"; Historic Site; King, William Frederick; Klotz, Otto Julius;** *National Atlas of Canada*; **Parks, National; Pearce, William; Plaskett, John Stanley**
Interior Plains: **British Columbia; Horton Plain; Peace River Lowland; Soil Classification; Spring**
Interior Plateau: **British Columbia; Fraser River; Sedimentary Rock**
Interior Platform: **Geological Regions; Mineral Resources**
interlibrary loan: **Genealogy; Libraries; National Library of Canada; Parliament, Library of**
"interlocking directorships": **Banking**
Intermedia: **Art, Contemporary Trends; Video Art**
intermediate wheatgrass: **Forage Crops**
interment: **Cemeteries; Funeral Practices**
Intermontane Belt: **Geological Regions**
Internal Security Operations: **Aid to (or of) the Civil Power**
International Air Services Transit Agreement: **Air Law & Space Law**
International Air Transport Assn: **Associations**
International Amateur Athletic Federation: **Track & Field**
International Amateur Theatre Assn: **Theatre, Multicultural**
International Animated Film Festival: **Film Festivals, Prizes**
International Assn for Religious Freedom: **Unitarians**
International Assn of Fish & Wildlife Agencies: **Canadian Wildlife Federation**
International Assn of Lions: **Chinese**
International Assn of Machinists: **Bengough, Percy; Russell, Robert Boyd**
International Assn of Machinists & Aerospace Workers: **Aerospace Industry; Machinery & Equipment Industry**
International Assn of Medical Museums: **Abbott, Maude E.S.**

International Astronomical Union: **Millman, Peter MacKenzie; Pearce, Joseph Algernon; Petrie, Robert Methven**
International Atomic Energy Agency: **Meagher, Blanche Margaret**
International Bible Students Assn: **Evangelism**
International Biological Program: **Cook, William Harrison; Environment; Fuller, William Albert; Iglulik Inuit; Mann, Kenneth Henry; Rigler, Frank Harold; Rowe, John Stanley**
International Bird Preservation Soc: **Canadian Wildlife Federation**
International Bitumen Co: **Bitumen**
International Board of United World Colleges: **Symons, Thomas H.B.**
international boundaries: **Alaska Boundary Dispute; Aroostook War; Ashburton-Webster Treaty; Boundaries; Boundary Waters Treaty; Brown, J.G., "Kootenai"; Forty-ninth Parallel; Fraser River Lowland; Fundy, Bay of/Gulf of Maine; Grand Falls, NB; Juan de Fuca Strait; Oregon Treaty; St Clair River**
International Bridge: **Gzowski, Casimir S.; Reid, Robert G.**
International Brotherhood of Electrical Workers: **Postal System**
International Brotherhood of Sleeping Car Porters: **West Indians**
International Children's Festival: **Citadel Theatre**
International Church of the Foursquare Gospel: **Evangelism**
International Civil Aviation Organization: **Air Law & Space Law; Airport; Safety Standards; Symington, Herbert J.; United Nations**
International Classification of Disease: **Psychiatry**
International Commission for the Northwest Atlantic Fisheries: **Fisheries History; Oceanography**
International Committee for the Conservation of the Industrial Heritage: **Archaeology, Industrial**
International Committee on Weights & Measures: **Time; Weights & Measures**
International Confederation of Free Trade Unions: **Bengough, Percy; Conroy, Pat; MacDonald, Donald**
International Congress of University Continuing Education: **Adult Education**
International Control Commissions: **Peacekeeping; Seaborn, James Blair**
International Council for Adult Education: **Kidd, J. Robbins**
International Council of Scientific Unions: **Environment; Physics**
International Court of Justice: **International Law; Read, John Erskine; United Nations**
International Covenant on Civil & Political Rights: **Human Rights; International Law; Legal Aid**
International Covenant on Economic, Social & Cultural Rights: **Human Rights**
International Date Line: **Time**
international debt: **Banking**
International Design Symposium: **Graphic Design**
International Development Assistance Program: **Strong, Maurice F.**
International Economic Assn: **Britnell, George Edwin**
International Electrotechnical Commission: **Safety Standards**
International Energy Agency: **Hydrogen; Wave Energy**
International Energy Development Corp: **Strong, Maurice F.**
International Express Mail: **Postal System**
International Festival of Children's Theatre: **Theatre for Young Audiences**
International Financial Society: **Hudson's Bay Company**
International Firearms Co: **Front de libération du Québec**

International Fisheries Commission: **Hazen, John Douglas**
International Fisheries Exhibition: **Wilmot, Samuel**
International Fisherman's Trophy: *Bluenose*; **Yachting**
International Foils Ltd: **Cap-de-la-Madeleine**
International Geographic Union: *National Atlas of Canada*
International Geophysical Year: **Ellesmere Island; North Pole; Physics**
International Grenfell Assn: **Grenfell, Wilfred T.; Macpherson, Cluny; Nain; Newfoundland; St Anthony**
International Harvester Canada Ltd: **Agricultural Implements Industry; Banking; Hamilton**
International Hydrodynamics Co Ltd: **Ocean Industry**
International Hydrological Program: **Environment; Hydrology**
International Ice Hockey Federation: **Canadian Olympic Hockey Team; Hockey, Ice**
International Ice Patrol: **Iceberg**
International Institute of Applied Systems Analysis: **Holling, C.S., "Buzz"**
International Jazz Festival: **Festivals**
International Journal of Ethics: **Brett, George S.**
International Labour Organization: **Labour Canada; Moore, Tom; Morris, Joseph; Shipping Industry**
International Labourers Union: **Italians**
International Ladies' Garment Workers' Union: **Clothing Industries; Jodoin, Claude**
International League Against Rheumatism: **Arthritis**
International Longshoremen's Assn: **Saint John**
International Maritime Organization: **Shipping Industry**
International Maritime Satellite Organization: **Satellite Communications**
International Meteorological Organization: **Stupart, Robert Frederic**
International Mineralogical Assn: **Mineral Naming**
International Minerals & Chemicals Corp (Canada) Ltd: **Potash**
International Nickel Co of Canada Ltd: **Agnew, John Lyons; Inco Ltd; Metallurgy; Richardson, James A., Sr; Science Centre; Stanley, Robert Crooks**
International North Pacific Fisheries Commission: **Fisheries Policy**
International Olympic Committee: **Olympic Games; Sports Organization, Amateur**
International Order of Good Templars: **Temperance Movement**
International Organization for Old Testament Studies: **MacKenzie, Roderick Andrew Francis**
International Organization for Standardization: **Consumer Standards; Safety Standards**
International Organization of Legal Metrology: **Weights & Measures**
International Paper Co: **Wood, Edward Rogers**
International Peace Park: **Waterton Lakes National Park**
International Planned Parenthood Federation: **Birth Control**
International Polar Years: **Ellesmere Island; Physics; Thomson, Andrew**
International Power Co: **Killam, Izaak Walton**
International Practical Temperature Scale: **Weights & Measures**
International Prime Meridian Conference: **Fleming, Sandford**
International Pulp, Sulphite & Papermill Workers Union: **Duggan, Alphonsus Gregory**
International Rapids: **St Lawrence River**
International Relations Committee: **Wyn Wood, Elizabeth**
International/Roger Du Toit: **CN Tower**
International Satellite Organization: **Satellite Communications**

International Satellites for Ionospheric Studies: **Satellite Communications**
International Sculpture Symposium: **Pauta Saila**
International Soc for Krishna Consciousness: **New Religious Movements**
international star catalogue: **Stewart, Robert Meldrum**
International Submarine Engineering Ltd: **Ocean Industry**
International Sugar Agreement: **Confectionery Industry; Sugar Industry**
international system of units: **Time; Weights & Measures**
International Telephone & Telegraph: **Guelph**
International Theatre Institute World Congress: **Theatre, English-Language**
International Union Against Tuberculosis: **Frappier, Armand**
International Union for the Conservation of Nature & Natural Resources: **Canadian Nature Federation; Canadian Wildlife Federation; Conservation; Endangered Plants; Environment; Fuller, William Albert; Parks, National; Strong, Maurice F.**
International Union of Bricklayers: **Charpentier, Alfred**
International Union of Geodesy & Geophysics: **Wilson, J. Tuzo**
International Union of Pure & Applied Chemistry: **Columbium**
International University Sports Federation: **World University Games**
International Vacations (Intervac): **Wardair International Ltd**
International Weightlifting Federation: **Weightlifting**
International Whaling Commission: **Arctic Animals; Whaling**
International Wine & Food Soc: **Cuisine**
international women's peace conferences: **Voice of Women**
International Women's Year: **Battle, Helen Irene; Women's Movement**
International Woodworkers of America: **Hodgson, Stuart M.; Morris, Joseph; Newfoundland Loggers' Strike**
interprovincial & interterritorial boundaries: **Boundaries; Continental Divide; Labrador Boundary Dispute; Lloydminster**
Interprovincial Bridge: **Bridges**
Interprovincial Council of Farm Women: **McNaughton, Violet C.**
Interprovincial Football Union: **Hamilton Tiger Cats**
Interprovincial Pipe Line Ltd: **Alberta; Computer Industry**
Interprovincial Rugby Football Union: **Football**
Interprovincial Rugby Union: **Montreal Concordes**
Interprovincial Standards Program: **Apprenticeship**
Interprovincial Steel & Pipe Corp Ltd: **Iron & Steel Industry**
Interprovincial Union of Farmers: **United Farmers of Québec**
interstellar medium: **Molecules in Interstellar Space**
Intervention: **Literary Periodicals in French; Social Work**
intimidation: **Censorship; Electoral Systems; Political Campaign**
intoxication: **Alcoholism; Criminal Law; Food Poisoning; Water-Borne Disease**
INTREPID: **Stephenson, William Samuel**
Inuit Broadcasting Corp: **Communications in the North; Native People, Communications**
Inuit Brotherhood: **Inuit Tapirisat of Canada**
Inuit Circumpolar Conference: **Berger, Thomas R.; Native People - Arctic**
Inuit Committee on National Issues: **Watt, Charlie**
Inuit Cultural Institute: **Eskimo Point, NWT**
Inuit Development Corp: **Native People, Economic Conditions**
Inuit dictionary: **Ungava Inuit**

Inuit Language Commission: **Native People - Arctic**
Inuktitut: **Canadian Broadcasting Corporation; Communications in the North; Cree Syllabics; Eskimo; Inuit; Inuit Art; James Bay Agreement; Native People, Communications**
invasion of privacy: **Privacy; Torts**
inventions: **Bell, Alexander Graham; Bombardier, J. Armand; Bull, Gerald Vincent; Desbarats, Georges-Edouard; Fenerty, Charles; Ferguson, Ivan Graeme; Fessenden, Reginald A.; Foulis, Robert; Gibson, William Wallace; Gisborne, Frederick Newton; Goodeve, Charles Frederick; Helava, Uno Vilho; Klein, George John; Leaver, Eric William; Leaver, Eric William; Patent; Patents, Copyright & Industrial Designs, Royal Commission on; Robb, F. Morse; Rogers, Edward Samuel; Stephenson, William Samuel; Turnbull, Wallace Rupert; Willson, Thomas L.**
Inverarden: **Cornwall**
Inverness Railway & Coal Co: **Inverness**
Investigator: **Arctic Exploration; McClure (M'Clure), Robert J. Le M.**
investment: **Balance of Payments; Bank of Canada; Bank Rate; Capital Formation; Stock & Bond Markets**
Investment Bankers' Assn of Canada: **Gundy, James Henry**
Investment Dealers Assn: **Stock & Bond Markets**
IODE competitions & awards: **Literary Prizes in English**
iodine: **Mineral**
iolite: **Gemstone**
ion: **Chemistry Subdisciplines**
Iona College: **University of Windsor**
Iona Station, Ont: **Galbraith, John K.**
Ionesco, Carmen: **Track & Field**
ionosphere: **Henderson, John Tasker; Physics; Satellite Communications; Space Technology**
Ipperwash Provincial Park: **Parks, Provincial**
Ipsas, Alta: **Romanians**
Ipswich sparrow: **Bird Sanctuaries & Reserves; Sparrow**
iridium: **Platinum**
Irie, Kevin: **Ethnic Literature**
iris: **Berkeley, Edith Dunington; Lily**
Irish, Blaine: **Film**
Irish & Maulson: **Parizeau, Gérard**
Irish Newfoundland Society: **Theatre, Multicultural**
Irish Rovers: **Television Programming**
iron: **Baking Industry; Dandelion; Maple Sugar Industry; Soil Classification; Spinach; Spring; Turnip**
iron lung: **Bell, Alexander Graham**
Iron Molders' Union: **Craft Unionism**
Iron Ore Co of Canada: **Bennett, William John; Iron & Steel Industry; Labrador City; Mulroney, M. Brian; Quebec; North Shore & Labrador Railway; Schefferville; Urban & Regional Planning**
iron oxides: **Ceramics; Metallurgy; Prince Edward Island; Soapstone; Vermilion River**
Iron Strand: **Nunatak**
iron sulphide: **Metallurgy**
ironmongery: **Art Education; Blacksmithing, French Canada**
irons: **Domestic Utensils**
ironstone china: **Ceramics**
ironweed: **Endangered Plants**
Iroquoian language family: **Native People, Languages**
Iroquoians: **Huron; Indian Art; Longhouse; Native People - Eastern Woodlands; Neutral; Petun; Saguenay River; Wintemberg, William John**
Iroquois: **Landymore, William Moss**
Iroquois, Lake: **Niagara Peninsula**
Iroquois, Upper Canada: **McIntosh, John**

Iroquois Confederacy: **Cayuga; Mohawk; Oneida; Onondaga; Seneca**
Iroquois dictionary: **Marie de l'Incarnation**
Iroquois engine: **Industrial Research & Development**
Iroquoise: **Sculpture**
Irvin, Arthur: **National Film Board**
Irvine River: **Elora**
Irving, Arthur: **Irving Group**
Irving, James: **Irving Group**
Irving, John: **Irving Group**
Irving, William N.: **Archaeology**
Irving family: **Business Elites**
Irving Oil Co: **Irving, K. C.; McCain, H. Harrison; New Brunswick**
Irving Pulp & Paper Ltd: **Irving, K. C.**
Irwin, Dave: **Skiing**
Irwin, John: **Book Publishing, English-Language**
Irwin, May: **Musical Theatre**
Isaacs, Avrom: **Art Dealers**
Isaacs Gallery: **Coughtry, Graham; Painting; Prent, Mark G.; Wieland, Joyce**
Isachsen, Gunerius: **Amund Ringnes Island**
Isachsen Dome: **Ellef Ringnes Island**
Isapik: **Inuit Art**
Isbister River: **Island Lake**
Isham, James: **Métis**
ISIS satellites: **Physics; Space Technology**
Iskut River: **BC Hydro; Mount Edziza Provincial Park; Stikine River**
Island Airport: **Toronto; Toronto Islands**
Island Copper Mine: **Port Hardy**
Island Falls, Sask: **Churchill River; Flin Flon**
Island Lake: **Nueltin Lake**
Island Telephone Co: **Bell Canada Enterprises Inc; TransCanada Telephone System**
island watersnake: **Endangered Animals**
Islander: **Pope, William Henry**
Islands, Bay of: **Corner Brook; Humber River**
Isle-de-Grâce, L': **Grosse Île**
Isle-Maligne, Qué: **Saguenay River**
Ismaili Muslims: **Africans; Islam; South Asians**
isobar: **Wind**
isonord: **Nordicity**
isopynum: **Endangered Plants**
isostatic uplift: **Annapolis Lowlands; Coastal Landform; Great Lakes; Igloolik Sites; Lake; Mountain Range; Northumberland Strait; Physiographic Regions - Appalachia**
isotope: **Chemistry Subdisciplines; Nuclear Energy; Nuclear Fusion; Nuclear Power Plants; Nuclear Safety; Physics; Thode, Henry George**
Israel, Werner: **Black Hole; Physics**
Issaurel, Salvator: **Alarie, Pierrette; La Palme, Béatrice; Simoneau, Léopold**
Issei: **Japanese**
Isthmus of Avalon: **Avalon Peninsula; Placentia Bay**
Istona, Mildred: **Chatelaine**
Itchen Lake: **Coppermine River**
Ithna-Ashariyah: **Africans**
Itsi Range: **Selwyn Mountains**
IUD: **Birth Control**
Ivaco Inc: **Iron & Steel Industry**
Ivakh, Onufrij: **Ukrainian Writing**
Ivanhoe Inc: **Steinberg, Samuel**
Ivanov, Igor: **Chess**
Ivens, William: **Pacifism**
Iverson, Bjorn: **Bobsledding**
Iverson, K.: **Computer-Assisted Learning**
Ivor Wynne Stadium: **Hamilton Tiger Cats**
ivory: **Beothuk; Brooman Point Village; Crafts; Edenshaw, Charlie; Folk Art; Gemstone; Inuit Art; Karoo Ashevak; L'Anse Amour Burial Site; Narwhal; Northwest Coast Indian Art; Osuitok Ipeelee; Pelly Bay; Prehistory; Thule Culture; Umiak; Walrus**
ivory gull: **Arctic Animals; Gull**

Ivy Lea, Ont: **Gananoque**
Iwaniuk, Wactaw (Wactor): **Ethnic Literature; Poles**
Izaak Walton Killam Hospital for Children: **Killam, Izaak Walton**

J

J.C.B. Grant Award: **Friedman, Sydney Murray**
J.D. Irving Ltd: **Irving, K. C.**
J.M. Dent & Sons: **Book Publishing, English-Language; *Canadian Forum***
J.O. Wisner, Son & Co: **Agricultural Implements**
J.P. Bickell Foundation: **Bickell, John Paris**
J.S. McLean Junior Farmer Scholarship: **McLean, James Stanley**
J.V. Clyne Bird Sanctuary: **Port Alberni**
Jack, Stephen: **Musical Theatre**
"Jack Canuck": **Cartoons**
Jack-in-the-pulpit: **Poisonous Plants**
jack-o'-lantern: **Pumpkin**
jack pine: **Forest Fire; Forest Harvesting; Mistassini, Lac; Ouimet Canyon; Pine; Prince Albert National Park; Pukaskwa National Park; Vegetation Regions - Boreal Forest or Taiga; Vegetation Regions - Eastern Temperate Forests**
jack pine budworm: **Manitoba**
Jackman, Arthur: **Jackman, William**
Jackman, T.: **Agricultural Economics**
Jackman Foundation: **Educational Foundations & Endowments**
Jacks, Ron: **Swimming, Speed**
Jackson, Daniel: **Grands Ballets Canadiens**
Jackson, Henry: **Silver, Domestic**
Jackson, J.N.: **Urban Studies**
Jackson, John: **Community**
Jackson, Roger: **Rowing**
Jacob, Suzanne: **Poetry in French; Short Fiction in French**
Jacobi, Otto: **Painting**
Jacobs, Mona: **Dene Nation**
Jacques & Hay: **Furniture, English, Scottish & American**
Jacques-Cartier, Détroit de: **Mingan, Îles de**
Jacques-Cartier, Mont: **Mégantic Hills; Physiographic Regions - Appalachia**
Jacques-Cartier, Rivière: **Laurentian Highlands**
Jacques-Cartier Bridge: **Bridges**
jade: **Mineral**
jail: **Child Welfare; Huron County Jail; Prison**
Jainism: **New Religious Movements**
Jamaicans: **West Indians**
James, Charlie: **Martin, Mungo**
James, Cyril: **McGill University**
James, Edwin: **Tanner, John**
James, Frances: **Music History**
James, Norman B.: **Autobiographical Writing in English**
James, William: **Photography**
James I of England: **Alexander, William; Easton, Peter; Mainwaring, Henry; Nova Scotia**
James II of England: **Albany River**
James & James: **Architecture, Development**
James Bay Native Development Corp: **James Bay Agreement**
James Bay Treaty: **Indian Treaties**
James Island, BC: **Deer**
James Lorimer & Co, Publishers: **Book Publishing, English-Language; Urban Studies**
James Richardson & Sons: **Richardson, James A., Jr; Richardson, James A., Sr**
James White Stable: **Thoroughbred Racing**
Jameson, Robert Sympson: **Jameson, Anna Brownell**
Jamieson, Laura: **Women's International League for Peace & Freedom**
Jamieson, Martha: **Stage & Costume Design**
Jamieson, Stuart: **Working-Class History**
Jang, Charlie: **Ethnic Literature**
Jani, Louis: **Judo**
Jansoone, Frédéric: **Saints**

Jardin botanique: **Arboretum; Botanical Garden; Herbarium; Raymond, Louis-Marcel**

Jardine, John: **Rexton**

Jardins de la République, Parc provincial des: **Heritage Trail**

jarosite: **Horton River**

Jarry Park: **Montreal Expos**

Jarvis, Don: **Painting**

Jarvis, Judy: **Choreography; Dance, Modern**

Jarvis, Ont: **Automobile Racing**

Jarvis, W.H.P.: **Exploration & Travel Literature in English**

Jarvis Collegiate Institute: **Public Art**

Jasmin, Claude: **Autobiographical Writing in French; Children's Literature in French;** *Littérature qui se fait;* **Novel in French;** *Pleure pas, Germaine*

jasper: **Gemstone; Silica**

Jasper House: **Jasper**

Jasper Park Lodge: **Brandtner, Fritz; Jasper**

Jauch, Ray: **Edmonton Eskimos**

Jautard, Valentin: **Literature in French - Criticism & Theory**

Javelin Foundry & Machine Works: **Doyle, John C.**

javelin throw: **Track & Field**

Javor, Pavel: **Czechs**

Jaworska, T.: **Poles**

Jaxon, Honoré Joseph: **Jackson, William H.**

Jean: **Allan Line**

Jean, Jocelyn: **Painting**

Jean A. Chalmers Choreographic Award: **Choreography; Dance History; Danny Grassman Dance Company; Fortier, Paul-André; Gradus, Lawrence; Grossman, Daniel W.; Lock, Édouard; Marcuse, Judith R.; Paula Ross Dance Company**

Jean d'Iberville, Qué: **St-Jean-sur-Richelieu**

Jeannin, Lac: **Iron & Steel Industry**

Jedinstvo (Unity): **Croatians**

Jeff Nicklin Trophy: **Parker, John D.**

Jeff Russell Trophy: **Golab, Anthony C.**

Jefferson Glass Co: **Glass**

Jeffery, Lawrence: **Drama in English; Theatre, English-Language**

Jeffery, R.L.: **Mathematics**

Jeffrey mine: **Asbestos, Qué; Gemstone**

Jégo, Jean-Baptiste: **Theatre, French-Language**

Jeldness, Olaus: **Ski Jumping; Skiing**

Jelinek, Maria: **Figure Skating**

Jelinek, Otto: **Figure Skating**

Jemseg River: **Gagetown**

Jenkins, George: **Hymns**

Jenkinson, Charles: **Hawkesbury**

Jenny: **Shipbuilding & Ship Repair**

Jenpeg, Man: **Winnipeg, Lake**

Jentel, Marie O.: **Mediterranean Archaeology**

jequirity bean: **Poisonous Plants**

Jérôme, Jean-Paul: **Plasticiens**

Jerusalem artichoke: **Biomass Energy; Vegetable**

Jervis, Robert: **Chemistry Subdisciplines**

Jesse Ketchum School: **Conacher, Lionel P.**

Jessie Dow award: **Suzor-Coté, Marc-Aurèlie de Foy**

Jessie Richardson Theatre Awards: **Theatre, English-Language**

Jessner, Irene: **Singing**

Jessop, John: **Education, History of**

Jesup-North Pacific Expedition: **Archaeology**

Jesuit Barracks: **Québec Citadel**

Jesuits: **Anthropology; Argenson, Pierre de Voyer d'; Art; Astronomy; Biard, Pierre; Biencourt, Charles de; Brandy Parliament; Brébeuf, Jean de; Cartography, History of; Catholicism; Charlevoix, Pierre-François-Xavier de; Chauchetiere, Claude; Christian Island; Christian Religious Communities; Concordia University; Curriculum Development; Des Groseilliers, Médard Chouart; Education, History of; Essay in French; Exploration & Travel Literature in French; Fur Trade; Georgian Bay; Huronia; Iroquois Wars;** *Jesuit Relations;* **Jogues, Isaac; La Brosse, Jean-Baptiste; La Peltrie, Marie-Madeleine de Chauvigny de; Lafitau, Joseph-François; Lake of the Woods; Lalemant, Charles; Lalemant, Jérôme; Laval, François de; L'Heureux, Jean-B.; Libraries; Lighting; Lithuanians; Lonergan, Bernard; Longhouse; MacKenzie, Roderick Andrew Francis; Manitoulin Island; Mohawk; Native People, Education; New France; Nursing; Painting; Port Dover; Private School; Religious Building; Saint-Jean, Lac; St Joseph Island; Ste Marie Among the Hurons; Saint Mary's University; Saint-Vallier, Jean-Baptiste de; Séminaire de Québec; Sillery; Silver, Church; Social Doctrine of the Roman Catholic Church; Theatre, English-Language; Theatre, French-Language; Theatre Education; Wine Industry**

Jésus, Île: **Montréal**

jet fighter: **Military Aviation & Aircraft**

jet stream: **Meteorology**

Jetté, Louis-Amable: **Cartier, George-Etienne**

Jetté, Rosalie: **Christian Religious Communities**

Jeu: **Drama in French; Literary Periodicals in French**

Jeune Scène: **Dubé, Marcel**

Jeunes Comédiens: **Drama in French**

Jeunesse étudiante catholique: **Catholic Action; Pelletier, Gérard**

Jeunesse ouvrière catholique: **Catholic Action**

Jeunesse rurale catholique: **Catholic Action**

Jeunesses patriotes: **Chartrand, Michel**

Jewell, Milton: **Painting**

jewelweed: **Poison Ivy; Touch-me-not**

Jewish Community Centre: **Theatre, Multicultural**

Jewish Council of Women: **Judaism**

Jewish Dialog: **Literary Magazines in English; Rosenblatt, Joseph**

Jim Baillie Nature Reserve: **Baillie, James L.**

jimsonweed (Jamestownweed): **Nightshade**

Joachim, Davis: **Guitar**

Joachim, Otto: **Choral Music; Orchestral Music**

job creation: **Labour Policy; Manufacturing**

job discrimination: **Work**

job mobility: **Work**

job security: **Collective Bargaining; Confederation of National Trade Unions; Franco-Americans; Office Automation; Postal Strikes; Teaching Profession**

Jodo Shinshu movement: **Religious Festivals**

Jodoin, René: **Film Animation**

Joe Batt's Arm: **Place-names**

Joel, A.H.: **Soil Science**

Joffre, Alta: **Alberta; Red Deer**

jogging: **Fitness; Snowshoeing**

Joggins, NS: **Fossil Animals; Nova Scotia**

Johannson, Sigurbjorn: **Ethnic Literature**

John, Alix: **Jones, Alice**

John A. Macdonald: **Icebreakers; Northwest Passage**

John Adaskin Project: **Music Education; Somers, Harry S.**

John B. Aird: **Lake Carriers**

John B. Parkin Associates: **Airport Architecture; Architecture, Development; Bank Architecture; Bregman & Hamann; Toronto City Hall**

John C. Williams Dory Shop: **Shelburne**

John C. Winston publishers: **Book Publishing, English-Language**

John Cabot: **Icebreakers**

John Drainie Award: **Ljungh, Esse W.**

John G. Diefenbaker Centre: **Saskatoon**

John Glassco Translation Prize: **Literary Prizes in English**

John Holden Players: **Theatre, English-Language**

John Howard Society: **Prison; Probation & Parole**

John Inglis Co Ltd: **Electrical Appliances Industry**

John Janzen Nature Centre: **Edmonton**

John Lovell & Son: **Book Publishing, English-Language**

John Molson & Sons: **Molson, John**

John Paul II, Pope: **Catholicism**

John S. Metcalf Co: **Grain Elevators**

John Young & Co: **Young, John**

Johnniebo: **Kenojuak Ashevak**

Johns, M.W.: **Physics**

Johns, Ted: **Blyth Festival**

Johnson, A.H.: **Philosophy**

Johnson, Albert: **Aklavik**

Johnson, Alexander: **Mathematics**

Johnson, Daniel, Jr: **Johnson, Daniel**

Johnson, Dave: **Swimming, Speed**

Johnson, Doug: **Loverboy**

Johnson, Guy: **Brant, Joseph**

Johnson, Harry G.: **Economic Nationalism; Economics**

Johnson, J.K.: **Autobiographical Writing in English**

Johnson, J.M.: **Fathers of Confederation**

Johnson, James: **Gananoque**

Johnson, Philip: **Architectural Styles**

Johnson, Pierre-Marc: **Johnson, Daniel**

Johnson, Thomas H.: **Icelanders**

Johnson, Tom: **Swimming, Speed**

Johnson, William Arthur: **Bovell, James**

Johnson Strait: **Vancouver Island**

Johnston, Basil: **Children's Literature in English**

Johnston, Dorothy Brooks: **Killam, Izaak Walton**

Johnston, James W.: **Baptists**

Johnston, Michael: **Vancouver Playhouse**

Johnston, Richard: **Choral Music; Music Education**

Johnston, Richard B.: **Archaeology**

Johnston, W.A.: **Geomorphology**

Joint Arctic Weather Stations project: **Northwest Territories**

Joint Centre on Modern East Asia: **York University**

joint custody: **Family Law**

Joint Metals Control Board: **Monture, Gilbert C.**

joint-stock company: **Hudson's Bay Company; Property Law**

joint tenancy: **Property Law**

Joliat, Aurèl: **Montreal Canadiens**

Joliat, Eugène: **Comparative Literature**

Joliette, Barthélemy: **Joliette**

Jolliffe, Michel: **Painting**

Jonas, George: **Ethnic Literature; Poetry in English**

Jonasson, Sigtryggur: **Icelanders**

Jones, Charles: **Brockville**

Jones, Chilion: **Fuller, Thomas**

Jones, Cliff: **Musical Theatre**

Jones, Daniel: **Brockville**

Jones, Edward: **Architecture, Development**

Jones, James E.: **Hymns**

Jones, John: **Jones, Peter**

Jones, Kelsey: **Choral Music; Opera; Songs & Songwriting**

Jones, Leonard: *Jones Case*

Jones, Mary Strachan: **Place-names**

Jones, Oliver: **Jazz**

Jones, Phyllis Jacobine: **Sculpture**

Jones, Sam: **Evangelism**

Jones Commission: **Macdonald, Angus L.; Nova Scotia**

Jones Falls: **Construction Industry, History**

Jones Sound: **Arctic Exploration; Baffin, William; Baffin Bay; Coastal Waters; Ellesmere Island**

Jonquière, Marquis de la: **Jonquière**

Jonsson, Einar Pall: **Ethnic Literature**

Jordan, Edward: **Piracy**

Jordan, Margaret: **Piracy**

Jordan, Ont: **Lincoln**

Jordan Station, Ont: **Lincoln**

Josenhans, Andreas: **Yachting**

Joseph, Lake: **Muskoka Lakes**

Joseph E. Seagram & Sons Ltd: **Bronfman Family; Seagram Co Ltd**

Joseph Hall Iron Works: **Oshawa**

Joseph Lally Trophy: **Canadian Lacrosse Hall of Fame**

Joseph's Prairie: **Cranbrook**

Josephsburg Colony: **Germans**

Josephson, Hannah: *Bonheur d'occasion*

Jost, George: **Skiing**

Joubin, Franc: **Hirshhorn, Joseph Herman**

Joudry, Patricia: **Drama in English; Theatre, English-Language**

Jour: **Harvey, Jean-Charles; Loranger, Jean-Aubert; Popular Literature in French**

Jourdain, Paul: **Music History**

Journal d'agriculture: **Barnard, Edouard-A.; Langevin, Hector-L.**

Journal de médecine de Québec: **Tessier, François-Xavier**

Journal de Montréal: **Newspapers; Péladeau, Pierre; Quebecor Inc**

Journal de Québec: **Cauchon, Joseph-Edouard; Newspapers; Péladeau, Pierre; Québec City; Quebecor Inc**

Journal of Canadian Fiction: **Literary Magazines in English; Literary Periodicals in English; Literature in English - Theory & Criticism**

Journal of Education: **Forrester, Alexander; Physical Education**

Journal of General Psychology: **Brett, George S.**

Journal of the Knights of Labor: **Wright, Alexander Whyte**

Journal of the Royal Astronomical Society of Canada: **Astronomy; McKellar, Andrew**

Journées thomistes: **Philosophy**

journeyman: **Apprenticeship in Early Canada; Craft Unionism; Leatherworking; Print Industry**

Joy Bay: **Pictographs & Petroglyphs**

Joybert: **Sculpture**

Joyner, Geoffrey: **Art Dealers**

Juan de Fuca Plate: **Earthquake; Geological Regions**

Juba, Stephen: **Ukrainians; Winnipeg**

Jubilee Auditoriums: **Alberta**

Juchereau dit de Saint-Ignace, Jean-François: **Guyon, Jean**

Judge, Peter: **Skiing**

Judges Act: **Judiciary**

Judica (Yehudit Zik): **Jewish Writing**

Judicature Acts: **Civil Procedure**

judicial decisions: **Law**

judicial power: **Constitutional Law**

Judith Jasin Award: **Benoît, Jacques**

Juet, Robert: **Hudson, Henry**

Jule, Walter: **Printmaking**

Julian calendar: **Orthodox Church; Religious Festivals**

Jull, O.: **Railway History**

Jumbo the elephant: **Grand Trunk Railway of Canada**

Jump, Edward: **Cartoons**

jumper: **Horse**

jumping: **Track & Field**

junco: **Sparrow**

June Bug: **Aviation**

Jung, Douglas: **Chinese**

Jung (Young), Casper: **Furniture, Country**

Jungkind, Walter: **Graphic Design**

Junior Forest Wardens: **Forest Ranger**

Juniper, NB: **Miramichi River**

Junkers aircraft: **Aviation; Bush Flying**

Juno Awards: **Boyd, Liona; Buck, Gary; Gagnon, André; Honours; Hunter, Thomas J.; Kuerti, Anton E.; Lightfoot, Gordon; Loverboy; McLauchlan, Murray; Murray, Anne; Music Awards & Competitions; Recording Industry; Rough Trade**

Juno Hall of Fame: **Snow, C.E., "Hank"**

Jupiter: **Meteor, Meteorite, Impact Crater; Moon**
Jupiter Theatre: **Greene, Lorne H.; Theatre, English-Language**
Jurassic period: **Bird Classification & Evolution; Dinosaur; Fossil Plants; Frog; Paleontology, History in Canada**
Jury, Wilfrid: **Ste Marie Among the Hurons**
Juste-au-Corps, NS: **Port Hood**
Justice Institute: **Community College**

K

Kabalarian Philosophy: **New Religious Movements**
Kagel, Mauricio: **Garant, Serge**
Kahgegagahbowh: **Copway, George**
Kahkewaquonaby: **Jones, Peter**
Kaien Island: **Prince Rupert**
Kaimei project: **Wave Energy**
Kain, Conrad: **Invermere; Robson, Mount**
Kakabeka Falls: **Grand Portage**
Kakfwi, Stephen: **Dene Nation**
Kakouchak: **Saint-Jean, Lac**
Kakwa River: **Rocky Mountains**
Kalamalka Lake: **Okanagan Valley; Vernon**
Kaleidoscope: **Theatre for Young Audiences**
Kaliski, S.F.: **Economics**
Kalium Chemicals Ltd: **Potash**
Kalman, Rolf: **Children's Literature in English**
Kalnins, Janis: **Music History**
Kaministiquia River: **Dulhut, Daniel Greysolon; Fort William; Thunder Bay**
Kaminuriak caribou herd: **Dubawnt Lake**
Kamloops Air Services: **Pacific Western Airlines Ltd**
Kamloops Lake: **Kamloops**
Kamloops Wawa: **Native People, Communications**
Kanadai Magyar Munkás (Canadian Hungarian Worker): **Hungarians**
Kanadai Magyarság (Canadian Hungarians): **Hungarians**
Kanader Adler: **Jewish Writing**
Kanadski Glasnik (Canada Herald): **Serbs**
Kanadský Slovák (The Canadian Slovak): **Slovaks**
Kananaskis River: **River**
Kanata, Ont: **Electronics Industry**
kaolin & kaolinite: **Clay; Indian Trade Goods**
Kapesh, An Antane: **Montagnais-Naskapi**
Kaplansky, Irving: **Mathematics**
Kapp, Joe: **British Columbia Lions**
kapton: **Canadarm**
Kapuskasing River: **Kapuskasing**
karat: **Gold**
Karate-doh: **Jiu-Jitsu**
Kareda, Urjo: **Tarragon Theatre**
Karl Pukara Accordian Orchestra: **Sudbury**
Karluk: **Bartlett, Robert Abram**
Karma Karoc: **Buddhism**
Karma Tinley Rinpoche: **Buddhism**
Karn & Co: **Piano Manufacturing**
Karngmalit Inuit: **Tuktoyaktuk**
karren: **Karst Landform**
karyotes: **Genetics**
Kassner, Eli: **Boyd, Liona**
Katchiwanooka Lake: **Kawartha Lakes**
Kater, Wolfgang: **Musical Instruments**
Kates, Joseph: **Science Council of Canada**
Kathleen Lakes: **Kluane National Park**
Katie Osborne Lilac Garden: **Botanical Garden**
Katski, S.: **Poles**
katsura: **Fossil Plants**
katydid: **Cricket**
Katz, Israel J.: **Folklore**
Kauffman Rubber Co: **Kitchener-Waterloo**
Kaufman, A.R.: **Birth Control**
Kaufmann, J.N.: **Philosophy**
Kaufmann, Walter: **Orchestral Music; Winnipeg Symphony Orchestra**
Kauk Harbour: **Nain**

Kaumajet Mountains: **Labrador Highlands**
Kawasaki, Mitch: **Japanese**
Kay, John: **Steppenwolf**
Kayll Lake: **Cosmology**
Kazville, Sask: **Romanians**
Keable Commission (Qué): **October Crisis**
Kealey, Gregory: **Marxism; Social History; Working-Class History**
Kean, A.D. "Cowboy": **Film**
Kearns, Lionel: **Poetry in English**
Kebeca Liberata medal: **Emblems of Canada; Medal**
Kechika River: **British Columbia; Rocky Mountain Trench**
Keefer, George: **Armed Forces - Air Force**
Keefer Terminal: **Thunder Bay**
Keele Peake: **Selwyn Mountains**
Keele Range: **Bluefish Caves**
Keele River: **Mackenzie River**
Keenan, Bill: **Skiing**
Keenlyside, David L.: **Archaeology**
Keewatin, Ont: **Climate Change; Kenora**
Keewatin Community College: **Manitoba; The Pas**
Keewatin Dist: **Drumlin; Dubawnt Lake; Periglacial Landform; Physiographic Regions - Canadian Shield Forest Lands; Place-names; Territorial Evolution; Tyrrell, James W.; Vegetation Regions - Arctic Tundra**
Keewatin Inuit Assn: **Inuit Tapirisat of Canada**
Keewatin Territory: **Hearst, William Howard**
Keffer, Karl: **Golf**
Kehiwin Reserve: **Dion, Joseph F.**
Kehoe, Alice B.: **Archaeology**
Kehoe, Thomas: **Archaeology**
Keillor, Elaine: **Musicology**
Keith, Alan: **Gymnastics**
Keith, John D.: **Pediatrics**
Keith, Marian (Mary Esther MacGregor): **Novel in English**
Keith Arm: **Great Bear Lake**
Kekerten, NWT: **Baffin Island; Whaling**
Kekertuk, NWT: **Baffin Island**
Keller, Terrence: **Painting**
Kellett, Henry: **Franklin Search; McClure (M'Clure), Robert J. Le M.**
Kelley, T.P.: **Donnellys, The**
Kellog Foundation: **Canadian Studies**
Kelly, John D.: **Printmaking**
Kelly James: **McLean Gang**
kelp: **Algae; Aquaculture; Seaweeds; Vegetation Regions - Coastal Marine Flora**
Kelsall, Karen: **Gymnastics**
Kelsey, Man: **Nelson River**
Kelsey Institute: **Saskatoon**
Kelso, Jack: **Swimming, Speed**
Kemano Reservoir: **Archaeology; Kitimat; Tunnels**
Kemeny, John: **Brittain, Donald**
Kemp, Hugh: **Radio Drama, English-Language**
Kempenfelt Bay: **Barrie; Simcoe, Lake**
Kenamu River: **Hamilton Inlet**
Kenins, Talivaldis: **Choral Music**
Kennaway, Joe: **Soccer**
Kennebec dialect: **Abenaki**
Kennebecasis River: **Millidge, Thomas Edward; Saint John River**
Kennedy, Clyde C.: **Archaeology**
Kennedy, D.M.: **Ginger Group**
Kennedy, Jennie Foster: **Butchart, Robert Pim**
Kennedy, Norman John: **Musicology**
Kennedy Channel: **Ellesmere Island**
Kenner, Hugh: **Literature in English - Theory & Criticism**
Kenneth G. Heffel Fine Art Inc: **Art Dealers**
Kenney, George: **Theatre, Multicultural**
Kenney Dam: **Nechako River**
Kenny, Mart: **Radio Programming**
Keno Hill, YT: **Yukon River**
Kénogami, Qué: **Jonquière**
Kenogami River: **Albany River**
Kenoran Orogeny: **Geological Regions**
Kensington, PEI: **Oral Literature in English; Prince Edward Island**
Kent, Larry: **Film**

Kent & Strathearn, Edward, Duke of: **Architecture, Development; Baillairgé Family; Montmorency; Mount Uniacke; Prince Edward Island**
Kent commission: **Magazines; Media Ownership; Newspapers; Politics & the Media; Southam Inc**
Kent House: **Montmorency**
Kentucky bluegrass: **Forage Crops; Grasses**
Kentucky coffee tree: **Vegetation Regions - Eastern Temperate Forests**
Kentville Regional Research Station: **Crop Research**
Kenyans: **Africans**
Kenyon, Walter A.: **Archaeology**
Keon, Dave: **Toronto Maple Leafs**
Keraronwe: **Snowshoeing**
kerosene: **Englehart, Jacob Lewis; Gesner, Abraham; Lighthouses; Lighting**
Kerr, Barbara Simpson: **Equestrian Sports**
Kerr, Donald: **Urban Studies**
Kerr, J.R.: **Almighty Voice**
Kerr, Mureil: **Music History**
Kerr, R.: **Olympic Games**
Kerr, Robert: **Place-names**
Kerr, Tom: **Neptune Theatre**
Kerr, Tom (trader): **Grande Prairie**
Kerrivan, Peter: **Masterless Men of Newfoundland**
Kerrobert, Sask: **Place-names**
Kertész, Sandor: **Theatre, Multicultural**
Kerwin, J.L.: **Physics**
Kesno Point: **French River**
kestrel: **Falcon**
Ketchem, Henry: **Chignecto Bay**
Ketchum's Patent Mower: **Agricultural Implements**
kettle: **Indian Trade Goods**
Kettle Rapids: **Nelson River**
Kettle Valley Railway: **Nelson; Penticton**
Key Publishers Co Ltd: **Magazines; Quill & Quire**
Keyano Swim Club: **Swimming, Speed**
Keyes, Carol: **Bobsledding**
Keyfitz, Nathan: **Demography**
Khaki University: **Adams, Frank Dawson; Adult Education; Tory, Henry M.; Wallace, William Stewart**
Khalsa Diwan Society: **Sikhism**
Khampo Gangra Drubgyudling meditation centre: **Buddhism**
Khan, Sharif: **Squash Racquets**
Khmer: **Southeast Asians**
Kicking Horse Flats: **Golden**
Kicking Horse River: **Hector, James**
Kidd, Adam: **Poetry in English**
Kidd, Kenneth E.: **Ste Marie Among the Hurons**
Kidd, Robert: **Archaeology**
Kidd, William: **Oak Island; Oral Literature in English; Piracy**
Kidd Creek Mines Ltd: **Canada Development Corp; Metallurgy; Mining; Prospecting**
Kierzkowski, Aleksander E.: **Poles**
Kiglapait Mountains: **Labrador Highlands**
Kikendatch Band: **Attikamek**
Kikino, Alta: **Métis Settlements**
Kilbourn, William: **Business History**
Kilburn, Weldon: **Marshall, Lois C.**
Kilian, Crawford: **Popular Literature in English**
Killam, Alta: **Stewart, Charles**
Killam, Dorothy: **Dalhousie University**
Killam Library: **Fairn, Leslie Raymond**
Killam Memorial Prize: **Killam, Izaak Walton**
killdeer: **Plover**
killer whale: **Animal; Arctic Animals; Cetacea; Hudson Bay; Lancaster Sound; Pacific Rim National Park; Québec; Walrus; Whale**
kiln: **Ceramics; Tobacco**
Kim, Andy: **Popular Music**
Kimsquit: **Bella Coola**
Kinal-Chevalier, Sylvie: **Dance History**
Kinbrook Island Provincial Park: **Brooks**
Kincolith, BC: **Nass River**
Kindersley, Robert: **Kindersley**
kinetics: **Chemistry Subdisciplines**

King, Basil: **Novel in English**
King, Bryan: **Purcell String Quartet**
King, Carlyle: **Literature in English - Teaching**
King, Charmion: **Gill, Robert**
King, Dave: **Canadian Olympic Hockey Team**
King, Jack: **Stage & Costume Design**
King, John: **Dent, John Charles**
King, L.V.: **Physics**
King, Mary Perry: **Carman, Bliss**
King, Philip: **Canada & Australia**
King, Victoria: **Peguis**
King, William: **Peguis**
King Christian Island: **Arctic Exploration**
King George's Sound: **Nootka Sound**
King George's War: **Rogers, Robert; War of the Austrian Succession**
King-Hamy chart: **Cartography, History of**
King William's Act: **Newfoundland Acts**
Kingdom of God on Earth: **Intellectual History; Mennonites; Methodism; Millenarianism**
"Kingdom of the Saguenay": **Donnacona; New France; Saguenay River**
kingfish: **Tuna**
Kingfisher: **Nootka**
Kingnait Mountains: **Cape Dorset**
kingnut hickory: **Vegetation Regions - Eastern Temperate Forests**
King's College (London): **University of Western Ontario**
King's College School: **Private School**
King's College (U of T): **Beaven, James; Chemistry; Clarke, James P.; Croft, Henry Holmes; LaFontaine, Louis-Hippolyte; Physics; Strachan, John; University of Toronto**
King's College (UNB): **Civil Engineering; d'Avray, 2nd Baron; Douglas, Howard; Engineering; Fredericton; Head, Edmund Walker; Mineral & Mining Engineering; University of New Brunswick**
King's Domain: **King's Posts; New France; Saint-Jean, Lac**
King's Head Inn: **Folk Art**
King's Highway: **Hotel**
King's Jubilee Medal: **Strickland, Edgar Harold**
King's Plate: **Queen's Plate; Thoroughbred Racing**
King's Playhouse: **Theatre, English-Language**
King's Printers: **Almanacs**
Kingsbury, Donald: **Popular Literature in English**
Kingsclear, NB: **New Brunswick**
Kingsclear Reserve: **Maliseet**
Kingscote, Anthony: **Parasitology**
Kingsford, William: **Historiography**
Kingsport, NS: **Sailing Ships**
Kingston, F. Temple: **Philosophy**
Kingston, NB: **Rexton**
Kingston Basin: **Ontario, Lake**
Kingston Boat Club: **Yachting**
Kingston Chronicle: **Macaulay, John**
Kingston Customs House: **Architectural Styles**
Kingston Mills, Upper Canada: **Technology**
Kingston Navy Yards: **Fort Henry**
Kingston-Pembroke Railway: **Kingston**
Kingston Penitentiary: **Irvine, Acheson Gosford; Prison; Revolutionary Industrial Unionism**
Kingston Post Office: **Architectural Styles**
Kingston Symphony: **Brott, Alexander**
Kingsville, Ont: **Bird Sanctuaries & Reserves**
Kinmount, Ont: **Icelanders**
Kinney Lake: **Robson, Mount**
kinnickinnick: **Bearberry; Plants, Native Uses**
Kino Québec: **Fitness**
Kinoosao, Sask: **Reindeer Lake**
Kinsella, W.P.: *Queen's Quarterly*
Kinsmen Aquatic Centre: **Edmonton**
Kioosta Reserve: **Edenshaw, Charlie**
Kiopini, Christian: **Painting**
Kipawa, Ont: **Adams, Thomas**
Kipawa mills: **Témiscaming**

Kirby, Michael: **Constitution, Patriation of; Fisheries Policy**
Kirby, Peter: **Emery, John**
Kirby House: **Niagara-on-the-Lake**
Kirby Memorandum: **Constitution, Patriation of**
Kirby Task Force: **Fisheries History**
Kireluk, Vic: **Billiards**
Kiriak, Elias: **Ukrainian Writing**
Kirikka, Mattii: **Sointula**
Kirkconnell, Watson: **Baptists; Ethnic Literature; Ukrainian Writing**
Kirke, James: **Kirke, David**
Kirke, John: **Kirke, David**
Kirke, Lewis: **Kirke, David**
Kirke, Thomas: **Kirke, David**
Kirkfield, Ont: **Mackenzie, William; Trent Canal**
Kirkland, J. Michael: **Architecture, Development**
Kirkland, Winnifred: **Kirkland Lake**
Kirkton, Ont: **Eaton, Timothy**
Kirkwood, Alexander: **Parks, Provincial**
Kirouac, Conrad: **Marie-Victorin, Frère**
Kirschner, Richard: **Shaw Festival**
Kirton, Doug: **Painting**
Kirwin, W.J.: **Dictionary**
Kispiox, BC: **Harris, Walter**
Kitamaat Village, BC: **Kitamaat**
"Kitchen Meeting": **Constitution, Patriation of**
Kitchener-Waterloo *Record*: **Honderich, Beland Hugh**
Kitchener wheat: **Wheeler, Seager**
kite: **Birds of Prey**
Kitikmeot Inuit Assn: **Inuit Tapirisat of Canada**
Kitiwin: **Ray, Carl**
Kitlope: **Kitamaat**
Kittegaryumiut: **Kittigazuit Site**
kittiwake: **Baffin Island; Bird Sanctuaries & Reserves; Gull; Wildlife Preserve**
Kitwancool Band: **Land Claims**
Kitwancool Reserve: **Duff, Wilson**
Kitwankul River: **Kitwanga Fort**
Kiviok: **Inuit Myth & Legend**
Kivitoo, NWT: **Baffin Island**
Kiyooka, Roy: **Ethnic Literature; Painting**
Klahoose: **Northern Georgia Strait Coast Salish**
Kleanza Provincial Park: **Terrace**
Kleefeld, Hans: **Logo**
Kleefeld, Man: **Hanover**
Kleena Kleene, BC: **Place-names**
Klein, Lothar: **Choral Music**
Klemtu, BC: **Bella Bella**
Klibansky, Raymond: **Philosophy**
Klimax Mine: **Coal**
Klinck, L.S.: **Agricultural Education**
Kline, John: **Kleinburg**
Klondike: **Whitehorse**
Klondike Days: **Festivals**
Klondike Gold Rush International Historical Park: **Yukon Territory**
Klondike Highway: **Carmacks; Dawson**
Klondike Plateau: **Periglacial Landform**
Klondike River: **Dawson; Prospecting**
Klondike Visitors Assn: **Dawson**
Kloss, Heinz: **German Writing**
Klotz, Lac: **Ungava Inuit**
Klunder, Harold: **Painting**
Klymasz, Robert B.: **Folklore; Musicology**
Kmeta, Ivan: **Ukrainian Writing**
Knapp, Budd: **Allan, Andrew E.F.**
knapweed: **Thistle; Weeds**
Knee Lake: **Hayes River**
knife: **Archaic; Clovis; Domestic Utensils; Fur Trade; Indian Trade Goods; L'Anse Amour Burial Site; Medicine Wheels; Northwest Coast Indian Art; Silver, Indian Trade; Tutchone**
Knight, David: **Novel in English**
Knight, James: **Prince of Wales's Fort**
Knight, Phyllis: **Autobiographical Writing in English**
Knight, Raymond: **Place-names**
Knight, Rolf: **Autobiographical Writing in English**
Knight Inlet: **Fjord; Waddington, Mount**
Knight Sugar Co: **Sugar Industry**
Knights of Columbus hostel: **Disasters**
Knister, Raymond: **Novel in English**
knitting machines: **Textile Industry**

Knob Lake: **Quebec, North Shore & Labrador Railway; Schefferville**
Knoiuszy, E.: **Poles**
knot: **Sandpiper**
knotted wrack: **Seaweeds**
Knowledge Network of the West Communications Authority: **Educational Broadcasting**
Knox College: **Caven, William; University of Toronto; Young, George Paxton**
Knudson, Niels Christian: **Painting**
Kobau, Mount: **Astronomy**
Kodlunarn Island: **Frobisher, Martin**
Koenig, Wolf: **Film Animation**
Koffler, Murray: **Shoppers Drug Mart**
Kohoutek, Comet: **Comet**
Koizumi, Kazuhiro: **Winnipeg Symphony Orchestra**
Kokanee Glacier Provincial Park: **Parks, Provincial**
Koldofsky, Adolph: **Hart House String Quartet**
Kolessa, Lubka: **Music History**
Kolin, Sask: **Czechs**
Kolinski, Mieczyslaw: **Musicology**
Kolisnyk, Peter: **Sculpture**
Komarno, Man: **Rockwood**
Komonen, Dave: **Long-Distance Running**
Komorus, Rudolf: **Music History**
Koocanusa, Lake: **Wardner**
Kootenay Forest Reserve: **Brown, J.G., "Kootenai"**
Kootenay language: **Native People, Languages**
Kootenay Plains: **Smallboy, Johnny Bob**
Kootenay Ranges: **Cranbrook**
Kootenay Reserve: **Kootenay**
Kootenay River: **Castlegar; Columbia River; Columbia River Treaty; Creston, BC; Fort Steele; Kootenay; Kootenay Lake; Trail; Vermilion River**
Kootenay Trout Hatchery: **Wardner**
Kootenay Valley: **Desert; Vegetation Regions - Cordillera**
korite: **Gemstone**
Korman, Gordon: **Literature in English**
Korn, Rochl: **Jewish Writing**
Kortum, F.: **Bank Architecture**
Koster, Wally: **Popular Music**
Kostyniuk, Ron: **Sculpture**
Koukdjuak River: **Nettilling Lake**
Kovar, Emile: **Nelligan, Emile**
Kovshun, Mykola: **Ukrainian Writing**
Kowalczyk, Anthony: **Saints**
Kowbel, Semen: **Ukrainian Writing**
Kraemer, Franz: **Music Broadcasting**
kraft pulp & paper: **La Tuque; Pulp & Paper Industry; Texada Island**
Kraglund, John: **Music Criticism**
kraken: **Mollusc**
Kralice Bible: **Czechs**
Kramer, Burton: **Graphic Design; Logo**
Kramer, Ken: **Globe Theatre**
Kramer, Sue: **Globe Theatre**
Krat, Pavlo: **Ukrainian Writing**
Kratochvil, Byron: **Harris, Walter E.**
Kraul, Earl: **Dance on Television & Film**
Kraus, Greta: **Aitken, Robert Morris**
Krever Commission: **Privacy**
Kreyer, Scott: **Toronto**
Krizanc, John: **Drama in English**
Kronika Tygodniowa (A Weekly Chronicle): **Poles**
Kroto, Harry: **Molecules in Interstellar Space**
Kru language: **Africans**
krypton: **Spring**
Ktamquk Ilnui Saquimawoutie: **Land Claims**
Ktinékétolékouac: **Sherbrooke**
Kubota, Nobuo: **Painting**
Kudelka, James: **Choreography; Dance on Television & Film; Grands Ballets Canadiens; National Ballet of Canada**
Kudryk, Vasyl: **Ukrainian Writing**
Kumwartok: **Inuit Art**
Kunghit Island: **Anthony Island Provincial Park**
Kunstmann II chart: **Cartography, History of**
Kuntz Brewery: **Kitchener-Waterloo**
Kunz, Alfred: **Choral Music**
Kuomintang: **Chinese**
Kuper, Jack: **Jewish Writing**

Kuper Island: **Gulf Islands**
Kuprejanov, George: **Chess**
Kurata, T.B.: **Walker, Edmund Murton**
Kurath, Gertrude P.: **Folklore**
Kuroshio Current: **Coastal Waters**
Kushner, Eva: **Comparative Literature**
Kutenay: **Kootenay**
Kuypers, Jan: **Industrial Design**
Kuznets cycle: **Business Cycles**
Kvietys, Yone: **Dance, Modern**
Kwakwakawock: **Kwakiutl**
Kwakwala language: **Kwakiutl; Northern Georgia Strait Coast Salish**
Kwatna: **Bella Coola**
Kwatna Inlet: **Bella Coola**
Kwok, Sun: **Black Hole**
Kybertec International Inc: **Diving, Underwater**
Kynoch Inlet: **Bella Bella**
Kyrijak, Illia: **Ukrainian Writing**

L

L. & P. Sawyer Co: **Agricultural Implements**
L-dopamine: **Seeman, Philip**
L.G. Beaubien et Cie: **Lévesque, Jean-Louis**
La Broquerie, Man: **Manitoba**
La Cave portage: **Ottawa River**
La Chasse, Pierre de: **Theatre, French-Language**
La Colle Falls: **Prince Albert**
La Conception mission: **Marquette, Jacques**
La Cosa chart: **Cartography, History of**
La Croix, Lac: **Grand Portage**
la Ferre, Marie de: **Saints**
La Ferté de la Madeleine, Abbé de: **La Prairie**
La Flamme, Rodolophe: **Riel, Louis**
La Forest, Lac: **Bienville, Lac**
La Gabelle, Qué: **St-Maurice, Rivière**
La Hève, Acadia: **Razilly, Isaac de**
La Jemerais, Sieur de: **La Vérendrye, Pierre**
LA LA LA: **Lock, Édouard**
La Lande, Jean de: **Saints**
La Loche, Lac: **Churchill River; Portage La Loche**
La Loche fur brigade: **Portage La Loche**
La Macaza, Qué: **Bomarc Missile Crisis**
La Montagne Reserve: **Bourgeoys, Marguerite**
La Nauze, Charles Dearing: **Sinnisiak**
La Patrie, Qué: **Musical Instruments**
La Pérade, Pierre-Thomas Tarieu de: **Verchères, Marie-Madeleine Jarret de**
La Pocatière, Qué: **Research Stations, Agricultural**
La Providence School: **Status of Women**
La Pylaie, Bachelot de: **Floras & Botanical Journals**
La Richardière, Testu de: **Cartography, History of**
La Roche, Marquis de: **Hog Farming; Sable Island**
La Roche Daillon, Joseph de: **Neutral**
La Rolanderie: **St Hubert Mission**
La Ronge, Sask: **Lac La Ronge; Saskatchewan; School Facilities**
La Sablonnière, Blanche de: **Theatre, English-Language**
La Salle, Qué: **Montréal**
La Salle Park: **Kingston**
La Slague: **Sudbury**
La Tour, Louis Bertrand de: **Pommier, Hugues**
La Vase portage: **North Bay**
La Vérendrye, François: **La Vérendrye, Louis-Joseph**
La Vérendrye, Jacques-René: **La Vérendrye, Pierre**
La Verendrye, Parc provincial de: **Parks, Provincial**
Labatt Brewing Co of Canada: **Biochemistry; Brewing Industry; Genetic Engineering; John Labatt Corp; Toronto Blue Jays**
Labatt Foundation: **Educational Foundations & Endowments**
L'Abbé, Maurice: **Mathematics**

Labelle, Elzéar: **Theatre, French-Language**
Labelle, Jean-Baptiste: **Music History**
Laberge, Lake: **Yukon River**
Laberge, Marie: **Governor General's Literary Awards; Theatre, French-Language**
LaBine, Charles: **LaBine, Gilbert**
Labor Advocate: **Thompson, Thomas Phillips**
Labour: **Historiography; Working-Class History**
Labour, Dept of: **Industrial Relations; King, W.L. Mackenzie; Labour Canada; Mitchell, Humphrey; Mulock, William; Wartime Prices & Trade Board**
Labour, Dept of (NS): **Nova Scotia**
labour code: **Employment Law**
Labour College of Canada: **Adult Education; Buller, Annie; Gauld, Bella Hall**
Labour Educational Assn of Ont: **Union Centrals, District & Regional**
Labour Force: **Statistics Canada**
Labour Gazette: **Industrial Relations**
Labour Progressive Party: **Communist Party of Canada; Rose, Fred; Ryerson, Stanley B.**
Labour Relations Act (NB): **Dysart, A. Allison**
labour standards: **Employment Law; Labour Law**
Labrador: **Icebreakers; Northwest Passage**
Labrador & Québec North Shore Railway: **Newfoundland**
Labrador Current: **Bonavista Bay; Coastal Waters; Davis Strait; Grand Banks; Labrador; Labrador Sea; Nova Scotia; Québec**
Labrador duck: **Duck; Endangered Animals; Wildlife Preserve**
Labrador Institute of Northern Studies: **Memorial University of Newfoundland**
Labrador Inuit Assn: **Inuit Tapirisat of Canada; Land Claims; Watt, Charlie**
Labrador Plateau: **Churchill River, Lab; Smallwood Reservoir**
Labrador retriever: **Dog**
Labrador Shelf: **Coastal Waters; Petroleum**
Labrador Trough: **Newfoundland**
labradorite: **Gemstone; Michikamau Lake; Mineral Naming**
Labrecque, J.C.: **Film**
Lac des Chats Portage: **Ottawa River**
Lac-des-Deux-Montagnes seigneury: **Oka**
Lac du Bonnet, Man: **Poles; Postal System**
Lac la Biche, Alta: **Métis; Steinhauer, Henry Bird**
Lac la Martre, NWT: **Dogrib; Martre, Lac la**
Lac Pelletier Provincial Park: **Parks, Provincial**
Lac Seul Reserve: **Seul, Lac**
L'Acadie, Qué: **Textile Industry**
Lacerte, Adèle: **Children's Literature in French**
Lach, Elmer: **Blake, Hector**
Lacharité, Normand: **Philosophy**
Lachenaie, Qué: **Daubigny, Victor-Théodule**
Lachine Bridge: **Reid, Robert G.**
Lachine Canal: **Dollier de Casson, François; Dunlop, William; Heritage Trail; Lake Carriers; Montréal; Working-Class History**
Lachine Rapids: **St Lawrence Lowland; St Lawrence River**
Lacolle, Qué: **Hunters' Lodges; Musical Instruments**
Lacombe, Alta: **Agricultural Research & Development**
Lacombe Citizen of the Year: **Fredeen, Howard**
Lacombe Hog: **Animal Breeding; Hog Farming**
Lacombe Home: **Lacombe, Albert; L'Heureux, Jean-B.**
Lacourcière, Luc: **Anthropology; Folklore; Nelligan, Emile; Oral Literature in French; Short Fiction in French**
Lacroix, Benoît: **Philosophy**

lacrosse equipment: **Native People, Economic Conditions; Sporting-Goods Industry**
Ladies' Morning Musical Club: **Forrester, Maureen; Québec**
Ladies' Prince of Wales Snowshoe Club: **Sports History**
ladle: **Northwest Coast Indian Art; Silver, Domestic; Woodenware**
Ladoo, Harold Sonny: **Lee, Dennis; Novel in English**
Ladue, Joseph: **Dawson**
Lady Manhattan & Kayser-Roth Canada Ltd: **Clothing Industries**
Lady's Book: **Drama in English**
Laflamme, Rodolphe: **Gallicanism**
Laflèche, Guy: **Essay in French**
Laforte, Conrad: **Folk Music, Franco-Canadian; Music History; Musicology; Oral Literature in French**
Lafortune, Ambroise: **Children's Literature in French**
Lafrance, Guy: **Philosophy**
Lafrance, Yvon: **Philosophy**
Lagacé, Mireille: **Music History**
Lagemodière, Julie: **Lagemodière, Marie-Anne**
Lagemodière, Reine: **Lagemodière, Marie-Anne**
lager: **Brewing Industry**
Laggan, Alta: **Lake Louise**
lagoon: **Grande Entrée, Île de; Lake; Miscou Island; Water Pollution**
Lagoya, Alexandre: **Boyd, Liona**
Lagueux, Maurice: **Philosophy**
Lahrman, Fred: **Diorama**
LaHurault: **Shipbuilding & Ship Repair**
Laidlaw Foundation: **Educational Foundations & Endowments**
Laing, G. Blair: **Art Dealers**
Laing, George: **Landscape Architecture**
Laing, Gertrude: **Chaput-Rolland, Solange**
Lajeunesse, M.-L.-C.-Emma: **Albani, Emma**
Lajeunesse, Marcel: **Intellectual History**
Lake, Kayll: **Black Hole**
Lake Erie, Essex & Detroit River Railway: **Walker, Hiram**
Lake Fleet Island: **Thousand Islands**
Lake Harbour, NWT: **Baffin Island; Fleming, Archibald Lang**
Lake Manitoba Railway & Canal Co: **Dauphin; Mann, Donald**
Lake Ontario Steel Co Ltd: **Iron & Steel Industry**
Lake St John Pulp & Paper Co: **Dolbeau**
Lake St Louis & Province Railway: **Montreal & Lachine Railroad**
Lake Shore Mines Ltd: **Kirkland Lake; Oakes, Harry; Ontario Northland Transportation Commission**
lake trout: **Char; Cuisine; Dubawnt Lake; Lake Superior Provincial Park; Mistassini, Lac; Rideau Lakes**
Lake Valley, Sask: **Devine, D. Grant**
lake whitefish: **Dubawnt Lake; Whitefish**
Lakefield, Ont: **Laurence, Margaret**
Lakehead College of Arts, Science & Technology: **Lakehead University**
Lakehead harbour: **Thunder Bay**
Lakehead Planning Board: **Thunder Bay**
Lakehead Region Conservation Authority: **Thunder Bay**
Lakehead Technical Institute: **Lakehead University**
Lakeland College: **Community College**
Lakelse Lake Provincial Park: **Terrace**
lakers: **Lake Carriers; Transportation**
Lakes Lillooet: **Salish, Interior**
Lakeshore Swim Club: **Lumsdon, Cliff; Marathon Swimming**
Lakota (Sioux): **Dakota (Sioux)**
Lalemant, Gabriel: **Ste Marie Among the Hurons**
L'Allier, Jean-Paul: **Book Publishing, French-Language**
Lalonde, Michèle: **Poetry in French**
Lamaque Mining Co: **Val-d'Or**
Lamarche, Marc-Antonin: **Literature in French - Criticism & Theory**
LaMarsh Research Program on Violence & Conflict Resolution: **York University**

lamb: **Animal Agriculture; Cuisine; Sheep Farming**
Lamb, Arthur Stanley: **Physical Education; Sports Organization, Amateur**
Lamb, Rael: **Ballets Jazz de Montréal**
Lamb, Thomas: **Industrial Design**
Lamb, W. Kaye: **Archives; Fraser, Simon; National Library of Canada**
Lambart, Evelyn: **McLaren, Norman**
Lambart, F.: **Logan, Mount**
Lambe, Lawrence M.: **Paleontology, History in Canada**
Lambert, George: **Singing**
Lambert, John: **Exploration & Travel Literature in English**
Lambert, Marcel: **Speaker**
Lambert, Paul: **Silver, Church; Silver, Domestic**
Lambert, Phyllis: **Architecture, Development**
Lambert, Wallace: **Second-Language Instruction**
Lambert Commission: **Economic Regulation**
Lamberts, Heath: **Shaw Festival**
Lambeth Conference: **Strachan, John**
Lambett, Adélard: **Oral Literature in French**
Lambrou, Lambros: **Alberta Ballet Company; Choreography**
lamb's-quarters: **Plants, Native Uses; Weeds**
Lambton Shield: **Mackenzie, Alexander (1822-92)**
Lamonde, Yvan: **Intellectual History; Philosophy**
Lamontagne-Beauregard, Blanche: **Poetry in French**
Lamontagne Committee: **Science Policy**
Lamontagne Ltée: **Turmel, Antoine**
Lamorille, Antoine: **Votive Painting**
lamp: **Lighthouses; Lighting; Silver, Church**
lamp chimney: **Glass**
lamp shell: **Brachiopoda; Fossil Animals**
Lampman, Sask: **Place-names**
Lamy, André: **Canadian Film Development Corp**
Lanark County Courthouse: **Perth**
Lancaster, James: **Lancaster Sound**
Lancaster, NB: **Saint John**
Lancaster bomber: **Aerospace Industry; Armaments; Bazalgette, Ian Willoughby; Mynarski, Andrew Charles; World War II**
Lancelot Press Ltd: **Small Presses**
Lancet Insurance Agency: **Canadian Medical Association**
Lanctôt, Gustave: **Archives; Intellectual History; Literature in French - Scholarship & Teaching; Oral Literature in French**
Lanctôt, Jacques: **Front de libération du Québec**
Lanctôt, Micheline: **Film**
land clearing: **Agricultural Soil Practices**
Land Commission Act (BC): **British Columbia**
Land Development Assn: **Agriculture History**
land management: **Agricultural Soil Practices; Soil Conservation**
land of the midnight sun: **Festivals; Midnight Sun**
land reclamation: **Delta; Holland Marsh; Soil Science; Sudbury; Tantramar Marsh**
Land Resource Research Institute: **Research Stations, Agricultural; Soil Science**
land tenure: **Seigneurial System**
land titles: **Funeral Practices; Property Law**
Land Use & Ownership, Royal Commission on (PEI): **Prince Edward Island**

land-use planning & change: **Agriculture & Food Policy; Building Codes & Regulations; City Politics; Floods & Flood Control; Heritage Conservation; Housing & Housing Policy; Landslide; Metropolitan Government; Municipal Administration; Regional Government; Remote Sensing; Soil Science; Spence-Sales, Harold; Urban & Regional Planning; Zoning**
landed immigrant: **Citizenship; Family Allowance; Latin Americans**
landing craft: **Armaments; Shipbuilding & Ship Repair**
landing tax: **Immigration**
Landlord & Tenant Act (NB): **Dysart, A. Allison**
Landron, Jean-François: **Silver, Church; Silver, Domestic**
Landry, Louis: **Children's Literature in French**
Landry, Napoléon: **Ethnic Literature**
Landry, Roger: *Presse*
Lands & Forests, Dept of (NS): **Nova Scotia**
Lands Directorate: **Physical Geography**
Lands End: **Beaufort Sea**
LANDSAT satellite: **Artificial Intelligence; Electronics Industry; Remote Sensing; Satellite, Artificial**
Lane, A.T.: **Cycling**
Lane, Gilles: **Philosophy**
Lane, Henry Bower: **Osgoode Hall**
Lane, Red: **Lane, Patrick**
Lang, R.J.: **Physics**
Langara, BC: **Lighthouses**
Lange, Lola: **Status of Women in Canada, Royal Commission on the**
Lange & Roberts: **Art Dealers**
Langelier, Charles-François: **Gallicanism**
Langevin, Adélard: **North-West Schools Question**
Langevin, Gilbert: **Poetry in French**
Langevin, Jean: **Catholicism**
Langford, James: **Silver, Domestic**
Langford Laboratories Ltd: **Veterinary Medicines Industry**
Langham, Michael: **Stratford Festival**
Langlade (Island): **Saint-Pierre & Miquelon**
Langlands, Robert: **Mathematics**
Langley, Henry: **Architectural Styles; Religious Building**
Langley, Thomas: **Langley**
Langlois, Georges: **Demography**
Langton, Anne: **Langton, Hugh Hornby; Women & Education**
language rights: **Canadian Unity, Task Force on; Education Policy; Ethnic & Race Relations; French in the West; Theatre, French-Language**
Lansdowne Park: **Ottawa, Ont; Ottawa Rough Riders**
L'Anse Amour, Lab: **Festivals**
Lanterne Canadienne: **Buies, Arthur**
Lantzville, BC: **Regionalism in Literature**
Lao: **Southeast Asians**
Lapalme, Robert: **Children's Literature in French**
Lapérouse, Comte de: **Prince of Wales's Fort**
lapidary art: **Gemstone; Rock & Mineral Collecting**
Lapierre, Eugène: **Opera**
lapis lazuli: **Gemstone**
Lapland longspur: **Biogeography**
Lapland rosebay: **Wildflowers**
Laplante, André: **Music History**
Lapointe, Alexis: **Trotteur, Alexis le**
Lapointe, Frank: **Printmaking**
Lapointe, Gatien: **Poetry in French**
Lapointe, Guy: **Montreal Canadiens**
Lapointe, Jeanne: **Status of Women in Canada, Royal Commission on the**
lapwing: **Plover**
Laramide Orogeny: **Geological Regions**
larceny: **Crime**
L'Arche: **Artists' Organizations**
L'Arche (the ark): **Vanier, Jean**
Larder Lake: **Gold Rushes**
Lareau, Edmond: **Comparative Literature, Canadian**
Laredo Strait: **Spanish**

large-flowered wintergreen: **Wildflowers**
large tooth aspen: **Aspen; Vegetation Regions - Eastern Temperate Forests**
largemouth bass: **Bass; Rideau Lakes; Thousand Islands**
LaRiviere, Hank: **Country & Western Music**
Larkin, Peter C.: **Canada House**
larkspur: **Poisonous Plants**
Laroche, Yves: **Skiing**
Larochelle, A.: **Plate Tectonics**
Larochelle, Emile: **Singing**
Larocque, François-Antoine: **Exploration & Travel Literature in French**
LaRoque, Charles: **Catholicism**
LaRose Mine: **Timmins, Noah A.**
Larrivée, Jean: **Musical Instruments**
Larrue, J.-M.: **Theatre, French-Language**
Larsen, Arthur: **Soaring**
Larter, Edward N.: **Genetics**
Lartigue, Jean-Jacques: **Catholicism; Ultramontanism**
LaRue, F.A.H.: *Soirées canadiennes*
LaRue, Hubert: **Folk Music, Franco-Canadian**
LaSalle Community College: **Clothing Industries**
Lasalle Conservatory: **Theatre Education**
Laser sailboat: **Industrial Design**
Lasermark: **Electronics Industry**
Lashburn, Sask: **Kenderdine, Augustus F.**
Lasserre, Fred: **Religious Building**
L'Assomption, Qué: **Research Stations, Agricultural**
L'Assomption, Rivière: **Joliette; St Lawrence Lowland**
Last Mountain Lake: **Bird Sanctuaries & Reserves; Wildlife Conservation & Management**
Latcholassie: **Inuit Art**
Latin language: **Classics**
latitude: **Forty-ninth Parallel; Surveying**
Latrobe, John: *Poussière sur la ville*
Latter Rain Movement: **New Religious Movements**
Lattimer, J.E.: **Agricultural Economics**
Laucke, Michael: **Guitar**
Laufer, Murray: **Stage & Costume Design**
Laughton, Stuart: **Canadian Brass**
laundered money: **Organized Crime**
Laura Secord Candy Shops Ltd: **John Labatt Corp**
Laure, Pierre: **Cartography, History of**
Laurel culture: **Betula Lake; Rainy River Burial Mounds**
Laurence, Jack: **Laurence, Margaret**
Laurendeau-Dunton Commission: **Bilingualism & Biculturalism, Royal Commission on**
Laurentian Archaic: **Prehistory**
Laurentian Autoroute: **Laurentian Highlands; Mirabel; Roads & Highways**
Laurentian Bobsledding Assn: **Bobsledding**
Laurentian Channel: **Earthquake; St Lawrence, Gulf of; Scotian Shelf**
Laurentian Museum & Arts Centre: **Sudbury**
Laurentide Air Service Ltd: **Bush Flying**
Laurentide Financial Corp: **National Bank of Canada**
Laurentide Ice Sheet: **Agassiz, Lake; Glaciation; Torngat Mountains**
Laurentide Mortgage Corp: **National Bank of Canada**
Laurentide Pulp & Paper Co: **Bush Flying**
Laurentides, Parc provincial des: **Laurentian Highlands; Montmorency Falls; Parks, Provincial**
Laurentides Railway Co: **Chapleau, J.-Adolphe**
Laureys, Henry: **Economics**
Laurie, Patrick: **Print Industry**
Laurie Wagon: **Bus Transportation**
Laurier House: **Underhill, Frank H.**
Laurier Palace Theatre: **Disasters**
Laut, Agnes: **Novel in English**
Lauzier, Louis-M.: **Oceanography**
Lauzon, François de: **St-François, Rivière**

Lauzon, Qué: **La Corriveau; Ocean Industry; Shipbuilding & Ship Repair; Swiss**

lava: **Garibaldi Provincial Park; Geological Regions; Helmcken Falls; Lake Superior Provincial Park; Mineral; Moon; Mount Edziza Provincial Park; Nass River; Plate Tectonics; Volcano**

Lavaill, Robert: **Popular Literature in French**

Laval, Qué: **Institut Armand-Frappier; Montréal**

Laval théologique et philosophique: **Philosophy**

Laval Trio: **Guitar**

Lavallé, Marcel: **Autobiographical Writing in French**

Lavallée family: **Musical Instruments**

lavender: **Herbs**

L'Avenir, Qué: **Dorion, Jean-Baptiste-Eric; Laurier, Wilfrid**

Laverdière, C.-H.: **Champlain, Samuel de**

Lavergne, Armand: **Nationalist League**

Lavigne, Arthur: **Music History**

Laviolette, Jack: **Montreal Canadiens**

Laviolette bridge: **Trois-Rivières**

Lavoie, Richard: **Film**

Law, Ronald: **Parasitology**

Law, Ruth: **Automobile Racing**

Law Journal: **Kennedy, William Paul McClure**

Law Reform Commission of Ontario: **Law of Evidence; Law Reform**

Law Soc of Alberta: **Distance Learning**

Law Soc of BC: **Associations**

Law Soc of Upper Canada: **Associations; Legal Education; Libraries; Osgoode Hall; University of Western Ontario; Wright, Cecil Augustus; York University**

lawn tennis: **Tennis**

Lawrence, William Dawson: *W.D. Lawrence*

Lawson, John: **Animal Breeding**

Lawson, May: **Singing**

Lawson, Smirle: **Football**

Lax, Gary: **Committee for an Independent Canada**

Laxer, James: **Lewis, David; New Democratic Party; Waffle**

Lay, Marion: **Swimming, Speed**

Laycock, Samuel: **Mental Health**

Laycoe, Hal: **Vancouver Canucks**

layoffs: **Employment Law**

lazaretto: **Tracadie, NB**

Lazo, BC: **Comox, BC**

Le Blanc, Eldridge: **Parizeau, Gérard**

Le Blanc, Stephen: **Stephenville**

Le Dain Commission: **Non-Medical Use of Drugs, Royal Commission on the**

Le Gardeur, Qué: **Dominion Arsenal**

Le Gros, Enid: **Ceramics, Contemporary**

Le Jeune, Louis: **Literature in French - Scholarship & Teaching**

Le Jeune, Oliver: **Blacks**

Le Magazine Maclean: **Lapointe, Paul-Marie**

Le Moyne, Charles: **Longueuil, Baron de**

Le Moyne, Pierre: **Iberville, Pierre Le Moyne d'**

Le Moyne family: **Bienville, Jean-Baptiste Le Moyne de**

Le Pan, Douglas: **Literature in English**

Le Raye, Charles: **Exploration & Travel Literature in French**

Le Roux, Guillaume: **Sinnisiak**

Le Royer de La Dauversière, Jérôme: **Saints**

Leadley, F. "Pep": **Football**

Leaf, Caroline: **Film Animation**

Leaf Basin: **Ungava Bay**

leaf miner: **Moth; Okra**

Leaf Rapids, Man: **Manitoba**

leaf roller: **Moth**

leafhopper: **Bug; Grape; Insect Pests; Parsnip; Plant Disease**

League for Human Rights: **Casgrain, Thérèse**

League for the Defence of Canada: **Chartrand, Michel**

League of Alberta Indians: **Callihoo, John**

League of Canadian Poets: **Authors & Their Milieu; Literature & Politics; Literature in English; Lowther, Patricia Louise; Rosenblatt, Joseph; Writers' Union of Canada**

League of Indians of Canada: **Native People, Political Organization & Activism**

League of the Five Nations: **Iroquois; Native People, Political Organization & Activism**

Leah Posluns Theatre: **Theatre, Multicultural**

Leaksdale, Ont: **Uxbridge**

Leamor Holdings Ltd: **Toronto-Dominion Bank**

Lear, Les: **Calgary Stampeders**

Learning, Walter: **Drama in English; Vancouver Playhouse**

lease: **Civil Code; Estate; Landlord & Tenant Law**

leasehold system: **Tenant League**

Leather Pass: **Yellowhead Pass**

leatherback turtle: **Endangered Animals; Turtle**

Leatherdale v *Leatherdale*: **Family Law**

leatherleaf: **Vegetation Regions - Cordillera**

Leavenworth, Hiram C.: **St Catharines**

Lebanese: **Arabs; Orthodox Church; Ottawa, Ont; Prince Edward Island**

Lebeau, Jean-Marc: **Dance on Television & Film**

Lebel, Andrée: **La Corriveau**

Leblanc, Hughes: **Philosophy**

Leblanc, Léopold: **Influence d'un livre**

LeBlanc, Raymond: **Ethnic Literature**

LeBlanc, Roméo: **Fisheries History**

Lebon, France: **Children's Literature in French**

LeBorgne, Reine: **Deyglun, Henri**

Lebourdais, Isabel: *R v Truscott*

Lebowitz, Michael: **Marxism**

LeCircuit: **Automobile Racing**

Lecker, Robert: **Literary Bibliography in English**

Leclair, Michel: **Printmaking**

Leclerc, Gilles: **Essay in French**

LeClercq, Chrestien: **Anthropology**

Leco Inc: **Plastics-Processing Industry**

l'Ecuyer, René: **Philosophy**

Ledge: **New Denver**

Ledingham, Robert: **Interior Design**

Ledoux, Lucie: **Children's Literature in French**

Leduc, André: **Film Animation**

Leduc, Hippolyte: **Leduc**

Leduc oilfield: **Fossil Plants; Harvie, Eric L.; Leduc; Manning, Ernest C.; Petroleum; Petroleum Industries; Pipeline; Sedimentary Rock**

Lee, Betty: **Little Theatre Movement**

Lee, Geddy: **Rush (music group)**

Lee, James Paris: **Firearm**

Lee, R.B.: **Anthropology**

Lee, Robert: **Iron & Steel Industry**

Lee, Thomas E.: **Norse Voyages**

Lee-Enfield rifle: **Armaments; Armed Forces - Militia & Army; Firearm**

Leech River gold flurry: **Photography**

Leechman, J. Douglas: **Archaeology; Dictionary**

leek: **Vegetable**

Lees, J.A.: **Exploration & Travel Literature in English**

Leese, Elizabeth: **Dance, Modern; Dance Education**

Leeson, Charles Roland: **Leeson, Thomas Sydney**

Leeson, John: **Oil City**

Lefebvre, Gilles: **Jeunesses musicales du Canada; Music History**

Leffingwell Crags: **Mackenzie King Island**

Lefort, Agnes: **Art Dealers; Printmaking**

Lefrançois, Alexis: **Poetry in French**

Lefroy, Mount: **Mountaineering**

Legal, Emile: **North-West Schools Question**

Legal, Roger: **Theatre, French-Language**

legal precedent: **Belcher, Jonathan; Criminal Law; Stare Decisis**

legal theory: **Jurisprudence**

Légaré, Huguette: **Theatre, French-Language**

Legault, Georges: **Philosophy**

Léger, Gabrielle Carmel: **Léger, Jules**

Léger, Viola: **Theatre, English-Language**

Legg, Stuart: **Daly, Thomas C.**

Leggo, William A.: **Desbarats, Georges-Edouard**

Legislative Assembly: **Constitution Act, 1982; Government; Provincial Government; Territorial Government**

Legislative Council: **Patriotes; Upper Canada**

legislative power: **Constitutional Law**

legislative rules: **Constitution**

legislature buildings: **Architecture; Government Building; Saskatchewan Legislative Building**

Legris, Renée: **Literature in French - Scholarship & Teaching**

legume: **Alfalfa; Clover; Endangered Plants; Faba Bean; Lentil; Lupine; Pea; Pulse Crops; Vetch**

Leica camera: **Midland**

Leigh, John: **Demasduwit**

Leighton, A.C.: **Graphic Design; Painting**

Leighton, David: **Banff Centre School of Fine Arts**

Leitinen, H.A.: **Harris, Walter E.**

LeJeune, Father: **Native People - Plateau**

Lekwiltok: **Kwakiutl; Northern Georgia Strait Coast Salish**

Lellis, Sylvio de: **Musical Instruments**

Lelouch, Claude: **Héroux, Denis**

LeMaich, Sue: **Billiards**

Lemaire, Jacques: **Montreal Canadiens**

Lemay, L.-Pamphile: *Evangeline*; **Literature in French; Poetry in French; Short Fiction in French**

Lemay & Leclerc: **Religious Building**

Lemieux, Germain: **Children's Literature in French; Folk Music, Franco-Canadian; Folklore; Oral Literature in French**

Lemieux, J.H.: **Jeunesses musicales du Canada**

Lemieux, Jacqueline: **Theatre Ballet of Canada**

Lemire, Maurice: **Essay in French**

Lemoine, Wilfrid: **Poetry in French**

Lemon, Frank: **Lost Lemon Mine**

Lemon Creek, BC: **Slocan**

Lemonde, Paul: **Frappier, Armand**

LeMoyne, James MacPherson: **La Corriveau**

Lenarduzzi, Bobby: **Soccer**

Lenarduzzi, Sam: **Soccer**

Leney, William S.: **Printmaking**

L'Enjoleur: **Lévesque, Jean-Louis**

Lennox, Charles Gordon: **Lennoxville**

Lennox, E.J.: **Architectural Styles; Architecture, Development; Toronto City Hall**

Lennox Island Reserve: **Prince Edward Island**

Lenoir, Joseph: **Literature in French - Scholarship & Teaching; Poetry in French**

Lentondal, Ginette: **Roux, Jean-Louis**

Leon & Thea Koerner Foundation: **Koerner, Leon J.**

Leonard, Lawrence: **Edmonton Symphony Orchestra**

Leonardville, NB: **Deer Island**

Lepage, François: **Philosophy**

LePage, Pierrette: **Mather, Bruce**

Lepage, Roland: **Tarragon Theatre**

Lepage Foundation: **Educational Foundations & Endowments**

Lépine, Alphonse T.: **Labour Party**

Lépine, Ambroise: **Nault, André; Riel, Louis**

Leprohon, J.-L.: **Leprohon, Rosanna E.**

Leprohons, Louis-Xavier: **Sculpture**

leprosy: **Chinese; Frappier, Armand; Montizambert, Frederick**

leptospirosis: **Water-Borne Disease**

L'Equille, Rivière: **Construction Industry, History**

LeRoi Mine: **Mining**

Leroux-Guillaume, Janine: **Printmaking**

LeRoy automobile: **Automotive Industry**

Les Cèdres, Rapide: **St Lawrence River**

Les Eboulements, Qué: **St Lawrence River**

Les Escoumins, Qué: **Basques**

Les Mines (Minas): **Canning; Grand Pré; Wolfville**

Les Saules: **Québec City**

Lesage, Edouardina: **Journalism**

Lesage Pianos Ltd: **Musical Instruments; Piano Manufacturing**

lesbianism: **Homosexuality; Maheux-Forcier, Louise; Rule, Jane V.; Women's Movement; Women's Organizations**

Leslie, Bailey: **Ceramics, Contemporary**

Leslie, John: **Philosophy**

Leslie, John (silversmith): **Jewellery & Silverware Industry**

Leslie & Garden: **Toys & Games**

Leslie Bell Singers: **Bell, Leslie R.**

Lespérance, Pierre: **Art Education**

Lessard, Etienne de: **Coudres, Ile aux; Ste-Anne-de-Beaupré**

Lessard, Lucille: **Archery**

lesser golden plover: **Migration; Plover**

Lesser Slave Lake Fort: **Rundle, Robert Terrill**

Lesser Slave River: **Athabasca River; Lesser Slave Lake**

Lesslie & Sons: **Coinage**

Lester B. Pearson Airport: **Architecture, Development**

Lester B. Pearson Building: **Gagnon, Charles**

Lester Pearson, Mount: **Place-names**

Lester Pearson College of the Pacific: **Downs, Barry Vance**

Letellier de Saint-Just, Luc: **Boucherville, Charles-Eugene Boucher de**

Letendre, Conrad: **Hétu, Pierre**

Letete, NB: **Deer Island**

Lethbridge *Herald*: **Alberta**

Lethbridge Irrigation District: **Oldman River**

Lethbridge Junior College: **University of Lethbridge**

Letondal, Henri: **Radio Drama, French-Language**

Letourneau, D.: **Film**

Letourneaux, J.-O.: **Book Publishing, French-Language**

Letter Carriers' Union of Canada: **Postal System**

letter of credit: **Commercial Law**

letter of marque: **Privateering**

lettering: **Germanic Fraktur & Calligraphy**

letterpress: **Print Industry**

Letters Patent: **Constitutional Law; Crown; Sovereign**

Lettres québécoises: **Literature in French - Criticism & Theory**

leukemia: **Axelrad, Arthur Aaron; Frappier, Armand**

leukotrienes: **Allergies**

Levac, Claude: **Theatre, French-Language**

Levasseur, François-Noël: **Ste-Anne-de-Beaupré**

Levasseur, Jean-Baptiste: **Sculpture**

Levasseur, Noël: **Religious Building; Sculpture**

Levasseur, Pierre-Noël: **Public Art; Religious Building**

Leveillé, Daniel: **Dance, Modern; Dance History**

Level Mountain: **Igneous Rock**

Levertov, Denise: **Poetry in English**

Lévesque, Albert: **Book Publishing, French-Language**

Lévesque, Beaubien Inc: **Lévesque, Jean-Louis**

Lévesque, Raymond: **Julien, Pauline**

Levey, James: **Hart House String Quartet**

Levi Strauss Canada Inc: **Clothing Industries**

Lévillé, Lionel: **Poetry in French**

Levine, Les: **Art, Contemporary Trends; Sculpture**

Levine, Saul V.: **New Religious Movements**

Levinge, Richard: **Exploration & Travel Literature in English**

Levitt, K.: **Economics, Radical**

Levy, Edwin: **Philosophy**

Levy, Gabriel: **Fashion Design**

Levy, Marv: **Montreal Concordes**

Levy Medal: **Foster, John Stuart**

Lewis, Glenn: **Art, Contemporary Trends**

Lewis, Ivor: **Printmaking**

Lewis, Maria: **Pacific Ballet Theatre**

Lewis Hills: **Long Range Mountains**

Lexicographical Centre for Canadian English: **Dictionary**

lexicology: **Translation**

LGL Ltd: **Gunn, William Walker Hamilton**

liability: **Delict; Torts; Traffic Law**

Liard Plain: **Rocky Mountain Trench**

libel: **Defamation; Gourlay, Robert F.; House of Commons; Journalism; Jury; Law & the Press; Newspapers; Violence; Woodsworth, J.S.**

Liberal: **Smith, Goldwin**

Liberal-Conservative Party: **Borden, Robert L.; Conservative Party; Greenway, Thomas; King, George Edwin; Macdonald, John A.; Monroe, Walter Stanley; National Policy; Province of Canada**

Liberal-Progressive Party: **Manitoba**

Liberal Reform Party: **Smallwood, Joseph R.; Squires, Richard Anderson**

liberalism: **Guibord Affair; Intellectual History; Laurier, Wilfrid; Macpherson, Crawford Brough; Nationalism; Trudeau, Pierre E.**

Liberator bomber: **Armed Forces - Air Force; Disasters**

libertarian socialism: **New Left**

libertarian tradition: **Education, Alternate**

Liberté: **St-Boniface**

Libling, Michener & Associates: **Religious Building**

Librairie de l'action française: **Book Publishing, French-Language**

Librairie St-Viateur: **Book Publishing, French-Language**

Librarie Beauchemin Ltée: **Book Publishing, French-Language**

Libre Parole: **Book Publishing, French-Language**

lichenology: **Botany History**

licorice: **Confectionery Industry**

Lidec: **Popular Literature in French**

Lidstone, Dorothy: **Archery**

Lieutenant-Governor medals: **Medal**

Lièvre, Rivière du: **Chemical Industries; Ottawa River**

life expectancy: **Aging; Death & Dying; International Economics; Native People, Social Conditions; Population**

life-support treatment: **Bioethics**

lifesaving stations: **Sable Island Horses**

Lifeson, Alex: **Rush (music group)**

Light Rapid Transit: **Urban Transportation**

light waves: **Physics; Spectroscopy**

lighter: **Shipbuilding & Ship Repair**

Lighthouse Park: **West Vancouver**

Lightstone, Pauline: **Donalda, Pauline**

lignin: **Chemistry**

lignite: **Coal; Coal Liquefaction; Estevan; Horton River; Northwest Coast Indian Art**

Ligue Anti-Alcoolique: **Temperance Movement**

Ligue des droits du français: *Action française*; **Intellectual History**

Ligue des institutrices catholiques de l'ouest: **Theatre, French-Language**

Ligue nationale d'improvisation: **Drama in French**

Ligue pour la défense du Canada: **Conscription; Laurendeau, J.-E.-André**

lilac: **Arboretum; Botanical Garden**

Lillian Massey Building: **Miller, George Martell**

Lillian Massey School of Household Science: **Benson, Clara Cynthia**

Lillooet (Indians): **Indian Art; Salish, Interior; Teit, James A.**

Lillooet Lake: **Lillooet**

Lillooet Reserve: **Salish, Interior**

lily-of-the-valley: **Lily; Poisonous Plants**

lima bean: **Vegetable**

Lime: **Popular Music**

lime: **Chemical Industries; Chemistry; Crop Research; Crops; Texada Island**

lime grass: **Weaving, Contemporary**

Limerick, Sask: **Romanians**

Limestone, Man: **Manitoba**

limnology: **Biology; Oceanography; Rawson, Donald Strathearn; Ricker, William Edwin; Vollenweider, Richard Albert**

Limoges, Camille: **Philosophy**

Limoilou: **Québec City**

limonite: **Iron Ore**

limpet: **Mollusc; Seashell**

linden: **Ornamentals**

Lindley, Harry: **Drama in English**

Lindner, Mositz: **Toys & Games**

Lindsay, A.W.: **Botany History**

Lindsay, Marie: **Cobham, Eric**

Lindsley, Halstead: **Lindsley, Thayer**

Line Creek Mine: **Sparwood**

Lineham, John: **Oil City**

linen: **Flax; Furniture, French; Pulp & Paper Industry; Quilt; Textile Industry**

linen press: **Furniture, Country**

liner: **Shipping Industry**

ling (burbot): **Fishing, Ice**

Lingan Mine: **Coal**

Linnamae, Urve: **Archaeology**

Linotype Co: **Print Industry**

linseed oil: **Flax; Vegetable Oil Industry**

Linton, George: **Hymns**

Lions, The: **North Vancouver**

Lions Gate Bridge: **North Vancouver; West Vancouver**

Lion's Head: **Bruce Peninsula**

Lipset, S.M.: **Sociology**

liqueur: **Distilling Industry**

liquid chromatography: **Chemistry Subdisciplines**

liquor: **Advertising; Alcoholism; Brandy Parliament; Bronfman Family; Christianity; Distilling Industry; Drug Use, Non-Medical; Food Legislation; Frontenac, Comte de; High Wines; Juvenile Delinquency; Medical Drug Abuse; Native People, Health; Native People, Social Conditions; Non-Medical Use of Drugs, Royal Commission on the; Northwest Coast; O'Keefe, Eugene; Prohibition; Prostitution; *Russell* Case; Smuggling; Temperance Movement; Whaling; XY Company**

liquor boards: **Distilling Industry; Hanna, David Blythe**

L'Islet, Qué: **Aide-Créquy, Jean-Antoine; Baillairgé Family; L'Islet-sur-Mer; Silver, Church**

L'Islet-St-Jean seigneury: **L'Islet-sur-Mer**

L'Islet-Station, Qué: **L'Islet-sur-Mer**

LISP: **Computer-Assisted Learning; Computer Science**

Lister, Pat: **Guitar; Musical Instruments**

Lister, Robert: **Rowan, William**

Listowel, Ont: **Place-names**

Literary Garland: **Drama in English; Leprohon, Rosanna E.; Literary Magazines in English; Literature in English; Moodie, Susanna; Poetry in English; Sangster, Charles**

Literary Guild: **Book Clubs**

Literary Miscellany: **Literary Magazines in English**

Literary Press Group: **Small Presses**

Literary Prize of Québec: **Tremblay, Marc-Adélard**

Litherland, A.E.: **Physics**

lithium: **Medical Drug Abuse; Nuclear Fusion; Québec**

lithography: **Art Education; Bayefsky, Aba; Kananginak Pootoogook; Lacroix, Richard; Printmaking**

Lithwick, N.H.: **Urban Studies**

Little Bad Man (Ayimisis): **Big Bear**

Little Billee Sketch Club: **Printmaking**

Little-Brown Canadian Children's Book Award: **Literary Prizes in English**

Little Clay Belt: **Haileybury; New Liskeard**

Little Cornwallis Island: **Cartography, History of; Zinc**

Little Current, Ont: **Manitoulin Island; Manitowaning**

Little Current Channel: **Tide**

Little Falls, NB: **Edmundston**

Little Falls (Ont): **Waterfall**

Little Gold Creek, YT: **Customs & Excise**

Little Placentia, Nfld: **Argentia**

Little Playgreen Lake: **Norway House**

Little Qualicum Falls Provincial Park: **Parksville**

Little Quill Lake: **Quill Lakes**

Little Saskatchewan Crossing: **Minnedosa**

Little Seldom, Nfld: **Place-names**

Little Shawinigan, Lac: **Shawinigan, Lac**

Little Smoky River: **Landslide**

Little Symphony Orchestra: **Medicine Hat**

Little Theatre Group: **Russell, John Alonzo**

Little Tracadie River: **Tracadie, NB**

Littler, William: **Music Criticism**

Liturgy of St John Chrysostom: **Catholicism**

Live Creek Mine: **Coal**

liverleaf: **Wildflowers**

Liverpool Bay (NS): **Liverpool**

Liverpool Bay (NWT): **Anderson River; Eskimo Lakes**

Liverpool Packet: **Privateering**

Livesay, Florence Randal: **Livesay, Dorothy**

Livesay, J.F.B.: **Livesay, Dorothy**

livestock: **Agricultural Exhibitions; Animal Agriculture; Animal Breeding; Animal Issues; Beef Cattle Farming; Couture, Joseph-Alphonse; Dairy Farming; Farm Law; Goat Farming; Hog Farming; Poultry Farming; Rabbit Farming; Sheep Farming**

livestock feed: **Apple; Barley; Beef Cattle Farming; Beet; Buckwheat; Canola; Cereal Crops; Distilling Industry; Farm Silo; Flax; Flour Milling Industry; Goat Farming; Grain Handling & Marketing; Millet; Oats; Oilseed Crops; Pea, Field; Potato; Rye; Soybean; Sunflower; Triticale**

Livestock Feed Assistance Act: **Canadian Livestock Feed Board**

Living Book: **Doukhobors**

Living Places: **Urban & Regional Planning**

Living Prairie Museum: **Manitoba**

Livingstone & Johnstone: **Clothing Industries**

Livius, Peter: **Carleton, Guy**

Llano culture: **Paleoindian**

Llewellyn, Marion: **Graphic Design**

Lloyd, Cecil Francis: **Essay in English**

Lloyd, George E.: **Barr Colonists; Lloydminster**

Lloyd Lake: **Clearwater River (Alta/Sask)**

Lloyds River: **Exploits River**

Lo, Ed: **Table Tennis**

loan: **Bank Rate; Commercial Law; Consumer Credit; Credit Unions; Educational Opportunity; Housing & Housing Policy; International Economics; Pawnbroking**

loan guarantees: **Labour Policy**

loansharking: **Organized Crime**

lobbying: **Assembly of First Nations; Cable Television; Canadian Federation for the Humanities; Continentalism; Economic Regulation; Fisheries History; Flour Milling Industry; Freedom of Information; Heaps, Abraham Albert; Lord's Day Alliance of Canada; Mental Health; Nova Scotia; Prejudice & Discrimination; Pressure Group; Prostitution; Psychology; Publications, Royal Commission on; Saskatchewan Wheat Pool; Second-Language Instruction; Voaden, Herman A.; White-Collar Crime; Women's Movement**

Lobchuk, Bill: **Printmaking**

Loblaw Groceries Co Ltd: **George Weston Ltd; Retail Trade**

Lobstick Lake: **Smallwood Reservoir**

Local Authorities Board (Alta): **Municipal Government; Urban Citizen Movements**

Local Church: **New Religious Movements**

Local Employment Assistance Program: **Labour Policy**

Local Government Boards: **Moose Jaw; Prince Albert; Regina**

Local Government Districts: **Manitoba**

local history: **Historical Societies; Oral History**

Local Initiatives Programs: **Labour Policy; Poverty; Theatre, English-Language**

local option: *Russell* Case; **Temperance Movement**

Local Prohibition case: **Peace, Order & Good Government**

Locarno Beach: **Prehistory; Vancouver**

Loch Leven reservoir: **Cypress Hills Provincial Park**

Lochhead, Douglas: **Literary Bibliography in English**

Lochleven, NS: **Inverness**

Lock, William: **Musicology**

Lock Gallery: **Art Dealers**

Lockeberg, Sigurd: **Ski Jumping; Skiing**

Lockheed aircraft: **Armed Forces - Air Force; Disasters**

lockout: **Labour Law; Strikes & Lockouts**

Lockport, Man: **Red River; St Andrews, Man**

locust: **Dawson, George M.; Grasshopper; Red River Colony**

lodgepole pine: **Banff National Park; Cypress Hills; Forest Fire; Forest Harvesting; Kananaskis Country; Mount Assiniboine Provincial Park; Pine**

Loebl, Eugen: **Roman, Stephen B.**

loess: **Aeolian Landform; Bluefish Caves**

Loft, F.O.: **Native People, Political Organization & Activism**

log booms & ships: **Forest Harvesting; Forest Harvesting; Raft; Transportation**

Logan, Harold: **Working-Class History**

loganberry: **Wine Industry**

Lögberg (The Tribune): **Icelanders**

logic: **Buddhism; Computer Science; Mathematics; Philosophy**

LOGO: **Computer-Assisted Learning**

Logos: **Catholicism**

logs & logging: **Algonquin Provincial Park; Balloon; Biomass Energy; Forest Harvesting; Forestry; Lumber & Wood Industries; Pollution; Timber Trade History**

Lohbrunner Alpine Garden: **Botanical Garden**

Loi sur le cinéma: **Film; Institut québecois du cinéma**

Lois Smith School of Dance: **Dance Education**

Lok, Michael: **Cartography, History of; Frobisher, Martin**

Lombardo, Carmen: **Lombardo, Guy**

Lombardo, Lebert: **Lombardo, Guy**

Lomonosov Ridge: **CESAR**

London, George: **Opera**

London & Gore Railroad Co: **Great Western Railway**

London & Port Stanley Railroad: **London**

London Asylum: **Bucke, Richard Maurice; Lett, Stephen; Tully, Kivas**

London Brewery: **Labatt, John**

London Canadian Investment Corp: **Gundy, James Henry**

London Dumping Convention: **Hazardous Wastes**

London Free Press: **Newspapers; Southam, William**

London Hunt Club: **Golf**

London Land Co: **Colvile, Eden**

London Life Insurance Co: **Insurance; London**

London Little Theatre: **Grand Theatre; Little Theatre Movement**

London Lords: **Jacobs, Jack**

London Regional Art Gallery: **Curnoe, Gregory R.; London**

London Regional Children's Museum: **Science Centre**

London Tecumsehs: **Baseball**

London Veterinary Correspondence School: **Veterinary Medicine, History**

Lone Pine, Hal: **Breau, Lenny**

Lonergan Research Centre: **Lonergan, Bernard**

Long, John: **Graphic Design**

Long Beach: **Pacific Rim National Park; Ucluelet**

Long Harbour, Nfld: **Newfoundland**

long-horned grasshopper: **Cricket; Grasshopper; Insect Classification**

Long Island: **Placentia Bay**

long jump: **Track & Field**

Long Lake (Cobalt Lake): **Cobalt, Ont**

Long Leg: **Dogrib**
Long Point (Nfld): **Port au Port Peninsula**
Long Point Provincial Park: **Parks, Provincial; Wildlife Preserve**
Long Pond, Nfld: **Conception Bay South**
Long Reach: **Saint John River**
Long Sault portage: **Dollard Des Ormeaux, Adam; Iroquois; Ottawa River**
Long Sault Rapids: **Rainy River Burial Mounds**
Long Spruce, Man: **Nelson River·**
long-tailed jaeger: **Arctic Animals; Jaeger**
longitude: **Astronomy; Cartography, History of; Klotz, Otto Julius; Stewart, Robert French**
Longmore, George: **Poetry in English**
Longpré, Bernard: **Film Animation**
Longpré, Catherine de: **Saints**
Longspoon Press: **Poetry in English; Small Presses**
longspur: **Bird Distribution & Habitat; Sparrow**
Longstreth, T.M.: **Children's Literature in English**
Longueuil, Qué: **Krieghoff, Cornelius D.; Longueuil, Baron de; Lower Canada; Montréal**
longwall: **Coal Mining; Ocean Mining**
loom: **Textiles, Woven; Weaving, Contemporary**
Loomer, Lorne: **Rowing**
Loram, C.T.: **McIlwraith, Thomas Forsyth**
loran: **Cambridge Bay; Cape Race**
Loranger, Francine: **Children's Literature in French**
Loranger, T.J.J.: **Federalism**
Lorcini, Gino: **Sculpture**
Lord Strathcona Memorial: **Public Art**
Lord's Day Act: **Christianity; Lord's Day Alliance of Canada**
Lord's Day Advocate: **Shearer, John George**
Lorenz curve: **Income Distribution**
Lorette, Man: **Italians**
Lorette Reserve: **Indian Art**
Loretteville, Qué: **Huron; Québec City**
Loretto Abbey: **Todd, Robert Clow**
LOREX: **CESAR; Oceanography**
Lorimer, J.: **Urban Studies**
Loring, Joshua: **Provincial Marine**
Lorne Pierce Medal: **Birney, A. Earle; Carman, Bliss; Davies, Robertson W.; Gérin, Léon; Leacock, Stephen; Literary Prizes in English; Pierce, Lorne A.; Pratt, E.J.; Roy, Gabrielle**
Lornex Mine: **Mining**
Lorrain, P.: **Physics**
Lortie, Bernard: **Front de libération du Québec**
Lortie, Jeanne d'Arc: **Essay in French**
Lotbinière, Louis-Théandre Chartier de: **Heraldry**
Lotbinière, Michel Chartier de: **Science**
Lotbinière, Qué: **Szilasi, Gabor**
Loth, Cedric: **Popular Literature in French**
Loto Québec: **Lottery**
Loucheux: **Aklavik; Arctic Red River, NWT; Fort McPherson; Old Crow; Old Crow Plain**
Louet, Lac: **Bienville, Lac**
Louis XIII of France: **Compagnie des Cent-Associés**
Louis XIV of France: **Armed Forces - Militia & Army; Beauharnois, Charles de; Callière, Louis-Hector de; Constitutional History; Demographic Data Collection; Fur Trade; Guitar; Honours; Horse; Intendant; Laval, François de; Law; Painting; Pilgrimage; Port Dover; Public Art; Sovereign Council; Truro**
Louis XV of France: **Art; Youville, Marie-Marguerite d'**
Louis XVI of France: **Painting**
louis d'or: **Coinage**
Louis Riel Métis Assn of BC: **Métis**
Louis S. St Laurent: **Icebreakers**
Louis St Laurent, Mount: **Place-names**

Louise Caroline Alberta, Princess: **Alberta; Artists' Organizations; Drama in English; Esson, James; Grant, James Alexander; Lake Louise; Lorne, Marquess of; Painting; Thoroughbred Racing**
Louiseville textile strike: **Picard, Gérard**
Louisiana: **Bienville, Jean-Baptiste Le Moyne de; Iberville, Pierre Le Moyne d'; La Salle, René-Robert**
Louisville, Qué: **Disasters**
lovage: **Plants, Native Uses**
Love, A.: **Botany History**
Love, B.I.: **Veterinary Medicine, History**
Love, D.: **Botany History**
Lovell, Jocelyn: **Burka, Sylvia; Cycling**
Lovell, John: **Literary Magazines in English**
Lovesick Lake: **Kawartha Lakes**
Lovettville, Alta: **Prairie West**
Lovin' Spoonful: **Popular Music**
Low, Colin: **Film Animation**
low pressure system: **Drought; Meteorology; Nova Scotia; Rain; Wind**
Lower, Bob: **Film, Documentary**
Lower Appalachian plateau: **Asbestos, Qué**
Lower Buckhorn Lake: **Kawartha Lakes**
Lower Canada College: **MacLennan, J. Hugh; Scott, Francis R.**
Lower Post, BC: **Kaska**
Lower Rideau Lake: **Rideau Lakes**
Lower Ship Harbour, NS: **Ship Harbour**
Lowery, R.T: **New Denver**
Lowes, Ray: **Bruce Trail**
Lowry, Margerie: **Lowry, C. Malcolm**
Lowther, Roy: **Lowther, Patricia Louise**
Loyalist College: **Belleville**
Loyalist Days: **Festivals**
Loyola College: **Concordia University**
Lozeau, Albert: **Literature & Politics; *Littérature qui se fait*; Poetry in French**
LRC train: **Railways, Contemporary**
LSAT: **Space Technology**
LSD: **Drug Use, Non-Medical**
Lubojanska, J.: **Poles**
Lucas, Alec: **Literature in English - Teaching; Short Fiction in English**
Lucas, Clarence: **Music History; Orchestral Music**
Lucas, Rex: **Company Town; Sociology**
Lucas, Rupert: **Radio Drama, English-Language**
Lucas, Steve: **Film, Documentary**
Lucerne, Qué: **Aylmer**
Luchkovich, Michael: **Ukrainians**
Lucier, Pierre: **Philosophy**
Luckenbooth heart: **Silver, Indian Trade**
Ludgate, Joe: **Salvation Army**
Ludwig, Jack: **Jewish Writing; Novel in English**
luge: **Bobsledding**
Lugg, Andrew: **Philosophy**
Luhovyj, Oleksander: **Ukrainian Writing**
Lulu Island: **Island; Richmond**
lumber: **Resource Rights; Winnipeg Commodity Exchange**
lumber camp: **Shanty**
Lumiuk: **Inuit Myth & Legend**
Lumonics Inc: **Electronics Industry**
Lumsdon, Kim: **Lumsdon, Cliff**
lunar calendar: **Moon; Religious Festivals**
lunar eclipse: **Astronomy; Cartography, History of**
Lunchbox Theatre: **Theatre, English-Language**
Lund, Blanche: **Lund, Alan**
Lund, Chris: **Photography**
Lundar, Man: **Icelanders**
Lundberg, H.: **Geochemistry**
Lundbreck Falls Provincial Park: **Parks, Provincial**
Lundstrom, Linda: **Fashion Design**
Lunenburg Bay: **Lunenburg**
lungfish: **Fossil Animals**
lungworm: **Parasitology**
lungwort: **Bluebell**
Lunn, Janet: **Children's Literature in English**
Luscar, Alta: **Fossil Plants**
Luscar Sterco Ltd: **Coal**

Lushes Bight, Nfld: **Place-names**
Lusitania: **Cunard Co**
Lussier, Denis: **Gaboury, Etienne-Joseph**
Lussier, Paul: **Printmaking**
lute: **Musical Instruments**
Luther College: **Lutherans; University of Regina**
Luther Theological Seminary: **Norwegians**
Lutheran Church of America: **Canadian Council of Churches; Danes; Lutherans**
Lutheran College: **Camrose; Norwegians; Ronning, Chester A.**
luvisols: **Soil Classification**
Luxton, W.F.: **Winnipeg Free Press**
Luxton Museum: **Harvie, Eric L.**
Lyall, Man: **Garson**
Lyall, Mount: **Oldman River**
Lybster Mills: **Textile Industry**
Lyell, Charles: **Exploration & Travel Literature in English**
Lyman Entomological Museum & Research Lab: **Entomology**
Lymbourne, Bob: **Ski Jumping; Skiing**
Lynch, Charles: **Journalism**
Lynch-Staunton Award: **Daudelin, Charles**
Lynn Lake, Man: **Manitoba**
Lynn Lake Mine: **Brown, Eldon Leslie**
Lynn Lake volcanic arc: **Geological Regions**
Lynn River: **Port Dover; Simcoe**
Lynx Lake: **Thelon River**
Lyonnais family: **Musical Instruments**
Lyric Arts Trio: **Aitken, Robert Morris; Morrison, Mary L.**
Lysenko, Vera: **Ethnic Literature**
Lysyk Inquiry: **Yukon Territory**
lythrum: **Flowers, Cultivated**

M

M. & L. Samuel, Benjamin & Co: **Samuel, Lewis**
M SAT: **Satellite Communications**
McAllister, D.E.: **Fish**
MacAlpine, C.D.H.: **Bush Flying**
McArthur, Peter: **Essay in English**
McArthur Hot Springs: **Spring**
McAulay, Malcolm: **Morrison, Donald**
McBirney, Mara: **Dance Education**
MacBride Museum: **Yukon Territory**
MacBrien, W.R.: **Armed Forces - Air Force**
McCabe, Michael: **Canadian Film Development Corp**
McCaffery, Steve: **Poetry in English**
McCain family: **Business Elites**
McCain Foods Ltd: **McCain, H. Harrison; New Brunswick**
McCain Group: **McCain, H. Harrison**
McCall, Ann: **Printmaking**
McCall, Christina: *Maclean's*; *Saturday Night*
McCall Field: **Airport Architecture**
McCalla, W.C.: **Botany History**
MacCallum, D.C.: **Medicine, History of**
MacCallum, J.M.: **National Gallery of Canada**
MacCallum, James: **Thomson, Thomas J.**
McCallum, John: **Economics**
MacCallum, W.G.: **Parasitology**
McCarter, R.: **Vancouver, Mount**
McCarter & Nairne: **Architectural Styles; Architecture, Development**
MacCarthy, Albert H.: **Logan, Mount; Mountaineering; Robson, Mount**
MacCarthy, Hamilton: **Sculpture**
McCarthy, Pearl: **Art Writing & Criticism**
McCaul, John: **Emblems of Canada**
MacClanahan, Anne: **Grenfell, Wilfred T.**
McClary, Dave: **Harness Racing**
McClary Mfg Co: **Copperware; Electrical Appliances Industry**
McClelland, John: **McClelland & Stewart Ltd**
McClelland & Goodchild Ltd: **Book Publishing, English-Language; McClelland & Stewart Ltd**
McClintock, Joel: **Water Skiing**
M'Clintock Channel: **Victoria Island**
McClung, Annie E.: **Women's Suffrage**

McClung, R. Wesley: **McClung, Nellie L.**
M'Clure Strait: **Banks Island; Island; Parry Channel**
McColl Frontenac Oil Co Ltd: **Petroleum Industries; Texaco Canada Inc**
McConnell Advertising: **Advertising**
McConnell Foundation: **Educational Foundations & Endowments**
McCool, Brian: **Music Education**
McCord Museum: **Montréal; Notman, William**
McCorkle, Donald: **Musicology**
McCormack, Ross: **Working-Class History**
McCormick, Robert R.: **Baie-Comeau**
McCormick's Ltd: **Confectionery Industry**
McCourt, Edward: *Great Lone Land*; **Regionalism in Literature**
McCowan, George: **Neptune Theatre**
McCready, Earl: **Wrestling**
McCreary, Man: **Poles**
McCullagh, George: *Globe & Mail*
McCulloch, Ernie: **Skiing**
McCulloch, Jack: **Speed Skating**
MacCulloh, Lewis Luke: **Drama in English**
McCully, Jonathan: **Fathers of Confederation**
McCurdy, F.B.: **Maritime Rights**
McCutcheon, Peter: **Guitar**
McCutcheon, Wallace: **Taylor, Edward Plunkett**
McDame, BC: **Kaska**
McDaniel, Grant: **Dance, Modern**
McDermot, Andrew: **Bannatyne, Andrew Graham Ballenden**
MacDermot, Galt: **Musical Theatre**
Macdonald, A.A.: **Fathers of Confederation**
McDonald, D.: **Wrestling**
MacDonald, D.K.C.: **Physics**
MacDonald, Daniel: **Campbell, William Bennett**
McDonald, David: **Royal Canadian Mounted Police**
MacDonald, Dettwiler & Associates: **Radar**
Macdonald, Donald: **Macdonald, William C.**
Macdonald, Ewan: **Montgomery, Lucy Maud**
McDonald, Garfield: **Track & Field**
MacDonald, George F.: **Archaeology**
Macdonald, Hotel: **Edmonton**
MacDonald, Irene: **Diving**
Macdonald, Mrs James: **Cuisine**
MacDonald, John: **Patterson, Walter; Prince Edward Island**
Macdonald, John: **Elbow**
Macdonald, Ross: **Popular Literature in English**
Macdonald Brier Tankard: **Curling; Northcott, Ronald C.; Watson, Ken**
MacDonald Building: **Miller, George Martell**
Macdonald-Cartier Freeway: **Thousand Islands; Windsor, Ont**
Macdonald College: **Agricultural Economics; Arboretum; Botanical Garden; Cameron, Thomas Wright Moir; Macdonald, William C.; Parasitology; Robertson, James Wilson; Soil Science**
McDonald Commission: **Inquiry into Certain Activities of the RCMP, Royal Commission of; Royal Canadian Mounted Police**
Macdonald Commission: **Barber, Clarence L.; Macdonald, Donald S.**
Macdonald Hall: **Macdonald, William C.**
Macdonald House (Winnipeg): **Manitoba**
Macdonald Institute: **Guelph; Literature in English - Teaching; University of Guelph**
Macdonald Manufacturing Co: **Toys & Games**
Macdonald-Stewart Art Gallery: **Guelph**
McDonald Stewart Foundation: **Educational Foundations & Endowments**
Macdonald Tobacco Co: **Macdonald, William C.**
McDonaugh, Pat: **Fashion Design**
MacDonell, Margaret: **Ethnic Literature**

McDonnell, Allan: **Shinguacôuse**
Macdonnell, Archibald: **Royal Military College of Canada**
MacDonnell, Richard G.: **Charlottetown Conference**
McDonnell Douglas aircraft: **Armed Forces - Unification; Military Aviation & Aircraft**
McDonnell Douglas Canada Ltd: **Aerospace Industry**
McDougall, Colin: **Literature in English; Novel in English**
McDougall, Duncan: **Pacific Fur Company**
McDougall, George: **Ranching History**
McDougall, Hart: **Heritage Canada Foundation**
McDougall, James: **Nechako River**
McDougall, John L.: **Renfrew**
McDougall, R.L.: **Literature in English - Teaching**
McDougall Commercial High School: **Edmonton Grads**
MacDougall Lake: **Back River**
McDougall Orphanage: **Walking Buffalo**
McDougall's Chute: **Matheson**
McDowell, Eugene A.: **Musical Theatre**
McDowell, F.D.: **Best-Sellers in English**
Mace: **A Mari usque ad Mare; Heraldry; House of Commons; Parliament, Opening of; Symbols of Authority**
McEachern, Allan: **Canadian Football League**
McEachran, J.M.: **Psychology**
Macedonian Orthodox Church: **Orthodox Church**
Macedonians: **Immigration**
McElcheran, William: **Sculpture**
McElhinney, S.: **Squash Racquets**
McEwan, John: **Sculpture**
McFadden, David W.: **Curnoe, Gregory R.; Literary Magazines in English**
McFadden Lumber Co: **Blind River**
McFarland, John I.: **McIvor, George Harold**
McFarland House: **Niagara-on-the-Lake**
McFarlane, James: **Ocean Industry**
Macfarlane, James: **Cuisine**
Macfarlane, R.A.: **Roads & Highways**
McGee, Timothy: **Musicology**
McGeer, Gerald G.: **On to Ottawa Trek; Vancouver**
McGeorge, Robert J.: **Literary Magazines in English**
McGhee, Robert: **Archaeology**
McGill, Andrew: **North West Company; Strachan, John**
MacGill, Elsie Gregory: **MacGill, Helen Gregory; Status of Women in Canada, Royal Commission on the**
McGill, James: **McGill University; North West Company**
MacGill, James: **MacGill, Helen Gregory**
McGill, John: **North West Company**
McGill Chamber Orchestra: **Brott, Alexander**
McGill Chemical Soc: **Chemistry**
McGill College: **McGill University**
McGill Conservatorium: **Music Education**
McGill Daily: **Starowicz, Mark**
McGill Daily Literary Supplement: **Kennedy, Leo; Poetry in English; Scott, Francis R.**
McGill Fence: **Early-Warning Radar**
McGill Fortnightly Review: **Kennedy, Leo; Poetry in English; Scott, Francis R.**
McGill Group: **Literature in English**
McGill Medical Museum: **Abbott, Maude E.S.**
McGill Social Science Project: **McGill University**
McGill University Arts Building: **Ostell, John**
McGill University Hockey Club: **Hockey, Ice**
McGill University Magazine: **University Magazine**
McGillite: **Mineral**
MacGillivray, Kenneth: **Roads & Highways**
McGowan, J.W.: **Physics**
McGrand, F.A.: **Humane Societies**

McGreevy, Thomas: **Langevin, Hector-L.**
McGreevy-Langevin scandal: **Tarte, Joseph-Israel**
McGregor, G.R.: **Armed Forces - Air Force**
McGregor, Gordon M.: **Automotive Industry**
MacGregor, James G.: **Autobiographical Writing in English**
MacGuigan Report (1977): **Prison**
Mach, Gerard: **Track & Field**
McHale, John: **Montreal Expos**
Machar, Agnes Maule. **Intellectual History; Novel in English**
Machault: **Diving, Underwater**
Machias Seal Island: **Bird Sanctuaries & Reserves**
Machiche, Lower Canada: **Loyalists**
machine gun: **Armaments; Bren Gun Scandal**
machine language: **Computer Science**
Machinery & Equipment Manufacturers Assn of Canada: **Construction Industry; Machinery & Equipment Industry**
McIlwraith, Jean Newton: **Drama in English; Theatre, English-Language**
MacInnis, Angus: **Ginger Group; MacInnis, Grace W.**
McIntosh, Allan: **McIntosh, John**
McIntosh, Dale: **Musicology**
McIntosh, John S.: **Musicology**
McIntosh Red apple: **McIntosh, John**
McIntyre, Colin: **Grands Ballets Canadiens**
McIntyre, James: **Ingersoll**
McIntyre, Paul: **Opera**
McIntyre Porcupine Mines Ltd: **Bickell, John Paris; Timmins**
McIntyre River: **Thunder Bay**
McIvor River: **Claire, Lake**
McJohn, Goldy: **Steppenwolf**
Mack, Theophilus: **Nursing**
MacKay, A.H.: **Botany History**
McKay, Alexander: **Pacific Fur Company**
McKay, Alexander G.: **Mediterranean Archaeology**
MacKay, Donald: **Business History**
Mackay, George Forrest: **Fraser, Graham**
McKay, Heather: **Squash Racquets**
Mackay, J.: **Poetry in English**
McKay, Jim: **Film Animation**
McKay, John: **Libraries**
McKay, Mount: **Thunder Bay**
Mackay, R.A.: **Public Administration**
Mackay, R.C.: *Mackay* **Case**
MacKay, Thomas: **Rideau Hall**
MacKay, William: **Cartography, History of**
McKay "Soles Sewing Machine": **Leatherworking**
McKean & Fairweather: **Architectural Styles**
McKee, J. Dalzell: **McKee Trophy**
McKenna, Fred: **Messer, Don, & the Islanders**
McKenna, W.J.: **Cod Liver Oil**
MacKenzie, Donald: **Pacific Fur Company**
MacKenzie, Donald: **Popular Literature in English**
McKenzie, Giselle: **Popular Music**
MacKenzie, Hugh: **Painting**
Mackenzie, Landon: **Painting**
Mackenzie, Nadine: **Children's Literature in French**
MacKenzie, Norman A.M.: **Wartime Information Board**
Mackenzie, Phillip: **Montagnais-Naskapi**
McKenzie, Roderick: *Grain Growers' Guide*
MacKenzie, Roderick: **Libraries**
Mackenzie, W. Roy: **Folk Music, Anglo-Canadian; Musicology; Songs & Songwriting**
Mackenzie Basin: **Geological Regions; Petroleum; Pond, Peter**
"MacKenzie" class destroyer: **Shipbuilding & Ship Repair**
Mackenzie Commission: **Official Secrets Act**

Mackenzie Dist: **Dease, Peter W.; Dubawnt Lake; Microblade Technology; Physiographic Regions - Canadian Shield Forest Lands; Separatism; Territorial Evolution; Vegetation Regions - Cordillera**
Mackenzie Forest Dist: **Mackenzie**
Mackenzie Hall: **Windsor, Ont**
Mackenzie Highway: **Archaeology, Salvage; Hay River, NWT; Roads & Highways**
Mackenzie River Basin: **Drainage Basin; Isbister, Alexander Kennedy; Resource Rights**
Mackenzie River Delta: **Land Claims; Mackenzie River**
Mackenzie River fur brigade: **Portage La Loche**
Mackenzie River Valley: **Hare (Indians); Land Claims; Northwest Territories; Periglacial Landform; Physical Geography**
McKeogh, Rita: **Art, Contemporary Trends**
Mackey, W.: **Oceanography**
McKillop, Brian: **Philosophy**
McKim, Anson: **Advertising**
McKim, Mead & White: **Bank Architecture**
Mackinac suspension bridge: **Huron, Lake**
McKinley, Ruth Gowdy: **Ceramics, Contemporary**
McKinnon, Alastair: **Philosophy**
MacKinnon, Archie: **Rowing**
McKinnon, Barry: **Poetry in English**
McKinnon, Catherine: **Messer, Don, & the Islanders**
MacKinnon, Colin: **Saint Francis Xavier University**
McKinnon, John: **Sculpture**
MacKinnon, Thomas: **Earnscliffe**
Mackintosh, W.A.: **Economics; Finance, Dept of**
Macklem, Michael: **Children's Literature in English**
Macklin, Madge: **Genetic Diseases**
Macklin, Sask: **Manske, Richard Helmuth Frederick**
McLachlan, Ian: **Novel in English**
McLaren, Jack: **Dumbells**
MacLaren, Roy: *Canadian Business*
Maclaren Power & Paper: **Electronics Industry**
McLauchlin, Daniel: **Arnprior**
McLaughlin, George: **McLaughlin, Robert Samuel**
McLaughlin, Robert: **McLaughlin, Robert Samuel**
McLaughlin Carriage Works: **McLaughlin, Robert Samuel; Oshawa**
McLaughlin, Elsie Motor Co, Ltd: **Automotive Industry; General Motors of Canada Ltd**
McLaughlin Planetarium: **McLaughlin, Robert Samuel; Royal Ontario Museum**
McLay, A.B.: **Physics**
McLean, A.: **Macdonald, John Sandfield**
MacLean, A.E.: **Maritime Rights**
McLean, A.J.: **Calgary Stampede**
McLean, Eric: **Music Criticism**
McLean, George: **Walking Buffalo**
McLean, Harry F.: **Merrickville**
McLean, Hugh: **Music History; Musicology**
McLean, John: **Ethnic Literature**
McLean, Kenny: **Rodeo**
MacLean, M.A.: **Vancouver**
Maclean, Neil John: **Thorlakson, Paul H.T.**
MacLean, Quentin: **Choral Music**
McLean, Ross: **National Film Board; Television Programming**
McLean Charitable Foundation: **Educational Foundations & Endowments**
Maclean Hunter Building: **Davidson, Robert C.**
Maclean-Thorlakson Surgical Clinic: **Thorlakson, Paul H.T.**
Maclean's Magazine Awards: **Literary Prizes in English**
McLeay, Franklin: **Theatre, English-Language**
MacLellan Strait: **Killinek Island**
MacLennan, J.C.: **Weights & Measures**
Macleod, Alistair M.: **Philosophy**

MacLeod, Colin M.: **Molecular Biology**
MacLeod, Donald G.: **Archaeology**
MacLeod, Jackie: **Canadian Olympic Hockey Team**
McLeod, John: **Cartography, History of**
MacLeod, John: **Molecules in Interstellar Space**
MacLeod, M.A.: **Falcon, Pierre**
MacLeod, N.A.: **Chess**
McLeod, Norma: **Musicology**
McLeod, Peter, Jr: **Chicoutimi**
McLeod, Wallace: **Armed Forces - Air Force**
McLeod, Young, Weir and Co Ltd: **Taylor, Edward Plunkett**
McLeod & Allen publishers: **Book Publishing, English-Language**
McLeod River: **Athabasca River**
McMahon Stadium: **Calgary Stampeders**
McMartin, Duncan: **Timmins, Noah A.**
McMartin, John: **Timmins, Noah A.**
MacMartin house (Perth): **Architecture**
McMaster Chamber Orchestra: **Hamilton**
McMaster Divinity College: **McMaster University**
McMaster University Health Services Centre: **Zeidler, Eberhard Heinrich**
MacMechan, Archibald: **Comparative Literature, Canadian; Essay in English; Literature in English - Teaching; Literature in English - Theory & Criticism**
McMenemy, J.: **Party System**
McMichael Collection: **Pauta Saila**
McMicking, Robert: **Overlanders of 1862**
McMicking, Thomas: **Overlanders of 1862**
MacMillan, Alexander: **Hymns**
Macmillan, Cyrus: **Children's Literature in English**
McMillan, David: **Photography**
Macmillan, Sandy: **Yachting**
MacMillan Bloedel office tower: **Erickson, Arthur C.**
Macmillan of Canada: **Authors & Their Milieu; Book Publishing, English-Language; Lee, Dennis; *National Atlas of Canada***
MacMillan Pass: **Yukon Territory**
MacMillan Theatre: **MacMillan, Ernest C.**
McMorrow, David: **Rough Trade**
McMullen, H.C.: **Calgary Stampede**
McMullen, John Mercier: **Book Publishing, English-Language; Historiography**
MacMurray, Katherine E.: **Pratt, Mary**
McMurray, William: **Fort McMurray**
McMurtry, Roy: **Constitution, Patriation of**
McNab, E.A.: **Battle of Britain**
McNair, "Buck": **Armed Forces - Air Force**
McNamara, Albert: **Art, Contemporary Trends**
MacNamara, Eugene: **Short Fiction in English**
McNaught, Kenneth: **Working-Class History**
Macnaughton, John: **Essay in English**
McNaughton Medal: **Ouimet, J.-Alphonse**
McNeil, G.: *McNeil* **Case**
McNeill, K.G.: **Physics**
MacNeish, Richard S.: **Archaeology**
McNutt, Alexander: **Nova Scotia 1714-84**
MacNutt, W.S.: **New Brunswick**
McPeek, Ben: **Opera**
McPhee, Colin: **Music History**
McPhee, Joseph: **Courtenay**
MacPherson, Fraser: **Jazz**
McPherson, Hugh: **Cod Liver Oil**
McPherson, M.: **Transportation, Royal Commission on**
McPherson Commission: **Transportation, Royal Commission on**
MacPherson Commission: **Railways, Contemporary; Transportation Regulation**
Macquarie, Lachlan: **Canada & Australia**
McQuesten, Leroy: **Forty Mile**
McRae, Robert: **Philosophy**

MacRae, Warren: **Messer, Don, & the Islanders**
McRobbie, Kenneth: *Mosaic*
McRoberts, Hugh: **Richmond**
macroeconomics: **Keynesian Economics**
Macskasy, Elod: **Chess**
Mactaggart, John: **Exploration & Travel Literature in English**
McTague, C.P.: **National War Labour Board**
Mactaquac, NB: **New Brunswick**
Mactaquac Power project: **Woodstock, NB**
Mactaquac Provincial Park: **Heritage Trail**
McTavish, Frobisher & Co: **Mackenzie, Alexander (1764-1820); North West Company**
McTavish, John G.: *Isaac Todd*; *Racoon*
McTavish, Newton: **Art Writing & Criticism; Essay in English**
McTavish Arm: **Great Bear Lake**
McTavish Reservoir Pumping Station: **Marchand, Jean-Omer**
McTeer, Maureen: **Clark, Charles Joseph**
McVicar Arm: **Great Bear Lake**
Madawaska River (NB): **Saint John River**
Madawaska River (Ont): **Arnprior; Cemeteries; McNab, Archibald; Ottawa River; St Lawrence Lowland**
Madoc, Ont: **Gold Rushes; Soapstone**
Madran, NB: **New Brunswick**
Madsen Red Lake Gold Mines: **Brown, Eldon Leslie**
madtom: **Catfish**
Mafia: **Organized Crime**
Magazine Maclean: **Langevin, André; Popular Literature in French**
Magdalen Island Co: **Grande Entrée, Ile de**
Magdalen Islands: **Lighthouses; MacEachern, Angus Bernard; Madeleine, Iles de la; Territorial Evolution; Wind Energy**
Magdalen Shallows: **St Lawrence, Gulf of**
magic: **Folklore; Religion**
magistrate's court: **Courts of Law; Nova Scotia**
magma: **Igneous Rock; Volcano**
Magnan, Charles-Joseph: **Exploration & Travel Literature in French**
magnesium: **Geological Regions; Metallurgy; Nepheline Syenite; Photography; Pidgeon, Lloyd Montgomery; Sedimentary Rock; Spring**
magnet: **Cobalt; Columbium**
Magnetawan, Ont: **Rayner, Gordon**
Magnetawan River: **Georgian Bay**
Magnetic Hill: **Moncton**
magnetic resonance: **McDowell, Charles Alexander**
magnetic tape: **Computer Industry; Computer Science; ECOLOG; Observatory; Print Industry; Video Art**
magnetite: **Iron & Steel Industry; Iron Ore; Mineral; Plate Tectonics; Prospecting**
magnetometer: **Petroleum Exploration & Production; Prospecting**
magnetosphere: **Northern Lights; Physics; Space Technology**
magnolia: **Endangered Plants**
Magog, Lake: **Mount Assiniboine Provincial Park**
Magog, Rivière: **Magog; St-François, Rivière**
Magog & Waterloo Railroad: **Magog**
Magog Cotton & Print Co: **Magog**
Magoon, H.A.: **Architecture, Development**
Magrath, Alta: **Grain Elevators**
Magyar Elet (Hungarian Life): **Hungarians**
Magyars: **Hungarians**
Maher v The Town of Portland: **New Brunswick School Question**
Maheu, Rivière: **Orléans, Ile d'**
Mahlstick Club: **Artists' Organizations; Printmaking**
mahogany: **Furniture, English, Scottish & American**
Mahogany Rush: **Popular Music**
Maid of the Mist: **Niagara Falls**
maidenhair: **Fossil Plants**

Maidstone, Sask: **Barr Colonists; Wesson, John Henry**
mail: **Allan, Hugh; Cunard, Samuel; Cunard Co; Maritime Shipping History to 1900; Postal System; Turnbull, Walter James**
mail opening: **Inquiry into Certain Activities of the RCMP, Royal Commission of; Intelligence Gathering; Privacy**
mail-order catalogue: **Advertising; Architecture, Development; Clothing; Eaton, Timothy; Furniture, Country; Postal System; School Facilities; Simpsons, Ltd; Simpsons-Sears Ltd**
Mailhot, Laurent: **Literature in French - Scholarship & Teaching**
Mailing, Phyllis: **Singing**
Maillard, Charles: **Cosgrove, Stanley Morel; Pellan, Alfred**
Maillard, Keith: **Novel in English**
Maillardville, BC: **Coquitlam**
Maillet, Andrée: *Amérique française*; **Children's Literature in French; Poetry in French**
Maillet, Marguerite: **Literature in French - Scholarship & Teaching**
Maillou, Joseph: **Maillou dit Desmoulins, Jean-Baptiste**
Maillou architectural plan: **Religious Building**
Mailloux, N.: **Psychology**
Main, O.W.: **Business History**
Main Channel: **Georgian Bay**
Mainguy Report: **Mainguy, Edmond Rollo**
Mainland Comox: **Northern Georgia Strait Coast Salish**
Mainland River: **Island Lake**
Mainmise: **Chamberland, Paul; Literary Periodicals in French; Popular Literature in French**
Mainse, David: **Evangelism**
Maison Alcan: **Affleck, Raymond Tait**
Maison Lamontagne: **Rimouski**
Maison Montmorency: **Lévesque, Georges-Henri**
Maisons du Québec: **Québec; Quiet Revolution**
Maitland, NS: *W.D. Lawrence*
Maitland River: **Goderich**
maize: **Archaic; Corn, Field; Palynology; Prehistory**
Major, Jean-Louis: **Literature in French - Scholarship & Teaching**
Major, Kevin: **Children's Literature in English**
Major, Leon: **Neptune Theatre**
Makah: **Nootka**
Makaryk, Iryna: **Ukrainian Writing**
Makivik Corp: **Inuit Tapirisat of Canada; Watt, Charlie**
Makkovik, Nfld: **Labrador Inuit**
Makwa Lake: **Loon Lake**
malacostraca: **Crustacean**
Malahat Review: **Literary Magazines in English; Literary Periodicals in English; Literary Prizes in English**
Malahat Ridge: **Malahat Pass; Victoria**
malaria: **Baldoon; Insect Pests; Medicine, History of; Parasitology; Rideau Canal; Veterinary Medicine**
Malartic, Comte de: **Malartic**
Malartic Goldfields Mine: **Malartic**
Malaspina, Alejandro: **Malaspina Expedition; Sutil & Mexicana**
Malbaie, Rivière: **La Malbaie**
Malcolm Island: **Sointula**
Malden, Upper Canada: **Girty, Simon**
Malden Asylum: **Lett, Stephen**
Malecite: **Maliseet**
Malépart, Germaine: **Gagnon, André**
Maley, S.R.: **Music Criticism**
Maligne Canyon: **Karst Landform**
Mallabar: **Stage & Costume Design**
mallard: **Cuisine; Duck**
Malle, Louis: **Héroux, Denis**
mallet: **Tools, Carpentry; Woodenware**
Mallet, Denis: **Sculpture**
Mallet, Jane: **Theatre, English-Language**
Mallet, Marilu: **Short Fiction in French**
Mallet-Paret, John: **Mathematics**
Mallette, Yvon: **Film Animation**
Mallory, J.R.: **Public Administration**
Mallorytown Glass Works: **Glass**

Mallorytown Landing: **St Lawrence Islands National Park**
Malnike language: **Africans**
malnutrition: **Medicine, History of; Native People, Health**
Malouf, Albert: **Land Claims**
Malouf, Pierre K.: **Drama in French**
Malouf Commission: **Drapeau, Jean**
"Malouidit": **Métis**
Malouin, Gérard: **Architecture**
Malouin-Gélinas, France: **Musicology**
Malpeque oyster: **Prince Edward Island**
malt: **Barley; Brewing Industry**
Maltby, W.L.: **Snowshoeing**
Malton, Ont: **Gordon, Crawford**
Malvina Collette, Sister: **Theatre, French-Language**
Mamas & the Papas: **Popular Music**
Mamawi Lake: **Claire, Lake**
mammalogy: **Cowan, Ian McTaggart; Fuller, William Albert; Tyrrell, Joseph B.**
mammoth: **Bluefish Caves; Paleoindian; Prehistory**
Man & Biosphere Program: **Environment; Parks, National**
Man & His World: **Expo 67; Montréal**
Man Drowned Himself Lake: **Place-names**
Man O'War Peak: **Labrador Highlands**
Manalta Coal Ltd: **Coal; Mannix, Frederick C.**
Mandarin language: **Ethnic Languages**
"mandarins": **Bureaucracy & Formal Organization**
mandatory supervision: **Probation & Parole**
Mandryka, Mykyta: **Ukrainian Writing**
M&S Coal Co: **Coal**
Mandy Mine: **Mineral Resources**
Manesokanjik Museum: **Lac-Mégantic**
manganese: **Ceramics; Cobalt; Iron & Steel Industry; Ocean Mining**
mange: **Mite; Veterinary Medicine, History**
Manhattan: **Arctic Exploration; Dunbar, I. Moira; Northwest Passage**
mania: **Psychiatry**
Maniates, M. Rika: **Musicology**
Manifest Destiny: **Geopolitics**
Manitoba Agricultural College: **University of Manitoba**
Manitoba Arts Council: **Manitoba; Manitoba Theatre Centre**
Manitoba Cat Club: **Cat**
Manitoba Centennial Concert Hall: **Winnipeg Symphony Orchestra**
Manitoba College: **Methodism; Patrick, William; University of Manitoba; University of Winnipeg**
Manitoba College of Pharmacy: **University of Manitoba**
Manitoba Council of Industry: **Gordon, Charles W.**
Manitoba Court of Appeal: **Constitution, Patriation of; Obscenity**
Manitoba Escarpment: **McLearn, Frank Harris; Physiographic Regions - Interior Plains; Riding Mountain National Park; Winnipegosis, Lake**
Manitoba Farm Bureau: **United Farmers of Manitoba**
Manitoba Federation of Agriculture: **United Farmers of Manitoba**
Manitoba Federation of the Visually Handicapped: **Blindness & Visual Impairment**
Manitoba Flood Agreement: **Land Claims**
Manitoba Forestry Resources Ltd: **The Pas**
Manitoba Free Press: **Dexter, A. Grant; Ferguson, George Victor; *Fort Frances Case*; Hayes, Kate S.; Sifton, Clifford; Spry, Graham; *Winnipeg Free Press***
Manitoba Government Telephones: **Dagger, Francis; Manitoba**
Manitoba Grain Act: **Canadian Pacific Railway; Grain Growers' Associations; Partridge, Edward A.**

Manitoba Grain Growers' Assn: **Grain Growers' Associations; Social Gospel; United Farmers of Manitoba**
Manitoba Highland Gathering: **Selkirk**
Manitoba Horticultural Society: **Skinner, Frank Leith**
Manitoba Hydro: **Electric Utilities; Manitoba; Southern Indian Lake**
Manitoba Indian Assn: **Prince, Thomas George**
Manitoba Indian Brotherhood: **Vesak, Norbert**
Manitoba Institute of Agrologists: **Stefansson, Baldur Rosmund**
Manitoba Legislature Building: **Government Building**
Manitoba maple: **Manitoba; Weeds**
Manitoba Medical College: **University of Manitoba**
Manitoba Métis Federation: **Métis**
Manitoba Museum of Man & Nature: **Diorama; *Nonsuch*; Science; Winnipeg**
Manitoba Music Festival: **Winnipeg**
Manitoba Opera Assn: **Opera; Winnipeg Symphony Orchestra**
Manitoba Plain: **Physiographic Regions - Interior Plains**
Manitoba Rolling Mills (Canada) Ltd: **Iron & Steel Industry; Selkirk**
Manitoba School for the Deaf: **Winnipeg**
Manitoba Society of Art: **Printmaking**
Manitoba Society of Artists: **Artists' Organizations**
Manitoba Stampede & Agricultural Exhibition: **Morris**
Manitoba Sugar Beet Growers Assn: **Siemens, Jacob John**
Manitoba Telephone System: **Manitoba; Mavor, James; Roblin, Rodmond P.; Telephones; TransCanada Telephone System**
Manitoba Theatre Workshop: **Theatre for Young Audiences**
Manitobah colony: **Portage la Prairie**
Manitoba's Mock Parliament: **Hind, E. Cora**
Manitou, Man: **McClung, Nellie L.**
Manitou Falls: **Seul, Lac**
Manitou Theatre: **Theatre, Multicultural**
Manitoulin, Lake: **Georgian Bay**
Manitouwabing, Lake: **Byelorussians**
Manitouwadge, Ont: **Gemstone**
Maniwaki, Qué: **Place-names**
Mann, A.: *Mann v the Queen*
Mann, Tony: **Graphic Design**
Mann Cup: **Canadian Lacrosse Hall of Fame; Lacrosse**
Manning, Edward: **Chamber Music**
Manning, Jo: **Printmaking**
Manning, Les: **Ceramics, Contemporary**
Manning Provincial Park: **Allison Pass; Cascade Mountains; Hope**
Mannix Co Ltd: **Lougheed, E. Peter; Mannix, Frederick C.**
Mannville, Alta: **Reid, Richard Gavin**
Manny, Louise: **Musicology**
Manny's Combined Reaper & Mower: **Agricultural Implements**
Manoir Richelieu: **La Malbaie**
Manor, The: **Grimsby**
Manouane, Qué: **Attikamek; St-Maurice, Rivière**
Manouane, Rivière: **Attikamek; St-Maurice, Rivière**
Manouane Band: **Attikamek**
Manpower & Immigration, Dept of: **Immigration Policy; Kent, Tom; Labour Policy**
Mansfield-Denham General: **Rubber Products Industry**
Mansfield Rubber Co: **Rubber Products Industry**
manslaughter: **Courts of Law; Homicide**
Mansouri, Lotfi: **Canadian Opera Co**
Mantario wilderness trail: **Whiteshell Provincial Park**
Mantell, Robert: **Theatre, English-Language**
mantid (mantis): **Insect Classification**
mantle lamp: **Lighthouses; Lighting**
Manual Construction Co: **Toys & Games**
manual training: **Education, Technical; Hughes, James Laughlin**

Manuel, Richard: **Band, The**
Manuels, Nfld: **Conception Bay South**
Manufacturer's Life Insurance Building (Toronto): **Sproatt and Rolph**
Manufacturers Life Insurance Co: **Literary Prizes in English; Macdonald, John A.**
Manufacturing Design Centre: **New Brunswick Research & Productivity Council**
manure: **Animal Agriculture; Biomass Energy**
Manville, John: **Asbestos, Qué**
Manyberries, Alta: **Research Stations, Agricultural**
Maoism: **Marxism**
MAPL code: **Recording Industry**
Maple Grove, Qué: **Hewton, Randolph Stanley**
maple leaf emblem: **Coinage; Decorations for Bravery; Emblems of Canada; Flag Debate; Folk Art; Logo; Silver, Domestic; Toronto Maple Leafs**
Maple Leaf Gardens: **Bickell, John Paris; Hewitt, Foster; Smythe, Constantine Falkland Cary**
Maple Leaf Hotel: **Connors, "Stompin' Tom"**
Maple-Meadows Industrial Park: **Maple Ridge**
maple sugar mold: **Woodenware**
maple syrup: **Crop Research; Festivals; Forestry; Maple Sugar Industry; Nova Scotia**
maps & mapmaking: **Thompson, David**
maps & mapping: **Burns, E.L.M.; Cartography, History of; Climate Information; Energy, Mines & Resources, Dept of; Fidler, Peter; Floods & Flood Control; Franquelin, Jean-Baptiste-Louis; Helava, Uno Vilho; Meteorology; *National Atlas of Canada*; Orléans, Ile d'; Painting; Pond, Peter; Printmaking; Québec; Remote Sensing; Weather Forecasting; Wilson, J. Tuzo**
Mara Lake: **Sicamous**
Marani, Lawson & Morris: **Bank Architecture**
Marani, Rounthwaite & Dick: **Bank Architecture; Marani, Ferdinand Herbert**
Marani & Morris: **Marani, Ferdinand Herbert**
Marathon, Ont: **Pukaskwa National Park**
"Marathon of Hope": **Fox, Terrance S.**
Marathon Realty Ltd: **Canadian Pacific Railway**
marathon running: **Long-Distance Running**
marble: **Furniture, English, Scottish & American; Laliberté, Alfred (artist); Mineral; Quarrying Industry**
March, Bill: **Mountaineering**
Marchak, Patricia: **Community**
Marchand, Clément: **Poetry in French**
Marchand, Olivier: **Poetry in French**
Marchessault, Jovette: **Novel in French; Theatre, French-Language**
Marconi, Guglielmo: **Mount Pearl; St John's; Signal Hill**
Marcotte house: **Architecture**
Marek's disease: **Veterinary Medicines Industry**
Margaree River: **Nova Scotia**
Margaret Eaton School: **Physical Education**
margarine: **Canola; Oilseed Crops; Soybean; Sunflower**
Margolin, Uri: **Comparative Literature**
Margolis, L.: **Parasitology**
Maria: **Moon**
Maria: **Catholicism**
Maria (schooner): **Sculpture**
Marian Congress (1947): **Catholicism**
mariculture: **Aquaculture**
Marie-Anne, Mother: **Saints**
Marie-Didace: **Survenant**
Marie-Léonie, Mother: **Saints**
Marie M. Maufils de St Louis, Mother: **Art Education**
marigold: **Flowers, Cultivated**
marijuana: **Drug Use, Non-Medical; Non-Medical Use of Drugs, Royal Commission on the; Organized Crime; Smuggling**
Marin, R.J.: **Postal System**

Marine, Dept of: **Fisheries History; Transport Canada; Transportation Agencies (Government)**
Marine & Fisheries, Dept of: **Armed Forces - Navy; Canadian Coast Guard; Cartography, History of; Dawson, William B.; Medal**
Marine Biological Station: **Taylor, George William**
marine biology: **Battle, Helen Irene**
Marine Building (Vancouver): **Architecture, Development**
marine chronometer: **Astronomy; Cartography, History of**
Marine Drive: **West Vancouver**
Marine Environmental Data Service: **Hydrography; Oceanography**
Marine Industries Ltée: **Locomotives & Rolling Stock**
Marine Navigation School: **Community College**
Marine Sciences Centre: **Dunbar, Maxwell John**
Marine Sciences Research Laboratory: **Memorial University of Newfoundland**
Marine Service: **Kingsmill, Charles Edmund**
marine worm: **Annelida; Berkeley, Edith Dunington**
Marino, Frank: **Popular Music**
Marion, Gilbert: **Printmaking**
Marion, Salomon: **Pewter; Silver, Domestic**
Marion, Séraphin: **Intellectual History; Literature in French - Scholarship & Teaching**
marionettes: **Daudelin, Charles; Hoedeman, Jacobus**
Mariposa Folk Festival: **Folk Festivals; McLachlan, Murray**
Marisat system: **Satellite Communications**
Maritain, Jacques: **Philosophy**
Maritime Academy of Music: **Musicology**
Maritime Archaic: **Forteau; Gemstone; Gros Morne National Park; Labrador; L'Anse Amour Burial Site; L'Anse aux Meadows; Nain; Okak; Port au Choix; Prehistory; Terra Nova National Park; Torngat Mountains**
Maritime Art: **Artists' Organizations**
Maritime Central Airways: **Aviation; Bush Flying**
Maritime Fishermen's Union: **Fisheries History**
Maritime Freight Rates Act: **New Brunswick; Regional Economics**
Maritime History Group: **Memorial University of Newfoundland**
Maritime Labor Herald: **McLachlan, James Bryson**
maritime law: **Federal Court of Canada; Law of the Sea; Shipping Industry**
Maritime Mining Record: **Drummond, Robert**
Maritime Museums: **Halifax; Vancouver**
Maritime Provinces Higher Education Commission: **New Brunswick**
Maritime studies: **Université Sainte-Anne**
Maritime Telegraph & Telephone Co: **Bell Canada Enterprises Inc; Telephones; TransCanada Telephone System**
Maritime union: **Atlantic Provinces; Gray, John Hamilton (PEI)**
Maritimes Basin: **Petroleum**
Maritimes' Forest Ranger School: **Community College; Forest Ranger**
Marjorie Lake: **Dubawnt River**
Markborough Properties Ltd: **Hudson's Bay Company**
Marker, C.P.: **Markerville**
Market Square: **Saint John**
Markevitch, Igor: **Orchestre symphonique de Montréal**
Markham, Ont: **Diving, Underwater; Motorcycle Racing**
Markham Bay: **Soapstone**
Markham wheat: **Saunders, Charles E.**
Markland: **Labrador; Norse Voyages**
Markland, NS: **Icelanders**
Markle, Andrew: **Trust Company**
Markle, Fletcher: **Literature in English; Radio Drama, English-Language**

Markle, Robert: **Drawing; Painting**
Markoosie: **Literature in English**
Marks, Joseph T.: **Union Centrals, District & Regional**
Marks & Spencer Canada Ltd: **Clothing Industries**
Marks Brothers: **Theatre, English-Language**
Markwell, Mary: **Hayes, Kate S.**
Marky, Paul de: **Peterson, Oscar E.**
Marlatt, Daphne: **Literary Magazines in English; Literature in English - Theory & Criticism; Poetry in English**
Marlboro, Alta: **Métis Settlements**
Marlborough, J.M.: **Spectroscopy**
Marlowe, Owen: **Nickinson, John**
Marlowe, Virginia: **Nickinson, John**
Marlyn, John: **Novel in English**
Marmaille: **Theatre for Young Audiences**
Marmet, P.: **Physics**
Marmette, Joseph-E.-E.: **Children's Literature in French; Novel in French; Poetry in French**
Marmette, Paul: **Railway Station**
Marmora, Ont: **Ontario**
Marmora Ironworks: **Cobourg & Peterborough Railway; Iron & Steel Industry**
Marois, Lauréat: **Printmaking**
Marois, Roger: **Archaeology**
Maronite Catholic Church: **Arabs; Catholicism**
Maroons: **Blacks**
Marpole: **Archaeology; Indian Art; Vancouver**
Marquart, Laurent: **Graphic Design**
Marquis wheat: **Craigie, John Hubert; Fife, David; Saunders, Charles E.; Wheat**
Marquise de Vandreuil: **Shipbuilding & Ship Repair**
Marr, Frances: **Adaskin, Harry**
marram grass: **Sable Island**
Marriage Act (Qué): **Family Law**
Married Women's Property Acts: **Women & the Law**
Marryat, Frederick: **Children's Literature in English; Exploration & Travel Literature in English**
Marryat, Sheila: **Radio Drama, English-Language**
Marsden, Jerry: **Mathematics**
marsh: **Annapolis Lowlands; Biogeography; Cattail; Erie, Lake; Fur Trapping, Contemporary; Grand Pré; Great Slave Lake; Holland Marsh; Manitoba, Lake; Minas Basin; Niagara Peninsula; Point Pelée National Park; South Nahanni River; Swamp, Marsh & Bog; Tantramar Marsh; Vegetation Regions - Pacific Coastal**
Marsh, Louis E.: **Lou Marsh Trophy**
marsh grass: **Furniture, French**
marsh hawk: **Hawk; Tantramar Marsh**
marsh hen: **Rail**
Marsh Point: **Hayes River; Nelson River**
Marshall, Grant: **Interior Design**
Marshall, J.S.: **Physics**
Marshallville, Nfld: **Lewisporte**
marshberries: **Cuisine**
Marshlands Reclamation Commission: **Nova Scotia**
Marsolais, Gilles: **Drama in French**
Martel, Suzanne: **Children's Literature in French; Popular Literature in English**
Martel family: **Musical Instruments**
Martijn, Charles A.: **Archaeology**
Martin, A.A.: **Printmaking**
Martin, Abraham: **Battle of the Plains of Abraham**
Martin, Carol: **Book Clubs**
Martin, Charles-Amador: **Music History; Religious Music**
Martin, Chester: **Historiography**
Martin, Felix: **Ste Marie Among the Hurons**
Martin, George: **Nicholson, Francis**
Martin, Gérard: **Literature in French - Scholarship & Teaching**
Martin, Jacqueline: **Theatre, French-Language**
Martin, Kent: **Film, Documentary**
Martin, Médéric: **Montréal**
Martin, Peter: **Book Clubs**
Martin, Peter (IOF): **Oronhyatekha**
Martin, Thomas Mower: **Printmaking**

Martin Bay: **U-boat Landings**
Martin Lake: **Martre, Lac la**
Martin-Orme pianos: **Piano Manufacturing**
Martineau, Edouard Alfred: **Toys & Games**
Martineau, Jean: **Bloc populaire canadien**
Martínez, Erik: **Ethnic Literature**
Martin's Point: **Campbellton, NB**
martyrs: **Jogues, Isaac; Saints; Scott, Thomas; Upper Canada**
Martyrs Shrine: **Brébeuf, Jean de; Ste Marie Among the Hurons**
Marvijenko, Teodor: **Ukrainian Writing**
Marxist-Leninism: **Literature in French; Marxism; New Left; *Parti pris***
Marxist-Socialism: **Communist Party of Canada**
Marxist Studies Centre: **Ryerson, Stanley B.**
Mary River: **Lancaster Sound**
Mary-Rousselière, Guy: **Archaeology**
Mary's Bay, NS: **Aquaculture**
Marystown, Ont: **Lucan**
Marysville, NB: **Fredericton**
Mascall, Jennifer: **Dance, Modern**
maser: **Laser**
maskinonge: **Muskellunge**
Maskinongé, Rivière: **St Lawrence Lowland**
Mason, S.G.: **Chemistry Subdisciplines**
Mason, "Skookum" Jim: **Carcross**
Mason & Risch Ltd: **Piano Manufacturing**
Masonic Hall: **Barkerville**
Masonic Memorial Temple (Montréal): **Archibald, John Smith**
masonry: **Architecture, Development; Bridges; Construction Industry, History**
masque: **Theatre, English-Language**
Mass: **Catholicism; Classics**
mass: **Weights & Measures**
mass media: **Art, Contemporary Trends; Communication Studies; Communications; Continentalism; Journalism; McLuhan, H. Marshall; Media Ownership; Native People, Communications; Native People, Political Organization & Activism; Politics & the Media; Radio Programming; Science & Society; Television Programming; Women's Movement**
Mass Media, Special Committee on the: **Davey, Keith; Magazines**
mass spectrometry: **McDowell, Charles Alexander**
massage parlor: **Prostitution**
Massassauga rattlesnake: **Georgian Bay Islands National Park; Rattlesnake**
Massawippi, Rivière: **Lennoxville**
Masset, BC: **Davidson, Robert C.; Edenshaw, Charlie; Queen Charlotte Islands**
Massett, Anthony: **Sculpture**
Massey, Alice: **Milne, David B.**
Massey, Charles Albert: **Massey, Hart A.**
Massey, Chester Daniel: **Massey, Hart A.**
Massey, Frederic Victor: **Massey, Hart A.**
Massey, Geoffrey: **Erickson, Arthur C.**
Massey, Ida: **Jewish Writing**
Massey, Walter Edward Hart: **Massey, Hart A.**
Massey Block (Winnipeg): **Browne, George, Jr**
Massey Foundation: **Architectural Competitions; Hart House String Quartet; Massey, Hart A.; Massey College; University of Toronto**
Massey-Harris Co Ltd: **Canada & Australia; Denison, Merrill; Film, Documentary; Gundy, James Henry; Massey, C. Vincent; Massey, Hart A.; Wood, Edward Rogers**
Massey-Lévesque Commission: **Art Galleries & Museums; Canada Council; National Development in the Arts, Letters & Sciences, Royal Commission on**
Massey Manufacturing Co: **Agricultural Implements; Business History; Massey, Daniel**

Massey Medals: **Architectural Competitions; Dunbar, I. Moira; Jenness, Diamond; Prus, Victor Marius**
Massey Tunnel: **Delta, BC**
Massey's Magazine: **Massey, Hart A.**
Massicotte, Edouard-Zotique: **Massicotte, Edmond-Joseph**
Master of the River: **Menaud maître-draveur**
Masters, D.C.: **Working-Class History**
Master's Gallery: **Art Dealers**
Masterworks of the Canadian Arctic: **Makpaaq, Vital**
mastitis: **Dairy Farming**
mastodon: **Paleoindian**
Matador Ranch: **Ranching History**
Matagami, Lac: **Nottaway, Rivière**
Matagami, Qué: **Urban & Regional Planning**
Matane, Qué: **Gaspé; St Lawrence River**
Matane Air Service: **Quebecair**
Matapédia Valley: **Mont-Joli; Painting**
Matawin, Rivière: **St-Maurice, Rivière**
matchlock musket: **Firearm**
materials analysis: **Franklin, Ursula Martius**
maternity benefits: **Employment Law; Postal Strikes; Status of Women in Canada, Royal Commission on the; Women's Movement; Work**
maternity care: **Birthing Practices; Women's Labour Leagues**
Matheson, John: **Flag Debate**
Matheson House: **Architecture, Development**
Mathew Moody & Sons: **Agricultural Implements**
Mathews, Brenda: **Davies, Robertson W.**
Mathews, Robin: **Canadian Studies; Literature in English - Teaching; Literature in English - Theory & Criticism**
Mathiassen, Therkel: **Archaeology**
Matière Chante: **Comtois, Ulysse**
Matinée symphoniques pour la jeunesse: **Pelletier, Wilfrid**
matrimonial property: **Family Law**
Matrix International Video: **Video Art**
Mattagami River: **Moose River**
Mattawa, Ont: **Dunlap, David Alexander**
Mattawa River: **Nipissing, Lake; North Bay**
Matthew, George F.: **Bailey, Loring W.; Science**
Matthews, Don: **British Columbia Lions**
Matthews, George: **Printmaking**
Matthews, J.: **Literature in English - Teaching**
Matthews, Ralph: **Community**
Matton, Roger: **Aubut, Françoise; Choral Music; Orchestral Music**
Maud, Ralph: **Hill-Tout, Charles**
Maugey, Axel: **Essay in French**
Maungwudaus: **Henry, George**
Maurault, Olivier: **Autobiographical Writing in French; Essay in French**
Maurault, Thomas: **Gill, Charles**
Maurer, Armand: **Philosophy**
Mauretania: **Cunard Co**
mausoleum: **Cemeteries**
Mawson, Thomas: **Calgary; Regina**
Max, John: **Photography**
Max Bell Foundation: **Educational Foundations & Endowments**
Max Sauer Memorial Award: **Curtin, Walter A.**
Maxine (M.C.A. Taschereau-Fortier): **Children's Literature in French**
Maxwell, Mary: **Baha'i Faith**
Maxwell, Moreau S.: **Archaeology**
Maxwell, Roberta: **Theatre, English-Language**
Maxwell, Thomas: *Canadian Business Review*
Maxwell, William S.: **Baha'i Faith; Maxwell, Edward**
Maxwell. W.R.: **Bush Flying**
Maxwell-Chalmers Motor Co of Canada: **Chrysler Canada Ltd**
May, Derek: **Film, Documentary**
mayapple: **Wildflowers**
Mayer, Uri: **Edmonton Symphony Orchestra**
Mayer-Oakes, William J.: **Archaeology**
Mayerovitch, Harry: **Graphic Design**

Mayers, H.G.: **Tennis**
Mayfair Glass Co: **Glass**
Mayland Heights Elementary School: **School Facilities**
Maynard, Fredelle: **Ethnic Literature**
Maynard, Richard J.: **Maynard, Hannah**
Mayne, R.C.: **Mayne Island**
Mayne, Seymour: **Jewish Writing**
Mayo, Alfred S.: **Mayo**
Mayo River: **Mayo**
mayor: **Municipal Government**
Mayureak: **Qaqaq Ashoona**
Mazaredo Sound: **Spanish**
Maze, Ida: **Jewish Writing**
Mazepa, Bohdan: **Ukrainian Writing**
Mazurette, Solomon: **Music History**
Mazzoleni, Ettore: **Royal Conservatory of Music of Toronto**
MD Management Ltd: **Canadian Medical Association**
Mead, Ray: **Painting**
Meade, Edward: **Literature in English**
meadow barley: **Vegetation Regions - Pacific Coastal**
Meadow Lake Provincial Park: **Cold Lake**
Meaford, Ont: **Northern Railway of Canada**
Meager, Mount: **Geothermal Energy**
Meagher, George: **Figure Skating**
Meagher's Rock: **Disasters**
Mealing, Stanley: **Working-Class History**
means test: **Legal Aid; Social Security**
Mears, Thomas: **Hawkesbury**
measles: **Abenaki; Biological Product; Carrier; Epidemic; Kittigazuit Site; Native People, Health; Nursing; Virus; Whaling**
measures: **Arpent; Weights & Measures**
meat: **Arctic Animals; Canada's Food Guide; Food Poisoning; Goat Farming; Hare; Veterinary Medicine**
Meat & Canned Foods Act: **Meat-Processing Industry**
Meat Inspection Act: **Commodity Inspection & Grading**
Mecham, G.F.: **Arctic Exploration**
Mechanical Contractors Assn of Canada: **Construction Industry**
Mechanics' Institutes: **Adult Education; Art Galleries & Museums; Croft, Henry Holmes; Education, Technical; Foulis, Robert; Gesner, Abraham; Ketchum, Jesse; Libraries; Literature & Politics; Miller, George Martell; Perley, Moses H.; Samuel, Lewis; Smith, Titus**
Mechanic's Magazine: **Desbarats, Georges-Edouard**
Mechtler, Guillaume: **Music History**
Médaille Pariseau: **Deslongchamps, Pierre**
Médaille Vincent: **Deslongchamps, Pierre**
medal of Confederation: **Hébert, L.-Philippe**
Medal of Service: **Cowan, Ian McTaggart; Karsh, Yousuf**
Medalta Potteries: **Ceramics; Medicine Hat**
Media Club of Canada: **Canadian Women's Press Club**
Media Watch: **Women's Movement**
Medical Act (Ont): **Medicine, History of**
Medical Arts Building (Toronto): **Marani, Ferdinand Herbert**
Medical Care Act: **Health Policy**
Medical Council of Canada: **Macpherson, Cluny; Medical Education; Medicine, Contemporary**
Medical Health Officers: **Urban Reform**
medical mining research: **Bickell, John Paris**
Medical Soc of NS: **Associations**
Medical Women's International Assn: **Federation of Medical Women of Canada**
Medicare: **Douglas, T.C.; Health Policy; LaMarsh, Judy V.; Lloyd, Woodrow S.; Manning, Ernest C.; Medical Education; Minority Government; Pearson, Lester B.; Psychiatry; Transfer Payments**

medicinal plants: **Alder; Aster; Bearberry; Botanical Garden; Botany; Carrot; Celery; Dandelion; Dock; Endangered Plants; Gentian; Geranium; Groundsel; Hawthorn; Herbs; Holly; Honeysuckle; Indian Pipe; Lady's Slipper; Mint; Mistletoe; Rhubarb; Trillium; Willow**
Medicine Hat College: **University of Calgary**
Medicine Hat *News*: **Alberta**
Medicine Lake: **Karst Landform**
Meduxnekeag River: **Woodstock, NB**
Meewasin Valley Authority: **Moriyama, Raymond; Saskatoon**
Mégantic, Mont: **Astronomy; Mégantic Hills**
Mégiscane, Rivière: **Nottaway, Rivière**
Meguma Zone: **Geological Regions**
Mehta, Zubin: **Orchestre symphonique de Montréal**
Meier, Rolf: **Comet**
Meighen Island: **Arctic Exploration; Fossil Plants**
Meikle, Christine: **Education, Special**
Meiklejohn, Robert: **Interior Design**
Meilleur, J.B.: **Chemistry**
meisols: **Soil Classification**
Mékinak, Rivière: **St-Maurice, Rivière**
Melançon, André: **Film**
Melançon, Claude: **Children's Literature in French**
Melançon, Joseph: **Poetry in French**
Mélanges religieux: **Bourget, Ignace; Langevin, Hector-L.**
Meldgaard, Jørgen: **Archaeology; Inuit Art**
Meldrum, G.H.: **Tennis**
Mélèzes, Rivière aux: **Koksoak, Rivière**
Melfi, Mary: **Italian Writing**
Melgund, Lord: **Minto, 4th Earl of**
Melkite Greek Catholic Church: **Arabs; Catholicism**
Mellon Creek: **Cactus**
Mellors Fine Art: **Art Dealers**
Meloche, Edouard: **Bourassa, Napoléon**
Meloche, F.-X.-E.: **Franchere, Joseph-Charles**
Melville, Sask: **Place-names**
Membertou: **Religious Music**
Membertou Reserve: **Native People, Communications**
Memorial Cup: **Canadian Olympic Hockey Team; Lafleur, Guy D.; Sports History**
Memorial Day: **National Holidays**
memorial societies: **Funeral Practices**
Memphrémagog, Lac: **Harris, Lawren S.; Magog; St-Benoit-du-Lac**
Memramcook, NB: **New Brunswick; Theatre, French-Language**
Ménard, Jean: **Essay in French**
Ménard, René: **Music History**
Menard automobile: **Wetaskiwin**
Menchini, Camillo: **Italian Writing**
Mendel Gallery: **Architectural Competitions; Saskatoon**
Mendelssohn pianos: **Piano Manufacturing**
menhaden: **Herring**
Menier, Henri: **Anticosti, Ile d'**
Ménière's disease: **McKenzie, Kenneth George**
Menihek Lakes: **Churchill River, Lab**
Mennonite Brethren Bible College: **Wiebe, Rudy H.**
Mennonite Brethren Church: **Evangelical Fellowship of Canada**
Mennonite Brethren College of Arts: **Wilfrid Laurier University**
Mennonite Central Committee (Canada): **Brethren in Christ; Mennonites**
Mennonite Central Committee (Man): **Peace Movement**
Mennonite Children's Choir: **Choral Music**
Mennonite Relief Sale (Ont): **New Hamburg**
Mennonite Reserve: **Germans; Mennonites**
Mennonite Village Museum: **Steinbach**
mental cruelty: **Family Law**
mental illness: **Biochemistry; Bucke, Richard Maurice; Criminal Law; Hincks, Clarence M.; Psychiatry**
mental retardation: **Barr, Murray Llewellyn**

mental telepathy: **New Religious Movements**
Menten, Maude L: **Biochemistry**
Menut, Jean-Baptiste: **Pewter**
Menut, Thomas: **Pewter**
meperidine: **Medical Drug Abuse**
Merasheen Island: **Placentia Bay**
Merasty, Angelique: **Birch-Bark Biting**
Mercer, M.S.: **Mont Sorrel**
Mercer's Cove: **Brunette Island**
merchandising: **Retail Trade**
Merchant Adventurers: **Newfoundland**
merchant marine: **Maritime Shipping History to 1900; Navy League of Canada**
Merchant Marine Ltd: **Shipbuilding & Ship Repair**
Merchants Bank of Canada: **Allan, Hugh Andrew Montagu; Bank Architecture**
Merchants Bank of Halifax: **Halifax; Royal Bank of Canada**
Mercier, Lac: **Mont-Tremblant**
Mercier, Margaret: **Dance on Television & Film**
Mercier, Serge: **Drama in French**
Merck, Sharp & Dohme Award: **Deslongchamps, Pierre**
Mercure, Monique: **Beaudin, Jean**
mercury-vapour lamps: **Lighthouses; Mercury**
Mercy Bay: **McClure (M'Clure), Robert J. Le M.**
Meredith, Morley: **Singing**
mergers: **Communications; Competition Policy; Consumer & Corporate Affairs, Dept of; Economic Nationalism; White-Collar Crime; Wholesale Trade**
meridians: **Surveying**
Merit Award of Québec: **Fashion Design**
merlin: **Falcon**
Merlinguesche (Merligash, Malagash), NS: **Germans; Lunenburg**
Mermaid Island: **Thousand Islands**
Mermaid Theatre: **Theatre for Young Audiences**
Mermet, Joseph: **Poetry in French**
Merrell Dow Pharmaceuticals (Canada) Inc: **Pharmaceuticals Industry**
Merrick, John: **Architecture, Development; Province House**
Merrick, William: **Merrickville**
Merril, Judith: **Popular Literature in English**
Merritt, Catharine Nina: **Drama in English**
Merritt, William H. (1855-1918): **Merritt**
Merritton, Ont: **Chemical Industries; Niagara Peninsula; Textile Industry**
Mersey Pulp & Paper Co: **Killam, Izaak Walton; Liverpool**
Mersey River: **Liverpool; Nova Scotia**
Mervin, Glen: **Rowing**
mescaline: **Drug Use, Non-Medical**
Mesgouez, Lac: **Mistassini, Lac**
Mesozoic era: **Alberta; Conifers; Dinosaur; Foothills; Forest; Geological Dating; Geological History; Kluane Ranges; McLearn, Frank Harris; Mollusc; Paleontology**
Mesplet, Fleury: **Book Publishing, French-Language; Literature in French - Criticism & Theory; Newspapers; Print Industry**
Mess, Suzanne: **Stage & Costume Design**
Messageries Dynamiques: **Quebecor Inc**
Messner, Pat: **Water Skiing**
Meta: **Translation**
Métabetchouane, Rivière: **Saint-Jean, Lac**
metabolism: **Baer, Erich; Diabetes Mellitus; Khorana, Har Gobind; Sourkes, Theodore Lionel**
metamorphic rock: **Geological Regions; Greenstone; Physiographic Regions - Cordillera; Soapstone**
metamorphosis: **Butterfly; Frog; Moth; Northwest Coast Indian Art**
metaphysics: **Philosophy**
Metayer, Maurice: **Nanogak, Agnes**

Metcalf, Eric: **Video Art**
Metcalfe, John S.: **Grain Elevators**
Meteorological Service of Canada: **Cameron, William Maxwell; Climate Information; Denison, Francis Napier; Kingston, George Templeman; McTaggart-Cowan, Patrick Duncan; Patterson, John; Physical Geography; Stupart, Robert Frederic; Thomson, Andrew; Time**
methadone: **Medical Drug Abuse**
methane: **Coal Demethanation; Coal Mining; Energy in Society; Hydrogen; Mining Safety & Health; Petroleum; Spring**
methanol: **Biomass Energy; Chemistry Subdisciplines; Coal Liquefaction; Hydrogen; Kitimat; Laser; Peat; Petrochemical Industry**
Méthe, Louise: **Children's Literature in French**
Methodist Book & Publishing House: **Book Publishing, English-Language**
Methodist Book Room: **Ryerson Press**
Methodist Magazine & Review: **Magazines**
Methodist Thousand Island Park:. **Thousand Islands**
Methye Portage: **Portage La Loche**
methyl alcohol: **Chemistry**
Métis Assn of Alberta: **Dion, Joseph F.; Métis**
Métis Assn of NWT: **Land Claims**
Métis Assn of Saskatchewan: **Norris, Malcolm Frederick**
Métis Betterment Act (Alta): **Callihoo, John; Métis; Métis Settlements**
Métis language: **Métis Settlements**
Métis National Council: **Métis; Native Council of Canada**
Métis sur Mer, Qué: *Empress of Ireland*
metric style manual: **Council of Ministers of Education, Canada**
Metro Toronto Police Force: **Policing**
Metroland Printing & Publishing: **Torstar Corp**
Metropolitan Demonstration School of Nursing: **Nursing**
Metropolitan Life Insurance Co: **Claxton, B. Brooke; Ottawa, Ont**
Metropolitan Toronto Central Library: **Architecture, Development; Libraries; Moriyama, Raymond; Suzuki, Aiko**
Metropolitan Toronto Planning Board: **Blumenfeld, Hans**
Metropolitan Toronto Zoo: **Arboretum**
Meunier, Claude: **Theatre, French-Language**
Meunier, Jean-Guy: **Philosophy**
Mexican Light & Power Co: **Wood, Edward Rogers**
Meyer, Art: **Biomass Energy**
Meyer, E.: **Botany History**
Meyers, D.C.: **Psychiatry**
Meyers, John: **Belleville**
Meyers' Creek: **Belleville**
Mezei, Kathy: **Literature in English - Theory & Criticism; Short Fiction in English**
Meziadin River: **Nass River**
mica: **Clay; Mineral; Prospecting; Soapstone**
Mica Bay: **Shinguacöuse**
Mica Creek: **British Columbia**
Mica Dam: **BC Hydro; Columbia River**
Michaelis-Menten equation: **Biochemistry**
Michaleshi, Bernard: **Graphic Design**
Michalos, Alex: **Philosophy**
Michalowska, B,: **Poles**
Michalyshyn, Peter B.: **Folklore**
Michaud, Josette: **Children's Literature in French**
Michaud, Oswald: **Musicology**
Michel, BC: **Sparwood**
Michel Underground Mine: **Coal**
Michelin Tires (Canada) Ltd: **Nova Scotia; Rubber Products Industry**
Michelle, Chief: **Salish, Interior**
Michelot, Alexis: **Sculpture**
Michener, Mount: **Place-names**
Michener, Norah: **Michener, D. Roland**
Michener Centre: **Red Deer**
Michibata, Glen: **Tennis**
Michigan, Lake: **Cartography, History of**
Michigan Basin: **Salt**

Michilimackinac Island: **Brock, Isaac; Dulhut, Daniel Greysolon**
Michipicoten Iron Mines Ltd: **Brown, Eldon Leslie**
Michipicoten Island: **Superior, Lake**
Michipicoten River: **Superior, Lake**
Michon, Jacques: **Literature in French - Scholarship & Teaching**
Micmac dictionary & grammar: **Maillard, Pierre**
Micmac Lake: **Dartmouth Lakes**
Micone, Marco: **Italian Writing**
microbiology: **Biology; Institut Armand-Frappier; Soil Science; Stanier, Roger Yate; Veterinary Medicine**
Micromedia Ltd: **Urban Studies**
microscope: **Medicine, History of**
microsurgery: **Klein, George John; Medicine, Contemporary**
Microsystems International Ltd: **Microchips & Transistors**
microwave: **Cable Television; Communications Technology; Computer Communications; Covington, Arthur Edwin; Electrical Appliances Industry; Laser; Molecules in Interstellar Space; Physics; Radar; Satellite Communications; Spectroscopy; Sun; Telephones**
Mid-Canada Line: **Early-Warning Radar; Helicopter**
mid-Labrador ridge: **Davis Strait**
Mid-Ocean Escort Force: **Battle of the Atlantic**
Middle Island: **Ontario**
Middle Musquodoboit, NS: **Musquodoboit Harbour**
Middle River: **Westville**
Middle West Pubnico Bus Builders: **Bus Transportation**
Middleton, Christopher: **Cartography, History of**
Middletown, BC: **Sparwood**
Midland Bay: **Midland**
Midland Railway of Canada: **Cox, George A.; Grand Trunk Railway of Canada; Midland**
Midland Superior Express: **Canadian National Railways**
Midnapore, Alta: **L'Heureux, Jean-B.**
Midnight Golf Tournament: **Festivals**
Midrex process: **Sidbec-Dosco Limitée**
Midway, BC: **Kettle Valley**
Midwest Airlines Ltd: **Pacific Western Airlines Ltd**
midwifery: **Birthing Practices; Women's Movement**
Midwinter Ceremonial: **Handsome Lake Religion**
Miers-Markham Report: **Art Galleries & Museums**
Miertsching, Johann: **Exploration & Travel Literature in English**
Miette River: **Jasper; Yellowhead Pass**
Mignault, Arthur: **World War I**
migrant workers: **Bunkhouse Men; Immigrant Labour; Industrial Workers of the World**
Migratory Birds Convention Act: **Aboriginal Rights; Anderson, Rudolph Martin; Game Bird; Harkin, James Bernard; Native People, Law**
Migratory Birds Convention Treaty: **Wildlife Conservation & Management**
Miguelez, Roberto: **Philosophy**
Migusha, Qué: **Fossil Animals**
Mikkelsen, Bernie: **Billiards**
Mikyo Dorje Institute: **Buddhism**
mildew: **Fungus**
Miles, John C.: **Long-Distance Running**
Miles Canyon: **Yukon River**
milfoil: **Weeds; Yarrow**
Milford, NS: **Scott, Ephraim**
Military Colonization Co: **Rodeo**
Military General Service Medal: **Medal**
Military Hospitals Commission: **World War I**
Military Police: **Police**
Military Service Council: **Biggar, Oliver Mowat**
Military Voters Act: **Franchise; Union Government**
militia: **Aid to (or of) the Civil Power; Armed Forces; Firearm; McNaughton, Andrew G.L.; Reserve Force of Canada**

Militia & Defence, Dept of: **Armed Forces - Air Force; Internment; Ministry of Overseas Military Forces**
milk & milk products: **Advertising; Agricultural Marketing Board; Animal Agriculture; Canada's Food Guide; Consumers' Association of Canada; Dairy Farming; Dairy Industry; Goat Farming; International Trade; Sheep Farming; Veterinary Medicine**
milk vetch: **Locoweed; Vegetation Regions - Cordillera**
Milky Way: **Native People, Religion**
mill: **Construction Industry, History; Flour Milling Industry; Lumber & Wood Industries; Sawmill; Technology**
Mill, Richard: **Painting**
'mill-bill': **Flour Milling Industry**
Mill Island: **Hudson Strait**
Mill of Kintail Museum: **Almonte; McKenzie, R. Tait**
Millar, Ian: **Equestrian Sports**
Millar, James F.V.: **Archaeology**
Millar, Margaret: **Popular Literature in English**
Millar, Terrance: **Equestrian Sports**
Millau, Gonzalo: **Ethnic Literature**
Mille-Iles, Rivière des: **Ottawa River; St-Eustache; St Lawrence River**
Mille Roches, Ont: **Long Sault**
Miller, Buzz: **Ballets Jazz de Montréal**
Miller, Charles: **O'Keefe, Eugene**
Miller, E.: **Physical Geography**
Miller, Elizabeth Russell: **Russell, Edward**
Miller, Henry: **Theatre, English-Language**
Miller, Henry C.: **Book Publishing, English-Language**
Miller, J.H.: *Miller & Cockriell* Case
Miller, Joey: **Musical Theatre**
Miller, Lewis: **Lewisporte**
Miller, Mark: **Music Criticism**
Miller, Michael: **Choral Music**
Miller, Orlo: **Donnellys, The**
Miller I map: **Cartography, History of**
Miller Pickering village: **Archaeology**
Millertown, Nfld: **Lewisporte**
Milligan, Henry: **Hart House String Quartet**
Milligan, James: **Opera; Singing**
milling: **Flour Milling Industry; Metallurgy**
Mills, Alan: **Singing**
Mills, Anthony J.: **Mediterranean Archaeology**
Mills, Frank: **Popular Music**
Mills, Fred: **Canadian Brass**
millstone: **Flour Milling Industry**
Milltown, NB: **St Stephen**
Milne, David, Jr.: **Milne, David B.**
Milne, W.S.: **Drama in English**
Milnes, H.: **German Writing**
Milton, Nfld: **Newfoundland**
Milton, Ont: **Brooks, Allan Cyril; Niagara Escarpment; Thoroughbred Racing**
Milton, William F.: **Exploration & Travel Literature in English**
mime: **Shaw Festival; Theatre for Young Audiences**
Minas Channel: **Cape Blomidon; Minas Basin**
Minden, Robert: **Photography**
Miner, Horace: **Anthropology**
Miner, Patricia: **Dance, Modern**
Mineral King Mine: **Invermere**
Mineral Resources of Ontario, Royal Commission on the: **Bell, Robert**
mineral rights: *Offshore Mineral Rights Reference*; **Real Estate; Resource Rights**
mineral waters: **Soft-Drink Industry**
mineralogy: **Geochemistry; Hunt, T. Sterry; Laflamme, Joseph-Clovis-Kemner; Rock & Mineral Collecting; Soil Science**
minerals: **Apricot; Cabbage; Cherry; Food Additives**
Miners' Festival: **Cobalt, Ont**
miner's lettuce: **Wildflowers**
Miners' Memorial Museum: **Glace Bay**
Miners' Mutual Protective Soc: **Union Centrals, District & Regional**

Minerve: **Book Publishing, French-Language; Couture, Guillaume; Intellectual History; Morin, Augustin-Norbert; Newspapers; Tardivel, Jules-Paul**
Mines, Dept of: **Energy, Mines & Resources, Dept of; Geological Survey of Canada; Monture, Gilbert C.; Petroleum Research & Development**
Mines, Dept of (Ont): **Prospecting**
Mines & Energy, Dept of (NS): **Nova Scotia**
Mines & Resources, Dept of: **Energy, Mines & Resources, Dept of; Geological Survey of Canada**
Mines & Technical Surveys, Dept of: **Cameron, William Maxwell; Energy, Mines & Resources, Dept of; Geological Survey of Canada;** *National Atlas of Canada*
minesweeper: **Shipbuilding & Ship Repair**
Mingan, Qué: **Basques; Jolliet, Louis**
Minifie, James M.: **Autobiographical Writing in English**
Minimum Wage Commission (Qué): **Francq, Gustave**
minister: **Government; House of Commons**
minke whale: **Grand Manan Island; Whale**
Minni, C.D.: **Italian Writing**
minor: **Family Law**
minority language rights: **Bilingualism; Constitution Act, 1982**
minority rights: **Native People, Law**
Minstrel: **Northern Dancer; Thoroughbred Racing**
Minto: **Icebreakers**
Minto, NB: **Fossil Plants**
Minto/Chipman area pits: **Coal**
Minto Cup: **Canadian Lacrosse Hall of Fame; Lacrosse**
Minto prizes: **Figure Skating**
Minto Skating Club: **Figure Skating**
Minville, E.: **Economics**
Miocene epoch: **Crow; Fossil Plants; Paleontology, History in Canada; Vegetation Regions - Boreal Forest or Taiga**
Mipawin, Sask: **Curling**
Miquelon Lake Provincial Park: **Waskahegan Trail**
Mirabel Airport: **Airport; Airport Architecture; Aviation;** *Montcalm Construction Case*; **Montréal; Ste-Scholastique**
miracle: **Nursing; Pilgrimage**
Miracle Mart: **Steinberg, Samuel**
Mirage Bay: **Nettiling Lake**
mirages: **Meteorology**
Miransky, Peretz: **Jewish Writing**
Mirimichi, Ont: **Pembroke**
MIRV: **Armaments**
Mirvish, Ed: **Royal Alexandra Theatre**
Miscou Harbour: **New Brunswick**
Miscou Point: **Miscou Island**
Mishnah: **Judaism**
Miska, John: **Ethnic Literature**
Misquuckkey: **Muskoka Lakes**
Miss Supertest: **Boating**
Missaguash River: **Fort Beauséjour**
missiles: **Armaments; Defence Research; Disarmament; Early-Warning Radar**
Missinaibi River: **Moose River**
mission boats: **Kelly, Peter Reginald; United Church of Canada**
Mission City, BC: **Italians; Mission**
Mission Junction, BC: **Mission**
Mission Reserve: **Paull, Andrew**
Missionary Church: **Anabaptists; Bible Schools; Evangelical & Fundamentalist Movements; Holiness Churches**
Missionary Sisters of Christian Charity: **Catholicism**
Missionary Soc of the Church in Canada: **Anglicanism**
Missionary Soc of the Methodist Church: **Dunlap, David Alexander**
Mississagi Forest Reserve: **Thomson, Thomas J.**
Mississagi River: **Blind River; Georgian Bay**
Mississauga: **Indian Treaties; Kawartha Lakes; Place-names; Thousand Islands; Toronto Islands**

Mississauga, Ont: **Architectural Competitions; Botanical Garden; Cement Industry; Electronics Industry; Lighthouses; Microchips & Transistors; Ocean Industry; Ontario; Ontario Research Foundation; Postal System; Railway Safety**
Mississauga City Hall: **Architecture, Development**
Mississauga News: **Advertising**
Mississauga Symphony Orchestra: **Neel, L. Boyd**
Mississippi River (Ont): **Carleton Place; Ottawa River; St Lawrence Lowland**
Mississippian period: **Fossil Plants; Lamprey; Nova Scotia; Paleontology, History in Canada**
Missisquoi, Baie: **Fenians**
Missouri Coteau: **Physiographic Regions - Interior Plains**
Mistahimaskwa: **Big Bear**
Mistassini, Rivière: **Dolbeau; Mistassini; Saint-Jean, Lac**
Mistassini (Indians): **Saint-Jean, Lac**
Mistassini Reserve: **Mistassini, Lac**
Mitchell, Donald: **Archaeology**
Mitchell, Howard T.: **Essay in English**
Mitchell, John: **Boundaries**
Mitchell, Ken: **Drama in English; Musical Theatre**
Mitchell, Louis: **Musical Instruments**
Mitchell, Man: **Hanover**
Mitchell, Ray: **Bowling, Indoor**
Mitchell, Roy: **Theatre, English-Language**
Mitchell, Thomas: **Photography**
Mitchell Lake: **Kawartha Lakes**
Mitchell's Corners, Ont: **Northern Railway of Canada**
Mitel Corp: **Electronics Industry; High Technology; Microchips & Transistors; New Brunswick; Print Industry**
Mitiarjuk: **Ungava Inuit**
mitrewort (bishop's cap): **Saxifrage; Wildflowers**
Miville, Pierre: **Swiss**
Mix, Wolf: **Soaring**
"mixed bloods": **Métis; Norquay, John; Prairie West; Red River Colony; Red River Rebellion**
mixed marriage: **Catholicism**
MIZEX: **Arctic Oceanography**
MLW-Worthington Ltd: **Bombardier Inc**
Moak Lake: **Thompson**
Mobil Oil Canada Ltd: **Ocean Industry; Petroleum Industries**
Mobile Command: **Allard, Jean-Victor; Armed Forces - Unification**
mobility rights: **Constitution Act, 1982**
moccasin flower: **Lady's Slipper**
mock orange: **Saxifrage**
Model School: **Hughes, James Laughlin**
modems: **Electronics Industry**
Modified Mercalli Intensity Scale: **Earthquake**
Moffat, Randall L.: **Moffat Communications Ltd**
mohair: **Goat Farming**
Mohawk College Singers: **Hamilton**
Mohawk Institute: **Shilling, Arthur**
Mohawk Oil Co Ltd: **Biomass Energy**
Moher, Frank: **Drama in English**
Mohs' scale: **Mineral; Soapstone**
Mohylianka, Daria: **Ukrainian Writing**
Moira River: **Belleville**
Moirs Ltd: **Confectionery Industry**
Moisan, Clément: **Comparative Literature; Comparative Literature, Canadian**
Moisie, Qué: **Moisie, Rivière**
molacology: **Mollusc**
molasses: **Beet; Sugar Industry**
molecule: **Biochemistry; Chemistry Subdisciplines; Genetics; Physics; Plastics-Processing Industry; Spectroscopy**
Molson Breweries of Canada Ltd: **Brewing Industry; Molson, Eric Herbert; Molson Companies Ltd**
Molson Foundation: **Literary Prizes in English**
Molson Lake: **Hayes River**
Molsons Bank: **Browne, George; Turner, Philip John**

Molt, Theodore F.: **Hymns; Music History**
molybdate: **Mineral**
Moment: **Acorn, Milton**
Monahan, Hugh: **Diorama**
Monarch, Alta: **Dutch**
monarch butterfly: **Migration**
Monarch Life Insurance Building (Winnipeg): **Smith, Ernest John**
monarchy: **Crown; Sovereign**
Monck, Viscountess: **Exploration & Travel Literature in English**
Moncton Arts Society: **Artists' Organizations**
Moncton Publishing Co Ltd: **Irving Group**
Moncton *Times-Transcript*: **Irving Group**
Mond Nickel Co: **Brown, Eldon Leslie; Stanley, Robert Crooks**
Monde: **Langevin, Hector-L.**
Monde illustré: **Massicotte, Edmond-Joseph; Nelligan, Émile**
Monde ouvrier/Labour World: **Francq, Gustave**
Mondelet, Charles: **Art Education**
Moneo, Gary: **Community**
Monet *dit* Bellehumeur, Marguerite: **Riel, Louis**
Monette, A.: **Philosophy**
Money, Ken: **Astronaut**
Money Point: **Cape North**
money supply: **Monetarism; Monetary Policy**
Monfrette, Claudine: **Charlebois, Robert**
Mongeau, Diane: **Chess**
Mongrain, Claude: **Sculpture**
Monière, Denis: **Essay in French**
monk: **Christian Religious Communities; St-Benoit-du-Lac**
Monk, Allan: **Opera**
Monk, Lorraine: **Photography**
monkey: **Biological Product**
monkshood: **Flowers, Cultivated; Poisonous Plants**
Monogram Glass Co: **Glass**
mononucleosis: **Virus**
monoplacophora: **Mollusc**
monopoly: **Cadet, Joseph-Michel; Canadian Pacific Railway; Competition Policy; Consumer & Corporate Affairs, Dept of; Economic Regulation; Forges Saint-Maurice; Irving Group; Media Ownership; Public Finance; Red River Rebellion; Shipping Industry; Tahltan; Telecommunications; Utilities; White-Collar Crime; Wholesale Trade**
Monsanto Canada Ltd: **Crop Research**
Monsarrat, Nicholas: **Popular Literature in English**
monstrance: **Silver, Church**
Mont-Laurier, Qué: **St-Jérôme**
Mont-Royal, Chalet du: **Public Art**
Mont-Royal metro station: **Daudelin, Charles**
Mont St-Hilaire, Qué: **Richelieu, Rivière**
Montage: **Hardy, Hagood**
Montagnards: **Choral Music**
Montagne de la grande traverse: **Edith Cavell, Mount**
Montagne-Tremblant, Parc de la: **Mont-Tremblant**
Montague Eastern Graphic: **Prince Edward Island**
Montague Harbour, BC: **Galiano Island**
Montague River: **Montague**
Montane Forest: **Forest Regions**
Montcalm: **Icebreakers**
Montcalm, Qué: **Québec City**
Montebello, Qué: **Bourassa, Henri; Papineau, Louis-Joseph**
Monteregian Hills: **Physiographic Regions - St Lawrence Lowlands; St Lawrence Lowland**
Montessori schools: **Education, Alternate; Education, Early-Childhood**
Montgomery, Henry: **Archaeology**
Montgomery, McMichael, Common, Howard & Ker: **Forsyth, Lionel Avard**
Montgomery Mine: **Coal**
Montgomery's Tavern: **Macdonald, John A.**
Montigny, Louvigny de: **Gill, Charles**
Montmarquette, Alfred: **Folk Music, Franco-Canadian**

Montmorency, Charles de: **Montmorency**
Montmorency, Rivière: **Laurentian Highlands; Montmorency Falls**
Montmorency Cotton Co: **Montmorency**
Montmorency ice cone: **Bobsledding; Montmorency Falls**
Montour, Pierre: **Popular Literature in French**
Montpetit, André: **Popular Literature in French**
Montpetit, Edouard: **Economics**
Montpetit, Francine: *Chatelaine*
Montreal: **Disasters**
Montréal, Île de: **Island; Lachine; Mance, Jeanne; Montréal; Ville-Marie**
Montreal AAA Winged Wheelers: **Hockey, Ice; Montreal Concordes; Stanley Cup**
Montreal Alouettes: **Calgary Stampeders; Edmonton Eskimos; Montreal Concordes**
Montreal Amateur Athletic Assn: **Football; Hodgson, George Ritchie; Montreal Concordes; Rubenstein, Louis; Schneider, J.G. Albert; Snowshoeing; Sports History; Sports Organization, Amateur; Swimming, Speed; Synchronized Swimming**
Montréal & Champlain Railroad Co: **Champlain & St Lawrence Railroad; Ostell, John**
Montreal & New York Railroad: **Champlain & St Lawrence Railroad; Montreal & Lachine Railroad**
Montreal & Occidental Railway: **Ste-Agathe-des-Monts**
Montréal Antiquarian & Numismatic Society: **Historic Site**
Montreal Arena: **Donalda, Pauline**
Montréal Art Assn: **Shepherd, Francis John**
Montreal Artists School: **Caiserman-Roth, Ghitta**
Montréal Board of Trade: **Allan, Hugh; Associations; Maxwell, Edward**
Montréal Botanical Garden: **Dansereau, Pierre; Marie-Victorin, Frère**
Montreal Brass Quintet: **Chamber Music**
Montreal Chamber of Commerce: *Canadian Business*
Montréal Children's Art Centre: **Lismer, Arthur**
Montreal Children's Art Centre: **Scott, Marian Mildred Dale**
Montréal Children's Hospital: **Fraser, F. Clarke; Goldbloom, Alton; Pediatrics**
Montréal Citizens Movement: **City Politics**
Montreal City Hall Annex: **Marchand, Jean-Omer**
Montreal City Passenger Railway: **Ostell, John**
Montréal Civic Party: **Drapeau, Jean**
Montréal Conservatory of Music: **Pépin, Clermont; Tremblay, Gilles**
Montreal Cotton Co: **Valleyfield**
Montréal Court House: **Ostell, John**
Montreal Cricket Club: **Tennis**
Montreal Curb Market: **Stock & Bond Markets**
Montréal Daily Advertiser: **Canada & Australia; Newspapers**
Montréal Daily Star: **Short Fiction in English; Skiing**
Montréal Daily Telegraph: **Fielding, William S.; Graham, Hugh**
Montréal Daily Witness: **Heavysege, Charles**
Montréal Eye & Ear Institution: **Ophthalmology**
Montréal Festivals: **Pelletier, Wilfrid**
Montreal Financial Times: **Financial Times**
Montreal Football Club: **Montreal Concordes; Rugby**
Montréal Forum: **Montreal Canadiens; Morenz, Howarth W.; Richard, J.-H.-Maurice**
Montreal Fox Hunt: **Equestrian Sports**

Montréal Gazette: **Cartoons; Guèvremont, Germaine; Harvey, Moses; Journalism; McMaster, Ross H.; Newspapers; Print Industry; Southam, William; Starowicz, Mark**
Montréal General Hospital: **McGill University; Medicine, History of; Nursing; Pediatrics; Roddick, Thomas George; Vaughan, Robert Charles**
Montréal harbour: **Bayfield, Henry Wolsey; Kennedy, John**
Montréal Herald: **Macdonald, Brian; Mitchell, Peter; Newspapers**
Montréal Humanist Fellowship: **Morgentaler, Henry**
Montréal Hunt Cup: **Allan, Hugh Andrew Montagu**
Montréal Ice Carnival: **Hockey, Ice**
Montréal International Airport (Dorval): **Airport; Airport Architecture; Disasters; Montréal; Noise**
Montreal International Y' Latvians: **Volleyball**
Montréal Jazz Workshop: **Bley, Paul**
Montréal Jockey Club: **Allan, Hugh Andrew Montagu**
Montreal Ladies Archery Club: **Sports History**
Montréal Lake: **Nordicity**
Montréal Light, Heat & Power Consolidated: **Forget, Joseph-David-Rodolphe; Forget, Louis-Joseph; Holt, Herbert S.; Hydro-Québec; Sweezey, Robert Oliver**
Montréal Locomotive Works: **Locomotives & Rolling Stock**
Montreal-McGill General Hospital Research Institute: **Biochemistry**
Montréal Manic: **Montréal; Soccer**
Montreal Maroons: **Conacher, Lionel P.; Hockey, Ice; Stewart, Nelson R.**
Montréal-Matin: **Loranger, Jean-Aubert**
Montréal Medical Institution: **McGill University; Medical Education; Medicine, History of; Nursing**
Montréal Métro: **Montréal**
Montreal Monthly Magazine: **Clothing**
Montréal Municipal Library: **Desrosiers, Léo-Paul**
Montreal Nail & Spike Works: **Business History**
Montréal Neurological Institute: **Elliott, K. Allan C.; Medical Research; Penfield, Wilder G.**
Montreal Ocean Steamship Co: **Allan, Hugh; Allan Line**
Montréal Olympic Athletic Club: **Lacrosse**
Montréal Opera Company: **La Palme, Béatrice; Music History**
Montréal Philharmonic Soc: **Music History**
Montreal *Pilot*: **Hincks, Francis**
Montréal Poetry Contest: **Literary Prizes in English**
Montréal Presbyterian College: **Huguenots**
Montréal Repertory Theatre: **Allan, Hugh Andrew Montagu; Little Theatre Movement; Plummer, A. Christopher O.; Theatre, English-Language**
Montréal River: **Superior, Lake; Timiskaming, Lake**
Montréal Rolling Mills Co: **McMaster, Ross H.; Stelco Inc**
Montreal Royals: **Baseball; Harvey, Douglas**
Montréal shipyards: **Muhlstock, Louis**
Montreal Star: **Art Writing & Criticism; Cartoons; Duncan, Sara Jeanette; Dunton, Arnold Davidson; Ferguson, George Victor; Graham, Hugh; Julien, O. Henry; McConnell, John Wilson; Magazines; Newspapers**
Montréal Stock Exchange: **Dunn, James Hamet; Forget, Joseph-David-Rodolphe; Forget, Louis-Joseph; Front de libération du Québec; Kierans, Eric W.; Stock & Bond Markets**
Montreal Street Railway Co: **Forget, Joseph-David-Rodolphe; Forget, Louis-Joseph**

Montréal Symphony Orchestra: **Brott, Alexander; Clarke, Douglas William; Claude, Renée; Couture, Guillaume; Forrester, Maureen; Music Broadcasting; Orchestral Music; Orchestre symphonique de Montréal; Tremblay, Gilles**
Montréal Technical School: **Archibald, John Smith**
Montreal Telegraph Co: **Telegraph; Telephones**
Montreal Tobogganing Club: **Bobsledding**
Montréal Trades & Labour Council: **Jodoin, Claude**
Montreal Tramways: **Forget, Joseph-David-Rodolphe**
Montreal Transcript: **Heavysege, Charles**
Montreal Trustco Inc: **Power Corp of Canada**
Montreal Type Foundry: **Print Industry**
Montréal University Settlement: **Gauld, Bella Hall**
Montréal Urban Community Police Force: **Policing**
Montréal Veterinary College: **Couture, Joseph-Alphonse; Daubigny, Victor-Théodule**
Montreal Wanderers: **Hockey, Ice; Keefer, Thomas C.; National Hockey League**
Montréal Women's Liberation Movement: **Women's Movement**
Montrealer: **Lyman, John G.; Painting**
Montrock, Ont: **Iroquois Falls**
Montrose, BC: **Trail**
Monument National: **Franchere, Joseph-Charles**
Moodie, J.W. Dunbar: **Moodie, Susanna**
Moodie, John: **Roads & Highways**
Moody, Dwight L.: **Evangelism**
Moody, Moore & Partners: **Architecture, Development**
Moody, Richard C.: **Douglas, James (1803-77); Port Moody; Richmond**
Moody, Robert V.: **Mathematics**
Moody, Sewell P.: **North Vancouver**
Moody, Thomas: **Northwest Coast Indian Art**
Moodyville, BC: **Americans; North Vancouver**
Moon: **Cartoons; Jefferys, Charles W.**
moon jelly: **Jellyfish**
Moon Lake: **Saskatoon**
Moonbeam, Ont: **Small Presses**
mooneye: **Herring**
Moonie, Esmie: **Radio Drama, English-Language**
"Moonies": **New Religious Movements**
"moonshine": **Prohibition**
Moore, A.H.: **Magog**
Moore, Bob: **Long-Distance Running**
Moore, Claudia: **Dance on Television & Film**
Moore, Dickie: **Hockey, Ice**
Moore, Samuel: **Print Industry**
Moore Business Forms: **Print Industry**
moorhen: **Gallinule; Game Bird**
Moos, Walter: **Art Dealers**
Moose Fort: **Moose Factory; Troyes, Pierre de**
moose-hair embroidery: **Indian Art**
moose hide: **Fur Trade; Mountain (Indians)**
Moose Jaw CFB: **Moose Jaw; Snowbirds**
Moose Jaw Collegiate Institute: **Kirk, Lawrence Eldred**
Moose Jaw Times: **Scott, T. Walter**
Moose Mountain Provincial Park: **Parks, Provincial**
Moose River, NS: **Disasters**
Moose River Basin: **Geological Regions**
Moose River Gold Mines, NS: **Musquodoboit Harbour**
Moosehead Breweries Ltd: **Brewing Industry**
Mooseland, NS: **Musquodoboit Harbour**
Mooswa, Alta: **Lindbergh**
Moppett, Ron: **Painting**
moquette: **Furniture, French**
Moral & Social Reform Council of Canada: **Social Gospel**
Morand, Paul: **Pewter; Silver, Domestic**
Morang, George: **Historiography; Hopkins, John Castell**

Moravian Brethren: **Czechs; George, Rivière; Haven, Jens; Killinek Island; Nain; Palliser, Hugh; Ungava Inuit**
Moravian Reserve: **Zeisberger, David**
Morawetz, Cathleen: **Mathematics**
Morden, Alvery: **Morden**
Morden Research Station: **Botanical Garden; Ornamentals**
Moreau, François: **Radio Drama, French-Language**
Moreau, Louis Zépherin: **Saints**
Moreau, Michel: **Film**
Morel de la Durantaye, Oliver: **Kamouraska**
Morell, PEI: **St Peters, PEI**
Morency, Pierre: **Poetry in French**
Moresby Island: **Hecate Strait; Queen Charlotte Islands**
Moretti, Pierre: **Film Animation; Laure, Carole**
Morey, Carl: **Musicology**
Morgan, Charles: **Philosophy**
Morgan, Henry: **Oak Island**
Morgan, Henry J.: **Archives; Literature in French - Scholarship & Teaching**
Morgan, James: **Gagnon, Clarence; Morgan, Henry**
Morgan, R.M.: **Logan, Mount**
Morgan Arboretum: **Arboretum; Botanical Garden**
Morien, NS: **Nova Scotia**
Morin, André: **Industrial Design**
Morin, Jean: **Graphic Design**
Morin, Marie: **Literature in French**
Morin, Michel: **Philosophy**
Moris, Joe: **Rossland**
Morisset, Gérard: **Art Writing & Criticism**
Morisset, Louis: **Television Drama, French-Language**
Morisset, Pierre: **Rousseau, Jacques**
Morlan, Richard E.: **Archaeology**
Morley, Alta: **McDougall, Elizabeth; Ranching History**
Morley, L.W.: **Plate Tectonics**
Morley, William: **Literary Bibliography in English**
Morleyville mission: **Stoney**
Morning Chronicle: **Newfoundland**
morphine: **Drug Use, Non-Medical; Medical Drug Abuse**
morphoedaphic index: **Rawson, Donald Strathearn**
morphology: **Biology; Botany; Language**
Morphy, William: **Carleton Place**
Morris, Alexander: **Manitoba**
Morris, Andrew: **Public Art**
Morris, Charles: **Charlottetown**
Morris, Edmund: **Watson, Homer R.**
Morris, James: **Postal System**
Morris, Michael: **Art, Contemporary Trends; Painting**
Morris, Patrick: **Newfoundland; Newfoundland Acts**
Morris, Teddy: **Football**
Morris River: **Morris**
Morrisburg, Ont: **Crysler's Farm; Disasters; St Lawrence Seaway; Upper Canada Village**
Morrish, A.H.: **Physics**
Morrison, Charlotte: **Nickinson, John; Theatre, English-Language**
Morrison, J.A.: **Physics**
Morrison, J.S.: **Chess**
Morrison, Joseph W.: **Crysler's Farm; War of 1812**
Morrison, R.H.: **Ukrainian Writing**
Morrison Hershfield Ltd: **Aerodynamics**
Morrissey, Stephen: **Poetry in English**
Morrow, Pat: **Mount Everest Expedition**
Morrow, Suzanne: **Figure Skating**
Morrow, William: **Dene Nation; Land Claims**
Morse, Barry: **Shaw Festival**
Morse, Larry: **Popular Literature in English**
mortality rate: **Birthing Practices; Childhood, History of; Death & Dying; Lower Canada; Population; Public Health**
Mortier Bay: **Marystown**
Mortimer-Lamb, Harold: **Bobak, Molly J.; Photography; Vanderpant, John**
Morton, Arthur Silver: **Horse**
Morton, Desmond: **Working-Class History**
Mosaic: **Festivals**

Mosca, Angelo: **Hamilton Tiger Cats**
Moseby, Lloyd: **Toronto Blue Jays**
Moser, Leo: **Mathematics**
Mosienko, Bill: **Bentley, Maxwell H.L.**
Moslems: **Islam**
mosque: **Arabs; Islam**
Mosquito Reserve: **Assiniboine**
moss animal: **Invertebrate**
Moss, John: **Humorous Writing in English**
Mossom Boyd & Co: **Business History; Timber Trade History**
mother carey's chickens: **Storm-petrel**
mother-of-pearl: **Mollusc; Seashell**
mother's allowance: **Edwards, Henrietta L.; Norris, Tobias Crawford**
Mother's Day vigil: **Peace Movement**
Mothers' Pension Act (BC): **Pension; Smith, M. Ellen**
Mothers' Pensions Act (Man): **Social Security**
Motion Picture Bureau: **Sparling, Gordon**
Motion Picture Bureau (Ont): **Film; Sparling, Gordon**
Motocross: **Motorcycle Racing**
Motor Coach Industries: **Bus Transportation**
Motor Vehicle Safety Act: **Consumer Law; Safety Standards**
Motor Vehicle Transport Act: **Transportation Regulation**
motorcycle gangs: **Organized Crime**
Mouchalagane, Rivière: **Manicouagan Réservoir**
Moulin, Rivière du: **Chicoutimi; Orléans, Ile d'**
Moulinette, Ont: **Long Sault**
mound builders: **Archaeology; L'Anse Amour Burial Site; Linear Mounds; Morden; Prehistory; Rainy River Burial Mounds; Serpent Mound**
Mounier, Emmanuel: **Philosophy**
Mount, Balfour: **Death & Dying**
Mount Allison College: **Lockhart, Grace Annie**
Mount Allison Conservatory: **Music Education**
Mount Currie, BC: **Salish, Interior**
Mount Currie Lillooet: **Salish, Interior**
Mount Currie Reserve: **Salish, Interior**
Mount Royal Community College: **Calgary; Methodism; Music Education; University of Alberta; University of Calgary**
Mount Royal Park: **Landscape Architecture**
Mount Royal Tunnel: **Locomotives & Rolling Stock; Tunnels**
Mount St Bernard College: **Saint Francis Xavier University**
Mount Seymour Provincial Park: **North Vancouver**
Mount Sinai Hospital & Research Institute: **Bregman & Hamann; Siminovitch, Louis**
Mountain, George J.: **Bishop's University; Mountain, Jacob**
mountain cranberry: **Vegetation Regions - Cordillera**
mountain-goat wool: **Chilkat Blanket; Native People - Northwest Coast**
mountain hemlock: **Garibaldi Provincial Park; Hemlock; Strathcona Provincial Park; Vegetation Regions - Cordillera**
mountain lion: **Biogeography; Cougar**
mountain pine beetle: **Forestry**
Mountain River: **Mountain (Indians)**
Mouré, Erin: **Poetry in English**
mourning dove: **Game Bird**
Mouse Island, Nfld: **Channel-Port aux Basques**
Mouvement contemporain: **Tremblay, Michel**
Mouvement de libération populaire: *Parti pris*
Mouvement laïque de langue française: **Godbout, Jacques**
"Mouvement littéraire de 1860": **Literary Periodicals in French; Literature in French - Scholarship & Teaching**
Mouvements coopératif desjardins: **Lévis**
Mowachat: **Nootka**
Mowry Sea: **Dinosaur Provincial Park**
Moyer, Samuel: **Germanic Fraktur & Calligraphy**

Moyer site: **Longhouse**
Moyie River: **Yahk**
Moyle, R.G.: **Literary Bibliography in English**
Mozambicans: **Africans**
MPB Technologies Inc: **Physics**
Muchalat: **Nootka**
Muchalat Inlet: **Nootka Sound; Vancouver Island**
Mud Creek, NS: **Wolfville**
mud dauber: **Wasp**
mud hen: **Coot; Rail**
mud pickerel: **Biogeography**
mud puppy: **Salamander**
Muddy River Indians: **Peigan**
Muddy Water Puppets: **Hirsch, John S.**
Muggs Island: **Toronto Islands**
Muir, Alexander: **Emblems of Canada**
Mukherjee, Bharati: **Blaise, Clark; Ethnic Literature**
Mukwina: **Maquinna**
Mulcaster, Wynona: **Painting; Sapp, Allen**
mule deer: **Banff National Park; Cypress Hills Provincial Park; Deer; Elk Island National Park; Grasslands National Park; Jasper National Park; Kootenay National Park; Mount Assiniboine Provincial Park**
Mulgrave, NS: **Canso, Strait of**
Mulgrave Road Co-op: **Theatre, English-Language**
mullein: **Poisonous Plants**
Mulleir brothers: **Public Art**
Mullen, Vic: **Country & Western Music; Messer, Don, & the Islanders**
Muller, Keith: **Industrial Design**
mullet: **Sucker**
Mulloy, L.W.: **South African War**
Mulloy, William: **Archaeology**
Mulock, Cawthra: **Royal Alexandra Theatre**
Mulock, R.H. "Red": **Royal Naval Air Service**
Multi-Cultural Festival: **Thunder Bay**
Multi-Plane aircraft: **Gibson, William Wallace**
Multiculturalism, Dept of: **Bilingualism & Biculturalism, Royal Commission on**
Multilateral Trade Negotiations: **Warren, Jack Hamilton**
Mulvihill, Man: **Swedes**
Mummers Troupe: **Theatre, English-Language**
mumps: **Biological Product; Epidemic**
Muncey Reserve: **Sunday, John**
Mundy Park: **Coquitlam**
mung bean: **Vegetable**
Mungo Martin Memorial: **Hunt, Henry**
Municipal Act (Ont): **Municipal Government**
Municipal Board (Ont): **Administrative Tribunals; Metropolitan Government; Municipal Government; Ontario; Urban Citizen Movements**
Municipal Commission (Qué): **Municipal Government**
municipal corp: **Improvement District**
Municipal Corporations Act (Province of Canada): **Ontario**
Municipal Court (Halifax): **Small Claims Court**
Municipal Government Act (Alta): **Calgary**
municipal incorporation: **Yarmouth**
Municipalities Funds: **Clergy Reserves**
Munk, W.H.: **Garrett, Christopher John Raymond**
Munk's Bay: **Danes**
Munn, William A.: **L'Anse aux Meadows**
Munro, Grant: **Dance on Television & Film; Film Animation**
Munro, Hugh: **Ferguson, Robert**
Munro, John: **Silver, Church**
Munro, W.B.: **Brandy Parliament**
Munro, Waldo: **Messer, Don, & the Islanders**
Munroe, Lorne: **Music History**
Munsch, Robert: **Children's Literature in French**
Munsinger, Gerda: **Munsinger Affair**
Munsterhjelm, Erik: **Children's Literature in French**
Mur, Dan: **Ukrainian Writing**

murder: **Courts of Law; Crime; Criminal Law; Duel; Front de libération du Québec; Homicide; Jury; La Corriveau; Laporte, Pierre;** *Miller & Cockriell* **Case; Organized Crime; Piracy; Pornography;** *R v Coffin;* **Sinnisiak; Violence**
Murdochville, Qué: **Gaspé; Murdoch, James Young; Resource Towns**
Murovych, Larysa: **Ukrainian Writing**
Murphy, Reverend Arthur: **Murphy, Emily**
Murphy, Arthur: **Theatre, English-Language**
Murphy, Michael: **Fenians**
Murphy, Rowley: **Thomson, Thomas J.**
Murphy Oil Co Ltd: **Webster, Lorne Campbell**
Murray, Albert: **Golf**
Murray, Charles: **Golf**
Murray, Dave: **Skiing**
Murray, Florence: **Medicine, History of**
Murray, John: **Printmaking**
Murray, John Wilson: **Popular Literature in English**
Murray, Margaret: **Lillooet**
Murray, Margaret (Ma): **Lillooet**
Murray, Margaret Polson: **Imperial Order of the Daughters of the Empire**
Murray Bay: **La Malbaie; Notman, William McFarlane**
Murray Map: **Cartography, History of**
Murray pine: **Biogeography**
murrelet: **Auk**
Murrell, John: **Alberta; Drama in English; Theatre, English-Language**
Murtle River: **Helmcken Falls**
"muscular Christianity": **Grant, George M.; Snowshoeing**
muscular dystrophy: **Disability; Thompson, Margaret Anne Wilson**
muscular hypertrophy: **Animal Breeding**
Musée d'art contemporain: **Borduas, Paul-Emile; Comtois, Ulysse; Hénault, Gilles; Montréal; Riopelle, Jean-Paul**
Musée de la civilisation: **Québec City**
Musée de la Province de Québec: **Canadian Museums Association; Sculpture**
Musée des beaux-arts de Montréal: **Art Education; Borduas, Paul-Emile; Children's Literature in French; Contemporary Arts Society; Ferron, Marcelle; Folk Art; Gagnon, Clarence; Jones, Hugh Griffith; Libraries; Maxwell, Edward; Montréal; Newton, Lilias; Riopelle, Jean-Paul; Silver, Church; Tonnancour, Jacques Godefroy de**
Musée du fjord: **La Baie**
Musée du Québec: **Beau, Henri; Comtois, Ulysse; Gagnon, Clarence; Québec City; Silver, Church**
Musée du Saguenay-Lac St-Jean: **Chicoutimi**
Musée du Séminaire de Québec: **Légaré, Joseph; Québec City**
Musée Louis-Hémon: **Saint-Jean, Lac**
Museum Assistance Program: **Art Galleries & Museums; National Museums of Canada**
Museum of Fine Arts: **Rimouski**
Museum of Indian Archaeology: **Ste Marie Among the Hurons**
Museum of Natural History: **Regina**
Museum of Science & Technology: *Silver Dart*
Museum of the Highwood: **High River**
Museum of the History of Medicine: **Drake, Theodore George Gustavus Harwood**
Musgrave, Susan: **Children's Literature in English; Ethnic Literature**
Musgrove, Alexander: **Printmaking**
Mushuau Innuts: **Montagnais-Naskapi**
"Music by Muzak": **CHUM Ltd; Western Dominion Investment Co Ltd**
musket: **Armaments; Indian Trade Goods; Iroquois Wars; Maliseet; Pine Point**

muskmelon: **Vegetable**
Muskoka River: **Georgian Bay; Huntsville; Muskoka Lakes**
Muskoka Road: **Huntsville**
Muskrat Falls: **Hamilton Inlet**
Muskrat River: **Pembroke**
Muskwa Ranges: **Rocky Mountains**
Muslims: **Arabs; Islam**
Musquakie: **Yellowhead, William**
Musquodoboit Valley: **Clay; Musquodoboit Harbour**
Musson Book Co: **Book Publishing, English-Language**
mustard: **Condiment Crops; Oilseed Crops; Poisonous Plants; Vegetable; Vegetable Oil Industry; Weeds**
mutation: **Genetics**
mutiny: **Mainguy, Edmond Rollo**
Muttart Conservatory: **Edmonton; Janvier, Alex S.**
mutton: **Animal Agriculture; Meat-Processing Industry; Sheep Farming**
Mutual Assured Distruction: **Science & Society**
Mutual Life Assurance Co of Canada: **Insurance; Kitchener-Waterloo**
My Fur Lady: **Theatre Education**
Myatt, W.E.: **Goldsmith, Oliver**
mycology: **Biology; Botany History; Fungus; Hughes, Stanley John; Mushroom & Puffball**
mycoplasma: **Plant Disease**
Myers, Lindsay: **Racquetball**
myna: **Starling**
Mynah Birds: **Young, Neil P.**
mystacocarida: **Crustacean**
Mystery Mountain: **Waddington, Mount**
myth: **Folklore; Inuit Myth & Legend; Oral Literature in English; Theatre for Young Audiences**

N

N.E. Thing Co Ltd: **Art, Contemporary Trends; Artists' Organizations; Baxter, J. Iain W.; Painting**
Na-Dene language stock: **Anthropology, Linguistics; Native People, Languages**
Naaman, Antoine: **Literary Bibliography in French**
NABU Manufacturing Corp: **Electronics Industry**
Nachvak Fjord: **Torngat Mountains**
Nackawic, NB: **New Brunswick**
Nadeau, Robert: **Philosophy**
Nadeau Report: **Collège d'enseignement général et professionnel**
Nader, G.: **Urban Studies**
Nagano, Manzo: **Japanese**
Nahnebahwequay: **Sutton, Catherine**
Nahwitti Lowland: **Vancouver Island**
Naikoon Provincial Park: **Queen Charlotte Islands**
nail: **Architecture, Development; Furniture, French; Indian Trade Goods; Technology; Tools, Carpentry**
Nairne, John: **La Malbaie**
Nakano, Takeo: **Ethnic Literature**
Nakash, George: **Karsh, Yousuf**
naled: **Ice**
"naluyuks": **Mumming**
naming practices: **Native People - Arctic**
Nanabozho: **Nanabozo**
Nanabush: **Nanabozo**
Nanaimo Biological Station: **Berkeley, Edith Dunington; Ricker, William Edwin; Strickland, John Douglas Hipwell; Zoology**
Nanaimo Lowland: **Saanich Peninsula; Vancouver Island**
Nanaimo Petroglyph Park: **Pictographs & Petroglyphs**
Nanaimo River: **Vancouver Island**
Nanakonagos, Moses: **Morrisseau, Norval**
Nanibijou (Sleeping Giant): **Thunder Bay**
Nanisivik Midnight Sun Marathon: **Long-Distance Running**
Nanisivik Mine: **Igulik Inuit; Lancaster Sound; Nanisivik**
Nankivell, Neville J.: *Financial Post*
Nansen Sound: **Axel Heiberg Island**

Nantis, Lac: **Ungava Inuit**
Napanee, Ont: **Agricultural Implements; Architecture; Cement Industry; Daly, Kathleen Frances**
Napanee Cement Co: **Technology**
Napatchie: **Kananginak Pootoogook; Qaqaq Ashoona**
naphtha & naphthenes: **Chemical Industries; Lighting; Petroleum**
Napier, Robert: **Cunard Co**
Napierville, Qué: **Hunters' Lodges**
Nappan, NS: **Research Stations, Agricultural**
Naramata, BC: **Little Theatre Movement**
narcissus: **Flowers, Cultivated**
narcolepsy: **Medical Drug Abuse**
Narcotic Control Act: **Criminal Procedure; Family Law**
narcotics: **Drug Use, Non-Medical; Medical Drug Abuse; Organized Crime; Rivard, Lucien; Royal Canadian Mounted Police**
Nares, George S.: *Challenger* **Expedition**
Nares Strait: **Arctic Archipelago; Baffin Bay**
Narrow Lake, Ont: **Bush Flying**
Narvaez Bay: **Spanish**
Naša Novine (Our News): **Croatians**
Naše Put (Our Way): **Croatians**
Nash, Phileo J.: **Archaeology**
Nash, Ronald J.: **Archaeology**
Nasha Meta: **Catholicism**
Nashwaak River: **Fredericton**
Nashwaaksis, NB: **Fredericton**
Naskapi Band of Schefferville: **Land Claims; Montagnais-Naskapi**
Naskapi-Montagnais Innu Assn: **Land Claims; Montagnais-Naskapi**
Naskaupi River: **Melville, Lake**
Nass-Gitksan: **Tsimshian**
Nastapoca, Rivière: **Hudson Bay**
Nastapoka Islands: **Hudson Bay**
Natal, BC: **Sparwood**
NATAL-74: **Computer-Assisted Learning**
Natashquan, Qué: **French Language**
Natashquan River: **Boundaries**
Nathan Phillips Square: **Urban Design**
Nathanson, Paul: **Nathanson, Nathan Louis**
Nation: **Canada First; Smith, Goldwin**
National: **Thompson, Thomas Phillips**
National Adjustment Grants: **Dominion-Provincial Relations, Royal Commission on; Equalization Payments**
National Aeronautical Collection: **National Museum of Science & Technology; Parkin, John Hamilton;** *Silver Dart*
National Aeronautical Establishment: **Canadarm; National Research Council of Canada; Thurston, Frank Russel**
National Affairs Monthly: **Buller, Annie; Ryerson, Stanley B.**
National Alliance for Red Power: **Native People, Political Organization & Activism**
National Archival Appraisal Board: **Canadian Historical Association**
National Arts Centre Orchestra: **Applebaum, Louis; Bernardi, Mario**
National Arts Council: **Loring, Frances N.**
National Assn for Photographic Art: **Patterson, Freeman W.; Photography**
National Athletic Training Camp: **Track & Field**
National Aviation Museum: **Avro CF-100 Canuck; Avro Jetliner; de Havilland Beaver; National Museum of Science & Technology; National Museums of Canada; Turnbull, Wallace Rupert**
National Battlefields Commission: **Crown Corporation; Historic Site**
National Bell Telephone Co: **Sise, Charles Fleetford**
National Book Festival: **Literary Prizes in English**
National Breweries Ltd: **Dawes, Norman James**
National Building Code: **Building Codes & Regulations; Earthquake; Housing & Housing Policy; Safety Standards**

National Cancer Institute of Canada: **Cancer; Medical Research**
National Capital Region: **Aylmer; Gatineau; Hull; Ottawa, Ont**
National Cenotaph: **National Holidays**
National Choreographic Seminars: **Dance Education; Dance History; Strate, Grant**
National Club: **Sproatt and Rolph**
National Committee on the Church & Industrial Society: **Ecumenical Social Action**
National Competitive Festival of Music: **Music Education**
National Conference Centre: **Federal-Provincial Relations**
National Congress of American Indians: **Pan-Indianism**
National Congress of Black Women: **West Indians; Women's Movement**
National Council of Canadian Labour: **Construction Industry**
National Council of Veterans Assns: **Army Benevolent Fund Board**
National Cultural Policy: **Conservation of Movable Cultural Property**
"national day of protest": **Morris, Joseph**
national debt: **Employment & Income, White Paper on; Public Debt**
national defence: **Aerospace Industry; Armed Forces; Defence Research; Distribution of Powers; Electronics Industry; Government; Imperialism; Public Debt; Taxation; Transportation**
National Defence Act: **Armed Forces - Air Force; Cadets; Capital Punishment; Courts of Law; Militia Acts**
National Defence College: **Dunlap, Clarence R.; Kingston; Military & Staff Colleges; Simonds, Guy G.**
National Defence Headquarters: **Armed Forces - Unification; National Defence, Dept of; Ottawa, Ont**
National Design Council: **Industrial Design**
National Employment Commission: **Purvis, Arthur Blaikie**
National Employment Service: **Labour Policy**
National Energy Policy: **Geopolitics; Lalonde, Marc; National Energy Board; Nationalism; Regional Economics; Separatism**
National Energy Program: **Andre, Harvie; Business Elites; Canadian-American Economic Relations; Chemical Industries; Economic Nationalism; Energy in Society; Energy Policy; Foreign Investment; Nationalization; New Democratic Party; Notley, W. Grant; Petroleum; Petroleum Industries; Resource Rights**
National Farm Products Marketing Council: **Agricultural Marketing Board; Agriculture, Dept of; Agriculture & Food Policy**
National Film, Television & Sound Archives: **Archives; Radio Drama, English-Language**
National Fire Code: **Building Codes & Regulations; Housing & Housing Policy; Safety Standards**
National Government: **Coaker, William F.; Morris, Edward P.; Squires, Richard Anderson**
National Health Grant Program: **Hospitals**
National Health Research & Development Program: **Medical Research**
National Heritage Day: **Heritage Canada Foundation**
National Historic Park: **Bellevue House; Cape Spear; Forges Saint-Maurice; Halifax Citadel; L'Anse aux Meadows; Newfoundland**
National Historic Site: **Bell, Alexander Graham; Kitwanga Fort; Louisbourg**
National Historic Sites Service: **Conservation of Movable Cultural Property; York Factory**
National History Project: **Canada Studies Foundation**
National Hockey Assn: **Hockey, Ice**

National Hockey League Players' Assn: **Eagleson, R. Alan; Lindsay, R.B. Theodore**

National Hockey League teams: **Calgary Flames; Edmonton Oilers; Montreal Canadiens; Québec Nordiques; Toronto Maple Leafs; Vancouver Canucks; Winnipeg Jets**

National Housing Act: **Building Codes & Regulations; Canada Mortgage & Housing Corp; Housing & Housing Policy; Urban & Regional Planning**

National Humanitarian Award: **Manning, Ernest C.**

National Indian Advisory Council: **Assembly of First Nations**

National Indian Brotherhood: **Assembly of First Nations; Deiter, Walter; Gros-Louis, Max; Manuel, George; Native Council of Canada**

National Indian Council: **Horn, Kahn-Tineta; Native Council of Canada**

National Industrial Design Council: **Art Education**

National Institute on Mental Retardation: **Education, Special**

National Labour Code: **Safety Standards**

National Lacrosse Assn: **Beers, W. George; Lacrosse**

National League: **Montreal Expos**

National Manufacturing Technology Information Centre: **National Research Council of Canada**

National Map Collection: **Archives; Cartography, History of**

National Museum of Canada: **Archaeology; Art Galleries & Museums; Creighton, M. Helen; McIlwraith, Thomas Forsyth; National Museum of Science & Technology; Russell, Loris S.; Wintemberg, William John**

National Museum of Natural History: **Zoology**

National Museums Act: **Archaeology, Salvage; National Museum of Natural Sciences**

National Native Women's Assn of Canada: **Native People, Political Organization & Activism**

National Oil Policy: **Energy, Royal Commission on; Energy Policy; Geopolitics; National Energy Board**

National Parks Act: **Heritage Conservation; Parks, National**

National Parole Board: **Probation & Parole; Solicitor General, Dept of**

National Photography Collection: **Archives**

National Physical Activity Week: **Fitness**

National Physical Fitness Act: **Physical Education**

National Postal Museum: **Postal System**

National Power Policy: **Energy Policy**

National Prehistoric Site Inventory: **Archaeology, Salvage**

National Railway Munitions Ltd: **Hungerford, Samuel James**

National Research Council Act: **Canadian Government Specifications Board**

National Revenue, Dept of: **Bourassa, Robert; Customs & Excise; Foundations; Revenue Canada**

National Science Library: **Art, Contemporary Trends; Wieland, Joyce**

National Sea Products Ltd: **Lunenburg**

National Seismograph Network: **Earthquake**

National Selective Service: **Status of Women; Wartime Home Front**

National Sport & Recreation Centre: **Rowing; Sports Organization, Amateur**

National Steel Car Corp: **Hamilton; Locomotives & Rolling Stock**

National Stud Farm: **Thoroughbred Racing**

National Symphony Orchestra: **Ottawa, Ont**

National Theatre School: **Gascon, Jean; Germain, Jean-Claude; Macdonald, Brian; Roux, Jean-Louis; Stage & Costume Design; Theatre, English-Language; Theatre Education**

National Topographic Survey: **Geological Survey of Canada; Treeline**

National Trades & Labor Congress: **Canadian Federation of Labour; Union Centrals, National**

National Training Act: **Community College; Students, Financial Aid to**

National Transcontinental Railway: **Canadian Government Railways; Grand Trunk Pacific Railway; Kapuskasing; Ontario Northland Transportation Commission**

National Transportation Act: **Air Law & Space Law; Canadian Coast Guard; Canadian Transport Commission; Communications Law; Railways, Contemporary; Safety Standards; Shipping Industry**

National Trust Co: **Flavelle, Joseph W.; Richardson, James A., Sr; Wood, Edward Rogers**

National Typographical Union: **Craft Unionism**

National Ukrainian Festival: **Dauphin**

National Unemployed Workers Assn: **Great Depression**

National Union of Provincial Government Employees: **Public-Service Unions**

National Union of Public Employees: **Canadian Union of Public Employees; Hartman, Grace**

National Union of Public Service Employees: **Canadian Union of Public Employees**

National War Service Funds Advisory Board: **Murdoch, James Young**

National War Services Committee of the YMCA: **Murdoch, James Young**

National Water Research Institute: **Canada Centre for Inland Waters**

National Wildlife Week: **Canadian Wildlife Federation; Miner, John T.**

National Youth Orchestra: **Feldbrill, Victor; Music History; Symonds, Norman**

Nationaliste: **Book Publishing, French-Language; Gill, Charles; Intellectual History; Nationalist League**

Nationalists: **Party System**

Native American Church: **Native People, Religion**

Native Brotherhood of British Columbia: **Calder, Frank A.; Kelly, Peter Reginald; Native People, Political Organization & Activism; Native People - Northwest Coast; Paull, Andrew**

Native Citizens' Directorate: **Native Council of Canada; Native People, Communications**

Native Counselling: **Probation & Parole**

Native Earth: **Theatre, Multicultural**

"Native of Hudson's Bay": **Métis**

Native People: **Native People, Communications**

Native People's Caravan: **Harper, Vern**

Native Sons of Canada: **Prejudice & Discrimination**

Native Theatre Productions: **Theatre, Multicultural**

native women's rights: **National Action Committee on the Status of Women**

Natkutsiak, William: **Nanogak, Agnes**

Nattiez, Jean-Jacques: **Musicology**

natural gas: **Automobile; Chemical Industries; International Trade; Iron & Steel Industry; Kitimat; Labrador Sea; Medicine Hat; Metallurgy; National Energy Board; Oil & Natural Gas; Petroleum; Petroleum Exploration & Production; Petroleum Research & Development; Scotian Shelf; Utilities**

Natural History Soc of Manitoba: **Broley, Charles Lavelle; Rowan, William**

Natural History Soc of Montreal: **Science**

Natural History Soc of New Brunswick: **Science**

Natural History Soc of Saint John: **New Brunswick**

Natural Resource Management Process: **Parks, National**

Natural Resources, Dept of (Man): **Manitoba**

natural selection: **Evolution**

Naturaliste canadien: **Dionne, Charles-Eusèbe; Provancher, Léon**

Naturalization Act: **Citizenship**

Nature Canada: **Canadian Nature Federation**

Nature Conservancy Area: **Garibaldi Provincial Park; Strathcona Provincial Park**

Nature Conservancy of Canada: **Wildlife Conservation & Management**

Naudville, Qué: **Alma**

Nautilus: **Taylor, George William**

Nautley River: **Nechako River**

Naval Dockyard: **Halifax**

Naval Research Establishment: **Mann, Cedric Robert**

Naval Reserve: **Reserve Force of Canada**

Naval Service, Dept of: **Oceanography; Wilson, John Armistead**

Naval Shipbuilding Branch: **Ambridge, Douglas White**

Naval Training Centre: **Cornwallis**

navette: **Silver, Church**

Navigable Waters Protection Act: **Hazardous Wastes**

navigation: **Air Law & Space Law; Astronomy; Boating; Buoy; Canadian Coast Guard; Cape Sable; Cartography, History of; Coastal Waters; Distribution of Powers; Foxe Basin; Hogg, Frank Scott; Hydrography; Jolliet, Louis; Migration; Montréal; North Cape; Oceanography; Radar; Steel, William Arthur; White Rock**

Navy Board Inlet: **Bylot Island**

Navy Island: **Thousand Islands**

Naylor, Bernard: **Choral Music**

Naylor, R.T.: **Business History**

Naylor, T.: **Economics, Radical**

NB Coal Ltd: **Coal**

NDWT: **Theatre, English-Language**

Neale, Cynthia: **Equestrian Sports**

Neatby Building: **Neatby, Kenneth William**

nebulae: **Observatory; Van den Bergh, Sidney**

nectarine: **Peach**

Neebing River: **Thunder Bay**

Needham, Richard: **Essay in English**

needle grass: **Poisonous Plants; Vegetation Regions - Cordillera**

Needs of Native People in an Urban Setting, Ontario Task Force on: **Native People, Urban Migration**

Neepawa, Man: **Brooker, Bertram Richard**

Neerlandia, Alta: **Dutch**

negligence: **Torts; Traffic Law**

negotiable instruments: **Commercial Law; Consumer Law**

"neighbourhood watch": **Police**

Neil, Al: **Art, Contemporary Trends**

Neilson, Henry Ivan: **Printmaking**

Neilson, John: **Almanacs; Book Publishing, English-Language; Lower Canada; Printmaking**

Neilson, Samuel: **Magazines; Printmaking**

Neilson, Terry: **Yachting**

Neish, Owen Rowland & Roy: **Parkin, John C.**

Nekt: **Kitwanga Fort**

Nelford, Jim: **Golf**

Nelles, H.V.: **Business History**

Nelligan, Kate: **Theatre, English-Language**

Nelson, Anne: **Brown, George**

Nelson, Harold: **Theatre, English-Language**

Nelson, Hugh: **Nelson**

Nelson, John: **Canadian Institute of International Affairs**

Nelson, Nels: **Ski Jumping; Skiing**

Nelson, Norman: **Purcell String Quartet**

Nelson, Robert: **Nelson River**

Nelson, Robert (1794-1873): **Lower Canada; Rebellions of 1837**

Nelson, Wolfred: **Cartier, George-Etienne; Lower Canada; Patriotes**

Nelson column: **Historic Site**

Nelson Head: **Banks Island**

Nelson House, Man: **Hudson Bay Railway; McIntosh, William**

Nelson Indians: **Kaska**

Nelson *News*: **Telegraph**

Nelsova, Zara: **Music History**

nematology: **Biology**

nemertea: **Flatworm; Invertebrate**

Némiscau, Lac: **Mistassini, Lac**

neo-Marxism: **Anthropology**

neodymium: **Geological Dating**

neon: **Chemistry; Laser; Spring**

Neon Products Ltd: **Pattison, James A.**

neoplasm: **Cancer**

Nepean, Ont: **Electronics Industry**

nephrite jade: **Gemstone; Greenstone; Rock & Mineral Collecting**

Nepisiguit, Acadia: **Bathurst; Denys, Nicolas**

Nepisiguit River: **Bathurst; Place-names**

Nepom, Shimon: **Jewish Writing**

nepotism: **Corruption**

Nepriklausoma Lietuva (Independent Lithuanian): **Lithuanians**

Neptune: **Low, Albert P.**

Nepveu, Pierre: **Literature in French - Scholarship & Teaching**

nervous system: **Botulism; Chiropractic; Diabetes Mellitus; Penfield, Wilder G.; Rossiter, Roger James**

Nerysoo, Richard: **Dene Nation**

Nesbitt-LaBine Mines: **LaBine, Gilbert**

Neskaitis, Violette: **Table Tennis**

Neskonlith Reserve: **Manuel, George**

Nesselroth, Peter W.: **Comparative Literature**

Netherlands Reformed Congregations: **Presbyterian & Reformed Churches**

Netherwood School for Girls: **New Brunswick**

Netla River: **Nahanni Butte**

Netly Creek & Marsh: **St Andrews, Man**

Netsilingmuit Inuit: **Netsilik Inuit**

nettle: **Plants, Native Uses; Poisonous Plants**

Nettler, Gwynn: **Criminology**

Neufchatel, Qué: **Québec City**

Neufeld, Dietrich: **German Writing**

Neufeld, E.P.: **Business History**

Neuman, Shirley: **Kroetsch, Robert; Literature in English - Theory & Criticism**

neurochemistry: **Elliott, K. Allan C.; Quastel, Judah Hirsch**

neuroendocrinology: **Chrétien, Michel**

neurology: **Penfield, Wilder G.**

neurosis: **Psychiatry**

neurosurgery: **Botterell, Edmund Harry; McKenzie, Kenneth George**

Neustadt, Ont: **Diefenbaker, John G.**

neutrality: **Acadia; American Revolution; Bloc populaire canadien; Cayuga; Mascarene, Paul; Onondaga; Pichon, Thomas; Woodsworth, J.S.**

Neutrality League: **Plaunt, Alan Butterworth**

neutron: **Nuclear Energy; Nuclear Fusion; Physics**

Neuville, Qué: **Architecture; Plamondon, Antoine**

Nevers, Edmond de: **Essay in French; Franco-Americans**

Nevitt, Barrington: **McLuhan, H. Marshall**

New, W.H.: *Canadian Literature*; **Short Fiction in English**

New Aiyansh, BC: **Nass River**

New Bothwell, Man: **Hanover**

New Brunswick Broadcasting Co Ltd: **Irving Group**

New Brunswick Council of Labour: **Union Centrals, District & Regional**

New Brunswick Courier: **Drama in English**

New Brunswick Electric Power Commission: **Dalhousie; Electric Utilities; Foster, Walter Edward; New Brunswick**

New Brunswick Historical Resources Administration: **Kings Landing Historical Settlement**

New Brunswick International Paper Co: **Dalhousie**
New Brunswick Magazine: **Literary Magazines in English**
New Brunswick Museum: **New Brunswick**
New Brunswick Publishing Co Ltd: **Irving Group**
New Brunswick Railway Co: **Irving, K. C.**
New Brunswick Telephone Co: **Bell Canada Enterprises Inc; New Brunswick; Telephones; TransCanada Telephone System**
New Canada Movement: **Plaunt, Alan Butterworth**
New Canadian Library: **Ross, Malcolm**
New Carlisle, Qué: **U-boat Landings**
New City Gas Co: **Ostell, John**
New College: **University of Toronto**
New Commonwealth: **Spry, Graham**
New Czech Theatre: **Theatre, Multicultural**
New Dance Group of Canada: **Dance, Modern; Dance History; Toronto Dance Theatre**
New Democracy Party: **Herridge, William Duncan**
New Denmark, NB: **Danes**
New Dominion Monthly: **Magazines**
New Edinburgh, Canada West: **Edwards, William Cameron**
New Era: **McGee, Thomas D'Arcy**
New Frontier: **Kennedy, Leo**
New Frontiers: **Acorn, Milton**
New Hanover: **New Caledonia**
New Hope, Upper Canada: **Hespeler**
New Horizons: **National Health & Welfare, Dept of**
New Iceland Reserve: **Gimli; Icelanders**
New Johnstown, Upper Canada: **Cornwall**
New Labrador Party: **Smallwood, Joseph R.**
New Leaf: **Book Clubs**
New Liberty: **Cahén, Oscar**
New Light movement: **Alline, Henry; Great Awakening**
New Music Concerts: **Chamber Music**
New Nijverdal, Alta: **Dutch**
New Party clubs: **New Democratic Party**
New Party Declaration: **Social Democracy**
New Place Centre: **Theatre, English-Language**
New Play Centre: **Theatre, English-Language**
New Play Soc: **Harron, Donald; Moore, Dora Mavor; Musical Theatre; Theatre, English-Language**
New Press: **Book Publishing, English-Language; Godfrey, Dave**
New Quarterly: **Horwood, Harold Andrew**
New Québec Crater: **Geological Dating; Meteor, Meteorite, Impact Crater; Québec**
New Québec Inuit: **Ungava Inuit**
New Regina Manifesto: **Social Democracy**
New Review: **Mladenovic, Milos**
New Ross, NS: **Ross Farm**
New Scandinavia, Man: **Erickson; Swedes**
New School of Art: **Coughtry, Graham**
New Star Books Ltd: **Literary Magazines in English**
New Stockholm, Assiniboia: **Lutherans**
"new town": **Alberta; Improvement District; Resource Towns; Spence-Sales, Harold; Thompson; Urban & Regional Planning**
New Union Singing Soc: **Music History**
New Waterford, NS: **Cape Breton Strikes, 1920s; Slovenes**
New Westminster Hyak Swim Club: **Swimming, Speed**
New Westminster penitentiary: **Prison**
New Westminster Royals: **Soccer; Turner, David**
New World: **Photography**
New World Island: **Notre Dame Bay**
New World Magazine: **Essay in English**
New York Life Insurance Co Building (Montréal): **Architecture, Development**
Newark, Upper Canada: **Newspapers; Niagara-on-the-Lake; Simcoe, Elizabeth P.; War of 1812**

Newboro, Ont: **Rideau Canal**
Newcastle Foundry & Machine Manufactory: **Massey, Daniel**
Newcomb, Simon: **Astronomy**
Newell, Lake: **Brooks**
NeWest Publishers Ltd: **Poetry in English**
NeWest Review: **Alberta; Literary Magazines in English**
Newfeld, Frank: **Children's Literature in English**
"Newfie" jokes: **Folklore**
Newfoundland: **Dog**
Newfoundland: **Disasters; Kean, Abraham (Abram)**
Newfoundland Agricultural Board: **Agriculture History**
Newfoundland & Labrador Hydro: **Electric Utilities; Wind Energy**
Newfoundland Brotherhood of Woodworkers: **Newfoundland Loggers' Strike**
Newfoundland Canal: **Grand Lake**
Newfoundland Capital Corp: **Steele, Harold Raymond**
Newfoundland Central Lowland: **Physiographic Regions - Appalachia**
Newfoundland Co-operative Union: **Duggan, Alphonsus Gregory**
Newfoundland Dockyard: **Shipbuilding & Ship Repair**
Newfoundland Federation of Labor: **Duggan, Alphonsus Gregory**
Newfoundland Fisheries Commission: **Commission of Government; Harvey, Moses**
Newfoundland Fisherman, Food & Allied Workers' Union: **Fisheries History**
Newfoundland Legislature Building: **Architecture**
Newfoundland Museum: **St John's**
Newfoundland Outport Nurses' Industrial Assn: **Crafts**
Newfoundland Patriot: **Parsons, Robert John**
Newfoundland Pulp & Paper Co: **Corner Brook**
Newfoundland Railway: **Bonavista; Channel-Port aux Basques**
Newfoundland Reference Re Continental Shelf: **Hibernia Case**
Newfoundland resettlement: **Brunette Island; Fogo Island**
Newfoundland School Soc: **Newfoundland**
Newfoundland Shelf: **St Lawrence, Gulf of**
Newfoundland Standard Time: **Time**
Newfoundland Telephone Co: **Bell Canada Enterprises Inc; Telephones; TransCanada Telephone System**
Newfoundland Timber Estates: **Lewisporte**
Newfoundland Trades & Labor Council: **Duggan, Alphonsus Gregory**
Newfoundland Writers Guild: **Literature & Politics**
Newman, Basil: **Exploration & Travel Literature in English**
Newman, Gerald: **Radio Drama, English-Language**
Newman, Jack: **Animal Breeding**
Newman, Red: **Dumbells**
Newport, BC: **Squamish**
Newport, Ont: **Welsh**
news conferences: **Parliamentary Press Gallery**
news manipulation & suppression: **Media Ownership**
Newscience: **Ontario Science Centre**
newsgathering: **Communications; Journalism; Telegraph**
Newspapers, Royal Commission on: **Media Ownership; Newspapers; Politics & the Media**
newsprint: **Foreign Investment; Forest Harvesting; Forestry; International Trade; Newspapers; Print Industry; Pulp & Paper Industry; Telephones**
Newsradio: **News Agencies**
newsreels: **Film; Sparling, Gordon**
newt: **Salamander**
Newton, BC: **Surrey**
Newton, Christopher: **Shaw Festival; Vancouver Playhouse**
Newton, Mount: **Saanich Peninsula**
Nexus: **Birney, A. Earle**
Nezavisna Drzava Hrvatska (The Independent State of Croatia): **Croatians**

Ngan, Wayne: **Ceramics, Contemporary**
niacin: **Cherry; Tomato**
Niagara, Ont (Niagara-on-the-Lake): **Libraries**
Niagara Apothecary: **Niagara-on-the-Lake**
Niagara College of Applied Arts & Technology: **St Catharines; Welland**
Niagara District Airport: **St Catharines**
Niagara Diversion Treaty: **Niagara Falls**
Niagara Escarpment Plan: **Bruce Peninsula**
Niagara Falls Art Gallery & Museum: **Kurelek, William**
Niagara Mail: **Kirby, William**
Niagara Parks Commission: **Arboretum; Gzowski, Casimir S.; Historic Site; Navy Island; Niagara Escarpment; Niagara Falls, Ont; Niagara Historic Frontier**
Niagara portage: **Queenston**
Niagara River Parkway: **Fort Erie**
Nichol, James: **Drama in English**
Nichol, John I.: **Parks, National**
Nicholas, Cindy: **Lumsden, Cliff; Marathon Swimming**
Nicholas, John: **Philosophy**
Nicholls, R.W.: **Physics**
Nicholson, J.W.A.: **Social Gospel**
Nicholson, James: *Dictionary of Canadian Biography*
Nicholson, L.H.: **Royal Canadian Mounted Police**
Nicholson Lake: **Dubawnt River**
Nicholsville, Nfld: **Deer Lake, Nfld**
Nickel Centre, Ont: **Sudbury**
nickel sulphide: **Metallurgy**
Nickerson, Eluid: **Cobourg**
Nickerson, William B.: **Archaeology**
Nickinson, John, Jr: **Nickinson, John**
Nickle Plate Mine: **Princeton**
"Nickle Resolution": **Honours**
Nickles Daily Oil Bulletin: **Petrochemical Industry**
Nickoloff, Bryon: **Chess**
Nicola, BC: **Architecture**
Nicola, Kamloops & Similkameen Railway: **Merritt**
Nicola Valley: **Desert; Merritt; Nicola-Similkameen; Ranching History; Salish, Interior; Vegetation Regions - Cordillera**
Nicola Valley Indian Administration: **Marchand, Leonard S.**
Nicolas, Louis: **Painting**
Nicolet, Jean: **Nicolet**
Nicolet, Qué: **Architecture**
Nicolet, R.R.: **CN Tower**
Nicolet, Rivière: **Arthabaska; Nicolet; St Lawrence Lowland; Victoriaville**
Nicoll, Marion: **Painting**
Nicolls, Gustavus: **Halifax Citadel**
nicotine: **Medical Drug Abuse; Pesticide**
Nictaux & Atlantic Railway: **Nova Scotia**
Nielsen, Julius "Duke": **Messer, Don, & the Islanders**
Nielson, Kai: **Philosophy**
Nielson, Roger: **Vancouver Canucks**
Nigel Island: **Balaklava Island**
Nigerians: **Africans**
night crawler: **Earthworm**
Nihilist Spasm Band: **Curnoe, Gregory R.**
Nikka Yuko Centennial Garden: **Lethbridge**
Nilsson, Ulf: **Winnipeg Jets**
NIMBUS satellites: **Remote Sensing**
Nimpkish Lake: **Vancouver Island**
Nincheri, Guido: **Public Art**
Ninerville, Man: **Germans**
92 Resolutions: **Aylmer, 5th Baron; Patriotes; Rebellions of 1837**
Nininger, James R.: *Canadian Business Review*
Ninstints, BC: **Anthony Island Provincial Park; Queen Charlotte Islands**
Niobec Inc: **Columbium**
niobium: **Columbium**
Niosi, Joe: **Niosi, Bert**
Niosi, Johnnie: **Niosi, Bert**
Niosi, Jorge: **Marxism**
Nipigon River: **Nipigon, Lake; Superior, Lake**
Nipissing: **Nicollet de Belleborne, Jean; Ste Marie Among the Hurons**

Nipissing College: **Laurentian University**
Nippon Shorinji Kempo: **Jiu-Jitsu**
Nirenberg, Louis: **Mathematics**
Nisbet, Thomas: **Furniture, English, Scottish & American**
Nisei: **Internment; Japanese**
Nishga: **Aboriginal Rights; Beynon, William; *Calder* Case; Calder, Frank A.; Land Claims; Nass River; Native People, Political Organization & Activism; Native-White Relations; Tsetsaut; Tsimshian**
Nishihata, Jessi: **Film, Documentary**
Nishnawbe Institute: **Pelletier, Wilfred**
Nisku, Alta: **Alberta Research Council**
Nisnevitch, Abraham: **Jewish Writing**
Nith River: **Paris**
Nitinat: **Nootka**
Nitobe Memorial Garden: **Botanical Garden**
nitrate: **Mineral**
nitric acid: **Acid Rain; Chemical Industries**
nitrogen: **Biotechnology; Chemistry; Chemistry Subdisciplines; Geological Dating; Mineral; Molecules in Interstellar Space; Mycorrhizae; Spring; Water Pollution**
nitrogen oxides: **Acid Rain; Pollution**
Niven, Frederick J.: **Autobiographical Writing in English; Best-Sellers in English**
Niverville, Man: **Grain Elevators**
No 26 Colliery: **Coal**
No 1765 Mine: **Coal**
No 1774 Mine: **Coal**
no-confidence motion: **King-Byng Affair; Minority Government; Parliament; Parliamentary Procedure**
"no fault" compensation: **Torts; Traffic Law**
no-see-um: **Fly; Midge**
"no taxation without representation": **Women's Suffrage**
NOAA satellites: **Remote Sensing; Satellite, Artificial; Space Technology**
Noah, William: **Inuit Art**
Nobel Prize: **Banting, Frederick G.; Best, Charles Herbert; Collip, James Bertram; Ethnic Literature; Herzberg, Gerhard; Macleod, John James Rickard; Pearson, Lester B.; Rutherford, Ernest; Sourkes, Theodore Lionel**
Noble, George: **Booth, John Rudolphus**
Noble, William C.: **Archaeology**
Noel, Jean-Guy: **Film**
Noel, N.P.R.: **Exploration & Travel Literature in English**
Noix, Ile aux: **Fortification**
Nokomis, Sask: **Place-names**
Noland, Kenneth: **Fauteux, André**
Nolin, Charles: **Riel, Louis**
Nomez, Nain: **Ethnic Literature**
None-Such Soda Water: **Soft-Drink Industry**
Nonosbawsut: **Demasduwit**
Non-Partisan Assn: **Vancouver**
nonprofit organizations: **Corporation Law**
nonproliferation: **Disarmament; Nuclear Safety**
non-trinitarian: **Christadelphians**
Noorduyn, R.B.C. "Bob": **Noorduyn Norseman**
Nootka Fault: **Earthquake**
Nootka rose: **Vegetation Regions - Pacific Coastal**
Nopiming Provincial Park: **Parks, Provincial**
Nor'-Wester: **Print Industry; Schultz, John Christian**
Noranda, Qué: **Astronaut; Beauchemin, Yves; Metallurgy; Rouyn-Noranda**
Noranda Award: **Clark, Howard Charles**
Noranda Research Centre: **Gauvin, William Henry**
Noranda Sales Corp Ltd: **Noranda Mines Ltd**
Nord, Rivière du: **Lachute; Laurentian Highlands; Ste-Agathe-des-Monts; St-André-Est; St-Jérôme**

Nordair Ltd: **Air Canada; Aviation; Hamilton; Quebecair; Thunder Bay; Transportation**
Nordbeck, Peter: **Art Education; Silver, Church; Silver, Domestic**
Nordegg, Alta: **Company Town**
Norden Society: **Swedes**
Nordenskiold River: **Carmacks**
Nordheimer Piano & Music Co: **Musical Instruments**
nori: **Algae; Seaweeds**
normal schools: **d'Avray, 2nd Baron; Dickie, Donalda J.; Forrester, Alexander; Saskatchewan; Secondary School; Status of Women**
Norman, Ont: **Kenora**
Norman, Percy: **Swimming, Speed**
Norman Acoustic Guitars: **Musical Instruments**
Norman Mackenzie Art Gallery: **Bloore, Ronald; Regina; Regina Five**
Norman McLeod Rogers: **Icebreakers**
Normandale, Ont: **Technology**
Normandin, Qué: **Research Stations, Agricultural**
Normick-Perron Inc: **Amos; La Sarre**
Norontair: **Sudbury; Thunder Bay**
Norpak Ltd: **Computer Industry; Electronics Industry**
Norquay Building: **Green, Blankstein, Russell**
Norrana: **Norwegians**
Norris, James: **James Norris Memorial Trophy**
Norris, John: **Music Criticism**
Norris, Ken: **Poetry in English**
Norris, T.G.: **Banks, Harold C.**
Norris Lake: **Rockwood**
Norrish, Ben: **Film**
Norse poetry: **Johnston, George B.**
North American Glass Co: **Glass**
North American Indian Brotherhood: **Calder, Frank A.; Marchand, Leonard S.; Native People, Political Organization & Activism; Paull, Andrew**
North American Life Assurance Co: **Gundy, James Henry**
North American Trust: **Webster, Lorne Campbell**
North Atlantic Treaty: **NATO; Wrong, H. Hume**
North Battleford, Sask: **Battleford; New Religious Movements; Prairie; Sapp, Allen; Saskatchewan River**
North Bentinck Arm: **Bella Coola**
North British Soc: **Halifax**
North Canadian Forest Industries: **Grande Prairie**
North Channel: **Georgian Bay; Manitoulin Island; St Joseph Island**
North Devon: **Devon Island**
North French River: **Moose River**
North Hatley, Qué: **Architectural Styles**
North Head, NB: **Grand Manan Island**
North Lake Provincial Park: **Heritage Trail**
North Magnetic Pole: **Bathurst Island; Boothia Peninsula; Geomagnetic Pole; Ross, James C.**
North Moose Lake: **Moose Lake**
North Mountain: **Annapolis Lowlands; Nova Scotia**
North Nahanni River: **Mackenzie River**
North Pacific Current: **Northwest Coast**
North Pacific Fur Seal Convention: **Fur Trapping, Contemporary; Sealing**
North Pender Island: **Gulf Islands**
North Point Reef: **North Cape**
North Rankin Nickel Mines: **Rankin Inlet, NWT**
North River: **Charlottetown**
North Saanich, BC: **Saanich Peninsula; Victoria**
North Saskatchewan River: **Saskatchewan River**
North Saskatchewan Trail: **Gladstone**
North Shore Railway Co: **Cauchon, Joseph-Edouard; Simpson, George; Trois-Rivières**
North Star Mines: **Kimberley**
North Star Mountains: **Kimberley**
North Street Terminal: **Railway Station**
North Temperate Zone: **Crops**

North Thompson River: **Thompson River**
North Toronto Collegiate: **Jamieson, Elmer**
North Vancouver Civic Centre: **Downs, Barry Vance**
North Virden-Scallion oil field: **Virden**
north-west angle of Nova Scotia: **Boundaries**
North West Angle Treaty: **Indian Treaties; Verner, Frederick A.**
North-West Canada Medal: **Medal**
North West Cattle Co: **Lane, George**
North West Georgia: **New Caledonia**
North West Pulp & Power Ltd: **Hinton**
North West River, Nfld: **Hamilton Inlet; Labrador Inuit; Melville, Lake; Montagnais-Naskapi**
North-West Territories: **Alberta; Assiniboia; Battleford; Dewdney, Edgar; Equal Rights Assn; Fort Battleford; Hudson's Bay Company; McDougall, William; North-West Mounted Police; North-West Schools Question; Patrick, Thomas Alfred; Regina; Royal Canadian Mounted Police; Saskatchewan; Territorial Evolution; Veterinary Medicine, History**
North West Trust Co: **Allard, Charles A.**
North Western Coal & Navigation Co: **Galt, Alexander T.; Lethbridge**
North-Western Territory: **Northwest Territories; Territorial Evolution**
North York, Ont: **Black Creek Pioneer Village; Ontario; Toronto; Whiten, Colette**
Northcote: **Batoche**
Northeast Channel: **Scotian Shelf**
Northeast Staging Route: **Northwest Territories**
Northern Aerial Mineral Exploration: **Bush Flying**
Northern Affairs, Dept of (Man): **Manitoba; Norway House**
Northern Affairs & Natural Resources, Dept of: **Indian Affairs & Northern Development, Dept of; Northwest Territories**
Northern Alberta Institute of Technology: **Edmonton**
Northern Alberta Railway: **Dawson Creek; Railway History**
Northern Aluminum Co: **Alcan Aluminium Ltd**
Northern Archaic: **Prehistory**
Northern Belt: **Geological Regions**
Northern Breweries Ltd: **Brewing Industry**
Northern Canada Power Commission: **Electric Utilities; Northwest Territories; Yukon Territory**
Northern College of Applied Arts & Technology (School of Mines): **Haileybury**
Northern Delight: **Theatre, Multicultural**
Northern Electric Co: **Winters, Robert H.**
Northern Games: **Festivals**
northern goshawk: **Hawk; Owl**
Northern Health Services: **Northwest Territories**
Northern Indian Lake: **Southern Indian Lake**
Northern Inland Waters Act: **Environmental Law**
Northern Journey: **Literary Magazines in English**
Northern Life: **Sudbury**
Northern Life Insurance Co: **Webster, Lorne Campbell**
Northern Light: **Theatre, English-Language**
Northern Light: **Icebreakers**
Northern Lights Community College: **Fort St John**
Northern Lights Folk Festival: **Sudbury**
northern liverwort: **Ouimet Canyon**
Northern locomotive: **Canadian National Railways; Locomotives & Rolling Stock**
Northern Messenger: **Magazines**
Northern Native Broadcast Access Program: **Communications in the North**
Northern Okanagan dialect: **Salish, Interior**
Northern Ontario Business: **Sudbury**

Northern Pacific Railway: **Greenway, Thomas; Roblin, Rodmond P.**
northern parula: **Warbler**
northern pike: **Pike; Rideau Lakes; Thousand Islands**
Northern Pipeline Agency: **Sharp, Mitchell W.**
Northern Québec Inuit Assn: **Land Claims; Watt, Charlie**
northern redbelly dace: **Minnow**
northern squawfish: **Minnow**
Northern Telecom Ltd: **Bell Canada Enterprises Inc; Computer Science; Electronics Industry; High Technology; Microchips & Transistors; Québec; Satellite Communications**
Northern Transportation Co Ltd: **Cornwall, James K.; Transportation Agencies (Government); Transportation in the North**
northern wheat grass: **Vegetation Regions - Prairie**
Northern Wings: **Quebecair**
Northey, Margot: **Comparative Literature, Canadian**
Northland School Div: **Métis Settlements**
Northlands Coliseum: **Edmonton Oilers**
Northlined Lake: **Nueltin Lake**
Northumberland: **Northumberland Strait**
Northumberland Ferries: **Prince Edward Island**
Northwest Arm: **Random Island**
Northwest Atlantic Fisheries Organization: **Fisheries Policy; Sealing**
Northwest Nitro Chemicals: **Medicine Hat**
Northwest Staging Route: **Whitehorse; Yukon Territory**
Northwood Pulp & Timber: **Chatham, NB**
Norton, Richard: **Prince of Wales's Fort**
Norton Sound: **Yukon Territory**
Norway haddock: **Québec**
Norway House Reserve: **Norway House**
Norway rat: **Owl; Rat**
Norwegian Lutheran Church: **Lutherans**
Norwood, Gilbert: **Essay in English**
Norwood, Robert: **Drama in English**
Norwood Wanderers: **Soccer**
Nose Creek: **Calgary**
Not a Love Story: **Women's Movement**
Not-for-Profit Corporations Act (Sask): **Corporation Law**
Notman & Fraser: **Fraser, John A.; Walker, Horatio**
Notman Photographic Archives: **Notman, William**
Notre-Dame-du-Bon-Conseil, Qué: **Cheese & Cheesemaking**
Notre-Dame-du-Lac Abbey: **Oka**
Notre-Dame (mountains): **Mégantic Hills**
Notre Dame University: **Nelson**
Nottawasaga Bay: **Christian Island; Georgian Bay; Robinson, Peter**
Nottawasaga River: **Collingwood; Georgian Bay**
Nottaway, Qué: **Senneterre**
Nottingham Island: **Hudson Strait; Ungava Inuit**
Nouveau Journal: **Lapointe, Paul-Marie**
Nouveau Monde: **Newspapers**
Nouvelle Aire: **Lock, Edouard**
Nouvelle barre du jour: **Barre du jour; Brossard, Nicole; Literary Periodicals in French**
Nouvelle compagnie théâtrale: **Drama in French; Theatre for Young Audiences**
Nouvelle relève: **Literary Periodicals in French; Relève**
Nouvelles soirées canadiennes: **Literary Periodicals in French**
Nouvelliste: **Trois-Rivières**
Nova, Aldo: **Popular Music**
Nova, Gary Lee: **Art, Contemporary Trends**
Nova Dance Theatre: **Dance, Modern**
Nova Dania: **Danes**
Nova Magnetics Ltd: **Nova Scotia Research Foundation Corp**
Nova Scotia Act: **Anglicanism**
Nova Scotia Assn of Architects: **Fairn, Leslie Raymond**

Nova Scotia Baptist Assn: **Acadia University**
Nova Scotia Barristers' Soc: **Associations**
Nova Scotia Board of Insurance Underwriters: **Associations**
Nova Scotia Centre of the Poetry Soc of England: **Literary Prizes in English**
Nova Scotia Chronicle: **Theatre, English-Language**
Nova Scotia Credit Union League: **MacDonald, Angus Bernard**
Nova Scotia duck tolling retriever: **Dog**
Nova Scotia Eastern Institute of Technology: **University College of Cape Breton**
Nova Scotia Fisheries Training Centre: **Nova Scotia**
Nova Scotia Forge Co: **Fraser, Graham**
Nova Scotia Fruit Growers' Assn: **Associations**
Nova Scotia Gazette & the Weekly Chronicle: **Drama in English**
Nova Scotia Glass Co: **Glass**
Nova Scotia Historical Soc: **Historical Societies**
Nova Scotia Institute of Natural Science: **Associations; Challenger Expedition; Science**
Nova Scotia Institute of Technology: **Halifax**
Nova Scotia Legislative Assembly: **Constitutional History**
Nova Scotia Legislature Building: **Architecture; Dumaresq, James Charles Philip**
Nova Scotia Light & Power Co: **Nova Scotia; Street Railways**
Nova Scotia Lumber Co: **Pipes, William Thomas**
Nova Scotia Magazine: **Literary Magazines in English; Magazines**
Nova Scotia Miner: **McLachlan, James Bryson**
Nova Scotia Museum: **Diorama; Nova Scotia; Ross Farm**
Nova Scotia Museum of Science: *Challenger* **Expedition**
Nova Scotia Nautical Institute: **Nova Scotia**
Nova Scotia Poetry Contest: **Literary Prizes in English**
Nova Scotia Power Commission: **Murray, George Henry; Nova Scotia; Tidal Energy**
Nova Scotia Power Corp: **Electric Utilities; Nova Scotia**
Nova Scotia Railway: **Howe, Joseph; Nova Scotia**
Nova Scotia Resources Ltd: **Nova Scotia**
Nova Scotia Society of Artists: **Artists' Organizations**
Nova Scotia Steel & Coal Co Ltd: **Bell Island; Cantley, Thomas; Carmichael, James William; Fraser, Graham; New Glasgow; Stairs, John Fitz-William; Sydney Mines**
Nova Scotia Sugar Refining: **Stairs, John Fitz-William**
Nova Scotia Teachers College: **Truro**
Nova Scotia Teachers' Union: **Coady, M.M.**
Nova Scotia Telegraph Co: **Gisborne, Frederick Newton**
Nova Scotia Telephone Co: **Telephones**
Nova Scotian Current: **St Lawrence, Gulf of**
Novaco Ltd: **Coal**
Novacor Chemical Co: **Petrochemical Industry**
Novakowsky, Nicholas: **Bison**
Noval Technologies Ltd: **Coal Demethanation**
Novalta Resources Ltd: **NOVA, An Alberta Corporation**
Novascotian: **Annand, William; Haliburton, Thomas C.; Howe, Joseph; Journalism; Libraries; Newspapers; Nova Scotia**
Novial: **Language**
Noxon, Gerald: **Radio Drama, English-Language**
NRC Prairie Regional Laboratory: **Biotechnology; Chemistry Subdisciplines; Lemieux, Raymond U.**
NRU reactor: **Lewis, Wilfrid Bennett; Physics**
NRX reactor: **Lewis, Wilfrid Bennett; Nuclear Energy; Physics**
Nu-West Development: **Development Industry**

nuclear chemistry: **Chemistry Subdisciplines; Yaffe, Leo**
nuclear engineering: **Aerospace Industry; Engineering**
nuclear fission: **Chemistry Subdisciplines; Nuclear Energy; Nuclear Power Plants**
nuclear magnetic resonance: **Bernstein, Harold Joseph; Chemistry Subdisciplines**
nuclear medicine: **Medicine, Contemporary**
nuclear physics: **Le Caine, Hugh; Physics**
nuclear weapons: **Armaments; Armed Forces - Unification; Bomarc Missile Crisis; Diefenbaker, John G.; Disarmament; Franklin, Ursula Martius; Harkness, Douglas S.; Hellyer, Paul T.; NATO; Nuclear Fusion; Nuclear Safety; Peace Movement; Political Campaign; Science & Society**
"nuclear winter": **Science & Society**
nucleotides: **Genetics**
Nuliayuk: **Inuit Myth & Legend**
nun: **Christian Religious Communities; Hôtel-Dieu**
Nunasi Corp: **Curley, Tagak**
Nunatsiakmiut Native Communications Soc: **Communications in the North; Native People, Communications**
Nunavut Territory: **Ittinuar, Peter F.**
Nureyev, Rudolf: **Dance History; Kain, Karen; National Ballet of Canada; Tennant, Veronica**
Nursery School & Child Laboratory: **Mental Health**
nursing homes: **Death & Dying; Health Policy; Social & Welfare Services**
nursing stations: **Grenfell, Wilfred T.; Northwest Territories; Nursing; Yukon Territory**
Nutana, Sask: **Saskatoon**
nutcracker: **Crow**
nutrition: **Agricultural Education; Dietetics; Drake, Theodore George Gustavus Harwood; Fish; Home Economics; International Development Research Centre; Population; Sourkes, Theodore Lionel**
Nutrition Soc of Canada: **McHenry, Earle Willard**
nuts: **Chestnut; Confectionery Industry; Walnut**
"Nuxalk Nation": **Bella Coola**
Nuytten, Phil: **Ocean Industry**
nylon: **Plastics-Processing Industry; Textile Industry**

O

Oak Ridge moraine: **Moraine; Ontario**
Oakbank, Man: **Springfield**
Oakes Garden: **Landscape Architecture**
Oakland automobile: **General Motors of Canada Ltd**
Oaks, Nathan: **Furniture, Country**
oath of allegiance: **Acadia; Doukhobors; Ontario**
Obed-Marsh Project: **Coal**
Obedjiwan, Qué: **Attikamek; St-Maurice, Rivière**
Oberon Press: **Book Publishing, English-Language; Poetry in English; Small Presses**
O'Billovich, Bob: **Toronto Argonauts**
Objectiv: **Leduc, Jacques**
Oblates: **Agriculture History; Belgians; Carrier; Catholicism; Christian Religious Communities; Fallon, Michael F.; Fort Resolution; Grandin, Vital-J.; Holman; Kelowna; Lac Ste Anne; Lacombe, Albert; L'Heureux, Jean-B.; Mission; Okanagan Valley; Ottawa, Ont; St Albert, Smallwood Reservoir; Taché, Alexandre-Antonin; Theatre, French-Language; Timiskaming, Lake; University of Ottawa; Ville-Marie**
O'Brien, Allan: **Halifax**
O'Brien, Ambrose: **Montreal Canadiens; Renfrew**
O'Brien, Cyril Cornelius: **Musicology**
O'Brien, Gordon: **Guitar**

O'Brien, Joe: **Harness Racing**
O'Brien, Oscar: **Music History**
obscurely segmented worm: **Invertebrate**
Observateur: **Magazines**
Observatory Art Centre: **MacLeod, Pegi Nicol**
obsidian: **Linear Mounds; Prehistory**
obstetrics: **Birthing Practices; Medicine, Contemporary**
OC Transpo: **Ottawa, Ont**
O'Callaghan, E.B.: **Lower Canada**
occupational health & safety: **Employment Law; Labour Law**
Ocean Dumping Control Act: **Environmental Law; Hazardous Wastes**
Ocean Falls Swim Club: **Swimming, Speed**
ocean laker: **Lake Carriers**
ocean ranching: **Aquaculture**
Ocean Ranger: **Climate & Man; Grand Banks; Royal Commissions**
ocean spray: **Plants, Native Uses; Vegetation Regions - Pacific Coastal**
ocean weather station: **Station PAPA**
O'Connor, Johnny: **Donnellys, The**
Odanak Reserve: **Obomsawin, Alanis**
Odawa: **Ottawa**
Odell, N.: **Vancouver, Mount**
Odelltown, Qué: **Hunters' Lodges**
Odeon Theatres: **Brockington, Leonard W.; Film; Nathanson, Nathan Louis**
Odin, Mount: **Baffin Island**
O'Donel, J.L.: **Catholicism**
O'Donnell, James: **Architectural Styles; Notre-Dame Church**
O'Donnell, William: **Harness Racing**
O'Donoghue, John: **O'Donoghue, Daniel J.**
Odrach, Fedir: **Ukrainian Writing**
Oeil: **Guèvremont, Germaine**
Oeufs, Ile aux: **Disasters**
Office de la langue française: **Translation**
office machines: **Electronics Industry; Office Automation**
Office of Dominion Statistician: **Demographic Data Collection**
Office of Equal Opportunities: **Status of Women**
Office of Native Claims: **Indian Affairs & Northern Development, Dept of**
Office of Science & Technology Policy (Sask): **Saskatchewan Research Council**
Official Development Assistance: **Agricultural Aid**
Official Languages Act (NB): **Bilingualism; Language Policy**
official languages of Canada: **Constitution Act, 1982; Distribution of Powers**
Official Opposition: **Caucus; Filibuster; Government; House of Commons; Leader of the Opposition; Monarchism; Parliamentary Procedure; Political Campaign; Separatism**
offset lithography: **Advertising; Postage Stamps; Print Industry**
Offshore Labrador Biological Studies: **Arctic Oceanography**
offshore resources: **Distribution of Powers; Environmental Law; Hecate Strait; *Hibernia* Case; Nova Scotia; Peckford, A. Brian**
Ogden, John: **Exploration & Travel Literature in English**
Ogden, Mount: **Gemstone**
Ogilvie, Doris: **Status of Women in Canada, Royal Commission on the**
Ogilvie, William: **White Pass**
Ogilvie Flour Mills Co Ltd: **Grain Elevators; Technology**
Ogilvie Mountains: **Yukon Territory**
Ogilvy-Renault: **Mulroney, M. Brian**
Ogoki Diversion: **Nipigon, Lake**
Ogoki River: **Albany River**
O'Hagan, Thomas: **Essay in English**
Ohienko, Ilarion: **Orthodox Church**
Ohitok: **Qaqaq Ashoona**
Ohlgren, Andy: **Skiing**
oil cake: **Agricultural Research & Development**
oil lamps: **Dorset Culture; Lighthouses**
Oil Pollution Prevention Regulations: **Environmental Law**

oil sands: **Alberta Oil Sands Technology & Research Authority; Alberta Research Council; Athabasca River; Bitumen; Fort McMurray; Mineral Resources; Petroleum; Petroleum Supply & Demand; Sulphur**
oil shale: **New Brunswick; Riverview**
oil spills: **Arctic Oceanography; Biological Oceanography; Conservation; Fundy, Bay of/Gulf of Maine; McTaggart-Cowan, Patrick Duncan; Razorbill; Remote Sensing; Sealing; Water Pollution; Wildlife Conservation & Management**
Oil Springs, Ont: **Petroleum Industries; Petroleum Research & Development**
Oilweek: **Petrochemical Industry**
Oiseau bleu: **Children's Literature in French**
Ojibwa Bible: **Jones, Peter**
Ojibwa dictionary: **Slovenes**
Ojibwa language & dialects: **Cree Syllabics; Native People, Languages**
Oka, T.: **Molecules in Interstellar Space; Physics**
Oka Hills: **St Lawrence Lowland**
Oka Reserve: **Algonquin**
Okak, Nfld: **Haven, Jens; Nain**
Okanagan: **Indian Art; Okanagan Valley; Ross, Alexander (1783-1856); Salish, Interior**
Okanagan Air Service: **Agar, Carlyle Clare**
Okanagan College: **Kelowna; Salmon Arm; Vernon**
Okanagan-Colville language: **Salish, Interior**
Okanagan Falls, BC: **Okanagan Valley**
Okanagan Helicopters Ltd: **Transportation**
Okanagan Highland: **Kettle Valley; Monashee Mountains**
Okanagan Lake: **Kelowna; Ogopogo; Salish, Interior; Vernon**
Okanagan Landing: **Vernon**
Okanagan Mountain Provincial Park: **Okanagan Valley**
Okanagan Range: **Cascade Mountains**
Okanagan River: **Columbia River; Okanagan Valley; Salish, Interior**
Oke, J.H.: **Golf**
Oke, Teddy: **Catherwood, Ethel**
O'Keefe Brewing Co Ltd: **O'Keefe, Eugene**
O'Keefe Centre: **National Ballet of Canada; Toronto**
Okotoks, Alta: **Calgary; Vanderpant, John**
Oktoberfests: **Festivals**
Old Age Assistance Act: **Old-Age Pension**
Old Age Pension Act: **Pension**
Old Age Security Act: **Old-Age Pension; Pension**
Old Angelo's: **Musical Theatre**
old Bath road: **Architecture**
Old Brewery Bay: **Orillia**
Old Cordilleran culture: **Prehistory**
Old Crow Mountains: **Old Crow Plain**
Old Crow River: **Old Crow; Old Crow Basin; Old Crow Plain**
Old Exchange Arts Centre: **Centaur Theatre**
Old Fort Brewing Company Ltd: **Brewing Industry**
Old Home Summer 10-Miler: **Long-Distance Running**
Old Lady's Ghost Creek: **Place-names**
Old Man on His Back Plateau: **Place-names**
Old Order Mennonite: **Germanic Fraktur & Calligraphy; Mennonites**
Old Perlican, Nfld: **Trinity Bay**
Old Port: **Québec City**
Old Post Office Museum: **Oakville**
Old Radicals: **Clear Grits**
Old Sun: **Blackfoot**
Old Sun, Jr: **Blackfoot**
Old Swan: **Blackfoot**
Oldfield, John: **Cartography, History of**
Olds School of Agriculture: **Agricultural Education**
Oldsmobile: **General Motors of Canada Ltd**
oleander: **Poisonous Plants**
O'Leary, Dostaler: **Essay in French**

O'Leary Commission: **Publications, Royal Commission on**
O'Leary Newfoundland Poetry Awards: **Literary Prizes in English**
Oleksandriv, Borys: **Ukrainian Writing**
Oligny, Odette: **Children's Literature in French**
Oligocene epoch: **Cypress Hills; Paleontology, History in Canada**
Oliphant, L.: **Exploration & Travel Literature in English**
Oliver, Al: **Montreal Expos**
Oliver, Bill: **Film**
Oliver, Murray: **Interior Design**
Oliver, Thelma: **25th Street Theatre**
Oliveriana chart: **Cartography, History of**
Olivier, François: **Children's Literature in French**
Olmstead, Bert: **Toronto Maple Leafs**
Olnick, Harvey J.: **Musicology**
Olsen, Dennis: **Elites**
Olsen, Phil: **Track & Field**
Olson, Charles: **Poetry in English**
Olson, Clifford R.: *R v Olson*
Olson, Gary: **Painting**
Olympia & York Developments Ltd: **Abitibi-Price Inc; Development Industry; Reichmann family**
Olympia Floor & Wall Tile: **Reichmann family**
Olympic Act: **Lottery**
Olympic Gymnasia: **Gymnastics**
Olympic Island: **Toronto Islands**
Olympic Rowing Basin: **Rowing**
Olympic Saddledome: **Calgary**
Olympic Stadium: **Montréal; Montreal Concordes; Montreal Expos; Soccer**
Omega: **Death & Dying**
Omineca Crystalline Belt: **Geological Regions**
Omineca gold rush: **Nechako River; Sekani; Skeena River**
Omineca Mountains: **Rocky Mountain Trench; Yukon Territory**
Omineca River: **Gold Rushes; Mackenzie**
Ommanney Bay: **Kennedy, William**
Onaping Falls, Ont: **Sudbury**
oncogene: **Cancer**
One Arrow Reserve: **Almighty Voice**
One Hundred Mile House, BC: **New Religious Movements**
Oné-Onti: **Gros-Louis, Max**
Oneida Reserve: **Handsome Lake Religion**
O'Neil, Bruce: **Painting**
O'Neill, Charles: **Music History**
O'Neill, Louis: **Dion, Gérard**
Only Paper Today: **Art Writing & Criticism**
Onondaga Escarpment: **Niagara Peninsula**
Onstage '81: **Theatre, English-Language**
Ontario: **Sailing Ships**
Ontario, Simcoe & Huron Railway: **Collingwood; Fleming, Sandford; Guarantee Act; Northern Railway of Canada; Railway History**
Ontario Advisory Council for the Disabled: **Watson, William**
Ontario Agricultural & Arts Assn: **Wilmot, Samuel**
Ontario Agricultural College: **Agricultural Economics; Agricultural Education; Agricultural Research & Development; Bethune, Charles James Stewart; Holland Marsh; Macdonald, William C.; McMurrich, James Playfair; Miller, George Martell; Physical Geography; Robertson, James Wilson; Soil Science; University of Guelph**
Ontario Air Service: **Sault Ste Marie**
Ontario Amateur Softball Assn: **Baseball**
Ontario Archaeological Soc: **Emerson, John Norman**
Ontario Arts Council: **Applebaum, Louis; Choreography; Dance History; Ontario; Small Presses**
Ontario Assn of Architects: **Architecture, Development; Marani, Ferdinand Herbert**
Ontario Bible College: **Bible Schools**
Ontario Bus Industries: **Bus Transportation**

Ontario Centre for Microelectronics: **Electronics Industry**
Ontario Club: **Sproatt and Rolph**
Ontario College of Education: **Althouse, John George**
Ontario College of Pharmacy: **Pharmaceuticals Industry; Saunders, William**
Ontario College of Physicians & Surgeons: **Aikins, William Thomas**
Ontario Commercial Registration Appeal Tribunal: **Regulatory Process**
Ontario Council of Regents: **Community College**
Ontario Council of University Libraries: **Libraries**
Ontario Court of Appeal: **Ontario**
Ontario Dental Assn: **Associations; Dentistry**
Ontario Deposit Insurance Corp: **Ambridge, Douglas White**
Ontario Educational Assn: **Associations**
Ontario Educational Communications Authority: **Educational Broadcasting**
Ontario Experimental Fur Farm: **Parasitology**
Ontario Federation of Agriculture: **Hannam, Herbert H.; United Farmers of Ontario**
Ontario Federation of Labour: **Burt, George**
Ontario Federation of Naturalists: **Hiking**
Ontario Fruit Growers' Assn: **Associations**
Ontario Geological Survey: **Geomorphology**
Ontario Geriatrics Research Soc: **Gerontology**
Ontario Grange: **Agriculture History; Morrison, James, "J.J."; United Farmers of Ontario**
Ontario Heritage Foundation: **Heritage Conservation**
Ontario Human Rights Commission: **Symons, Thomas H.B.**
Ontario Hydro-Electric Power Commission: **Beck, Adam; Electric Power**
Ontario Institute for Studies in Education: **Canadian Studies; Computer-Assisted Learning; Kidd, J. Robbins; University of Toronto**
Ontario Jockey Club: **Seagram, Joseph E.; Taylor, Edward Plunkett; Thoroughbred Racing**
Ontario Lacrosse Assn: **Conacher, Lionel P.**
Ontario Ladies College: **Miller, George Martell**
Ontario Marketing Board: **Agriculture History**
Ontario Medical Assn: **Canniff, William**
Ontario Medical College for Women: **Medicine, History of; Stowe-Gullen, A. Augusta**
Ontario Métis & Non-Status Indian Assn: **Harper, Vern; Métis**
Ontario Native Women's Assn: **Native People, Urban Migration**
Ontario New Universities Library Project: **Libraries**
Ontario Northland Communications: **Ontario Northland Transportation Commission**
Ontario Palliative Care Assn: **Death & Dying**
Ontario Paper Co: **Ambridge, Douglas White**
Ontario Parliament Buildings: **Toronto**
Ontario Place: **Canadian National Exhibition; Ferguson, Ivan Graeme; *Haida*; Toronto Symphony; Zeidler, Eberhard Heinrich**
Ontario Plain: **Niagara Peninsula**
Ontario Potters Assn: **Ceramics, Contemporary**
Ontario Professional Organizations Committee: **Economic Regulation**
Ontario Provincial Air Service: **Bush Flying**
Ontario Provincial Lunatic Asylum: **Clarke, Charles Kirk; Workman, Joseph**
Ontario Provincial Museum: **Archaeology; Boyle, David; Wintemberg, William John**

Ontario Provincial Police: **Casson, Alfred Joseph; Policing**
Ontario Psychogeriatric Assn: **Gerontology**
Ontario Railway & Municipal Board: **Dagger, Francis**
Ontario Rugby Football Union: **Football; Hamilton Tiger Cats**
Ontario-St Lawrence Development Commission: **Upper Canada Village**
Ontario School of Agriculture: **Agricultural Education; Agricultural Research & Development; University of Guelph**
Ontario School of Art & Design: **Schreiber, Charlotte Mount Brock**
Ontario Securities Commission: **Drew, George A.**
Ontario Soc for Crippled Children: **Watson, William**
Ontario Soc of Artists: **Art Education; Artists' Organizations; Bush, John H.; Forster, John Wycliffe Lowes; Fraser, John A.; MacDonald, James Edward Hervey; Manly, Charles MacDonald; O'Brien, Lucius R.; Ontario College of Art; Printmaking**
Ontario Summer Games: **Peterborough**
Ontario Teachers' Federation: **Federation of Women Teachers' Assn of Ontario**
Ontario Trappers Assn: **Fur Trapping, Contemporary**
Ontario Universities Athletic Assn: **Football**
Ontario Veterinary Assn: **Smith, Andrew; Veterinary Medicine, History**
Ontario Veterinary College: **McGilvray, Charles Duncan; Parasitology; Rutherford, John Gunion; University of Guelph; Veterinary Medicine; Veterinary Medicine, Education; Veterinary Medicine, History**
Ontario Veterinary Medical Assn: **Veterinary Medicine, History**
Ontario Waste Management Corp: **Chant, Donald Alfred**
Ontario Winter Games: **Thunder Bay**
Ontario Workman: **Hewitt, John**
Ookpik Carnival: **Festivals**
Oolichan Books: **Regionalism in Literature**
Oowekeeno (Owikeno): **Bella Bella**
Oowekyala language: **Bella Bella; Kwakiutl**
Opabinia: **Burgess Shale Site**
Opasquia Indian Days: **Festivals**
open-area schools: **Education, Early-Childhood; School Facilities**
Open Circle: **Theatre, English-Language**
open-hearth process: **Dominion Foundries & Steel, Ltd; Iron & Steel Industry; Sydney Steel Corp**
Open Learning Institute: **Community College; Distance Learning**
Open Letter: **Bowering, George; Davey, Frank; Literary Magazines in English; Literature in English - Theory & Criticism**
open-line radio: **Webster, Jack**
open-pit mining: **British Columbia; Coal Mining; Rocky Mountains**
Open Studio: **Printmaking**
Opera Canada: **Music History**
Opéra de chambre du Québec: **Opera**
Opéra de Montréal: **Music History; Opera**
Opéra du Québec: **Music History; Opera; Place des Arts; Simoneau, Léopold; Vickers, Jonathan S.**
Opera Festival Assn: **Canadian Opera Co**
Opera Guild of Montréal: **Donalda, Pauline; Quilico, Louis**
opera houses: **Concert Halls & Opera Houses; Theatre, English-Language**
Operation *Blockbuster*: **Battle of the Rhineland**
Operation *Dismantle*: **Peace Movement**
Operation *Muskox*: **Baker Lake**
Operation *Oil*: **McTaggart-Cowan, Patrick Duncan**
Operation *Overlord*: **Normandy Invasion**
Operation *Umbrella*: **Rainmaking**

Operation *Veritable*: **Battle of the Rhineland**
operetta: **Musical Theatre; Theatre, French-Language**
ophiuroids: **Echinodermata**
Opimian Soc: **Cuisine**
Opinaca River: **James Bay Project**
Opinion publique illustré: **Cartoons; Literary Periodicals in French; Magazines; Mousseau, Joseph-Alfred**
opium: **Chinese; Drug Use, Non-Medical; Medical Drug Abuse; Medicine, History of; Pharmaceuticals Industry**
Opocopa, Lac: **Moisie, Rivière**
Oppenheimer, David: **Vancouver**
Opportunities for Youth: **Labour Policy; Poverty; Theatre, English-Language**
optical fibre: **Cable Television; Computer Communications; Laser; Telidon**
optical glass: **Phillips, W. Eric**
optical telescope: **Chant, Clarence Augustus**
opticon: **Education, Special**
optics: **Meteorology; Photography; Physics**
Opus Dei: **Secret Societies**
Oracle: **Folklore**
Orangemen's Day: **National Holidays**
Orangeville, Ont: **Niagara Escarpment; Place-names**
oratorio: **Religious Music**
Orchard, William J.: **Archaeology**
orchard grass: **Forage Crops**
orchards: **Annapolis Lowlands; Cuisine; Okanagan Valley; Osoyoos; Penticton; Sharp, Francis Peabody**
Orchestre symphonique de Québec: **Arts Funding; Léveillée, Claude; Orchestral Music; Pelletier, Wilfrid; Québec City**
ORDCO Technology Ltd: **Ontario Research Foundation**
Order of Baronets: **Nova Scotia**
Order of Friars Preachers: **Collège dominicain de philosophie et de théologie**
Order of Presentation Sisters: **St John's**
Order of Sleeping Car Porters: **West Indians**
Order of the Holy Cross: **Christian Religious Communities**
Order Paper: **House of Commons; Parliamentary Procedure**
Orders of Prohibition: **White-Collar Crime**
Ordnance Land: **Rondeau Provincial Park**
Ordovician period: **Echinodermata; Mineral Naming; New Brunswick; Paleontology, History in Canada; Trilobite; Wilson, Alice E.**
Ordre mondial des gourmets: **Cuisine**
Ordre royal et militaire de Saint Louis: **Croix de Saint Louis**
Oregon: **New Caledonia**
Oregon: **Chinese**
Oregon box: **Vegetation Regions - Cordillera**
Oregon grape: **Plants, Native Uses**
Oregon wintergreen: **Vegetation Regions - Cordillera**
Orenda: **Native People, Religion**
Orenda engine: **Industrial Research & Development**
Orford, Mont: **Mount Orford Park**
Orford Art Centre: **Guitar; Jeunesses musicales du Canada; Mount Orford Park**
Orford Refining Co: **Sudbury**
organ & organ music: **Gilbert, Kenneth; Labrosse, Paul-Raymond Jourdain; Musical Instruments; Musicology; Pewter; Religious Music; Robb, F. Morse**
organ transplantation: **Bioethics; Medical Ethics; Medical Jurisprudence; Medicine, Contemporary**
organic chemistry: **Chemistry Subdisciplines; Harding, Victor John; Khorana, Har Gobind; Lemieux, Raymond U.; Wiesner, Karel**
organic synthesis: **Deslongchamps, Pierre**

Organization for Economic Cooperation & Development: **Agricultural Aid; Economic Forecasting; Education Organization; Hazardous Wastes; Ostry, Sylvia; School Systems; Science Policy**
Organization of Ontario with Self-help Tactics: **Blindness & Visual Impairment**
oriental poppy: **Flowers, Cultivated**
Original Discovery no 1: **Oil City**
Orkney, James: **Furniture, English, Scottish & American**
ornithology: **Baillie, James L.; Biology; Broley, Charles Lavelle; Cinq-Mars, Lionel; Cowan, Ian McTaggart; Rowan, William; Taverner, Percy A.; Tyrrell, Joseph B.**
Ornstein, Robert: **Literature in English**
Oromocto Band: **Land Claims**
Oromocto Reserve: **Maliseet**
Oromocto River: **Oromocto**
orphanage: **Child Welfare; Grenfell, Wilfred T.; Nursing; Pentecostal Movement; Spencer, David; Walking Buffalo**
Orpheum Theatre: **Heritage Conservation; Vancouver**
Orr, Rowland B.: **Archaeology**
Orsainville, Qué: **Québec City**
Orser, George W.: **Baptists**
Orser, William: **Hartland**
orthoclase: **Mineral**
orthoptics: **Optometry**
Orwell Corner, PEI: **Prince Edward Island**
Osborne, Gwendolen: **Ballet**
Osborne, Henry: **Newfoundland**
Osborne, Lyndal: **Printmaking**
Osborne, Stanley L.: **Hymns**
Osburne, Marg: **Messer, Don, & the Islanders**
Osgoode Hall Law School: **Law & Society; Legal Education; Osgoode, William; Osgoode Hall; Wright, Cecil Augustus; York University**
Oshawa Generals: **Canadian Olympic Hockey Team; Orr, Robert G.**
Oshawa *Vindicator*: **Firearm**
Oshweken, Ont: **Indian Art**
Osisko, Lac: **Rouyn-Noranda**
Osler & Harcourt: **Wilson, Bertha**
Osler Library: **Osler, William**
osmium: **Platinum**
Osnaburgh, Upper Canada: **Macdonell, Miles**
Osoyoos Lake: **Okanagan Valley; Osoyoos**
Ossant, Lac: **Bienville, Lac**
ossuary: **Archaeology; Feast of the Dead**
osteichthyes: **Fish**
Ostenfeld, Man: **Danes**
osteoporosis: **Estrogen**
Ostiguy, Jean-René: **National Gallery of Canada**
ostracoda: **Crustacean**
ostrich fern: **Fiddlehead Greens**
O'Sullivan, Michael: **Nursing**
O'Sullivan, Shawn: **Boxing**
Otanabee, Upper Canada: **Fife, David**
Otis Elevator Co: **Architecture, Development; Hamilton**
Otonabee River: **Autobiographical Writing in English; Canoeing; Kawartha Lakes; Peterborough; Traill, Catharine Parr; Trent Canal**
Otoskwin River: **Attawapiskat River**
Ottawa, Arnprior & Parry Sound Railway: **Booth, John Rudolphus**
Ottawa '67s: **Ottawa, Ont**
Ottawa & Prescott Railway: **Shanly, Walter**
Ottawa Art Assn: **Brownell, Peleg Franklin**
Ottawa Art School: **Brownell, Peleg Franklin**
Ottawa Capital Marathon: **Sports History**
Ottawa Citizen: **German Writing; Southam, William**
Ottawa City Hall: **Archambault, Louis; Architecture, Development**
Ottawa Civic Hospital: **Mitchell, Charles Alexander**
Ottawa Country Club: **Golf**
Ottawa Drama League: **Theatre, English-Language**
Ottawa Electric Co: **Bronson, Erskine Henry**

Ottawa Free Press: **Hayes, Kate S.;** *Ottawa Journal*
Ottawa General Hospital: **Bregman & Hamann; Labelle, Huguette**
Ottawa Glass Works: **Glass**
Ottawa Improvement Commission: **Ahearn, Thomas**
Ottawa International Airport: **Airport Architecture; Archambault, Louis**
Ottawa Islands: **Hudson Bay; Ungava Inuit**
Ottawa Journal: **Brittain, Donald; Grey Cup; O'Leary, M. Grattan; Smart, Elizabeth; Smith, Irving Norman**
Ottawa Little Theatre: **Literary Prizes in English; Little Theatre Movement; Scott, Duncan Campbell**
Ottawa Naturalist: **Ami, Henri-Marc; Taylor, George William**
Ottawa Planning Board: **Ottawa, Ont**
Ottawa Power Co: **Bronson, Erskine Henry**
Ottawa Public Library: **Burpee, Lawrence Johnston**
Ottawa Research Station: **Flowers, Cultivated; Ornamentals**
Ottawa River Canal: **Canals & Inland Waterways**
Ottawa River Solar Observatory: **Sun**
Ottawa St Brigid's: **Ottawa Rough Riders**
Ottawa Senators: **National Hockey League; Ottawa Rough Riders; Stanley Cup**
Ottawa Silver Seven: **Stanley Cup**
Ottawa Ski Club: **Ski Jumping**
Ottawa Town Planning Commission: **Cauchon, J.-E.-Noulan**
Ottawa Trades Council: **O'Donoghue, Daniel J.**
Ottawa Typographical Union: **O'Donoghue, Daniel J.**
Ottawa Valley: **Champlain Sea; Labelle, F.-X.-Antoine; Oral Literature in English; Ottawa, Ont; Pulp & Paper Industry; St Lawrence Lowland; Timber Slide; Timber Trade History**
Ottawa Valley Power Co: **Killam, Izaak Walton**
Otter Creek, Nfld: **Happy Valley-Goose Bay**
Otter Lake: **Erickson**
Otterville, Ont: **Innis, Harold A.**
Ottey, Milt: **Track & Field**
Ouchterlony, David: **Choral Music**
Ouellet, Fernand: **French Canadian Nationalism**
Oughton: **Baldoon**
Ouiatchouane, Rivière: **Parc de Val-Jalbert; Saint-Jean, Lac**
Ouimet, André: **Fils de la Liberté**
Ouimetoscope: **Ouimet, L.-Ernest**
Oulton, Robert T.: **Summerside**
Ounontisaston: **Neutral**
Our Generation: **New Left**
Outaouaise: **Sculpture**
Outardes, Rivière: **Baie-Comeau**
Outchibou: **Ojibwa**
Outer Space Treaty: **Air Law & Space Law**
Outlander: **Survenant**
outlaws: **Donnellys; McLean Gang; Masterless Men of Newfoundland**
Outlaws, the: **Organized Crime**
Outlook, Sask: **Lutherans**
Outlook College: **Norwegians**
Outlook Conference: **Wesson, John Henry**
Outpost Nursing Committee: **Crafts**
Outram, Richard: **Literature in English**
Ouvrard, René: **Novel in French**
Ouzounian, Richard: **Festival Lennoxville; Manitoba Theatre Centre**
oval-leaved blueberry: **Vegetation Regions - Cordillera**
ovenbird: **Biogeography; Warbler**
Ovens, Raymond: **Purcell String Quartet**
ovens & ovenware: **Domestic Utensils; Electrical Appliances Industry; Nepheline Syenite**
Overseas Book Centre: **Kidd, J. Robbins**
Overseas Institute: **Kidd, J. Robbins**
overtime: **Employment Law**
OVO: **Photography**
ovum: **Family Law**

Owen, Edward Campbell Rich: **Owen Sound**
Owen, William: **Campobello Island**
Owen, William F.: **Bayfield, Henry Wolsey; Cartography, History of; Georgian Bay**
Owen Sound: **Poetry in English**
Owen Sound Portland Cement Co: **Butchart, Robert Pim**
Owen Sound Summer Folk Festival: **Folk Festivals**
Owenite community: **Co-operative Movement (See Addendum, page 1992)**
Owens, Joseph: **Philosophy**
Owens Art Institute: **Art Education**
Owl: **Children's Literature in English**
oxbow: **Lake; River Landform**
Oxbow, Sask: **Allen, Ralph**
Oxbow Lake: **Saskatoon**
Oxen Pond Botanic Park: **Memorial University of Newfoundland**
Oxfam Canada: **Agricultural Aid; Canada-Third World Relations**
Oxford, Upper Canada: **Woodstock, Ont**
Oxford House, Man: **Steinhauer, Henry Bird**
Oxford Lake: **Hayes River; Manitoba**
Oxford University Press: **Book Publishing, English-Language; Lane, Patrick**
Oxford Village, Upper Canada: **Ingersoll**
oxide: **Mineral**
Oxley Ranch: **Ranching History**
oxygen: **Chemistry; Chemistry Subdisciplines; Crop Research; Iron & Steel Industry; Molecules in Interstellar Space; Spring**
oyster drill: **Whelk**
Oyster Harbour: **Ladysmith**
Oyster River: **University of British Columbia**
Ozawa, Seiji: **Toronto Symphony**
Ozette: **Nootka**
ozone: **Pollution**

P

P. Burns & Co: **Meat-Processing Industry**
P.J. Gardiner Institute of Small Business Studies: **Memorial University of Newfoundland**
Pablum: **Drake, Theodore George Gustavus Harwood; University of Toronto**
Pacaud, Ernest: *Soleil*
pacemaker: **Computer Systems Applications; Heart Disease; Nuclear Energy; Platinum; Safety Standards**
pacer: **Harness Racing; Horse**
Pachena, BC: **Lighthouses**
Paci, Frank: **Ethnic Literature; Italian Writing**
Pacific Centre: **Vancouver**
Pacific Coach Lines: **Bus Transportation**
Pacific Coast Baseball League: **Edmonton**
Pacific Coast Terminal: **Port Coquitlam**
Pacific coastal strawberry: **Vegetation Regions - Pacific Coastal**
Pacific Coliseum: **Vancouver Canucks**
Pacific Creek: **Athabasca Pass**
Pacific Great Eastern Railway: **Ashcroft; Brewster, Harlan Carey; British Columbia Railway; Dawson Creek; Johnson, Byron Ingemar; North Vancouver; Oliver, John; Prince George; Quesnel; Vancouver; Woodward, Charles**
Pacific locomotive: **Locomotives & Rolling Stock**
Pacific Marine Training Institute: **Community College**
Pacific National Exhibition: **Basketball; Japanese; Vancouver**
Pacific ocean perch: **Fisheries; Scorpionfish**
Pacific Oceanographic Group: **Tully, John Patrick**
Pacific Petroleums Ltd: **McMahon, Francis M.P.**
Pacific Plate: **Earthquake**
Pacific Shelf: **Geological Regions**
Pacific Station: **Hornby Island**

Pacific Vocational Institute: **Community College**
pack ice: **Cabot Strait; Glace Bay; Labrador Sea; Parry Channel; Sea Ice**
Packaging & Labelling Act: **Consumer Standards; Consumers' Association of Canada**
Packard, Frank L.: **Best-Sellers in English; Popular Literature in English**
PACXnet: **Electronics Industry**
Paddle Prairie, Alta: **Métis Settlements**
paddlefish: **Endangered Animals**
paddlewheeler: *Accommodation;* **Beaver; Steamboats & Paddlewheelers**
Page, Graeme: **Canadian Brass**
Pagé, Jacques: **Silver, Church; Silver, Domestic**
Page, James E.: **Association for Canadian Studies; Canadian Studies; Symons, Thomas H.B.; Women & Education**
Pagé, Pierre: **Literature in French - Scholarship & Teaching**
Page, Robert: **Committee for an Independent Canada**
Page & Steele: **Architectural Styles**
Page-Hersey Tubes Ltd: **Stelco Inc**
Pahtahsega: **Jacobs, Peter**
Paikeday, T.M.: **Dictionary**
Paiment, André: **Theatre, French-Language**
Painchaud, Paul: **Essay in French**
Paint & Drawing Council of Canada: **Artists' Organizations**
Paint Pots: **Spring**
Paintearth Mine: **Coal**
pak-choi Chinese cabbage: **Vegetable**
Pakenham, Alma V.C.D.: **Rattenbury, Francis M.**
Pakistanis: **Prejudice & Discrimination; South Asians**
Palace Grand Theatre: **Dawson**
Palais de Congrès: **Hull; Prus, Victor Marius**
Palais de Justice: **Cormier, Ernest; Daudelin, Charles**
Palais Royale: **Niosi, Bert**
Palardy, Jean: **Art Writing & Criticism; Film**
paleobotany: **Botany History; Fossil Plants; Stewart, Wilson Nichols**
Paleocene epoch: **Bird Classification & Evolution; Fossil Plants**
paleoecology: **Palynology**
Paleoeskimo: **Bloody Falls; Brooman Point Village; Igloolik Sites; Labrador; Okak; Port Refuge; Pre-Dorset; Prehistory; Terra Nova National Park**
Paleolithic era: **Fishing, Ice**
Paleozoic era: **Alberta; Brachiopoda; Geological Dating; Geological History; Kluane Ranges; Mollusc; Paleontology, History in Canada; Physiographic Regions - Arctic Lands; St Lawrence Lowland; Southampton Island; Trilobite; Wilson, Alice E.**
Palestine, Man: **Gladstone**
Palestinians: **Arabs; Orthodox Church**
Palgrave, Ont: **Milne, David B.**
Pali texts: **Buddhism**
palisade: **Fortification**
Palisade Lake Dam: **Agar, Carlyle Clare**
palladium: **Platinum**
Palladium: **Whelan, Edward**
Palliative Care Foundation: **Death & Dying**
Palliser Distillers: **Lethbridge**
Palliser Formation: **Sedimentary Rock**
Palliser Pass: **Great Divide Trail**
Palliser Triangle: **Drought; Palliser Expedition**
Palmason, Diane: **Long-Distance Running**
Palmer, Bryan: **Marxism; Social History; Working-Class History**
Palmer, D.D.: **Chiropractic**
Palmer, Dorothea: **Birth Control**
Palmer, Eli J.: **Photography**
Palmer, Olive Freeman: **Diefenbaker, John G.**
palouse prairie: **Vegetation Regions - Prairie**
palsa: **Periglacial Landform; Permafrost**
Pampalon, Alfred: **Saints**
Pan-Am Swimming Pool: **Winnipeg**

Pan-Indian powwow: **Folk Dance**
Panaccio, Claude: **Philosophy**
PanArctic Oils Ltd: **Disasters; Petroleum Industries**
PanCanadian Petroleum Ltd: **Canadian Pacific Railway**
pancreas: **Diabetes Mellitus; Insulin; Wesbrook, Frank Fairchild**
Pandora: **Oceanography**
Pandora Expedition: **Tookoolito, "Hannah"**
Panet, Bernard-Claude: **Taschereau, Elzéar-Alexander**
Panet, Marie: **Taschereau, Elzéar-Alexander**
Pangea Continent: **Geological Regions; Plate Tectonics**
Pangman, Peter: **Pangman, Bastonnais**
Pangnirtung Fjord: **Pangnirtung**
Pangnirtung Pass: **Baffin Island**
Panitch, Leo: **Marxism**
Panko, William: **Folk Art**
Pannell, Raymond: **Opera**
Panorama Ski Resort: **Invermere**
pansy: **Violet**
Pap test: **Cancer; Hilliard, Anna Marion; Medicine, Contemporary**
Papachristidis Maritime Inc: **Shipping Industry**
paper: **Corn, Field; Flax; Nepheline Syenite; Northwest Coast Indian Art; Postage Stamps; Price, William (1867-1924); Pulp & Paper Industry; Quarrying Industry; Sedge; Soapstone**
Paper Control Tribunal: *Fort Frances Case*
paper money: **Flax; Playing-Card Money; Shinplasters**
Paperk, Josie: **Inuit Art**
Papin, Joseph: **Parti rouge**
Papineau, Gèrin-Lajoie, LeBlanc, Edwards: **Airport Architecture**
Pâquet, Benjamin: **Taschereau, Elzéar-Alexander**
Paquet, Léonce: **Philosophy**
Paquette, Vincent: **Film**
Paquin, Ubald: **Popular Literature in French**
Parachute: **Art, Contemporary Trends**
Parachute Centre: **Art Writing & Criticism**
Paradis, Alodie-Virginie: **Saints**
Paradis, Father: **Timiskaming, Lake**
Paradis, Roland: **Silver, Church; Silver, Domestic**
Paradis, Suzanne: **Poetry in French**
Paradise Mine: **Invermere**
paraffin: **Lighting; Petroleum**
Paraffine oil: **Lighting**
Paragon Insurance of Canada Ltd: **Webster, Lorne Campbell**
Paragon Sales book: **Print Industry**
Parallel: **Literary Magazines in English**
Parallelogramme: **Art, Contemporary Trends**
paralytic shellfish poisoning: **Molluscan Resources**
paraplegia: **Disability; Injury & Prevention**
parasite: **Animal Agriculture; Ant; Arachnida; Beetle; Butterfly; Crop Research; Crustacean; Cuckoo; Duck; Fish; Flatworm; Flea; Fly; Food Poisoning; Fungus; Grasshopper; Lamprey; Leech; Louse; Mistletoe; Mite; Mollusc; Morning Glory; Nematoda; Paintbrush; Parasitology; Perch; Pike; Tick; Virus; Warbler; Wasp; Water-Borne Disease; Yeast**
pardon: **Royal Prerogative of Mercy**
Paré, Jean: *Actualité; Gutenberg Galaxy*
Paré, Roger: **Children's Literature in French**
Parent, Alphonse-Marie: **Quiet Revolution**
Parent, Lac: **Nottaway, Rivière**
Parent, Louis-Joseph: **Sculpture**
Parent Commission: **Collège d'enseignement général et professionnel; Music Education; Québec; Quiet Revolution; Sociology**
parent-education programs: **Social & Welfare Services**
parental benefits: **Women & the Law**
Parents' Information Bureau: **Birth Control**
Parian porcelain: **Ceramics**
Paris Convention: **Hazardous Wastes**

"Paris Four": **Rowing**
Paris Peace Conference: **Biggar, Oliver Mowat; Borden, Robert L.; Christie, Loring C.; Commonwealth; Doherty, Charles Joseph; Sifton, Arthur L.; Treaty of Versailles**
Parish Schools Act: **Lower Canada**
Parisien, Norbert: **Schultz, John Christian**
Parizeau: **Oceanography**
Parizeau, Jacques: **Parizeau, Gérard**
Parizeau, Marcel: **Architectural Styles; Architecture, Development; Barbeau, Marcel**
Parizeau, R.: **Parizeau, Gérard**
Park, Dorothy Allan: **Singing**
Park Gallery: **Painters Eleven**
Park Lake Provincial Park: **Parks, Provincial**
Park Royal (Vancouver): **Development Industry**
Park Steamship Co: **Shipbuilding & Ship Repair**
Park Valley, Sask: **Campbell, Maria**
Parkdale, PEI: **Prince Edward Island**
Parker, Alfred J.: **New Religious Movements**
Parker, David: **Medicine, History of**
Parker, Harley: **McLuhan, H. Marshall**
Parker, I.: **Economics, Radical**
Parker, Raymond: **Biological Product; Connaught Laboratories Ltd**
Parkin, Edmond T.: **Parkin, John B.**
Parkinsonian syndrome: **Influenza**
Parkinson's Disease: **Disability; Seeman, Philip; Sourkes, Theodore Lionel**
parkland: **Alberta; Waskahegan Trail**
Parkman, Francis: **Historiography**
Parks, Francis: **Parksville**
Parks Canada: **Archaeology; Bellevue House; Conservation of Movable Cultural Property; Diving, Underwater; Fort Walsh; Gaspé, Qué; Heritage Conservation; Indian Affairs & Northern Development, Dept of; Landscape Architecture; L'Anse aux Meadows; Louisbourg; Lower Fort Garry; Mingan, Iles de; Niagara Historic Frontier; Parks, National; Restigouche; Richelieu, Rivière; Rocky Mountain House National Historic Park; St Lawrence Seaway; Trent Canal; Trois-Rivières; York Factory**
Parkwood Stables: **Thoroughbred Racing**
Parliament, Opening of: **Speech from the Throne**
Parliament Building (Qué): **Huot, Charles**
Parliament Hill: **Centennial Year; Constitution, Patriation of**
Parliamentarians for World Order: **Peace Movement**
parliamentary debate: **Committees; *Hansard*; House of Commons**
parliamentary democracy: ***Alberta Press Act* Reference; Constitutional Law; Crown; Monarchism**
parliamentary secretary: **Committees; House of Commons**
parliamentary supremacy: **Constitutional History**
parliamentary system: **Conservatism; English; Government; Party Financing**
Parlow String Quartet: **Chamber Music; Parlow, Kathleen**
Parnassian movement: **Poetry in French**
parole: **Probation & Parole**
Parr, Joy: **Social History; Working-Class History**
Parr Town, NS: **Saint John**
Parrot, Jean-Claude: **Postal Strikes**
Parrsboro, NS: **Gesner, Abraham; Minas Basin**
Parry Island Ojibwa band: **Pegahmagabow, Francis**
parsley: **Herbs; Vegetable**
Parsnip River: **Mackenzie; Peace River**
Parsons, Bruce: **Art, Contemporary Trends**
Parsons, Buzz: **Soccer**
part-time students: **Community College; Concordia University; York University**

part-time work: **Fisheries; Postal Strikes; Status of Women; Status of Women in Canada, Royal Commission on the; Teaching Profession; Women in the Labour Force; Work**
Parti-Acadien: **New Brunswick**
Parti démocratique: **Parti rouge**
Parti fermier-progressiste du Québec: **United Farmers of Québec**
Parti national populaire: **Roy, Fabien**
Parti ouvrier: **Francq, Gustave; Verville, Alphonse; Working-Class History**
Parti socialiste du Québec: **Chartrand, Michel**
ParticipAction: **Physical Education; Sports History**
participatory democracy: **New Left**
particle-accelerator: **Physics**
particle board: **Forestry; Lumber & Wood Industries**
Partnenais, Anatole: **Sculpture**
partnership: **Civil Code; Corporation Law; Fisheries**
partridge: **Bird Classification & Evolution; Cuisine; Game Bird; Hunting**
Partridge, David: **Printmaking; Sculpture**
Partridge, Henry: **Partridge, Edward A.**
Partridge Island: **American Revolution; Foulis, Robert**
partridgeberry: **Cuisine; Newfoundland**
Partz, Felix: **Art, Contemporary Trends**
parvovirus: **Veterinary Medicine**
Pascal: **Computer-Assisted Learning; Computer Science**
Pasco, Duane: **Diesing, Freda**
Pasley Bay: **Boothia Peninsula**
Pasquia Hills: **Winnipegosis, Lake**
Pasquia (Man): **The Pas**
Pass Lake, Ont: **Danes**
Passage Harbour: **Come By Chance**
Passage Holdings Inc: **Canada Steamship Lines Inc**
Passamaquoddy: **St Andrews, NB**
Passe-Temps: **La Liberté, Alfred (musician); Music History**
Passfield, Loreen: **Marathon Swimming**
Passover: **Judaism**
passport: **Citizenship**
pasteurization: **Ontario; Technology**
pasture: **Agriculture History; Beef Cattle Farming; Crops; Forage Crops**
Pat Lowther Memorial Award: **Literary Prizes in English; Lowther, Patricia Louise**
Patel, C.K.N.: **Laser**
Patel, Ishu: **Film Animation**
paten: **Silver, Church**
paternity: **Family Law**
paternity benefits: **Women's Movement**
Pathfinder group: **Armed Forces - Air Force**
pathmaster: **Roads & Highways**
pathology: **Abbott, Maude E.S.; Biology; Boyd, William; Canniff, William; Osler, William; Persaud, Trivedi Vidhya Nandan; Veterinary Medicine**
patience plant: **Touch-me-not**
Patricia Airways & Exploration Ltd: **Bush Flying**
Patricia Bay, BC: **Geological Survey of Canada; Mann, Cedric Robert**
Patrick, A.P.: **Oil City**
Patrick, Bill: **Diving**
Patrie: **Harvey, Jean-Charles; Loranger, Jean-Aubert; Morin, Léo-Pol; Popular Literature in French; Tarte, Joseph-Israel**
Patriot: **Photography**
Patrons of Industry: **Agriculture History; Morrison, James, "J.J."; Partridge, Edward A.**
Patry, P.: **Film**
Patterson, A.P.: **Maritime Rights**
Patterson, Tom: **Neptune Theatre; Stratford Festival**
Patterson Bros: **Agricultural Implements**
Patterson Candy Co: **Confectionery Industry**
Patterson Lake: **Clearwater River (Alta/Sask)**

Patterson Medal: **Patterson, John; Stewart, Robert William; Thomson, Andrew**
Pattison, Nellie Lyle: **Popular Literature in English**
Pattison, William: **Tourism**
Paul, Henri: **Photography**
Paul Reserve: **Stoney**
Paul-Sauvé, Parc: **Oka**
Paul Taylor Dance Co: **Grossman, Daniel W.**
Paulassie: **Kananginak Pootoogook**
Paulatuk, NWT: **Mackenzie Inuit; Northwest Territories**
Paulette caveat: **Dene Nation**
Paulson, Jamie: **Badminton**
Pavey, Kathleen: **Milne, David B.**
Pavilion Reserve: **Salish, Interior**
pax: **Silver, Church**
Payette, Lise: **Television Programming**
payment for evidence: ***R v Olson***
Payne, Lac: **Ungava Inuit**
payroll: **Computer Systems Applications; Office Automation**
Pays laurentian: **Essay in French**
Pays théâtral: **Germain, Jean-Claude**
Paysana: **Guèvremont, Germaine**
Payzant, Geoffrey: **Gould, Glenn H.; Musicology**
Payzant, John: **Great Awakening**
PCBs: **Hazardous Wastes; Veterinary Medicine; Water Pollution**
pe-tsai Chinese cabbage: **Vegetable**
Peabody, Francis: **Chatham, NB**
Peace Arch News: **White Rock**
Peace-Athabasca Delta: **Slave River; Wood Buffalo National Park**
Peace Bridge: **Fort Erie**
Peace Hills: **Wetaskiwin**
Peace of Vereeniging: **South African War**
peace pipe: **Calumet**
Peace Point: **Peace River, Alta**
Peace River Canyon: **Dinosaur; Peace River**
Peace River coalfield: **Coal Mining**
Peace River Crossing: **Peace River, Alta**
Peace River hydroelectric project: **Dawson Creek; Peace River**
Peace Tower: **Parliament Buildings; Price, F. Percival**
Peach Bowl Convention Centre: **Penticton**
Peacock, Edward: **Maxville**
Peacock, Kenneth: **Folk Music, Anglo-Canadian; Musicology**
peanut: **Oilseed Crops**
Pearce, Bob: **Rowing**
Pearce Lake: **Schefferville**
pearl: **Mineral; Seashell**
Pearl, James: **Mount Pearl**
Pearl, Kenny: **Toronto Dance Theatre**
pearl ash: **Potash**
Pearse, Peter: **Fisheries Policy**
Pearson, F.S.: **Mackenzie, Alexander (1860-1943)**
Pearson, Richard N.: **Archaeology**
Pearson & Marchand: **Parliament Buildings**
Pearson Cup: **Baseball**
Pearson medal for peace: **Lévesque, Georges-Henri**
Peart, Neil: **Rush**
Peary caribou: **Arctic Archipelago; Caribou; Prince of Wales Island; Somerset Island; Stefansson Island; Vegetation Regions - Arctic Tundra**
Peberdy, Harold: **Film Animation**
Peck, Brian: **Postal System**
Peck, Robin: **Sculpture**
Peck Rolling Mills: **Lang, Charles Benjamin**
pectin: **Apple**
Pedder Bay: **Downs, Barry Vance**
Pedersen, Paul: **Musicology**
Pedestal: **Women's Movement**
pediment: **Desert; River Landform**
pedology: **Soil Science**
Peekaboo Corner, NB: **Place-names**
Peel Channel: **Mackenzie River**
Peel River: **Fort McPherson; Yukon Territory**
Peel Sound: **Ross, James C.**
Peepeekesis Reserve: **Deiter, Walter**
Peggy's Cove, NS: **St Margaret's Bay**
Péghaire, J.: **Philosophy**
Pegis, Anton: **Philosophy**
Pei, I.M.: **Bank Architecture; Place Ville Marie**

Peigan Reserve: **Smallboy, Johnny Bob**
Pekisko, Alta: **Lane, George**
pelargonium: **Flowers, Cultivated**
Pélican: **Iberville, Pierre Le Moyne d'**
Pelican Rapids: **Slave River**
Pelland, Louis: **Radio Drama, French-Language**
Pellegrin, Gabriel: **Cartography, History of**
Pelletier, Albert: **Book Publishing, French-Language; Literature in French - Criticism & Theory**
Pelletier, Alexandrine: **Pelletier, Gérard**
Pelletier, Denise: **Roux, Jean-Louis**
Pelletier, Georges: ***Devoir***
Pelletier, Gilles: **Deyglun, Henri**
Pelletier, Pierre-Yves: **Graphic Design**
Pelletier, Romain-Octave: **Champagne, Claude**
Pelly, John H.: **Back River; Pelly Bay**
Pelly Lake: **Back River**
Pelly Mountains: **Liard River**
Pelly River: **Yukon River; Yukon Territory**
Péloquin, Claude: **Poetry in French**
Pemberton, Joseph: **Cartography, History of**
Pemberton Valley: **Salish, Interior**
Pembina, N Dak: **Red River Colony**
Pembina Hills: **Notre Dame de Lourdes**
Pembina oil field: **Alberta; Petroleum**
Pembina Resources Ltd: **Mannix, Frederick C.**
Pembina River (Alta): **Athabasca River**
Pembina Triangle: **Manitoba**
Pembroke: **Cook, James**
"Pemmican Proclamation": **Pangman, Bastonnais; Red River Colony**
Pen & Pencil Club: **Artists' Organizations; Harris, Robert**
Penacook: **Abenaki**
pence: **Money**
Pend-d'Oreille River: **Trail**
Pender, Daniel: **Balaklava Island**
Pendergast, James F.: **Archaeology**
pendulum: **Time**
Penelhum, Terence: **Philosophy**
Penetangore, Ont: **Kincardine**
Pengilly, Gordon: **Drama in English**
Penguin Books Canada Ltd: **Poetry in English**
Penguin Theatre: **Ottawa, Ont**
Penhallow, D.P.: **Botany History**
penicillin: **Allergies; Connaught Laboratories Ltd; Influenza; Medicine, Contemporary**
penitentiary: **Distribution of Powers; Kingston; Prison**
Penmarvian: **Paris**
Pennée, Georgina: ***Anciens Canadiens***
Penner, Jacob: **Russell, Robert Boyd**
Penner Report: **Native People, Government Policy**
Penney, Jennifer: **Dance History**
pennies: **Coinage**
Pennsylvania Dutch: **Furniture, German; Mennonites; Uxbridge**
Pennsylvanian period: **Fossil Plants; Lamprey; Nova Scotia; Vertebrate**
Penny, Evan: **Sculpture**
Penny, William: **Eenoolooapik; Franklin Search**
Penny Ice Cap: **Auyuittuq National Park**
Penobscot: **Abenaki; Micmac; Shaking Tent**
Penobscot Assn: **St Andrews, NB**
Penokean Fold Belt: **Geological Regions**
pension funds: **Mutual Funds; Trust**
pension indexing: **Lewis, David**
Pensions & National Health, Dept of: **Public Health**
Pentateuch: **Judaism**
Pentecostal Assemblies of Canada: **Evangelical Fellowship of Canada; Pentecostal Movement**
Pentland, H.C.: **Economics, Radical; Working-Class History**
Pentlatch: **Northern Georgia Strait Coast Salish**
Penumbra Press: **Small Presses**
Penutian language stock: **Native People, Languages**
peony: **Flowers, Cultivated**
People for Sunday Assn of Canada: **Lord's Day Alliance of Canada**
People's Party: **Bond, Robert; Morris, Edward P.**

"Peoples' Poet Award": **Acorn, Milton**
Pépin, Joseph: **Sculpture**
pepperroot: **Plants, Native Uses**
Pequawket dialect: **Abenaki**
Pequegnat, Arthur: **Clocks & Watches**
Percheron horse: **Horse; Lane, George**
percussion cap: **Firearm**
Percy, H.R.: **Short Fiction in English**
Performing Arts Centre: **University of Lethbridge**
Performing Arts in Canada: **Theatre, English-Language**
Performing Rights Organization of Canada: **Music History; Orchestre symphonique de Montréal; Recording Industry**
Performing Rights Organization of Canada Ltd: **Garant, Serge**
Péribonca, Rivière: **Saguenay River; Saint-Jean, Lac**
Perimeter Airlines: **Manitoba**
periodic table: **Geochemistry**
Periodical Distributors of Canada: **Literary Prizes in English**
Periodical Writers's Assn of Canada: **Writers' Union of Canada**
peristerite: **Gemstone**
Periwinkle Press: **Tanabe, Takao**
Perkins, F.: **Figure Skating**
Perkins, Kenneth: **Orford String Quartet**
Perl, Shabtai: **Jewish Writing**
Perley, George H.: **Ministry of Overseas Military Forces**
Perley, William: **Booth, John Rudolphus**
Permian period: **Beetle; Fossil Plants; Geological History**
Perrault, Jean-Baptiste: **Exploration & Travel Literature in French**
Perrault, Joseph-François: **Exploration & Travel Literature in French**
Perrault, Joseph-Julien: **Choral Music**
Perré, Henri: **Watson, Homer R.**
Perreault, Claude: **Zoology**
Perrier, Luc: **Poetry in French**
Perrin, H.C.: **Hymns**
Perron, Clément: **Film**
Perry, Norm: **Football**
Perry, P.J.: **Jazz**
Perry, Peter: **Clear Grits**
Perry's Corners, Ont: **Whitby**
Persephone Theatre: **Musical Theatre; Theatre, English-Language**
Pershing II missile: **Peace Movement**
Persian language: **Iranians; Language**
Persico, E.: **Physics**
Personal Insurance Co of Canada Ltd: **Webster, Lorne Campbell**
Personal Property Security Act: **Commercial Law**
personnel carriers: **Armed Forces - Unification**
perthite: **Gemstone**
Perticarini, Romano: **Italian Writing**
pertussis: **Biological Product; Connaught Laboratories Ltd**
Pesach: **Judaism**
Pest Control Products Act & Regulations: **Environmental Law; Food Legislation**
Pestieau, Joseph: **Philosophy**
Pétainism: **Philosophy**
Petawawa, Ont: **Ottawa River**
Petawawa National Forestry Institute: **Forestry**
Petawawa River: **Ottawa River; Petawawa, CFB**
Petch, Steve: **Tarragon Theatre**
Peter Jackson Trophy: **Golf**
Peter Martin publishers: **Book Publishing, English-Language**
Peter Pond Lake: **Churchill River**
Peterborough Canoe Co: **Peterborough**
Peterborough *Examiner*: **Davies, Robertson W.**
Peters, David: **Graphic Design**
Peters, Eliza: **Nickinson, John**
Peters, Fred: **Graphic Design**
Peters, James: **Photography**
Petersen, Len: **Allan, Andrew E.F.**
Petersfield, Man: **St Andrews, Man**
Peterson, Colleen: **Country & Western Music**
Peterson, Eric: **Humorous Writing in English; Theatre, English-Language**
Peterson, Garry: **Guess Who**
Peterson, Margaret: **O'Hagan, Howard**
Peterson, Roy: **Cartoons**
Peterson, William: **Capper, Stewart Henbest; McGill University**
Petit Chocpiele, NB: **Barns**

Petit Hermine: **Cartier, Jacques**
Petit Journal: **Germain, Jean-Claude; Harvey, Jean-Charles**
Petit Mécatina, Rivière du: **Boundaries**
Petit Messager du Très-Saint-Sacrement: **Nelligan, Emile**
Petit Séminaire de Québec: **Music History; Roy, Camille; Séminaire de Québec**
Petit train du nord: **Laurentian Highlands**
Petitcodiac River: **Chignecto Bay; Moncton; Riverview; Tide**
Petite Nation, Rivière de la: **Ottawa River**
Petite Nation seigneury: **Ottawa River; Papineau, Louis-Joseph**
Petite Rivière: **Petite Rivière, NS**
Petitjean, Léon: **Drama in French; Theatre, French-Language**
Petitot, Emile F.S.J.: **Slavey (Slave)**
Petitot River: **Liard River**
Petits Dessins: **Popular Literature in French**
Peto, Brassey, Jackson & Betts: **Grand Trunk Railway of Canada**
Petrie, Graham: **Novel in English**
petrified wood: **Gemstone**
Petrofina: **Chemical Industries; Steinberg, Samuel**
petroglyphs: **Betula Lake; Hornby Island; Inuit Art; Metlakatla Pass Sites; Ogopogo; Pictographs & Petroglyphs**
petrographic (polarizing) microscope: **Mineral**
petrography: **Rock**
Petroleum Administration Act: **Energy Policy; Resource Rights**
petroleum geology: **McLearn, Frank Harris**
Petroleum Incentives Program: **Economic Nationalism; Petroleum Industries**
Petroleum Park: **Wainwright**
petroleum-pricing issue: **Alberta; Lougheed, E. Peter; Pressure Group**
Petrolia, Ont: **Englehart, Jacob Lewis; Petroleum Research & Development**
Petromont consortium: **Chemical Industries**
Petrone, P.: **Henry, George**
Petrosar: **Sarnia**
Pettipas, Leo F.: **Archaeology**
Pettipiece, R.P.: **Union Centrals, District & Regional**
Pettkus v Becker: **Family Law; Property Law**
petunia: **Flowers, Cultivated**
Peyton, John: **Shawnandithit**
pH: **Acid Rain; Water Treatment**
Phanerozoic time: **Geological History; Geological Regions**
pharmacology: **Biology; Seeman, Philip**
Pharmaprix: **Steinberg, Samuel**
phenobarbital: **Pharmaceuticals Industry**
phenolic resin: **Lumber & Wood Industries**
phenomenology: **Philosophy**
Philadelphia Co: *Hector*; **Pictou**
philately: **Postage Stamps; Stamp Collecting**
Philibert, Nicholas: **Golden Dog**
Philip, Prince: **Newton, Lilias; Queen's Plate**
Philips Prize: **Literary Prizes in English**
Phillips, Alfie: **Diving**
Phillips, Bruce: **Journalism**
Phillips, George: **Glass**
Phillips, Paul: **Working-Class History**
Phillips, R.A.J.: **Heritage Canada Foundation**
Phillips, Robin: **Grand Theatre; Stratford Festival**
Phillips, Stu: **Country & Western Music**
Phillips, W.P.: **Crop Research**
Phillips, William: **Baseball**
Phillips, William (trumpeter): **Canadian Brass**
Phillips, Ziba: **Maitland**
Phillips Curve: **Economics**
Phillips Square: **Birks, Henry; Toronto City Hall**
Philp, O.B.: **Snowbirds**
Philpot, Terry: **Musical Instruments**
Phoenix: **Classics**
Phoenix (ship): *Breadalbane*

phonograph: **Bell, Alexander Graham**
phonology: **Language**
phosphate: **Mineral**
phosphorus: **Agricultural Soil Practices; Chemical Industries; Chemistry Subdisciplines; Dandelion; Iron & Steel Industry; Maple Sugar Industry; Mineral; Newfoundland; Okra; Onion; Soil Science; Water Pollution**
Photo Canada: **Art Writing & Criticism**
photo-electric arts: **Ontario College of Art**
photo-engraving: **Magazines**
photochemistry: **Chemistry Subdisciplines**
photocopying: **Authors & Their Milieu; Copyright Law**
photoelectric cell: **Bell, Alexander Graham**
photogrammetry: **Cartography, History of; Deville, Edouard Gaston; Helava, Uno Vilho; Soil Science; Surveying; Wheeler, Arthur Oliver**
photographic film: **Silver**
Photographic Soc of America: **Helders, Johan (John) A. J.**
photographic zenith tube: **Time**
photojournalism: **Curtin, Walter A.; Gaudard, Pierre; Lambeth, Michel; Photography; Spremo, Boris; Taconis, Kryn; Vanderpant, John**
photons: **Black Hole; Observatory**
photosphere: **Sun**
photosynthesis: **Algae; Blue-green Algae; Fossil Plants; Lake; Ocean; Plant; Solar Energy; Vegetation Regions - Coastal Marine Flora**
phototypesetter: **Print Industry**
photovoltaic cells: **Solar Energy**
physical chemistry: **Chemistry Subdisciplines**
physical cruelty: **Alimony; Family Law**
Physicians' Services Inc: **Foundations; Health Policy**
physiotherapy: **Arthritis; Health Policy; Status of Women**
phytopathology: **Plant Disease**
Piaget, Jean: **Literature in English**
Piapot Reserve: **Sainte-Marie, Buffy**
Piasetski, Leon: **Chess**
Pic River: **Superior, Lake**
Picard, Bernard: **Dance on Television & Film**
Picard, Jean-Claude: **Jeunesses musicales du Canada**
Picard, Laurent: **Newspapers**
Piccadily Head Provincial Park: **Port au Port Peninsula**
Piché, Alphonse: **Poetry in French**
Pick Eyes, Nfld: **Place-names**
Pickering, Ont: **Energy Policy**
Pickering College: **Newmarket**
picketing: **Labour Law; Strikes & Lockouts**
Pickett, A.D.: **Crop Research**
pickleweed: **Vegetation Regions - Pacific Coastal**
pickling: **Condiment Crops; Fruit & Vegetable Industry**
Pickthall, Marjorie: **Drama in English; Pierce, Lorne A.; Poetry in English**
Picton, Thomas: **Picton**
Pictou Academy: **McCulloch, Thomas; Pictou**
Pictou County Court House: **Stirling, David**
Pictou Harbour: *Samson*
Pictou Lobster Carnival: **Festivals**
Picture Loan Soc: **Duncan, Douglas M.; MacLeod, Pegi Nicol; Muhlstock, Louis**
Picture Loan Society: **Town, Harold Barling**
Pidcock, Reginald: **Courtenay**
Pidgeon Process: **Metallurgy**
piedmont: **Foothills**
Piedmont Appalachians: **Arthabaska; Drummondville; Victoriaville**
Pierce, Edward Mitchell: **Cannington Manor**
Pierre Laporte Bridge: **Québec City**
Pierre Radisson: **Icebreakers**
Pierron, Jean: **Painting**
Piers, Harry: **Archaeology**
Piette, Robert: **Children's Literature in French**
pig: **Animal Agriculture; Hog Farming; Salmonella**

"pig boats": **Lake Carriers**
pig iron: **Algoma Steel Corp Ltd; Hamilton; Iron & Steel Industry**
Pigeon, Louis-Philippe: *Calder* **Case**
Pigeon Island: **Lighthouses**
Pigeon Lake: **Kawartha Lakes**
Pigeon Lake Mission: **Rundle, Robert Terrill**
Pigeon River: **Boundaries; Grand Portage; Superior, Lake; Waterfall**
pigging: **Pipeline**
Piggott, Joseph: **Apprenticeship**
"piggyback" transportation: **Canadian National Railways; Forest Harvesting; Manitoba; Transportation**
pigments: **Cadmium; Chromium; Crafts; Mining; Molybdenum; Sulphur; Titanium**
pignut hickory: **Endangered Plants; Vegetation Regions - Eastern Temperate Forests**
Pigwacket: **Abenaki**
pigweed: **Weeds**
Pike, Gilbert: **Princess Sheila**
Pike, Warburton: **Exploration & Travel Literature in English**
Pike Bay: **Fishing Islands**
Pike Lake: **Saskatoon**
pikeperch: **Walleye**
Pikogan, Qué: **Amos**
pilchard: **Fisheries History; Herring**
Pile O' Bones Creek: **Regina**
pileated woodpecker: **Mont St-Hilaire Nature Conservation Centre; Woodpecker**
Pilgrim Holiness Church: **Baptists**
pill bug: **Crustacean**
Pilon, Jean-Guy: *Liberté*; **Ouellette, Fernand**
PILOT: **Computer-Assisted Learning**
pilot whale: **Saguenay River; Whale**
Pilote, François: **Agricultural Education**
piloting: **Bic, Île du**
pimp: **Prostitution**
pin cherry: **Cuisine; Newfoundland; Poisonous Plants**
pin oak: **Oak; Vegetation Regions - Eastern Temperate Forests**
Pinawa, Man: **Winnipeg River**
Pincher Creek, Alta: **Chinook; Lacombe, Albert; L'Heureux, Jean-B.; Peigan**
Pinchgut Tickle: **Place-names**
Pinchi Lake: **Mercury**
Pine Days: **Festivals**
Pine Falls, Man: **Manitoba; Winnipeg River**
pine grass: **Vegetation Regions - Cordillera**
Pine Hill Divinity Hall: **Falconer, Robert Alexander; Grant, John Webster; Nova Scotia**
pine marten: **Barachois Pond Provincial Park; Gros Morne National Park; Martre, Lac la**
pine oil: **Lighting**
Pine Point Mines: **Fort Resolution; Pine Point; Stavert, Reuben Ewart**
Pine River: **Peace River; Pine Pass**
pine tar: **Canoe, Birchbark; Cross-Country Skiing**
Pinehill Library: **Dumaresq, James Charles Philip**
Pineimuta River: **Attawapiskat River**
Pinetree Line: **Early-Warning Radar; Happy Valley-Goose Bay**
ping-pong: **Table Tennis**
Pinkham, Joan: *Nègres blancs d'Amérique*
Pinoteau, Claude: **Héroux, Denis**
Pinsky, Alfred: **Savage, Anne Douglas**
Pinze, Leveright: **Poles**
Pioneer: **Anson Northup**
Pioneer Days: **Steinbach**
Pioneer Days Museum (Edmonton): **Brown, Ernest**
Pioneer Days (Saskatoon): **Festivals**
Pioneer Mills: **North Vancouver**
Pioneer Women: **Judaism**
Pipe Line Contractors Assn of Canada: **Construction Industry**
pipes & pipestems: **Calumet; Indian Art; Indian Trade Goods; Prehistory; Quillwork**
piping: **Milk River**
piping plover: **Plover**
pipsissewa: **Wintergreen**
Pirlot, Paul: **Philosophy**
Pisces IV: **Oceanography**
Pisiquid, NS: **Windsor, NS**
pissenlit: **Dandelion**

pistol: **Duel; Firearm; Shooting**
pit house: **Boyd's Cove; Native People - Plateau; Prehistory**
pit viper: **Rattlesnake**
Pitaloosie: **Pauta Saila**
pitch pine: **Endangered Plants; Pine; Thousand Islands**
pitchblende: **LaBine, Gilbert; Metallurgy; Radium; Uranium**
Pitt River: **Port Coquitlam**
Pittman, Al: **Children's Literature in English**
Pitt's Horse Power: **Agricultural Implements**
Pivniki, Mila: **Mulroney, M. Brian**
Pizzolongo, Lina: **Quilico, Louis**
Place Bonaventure: **Affleck, Raymond Tait**
Place d'Armes: **Architecture, Development; Sculpture; Urban Design**
Place Desjardins: **Urban Design**
Place du Portage: **Hull**
Place Royale: **Public Art; Québec City**
Place St Joseph: **Sudbury**
Place Viger: **Canadian Pacific Railway**
plague: **Veterinary Medicine**
plaice: **Flatfish; Hudson Bay; Madeleine, Iles de la; Newfoundland**
plains: **Physiographic Regions - Interior Plains; Prairie; Soil Conservation**
Plains Cree: **Big Bear; Cree; Native People, Political Organization & Activism; Sapp, Allen**
Plains of Abraham: **Battle of the Plains of Abraham; Québec City**
plainsong: **Religious Music**
plaintiff: **Civil Procedure; Torts**
Plamondon, Luc: **Claude, Renée**
Planck's constant: **Physics**
plane: **Tools, Carpentry**
plane crashes: **Disasters**
planetarium: **Science Centre**
plank roads: **Cobourg & Peterborough Railway; Roads & Highways; Technology**
planks: **Timber Trade History**
Planned Parenthood Federation of Canada: **Birth Control**
Plano culture: **Fisherman Lake; Paleoindian; Prehistory**
planograph: **Printmaking**
Plant Biotechnology Institute: **National Research Council of Canada**
plant breeding: **Corn, Field; Downey, Richard Keith; Goulden, Cyril Harold; Oilseed Crops; Saunders, Charles E.; Triticale**
plant systematics: **Cinq-Mars, Lionel**
plantain: **Weeds**
Plante, Raymond: **Children's Literature in French**
Plaskett, Joseph F.: **Regina Five**
plasma: **Physics**
plaster: **Architecture, Development; Art; Fafard, Joseph; Gypsum; Laliberté, Alfred (artist)**
Plastomer Inc: **Plastics-Processing Industry**
plate: **Glass; Pewter; Silver, Domestic**
plate steel: **Algoma Steel Corp Ltd; Dominion Foundries & Steel, Ltd**
platforms: **Geological Regions**
PLATO: **Computer-Assisted Learning**
Platt, Samuel: **Salt**
Playboy: **Pornography**
Playgreen Lake: **Manitoba; Nelson River**
Playhouse Theatre Centre: **Vancouver**
Playtner, Henry: **Clocks & Watches**
Playwrights Canada: **Literature & Politics; Small Presses; Theatre, English-Language**
Playwrights Co-op: **Hendry, Thomas B.; Peterson, Leonard B.; Theatre, English-Language; Theatre for Young Audiences**
Playwrights Colony: **Hendry, Thomas B.**
Playwrights Union of Canada: **Writers' Union of Canada**
playwriting: **Theatre Education**
plebiscite: **Bloc populaire canadien; Conscription; Prohibition; Referendum**

Pleistocene epoch: **Arctic Animals; Bitumen; Bluefish Caves; Coastal Landform; Geomorphology; Hunting; Ice Age; Northwest Territories; Opossum; Yukon Territory**
Plessisville, Qué: **Festivals**
Pleurondon, Marius: **Sculpture**
Plotek, Leopold: **Painting**
plotter: **Helava, Uno Vilho**
plow: **Agricultural Implements; Agricultural Implements Industry; Agricultural Soil Practices; Technology**
plowing match: **Sports History**
Plum Creek: **Souris, Man**
Plumbers' Union: **Verville, Alphonse**
plumbing: **Copper; Lead; Safety Standards**
plunger: **Domestic Utensils**
Plunkett, Al: **Dumbells**
Plunkett, Merton: **Dumbells**
PLURA: **Ecumenical Social Action**
plural voting: **Local Elections**
pluralism: **Philosophy;** *Refus Global*
Plus 15: **Architecture, Development; Urban Design**
Pluto: **Moon**
plutonium: **Chalk River; Nuclear Energy; Nuclear Research Establishments; Nuclear Safety**
Plymouth automobile: **Chrysler Canada Ltd**
plywood: **Forestry; Lumber & Wood Industries; MacMillan, H.R.**
pneumatic tire: **Rubber Products Industry; Technology**
pneumoconiosis: **Coal Mining**
pneumonia: **Air Pollution; Death & Dying; Hospitals; Influenza**
poaching: **Miramichi River**
Poce, Paul: **Track & Field**
Pocklington, Peter: **Calgary Flames; Edmonton Oilers; Trust Company**
Podbrey, Maurice: **Centaur Theatre**
podzols: **Soil Classification**
"Poets of Confederation": **Poetry in English**
Poile, Bud: **Vancouver Canucks**
poinsettia: **Flowers, Cultivated; Poisonous Plants**
Point, Pierre: **University of Windsor**
Point Aconi Pit: **Coal**
Point de Meuron: **Fort William**
Point Edward, Ont: **Sarnia**
Point Ellice: **Disasters**
Point Grey: **Archaeology; University of British Columbia; Vancouver**
Point Henry: **Fort Henry**
Point Lake: **Coppermine River**
Point Lance: **St Mary's Bay**
Point Lepreau: **MacLean, John Angus; New Brunswick; Nuclear Power Plants; Nuclear Safety**
Point McNicoll, Ont: **Georgian Bay**
Point Pleasant Park: **Halifax**
Point Riche: **French Shore**
Point Separation: **Mackenzie River**
Pointe-à-Callière: **Art; Montréal**
Pointe à l'Orignal: **L'Orignal**
Pointe Amour: **Forteau**
Pointe au Baril: **Maitland**
Pointe-au-Père (Father Point): **Bic, Ile du; Disasters; Lighthouses**
Pointe-au-Pic, Qué: **La Malbaie; Rugs & Rug Making**
Pointe-aux-Trembles, Qué: **Huguenots**
Pointe-Claire, Qué: **Pulp & Paper Industry**
Pointe-Claire Swim Club: **Swimming, Speed**
Pointe de Lévy: **La Corriveau**
Pointe-des-Savages: **Campbellton, NB**
Pointe-Gatineau, Qué: **Gatineau**
Pointe-Lévy, Qué: **Leatherworking**
Pointe-Lévy Hospital: **Tessier, François-Xavier**
Pointe Louis-XIV: **James Bay**
Pointe Noire: **Iron & Steel Industry**
Pointe-Rochelle: **Campbellton, NB**
Pointe-St-Charles, Qué: **Canadian National Railways; Le Ber, Pierre**
Pointe-St-Pierre, Qué: **Gaspé, Qué**
Pointed Mountain: **Northwest Territories**
Pointépienu: **Dance, Modern**
Poirier, Claude: **Children's Literature in French; Popular Literature in French**
Poirier, Michelle: **Children's Literature in French**
poison-control centres: **Pharmaceuticals Industry**

poison hemlock: **Poisonous Plants**
poison oak: **Poison Ivy**
poisoning: **Alcoholism; Botulism; Death & Dying; Food Poisoning; Injury & Prevention; Molluscan Resources; Salmonella**
Poitras, Edward: **Art, Contemporary Trends**
poker: **Gambling**
Polanyi, Michael: **Polanyi, John C.**
"Polar Bear Express": **Cochrane, Ont; Moosonee**
Polar Bear Provincial Park: **Parks, Provincial**
polar cod: **Arctic Animals**
Polar Continental Shelf Project: **Arctic Oceanography; Energy, Mines & Resources, Dept of**
polar desert: **Arctic Archipelago**
Polaris Charter Co Ltd: **Ward, Maxwell W.**
Polaris Mine Project: **Architecture, Development**
Poldaas, Jaan: **Painting**
pole vault: **Apps, C.J. Sylvanus; Lyon, George S.; Track & Field**
Polgar, Tibor: **Opera**
police harassment: **Prejudice & Discrimination**
Policies & Priorities Committee: **Cabinet**
poliomyelitis: **Connaught Laboratories Ltd; Disability; Disasters; Epidemic; Medicine, Contemporary; Virus**
Polish Orthodox Church: **Orthodox Church**
political dissent: **Crime**
Political Equality League of Manitoba: **Beynon, Francis Marion**
political parties: **Action libérale nationale; Bloc populaire canadien; Communist Party of Canada; Conservative Party; Co-operative Commonwealth Federation; Créditistes; Labour Party; Leadership Convention; Liberal Party; New Democratic Party; Parliament; Parti bleu; Parti canadien; Parti national; Parti Québécois; Parti rouge; Party System; Progressive Party; Rhinoceros Party; Social Credit; Socialist Party of Canada; Union Nationale**
Political Process Financing Act: **Hatfield, Richard B.**
political theatre: **Theatre, French-Language**
polje: **Karst Landform**
poll axe: **Timber Axe**
poll tax: **Municipal Finance**
Pollack, W.H.: **Chess**
pollen record: **Beringia; Bluefish Caves; Climate Change; Palynology; Treeline**
polling division: **Electoral Systems**
pollock: **Cod; Westport**
Pollock, Sharon: **Alberta; Drama in English; Festival Lennoxville; Governor General's Literary Awards; Jewish Writing; Literature in English; Theatre, English-Language**
Pollock Gallery: **Morrisseau, Norval**
Pollok, Gilmour & Co: **Timber Trade History**
polls: **Political Campaign; Privacy; Public Opinion; Wartime Information Board**
pollywog: **Frog**
Polo Park Shopping Centre: **Green, Blankstein, Russell**
polonium: **Uranium**
Poltimore, Qué: **Mineral Naming**
Polunin, N.: **Botany History**
polyesters: **Textile Industry**
polyethylene: **Chemical Industries; Greenhouse Crops; Petrochemical Industry; Plastics-Processing Industry**
polygamy: **Han; Mormon Church; Native People - Arctic; New Religious Movements**
Polymer Corp Ltd: **Ambridge, Douglas White; Berkinshaw, Richard Coulton; Chemical Industries; Munitions & Supply, Dept of; Sarnia**
polynya: **Arctic Animals; Arctic Archipelago; Baffin Bay**
polyplacophora: **Mollusc**

polypropylene: **Chemical Industries; Plastics-Processing Industry; Textile Industry**
Polysar Ltd: **Canada Development Corp; Chemical Industries; Sarnia**
polystyrene: **Chemical Industries; Plastics-Processing Industry**
Pomerleau, R.: **Botany History**
Pond Inlet: **Baffin Island; Bylot Island; Iglulik Inuit; Lancaster Sound**
ponderosa pine: **Pine; Vegetation Regions - Cordillera**
pondskater: **Bug**
Pontac Inn: **Theatre, English-Language**
Pontiac & Pacific Railway Co: **Chapleau, J.-Adolphe**
Pontifical Institute of Mediaeval Studies: **Classics; Philosophy**
Ponton, Joseph-Noé: **United Farmers of Québec**
Pontypool, Ont: **Welsh**
pool: **Billiards; Chenier, Georges; Thorburn, Clifford C.D.**
Poole, Jack: **Development Industry**
poor law & poorhouse: **Social Security**
poorwill: **Nighthawk**
Pootoogook: **Kananginak Pootoogook**
popcorn: **Confectionery Industry; Vegetable**
Pope, Carole: **Rough Trade**
Pope, Georgina F.: **South African War**
Pope, Joseph: **A Mari usque ad Mare; External Affairs, Dept of; Summerside**
Pope, Matthew: **Furniture, Country**
poplar borer: **Beetle**
Poplar River Dam: **Coronach**
Poplar River Mine: **Coal**
Pople, J.A.: **Bernstein, Harold Joseph**
poppy: **Poisonous Plants; Remembrance Day; Vegetation Regions - Arctic Tundra; Wildflowers**
popular culture: **Folklore**
Popular Front: **Bland, Salem G.**
porcelain: **Ceramics; Nepheline Syenite**
Porcépic: **Literary Magazines in English**
Porcupine Hills (Alta): **Alberta; Head-Smashed-In Buffalo Jump**
Porcupine Hills (Man-Sask): **Winnipegosis, Lake**
Porcupine Lake: **Bickell, John Paris; Gold; Prospecting; South Porcupine; Timmins, Noah A.**
Porcupine Plateau: **Old Crow Plain; Yukon Territory**
porcupine-quill work: **Indian Art; Kutchin**
Porcupine River: **Old Crow; Old Crow Plain; Yukon River**
pork: **Animal Agriculture; Cuisine; Food Poisoning; Hog Farming; Insulin; Meat-Processing Industry**
pork barrel: **Corruption**
porpoise: **Coudres, Ile aux; Dolphin & Porpoise; Micmac; Saguenay River**
Porsild, Robert T.: **Porsild, A. Erling**
port: **Wine Industry**
Port-Alfred, Qué: **La Baie**
Port Alice, BC: **Landslide; Urban & Regional Planning**
Port Arthur, Ont: **Beatty, Henry; Canadian Pacific Railway; Grain Elevators; Lakehead University; *Noronic*; Shipbuilding & Ship Repair; Thunder Bay**
Port Arthur Hills: **Physiographic Regions - Canadian Shield Forest Lands; Thunder Bay**
Port au Port Bay: **Port au Port Peninsula**
Port aux Basques, Nfld: **Channel-Port aux Basques**
Port Barrington, NS: **Port Hood**
Port Bralsant, NWT: **Tuktoyaktuk**
Port Burwell, NWT: **Killinek Island**
Port Carling, Ont: **Muskoka Lakes**
Port Clements, BC: **Queen Charlotte Islands**
Port Dalhousie, Ont: **Niagara Peninsula**
Port Dover & Lake Huron Railway: **Grand Trunk Railway of Canada**
Port Essington, BC: **Skeena River**
Port Fourchu: **Yarmouth**
Port Hawkesbury, NS: **Canso, Strait of; Cape Breton Island**

Port Hilford, NS: **Carter, Wilfred A.C.**
Port Hill, PEI: **Prince Edward Island**
Port La Joie: **Charlottetown**
Port Leopold: **Lancaster Sound**
Port Mann Bridge: **Surrey**
Port Matoon Assn: **St Stephen**
Port-Menier, Qué: **Anticosti, Ile d'**
Port-Nouveau-Québec, Qué: **George, Rivière; Torngat Mountains**
Port of Montréal: **Grain Elevators; Montréal; St Lawrence River; Tarte, Joseph-Israel; Transportation Agencies (Government)**
Port of Québec: **Blanchet, François; Tessier, François-Xavier**
Port of Sept-Iles: **St Lawrence River**
Port of Toronto: **Ontario**
Port Perry, Ont: **Chiropractic**
Port Radium, NWT: **Geological Survey of Canada; Mackenzie River**
Port Renfrew, BC: **Pacific Rim National Park; West Coast Trail**
Port Robinson, Ont: **Niagara Peninsula**
Port Rossignol: **Denys, Nicolas; Liverpool**
Port Sandfield, Ont: **Muskoka Lakes**
Port Severn, Ont: **Trent Canal**
Port Talbot, Ont: **Talbot, Thomas; Welsh**
Port Weller, Ont: **Shipbuilding & Ship Repair; Welland Canal**
Portage & Main: **Bank Architecture; Smith, Ernest John; Winnipeg**
Portage-du-Fort: **Ottawa River**
Portage la Prairie Daily Graphic: **Manitoba**
Portage Plain: **Brown, J.G., "Kootenai"; Manitoba; Portage la Prairie**
Porte, John: **Aviation**
Porte Sainte Marguerite: **St Margaret's Bay**
Porteous, Cameron: **Stage & Costume Design**
Porteous house: **Brymner, William**
porter: **Brewing Industry**
Porter, Edward: **Printmaking**
Porter Commission: **Banking & Finance, Royal Commission on**
Portland, NB: **Saint John**
Portland Canal: **Alaska Boundary Dispute**
Portland Inlet: **Nass River**
Portland Point (NB): **Saint John**
Portlock, Nathaniel: **King George's Sound Company**
Ports Canada: **Shipping Industry; Transportation**
Portugais, Louis: **Film**
Portugal Cove, Nfld: **Children's Literature in English**
positivism: **Atheism & Agnosticism; Sociology**
positron: **Physics**
Post, Jordan: **Silver, Domestic**
Post Office Act: **Censorship**
Post Office Dept: **Canada Post Corp; Lampman, Archibald; Turnbull, Walter James**
post offices: **Government Building**
Postal Union of the Americas & Spain: **Postal System; Turnbull, Walter James**
posters: **Advertising; Censorship; Graphic Design; Political Campaign; Public Art**
Postup-Progress: **Catholicism**
Postville, Nfld: **Labrador**
pot: **Copperware; Domestic Utensils**
Potash Corp of Saskatchewan: **Barter; Chemical Industries; Crown Corporation; Potash**
potassium: **Dandelion; Geological Dating; Kohlrabi; Maple Sugar Industry; Nuclear Power Plants; Onion; Parsnip; Radish; Spring; Turnip**
Potawatomi: **Currie, Walter; Odjig, Daphne; Ottawa**
potherb: **Beet**
Potlatch Publications Limited: **Small Presses**
Pottawattomi River: **Owen Sound**
Potterton, Gerald: **Film Animation**
pottery: **Archaic; Brockinton; Ceramics; Ceramics, Contemporary; Clay; Folklore; Indian Art; Kavik, John; Masks; Medicine Hat; Neutral; Prehistory; St-Denis**
Pottier Report: **Nova Scotia**

Potts, Lyman: **Music Broadcasting**
Pouce Coupé River: **Peace River**
Poulain, Jacques: **Philosophy**
Poulin, Julien: **Video Art**
Poulin, Roland: **Sculpture**
Poulin de La Fontaine, Maurice: **St-Maurice, Rivière**
Pouliot, Adrien: **Science**
poultry: **Salmonella**
poultry feed: **Buckwheat; Soybean**
Pound, Dick: **Swimming, Speed**
Poundmaker Reserve: **Big Bear**
pounds: **Money**
Poupart, Jean-Marie: **Children's Literature in French; Novel in French**
Pourquoi pas?: **Theatre, French-Language**
Povungnituk, Qué: **Inuit Art; Inuit Co-operatives; Ungava Inuit**
Povungnituk Co-operative: **Sivuarapik, Charlie**
Powell, Israel Wood: **Powell River**
Powell, R.B.: **Tennis**
Powell Lake: **Lake; Powell River**
Powell River Paper Co Ltd: **MacMillan Bloedel Ltd**
Powell Street (Vancouver): **Japanese**
power: **Utilities**
Power of Attorney: **Attorney**
power takeoff: **Technology**
powerboat: **Boating; Valleyfield**
Pozer, George: **St-Georges**
Prague, Alta: **Czechs**
Prairie Agricultural Machinery Institute: **Humboldt**
Prairie Bible Institute: **Bible Schools**
prairie chicken: **Cuisine; Endangered Animals; Game Bird; Grouse**
Prairie Farm Commodity Coalition: **Agriculture & Food Policy**
Prairie Justice Research Consortium: **Criminology**
prairie lily: **Lily; Wildflowers**
prairie parsley: **Endangered Plants**
Prairie Provinces Economic Council: **Federal-Provincial Relations**
prairie rose: **Rose; Wildflowers**
Prairie Wildlife Interpretation Centre: **Wildlife Preserve**
prairie wolf: **Coyote**
Prairies, Lac des: **Manitoba, Lake**
Prairies, Lake of the: **Assiniboine River**
Prairies, Rivière des: **Montréal; Ottawa River; St Lawrence River**
Prangnell, Peter: **Architecture, Development**
Prat, Louis: **Sculpture**
Pratiques théâtrales: **Drama in French**
Pratt, Babe: **Toronto Maple Leafs**
Pratt, Charles Edward: **Architectural Styles; Thompson, Berwick, Pratt & Partners**
Pratt & Whitney Aircraft of Canada, Ltd: **Aerospace Industry; Mechanical Engineering; Québec**
Pratte et Cie: **Piano Manufacturing**
prawn: **Crustacean Resources; Shrimp**
pre-emptions: **Colonization Companies**
Préambule: **Popular Literature in French**
Prebus, A.F.: **Burton, Eli Franklin**
Precambrian time: **Cnidaria; Echinodermata; Fossil Plants; Geological History; Geological Regions; Geomorphology; Invertebrate; Paleontology; Physiographic Regions - Canadian Shield Forest Lands; St Lawrence Islands National Park; Shield**
precatory bean: **Poisonous Plants**
Precious Metals Marking Act: **Jewellery & Silverware Industry**
precipitation: **Chinook; Climate; Climate Information; Hail; Rain; Weather Forecasting; Wind**
predestination: **Jansenism**
prefabricated units: **Architecture, Development; Bank Architecture; Bridges; Native People, Economic Conditions**
preferred shares: **Corporation Law; Stock & Bond Markets**
Préfontaine, Claude: **Drama in French**
Préfontaine, Fernand: **Loranger, Jean-Aubert; *Nigog***
Préfontaine, Yves: **Poetry in French**

pregnancy: **Abortion; Birth Control; Birthing Practices; Child Abuse; Diabetes Mellitus; Harding, Victor John; Medicine, Contemporary; Women's Movement**
preliminary hearing: **Criminal Procedure**
Premarin: **Estrogen**
premeditation: **Criminal Law**
Premier Choix/First Choice: **Quebecor Inc**
Premier Range: **Place-names**
Premier Steel Mills Ltd: **Stelco Inc**
Premonstratensians: **Belgians**
Prenor Group Ltd: **Caisse de dépôt et placement du Québec; Webster, Lorne Campbell**
Prentice, A.: **Social History**
Prentiss, Alta: **Red Deer**
Presbyterian College: **Pidgeon, George Campbell**
Presbyterian Record: **Scott, Ephraim**
Présence francophone: **Literary Periodicals in French**
Presentation Convent: **Purcell, James**
preservation: **Conservation; Conservation of Movable Cultural Property**
Presqu'Amérique: **Literary Periodicals in French**
Presqu'ile Provincial Park: **Parks, Provincial**
press associations: **Canadian Press; News Agencies**
press council: **Newspapers**
Press News Ltd: **Canadian Press**
Press Porcépic: **Godfrey, Dave**
Presses de l'Université de Montréal: **Literature in French - Criticism & Theory**
Presses de l'Université du Québec: **Literary Periodicals in French**
Presses de l'Université Laval: **Book Publishing, French-Language; Dictionary of Canadian Biography; Literature in French - Criticism & Theory**
Preston, M.H.: **Physics**
Preston, Ont: **Cambridge; Clocks & Watches; Toys & Games**
Preview: **Northern Review; Page, Patricia Kathleen; Poetry in English**
Préville, Qué: **Spence-Sales, Harold**
Prévost, André: **Music History; Orchestral Music; Papineau-Couture, Jean; Songs & Songwriting**
Prévost, Eugène: **Saints**
Prévost, Françoise: **L'Orignal**
Prévost, P.E.: **Franchere, Joseph-Charles**
Prevost, Robert: **Stage & Costume Design**
Price, Barrington: **Keremeos**
Price, Bruce: **Hotel; Railway Station**
Price, Harry I.: **Canada's Sports Hall of Fame**
Price, Norman: **Graphic Design; Printmaking**
Price Brothers & Co: **Alma; Grand Falls, Nfld; Jonquière; Price, William (1867-1924); Symington, Herbert J.**
price discrimination: **Competition Policy**
price fixing: **White-Collar Crime**
price freeze or control: **Wage & Price Controls; Wartime Prices & Trade Board**
Price Mountain: **Garibaldi Provincial Park**
Pricket, Abacuk: **Hudson, Henry**
prickly pear: **Cactus; Desert; Okanagan Valley; Vegetation Regions - Cordillera**
prickly rose: **Rose**
Priestman, Brian: **Edmonton Symphony Orchestra**
Priestner, Cathy: **Speed Skating**
Priest's Mills: **Alexandria**
primates: **Anthropology**
prime lending rate: **Interest**
prime time: **Broadcasting, Radio & Television**
Primeau, Joe: **Conacher, Charles W.**
primitive art: **Folk Art**
primogeniture: **Property Law**
primrose: **Flowers, Cultivated; Poisonous Plants; Shooting Star**
Prince Albert penitentiary: **Prison**
Prince Albert Pulp Co: **Prince Albert**

Prince Albert Sound: **Victoria Island**
Prince Arthur's Landing: **Thunder Bay**
Prince Edward Island Development Corp: **Urban & Regional Planning**
Prince Edward Island Railway: **Canadian Government Railways**
Prince Edward Island Temperance Federation: **Jones, John Walter**
Prince Leopold Island: **Somerset Island**
Prince Mine: **Coal**
Prince of Wales College: **Prince Edward Island; University of Prince Edward Island**
Prince of Wales Northern Heritage Centre: **Conservation of Movable Cultural Property; Northwest Territories; Yellowknife, NWT**
Prince of Wales Strait: **McClure (M'Clure), Robert J. Le M.**
Prince Regent Inlet: **Arctic Exploration; Gulf of Boothia; Parry, W. Edward**
Prince Rupert: **Helmcken, John Sebastian**
Prince Rupert Fishermen's Co-operative Assn: **Fisheries History**
Prince Shoal: **Lighthouses**
Princess Colliery: **Sydney Mines**
Princess Margaret Mountains: **Axel Heiberg Island**
Princess Royal Channel: **Kitamaat**
Princess Sophia: **Disasters**
Princetown, PEI: **Malpeque**
Principal Meridian: **Meridian, First or Principal**
Pringle, R.W.: **Physics**
Print & Drawing Council of Canada: **Printmaking**
Print Measurement Bureau: **Advertising**
printing press: ***Edmonton Journal*; Magazines; Newspapers; Oliver, Frank; Print Industry; Printmaking; Sports History; Theatre, French-Language**
Priorities & Planning Committee: **Budgetary Process; Prime Minister**
prism: **Rainbow; Spectroscopy**
Prism International: **Literary Magazines in English**
Prisme: **Popular Literature in French**
Prisme d'yeux: **Archambault, Louis; Pellan, Alfred; Tonnancour, Jacques Godefroy de**
Prison Gate Home: **Salvation Army**
Privacy Act: **Law & the Press; Social Insurance Number**
Privacy Commissioner: **Ombudsman**
private enterprise: **Advertising; Competition Policy; Fisheries Policy; Public Ownership; State**
private law: **Civil Code; Courts of Law; Distribution of Powers; Law; Torts**
private member: **House of Commons; Parliamentary Procedure**
Privateer's Wharf: **Heritage Conservation**
"privatization": **Nationalization**
Privileges & Elections, Standing Committee on: **House of Commons**
Privy Seal: **Consumer & Corporate Affairs, Dept of; Symbols of Authority**
Prix Anik: **Dufresne, Guy**
Prix Borduas: **Comtois, Ulysse; Giguère, Roland; Molinari, Guido**
Prix David: **Bessette, Gerard; Children's Literature in French; Dubé, Marcel; Ferron, Jacques; Grignon, Claude-Henri; Guèvremont, Germaine; Lasnier, Rina; Literary Prizes in French; Morin, Paul; Potvin, Damase; Roy, Camille; Roy, Gabrielle**
Prix de la critique québécoise: **Arcand, Denys; Film Festivals, Prizes**
Prix de la revue *Études françaises*: **Literary Prizes in French**
Prix de l'académie Charles-Cros: **Vigneault, Gilles**
Prix de musique Calixa-Lavallée: **Alarie, Pierrette; Aubut, Françoise; Carignan, Jean; Leyrac, Monique; Papineau-Couture, Jean; Pépin, Clermont; Quilico, Louis; Tremblay, Gilles**

Prix de poésie de la société des poètes canadiens-français: **Literary Prizes in French**
Prix de poésie du Québec: **Brault, Jacques**
Prix de poésie Marie Lemelin: **Literary Prizes in French**
Prix Denise-Pelletier: **Vigneault, Gilles**
Prix des Vikings: **Panneton, Philippe**
Prix d'Europe: **Gilbert, Kenneth; Morin, Léo-Pol**
Prix du Cercle du Livre de France: **Literary Prizes in French**
Prix du Ministre: **Archambault, Louis**
Prix du Québec: **Bessette, Gerard**
Prix Duvernay: **Brault, Jacques; Charbonneau, Robert; Ethier-Blais, Jean; Ferron, Jacques; Guèvremont, Germaine; Lasnier, Rina; Literary Prizes in French; Roy, Gabrielle**
Prix Esso du Cercle du Livre de France: **Literary Prizes in French**
Prix Félix-Leclerc: **Charlebois, Robert**
Prix France-Canada: **Beaulieu, Victor-Levy; Brault, Jacques; Kattan, Naim; Lasnier, Rina; Literary Prizes in French**
Prix France-Québec: **Giguère, Roland; Loranger, Jean-Aubert**
Prix France-Québec Jean Hamelin: **Literary Prizes in French**
Prix Jean-Beraud-Molson: **Beaulieu, Victor-Levy**
Prix Jean-Béraud-Molson: **Literary Prizes in French**
Prix Jules-Léger: **Mather, Bruce**
Prix Philippe-Hébert: **Daudelin, Charles; Hébert, L.-Philippe**
Prix René-Barthélemy: **Crum, George**
Prix Robert-Cliche: **Literary Prizes in French**
Prix Sully-Olivier de Serres: **Guèvremont, Germaine**
Prix Victor-Morin: **Dubé, Marcel; Gascon, Jean; Germain, Jean-Claude; Roux, Jean-Louis; Tremblay, Michel**
Pro Musica Soc: **Charpentier, Gabriel**
Probate or Surrogate Court: **Courts of Law**
Probe Post: **Pollution Probe Foundation**
Proch, Don: **Printmaking; Sculpture**
Procor, Ltd: **Locomotives & Rolling Stock**
ProCoro Canada: **Choral Music**
Procter, Henry A.: **Proctor, Henry; War of 1812**
Procter & Gamble Inc: **Advertising; Grande Prairie; Hamilton**
Proctor, Alexander Phimister: **Sculpture**
Proctor, George: **Musicology**
procuring: **Prostitution**
producer gas: **Coal Gasification**
Productions Réalisations Indépendants de Montréal Inc: **Video Art**
Professional Institute of the Publice Service of Canada: **Postal System**
Professional Native Artists Inc: **Janvier, Alex S.**
Professional Native Indian Artists' Assn: **Odjig, Daphne**
Professional Program of the Royal Winnipeg Ballet: **Dance Education**
profit-sharing: **Work**
profiteering: **Cadet, Joseph-Michel; Grande Société**
Programme catholique: **La Flèche, Louis-François; Tarte, Joseph-Israel**
Programme de restauration sociale: **Social Doctrine of the Roman Catholic Church**
Programme of Equal Opportunity (NB): **Hatfield, Richard B.; New Brunswick; Robichaud, Louis J.**
Progressive Arts Club: **Theatre, English-Language**
Progressive Farmers of Québec: **United Farmers of Québec**
Prohibition case: **Peace, Order & Good Government**
Project Eole: **Wind Energy**
Project North: **Ecumenical Social Action**
Project Ploughshares: **Ecumenical Social Action; Peace Movement; Voice of Women**
prokaryotes: **Genetics**
Promenades de l'Outaouais: **Gatineau**
promissory notes: **Commercial Law**

Promodev Soc: **Mont-Tremblant**
propaganda: **Anti-Reciprocity Movement; Film, Documentary; Public Art; Radio Programming**
propane: **Automobile; Balloon; Lighting; Petroleum; Petroleum Exploration & Production**
property damage: **Delict**
property rights: **Constitution, Patriation of; Crime; Distribution of Powers; Economics; Real Estate**
property tax: **Alberta; Education, History of; Municipal Administration; Municipal Finance; Municipal-Provincial Relations; New Brunswick; Real Estate; Separate School; Social Security**
Prophet, Ronnie: **Country & Western Music**
Prophetic Bible Institute: **Aberhart, William; Bible Schools; Evangelical & Fundamentalist Movements; Manning, Ernest C.**
Proprietary Assn of Canada: **Pharmaceuticals Industry**
prosody: **Language**
Protecteur du citoyen: **Ombudsman**
Protection of Life Project: **Bioethics; Medical Ethics**
Protective Assn for Indians & their Treaties: **Native People, Political Organization & Activism**
protein: **Allergies; Animal Agriculture; Canola; Cheese & Cheesemaking; Diabetes Mellitus; Flax; Forage Crops; Genetic Engineering; Genetics; Molecular Biology; Onion; Potato; Pulse Crops; Sunflower; Triticale; Vegetarianism; Virus; Wheat**
Proterozoic time: **Geological History; Geological Regions; Plate Tectonics**
Protestant Orphanage (Victoria): **Spencer, David**
Protestant Protective Assn: **Equal Rights Assn**
Protestant Reformed Church: **Presbyterian & Reformed Churches**
"Protestant Rights" Party: **Thorburn, Robert; Winter, James Spearman**
Protestant Royal Education Board (Lower Canada): **Education Policy**
"Protestant work ethic": **Calvinism**
Protestantism: **Anabaptists; Baptists; Bible Schools; Brethren in Christ; Calvinism; Christianity; Congregational Churches; Doukhobors; Evangelical & Fundamentalist Movements; Evangelical Fellowship of Canada; Evangelism; Folk Art; Great Awakening; Holiness Churches; Huguenots; Hutterites; Jesuits' Estates Act; Lutherans; Marriage & Divorce, History of; Mennonites; Methodism; Native People, Education; Newspapers; Orange Order; Pentecostal Movement; Presbyterian & Reformed Churches; Prostitution; Salvation Army; Social Gospel; Sunday Schools; Theatre, English-Language; United Church of Canada**
prothonotary warbler: **Rondeau Provincial Park; Warbler**
protistology: **Biology**
proton: **Northern Lights; Nuclear Energy; Nuclear Fusion; Physics**
proton accelerator: **Foster, John Stuart**
Proudfoot, William: **Bank of Upper Canada**
Proulx, Jean-Baptiste: **Children's Literature in French; Exploration & Travel Literature in French; Theatre, French-Language**
Proulx, Jeanne: **Literary Bibliography in French**
Provancher Soc of Natural History: **Bird Sanctuaries & Reserves**
Provencer, Norbert: **Taché, Alexandre-Antonin**
Provident Assurance Co: **Turmel, Antoine**
Provider: **Shipbuilding & Ship Repair**
Province House (PEI): **Charlottetown**
Province of Avalon: **Calvert, George; Ferryland**
Province of Québec Assn of Architects: **Architecture, Development**

Provincial Academy of Arts & Sciences: **University of New Brunswick**
Provincial Agricultural Soc (NS): **Young, John**
Provincial Archives of Alberta: **Brown, Ernest; Edmonton**
Provincial Archives of British Columbia: **Archives**
Provincial Archives of Manitoba: **Winnipeg**
Provincial Archives of New Brunswick: **New Brunswick**
Provincial Building (Sask): **Saskatoon**
Provincial Court House (BC): **Vancouver**
Provincial Exhibition of Manitoba: **Brandon**
Provincial Federation of Labour of Québec: **Union Centrals, Québec**
Provincial Franchise Committee (Qué): **Casgrain, Thérèse; Gerin-Lajoie, Marie**
Provincial Historic Park (Sask): **Wood Mountain**
Provincial Horticultural Research Station (Alta): **Brooks**
Provincial Institute of Technology & Art (Alta): **Bates, Maxwell; Glyde, Henry George; Kerr, Illingworth H.; Macdonald, J.W.G., "Jock"**
Provincial Land Use Commission (PEI): **Prince Edward Island**
Provincial Museum of Alberta: **Conservation of Movable Cultural Property; Diorama; Edmonton**
Provincial Offences Court: **Courts of Law**
provincial paramountcy: **Constitution Act, 1867**
Provincial Parks & Protected Areas Act (Alta): **Parks, Provincial**
"provincial rights": **Constitutional History**
Provincial Synod of the Church of England & Ireland in Canada: **Anglicanism**
Provincial Transport Co: **Desmarais, Paul**
Provincial Workmen's Assn of Nova Scotia: **Canadian Federation of Labour; Drummond, Robert; Union Centrals, District & Regional**
provisional government: **Bannatyne, Andrew Graham Ballenden; Red River Rebellion; Riel, Louis; Smith, Donald A.**
Provost, Alta: **Gallagher, John P.**
Provost, René: **Theatre, French-Language**
Pruche, Benoit: **Philosophy**
Prudential Insurance Co of America: **Reppen, John R.**
Prus, Maria Fisz: **Prus, Victor Marius**
Pryce, M.H.L.: **Physics**
pseudogout: **Arthritis**
pseudoscorpion: **Arachnida**
psilocybin: **Drug Use, Non-Medical**
psoriasis & psoriatic arthritis: **Arthritis**
Psychiatric Nurses' Assn of Canada: **Nursing**
psyllid: **Bug**
pterosaur: **Dinosaur**
P'tits enfants Laliberté: **Germain, Jean-Claude**
Public Accounts Committee (Qué): **Duplessis, Maurice Le Noblet**
Public Archives of Manitoba: **Manitoba**
Public Archives of Nova Scotia: **Messer, Don, & the Islanders; Nova Scotia**
Public Health, Dept of (NS): **Nova Scotia**
Public Health Act: **Health Policy**
Public Health Grants: **Medical Research**
public housing: **Halifax Relief Commission; Housing & Housing Policy**
Public Initiatives Program: **Telidon**
Public Instruction, Dept of (Qué): **Boucherville, Charles-Eugene Boucher de; Potvin, Damase**
Public Interest Advocacy Centre: **Pressure Group**
"Public Lending Right": **Writers' Union of Canada**
Public Order (Temporary Measures) Act: **October Crisis**
Public Petroleum Assn: **Nationalism**

Public School Act (BC): **British Columbia**
Public Schools Act (Man): **Teaching Profession**
Public Schools Act (PEI): **Davies, Louis Henry**
Public Service Acts: **Public Service; Public Service Commission; Public-Service Unions; Status of Women**
Public Service Alliance of Canada: **Postal System; Public-Service Unions**
Public Service Board (Qué): *Dionne* **Case**
Public Service of Canada Merit Award: **Fredeen, Howard**
Public Service's Outstanding Achievement Award: **Hodgson, Stuart M.**
Public Utilities Boards: **Telephones**
Public Works, Dept of: **Architectural Styles; Architecture, Development; Art Dealers; Railway Station; Scott, Thomas S.**
Public Works, Dept of (Ont): **Tully, Kivas**
Publications Les Affaires (1979) Inc: *Affaires*
Puccetti, Roland: **Philosophy**
Puce, George: **Track & Field**
pucoon: **Plants, Native Uses**
puffball: **Mushroom & Puffball**
Puget's Sound Agricultural Co: **Agriculture History; Craigflower Manor & Schoolhouse**
Pugh, Kevin: **National Ballet School**
pugnose minnow: **Endangered Animals; Minnow**
pugnose shiner: **Endangered Animals**
Pugsley, W.H.: **Autobiographical Writing in English**
Pugwash Conferences: **Eaton, Cyrus S.; Peace Movement; Pugwash**
Puhl, Terry: **Baseball**
pulamons: **Fishing, Ice**
Pulfer, Ken: **Electroacoustic Music**
Pulford, Ted: **Pratt, Mary**
Pulitzer Award: *Edmonton Journal*; **Journalism**
Pullen, Wayne: **Archery**
Pulp & Paper Research Institute of Canada: **Chemistry Subdisciplines; Forestry; Gauvin, William Henry; Maass, Otto; Pulp & Paper Industry; Science**
Pulp Press International 3-Day Novel Writing Contest: **Literary Prizes in English**
puma: **Cougar**
pumice: **Volcano**
pumps: **Machinery & Equipment Industry**
Punch in Canada: **Cartoons**
punched-card technology: **Computer Systems Applications**
punishment: **Crime; Criminal Procedure; Prison; Student Rights**
Punjabi language: **Ethnic Literature; Hinduism**
Punkeydoodles Corners, Ont: **Place-names**
puppetry: **Theatre, English-Language; Theatre for Young Audiences**
Purcell Mountains: **Columbia Mountains; Glacier National Park; Invermere; Kootenay Lake**
Purdie, J.E.: **Evangelism**
Purdy, William: **Lindsay**
Purdy, William (chemist): **Chemistry Subdisciplines**
Purdy's Mills, Ont: **Lindsay**
Puritans: **Calvert, George; Congregational Churches**
purple finch: **Biogeography**
purple laver: **Seaweeds**
purple saxifrage: **Biogeography; Saxifrage**
purse seine: **Fisheries; Fisheries History**
purslane: **Weeds**
puschkinia: **Flowers, Cultivated**
Putnam, Donald F.: **Geography**
Pylypiw, Ivan: **Ukrainians**
Pylyshyn, Zenon: **Philosophy**
Pyper, C.B.: **Essay in English**
pyramid schemes: **Competition Policy; White-Collar Crime**
pyrargyrite: **Mineral**
pyrethrum: **Pesticide**
pyrite: **Gold; Iron & Steel Industry; Sulphur**

pyrochlore: **Columbium**
pyrophyllite: **Soapstone**
pyroxene: **Mineral; Soapstone**
pyrrhotite: **Iron & Steel Industry; Mineral**
pyx: **Silver, Church**

Q

Qajartalik, Qué: **Pictographs & Petroglyphs**
QIT-Fer et Titane Inc: **Titanium**
Quadra: **Walbran, John Thomas**
Quadra (CCGS): **Station PAPA**
Quadra Rocks: **Spanish**
quahog: **Clam**
Quaker Oats Co of Canada Ltd: **Peterborough**
quality control: **Industrial Quality Control; Institut Armand-Frappier; Pharmaceuticals Industry**
"quality of life": **Franklin, Ursula Martius; Medical Ethics**
"quality of working life": **Corporatism; Work**
Quality Records: **Selkirk Communications Ltd**
quantum theory: **Black Hole; Chemistry Subdisciplines; Gordon, Andrew Robertson; Physics**
Qu'Appelle, Sask: **North-West Rebellion**
Qu'Appelle Valley: **Indian Head**
quarantine: **Animal Agriculture; Couture, Jean-Alphonse; Epidemic; McEachran, Duncan; Plant Disease**
Quarantine Island: **Grosse Île**
quark hypothesis: **Physics**
Quarry: **Fox, Gail; Literary Magazines in English**
Quarry Press: **Small Presses**
quartz: **Clay; Diamonds of Canada; Iron & Steel Industry; Mineral; Sedimentary Rock; Silica; Soapstone**
quartz crystal: **Time**
Quaternary period: **Cypress Hills; Drumlin; Foothills; Geomorphology; Nunatak**
Québec, Montreal, Ottawa & Occidental Railway: **Senécal, Louis-Adélard**
Québec Aces: **Beliveau, Jean**
Québec Airways: **Disasters**
Québec/Amérique: **Book Publishing, French-Language; Popular Literature in French**
Québec Assembly of Bishops: **Dion, Gérard**
Quebec Bank: **Coinage**
Québec Battlefields Commission: **Historic Site**
Québec Bridge: **Bridges; Québec Bridge Disasters; Québec City**
Québec Bulldogs: **Hockey, Ice; Malone, M. Joseph**
Québec-Canada Council of Ministers: **Sovereignty-Association**
Québec-Cartier Mining Co: **Iron & Steel Industry**
Québec-Cartier Railway: **Railways, Contemporary**
Quebec Central Railway: **Lac-Mégantic; Ste-Marie**
Québec Charter of Rights & Freedoms: **Human Rights**
Québec Chronicle-Telegraph: **Advertising**
Québec Conferences (1943): **World War II**
Québec Court of Appeal: **Constitution, Patriation of; Official Secrets Act**
Québec Deposit & Investment Fund: **Caisse de dépôt et placement du Québec**
Québec Federation of Labour: **Construction Industry; Murdochville Strike; Public-Service Unions**
Québec flag: **Duplessis, Maurice Le Noblet**
Quebec Gazette/La Gazette de Quebec: **Advertising; Book Publishing, English-Language; Brown, William; Literature in French; Newspapers**
Québec Gazette/La Gazette de Québec: **Parent, Etienne**
Quebec Gazette/La Gazette de Quebec: **Photography**

Québec harbour: **Bayfield, Henry Wolsey**
Québec Harmonic Soc: **Germans; Music History**
Québec Jewellers Corp: **Jewellery & Silverware Industry**
Québec-Lac Saint-Jean Railway: **Roberval**
Québec Literary Competition: **Benoît, Jacques; Charbonneau, Robert; Le Moyne, Jean; Literary Prizes in English**
Québec Magazine: **Literary Magazines in English; Printmaking**
Québec Mercury: **Intellectual History; Newspapers; Tarte, Joseph-Israel**
Québec Music Hall: **Baillairgé Family**
Québec National Library: **Montréal**
Québec North Shore Paper Co: **Baie-Comeau**
Québec Press Gallery: **Potvin, Damase**
Québec-Presse: **Popular Literature in French**
Québec prison: **Baillairgé Family; Bernier, Joseph-Elzéar**
Québec-Productions: **Film**
Québec Provincial Police: **Policing**
Quebec Pulp & Paper Mills: **Parc de Val-Jalbert**
Quebec Railway, Light & Power Co: **Forget, Joseph-David-Rodolphe**
Québec Remparts: **Lafleur, Guy D.**
Québec Resolutions: **Nova Scotia; Québec Conference; Tupper, Charles**
Québec Revenue Act: **Constitutional History**
Québec Rugby Football Union: **Football**
Québec Science: **Science; Science & Society**
Québec Seminary: **Séminaire de Québec**
Québec Soc of Artists: **Printmaking**
Québec Streams Commission: **Gouin, Réservoir; Parent, Simon-Napoléon**
Québec Teachers' Corp: **Confederation of National Trade Unions; Public-Service Unions**
Québec-Téléphone Co: **Turmel, Antoine**
Québec Tercentenary Medal: **Medal**
Québec Turf Club: **Thoroughbred Racing**
Québec United Fishermen: **Fisheries History**
Québec Winter Carnival: **Festivals**
Québécoises deboutte: **Women's Movement**
Queen Anne's War: **War of the Spanish Succession**
Queen Charlotte: **Queen Charlotte Islands**
Queen Charlotte, BC: **Queen Charlotte Islands**
Queen Charlotte Strait: **Vancouver Island**
Queen Charlotte weasel: **Endangered Animals**
Queen Elizabeth II Silver Jubilee Medal: **Laidler, Keith James; Medal; Symons, Thomas H.B.; Trigger, Bruce G.**
Queen Elizabeth 2: **Cunard Co**
Queen Elizabeth Foreland: **Place-names**
Queen Elizabeth Hospital (Charlottetown): **Prince Edward Island**
Queen Elizabeth Hospital (Montréal): **Astronaut**
Queen Elizabeth Hospital (Toronto): **Berkinshaw, Richard Coulton**
Queen Elizabeth Hotel: **Brandtner, Fritz; Canadian National Railways**
Queen Elizabeth-Lac Cardinal Provincial Park: **Peace River, Alta**
Queen Elizabeth Park (Vancouver): **Arboretum**
Queen Elizabeth Planetarium: **Astronomy**
Queen Elizabeth Theatre: **Affleck, Raymond Tait; Lebensold, Fred David; Vancouver; Vancouver Playhouse; Vancouver Symphony Orchestra**
Queen Maude Gulf: **Bird Sanctuaries & Reserves**
Queen Street Mental Health Centre: **Whiten, Colette**
Queen Victoria Park: **Niagara Falls**

Queen Victoria Treaty Protective Assn: **Native People, Political Organization & Activism**
Queen's Bush: **Americans**
Queen's College (Kingston): **Bell, Alexander Melville; Botanical Garden; Queen's University**
Queen's College (Wolfville): **Acadia University**
Queen's Park: **Hippies; Royal Ontario Museum**
Queen's Printer: **Begg, Alexander; Desbarats, Georges-Edouard; *Hansard*; Supply & Services, Dept of**
Queen's Theological College: **Queen's University**
Queen's University Gaels: **Kingston**
Queensware: **Ceramics**
Quen, Jean de: **Sept-Iles**
Quesnel, Jules M.: **Quesnel**
Quesnel Highlands: **Columbia Mountains**
question period: **Committees; House of Commons; Parliamentary Procedure**
Quetico Provincial Park: **Atikokan; Parks, Provincial; Pictographs & Petroglyphs**
Quetico Residential Conference & Training Centre: **Adult Education**
Quévillon, Lac: **Nottaway, Rivière**
Qui a vu le vent: **Who Has Seen the Wind**
Quick Canadian Facts: **Popular Literature in English**
quicklime: **Limestone**
quicksilver: **Mercury**
Quidi Vidi Lake: **St John's Regatta**
Quidoz Pianos: **Piano Manufacturing**
Quilico, Gino: **Quilico, Louis**
Quill Lake, Sask: **Quill Lakes; Slovenes**
quillback: **Sucker**
quinine: **Pharmaceuticals Industry**
Quinte, Bay of: **Belleville; Deserontyon, John; Iroquois; Loyalists; Mohawk; Ontario, Lake; Picton; Trenton, CFB**
Quintette Mine: **Coal**
Quintette Mountain: **Rocky Mountains**
Quinton, Sask: **Deutsch, John Hames**
Quinze, Rivière des: **Technology**
Qumak, Thomassie: **Ungava Inuit**
Qur'an (Koran): **Islam**

R

R v Workman & Huculak: **Criminal Investigation**
R v Wray: **R v Olson**
R.S. Williams & Sons: **Music History**
Rabbit Creek: **Klondike Gold Rush**
rabbit-foot clover: **Poisonous Plants**
Rabbit Lake: **Uranium**
rabbitbrush: **Desert; Vegetation Regions - Cordillera**
Rabbitkettle Hot Springs: **Spring**
Rabenstein, Dallas L.: **Chemistry Subdisciplines**
rabies: **Biological Product; Connaught Laboratories Ltd; Veterinary Medicine; Veterinary Medicines Industry; Virus**
Rabin, Linda: **Dance, Modern; Dance History; Grands Ballets Canadiens**
Rabinovitch, Isaiah: **Jewish Writing**
Rabinovitch, S.: **Education, Special**
Rabu, Renald: **Pacific Ballet Theatre**
RACAR: **Art Writing & Criticism**
Raccoon: **World War II**
Race Rocks: **Lighthouses**
racetracks: **Edmonton; Harness Racing; Horse; Thoroughbred Racing**
Racey, Arthur: **Cartoons**
Rached, T.: **Film**
Racicot, Marcel: **Film Animation**
Racicot, Réal: **Film Animation**
Racine, Jean-E.: **Autobiographical Writing in French**
Racine, Luc: **Poetry in French**
radar satellite: **Satellite, Artificial; Satellite Communications; Space Technology**
Radford, Tom: **Film, Documentary**

radiation: **Cancer; Chemistry Subdisciplines; Climatology; Energy; Injury & Prevention; Meteorology; Molecules in Interstellar Space; Nuclear Energy; Nuclear Power Plants; Nuclear Research Establishments; Nuclear Safety; Observatory; Solar Energy; Spectroscopy; Spinks, John William Tranter**
radiation chemistry: **Chemistry Subdisciplines**
radiation exposure: **Work**
Radiation Protection Bureau: **Medical Devices Industry**
radiation therapy: **Cancer; Medical Devices Industry; Physics**
Radin, Paul: **Folklore**
Radio Broadcasting, Royal Commission on: **Aird, John; Canadian Broadcasting Corporation**
Radio-Canada: **Arcand, Denys; Beaulne, Guy; Communications; Franco-Ontarians; Lapointe, Paul-Marie; Morel, François; October Crisis; Ouellette, Fernand; Pépin, Clermont; Perrault, Pierre; Radio Drama, French-Language; Renaud, Jacques; Television Drama, French-Language; Television Programming; Tremblay, Michel**
Radio-Canada International: **Canadian Broadcasting Corporation; Lévesque, René; Music Broadcasting**
Radio-City cinema: **Comédie-Canadienne**
Radio Forums: **Adult Education**
Radio-Québec: **Broadcasting, Radio & Television; Communications in Québec; Educational Broadcasting; Johnson, Daniel; New Brunswick; Television Drama, French-Language**
Radio Sunday School: **Aberhart, William**
radio telescope: **Observatory; Radar**
radioactive decay: **Geological History; Physics**
radioactive tracers: **Cobalt**
radioactive waste: **Hazardous Wastes; Pollution**
radioactivity: **Boyle, Robert William; Geological Dating; Geological History; McLennan, John Cunningham; Nuclear Energy; Nuclear Fusion; Nuclear Power Plants; Petroleum Exploration & Production; Physics; Plate Tectonics; Prospecting; Rutherford, Ernest; Uranium**
radioautography: **Leblond, Charles Philippe**
radiocarbon dating: **Aeolian Landform; Brooman Point Village; Debert; Glaciation; L'Anse Amour Burial Site; L'Anse aux Meadows; Old Crow Basin; Prehistory**
radioisotopes: **Cobalt; Hazardous Wastes; Hydrogen; Nuclear Energy; Ocean; Physics; Radium; Soil Science; Spinks, John William Tranter**
radiology: **Laurence, George C.; Veterinary Medicine**
radiometric dating: **Geological Dating; Geological History; Volcano**
radiometric survey: **Geological Survey of Canada**
Radiotelegraph Act: **Broadcasting, Radio & Television**
Radium Hot Springs: **Invermere; Kootenay National Park**
Radler, Nancy: **Dance, Modern**
radon: **Mining Safety & Health; Spring**
Radville, Sask: **Ljungh, Esse W.**
Rae, Fraser: **Exploration & Travel Literature in English**
Rae Isthmus: **Melville Peninsula**
Rae Lake: **Great Bear Lake**
Rae Lakes, NWT: **Dogrib**
Rae River: **Coronation Gulf**
Raffeix, Pierre: **Cartography, History of**
Raffi: **Oral Literature in English**
Ragged Range: **Selwyn Mountains; South Nahanni River**

Raglan Mountains: **Queen Elizabeth Islands**
Ragueneau, Paul: *Jesuit Relations*
Ragweed Press Inc: **Small Presses**
ragwort: **Endangered Plants; Groundsel; Nova Scotia**
Rahnefeld, Gunther: **Animal Breeding**
rails: **Champlain & St Lawrence Railroad; Railways, Contemporary; Railways, Track & Yards;** *Samson*
railway accidents: **Disasters; Grand Trunk Railway of Canada**
Railway Act: **Communications Law; Safety Standards; Telephones**
Railway Committee of the Privy Council: **Transportation Regulation**
Railway Police: **Police**
railway post offices: **Postal System**
Railway Rates Regulation: **Transportation Regulation**
railway tunnel: **Hobson, Joseph; Keefer, Samuel; Shanly, Francis; Tunnels**
Railways & Canals, Dept of: **Henry, R.A.C., "Red"; Transport Canada; Transportation Agencies (Government); Trent Canal**
Rain Deer Lake: **Reindeer Lake**
rain gauge: **Hydrology**
Rainbow Animation: **Film Animation**
Rainbow Bridge: **Niagara River; Wyn Wood, Elizabeth**
Rainbow Lake, Alta: **Fossil Plants; High Level**
Rainbow Stage: **Hendry, Thomas B.; Musical Theatre**
rainbow trout: **Huron, Lake; Trout**
Rainbow Valley: **Yellowknife, NWT**
Raine, Douglas: **Popular Literature in English; Stratford Festival**
Raine, Herbert: **Printmaking**
Rainer pianos: **Piano Manufacturing**
Raines, Tim: **Montreal Expos**
Rainy River: **Archaeology; Fort Frances; Rainy Lake; Thompson, David**
Rajan, Tillottama: **Literature in English - Theory & Criticism**
Rajneeshism: **New Religious Movements**
raku: **Ceramics, Contemporary**
Raleigh: **Gilbert, Humphrey**
Ralliement des créditistes: **Caouette, J.-D.-Réal; Créditistes; Roy, Fabien**
Ralliement national: **French Canadian Nationalism; Separatism**
Ralston, Alta: **Defence Research**
Ram hull: **Armaments**
Ram tank: **Armaments**
Rama Reserve: **Jacobs, Peter; Orillia; Shilling, Arthur; Theatre, Multicultural**
Ramadan: **Islam**
Ramah Bay: **Torngat Mountains**
Ramakrishna Mission: **Hinduism**
Ramirez, Bruno: **Italian Writing**
Rampart House, NWT: **Old Crow**
Ramparts: **Mackenzie River**
Ramsar Convention for the Conservation of Wetlands: **Bird Sanctuaries & Reserves**
Ramsay, D.A.: **Physics**
Ramsay, Lady Patricia: **Calgary Stampede**
Ramsay, W.A.: **Airport Architecture**
Ramsden, Peter G.: **Archaeology**
Ramsey, Frances: **Fort Frances; Simpson, George**
Ramsey, Lake: **Sudbury**
Randazzo, Peter: **Dance, Modern; Toronto Dance Theatre**
Randin, Hugues: **Superior, Lake**
Randolph, Man: **Hanover**
Random, Nfld: **Newfoundland**
Random Sound: **Random Island**
range finder: **Phillips, W. Eric; Surveying**
rangeland: **Cactus; Crops; Grasshopper; Remote Sensing; Soil Science; Vegetation Regions - Prairie; Wildlife Preserve**
Rangeland Derby: **Calgary Stampede**
Rankin, Alexander: **Cunard, Joseph**
Rankin, John: **Rankin Inlet, NWT**
Rankin Inlet: **Hudson Bay; Rankin Inlet, NWT**
Ranklin, McKee: **Theatre, English-Language**

Ranvoyzé, I.-François: **Jewellery & Silverware Industry; Ste-Anne-de-Beaupré; Silver, Church; Silver, Domestic**
Raoul-Blanchard, Mont: **Laurentian Highlands**
rape crisis centres: **Social & Welfare Services; Status of Women**
rape plant: **Canola**
rapeseed oil: **Downey, Richard Keith; Lighting; Vegetable Oil Industry**
Rapid River: **Lac La Ronge**
Rapoport, Janis: **Jewish Writing**
Rasco's Hotel: **Hotel**
Rasetti, F.: **Physics**
Rasky, Harry: **Film, Documentary**
Rasmussen, Knud: **Archaeology; Ethnic Literature; Netsilik Inuit**
rasp: **Tools, Carpentry**
raspberries: **Berries, Cultivated; Berries, Wild; Biogeography**
Raspberry Pass: **Mount Edziza Provincial Park**
Rassemblement pour l'indépendance nationale: **Bourgault, Pierre; Separatism**
Rassemblement pour l'indépendance nationale: **Aquin, Hubert**
Rastafarians: **Millenarianism; West Indians**
Rat Pass: **Permafrost**
Rat Portage, Man: **Kenora**
ratfish: **Chimaera**
Rathburn, Eldon: **Orchestral Music**
Rathwell case: **Property Law**
rationing: **Distilling Industry; Wartime Home Front**
Raudot: **Sculpture**
Raulston, Ont: **Domestic Utensils**
Ravelston Corp Ltd: **Argus Corp Ltd**
Ravenscrag, Sask: **Fossil Plants**
Ravitch, Melech: **Jewish Writing**
Ravitz, Paula: **Dance, Modern**
rawhide: **Babiche; Furniture, French; Medicine Bundles; Parfleche; Shaganappi**
Ray-O-Vac Corp: **Inco Ltd**
Raymond, Alta: **Place-names**
Raymond, Gérard: **Popular Literature in French; Saints**
Raymond, Maxine: **Bloc populaire canadien**
Raymond Sewing Machine Co: **Guelph**
Raynauld, André: **Economics**
rayon: **Textile Industry**
Rayside-Balfour, Ont: **Sudbury**
Razorback Mountain: **Torngat Mountains**
RCA Canadian Research & Development Laboratories Ltd: **Physics**
RCA Inc: **Baker, Carroll; Industrial Research & Development; Physics; Satellite Communications**
RCAF Flyers: **Olympic Games**
RCAF Hurricanes: **Gaudaur, Jacob G., Jr**
RCAF Memorial: **Prus, Victor Marius**
RCMP: **Royal Canadian Mounted Police**
RCMP Security Service: **Inquiry into Certain Activities of the RCMP, Royal Commission of**
RDC Ltd: **Biomass Energy**
Re-Mar Investment Management Corp: **Trust Company**
Re:Sounding: **Poetry in English**
Rea, John: **Opera**
Rea Point: **Disasters**
Read, Frank: **Rowing**
Readers Club of Canada: **Book Clubs**
Reader's Digest: **Committee for an Independent Canada; Magazines**
real servitudes: **Property Law**
realgar: **Mineral**
reaper: **Agricultural Implements; Agriculture History**
Reaume, Arthur: **Windsor, Ont**
Rebel: **Canadian Forum**
Réboul, Oliver: **Philosophy**
receivership: **Corporation Law**
Recherches sociales: **Scott, Francis R.**
Recherches sociographiques: **Intellectual History; Sociology**
Récollets: **Art; Catholicism; Christian Religious Communities; Education, History of; Essay in French; Fur Trade; Hennepin, Louis; Luc, Frère; Native People, Education; Religious Building; Ste Marie Among the Hurons; Saint-Vallier, Jean-Baptiste de; Trois-Rivières**

recombinant DNA technology: **Bioethics; Genetics**
Reconstruction Party: **Conservative Party; Great Depression; Party System; Stevens, Henry Herbert**
Recorder's Court: **Architecture, Development**
records management: **Archives; Library Science**
recycling: **Conserver Society; Energy in Society; Pollution; Waste Disposal**
red alder: **Alder; Vegetation Regions - Pacific Coastal**
red algae: **Algae; Biology; Fossil Plants; Vegetation Regions - Coastal Marine Flora**
Red Bank, NB: **Miramichi River**
Red Bobs wheat: **Wheeler, Seager**
red cabbage: **Cabbage; Cuisine**
red clover: **Clover; Forage Crops**
Red Cross Horse Show: **Queen's Plate**
Red Deer *Advocate*: **Alberta**
Red Earth Forks, BC: **Princeton**
red elderberry: **Vegetation Regions - Pacific Coastal**
red fescue: **Vegetation Regions - Pacific Coastal**
Red Fife wheat: **Agricultural Research & Development; Fife, David; Manitoba; Peterborough; Saunders, Charles E.; Wheat**
red fox: **Arctic Animals; Forillon National Park; Fox; Fundy National Park; Grasslands National Park; Kejimkujik National Park; Kouchibouguac National Park; La Mauricie National Park**
Red Hot Video: **Pornography**
red huckleberry: **Vegetation Regions - Cordillera**
Red Indian Lake: **Demasduwit; Exploits River**
"Red Indians": **Beothuk**
Red Lake: **Bush Flying; Tyrrell, James W.**
Red Lake, Ont: **Iron & Steel Industry; Nordicity**
red maple: **Maple; Vegetation Regions - Eastern Temperate Forests**
Red Mountain: **Rossland**
red mountain heather: **Vegetation Regions - Cordillera**
red mulberry: **Vegetation Regions - Eastern Temperate Forests**
red oak: **Oak; Plants, Native Uses; Vegetation Regions - Eastern Temperate Forests**
red ochre: **Agawa Bay; Bell Island; Beothuk; Kutchin; La Mauricie National Park; L'Anse Amour Burial Site; Northwest Coast Indian Art; Prehistory; Rainy River Burial Mounds**
"Red Paper": **Cardinal, Harold; Snow, John**
Red Pheasant Reserve: **Sapp, Allen**
red pine: **Forest Fire; Huron, Lake; Pine; Vegetation Regions - Eastern Temperate Forests**
red pipestone: **Linear Mounds**
Red Power: **Pan-Indianism**
Red River Brigades: **Morris; Souris, Man**
Red River Community College: **Clothing Industries; Manitoba**
Red River Exhibition: **Festivals**
Red River Expeditionary Force: **Butler, William Francis; Irvine, Acheson Gosford; Macleod, James F.; Riel, Louis; Winnipeg River; Wolseley, Garnet J.**
"Red River Frame": **Architecture, Development**
Red River Jig: **Métis Settlements**
Red River Transportation Co: **Hill, James J.**
Red Rock, Ont: **Nipigon, Lake**
red snapper: **Scorpionfish**
red sore: **Pike**
red spruce: **Spruce; Vegetation Regions - Atlantic Coastal**
red squirrel: **Lake Superior Provincial Park; Wood Buffalo National Park**
red-tailed hawk: **Hawk; Owl**
red tape: **Bureaucracy; Bureaucracy & Formal Organization; Freedom of Information; Kahane, Anne; Pollution**
Red Wing: **Aviation**

red-winged blackbird: **Biogeography; Blackbird; Conservation**
Redbird, Duke: **Ethnic Literature**
Redbirds: **Skiing**
redbud: **Endangered Plants**
Redeemer's Voice: **Catholicism**
Redemptorists: **Belgians; Catholicism**
redfish: **Coastal Waters; Fisheries; Fisheries History; Grand Banks; Prince Edward Island**
Redford, Donald: **Mediterranean Archaeology**
redhorse: **Sucker**
Redinger, Walter: **Sculpture**
Redman wheat: **Goulden, Cyril Harold**
Redmond, Lawrence: **Plastics-Processing Industry**
Redpath, Peter: **Science**
Redpath Industries: **John Labatt Corp**
Redpath Museum: **Hutchison, Alexander Cowper**
redpoll: **Finch**
redroot: **Endangered Plants**
Redsell, James Matthew: **Musical Instruments**
redside dace: **Minnow**
redstem ceanothus: **Vegetation Regions - Cordillera**
Redstone River: **Mackenzie River; Mountain (Indians)**
reductionism: **Science & Society**
Redvers, Sask: **Danes**
Redwater, Alta: **Japanese**
Redwater oil field: **Alberta; Harvie, Eric L.; Sedimentary Rock**
redwood: **Fossil Plants**
reed: **Biogeography**
Reed, William: **Choral Music**
reed canary grass: **Forage Crops**
Reeks, H.: **Botany History**
Reeve, John: **Ceramics, Contemporary**
Reeves, Gladys: **Brown, Ernest**
reference books: *Canada & Its Provinces*; **Dictionary;** *Dictionary of Canadian Biography;* **Encyclopedia;** *Encyclopedia of Music in Canada;* **Popular Literature in English**
refining: **Computer Systems Applications; Energy in Society; Metallurgy**
reform Darwinism: **Social Gospel**
Reform Party: **Howe, Joseph; Journalism; Little, Philip Francis; McGee, Thomas D'Arcy; Mowat, Oliver; Nova Scotia**
reformatory: **Child Welfare; Prison**
Reformed Episcopal Church: **Anglicanism**
Reformed tradition: **Presbyterian & Reformed Churches**
refractometer: **Mineral**
refrigerators & refrigeration: **Agriculture History; Crop Research; Electrical Appliances Industry; Locomotives & Rolling Stock; Meat-Processing Industry; Technology**
refuse: **Waste Disposal**
Regal Toy Ltd: **Toys & Games**
regatta: **Canoeing; Dartmouth Lakes; Lake of the Woods; Rowing; St John's Regatta; Valleyfield**
regeneration: **Salamander; Seashell**
Regent College: **Evangelical & Fundamentalist Movements; University of British Columbia**
Regent Park: **Carver, Humphrey S.M.**
Regent wheat: **Goulden, Cyril Harold**
"reggae" music: **West Indians**
Régie de l'assurance-automobile: **Québec**
Régie des rentes: **Québec**
Régie des services publics: **Communications in Québec**
Regina College: **University of Regina; University of Saskatchewan**
Regina College Conservatory: **Music Education**
Regina College of Art: **Bloore, Ronald; Regina Five**
Regina Exhibition Grounds: **On to Ottawa Trek**
Regina Indian & Métis Friendship Centre: **Deiter, Walter**
Regina Leader: **Davin, Nicholas Flood; Hayes, Kate S.; Journalism; Scott, T. Walter**
Regina Leader-Post: **Armadale Co Ltd**
Regina Manifesto: **Co-operative Commonwealth Federation; Economics, Radical; Plaunt, Alan Butterworth; Underhill, Frank H.**

Regina Modern Dance Works: **Dance, Modern; Dance History**
Regina Plains Community College: **Regina**
Regina Roughriders: **Football**
Regina Rugby Club: **Saskatchewan Roughriders**
Regionair: **Quebecair**
Regional Arts Council: **Theatre, French-Language**
Regional Development Incentives Act: **Regional Economics**
Regional Economic Expansion, Dept of: **Agricultural Economics; Regional Development Planning; Roads & Highways**
Regional Industrial Expansion, Dept of: **Regional Development Planning; Tourism**
Regiopolis College: **Macdonell, Alexander**
Regis College: **Lonergan, Bernard; MacKenzie, Roderick Andrew Francis**
Registered Homeownership Savings Plans: **Housing & Housing Policy**
Registered Retirement Savings Plans: **Pension**
Registrar General, Dept of the: **Consumer & Corporate Affairs, Dept of**
regosols: **Soil Classification**
Regroupement de l'association des amblyopes et aveugles du Québec: **Blindness & Visual Impairment**
Regulation 17 (Ont): **Bourassa, Henri; Ferguson, G. Howard; Ontario Schools Question; Paquet, Louis-Adolphe**
Regulation Reference of the Economic Council of Canada: **Economic Regulation**
"regulatory offences": **Criminal Law**
Regulatory Reform, Task Force on (Peterson Committee): **Economic Regulation**
rehabilitation: **Disability; Social & Welfare Services; Workers' Compensation**
Reibl v Hughes: **Medical Ethics**
Reichenbach, Oliver: **Théâtre du nouveau monde**
Reichert, Don: **Painting**
Reid, Dennis: **National Gallery of Canada**
Reid, Dorothy: **Children's Literature in English**
Reid, Leslie: **Printmaking**
Reid, N.H.: **Logan, Mount**
Reid, T.M.: **McKee Trophy**
Reid, William D.: **Genealogy**
Reid-Newfoundland Co: **Morine, Alfred Bishop; Reid, Robert G.**
Reimer, Bill: **New Religious Movements**
Reinblatt, Moe: **Printmaking**
reincarnation: **Hinduism; New Religious Movements**
reindeer: **Caribou; Stefansson, Vilhjalmur**
Reindeer: **Shipbuilding & Ship Repair**
Reindeer River: **Reindeer Lake**
Reinel, Pedro: **Cartography, History of**
Reis, Kurt: **Manitoba Theatre Centre**
Reiss, Timothy J.: **Comparative Literature**
Reiter's syndrome: **Arthritis**
Reitman, Ivan: **Film**
Reiyukai Soc of British Columbia: **Buddhism**
relapsing fever: **Insect Pests; Louse; Parasitology**
Relations des jésuites: *Jesuit Relations*
Relations industrielles: **Dion, Gérard; Industrial Relations**
Relations of Labour & Capital, Royal Commission on the: **Armstrong, John; Work; Workers' Compensation; Working-Class History**
relativity: **Cosmology**
Reliable Toy Ltd: **Toys & Games**
Reliance Toy Co: **Toys & Games**
Relief Camp Workers Union: **Great Depression**
relief measures: **Ecumenical Social Action; Government; Great Depression; Labour Policy; Macdonald, Angus L.; MacMillan, William Joseph Parnell; Prejudice & Discrimination; Purvis, Arthur Blaikie; Social Security**

relief printing: **Print Industry; Printmaking**
reliefs: **Architecture, Development; Bornstein, Eli**
Religieuses hospitalières: **Hôtel-Dieu**
Religion-Labour Council: **Ecumenical Social Action**
religious broadcasting: **Christianity**
religious fanaticism: **Gavazzi Riots**
religious instruction: **Bible Schools; Christianity; Education Policy; Sunday Schools**
Religious Orders: **Christian Religious Communities**
religious revival: **Alline, Henry; Evangelism; Great Awakening; Holiness Churches; McPherson, Aimee Semple; Pentecostal Movement**
Religious Societies Lands Act (Alta): **Corporation Law**
Religious Society of Friends: **Quakers**
religious supremacy: **Ultramontanism**
religious theatre: **Theatre, French-Language**
reliquary: **Silver, Church**
remand centre: **Prison**
Rembe, Heinrich: **German Writing**
Renaissance Film Co: **Film**
Renaissance International: **Evangelism**
Renard, Alphonse: *Challenger Expedition*
Renaud, André: **Literature in French - Scholarship & Teaching**
Renaud, Bernadette: **Children's Literature in French**
Renaud, Emiliano: **Music History**
Renaud, Jeanne: **Dance History**
Rencontre québécoise internationale des écrivains: **Ouellette, Fernand**
René-Levasseur Island: **Island**
Renews, Nfld: **Vaughan, William**
Renison College: **University of Waterloo**
Reno, Mike: **Loverboy**
Renown wheat: **Goulden, Cyril Harold**
Repentigny, Qué: **Montréal; Religious Building**
Repentigny, Rodolphe de: **Plasticiens**
Report & Collections of the Nova Scotia Historical Society: **Historical Societies**
Representation Act: **Redistribution**
reproduction rights: **Chambers, Jack; Copyright Law**
reproductive technology: **Medical Ethics**
"république du Madawaska": **Edmundston; New Brunswick**
Repulse Bay, NWT: **Iglulik Inuit; Inuit Art**
Requiem: **Literary Periodicals in French; Popular Literature in French**
Rescue Homes: **Salvation Army**
research & development: **Agricultural Research & Development; Alberta Oil Sands Technology & Research Authority; Animal Breeding; Business Management; Canada-US Automotive Products Agreement; Coal; Crop Research; Cuisine; Defence Research; Electronics Industry; Environment; Industrial Research & Development; Industry; Medical Devices Industry; Medical Research; National Research Council of Canada; Petroleum Research & Development; Research, Provincial Organizations; Science Policy; Scientific Research & Development; Telecommunications; Transportation Research Centres**
research & experimentation upon human beings: **Medical Ethics**
Research Development Corp: **Lowden, John Alexander**
Research Enterprises Ltd: **Burton, Eli Franklin; Leaver, Eric William; Munitions & Supply, Dept of; Phillips, W. Eric; Physics**
Research Institute, Hospital for Sick Children: **Lowden, John Alexander; Rothstein, Aser**
Research Program in Strategic Studies: **York University**
Réseau de résistance: **Renaud, Jacques**
Reserve Mines, NS: **Tompkins, James J.**

resin: **Muskeg; Petroleum; Plastics-Processing Industry**
Resnais, Alain: **Bujold, Geneviève**
Resolute: **McClure (M'Clure), Robert J. Le M.**
Resolution Island: **Hudson Strait; Wind**
Resources & Development, Dept of: **Halifax Citadel**
Resources for Feminist Research: **Women's Studies**
Resources Investment Corp: **Nationalization**
Restigouche Channel: **Chaleur Bay**
Restigouche Gallery: **Campbellton, NB**
restraint of trade: **Consumer & Corporate Affairs, Dept of**
retinal photography: **Ophthalmology**
retirement: **Aging; Work**
Retraite St-Bénoît: **Nelligan, Émile**
Retty, J.A.: **Schefferville**
Returning Officer: **Electoral Systems**
Revell, Guy: **Figure Skating**
Revell, Viljo: **Architecture, Development; Toronto City Hall**
Revelstoke Canyon Dam: **Castlegar; Revelstoke**
Revelstoke Ski Club: **Ski Jumping**
Reversing Falls: **Fundy, Bay of/Gulf of Maine; New Brunswick; Saint John; Saint John River; Tide; Waterfall**
Review of Historical Publications Relating to Canada: **Historiography; Wrong, George M.**
Review/Revue: **Musicology**
Reville, Ralph H.: **Golf**
revolver: **Firearm**
Revue canadienne: *Angéline de Montbrun*; **Art Writing & Criticism; Book Publishing, French-Language; Literary Periodicals in French**
Revue nationale: **Essay in French**
Revue socialiste: **Ferron, Jacques**
revues: **Deschamps, Yvon; Dumbells; Musical Theatre; Television Drama**
Rexdale, Ont: **Fur Trapping, Contemporary**
Reynolds, J.B.: **Literature in English - Teaching**
Reynolds, William: **Curling**
Reynolds Aluminum Co of Canada: **Baie-Comeau; Cap-de-la-Madeleine**
Reynolds Museum: **Wetaskiwin**
Rh factor: **Biological Product; Pediatrics; University of Manitoba**
rheumatic fever: **Heart Disease**
rheumatism: **Arthritis**
Rhineland Consumers Co-operative Ltd: **Siemens, Jacob John**
rhinitis: **Allergies**
Rho, Adolphe: **Leduc, Ozias**
Rhodenizer, V.B.: **Literature in English - Teaching**
Rhodes Curry Co: **Pipes, William Thomas**
Rhodesians: **Africans**
rhodium: **Platinum**
rhodonite: **Gemstone; Mineral**
Rhys, Horton: **Concert Halls & Opera Houses**
ribbon snake: **Kejimkujik National Park**
ribbon worm: **Flatworm**
Ribeiro, Diogo: **Cartography, History of**
Ribes, René: **Archaeology**
riboflavin: **Cherry; Tomato**
Ricard, François: *Liberté*
Ricardou, Jean: **Novel in French**
Rice Lake: **Canoeing; Foster, Harold; Island; Serpent Mound; Sunday, John; Trent Canal**
Rice Lake bridge: **Cobourg & Peterborough Railway**
Rich, E.E.: **Hudson's Bay Record Society**
Richard, Henri: **Hockey, Ice**
Richard, Jean-Jules: **Novel in French**
Richard, René: **Roy, Gabrielle**
Richard Smith: **Steamboats & Paddlewheelers**
Richards, A. Robert: *Fiddlehead*
Richards, David Adams: **Novel in English**
Richards, George: **Garibaldi Provincial Park**
Richardson, Arnold: **Richardson, Ernie**

Richardson, Bond & Wright: **Owen Sound**
Richardson, Garnet: **Richardson, Ernie**
Richardson, J.: **Botany History**
Richardson, Michael: **Popular Literature in English**
Richardson, Wes: **Richardson, Ernie**
Richardson Mountains: **Earthquake; Mackenzie River; Old Crow Plain**
Richbucto River: **Rexton**
Richelieu & Ontario Navigation Co: **Forget, Joseph-David-Rodolphe; Forget, Louis-Joseph; Senécal, Louis-Adélard**
Richelieu Steamboat Co: **Canada Steamship Lines Inc**
Richer, Luther: **Public Administration**
Richer-Lortie, Lyse: **Musicology**
Richibucto, NB: **New Brunswick; Northumberland Strait**
Richman, T.R.: **Exploration & Travel Literature in English**
Richmond, Qué: **St-François, Rivière**
Richmond, Upper Canada: **Windsor, Ont**
Richmond Gulf: **Guillaume-Delisle, Lake**
Richmond Hill Dynes: **Baseball**
Richter magnitude scale: **Earthquake**
Riddez, Mia: **Television Drama, French-Language**
Rideau Aquatic Club: **Amyot, Francis**
Rideau Canoe Club: **Amyot, Francis**
Rideau Centre: **Ottawa, Ont**
Rideau Falls: **Ottawa, Ont**
Rideau Hall Rebels: **Stanley, Frederick Arthur**
Rideau Regional Centre for Retarded Children: **Smiths Falls**
Rideau River: **Kemptville; Newman, Leonard Harold; Ottawa, Ont; Rideau Lakes; St Lawrence Lowland**
Rider-Rider, William: **Photography**
"riding": **Electoral Systems**
Riding Mountain: **Winnipegosis, Lake**
Ridley, Frank: **Archaeology**
Ridout, Thomas G.: **Bank of Upper Canada**
Riedesel, Baroness von: **Germans**
Riel House: **Manitoba**
rifle: **Armaments; Firearm; Shooting**
Rigaud Mont: **St Lawrence Lowland**
Riggall, Bert: **Russell, Andy**
"right of eminent domain": **Nationalization**
right of peaceful assembly: **Student Rights**
right to strike: **Public Service**
right whale: **Arctic Animals; Grand Manan Island; Whale**
Rigolet, Nfld: **Churchill River, Lab; Hamilton Inlet**
Rikka: **Ethnic Literature**
rime: **Ice**
Rimmer, Karen: **Dance, Modern**
Rimouski Airlines: **Quebecair**
Rinfret, Edouard-Gabriel: **Literary Bibliography in French**
ringed seal: **Arctic Animals; Lancaster Sound; Seal**
Ringness, Charles: **Printmaking**
Ringuet: **Panneton, Philippe**
ringworm: **Mold**
Rio Algom Ltd: **Elliot Lake; Iron & Steel Industry; Winters, Robert H.**
Riopelle, Françoise: **Dance History**
Riordon Pulp & Paper Co: **Edwards, William Cameron; Témiscaming**
Riot Act: **Riot; Vancouver**
Rioux, Marcel: **Community; Essay in French**
Rioux Report: **Art Education; Music Education**
rip tide: **Cape Blomidon; Tide**
riparian ownership: **Sportfishing**
Rising Tide Theatre: **Theatre, English-Language**
risk: **Insurance; Interest; Medical Jurisprudence**
Risk, Sydney: **Theatre, English-Language**
Rist, John: **Philosophy**
Ristvedt-Handerek, Milly: **Painting**
Ritchie, Ella: **Ritchie, Eliza**
Ritchie, J.W.: **Fathers of Confederation**
Ritchie, Mary: **Ritchie, Eliza**
Ritchie, Roland A.: *McNeil Case*

Rittenhouse, David: **Festival Lennoxville**
Ritter, Erika: **Drama in English**
Rittinger, John A.: **German Writing**
ritual: **Death & Dying; Folklore; Religion**
Rivard, Adjutor: **Autobiographical Writing in French**
Rivard, Gilles: **Children's Literature in French**
River Brethren: **Brethren in Christ**
river lot: **Agriculture History; Fidler, Peter; Seigneurial System**
Riverbend, Qué: **Alma**
Riverdale, North-West Territories: **Saskatoon**
Rivermead Cup: **Golf**
Rivers Inlet: **Bella Bella**
Rivière du Chêne seigneury: **St-Eustache**
RNA: **Molecular Biology; Virus**
RO/RO (roll on-roll off) transportation: **Ferries; Transportation**
road racing: **Automobile Racing; Motorcycle Racing**
Roads to Resources Program: **Hamilton, F. Alvin G.; Roads & Highways; Yukon Territory**
Robb, Alta: **Fossil Plants**
Robb, James: **Science**
Robb Wave Organ: **Robb, F. Morse**
Robbins, John D.: **Essay in English**
Robe & Hall: **Architecture, Development**
Roberge, Guy: **National Film Board**
Robert, Guy: **Essay in French**
Robert, P.: **Philosophy**
Robert, Serge: **Philosophy**
Robert Flaherty Award: **Film, Documentary**
Robert Harris Memorial Gallery & Library: **Harris, Robert**
Robert McLaughlin Gallery: **Eyre, Ivan K.; Luke, Alexandra; Painters Eleven**
Robert Simpson Co: **Architecture, Development; Simpson, Robert**
Robert Watson Co: **Confectionery Industry**
Robert Young House: **Almonte**
Roberts, David: **Sproatt and Rolph**
Roberts, Helen: **Ethnic Literature**
Roberts, J.M.: **Dieppe**
Roberts, Latham: **Autobiographical Writing in English**
Roberts, Sarah Ellen: **Autobiographical Writing in English**
Roberts, Theodore Goodridge: **Novel in English**
Roberts Bank superport: **Delta, BC; Shipping Industry; Vancouver**
Roberts Gallery: **Art Dealers; Painters Eleven**
Robertson, A. Bruce: **Vancouver, Mount**
Robertson, Alexander: **Canada & Australia**
Robertson, Barbara: **Children's Literature in English**
Robertson, Colin: **North West Company; Robson, Mount**
Robertson, Gideon: **Winnipeg General Strike**
Robertson, J.K.: **Physics**
Robertson, John Charles: **Essay in English**
Robertson, Robbie: **Band, The; Guitar**
Robertson & Ensor: **Art Dealers**
Robertson Brothers Ltd: **Confectionery Industry**
Robertson Collection (Regina): **Musical Instruments**
Robichaud, Michel: **Fashion Design**
Robidoux, Réjean: **Literature in French - Scholarship & Teaching**
Robillard, Yves: **Art, Contemporary Trends**
Robilschek, Ray: **Stage & Costume Design**
Robin, Martin: **Working-Class History**
Robin Bros fishing company: **Caraquet; New Brunswick**
Robin Hood Flour Co Ltd: **McIvor, George Harold**
Robinson, Christopher: **Newmarket**
Robinson, Gladys: **Speed Skating**
Robinson, Graydon: **Bowling, Indoor**
Robinson, Helier J.: **Philosophy**
Robinson, Jeanne: **Dance, Modern**
Robinson, Spider: **Popular Literature in English**

Robinson, T.M.: **Philosophy**
Robinson, Tedd: **Dance, Modern**
Robinson, W.A.: **Railway History**
Robinson, W.B.: **Indian Treaties**
Robinson-Huron Treaty: **Indian Treaties; Native People - Eastern Woodlands**
Robinson-Superior Treaty: **Indian Treaties; Native People - Eastern Woodlands; Shinguacôuse**
Robitaille, Louis: **Dance on Television & Film**
Roblin News: **Manitoba**
Robson, Albert H.: **Printmaking; Thomson, Thomas J.**
Robson, Fred: **Speed Skating**
Robson, J.M.: **Physics**
Robson, John: **Philosophy**
Robson Square: **Architecture; Shrum, Gordon M.; Urban Design; Vancouver**
Roby, John: **Musical Theatre**
Roby, Yves: **Business History**
Roby Kidd Award: **Adult Education**
Roch, Ernest: **Graphic Design**
Rochdale College: **Hippies; Pelletier, Wilfred**
Roche Fendue portage: **Ottawa River**
Roche Percée, Sask: **Saskatchewan**
Roches moutonnées: **Glaciation**
Rochon, Esther: **Popular Literature in French**
rock art: **French River; La Mauricie National Park; Lake of the Woods; Lake Superior Provincial Park; Metlakatla Pass Sites; Pictographs & Petroglyphs**
Rock Creek gold rush: **Princeton**
rock crystal: **Mineral Naming**
rock elm: **Elm; Timber Trade History**
rock flour: **Fjord**
Rock Forest, Qué: **Sherbrooke**
Rock Partridge Lake: **Kasba Lake**
Rock Pile Feast: **Sarcee**
rock rabbit: **Pika**
Rockcliffe Airport: **Ottawa, Ont**
Rockcliffe Park: **Ski Jumping**
rocket: **Electronics Industry; Physics; Space Technology**
rockfish: **Scorpionfish**
Rockhead's Paradise: **Jazz**
Rockland, Ont: **Edwards, William Cameron; Theatre, French-Language**
Rockland Shopping Centre: **Prus, Victor Marius**
rockling: **Cod**
Rockport, Ont: **Thousand Islands**
rockweed: **Algae**
Rockwood Academy: **Barns**
Rockwood Asylum: **Clarke, Charles Kirk**
Rocky Mountain Breweries Ltd: **Brewing Industry**
Rocky Mountain Development Co: **Oil City**
Rocky Mountain House: **Butler, William Francis; L'Heureux, Jean-B.; Rundle, Robert Terrill**
Rocky Mountain juniper: **Juniper; Vegetation Regions - Cordillera**
Rocky Mountain Rangers: **Brown, J.G., "Kootenai"**
Rocky Mountain spotted fever: **Tick**
Rocky Mountain wolf: **Endangered Animals**
Rocky Mountains Park Act: **Heritage Conservation; Parks, National**
Rocquet Report: **Collège d'enseignement général et professionnel**
rod steel: **Sidbec-Dosco Limitée**
Roden Bros Glass Co: **Glass**
rodenticide: **Pesticide**
roe: **Newfoundland**
Roebuck, Arthur: **Oshawa Strike**
Roeder, Robert: **Black Hole; Cosmology**
Rogel, Joseph: **Jewish Writing**
Rogers, A.B.: **Rogers Pass**
Rogers, Doug: **Judo**
Rogers, E.B.: **MacKay, Robert Alexander**
Rogers, Edward S.: **Archaeology**
Rogers, Edward Samuel, II: **Rogers, Edward Samuel**
Rogers, Melville: **Figure Skating**
Rogers, Stan: **Folk Festivals**
Rogers, Steve: **Montreal Expos**
Rogers, Tim: **Musicology**
Rogers, Timothy: **Newmarket**
Rogers Cablesystems Inc: **Rogers Telecommunications Ltd**

Rogers Majestic Co: **Rogers, Edward Samuel**
Rogerson, John: **Sculpture**
Rogge, Bianca: **Dance, Modern**
Rohmer, Richard: **Best-Sellers in English; Book Publishing, English-Language; Literature & Politics; Popular Literature in English**
Roland, C.G.: **Scarlett, Earle P.**
Roland, Man: **4-H Clubs**
Rolin Art Centre: **Port Alberni**
Rolland Co: **St-Jérôme**
Rolland-Germain, Frère: **Botany History**
rolled steel: **Dominion Foundries & Steel, Ltd; Iron & Steel Industry; Railways, Track & Yards**
Rollet, Marie: **Hébert, Louis**
Rollin, Henri: **Drama in French; Theatre, French-Language**
Rollin, Paul: **Sculpture**
Rolling River: **Erickson**
Rollins, Al: **Broda, Walter**
Rolpf, John: **Parasitology**
Rolph, Ernest Ross: **Sproatt and Rolph**
Rolph, John: **Reform Movement in Upper Canada; St Thomas; Workman, Joseph**
Rolphton, Ont: **Electric Power; Nuclear Energy**
Rolston, Thomas: **Edmonton Symphony Orchestra**
Roma, Alta: **Railway History**
Roman, Zoltan: **Musicology**
Roman Catholic Church: **Catholicism**
Roman Catholic index of forbidden books: **Guibord Affair; Institut canadien**
Romanian Orthodox Episcopate of America: **Orthodox Church**
Romanow, Roy J.: **Constitution, Patriation of**
Romen, Levko: **Ukrainian Writing**
Romero, Hugo: **Dance on Television & Film**
Romm, Ronald: **Canadian Brass**
Ronfard, Jean-Pierre: **Drama in French**
Rooke, Leon: **Humorous Writing in English; Short Fiction in English**
room-and-pillar mining: **Coal Mining; Salt**
Roos, Celine: **Chess**
Roos, Charles: **Film**
Roos, Len: **Film**
Roosevelt elk: **Strathcona Provincial Park**
Roosters' Comb: **Golden Hinde**
Roper, E. June: **Dance History**
Roper, Edward: **Exploration & Travel Literature in English**
Roper, Elmo: **Social Gospel**
Roper, G.: **Literature in English - Teaching**
Rosary: **Catholicism**
Rose, George Maclean: **Book Publishing, English-Language**
Rose, Hilda: **Autobiographical Writing in English**
Rose, Paul: **Front de libération du Québec**
Rose, Peter: **Architectural Styles; Architecture, Development**
Rose, Sheldon: **Drama in English**
Rose-Belford's Canadian Monthly & National Review: **Book Publishing, English-Language; Literary Magazines in English; Literary Periodicals in English; Literature in English**
rose quartz: **Gemstone; Silica**
Rosebank Cottage: **Ross Farm**
Rosedale, Man: **Poles**
Rosedale, Valerie: **Harron, Donald**
Roselyn Mine: **Coal**
rosemary: **Herbs**
Rosenberg, Judah: **Jewish Writing**
Rosenberg, Neil: **Musicology**
Rosenboom, David: **Musicology**
Rosenfarb, Chava: **Jewish Writing**
Rosenfeld, Man: **Germans**
Rosevear, Robert: **Music Education**
rosewood: **Furniture, English, Scottish & American**
Rosh Hashanah: **Judaism**
rosin oil: **Lighting**
Ross, A.M.: **Railway Station**
Ross, Alexander: **Business Elites; *Canadian Business***
Ross, Arthur H.: **Art Ross Trophy**
Ross, Charles: **Firearm**
Ross, E.: **Urban Studies**

Ross, Earl: **Automobile Racing**
Ross, Frank: **Turner, John N.**
Ross, J.H.: **Chemistry Subdisciplines**
Ross, James H.: **Baseball**
Ross, John: **Exploration & Travel Literature in English; North West Company**
Ross, P.D.: **Grey Cup; *Ottawa Journal***
Ross, W.E. Dan: **Popular Literature in English**
Ross, W.W.E.: **Literature in English**
Ross, William: **Ross Farm**
Ross Aboretum: **Botanical Garden**
Ross & Macdonald: **Railway Station; Union Station**
Ross & MacFarlane: **Hotel**
Ross House: **Manitoba**
Ross rifle: **Armaments; Armed Forces - Militia & Army; Firearm; World War I; World War II**
Ross River: **Yukon Territory**
Ross River, YT: **Kaska**
Rosseau, Lake: **Muskoka Lakes**
Rossignol, Lake: **Nova Scotia**
Rossville, Man: **Evans, James; Norway House**
Rosthern, Sask: **Germans; Ukrainians; Wheeler, Seager**
rotary press: **Printmaking**
rotary snowplough: **Railway History**
rotenone: **Pesticide**
Roth, Evelyn: **Art, Contemporary Trends**
Rother, Bland & Trudeau: **Architecture, Development**
Rothesay, NB: **Turnbull, Wallace Rupert**
Rothesay Collegiate: **New Brunswick**
Rothmans Merit Award for Literature: **Literary Prizes in English**
Rotstein, Abraham: *Canadian Forum*; **Committee for an Independent Canada; Economics; Intellectual History**
Rottenburg, George: **Cartography, History of**
Rotz, John: **Cartography, History of**
Rouch, Jean: **Jutra, Claude**
Roue, William J.: *Bluenose*
Rouge, Rivière: **Laurentian Highlands; Ottawa River**
Rougemont, Qué: **St Lawrence Lowland**
rough-legged hawk: **Banks Island; Hawk**
Rougier laboratories: **Pharmaceuticals Industry**
Rouillard, Jacques: **Social History**
Rouleau, Ernest: **Marie-Victorin, Frère**
Rouleau, Joseph: **Singing**
roulette: **Gambling**
Roulotte: **Deschamps, Yvon**
Roulston, Keith: **Blyth Festival**
Round Table Quarterly: **Walker, B. Edmund**
round whitefish: **Dubawnt Lake; Whitefish**
roundworm: **Animal Agriculture; Nematoda**
Rous & Mann: **Graphic Design**
Rousseau, Alfred: **Radio Drama, French-Language**
Rousseau, Benjamin: **Curling**
Rousseau, François: **Art, Contemporary Trends**
Rousseau, Joseph: **Suzor-Coté, Marc-Aurèlie de Foy**
Rousseau, Ont: **Icelanders**
Rousseau-Vermette, Mariette: **Public Art**
Roussel, Timothée: **Golden Dog**
Routhier, Adolphe-Basile: **Exploration & Travel Literature in French; Literature in French; Literature in French - Scholarship & Teaching; *O Canada***
Routier, Simone: **Autobiographical Writing in French; Poetry in French**
Rouvière, Jean-Baptiste: **Sinnisiak**
Rouyn, Jean-Baptiste de: **Rouyn-Noranda**
row house: **Condominium**
rowan: **Mountain Ash**
Rowat, D.C.: **Public Administration**
Rowe, Nelly: **La Palme, Béatrice**
Rowe, Peter: **Film, Experimental**
Rowe, Richard D.: **Pediatrics**
Rowe Report: **Nationalism**

Rowell, Newton W.: **Dominion-Provincial Relations, Royal Commission on; League of Nations Society; World War I**

Rowell-Sirois Commission: **Deutsch, John Hames; Dominion-Provincial Relations, Royal Commission on; St Laurent, Louis Stephen**

Rowley, Kent: **Parent, Madeleine**

Roxy Petroleum: **Hudson's Bay Company**

Roy, André: **Poetry in French**

Roy, Antoine: **Literature in French - Scholarship & Teaching**

Roy, Carmen: **Musicology; Oral Literature in French**

Roy, James: **Blyth Festival; Manitoba Theatre Centre**

Roy, Jean: **Philosophy**

Roy, Jean-Claude: **Université Sainte-Anne**

Roy, Jean-Louis: *Devoir*

Roy, Jean-Pierre: **Baseball**

Roy, Joseph-Edmond: **Historiography**

Roy, Léo: **Music Criticism; Music History**

Roy, Louis: **Print Industry**

Roy, Michel: *Devoir; Presse*

Roy, Narcisse: **Silver, Indian Trade**

Roy, Pierre-Georges: **Genealogy**

Roy, Régis: **Theatre, French-Language**

Roy Thomson Hall: **Concert Halls & Opera Houses; Erickson, Arthur C.; Massey Hall; Toronto; Toronto Symphony**

Royal, Mont: **Physiographic Regions - St Lawrence Lowlands; St Lawrence Lowland**

Royal Alexandra Hospital (Fergus, Ont): **Groves, Abraham**

Royal Architectural Institute of Canada: **Archambault, Louis; Archibald, John Smith; Architectural Competitions; Architectural Practice; Architecture, Development; Chaussé, Joseph-Alcide; Fairn, Leslie Raymond**

Royal Assent: **Sovereign; Speaker**

Royal Astronomical Soc of Canada: **Associations; Astronomy; Chant, Clarence Augustus; Douglas, Alice Vibert; Hogg, Frank Scott; Hogg, Helen B.; King, William Frederick; Pearce, Joseph Algernon; Science**

Royal Bank Plaza: **Architecture, Development; Bank Architecture**

Royal Canadian Academy of Arts: **Art Education; Artists' Organizations; Drawing; Franchere, Joseph-Charles; Group of Seven; National Gallery of Canada; Painting; Printmaking**

Royal Canadian Air Force: **Armed Forces; Helicopter; Leckie, Robert; Reserve Force of Canada; Uniforms**

Royal Canadian College of Organists: **Religious Music**

Royal Canadian Geographical Soc: **Geography; Jenness, Diamond**

Royal Canadian Henley Regatta: **Fear, Alfred Henry; Rowing; Wright, Joseph, Sr**

Royal Canadian Infantry School: **Dextraze, Jacques A.**

Royal Canadian Institute: **Associations; Carpmael, Charles; Fields, John Charles; Literary Magazines in English; McIlwraith, Thomas Forsyth; McLennan, John Cunningham; Manery, Jeanne Fisher; Mathematics; Tully, Kivas**

Royal Canadian Mint: **Gaboury, Etienne-Joseph; Medal; Minting; Supply & Services, Dept of; Winnipeg**

Royal Canadian Navy: **Armed Forces; Brodeur, Louis-Philippe; Helicopter; Kingsmill, Charles Edmund; Landymore, William Moss; Steele, Harold Raymond; Uniforms**

Royal Canadian Regiment: **Lombardo, Guy**

Royal Centre: **Vancouver**

royal charter: **Literary & Historical Soc of Québec; Royal Winnipeg Ballet**

Royal College of Dental Surgeons: **University of Toronto**

Royal College of Physicians & Surgeons of Canada: **Farquharson, Ray Fletcher; Medical Education; Medical Ethics; Medicine, Contemporary; Ophthalmology; Psychiatry**

Royal Columbian Hospital: **New Westminster**

Royal Conservatory Opera Co: **Canadian Opera Co; Crum, George**

Royal Conservatory's Eaton Graduating Scholarship: **Marshall, Lois C.**

Royal Edward: **Sculpture**

Royal Electric Co: **Electric Power**

Royal Gazette: **Blacks**

Royal George Theatre: **Shaw Festival**

Royal Hamilton Conservatory of Music: **Hamilton**

Royal Horse Show: **Day, James; Elder, James; Equestrian Sports**

Royal Inland Hospital: **Kamloops**

Royal Institution for the Advancement of Learning: **McGill University**

Royal Life Saving Soc of Canada: **Boating**

Royal Lyceum Theatre: **Nickinson, John**

Royal Manitoba Winter Fair: **Brandon**

Royal National Mission to Deep-Sea Fishermen: **Grenfell, Wilfred T.; St Anthony**

Royal Naval College of Canada: **Armed Forces - Navy; Military & Staff Colleges**

Royal North-West Mounted Police: **North-West Mounted Police; Pearkes, George R.; Royal Canadian Mounted Police; Whaling**

Royal Philatelic Society of Canada: **Stamp Collecting**

Royal Prerogative: **Law; Prerogative Powers**

Royal Red Cross: **Smellie, Elizabeth Lawrie; South African War**

Royal Roads Military College: **Military & Staff Colleges; Oceanography**

Royal School of Church Music: **Religious Music**

Royal Securities Corp: **Aitken, W. Maxwell; Killam, Izaak Walton; Stairs, John Fitz-William**

Royal Society of Arts: **Fairn, Leslie Raymond; Houston, James Archibald**

Royal Style & Titles Act: **Sovereign**

"Royal Twenty Centers": **Unemployment Relief Camps**

Royal Victoria Hospital: **Archibald, Edward William; Bethune, H. Norman; Death & Dying; Penfield, Wilder G.; Stephen, George**

Royal Winnipeg Ballet School: **Moroni, David Lee**

Royal Winter Fair: **Agricultural Exhibitions; 4-H Clubs**

Royale, Île: **Agriculture History; Beaucours, Josué Dubois Berthelot de; Cape Breton Island; Louisbourg; Maillard, Pierre; Nova Scotia 1714-84; Treaty of Paris (1763); Treaty of Utrecht; Verville, Jean-François Du Verger de**

Roz, Lac: **Bienville, Lac**

Rozeboom, William: **Philosophy**

Rubble Creek: **Rockslide**

Rubbo, Michael: **Film, Documentary**

rubella: **Biological Product; Virus**

Rubenstein, Burton: **Film, Experimental**

rubidium: **Geological Dating**

Rubinoff, Lionel: **Philosophy**

Rudnyckyj, J.B.: **Linguistics**

Rue de Bleury: **Lighting**

Rue des Forges: **Trois-Rivières**

Rue du Palais: **Hôtel-Dieu**

Rue Notre-Dame: **Trois-Rivières**

Ruest, Paul: **Theatre, French-Language**

ruffed grouse: **Game Bird; Grouse; New Brunswick**

Ruhnke, G.N.: **Soil Science**

Rule Against Perpetuities: **Trust**

Rules of Court: **Civil Procedure**

Rules of Practice: **Civil Procedure**

rum: **Alcoholism; Distilling Industry; Mauger, Joshua**

rum-running: *I'm Alone*; **Liverpool; Prohibition**

Rumble, John: **Equestrian Sports**

Rumilly, Robert: **Book Publishing, French-Language; Historiography**

Rundle Formation: **Sedimentary Rock**

Rungius, Carl: **Banff; Glenbow Museum**

running: **Long-Distance Running; Track & Field**

running pine: **Club Moss**

Runnymede Library: **Lyle, John M.**

Rupert Bay: **Nottaway, Rivière**

Rupert House, Qué: **Diamond, Billy; Rupert, Rivière de; Troyes, Pierre de**

Ruprecht, Hans-George: **Comparative Literature**

Rural Co-operator: **United Farmers of Ontario**

Rural Electrification Assn (Alta): **Strom, Harry Edwin**

Ruse, Michael: **Philosophy**

Rush, Tom: **Cockburn, Bruce**

Ruskin, BC: **Mission**

Russel, Colin K.: **Penfield, Wilder G.**

Russell, Ernestine: **Gymnastics**

Russell, G.L.: **Green, Blankstein, Russell**

Russell, Gyrth: **Printmaking**

Russell, I.C.: **Logan, Mount**

Russell, Lawrence: **Drama in English**

Russell, Peter: **Upper Canada**

Russell, R.D.: **Physics**

Russell, Welford: **Choral Music**

Russell, William A.: **Archaeology**

Russell Agricultural Soc: **Edwards, William Cameron**

Russell automobile: **Automotive Industry**

Russell Resolutions: **Gosford, 2nd Earl of; Lower Canada; Patriotes; Rebellions of 1837**

Russian American Fur Co: **Promyshlennik**

Russian Orthodox Church: **Orthodox Church; Russians; Ukrainians**

Russian wild ryegrass: **Forage Crops**

rusts: **Asparagus; Biology; Craigie, John Hubert; Crop Research; Fossil Plants; Fungus; Goulden, Cyril Harold; Neatby, Kenneth William; Newton, Margaret; Newton, Robert; Wheat**

Ruth Schwartz Memorial Award: **Literary Prizes in English; Richler, Mordecai**

ruthenium: **Platinum**

Rutherford Library: **Rutherford, Alexander C.**

rutile: **Titanium**

Ruttan, R.F.: **Biochemistry**

Ruysch map: **Cartography, History of**

Ruzicka, Bob: **Country & Western Music**

Ryan, D.E.: **Chemistry Subdisciplines**

Ryan, James: **Nine-Hour Movement**

Ryan, Joe: **Skiing**

Ryan, Joe (Winnipeg Blue Bombers): **Football**

Ryan, Oscar: **Drama in English**

Ryan, Peter: **Automobile Racing**

Ryder, Gus: **Lumsdon, Cliff**

Ryder, Norman B.: **Demography**

Ryerson, George Sterling: **Red Cross Society**

Ryerson Act: **Ryerson Polytechnical Institute**

Ryerson Fiction Award: **Literary Prizes in English**

Ryerson Theatre Canadian College of Dance: **Dance Education**

S

S.R. Gent & Corah Ltd: **Clothing Industries**

Saanich, BC: **Saanich Peninsula; Victoria**

Saanich Inlet: **Saanich Peninsula; Victoria**

Saanichton Research & Plant Quarantine Station: **Ornamentals**

Sabatier, Charles W.: **Music History**

Sabbath: **Judaism; Lord's Day Alliance of Canada**

Sabia, Laura: **Italians; Status of Women in Canada, Royal Commission on the**

sable fish: **Aquaculture**

Sables, Lac des: **Ste-Agathe-des-Monts**

Sables, Rivière aux: **Jonquière**

Sabourin, Jean-Guy: **Drama in French**

Sabre aircraft: **Military Aviation & Aircraft**

saccharin: **Soft-Drink Industry**

Sacerdotal Commission on Social Studies: **Social Doctrine of the Roman Catholic Church**

Sachs Harbour: **Banks Island; Copper Inuit**

Sachs River: **Banks Island**

Sackbut synthesizer: **Electroacoustic Music; Le Caine, Hugh**

Sackville, NS: **Halifax**

Sackville Daily News: **Halifax**

Sackville River: **Nova Scotia**

Sacouman, R. James: **Marxism**

sacraments: **Anabaptists; Anglicanism; Catholicism; Christianity; Lutherans; Mennonites**

saddle-bronc riding: **Rodeo**

Saddle Island: **Red Bay**

Saddle Lake, Alta: **Steinhauer, Ralph G.**

Saddle Lake Indian School: **Janvier, Alex S.**

"saddlebag preachers": **Alline, Henry; Methodism**

sadeku: **Carrier**

Sadowska, Konrad: **Ceramics, Contemporary**

Sadowska, Krystyna: **Ceramics, Contemporary**

saengerfests: **Kitchener-Waterloo**

Safeway Stores Ltd: **Canada Safeway Ltd**

Saga: **Popular Music; Recording Industry**

Sagard-Théodat, Gabriel: **Anthropology; Botany History; Literature in French; Music History**

Sagawitchewan River: **Island Lake**

Saginaw River: **Huron, Lake**

Saglek Bay: **Geological Dating; Torngat Mountains**

Saglouc, Qué: **Inuit Art**

Saguenay: **Nelles, Percy Walker**

Saguenay depression: **Nordicity**

Saguenay Fjord: **Fjord**

Saguenay Power Co: **Technology**

Saia, Louis: **Theatre, French-Language**

Saidye Bronfman Award: **Ceramics, Contemporary; Weaving, Contemporary**

Saidye Bronfman Centre: **Caiserman-Roth, Ghitta; Theatre, Multicultural**

Sail-by-the-wind-sailor: **Jellyfish**

Saila: **Pauta Saila**

sailing: **Boating**

"Sailing Directions": **Hydrography**

St Albert le Grand conference: **Philosophy**

St-André d'Argenteuil, Qué: **St-André-Est**

St Andrews Biological Station: **Passamaquoddy Bay; Physical Oceanography; Zoology**

St Andrew's College (Man): **Orthodox Church; University of Manitoba**

St Andrews College (Ont): **Harris, Lawren S.**

St Andrew's College (PEI): **MacEachern, Angus Bernard**

St Andrew's Hall: **University of British Columbia**

St Andrew's Institute: **Social Gospel**

St Andrews Locks: **St Andrews, Man; Selkirk**

St Andrew's Society of Winnipeg: **Highland Games**

Ste-Anne, Mont: **Québec City**

Ste-Anne, Rivière: **St Lawrence Lowland**

Ste-Anne-de-Bellevue, Qué: **Agricultural Education; Arctic Oceanography; Bridges**

Ste-Anne-de-Danville, Qué: **Johnson, Daniel**

Ste-Anne-de-la-Perade, Lower Canada: **Dorion, Jean-Baptiste-Eric**

Ste-Anne-de-Sabrevois, Qué: **Bessette, Gerard**

Ste-Anne Mission: **Restigouche**

Ste Anne's Day: **Pilgrimage**

St Anne's Point: **Fredericton**

St Anns Harbour: **McLeod, Norman; St Anns**

St-Anselme, Qué: **Laflamme, Joseph-Clovis-Kemner**

St Anthony's Fire: **Veterinary Medicines Industry**

St-Antoine, Nfld: **St Anthony**
St-Augustin, Marie-Catherine de: **Saints**
St-Augustin, Rivière: **Boundaries**
St-Augustin-de-Portneuf, Qué: **Petitclair, Pierre**
St Bonaventure's College: **Mullock, John Thomas; Purcell, James**
St-Boniface Basilica: **Manitoba**
St-Boniface Museum: **Furniture, Country; Manitoba**
St-Bruno, Mont: **St Lawrence Lowland**
St Catharines Parachuting Club: **Parachuting, Sport**
Ste-Catherine-de-Fossambault, Qué: **Garneau, H. de Saint-Denys; Hébert, Anne**
St Catherines: **Station PAPA**
St Catherine's Milling case: **Aboriginal Rights; Indian Treaties**
Ste-Cecile-de-Frontenac, Qué: **Dion, Gérard**
Ste-Cécile-de-Rome, Marie de: **Saints**
St Charles, Joseph: **Hébert, Adrien**
St-Charles, Rivière: **Québec City; Shipbuilding & Ship Repair**
St Charles Country Club: **Knudson, George**
St-Charles Mission: **Ste Marie Among the Hurons**
St-Charles seigneury: **St-Charles-sur-Richelieu**
St Clair Beach, Ont: **Windsor, Ont**
St Clair College of Applied Arts & Technology: **Chatham, Ont; Windsor, Ont**
St Clair Processing Corp Ltd: **Petrochemical Industry**
St Clair Reserve: **Sarnia**
St Clair Tunnel: **Locomotives & Rolling Stock; Sarnia**
St Claude, Man: **Architecture**
St Clement's, Man: **Poles**
St Cloud, BC: **Ashcroft**
St Columban, Qué: **Hall, Emmett M.**
Ste-Croix, Ile: **Associations; Monts, Pierre Du Gua de**
St Croix Courier: **Clarke, George Johnson**
St Cyr, Marcel: **Orford String Quartet**
St David's, Ont: **Wine Industry**
St Davids gorge: **Niagara Peninsula**
St David's Soc: **Welsh**
Saint-Denis, Michel: **Theatre Education**
St-Donat, Qué: **Disasters**
St Dunstan's University: **Prince Edward Island; University of Prince Edward Island**
St Eleanors, PEI: **Slemon Park; Summerside**
St Elias Mountains: **Glaciation; Kluane Ranges; Logan, Mount; Lucania, Mount; Vancouver, Mount; Yukon Territory**
St Elmo, Ont: **Maxville**
St-Eloi, Qué: **Godbout, Joseph-Adélard**
St-Esprit Mission: **Ste Marie Among the Hurons**
St Eustache, Man: **Physics**
Sainte-Famille, Mont: **Hôtel-Dieu**
Ste-Flavie, Qué: **Intercolonial Railway**
Ste-Foy, Qué: **Battle of Ste-Foy; Centre de recherche industrielle du Québec; Québec City; Research Stations, Agricultural; Université Laval**
St-François, Lac: **St-François, Rivière; St Lawrence River; Valleyfield**
St François Xavier, Man: **Grant, Cuthbert**
St-François-Xavier mission: **Chauchetiere, Claude; Marquette, Jacques; Tekakwitha, Kateri**
Saint Gelais & Tremblay: **Religious Building**
St George, Ont: **Hoodless, Adelaide**
St Georges Bay: **Canso, Strait of**
St George's Bay: **Port au Port Peninsula; Stephenville**
St George's Cathedral Choir: **Kingston**
St George's Day: **English; National Holidays**
St-Georges-de-Beauce, Qué: **Pépin, Clermont**
St George's School for Child Study: **Mental Health**
St George's Soc: **Samuel, Lewis**
St-Gregoire, Mont: **St Lawrence Lowland**

Ste-Hélène, Île: **Montréal; Science Centre**
St-Hilaire, Canada East: **Disasters**
St-Hilaire, Mont: **Mont St-Hilaire Nature Conservation Centre**
St-Hilaire-le-Dorset, Qué: **Ouimet, Gédéon**
St-Hubert, Qué: **Armed Forces - Unification; Laporte, Pierre; Montréal**
St-Hubert Airport: **Montréal**
St-Ignace mission: **Brébeuf, Jean de; Marquette, Jacques**
St Jacobs, Ont: **Technology**
St James, René: **Sculpture**
Saint-Jean, Ernest: **Theatre, French-Language**
St-Jean, Lac: **Gemstone; Notman, William McFarlane; Rainmaking; Szilasi, Gabor**
St-Jean, Qué: **Canals & Inland Waterways; Glass; Locomotives & Rolling Stock; Research Stations, Agricultural; Toys & Games**
St-Jean, Rivière: **St Lawrence River**
St-Jean-Baptiste, Qué: **Québec City**
St-Jean-Baptiste Day: **Festivals; National Holidays**
St-Jean-Port-Joli, Qué: **Aubert de Gaspé, Philippe-I.-F.; Aubert de Gaspé, Philippe-J.; Sculpture**
St-Jean-Vianney, Qué: **Landslide**
St Jerome's College: **University of Waterloo**
St-Joachim, Qué: **Agricultural Education; Aide-Créquy, Jean-Antoine; Disasters; Education, Technical**
St John, Island of (Ile St-Jean): **British North America; *Hector*; Loyalists; Patterson, Walter; Prince Edward Island; Territorial Evolution**
St John Ambulance Assn: **Hodgetts, Charles A.**
Saint John Customs House: **Architectural Styles**
Saint John *Evening Times-Globe*: **Irving Group**
Saint John Foundry: **Foulis, Robert**
Saint John harbour: **Saint John; Saint John River**
Saint John Philharmonic Soc: **Music History**
Saint John Port of Registry: **Millidge, Thomas Edward**
Saint John Shipbuilding & Dry Dock Co Ltd: **New Brunswick; Ocean Industry; Shipbuilding & Ship Repair**
Saint John *Telegraph Journal*: **Irving Group**
St John's College: **Machray, Robert; Manitoba; Scots; University of Manitoba**
St John's Daily News: **Newfoundland**
St John's Day Celebrations: **Festivals**
St John's Evening Telegram: **Horwood, Harold Andrew; Lloyd, William Frederick; Newfoundland**
St John's Free Press & Daily Advertiser: **Newfoundland**
St John's General Hospital: **Newfoundland**
St John's harbour: **Cook, James; English**
St John's Royal Gazette: **Newfoundland**
St Johns (St-Jean), Qué: **Toys & Games**
St Johns Stone Chinaware Co: **Toys & Games**
St John's Technical High School: **Phillips, Walter J.**
St John's wort: **Insect, Beneficial; Poisonous Plants; Weeds**
St Joseph, Lake: **Albany River**
St Joseph, Mother de: **Singing**
St Joseph Channel: **St Joseph Island**
St-Joseph de la Montagne Oratory: **Lac-Mégantic**
St-Joseph mission: **Ste Marie Among the Hurons**
St Joseph River: **Muskoka Lakes**
St Joseph's College: **University of Alberta**
St Josephs Colony: **Germans**
St Joseph's Island: **Christian Island**
St Joseph's Oratory: **Pilgrimage**
St Joseph's University: **Beau, Henri**
Ste-Jovite, Qué: **Automobile Racing**
St-Lambert, Qué: **Daudelin, Charles; Place-names**
St-Lambert Bilingual School Study Group: **Second-Language Instruction**

St Laurence Cement Inc: **Cement Industry**
St Laurent: **DeWolf, Harry George**
St-Laurent, Île de: **Orléans, Ile d'**
St-Laurent, Qué: **Montréal**
"St Laurent" class destroyer escort: **Armaments; Shipbuilding & Ship Repair**
St Laurent commune: **Dumont, Gabriel**
St Laurence: **Sailing Ships; Shipbuilding & Ship Repair**
St Lawrence, Nfld: **Newfoundland**
St Lawrence Centre: **Stage & Costume Design; Theatre, English-Language**
St Lawrence College of Applied Arts & Technology: **Brockville; Cornwall**
St Lawrence Dry Dock: **Shipbuilding & Ship Repair**
St Lawrence Glass Co: **Glass**
St Lawrence Parks Commission: **Niagara Historic Frontier**
St Lawrence Platform: **Geological Regions; St-Maurice, Rivière**
St Lawrence rapids: **Prescott**
St Lawrence Seaway Authority: **Crown Corporation; Transport Canada; Transportation Agencies (Government)**
St Lawrence Ship Channel: **Kennedy, John**
St Lawrence Sugar Refineries Ltd: **McConnell, John Wilson**
St Lawrence Warehouse, Dock & Wharfage Co: **Macdonald, John A.**
St-Lazare, Man: **Royal Canadian Mounted Police**
St Leonard, NB: **New Brunswick**
St-Léonard, Qué: **Bill 63; Montréal; Theatre, French-Language**
St-Lin, Qué: **Architecture; Bus Transportation**
St-Louis, Lac: **Ottawa River; St Lawrence River**
St-Louis-des-Illinois: **Fur Trade**
St-Louis-du-Ha! Ha!, Qué: **Place-names**
St-Louis mission: **Brébeuf, Jean de**
St Louis River: **Superior, Lake**
Ste-Luce, Qué: ***Empress of Ireland***
St-Malo, Qué: **Québec City**
St Malo Provincial Park: **Parks, Provincial**
St Margaret's CFS: **Chatham, NB**
Ste-Marguerite, Qué: **Skiing**
Ste-Marguerite, Rivière: **Saguenay Provincial Park**
Ste-Marie, Ile: **Orléans, Ile d'**
Ste-Marie de la Beauce, Lower Canada: **Taschereau Legal Dynasty**
Sainte-Marie Prize in History: **Literary Prizes in English**
St Mark's College: **University of British Columbia**
Ste Marthe, Sask: **Fafard, Joseph**
Saint-Martin, Fernande: ***Chatelaine***
St Mary River: **Blood; Lethbridge**
St Mary River Irrigation Project: **Prairie Farm Rehabilitation Administration**
St Mary's, Ont: **Eaton, Timothy; Harrison, David Howard; Hincks, Clarence M.; Kennedy, Theodore; Place-names**
St Marys Bay: **Brier Island**
St Mary's Foundry: **Shipbuilding & Ship Repair**
St Mary's Girls' School: **Dumaresq, James Charles Philip**
St Mary's Junction, Ont: **Railway Station**
St Mary's Reserve: **Kootenay**
St Mary's River: **Sault Ste Marie; Superior, Lake**
St Mary's River Canal: **Canals & Inland Waterways; St Lawrence Seaway**
St-Maurice Valley: **Bush Flying; Chemical Industries; Pulp & Paper Industry**
St Michaels, Nfld: **Printmaking**
St Michael's College: **Charbonnel, Armand-F.-M. de; Kelly, Leonard; Mahovlich, Francis W.; University of Toronto**
St Michael's Majors: **Canadian Olympic Hockey Team**
St-Michel, Mont: **Arthabaska**
St-Michel-des-Vieilles-Forges: **Trois-Rivières**
Saint-Onge, Paule: **Autobiographical Writing in French**

St-Ours, Qué: **Canals & Inland Waterways**
St Patrick, Mount: **Cape Scott Provincial Park**
St Patrick's Day: **National Holidays**
St Paul, Alta: **Janvier, Alex S.**
St Paul, Minneapolis & Manitoba Railroad: **Hill, James J.; Smith, Donald A.; Stephen, George**
St-Paul, Rivière: **Boundaries**
St Paul des Cris: **Lacombe, Albert**
St Paul des Métis: **Lacombe, Albert; Métis**
St Paul University: **University of Ottawa**
St Paul's Bay: **Norse Voyages**
St Paul's College (Man): **University of Manitoba**
St Paul's College (Ont): **University of Waterloo**
Saint-Père, Agathe de: **Status of Women**
St Peters, NB: **Bathurst**
St Peters Bay (NS): **St Peter's, NS**
St Peters Bay (PEI): **St Peters, PEI**
St Peter's Canal: **Canals & Inland Waterways; St Peter's, NS**
St Peter's College seminary: **University of Western Ontario**
St Peters Colony: **Germans; Humboldt**
St Peters Inlet: **St Peter's, NS**
St-Pierre, Annette: **Theatre, French-Language**
Saint-Pierre, Arthur: **Children's Literature in French**
St-Pierre, Comte de: **St Peters, PEI**
Saint-Pierre, Marcel: *Barre du jour*
St Pierre Bank: **Grand Banks**
St-Pierre-de-la-Malbaie, Qué: **Percé**
St-Pierre-de-la-Rivière-du-Sud, Qué: **Blanchet, François**
St-Pierre Mission: **Ste Marie Among the Hurons**
St Pierre race course: **Lacrosse**
St Regis Akwesasne Reserve: **Handsome Lake Religion; Iroquois; Mohawk**
St Regis Ltd: **Hinton**
St-Roch, Qué: **Québec City**
St-Roch-des-Aulnaies, Qué: **Aide-Créquy, Jean-Antoine; Musical Instruments**
St Rose Mine: **Coal**
St-Sauveur, Qué: **Laurentian Highlands; Québec City**
St Shotts, Nfld: **St Mary's Bay**
St Stanislaus Credit Union: **Poles**
St Stephen, NB: **New Brunswick**
St Stephen's College: **University of Alberta**
St-Sulpice, Qué: **Lacombe, Albert**
Ste-Thérèse, Qué: **Disasters; Piano Manufacturing; Place-names**
St Thomas Aquinas Soc: **Prince Edward Island**
St Thomas More College: **Communication Studies**
St Thomas University: **University of New Brunswick**
St-Vincent-de-Paul, Qué: **Quévillon, Louis-Amable**
St Vincent de Paul Soc: **Charbonnel, Armand-F.-M. de**
St Vincent's, Nfld: **St Mary's Bay**
St Vital, Man: **Nault, André; St-Boniface**
Saito, Satashi: **Ceramics, Contemporary**
saki: **Mold**
Sakowska, Krystyne: **Poles**
Salaberry, Charles-René de: **Riel, Louis**
Salaberry-de-Valleyfield: **Valleyfield**
salad oil: **Oilseed Crops; Soybean**
Saladin: **Piracy**
salal: **Berries, Wild; Cape Scott Provincial Park**
saldid: **Bug**
sale: **Civil Code**
Sale of Goods Act: **Commercial Law**
Salermiut Range: **Torngat Mountains**
sales tax: **Brewing Industry; Confectionery Industry; Distilling Industry; Jewellery & Silverware Industry; Johnson, Byron Ingemar; Manning, Ernest C.; Municipal Finance; Native People, Law; Taxation**
salicylic acid: **Herbs**
Salisbury, NB: **Parkin, George R.**
Salisbury, Richard Frank: **Anthropology**
Salisbury Island: **Hudson Strait**

Salish: **Bella Coola; Cartoons; Central Coast Salish; Children's Literature in English; Esquimalt; Galiano Island; Hill-Tout, Charles; Northern Georgia Strait Coast Salish; Ogopogo; Saanich Peninsula; Sidney**
Salishan linguistic family: **Native People, Languages**
Salivarova, Zdena: **Skvorecký, Josef**
Salk, Joseph: **Biological Product**
Salk vaccine: **Connaught Laboratories Ltd**
Sallirmiut Inuit: **Sadlermiut Inuit**
Sallualuk, Eli: **Inuit Art**
Salmo River: **Salmo**
Salmon, Peter: **Swimming, Speed**
Salmon Festival: **Campbellton, NB**
Salmon River, BC: **Salmo**
salmonberry: **Berries, Wild; Cape Scott Provincial Park; Vegetation Regions - Pacific Coastal**
Salmonid Enhancement Program: **Aquaculture**
salmonidae: **Char; Grayling; Salmon; Trout; Whitefish**
Salon du printemps: **Beau, Henri**
Salon international du livre de Québec: **Literary Prizes in French**
salsify: **Vegetable**
SALT: **Disarmament**
Salt Fish Board: **Fisheries History**
salt-fish trade: **Bait Acts; Bay Roberts; Dry Fishery; Fisheries History; Fisheries Policy**
salt grass: **Vegetation Regions - Prairie**
salt-marsh starwort: **Vegetation Regions - Pacific Coastal**
Salt Records: **Ian & Sylvia**
Saltcoats, Sask: **Patrick, Thomas Alfred**
Salter, George: **Moncton**
Salter, Joseph: **Moncton**
Salter & Allison: **Religious Building**
Saltsman, Max: **Committee for an Independent Canada**
Salutin, Rick: **Drama in English; Jewish Writing; Neptune Theatre**
Salvatore, Filippo: **Italian Writing**
Salverson, Laura Goodman: **Ethnic Literature; Icelanders; Novel in English**
samarium: **Geological Dating**
Sambro Island: **Lighthouses**
Samchuk, Ulas: **Ukrainian Writing**
Samedi: **Laberge, Albert; Nelligan, Emile**
samphire: **Biogeography**
Sampson-Matthews: **Printmaking**
Samson V: **Steamboats & Paddlewheelers**
Samuel, Constance: **Figure Skating; Wilson, Montgomery**
Samuel, Mark: **Samuel, Lewis**
Samuel French (Canada) Ltd: **Drama in English**
San José Scale Act: **Fletcher, James**
San Juan: **Basques; Diving, Underwater; Red Bay**
San Juan Island: **Joint Commission; Treaty of Washington**
Sanavik Co-op: **Oonark, Jessie**
Sanche, Wilfrid: **Theatre, French-Language**
sand dab: **Flatfish**
sand dollar: **Echinodermata; Sea Urchin**
sand dropseed: **Vegetation Regions - Prairie**
sand grass: **Vegetation Regions - Prairie**
sand hopper: **Crustacean**
Sand Point Reserve: **Morrisseau, Norval**
sandberry: **Bearberry**
Sandemose, Aksel: **Ethnic Literature**
sanderling: **Sandpiper**
Sanders, Byrne Hope: *Chatelaine*
Sandham, Henry: **Painting; Printmaking**
sandhill crane: **Crane; Game Bird; Lake Superior Provincial Park; Whooping Crane**
Sandilands Provincial Forest: **Springfield**
Sandspit, BC: **Queen Charlotte Islands**
sandstone: **Badlands; Hoodoo Rock; Plate Tectonics; Quarrying Industry; Sedimentary Rock**

Sandwell, Bernard K.: **Essay in English;** *Financial Times;* **Magazines;** *Saturday Night;* **Theatre, English-Language**
Sandwich, Ont: **Architecture; Mountain, Jacob; Technology; Windsor, Ont**
sandwort: **Endangered Plants**
Sandy Lake, Ont: **Ray, Carl**
Sandy Lake (Nfld): **Grand Lake**
Sandyford Place: **Hamilton**
Sanger, David: **Archaeology**
Sanjo: **Koreans**
sanitary landfill: **Pollution; Solid Waste; Waste Disposal**
sanitation: **Cuisine; Cuisine; Public Health; Water Treatment**
Sans Sault Rapids: **Mackenzie River**
Sansei: **Japanese**
Sanskrit language: **Buddhism; Hinduism; Religion**
Sanson, NB: **Botany History**
Santa Cruz map: **Cartography, History of**
Sappington, Margo: **Pacific Ballet Theatre**
sapsucker: **Woodpecker**
Sarcee Reserve: **Calgary**
Sargent, B.W.: **Physics**
Sarkány, Stéphane: **Comparative Literature**
Sarnia Bay: **Sarnia**
Sarnia Drama League: **Theatre, English-Language**
Sarnia Imperials: **Football**
Sarsaparilla: **Soft-Drink Industry**
SARSAT project: **Space Technology**
Sarto, Man: **Hanover**
Sarvaqtuungrmiut group: **Makpaaq, Vital**
Sasaki, Senju: **Buddhism; Judo**
Saskatchewan Centre for Community Studies: **Sociology**
Saskatchewan Centre of the Arts: **Concert Halls & Opera Houses; Regina**
Saskatchewan Co-operative Elevator Co: **Co-operative Movement (See Addendum, page 1992); Dunning, Charles Avery; Grain Growers' Associations; McPhail, Alexander James; Saskatchewan Wheat Pool**
Saskatchewan Conservation House: **Energy in Society**
Saskatchewan Educational Communications Corp (SaskMedia): **Educational Broadcasting**
Saskatchewan Equal Franchise League: **McNaughton, Violet C.**
Saskatchewan Farmers' Union: **United Farmers of Canada**
Saskatchewan Glacier: **Columbia Icefield**
Saskatchewan Government Telephones: **Dagger, Francis**
Saskatchewan Grain Growers' Assn: **Grain Growers' Associations; McNaughton, Violet C.; McPhail, Alexander James; Social Gospel; United Farmers of Canada; Wesson, John Henry**
Saskatchewan Herald: **Newspapers; Print Industry**
Saskatchewan History: **Ahenakew, Edward**
Saskatchewan Indian Assn: **Native People, Political Organization & Activism**
Saskatchewan Indian Cultural College: **Stump, Sarain**
Saskatchewan Indian Federated College: **Community College; University of Regina**
Saskatchewan Métis Soc: **Métis**
Saskatchewan Museum of Natural History: **Diorama; Paleontology, History in Canada**
Saskatchewan Native Writers' Contest: **Literary Prizes in English**
Saskatchewan Native Youth Movement: **Native People, Political Organization & Activism**
Saskatchewan Plain: **Physiographic Regions - Interior Plains**
Saskatchewan Power Corp: **Coal; Coal Gasification; Coronach; Electric Utilities; Estevan; Saskatchewan; Wind Energy**
Saskatchewan Provincial Police: **Perry, A. Bowen**
Saskatchewan Summer School of the Arts: **Kroetsch, Robert**

Saskatchewan Teachers' Federation: **Lloyd, Woodrow S.**
Saskatchewan Technical Institute: **Moose Jaw**
Saskatchewan Telecommunications: **Telephones; TransCanada Telephone System; Utilities**
Saskatchewan Transportation Co: **Bus Transportation; Saskatoon**
saskatoon: **Berries, Wild; Cinq-Mars, Lionel; Cuisine; Pemmican**
Saskatoon City Hall: **Murray, Robert**
Saskatoon Island Provincial Park: **Parks, Provincial**
Saskatoon *Star-Phoenix*: **Armadale Co Ltd**
Saskatoon Symphony Orchestra: **Adaskin, Murray**
Saskatoon Technical College: **Printmaking**
sassafras: **Plants, Native Uses; Point Pelée National Park; Rondeau Provincial Park; Vegetation Regions - Eastern Temperate Forests**
Sasseville, François: **Art Education; Silver, Church**
Satan's Choice: **Organized Crime**
Satellite Doppler System: **Cartography, History of**
satellite photography: **Aeolian Landform; Cloud; Geography; Helava, Uno Vilho; Iceberg; Physical Geography**
satellite tracking: **Cold Lake**
Sather, Glen: **Edmonton Oilers**
satinwood: **Furniture, English, Scottish & American**
Saturna Island: **Gulf Islands**
Saucier, Joseph: **Recording Industry**
Sauer (Sower), Christopher: **Almanacs; Printmaking**
sauger: **Manitoba; Perch; Walleye**
Saul, John: **Marxism**
Saulnier, Denise: **Graphic Design**
Saulnier, Jean-Pierre: **Germain, Jean-Claude**
Sault de Gaston: **Sault Ste Marie**
Sault-St-Louis, New France: **Lafitau, Joseph-François**
Sault Ste Marie Greyhounds: **Gretzky, Wayne**
Saulteaux: **Fort Qu'Appelle; Midewiwin; Ojibwa; Parks, Provincial; Peguis; Tanner, John**
Saumon, Rivière au: **Lennoxville**
Saunders, A.P.: **Saunders, Charles E.**
Saunders, Charles: **Battle of the Plains of Abraham**
Saunders, Charles R.: **Popular Literature in English**
Saurel, Pierre de: **Sorel**
Saut de la Chaudière: **Chaudière, Rivière**
Sauvageau, Charles: **Music History**
Sauve, Arthur: **Duplessis, Maurice Le Noblet**
Savage, George: **Silver, Domestic**
Savage, Roger: **Printmaking**
Savage & Lyman: **Birks, Henry**
Savan, David: **Philosophy**
Savanne River: **Grand Portage**
Savard, Guy: **Iron & Steel Industry**
Savard, Pierre: **Intellectual History; Literature in French - Scholarship & Teaching**
Savard, Serge: **Montreal Canadiens**
Savary, Claude: **Philosophy**
Save Our Streams: **Endangered Animals**
Savings & Investment Group: **Tardif, Jean-Paul**
savings bank: **Bank Rate**
Savings Bank Act (Qué): **Bank Rate**
Savoie, Maurice: **Ceramics, Contemporary**
Savoie, Robert: **Printmaking**
Savoie Apartment Bldg: **Prus, Victor Marius**
savory: **Condiment Crops**
SAW: **Art Dealers**
Sawai, Noboru: **Printmaking**
sawdust: **Biomass Energy; Lumber & Wood Industries**
sawfish: **Ray**
saws: **Sawmill; Technology**
Sawyer, Paul: **Pediatrics**
Sawyer-Massey Co: **Agricultural Implements**
saxophone: **Jazz**
Sayer, Pierre-Guillaume: **Hudson's Bay Company; Red River Colony**
Sayer Trial: **Grant, Cuthbert**

Saywell, John: *Canadian Historical Review*
scabies: **Mite**
"scabs": **Jones, John Walter; Strikes & Lockouts**
Scalero, Rosario: **Pépin, Clermont**
scallop-dragging: **Fisheries**
scandals: **Baie des Chaleurs Scandal; Bren Gun Scandal; Munsinger Affair; Pacific Scandal; Rivard, Lucien**
Scandinavian Reserve: **Erickson**
Scandinavians: **Alberta; Camrose; Danes; Erickson; Ethnic Literature; Icelanders; Immigration; Minnedosa; Moose Jaw; New Brunswick; North Bay; Norwegians; Prairie West; Prince Edward Island; Regina; Religious Building; Rockwood; Saskatchewan; Saskatoon; Swedes; Thunder Bay; Wetaskiwin**
scaphopoda: **Mollusc; Seashell**
scapolite: **Gemstone**
scapulomancy: **Native People - Subarctic**
Scarborough, Ont: **Buddhism; Ontario; Religious Building; Toronto**
Scarborough Bluffs: **Landslide; Ontario, Lake; Toronto Islands**
Scarborough Civic Centre: **Moriyama, Raymond**
Scarborough College: **Architecture; University of Toronto**
Scargill, M.H.: **Dictionary; Linguistics**
scarlet fever: **Anderson River; Nursing; Sarcee; Whaling**
Scarlet Point: **Balaklava Island**
scarlet runner bean: **Vegetable**
scarlet tanager: **Algonquin Provincial Park; Tanager**
Scene Changes: **Theatre, English-Language**
Schaeffer, Myron: **Electroacoustic Music**
Schaeffer, Pierre: **Saint-Marcoux, Micheline Coulombe**
Schaffer, Urlich: **German Writing**
Schawlow, Arthur L.: **Laser**
Scheckter, Jody: **Villeneuve, Gilles**
scheelite: **Mineral; Tungsten**
Scheffer, Lionel: **Schefferville**
Scheissler, R.: **Chemistry Subdisciplines**
Schenley Trophy: **Canadian Football Hall of Fame & Museum; Honours**
Schilke, Renold: **Canadian Brass**
Schiller, Joseph: **Wine Industry**
Schindler, Joseph: **Silver, Indian Trade**
Schindler family: **Silver, Domestic**
schist: **Mineral Naming; Prospecting**
schizophrenia: **Psychiatry; Seeman, Mary Violette**
Schleeh, Hans: **Sculpture**
Schlegel, Elfi: **Gymnastics**
Schleimer, Joe: **Wrestling**
Schneid, Miriam: **Jewish Writing**
Schneider, J.M.: **Kitchener-Waterloo**
Schneider, Mary: **Poles**
Schoenauer, Norbert: **Urban & Regional Planning**
Schofield, John: **Railway Station**
Scholastic TAB Publications Ltd: **Book Clubs**
Scholes, Lou: **Rowing**
School Act (Man): **Manitoba**
School Act (Ont): **Ryerson, A. Egerton**
School Act (Province of Canada): **Education, History of**
School Act (Sask): **Anderson, James Thomas Milton**
School Attendance Act (Man): **Manitoba**
school cars: **Canadian National Railways**
School for the Deaf (Saskatoon): **Anderson, James Thomas Milton**
School for the Performing Arts: **Citadel Theatre**
School of Agriculture (NS): **Nova Scotia Agricultural College**
School of Agriculture of Oka: **Agricultural Education**
School of Agriculture of Ste-Anne-de-la-Pocatière: **Agricultural Education**
School of Comparative Medicine & Veterinary Science: **Daubigny, Victor-Théodule; Veterinary Medicine, History**

School of Dramatic Arts: **Theatre, French-Language**
School of Horticulture: **Nova Scotia Agricultural College**
School of Practical Science: **Architecture, Development; Chemical Engineering; Civil Engineering; Loudon, James; Mineral & Mining Engineering; Technology; University of Toronto**
School of Technology: **Loudon, James**
School of the Toronto Dance Theatre: **Dance Education**
School of Veterinary Medicine of Montréal: **Daubigny, Victor-Théodule**
schooner: *Bluenose*; **Fisheries History; Lunenburg; Mackinaw Boat; Nova Scotia; Pinky Schooner; Sailing Ships**; *St Roch*; *Sutil & Mexicana*
schrank: **Furniture, German**
Schreiber, Collingwood: **Architecture, Development**
Schreiber, Weymouth: **Schreiber, Charlotte Mount Brock**
Schreibman, Phil: **Musical Theatre**
Schreiner, Michael: **Musical Instruments**
Schreyer, Lily: **Schreyer, Edward R.**
Schroeder, Andreas: **German Writing; Short Fiction in English**
Schubert Choir: **Music History**
Schultz, Marvin: **Archaeology**
Schultz Lake: **Thelon River**
Schwardschild radius: **Black Hole**
Schwengers, B.P.: **Tennis**
science & religion: **Intellectual History**
Science for Peace: **Franklin, Ursula Martius**
Science Forum: **Science; Siminovitch, Louis**
Science North: **Science Centre**
Science Secretariat of Canada: **Forward, Frank Arthur**
Scientific & Industrial Research Council of Alberta: **Alberta Research Council**
Scientology: **New Religious Movements; Religion**
scilla: **Flowers, Cultivated**
scintillometer: **Mineral; Prospecting**
Scobie, Hugh: **Almanacs; Drama in English; Printmaking**
Scobie, Stephen: **Humorous Writing in English; Literature in English - Theory & Criticism; Poetry in English**
Scoggan, H.J.: **Botany History**
"scorched-earth policy": **Fur Trade**
scorpionfly: **Insect Classification**
Scotchfort Reserve: **Prince Edward Island**
Scotia Square: **Halifax**
Scotia-Toronto Dominion Leasing Ltd: **Toronto-Dominion Bank**
Scotiabank: **Bank of Nova Scotia**
Scots Bay: **Cape Blomidon**
Scots pine: **Forestry**
Scott, Amy: **Scott, Francis R.**
Scott, David: **Cape Scott Provincial Park**
Scott, Frederick G.: **Scott, Francis R.**
Scott, Gail: **Literature in English - Theory & Criticism**
Scott, George Gilbert: **Architecture, Development**
Scott, Jack: **Essay in English; Journalism**
Scott, James: **Film**
Scott, John: **Drawing; Painting**
Scott, Michael: **Film, Documentary**
Scott, Richard: **Province House**
Scott, Robert A.: **Painting**
Scott, Vince: **Hamilton Tiger Cats**
Scoudouc River: **Shediac**
scouler willow: **Vegetation Regions - Pacific Coastal**
Scourge: **Diving, Underwater; Ontario, Lake**
scouring rush: **Horsetail; Plants, Native Uses**
scrap iron & steel: **Iron & Steel Industry; Sidbec-Dosco Limitée**
scrapers: **Clovis; Medicine Wheels; Microblade Technology; Neutral**
Scratching River, Man: **Morris**
scree: **Kluane Ranges; Periglacial Landform; Rockslide**
screen printing: **Newspapers; Print Industry; Printmaking**
Scribbler: **Drama in English**

scrip: **Indian Treaties; Métis; Native People, Law**
script: **Germanic Fraktur & Calligraphy**
Scriver, Charles: **Pediatrics**
scuba diving: **Biological Oceanography; Diving, Underwater; Georgian Bay Islands National Park; Pacific Rim National Park**
Scugog Lake: **Kawartha Lakes; Lindsay**
Scugog River: **Lindsay**
sculling: **Rowing**
Sculptors' Soc of Canada: **Artists' Organizations; Sivuarapik, Charlie; Wyle, Florence**
Scurfield, Ralph: **Development Industry**
scurvy: **Arctic Exploration; Cartier, Jacques; Donnacona; Great Depression; Hospitals; St Croix River; Troyes, Pierre de; Vegetarianism**
scythe: **Agricultural Implements**
sea anemone: **Cnidaria; Fundy National Park**
sea butterfly: **Mollusc**
Sea Cadets: **Navy League of Canada**
Sea Clipper: **Jackman, William**
sea coal: **Sydney**
sea cucumber: **Echinodermata**
sea fan: **Coral**
Sea Forest Plantation: **Cupids**
sea goddess: **Inuit Myth & Legend**
sea gooseberry: **Invertebrate**
sea hare: **Mollusc**
Sea Island: **Island; Richmond**
sea lily: **Echinodermata; Fossil Animals**
sea pen: **Cnidaria**
sea plantain: **Vegetation Regions - Pacific Coastal**
sea rocket: **Vegetation Regions - Coastal Marine Flora**
sea scallop: **Fisheries History; Scallop**
sea shanties: **Folk Music, Anglo-Canadian**
sea slug: **Mollusc**
sea squirt: **Invertebrate**
sea star: **Starfish**
sea thrift: **Endangered Plants**
sea trout: **St Mary's River; Trout**
sea worm: **Burgess Shale Site**
Seaboard Life Insurance Co: **Allard, Charles A.**
Seagram Gold Cup: **Golf**
Seagram Museum: **Myers, Barton**
Seagram Stables: **Seagram, Joseph E.; Thoroughbred Racing**
Seal Books First Novel Award: **Literary Prizes in English**
Seal Cove, NB: **Grand Manan Island**
Seal Cove, Nfld: **Conception Bay South**
Seal Island: **Lighthouses**
seal oil: **Arctic Animals; Lighthouses**
Seal River: **Chipewyan**
sealer: **Sailing Ships**
sealskin: **Cross-Country Skiing; Kayak; Mukluk; Ookpik**
Seaman, Byron: **Calgary Flames**
Seaman, Daryl: **Calgary Flames**
seamount: **Ocean**
seance: **New Religious Movements**
Search & Rescue: **Armed Forces - Air Force; Boating; Canadian Coast Guard; de Havilland Otter; Helicopter; Icebreakers; May, W.R., "Wop"; Military Aviation & Aircraft; Space Technology; Spinks, John William Tranter; Station PAPA; Trenton, CFB**
search & seizure: **Official Secrets Act**
Search-for-a-New-Alberta-Novelist Competition: **Literary Prizes in English**
search warrant: **Criminal Investigation**
searchlight: **Lighting**
Sears Canada Ltd: **Retail Trade**
Seary, E.R.: **Linguistics**
Seasat satellite: **Radar; Remote Sensing**
seaside arrow grass: **Vegetation Regions - Pacific Coastal**
Season in the Life of Emmanuel, A: **Saison dans la vie d'Emmanuel**
seasonal unemployment: **Labour Policy; Unemployment**
seat belts: **Automobile**
"seat sales": **Transportation Regulation**

Seccombe family: **Quill & Quire**
Secession churches: **Presbyterian & Reformed Churches**
Sechelt: **Northern Georgia Strait Coast Salish**
Second City: **Theatre, English-Language**
Second Narrows Bridge: **Disasters; North Vancouver**
Secondary Education Act (Sask): **Education, Technical**
secret ballot: **Political Campaign; Prince Edward Island**
sect: **New Religious Movements; Racism**
secular institute: **Christian Religious Communities**
securities: **Bank of Canada; Economic Regulation; Mutual Funds; Public Debt; Stock & Bond Markets**
Securities Acts: **Corporation Law**
Security, Royal Commission on: **Royal Canadian Mounted Police**
security & intelligence: **Armed Forces - Militia & Army; CHUM Ltd; Commercial Law; Crime; Freedom of Information; Gouzenko, Igor S.; Inquiry into Certain Activities of the RCMP, Royal Commission of; Intelligence Gathering; Police; Policing; Rogers Telecommunications Ltd; Royal Canadian Mounted Police**
SED Systems Inc: **Electronics Industry; Satellite Communications**
Sedgwick, Robert: **Annapolis Royal**
sediment core: **Climate Information**
sedimentation: **Agricultural Soil Practices; Coastal Landform; Endangered Animals; Hydrology; Lake; Okanagan Valley; Physiographic Regions - Interior Plains; Remote Sensing**
sedimentation process: **Water Treatment**
sedition: **Crime; Front de libération du Québec; Gourlay, Robert F.; Jury; Rose, Fred; Violence; Winnipeg General Strike**
seditious conspiracy: **Parent, Madeleine; Russell, Robert Boyd**
seditious libel: **McLachlan, James Bryson**
Sedna the sea goddess: **Inuit Myth & Legend; Kiugak Ashoona; Native People, Religion**
seduction: **Jury; Women & the Law**
seed certification: **Agriculture, Dept of**
Seed Control Act: **Commodity Inspection & Grading**
seed ferns: **Fossil Plants**
seed selection: **Agriculture History**
seed treatment: **Oilseed Crops**
seeder: **Agricultural Implements; Agricultural Implements Industry**
seeds: **Barley; Canola; Foreign Aid; Grain Handling & Marketing; Port-Royal; Prince Edward Island; Reforestation; Research Stations, Agricultural; Saunders, Charles E.; Smith, Titus; Tobacco-Products Industry**
Seel, Else: **German Writing**
Seen From Afar: **Blood**
Segal, Derek: **Tennis**
Segal, J.I.: **Jewish Writing**
segregation: **Blacks; Prejudice & Discrimination; Women in the Labour Force**
Seguin, Maurice: **Historiography**
Séguin, Robert-Lionel: **Folklore**
Segwun: **Gravenhurst**
Sehon, A.: **Biochemistry**
Seibner, Herbert: **Printmaking**
seiching: **Winnipeg, Lake**
Seine River: **St-Boniface**
seismic reflection: **Sonar**
seismograph: **Denison, Francis Napier; Petroleum Exploration & Production**
seismology: **Acoustics; Plate Tectonics**
Seitz, Ernest: **Music History**
select committee: **Committees; Parliamentary Procedure**
self-defence: **Criminal Law; Jiu-Jitsu; Judo; Torts; Women's Movement**
self-dumping carriers: **British Columbia; Lake Carriers; Shipping Industry**
Selfridge, Tom: **Aviation**

Selkirk, George: **Baseball**
Selkirk College: **Castlegar; Nelson**
Selkirk locomotive: **Locomotives & Rolling Stock**
Selkirk wheat: **Agricultural Research & Development**
Sellman, Dallas: **Art, Contemporary Trends**
Semchishen, Orest: **Photography**
Semeur: **Book Publishing, French-Language**
Semeur canadien: **Huguenots**
Semiahmoo Bay: **White Rock**
semiconductors: **Computer Industry; Electronics Industry; Microchips & Transistors**
Séminaire de Montréal: **Oka**
Séminaire de Nicolet: **Aubert de Gaspé, Philippe-I.-F.**
Séminaire de St-Hyacinthe: **L'Heureux, Jean-B.; Ultramontanism**
Séminaire de Saint-Sulpice: **Montréal**
Séminaire des missions étrangères de Québec: **Séminaire de Québec**
Séminaire St-Charles Borromée: **Université de Sherbrooke**
Seminary of the Holy Spirit: **Catholicism**
semiotics: **Literature in French - Criticism & Theory**
semipalmated sandpiper: **Fundy, Bay of/Gulf of Maine; Sandpiper**
semolina: **Wheat**
Semple, Robert: **McPherson, Aimee Semple**
Senate Banking Committee: **Pressure Group**
Seneca College: **Association for Canadian Studies; Clothing Industries**
Senécal, Irène: **Art Education**
Senéchaussée: **Government Building**
Senn, Fritz: **German Writing**
Senn, H.A.: **Botany History**
Senneterre, Henri de: **Senneterre**
Senneville, Qué: **Maxwell, Edward**
Senoff, C.V.: **Chemistry Subdisciplines**
Sens, Al: **Film Animation**
Sentinel: **Hewitt, John**
Sentol Systems: **Leaver, Eric William**
separatist manifesto: **Communications**
Sephardic Jews: **De Sola, Alexander Abraham; Spanish**
sepia ink: **Cuttlefish**
Sept Iles People: **Montagnais-Naskapi**
Septuor Haydn: **Chamber Music; Music History**
Sepúlveda, Ramóu: **Ethnic Literature**
Serbian Orthodox Church: **Orthodox Church**
Serbo-Croats: **Serbs**
SERENA: **Birth Control**
Sergeant-at-Arms: **House of Commons; Parliament, Opening of**
serigraphy: **Print Industry; Printmaking**
Sernine, Daniel: **Children's Literature in French; Popular Literature in French**
serpentine: **Greenstone; Inuit Art; Soapstone**
Servais-Maquoi, Mireille: **Essay in French**
Service Ciné-photographie: **Film**
Service des parcs de la ville de Montréal: **Botanical Garden**
Servites: **Italians**
Sesimiz (The Voice): **Turks**
SETI: **Science & Society**
Sétian, Nerses M.: **Catholicism**
Seton Lake: **Lillooet; Salish, Interior**
Seton Lake Reserve: **Salish, Interior**
settlement houses: **Urban Reform**
"settlers' effects": **Crow's Nest Pass Agreement**
settlor: **Trust**
setup: **Winnipeg, Lake**
Seven Islands Reserve: **Sept-Iles**
Seven Oaks House: **Manitoba**
'76 Ranch: **Ranching History**
Severn Lake: **Severn River**
Severn River: **Georgian Bay; Orillia; Trent Canal**
sewage: **Biomass Energy; Lake; Soil Science; Solid Waste; Water Pollution**
Seward Glacier: **Vancouver, Mount**
Sewell, John: **Populism; Urban Reform**
Sewell, Richard: **Printmaking**
sewing machine: **Clothing Industries; Leatherworking**

sewing tools: **L'Anse aux Meadows**
sex chromosone: **Barr, Murray Llewellyn**
sex education: **Christianity; Education Policy; Family Studies; Woman's Christian Temperance Union**
sex ratio: **Population**
sex-role stereotyping: **Women & Education**
sexing: **Dairy Farming**
sexism: **Drama in English; Fascism; Prostitution; Status of Women; Teaching Profession; Women's Movement; Women's Studies**
sextant: **Cartography, History of; Hogg, Frank Scott**
sexual behaviour: **Hippies; Prostitution**
sexual equality: **Constitution, Patriation of; Women & the Law**
sexual intercourse: **Marriage & Divorce, History of; Rape; Sexual Abuse of Children; Sexually Transmitted Disease**
sexual offence: **Canadian Advisory Council on the Status of Women; Child Abuse; Courts of Law; Crime; Juvenile Delinquency; Rape; Status of Women; Women & the Law**
Seymour Mountain: **North Vancouver**
SG-N-D Grey Gull: **Helicopter**
Shabbat: **Judaism**
shad: **Coastal Waters; Cuisine; Herring; Miramichi River**
Shade, Absalom: **Galt**
Shade's Mill, Upper Canada: **Galt**
shadow cabinet: **House of Commons**
Shaffer, Ivan: **Literature & Politics**
shaft furnace: **Sidbec-Dosco Limitée**
shagbark hickory: **Point Pelée National Park; Thousand Islands; Vegetation Regions - Eastern Temperate Forests**
Shah-wun-dais: **Sunday, John**
Shaheen: **Ethnic Literature**
Shaheen, Elias: **Catholicism**
Shakespeare, Ont: **Place-names**
Shakwak Valley: **Kluane Ranges**
shale: **Badlands; Bell Island; Burgess Shale Site; Clay; Devon Island; Ellef Ringnes Island; Geological Regions; Hoodoo Rock; Innuitian Region; Mineral; Niagara Falls; Northwest Coast Indian Art; Paleontology, History in Canada; Random Island; St Lawrence Lowland; Sedimentary Rock**
shallot: **Vegetable**
Shallow Lake, Ont: **Cement Industry**
Shampers Bluff, NB: **Patterson, Freeman W.**
Shamrock Players: **Theatre, Multicultural**
Shandro, Andrew: **Ukrainians**
Shandro, Nikon: **Shandro**
Shapinker case: **Canadian Charter of Rights & Freedoms**
Shapiro, Lionel: **Best-Sellers in English**
Shapiro, Norman: *Kamouraska*
shared-cost programs: **Government; Taxation**
shared jobs: **Work**
shares: **Banking; Condominium; Corporation Law; Farm Law; Fisheries; Mutual Funds; Property Law; Stock & Bond Markets**
Sharland, Joseph B.: **Music History**
Sharon, Lois & Bram: **Oral Literature in English**
Sharon, Ont: **Hymns**
Sharon Temple: **Folk Art**
Sharp, Edith: **Children's Literature in English**
Sharp, G.L.T.: **Thompson, Berwick, Pratt & Partners**
Sharp & Thompson: **Religious Building; Thompson, Berwick, Pratt & Partners**
sharp-tailed grouse: **Cypress Hills Provincial Park; Game Bird; Grouse**
Shasta daisy: **Flowers, Cultivated**
Shatford Brothers Ltd: **Shatford, Sidney S.**
shatrag: **Dartmouth Lakes**
Shatto, Cindy: **Diving**
Shaughnessy, Frank: **Baseball; Football**
Shaunavon, Sask: **Coal Gasification**

Shaunnesy, Arthur: **Hunt, Henry**
Shaver Poultry Breeding Farms Ltd: **Poultry Farming**
Shaw, Joseph: **Ginger Group**
Shaw, Joseph W.: **Mediterranean Archaeology**
Shaw, M.: **Crop Research**
Shaw, Robert: **Expo 67**
Shawbridge, Qué: **Skiing**
Shawinigan Carbide: **Chemical Industries**
Shawinigan Chemicals Ltd: **Chemistry; Shawinigan**
Shawinigan Cotton: **Shawinigan**
Shawinigan Falls, Qué: **Alcan Aluminium Ltd; Shawinigan; Technology**
Shawinigan River: **Shawinigan, Lac**
Shawinigan Water & Power Co: **Chemical Industries; Shawinigan**
Shawnigan Lake: **Hughes, Edward John; Malahat Pass**
Shea, Ambrose: **Fathers of Confederation**
Shea, William: **Philosophy**
Sheardown, John: **Taylor, Kenneth Douglas**
Shearer, Margaret: **Synchronized Swimming**
Shebandowan, Ont: **Nickel**
Shebeski, Leonard H.: **Genetics**
Sheeguapik: **Sivuarapik, Charlie**
sheep & cattle herding: **Dog**
sheep laurel (sheepkill): **Poisonous Plants**
sheepskin: **Leatherworking**
sheet metal: **Algoma Steel Corp Ltd; Dominion Foundries & Steel, Ltd; Iron & Steel Industry; Silver, Domestic**
Sheffield, NB: **Maugerville**
Shefford, Mont: **Biogeography; St Lawrence Lowland**
Sheguiandah site: **Archaeology**
Sheila Na Geira: **Princess Sheila**
Shekter, Mark: **Musical Theatre**
Shell Committee: **Cantley, Thomas; World War I**
shell midden: **Archaeology; Galiano Island; Metlakatla Pass Sites; Nova Scotia; Prehistory; Teacher's Cove**
Shellmouth Dam: **Manitoba**
shells: **Dominion Arsenal; Fortification**
shelterbelt: **Agricultural Soil Practices; Climate & Man; Drought; Manitoba; Motherwell Homestead; Prairie Farm Rehabilitation Administration**
sheltered workshop: **Disability; Education, Special; Social & Welfare Services**
Shepherd, John: **Musicology**
Shepody Bay: **New Brunswick**
Sheppard, David: **Almonte**
Sheppard, E.E.: **Journalism;** *Saturday Night*
Sheppard, Roy: **Fitness**
Sheppard's Falls, Upper Canada: **Robinson, Peter**
Sheraton chair: **Furniture, Country**
Sheraton Hotels: **Four Seasons Hotels Ltd**
Sherbourne Lanes: **Myers, Barton**
Sherbrooke, NS: **St Mary's River**
Sheridan College of Applied Arts & Technology: **Clothing Industries; Crafts; Oakville**
Sheridan Park Research Community: **Ontario Research Foundation; Petroleum Research & Development**
Sherlock-Manning Piano Co: **Heintzman & Co Ltd; Piano Manufacturing**
Sherman, Clifton: **Sherman, Frank Albert**
Sherman, Francis: **Poetry in English**
Sherman, Leah: **Savage, Anne Douglas**
Sherman Mine: **Iron & Steel Industry**
Sherring, William: **Long-Distance Running**
Sherritt Gordon Mines Ltd: **Brown, Eldon Leslie; Chemical Engineering; Chemical Industries; Lindsley, Thayer; Metallurgy**
Sherritt Mint: **Medal**
sherry: **Alcoholism; Wine Industry**
Sherry, Helen Davies: **Singing**
Sherwin-Williams Co of Canada, Ltd: **McMaster, Ross H.**

Sherwood, Henry: **Province of Canada**
Sherwood, William Albert: **Art Writing & Criticism**
Sherwood Park, Alta: **Alberta; Janvier, Alex S.**
Shevenel, R.H.: **Psychology**
Shewart, Walter: **Industrial Quality Control**
Shia Muslims: **Islam**
Shield Archaic: **Prehistory**
shields: **Coppers; Indian Art; Native People - Plains**
Shields, Carol: **Novel in English**
Shields, Dorothy: **Dictionary**
shigellosis: **Water-Borne Disease**
shillings: **Money**
Shimbashi, Zenkichi: **Japanese**
Shin Issei: **Japanese**
Shinbrott, Marvin: **Mathematics**
shingles & shakes: **Architectural Styles; Architecture, Development; Forestry; Timber Trade History**
shinny (shinty): **Hockey, Ice**
Shiomi, Rick: **Theatre, English-Language**
Shipman, Nell: **Film**
Shipman's Corners, Upper Canada: **St Catharines**
Shippegan, NB: **Université de Moncton**
Shippegan Island: **Lamèque, Île**
Shippegan Sound: **Lamèque, Île**
ship's masts: **Oromocto; Timber Axe; Timber Trade History**
Shipshaw, Rivière: **Saguenay River**
shipworm: **Mollusc**
shipwrecks: **Baffin Island Inuit; Basques; Bic, Île du;** *Breadalbane;* **Bruce Peninsula; Coinage; Disasters;** *Empress of Ireland;* **Lake Carriers; Ocean Industry; Sable Island; Saint-Pierre & Miquelon**
Shirley Bay, Ont: **Industrial Research & Development**
Shirt, Pauline: **Harper, Vern**
Shkolnikov, A.S.: **Jewish Writing**
Shoctor, Joseph, H.: **Citadel Theatre**
shoes: **Footwear Industry; Leatherworking; Native People, Economic Conditions**
shoplifting: **Crime**
shopping centres: **Civil Engineering; Native People, Economic Conditions; Retail Trade**
shore pine: **Vegetation Regions - Pacific Coastal**
Shoreham, NS: **Chester**
Short, Richard: **Art; Drawing; Painting; Topographic Painters**
short-awned porcupine grass: **Vegetation Regions - Prairie**
Short Hills: **Niagara Peninsula**
shorthead sculpin: **Endangered Animals**
Shortt, Adam: **Economics; Encyclopedia**
Shortt, Terry: **Diorama**
shortwave radio: **Canadian Broadcasting Corporation; Music Broadcasting; Telecommunications**
shot-put: **Highland Games; Track & Field**
shotgun: **Firearm; Shooting**
Shotwell, James T.: **Historiography**
Shoub, Mac: **Radio Drama, English-Language**
Shouldice, Larry: *Littérature qui se fait*
show jumping: **Equestrian Sports**
shrine: **André, Brother; Lac Ste Anne; Pilgrimage; Ste-Anne-de-Beaupré; Ste Marie Among the Hurons**
Shriner, Michael: **Guitar**
Shrubb, Alfred: **Bowling, Indoor**
Shterenberg, Nava: **Chess**
Shtern, Sholem: **Jewish Writing**
Shu, Albert: **Fashion Design**
Shube, Anson D.: **New Religious Movements**
Shubenacadie, NS: **Nova Scotia**
Shubenacadie Canal: **Canals & Inland Waterways; Dartmouth Lakes**
Shubenacadie mission: **Le Loutre, Jean-Louis**
Shubenacadie River: **Clay; Nova Scotia**
Shubert, Catherine: **Overlanders of 1862**
Shulman, Morton: **Best-Sellers in English**
Shumka Dancers: **Theatre, Multicultural**

Shupe, Isaac: **Domestic Utensils**
Shuster, Frank: **Wayne & Shuster**
Shuswap: **Indian Art; Kamloops; Manuel, George; Salish, Interior; Salmon Arm; Teit, James A.**
Shuswap Highlands: **Columbia Mountains; Monashee Mountains**
Shuswap Lake: **Eagle Pass; Salmon Arm; Sicamous; Thompson River**
Shuswap Reserve: **Kootenay**
Shutt, Frank T.: **Science; Soil Science**
Shutt, Michael: **Guitar**
Shuttleworth, E.B.: **Pharmaceuticals Industry**
Shuttleworth, William: **Baseball**
Sibley, Joseph: **Furniture, Country**
Sibley Peninsula: **Silver Islet; Thunder Bay**
side-looking radar: **Dunbar, I. Moira; Remote Sensing**
siderite: **Iron & Steel Industry**
Siderno group: **Organized Crime**
Siderurgie du Québec: **Sidbec-Dosco Limitée**
Sidey brothers: **Golf**
Siding 16, North-West Territories: **Wetaskiwin**
Siding 29, North-West Territories: **Banff**
Sidney, F.W.: **Sidney**
Sidney Island: **Sidney**
Sidney Williams, Mount: **Gemstone**
Siebens Oil & Gas Co: **Hudson's Bay Company; Mingan, Îles de**
Siebert, Babe: **Stewart, Nelson R.**
Sievert, Lou: **Gymnastics**
Sifton family: **Armadale Co Ltd**
Sigma Mine: **Val-d'Or**
Sigmund Samuel Canadiana Building: **Royal Ontario Museum**
sign language: **Auditory Impairment; Native People - Plains**
Sigurdson, Frank: **Gaboury, Etienne-Joseph**
silage: **Agricultural Implements Industry; Agriculture & Food; Alfalfa; Animal Agriculture; Cereal Crops; Faba Bean; Farm Silo; Forage Crops; Ontario**
Silcox, David P.: **Town, Harold Barling**
silicate: **Mineral**
silicon: **Mineral**
"Silicon Valley North": **Electronics Industry**
silicosis: **Air Pollution; Banting, Frederick G.; Mining Safety & Health**
silk: **Crafts; Textile Industry**
silk-screen printing: **Curnoe, Gregory R.; David, Joe; Kananginak Pootoogook; Lacroix, Richard; Onley, N. Antony; Print Industry; Printmaking; Thompson, Arthur**
silt & siltstone: **Badlands; Claire, Lake; Delta; Devon Island; Erie, Lake; Northumberland Strait; Sand & Gravel; Saskatchewan River**
Silurian period: **Forest; Fossil Plants; McLearn, Frank Harris; Paleontology, History in Canada; Vertebrate**
Silver, Greg: **Graphic Design**
Silver, Philip: **Stage & Costume Design**
Silver City, North-West Territories: **Golden**
silver fox: **Fur Farming; North Cape; Summerside**
silver iodide: **Cloud; Hail; Rainmaking**
Silver King Mine: **Nelson**
silver maple: **London; Maple; Ornamentals; Vegetation Regions - Eastern Temperate Forests**
Silver Star Provincial Park: **Okanagan Valley**
Silver Stars: **Snowbirds**
Silver Tractors: **McLauchlan, Murray**
Silverdale, BC: **Mission**
silverfish: **Insect Classification; Insect Pests**
Silverman, Stanley: **Musical Theatre**
silversmithing: **Art Education**
Silverton, BC: **New Denver**
silverware: **Jewellery & Silverware Industry; Silver, Church; Silver, Domestic**
Silvester, Frederick: **Toronto Mendelssohn Choir**
Simard, Jean: **Novel in French**

Simard, Lac: **Ottawa River**
Simard, René: **Recording Industry**
Simchovitch, Simcha: **Jewish Writing**
Simcoe County Jail: **Huron County Jail**
Simcoe Day: **Festivals; National Holidays**
Simcoe Memorial. **Wyn Wood, Elizabeth**
SIMFAC: **Space Technology**
Similkameen, BC: **Princeton**
Similkameen Okanagan dialect: **Salish, Interior**
Similkameen Valley: **Allison Pass; Desert; Keremeos; Nicola-Similkameen; Princeton; Salish, Interior; Vegetation Regions - Cordillera; Wine Industry**
Simkins, Howard: **Painting**
Simmins, Richard: **Regina Five**
Simmonds, Sarah: **Millidge, Thomas Edward**
Simmons, J.: **Urban Studies**
Simmons, R.: **Urban Studies**
Simmons, Ray: **Messer, Don, & the Islanders**
Simon case: **Indian Treaties**
Simon & Pierre Publishing Co Ltd: **Small Presses; Theatre for Young Audiences**
Simonds, James: **Saint John**
Simpson, A.: **Golf**
Simpson, Albert B.: **Bible Schools; Evangelical & Fundamentalist Movements**
Simpson, Bruce: **Track & Field**
Simpson, Leo: **Humorous Writing in English; Novel in English**
Simpson, Thomas: **Dease, Peter W.; Franklin, John; Victoria Island**
Simpson Tower: **Bregman & Hamann**
SIMULA: **Computer Science**
Simumbra lamp: **Lighting**
Sinclair, Benjamin: **Rundle, Robert Terrill**
Sinclair, G.W.: **Paleontology, History in Canada**
Sinclair, Lister: **Allan, Andrew E.F.; Drama in English; Festival Lennoxville; Radio Drama, English-Language; Theatre, English-Language**
Sinclair, Margaret: **Trudeau, Pierre E.**
sines & cosines: **Mathematics**
Singaporeans: **Malaysians**
Singer, Jacques: **Vancouver Symphony Orchestra**
single parents: **Family; Marriage & Divorce; Poverty; Women in the Labour Force**
Singleton, Gordon: **Cycling**
sinkhole: **Karst Landform**
Sintaluta, Man: **Partridge, Edward A.**
Siouan linguistic family: **Assiniboine; Iroquois; Native People, Languages**
Sioux: **Dakota (Sioux); Dumont, Gabriel; Hennepin, Louis; Minnedosa**
Sioux Lookout, Ont: **Bush Flying; Native People, Communications; Seul, Lac; Theatre, Multicultural**
Sipiwesk Lake: **Manitoba; Nelson River**
Sir Donald, Mount: **Mountaineering**
Sir Frederick Fraser School: **Blindness & Visual Impairment**
Sir George Williams University: **Caiserman-Roth, Ghitta; Concordia University; Layton, Irving P.; Religion**
Sir James MacBrian, Mount: **Mackenzie Mountains**
Sir John Franklin: **Icebreakers**
Sir Robert Peel: **Hunters' Lodges**
Sir Sandford Fleming College of Applied Arts & Technology: **Conservation of Movable Cultural Property; Lindsay**
Sir Wilfred Grenfell College: **Corner Brook; Newfoundland**
Sir Wilfrid, Mont: **Laurentian Highlands**
Sir Winston Churchill Provincial Park: **Alberta**
Sir Winston Churchill Trophy: **Football**
Sirois, Joseph: **Dominion-Provincial Relations, Royal Commission on**
Sirois, Serge: **Drama in French**
siskin: **Finch**
Siskind, Jacob: **Music Criticism**

Sisterhood of St John the Divine: **Christian Religious Communities**
Sisters Hospitallers: **Mance, Jeanne**
Sisters of Charity: **Christian Religious Communities; Mount Saint Vincent University**
Sisters of Providence: **Christian Religious Communities**
Sisters of Saint Anne: **Christian Religious Communities; Literature in French - Scholarship & Teaching**
Sisters of Saint Joseph: **Catholicism; Charbonnel, Armand-F.-M. de; Christian Religious Communities**
Sisters of the Holy Names of Jesus & Mary: **Christian Religious Communities; La Liberté, Alfred (musician); Marie-Rose, Mother**
Sisters of the Immaculate Conception: **Lithuanians**
Sisters Servants of Mary Immaculate: **Catholicism**
Sitka alder: **Alder; Vegetation Regions - Cordillera**
Sitka mountain ash: **Vegetation Regions - Cordillera**
Sitka spruce: **Forest Harvesting; Pacific Rim National Park; Queen Charlotte Islands; Spruce; Timber Trade History; Vegetation Regions - Pacific Coastal**
Situations: **Ferron, Jacques**
"Six & Five" legislation: **Labour Relations**
Six Mile Lake: **Milne, David B.**
Six Nations Confederacy: **Dekanahwideh; Deskaheh; Native People, Political Organization & Activism**
Six Nations Indian Pageant: **Festivals**
Six Nations Pageant: **Theatre, Multicultural**
Six Nations Reserve: **Brantford; Cayuga; Elmira; Folk Dance; Handsome Lake Religion; Iroquois; Kitchener-Waterloo; Mohawk; Monture, Gilbert C.; Onondaga**
Sixteen Mile Creek: **Oakville**
Sixty Eight publishing: **Škvorecký, Josef**
Sixtymile, YT: **Fort Reliance**
Sjelderup, Gunnar: **Ski Jumping**
Skae's Corners, Upper Canada: **Oshawa**
Skagit Range: **Cascade Mountains**
Skagit Valley: **Allison Pass; Cascade Mountains**
Skaha Lake: **Okanagan Valley; Penticton**
Skakel, Alexander: **Logan, William E.**
Skalbania, Nelson: **Calgary Flames; Edmonton Oilers**
skate: **Ray**
Skate Canada: **Figure Skating**
skates: **Dartmouth Lakes; Ice Skating; Roller Skating; Sporting-Goods Industry**
skating: **Figure Skating; Ice Skating; Laurentian Highlands; Rideau Canal; Roller Skating; Speed Skating**
Skeena Air Transport: **Pacific Western Airlines Ltd**
Skeena Treasure House: **Ksan**
skeet shooting: **Shooting**
Skerring, B.: **Olympic Games**
Ski-doo: **Bombardier, J. Armand; Bombardier Inc**
ski plane: **Bush Flying; de Havilland Otter; Klein, George John**
skid road: **Forest Harvesting; Timber Axe; Timber Trade History**
Skidegate, BC: **Kelly, Peter Reginald; Queen Charlotte Islands**
skin boat: **Kayak; Prehistory**
skin tent: **Prehistory; Tipi**
skink: **Lizard**
skipjack: **Mackerel**
skiwear: **Clothing Industries; Sporting-Goods Industry**
Sklar Manufacturing Ltd.: **Heintzman & Co Ltd**
"Skookum Jim": **Carcross; Klondike Gold Rush**
Skookumchuck Reserve: **Salish, Interior**
Skookumchuk, BC: **Religious Building**
Skorupskyj, Volodymyr: **Ukrainian Writing**

Skreslet, Laurie: **Mount Everest Expedition**
Skrien, Dave: **British Columbia Lions**
skua: **Bird Classification & Evolution; Jaeger**
Skungwai Island: **Queen Charlotte Islands**
skunk cabbage: **Plants, Native Uses; Pollination**
skydiving: **Parachuting, Sport**
skyscraper: **Architecture, Development**
Slade, Bernard: **Theatre, English-Language**
Slade, John: **Twillingate**
Sladen, Douglas: **Exploration & Travel Literature in English**
slag: **Metallurgy; Sudbury**
slander: **Defamation; Jury; Law & the Press**
slash-and-burn: **Agriculture History; Conservation; Forest Harvesting**
slate: **Asbestos, Qué; Flour Milling Industry**
slate weapon: **Prehistory**
Slater, Patrick: **Best-Sellers in English**
Slater Shoes: **Lévesque, Jean-Louis**
Slatter, John: **Music History**
Slave Lake, Alta: **Lesser Slave Lake**
Slave Province: **Geological History**
Slavs: **Byelorussians; Czechs; Prejudice & Discrimination; Toronto; Ukrainians; Winnipeg**
Slavutych, Yar: **Ukrainian Writing**
SLBM: **Armaments**
Sleeman, George: **Baseball**
Sleeper Islands: **Hudson Bay; Ungava Inuit**
Sleeping Giant: **Thunder Bay**
sleeping sickness: **Parasitology**
sleigh: **Roads & Highways; Street Railways; Technology; Toys & Games**
sleigh bed: **Furniture, English, Scottish & American**
Slemon, Peter: **Musicology**
Sliammon: **Northern Georgia Strait Coast Salish**
Sliammon Creek: **Northern Georgia Strait Coast Salish**
slippers: **Footwear Industry; Leatherworking**
slippery (red) elm: **Vegetation Regions - Eastern Temperate Forests**
Slocan Lake: **New Denver; Slocan**
Slocan Valley: **Sandon**
Slocum, Joshua: **Brier Island**
Sloggett, Paul: **Painting**
sloop: **Maugerville; Pinky Schooner; *Racoon***
Slopen, Beverly: **Popular Literature in English**
slough: **Lake**
slough grass: **Vegetation Regions - Prairie**
Slovenska država (Slovenian State): **Slovenes**
Slovenské Slovo (Slovak Word): **Czechs**
Small, Alastair M.: **Mediterranean Archaeology**
Small, Ambrose: **Grand Theatre**
Small, Holly: **Dance, Modern**
Small, John: **Duel**
Small, Sam: **Evangelism**
Small Loans Act: **Law & Society**
smallmouth bass: **Algonquin Provincial Park; Bass; Rideau Lakes; Thousand Islands**
smallpox: **Abenaki; Acadia; Assiniboine; Biological Product; Blackfoot Nation; Brébeuf, Jean de; Carrier; Charlottetown; Chipewyan; Cluny Earthlodge Village; Cree; Disasters; Epidemic; Gimli; Haida; Health Policy; Hôtel-Dieu; Huron; Icelanders; Macpherson, Cluny; Native People, Health; Neutral; Nootka Sound; Nursing; Old Crow; Peigan; St Albert; Sarcee; Stoney; Trinity; Virus; Youville, Marie-Marguerite d'**
Smallwood Mine: **Labrador City**
Smart, William: **Sunday Schools**
"Smashers": **Tilley, Samuel L.**
Smellie, David: **Pewter**
smelters: **Acid Rain; Energy in Society; Metallurgy; Pollution; Rouyn-Noranda; Trail**
Smieja, Florian: **Poles**
Smith, Alta: **Railway Station**
Smith, Andréa Ciel: **Dance, Modern**

Smith, Becky: **Swimming, Speed**
Smith, Bob: **Music Criticism**
Smith, Carter, Parkin: **Smith, Ernest John**
Smith, Carter & Searle: **Architecture, Development**
Smith, Cecil: **Figure Skating**
Smith, David: **Tourism**
Smith, David S.: **Morgan, Henry**
Smith, Dorothy: **Marxism**
Smith, E. Norman: **Ottawa Journal; Smith, Irving Norman**
Smith, Eden: **Architecture, Development**
Smith, Ethel: **Track & Field**
Smith, Gustave: **Music History**
Smith, H. "Okanagan": **Okanagan Valley**
Smith, H.A.: **Scott, Francis R.**
Smith, Harlan I.: **Archaeology**
Smith, Hooley: **Stewart, Nelson R.**
Smith, James: *Marco Polo*
Smith, John Ivor: **Sculpture**
Smith, John Meredith: **Meredith, John**
Smith, M.: **Molecular Biology**
Smith, Morley: **Industrial Design**
Smith, Neville: **Graphic Design**
Smith, Nicholas: **Autobiographical Writing in English**
Smith, Peter: **Port Hope**
Smith, Philip: **Business History**
Smith, R. Harlan: **Country & Western Music**
Smith, Ray: **Humorous Writing in English; Novel in English; Short Fiction in English**
Smith, S.: **Physics**
Smith, Scott: **Loverboy**
Smith, Shannon: **Swimming, Speed**
Smith, Stuart L.: **Science Council of Canada**
Smith, Tricia: **Rowing**
Smith, Wilfred Cantwell: **Religion**
Smith, Wilfred I.: **Archives; Oral History**
Smith, William: **Baseball**
Smith, William A.: **De Cosmos, Amor**
Smith & Rhuland: *Bluenose*
Smith Arm: **Great Bear Lake**
Smith Brothers: **Bus Transportation**
Smith Carter Partners: **Smith, Ernest John**
Smith Mountain: **Powell River**
Smith Sound: **Ellesmere Island Archaeological Sites; Random Island**
Smithers, BC: **Fossil Plants**
Smithfield, Ont: **Research Stations, Agricultural**
Smith's Creek: **Port Hope**
Smithville, Ont: **Shrum, Gordon M.**
smog: **Automobile; Pollution**
Smoking Hills: **Horton River**
smoking (preservation): **Cap aux Meules, Ile du; Dark Harbour; Meat-Processing Industry; Smokehouse**
Smoky Lake, Alta: **Erasmus, Peter**
smoky quartz: **Silica**
Smoky River: **Coal Mining; Peace River, Alta**
Smoky River Coals Ltd: **Coal**
smooth sumac: **Poison Ivy; Sumac; Vegetation Regions - Cordillera**
Smotrych, Oleksander: **Ukrainian Writing**
SMT (Eastern) Ltd: **Bus Transportation; New Brunswick**
Smucker, Barbara: **Children's Literature in English; Children's Literature in French**
smuts: **Fungus**
Smyth, Hervey: **Drawing; Painting; Topographic Painters**
Smyth, James C.: **Halifax Citadel**
Smyth, Thomas: **Smiths Falls**
Smythe, Stafford: **Smythe, Constantine Falkland Cary; Toronto Maple Leafs**
Snafu Creek: **Place-names**
Snag Creek: **Snag**
Snag Junction, YT: **Snag**
Snake Island: **Toronto Islands**
snakebite: **Rattlesnake; Snake**
snakefly: **Insect Classification**
snakeroot: **Poisonous Plants**
snapdragon: **Ornamentals**
snapping hazel: **Witch Hazel**
Snare Lake: **Dogrib**
Snare River: **Great Slave Lake; Mackenzie River; Yellowknife, NWT**

Snelling, Derek: **Swimming, Speed**
Snider-Enfield rifle: **Firearm**
Snively, Agnes: **Nursing**
SNOBOL: **Computer Science**
snooker: **Billiards; Chenier, Georges; Thorburn, Clifford C.D.**
Snooks Harbour, Nfld: **Random Island**
Snorri Thorfinnsson: **Icelanders**
Snow, J.T.: **Domestic Utensils**
Snow, John: **Printmaking**
snow & snowfall: **Aerodynamics; Algae; Avalanche; Blizzard; Climate Information; Cloud; Hydrology; Ice; Klein, George John; Language; Manitoba; Nova Scotia; Ontario; Pollution; Québec; Smallwood, Charles**
snow bunting: **Arctic Animals; Bunting**
Snow Dome: **Columbia Icefield**
snow goose: **Arctic Animals; Banks Island; Goose; Hudson Bay; Hunting; Québec; St Lawrence River**
Snow Lake, Man: **Flin Flon; Resource Towns**
snow-on-the-mountain: **Poisonous Plants**
snow removal: **Climate & Man; Railway History; Roads & Highways**
Snow Valley Ski Area: **Fernie**
snowberry: **Vegetation Regions - Pacific Coastal**
Snowbird Lake: **Kasba Lake**
snowbush ceanothus: **Vegetation Regions - Cordillera**
Snowdrift River: **Great Slave Lake**
Snowfest: **Peterborough**
snowflea (collembola): **Insect Classification**
snowshoe hare: **Barachois Pond Provincial Park; Cape Breton Highlands National Park; Gros Morne National Park; Hare; Hare (Indians); Owl; Terra Nova National Park**
snowy grouper: **Bass**
snowy owl: **Banks Island; Migration; Owl**
snuff & snuffboxes: **Silver, Domestic; Tobacco**
Snukal, Sherman: **Theatre, English-Language**
Snyder, Lester L.: **Diorama**
So Little for the Mind: **Neatby, Hilda M.**
soap operas: **Radio Drama, French-Language; Radio Programming; Television Drama**
soapberry: **Berries, Wild**
Sobey, John William: **Sobey, William Macdonald**
Sobey Stores Ltd: **Provigo Inc; Sobey, William Macdonald**
Soccio, Gino: **Popular Music**
Social Planning Council of Metropolitan Toronto: **Marshall, Kenric Rudolphus**
Social Reform Council of Canada: **Patrick, William**
Social Science Research Council: **McIlwraith, Thomas Forsyth; Social Science**
Social Service Council of Canada: **Social Gospel**
Social Services Council of Ontario: **Dunlap, David Alexander**
Social Welfare Court (Qué): **Courts of Law; Family Court**
Socialisme: **Vadeboncoeur, Pierre**
Socialist International: **New Democratic Party**
Socialist Youth Movement: **Buller, Annie**
Société canadienne d'opérette: **Music History**
Société canadienne de théologie: **Religion**
Société canadienne d'histoire naturelle: **Marie-Victorin, Frère**
Société d'archéologie du Québec: **Archaeology**
Société de fiducie du Québec: **Caisse populaire**
Société de musique canadienne: **Canadian League of Composers**
Société de musique contemporaine du Québec: **Chamber Music; Mather, Bruce; Music History; Papineau-Couture, Jean; Pelletier, Wilfrid; Tremblay, Gilles**

Société de Notre-Dame de Montréal: **Mance, Jeanne; Ville-Marie**
Société de philosophie du Québec: **Philosophy**
Société de philosophique de Montréal: **Philosophy**
Société de production et de programmation de spectacles: **Arsenault, Angèle**
Société de protection des plantes du Québec: **Entomology**
Société d'éducation des adultes: **Lévesque, Georges-Henri**
Société des artistes professionels du Québec: **Artists' Organizations**
Société des arts, sciences et lettres de Québec: **Potvin, Damase**
Société des auteurs: **Roux, Jean-Louis**
Société des concerts symphoniques de Montréal: **Pelletier, Wilfrid**
Société des dix: **Desrosiers, Léo-Paul**
Société des écrivains canadiens: **Charbonneau, Robert; Literature & Politics; Literature in French - Scholarship & Teaching**
Société des frères chasseurs: **Lower Canada**
Société des graphistes du Québec: **Graphic Design**
Société des loteries et courses du Québec: **Lottery**
Société des traversiers du Québec: **Ferries**
Société des vingt-et-un: **La Baie**
Société d'opéra français: **Opera**
Société du parler français au Canada: **Dictionary; Intellectual History; Roy, Camille**
Société entomologique du Québec: **Entomology**
Société générale de financement: **Chemical Industries; Filion, Gérard; Lesage, Jean; Pepin, Marcel; Québec**
Société générale de publications Inc: **UniMédia Inc**
Société historique de Québec: **Literary Prizes in French**
Société historique de St-Boniface: **Theatre, French-Language**
Société historique du Saguenay: **Chicoutimi**
Société internationale pour la musique contemporaine: **Garant, Serge**
Société musicale Ste-Cécile: **Dessane, M.-H.-Antoine**
Société pour l'encouragement des sciences et des arts en Canada: **Artists' Organizations; Légaré, Joseph**
Société québécoise de science politique: **Political Science**
Société symphonique de Québec: **Arts Funding; Orchestral Music**
Societies Act (Alta): **Corporation Law**
Society for Development, Justice & Peace: **Strong, Maurice F.**
Society for General Physiologists: **Rothstein, Aser**
Society for Promoting Christian Knowledge: **Anglicanism**
Society for the Propagation of the Gospel in Foreign Parts: **Anglicanism; Newfoundland**
Society for the Study of Architecture in Canada: **Architecture, Development; Heritage Conservation**
Society for the Study of Social Problems: **Criminology**
Society of Canadian Artists: **Artists' Organizations; Eaton, Wyatt; Edson, Aaron Allan**
Society of Canadian Limnologists: **Rigler, Frank Harold**
Society of Canadian Painter-Etchers & Engravers: **Artists' Organizations; Printmaking; Wood, William John**
Society of Chemical Industry: **Chemistry**
society of common life: **Christian Religious Communities**
Society of Equity: **Wood, Henry Wise**
Society of Friends: **Quakers**
Society of Limners: **Pavelic, Myfanwy Spencer**
Society of St John the Evangelist: **Christian Religious Communities**
Society of St Margaret: **Christian Religious Communities**
Society of Typographic Designers: **Graphic Design**

Sock-a-jaw-wu: **Stump, Sarain**
sockeye salmon: **Chilcotin; Pacific Salmon; Salish, Interior**
soda ash: **Quarrying Industry; Salt**
sodalite: **Gemstone**
Sodarcan management: **Parizeau, Gérard**
Soddy, Frederick: **Chemistry Subdisciplines; Rutherford, Ernest**
sodium: **Maple Sugar Industry; Nuclear Power Plants; Soil Classification; Spectroscopy; Spring; Turnip**
Soeurs de Miséricorde: **Christian Religious Communities**
softball: **Baseball; Sports History**
software: **Computer Industry; Computer Science; Computer Systems Applications; Copyright Law**
softwood: **Chestnut; Forestry; Furniture, Country; Furniture, German; International Trade; Lumber & Wood Industries; Maritime Shipping History to 1900; Pulp & Paper Industry; Woodenware**
Sogebry Ltd: **Caisse de dépôt et placement du Québec**
Sohier, G.H.: **Sculpture**
soil mechanics: **Civil Engineering; Hydrology; Legget, Robert Ferguson**
Soils Group: **Soil Science**
Sokoki: **Abenaki**
solar eclipse: **Astronomy; Chant, Clarence Augustus; Covington, Arthur Edwin; Plaskett, John Stanley; Sun**
solar emissions: **Covington, Arthur Edwin; Observatory**
Solar Energy Soc of Canada: **Solar Energy; Wind Energy**
Solar Maximum Satellite: **Canadarm**
solar radiation: **Climate; Climate Information; Climatology; Desert; Lake; Meteorology; Ocean**
Solar Stage: **Theatre, English-Language**
solar system: **Astronomy; Meteor, Meteorite, Impact Crater**
solar time: **Time**
solar wind: **Northern Lights**
Solaris: **Literary Periodicals in French; Popular Literature in French**
soldier settlement Act: **Veterans' Land Act**
Soldiers' Civil Re-establishment, Dept of: **National Health & Welfare, Dept of**
sole: **British Columbia; Flatfish; Québec**
sole proprietorship: **Corporation Law**
Solidarity Coalition: **Bennett, William R.**
solitary confinement: **Miller & Cockriell Case**
Solomon, Michel: **Jewish Writing**
solonetz: **Soil Classification**
sols: **Coinage**
solvents: **Coal Liquefaction; Crafts; Petrochemical Industry**
somatic cells: **Genetics**
Somerset, Duchess of: **Exploration & Travel Literature in English**
Somerville, C.R. "Sandy": **Golf**
Sommer, Richard: **Poetry in English**
Sono Nis Press: **Small Presses**
Sons of England: **English; Samuel, Lewis**
Sons of Freedom: **Doukhobors**
"Sons-of-Mitches": **Oshawa Strike**
Sons of the Clergy Islands: **Place-names**
Soo Line Railroad Co: **Canadian Pacific Railway**
Soper, W.Y.: **Ahearn, Thomas**
Soper River: **Soper, J. Dewey**
Soper's ringed seal: **Soper, J. Dewey**
Sorby, Thomas Charles: **Hotel; Railway Station**
Sorenson, Gerry: **Skiing**
Sorestad, Glen: **Regionalism in Literature**
sorrel: **Dock**
Sortilèges: **Folk Dance**
Sorviluk Range: **Torngat Mountains**
Soscumica, Lac: **Nottaway, Rivière**
Sotheby's: **Art Dealers**
Sotho language: **Africans**
Soto Zen: **Buddhism**
Soublière, Roger: **Barre du jour**

Soucy, François: **Art, Contemporary Trends**
Souharissen: **Neutral**
Soulanges Canal: **Canals & Inland Waterways**
soulcatcher: **Northwest Coast Indian Art**
Soulières, Robert: **Children's Literature in French**
sound: **Acoustics; Aerodynamics; Noise; Telecommunications**
Sound Heritage Series: **Oral History**
sound synthesizers: **Electroacoustic Music**
sour gas: **Petroleum; Sulphur**
sour gum: **Vegetation Regions - Eastern Temperate Forests**
Sour Lemon: **Soft-Drink Industry**
Sourdough Rendezvous: **Festivals**
Souriquois: **Micmac**
Souris, Lake: **Souris River**
Souris Valley Mine: **Coal**
sous: **Coinage**
South Africans: **Africans**
South Bentinck Arm: **Bella Coola**
South Bolton, Qué: **Soapstone**
South Detroit, Upper Canada: **Windsor, Ont**
South Eastern Railway: **Farnham**
South Indian Orthodox Church: **Orthodox Church**
South Island: **Toronto Islands**
South Moose Lake: **Moose Lake**
South Mountain: **Annapolis Lowlands; Nova Scotia**
South Nation River: **Landslide; Ottawa River; St Lawrence Lowland**
South Pender Island: **Gulf Islands**
South Saskatchewan River: **Saskatchewan River**
South Saskatchewan River Development Project: **Diefenbaker Lake; Prairie Farm Rehabilitation Administration**
South Surrey, BC: **Surrey**
South Témiscaming, Qué: **Témiscaming**
South Thompson River: **Thompson River**
South Twillingate Island: **Twillingate**
Southam, G. Hamilton: **National Arts Centre**
Southam-Maclean Publications Ltd: **Financial Times**
Southam News Service: **News Agencies**
Southeastern Railway: **Hungerford, Samuel James**
Southend, Sask: **Reindeer Lake**
Southern Alberta College of Art: **Janvier, Alex S.**
Southern Alberta Institute of Technology: **Aerospace Industry; Calgary**
Southern Alberta Opera Assn: **Alberta**
Southern Alberta Pioneer Women & Old Timer's Assn: **McDougall, Elizabeth**
Southern Cross: **Disasters**
Southern Okanagan Lands Project: **Oliver; Osoyoos; Penticton**
Southern Province: **Geological Regions**
Southern Shelf: **Geological Regions**
Southern Tsimshian language: **Tsimshian**
Southesk, James C.: **Exploration & Travel Literature in English; Stoney**
Southport, PEI: **Charlottetown**
Sovereign Bank of Canada: **Holt, Herbert S.**
sovereigns: **Coinage; Queen's Plate**
sovereignty: **Aboriginal Rights; Armed Forces; Bernier, Joseph-Elzéar; Boundaries; Communications; Deer Island; Economic Nationalism; Ellesmere Island; Grise Fiord; Hibernia Case; Hudson Bay; Icebreakers; Low, Albert P.; St Roch; Shield; State; Sverdrup Islands; Whaling; Yukon Field Force**
Sovremennik (Contemporary): **Russians**
sow bug: **Crustacean**
soy sauce: **Mold**
spa: **St Catharines**
Space Research Corp: **Bull, Gerald Vincent**
space science: **Astronomy**
Space Sciences Centre: **Edmonton; Science Centre**

Spadina Freeway: **Automobile; Davis, William G.**
Spadina Subway: **Wieland, Joyce**
spangle grass: **Vegetation Regions - Prairie**
Spanish Bay: **Sydney**
Spanish dollar: **Money**
Spanish flu: **Influenza**
Spanish Language Theatre: **Theatre, Multicultural**
Spanish River: **Georgian Bay**
Spar Aerospace Ltd: **Canadarm; Electronics Industry; Industrial Research & Development; Québec; Satellite Communications**
Sparks Street: **Bank Architecture; Urban Design**
Sparling, Alta: **Camrose**
Sparrow: **Steppenwolf**
sparrow hawk (American kestrel): **Falcon; Québec**
Sparshott, Francis: **Humorous Writing in English; Literature in English - Theory & Criticism; Philosophy**
Spatsizi Wilderness Park: **Stikine River**
spatterdock: **Water Lily**
SPCA: **Humane Societies**
"speakeasy": **Prohibition**
speaking in tongues: **Charismatic Renewal; Pentecostal Movement**
spear grass: **Vegetation Regions - Prairie**
spear throwing: **Sports History**
Spears, Borden: **Newspapers**
spears & spearpoints: **Beothuk; Calgary; Chilcotin; Debert; L'Anse Amour Burial Site; Prehistory**
Special Areas Board (Alta): **Urban & Regional Planning**
Special Commissioner for Defence Projects in the Northwest: **World War II**
special committee: **Committees; Parliamentary Procedure**
special interest groups: **Advertising; Animal Issues; Pressure Group; School Boards**
"special status": **Federalism; Opting-Out; Quiet Revolution**
speckled trout: **Char**
spectrophotometry: **Hogg, Frank Scott**
spectroscopic binary: **Harper, William Edmund; Petrie, Robert Methven**
Spectrum Mountains: **Mount Edziza Provincial Park**
speech impairment: **Auditory Impairment**
Speed River: **Guelph**
speedboat regatta: **Valleyfield**
Speers, R.L. "Jim": **Thoroughbred Racing**
speleology: **Cave**
Spelt, Jacob: **Urban Studies**
spelunking: **Cave**
Spence, Francis S.: **Temperance Movement**
Spence, Michael W.: **Archaeology**
Spence, Thomas: **Portage la Prairie**
Spencer, Aubrey George: **Wix, Edward**
Spencer, Christopher: **Spencer, David**
Spencer, Elizabeth: **Short Fiction in English**
Spencer, George V.: **Royal Canadian Mounted Police**
Spencer, Henry: **Ginger Group**
Spencer, J.W.: **Geomorphology**
Spencer, Michael: **Canadian Film Development Corp**
Spencer carbine: **Firearm**
Spencer repeating rifle: **Firearm**
Spencer's Island: *Mary Celeste*
Spences Bridge, BC: **Native People - Plateau; Teit, James A.**
Spettigue, Douglas O.: **Autobiographical Writing in English; Grove, Frederick Philip**
sphalerite: **Mineral**
Spicer, Jack: **Poetry in English**
spices: **Food Additives; Herbs**
Spickett, Ron: **Painting**
spider (skillet): **Domestic Utensils**
spike bent grass: **Vegetation Regions - Pacific Coastal**
spinal cord: **Chiropractic; Vegetarianism**
spindle whorl: **L'Anse aux Meadows**
spinel: **Mineral**
Spiral Tunnels: **Kicking Horse Pass; Tunnels**
Spirale: **Literary Periodicals in French**

Spirit of the Buffalo: **Native People, Religion**
spiritualism: **King, W.L. Mackenzie; New Religious Movements**
spiroplasma: **Plant Disease**
spit: **Domestic Utensils**
Spitfire: **Steamboats & Paddlewheelers**
splake: **Char; English Language**
Split Lake: **Nelson River**
Split Point: **Conception Bay**
sponge iron: **Sidbec-Dosco Limitée**
spoolwoods: **Timber Trade History**
spoon: **Northwest Coast Indian Art; Pewter; Woodenware**
Spooner, James: **Art Dealers**
Sport Canada: **Hoffman, Abigail; Jerome, Harry W.; Racquetball; Sports Organization, Amateur; Track & Field**
Sport for Canadians, Task Force on: **Sports Organization, Amateur**
Sports Federation of Canada: **Sports Organization, Amateur**
Sports Pool: **Lottery**
sportswear: **Clothing Industries; Sporting-Goods Industry**
Spotted Island: **Jackman, William**
spotted owl: **Endangered Animals; Owl**
spotted turtle: **Georgian Bay Islands National Park; Point Pelée National Park; Turtle**
Spouses' Allowance: **Old-Age Pension; Poverty; Social Security**
Spraggett, Kevin: **Chess**
Spray Lakes Reservoir: **Mount Assiniboine Provincial Park**
spring beauty: **Plants, Native Uses**
Spring Thaw: **Moore, Dora Mavor; Moore, Mavor**
springbank clover: **Vegetation Regions - Pacific Coastal**
Springer, BC: **Slocan**
Springhill & Parrsboro Coal & Railway Co Ltd: **Springhill**
Springhill Meteor Observatory: **Astronomy**
springtail (collembola): **Insect Classification**
Sproat Lake: **Pictographs & Petroglyphs; Port Alberni; Vancouver Island**
Sproatt, Henry: **Sproatt and Rolph**
Sproule, J.C.: **Cree Lake**
Sproule, Robert A.: **Printmaking**
spruce bark beetle: **Forestry**
spruce budworm: **Fundy National Park; Invertebrate; Manitoba; Vegetation Regions - Atlantic Coastal**
Spruce Falls Power & Paper Co: **Kapuskasing**
spruce grouse: **Algonquin Provincial Park; Game Bird; Grouse; Migration**
Spruce Meadows: **Equestrian Sports; Horse**
spruce root: **Davidson, Florence Edenshaw; Northwest Coast Indian Art**
Spruce Woods Provincial Forest: **Shilo, CFB**
Spruce Woods Provincial Park: **Brandon; Parks, Provincial**
SPSS: **Computer Science**
spurges: **Poisonous Plants; Weeds**
Spuzzum, BC: **Salish, Interior**
spying: **Gouzenko, Igor S.; Official Secrets Act; Pichon, Thomas; Rose, Fred; Stephenson, William Samuel**
Squally Reach: **Malahat Pass**
Squamish (Indians): **Central Coast Salish; George, Dan**
Squamish Valley: **Central Coast Salish; Squamish**
Square Deal: **Literary Magazines in English**
Square Deal Grain Co: **Partridge, Edward A.**
square-rigger: **Sailing Ships**
square root: **Computer Systems Applications**
squared timber: **Huntsville; Labour Policy; Lower Canada; Ottawa, Ont; Ottawa River; Shediac; Timber Axe; Timber Trade History; Wright, Philemon**
squashberries: **Cuisine**
squaw-weed: **Groundsel**
squawfish: **Minnow**

squawroot: **Georgian Bay Islands National Park**
Squid-Jiggin' Grounds: **Scammell, Arthur Reginald**
Squires, The: **Young, Neil P.**
Squirrel: **Gilbert, Humphrey**
Squirrel Cove, BC: **Northern Georgia Strait Coast Salish**
Squohomish: **Squamish**
Sri Lankans: **Ethnic Literature; South Asians**
St-Jean, Île (Island of St John): **Agriculture History; Charlottetown; Festivals; Fort Amherst; Treaty of Utrecht**
Staebler, Edna: **Cuisine; Popular Literature in English**
Stafford, Jan: *Barre du jour*
Stage-Coach Players: **Theatre for Young Audiences**
Stage Society: **Plummer, A. Christopher O.**
Stage West: **Theatre, English-Language**
stagecoach: **Roads & Highways**
Stagiaire: **Legal Education**
stained glass: **Glass, Stained; Public Art**
stainless steel: **Canadarm; Chromium; Iron & Steel Industry; Nickel**
Stairs, John: **Piracy**
Stairs, William: **Stairs, John Fitz-William**
stampede: **Calgary Stampede; Rodeo**
Stampede Park: **Calgary**
Stand Off, Alta: **Red Crow**
Standard, Alta: **Danes**
Standard Bank of Canada: **Canadian Imperial Bank of Commerce**
Standard Broadcast News: **News Agencies; Western Dominion Investment Co Ltd**
Standard Broadcasting Corp Ltd: **Dominion Stores Ltd; Western Dominion Investment Co Ltd**
Standard Church of America: **Holiness Churches; Horner, Ralph C.**
Standard Shirt Co: **Gordon, Charles Blair**
Standard Stock & Mining Exchange: **Stock & Bond Markets**
standard time: **Fleming, Sandford; Time**
Standard Wood Chemical Ltd: **McConnell, John Wilson**
standardbred: **Harness Racing; Horse**
standards: **Building Codes & Regulations; Metric Conversion; Safety Standards; Time; Weights & Measures**
Standards Council of Canada: **Canadian Government Specifications Board; Industrial Quality Control**
standing committee: **Committees; Parliamentary Procedure**
standing orders: **Closure; Parliamentary Procedure**
Stanfield's Ltd: **Truro**
Staniszkis, Joanna: **Weaving, Contemporary**
Stanley: **Icebreakers**
Stanley, Arthur: **Stanley, Frederick Arthur**
Stanley, G.M.: **Geomorphology**
Stanley, William: **Stanley, Frederick Arthur**
Stanley Park: **Hippies; Vancouver**
Stansbury, Joseph: **Poetry in English**
Stanstead, Qué: **Automotive Industry**
Stanstead Wesleyan College: **Methodism**
Stanton, NWT: **Anderson River**
Staples, Kevan: **Rough Trade**
star: **Astronomy; Black Hole; Douglas, Alice Vibert; Galaxy; Harper, William Edmund; Hogg, Helen B.; McKellar, Andrew; Petrie, Robert Methven; Plaskett, John Stanley; Stewart, Robert Meldrum; Sun; Van den Bergh, Sidney**
Star Channel: **Pay Television**
Star City, Sask: **Religious Building**
Star Husband: **Native People, Religion**
Star of Courage: **Decorations for Bravery**
Starblanket, Noel: **Assembly of First Nations**
Starfighter aircraft: **Military Aviation & Aircraft**
Stark, T. James: **Peace Movement**

Stark effect: **Foster, John Stuart**
Starlab: **Observatory**
Staron, G.: **Poles**
Starr, Lucille: **Country & Western Music**
Starr, Michael: **Oshawa**
Starr Manufacturing Co: **Dartmouth Lakes**
START: **Disarmament**
starvation: **Big Bear; Fur Trade; Kavik, John; Vegetarianism**
Stasas Eagles: **Edenshaw, Charlie**
Stastney brothers: **Québec Nordiques**
Stations of the Cross: **Catholicism; Pilgrimage**
Statistical Act (1848): **Demographic Data Collection**
Statistical Soc of Canada: **Mathematics; Statistics**
Statistics Act: **Privacy; Statistics Canada**
statutes & charters of Britain: **Constitutional Law**
statutory holidays: **Employment Law; National Holidays**
Staub, Marie-Clément: **Saints**
Staudt, Linda: **Long-Distance Running**
Stave Falls, BC: **Mission**
Steacie Memorial Fellowship: **Suzuki, David Takayoshi**
steacyite: **Mineral Naming**
Stead, Robert J.C.: **Best-Sellers in English; Novel in English**
steam locomotive: **Canadian National Railways; Locomotives & Rolling Stock**
steam power: **Sawmill; Technology**
Stearns, Linda: **Grands Ballets Canadiens**
Stechyshyn, Myroslav: **Ukrainian Writing**
Stedman fractionating column: **Stedman, Donald Frank**
Steed, Judy: **Film, Experimental**
steel & steelmaking: **Algoma Steel Corp Ltd; Architecture, Development; Bridges; Dominion Foundries & Steel, Ltd; Forges Saint-Maurice; Iron & Steel Industry; Iron & Steel Industry; Sidbec-Dosco Limitée; Sydney Steel Corp**
Steel Co of Canada, Ltd: **Hobson, Robert; Nanticoke; Sefton, Lawrence F.; Stelco Inc**
Steele, J.: **Canadian Studies; Literature in English - Teaching**
Steele, Lisa: **Art, Contemporary Trends; Video Art**
Steele Glacier: **Steele, Mount**
Steele Narrows Historic Park: **Loon Lake**
Steelhead, BC: **Mission**
steelhead trout: **Dean River; Trout**
Steen, Dave: **Track & Field**
Steep Rock Iron Ore: **Eaton, Cyrus S.**
Steep Rock Lake: **Atikokan; Geological Dating**
steeplechase: **Equestrian Sports; Olympic Games; Snowshoeing; Thoroughbred Racing; Track & Field**
steer: **Animal Agriculture; Beef Cattle Farming**
Steeves, Dorothy: **Women's International League for Peace & Freedom**
Steeves, W.H.: **Fathers of Confederation**
Stefansson-Anderson Arctic Expedition: **Archaeology**
Stegner, Wallace: **Short Fiction in English**
Stein, David Lewis: **Novel in English**
Steinberg, Ben: **Choral Music**
Steinberg, Jack: **Archaeology**
Steinberg, Robert: **Mathematics**
Steiner schools: **Education, Alternate**
Steinhauer, Eugene: **Native People, Communications**
Stelck, Charles R.: **Paleontology, History in Canada**
Stellarton, NS: **Co-operative Movement (See Addendum, page 1992); Sobey, William Macdonald**
Stelmach, Natalie: **Billiards**
Stelter, G.A.: **Urban Studies**
STEM: **Klein, George John**
stem turnip: **Kohlrabi**
Stenhouse, Patti: **Swimming, Speed**
Stennett, William: **Silver, Domestic**
Stent & Laver: **Parliament Buildings**

Stephen Leacock Memorial Medal: **Birney, A. Earle; Davies, Robertson W.; Gotlieb, Sondra; Humorous Writing in English; Leacock, Stephen; Literary Prizes in English; Nicol, Eric**
stereograph: **Photography**
Stereometrical Tableau: **Baillairgé Family**
stereoscope: **Esson, James**
stereotype: **Newspapers**
sterilization: **Bioethics; Birth Control; Medical Ethics**
Sterling Newspapers: **Black, Conrad M.; Western Dominion Investment Co Ltd**
Stern, Max: **Art Dealers; Hughes, Edward John**
Sternberg, Charles H.: **Paleontology, History in Canada**
Sternberg, Levi: **Paleontology, History in Canada**
steroids: **Veterinary Medicines Industry**
Stettler, Alta: **CHUM Ltd**
Stevens, Paul: **Children's Literature in French**
Stevens, Peter: **Literary Bibliography in English**
Stevens, Warren: **Football**
Stevens Lake: **Nelson River**
Stevenson, A.: **Hymns**
Stevenson, Lionel: **Literature in English - Theory & Criticism**
Stevenson, Raines, Barret, Hutton, Seton & Partners: **Airport Architecture**
Stevenson, W.L.: **Alberta**
Stevenson, William: **Best-Sellers in English; Stephenson, William Samuel**
Stevenson Field: **Airport Architecture**
Steveston, BC: **Japanese; Richmond**
Stewart, A.T.: **Physics**
Stewart, BC: **British Columbia; Coast Mountains**
Stewart, George: **McClelland & Stewart Ltd**
Stewart, George, Jr: **Literary Magazines in English**
Stewart, Harriet Starr: **Mount Allison University**
Stewart, Helen: **Swimming, Speed**
Stewart, Mary: **Swimming, Speed**
Stewart, Reginald: **Music History**
Stewart, Ron: **Sawchuk, Terrence G.**
Stewart, Thomas Alexander: **Stewart, Frances**
Stewart, William: **Morrice, James Wilson**
Stewart & Morrison Ltd: **Logo**
Stewart River: **Mayo; Yukon River**
stibnite: **Antimony**
stick insect: **Insect Classification**
Stieb, Dave: **Toronto Blue Jays**
Stikine Plateau: **British Columbia**
Stikine Ranges: **Cassiar Mountains**
stills: **Prohibition**
stimulant: **Medical Drug Abuse; Sports Medicine**
Stine, Anne: **L'Anse aux Meadows**
Stinson, Katherine: **Postal System**
Stinson, Margaret Rose: **Interior Design**
Stirling, Bummer: **Football**
stoat: **Weasel**
Stobbe, Gordon: **Musical Theatre**
Stobie, Margaret: **Grove, Frederick Philip**
stock car racing: **Automobile Racing; Beck, Gary**
stock companies: **Theatre, English-Language**
stock-watering reserve: **Ranching History**
stocker operation: **Beef Cattle Farming**
Stockholm, Sask: **Swedes**
Stockton, D.: **Wrestling**
Stockwell, C.H.: **Shield**
Stockwell, Francis: **Anticosti, Ile d'**
Stoermer Bell Foundry: **Musical Instruments**
Stokes, A.B.: **Psychiatry**
STOL aircraft: **Technology**
Stone, Edgar: **Theatre, English-Language**
Stone, H.C.: **Bank Architecture**
Stone, Joel: **Gananoque**
Stone, Kay: **Folklore**
Stone, L.: **Urban Studies**
Stone, Paddy: **Dance History**

stone circles: **British Block Cairn & Suffield Tipi Rings; Medicine Wheels**
stone sheep: **Mount Edziza Provincial Park; Mountain Sheep**
stone tools: **Bluefish Caves; Clovis; Cree; Debert; Edmonton; Ellesmere Island Archaeological Sites; Head-Smashed-In Buffalo Jump; Thule Culture**
stonefish: **Sculpin**
Stoneman, Bill: **Montreal Expos**
Stonetown: **Station PAPA**
Stonewall, Man: **Rockwood**
stoneware: **Ceramics; Clay**
stonewort: **Algae**
Stoney Creek, Ont: **Federated Women's Institutes of Canada; Hamilton**
Stoney Creek, Sask: **Melfort**
Stoney Creek (Alta): **Camrose**
Stoney Creek (BC): **Bridges**
Stony Lake: **Kawartha Lakes**
Stony Mountain, Man: **Fossil Animals; Rockwood**
Stony Mountain Penitentiary: **Big Bear; Irvine, Acheson Gosford; Prison**
stook: **Gambling**
storage chest: **Furniture, German**
Stork Derby: **Millar, Charles Vance**
storm: **Blizzard; Disasters; Thunderstorm; Tornado**
Storm, George: **Thomas, William**
Storm, William G.: **University College**
Storm Mountain: **Vermilion Pass**
Stornoway: **House of Commons**
Storstad: **Disasters**
Story, G.M.: **Dictionary; Folklore**
Story, Norah: **Encyclopedia**
Story Theatre: **Theatre, Multicultural**
Stothart, John G.: **Animal Breeding**
Stott, Denis: **Education, Special**
Stoughton, Sask: **Curling**
Stovin Island: **Thousand Islands**
Stowe, John: **Stowe, Emily H.**
Strabane, Ont: **Stewart, Charles**
Stracey, Barbara: **Equestrian Sports**
Strachan, Mount: **West Vancouver**
Straiton, John: **Film Animation**
Straits of Mackinac (Mackinaw): **Huron, Lake; Mackinaw Boat**
Straits Salish: **Central Coast Salish**
Strakhovsky, Leonid I.: **Russians**
Strangway, David W.: **Moon**
Strasbourg, Sask: **Place-names**
Strassburg, Ont: **Place-names**
Stratégie: **Literary Periodicals in French**
Stratford, Philip: **Comparative Literature, Canadian; Translation**
Stratford, R.K.: **Petroleum Research & Development**
Stratford Beacon-Herald: **Dair, Carl**
Stratford Music Festival: **Gellman, Steven**
Strathcona, 1st Baron: **Smith, Donald A.**
Strathcona, Alta: **Edmonton**
Strathcona, Ont: **Technology**
Strathcona Cup: **Curling**
Strathcona Park Lodge: **Strathcona Provincial Park**
Strathcona Science Park: **Edmonton**
Strathcona Sound: **Inuit Art; Nanisivik**
Strathcona Trust: **Physical Education**
Strathy, George W.: **Music History**
stratigraphy: **Paleontology, History in Canada**
Stratton, Allan: **Drama in English; Theatre, English-Language**
stratus: **Cloud**
Straumfiord: **Norse Voyages**
straw: **Biomass Energy**
Straw Hat Players: **Gill, Robert; Reid, D. Kate**
strawberry: **Berries, Cultivated; Berries, Wild; Cuisine; Fruit & Vegetable Industry; Rose**
Strazhilova Choir of Toronto: **Serbs**
Streatfeild, Simon: **Purcell String Quartet**
Streetheart: **Popular Music**
streetwalking: **Prostitution**
Stretching Tree: **Native People, Religion**
Strickland, Samuel: **Autobiographical Writing in English; Exploration & Travel Literature in English; Moodie, Susanna**

strikebreaking: **Aid to (or of) the Civil Power; Policing; Strikes & Lockouts**
strip farming: **Prairie Farm Rehabilitation Administration**
strip mining: **Coal Mining; Coronach**
striped bass: **Bass; LaHave River Estuary**
stromatolites: **Superior, Lake**
Strong, Daniel: **Black Creek Pioneer Village**
Strong-Hearth, Karen: **Cycling**
strontium: **Franklin, Ursula Martius; Geological Dating**
stroud: **Fur Trade**
Struc, Roman: **Comparative Literature**
structural geography: **Adams, Frank Dawson**
structural steel: **Architecture, Development; Construction Industry, History**
Structure of Canadian Industry, Task Force on the: **Gordon, Walter L.**
Structurist: **Painting**
Struk, Danylo: **Ukrainian Writing**
Stuart, David: **Kamloops; Kelowna; Okanagan Valley; Penticton; Vernon**
Stuart, James: **Act of Union**
Stuart, John: **Okanagan Valley**
Stuart Lake: **Agriculture History; Carrier; Prince George**
Stuart River: **Nechako River**
Stuartburn, Man: **Ukrainians**
stucco: **Gypsum; Quarrying Industry; Texada Island**
Stud Horse Creek: **Fort Steele**
Student Christian Movement: **Christianity**
student employment: **Labour Policy**
Student Union for Peace Action: **New Left**
Students for a Democratic University: **New Left**
Studies in Canadian Literature: **Literary Periodicals in English; Literature in English - Theory & Criticism**
Studies in Political Economy: **Sociology**
Studio Building (Toronto): **Daly, Kathleen Frances**
Studites & Studite Nuns: **Catholicism**
Stukely, Lac: **Mount Orford Park**
Stukus, Annis: **British Columbia Lions**
stumper: **Agricultural Soil Practices**
Stumpf, Carl: **Musicology**
Sturgeon Lake (Ont): **Kawartha Lakes**
Sturgeon River (Alta): **St Albert**
Sturgeon River (Ont): **French River; Nipissing, Lake; Sturgeon Falls**
Sturgeon-weir River: **Churchill River**
subalpine fir: **Strathcona Provincial Park; Vegetation Regions - Cordillera**
Subalpine Forest: **Forest Regions**
subalpine larch: **Vegetation Regions - Cordillera**
subculture: **Hippies; Juvenile Delinquency**
Subercase, Daniel d'Auger de: **Theatre, French-Language**
submarine chaser: **Shipbuilding & Ship Repair**
submarine detection: **Boyle, Robert William**
submarines: **McBride, Richard; Ocean Industry; U-boat Landings; World War II**
subsurface rights: **Real Estate**
subversive activity: **Intelligence Gathering**
succession duties: **Equalization Payments; Taxation**
succulent: **Cactus**
Such, Peter: **Novel in English**
Sucker Creek Reserve: **Cardinal, Harold**
sucrose: **Lemieux, Raymond U.**
Sudbury Basin: **Geological Regions; Murray, Alexander; Platinum; Sudbury**
Sudbury Theatre Centre: **Sudbury; Theatre, English-Language**
Suddon, Alan: **Children's Literature in English**
Sudeten Germans: **Germans**
Suffield, CFB: **Archaeology, Salvage**
Suffield Experimental Station: **Defence Research**
Suffield gas field: **Petroleum**
suffrage: **Electoral Systems; Franchise; Women's Suffrage**

sugar beet: **Beet**
Sugar Cane Reserve: **Williams Lake**
sugar maple: **Biogeography; Furniture, French; Laurentian Highlands; Maple; Maple Sugar Industry; Plant Classification; Rondeau Provincial Park; Vegetation Regions - Atlantic Coastal; Vegetation Regions - Eastern Temperate Forests**
sugaring off: **Festivals; Maple Sugar Industry**
Sugarloaf Mountain: **Campbellton, NB; Cape North**
Sugluk, Qué: **Native People, Communications**
Suknaski, Andrew: **Ethnic Literature; Regionalism in Literature**
sulky cart: **Harness Racing**
Sullivan, Alan: **Best-Sellers in English; Children's Literature in English; *Menaud maître-draveur***
Sullivan, Francis C.: **Architecture, Development**
Sullivan, Françoise: **Automatistes; Dance History**
Sullivan, J.A. "Pat": **Internment**
Sullivan, John W.: **Palliser Expedition**
Sullivan Mine: **Kimberley; Mining; Prospecting; Zinc**
Sullivan Mountains: **Kimberley**
Sulpetro Ltd: **Banking; Petroleum Industries**
sulphate: **Karst Landform; Mineral; Spring**
sulphide: **Mineral; Spring**
Sulphide, Ont: **Technology**
sulphosalt: **Mineral**
sulphur dioxide: **Chemistry Subdisciplines; Metallurgy**
Sulphur Mountain: **Parks, National; Walker, Edmund Murton**
sulphur oxides: **Acid Rain; Pollution**
sulphuric acid: **Acid Rain; Chemistry; Metallurgy; Pesticide; Technology**
Sulpicians: **Bourgeoys, Marguerite; Bourget, Ignace; Cartography, History of; Catholicism; Charbonnel, Armand-F.-M. de; Christian Religious Communities; Dollier de Casson, François; Gallicanism; Laval, François de; Maguire, Thomas; St Clair, Lake; Timiskaming, Lake; Ville-Marie; Youville, Marie-Marguerite d'**
Sulte, Benjamin: *Histoire des Canadiens-français 1608-1880*; **Intellectual History; Literature in French - Scholarship & Teaching**
Sumas Mountain: **Clay**
summary conviction: **Criminal Procedure**
summer fallow: **Agricultural Soil Practices; Agriculture History; Crops; Drought; Mackay, Angus; Remote Sensing; Saskatchewan**
Summer Research Institute: **Mathematics**
summer savoury: **Herbs**
Summer Stakes: **Northern Dancer**
summer stock: **Prince Edward Island; Theatre, English-Language**
"summer villages": **Alberta**
Summerland, BC: **Crop Research; Research Stations, Agricultural**
Summers, Robert: **Corruption**
Summerside CFB: **Canadair CL-28 Argus; Slemon Park; Summerside**
Summerside Journal-Pioneer: **Prince Edward Island**
summons: **Civil Procedure**
Sumner, Wayne: **Philosophy**
Sun Life Assurance Co of Canada: **Insurance**
Sun Publishing Co: **Media Ownership; *Sun***
sun spider: **Invertebrate**
Suncor Inc: **Alberta; Bitumen**
Sunday Express: **Quebecor Inc**
Sunday shopping: **Lord's Day Alliance of Canada**
Sundberg, E.: **Ski Jumping**
sundew: **Carnivorous Plants**
sunfish: **Bass**
Sunim, Samu: **Buddhism**
Sunni Muslims: **Islam; South Asians**
Sunnyside Auto Body Works: **Bus Transportation**
Sunnyside (Dugald), Man: **Springfield**
Sunset Lodges: **Salvation Army**

sunshine: **Alberta; Climate Information; Okanagan Valley; Urban Effect on Climate**
"Sunshine Coast": **Sechelt Peninsula**
Sunshine Theatre Co: **Kelowna**
Sunshine Village: **Mount Assiniboine Provincial Park**
sunspot: **Northern Lights; Sun**
Sunwheat Biscuits: **Drake, Theodore George Gustavus Harwood**
Super Constellation aircraft: **Trans-Canada Airlines**
superheterodyne principle: **Fessenden, Reginald A.**
Superior Council: **Sovereign Council**
Superior Council of Education: **Collège d'enseignement général et professionnel**
Superior Courts: **Courts of Law; Film Censorship; Supreme Court of Canada; Tax Court of Canada**
Superior Highlands: **Ontario**
Superior Province: **Geological History; Geological Regions; Mineral Resources**
supernovae: **Van den Bergh, Sidney**
Superpanner: **Haultain, Herbert Edward Terrick**
superport: **Delta, BC; Nova Scotia; Shipping Industry**
supply & demand: **Energy Policy; Income Distribution**
Supreme Court Act: **Courts of Law; Judicial Committee of the Privy Council; Supreme Court of Canada**
Supreme Court of BC: **Courts of Law; Stickeen Territory**
Supreme Court of Canada building: **Architecture, Development**
Supreme Court of NB: **New Brunswick**
Supreme Court of Nfld: **Constitution, Patriation of; Courts of Law**
Supreme Court of NS: **Courts of Law; Nova Scotia**
Supreme Court of Ont: **Abortion**
Supreme Court of PEI: **Family Court; Small Claims Court**
Supreme Court of Sask: **Nursing**
Supreme Court of the NWT: **Courts of Law**
Supreme Court of the YT: **Yukon Territory**
Supreme wheat: **Wheeler, Seager**
Sures, Jack: **Ceramics, Contemporary**
surfbird: **Plover; Sandpiper**
surfgrass: **Vegetation Regions - Coastal Marine Flora**
surgery: **Archibald, Edward William; Bethune, H. Norman; Cancer; Gray, Jessie Catherine; Health Policy; Heart Disease; Hospitals; Laser; Malloch, Archibald Edward; Medicine, Contemporary; Ophthalmology; Salter, Robert Bruce; Veterinary Medicine**
Surintendant de l'instruction publique: **Intellectual History**
surrogate motherhood: **Bioethics; Medical Ethics**
surveillance: **Aid to (or of) the Civil Power; Intelligence Gathering; Law & the Press; Policing**
suspended sentence: **Criminal Law; Probation & Parole**
suspension bridge: **Bridges; Huron, Lake; Keefer, Samuel; Montmorency Falls; Québec City; Windsor, Ont**
Sussan, Walter: **Soldiers of Fortune**
Sussex, NB: **Weldon, Richard Chapman**
Susskind, Walter: **Toronto Mendelssohn Choir; Toronto Symphony**
Sutherland, Hugh: **Schultz, John Christian**
Sutherland, James T.: **International Hockey Hall of Fame**
Sutherland, Ronald: **Comparative Literature; Comparative Literature, Canadian**
Sutherland, Sask: **Saskatoon**
Sutton, Eric: *Survenant*
Sutton, William: **Sutton, Catherine**
Sutton Ridges: **Physiographic Regions - Interior Plains**
Sverdrup Basin: **Geological Regions; Geothermal Energy; Innuitian Region; Prince Patrick Island**
Svitlo: **Catholicism**
Swadesh, M.: **Thomas, Alexander**
Swaffield, Walter: **Film Animation**
Swallow: **Gilbert, Humphrey**

Swampy River: **Koksoak, Rivière**
Swan, Scott: **Festival Lennoxville**
Swan Hills: **Fossil Plants**
Swan Lake, Man: **Gaboury, Etienne-Joseph**
Swan Lake (BC): **Okanagan Valley; Swan**
Swan River, Man: **Murphy, Emily**
Swan River (Alta): **Lesser Slave Lake**
Swan River (Man): **Manitoba**
Swan River Report: **Manitoba**
Swartzman, Roslyn: **Printmaking**
Swastika, Ont: **Oakes, Harry; Ontario Northland Transportation Commission; Place-names**
swather: **Agricultural Implements Industry**
sweatshop: **Status of Women; Women in the Labour Force; Work; Wright, Alexander Whyte**
Swede turnip: **Rutabaga**
Sweeney, Robert: **Duel**
sweet almond: **Poisonous Plants**
sweet basil: **Herbs**
sweet chestnut: **Chestnut; Vegetation Regions - Eastern Temperate Forests**
sweet cicely: **Biogeography**
sweet clover: **Clover; Forage Crops**
sweet-clover poisoning: **Schofield, Francis William; Veterinary Medicine**
sweet marjoram: **Herbs**
sweet pignut hickory: **Vegetation Regions - Eastern Temperate Forests**
sweet sorghum: **Biomass Energy**
sweet William: **Phlox**
sweetgrass: **Plants, Native Uses**
Swerdlow, Elizabeth: **Musical Theatre**
Swerdlow, Robert: **Musical Theatre**
Swift, J.W.: **Folk Art**
swift fox: **Endangered Animals; Fox**
swimmer's itch: **Invertebrate; Water-Borne Disease**
swine: **Hog Farming; Veterinary Medicines Industry**
swing: **Jazz**
Swinton, George: **Art Writing & Criticism; Painting**
Swinton Park, Ont: **Hannam, Herbert H.**
Swiss chard: **Beet; Vegetable**
Swiss Germans: **Hespeler**
Switzer, K.: **Humane Societies**
swivel gun: **Firearm**
Sword Street Press: **Printmaking**
swordfish: **Cuisine; Nova Scotia**
Sxayxway mask: **Northwest Coast Indian Art**
sycamore: **Fossil Plants; Vegetation Regions - Eastern Temperate Forests**
Sydenham, Canada West: **Owen Sound**
Sydenham Glass Co: **Glass**
Sydenham River: **Dresden; Owen Sound; Wallaceburg**
Sydney Post-Record: **Nova Scotia**
syllabics: **Cree Syllabics; Print Industry**
Sylvain, Isabelle: **La Corriveau**
Sylvain, Philippe: **Intellectual History**
Sylvan Lake, Alta: **Cardinal, Douglas J.; Co-operative Movement (See Addendum, page 1992)**
Sylvan Lake Provincial Park: **Parks, Provincial**
sylvatic plague: **Flea**
Sylvester auto-thresher: **Technology**
Sylvestre, Daniel: **Children's Literature in French**
Sylvestre, Guy: **Literature in French - Criticism & Theory; Literature in French - Scholarship & Teaching; National Library of Canada**
sylvite: **Mineral**
symbiosis: **Biology; Cnidaria; Fossil Animals; Louse; Mycorrhizae**
Symington Yards: **Manitoba; St-Boniface**
Symmes Inn: **Architecture; Hotel**
Symonds, Nelson: **Guitar; Jazz**
Symons, Harry Lutz: **Essay in English**
Symons, Robert: **Diorama**
Symons, Scott: **Novel in English**
Symons Report: **Canadian Studies; Symons, Thomas H.B.**
Syms, E. Leigh: **Archaeology**
synagogue: **Judaism; Samuel, Lewis**

Syncrude Canada Ltd: **Bitumen; Clark, Karl Adolf; Imperial Oil Ltd; Megaprojects; Petroleum Research & Development**
syndicalism: **Industrial Workers of the World; Revolutionary Industrial Unionism; Working-Class History**
Syndicat des métallos: **Chartrand, Michel**
Syndicat national du cinéma: **Brault, Michel**
Synge, J.L.: **Physics**
syntax: **Language**
Syntax (Calgary International Artists' Contact Centre): **Art, Contemporary Trends**
synthetic-aperture radar: **Radar; Remote Sensing**
synthetic oil: **Bitumen; Fort McMurray; Petroleum Supply & Demand; Shell Canada Ltd**
synthetic rubber: **Chemical Industries; Petrochemical Industry; Rubber Products Industry; Sarnia**
syphilis: **Mercury; Sexually Transmitted Disease**
Syrian Orthodox Church: **Orthodox Church**
Syrians: **Arabs; Immigration**
Sysak, Juliette A.: **Juliette; Television Programming**
Sysco: **Sydney Steel Corp**
Szanto, George: **Comparative Literature**
Szatmari, John: **Ethnic Literature**
Sznycer, Bernard: **Helicopter**
Sztehlo, Zoltan: **Equestrian Sports**

T

T-D Realty Co Ltd: **Toronto-Dominion Bank**
T.W. Graham & Co: **North Vancouver**
tabac canadien: **Tobacco-Products Industry**
Tableau, Pierre-Antoine: **Exploration & Travel Literature in French**
Tabor, Nfld: **Gemstone**
Taché, Joseph-Charles: *Forestiers et voyageurs*; **Short Fiction in French;** *Soirées canadiennes*
Taché, Louis-Hippolyte: **Literature in French - Scholarship & Teaching**
Taché family: **Kamouraska**
Taconian Orogeny: **Geological Regions**
Tae Kwon Do: **Koreans**
Tafler, David: *Financial Times*
Tagish Charley: **Carcross; Klondike Gold Rush**
Tagish Lake: **Yukon River**
Tahir, M. Athar: **Ethnic Literature**
Tahltan bear dog: **Dog**
Tahltan Highlands: **Mount Edziza Provincial Park**
Tahn, Andras: **25th Street Theatre**
Tahontaenrat: **Huron**
Tahsis, BC: **Nootka Sound**
Tahsis Inlet: **Nootka Sound**
taiga: **Vegetation Regions - Boreal Forest or Taiga**
Taignoagny: **Translation**
Tail of the Grand Banks: **Fisheries Policy**
tailings: **Metallurgy**
Tait, W.D.: **Psychology**
Takahashi, Phil: **Judo**
Takashima, Shizuke: **Children's Literature in English**
Takhini Hot Springs: **Spring**
Talbot, Don: **Swimming, Speed**
Talbot, E.A.: **Exploration & Travel Literature in English**
Talbot Dispensary: **Medicine, History of**
Talbot Settlement: **Colonization Companies; Talbot, Thomas**
talc: **Mineral; Soapstone**
talik: **Permafrost**
Talio: **Bella Coola**
Talirunili, Joe: **Inuit Art**
tall Oregon grape: **Vegetation Regions - Cordillera**
Talluliyuk: **Inuit Myth & Legend**
Talmud: **Judaism; Plaut, Gunther W.**

Talonbooks: **Book Publishing, English-Language; Literary Magazines in English; Poetry in English; Small Presses; Theatre, English-Language; Theatre for Young Audiences**
Taltson River: **Great Slave Lake; Mackenzie River**
talus: **Kluane Ranges; Periglacial Landform; Rockslide**
Tamahnous: **Theatre, English-Language**
tamarack: **Larch; Laurentian Highlands**
Tamasauskas, Otis: **Printmaking**
Tamil language: **Hinduism**
Tancook Island: **Mahone Bay**
Tandy, Jessica: **Cronyn, Hume**
Tanguay, Cyprien: **Genealogy**
Tanguay, Eva: **Musical Theatre**
tank car: **Locomotives & Rolling Stock; Petroleum Exploration & Production**
tankers & supertankers: **Coastal Waters; Shipping Industry**
tanks: **Armaments; Armed Forces; World War II**
Tanner, John: **Minnedosa**
Tanner, V.A.: **Labrador**
Tanner's Crossing, Man: **Minnedosa**
tannery: **Footwear Industry; Leatherworking**
tannin: **Alder; Bearberry; Larch; Leatherworking**
Tanquary Fjord: **Ellesmere Island**
Tantalum Mining Co of Canada Ltd: **Tantalum**
Tantalus Butte: **Yukon Territory**
Tantramar River: **Tantramar Marsh**
Tanzanians: **Africans**
Taoism: **Buddhism**
tapestry: **Furniture, French; Pangnirtung; Weaving, Contemporary**
tapeworm: **Animal Agriculture; Flatworm; Perch; Pike**
Tapp, Gordie: **Television Programming**
Taqramiut Nipingat Inc: **Native People, Communications**
tar sands: **Alberta Oil Sands Technology & Research Authority; Alberta Research Council; Athabasca River; Bitumen; Clark, Karl Adolf; Fort McMurray; Mineral Resources; Petroleum; Petroleum Supply & Demand; Sulphur; University of Alberta**
Tardi, Henri: **Holman**
Tardif, Marc: **Québec Nordiques**
Tarfu Creek: **Place-names**
Tariff Board: **Automotive Industry; Courts of Law; Elliott, George Alexander; McDougall, Pamela Ann**
tarragon: **Sagebrush**
Tarrantines: **Micmac**
tartans: **Scots**
Tarxien Co Ltd: **Plastics-Processing Industry**
Taschereau, Gabriel-Elzéar: **Taschereau Legal Dynasty**
Taschereau, Henri-Elzéar: **Taschereau Legal Dynasty**
Taschereau, Henri-Thomas: **Pope, Maurice Arthur; Taschereau Legal Dynasty**
Taschereau, Jean-Thomas (1778-1832): **Taschereau, Elzéar-Alexander; Taschereau Legal Dynasty**
Taschereau, Jean-Thomas (1814-1893): **Taschereau Legal Dynasty**
Taschereau, Joseph-André: **Taschereau Legal Dynasty**
Taschereau, Robert: **Taschereau Legal Dynasty**
Taschereau, Thomas-Jacques: **Ste-Marie**
Taschereau-Fortier, M.C.A.: **Children's Literature in French**
Tascona, Tony: **Printmaking**
Tassé, Gilles: **Archaeology**
Tassé, Michel: **Popular Literature in French**
Tasu, BC: **Queen Charlotte Islands**
Tatanga Mani: **Walking Buffalo**
Tatimagana: **Alikomiak**
tatooing: **Bayefsky, Aba; Kutchin; Native People - Arctic; Native People - Plateau**
Tatshenshini River: **Kluane Ranges**
Tattanoeuck: **Augustus**

tattler: **Sandpiper**
TAUM project: **Artificial Intelligence**
Tavernier, Albert: **Theatre, English-Language**
Tax Act: **Housing & Housing Policy**
Tax Appeal Board: **Tax Court of Canada**
tax concessions: **Housing & Housing Policy; Labour Policy; Magazines; Public Finance**
tax credits: **Municipal Finance; Party Financing**
tax deductions: **Taxation**
tax evasion: **Underground Economy; White-Collar Crime**
tax exemptions: **Biomass Energy; Credit Unions; Municipal Finance; Native People, Law; Taxation**
tax fraud: **Intelligence Gathering**
tax reform: **Artists' Organizations; Gosling, William Gilbert; White Paper**
Tax Rental Agreement: **Welfare State**
Tax Review Board: **Justice, Dept of; Tax Court of Canada**
taxi: **Regulatory Process; Transportation**
taxidermy: **Brooks, Allan Cyril; Dionne, Charles-Eusèbe**
taxonomy: **Biogeography; Biology; Botany; Entomology; Paleontology; Parasitology**
Tay River: **Perth**
Taylor, A.: **Logan, Mount**
Taylor, Art: **Long-Distance Running**
Taylor, BC: **Fort St John**
Taylor, F.B.: **Geomorphology**
Taylor, Henry Seth: **Automotive Industry**
Taylor, McDougald & Co Ltd: **McDougald, John Angus**
Taylor, Malcolm: **Public Administration**
Taylor, N.J.: **Saskatchewan Roughriders**
Taylor, Richard: **Humane Societies**
Taylor, S. Allan: **Stamp Collecting**
Taylor, William E., Jr: **Archaeology**
Taylor-Corbett, Lynne: **Ballets Jazz de Montréal**
Taylor Field: **Saskatchewan Roughriders**
Tazewell, Samuel O.: **Printmaking**
Teachers' College (NB): **University of New Brunswick**
Team Canada: **Canada-Soviet Hockey Series, 1972**
Techman Engineering: **Mannix, Frederick C.**
Technical & Vocational Training Act: **Education, Technical; Labour Policy**
Technical Education, Royal Commission on: **Robertson, James Wilson**
Technical Education Act: **Education, Technical**
Technical Service Council: **Haultain, Herbert Edward Terrick**
Teck Corp: **Coal; Ontario Northland Transportation Commission**
Tecumseh, Ont: **Windsor, Ont**
Tecumseh Cup: **Snowshoeing**
Tecumseh Press Ltd: **Small Presses**
Teeling, William: **Exploration & Travel Literature in English**
Tegler Building: **Architecture, Development**
Télé-métropole Inc: **Media Ownership**
Télé-université: **Distance Learning; Université du Québec**
Telecable Videotron Ltée: **Cable Television; Media Ownership**
Telecom Canada: **Satellite Communications; Telecommunications**
Teleglobe Canada: **Communications, Dept of; Postal System**
Telegram Corp Ltd: **Baton Broadcasting Inc**
Telegraph Creek, BC: **Stikine River; Tahltan**
Teleguide: **Torstar Corp**
telephone equipment: **Computer Systems Applications; Electronics Industry; Industrial Research & Development; Technology; Telidon**
Telephone Systems, Special Committee on: **Dagger, Francis; Mulock, William; Sise, Charles Fleetford**

Telesat Canada: **Communications, Dept of; Communications in the North; Ouimet, J.-Alphonse**
telescope: **Astronomy; Chant, Clarence Augustus; Molecules in Interstellar Space; National Museum of Science & Technology; Observatory; Spectroscopy**
television sets: **Consumer Standards; Electronics Industry**
Telgmann, Oscar F.: **Drama in English; Music History**
Temagami, Lake: **Temagami**
Témiscamingue, Lac: **Boundaries; Témiscaming; Timiskaming, Lake; Ville-Marie**
Témiscouata portage: **Rivière-du-Loup**
Témiscouata Railway: **Rivière-du-Loup**
Témiscouata Valley: **Rivière-du-Loup**
Temiskaming & Northern Ontario Railway: **Cobalt, Ont; Cochrane, Ont; Englehart, Jacob Lewis; New Liskeard; Ontario Northland Transportation Commission; South Porcupine; Temagami**
Temiskaming Colonization Railroad: **Timiskaming, Lake**
tempeh: **Mold**
Temperance Act (Ont): **Drury, Ernest Charles**
Temperance & Moral Reform, Dept of: **Chown, Samuel Dwight**
temperature: **Climate Information; Cloud; Urban Effect on Climate; Weather Forecasting; Weights & Measures**
temperature inversion: **Air Pollution; Fog**
Templar Channel: *Tonquin*
Temple, Mount: **Mountaineering**
Temple Building: **Architecture, Development**
Templeton, Qué: **Gatineau**
Temporary Government Act: **North-West Territories Act**
Ten Centuries Concert: **Mather, Bruce**
Ten Days for World Development: **Ecumenical Social Action**
tenant: **Land Question, PEI; Landlord & Tenant Law**
tenement: **House**
Tener, G.: **Molecular Biology**
teratology: **Fraser, F. Clarke; Pharmaceuticals Industry**
terephthalate: **Plastics-Processing Industry**
Tereszczenko, Jan: **Long-Distance Running**
Terminal City Dance Research: **Dance, Modern; Dance History**
tern schooner: **Shipbuilding & Ship Repair**
Terra Nova River: **Newfoundland**
Terra Transport: **Bus Transportation**
Terrasse, Jean: **Essay in French**
Terrasses de la Chaudière: **Hull**
terrazzo: **Architecture, Development; Quarrying Industry**
Terre de chez Nous: **Filion, Gérard**
Terrebonne, Qué: **Agricultural Implements**
Territorial Court of the YT: **Courts of Law**
Territorial Grain Growers' Assn: **Grain Growers' Associations; Motherwell, William R.**
Territorial Library: **Northwest Territories**
Territorial Library & Archives: **Yukon Territory**
Terroir: **Literary Periodicals in French; Poetry in French; Potvin, Damase**
Terror: **Franklin, John; McClure (M'Clure), Robert J. Le M.**
Terror Colt: **Thoroughbred Racing**
Terry Fox: **Shipbuilding & Ship Repair**
Terry Fox Fund: **Medicine, Contemporary**
Tertiary period: **Biogeography; Cypress Hills; Foothills; Gemstone; Paleontology, History in Canada; Prince Patrick Island; River Landform; Sverdrup Islands**
Teshima, Ted: **Moriyama, Raymond**
Teslin, YT: **Yukon Territory**
Teslin Lake: **Yukon River**
Teslin River: **Yukon River**
Tessier, Albert: **Film; Film, Documentary**

Test Oath: **Constitutional History; Province of Quebec, 1763-91; Quebec Act**
Teswahno: **George, Dan**
tetanus: **Animal Agriculture; Biological Product; Connaught Laboratories Ltd**
Tête-de-Boule: **Attikamek**
Tête Jaune: **O'Hagan, Howard; Yellowhead Pass**
Têtes de pioche: **Brossard, Nicole; Literary Periodicals in French**
Tetlichi, John: **Fort McPherson**
Tetragona, Mount: **Torngat Mountains**
tetralogy of Fallot: **Heart Disease**
Tétreau, Jean: **Popular Literature in French**
Tétreault, Pierre Léon: **Printmaking**
Teulon, Man: **Rockwood; Swedes**
Teviskes Ziburai (Lights of the Homeland): **Lithuanians**
Texas fever: **Veterinary Medicine**
textbooks: **Authors & Their Milieu; Book Publishing, English-Language; Book Publishing, French-Language; Canada Studies Foundation; Commercial Law; Curriculum Development; Dickie, Donalda J.; Education Policy; Environment; Pierce, Lorne A.; Psychiatry; Science & Society; Women & Education; Women's International League for Peace & Freedom**
Textile Labelling Act: **Consumer Law**
Thames River: **Chatham, Ont; Disasters; Ingersoll; London; Loyalists; Moraviantown; Oneida; Ontario; St Clair, Lake; Woodstock, Ont**
Thamesville, Ont: **Zeisberger, David**
Thanadelther (Slave Woman): **Chipewyan**
Thatcher wheat: **Agricultural Research & Development; Wheat**
Thauberger, David: **Painting**
Thavenet, Marguerite de: **Hertel de La Fresnière, Joseph-François**
Thayendanegea: **Brant, Joseph**
The Bend, NB: **Moncton**
The Ferry, Upper Canada: **Windsor, Ont**
The Forty, Upper Canada: **Grimsby**
The Hawk, NS: **Cape Sable Island**
The Investors Group: **Power Corp of Canada**
The Outlet: **Magog**
The Prophet: **Tecumseh**
The Rapids, Upper Canada: **Sarnia**
The Royal George: **Sculpture**
The Swan: **Blackfoot**
The Twelve, Upper Canada: **St Catharines**
The Valhallas Provincial Park: **New Denver; Slocan**
Theatre 3: **Theatre, English-Language**
Theatre 77: **Hendry, Thomas B.; Hirsch, John S.; Manitoba Theatre Centre; Pinsent, Gordon E.**
Théâtre à l'ouvrage: **Drama in French**
Théâtre Antonin-Artaud: **Germain, Jean-Claude**
Theatre Aquarius: **Hamilton**
Theatre Calgary: **Theatre, English-Language; Theatre for Young Audiences**
Theatre Canada: **Little Theatre Movement; Theatre, English-Language**
Théâtre carrousel: **Drama in French**
Théâtre-Club: **Drama in French**
Théâtre d'aujourd'hui: **Drama in French**
Théâtre de carton: **Theatre for Young Audiences**
Théâtre de cuisines: **Drama in French**
Théâtre de la Place Ville-Marie: **Drama in French; Tremblay, Michel**
Théâtre de la société: **Drama in French; Music History**
Théâtre de l'ermitage: **Automatistes; Borduas, Paul-Emile**
Théâtre de l'eskable: **Theatre, French-Language**
Théâtre de l'île: **Hull**
Théâtre de l'oeil: **Theatre for Young Audiences**
Théâtre de Montréal: **Germain, Jean-Claude**
Théâtre de quartier: **Drama in French**

Théâtre de quat'sous: **Deschamps, Yvon; Drama in French**
Théâtre d'environnement intégral: **Drama in French**
Théâtre des compagnons: **Théâtre du rideau vert**
Théâtre des confettis: **Theatre for Young Audiences**
Théâtre des pissenlits: **Theatre for Young Audiences**
theatre design: **Lebensold, Fred David**
Théâtre d'essai: **Roux, Jean-Louis**
Théâtre du gesù: **Drama in French**
Théâtre du Lazarre: **Deyglun, Henri**
Théâtre du même nom: **Germain, Jean-Claude; Theatre, French-Language**
Théâtre du nouvel-Ontario: **Sudbury**
Théâtre du p'tit bonheur: **Theatre, French-Language**
Théâtre du sang neuf: **Drama in French**
Théâtre euh!: **Drama in French**
Théâtre expérimental de Montréal: **Drama in French**
Théâtre expérimental des femmes: **Theatre, French-Language**
Theatre Five: **Theatre for Young Audiences**
Theatre History in Canada: **Literary Periodicals in English; Theatre, English-Language**
Theatre Hour: **Theatre for Young Audiences**
Theatre in the Dell: **Musical Theatre**
Théâtre les gens d'en bas: **Theatre, French-Language**
Theatre London: **Grand Theatre; Hutt, William**
Théâtre lyrique de Nouvelle-France: **Opera**
Théâtre lyrique du Québec: **Opera**
Theatre New Brunswick: **New Brunswick; Theatre for Young Audiences**
Theatre Newfoundland & Labrador: **Theatre, English-Language**
Theatre of Action: **Little Theatre Movement**
Théâtre parminou: **Drama in French; Theatre, French-Language**
Theatre Passe Muraille: **Blyth Festival; Drama in English; Ondaatje, Michael; Theatre, English-Language; Thompson, Paul; Wiebe, Rudy H.**
Théâtre petit à petit: **Drama in French**
Theatre Plus: **Theatre, English-Language**
Théâtre populaire du Québec: **Theatre, French-Language**
Théâtre soleil: **Theatre for Young Audiences**
Théâtre Stella: **Deyglun, Henri**
Theatre Under the Stars: **Theatre, English-Language**
Théâtre universitaire canadien: **Deschamps, Yvon**
Theatres & Amusement Act (NS): *McNeil Case*
Theau, Jean: **Philosophy**
theft: **Computer Communications; Computers & Society; Inquiry into Certain Activities of the RCMP, Royal Commission of; Juvenile Delinquency; Medical Drug Abuse; Robbery**
Theismann, Joe: **Toronto Argonauts**
Thelon Basin: **Geological Regions**
Thelon Game Sanctuary: **Thelon River**
Thelon Plain: **Drumlin**
theocracy: **Lower Canada**
theodolite: **Surveying**
Theodore, Sask: **Railway Station**
theology: **Burwash, Nathanael; Philosophy; Religion; Women's Studies**
theorem: **Mathematics**
Théorêt, France: **Novel in French; Poetry in French**
theoretical chemistry: **Chemistry Subdisciplines**
theory of computation: **Computer Science**
theory of relativity: **Astronomy; Black Hole**
Theratron machine: **Lewis, Wilfrid Bennett**
Thérien, J.A.: **Literary Prizes in French**

Thério, Adrien: **Literature in French - Scholarship & Teaching**
thermal energy: **Electric-Power Generation; Hydroelectricity**
"thermal oasis": **Ellesmere Island**
thermodynamics: **Chemistry Subdisciplines; Climatology; Meteorology; Physics; Weather Forecasting**
thermokarst: **Permafrost**
Therrien Committee: **Pay Television**
Thesen, Sharon: **Humorous Writing in English; Poetry in English**
Thessalon, Ont: **Buck, Gary; Woodward, Charles**
Thetis Island: **Gulf Islands**
Theytus Books: **Small Presses**
thiamine: **Tomato**
Thibaudeau, Colleen: **Reaney, James C.**
Thibault, Jean-Baptiste: **Lac Ste Anne; Riel, Louis**
Thibert, Patrick: **Sculpture**
thick-billed murre: **Baffin Island; Murre**
thimbleberry: **Berries, Wild; Vegetation Regions - Pacific Coastal**
thinleaf (mountain) alder: **Alder; Vegetation Regions - Cordillera**
Third Crossing (of the Whitemud): **Gladstone**
Thirsk, Robert: **Astronaut**
Thirty Acres: Trente Arpents
Thirty Thousand Islands: **Georgian Bay; Island; Parry Sound**
Thistle, Loretta: **Music Criticism**
Thistle Club: **Curling**
Thistledown Press Ltd: **Poetry in English; Small Presses**
Thlewiaza River: **Nueltin Lake**
Thom Bay, NWT: **Boothia Peninsula**
Thomas, C.P.: **Architectural Styles; Thomas, William Tutin**
Thomas, Clara: *Backwoods of Canada*
Thomas, Lillian: **Drama in English; Women's Suffrage**
Thomas, Morley K.: **Hare, Frederick Kenneth**
Thomas, Philip J.: **Folk Music, Anglo-Canadian; Musicology**
Thomas automobile: **Automotive Industry**
Thomas Davidson Manufacturing Co: **Toys & Games**
Thomas Equipment Ltd: **McCain, H. Harrison**
Thomas House: **Oakville**
Thomas Killam & Co: **Killam, Thomas**
Thomas Nelson & Sons Ltd: **Book Publishing, English-Language**
Thomism: **Fairweather, Eugene Rathbone; Lachance, Louis; Paquet, Louis-Adolphe; Philosophy; Psychology; Régis, Louis-Marie**
Thompson, BC: **Rossland**
Thompson, Charles J.: **Thompson, Berwick, Pratt & Partners**
Thompson, D.: **Botany History**
Thompson, Don: **Bickert, Edward Isaac; Jazz**
Thompson, E.P.: **Social History**
Thompson, Earl: **Olympic Games**
Thompson, Homer A.: **Mediterranean Archaeology**
Thompson, J. Antonio: **Musicology**
Thompson, J.W.: **Bush Flying**
Thompson, James Scott: **Thompson, Margaret Anne Wilson**
Thompson, John: **Poetry in English**
Thompson, John F.: **Thompson**
Thompson, Judith: **Drama in English; Tarragon Theatre; Theatre, English-Language**
Thompson, Kent: **Short Fiction in English**
Thompson, Ross: **Rossland**
Thompson Citizen: **Manitoba**
Thompson (Indians): **Bearberry; Indian Art; Salish, Interior; Teit, James A.**
Thompson Plateau: **Cascade Mountains**
Thomsen River: **Banks Island**
Thomson, Charles W.: *Challenger* **Expedition**
Thomson, D.L.: **Estrogen**
Thomson, David F.: **Printmaking**
Thomson, Hugh C.: **Book Publishing, English-Language**
Thomson, McKinnon: **Bickell, John Paris**

Thomson, William J.: **Printmaking**
Thoreau, Henry David: **Exploration & Travel Literature in English**
Thorfinnr Thordarson: **Karlsefni**
thorite: **Mineral**
thorium: **Mineral; Nuclear Energy; Nuclear Power Plants; Nuclear Research Establishments**
Thorn, Jonathan: *Tonquin*
thornapple: **Nightshade**
Thorneloe University: **Laurentian University**
Thornhill, Ont: **Baha'i Faith**
Thornton, John: **Cartography, History of**
Thornton, Peter: **Architectural Styles; Architecture, Development**
Thorpe, Robert: **Gore, Francis; Upper Canada**
Thorsteinsson, Thorsteinn: **Ethnic Literature**
Thorvaldr Ericsson: **Norse Voyages**
Thorvaldson Lake: **Thorvaldson, Thorbergur**
Thrasher, Anthony Apakark: **Ethnic Literature**
Three Forks, BC: **New Denver**
Three Pence Beaver: **Postage Stamps**
Three Persons, Tom: **Calgary Stampede**
Three Rivers Dam: **Oldman River**
Three Sisters: **Piracy**
Three Suns: **Blackfoot**
three-toed woodpecker: **Barachois Pond Provincial Park; Woodpecker**
Three's A Crowd: **Cockburn, Bruce**
threshing machine: **Agricultural Implements; Agricultural Implements Industry; Agriculture History**
Throat Singing: **Native People - Arctic**
Thrust: **Evangelical Fellowship of Canada**
Thule Archaeology Conservation Project: **Archaeology, Salvage**
Thunder Bay Thunderbolts: **Swimming, Speed**
Thunder Cape: **Thunder Bay**
Thunder Creek: **Moose Jaw**
Thurso, Qué: **Place-names**
Thwaites, Reuben Gold: *Jesuit Relations; Mémoires de l'Amérique septentrionale*
thyme: **Herbs**
thyroid disease: **Medicine, Contemporary**
Ti-Jean: **Folklore**
Tibo (Gilles Tibault): **Children's Literature in French**
tidal wave: **Disasters; Lighthouses**
tide tables: **Dawson, William B.; Hydrography**
Tidler, Charles: **Drama in English; Theatre, English-Language**
Tidnish Bridge, NB: **Tidnish**
Tier Building: **Stoughton, Arthur Alexander**
tiercel: **Peregrine Falcon**
Tiffany, Silvester: **Almanacs**
Tignish, PEI: **Prince Edward Island**
Tigrinya language: **Africans**
Tihanyi, Jeno: **Baumann, Alex**
Tiktaliktak: **Inuit Myth & Legend**
Tilbury Island: **Delta, BC**
tile: **Architecture, Development; Clay; Medicine Hat; St Lawrence Lowland; Silica**
Tilford Gardens: **North Vancouver**
till: **Banks Island; Cape Spear; Drumlin; Glaciation; Island; Moraine; St Lawrence Lowland; Surrey**
Tillenius, Clarence: **Diorama**
Tillicum Theatre: **Theatre, Multicultural**
Tilston, Man: **Manitoba**
Tilt Cove: **Bennett, Charles James Fox**
timber: **Architecture, Development; Bridges; Grain Elevators; Norse Voyages**
timber rattlesnake: **Endangered Animals; Rattlesnake**
timber wolf: **Animal; Kluane Ranges**
timberline: **Mackenzie Mountains; Treeline**
Time (Canada): **Committee for an Independent Canada; Gaudard, Pierre; Magazines**
Time Air Ltd: **Alberta**

"Time-Reader's Digest Act": **Publications, Royal Commission on**
time scale: **Geological History**
time zones: **Fleming, Sandford; Time**
Timmins, Henry: **Timmins, Noah A.**
Timmis, R.S.: **Equestrian Sports**
timothy grass: **Forage Crops**
tin: **Kimberley; Pewter; Wyn Wood, Elizabeth**
Tin Flute: Bonheur d'occasion
Tindastoll, North-West Territories: **Markerville**
Tinning, Campbell: **Ogilvie, Will**
tinsmithing: **Art Education**
Tintamarre National Wildlife Reserve: **Tantramar Marsh**
Tintin: **Popular Literature in French**
"Tiny Perfect Mayor": **Crombie, David**
Tip Top Tailors: **Clothing Industries**
Tipperary Creek: **Saskatoon**
TIPS: **Criminal Investigation**
Tirol, Marcel: **Literary Bibliography in French**
TIROS satellites: **Remote Sensing**
Tish: **Bowering, George; Literary Magazines in English; Poetry in English**
Tisseyre, Pierre: **Book Publishing, French-Language**
title: **Commercial Law**
titmouse: **Chickadee**
Tlingit: **Chilkat Blanket; Malaspina Expedition; Raven Symbolism; Stikine River; Tagish; Tutchone**
Tlupana Inlet: **Nootka Sound**
Toad Mountain: **Nelson**
toadstool: **Mushroom & Puffball**
Tobacco Enquiry Committee: **Archibald, Edgar Spinney**
Tobacco Indians: **Petun**
Tobacco Plains Reserve: **Kootenay**
Tobermory, Ont: **Bruce Peninsula; Bruce Trail; Escarpment; Ferries; Georgian Bay; Wildlife Preserve**
Tobin Lake: **Saskatchewan River**
Tobique Reserve: **Maliseet**
Tobique River: **Saint John River**
tobogganing: **Bobsledding**
Tod, John: **Oak Bay**
Tod House: **Oak Bay**
Tod Inlet: **Butchart, Robert Pim**
Todd, Frederick: **Landscape Architecture**
Todd, Isaac: **North West Company**
Todd, J.L.: **Parasitology**
Todd, W.E.C.: **Belcher Islands**
Toews, Clint: **German Writing**
Toews, Gerhard: **German Writing**
tofu: **Mold**
tokens: **Coinage; Montreal & Lachine Railroad**
Tokumm Creek: **Vermilion River**
Tokyo Round of trade talks: **International Trade**
Tolfrey, F.: **Exploration & Travel Literature in English**
toll levying: **Roads & Highways; Timber Slide**
Tolmie, Mount: **Medicine, History of**
toluene: **Chemical Industries; Chemistry**
Tom Longboat Award: **Morris, Alwyn**
Tom Thompson Memorial Gallery: **Owen Sound**
Tomcik, Andy: **Graphic Design**
Tomkins, George S.: **Canada Studies Foundation**
Tonge, Griselda: **Cottnam, Deborah**
Tonge, William Cottnam: **Nova Scotia**
Tonnancour manor: **Trois-Rivières**
Tonty, Lorenzo de: **Tonty, Henri de**
Toodoggone River: **Cassiar Mountains**
Tookoome, Simon: **Inuit Art**
tooth shell: **Mollusc; Tahltan**
toothwort: **Wildflowers**
topaz: **Mineral**
topographic maps: **Cartography, History of; Remote Sensing**
topology: **Mathematics**
Toppings, Glenn: **Art, Contemporary Trends**
Topsail, Nfld: **Conception Bay South**
Toquat: **Nootka**
toque: **Clothing; La Tuque**
tor: **Periglacial Landform**
Tor Bay: **Basques**
Torah: **Judaism; Plaut, Gunther W.**
Torbett, Charles W.: **Printmaking**
Tordom Corp International: **Toronto-Dominion Bank**
Torngarsuak Mountain: **Torngat Mountains**

Torok, Alan: **Guitar**
Toronto: **Locomotives & Rolling Stock; Northern Railway of Canada**
Toronto, Grey & Bruce Railway: **Railway History**
Toronto, Hamilton & Buffalo Railway: **Hamilton**
Toronto, Hamilton & Niagara Electro-Magnetic Telegraph Co: **Telegraph**
Toronto Allied Printing Trades Council: **Print Industry**
Toronto Amateur Photographic Assn: **Photography**
Toronto & District Trades & Labor Council: **Simpson, James**
Toronto and Georgian Bay Ship Canal: **Tully, Kivas**
Toronto & Nipissing Railway: **Railway History**
Toronto Arenas: **National Hockey League**
Toronto Art Students' League: **Drawing; Manly, Charles MacDonald; Printmaking**
Toronto Arts Productions: **Hirsch, John S.**
Toronto Astronomical Club: **Astronomy; Science**
Toronto Asylum: **Lett, Stephen**
Toronto Balmy Beach: **Ottawa Rough Riders**
Toronto Baptist College: **Baptists; McMaster, William; McMaster University**
Toronto Bay: **Hanlan, Edward**
Toronto Blizzard: **Croatians; Soccer**
Toronto Board of Control: **Urban Reform**
Toronto Board of Trade: **Associations; Berkinshaw, Richard Coulton; Chamber of Commerce**
Toronto Buddhist Federation: **Buddhism**
Toronto Bureau of Municipal Research: **Wickett, Samuel Morley**
Toronto Camera Club: **Artists' Organizations; Photography**
Toronto Canoe Club: **Canoeing**
Toronto Central Y' Estonians: **Volleyball**
Toronto Central YMCA: **Goulding, George Henry**
Toronto Children's Players: **Earle, David**
Toronto City Hall (1890): **Architectural Styles; Architecture, Development**
Toronto City Hall (1899): **Reid, George A.; Toronto**
Toronto Coliseum: **Equestrian Sports**
Toronto Conservatory of Music: **MacMillan, Ernest C.; Parlow, Kathleen; Pentland, Barbara L.; Royal Conservatory of Music of Toronto; Smith, J. Leopold; Vogt, A.S.; Waddington, Geoffrey; Walter, Arnold Maria; Weinzweig, John J.; Willan, J. Healey**
Toronto Conservatory of Music Choir: **Toronto Mendelssohn Choir**
(Toronto) Conservatory String Quartet: **Chamber Music**
Toronto Conservatory Symphony Orchestra: **Toronto Symphony**
Toronto Convention Centre Complex: **Canadian National Railways**
Toronto Daily News: **Newspapers**
Toronto Daily Star: **Hewitt, Foster**
Toronto-Dominion Centre: **Architecture, Development; Bank Architecture; Bregman & Hamann; Fafard, Joseph; Parkin, John B.**
Toronto Empire: Globe & Mail; **Newspapers**
Toronto Examiner: **Hincks, Francis**
Toronto Festival of Storytelling: **Folk Festivals**
Toronto Field Naturalists' Club: **Baillie, James L.**
Toronto Flying Club: **Curtis, Wilfred Austin**
Toronto Free Theatre: **Hendry, Thomas B.**

Toronto General Hospital: **Botterell, Edmund Harry; Clarke, Charles Kirk; Cox, George A.; Flavelle, Joseph W.; Gray, Jessie Catherine; Hospitals; McKenzie, Kenneth George; Medicine, History of; Nursing; Wyle, Florence**

Toronto General Trust Building: **Miller, George Martell**

Toronto Globe: **Bengough, John W.; Brown, George; Campbell, W. Wilfred; Cycling; Davin, Nicholas Flood; Duncan, Sara Jeanette; Essay in English;** *Globe & Mail;* **Harris, Robert; Journalism; Lampman, Archibald; Literature in English; Macdonald, John A.; Newspapers; Print Industry; Province of Canada; Scott, Duncan Campbell; Willison, John S.**

Toronto Granite Club: **Olympic Games**

Toronto Guild of Civic Art: **Public Art**

Toronto harbour: **Disasters; Toronto; Toronto Islands**

Toronto Hilton: **Hotel**

Toronto Historical Board: **Heritage Conservation**

Toronto Hydro: **Gardiner, Frederick Goldwin**

Toronto Incandescent Light Co: **Nicholls, Frederic**

Toronto Independent Dance Enterprise: **Dance History**

Toronto Indian Friendship Centre: **Currie, Walter**

Toronto Industrial Exhibition: **Canadian National Exhibition; Medal; Urban Transportation**

Toronto International Airport: **Airport; Airport Architecture; Archaeology, Salvage; Archambault, Louis; Disasters; Noise; Toronto**

Toronto International Festival: **Opera**

Toronto International Film Studios: **Kleinburg**

Toronto Life: **Magazines**

Toronto Light Binder: **Massey-Ferguson Ltd**

Toronto Lithographing Co: **Graphic Design**

Toronto Magnetic Observatory: **Astronomy**

Toronto Mail: **Armstrong, John; Davin, Nicholas Flood;** *Globe & Mail;* **Journalism; Newspapers**

Toronto Mail & Empire: **Canadian Women's Press Club;** *Globe & Mail;* **Hopkins, John Castell; Journalism; Newspapers**

Toronto Mercantile League: **Fear, Alfred Henry**

Toronto Meteorological Observatory: **Carpmael, Charles; Denison, Francis Napier; Indian Summer; Kingston, George Templeman**

Toronto Metros-Croatia: **Croatians; Soccer**

Toronto News: **Journalism; Newspapers; Thompson, Thomas Phillips; Willison, John S.**

Toronto Normal School: **Armstrong, William; Art Education; Hind, Henry Y.; Hughes, James Laughlin; Physical Education; Ryerson Polytechnical Institute**

Toronto Olympic Club: **Hoffman, Abigail; Long-Distance Running**

Toronto Opera Festival: **Stratas, Teresa**

Toronto Ornithological club: **Baillie, James L.**

Toronto Palliative Care Working Group: **Death & Dying**

Toronto Parkdale Canoe Club: **Football**

Toronto Passage: **Georgian Bay; Toronto**

Toronto Philharmonic Soc: **Clarke, James P.; Music History**

Toronto Post Office: **Architectural Styles**

Toronto Public Library: **Libraries; Popular Literature in English; Red Cross Society; Robertson, John Ross; Samuel, Lewis**

Toronto Reaper & Mower Co: **Agricultural Implements; Massey, Hart A.**

Toronto Research Group: **Nichol, bp**

Toronto St Pats: **Hockey, Ice; Smythe, Constantine Falkland Cary; Toronto Maple Leafs**

Toronto Savings & Loan Co: **Wood, Edward Rogers**

Toronto Savings Bank: **Charbonnel, Armand-F.-M. de; O'Keefe, Eugene**

Toronto School of Medicine: **Aikins, William Thomas; Bovell, James**

Toronto School of Theology: **University of Toronto**

Toronto Senior Argonauts: **Lou Marsh Trophy**

Toronto Skating Club: **Dance History**

Toronto Soc of Artists: **Howard, John George**

Toronto South Asian Review: **Ethnic Literature**

Toronto Star Weekly: *Star Weekly*

Toronto Stock Exchange: **Comfort, Charles F.; Graham, Howard Douglas; Hime, Humphrey Lloyd; Ontario; Stock & Bond Markets**

Toronto Street Railway: **Mackenzie, William**

Toronto String Quartette Club: **Chamber Music**

Toronto Studio Club: **Photography**

Toronto subway: **Tunnels**

Toronto Sun: **Maclean Hunter Ltd; Newspapers; Official Secrets Act**

Toronto Sunday World: **Denison, Flora MacDonald**

Toronto Telegram: **Baillie, James L.; Newspapers; Pidgeon, George Campbell; Robertson, John Ross**

Toronto Tip Tops: **Sports History**

Toronto Toros: **Mahovlich, Francis W.**

Toronto Trades & Labor Council: **Armstrong, John; O'Donoghue, Daniel J.**

Toronto Trades Assembly: **Hewitt, John; Union Centrals, District & Regional**

Toronto Transportation Commission: **Urban Transportation**

Toronto Truck: **Theatre, English-Language**

Toronto Type Foundry: **Print Industry**

Toronto Typographical Union: **Print Industry**

Toronto Western Hospital: **Stowe-Gullen, A. Augusta**

Toronto Women's Literary Club: **Stowe, Emily H.; Women's Suffrage**

Toronto Workshop Productions: **Luscombe, George; Theatre, English-Language**

torpedo carriers: **Military Aviation & Aircraft**

Torrens system: **Property Law**

Torrey, John: **Floras & Botanical Journals**

Torrington, Frederick Herbert: **Music History**

Totem Marina (Shuswap Lake): **Hunt, Henry**

Touchwood, Alta: **Métis Settlements**

Tougas, Gérard: **Literature in French - Scholarship & Teaching**

Tough, George: **Kirkland Lake**

Tough, Thomas B.: **Kirkland Lake**

Toulinguet, Marie: **Music History**

Toumine, Nesta: **Moroni, David Lee**

Toupin, Fernand: **Plasticiens**

Touraine, Qué: **Gatineau**

Touram Inc: **Air Canada**

Tovell, Rosemarie: **Art Writing & Criticism**

Tovell, Vincent: **Music Broadcasting**

Tower Mortgage Ltd: **Trust Company**

towhee: **Sparrow**

Town & Rural Planning Act (Alta): **Urban & Regional Planning**

town gas: **Coal Gasification**

town house: **House**

town planning: **Guelph; Spence-Sales, Harold; Urban & Regional Planning; Vancouver**

Town Planning Institute of Canada: **Adams, Thomas; Cauchon, J.-E.-Noulan**

Town Plot, Upper Canada: **Woodstock, Ont**

Town Tavern: **Jazz**

Town Trust Commission: **Peterborough**

Towns & Cities Act (Qué): **Québec**

Townsend, Cathy: **Bowling, Indoor**

Townsend, Graham: **Country & Western Music; Messer, Don, & the Islanders**

Townsendia daisy: **Endangered Plants**

Townshend, George: **Cartoons**

toxicology: **Biology; Pesticide; Pharmaceuticals Industry**

toxoids: **Biological Product; Connaught Laboratories Ltd**

Toy Soldier Novelty Co: **Toys & Games**

Toye, William: **Children's Literature in English; Literature in English - Theory & Criticism; Popular Literature in English;** *Tamarack Review*

tractor: **Agricultural Implements; Agricultural Implements Industry; Agriculture History; Massey-Ferguson Ltd**

Tracy, Marquis de: **New France; Swiss**

Tracy, Qué: **Iron & Steel Industry**

Trade & Commerce, Dept of: **Agricultural Aid; Sharp, Mitchell W.; Warren, Jack Hamilton**

Trade Practices Act (BC): **Retail Trade**

trade unions: **Advertising; Aerospace Industry; AFL-CIO; Arvida Strike; Canadian Federation of Labour; Cape Breton Strikes, 1920s; Chemical Industries; Class & Politics; Clothing Industries; Collective Bargaining; Communist Party of Canada; Company Town; Conspiracy; Construction Industry; Co-operative Movement (See Addendum, page 1992); Corporatism; Electoral Behaviour; English; Fisheries History; Industrial Relations; Knights of Labor; Labour Law; Labour Market; Labour Organizations; Labour Relations; Machinery & Equipment Industry; Montréal; Murdochville Strike; Newfoundland Loggers' Strike; Newspapers; Nine-Hour Movement; Oil, Chemical & Atomic Workers International Union v Imperial Oil Ltd et al; One Big Union; Oshawa Strike; Party Financing; Print Industry; Public-Service Unions; Revolutionary Industrial Unionism; Saskatchewan; Social Security; Songs & Songwriting; Strikes & Lockouts; Union Centrals, National; Women in the Labour Force; Workers' Compensation; Working-Class History**

trade unions, Catholic: **André, Brother; Confederation of National Trade Unions; Québec Shoe Workers' Strike; Union Centrals, National**

trade unions, Christian: **Calvinism; Construction Industry**

Trade Unions Act: **Strikes & Lockouts; Working-Class History**

Trade Unions Act (NS): **Cape Breton Strikes, 1920s**

Trades & Labour Councils: **Union Centrals, District & Regional**

Trades Journal: **Drummond, Robert; Union Centrals, District & Regional**

Trading River: **Attawapiskat River**

traffic accidents: **Alcoholism; Delict; Disasters; Injury & Prevention**

traffic control: **Computer Systems Applications; Policing**

traffic engineering: **Roads & Highways**

trailing arbutus: **Mayflower**

trailing snowberry: **Vegetation Regions - Cordillera**

Traill, Thomas: **Traill, Catharine Parr**

Training & Re-establishment Institute: **Ryerson Polytechnical Institute**

tram: **Chilkoot Pass; Street Railways; Urban Transportation**

Tramping Lake: **Germans**

Tramplin, Morgan J.: **Archaeology**

tranquilizers: **Medical Drug Abuse; Pharmaceuticals Industry; Women & Health**

trans-Atlantic cable: **Cabot Strait; Canso; Cape North; Heart's Content; Newspapers; Telecommunications**

Trans-Canada: **Quebecor Inc**

Trans-Canada Corp Fund: **Desmarais, Paul**

Trans-Canada Theatre Society: **Theatre, English-Language**

Trans Mountain Pipe Line Co Ltd: **Alberta**

trans-Pacific cable: **Fleming, Sandford; Mulock, William**

Trans-Québec & Maritimes Pipelines: **Utilities**

Trans-Québec Autoroute: **Sherbrooke**

Transair: **Manitoba**

Transalta Utilities Corp: **Coal**

Transcendental Meditation: **New Religious Movements**

Transcona shops: **Manitoba**

Transcontinental Railway Commission: **Parent, Simon-Napoléon**

Transfer of Duties Act: **Government Organization, Royal Commission on**

transferable ballot: **Local Elections**

Transformer: **Native People, Religion**

transistor: **Microchips & Transistors; Physics; Science & Society**

transit telescopes: **Time**

transits: **Surveying**

transits of Venus: **Astronomy**

transponder: **Satellite Communications; Space Technology**

Transport, Dept of: **Airport; Airport Architecture; Aviation; British Commonwealth Air Training Plan; Canadian Coast Guard; Snag; Stephenville; Transportation Agencies (Government)**

Transport Development Centre: **Transportation Research Centres**

Transportation Advisory Board: **Fowke, Vernon Clifford**

traplines, traps & snares: **Fur Trapping, Contemporary**

Trapper Nelson Packboard: **Camping**

Trappers' Festival: **Manitoba**

trapper's tea: **Labrador Tea; Poisonous Plants**

Trappist Agricultural Institute: **Veterinary Medicine, History**

Trappists: **Agricultural Education; Cheese & Cheesemaking; Christian Religious Communities; Mistassini; Oka; Tracadie, NS**

trapshooting: **Shooting**

Trasov, Vincent: **Art, Contemporary Trends**

Travail: **Pelletier, Gérard**

Travailleur: **Potvin, Damase**

Traves, Tom: **Business History**

trawler: **Fisheries; Fisheries History; Lunenburg; Marystown; Nova Scotia**

treadmill: **Agricultural Implements**

treasury bills: **Bank Rate; Banking; Interest; Monetary Policy; Winnipeg Commodity Exchange**

Treasury Branch: **Graphic Design**

Treaty No 1: **Indian Treaties; McKay, James**

Treaty No 2: **McKay, James**

Treaty No 3: **Aboriginal Rights; Indian Treaties; McKay, James; Verner, Frederick A.**

Treaty No 4: **Fort Qu'Appelle**

Treaty No 5: **McKay, James**

Treaty No 6: **Assiniboine; Big Bear; Erasmus, Peter; Indian Treaties; McKay, James; Poundmaker; Stoney**

Treaty No 7: **Blackfoot; Blackfoot Nation; Blood; Brooks; Crowfoot; Denny, Cecil E.; L'Heureux, Jean-B.; Macleod, James F.; Macleod, Mary I. Drever; Peigan; Potts, Jerry; Red Crow; Sarcee; Walking Buffalo**

Treaty No 8: **Beaver (Indians); Dene Nation; Indian Treaties; Métis; Slavey (Slave); Yellowknife (Redknives, Copper)**

Treaty No 9: **Indian Treaties**

Treaty No 11: **Dene Nation; Indian Treaties; Slavey (Slave)**

Treaty of Aix-la-Chapelle: **War of the Austrian Succession**

Treaty of Paris (1814): **French Shore**

Treaty of St Germain: **Québec City**

Treaty of Sévres: **Chanak Affair**

Tredwell, Charles: **L'Orignal**

Tredwell, Nathaniel: **L'Orignal**

Tree Frog Press: **Children's Literature in English**

Tree Fruit Board (BC): **Agriculture History**

tree nursery: **Drought; Indian Head; New Brunswick; Prairie Farm Rehabilitation Administration**

tree rings: **Climate Change; Climate Information; Drought; Trees**
Tree River: **Alikomiak; Coronation Gulf**
treen: **Woodenware**
Treleavan, Dave: **Committee for an Independent Canada**
Tremaine, Marie: **Literary Bibliography in English; Literary Bibliography in French**
Trémaudan, Auguste-Henri de: **Métis; Theatre, French-Language**
Tremayne, W.A.: **Drama in English; Theatre, English-Language**
Tremblant, Mont: **Mount Tremblant Provincial Park**
Tremblay, Gaston: **New Religious Movements**
Tremblay, Georges-Edouard: **Rugs & Rug Making**
Tremblay, Jean-Louis: **Drama in French**
Tremblay, Jules: **Poetry in French**
Tremblay, Thomas: **Constitutional Problems, Royal Commission of Inquiry on**
Tremblay Commission: **Constitutional History**
trembling aspen: **Aspen; Vegetation Regions - Atlantic Coastal; Vegetation Regions - Cordillera; Vegetation Regions - Eastern Temperate Forests**
trench fever: **Insect Pests**
Trenche, Rivière: **St-Maurice, Rivière**
Trent River: **Ontario, Lake; Trent Canal**
Trenton, NS: **Fraser, Graham; Locomotives & Rolling Stock**
Trenton, Ont: **Armed Forces - Air Force; Film; Trent Canal; Trenton, CFB**
Trepassey, Nfld: **Piracy; Roberts, Bartholomew; Vaughan, William**
trespass: **Criminal Investigation; Torts**
Trevor, Leslie: **Graphic Design**
Tri-University Libraries: **Libraries**
Triads, the: **Organized Crime**
trial: **Civil Procedure; Criminal Procedure**
triangulation: **Surveying**
Triano, Dom: **Guitar**
Triassic period: **Annapolis Lowlands; Beetle; Bird Classification & Evolution; Fly; Fossil Plants; Frog; Geological History; Nova Scotia; Paleontology, History in Canada; Petroleum; Vertebrate**
TriBACH Festival: **Marshall, Lois C.**
"Tribal" class destroyer: **Armaments; Haida; Shipbuilding & Ship Repair; World War II**
Tribune: **Buller, Annie**
Tribune, La: **Marcotte, Gilles**
trichina worm: **Nematoda**
trichinosis: **Food Poisoning**
Trickster myth: **Native People, Religion**
Tridentine rite: **Catholicism**
Trifunov, James: **Wrestling**
trigonometry: **Computer Systems Applications; Mathematics**
Trimble, Jim: **Hamilton Tiger Cats**
Trinidad & Tobago Assn Drama Committee: **Theatre, Multicultural**
Trinidad Electric Co Ltd: **Stairs, John Fitz-William**
Trinidadians: **West Indians**
Trinity College School: **Bethune, Charles James Stewart; Blackwood, David L.; Bovell, James; Canada Studies Foundation; Port Hope**
Trinity College (U of T): **Anglicanism; Berkinshaw, Richard Coulton; Bovell, James; Brett, George S.; Child, Philip Albert; Fairweather, Eugene Rathbone; Hare, Frederick Kenneth; Hind, Henry Y.; MacGill, Helen Gregory; Rugby; Strachan, John; University of Toronto**
Trinity Square Video: **Video Art**
Trinity Western College: **British Columbia; Thompson, Robert N.**
tritium: **Hydrogen; Nuclear Energy; Nuclear Fusion**
TRIUMF: **National Research Council of Canada; Physics; University of British Columbia**
Triumph: **Popular Music**
trivet: **Domestic Utensils; Folk Art**

Trofimenkoff, S.M.: **Social History**
trolley: **Urban Transportation**
Trollope, Anthony: **Exploration & Travel Literature in English**
Trotskyism: **Marxism**
Trott, Elizabeth: **Philosophy**
trotter: **Harness Racing**
Trotter, J.: **Chemistry Subdisciplines**
Trottier, Pierre: **Poetry in French**
Troubadour: **Folklore**
Troupe des Trieze: **Drama in French**
Troupe Oxygène: **Theatre, French-Language**
trousers: **Arctic Animals; Clothing**
Trout, Edward: **Trout, Jennie**
Trout Festival: **Flin Flon**
Trout Lake: **North Bay**
Trower, Peter: **Regionalism in Literature**
Troyes, Rivière de: **Eau Claire, Lac à l'**
truancy: **Juvenile Delinquency**
Truax, Barry: **Electroacoustic Music**
Trudeau, Charles: **Baseball**
Trudeau, Jean-Baptiste: **Exploration & Travel Literature in French**
Trudeau, Justin: **Trudeau, Pierre E.**
Trudeau, Michel: **Trudeau, Pierre E.**
Trudeau, Sasha: **Trudeau, Pierre E.**
Trudel, François-Xavier-Anselme: **Castors**
Trudel, Jean: **National Gallery of Canada**
Trudel, Marcel: **Book Publishing, French-Language; Des Sauvages, ou, Voyage de Samuel Champlain; Dictionary of Canadian Biography; Historiography; Intellectual History**
True North Records: **McLauchlan, Murray**
"true-steel": **Flour Milling Industry**
Truelove Lowland: **Devon Island**
Trueman, Albert: **National Film Board**
trumpet flower: **Endangered Plants**
trumpet honeysuckle: **Honeysuckle; Vegetation Regions - Cordillera**
Trumpeter: **Thoroughbred Racing**
trumpeter swan: **Nahanni National Park; Swan**
Truscott, Steven: **R v Truscott**
Truss, Jan: **Children's Literature in English**
Trustee Acts: **Trust**
Try-Davies, J: **Hensley, Sophia Margaretta**
Tryggvason, Bjarni: **Astronaut**
Tryon, PEI: **Lea, Walter Maxfield**
Tsaika dance series: **Bella Bella**
Tsawwassen, BC: **Delta, BC**
Tsimpsean Peninsula: **Metlakatla Pass Sites**
Tswana language: **Africans**
Ttatanaka, Bill: **Japanese**
tuberculosis: **Bethune, H. Norman; Biological Product; Bryce, Peter Henderson; Fort Resolution; Hospitals; Medicine, Contemporary; Medicine, History of; Native People, Health; Nova Scotia; Nursing; Public Health; Veterinary Medicine**
Tuchmaier, Henri: **Essay in French**
Tuck, James A.: **Archaeology**
Tucker, Lloyd: **Cowan, Gary**
Tudhope automobile: **Automotive Industry**
Tudor Singers of Montreal: **Choral Music**
tufted hair grass: **Vegetation Regions - Pacific Coastal**
tug: **Forest Harvesting; Great Bear Lake; Great Slave Lake; Mackenzie River; Shipbuilding & Ship Repair; Shipping Industry; Timber Trade History**
tug-of-war: **Highland Games; Sports History**
Tuktoyaktuk Peninsula: **Beaufort Sea; Eskimo Lakes; Pingo**
Tulameen River: **Princeton**
tularemia: **Muskrat; Tick; Veterinary Medicine**
tule-mat lodge: **Kootenay; Native People - Plateau; Nicola-Similkameen; Salish, Interior**
tulip: **Festivals; Flowers, Cultivated; Rondeau Provincial Park**
tulip tree: **Biogeography; Vegetation Regions - Eastern Temperate Forests**

Tulles, Pallister & McDonald: **Furniture, English, Scottish & American**
Tulluq: **Inuit Art**
Tully, Sidney Strickland: **Drawing**
Tumbler Ridge, BC: **Dawson Creek**
tumor: **Auditory Impairment; Cancer; Medicine, History of; Virus**
Tundra Books Inc: **Children's Literature in English; Small Presses**
tundra polygons: **Periglacial Landform; Physiographic Regions - Arctic Lands**
tundra vole: **Arctic Animals**
Tungavik Federation of Nunavut: **Land Claims**
tungstate: **Mineral**
Tunkers: **Brethren in Christ**
Tunnel Mountain: **Banff Centre School of Fine Arts**
tupiq: **House**
Tupper, J. Stewart: **Macdonald, Hugh John**
turbine: **Aerodynamics; Coal Gasification; Copper; Industrial Research & Development; Machinery & Equipment Industry; Nova Scotia**
Turbo Research Ltd: **Aerospace Industry**
Turbo Resources Ltd: **Banking**
turbot: **Flatfish; Newfoundland**
Turgeon, Pierre-Flavien: **Taschereau, Elzéar-Alexander**
Turgov, Morley: **Ethnic Literature**
Turini, Ronald: **Music History**
turkey, domestic: **Agricultural Marketing Board; Cuisine; International Trade; Manitoulin Island; Poultry Farming**
turkey, wild: **Bird Classification & Evolution; Game Bird; Wildlife Conservation & Management; Wildlife Preserve**
Turnbull, Christopher: **Archaeology**
Turnbull, Gael: **Poetry in English**
Turnbull, Jane Mason: **Literature in French - Scholarship & Teaching**
Turner, Barry: **Molecules in Interstellar Space**
Turner, Beeton & Co: **Turner, John Herbert**
Turner, Edward R.: **Musical Instruments**
Turner, G.H.: **Botany History**
Turner, James: **Turner Valley**
Turner, Robert: **Turner Valley**
Turner, Robert (composer): **Choral Music; Opera**
Turner, Stan: **Armed Forces - Air Force**
Turner-Trudeau formula: **Constitutional Law**
Turnor, Philip: **Thompson, David**
turnpike: **Roads & Highways**
Turnstone Press: **Poetry in English; Small Presses**
turnvereins: **Kitchener-Waterloo**
Turtle Mountain: **Frank Slide; Rockslide**
Turtle Mountain Provincial Park: **Parks, Provincial**
Tuscarora: **Iroquois; Wine Industry**
tusk shell: **Mollusc; Seashell**
tussock sedge: **Vegetation Regions - Arctic Tundra**
Tutela Heights, Ont: **Bell, Alexander Melville**
Tutton & Duncans Foundry: **Technology**
tuya: **Volcano**
Tuz, Tamas: **Ethnic Literature**
TV Guide: **Magazines; Southam Inc**
TV Hebdo: **Southam Inc**
TV Ontario: **Broadcasting, Radio & Television; Ontario; Video Art**
TVA (Télédiffuseurs Associés): **Broadcasting, Radio & Television; Communications in Québec; Television Programming**
TVEC: **Pay Television**
Tweed, Tommy: **Allan, Andrew E.F.**
Tweedsmuir, 1st Baron: **Buchan, John**
Tweedsmuir Provincial Park: **Archaeology; British Columbia**
Twelve, Brother: **Valdes Island**
Twelve Mile Creek: **St Catharines**
20 Cents Magazine: **Curnoe, Gregory R.**
Twin Falls: **Waterfall**
Twin Gorges: **Northwest Territories**

Twin-Plane aircraft: **Gibson, William Wallace**
twinflower: **Biogeography; Wildflowers**
Twiss brothers: **Clocks & Watches**
2-4-D: **Pesticide**
Tyara maskette: **Inuit Art**
tyee salmon: **Campbell River, BC**
Tyler, S.A.: **Fossil Plants**
Tyndall, Man: **Religious Building**
Tyndall Stone: **Garson; Manitoba; Quarrying Industry**
typesetting: **Advertising; Communications; Computer Systems Applications**
typewriter: **Computer Communications; Hind, E. Cora**
typhoid: **Acadia; Biological Product; Medicine, History of; Nursing; Salmonella; Social Security; Water-Borne Disease**
typhoon: **Wind**
typhus: **Biological Product; Disasters; Epidemic; Grosse Ile; Influenza; Insect Pests; Louse; Nursing; Parasitology; Province of Canada; Whaling**
typography: **Dair, Carl; Graphic Design**
Tyrell, Thomas: **Pichon, Thomas**
Tyrrell, Edith: **Autobiographical Writing in English**
Tyrrell Medal: **Careless, J.M.S.; Literary Prizes in English; Lower, Arthur R.M.**
Tyrrell Museum of Paleontology: **Drumheller**
Tyrrell Red Lake Mines: **Tyrrell, James W.**
Tyson, Ian D.: **Ian & Sylvia**
Tyson, John: **Industrial Design**
Tyson, Sylvia: **Ian & Sylvia**
Tyyska, Alan E.: **Archaeology**

U

UAP Inc: **Turmel, Antoine**
Uashau Innuts: **Montagnais-Naskapi**
UBC Players Club: **Theatre Education**
UBC Thunderbirds: **Football**
UFA: **Co-operative Movement (See Addendum, page 1992)**
UFOs: **Millman, Peter MacKenzie; Science & Society**
Uganda: **Mainguy, Edmond Rollo**
Ugandans: **Africans; Immigration; Refugees**
Uguay, Marie: **Poetry in French**
Ukrainian Catholic Church: **Catholicism; Manitoba; Ukrainians**
Ukrainian Children's Theatre: **Theatre, Multicultural**
Ukrainian Cultural Heritage Village (Alta): **Architecture, Development**
Ukrainian Dramatic Ensemble: **Theatre, Multicultural**
Ukrainian Easter eggs: **Folk Art; Ukrainians**
Ukrainian Greek Orthodox Brotherhood: **Orthodox Church**
Ukrainian Greek Orthodox Church of Canada: **Manitoba; Ukrainians**
Ukrainian Museum of Canada: **Saskatoon**
Ukrainian Orthodox Church: **Orthodox Church**
Ukrainian Record: **Catholicism**
Ukrainski Visti: **Catholicism**
ulcer: **Psychology; Stress**
Ultramar Canada Inc: **Québec City**
ultrasound: **Acoustics; Boyle, Robert William; Medicine, Contemporary; Optometry**
ultraviolet radiation: **Fossil Plants; Observatory; Remote Sensing; Solar Energy; Spectroscopy**
Uluksuk: **Sinnisiak**
umbrella plant: **Biogeography**
Umik: **Igloolik**
U'mista Cultural Centre: **Kwakiutl**
UN: **United Nations**
UN Atomic Energy Commission: **Laurence, George C.; McNaughton, Andrew G.L.**
UN Commission on refugees: **Refugees**
UN Committee on the Peaceful Uses of Outer Space: **Air Law & Space Law**
UN Conference on the Human Environment: **Environment; Strong, Maurice F.**

UN Conference on Trade & Development: **Canada-Third World Relations; Shipping Industry**
UN Convention on the Law of the Sea: **Law of the Sea; Shipping Industry**
UN Emergency Force: **Burns, E.L.M.; Peacekeeping; Suez Crisis**
UN Environment Program: **Conservation; Environment; Hare, Frederick Kenneth; Strong, Maurice F.**
UN Food Administration Organization: **Agricultural Products Board**
UN Fund for Population Activities: **Birth Control**
UN Inter-Governmental Maritime Consultative Organization: **Safety Standards**
UN Interim Fund for Science & Technology for Development: **Environment**
UN Special Committee on Palestine: **Rand, Ivan Cleveland**
UN Technical Assistance Administration: **Keenleyside, Hugh L.**
UN Treaty Series: **Treaty-Making Power**
UN World Heritage Site: **Anthony Island Provincial Park; Burgess Shale Site; Dinosaur Provincial Park; Head-Smashed-In Buffalo Jump; Kluane National Park; L'Anse aux Meadows; Nahanni National Park; Queen Charlotte Islands**
Uncle Tom's Cabin Museum: **Dresden**
undersea cable: **Cabot Strait; Canso; Cape North; Fleming, Sandford; Gisborne, Frederick Newton; Heart's Content; Icebreakers; Telecommunications**
undersea vehicles: **Batfish; Ocean Industry; Submersible**
Understanding Media: **Gutenberg Galaxy**
Underwater Panther: **Indian Art**
Unemployment Insurance Act: **Labour Policy; Poverty; Social Security; Women & the Law**
Unemployment Insurance Commission: **Social Insurance Number**
UNESCO: **Environment; Grierson, John; Literacy; Riopelle, Jean-Paul**
UNESCO Cell Physiology Commission: **Rothstein, Aser**
UNESCO International Geological Correlation Program: **Environment**
UNESCO World Conference on Adult Education: **Kidd, J. Robbins**
UNESCO World Heritage Convention: **Parks, National**
Ungava Crater: **Québec**
Ungava Dist: **Territorial Evolution**
Ungava lemming: **Mammals**
Ungava Peninsula: **Hudson Strait; Physiographic Regions - Arctic Lands**
Uniacke House: **Mount Uniacke; Nova Scotia**
Unification Church: **New Religious Movements; Religion**
Unified Family Court: **Courts of Law**
Uniform Law Conference of Canada: **Commercial Law; Law of Evidence**
Uniform Personal Property Security Act: **Commercial Law**
Uniform Site Designation: **Archaeology**
Union (boat): **Hawkesbury; Steamboats & Paddlewheelers**
Union (periodical): **Bugnet, Georges-C.-J.**
Union Bank of Halifax: **Killam, Izaak Walton; Stairs, John FitzWilliam**
Union Bank of Prince Edward Island: **Bank of Nova Scotia**
Union Bay, BC: **Dunsmuir, Robert; Vancouver Island**
Union Bill of 1822: **Papineau, Louis-Joseph**
Union Bridge: **Bridges**
Union Carbide Canada Ltd: **Chemical Industries; Petrochemical Industry; Plastics-Processing Industry**
Union catholiques des cultivateurs: **Agriculture History; Filion, Gérard; Rural Society, Québec; United Farmers of Québec**
Union College: **Grant, John Webster; Scott, Robert Balgarnie Young**

Union des artistes: **Music, Profession of**
Union des cultivateurs du Québec: **United Farmers of Québec**
Union des écrivains québécois: **Brossard, Nicole; Godbout, Jacques; Literature & Politics**
Union des électeurs: **Caouette, J.-D.-Réal; Créditistes**
Union des producteurs agricoles: **Rural Society, Québec**
Union generale des etudiants de Québec: **New Left**
Union Jack: **Emblems of Canada; Flag Debate**
Union Nationale Métisse St-Joseph de Manitoba: **Métis**
Union of New Brunswick Indians: **New Brunswick**
Union of Nova Scotia Indians: **Land Claims**
Union of Regular Baptist Churches: **Evangelical & Fundamentalist Movements**
Union of Saskatchewan Indians: **Native People, Political Organization & Activism**
Union of Spiritual Communities of Christ: **Doukhobors**
Union Oil Co of Canada Ltd: **Coal**
Union Station, Ottawa: **Lyle, John M.; Parkin, John B.**
Union Station, Winnipeg: **Railway Station**
Union Station (2nd), Toronto: **Railway Station**
Union Steamships: **Vancouver**
Union Stockyards: **St-Boniface**
Union typographique Jacques-Cartier: **Francq, Gustave**
Uniroyal Ltd: **Kitchener-Waterloo; Rubber Products Industry**
unit train: **Coal; Coal Mining; Railways, Contemporary; Transportation**
United Aircraft: **Union Centrals, Québec**
United Automobile Workers: **Aerospace Industry; Burt, George; Chemical Industries; Industrial Unionism; McDermott, Dennis; Machinery & Equipment Industry; Millard, Charles Hibbert; Oshawa Strike; Windsor Strike**
United Baptist Church: **Wolfville**
United Brotherhood of Carpenters & Joiners: **Newfoundland Loggers' Strike**
United Co-operatives of Ontario: **United Farmers of Ontario**
United College: **Academic Freedom; Methodism; University of Winnipeg**
United Danish Lutheran Synod: **Danes**
United Electrical Workers: **Electrical Appliances Industry; Jackson, Clarence Shirley**
United Empire Loyalist: **Loyalists**
United Farm Women: **United Farmers of Ontario**
United Farm Women of Alberta: **United Farmers of Alberta**
United Farm Workers: **McDermott, Dennis**
United Farm Young People: **United Farmers of Ontario**
United Farmers' Co-operative: **Co-operative Movement (*See* Addendum, page 1992); Good, William Charles; Hannam, Herbert H.; Morrison, James, "J.J."; United Farmers of Ontario**
United Farmers of Saskatchewan: **Class & Politics**
United Farmers' Party: **New Brunswick**
United Fishermen & Allied Workers Union: **Fisheries History**
United Food & Commercial Workers International Union: **Fisheries Policy**
United Garment Workers of America: **Clothing Industries**
United Grain Growers: **Brownlee, John E.; Grain Growers' Guide; Manitoba; United Farmers of Alberta**
United Hetman Organization: **Ukrainians**
United Irishmen: **Secret Societies**
United Jewish Appeal: **Judaism**

United Keno Hill mine: **Yukon Territory**
United Maritimes Fishermen's Co-operative: **Coady, M.M.; Fisheries History**
United Mine Workers of America: **Barrett, Silby; Cape Breton Strikes, 1920s; Coal; Company Town; Conroy, Pat; MacDonald, Donald; McLachlan, James Bryson; Union Centrals, District & Regional**
United Mine Workers of NS: **Barrett, Silby**
United Missionary Church: **Evangelical & Fundamentalist Movements**
United Nations Assn: **Gordon, J. King**
United Oilseed Products Ltd: **Crop Research**
United Parcel Service: **Transportation**
United Presbyterian Seminary: **Caven, William**
United Press Canada Ltd: **News Agencies**
United States Mountains: **Innuitian Region**
United Steelworkers of America: **Industrial Unionism; Machinery & Equipment Industry; Murdochville Strike; Sefton, Lawrence F.; Sydney**
United Textile Workers of America: **Parent, Madeleine**
United Theological College: **Academic Freedom; Gordon, J. King; Pierce, Lorne A.; Scott, Robert Balgarnie Young**
United Way: **Birth Control; Foundations; Social & Welfare Services; Victorian Order of Nurses**
"Unity '84": **Fisheries Policy**
Universal Declaration of Human Rights: **Educational Opportunity; Human Rights; International Law; Prejudice & Discrimination**
Universal Negro Improvement Assn: **West Indians**
Universal Postal Union: **Postal System; Turnbull, Walter James**
Universal Radio of Canada: **Evangelism**
University Affairs: **Association of Universities & Colleges of Canada**
University Alumnae: **Little Theatre Movement**
University Bridge (Saskatoon): **Bridges**
University College (Man): **University of Manitoba**
University Dramatic Club of Montréal: **Theatre Education**
University League for Social Reform: **Economic Nationalism**
University Magazine: **Drama in English**
University of Alberta Hospital: **Computer Systems Applications; Dietetics; Thompson, Margaret Anne Wilson**
University of Alberta National Awards in Letters, Music, & Painting & the Related Arts: **Literary Prizes in English**
University of Alberta Press: **University of Alberta**
University of British Columbia Medal for Popular Biography: **Literary Prizes in English**
University of British Columbia Museum of Anthropology: **British Columbia; Duff, Wilson; Musical Instruments; Northwest Coast Indian Art; Reid, William R.**
University of McGill College: **McGill University**
University of Manitoba Medical College Block: **Stoughton, Arthur Alexander**
University of Manitoba Science Building: **Stoughton, Arthur Alexander**
University of Ottawa Quarterly: **Literary Periodicals in French**
University of St Jerome College: **University of Waterloo**
University of St Michael's College: **Catholicism**
University of Saskatchewan Hospital: **Nuclear Energy**
University of Saskatchewan Playwriting Competition: **Literary Prizes in English**

University of Sudbury: **Folk Music, Franco-Canadian; Laurentian University**
University of Toronto Act (Ont): **University**
University of Toronto Grads: **Olympic Games; Smythe, Constantine Falkland Cary**
University of Toronto Memorial Tower: **Sproatt and Rolph**
University of Toronto Press: **Book Publishing, English-Language; *Canadian Journal of Economics & Political Science*; *Dictionary of Canadian Biography*; *Encyclopedia of Music in Canada*; Graphic Design; Social History; University of Toronto**
University of Trinity College: **Medicine, History of; Music History; Royal Conservatory of Music of Toronto**
University of Western Ontario President's Medals: **Literary Prizes in English**
University of Windsor Review: **Literary Magazines in English**
University Press New Brunswick Ltd: **Irving Group**
"University Without Walls": **Heritage Canada Foundation**
unlawful assembly: **Riot**
unlawful associations: **Communist Party of Canada**
Unorganized Territory: **British Columbia**
unsegmented worms: **Invertebrate**
Uplands Airport: **Ottawa, Ont**
Upper Canada Academy: **Methodism; Ryerson, A. Egerton; Steinhauer, Henry Bird**
Upper Canada College: **English; Howard, John George; Leacock, Stephen; Newman, Peter C.; Parkin, George R.; Robertson, John Ross**
Upper Canada Gazette: **Newspapers; Print Industry**
Upper Canada Guardian: **Willcocks, Joseph**
Upper Canada Veterinary College: **Bovell, James; McEachran, Duncan; Smith, Andrew**
Upper Canadian Law Journal: **Gowan, James Robert**
Upper Fort Garry: **Winnipeg**
Upper Gullies, Nfld: **Conception Bay South**
Upper Hot Spring: **Spring**
Upper Levels Highway: **West Vancouver**
Upper Liard, YT: **Kaska**
Upper Melbourne, Qué: **Coburn, Frederick Simpson**
Upper Musquodoboit, NS: **Musquodoboit Harbour**
Upper Rideau Lake: **Rideau Lakes**
Upper South River, NS: **MacMillan, Alexander Stirling**
Upshaw, Willie: **Toronto Blue Jays**
Upton, Qué: **Longpré, Ephrem**
Uptown Theatre: **Volkoff, Boris V.**
uraninite: **Metallurgy; Mineral**
Uranium Canada Ltd: **Energy, Mines & Resources, Dept of**
Urban, Keith: **Dance, Modern**
Urban Development Institute: **Construction Industry**
Urban History Review: **Historiography; Urban Studies**
urban mapping: **Cartography, History of**
Urban Municipalities Act (Sask): **Saskatoon**
Urban Transportation Development Corp (Ont): **Ontario; Ontario Northland Transportation Commission; Subways & Light Rapid Transit; Transportation**
Urbanyi, Pablo: **Ethnic Literature**
Urbina, José Leandro: **Ethnic Literature**
Urdu language: **Ethnic Literature**
Urquhart, Alasdair: **Philosophy**
Urquhart, M.C.: **Buckley, Kenneth Arthur Haig**
Ursulines: **Christian Religious Communities; Education, History of; La Peltrie, Marie-Madeleine de Chauvigny de; Maguire, Thomas; Marie de l'Incarnation;** *cont...*

Native People, Education; Nursing; Religious Building; Roberval; Trois-Rivières; University of Western Ontario
Usher, Robert A.: **Pediatrics**
Ussher, John Tannatt: **McLean Gang**
usufruct: **Property Law**
usury: **Interest**
Utah honeysuckle: **Vegetation Regions - Cordillera**
UTEC: **Computer Science**
Utility Valley Mine: **Coal**
Utkuhikhalingmiut people: **Anguhadluq, Luke**
Utopia, Lake: **Place-names**

V

Vac, Bertrand: **Literary Prizes in French**
vacations & vacation pay: **Employment Law**
Vacca, Hector: **Sculpture**
vaccines & vaccination: **Animal Agriculture; Beef Cattle Farming; Biological Product; Connaught Laboratories Ltd; Dairy Farming; Epidemic; Frappier, Armand; Genetic Engineering; Influenza; Institut Armand-Frappier; Medicine, Contemporary; Medicine, History of; Veterinary Medicines Industry; Virus**
Vaches, Île aux: **La Vérendrye, Pierre**
Vachon, André: *Dictionary of Canadian Biography*
vacuum-tube: **Technology**
Vághy String Quartet: **Chamber Music**
vagrancy: **Crime; Prostitution**
Vaillancourt, Jean: **Novel in French**
Vaillancourt, Michel: **Equestrian Sports**
Vaillancourt, Pauline: **Marxism**
Vaitonis, Paul: **Chess**
Val-David, Qué: **Printmaking**
Val-Jalbert, Qué: **Parc de Val-Jalbert; Saint-Jean, Lac**
Val Marie, Sask: **Horse; Prairie Dog**
Valcartier, Qué: **Laser**
Valcke, Louis: **Philosophy**
Valcourt, Qué: **Snowmobile**
Valdés, Cayetano: **Cartography, History of; Kwakiutl; Spanish Exploration;** *Sutil & Mexicana*
Valdmanis, Alfred A.: **Smallwood, Joseph R.**
Valentine, William: **Photography**
Valgardson, William D.: *Dalhousie Review*; **Ethnic Literature; Icelanders; Short Fiction in English**
Valin Massif: **Saguenay Provincial Park**
Vallance, Hugh: **Architectural Styles**
Vallard map: **Cartography, History of**
Vallerand, Claudine: **Children's Literature in French**
Valley East, Ont: **Sudbury**
Valleyview, Alta: **Landslide**
Vallières, Jean: **Guitar**
Vampire aircraft: **Armed Forces - Air Force; Military Aviation & Aircraft**
Van Bridge, Tony: **Shaw Festival; Stratford Festival**
Van Courtland, Ida: **Theatre, English-Language**
Van de Graaff accelerator: **Physics**
van den Berg, Jan: **Soldiers of Fortune**
van der Rohe, Ludwig Mies: **Bank Architecture**
Van Dusen, W.J.: **MacMillan, H.R.**
Van Dusen Botanical Display Garden: **Botanical Garden**
Van Fraassen, Bas: **Philosophy**
van Ginkel, Blanche: **van Ginkel, H.P.D., "Sandy"**
van Hamel, Martine: **National Ballet School**
Van Kranendonk, J.: **Physics**
van Rjndt, Phillippe: **Popular Literature in English**
Van Schendel, Michel: **Poetry in French**
Van Stolk, Mary: **Child Abuse**
Van Straubenzie, Bowen: **Batoche**
van Vogt, A.E.: **Popular Literature in English**
vanadium: **Iron & Steel Industry; Mineral**
Vananda, BC: **Texada Island**

Vance, Christie MacDonald: **Comparative Literature**
Vance, Dennis: **Art, Contemporary Trends**
Vance, Eugene: **Comparative Literature**
Vancouver: **Station PAPA**
Vancouver Amateur Swim Club: **Swimming, Speed**
Vancouver Aquarium: **Reid, William R.**
Vancouver Art Gallery: **Art Writing & Criticism; Erickson, Arthur C.; Falk, Gathie; Smith, Gordon Appelbe; Video Art**
Vancouver Arts, Science & Technology Centre: **Science Centre**
Vancouver Board of Parks & Recreation: **Botanical Garden**
Vancouver Chamber Choir: **Choral Music**
Vancouver City Archives: **British Columbia**
Vancouver Coal Mining & Land Co: **Nanaimo**
Vancouver Daily Province: **Sun**
Vancouver Daily Star: **Odlum, Victor W.**
Vancouver District Trades & Labor Council: **Bengough, Percy**
Vancouver *Evening Journal*: **Martin, Joseph**
Vancouver Film Society: **King, Allan W.**
Vancouver Game Farm: **Langley**
Vancouver General Hospital: **Dietetics; Mussallem, Helen K.**
Vancouver *Guardian*: **Martin, Joseph**
Vancouver harbour: *Beaver*
Vancouver International Airport: **Richmond; Vancouver**
Vancouver International Festival: **Opera; Theatre, English-Language**
Vancouver International Marathon: **Long-Distance Running**
Vancouver Island Board of Trade: **Parks, Provincial**
Vancouver Island marmot: **Endangered Animals; Mammals; Marmot**
Vancouver Liberation Front: **Hippies**
Vancouver Little Theatre: **Little Theatre Movement**
Vancouver Millionaires: **Stanley Cup; Taylor, Frederick W.**
Vancouver Museum & Planetarium: **British Columbia**
Vancouver New Music Society: **Chamber Music**
Vancouver News-Herald: **Berton, Pierre; Vancouver**
Vancouver Playhouse Acting School: **Theatre Education**
Vancouver Police Force: **Policing**
Vancouver Province: **Essay in English; Media Ownership; Nicol, Eric**
Vancouver St Andrew's Soccer Club: **Turner, David**
Vancouver School of Art: **Bell, Alistair Macready; Binning, Bertram Charles; Davidson, Robert C.; Diesing, Freda; Kerr, Illingworth H.; Printmaking; Raginsky, Nina; Shadbolt, Jack Leonard; Tanabe, Takao; Varley, Frederick H.**
Vancouver School of Decorative & Applied Arts: **Hughes, Edward John; Macdonald, J.W.G., "Jock"**
Vancouver School of Technology: **University of British Columbia**
Vancouver Sun: **Cartoons; Hutchison, W. Bruce; Journalism;** *Sun*; **Webster, Jack**
Vancouver Trades & Labour Council: **Gutteridge, Helena Rose**
Vancouver Whitecaps: **Soccer**
Vancouver Women's Caucus: **Women's Movement**
Vancouver Women's Health Collective: **Women & Health**
Vancouver World Exhibition: **Science Centre**
Vancouver's Island: **British North America; Territorial Evolution**
Vanderburg, Helen: **Synchronized Swimming**
Vanderhaeghe, Guy: **Short Fiction in English**
Vanderveken, Daniel: **Philosophy**
Vangelisti, Guglielmo: **Italian Writing**
Vanguard: **Art, Contemporary Trends; Art Writing & Criticism**

Vanguard Institute: **Thompson, Robert N.**
Vanier, Denis: **Poetry in French**
Vanier, Ont: **Rowing**
Vanier, Pauline: **Vanier, Georges-P.**
Vanier Cup: **Football**
Vanier Institute of the Family: **Family Studies; Penfield, Wilder G.**
Vanier School of Nursing: **Labelle, Huguette**
Vansittart, Henry: **Woodstock, Ont**
Vantage Arts Academy Award: **Centaur Theatre**
Vapaa Sana: **Finns**
Varennes, Qué: **Chemical Industries; Hydrogen; Nuclear Fusion**
variable-pitch propeller: **Turnbull, Wallace Rupert**
Variétés lyriques: **Music History; Simoneau, Léopold**
Varin, Jacques: **Silver, Domestic**
Varsity: **Allan, Andrew E.F.**
Varsity Stadium: **Football; Toronto Argonauts**
varying lemming: **Arctic Animals**
Vasa Order of America: **Swedes**
Vaseux Lake: **Okanagan Valley**
Vastokas, Romas: **Archaeology**
vaudeville: **Music History**
Vaudreuil, Qué: **Musical Instruments; Sculpture**
Vaughn, Ont: **Kleinburg**
Vaux, Calvert: **Landscape Architecture**
Vaux, George: **Geomorphology**
Vaux, William S.: **Geomorphology**
Vazan, Bill: **Art, Contemporary Trends**
veal: **Animal Agriculture; Beef Cattle Farming; International Trade**
Vedder Crossing, BC: **Chilliwack, BC**
Vedette aircraft: **Aerospace Industry**
Vegreville, Alta: **Brown, Ernest; Mazankowski, Donald Frank; Research Stations, Agricultural**
Véhicule Art: **Video Art**
Véhicule Press: **Art Writing & Criticism; Poetry in English; Small Presses**
Veith, William: **Silver, Domestic**
Velma Springstead Trophy: **Magnussen, Karen D.**
velocipede: **Cycling**
Veltri, Giovanni: **Italians**
Veltri, Vincenzo: **Italians**
velvet ant: **Wasp**
vending machines: **Retail Trade**
Vendôme station: **Ferron, Marcelle**
veneer: **Forest Harvesting; Forestry; Furniture, English, Scottish & American; Lumber & Wood Industries**
venereal disease: **Public Health; Sexually Transmitted Disease**
Venn Passage: **Metlakatla Pass Sites**
Venne, Stéphane: **Arcand, Denys; Claude, Renée**
Venning, Eleanor: **Biochemistry**
venom: **Allergies; Rattlesnake; Snake; Spider**
Vent, Butte du: **Cap aux Meules, Île du**
Ventura aircraft: **Armed Forces - Air Force**
Venture: **Sailing Ships**
venture corporations: **Small Business**
Venture gas field: **Coastal Waters; Nova Scotia**
Venus: **Astronomy**
verbena: **Flowers, Cultivated**
Verchères, François Jarrett de: **Verchères, Marie-Madeleine Jarret de**
Verchères, Qué: **Lavallée, Calixa; Sculpture**
Verdun, Qué: **Douglas, James (1800-86); Duel**
Vergilian Bibliography: **Classics**
Verier, Étienne: **Drawing**
Verigin, John J.: **Doukhobors**
Vérité: **Couture, Joseph-Alphonse; Tardivel, Jules-Paul**
Vermilion, BC: **Princeton**
Vermilion River: **Dauphin**
Vermilion School of Agriculture: **Agricultural Education**
vermillion: **Mercury**
Vermillon, Rivière: **St-Maurice, Rivière**
vermouth: **Alcoholism**
Verne, Rudolph: **Skiing**
Vernon, George Forbes: **Vernon**

Vernon, Lake: **Huntsville**
Vernot, George: **Swimming, Speed**
Verrall, Robert: **Film Animation**
Verreau, Hospice-Anselme: **Theatre, French-Language**
Verte, Baie (NB): **Boundaries**
Verte, Île: **Lighthouses**
vertical migration rythm: **Blue-green Algae**
Vesta Mine: **Coal**
Vestnik (Herald): **Russians**
Veteran's Allowances: **Public Finance**
Veterans Charter: **Veterans Affairs, Dept of**
Veterans Rehabilitation Act: **Students, Financial Aid to**
Veterinary Infectious Diseases Organization: **Animal Breeding; Genetic Engineering; Veterinary Medicine; Veterinary Medicines Industry; Virus**
Veterinary Remount Establishment: **Veterinary Medicine, History**
Veterinary Science Co: **Veterinary Medicine, History**
Vetrapharm: **Veterinary Medicines Industry**
Vézina, Charles: **Ste-Anne-de-Beaupré**
Vézina, Joseph: **Music History**
Vézina, Medjé: **Poetry in French**
Viatorians: **Christian Religious Communities**
Viatte, Auguste: **Intellectual History; Literature in French - Scholarship & Teaching**
Viau, Roger: **Novel in French**
Viau Ltée: **Confectionery Industry**
Vickers, Chris: **Archaeology**
Vickers aircraft: **Parkin, John Hamilton; Trans-Canada Airlines**
Vicky Metcalf Award: **Literary Prizes in English**
Victor Publishing Co Ltd: **Furniture & Fixture Industry**
Victor Talking Machine Co: **Music Education**
Victoria: **Disasters**
Victoria, PEI: **Prince Edward Island**
Victoria & Grey Trust: **Jackman, Henry N.R.**
Victoria Brewery: **O'Keefe, Eugene**
Victoria Bridge: **Bridges; Construction Industry, History; Grand Trunk Railway of Canada; Hobson, Joseph; Keefer, Thomas C.; Notman, William; Photography**
Victoria Chamber Opera Co: **Alarie, Pierrette**
Victoria Charter: **Constitutional Law**
Victoria College: **University of British Columbia; University of Victoria**
Victoria College of Art: **Wise, Jack M.**
Victoria College (U of T): **Birge, Cyrus Albert; Blewett, George J.; Burwash, Nathanael; Canniff, William; Cobourg; Frye, H. Northrop; Malloch, Archibald Edward; Ryerson, A. Egerton; University of Toronto**
Victoria Conference: **Constitution, Patriation of**
Victoria Conservatory of Music: **Victoria**
Victoria Cougars: **Stanley Cup**
Victoria Foundry & Machine Shops: **Technology**
Victoria Gazette: **Print Industry**
Victoria Hall: **Theatre, English-Language**
Victoria harbour: **Maynard, Hannah; Victoria**
Victoria Harbour, Ont: **Georgian Bay**
Victoria Hospital (London): **Nuclear Energy**
Victoria Lumber & Manufacturing Co: **MacMillan, H.R.**
Victoria Machinery Depot Ltd: **Shipbuilding & Ship Repair**
Victoria Magazine: **Literary Magazines in English; Moodie, Susanna**
Victoria Memorial Museum: **Anthropology; Archaeology; National Museum of Natural Sciences; Wintemberg, William John**
Victoria of England: **Acadia University; Bell-Smith, Frederic Marlett;** *Breadalbane*; **British Columbia; Coinage; Edwards, William Cameron; Emblems, Provincial & Territorial; Evans, Thomas Dixon Byron;** *cont...*

Grant, James Alexander; Gzowski, Casimir S.; Hébert, L.-Philippe; LaFontaine, Louis-Hippolyte; National Museum of Man; New Caledonia; New Westminster; Ottawa, Ont; Postal System; Queen's Plate; Queen's University; Regina; Royal Military College of Canada; St John's; Sculpture; Sovereign; Stamp Collecting; Sutton, Catherine; Swan, Anna H.; Thompson, John S.D.; Thoroughbred Racing; Tookoolito, "Hannah"; Victoria; Victoria Cross; Victoria Day; Victoria Island; Victorian Order of Nurses; Victoriaville; Watson, Homer R.

Victoria Park: **Queen's Plate**
Victoria Philharmonic Soc: **Music History**
Victoria Rink (Montréal): **Figure Skating; Ice Skating**
Victoria Rink (Saint John): **Speed Skating**
Victoria River: **Exploits River**
Victoria School of Art & Design: **Leonowens, Anna H.; Lismer, Arthur**
Victoria School of Fine Art: **Ritchie, Eliza**
Victoria-Sidney Railway: **Sidney**
Victoria Strait: **Netsilik Inuit**
Victoria *Times*: **Hutchison, W. Bruce**
Victoria University: **Dunlap, David Alexander**
Victory Aircraft Ltd: **Aerospace Industry; Bickell, John Paris; Munitions & Supply, Dept of**
Victory Bonds: **Canada Savings Bonds; Wartime Home Front**
victory garden: **Wartime Home Front**
Victory Loan Campaign: **Gundy, James Henry; Radio Programming; World War I**
Victory Point: **Franklin, John**
Video Guide: **Art Writing & Criticism**
Video Inn: **Video Art**
Vidéo Véhicule: **Video Art**
videodisc & videotape: **Communications in the North; Distance Learning; Pornography; Television Drama; Theatre, English-Language; Video Art**
Vidéographe: **Video Art**
videotex: **Communications; Electronics Industry; Libraries; Newspapers; Southam Inc; Telidon**
Vie des arts: **Art Writing & Criticism**
Vielles-Forges: **St-Maurice, Rivière**
Vienna Convention on Diplomatic Relations: **International Law**
Vienna Convention on the Law of Treaties: **International Law**
Vienneau, Azor: **Diorama**
Vietnam War: **Seaborn, James Blair**
Vietnamese: **Southeast Asians**
Vieux-Poste: **Sept-Iles**
Viger, Denis-Benjamin: **Garneau, François-Xavier**
Viirlaid, Arved: **Ethnic Literature**
Viking, Alta: **Mazankowski, Donald Frank**
Viking satellite: **Space Technology**
Vikings: **Bjarni Herjolfsson; Dog; Eric the Red; Leif Ericsson; Norse Voyages**
Village Island: **Kwakiutl**
Village Players: **Moore, Dora Mavor**
Village Québécois d'Antan: **Drummondville**
Village Service Act (NS): **Nova Scotia**
Villebon, Joseph Robinau de: **Fredericton**
Villemaire, Yolande: **Novel in French; Poetry in French**
Villeneuve, Alta: **Callihoo, Victoria**
Villeneuve, Jocelyne: **Children's Literature in French**
Vinal, Harold: **Poetry in English**
Vinay, Jean-Paul: **Dictionary; Linguistics**
Vincent Massey Awards for Excellence in the Urban Environment: **Urban Design**
Vinci, Ernesto: **Singing**
vine maple: **Maple; Vegetation Regions - Cordillera**
Vineberg, A.M.: **Heart Disease**
Vineland, Ont: **Crop Research; Germanic Fraktur & Calligraphy; Lincoln; Research Stations, Agricultural**

Vineland Horticultural Station: **Wine Industry**
Viner, Jacob: **Economics**
vines: **Grape; Norse Voyages; Wine Industry**
Vining, Charles: **Wartime Information Board**
Vining, L.C.: **Biochemistry**
Vinland: **Karlsefni; Norse Voyages**
Vinland Map: **Cartography, History of**
vinyl: **Petrochemical Industry; Plastics-Processing Industry**
vinyl chloride: **Environmental Law**
viol: **Musical Instruments**
viola & viola music: **Chamber Music; Musical Instruments**
Violet, Ont: **Perry, A. Bowen**
Violi, Paul: **Organized Crime**
violin & violin music: **Chamber Music; Haendel, Ida; Jehin-Prume, Frantz; Musical Instruments; Staryk, Steven**
viper: **Snake**
Virden-Roselea oil field: **Virden**
Virgo, Sean: **Literature in English; Short Fiction in English**
Virus: **Art Writing & Criticism**
Viscount Melville Sound: **Arctic Exploration; Island; Parry Channel; Physiographic Regions - Arctic Lands; Prince of Wales Strait; Victoria Island**
visible radiation: **Remote Sensing; Solar Energy; Sun**
visions: **False Face Society; Kootenay; Medicine Bundles; Native People, Religion; New Religious Movements; Salish, Interior; Seneca; Sun Dance**
visitation rights: **Family Law**
visual impairment: **Blindness & Visual Impairment; Education, Special**
visual training: **Optometry**
vital statistics: **Demographic Data Collection; Family Studies**
Vital Statistics Act: **Names**
Vital Statistics Act (Man): **Death**
vitamins: **Animal Agriculture; Apricot; Baking Industry; Beet; Cabbage; Canada's Food Guide; Chemistry Subdisciplines; Cod Liver Oil; Dandelion; Food Additives; Kale; Okra; Onion; Peach; Pepper; Potato; Radish; Spinach; Tomato; Turnip; Vegetarianism**
Vitez, Gyorgy: **Ethnic Literature**
Vitré, Denis de: **Trois-Pistoles**
Vivier, Claude: **Chamber Music; Choral Music**
Vivre: **Quebecor Inc**
VLB Éditeur: **Beaulieu, Victor-Levy; Book Publishing, French-Language**
VLM troupe: **Leclerc, Félix**
Vocational & Rehabilitation Research Institute: **Education, Special**
Vocational Education Act (Ont): **Career Counselling**
vocational training: **Apprenticeship in Early Canada; Community College; Construction Industry; Education, Higher; Education, Special; Education Policy; Labour Policy; Opting-Out; Regional Development Planning; Ryerson Polytechnical Institute; Secondary School**
Vocational Training Co-ordination Act: **Apprenticeship**
Vogan, Nancy: **Musicology**
Vogel, Vic: **Jazz**
Voice: **Puttee, Arthur**
Voices: **Poetry in English**
Voix Acadienne: **Prince Edward Island**
Voix et images du pays: **Literary Periodicals in French**
Volkov, G.M.: **Physics**
Volkova, Vera: **Moroni, David Lee**
Voltigeurs, Parc des: **Drummondville**
Voluntary Disclosure Registry: **Adoption**
volunteering: **Canadian Coast Guard; Climate Information; Death & Dying; Fitness; 4-H Clubs; Girl Guides; Historical Societies; Hospitals; Influenza; Marshall, Kenric Rudolphus; Navy League of Canada; Political Participation; Red Cross Society; Royal Ontario Museum**

Von Borstel, R.C.: **Genetics**
Von Der Ohe, Katie: **Sculpture**
von Kunits, Luigi: **Music Broadcasting; Toronto Symphony**
von Schoultz, Nils: **Macdonald, John A.**
Vonarburg, Elisabeth: **Popular Literature in French**
Voodoo aircraft: **Military Aviation & Aircraft**
Vorsklo, Vira: **Ukrainian Writing**
Voss, Carl: **Calder Trophy**
vote buying: **Corruption**
voting: **Elections; Electoral Behaviour; Electoral Systems; Franchise; Local Elections; Native People, Political Organization & Activism; Parliamentary Procedure; Political Campaign; Public Opinion; Quiet Revolution; Referendum; South Asians; Women's Suffrage**
Voûtes du Palais: **Québec City**
VOWR: **Evangelism**
Voyageur: **Sudbury**
Voyageur Canoe Pageant: **Heritage Conservation**
Voyageur Enterprises Ltd: **Bus Transportation; New Brunswick**
Vranešić, Zvonko: **Chess**
Vujošević, Smilja: **Chess**
Vukadinov, Milan: **Chess**

W

W. Bell & Co: **Piano Manufacturing**
W. Ross Macdonald School: **Blindness & Visual Impairment**
W.A.C. Bennett Dam: **BC Hydro; Mackenzie; Sekani**
W.C. Edwards & Co: **Edwards, William Cameron**
W.C. Wood Co: **Guelph**
W.E. Phillips Ltd: **Phillips, W. Eric**
W.H. Smith Booksellers: **Authors & Their Milieu**
W.J. Hughes Glass Co: **Glass**
W.R. Johnstone & Co: **Clothing Industries**
Wa Wa Ta Native Communications Soc: **Native People, Communications**
Waba Lodge: **Arnprior**
Wabamun Lake: **Fossil Plants**
Wabana, Nfld: **Bell Island**
Wabana Mine: **Mineral Resources**
Wabanaki: **Children's Literature in English; Micmac**
Wabasca River: **Bitumen; Peace River**
Wabi Creek: **New Liskeard**
Wabush, Nfld: **Labrador**
Wabush Lake: **Iron & Steel Industry**
Wabush Mines: **Iron & Steel Industry**
Waddell, James: **Furniture, English, Scottish & American**
Waddens, Jean-Etienne: **North West Company**
Waddington, Alfred: **Waddington, Mount**
Wade, Brian: **Drama in English**
Wade, George: **Country & Western Music**
Wade, Mason: **Intellectual History**
Wadhope, Man: **Postal System**
Wadow, Isidore: **Debassige, Blake R.**
Waelti-Walters, Jennifer: **Comparative Literature**
wage stabilization: **National War Labour Board; Wartime Prices & Trade Board**
Wager Bay: **Waterfall**
wages: **Apprenticeship; Business Management; National Income; Postal Strikes; Real Wages; Women's Movement**
Waghorne, A.C.: **Botany History**
Wagmatcook Band: **Land Claims**
Wagner, John: **Canada & Australia**
wagtail: **Pipit**
Wah, Fred: **Literary Magazines in English; Literature in English - Theory & Criticism; Poetry in English**
Wahn Report: **Economic Nationalism**
Wainfleet, Ont: **Niagara Peninsula**
Wainwright, William: **Wainwright**
Wakan: **Native People, Religion**
Wakashan linguistic family: **Bella Bella; Kitamaat; Kwakiutl; Native People, Languages; Nootka; Vancouver Island**
Wakaw, Sask: **Diefenbaker, John G.**

wake: **Funeral Practices**
Wakefield, Qué: **National Museum of Science & Technology**
Wakeham Bay, Qué: **Inuit Art; Ungava Inuit**
wakerobin: **Trillium**
Walcot, Isabella: **Nickinson, John**
Walcott, Charles D.: **Burgess Shale Site; Paleontology, History in Canada**
Walden, Ont: **Sudbury**
Waldorf schools: **Education, Alternate**
Waldseemüller map: **Cartography, History of**
Wales, Prince of (Edward VII): **Beers, W. George; Cobourg & Peterborough Railway; Emblems of Canada; Medal; Oronhyatekha; Photography; Princeton; Royal Tours; St John's Regatta; Timber Slide**
Wales, Prince of (Edward VIII): **Prince of Wales Trophy; Royal Tours**
Wales, Prince of (George IV): **Cornwall**
Wales, William: **Astronomy**
Walker, Alan: **Musicology**
Walker, George F.: **Drama in English; Literature in English; Musical Theatre; Theatre, English-Language**
Walker, Hovenden: **Disasters**
Walker, J.B.: **Cartoons**
Walker, Norma Ford: **Genetic Diseases; Thompson, Margaret Anne Wilson**
Walker, Thomas Hollis: **Warren, William Robertson**
Walker Bay: **Victoria Island**
Walker Report on Public Education Finance: **Nova Scotia**
Walkerville, Ont: **Americans; Walker, Hiram**
Walkerville Wagon Co Ltd: **Automotive Industry**
Walking Crow: **Old Crow**
Wall, Jeff: **Art, Contemporary Trends**
Wall, John H.: **Paleontology, History in Canada**
Wall, Nick: **Thoroughbred Racing**
Wallace, Clarke: **Morrison, Donald**
Wallace, George: **Sculpture**
Wallace, Herbert: **Native-White Relations**
Wallace, Ian: **Art, Contemporary Trends**
Wallace, Lake: **Sable Island**
Wallace, T.H.: **Canoeing**
Wallace, W.T.: **Graphic Design**
walleyed pike: **Saint-Jean, Lac**
Wallis Tractor: **Massey-Ferguson Ltd**
Walloons: **Belgians**
Wallot, Jean-Pierre: **Historiography; Intellectual History; Literary Bibliography in French**
Walmsley, Tom: **Drama in English; Tarragon Theatre; Theatre, English-Language**
Walrond Ranch: **Ranching History; Rodeo**
Walrus Island: **Sadlermiut Inuit**
Walsh, Edward: **Printmaking**
Walsh Glacier: **Lucania, Mount; Steele, Mount**
Walter v Attorney-General of Alberta: **Communal Properties Act Case**
Walter, Dorothea: *Trente Arpents*
Walter, Felix: **Poetry in English**; *Trente Arpents*
Walter Baker Co of Canada: **Confectionery Industry**
Walter C. Mackenzie Health Science Centre: **Zeidler, Eberhard Heinrich**
Walter Hall: **Orford String Quartet**
Walter Klinkhoff Gallery Inc: **Art Dealers**
Walter M. Lowney Co: **Confectionery Industry**
Walters, Angus J.: *Bluenose*
Waltner-Toews, David: **German Writing**
Wanderers' Amateur Athletic Assn: **Halifax**
Wandering Spirit Survival School: **Harper, Vern**
"wane" (bevel): **Timber Trade History**
Wánkowicz, Melchior: **Ethnic Literature**
Wanzer mechanical lamp: **Lighting**
Wanzer Sewing Machine Co: **Lighting**
wapato: **Plants, Native Uses**
Wapella, Sask: **Bronfman Family; Kidd, J. Robbins**

Wapiabi Formation: **Sedimentary Rock**
Wapomeo Island: **Thomson, Thomas J.**
Wapta Icefield: **Bow River**
Wapussakatoo Mountains: **Labrador City**
Waputik Mountains: **Bow River**
war & rebellion: **American Civil War; American Revolution; Iroquois Wars; Korean War; North-West Rebellion; Rebellions of 1837; Riel Rebellion; Seven Years' War; South African War; War of 1812; War of the Austrian Succession; War of the Spanish Succession; World War I; World War II**
war artists: **Bayefsky, Aba; Bobak, B.J., "Bruno"; Bobak, Molly J.; Brittain, Miller G.; Colville, Alexander; Comfort, Charles F.; Goldhamer, Charles; Hughes, Edward John; Jackson, A.Y.; Nichols, Jack; Ogilvie, Will; Pepper, George Douglas; Printmaking; Roberts, W. Goodridge; Schaefer, Carl F.; Shadbolt, Jack Leonard**
war canoes: **Kwakiutl**
War Emergency Training Program: **Education, Technical**
war labour code: **National War Labour Board**
War Metals Research Board: **Forward, Frank Arthur**
"War of the Boundary Lines": **Boundaries**
war pipe: **Calumet**
War Savings Stamps & Certificates: **Canada Savings Bonds; Wartime Home Front**
War Supply Board: **Borden, Henry; Henry, R.A.C., "Red"**
War Trophies Building: **National Museum of Man**
warble fly: **Fly; Insect, Beneficial; Parasitology**
Warburton, George: **Exploration & Travel Literature in English**
ward: **Municipal Government; Urban Reform**
Ward, Abel R.: **Smiths Falls**
Ward, David: **Toronto Islands**
Ward, Norman: **Essay in English**
Ward, W.J.: **Ginger Group**
Ward Hunt ice shelf: **CESAR**
Warde, Henry: **Duel**
Warden, John: **Fashion Design**
Wardlaw Block: **Atchison, John D.**
Wardle, R.A.: **Zoology**
Wardner, James F.: **Wardner**
wardrobe: **Furniture, Country; Furniture, German**
Ward's Island: **Toronto Islands**
Warfield, BC: **Trail**
Warkov, Esther: **Painting**
warm front: **Fog**
Warnaco of Canada Ltd: **Clothing Industries**
Warrack, David: **Musical Theatre**
warrant: **Gun Control**
warranty: **Consumer Law**
Warren, H.V.: **Geochemistry**
Warren, J.B.: **Physics**
Warren, L., "Jack": **Morrison, Donald**
Warren, Mary Schaffer: **Banff**
Warren, P.S.: **Paleontology, History in Canada**
Warren, R. Michael: **Postal System**
Warren, Samuel: **Musical Instruments**
Warren, Samuel P.: **Music History**
Warren, William: **Religious Music**
Warren & Wetmore: **Railway Station**
Warrillow, James K.: *Financial Post*
Wartime Housing Ltd: **Architecture, Development; Canada Mortgage & Housing Corp; Housing & Housing Policy**
Wartime Industries Control Board: **Berkinshaw, Richard Coulton; Borden, Henry**
Wartime Oils: **Petroleum Industries**
wartime registration program: **Labour Policy**
Wartime Shipping Ltd: **MacMillan, H.R.**
warts: **Virus**
Wasaga Beach, Ont: **Georgian Bay**
Wasaga Beach Provincial Park: **Parks, Provincial**
Wascana Centre: **Regina**

Wascana Institute of Applied Arts & Sciences: **Regina**
Wascana Lake: **Regina**
Wascana Park: **Science Centre**
Wascana Review: **Literary Magazines in English**
Washburn, Bradford: **Lucania, Mount**
Washington, Mount: **Comox, BC**
Waskahegan Trail Assn: **Hiking**
Waskesiu, Sask: **Prince Albert National Park**
Wasserman, Dora: **Theatre, Multicultural**
Wassermann, Charles: **German Writing**
wastepaper: **Pulp & Paper Industry**
Wastewater Technology Centre: **Canada Centre for Inland Waters**
Waswanipi, Rivière: **Nottaway, Rivière**
Watch Tower Soc: **Jehovah's Witnesses**
water birch: **Birch; Vegetation Regions - Cordillera**
water-diversion schemes: **Red Deer River**
water gas: **Coal Gasification; Foulis, Robert**
water hemlock: **Poisonous Plants**
water ouzel: **Dipper**
water pipit: **Baffin Island**
Water Quality Agreement Act: **Vollenweider, Richard Albert**
Water Safety Service: **Red Cross Society**
water transportation: **Canoe, Birchbark; Ferries; Kayak; Sailing Ships; Shipping, Maritime; Steamboats & Paddlewheelers; Transportation; Transportation in the North**
water vapour: **Chinook; Cloud; Fog; Ice; Urban Effect on Climate**
waterboatman: **Bug**
watercress: **Vegetable**
Waterhen River: **Winnipegosis, Lake**
Waterloo, Ont: **Kitchener-Waterloo; Myers, Barton**
Waterloo College of Arts: **University of Waterloo; University of Western Ontario; Wilfrid Laurier University**
Waterloo Gasoline Engine Co: **Agricultural Implements**
Waterloo Lutheran University: **University of Waterloo; Wilfrid Laurier University**
Waterman, Douglas: **Video Art**
watermelon: **Vegetable**
Waters, Allan: **CHUM Ltd**
Waters, F.W.: **Philosophy**
waterthrush: **Warbler**
Waterton, Betty: **Children's Literature in English**
Waterville, NS: **Nova Scotia**
Waterville, Qué: **Baptists**
Waterways, Alta: **Athabasca River; Transportation in the North**
WATFOR: **Computer Science**
Watkin, Edward: **Railway History**
Watkins, Mel: *Canadian Forum*; **Economics; Economics, Radical; Foreign Ownership, Task Force on; Waffle**
Watkins Task Force: **Economic Nationalism; Foreign Ownership, Task Force on**
Watson, Frank: **Watson Lake**
Watson, J. Wreford: **Urban Studies**
Watson, W.D.: **Holland Marsh**
Watson, William R.: **Art Dealers**
Watt, Frank: **Working-Class History**
Watt, Tom: **Winnipeg Jets**
Watters, R.E.: **Klinck, Carl; Literary Bibliography in English; Literature in English - Teaching**
Watts, Eugene: **Canadian Brass**
Waugh, Frederick: **Archaeology**
Waves: **Literary Magazines in English**
Wawa, Ont: **Iron & Steel Industry; Pictographs & Petroglyphs**
Way, The: **New Religious Movements**
Wayagamack Pulp & Paper Co: **Cap-de-la-Madeleine**
Wayman, Tom: **Humorous Writing in English; Literature in English; Poetry in English;** *Queen's Quarterly*
wayside crosses: **Catholicism; Folk Art**
Weadick, Guy: **Calgary Stampede; Rodeo**

Weasel snowmobile: **Klein, George John**
weather station: **Cornwallis Island; Snag; Station PAPA**
weather vanes: **Folk Art**
Weaver, Robert: **Poetry in English; Short Fiction in English;** *Tamarack Review*
weaving: **Chilkat Blanket; Dog; Northwest Coast Indian Art; Public Art; Textile Industry**
web press: **Newspapers**
Webb, Brian: **Dance, Modern**
Webb, Matthew: **Marathon Swimming**
Webb, Zerafa, Menkes, Housden Partnership: **Architecture, Development; Bank Architecture; CN Tower**
Webber, John: **Topographic Painters**
Weber, Anna: **Folk Art; Germanic Fraktur & Calligraphy**
Weber, George: **Printmaking**
Weber, Hans: **Buckler, Ernest; CESAR**
Weber & Co: **Piano Manufacturing**
Webling, Peggy: **Exploration & Travel Literature in English**
Webster, Harold: **Track & Field**
Webster, J.: **Medicine, History of**
Webster, J.C.: **New Brunswick**
Webster, Norman: **Book Clubs**
Wedgeport, NS: **Nova Scotia**
Week: **Art Writing & Criticism; Essay in English; Literary Magazines in English; Literary Periodicals in English; Literature in English - Theory & Criticism; McMurrich, James Playfair; Roberts, Charles G.D.; Smith, Goldwin**
Weekes, William: **Upper Canada**
Weekly Sun: **Smith, Goldwin**
Weider, Jozo: **Collingwood**
Weimar map: **Cartography, History of**
Weiner, Andrew: **Popular Literature in English**
Weintraub, William: **Popular Literature in English**
Weinzweig, Helen: **Novel in English**
Weir, Charles: **Musical Theatre**
Weir, G.: **Nursing**
Weir, Lorraine: **Literature in English - Theory & Criticism**
Weir, Robert Stanley: *O Canada*
Weiselberger, Carl: **German Writing**
Weissner, F.: **Waddington, Mount**
Welch, Cyril: **Philosophy**
Welch Construction Co: **Italians**
Weld, Isaac: **Exploration & Travel Literature in English**
Welland Canal Co: **Allan, William; Upper Canada**
Welland County Courthouse: **Tully, Kivas**
Welland-Crowland War Memorial: **Wyn Wood, Elizabeth**
Welland Railway: **Port Colborne; St Catharines**
Welland River: **Welland**
Wellesley Hospital: **Bruce, Herbert Alexander**
Wellesley-Pole, Mary Charlotte Anne: **Bagot, Charles**
Wellesly Island: **Thousand Islands**
Wellington, BC: **Dunsmuir, Robert**
Wellington Channel: **Beechey Island**
Wellman, Saul "Sol": **Mackenzie-Papineau Battalion**
Wells, BC: **Barkerville**
Wells, Caroline Louisa Josephine: **Dentistry**
Wells, John: **Architecture, Development; Art**
Wells, Kenneth McNeil: **Essay in English**
Wells & Richardson: **Rugs & Rug Making**
Wells Gray Provincial Park: **Columbia Mountains; Helmcken Falls; Igneous Rock; Parks, Provincial**
weloganite: **Mineral**
Welsh, Peter: **Horse**
wendigo: **Char**
Wentworth, John: **Council of Twelve**
Werlich Manufacturing Co: **Toys & Games**
Wesley band: **Stoney**
Wesley College: **Academic Freedom; Browne, George, Jr; Icelanders; Lower, Arthur R.M.; Methodism; Pickersgill, John W.; University of Manitoba; University of Winnipeg**
Wesleyan Church: **Baptists**

Wesleyan Methodist Church: **Baptists; Horner, Ralph C.; Huntsville**
Wesleyville, Nfld: **Blackwood, David L.**
Wesson, Paul: **Cosmology**
West, Comet: **Comet**
West, Lynn: **Guitar**
West, Tom: **Guitar**
West Banff Co-operative: **Inuit Co-operatives**
West Coast Review: **Ethnic Literature; Literary Magazines in English**
West Coast Tribal Council: **Nootka**
West Country Merchants: **Newfoundland**
West Edmonton Mall: **Retail Trade**
West Greenland Current: **Davis Strait; Labrador Sea**
West Hawk Lake: **Whiteshell Provincial Park**
West Head: **Bay d'Espoir**
West Prairie River: **Lesser Slave Lake**
West River: **Charlottetown**
West River, NS: **McCulloch, Thomas**
West Road (Blackwater) River: **Fraser River**
Westar Mining Ltd: **Coal**
Westbury, G.H.: **Autobiographical Writing in English**
Westcoast Actors' Society: **Theatre, English-Language**
Westcoast Transmission Co: **Mackenzie Valley Pipeline; McMahon, Francis M.P.**
Westendorp v The Queen: **Prostitution**
Westerkamp, H.: **World Soundscape Project**
Western Air Command: **Cameron, William Maxwell**
Western Associated Press: **Telegraph**
Western Bank: **Lunenburg**
Western Bay, Nfld: **Pratt, E.J.**
Western Bible College: **Evangelism**
Western Board of Music: **Music Education**
Western Broadcasting: **Media Ownership**
western buttercup: **Vegetation Regions - Pacific Coastal**
Western Canada Airways Ltd: **Bush Flying; Dickins, C.H. "Punch"**
Western Canada Aviation Museum: **Helicopter**
Western Canada Basin: **Petroleum; Petroleum Supply & Demand**
Western Canada Concept: **Separatism**
Western Canada Conference of the Evangelical United Brethren Church: **United Church of Canada**
Western Canada League: **Baseball**
Western Canada Lottery Foundation: **British Columbia; Lottery**
Western Canada Steel Ltd: **Iron & Steel Industry**
Western Canadian Veterinary Assn: **Veterinary Medicine, History**
Western Clarion: **Buller, Annie**
Western College of Veterinary Medicine: **Rowsell, Harry Cecil; Smith, David Laurence Thomson; Veterinary Medicine, Education**
Western Counties Railway: **Nova Scotia**
Western Dance Theatre: **Seymour, Lynn; Vesak, Norbert**
Western Development Museum: **Heintzman & Co Ltd; Saskatoon; Yorkton**
western flowering dogwood: **Dogwood; Vegetation Regions - Cordillera; Vegetation Regions - Pacific Coastal**
Western Football Assn: **Soccer**
Western Foundation for Advanced Industrial Technology: **British Columbia Research Council**
Western Front: **Art, Contemporary Trends; Artists' Organizations; Video Art**
Western Grain Stabilization Act: **Agriculture & Food Policy**
Western Grain Transportation Act: **Crow's Nest Pass Agreement**
Western Guard: **Racism**
western hemlock: **Forest Harvesting; Garibaldi Provincial Park; Glacier National Park; Hemlock; Pacific Rim National Park; Strathcona Provincial Park**
Western Hockey League: **Vancouver Canucks**
Western Horse Marketing Co-operative: **Horse**

Western Hospital: **Ritchie, Octavia Grace; Seeman, Mary Violette**
Western Intercollegiate Football League: **Football**
Western Interprovincial Football Union: **Canadian Football League**
Western Irrigation District: **Bow River**
Western Junior Hockey League: **Medicine Hat**
Western Labour Conference: **One Big Union**
western larch: **Larch; Vegetation Regions - Cordillera**
Western Leaseholds, Ltd: **Harvie, Eric L.**
Western Minerals, Ltd: **Harvie, Eric L.**
Western Music Company Ltd: **Religious Music**
Western Oil Examiner: **Gray, James H.**
Western Ontario Mustangs: **Football**
western prince's pine: **Biogeography**
Western Producer: **Co-operative Movement (*See* Addendum, page 1992); McNaughton, Violet C.; Saskatchewan Wheat Pool; Saskatoon**
Western Producer Prairie Books: **Book Publishing, English-Language; Saskatchewan Wheat Pool; Saskatoon**
Western Realty: **Belzberg, Samuel**
western red cedar: **Allergies; Cedar; Forest Harvesting; Garibaldi Provincial Park; Glacier National Park; Northern Georgia Strait Coast Salish; Pacific Rim National Park; Plants, Native Uses; Strathcona Provincial Park; Timber Trade History; Vegetation Regions - Pacific Coastal**
western sword fern: **Vegetation Regions - Cordillera; Vegetation Regions - Pacific Coastal**
Western University of London: **University of Western Ontario; University of Windsor**
western wheatgrass: **Vegetation Regions - Prairie**
western white pine: **Pine; Vegetation Regions - Cordillera**
western yew: **Vegetation Regions - Pacific Coastal; Yew**
Westhues, Kenneth: **Community**
Westinghouse Canada Ltd: **Barter; Business History; Electrical Appliances Industry; Hamilton**
Westmain: **Eastmain**
Westman & Baker: **Print Industry**
Westminster Hall: **Pidgeon, George Campbell**
Westminster Hall: **Literary Magazines in English**
Westminster Institute for Ethics & Human Values: **Bioethics; Jurisprudence; Medical Ethics; Medical Research; Philosophy**
Westminster Press: **Book Publishing, English-Language**
Westmorland Bank: **Moncton**
Westmount: **Architecture; English; Montréal**
Westmount Public School (Montréal): **Larose, Ludger**
Weston, Abijah: **Bronson, Henry Franklin**
Weston, Galen: **Weston, W. Garfield**
Weston, Garry: **Weston, W. Garfield**
Weston, George: **Weston, W. Garfield**
Weston shops: **Manitoba**
Westwater Research: **Fox, Irving Kingsbury**
Wetaskiwin Free Lance: **Edwards, Robert C.**
Wetmore, George Ludlow: **Wetmore, Andrew Rainsford**
Wettlaufer, Boyd N.: **Archaeology**
Weymontachingue, Qué: **Attikamek; St-Maurice, Rivière**
Weymouth, George: *Discovery*
Weymouth Free Press: **Armstrong, Ernest Howard**
Whale, Robert R.: **Art**
Whale Cove, NWT: **Caribou Inuit**
whale oil: **Basques; Lighthouses; Trois-Pistoles**
Whale rivers: **Guillaume-Delisle, Lake**
whaleback: **Lake Carriers**
whalebone: **Karoo Ashevak; Umiak**
whaler: **Sailing Ships**
Whaley, Royce & Co Ltd: **Music History**

Whalley, BC: **Surrey**
Whalley, George: **Literature in English - Theory & Criticism**
Whalley, John: **Economics**
Wharton Lake: **Dubawnt River**
wheat germ: **Flour Milling Industry**
wheat pools: **Agriculture History; Alberta Wheat Pool; Saskatchewan Wheat Pool; Wheat**
wheat stem sawfly: **Crop Research; Wheat**
wheatgrass: **Biogeography; Vegetation Regions - Cordillera**
wheel animal: **Invertebrate**
wheel-lock musket: **Firearm**
wheel of fortune: **Gambling**
wheelchair: **Klein, George John**
Wheeler, Anne: **Film, Documentary**
Wheeler, Orson: **Sculpture**
Wheeler brothers: **Cross-Country Skiing**
Whelan, Eugene: **Agriculture & Food Policy**
Whidden, Howard P.: **McMaster University**
Whig Standard: **Kingston**
whippoorwill: **Nighthawk**
Whirlpool Rapids Bridge: **Niagara Falls, Ont**
Whirlpool River: **Athabasca Pass**
whisky: **Alcoholism; Bronfman Family; Cuisine; Distilling Industry; Labatt, John S.; O'Keefe, Eugene; Sunday, John; Walker, Hiram**
whisky fort: **Calgary; Whoop-up**
whisky jack (gray jay): **Animal; Jay**
whisky trade: **Brown, J.G., "Kootenai"; Cypress Hills; Fort Macleod; Wood Mountain**
Whistler Mountain: **Garibaldi Provincial Park; Squamish**
whistling swan: **Arctic Animals; Banks Island; Swan**
Whitbourne, Richard: **Trinity**
Whitby Gazette: **Cartoons**
Whitby-Port Perry Railway: **Whitby**
Whitchurch, Ont: **Germans**
White, Ben: **Harness Racing**
White, Charles Henry: **Printmaking**
White, Cliff: **Skiing**
White, George: **Photography**
White, James: **Saint John**
White, John: **Duel**
White, John (painter): **Art**
White, Nancy: **Musical Theatre**
White, Peter: **Pembroke**
White, Thomas: **White Pass; World War I**
white ant: **Termite**
white ash: **Ash; Ornamentals; Vegetation Regions - Eastern Temperate Forests**
White Bay: **French Shore**
White Bear Reserve: **Assiniboine**
white cedar: **Botany History; Cypress; Donnacona**
white clover: **Clover; Forage Crops**
White Dog Festival: **Dog**
white elm: **Elm; Manitoba; Vegetation Regions - Eastern Temperate Forests**
White Farm Equipment: **Agricultural Implements Industry**
White Fish Lake Reserve: **Erasmus, Peter; Steinhauer, Henry Bird**
White Horse Plain: **Falcon, Pierre; Grant, Cuthbert**
White Island Reef: **Lighthouses**
white lady's slipper: **Endangered Plants**
white-leaved rhododendron: **Vegetation Regions - Cordillera**
white lily: **Trillium**
White Man's Pass: **Exploration**
White Niggers of America: **Nègres blancs d'Amérique**
white oak: **Oak; Timber Trade History; Vegetation Regions - Eastern Temperate Forests**
white (paper) birch: **Birch; Forest Fire; Laurentian Highlands; Mistassini, Lac; Pukaskwa National Park; Saguenay Provincial Park; Vegetation Regions - Atlantic Coastal; Vegetation Regions - Eastern Temperate Forests**
White Pass & Yukon Route Corp: **Whitehorse**
white pelican: **Pelican; Prince Albert National Park; Slave River**
White Pelican: **Watson, Sheila**

white perch: **Bass**
white pine: **Algonquin Provincial Park; Barachois Pond Provincial Park; Botany History; Dumoine, Rivière; Forest Fire; Furniture, French; Huntsville; Huron, Lake; Laurentian Highlands; Pine; Rondeau Provincial Park; Vegetation Regions - Atlantic Coastal; Vegetation Regions - Eastern Temperate Forests**
white pine blister rust: **Vegetation Regions - Atlantic Coastal**
White River (Ont): **Superior, Lake**
White River (YT): **Yukon River**
white spruce: **Biogeography; Cypress Hills; Forest Fire; Forest Harvesting; Laurentian Highlands; Mistassini, Lac; Spruce; Vegetation Regions - Atlantic Coastal; Vegetation Regions - Boreal Forest or Taiga; Vegetation Regions - Cordillera**
White Star Line: **Cunard Co; Disasters**
white-tailed deer: **Anticosti, Ile d'; Biogeography; Cape Breton Highlands National Park; Caribou; Cuisine; Cypress Hills Provincial Park; Deer; Fundy National Park; Lake Superior Provincial Park; Parasitology; Riding Mountain National Park; Rondeau Provincial Park**
white-tailed jackrabbit: **Hare**
white-tailed ptarmigan: **Game Bird; Ptarmigan; Strathcona Provincial Park; Yoho National Park**
white trillium: **Biogeography; Endangered Plants; Trillium**
white water lily: **Nova Scotia; Water Lily**
white whale: **Beluga Whale**
White Wing: **Aviation**
Whiteaves, J.F.: **Paleontology, History in Canada**
whitebark pine: **Garibaldi Provincial Park; Kananaskis Country; Pine; Vegetation Regions - Cordillera**
Whiteboys: **Secret Societies**
Whitefish Bay Reserve: **Sioux Narrows**
Whitefish River: **Superior, Lake**
Whitehead, Alfred: **Choral Music; Hymns; Music History**
Whitehead, Paxton: **Shaw Festival; Vancouver Playhouse**
Whitehern: **Hamilton**
Whitehorse Copper Mine: **Yukon Territory**
Whitehorse Rapids: **Whitehorse**
Whitemouth, Man: **Poles**
Whitemud Formation: **Clay**
Whitemud River: **Gladstone**
Whites' Corners, Canada West: **Partridge, Edward A.**
Whitesand River: **Assiniboine River; Quill Lakes**
Whiteshell Forest Reserve: **Rennie**
whitesided dolphin: **Dolphin & Porpoise; Grand Manan Island**
Whitewood, Sask: **Cannington Manor**
Whitewood Mine: **Coal**
whiting: **Cod**
whitloof: **Vegetable**
Whitman, Walt: **Exploration & Travel Literature in English**
Whitney, C.J.: **Grand Theatre**
Whitney Syndicate: **Nova Scotia**
Whittall, Beth: **Swimming, Speed**
Whittome, Irene: **Art, Contemporary Trends; Printmaking**
Wholdaia Lake: **Dubawnt River**
Whonock Lake Municipal Park: **Maple Ridge**
Whyac, BC: **Thompson, Arthur**
Whyte, Ernest: **Songs & Songwriting**
Whyte, Peter: **Banff**
Whyte, Phyllis: **Dance, Modern**
Whyte Packing Co: **Meat-Processing Industry**
Wickenden, R.T.D.: **Paleontology, History in Canada**
wicker: **Furniture, English, Scottish & American**
Wickson, Mildred: **Dance Education**
Widdowson, J.D.A.: **Dictionary**
widgeon: **Bird Sanctuaries & Reserves; Duck**
Widmer, Christopher: **Medicine, History of**
Wiebe, Menno: **German Writing**

Wigate, John: **Cartography, History of**
Wightman, Edith M.: **Mediterranean Archaeology**
Wiitasalo, Shirley: **Painting**
Wikwemikong Unceded Reserve: **Bell, Leland; Manitowaning; Odjig, Daphne; Ottawa**
Wilberforce Colony: **Lucan**
Wilcocke, Samuel Hull: **Drama in English**
Wild, Eric: **Hymns**
wild barley: **Poisonous Plants; Vegetation Regions - Prairie**
wild bergamot (mint): **Plants, Native Uses**
wild buckwheat: **Buckwheat; Weeds**
wild canary: **Warbler**
wild cat: **Bobcat; Cougar; Lynx**
wild cherry: **Plants, Native Uses**
wild-cow milking: **Rodeo**
wild crabapple: **Plants, Native Uses**
wild ginger: **Plants, Native Uses; Wildflowers**
Wild Horse Creek: **Brown, J.G., "Kootenai"; Fort Steele**
Wild Horse gold rush: **Fort Steele**
wild lettuce: **Poisonous Plants**
wild oats: **Oats; Weeds**
wild onion: **Plants, Native Uses**
wild rose: **Rose**
wild rye: **Poisonous Plants**
"wildcat" well: **Petroleum Exploration & Production**
Wilde, Patricia: **Ballet**
wilderness areas: **Alberta; Avalon Peninsula; Environmental Law**
Wildwood Park: **Green, Blankstein, Russell**
Wilkes, Debbie: **Figure Skating**
Wilkin, Mike: **Children's Literature in French**
Will, John: **Printmaking**
Willards Chocolate Co, Ltd: **Confectionery Industry**
Willard's Hotel: **Hotel**
willet: **Sandpiper**
Willet Flour Mills: **Chambly**
Willet Textile Mills: **Chambly**
Willett, Mahlon: **Textile Industry**
William, Chief: **Williams Lake**
William III of England: **Newfoundland**
William IV of England: **King William Island**
William Clark Co: **Meat-Processing Industry**
William Davies Co: **Canada Packers Inc; Flavelle, Joseph W.; Meat-Processing Industry**
William H. Verity & Sons: **Agricultural Implements**
William Henry, Lower Canada: **Sorel**
William Henry Drummond National Poetry Writing Contest: **Literary Prizes in English**
William M. Jennings Award: **Vezina Trophy**
William Neilson Ltd: **Confectionery Industry**
William Notman & Son: **Fraser, John A.; Notman, William; Notman, William McFarlane**
William Price & Sons: **Price, William (1789-1867)**
William Scott & Son: **Suzor-Coté, Marc-Aurélie de Foy**
William Southam & Sons: *Edmonton Journal*
William Tabler & Campeau: **Hotel**
Williams, Amos: **Shelburne**
Williams, Arthur T.H.: **Batoche**
Williams, E. Hector: **Mediterranean Archaeology**
Williams, Glyndwr: **Graham, Andrew**
Williams, John: **Motorcycle Racing**
Williams, John Handbury: **Sports Organization, Amateur**
Williams, M.Y.: **Paleontology, History in Canada**
Williams, Penny: *Prochain Épisode*
Williams, R.S.: **Piano Manufacturing**
Williams, Thomas: **Williams, Eleazer**
Williams, V.A.S.: **Mont Sorrel**
Williams, William: **North West Company; Simpson, George**
Williams Commission: **Privacy**
Williams Creek: **Gold Rushes**
Williams culture: **Brockinton**
Williams No 1: **Petroleum Industries**
Williamsburg Canal: **Canals & Inland Waterways**
Williamstown, Ont: **Thompson, David**

Willingdon Arts Competitions: **Willingdon, 1st Marquess of**
Willingdon Cup: **Golf**
Willis, A.P.: **Piano Manufacturing**
Willis, J. Frank: **Radio Drama, English-Language; Radio Programming**
Willis & Co Ltd: **Musical Instruments**
Willison's Monthly: **Willison, John S.**
Willistead Manor: **Windsor, Ont**
Williston, Ray: **Williston Lake**
Williston Basin: **Manitoba**
Willmore Wilderness Provincial Park: **Alberta; Grande Cache**
Willmot, D.G.: **Molson, Eric Herbert**
Willowdale, Ont: **Association for Canadian Studies; Evangelical Fellowship of Canada; Lawn Bowling**
wills: **Family Law; Millar, Charles Vance; Property Law; Solicitor; Trust**
Wills, Frank: **Architectural Styles; Architecture, Development; Christ Church Cathedral; Medley, John**
Willson, Bruce: **Committee for an Independent Canada**
Wilmeth, Roscoe: **Archaeology**
Wilmot, Lemuel Allen: **Florenceville**
Wilmot, R.D.: **Fathers of Confederation**
Wilmot, S.S.: **Uxbridge**
Wilson, A.W.G.: **Geomorphology**
Wilson, Alex: **Track & Field**
Wilson, Andrew H.: **Patents, Copyright & Industrial Designs, Royal Commission on**
Wilson, Anne Elizabeth: *Chatelaine*
Wilson, Bruce: **Soccer**
Wilson, Charles: **Choral Music; Opera; Songs & Songwriting**
Wilson, Charles (Mayor of Montréal): **Gavazzi Riots**
Wilson, David: **Literature in English - Theory & Criticism**
Wilson, Ethel: **Novel in English; Pacey, W.C. Desmond**
Wilson, Fred: **Philosophy**
Wilson, Herb: **Ballets Jazz de Montréal**
Wilson, Hiram: **Henson, Josiah**
Wilson, John: **Wilson, Bertha**
Wilson, Lois M.: **United Church of Canada**
Wilson, Milton: *Canadian Forum*
Wilson, Robert: **Kroetsch, Robert; Literature in English - Theory & Criticism**
Wilson, Serge: **Children's Literature in French; Popular Literature in French**
Wilson, Thomas Edmund: **Lake Louise**
Wilson, William: **Hudson, Henry**
Wilson-McCallister Duo: **Guitar**
Wilson MacDonald Poetry Socs: **MacDonald, Wilson P.**
Winchester carbine: **Firearm**
wind chill: **Arctic Animals; Blizzard; Wind**
wind flower: **Anemone**
wind tunnel: **Aerodynamics; Klein, George John; Parkin, John Hamilton; Turnbull, Wallace Rupert**
Windermere Lake: **Invermere**
Windeyer, Walter: **Yachting**
Windfields Farms Ltd: **Taylor, Edward Plunkett; Turcotte, Ron**
windmill: **Construction Industry, History; Electric-Power Generation; Ste-Scholastique**
Windsor-Annapolis Railway: **Kentville**
Windsor chair: **Furniture, Country**
Windsor-Detroit International Freedom Festival: **Windsor, Ont**
Windsor Distillery & Flouring Mill: **Walker, Hiram**
Windsor Ford V8s: **Basketball**
Windsor Hotel (Montréal): **Hotel; Notman, William**
Windsor Mills, Qué: **Pulp & Paper Industry**
Windsor *Star*: **Southam, William**
Windsor Station (Montréal): **Railway Station**
Winkler, Valentine: **Winkler**
Winn, C.: **Party System**
Winnipeg Arena: **Winnipeg Jets**

Winnipeg Art Gallery: **Architectural Competitions; Da Roza, Gustavo Uriel; Eckhardt-Gramatté, S.C. Sonia; Milne, David B.; Photography**
Winnipeg Auditorium: **Winnipeg Symphony Orchestra**
Winnipeg Automobile Club: **Automobile Racing**
Winnipeg Ballet: **Farrally, Betty; Orchestral Music; Royal Winnipeg Ballet; Spohr, Arnold T.**
Winnipeg Ballet Club: **Lloyd, Gweneth**
Winnipeg Basin: **Red River Colony**
Winnipeg Beach, Man: **St Andrews, Man**
Winnipeg Children's Hospital: **Pediatrics**
Winnipeg Chilean Assn: **Latin Americans**
Winnipeg Citizen: **Laurence, Margaret; Newspapers**
Winnipeg City Hall: **Architectural Competitions**
Winnipeg Clinic Research Institute: **Thorlakson, Paul H.T.**
Winnipeg Declaration: **Co-operative Commonwealth Federation; Lewis, David**
Winnipeg Falcons: **Hockey, Ice**
Winnipeg Flying Club: **Airport Architecture**
Winnipeg Folk Festival: **Folk Festivals; Folklore**
Winnipeg Football Club: **Rugby**
Winnipeg General Hospital: **Kahane, Anne**
Winnipeg goldeye: **Animal; Cuisine**
Winnipeg Grain Exchange: **McIvor, George Harold; Partridge, Edward A.; Richardson, James A., Sr**
Winnipeg "Group of Seven": **Beardy, Jackson**
Winnipeg Hydro: **Manitoba**
Winnipeg Industrial Exhibition: **Horse**
Winnipeg International Airport: **Airport Architecture; Green, Blankstein, Russell; Kahane, Anne; Noise; St Andrews, Man**
Winnipeg Little Theatre: **Little Theatre Movement; Ljungh, Esse W.; Manitoba Theatre Centre; Russell, John Alonzo**
Winnipeg Magazine: **Quebecor Inc**
Winnipeg Male Voice Choir: **Music History**
Winnipeg Mennonite Theatre: **Theatre, Multicultural**
Winnipeg Meridian: **Meridian, First or Principal**
Winnipeg Post Office: **Green, Blankstein, Russell**
Winnipeg Press Club: **Musical Theatre**
Winnipeg Rh Institute: **Biological Product**
Winnipeg Rugby Football Club: **Winnipeg Blue Bombers**
Winnipeg School of Art: **FitzGerald, Lionel LeMoine; Freedman, Harry; Johnston, Francis Hans**
Winnipeg Shamrocks: **Olympic Games**
Winnipeg Square: **Smith, Ernest John**
Winnipeg Stadium: **Winnipeg Blue Bombers**
Winnipeg Stock Exchange: **Stock & Bond Markets**
Winnipeg Sun: **Manitoba; Quebecor Inc**
Winnipeg Tigers: **Winnipeg Blue Bombers**
Winnipeg Trades & Labor Council: **Winnipeg General Strike**
Winnipeg Tribune: **Allen, Ralph; *Winnipeg Free Press***
Winnipeg Victories: **Stanley Cup**
Winnipeg Videon Inc: **Moffat Communications Ltd**
Winnipeg Women's Canadian Club: **Literary Prizes in English**
Winnipeg Zoo: **Manitoba**
Winokapau Lake: **Churchill River, Lab**
Winter, H.W.: **Furniture, Country**
Winter, Henry: **Film**
Winter Ceremonial: **Bella Bella; Native People, Religion**
winter construction: **Construction Industry, History; Pipeline**
Winter Garden Theatre: **Theatre, English-Language**

Winter Guardian Spirit Dance: **Native People - Plateau**
Winter Harbour: **Northwest Territories**
winter moth: **Conservation**
"winter roads": **Champlain, Lake; Manitoba; Northwest Territories**
winter squash: **Vegetable**
winter-works programs: **Labour Policy**
Winterlude: **Canadian Ski Marathon; Festivals**
Winters, L.M.: **Animal Breeding**
Winton horseless carriage: **Roads & Highways**
wire services: **News Agencies**
wirephoto: **Stephenson, William Samuel**
wiretap: **Intelligence Gathering; Official Secrets Act; Privacy**
Wisconsinan ice sheets: **Cypress Hills; Glaciation; Great Lakes**
Wiseman, Morley: **Pacific Ballet Theatre**
Wisler, Clark: **Archaeology**
witch: **Flatfish**
withholding tax: **Taxation**
Witkin, Stephen: **Musical Theatre**
Witless Bay: **Puffin**
witness: **Civil Procedure; Criminal Investigation**
"Witness Against War" manifesto: **Pacifism**
Witt, Laszlo: **Chess**
Wittington Investments Ltd: **George Weston Ltd**
Witton, Henry Buckingham: **Working-Class History**
Wizard Lake oil field: **Petroleum**
Wizard of Miramichi: **Oral Literature in English**
WNOBS: **Theatre, English-Language**
Wobblies: **Industrial Workers of the World**
Wodicka, Ulrich: **Graphic Design**
Wodiczko, Krzysztof: **Art, Contemporary Trends; Poles**
Wojciechowski, Jerzy: **Philosophy**
Wolf Lake: **Bitumen**
Wolf Lake, Alta: **Métis Settlements**
Wolf Ritual: **Nootka**
Wolfall, Robert: **Anglicanism**
Wolfe Island: **St Lawrence River**
Wolfe's Cove: **Tunnels**
wolframite: **Tungsten**
Wollaston Peninsula: **Victoria Island**
Wolof language: **Africans**
Wolseley, Sask: **Place-names**
Woltjen/Udell Gallery: **Art Dealers**
Woman Worker: **Women's Labour Leagues**
Woman's Art Assn of Ottawa: **Brownell, Peleg Franklin**
Woman's Baptist Missionary Union: **Norris, Hannah Maria**
Women Against Pornography: **Pornography**
women & sport: **Hoffman, Abigail; Jones Konihowski, Diane; Sports History; Track & Field**
Women in Science & Engineering: **Women's Movement**
Women Painters of Western Canada: **Artists' Organizations**
Women's Art Assn: **Artists' Organizations; Crafts; Stevens, Dorothy**
women's centres: **Social & Welfare Services; Status of Women**
Women's College Hospital: **Gray, Jessie Catherine; Hilliard, Anna Marion**
Women's Institutes: **Federated Women's Institutes of Canada**
Women's Inter-Church Council: **Ecumenical Social Action**
Women's Medical College (Kingston): **Medicine, History of; Ritchie, Octavia Grace; Smith-Shortt, Elizabeth; Trout, Jennie**
Women's Medical College (Toronto): **Medicine, History of; Stowe, Emily H.; Stowe-Gullen, A. Augusta**
Women's missionary societies: **Status of Women; United Church of Canada**
Women's Press: **Book Publishing, English-Language**
women's shelters: **Campbell, Maria; Women & the Law**
Women's University Club: **MacGill, Helen Gregory**
Women's War Conference: **Status of Women**

Women's Work in Canada: **Edwards, Henrietta L.**
Wonderful Grand Band: **Theatre, English-Language**
Wood, Alan: **Painting**
Wood, Ann: **Strachan, John**
Wood, G. Wallace: *Canadian Business*
Wood, Gundy & Co: **Gundy, James Henry**
Wood, H.: **Steele, Mount**
Wood, Stan: **Ferguson, Maynard**
Wood, W.: **Steele, Mount**
Wood, W.C.: **Electrical Appliances Industry**
Wood, W.P.: **Drama in English**
wood alcohol: **Biomass Energy**
wood betony: **Lousewort**
wood chips: **Biomass Energy; Lumber & Wood Industries; Pulp & Paper Industry**
wood frog: **Biogeography; Frog**
Wood Islands, PEI: **Northumberland Strait; Prince Edward Island**
Wood Lake: **Okanagan Valley**
wood louse: **Crustacean**
Wood River: **Athabasca Pass**
wood warbler: **Bird Distribution & Habitat; Warbler**
Woodbend oilfield: **Alberta**
woodbine: **Honeysuckle**
Woodbine Park: **Queen's Plate; Thoroughbred Racing**
Woodburn, A.S.: *Ottawa Journal*
woodchuck: **Marmot**
Woodhead, W.D.: **Essay in English**
woodland caribou: **Caribou; Debert; Endangered Animals; Nahanni National Park; Pukaskwa National Park**
Woodland culture: **Prehistory**
Woodrow, Paul: **Art, Contemporary Trends**
Woods, Holly: **Toronto**
Woods, J.: **Firearm**
Woods, John: **Philosophy**
Woods, R.J.: **Spinks, John William Tranter**
Woods, Sara: **Popular Literature in English**
Wood's New Self-Raking Reaper: **Agricultural Implements**
Woodside National Historic Park: **Heritage Trail**
Woodstock College: **Baptists; McMaster, William; McMaster University**
Woodstock Reserve: **Maliseet**
Woodstock *Sentinel*: **Pattullo, T. Dufferin**
Woodsworth Building: **Smith, Ernest John**
Woodward, Charles N.W.: **Woodward, Charles**
Woodward Stores Ltd: **Woodward, Charles**
Wookey, Bush & Winter: **Rayner, Gordon**
wool: **Goat Farming; Northwest Coast Indian Art; Occupational Disease; Quilt; Sheep Farming; Textile Industry; Weaving, Contemporary**
Woolf, George: **Thoroughbred Racing**
Woolford, John Elliot: **Printmaking**
woolly fernweed: **Wildflowers**
Woolverton, Charles: **Landscape Architecture**
Woonton, G.A.: **Physics**
Wopmay Mountain Belt: **Geological History; Geological Regions**
word processing: **Computer Industry; Computer Systems Applications; Electronics Industry; Office Automation**
Wordplex International Inc: **Canada Development Corp**
Wordsworth, Lucy: **Women's International League for Peace & Freedom**
"Work & Wages" program: **Great Depression**
work bee: **Corvée; Quilt; Sports History**
work camps: **Prison; Unemployment Relief Camps**
Work Point: **Esquimalt**
work sharing: **Labour Policy**
work stoppages: **Strikes & Lockouts**
work-to-rule: **Postal Strikes; Strikes & Lockouts**
Workers' Education Assn: **Adult Education**

Workers Experimental Theatre: **Theatre, English-Language**
Workers' Party of Canada: **Buhay, Rebecca; Communist Party of Canada**
Workers' Unity League: **Cohen, Jacob Laurence; Great Depression; Industrial Unionism; McLachlan, James Bryson; On to Ottawa Trek; Revolutionary Industrial Unionism; Union Centrals, National**
Working Girls' Assn: **Edwards, Henrietta L.**
Workingmen's Protective Assn: **Union Centrals, District & Regional**
Workman, Ted: **Canadian Football League**
Workmen's Compensation Act (Ont): **Canadian Manufacturers' Association; Social Security; Workers' Compensation**
Workmen's Compensation Board (Ont): **Wright, Alexander Whyte**
Workshop 14: **Little Theatre Movement**
World Alliance of Reformed Churches: **Pidgeon, George Campbell; Presbyterian & Reformed Churches; United Church of Canada**
World Bank: **Agricultural Economics; Environment; International Economics; Standard of Living**
World Climate Program: **Climatology**
World Council of Churches: **Baptists; Canadian Council of Churches; Christian Church (Disciples of Christ); Christianity; Fairweather, Eugene Rathbone; Pidgeon, George Campbell; Presbyterian & Reformed Churches; Strong, Maurice F.; United Church of Canada**
World Council of Indigenous Peoples: **Manuel, George; Native People, Political Organization & Activism**
World Culinary Olympics: **Cuisine**
World Federalists of Canada: **Peace Movement**
World Film Festival: **Festivals; Film Festivals, Prizes**
World Food Program: **Agricultural Aid**
world government: **Baha'i Faith**
World Grain Exhibition & Conference: **Archibald, Edgar Spinney**
World Health Organization: **Birthing Practices; Canada Centre for Inland Waters; Chisholm, G. Brock; Disability; Environment; Frappier, Armand; Mussallem, Helen K.; Water-Borne Disease**
World Hockey Assn: **Edmonton Oilers; Québec Nordiques; Winnipeg Jets**
World Marxist Review: **Ryerson, Stanley B.**
World Meteorological Organization: **Climatology; Environment; Sea Ice; Thomson, Andrew; Weather Forecasting**
World Methodist Council: **United Church of Canada**
world monetary system: **International Economics**
World Nickel Conference: **Sefton, Lawrence F.**
World Peace Council: **Endicott, James**
World Student Relief: **Pelletier, Gérard**
World Theatre Mosaic: **Theatre, English-Language**
World Wildlife Fund: **Conservation; Endangered Animals; Environment; Strong, Maurice F.; Wildlife Conservation & Management**
World's Fair: **Expo 67**
World's Professional Marathon Championship: **Longboat, Thomas C.**
Wormington, H. Marie: **Archaeology**
worms: **Annelida; Devon Island; Flatworm; Insect Pests; Moth; Nematoda; Parasitology**
wormwood: **Alcoholism; Sagebrush**
Worobetz, Stephen: **Ukrainians**

Worth Commission (Alta): **Education, Alternate**
Worthington, Frank: **Soldiers of Fortune**
Worthington, G.H.: **Hotel**
Worthington, James: **Sudbury**
wreckfish: **Bass**
Wright, Edward: **Cartography, History of**
Wright, J.J.: **Canadian National Exhibition**
Wright, James V.: **Archaeology**
Wright, Judith: **Swimming, Speed**
Wright, Richard: **Literature in English; Novel in English**
Wright, Ruggles: **Timber Slide**
Wright, Walter: **Ophthalmology**
Wright, William H.: **Kirkland Lake**
Wright-Hargreaves Mines, Ltd: **Kirkland Lake**
Wrightstown, Lower Canada: **Hull**
Wrigley, NWT: **Northwest Territories**
Wrinch, Mary: **Hutchinson, Leonard**
Writer's Development Trust: **Gibson, Graeme; Literary Prizes in English**
Writers Exchange Fellowship to Scotland: **Gibson, Graeme**
Writers Guild of Alberta Awards: **Literary Prizes in English**
wrongful dismissal: **Employment Law**
wrought iron: **Architecture, Development; Bridges; Construction Industry, History; Lighting**
Wuensch, Gerhard: **Music History**
Wunnummin Lake: **Winisk River**
Wyatt, Charles B.: **Gore, Francis**
Wyatt, F.A.: **Soil Science**
Wyatt, G.: **Molecular Biology**
Wycliffe College: **Fleming, Archibald Lang; University of Toronto**
Wyczynski, Paul: **Literary Bibliography in French; Literature in French - Scholarship & Teaching**
Wye Marsh Wildlife Interpretive Centre: **Heritage Trail; Midland**
Wyers, Jan: **Folk Art**
Wyman, Max: **Music Criticism**
Wynand, Derk: **German Writing**
Wynkeham-Martin, S.F.: **Parachuting, Sport**

X-Y-Z

X-ray: **Balloon; Chant, Clarence Augustus; Chemistry Subdisciplines; Computer Systems Applications; Gray, Joseph Alexander; Laurence, George C.; Mineral; Nuclear Safety; Observatory; Pipeline; Pollution; Spectroscopy**
X-ray machines: **Medical Devices Industry**
xenon: **Lighthouses; Spring**
xerographic printers: **Computer Systems Applications; Print Industry**
Xerox Canada Inc: **Toronto**
Xerox Research Centre of Canada Ltd: **Physics**
xonotlite: **Gemstone**
XWA Montréal: **Communications in Québec**
xylenes: **Chemical Industries**
Yale, BC: **Cariboo Road; Dewdney, Edgar; Semlin, Charles A.**
Yale Convention: **Blacks**
Yamaska, Mont: **Granby; St Lawrence Lowland**
Yamaska, Rivière: **Cowansville; Farnham; Floods & Flood Control; Granby; St-Hyacinthe; St Lawrence Lowland**
Yanovsky, Zal: **Popular Music**
yardang: **Aeolian Landform**
Yardbird Suite: **Jazz**
yarding: **Forest Harvesting**
Yardley Jones, John: **Welsh**
Yarmouth Duck & Yarn Co: **Lovitt, William Dodge**
yarn: **Clothing Industries; Rugs & Rug Making; Textile Industry; Weaving, Contemporary**

Yarrows Ltd: **Shipbuilding & Ship Repair**
Yarwood, Walter: **Painters Eleven; Painting**
Yates Memorial Centre: **Lethbridge**
Yatze Reserve: **Edenshaw, Charlie**
Ye Sa To Native Communications Soc: **Native People, Communications**
Yeddeau, David: **Dance History**
Yee, Paul: **Ethnic Literature**
yellow birch: **Birch; Cape Breton Highlands National Park; Furniture, French; Saguenay Provincial Park; Vegetation Regions - Atlantic Coastal; Vegetation Regions - Eastern Temperate Forests**
yellow-breasted chat: **Warbler**
yellow cedar (yellow cypress): **Garibaldi Provincial Park**
yellow cypress: **Cypress; Vegetation Regions - Pacific Coastal**
Yellow Grass marshes: **Souris River**
yellow grub: **Perch; Pike**
yellow lady's slipper: **Endangered Plants; Lady's Slipper**
yellow mountain aven: **Drummond, Thomas**
yellow perch: **Erie, Lake; Perch; Rideau Lakes; Thousand Islands**
yellowcake (uranium): **Nuclear Power Plants**
Yellowhead Highway: **Alberta; Skeena River; Yellowhead Pass**
Yellowhead Lake: **Yellowhead Pass**
Yellowknife Bay: **Great Slave Lake**
Yellowknife River: **Great Slave Lake**
yellowlegs: **Sandpiper**
yellowtail: **Flatfish**
yellowthroat: **Warbler**
Yeo, Leslie: **Shaw Festival**
Yeomans, Amelia: **Women's Suffrage**
Yevshan Ukrainian Folk-Ballet: **Saskatoon**
Yiddish Drama Group: **Theatre, Multicultural**
Yiddish language: **Ethnic Literature; Jewish Writing; Judaism; Language; Women's Labour Leagues**
yoga: **Hinduism; New Religious Movements**
Yoho Glacier: **Waterfall**
Yoho River: **Takakkaw Falls**
Yom Kippur: **Judaism**
Yonge Main Store Ltd: **Canadian Tire Corp, Ltd**
Yonge Street: *Financial Times*; **Roads & Highways; Toronto**
Yorath, C.J.: **Saskatoon**
York, Ritchie: **Music Criticism**
York, Upper Canada: **Allan, William; Autobiographical Writing in English; Bank of Upper Canada; Duel; Family Compact; Government Building; Ketchum, Jesse; Literary Magazines in English; Mackenzie, William Lyon; Put-In-Bay; Sheaffe, Roger Hale; Simcoe, Elizabeth P.; Strachan, John; Toronto; War of 1812**
York Band: **Music History**
York City, North-West Territories: **Yorkton**
York Club: **Sproatt and Rolph**
York Farmers' Colonization Co: **Yorkton**
York Fort (York Factory): **Henday, Anthony**
York Hospital: **Hospitals; Medicine, History of**
York Mechanics' Institute: **Ketchum, Jesse**
York Printer's Union: **Toronto**
York-Toronto Joint Program: **Transportation Research Centres**
York Toy Novelty Co: **Toys & Games**
York Typographical Soc: **Print Industry**
York Winds: **Chamber Music**
Yorkdale subway station: **Hayden, Michael**
Yorkton International Film Festival: **Film Festivals, Prizes**
Yorkville Archery Club: **Archery**
Yoruba language: **Africans**
Yoshida, Yuki: **Japanese**
Young, George: **Marathon Swimming**

Young, John: **Great Western Railway**
Young, Lily: **Golf**
Young, Robert: **Painting**
Young, Scott: **Smythe, Constantine Falkland Cary; Young, Neil P.**
Young, Thomas: **Huron County Jail**
Young, Walter: **Long-Distance Running**
Young, Walter (social scientist): **Working-Class History**
Young Canada Works: **Labour Policy**
Young Canadian Writers Award: **Literary Prizes in English**
Young Canadians: **Baseball**
Young Catholic Students Group: **Sauvé, Jeanne-M.**
Young Co: **Theatre for Young Audiences**
Young Communist League: **Rose, Fred**
Young Men's Hebrew Assn: **Judaism**
Young Offenders Act: **Juvenile Delinquency; Prison**
Young People's Theatre: **Hirsch, John S.**
Young Women's Hebrew Assn: **Judaism**
Young's sawmill (Ottawa): **Technology**
Youth for Christ: **Ambrose, Tommy; Templeton, Charles B.**
Youth Training Act: **Education, Technical; Students, Financial Aid to**
Youtheatre: **Theatre for Young Audiences**
Youville, François d': **Youville, Marie-Marguerite d'**
Yugoslavs: **Croatians; Serbs; Slovenes**
Yukon Consolidated Gold Corp: **Dawson; Yukon Territory**
Yukon Indian Brotherhood: **Land Claims**
Yukon Regional Library System: **Libraries**
Yukon Southern Air Transport: **McConachie, G.W. Grant**
Yukon telegraph line: **Nechako River**
Yukon Territory Act: **Territorial Government; Yukon Territory**
Yuquot, BC: **Malaspina Expedition; Nootka Sound**
Zacks, Samuel J.: **Etrog, Sorel**
Zairians: **Africans**
Zakuta, Leo: **Working-Class History**
Zama, Alta: **Native People, Economic Conditions**
Zambians: **Africans**
Zamparo v Brisson: **Medical Ethics**
Zaslow, Morris: **Nordicity**
Zayas Island: **Dundas Island**
Zbura, Ivan: **Ukrainian Writing**
Zeballos, BC: **Leckie, John E.**
ZEEP reactor: **Klein, George John; Laurence, George C.; Lewis, Wilfrid Bennett; Nuclear Energy**
Zeidler Roberts Partnership: **Zeidler, Eberhard Heinrich**
Zelenak, Ed: **Sculpture**
Zeller, Ludwig: **Ethnic Literature**
Zeller's Inc: **Hudson's Bay Company; Retail Trade; Thomson Group**
Zen Lotus Soc: **Buddhism**
Zend, Robert: **Ethnic Literature**
Zia, Abdul Qavi: **Ethnic Literature**
Zieroth, Dale: **Ethnic Literature**
Zimmerman, Carle: **Community**
Zimmerman, Samuel: **Banking**
Zinor Holdings: **Noranda Mines Ltd**
Zionism: **Jewish Writing; Judaism**
zircon: **Geological Dating; Mineral**
zirconium: **Mineral**
Zontal, Jorge: **Art, Contemporary Trends**
zoological journals & societies: **Entomology; Fry, Frederick Ernest Joseph; Parasitology; Zoology**
Zuck, Tim: **Painting**
Zujewskyj, Oleh: **Ukrainian Writing**
Zuk, Radoslav: **Religious Building**
Zulu language: **Africans**
Zumthor, Paul: **Comparative Literature**
Zurich, Ont: **Swiss**
Zwicker, Leroy: **Art Dealers**
Zymaize experiment: **John Labatt Corp**

THE CANADIAN ENCYCLOPEDIA

Designed by David Shaw & Associates, Toronto

*Typeset by Printing Services, University of Alberta
in 8 point Latine*

Colour separations by Zenith Graphics

Film assembly by Ronalds-Federated Western Ltd., Vancouver and Edmonton

Printed by Imprimerie Ronalds, Montréal

*Paper (Rolland 50 lb S.T. Encyclopedia Opaque)
manufactured by Rolland Paper Mills, St. Jérôme, Qué*

Bound by The Bryant Press Ltd., and T.H. Best Printing Co. Ltd., Toronto

*Cloth (Riverside Linen and Bayside Linen)
manufactured by Columbia Finishing Mills, Cornwall, Ont*

Slipcases by Fielder Paper Box, Toronto

Cartons designed and manufactured by Domtar Packaging, Inc., Edmonton/Toronto

Packaging by Britman Industries, Oshawa, Ont

Emily Carr

Margaret Lauren

William Lyon Mackenzie King

Sir Alexander Mackenzie

Wayne Gretzky

J. S. Woodsworth